"AND I WAS THERE"
PEARL HARBOR AND MIDWAY—
BREAKING THE SECRETS

Pearl Harbor. 7 December 1941. Japanese bombs and torpedoes slam into the battleships of the Pacific Fleet as Commander Edwin T. Layton leaps up the stairs to his second-floor office. "Ah," says Captain Willard Kitts, the staff gunner officer, "here's the man we should have been listening to all along."

Why did the Japanese attack? How had they inflicted the greatest military defeat in American history? What had gone wrong?

"And I Was There" is the first book by a top-ranking American navy officer to answer these questions. Admiral Layton scrupulously kept these secrets to himself—for forty-three years—until recently, when the government released half a million classified documents from its intelligence archives. Layton's revelations are incredible. He names those who knew about Japanese intentions, how they acquired their knowledge, and how they misused it.

Acclaim for
"And I Was There"

"Admiral Layton's book offers a new analysis based on declassified documents."

—The Associated Press

"(It) paints Kimmel as the unwitting scapegoat . . . It's a picture of bitter feuding within the naval intelligence organization and the service's high command."

—*St. Petersburg Times*

"Layton contends that unknown to Mr. Roosevelt, the bureaucratic fighting meant vital intelligence that could have alerted Pearl Harbor was denied Layton—and Admiral Kimmel."

—*Journal of Commerce*

"Rarely has a book righted an old wrong before it is published, but the memoirs of Adm. Layton . . . have accomplsihed this feat."

—Baltimore *Sun*

"Layton's dramatic and sometimes thrilling book can be read as a case history of a problem that affects us even more widely nowadays than it did in 1941— the problem of communications within large organizations."

—*The New Yorker*

"No one reading Admiral Layton's book can afford to ignore the documentation he appends. . . . Until someone authoritatively refutes Admiral Layton, if at all possible, his is the last word on the subject."

—CAPTAIN EDWARD L. BEACH, U.S.N. (Ret.),
Naval Institute *Proceedings*

BOOKS BY JOHN COSTELLO:

The Battle for Concorde (with Terry Hughes, 1971)
D-Day (with Warren Tute and Terry Hughes, 1974)
The Concorde Conspiracy (with Terry Hughes, 1976)
Jutland 1916 (with Terry Hughes, 1976)
The Battle of the Atlantic (with Terry Hughes, 1977)
The Pacific War (1981)
Love, Sex and War—Changing Values 1939–45 (1985)

BOOKS BY ROGER PINEAU:

A Picture History of the Pacific War (with Robert Sherrod, 1952)
Midway, the Battle That Doomed Japan (with Mitsuo Fuchida, Masatake Okumiya, and Clarke H. Kawakami, 1955)
The Divine Wind (with Rikihei Inoguchi and Tadashi Nakajima, 1958)
Japanese Destroyer Captain (with Tameichi Hara and Fred Saito, 1961)
The End of the Imperial Japanese Navy (with Masanori Ito and Andrew Y. Kuroda, 1962)
The Japan Expedition, 1852–4: The Personal Journal of Commodore Matthew C. Perry (Ed., 1969)
"Isoruku Yamamoto" in *The War Lords* (Ed. Sir Michael Carver, 1976)

"And I Was There"

Pearl Harbor and Midway—
Breaking the Secrets

*by Rear Admiral Edwin T. Layton, U.S.N. (Ret.),
with Captain Roger Pineau, U.S.N.R. (Ret.),
and John Costello*

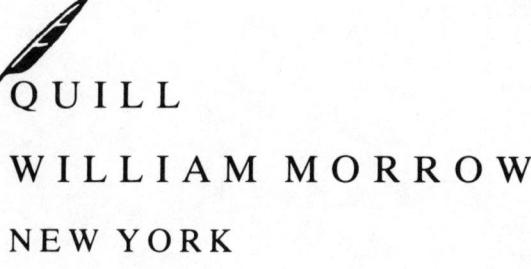

QUILL

WILLIAM MORROW

NEW YORK

In recognition of the unsung heroes
of radio intelligence
in the United States Navy

Library of Congress Cataloging-in-Publication Data

Layton, Edwin T., 1903–
  "And I was there."

  Bibliography: p.
  Includes index.
  1. Layton, Edwin T., 1903– . 2. Pearl Harbor
(Hawaii), Attack on, 1941—Personal narratives, American.
3. Midway, Battle of, 1942—Personal narratives,
American.   4. United States. Navy—Biography.
5. Admirals—United States—Biography. I. Pineau,
Roger, 1916– . II. Costello, John. III. Title.
D767.92.L39   1987   940.54'26'0924 [B]   86-21199
ISBN 0-688-06968-1 (pbk.)

Printed in the United States of America

First Quill Edition

1 2 3 4 5 6 7 8 9 10

BOOK DESIGN BY BERNARD SCHLEIFER

Acknowledgments

COMPLETING THE PROJECT that the late Admiral Layton began so many years ago in the densely packed handwritten pages of his notebooks has required the assistance and cooperation of many people. Foremost of them are his surviving wartime colleagues and his widow, Miriam. She not only encouraged her husband to make the decision to commit his story to print and assisted with the preparation of early manuscript drafts, but after his death continued to sustain his collaborators by making available all his research notes and papers in addition to providing them with gracious hospitality. Mrs. Layton has also read the final manuscript and provided insightful comment on it.

Admiral Arleigh Burke, who has initiated so many significant projects, inspired Admiral Layton and us to undertake the writing of this book. We have benefited from his sound advice and encouragement. Others strongly supportive of this project have been Rear Admiral John Butts, U.S.N., Rear Admiral P. W. "Pete" Dillingham, Rear Admiral William C. Mott, Rear Admiral L. Robert Schulz, Rear Admiral Robert H. Weeks, all U.S.N. (Ret.). Captain Raymond P. Schmidt, U.S.N.R., with his knowledge of radio intelligence history, has contributed greatly to this work and, with his wife, Roberta, devoted many hours to a critical reading of the manuscript.

Friends and colleagues of Admiral Layton who have given generously of their time and knowledge are many. We are especially grateful to the late Captain Thomas H. Dyer, his naval academy classmate, cryptologist, and mathematician par excellence; and Captain Wesley A. "Ham" Wright, U.S.N., who has shared with us his acute recollections, lively humor, and vast cryptanalytic lore.

Others who shared with us their wartime Cincpac experience and memories of Admiral Layton include Rear Admiral D. M. "Mac" Showers; Captains John G. Roenigk, Arthur L. Benedict, Forrest R. "Tex"

5

Biard, Allyn Cole, Robert E. Hudson, Wilfred J. Holmes, Willis L. Thomas, and Gilven M. Slonim, all U.S.N. (Ret.); Brigadier General Bankson Holcomb and Colonel Alva B. Lasswell, U.S.M.C. (Ret.); and Commander H. M. Anthony, U.S.C.G. (Ret.). We are also indebted to Rear Admiral Kemp Tolley; to Captain H. Arthur Lamar, wartime aide to Admiral Nimitz; to Pauline Birtley, widow of Captain Thomas B. Birtley; and Betty Lee Watts, widow of Captain Ethelbert Watts, for information each provided.

The book has benefited from the insights provided by Phil Cate, Eunice Willson Rice, and Fred C. Woodrough, Jr. These former civilian employees of OP-20-GZ have perceptively helped to flesh out the archival record.

We are grateful also to Captain Thomas Kimmel (son of Admiral Kimmel) and his son Tom Kimmel. They have given us access to many of the admiral's papers and provided informed advice. Mrs. Janet Elerding, daughter of Captain Joseph J. Rochefort, generously made her father's private document collection available, as did the Dyer family. We are grateful to Commander Howard McCollum, son of Admiral McCollum, for placing useful papers and records at our disposal.

Professor E. B. Potter and John Lundstrom have generously made available their correspondence with Layton and his critiques of key issues. Keiji Miyoshi, formerly an intelligence officer in the imperial Japanese navy, has been an unstinting source of answers to many questions. Robert Haslach and James Rusbridger have magnanimously shared with us the fruits of their respective research into the Dutch and British intelligence services. Paul M. Stillwell has kindly made available records from the U.S. Naval Institute's comprehensive oral history program.

Although the interpretation of the recently declassified documentation is that of the authors, we are grateful for the advice and help given by Professor Warren Kimball of Rutgers University, Professor Forrest C. Pogue of the Eisenhower Institute, Dr. John W. Chapman of Sussex University, Dr. Martin Gilbert of Oxford, and Dr. David Reynolds of Cambridge University. Professor Raymond G. O'Connor, formerly of the Naval War College and Stanford University; Professor Gerald Wheeler, formerly of San Jose State University; and Bill Williams, latterly with *The Washington Post*, have given valued professional critiques of the final manuscript.

The staffs of many federal archives have responded promptly and helpfully over the years to many requests for documents. They include: the National Archives in Washington, D.C., and its subsidiary repositories at Suitland, San Bruno, and Laguna Niguel; the National Personnel Records Center, St. Louis; the Franklin D. Roosevelt Library, Hyde Park, N.Y.; and the Naval Historical Center and the Self-Defense Force Historical Center in Japan.

The Naval Security Group and the National Security Agency have released vast quantities of wartime intelligence material and both Admiral Layton and his coauthors have been privileged to have received invaluable assistance from the members of the historical departments at these organizations and other officials of Britain's ministry of defence.

In these massive and seemingly impersonal organizations we have discovered helpful friends who have made our research easier by the personal interest they have given this project. To name some is to risk omitting others who are equally deserving, but we are particularly grateful to Michael Anderson, B. F. "Cal" Cavalcante, Fred Close, Martha Crawley, Robert Cresswood, Charles R. Haberlein, Jr., Terri Hammet, Richard von Doenhoff, Deborah Edge, Hisao Iwashima, Rose Mary Kennedy, Raymond E. Lewis, William H. Lewis, Barbara A. Lynch, Sally Marks, Katherine Nicastro, Diane Nixon, Neal Petersen, Robert Parks, Edward Reese, John C. Reilly, Jr., Lieutenant Commander Robert J. Schultz, U.S.N., John Taylor, Jim Trimble, and John E. Vajda.

The Public Records Office, England; the New Zealand National Archives, Auckland; the Australian War Memorial, Canberra; the Imperial War Museum in London; the Bundesarchiv, Frieberg; the Admiralty Library, London; and the Military History Section of the Royal Netherlands Army have also been the sources of new documentation. The staff of the Library of Congress, especially the Japanese section of the Orientalia Division, has answered our many calls on their expertise with promptness and precision.

Admiral Layton would have wished us to extend a particular expression of gratitude to the librarians of the U.S. Navy Postgraduate School, Monterey, for all the assistance they gave to his researches. The New York Public Library and the Columbia University Library have also served as valued sources of published material. The University of Wyoming Library afforded us information from its Archive of Contemporary History.

Others who have helped with this project are those with special knowledge, wartime experience, or authors of important source works. Friends and relatives of Admiral Layton and his two coauthors have assisted with information and translations, or have generously contributed to logistical support. Our gratitude is extended to Captain Edward L. Beach, U.S.N. (Ret.), Joan and Richard Bergsund, Patrick Beasely, Clay Blair, Jr., William C. Bodie, Commander Masataka Chihaya, Paul Crosley, Robert T. Crowley, George M. Elsey, Admiral Sir Morgan Giles, Dr. Ruth Harris, Douglass Hubbard, Henry and Julienne Hubbard, Stephen Hubbard, Gerald P. Jantzi, Ernest Kroll, Andrew Y. Kuroda, Lieutenant Commander L. B. Luchenbach, U.S.N., Catherine Magistretti, Richard and Virginia Morrall, Kenneth J. Nichols, Captain Wyman Packard, U.S.N. (Ret.), Lawrence Pratt, Commander Ernest Saftig, U.S.N. (Ret.), Robert Sherrod, Charles A. "Sandy" Sims, Riley Sunderland, Anna Del Valle, Robin and Julia Wight, and Thomas F. Troy.

The copy-editing and production staff of William Morrow have met impossible deadlines with graceful competence, and we are especially grateful to assistant editor Elizabeth Terhune. We should like to thank

Victoria Klose and freelancer David Falk for their judicious copy editing, Bernard Schliefer for designing the book, Cheryl Asherman for her striking cover, and Richard Natkiel of London whose cartographic skills provided the maps.

Maxine Pineau earned our gratitude for having let World War II be waged again on her home front in the 1980s. She not only kept Layton's collaborators nourished but her expertise with the word processor greatly facilitated the production of the final manuscript.

A very special category of our appreciation must be reserved for two friends without whose help this book would never have been realized in its present form. One is Bruce Lee, prescient editor extraordinaire, who inspired and guided the project to its successful conclusion. The other, though his name appears in these pages, has requested anonymity. That request is honored, but we want him to know that his comments and suggestions, based on deft command of our language and thorough knowledge of communications intelligence, have contributed greatly to the authority and accuracy of Admiral Layton's story.

In the quarter century of our life together, my husband relived over and over the events of his naval career, particularly the period of duty as intelligence officer for Admiral Nimitz. I became almost as familiar with the day-to-day happenings as if I had been there—and in the retelling his memory remained fresh.

He fairly seethed with pent-up emotions surrounding the trauma of having gone through all but one of the Pearl Harbor investigations and of hearing some of his fellow officers verbally coerced into testifying falsely. Our countless evenings of conversation fulfilled his need to give vent to his outrage at the cover-up in Washington, and at the sacrifice of Admiral Kimmel and General Short.

Time and again Edwin was urged to write his experiences. Though he was reticent, he finally came to the conviction that he owed one more contribution to his country. The gradual release of top secret documents in the National Archives helped persuade him to reveal the true version of events. Proof of his statements was assured via copies of actual messages as more and more papers were freed. He felt history required that he produce a record of what really happened as only he could tell it because he was there, living it all.

With two friends whose professional qualifications he respected and admired, my husband agreed to recount, tape record, and write his experiences for the benefit of historians and the future generations of Americans who will love their country as much as he did.

—MIRIAM P. LAYTON

Carmel, California
July 1985

Contents

Charts

"And I Was There"

THE PACIFIC WAR—1941: The Japanese Conquest

Kamchatka

ATTU   ATKA   KISKA   Aleutian Islands

Kurile Is
ETOROFU
Hitokappu B
Hokkaido

**26 Nov 1941
Nagumo's fleet
sails**

**4 Dec
Refuelling
point**

7 Dec 1941

**Japanese carrier
strike force**

**16 Dec
Part of fleet
to Wake I in
support of attack**

**0600 hrs, 7 Dec 1941
Air strike on
Pearl Harbor launched**

P   A   C   I   F   I   C

MIDWAY

MARCUS

**8 Dec
Wake I attacked
23 Dec
surrendered**

WAKE

O   C   E   A   N

Hawaiian Is
OAHU
PEARL HARBOR   HAWAII

Mariana
Islands
SAIPAN
GUAM

ENIWETOK   KWAJALEIN
TRUK   **Marshall
Islands**
MAJURO
MAKIN
ne Islands   TARAWA   **Gilbert
Is**

PALMYRA
CHRISTMAS

Line Islands

NAURU   OCEAN I
RALTY   JARVIS   MALDEN
NEW IRELAND
BRITAIN   RABAUL
BOUGAINVILLE   NANUMEA   **Phoenix Is**   VICTORIA
Solomon Is   **Ellice
Is**   **Tokelau Is**   CAROLINE
NEW
GEORGIA   GUADALCANAL
SBY   SANTA CRUZ IS   SUVOROV
Samoa Is

CORAL SEA   ESPIRITU SANTO
AIRNS   **New
Hebrides**   EFATE   **Fiji
Is**   **Cook Is**   **Society Is**   TAHITI
SUVA
**New
Caledonia**   **Tonga Is**   RAROTONGA
ROCKHAMPTON   NOUMEA   TUBUAI

BRISBANE
NORFOLK   KERMADEC IS

h Wales
SYDNEY
CANBERRA

**TASMAN
SEA**   AUCKLAND
ELBOURNE
WELLINGTON
Tasmania   **NEW ZEALAND**
CHRISTCHURCH

International date line (Monday) (Sunday)

THE PACIFIC WAR—1942–45: The Allied Offensives

Kamchatka

Sakhalin

Kurile Is

ETEROFU

Hokkaido

ATTU
KISKA
ATKA
Aleutian Islands

15 Aug
1943

North Pacific Area

18 April 1942
Doolittle's air raid on Tokyo
from carrier task force

P   A   C   I   F   I   C

MARCUS

MIDWAY

Pacific Ocean Areas
(Nimitz)

Hawaiian Is
OAHU
PEARL HARBOR
HAWAII

WAKE

Central Pacific Area

Mariana
Islands
SAIPAN 15 July 1944
GUAM 21 July 1944

O   C   E   A   N

ENIWETOK
17 Feb 1944

.1 Feb 1944
KWAJALEIN

TRUK

**Marshall
Islands**

MAJURO

MAKIN

PALMYRA

Line

CHRISTMAS

ne   Islands

TARAWA
20 Nov 1943

Gilbert
Is

Islands

JARVIS

MALDEN

28 Feb 1944

NEW IRELAND

NEW
BRITAIN   RABAUL

BOUGAINVILLE

NEW
GEORGIA

ESBO

GUADALCANAL

NAURU

OCEAN I

NANUMEA

Solomon Is

Ellice
Is

7 Aug 1942

SANTA CRUZ IS

Phoenix Is

Tokelau Is

VICTORIA

SUVOROV

CAROLINE

Samoa Is

C O R A L   S E A

CAIRNS

ESPIRITU SANTO

New
Hebrides

EFATE

Fiji
Is

SUVA

New
Caledonia

NOUMEA

ROCKHAMPTON

BRISBANE

NORFOLK

Cook Is

RAROTONGA

Tonga Is

KERMADEC IS

TAHITI

Society Is

TUBUAI

South Pacific Area
(Ghormley, Halsey later)

SYDNEY
CANBERRA

MELBOURNE

**T A S M A N
S E A**

AUCKLAND

WELLINGTON

NEW ZEALAND

CHRISTCHURCH

International date line (Monday)
(Sunday)

1

"I Was There"

"**P**EARL HARBOR is under air attack, sir."
That Sunday morning telephone call from the duty yeoman in my office at Pacific Fleet headquarters was the most stunning message of my life. At my home near Diamond Head, fifteen miles east of Pearl Harbor, there had been no sound of planes, bombs, gunfire, or any other indication that Japan had brought war to the Hawaiian island of Oahu.

"I'll be right there," I replied, and began pulling on my clothes of last evening. Almost immediately an expected phone call came from my Kalanianaole Highway neighbor Lieutenant Paul Crosley. He was flag secretary to Admiral Husband E. Kimmel, commander in chief of the United States Pacific Fleet, and I was fleet intelligence officer. "Be out front, Eddie," he hollered. "I'll pick you up in three minutes."

Mrs. Crosley was driving as the huge roadster paused at the curb and I jumped into the rumble seat. We roared off in their striking blue sixteen-cylinder Cadillac, with its white-sidewall tires. We must have been doing sixty as we flew into the eastern outskirts of Honolulu. The scene was eye-catching enough to attract a motorcycle cop who overtook us with his red light flashing.

Before he could say a word about our speeding, I yelled that Pearl Harbor was under air attack, we were fleet staff officers, and we needed his help to get out there immediately. At that moment the policeman's radio blared news of the air raid. He motioned us to follow, flipped on his siren, and shot ahead, leading the way along the hill route skirting the city. As Crosley later recalled, "We must have been the only private parties who ever drove through the Punchbowl area at eighty miles an hour."

Smoke billowed skyward as we approached the naval base. At the Schofield barracks intersection, traffic was completely blocked. Our cop-

17

guide veered off the highway and led us bumping and bouncing over a rough stretch of terrain and into the navy yard just as the second wave of Japanese planes came screaming in.

I dashed into the submarine base administration building and leaped up the stairs toward my second-floor office. Several officers were conferring in the corridor. Captain Willard Kitts, the staff gunnery officer, spotted me and called out, "Ah, here's the man we should have been listening to all along."

The middle of an air raid, with the rat-a-tat-tat of machine guns on the submarines in the slip below our windows, was hardly a moment for philosophic reflections. As fleet intelligence officer, my job was to keep the commander in chief informed of when, where, how, and in what strength a potential enemy attack might be anticipated.

Until that very Sunday morning we had not known the whereabouts of the main Japanese aircraft carriers. On the 2 December intelligence sheet I had written "Homeland waters?" for their location. This prompted an exchange with Admiral Kimmel which, in the event, was a dreadful irony.

"What? You don't know where the carriers are?" Kimmel had erupted.

"No, sir," I replied.

"You haven't any idea of where they are?"

"No, sir. That's why I have 'Homeland waters' with a question mark. I don't know."

"You mean to say that you, the intelligence officer, don't know where the carriers are?"

"No, sir, I don't."

"You mean they could be coming around Diamond Head, and you wouldn't know it?"

"Yes, sir, but I hope they'd have been sighted before now."

"I understand." Kimmel said, with a twinkle in his eye that kidded me for losing track of a substantial part of the Japanese fleet.

I have since worn a hole in the seat of my trousers kicking myself for not reminding Kimmel then and there about the translation I had given him several months earlier. It was from a Japanese book, *When We Fight,* published in 1933, and it had predicted that in the event of war with the United States, the Japanese fleet would attack Pearl Harbor.

The numbing memory of those terrible first hours of the Pacific war came flooding back to me during the measured ritual of the formal surrender ceremony on board battleship *Missouri* the morning of 2 September 1945.

Scudding gray clouds swirled over the long lines of Allied naval vessels that crowded Tokyo Bay. The early morning mists had lifted by the time that General Douglas MacArthur came on board *Missouri* shortly after 0800, but a sullen sky continued to threaten the anchorage. The waters of the great bay were eerily still and black, dancing with reflections of the lean hulls of 260 assembled warships, an awesome demonstration of the military might that had been marshaled to defeat Japan.

At the appointed hour of 0900, an American destroyer bearing the eleven-man Japanese delegation closed the battleship's starboard side. The emperor's burden of capitulation appeared to weigh heavily on the shoulders of the foreign minister. It was impossible not to feel sympathy for this frail figure in frock coat and top hat who labored so painfully up the companion ladder. Mamoru Shigemitsu had lost his left leg to a Communist bomb years before, and we watched in agonized silence as he limped across the quarterdeck below number two gun turret. Alongside him stood General Yoshijiro Umezu, the chief of the imperial general staff, whose stony detachment betrayed a warrior's distaste for submitting to the ultimate military indignity.

When MacArthur called on them to "conclude a solemn agreement," the minister and general were the first to sign, followed by the supreme commander and the officers representing all the Allied nations. The final surrender document had been laid out before the Japanese delegation on an old mess table that, to one observer, seemed to have been transformed by a green felt cloth into an altar of peace. In an auspicious epilogue to MacArthur's final prayer for world peace, the sun burst through the cloud layers just before hundreds of Allied planes roared overhead.

Many diverse elements had conspired to ensure that I was one of the few people to be present at both the opening and closing events of the war in the Pacific. Although I had labored long and hard in the intervening four and a half years to help America win that war, I still felt a curious sympathy for Japan and its people. From the day I first arrived in Japan sixteen years earlier, their proud nationalism had impressed me, even though it had led them into horrific wartime deprivations and the finality of a bitter defeat.

My view of the actual moment of surrender was obscured by ranks of senior officers crowded in front of me. Still I counted myself very fortunate to be present as the personal guest of Admiral Chester W. Nimitz, whom I had served as fleet intelligence officer throughout the war. But my personal relief that Japan and the United States were finally at peace was rudely shaken by another memorable event that day. Unlike the surrender ceremony, this experience was intensely personal and bitter—and totally unexpected.

As a member of the Pacific Fleet commander's official entourage, I was quartered on board his flagship *South Dakota*. That evening, after we had finished dinner and were relaxing with a game of acey-deucey in the wardroom, Admiral Richmond Kelly Turner, another personal guest of Nimitz, strode in.

The war had made "Terrible" Turner a naval legend. As commander of Nimitz's amphibious forces, he had executed all our landing operations from Guadalcanal to Iwo Jima with brilliant distinction. But few who worked closely with him in these operations could forget—or forgive—his stormy temper, overbearing ego, and celebrated bouts with the bottle. From the manner in which he entered the wardroom that evening, it was evident that he was stoked up. He soon galvanized the wardroom with the reason for his celebration.

"Did you see the navy department's release about the findings of the Pearl Harbor court of inquiry?" he demanded, his booming voice stopping all conversation. "They said that goddamned Kimmel had all the information and didn't do anything about it. They should hang him higher than a kite!"

Turner continued to hold forth. Time and again he said, "Kimmel was given all that information and didn't do anything about it."

I sat there stunned. I knew that what he was saying was not only untrue, but a monstrous slur on my former commander in chief.

Turner's gloating denunciation was not the first venting I had been exposed to of the internecine feud that had flared up time and again in the upper reaches of the navy. Its ramifications were to divide a generation of senior officers and help fuel a mounting political and historical controversy over who was to blame for the events leading to the disaster at Pearl Harbor on 7 December 1941.

The feud was rooted in the classic power struggle that has been endemic in military organizations since men first answered the call to arms: the struggle over who should control military intelligence. The resurgence of the old fight had caused divisions in the navy department, between the office of naval intelligence (ONI) and office of naval communications (ONC), during the critical year between the spring of 1941 and the early summer of 1942. Not only had it made a major contribution toward ensuring that the Japanese succeeded with their surprise attack, but had almost cost us the battle at Midway. In truth it had plagued our military commands throughout World War II—and it is still going on today.

It was ironic that on the first night of official peace I found myself walking into the flames of another such controversy. Having been Admiral Kimmel's fleet intelligence officer on 7 December 1941, and having testified at all but one of the secret wartime inquiries into Pearl Harbor, I knew that Turner's bald assertions were scandalously untrue. Admiral Kimmel had been a victim of circumstances and became a convenient scapegoat in order to cover up navy department derelictions.

Responsibility for this failure bore heavily on Turner who, in his capacity as chief of war plans, had been the forceful junior member of the triumvirate who virtually ran the office of naval operations throughout 1941. He had arrogated to himself many of the traditional functions of the office of naval intelligence and to protect his errors of judgment and conceal the collective culpability of the most senior officers in the navy,

Turner had played a leading part in the campaign to pillory a fellow officer and fine commander of the fleet.

Turner repeated his rant: "They should hang him higher than a kite!" And I, boiling with indignation, had to correct him. "Admiral," I said, "I'm sorry. But Kimmel did not have that information. You say that he did. I know that he did not, and I was there."

"Who are you?" demanded the four-star admiral, with the fury of a bull stopped in mid-charge. I identified myself as Kimmel's intelligence officer at the time, saying that I knew what had happened and why. Before I could finish, Turner came roaring across the room bellowing, "Are you calling me a liar?" He grabbed at my throat. We were stopped from fisticuffs only by the swift intervention of *South Dakota*'s skipper, Captain Emmet P. Forrestel, who parted us. Later I pondered the incongruity of four stripes mixing it up with four stars.

For all his lustrous war record as an amphibious commander, Admiral Turner that evening had lived up to his other reputation as an opinionated, stubborn fool. There he was, hanging Kimmel by his fingernails, when the truth—as we both well knew—was that Turner had failed to relay to the fleet commander at Pearl Harbor the vital intelligence that might have averted the disaster. Despite his loudmouthed bluster in the wardroom of *South Dakota,* the former director of war plans was later obliged to admit under oath that his assertion was wrong,[1] but he was never to concede his own errors of judgment. It was already too late to rectify the harm done to Admiral Kimmel. His reputation had already been sacrificed in order to placate the wartime outrage of the American people and save the prestige of United States military leadership.

Turner's behavior was unforgiving—and unforgivable. One of the first things I learned on entering the navy was the primary principle of command, that an officer bears personal responsibility for ensuring that his orders are carried out. Turner, instead, blamed his subordinates, maintaining that they had assured him that Admiral Kimmel was "receiving the same decrypted information" available in Washington.[2] A simple check of his own signal logs would have revealed that we had *not* received some of the most essential and important pieces of intelligence that became available to the navy department during four months preceding the Japanese attack.

Military commanders seldom if ever receive enough intelligence—evaluated information on which they can rely when making strategic and tactical decisions. Yet, by any objective measure, Admiral Kimmel was cheated. Intelligence is always a matter of trying to assemble a jigsaw puzzle with missing pieces. But my task in the weeks before 7 December 1941 had been frustrated because Washington had failed to relay to us vital pieces of the intelligence jigsaw that we at Pearl Harbor were still missing. Had those pieces arrived in time, they would have provided us with clues that the impending Japanese attack was a probability rather than a remote possibility.[3]

We had no way of knowing that much additional information was being denied us.[4]

I had been personally assured in May 1941 by the office of naval intelligence in Washington that we would be sent every piece of pertinent information. So when I eventually learned the truth, I was shocked at the extent to which we had been shortchanged. That discovery raised serious questions in my mind about who in the navy department knew what and when they knew it, questions that had to remain publicly unanswered until the declassification of wartime intelligence records made it possible to break the inside secret story of Pearl Harbor and Midway.

Intelligence is a perishable commodity. Battles are won and lost and campaigns decided often on the basis of which side is most proficient in the use of intelligence—that is, the acquisition, evaluation, *and* dissemination of military information in time for commanders to act upon it. No matter how accurate the information, it is militarily useless if it is not *made available* soon enough for command decisions.

The Japanese attack on Pearl Harbor succeeded not just because of their audacious planning and skillful execution, but also, as we shall see, from a dramatic breakdown in our intelligence process.

That breakdown was related directly to feuding among high-level naval officers in Washington. The 7 December catastrophe should have served to quell the feuding and provide a lesson against such failures in the future. It is therefore shocking that, within six months of the Pearl Harbor disaster, continued feuding in Washington almost caused us to lose the tide-turning battle at Midway in June 1942. It is indicative of the extent and seriousness of those failures that the full details in both instances have been so successfully concealed from public scrutiny and understanding for so long.

2

The Undeclared War

WHEN THE IDEA OF a naval career struck me, like most boys I saw myself only on the bridge of a battleship, where a sailor belongs, never deskbound as a pen pusher. The idea surely arose during my early childhood in the river town of Nauvoo, Illinois. Holiday boat trips on the Mississippi with my grandfather heightened my early nautical interests. Like most aspiring midshipmen, I could not imagine swerving from the notion that a sailor's proper place is at sea. The gallant image persisted during academy years, and after my difficulties in getting there, I was not about to buck tradition.

In high school my favorite writing topic was Annapolis and the naval academy. My determination to go there was influenced by natural rivalry with my older brother, Clyde, who always talked of going to West Point. Each November we bet part of our meager allowance on the Army-Navy football game. Army usually won, but that did not put me off the navy. When Clyde enlisted in the army right out of high school, I determined to get into the naval academy as soon as possible.

On the recommendation of our congressman, a family friend, and a customer on my newspaper route, I took the competitive examination in 1920. I was seventeen, a year younger than the four other Illinois candidates. It wasn't very competitive because the others failed to show up. All that I had to do was to pass the written exam, or at least that's what I thought. Naval regulations also required a physical examination, however, and I was rejected for being underweight. I went to Washington to apply in person for a waiver so that I could try again.

While I was sitting in an office of the navy department waiting for them to straighten out my qualifications, an old pharmacist's mate gave me some good advice. "Son, I've got a word for you," he said. "They aren't going to do anything about this until your congressman calls to say he'd like to have them fix it. I've seen your report, you just haven't got your weight up. Before you take the physical again, eat a few pounds of bananas."

So I telephoned my father, who telephoned our congressman, and then things happened. I ate a dozen or so bananas, put on two and a half pounds, took another physical examination, and got the waiver.

I expected discipline and regimentation at Annapolis and was not disappointed, but it was a far cry from Illinois home life. I became acquainted with classmates from all parts of the country: Tommy Dyer from Kansas, Tom Huckins from Wisconsin, Dan McCallum from Idaho, and Bertie Watts from Pennsylvania all were friends throughout undergraduate years, and our careers became interwoven in intelligence. Also in our class of 1924 was the bookish Hanson G. Baldwin who left the navy to make his name as a historian and military correspondent for *The New York Times*. A year ahead of us was Arleigh Burke, who wrestled in school as a lightweight but was an unquestioned heavyweight in wartime destroyer squadrons, and went on to become an outstanding chief of naval operations.

Younger and smaller than most of the class, I did not go in for athletics any more than was necessary, but Dyer and I were both in the Radiator Club, which, instead of engaging in strenuous sports, was devoted to sitting around on chilly days on warm radiators swapping dirty stories. Dramatics interested me, and being slight of build, I won a lead role as the vamp in one of the annual productions. Classmates never let me forget it. But as it turned out the role playing was good experience for a couple of counterintelligence assignments later in my naval career.

We all learned how to give orders, the hard way, by taking them for three years from upperclassmen, and then having a glorious year of being first classmen ourselves. Among all our varied studies in those four years, one subject never covered was naval intelligence. Surprising as that seems today, when so much emphasis is placed on intelligence, it was never even mentioned in any academy class. Intelligence was something that an aspiring midshipman of my day never thought about. In a navy in which war college tactical courses were largely devoted to refighting World War I engagements, like Jutland with its nineteenth-century principles, intelligence was ignored by officers striving for flag rank.

My first awareness of anything remotely connected with naval intelligence did not come until six months after I was out of the academy. Upon graduation in June 1924 I was delighted and proud to be assigned to duty in battleship *West Virginia*. The following January we steamed into San Francisco Bay with two other new battleships to serve as hosts for the annual visit of Japan's cadet training squadron.

It was at first incongruous to me that we would send three of our newest and biggest battleships as hosts to three old armored cruisers, survivors of the Russo-Japanese War. Then I realized that it was done to overawe and impress our visitors with the might of the United States.

As a lowly ensign I was among the junior officers detailed to escort our opposite numbers, who had just completed four years at Etajima, the Japanese naval academy. I had never met any Japanese. These eager and friendly young men surprised me by their command of English, which they spoke with ease and fluency, not at all in textbook fashion. The few who didn't know English could converse in excellent French. I was embarrassed to realize that not one of our officers could speak a single word of Japanese, and it dawned on me what it means to "lose face." The United States might have more and bigger warships, but I was more impressed by the discovery that the Japanese could communicate in our language.

That did not prevent us from having a good time. My Japanese companion was eager to visit a speakeasy and a nightclub, so I took him to one of each. At the nightclub, he produced from his raincoat pocket a bottle of genuine scotch, literally "just off the boat." This, at the height of the Prohibition era, won the hearts of the nightclub manager and staff, and the visitor from Japan was soon made the center of attention by the entertainers.

By the time the Japanese squadron was steaming out through the Golden Gate, I was writing to the navy department. My brash letter suggested that on such visits we should have someone present who spoke Japanese; and that if there was no such policy there should be. I even volunteered to learn Japanese myself.

Back came an official letter pointing out that there already existed a Japanese language program for officers who had completed five years of sea duty. I later learned that it had been started in 1910 and, after wartime interruption, resumed in 1920, and that an average of two officers a year entered the program, including a marine every third year. Then and there, it became my goal to get into that program. After battleship duty and four years in four-stack destroyer *Chase,* my assignment to the Japanese language program came through in June 1929.

In my youthful enthusiasm, it did not even occur to me that naval intelligence was not a stepping-stone toward advancement. Alternating tours of sea duty with the fleet and staff assignments ashore was still the traditional way up the naval ladder. Intelligence duty was suitable for reservists and dilettantes, but it was just marking time for career officers for whom gunnery and navigation were surer routes to flag rank.

This attitude had prevailed even after World War I had demonstrated how the revolution in communications had changed the nature of military intelligence. Until the development of electrical transmission in the nineteenth century, military orders and reports were sent by couriers or visual signals. Messengers were still being waylaid during our Civil War campaigns, as they had been since the days of the ancient Greeks, for the secrets they carried could have decisive influence on the outcome of battles. The basic principle remained the same when military organizations adopted the new systems of transmission. Telegraphs and telephones were tapped—anyone within range could pick up wireless transmissions—multiplying the opportunities for waylaying secret messages.

In the context of naval operations, radio solved the age-old problem of how to direct widely scattered forces at sea, which, until World War I, had relied on flags and scouting vessels for relaying orders and collecting intelligence. But electronic communications introduced new problems. For the first time it became possible for admirals ashore to intervene directly in fleet operations, and complex ciphers and codes were needed to protect radio transmissions from hostile listeners.

Because the terms *cipher* and *code* are not always clearly understood or precisely used, a simple definition of the two words may be appropriate. A rule of thumb used by Captain Wesley A. Wright, one of the navy's noted World War II cryptanalysts, is that the cipher changes the text "letter by letter," and a code makes the change "idea for idea."[1]

As codes and ciphers became valuable adjuncts of communications and intelligence-gathering, there developed a tremendous need and demand for breaking them. There also developed the arcane science of *cryptology* (from the Greek *kryptos,* "hidden," and *logos,* "word"), which deals with methods of secret communications, and *cryptanalysis,* which is its application. Cryptology includes signal security (protecting one's own communications) and signal intelligence (acquiring information by nullifying the enemy's signal security). *Cryptography* is the process of encoding (or enciphering) messages intended to be decoded (or deciphered) only by those to whom they are addressed.

Cipher systems involve cryptographic treatment of textual units of constant and equal length, usually single letters, but sometimes pairs or three-letter sets. The two basic classes of ciphers are those created by transposition (rearrangement of the plain-text letters without changing their identity), and those created by substitution (replacement of the plain-text letters without change in their sequence). When number groups are used in substitution, a further variation of the system can be achieved by the superimposition of a set of prearranged additives, making the solution more complicated for eavesdroppers.

In diplomatic and military communications, where secrecy is of the utmost importance, a message may be protected by a combination of encoding and enciphering, or superencipherment. Identical code books listing the equivalent number or letter groups are held by the legitimate communicators, who also possess the "key," which identifies the method they are using to encipher their message. Before a third party can break into their communications, the key used to encipher their code must first be identified. The more frequently it is changed, the more secure the system of communications.

Even when the contents of an intercepted communication cannot be read by cryptanalysis, it can be made to yield important intelligence by means of a process called traffic analysis. This involves making deductions from an analysis of messages transmitted—on the basis of from whom each message was sent and to whom it is addressed—a process that often does not require knowledge of the cipher key since the originator and designee are usually transmitted in a simple code to facilitate identification. Further, radio direction finding can pinpoint the location of transmission, and other factors such as a transmission's length, its routing, and the volume of traffic can also yield important clues to the general nature and contents and precedence of a message.

The Japanese navy has the distinction of having first made use of radio traffic analysis as a technique in war. In 1904, during the Russo-Japanese War, radio-equipped Japanese warships intercepted a message sent by a squadron of the czar's Vladivostok fleet, which was cruising secretly south of Tokyo Bay.[2]

World War I proved that, even with modern technology, there was still nothing like "intercepting the messenger," be it human courier or invisible radio waves. "We found, in the enemy's communications, information which was always truthful, obtained without risk of human lives, without expense, with a speed and surety that no other intelligence organization was able to equal" was the evaluation of Colonel Marcel Givierge, chief of the French army's cipher division in World War I.[3]

The interception and breaking of a potential enemy's codes and ciphers therefore became a vital intelligence function. The advantage of such "radio intelligence" is that it is timely, pertinent, and reliable, and very cost-effective. This was attested to by the successes of World War I. The Russians solved the German naval cipher in 1914, the British applied radio intelligence in the 1916 naval clash at Jutland, and in 1918 the U.S. Army broke into German military communications with a captured trench code.[4]

World War I demonstrated that the key to effective radio intelligence was detailed knowledge of an enemy's communications systems based on analysis of the frequencies, the designators of the addressee and originator of messages, the transmission routines followed, and even the idiosyncrasies of individual radio operators. To be effective such activity requires an extensive and strategically located series of listening posts for interception and direction finding, in addition to the assembly of a team of analysts skilled enough to recognize when an enemy might be sending deceptive messages.[5]

The arcane business of electronic interception, deception, and code breaking was born in World War I, and had its adolescence in World War II when it became known as communications intelligence, or comint. During this time, we were dependent on human ears to pick out radio signals. Enormous applications of time and brainpower were applied to break ciphers and analyze traffic when intercepted messages defied our best efforts to break through their secrets.

After World War II, with the onset of the cold war, comint became sigint (signals intelligence), a term that includes all forms of electronic intelligence emissions, including radar. Today, satellites are used like giant electronic ears hovering out in space providing surveillance of the vast range of global radio transmissions. Some of the world's most powerful computers are employed to sift through the mass of electronic traffic and penetrate the increasingly elaborate cipher systems with which countries try to guard their most sensitive communications.

For all practical purposes the history of American comint activity begins with our entry into World War I, when codes and ciphers were naïve by current standards. Prior to that time neither the army nor the navy had any organization for intercepting foreign communications. The army set up our first organized code-breaking office in June 1917 under Herbert O. Yardley. This cipher bureau, called MI-8, worked with the British and French through the end of the war. Cryptographic techniques were primitive: Ciphers were broken and code values recovered entirely by hand. Starting with just 3 assistants, by 1918 Yardley's staff had increased to 150, with an annual budget of $100,000.[6] To provide suitable recruits for cipher work, 80 officers were sent to Aurora, Illinois, for a crash course of study under William F. Friedman, then in his mid-twenties and already an acknowledged genius at cryptanalysis (he invented the word), who was on the staff of the nearby Riverbank Laboratories. This scientific hothouse had been founded by George Fabyan, an eccentric millionaire, one of whose consuming passions was to demonstrate by comparative word analysis that Francis Bacon was the real Shakespeare.[7]

Russian-born Friedman had joined the Riverbank community as a geneticist but his interests had moved to code breaking and cryptography, which became his life work. The first demonstration of his innate ability came when he worked out the solution to the British army's so-called Plett cipher from a few sample messages. Our army was sufficiently impressed by his ability that it commissioned him a lieutenant and sent him to France in June 1918, where he helped provide the solution of a major German army cipher in time to contribute to the final Allied victory on the western front. When the war ended he returned to Riverbank in April 1919, but by the beginning of 1921 the army had lured him back as a civilian cryptographer with the war department. In Washington, Friedman provided the new code system for the military staff, so when the Signal Intelligence Service was created ten years later in 1931, he was the natural choice to be its first director.[8]

Although radio intelligence had proved its intelligence potential long before 1918, our navy was slow in entering the field. We relied on Great Britain and the pioneering naval code-breakers of the Admiralty led by Captain William R. "Blinker" Hall. Our only comint activity had been to establish a direction-finding network along the Atlantic seaboard to track U-boats. We did, however, build up a code and signal section, an integrated security organization for the compilation, production, distribution, and safeguarding of our own codes and ciphers.

Not until the closing stage of World War I was President Wilson finally persuaded by the secretary of the navy to set up a $100,000 fund for code-breaking operations. The fund—worth more than $1 million in present-day terms—was so secret that it was deposited in a local Washington bank to the personal credit of the director of naval intelligence. Checkbook stubs were the only records kept, and the balance was transferred to the personal custody of each succeeding head of naval intelligence in order to conceal the fund from congressional scrutiny. There was strong distaste at the time for involvement in what many officers regarded as an ungentlemanly profession.[9]

That secret slush fund continued to support our naval code-breaking activities for more than a decade, and it still amounted to $65,000 in June 1931. An acting director of ONI, Captain William Baggaley, stricken by a fit of conscience, prompted by then Secretary of State Henry L. Stimson's 1929 sanction against "reading other gentlemen's mail,"[10] returned the balance to the Treasury. One naval cipher expert characterized the move as "a great mistake," saying, "It is a safe bet that one year hence when he leaves, his reliefs for many years to come will bemoan the fact that their hands have been tied by lack of funds to prosecute urgent secret tasks."[11]

Yardley's postwar cipher bureau, which was financed by the army and the State Department, had to move out of the District of Columbia because the State Department funds could not legally be spent there. It moved to New York City and set up shop as our first permanent code-breaking organization in a four-story brownstone just off Fifth Avenue, and became known as the Black Chamber. Yardley's first major assignment was to break Japanese codes, since we were interested in that country's naval expansion. Yardley had been instrumental in maneuvering Japan into accepting the inferior naval status imposed by the 1921 Washington Naval Conference. By reading Tokyo's secret telegraphic instructions to its delegation, the Americans knew the limits allowed the Japanese representatives and were able to maneuver them into accepting the end of a 5:5:3 capital-ship tonnage ratio with Britain and the United States. This American advantage was the equivalent of knowing the opponent's cards in a poker game, and it enabled us to win an agreement to a naval limitation treaty that sank more battleships than any fleet engagement in history.

In May 1929, Yardley's New York establishment was closed after Secretary of State Stimson's injunction against reading other people's mail. The military intelligence division of the army, which had been subcontracting its cryptanalytic work to Yardley, now transferred this work and responsibility to the chief signal officer. Civilian cryptanalyst Friedman was placed in charge of a new organization, the Signal Intelligence Service, which was to set up to combine the duties of the defunct cipher bureau with those of the Cipher Compilation Service. This was one forerunner of our present-day Armed Forces Security Agency and the National Security Agency.

While the United States continued to make steady progress following a slow start, the Japanese failed to maintain the early advantage gained by being the first nation to apply comint, and after World War I Japan found herself at a complete disadvantage in both diplomatic negotiations and naval intelligence. It was not until 1923, after her Kwantung army in Manchuria became concerned about the Soviet threat to the extensive Japanese mining and railway concessions in China, that Japan undertook a serious comint effort.

Captain Jan Kowalewski, the Polish army staff's code expert, was invited to Tokyo to give a series of lectures on cryptology. (It is interesting to note that Britain also benefited from Polish cryptographic help that contributed to the breaking of the principal German cipher systems in World War II, which relied on the so-called Enigma machine.) His select group of students consisted of six army and three naval officers, one of whom was Commander Risaburo Itō, a naturally gifted code breaker.[12]

While serving as communications officer with the Japanese Mediterranean force attached to the Royal Navy in World War I, Itō had single-handedly broken the Playfair code system used by the British allies as an army field cipher. That success persuaded the Japanese to upgrade the security of their own code systems. Itō was also to translate Yardley's *The American Black Chamber,* which became an instant best seller in Japan. Later, as head of the communications section of the navy general staff, he would play an instrumental part in designing the "Red" and subsequently the "Purple" machines that were to be used for enciphering Japan's most secret diplomatic traffic.

The natural Japanese predilection for secrecy was greatly magnified in the armed services, where the zeal for security so dominated communications intelligence as to severely hamper its development. The first organized *tsushintai* (radio intercept unit) was established in the navy ministry in 1929. This "special chamber" consisted of Lieutenant Commander Kyujino Nakasugi (a Kowalewski student), two other officers, and three typists. Not until the mid-1930s was there any large-scale expansion of radio intelligence work in the Japanese navy, and even six years later the section was being run by only nine naval staff officers. The entire field of intelligence in general, despite its importance, was traditionally a hushed subject in the imperial navy. There was no mention, let alone classroom discussion, of it at the naval academy, and career officers usually stayed away from intelligence duty when they could, as it was not considered useful to advancement.[13]

During these early stages most of the officers assigned to comint had been career men. In the growing wartime establishment, however, the majority of the staff were *yobigakusei* (reserve officers) fresh from colleges, most of whom had majored in foreign languages. By the end of the war, women and nisei were being recruited. When it came to communications intelligence, most regular officers were unaware even of the words for it—*tsūshin chōhō*. The secret clique excluded outsiders to the extent that it was virtually unknown to all but those who worked in it and the very limited number of recipients of its product, who probably numbered no more than a dozen or so in the entire navy.

This obsession with security was not peculiar to the Japanese navy. It also impeded the development of radio intelligence and the proper understanding and use of it in our own navy. Nevertheless, thanks to the dedication and foresight of successive postwar ONI directors, by 1929 our navy finally began to catch up with the British in realizing the importance of communications interception and code breaking. This progress had been achieved through strenuous efforts in cryptanalysis, financed with ONI's secret slush fund, and occasionally requiring resort to burglary. Such involvements made the whole operation suspect in the eyes of many conservative naval officers, especially those who lacked experience in and understanding of intelligence.

As codes and ciphers became increasingly sophisticated, complicating the cryptanalytic efforts of every nation, there was a practical limit to the amount of effort that could be expended in attempting to decipher intercepted traffic. The point was reached where it became desirable, whenever possible, to circumvent the laborious cryptanalysis process by surreptitious means—theft. There was risk involved in such "black bag jobs," as the stealing of foreign codes was dubbed, but the saving in manhours spent at conventional code breaking justified the risk.

In the decade before the State Department's injunction against reading other nations' code traffic, our navy had become very proficient in this less than gentlemanly activity. In the spring of 1920 the secret ONI fund had financed a major undercover operation that involved not just one but a whole series of break-ins at the Japanese consulate in New York City. The FBI reported that a Japanese naval officer was masquerading there as the vice-consul. A counterespionage squad picked the locks of his office door and a combination safe.

The operation required more than one visit. It was slow going with the cameras of that day to photograph the voluminous code book of the Japanese fleet. It took even longer for ONI to find a reliable and discreet linguist to translate the book. Eventually the director persuaded Dr. Emerson J. Haworth and his wife, both Japanese linguists, to take on the mammoth task. They were paid from the slush fund, which also provided special kana (Japanese syllabary) dictionaries, and grammar books.[14]

The Haworths spent nearly four years translating the code book. That material was updated with more photos taken in a second round of break-ins at the New York consulate in 1926 and 1927. Further translation and retyping resulted in two manageable volumes, bound in red buckram, from which the Japanese code acquired its American color designation, the Red code.

This Red code book was handed over to the Code and Signal Section of the office of naval communications, which managed signal traffic and maintained the security of our own codes and ciphers. In 1924 that duty was expanded to include an effort to break foreign codes and ciphers. Until that time our navy had had no organized code-breaking program. What began as a one-man unit became the nucleus of an operation that was to grow into a radio intelligence organization of more than five thousand in World War II.

A cryptographic section was established late in 1923, not primarily for the purpose of deciphering codes and ciphers of foreign nations, but to analyze our own and suggest improvements. Its original function was "to work side by side with the code desk in a sort of advisory capacity." But in January 1924, Lieutenant Laurence F. Safford was appointed as head of a cryptographic section that comprised one cryptanalyst and two typists. This little group soon realized the possibility offered by the Red Book and began work on intercepted Japanese radio traffic, with "remarkable success."[15] To disguise its true function it was known simply as the research desk.

Safford, who was destined to become the "father" of naval cryptography, was an earnest character whose most remarkable feature was his eyes, which were constantly darting back and forth, as if watching out for some danger. He had been plucked by the sheerest chance of the naval bureaucracy from a humdrum command of a Yangtze River mine-sweeper. Although he had ranked fifteenth in the 1916 class at Annapolis, the communications establishment would always look upon him as an outsider because he did not fit the starched image of a smart naval academy officer. Safford's uniform was always rumpled, as if he had slept in it. According to Mrs. Eunice Rice Willson, a longtime member of the OP-20-G staff, "His hair seemed permanently to be standing on end as if he had been scratching his head in perplexity. He spoke in little bursts, unconnected phrases that unnerved his listeners and brought universal admiration from us for his secretary's ability to produce a coherent memorandum from his dictation."[16] But Safford's natural flair for mathematics and affinity for mechanical devices made him an effective promoter of the navy's nascent code-breaking efforts. He acquired the affectionate nickname "Saffo" and his staff took pride in their boss. "A mad genius" whose eccentricities, according to one of his staff, caused many to laugh and underestimate his abilities, he nevertheless had a "single-minded devotion to duty."[17]

While Safford quickly discovered an innate talent for cryptography, his introduction and grounding in that arcane science was provided by his assistant, Miss Agnes Meyer. She was an enigmatic but brilliant crypt-analyst, who was thirty-two and working as a code clerk in the navy department in 1921 when she solved a sample cipher that cryptologist Edward H. Hebern had considered unbreakable.

Hebern was so impressed by her solution that in 1923 he hired the lady away for his new code-machine business in California. Within a year she left Hebern's employ, married Michael B. Driscoll, a Washington attorney, and was back with the navy, initiating Safford into the mysteries of cryptology. A woman in a man's world, the patrician "Miss Aggie," as friends still called her, was tall, slender, quiet, and extremely dedicated. She not only trained most of the leading naval cryptanalysts of World War II, but they were all agreed that none exceeded her gifted accomplishments in the business. Injuries sustained in a bad auto accident in 1937 required her to use a cane for the rest of her life, but she continued to work miracles, as we shall see, in breaking Japanese and German codes and ciphers throughout World War II.[18]

Safford's tiny clandestine outfit, located in room 1621 of the old navy department building, was charged with the highly sensitive task of using ONI's pilfered code book to open a new source of intelligence on the Japanese navy. The possession of the imperial navy's most secret cryptographic system, in turn, became justification for ONC to encourage Safford's outfit to develop cryptanalytic techniques, and establish a Pacific network of radio intercept stations. With the indulgence of both the director of naval communications and the director of naval intelligence, the research desk thrived under Safford. There was little concern for the day when its jealous parents might vie for their offspring's loyalty.

Safford emphasized the importance of the Red Book as the foundation of our navy's penetration of Japanese naval secrets. "We had only to solve the ciphers used with this code in order to decrypt messages," he wrote. "If we had been faced at the beginning with the task of solving the cipher plus an unknown code, it might have been too much for us and, at least, it would have slowed our early efforts."[19] The daily work load was enough to keep the small staff fully occupied, but there were additional problems. Safford still had to extend an intercept network, develop working methods, acquire a staff of trained cryptanalysts, and find more linguists. He also had to plan against the day when Japan would introduce new ciphers. To acquire further cryptographers, Safford ingeniously circulated practice cryptograms and other puzzles throughout the navy. Applicants who submitted the best solutions were earmarked for duty in his research section as the organization grew.

Safford's day-to-day burdens were eased in 1925 when Lieutenant (j.g.) Joseph J. Rochefort was assigned to the research desk. The newcomer was a lean, intense man whose gentle manner belied a fierce tenacity and independent cast of mind that resulted from competing as an

outsider in a navy dominated by Annapolis men. Unlike most of his contemporaries, Rochefort was not a naval academy graduate, but had enlisted in the navy during World War I after attending the University of
California. He made a fine partner for Safford and both officers learned
the code-breaking skills of the insightful Miss Aggie.

Under the stringent "Manchu" rules of the day, which required officers to alternate duty ashore with service afloat, Safford was sent back
to sea in February 1926, and Rochefort took his place. Before the end of
his first tour, Safford had instituted the first course to train naval officers
in cryptanalysis. One of the earliest students was Ensign Joseph N.
Wenger who recalled as an admiral that he had been selected by his commanding officer because he was the only eligible candidate whose family
lived in Washington and could therefore "afford to live there on an ensign's pay."[20]

Rochefort was in charge of the research desk when the first Red Japanese naval messages were broken, and it was Miss Aggie who was responsible for the initial solutions of the current Japanese cipher key that
unlocked the code. This was no small achievement, because the two-vol-
ume Red Book contained some 100,000 code groups, with as many as 3
groups assigned to each Japanese word or expression. The Japanese instructions for the code stated that it was never to be used without superencipherment.

When the first solution of the cipher used with the Red Book code
was made in 1926, the Japanese employed only one cipher of a relatively
simple nature and each key remained in effect for several weeks. Each
succeeding cipher, however, grew more complex than its predecessor and
the keys began to be changed more frequently. The keys associated with
specific ciphers were often solved by officers under instruction, but
Rochefort's unit was never able to exploit more than a very small fraction
of the messages, because the navy was so desperately short of Japanese
translators.[21]

Safford had returned from sea duty to take over the helm at the research desk when Rochefort left for Japan in the summer of 1929. By the
following year the unit was ready to monitor Japan's naval exercises. The
grand fleet maneuvers that spring saw virtually every ship in the imperial
navy put to sea. The vast operation was nevertheless managed with such
secrecy that not even our naval attaché in Tokyo had any advance warning. The first indication that "something was up" came on 18 May with a
sudden increase in Japanese radio traffic picked up by Guam, one of our
Pacific listening stations.[22] (Others were at Shanghai, Peking, and
Olongapo or Cavite in the Philippines.) But Washington knew nothing of
the Japanese fleet maneuvers until more than a week later when a courier
suddenly delivered hundreds of radio intercepts.

The inefficiency of prewar American naval communications, tragically
to be repeated in December 1941, found the commandant on Guam ne-

glecting to report the Japanese activity because he assumed ONI was so well informed that he did not need to tell them. He even complained that Washington had failed to alert him in advance of the Japanese maneuvers![23]

Safford seized this heaven-sent opportunity to prove to a skeptical navy department the enormous potential of radio intelligence. All hands turned to on the mass of accumulated traffic. Mrs. Driscoll again made the first significant break in the Red code, and other keys then fell out with comparative ease. Our major problem remained not cryptanalysis but translation, since the unit's only linguist at the time was the venerable Dr. Haworth. Many of the routine messages, however, did not require knowledge of Japanese, and much of that work was done by apprentice cryptanalyst Lieutenant Joseph N. Wenger.

The rich intelligence haul made from the intercepts of Japan's 1930 naval maneuvers was officially compared to "exploring virgin territory" since no one in our navy at the time had any idea of the professional concepts, communication routines, or even the battle tactics of the Japanese fleet.[24] By assembling the decrypts, we were able to learn a great deal about how Japan intended to conduct any naval war against us. The capture of Guam and the Philippines were the subject of early "victory" announcements, and the intercepts revealed a mock air raid on Tokyo from American carriers. Their maneuvers concluded that year with what was proclaimed as the "constructive" defeat of the Pacific Fleet, an indication that even in 1930 the imperial navy already considered itself capable of defeating the U.S. Navy in the western Pacific.[25]

After Captain Royal E. Ingersoll, head of the navy's war plans division, had spent six weeks reconstructing the Japanese order of battle, he made "the most astonishing discovery."[26] Their naval intelligence had apparently succeeded in obtaining a very accurate picture of the latest modifications in our war plan Orange. These were current contingency plans for a Pacific war as rehearsed that year by our military war colleges.

The cryptographic section's code-breaking triumph was communicated to the secretary of the navy in a secret memorandum of 31 January 1931, which claimed that we had achieved "as complete ascendency over the Japanese navy in the matter of radio intelligence as the British navy had over the German navy in the World War."[27] Because of the interdepartmental rivalry already stirring in regard to radio intelligence, however, Captain Harry A. Baldridge, the director of ONI, was not made privy to this vital news. Admiral William V. Pratt, the chief of naval operations, outrageously believed he "could not trust" his subordinate and he warned, *"One suspicion on the part of the Japanese would undo the accomplishment of seven years* [emphasis in original]."[28] What misuse Pratt thought Baldridge might make of the information one can only imagine, but it suggests that a bitter feud was already festering in the navy department.

The United States had won a major victory in what Safford was to call "the undeclared war" against the Japanese.[29] Yet this success sparked another undeclared war at home as a long struggle for control of this valuable new source of intelligence began within the navy department. Nominally the research desk was organizationally under the purview of the office of naval communications, but its raison d'être was exploitaion of Japanese naval communications for intelligence purposes. These were accessible only through the Red Book and Japanese linguists, both of which had been funded entirely by the office of naval intelligence.

While the office of naval intelligence had turned over its Red Book asset to naval communications, it had been "with the agreement and expectation that it [ONI] would be furnished the information obtained by the use of this code."[30] But this expectation was not to be fulfilled. A year after its inception the cryptographic section had become the center of an administrative dispute. Soon after Rochefort took charge of the research desk he noted that "several attempts" were made to bring the section over to the office of naval intelligence. The takeover efforts failed because of the "strong opposition" of the director of naval communications.[31]

The result was that by 1930 naval intelligence was being denied the information obtained from the Japanese fleet exercises, because chief of naval operations Admiral Charles F. Hughes sided with the director of naval communications. The rationale offered for ordering the director of naval communications "to show intercepted messages to him[self] and to no other person" was that Hughes "thought he could not trust his director of naval intelligence."[32]

The necessity for keeping the cryptographic section's work a tight secret was undoubtedly a result of several occasions when the Japanese had changed their codes and ciphers, apparently as a result of becoming suspicious of eavesdropping. According to a 1932 memorandum written by Rochefort to Captain Joseph V. Ogan, the acting director of naval intelligence, "several instances of this sort are a matter of record." Rochefort reported that "one happened while I was in the section and the net result was that one year's work went for naught and we were forced to start over from the beginning."[33]

Rochefort's "personal opinion" on the origins of the feud was that "the Cryptography Section has been and is being used by the officers concerned to further their own ends."[34] Nine years before the Japanese attack on Pearl Harbor this warning had identified one of the principal factors that caused us to be so badly surprised at Pearl Harbor: "Instead of handling the information obtained in such a way that the Navy will benefit, they are prone to handle it in order to obtain personal recognition."[35]

The astonishing decision that denied naval intelligence direct access to our most important source of intelligence about the Japanese navy was not rescinded until 1933, when it was agreed that radio intelligence would continue to come under the control of the office of naval communications "at least in peacetime."[36] This made it inevitable that when war clouds began gathering over the Pacific the old feud would be revived. When the war plans division waded in to make the struggle for control of communications intelligence a three-way fight during 1941, its consequences were to contribute to the disaster of 7 December.

3

"Keep the Dogs Yapping"

U NTIL I REPORTED to the flagship in December 1940, I was unaware that the Pacific Fleet had never had a full-time intelligence
officer. The job was normally assigned as additional duty to another member of the staff. To my further astonishment, I found that the
sturdy safe built into battleship *Pennsylvania*'s bulkhead as repository for
the fleet's most secret documents contained just eighteen file folders; and
most of them were empty!

One contained several newspaper clippings from the early 1920s on
South Africa, and three held military dossiers about France, totally unrelated to the Pacific. In only one did I discover *any* information about
Japan. This was ONI Monograph 49, which, although kept meticulously
up to date, provided only the broadest of generalities about the imperial
navy. It had languished in the safe for years protected by its red-stamped
cover, which read, TO BE REMOVED ONLY IN THE EVENT OF WAR.

The discovery that the Pacific Fleet command had been given no up-
to-date military information on Japan was a major disappointment, to say
the least. It was my duty as fleet intelligence officer to brief the commander in chief, Admiral James O. Richardson, on the movements, dispositions, and intentions of the Japanese navy in the Pacific. I realized
that, with the worsening relations between Tokyo and Washington, the
lack of adequate intelligence could leave me sitting on a very sharp spike.

The fact that our intelligence cupboard was so bare spurred my efforts
to remedy the appalling situation. In two tours of duty in Japan I had
become convinced that their armed forces were highly trained, and well
informed about us. Their navy would certainly be a formidable adversary
if and when it came to a fight.

My feeling of apprehension about Japan then was similar to what I
had felt eleven years earlier when I arrived at Kōbe for three years of
language study. As I walked down the ship's gangway and onto Japanese

soil for the first time, it was an unsettling, and at the same time an exciting, experience to be in a totally foreign world.

Until that moment my only naval experience even touching on intelligence had consisted of a few weeks spent at the office of naval intelligence a month earlier, being briefed for my language studies. Fortunately, the other naval officer being sent to study Japanese in 1929 was Joseph Rochefort. Our lifelong friendship began that August on board steamer *President Adams* when the long Pacific crossing gave me the chancé to get acquainted with him, his attractive wife, and their infant son. Rochefort was one of only three married officers ever chosen for language study in Japan; his selection came after he had completed a tour of duty as executive officer of destroyer *Macdonough* based in San Diego following two years in the Code and Signal Section in Washington.

Throughout our three years of study in Japan, Rochefort never once mentioned his involvement with the navy's secret code-breaking operations. Not knowing of his experience with Japanese codes and communications, I was surprised at his apparent familiarity with the country. My knowledge of Japan and its people was extremely sketchy. From a tourist magazine I had learned that a woman's hairstyle indicated her marital status. This wasn't much, but it was of vital interest to a young man starting a three-year stay in that strange country.

In Tokyo I reported to Captain Joseph Vance Ogan, the bluff naval attaché. "Layton," he snapped, "I don't know anything about this language, but I understand it's difficult." Looking me square in the eye, he cautioned, "You have only two duties to perform: One, study and master the Japanese language; two, stay out of trouble. If you fail in either, I'll send you home in the next ship. You are not to engage in any spying or other espionage activity. Don't think of yourself as some Nathan Hale or anything like that. Keep your nose clean. Oh, yes, payday is once a month. Other than that, I don't want to see you. Good-bye."

These words were echoed by his assistant, Lieutenant Commander Arthur H. McCollum, who was to supervise our language instruction. He had been born in Japan, and had completed the language course five years earlier, so I took seriously his warning never to "engage in anything that could be construed as intelligence activity." McCollum was a stocky, affable man, the kind who would give a newcomer a cold dry martini and add a warm invitation to dinner.

I appreciated such kindnesses because prewar Japan had a mania about spies, and a foreign naval officer could be very lonely there. The lengths to which the Japanese went to prevent espionage were evident in the extensive areas around military and naval bases designated "fortified zones." On the sandy shore of Tokyo Bay, I was dumbfounded to see at the monument of Commodore Matthew C. Perry a badly done sign, in "Jap-lish," reading PHOTOGRAPHY NO BECAUSE HERE. We were told that any picture of the monument might include beaches that could be used in an amphibious landing.

This national sense of diligence was embodied in the person of our language instructor and closest Japanese contact, Naoe Naganuma, an ambitious young Japanese scholar, our *sensei*—"teacher." He introduced us to the complex language the way a child is taught, through hearing. This was relatively painless, since Japanese is one of the easier languages to comprehend in simple spoken form, although no modern language is more difficult to read and write. The writing, which used Chinese characters, was adopted in Japan and superimposed upon the independently developed spoken language. Each character, or *kanji* (literally, "Chinese ideograph"), has two or more pronunciations in Japanese.

After we were able to understand a little Japanese, Naganuma had us go to a movie house showing American silent films. There a *benshi*—movie interpreter—gave the gist in colloquial Japanese, speaking from a dais adjacent to the screen. Conversation became much easier for us after hearing these shows repeated time after time.

When we had a basic grasp of the language, we went to live away from the capital for a while. My choice was the isolated town of Beppu, in the Kyūshū region; it was four hundred miles southwest of Tokyo, across the Inland Sea. Foreigners, like the Japanese themselves, were kept under constant official scrutiny from the ubiquitous "police box." Nobody passed by without recognition, and it always seemed that the police looked for any opportunity to blackmail foreigners.

Even in remote Beppu I had a "personal" spy who not only dogged my tracks but also pestered my servant, and became a real nuisance. If I went for a walk, my Japanese shadow followed. After a time I began harassing him by going into bars and leaving before he had finished his beer. Then one day I confronted him: "Stop pestering me, and I'll not leave the bar until you finish your beer. But don't hang around my house." The bargain appealed to him, as a beer drinker, and he was less of a bother after that.

While I was living in Beppu, if the Japanese fleet happened to anchor in the spacious harbor it was impossible for me not to observe naval activities, which I did with great interest. The crews came ashore with artillery for exercises, charging up and down the mountains above the beach. It left me with the indelible impression that the Japanese never rest.

Whenever the fleet was in I played a vicarious sort of game with the Japanese officers in the local geisha houses. It was the custom for the proprietor to present an *akagami* (literally, "red paper") naming all available *geisha* ("talented persons") in order of their popularity. I knew that if an officer selected a girl who was already engaged, her patron would have to pay double if he chose to keep her more than an hour. So I would request all of the most popular girls, knowing that they would be busy, in each case causing the patron's bill to be doubled. It always tickled the geisha to see my ruse in action, and they squealed with delight.

My favorite geisha was Ko-ume ("Little Plum"), an excellent conversationalist, full of modern slang, who gave enjoyable company and inexpensive conversation instruction. Occasionally, however, a Japanese officer would *akagami* me by asking for her. It would then cost me double to talk with her after the first hour, but it increased my popularity with Ko-ume.

Such antics with foreigners became noticeably less popular, and suspicion of Americans increased markedly in 1931, after an unsuccessful attempt on the life of Prime Minister Yuko Hamaguchi by ultranationalist Japanese societies. These groups included many junior naval officers who reacted with violence to the government's failure to achieve an increase in capital-ship construction, whereby Japan's battleship strength was constrained by treaty to 60 percent of the tonnage ratio of the American and British fleets.

The nationalists gained support, and popular hostility toward the United States increased after publication of *The American Black Chamber*.[1] Yardley's account revealed how he had apparently tricked Japan into accepting a position of naval inferiority at the Washington Naval Conference ten years earlier. Throughout June, Japanese newspaper headlines blazed with the author's amazing claim that the American government had read thousands of secret official Japanese messages since 1917. Yardley had exacted his revenge for being put out of a job two years early by the State Department's temporary code-breaking ban by revealing details of American cryptanalytic activities. Existing laws made it impossible for the government to prosecute its erstwhile master code breaker, and he profited handsomely from his revelations.

Japan's foreign ministry, which had also contributed to his enrichment, would have been glad to see Yardley tried and sentenced. A secret memorandum circulated within the ministry denounced the book's publication as "a flagrant act of bad faith."[2] It condemned not the United States government, but Yardley himself because the previous year Japan's ambassador in Washington had paid him seven thousand dollars for copies of the Black Chamber cables and methods. The secret bargain had included a stipulation that Yardley would make no public revelation of how the Japanese government had been tricked into the unpopular disarmament straitjacket.

The real cost of Yardley's escapade was not just that it caused the moderate Japanese government to lose face but that he had revealed very precisely how we had broken Tokyo's secret cables. Alerted to American code-breaking successes, the Japanese became more secretive than ever. Not only did they intensify their own code security, but they made their naval call signs more complex by assigning their warships more letters and changing these identifiers more frequently. They were also stimulated to renewed assaults on American cipher traffic.

Our naval systems then became a special target. The Japanese had learned a great deal about our call signs and shortwave transmission systems beginning in 1926 when light cruiser *Yubari* and tanker *Sata* had shadowed our annual naval maneuvers. They had discovered that we had shifted our traffic from medium- to shortwave radio, and they had valuable clues about our fleet organization, call signs, and communication techniques.

Moreover, I saw at first-hand how the furor over Yardley's exploits had increased Japanese xenophobia. Democracy in Japan was already being severely tested in 1932, my final year of language study, as attacks mounted against western-style politicians in the Diet. On 18 September 1931 headstrong generals of the Kwantung army in Manchuria engineered an "incident" on the Japanese railway line at Mukden. Blaming it on the Chinese Nationalists, they used it as an excuse to begin a military take-over of the northern province.

While the League of Nations fumed impotently against Japanese aggression, the Kwantung army moved swiftly to occupy the whole of Manchuria. Secretary of State Stimson called for sanctions, but President Hoover shied from "sticking pins in tigers."[3] Without United States support, the international move against Japanese aggression in China foundered, giving encouragement to other would-be aggressors such as Hitler and Mussolini.

Undeterred by this barrage of diplomatic paper bullets, Japan's mainland adventure accelerated when her naval units moved to occupy the international port of Shanghai in January 1932. Two months later Manchuria became a "made in Japan" puppet state, Manchukuo. It was not enough, however, to prevent the May assassination of Premier Tsuyoshi Inukai. His moderate cabinet had not moved swiftly enough for the ultra-nationalists in its Manchurian takeover. Succeeding cabinets in Tokyo were committed to supporting the smoldering mainland conflict and the rising mood of military belligerency.

The ominous trends were forcefully impressed on Ambassador Joseph Clark Grew, who had arrived in Tokyo in June 1932 during the final months of my language studies. Grew was an old-school diplomat whose qualifications for the Japan post included a visit there as a child. His wife was a descendant of Commodore Matthew C. Perry, who had successfully opened the door to American-Japanese diplomatic relations in the 1850s.

Notwithstanding his credentials, our new ambassador was not even accorded common courtesy at his maiden public speech in Tokyo, presented to the annual dinner of the America-Japan Society. I was as shocked as Grew must have been by the vice-president's introductory remarks. They were the most insulting words of welcome I have ever heard. He concluded with an abusive demand for "direct answers to my questions on U.S.-Japanese relations, and not just another 'hands-across-the-sea' speech."

Grew earned my instant admiration and lasting respect by his deft response, which he delivered with dignity and incredible restraint. He began by saying that when he was a child, a friend had thrown a firecracker at him which had impaired his hearing. "So, since I could not hear anything the vice-president said," he told the audience, "I will not be able to respond to any of his remarks." Grew then returned to his prepared "hands-across-the-sea" speech. It was received with sustained applause by all the Americans and most of the Japanese, for whom rudeness to invited guests is an unpardonable breach of etiquette.

In February 1933, after Japan responded to a sustained chorus of international condemnation by walking out of the League of Nations, Ambassador Grew minced no words in reporting his frank estimate of the national mood. "The military themselves, and the public through military propaganda, are prepared to fight rather than surrender to moral or other pressures from the West," he cabled Washington.[4] When Japan left the league, she did not relinquish control of Germany's former Pacific islands that had been mandated to her "peaceful" custody after World War I.

In the internal upheavals that set Japan on the road to war, I had my own brush with the rising tide of ultranationalist violence. The date, 15 May 1932, is clear in my memory as the night Premier Inukai was assassinated. And that evening I was in Tokyo's Florida Dance Hall. I was standing at the bar having a beer when a Japanese tough swaggered up and deliberately knocked over my glass. The other patrons turned to see my reaction. "You would do well to learn your manners," I said, and ordered another beer.

When it was served, the bully, still at my side, spit in the glass. Infuriated, I whacked him a blow that sent him sprawling. "Do you want to fight now or later?" I challenged, but he just lay there, stunned. So I dropped my calling card on him and went on my way.

Next morning, to my surprise, the police came to my home asking about the incident with a mug shot of a man named Okamura. "You mean, that gangster at the Florida Dance Hall? Sure, I saw him there yesterday evening." They were trying to connect him with the previous night's assassination of the prime minister. As it turned out, I was the bully's alibi, and he later sent me a note of thanks. It occurred to me that my new gangster "friend" might be a useful source of intelligence, but I had been warned against playing spy. After this brush with the authorities I was careful to avoid any further such adventures during my last six months of language study.

In September 1932 I received orders to report for duty at ONI upon completion of my studies, but that was suddenly changed by a cable in early October ordering me to temporary duty in Peiping (the Nationalist name for Peking from 1928 to 1949) as assistant naval attaché at the American legation.

In the past several months the Japanese legation guard had twice marched out of their area (contrary to international rules) on pretext of conducting "night maneuvers," hoping to provoke an incident that would provide an excuse for occupying the city. Our legation had protested the violation of protocol, but the Japanese excuse was that they had no one who spoke English. I was brought in to maintain liaison with the Japanese legation guard and prevent future misunderstandings. As part of this mission, I also called on other legation guard commanders and had an opportunity for intelligence gathering in a trip to Harbin, in Manchuria, which included a visit to the nearby Port Arthur naval base. I made notes of all the details of the docks, repair yards, and facilities, but did not want to carry this compromising information on the rest of my journey. Accordingly, I mailed it by ordinary post from Dairen, addressed to myself in Peiping, affixing something less than the required amount of postage. Having postage due, the package would have to be receipted for by each postal handler until it reached me.

After learning that I played poker, the naval attaché, Cleveland Mc-Cauley, gave me the most unusual intelligence assignment of my career: "I'd like for you to sit in on a particular game of poker players. They are the crew of Marshal Chang Hsueh-liang's personal Ford trimotor airplane. Sometimes the marshal himself joins, so I want you to get acquainted, be a part of the game, and keep your ears open. I have no funds for this sort of thing so you'll have to use your own money. What you win is yours, and what you lose is yours, so play carefully."

I got into the nightly game and became well acquainted with the regulars, who played a wide-open, no-limit game that began about eleven in the evening and went on most of the night. Playing in that kind of game on a lieutenant's $175 per month was bound to be exciting.

When Chang Hsueh-liang, the young Chinese warlord who was shortly to demonstrate his independence of Chiang Kai-shek by kidnapping the generalissimo in 1937, played, there was an unwritten rule: One never called his hand. It was OK to raise him, but never just call him, because he might not have the winning hand, and that would cause him to lose face. Then he would be uncomfortable. That taught me more about "face."

In fact, that taught me to develop a rule of my own: Do not even sit in when the marshal is playing. He bet money as if it were nothing at all. The Chinese yuan was not worth very much, but in huge quantities they mounted up. All gambling debts were paid off the following day, in Chinese currency. One time I was paying off the head of the Peking Power and Light Company, and he "rang out" each coin to make sure that it was not counterfeit. If it did not ring true as he dropped it on the table, he would return it for replacement.

I managed *not* to lose my shirt, and the conversation often provided snippets of information that were always of interest and sometimes of use to my mission. After four months in Peiping, where it became increasingly dangerous for westerners as the fighting in Manchuria spread southward, it was a relief to return to the United States in February 1933.

I reported to ONI in Washington during one of the periodic interoffice spats between ONC and ONI. Successive chiefs of naval operations had appeared to encourage the feuding, figuring that it was beneficial to have the two sections fiercely competitive on the principle of "Keep the dogs yapping; they'll go after the foxes better."

Captain Hayne Ellis, then director of naval intelligence, informed me, "Layton, you were scheduled to go to naval communications, where Japanese linguists are sorely needed. They like to have our language students help out their few civilian translators, but we never get any credit for that, so I'm going to put you to work here. We need a study of Japan's electric power distribution network, showing strategic targets; a bombing plot, in the event of war."

I gathered what little information about Japan was then available at ONI, mostly from maps, and added details recalled from my recent duty. My effort was a beginning, but much more was needed, and the work was continued by others with information gathered on strategic industries and port installations. The power-grid work I started developed into a project that eventually was applied in the 1945 strategic bombing raids on Japan.

During my work on the Japanese power-grid system, the interoffice feud cooled off sufficiently for me to be assigned to naval communications. There I received my first introduction to the mysteries of radio intelligence and the intriguing "black chamber" world of cryptanalysis as a translator in the Code and Signal Section then designated as OP-20-G (naval communications was OP-20 and the cryptographic unit was listed alphabetically as G). My new colleagues were all engaged in quiet but frantic activity in anticipation of that summer's annual Japanese fleet exercise. This was to be a crucial test for our expanding Pacific direction-finding network and our ability to read Japan's new naval code system, which had superseded the Red Book at the end of 1930.

It had taken more than three years of incredible mind-boggling work to break a complex code and cipher system by pure cryptanalysis—the hard way. No other code breakers had ever achieved such a breakthrough. This was the greatest challenge and success in the unostentatious but spectacular career of Mrs. Agnes Meyer Driscoll. At the start she and her colleagues had faced the seemingly impossible task of stripping away a two-tier layer of protective encipherment, and then working out the meanings of a code made up of some eighty-five thousand basic groups.

It was a measure of the bad blood left by the interoffice feud that the director of naval communications was determined not to ask for ONI assistance in the form of black-bag jobs, except as a last resort. Instead, the Blue Book solution was to be a test of his cryptanalysts' ability to confront a wartime situation, in which there would be no Japanese consulate to break into. Miss Aggie and the OP-20-G team had "to work out their own salvation" by compiling the new code from scratch.[5] The code groups had to be solved individually, one at a time. These were, and were then entered in the Blue Book (named for the color of its binding), with solutions added by hand in both Japanese characters (*kanji*) and English translations.

The assault on Blue was led by Mrs. Driscoll, to whom it was an article of faith that any man-made code could be broken by a woman! One of her male colleagues marveled at her quiet ability as a "first-class cryptanalyst."[6] She was the first to spot that a new code had been instituted. This occurred in the fall of 1931, six months after Tommy Dyer, my academy classmate, had joined OP-20-G as a trainee to work on solutions to the old Red code. He was not making very fast progress the day that Mrs. Driscoll looked over his shoulder, took a work sheet from his hand, and remarked, "The reason you're not getting anywhere is because this is a new code."[7] The Red Book was a three-kana system, and she recognized through her uncanny grasp of cryptology that the piece Dyer was working on had to be a four-kana system. Even with this discovery, it was slow, painful, laborious work before the code was broken.

While it went on, Dyer and Lieutenant Joseph Wenger, his immediate superior who had recently returned from running the Manila intercept station, looked for ways to improve the situation. Wenger had learned that Remington-Rand had just produced punch-card equipment that could handle alphabetic information, but investigation showed that it did not fill our requirements.

It was Dyer, however, who after five months of pencil-pushing drudgery, came up with an ingenious labor-saving solution. He found a way to use IBM tabulating machines to ease the burden of sifting through the myriad possible solutions of the code group. This was in the biting days of the Depression but Wenger and Dyer managed to talk the Bureau of Ships into providing five thousand dollars to rent the IBM equipment. They were also able to hire two key-punch operators, and things began looking up.

After ten years of pencil-pushing, Mrs. Driscoll was initially unenthusiastic about having her task mechanized until the breakthrough into the Japanese navy's Blue system came in September 1931 after she had worked out the key to the cipher's principal transposition. By then it was clear that although it was a two-part code unlike the predecessor, it used essentially the same vocabulary and phraseology as the old Red Book. The use of the IBM tabulating machine made it easier to keep track of changing cipher keys and speeded up penetration of new systems. Long before the introduction of computers, the sorting techniques that Dyer devised and pioneered enabled the United States to forge ahead of Britain in cryptology; it earned him the accolade "the father of machine cryptanalysis."[8]

In spite of the growing application of machine analysis, however, human errors such as repeated transmissions of the same message still produced the fastest code breaks. "We found we could always trust the Japanese themselves to do something that would assist us in the solutions of their systems," Safford asserted. *"They never failed us!"*[9]

Our experience in breaking the Japanese Blue code was a lesson to us of what is likely to happen if great care is not taken to avoid standard form and phraseology in secret dispatches. That such a fundamental slip was made by Japan was ironic, because it occurred at the very time when they were stepping up their own code-breaking activity in the wake of the Yardley scandal. Their target was not just U.S. communications, but also those of China.

Toward that end an intercept unit, the "X Facility," had been set up within the special naval landing force at Shanghai. With this unit, Lieutenant Commander Tsunezo Wachi and a Lieutenant Yamada, an expert in Chinese codes, succeeded early in 1932 in decryptions that enabled Japanese carriers to make a preemptive strike against Nationalist airfields at Ch'ang-sha. For this achievement, Wachi and Yamada were awarded the Order of the Golden Kite, Japan's highest military decoration. This demonstration of the tactical value of radio intelligence resulted in the naval general staff's establishing a Tenth Section devoted to communications.[10]

This expanded facility concentrated its efforts on the United States Pacific Fleet. Tanker *Erimo* was sent out to spy on our 1932 autumn maneuvers, and reported that the Pacific Fleet was using a Hebern cipher machine—whose system the Japanese promptly penetrated. It was a short-lived triumph, however, because we had discovered for ourselves that the machine's rotary system was too vulnerable to sustained cryptanalysis. It had been abandoned in favor of the so-called strip cipher in which the encipherment, resulting from sliding card strips printed with various alphabetic arrangements, afforded great security because the alphabets could be changed easily and frequently.[11]

The Japanese naval code breakers also paid increasing attention to the United States diplomatic traffic, which was transmitted to the Far East on naval circuits. They tried to penetrate our one-volume State Department Gray code the "hard way." After analyzing the frequency of vowels and key words, they discovered that "NADED" meant "stop," and similarly worked out the groups for words such as "is," "that," "are," and so on, but progress was slow. With help from the Tokyo *kempeitai* (military police), scraps of message tapes were salvaged from American embassy wastebaskets. In this way original State Department telegrams could be compared with the intercepts to permit recovery of a substantial number of cipher keys.[12]

The technique was used not only by the Japanese. Other nations and people had rifled trash heaps throughout history, and ONI received regular shipments of bags filled with scraps from the Japanese consulate in New York. Our linguists worked over these treasures to find many things of interest including travel itineraries of staff members. In one bag salvaged from Japan's New York consulate they discovered details of our design for variable-pitch propellers. But the Japanese appear to have had a special talent for processing scraps of paper, and by the end of 1932 they had recovered some five thousand code groups. To expedite their penetration, the Japanese turned to black-bag jobs, the last resort of the code-breaking fraternity—if you can't break 'em, pinch 'em.[13]

At the beginning of 1933 a certain tailor in Kōbe became a frequent visitor to the American consulate, gaining the trust, as well as the tailoring business, of the staff. He was soon doing other chores for the staff besides making their clothes. No one suspected that he was a *kempeitai* in disguise, or he would not have been allowed free run of the consul's office where the code safe was located. This resourceful "tailor" bribed a staff member to get a wax imprint of the safe key. On a Saturday night in late April, while the American diplomat was celebrating a lovely spring evening at the Gion geisha house, a special squad broke into his office, opened the safe, and photographed the code books.

The operation was so skillfully conducted that there were no traces of the break-in—and the United States' Gray code was thenceforth shared with the Japanese navy's Tenth Section. This success encouraged the *kempeitai* to set up a special unit of safecrackers, photographers, and technicians to cooperate with the navy in breaking into foreign consulates. Squads of judo-men patrolled outside to create diversions if necessary. As a result, the British foreign office's top-secret interdepartmental code was also soon being read in Tokyo as readily as in London, after a clandestine nighttime visit to his majesty's consulate in Ōsaka.[14]

A break-in at the office of the U.S. naval attaché in Tokyo was—fortunately for us—bungled, leading Washington to suspect that the Japanese were pinching American methods as well as our codes, and that the navy's current system—an early version of the strip cipher—had been compromised. Security was tightened and the introduction by mid-1933 of a more complex system sent the imperial navy's Tenth Section back to square one as far as our secret naval communications were concerned. Since no American break-ins had been made to pinch their Blue code, the Japanese did not suspect that we were reading any communications encrypted in their high-level naval command systems.[15]

Before leaving OP-20-G for sea duty in the summer of 1933, I had assisted in the analysis of information obtained from the Japanese naval codes from which we gained "an extraordinarily accurate picture of the organization of all Orange [Japanese] naval forces." According to the report of the Asiatic Fleet commander in chief, the important lesson learned was that "in the matter of training and preparation for war, the Japanese navy was at least equal to our own."[16]

My brief but fascinating introduction into code breaking ended in June 1933, when I joined *Pennsylvania.* For the first of my two tours of duty in the battleship I was a division officer in charge of number four turret. My classmate Tommy Dyer was also to be my shipmate for the next three years and friendly rival as captain of number three turret. Lieutenant Wesley A. "Ham" Wright came on board *Pennsylvania,* fresh from cryptanalytic training in OP-20-G, in 1936. This was shortly before Rochefort arrived, when Admiral Joseph M. Reeves moved his staff into the battleship, which became Pacific Fleet flagship. This curious coincidence brought together in the same ship the four of us who five years later would find ourselves working alongside each other in the critical months leading up to Pearl Harbor and on through the Battle of Midway.

We always looked back on our battleship duty together as an interesting twist of fate. The coincidence was heightened by the fact that *Pennsylvania*'s skipper was Captain Russell Willson, who had been director of naval communications in World War I. Moreover, when Rochefort came on board, in addition to his duties as assistant operations officer, Pacific Fleet, he was also staff intelligence chief. Joe was praised as a "general encyclopedia of information and usefulness" by Reeves, who formally commended him as "one of the most outstanding officers of his rank," whose "judgment and ability are truly remarkable."[17] Although Reeves noted in his report that Rochefort was not a naval academy graduate, he stated that "this makes his ability and performance of duty all the more remarkable" and that Joe was "destined to advance to positions of high rank and great responsibility."[18]

Rochefort had particularly impressed his commander in chief for the acumen he had shown as his intelligence officer. Whenever we were in port Joe had worked closely with the naval district officers to keep track of attempts to subvert enlisted men in local Communist cells, and Japan's increasing espionage efforts. When the San Pedro coast guard reported that the local Japanese fishing boats were sending coded radio messages, Joe put Ham Wright—fresh from the OP-20-G cryptanalyst training course—onto the investigation.

Wright was eager to demonstrate his newly acquired skills and worked through one Friday night with the coast guard. The code came apart before dawn, only to reveal that the Japanese were exchanging information no more sinister than reporting schools of fish. But Ham missed the Saturday morning inspection, arousing the wrath of Captain Willson.[19]

Wright explained how he had become engrossed in breaking the intercepts, only to be given further hell for "fooling around with that stuff." When Ham respectfully reminded Willson that he had once been involved in the business himself, the captain replied, "Yes, but I had the good sense to get out of it."[20] This was symptomatic of the lack of regard for cryptography and radio intelligence in the pre-World War II navy—even from an officer who should have been well informed. It was ironic that his daughter, Eunice Willson, was to be employed as a civilian crypt-analyst in OP-20-G during the war.

Rochefort's many remarkable attributes included his marvelous talent for getting people to help when there was a job to be done. During our *Pennsylvania* days he got me involved on two separate occasions in extra-curricular activities that were not only interesting but also turned out successfully.

In the fall of 1934, Joe told me what was on his mind: "There's a Lieutenant (j.g.) Cecil H. Coggins, a doctor, over at Long Beach, who works with Eleventh Naval District and ONI's undercover organization, keeping track of what's going on in the Japanese community. He's just learned that the Japanese naval tanker that came in today has some special film they intend to show to the local Japanese association tomorrow night. We suspect that the film is subversive, and I'd like to have you help the undercover boys in this matter."

The Japanese Citizens Patriotic Society had rented an auditorium in Long Beach from Shell Oil and had the right to deny entry to any non-member—namely me. The auditorium had no projection booth, so the two film projectors would be exposed. Following the suggestion of an ONI agent, I posed as a fire insurance inspector. I took along a fire ex-tinguisher and said that I was there to enforce regulations against smok-ing in the auditorium during the film show. False credentials provided apparent authority for me to protect Shell Oil interests. Before the meet-ing I showed the local chairman these papers, feigning no knowledge of Japanese, but he wanted me to clear out. I refused to leave, saying, "Me no here, no movies." By this time some three hundred people had ar-rived, so I stayed, and I went around telling the crowd to put out ciga-rettes.

The films were pretty corny, with their strident message that the em-peror system was best and democracy was no good. Designed to arouse Japanese patriotism, one showed "brave Japanese soldiers" assaulting Chinese positions, troops atop a wall waving a Japanese flag and shouting "Banzai." Another showed contempt for American democracy, with co-medians doing takeoffs of FDR and his mannerisms. An animated car-toon depicted J. P. Morgan pushing a wheelbarrow full of money over the bodies of the poor.

In the course of the evening an inquisitive Japanese seaman from the tanker turned my fire extinguisher upside down and got a face full of foam for his trouble. I had to clean up the mess but received five dollars from the local chairman for my trouble. The doctor, ONI agent, and I drank that up in a Long Beach bar to celebrate the successful conclusion of my first undercover operation.

This exploit led to another counterintelligence mission for me the following year. We were steaming at sea, en route to San Francisco as part of a fleet maneuver, when Joe Rochefort again sent for me. Once his cabin door closed, he briefed me about a Japanese spy operating in the Dutch Harbor area of the Aleutians. Admiral Reeves wanted the spy "out of the way" before he could observe and report on the arrival of our forces for Fleet Problem 16. My orders were to leave ship at Hunters Point Navy Yard, take a train for Seattle, proceed to Bremerton, and there board navy tanker *Brazos,* which was sailing to Dutch Harbor in advance of the other ships involved in the fleet problem.

Early one May morning *Brazos* anchored in Unalaska Bay and, wearing civilian clothes, I slipped ashore at Illilliuk, the civilian community. The naval base of Dutch Harbor is located on a small island in the bay. By prearrangement I went to the postmaster, who was also the federal judge, and presented my credentials. When he had heard my mission, he told me that there was only one Japanese local, a Mr. Shimizu from Seattle. He had to be the man.

We managed to put Shimizu behind bars on a charge of illegally selling alcohol, along with his prostitute girl friend "contact," by turning up evidence that they were both involved in espionage. I was able to radio a message to the fleet flagship: "For Joe—mission accomplished." Later I learned that when their jail terms were up, Shimizu and the whore were deported from Alaska as undesirable aliens. The cash expenditure for this successful counterintelligence mission was modest by any standard: two dollars for Shimizu's bottle of bad booze and two dollars for a mail orderly to compromise the whore!

The naval authorities approved of my performance in this job, but my Japanese language colleague and friend Forrest R. Biard, who was serving in cruiser *New Orleans* during the fleet problem, reported afterward that there were many disgruntled sailors as a result of my successful mission. As he tells it, during shore leave at Illilliuk the gobs were "doing the town" and learned that the only prostitute was in jail. At least one of the sailors, under a full head of steam, proceeded to the jailhouse and demanded to be permitted to go her bail, shouting that he wanted "some of that Alaskan stuff."[21]

It brought back pleasant memories to recall my shipmates in December 1940, when I rejoined that same *Pennsylvania* battleship as Pacific Fleet intelligence officer. In the earlier tour my turret had won the ship's first E for gunnery excellence. But whereas gunnery is a matter of technique in which one goes by the book, I had no manuals and no margin for error as I set about to familiarize myself with all available background information on Japan's Combined Fleet.

4

Code Breaking and Kabuki

THE PALM-FRINGED ATOLLS of the western Marshalls were the nearest Japanese territory to our Pearl Harbor base and therefore the most immediate potential danger to our security. Ever since my time in Tokyo I had suspected that they were being fortified as military bases. One of the biggest islands, Jaluit, was just over two thousand miles southwest of Hawaii and its proximity as a possible enemy base made it a priority in my intelligence mission to find out what Japan might be doing in the mandates. The islands of the Japanese mandate, sprawling across the central Pacific, offered ideal jumping-off points from which their powerful surface and submarine fleet could sally forth to sever our communication lines to the Philippines—or even to raid Hawaii.

As soon as I was established in my new billet, I visited the Fourteenth Naval District's communications intelligence unit, which was then located on the second deck of Building No. 1 in the navy yard at Pearl. This was one of the navy's three prewar centers that specialized in the interception, cryptanalysis, and translation of Japanese radio communications. Tommy Dyer had started the unit in 1936 as a one-man operation. He eventually received radio operators and then a language officer, as well as additional cryptanalysts. Dyer was to remain there throughout the war as chief cryptanalyst, but the officer in charge of the communication intelligence unit on Oahu, Station Hypo, was Lieutenant Commander Thomas B. Birtley. He and Lieutenant Ranson Fullinwider were the only Japanese language officers and it was evident that the outfit was understaffed and overworked. I offered to help in any way I could. When Dyer said that minor systems always needed work Birtley suggested I could try my hand at solving an auxiliary address cipher. I plunged right in at every spare moment to assist Birtley, and work over several hundred intercepts of what he had designated the WE WE (pronounced WEH WEH) cipher.

It was a simple substitution system and I quickly found that there were altogether too many "soft sound" indicators being used for it to be pure Japanese text. Also "hard sound" indicators were being assigned to kana (the Japanese phonetic syllabary), which in Japanese words never carry those inflections. My analysis showed a presence of the "P" sound in un-Japanese positions in what appeared to be proper names. They appeared to fit with names such as "PA"rao (Palau) and Pona"PE" which were islands in the Carolines and Marshalls.

The cipher continued to break down. As I recovered each new value, specific units were addressed such as the Saipan defense force, Ponape garrison force, Kwajalein submarine base, and Palau landplane base. I plotted each recovery on a chart and, when the picture of a Japanese military buildup became clear, rushed the material to the Pacific Fleet commander in chief. Admiral James O. Richardson was skeptical at first, but after I had explained it in detail, and demonstrated the decryption process, he accepted the validity of this intelligence and recognized its strategic significance.

"Now we know," Richardson said, "that the Japs are secretly violating their mandate for administering those islands. We have been trying to find out what's going on out there for twenty years, and here you've done it in twenty days."

I was impressed with the admiral's quick grasp and flattered by the encouragement he gave me as the "new boy" on his staff. Richardson had relieved Admiral Claude C. Bloch as commander in chief, United States Fleet, in January 1940. It had been a trying year for the rangy admiral from Texas. He was a battleship sailor by training and inclination who—despite a succession of senior shore appointments, including a spell as presidential aide—still firmly believed that "the business of a naval officer is on the sea."[1]

Formerly the Pacific Fleet's battle force commander, Richardson had assumed command of the fleet in a critical year that saw President Roosevelt nudge an isolationist Congress into reluctant support for Britain in the fight against Hitler. The U.S. Navy edged toward an undeclared war against U-boats in the Atlantic while Germany's spectacular spring blitzkrieg through western Europe had acted as a spur to Japan's aggressive intentions in the Far East.

Diplomatic pressure was being exerted by Tokyo to force Britain to close the Burma Road in preparation for an all-out drive against the Chinese Nationalists. Anticipating that this might trigger an American oil embargo, the Japanese government was trying to squeeze massive new petroleum concessions from the Netherlands East Indies. To the British and to the Dutch government in exile in London, the dispatch of a powerful American naval force to support the empty fortress of Singapore appeared to offer the only hope of resisting Japan's insistent demands.

Secret talks among American, British, Dutch, and Australian staff officers at Singapore during April 1940 had failed to convince the American chiefs of staff of the strategic necessity, or political advisability, of sending warships to defend European colonial territory in the Far East. But in a symbolic gesture of support for Britain, President Roosevelt directed the Pacific Fleet to conduct its spring maneuvers in Hawaiian waters. Richardson then found that he was ordered to keep the fleet indefinitely at Pearl instead of returning to the west coast.

Japan's growing belligerency in the Pacific persuaded Richardson that his fleet would be less exposed back at San Diego. He felt that the navy was increasingly becoming hostage to the State Department's Far East policy, without considering the danger that provoking Japan would involve the United States in a two-ocean war, when we had only a one-ocean fleet. But when Richardson questioned the wisdom of keeping his ships away from their west coast base "until further notice" and possibly inviting a Japanese attack, Admiral Harold R. Stark, the chief of naval operations, informed him that the fleet was stationed at Pearl as a "deterrent" to Japan.[2]

Richardson, whose determination matched his convictions, flew to Washington in July 1940 to protest that the basing of the fleet at Pearl Harbor "was undertaken under a completely false premise."[3] Stark's polite refusal to rescind the order convinced Richardson that the president was keeping the fleet in Hawaiian waters to satisfy the Far East desk of the State Department who "did not ask their senior military advisers whether it would accomplish such an end."[4]

Richardson's belief that politicians, rather than admirals, were dictating United States naval strategy appeared to be confirmed when he was told that the fleet could not return to San Diego because this would be taken as a climb-down in Tokyo. Nor were his fears eased by the announcement of an American embargo of strategic exports to Japan, including scrap iron.

When the Japanese signed their tripartite pact with Germany and Italy in September 1940, precipitating yet another increase in tension, Richardson took off for Washington again to confront Roosevelt during his October reelection campaign. He had not chosen the best time to force a showdown with a president in the midst of an unprecedented third-term campaign. Roosevelt was facing a strong isolationist challenge and had many political promises to keep, not least of which was to satisfy the strong public demand that there was going to be no sellout of the Chinese Nationalists to the Japanese.

After a "hot and heavy confrontation," according to Richardson, Roosevelt terminated the discussion with an expression of pained surprise, saying, "Joe, you just don't understand."[5]

Richardson nonetheless returned to Hawaii convinced that his forceful presentation had "shocked" Roosevelt into reconsidering his naval policy. It came as a stunning blow, therefore, when Richardson learned in late January 1941 that he was to be relieved. The president had evidently decided to put the demands of diplomacy above those of prudent strategy.

Rear Admiral Husband E. Kimmel, the commander of the battle force cruisers, was promoted to CinC U.S. Fleet over officers senior to him. Handpicked by Roosevelt, who had known him in his years as assistant secretary of the navy, Kimmel had earned the reputation of a hard-driving, conscientious officer, who demanded as much from his staff as from himself. Richardson invited him to flagship *Pennsylvania,* then at sea, for preliminary conversations the last week of January, and it was then that I met Kimmel. We were out on exercises when his flagship, cruiser *Honolulu,* came abeam, and the admiral came over in his whaleboat. The sea was running so heavy that climbing the ship's ladder seemed risky, so *Pennsylvania*'s crane hoisted the whaleboat right on board. After a while, Richardson summoned me and said, "Tell Admiral Kimmel what you told me about Japanese remilitarization of the mandates." I excused myself to get maps from the safe, and returned to give my presentation.

Following the transfer of command, Admiral Kimmel asked to see my mandates charts again. I spread them out in his office for a review of the entire procedure. He was intrigued by the WE WE cipher and wanted the details about how it was broken. I did not know if he was previously familiar with radio intercept material, but his first-rate analytical ability impressed me. He seemed to appreciate the importance of the information, so much so that a week later he had me repeat the briefing for his staff.

What neither Kimmel nor I knew was that the navy department in Washington was still totally ignorant of the full extent of Japan's military preparations in the mandates. At the time of our conference at sea I assumed that since OP-20-G had received the same intercepts they must have made the same evaluation of them. We were to learn nearly three months later that they had completely ignored the WE WE cipher and its important intelligence. That omission alone was a telling indication that the navy department in Washington was not making comprehensive or complete intelligence evaluations of Japanese preparations for war.

Intelligence, as defined by *Webster's Third New International Dictionary,* is "evaluated information concerning an enemy or possible enemy or a possible theater of operations and the conclusions drawn therefrom."[6] That definition is inadequate because it covers only two of the three essential elements of intelligence. It comprehends acquisition and evaluation, but it omits the vital third element—dissemination. Information can be acquired and evaluated until hell freezes over, but it does not become intelligence until delivered to the commanders who can make proper use of it.

Prior to World War II our principal sources of intelligence on the

Japanese navy were the intercepts of their radio traffic made by our network of listening posts and processed in the three cryptanalysis centers. The Pacific Fleet's communications intelligence unit was code-named Station Hypo after the "H" of Heeia on the east side of Oahu where its radio intercept towers were located. It had been established in 1936, twelve years after the first navy intercept station had been set up in the U.S. consulate in Shanghai.[7] In 1925 a station had been set up to monitor Japanese diplomatic radio traffic in Peking, the same year that a temporary listening post had been established at Wailupe east of Honolulu.

The first fleet radio intelligence units had been started in 1927 at Guam and Olongapo in the Philippines under the Asiatic command. Station Cast, as it was designated even before its move to Cavite, was to establish the units as satellite outposts. When Cast was under the command of Lieutenant Joseph N. Wenger, there had been no staff, or time, for anything more than intercepting Japanese communications and rudimentary traffic analysis. But in 1934 he had been succeeded by Lieutenant T. A. Huckins whose assistant, Lieutenant E.S.L. Goodwin, "realized that he was being given a free hand." Goodwin continued the code-breaking work he had started in Washington. His "remarkable piece of work" on the Japanese fleet maneuvers was praised in Washington in a report that noted, "With adequate and capable personnel this unit is capable of furnishing considerable information."[8] Goodwin then established the precedent that led to a 1935 decision by Safford—back from sea and again in his old job—that the intercept stations should establish their own cryptanalytic bureaus.

The real front-line warriors in the secret radio war were not the cryptanalysts, however, but the enlisted men who manned the headsets of our receivers at these intercept stations. This required more radiomen who were adept at rapidly recording the Morse code equivalents of the Japanese kana characters. This was no mean feat, for the international Morse code A = (.—) was the kana "I," our C = (—.—.) was kana "NI," and so on. Two dozen Japanese combinations were unique to kana, although both systems shared Arabic numerals.

In 1924 the navy had only two operators who could carry out this task. To overcome this obstacle, Safford that same year had persuaded the Underwood Typewriter Company to develop a special hybrid machine to his own design. This printed the equivalent Japanese character from the dot-dash combination, which took care of the twenty-six-letter Roman alphabet. The other twenty-four unique kana combinations were typed using the upper-case shift key.[9]

The hybrid kana typewriters, at $160 each, were a high-ticket item for the time. Only a few could be purchased. Those that were sent out to our two fleets operating in the Pacific proved that skilled radio operators could quickly become proficient in recording Japanese Morse. But it was still necessary to increase the number of radiomen familiar with Japanese communications and able to take down kana by hand. Commencing in 1928, OP-20-G operated four-month instruction classes for front-line radio operators. They were conducted under conditions of great secrecy in a specially constructed classroom on top of the navy department building in Washington.

The "roofers," or On the Roof Gang (OTRG) as they came to be known, were the "ears" of our radio intelligence system at the chain of naval stations that encircled the North Pacific. The principal listening posts were established over the next decade at Shanghai in China, Guam in the Marianas, Marivele in the Philippines, Heeia on Oahu, and Bainbridge Island near Seattle The roofers manned the headsets and scanned the airways, taking down on message pads the torrent of Japanese Morse. These were relayed—depending on the location of the station—by courier pouch or secure cable line to the three centers where cryptanalysts and translators attempted to break out the messages into plain English. When this was not possible, direction-finding and traffic analysis was applied to extract whatever intelligence could be gleaned from a steadily increasing volume of intercepted Japanese traffic.

The nerve center of our radio intelligence operation was OP-20-G. Code-named Station Negat from the "N" of the navy department building, its maximum prewar staff of sixty civilians and servicemen operated from ten cramped office spaces on the first and second "decks" (floors) of wing number six. The now-demolished three-story World War I complex included the nine wings of the look-alike war department building. Until the Pentagon was completed in 1943, this sprawling four-block-long complex that reached back to the Reflecting Pool from the south side of Constitution Avenue housed the headquarters of our armed services.

Station Negat was my assignment when I returned from China in the early summer of 1936. In June, I took over from Birtley as chief of OP-20-GZ, the translation section. It was my responsibility to see that the decrypts made by OP-20-G were turned into plain English, and my small staff consisted almost entirely of civilian linguists.

My job was not solely translating. In the summer of 1936, I was able to assist with the analysis on a series of decrypts that turned out to be the intercepted radio reports on the postmodernization trials of battleship *Nagato*. To my surprise, these revealed that this rehabilitated World War I dreadnought had made better than 26 knots with her rebuilt turbines. This information also created concern in our war plans division where it was believed that the old *Mutsu* class, to which *Nagato* belonged, was good for only 23½ knots. Our new battleships—then in the blueprint stage—had accordingly been planned for a top speed of 24 knots. Captain Royal E. Ingersoll, from war plans, came down to check our information that *Nagato,* in several full-power runs, had indeed exceeded 26 knots.[10]

This timely intelligence enabled the navy general board to change the design of our *North Carolina*-class battleships to allow for speed of twenty-seven knots—and to provide an even greater margin, with a speed of twenty-eight knots for all later classes. This would give our naval task forces a one-knot superiority over their Japanese opponents. This single piece of radio intelligence gave our new battleships an important tactical wartime advantage. Safford, now promoted to head of OP-20-G, was amply justified in claiming that this coup "paid for our peacetime RI organization a thousand times over."[11] It was during my stint as head of the translation section of OP-20-G that I came to appreciate the magnitude of the contribution being made to our code-breaking effort by Mrs. Driscoll.

I had been warned not to patronize Madam "X," as her colleagues sometimes referred to her, because she was sensitive to her role as a woman in a man's world. Because of this she kept to herself as much as possible and none of us was ever invited to socialize with her and her lawyer husband. While she could be warm and friendly, she usually affected an air of intense detachment, which was heightened by her tailored clothes and shunning of makeup. It was surprising to hear Miss Aggie curse, which she frequently did—as fluently as any sailor whom I have ever heard.

In the navy she was without peer as a cryptanalyst. Some of her pupils, like Ham Wright, were more able mathematicians but she had taught cryptanalysis to all of them, and none ever questioned her superb talent and determination in breaking codes and ciphers. She understood machines and how to apply them. In 1937 she would share the fifteen-thousand-dollar prize granted by the Senate for her contribution to developing a cipher machine with Lieutenant Commander William F. Gresham.[12] But her principal talent was her ability to get to the root of a problem, sort out its essential components, and find a way to solve it. Among her uniformed naval colleagues, she was held in the highest esteem throughout her long career, which continued from the office of naval communications to the Armed Forces Security Agency, and then to the National Security Agency, before she retired in 1959.

My first encounter with Miss Aggie's formidable intellect occurred when she came to me one morning with a large piece of graph paper and asked, "Lieutenant Layton, does this make any sense?" She had marked the paper with zigzag staircases of letters in different color inks. Not being a Japanese linguist, she pointed along the letters on one of the staircases, and asked if it said anything in Japanese. I told her that it did not because there were too many vowels. Then she traced out another zigzag, which read "TO-MI-MU-RA;" I told her that this one made sense. It could be a Japanese name, "Tomimura." When she shook her head at that idea, I suggested that the "mura," which means town, has an alternate reading of "son," so it might also be rendered Tomison, or Thompson. She stopped me later as I was passing her desk on my way to lunch. "Lieutenant Layton, I want to thank you. You helped me solve part of a cipher that has been bothering me for some time. The name is Thompson."

The Thompson, the "Tomimura" whose name appeared in the intercepted Japanese foreign office traffic, after a secret investigation instigated by naval intelligence, was identified as a Pacific Fleet radioman. The American who was his accomplice and referred to as Agent K in the same message turned out to be John S. Farnsworth, a cashiered navy officer. It was he who had masterminded an espionage ring that turned over engineering and gunnery secrets, including the blueprint of the model D-4 bombsight, to Japan. Toshio Miyazaki and Akira Yamaki, the Japanese navy lieutenants who had been their contacts, were legally in the United States as language students.[13]

Farnsworth and Thompson were arrested in 1936. Although the evidence that unmasked Harry H. Thompson and led to the pair's apprehension could never be presented in court, they were convicted the following year of conspiring to violate federal espionage laws and each sentenced to four to twelve years in prison.

The whole affair had underscored the importance of maintaining the closest cooperation between the offices of naval communications and naval intelligence, and relations between the two had been considerably improved—during my eight months in OP-20-GZ, the translation section—by Captain William D. Puleston. Although naval communications still maintained administrative responsibility for OP-20-G, it was ONI that had the responsibility for disseminating the final product of the growing number of intercepted Japanese radio communications.

Like Captain Alfred T. Mahan, the nineteenth-century American naval strategist whom he studied and wrote about, Puleston was a thinking man's sailor. In addition to advocating the establishment of a national war college for senior officers of both armed services, he was one of the moving forces in expanding our secret radio war against the Japanese during his three-year tenure as director of ONI, which began in 1934. He was assisted by Commander Ellis M. Zacharias, his Far East section chief, who was one of the few Jewish naval academy graduates of his generation. Duty as a language student and later as assistant naval attaché in Tokyo had persuaded Zacharias that sooner or later we would have to fight the Japanese for control of the Pacific.

I came to know "Pulie," as we affectionately called him, quite well during the final six months of his productive tenure as ONI director. He was brilliant in addition to being energetic, and my already high respect for him was increased after an incident I witnessed on Christmas Eve 1936.

When Puleston came to offer those of us on duty a seasonal greeting, he found himself barred from access to our section by the armed marine guarding the door to our office, because the DNI's name was not on the official list. Overhearing the rising voices outside, I rushed to his rescue, just in time to find that the marine guard had drawn his pistol. "This gun is aimed at your belt, sir," the guard said. "If you step forward, I'll fire. Those are my orders."

Pulie was standing stock still, livid, and mad as hell. Upon my assurance that this was the director of naval intelligence and that he was authorized to enter, the guard stood aside. But Puleston, not ready to settle for that, took the guard's name and that of his commanding officer. Thereupon his stern manner softened and he congratulated Private Leo S. Schmidt for his diligence, said that he would have put him on report had he done otherwise, and announced that he was going to recommend him for promotion, which he did.

That was typical of Pulie, who was responsible for recommending my appointment as assistant naval attaché in Tokyo, which came through in February 1937.

I arrived in Japan that spring at the height of the cherry blossom season, when most Japanese love to stroll the countryside for *hanami*—flower viewing. That seasonal mood contrasted sharply, however, with the increasing aggressiveness of Japanese militarists and the jingoistic headlines. The army could do no wrong; the Chinese were "insincere and violently anti-Japanese." There was no opposition press to provide any kind of balance.

The invidious effect of the headlines upon the people was plain to see. One day I was sitting on a bench in Tokyo's Shinagawa Station, awaiting a connecting train, when I overheard two men discussing the news.

"I see we are sending troops to China."

"We don't need to send troops over there. All we have to do is send a bunch of boy scouts to kick those Chinese heads in. That would do it."

"I'm not so sure. It might take a little more than boy scouts to do the job."

The last speaker's touch of moderation was a rapidly vanishing trait of the Japanese man in the street. Everyone was being swept up in the extreme spirit of nationalism fostered by the state-controlled press and radio. In June a moderate cabinet fell victim to army factionalism. Prince Fumimaro Konoye's administration tried to reconcile conflicting interests. This was an impossible goal in the face of ultranationalist patriotic societies which championed the wayward army commanders in northern China. Within a month the Kwantung army widened the war in China, and Konoye's policies were derailed.

On 7 July 1937 the young anti-Japanese officers of the Chinese 29th Route Army, dissatisfied with "local agreements," attacked the neighboring Japanese army unit. Their intention had been reported to Washington by the assistant naval attaché at the American legation in Peiping. That message was intercepted by Japanese naval intelligence and reported to Tokyo, where army headquarters ignored the warning.

That same night Chinese and Japanese army units collided at Peiping's historic Marco Polo Bridge. The ensuing skirmish was a fuse igniting a full-scale but undeclared war on the mainland. Within three weeks Nationalist Chinese forces and the Japanese army were locked in a series of pitched battles. By August 1937 fighting had spread to Shanghai, and Konoye ordered a partial mobilization for a "war of chastisement." His last-ditch effort to prevent Japan from becoming committed to a continental war collapsed after Japanese army code breakers intercepted Chinese government messages revealing that Konoye was planning to bargain with the Nationalists. The prime minister's emissary was arrested as he was about to set off for Nanking.

The generals got their war. Konoye put the best face on his sandbagged position by claiming that the mainland fighting involving Japanese troops was just another "China incident." Ambassador Grew warned Washington that it was now too late to halt the conflict with "paper bullets." High explosives, however, almost started a real war with real bullets between Japan and the United States on 12 December 1937. That Sunday afternoon Japanese naval planes screamed down over the Yangtze River to bomb and sink U.S.S. *Panay,* which was evacuating the U.S. embassy staff from the besieged Nationalist capital of Nanking.

It was an anxious time for us in the embassy in Tokyo. Ambassador Grew, remembering how the Spanish-American War had broken out in 1898 after the sinking of the *Maine* in Havana Harbor, expected a declaration of war from Washington and ordered his staff to begin packing. The days that followed brought a hectic round of activity in the attaché's office as we tried to ascertain the facts and await the outcome. It was shocking to hear intelligent Japanese friends reveal their sincere and unanimous belief that the whole affair was "Chinese propaganda!" just as the screaming headlines proclaimed. On the other hand, our embassy was deluged with expressions of shame and regret from people of all walks of life. One well-dressed Japanese lady came to Ambassador Grew's office with flowers, made a brief speech of apology, and cut off her hair as a public act of penance.

The Tokyo government quickly moved to defuse the tense situation with a hasty apology, offer of indemnity, and assurances that it was an unfortunate case of mistaken identity. The *Panay* sinking and the savage rape of Nanking caused irreparable damage to Japanese-United States relations. These crises were aggravated, ironically, by the recent success of Japanese naval code breakers.

In 1936 the *kempeitai* had supplied the Japanese navy with codes from the British consulate in Ōsaka. In the fall of 1937, even before the American Brown code had been put into operation, photographic copies of the new State Department cipher together with a military strip system had been secretly obtained from the consulate in Kōbe. The Japanese were therefore able to read sufficient of the diplomatic codes to get the American and British assessments of events. Our secret cables differed dramatically from their official representations and their decrypts of our cables persuaded the Japanese that foreign diplomats were deliberately distorting their reports.

The *Panay* crisis brought an extra chill to the Tokyo winter. Japanese authorities became noticeably more circumspect in their official attitudes and dealings with us. The widening war in China made the gathering of intelligence even more difficult as military mobilization resulted in tighter censorship and security measures. Our sources were reduced to tidbits gleaned from a few military magazines and *gogai* (newspaper extras) sold on the street, and we were still being warned by our superiors to be careful about overstepping the bounds of diplomacy and discretion.

Our Japanese office boy regularly brought in a monthly newssheet issued by his "mobilization center." Once in a while it had squibs of naval news not appearing in newspapers or magazines. Shortly before our 1939 naval maneuvers off the Hawaiian Islands, I noticed an item rescheduling the routing of six Japanese naval tankers to California to load fuel oil. I reported this to ONI by diplomatic cipher, noting that the tankers were probably being diverted to monitor radio transmissions from our maneuvers. When the boy stopped bringing in the newssheets, I asked about them, and he said that they had been discontinued. I did not then know about the *kempeitai* break-in and code theft at Kōbe, and so did not realize that the Japanese authorities had been alerted to the newssheet as an intelligence source by reading my coded cable.

Courtesy calls to the Navy Ministry also became less frequent. I regretted this as I had struck up many friendships during official calls at the old Victorian red-brick building in Kasumigaseki, a district of official ministries and bureaus south-southwest of the imperial palace grounds. There I had met many Japanese naval officers whose names would become well known in World War II. Foremost among these was Vice Admiral Isoroku Yamamoto, who was then naval vice-minister.

We had worked closely with Yamamoto's office during the July 1937 search for Amelia Earhart, a matter in which they cooperated politely, but only halfheartedly. On one visit to naval headquarters I stopped in to greet Yamamoto's friendly aide, Captain Yasuichiro Kondo, who invited me to pay my respects to the admiral.

The admiral rose from the plain wood desk and greeted me cordially with a brisk but firm handshake. I knew he enjoyed chatting with me in Japanese, which my boss, Captain Bemis, did not speak. Yamamoto's manner was poised and cultured, but warm. He motioned me to a chair. The walls of his sparsely furnished office were bare except for a *kakemono* and a large map of the world.

He provided me with a perfect opening: "What can I do for you, Layton-san?"

"Admiral, I've been reading in the newspapers about those naval tankers *Tsurugizaki* and *Takasaki* that you're building."

"Yes. What about them?"

"Sir, I was wondering why their construction is taking so long."

He bristled slightly. "What do you mean by that?"

"Well, sir, yesterday's paper reported that a ten-thousand-ton, twenty-one-knot tanker had been completed by a civilian shipyard in five months and twenty-four days. So I wondered why it was taking so much longer to build naval tankers; I thought they would be completed by now."

I sensed that his initial geniality was fading. This had to be a sensitive matter, but he waved it off, saying, "Oh, I don't know such details. I can't be bothered with things like that." So we dropped that subject and our conversation moved to other things. (I later learned that the two tankers—still on the slipways—were even then being converted into aircraft carriers *Shōhō* and *Zuiho.*)

He asked if I liked kabuki. That highly stylized theater was one of my favorite Japanese entertainments. I told him how seven years earlier, during my language-study years, our *sensei* had taken us to kabuki as part of training. I had acquired a real fondness for it, but found *noh* drama hard to comprehend. Yamamoto said he looked forward to seeing me soon at a theater party he was planning for some of the naval attachés. On that pleasant note I departed.

Soon after our encounter over the mysterious tankers, he invited me to an evening of kabuki. When we were in our places in the theater he indicated adjoining vacant seats, explaining that other attachés were invited, but they didn't show up. That gave me an opportunity to converse with him at great length, but we talked only about theater. He seemed to appreciate my sincere interest in his country, that I had studied its history and its culture as well as the language—just as he had done as a language student and Japan's naval attaché in Washington in 1926. I felt we had a kind of kinship through our work and mutual interests.

Yamamoto asked about my first kabuki of a decade ago, which was still vivid in memory. My initial impression of kabuki had been that it was pretty weird; but it had really moved the Japanese. At thrilling points in the play, people in the audience had stood up and shouted such things as "That's what I'm here for!" "That's what I came for!" "That's what I've been waiting for." I told Yamamoto of the dignified-looking man who had been seated next to me, a complete stranger, who had been so moved at one denouement that he grabbed my shoulder and, cheeks streaming with tears, cried out, "Isn't it saaaad?" Yamamoto chuckled.

My evening with Yamamoto was also memorable for the program which included famed actor Kimburo doing his lion dance. We also saw *Musume Do-jo-ji (The Dojo Temple Maiden),* about the dedication of a temple bell. The priest has lustful designs on a maiden who is actually a devil in disguise. She suddenly turns into a devil right there on the stage, all red and fiery, and you think she is really on fire. Yamamoto displayed no emotion during the plays, but he obviously enjoyed them and wanted to know if the burning devil distressed me. It did not, but it certainly moved the audience, who shrieked with delight.

Our next social encounter was in the autumn of 1938 when Yamamoto invited me to a formal *kamoryo* (duck-netting) party. The guests at this were strictly blue-water naval officers. It was held at Hama *rikyū*, a detached palace, about a mile south of the main imperial palace in Tokyo. Part of the grounds had been set aside as a *kamoba,* a series of shallow canals where wild duck, lured by corn and tame decoys, were the quarry of the hunt. The object was to catch them, rather like giant butterflies, by deft use of long-handled nets. A rustic reed-covered hut on the embankment served as a base where the main party drank and played bridge while the hunt was carried on by groups of four. Eventually, when everyone had either caught a duck or given up, we all dined on delicious duck sukiyaki.

After our group had taken our turn with the nets, Yamamoto invited us to join him in a rubber of bridge. He was a skillful player who made clever ruffs and enjoyed winning all three rubbers. He accepted our congratulations and reminded us, mischievously, "Science and skill will always win over luck and superstition."

The favorite drink of senior Japanese officers before the war was John Begg scotch whisky, which was bottled in a squat ceramic jug. At the duck hunt it flowed as freely as the water in the canals outside. But while our host appeared to consume as many glasses as his guests, I later found out that Yamamoto had pulled the old Chinese trick of drinking cold tea.

The foreign naval and army attachés frequently were guests at social affairs, but we were never invited to air displays and army maneuvers, nor were we permitted to visit naval bases, air stations, or dockyards. The Japanese went to extreme lengths to conceal their warship construction. Outside their shipyards they erected huge screens of bamboo and canvas around the ways on which two big new superbattleships and carriers were being built. Every building site and military area was designated a fortified zone, where even casual visitors were often arrested on sight.

One of Japan's most guarded concerns was its trust territories in the mid-Pacific. A cable from the director of naval intelligence early in 1938 directed the naval attaché to obtain information about the possibility that Japan was militarizing these atolls, especially the Marianas, Carolines, and Marshalls, in defiance of the League of Nations' mandate. I was given the assignment and set about to book passage to the mandates, to try to find out whether seaplane and submarine bases had been constructed.

Armed with the schedule of sailings, I repeatedly visited the only steamship line offering passenger service to the islands to secure passage. I was told that each and every sailing was booked solid for the entire year. When I protested the "completely sold out" excuse, the senior passenger agent courteously but firmly informed me that he was under standing instructions "not to sell any foreigners passage to the mandated islands under any circumstances whatsoever."

Despite all Japanese protests to the contrary, American suspicion of clandestine militarization had been aroused as early as 1923 when Earle Ellis, a marine corps undercover agent, had disappeared in the mandates after gaining passage to the islands on pretense of doing nature studies. Japanese authorities had informed our naval attaché only that Ellis had died of unknown causes on the island of Palau, in the western Carolines.

Chief Pharmacist Lawrence Zembsch, of the American naval hospital in Yokohama that had been established in World War I, was sent to investigate the circumstances of Ellis's death. Zembsch returned with the major's ashes, but in a stupor, apparently drug-induced, and suffering from amnesia. He was hospitalized, with some hope that his recovery might clear the mystery. Unfortunately, Zembsch was killed in the naval hospital when it was destroyed in the great earthquake of 1 September 1923.

Although I never got within a thousand miles of the mandates, the authorities, somehow, did not object to my having a summer residence in Hayama, a "fortified zone" south of Tokyo, near the emperor's summer palace. As it happened, my *besso*—beach cottage—was under the aerial path of aircraft making test flights from nearby Yokosuka naval base. The planes flew so close on takeoff and landing that I did not even need binoculars to make out their details.

We had a report from Chungking about a crashed Zero: It was so light that two men could pick up a wing section. Powerfully armed and highly maneuverable, it had shot down many Russian-built I-15 fighters of the Chinese Nationalists. So when I spotted an unfamiliar aircraft overhead I felt immediately that it must be one of the new Zeros. It was also evident from the deft maneuvering of these planes that their pilots were far more skillful and better trained than was popularly believed.

Another advantage of summer living at Hayama for an intelligence officer was that my daily commuter train to Tokyo passed over the big railroad marshaling yards at Shinagawa. From the carriage window I could observe tanks, trucks, artillery, and troops being loaded on railcars for onward shipment to China.

Our commercial attaché and his staff were very helpful when it came to compiling intelligence reports, but we American attachés were never as effective as the British, who had fewer rules restraining their activities and conduct. While I was in Tokyo a new British naval attaché arrived, fully equipped with Leica camera and telephoto lens. When his ship docked at Kōbe, *Chiyoda* was in harbor. He poked his long lens through a cabin porthole and took the first pictures of a *Chiyoda*-class seaplane carrier to reach the West.

On a trip to Shanghai I once missed an excellent opportunity to photograph the new cruiser *Toné.* She was coming in from builder's trials when our passenger liner, *Empress of Asia,* put into Nagasaki for coal. We were held up at the entrance to the harbor to let *Toné* enter ahead of us. She was of the *Chikuma* class, with four turrets forward, and a floatplane-handling deck aft. Our people had never been close enough to obtain accurate information about these hybrid cruisers and it would have been easy to snap pictures of her from my cabin. But I had been officially discouraged from having a camera, "the sure sign of a spy."

The paranoid Japanese concern with security contrasted with the ease with which their attachés and undercover agents were able to operate in the United States. After 1937 the naval staff in Tokyo was faced with having to plan for a war against the United States that might come sooner rather than later. They concluded that more information was needed about their potential enemy.

Reliance on civilian spies had been most unsatisfactory for providing military information about the United States. Their reports included such stupid and useless things as "American warships carry women dressed as men," or "Since these men in the Navy have volunteered in the service just to have a free round-the-world trip, they will take to their heels when a war breaks out."[14] As a result, the naval attaché's office in Washington had been expanded during the 1930s. The Third Section of the imperial navy staff, which directed intelligence operations, had begun recruiting and training navy men as spies and sending them to the United States as undercover agents. Posing as language students, their mission had been to collect technical data about warship construction, radio communications, naval training, and weapons as well as details about American readiness for war.

One of their most successful naval undercover agents was a Lieutenant Commander Togami whose novel mission was to set up a mobile radio intelligence unit and collect detailed operational data on the U.S. Navy. Four years earlier our own office of naval intelligence had attempted a similar operation when four specially trained officers posing as civilian meteorological scientists had spent a year on board American Lines ships making passages to and from Japanese ports in the Far East.[15]

While our first use of mobile radio intelligence units had proved relatively unsuccessful, the Japanese, because they were able to conduct their clandestine operation ashore, had better luck. After sailing from Yokohama for Seattle early in 1937, accompanied by an expert radio operator, Togami spent six months in the Japanese embassy in Washington studying radio intercept methods and exercise routines at American naval establishments. His assistant purchased a high-powered shortwave radio receiver, and they set off on an eighteen-month motor tour—with the set concealed in the trunk of their car.[16]

A carefully planned itinerary took them to our main bases where, from rented houses, they eavesdropped on radio signals sent from ship to shore during maneuvers and routine operations. From hundreds of hours of patient listening, they compiled a dossier on American naval operations that revealed, among a wealth of useful intelligence data, that the American and Japanese navies employed similar fire-control methods, and that U.S. naval ships consumed three times as much fuel in training and were far superior in communications.

The haul of intelligence data, when analyzed in Tokyo, also told Japan's naval planners that the U.S. Navy was weak in night-fighting skills. This was of extreme interest and importance to the planners because for years they had placed considerable emphasis on training in night-battle tactics. Their resultant skill paid great dividends during the first year of the war in the Pacific when Japanese warships repeatedly outfought ours in night actions.

One other most significant observation made by the Japanese naval visitors to American shores pertained to a detail of our annual training schedules. They noted that fighting efficiency in the American fleet reached a peak in June each year, whereas the Japanese navy peaked in December.[17]

This kind of technical information was entirely inaccessible to American naval officers in Japan—and we were not encouraged to try snooping. Our naval attaché, Captain Bemis, frequently warned me in ominous tones, "Keep your hands out of that, boy!" This gave me the impression that we must have extensive undercover intelligence operations in Japan—which I later learned was just not so. The *kempeitai* managed to eliminate every one of our prewar undercover agents. Nevertheless, I contributed some useful intelligence in the fall of 1937 from newspaper communiqués about a Japanese air strike against the mainland. Our assistant naval attaché for air, Lieutenant Commander Frank Bridget, and I were able to determine that the flights had originated in Formosa. His report to Washington emphasized that this brilliant operation demonstrated the strategy of preemptive strikes and showed the capabilities of the Japanese naval air force.

My friend Bridget was an insightful and intuitive man of vast good humor. He enjoyed a drink of good whiskey now and then, which often got him into hot water with our straitlaced naval attaché, Captain Bemis. Frank had undertaken on his own an exhaustive study of the technical ability of Japanese naval aviators. At my recommendation he had taken a house next to mine in Hayama. Together we observed Japanese planes operating from nearby Yokosuka naval air station. We saw type 96 twin-engine bombers after takeoff, on landing approaches, flying singly and in formation, and we knew that their pilots were superbly trained.

Frank's report set out in great detail the skill of Japanese pilots and the performance of their planes. He concluded that men and equipment were superior to our previous reports, and that our own air outfits should know this. Since all his sources of information were public, the report noted that the Bureau of Aeronautics in Washington need not even classify its distribution.

This report proved how wrong were the assumptions current in Washington before the war that Japanese pilots could not fly and shoot straight because of their "weak" eyes. It might have dispelled such racial illusions and have had far-reaching effect on our state of preparedness three years later. But the evening that Bridget presented it to the naval attaché for forwarding to Washington in November 1938, he went out on the town to celebrate, and got drunk. This was reported to Bemis, who was furious. He not only placed Bridget under military arrest, but also gave him an unsatisfactory fitness report—a career blight. Further, in his anger, Bemis refused to sign or forward the report on Japanese naval aviation.

Bridget, in desperation, requested that it go out anyway under his own signature. Bemis refused, saying, "We do not issue reports signed by an assistant," and put the document in his safe. When I left Tokyo five months later, the report was still there, and it never was circulated by the Bureau of Aeronautics. I doubt that it ever reached Washington.

Such bureaucratic foolishness in a naval officer was astonishing, especially in light of the deteriorating diplomatic situation during my final year in Tokyo. Konoye was still struggling to keep his cabinet in power by a political balancing act, trying to bring the China war to a close, eliminate Chiang Kai-shek's Nationalist government, and establish a "new order" in the Far East. The tightrope he walked was already swaying precariously over the chasm of a general Pacific war when I was recalled from Tokyo in the spring of 1939 to assume command of my first ship, minesweeper *Boggs*.

It was during that summer, when *Boggs* put into San Diego, that I ran across Captain Zacharias, who was then running the intelligence office for the Eleventh Naval District. We had become friendly two years before during my spell as OP-20-GZ when "Zach" had headed ONI's Far East desk. As fellow language officers we shared a mutual interest in Japan and now he was anxious to hear the latest news about my time in Tokyo. I also soon discovered that he was talent scouting in anticipation of achieving his ambition to become director of naval intelligence.

We had been casually swapping Japan stories and Zach was squeezing fresh-plucked limes for our daiquiris when, quite suddenly, he asked, "How would you like to be fleet intelligence officer?"

I had never even thought of such a thing, and said so. Zach smiled and, in his conspiratorial way, explained that he had been "talking with people in Washington" about the need for a specialist intelligence officer on the fleet staff at Pearl Harbor. He was convinced that war with Japan was just over the horizon and that the fleet needed an intelligence officer who was a Japanese linguist. Whoever got the job would be the busiest man on the staff when the inevitable conflict broke out in the Pacific.

To my astonishment, Zacharias had already put my name forward for the job, even recommending that I should have an assistant. Had I any ideas about who would be a good assistant? In fact, I had, and named Bob Hudson. A number of us had learned the language, but of all my linguist colleagues, Hudson knew the Japanese people and their psychology best. Zacharias seemed to enjoy my surprise at the whole idea, commended my choice of Hudson, and said that we should keep thinking about it.

I was not surprised, therefore, when the following year orders came for me to report to flagship *Pennsylvania* as fleet intelligence officer. Hudson joined shortly afterward as my assistant. Nor was I surprised to find that Zach had preceded me to Pearl, for sea duty as captain of heavy cruiser *Salt Lake City*. He had no official intelligence function with regard to the Pacific Fleet, but retained his passion for "cloak and dagger" activities. He would drop into my office whenever he was ashore, apparently because he had been given a "commission to continue intelligence work."[18] I sometimes wondered if Zacharias thought that his pushing me for the fleet intelligence billet might provide him with a direct line to Admiral Kimmel. If he entertained such a notion, it was dashed after his one and only attempt to brief Kimmel in April 1941.

Shortly after Zach had brought his cruiser to San Francisco in February he encountered our old friend Admiral Kichisaburo Nomura en route to Washington to become Japan's new ambassador. Later, Zacharias would testify at the 1945 Pearl Harbor congressional inquiry that he had requested a chance to brief Kimmel after this encounter. Specifically he claimed that he had warned Kimmel of the need for long-range air patrols to guard against the dangers of an air strike against Pearl Harbor.[19]

Captain William W. Smith, Kimmel's chief of staff, who was also present at the meeting, testified that there had never been any mention of an air attack. He described Zacharias's sworn recollections as "clairvoyance operating in reverse."[20]

5

"When We Fight"

THREE MONTHS BEFORE I left Tokyo, I had attended a farewell gathering in January 1939 for the British naval attaché, Captain Bernard Rawlings. "I suppose you're a little sad to be leaving Japan?" I said to him when we were making our farewells.

"No, Layton. The next time I see the little yellow buggers, I hope it will be through the sights of a fourteen-inch gun!"

That wish was to be granted exactly six years later. In January 1945, as Rear Admiral Sir Bernard Rawlings, he flew his flag in battleship H.M.S. *King George V* as commander of the British task force sent out to the Pacific to operate with our fleet in the final months of the war.

The seriousness of the British naval attaché's parting salvo did not strike me until nearly two years after I had left Tokyo myself. In April 1941, while assembling a background brief on Japan's fleet for Admiral Kimmel, I came across some translations I had made to keep up my Japanese while skipper of *Boggs*. Among them was a book by the popular naval author Shinsaku Hirata, published in Tokyo seven years earlier. Its title—*Warera Moshi Tatakawaba*—struck me as significant because it translated as not "If" but "When We Fight."

The book included a vivid portrayal of the American fleet commander at Pearl Harbor worrying about the "fearsome" possibility that Japan would send "a fast striking force of cruisers and aircraft carriers" that would be "truly matchless and invincible!" The author's speculative conclusion struck me as remarkably perceptive since it had been drawn from knowledge of our naval exercises:

> Whether such a surprise raid could be organized only the Japanese Naval General Staff knows. During an American fleet problem off Hawaii some years ago, a carrier striking force sent flights of planes to attack after they had penetrated to seventy or eighty miles off

70

Hawaii. Aided by rain squalls these planes were able to surprise the "defenders" and carry out an effective bombardment of Pearl Harbor, theoretically destroying that major naval base.[1]

I was so impressed by Hirata's thesis that, under the pen name Tomomasa Emura, I submitted a translated summary to several magazines in October 1940, with a cover letter that ended, "Whether or not it is a preview of Japanese-American naval warfare is a matter for history to determine." I received the rejection slips philosophically but, after history had indeed determined the matter on 7 December 1941, I could not help wondering if any of those magazine editors remembered my translation and regretted as much as I did their decision not to publish it.

It would be going too far to suggest that *When We Fight* inspired the Pearl Harbor attack, but author Hirata's speculation had been founded on some knowledge of our naval maneuvers in which carrier-based planes had demonstrated it was possible to carry out a "successful" surprise attack on Hawaii. Within three years a Pearl Harbor concept was part of the Japanese naval war college study, "Strategy and Tactics Against the United States."[2]

In the early 1930s the very idea of an assault on Hawaii was enough to raise the eyebrows of Japanese naval traditionalists. While a surprise attack on Port Arthur in 1904 had worked for Japan in the Russo-Japanese War, it did not seem appropriate three decades later against a nation as powerful as the United States. Naval analysts in Tokyo knew that since 1907 America's war strategy—the so-called Orange plan—had envisaged a decisive confrontation west of the Marshalls.

Japan's answer to our Orange plan, which had been drawn up when our Pacific Fleet was numerically superior to Japan's Combined Fleet, was the doctrine of *yōgeki sakusen* ("ambush operations"). This called for their powerful submarine fleet to whittle down our advancing battle line before the final slugging match.[3] But even in 1940 when their battle line exceeded ours, Yamamoto, who knew America better than any other Japanese admiral, saw the strategic weakness of this doctrine. He made no bones about the desirability of avoiding such a confrontation that would result in war with the United States. He knew that if it came to a prolonged fight, the Pacific Fleet would not sortie to challenge the Combined Fleet to "the decisive battle" until we had built up our superiority.

It had been apparent to all observers during the late 1930s that Yamamoto's life was in danger. Being acquainted with him professionally and socially, and feeling a friendly kinship with him through the similarity of our interests, I watched his activities with a special interest. I had seen at first hand how as vice-minister of the navy he had risked his popularity and even his life to steer successive governments away from confrontation with the United States over the war in China. He had been marked by the right wing for his opposition to the tripartite pact, and he had been a stubborn opponent of war with the United States and Great Britain.[4]

During the spring of 1939 and into the summer, reports of plots against Yamamoto became increasingly lurid, and the campaign to drive him out was violent, with some threatening that "if he does not mend his ways he will be got rid of, with explosives or a bomb if necessary."[5]

When, for his own safety, on 30 August he was given command of the Combined Fleet, Yamamoto realized that a clash with the United States had become all but inevitable. Konoye's new-order-for-Asia policy in 1940 had aligned Japan with Germany and Italy in the tripartite pact. The parties were bound by the treaty to come to each other's aid if any one of them was attacked by a power "not involved in the European war or in the Sino-Japanese conflict."

"If we are ordered to do it," Yamamoto had told the prime minister to his face, on the eve of the signing of the tripartite pact on 27 September, "then I can guarantee to put up a tough fight for the first six months, but I have absolutely no confidence as to what would happen if it went on for two or three years. It's too late to do anything about the tripartite pact now, but I hope at least you'll make every effort to avoid war with America."[6]

Distrustful of politicians but loyal to duty, Yamamoto set out to modify the naval staff's *yōgeki sakusen* doctrine into a quick-victory strategy for Japan in the impending naval war. As a young man he had hitchhiked around the United States. He had been mightily impressed with the power manifest in the Pittsburgh steel mills, the Detroit auto factories, the Kansas wheat fields, and above all by the Texas oil fields. More than any other Japanese, Yamamoto had come to appreciate that *Beikoku*, "rice country," their descriptive word for the United States as a land of abundant resources, was correct.

If it should come to war with the United States, Japan's best chance, as Yamamoto saw it, was a quick knockout blow to immobilize the enemy's battle fleet and neutralize American naval power long enough for Japan to secure the natural resources and defenses of southeast Asia and the western Pacific.

Surprisingly, the stationing of our fleet in Pearl Harbor offered the best opportunity for achievement of this goal. The scenario conjured up by Hirata's 1933 tract had been given theoretical shape with a 1936 study at the imperial navy war college of an attack on Hawaii. It became practicable after the impressive demonstration of Japanese carrier planes in the spring naval maneuvers of 1940. But it was the British naval air attack on the Italian fleet in Taranto harbor on 12 November that finally crystallized the concept into a nine-page outline by Yamamoto "Views on Preparations for War," which contains his first formal suggestion of an air attack on Hawaii. He submitted this paper to Navy Minister Koshiro Oikawa in strict confidence on 7 January 1941.[7]

Yamamoto also gave this secret outline to Rear Admiral Takijiro Ohnishi, the tactical genius of Japanese naval aviation, for study and evaluation. Within six weeks Ohnishi had concluded that the operation, though risky, was feasible—but only *if* surprise could be achieved. The working out of operational details was turned over to Commander Minoru Genda, the resourceful thirty-six-year-old tactical aviator on the staff of Vice Admiral Chuichi Nagumo's newly formed First Air Fleet.

Genda, a naval attaché in London at the time of the Royal Navy's successful torpedo plane attacks on the Italian battleships, had made a firsthand study of the techniques employed. If twenty-one British carrier planes could cripple three Italian capital ships, he reasoned, then two hundred Japanese aircraft should be able to put most, if not all, of the Pacific Fleet out of commission.

It took two months for Genda to work up his draft tactical study for the attack on Pearl Harbor. Meanwhile, the secrecy that was essential for any chance of success came perilously close to being blown. On 27 January, Ambassador Grew sent to Washington a report that the Peruvian minister had been told "from many sources, including a Japanese source, that in the event of trouble's breaking out between the United States and Japan, the Japanese intend to make a surprise attack against Pearl Harbor with all their strength and employing all their equipment."[8]

This information was relayed to Kimmel on 1 February, the day when he assumed command of the Pacific Fleet. With it came an assessment by my old boss, Commander McCollum, now head of ONI's Far East section: "Naval Intelligence places no credence in these rumors." Such a casual dismissal, even of cocktail party gossip, was surprising given the current concern of the war plans division that if "war eventuates with Japan, it is believed easily possible that hostilities would be preceded by a surprise attack upon the Pacific Fleet in the naval base of Pearl Harbor."[9]

Admiral Stark had evidently been alarmed enough by this scenario to have the secretary of the navy alert the war department on 24 January 1941 that the "inherent possibility of a *major disaster to the fleet or naval base* warrant taking every step, as rapidly as can be done, as will increase the joint readiness of the Army and Navy to withstand a raid [emphasis added]." The memorandum, which originated from the director of war plans, drew attention to "air bombing attack" and "air torpedo plane attack" as the principal dangers threatening Pearl Harbor, since precautions had already been taken against submarines, mines, and "bombardment by gunfire."[10]

Admiral Turner, the recently installed head of war plans, was to persistently claim—after the event—that he had predicted Japan might attack Oahu with planes launched from "a striking force of carriers." It is all the more astonishing therefore, that Turner authorized a dispatch so dismissive of just such a possibility a week after his memorandum had been circulated.

Whether there had been some kind of a real leak in Tokyo has never been established. It was later learned, however, that the rumor had reached Grew from a Japanese member of the Peruvian embassy's staff who had apparently picked it up from her chauffeur boyfriend. But what was dismissed in Washington as fantastic gossip struck a chord that brought to my mind the Hirata translation, containing his imaginative account of the air attack on Pearl Harbor, that I had tried to get published five months earlier. I was reminded by the Peruvian rumor to show it to Kimmel.

When the admiral returned the translation, we discussed various points about the piece and Kimmel asked if I thought that Hirata had written from an official or semiofficial point of view, and whether the Japanese would consider such a risky undertaking. Considering the Japanese mania for secrecy, I doubted that the author was reflecting official Japanese naval opinion. But I pointed out that the possible would become probable only if they thought that such an attack could succeed. We had to remember that, historically, Japan's actions did not follow orthodox military strategy, and that the Japanese had made a similar preemptive surprise attack on Port Arthur in 1904 during the war with Russia.

Finally Kimmel sent for his war plans officer, Captain Charles H. McMorris, and asked what he thought about the chances of a Japanese strike at Pearl Harbor. Soc (his sobriquet was a tribute to his Socratic wisdom) admitted that, as operations officer at Pearl since 1939, he had considered this possibility. His conclusion was that although it was possible, the Japanese would be deterred by the huge risk involved. But however remote the possibility might appear, he said, we had to admit that the British strike on the Italian fleet at Taranto the previous November had shown that an airborne torpedo attack on anchored ships could be devastating.

Pearl Harbor was not equipped with antitorpedo nets. In January, however, Washington had considered providing them, but the plan had fallen by the administrative wayside. That the Japanese might have in mind a carrier strike against us was an option that we considered. But no information was received subsequent to the dismissive 1 February report from Washington that gave me any grounds for uprating what was only a *possibility* into a *probability*.

Furthermore, in the week before being relieved, Richardson also had expressed his concern about fleet security in the face of "surprise raids on Pearl Harbor," in a report in which Kimmel collaborated.[11] In a letter of 15 February the chief of naval operations told Kimmel that Washington analysts had determined that antitorpedo nets were not necessary since the waters of Pearl Harbor, unlike Taranto, were too shallow for making an effective aerial torpedo attack.[12] Admiral Bloch, commandant of the Fourteenth Naval District, concurred.

Stark's letter had emphasized that his main concern was the threat of enemy submarine attacks and mining at Pearl Harbor, not an air attack. Kimmel, nevertheless, had issued a 15 February order to the fleet which noted that, in addition to these dangers, "a declaration of war might be preceded by:

1. a surprise attack on ships in Pearl Harbor
2. a surprise submarine attack on ships in operating area
3. a combination of these two."[13]

This focus on seaborne threats naturally loomed larger in the minds of surface unit commanders, but bombing and aerial torpedoes were rated a far greater menace in the calculations of air commanders. The vulnerability of Pearl Harbor to a carrier-borne air strike had been demonstrated as recently as March 1938, when Admiral Ernest J. King had launched a successful air strike from *Saratoga,* to conclude Fleet Problem XIX. The alarming ease with which this attack had been executed was still fresh in the minds of Major General F. L. Martin, head of the Hawaiian army air corps, and Rear Admiral Patrick L. N. Bellinger, head of the Hawaiian naval air patrol.

"It appears that the most likely and dangerous form of attack on Oahu would be an air attack," they warned in a joint report of 31 March 1941, which would later appear to be a remarkable piece of prophecy. "At present such an attack would most likely be launched from one or more carriers which would probably approach inside of three hundred miles," they predicted, advising that it would come at sunrise since "in a dawn air attack there is a high probability that it could be delivered as a complete surprise."[14]

Coincidentally, on 1 April (the day after the Martin-Bellinger report was issued) CNO sent a caution to all commands that "past experience" showed that Axis powers preferred to launch attacks on Saturdays, Sundays, or national holidays, and that all commands "should take such steps on such days to see that proper watches and precautions are in effect."[15]

Little did Martin and Bellinger realize that on the other side of the Pacific, Lieutenant Commander Genda's secret feasibility study of the Hawaii attack proposal was reaching identical conclusions. To defend against a dawn raid, the commanders responsible for the air defenses of Hawaii advised that it was "desirable" to organize daily air patrols "as far as possible to seaward through 360 degrees to reduce the probabilities of surface or air surprise." But Martin and Bellinger recognized that the demands of effective defense could not be reconciled with the shortages of aircraft and personnel, both army and naval, in Hawaii. Accordingly, this limited the "desirable" around-the-compass, long-range air patrols to those times when "*intelligence* indicates that a surface raid is probable [emphasis added]."[16]

Despite repeated pleas from Admiral Kimmel and Lieutenant General Walter C. Short, the army commander in Hawaii, Washington refused to make any more planes or other matériel available for adequate long-range surveillance. This is all the more surprising because Admiral Turner would testify at the congressional hearings on Pearl Harbor in 1945 that the Martin-Bellinger report of 31 March 1941 was endorsed at the highest levels in Washington.

"We agreed thoroughly with it, approved it, and it was very gratifying to see that officers in important commands out there had the same view of the situation as was held by the war and navy departments."[17] While this was Turner's position in 1945, it may be asked why he and the other military leaders in Washington did not see to it that Pearl Harbor received the planes and the intelligence that could and should have been sent out to us before December 1941?

This question has two answers. The simple one is that Washington was looking in the wrong direction, toward Europe, and not properly evaluating the Pacific situation; nor were they paying any attention to the advice of commanders in the field. The complex answer is to be found in the breakdown of the intelligence process in Washington in the critical months of 1941 as Japan and the United States drifted closer to war.

Accurate information about our fleet was one of the keys to the success of Japan's attack on Pearl Harbor. It was a tragic paradox that while our intelligence was far more extensive, it still failed to provide us with an adequate warning of the attack. In a sequence of events that bore an uncanny resemblance to a Greek tragedy, our intelligence advantage was thrown away: Washington was doomed, as if by some fatal curse, to ignore, misinterpret, or neglect to relay to Pearl Harbor the vital clues that would have saved the battle fleet. By the same token, General Douglas MacArthur, despite a ten-day warning of the threat of an imminent strike on the Philippines, lost his air superiority in a bombing raid *nine* hours *after* the Pearl Harbor attack.

Never in history had a nation steered into a confrontation with a rival power with more information about the general intentions of the potential enemy than the United States had about Japan on the eve of the Pacific war. But our leaders in Washington gambled on the assumption that our eavesdropping on Tokyo's diplomatic traffic would provide an early warning of their moves—even though we had lost our ability to tap into their army and naval communications.

It is all the more astonishing that such a fundamental miscalculation occurred after Washington had been reading the Japanese diplomatic and naval ciphers for more than a decade. By a combination of code breaking, direction finding, and traffic analysis it had been possible to predict every movement of Japan's fleet until 1940. It was in October that year that the chief of naval operations issued the warning: "During the past year and a half, however, the major Orange naval cryptographic systems have undergone radical changes, resulting in a temporary reduction in the intelligence obtained by cryptanalytical means."[18]

Japan's first counterstrike against our cryptanalysts in the secret radio intelligence war had been made on 1 November 1938 when a new code superseded their eight-year-old Blue Book. The change was apparently a direct response to warnings by Japan's naval commander in China that their high-level administrative code system was no longer secure.[19]

The new cipher system was designated "AD" from its similarity to the "A" version of the Blue Book, but it still meant that all the code values recovered by us over the past eight years had to be scrapped. The entire system—code and new cipher forms, as well as keys—had to be reconstructed from scratch. This required the recovery of the four thousand keys that were changed every four months, in addition to finding the solution of the transposition form that was changed every ten days.

The arduous task was assigned by Safford to Commander Dyer's cryptographic unit at Pearl Harbor. Hypo's staff was increased to four officers to cope, but the problem, according to a contemporary report, was "one of quantity and time rather than difficulty."[20]

After a year's effort, Dyer's team at Pearl Harbor had reached the point in November 1940 that the "AD" system was beginning to produce intelligible text when Japan made another major change in the underlying code. Unlike the first version, the new edition of the code book appeared to have a circulation limited to flag officers. There were comparatively few messages transmitted over the next twelve months and fewer intercepts could be made. Although Hypo continued to concentrate exclusively on what was designated as the "NL" system until the second week of December 1941, it consumed many thousands of valuable hours of cryptanalytic effort for no intelligence return. Only some two hundred intercepts were ever made, a totally inadequate number for the effective penetration of any cipher system.[21]

While the Pacific Fleet's communications intelligence unit was left to wage its fruitless struggle with the so-called flag officers system, navy department cryptanalysts had turned their attention to a new "Operations Code" that had come into use on 1 June 1939. This "AN" cipher, later to be designated JN-25, was radically different from any other so far employed by the Japanese navy. It was a five-numeral, two-part code, consisting of 33,333 groups in the "dictionary book," to each of which were added, by false arithmetic (no borrowing or carrying) a five-digit number selected in sequence according to the start key from a second book of random additives. The resulting encipherment consisted of a series of five-digit numbers divisible by three to provide a convenient check against garbles.

The assault on the three entities that made up the JN-25 system had been spearheaded by the redoubtable Mrs. Driscoll. The three parts of the system were (1) the code itself, (2) the current additive book, and (3) the system of encrypting that was indicated at the beginning of the message, the starting point in the stream of additives.[22] Not until after the initial breakthrough had been made in the fall of 1939 did the most laborious and time-consuming task of recovering the additives and code groups begin. The OP-20-G cryptanalysts under Lieutenant E.S.L. Goodwin labored for a year compiling code book and additive tables in blank ledger books. The columns, five-digit groups, and their appropriate Japanese characters and English translation were entered one by one with medieval patience by civilian linguists Phillip H. Cate and Fred C. Woodrough, Jr.

After the cryptographic section had been "banging its head into the wall over the 5-digit system" the first JN-25 decrypts were finally made two months after Goodwin left in September 1940.[23] By the end of the year the first "A" version of the code, which had by then been in use for eighteen months, had been solved. Then on 1 December 1940 it was superseded by the "B" version. Five successive cipher books had been used during the life of JN-25A, but the fifth was to be in effect during the first two months of JN-25B. This facilitated both the recognition of the change and the rapid recovery of some two thousand values for the new code book. But once the new additives came into use in January 1941, progress slowed until the "difference table" produced by the IBM tabulating machines was used to speed up the recovery process.[24]

Japan's drastic code changes at the end of 1940 left us unable to read anything in their main naval cipher systems until well into 1941. Only their merchant ship code continued to be "99% readable." Even their "Material Code System," labeled "HE," which contained details of naval housekeeping and supply, required six months' work before it could be reread for items of minor importance. Japan's "Intelligence Code System," considered unlikely to be of "any great value as far as current information," was given an even lower priority.[25]

So the critical year of 1941 began with an almost total blackout of Japanese naval intelligence. Safford's five officers and two civilian cryptanalysts were also obliged to divide their labors trying to crack the German naval Enigma used by the U-boats on the Atlantic, while laboring over the machine cipher employed by the Japanese naval attachés. In addition to their main assault on the JN-25 operational code, OP-20-G had to divert efforts to helping the army penetrate Japan's diplomatic traffic.

The army's Signal Intelligence Section led by Colonel William F. Friedman had made their first breakthrough into Tokyo's most secret diplomatic cipher in September 1940 within a week of the navy cryptanalysts' initial decryption of JN-25. This was a remarkable simultaneous feat of cryptography by the two teams, since the Japanese foreign ministry had also introduced its new cipher in February 1939, five months before the navy. Newly released documentation reveals that—contrary to what has previously been written about the army's singular triumph—it was not accomplished without assistance from the navy.[26]

The relatively small SIS team had begun to work on Japan's main diplomatic communications in 1932, after achieving a partial success with the German and Italian government ciphers only three years after the State Department's injunction against reading "other gentlemen's mail." Friedman's special expertise was in machine enciphering systems. He had patented the electrically controlled rotors that became the heart of the cipher machine that was our most secure and widely used coding device throughout World War II. The development of the Sigaba, as the army called the machine, known in the navy as the ECM, was also being paralleled in Japan.[27]

The Japanese navy was evidently spurred to develop an electric coding machine in the aftermath of the revelations of Yardley's book about our Black Chamber. In 1935 its use first became apparent to the OP-20-G cryptanalysts who encountered cipher traffic which Mrs. Driscoll analyzed as having been generated by a machine. She quickly developed a method of manual decryption for "M1," as the Japanese device was named. It involved the use of a graph-paper diagram against which she slid the recovered cipher sequence on a long strip of graph paper, enabling the substitution generated by the machine to be manually recorded. It was by this technique that Miss Aggie had first identified the word "Tomimura," which had led to the capture of our navy spies in 1936.[28] Our cryptanalysts were naturally anxious to reconstruct their own version of the device, none more so than Lieutenant Jack S. Holtwick who had helped Mrs. Driscoll crack "M1." When it became apparent that this traffic was being exchanged with the Japanese naval attaché in Washington, surveillance of his Alban Towers apartment was conducted. This picked up mysterious clicking. On the assumption that this noise was produced by the coding machine, an elaborate break-in was arranged.

While the attaché was being royally entertained by Commander Zacharias and his wife at dinner on an evening in July 1935, Holtwick and a chief radioman called McGregor, posing as electricians, conducted a detailed examination of the Japanese officers' residence-cum-office in the imposing building that dominates the intersection of Massachusetts and Wisconsin avenues. No sign of either an electrical or mechanical coding device was found. So (contrary to what other writers have claimed) Holtwick had to draw on his own ingenuity and Mrs. Driscoll's cryptanalysis in order to design his own version of the machine.[29]

This analog worked well enough to decrypt the Japanese navy's machine cipher until it was abandoned in 1938. But the real value of the "M1" machine was that it gave Friedman's team a headstart in constructing the device that would imitate the "M3" machine, which was then being used by the Japanese foreign ministry in 1935 to encode its most confidential communications. By 1936 it was enabling us to read Tokyo's diplomatic messages on a regular basis. At the suggestion of one of Friedman's staff the colors of the primary spectrum were adopted as identifiers and the "A" enciphering device was thenceforth dubbed the "Red machine"—not to be confused with the Japanese navy's Red code book. The Red machine remained in use for communications between Tokyo and its principal embassies until February 1939. A decrypt late in 1938 forewarned us of an impending change by revealing that a cipher expert named Okamoto was being sent to nine of Japan's most important embassies to install a type "B" machine.[30]

The new encoding device, like its predecessor, had been developed by Captain Risaburo Itō. Designated *97-shiki O-bun Injiki,* or "Alphabetical Typewriter 97," its number was adopted from the year of its invention, 1937, which was the ninety-seventh year of the twenty-fifth century according to the ancient Japanese calendar. It represented a radical departure from the German Enigma and our Sigaba electrical encoding devices because it was not based on rotors, but a battery of six-level, twenty-five-point telephone exchange stepping switches with a plugboard to set up the key. A typewriter keyboard was used to enter the message in kana with a three-letter code for numerals and the enciphered communication was printed out by a second electric typewriter. The millions upon millions of possible cipher combinations made possible by switch and plug settings convinced its inventor—and the Japanese foreign ministry—that the Type 97 code system was unbreakable.

The intercept of a Red message sent from Tokyo on 18 February 1939 announced that the new cipher system would come into operation two days later.[31] Following the precedent set for the Red machine, Friedman adopted the cover-name "Purple" for the new system and immediately launched into an intensive eighteen-month effort to unravel this cipher and construct a new decoding device.

"The volume of messages in the new system gradually increased," according to Frank B. Rowlett, Friedman's specialist on Japanese codes, "until in mid April it was clear that the new machine had virtually replaced the old on the major diplomatic circuits."[32] Because the Japanese continued using the old system after transferring the Red machines to less important embassies around the world, we continued reading part of Japan's diplomatic traffic. This provided important help to Friedman's SIS cryptanalysts, since there was some overlap between the communications sent in Red and Purple. But the most important intercepts exchanged between Tokyo and Berlin, London and Washington piled up unread, and the pressure on Friedman and his team increased as Europe lurched toward war in 1939.

Analysis of this traffic had revealed that while Purple was a more complex encipherment than Red, both were based on a system that divided the twenty-six letters of the Roman alphabet into subsets of six and twenty elements. This was the discovery that provided the key by which Friedman and his analysts began to unlock the new cipher. But recovering the "sixes" proved a slow pencil-and-paper effort that dragged on until August 1940 when Larry Clark, a civilian cryptanalyst recruited by Friedman, hit on the notion that the Japanese had used telephone stepping switches instead of rotors as the enciphering mechanism. Within a month Friedman's team, by a process of trial, error, and mathematical calculation, produced a blueprint for a device that duplicated their conception of the Japanese machine. The first Purple analog was actually built by navy technicians at the Washington Navy Yard. By the second week in September the current keys to the Purple cipher had been recovered and the rat's nest of wiring and chattering relays housed in a makeshift black wooden box finally rewarded the months of ingenious labor by producing the first decrypts of Tokyo's most secret diplomatic messages.

The enormous mental effort put Friedman temporarily in the hospital with a breakdown. But the full measure of his team's remarkable achievement came five years later after the dissection of remains of a captured Japanese "B" machine revealed that of the several hundred connections in their analog, only two were wired differently from the Japanese machine's. The Purple machine, of which five were eventually constructed, also proved more reliable than the Japanese originals in eliminating garbled code groups. The total cost of the hardware in the first two navy-built analogs was $684.65—an investment that was minuscule when measured against the return.[33]

The ability of Friedman's army team to read the high-level Japanese diplomatic communications greatly enhanced their status. As one of its key members, Frank Rowlett, put it, "The chief signal officer liked to refer to us as magicians."[34] This name stuck and the term Magic came into general use with reference to all cryptographic intelligence, even after we had adopted the British practice of formally classifying it as "ultrasecret" information, or simply as "Ultra."

Magic was considered so vital that by the beginning of 1941 it had been hedged with a fetish of secrecy so overwhelming that its value as intelligence began to erode. Apart from the operational heads in the war and navy departments, it was made available only to the president and his secretaries of state, navy, and war. Information derived from the diplomatic intercepts was only sporadically to be sent out to Admiral Kimmel.

Although the army had yet to penetrate any of the Japanese military ciphers, and the navy cryptanalysts were still battling to get back into the Japanese naval codes, the ultrasecret mystique of the intelligence derived from the Purple machine created a sense of infallibility in Washington, as if we possessed a "magic wand" with which to divine Japanese intentions. Control of such a potent source of information in a command setup is never more critical than when it falls into the hands of ambitious and determined officers.

The newly declassified records reveal hitherto unknown details about how this intelligence was abused. It is now clear that ranking officers use Magic to further their own authority at the expense of its proper dissemination as the crisis with Japan worsened. The consequences disastrous.

6

Pacific Overtures

DESPITE THE MOUNTING TENSION between Washington and Tokyo at the beginning of 1941, on 31 January when Japanese liner *Kamakura Maru* entered Honolulu harbor escorted by two American destroyers, she was roundly greeted. Her distinguished passenger, Admiral Kichisaburo Nomura, was visiting Honolulu for the day en route to his new post as ambassador to the United States. Civilian and military leaders were waiting to greet him when the ship docked at eight that Friday morning. I was with Admiral Richardson because he knew of my friendship with Nomura and had assigned me as his honorary aide for the visit.

I had first met Nomura during my student days in Japan in 1931, when he was director of naval intelligence. We became friends six years later while I was in Tokyo as assistant naval attaché, when he was Japan's foreign minister. Tall, moon-faced, suave, poker-playing, bourbon-drinking, chain-smoking Nomura was a sincere friend of the United States. He had been naval attaché in Washington during World War I, and had many personal friends in America.

His day in Honolulu was busy, and I was at his side throughout the full schedule, which included visits to the governor and flagship *Pennsylvania,* a chamber of commerce lunch at the Royal Hawaiian Hotel, a memorial church service, and a United Japanese Society dinner honor at the Sunchoro tea house.

ited Japanese Society had plainly not expected me to be pres-
Nomura's opening words were, "Leftenant Commander
friend and is my guest. I am on my way to Washing-
nd straighten out any problems between our
Leftenant Commander Layton to be present
s and speeches here because I have nothing to
him to know and assure his government that I

82

Despite his tight schedule, we had some opportunities that busy day for friendly conversation, and I was impressed by Nomura's clear sincerity and genuine concern for the drift of events. He thanked me warmly as we parted late that night and he boarded *Kamakura Maru* for San Francisco.

Nomura was one of the few senior Japanese officials I knew who had real affinity for and understanding of the United States. His appointment at this critical time was a signal of Tokyo's attempt to calm American concern. If anyone could have done it, Nomura was that man.

He arrived in Washington on 12 February 1941 and was at the White House two days later to present his credentials and have candid discussions with President Roosevelt on the key issues dividing their two nations. Diplomatically naïve, Nomura was so eager to succeed in his mission to reach a speedy settlement with the United States that he was ready to accept commitments that his cabinet could not possibly have sold to the military. His first meeting was marked by much cordiality and personal friendliness, since the president considered the admiral to be an old navy friend. Even Secretary of State Cordell Hull, who made no bones about his abiding distaste for the Japanese, warmed to Nomura's eagerness to restore friendly relations.

The ambassador reported to Tokyo that Roosevelt was principally concerned that Japan might move into the French Indochina area and that Germany and Italy would force Japan into war by orchestrating another *Panay* incident. The president had reassuringly told him that, provided outstanding differences over Japan's aggression in China could be settled, there was "plenty of room in the Pacific for everybody."[1]

At the beginning of April 1941 the chances for reaching a settlement of long-standing differences between Japan and the United States seemed brighter than they had ever been as a result of Nomura's arrival and the president's favorable reaction to his initial overtures. The Roosevelt administration had a specific reason for welcoming any sign of a thaw in relations with Tokyo. Washington was wrestling with one of America's perennial strategic dilemmas: how to defend the nation and fight a two-ocean war with a one-ocean navy. With Britain having been at war with Germany for a year and a half, our military leaders had adopted an Atlantic first commitment that was implicit in their latest "Rainbow 5" contingency war plan.

The army and navy had jointly developed five plans for the principal war contingencies with our foes and allies designated by colors so that Rainbow was chosen as an appropriate code name. By the spring of 1941 it had become increasingly clear that only Rainbow 5, which envisaged dealing with Germany in the Atlantic and holding Japan in the Pacific, would meet the emerging global crisis. Rainbow 5 had itself evolved from an October 1940 memorandum of Admiral Stark that urged the adoption of the navy's Plan D (for dog), which anticipated entering the naval beside Britain if necessary. This had persuaded the army toward lantic strategy in support of Britain's war against the Axis powers. The logistical balance for this plan had already been set by Roosevelt's ingenious fiscal sleight of hand "to get rid of this silly, foolish dollar sign" by lending the British whatever arms and supplies they needed under a lend-lease bill.[2] It had been fought through Congress against the vociferous opposition of the isolationists, and by March was passed into law.

America's increasing commitment to Britain, however, produced growing German pressure on Japan to launch a diversionary attack against British territory in the Far East. To assure Hitler that this was Tokyo's intention, the pro-Axis foreign minister, Yosuke Matsuoka, undertook the long trans-Siberian railway trip to Berlin in April. He left without being told that Prime Minister Konoye was engaged in a conflicting secret diplomatic initiative to reach an accord with the United States, aimed at nipping in the bud a potential Anglo-American alliance in the Far East.

Konoye's highly unorthodox diplomatic maneuver had begun stealthily in December 1940 with the recruitment of two Roman Catholic priests, Bishop James E. Walsh and Father James M. Drought, of the Maryknoll Mission. While they had been visiting Tokyo just before Christmas 1940, their isolationist anti-Roosevelt sympathies had been skillfully played upon by Colonel Takeo Iwakuro of the military affairs bureau and Tadeo Ikawa, a banker and confidant of Konoye. By the time they left Tokyo the priests had become committed to undertaking a two-man private peace mission whose objective was to strike a deal with Washington that would facilitate Konoye's schemes for a "new order" in Asia without the invoking of American economic reprisals.

Since Japan relied on the United States for more than 90 percent of her oil needs, Konoye's initiative was given a special urgency in January 1941 after Secretary of State Hull threatened her with extensive economic reprisals if Japan went any further toward extending herself in the western Pacific by force of arms. Drought and Walsh returned home to enlist the sympathetic consideration of Postmaster General Frank C. Walker, the leading Roman Catholic in Roosevelt's administration.

Not until the arrival of Admiral Nomura was Walker able to persuade the secretary of state to consider secret negotiations with the new Japanese ambassador. These negotiations were to be based on a "draft understanding" prepared by the two priests that purported to rationalize aggression in China. This document, which the State Department "John Doe Memorandum" was ostensibly formulated by But it had actually been drafted in consultation with followed them back from Japan in the role of

ications of Japan's military attaché in Washcoded until the middle of the war, reveal the and Walsh—who were referred to as John Doe by the State Department—were being manipulated by Konoye's aides and by Taro Terasaki, Japan's spymaster in Washington. "We decided, therefore, first to feel our way from behind the scenes," the military attaché reported from the Washington embassy on 16 April 1941: "In this respect Iwakuro and Ikawa were assigned to sounding out the contacts we made in December [i.e., Walsh, Drought, and Walker] and then have the ambassador confirm the results obtained."[3]

Consistent with Konoye's demands for utmost secrecy, a series of evening meetings took place in late March for which the portly Ambassador Nomura smuggled himself in and out of Secretary Hull's Carlton Hotel suite through the service entrance. These clandestine sessions appeared to Nomura, at least, to have made such progress toward resolving issues that by 16 April he reported enthusiastically to Konoye that an accord was imminent.

The ambassador's optimism was also reflected in that day's report by Japan's military attaché, which acknowledged encouragement given Japan by Charles Lindbergh and his isolationist friends with their antiwar rallies. As a result of their assistance Roosevelt was thought to be "bowing to the pressure" of public opinion.[4] The intercepted communications reveal frequent contacts by leaders of the isolationist lobby with Japanese and Germans, as well as the surprising extent to which the celebrated aviator hero was subject to the influence of intermediaries in the pay of Berlin and Tokyo.[5]

The reports from Washington combined to persuade Konoye that the "John Doe Memorandum" of understanding had been accepted as a basis for opening negotiations. Japan's premier was simply deluding himself. Since the memorandum proposed that the United States recognize Japanese authority over a large part of China, and pressure Chiang Kai-shek to accept a peace treaty, it was dismissed by Secretary Hull as "much less accommodating than we had been led to believe it would be and all that the most ardent Japanese imperialist could want."[6] The State Department's counterproposal was a four-point American demand that Japan respect the territorial integrity of China, support the open-door principle of equal commercial opportunity, abide by the status quo in the western Pacific, and detach herself from the tripartite pact. Hull's "Four Principles," as these demands came to be known, ran diametrically counter to Konoye's proposals.

The rosy April twilight that flooded into Hull's hotel suite during their clandestine evening sessions suffused the conversations between the two men with warm feelings for one another, which disguised the extent of the gulf that separated Tokyo and Washington. Nomura's advancing deafness and his painful determination to maintain cordial relations led him to overstress American willingness to negotiate on the basis of the "draft understanding." For his part, Hull failed to appreciate that Tokyo's pact with Hitler and Mussolini was a major stumbling block, or just how in-

transient Japan's army leadership was over the China issue. With the
fire-breathing Matsuoka in Berlin cementing Tokyo's alignment with Nazi
Germany at the same time, our State Department was receiving conflicting signals.

After Nomura's early optimistic reports, Konoye hoped to reach an
agreement with Washington before Matsuoka's return to Tokyo resulted
in his pressure for a closer alliance with Germany. But these hopes
foundered when the army refused any concessions over the China issue
and the foreign minister came back with promises to keep to Hitler, plus
a neutrality pact with the Soviet Union. "Japan can straighten out the Far
East and Germany will handle Europe," Stalin had promised the diminutive Matsuoka at Moscow's central station. "Later, together all of us will
deal with America."[7]

After forty years, documents have emerged from the declassified American archives that shed new light on the events of 1941. One of the most
significant must be a Japanese radio intercept of 11 December 1940—not
decrypted until 1945—which reveals an astonishing Axis intelligence coup
that undoubtedly helped precipitate Japan down the road to Pearl Harbor.[8]

The capture of a British steamer in the Indian Ocean by a German
surface raider on 11 November has been a hitherto overlooked incident.
But now its consequences can be seen to have had an important impact
on Tokyo's foreign policy. Although the tripartite pact had been signed in
September, Japan was still hesitant to provide Hitler with all the assistance he was asking for to take the naval war against Britain into the
Far East. Supply ships for the German raiders had been operating from
Japanese ports but the foreign minister wanted far closer cooperation
with Hitler. In this Matsuoka had the support of Nobutake Kondo, vice-
chief of the imperial naval general staff, who forcefully argued that since
the German navy, only one tenth the size of the British, had succeeded in
taking over Norway, then the Japanese navy, with its superior odds, had
little to fear from the Anglo-American fleet in a southward move against
the Netherlands East Indies.

Kondo urged that Prime Minister Konoye must now "openly embrace
the Axis powers."[9] The German naval attaché to Japan reported on 13
September that "a transformation has taken place in the views of fleet
commander in chief Yamamoto, who until now has always taken a pro-
Anglo-Saxon attitude." Rear Admiral Paul Wenneker, an astute observer
of Tokyo politics, ascribed the change to "the continually worsening relations with the USA and the tremendous armament program they have
initiated over there." Wenneker, therefore, predicted Japan would "resolve Far Eastern problems before this has been completed."[10] Hitler
pressured Japan for a more pro-German policy in the Far East, especially
for assistance with commerce raiding on British ships. On 14 November

1940 Admiral Erich Raeder, commander in chief of the German navy, summoned Admiral Yoshikazu Endo, Japan's naval attaché in Berlin, and urged him to cooperate in the submarine war in the Atlantic, bases in the mandates "for use in secret replenishment and repairs of warships operating in the Pacific," and "intelligence regarding movements" of British warships and merchantmen.[11]

Despite Endo's cautioning Tokyo that it would be "advantageous" to give assistance "in utmost secrecy to German naval operations," the naval staff was still uncertain about throwing in its lot with the Axis. They tactfully refused to send submarines into the Atlantic while requesting detailed German plans for secret bases in the Marshalls. But they enthusiastically offered to share intelligence information "to foster the exchange between navies."[12]

The true extent of Japanese assistance to the German commerce-raiding operations in the Pacific is still disputed because "the extent of the help given the German navy is wrapped in a veil of deep secrecy," according to *Senshi Sōsho,* Japan's official war history. "Whatever cooperation between the Japanese and German navies may have been, however, it is certain that it was not such as to have had great effect," it asserts. But this "official" denial is belied by captured German naval records. They reveal that after the fall of 1940 the Kriegsmarine's armed merchant cruisers were regularly using bases in the Marianas, Carolines, and Marshalls for refit and supply.[13]

For the first time, with the release of the Japanese naval attaché intercepts, it is possible to document how close this cooperation must have been, because it brought Tokyo an intelligence bonanza that included Royal Navy and British merchant ship ciphers, in addition to top-secret war cabinet papers detailing the parlous state of Britain's Far East defenses.[14]

This priceless information was discovered in the sixty packets of confidential government mail that the British steamer *Automedon* was carrying from London to Singapore when she was captured by the German raider *Atlantis* on 11 November 1940. The importance of the secret mail was at once appreciated by the intelligence officer of Schiff 16, as the armed merchantman was code-named. At a rendezvous in the mandates it was transferred from *Atlantis* to the Norwegian prize supply ship *Ole Jacob*—contrary to international law, which prohibited regular use of neutral ports by warships. *Ole Jacob* arrived in Kōbe on 4 December when her Norwegian crew was removed in the dead of night to German liner *Scharnhorst* to prevent its contacting any Allied agents and telling of the *Automedon*'s capture.[15]

Couriers from the German consulate general in Kōbe accompanied the large chest of top-secret British documents to Tokyo, and, on 9 December, Admiral Wenneker, the naval attaché, skimmed through them. He at once appreciated the explosive significance of the minutes of a

British war cabinet meeting on the Far East that had been held on 15 August 1940. The papers were sent off that afternoon by special courier to Berlin after Wenneker radioed a summary by a top-secret Enigma cipher that was never cracked by the British.

The importance of the papers as Wenneker read them was that Churchill's cabinet had decided that the British were "unable to send a fleet to the Far East," and so "must avoid 'open clash' with Japan" until military cooperation with the United States was assured. The British would not go to war even if Japan attacked Thailand or Indochina. Instead, efforts would be made to buy off Tokyo with "general concessions"—including abandoning Singapore and making a deal over Malaya.[16]

Four days later, after the material had been evaluated by the naval staff in Berlin, the British documents were passed to the Japanese naval attaché in Germany. He summarized their contents in an 11 December message to Tokyo. Next morning Wenneker handed copies to members of the Japanese naval staff, whose reaction was one of "extraordinary interest."[17] That evening Admiral Kondo sent for the German naval attaché and repeatedly expressed his thanks for such priceless intelligence.

It was not that Japan did not know about the defenselessness of Singapore, but now they were sure that the British government had committed itself to a policy of appeasement if Tokyo stepped up the diplomatic pressure. This sensational intelligence reduced many of Japan's uncertainties about how to proceed with their strategic and diplomatic plans for realization of their "new order" in southeast Asia. Konoye now saw the possibility that diplomacy alone could achieve this goal; but only if an Anglo-American Far East alliance could be prevented. The Japanese navy could then prepare for its southward advance with no opposition from the weak British and Dutch forces. The strength of the Combined Fleet could instead be directed to dealing with the United States Pacific Fleet, when and where it suited Japan.

Konoye's secret diplomacy was intended to drive a wedge between Great Britain and the United States. His plan survived its first test when Churchill responded to the increasingly chill winds blowing from Tokyo by cabling Roosevelt on 15 February that there were "drifting straws" indicating "Japanese intentions to make war on us."[18] His fear was that Australia might be invaded by a Japanese war machine fueled by the oil from the Dutch East Indies. During the round of ABC-1 (American-British-Canadian) staff talks that month in Washington, however, Admiral Stark repeatedly rejected Churchill's call for American warships in Singapore.

General George C. Marshall concurred. Such a move would have been a concession to General Douglas MacArthur's repeated pleas to reinforce the Philippines. The chief of the army was convinced that to reverse the twenty-year-old U.S. policy not to make major defense commitments west of Hawaii would be "a strategic error of the first magnitude."[19] Thus British alarms that Japan was about to move into the East Indies to invade Australia failed to bring about a joint defensive alliance because Roosevelt was advised that their loss, together with that of the Philippines, could be "absorbed without leading to final disaster."[20]

Churchill next sought to tie Britain's Far East interests to those of the United States. He urged Roosevelt to issue a formal declaration that any attack on British or Dutch territory would bring the United States to their defense. This would "inspire the Japanese with fear of a double war."[21] But the president shied away. He needed the backing of American public opinion and his cabinet for such strong talk, and he had neither. Roosevelt, who had deliberately not told Churchill about Nomura's overtures, advised Hull to temporize in the clandestine April meetings and agreed with the secretary of state's suggestion that the navy embark on a series of flag-waving cruises in the Pacific.

Talking softly and carrying a big stick might have worked for Theodore Roosevelt at the turn of the century when our fleet outnumbered Japan's, but four decades later Ambassador Grew was soon warning that a show of naval strength in the Pacific could only increase the risk of war. Admiral Stark reminded the president in February that "the Pacific Fleet is now weaker in total tonnage and aircraft than the Japanese navy."[22] Nevertheless, the president insisted that a squadron of four cruisers be sent to show the flag in Australian waters, and in April he wanted to dispatch another force "to keep them popping up here and there, and keep the Japs guessing."[23] This put additional demands on the Pacific Fleet, whose value as a deterrent was also threatened by the urgent need to reinforce the Atlantic. What Stark termed the "many conflicting and strong cross currents and tide rips" in the policy debate in Washington alerted Kimmel that he might soon lose three of his battleships and their escorts in order to bolster Admiral Ernest J. King's forces on the other side of the globe.

As the Pacific Fleet's commander in chief, Kimmel vigorously protested the proposed reduction of one quarter of his strength. Stark replied that the situation was "critical in the Atlantic," but the president felt that the Far East situation also was sufficiently critical. Therefore, Stark settled for the transfer of only a single cruiser and one destroyer division. He wanted to avoid giving "any signs of seriously weakening the forces in the Pacific" until the outcome of Matsuoka's Berlin visit and Japan's intervention in Indochina became clearer.[24]

That the president and his chiefs of staff were planning a further reduction in Pacific Fleet strength to meet the worsening situation in the Atlantic was not simply because of their commitment to the "Atlantic first" strategy. When that decision had been made in April, they were also taking account of Nomura's secret negotiations. Although no one in the administration was under any illusion that Tokyo was holding forth an olive branch, the twig proffered by the genial ambassador was at least a sign that the slide to all-out confrontation in the Pacific might be averted by some skillful diplomatic footwork.

The prospect of a thaw in relations between Tokyo and Washington lulled the navy and army staffs in Washington into making a fatal error. Only three months earlier the possibility of a surprise enemy strike at Pearl Harbor had persuaded Admiral Turner and the chief of naval operations to press the war department to approve a plan of "joint readiness for immediate action in defense against surprise attacks."[25] But by April, the director of war plans appears to have revised his strategic opinions.

The about-face by Turner began when he met with Nomura on 12 March and received the ambassador's assurances "against further aggressive moves by the military forces of Japan."[26] Then on 3 April he received an army staff report which painted a very reassuring picture of the strength of our Pacific defenses. According to the army planners, "due to its fortification, its garrison and its physical characteristics," Oahu was claimed "to be the strongest fortress in the world."[27] Sabotage, according to the army, was the main threat to Pearl Harbor because, they predicted, "with adequate air defense, enemy carriers, naval escorts and transports will begin to come under air attack at a distance of approximately 750 miles."[28] Such a forecast was wildly optimistic when the Hawaiian command at the time could muster only a handful of obsolescent bombers against an attacking enemy fleet—and none had the range to operate so far from shore. Turner evidently chose to ignore this potentially fatal piece of wishful thinking, nor was it raised by General Marshall when Stimson and he reviewed Pearl Harbor's defenses with Roosevelt in their White House meeting of 24 April.

The chief of staff of the army assured the president that Hawaii was impregnable, whether there were any ships left there or not; that land defense was amply sufficient, together with the air defense, to keep off the Japanese; and that the air defense "could always be reinforced from the mainland of America."[29] How, someone might have wondered, would an island fortress be reinforced and supplied without control of the sea?

Kimmel, however, was not made privy to this astonishing piece of military hyperbole. There was no mention of it in any of the confidential letters he was receiving from Admiral Stark—or he would have been the first to demolish Washington's false premise. He would certainly have responded to the concerns about the security of the fleet, which were raised by Stark's letter of 4 April alerting him to the "tremendous issues at stake," which "at any moment would precipitate action," because "just what the Oriental *really* plans, none of us can be sure."[30]

Yet because we were not being sent any diplomatic Magic, neither Kimmel nor I had any way of knowing what dire intelligence prompted Washington's fears. The chief of naval operations was not merely failing to provide information, but was resorting to platitudes to refer to insoluble strategic dilemmas. Furthermore, Kimmel found himself in the unenviable position of a fleet commander who would be stripped of ships should war break out in the Atlantic.

"I do not know that we have missed anything, but if there is any doubt as to whose responsibility it is to keep the commander-in-chief fully informed with pertinent reports on subjects that should be of interest to the fleet," he had already written to Stark on 18 February, "will you kindly fix that responsibility so that there will be no misunderstanding?"[31]

Kimmel's postscript had reminded Stark to ensure we received "information of a secret nature." In the light of subsequent events, Stark's response, "ONI is fully aware of its responsibility in keeping you adequately informed," turned out to be a hollow assertion.[32] Kimmel was justfiably uneasy despite Washington's assurance. He repeatedly asked me whether I thought that we were receiving all the diplomatic intelligence available to Washington, and I agreed to make my own personal efforts to find out.

I took the matter up directly with my opposite number in the navy department. On 11 March, I penned a personal letter for hand-delivery by courier to my former boss and old associate from the Tokyo embassy, Commander McCollum who was then head of the Far East Section in ONI. I frankly expressed my concern and Kimmel's belief that we were being shortchanged on diplomatic intelligence and urged him to make sure that he sent us intercepted Japanese traffic on a regular basis. As the political situation with Japan was becoming increasingly tense, I also suggested to McCollum that Station Hypo be allowed to retain two of its most experienced Japanese language officers who were "doing exceptionally well," but were coming due for sea duty.

More than a month went by before I received his "Dear Eddie" letter by locked courier pouch on the Pan Am Clipper. Despite its amicable tone, McCollum gave what amounted to a stinging formal brush-off to both my requests. Washington, he maintained, was responsible for "evaluating the political situation" and "matters of security, et cetera, which would be very difficult to solve" made it impractical to send us diplomatic intercepts. As he put it:

> I should think that forces afloat should, in general, confine themselves to the estimates of the strategic and tactical situations with which they will be confronted when the time of action arrives. The material you mention can necessarily have but passing and transient interest as action in the political sphere is determined by the government as a whole and not by the forces afloat.[33]

Washington's decision that diplomatic intelligence was "none of Pearl Harbor's business" was to have fatal repercussions eight months later.

7

"On the Mat"

I N SPITE OF THE REBUFF I received from Washington to my request for diplomatic intelligence, my hopes that it would now be possible to get the full intelligence picture for Admiral Kimmel were raised on 15 May when my longtime friend Joe Rochefort arrived at Pearl Harbor to relieve Tom Birtley as head of Station Hypo. I could not have wished for a better and more understanding colleague in a difficult situation.

My opportunity for close cooperation with Station Hypo at Pearl Harbor had been facilitated in April when Kimmel moved his headquarters ashore from the crowded cabin space in flagship *Pennsylvania*. Cincpac offices were established at the submarine base, on the second deck of the headquarters building. Our office windows looked out on the sub pens below and over to Ford Island with its majestic line of steel dreadnoughts moored at Battleship Row. Across Southeast Loch was the comint nerve center for the Pacific Fleet, housed in the Fourteenth Naval District headquarters building at the naval shipyard. Rochefort was therefore nominally under Admiral Bloch's command, but had special orders also to report direct to Admiral Kimmel.

I visited Rochefort's shop whenever possible, to sound out his opinion and keep abreast of the latest code-breaking developments. Such opportunities were not as frequent as I would have liked, because Kimmel, even after his own headquarters were set up ashore, spent a lot of time at sea. I was shown how the intercepts would be submitted first to traffic analysis by Lieutenant Thomas A. Huckins, my naval academy classmate, or Lieutenant John A. Williams. From its external attributes—the sender of the message and the call sign of its addressee as well as any radio direction-finding information on the transmission—these two officers distilled observations about Japanese naval activities, which were delivered to me each day in summary form.

After traffic analysis, the intercepts were sorted for duplication before being examined to recover additives, code entries, and plain language. The sheets were also scanned for any errors or repetitions made by Japanese radio operators that might aid in our cryptanalysis. The place was jammed with tables of every kind filled with boxes of punched cards and printouts that spewed forth from a row of IBM tabulating machines. These electromechanical sorting devices, the precursors of the modern computer, had somehow been acquired since 1936 by Tommy Dyer, Rochefort's quiet but determined second in command, who ranked as the navy's foremost officer cryptanalyst.

In the interest of security, Rochefort insisted that Hypo's official designation be changed from Communications to Combat Intelligence Unit. When his staff was moved to the underground basement of the headquarters building that summer, an armed guard was posted at its only entrance. "The dungeon" as it was known, did not even have windows, and the air-conditioning system was notoriously temperamental. In the months before war broke out Joe was constantly battling technical problems such as the lack of a teleprinter line to their radio receiving station. Couriers, sometimes even Rochefort himself, had to make the thirty-mile drive to Heeia to collect the intercepted Japanese radio messages. Not until the radio masts were relocated to a site on the west side of Oahu in 1942 was this hand-carried system remedied.

The lack of an adequate and rapid communications link between Oahu, Midway, Samoa, and Dutch Harbor also plagued the operation of the mid-Pacific radio direction-finding (D/F) network, which also came under Rochefort's command. He had complained to Washington that "poor apparatus and lack of suitable control facilities" made our D/F "the weak point of our Communication Intelligence set up." The Pacific D/F capability was so inadequate that Washington had made arrangements with Pan American Airways to requisition their network of stations in the event of war.[1]

The poor performance of Pearl Harbor's direction finding was particularly worrisome because it was the only means we had of pinpointing the movement of Japanese naval vessels while Hypo was still laboring to break into their flag officers cipher. Although a Red machine had been sent out to Hypo, it was not utilized because there was no local traffic in this diplomatic code. Much more serious was that the Purple machine originally destined for Pearl Harbor had been diverted in January to the British. It became part of a trade involving top-secret information in which we received the keys to the German Enigma cipher. Then to add insult to injury, the Royal Navy code breakers in Singapore turned over all their recoveries in the five-numeral system to the Asiatic Fleet. This was especially galling since Station Cast had received a Purple machine. Until 5 March, when the British made the delivery of the keys to unlock JN-25 to Cavite, OP-20-G had retained exclusive right to work on the JN-25 operational code.[2]

When Station Cast informed Washington that they now intended to make JN-25 their first priority, there was a twofold objection. They were told by OP-20-G that their cryptographic unit "was not sufficiently supplied with the necessary statistical machinery," and that it had been intended to "transfer this attack to Pearl Harbor in July."[3] But Cast's claim prevailed over Hypo's. On 24 April, Hypo was the information addressee of a dispatch instructing the rival unit that it should concentrate on breaking the current JN-25 cipher, and that "project will not be transferred to fourteenth as previously planned."[4] Rochefort's arrival at Hypo a month later raised hopes that he might win a reprieve from their fruitless slog against the Japanese flag officers code. But this was dashed by a 2 May order from Washington that his unit would continue exclusively on the admirals system, or AD, as the flag officers code was designated.

The net result of Washington's code-breaking trade with the British was frustration for Rochefort and the navy's best cryptanalysts: Dyer and Wright. It was also ultimately to prove disastrous for the Pacific Fleet. For nine more months the Hypo team would obediently beat their heads against the stone wall of the Japanese admirals code with negative results. They were also cut out of direct access to Japan's high-level diplomatic traffic. There were comparatively few exchanges between Washington and Cast on the dedicated radio network on which the navy's three cryptographic centers swapped technical information using a secure cipher system code-named Copek. Nor was Hypo provided with the current keys for the "J" series of transposition ciphers which were used for the most secret communications by Japan's consulates. The only Japanese diplomatic systems that Rochefort's outfit was equipped for were the low-grade ciphers designated "PA-K2" and "LA," used for routine "housekeeping" traffic.

Just how badly Washington had goofed in dividing its cryptographic resources would become apparent after 7 December 1941. The frantic search for missed radio intelligence clues to the Japanese attack revealed that many of them were contained in the J-19 cipher used by Japan's consul in Honolulu to send Tokyo an ever-increasing flow of ships-in-harbor reports. But even these could not be decrypted by Hypo cryptanalysts only fifteen miles away. Because of the priority given to the Purple traffic in Washington, they had been accumulated unread and for the most part unbroken.

The decision to give the Asiatic Fleet priority over Pearl Harbor for one of the precious hand-built Purple machines reflected Washington's belief that the Philippines were more exposed to the Japanese threat, as well as better placed to intercept Tokyo's radio signals. But the denial of access to Hypo of the main Japanese operational cipher which resulted from the wrangling over JN-25 was a major blunder. With all the other pressures on the cryptanalysts at Washington and Cavite, the JN-25B system was never—as far as our navy was concerned—to yield more than a partial readability before war broke out.[5]

As we shall see, the intelligence that might have been extracted from JN-25 could have been instrumental in forestalling Japan's attack. By the middle of 1941 it had become the Japanese navy's principal operational system. We now know that the "A" version had become readable in little more than a year. Less than five months after being authorized to tackle the "B" version, Rochefort's team was reading enough of the messages to be able to predict the Japanese plan to invade Midway.

If Hypo had set to work on JN-25 as originally intended in July, it is probable that the cipher could have been penetrated in time—especially with the cooperation of the cryptanalysts at Cavite and Singapore—for the course of history to have been changed. This could be why the various Pearl Harbor inquiries dealt only with our ability to read the Purple traffic, and avoided all but the vaguest references to JN-25. It could also explain why not a single American or British JN-25 decrypt made in 1941 has yet been declassified—despite repeated official requests made by the authors and other historians.

At the time, neither Rochefort nor I realized the extent to which Hypo's cryptanalytic resources were being squandered for the greater part of 1941. We received hints from new arrivals from Washington of the huge successes that had been achieved with Japan's diplomatic ciphers. Too late it became clear that the Pacific Fleet's access to important intelligence about our potential enemy had fallen hostage to the running feud that flared and sputtered in the navy department that spring and summer. But it should have been apparent from the decision to put Rochefort in charge of Hypo. Assigning the only naval officer who was fully qualified in both Japanese and cryptanalysis to Pearl Harbor, with the promise of a handpicked team, was an attempt by his old colleague Commander Safford to give the fleet an independent access to radio intelligence, free of the navy department feuding.

Later I was astonished to discover the true extent of the interdepartmental warfare. It actually threatened the second deck of the navy department building in Washington with an incipient mutiny because of the discontent of certain communications and intelligence officers. It shaped the climate of hostility in which intelligence went unevaluated and the special needs of the Pacific Fleet to be kept informed were submerged in furious personal rivalries.

The conflict and jealousy that soured the spring air on Constitution Avenue were not caused by the old feud between the offices of naval communications and naval intelligence for control of the code-breaking product. That had finally been settled. The previous fall Admiral Stark had written an administrative directive that set out, for the first time, the responsibilities of the sections that made up the office of naval operations. The CNO staff manual of 23 November 1940 required that the director of naval communications (OP-20) had to defer to the director of naval intelligence (OP-16), who was charged with securing "all classes of pertinent information pertaining to naval and maritime matters."[6]

The products of OP-20-G's code breaking were therefore clearly "pertinent information" which ONI was authorized to "*evaluate* and disseminate as advisable [emphasis added]."[7] But no sooner had this conflict of interests been settled than a new area of contention appeared. The gauntlet was thrown down by Rear Admiral Richmond Kelly Turner, the recently appointed director of war plans (OP-12), whose own duties were already so extensive that they were divided into two sections—one for "preparing war and operational plans," and the other for developing policies and projects in support of those plans—in addition to preparing directives on a wide range of subjects. Nowhere in Stark's memorandum was there any mention that the war plans division was to evaluate and disseminate intelligence, although both were important collateral considerations in planning for war.[8]

Stark's solomonic division of his staff's authority had not suited Turner, who had been personally selected with promotion to admiral as "the right man" to head the most important section in the navy department.[9] At fifty-five, Turner finally found himself close to becoming the heir apparent to the job of ultimate naval authority, to which he had aspired since he graduated fifth in the 1908 class at Annapolis. Lean and quick-acting and over six feet tall, he cut an imposing figure, with lantern jaw and beetling black brows that gave him a Mephistophelean aspect. Turner was intimidating both in appearance and personality.

"Abrasive as a file" was how a junior navy department officer described the new director of war plans.[10] Turner's competitiveness, which had made him a model midshipman, left him always resentful of having failed to win top place at Annapolis. This drove him to dominate his equals and bitterly resent anyone who opposed him. A relentless taskmaster, he was called "Terrible Turner" behind his back, with good reason.

Stark, however, called him "invaluable,"[11] which provides the best clue to the relationship that Turner quickly established with the chief of naval operations. By relieving Stark of memorandum writing and detailed staff work, he was valued for being a determined "fixer" when it came to getting things pushed through the slothfully bureaucratic peacetime navy department.

Turner was the navy's Patton. They both possessed that amalgam of military brilliance, opinionated paranoia, and instinctive courage that leads men into enemy gunfire; but their immoderate self-assertion soured cooperation down the ladder of command. Like many men supremely confident of their own abilities, Turner made no point of trying to make people like him, but commanded a high degree of respect by the manner in which he had mastered his profession.[12]

Turner had little knowledge of the intelligence process, but rated himself an expert on Japan after visiting Tokyo and the Yokosuka naval base in 1939 as captain of the cruiser *Astoria,* which had borne home the ashes of Ambassador Hiroshi Saito. But as soon as he moved into the war plans division, despite Stark's demarcating memorandum, he conceived it to be the function of war plans to give "the major strategic overall picture for the use of my superiors and disseminate that."[13]

Turner was tapped for flag rank by the December 1940 selection board. But he became the kind of admiral "who could not come ashore in a launch without giving detailed orders to the coxswain."[14] It was the same with intelligence. Although he had no experience in evaluation, the new director of war plans assumed his judgment was superior to the ONI staff's when it came to analyzing and interpreting strategic information. He maintained that the officers in his division were "more experienced than the officers in naval intelligence who generally were more junior, and were trained rather [sic] for the collection and dissemination of information, rather than its application to a strategic situation."[15]

Within a month of his becoming head of war plans, Turner's forceful presentation of his case persuaded Stark to issue a second 1940 Alnav (instruction to all ships and stations) that further undercut ONI's authority: "Certain evaluations can only be made by competent specialists beyond the ability of the division of naval intelligence."[16] The director of war plans then moved swiftly to take advantage of the interregnum existing in ONI when Captain Jules J. James became acting director in December 1940.

James naturally resented the encroachment on his turf. So in addition to preparing the series of fortnightly global naval intelligence summaries that were frequently out of date before they reached the fleet by mail, James continued issuing a weekly digest by radio. This brought Turner storming into his office to demand that "ONI make no estimate of prospective enemy intentions to CNO, but furnish information to war plans who would make the required estimate." James icily reminded him that "existing printed organization instructions of CNO required Intelligence to make these estimates."[17]

This was the kind of interference that the aggressive Turner could not brook. He wanted to do all the roaring and not be roared at by anybody. But he was temporarily diverted from counterattacking by the preparations for the ABC-1 staff talks. In February he returned to the offensive and without any reference to ONI issued a dispatch that predicted that the Japanese were going north to invade Siberia. This forecast contrasted with the latest bulletin sent out by the head of the ONI Far East desk. Captain McCollum's estimate pointed toward a forthcoming Japanese move south into Indochina.

Turner sent for the head of the Far East section to demand an explanation and apology. "I think I made him rather angry when I suggested that maybe he was privy to some intelligence that I certainly didn't have," McCollum recalled of the confrontation, which brought instructions "that hereafter War Plans would do all the evaluating of probable enemy intentions and that we had to be particularly careful that the director of war plans got all the pertinent information."[18]

An appeal was made to Stark, who according to McCollum accepted that "it was the function of ONI to talk about intentions; it was in the manual." But "he thought that in the interests of coordination, Turner was the man to do the coordinating."[19] Since Turner was already overextended in his duties, he set up what amounted to his own three-man intelligence section. But the officers he appointed were as inexperienced as he was in evaluating information. All they did was beat a path down the corridor to ONI offices, pick the brains of intelligence people, and carry the word back to Turner, who began distributing his own digests and summaries.

It was "a futile business" for the officers in ONI. They resented that Turner's coordinating role enabled him "to keep his hand on our gullets" and maintain a stranglehold on their output.[20] This was the situation in March when the battle flared again with the arrival of the forceful new director of ONI, Captain Alan C. Kirk. Fresh from the exhilarating duty of monitoring the real war as naval attaché in London, Kirk had been impressed by the effective meshing of the British navy's intelligence and war planning organizations in the Combined Operations Intelligence Centre. He saw no reason why such a joint unit should not be set up in Washington.

Turner, too, saw the potential of such a clearinghouse for intelligence—but he wanted to run the whole show. The director of war plans also had the advantage both of rank and of access to Stark's ear, plus the support of CNO's pliant deputy, Rear Admiral Royal E. Ingersoll.

"Kirk wasn't any weak sister," according to McCollum. "He immediately went in to bat, and he and Turner were on the mat all the time. The DNI was fighting to maintain the integrity of his section, but losing out. Every time he'd go in to bat, he'd strike out on it."[21] For the entire eight months that Kirk remained captain of the ONI team, the struggle with war plans was to flare and sputter with all the embittered rivalry of a grudge match, sown by personal venom.

"There was some harassment in this office of mine," Kirk would later concede with remarkable understatement, "because we had charge of what was called Magic."[22] So while ONI and war plans battled for control of strategic intelligence, Rear Admiral Leigh Noyes, the communications chief, claimed responsibility for disseminating the actual intelligence to its limited circle of recipients in the navy department and White House. Noyes required all his good nature to cope with Turner, who would often bark his complaints about Noyes "and his God-damn secrets."[23]

When Turner bullheadedly began preparing his own intelligence estimates and sending them out—according to McCollum "without reference to or consideration by ONI at all"—a showdown with Kirk became inevitable. The shootout for control of the intelligence function took place in April 1941. After listening to the stormy confrontation in his office, Ingersoll took the antagonists to Stark where "the points at issue were reviewed." Kirk maintained that "the office of naval intelligence was responsible for interpreting possible enemy intentions after evaluating information received from whatever source." He argued that ONI was "comparable to G-2 in the war department general staff in these respects, and should likewise prepare that section of a formal estimate known as Enemy Intention."[24]

Turner contested this. He argued that "war plans division should prepare such sections of the estimate and should interpret and evaluate *all* information concerning possible hostile nations from *whatever* source received."[25] In a monumental overstatement of the war plans division's role, he insisted that ONI "was solely a collecting agency and a distributing agency, and was not charged with sending out any information which would initiate any operations on the part of the fleet, or fleets anywhere."[26]

Stark had no stomach for refereeing a knock-down drag-out fight on his staff. His exterior affability concealed the fact that he was a shrewd member of the president's inner circle. He had been friends with Roosevelt since 1914 when, as a junior captain, he had demonstrated his independence by tactfully refusing the then assistant secretary of the navy's attempt to navigate his destroyer off the rocky Maine coast. Pink-cheeked, with a mop of white hair, Stark looked like a superannuated schoolboy. His administrative ability and powers of persuasion had won support on Capitol Hill for the president's soaring naval budgets, and he was an astute manipulator in staff conferences. But "Betty" Stark lacked the stern fiber necessary for a battle commander. Secretary of War Stimson regarded him as "a timid and ineffective man to be in the post he holds."[27]

Stark, however, was not so much dominated as impressed with Turner's genuine abilities, which he had demonstrated by reworking Stark's original "Dog" memorandum into the full-fledged Rainbow 5 war plan. Given Stark's admiration for Turner, he had every reason therefore to resolve the feud in the war plans division's favor by fudging the original demarcations that he had established earlier. He therefore let it be known that he had "approved the position" taken by the director of war plans. Kirk had no choice but to admit defeat, and "so advised my principal chiefs."[28]

It was also typical of Stark, the compromiser, that he carefully avoided publicizing his volte-face over the control of communications by revising the staff manual. This created a dangerous area for confusion about responsibility for disseminating directives, which was later described by Turner's official biographer as "an administrative error."[29] It also gave Turner the opportunity to shirk blame for the intelligence failures that left the door wide open for the Japanese attack on Pearl Harbor.

In later years, the maneuvering to avoid responsibility for Pearl Harbor was not confined to the highest levels of the navy department. It extended right down the chain of command. For example, I retained a copy of the 1940 manual titled *ONI 11* that described in detail the function of intelligence. From time to time changes and updates were made and one day in 1943, the fleet's publications officer, a Lieutenant Robert G. Bidwell, came around saying he had changes for the ONI manual. It was stored in my safe. He made the changes, and I put it back in the safe without examining it, as I was busy at the time. Sometime later I opened it and found that the entire section having to do with "duties and responsibilities" of ONI and fleet intelligence officers had been removed, and no new pages had been added. There no longer was anything on that subject in the manual, and that day in 1943 Bidwell had evidently been acting on instructions from the navy department.

I asked Bidwell about replacement pages. He said none were furnished. I sent him out to see if, by chance, some ship had not yet entered the changes, so I could get the old pages before they were burned (as ours had been). We searched high and low, trying to find one copy, but failed. During the 1945 congressional investigation on Pearl Harbor, where a central issue was who bore the responsibility for the intelligence function, what had previously been on those blank pages could have been important evidence for countering Turner's charges of shirking of responsibility.

When I was called to testify, I originally intended to raise the WE WE cipher affair and the neglect of Japan's fortification of the mandates. The surly CNO message and Kimmel's reply were a good example of how Washington had failed to properly carry out the intelligence function in mid-1941. But I was told by the Judge Advocate General's Office, which previewed my case, that I could not introduce data going back beyond July 1941. This decision, I believe, is another example of the extent to which the navy department went to try to conceal its sorry role in the debacle that overtook the fleet on 7 December.

Certainly Turner had plenty to conceal. He was vehemently unforgiving of officers who defied him. He continued to harass Kirk as he tried to turn ONI into nothing more than an intelligence drop-box. By May 1941 the increasing interference of war plans in what ONI officers regarded as their prerogative in intelligence matters caused deep resentment. One of the fortnightly summaries on which Kirk had handwritten "In my view the Japs will jump pretty soon" had been returned from "coordination" by war plans with the bold scrawl, "I don't think that the Japs are going to jump now or ever! R.K.T."[30]

Turner's confidence in his exclusive ability to forecast Japan's moves, while they provoked Kirk and McCollum to fury, were apparently being taken seriously by the Asiatic Fleet commander. "If Japan starts a war in the immediate future it will be against Russia," Admiral Thomas C. Hart reported back in a dispatch of 25 June.[31] "Success against Russia will be necessary before Japan makes an advance to the south."[32] Kirk ordered his Far East section to invite Hart's attention to a list of the latest intelligence that indicated that if Japan moved it would be southward, not north. "Consider your analysis not now justified in view of these factors," he ended his dispatch—to which Turner appended a petulant "But this does not rule it out as an eventuality."[33]

Such pronouncements vitiated the impact of McCollum's accurate estimates and reveal how Turner tried to dictate strategic intelligence. ONI often found itself in the unenviable position of having no say about enemy intentions, but being accountable if war plans made a wrong evaluation. It left many of those in the junior echelons feeling they had been "robbed" of their main intelligence function—evaluation. The bad blood between the divisions did nothing to encourage the cooperation so essential to the complex function of turning raw data into meaningful intelligence.

Meanwhile, the internal struggle among the CNO staff amounted to a progressive takeover by the abrasive war plans director of many of the functions and responsibilities of Stark himself. "There had grown up in the office of the chief of naval operations a coterie," explained McCollum, who as ONI Far East section head observed the struggle at close quarters. "Stark, Ingersoll, and Turner became a sort of 'triumvirate.' Turner would bring in the ideas and the other two would endorse them—frequently without referring to anyone else on the staff."[34]

As in all triumvirates, one member exerted a dominating influence. In this case it was Richmond Kelly Turner, who aggressively promoted his own intelligence evaluations and made arbitrary decisions on their dissemination, knowing that he could count on Stark to rubber-stamp them. This situation created a climate of embittered indifference and uncertainty in the subordinate divisions of the navy department that was ultimately to prove disastrous for the Pacific Fleet. Shorn of its evaluative function, ONI was unable to heed Puleston's prophetic 1934 admonition that "constant and careful study of the daily course of Orange radio activity cannot be overemphasized in its importance as a barometer of the hostile intentions of that nation."[35]

It was one of the tragic ironies of 1941 that the Japanese were to heed this wise advice more closely than Washington. Although their comint organization was not able to break into any of our ciphered communications, our own observation of the pattern of their radio transmissions had revealed that their communications units doubled as shore-based radio transmitting and receiving stations, as well as radio intelligence intercept and direction-finding stations. Everything was fed into a central control at Owada on the outskirts of Tokyo, where the Japanese navy's crypt-

analysis section was located. This was the Japanese naval staff's counter-
part of OP-20-G, and it had developed along lines remarkably similar to
our own.[36]

Unlike our decentralized setup of OP-20-G, with its two satellite units
at Pearl and Cavite, which also carried out decryption and traffic analysis,
the Japanese radio intelligence unit relied on the Owada nerve center to
exploit both its strategic direction finders and radio intercepts. Its listen-
ing-post network extended out from Tokyo like the invisible spokes of a
giant wheel which reached south from the Kuriles, along the main islands, down through Formosa, and east out across the mandates.

Just after war broke out in Europe in the fall of 1939, the Japanese
had the opportunity to test their radio intelligence operation by monitoring our Pacific Fleet maneuvers then being conducted in the Hawaiian
area. They made the most of this chance to snoop data on our operations
and tactics by increasing their intercept station staff on Jaluit. They also
rerouted seaplane tender *Kamoi* and sent naval tankers to load fuel oil at
Los Angeles in order to traverse our maneuver area. From that time on,
their radio intelligence organization remained on a combat-ready basis.
The large volume of data they gathered throughout 1940 enabled them to
update their plan for operations against the United States.[37]

The major difference between Japan's radio intelligence operation
and ours was that while our navy department became locked in internal
conflict over the control of intelligence, by 1941 their naval staff was gearing up to fight a war.

8

The Biggest Rattlesnake

THERE IS AN OLD cowboy saying: "The nearest rattlesnake is always bigger." It illustrates perfectly how the intelligence evaluations made at Washington and Pearl Harbor differed throughout 1941. The polarity, which had been aggravated by the feud within the navy department, was now further worsened on 27 May when Roosevelt declared a state of "unlimited national emergency" and warned Americans in a radio broadcast that war was "coming very close to home."[1]

To Admirals Stark and Turner, both of whom had played such a leading role in drafting the "Atlantic first" strategy, compared to the German submarines Japan was a distant menace. The president was calling the U-boats "the rattlesnakes of the Atlantic." They threatened to cut the lend-lease supply line to Britain. But from Admiral Kimmel's point of view the German submarines were less of a menace than a Japanese battle fleet, which could sortie from bases in the Marshall Islands, less than two thousand miles southwest of Pearl Harbor. But if we had known just how closely Axis agents had been studying the Pacific Fleet ever since the early spring, the Japanese rattlesnake would have appeared even larger.

Since February Admiral Yamamoto had been planning and coordinating the massive naval air operation that depended on the skillful application of intelligence in order to realize his strategic gamble for control of the western Pacific. Above his table on board flagship *Nagato* hung a detailed map of the American naval base on Oahu, marked with anchorages, defenses, and fuel-storage depots. In his desk drawer was a weighty volume titled *The Habits, Strengths, and Defenses of the American Fleet in the Hawaiian Area*, a bible of data on warship movements, water depths, and air and sea patrol patterns that were constantly updated by reports from Japanese agents in Hawaii.

Yamamoto's most valuable source of such information was the consulate at Honolulu. On 27 March 1941 the two-story white building on

Nuuanu Avenue became the base of operations for the Japanese navy's espionage effort when a junior diplomat known as Tadashi Morimura arrived at the consulate to take up his mission of collecting information essential to the fleet's destruction.

Morimura was the alias of twenty-eight-year-old former Ensign Takeo Yoshikawa. It also literally gave a new lease on life to a naval officer whose career had been terminated by stomach cancer. Yoshikawa had been recruited by the intelligence division of the naval general staff and trained for four years as an undercover agent for American operations. A slim, personable man, with an infectious politeness, he attracted little attention among the many Japanese Americans of Oahu.

At the consulate, however, where "Morimura" was assigned a desk in the vice-consul's office, it was curious—as one of the nisei female clerks was later to admit—that Otajiro Okuda's new assistant paid little attention to his duty of administering expatriate affairs. He was often late arriving for work and was seldom at his desk in the afternoon. Once Miss Kimie Doue saw a map of Oahu spread on his desk, and she often saw him leave the consulate in a taxi driven by John Mikami, who worked out of a stand on Vineyard Street. Another clerk would recall that Morimura sometimes arrived wearing an aloha sports shirt and was driven away in the car of Richard Kotoshirodo, who once admitted that the trips were to "military places."[2]

Although the Honolulu consulate was staked out by both the FBI and the Fourteenth Naval District intelligence office, it was not until after war broke out that interrogation of the taxi driver Mikami and clerk Kotoshirido revealed how extensive had been the assistance they gave to Yoshikawa's espionage activities. Both admitted making frequent trips with him to observe the local airfields, or to the Sunchoro tea house at Aiea Heights and the Punchbowl overlooking Pearl Harbor where they "looked at the view."[3]

During the latter half of 1941 his reports on the movements of the Pacific Fleet would be relayed by the consul in the J-19 cipher to the foreign ministry. To preserve the secrecy of the Pearl Harbor attack plan, neither Nagao Kita nor Yoshikawa was informed of the special importance that was attached to these reports.

In fact every port and naval base in the United States as well as the Panama Canal, the Philippines and the British, Dutch, and Australian territories in the Far East were already under intensive surveillance. By 1941, FBI director J. Edgar Hoover was keeping detailed files on some 342 suspected Japanese agents operating throughout the United States. Their movements were monitored, as it was widely believed that many were engaged in espionage directed from the Japanese embassy in Washington and Japan's main consulates in New York, Los Angeles, San Francisco, and Honolulu. Many of the suspects were nisei on the west coast who belonged to one of the patriotic societies with close links to Tokyo.

Especially close watch was also being kept on those Japanese who met with known Nazi agents.[4]

It was evident by 1941 that there was increasing cooperation between the undercover operatives of the Axis powers, but Hoover was to drop the ball completely when the British sent over to the United States their double agent known as Tricycle, who had been ordered to Berlin to undertake an espionage mission to Hawaii. Dusko Popov—and revisionist Pearl Harbor historians—have made much of the claim that Popov's mission had warned Roosevelt of the Japanese plan to attack the Pacific Fleet. Popov asserted that the straitlaced Hoover underrated the importance of the intelligence concealed in the microdot questionnaire he was given by his German contact in Lisbon. He also clashed with Hoover over his philandering and high-spending ways.[5]

Newly released FBI files, however, reveal that Hoover had more than enough justification for regarding Popov's credentials as suspect. When he had arrived in the United States he had received an unreported eighteen-thousand-dollar payoff from a local German Abwehr agent.[6] Popov did, however, hand over his questionnaire with its misspelled list of Hawaiian military installations drawn up by his German paymasters at the request of Tokyo. But only about a third of the questions dealt specifically with Hawaii; the rest related to general intelligence about United States war production.

Hoover and his aides therefore failed to see any special significance in the document. They were more concerned with claiming credit for uncovering the microdot technique. This formed the basis of Hoover's "Strictly Confidential" report to the White House on 3 September. The president received only the first page of the questionnaire, which did not include any reference to Hawaii. Hoover did not communicate the entire Popov microdot document to either naval or army intelligence, despite a 1940 agreement by which the FBI pledged to cooperate with the military intelligence to counter Axis espionage. His failure represented another American fumble on the road to Pearl Harbor.[7]

The FBI, however, was more diligent in its pursuit of potential Japanese agents, especially the dozens of naval officers who had arrived in the late thirties claiming to be language students or technical experts."[8]

In addition to spying on navy bases and armaments factories by the Japanese, there was another general level of espionage conducted by naval officers posted to the United States to study English. Whereas our own naval officers sent to Japan at this time to study the language numbered about three or four per year, Tokyo was sending them by the dozens to the United States. They reported for a few weeks to the embassy in Washington, where they would be briefed by Second Secretary Taro Terasaki, who by 1941 had become the mastermind of Japan's entire espionage network in the western hemisphere.

Terasaki, whose brother was a ranking official in the Japanese foreign ministry, had studied at Brown University and gleaned valuable information from former classmates who were now in the State Department. We can now see from recently declassified FBI documents, and the signal traffic of Japan's military attachés, just how extensive this espionage was. Terasaki reported to Tokyo that, in addition to the isolationist supporters of Charles Lindbergh's America First campaign, his agents were also cultivating "very influential Negro leaders" in anticipation of stirring up racial discontent "to stall the program of U.S. plans for national defense and the economy as well as sabotage."[9] Special attention was also paid to nisei working in the west coast aircraft factories and to their relatives in the U.S. Army.

Terasaki ordered the naval agents to enroll at universities and technical institutes, principally in the vicinity of west coast ports. The naval attaché maintained a branch office in New York, known as the "inspector's office," where the FBI investigation found that disbursements for the development of intelligence amounted to half a million dollars a month, a staggering sum for those days. Much of this was spent to obtain technical information and to buy aircraft parts, radios, and tools, apparently only for examination. Two officers assigned to the New York inspectorate had been meeting with a German agent, code-named "Steamer," in the Nippon Club where they shared American scientific and technical information.[10]

The major effort was centered on the west coast. In San Francisco, outposts of large Japanese corporations such as the Yokohama Specie Bank, Mitsubishi Shoji Kaisha, and Nippon Yusen Kaisha provided protection and a channel of communications for the imperial navy's undercover agents. The Los Angeles headquarters of the North American branch of the Nippon Kaigun Kyokai (Japanese Naval Association) collaborated with the language officers to obtain information about naval bases and defense plants. In Los Angeles a Dr. Takashi Furusawa and his wife Sachiko (known as the mother of the Japanese navy), members of the Japanese Political Society, ran a clearinghouse for information collected by these undercover Japanese naval officers.

Lieutenant Commander Itaru Tachibana was one of the most active of the "language students." He lived in Los Angeles, used the name Yamato as an alias, and operated a string of brothels for his cover and added income, while spying under orders of Commander Nagasawa, the local representative of the naval attaché.

Tachibana came to the attention of the Eleventh Naval District intelligence office in early 1941 through, of all people, Al D. Blake, also known as Keeno, King of the Robots, from the world record he had set by standing motionless for one hour and twenty-seven minutes. He was a sometime vaudeville performer whose robot act got him occasional jobs at fairs and store openings. He had spent four years in the navy before playing a bit role in Charlie Chaplin's 1917 movie *Shoulder Arms,* where he became acquainted with the star's valet-chauffeur, Toraichi Kono.[11]

When they met by chance again in 1940, Blake was broke and jobless, and Kono was "chauffeur" to Tachibana. Tachibana offered Blake five thousand dollars if he could produce classified naval information. First, however, Tachibana wanted proof of Blake's naval connection and a sample of the sort of data he claimed he could provide. Blake, now realizing that he was beyond his depth, went to the FBI in Los Angeles with this story, saying that he had led Tachibana on out of patriotism, intending to expose him. He confessed that he had no buddy in the fleet, but that he did need money, and offered his full cooperation. The FBI notified the local office of naval intelligence headquarters who cabled Pearl Harbor and asked for cooperation.

Most of Admiral Kimmel's staff wanted nothing to do with this "cops and robbers" caper, feeling that the Fourteenth Naval District could handle it, and seeing no need for Cincpac involvement. Because of my previous experience with undercover operations, I urged that we cooperate. I explained that we could easily arrange for Blake to get faked classified information. That would bolster his position with Tachibana, and at the same time feed bum dope to the Japanese, and perhaps help catch some of their spies. Kimmel approved, saying, "Why not? If we can catch spies, and at the same time lead the Japanese astray, I think it's a good idea. You go ahead with it, Layton."

We arranged for Blake to write to his "buddy Paul Mitchell" in *Pennsylvania,* saying, "We can make a heap of dough if you cooperate." A naval agent in Honolulu posed as "Mitchell" who corresponded on *Pennsylvania* letterhead stationery telling how fed up he was with the navy, how much he needed money, and that he was eager to see his pal Al and hear more about the money. Tachibana was so impressed by the "Mitchell" letter that he booked passage for Blake on *President Garfield,* which sailed for Honolulu shortly after noon on 25 April.

As if Blake was not involved enough, he made shipboard acquaintances of four Nazis and decided to play "boy spy" with them. One of them brawled with Blake, but he got clear of the Nazis when they were arrested after the captain reported the incident to a passing Canadian cruiser 29 April, the night before entering Oahu.

Meanwhile, we had prepared for Blake's arrival. When he stepped ashore and hailed a taxi, a naval agent was at the wheel. They went directly to the Alexander Young Hotel, where a room—specially wired with a recording machine—was reserved. We also had a cover for him, and a cover for the cover. If the Japs tailed him, we'd have a tail on them. At Pearl Harbor, Bill Kitts, the staff gunnery officer, helped me prepare some bait documents on fleet gunfire practices.

Blake spent enough time doing Honolulu with his "buddy" to be seen in the right places, before returning to the mainland with his "delivery." On 15 May, Tachibana, accompanied by another "language student," carried the material to the Japanese embassy in Washington. The naval attaché liked it so much that he authorized a second Blake mission to Honolulu. We had arranged his reception as before.

We were doctoring bait for the second delivery when out of the blue I got a call from the ONI office in Honolulu saying that Blake had blown his cover. He had run across a woman friend from his old vaudeville days, dined her, and got her up to his room. There, midst amours, he bragged of being an intelligence agent. Our microphones had recorded everything he blabbed.

My yeoman, Hedges R. Keene, fetched Blake from Honolulu to my office, where I read him the riot act. I told him his Hawaiian holiday was over, that we knew all about his hotel-room indiscretions, and that he was on his way home. I made it clear that if he created any further fuss, we would notify the woman's husband. Meanwhile, an ONI agent visited her home at Waianae, ensuring her silence in exchange for our not giving her husband a copy of the hotel-room recording.

Back in Los Angeles, Blake made the second delivery to Tachibana, who was arrested by the FBI after it obtained Department of State approval. His property was seized and three of the navy's best translators were rushed to Los Angeles to screen the voluminous papers. Further confirmation of Tachibana's espionage activity came from the code breakers in Washington who intercepted a message from the Japanese consul in Los Angeles asking the embassy in Washington to subsidize Kono and "friends" to the tune of twenty-five thousand dollars "in view of the fact that he might give evidence unsatisfactory to Tachibana."[12]

Among Tachibana's effects was a suitcase belonging to Lieutenant Commander Sadatomo Okada, another "language officer" suspected for many months of being engaged in espionage activities, and who was rounded up for deportation. It contained a great quantity of data relating to national defense in the Pacific northwest: data on antiaircraft defenses for the Boeing aircraft plant in Seattle, details of naval ships under construction, times of warship arrivals and departures, test data on naval aircraft, records of movements of troops at military establishments, production data on national defense factories, and aerial photographs of naval and army bases as well as war plants.[13]

The haul of intelligence material was so extensive and incriminating that Secretary of the Navy Frank Knox wanted Tachibana, Okada, and another language officer named Yamada to be charged with conspiracy to violate our espionage statute. Washington's diplomatic wheels, however, soon began turning and this charge was tempered. Ambassador Nomura personally intervened to request that "the Tachibana incident be dealt with from the standpoint of the current political trend."[14]

On 21 June, escorted by a posse of FBI agents, Tachibana boarded *Nitta Maru* en route to Tokyo. There his talents were to be put to use by the Third Section (intelligence) in supervising and analyzing the flow of information from the consulate in Honolulu. To protect remaining naval agents in the United States, instructions went out from the foreign ministry that they should be appointed naval attachés to give them diplomatic immunity.

The Tachibana case represented the culmination of several years of counterintelligence operations by the navy in unofficial collaboration with the FBI. The headquarters of the Twelfth Naval District at San Francisco was the most active center of these operations. While the detailed counterintelligence files kept by the district intelligence office for the prewar years have been recalled by the navy, station signal logs and the testimony of former staffers confirm that the office was engaged in extensive counterintelligence operations against the Japanese community on the west coast. Not only was it responsible for monitoring all the transpacific telephone calls from a Market Street office adjacent to the main San Francisco telephone exchange, but it was also tapping telephones in offices and hotel rooms used by members of the local Japanese business community.[15]

The evidence of extensive espionage discovered in these and similar operations on the west coast probably influenced Roosevelt when he issued a controversial emergency executive order two months after Pearl Harbor that resulted in the rounding up of Japanese Americans and packing them off to detention camps. Commander Robert E. Lawrance, the deputy intelligence officer for the Twelfth Naval District, was responsible for directing the undercover surveillance of Japan's suspected espionage network. With the promise of a lieutenancy in the naval reserve, he hired William L. Magistretti—a twenty-year-old student of Japanese at the University of California at Berkeley, who had studied at the Imperial University in Tokyo. Lawrance made it clear that the job required illegal entries and break-ins that amounted to burglary, a felony offense, and that if Magistretti was caught in the act the navy would have to disown him. Magistretti patriotically accepted the job, nevertheless, and participated in a number of successful break-ins, starting in 1938. But he finally quit when the promised commission never materialized, joined the office of strategic services (OSS) in 1943, and served in the China-Burma-India theater for the rest of the war.[16]

To assist Magistretti, a civilian named Seeman Gaddis was engaged to pick the locks of offices of Japanese cultural centers, organizations, and businesses in the San Francisco area. An ex-flatfoot known as Soapy, he was an employee of a private detective agency run by Gene Kerrigan, who was under contract to carry out these break-ins for the Twelfth Naval District. In addition to discovering hundreds of pornographic pictures, which many Japanese businessmen kept locked in their desks, the break-ins by Gaddis and Magistretti produced a useful flow of intelligence about the extent of Japan's surveillance of naval and army bases on the west coast.

In 1940 they conspired to obtain a copy of the imperial navy's mobilization codes for the merchant marine from a Japanese ship in San Pedro. During a "customs inspection" Gaddis planted and "discovered" narcotics in the captain's safe, thereby providing an excuse for removal of its contents, over furious protests by the Japanese skipper. Magistretti identified the merchant-ship code book, which was quickly photographed in a dockside warehouse, and the contents of the safe were returned.[17]

Getting the merchant-ship code was a windfall for ONI. Even though the Japanese switched codes as soon as the ship's captain reported that it had been compromised, possessing an entire code was always useful for comparison purposes. This American success, however, was only a drop in the bucket compared with the information Japan's undercover agents like Tachibana were getting in the United States. In contrast to Japan, we were a free country with none of the police-state controls and restrictions that I had discovered made intelligence gathering so difficult when I was assistant naval attaché in Tokyo.

The United States armed services were constitutionally restrained from conducting extensive counterintelligence activities such as phone tapping against civilians. Such operations had to be conducted on an unofficial and ad hoc basis, but it is now clear that enterprising intelligence officers in naval districts such as San Francisco took it upon themselves to organize quite extensive covert surveillance operations with the connivance—if not approval—of the ONI and FBI in Washington.

Once the Pacific Fleet had moved to Pearl Harbor in 1940, it was realized by the local district intelligence office and by the ONI in Washington that that base would certainly become the focus of Japanese espionage. Nevertheless, the monitoring of telephone and cable traffic to and from Honolulu was far less extensive than that conducted in San Francisco.

This was not through any lack of zeal on the part of Captain Irving H. Mayfield, Fourteenth Naval District intelligence officer, but because telegraph companies in Honolulu insisted on hewing to the statutes which made the disclosure of communications a federal crime. On his own initiative Mayfield, in an ingenious bid to bypass the regulations, had enlisted the aid of local telephone authorities. They provided telephone sets modified with live microphones, which were installed in the Japanese consulate by two warrant officers in phone company uniforms who drove up in a phone company truck. The same team used street cables to route the taps on the consulate switchboard to a nearby Nuuanu Heights residence where Mayfield had set up a listening station equipped with recording machines.[18]

The eighteen-month eavesdropping operation on the Honolulu consulate had failed to provide us with any hard evidence of Japan's special interest in Pearl Harbor. It was to be expected that they would be interested in watching our main Pacific Fleet base, but apart from confirming that their diplomats were engaged in a general surveillance, our investigation uncovered nothing that singled out their agent Yoshikawa for special attention by Captain Mayfield's office before December 1941.[19]

Our main concern was with preventing unauthorized snooping at sea. An attempt had been made by the coast guard in 1939 to deprive Japanese nationals from operating fishing boats in the waters off Diamond Head, but the wanderings of one additional Japanese among the 150,000 already living on Oahu attracted no special attention. Using his cover name Morimura, Yoshikawa had set to work promptly and effectively, a professional naval observer who knew exactly what was needed and how to obtain and report it. His casual strolls, auto rides, and even sightseeing plane trips were not as casual as they seemed. All his intelligence data were being channeled to Admiral Yamamoto's planning team.

As the Pearl Harbor attack concept moved from studies by Ohnishi and Genda to full operational treatment by the Combined Fleet staff, details about Pearl Harbor's water depths, ship movements, and fleet routine became increasingly important to the Japanese. The problems were broken down into four categories: operations and supply, communications and intelligence, navigation and meteorology, and air and submarine aspects. By April 1941 a major reorganization was under way that greatly facilitated Yamamoto's still-evolving plan. This was the creation of a First Air Fleet, which saw the effective marshaling of more than two hundred carrier-based planes under a single commander.[20]

The overall plan—designated Operation Z in honor of the signal flag used by Admiral Heihachiro Togo at the Battle of Tsushima—was still known to only a few members of Yamamoto's staff. Serious operational planning could not begin until the imperial general staff resolved differences in strategic policy. The army still wanted a northward advance against the Russians in Siberia and an all-out commitment to conclude the long war in China. The navy argued for a southward assault to seize the oil and other natural resources of the Dutch East Indies, which Japan would need if her expansionist policies led to a severing of trade with the United States. This was the major issue confronting the Japanese cabinet which, by the end of June 1941, still had not authorized the imperial general staff to begin any formal planning for war.

9

Dropping the Ball

WHILE NEITHER KIMMEL nor I yet suspected the danger of the Japanese rattlesnake that was literally "in our backyard" at Pearl Harbor, by the late spring of 1941 we were paying very careful attention to the one that menaced us from the mandated islands. At the beginning of May, I prepared for the admiral and his staff detailed charts of the larger mid-Pacific atolls showing where I believed that Japan had illegally established military installations. The evidence had been provided from monitoring their radio traffic, careful submarine surveillance, and occasional help from Pan American Airways, whose flying boats passed close to the Japanese-held islands on their way across the Pacific. Reports had also been gathered from our agents who solicited information from merchant seamen in ports throughout the Far East.

All this information built up to a disturbing picture. On Kwajalein and Jaluit in the Marshalls there was evidence that seaplane and submarine bases had been blasted out of the coral lagoons. At Ponape in the Carolines, transmitting towers rose high above the palm trees. Airstrips capable of handling long-range bombers had been bulldozed across the cane fields of Saipan in the Marianas. And a deep-water anchorage at Truk offered an advance base big enough to shelter the entire Japanese Combined Fleet.

The most productive source of accurate information on Japanese military activities in these islands had come from radio intelligence as a result of my work on the low-priority WE WE cipher for Hypo. Its revelations had impressed Kimmel, as they had Richardson, and he readily agreed to follow up my inquiry about how Stark viewed the Japanese activity in the mandates when he left at the end of May for conferences in Washington at the navy department. Accompanied by Captain Charles H. McMorris, his war plans chief, Kimmel carried a carefully considered letter that he had written on 26 May. It listed shortcomings in fleet strength and personnel, patrol planes, and antiaircraft defenses.

"No policy today is better than the force available to enforce it," Kimmel cautioned in his letter, adding, "While this is well recognized in principle, it is apparently lost sight of in practice."[1] His sharpest criticism was that with "the rapid developments in the international picture, both diplomatic and military," a "marked improvement" was needed to provide the fleet with "timely information."[2] So Kimmel made it a first order of business to raise the issue of mandates intelligence with the navy department.

On the day Kimmel arrived in Washington, 4 June 1941, a top-secret message was delivered at fleet headquarters, Pearl Harbor, which read:

> It has come to the attention of CNO that the Pacific Fleet intelligence officer has in his possession certain vital information dealing with the militarization of mandated islands by Japan, which he has not seen fit to report to CNO or to ONI. You will immediately send this information to this office in this same cipher system.[3]

Never had I seen such an invidious naval message. But I responded promptly, summarizing all the intelligence I had in three closely spaced pages. The last paragraph noted that *all* of this information came from Station George (Guam) intercepts addressed to CNO (OP-20-G), copy to Station Hypo. Although none of them had been specifically addressed to the commander in chief, U.S. Pacific Fleet, as fleet intelligence officer, I had "examined this material for tactical information of value to the fleet," in accordance with current signal procedure.

It was inconceivable to me that the chief of naval operations might be unaware of the intelligence contents of intercepts sent to his office. But after that dispatch it became clear that no one in Washington had paid proper attention to the Guam WE WE cipher intercepts. Had anyone looked at them, the wealth of intelligence data contained in the originator and addressees would have impelled them to bring it to the attention of OP-20-G, and thence to ONI and CNO. Perhaps even Admiral Turner would have been awakened to the reality of Japan's preparations for a southward advance. But no one in Washington had even bothered to examine the raw intercepts—let alone decrypt, translate, evaluate, and disseminate them.

This failure was just one example of the underlying flaw in the intelligence procedures of the office of naval operations in Washington. During the latter part of May our direction-finding stations, and our analysis of radio traffic, had revealed that Japan was conducting major naval exercises in the mandates. Carrier *Ryūjō,* and possibly *Hiryū,* as well as half the submarine fleet were taking part. Apparently Fourth Fleet had played the role of enemy, attempting to invade the Marshall Islands against defending submarines and land-based planes. After the exercise the ships visited Wotje, Kwajalein, and Jaluit before returning to their normal operating waters by the end of June.[4]

Since Washington appeared to have discounted the importance of these Japanese maneuvers in the mandates, when Kimmel returned I asked him about it, and about my "blast" from CNO. He told me that when the question of the militarization of the mandates came up, Admiral Stark said he had never heard of it. His ONI director, Captain Kirk, and his assistant, Commander McCollum, were summoned. They had to admit that they knew nothing about a Japanese military buildup in the mid-Pacific islands. The raw information was finally found in the files, but nothing had been done with it. Coming hard on the heels of ONI's defeat in the face-off with Turner, Kirk and McCollum were especially irritated to have this new failure exposed to CNO. Their rude blast at me was a cover-up for both their injured pride and the intelligence blunder.

My copy of the Pacific Fleet staff instructions clearly stated that the intelligence officer "directs assembly of enemy information and evaluates the same; disseminating to the various members of staff, indicating where action is required."[5] This is precisely what I had done. There was no way of my knowing that Washington was not properly evaluating the same information when they received it.

The WE WE affair must have been acutely embarrassing for Stark. He had promised to keep Kimmel "adequately informed" and ONI had now been caught on one foot. That OP-20-G had so obviously dropped the ball early in 1941 was indicative of the kind of blunders that accumulated over the coming months into a major disaster.

The WE WE foul-up was just one of a series of jolts that Kimmel received in Washington. Even while he had been en route by air back to the west coast, the first copies of the joint army-navy Rainbow 5 war plan were being circulated to the Pacific naval commands. The policy directive announced that "since Germany is the predominant member of the Axis powers, the Atlantic and European area is considered to be the decisive theater." This meant that American strategy focused still on the Atlantic, and it did not take Kimmel long to discover that it was a course that the navy department intended to hold to at the expense of the Pacific.

"If Japan does enter the war, the military strategy in the Far East will be defensive"[6] was the constraint that the Rainbow 5 plan imposed on Kimmel. In discussions with Turner, he had made no bones about the inadequacy of his assigned fleet for the tasks expected of it. The plan required his fleet to divert enemy strength by undertaking to "capture . . . positions in the Marshalls, destroy Axis sea communications, and protect the territory of the associated powers."[7] But Turner, who was now making contingency plans for a possible American involvement in the naval war against Germany in the Atlantic, could offer no prospects of sending more ships to the Pacific. Kimmel protested that his forces were inferior to the Japanese fleet in every category of fighting ship, and that he lacked the support vessels needed to operate across the vast distance of the Pacific.

To contest a Japanese advance in the Pacific, Kimmel had only one fast-carrier task force, one amphibious task force, and one battleship task force. Twenty-five percent of the fleet's April strength had been whittled away when a carrier, three battleships, four cruisers, and eighteen destroyers had been transferred to the Atlantic in May. The fleet's operating range was restricted by a lack of oilers, a weakness that must have been obvious to the Japanese. Lastly, Kimmel's ships were undermanned, and many more aircraft and antiaircraft batteries were needed to properly defend the Pearl Harbor base.

Such inadequacies, serious though they were, worried Kimmel less than Stark's new and astonishing proposal. Stark was planning to remove an additional detachment of three battleships, four cruisers, two squadrons of destroyers, and a carrier and send them to the Atlantic. Appalled by the prospect, Kimmel had made a vigorous protest against it during his 9 June meeting with Roosevelt. In presenting his views about the fleet's presence at Pearl Harbor, Kimmel had argued, "Once the fleet was placed there, for the assumed purpose of exerting a deterrent effect upon Japan, it was not maintaining a consistent policy thereafter to weaken the fleet, visibly and plainly, by diversion of powerful units to the Atlantic."[8]

Stark and the president took the point. The proposed reductions were canceled. Kimmel had good reason to hope that both the White House and the navy department had now clearly grasped his view of the strategic situation.

While Kimmel's forceful presentation in the White House had prevented any further sapping of his fleet strength, he was unsuccessful in persuading the navy department that there was a pressing need to increase his intelligence input. Our ability to eavesdrop on Japan's diplomatic traffic was not brought up in his meetings with either Turner or Kirk. So Kimmel was to remain ignorant of the scope and limitations of the Magic operation, the surest gauge of Japanese intentions available to his superiors in Washington.

The failure of Turner and Kirk to brief Kimmel on the subject was an indication of the extent to which Magic secrecy had become a fetish by the middle of 1941. This was the result of a series of scares and slipups in handling of the material. These began in March 1941 when the State Department "lost" a Magic memorandum. The same month another one was found in the wastepaper basket of the president's military aide.[9]

The alarm bells rang loudest on 5 May 1941 when message 192 from the foreign ministry in Tokyo to the embassy in Washington was translated: "According to a fairly reliable source of information it appears almost certain the United States government is reading your code messages. Please let me know whether you have any suspicion of the above"[10]

The Japanese military leaders must have reacted with as great a concern as the navy department to the flurry of diplomatic messages from

Nomura. In rapid succession he asked for the "source," assured Japan's minister of his "stringent precautions," promising "investigations" to track any possible leak. It was soon evident from an intercepted message to Japan's Berlin embassy that the "reliable source" was the German foreign minister. The ambassador was requested to find out more information "so that we might take appropriate action."[11]

Forty-eight hours later all Japanese embassies were ordered to put new code routines into operation. Then on 20 May the panic eased after Nomura informed Tokyo, "Though I do not know which ones, I have discovered that the United States is reading some of our codes." The leak had evidently been traced to some source other than Purple, which remained in use. There must have been some residual concern that top-level diplomatic traffic might still be subject to eavesdropping, however, because the ambassador cryptically added, "As for how I got this intelligence, I will inform you by courier or another safe way."[12]

Precisely what codes Nomura believed we were reading, and how the leak occurred, remained a mystery. Nevertheless, Tokyo continued to use Purple for its most sensitive diplomatic communications throughout the war, in the apparent belief that its complex cipher system remained secure. Japan's armed forces, however, committed no important military data to Purple. This was a major blow to our military intelligence chiefs in Washington who apparently maintained an unshaken faith that the diplomatic circuits would provide them with advance notice of the time, date, and target of any Japanese attack.

Piecing together evidence from recently declassified data on both sides of the Atlantic, it emerges that the German warning to Tokyo probably originated from a successful break into one of Britain's cipher systems. A wartime investigation ordered by the foreign office in London revealed that a cipher clerk in the British embassy in Washington on 30 April had made the fatal error of encoding his ambassador's secret bulletin in a low-grade cipher intended for use only by the ministry of aircraft supply. This was picked up by a code-breaking unit in the German embassy, located a mile to the east on Massachusetts Avenue, and relayed to Berlin.

That message to London, which might have blown the whole Magic operation, contained the gist of a Purple intercept. It was reporting a policy accord that Japan had reached four days earlier with Foreign Minister Joachim von Ribbentrop in Berlin. The State Department had sent the Magic report to the British embassy. The irony of the affair was that the British cryptanalysts at Bletchley Park's code and cipher school were already becoming proficient with their recently delivered Purple machine, and had probably broken out the message for themselves.[13]

We Americans were left equally baffled as to the source of these leaks, and our British colleagues were not about to reveal they had dropped the ball. The panic caused by direct evidence that the Japanese, for the first time, suspected that their codes were being intercepted was matched only by our relief when they did not institute an immediate code change. But the incident had prompted a lid to be clamped on the handling and distribution of Magic material. That connection was reinforced after an August report from Ambassador Grew that our State Department codes might be prejudiced. His concern was aroused after a pro-American Japanese foreign ministry official asked Grew to communicate the information he had given in a code that Japan's military cryptanalysts could not read. He advised the astonished ambassador that the embassy had only "one code which is considered unbreakable."[14]

Even before the August scare the army staff had screwed down security. In May they refused to continue accepting responsibility for delivering messages to the White House. Until that point the war and navy departments had rotated this delivery on a monthly basis. Now they resorted instead to presenting only an oral briefing. During the navy's turn, in June, the president specifically asked to see the individual messages, and his naval aide made them available. He continued to do so in subsequent months when the army "sent nothing to the White House."[15]

That the commander in chief could be denied details of vital intelligence for a whole month—a situation that recurred in the fall, according to a formerly secret wartime army report—must once and for all cast doubt on the credibility of the argument that an omniscient Roosevelt had advance warning of the Pearl Harbor attack. It also indicates the extent to which access to Magic was willfully regulated by the officers responsible for its dissemination. This was certainly true for the Pacific Fleet, and it was action by Adolf Hitler rather than the navy department that set in motion the events that resulted in our being sent our first Purple diplomatic decrypts.

The shock of a six-thousand-gun German barrage on 22 June 1941, followed by a tidal wave of tanks and armored vehicles pouring into Russia, plunged Japan into another cabinet crisis. And it started a train of events that set the seal on a secret Anglo-American alliance in the Far East. News of the German attack sent the Japanese foreign minister to the imperial palace to win the emperor's backing for a Siberian adventure. Matsuoka was eager to renege on his two-month-old pledges to Stalin. But the army staff had no intention of taking on Soviet tanks and planes until they could be quite sure of German victory. And the naval staff was dead set against any war in the north, since their planning was now gearing toward a rapid southward thrust to secure Dutch East Indies oil in anticipation of further deterioration of relations with the United States.

Coincident with the German attack on Russia, Roosevelt proposed an offer of lend-lease aid to the Soviet Union, and Secretary of State Hull rejected Nomura's latest diplomatic overture, questioning the good faith of Japan's foreign minister.

Matsuoka took this as a personal insult. He called for termination of all discussions with Washington, radioing Berlin, "Japan is preparing for all possible eventualities as regards the USSR in order to join forces with her [Germany] in active crushing of the communist menace."[16] Japan's ambassador was told to inform Ribbentrop that the "Japanese government have [sic] decided to secure 'points d'appui' in French Indochina to enable Japan further to strengthen her pressure on Great Britain and the United States of America."[17]

The decrypt of this belligerent message aroused the secretary of state to the possibility of war breaking out in the Far East. It concluded, "We Japanese are not going to sit on the fence while you Germans fight the Russian."[18] The Purple traffic on the Tokyo-Berlin and Tokyo-Washington circuits revealed to Washington that Konoye's cabinet was not yet prepared to jump off the fence into war.

Roosevelt could readily imagine the turmoil swirling around Japan's leaders, since he was also having to deal with dissension in his cabinet. Interior Secretary Harold L. Ickes, in his capacity as "Petroleum Coordinator," urged the cabinet on 23 June to initiate an immediate oil embargo because "Japan is so occupied with what is happening in Russia, and what may happen in Siberia, that she won't venture a hostile move against the Dutch East Indies."[19] A week later when Ickes threatened to resign if Japan's oil supply was not shut off, the president chided him, "I think it will interest you to know that the Japanese are having a real drag-down and knock-out fight among themselves for the past week trying to decide which way they are going to jump."[20]

The president apparently believed that any further economic sanctions by the United States might prompt Japan to jump south to grab alternate oil supplies. He reminded his irascible secretary of the interior, "I simply have not got the navy to go around, and every little episode in the Pacific means fewer ships in the Atlantic."[21] Roosevelt's fears were raised by Purple decrypts revealing that the Vichy French were being pressed by Tokyo for air and sea bases at Saigon and Camranh Bay.

On 2 July 1941 the Japanese finally made up their minds. An imperial conference that Friday took the momentous decision for a policy of southward expansion, "no matter what obstacles may be encountered." Konoye's prepared statement of the cabinet position had rejected Matsuoka's advocacy of an immediate attack on Russia in favor of advancing "southward in order to firmly establish a basis for her self-existence and self-protection."[22] A "joint protectorate" with the French in Indochina was to be established. It would provide the army with a base for launching northward against Nationalist China, west against Thailand and Burma, and south to threaten Malaya.

Konoye was still counting on a diplomatic blitzkrieg to influence the British to return to their policy of appeasement. As a precaution, however, two million more troops were to be conscripted and armament production increased. The prime minister left no doubt about Japan's ultimate intention to secure the "liberation of southeast Asia"—by force, if diplomacy failed. "Preparations for war with Great Britain and the United States will be made," he announced, stating that Japan must be prepared to take this ultimate step to achieve her national destiny.

The emperor's assent for Konoye's plan was automatic. But the decision was not acceptable to Matsuoka, who was attracting the tag of "Hitler's office boy." He kept calling for a strike north until he was forced out as foreign minister on 17 July. But if replacing the firebrand Matsuoka with the more temperate Admiral Teijiro Toyoda was intended by Konoye to strike a harmonious note in Washington, it was drowned out by saber-rattling demands revealed in the Magic decrypts of Japan's diplomatic traffic.

Washington's mounting concern at developments in Tokyo became apparent to us at Pearl Harbor ten days before Matsuoka's removal. On 7 July, Kimmel had been sent two messages containing an up-to-date digest of Tokyo's more belligerent signals. Although we knew nothing about the scope of the Magic operations, it was clear to me that this information could have been obtained only by intercepting Japan's most secret diplomatic communications.

This welcome diplomatic intelligence enabled us to keep abreast of the advancing seriousness of the Indochina crisis. The Magic summaries we received clearly set out the timetable of Japan's "determination to get bases" from the Vichy government. A 1 July intercept warned that Japanese cargo vessels in American waters were to be rushed through the Panama Canal by the third week of the month. Intercepts made the following day from the Tokyo-Berlin circuit revealed that "Japan is preparing for all possible eventualities regarding the Soviets in order to join forces with Germany." Broad hints of a possible attack in Siberia reinforced their ambassador's earlier assurance that "Japan will not sit on the fence."[23]

On 15 July another CNO message based on Magic told us that Tokyo had decided "to use force" to get Indochina air and naval bases if the French objected. They wished "to avoid friction with Britain and particularly the United States if possible, but risk is necessary."[24] Two days later another message gave us the full terms of Tokyo's ultimatum, including the deadline, stated as "army planning advance on about twenty July."[25] We received a Purple decrypt of 16 July warning Japan's Hanoi and Saigon legations to "burn codes" and evacuate personnel by sea a week later. Ominously it stated, "Japan intends carry out plans by force if opposed or if British or United States intervenes."[26]

During the July crisis Washington kept Kimmel posted on diplomatic intelligence. We also received other important decrypts directly from Station Cast at Cavite where the Purple machine was used to good effect. On 14 July, following Matsuoka's forced resignation, we were told that Tokyo had advised all consulates, "Although cabinet has changed there will of course be no departure from the principle that tripartite pact forms keystone of Japan's national policy." From the same source, we learned a week later that the Japanese army had "decided to advance [into northern Indochina] regardless of whether demands accepted or not."[27]

We did not know it at the time, but this was the last piece of Purple diplomatic intelligence that Kimmel was to receive for more than four months. We were cut off from Magic, ostensibly for security reasons, a decision that was completely unknown to Kimmel, Rochefort, and me. The lack of this high-level diplomatic information seriously hampered our ability to assemble all the pieces of the intelligence jigsaw puzzle. Having received diplomatic coverage in July, and having been assured that we would be supplied with any information of importance to the Pacific Fleet, we never dreamed that Washington had been collecting Japanese intercepts that would have alerted us to the immediate danger far beyond any warnings of war we received from Washington.

During the Indochina crisis, for example, we received enough diplomatic information from Magic for me to provide Kimmel with a far more accurate picture of the Far East situation than he ever got from Admiral Stark's personal letters, whose intelligence was devalued by both the ten-day-long postal delays and CNO's attempt to disguise the uncertainty of his own evaluations. The chatty style of his personal communications to his Pacific Fleet commander veered wildly among cheerful reassurance, painful obfuscation, and hesitant alarm.

To Kimmel, whose mind worked with a well-ordered precision, the overwhelming vagueness of Stark's communications as the first major Far East crisis of 1941 boiled to a head, was exasperating and unsettling.

On 13 July he had received CNO's letter with Stark's "unmistakable deduction" that "the Japanese government has determined upon its future policy," which "probably involves war in the near future." An advance against the British and Dutch could "not be ruled out," but Stark believed "that Jap activity in the south will be for the present confined to seizure and development of naval, army, and air bases in Indochina."[28]

Stark's vagueness, characterized by an earlier opinion—"What will happen in the Pacific is anyone's guess,"—disturbed Kimmel. It cannot, therefore, have come as a complete surprise, discouraging though it was, when he received Stark's 24 July enjoinder: "Obviously the situation in the Far East continues to deteriorate; this is one thing that is factual."[29] In the circumstances, this must surely rate as some of the most remarkably worthless reading ever to emerge from Washington.

Stark's confusion throughout the July crisis reflected the continuing conflict between the war plans division and ONI in evaluating Japan's likely response to a freeze by the United States on trade with the Axis powers. When the question of economic sanctions was raised, Stark had "opposed it just as strongly as I could." His fear that an oil embargo presented the possibility of a strike at Borneo was reinforced by a frank "admiral to admiral" chat with Nomura on 24 July. "If the Russians are well beaten down, I think it highly probable that they will move into Siberia," CNO wrote, echoing the conviction of the war plans chief that Japan would still strike northward. Stark's 26 July letter concluded with a singularly imprecise "Just where it will all end I do not know."[30]

Stark's underlying pessimism also echoed the alarm sounded in a 19 July memorandum from his director of war plans. "An embargo would probably result in a fairly early attack on Malaya and the Netherlands East Indies, and possibly would involve the United States in early war in the Pacific" was Turner's assessment. His advice that "trade with Japan not be embargoed at this time" was forwarded by CNO to the president with the note "I concur in general."[31]

The day that Roosevelt received this caution from the navy dispatch, he also saw a Magic intercept of 20 July which confirmed that Japan's army had "decided to advance on 24th regardless of whether demands accepted or not."[32] This forewarning of impending aggression persuaded a majority of the president's advisers that they had to force some kind of showdown with Tokyo.

On Monday, 26 July, twenty-four hours after Japanese troops marched across the borders of Indochina, the State Department announced the freezing of all Axis funds in the United States—and therefore trade with the United States. But Roosevelt, heeding State's advice, spoke carefully on the issues involved. To allay the navy's concerns, which were reinforced by Churchill's fears that the American sanctions might force the Japanese to run amok, the president personally reassured Nomura that he did not yet intend the blanket embargo on trade to include oil exports. Nonetheless, Secretary of the Interior Harold L. Ickes and anti-Japanese hard-liners in the State Department (led by Far East desk head Dr. Stanley K. Hornbeck) seized their chance to interpret the freeze order as an oil embargo. This was contrary to the president's assurances to the Japanese ambassador and his remark to Ickes that his intention was only to "slip the noose around Japan's neck and give it a jerk now and then."[33]

The New York Times interpreted the freeze as "the most drastic blow short of war." This view was reinforced by the army's announcement the same day that General Douglas MacArthur was being recalled to active duty as commander in chief of U.S. forces in the Far East. This signaled the beginnings of a major reinforcement of our military strength in the Philippines as a strategic barrier to deter a Japanese southward move to grab the oil reserves of the Dutch East Indies.

It was a move that reversed the strategic doctrines of both the Rainbow 5 war plan and a twenty-year-old policy *not* to make any major commitment of American forces west of Hawaii. As far as the Pacific Fleet was concerned, the Cavite base outside Manila did not have adequate repair facilities or fuel reserves to act as a forward base. So General

MacArthur would be faced with defending the Philippines with untrained troops at the end of an exposed and insufficient ocean supply line.

It was a military commitment that neither the army nor our already overstretched fleet at Hawaii could fulfill. Within four short months the Japanese would prove the point.

By declaring an embargo on the Axis, the president had allowed diplomatic pressures to override the prudent dictates of military strategy. Against the advice of the navy department, a presidential decision had been made to shift our front line of defense five thousand miles westward across the reaches of the Pacific Ocean. This decision invited all the risks attendant on launching a military buildup on the front doorstep of an adversary's intended domain.

10

A Ridiculous Situation

THE FREEZING OF AXIS FUNDS, which was to cut off Japan's trade with the United States, was a move that might have precipitated hostilities in the Pacific. But Washington gave Pearl Harbor only six hours' notice of the announcement. The message that arrived first thing that Saturday, addressed jointly to Admiral Kimmel and General Short, advised them that "at 1400 GCT July twenty-sixth United States will impose economic sanctions against Japan," and went on to say that the Philippine militia was to be called to active service, and that American merchant ships would be prohibited from sailing for Japanese ports. Nonetheless, although "immediate hostile reaction by Japan through the use of military means" was not anticipated, the Hawaiian commanders were alerted to "take appropriate precautionary measures against possible eventualities."[1]

No clue whatever was offered to what the "possible eventualities" might be. As a fleet alert, therefore, the 25 July warning, which it later emerged had been drafted by Admiral Turner, was full of shortcomings. It conflicted with an earlier dispatch that Kimmel had received on 3 July. That was a notification that Japanese merchant ships were to be clear of American ports within three weeks, when "unusually reliable Chinese sources" had predicted that Japan would attack Russia. It was beginning to look to us as though the navy department was crying wolf without a proper evaluation of the direction, size, and significance of the threat.

"What are you going to do? Be ready to shoot in all directions at once?" was the angry reaction of Commander McCollum in Washington when he found that Turner's 26 July alert had been issued without any reference to ONI.[2] For a month the head of the Far East section, whose job it was to assess incoming Japanese intelligence, had been disputing Turner's fixation—based on no good evidence—that the Japanese were about to abrogate their neutrality treaty and attack Russia. Turner was

123

apparently "bemused," according to McCollum, by the German attack on the Soviet Union, which had coincided with the alarms flooding in from the Nationalist Chinese. Chiang Kai-shek was claiming he needed more lend-lease aid to meet a supposed Japanese offensive that was about to develop on the mainland.

"Turner had the theory that Russia was going to fold up momentarily, and he figured out that the Japanese would plunge into Siberia," Mc-Collum explained. "This thinking within the navy department tied Japan to Hitler's tail, even though the Japanese never considered themselves as a satellite to anybody."[3] So without referring to ONI, the war plans director had persuaded Stark to fire off his 3 July alert of Japan's impending attack on Russia, with its confused warning that their fleet "is capable of movement either south or north" and "a definite move by the Japanese may be expected during the period."

Turner's insistence on sending out war warnings based on his own hunches forced the navy department into making incorrect evaluations of Japanese intentions. Turner's warnings conflicted wildly with McCollum's more sober estimates, which were sent to commanders in his fortnightly intelligence summary and predicted an imminent Japanese move into Indochina. The arrogant refusal of the chief of war plans to consult with McCollum left ONI officers in the outrageous situation of not having "any information as to what our own government was doing, because we frequently picked it up only as a result of the decoding of the Japanese diplomatic ciphers." As McCollum later observed, "To say that the guy who has the job of trying to figure things out that he [sic] cannot be told what action has been ordered was ridiculous."[4]

It was only because Kimmel had received some dispatches from Washington based on Purple in July that our predicament was not worse. From these gleanings I had been able to assemble a reasonably accurate picture of the immediate Japanese objectives in Indochina and to estimate their probable naval movements. Therefore, I felt confident in briefing Kimmel's Pacific Fleet staff conference on the morning of 26 July with the scenario I had constructed of what Japanese naval forces were at sea that weekend to support Tokyo's diplomatic demands on the French. We had the details of Japan's ultimatum to the Vichy government, so we knew their precise military objectives. That it was clearly a limited military operation was supported by their Magic intercept of 15 July saying that they hoped to make the moves "peacefully with French agreement if possible," and with the express intent "to avoid friction with Britain and particularly the United States."[5]

In contrast to what would happen later, during the weeks preceding the July crisis the intelligence Kimmel received from Magic sources provided us with all the information we needed to keep us abreast of diplomatic as well as military developments. This intelligence put Turner's idiosyncratic viewpoint into perspective. It enabled Kimmel to have the big picture of developments in Washington and Tokyo. At the same time, it provided me with an overall framework within which I could assemble the detailed pieces of data necessary to work out the dispositions of Japanese naval forces.

The diplomatic information was especially valuable because our naval cryptanalysts were still trying for a breakthrough into Japan's fleet code systems. We had to rely on this for our radio intelligence and for the task of identifying individual call signs from more than fifteen thousand designators. This was complicated, because the Japanese navy had made its annual designator changes on 1 May 1941. In less than two months, however, Rochefort's team had managed to find attributions for enough of the two-kana-numeral call signs to make dependable identifications of many units appearing in the radio traffic. We could not track all the important elements, notably the carrier divisions, but we managed to slot together from other sources some key units that were likely to be deployed in the takeover of Indochina bases. We were also reassured to find no new revision of call signs, another indication that Japan was not contemplating an immediate plunge into outright war.

Our main concern was to locate Japan's carriers, since they would provide the best clue to the movements of her naval forces. But the designators for most of the aircraft carrier divisions had not appeared for a week or more as either originators or addressees. This could mean either that the carriers were not at sea or that they were observing strict radio silence to keep their operations secret. By the summer of 1941 we had become pretty familiar with the pattern of their radio transmissions as well as the overall organization of Japan's naval operations. So although we could not read the codes in which their messages were transmitted, traffic analysis and radio direction-finding pinpointed the location of radio sending stations or units, and evaluated message flow for frequencies, volume, and addressees.

The most important intelligence culled from analysis of radio traffic during the weeks leading up to the July crisis were indications that the Japanese fleet was undergoing a major reorganization. Unknown to us, a new First Air Fleet had been created on 10 April 1941, under command of Admiral Chuichi Nagumo. Hints of this new command were first noted by Rochefort's analysts. Its significance, however, was not appreciated until early 1942. There was not sufficient traffic to allow us to reliably plot the pattern of its operations, but we recognized that this air fleet had authority over all eight aircraft carriers and attached units, together with an escort force of at least sixteen destroyers.

The creation of this fleet signified a new Japanese emphasis on naval air power; and because our Pacific Fleet had only three aircraft carriers, this new force presented a formidable threat. While we did not know when the First Air Fleet would operate as a combined force, our analysts determined that it was made up of four divisions having two carriers apiece, with each division having three or four destroyers to guard its planes. We predicted that, in conformity with our knowledge of their current naval doctrine and thinking, the First Air Fleet would play a supporting role in operations with the battle fleets. These were the days in the U.S. Navy when carriers and their planes were still thought of primarily in terms of scouting and reconnaissance. Aircraft carriers had been used on offensive missions in naval fleet problems as early as 1929 and as recently as 1940, before headquarters were moved to Pearl Harbor. But in the summer of 1941 battleship sailors still ruled the waves.

We linked Nagumo, the First Air Fleet commander in chief, with Carrier Division 1, which consisted of flagship *Kaga* and *Akagi,* as being the crack unit. They were Japan's biggest carriers, and operated with Destroyer Division 7. Like our *Lexington* and *Saratoga,* these thirty-thousand-ton flattops had been converted on the ways from a battleship and battle cruiser. Carrier Division 2 was made up of the newer *Sōryū* and *Hiryū,* and was linked with Destroyer Division 23; Carrier Division 3, light carriers *Ryūjō* and *Hosho,* was teamed with Destroyer Division 17. Carrier Division 4, made up of the fleet's newest twenty-thousand-ton carriers, *Shōkaku* and *Zuikaku,* was in tandem with Destroyer Division 3. Two converted merchantmen, *Horyu Maru* and *Kasuga Maru,* constituted what seemed to be an auxiliary carrier force, which we designated Carrier Division 5.[6]

The battleships and cruisers of Combined Fleet we knew were organized into First Fleet, or battle force; and Second Fleet, the scouting force. A Third Fleet, a blockade and transport force, consisted of a light cruiser, a dozen destroyers, tenders, transports, and miscellaneous vessels. So when our analysis of radio transmissions in the weeks leading up to 26 July revealed that, despite the potential power of the new First Air Fleet, two divisions of its carriers were assigned to support First and Second Fleet operations, we were confident that no major expedition was at sea.[7]

Rochefort's daily summaries of intelligence, derived from traffic analysis, indicated that at least one carrier division was with the scouting force in the South China Sea. This became even more of a certainty when we considered what had happened in February 1941, when the Japanese decided to mediate the French Indochina-Thailand border dispute with a show of naval force. At that time the Second and Third fleets, along with their carriers, had been sighted steaming southward. It was therefore a good bet that the Japanese would send a similar force south again in July. Since this time it seemed to be a Second Fleet show, we assumed that Carrier Division 2 would again be part of this operation to cover the occupation of the Indochina bases.[8]

Confirmation that such a task force was under way was evident from intelligence received from our consuls and naval attachés in Shanghai. The concentration of Japanese naval forces was also confirmed by the latest sighting reports from the ONI network of our seventeen under-cover observers in Far East ports. A low volume of Japanese naval radio traffic during the second part of July suggested that most of the Com-bined Fleet was probably still in home waters. *The New York Times* on 8 July supported this with reports from its Tokyo correspondent that most of the fleet was at anchor off Yokohama "without any attempt at se-crecy."

Only after the war was the accuracy of our July traffic analysis esti-mates finally confirmed. Interrogations of Japanese pilots revealed that *Sōryū* and *Hiryū* had spent the two-thousand-mile trip south to Indochina waters and back conducting continual exercises. What we had not guessed was that while Carrier Division 2 was en route back to Japan, it had rendezvoused with carriers *Akagi* and *Kaga* to practice combat ma-neuvers against Carrier Division 1. These mock attacks were an impor-tant operational test of techniques that the same pilots and planes would use for the attack on Pearl Harbor five months later.

The Indochina crisis was also an important test of our own ability to forecast enemy operations in time to be able to meet them. By coinci-dence, at 0400 that Saturday, 26 July 1941, Kimmel's revised war plan for the Pacific Fleet came into effect. To fulfill the broad directives of the Rainbow 5 war strategy, the fleet would be used to "check any Japanese moves toward the eventual capture of Malaysia (including the Philip-pines) and Hong Kong," or "the capture of Guam and other outlying positions."[9]

Kimmel developed his plan on the assumption that the Pacific Fleet's numerical inferiority to Combined Fleet would preclude a decisive con-frontation. The fleet's principal mission would therefore be "diverting the enemy strength away from the Malay barrier, through the denial and capture of positions in the Marshalls." Until hostilities were imminent, one of our main tasks was to "guard against surprise attack by Japan."[10]

So at his staff conference on the morning of 26 July, although he agreed with the estimates from Washington and from his staff that hostile moves by Japan would be limited to local demonstrations off the Indo-china coast by a part of the Combined Fleet, Kimmel agreed with Admi-ral Bloch on the "advisability" of increasing our long-range air searches. Bloch, the commander in chief of the Fourteenth Naval District, who had preceded Richardson as fleet commander, believed that a surprise attack on Pearl Harbor was a very remote possibility, but he felt it prudent to initiate contingency air defense measures. Planes took off at dawn the next day on a series of long-range patrols five hundred miles to the west-southwest, toward Jaluit, to intercept any Japanese force that might be sneaking in to attack from their secret bases in the Marshalls.

Simultaneously, General Short reacted to Washington's 25 July alert by placing his forces on a "half alert against sabotage."[11] The air recon-naissance continued through the weekend until the absence of "untoward eventualities" persuaded Kimmel and Short to step down their alert. Japan had occupied Indochina naval bases at Camranh Bay and Saigon, and air bases at Phnom Penh, Bien-hoa, and Saigon, but despite Turner's fears, the Tokyo government appeared to be waiting to test the impact of American economic sanctions before embarking on any hostile adventures in Siberia or anywhere else.

Kimmel nevertheless continued to regard the Pacific Fleet as being on a wartime footing because, after 26 July, there was no doubt in our minds at Pearl Harbor about the ultimate consequence of the embargo. Sooner, rather than later, Japan would move southward from her newly acquired bases in Indochina to seize alternative oil supplies from the Netherlands East Indies and Malaya? The Indochina crisis had, therefore, raised a number of serious concerns for Kimmel. What would be the role the fleet was expected to play now that tension between Japan and the United States had been hiked up several notches by the embargo? What was the significance of the occupation of bases in Indochina, which shortened the striking distance between Japanese forces and Malaya?

Kimmel voiced these concerns in a 26 July letter to Admiral Stark. It stressed the "importance of keeping the commander in chief advised of department policies and decisions, and changes of policies and decisions to meet changes in the international situation." Kimmel asked to be informed of what plans Washington had for "mutual support" if Japan attacked British or Dutch territory.[12]

Stark's acknowledgment of 8 August was as brief as it was evasive. He promised that "we shall go through it paragraph by paragraph" and that he was "glad to get an occasional check of this sort."[13] Meanwhile, Kimmel's fears about his fleet's strength were exacerbated by another brief CNO letter, dated 25 July, informing him that the president was considering that "you may be called upon to send a carrier load of planes to one of the Asiatic Russian ports."[14] It was incredible that anyone in Washington would even consider jeopardizing one of our precious carriers on such a risky mission. Kimmel fired back at once that the "entire Pacific Fleet" would be needed to ensure its safety. Moreover, "in the tense situation it would be tantamount to initiation of a Japanese-American war. . . .

"If for reasons of political expediency, it has been determined to force Japan to fire the first shot," Kimmel concluded acidly, "let us choose a method that will be more advantageous to ourselves. Certainly an operation such as that proposed is far less likely to bluff Japan into acquiescence or inactivity that it is to disturb her to the point of hostile use of bombs, torpedoes, and guns."[15]

Kimmel's distaste for what he considered to be Roosevelt's madcap schemes was increased by the confused "thinking out loud" letter of 31 July addressed by Stark to Captain Charles M. Cooke, Jr., with copies to Kimmel and Hart. "Savvy" Cooke of flagship *Pennsylvania* had preceded Turner as Stark's confidant and director of war plans.

The letter was charged with Stark's confusion about whether the embargo would ultimately send Japan charging south to seize the alternative oil supplies of the Dutch East Indies. Roosevelt's erratic course was his main gripe. "To some of my very pointed questions, which all of us would like to have answered, I get a smile or a 'Betty, please don't ask me that,'" Stark complained. He wearily admitted that he had offered to resign more than once. "Policy seems to be something never fixed, always fluid and changing." This also revealed the astonishing degree to which CNO had become dependent on the erratic intelligence estimates of his director of war plans. Turner's incorrect forecast that Japan would soon invade Vladivostok and Russia's maritime provinces was passed on with the comment, "He may be right. He usually is."[16]

It was bad enough being in Pearl Harbor and realizing that the navy department was so confused about what would happen next. But Kimmel was dismayed to learn that Roosevelt was not even confiding in his chief of naval operations. Kimmel knew the president was adept at using affability to sidestep awkward issues and Admiral Stark was not the only senior member of the administration to complain. Supreme Court Chief Justice Felix Frankfurter observed the president's preference for looking at problems through the wrong end of a telescope because "it makes things easier to bear."[17]

Cabinet members did not bear the burden so lightly. They were often exasperated by Roosevelt's penchant for reaching critical policy decisions in long, rambling monologues that went largely unrecorded. It was what Secretary of War Stimson called "the topsy turvy, upside-down system of poor administration" by which the United States was governed.

To the British ambassador, such decision making was more like "a disorderly day's rabbit shooting" than sound government.[18] Lord Halifax's complaint to London about Roosevelt's studied evasiveness is especially revealing. He had been upset because, during the several ABC-1 staff talks in March 1941, the Americans had refused to enter into the most tentative of military commitments in the Far East. Then, despite broad general agreement at joint staff discussions with the Dutch at Singapore in May, the American chiefs of staff still refused to endorse any formal mutual defense pact against Japan. But, as Lord Halifax reported to London, Roosevelt's announcement of 26 July concerning American economic sanctions against Japan had changed all that.

Kimmel was guessing right. To enforce the new sanctions, Washington had to reconsider the desirability of a defensive alliance in the Far East. Some Anglo-American agreement on joint defensive measures to hold the Malay Barrier-Philippine defense line was now not merely desirable, but given Japan's naval superiority and lack of oil supplies, it was essential.

Churchill had appreciated the strategic implications of the American embargo far more clearly than the foreign policy makers in Washington.

With the U-boats in the Atlantic threatening to gnaw through Britain's fuel line to the United States, the prime minister knew just how the Japanese viewed the prospects that their war machine would be drained of its offensive and defensive capability as their planes ran out of gas and their warships were confined to port for lack of fuel. Although the Dutch and British readily agreed to join in with the economic embargo, the prime minister warned Roosevelt that measures were needed to stop the Japanese who were ready to "run amok."[19] Japan had to import all but 12 percent of her oil, 80 percent of it in 1941 coming from the United States. In the year ending March 1941, imports reached an all-time high of nearly twenty-three million barrels of crude, and fifteen million of refined petroleum. The Japanese had been stockpiling oil, but it was calculated that with naval consumption alone running at three hundred thousand tons a month, the reserves on hand would last less than a year even with stringent civilian rationing.

Washington's failure to make this calculation must be counted as one of the major intelligence blunders of history. This was especially true after Magic provided the clear warning in a 31 July Tokyo-Berlin intercept. "To save its very life," Ambassador Oshima was told, Japan "must take immediate steps to break asunder this ever strengthening chain of encirclement which is being woven under the guidance and with the participation of England and the United States, acting like a cunning dragon seemingly asleep."[20] For all its quaint phraseology, this message was a blunt expression of Japan's intention: to advance southward and seize alternative supplies if diplomacy failed to quickly reopen the tap on American oil.

It appears that no one in Washington was alerted by this Magic intercept to the fact that the Japanese government had now been forced onto a deadline for reconciling its national policy objectives. The State Department therefore made a bad miscalculation when it launched into a carrot-and-stick diplomacy in the expectation that the resumption of oil supplies would serve as the reward, while the Anglo-American military buildup in the Far East would provide the threat.

The reality, however, was that our foreign policy toward Japan was now forced into the dangerous posture of allowing diplomatic policy to dictate military strategy. We lacked the military strength to enforce the embargo. To meet the two-ocean Axis menace with a one-ocean navy and avoid the objections of an isolationist Congress, Roosevelt was now forced into a secret commitment to Britain. And this led both nations into a Far East deterrent strategy that was as unfounded as it was to prove catastrophic.

11

Deceptive Deterrents

O N 2 AUGUST 1941 Roosevelt put to sea in the presidential yacht *Potomac.* He was going on a well-publicized "fishing trip." But out of sight of the New England coast, he transferred from the yacht to heavy cruiser *Augusta,* where his military chiefs were already on board. Their mission was to be one of the most consequential, but little understood, meetings in history; it would be held in foggy Placentia Bay on the bleak southern coast off Newfoundland.

Meanwhile, Winston Churchill and his advisers were steaming at high speed westward across the Atlantic on board the Royal Navy's newest battleship, *Prince of Wales.* Still bearing the scars of her gunnery duel the past May with the German battleship *Bismarck, Prince of Wales* was relying on Enigma decrypts of U-boat signals to dodge German wolf packs. On Saturday, 9 August 1941, she hove to a short haul from where *Augusta* and her escorts swung at anchor off the village of Argentia and its nearby lend-lease airstrip.

Within hours of the battleship's arrival Roosevelt and Churchill met for the first time as president and prime minister on board *Augusta.* They quickly discovered a strong personal rapport and struck an overall agreement on strategy. The American chiefs of staff, led by General George C. Marshall and Admiral Harold R. Stark, with General "Hap" Arnold and Admiral Richmond K. Turner in attendance, conferred with the British chiefs led by Admiral Sir Dudley Pound and General Sir John Dill, to hammer out what Roosevelt carefully laid down as being "broad principles which should guide our policies along the same road."[1]

During the first round of discussions, the British military leaders found themselves in the same ship but not yet "in the same boat" concerning an agreement on the terms of an overall alliance they hoped for with the United States. Churchill was disappointed to learn that his team could not get an American commitment to send warships into the Mediterranean, or to commence the convoying of Britain's merchant shipping beyond the American neutrality zone all the way across the Atlantic. But when it came to the Pacific it was a different matter. The British delegation was encouraged to find that American military policy against Japan had undergone a complete revision since the strategic stalemate of the May staff conversations in Singapore. They were delighted to discover that Washington's embargo on Axis trade was forcing the American chiefs of staff to accept the need for establishing a powerful military and naval force in the Far East as a deterrent against Japan.

"We are now trying to build up the defense of the Philippines as a direct defense to the Indian Ocean and Singapore," Admiral Stark told a joint meeting on board *Prince of Wales* on Monday, 11 August.[2] "Could the British rearrange their schedules to help out on this?" Marshall explained that the recent American decision to bolster the defenses of Manila and the Asiatic Fleet could be made only if the scheduled lend-lease shipments of antiaircraft batteries and heavy bombers originally destined for Britain could be redirected across the Pacific to General MacArthur.

In the horse trading that followed, Marshall went far beyond the limited commitments to Far East defense which had been agreed to at the ABC-1 staff talks in March and which were the basis of the Rainbow 5 strategic war plan. Pound and Dill fell all over themselves to accommodate the American request. They believed that they were getting the best of a bargain in which bombers and antiaircraft guns were to be traded for a massive American buildup in the Philippines. Visions of the Pacific Fleet in Manila Bay, only three days' steaming from the still-vacant battleship berths at the Singapore naval base, prompted Admiral Pound's enthusiastic endorsement that "a strong defense of the Philippine Islands directly strengthens the defense of Singapore and the Netherlands East Indies."[3] A speedy buildup of MacArthur's forces was also entirely in accord with the sentiments Churchill had expressed in his after-dinner speech on board *Prince of Wales* the previous evening; he had called on the United States to join with Britain and Russia in issuing a final ultimatum to Japan.

Churchill's comments had been received with as much vocal approval by our military staff as by their British hosts. But outside the euphoria in *Prince of Wales*'s oak-paneled admiral's quarters, Roosevelt knew that the full-blooded declaration of mutual alliance that the prime minister sought would not play well with his congressional foes on Capitol Hill.

So the publicly announced result of the conference was restricted to the so-called Atlantic Charter declaration of the British and American agreement to uphold Roosevelt's Four Principles of Freedom that were later to be incorporated into the United Nations Charter. The declaration's euphoric rhetoric, however, camouflaged a more far-reaching military arrangement by the United States, which was not committed to writing. Just what the prime minister and president agreed to in their private sessions was a matter of concern to General Arnold, one of the leading participants in the conference. "I can't make up my mind as yet whether most of us are window dressing for the main actors, or whether we are playing minor roles in the drama," he noted disparagingly, the more so because he had been instrumental in hammering out substantive military details. Alluding to some secret accord, which Arnold termed the "epoch-making" outcome of the conference, he wrote, "What the President and the Prime Minister had to say when together I know not."[4]

The chief of the army air force knew better than anyone that Churchill would not have agreed to release badly needed bombers and anti-aircraft batteries to MacArthur without the quid pro quo that they would indeed be employed as a "direct defense to the Indian Ocean and Singapore.[5] There may have been failure to agree on convoying, or the intended British occupation of the north African French port of Dakar, but when the warships carrying the prime minister and president sailed from Placentia Bay on 14 August, Arnold believed firmly that the military leaders were in total accord on "the handling of Japan if that nation moved farther southward."[6]

The pact on "handling Japan" would indeed turn out to be "epoch-making"—but not in the way the participants intended. The volte-face on strategy in the Pacific resulted in a disastrous strategic miscalculation for the United States, because the belief that a scratch force of American bombers and a few British warships could be transformed by diplomatic bluff into a "big stick" that would force the Japanese to halt their southward advance was a gamble doomed to failure. By embarking on a deterrent policy before the military forces were installed in the Philippines to make it credible, Britain and the United States succeeded in making the concept of a preemptive strike an attractive option to the Japanese.

It was also ironic that the conference should have settled on aircraft rather than battleships as the prescription for dissuading Japan from launching an essentially maritime adventure. But the chiefs of our armed forces had placed their military bets, believing that General Arnold's Flying Fortress bombers were the right strategic chips with which to gamble the defense of Anglo-American territory in the Far East, that the B-17s would be an effective deterrent to Japanese aggression. The long-range bombers, which otherwise would have been on their way to Britain, were accordingly diverted to the Philippines. They were to be backed up by Churchill's pledge to send a squadron of modern battleships and carriers to Singapore.

Getting adequate deterrent forces out to the Far East was going to take many months, so Churchill readily accepted Roosevelt's assurance that the State Department would be able to "baby them [the Japanese] along"[7] until then. Despite foreign office protests that he was making an unprecedented abrogation of British diplomatic independence, Churchill issued instructions that future negotiations with the Japanese were in the hands of the State Department. Did this mean that if the "babying along" failed, the Americans would be committed to fight Japan even if American territory was not attacked first?

In later years it would be a favorite charge by the isolationists that Roosevelt had, indeed, made just such a secret and unconstitutional pact with Churchill at Argentia. Exactly how far the president went in his private sessions with the British prime minister may never be known, but a logical assessment of the situation suggests that some deal was struck that amounted to a de facto Anglo-American alliance against Japan that was never submitted to Congress for ratification. Although Roosevelt would not have run afoul of the constitutional restraints until he was actually called upon to honor the guarantees he had given Churchill, we shall see how he came perilously close to doing just that by 4 December 1941.

Churchill's rejection of a foreign office minute that Britain had abrogated her traditional rights of independent negotiation with Japan, without signing a formal accord with the United States, was one indication of the unwritten alliance. Another was the considerable risk that the prime minister had run in making a seven-thousand-mile round trip across the U-boat-infested Atlantic, which was hardly justified by the idealistic window-dressing of the Atlantic Charter. Noble and inspiring though its ringing phrases were, the document did not amount to any tangible furtherance of Britain's war aims—and it was also unsigned.

The best evidence that the isolationists were right is contained in the minutes of the Joint Army-Navy Board. Chaired by Admiral Stark throughout 1941, the same top military brains that had attended the Argentia conference continued to meet every two weeks, and they were final arbiter of American strategic planning. The minutes of these Joint Board meetings subsequent to August 1941 show how the supreme military council of the United States put a de facto Anglo-American alliance against Japan into effect by making preparations to commit our forces to a war even if it was British rather than our territory that the Japanese struck first. The records now available confirm that the board members were making their plans on the assumption that America would be at war if Japan attacked British, but not United States, territory first.

The nature of the commitments that Roosevelt had given to Churchill were questioned at the first full joint board meeting after Argentia. General Marshall, on 4 September, voiced concern that "the president might direct the British be given a seat on the Joint Board."[8] This unprecedented recognition of the fraternity of Anglo-American military interest was something that the army chief was determined to resist.

When the board next convened on 14 September, Turner outlined the navy's plans for dealing with "offensive operations" by the Japanese—not just concerning the Philippines but taking into account joint operations with British and Dutch forces to defend Malaya. A month later, on

10 October, the board discussed and approved a strategic critique submitted by the British chiefs of staff and agreed to a list of fuel and bomb depots being established at Far East air bases belonging to Britain, Australia, and the Netherlands.

If there was any doubt that a de facto Anglo-American alliance was already in existence, it was removed for the members of the Joint Board at their 3 November session at which Admiral Stark clearly let it be known that we would go to war if Japan launched full-scale offensive operations: "In the case of a Japanese attack against either the Philippines or British or Dutch possessions, the United States should resist the attack. In case of a Japanese attack against Siberia, Thailand or China through Yunnan, the United States should not declare war."[9]

From the context of this statement, there can be no doubt about the true implication of Stark's recommendation that our forces "should resist" a Japanese attack on the territory of foreign powers with whom at that point we had no congressionally ratified alliance. That there was no question about the board's intentions is evident from Admiral Ingersoll's meeting notes. "Yes" is checked against "War" in only two of five possibilities—that Japan attacked the Philippines and "British or Dutch Malay."[10]

It is now abundantly clear what Roosevelt meant when he told the British ambassador on the evening of 2 December that "we shall all be in it together."[11] The military leadership in Washington was already basing its contingency planning for war on that premise.

That Roosevelt *did* provide Churchill with what amounted to a potentially unconstitutional assurance of alliance became public knowledge six months later. To the consternation of presidential aide Harry Hopkins, on 17 January 1942, the prime minister felt obliged to allude to the agreement in defending himself against a censure motion in the House of Commons. To the charge that Britain's colonies in the Far East had been inadequately guarded, Churchill asserted he had taken care that Britain "should not be exposed single-handed to the Japanese onslaught."[12] Choosing his words with caution lest he let the cat out of the bag and embarrass the president, he insisted there had been no neglect because of "the probability since the Atlantic conference at which I discussed these matters with Mr. Roosevelt, that the United States, even if not attacked herself, would come into a war in the Far East." His "expectation"—as he put it—was "reinforced as time went on" and "one had greater assurance that if Japan ran amok in the Pacific, we should not fight alone." Nor, as Churchill reminded his detractors, had his confidence in the United States been "falsified by events."[13]

The prime minister's 1942 statement that hinted at the true extent of this clandestine military cooperation against Japan set alarm bells ringing in the White House and brought an attack from Senator Burton K. Wheeler who had been one of the most vocal spokesmen of the isolationists. On 21 February, Harry Hopkins sent the president a memorandum warning that "some day soon Wheeler and his crowd may pick it up." They did.[14]

At the 1945 Pearl Harbor hearings it was repeatedly charged that the president had exceeded his constitutional powers in making a secret alliance with Britain. But although considerable evidence was cited, the full records of the Joint Board meetings were not made available to the hearings. As a result the majority determined that no such commitment had been made.

This refusal to release the records was an understandable effort to protect Roosevelt against charges that he had acted unconstitutionally. But the most damaging aspect of the original conference was the failure of Admiral Stark to immediately inform the Pacific Fleet commander of the true implications of the new Anglo-American strategy against Japan. The failure to pass on such a critical bit of information was inexcusable.

In hindsight, it was all the more astonishing because of Kimmel's urgent request of Stark to learn "what arrangements" existed for cooperation with the British and Dutch naval forces in the event that fighting broke out in the Far East. The question was ignored altogether by the chief of naval operations in his 21 August letter which, nonetheless, expressed a growing concern about "the seriousness of the Pacific situation which continues to deteriorate."[15]

Admiral Kimmel was relieved, however, that CNO's first lengthy dispatch since the Churchill-Roosevelt meeting did not request another transfer of Pacific Fleet ships to strengthen our Atlantic naval forces. Nor did it call for sending reinforcements to Admiral Hart's tiny Asiatic Fleet in Manila, although it was now dangerously exposed to Japanese warships, which were operating from newly acquired bases in Indochina.

The events of July had convinced Kimmel that there could be no reining in our preparations for the fleet's assigned mission under the original Rainbow 5 war plan: to conduct a sortie toward Japanese bases in the Marshalls to draw their forces away from the Philippines and the Malay Barrier. There could be no letup in the intensive schedule of training operations needed to bring ships and men up to battle readiness. The problem, however, was more than just keeping men, ships, and equipment in good physical condition and readiness. There were the equally important considerations of morale and spirit. Most of the sailors in Hawaii were long separated from home and loved ones. The fleshpots of Honolulu could offer little more than temporary solace. There was a limit in peacetime as to how long men could be kept on watch-and-watch duty.

Throughout the summer of 1941 Kimmel's hard-driving schedule of operations kept at least one—and often two—of the fleet's task forces at sea. Port calls were necessary for replenishment and crew morale, but it is often forgotten that at no time during 1941 were *all* the ships of the fleet in Pearl Harbor.[16] Maximum security measures, consistent with the maintenance of the training program, were kept in effect after July. But to effect the critical transition of the fleet from intensive training to all-out war measures was a matter of timing. To determine when that moment was at hand, the fleet commander had to rely on the intelligence he received from Washington.

"When would Japanese-American relations reach the point that all training should cease and all-out war dispositions should be made?"[17] That was the question that Kimmel was constantly asking himself, as relations between Japan and the United States worsened.

This was the very time when we needed all the intelligence—especially diplomatic intelligence—that we could lay our hands on. But not one single piece of the Magic by which Washington was monitoring this policy of "babying along" Tokyo's diplomats was relayed to us at Pearl Harbor from August through November. Nor did we know why the decrypts were not sent to us. After Kimmel had received the July Magics, I had remained confident that ONI's Far East section was living up to their promise to us the previous April that we would get *all* diplomatic intelligence relevant to the fleet.

Those determined to blame the president for a conspiracy to get the United States into the war against Hitler "by the back door" claim that Admiral Kimmel was denied this Magic intelligence on the direct orders of the White House.

While there can be no doubt now that Roosevelt exceeded the limits of his executive authority in the assurances he gave Churchill, that the United States would go to war if British territory in the Far East was attacked, there is no evidence that any presidential directive was issued restricting the flow of intelligence to Pearl Harbor—or anywhere else. The decision to limit the type of intelligence sent to overseas commands, in fact, appears to have been a bureaucratic one. The reason for it was a genuine fear that Washington's secrets were leaking to the Japanese.

12

Shortchanged

I N VIEW OF THE fatal consequences of the de facto Anglo-American military alliance against Japan, it was a curious twist of fate that Japan had somehow penetrated our heavy curtain of secrecy in order to correctly estimate the significance of the Argentia conference. This startling revelation emerged from the intercept of Ambassador Nomura's 7 August report to Tokyo that Japanese-American relations were "extremely critical" since "the president accompanied by high army and navy officials is meeting with Churchill."[1]

The Purple decrypt of Ambassador Nomura's report, which had been sent a full *three days* before the first meeting between Roosevelt and Churchill, alerted the foreign minister that the Argentia conference would be proof that "careful preparations are being made to counter our every move." These fears were confirmed the following day by Japan's London envoy. In a cable that was also intercepted, Tokyo was informed that presidential aide Harry Hopkins was accompanying Churchill's party and that Marshall, Stark, and King would participate in the conference in which the Far East was to be one of the principal topics.[2]

The Japanese military attaché in Washington also roused the army's concern with his report that such a high-level meeting could mean only one thing: "closer arrangements for a joint Anglo-American participation in the war."[3] Although this message was intercepted too, it was in a code that could not be read until 1943. But the two Purple decrypts were alarming enough evidence that Japan had advance warning of the Churchill-Roosevelt meeting. So was Tokyo's 9 August instruction to Nomura to press the White House for a meeting with Japan's prime minister "immediately upon President Roosevelt's return."[4] The sources of the leak were never pinpointed, but the incident served to reinforce Washington's security fetish.

When I became Pacific Fleet intelligence officer in December 1940, I had been impressed by my having to swear an oath of secrecy. There were very strict regulations limiting the supersecret comint only to the commander in chief and those few members of his staff who had also been sworn to secrecy. For those other staff members who had not been cleared, I prepared a special intelligence summary that was given an A-1 rating, but no identification as to its source. So great was our concern for these secrets that when Kimmel added his war plans officer to the comint list, I could not brief Captain McMorris on the material until the admiral gave me handwritten authority.[5]

Measures to protect our own communications channels for Magic were every bit as strict. Intercepted Japanese signals, even though they could not be broken, were relayed after reencipherment on a special radio circuit code-named Copek. Messages containing references to radio intelligence used the regular naval communications network. But all such communications had to be sent by our electric cipher machines (ECM) in a special cipher, which could be deciphered only by the command holding the correct rotors for that cipher. The rotors were issued to commands according to rank. A rear admiral (two stars), for example, rated a set that enabled him to read messages sent out for commands of his rank. When such messages were received by the communications office, they could identify only that this was a special cipher. It was then passed to the fleet security officer. At Cincpac, he alone would be responsible for using the special machine and code wheels to break out the message to be hand-delivered to the admiral, his chief of staff, or, if so directed by Kimmel, passed on to me.

The August 1941 security flap in Washington came hard on the heels of a top-secret army inquiry after the State Department reported fears that its codes "had already been broken by one or more foreign governments."[6] Investigation revealed that these fears were groundless, but General Marshall ordered a general tightening up of security where codes and communications were involved.

It was against this paranoid background of investigations and new directives intended to reduce the risk of leakage of our most secret information that the custodians of Magic evidently concluded that even the navy's flag-officer rotor system, which had previously been considered far more secure than the army or State Department code systems, could not now guarantee sufficient protection for their most vital intelligence source. While based on the sound principle of restricting secret information on a "need to know" basis, it negated Magic's informational value as practical intelligence since it was subsequently denied to the Pacific Fleet. Admiral Kimmel was the one overseas commander above all others who had a need to know and act on Magic.

After 7 December, however, no one wanted to acknowledge responsibility for having shut off our Pearl Harbor headquarters from the intelligence that could have saved the Pacific Fleet. At the seven secret wartime inquiries, and again during the public testimony at the congressional hearings held in 1945, a parade of senior staff officers denied any direct responsibility for setting the policy. Such reticence, even in 1945, suggests a realization by these officers that the December disaster might have been prevented if Admiral Kimmel had received detailed intelligence based on Purple diplomatic traffic.

Their testimony was understandably evasive, patently confused, and often conflicting about whether the ban on sending Magic overseas was the result of specific orders, or just a consensus action. But there was general agreement that as relations between Washington and Tokyo grew more strained, increasingly stringent measures had been put into effect by both navy and military intelligence organizations to prevent the Japanese from getting "any inkling" that we could read their diplomatic communications.[7]

Colonel Rufus Bratton, chief of the Far East section of military intelligence, Captain McCollum's opposite number in the army, testified before the congressional committee that orders from the army chief of staff "prevented me from transmitting any Magic to overseas commanders."[8] General Marshall challenged this assertion. He insisted that he could "recall giving no such specific instructions."[9]

Admiral Stark also denied issuing orders preventing transmission of Magic to Admiral Kimmel. He explained that he had tried to incorporate it into his "personal letters." The former chief of naval operations claimed he "would have far rather sent him too much than too little." So great was the secrecy surrounding Magic, and so complete Admiral Turner's control of intelligence, that Stark admitted that he had been led to believe by his chief of war plans that Pearl Harbor could translate, as well as intercept, the Japanese diplomatic messages.[10]

"I inquired on two or three occasions as to whether or not Kimmel could read certain dispatches, when they came up and which we were interpreting," Stark testified, ". . . and I was told that he could."[11] Admiral Turner maintained that this was indeed "my impression at the time" because he had been assured by the director of naval communications in "March or April" 1941 that Kimmel was not only "getting as much as we were" but "he was getting it sooner than we were."[12]

Such oversight on the part of the director of war plans, who was known for poking his nose into everyone's pie, reveals he was either a fool or a liar. This was not in keeping with the character of Turner, who had taken a crash course in music in order to be able to bawl out the band on his cruiser,[13] and whose war plans staff had been used to his raging against Noyes "and his God-damn secrets!"[14] Turner, moreover, not only had access to the daily Magic summaries, but insisted on reviewing all operational intelligence sent to us at Pearl Harbor.

Turner's professed ignorance was essential to his denial of all responsibility for what intelligence was made available to us at Pearl Harbor before 7 December 1941. It put Noyes on the spot when he was sworn as a witness at the secret 1944 naval court of inquiry. At first the former director of naval communications was carefully evasive about precisely what assurances had been given to his buccaneering superior. After repeated questioning, he eventually conceded that Turner raised the matter of who was getting what in "almost daily" meetings that "continually discussed" the status of decrypting. Turner, therefore, "should have understood."[15]

Under cross-examination Noyes went even further. He testified that it was his remembrance that when the director of war plans "asked what was our setup in regard to intercepted messages," it was "fully explained to him." Pressed whether he had ever given the chief of war plans "any impression that the commander in chief of the Pacific Fleet was getting information of the type contained in the Purple code intercepts," Noyes refused to be budged from his equivocal "Not intentionally."[16]

This refusal to actually blame a brother admiral let Turner off the hook. The former war plans chief maintained his assertion that Kimmel "had everything we had"—as he had so brazenly tried to outface me on the night of the surrender ceremony with his claim that Pearl Harbor could read the Japanese diplomatic traffic!

Four months later, however, on 21 December 1945, Turner was called to answer the glaring conflict in testimony that was revealed when the congressional investigating committee gained access to the secret record of the naval court of inquiry. Then the former war plans chief was forced to admit that he "was entirely in error as regards the diplomatic codes."[17]

Turner then tried to cover up the magnitude of the consequences of his error in a cloud of self-assertiveness that befitted his public stature as one of the heroic leaders of the Pacific campaign. Like a cuttlefish ejecting ink to escape danger, he blew a bombastic smokescreen that enabled him to dart for cover behind the failures of the intelligence specialists whose function he had so tenaciously usurped in 1941. None of his former subordinates had the courage to take on the fire-breathing four-star admiral who had successfully masterminded the navy's wartime amphibious operations. No witness dared to expose the extent to which the director of war plans and his three-man "coordinating" group effectively maintained a stranglehold on the intelligence that went out to the fleet.

Turner was thereby allowed to escape with his reputation, if not honor, intact by claiming that he "did not know the details at all of the decryption methods or codes." Noyes was supposedly confused or had "misunderstood what I was trying to get at."[18] Turner could not recall whether Noyes had "specified diplomatic intercepts" in their discussion four years earlier, and Turner double-talked at the inquiry, saying that confusion about the actual decrypting process had given them both a false impression about precisely what information Kimmel was receiving.[19]

Turner's deceptive and evasive responses in December 1945 betrayed an ignorance that was highly unlikely, or a deception that was highly obvious. But since none of his former colleagues was going to "spill the beans," he confused the congressional investigators, who tried to chip away at his granitelike composure.

Such confusion of terms might have been excusable in a layman. But it suggests a lack of credibility in a ranking admiral with a formidable reputation for excessive attention to detail. The committee's senior counsel was moved to ask how it was possible for him to have discharged his duty to keep the fleet commanders fully advised of intelligence indicating the possibility of war. "You could not do that," William D. Mitchell asked Turner with deliberate sarcasm, "unless you knew precisely just what they had and what they needed from you. Isn't that so?"[20]

"No, sir; that is not correct. It was not my duty to inform commanders in chief as to intelligence," Turner shot back. "Sending intercepts, or summaries of intercepts, or evaluating them as to authenticity or probability, was not war plans province and we never under any circumstance sent such information out."[21]

To anyone who is familiar with the mutinous conditions provoked by Turner's interference in the intelligence process on the second deck of the navy department throughout 1941, his barefaced denial of any responsibility for its consequences was as outrageous as it was untrue. Not only had he ridden roughshod over the functions and sensibilities of two directors of naval intelligence, but he had sent out false warnings and interfered with estimates without any reference to the very department whose duty it was to evaluate the extent and direction of the Japanese threat. Only because Stark and Ingersoll had resisted making any written change in the naval operations manual was Turner able to outface the charge of culpability for the intelligence debacle that led to disaster at Pearl Harbor.

In 1961 Turner died with his lies caught in his throat. The other officers who, in 1941, comprised the upper echelon of the naval staff in Washington closed ranks to protect his and their own reputations, intending to take the secret to their collective graves. Fortunately, five years after Turner's death, one of them—Captain McCollum—decided that posterity deserved the truth. Then retired, and a distinguished rear admiral, the former head of ONI's Far East desk provided the U.S. Naval Institute with a graphic personal account of the temper and tempests that followed Turner's rise to power as the domineering member of the triumvirate that ran the office of naval operations throughout 1941.

McCollum's chief, ONI director Admiral Kirk, had repeatedly protested this usurpation of their role by war plans. At the height of his battle with Turner in May, it was clear to both McCollum and Kirk that if Turner's arbitrary authority was not formalized, they would be in a position to be blamed for anything that went wrong as a result of the inaccurate estimates that war plans was sending out to the commands without consulting ONI.

Captain McCollum took it upon himself to attempt to resolve the feud between naval intelligence and the war plans division that was poisoning the air on the navy department's second deck, and throttling off the fleet at Pearl Harbor from an adequate flow of properly evaluated intelligence. In a personal interview with Admiral Ingersoll, McCollum sought to enlist his support in persuading Admiral Stark to regularize the procedures Turner was controlling by oral fiat. Ingersoll's deputy was a mild, soft-spoken, thoughtful officer whom Kirk believed to be his only ally in the upper reaches of the naval staff.

McCollum patiently detailed what was going wrong. War plans was sending out its own, often wildly incorrect estimates without any reference to himself or the ONI director. He pointed out the inconsistencies of this conduct with the procedures and responsibilities laid down by the CNO manual. The dangers were self-evident. McCollum reminded Ingersoll of the procedure, similar to the army's, that had been followed by the navy until Turner arrived—for ONI to do the evaluating. Ingersoll was not sympathetic. His hackles rising, he insisted on knowing all about the army practice, but observed that the navy did not do it that way.[22]

"Admiral, if that's the case, how about issuing an order in writing amending that part of the ONI manual?" McCollum ventured. The usually affable Ingersoll was set alight by this apparent attempt by a subordinate to dictate CNO policy.

"Get the hell out of here," roared the admiral. "A verbal [sic] order is enough!"[23]

This abrupt dismissal ended any further efforts by the ONI staff to have the intelligence responsibility of the war plans directorate committed to writing. Since the manual was not amended, Richmond Kelly Turner was allowed to deny his responsibility for failing to keep Admiral Kimmel fully informed with all the pertinent intelligence that was available in Washington. Stark and Ingersoll had knowingly sanctioned Turner's insistence on "coordinating" the final evaluation of operational intelligence. Their tacit acceptance of his role and oral instruction was not on the record. So four years later when the former war plans director professed ignorance of just what intelligence Pearl Harbor received, the opportunity was lost to roast him over the glowing coals of his admitted dereliction.

It was indeed a measure of Turner's influence in the triumvirate that ran naval operations that by the fall of 1941 Stark had been impressed enough by his forcefulness and apparent command of intelligence to let him control ONI's function without need for a written directive. It was a situation that placed McCollum in an unenviable predicament: "We were told in effect, all right, if there's anything wrong with the evaluation, you guys did it, and you guys and not war plans must take the onus [blame]."[24]

Turner, by omission or commission, therefore played a leading part in shutting off Pearl Harbor from the best source of intelligence. He diminished our ability to judge Japan's plans and intentions affecting the Pacific Fleet. The secondhand evaluations sent out by Stark, which he claimed were based on Magic, were more confusing than helpful. They were certainly no substitute for the full decrypts in our efforts to analyze Japan's situation, especially considering the extent to which Stark was influenced by Turner's idiosyncratic views. Moreover, neither Kimmel nor I had any indication that important Magic information that vitally concerned the fleet was being withheld from us after 20 July.

The biggest intelligence loss that resulted from our being denied access to Magic was the opportunity to monitor the traffic in the J-19 code between Tokyo and Japan's Honolulu consulate. Hypo intercepts were forwarded on to Washington unread by Pearl Harbor because of Rochefort's instruction to leave the diplomatic ciphers to Washington. And in Washington they were given a low priority. When they were eventually decrypted, information that would have been very pertinent did not reach us. Evidently Turner and his "expert" three-man intelligence committee did not consider it important for the Pacific Fleet to know that the Japanese consulate in Honolulu was paying unusually close attention to the fleet anchorage and shipping movements in Pearl Harbor.

The intelligence officer on the spot must always assess the scope of the overall picture. In trying to fit together the strategic jigsaw puzzle in the fall of 1941, I had lacked vital information about Japan's diplomatic intentions. I was unaware at the time that these facts were available in Washington or that Magic had uncovered clues that the naval war planners in Tokyo were paying special attention to Hawaii. The tragedy was that even those vitally illuminating pieces of intelligence concerning Pearl Harbor were not passed on to us.

Washington was twice as far away from the uncoiling snake of Japanese military power as we were in Hawaii. When it came to preparing strategic estimates, the vast distances involved in the Pacific induced a dangerous illusion in the minds of the analysts in Washington as to Pearl Harbor's security. They pored over their maps and made neat strategic calculations about where and when Japan was most likely to attack: the Philippines, Malaya, and the Dutch East Indies were obvious targets. In spite of Turner's earlier concerns, Hawaii and not Pearl Harbor did not rate so highly on his danger list after he became convinced that the Japanese would attack Russia in the summer of 1941.

When I found out, a couple of years later, how we had been shortchanged, I was astonished and outraged. Had I been similarly negligent, and willfully withheld information critical to the safety of our fleet, I would have been court-martialed—and would have deserved to be shot!

Yet senior members of the naval staff who bore the real burden for the intelligence failures that led directly to Pearl Harbor were not court-martialed, not reprimanded, not in any way taken to task for their part in the debacle. They all remained on active duty. Indeed, they advanced in rank, prestige, and glory throughout the war. There was no taint or tarnish on their careers. Being in Washington, they were too close to the White House and the rest of the bureaucracy to attract the finger of scorn. Furthermore, and most important, convenient scapegoats were available. It was easier and safer to blame the commanders on the spot at Pearl Harbor: Admiral Kimmel and General Short.

13

"Waves of Strife"

I N THE FINAL MONTHS of peace in 1941, my duty as fleet intelligence officer obliged me to do more than merely be a conduit for strategic information that others sent. It also required predicting where there were gaps that could be filled by collecting intelligence from local sources. My involvement in the Tachibana case, four months before, had taught me that Honolulu, with its large Japanese population rubbing shoulders daily with white hats on liberty, was fertile territory for espionage.

Japan's consulate was on Nuuanu Avenue. The official diplomatic list showed only five assistant consuls. According to the Fourteenth Naval District Intelligence Office and FBI reports, however, it was home base for more than two hundred subconsular agents scattered throughout the territory of Hawaii.[1] At least forty of them were being monitored for espionage activity as they mingled with the 160,000 Japanese-Americans who, besides running most of the fruit and vegetable business of the island, owned more than half the licensed bars in Honolulu, plus many of the legal and illegal brothels that attracted large numbers of off-duty sailors.

Apart from the lure of the Honolulu red-light district, there was a repetitive humdrum to the life-style of the uniformed Americans on Oahu. Off-hours for the enlisted men were usually spent in a service club or in crowded bars and clip joints. These ranged from the few fancy spots at fashionable hotels to a favorite servicemen's hangout like Lousy Lui's at the two-bit end of Waikiki. In this joint there existed an undercurrent of uneasy suspicion that mingled with the tobacco smoke and alcohol fumes. Like many of the bar owners, Lousy Lui was Japanese, but born in the islands, so he was an American citizen. Since his parents were born in Japan, that also made him a citizen of Japan under Japanese law. Rumor had it that he was a military intelligence agent for the Japanese.

146

Walter Davenport from *Colliers* magazine described the nervous confidence that infused the large service population on the island during its last months of peace:

> The enlisted men grouse about military life, and talk more Jap. Their speculations about war are always on the optimistic side. Oahu is a 604-square-mile fort bristling with eight-, twelve-, and fourteen-inch guns, and the Pacific Fleet is no slouch. Pearl Harbor, Manila, and Singapore know hour by hour where every American and British ship is, between the Panama Canal and the Red Sea. So, militarily we have nothing to be concerned about in the summer of 1941.[2]

While the FBI labored with the near hopeless task of trying to weed the real spies out of a local population of which more than a third was Japanese and potentially suspect, the navy tried to control the sampan fleet. Based at Kewalo Basin, due south of Punchbowl crater, about twelve miles from the entrance to Honolulu harbor, the sampans were sturdy diesel-powered fishing vessels, up to eighty feet long, manned by tough Japanese fishermen. They ranged out five hundred miles to sea in search of tuna, and repeatedly had to be chased from the waters south and west of Pearl Harbor where the fleet exercised. All vessels trespassing within three miles of Diamond Head were stopped and questioned. No Japanese-Americans were permitted to work within naval reservations, but many navy wives had Japanese maids and cooks. So undercover agents for the consulate, like Yoshikawa, probably had little difficulty picking up inside information on fleet movements.

Even with all these precautions afloat and ashore, neither the FBI nor military counterintelligence officers could do anything to bring charges of illegal activity against the Japanese navy's most active spy. Ensign Yoshikawa, under the guise of consulate official Morimura, was able to drive right up to military installations and take air-taxi flights that provided him detailed bird's-eye photographs of our fleet's anchorage. Yoshikawa's phone calls were being tapped as part of the Fourteenth Naval District Intelligence Office's bugging of the consulate. But since we could not read the consulate's enciphered cable traffic, we had no idea of how extensive an espionage operation he was running at the time.[3]

In the midst of the July crisis there had been a flurry of code burning at the Japanese consulate. Mayfield advised General Short that the military police should round up the 217 assistant consuls for violating the act that required the registration of foreign agents. Local FBI agents Shivers and Tillman had already submitted enough evidence to the attorney general's office to commence prosecution against 40 of them with the navy's blessing. But a 25 July letter from the secretary of war halted institution of legal proceedings in favor of a warning. General Short had cabled that "prosecution at this time would unduly alarm the entire population and jeopardize the success [of] our current campaign to secure [the] loyalty of the Japanese population."[4]

Mayfield's concern about Japanese espionage echoed a five-year-old memorandum from the president. On 10 August 1936, Roosevelt had sent a memorandum to the chief of naval operations suggesting that "every Japanese citizen or non-citizen on the island of Oahu who meets Japanese ships or has any connection with their officers or men should be secretly identified" and listed for placement "in a concentration camp in the event of trouble." The memo went on to consider the Japanese population of all the other Hawaiian Islands, and asked for "further recommendations after studies have been made."[5]

The studies revealed the magnitude of the espionage threat, but by 1941 Roosevelt's concern for Tokyo's sensibilities resulted in the administration's blocking efforts by the House Un-American Activities Committee to conduct its planned September hearings into Japanese subversion. The committee's chairman, Martin Dies of Texas, had made headlines earlier in the year with the exposure of German activities. Now he was sounding the alarm about the "potential Japanese spy system" and telling the press that he intended "to rouse the whole American people into a sense of impending crisis."[6]

The State Department, however, was more alarmed that the "exhaustive investigation" proposed by Dies would inflame our critical relations with Tokyo. The president himself intervened to urge Dies to abandon his intention to call fifty-two witnesses to testify about Japan's undercover operations in the United States. This muffling by the White House could not prevent Senator Guy M. Gillette of Iowa from introducing a resolution on 2 October citing "the activities of Japanese consular officials in Hawaii and the western United States" as alarming evidence of the need for a full-scale investigation.[7] Any public hearings would have drawn attention to Tachibana's espionage ring and all its implications. The case would also have raised many difficult questions in the press about the extent to which naval intelligence officers had become involved in surveillance operations against American citizens.

My involvement in April with the Tachibana affair, nevertheless, had taught me that if a broken-down Hollywood actor could be engaged in espionage, Honolulu was obviously ripe for exploitation by agents of Japan. With this in mind, I instructed my yeoman, Keene, to make periodic checks of the downtown streets and bars, wearing old clothes. While his forays as my personal listening resource did not uncover any startling plots, they did confirm that the increasing incidence of brawling and dissolute behavior was an open invitation to Japanese agents.[8] The strain of keeping Pacific Fleet sailors so far from their mainland homes and loved ones was beginning to tell.

Morale was becoming a major concern for Admiral Kimmel. Because of the rigorous sea-training schedule, he demanded that more facilities be provided ashore. A new fleet recreation center, commissioned on 1 August, included an enormous beer bar, ten bowling alleys, eleven pool tables, and a six-thousand-seat arena for boxing matches and movies. A rotation of stateside cruises enabled some sailors to arrange family reunions.

Sustaining the morale of his men was yet another telling indication of the responsibilities and concerns that the Pacific Fleet commander was carrying. It was a burden aggravated by Washington's apparent indifference to his repeated requests for more personnel and escort ships. The fleet desperately needed twenty thousand additional men to bring the crews up to their full wartime complements. "We are ready to do our damnedest," he wrote to CNO Stark on 12 August, but this assurance was accompanied by still another plea that Washington keep him adequately informed. "You will probably have information sooner than I do which will warrant the cancellation of such cruises and I shall of course expect advice or orders from you on the subject."[9]

Although Admiral Kimmel was not given the advice he sought, it was apparent to us that tension was increasing between Washington and Tokyo. An Opnav dispatch had already alerted us that the "Japanese [are] rapidly completing withdrawal from world shipping routes."[10]

The focus of Washington's concern, as I soon discovered, was on the other side of the Pacific. On 26 August the first nine B-17s, which had stopped over in Hawaii, took off to make the long overwater haul via Wake, Midway, and Ocean Island, then south to Australia. Then they would head north to the Philippines. There was considerable apprehension that if the Japanese learned of the flight they might attempt to interfere with this first demonstration that air reinforcement for MacArthur was practicable.

In preparation for the departure of these planes, I was called upon to furnish the army air command on Hawaii with all available information on weather conditions and bases, including some highly secret information we had from the Dutch regarding their air bases in the East Indies. A special watch was kept by Hypo's listening posts for radio transmissions emanating from the Marshalls for any indications of hostile intentions as the bombers flew within range of Japanese air bases there. If Tokyo raised objections, the war department had ready a special press announcement that this was a normal operation involving the replacement of obsolescent aircraft.

It proved to be an unnecessary precaution. All nine Flying Fortresses arrived at Clark Field by 12 September, apparently unspotted by Japan. Secretary of War Stimson was ecstatic. The success of this first flight was seen as giving the army the opportunity "to get back into the islands in a way it hadn't been able to for years." Stimson pressed for an immediate increase in the B-17 production rate. MacArthur was given priority for the bombers, even though they had long been regarded as an essential adjunct of Hawaiian defense. An army air force memorandum of 26 August set quotas for a force of at least 128 Flying Fortresses in the Philippines by February 1942, with twice that number by the end of the year. It was also planned to then begin supplying B-17s for three bombardment groups based on Oahu, to guard against what was prophetically described as a "diversionary" Japanese attack on Pearl Harbor. The same staff paper, however, allowed that the three groups of 204 long-range bombers were the "barest minimum," and that "in the face of a major attack by large forces, it is questionable that this force would be adequate."[11]

The importance of that estimate should have been realized in Washington because it was reinforced by a still more telling report from the Hawaiian air force headquarters that had been issued only a few days earlier. This "Plan for the Employment of Bombardment Aviation in the Defense of Oahu," dated 20 August, had been drawn up on General Arnold's orders. He called for an update of the March study of the island's air defenses, which had been prepared by General Martin and Admiral Bellinger. The new report predicted the threat of an aerial attack, with astonishing accuracy, and estimated that the Japanese "can probably employ a maximum of 6 carriers against Oahu." Underlined for particular emphasis, on page 5, was the forecast that an "*early morning attack is, therefore, the best plan of action to the enemy.*"[12] A minimum of thirty-six B-17s "would be required to disable and destroy the carriers," but Martin's recommendation was for "immediate consideration to the allotment of one hundred and eighty." This was a "small force when compared with the importance of this outpost," and one that they pointed out could be provided "at less cost to the government than the cost of a modern battleship."[13]

The report from the army's Hawaiian air commanders urged that the planes be made available "as soon as possible."[14] The number of planes General Martin called for was only twenty fewer than the long-range bomber strength recommended for the Hawaiian command by Arnold's own staff, and his report warned that "under no circumstances could the Hawaiian bombardment force be reduced without gravely endangering the security of the Pacific coast."[15]

Yet with every available B-17 being rushed to the Philippines, not even the minimum recommended force of thirty-six was allocated to our local army air command. General Marshall testified that he had "given Hawaii all we could afford to give them up to that time,"[16] but as of November only a dozen of the long-range bombers remained on the island. General Martin had the frustration of seeing airfields, which he believed were critical for the defense of Pearl Harbor, turned into mere refueling stops for bombers heading out to MacArthur's air force.

To the extent that Washington planners were thinking about Pacific requirements at all during the fall of 1941, it appears that they were concentrating on a deterrent force of American bombers in the Philippines. They would not have been so complacent had they known that the main target of this deterrence—Japan's Combined Fleet—was focusing its attention, not on Singapore or Manila, but the Pacific Fleet in Pearl Harbor. On 7 August the naval staff in Tokyo had again considered Yamamoto's plan to attack the Pacific Fleet in harbor as an opening move in a war that most admirals had come to regard as inevitable. Even the more conservative members of navy chief Osami Nagano's staff appreciated the need for attempting a knockout opening blow against the United States. But they postponed the final decision on the Pearl Harbor attack plan until after the concept had been tested on the plotting boards at Combined Fleet's annual war games, which had been delayed, at Yamamoto's request, until the first week in September.

The prospect that their ships, planes, and tanks might be immobilized by fuel starvation galvanized the conference at imperial general headquarters on 15 August. This time it was the navy that called for urgent completion of war planning against Britain and the United States. Four days later the basis of a joint operational plan was established after naval observers participated in army war games which rehearsed the blueprint for military conquest of southeast Asia.

It was masterminded by Colonel Masanobu Tsuji, a brilliant but fanatical member of the army staff, who clearly appreciated the navy's priority for a speedy invasion schedule. Two months were scheduled for the capture of Manila, three for Singapore, and five for Burma. Simultaneous operations were to be conducted against the Dutch East Indies to bring their rich oil fields under Japanese control within the fourth month, between the opening of the war and the occupation of Java.[17]

While imperial general headquarters was fixing mid-October as the deadline for completing war preparations, Konoye was attempting to recover initiative on the diplomatic front. On 18 August, two days after Nomura had advised Tokyo that the Churchill-Roosevelt summit was an indication of Britain's hope for "a Japanese-American war started by the back door,"[18] the prime minister pressed our ambassador for a face-to-face meeting with the president. Grew supported the idea, advising Washington that it was worthy of "very prayerful consideration" because of the "incalculable" benefits that might flow from a Pacific summit.[19]

Still flushed with the success of his Churchill meeting, Roosevelt had not at first ruled out the idea of a Konoye meeting in Alaska or Hawaii in his 17 August talk with Nomura. The ambassador's hopes for pulling off a 15 October tête-à-tête between the president and prime minister at Juneau were soon washed out by the State Department's insistence that a prior condition for any summit would be Japan's agreement to withdraw their forces from China and abandon the tripartite pact.

Konoye believed that such thorny issues should be reserved for a face-to-face meeting. A note of desperation crept into his 26 August instructions to Nomura that he would consider Hawaii as a possible venue for a Pacific summit and self-effacingly he offered to withdraw Japanese troops from Indochina when "a just peace is established in the Far East."[20]

Prime Minister Konoye's hopes that a Pacific summit might halt the momentum of Japan's preparations for war were fading fast. He faced the impatient admirals and generals in a 3 September liaison conference, and they wanted cabinet approval for the Outline Plan for the Execution of the Empire's National Policy.[21] This characteristically Japanese euphemism was the bureaucratic title of the tentative war plan that the army and navy had agreed to weeks earlier. There was nothing euphemistic, however, about the blunt exchanges with which the prime minister was assailed during the seven-hour meeting. Konoye repeatedly stressed the need for more time to arrange his personal meeting with President Roosevelt, but the military chiefs insisted on setting a limit and deadline for negotiations.

"Although I feel sure we have a chance to win a war right now, I am afraid that the chance will vanish with the passage of time," warned navy chief Nagano.[22] Next day the cabinet met to approve the list of "minimum" demands and "maximum" concessions that were intended to severely curtail Konoye's room for diplomatic maneuver. Japan's right to station troops in China or Indochina was nonnegotiable, being essential to her defense. But Konoye could promise not to use them against neighboring areas if Washington agreed to terminate all aid to Chiang Kaishek. The prime minister was to tell the United States that Japan would "guarantee the neutrality of the Philippine Islands," abide by her treaty not to attack Russia, and might even be prepared to interpret her tripartite pact obligations "independently." But the military firmly rejected any other concessions. The crux of the cabinet decision was contained in its opening paragraph, which asserted that Japan, "for the purpose of self-defense and self-preservation, will complete preparations for war." The last ten days of October were set as a tentative deadline for diplomacy, after which Japan "resolved to go to war with the United States, Great Britain, and the Netherlands if necessary."[23]

On 6 September the cabinet declaration was to receive the stamp of irreversible national policy in the conference chamber at Tokyo's imperial palace. The small, bespectacled emperor sat silently on a dais as his ministers and senior officers rehearsed the now familiar arguments in the flat, baleful tones demanded by the solemnity of this formal occasion. Emperor Hirohito heard how the military planned to achieve Japan's national objectives and that they were preparing for "war with the United States, Great Britain, and the Netherlands to expel their influence from east Asia, to establish a sphere for the self-defense and self-preservation of our empire, and to build a new order in Greater East Asia."[24]

In a preconference briefing the day before, the emperor had expressed his regret to Konoye that the cabinet "placed war preparations first and diplomatic negotiations second."[25] Army chief of staff General Hajime Sugiyama had assured the emperor that the "operation in the south Pacific could be disposed of in three months." But when Hirohito pressed Sugiyama about the chances of victory, he would give no guarantee that Japan could be certain of winning. Navy chief Nagano predicted a long war and he foresaw that it would be "impossible to expect a surrender from the United States." The best they could hope for was that a lightning conquest of southeast Asia, and a defensive perimeter of Pacific island bases, could secure an invincible position for Japan, thereby permitting her diplomats to negotiate from a position of strength to bring the war to an end.[26]

Such were the inherent contradictions in cabinet policy that Baron Yoshimichi Hara, in his role as president of the privy council, raised the next morning at the imperial conference. The silent evasiveness of Admiral Nagumo and General Sugiyama, who would not provide direct answers, finally moved Hirohito to break with centuries-old tradition of no direct participation in the council. Suddenly he uttered a shrill demand to know why military action was taking precedence over diplomacy. Then, to the further astonishment of all present, Hirohito drew a paper from his pocket and read in a piping voice a *waka* (or *tanka,* a thirty-one-syllable poem) composed by his grandfather, the enlightened Emperor Meiji:

> *Yomo no umi*
> *mina harakara to*
> *omou yo ni,*
> *Nado namikaze no*
> *tachisawaguran?*

(Since all seas of the world are brothers,
Why do winds and waves of strife rage so violently?)[27]

Hirohito declared that he was only "striving to introduce into the present Emperor Meiji's ideal of international peace." But this unprecedented interruption from the throne brought an awestricken silence that was finally broken by Nagano's expressing his "trepidation" at his majesty's displeasure with the supreme command. He assured the emperor that they recognized "the importance of diplomacy, and advocated a resort to arms only when there seemed no other way out."[28]

When the momentous conference finally adjourned at noon "in an atmosphere of unprecedented tenseness,"[29] Konoye had secured another slender chance to establish agreement with the United States. The prime minister had been given until 16 October to achieve a diplomatic breakthrough.

With less than six weeks in which to overcome the hurdle of Washington's latest demand that "fundamental and essential questions" be resolved, he summoned the American ambassador that very night to a clandestine meeting at the house of his mistress. His case for a summit with Roosevelt made a powerful impression on Grew. He cabled the State Department the next day of the premier's new willingness to "conclusively and wholeheartedly" accept the four principles enunciated by Hull during the secret April talks as a basis for reopening serious discussions.[30]

While not diminishing the obstacles to reaching any agreement, the ambassador warned that Konoye "saw the handwriting on the wall and realized that Japan was on the brink of an abyss and wanted, if possible, to reverse the engines."[31] He reinforced this view in a personal letter of 22 September to Roosevelt warning that the "alternative to reaching a settlement now would be the greatly increased probability of war—Facilis descensus Averno est."[32] The letter with his classical allusion to how easy it was to fall into hell did not reach the White House until after Konoye's cabinet had itself fallen. This well-intentioned bid to assist Konoye in putting the engines of the Japanese war machine into reverse did not succeed, because Roosevelt's attention had been diverted from the Pacific by events in the Atlantic.

On 4 September, America had come close to the brink of war with Germany when a U-boat attacked destroyer *Greer.* Roosevelt promptly accused Hitler of "piracy." Stark dashed off a pessimistic letter that alerted Kimmel to the imminent possibility of war's breaking out in the Atlantic. "We are all but, if not actually in it," he wrote on 22 September (the same day that Grew was writing Roosevelt).[33] So, while the navy battened down to convoy British ships and shoot hostile submarines on sight, Secretary Hull and the State Department hard-liners, led by its Far East specialist Dr. Stanley K. Hornbeck, misinterpreted Konoye's apparent willingness to negotiate as an indication that the American sanctions were biting deeply at Japan's economy. They concluded, wrongly, that it was only a matter of months before the military leaders in Tokyo would be forced to withdraw their forces from the mainland. This mistaken policy was further encouraged by the memory of how stonewalling tactics had succeeded at the Washington disarmament conference twenty years earlier, and it was reinforced by our ability to monitor Japan's diplomatic traffic. But the Purple decrypts, as early as September, were already indicating that, unlike 1921, Japan was in no mood to be bluffed into another retreat.

Yamamoto's strategy to attack Pearl Harbor had been transformed from a staff blueprint into a practical plan. Most of the technical and tactical details were ready by 11 September, when the annual map maneuvers began behind the wrought-iron gates of the naval war college in suburban Tokyo. As colored markers were laid out over large charts of the western Pacific and China Sea, it became evident that this might be their last full-scale dress rehearsal before war. Ten days of intensive wargaming tested all the interlocking naval operations and their ability to effect a swift Japanese takeover of southeast Asia. The staffs of Third Fleet and Eleventh Air Fleet rehearsed the invasion of the Philippines and the conquest of Borneo; the Second Fleet staff practiced moving from the Pescadores to cover the invasion of Malaya; and the Fourth Fleet practiced its attacks on Wake Island and Guam.

Only thirty of more than a hundred staff officers who participated in the map maneuvers were allowed into the college's closely guarded east wing room where the charts of Hawaii were laid out. Yamamoto himself supervised these briefings. Operation Z, as the planned attack was code-named, was conducted under close scrutiny of the still skeptical naval general staff. Admiral Matome Ugaki, Yamamoto's own chief of staff, commanded the Blue Fleet (Japanese) force of two carrier divisions, two battleships, three cruisers, escorted by destroyer flotillas, and tankers, which set out for "Pearl Harbor." On the first run-through he met with disaster during a daylight approach when the Blue force was intercepted by "American" aircraft, which "sank" two carriers. Only minor damage was inflicted on the Red Fleet at Pearl Harbor, while Ugaki's force had paper losses of one third of its air and sea strength.[34]

The umpires concluded that the Hawaiian operation was too risky. This was too quick a rush to judgment for Yamamoto. A second tabletop run-through was held the same afternoon; but this time the Blue Fleet's route was adjusted to bring it within striking distance of Oahu during darkness for launching planes at first light. This time the carrier strike arrived undetected and "sank" four Red battleships. Defending Red planes managed to launch a counterstrike, which the umpires credited with sinking one Blue carrier.[35]

The plotting-table maneuvers underscored both the risks and rewards of Operation Z, leaving the naval staff still in doubt about the wisdom of sanctioning the operation. Even Yamamoto's own staff was not in unanimous agreement. Some tactical details remained to be ironed out, and a few officers doubted that the necessary element of surprise could be achieved. In the few weeks remaining before the mid-October deadline of Japan's war plan, it became a race against time to win over naval staff chief Nagano and solve the problems of how bombs and torpedoes could be modified for maximum effectiveness against Pearl Harbor targets.

The order went out to speed up the development of sixteen-inch shells and bombs to penetrate the thick steel of American battleships. Wooden boxlike baffles were attached to the fins of standard torpedoes to prevent their plunging into the mud of shallow Pearl Harbor. While technical details were being worked out, pilots trained intensively to fine-tune their bombing skills and drop torpedoes low enough and close enough to hit their targets.[36]

In the southern Honshū city of Kagoshima naval planes buzzed in low over Yamagataya department store to make bombing runs on target vessels in the bay. This practice site in the shadow of active Sakurajima volcano was selected for its topographical similarity to Pearl Harbor. Off the nearby naval base of Kanoya, at the tip of Kyūshū, the obsolete battleship *Settsu* was anchored in Ariake Bay as a target for dive-bomber pilots. Safety regulations were ignored, at a cost of at least one plane, in order to perfect steep dives and low-level pullouts and improve bombing accuracy. Off the rocky coast of Shikoku, the smallest of Japan's main islands, the two-man midget submarines practiced making submerged attacks with their temperamental craft.

Midget submarine attacks had been incorporated almost as an afterthought by Yamamoto, against strong argument by some of the Combined Fleet staff that they might prematurely divulge the whole plan. But the objectors were silenced on 9 October, when after five days of map maneuvers on board battleship *Nagato* in Hiroshima Bay, the whole operation was successfully rehearsed with the midget submarines of the Sixth Fleet participating for the first time.

"Some of you may object but, so long as I am commander in chief, I'm intent on going ahead with the raid," declared Yamamoto in an appeal to the loyalty of the Combined Fleet staff officers on the assumption that the raid was on.[37] This was not easy when his principal critic was the First Air Fleet commander whose carriers were to carry out the surprise attack. Admiral Chuichi Nagumo had sent a delegation with a written plea stressing the inherent risks in attacking Pearl Harbor. He reminded Yamamoto that the eventual necessity of a compromise peace made it advisable "to avoid anything like the Hawaiian operation that would put America's back up."[38]

Compromise was not an issue to be weighed by the members of imperial general headquarters as they prepared to march Japan into war with the United States. For more than a year Japanese foreign policy had been effectively controlled by the military leadership through the "liaison conferences," which virtually dictated cabinet decisions. So as Konoye's diplomatic overtures to Washington stalled, the army faction, led by War Minister Hideki Tojo, lost no time making it clear that they had had enough of diplomacy.

An assassination attempt on the prime minister on 16 September was another indication of how shakily Konoye clung to his office. In a frantic bid for a face-to-face meeting with Roosevelt, he instructed Ambassador Nomura to hold out the chance of a virtual abnegation of the tripartite pact, neutralization of Indochina, and reduction of troops in China. It was an offer born of desperation, since on 25 September Tojo had flatly refused to consider even a token troop withdrawal from China. The war minister's insistence that the "way of diplomacy is not always a matter of concession; sometimes it is oppression," was characteristic of the hardline general whose sobriquet was the Razor.[39]

The State Department was not prepared to back down either. Hull continued to stall the Japanese ambassador. Meanwhile, Nomura lobbied senior officials in the navy department in addition to making his regular diplomatic rounds. The feverish tone of Konoye's instructions to his emissary was plain in the Purple decrypts that reached the secretary of state each day, but its impact appears to have been lost on Washington policymakers. References to the first anniversary of the tripartite pact as a "turning point" and that "the situation is all the more grave" were dismissed along with Konoye's allusion to the pressure he was under from "the advocates of anti-Americanism."[40]

While Washington stalled, Tokyo speculated. It was believed that Secretary Hull harbored strong doubts about the "trustworthiness of Prince Konoye." What the Japanese did not suspect was that Hull's conviction was reinforced almost daily by Magic decrypts. These revealed that Nomura's eagerness to clutch at any straw was getting him sharp rebukes from his foreign minister "not to add or detract a jot or tittle on your *own* without first getting in contact with me."[41]

The Purple decrypts, translated by army and navy linguists untutored in the subtle nuances of diplomatic Japanese, confronted the secretary of state with language that was often far stronger than intended. He paid more attention to these than to Nomura's more studied official representations because Hull was also reading the ambassador's reports, which frequently put too optimistic a construction on the United States' willingness to negotiate. Eavesdropping on the Purple traffic that flashed back and forth between Tokyo and Washington depreciated the normal diplomatic process. The State Department's long-held belief in Tokyo's fundamental duplicity was confirmed by Magic decrypts from Japan's other embassies in the Far East, which revealed the steadily mounting southward momentum of their military buildup in Indochina.

Confident that Magic had betrayed Tokyo's two-faced policy, Hull procrastinated for three weeks before Ambassador Nomura was summoned to the State Department on 3 October. He received an "oral statement" that amounted to a final rejection of Konoye's hoped-for summit. "Since it appears that although Japan agrees with the United States regarding principles, she differs on their application," Nomura cabled the foreign minister dispiritedly. "The United States is doubtful about holding a meeting of the two heads of state."[42]

Tojo denounced Hull's four principles in a stormy liaison conference the next day at which navy chief Nagano joined the demand for "quick action."[43] Konoye had to rein in his ambassador from making any concessionary proposal. Three days later the army high command met and concluded that "war is inevitable."[44]

There was a simultaneous hardening of positions in Washington. After the 6 October meeting of the president's inner cabinet, the secretary of war told Hull that without a troop withdrawal from China "no promises of the Japs based on words would be worth anything."[45] If there was any doubt that another major crisis was boiling up with Tokyo, it should have been dispelled by the diplomatic traffic. On 10 October, Nomura was told that the "decisive stage" of negotiations had been reached "and the situation does not permit of this senseless procrastination."[46] The ambassador's desperation was visible in the Purple decrypt of his reply that "they are not budging an inch."[47] That cable prompted Konoye to summon Grew to tell him that time was running out. Konoye said that the Japanese ambassador in Washington was "very fatigued" and that his replacement was under "serious consideration."[48]

A secret cabinet session was held the next day in the prime minister's home. The navy and army ministers were adamant in their refusal to shift the 15 October deadline for negotiations. After this meeting Konoye sent a final urgent plea to Nomura to do everything to get a breakthrough: "The situation at home is fast approaching a crisis and it is becoming absolutely essential that the two leaders meet if any adjustment of Japan-U.S. relations is to be accomplished."[49]

The polite generalities with which Nomura's last-minute pleading had been greeted by Hull left Konoye with no option but to resign his cabinet on 16 October, when the deadline set by the military expired. The emperor was taken by surprise—as was Washington, where the State Department should have known by the swiftness of Konoye's fall from power that time was now of the essence to Japan's military leadership. If that was not enough, the appointment of the war minister to form a new government was another sign.

By calling on General Tojo to take over, Hirohito was placing responsibility squarely on the army leadership. What Magic did not reveal was that the emperor sternly admonished the new prime minister to make a last effort at a diplomatic solution. The new foreign minister, Admiral Teijiro Toyoda, was accordingly instructed to prepare for a final attempt at opening negotiations with the United States. This brought Tojo under criticism from the navy minister, whose admirals were alarmed by the oil situation. He warned the new cabinet, "The situation is urgent; we must have a decision one way or the other."[50]

The fall of the Konoye government had not been unanticipated in Washington. But its timing was a surprise, because it had not been foreshadowed by Magic. This should have been a timely lesson that the Purple diplomatic traffic would not provide advance warning of every move Tokyo made. The crisis, nonetheless, was judged sufficiently serious for the president to cancel his regular Thursday cabinet meeting. Instead he called an emergency conference of what he liked to call his war council. This consisted of the secretaries of state, war, and the navy; the service chiefs; and his indispensable aide Harry Hopkins. The group's deliberations resulted in another alert message to overseas army and naval commands.

Since the Pacific Fleet command had received no diplomatic decrypts since mid-July, the CNO dispatch arriving on the afternoon of 17 October came as a surprise. It was in our most secure naval code, addressed to Admiral Kimmel with instructions to forward it to General Short. It warned of "a grave situation" created by the resignation of the Japanese cabinet; that there was "a strong possibility" of an attack on Russia; and that, since "the U.S. and Britain are held responsible by Japan for her present situation, there is also a possibility that Japan may attack. . . ." Kimmel was accordingly directed to "take due precautions including such preparatory deployments," but not so as "to disclose strategic intentions nor constitute provocative actions against Japan."[51]

As with the July alert, that Friday afternoon's dispatch left Kimmel at some loss as to just what "preparatory deployments" the emergency demanded. The intelligence picture we had assembled was lacking the diplomatic information that could have provided us with valuable clues about the broad framework of Tokyo's intentions. The only diplomatic intelligence Kimmel had received since July were the vague and often conflicting statements made by Admiral Stark in his letters. Stark had sounded an optimistic note to Admiral Hart in Manila, who was a joint addressee of a 22 September letter, which stated that "the Japanese appear to be making some effort at reaching a satisfactory solution." Yet the following day he wrote informing Kimmel that "conversations with Japan have reached an impasse," and that a "strong warning and a threat of hostile action" would be the "next step" to counter Japanese submarines prowling off U.S. territory.[52] Stark's pessimism was reinforced, as evidenced by his letter to Kimmel of 29 October, after a meeting with Nomura. "He usually comes in when he begins to feel near the end of his rope," CNO warned. "There is not much to spare at the end now."[53]

These Delphic insights into the diplomatic turmoil alerted us at Pearl Harbor to the fact that negotiations with Japan were running out of sand. But they were no substitute for the access we were being denied to the Purple decrypts. There was no way we could judge how likely was CNO's prediction of the "strong possibility" that Japan might attack Russia, or, for that matter, any of our outlying island bases. Instead, we had to take the intelligence we were given at face value. This left us to make our best estimate on the assumption that if Japan was about to make any offensive moves, the targets would be on the other side of the Pacific.

The reaction of the Hawaiian commands to the October alert simply reflected the scenario as Washington relayed it to us. General Short was to testify in 1944 that his second alert in three months of an attack on Russia "weakened as far as I was concerned the probability of an immediate war between the U.S. and Japan,"[54] and so this command merely tightened up "all our guards against sabotage."[55] Kimmel was also under the impression that the threat, such as it might materialize, was on the far side of the Pacific. His principal deployment, therefore, apart from ordering six submarines to be ready to depart for Japanese waters at short notice, was to send twelve more patrol planes to Midway. Additional marines and defenses were also ordered sent to the outlying islands, and the departure of battleship *West Virginia* for refit at Puget Sound was postponed indefinitely.[56]

In a letter dated 22 October, Admiral Kimmel reported his measures taken in response to the alert of the sixteenth. He also informed CNO that he had ordered "some additional security measures in effect in the operating areas outside Pearl Harbor," and that Admiral Pye's battle force was put on twelve hours' notice. Stark acknowledged this two weeks later, saying, "OK on the dispositions you made in connection with recent change in the Japanese Cabinet."[57]

The Pacific Fleet's dispositions might have been dramatically different if Washington had not denied us another vital piece of Magic intelligence. This was an intercepted instruction from Tokyo to the Honolulu consul requesting very detailed reports of the fleet anchorage. It had been circulated in Washington a full week before the mid-October alert. Had we received it at Pearl Harbor at any time before 7 December it would have alerted us to the rattlesnake lurking in our backyard. Tragically, no one on the CNO staff who read it bothered to evaluate its significance.

14

"Affirmative Misrepresentation"

T
HE WAR GAMES in Tokyo that first tested Yamamoto's daring concept of attacking Pearl Harbor persuaded the naval staff that they needed more detailed intelligence about the status and movements of the Pacific Fleet. The task of obtaining the information fell upon the naval staff's Third Bureau.

Comparable to our office of naval intelligence, its best man was its deputy chief, Captain Kanji Ogawa, a former assistant naval attaché in Washington. His mouselike demeanor concealed an encyclopedic knowledge of the United States that he had acquired through skillful espionage. It was Ogawa who had been instrumental in bringing into the Third Bureau one of his former undercover agents, Lieutenant Commander Itaru Tachibana.

This was none other than the former brothel keeper and Japanese agent in Los Angeles, whose spying had been uncovered in a counterintelligence operation in which I had played a small part. Tachibana's unceremonious expulsion from the United States, instead of being made to stand trial for espionage, was a diplomatic concession to American-Japanese relations that we would regret later. He returned home and put all the information he had garnered to good use, becoming one of Ogawa's principal assistants as an expert on our naval practices.[1]

Because of his expertise, Tachibana had been one of the privileged handful of officers whom Yamamoto had permitted to observe the Pearl Harbor map exercises. And Tachibana subsequently played a leading role in assembling the detailed intelligence that was to make the attack possible. The Third Bureau already knew, from the reports of agents in Honolulu and their traffic analysis of American radio signals, that our task forces usually sortied from Hawaii on a weekly rotation on Mondays or Tuesdays. This schedule indicated that the best opportunity for catching a majority of the fleet in harbor would be on a Sunday. But for

Yamamoto's plan to succeed, it was essential to know not only when the fleet was in port, but the precise locations of where the American warships were berthed or anchored within the harbor.

To obtain the information that the Japanese pilots would need to perfect their bombing and torpedo attack training, Tachibana drafted a dispatch and Ogawa approved it. The "strictly secret" signal addressed to their consul general in Honolulu was transmitted on 24 September by Japan's foreign ministry, at the express request of navy ministry:

> 1. The waters (of Pearl Harbor) are to be divided roughly into five sub areas. (We have no objection to your abbreviating as much as you like.)
> Area A. Waters between Ford Island and the arsenal.
> Area B. Waters adjacent to the island south and west of Ford Island. (This area is on the opposite side of the island from Area A.)
> Area C. East Loch.
> Area D. Middle Loch.
> Area E. West Loch and the communicating water routes.
>
> 2. With regard to the warships and aircraft carriers, we would like to have you report on those at anchor (these are not so important), tied up at wharves, buoys, and docks. (Designate types and classes briefly. If possible we should like to have you make mention of the fact when there are two or more vessels alongside at the same wharf.)[2]

This instruction put an invisible grid over Pearl Harbor. Clearly it was intended as an overlay for planning bombing attack targets—hence it came to be known as the "bomb plot message."

Its significance was immediately appreciated by Ensign Yoshikawa, the Third Bureau's resident agent in Honolulu, who was posing as an assistant secretary at the consulate. Previously, he had been asked only to report the *movements* of the fleet. Now the grid system meant that naval intelligence in Tokyo was interested in having accurate positions of the warships when they were in harbor. Yoshikawa was convinced that this meant that some operation, possibly even an invasion of Hawaii, was being contemplated. Accordingly, five days later Consul Kita cabled a modification that effectively filled in additional grid locators to make the reports even more precise:

> The following codes will be used hereafter to designate the location of vessels:
> 1. Repair dock in the navy yard (The repair base referred to in my message to Washington #48): KS
> 2. Navy dock in the navy yard (Ten Ten Pier): KT

3. Moorings in the vicinity of Ford Island: FV
4. Alongside at Ford Island: FG (east and west sides will be designated A and B respectively)[3]

This second signal was not decrypted by the navy until 10 October, a day after the army had broken out the original bomb plot message. The reason for the long delay between interception and translation was that the navy and army commands on Oahu were responsible only for the collection and forwarding of the diplomatic traffic. The original bomb plot message had not reached Washington for twelve days. Like all the army intercepts it was pouched and sent by mail—in this case the Pan Am Clipper flight had been delayed by bad weather. Then both it and the second message had awaited decryption, because the J-19 consular code in which they had been transmitted had been given a lower priority than Purple.

By a trick of fate as it turned out, the decision of the Japanese foreign ministry not to equip the Honolulu consulate with the Purple system proved to be an unintentional factor in helping to conceal the attack. Five times as many espionage messages were read from Japan's Philippines consulate between September and December 1941 primarily because Manila was transmitting them in Purple.[4]

The downgrading of the Honolulu consular traffic as a potential source of information by Washington might have had less serious consequences if Hypo's cryptanalysts had been assigned to decode the messages Tokyo exchanged with Japan's local consulate. That the "biggest snake is the one nearest you" was, after all, one of the considerations in Washington's sending a Purple decoding machine to Manila.

This meant that the Pacific Fleet, the principal instrument of our military power in the Pacific, was not equipped to monitor the enemy beyond its harbor wall. The situation was all the more surprising because, a month earlier, a Purple decrypt had pinpointed the Honolulu consulate as a potential source of espionage. This information was understandably concealed from the 1945 congressional hearings, and was to remain a secret for more than forty years.

The Purple decrypt in question reveals that, on 2 September, five weeks before the bomb plot messages were decrypted, the foreign ministry had instructed its Washington embassy that the "naval authorities" had made the following request: "They would like to have you insist at this time upon a member of your staff going to Hawaii in the capacity of a courier."[5]

This message was "highly significant," as is pointed out in the hitherto classified 1942 U.S. Navy analysis of the pre-December signal traffic: "If the Japanese Navy demanded a special courier to and from Hawaii at this time, and insisted it be a diplomatic agent rather than a naval officer for better security," there could only be one objective in mind—Pearl Harbor.[6]

That the significance of the courier message was entirely lost, even after another intercept two days later from Honolulu addressed to Captain Ogawa, demonstrates again the poor quality of intelligence analysis that was being carried out in Washington. The message to Ogawa read, "The matter in question should be . . . no later than the end of September. Please advise me."[7] This J-19 message, decrypted in Washington on 26 September, was clear proof of the involvement of the deputy chief of Japan's naval intelligence. It could have been interpreted only as a suspicious espionage operation whose likely focus was the Pacific Fleet.

Neither the Fourteenth Naval District nor our headquarters was ever told about these early signs that Japanese naval intelligence was focusing on Pearl Harbor. Washington's failure to keep the local commands informed of these activities after they had been discovered was tantamount to folly. It was all the more so when the two so-called bomb plot messages were decrypted two weeks later.

The Magic summaries made their rounds of the most senior army and navy staff officers on 9 and 10 October. The first indication that the Japanese had imposed an invisible bombing grid on Pearl Harbor had been asterisked as "an interesting message" by Lieutenant Commander Alwin D. Kramer, who as OP-20-GZ was in charge of the translation section in the navy department. On the gist sheet that he circulated with the daily Magics until the end of the month, when the pressure of work forced him to abandon the practice, Kramer drew attention to the Honolulu signal in a note that read, "Tokyo directs special reports on the ships in Pearl Harbor which is divided into five areas for the purpose of showing exact locations."[8]

Although the second message that circulated the following day was not singled out with an asterisk, it was another example of Washington's lack of concern about Pearl Harbor. Even after the courier messages, neither the director of naval intelligence, nor the chief of war plans, nor the chief of naval operations appreciated that the bomb plot messages were sufficiently worthy of note to relay this intelligence to Pearl Harbor. Their cover-up in public began at the 1945 congressional hearings. They professed not to remember, or assumed that the information was available to us merely because it had been relayed to Admiral Hart at Manila. This was because Station Cast *was* working on Japanese diplomatic ciphers. Kramer, who should have known that Station Hypo could not decrypt J-19, testified that he was under the "impression" that such messages to the Asiatic Fleet were sent "either as an action addressee or information addressee to Admiral Kimmel."[9]

Admiral Noyes, the director of naval communications, was to testify that if Station Cast's cryptanalysts in the Philippines got stuck translating a certain intercept, they had only to radio Washington on the secure

Copek circuit for the translation. But Rochefort's cryptanalysts at Pearl Harbor had been specifically *excluded* from working on any diplomatic intercepts, because Washington evidently believed it was unnecessary to make Rochefort an information addressee of anything to do with diplomatic traffic. Noyes, however, was obliged to concede reluctantly in testimony to the Pearl Harbor hearings that Kimmel was *not* provided this information. He was asked if the consular decrypts had been sent to Kimmel as an information addressee:

"It wouldn't be sent out for information to anybody," Noyes replied.

Nor was the army sending out Magic information to General Short. The army's chief of military intelligence, Major General Sherman Miles, dismissed his G-2 section's failure to acquaint Short with the significance of the bomb plot decrypt by claiming that it was "one of a great number of messages being sent by the Japanese to various parts of the world in their attempt to follow the movements of our naval vessels."[10] But when Miles was challenged and asked to point to any other message that was so specific, he was obliged to admit, "I have not found any, sir, similar to this in the sense of dividing any particular waters."[11]

Colonel Rufus S. Bratton, who at the time was chief of the Far East section of G-2, testified that he believed these two messages indicated the Japanese were showing "an unusual interest in the port of Honolulu." He said he had "discussed this with my opposite numbers in the navy on several occasions."[12] They concluded that the subdivision of Pearl Harbor into areas might be "a device to reduce the volume of radio traffic . . . a plan for sabotage . . . a plan for a submarine attack . . . *or it might be a plan for an air attack.* [emphasis added]."[13]

Why had this vital evaluation of intelligence in Washington not been sent to us at Pacific Fleet headquarters? With the advantage of hindsight this is what both Admiral Kimmel and the 1945 congressional investigators wanted answered. It never was.

Admiral Stark denied ever seeing the bomb plot message. He claimed that if he had, he would have regarded it as "just another example of their [the Japanese's] great attention to detail."[14] Admiral Turner also claimed "no recollection of ever having seen that dispatch of 24 September." And if he had, he said, he would have referred it to the director of naval intelligence rather than "have initiated a dispatch on that subject myself."[15]

Turner's denials increase rather than excuse his responsibility. He had made himself CNO's self-appointed arbiter of what intelligence was relayed by Washington to the Pacific commands. His omission to note the importance of the bomb plot message was compounded because it arrived in Washington at a time when his authority over ONI was undisputed. The usurpation of the naval intelligence function by the director of war plans had finally driven the DNI three weeks earlier to petition the assistant secretary of the navy for a transfer to sea duty.

"We were clashing right along," Captain Kirk would record of his unhappy tenure as DNI.[16] His weeks in office as a lame-duck DNI were not made any easier. His knowledgeable Far East section chief, McCollum, was on duty in London and Kirk had to work alongside his own successor. The new DNI, Rear Admiral Theodore S. Wilkinson, was Admiral Stark's personal choice for the job. His appointment was unexpected, "the penalty of selection" as he wrote to Rochefort. But the appointment was not the "grand job" he anticipated.[17] He was the third officer to be appointed to the embattled ONI directorship in twelve months. He had graduated at the top of his class at the naval academy, which included Kirk, and he was the first officer of his class to make flag rank. Affable as well as brilliant, Wilkinson had received the Medal of Honor for bravery at Vera Cruz in 1914 and, with his accumulated years of naval staff duties, he came to the job with all the right qualifications— *except* firsthand experience in the job. It was experience that was so essential for the proper functioning of the office of naval intelligence.

In contrast to the assertive Kirk, Ping Wilkinson knew how to serve up advice at staff meetings without ruffling feathers. He did this with the same smooth assurance with which he partnered Under Secretary of the Navy James V. Forrestal on the tennis courts of the exclusive Chevy Chase Club. But his lack of intelligence experience was seen by many in ONI as yet another reflection of the lack of respect accorded to their profession by the naval staff. Moreover, he had no doubts that his first duty was to spread oil on the troubled waters between war plans division and ONI.

It was at this juncture that Kirk and Captain Howard D. Bode, one of ONI's most conscientious officers and then head of foreign intelligence, wanted to inform Kimmel of the bomb plot decrypts. So did Commander Safford. He claimed that he actually drafted a message to Rochefort that instructed Pearl Harbor to start decrypting the traffic from the local Japanese consulate. But he was stopped from doing so by Noyes, who told him that he was "not going to tell any district commandant how to run his job!"[18]

Wilkinson was caught in a dilemma. He lacked the necessary specialist's knowledge, and he had no backing from Captain McCollum, who was to return to Washington a week later. So he did nothing. Nevertheless, he was the only member of the naval staff who testified at the 1945 congressional hearings to being aware of a message that, even with his lack of intelligence background, he assumed was "part of a general information system established by the Japanese."[19] He insisted, however, that there had never been any discussion of whether the bomb plot signal should be relayed to the Pacific Fleet because it appeared to him "as an illustration of the nicety of detail of intelligence the Japanese were capable of seeking and getting."[20]

It was indeed this "nicety of detail" that separated the two courier reports, and the bomb plot messages, from those being sent by Japan's consulates in Manila, Panama, and the west coast ports. No other reports divided an American base with such detail into sectors. No other area rated Tokyo's request for couriered information or such precise details as whether two or more vessels were alongside the same wharf or anchored together. And in the weeks that followed, an ominous change in the character of the information requested by Tokyo about Pearl Harbor made it stand out from all the other Japanese espionage traffic uncovered by Magic decrypts. The very specificity of these messages should have drawn careful attention. They were, in their own right, beyond the realm of reasonable suspicion.

Unlike Japan's consulates in Panama, Manila, or Seattle, the one in Honolulu was no longer directed merely to ascertain the general whereabouts of the ships of the Pacific Fleet. Washington knew that the naval intelligence section in Tokyo wanted the locations of our warships when they were in harbor. During the next month, Consul Kita was told that because "relations between Japan and the United States are most critical," his "ships-in-harbor report was to be made twice a week," with "extra care to maintain secrecy."[21] Three days later another area, N, was added to the grid. On 20 November, special reports were asked for about bases "in the neighborhood of the Hawaiian military reservation."[22] Four days later Kita was told to report the exact locations of our warships "even when there are no movements."[23] The tragedy of all this was that only a handful of Kita's reports were even translated before 7 December. This clearly indicates the low priority Washington gave them as intelligence.

As I have said earlier, none of the original bomb plot signals, or any of the decrypts that were made that betrayed Japan's increasing interest in Pearl Harbor, was communicated directly (or indirectly) to Admiral Kimmel or Admiral Bloch, the district commander. It does not require any remarkable foresight to discern the significance of this information. Repeated transmissions of such detailed ships-in-harbor locations could have had no usefulness unless the Japanese were planning to execute an attack on our fleet while it was in port. Why? Such detailed reports lost all value once the ships sailed from the carefully designated berths.

If the suspicions of naval intelligence officers were aroused to this possibility, as Colonel Bratton and Commander Safford's evidence suggests, then the failure of the office of naval operations to ensure that the bomb plot messages were sent to us at Pearl Harbor was blind stupidity at the least, and gross neglect at best.

The tragedy of Pearl Harbor also might have been avoided if only the attempt by the Joint Board to set up a body to coordinate army and navy intelligence functions had been successful. On 26 September, two days after the first bomb plot message had been transmitted, the ranking members of naval and army war plans and intelligence divisions sat down for their first meeting. Their goal was to establish a system for coordinating and handling important strategic and tactical information. But it was shattered by a bitter dispute. Brigadier General Leonard T. Gerow, the army chief of war plans, proposed that the joint committee assume responsibility to "collate, analyze and interpret information with its implications, to estimate hostile capabilities and probable intentions."[24]

Admiral Turner, like many naval officers of his generation, harbored a hearty distrust of his sister service. He disagreed with any proposal for joint evaluation. He argued that the committee be restricted to the "presentation of such factual evidence as might be available, but to make no estimate or prediction."[25] "Admiral Turner was practically Naval Operations," General Miles, the army intelligence chief would testify later. "Neither Gerow nor . . . myself could get very far with him."[26]

So the first session of the committee to coordinate intelligence adjourned in a state of rancorous deadlock that 26 September. It did not meet again until 9 December. But for Turner's bullheadedness, it would have reconvened to "analyze and interpret" intelligence—such as the bomb plot messages—that vitally affected joint commands such as Hawaii. It would have noted the accelerating volume and focus of Tokyo's communications with their Honolulu consulate. And this could have resulted in a proper evaluation and warnings to Admiral Kimmel and General Short.

"Knowledge of these intercepted Japanese dispatches," Kimmel testified, "would have radically changed the estimate of the situation made by me and my staff." Whether it would have enabled us to spring an "ambush on the Japanese striking force as it approached Hawaii"[27] is a matter of debate. But it is difficult to argue that in any recasting of events—if we had been alerted to the bomb plot messages—Kimmel would have left his battleships to become sitting-duck targets. One certain result would have been his giving greater priority to interception and decryption of the J-19 messages sent from the Honolulu consulate. (This alone would have changed events.) Or if Hypo had been allowed to participate—as Safford wanted—in decrypting, instead of merely intercepting, the Honolulu consulate's traffic, we would quickly have become aware of the increasing extent, detail, and urgency of the ships-in-harbor reports. It is most unlikely that I, or anyone else on Kimmel's staff, would ever have dismissed this intelligence as being merely a "nicety of detail."

Whatever the reason for the naval staff's dereliction, Washington's failure to relay the bomb plot messages to Pearl Harbor added up to what Kimmel called "affirmative misrepresentation."[28] We had asked Washington repeatedly for all intelligence relevant to the fleet. We had been assured repeatedly that we would have it. We believed that we were receiving it. Our estimates and actions were made on this basis. But the failure to relay these vital pieces of intelligence to us deprived us of essential facts and misled us when it came to our assessing the possibility of a Japanese attack on Pearl Harbor.[29]

15

"Imperfect Threats"

B ESIDES BEING DENIED vital information from intelligence sources in Washington, Kimmel faced another handicap. He had to depend on CNO's personal letters for a glimpse into the world of diplomatic news. Unfortunately, these letters were deceptive in their reassuring tone.

For example, on 17 October, Stark wrote to Kimmel, "Personally I do not believe the Japs are going to sail into us and the message I sent you merely stated the possibility," adding that Washington was working "to maintain the status quo in the Pacific."[1] Such a message, which arrived at Pearl Harbor a week after we had been warned about the "grave situation" alert (Stark's letter was written the day after the alert), was hardly reassuring as to the reliability of Washington's alarums.

Kimmel had been surprised by Stark's abrupt retreat from the alert triggered by the fall of the Konoye cabinet. We did not know that Washington's fear of immediate Japanese action had been removed by the Purple decrypt of 18 October in which Tokyo assured Ambassador Nomura, "Regardless of the make-up of the new cabinet, negotiations with the United States shall be continued."[2] And Turner, who had drafted the alert message, was to admit later, "I did not believe that there would be any possibility of war for at least a month."[3]

The only hint of Washington's overview of the new diplomatic situation was Stark's assurance that he saw "eye to eye" with the naval liaison officer at the State Department, who advised Stark not to "overestimate the importance of the recent changes in the Japanese cabinet." Captain Roscoe E. Schuirmann's memorandum echoed the opinion of Dr. Stanley K. Hornbeck, who warned Secretary of State Hull not to be fooled into negotiating "the bill of goods" to save the moderate members of the cabinet in Tokyo. According to Hornbeck's view, Japan's foreign policy was already hostage to military extremists. He believed their next aggressive move was going to be dictated by opportunism, and whether this was north or south would depend on "the course of the war in Russia."[4]

This was the only piece of detailed diplomatic analysis that Kimmel received from CNO in a three-month period, and its impact on him was doubly unfortunate. The memo betrayed the State Department's lack of a sense of urgency and its mistaken assumption that Tokyo's actions would be tied to Hitler's war against the Soviet Union. Its on-again, off-again tone was characterized by its recital of the army's fears that the Japanese might raid Wake Island to disrupt the flights of B-17 bombers to the Philippines. While Stark believed that such an attack was "extremely improbable," he nevertheless cautioned that "a carefully planned raid on any of these island carriers in the Pacific might be difficult to detect."[5]

The implication that Kimmel drew from this letter was that from his depleted resources of men, ships, and planes, he was now expected to provide protection for the army bombers on their way to reinforce the Philippines. It was another galling reminder of the degree to which our strategic priorities in the Pacific had undergone a complete reversal: The United States' front line of defense had effectively been moved five thousand miles westward across the Pacific. Hawaii's strategic priorities had given way to the Philippines. Washington evidently saw Pearl Harbor as being only a way station to ferry B-17s to build up MacArthur's forces. "We turned our endeavor to set up sufficient force in the Philippine Islands to guard the islands to be a threat to any Japanese movement through the South China Sea," General Marshall was to concede four years later. "We turned from the meeting of the demands of Hawaii and fulfilling the Martin-Bellinger request for 190 B-17s."[6]

Admiral Kimmel was never properly advised about this reversal of American Pacific strategy—even though it had been decided at the Argentia summit and endorsed by the Joint Board. The 19 September meeting of what was effectively the supreme war council of the United States had agreed to accelerate the military buildup in the Philippines at the expense of Pearl Harbor. The board "concurred" with the army chief of staff's view that this "would have a profound strategic effect and that it might be the decisive element in deterring Japan from undertaking a Pacific war."[7]

Marshall would later explain the decision, testifying, "If we could make the Philippines reasonably defensible, particularly with heavy bombers in which the air corps had at that time great faith, we felt that we could block the Japanese advance and block their entry into the war by their fear of what would happen if they couldn't take the Philippines."[8]

But we did not know about this decision. Nor did we know that Washington believed that "the Japanese could not dare to attempt to move to the south of the Philippines, or to make a naval attack."[9] Washington's notion of its new Pacific military capability had taken off into a flight of strategic fantasy. And the secretary of war hand-delivered it to the White House on 21 October 1941.

"A strategic opportunity of the utmost importance has suddenly arisen in the southwestern Pacific. Our whole strategic possibilities of the past twenty years have been revolutionized," Stimson enthusiastically informed the president. "From being impotent to influence events in the area, we suddenly find ourselves vested with the possibility of great effective power. Indeed, we hardly yet realize our opportunities in this respect."[10] The "possibilities" that so excited Marshall and the secretary of war were graphically demonstrated by red and blue circles penciled onto an accompanying chart of the Far East. Those that radiated north from the Philippines and south from Vladisvostok implied that by using Russian airstrips, we would bring all the home islands of Japan within reach of aerial attack by the army's four-engine bombers, which had a thousand-mile range.

Stimson's allusion to the possibility of American planes raining destruction over Tokyo actually left Roosevelt "a bit bewildered."[11] But the secretary of war's enthusiastic belief was that the B-17 bomber force "had changed the whole picture in the Asiatic area."[12] Within weeks, even MacArthur was cabling Marshall for target maps for "the location of 600 industrial objectives, in Japan proper."[13]

This was the first time—but not the last—that our military was bemused by the supposed deterrent value of strategic bombing. But in the autumn of 1941 two major flaws ought to have caused Marshall to question this new strategy: The doctrine was untried, and it depended on the Japanese to take no military action until enough bombers had been rushed to the Philippines to put it into effect.

The magnitude of military miscalculation in Washington is apparent in Stimson's memorandum. Its premise was based on the army air staff's calculation that 128 B-17s would be sufficient to defend the Philippines. "Yet even this imperfect threat, if not promptly called by the Japanese, bids fair to stop Japan's march to the south and secure the safety of Singapore," the secretary of war confidently predicted, "with all the revolutionary consequences of such action."[14]

Four years later Marshall admitted the folly of the strategic gamble he had supported: "Although we now think in terms of thousands [of bombers], at that time 100 was a very large figure."[15] Production rates were so low that by the beginning of December fewer than fifty planes could be sent to the Philippines. Yet our military staff had become entranced with the strategic bombing doctrine. It was believed, as Marshall himself was to testify, that only a few score bombers were adequate so "that we would probably deter the Japanese from making an attack."[16]

So Stimson's "strategic opportunity" became, in effect, a monumental blunder. From the time the first B-17 touched down in the Philippines at the beginning of September, until the moment Japan's surprise attack exploded their strategic miscalculation three months later, our leaders in Washington were transfixed by their Far East deterrent strategy. They believed that every B-17 that droned its way from Hawaii to Midway and on via Wake and Samoa to the Philippines would add another nail to the club MacArthur would use to cow Japan. The State Department's "babying along" of Tokyo was focused on the production timetables of the Boeing Aircraft Company instead of the increasing signs of Japanese impatience that diplomacy was failing to yield them results.

"As you well know, however, the final success of the operation lies on the knees of the gods," Stimson had reminded Roosevelt, "and we cannot tell what explosion may momentarily come from Japan."[17] What the secretary of war did not know was that three days before he wrote these prophetic words, the fuse that was to ignite the Pacific explosion had been lit. The naval staff in Tokyo was presented with an ultimatum on 10 October. It was delivered by Admiral Yamamoto's senior staff officer Captain Kameto Kuroshima. He carried the blunt message from the fleet's indispensable commander in chief that either they give their approval to the plan to attack Pearl Harbor with the full force of six aircraft carriers, or they face the prospect of his resignation, along with his entire staff. Navy chief Nagano capitulated. The Pearl Harbor operation was officially made part of Japan's overall war plan. The only proviso was that it must not interfere with the main thrust of Japan's southward offensive.

Yamamoto had played a blackmailing hand to overcome naval staff opposition. It was a measure of his skill as a master poker player and an ominous omen that he now considered war with the United States inevitable. Only a month earlier he had secretly cautioned Premier Konoye that if negotiations with the United States failed, "I can promise to give them hell for a year or a year and a half, but can guarantee nothing as to what will happen after that."[18]

"Yet in a letter of 24 October to the new navy minister, the Combined Fleet CinC struck a decidedly different tone. "When one views the situation as a whole, it is obvious that a collision between Japan and America should be avoided," Yamamoto advised Vice Admiral Shigetaro Shimada, the navy minister. But Yamamoto was a realist who doubted that "now Japan has been driven to its present situation," it might be too late to change course. He insisted that "if the situation is going to force us into action," then the Pearl Harbor operation, conceived though it had been "in desperation," was the only viable strategy. "I feel, as officer in command of the fleet, that there will be little prospect of success if we employ the normal type of operations," he concluded, repeating his threat of resignation.[19]

Yamamoto, however, had no intention of employing normal operations. His victory over the naval staff now secured, he sailed a week later with the Combined Fleet for the broad reaches of Tosa Bay on the southerly island of Shikoku to conduct a final series of maneuvers. While Admiral Nagumo's First Air Fleet completed preparations for a final dress rehearsal of the Pearl Harbor attack on 3 November, Yamamoto was summoned to Tokyo to brief the navy minister.

After the commander in chief left, Admiral Ugaki, his chief of staff, remained on board battleship *Nagato*. He began that day's diary entry on a confident note. "Everything is OK," he wrote. Then, reflecting on the ambition of the undertaking, his self-restraint cracked: "Die, die all of you! I, too, will die for my country."[20]

Under cover of darkness in the small hours of 4 November, Admiral Nagumo's carrier striking force made a high-speed run to the southwest to within two hundred miles of the southernmost tip of Kyūshū before launching planes to make practice strikes against Ariake Bay. While Commander Mitsuo Fuchida led the full complement of aircraft in mock raids against the town of Saeki, Ugaki and the staff on the flagship polished their final drafts of the army and navy agreement for Yamamoto's war plan.

X-day was set for the first week in December. A full moon between midnight and dawn would give the various invasion forces the visibility they needed to get into position to attack. The first Sunday of the month was also considered the ideal time to catch the Pacific Fleet in harbor and unawares. On 5 November the war directive itself was issued by imperial general headquarters: "In the interest of self-defense and survival, the empire is due to open hostilities with the United States, Britain, and Holland in the first ten days of December. Preparations are to be completed for the various operations involved."[21]

The hundred pages of Yamamoto's operational order number 1, which he had submitted personally to the navy staff in Tokyo two days later, was issued the same day. Far more comprehensive than a simple plan for opening hostilities, it was the naval blueprint for the first six months of war. Seven hundred copies were printed under tight security, an astonishingly large number for a top-secret war plan. As a precaution, the final section detailing the Pearl Harbor plan was detached. Copies of it were held under even tighter security for distribution to only the commanders of Nagumo's striking force.[22]

Coincident with the issue of his operational orders, Yamamoto also took care to draw a tight cloak of secrecy around radio communications of the Combined Fleet.

We soon became aware of these new procedures at Pearl Harbor. On 1 November, Rochefort reported that the call signs of all seagoing commands and warships had been changed as of midnight, Tokyo time. This caused us no undue alarm. The last major change had been made in May and the imperial navy routinely revised its call signs every six months. We had been anticipating the switch, because they had introduced new call signs for all shore stations at the beginning of October. But because the Hypo cryptanalysts had still made no progress with the Japanese flag officer code, and lacked the current keys Washington had recovered to the JN-25 fleet operational cipher, our ability to track their naval units was once again curtailed.

The relatively high volume of traffic, however, enabled Hypo's traffic analysts to make speedy progress toward establishing some key call signs, of which there were an estimated twenty thousand new warship identifier codes used in radio transmissions. Within twenty-four hours Rochefort's daily traffic analysis summary reported "casual identification" of many units, although the Japanese were evidently using as many as seven call signs for each major unit.[23]

Despite this effort at concealment, the Japanese could not hide the signature of certain radio operators. The ears of our On the Roof Gang manning the Wahiawa listening station had by now become so attuned that they easily picked out one of the ham-fisted telegraphists on carrier *Akagi* who played the Morse key as if he were sitting on it!

On 3 November, Rochefort reported an important discovery. One of the addressees had been broken out as *Ichi Kōkū Kantai,* literally the "First Air Fleet." Based upon this, and together with other analyses, Joe was certain that it indicated "an entirely new organization of the naval air fleets.[24]

We guessed from the volume of traffic addressed to the Japanese carriers on their tactical circuits that some major Combined Fleet exercise must be taking place across the Pacific. But there was no evidence in the radio traffic that they were preparing for an attack on United States territory. Our suspicions might have been aroused had we known more about the innocent-looking steamer that docked at Honolulu Harbor on the morning of 1 November. She had just crossed the Pacific undetected, using the northerly route selected for the Japanese carrier striking force. The stormy waters to the north and west of Hawaii were empty of our merchant shipping which, since September, had been routed to the south of Hawaii as a safety measure. *Taiyo Maru* had proved to the satisfaction of the naval officers traveling incognito on board that it was possible to approach to within two hundred miles of Pearl Harbor without risk of being spotted by our naval patrol planes.

The ship was staked out by the local ONI and FBI agents as soon as she tied up. Yet careful monitoring of her visitors did not reveal that Consul General Kita's frequent visits were for the purpose of relaying detailed intelligence reports. The naval officers remained on board, carefully making note of the number and direction of daily air patrols.

Our ONI and FBI agents might have been more suspicious about the role the consul was playing if they had paid more attention to the peripatetic journeyings of his energetic third secretary, Yoshikawa, alias Morimura.

The Fourteenth Naval District had failed to watch closely either Yoshikawa or one of his resident spies who had been identified as a

"Class A Nazi suspect" by Captain Mayfield's office in July 1940. It was astonishing that such an obvious agent as Fritz Kuehn was overlooked. He had paid frequent trips to Japan after settling in Honolulu in 1936 to run a steel furniture business that soon failed. The former naval policeman and ex-Nazi, who had been jailed twice before leaving Germany, also owned "considerable real estate" and lived well with two homes— one a Lanikai beach house. Kuehn appeared to have no visible means of support other than his wife's beauty parlor. But his file noted that he had received suspiciously large payments through the local Japanese consulate.[25]

The forty-six-year-old Kuehn, who used the code-name "Jimmie," would later confess to supplying Consul Kita with "perfectitiously information" about the Pacific Fleet. Kuehn had fallen under suspicion the previous year when he began cultivating acquaintances among naval officers. But he was not tailed when he drove his brown roadster up to the Japanese consulate in the fall of 1941 to submit the complex signal system that would enable him to report fleet movements from his beach house by lights and using a radio transmitter. He received $14,000 for his services, the money delivered to his home on an October Sunday by a Japanese contact named Kyogoku, who had come to brief him on the important mission. The mysterious caller was to be identified by Kuehn's stepson as none other than Yoshikawa.[26]

If our counterintelligence operations on Oahu failed to apprehend Yoshikawa and his network it was because their elaborately orchestrated spying had not been detected. Nor had the young Japanese diplomat actually infringed any law that would have enabled the local FBI to bring charges. But there could be no such excuses for Washington's failure to evaluate and alert the overseas commands of the Magic intelligence that clearly indicated Japan's acceleration toward belligerency.

On 2 November a Purple decrypt from Tokyo alerted Ambassador Nomura—and our own military leaders and diplomats—that the cabinet "in a meeting on the morning of the 5th" would issue new instructions for resuming negotiations. "This will be our government's last effort to improve diplomatic relations," it warned. "The situation is very grave. When we resume negotiations, the situation makes it urgent that we reach a decision at once."[27]

This message signaled in unequivocal terms that Japan was about to embark on a final attempt at diplomacy. It had resulted from more than ten days of stormy liaison conference meetings in Tokyo during which Tojo had struggled to reconcile the hard-line militarists—who called for immediate war preparations—with the emperor's instruction to his new premier to "go back to blank paper," to give diplomacy one final chance.

Not until the end of October had the military leaders been persuaded to give their diplomats until the third week of November to arrange a settlement that could lead to the resumption of American oil shipments to Japan. In doing so, the military again rejected Hull's four principles for guaranteeing China's autonomy, as a basis for negotiation. They insisted that there was to be no backing out of their tripartite pact obligations, and refused to remove their troops from Indochina or China until after twenty-five years.

This was the basis of Japan's so-called "A" Proposal, which represented Tokyo's minimum demands and maximum concessions. Tojo continued to argue for a more flexible negotiating position. On 5 November he finally succeeded in wringing cabinet approval for a "B" proposal. This was a *modus vivendi,* a temporary accommodation that was to be put forward only if the terms and conditions of "A" proposal were rejected.

Our ambassador in Tokyo had relayed the information that the new cabinet was being given a stormy ride by its service ministers who wanted action, not more diplomacy. On 3 November, Grew advised the State Department that even Tojo might not be able to hold down the pressure building within his cabinet. His cable warned of "an all out, do or die attempt to render Japan impervious to foreign embargoes, even risking national hara-kiri rather than cede to foreign pressure."[28]

In Washington the next day the senior members of our army and navy staffs wrestled in their 3 November joint meeting with the problem of how to prevent a premature explosion in the Pacific before MacArthur had been adequately reinforced. They considered a toughly worded State Department policy paper that advocated stepping up aid to China and issuing a firm ultimatum to Japan.

"Mr. Hull is of the opinion that there was no use to issue any additional warnings against Japan if we can't back them up," Marshall advised the Joint Board. The army chief reminded the meeting that they still did not have enough military resources in the Philippines to back up any ultimatum to Japan. He reminded the board that it had committed the United States to an Atlantic-oriented strategy. Any flare-up in the Far East would detract from Britain's ability to continue the fight against Germany. Not until mid-December would MacArthur have sufficient bombers to provide the "impressive strength" needed to "have a deterrent effect on Japanese operations."[29]

Admiral Ingersoll was all for rejecting Hull's hard-line policy proposal. He accused the State Department of being "under the impression that Japan could be defeated in military action in a few weeks."[30] The chief of naval operations concurred. Stark also pointed out that it would be impossible to provide enough tankers to support offensive operations by the Pacific Fleet without causing a major fuel crisis in the United States. "Assuming that the fleet could be moved to the Far East," CNO warned, "no repair facilities are available at either Manila or Singapore."[31]

Facing this dilemma, Marshall concluded, "It would take some very clever diplomacy to save the situation." Marshall suggested making "certain minor concessions which the Japanese could use in saving face." The Joint Board therefore resolved to reject the State Department's hard-line proposals. Instead, the board would send the president its own memorandum spelling out the strategic realities and dangers in the Pacific. The board opposed "the issuance of an ultimatum to Japan." Instead it advocated that they "put off hostilities with Japan as long as possible" by suggesting agreements "to tide the situation over for the next several months."[32]

The need to avoid any acts that might provoke Japan into war was stressed throughout a six-point memorandum, over the joint signatures of Marshall and Stark, that went to the White House on 5 November. "The only current plans for war against Japan in the Far East are to conduct a defensive war in cooperation with the British and the Dutch," it declared.[33] The president was advised that the Philippine-based strategic bombers could not become a "positive threat" until mid-December, and they would not reach their projected strength until February or March 1942 when the "potency of this threat will have reached the point where it might well be the deciding factor in deterring Japan."[34]

Meanwhile, Purple decrypts had revealed that Japan's consulate in Manila—paying close attention to every B-17 arrival—was keeping Tokyo posted on the accelerating pace of MacArthur's military buildup. That Japan anticipated Washington might be intending to threaten the home islands from the air was evident in a 4 September circular put out to the Japanese consulates on the west coast from the embassy in Washington asking for investigation of the "possibility the United States is preparing for the eventuality when a considerable bombing force will have to be transferred to the (Siberian?) area."[35]

Their military attaché in Berlin was simultaneously ordered to collect German data on the Flying Fortress raids flown by the Royal Air Force that summer. The Luftwaffe reported the poor performance of the few British B-17s in raiding Berlin. Military analysts in Tokyo were therefore soon able to discount the strategic bombing threat on which our military leaders had placed so much faith as a deterrent.

General Marshall's own staff was also beginning to come to the same conclusion. Their 21 November appraisal entitled "Strategic Air Offensive Against Japan" cautioned that "we are going much too far on the offensive side" for the "smallness of the proposed army air force in the Philippines." It concluded that the inflammability of Tokyo had been "considerably overestimated" in MacArthur's plans for "general incendiary attacks to burn up the wood-and-paper structures of the densely populated Japanese cities."[36]

Hundreds of target maps had already been dispatched to the Philippines, but the limited range of the B-17s necessitated their landing in Russia after bombing the Japanese home islands. Negotiations to land at

Russian airfields around Vladivostok had been dragging on with Kremlin officials since 11 October. And Stalin steadfastly refused to sanction their use by American planes.

Just before Richard Sorge's espionage ring was exposed on 14 November, the Soviet master spy had confirmed to Stalin that Japan was committed to a southward advance. This had permitted Stalin to issue the orders recalling the Red Army's Siberian divisions in time to join the defense of Moscow. With the desperate battle for Moscow looming, the Russians feared that any agreement for our bombers to use their bases might trigger a retaliatory attack by Tokyo across the now weakly guarded Manchurian frontier.

While Stalin's noncooperation was stalling the Anglo-American ability to directly menace Japan, Britain's seaborne contribution to the defense of the South Pacific was also losing its credibility. Churchill had promised to send a "formidable, fast, high-class squadron" to Singapore.[37] But objections by the Admiralty had reduced this to a one-carrier task force.

"There is nothing like having something that can catch and kill anything," the prime minister had nonetheless cheerfully cabled Roosevelt on 2 November, a week after battleship Prince of Wales sailed on the first leg of her long haul halfway around the globe.[38] "The firmer your attitude and ours, the less chance of their taking the plunge," Churchill assured the president.[39]

The prime minister's optimism was in no way dampened the next day by the news that the aircraft carrier that had been assigned to the squadron had run aground on a reef off Bermuda. Neither Admiral Sir Tom Phillips, flying his flag in the battleship, nor the prime minister reconsidered the danger to the task force if it proceeded to Singapore without air cover. Phillips, like most Royal Navy gunnery officers of his generation, had repeatedly insisted, as vice-chief of the naval staff, that "bombers were no match for battleships."

When Prince of Wales put into Capetown on 16 November, South African Prime Minister Jan Christian Smuts cabled London, "If the Japanese are really nippy, there is an opening here for a first-class disaster."[40] Neither Phillips nor Churchill paid heed to his keen strategic instincts. The veteran Boer general saw the strategic folly of sending a weak force steaming into waters dominated by Japan's overwhelming sea and air supremacy.

The British prime minister's continued expectation that a one-battleship squadron could strike awe into the militarists in Tokyo was yet another link in the fatal chain of strategic illusion. Our own military leaders were blind to the ominous indications that Japan was moving to call the Anglo-American bluff—months before either the sea or air forces became a credible military force. By the end of the first week in November the warnings could be read in almost every line of the Purple decrypts of the messages sent to the Japanese embassy on Massachusetts Avenue from the foreign ministry in Tokyo.

On 4 November, Ambassador Nomura was informed that diplomat Saburo Kurusu was coming to Washington because of the "gravity of the present negotiations."[41] The arrival of a special envoy gave specific warning that this truly was a last-ditch diplomatic effort at negotiation. It removed any doubt that if the current discussions led nowhere, "relations between our two nations will be on the brink of chaos."[42]

In a four-part message the next day, the terms of Japan's "last possible bargain" were spelled out to Nomura. His instructions were that "there will be no room for personal interpretation."[43] "A" proposal for a permanent settlement that was transmitted on 5 November not only contained the very narrow limits within which Japan was prepared to negotiate, but her ambassador was ordered to present it "at the earliest possible moment." He was told, "Speed is an absolutely essential factor."[44]

The cable also contained "B" proposal for a temporary accommodation, which was to be put forward only if there was "a remarkable difference between the Japanese and American views." Nomura was left in no doubt that this was his government's "final step." Time was "exceedingly short," and the situation "very critical." He was told that "absolutely no delays" were permitted, and that it was vital that "all arrangements for the signing of this agreement be completed by the 25th of this month."[45]

Just under three weeks now remained for Ambassador Nomura to pull off what the Japanese foreign minister admitted would be a "difficult order."[46] The ominous drumbeat of impending belligerency was heard in the carefully specified deadline of 25 November, the day appointed by Yamamoto for the striking force to set sail for Hawaii. But even this did not rouse any immediate appreciation of the true dimension of the crisis in Washington.

Magic's forewarnings, it seems, had drained the situation of all urgency. Nomura arrived at the State Department on Friday morning to deliver proposal "A." Hull was cordial, but did not believe that it offered "any real recessions from the position consistently maintained by the Japanese government." The secretary of state did, however, warn Roosevelt's inner cabinet that afternoon that "relations were extremely critical and . . . we should be on the lookout for a military attack anywhere by Japan at any time."[47]

The chief of naval operations allowed only a vague echo of the strident urgency of the Magic decrypts to creep into the message he sent off to Kimmel that same day. "The big question is—what next?" was how Stark began another of his epistles. This one was concerned mainly with turning down Kimmel's recent requests for more destroyers and the new battleships *North Carolina* and *Washington*.[48] He did allow, however, that dealing with Japan "continually gets worser and worser."

Three days earlier we had received notice that Japan was recalling all her merchant ships from the western hemisphere.[49] But no dispatch told us of the most specific intelligence Washington had yet received of

Japan's timetable for war. If Kimmel had been informed of Tokyo's 25 November deadline for negotiations, we might have been more concerned at the sudden disappearance of radio traffic addressed to their carriers.

Instead, Stark sent another of his Delphic warnings that "a month may see, literally, most anything."[50] Considering that this letter was dated 7 November, his prediction, "It doesn't look too good," proved to be one of CNO's more accurate utterances on the situation.

16

"What Will We Do?"

I̲T̲ ̲W̲A̲S̲ ̲A̲ ̲S̲T̲R̲I̲K̲I̲N̲G̲ incongruity of our naval intelligence setup that while Washington was able to intercept, decrypt, and translate Japan's high-level diplomatic traffic within a day or so, it took more than a week for the letters from CNO to reach Pearl Harbor by mail. So Stark's 7 November letter, with its vapid prediction that "anything" could happen with Tokyo in a month, crossed in transit with Kimmel's urgent question: "If they [the Japanese] do embark on such an adventure and Britain and the Dutch East Indies declare war on Japan, what will we do?"[1]

We believed that the imperial navy was clearly preparing for hostile operations. This was evident from the surge in tactical signal traffic from the Combined Fleet's early November exercises and indications of an acceleration of their military buildup in the mandated islands. Yet it seemed to me that naval intelligence in Washington continued to ignore the growing threat posed by naval and air bases in the Marshalls and Carolines. Remembering how they had neglected the WE WE cipher earlier in the year, on 6 November we sent off our latest analysis of Japanese bases and aircraft in the mandates to the chief of naval operations.

"You will note, of course, that our estimate differs considerably from the one prepared by Washington," Kimmel advised Stark. "I doubt very much if the navy department effort has had the care expended upon it that we have given."[2] Our concern was that Japan had already illegally garrisoned and established facilities for both submarines and aircraft in these strategically located islands.

We knew that Truk, with its fine deep-water anchorage, at the heart of the Caroline archipelago, was already in use as an operating base for the Fourth Fleet. My estimates—based on the number of reconnaissance flights being made over Britain's neighboring Gilbert Islands—were that somewhere between 62 and 268 aircraft were operating throughout the mandates.

At the west end of the thousand-mile necklace of coral islands that strategically straddled our Pacific line of communications were the Palaus. We knew that at least two seaplane bases, an airstrip, gun batteries, and barracks had been built there to guard the excellent anchorage. To the east in the Marshall chain was Jaluit, some eight hundred miles south of our highly vulnerable base at Wake atoll. In addition to a pair of four-hundred-foot radio towers that eavesdropped on our communications, Jaluit was equipped with two landing fields, seaplane slips, shore batteries, and antiaircraft guns. The fortification of the mandates, as a launching point for a submarine or surface offensive against our fleet, was a logical strategic move by the Japanese.

One of the basic axioms of intelligence work is to put yourself into the enemy's shoes and try to figure out what he would do. This was how I approached the task of assembling the information on the mandates. And it was the picture of Japanese movements that I gave to Admiral Kimmel in my daily briefing. Also, several times a day I would discuss the latest traffic analysis findings with Joe Rochefort.

During these consultations, I was often reminded how painfully reliant we were on the inexact science of traffic analysis. Hypo was still unable to read any of the major naval code systems. The extent and accuracy of intelligence derived from traffic analysis had certain limitations—as we would learn later—because it was based on the technique of identification by association. To identify an unknown Japanese unit, we monitored its activities on one of the two hundred radio circuits and the traffic—a broad term for communications carried by radio frequency circuits—the unit was associated with.

Japan's unique naval communications system was both a help and a hindrance to this technique. Their commanders did not normally communicate with one another directly, except in tactical situations. Administrative and command traffic was usually transmitted up a chain of command to the nearest shore station, which sent out the signal for all addressees on an umbrella broadcast, usually repeated several times. While our performance in traffic analysis over a long period was pretty good, we were less accurate in divining the details of an opponent's day-by-day moves, especially if new call signs and circuits were introduced, as they had been at the beginning of November.

Yet the peculiar nature of the Japanese communications setup could often yield surprisingly precise intelligence. If for example a carrier division at Kure, in the southwest of Honshū, was ordered to proceed to the northern port of Ominato, it would send a movement report to Kure and another to the navy's main reporting division in Tokyo. A call would then be put out to the naval station in Ominato, which would be rebroadcast by both Tokyo and Ominato. So by comparing the addressees, even though the actual coded message could not be read, it was a simple matter to forecast that the carrier division was proceeding from Kure to Ominato.

I kept an extensive card file in my office listing Japanese naval units and commands. Whenever a new unit appeared on the sheets sent up from Rochefort's outfit, I could thumb through my tickler file on which I noted the latest sightings and radio estimates and pencil in the most likely ship or command involved. Filling in my record cards every day enabled me to draw up a location sheet and chart up-to-date positions and likely movements of the majority of Japanese fleet units.

I had frequent exchanges with Rochefort on call sign recoveries after their November call sign change revealed that certain fleet units had apparently been transferred to other commands. Each fleet circuit—which we called a "mother"—had certain "chickens" under its radio "wing." Some of these chickens no longer turned up with their usual mother, but were calling the mother address of other fleets. This was unusual. When these new commanders began addressing the subordinates of another command, like the First Fleet destroyers that appeared in Second Fleet traffic, it was a sign that they had assumed direct tactical control over them for some impending operations.

A fleet intelligence officer always has to establish a framework for defining the scope of the strategic picture. Within it he can assemble scattered elements to piece together an overall pattern, rather like a jigsaw puzzle. We could never expect to have all the pieces, but that November we had received no Magic dispatches—from either Washington or Cavite. Our attention was, therefore, concentrated on the region bounded by the South China Sea on the west and the Marshall Islands to the east. Those pieces of the puzzle that we possessed fit neatly into this framework. As we saw it, a Japanese offensive move was shaping up against Malaya. It was possible that it was also directed against the Philippines, and there was a strong defensive and offensive capability in the mandates.

Rochefort's communications intelligence summary was delivered to my office each day around 0700. I would take it to Admiral Kimmel an hour later with my own daily briefing. In reading it, he would mark or underline in pencil the items he considered important. The admiral would ask me for clarification or more information, and then initial the paper. His chief of staff, Captain William W. "Poco" Smith, was usually present during my presentation, and if a crisis was building, the senior war plans officer and the senior operations officer would be called in to discuss my reports.

Admiral Kimmel always encouraged his officers to express themselves. I took full advantage of this to offer my opinions. There were also meetings almost daily in which I briefed, so that staff officers did not have to read through the entire material. When our other task force commanders were in port—they usually operated at sea for two weeks and in port for one week—Kimmel had me give them a review of events that had occurred in their absence. There were general discussions covering Japanese intentions and how we could counter them. Particular attention was always paid to the mandates, and General Short was present at several of the sessions during which we discussed the threat these island bases posed to Hawaii.

The picture that we constructed in November pointed unmistakably to a Japanese buildup for naval operations to the south. It was confirmed by the sightings in November of an increasing number of transports by our observers in Chinese ports. Our naval attachés and merchant skippers also added their reports of Japanese troopships departing southward from Shanghai. Again, this fit neatly into our overall picture formed by our traffic analysis.

During the first week of November, we discovered that Jaluit radio activity had increased dramatically, and circuit congestion revealed "heavy concentrations" in the Marshalls.[3] My discussions with Admiral Kimmel and his chief of war plans, Captain Charles H. "Soc" McMorris, increasingly focused on the recent changes in the Japanese tactical organization. It was also evident that a large amount of the Combined Fleet traffic was appearing, as Rochefort reported, "with secret (tactical) calls in use."[4] This was another indicator of naval forces making ready for some major operation. During the second week of November radio activity in the mandates continued at a high level, and the pattern of Combined Fleet traffic continued to point to a major reorganization. On 9 November carrier *Akagi,* flagship of the newly identified First Air Fleet, was picked up at Sasebo, and transmissions from Carrier Divisions 3 and 4 indicated that they were also heading for home ports after their recent exercises with the battleships.[5]

Then, during the next five days, there was such a decline in traffic on the naval air circuits that Rochefort reported that the "carriers remain relatively inactive."[6] We deduced that the Japanese carriers were probably replenishing prior to operating with the Second Fleet. It remained the single most active originator of traffic throughout the third week of November.[7] On Monday, 17 October, Rochefort's daily summary confirmed that the "carriers are mostly in the Kure-Sasebo area, with the exception of a few which are operating in the Kyushu area."[8] Over the next twenty-four-hour period several messages were picked up addressed to the carrier divisions from Tokyo, from which we concluded, "No movement from home waters."[9]

Our estimate was dead wrong! That very afternoon, Admiral Yamamoto delivered a rousing send-off speech on *Akagi*'s flight deck in Saeki Bay. As dusk fell, the six blacked-out carriers slipped out to sea bound for a secret assembly point at Tankan Bay (Hitokappu Wan) in the foggy remoteness of the Kurile Islands.

Strict radio silence was observed by the Japanese carriers, so our radio intelligence network did not detect the first move of the powerful force that was to attack Pearl Harbor. The Big Boss—as we called Yamamoto—continued sending out many messages to Second Fleet, which we assumed would operate with carriers because on 23 November

Rochefort reported that "Cardiv 3 [carrier division] definitely associated with 2nd Fleet operations."[10]

All our traffic analysis continued to show that preparations were being made for a southward advance through the South China Sea, under cover of Indochina airfields, with Malaya, the Dutch East Indies, and possibly the Philippines being the probable objectives.[11] The Third Fleet was also such a frequent addressee that we believed it must be the main amphibious invasion force, because it appeared prominently in communications with the commander of shore-based air units in Indochina.[12] Station Cast from Cavite estimated Carrier Division 3 could be in the Palaus, but Rochefort and I remained convinced that at least one of its carriers would operate as far east as the Marshalls. I so informed the commander in chief.

We were wrong in our deductions about the Japanese carriers. It was a tragic example of how reliance on traffic analysis alone can lead to error. The pattern of Japanese carrier radio circuits indicated that each division customarily kept its same destroyer division. We therefore assumed that even if their "mother" did not turn up in the traffic, the appearance of her "chickens" would indicate the presence of a carrier division. On 16 November "associations" had been noted by Hypo that indicated carriers were in the mandates as a result of interceptions from the Marshalls of the call sign of a division of destroyers which "has been or is operating with carrier division."[13]

While such analysis did not prove that the mother carriers were with their chickens, we decided they were, because other addressees associated with Japanese carrier traffic had also dried up that week. When Rochefort reported on 23 November that "yesterday a number of dispatches associated Cardiv 3 with CinC 3rd Fleet,"[14] we had no way of knowing that it was actually the small carriers of division 4 that were heading for Formosa. The large carriers of division 3 were already in the Kurile Islands with Carrier Division 1 and were making final preparations for the long voyage across the Pacific to Hawaii.

Twenty-four hours later what appeared to be exchanges between Jaluit and commander carriers persuaded Rochefort there was a definite indication that "one or more Cardivs are present in the Mandates."[16] This was far and away the most potent danger to Pearl Harbor. Again, it fit in with the overall picture of the forces in the Marshalls as being the easterly component of the large task force that was building up to conduct the southward advance and attack the Philippines and Malaya. This conclusion came from an association of the call signs of many Second Fleet warships with the addressees of base commands in Formosa, Hainan, and French Indochina.[17]

By 20 November, Rochefort was convinced that the task force assembling under control of the Second Fleet was so massive that it "will comprise a good portion of the navy."[18]

Although on 24 November, Rochefort was cautioning "no definite indications of location of carriers,"[19] Hypo's traffic analysts predicted that at least one, and possibly two, of the Japanese carrier divisions would probably be associated with the movement and that one might be heading from Japan for the Marshalls. Kimmel was following these reports very closely, the assumption being that wherever the carriers were located would highlight the main thrust of the Combined Fleet.

At my briefing with Kimmel that Wednesday, he told me to ask Rochefort to confirm his estimates of the carrier locations with the other intercept stations. When Joe reported that no one had so far commented on it via the secure cryptographic radio circuit, Kimmel directed me to send a Copek dispatch setting forth his observations and our conclusions drawn from the Hypo summaries. Two days later Station Cast confirmed our general picture that Japan was building up for a southward thrust. They also predicted that a task force was "expected to operate in the Mandates." This included battleships, cruisers, Destroyer Division 23, and at least one unit of Carrier Division 3—*Ryujo*.[20]

The intelligence estimates of the extensive Japanese forces massing on the other side of the Pacific coincided with the arrival that 24 November on Kimmel's desk of the letter dated 14 November from CNO, which equivocally told him "what we will do in the Far East remains to be seen."[21] The letter also included a copy of the Stark-Marshall memorandum of 5 November to the president, which proved to be more unsettling. It was the first indication that a strategic tug-of war was going on in Washington. Kimmel was, however, reassured by their strong plea to the president that "no ultimatum" be sent to Tokyo and the statement that for two months, at least, war "should be avoided while building up defensive forces in the Far East."[22] He took this as a clear indication that the military leadership in Washington hoped to postpone hostilities until the spring of 1942.

The Stark-Marshall memorandum was also Kimmel's first direct confirmation that the Joint Board recognized that because of Pacific Fleet's inferiority it was unable to "undertake an unlimited strategic offensive." Ten days earlier Kimmel had tried once again to explain his predicament to Stark. Kimmel was concerned that the situation in the Pacific was rushing to a showdown, and he put his concerns bluntly: "We must be in a position to minimize our own losses, and to inflict maximum damage to Japanese fleet, merchant shipping, and bases. . . . I must insist that more consideration be given to the needs of the Pacific Fleet."[23]

The measure of reassurance that Kimmel gained from the knowledge that the strategic realities we faced were finally recognized in Washington was diminished by his alarm at the memorandum's confirmation that the United States would go to war if Japan attacked British and Dutch territory, or began a movement into Thailand that threatened to become an invasion of the Malay Peninsula.[24]

That was precisely what our intelligence indicated that the Japanese naval task forces were preparing to do. But Washington's determination to avoid a showdown with Japan, while at the same time committing us to war if Malaya was attacked, exposed a dangerous strategic contradiction. It became a hot topic of "corridor gossip"[25] at headquarters. We could only hope that the State Department would make some accommodation in the negotiations with Japan that would give us the time needed to get the reinforcements Kimmel had requested.

Such hope was not encouraged by an alert flashed out that Monday afternoon from Washington to all the Pacific commands: "Chances of favorable outcome of negotiations with Japan very doubtful. This situation coupled with statements of Japanese government and movements their naval and military forces indicate in our opinion that surprise aggressive movement *in any direction* including attack on Philippines or Guam is a possibility [emphasis added]."[26]

In the absence of any of the diplomatic intelligence, the failure of the warning to specify just what the threat was negated its urgency at fleet headquarters. So did the injunction for observing "utmost secrecy" so as not to "complicate an already tense situation." The dispatch did, however, appear to confirm that the naval staff had made an identical evaluation of the impending southward movement of hostile naval forces. That a warning had been sent at all was also confirmation of my belief that Japan probably would not risk a southward advance if the Philippines or Guam remained free to attack their right flank. It was not in keeping with the historical record of their military operations.[27]

The estimate that I gave the commander in chief that weekend allowed that some aggressive movement might be imminent from the two powerful task forces assembling five thousand miles across the Pacific. Although both were under the authority of the Second Fleet command, it was already clear that the most powerful one was likely to proceed south from the Formosa-Hainan-Bako area into the South China Sea, aiming at the Isthmus of Kra at the neck of the Malay Peninsula in the Gulf of Siam. The other task force was more likely to travel via the Palaus, in the western Carolines, with the intention of threatening the Dutch East Indies. Once such a movement got under way, I felt, it would not be long before they attacked the Philippines. Our growing air force posed a threat to their line of communications if we took action to assist the British and the Dutch.[28]

After my briefing, Kimmel considered the situation sufficiently urgent to instruct me to personally take the alert over to General Short. When I arrived at Fort Shafter shortly past noon, I found him listening to the midday radio news. After reading the dispatch, he quizzed me about Guam's defenses. Apart from the occasional plane, I explained, the navy had dismantled all coast defense guns in accordance with the League of Nations Naval Limitation Treaty of 1922 which did not permit fortification of the island. The meeting ended with the general expressing his disapproval of the consequences of having appeased Japan too much. I reflected on this on my way back to Cincpac headquarters to report my mission had been completed.

General Short's anger would have been still greater had he known that, even as we spoke, our military leadership in Washington was preparing a deal that, on the face of it, appeared very much like appeasement. It would urge the White House to make a temporary accommodation with Tokyo to forestall a possible breakdown in negotiations. Three days earlier a memorandum from General Gerow, the chief of army war plans, had stressed "the grave importance to the success of war effort in Europe that we reach a *modus vivendi* with Japan."[29] The naval staff had also given its support to the *modus vivendi* plan as a way of buying more time to get the fifty more bombers and the troop convoys across the Pacific. Since Marshall was absent from Washington that Monday on a long weekend, Stark had taken the initiative to order the drafting of another appeal to Roosevelt to do everything to continue negotiations despite clear warnings from the Magic decrypts that Tokyo was about to break them off for lack of progress.[30]

The realization that it was going to take more than fifty B-17s and a few thousand more American soldiers in the Philippines to stop Japan from taking the plunge was already beginning to dawn on our military leaders. That Monday, Stark was to dictate a letter that apprised Kimmel of the "gravity of the situation" as viewed by the president and secretary of state. "Neither would be surprised over a Japanese surprise attack," CNO warned. "From many angles an attack on the Philippines would be the most embarrassing thing that could happen to us."[31] And once again Stark watered down the urgency of his warning by confessing, "I do not give it the weight others do."

This letter reached fleet headquarters only four days before the Japanese attack. Stark's final attempt to represent the urgency of the situation as he saw it gave a less than adequate picture as negotiations with Japan entered their final round. But the confusion in his dispatch was symptomatic of the uncertainty of our military leaders as the United States faced a crisis as great as any in our history. Instead of providing Kimmel with a reasoned evaluation of the intelligence that indicated the awesome extent to which American strategy in the Pacific was coming unstuck, the chief of naval operations wrapped his fears in a flurry of conflicting statements: "I won't go into the pros or cons of what the United States may do. I will be damned if I know. I wish I did. The only thing I do know is that we may do most anything and that's the only thing I know to be prepared for; or we may do nothing—I think it is more likely to be 'anything.'"[32]

17

Negotiations On

IN AN UNPRECEDENTED DISPLAY of army-navy unity, General Marshall and Admiral Stark reinforced the Joint Board's warning against any ultimatum to Japan until the Anglo-American force was a credible deterrent. The State Department was obliged to concede its hard-line attitude and the imbalance of United States foreign policy had been redressed by sound military strategy. But it was too late. By the middle of November it was obvious in Washington that Tokyo was not going to endure three more months of diplomatic procrastination while their oil reserves drained away and our strategic bombing force grew strong enough to threaten the Japanese home islands.

Magic revealed the increasingly impatient directions Tokyo was giving its Washington embassy. The assignment of Saburo Kurusu, an experienced diplomat with an American wife, to assist Ambassador Nomura was another sign of the Japanese cabinet's determination to speed up the diplomatic process. Our analysts in Washington had calculated that the Japanese objective must be the restoration of oil supplies by negotiation with the United States, or the seizure of alternate sources in the Dutch East Indies. That Kurusu did not rate his chances highly had been publicized on 10 November. *The New York Times* correspondent in Manila reported the envoy's remark that he was "going to Washington, but [I] have no great hopes for a successful conclusion to negotiations."[1] Tokyo's swift response by cable to Kurusu expressing the foreign minister's displeasure with his comments circulated with the Magics three days after his arrival in Washington on 15 November.[2]

Kurusu's indiscretions did not add warmth to his welcome in Washington; nor did they enhance the State Department's hope for a successful outcome of the new round of negotiations. Although he read Tokyo's protests in the Purple decrypts "that the United States takes this lazy and easy-going attitude,"[3] Secretary Hull had been stalling the Japanese ambassador for a week. Japanese patience was wearing thinner by the day. Two days after Nomura formally had presented the "A" proposal for a full settlement on 10 November, Hull countered with an "oral" statement that prior approval was needed from Chiang Kai-shek before the matter of China could be discussed. It came as no surprise that Nomura reported that this "fell far short of Japanese anticipation,"[4] and Magic eavesdropping revealed the embassy's preparations to begin repatriating diplomatic personnel by sea.

On 15 November, Hull had another hour-and-a-half meeting with the ambassador. Hull held out some prospect of agreement on trade concessions. After offering this small carrot of hope, he insisted on withholding his formal reply to the other two points of the "A" proposal until Tokyo had responded to his demand for recognition of his four principles. The secretary of state then sprang a new, but not unexpected, condition. "If Japan succeeds in coming to an agreement with the United States," he told Nomura, "she would not find it necessary to hold onto the tripartite pact."[5]

Two days later Magic revealed that the American offer of trade concession had not been enough of an inducement for Tokyo to continue negotiations. The decrypt of Tokyo's response to the ambassador's assurance that he would "do my very best with infinite patience"[6] was a brusque reminder that "the fate of our empire hangs by a slender thread of a few days, so please fight harder than you did before." There was to be "no change" in the 25 November "deadline set for the solution of these negotiations."[7]

The day set for the diet (national assembly) to reconvene in Tokyo struck no particular chord of urgency in the minds of the Far East analysts in the State Department. Washington had no way of knowing that 25 November was also the day the Pearl Harbor striking force was due to put to sea.

The foreign minister's 15 November cable did contain Tokyo's instructions to give up on the "A" proposal and present their "B" plan. Once again Magic's forewarning of Japan's fall-back position appears to have reduced, rather than heightened, State Department concern in Washington. Yet it should have been clear that negotiations were now moving toward a climax in the message to the newly arrived Kurusu that expressed exasperation at the "laxness" of the U.S. government's "stalling for time" when "the crisis was fast approaching."[8]

Stalling was precisely what the secretary of state was being requested to do by our army and naval leaders. But Hull's patience was also faltering. So was his health. After eight years of navigating American foreign policy through increasingly stormy waters at home and overseas, the six months of fruitless negotiation with Nomura had left the seventy-year-old Cordell Hull weary of the diplomatic process in general and of Japan's envoys in particular. He took an instant dislike to the portly, bespectacled Kurusu when he arrived with Nomura at the State Department on Monday, 17 November.

If the secretary of state was terse, Roosevelt, who had postponed his annual Thanksgiving trip to the retreat in Warm Springs, Georgia, was at his most affable. For an hour and a half the talk ranged over the three points on which a breakthrough had to be found to end the deadlock: equality in commerce, the tripartite pact, and the evacuation of Japan's forces from the Chinese mainland. Hull's customary denunciation of the Japanese government's "Hitlerian policy of expansion" was interrupted by Kurusu. He sought to inject a note of urgency by warning of an "imminent explosion" unless an accord was reached.[9]

"There is no last word between friends," the president chipped in, offering to remain in Washington through that weekend to further the discussions. The two Japanese envoys seized on this indication of American willingness to cable Tokyo for permission to advance the *modus vivendi* proposal. They dutifully reported that "it seems very clear that they are of a mind to bring about a compromise after making sure of our peaceful intentions," speculating that the new receptivity was because "the United States has turned more and more than ever toward the Atlantic of late."[10]

In this the Japanese envoys were at least partially correct.

The aftershock of the 31 October torpedoing of destroyer *Reuben James*, which sank with 115 crew members, was still being absorbed by legislators on Capitol Hill. Roosevelt had immediately cashed in on the public outrage against Germany to order the arming of all American merchant ships. But our first service casualties of the war brought demonstrators parading in front of the White House railings, with placards calling for the president's impeachment. Isolationist leader Charles Lindbergh was attracting huge crowds at fall rallies that vociferously protested Roosevelt's support for Britain.

The drift into a shooting war in the Atlantic had been another powerful argument for the joint army-navy memorandum of 5 November that urged the president to make concessions to Japan to avert a simultaneous explosion in the Pacific. The strategic logic of Roosevelt's military advisers was endorsed by a 13 November cable from John Hay Whitney, the London representative of Colonel William J. "Wild Bill" Donovan, the coordinator of intelligence for the White House. It succinctly summarized Churchill's priorities for American intervention:

1. every week sooner we come in will reduce the war by one month
2. order of choice:
    a. United States without Japan
    b. United States and Japan both in war
    c. neither at war
    d. Japan without America (this possibility unthinkable!)[11]

After months of ducking the issue, Roosevelt now faced a clear-cut choice between satisfying the demands of either diplomatic principle or military strategy. Against stiff isolationist opposition, the president had successfully nudged the United States into an undeclared war with Germany in the Atlantic, and an unratified mutual defense pact with Britain in the Pacific. But the Joint Board's Atlantic-oriented strategy made it imperative to avoid a military showdown with Japan while MacArthur's forces lacked the strength to constitute an adequate deterrent. Three more months were needed—and Russian agreement—before a strategic bomber offensive could be launched against the Japanese islands. A pre-emptive strike by the United States against either Axis power would plunge us into a two-ocean war because of the tripartite pact. While this may not have been the worst-case scenario for the British, it was the strategic nightmare that haunted our military leaders throughout 1941.

These were the conflicting demands of military and diplomatic reality that caused the State Department, for the first time in two decades, to reappraise the wisdom of its hard-line stand against the Japanese. At the 17 November meetings, Kurusu, on his own initiative, asked Hull "if the Japanese were now to withdraw their troops from Indochina, could the United States ease their oil and economic pressure to the point of sending small quantities of oil?" That same evening the secretary of state told the British minister in Washington that the idea was "attractive enough to warrant its being tried at least."[12]

In fact the rationale for an American proposal along very much the same lines had already been set out in a memorandum that same morning by the president's confidant, Henry Morgenthau. The forceful secretary of the treasury strongly supported such a plan, and the memorandum, which had been drawn up by Morgenthau's adroit young aide, Harry Dexter White,[13] was entitled "An Approach to the Problem of Eliminating Tension with Japan and Insuring the Defeat of Germany."

The proposal was intended to provide a plan for the release of the Pacific Fleet for operations against Germany in the Atlantic. It envisaged a withdrawal of Japanese troops from Indochina and a phased pullout from China geared to a progressive lifting of America's oil and trade embargo. In effect, it fleshed out Roosevelt's October idea for buying time by offering Japan a six-month truce—"some oil and rice now—more later"—in return for not sending any more troops into Indochina, plus an agreement "not to invoke tripartite pact even if U.S. gets into European war."[14]

The State Department had resisted any compromise with Japan at the beginning of the month. Now the pressures had built to such an extent that Roosevelt was pressing Hull into just such an accord as a means of defusing the dynamite keg in the Pacific. This was evident from Nomura's 18 November cable to Tokyo, which quoted the secretary of state proposing a return to the status quo before July:

I mean Japan should evacuate southern French Indochina, and in return the United States should rescind the freezing order. If the atmosphere remains calm in this manner, there will be no need of sending warships to Singapore or strengthening military facilities in the Philippines. Then we should like to continue talks.[15]

This statement makes it clear that the secretary of state was not simply preempting Tokyo's next diplomatic move. He was also prepared to consider including the Anglo-American deterrent as a bargaining chip to entice Tokyo into another round of negotiations. When he leafed through the Magic summaries three days later, he saw that Nomura and Kurusu had suggested postponing their B proposal to try for "a practical settlement.[16]

But Tokyo would brook no delay. Nomura was told curtly on 19 November to "please present our B proposal of the imperial government and no further concessions can be made." If the American government could not be persuaded to agree by the deadline—now only a week away—"the negotiations will have to be broken off."[17] The ambassador protested that this would "bring about a situation full of dynamite,"[18] but he was given no choice. Reluctantly, therefore, Nomura set off with Kurusu for the State Department on Thanksgiving Day 1941 to present Japan's own *modus vivendi* proposal.

On the morning of 21 November, Hull was careful to give Nomura no indication he had known for over a week the terms of Tokyo's B proposal. According to the Japanese ambassador's report, he was "glad to see both me and Ambassador Kurusu."[19] It was clear that American aid to Chiang Kai-shek was still a major stumbling block. Hull promised to "think over this proposal you have brought me fully and sympathetically." The next day brought further discussions on the general subject of peace. To try to defuse the issue of Tokyo's treaty obligations to Germany and Italy, Kurusu promised that any agreement with the United States would "outshine the tripartite pact." But Hull stressed that Japan must cut its ties with Germany first. He deferred any final decision until after consultation with representatives of Britain, China, and the Dutch government in exile.[20]

Despite Kurusu's complaint that there had been a "complete evasion" of details, Hull had been sympathetic enough to encourage Japan's envoys to anticipate that the weekend would bring a firm American proposal for a temporary accommodation. On the strength of their optimistic reports, Tokyo agreed to extend its deadline four days, despite "reasons beyond your ability to guess why we wanted to settle Japanese-American relations by the 25th."[21] This in itself was a major concession. It indicated that Tokyo was still prepared to seek a diplomatic way out—even after the striking force sailed. But Japan's envoys—and also those who read Magic in Washington—were left in no doubt that they had to get any *modus vivendi* sealed by 29 November. The Magic decrypt read,

"This time we mean it, that the deadline absolutely cannot be changed. After that *things are automatically going to happen.* [emphasis added]."[22]

The third week of November concluded in Washington and Tokyo on a cautiously optimistic note. The State Department was "clutching at straws" in what Hull later characterized the "desperate effort to get something worked out that might stay the hand of the Japanese army and navy for a few days, or a few weeks." Indeed, it appears that that week-end Washington and Tokyo had not given up hope that some temporary accommodation to avert war might be reached.[23]

Working through Saturday and Sunday, State Department officials hammered together a compromise proposal that, while it went against the grain of Dr. Hornbeck's principles, could not be regarded as a sellout of Chiang Kai-shek, or an appeasement to Japanese aggression. The final draft of this compromise proposal was on the secretary of state's desk first thing Monday morning. In return for restoring commercial relations and "a required quantity of oil" for civilian use,[24] Japan would be expected to pull back troops from southern Indochina, set a twenty-five-thousand-man limit to her forces in Indochina, and refrain from further "armed advancement" for three months while negotiations continued to settle the major issues. The proposal stopped short of proposing that lend-lease aid to China be halted, or simply not accelerated. It put forward the Philippines as a site for Sino-Japanese peace talks without direct American involvement. To soothe Chiang Kai-shek's fears of the actual *modus vivendi,* terms were to be accompanied by a ten-point list of the main issues to be negotiated as part of any long-term settlement.

Contrary to the views of some historians, we know now from an unofficially retained memorandum, whose State Department original was destroyed, that Hull regarded the *modus vivendi* as an "important factor in facilitating the conversations and avoiding a breakdown" with Japan. He believed that it would be "giving our army and navy what they solemnly and most urgently represented as an urgent need for several weeks more time in which to get ready to defend on two-ocean fronts."[25]

The secretary of state believed "that to give Japan the privilege for ninety days of purchasing lower grade products in the amount of some two million tons, plus some flour and cotton and certain other foodstuffs, would be in entire accordance with a policy of gradually moving toward a peaceful basis for ninety days in return for a tremendous movement in that direction on the part of Japan."[26]

Hull's willingness to try for a quid pro quo in which the United States made "absolutely microscopic" concessions in return "for what I was asking of Japan," anticipated that Magic would monitor Japan's compliance. As the secretary of state put it:

> It was at this most critical stage with possible war on both fronts threatening that I formally made this proposal in reply to that of the

Japanese. The truth is that the benefits to this government, if the chance for an agreement had been realized—and, of course, it was only a chance—would alone more than have justified the concessions offered to Japan for 90 days.[27]

Given Hull's commitment, as we now know it to have been, the American *modus vivendi* would not have been impossible to reconcile with the proposals already on the negotiating table for Japan. It was ironic, therefore, that the Friday Purple decrypts from Tokyo were instrumental in renewing Hull's fears that the Japanese were about to stiffen their terms. A repetition of the deadline notice heightened the negative impact of a cable reminding Nomura that "cessation of aid to Chiang Kai-shek . . . and at the same time the supply of American petroleum is the most essential condition."[28]

This same decrypt accounted for the lack of optimism in Roosevelt's cable to Churchill informing him of the American *modus vivendi* terms: "This seems to me to be a fair proposition, but its acceptance or rejection is really a matter of internal Japanese politics. I am not very hopeful and we must all prepare for trouble very soon."[29]

Such was the backdrop of tension and uncertainty on 25 November when the president met with the secretaries of war, state, and navy along with the service chiefs. The war council lived up to its name that Tuesday morning—even though the United States was still at peace. Before the conference even started, Hull took care to show the text of the final *modus vivendi* to Stimson and Knox. It had already been approved by both Stark and Marshall, and with the proviso that its presentation would not stop the flow of aircraft and troop convoys to the Philippines.

"It adequately safeguarded our interests," Stimson recorded.[30] Although he had doubts that the Japanese would go along with all the details, he strongly favored any measure that would buy more time for our Pacific buildup. This was evidently the view of the war council, because the main focus of the discussion that Tuesday was not whether America should make an attempt at a temporary accommodation, but what to do if the Japanese rejected it. Stimson's notes reveal that the Far East crisis crowded out any discussion of the Atlantic situation. Roosevelt feared that if negotiations with Japan were broken off after the Friday deadline, "we were likely to be attacked perhaps as soon as next Monday for the Japanese are notorious for attacking without warning."[31]

The "difficult proposition" that would then confront the United States, as the president put it, "was how we should maneuver them into the position of firing the first shot without allowing too much danger to ourselves."[32] This was not necessarily an anticipation of United States belligerence, as some revisionist historians have misquoted it. Roosevelt was more likely expressing an appreciation of the political reality "that in

order to have the full support of the American people it was desirable to
make sure that the Japanese be the ones to do this so that there should be
no doubt in anyone's mind as to who were the aggressors."[33]

Neither Hull's nor Stimson's records indicate that there was any discussion of dropping the *modus vivendi* that day. The secretary of state's
prime concern seems to have been how to deal with the Chinese and their
supporters. They were already being bombarded by telegrams from
Chiang Kai-shek protesting the anticipated deal with Tokyo. (This was in
response to the meeting of the previous day in which the secretary of
state had patiently justified the proposed ninety-day temporary accommodation in an hour-long briefing with the Chinese, British, Dutch, and
Australian representatives in Washington.)

While the other envoys agreed to refer the plan to their governments,
only the Chinese ambassador, Dr. Hu Shih, had strongly protested the
plan. He argued that five thousand rather than twenty-five thousand
should be the limit on Japanese troops allowed to remain in southern
Indochina. Hull's conviction that this typified China's selfish attitude and
"lack of a disposition to cooperate"[34] was reinforced by the telegrams
from Chungking that flooded Washington that day. Hull was deeply af-
fronted by these "numerous hysterical cables to different cabinet officers." He regarded them as an intrusion "into a delicate situation with
no idea of what the facts are."[35]

So when the Chinese ambassador arrived for his Tuesday evening
meeting, the secretary of state's official demeanor barely concealed his
displeasure. Hull wanted to scotch rumors of an impending appeasement.
He was equally determined to set out the hard facts justifying the cabinet's decision to go ahead with the *modus vivendi* despite Chiang's "hysterical" protests. Hu Shih was firmly told, "Our proposals would relieve
the menace of Japan in Indochina to the whole south Pacific area."[36]
Hull stressed the temporary nature of the accommodation's ninety-day
time limit and said that "the limited amount of more or less inferior oil
products that we might let Japan have during that period would not, to
any appreciable extent, increase Japanese war and naval preparations."[37]

According to State Department minutes of the session, Hull warned
the Chinese ambassador, "We can cancel this proposal, but it must be
with the understanding that we are not to be charged with failure to send
our fleet into Japanese water, if by chance Japan makes a military drive
southward." Aside from this firm statement of policy, the secretary of
state gave no indication that he was even considering abandoning the
approved *modus vivendi*—and the ambassador left after promising to
send a "fuller explanation" to calm Chiang Kai-shek's fears.[38]

If ever there was a moment in a nation's history that called for a full,
calm, and reasoned application of intelligence to guide its interlocked
military and diplomatic destiny, that moment dawned in Washington on
26 November 1941.

On that fateful Wednesday an event occurred that caused the president to overrule his diplomatic and military advisers to stop negotiations with Japan dead in the water. Given the previous day's agreement of the war council on the terms for the temporary accommodation, Roosevelt's volte-face was unexplainable. It was tantamount to courting disaster.

What event prompted the president's momentous decision? The evidence has to be examined afresh in the light of newly uncovered documentation that casts grave doubts on the credibility of the versions of events that have been accepted for more than forty years.

18

Negotiations Off

O N THE AFTERNOON OF 26 November the secretary of state quashed any possibility of compromise.

The Japanese envoys had arrived in Hull's office that afternoon expecting to be handed details of an accommodation based on Roosevelt's formula of "some oil now, more later." Instead, they got only an uncompromising ten-point declaration of absolute conditions that had to be met before the United States would consider resuming trade or lifting its oil embargo.

The two ambassadors were "dumbfounded." Hull's declaration left their expectations in ruins. Shaking with frustration and pent-up anger at this apparent reversal, Nomura argued back "furiously." He said that the United States' return to hard-line principles could be interpreted only as an ultimatum in Tokyo. But the secretary of state remained "as solid as a rock."[1] And it was just the type of ultimatum that Marshall and Stark had tried to avoid being sent to Japan for at least three more months.

Dropping the *modus vivendi* might not have been an "ultimatum" in diplomatic terms, but in the circumstances it came close. Magic decrypts of Japan's diplomatic communications had already revealed a seventy-two-hour deadline for negotiations to be completed and an accord signed. So the decision to withdraw previously discussed possibilities of a compromise and merely list the issues dividing Tokyo and Washington was not exactly going to assist the diplomatic process. Hull certainly knew this because, around 9 A.M. that Wednesday he had telephoned the war department to alert Stimson that he was about "ready to kick the whole thing over."[2]

In written testimony to the 1945 congressional investigating committee Hull later claimed that it was his decision to abandon the *modus vivendi* because he had come to the conclusion that morning that it was "perfectly evident" even a temporary accommodation with Japan was "not feasible." It would cause the collapse of Chinese morale. In his memoirs Hull claimed that his decision to advise the president against a temporary accommodation had been influenced by the lukewarm attitude of the British as expressed in an overnight cable from London in which Churchill asked, "What about Chiang Kai-shek? Is he not having a very thin diet?"[3]

Churchill's sudden concern for the Chinese was, indeed, a surprise. He was never a noted supporter of the Nationalist Chinese. Recently declassified British cabinet papers indicate that he appeared content to leave negotiations with Japan to the United States. "My own feeling is that we might give Hull the latitude he asks," the prime minister had told the foreign secretary. "Our major interest is: no further encroachments and no war, as we have already enough of the latter."[4]

Confidential British foreign office assessments confirm that "the President and Mr. Hull were . . . fully conscious of what they were doing." Churchill would later try to suppress the 1943 report by Britain's last ambassador to Tokyo, who condemned the way the State Department had handled the negotiations. "I consider," Sir Robert Craigie wrote, "that had it been possible to reach a compromise with Japan in December 1941 involving the withdrawal of Japanese troops from Indochina, war with Japan would not have been inevitable."[5] His views were regarded by the foreign office as a "pretty sweeping indictment of U.S. policy," and they did not please Churchill.

"It is a very strange document and one which should be kept most scrupulously secret," Churchill noted on the report. "A more one-sided pro-Japanese account of what occurred I have hardly ever read. . . . He also writes of the breach with Japan as if it were an unmitigated disaster. . . . It was a blessing that Japan attacked the United States and thus brought America wholeheartedly into the war."[6]

Churchill's reaction is significant. But whether war could or could not have been averted *if* the *modus vivendi* had been presented is less important than the reason for Hull's abandoning it. Policy was reversed overnight. The reversal was so sweeping in its implications that the president must have had a direct hand in it. And the prime minister was quick to distance himself from Hull's suggestion that he might have influenced the fateful decision to drop the *modus vivendi*. "I understood the dangers attending the thought 'the British are trying to drag us into war,'" he wrote in his 1950 memoir. "I therefore placed the issue where it belonged, namely in the president's hands."[7]

Hull's 1945 interpretation of the events of 25 November may have been colored by his fury at Japan's attack. New documentation has come to light, however, that casts serious doubt on the hitherto accepted official version in his memoirs. Far from initiating the dropping of the *modus vivendi*, says an aide who was in his office at the time, the secretary of state was the reluctant executor of a presidential order.

During the critical days before the policy reversal, Landreth Harrison recalls, Hull was summoned to an urgent meeting with the president. He returned to the State Department, which was then housed in what is now the executive office building adjacent to the White House, "very agitated" and muttering that "those men over there do not believe me when I tell them that the Japs will attack us. You cannot give an ultimatum to a powerful and proud people and not expect them to react violently."[8]

Despite what he later recorded for posterity, Hull's reluctance to abandon the *modus vivendi* proposal was evident in a revealing memorandum. He dictated it on 27 November in response to a letter from Dr. Hornbeck, who would later give five-to-one odds against Japan's going to war. Hornbeck had written to Hull to reassure his boss that "in days to come you will look upon the *decision which was made* and the action you took yesterday with great satisfaction [emphasis added]."[9]

Hornbeck's choice of words indicates that the secretary's action had been decided for him by the president. The letter (which was later removed from the State Department records) suggested that the *modus vivendi* had only a "small chance" of success because the Japanese would have balked at what he described as a "not . . . completely honest document" that was intended to "give us more time to prepare our weapons of defense."[10]

Hull did not accept Hornbeck's oily contentions at all. "We differ so entirely, however, that I must in writing offer my dissent," the secretary of state replied. He continued:

> It is no answer to the question of whether this proposal [the *modus vivendi*] is sound and desirable at this most critical period to say that it probably would not have been accepted by Japan in any event; nor to say I would have been widely criticized in the astounding theory of selling China down the river of appeasement. If that sort of demagoguery stuff would be rung into this sort of undertaking, then there could never be a settlement between countries except at the point of a sword.[11]

It is evident that Hull was making a serious effort to reach a settlement with Tokyo until the afternoon of 26 November 1941. Why the *modus vivendi* was called off now becomes of greater historical importance than whether a temporary accommodation with Japan could have averted war.

Apart from Hull's testimony about his professed reluctance to upset Chiang Kai-shek, the generally accepted story about what caused the president's dramatic change of heart was supplied by the diary kept by the secretary of war. While it purports to be an accurate record, it is a carefully typed up reconstruction of events. According to Stimson the key event on the morning of 26 November was Stimson's telephone call to the

White House sometime around nine. This was put through *after* he had called the State Department about the protest he had received from Chiang Kai-shek, only to be told by Hull that "he had just about made up his mind to give up the whole thing in respect to a truce and simply tell the Japanese that he had no further action to propose."[12]

"A few minutes later I talked to the President over the telephone," Stimson's diary continues. "I asked him whether he had received the paper which I had sent him over last night about the Japanese having started a new expedition from Shanghai down toward Indo-china." This was the news of the Japanese convoy of "30, 40, or 50 ships" sighted "south of Formosa." According to Stimson the president was "shocked and at once took it as further evidence of bad faith on the part of the Japanese."[13] His diary paints an even more dramatic reaction: "He fairly blew up—jumped up into the air, so to speak, and said he hadn't seen it and that changed the whole situation. . . . I at once got another copy of the paper I had sent last night and sent it over to him by special messenger."[14]

The "evidence of bad faith on the part of the Japanese" that supposedly played such a large part in influencing the president's decision to drop the *modus vivendi* was an intelligence report that Stimson had found waiting for him the previous afternoon after he had returned from the White House war council meeting. According to his diary it was news that a Japanese "expedition had started" with five divisions of troops arriving at Shanghai. "There they had embarked on ships—30, 40, or 50 ships—and have been sighted south of Formosa."[15]

Stimson's chronology of events depends on Roosevelt's not having received this information on the afternoon of 25 November. Yet it is puzzling that a top-secret report containing Magic information failed to reach the White House. Even more curious is why the notoriously short-fused Hull had not "jumped up into the air" himself that same afternoon when the secretary of war had called him and "told him about it and sent copies to him and to the President of the message from G-2."[16]

The secretary of state did not appear to have considered Stimson's report to be sufficient evidence of Japanese treachery to evoke his sympathy an hour or so later when the Chinese ambassador arrived to protest the decision to proceed with the *modus vivendi*. Nor did Stimson himself consider the intelligence of such urgent importance to call the President directly. Hull made no mention of the Japanese convoy in either his regretful memorandum to Hornbeck or in his 1945 testimony explaining why the *modus vivendi* proposals were abandoned.

What makes it more unlikely that the day-old intelligence was evidence of Japanese treachery alarming enough to shock the president into reversing the course of American diplomacy was the recent discovery of the original message that was sent to the White House. Dated 25 November, it makes reference not to "30, 40, or 50 ships," but to only "ten to thirty troopships." Nor were they at sea. The actual message refers to nothing more explosive than *"a more or less normal movement"* of these transports which were *"in the Yangtse River below Shanghai* [emphasis added]."[17]

Stimson's diary states, moreover, that the convoy movement had been anticipated. Its arrival had been forewarned in a month-old Magic intercept. Enclosed with his letter was the latest British Far East intelligence estimate that predicted nothing more alarming than that "Japan will make a last effort at agreement with U.S.A." The worst scenario was that Tokyo might order troops into Thailand *if* negotiations with the United States broke down.[18]

The message did reach the White House. Attached to it is a cryptic note, dated 27 November from Major General Edwin M. "Pa" Watson, to the effect that he had found it "in the inside pocket of a very distinguished gentleman."[19] The very fact that the message now resides in the recently declassified "Safe File" of the former secretary of war must cast doubt on Stimson's official account. That the president did not know of its contents until the morning of 26 November seems most unlikely. All the indications are that the "very distinguished gentleman" could have been none other than Roosevelt himself.

Stimson's account of the "missing" report seems to have been a cover story for some more important secret information. This seems certain, because his 26 November "duplicate," which was also hand-delivered to the White House, contains an additional line: "Later reports indicate that this movement is already under way and ships have been seen south of Formosa."[20] Yet the actual G-2 intelligence report referred to the ships at anchor below Shanghai, and the penciled notes made by the secretary of war record "no new direct reports of captains at sea—since the five ships capt[ain]s last reported from Shanghai."[21]

Neither the timing nor the implicit threat of Stimson's report is such that it can have been the fateful instrument that caused the president to reverse American policy. But it is equally plain that an alarming piece of intelligence warning of imminent hostile Japanese action must have reached the White House between the evening of 25 November and nine the following morning.

"On November 26 there was received *specific evidence* of the Japanese intention to wage offensive war against Great Britain and the United States [emphasis added]," was how it was described in 1944 by the army board set up to investigate Pearl Harbor. Significantly, however, the army investigators, unable to establish this evidence more precisely, did not link it to Stimson's Shanghai convoy, which was identified as a report of "the concentration of units of the Japanese fleet at an unknown port ready for offensive action."[22]

Such imprecision did not satisfy Admiral Kimmel. At the navy court of inquiry, which sat simultaneously with the army's investigation, he finally won the right to cross-examine Admiral Stark on this critical issue.

Kimmel asked his former chief, "Do you recall whether on or about 26 November you received information from the office of naval intelligence that gave specific evidence of Japan's intention to wage offensive war against Britain and France?"[23] Although the tribunal was sitting in secret, Stark insisted that to answer this question would "involve the disclosure of information detrimental to the public interest." The court came to his rescue by ruling that he need not reveal any "state secrets."[24]

That the former chief of naval operations successfully claimed executive privilege to conceal the precise nature of the catalyst of 26 November was most revealing. It indicates that it was intelligence that did not originate from naval or army sources. Knowledge of whatever information Roosevelt received of Japan's bad faith must have been restricted to the most intimate circle of presidential advisers. If Stark and Marshall knew, they were not saying. Time and again during the 1945 congressional hearings they sidestepped questions, which like Kimmel's a year earlier sought to pinpoint what intelligence had prompted the president to abandon the *modus vivendi.*

Marshall repeatedly had "no specific recollection" of what he had talked about in the flurry of telephone calls put through the White House switchboard that Wednesday morning.[25] Stark admitted, "We were playing for time," but he was "unable to separate and clarify just what happened on the dates around the 25th."[26] Such opacity of memory is surprising. Within a few hours they were framing the warnings that put the armed forces onto a war alert, but four years later they could not recall with any precision what it was that triggered their actions.

There is a further clue that the "missing" intelligence may have reached the White House through the secret channel of the British security coordination organization headed by Sir William "Intrepid" Stephenson. Colonel James Roosevelt, the president's son, was dispatched to Stephenson's New York headquarters that afternoon with a message that resulted in a cable to Churchill in London the next day: "Negotiations off. Services expect action within two weeks." This might have been a response to some vital intelligence that was also received via the same highly confidential channel.[27]

There is another indication that news of Japan's treachery had come to the president directly from Churchill. The cover note to the American embassy in London of 26 November that supposedly enclosed Churchill's "thin diet for Chiang Kai-shek" telegram was marked "Most Secret." It apologized for the "lateness of the hour" of its delivery—around three A.M.—yet nothing it contained, at least as we now see it, can have warranted disturbing the American embassy in mid-slumber. It could have waited until London office hours next morning and still reached Washington at the start of the 26 November business day.

The prime minister's cable, furthermore, specifically refers to a message from Roosevelt "received to-night." If—as the official record would have us believe—this was the "President to Former Naval Person" (as the two familiarly addressed one another) message detailing the final *modus vivendi* proposals, this is a glaring inconsistency. Roosevelt's message had been delivered to Downing Street by the American embassy messenger that morning and the foreign office copy of the same cable was received directly from the British embassy in Washington at 1300 that afternoon.[28]

It is unlikely that Churchill, who set so much store by his direct line to Roosevelt, would have confused information from the White House that was nearly twenty-four hours old with a message that required an immediate response—even to the point of rousing American embassy staff at three in the morning. Yet if there was a second cable, as Churchill's response appears to indicate, it is not in the files.

The evidence points, therefore, to another exchange made that night between London and Washington—for which the "thin diet" cable served as a convenient cover. Especially significant, given this inconsistency in the declassified records, is that Japanese intelligence reports in the prime minister's confidential files remain "closed for 75 years." Repeated requests for their release, or even privileged access, have been repeatedly rebuffed at cabinet level "because it would not be in the national interest at this time."[29]

What can be so secret after forty years that Britain's cabinet continues to deny access to documents that could resolve an important discrepancy in the historical record? Until they are opened there is a strong presumption that the closed files in London concern some additional warning of Japanese "treachery" that reached the White House on the morning of 26 November.

Whatever the intelligence was it had to be specific, credible, and from an undisputed source—such as details of the Japanese army or navy war plans. It must be remembered that seven hundred copies of Yamamoto's operational order number 1 were circulating by the second week in November. Moreover, an even larger number of the army's plans had been sent out—including copies to the Japanese embassy in Bangkok.[30] British or Dutch agents may have gained access to a copy of Japan's war plans.

Soviet agents had tapped the highest levels of power in Tokyo. Their master spy, Richard Sorge, had been arrested a month earlier. But many members of the Communist ring in Tokyo were as yet undetected—including one who was a member of the imperial family. The Russians are also known to have penetrated Japan's Moscow and Bangkok embassies. Moreover, since the German army was poised for Hitler's "final offensive" toward Moscow, it was in Stalin's interest to ensure that Japan became embroiled in a war to prevent another attack in Siberia. It was even more important since the seven Red Army divisions that had been guarding the Nomonhan front against another Japanese attack from Manchuria had been withdrawn for the final defense of Moscow.

It is also interesting to note that Stalin betrayed a remarkable certainty about the imminence of Japan's attack on Malaya to General Sikorski when the Polish military mission visited the Kremlin on 4 December. And General Marshall, in his 1945 testimony, made an oblique reference to secret information the Russians gave exclusively to the British.[31]

It is possible, therefore, that the Russians possessed details of the Japanese war plans. The prime minister might have obtained his information about Japan's impending attack plan from a British penetration of Soviet cipher traffic. There has not been any release of information on any wartime successes in penetrating the Russian cipher code systems. Their ciphers were difficult to break because of their reliance on slow but secure one-time code pads. But if the warning of Japan's treachery had been broken out of some undercover Soviet agent's radio report it would have had the necessary credibility—and that would explain why it is "not in the national interest" for the British government to make the information available.

The British have so far refused to release *any* of their Japanese Ultra intelligence. When combined with the seventy-five-year classification of part of Churchill's records dealing with the Far East, this could mean that the missing intelligence of 26 November is connected with parallel records that also remain classified in the Australian archives. These appear to cover the disappearance of light cruiser H.M.A.S. *Sydney* a week earlier. This celebrated fighting ship, which had outgunned and sunk an Italian cruiser in the Mediterranean, sank with all hands in an encounter with the German merchant raider *Kormoran* off the coast of western Australia."[32] The *Sydney*'s loss has still to be satisfactorily explained, since the *Kormoran* also sank, but most of her crew survived in their lifeboats.

There were also reports of unidentified planes in the vicinity of the action.[33] This raises suspicion that one of the aircraft-carrying Japanese submarines might have assisted in the cruiser's destruction. Churchill would have been reluctant to make the sinking of an Australian cruiser by a Japanese submarine a *casus belli* while America's commitment to war was still in doubt. It therefore would have suited the designs of all sides—including Japan—to hush up the affair.

Information that the Japanese might have been implicated in the sinking of the Australian cruiser, by itself, would probably not have provided sufficient evidence of Tokyo's treachery to prompt Roosevelt to abandon the *modus vivendi*. But it would have been yet another indication of Japan's belligerency. It would have been an even clearer indication of Tokyo's treacherous intent and acceleration of war preparations if taken into account with intercepts of the Japanese navy's main operational cipher.

On the evening of 20 November, Tokyo's main naval radio station transmitted a preliminary war alert that notified all fleets: AT 0000 ON 21 NOVEMBER CARRY OUT SECOND PHASE OF PREPARATIONS FOR OPENING

HOSTILITIES.[34] This message *was* picked up by our navy's radio intelligence network because it has been discovered in among the quarter million recently declassified Japanese naval intercepts. No JN-25 traffic that was actually decrypted *before* war broke has yet been made available and the completely translated version, dated 26 November 1945, provides no real clue about how much of the message might have been broken out in 1941. Although Safford testified that about 10 percent of JN-25 was being read throughout that year, on 1 November the work of the cryptanalysts in OP-20-G and Station Cast had been made more difficult by the introduction of a new additive book.

We now know, however, that our navy was not alone in being able to read the Japanese naval cipher systems. The five-digit operational cipher we knew as JN-25 had also been extensively penetrated by the British and the Dutch. Britain's attack on JN-25 was concentrated at their Far East Combined Bureau (FECB), which was based in Singapore, with an outpost on Stonecutter's Island, Hong Kong. One of the tantalizingly few references to the work of the FECB in the recently published three-volume official history *British Intelligence in the Second World War* notes that "beginning with the Fleet cypher, the new cyphers began to yield" to the interservice code-breaking team in September 1939.[35] Together with the assertion that it remained possible "to keep track of her main naval movements," this suggests that the Royal Navy's successful penetration of JN-25 was equal to, or might even have exceeded, the reading of Japan's main naval operational cipher by our own cryptanalysts.

The Dutch also maintained a remarkably efficient but much smaller code-breaking operation attached to their military headquarters on Java. Under the direction of cryptanalyst Lieutenant Colonel J. A. Verkuyl and his deputy, Captain J. W. Henning, their *Kamer 14* at Bandung was, by 1941, reading the Red diplomatic machine code and the J-19 consular ciphers as well as penetrating the five-digit Japanese fleet system. While Purple intercepts could not be read, they were forwarded to the British code breakers in Singapore under the orders given General Hein ter Poorten, the Dutch commander in chief in the Far East, to cooperate fully with the British.

General ter Poorten, moreover, is on record as asserting that his *Kamer 14* code breakers provided him with intelligence reports that "showed Japanese naval concentrations near the Kuriles."[37] Unfortunately, all the Dutch decrypts were burned in the retreat from Bandung, but according to a civilian member of his intelligence staff, this information was derived from the sailing order to the Pearl Harbor strike force.[38] Since there were no Dutch submarines on patrol so far north, and Nagumo's carriers had been observing strict radio silence ever since they sailed for the secret rendezvous in Hitokappu Wan a week earlier, interception of the message would have been the only source of information that there was a Japanese fleet in the Kuriles.

All Japan's orders to the Pearl Harbor strike force were destroyed at the end of the war, but a reconstruction of events obtained from its surviving commanders in 1945 confirm that such a sailing message was indeed transmitted on 25 November. According to Captain Fuchida's recollection it was worded that "the task force will move out of Hitokappu Wan on 26 November and proceed without being detected to the evening rendezvous point (latitude 40 degrees north, longitude 170 degrees west) set for 3 December where refueling and supply will be carried out as quickly as possible."[39]

The original transmitted message would have given the final refueling point coordinates in a special designator code, so any decryption made in 1941 would not necessarily have revealed that a Japanese task force had sailed for the mid-Pacific. To the Dutch, therefore, the intercept of this message would have indicated that the most likely target of a force assembling in Hitokappu Wan was the Soviet Union. In fact, Ter Poorten's account reveals that his intelligence staff was convinced that Japan might repeat the 1904 surprise attack on Port Arthur with a raid on Vladivostok. As Captain Henning himself wrote: "That war was imminent was clear to us, but I am sure that there has never been talked [sic] directly about an attack on Pearl Harbor."[40]

What is also clear from the JN-25 file in the National Archives is that we evidently did not pick up Yamamoto's 25 November sailing message. It is therefore likely that this vital piece of intelligence could have been passed on from the Dutch only by the British, whose FECB cryptanalysts might also have intercepted it at Singapore. If they did—and the timing appears remarkably coincident—it could have been the final proof that Japan was negotiating treacherously and the evidence that prompted Roosevelt's decision to drop further negotiations with Tokyo. Taken in conjunction with the 21 November message about "opening hostilities," and the suggestion of Japan's involvement in sinking the Australian cruiser, the news that a Japanese task force had been ordered to put to sea on 26 November would have provided the president with a very clear picture of Tokyo's duplicitous intent.

That it was London, not Washington, which was evidently able to assemble these three pieces of intelligence into a war warning would have justified Churchill in sending his "urgent" message around to the American embassy in the small hours of the morning of 26 November. If Yamamoto's sailing order was relayed to the White House—even though it did not give a specific indication that Pearl Harbor was a target—it would explain why Roosevelt's closest aides were so reluctant to be specific about the nature of the "war warning" that reached Washington that same morning.

19

"Future Action Unpredictable"

T HE PRECISE NATURE of the alarming intelligence that arrived in the White House on the morning of 26 November may remain in doubt. But for the detective seeking clues, its impact on the president was obvious to early morning visitors. "He had not touched his coffee," Treasury Secretary Morgenthau noted. "He was talking to Hull and trying to eat his food at the same time, by the time he finished his conversation, his food was cold, and he didn't touch it."[1]

It was a long and agonizing morning for Roosevelt and his war council. The White House switchboard records reveal that the lines were busy as the president consulted with his closest confidants. The dilemma that confronted them was that if they abandoned the *modus vivendi* seventy-two hours before Tokyo's stated deadline for the completion of negotiations, they could force Japan into opening hostilities. Stimson favored a preemptive attack against the Japanese. But the president could not risk such an action because the isolationist opposition in Congress could successfully accuse him of engineering the war.

Yet if Japan attacked after the negotiation of a temporary settlement with Tokyo, Roosevelt would be branded as an appeaser. This would make it more difficult for the president to rally the Congress to fulfill the secret guarantees he had made to the British prime minister. To do nothing except wait for the blow to fall, while it would facilitate winning votes on Capitol Hill to fight Japanese aggression, could expose the president to a charge of dereliction of his duty as commander in chief.

The president and his advisers resolved that there really was no way out of the dilemma. They had to abandon the *modus vivendi* and accept "letting the Japanese fire the first shot," as Stimson put it. To avoid the issue of dereliction if the American bases in the Philippines were attacked, unprecedented steps were necessary to cover up the nature and extent of the warning received by the White House. The charade over the secretary of war's "missing" report, and Stark's and Marshall's inability to recall what they discussed during their busy exchange of telephone calls that morning, were all part of this camouflage operation.[2] The necessity for concealing *any* clue that the White House received any specific intelligence about Japan's intention to go to war was to be intensified by the political aftermath of Pearl Harbor, which overshadowed the disaster that also befell MacArthur in the Philippines.

The message establishing Japan's Friday deadline had threatened that "things are automatically going to happen." So on that Wednesday morning our military leadership had to face a situation in which the Japanese had called their bluff on the Anglo-American plans of deterrence. They were now trapped. Like a chess player who sees no escape from checkmate, they could only hope to gain time. Even if Japan's attack could not be postponed until the end of December, as they had initially calculated, even a delay of a week or two would ensure that the troop convoys steaming across the Pacific, and the B-17 bombers on the west coast, could reach the Philippines before the blow fell.

The prospect of war within a few days galvanized the top echelons of the war and navy departments that morning. At ten-thirty an emergency conference was held in Marshall's office to hear him warn that the president and secretary of state believed that upon the termination of the talks with the Japanese envoys, Tokyo "will soon cut loose" with "an assault on the Philippines."[3] Marshall's principal concern was what instructions should be issued to cover the emergency caused by the breakdown in negotiations, which might not bring an immediate declaration of war. "We know a great deal that the Japanese are not aware we know," Marshall announced, adding significantly "and *we are familiar with their plans to a certain extent* [emphasis added]."[4]

Marshall decided that Tokyo should be warned as soon as possible that if Japanese troops proceeded into Thailand, to the west of a demarcation line 100 degrees east or 10 degrees south, our vital interests would be "imperiled." But this required that MacArthur had to be given a "war warning" on which he could act without precipitating hostile moves that would invite a Japanese attack before reinforcements reached the Philippines.

It was agreed that "prior to a state of war" that MacArthur was to be "directed," not merely "desired," to carry out orders "to attack threatening convoys."[5] He was told to begin the reconnaissance flights over Japanese bases in Formosa, even at the risk of provoking a shooting match. The navy was to be asked to use its two Pacific fleet carriers to ferry pursuit planes from Hawaii to Wake and Midway so that the upcoming flight of forty-eight B-17 bombers could be assured of adequate fighter protection.

After agreement on the need for the war warning, the next priority item was the plan to have the navy rush extra fighters to Wake and Midway. This was discussed at the meeting of the Joint Board that the army chief of staff chaired an hour later, just before he took a plane to observe army maneuvers in South Carolina. It was also agreed that in view of the worsening situation, and recent Japanese flights over our island outposts in the western Pacific, a full-scale aerial reconnaissance must be made of Japan's bases in the mandates. General Arnold agreed to provide two high-flying B-24 bombers to photograph Jaluit and Truk. When the meeting broke up shortly before midday, Stark radioed to Admiral Kimmel, informing him of the impending photoreconnaissance mission and also directing him to arrange for his two carriers to transport the twenty-five planes and ground crews to Wake and Midway "as soon as possible."[6]

That Stark, as well as Marshall, agreed to reduce the fighter strength at Pearl Harbor by half, and to run the risk that "there will be nothing left at Hawaii until replacements arrive,"[7] was in itself evidence that whatever warning of Japan's war moves had been received in Washington, it contained no hint of an attack on Pearl Harbor. There was, however, every indication that some specific warning had been received of an impending attack on the Philippines.

Roosevelt himself dispatched a cabled alert that afternoon to his old friend Francis Sayre, our commissioner in Manila. Admiral Hart certainly took Sayre's alert to be a war warning because, as he noted in his diary, its source was "straight from the horse's mouth."[8] The Asiatic Fleet commander had no doubt about the urgency of the looming danger. A CNO dispatch sent out the same afternoon directed him to begin unrestricted submarine warfare as soon as "formal war eventuates."[9] He was also instructed to begin consultations with British and Dutch liaison officers to coordinate joint operating procedures because the "situation will be far more complex *if hostilities ensue without a formal declaration of war* [emphasis added]."[10]

While this message was another indication of the extent of prearranged Anglo-American military cooperation, it was also a telling sign that the focus of Washington's strategic priorities in the Pacific was not Hawaii. Almost twenty-four hours slipped by and it was well into 27 November before Pearl Harbor received its alert that relations between the United States and Japan were sliding toward a rupture.

According to Stimson's diary, that Thursday began "first thing in the morning" with his phone call to the secretary of state. Hull told him "he had broken the whole thing off," and that he had "washed my hands of it and it is now in the hands of you and Knox—the Army and Navy."[11] The secretary of the navy and the chief of naval operations then hurried over to the war department for consultations with Stimson and General Gerow, who was standing in for Marshall while he was away on maneuvers. They agreed with Stark's proposed draft of a joint army-navy memorandum detailing the reinforcements currently on their way to MacArthur. The memo urged the president that "the most essential thing now, from the United States viewpoint, is to gain time."[12] For the second time that month Roosevelt was to be advised against giving an ultimatum to Japan "prior to the completion of the Philippine reinforcement," and that "military counter-action be considered" only if Japan attacked.[13]

The secretary of war was sympathetic to the memo, but "didn't want it at any cost of humility on the part of the United States or of re-opening the thing which would show a weakness on our part."[14] The more immediate priority was sending "the final alert" to the Pacific commands.

The president telephoned his approval. The war warnings were drafted with General MacArthur and Admiral Hart as their prime recipients. Stimson believed that the Philippines had been put on "quasi alert" the day before, so now all that was necessary was to issue instructions that they be "on the *qui vive* for any attack."[15] The army warning incorporated the latest State Department position subject to the president's constraint that it must be the Japanese who fired the first shot. However, the wording of the army alert, which was sent out late that afternoon, cushioned its urgency and impact.

"Negotiations with Japan appear to be terminated," it began, making no mention of war, leaving open the possibility—albeit a slender one— that "the Japanese Government might come back and offer to continue." It specified no likely targets of attack, merely stating that "Japanese future action unpredictable but hostile action possible at any moment." So while MacArthur and Short were ordered to initiate "reconnaissance and other measures," they were "not repeat not to alarm civil population or disclose intent." The message repeated, no fewer than three times, that Japan had "to commit the first overt act," before "offensive action" was undertaken."[16]

General Short therefore interpreted the dispatch, not as a full-blown war warning, but an alert against Japanese sabotage on Hawaii. It was, according to his testimony, "no more than saying that Japan was going to attack some place."[17]

Stronger terms were favored by the navy department after Stark "pondered almost an entire forenoon" over its wording. To the CNO staff Japanese aggression was "expected" rather than "a possibility," and so they decided on "language which we thought was strong enough to indicate to them that Japan was going to strike."[18]

Admiral Turner, as chief of war plans, was given primary responsibility for drafting the dispatch. Never a man to chop phrases too finely, he put the phrase "war warning" up front "to express the strong conviction on the part of the department that war was surely coming."[19] Furthermore, he was evidently so certain where the first blows would fall that he listed targets on the other side of the Pacific. While this impressed on the Asiatic Fleet commander the immediacy of the danger, it softened the warning's impact for us at Pacific Fleet headquarters, four thousand miles from the scene of the proposed attack.

While minds in Washington that evening were struggling to make the English language convey the complex nuances of diplomatic and military intelligence, the Japanese were having their own communications difficulties. Yet another example of the urgency gripping Tokyo was the foreign ministry's resorting to the transpacific telephone lines to try to clarify the situation. A clumsy group of code words was employed in which the secretary of state became Miss Umeko, the president Miss Kimiko, and the negotiations "matrimonial questions." Kurusu reported that his meeting that afternoon with Miss Kimiko "wasn't much different from what Miss Umeko said yesterday, "and that the 'southward matter' was 'the monkey wrench.'"[20]

American monitoring of this incongruous conversation, during which Ambassador Kurusu broke into laughter at its inanity, yielded one deadly accurate piece of intelligence. Kurusu was told several times that in "the matter pertaining to arranging a marriage—'don't break them off.'"[21] This should have alerted Washington that the Japanese government had ordered its envoys to keep up the pretense of diplomatic negotiation as a cover for its preliminary war moves.

While it was evident to the intelligence analysts in the navy department, as it was to us at Hypo, that Japanese invasion and support forces were preparing for a southward advance, there had still been no hint in any of the intercepted communications about the carrier force heading toward Hawaii.

That evening, some eight hundred miles from Japan, out in the northern Pacific, the ships of Admiral Nagumo's *Kido Butai* (literally Mobile Force but more accurately Striking force) were rolling and pitching their way eastward. Despite the rising heavy seas the *Kido Butai*'s oil-hungry destroyers and four carriers had successfully completed their first scheduled refueling operation.

"A good beginning," Commander Tomatsu Oishi noted in his diary. Lookouts had been increased after the Kwajalein radio relayed a report from cruiser *Katori* that an American light cruiser, escorting five transports, had been spotted east of Saipan.[22] This was *Boise* shepherding a convoy of troop reinforcements toward the Philippines—but her captain did not make a sighting report of the Japanese ships until his force reached Manila a week later, on 4 December.

Tokyo naval radio center was also keeping Nagumo posted about the rapidly deteriorating state of diplomatic negotiations. "The striking force hopes the political situation continues until the 8th–9th," staff officer Commander Kikuichi Fujita on heavy cruiser *Toné* confided to his diary. "The activity of the diplomats must not cease because it will cause a relaxation of American vigilance."[23]

Like everyone on board the *Kido Butai,* Fujita appreciated that secrecy and air power were the twin factors on which their do-or-die mission depended. So far both vital elements were intact.

The highly trained First Air Fleet in the six carriers under Nagumo's command counted on their two-to-one superiority in this category to overwhelm the Pacific Fleet, in or out of Pearl Harbor. But if it came to an old-fashioned slugfest, the Japanese would lose their advantage over our carriers. Outgunned by our sixteen-inch shells, against their fourteen-inch projectiles, Nagumo's two escorting battleships, *Hiei* and *Kirishima,* would have only their superior speed to save them from the four-to-one superiority of the Pacific Fleet's battle line. Despite their better torpedoes and speed advantage, his two cruisers and nine destroyers would be outgunned by Kimmel's eighteen cruisers and twenty-nine destroyers.

The *Kido Butai* had to catch the Pacific Fleet in Pearl Harbor. Thus any premature discovery during the first ten days of the mission meant Nagumo would have to abort the mission. He had to count on stealth and surprise. Three large submarines, each with a floatplane in a waterproof hangar, scouted two hundred miles ahead of the striking force, which was restricted to less than fourteen knots speed so that its seven accompanying oilers could keep up. So vital was the preservation of secrecy that Nagumo had given orders that the key of every radio transmitter was to be "sealed or removed" to prevent any accidental radio transmission that might alert enemy listening stations to their approach.[24]

After sailing from Saeki Bay nine days earlier, the *Kido Butai* had had no radio contact, other than listening in on the three shortwave bands and single ultralong wavelength of the number 1 station of the Tokyo signals unit.[25] These were the invisible threads by which the striking force could still be reined back—if a last-minute agreement on the *modus vivendi* was reached with the United States. It was also the link by which Nagumo would be ordered into the final, unstoppable charge to attack Pearl Harbor.

As cruiser *Toné* heaved her long fo'c'sle in and out of crashing gray seas, staff officer Fujita speculated on the odds against the momentous mission of which he was a small part:

> I think this sortie is going to be like going into the tiger's lair to get her cubs. We cannot expect success unless the attack is a total surprise and the enemy is unprepared. It is most important therefore not to encounter any vessel on the trip, either a warship or merchantman of any other nation. That is why a great deal of attention has been paid to the selection of our fleet formation. Still we cannot afford the risk of a chance encounter. The only thing we can do is to pray for heaven's help to prevent this.[26]

Heaven did not answer Fujita's prayers. As it turned out, it was Soviet self-interest rather than divine intervention that let the Japanese striking force reach its target without being detected.

20

"Going to Be in a Fight"

T HE SUN WAS DIPPING into the Waianae Hills beyond Pearl Harbor's west loch late in the afternoon of 27 November. That Thursday had been a busy one of coming and going for briefings at the submarine base headquarters of the Pacific Fleet. The CNO dispatch that had arrived overnight brought about almost continuous conferences. In addition to his own staff, Admiral Kimmel met with General Short and his air officers to make arrangements to provide additional fighter cover at Wake and Midway islands to ensure the safe arrival of the B-17s in the Philippines.

Washington's instruction to transfer up to half of Hawaii's P-40 pursuit planes to Wake and Midway was taken by Kimmel as a clear sign that the army and navy staffs "did not consider hostile action on Pearl Harbor imminent or probable."[1] Short insisted on retaining control of all army aircraft, so it was decided to substitute two-Oahu-based marine squadrons so that Kimmel could retain undivided command of the forces garrisoning the outlying islands.

Admiral Halsey's *Lexington* task force was designated to ferry the first mission to Midway. He left the all-day session at 1800 hours, feeling, in his own words, "that we were going to be in a fight." To keep up the appearances of a routine operation, Halsey would sortie with three of the battleships. The slow, old battlewagons would then be detached at the first opportunity. He assured his academy classmate Kimmel, "If I have to run I don't want anything to interfere with my running."[2]

Shortly after Halsey left the headquarters building, I learned that a top-secret and urgent dispatch had just come in. I at once went into the communications office down the corridor and was shown the tape copy of a war warning. As I scanned the smudged tape spewing out of the decoding machine that was reserved for our most secret communications, I was instantly galvanized by the message:

This dispatch is to be considered a war warning. Negotiations with Japan looking toward stabilization of conditions in the Pacific have ceased and an aggressive move by Japan is expected within the next few days. The number and equipment of Japanese troops and the organization of naval task forces indicate an amphibious expedition against either the Philippines Thai or Kra peninsula or possibly Borneo. Execute an appropriate defensive deployment preparatory to carrying out tasks assigned in WPL 46. Inform District and Army authorities. A similar warning is being sent by War Department. Spenavo [Special Naval Observer in London] inform British. Continental districts Guam, Samoa directed to take appropriate measures against sabotage.[3]

When I read "This dispatch is . . . a war warning," it gave me a jolt; I had never seen such a message before. It struck me that there was no mention of Guam as a target this time. Someone else saw this too, and commented, "They probably figured Guam was going to fall anyway, so it wasn't worthwhile putting it in." There was barely time to reread the dispatch, let alone formulate my thoughts about its full implications, before Admiral Kimmel sent for me.

My first reaction to the warning was that it agreed precisely with my own estimates. I believed that the Japanese would continue their push southward and I was apprehensive that they would not risk leaving our Philippine forces on their flank. This was how I summarized the situation to Admiral Kimmel. Our initial discussion was brief, because he wanted the message paraphrased and delivered immediately to General Short.

Recasting the words of top-secret communications was standard procedure to protect the security of our ciphers. It took three attempts before the communications officer and I were satisfied that we had the meaning accurately conveyed. By this time the admiral was in conference and his office door was closed, a do-not-disturb signal that all his staff had learned to respect.

When the door finally opened, I entered and found him deep in conversation with half a dozen of his senior staff. While he interrupted his discussion to satisfy himself that my version of the war warning conveyed the urgency of the original tape, Admiral Bloch's chief of staff arrived. General Short had insisted that no copies were to be made of the army's war warning, which had arrived an hour and a half earlier, and Captain John Bayliss Earle had hand-carried the original over from the Fourteenth Naval District headquarters in Honolulu.

"This is the same dispatch in substance that we have just received," Kimmel announced as he passed it around to his staff for comment. We immediately noted that it was not so strongly worded as the navy's, because of its concluding instruction: "Undertake no offensive action until Japan has committed an overt act. Be prepared to carry out tasks assigned in WPL 46, so far as they apply to Japan in case hostilities occur."[4] After some discussion about the similarity and differences in the two dispatches, Kimmel returned my paraphrase of the navy's warning and ordered, "Get this to General Short right away."[5]

As I left the office, I chatted with Lieutenant Harold J. Burr, naval liaison officer at Fort Shafter, who had accompanied Captain Earle. At their suggestion I gave Captain Earle the paraphrase so that he could deliver it to the general on his return. It seemed like a good idea at the time. But it displeased Kimmel when he later found that I had not carried out his orders precisely. There was never any doubt in my mind that General Short had received it, however, because on my way home late that evening I encountered convoys of trucks and troops on the move.

I assumed that the army was going to a full condition of readiness, and that Short's troops were going to man antiaircraft batteries and set up mobile weapons around Pearl Harbor and other strategic points. Later I found out that General Short had only ordered a number 1 alert. Unlike the navy, which starts with number 3 and builds to a full number 1 alert, the army's number 1 was their lowest state of readiness and that was a precautionary deployment against sabotage.

"The danger of sabotage was paramount in my mind, and seemed to me the chief danger which the war department feared," was how Short himself later justified his lack of preparedness against enemy air attack or landings.[6] The same signal had been addressed to all army commanders; however, Short's emergency staff meeting that afternoon had concluded that warning of "hostile action" as it applied locally on Oahu could only refer to the threat of "internal disorder."[7] The morning had been spent arranging with the navy—at the army chief of staff's direction—the transfer of aircraft from Hawaii to the outlying islands. This in itself was taken as confirmation that Hawaii was not in any immediate danger, nor had it been listed as a possible target for attack. In the absence of any other intelligence to the contrary, General Marshall himself was later to admit, "We were reasonable in our assumption" in the circumstances.[8]

It was a decision reinforced that evening by another dispatch, specifically addressed to Hawaiian headquarters, reminding Short that "subversive activities may be expected." This second alert, for the information of "commanding general and chief of staff only," added further support to Short's decision with its cautionary injunction "not to alarm civil population."[9] Washington was evidently more concerned about possible charges from Tokyo that Japanese residents of the islands were subjected to undue harassment than defending Pearl Harbor against external attack. So every effort was made to restrict the antisabotage measures to our bases and military airfields. Consequently, planes were grouped together to make them easier to guard with minimum troop deployments, and the ammunition for antiaircraft batteries was kept locked in the munition bunkers.

The charges that General Short "must have known" the Japanese would attack without warning, which were leveled against him by Stimson four years later, were grossly unfair. Unfounded too was the statement by the former secretary of war that the Hawaiian command "betrayed a misconception of his real duty that went beyond belief."[10] Indeed, one of the measures that Short took was to order the newly arrived mobile army radar units to begin operations an hour before dawn and continue until 7 A.M.

Stimson's bald assertions appear to have been part of the smokescreen of blame thrown up by Washington to absolve itself of any responsibility. There was never a hint in any intelligence received by the local command of any Japanese threat to Hawaii. Our air defenses were stripped on orders from the army chief himself. Of the twelve B-17s on the island, only six could be kept in the air by cannibalizing the others for spare parts. Hickam Field had been reduced to a refueling station for the long-range bombers on their way to the Philippines. And General Martin's aircrews had been committed, not to long-range defensive patrols, but to pilot training so as to enable the Flying Fortresses to navigate the long ocean-hops to the Philippines.

The secretary of war's bigoted condemnation of a field commander who fulfilled his duty as directed overlooked the war department's own failure to intervene *if* it really had considered Short's reported anti-sabotage efforts an inadequate response to the 27 November alert. General MacArthur had likewise informed Washington that his air reconnaissance had been "intensified and extended."[11] And since General Marshall had seen Short's dispatch confirming that he had been "alerted to prevent sabotage,"[12] Short could presume that Marshall agreed with his state of alert. It was only with the advantage of hindsight in December 1945 that Marshall admitted reproachfully, "That was my opportunity to intervene and I did not do it."[13]

Admiral Stark, even if he had felt differently from Marshall, had no opportunity to intervene. But Stark's director of war plans "did not even consider it necessary" to issue a further warning. Turner was to insist that there was no "possibility of misinterpreting that sentence." But the sentences following "This dispatch is to be considered a war warning" did not rule out further negotiations, and precautionary measures were urged "in order not to complicate an already tense situation."[14]

"We expected all military services and outlying detachments to act in every way as if we were actually at war, except making attacks on the enemy, if encountered, or initiating movements against enemy forces," was how Turner characterized the anticipated response to his so-called war warning.[15] But he appears to have ignored the cardinal rule: Warnings to a field commander are always read and acted upon within the local context.

In sizing up the situation that confronted us at Pearl Harbor in the twenty-four hours following the receipt of the 27 November navy and army war alerts, Admiral Kimmel had neither the advantage of Turner's ex post facto second-guessing nor the full context of the diplomatic intelligence in which the chief of war plans framed his warning.

Only in one respect was the army warning, which was formally relayed by CNO on the twenty-eighth, more specific: It instructed the Hawaiian commanders to "be prepared to carry out tasks assigned in WPL 46."[16] Turner later claimed that his use of the phrase "defensive deployment" should have been interpreted by Kimmel as requiring him to immediately order the Pacific Fleet to carry out its preliminary war plan task of protecting our sea communications "by escorting, covering, and patrolling as required by circumstances and by destroying enemy raiding forces."[17] But Turner's supposedly all-embracing warning omitted any reference to the threats that might be developing within range of the Hawaiian Islands.

The Philippines, Thailand, and the Isthmus of Kra had indeed been identified as "probable" Japanese objectives, with Borneo as the only other "possible" target. All these locations were five thousand miles from Hawaii, which was not even mentioned. The supposedly comprehensive war warning did not even pick up the phrase "an aggressive movement *in any direction* [emphasis added],"[18] which had been used in the alert sent out by Washington three days earlier. Since we received no better information, we assumed that the dropping of this general threat meant that new information must have enabled Washington to be more specific about the Japanese objectives.

With justification Kimmel was later to complain, "The phrase 'war warning' cannot be made the catch-all for all the contingencies hindsight may suggest."[19] Given the intelligence picture, as we had been able to piece it together in the context of the alerts we had received, there was nothing illogical or derelict about his conclusion that "an air attack on Pearl Harbor or anything other than a surprise submarine attack was most improbable."[20]

While our overall picture indicated to Kimmel that "war with Japan was closer than it had been before," there was nothing we had received from Washington or any other source to suggest that it was looming over the Hawaiian horizon.[21] Had we been receiving the Magic intercepts, or even been told about either of the two negotiating deadlines, the dropping of the *modus vivendi,* and the secretary of state's trenchant ten points delivered to the Japanese the day before, the realization that the rupture of diplomatic relations was imminent would have been inescapable.

It was also the third occasion in four months that Washington had flashed an alert to the Pacific Fleet. So, in weighing whether the war would break out in a matter of hours, days—or would again be averted by more negotiations—Kimmel took account of the most recent dispatch from Stark and its enclosed memorandum urging that the president avoid war and that "no ultimatum be delivered to Japan."[22]

Not until the next day, 28 November, with the arrival of our first piece of Magic diplomatic intelligence in four months, did we have any hint that our relations with Japan might be hovering really close to the brink of war. The so-called wind code message on shortwave Tokyo radio was not intended by Tokyo as a war warning per se. Such a message would be an emergency alert to Japan's embassies that there was a "danger of cutting international relations" between Japan and whatever country was specified by a sequence of code words:

1. HIGASHI NO KAZE AME (east wind rain) would mean Japan-US relations in danger
2. KITA NO KAZE KUMORI (north wind cloudy) Japan-USSR relations in danger
3. NISHI NO KAZE HARE (west wind clear), Japan-British relations in danger.[23]

A similar message to "destroy all codes and papers" when "diplomatic relations are becoming dangerous"—also using the same country designators, *Higashi, Kita,* and *Nishi*—was also sent out by Tokyo at the same time.[24] But the importance of this was overshadowed in Washington by the wind code message, because it was decrypted within hours of the expiration of Tokyo's 29 November deadline. That juxtaposition gave many senior staff officers the notion that the receipt of an "east wind rain" broadcast would be tantamount to Japan's declaring war on the United States.

While the crisis was deemed serious enough to warrant sending us some Magic information, it was unfortunate that the opportunity was missed by Washington to provide us with a more informative diplomatic intelligence. Had they done so, it might have prompted us to take more heed of a signal received from British intelligence headquarters at Singapore that "Japan will commence military operations on 1 December against the Kra Isthmus."[25]

This message, which I rated as less than reliable, might have seemed more important had we been given the intelligence decrypted in Washington from Tokyo's message praising the "superhuman efforts" of the two ambassadors. It went on to say that the "humiliating proposal" delivered by Hull was "quite unexpected and regrettable" and that in "two or three days" it was "inevitable" that *"negotiations will be 'de facto' ruptured* [emphasis added]." Nomura and Kurusu were, however, instructed to continue placatory overtures so as not to "give the impression that the negotiations are broken off."[26]

The importance of this message cannot have been lost on Roosevelt and his advisers. They had gathered for their morning session around the presidential bedside to review the "dangerous possibilities." Roosevelt had to decide among three courses of action: "to do nothing; to make something in the nature of an ultimatum again, stating a point beyond which we would fight; third, to fight at once."[27] Stimson was all for fighting, but Marshall and Stark wanted "no immediate action which would lead to immediate hostilities." Their appeal for more time to complete the Philippine buildup had already been overtaken by events.

At noon a more formal meeting of the war council agreed that "if the Japanese get into the isthmus of Kra, the British would fight" and the United States was "committed to join them." The "whole chain of disastrous events," Stimson recorded, would be set in motion if the Japanese expeditionary force, reportedly assembling for a southward advance, "was allowed to round the southern point of Indochina."[28] Hull was of the opinion that the Japanese "might make the element of surprise a central point in their strategy and also might attack at various points simultaneously with a view to demoralizing efforts of defense and coordination."[29] But his point was apparently not taken to heart by the navy or army chiefs. They were evidently still preoccupied with gaining time to reinforce the Philippines. But it was agreed that if the Japanese naval forces advanced past "a certain point, we should have to fight."[30] No ultimatum defining that boundary was to be sent yet to Tokyo.

Halfway around the world a Japanese task force was steaming toward a demarcation line that would have figured prominently in any accounting of American interests: the 180-degree line of longitude that divided the eastern from the western hemisphere.

"Tense since yesterday," staff officer Fujita noted in his diary. "Today we heard from the naval general staff that they had now lost hope for a resolution of U.S.-Japanese relations after America suddenly changed its attitude on 26th and became unyielding."[31]

The ships of the *Kido Butai* were clawing through thick fog. But the greatly increased collision hazard was not the only worry that that day brought Nagumo. Tokyo had radioed "concern that we might run into a Soviet merchant ship bound from San Francisco to the Far East."[32]

This intriguing reference in the official Japanese war history—*Hawai Sakusen* (*Hawaii Operation*) *Senshi Sosho* (*War History Series*) Vol. 10— is confirmed by a firsthand wartime account. But it has been overlooked by every American historian. Investigation of the War Shipping Administration records reveals that the freighter was almost certainly *Uritsky*, which had sailed under the Golden Gate days earlier with a cargo of vital military lend-lease supplies. The steamer's course for Vladivostok would intersect with the *Kido Butai*'s intended track somewhere to the northwest of the Hawaiian Islands.[33]

Just how naval headquarters in Tokyo could have known the precise course of a Russian merchantman raises many intriguing questions. For example, why was Nagumo not ordered to sink the freighter on sight? He had been ordered to dispose of all other vessels. Or, did the information about the *Uritsky*'s course and destination come from the Japanese consulate in San Francisco? Since the route to Vladivostok passed close to waters patrolled by Japan, Tokyo might have been advised, as a precaution and courtesy, of the Russian freighter's imminent passage across the north Pacific. But there is no record in the intercepts of the San Francisco consul's relaying such information. Significantly, however, within hours of the alert's being flashed out to the *Kido Butai,* Tokyo cabled the San Francisco consulate to make "full reports" on the departure of "all" ships that were leaving the west coast and heading into the Pacific.[34] This suggests that Japan's naval staff received news of *Uritsky* from another source and that this prompted the message to San Francisco.

How the Japanese found out about a Russian freighter plowing a lonely course across the vast emptiness of the north Pacific, so that they knew its course and speed precisely enough to predict that it would collide with the *Kido Butai,* becomes an issue of extraordinary significance. It seems highly unlikely that an officer of the naval staff in Tokyo could simply have stumbled across *Uritsky*'s sailing orders. This raises the probability that *Uritsky*'s course must have been given to the Japanese by the Russians themselves. This deduction then leads to the logical assumption that Soviet intelligence *knew* precise details of the course to be taken across the northern Pacific by Nagumo's striking force!

If they did, it would have been logical for Stalin to order that Tokyo be told about the *Uritsky.* He needed to avoid provoking an incident at a critical juncture for both countries. He also had to ensure that the freighter's lend-lease cargo of tanks and planes reached Vladivostok safely so they could be shipped via the trans-Siberian railroad in time for the last-ditch stand to save Moscow.

If the Russians had succeeded in penetrating Japan's tight naval security, then it might well have been Stalin himself—or intercepted Soviet signal traffic—that had been the source of the critical intelligence that had jolted the White House early on the morning of 26 November.

21

"Self-deception"

A T 0800 ON FRIDAY, 28 November, carrier *Enterprise* led the procession of battleships, cruisers, and destroyers that was Task Force 8 into the narrow channel leading out of Pearl Harbor. Once they were in open seas, Admiral Halsey split off the three battlewagons and set course for Wake with three heavy cruisers and nine destroyers. "The *Enterprise* is now operating under war conditions," her captain ordered the carrier's crew. At Halsey's instruction all torpedoes and bombs were armed. All ships in the task force were directed "to regard any submarine seen as hostile and sink it . . . [and] shoot down any plane seen in the air . . . not known to be one of our own."[1]

Admiral Kimmel anticipated that the main danger was attack from Japanese submarines. That morning he issued a fleet directive calling for extreme vigilance. Our warships were to "depth bomb all contacts expected to be hostile in the fleet operating areas."[2] The factor that carried the most weight in influencing his decisions was the directive received from Washington to use his two carriers to ferry fighter reinforcements to the outlying islands. Kimmel could only regard this as a sure indication that "no attack on Pearl Harbor could be expected in the immediate future." Just getting to Wake and back would take a week.

Since speed was essential in this mission, Halsey had elected not to take along the plodding battlewagons. Without carrier air cover as protection against torpedo plane attack, battle force commander Vice Admiral William Pye agreed, it made no tactical sense to keep his battleships at sea. In Pearl Harbor the shallow water, based on studies prepared by the naval staff, was thought to render the danger of such attack negligible. At their berths, the battleships were also expected to be protected by army fighters and antiaircraft batteries.[3]

Kimmel's principal concern was readying the fleet to carry out the assigned mission under War Plan 46, to "prepare to capture and establish

222

control over Caroline and Marshall islands area, and to establish an advanced fleet base in Truk."[4] For months I had been gathering all the information I could on Japanese forces and bases in the mandates. The admiral periodically incorporated my intelligence reports into his daily memorandum: "Steps to Be Taken in Case of American-Japanese War Within the Next 24 Hours."[5]

If a Japanese attack was pointed at Hawaii, then strategic logic and our best intelligence suggested that it would develop from the deep-water anchorage of one of the large atolls in the mandates. Jaluit was slightly more than two thousand miles southwest of Pearl Harbor. We knew from analysis of Japan's radio traffic that a powerful force of submarines was based there, and there were indications that "at least one carrier division unit" was heading toward the Marshalls.[6]

Rochefort and I badly needed confirmation of our suspicions that a powerful Japanese task force was assembling within striking distance of Pearl Harbor. Kimmel was therefore pleased to receive that Friday morning the memorandum describing my conference with General Martin on the army's intended high-level reconnaissance by specially modified B-24 bombers. We had agreed that they were to fly over the Marshalls from Wake on missions that would also cover Truk and Ponape.[7]

Photoreconnaissance was expected to settle the difference between the Hypo and Cast traffic analyses about whether one or two Japanese carriers were already in, or heading toward, the Marshalls. But until the dispute had been resolved, Kimmel had to make his plans on the assumption that the main danger to Pearl Harbor in the event of war was an enemy task force steaming out to make a surprise attack from the southwest. That was the primary focus of our concern. Kimmel's orders to dispatch the carriers to Wake and Midway was seen as fitting neatly in with the need to step up the surveillance of the southwestern approaches to Oahu as well as reinforcing the outlying islands.

"It permitted a broad area to be scouted for signs of enemy movement along the path of advance of these task forces to the islands and their return," Kimmel later explained. "In addition they would be in an excellent position to intercept any enemy force which might be on the move."[8] Although Kimmel was to be severely censured for failing to carry out the basic war plan, the demands of WPL 46 were precisely met by his decision to send Admiral Halsey's Task Force 8 to Wake, and a week later *Lexington* and Task Force 12 (commanded by Rear Admiral John H. Newton) to Midway, while Vice Admiral Wilson Brown's cruisers of Task Force 5 headed south to conduct landing exercises at Johnston Island, which lay a third of the way between Hawaii and the easternmost of the Marshalls.

Each task force was directed to send out air patrols night and morning to scour the southern and western Pacific approaches to Oahu. To increase our surveillance of these waters, which intelligence estimates showed to be the most logical direction for a Japanese threat to Pearl Harbor, Kimmel also ordered them swept by two squadrons of PBY-5 patrol planes. On Thursday the unit based on Midway had departed for Wake to conduct a 525-mile-wide sweep search en route. On Sunday the patrol wing scheduled to replace them took off from their Ford Island base and headed south to Johnston Island to refuel before heading northwest to Midway, whence they conducted daily 500-mile deep-ocean reconnaissance.

In the week before 7 December the navy aircraft scoured over two million square miles of the Pacific without spotting a single Japanese warship. Yet Kimmel was still censured for failing to conduct adequate longrange air patrols.

Only round-the-compass, deep-ocean reconnaissance, as agreed to in April 1941 in the Martin-Bellinger report, could have guaranteed Pearl Harbor adequate advance warning of the approach of hostile forces. But eight months had elapsed since the plan had been submitted to Washington, and neither Admiral Bellinger nor General Martin had enough aircraft to collectively operate anything approaching a full 360-degree air patrol on a daily basis.

Only 6 army B-17s were flyable. The navy had only 81 long-range PBY amphibians. Crew and plane fatigue on the punishing sixteen-hour, seven-hundred-mile forays cut by one third a patrol wing's effective strength. It would have required at least 250 PBYs to maintain a comprehensive daily surveillance. This was more than three times the number Bellinger commanded, and 54 of his 81 planes were new arrivals. Their partly trained crews had no spare parts for their twin-engine PBY-5 Catalinas.

The Cats, as the crews affectionately called their amphibians, were less feline than dragonflylike with their large wings and bulbous observation blisters. Ungraceful they were, but each could search an 8-degree wedge of ocean to a distance of over seven hundred miles. This was more than enough range to spot an approaching task force a full day before its carrier planes were within striking distance of Pearl Harbor, but with fewer than thirty planes available for continuous daily operations, only a 144-degree sector of the approaches to Oahu could be covered, leaving 60 percent of the compass unguarded.

Kimmel's dilemma was not simply which third of the approaches to cover. He had been ordered by Washington, "not once but twice," to be prepared to carry out raids on the Marshalls, for which long-range aerial reconnaissance was an essential precursor of fleet operations. He could not afford to fritter away patrol plane resources. "Had I directed their use for intensive distance searches from Oahu," Kimmel was to testify, "I faced the peril of having these planes grounded when the fleet needed them and when the war plan was executed."[9]

Wartime inquisitors and postwar historians have repeatedly condemned Kimmel for not conducting more extensive air searches. Their comments reveal little appreciation for the circumstances behind his decision to concentrate his attention mainly on the southwestern sector.

Lack of aircraft and too much geography imposed severe restraints on the Pacific Fleet's operational capabilities. Assume that Pearl Harbor is the center of a circle that represents a compass rose. Directly south of the waters where our warships exercised lay the Line Islands—Palmyra, Christmas, and Victoria—which were some fifteen hundred miles from Hawaii, the same distance that these atolls lay north of Tahiti. Some five hundred miles to the southwest of the Hawaiian chain lay Johnston Island—and fifteen hundred miles southwest of this American sandspit was the easternmost Japanese territory in the Marshall Islands. Just over two thousand miles due west of Pearl Harbor was Wake Island, a vital stepping stone to Guam and the Philippines. Fifteen hundred miles northwest of us was Midway. To the north lay the empty vastness of the northern Pacific, an area of frequent depressions that swept the storms and fogs south from the Aleutian Islands and the rocky Alaskan coastline.

Looking out from the center of the compass at Pearl Harbor it was obvious therefore that our attention would be focused to the southwest. It was the direction of the Japanese bases in the Marshall and Caroline islands. These were the obvious jumping-off points for a Japanese advance toward New Guinea and Australia. They were also a roadblock to our seaborne communications with the Philippines. So when it came to immediate threats, Kimmel had to take into account Jaluit in the eastern Marshalls. It was less than five days' hard steaming away for a fast-striking force. Given the superiority of the Japanese carrier fleet and the signs of the recent buildup in the mandates, it was clear that the Pacific Fleet's first priority was to guard against an attack from the southwest sector.

Kimmel had no precise indication of when war was going to break out, and his air commander was to testify that "any adequate search was impossible for more than a few days."[10] In consultation with his staff, Kimmel determined that the most vital areas for aerial reconnaissance were south from the Line Islands, swinging southwest toward the Marshalls and Carolines, thence westward through Wake to Midway in the northwest. Transposing the compass rose onto a clock face, this meant that while the sectors between 6 and 11 were thoroughly covered by air patrols during the next ten days, the rest were only intermittently searched. The decision to leave the 12 o'clock sector unpatrolled was a calculated risk, taken by professional naval officers acting on the best information that was available to them. Unfortunately, the Japanese either guessed our predicament or knowingly took advantage of it, because they attacked from the north—an area uncovered by aerial reconnaissance.

During the July 1940 alert Admiral Richardson had ordered deep-ocean air patrols to cover the sector from west to northwest. That was the sector from which Pearl Harbor had been successfully attacked during the 1938 fleet problem. But even if Kimmel had repeated his predecessor's action, as his critics later charged he should have, patrols would *still* have missed the Japanese striking force running down from due north.

At no time did Kimmel receive any intelligence, or hint, that there was any threat to Pearl Harbor from any direction but from the southwest. He believed that any Japanese sortie from the Marshalls that attempted an end run to the south or north would have been spotted by the patrol wings of Catalinas dispatched that weekend to Midway, Wake, and Johnston Island. Nor were the remaining forty-nine PBYs unemployed. During the next ten days, in addition to training flights, they mounted patrols to the north and northwest of Oahu as well as executing a daily dawn reconnaissance over the fleet's exercise area three hundred miles south of Pearl Harbor.

"I took account of my probable future needs and of my orders from the navy department," was how Kimmel justified his deployment. "I decided that I could not risk having no patrol plane force worthy of the name for the fleet's expected movement into the Marshalls."[11] Given the information he possessed, the demands of his war plan, the shortage of aircraft, and the geographical constraints he faced, Kimmel could not have made any other decision.

That was the conclusion of the admirals who sat from July to October 1944 as the navy court of inquiry. It was not only a judgment of his professionally qualified peers, but because the court sat in secret session it was not subject to political pressures. Their verdict was a vindication of his decision: "The omission of this reconnaissance was not due to oversight or neglect. It was the result of a military decision, reached after much deliberation and consultation with experienced officers and after weighing the information at hand and all the factors involved."[12]

Such an exoneration of the admiral who had already been publicly made the scapegoat for the Pearl Harbor disaster sat badly with then Secretary of the Navy James V. Forrestal. He suppressed the navy inquiry's report until it had been reviewed by other flag officers. Admiral King, who was then chief of naval operations, found it expedient to leave his fellow admiral in purgatory rather than expose the navy department's blunders.

The facts as we had them at Pacific Fleet headquarters in the first week of December 1941 left Kimmel no choice but to concentrate our sea and air searches to the southwestern and northwestern approaches to Oahu. Throughout that last Saturday and Sunday of peace I worked nonstop to meet the deadline set by the admiral for a comprehensive and detailed estimate of the whereabouts of every major Japanese air and surface unit for his Monday morning staff conference.

Rochefort and I spent a great deal of time comparing notes. But it was clear that despite the best efforts of his traffic analysts there were some big question marks. No further evidence of the carrier division in the mandates had been received since the 27 November communications intelligence summary. Joe was concerned, moreover, that the Japanese might be stealing a march on us. His report the next day stated that *their* radio intelligence network was "operating at full strength," and he had typed in bold capitals, "IS GETTING RESULTS."[13]

On 30 November, as I sat in my office typing up my report, because Yeoman Keene was off duty that Sunday afternoon, I shared Joe's concern that much of the day's intercepted traffic appeared to be repeats of previous transmitted messages. Some were four days old. Two vital pieces of radio intelligence that I confidently incorporated in my report later turned out to be miscalculations. One was to put *Hiei* and *Kongo* in with the southern task force off Formosa, because radio messages addressed to the two battleships appeared to link them with the Second Fleet. The other concerned carrier *Akagi*.

Rochefort's communications intelligence summary for 30 November had noted: "The only tactical circuit heard today was one with *Akagi* and several *marus*."[14] But we did not take these isolated communications as evidence that the other carrier divisions we thought were in home waters were also out because the low power of such transmissions thwarted accurate direction finding by Hypo's shaky system. The report appears anyway to have been a misidentification of call signs. Although *Akagi* and the two battleships were in fact at sea in the north Pacific, the *Kido Butai* was under orders to observe strict radio silence with transmitter switches sealed off—a fact recently reconfirmed by Admiral Genda.[15]

There was no doubt in my mind about the critical importance of the memorandum that I headed "Location of Japanese Fleet Units."[16] The evidence that most of their fleet had been concentrated into two huge task forces was an unmistakable signal that five thousand miles away across the Pacific an unstable powder keg might blow up. The alerts we had received from Washington, our own intelligence picture, and the dictates of geography indicated that the fuse that had been set led directly from the Japanese naval bases in Formosa and Hainan Island to the Isthmus of Kra, Malaya, the Dutch East Indies, and probably the Philippines. But just where the spark would be struck to ignite the explosion was still an open question.

When I reviewed the evaluation that I had worked on all weekend, I was struck by the enormous responsibility I bore for those five typewritten pages. The alarming thought had already crossed my mind that much of the report—which would determine the disposition of the Pacific Fleet in the countdown to war—was nothing more than guesswork. Inspired, perhaps, but it was guesswork nonetheless, because it was founded on analysis of naval signals whose encoded messages we could not decipher.

This was why my estimate was prefaced, "From best available information units of Orange fleet are *thought* to be located as listed below
[emphasis added]."[17]

The pattern that emerged from the dispositions of the Japanese
fleet—from those pieces that we had been able to lock into place as well
as from those that were still missing—was disturbing. This applied especially to half their carrier forces. We could locate them only in the negative sense—that we did not have any confirmation of their precise
whereabouts.

The jigsaw puzzle we had assembled at Pearl Harbor by 30 November
revealed that two main task forces had gathered under the loose command of the Second Fleet. The previous week's confirmation that had
come from Cavite's traffic analysts was that one of these forces,
spearheaded by a considerable number of submarines, was heading for
the mandates. From there they would be in position either for offensive
operations against the Pacific Fleet or to cover the flank of the main force
then concentrating for an advance toward Malaya and the Philippines.
Although the carriers had not been heard of for more than two weeks,
Station Cast agreed with the Hypo analysis that transmissions indicated
that at least one division was associated with the force in Formosan ports.
Another force was heading for the Palaus. Cavite, however, had not been
able to confirm, or discount, Rochefort's estimate that at least one auxiliary carrier was already in the mandates.

So in making my final estimate for Kimmel, I deliberately omitted
from my location sheet two Japanese carrier divisions, although I had
placed two others in the vicinity of Formosa and I put a question mark
beside the placement of the auxiliary carrier in the Marshalls. All the
Japanese warship locations in my estimate, with the exception of sightings
of transports and light cruisers and the submarines, had been based on
nothing more positive than our analysis of the enemy naval radio circuits.
Nobody knew better than Rochefort and I that intelligence derived from
traffic analysis could be inconclusive, sometimes contradictory, and very
often incomplete. Yet barring planned deception—and there was no evidence of this beyond the duplication of previous messages—we believed
that traffic analysis had given us a broadly accurate picture.

Contrary to popular myth and the assumptions of many historians,
there was no sustained deception plan put into operation by Japan. They
did not, for example, reassign carrier call signs to destroyers in the inland
sea.[18] It was only assumed that they did by a certain section of the naval
staff in Washington, which assumption was given official credence in the
navy's secret publication CSP-1494-A as part of the effort to discredit
Rochefort in the spring of 1942. *Black Magic in Communications* was
the title of this paper. And in the chapter headed "Did the Japanese
Paint Us a Picture?" it suggested that the Hypo analysts had been taken
in by radio deception.

"The Japs did not even attempt deception," was Joe's angry rejection of the charge that he had been "painted a picture." "There was plenty of deception out here, but it was all self-deception."[19] That self-deception on our part was encouraged by the increased precautions of the Japanese to protect their radio security in the first week of December by using multiple addresses and blanket coverage as well as signals that were addressed to nobody from nobody. The Japanese evidently believed that the overnight change in call signs was concealment enough. Although Rochefort was able to report that within twenty-four hours Hypo had recovered partial identification of "over 200 hundred service calls,"[20] we both knew that having to reidentify nearly twenty-thousand indicators would make positive identification of the "missing" carriers even more problematical.

When all but one of the carriers had vanished from radio traffic after they had returned from the fleet exercises after the first week of November, the logical explanation was that they had returned to port and inactive status, just as they had done for a time in October. It was not unusual for traffic to vanish on the carrier circuits when they were in harbor. Once their planes had been flown off on approach to their home ports—as we ourselves did—there would be no more of the ship-to-air communications that were the giveaway of carriers.

So when Carrier Divisions 1 and 2 air traffic and identifiers dried up in mid-November, the assumption was that they were in port replenishing for operations. As for the other carriers, transmission addressed to the Second Fleet over the previous ten days indicated that at least one other division, and probably two, was associated with the large task force assembling in Formosan waters. We had later to discover that we misidentified the big carriers of Division 3 as the small ones of Division 4. Only the weaker force was in fact participating in the southern operations, because Carrier Division 3 was actually part of the striking force. Identification of call signs from a destroyer division that formerly acted as plane guards led Rochefort to assume that "one or more of the carrier divisions were in the Mandates."[21] But the apparent lack of calls to the four other carriers, including flagship *Kaga*, became a subject of debate in Hypo.

Since the previous Friday an intense watch was being kept by Hypo's listening station to try to find the carrier frequencies. Our On the Roof Gang listeners were by now familiar with the "fists"—the characteristic use of the Morse key—of many radiomen of the Combined Fleet. But there was no traffic intercepted from flagship *Kaga*. Rochefort and I chewed over his 2 December report the next day, which stated that traffic was "at a low ebb" and there was "almost a complete lack of information on the carriers."[22]

Hypo's two traffic analysts were split. Lieutenant Huckins agreed with our conclusion that absence of carrier call signs was because they were tied up at their piers in Japan awaiting orders to sail. But Lieutenant

John A. Williams was sure something was going on.[23] Nobody had any hard evidence, and the lack of any of the other carrier call signs identified with the Second Fleet task forces encouraged the view that Carrier Divisions 1 and 2 were still in harbor at Kure. That is why they were omitted from my 1 December location sheet. But the possibility that they might be involved in the eastern task force in the mandates and ready to conduct offensive operations against Hawaii from the southwest was causing some of us to sprout gray hairs.

We agreed it was possible that the four "lost" carriers had sailed under sealed orders and were observing strict radio silence, as they had during the week they had covered the operations in Indochina that July. Radio silence alone would have been a giveaway *if* they had been identified in the other communication traffic. But when the buildup came during November, they were not addressed. The fact that they were apparently unconnected with the Second Fleet task forces and operating no radio, whether as originators or addressees, led us to the belief, erroneous as it was, that these carriers would not be participating in the forthcoming movements and were preparing for some other operation.

It would have been very different if they had been addressed in *any* one of the thousands of messages sent out from the naval general headquarters in the previous weeks. For if they had been observing radio silence and made no response, it would have been a clear sign that they were at sea. But without such indications, or reliable witnesses to their sailing, our intelligence led us to conclude throughout the next six days that half the Japanese carrier fleet was still in home waters.

While we did not know it at the time, Jack Williams was right. The "missing" Japanese carriers were at sea, observing radio silence—and *were* being addressed. It was just that we did not know what we were looking for. The overnight switch in the two-kana-hyphen-numeral designators made an already difficult task more like hunting for a needle in a haystack—but without even knowing what a needle looked like!

That evening, as the *Kido Butai* crossed the 180-degree longitude line into the western hemisphere, Admiral Nagumo, concerned that they were now within range of American air searches from the Aleutian island of Kiska, flashed a light signal to all ships. Watchkeepers were urged to maintain a "careful lookout for enemy ships including ones that might pursue us from the rear."[24]

We had no way of knowing that the Pearl Harbor attack group that had sailed from Tankan Bay five days earlier was designated as the *Kido Butai*. Since it was not making any transmissions at all, it did not provide us with any signals from which to take a direction-finder bearing, or to compare a "fist," or designator, reference; so we could not make a match with any one of the thousands of new call signs. Hypo's IBM machines and tray of punch cards had been rendered useless by the 1 December change in call signs.

The clues that might have unmasked the striking force's "SU TE 9" call sign had in fact already been intercepted in the JN-25B fleet code.[25] They had been picked up early on the morning of 17 November by our largest listening facility at Bainbridge Island off the Washington coast. This intercepted message, and another one of 24 November, relayed the latest revisions in the unit identifiers. But the fleet code was unavailable to Rochefort's team.

If Hypo had received the latest recoveries of the JN-25 additives and code book recoveries as scheduled at the beginning of November, Rochefort might have had a slim chance to get into the navy's operational cipher. But the painstakingly handwritten code sheets that he needed for this work lay sealed in the hold of a transport whose departure for Honolulu from San Diego had been delayed by three weeks.[26]

The JN-25 fleet operational code was part of the 90 percent of the Japanese naval traffic that was closed to Rochefort's code breakers. They had continued their fruitless battle concentrating on the flag officers cipher, as Washington had ordered, in addition to the low-grade administrative and weather traffic.

Meanwhile, the Negat cryptanalysts in Washington, and those at Station Cast in Cavite, were breaking into JN-25B. According to Safford, intercepts in this code were "partly readable" by December 1941, at which time the Japanese introduced a new book of random additives to encipher the five-digit code.[27] Exactly what information was being gleaned from the operational cipher at this stage in Washington or Cavite is difficult to establish.

The recent discovery of a batch of intercepts covering the period from June to November 1941 that were buried amid approximately three hundred thousand wartime Japanese naval messages declassified to date has finally made it possible to see what intelligence could have been recovered *if* Hypo had been permitted to work on the JN-25 traffic.

The translations of the decrypts were reworked in 1945. They do not give a precise indication of what was known in 1941 by our naval cryptographic teams in OP-20-G, Cavite, or the cryptanalysts of Britain's Far East Combined Bureau at Singapore. But they do show which of the Combined Fleet dispatches were picked up and these reveal their enormous *potential* intelligence value as clues to Japan's operational intentions, *including* indications that an attack force of carriers was heading for an unknown target.

All our speculation is based on Safford's assertion of the partial readability of the JN-25 B cipher. According to the estimate of Dyer and Wright, this amounted to about 10 percent. This does not mean that 10 percent of the intercepts in Japan's main operational fleet code were then being decrypted, or even that a tenth of each and every communication in the five-digit cipher was translated into meaningful English. But it does suggest that on average, 10 percent of *each* message that could be broken was yielding some information, even if fortuitous and disconnected.[28]

There can be no doubt that Washington therefore must have had some fragmentary intelligence from the Japanese fleet cipher. What it was or how significant is impossible to assess because, to date, *not one single original decrypt made at the time of any JN-25 message has been found or declassified.* And it should be noted that none was considered or produced by any of the Pearl Harbor inquiries or the 1945 congressional investigations. This does not *necessarily* suggest that an embarrassingly important piece of the intelligence puzzle was missed and therefore has been covered up by Washington. But it is surely another example of how reluctant the naval staff was to reveal that there could have been some additional clues to Japan's intentions from the JN-25 intercepts and that they were either ignored or overlooked like the bomb plot message in the J-19 consular traffic.

The intercepted pre-Pearl Harbor JN-25 signal traffic for the month before 7 December is highly illuminating. The question is how much intelligence was broken out of these messages at the time. Certainly even such a partial decryption as the 10 percent of the traffic claimed by Safford could have provided us with some precise information on those naval movements that led directly to an attack.

The November 1941 JN-25 traffic vibrated with indications of war: On 14 November Japanese merchant shipping is alerted that "wartime recognition signals" will be effective on 1 December.[29] Next day the Combined Fleet is advised of the distribution of new code books;[30] the following day the "Combined Fleet Special Call List for Wartime Use" is announced.[31] On 19 November a destroyer division requests its copy of the "Combined Fleet Battle Plan,"[32] and the same day a cruiser requests its copy of "Striking Force Operational Order No. 5."[33] The next day an oiler reports that she'll finish loading fuel and aviation gasoline by 21 November and join the striking force by the twenty-seventh.[34]

A strict military cordon is drawn around personnel assembling on Hainan Island 20 November "until further notice" because of a "leakage of secret information."[35] On the twenty-first a top-secret Combined Fleet signal is radioed "at 0000 on 21 November, repeat 21 November, carry out second phase of operations for opening hostilities."[36] On 29 November all naval forces in the mandates are ordered to "maintain battle condition shortwave silence."[37]

Even more revealing are the half dozen signals intercepted in the final weeks of November that update the call signs for the commanders about to be involved in the upcoming operations. These allocate the new two-kana-numeral identifiers to all the operational, support, and submarine forces.[38] These list designators for an E Force, an H Force, an M Force, an N Force, an AA Occupation Force, a G Force, an AF Commerce Destruction Unit, as well as the Main Force, an Advance Expeditionary Force, and the *Kido Butai*—Striking Force. The importance of the last is evident, because its flagship is allocated a second call sign, as is its Supply Unit.

The ability to decrypt even 10 percent of this type of traffic in the final weeks of November should have given both Washington and Cavite—not to mention the British—considerable opportunity to uncover some key elements of Japan's naval war plans. Although Safford asserted in 1945 that the "5-numeral system yielded no information which would arouse even a suspicion of the Pearl Harbor raid," it could have provided some indication both of the forces involved and potential targets before the new cipher additives came into use on 1 December.

In 1945 the translator of these messages took pains to note that in 1941 the following was not known: E equaled Malaya; H, the Dutch East Indies; M, Manila (the Philippines); N, Nippon (Japan); AA, Wake Island; G, Guam; and AF, Midway. But to the intelligence officer, the letters chosen by the Japanese indicate a surprising trust in the security of their own codes. With the exception of Wake and Midway they show a direct alphabetic association with their geographic destinations! Even if this self-evident association was not apparent, then merely by allocating the forces on a map, according to their likely targets, could have shown the Japanese strategic objectives in the Far East.

More important, this would have left the targets of the so-called main force of battleships and a striking force which could be presumed to contain carriers, unaccounted for. Since the main force was not allocated any supply units, and the striking force was assigned two of them, it could have been readily inferred that the former would support the E, H, and M operations, which were within range of the naval bases in Formosa and Indochina. The *Kido Butai*, on the other hand, was destined for some long-range operation.

Precisely what its mission was would not have been clear even if the decrypts had been broken in full. But some clues could have been pieced together from the series of ships-in-harbor updates relayed to the *Kido Butai* by Tokyo via Honolulu. The JN-25 intercepts reveal that at least one was picked up and sent to Washington. It was a 27 November report from Consul Kita saying that "4 destroyers left AIO the evening of 16 November."[39] Since none of the operational messages was addressed to individual carrier divisions, this in itself might have been taken as an indication that they were collectively involved with the operational objectives of a striking force that required two support forces. This would have been another clue that the Japanese were planning a strike at some distant American territory, probably in the Pacific, and possible targets included the West Coast, Panama, and our Hawaiian base.

While none of the signals give any *specific* indication that Pearl Harbor was going to be attacked, they contain clear pointers in that direction. They also show the intention of Japan's forces to attack Malaya, Guam, the Dutch East Indies, and the Philippines. What still remains a mystery, until the 1941 decrypts become available, is how much of this was known, or deduced, by the naval staff in Washington. If only a fraction of this had been available to us at Pearl Harbor, it would have answered Kimmel's doubts about the direction of Japan's belligerent intentions and so galvanized the level of the alert at Pearl Harbor.

During that final week one of the main problems that both Kimmel and I faced was having to evaluate evidence when we did not even have the diplomatic background about what Japanese policy really was. It was clear that the bulk of Japan's naval strength was being concentrated into task forces. It was self-evident days before we received the alert from Washington that Japan's probable targets of attack were Malaya, the Isthmus of Kra, Thailand, and possibly the Philippines. It needed no strategic genius to see that. But we knew that the Japanese had a propensity for always trying to get something for nothing. As Kimmel and I rationalized, it was possible that their forces were cover for another operation such as their July takeover of bases in Indochina. This time, it seemed, their objective might be Thailand, knowing that if they got in there and we took no action, they would be strategically well placed for another move southward. The same was true for the Dutch East Indies.

On four or five occasions during that final week of peace, we tried to resolve the uncertainty concerning Japanese objectives. However, the lack of diplomatic intelligence about Tokyo's overall intentions, and our own uncertainty of precisely what action the president would order if British but not American territory was attacked, bore heavily upon us.

"I wish I knew what we were going to do," Admiral Kimmel said to me during our discussions that week.[40] That he repeated this five or six times was a measure of his frustration and worry about being kept in the dark by Washington.

The Pacific Fleet dispositions had been made according to the intelligence picture as I had been able to assemble it. We knew that war was over the horizon—both literally and figuratively. But just how close it was we were never told. What we did know was that the main thrust of the Japanese offensive was going to be directed at Malaya, Thailand, or the Philippines—territories five thousand miles away. Just as Washington was to be mesmerized by the nest of vipers believed to be about to uncoil across the South China Sea toward the Philippines, our attention at Pacific Fleet headquarters was focused on the rattlesnake nearest to Pearl Harbor: the probability that a hostile task force was preparing to strike at us from Kwajalein—less than two thousand miles to the southwest.

We were unaware of the danger that was approaching us from the north. That Washington's collective back remained turned was, in hindsight, an appalling testament of mortal stupidity, shortsightedness, and plain bad luck.

*   *   *

The seeds of the disaster that was about to occur had been sown as Admiral Richardson had predicted the year before, when our foreign policy was allowed to dictate military strategy. This situation had resulted in a disastrous deterrent posture. Our bluff was called when the failure of Tokyo's diplomatic efforts to restore its flow of oil made a preemptive strike an attractive option as a way to save Japan's face. Myopically unaware of the magnitude of its strategic miscalculation, Washington had blundered by failing to keep the fleet adequately informed during the rush of diplomacy. The result was that neither they, nor we, were aware of the extent to which the principal instrument of our power in the Pacific had now become the target for attack.

The stage was set for the attack on Pearl Harbor by 1 December. The final six days were in effect little more than a remorseless countdown to disaster.

22

Countdown to War

1 DECEMBER   *"It May Be Worse Next Week"*

Kido Butai

A RADIO SIGNAL from Tokyo naval headquarters had alerted Admiral Nagumo's *Kido Butai* the previous evening that "AMERICA HAD SUDDENLY CHANGED ITS ATTITUDE ON 26TH AND BECAME ABRUPTLY UNBENDING." A rupture of diplomatic negotiations was therefore inevitable.[1]

After learning of this report, staff officer Fujita in cruiser *Toné* declared in his diary his relief that "the opening of hostilities was inevitable" because they "could now devote themselves to the operation without any anxiety."[2]

Ohnishi noted in his diary after seas moderated enough to permit refueling under cloudy skies that "a divine grace is bestowed on us." The only snag so far was that one of the scouting submarines had developed bearing trouble and had dropped behind during the night. The loss of one of the three scouts required all watchkeepers to increase their vigilance. Binoculars were locked on the gray horizon ahead for any sign of the Soviet freighter that all lookouts had been warned to expect on an intersecting course.

In the small hours they had sailed over the dark ocean's invisible 180-degree line of longitude into the western hemisphere.

"This force has now entered the supposed zone of air searches from Kiska and Midway," Nagumo signaled by blinker lights. The gods were evidently smiling on the *Kido Butai* because southerly winds and calm seas facilitated refueling.[3] Just over seventeen hundred miles to the southeast lay a still unsuspecting Pearl Harbor.

236

Staff officer Fujita's optimism was rising: "The radio signal for the beginning of hostilities has been received, Hawaii intelligence has begun to arrive, and now everything is going as hoped for."[4]

Pearl Harbor

Intelligence about Japanese war preparations reinforced our view at Pacific Fleet headquarters that some assault was imminent on the other side of the Pacific.

Our belief was supported by a relay from Station Cast—the second piece of diplomatic Magic we had received within a week—of the decrypt of a Purple message of 29 November from Japan's Bangkok embassy: "Absolutely reliable agent in Bangkok reports that on 29th conferences were in progress considering plans to force the British to attack Thai at Padang Base near Singora as countermove to Japanese landing at Kota Bharu."[5]

Such clear indications of the imminence of hostilities increased my apprehension as to how Kimmel would react to the lack of information about the Japanese carrier dispositions in my location sheet. So I called Rochefort first thing on Monday to see if anything had come in overnight.

I was concerned to hear that all the Japanese service call signs afloat had changed promptly at midnight. Now we understood why they had been retransmitting so much old traffic in the preceding days; it had been a cover for the switch.

The portents were ominous: First, we had detected their naval exercises in the middle of November; second, we had tracked the formations of the large task forces being formed; third, the call signs had changed again. It all added up to the launching of offensive operations in the very near future.

Traffic analysis indicated that many of the Combined Fleet units were changing their locations. Joe told me to expect more alterations. He suggested I postpone my disposition report one more day so that it would reflect the latest information. I called Kimmel's aide and asked him to inform the admiral that the information he wanted that morning was changing all the time and that my report would be much more meaningful if he could allow me one more day.

The reply was affirmative. I called Joe and told him I would work on it all night if necessary. But he had to get me his latest report first thing in the morning so that I could review my disposition chart before presenting it to the admiral.

As soon as I had Rochefort's latest intelligence summary, I went to see Admiral Kimmel. He shared my concern when he read Joe's assessment: "The fact that service calls lasted only one month indicates an additional progressive step preparing for active operations on a large scale." I witnessed Kimmel's obvious concern. He underlined that sentence as he read it.

The tenseness was also apparent when he noted "No change" in the section dealing with Japan's carriers. He shared my concern that they would be the most dangerous element of a striking force that might already be assembling in the Marshalls for an offensive move against Pearl Harbor. Our concern would have been far greater had we received the intelligence contained in another intercept that had also been broken by army cryptanalysts from a Purple message sent from Tokyo to Berlin only twenty-four hours earlier. It clearly pointed to Japan's being on the brink of war. Its significance could not have been overlooked in the navy and war departments, but it was not considered necessary to inform the Pacific Fleet.

Washington

"Say *very secretly* to them that *there is extreme danger that war may break out* between the Anglo-Saxon nations and Japan through some clash of arms, add that the *time of this war may come quicker than anyone dreams* [emphasis added]," was how Baron Hiroshi Oshima, Japan's ambassador in Berlin, was instructed to present the situation to the Nazi government. He was to reassure the fuehrer that "*by our present moves southward* we do not mean to relax our pressure against the Soviet [Union] and that if Russia joins hands tighter with England and the United States resists us, we are ready to turn upon her with all our might [emphasis added]."[6]

Any doubt remaining in Washington about what Tokyo was about to do ought to have been dispelled that Monday by that decrypted message. It had been sent that day to Nomura and Kurusu, and it was broken within hours of its interception by the navy. Nomura and Kurusu had been alerted that the deadline for negotiations had come and gone, yet "*to prevent the United States from becoming unduly suspicious* we have been advising the press and others that though there are some wide differences between Japan and the United States, the negotiations are continuing. The above for your information only [emphasis added]."[7]

The two envoys were told to "make the necessary representations" as a cover for Tokyo's withholding of a response to the United States' rebuff of the *modus vivendi* the previous Wednesday. They dutifully did so at a meeting that day with the secretary of state at which Hull took a firm line and reminded them that the American government was not "going to go into partnership" with Japan's military leaders.[8]

On their return to the Japanese embassy they found a circular cable advising that their "officers in London, Hongkong, Singapore, and Manila have been instructed to abandon the use of the code machines and to dispose of them." The Washington embassy's code machines were to remain intact for the time being. Nomura was advised that when he "faced the necessity of destroying codes," he should contact the naval attaché who had the appropriate chemicals "on hand for this purpose."[9]

A proper intelligence evaluation of these messages would have indicated that Japan's diplomats were being instructed to play for time while Japanese military forces were being deployed for an attack on the United States. But this conclusion does not appear to have been drawn. The decrypt of Nomura's reply was not sent to Admiral Kimmel.

Captain McCollum, however, had already become concerned that Japan was lurching toward hostilities. That Monday morning he had put the finishing touches to his three-page résumé of the outstanding military and political moves made by Japan during the past two months. It summarized all available intelligence about Japan's war preparations. The head of naval intelligence's Far East section reviewed the memorandum with Admiral Wilkinson. Then McCollum accompanied DNI to CNO's office where Ingersoll and Turner were also present, along with Admiral Noyes and Rear Admiral R. M. Brainard, director of ships movements division.

McCollum briefed the admirals from his report, which listed the southward movement since mid-November of Japanese transports carrying veteran troops from northern China to Formosa, Hainan, Haiphong, and Shanghai. These ports were "reported crowded with Japanese transports unloading supplies and men."[10] McCollum drew the attention of those gathered in Stark's office to Japan's recent docking of warships and the requisitioning of merchantmen, the air reinforcement of the mandates, and the air and submarine surveillance of Guam. As additional evidence of the direction and scale of Japan's intended operations, he pointed to the size of the two large naval task groups under the command of the Second Fleet whose CinC "expects to be in Southern Formosa by 3 or 4 December."

McCollum pulled no punches in underlining that Japanese war preparations were nearing completion. Magic had revealed that their consular officials in the Philippines, and in British and Dutch territories, were being evacuated. So were Japanese diplomats and citizens in the United States and Canada. They had been instructed to apply for berths in steamers that were being sent to the west coast to collect them.

The intelligence and espionage section headed by Taro Terasaki in the Washington embassy had also been ordered to pack up in preparation for transfer to Rio de Janeiro, where the government was sympathetic to the Axis. Other Purple traffic had revealed that sabotage agents had been infiltrated into Singapore. The Bangkok embassy had been turned into an undercover military nerve center. And Japan's consul general in Shanghai had "informed his government that all preparations are complete for taking over the physical property in China belonging to the British, American and other enemy nationals."[11]

McCollum knew that he was sticking his neck out by asking whether or not the fleets in the Pacific had been "adequately alerted." But he did so, he later recalled, because he had decided that "war or a rupture of diplomatic relations was imminent." Stark and Turner, he said, both gave him "categorical assurance" that "dispatches fully alerting the fleets and placing them on a war basis" had been sent.[12] This came as a surprise to the head of the Far East section. It was the first he had heard about it. The whole point of McCollum's drawing up his memorandum was to convince the director of war plans that it was high time that war warnings were sent out to the Pacific commands.

After this meeting Stark went to the White House. At Hull's urging, Roosevelt had cut short his brief Thanksgiving break at his Georgia retreat at Warm Springs. The presidential train pulled into the Washington freight yard shortly after eleven that morning. The secretary of state spent an hour discussing the worsening situation.

Magic had revealed a plot by Tokyo to trick the British into making a preemptive occupation of Thailand's territory on the Isthmus of Kra to clear the way for the impending Japanese invasion of Malaya. And Roosevelt was concerned about the commitment he had made to Churchill if the Congress should react negatively to a presidential call for declaring war on Japan before American territory had been attacked. That problems were mounting for Roosevelt was evidenced by his telling Treasury Secretary Morgenthau, who telephoned after his meeting with Stark, to go ahead and float $1.5-billion worth of government financing that Thursday, because "it may be worse next week." The president "could not guarantee anything" and insisted, "It is all in the laps of the gods."[13]

Just how much was "in the laps of the gods" was precisely what the British ambassador wanted to ascertain when he arrived a few minutes later for a working luncheon. The foreign office had instructed Lord Halifax to "ask for an urgent expression" of American views in the event that Thailand was occupied and Malaya invaded.

"You will realize," Lord Halifax was reminded by the 29 November cable, "how important it is to ensure ourselves of American support in the event of hostilities." Churchill had also sent a "Former Naval Person" telegram the previous day expressing his fears about the worsening situation. It was intended to prod Roosevelt to issue an ultimatum to Tokyo: "I beg you to consider whether, at the moment you judge right, which may be very near, you should not say that any further Japanese aggression would compel you to place the gravest issues before Congress."[14]

Roosevelt wanted to delay placing "the gravest issues" before a divided House and Senate. So he told Halifax that he wanted Tokyo's reaction to his formal question about the troop transports heading south from Shanghai before issuing any joint declaration with Britain. The president did, however, discuss the possibility of using the B-17 bombers in the Philippines, in conjunction with Anglo-American naval forces, for a long-distance blockade, "which of course means shooting." But Halifax could report only that Roosevelt, "in an aside," had said "that in the event of an attack on ourselves or the Dutch, we should obviously be all in it together."[15]

A presidential "aside" over the lunch table fell far short of the unqualified guarantee that Churchill and his ambassador were seeking. As Halifax conveyed it to London, Roosevelt was still far from unequivocal when he stated that Britain "could certainly count on [U.S.] support, though it might take a short time, a few days, to get things into political shape here."[16]

Getting "things into political shape" was interpreted, correctly, as a euphemism for Roosevelt's still having to do some fancy footwork on Capitol Hill in the event that Japan did not fire her first shots simultaneously at the Stars and Stripes when she opened up on the Union Jack. The president sent word to the secretary of state to coordinate with Stimson and Knox on the preparation of a message that would secure congressional backing. This might prove necessary for American involvement should the first Japanese salvos explode on United States territory or ships.

The president retired at eleven that evening of 1 December, unaware that while he slept, his political and military dilemma was about to be resolved for him in Tokyo.

2 DECEMBER   *"Now We Have Come This Far, Will We Succeed?"*

Tokyo

As midnight struck in Washington, it was two in the afternoon of 1 December in Japan. This was the hour appointed for the emperor to ascend the dais in room 1 east of the imperial palace where Prime Minister Tojo was to explain how every effort to bring about "an adjustment in relations with the United States" had failed. The objectives of Japan's national policy made it necessary to go to war. Regrettable though this was, Tojo claimed, the nation was united to the death to break through the crisis. For another two hours wooden rhetoric supporting the prime minister was spoken by the senior members of the cabinet and the service chiefs. This time there was no interruption by the throne. Privy Council president Baron Yoshimichi Hara, speaking for the impassive emperor, accepted the fact that "the proposal before us cannot be avoided in the light of present circumstances."[17]

"At this moment our empire stands at the threshold of glory or oblivion," Tojo declared before adjourning the historic imperial conference with an expression of his "resolve that the nation will go on to victory, make an all-out effort to achieve our war aims, and set his majesty's mind at ease.[18]

Imperial general headquarters was a beehive of activity that evening. Alarming news had been received that a transport plane had crashed that afternoon in Nationalist-held territory in Kwantung province in China. On board was a major who had been carrying the secret war order to the Twenty-third Army headquarters in Canton. If his papers were discovered by Chiang Kai-shek's soldiers, and then relayed to London or to Washington, the British and Americans might launch a preemptive attack on Japan.

With a fatalism characteristic of the Orient, the warlords of Tokyo decided it was too late to do anything except "close one's eyes and pray to the Gods."[19] Next morning the army and navy chiefs went to the palace to formally request the emperor's approval for a war order in his name confirming that X-day was to be 8 December. On that night a full moon would illuminate the intended attack zones from midnight to sunrise.

Imperial authorization was granted. That afternoon, the powerful transmitters of the Tokyo signals unit Station 1 flashed out simultaneously on four different wavelengths the code-message: NIITAKA YAMA NO-BORE 1208.

The prearranged signal, which meant "Climb Mount Niitaka on the eighth day of the twelfth month," was picked up by the U.S. Navy's tall antennas on Bainbridge Island in Puget Sound. Precisely how much of the JN-25 message was decrypted that Tuesday is still unclear. But its significance was fully appreciated later by a navy translator in 1945: "This was undoubtedly the prearranged signal for specifying the date for the opening of hostilities. The significance of the phrase is interesting, however, in that it is so appropriately used in this connection. Niitaka-yama is the highest mountain in the Japanese empire."[20]

Kido Butai

"I have accepted an awesome assignment; with stronger will I might have refused it," Admiral Nagumo confided to his aide. "Now we have come this far, will we succeed?"[21] The chances that they would succeed were looking better every day. They had received a radio message from Tokyo the previous evening that repeated the Honolulu consulate's Friday report on the disposition of the fleet at Pearl Harbor:

Two battleships (OKLAHOMA, NEVADA), 1 aircraft carrier (ENTER-
PRISE), 2 heavy cruisers, 12 destroyers sailed. The force that had
departed on 22 November returned to port. Ships at anchor Pearl
Harbor p.m. 28 November were 6 battleships (2 MARYLAND class, 2
CALIFORNIA class, 2 PENNSYLVANIA class), 1 aircraft carrier (LEX-
INGTON), 9 heavy cruisers (5 SAN FRANCISCO class, 3 CHICAGO
class, 1 SALT LAKE class), 5 light cruisers (4 HONOLULU class, 1
OMAHA class)

"I pray that the American fleet remains thus on X-day," Fujita noted in
his diary.[22]

Pearl Harbor

While Admiral Nagumo was getting up-to-the-minute information on
our movements, Admiral Kimmel was getting no intelligence about the
Japanese carriers.

"Almost a complete lack of information on the carriers today,"
Rochefort reported. "Since over 200 service calls have been partially
identified since the 1st of December and not one call has been recalled, it
is evident that carrier traffic is at a low ebb."[23]

Even as I was reviewing my revised disposition report that morning,
Joe called in new changes. I made the alterations and additions in pencil,
but there was still no hard information on the two carrier divisions we
believed were still in Japan. There was no traffic—or traffic analysis—to
or from these carriers or their commanders. Nor were these divisions
information addressees of any messages, with the exception of the supply-
type signal to *Akagi* two days earlier. Before taking the location sheet to
the admiral, I called Joe once again. He confirmed there had not been
any direct information on carriers for a long time; therefore he couldn't
give them a precise disposition, but the majority opinion of his analysts
was that they were still in home waters. So I wrote down, "Unknown—
home waters?"

The admiral read my report very carefully. It did not escape his eagle
eye that I had left out most of their carriers from my location sheet. His
concern became very vocal.

"What! You don't know where the carriers are?"

I explained that I had omitted them because neither carrier division 1
nor 2 had been identified as an originator or addressee in recent radio
traffic.

"Well, where do you estimate they are?"

I explained that there was no recent or good indication of their locations, but that if I had to guess, I would put them in "home waters,"
probably in the vicinity of the Kure naval base. I admitted that the pre-

sumption that they were in "home waters" was based on no hard evidence, but was an estimate deriving from past observations.

"Then you don't really know where Carrier Division One and Carrier Division Two are?"

"No, sir, I do not. I think they are in home waters, but I do not *know* for sure where they are. But I feel pretty confident of the location of the rest of the units."

The admiral then looked at me, as sometimes he would, with a stern countenance and an icy twinkle in his penetrating blue eyes.

"Do you mean to say they could be rounding Diamond Head and you wouldn't know it?"

"I hope they would have been spotted before now," I replied weakly.

Admiral Kimmel was often sharply ironic when he wanted to drive home a point. This exchange, which I recalled during my testimony at the various Pearl Harbor inquiries, was to attract unfortunate accusations of levity on the admiral's part by hostile examiners. But at the time it left me painfully aware that my commanding officer was extremely concerned about this serious gap in my report.

If the continued silence of the carriers created a gaping hole in our intelligence estimate, there was plenty of traffic intercepted from the Second Fleet's tactical circuits. This enabled me to tell Kimmel with some confidence that a large part of the Second and Third fleet units was probably already under way in the China Sea. Since one carrier division was also definitely southbound, and another appeared to be associated with signals exchanged with Tokyo, I estimated, wrongly, that the third carrier division must also be accompanying the fourth division south.

Had Hypo been able to read the Japanese diplomatic traffic and see how closely the local consulate was reporting the fleet dispositions in Pearl Harbor, our estimates would have been different. That Tuesday Rochefort received a hand-delivered envelope marked SECRET from Captain Mayfield's district intelligence office in Honolulu. It enclosed a note from his assistant, Lieutenant Yale Maxon, advising that the office had available "through a very confidential source known to you, rechecks on cables received from time to time by the principal Orange establishment."[24]

Mayfield's cryptic allusion was to the manager of the local RCA office who began turning over copies of the consulate cables after he had been ordered to do so by David Sarnoff, the head of RCA. Sarnoff had paid a November visit to Honolulu during which Mayfield had managed to persuade him that it was in the national interest that the navy obtain access to the Japanese consul's communications.[25]

Had Rochefort received notice from Washington of the so-called bomb plot messages with their grid system for reporting the ships moored in Pearl Harbor in October, he would certainly have been alerted to the importance of monitoring the consulate traffic. But Washington had never sent us the bomb plot messages, and had specifically instructed Hypo to concentrate on naval matters.

The basic keys for unlocking the J-19 code were available to Rochefort's unit, but Hypo had not been keeping up with the traffic and did not have the current cipher, because all the intercepted messages had been previously forwarded to Washington. There was also only one member of Joe's outfit with any previous experience in breaking the consular systems,[26] so the offer from Mayfield was not immediately accepted.

The very same day, however, the Japanese consulate was ordered to burn its J-19 code manuals and resort to the PA-K2 code, which was a much simpler system. Then, as chance would have it on the next day, the first cables decrypted were routine consular housekeeping traffic sent in PA-K2, but before the J-19 code had been abandoned.[27] So the first messages to be broken were of "absolutely no value." As a result, the RCA messages were given a low priority in Hypo.

Rochefort's unwitting neglect of a source of potentially valuable intelligence in the final days before the Japanese attack was typical of the comedy of errors that bedeviled our operations. Another was the chance discovery that deprived us of the DIO's "direct line" into the nerve center of Japan's local espionage operation. A lineman of the Mutual Telephone Company of Hawaii making a routine check of the poles outside 1742 Nuuanu Avenue uncovered the two wiretaps, and this was reported to the FBI—who were also independently monitoring the consul's lines.

The DIO was immediately alerted by the FBI. Captain Mayfield's annoyance at the failure of the FBI to inform him that they were eavesdropping on the Japanese was exceeded by his concern that the discovery might trigger an international incident for which the navy would be blamed. Orders were issued to stop the operation immediately. Warrant Officer Ted Emmanuel offered to resign from the navy in order to continue listening in. But at 1600 he had to pull the plugs and "bade adieu to my friend of 22 months' standing."[28]

Actions that Japan might consider hostile also preoccupied Admiral Kimmel. "You will note that I have issued orders to the Pacific Fleet to depth bomb all submarine contacts in the Oahu operating area," he informed Stark in a postscript to a long letter that detailed the steps he had taken to reinforce the outlying islands.[29] After a morning conference with General Short to discuss the construction of army airfields in Fiji and New Caledonia, the admiral was worried that his resources were being stretched too thin.

"Too much diversion of effort for defense will leave us an inadequate force with which to take the offensive," Kimmel warned Stark.[30] The fleet's cruisers were now deployed on convoy duties, and his concluding postscript was a harbinger of disasters to come: "I realize of course that the demands for transpacific escorts may decrease if it becomes impossible to route ships to Manila, but it will still be necessary to supply the Asiatic fleet and our allies in the Far East."[31]

Washington

The problem of how to ensure that Congress would accept the British and Dutch as allies if Japan did not attack the United States continued to nag Roosevelt. The president and his war council dared not risk revealing the extent of the military commitments already made by the Joint Board. So Roosevelt began to plan a speech that would be an appeal for congressional support to warn Japan that offensive operations against British or Dutch territories would be considered a threat to the vital interests of the United States.

The drafting of this critical address began after that morning's White House conference. The secretaries of the navy and war had discussed the latest intelligence report that a Japanese expeditionary force was landing troops near Saigon. Stimson regarded the news as providing "a little respite."[32] Under Secretary of State Sumner Welles, acting as deputy for an indisposed Hull, was directed to send a stiff note to Tokyo demanding an explanation for the "very rapid and material increase" that "would seem to imply the utilization of these forces by Japan for the purposes of further aggression."[33]

Roosevelt knew that more Japanese aggression in Indochina would not win votes for his intended plea to Congress. A public opinion survey taken that week showed that while 69 percent of the nation was willing to risk war to halt Japanese aggression, only 51 percent believed that this would involve hostilities.[34] An assault on American territory or ships was needed to fire up public and congressional outrage.

There was no doubt that Japan must be targeting the Philippines. But Tokyo had shown a preference for step-by-step aggression and might be planning to grab British territory as an opening move that would not rouse the United States. To guard against this eventuality, that afternoon Roosevelt took the extraordinary step of ordering the navy to provide a series of lures for the Japanese tiger.

"The president directs that the following be done as soon as possible and within two days."[35] That was how Stark began one of the strangest orders a chief of naval operations had ever dispatched. His wording was evidently intended to leave Admiral Hart, commander of the Asiatic Fleet in Manila, with no doubt as to the origins of the madcap operation that he was being ordered to arrange.

Charter three small vessels to [sic] for quote defensive information patrol unquote. Minimum requirements to establish identity as United States men of war are commanded by a naval officer and to mount a small machine gun would suffice. Filipino crews may be employed with minimum number of naval ratings to accomplish purpose which is to observe and report by radio Japanese movements in West China Sea and Gulf of Siam.[36]

By quoting Roosevelt's term "defensive information patrol," Stark was disassociating himself from a mission that he knew was foolhardy and unjustified from a military standpoint. In any case, three days earlier, Stark had obtained presidential approval for ordering Admiral Hart to send out aerial reconnaissance to check on the southward movement of the Japanese expeditionary force: "For security of our position in the Philippines desire you cover by air the line Manila-Camranh Bay on three days commencing receipt of this dispatch."[37]

A copy of this dispatch had been sent to Kimmel for information. But Kimmel was not included as an addressee for the dispatch about the "defensive information patrol" by three small vessels. Nor was he made privy to the one that followed it only minutes later that advised Hart that "it is very important that you exchange full military information with the British and Dutch naval commanders-in-chief except in cases where you consider it definitely inadvisable."[38]

The omission of Kimmel from these two signals was another indication of the extent to which Washington kept us in the dark. Understandably, Stark might have been reluctant to let Kimmel in on Hart's "fish bait" operation, whose purpose was apparent from his orders not to risk any naval vessels.

The sacrificial nature of the operation—which required expendable vessels with Filipino crews—was the direct result of the wavering by President Manuel Luis Quezon y Molina to commit the Philippines to fight. If Filipino crewmen were to be killed as the result of Japanese military action, it was assumed that Quezon would have no choice but to support the Americans. Roosevelt's specific instructions as to where the "goats" were to be tethered—with one south of Hainan, another off the Indochina coast, and the third south of Cape Cambodia—were intended to ensure that they lay directly in the path of any Japanese naval force advancing south toward Malaya. That the vessels were to sail within forty-eight hours meant that the "bait" was to be laid by Friday.

Hart's response to Roosevelt's subterfuge was less than enthusiastic. He replied that it was "improbable that [we] can start any chartered craft within two days." But since it was a presidential order, the command's steam yacht was selected as one.[39] The very idea that the sleek, two-funneled *Isabel* should be sunk like another *Panay* offended the Asiatic Fleet commander, who used his yacht for weekend cruises around Manila Bay. He informed Stark that "she is too short radius to accomplish much and since we have few fast ships her loss would be serious."[40] With a heavy heart Admiral Hart watched the *Isabel* pull away from the Cavite pierhead on the following day. He was convinced he would never see his "holiday flagship" again.

Two days later *Isabel* was twenty-two miles off the coast of Indochina when she was spotted and buzzed by Japanese patrol planes. When it was clear from her skipper's radio reports that the Japanese were not going to take the bait and attack, Hart recalled her. Meanwhile, at the Cavite naval base two chartered schooners, *Molly Moore* and *Lanikai,* were being readied for their mission with a cannon, World War I machine guns, and a radio set that could receive but not transmit.

Lanikai's skipper was Lieutenant Kemp Tolley, an eager young officer, but neither he nor the Filipino volunteers who had jumped at the chance to don navy uniforms would have been so enthusiastic if they had realized that they were to become fish bait. However, because neither schooner was ready to sail until the morning that war broke out, Kemp Tolley survived.[41]

London

Churchill was unaware of Roosevelt's scheme. The British cabinet's Defense Committee met that afternoon to consider Halifax's report. Evidently, the American president's unofficial assurance that, in the event of an attack upon the British or Dutch, "we should obviously be all in it together" was not a sufficient guarantee of support for the British to issue ironclad commitments to Thailand or the Dutch. Although Roosevelt had told the ambassador that such commitments would have his full support, Churchill needed to be "quite sure of the American attitude."[42]

Lord Halifax was instructed, in effect, to pin the president down by asking if "we would have the armed support of the United States if our action resulted in hostilities with Japan" before the British gave guarantees to the Thai prime minister that they would intervene to prevent the Japanese task force's reaching the Isthmus of Kra to invade Thailand. Until Roosevelt had provided such assurances, Churchill advised the foreign secretary that "settled policy" was "not to take forward action in advance of the United States."[43] This left the suave Anthony Eden with the difficult task of explaining to the Royal Netherlands government in exile that their forces in the Dutch East Indies might have to play the role of fall guy to a Japanese attack.

If only Dutch territory was attacked, the prime minister's memorandum stated, "we should do nothing to prevent the full impact of this Japanese aggression presenting itself to the United States." The Netherlands foreign minister was to be reassured that if the Americans declared war on Japan, "we will follow within the hour." Moreover, if "after a reasonable interval, the United States is found to be incapable of any decisive action, even with our immediate support we will nevertheless, although alone, make common cause with the Dutch."[44]

3 DECEMBER *"Scary Reports"*

Tokyo

Premier Tojo's cabinet agreed that Foreign Minister Togo's final reply to the United States would be delivered *prior* to the launching of military operations. This was in response to repeated cautions from the emperor that Japan had signed the Hague Convention and must adhere to Article I, which required that "hostilities . . . must not commence without an explicit warning, in the form of either a reasoned declaration of war or of an ultimatum with conditional declaration of war."[45] But the fourteen-part message, whose wording was approved at the next day's liaison conference, made no such specific declaration. Foreign Minister Togo, however, believed it "clearly signified a cessation of peace."

Kido Butai

Some fifteen hundred miles northeast of its objective, Nagumo's striking force had run into the first really big storm since leaving Tankan Bay. A petty officer was washed overboard from carrier *Kaga*; heavy seas ruled out any refueling throughout the day. Nagumo, however, could take some comfort from the fact that the thick weather would also thwart any American air patrols flying south from the Aleutians.

The chances that the *Kido Butai*'s mission would be discovered through interception of any of the signals that were being addressed to it by Tokyo were greatly decreased that day. At midnight the Japanese navy switched over to the new number 8 additive book of random five-digit number groups for its JN-25 fleet code. It is still not clear how much of the system the Washington or British code breakers were able to read even prior to the changeover. But it is possible that OP-20-G had an inkling of the change, since we had intercepted a signal from the navy ministry forty-eight hours earlier directing, "Starting 4 December 1941 additive system #8 of Naval Code D will be used, and additive system #7 will be discontinued."[47]

Pearl Harbor

Once again during my morning briefing I had to inform Admiral Kimmel that we still had no information on the carriers. The extensive use of alternate call signs by the Japanese was taxing the efforts of Hypo's cryptanalysts. There was also activity on the Fourth Fleet circuits in the Marshalls, and Rochefort had a hunch that the Second and Third fleets were already under way. But he did not have any radio intelligence to verify it.

I was in my office that Wednesday afternoon when Kimmel sent for me again. He showed me an Opnav dispatch sent to the Asiatic Fleet and addressed to him for information. This was only the third Magic decrypt that we had received since July. It was an instruction from Tokyo ordering the legations at London, Hong Kong, Singapore, and Manila "to destroy Purple machine." It also advised us that the previous day "Washington also directed destroy Purple."[48]

"What is Purple?" the admiral asked. I told him that I didn't know. But after leaving Kimmel, I approached Lieutenant Herbert M. Coleman, the fleet security officer. He had recently come from Washington and was able to tell me that Purple was a Japanese electrical coding machine. I then informed the admiral that the Japanese destruction of their code machines must indicate they were preparing for any or all eventualities. But since most of the embassies, with the exception of London and Washington, were in the Far East, we believed the Magic decrypt was further evidence that Japan was preparing to launch operations in this area. This was confirmed by receipt of another dispatch from Washington quoting "highly reliable information" that the same Japanese outposts had been ordered "to destroy most of their codes and ciphers at once and to burn all other important confidential and secret documents."[49]

The Honolulu consulate was not mentioned. And we did not know if it had one of the Purple machines; but it was not until the next day that I received word from Rochefort that the local Japanese diplomats were also burning their codes. That news was relayed by Captain Mayfield from the FBI who had picked up confirmation on the telephone line they were still tapping to the consulate's kitchens.

When Rochefort called me with the news, I said, "That fits the picture that the Japanese are preparing for something by destroying their codes."[50] I at once gave the information to the admiral. Later, Kimmel was to be accused, unjustly in my view, of failing to let General Short know about the first message about destroying the Purple machines during their Wednesday afternoon conference. But Kimmel was abiding by the strict regulations governing dissemination of radio intelligence and, moreover, was unaware that the army had not informed Short about Purple, either. Anyway, the Purple information did not appear to be "vitally important" because it was not until the *next day* that Kimmel got news of the code burning in the local consulate.[51]

Furthermore, at least two of Short's staff did have the intelligence almost as soon as we did. Rochefort had informed his opposite number in the army that the Japanese were destroying important papers and code books, not only in Honolulu, but everywhere else.[52] I also communicated the same information to Colonel Edward W. Raley at Fort Shafter, although I was careful not to mention the Purple machine to him because this would have meant breaking our strict security regulations.

If both the navy and army commands, in addition to fleet headquarters, failed to make the correct deductions about the code burning, it was because we were becoming immune to what Kimmel called "scary reports."[53] At the time, there were no other clues that Oahu was in danger and the mere fact that there was a bonfire of papers in the embassy was not enough by itself to trigger our apprehension.

Washington

By sending us snippets of Magic out of context, the navy department had overlooked one of the cardinal rules of intelligence: A local commander can only react to information in the context of his immediate situation. Washington had the advantage of construing Tokyo's order to destroy the Purple machine in the broader framework. Stark believed that the message was "one of the most important dispatches we ever sent. We felt that war was a matter of time."[54]

Admiral Ingersoll went so far as to claim that the inclusion of the Japanese Washington embassy in Tokyo's signal clearly indicated that "the first aggressive Japanese move would include us and this was only to emphasize all of the previous dispatches that war with Japan was imminent."[55] Turner was to testify he believed there would be "war within two or three days," because, "the destruction of codes in that manner and in those places in my mind and experience is a sure indication of war with those nations in whose capitals or other places those codes are destroyed."[56]

Yet despite Turner's claim to omniscient farsightedness, the items about Magic reached us as the result of extraordinary circumstances rather than as the result of careful thought on the part of war plans division. McCollum was responsible for drafting the message about "highly reliable information."[57] The wording had been necessarily cautious in order for the director of naval intelligence to be able to issue it on his own authority without risking Turner's wrath.

"We could only send information out, without the approval of War Plans, if it contained nothing but pure facts," Wilkinson was later to explain. "We were prohibited from saying 'Invite your attention that this is a prelude to war.' We could not say that, but we could state a fact. This is what we did."[58]

I later found out that it had been Captain Safford, himself, who was responsible for the dispatch that mentioned Purple. After seeing the original decrypt he realized the importance of the order to destroy the codes. He telephoned McCollum to know what ONI was doing "to get a warning out to the Pacific Fleet."[59]

When Safford sensed from McCollum's tone that the Far East section desk might have difficulty sidestepping Turner, he decided to have a go himself even though it meant that he risked "overstepping the bounds." By drafting his own message, and by incorporating a reference not only to Purple but also giving the Japanese circular number, Safford flouted all the rules of security. He later testified that he had couched the dispatch "in highly technical language" because he knew that Coleman was the one officer at Pearl Harbor who would know its real importance.[60]

Tragically for us, the risks that Safford ran in exposing the extent of our code breaking were to no avail. The true importance of his dispatch was lost on Pacific Fleet headquarters because neither Kimmel nor I had any proper appreciation of the diplomatic intelligence picture.

It was a miscalculation that was compounded by Turner's assumption that Kimmel did know all about Magic. Any further war warnings were unnecessary. "The fact that this was going out in this manner" he considered was "all that was necessary to insure that the commanders-in-chief and the commandants of the fourteenth [Pearl Harbor] and sixteenth [Manila] naval districts thoroughly understood the urgency of the situation."[61]

That understanding, which the navy department and many historians have failed to appreciate, was dependent on the perspective that Washington received because of its daily access to Magic. Admiral Kimmel had been denied this essential knowledge. Meanwhile, the Sixteenth Naval District at Manila had an operating Purple machine. As I have said before, context is an essential factor in transforming information into intelligence.

For those who were eavesdropping on Tokyo's secret communications on a daily basis—such as the naval aide in the White House—it was obvious that the code-destruct decrypt was a sign that war was "going to break out," and that we were "going to be attacked."[62]

"Mr. President, this is a very significant dispatch," was how Captain John R. Beardall, Jr., recalled drawing Roosevelt's attention to these particular messages.

"When do you think it is going to happen?" Beardall inquired after Roosevelt had read the translation.

"Most any time," the president replied.[63]

The indications in Magic that war was looming a matter of days, or even hours, away brought the British ambassador back to the White House shortly after seven that evening. Halifax was under direct instruction from London to nail the president down once and for all on what American support Britain could count on if Japan attacked. Roosevelt finally assured the ambassador, in the presence of Under Secretary of State Sumner Welles, that he really did mean "armed support."

The president evidently felt more comfortable in giving such an unequivocal commitment because of his belief that three small vessels flying the Stars and Stripes were heading for a collision with the Japanese invasion forces. If this was so, no mention was made to the British ambassador. But Roosevelt did hint that the latest intelligence showed that the Japanese were heading for the Dutch East Indies and that "action of this kind would prove more easy of presentation to United States public opinion on the ground of threat to the Philippines by encirclement."[64]

That afternoon the secretary of the treasury had found Roosevelt buoyed up.

"I think the Japanese are doing everything they can to stall until they are ready," Roosevelt said. He also advised Morgenthau that he was "talking with the English about war plans." He was convinced that "the Japanese were running around like a lot of wet hens" after his formal inquiry about the increase in their Indochina forces.[65]

The president's speculation about Japan's confusion was probably the result of an earlier visit from an acquaintance of his, a minister named Dr. E. Stanley Jones. Like the Maryknoll fathers, the Reverend Dr. Jones was another cleric trying to bridge the widening chasm between Washington and Tokyo. Jones had arrived that morning at the White House, an unlikely emissary of the Japanese embassy. He brought with him a letter that urged Roosevelt to revive the *modus vivendi* in an appeal directly to the emperor over the head of Prime Minister Tojo.

The plea had originated from special envoy Kurusu, but the letter was drafted by Hidenari Terasaki. The involvement of the Japanese embassy's second secretary gave Roosevelt grounds for suspicion. Terasaki and his American wife were under FBI surveillance as the known heads of Japan's espionage operations in the United States. Roosevelt nonetheless told Jones that he was considering the appeal and Jones should tell Terasaki that "his secret is safe."[66]

4 DECEMBER   *"War Within Forty-eight Hours"*

Tokyo

Roosevelt may have assumed that confusion reigned in Tokyo, but the only "wet hens" were in the European section of the foreign ministry. For four days they had been awaiting word from the ambassador in Berlin that Hitler would accept a reinterpretation of the tripartite pact that would commit Germany to war providing Japan was the aggressor rather than the victim.

"Delay regrettable, but unavoidable," Ambassador Hiroshi Oshima had cabled the previous afternoon. Article 3 of the tripartite pact required the partners to come to each other's mutual aid only if they were attacked by a foreign power. Mussolini had already agreed to a modification of the article because of the "bullheadedness of the United States and the meddlesome nature of President Roosevelt." But he did not want Italy left on a limb and he needed to "confer with Germany on this point."[67]

Hitler, however, had neither the time nor inclination to mince legal niceties with the Japanese envoy at a time of great crisis for the Third Reich. He had left Berlin for his advance headquarters to revive the "final" offensive to take Moscow. It was stalling in the snows outside the Soviet capital. His foreign minister was left to handle the politely persistent Oshima.

"As I have told you before," Ribbentrop assured the Japanese ambassador, "we cannot give an official reply until the fuehrer has given his approval."[68] He would only "assume that there will be no objections."

Ribbentrop knew better than to badger the fuehrer with Japan's request at a time that the Wehrmacht's grand strategy was running up against unexpectedly stiff Russian resistance. Hitler's answer would be a sour reminder that the fresh Red Army division blocking his advance on Moscow had been released from border duty in Siberia by Tokyo's decision to advance southward.

With or without the support of her Axis partners, Japan had already taken the decision for war. Admiral Yamamoto that morning was summoned to the imperial palace. "The task facing the Combined Fleet is of the utmost importance," the emperor told him, "and the whole fate of our nation will depend on the outcome."[69] That afternoon the troopships and escorts of the Southern Expeditionary Force sailed from the harbors of Hainan Island. Their destination was the Isthmus of Kra, from where the invasion of Malaya and Thailand was to be launched.

Kido Butai

The Japanese warships had bucketed through another night of heavy rain and stormy seas. It was, as Fujita recorded it, weather "made to order" for not being sighted. On the other side of the coin, "refuelling is impossible and the heavy rolling and pitching of the battleship makes her crew distressed and suffer."[70]

There was some consolation when Nagumo received the Honolulu consulate's Saturday report. The ships in harbor were listed precisely according to the alphabetic designators of the "bomb plot," and it also advised, "No changes to 2 December Hawaiian Time. No signs of any standby condition observed, crews going about as usual."[71]

After eight days on a straight easterly course across the North Pacific, an hour after sunrise that morning the *Kido Butai* reached "Point C," some one thousand miles north-northwest of the Hawaiian chain and it hauled around onto a southeasterly track to begin its approach to the islands. *Akagi*'s signal lamp blinked out a lengthy message from Nagumo, which began:

Although the opening of hostilities is ordered for 8 December the situation in the Far East is growing increasingly urgent and it is difficult to tell when war will break out. At present we have no impression of a change in the state of alert of the enemy forces in the Hawaiian area. There is no indication that the movement of the *Kido Butai* has been detected and while it is difficult to predict the enemy intentions we shall have to be particularly vigilant.[72]

Within minutes the alert had been relayed to all the ships in the force. It was followed by the latest report of the American ships in Pearl Harbor, an update on refueling plans, and courses to be taken on the return trip after the attack. The clear reception of Hawaiian radio broadcasts not only gave the crews a taste for their prey but provided important weather data and confirmation that the islands were still ignorant of the approaching danger.

Pearl Harbor

The summary that I took to Admiral Kimmel that morning revealed that the Tokyo radio intelligence center had been busily sending out urgent reports to major commanders. We had also observed an important change in the pattern of traffic. The Takao station on Formosa had adopted Radio Tokyo's call sign and was handling fleet traffic on the high-speed circuits. According to Rochefort's "Running Hypo Chronology," which was located recently in his private papers and has never been fully explained, he believed "the large number of high-precedence messages and general distribution might indicate that the entire [Japanese] navy is being prepared for drastic action."[73]

From this evidence, and from the lack of messages originating from CinC Second Fleet, and CinC Third Fleet, we concluded that these forces must have put to sea and were observing radio silence in order not to betray their positions. They were still receiving messages but were not themselves sending. The Japanese had not found out the little trick we used of omitting the originator during operations. We taught them that later in the war after which they dutifully followed it, much to our chagrin because it made tracking an operational force observing radio silence impossible.

On Thursday evening we learned that our naval station at Guam had been ordered to "destroy all secret and confidential publications and other classified matter which is necessary for current purposes and special intelligence." They were also put on the alert to be "prepared to destroy instantly all classified matter you retain in event of emergency."[74]

In isolation this message was not judged by Kimmel as particularly ominous. Guam, which was under command of the Asiatic Fleet, was both indefensible and an anticipated Japanese target. The naval station there was part of our radio intelligence setup and had some very secret code material that Kimmel reasoned the navy department "wanted destroyed because they never should have had them."[75]

Admiral Kimmel might have been more concerned if Washington had informed him that Guam was *not* an isolated recipient of such drastic orders.

Washington

Earlier that day two dispatches similar to the one sent Guam had been sent to our naval attachés in Tokyo, Bangkok, Peiping, and Shanghai, as well as to our observers in Peiping and Tientsin. They were ordered to report the destruction of the code systems "at discretion" with the plain-language signal "Jabberwock" and the burning of confidential papers with the word "Boomerang."

The Japanese had chosen the code word *"Haruna"* as their confirmatory signal, indicating compliance with similar orders. It was the stream of *Haruna*s from their consulates and embassies that had prompted McCollum to ask Safford to draft the code-destruct dispatches for our legations in the Far East.[76]

Safford felt "officially responsible" for stripping ship, but his original strongly worded order to Guam had to be toned down by the over-cautious director of naval communications, Admiral Noyes. He was fearful that Turner might regard it as an action signal and veto its transmission. In a reference to what he termed "the war between war plans and ONI," McCollum noted that even the transmission of these dispatches "was accomplished with some difficulty."[77]

In this way Kimmel was not even made an information addressee for the orders shutting down our entire naval intelligence network in the Far East in anticipation of imminent Japanese attacks. This was a telling revelation that Washington did not regard Pearl Harbor as under any immediate threat.

There can be no doubt that by Thursday even the junior echelons of the navy department knew that war was imminent. At that morning's meeting of the Defense Communication Board, Captain Joseph Redman—Noyes's astute deputy—agreed wholeheartedly with Colonel Sadtler's prediction that "we will have war within 48 hours."[78]

Amazingly enough, it was not Japan's preparations for war but those of America that made the newspaper headlines that day. In a sensational scoop the isolationist Chicago *Tribune* revealed the details of General Marshall's "Victory Program" for committing a ten-million-man army to defeat Germany on the ground in Europe. Some cabinet members wanted the *Tribune*'s owner, Colonel Robert R. McCormick, put on trial for treason. His virulently anti-Roosevelt paper had published the army's documents, which had mysteriously been delivered to Senator Burton K. Wheeler of Montana, one of the leading champions on Capitol Hill of the isolationist cause.

The storm whipped up by the publication of the *Tribune*'s article headlined "FDR'S WAR PLANS" emphasized the magnitude of the president's dilemma. How could he confront the probability of a Japanese attack? Roosevelt reiterated the problem in a late-night meeting with the British ambassador as they discussed the issue of when to send an ultimatum to Japan. Churchill had wanted a parallel warning to include Thailand, Malaya, and the Dutch East Indies. The president, mindful of the address he was preparing for Congress, insisted he must make his declaration first.

"On account of political considerations here," Halifax reported, it was important "that this action should be based on independent necessities of the United States defense, and not appear to follow ourselves." The president also raised with the ambassador the clandestine letter he had received from Kurusu via the Reverend Dr. Jones the day before. Roosevelt felt that an appeal direct to the emperor "would strengthen his general case if things went wrong." While the president confirmed that he had indeed meant what he said about armed support extending to a British preemptive move to prevent a Japanese invasion of Thailand, the "character of this armed support must be decided by the [military] chiefs."[79] But Halifax was concerned about having to report yet again the presidential inclination to postpone the public declaration that would actually put the United States in the same boat as Britain in the Far East.

Time was running out faster than the president appreciated.

Royal Netherlands Navy submarines spotted a Japanese invasion force heading south. The Dutch overreacted when the Java command called on the Australian government to put into operation their joint part in the Rainbow 5 war plan. For twelve hours while the Australian cabinet met to discuss and defuse the situation the American military attaché held off sending the alert message to the Philippines.

5 DECEMBER *"It Could Mean One Thing"*

Tokyo

Late that evening—it was already Saturday across the international date line in Japan—the foreign ministry transmitted the pilot message that alerted their embassy in Washington to expect the final reply to the American ten-point proposal next day. The previous afternoon the vice-chief of the naval general staff, Vice Admiral Seiichi Ito, accompanied by Lieutenant General Shinichi Tanaka, the chief of the army general staff operations bureau, had called on the foreign minister to request a half-hour delay in the delivery of the fourteen-part message breaking off diplomatic relations with the United States.

Without revealing an operational secret they insisted that Togo (who did not know of the Pearl Harbor attack) ensure that their Washington embassy did not deliver the final Japanese message to the State Department until one o'clock the following afternoon in Washington.

Manila

British Admiral Sir Tom Phillips, who had arrived at Singapore forty-eight hours earlier with the *Prince of Wales,* flew in for a council of war. He met with General MacArthur and Admiral Hart to agree on a joint war strategy.

"Nothing would please me better than if they would give me three months and then attack me here," MacArthur told Phillips, listing the bombers and troops already on their way across the Pacific. Until then his plan was "in the nature of an improvisation." But the general had "every confidence that we can defend this place." Echoing Churchill's defiant words that he was "going to fight on the beaches" and "fight to the destruction on the shore lines," MacArthur predicted he had "nothing to fear at all" with his 112 tanks, his 125,000-man Filipino army, and his "ace unit" of B-17 bombers.[80]

The British admiral was impressed by MacArthur's vaunted air power. Phillips agreed that Britain's Far East fleet would base itself in Manila, rather than Singapore, for offensive operations against the Japanese. "Clearly, until you have a fleet you can't do much except act on the defensive," the admiral told Hart. "And it is quite clear that to stick your head out where the enemy is with a very inferior force would be foolish."[81]

That afternoon an RAF reconnaissance patrol over the Gulf of Siam spotted a Japanese convoy steaming southwest of the tip of Indochina. The news prompted Admiral Phillips to cut short the conference and make arrangements to fly back to Singapore next day "to be there when the war starts."

Four days later Phillips was to lose his battleship—and his life—in a tragic demonstration of the truth of his words to Hart.

The British report put Manila on notice that a Japanese invasion of the Isthmus of Kra was probably only days away. That same afternoon Admiral Hart received a cable from Captain John M. Creighton, the U.S. naval observer in Singapore, quoting a signal received from London by Air Vice Marshal Brooke Popham, the British commander in chief in Malaya:

We have now received assurance of armed support in cases as follows:

(A). We are obliged to execute our plans to forestall Japs landing Isthmus of Kra or take action in reply to Nips invasion in any other part of Siam.
(B). If Dutch Indies are attacked and we go to their defense.
(C). If Japs attack us [sic] the British.

Therefore without reference to London put plan in action if first you have good info[rmation] Jap expedition advancing with the apparent intention of landing in Kra, second if Nips violate any part of Thailand.

If N[etherlands] E[ast] I[ndies] are attacked put into operation plans agreed upon between British and Dutch.[82]

The apparent guarantees of American military support were a lightning bolt from the blue to Admiral Hart. Forty-eight hours earlier he had been instructed only to "exchange full military information with the British and Dutch naval commanders."[83] This was the first he had heard of any commitment that he would have to fight even if American territory was not attacked.

The Asiatic Fleet commander shot off an urgent cable to the navy department: "Learn from Singapore we have assured British armed support under three or four eventualities. Have received no corresponding instructions from you."[84]

No official instructions were forthcoming. None had been drafted. Until the president made his appeal to Congress for an ultimatum to Japan, the only assistance the navy department knew about was an informal one.

Apparently, the British chiefs of staff in London had jumped the gun or were trying to force Roosevelt's hand. They also sent a similar message to their Middle East headquarters in Egypt. This one was responsible for the warm welcome that Colonel Bonner Fellers was to receive upon his arrival in Cairo.

"Bonner, you will be in the war in twenty-four hours," Air Marshall Sir Arthur Longmore told the American military observer the following morning. "We have a secret signal Japan will strike the U.S. in twenty-four hours." The colonel was amazed. He knew nothing about Japanese-American relations having reached the breaking point. He toyed with the idea of relaying a report to Washington, but did not send it. After thinking it over, he decided that if the British knew about the attack, we also knew about it.[85]

Admiral Hart, however, was better informed, thanks to the Purple machine and Station Cast's cryptanalysts. He had already given the orders the day before to disperse his meager fleet. The cruisers and destroyers were sent south, out of range of Japanese air attacks. The night before, Japanese planes began flying brazenly over the coast of Luzon and he had come to the conclusion that if Japan intended to launch an assault on the British and Dutch, they must simultaneously invade the Philippines.

"My own estimate was that they would not leave us on their flank," Hart was to testify. "Consequently, they would attack."[86] Unfortunately, Kimmel's headquarters was not an information addressee of Hart's signal asking Washington to confirm the guarantees of armed support that had been given the British. Admiral Kimmel had already asked the same question and received no answer.

Kido Butai

Visibility was poor, but the seas were calm that day. Nagumo's meteorologists were having difficulty accurately forecasting the changeable conditions. A leaden cloud base eased the admiral's constant worry about being spotted. Another Honolulu intelligence report, less than a day old, also gave comfort, because it revealed that the Americans were making only "occasional" long-range flights from Oahu.

This reassuring intelligence did not relax the vigilance on the warships. It had been stepped up after Combined Fleet headquarters radioed precise orders on how Nagumo was to deal with any unexpected encounters. These had been relayed by signal lamp to all the commanding officers in the force:

1. A warship which sights the enemy or third-nation warships or merchant ships, must recognize the need for concealing our plans and so will immediately render it incapable of signaling and if necessary will attack and sink it.

2. Panamanian, Norwegian and Greek ships shall be treated as hostile enemy shipping.[87]

The orders to deal ruthlessly with vessels of countries closely associated with Britain and the United States *excluded* those flying the Soviet flag. It was on this day that the *Kido Butai* finally encountered a "vessel of a third nation," as it was cryptically described by a former Japanese navy intelligence officer.[88]

"Those in command of the task force watched the progress of the ship in question, a merchantman, with an extraordinary degree of tension," Hiroyuki Agawa wrote in his definitive biography of Admiral Yamamoto. "Had it shown any signs of radioing a report on the movements of the task force to anyone else, it would probably have found itself at the bottom of the sea within a few minutes."

Significantly, perhaps, neither Volume 10 of *Senshi Sosho*, the official Japanese history, nor an enlisted man's wartime account, *Southern Cross*, which both refer to the receipt of the alert that a Soviet freighter would be encountered, makes any reference to an actual sighting. That it took a quarter of a century for the Japanese government to publicly confirm the interception is consistent with Japan's reluctance to make any official admission of events that would open new questions about the attack on Pearl Harbor.

Tokyo's instructions to Nagumo suggest that the Soviet Union was the only "third nation" that could be trusted to keep silent about sighting the *Kido Butai*. This can be the only explanation of why this ship was allowed to go on its way. There is no indication that the admiral even considered it necessary to make a precautionary boarding of the ship to remove its radio. That no crew members have ever come forward to tell the story of this remarkable mid-ocean meeting only two days before Pearl Harbor is further confirmation that the ship was from Russia, and not from Peru, which was the only other nation whose ships were still on the North Pacific route to Japan.

The timing and the location of the contact reveal that the vessel sighted by the *Kido Butai* could have been only *Uritsky*. The twelve-hundred-ton freighter had sailed from San Francisco on 28 November and, according to port records, had made a brief stopover at Portland, Oregon, the previous Sunday.[89]

The fact that Tokyo had issued the alert at all and that the *Kido Butai* ran into the Russian ship, which was some nine hundred miles south of the shorter great circle track to Vladivostok from the west coast, suggests that the Japanese had some tipoff. This could have come only from the Russians who were the only ones who knew that *Uritsky* was so heavily laden that their small freighter would be routed on a course unusually far south from the heavy weather off the Alaskan coast. The warning and the contact indicate a hitherto unsuspected degree of collusion between Moscow and Tokyo. If the *Uritsky* did sight the *Kido Butai* that last Friday of peace in the Pacific, her master did not make the customary sighting reports in plain Morse on the recognized international shipping frequencies. They could have been made after the freighter was safely out of range of the Japanese fleet. Although no such reports were picked up, it is probable that the *Uritsky* would have reported such important military intelligence by secret Soviet cipher transmissions outside the standard frequencies.[90]

Mysterious radio signals have even led some into the assertion that the navy tracked the Japanese fleet's advance on Pearl Harbor. While such charges cannot be made to fit the facts, it has been known since the war that the radio operator of S.S. *Lurline* did report receiving messages on the lower marine frequencies on the Matson liner's second and third nights out from Los Angeles on passage to Honolulu. The liner's relatively unsophisticated direction-finding apparatus placed the signals "north and west" of Hawaii. This was also in the general direction of Japan—or Vladivostok. Although the operator positively identified one station call sign as "JCS" Yokohama, it appeared the signals were being repeated by small craft. Their apparent mid-Pacific origination could be explained by atmospheric anomalies—or misidentification of the daily position reports radioed out by *Uritsky*.[91]

If the Russian freighter was the source of these signals, then this would explain why the *Kido Butai* survivors—and the record—deny that the Japanese force ever broke radio silence. It would certainly be astonishing if Admiral Nagumo had permitted a breach of operational orders that could have put the whole operation in jeopardy. But the gullibility of those uninitiated in radio intelligence has been fed by the "revelations" in 1982 of a so-called Seaman Z. He was later identified as Robert D. Ogg, who in 1941 was a seaman first class attached to the Twelfth Naval District Intelligence Office in San Francisco. A year after his story had made newspaper headlines, Ogg provided a detailed deposition to Commander Irwin G. Newman, U.S.N.R. (Ret.), of Naval Security Group Command.[92]

When Ogg's deposition was declassified by the National Security Agency in 1984, it became clear that his recollections were not as specific, or as sensational, as certain revisionist historians had tried to make them out to be. The transmissions were allegedly picked up by commercial radio companies on Wednesday, Thursday, and Friday, 3–5 December and, according to Ogg's statement, contained "no reference that it was a carrier force rather than a fishing force."[93] More important, he conceded that they might not even have been Japanese (Ogg does not speak the language). Under questioning by an experienced naval officer, Ogg admitted that their language was never precisely identified to him at the time and that "they just said these were Japanese and I presumed the language . . . but I'm not sure of that either."[94]

Since the radio signals were on a lower frequency than those which the Japanese used for their transmissions, it is likely that they could have been misidentified. They could have been Russian, because the Soviet Union's merchant ships did not transmit or receive on the standard international bands. It is probable that the bearings "on these odd frequencies" were determined only by an approximate triangulation from shore stations in an "area east of the International date line."[95] This is an enormous expanse of ocean, so it is possible that Russian signals were also picked up from a second Soviet freighter, the *Pavlov Vinogradov*, which was also crossing the North Pacific after sailing from Los Angeles on the sixth of November.[96]

Another bit of circumstantial evidence pointing toward a possible collusion between Tokyo and Moscow suggests that Stalin had a very precise knowledge of how, when, and where the war in the Pacific would break out.

One of the passengers on board the last Pan Am flight across the Pacific was Maksim Litvinov, the newly appointed Soviet ambassador to the United States. He was the Gromyko of his day. Beaming for the photographers, he stepped ashore with his wife from the Boeing flying boat *China Clipper,* which docked at Honolulu that Friday afternoon. That Litvinov managed to reach the west coast safely and arrive in Washington on the very day that war burst upon the Pacific may have been a curious coincidence. But it may be yet another indication that Stalin knew far more about the Japanese strategic plans than he chose to reveal to either Churchill or Roosevelt. It was certainly very much in the strategic interests of the Soviet Union that the Japanese become embroiled in war with the United States.

Pearl Harbor

Our attention that Friday morning at Pacific Fleet headquarters was focused on the western side of the Pacific. Tokyo radio circuits had been sending out messages at a very high rate for the past twenty-four hours. From the continued absence of Second or Third fleet originators in any of the traffic, Rochefort was certain that these forces were already at sea and heading south.[97]

This was the up-to-date intelligence that was given to Rear Admiral John H. Newton who sailed in the morning in *Chicago* to provide the heavy cruiser escort for carrier *Lexington* in Task Force 12. The mission of this task force was to ferry the marine fighter reinforcements to Midway and carry out extensive reconnaissance sweeps of the northwestern approaches to the Hawaiian Islands. Newton, who was the commander of the fleet's cruiser forces, left harbor believing that the "greatest menace" he faced was the threat of submarine attack.[98] It was a concern shared by Admiral Wilson Brown, who later in the day set course for Johnston Island with Task Force 5.

At this point, the disposition of Kimmel's forces was as follows: All the carriers were at sea with specific missions. All the heavy cruisers and more than one half of the fleet's destroyers were at sea protecting the carriers. Only the battle force—the old, slow battleships with their escorts of light cruisers and destroyers—was still at Pearl Harbor.

Meanwhile, our suspicions that the Japanese were concentrating on prowling Hawaiian waters was not considered in itself an especially urgent indication of the imminence of war. Our own boats were on surveillance missions off their home islands. And yet the worry about their submarines had been growing ever since Hypo had detected the easterly movement of Japan's main submarine flotillas toward the Marshalls. The previous night an unidentified submarine had been reported off Hawaii, and that afternoon destroyers picked up two suspicious underwater contacts barely five miles south of Diamond Head.

The newly issued fleet standing orders authorized offensive action against potentially hostile submarines detected in the vicinity of our base and exercise areas. That Friday afternoon the captain of destroyer *Selfridge* had made a sonar contact, but decided not to release any depth charges. As long as we remained at peace with Japan, the prospect of sparking an incident that might ignite war made skippers wary of taking such decisive action.

This was yet another instance of the problems that Kimmel faced when it came to operating a peacetime fleet under what were becoming wartime conditions. His concern was how to effect the transition without provoking an incident that would precipitate hostilities on his doorstep.

Washington

Kimmel would have been more worried had he been informed that intelligence was reaching Washington that convinced some senior officers that hostilities were not a matter of chance, but absolute certainty.

Ever since Tuesday, when Magic had revealed that the Japanese had ordered their diplomatic missions to destroy their code books and machines, Tokyo's winds code alert had assumed a vital new importance in the minds of certain ranking generals and admirals. It was now regarded as the trigger by which Japan would communicate its final decision for peace or war.

All naval radio stations were ordered to institute special watches. The On the Roof Gang operators were instructed to monitor every Japanese weather broadcast for any combination of words that might resemble the "east wind rain" code signal.

One unforeseen result was that OP-20-G's work load increased suddenly and dramatically. Bales of falsely identified winds alerts were relayed to Washington for analysis. This added to the work load of Captain Safford's already overburdened team, and it further diverted his attention and resources from the more critical work of penetrating the Japanese naval code systems.

The pressure was such that Admiral Noyes, the director of naval communications, made a daily check for anything remotely resembling a winds execute message. As Safford put it: "Higher Authority began heckling me as to the possibility of having missed it."[99]

The navy department attached such special importance to the three winds code alerts that they were typed up on small reminder cards that made it clear which country's relations with Tokyo were "in danger."

HIGASHI NO KAZE AME (EAST WIND RAIN) = JAPAN-US
KITA NO KAZE KUMORI (NORTH WIND CLOUDY) = JAPAN-USSR

NISHI NO KAZE HARE (west wind clear) = japan-british[100]

These prompt cards were prepared at the direction of Admiral Noyes by Lieutenant Commander Alwin D. Kramer who was head of translation in OP-20-GZ. They were intended to be kept in the pockets of the five most senior officers in the navy department. Admiral Noyes, realizing that he would be the person who would flash the word that we were at war, had ordered Captain Safford to have couriers standing by round the clock to get word out to them as soon as OP-20-G translated a winds alert signal.[101]

This is precisely what appears to have happened. It was either that Thursday or Friday. But just which message it was and whether it was a genuine winds alert has been fiercely debated ever since. The debate is related in full in the Notes section of this book, but what is important is that Safford testified at the 1944 naval court of inquiry that an "east wind rain" intercept was received on either 4 or 5 December.

Besides Safford's account, there is a blank page (No: JD7001) in the Japanese diplomatic intercepts file,[102] plus the testimony of Colonel Otis K. Sadtler. This thirty-one-year veteran was a Signal Corps officer, who occupied the same sort of supervisory position in the army signal intelligence operations section as Safford did in naval intelligence. As opposite numbers they had learned to work closely together, forgetting the interservice barrier that so many of their fellow officers failed to surmount. Sadtler's compellingly forthright and precise testimony makes it clear that a winds code alert was received Friday morning, 5 December.

"About 9 or shortly thereafter on Friday, December 5, Admiral Noyes telephoned me to the effect that the message was in," Sadtler asserted.[103] It had to be that morning because the day before he had spent all morning at the weekly Defense Communications Board meeting.

The intercept that prompted Noyes to call Sadtler was, according to a letter written by Safford in 1943, confirmed by Kramer's reply to it, which was written *six months* before either of them was called upon to give any testimony. That it was an intercept from the Maryland Station M appears certain, because it was not a plain-language broadcast, but a kana transmission in Morse.[104]

According to Safford's letter the Japanese naval radio station had broadcast "Higashi no kaze ame. Mishi [sic] no kaze hare."[105] The wording appeared to match exactly the emergency-alert reminder cards that Japanese relations with *both* Britain and the United States were in danger. After the teletype machine had spewed out the message, the watch officer, who was not a linguist, thought it matched the correct wording but "was not sure of it." He telephoned Kramer, who "arrived early in the morning and verified it."[106]

When Safford came into his office shortly before 0800 that morning, he recalled how Lieutenant A. A. Murray had come in "with a big smile on his face and a piece of paper in his hand and said: 'Here it is!' as he handed me the original yellow teletype sheet with the significant Winds underscored and the meaning in Kramer's handwriting at the bottom." Safford immediately had five copies typed up and distributed to the same officers who had been provided with the winds code prompt cards and then went to discuss the matter with Admiral Noyes.[107]

"As I remember it," Noyes was to testify in 1944, before the naval court of inquiry, "we received some outside information which afterwards turned out not to be correct."[108] The director of naval communications subsequently became even more vague, but admitted that the intercept he got that morning "was taken to mean that an execute of this 'Winds Message' had been received."[109]

That was certainly the impression Noyes conveyed in his telephone conversation, as Sadtler recalled it: "I asked him which one, and he told me that it was the word that implied a break between Japan and Great Britain." Sadtler regarded that phone call as "the most important message I ever received." He hurried to the office of the chief of military intelligence to tell General Sherman Miles that "the word is in."[110]

Colonel Rufus S. Bratton was called in. The army's Far East director of military intelligence was told by Sadtler, "Diplomatic relations between Japan and Great Britain are in danger." The head of the army Far East section then pulled one of the navy winds code prompt cards out of his pocket and asked "which one of those words it was."[111] Since Sadtler knew no Japanese, he went back to his office to use his secure navy telephone to confirm that it was not another false alert.

Noyes, who knew no Japanese either and had no time to verify the winds code message because he was on his way to Stark's morning meeting, insisted the intercept "meant Japan and Great Britain." Sadtler went back to Miles and confirmed that the message received was "definitely meaning Japan and Great Britain" and that verification would be given later.[112]

Sadtler did not wait for verification. Although he had not seen the intercept, its indication of the imminence of war was obvious to him. Bratton was also certain that in conjunction with the codes-destruct signals "it could mean one thing, and that was war."[113]

Sadtler knew that Japan's ambassador in the United States had been instructed to keep one of his two Purple cipher machines in operation but that their London embassy had been ordered to destroy both. This was a sure sign to him that relations with Britain were already at an end and that a rupture with the United States was only days, or hours, away. Sadtler regarded the winds alert therefore as further confirmation that "we were going to have war in a very short time."[114]

Filled with concern and apprehension, Sadtler drafted what he considered an appropriate alert to be sent out immediately to the Pacific army commanders: "Reliable information indicates war with Japan in the very near future. Take every precaution to prevent a repetition of Port Arthur. Notify Navy." But General Gerow rejected it because he believed that "the various departments had been adequately warned."[115]

Sadtler's initiative ran out of gas because Noyes never telephoned confirmation that the winds alert was genuine. Meanwhile, Bratton had telephoned McCollum, his opposite number. The navy's Far East section had not yet been told about the intercept.

False or not, that Friday morning call from the navy department sent a current of concern around the war department because everybody, as Sadtler put it, "knew about that winds message."[116] General Miles himself authorized the sending of a dispatch to the Panama command that warned, "U.S.-Japanese relations strained. Will inform you if and when severance of Japanese relations imminent."[117] But it was not given a priority stamp, and so it was not transmitted for forty-eight hours!

Bratton had a nagging concern about the winds alert. He was able to obtain Miles's approval for a signal to General Short's headquarters advising the Hawaiian command's intelligence officer, "Contact Commander Rochefort immediately thru [sic] Commandant Fourteen Naval District regarding broadcasts from Tokyo reference weather."[118] Rochefort was not able to confirm or deny anything, because no warning that a winds alert had been received was ever sent out to us at Pearl Harbor.

Even if Noyes ultimately decided the winds alert was false, it also prompted a Friday morning meeting between admirals Turner and Ingersoll to review the situation. Turner later testified that there was a "50-50" chance of a "heavy raid" on Pearl Harbor. "What more ought to be done?" he claimed to have asked Ingersoll. "Should we send more dispatches or what?"[119]

Ingersoll was of the opinion that this was unnecessary because "everyone" in the navy had expected war with Japan for twenty years. He was prepared to concede, however, that the burning of their codes certainly made it seem more imminent and that he "expected to be at war very shortly."[120]

After Ingersoll, according to Turner, had concluded that "everything had been done covering the entire situation that ought to be done," the two admirals went to the CNO's office. Stark also did not merely "expect," but proclaimed that he "knew," war was a probability.[121] Nonetheless, he "stood together" with Marshall on the need to "gain time" for the reinforcements, already on their way to reach the Philippines. After Stark's flag secretary emphasized the dangers of crying wolf with more warnings, the triumvirate was "unanimous" in the conclusion that their earlier alerts to the fleet were "sufficient."[122]

McCollum, however, did not believe that sufficient notice of Japan's belligerent intent had been given the overseas commands. According to his testimony at the 1945 congressional inquiry and his oral history mentioned earlier, he condensed the indications of war from his 1 December memorandum, into a dispatch and (so Safford claims) added the winds alert and an interpretation for good measure. Then he took his message up to Wilkinson.

"Wilkinson approved the message and discussed it with Admiral Noyes," Safford claimed. He saw the McCollum alert at about 1500 that day. And he was present when Noyes dismissed it as "an insult to the intelligence of the commander in chief [Kimmel]."[123]

"I do not agree with you," Admiral Wilkinson had replied. "Admiral Kimmel is a very busy man, with a lot of things on his mind, and he may not see the picture as clearly as you and I do."[124]

Safford recalled how Wilkinson then left to "get it released by the front office"—meaning Turner, the director of war plans.[125] It was not until two years later that Safford realized while reading the Roberts Commission testimony that McCollum's warning had never been sent. It prompted Safford's search for the missing winds alert and ultimately his crusade to set the record straight by showing how "Admiral Kimmel was a scapegoat from the start."[126]

While McCollum later admitted that he had tried hard to get another war warning sent out on "either 4th or 5th" December,[127] he denied that it had been inspired by a winds alert. He testified that he had used his memorandum for drafting a war warning, which Wilkinson had approved. However, it had stuck in the throat of the director of war plans.

Turner took a dim view of anyone telling him how to perform, especially since his morning conference had been "unanimous" in its agreement that his 27 November warning was "sufficient."[128] McCollum had yet to see this dispatch. Otherwise he might not have continued to press for his own version. Eventually Turner sourly took the new draft. He "made a number of changes in it, striking out all except the informational parts of it."[129] McCollum protested this emasculation. "Finally, I raised so much sand in Turner's office that he showed me the dispatch," McCollum would recall.[130]

"Well, good gosh, you put in the words 'war warning,'" McCollum exclaimed with surprise. "I do not know what could be plainer than that, but nevertheless I would like to see mine go too."[131]

"Well, if you want to send it, you either send it the way I corrected it, or take it back to Wilkinson and we will argue about it," Turner snapped.

Turner later testified that McCollum "tore up his proposed dispatch," saying, "That is enough."[132] It was his contention that the 27 November warning was indeed "covering the entire situation."[133]

According to McCollum, he returned with the penciled draft to try to persuade Wilkinson to reason with Turner about the necessity of sending out an updated message that war was imminent. "Leave it here with me for a while," McCollum said he was told.[134]

McCollum's dispatch was never sent. No copies of his draft survived to show how we might have interpreted it at Pearl Harbor. But it is hard not to believe that his detailed war indications based on Magic, or Sadtler's punchier warning with its reminder of Japan's historic preference for surprise attack, would have directed Kimmel's attention to the imminence of war with Japan.

If a 5 December winds alert was removed from the files, the resulting documentation and testimony it generated indicate two things. First, some army and naval officers doubted the adequacy of Washington's two formal war alerts. Second, other army and naval officers were determined to cover up their efforts to stop another warning's being sent out. So although Safford was left hanging by his unsupported testimony, the navy department had to go to extreme lengths to demonstrate the message's nonexistence.

Charges were made in 1945, and confirmed to the authors recently by a brother officer and neighbor, that Captain Kramer was "persuaded" to modify his testimony about the winds message by the threat of permanent confinement in a psychiatric ward. Then there are affidavits from scores of On the Roof Gang radio operators. Their claims are astonishingly identical, saying they did not know about the winds messages "until I read about it in the newspapers."[135] Such uniformity suggests that their answers might have been dictated.

Perhaps the most telling indication of the rationale behind the official effort to deny there ever was a winds intercept is contained in the recently released waspish memorandum from the naval liaison officer appointed to assist the congressional investigation. On 13 February 1946, after the hearings had been safely concluded, Lieutenant Commander John F. Baecher advised the secretary of the navy that awarding Safford the Legion of Merit for his wartime work was "inappropriate." On the other hand, Baecher maintained, Captain Kramer deserved a higher decoration "because the effect of his testimony was to support the integrity of the higher command of the Navy."[136]

The recent release of the massive amount of the documentation generated by Baecher's office in 1945 is in itself a tangible example of the extent to which the "integrity of the higher command" was felt to be at stake. It also demonstrates how great were the steps taken to conceal the navy department's collective responsibility for Pearl Harbor.

It was also ironic that on Friday, 5 December 1941, the war alarm was sounding more loudly at the navy and war departments than at the Japanese embassy thirteen blocks away on Massachusetts Avenue. The Japanese ambassador and his special envoy still had no real knowledge of their government's commitment to hostilities. This is evident from the two requests they made that day to Tokyo. The first was to "delay for a while yet the destruction of the one code machine,"[137] and the other was to try to postpone the departure of Terasaki, who had been instructed to "leave by plane within the next couple of days."[138]

The requested delay in the second secretary's departure for Mexico had less to do with "the importance of his intelligence set-up" than Kurusu's hope that the White House might yet respond to his personal appeal to Roosevelt. Two days earlier Nomura had advised the foreign ministry about the Reverend Dr. Jones's mission: "Terasaki had Stanley Jones, with whom he is on the most intimate terms, call upon Roosevelt."[139] This message shows that Jones's intervention was neither as disinterested, clandestine, nor unofficial as some recent historians have suggested.

Nomura did, however, confirm that "the president clearly hopes for peace" and was considering some sort of "emergency diplomatic means."[140] That some emergency appeal was needed to break the diplomatic impasse was apparent to both Nomura and Hull when they met that Friday morning at the State Department. The Japanese envoys were to present Tokyo's response to the United States' diplomatic note expressing concern about Japan's military buildup in Indochina. Premier Tojo's curt answer to an "exaggerated" report was that Japanese troops were taking "precautionary measures" in response to "frequent signs" of Chinese movements along the frontier.[141]

Hull dismissed the claim that Japanese troops were in Indochina for purposes solely of defense. A sharp exchange of views concluded with Nomura's plea to Hull that "there must be wise statesmanship to save the situation."[142] To the ambassador's candid observation, "This isn't getting us anywhere," Hull retorted that "we are not looking for trouble, but at the same time we are not running away from menaces."[143]

The acrimonious tenor of the meeting convinced Hull that it was time for the department to instruct our diplomats in the Far East to make preparations for the destruction of secret papers and closing down "in the event of a sudden emergency cutting-off of communications with the department."[144]

Hull's mood of pessimistic resolution was apparent when the secretary of state reported the increasing strain in Japanese-American relations to Friday afternoon's cabinet meeting. "With every hour that passes I become more convinced that they are not playing in the open," Hull told the meeting. According to Secretary of Labor Frances Perkins, the administration's ranking woman, the situation was "ticklish." Navy Secretary Knox then revealed the riveting information that "very secret information" led the navy to believe a Japanese fleet was at sea, heading south and "going to do something."[145]

Singapore was mentioned. The president confirmed that the British base was the "presumed objective," although he could not be certain that they might not also strike elsewhere, even the Aleutians. "What shall we do?" was the question Roosevelt posed to his cabinet. "If they proceed south towards Singapore, what's the problem for the United States? What should the United States do?" According to the Perkins account he wanted a straw poll of their opinions, not a formal policy vote. "It is a terrible problem," the president said as he told them he was "just checking to see how your minds are operating. . . . It's a terrible problem. I hope I won't have to act on it, or settle it, but we may have to."[146]

The secretary of labor was one of those who declared she thought we should go to the aid of the British if Singapore was attacked. But the immediacy of war came as a shock to her. The cabinet came out with a clear majority in favor of standing by Britain if it came to a fight. Roosevelt could take some comfort in the vote. He knew that his critical appeal for congressional support for a full-fledged ultimatum to Japan could not be postponed for long.

That afternoon the secretary of state left with the president a twenty-seven-page draft of the proposed address to Congress in anticipation that he might have to send it up to Capitol Hill as soon as the legislators returned from their weekend break. In reading the recently surfaced document, one can see that its very length and convoluted logic indicate the problem that Roosevelt would face in getting a declaration of war if Japan did not attack the United States.

"I have to report to you a serious danger which is threatening this country and its interests in the Far East," the address began. A dozen pages cataloging and condemning Japanese expansionism, and Tokyo's adherence to the Axis pact, concluded, "Simply stated, what we are confronted with in the Far East is a repetition of the strategy pursued by Hitler in Europe." After attempting to "subjugate China" and invading Indochina, Japan "now threatens with imminent attack various neighboring areas, not excluding the Philippines." After eight months of negotiations the "Japanese government have given no indication of a clear-cut desire to follow the course of peace."[147]

There would be a direct threat to American security and interests if Japan were to become "established in Singapore or the Netherlands East Indies or, were she to dominate China, the lines of communication between the United States, China and other peace-loving nations would be cut." The question that Roosevelt planned to ask in Congress was "whether the United States is or is not to stand by while Japan goes forward with a program of conquest by force." Permitting further Japanese aggression would not only destroy American commercial interests but the "farsighted experiment" of impending Philippine independence. It would "forever terminate the prestige and influence of the United States . . . throughout the Orient." Roosevelt was to remind Congress that "we are pledged to aid those countries," who were defending themselves against "Hitlerism," and express his "full confidence that it is within our capacity to withstand any attack which anyone may make upon us."[148]

Precisely what pledges he had given to the British were left unstated, but they were implicit in his concluding sentence: "As commander-in-chief, I have given appropriate orders to our Forces in the Far East." Whether a majority of Congress would have backed the "appropriate orders" that the president had already issued was never put to the test. But his intention to brand the Japanese as "no better than the Nazi leaders" who asserted their "right to world conquest," to establish "slave states" in a "rule of merciless horror matched only by that of Hitlerized Germany," would undoubtedly have rallied support from the American public.[149]

Whatever rhetorical salvos the president was toying with that Friday, his main objective was still to delay firing them. He knew that his military chiefs needed every day that could be bought to get more reinforcements to the Philippines. Two troop convoys were already in mid-Pacific. The first flight of the forty-eight B-17 bombers, which would more than double General MacArthur's strategic bombing capability, were only twenty-four hours from taking off from airfields on the west coast.

Roosevelt had told his cabinet that Friday that he still had one more diplomatic card to play. This was an appeal to the emperor of Japan himself—the first direct communication from an American president since Millard Fillmore sent his famous greeting of "peace and friendship" with Commodore Matthew C. Perry in 1853. Whether a similar ploy would prove effective eighty-eight years later was much more doubtful. But the president now realized that the time had come to make his final bid to avert war.

6 DECEMBER   *"The Japanese Won't Attack Us"*

Tokyo

At 1000 Tokyo time that morning the main naval radio station at Owada relayed Admiral Yamamoto's eve of war message to all the ships under his command. It was the solemn promise given on behalf of his men to the emperor: "I humbly accept your Majesty's order and promise that every officer and man of the Combined Fleet is ready to give his body and soul to achieve the goal of this expedition in answer to the Imperial Command."[150]

Kido Butai

Cloudy skies concealed the noonday sun. Nagumo's force crossed the "last hurdle," as staff officer Fujita called the seven-hundred-mile limit of long-range air patrols from the Hawaiian Islands. But that weekend none of our PBYs was scheduled to patrol north of Oahu. The final refueling of the carrier's destroyer escorts went ahead without a hitch. The last of the accompanying oilers dropped behind and all hands busied themselves with preparations for battle.

Water, which had been rationed to preserve fuel, was now made available for bathing for the first time since leaving Tankan Bay. Each ship held prayer meetings so that their crews could enter into battle clean in spirit as well as body.

Just before dawn a message had been received from submarine *I-72*, which had been scouting off Maui, that the "American Fleet is not in ALL [the code designates for Lahaina Bay]."[151] A final reconnaissance was to be made the following morning to confirm that none of the Pacific Fleet was in its alternative anchorage. Commander Genda prepared for the final aircrew briefings on the assumption that the air fleet would be attacking Pearl Harbor.

That afternoon the *Kido Butai* hauled around onto a course due south and increased speed to twelve knots for the final high-speed night run to the dawn launching point for the air attack. The "D G" code flags were broken out on *Akagi*'s masthead to signify the message that Admiral Togo had flown thirty-seven years earlier at the Battle of Tsushima Strait: THE FATE OF OUR NATION DEPENDS ON THIS BATTLE—ALL HANDS WILL EXERT THEMSELVES TO THEIR UTMOST.[152]

The flagship's crew cheered as they went to battle stations. That evening, the receipt of Tokyo's relay of the Honolulu consulate's latest report indicated there were no unusual American activities or air patrols. Admiral Nagumo finally began to believe that his force had a good chance to emulate Togo's stunning 1904 naval victory.

The overall plans were carefully scheduled to enable the *Kido Butai* to achieve the maximum of surprise by making the first strikes. But that afternoon Combined Fleet headquarters relayed that army pilots flying from Indochina had "shot down a British seaplane to the westward of FGU [the Japanese coordinates for the southernmost tip of Indochina]."[153]

The first blood spilled in the Pacific war belonged to a Royal Australian Air Force pilot from the Kota Bharu airfield on Malaya's north coast. Nevertheless, he had managed to radio a warning that the large Japanese convoy was rounding Cambodia Point heading east before his twin-engine Hudson crashed into the Gulf of Siam.

Pearl Harbor

All the intelligence we had been able to assemble at Pacific Fleet headquarters indicated that the South China Sea was about to become the cockpit of war. It was the focus of my attention that Saturday. At my daily briefing shortly after 0800 I had drawn to Admiral Kimmel's attention that an invasion of Siam or Malaya was imminent. The continued absence of carrier transmission suggested that one or more divisions were tied up in the southward advance.

We had received confirmation early that morning from the Asiatic Fleet that a "25 ship convoy with an escort of 6 cruisers and 10 destroyers" had been sighted off the southernmost tip of Indochina. Not far behind was another convoy of "10 ships with 2 cruisers and 10 destroyers," also on a westerly course. Thirty more transports and a large cruiser had been spotted in Camranh Bay. Admiral Hart's estimate was that "all forces will make for Kohtron"—the narrow of the Isthmus of Kra on the frontier between Siam and British Malaya.[154]

If the Japanese convoys maintained their present course and speed, I calculated, the invasion would hit the beaches early the following day. Siam and Britain would then be at war, and I was concerned that the Japanese might also be planning a simultaneous attack on the Philippines. I did not believe Japan would risk leaving her flank exposed.

After my briefing Admiral Kimmel called in his staff to discuss the situation. Meanwhile, he sent me to get the opinion of Admiral Pye, the battle force commander.

The trip by gig across the harbor to *California* was a welcome break from the mounting tension at the submarine base. It was a glorious day, and the flagship of the battle force was moored in majestic isolation off Ford Island at the head of Battleship Row. I found the admiral, Rear Admiral Pye, and his acting chief of staff on *California*'s quarterdeck. I handed them the dispatch containing the report of the Japanese convoys heading into the Gulf of Siam, and the many naval vessels, including submarines, sighted off the Indochina coast. They both read it and concluded that Japan was probably not going to attack the British but would occupy a position in the Gulf of Siam as an advance base to operate from, probably against the Burma Road.

They asked me what fleet intelligence made of the latest reports. I told them frankly and very definitely that I considered the movement to the Gulf of Siam to be extremely significant. I did not believe that they would stop at the Burma Road. Japan's real objective was farther south, probably the oil of the Dutch East Indies. They might not leave our forces in the Philippines unengaged on their flank. My belief was they would take us out on the way down, and we would be at war.

Pye and his chief of staff were very doubtful about my strategic estimate. "Oh, no. The Japanese won't attack us," Pye told me. "We're too strong and powerful."

After I had returned to headquarters and filed the message, I reported to Admiral Kimmel. He was anxious to know Pye's reaction. When I had explained their confident rejection of my estimate about an attack on the Philippines, he said, "I want you to repeat that again." As I did so the admiral looked straight through me. He then snorted as if disappointed at Pye's response.

Even if Kimmel was inclined to share my fears about an attack on the Philippines, any thought that the Japanese might also hit Pearl Harbor at that time was far from our minds. But while I had been with Pye, Kimmel, after assessing the latest intelligence, had discussed the advisability of sending the battle force to sea as a precautionary measure for commencing war operations.

Kimmel discussed the idea with his chief of staff, Captain William "Poco" Smith; his operations officer, Captain Walter DeLany; and Captain Charles E. "Soc" McMorris, the war plans officer. But they concluded that without the carriers and protective air cover the battleships would be too vulnerable at sea. Moreover, sending the fleet out on a weekend would cause just the sort of alarm that the army war warning had cautioned against. It would also be an unnecessary drain on the fleet's fuel reserves. These were earmarked for long-range operations against the Japanese bases in the Marshalls. Kimmel's primary concern was to have the fleet ready for an offensive sortie as soon as hostilities broke out.

The admiral's extended conference broke up just before 1400. As I was late for lunch at the wardroom mess, I made my apologies to the senior officer present. He happened to be the fleet gunnery officer, Captain Willard A. Kitts, Jr. I explained that I had been delayed because Kimmel had sent me to Pye with an urgent dispatch. During lunch several of the staff asked me what I thought about the news of Japanese troop transports steaming into the Gulf of Siam. I repeated my assertion that they would not leave the Philippines on their flank and that we would probably be at war the next day.

"Ah, Layton and his Saturday crisis," was how Captain Kitts ribbed me, referring to my predictions at the mess lunch a week earlier that a serious crisis was brewing. I assured him that in my view the situation was a lot more ominous this weekend.

Late that afternoon, my conviction that we would shortly be at war was reinforced when Rochefort called to inform me that the Japanese consulate in Honolulu had been burning codes and official papers. Joe explained that Mayfield had gotten the information. While I did not know specifically about the telephone tap on the consulate's kitchen, I guessed that the FBI had a very reliable internal source of information, which Joe liked to refer to as "inside the horse's mouth."

Rochefort told me he had already drafted a cable to advise Opnav: "Believe local consul has destroyed all but one system."[155] But the Fourteenth Naval District Communications Office—in an unwise economy measure—sent the dispatch out "deferred status." In this case, a piece of important intelligence from Honolulu did not reach Washington until after the Japanese attack.

Although I was not sent a copy of the message, I did consider it significant enough to alert Kimmel's duty officer. The admiral was not immediately available, and later he could not recollect whether he had received my report about the code burning. Even if he had been given the message, it was not the first time we had had information that the Japanese consulate was burning codes. Without being able to read it in the context of the increasing number of ships-in-harbor reports being made by Consul Kita, Kimmel testified, he would not have regarded the code burning as "very vital." It merely reinforced what we had already been told by Washington.[156]

What might have proved another vital clue to the impending Japanese attack was also missed that evening, because we had never been alerted to the Kita messages. It surfaced around 1800, when I received a telephone call from Captain Mayfield. He wanted to know whether I would be going to my office on Sunday. When I said that I would be in the next day, he asked me to stop by Fourteenth Naval District headquarters. I asked if I should come down to Honolulu that evening, but was told no. It was apparent that he would not have the information on which he wanted my opinion until the next morning.

It was a year before I discovered that the reason for his call was to discuss the transcript of a transpacific telephone call supposedly made by a Tokyo newspaper to one Mrs. Mori, a Honolulu resident. She was the wife of a local Japanese dentist, who had already come under FBI surveillance. At fifteen dollars for three minutes' time, the two-hundred-dollar cost of the call had aroused suspicions that it must be connected with an espionage operation, the more so since Mrs. Mori had been questioned in code that referred to flowers in bloom and the latest weather conditions. She also supplied information on the movements of the Pacific Fleet and was asked, "Are airplanes flying daily?" and "What about the searchlights?"[157]

When the FBI translated the Mori call that afternoon, the local bureau chief, Robert L. Shivers, was convinced that the call had important "military significance."[158] He telephoned Mayfield's office. The DIO was not there, but when told about the Mori call he decided that it probably was a hidden code. But because all the references were to the Hawaiian Islands he concluded it could not be urgent because "there was nothing in the message in line with previous information indicating Japanese movements."[159] And so he postponed any further action until he could discuss its possible significance with me the next day.

After receiving Shivers's call, Lieutenant Colonel George W. Bicknell, Short's assistant G-2 of the Fort Shafter intelligence section, decided the Mori intercept did warrant immediate evaluation. He drove downtown to pick up a transcript and then persuaded his chief, Lieutenant Colonel Kendall J. Fielder, that it was important enough to delay General Short's departure to a dinner engagement to discuss its significance.

A brief discussion on the porch of the general's quarters was unable to "make heads nor tails of it." Short concluded that although it looked "very fishy" it was "nothing very much to get excited about."[160]

General Short and Captain Mayfield might have become very excited about that Mori message if army or navy intelligence officers on Oahu had known as much as Washington did about the kinds of messages that had been passing back and forth between Tokyo and the local Japanese consulate. Only three days earlier Hypo's cryptanalysts had gotten their first chance to break into that traffic. Unfortunately for us, Rochefort's team had not been assigned the task of cracking any diplomatic intercepts. Unfamiliarity with the consular ciphers and bad luck conspired to keep us from unlocking the potentially vital intelligence they contained.

Warrant Officer Farnsley C. Woodward, the only Hypo cryptanalyst with any experience in the Japanese diplomatic cipher systems, had started on Wednesday with the cables in the low-grade LA cipher. By Thursday afternoon most of these turned out to be routine administrative matters, which he described as "junk."[161] By Friday afternoon Woodward had moved on to tackle the PA-K2 traffic, which the consulate had been using for its confidential messages after burning its J-19 code books that Tuesday.

If Hypo had possessed all the latest key recoveries, the decryption process would have involved about six hours' work to break out the traffic for a whole day. By Saturday Rochefort could have provided me with most of that week's detailed twice-a-day fleet reports that Kita was cabling to Tokyo, and Kimmel—who was already toying with the idea— would almost certainly have sent the battle force to sea.

But Hypo did not have the key recoveries that would have speeded up the process. Because Rochefort was not supposed to tackle any diplomatic intercepts, he could not ask Washington for them without risking a flap. Woodward therefore set to work from scratch and tried to break out the keys himself. This was not a difficult task, given enough traffic. But he also handicapped himself. In the preliminary step of lining up the message text prior to commencing the columnar decoding process, he erroneously set up the messages backward. As fate would have it, four days of wrestling with the seemingly indecipherable messages passed before he discovered his simple error.

So Woodward did not break out a single PA-K2 cable until the Wednesday following the attack.[162] It was yet another human error in a string of similar miscalculations that denied us last-minute intelligence that a Japanese striking force was steaming toward Pearl Harbor. It was a failure that bore heavily on Woodward.[163]

One message that was contained in the first batch Rochefort saw was Kita's 2 December report, which Woodward put aside because he lacked the current key to the J-19 cipher. Instead he turned to the subsequent messages in the simple PA-K2 code. It was a bad mistake because this one report could have proved an even more accurate indicator that the Japanese were contemplating a Taranto-style torpedo plane attack on Pearl Harbor:

> In view of the present situation, the presence in port of warships, airplane carriers and cruisers is of the utmost importance. Hereafter, to the utmost of your ability, let me know day by day. Wire me in each case whether or not there are any observation balloons above Pearl Harbor or if there are any indications that they will be sent up. Also advise whether or not the warships are provided with anti-torpedo nets.[164]

This message was fated not to reach the Washington cryptanalysts until 23 December. With no intimation of the explosive intelligence it might contain, the army communications center at Fort Shafter, which had received instructions not to give priority to J-19 messages, were economists on their cables and so the intercept was sent off by surface mail!

While there is no certainty that this message would, by itself, have changed the course of history, both the loss of this message and Woodward's error denied us access to intelligence that might have sounded the alarm. Any of the Kita reports would, at the very least, have brought an increase in the level of alert on Oahu. Air patrols would probably have been stepped up, and Kimmel might well have reversed his decision not to send the battle fleet to sea.

The first message that could have tipped the balance was contained in a lengthy RCA message of 3 December in which Consul Kita relayed to Tokyo in PA-K2 cipher the elaborate methods by which Yoshikawa's agent Fritz Kuehn proposed to send his reports to Japanese army intelligence. His proposed system for signaling to a Japanese submarine offshore was a characteristically Teutonic "belt and suspenders" operation. It involved a complex array of prearranged light patterns at night, Roman numerals on a boat sail by day, bonfire signals, and even want ads to be broadcast by a local radio station.

The lights message, as it came to be known, was the first PA-K2 cable that Woodward picked and the one on which he labored so unsuccessfully until 10 December. If he had broken it out, it would have been an inescapable sign of the attention that Tokyo wanted paid to the Pacific Fleet:

MEANING		SIGNAL
Battleship divisions including scouts and screen units	Preparing to sortie	1
A number of carriers	Preparing to sortie	2

Battleship divisions	All departed between 1st and 3rd	3
Carriers	Several departed between 1st and 3rd	4
Carriers	All departed between 1st and 3rd	5
Battleship divisions	All departed between 4th and 6th	6
Carriers	Several departed between 4th and 6th	7
Carriers	All departed between 4th and 6th	8

Kuehn did not know of the impending attack. He had devised his reporting system to be equally applicable to the first week of any month. But if we had seen this cable that Saturday we would have evaluated it in the context of the worsening diplomatic situation and my hunch that Japan would attack the Philippines as well as the Isthmus of Kra. Although not specifically intended to refer to 6 December, the reference to the sixth as the last date the Japanese wanted to know what ships had sailed from Pearl Harbor would have had very special significance that Saturday. It would have exactly tied in with my belief that war would break out the next day, 7 December.

The impact of this lights message as an indication of Japan's focus on the Pacific Fleet anchorage would have been even greater had Hypo's cryptanalysts managed to break out either of the Japanese consul's ships-in-harbor reports made on Thursday and Friday. Any suspicions aroused by the lights message could only have been increased if we had read these messages in conjunction with Tokyo's reminder to Kita that very day to "please *wire immediately* re the latter part of my #123 (. . . . . . .) the *movements of the fleet subsequent to the fourth* [emphasis added]."[166]

The two reports that Kita sent that same day would have opened our eyes to the possibility of an air attack. One answered Tokyo's 2 December request about Pearl Harbor's aerial defenses: "At the present time there are *no signs of barrage balloon equipment.* . . . In my opinion the *battleships do not have torpedo nets* [emphasis added]." It called our attention to the obvious: "I imagine that in all probability there is *considerable opportunity* left to take advantage for a surprise attack." The second message would have emphasized the point because it listed the "9 [sic] battleships, 3 light cruisers, 3 submarine tenders, 17 destroyers and . . . 4 light cruisers, 2 destroyers lying at dock." This final report concluded, "It appears that *no air reconnaissance is being conducted* by the fleet air arm [emphasis added]."[167]

These were vital clues of an impending air attack on the Pacific Fleet. But the information was fated never to become intelligence, because it remained hidden in the PA-K2 code until after the raid. Of greater significance was the fact that Washington had already unlocked information from earlier Kita reports that could have been an equally important harbinger of what was to come. This information was never turned into intelligence, and, instead of being relayed to Pearl Harbor, it joined the accumulating Magic files in the safes of the war and navy departments.

Washington

The terrible irony of the Kita messages is this: The cryptanalysts in OP-20-GY and the army's Signal Corps special intelligence section had no trouble reading the Japanese J-19 or PA-K2. But the consular ciphers had a low priority and although several had been broken out that week none was relayed to Pacific Fleet headquarters.

Among them was a three-week-old J-19 report of 18 November that listed every major warship in harbor that day. Significantly, it also detailed the speed, procedures, and the time it took—nearly an hour—for five destroyers to enter through the channel and reach their moorings.[168]

On Wednesday, Tokyo's 15 November request for its Honolulu consulate to report "twice a week" and "take extra care to maintain secrecy" was translated by the navy.[169]

On Thursday the army had broken out the 18 November instruction for Kita to "investigate comprehensively the fleet [air] bases in the neighborhood of the Hawaiian military reservation." Twenty-four hours later the readers of Friday's Magics knew that "great secrecy" was to be used to investigate vessels anchored in "Area 'N' Pearl Harbor"; and what was mistranslated as "Manila Bay" was in the context clearly Mamala Bay, which was adjacent to the port of Honolulu itself.[170]

That same day OP-20-GZ read a five-day-old instruction to Kita that should have been seen as an even more explicit clue to Tokyo's increasing concern with Pearl Harbor: "We have been receiving reports from you on ship movements, but in future will you also report *when there are no movements* [emphasis added]."[171] If this had been properly evaluated in conjunction with the other available messages, this was the *one* that was the real giveaway. But apparently no one in the navy department stopped to reflect why Japanese naval intelligence was as interested in knowing what warships were actually *in* Pearl Harbor as they were in those that put to sea.

The failure to relate these recently decrypted messages with the earlier "bomb plot" signal, and so to appreciate what set them apart both in volume and specificity from the espionage reports that were intercepted from the Japanese consulates in Seattle and Manila, was indicative of just how badly the evaluation and dissemination—two of the three functions necessary to turn raw information into meaningful intelligence—had broken down. The extent of this failure was to be recognized by the navy in its own secret analysis, made in September 1942. Understandably, it was not released until nearly forty years after the 1945 congressional hearings.

This report demonstrated how a simple statistical calculation would have yielded the "interesting point" that while Seattle and Panama accounted for only six and eighteen intercepted shipping reports in the months of August through November 1941, fifty-five related to Manila and *sixty-eight to Pearl Harbor*. Naval intelligence's own analysis underscored the magnitude of its failure to see what was staring it in the face for nearly a month before war broke out:

> The significant point is that the Japanese government did not treat the Honolulu and Manila reports as routine matters, but continually kept trying to elicit more information from its representatives. The acceleration of messages from Honolulu and Manila in November was another identification of war preparations.[172]

The lack of any systematic evaluation of Japan's consular diplomatic traffic was not an excuse that justified the subsequent pillorying of Admiral Kimmel and General Short. Their reputations, and the 2,335 servicemen who died at Pearl Harbor, became the victims of Washington's failure to recognize the significance of the Kita messages.

The intelligence breakdown was compounded on 6 December when the intuition of one of OP-20-GZ's newest recruits succeeded in uncovering one of the clues that had been missed by trained intelligence officers and the most senior admirals on the naval staff. The tragedy was that her discovery of last-minute intelligence that might have warned the Pacific Fleet of the incoming attack was not only dismissed, but was ignored until Monday morning.

Mrs. Dorothy Edgers had been working in OP-20-GZ but a few weeks when the Honolulu consulate's three-day-old lights message landed on her desk that Saturday morning. It was part of a batch of diplomatic decrypts awaiting translation into English.

"At first glance, this seemed to be more interesting than some of the other messages I had in my basket," she was to tell the 1944 navy court of inquiry. "I selected it and asked one of the other men, who were also translators working on the other messages, whether or not it shouldn't be done immediately."[173]

The person who gave her permission to go ahead was her brother, Fred Woodrough, who had been one of naval communications' leading civilian Japanese linguists for more than four years. He had recommended his sister for a translator's job because after thirty years in Japan she was "much more fluent" in the language.[174] Navy bureaucrats, however, had offered her "practically beginner's pay." But Dorothy, unlike her quiet and introspective brother, was a spirited extrovert. A "born salesman," she had successfully argued that her fluency with the language entitled her to pay equal to the other translators'.

At the congressional hearings in 1945 Dorothy Edgers was to be portrayed as inexperienced and timid by Lieutenant Commander Kramer, for whom she worked in OP-20-GZ. Nothing could have been further from the truth. Significantly, Mrs. Edgers was *not* called on to testify before the congressional committee.

Dorothy was not the kind of woman to be easily brushed aside when she decided something was important—and that was how the lights message struck her. When she found it contained some garbles, she went off to find a crippie to straighten them out. The message was not returned to her desk until around 1230 Saturday and Dorothy could easily have left it there until Monday, because it was past the hour when civilian translators ended weekly work.

Dorothy Edgers was not like that. She went to find Kramer and tried to interest him in the intercept. After a glance, OP-20-GZ told her he did not think it was of "sufficient importance" to warrant her staying behind to complete the translation. So she went back to ask her brother's advice.

"What do you think?" Fred recalls her asking. She showed him the message with its instruction about signal lights and the Pacific Fleet's movements through the "6th." "I remember reading it quickly and saying, 'Yes, I think you should stay and do this.'" Woodrough recalls, although he admitted he "wasn't about to stay and do it myself."[175]

So Dorothy Edgers stayed behind and completed the first translation, which she finished around 1400. It made so much of an impression on her that three years later she was still able to recall all its salient points. The message revealed "how they were going to communicate from Honolulu to the parties interested the information on our fleet movements." She recollected that it had to "do with lights in the window of a certain house, and there was also something about newspaper advertising."[176]

Kramer was not in the office when Mrs. Edgers left, but since "he knew I was working on it," she entrusted it to Chief Clerk Harold L. Bryant, "whose job it was to edit the messages and write them up." But that was as close as this important information came to becoming intelligence.

"On Monday morning that message was still on Kramer's desk," Fred Woodrough asserts. "He had not looked at it. It was quite possible that the English would have had to be smoothed out, but the essential translating work was done."[177]

Commander Kramer, whose responsibility as OP-20-GZ was to review all intercepts for further evaluation, was to deny any recollection of Mrs. Edgers's translation when he was questioned by the congressional investigating committee in 1945. Yet he was obliged to concede that he must have failed to give it proper scrutiny because in the "10 to 15 seconds" that he admitted that he might have studied it that afternoon he decided it was "not materially different from the information we had already." According to Kramer, Mrs. Edgers "was still unfamiliar with the practices and procedures of my office," and he denied that she had ever "invited" his attention to the message that morning. Moreover, he sought to cast doubt on her translation by claiming that he had subsequently to spend three days "clearing and working with this message" before it was readable.[178]

When asked whether he would have considered the lights' message an important piece of intelligence, Kramer conceded, "If I had seen it Saturday afternoon, I most certainly would have."[179] That admission explains why his testimony was at odds with that of Mrs. Edgers and the recollections of her brother. Dorothy's original worksheet had disappeared by 1945. The only remaining documentary evidence is Kramer's polished translation of 11 December stamped TOP SECRET ULTRA, which was not sent to Pearl Harbor.

The lights message did not get the attention it warranted from Kramer because it was in a low-grade PA-K2 consular cipher. He appears to have been obsessed with the high-priority Purple traffic that afternoon. As one of Woodrough's staff observed: "Al was not the ideal man for the job at that time." Like many perfectionists he could not distinguish details from important issues. He could never give a short answer and would weigh all the pros and cons. "Sometimes he couldn't give a decision at all—and didn't."[180]

Many of the crippies were first-rate bridge players; it was a skill that went with the job. But when Kramer joined an occasional off-duty game with them, they noticed, he was always the last one to play his hand. He would ponder his cards, trying the patience of his partners, apparently laying out his whole strategy. "If everything went the way he figured, with everyone discarding as he allowed, he would play the next card," Woodrough remembered. "But if there was the slightest variation he would have to go back into his trance again."[181]

During those critical weeks of November and December 1941 the shortage of manpower had been exacerbated by watching for the winds messages. OP-20-GZ and its overstrung chief were under constant strain. The pressure on Kramer was often as imaginary as it was real. "Al would take even the most trivial piece of traffic and devote the same amount of time changing a comma here and a period there, as he would spend on an important message," Fred Woodrough recalled. He often wondered why his boss "got stuck on things" and assumed that the strain of his job contributed to his hospitalization just before the congressional hearings in

1945.[182] Kramer's perfectionism soon came to border on an obsession. It slowed up the whole translation process, because he would not let a message be released until he had personally reviewed it to assure himself it was letter perfect.

Kramer was operating under considerable pressure even before December. Earlier in the year he had participated in several ONI "black bag" operations directed against the office of the Japanese consul in New York. After one of these break-ins early in 1941, Kramer—who had processed the films in his own darkroom—called in Lieutenant Robert H. Weeks, his next-door neighbor and fellow member of OP-20-G, to see the latest haul. When a knock was heard at the door, Weeks recalled how they had to keep the visitor outside while they quickly scooped up the prints of Japanese code books: The caller chanced to be Japan's naval attaché in Washington, with whom Kramer maintained a friendship.

Woodrough observed how on several of the mornings after Kramer arrived in the OP-20-GZ office wearing tennis shoes and looking bleary eyed, a spate of new code breaks had shortly followed. Which ciphers benefited from Kramer's nocturnal excursions in New York are unclear. But the black-bag jobs were evidently sufficiently productive for Kramer to write a revealing confidential memorandum in 1945, in anticipation of his appearance before Admiral H. Kent Hewitt's naval inquiry into the Pearl Harbor attack. "I see no purpose in disclosing the N.Y. period activity that would be pertinent to the investigation," he wrote cryptically. "Such disclosures could only result in compromising the status of certain individuals who contributed, as well as seriously harming [sic] possible further activities in this line."[183]

Kramer, therefore, was overstressed throughout 1941. He put in tough hours and constantly munched on chocolate bars, dropping crumbs around his desk which attracted mice. In spite of being overworked, he was obsessed with achieving perfect translations and would not release even the most unimportant consular decrypt until he had personally satisfied himself that it was absolutely correct. This slowed up the whole process of translating the Japanese naval intercepts and Magics. His lack of organization was evident from his cluttered desk with its piles of partially translated decrypts awaiting his critical analysis and approval.

"When the volume of intercepts was very high, the stuff just piled up in a basket," Woodrough recalled. "Whoever was ready would take the top one and translate it. We picked whichever one had the highest priority, and Purple got top priority."[184] In such circumstances, his sister's translation had only a slim chance of getting past Kramer's supercritical eye during the hectic rush that overtook him during the final afternoon of peace.

That Saturday the navy's cryptanalytic effort was concentrated on the high-priority Purple message that contained Japan's formal rejection of Hull's ten-point proposal of 26 November. The clues that Japan's reply was about to arrive were contained in two pilot messages that had been intercepted by the navy's west coast listening station at Bainbridge Island on Puget Sound at around 0700 that day. As it was an even-numbered date and therefore the army's duty day for translating Purple, OP-20-G routed the intercepts to the Signal Corps Special Intelligence Section in the war department at midday. Two hours later the Purple machine had spewed out the plain Japanese text, which was rapidly translated.

The first pilot message advised Nomura that the "situation was extremely delicate," and that he would receive a communication in fourteen parts, which he was to "keep secret for the time being." The ambassador was to "put it in a nicely drafted form and make every preparation to present it to the Americans just as soon as you receive instructions."[185] It was followed by a second dispatch that instructed, "In the preparation of an aide memoire be absolutely sure not to use a typist or any other person. Be most extremely cautious in preserving secrecy."[186]

When the pilot messages reached the desk of Colonel Rufus Bratton, at around 1400, the head of military intelligence's Far East section realized he faced a logistical problem. Unlike the navy, the army cryptanalysts were not yet on a twenty-four-hour shift. Bratton had to get General Miles's permission to ask the navy to help out. By the time this had been arranged with Safford and Kramer, the intercepts of the first parts of Tokyo's long message were already chattering in on the OP-20-G teleprinters from Bainbridge Island.

Tokyo had begun transmitting its detailed instructions to Ambassador Nomura just after noon. By three that afternoon, all except the final, fourteenth part were being processed by the navy code breakers. Although they were not sent in sequential order, the first thirteen parts had been transmitted in English. There could be no mistaking that this was a final statement of Japan's position because the ambassadors were given no room for misinterpretation.[187]

Typists lent by the army prepared the final copies. All Kramer had to do was to ensure that the message was assembled in logical order. This made it all the more surprising that Kramer did not give proper attention that afternoon to Mrs. Edgers's translation.

Even if the lights message had gotten off Kramer's desk and out to McCollum's analysts, there is no guarantee that it would have reached us at Pearl Harbor in time. It was not just Kramer who was overworked. The whole OP-20-G staff was overstretched and dividing its manpower resources among the Japanese diplomatic messages, the JN-25 naval code, and the tracking of potentially hostile U-boats in the Atlantic.

Two weeks of fifteen-hour workdays had left Safford physically drained and approaching a state of nervous exhaustion as well. An unwelcome new problem had kept him in the office until late the previous evening: An inventory by the Registered Publications Section had confirmed that Wake Island held copies of virtually every secret code and

cipher system the navy possessed. Safford, whose responsibilities also included ensuring the security of naval communications systems, labored
late into the night checking the list. Before leaving for home in the small
hours of Saturday, he drafted an urgent warning to go to the Pacific Fleet
commander to order the destruction of all confidential systems "in view
of the imminence of war."[188]

When he returned to the office on Saturday morning, Safford took the
draft message straight to Captain Joseph R. Redman. But he was unable
to persuade the assistant director of naval communications to release a
dispatch that warned of war without the approval of his superior, Admiral Noyes. This was despite Redman's prediction the previous Saturday:
"If the Japs don't strike us this weekend, I'll eat my shirt."[189]

Admiral Noyes was attending the daily briefing for the secretary of
the navy. Stark and Turner were also present when Knox asked, "Are
they going to hit us?"

"No, Mr. Secretary," Turner declared. "They are going to attack the
British. They are not ready for us yet."[190]

Turner's certainty that Japan would not attack the United States impressed the reticent Admiral Leigh Noyes. Several hours later when Safford went to the director of naval communications to ask why he had still
not sent out his warning, according to Safford's testimony a stormy exchange took place in the DNC's office.

"What do you mean by using such language as that?" Noyes shouted,
pointing to the message. As drafted, it would have impinged on Admiral
Turner's authority because it warned that war was imminent.

"Admiral, the war is just a matter of days, if not hours," Safford
replied, standing his ground.

"You may think there is going to be a war, but I think they are bluff-
ing," Noyes snapped back.

"Well, Admiral, if all these publications on Wake are captured we will
never be able to explain it."[191]

Safford's point was not lost on his superior. But Noyes, fearful of
igniting Turner's wrath, insisted on toning down the dispatch. In deference to the authority of war plans, it omitted all reference to the imminent outbreak of hostilities. Nor was it sent direct to Wake but only to
Pacific Fleet headquarters and the Asiatic Fleet command for information.

When it arrived at Pearl Harbor, as a "deferred priority" cable,
shortly before midnight, what might have been seen as a last-minute war
warning from Washington was shorn of any sense of urgency. It read
more like a routine administrative message:

> In view of the international situation and the exposed position of
> our outlying Pacific islands you may authorize destruction by them
> of secret and confidential documents now or under later conditions

of greater emergency. Means of communication to support our current operations and special intelligence should of course be maintained until the last moment.[192]

The attempt to goad Admiral Noyes into sending a last-minute alert to Pearl Harbor had been Safford's last effort on a tension-filled day. Secure in the knowledge that the first thirteen parts of the final Japanese message were in the process of being decrypted, he announced at 1630 that he was going home. Safford intended to take a badly needed rest for the remainder of the weekend. He had every confidence that Commander George W. Linn, a proficient cryptanalyst and his "best man on the watch side," would be able to handle all eventualities in OP-20-G.[193]

As Safford joined the exodus of afternoon duty officers on Constitution Avenue, the war department's communications center received a report from their observer in Singapore. Patrols of the Royal Air Force had spotted the two Japanese invasion forces south of Cambodia Point steaming west.[194] Streetlamps were blinking on and the gray shadows of a winter dusk were enveloping the White House when the gaunt form of the British ambassador climbed out of his Rolls-Royce.

Lord Halifax had come to try to get the president's agreement for a preemptive British strike against the Japanese convoys steaming toward the Isthmus of Kra. Roosevelt offered both reassurance and evasion. He told the ambassador, "If we saw Japanese transports steaming west or southwest across the Gulf of Thailand [Siam] we should obviously attack them since they must either be going for Thailand or Malaya." But when Halifax indicated that this did not answer the question of whether the United States would respond with immediate armed support, Roosevelt said that "he would not cross that bridge before we came to it, and that you could not tell exactly how the thing was going to start."[195]

After receiving Halifax's cable, Churchill that same evening sent an urgent minute to the foreign secretary and chiefs of staff. It claimed that Roosevelt's answers were "very satisfactory" and that "this removes all political difficulty for initiating Naval or Air action and I agree with [the] President that we 'should obviously attack Japanese transports.' . . . Attack is therefore solely one of naval opportunity and expediency. Admiral Phillips should be made fully aware of all these telegrams from the United States." To nail down Roosevelt's commitment, the prime minister drafted a cable instructing Halifax to advise the president "we should be justified in attacking at sea" any Japanese expedition because "we understand we can rely on armed support of the United States if we become involved in hostilities with Japan. . . ."[196] Roosevelt had now been put squarely on the line. Whether he would have actually honored the guarantees Churchill believed he had given without congressional approval was never put to the test because the Japanese attacked Pearl Harbor before this telegram could be sent.

The uncertainty about what was going to happen charged the president's inner circle in Washington. The latest estimate from military intelligence was that the "most probable line of action for Japan is the occupation of Thailand."[197]

Secretary of War Stimson had earlier canceled a weekend trip to join his wife in Long Island. He had spent the day closeted with General Marshall because the "atmosphere indicated that something was going to happen."[198]

Roosevelt concurred. After receiving a phone call that morning from Secretary Knox reporting the sightings of the Japanese convoy, the president told his budget director, Harold Smith, "We might be at war with Japan, although no one knew."[199] From London the president's special envoy, Averell Harriman, had cabled that in the event of a Japanese attack, Churchill would "postpone taking any action—even though the delay might involve some military sacrifice—until the president has taken such action, as under the circumstances, he considers best."[200]

The prime minister was most anxious not to hurt Roosevelt's chances of persuading Congress to declare war if Japan did not attack the Philippines. Churchill, however, promised that once the president had moved, he would act, "not within the hour, but within the minute."[201] How best to coordinate the moves between the White House and Downing Street was the topic of the half-hour meeting early that evening with the British ambassador. The discussions between Halifax and Roosevelt also included William Casey, Australia's minister for external affairs in Washington.

The Australian cabinet, after a premature precipitation of the joint war plan by the Dutch had been narrowly averted—and when such an outbreak would have spoiled Roosevelt's plans—had confirmed that they would join in issuing an ultimatum to Japan. It had already been agreed that the United States and Britain would issue parallel warnings, but Australia's prime minister insisted that Roosevelt not only approve the text but also give the "signal for actual delivery of the warning."[202] Casey's cable to Canberra that evening set out Roosevelt's carefully plotted moves:

1. President has decided to send message to Emperor
2. President's subsequent procedure is that if no answer is received by him from Emperor by Monday evening (December 8)
   a. he will issue his warning on Tuesday afternoon or evening.
   b. warning or equivalent by British or others will not follow until Wednesday morning, i.e., after his own warning has been delivered repeatedly in Tokyo and Washington.[203]

Grace Tully, the president's personal secretary, was summoned from a cocktail party and Roosevelt dictated his telegram for the emperor. In keeping with the draft agreed upon with Secretary Hull earlier in the week, it opened with a reminder that almost a century earlier one of the president's predecessors had extended the "offer of friendship." Then it detailed the "deep and far-reaching emergency" that prompted a second historic epistle. The president addressed the issues indirectly. Regarding the Japanese military buildup in Indochina, he said it was "only reasonable that the people of the Philippines, of the hundreds of islands of the East Indies, of Malaya and Thailand are asking themselves whether the forces of Japan are preparing or intending to make an attack in one or more of these many directions." Roosevelt compared their situation to sitting "on a keg of dynamite." After giving assurances that the United States had no hostile intentions, "for the sake of humanity" he appealed to the emperor to "give thought in this definite emergency to the ways of dispelling the dark clouds . . . to restore traditional amity and prevent further death and destruction in the world."[204]

"Shoot this off to Grew," the president's note directed Hull. "I think it can go in gray code—saves time—I don't mind if it gets picked up." As he wryly observed to one of Mrs. Roosevelt's dinner guests that evening, "This son of man has just sent his final message to the son of God."[205]

Shortly after eight thirty the Japanese embassy telephoned to Ambassador Kurusu news of the president's cable. He was guest of honor at the dinner being given at Evermay, the lavish Georgetown estate of millionaire industrialist and former U.S. envoy to Poland Ferdinand Lammot Berlin. Among the guests was Colonel William J. "Wild Bill" Donovan, the president's Coordinator of Information. He noted Kurusu's candid reaction to Roosevelt's cable: Kurusu called it "a clever move" that would cause "headaches in Tokyo and more thinking."[206]

The dinner parties at the White House and Evermay were in midmenu that evening when Commander Kramer was finally satisfied with the punctuation in Japan's fourteen-part message. He telephoned Admiral Wilkinson for permission to send it out to the Magic recipients. The director of naval intelligence was also hosting a dinner party, at his Arlington home, for General Miles and Rear Admiral John R. Beardall, the president's naval aide. But Kramer failed to reach Stark or Turner. The chief of naval operations was at the National Theater and the chief of war plans was apparently out exercising the brood of Lhasa terriers that he and his wife raised as a hobby.

According to Kramer's testimony, he crossed them off the navy's distribution list when he made the decision to act as courier himself and deliver the remaining Magic pouches around to the other recipients. He called his wife, who drove over from their Arlington home to the navy department. Their first stop was the White House, at around nine thirty, where Kramer dropped off the locked pouch at the Situation Room. He told Beardall's assistant to deliver it at once.[207]

Lieutenant Lester R. Schulz had been a member of the presidential entourage for only two weeks. Still unfamiliar with the White House routine, he had been alerted, however, to the need to take the Magic pouch immediately to the president, who was expecting it. The president had slipped away from the violin recital that was entertaining his wife's dinner party. He was in his study toying with his stamp collection and chatting with Harry Hopkins. After he was ushered in, Schulz crossed to Roosevelt's desk, unlocked the pouch, and pulled out the papers. Hopkins paced back and forth as Roosevelt pored over the typewritten pages of the first thirteen parts of the message they both knew Tokyo intended to be its last word to Washington.

"The Government of Japan, prompted by a genuine desire to come to an amicable understanding with the Government of the United States," was how Tokyo prefaced statements intended to demonstrate the "utmost sincerity" of the efforts that they had made since April to "insure the stability of East Asia and to promote world peace, and thereby to enable all nations to find a proper place in the world."[208]

Half the document was a self-justificatory analysis of "the China question" as the principal issue in contention and one over which the Japanese government claimed it had "showed a most conciliatory attitude." The United States and Britain were repeatedly accused of conspiring with Chiang Kai-shek to obstruct "constructive endeavors" to stabilize the Far East and "realize the ideal of common prosperity in cooperation with these regions." Washington was accused of being the intransigent negotiator "always holding fast to theories in disregard of realities and refusing to yield an inch on its impractical principles." The American government, moreover, was charged with "scheming for the extension of the war" by "aiding Great Britain and preparing to attack, in the name of self-defense, Germany and Italy, two powers that are striving to establish a new order in Europe."[209]

The president's practiced eye filleted the bones of Japan's position from the obsequious diplomatic phrases. Such a bald accusation of American bad faith could indicate only that Tokyo was intending to rupture relations. Japan's communication concluded: "Therefore, viewed in its entirety, the Japanese Government regrets that it cannot accept the proposal as a basis for negotiation."[210]

"This means war" was Roosevelt's immediate reaction to this clear statement of impending Japanese belligerence. He did not necessarily mean that he thought the United States was going to be attacked, but that we would be at war because of his pledge to support the British in the event of an assault on them by the Japanese. His observation was later to be misconstrued as a dramatic declaration. But it was a low-key reaction given the offensive tone of Tokyo's note, as Schulz's own recollection makes clear: "The President then turned toward Mr. Hopkins and said in substance—I am not sure of the exact words, but in substance—'This means war.'"[211]

The absence of any sensational, sinister intent on the president's part is evident. The presence of the young naval officer did not inhibit five minutes of frank exchange that Schulz subsequently recalled for the congressional investigators.

Hopkins suggested that since war was coming anyway, "it was too bad that we could not strike the first blow and prevent any sort of surprise." Roosevelt was adamant. "No we can't do that. We are a democracy and a peaceful people," he said, raising his voice. "But we have a good record."

There was no mention of Pearl Harbor or of anyplace other than Indochina. Nor was there any indication that war would begin "tomorrow." Schulz's impression was that the president was determined to "stand on that record" and he appreciated that "we could not make the first move."[212]

Schulz was still in the study when Roosevelt tried to reach Admiral Stark only to be told he was at a performance of *The Student Prince*. The president decided not to have him paged because it would cause too much public concern. He announced that he would reach the admiral later, handed the papers back, and Schulz was ushered out.[213]

It was around ten o'clock before the Kramers reached the Wardman Park Hotel in northwest Washington where the secretary of the navy resided. After studying the fifteen pages for twenty minutes in his suite, Knox made "a number of phone calls including Mr. Hull."[214] Security prevented a discussion of Magic on open lines, so it was arranged that they would meet with Stimson in the State Department at ten the next morning to discuss Japan's reply. Kramer was instructed to be there.[215]

Driving from northwest Washington over Memorial Bridge into Virginia took another half hour. It was eleven-twenty before Kramer rang the doorbell at the Wilkinson house on Arlington's North Uhle Street.[216] The admiral was entertaining General Miles and Admiral Beardall as well as two Vichy French naval officers, so they discreetly adjourned to the privacy of his study before unlocking the leather pouch. He discussed its contents with Miles and Beardall. But apparently neither navy nor army intelligence head believed the thirteen parts merited immediate action. This must be considered somewhat surprising in view of the president's reaction and their admission later that they had agreed "it certainly looked as though the Japanese were terminating negotiations."[217]

According to Kramer's account, Wilkinson put in a call to the chief of naval operations, who had by then returned from the theater.[218] Later, Stark was to be vague in his recollection of whether he discussed the receipt of the Japanese diplomatic communication with Wilkinson. He was unable to recollect if it was before or after he had received a phone call from the White House. Stark was nevertheless to insist that he would not have regarded it as "anything that required action." Certainly no action was taken—if it was considered—to issue a final war alert that night to the Pacific commands.[219]

Admirals Ingersoll and Turner would both testify later that they recalled reading the thirteen-part dispatch late that evening—and also deciding that no action was necessary. Their certainty was curious, considering that Kramer claimed he had made no delivery to either of them. Their telephones were not answered before he set out on his drive around Washington, and it would have been beyond the abilities of Kramer's car to reach the phenomenal speed required to go out to Chevy Chase, where Turner lived, then on to Ingersoll's house, and to have gotten back to the navy department by half past midnight when the Magic papers were safely back in the OP-20-G safe. After the watch officer assured him that the fourteenth and final part of the Japanese message had not yet been intercepted, Mrs. Kramer was finally able to drive her exhausted husband home to bed around one.[220]

While Kramer had been making the rounds of the navy's Magic recipients, Bratton was discharging a similar duty for those on the army list. A bearlike man of professorial mien, Bratton was one of the most capable G-2 officers and would have made general if he had not heeded the request to remain in Washington when relations with Japan nose-dived that November.[221] In addition to his communications duties, Bratton was also the head of the army military intelligence division's Far East section. It was a post that he was well qualified to fill. He had spent four years in Japan, first as a language student, then in Japan's General Staff College, and later as military attaché at our Tokyo embassy. After commanding an infantry battalion, Bratton was briefly professor of military science and tactics at the University of Idaho before joining the general staff's G-2 section in 1937.

Bratton, therefore, was well informed of the seriousness of the situation. After delivering the pilot message that Saturday afternoon to the secretary of state, the secretary of war, and General Marshall, he had returned to his office to wait for navy to finish decoding and typing up the thirteen parts of the Tokyo message. At the 1944 army court of inquiry, Bratton was to testify under oath, "without equivocation and without qualification,"[222] that around ten that evening he had made another round to deliver the thirteen parts of Tokyo's final message to Generals Marshall, Miles, and Gerow.

"It was my practice to deliver them their copies before I went to the State Department" was Bratton's recollection of his second trip around the war department. He claimed he had given Marshall's locked pouch to Colonel Bedell Smith before leaving the one for Secretary Hull with the watch officer at the State Department at ten-thirty.[223] Smith, who was not cleared to receive Magic, was told that the pouch contained an important document that was to go to Marshall straightaway. Bratton thought Marshall's aide had understood the priority because "if it had been otherwise, it would have registered in my memory."[224]

It was Bratton's testimony that persuaded the army's secret board of investigation in 1944 that General Marshall and his principal aides must therefore have been aware of the contents and implications of the thirteen-part message that evening. This led them to issue their indictment of the chief of staff of the army who "failed . . . to get General Short on the evening of December 6th and the early morning of December 7th, the critical information indicating an almost immediate break with Japan, though there was ample time to have accomplished this."[225]

A year later, however, when Bratton appeared before the congressional investigating committee, he had revised his testimony. He was chased around Germany in 1945 by a staff officer and confronted with affidavits sworn by Bedell Smith, Gerow, and the other former war department staff officers "to the effect that they did not receive these pouches from G-2 on the night of the 6th."[226] Confronted by the denials of his brother officers, Bratton signed an affidavit in a Paris hotel that effectively negated his previous testimony.

There was an evident note of reluctance in Bratton's admission that "in the light of the evidence before me now it seems advisable to modify some of my statements."[227] That "evidence" was the phalanx of his brother officers contradicting his previous testimony. As a member of the West Point class of 1914, Bratton appears to have been influenced by the military academy's code of loyalty, which caused him to put the reputations of brother officers before respect for the truth. The discomfort that this caused Bratton was apparent in the less than convincing rationale for changing his testimony that he gave the probing minority counsel at the 1945 congressional hearings: "I know all of these officers; they are men of honor and integrity, and if they say that they didn't receive the pouches from me or Colonel Dusenbury, or one of my assistants, then my recollection must have been at fault and I so admit."[228]

Yet only a few months later in Japan, Bratton was to assure Colonel Raymond Orr, a fellow officer on General MacArthur's staff, that Marshall *was* more than aware of the implications of the thirteen-part message (see Orr affidavit in Authors' Notes). He explained that he had tried to deliver it personally to the army chief of staff that night. That afternoon, moreover, Bratton had vainly tried to persuade Marshall to issue another alert to the Pacific commands. But Marshall had refused, and he left for his quarters at Fort Myer after telling Bratton that he "did not want to be disturbed."[229]

Whether Marshall was "disturbed"—and by what news—must be a matter for valid speculation. The army chief of staff later demonstrated a surprising inability to recollect where he was, or what he did, in the critical hours of Saturday night and early Sunday morning.

For over a week Marshall's head of military intelligence, General Miles, had "considered war as very probable if not inevitable."[230] It was looming so close that Saturday afternoon when Marshall left the office, he could not have been unaware that it might occur sooner rather than later. The war department had received news that two large Japanese invasion convoys were only hours away from the Malaya Peninsula. Marshall himself had been party to the president's pledges to fight alongside the British. An attack on the Philippines could not be ruled out. Magic had revealed that the Japanese were keeping a careful note of MacArthur's strategic bombers, and the latest diplomatic indications were that Tokyo was about to rupture relations with the United States.[231]

Yet General Marshall's testimony presents a detachment, as the hour of supreme national crisis approached, from this momentous event that was as surprising as it was uncharacteristic of the country's most senior military officer. Under cross-examination, however, the chief of the army conceded that standing orders were "if anything came up at night on which I could act that night, on which it was necessary I should act that night, it should be brought to my attention immediately."[232] Yet Marshall managed to evade admitting whether he had received any information by courier or telephone that evening; he was even uncertain about his whereabouts.

"I think I was at home," Marshall testified before the congressional committee. "I am not certain about that. I had no formal engagement, and we practically did not get out at all, except to the movies." But while he could not even recall which of his orderlies was on duty that evening, he was "certain" that Colonel Bratton had not made a Magic delivery to Fort Myer. Nor, apparently, did anyone else. In fact Marshall agreed that he had gone to bed that night "without any knowledge that the Japs were sending any reply at all."[233]

Marshall, nonetheless, cannot have left the war department in ignorance of the pilot message foreshadowing Tokyo's reply that was circulated in the early afternoon. If Bedell Smith had received the pouch, as it was claimed he did, he would have sent it by courier to Fort Myer. Still more difficult to believe is that if Roosevelt had tried to reach Stark, which he did, he would not have tried to reach Marshall to consult about the thirteen-part message that had caused him to remark, "This means war."

The only possible explanation of why Marshall might not have received the thirteen-part message was given by General Miles. After seeing Admiral Wilkinson's pouch, Miles testified, he had decided that it was of "little military significance,"[234] since Japan's rejection of Hull's ten points plan as a basis for negotiations "had been expected and discounted for some time."[235] Accordingly, Miles "contented himself that night by calling Colonel Bratton at his home about 11:30 P.M., and assuring myself that a full reply would be disseminated next morning on Sunday and that he and I would be in our offices then."[236]

Although he "could not remember exactly what was decided between Colonel Bratton and myself that night," Miles testified, he "saw no reason for alerting or waking up the Chief of Staff." Yet, in apparent contradiction, Miles also admitted that his telephone conversation with Bratton "satisfied me that the messages *were being delivered* or would be delivered early next morning when the complete message was in [emphasis added]."[237] According to Bratton's original testimony he had indeed made his delivery of the Magic pouches to Marshall's aide, and to the secretary of state, nearly two hours earlier!

Such inconsistencies must be considered in conjunction with the affidavits of senior staff officers which deny that Bratton had ever made that delivery. Serious doubt is therefore cast on the veracity of both Miles's and Marshall's stories. Either the army's Magic delivery system broke down that Saturday evening—or General Marshall believed he needed an alibi to deny receiving the thirteen-part message. The latter is more probable, because of the evidence indicating that the chief of the army did not spend the evening at his quarters, or retire to bed too early to be disturbed.

A headline in the Washington *Times Herald* that 7 December reported MARSHALL GOES TO VETS REUNION. It appears that the army chief of staff had attended a reunion dinner of World War I veterans that evening.

This explains why Marshall was so unwilling to recollect that he was actually within a few blocks of the White House that evening, and that he may have been summoned to see the president for a final review of the military situation in the Far East. That possibility appears likely, because of the recent release of a statement by James G. Stahlman, then a reserve officer, who was in naval intelligence and a longtime friend of Frank Knox. Stahlman recalls that on the night that the secretary of the navy returned from his fact-finding visit to Pearl Harbor, a week after the attack, his anger and shock prompted a surprisingly frank admission: "He told me that the following had sat for a considerable portion of the night of December 6 at the White House, anticipating a Jap strike somewhere: FDR, Hopkins, Stimson, Marshall, Knox, with John McCrea [Stark's aide] and Frank Beatty [Knox's aide]."[238]

There is no evidence in the official record that any of the president's war council were admitted to his presence that evening. According to the Usher's record at the White House, Roosevelt retired at a quarter to midnight. But this does not mean that a vigil did not take place. It means only that it was not recorded. It is only logical that Roosevelt would have wanted to take stock of the situation with the key members of his war council.

If the president did summon a late-night council of war, then it was apparently not attended by the secretary of state. This may have been because of his poor health, but it might also have been another indication of the extent to which he was being excluded from Roosevelt's inner circle. The reasons were apparent enough from the confidential report on events prepared a few weeks later by the president's closest aide.

"Hull wanted peace above everything," Hopkins noted cryptically. "It is true that Hull told the Secretaries of War and Navy that he believed that Japan might attack at any moment. On the other hand, up to the very last day, he undoubtedly had hopes that something could be worked out at the last moment."[239] Roosevelt blamed Hull for the "weakness in our policy" and for his inability to "be specific" over guarantees to the British and Dutch. The president had complained to Hopkins on more than one occasion during those final weeks of peace that the secretary of state "always ducked the question" and "would never envisage the tough answer to the problem that would have to be faced if Japan attacked, for instance, either Singapore or the Netherlands East Indies."[240]

Whether Roosevelt and his key aides "deliberately sat through the night of 6 December 1941, waiting for the Japs to strike somewhere" as Stahlman maintained—or just conversed on the telephone, it was clear that the time had come to find that "tough answer." That is why Assistant Secretary of State Adolph Berle wondered in his diary whether that Saturday would go down in history as "the day, when in practice, the war really started."[241] He had spent the morning working on the message that Hull was preparing for the president to send to Congress.

After taking his daughters to see the matinee performance of *The Student Prince,* Berle returned to the State Department around seven. He noted that half an hour later "Army Intelligence reported that they had intercepted the text of the reply which Japan was to make."[242] His 6 December diary entry appears to corroborate Bratton's 1944 testimony that he *did* make his second Magic delivery that evening:

> It was not only a flat turn down, but a coarse and gratuitous and insulting message as well. Bad as this was, the accompanying message, likewise intercepted, was worse. The Japanese envoys were to keep this message locked up in their safe and present it only on receipt of a signal; and during this time the final dispositions were to be completed.
>
> We worked up the text of a message; and I turned in to bed about one A.M., feeling very uneasy. The waltzes of "The Student Prince" seemed like a dirge of something that may have existed once, but certainly had very little relation to anything one knew today.[243]

Berle's reaction to the Japanese thirteen-part message contradicts both the testimony and evaluations made by General Miles and Admiral Wilkinson. Those who burned midnight oil in the State Department grasped, as the president had, its ominous significance. This makes it difficult to understand how the heads of naval and army intelligence could conclude that the decrypts of the Tokyo message were "not of great military significance" without the final, fourteenth part of Japan's final message.[244]

Evaluation of the intelligence that was available to Washington that Saturday night should have revealed that the fuse to the Pacific powder keg was burning down. The war department had been alerted that the British had given orders to their Far East commander for Operation Matador. This was a preemptive occupation of the Isthmus of Kra to forestall the arrival of Japanese invasion forces at the Singora and Patani beachheads. In either event the United States would be sucked into the war because of the assurance that Roosevelt had given, and the contingency plans to which the Joint Board had agreed.[245]

The only two pieces of the intelligence puzzle that the war and navy departments did not have that Saturday night were the precise hour that Japan would commence hostilities—and how soon America would be involved in the actual fighting.

If Japan did not attack the Philippines or some other outpost, the president would have to persuade the nation to honor his commitment to fight. That was why Adolph Berle labored into the early morning hours of 7 December to have the statement for Congress ready for approval of Hull, Stimson, and Knox at their scheduled 10 A.M. meeting that Sunday. That document and its accompanying ultimatum to Tokyo was what consumed the president and his army and naval advisers that Saturday night. So whether he went to the White House on the way home, or conversed in only general terms by telephone with the president, it is improbable that General Marshall went to bed in the blissful state of ignorance to which he testified later.

Contrary to his professed aloofness from the climactic hours of the crisis, Marshall had spoken to General Arnold that afternoon after Arnold arrived at the west coast to get the forty-eight B-17s off to Hawaii on the first leg of their long flight to the Philippines. "These damn fellows don't realize how serious this thing is," Hap Arnold had telephoned.

"Well, you are there and they are your people," his chief of staff retorted. "You start them out."[246]

Arnold did as he was ordered. The first group of unarmed Flying Fortresses took off for Hickam Field, Oahu, that evening.

Marshall's subsequent downplaying of his anticipation that war would break out the next day apparently was an attempt to justify why he took a longer than usual Sunday horseback ride that kept him out of the war department until midmorning that day. His absence from the office was to play a crucial part in the failure to get the last-minute warning to Pearl Harbor and could be construed as a dereliction of duty.

The effort to divert investigators from a collective charge of dereliction against the most senior officers in the war and navy departments appears to have been responsible for the conflicting testimony of the staff officers about how much they knew, or surmised, of Japanese intentions from the intelligence that was in their hands that Saturday evening. Whereas the evaluations made by the State Department pertained to diplomatic and political considerations, Marshall and Stark were the men primarily responsible for keeping the overseas commands informed.

Nor should it be forgotten that the inquiries by both the army and navy in 1944, which weighed all the evidence then available in secret hearings that were free of political manipulation, censured both the chief of naval operations and the chief of the army for their failure to pass on vital intelligence to their Hawaiian commanders. It is also surely significant that Secretary Knox, who never testified and who died before the 1945 congressional investigation began, arrived in Pearl Harbor three days after the attack convinced that another war alert *had* been sent out to our Pacific commands on the evening of 6 December.

In spite of the secretary of the navy's impression, no such warning was received by Admiral Kimmel or General Short. Had such a dispatch been received, it would probably have persuaded Kimmel to reject Admiral Pye's complacency and send the battle fleet to sea. A late-afternoon conference with his chief of war plans and operations officer had revived Kimmel's uneasiness. It led to a discussion about whether he should order a sortie that night at the risk of alarming the local population.[247]

Kimmel's unease was not translated into action. It probably would have been if he had received the warning that Knox assured him and *myself* that he believed had been sent from Washington that night. The failure to send out any eleventh-hour alert on 6 December has been inflated by revisionist historians into a deliberate conspiracy by Roosevelt to deny Pearl Harbor warning so that the nation would enter World War II united and inflamed by the Japanese attack on the Hawaiian Islands.

All the new evidence that has been gathered for this account shows beyond any reasonable doubt that our leaders in Washington *knew* by the evening of 6 December that Japan would launch into war in a matter of hours rather than days. Not a shred of evidence has been uncovered from all the declassified intelligence files to suggest that anyone suspected that Pearl Harbor would be a target. But there was more than enough justification to have sent out an urgent and more precise eleventh-hour war alarm to the Pacific commands. Worse, we shall see how the failure to disseminate even the last-minute intelligence continued to deny us the clues that would have warned of the attack.

Imperial Japan: As language course lieutenants Rochefort (above left) and Layton (above right) in 1931 were attached to the U.S. embassy in Tokyo as McCollum and Zacharias (below second row, right and far right) had been ten years earlier.

The Code Breakers: Laurence F. Safford (above left) was head of the navy's OP-20-G cryptographic unit. His experience with Japanese machine codes assisted William F. Friedman's (above right) army team in constructing the first Purple decoding machine (below) in 1939.

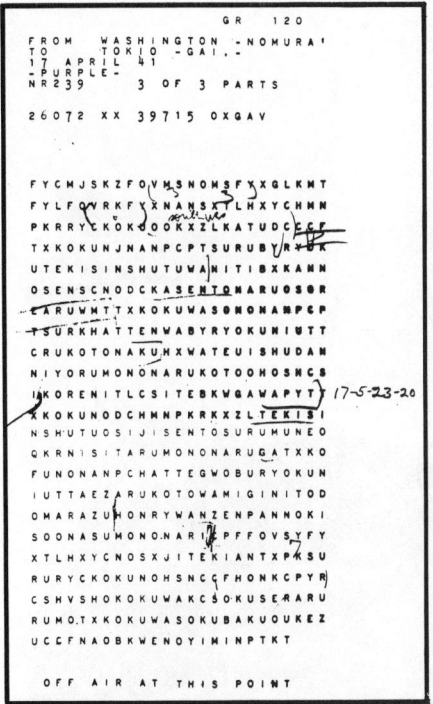

Left facsimile:

```
                    GR   120
FROM    WASHINGTON -NOMURA'
TO      TOKIO -GAI .-
17 APRIL 41
-PURPLE-
NR239       3 OF 3 PARTS

26072 XX 39715 OXGAV


FYCMJSKZFOVMSNOHSFXXGLKMT
FYLFOVRKFXXNANSXTLHXYCHMN
PKRRYCKOKOOKXZLKATUDCECF
TXKOKUNJNANPCPTSURUBYR+UK
UTEKISINSHUTUWANITIBXKAMN
OSENSCNODCKASENTONARUOSOR
CARUWMTTXKOKUWASOHONAMPCP
TSURKHATTENWABYRYOKUNIUTT
CRUKOTONAKUHXWATEUISHUDAN
NIYORUMONONARUKOTOOHOSNCS
IAKORENITLCSITEBKWGAWAPYT
XKOKUNODCHMNPKRKXZLTEKISI
NSHUTUOSIJISENTOSURUMUNEO
QKRNISITARUMONONARUGATXKO
FUNONANPCHATTEGWOBURYOKUN
IUTTAEZARUKOTOWAMIGINITOD
OMARAZUHONRYWANZENPANNOKI
SOONASUMONONARIHPFFOVSYFY
XTLHXYCNOSXJITEKIANTXPKSU
RURYCKOKUNOHSNCCFHONKCPYR
CSHVSHOKOKUWAKCSOKUSERARU
RUMO.TXKOKUWASOKUBAKUOUKEZ
UCCFNAOBKWENOYIMINPTKT

OFF AIR AT THIS POINT
```

Handwritten annotations: 17-5-23-20

Right facsimile:

```
From: Washington (Nomura)
To:   Tokyo
April 17th, 1941.

#239.        (Part 3 of 3)

             Secret outside the department.

     VI.  The activities of our two countries in the Southwestern

Pacific:

             Since there is the danger that an advance southward
militarily by our Empire would lead to war between the United States
and Japan, it is held that our progress in that direction must be
conducted by peaceful means without resorting to the sword. It has
been made clear to me that if we do thus, the United States will support
our economic penetration thither. I must emphasize that this premise
is the one and only basis of the present proposal for an understanding.

     VII.  The policy of the Two Nations Concerning the

Political Stabilization of the Pacific:

             Through this clause the countries of Europe will suffer
some reverses but our Empire will have all to gain and nothing to lose.


             (Message incomplete)


(Copy sent to G-2, 12:00 noon, April 19th)


16448                          Trans. 4-19-41 (7,

ARMY
```

The Purple Code: Japan's top secret diplomatic communications, such as this message to its Washington ambassador as sent (above left) and decrypted (above right), were enciphered on an electric typewriter connected to a Type 97 coding machine similar to the device (below) captured on Guam in 1944.

Anglo-American Deterrent: At the Atlantic Charter summer conference, Roosevelt, Churchill, and military advisers, including Admiral King, General Marshall, and General Dill (above), agreed to a secret defense pact based on a strategic bomber force in the Philippines.

Marching to Different Drums: General MacArthur (above right) prepared to threaten Japan with preemptive B-17 bomber raids (above left) by 1942 while Secretary Hull (below) babied along ambassadors Nomura and Kurusu. But Tokyo's patience ran out before the deterrent became credible.

Kept in the Dark: Admiral Kimmel and General Short were not informed that the focus of American strategy in the fall of 1941 had shifted from defense based on the Pacific Fleet in Pearl Harbor (below, note prominence of oil storage tanks in upper left) to a strategic bomber deterrent five thousand miles away in the Philippines.

Vulnerable Fortresses: The Pacific Fleet battleships on prewar maneuvers were destined to become floating targets rather than bulwarks of naval power. Too slow to operate with the carriers, the battle fleet was left behind by Admiral Halsey when he sortied in the first week of December 1941 to ferry fighter plane reinforcements to Wake.

A Knockout Blow: Admiral Yamamoto (above right—a posthumous silk painting Roger Pineau rescued from Japan in 1949) believed an air attack led by Admiral Nagumo (above left) was the best chance for Japan's navy—which included powerful 10,000-ton cruisers (below)—to win a quick victory over the United States.

The *Kido Butai*: *Akagi* and three of Nagumo's six carriers shortly before the striking force set sail for Hawaii on 26 November 1941.

The Feud on the Second Deck: Admiral Turner (above left), appointed by Admiral Stark (above center) as director of war plans, fought DNI Captain Kirk (above right) for control of cryptanalytic information. After Admiral Wilkinson (below left) became DNI in October 1941, Turner vetoed all operational dispatches from Commander McCollum (below center) and DNC Admiral Leigh Noyes (below right). NAVAL HISTORICAL CENTER

Missed Clues: Kramer (above left), head of OP-20-G translation section, neglected the true significance of the so-called bomb plot decrypt (below left) and the "lights message" (below right) translated by Mrs. Dorothy Edgers (above right) on the eve of Japan's attack.

From: Tokyo (Toyoda)
To: Honolulu
September 24, 1941

#83

      Strictly secret.

      Henceforth, we would like to have you make reports concerning vessels along the following lines insofar as possible:

      1. The waters (of Pearl Harbor) are to be divided roughly into five sub-areas. (We have no objections to your abbreviating as much as you like.)

      Area A. Waters between Ford Island and the Arsenal.

      Area B. Waters adjacent to the Island south and west of Ford Island. (This area is on the opposite side of the Island from Area A.)

      Area C. East Loch.

      Area D. Middle Loch.

      Area E. West Loch and the communicating water routes.

      2. With regard to warships and aircraft carriers, we would like to have you report on those at anchor, (these are not so important) tied up at wharves, buoys and in docks. (Designate types and classes briefly. If possible we would like to have you make mention of the fact when there are two or more vessels alongside the same wharf.)

23260
ARMY   Trans. 10/9/41 (S)

T   K   TOP SECRET [ULTRA]

From: Honolulu (Kita).
To : Tokyo.
3 December 1941
(PA-K2)

#245 (In 2 parts, complete)

      (Military secret).

      From Ichiro Fujii to the Chief of #3 Section of Military Staff Headquarters.

      1. I wish to change my method of communicating by signals to the following:

      I. Arrange the eight signals in three columns as follows:

Meaning		Signal
Battleship divisions including scouts and screen units	Preparing to sortie.	1
A number of carriers	Preparing to sortie.	2
Battleship divisions	All departed between 1st and 3rd.	3
Carriers	Several departed between 1st and 3rd.	4
Carriers	All departed between 1st and 3rd.	5
Battleship divisions	All departed between 4th and 6th.	6
Carriers	Several departed between 4th and 6th.	7
Carriers	All departed between 4th and 6th.	8

JD-1: 7370 SECRET   (continued)   (M) Navy Trans. 12-11-41 (7)

TO RA! TO RA! TO RA!: A Japanese Kate (above), armed with a specially modified bomb, heading in with the second wave to attack an already crippled Battleship Row, while *Nevada* (below center) manages to limp across the harbor.

Battleship Row: As seen from the cockpit of an attacking plane (above) and at sea level (below) as *Arizona* blazes after the magazine explosion in *Tennessee* and *West Virginia*.

The Men of Station Hypo: The leadership of Rochefort (above left) inspired cryptanalysts like Wesley A. Wright (above right) and the ex-bandsmen of battleship *California* (below), who ran the I.B.M. punch-card machines.

Negat Versus Hypo: The reorganization of OP-20-G by Joseph R. Redman (above left), the new director of naval communications, and his brother, John R. Redman (above right), threatened the independence and integrity of Rochefort and his deputy, Thomas H. Dyer (below, at his pinup desk).

(32) (40) , MAY 1942

→ ALL MESSAGES PRIORITY WHILE UP ABOVE URGENT

Ø1 Ø1 44
COM 14 → COMB. JALUIT RADIO SENT "U.S. RADIO INTELLIGENCE
(Ø1ØØ 1MAY) REPORT — 14 NAVAL AIRCRAFT HEARD, APPARENTLY
FOR UNITS SORTIEING.
AN AIR PATROL COVERING A SORTIE. COM GREATLY INCREASED
INTEREST IN AIR OPERATIONS IN HAWAIIAN, ALASKAN AND SAMOAN
AREA BEING SHOWN BY JAPANESE RECENTLY. ALSO ON 25 APRIL
TOKYO REPORTED THAT FLEET UNITS HAD RETURNED TO PEARL
HARBOR, (FROM DOLITTLE RAID) AS EVIDENCED BY TRANSMISSIONS
FROM SOME 20 CARRIER BASED AIRCRAFT, INDICATING THEIR RETURN
TO PEARL HARBOR.

Ø111X5 — Ø1 11 38 — Ø11 1Ø8   ((CI. SUMMARY FOR R.I.
COM 14 → OPNAV, BELCONNEN, C.T.F 16. UNIT IN CTF 16.))
©....."MO" CAMPAIGN NOW UNDERWAY INVOLVES SOUTH EAST NEW
GUINEA AND LOUISIADE ARCHEPELAGO. SUGGEST MORESBY FOR
"MO". FORCES INVOLVED WILL CONSIST OF CARDIV 5, CRUDIV 5 LESS
NACHI, GUNBOAT DIVISION 8, CRUDIV 18 AND DESRON 6 AVAILABLE.
NEW BRITAIN AIR, KNOWN AS 5TH AIR ATTACK FORCE, CONSISTING
OF TAINAN AIR, 4TH AIR, AND YOKOHAMA AIR. FIRST TWO
HAVE LAND BASED BOMBERS AND FIGHTERS, LAST ONE MADE
UP OF SEAPLANES AND FLYING BOATS, TOTAL SHORE BASED AIR
BELIEVED 15 BOMBERS, 18 VP AND UNKNOWN FIGHTERS .... LIGHT
FORCES ENROUTE OPERATING AREA DESPITE MSG GIVING TOWNSVILLE
AS REFERENCE POINT. DO NOT BELIEVE AUSTRALIA IS TARGET
OF THESE OPERATIONS IN IMMEDIATE FUTURE EXCEPT FOR
SUBMARINES. CINC 4TH FLEET IS IN IMMEDIATE COMMAND OF OPERATIONS.
(D) FIGHTING UNITS IN HOME YARDS PLUS FOLLOWING FORCES ARE
AVAILABLE FOR OTHER OFFENSIVE OR DEFENSIVE TASKS: BATDIVS
1 AND 2 x CRUDIVS 4 AND 7 x KAGA x SORYU x (OTHER CARRIERS
IN YARD ON A 2-3 DAY SAILING-ORDER BASIS) AND AN UNKNOWN
NUMBER OF DESTROYERS. IN VIEW OF GREAT INTEREST
SHOWN BY TOKYO IN PALMYRA, SAMOA — CANTON AREA RECENTLY,
OF THE PRIMARY AND URGENT RADIO INTELLIGENCE ATTENTION
TO ABOVE AND HAWAIIAN AREAS AND THE RECENT RECONNAISSANCE
OF BAKER - HOWLAND ISLANDS, ESTIMATE PART, OR ALL, OF THE
ABOVE UNITS WILL COVER THE "MO" CAMPAIGN WITH POSSIBLE
RAIDS ON SAMOA AND SUVA AREAS. IN EARLY APRIL THE KAGA
TOLD TO EXPEDITE REPAIRS AS WAS SCHEDULED FOR OPERATIONS IN
THE NEW GUINEA AREA. VARIOUS RADIO INTELLIGENCE STATIONS
HAVE RECENTLY SHOWN INTEREST IN ALEUTIANS. BEST INDICATIONS
OF FUTURE OPERATIONS IS TOKYO'S ASSIGNMENT OF NEW NAME PLACE
DESIGNATORS; LAST JANUARY NEW ONES ISSUED FOR PLACES IN THE
ALEUTIANS, INDICATING THAT AREA FOR FUTURE OPERATIONS. FOR
THAT REASON SECOND CHOICE FOR OPERATIONS OF AVAILABLE FORCES
IS A RAID ON THE ALEUTIANS BUT THIS CONSIDERED UNLIKELY AT
THIS TIME BUT CERTAINLY PROBABLE AT A LATER DATE. CINC
2ND FLEET WILL COMMAND AVAILABLE FORCE. CINC 1ST FLEET IS
STILL IN COMMAND OF SCREENING FORCES IN HOME WATERS "

Coral Sea Action: The Hypo (Com 14) summary of 1 May that predicted the Japanese naval forces' "MO" operation in the author's reconstruction (above) of the Cincpac signal log. An enemy pilot's view of the attack on *Lexington* that cost Admiral Fletcher (lower right) the carrier.

Midway Victory: Hypo cryptanalysts (above, starred) reveal more clues about "AF." But even after the battle began (upper right—a Japanese torpedo scoring a direct hit on *Yorktown*) radio intelligence failed to warn that *Yamato* (lower right) was leading the battle fleet into action.

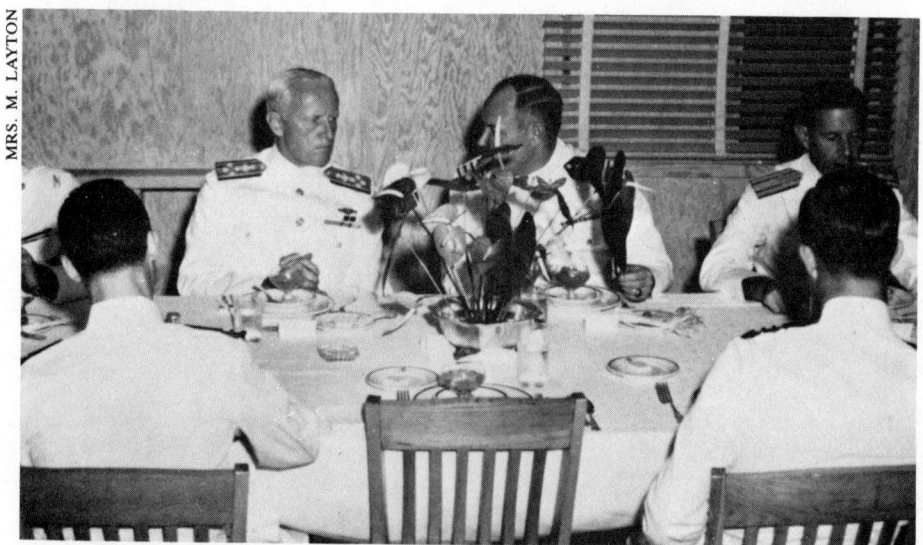

Cincpac Headquarters: The author in the plotting room (above) and Nimitz dining in the Makalapa mess with his staff (below) and Admiral Spruance at the extreme right.

The Winning Team: Admiral Halsey (above left) rotated command of the fleet with Admiral Spruance (center), and Admiral Turner (above right) commanded amphibious operations. The Battle of the Philippine Sea (below) on 14–15 June 1944 was the beginning of the end for the Japanese navy.

Strategic Decisions: The navy's mid-Pacific offensive and devastating submarine campaign (above) were defeating Japan by mid-1944. But MacArthur argued successfully for a Philippine invasion at the July conference with Roosevelt and Nimitz (below) at Pearl Harbor.

Victory off the Philippines: The two-day Battle for Leyte Gulf decimated the remaining forces of the once-mighty Combined Fleet. *Yamato* (above), under air attack off Samar, and carrier *Zuiho* (below), sunk off Cape Engano.

Surrender at Tokyo: The author (above), appropriately armed, accompanied Nimitz and Halsey (left) to the Yokosuka naval base the day before the formal capitulation (below) on board *Missouri*—Layton, arrowed, back row.

23

Day of Infamy

Pearl Harbor *6:30 P.M. local time*
(13 hours 23 minutes before the attack)

I T WAS 1830 in Honolulu, the end of another lazy afternoon, and the second weekend of low-level alert at the island's army and naval bases found most service personnel off duty. Enlisted men were flocking as usual to the bars, dance halls, and pinball parlors of the waterfront. At the officers clubs and the verandahed dining rooms of the Waikiki hotels, tables were being taken for a leisurely evening.

General Short and his wife attended a charity dinner-dance at the Schofield Barracks officers club. Admiral Kimmel, more wisely than he appreciated at the time, had turned down an invitation to cocktails at the Japanese consulate. Instead, he went straight to the Halekulani Hotel for a small dinner party hosted by his successor as cruiser force commander, Rear Admiral Herbert F. Leary.

That evening I was with a group of officers and their wives who gathered to dine and dance in the tropical splendor of the Royal Hawaiian Hotel. Beyond the terrace, the lights of Waikiki's palm-fringed crescent stretched away like a Hollywood set. The mood and music almost made me forget my preoccupation with the events on the far side of the Pacific that were rushing to shape our nation's destiny. But at midnight the familiar refrain of the "Star-Spangled Banner," which ended the dancing, brought me back to reality. As I stood to attention I was suddenly overcome with the urge to yell "Wake up, America!"

On that last evening of peace our military installations on the island betrayed few indications that the island was already on war alert; everything had been carefully concealed to avoid alarming local residents. At Hickam and Wheeler airfields armed guards patrolled the rows of aircraft that were parked wingtip to wingtip. The duty air commander had arranged to pay for radio station KGMB to remain on the air all night so that its broadcasts would help guide the first flight of a dozen B-17s that were due to fly in from the mainland at around 0800.

Pearl Harbor was ablaze with light. The main attraction for white hats without liberty was the band championship at the new fleet recreation center. Only one officer and a switchboard operator were on duty at the Naval Control Center on Ford Island, where only seven PBY patrol planes had been scheduled for dawn antisubmarine patrol off the south coast of Oahu. The only concession to additional vigilance was the army's mobile radar trucks on the northern heights of Oahu. They were under orders to start operating two hours before dawn the next morning.

Yet even if the radars had been reaching out into the dark waters north of the island during those last hours of peace, their 132-mile ground-to-air range could not have reached the Japanese warships. They were still more than 200 miles away. A light cruiser and four destroyers scouted 3 miles ahead of the main force. The six carriers that bore the three hundred aircraft that were to deliver the actual strike were guarded by a phalanx of battleships, heavy cruisers, and destroyers.

Clouds masked the waning full moon through the long dark hours that the *Kido Butai* charged southward at twenty-four knots. Flight crews dozed fitfully as mechanics labored with the bombing and arming of the planes. The first hours of the new day had brought a reassuring piece of intelligence relayed from Honolulu: "No unusual condition was observed concerning the fleet."[1]

The fateful race of events that conspired to make that Sunday a day which would live in infamy were unwinding.

Washington   *7:30 A.M. local time*
                  (5 hours 53 minutes before the attack)

When Commander Kramer arrived at OP-20-GZ shortly after 0730 on Sunday, he found the fourteenth part of Tokyo's diplomatic message, which had been received an hour earlier. "Obviously it is the intention of the American Government to conspire with Great Britain," it began, and continued in the same accusatory vein. It ended with "regrets" that the Japanese government "cannot but consider that it is impossible to reach an agreement through further negotiations."[2]

After Kramer discussed the latest message with Commander McCollum, they together took it to Admiral Stark. The "virulence and tenor of the language" of the entire fourteen parts[3] was a clear indication to McCollum "that we could expect war."[4] But Stark said, "No, I don't think any further warning is necessary."[5]

Kramer hurried off on foot to hand-deliver the latest Magics to the White House and State Department. The president, who had anticipated the fourteenth part's final rejection, remarked—almost casually—"that it looked as though the Japanese are going to sever negotiations."[6]

Pearl Harbor   *3:42 A.M. local time*
(4 hours 11 minutes before the attack)

The moon broke through the patchy overcast shrouding Kaenapapuaa Point to illuminate the black waters off Pearl Harbor. The light silhouetted the vertical stalk of a periscope approaching the outermost line of buoys that marked the route into Pearl Harbor. An alert lookout on one of two Channel Entrance Patrol minesweepers guarding the boom defense nets reported the sighting "1 3/4 miles south of the entrance buoys."[7] It was one of the five midget submersibles that had cast off two hours earlier from their mother submarines.

"Sighted submerged submarine on westerly course. Speed nine knots," the minesweeper *Condor* signaled by blinker lamp to the four-stack destroyer *Ward,* which was duty patrol destroyer that night.[8]

Lieutenant William W. Outerbridge swung his ship around onto the bearing, ordered general quarters, and commenced a sonar sweep. An hour later when no contact had been made, the net boom at the channel entrance was opened and the two minesweepers steamed through. They were followed into the protected channel by at least two Japanese midget submarines.

No sighting report reached the Naval Control Center on Ford Island. When no contact was made, the duty officer at the Bishop's Point naval radio station concluded that *Ward*'s report was another false alarm by a jumpy destroyer skipper.

Kido Butai   *4:00 A.M. local time*
(3 hours 53 minutes before the attack)

Dawn was less than two hours away when the flight crews were roused. After donning their "thousand stitch," good-luck waistbands, the fliers ate a celebratory breakfast of red snapper and rice, washed down with toasts of sake. Word quickly spread that the one Honolulu radio station that had stayed on the air all night was still playing its soft music. This was an unmistakable sign that their mission would achieve the surprise essential to success.

The *Kido Butai* was still some 230 miles due north of Oahu when aircrews crammed into the dimly illuminated briefing rooms. Even *Akagi*'s "was not large enough for all the men, some of whom had to stand out in the passageway," according to Commander Mitsuo Fuchida, who was to lead the attack. "On the blackboard was written the positions of ships in Pearl Harbor as of 0600 December 7."[9]

Washington *9:30 A.M. local time*
(3 hours 53 minutes before the attack)

Colonel Bratton arrived at the Munitions Building shortly before nine. He was reading the fourteenth part of the Tokyo message and comparing it with the previous afternoon's thirteen parts when he was handed a much shorter message that had just been decrypted: "Will the ambassador please submit to the United States Government (if possible the Secretary of State) our reply to the United States at 1:00 p.m. on 7th, your time."[10]

"This immediately stunned me into frenzied activity because of its implications," Bratton testified. "The vital factor in my mind was the date and hour of delivery of the 14-part message."[11] That Tokyo would want a diplomatic message delivered on a Sunday was unusual enough, but the specific timing was its real significance. Dawn was an ideal time to launch a surprise attack, and a brief look at a time chart left Bratton "convinced the Japanese were going to attack some American installation in the Pacific Area."[12]

It did not occur to him that Pearl Harbor was at risk because one o'clock Washington time was well after dawn in Hawaiian time. Furthermore, Bratton shared the general belief that the fleet had gone to sea "because that was part of the war plan."[13] The deadline did, however, fall before the sun was due to rise over Guam and the Philippines and he felt strongly that another war warning ought to be sent out. He telephoned his chief of military intelligence at home. General Miles was concerned enough to leave right away for the Munitions Building. There he consulted with Bratton and General Gerow. But while they agreed that an alert should be sent out, neither of them had the authority to issue a command message without approval of General Marshall.

At 0930 Bratton put in a phone call to the chief of staff's Fort Myer quarters. But Marshall was out on his Sunday morning canter along the Potomac. An urgent message was left with his duty officer for the general to call the war department as soon as he returned.

Tokyo *11:30 P.M. local time*
(3 hours 53 minutes before the attack)

The code clerks at the American embassy had finished decoding Roosevelt's appeal to the emperor. The president's triple-priority telegram had been delayed ten hours by the Censorship Office of the Ministry of Communications. To impress the foreign minister with its importance and make up for lost time, Ambassador Grew asked to be received immediately by the foreign minister. An hour later he was urging Togo to arrange for him to see the emperor. Although he knew that protocol ruled out such an audience, Grew left the foreign minister confident that the president's cable would at least reach the imperial palace that night.[14]

Washington *10:30 A.M. local time*
(2 hours 53 minutes before the attack)

General Marshall finally called the war department. The chief of staff would later not recall speaking with Bratton, who testified that he had offered to make the twenty-minute trip out to Fort Myer to discuss "an important message."[15] According to him, Marshall insisted that it could wait until he came down to the office.[16]

At about the same time, Kramer arrived back in his office, from his brisk walk from the State Department. The decrypt of the deadline message was on his desk. He made a quick calculation "to get a picture of how this 1 o'clock Washington message tied up with the movement of the big Japanese convoy moving down the coast of French Indochina."[17] Kramer decided that it was probably timed to coincide with the beginning of an amphibious operation shortly before dawn on the north coast of Malaya.[18]

Then the watch officer brought him a plain-language intercept. Kramer quickly realized that it was a true winds alert message, which he hastily translated: "Relations between Japan and England are not in accordance with expectations."[19] Later he discovered that he had erred in his translation of the word *higashi* (east), which was their code for the United States.

A correct reading might have sparked a more urgent reaction when he took the message up to Stark's office. Captain McCollum ventured that the 1300 deadline was tied up with some Japanese movement in the southwest Pacific. The message was nonetheless considered sufficiently urgent for Kramer to be directed to take it immediately to the White House and make the army's delivery to the secretary of state. As Kramer set off "at the double,"[20] McCollum pointed out to Stark that 1300 in Washington was "very early in the morning in the Far East."[21] They chewed over the implications of this fact and concluded that "it was timed for operations in the Far East and possibly Hawaii."[22]

Wilkinson, according to McCollum, made the only positive suggestion. "Why don't you pick up the telephone and call Kimmel?" he asked Stark.[23] Considering the security-mindedness of the office of naval operations, McCollum was surprised to see Stark actually lift the receiver. Then he shook his head and said, "No, I think I will call the president."[24]

The White House switchboard regretted that Roosevelt was engaged.

The emergency meeting in Stark's office was over by the time that Admiral Turner arrived at the navy department at 1115. The chief of war plans, surprisingly, testified later that he had not been informed of the deadline message, and that Stark had discussed only matters relating to what the Asiatic Fleet would do in the event that war broke out.

Kramer, after dropping off the morning's Magic pouch for the president, went directly to the State Department, where he found that the secretaries of war, navy, and state were in mid-conference. He emphasized again that the deadline in the Japanese message coincided with "a few hours before sunrise off the north Malayan coast at Kota Bharu."[25]

Kido Butai   *5:00 A.M. local time*
(2 hours 53 minutes before the attack)

The aircrews of the first attack wave, with *hachimaki* headbands tied onto their flying helmets, were clambering into their cramped cockpits. As the battle ensigns were broken out from *Akagi*'s masthead, Fuchida accepted the traditional bandana worn by warriors in battle from the flagship's crew. It bore the Japanese characters for *Hissho*—"certain victory."

At 0530 a pair of seaplanes were catapulted off the two heavy cruisers that were steaming ahead of the carriers. Their mission was to stealthily fly a reconnaissance over Pearl Harbor and the fleet's alternative Lahaina anchorage and radio back positive confirmation of the fleet's position.

For twenty minutes the other aircrews sat in their machines on the pitching decks, waiting for the predawn murk to clear sufficiently to take off. Spray lifted over the decks of the carriers as the force turned into the easterly wind to begin launching just before 0600.

Green signal lamps flashed, engines burst into life, and chocks were pulled to allow the first plane to roll. The crowded decks left the leading Zeros very little room for a takeoff run. After catching their breath as the first plane dipped perilously low over *Akagi*'s bucking bow, cheers rang out as the fighter clawed its way aloft.

During the next fifteen minutes, fighters, bombers, and torpedo planes swarmed up from the six carriers—some barely scraping the spume-flecked waves. Only 1 Zero pilot failed to make the tricky takeoff synchronization and ditched. The other 183 aircraft wheeled overhead as the first attack wave took up its carefully ordered formation.

Five minutes later Fuchida's bomber roared over the flagship's bow to lead the aerial armada, his orange commander's marker light vanishing into the clouds. Setting course due south, Fuchida climbed through the heavy overcast and burst into the dawn sunlight. It flashed off the burnished wings of the forty-nine high-level bombers following in formation. Then came the fifty-one dive bombers, the forty torpedo planes, and the forty-three escorting Zero fighters. Fuchida's navigator estimated that with the help of the strong tailwind they would be approaching their target in just over an hour and a half.

After returning to a southerly course after the first attack wave had been launched, Nagumo ordered his force to head into the wind to launch the second wave. It had taken less than three quarters of an hour to get planes up from the hangars and ready for launching. As the flight deck crews cheered and madly waved their caps, the fifty-four bombers and seventy-eight dive bombers rumbled off into the mile-high cloud base.

As Admiral Nagumo stoically watched their departure, even his confidence was rising that the huge aerial armada of 350 planes really would be able to pull off a spectacular attack.

Washington   *11:25 A.M. local time*
(1 hour 58 minutes before the attack)

Nearly two hours had elapsed from the receipt of the deadline message to the time that General Marshall arrived at his office. When Miles and Bratton appeared, the chief of the army insisted on reviewing the full fourteen-part message while they waited impatiently to give him the more urgent decrypt. Only then were they able to explain why they "were convinced it meant Japanese hostile action against some American installation in the Pacific at or shortly after 1 o'clock that afternoon."[26]

MacArthur's forces were seen as the obvious target, although no invasion convoys had been sighted heading south from Formosa and there was some doubt that Japanese bombers had the range to reach Manila. But 1300 Washington time would be an hour before dawn in the Philippines. As a precautionary measure, Miles urged that warnings also be transmitted to all our military commands in the Pacific, including Hawaii, Panama, and the west coast.[27]

Marshall eventually agreed that another alert should be "sent at once by the fastest possible means."[28] On a piece of scratch paper, he later testified, he wrote out the dispatch in longhand before calling Admiral Stark on the White House telephone system to inform him "in a guarded way."[29] But, according to Marshall, the admiral's first reaction was that another war warning would be unnecessary because "we had sent them so much already," and he "hesitated to send more."[30]

After a few minutes' reflection Stark changed his mind. A minute or so later he suggested that a joint dispatch could go out by the naval communications system. When Marshall said he "could get it through very quickly,"[31] Stark replied that the Pacific army commanders should be advised "to inform their naval opposites."[31]

Despite the "awful urgency" about beating the deadline, which was little more than an hour away, for security reasons Marshall did not want to use the scrambler telephone. If he had done so, he testified, he would have given priority to MacArthur, then Panama.[33] As Bratton left with the draft dispatch for the signal center, the chief of the army told him, "If there is any question of priority, give the Philippines first priority."[34]

Time was running out, as Bratton well appreciated. When he arrived at the signal center he was "very much exercised," according to Colonel

Edward F. French who was in charge of the army's signal center.[35] Bratton had to translate Marshall's hastily scrawled dispatch, which read:

> Japanese are presenting at one p.m. eastern standard time today what amounts to an ultimatum. Also they are under orders to destroy their code machine immediately. Just what significance the hour set may have we do not know but be on the alert accordingly. Inform naval authorities of this communication. Marshall.[36]

When Bratton returned to Marshall's office to confirm that the dispatch had been sent, he was told to go back and check with French how long it would take to be delivered to the addressees. Bratton was told by French that it would take "about 30 or 40 minutes."[37] The chief of the army seemed satisfied with this—even though he must have realized that with the decoding necessary the dispatch would not have reached the Pacific commanders until late in the hour before the deadline was due to expire.

Marshall might have changed his mind about using the navy facilities, or his scrambler telephone, to reach General Short if French had reported that heavy static had blacked out the army's radio circuits to Honolulu since 1030. When French learned of this holdup, he decided to send the message to Hawaii using his teleprinter link to the Western Union Washington office. He reasoned that the message would be relayed from San Francisco via the RCA radio station, which had four times the power of the army's and would be able to break through the atmospherics. He also anticipated that this would save time, because he had heard that RCA was installing a direct connection to Fort Shafter.

Unfortunately, the army teleprinter circuit link on Oahu was not yet in operation. This contributed to French's second miscalculation. Because the coded telegram containing Marshall's warning had been inadvertently sent out without a priority designation, when it reached the RCA Honolulu office at three minutes after the deadline had expired in Washington, it was pigeonholed for routine delivery to Fort Shafter.

Task Force 8   *6:00 A.M. local time*
(1 hour 3 minutes before the attack)

Approximately the same distance west of Pearl Harbor as the *Kido Butai* was north that morning, carrier *Enterprise* was steaming for home port after delivering the fighters to Wake Island. At dawn Admiral Halsey sent up a search patrol, and a flight of Dauntless dive bombers was being prepared to make the trip to Oahu in anticipation that Task Force 8 would reach harbor that evening.

Pearl Harbor   *6:30 A.M. local time*
                   (1 hour 23 minutes before the attack)

Off the entrance channel the skipper of *Antares*, a supply vessel with a lighter in tow, spotted what he thought was the conning tower of a small submarine having difficulty keeping submerged. The highly suspicious object was also sighted by the helmsman on destroyer *Ward*. Roused from his bunk, Lieutenant William W. Outerbridge immediately had his men open fire and ordered full speed to ram, while depth charges were hurled overboard.

"We have attacked, fired upon, and dropped depth charges upon sub operating in defensive area," Outerbridge radioed to the commandant of the Fourteenth Naval District.[38] After attempting to ram the underwater craft and observing a patch of oil, Outerbridge failed to file a detailed report because he steamed off to chase away a suspicious sampan from the restricted waters.

The naval radio station at Bishop's Point acknowledged *Ward*'s report, but no alarm bells were rung at Fourteenth Naval District or Pacific Fleet headquarters. Nor were they set off by a second radio message received half an hour later from one of the pilots of the dawn PBY patrol who claimed to have "sunk a submerged submarine one mile off the entrance to Pearl Harbor."[39]

Washington   *12:00 noon local time*
                 (1 hour 23 minutes before the attack)

The conference among the secretaries of state, war, and navy in Hull's office was breaking for lunch after a grim hour and a half devoted to polishing the presidential address to Congress. From the Magic reports whose delivery by Kramer had interrupted their meeting, Hull was convinced that "zero hour was a matter of hours, perhaps minutes" away.[40] After the Japanese envoys had telephoned to request a meeting, Stimson noted, Hull was certain that "the Japs are planning some deviltry."[41]

Now the main concern of the three secretaries was "wondering where the blow will strike." They all agreed that the United States' objective was "to hold the main people who are interested in the Far East together."[42] To this end Hull dictated a draft of an ultimatum to go to Japan:

> In view of the vital interests of the United States and of the British Commonwealth and Netherlands East Indies, the movement of any Japanese expeditionary force into waters in close proximity to the Philippine Islands or into the China sea south of latitude 10 degrees

north, will of necessity be considered a hostile act directed against the governments concerned.[43]

Fort Shafter   *7:00 A.M. local time*
              (53 minutes before the attack)

The navy's submarine alert was not communicated to the duty officer at army headquarters. Had this contact been made, more attention might have been paid at Fort Shafter to another contact report that was received by the Information Center shortly after 0700.

The telephone call came from the Opana Mobile Radar Unit stationed at Kahuku Point twenty-eight miles north of Honolulu, where Privates Joseph L. Lockard and George F. Elliott had been operating their primitive radar set since 0400. The radar would have been switched off at the appointed time of 0700 if the breakfast truck had arrived on time.

On the hour Elliott noticed "something completely out of the ordinary on the radar screen."[44] Such a large green blip had flipped up on the oscilloscope of the primitive SCR 270B set that he thought something must be wrong. After a few minutes' checking for possible faults from the flickering green spoke of the oscilloscope he concluded that "it must be a flight of some sort."[45] The two soldiers went to the plotting board to transfer the distance and bearing from the etched Lucite over the screen. It indicated more than fifty planes were bearing down on the island from just over 130 miles to the north.

When Lockard called the Information Center to report "the biggest sighting he had ever seen,"[46] he omitted to pass on his estimate of how many aircraft it represented. As fate had arranged it, the duty pursuit officer to whom the call was routed was inexperienced. Knowing that the flight of B-17s was expected at around 0800, he assumed that this was what the radar operators were tracking.

"Well, don't worry about it," Lockard was told.[47] The irony was that our dozen four-engine bombers were then less than two hundred miles behind the Japanese. Like Fuchida's, the B-17 flight from the west coast was also using the KGMB radio station's music broadcast to home in to the island.

The radar crew nonetheless continued to plot the approach of the incoming planes until they were less than twenty miles off, when the backwave from the mountains scrambled the blips.

In a second breakdown of interservice cooperation that morning, Fort Shafter did not relay the sighting to either naval headquarters. So the last chance to have triggered an alert was lost.

Washington   *12:30 P.M. local time*
               (53 minutes before the attack)

At the Japanese embassy Ambassador Nomura impatiently waited for the fourteen-part reply to be typed up so that he could keep his appointment at the State Department. Obedient to Tokyo's instructions not to use an ordinary typist, a diplomatic secretary had been slowly pecking his way through the lengthy message. Nomura realized that he would not now be able to make the deadline, and the embassy called Hull's office to request a three quarters of an hour postponement.

Downtown at the White House, the president was informing the Chinese ambassador of his personal appeal to the emperor. "This is my last effort for peace," Roosevelt told Hu Shih. "I am afraid it may fail."[48]

Fourteenth Naval District Headquarters   *7:15 A.M. local time*
                                             (38 minutes before the attack)

Half an hour of telephone exchanges between Admiral Bloch's and Admiral Kimmel's staff officers failed to resolve whether hostile submarines were attempting to penetrate Pearl Harbor. When he was informed, at 0715, of the sightings, Bloch was inclined to share the opinion of his staff officers that *Ward*'s reported depth-charge run was just another false alarm.

That it took the harbor duty destroyer *Monoghan* only three quarters of an hour to raise steam and get under way was an indication of how swiftly more than eighty vessels could have gone to general quarters even if the alert had been given shortly after seven. The battle force was just awakening to the relaxed routine of another Sunday. Only three quarters of the crews were aboard and many ships had scuttles and watertight hatches unclipped.

It was a situation that Kimmel must have mentally measured as he stood unshaven and undressed and responded to the telephone call from his duty officer. He was inclined to agree with Commander Vincent Murphy, his assistant war plans officer, that it was nothing major. But whatever doubts he might have entertained about the validity of *Ward*'s reports, Kimmel abandoned breakfast and promised to be "right down" to his submarine base headquarters as soon as he was shaved and dressed.

Neither Kimmel nor the duty officer rated the situation as serious enough to rouse the rest of the headquarters staff. I did not discover until much later that awful morning that we had ignored what—in hindsight— were clearly the underwater outriders of the main attack.

The reaction might well have been different if Stark had not had second thoughts and had called up an hour earlier to inform us about the one o'clock deadline. And there would still have been just enough time for a general quarters alert if static and the exigencies of the commercial telegraph system had not delayed Marshall's cable to General Short. At the very least such a warning could have galvanized the island's anti-aircraft and fighter defenses soon enough to have spared the battleships the worst. And in all likelihood they would not even have been in harbor overnight had Kimmel received the warning from Washington that Secretary Knox believed had been relayed to him the previous evening.

Again left in the dark as to the general picture that indicated Japan was about to take the plunge into hostilities, Kimmel had to evaluate in isolation the intelligence concerning a submarine attack. He decided to await verification of the *Ward* and PBY reports and was still hopeful that the flap would blow over in time for him to make his regular Sunday golf date with General Short.

Tokyo   *3:00 A.M. local time*
   (23 minutes before the attack)

An hour after conferring with Prime Minister Tojo on the delicate issue of how to handle a message addressed personally to the emperor from the president of the United States, the foreign minister was driven through the tall gates of the imperial palace. Despite the appalling earliness of the hour, Lord Privy Seal Marquis Koichi Kido had roused the emperor from his bed.

Whether Hirohito knew that the Pearl Harbor attack was scheduled to be already taking place is not certain, but while a melodramatic scene was being played out in the ornate council chamber, the opening shots of the Pacific War were being fired by Japanese warships off the north coast of Malaya.

Kota Bharu   *12:00 midnight local time*
   (23 minutes before the attack)

It was pouring rain at midnight when the most southerly of General Yamashita's invasion convoys arrived off the small fishing port of Kota Bharu. Ahead of schedule, four destroyers and a light cruiser commenced blasting away at the pillbox defenses manned by the 9th Division of the Indian army guarding the beachhead at the mouth of the Kelantan River on the north coast of Malaya.

"Someone's opened fire," the commander of the local airfield told Royal Air Force headquarters in Singapore when he telephoned for permission to scramble his planes.

"Go for the transports, you bloody fools!" was the abrupt reply.

Roused from his bed, the British governor, Sir Shento Thomas, sleepily told army commander General Arthur Percival, "Well, I suppose you'll shove the little men off."[49]

Air Raid Pearl Harbor *7:35 A.M. local time*
(18 minutes before the attack)

Unspotted by any American, the floatplane from the cruiser *Chikuma* winged its way north of Pearl Harbor and radioed back to the *Kido Butai,* "Enemy formation at anchor. Nine battleships, one heavy cruiser, six light cruisers are in harbor."[50] This was followed by a detailed report of the wind and cloud conditions over the target. Simultaneously the *Tonē's* plane signaled from over Maui that there were no American warships in the Lahaina anchorage.

The report was relayed to Fuchida, whose plane was less than twenty-five miles north of Oahu. He was straining through binoculars to penetrate the cloud breaks for a glimpse of the island's peaks. The Hawaiian radio station that had so accurately and unwittingly acted as his guide had just promised a warm, clear, sunny day when he was rewarded with his first sight of the terrain that had become so familiar from intense study of maps and photographs.

"All of a sudden the clouds broke, and a long line of coast appeared," Fuchida was to recall. "We were over Kahuku Point, the northern tip of the island, and it was now time for our deployment."[51] Then came the only snag in the otherwise clockwork precision of the strike.

Fuchida, certain that one flight of torpedo bombers had not seen the flare he fired to send them in to attack an unalerted Pearl Harbor, fired another "Black Dragon." The wing leader of the dive bombers mistook the timing, and thought he had just witnessed the two-flare signal for a diversionary attack on Hickam Field and the naval strip at Ford Island. The dive bombers peeled away, climbed to twelve thousand feet, and came screaming down on our unsuspecting bases. Surprise was so complete that this hitch in the rehearsed precision of the raid was to make little difference.

"Notify all planes to attack," Fuchida ordered his radio operator.

The "TO, TO, TO" signal—an abbreviation for *totsugeki* ("charge")—was flashed out as Fuchida's bomber swung around Barbers Point. Seconds later, at 0753, the prearranged code signal, "TO RA, TO RA, TO RA," was tapped out over the airwaves.[52] It was picked up over five thousand miles away by the aerials of the Combined Fleet flagship in the inland sea.

Admiral Yamamoto was engrossed in a round of *shogi* with his chief of staff. After receiving the message that complete surprise had been achieved, he continued clicking his counters across the hatched game board. The same traditional impassivity was not manifested by his pilots as they swept over the jewel-green checkerboard of Oahu's cane fields and pineapple plantations to rain destruction on the airstrips that were supposed to be the front line of Pearl Harbor's defense.

At Wheeler Field explosions and strafing runs tore apart the rows of parked fighters. On Ford Island bombs plastered the flying-boat slips, sending blazing chunks of PBYs roaring around like comets.

The torpedo bombers with their menacing instruments of destruction crowned by strange wooden boxes came looping in around Ford Island. Peeling off in pairs, they headed toward the line of battlewagons. The raid erupted with such sudden fury that it was vital minutes before those on board the helpless warships grasped what was happening.

Along Battleship Row the forenoon watch had just been piped to breakfast. Smartly drilled color parties were lined up on the fantails awaiting the bugler to signal the hour to break out ensigns. But the calls and the gentler sound of chiming chapel bells drifting across the harbor were abruptly drowned by the rattle of machine gun fire, the whistle of falling bombs, and the sickening crump of torpedo explosions.

The first "Kate" torpedo plane raced in so low over *Nevada* that it shredded the half-hoisted ensign with cannon fire. The sternmost battleship's astonished band continued to thump out a few more bars of "The Star-Spangled Banner" without missing a beat. Like a bloated steel lance the plane's torpedo splashed into the harbor abaft of *Arizona,* which was moored ahead. On board *Maryland* a seaman in the superstructure managed to break out a machine gun belt to open fire on two approaching torpedo planes.

The round of explosions that rocked Ford Island also roused the commander of the 2nd Patrol Wing. He broadcast an alarm from the control tower at 0758: "Air raid Pearl Harbor. This is not drill."[53] Within a couple of minutes the shrill cry of alarm was taken up by the naval radio station, which began flashing it out to the United States.

The Kates attacked in tandem, and moments later torpedoes had slammed into *Oklahoma* and *West Virginia.* High aloft, Fuchida was encouraged by "tiny white flashes of smoke [and] wave rings in the water" as the assault concentrated on the outermost of the three pairs of battleships.[54]

Kimmel was still in his dressing gown at just before 0800 when he took a call from the duty officer reporting that *Ward* had stopped a suspicious sampan. Murphy was still speaking when Kimmel's yeoman rushed in to tell him that the signal tower was broadcasting that the attack was no drill.

Kimmel had not yet finished buttoning his white jacket as he rushed outside. He stood transfixed for a few moments on the neighbors' lawn where he had a clear view of the planes circling over the harbor like angry hornets. "I knew right away that something terrible was going on," Kimmel would recall, "that this was not a casual raid by just a few stray planes."[55]

The first explosions rocked the underground headquarters of Station Hypo where Lieutenant Wesley "Ham" Wright was the duty officer that Sunday morning. The man he sent upstairs to check what was going on was Lieutenant John A. Williams, the only traffic analyst who had argued that the long radio silence of the Japanese carriers meant they were at sea. Williams must also have been the only man at Pearl Harbor that morning who was not surprised to see that the wheeling and diving planes had orange roundels on their wings. "They're Japanese aircraft and they're attacking Pearl Harbor," he came down to tell Wright in a flat voice.[56]

My astonishment was complete when, at about the same time, my yeoman called me with the shocking news. At first I found it difficult to grasp, because the sight and sound of the fury erupting at Pearl Harbor was shut off from my house by the drop curtain of Diamond Head.

Minutes later my neighbor Lieutenant Paul Crosley picked me up in his Cadillac roadster. As we hurtled down into Honolulu, the nightmare grew larger the closer we came to the naval base, which radiated terrible explosions. I remember feeling that this was just a bad dream that could not be true.

Tall columns of smoke were rising from Battleship Row. Prompt flooding of the magazines had saved *West Virginia*. But in the first quarter hour a combined strike by bombs and torpedoes had caught the great battleship astern of her. *Arizona* erupted in a volcanic sheet of flame as her forward magazines ignited.

At the head of the row torpedoes had ripped open *Oklahoma*'s port side. She turned turtle within minutes, entombing more than four hundred crew members.

Waterspouts from bombs and torpedoes continued to burst skyward. Overhead the increasing number of black mushrooms of exploding anti-aircraft shells were a hopeful indication that our gunners had recovered from their initial shock and were fighting back. Fuchida's plane was hit "as if struck by a huge club." A few holes and a severed control cable, however, did not stop the leader's bombing run over *Maryland*. Four missiles plummeted down to become "poppy seeds and finally disappeared just as two white flashes of smoke appeared on and near the ship."[57]

Maryland was saved by her stoutly armored deck. Like *Tennessee* astern, her inboard position also protected her. While far from unscathed, the pair were the least damaged of all the battleships. Not so the battle force flagship. At her isolated forward berth *California* took two torpedoes and was settling by the head. *Nevada*, at the rear of Battleship Row, was struggling to get under way. She had cast off her moorings and every gun that could be trained aloft was firing at the dive bombers that swarmed down on her.

A little under half an hour after the attack began, its fury began to abate when the first wave of planes flew off. Across the harbor, destroyer *Helms* ran down and damaged another midget submarine, which would later beach and a single member of her two-man crew survive to surrender.

During the twenty-minute lull Admiral Kimmel reached his headquarters at the submarine base, while Crosley and I were still fighting our way through traffic with the help of a friendly motorcycle policeman.

Washington *1:30 P.M. local time*

Just as the first wave of the Japanese attack was beginning to lose its fury, the electrifying news began circulating in Washington.

"My God!" Secretary Knox exclaimed when he was handed the dispatch. "This can't be true, this must mean the Philippines."[58] But Stark himself confirmed it. "No, sir, this is Pearl."[59]

Knox immediately put in a call to the White House. Roosevelt was lunching with Hopkins in his Oval Room study. His aide also believed there must be some mistake: "Surely Japan would not attack in Honolulu?"[60]

Shortly after two the president managed to reach the secretary of state. Hull was shocked. But he agreed to receive the Japanese envoys who had just arrived in his anteroom. Roosevelt advised him not to tell them about the raid but "to receive their reply formally and coolly bow them out."[61]

After he glanced at their copy of the fourteen-part message, Hull's anger burst forth. "In all my fifty years of public service," he told the astonished diplomats, "I have never seen such a document that was more crowded with infamous falsehood and distortions."[62] Nomura and Kurusu, who had not been told of the attack, bowed themselves out in an embarrassed fluster. A department official overheard Hull muttering under his breath as the door closed, "Scoundrels and piss-ants."[63]

At about this time the news that had stunned official Washington was being broadcast to shocked American citizens. From coast to coast, radio stations were breaking into their Sunday afternoon broadcasts to report that Pearl Harbor was under attack by Japanese aircraft.

Pearl Harbor *8:40 A.M. local time*

While Admiral Bloch was telephoning an eyewitness account of the raid to the secretary of the navy, the second wave of the Japanese attack came winging in over Honolulu.

"He could look through a window," as Knox was to relate, "and see smoke and flames from the ships still burning in the harbor."[64]

The renewal of the raid's intensity coincided with the arrival of the first of the B-17s flying in from the west coast. Unarmed and down to their last gallons of fuel after the fourteen-hour flight, the pilots nonetheless managed to land their bombers by scattering to airfields all over the island.

A hot reception also greeted the eighteen Dauntless dive bombers that had flown off *Enterprise* an hour earlier. One was shot down by our own gunfire, and four by Japanese Zeros.

Not a single navy pilot managed to get aloft as 140 Japanese dive bombers and high-level bombers swept in from the east. Battling fearful odds, a handful of army pursuit planes did climb off from Bellows Field to knock eleven enemy planes out of a sky that was now being punctuated by the puffs of antiaircraft fire.

Retaliation came too late to save the battleships. Kimmel stood by the window of his office at the submarine base, his jaw set in stony anguish. As he watched the disaster across the harbor unfold with terrible fury, a spent .50-caliber machine gun bullet crashed through the glass. It brushed the admiral before it clanged to the floor. It cut his white jacket and raised a welt on his chest.

"It would have been merciful had it killed me," Kimmel murmured to his communications officer, Commander Maurice "Germany" Curts.[65]

Later that day the admiral would show me the bullet and explain that although the practice was to turn over all captured enemy matériel to fleet intelligence, he would like to keep it.

The second wave of the attack was reaching its peak when destroyer *Monoghan* managed to ram a single midget submarine that was coolly firing a torpedo at the tender *Curtiss,* which was moored in the middle loch. The Japanese dive bombers concentrated their efforts on *Nevada* as she crawled past the blazing wreckage of Battleship Row. Her defiance was gamely cheered on by the men waiting to be rescued from the overturned *Oklahoma.*

Some *Arizona* survivors were picked up and helped man *Nevada*'s guns as the defiant battlewagon continued to fight off her attackers. The tugs that hurried out to prevent the listing battleship from sinking and blocking the main channel somehow managed to beach it at Waipo Point. It was the tugs' fire pumps that fought the flames that were threatening to engulf the battleship after her own fire main was knocked out by a bomb.

Nevada's dash for safety drew the Japanese bombers away from *Pennsylvania,* which was helplessly chocked up in the Number 1 Dry Dock. One bomb did penetrate the flagship's boat deck. Another bomb blew the bows off destroyer *Shaw* which was sharing the dock with the battleship and destroyer *Cassin.* The dry dock was flooded to douse the flames, but the intense heat of the burning fuel oil ignited the magazines and torpedo stores of both thin-hulled destroyers.

Ten minutes before this terrific explosion rocked the southern end of the harbor, which occurred just after 0900, Crosley and I roared up to Pacific Fleet headquarters across the loch from the dry dock. Under such terrible circumstances, with antiaircraft gunfire blasting up from the submarines, there was no satisfaction in being greeted as the "man we should have been listening to." I felt numb, and very sick.

The atmosphere was one of general shock and electric wonder about what was going to happen next. Everyone was stunned. Even my yeoman, who was normally as steady as a rock, was jittery as he handed me the intelligence log that he had been keeping. It detailed the progress of the attack and listed the ships hit so far, those that were sinking, and others that were asking for assistance. It made me feel physically ill just to read it.

Looking out of my window, it was even more horrible to see *Oklahoma* upside down and *Arizona* ablaze. Seaplanes were burning like torches on the ramp at Ford Island.

I knew that men were out there dying. Oil was burning on the water and the sky was a pall of black smoke. Such a terrible scene of destruction was impossible ever to forget. There was another pyre rising over the hill from the marine corps field at Ewa. My log said that Wheeler Field had been knocked out and most of its planes destroyed. Kaneohe naval air station on the west side of the island was out of commission and under attack.

Captain McMorris arrived at 0900 and immediately asked to see me. When I entered his office down the corridor I found the chief of war plans with Murphy and other members of his staff. They all looked at me as though it was a court-martial.

"Well, Layton, if it's any satisfaction to you, we were wrong and you were right," McMorris declared.

Of course I had been saying for weeks that Japan was planning aggressive moves, but it had not been my prediction at any time that they would open hostilities with an attack on Pearl Harbor. "Sir," I said, "it is no satisfaction to me whatsoever."

The *Cassin* and *Downes* were exploding in the dry dock as this exchange took place. It made me feel terrible. I excused myself and left to return to my office.

Now that the whole of Battleship Row lay under a billowing black cloud and a big blaze was raging in the dry dock, the Japanese bombers turned their attention to the northern side of Ford Island. During the final phase of their raid they damaged three light cruisers and sank the old battlewagon *Utah,* which was serving as a target ship.

It was during this final round that Ham Wright telephoned me from Hypo to tell me that they had just gotten a direction-finder bearing on radio signals made by the Japanese force. It was a "bilateral," a two-way reading of either 363 degrees or 183 degrees—this could mean that the carriers we had been trying to locate for so long were either due north or due south of us.

I wanted to know why the seventy-five-foot antenna of our top-secret CKK-X direction finder concealed high on a jungled peak to the north of Pearl Harbor could not give us a more accurate fix. "We can't get in communication with them," Wright told me. It later turned out that our telephone lines to it were army circuits. They had pulled the plugs on us when the emergency began and had not given us any warning.

When I went down to the operations room plot to lay down the two bearings, Admiral Kimmel came in. He was white and shaken, but determined to find a way of hitting back without delay. He wanted to know where the Japanese force was, and became uncharacteristically testy when I could not tell him whether the enemy carrier force was north or south.

"Goddammit! We're under attack here, everybody knows we're under attack," the admiral erupted. "Here you are, the fleet intelligence officer, and you don't even know whether they're north or south. For Christ's sake!"

The world had exploded in his face and I could not blame the admiral. If he had known at that moment that Washington had withheld vital intelligence from him, I believe he would have had a stroke then and there. The battleships were burning, ships were exploding, men were dying— and he was the man responsible. He had received no warning and then I was unable to tell him where our tormentors were. It was too much to ask any man to remain calm under such dreadful pressure.

All through the morning we had been receiving confusing and conflicting intelligence. Some army units were reporting an invasion had begun. "Enemy troops landing on north shore. Blue overalls with red emblems" was one message we received. Another reported paratroops landing on Barbers Point. It later transpired that both false reports had been triggered by a mechanic in dungarees who had parachuted to safety after his seaplane had been shot down by the Japanese.[66]

The confusion was awful and inexcusable—and I felt bad about it. We would have been able to resolve our dilemma over where the carriers were if only Fort Shafter had relayed us the bearings plotted by the Opana radar truck. But they did not. The only report in which I had any confidence was Rochefort's. He telephoned me briefly as the raid was in its dying moments to tell me that the *Akagi* was the flagship of the attacking force.

"How do you know it's *Akagi*?" I asked. Joe explained, "It's the same ham-fisted radio operator who uses his transmitting key as if he is kicking it with his foot." But it was not much help to Kimmel that morning to know that the *Akagi* was two hundred miles away if I could not tell him whether the Japanese were north or south.

Captain McMorris was of the opinion that the Japanese must have come from the mandates and were therefore to southward. If so, Halsey's task force was within striking distance. Accordingly, at 1046 Kimmel radioed Task Force 8: "DF bearings indicate enemy carrier bearing 178 from Barbers Point."[67]

Shortly afterward four army bombers managed to get off from Hickam Field to begin searching the waters south of Barbers Point. They discovered *Minneapolis* steaming in the fleet exercise area. Such was the confusion that the heavy cruiser's report, "No carriers in sight," became garbled in translation to "Two carriers in sight."[68] That afternoon a PBY patrol returning from Midway mistakenly bombed a cruiser of Admiral Wilson Brown's task force, which was also south of Oahu.

Yet despite Kimmel's anger and frustration in his impatience to hit back, our confused intelligence picture that sent Halsey off on a fruitless chase to the south undoubtedly saved his force from destruction by the vastly superior Japanese striking force. This was no comfort to the fleet's pugnacious fighting admiral who returned to a still-smoking Pearl Harbor the next day vowing, "Before we're through with 'em, the Japanese language will be spoken only in hell."[69]

Washington   *3:00 P.M. local time*

While the attack on Pearl Harbor was approaching its climax, Stimson, Knox, Hull, Stark, and Marshall gathered for their first real council of war in the White House. Roosevelt was firmly in command of the situation, firing off a succession of orders for guarding military installations, grounding private planes, and instructing the FBI to begin rounding up Japanese and German aliens.

Underpinning the brusque confidence of a commander in chief at war was Roosevelt's realization that Japan's attack had taken him off the strategic and political hook on which his guarantees to Britain had impaled him. The president knew that whatever the magnitude of the disaster that had so swiftly and unexpectedly overtaken the Pacific Fleet, the attack had silenced the isolationists and united Americans in a war fever that no address to Congress could have achieved.

The president had already decided in favor of a short speech asking for a declaration of war the next morning when he was interrupted by a call from across the Atlantic. After Ambassador John G. Winant had spoken, the gruff voice of Winston Churchill came on the line. Both had been dining at the prime minister's country retreat at Chequers when the nine o'clock BBC news bulletin had reported the attack on Pearl Harbor.

"Mr. President, what's all this about Japan?" Churchill asked. "It's quite true," Roosevelt said. "They have attacked Pearl Harbor. We are all in the same boat now." The prime minister told him about the landings in northern Malaya and they agreed that he would make a simultaneous declaration of war against Japan the next day in the House of Commons.[70] (In fact, WSC jumped the gun by declaring two hours before FDR.)

Manila   *4:00 A.M. local time*

It was a full hour since Admiral Hart had been roused with news that Pearl Harbor was under attack. General MacArthur's first reaction had been to exclaim, "Pearl Harbor! It should be our strongest point."[71]

Forty minutes later, as the general was dressing, he took a call from war plans in Washington. General Gerow warned him that he "wouldn't be surprised if you get an attack there in the near future."

At 0400 that morning General Lewis Hyde Brereton, MacArthur's air commander, put his aircrews on standby alert. He also requested permission to send his B-17s on a preemptive strike against air bases in Formosa. Had this raid been allowed to take place, it would have caught Japan's intended dawn strike against Manila grounded by early morning mist. But MacArthur was apparently under the impression that "my orders were explicit not to initiate hostilities against the Japanese."[72]

Inexplicably MacArthur failed to seize the initiative—even after he had been ordered to initiate his war plan, and Japanese carrier aircraft had just bombed a seaplane tender early that morning in the Davao Gulf. His failure to act had a swift retribution in the disaster that overtook the Philippines seven hours after the last bomb fell on Pearl Harbor.

Pearl Harbor   *10:00 A.M. local time*

After the last Japanese bomber had flown off northward, Fuchida's damaged plane continued to circle high above Pearl Harbor photographing the carnage: "I counted four battleships definitely sunk and three severely damaged and extensive damage had also been inflicted upon other types of ships. The seaplane base at Ford Island was all in flames, as were the airfields, especially Wheeler Field."[73]

The pyre of dense black smoke that snaked thousands of feet into the clear sky was an awesome symbol of Japan's tactical victory and our defeat. The acrid stench of destruction haunted us that morning, punctuated by sporadic explosions and the flickering fires of burning ships and blazing oil. Our attackers might have flown off, but the havoc they had wreaked continued to grow as the nightmare translated itself into statistical reality with the ever-lengthening lists of casualties and the bill of destruction.

The final death toll, including 68 civilians, was to reach 2,403—nearly half of them were lost in *Arizona*.[74] All told, some 1,178 were wounded—many of them burn victims whose lives were saved by the doctors who waged a successful battle against infected burns with the new antibiotic sulfanilamide.

The attack had cost the fleet eighteen operational warships. Four battleships and *Utah* had been sunk; four were severely damaged and only two were locally repairable. Three light cruisers, three destroyers, and three auxiliary craft had been put out of action, sunk, or wrecked beyond repair. The navy had lost thirteen fighters, twenty-one scout bombers, and forty-six patrol planes in addition to *Enterprise*'s four dive bombers. The army air force losses were even more punishing: eighteen bombers—including four B-17s—and fifty-nine fighters. In addition there was extensive damage to airfields and installations.

The death and destruction did not end when the bombs stopped falling. Thousands of our men spent the day battling the flames as small craft, captains' gigs, and admirals' barges were pressed into service dodging the pools of burning oil to snatch fuel-blackened survivors from the water. For two days rescue teams and divers waged an agonizing struggle to cut their way into compartments where trapped men could be heard tapping desperately until air ran out. Only thirty-four out of the four hundred entombed in the capsized *Oklahoma* could be extricated alive.

Around 1100 the commander and staff officers of the battle force reported to Kimmel's headquarters. While I was checking the operations plot, I saw a short, heavyset officer with a vice admiral's shoulder flashes, still wearing a life jacket, his whites spotted with fuel oil, his face blackened by smoke and soot. His eyes were almost shut; he looked dazed as he stared off into space, not saying a word.

It was Admiral Pye, who had assured me, almost twenty-four hours earlier to the minute, that the Japanese would not attack us because "we were too strong and powerful."

Fort Shafter   *11:45 A.M. local time*

Tadeo Fuchimaki, the RCA messenger who had been delayed for more than an hour and a half in the panicky traffic jams, finally gunned his motorbike up to the gates of Fort Shafter. General Short's staff was preoccupied with preparing for the possibility of another Japanese air raid and making precautionary deployments against a possible invasion.

The communications staff was flooded with incoming and outgoing reports, so it was almost four hours before anyone thought of decoding the low-priority cable from Washington.

When Short finally saw a copy of Marshall's warning, it was nearly eight hours old. Predictably, he about went through the roof.

Shortly afterward Kimmel angrily crumpled his copy of the dispatch and hurled it into the wastebasket.[75]

Military annals have provided few more glaring examples of information that arrived too late to change the course of history. To his dying day Admiral Kimmel considered the delayed warning of Tokyo's one o'clock deadline as the most shocking example of Washington's mishandling of the whole matter of intelligence. Even if we had known of it that afternoon, I suspect we would have taken little comfort in the fact that the commander of Japan's striking force was also making his own blunder. It would rob the *Kido Butai*—and Japan herself—of the chance of a still more stunning victory.

Kido Butai   *12:00 noon local time*

Fuchida's bomber was the last plane to be recovered by *Akagi,* shortly before 1200. He rushed up to the bridge in his flying gear to deliver an enthusiastic report that four battleships had been sunk and four damaged. Admiral Nagumo wanted to know two things: Had the Pacific Fleet been sufficiently damaged to put it out of operation for six months, and where were the American carriers?

Fuchida estimated the "main force" of the Pacific Fleet would not venture out for six months, but he did not know where the American flattops were. Instead, he proposed launching another strike as quickly as possible to wipe out Pearl Harbor's oil storage farms and dockyard installations.

While the planes were being refueled and bombed up for departure, Fuchida went to the briefing room where his pilots were making their attack reports. Up on *Akagi*'s bridge Nagumo debated the tactical wisdom and strategic necessity of sending out another attack. He believed strongly that he had achieved his main objective of protecting Japan's invasion forces and the mandated islands from a flank attack for at least six months, possibly even longer.

Commander Genda, however, disagreed. He urged another strike, which could deliver a knockout blow to an already stunned opponent. But without knowledge of the whereabouts of the American carriers, Nagumo argued, he would be risking three quarters of the Combined Fleet's carrier strength just to wipe out static facilities. His staff was more conservative in weighing the strategic advantage to be gained against what they saw as the tactical odds against them. Only nine planes had been lost in the first attack wave, but twenty had failed to return from the second wave. Even heavier losses could be expected from antiaircraft and fighter defenses that would be thoroughly alerted to an afternoon raid. Another factor that contributed to Nagumo's decision to cancel preparations for a third attack was his concern that "to remain within range of enemy land-based planes was distinctly to our disadvantage."[76]

"The objective of the Pearl Harbor operation has been achieved" was how Rear Admiral Ryunosuke Kusaka silenced Fuchida, who had dashed back up to the bridge to protest. "Now we must prepare for other operations ahead,"[77] insisted Nagumo's chief of staff.

As far as the imperial general staff was concerned, Nagumo had indeed successfully discharged his part in its master plan for the conquest of the Far East. But other Japanese naval officers knew better. Yamamoto's chief of staff, Rear Admiral Ugaki, compared Nagumo's decision to "the quick pace of a fleeing thief" who was "contented with a humble lot." Commenting on the lost opportunity in his diary the next day, Ugaki observed, "In a situation where we lost only thirty planes the most essential thing is to exploit the achieved results of the attack."[78]

The failure of the Japanese to attack us again, as we expected them to do that afternoon, was their biggest strategic miscalculation since the decision to start the war. Destruction of the huge collection of exposed oil tanks at the southwest corner of the southeast loch would have ensured them a far greater victory than sinking the battleships.

The lack of fuel—and shortage of tankers to resupply the base—would have prevented any of our carrier task forces from operating in the western Pacific for more than six months. As Kimmel himself was to testify, "It would have forced the withdrawal of the fleet to the [west] coast because there wasn't any oil anywhere else out there to keep the fleet operating."[79]

Pearl Harbor   *1:00 P.M. local time*

We were still awaiting another Japanese assault when the afternoon began with news that Guam had been raided by bombers from nearby Saipan. They sank the naval auxiliary *Penguin* in Apia Harbor.

Minutes later came the disheartening news that Wake had been bombed and strafed. The attack cost the marine garrison seven of their newly delivered fighters and a large part of their gasoline stockpile. Pan Am's flying boat, *Philippine Clipper,* however, had managed to escape from the atoll's lagoon with only minor damage. While enroute to Midway the pilot radioed sighting a Japanese cruiser and destroyers that were clearly heading to invade the lonely marine outpost.

News had also been received that Singapore had been bombed and that Britain's colony at Hong Kong had suffered a series of heavy air raids. At Shanghai the Japanese had captured our gunboat *Wake* and imprisoned her crew. There had been two bombing attacks so far on the Philippines—but MacArthur was still refusing to allow his B-17 force to make a counterstrike on Formosa.

As the reports came in to Pacific Fleet headquarters, it was becoming clear that all Japan's attacks had been carefully synchronized with the raid on Pearl Harbor. But it was not until well into the afternoon that I was finally able to tell Kimmel with certainty that our attackers had come in from the north. The information was less vital than it might have been during the morning, because with each hour that passed it was becoming apparent that we were to be spared another strike.

The answer to the question that had caused Admiral Kimmel to flare up that morning was provided by a "plot board" and pilot's navigation sheet that had been recovered from a Japanese plane that crashed into the seaplane tender *Curtiss*. It was marked with the plane's attack course and his return route to the carriers, some two hundred miles to the north of Oahu. Like Marshall's war warning, this information came too late to influence events. But a far more valuable piece of intelligence emerged from this bloodstained package. It was a temporary call-sign card for all the ships that comprised the striking force.

The documents confirmed the report brought back by a dispatch rider sent out to the secret direction-finding station. So when Admiral Kimmel sent for me late that afternoon, I was able to give him the exact composition of the enemy force, which was by then far to the northwest and out of reach of our planes and ships.

It was then that Kimmel apologized to me for blowing up earlier. "I know direction finders are bilateral," the admiral explained. "but I know we had one that gave good bearings and I didn't understand how they didn't get through this morning." I thanked him and explained that he had every right to lose his temper with me, although I regretted that it was the army that had pulled our connections with the direction-finding station.

Washington   *8:30 P.M. local time*

The full membership of Roosevelt's cabinet assembled in the White House Oval Room to hear the president give a solemn summary of the day's events. "It was obvious to me that Roosevelt was having a dreadful time just accepting the idea that the navy had been caught unaware," Frances Perkins would recall.[80]

The president drew a historic parallel with Lincoln's cabinet meeting on the eve of the Civil War. He regretted to have to report that casualties "were extremely heavy."[81] Stimson urged that the president use the occasion before Congress to make a joint declaration of war, including Hitler, on "evidence that Germany had pushed Japan into this."[82] But Roosevelt was too shrewd for such a gamble. A double declaration would allow the isolationists to charge that he had engineered the fight with the Japanese. So the cabinet agreed to wait and see whether Hitler carried out the promises made by Ribbentrop to the Japanese ambassador.

At half past nine that evening the Democratic and Republican leaders of Congress were ushered into the meeting. Once again Roosevelt rehearsed the terrible catalog of the day's disasters. Outside the White House portico, which was usually well lighted but now was darkened as a precaution against air raids, the crowd that had been milling around the Pennsylvania Avenue railings all afternoon broke into another chorus of "God Bless America" as the meeting broke up.

One final shock was in store for the president before the day came to a close. A Japanese attack on the Philippines had been looming large in the strategic calculations made by the president and his advisers ever since 26 November. General MacArthur, unlike Kimmel and Short, not only had Purple intelligence, but he had been repeatedly warned that an attack was coming. So when the news arrived at the White House just before midnight that an air raid had wiped out most of the Philippines air force, it fell all the harder on Roosevelt.

It was a reprise of Pearl Harbor. The Japanese planes from Formosa swept in in well-coordinated waves to strafe and bomb Clark Field and the other airstrips north of Manila at lunchtime. General Brereton's planes were swallowed like sitting ducks in a holocaust of exploding bombs and blazing gasoline. In less than half an hour, three quarters of the fighters in MacArthur's command had been reduced to charred skeletons. The only four-engine bombers of his vaunted deterrent force that survived were the seventeen B-17s that had been evacuated south to Mindanao the previous day.

In strategic terms the Japanese raid at midday on the Philippine airfields was a far greater triumph than the attack on Pearl Harbor. At a single blow it had removed our ability to strike back and guaranteed the success of the impending Japanese invasion of the islands.

Roosevelt appreciated these strategic implications as soon as he was handed the dispatch from MacArthur's Manila headquarters. It reached him just after midnight. The president was at the time unwinding from the day's traumas with Edward R. Murrow. The broadcaster was to recall how the president's anger and dismay boiled that so many planes had been destroyed "on the ground, by God, on the ground!"[83]

The president must have wondered whether some terrible curse stalked his commanders in the Pacific to bring off such a Greek tragedy. For while the attack on Pearl Harbor was unexpected and explainable by a breakdown of our military intelligence, it was inexplicable that the thrice-warned MacArthur should have been trapped in the same fate nine hours after the first bombs fell on Pearl Harbor.

"Our general and leaders committed one of the greatest errors possible to military men," observed one of the B-17 pilots, "that of letting themselves be taken by surprise."[84] Why Admiral Kimmel and General Short were to be so publicly and immediately pilloried for a disaster they were powerless to prevent, when General Douglas MacArthur escaped *any* charge of accountability, is a question that has never been satisfactorily answered.

24

"Hard for Us to Take"

A SOMBER MOOD hung over Pacific Fleet headquarters after the attack. Updated casualty reports on Monday morning magnified the enormity of the disaster. Firefighters continued to douse flames that still licked the blackened skeletons of the wrecks, while engineering parties picked their way through the bowels of damaged warships to prepare for a monumental salvage operation. Alongside them rescue parties labored in the reeking hulls to reach survivors still trapped in compartments.

Dense smoke continued to rise from the wrecks along Battleship Row. We were spared the sight; the paint that had been used to hurriedly effect a blackout of the submarine base windows had been applied to the interior surface of the glass, but we had to endure the stifling fumes that intensified the cloying odor of burnt oil that hung over the harbor. This was the depressing setting in which Admiral Kimmel assembled his staff that Monday to announce his plans to commence offensive operations against the Japanese.

Kimmel had not forgotten, even if many of us had, that he still possessed a powerful fleet. The destruction of the battle force as a fighting unit seemed more stunning at the time than it actually turned out to be. This was the result of the prominent role that prewar naval strategists had foreseen for the battleship. Pearl Harbor may have been a disaster, but it was a long way from being the knockout blow that Yamamoto had intended. The Pacific Fleet could still send to battle two task forces with undamaged carriers. Meanwhile, the nucleus of a third task force was steaming at high speed toward Pearl Harbor in the shape of carrier *Saratoga*. Furthermore, a formidable force of nine heavy cruisers had been spared, and all but two of the light cruisers and three of the fleet destroyers had survived. And so had *all* our submarines.

The immediate task facing the fleet was to shake off shock and con-

325

fusion. It still marred the operational efficiency of those units that were at sea that Monday. Admiral Wilson Brown with *Indianapolis* had added his heavy cruisers to Task Force 12. But most of the morning was wasted while *Lexington*'s planes investigated an enemy sighting report that turned out to be heavy cruiser *Portland*. Task Force 12 was recalled to Pearl at noon. But another false report sent Brown haring south again after hearing that Johnston Island was under attack. It, too, was a false alarm.

North of Oahu, Rear Admiral Milo F. Draemel's light cruisers, reinforced by heavy cruiser *Minneapolis,* were spending the first of two days fruitlessly trying to track down the retreating Japanese striking force.

The southwestern approaches of Oahu were being scoured by Halsey's force. After putting in for refueling that evening, Task Force 8 sailed again at dawn on 9 December to continue the search. It was to be two more days before *Enterprise*'s planes caught and sank Japanese submarine *I-70*. Accounting for one of Japan's two-thousand-ton oceangoing submarines was some consolation for Admiral Halsey, whose thirst for revenge had been inflamed by the scene of disaster he had witnessed at Pearl Harbor.

The wild chasing of our tail in the immediate aftermath of the attack may have been excusable, but it was doing nothing to help Kimmel to hit back. I was very conscious of the need for more detailed information about the precise whereabouts of the enemy carriers. Kimmel wanted to know what the prospects were of their launching more attacks, if not on Oahu then on Wake or Midway. The intelligence that I had been able to garner from the Japanese pilot's salvaged logbook convinced me that an examination of an aircraft radio might provide more useful clues about call signs and frequencies.

So I called up Captain Mayfield and told him that we wanted to obtain a radio from one of the downed planes as soon as possible. He sent out one of his work crews to find a suitable specimen. Naturally, I anticipated that the radio set alone would suffice, but Warrant Officer Ernest Saftig, who had been detailed to carry out my request, had more ambitious ideas. After his crew selected a crashed three-man bomber in a cane field not far from Pearl, they loaded it onto a flatbed truck that they borrowed from the sugar plantation, and drove it up in front of the submarine base that morning.

When Saftig came to my office that Monday morning to tell me he had something for me, I asked him where the radio was.

"Outside the front door of headquarters, sir."

"Why the hell didn't you bring it up?"

"Because it's still attached to the plane, sir."

When I got outside, I saw what he meant. The plane had nose-dived into the ground when it crashed, telescoping its forty-foot fuselage into an accordionlike lump of metal along with its three-man crew. The hot

Hawaiian sun had already created a powerful reaction in the compressed corpses and Saftig, a former policeman and FBI agent, wanted to know from which part he should begin digging out the radio and also its documents. He would later prove so adept at such unpleasant tasks that I asked Mayfield to assign him to getting the papers from the midget submarine that was salvaged from the harbor.[1]

While we were standing by the debris, Admiral Kimmel came down and asked what was going on. When I explained my predicament, his face cracked into a grin. It was probably the first time since Saturday night that he had smiled.

In Washington, President Roosevelt had painfully climbed the podium in the House of Representatives on the arm of his uniformed son James, who was a marine captain.

"Yesterday, December 7, 1941—a date which will live in infamy—the United States was suddenly and deliberately attacked by the naval and air forces of the Empire of Japan" was how Roosevelt opened his address. His ringing phrase was to engrave itself not only on the conscience of the nation but forever on this particular page of history. After reciting the solemn litany of the "unprovoked and dastardly attack," the president warned that "there is no blinking at the fact that our people, our territory and our interests are in grave danger." But he promised that "with the unbounding determination of our people we will gain the inevitable victory."[2]

Within an hour Congress passed the war resolution, with only a single dissenting vote. Two hours earlier Churchill beat the United States to the punch with the formal announcement in the House of Commons that Britain was now at war with Japan. Declaring to the war cabinet his intention to visit Washington as soon as possible to secure an American commitment to the Atlantic war, he brushed aside advice that it might be too soon to put such direct pressure on their new ally: "Oh, that's the way we talked while we were wooing her—now that she's in the harem, we can talk to her quite differently."[3]

Roosevelt was reluctant to welcome the British prime minister until the United States was formally at war with Germany. Japan's attack had solved only half the president's strategic dilemma. For three days the two Allied leaders anxiously waited for Hitler to take the plunge and commit us to the global struggle. The fuehrer's declaration of war, when it came on 11 December, was not so much prompted by a desire to honor the tripartite pact—the German general staff saw little military advantage in taking on the United States just to please Japan. But Hitler was determined to beat the hated Roosevelt into the ring. He did so after the German chargé d'affaires in Washington apparently fell for a skillful leak from the White House on 10 December reporting that "within 24 hours the U.S. will declare war on Germany."[4]

The president knew that he could rely on Hitler's pique to avoid a

time-consuming debate on Capitol Hill. He had skirted a potentially divisive issue by telling reporters that Germany and Italy already "consider
themselves at war with the United States at this moment."[5] But Roosevelt was equally determined not to squander the new mood of national
unity. He would not wait for his isolationist opponents on Capitol Hill to
cash in on the public outrage over Pearl Harbor by demanding the heads
of those who were to blame.

The secretary of the navy was also keenly attuned to the political
mood. He resolved on the night of the attack to make a personal visit to
Oahu "to determine the extent of the damage and if possible to find out
why the Japanese had caught the U.S. forces unprepared." He hoped
thereby to avert the "prospect of a nasty congressional investigation."[6]
By 9 December he had obtained Roosevelt's approval for a visit. Its principal purpose, according to his aide, Captain Frank E. Beatty, was "for
an inspection of the terrific damage with a view to placing the responsibility for the unprepared condition in which the attack had caught our
forces."[7]

The navy's first Pearl Harbor inquiry got under way when the secretary of the navy's party boarded a plane for the west coast at the Ana-
costia naval air station on the afternoon of 10 December. In addition to
Beatty, the party included Joseph W. Powell, a vice-president of Beth-
lehem Shipbuilding Company, and Knox's special assistant, Lieutenant
Commander Edward A. Hayes. The ad hoc investigating team was supposed to parallel a similar army inquiry. But the war department's preliminary investigation came to an unfortunate end when a plane carrying
Colonel Charles W. Bundy, of the war plans division, crashed into the
High Sierras en route to the west coast.

The navy Lockheed, however, made it safely through to San Diego
despite severe icing and turbulent winter weather. At the naval base the
party transferred to a four-engine PB2Y Coronado flying boat. After his
bumpy ride from Washington, the secretary of the navy's confidence in
weather forecasts had worn thin. "That's just fine, son, but just you come
along with me," he told the base aerological officer, who had just promised a smooth trip across the Pacific.[8] The unfortunate officer had no
choice but to comply. He endured having to stand all the way because the
giant flying boat was so tightly packed with blood plasma and serum for
burn victims on Oahu that it had to make two takeoff runs before un-
sticking from the water.

Even before Knox's mission was communicated to Pacific Fleet headquarters, Kimmel anticipated that he would probably be relieved of command. It was the old naval principle that defeated admirals were expected
to go down with their ship. The first sign that the navy department had
lost confidence in him came in the shape of a panicky 9 December dispatch from Stark warning that another raid was imminent. It could "render Hawaii untenable as a naval base in which eventuality it is believed

Japanese have forces suitable for initial occupation of islands other than Oahu including Midway, Maui and Hawaii."[9] It was instructional, rather than advisory. Kimmel was told that "until defenses are increased it is doubtful if Pearl should be used as a base for any except patrol craft, naval aircraft, submarines or for short periods when it is reasonably certain that Japanese attacks will not be made."[10] The message was most certainly not the way Kimmel saw the situation.

According to Commander Safford, who told Noyes that "at a time like this somebody should keep his head," the dispatch had been sent as a result of an overhasty evaluation of the situation by Turner and the war plans division. Safford, as head of OP-20-G, had assured Noyes, the director of naval communications, that the Pearl Harbor attack "was a hit-and-run affair," because the pattern of Japanese signal traffic indicated that now that they had accomplished their objective they were proceeding with the conquest of southeast Asia.[11]

After reviewing the latest radio intelligence with Rochefort, I was able to give much the same estimate to Kimmel. Following my briefing next morning, he tried to correct Stark's pessimistic assumptions by requesting replacement aircraft and assuring him that "our heavy losses have not seriously depleted our fast striking forces nor reduced morale and determination."[12]

Morale and determination, however, were not going to be enough to reverse the tide of the Japanese advance. We realized that fact on Wednesday when we received the news that the British battleship *Prince of Wales* and battle cruiser *Repulse* had been sunk by air attack off the coast of Malaya. Meanwhile, Japanese bombers devastated our Asiatic Fleet's base at Cavite in the Philippines.

Nonetheless, Kimmel worked that afternoon on putting the finishing touches to his revised war plan for beginning offensive operations. It was typical of the admiral that he intended to waste no time in getting the secretary of the navy's approval to hit back quickly and hit back hard with a dispatch to the chief of naval operations:

> With the losses we have sustained, it is necessary to revise completely our strategy of a Pacific war. The loss of battleships commits us to the strategic defensive until our forces can be built up. However, a very powerful striking force of carriers, cruisers and destroyers survives. These forces must be operated boldly and vigorously on the tactical offensive in order to retrieve our initial disaster.[13]

Kimmel had picked himself up, dusted off the ashes of defeat, and was preparing for the next round. The depleted fleet might not be strong enough now—if it ever was—to go steaming across the Pacific to the aid of the Philippines, but it could still project its power to secure those island bases such as Samoa, Fiji, and New Caledonia, which were essential to protect our line of communications with Australia and New Zealand.

To this extent the admiral accepted that Japan's attack had put us on the defensive "and that is hard for us to take."[14] He decided that another raid on Oahu was possible, but not probable, because "the logistic requirements render such an operation unlikely." As Kimmel saw it the principal threat was from submarines and raids by fast-carrier striking forces. He therefore proposed keeping two of his three carrier groups constantly at sea for search and strike operations while the remaining task force guarded the approaches to Oahu or entered harbor for replenishment. The surviving battleships, which were not fast enough to keep up with the carriers (and this was very important but largely ignored by historians), were to be sent to the west coast. This would relieve the congestion in Pearl Harbor and protect the ocean convoy route to Hawaii. Kimmel intended to rely on our submarines to take the war to Japanese waters, and to guard the waters off Wake and Midway. The arrival of new planes and antiaircraft batteries would augment the defense of the fleet base against further raids, with the army and navy sharing an extensive offshore surveillance of the Hawaiian Islands.[15]

The strategy that Kimmel drew up in those first dark days of war was to prove so sound that it governed Pacific Fleet operations for the first six months of the war.

After Guam fell on 10 December and news came that the Japanese were moving south of the Marshalls into the Gilbert Islands, the priority for Soc McMorris and the war plans staff was to draw up plans for sending an expedition to secure Wake Island. An attack there was anticipated to be imminent.

Preparations for the relief of Wake were occupying Kimmel and his staff on 11 December when the secretary of the navy arrived. His Coronado landed at Kaneohe Bay early that Thursday morning. The burned-out hangars and wrecked planes at the naval air station on the northeast coast of Oahu were an unwelcome foretaste for the former newspaper publisher, who had spent most of a wakeful night huddled for warmth in flying gear and blankets.[16] On the drive into Honolulu the ferocity of the Japanese attack was evident from the wreckage of strafed cars and the beached midget submarine.

To preserve the "investigative nature" of his visit, Knox had given orders that "he would not be the guest of any senior officer."[17] Instead the party was driven to the Royal Hawaiian Hotel where they were met by Admiral Kimmel, who escorted them to his submarine base headquarters. Even Knox, the veteran Rough Rider who had charged with Teddy Roosevelt up San Juan Hill during the Spanish-American War, was shocked to his boots by the shambles of Battleship Row. Everywhere Knox looked, he noted men laboring to clear up the debris, removing corpses, and making defenses against another attack.

The loss of three quarters of the battle force was shocking enough, but the heavy toll in American lives was still more disturbing. Knox was told that six hundred servicemen had been buried that morning in a mass grave. On the ferry across to Ford Island he was able to see for himself the oil-soaked bodies being fished from the scorched flotsam drifting in the harbor. The terrible price that we had paid for unpreparedness was measured in the suffering Knox witnessed during his tour of the wards at Hospital Point where some survivors were "so terribly burned and charred as to be beyond recognition." He later confided to his naval aide that "the sight of those men made me as angry as I have ever been in my life."[18]

At fleet headquarters, Knox listened quietly to a thorough review of events by Kimmel. During the course of this briefing, Captain Beatty recorded that a staff officer "made a strong, fervent plea for the dispatch of an expedition to reinforce Wake Island with planes, men and material, but no decision was reached." This first briefing dwelt mainly on the damage the Japanese inflicted, and the secretary of the navy tried to grasp why their attack had taken us by surprise. Knox later commented on "the willingness of those in responsible positions to assume their share of the blame."[19] But when it came to pinpointing responsibility, Kimmel was careful to emphasize that he had received no advance intelligence that he might be under threat of attack.

This appeared to astonish the secretary of the navy. He had carefully studied all the dispatches and background intelligence before leaving Washington. "Did you get Saturday night the dispatch the navy department sent out?" he asked.[20] Kimmel denied receiving any war warning after 27 November. The secretary of the navy declared emphatically, "Well, we sent you one."[21]

Kimmel's denial also surprised Captain Beatty, whose "particular quest was to fathom the failure in delivery of a message ordered sent to Admiral Kimmel."[22] One of the first questions the naval aide asked every staff member from then on was "Did you receive our message of the sixth?"

My first reaction when I heard the question was to think they must be mistaken. Surely they meant the warning sent on Sunday, 7 December, in Marshall's deadline dispatch that did not reach us until after the attack was over. That was also the impression gained by Kimmel's chief of staff Soc McMorris, who was to testify later about hearing Knox make reference to the message.

Poco Smith, like Kimmel and other staff members present, nonetheless distinctly recalled Knox's referring to a "warning message" that was sent from Washington "*on the Saturday* preceding Pearl Harbor [emphasis added]."[23] It does not appear that he was confusing it with Marshall's 1 P.M. deadline warning, because even if it had reached our headquarters it would have given no time for the fleet to have sortied.

Knox's impression that there had been an adequate warning message sent that Saturday night would have been in keeping with the president's

"This means war" reaction to the Magic decrypt of the Japanese diplomatic message earlier that evening. It would also tie in with the claim by Knox's confidant, James G. Stahlman, that the secretary of the navy admitted to him that a late-night council of war took place in the White House on the eve of the Pearl Harbor attack. But if the council had agreed to send out a warning—as Knox's statements that Thursday afternoon appear to indicate—no such dispatch was ever sent out; nor was any trace of a draft to show up in navy department files.

So when Beatty arrived in the intelligence section that afternoon, he quizzed me about the missing war warning. I could only deny that we had received one. I also showed him the photographs of the attack taken by navy photographers, which Kimmel had ordered me to release to no one without his authority.

When Knox came along to look at the pictures, his mood was detached. He showed the curiosity of a not-too-aggressive news reporter who was nevertheless determined to collect all the facts. My impression was that he blustered, but not in an angry way. He was one of those people who wanted to know everything about everything. He insisted on seeing every picture and knowing about each one. How did I get them? Whom did they belong to? Did anybody else have copies? I was sure he was checking to see if any had been released yet and I had the feeling that he would have liked to have them for the *Chicago Daily News*. But the appearance of any single one of them on the front page of a newspaper back home would have done nothing for national morale.

In the course of his brief visit of my office Knox asked me the same question he had asked Kimmel: "Did you get our message?"

"What message?" I asked.

"We sent a message to you telling you to be alert for an attack," he replied.

I could only respond "Sir, as far as I know we never got one; at least I never saw it.'"

I remember thinking at the time of this exchange that the secretary of the navy was not so dumb as to be referring to the deadline message of 27 November, or the deadline dispatch of Sunday. He was certainly under the impression that some warning had been drafted the night before the attack. But what it was he did not specify. And it was not my position to ask.

Knox then went off to meet General Short, who had come down to Kimmel's quarters. They had a brief meeting before the secretary of the navy left for dinner at the blacked-out Royal Hawaiian Hotel with the governor, Joseph B. Poindexter. Next morning, Knox went to Fort Shafter for a longer session, which, according to Short, did not "indicate in any way he was not satisfied."[24] That afternoon his party made another stopover at fleet headquarters to collect the photographs, Japanese *hachimaki* bandanas, and spent bullets before departing for Kaneohe where the flying boat was waiting to take them back to mainland.

After just thirty-two hours of "fact finding," which raised more questions than were answered, Knox was confident that he could report to the president. The first remark that the secretary of the navy made to Beatty after takeoff was "Frank, you will be glad to hear that a decision was finally reached and the relief force for Wake will soon be on its way."[25] Then Knox went up to the navigator's compartment to work on the plotting table and prepare the first draft of a document that was to have far-reaching consequences.

"The navy must lead the way. Speed up" was the message that the secretary of the navy had sent to all ships and shore commands three days earlier. That Friday evening, as a blacked-out flying boat droned its way back to the mainland, Knox knew that he was faced with trying to reconcile two conflicting demands: First, he had approved Kimmel's plan for the relief of Wake Island. Second, if the admiral was prematurely removed from his command, it would prejudice the whole operation—which was vital to restoring the confidence of the fleet. Deep though his love for the navy was, Knox was first and foremost a politician. He was well aware of the damage that could be done the administration if the demand for a public accounting of the disaster was not met promptly.

The first hints of a nasty congressional investigation, which his trip was supposed to head off, surfaced while he was traveling back to Washington. The first rumblings had been voiced on Thursday by Republican senators asking why the president had not yet made a full statement of why Pearl Harbor was surprised. There was also the danger of a major interservice fight in the offing.

"We are doing our best to keep from having a row with the Navy," Stimson noted in his diary. "There is bitterness on both sides over the failure at Hawaii and the younger, less responsible—and some of the irresponsible older men—are all trying to throw the burden on the other Department."[26]

While Knox was preparing to take steps to save the administration from a two-front battle, the marines on Wake Island, unaware that their fate would hang on the secretary of the navy's report, were digging in to face a Japanese assault. After surviving a third day of heavy air raids, lookouts on Peacock Point that night spotted the blinking lights of the approaching invasion force. Major James P. Devereux called his five-hundred-strong garrison to general quarters.

Just before dawn the first Japanese shells began exploding on the sandy spit of land, panicking the atoll's population of gooney birds. Seventy-five minutes later the Japanese warships, led by Admiral Sadamichi Kajioka's two light cruisers and four destroyers, escorted four troopships close in to the outer reef to begin loading the landing barges. This miscalculation brought them within range of the active marine batteries. Minutes later *Yubari* was hit. As the flagship cruiser limped off, the gunners on tiny Peale Island at the north of the lagoon landed a salvo

squarely on destroyer *Hayate*. After a fierce explosion it broke in two and
sank.

Cheering broke out to celebrate the first American sinking of a Japanese warship. "Knock it off you bastards and get back to your guns,"
bellowed Platoon Sergeant Henry Bedell. "Wha' d'ya think this is, a ball
game?"[27] Spurred on by this success, the battery succeeded in hitting
another destroyer and setting a transport on fire. As the Japanese invasion force hurriedly withdrew under cover of smoke, Wake's four surviving Wildcats took off. Carrying a pair of bombs apiece, they made
repeated shuttle runs and managed to sink another destroyer before Kajioka put discretion before valor and was "temporarily forced to retire."[28]

The news of the victory by the Wake garrison that Friday brought
elation to Pacific Fleet headquarters. It raised Kimmel's hopes that the
temporary respite the marines had bought would allow him to mount his
full-scale relief operation. The knowledge that the Japanese would now
probably allocate a much bigger support force for any second invasion
attempt was a vindication of Kimmel's original war plan: to strengthen
Wake's defenses in order to provide him with the "opportunity to get at
naval forces with naval forces."[29]

To turn the temporary Wake victory to our strategic advantage, Kimmel directed McMorris to plan to bring every ship we had into the relief
operation. The tiny atoll was to become the bait—just as Midway would
six months later—to lure the Japanese into a trap. It was a bold and
tactically imaginative scheme. It involved all three carrier task forces:
Brown with *Lexington* would make a diversionary raid on Jaluit to pin
down enemy air and surface forces in the Marshalls. Halsey's Task Force
8 with *Enterprise* would operate west of Johnston Island as cover for
Oahu and long-range support for the actual relief expedition. The expedition itself would be led by *Saratoga*, which would provide the striking
punch to ensure that seaplane tender *Tangier*, loaded with ammunition
and supplies, could steam in to reinforce the Wake garrison.

The three-pronged operation could not begin immediately. It had to
await the arrival of *Saratoga*, which was on passage from the west coast
with another marine corps fighter squadron. Rear Admiral Aubrey Fitch,
who was flying his flag in the *Sarah*, was the natural choice to lead the
critical relief force. But Kimmel, perhaps overconscious of how his own
leapfrog promotion to commander in chief had been resented in the fleet,
decided to assign the overall command to Rear Admiral Frank J.
Fletcher. Although totally inexperienced in conducting air operations,
Fletcher was nevertheless the ranking flag officer; his division of heavy
cruisers had returned from patrol to Pearl to refuel on 10 December.

The Pacific Fleet's ambitious Wake operation, if it succeeded, might
redeem Admiral Kimmel's damaged reputation. Perhaps that is why it
was to be doomed by the decisions that were about to be made in Washington.

Knox's plane landed Sunday evening—a week to the day since the Japanese attack. His twenty-nine-page report, which had been prepared on a borrowed portable typewriter during the flight, was taken straight to the White House by the secretary of the navy. The lateness of the hour and urgency that attached to its delivery are attested to by Roosevelt's scrawled notation: "1941—given me by F.K. 10 PM Dec 14 when he landed here from Hawaii."[30]

After his meeting with the president, Knox—according to James Stahlman—unwound from the tensions of his trip to Pearl Harbor by recounting details of the eve-of-war vigil at the White House. The secretary of the navy also confessed that "the damage was so horrendous" that he had not detailed everything in his report for fear of some leak: "He said that if the American people knew what had happened at Pearl, they would panic and the war would be over before we ever got into it."[31]

Knox's assessment of the damage was horrendous enough to knock some stuffing out of the normally resilient Roosevelt. Treasury Secretary Morgenthau found him in very low spirits after he had been closeted with the secretary of the navy "all night and day."[32] With a skillful economy of words, Knox had laid out the facts as he found them. He was carefully evenhanded. He avoided loading all the blame for the disaster onto Kimmel or Short. But he could not disguise his belief that the success of the Japanese attack was due to the "lack of a state of readiness against such an air attack, by both branches of the service."[33]

This unreadiness, as Knox's report made clear, was partly attributable to the denial of much of the Magic intelligence to the local commander, plus their lack of adequate numbers of fighters and antiaircraft guns. Responsibility for these failures could be fixed only in Washington. While his report did not exonerate the Hawaiian commanders, it fell far short of leveling charges of dereliction, which both Kimmel and Short were soon to face.

Knox also submitted his recommendations to the president on the steps that he felt were essential to restore public confidence and the navy's morale. The most important of these was that a board of inquiry be set up to investigate the Pearl Harbor attack. While Knox may have had reservations about replacing Kimmel before the completion of the Wake operation, the report conceded that he would have to go, because his name was linked with the disaster. So while he was reluctant to remove the admiral from his command pending outcome of any investigation, Knox proposed to effect a dramatic reorganization of the navy by removing from Kimmel his administrative responsibility as commander in chief U.S. Fleet. Admiral Ernest J. King—then commander of the Atlantic Fleet—was to be recalled to the navy department as the new commander in chief U.S. Fleet.[34]

Roosevelt endorsed the appointment. This decision diminished Stark's authority, although he remained CNO for the time being. To have replaced him would have made it appear that he was to blame for the Pearl Harbor disaster. The president and Knox were confident that King's reputation as an uncompromising admiral and one of the fleet's most able organizers would help restore public confidence in the navy. After a long discussion at the White House that Monday, it was agreed that both the secretary of war and navy would hold immediate press conferences and release those parts of Knox's report that would not reveal anything of advantage to the Japanese. The objective was to set people's minds at rest by minimizing the extent of the damage, and by providing assurances that the two services shared equal responsibility for the disaster, which would be the subject of a full investigation.

"Knox agrees with me that there had been remissness in both branches of the service," Stimson recorded. His 15 December diary entry emphasized how they were both "very anxious not to get into any inter-departmental scraps, but to keep the thing on a basis of no recrimination but inflexible responsibility and punishment."[35]

That afternoon the secretary of the navy treated the press to a bravura performance, which avoided any suggestion of individual blame. Sticking closely to his agreed brief, Knox admitted only that *Arizona,* three destroyers, and an auxiliary vessel had been sunk besides the target ship *Utah.*

"In the Navy's greatest hour of peril, the officers and men of the fleet exhibited magnificent courage and resourcefulness,"[36] Knox declared. He admitted that the "services were not on the alert against surprise attack." Since it was impossible to reveal his concern that we had been denied Magic intelligence, and would have been imprudent to indicate the lack of anti-aircraft defenses, the impression Knox conveyed in his report to the press inevitably pointed a finger of blame directly at Kimmel and Short.

That was how many newspapers interpreted Knox's report, even though he had announced that the president was immediately going to initiate a "formal investigation" to ascertain *if* there had been "any dereliction of duty."[37] At his press conference Knox had insisted that action against the local commanders was to await "the facts and recommendations made by this investigating board."[38] But the very next day he went back on his word.

The decision to peremptorily remove Kimmel from his command was prompted by pressures put on Knox that evening. The president wanted "to appoint a commission consisting of two army and two navy officers and a civilian to investigate the responsibility for the losses and to make recommendations."[39] This meant that the Hawaiian commanders would be expected to fulfill their war duties while undergoing a full-blown investigation into their conduct. The secretary of the navy also acceded to Stimson's wishes to speed up the process and to accept Justice Owen J. Roberts to head the special commission of inquiry.

Roberts, who had made his reputation in 1923 as the special prosecutor in the celebrated Teapot Dome scandals, was Roosevelt's choice. As an associate justice of the Supreme Court, the president knew, Roberts would have the trust of the public. And since he had been a leading supporter of the pro-interventionist Committee to Aid America by Aiding the Allies, Roosevelt had every confidence that the judge would pay due attention to the need to preserve national unity behind the war effort. The White House was especially anxious to squash the insidious isolationist rumors that Japan had been manipulated into an attack to provide the president with his excuse for joining Britain in the war against Hitler.

When the war council resumed its deliberations in the presidential study at nine the next morning, Stimson had not only won Knox's agreement to Roberts, but had picked his nominees for the commission: Major General Frank B. McCoy, one of Marshall's trusted aides, and Brigadier General Joseph T. McNarney, a ranking air corps officer, who was recommended by the chief of the army. Knox had selected Admiral William H. Standley, a former chief of naval operations, and Rear Admiral Joseph M. Reeves, an engineering officer who had come out of retirement to take charge of the navy's end of lend-lease to Britain. Apart from Standley, therefore, the supposedly independent members of the investigating commission all had ties and owed favors to the administration.

The names of the commission members were not due to be announced until 17 December—the next day. But its mission was prejudiced—some were to say preempted—by the announcement on 16 December that the Hawaiian commanders were to be replaced. Knox's mind was made up at a White House meeting that Tuesday morning, at which the president approved the appointment of Rear Admiral Chester W. Nimitz as the new commander in chief of the Pacific Fleet. Roosevelt stressed the need for urgency.

"Tell Nimitz to get the hell out to Pearl and stay there till the war is won," Roosevelt had directed the secretary of the navy. But when Knox hurried back to the navy department to inform the chief of the bureau of navigation about his new appointment, Nimitz was astonished by the decision.[40] He protested that it would take a week to wrap up his current work. But the secretary of the navy wasted no time in breaking the news.

Simultaneously came the announcement that afternoon from the secretary of war that General Short and General Martin were being relieved. Stimson, who declared he was "side by side with Knox as to the absence of preparedness on December 7th," cited the need to avoid "a situation where officials charged with the responsibility of the vital naval base would otherwise in this critical hour also be involved in the searching investigation ordered yesterday by the president."[41]

The summary removal of the Hawaiian commanders *before* the presidential investigating team had even been formally announced had the effect of branding Kimmel and Short with a public charge of dereliction. It served to draw attention away from any responsibility that Washington might bear for the Pearl Harbor disaster. It smacked of firing the office boys to conceal skullduggery in the boardroom.

25

"Sold Down the River"

THAT TUESDAY AFTERNOON, 16 December, I was shaken to see a copy of the dispatch informing Admiral Kimmel that he was to relinquish his command "effective 3 p.m. on December 17."[1] I immediately went down to his office. There was no one there except a marine orderly who would only say that the admiral had "retired to his quarters."

At three the following afternoon there was a terse formal handover. Admiral Pye had been designated temporary commander in chief. Each man faced the other, read his orders, and shook hands. Then Kimmel left the headquarters building after quietly bidding farewell to staff. We were as downhearted as he was. Although his dismissal was not unexpected, we all regarded it as premature. We wondered what would happen to the Wake operation. It may be an established American tradition that losing baseball teams have their manager fired, but not during the first game of the World Series.

The choice of Admiral Pye as temporary fleet commander also surprised us—and no one was more surprised than I. It was impossible not to reflect on the part that he had played in the disaster on the eve of the raid by dismissing my estimate with such certainty and saying that Japan would not attack the United States.

While we were apprehensive about Kimmel's departure, we realized that he had been the victim of fate. But none of us expected that he would get the raw deal that was to be meted out to him by Washington. Nor did Kimmel himself.

"Immediately after Pearl Harbor," Kimmel was later to reflect, "I felt that, no matter how hard and how conscientiously I had tried, I had not been smart enough, and to that extent, must accept blame for Pearl Harbor." But he fully expected to be assigned another command. He was assured as much in a sympathetic 29 December letter from Admiral

338

Stark: "Don't worry about our finding duty for you. I value your services just as much as I ever did and more and I say this straight from the heart as well as the head."[2]

But within a month, Kimmel had been forced into retirement. Being made Washington's scapegoat was a fate that a fine admiral did not deserve. "It is an age-old tradition that the commanding officer of a ship is liable if the ship is lost. For this reason, Admiral Kimmel must be held responsible for his losses at Pearl Harbor,"[3] Joe Rochefort was to observe. "However, if these losses were due in part, or in whole, to errors by his superiors, then those superiors must be held responsible."[4]

It was to be several years before the awful truth of Washington's errors began to emerge. When Kimmel discovered how appalling they were, he became fighting mad at the wrong he had been done and the indignity he had been forced to suffer: "Since learning that definite information of the Japanese intentions to attack the United States was in the hands of the War and Navy Departments and was not supplied to me, I now refuse to accept any responsibility for the catastrophe."[5]

At the moment Kimmel stepped out of the submarine base building for the last time on 17 December, the responsibility for the Pacific Fleet passed temporarily to Admiral Pye. Rather than operating through Kimmel's staff, Pye preferred to work with his team, which had become homeless as the result of the damage to *California*. But Pye had to rely on us for intelligence and to operate through the war plans section, which had planned the Wake operation.

It was not a happy arrangement. While Pye could not be faulted for his knowledge of strategy, McMorris and I soon found out that the shock of losing his battle force had shaken his confidence and decisiveness. Kimmel's bold decision to commit all three carrier task forces to the Wake operation rode unhappily with him. It was characteristic of Kimmel to seize the initiative. But Pye was a more cautious commander who preferred to wait and see what the enemy would do before making his moves.[6]

This was a luxury that our temporary commander in chief could not afford. Nor was fleet intelligence in a position yet to predict from radio intelligence, or code breaking, what the Japanese would do, or precisely how many of their warships would be committed in their second attempt to take Wake.

On 17 December, Rochefort had finally been given the go-ahead from Washington to abandon the unbreakable Japanese flag officers code. He was to "commence solution" of the current JN-25 ciphers, but it would be three weeks before the enemy's main operational code began yielding up its secrets.[7]

The task facing Tommy Dyer and Ham Wright was, however, made easier by a message that came in shortly afterward from Station Cast in Manila. This message that the Japanese had inadvertently duplicated in the JN-25 code and again in plain text "confirmed indicator subtractor already recovered by mathematical elimination PM code remains unchanged."[8] This confirmed that the cipher changes ordered in JN-25 on 2 December were limited to the five-figure additives. The main code book was unchanged. And by a happy coincidence, Hypo's copy of the code book recoveries were unloaded that day from a shipment that had been en route from Washington since early November. (The reasons for that slow shipment were typical bureaucratic ones.) Cryptanalysts at Cast transmitted the subtractor and additive recoveries for the current period on the secure Copek line from the Philippines, and Rochefort's team began their assault on JN-25 right away.

Unfortunately, I could give Admiral Pye no assurances the next day about how soon Hypo's code-breaking efforts would begin producing the information he needed so desperately. All I could do was to brief him about the conclusions I had drawn concerning the whereabouts of the Japanese striking force that were based on the documents taken from the bomber that had crashed in the cane field. From them we could be certain that the striking force of six carriers, two battleships, and two heavy cruisers outnumbered us two to one. But my estimate was that most of the enemy force would be returning to Japan for replenishment, and that only one or two carriers would have been detached to ensure the capture of Wake.

Admiral Pye's worry was that instead of springing a trap, to continue with Kimmel's operation could send all our forces steaming into a Japanese ambush. This concern had been raised by Admiral Wilson Brown three days earlier when Task Force 11 was refueling at Pearl prior to sailing with *Lexington* to carry out the diversionary raid on Jaluit. There was a possibility that a powerful land-based air force had already been flown into the easternmost island of the Marshalls. And this had persuaded Kimmel to give Brown the option of shifting his objective to Makin in the Gilberts, or retiring if circumstances dictated. Brown's confidence in the ability of his force to defend itself against planes was further shaken when gunnery practice the next morning revealed that most of the antiaircraft ammunition for his cruisers was defective.

One of Kimmel's final acts as fleet commander was to brief Admiral Fletcher on Tuesday before he sailed with *Saratoga* to make the trip of just over a thousand miles due west to Wake. After Fletcher had departed, Halsey's Task Force 8 entered Pearl Harbor for badly needed refueling and replenishment that was to take four days. The next morning, as the sad transfer ceremony was taking place at the submarine base, Fletcher's force joined up with the oiler *Neches* and seaplane tender *Tangier* which had left Pearl the day before.

Admiral Kimmel had done all that he could. He had disposed his forces for a decisive naval engagement. As we had predicted—but could not confirm—the Japanese were preparing to steam right into the trap that had been set for them by detaching two carriers from their striking force and sending four heavy cruisers northeast from Truk to cover the Wake landing. But while Kimmel was not permitted to remain in charge of his operation, the Japanese gave Admiral Kajioka an opportunity to save face. He was scheduled to sail in command of the invasion force from Kwajalein where his flagship *Yubari* was being patched up. In company with two light cruisers he would escort the transports carrying two thousand battle-hardened veterans of the imperial navy's Special Naval Landing Force on the three-hundred-mile trip north to Wake.

The strategy that Kimmel hoped would provide a badly needed Christmas victory celebration for Americans was shaping up according to plan. But a drama of a very different kind was being arranged in Washington.

That Wednesday morning Justice Roberts held his first informal meeting with Knox and Stimson in the secretary of war's office. In circumstances that must appear highly prejudicial to the objectivity of an impending investigation, guidance was given as to the terms and nature of his inquiry by two of the principal parties. On Thursday morning at ten, without waiting for one of its members, the Roberts Commission got down to business at the war department. That they began work without defining their terms of reference, or waiting for Admiral Standley, who was delayed traveling to Washington, was another sign of how the Roberts Commission was "packed" on the side of the vested interests in Washington. Justice Roberts himself was known to be friendly with the president; Admiral Reeves was beholden to Roosevelt for his lend-lease post; McCoy was a trusted thirty-year confidant of Marshall; and McNarney was an ambitious young member of the army staff in search of promotion. The recorder lacked any court-martial experience. Lastly, a marine corps colonel, without extensive legal expertise, was made provost marshal.

When Admiral Standley finally arrived, he was concerned to find that none of the witnesses had been sworn and that he was expected to serve alongside General McNarney, a ranking member of the army staff whose interests were clearly less than impartial. General Marshall, assisted by the chief of war plans General Gerow, was giving details of the warnings sent to the Hawaiian command. A clubby atmosphere, more appropriate to a mess than a judicial investigation, prevailed. Stark or a member of his team was in attendance during the entire proceedings; they presented their case in the same easy manner that was not conducive to proper cross-examination.

Even if there had been any questioning, no full record was being kept of the questions—or answers. This was too much for the upright Standley. He protested the absence of sworn testimony and a recorder to keep a verbatim transcript. He was puzzled that an associate member of the Supreme Court should permit such informal and ad hoc procedures on an investigation of such importance. After Stark had completed his presentation and withdrawn, Standley pressed for the commission to seek congressional authorization to subpoena witnesses and administer oaths. This was agreed and a special bill hurriedly drafted to go to Capitol Hill.

Yet when Justice Roberts called the meeting to order for the second day on 19 December, witnesses continued to give unsworn testimony and still no written account was taken of the case presented by the heads of naval and army intelligence. Although history was denied a detailed record, perhaps intentionally, Admiral Wilkinson prepared verbatim notes of the proceedings in a "top secret" aide-mémoire. The full text of this memorandum, annotated in Turner's writing and located in his file in the fall of 1984, gives a fuller record of what went on than does the abbreviated summary of the official Roberts Commission report.[9]

The Wilkinson memorandum for the CNO was evidently prepared for immediate circulation that afternoon to Admirals Stark, Ingersoll, and Turner. The document is, in itself, a pertinent indication of the way in which the ranking navy and war department officers were attempting to rig the commission's findings in their favor. It reveals that they sought to divert investigation of their considerable sins of omission by exaggerating the lesser omissions of the Hawaiian commanders.

Wilkinson recounted how he had been accompanied by Captain McCollum to the munitions building where he found General Miles and Colonel Bratton already present in the boardroom. His digest of the evidence of the morning of 19 December suggests that there was a certain degree of collusion and deliberate misstatement in what appears to have been a collaborative effort by army and navy to convey the impression that *no* intelligence had been withheld from Admiral Kimmel or General Short.

"The Commission stated that they wished the Army and Navy intelligence to *cooperate* in their answers" was how Wilkinson reported the opportunity that was given them to line up a unified testimony [emphasis added].[10] This was facilitated because Roberts permitted them to sit in on each other's testimony. Miles, after giving a rundown on the instruction that had been given to the Hawaiian command in the month preceding the attack, "described at some length the events in General Marshall's office, including the sending of the subsequently delayed dispatch to General Short on the morning of Sunday, December 7th."[11]

Speaking from his own experience in the Hawaiian command, Miles said, he concluded "that a successful raid *was possible* against a garrison which *had not been warned,* but was not possible against a garrison that had been warned [emphasis added]."[12] Given the choice between assuming that either the local commands had *not* received adequate warning, or that their commanders were derelict, the majority of the commission chose the latter explanation without questioning it.

Wilkinson was then asked about what information and communications had been sent to the Pacific Fleet in the months before the attack. The discursive reply was intended to convey the impression that Kimmel was as well informed as the navy department: "As to the actual interchange of messages relating to intelligence, in general the sources reported their information to the Commander-in-Chief of the Asiatic Fleet and in forwarding it the Commander-in-Chief Pacific *was usually* advised [emphasis added]."[13]

The chief of naval intelligence then listed the seven-point summary of the indications pointing to war that McCollum had drafted on 1 December. But it was not pointed out that transmission of McCollum's list to Pearl Harbor had effectively been blocked by Turner. Instead, Wilkinson gave the commission the clear impression that the Pacific Fleet was far better informed about the imminence of Japan's intentions to commence hostilities than it actually was. He misled them by listing McCollum's 1 December memorandum—the fact that it was mentioned at all obviously rankled Turner, who struck it through on his copy of Wilkinson's minutes.

In the course of discussing radio intelligence decrypts concerning the two Japanese task groups massing in the South China Sea and the mandated islands, Wilkinson was careful to point out that "nothing in this item made us forecast a movement as far east of the Mandated area as Hawaii."[14] Roberts, significantly, wanted to know how far away these islands were from Hawaii. The director of naval intelligence, perhaps inadvertently, in his answer added two hundred miles (almost a whole day's steaming for a task force) to the distance from Pearl Harbor to Jaluit.

"Without mentioning particular dispatches," Wilkinson told the commission, "we had assured ourselves that all of this information had either passed through the CinC Asiatic and Pacific Fleets or, if not, it had been furnished them from the Department." Such reticence in mentioning diplomatic intelligence was surprising because Wilkinson noted "*the meeting was discussing Magic freely,* but stated that they would be most careful that no mention of it would be made [emphasis added]."[15]

Yet the only "particular dispatches" that Wilkinson made reference to were those of 3 December, relating to the code burning at the Japanese embassies. (This paragraph has also been struck out in Turner's copy of the report.)

Since Wilkinson was aware that the Roberts Commission knew about, and understood, the importance of Magic, his repeated declaration that Kimmel "had as much information as we had" was so misleading as to be a deliberate lie. But he was careful to point out, "I myself could not expect that he and his staff would infer positively a raid on Hawaii any more than we had been able to do from the same information."[16]

What Roberts was *not* told, however, was that the Pacific Fleet did *not* have access to the *same* information that Washington possessed. Wilkinson chose not to reveal that the navy department had ignored the importance of the bomb plot messages and other important Magic intelligence by not relaying them out to Hawaii. His testimony was geared—as had been Stark's and Marshall's the previous day—to reinforcing the contention that the Hawaiian commands had been given all the intelligence available in Washington.

The presidential commission of inquiry was apparently ready to accept the unrecorded and unsworn word of senior officers. Roberts himself was to concede that no attempt was made to examine the actual intelligence records, which would have told a very different story. "The Magic was not shown to us. I would not have bothered to read it if it had been shown to us," Roberts was later to admit. "All I wanted to know was whether the commanders had been advised of the criticalness of the situation. . . . The commission found that they had ample warning."[17]

Justice Roberts, it seems, had made up his mind about where the blame must fall by the time the commission had finished hearing the unsupported statement by the director of naval intelligence. At midday Friday, the inquiry adjourned to pack for their scheduled four o'clock takeoff on the first leg of a two-and-a-half-day flight to Hawaii.

The next day, while the investigators were in mid-flight, Admiral Halsey's Task Force 8 had steamed out of Pearl to guard the western approaches to Oahu. Now the navy began to pay the price for the premature removal of Admiral Kimmel.

On Saturday morning the relief force under Admiral Fletcher was approaching the halfway point of its passage to Wake. Shortly after 1200 on 20 December, Admiral Wilson Brown decided that to press on with his raid on Jaluit might cost him the loss of *Lexington* to air or submarine attack. So he independently exercised the option he had been given to raid Makin as an alternative target. At Pacific Fleet headquarters we had received what turned out to be a greatly exaggerated report of the Japanese forces occupying the Gilberts. Traffic analysis suggested that a big seaplane tender and the Yokohama Corps of the naval air fleet had already reached Makin.[18] Although there was no way of confirming this, I told Admiral Pye that this might mean that anywhere from twenty to two hundred planes were already in a position to threaten Task Force 11. Hypo had also identified the Japanese submarine force commander as being garrisoned at Jaluit. The threat of Brown's force steaming into a possible underwater ambush added to the concern that was swirling around the operation at headquarters.

Admiral Pye, very conscious that he was merely keeping the command seat warm for Admiral Nimitz, decided that he could not risk the loss of any of the carriers. He sent a dispatch ordering Brown north to support Fletcher. At the same time he instructed Fletcher to undertake a refueling operation the next day. Although it was not strictly necessary, Pye wanted to provide a fixed rendezvous point for Brown's force to join up with Fletcher.[19]

The responsibility for this decision to refuel was to be hotly debated. Regardless of whether it was at Pye's or Fletcher's initiative, it disastrously delayed the approach to Wake. Pearl Harbor was receiving urgent cables from the marine commander on Wake that his men were coming under increasingly heavy air attack. One of these reports identified carrier-based dive bombers, which confirmed my estimate that part of the Pearl Harbor striking force had been detached. The news added more fuel to Pye's alarm. He at once informed the chief of naval operations of his revision in the Wake plan in a cable that emphasized his primary concern was the maintenance of the fleet's strength to defend Hawaii. Stark not only confirmed the priority, but cabled that Admiral King—the newly installed commander in chief of the U.S. Fleet—considered Wake Island a liability.

Pye was thereby duly authorized to use his discretion to order an evacuation, rather than attempt a reinforcement. Admiral Kajioka's invasion force set sail the same day from Kwajalein. The next morning *Saratoga* was just six hundred miles northeast of Wake when Fletcher commenced a ten-hour refueling operation that according to ships' logs was unnecessary. If Fletcher had continued a twenty-knot run to Wake, Task Force 14 would have been within range the next day to smash Kajioka's invasion force when it steamed into position to commence its second landing attempt.

The small hours of 23 December, local time, found a much battered marine garrison on Wake preparing to make a final stand in anticipation of reinforcements arriving. A week of repeated air bombardment had knocked out half their gun batteries and cost them all their fighter planes. This time the Japanese landing barges took care to make simultaneous assaults out of the line of fire of the surviving batteries.

At 0250, Wake command flashed out, "Enemy apparently landing." Over the next two hours bitter hand-to-hand fighting erupted. The outnumbered marine garrison was steadily overwhelmed by the numbers of Japanese coming ashore. "The enemy is on the island," Wake command signaled at 0500. "The issue is in doubt."[20]

At Pacific Fleet headquarters, Pye and his chief of staff, Admiral Draemel, were debating with Captain McMorris what to do. Soc McMorris was strongly of the opinion that Fletcher should press the attack and that Brown should steam up in support. But Task Force 14 was still 425 miles northeast of Wake while Fletcher was attempting to top off the bunkers of four destroyers whose tanks were already three quarters full. But heavy swells repeatedly parted the oil hoses. Task Force 11 was twice as far away to the southeast, and Halsey's Task Force 8 was some 100 miles west of Midway, too far away to intervene. It would take twelve hours for Fitch's *Saratoga* to get within range for an air strike. And it would be a full day before *Lexington*'s planes could be brought into the action. McMorris pointed out the tactical advantages of Fletcher's position. Halsey's *Enterprise* could be brought south to assist, or to cover Fletcher's retirement if necessary. But no matter how you viewed it, the Japanese would have been trapped from three sides.

Pye's lack of resolution and his determination not to risk any of his three carriers resulted in a series of conflicting orders to Fletcher. After agreeing with McMorris's plan, Pye's feet got progressively colder about the whole operation. The result was confusion and indecision. It sapped the confidence of the commander on the spot. The first dispatch sent to Fletcher instructed him to make full speed to bring *Saratoga* within two hundred miles of Wake and then launch a search and attack strike. Hardly had that order been received than it was countermanded. Now Fletcher was told that seaplane tender *Tangier* was to make a high-speed unescorted run into the atoll and evacuate its surviving defenders. Within the hour even this halfhearted rescue attempt was canceled.

At 0911, some twenty minutes before the news of Wake's surrender was received at headquarters, Pye sent out an order recalling Fletcher and Brown to Pearl Harbor. Some of the marine fliers on *Saratoga*, who had been destined to fly their aircraft to join their comrades on Wake, were nearly mutinous. Some threatened to get in their planes and fly off regardless. But Fletcher was not cut out for a Nelsonian gesture of "putting the telescope to his blind eye."[21] Those who think he could and should have taken more aggressive action—and who point especially to his refueling delay—have concluded that Fletcher had a yellow streak down his back. They claimed he did not proceed at his task force's best speed, using refueling to wait for a chance to withdraw from the operation. What is clear is that on board *Saratoga*, Admiral Fitch, who probably was the most experienced carrier admiral in the navy, was more disconcerted to be recalled. When during the discussion on *Saratoga*'s bridge it was suggested that Fitch should ignore the dispatch, he retired to his cabin lest his staff should seek to persuade him to defy his orders.[22]

Whether Fletcher intentionally prolonged his refueling or not, it was Pye's apprehension about the Japanese carriers that finally lost us Wake. Pye's decision also ended any chance of delivering a smashing surprise blow against the Japanese naval forces which, as it turned out later, did not suspect that within two weeks of their raid on Pearl Harbor the Pacific Fleet was capable of striking back.

Admiral Pye, who "ordered the retirement with extreme regret," was not prepared to run any risks, however much he tried to disguise it. "The use of offensive action to relieve Wake had been my intention and desire," he was to explain in his report to the chief of naval operations. "But when the enemy once landed on the island, the general strategic situation took precedence, and the conservation of our naval forces became the first consideration."[23]

The tragedy was that Kimmel's strategy had worked perfectly to bring about the conditions for a spectacular American victory. Our three carriers and superior cruiser striking power would have been concentrated against two Japanese carriers and heavy cruisers. But by putting strategic caution before tactical calculation, Pye had deprived the navy of the chance to catch the enemy unawares in much the same circumstances as we were able to do at Midway six months later. A December victory at Wake, moreover, would have been a stunning blow to Japan. It would have been a decisive demonstration that Yamamoto's grand strategy had failed to knock the fight out of the Pacific Fleet for a six-month period as Nagumo claimed. It would have opened the way to a transpacific relief of Corregidor and the Philippines. And it would have rallied the navy and provided a tremendous boost to the morale of the American people who were facing a bleak Christmas.

The lost opportunity at Wake would also have helped redeem Admiral Kimmel's reputation. But the collapse of the operation that he had masterminded, on the very day that the Roberts Commission members flew into Honolulu to begin their investigation, did nothing to enhance the reputation of the former commander in chief.

The members of the presidential investigating commission established themselves at the Royal Hawaiian Hotel on 22 December. That Monday afternoon they began drawing up a list of the army and navy officers they wished to interview. At nine the next morning Justice Roberts began the formal part of his investigation at Fort Shafter. General Short appeared for questioning with no legal adviser, because he regarded himself as "absolutely not guilty in any sense."[24] He had assembled a formidable array of documentation to prove there had been no dereliction of duty as far as he was concerned. Short explained why he regarded the 27 November war warning as an alert against sabotage. Although he conceded that he "made a very serious mistake when we didn't go to an alert against an all out air attack,"[25] he said that it was because he had received no intelligence or any other warning from Washington indicating the possibility of such an attack.

The investigators therefore had to judge the degree to which Short could have been expected to read between the lines to divine the probability of a Japanese raid and to have increased the preparedness necessary to counter it. After the assurances they had received four days earlier in Washington that the Hawaiian commanders were more familiar than they actually were with the overall intelligence picture, it was inevitable that the commission members were less inclined to give either Hawaiian commander the benefit of the doubt.

There was, moreover, a significant shift in the way that Roberts conducted his inquiry. In Washington the witnesses from the war and navy departments had been permitted to sit in during each other's testimony, and were even directed "to cooperate in their answers."[26] But neither Short nor Kimmel was permitted this privilege. This helped foster the impression of a lack of cooperation between the local commands, which compared unfavorably with the impression that had been given by the service chiefs in Washington. The Roberts Commission was to make a great point of this later as a contributory cause of the disaster.

After a break for Christmas, Justice Roberts resumed the chair in Fort Shafter to continue questioning army witnesses. Not until 27 December did the inquiry move to the wardroom lounge of the submarine base to begin a long interrogation of Admiral Kimmel. Unlike Short, the former commander in chief had brought his old friend Rear Admiral Robert Theobald—the fleet destroyer force commander—to assist in the presentation of his case.

"Of course you are not here in the capacity of a defense counsel because you and Admiral Kimmel both understand that no charges have been preferred against him; he is not in the status of a defendant," Roberts assured Theobald. But after the former commander in chief had presented his statement of events, he believed that Roberts's questioning assumed the manner of "a trial lawyer in a lower court."[27]

Kimmel, however much he was reassured to the contrary, could not but see himself in the position of a defendant. To explain and justify the decisions he had made after receiving the 27 November war warning, he had repeatedly to explain technicalities, and justify decisions that were based on these, to a nonnaval inquisitor. Hindsight—and Roberts's assumptions that Kimmel knew as much secret intelligence as Washington—made many of the admiral's decisions appear derelict. Of all his "omissions," none appeared in such a bad light as his belief that the battleships in harbor were not in danger from torpedo attacks, his failure to order round-the-compass air patrols, and to appreciate the significance of the code burning at the Japanese consulate.

Lack of sleep and the strain of having to prepare a full report on the disaster without adequate staff further contributed to the impression Kimmel made as a witness. His pride bristled frequently at having his arguments challenged by a landlubber and the two army members of the commission. "McNarney was a lying s.o.b. who had no more morals than a crawling snake," he would later complain.[28] Admiral Standley, who appears to have been the only commission member sympathetic to the former commander in chief, regarded the fast-talking Admiral Reeves as very antagonistic to Kimmel and Short.

That antagonism surfaced in a nasty exchange when Kimmel, after discovering the inadequacy of the stenographic record—which omitted his entire first statement—asked for permission to correct it. Roberts was very opposed to what he saw as an attempt by the admiral to "interlard things that you did not say."[29] It was the intervention of Admiral Standley that permitted Kimmel to make parallel corrections in the text and append his fully corrected statement as an addendum. According to a memorandum left by Standley, it appears that Justice Roberts and a majority of his fellow commission members had been convinced by what they heard before leaving Washington that the local commanders must be guilty of some major dereliction. Standley did not agree, then or later: "I felt that, with all the information available to them in Washington, Admiral Stark and General Marshall were equally culpable."[30]

I was called before the Roberts Commission on 2 January. The evidence I contributed showed how radio intelligence and traffic analysis left us in the dark about the whereabouts of the main enemy carrier forces, although it had revealed the buildup of the main Japanese forces in the China Sea and the mandates. In my view, I said, the dispatches we had received from Washington "gave rise to the firm belief that some action by Japan was impending" in the Far East, but gave us no specific indication that there was even an indirect threat against Hawaii.[31]

Admiral Standley then raised the question of whether the navy department might have had more information than we had access to. "From my knowledge, they have sir, but I do not know how much," I replied.[32] That was as far as I felt that I could go at the time. Later, I found out that Standley's suspicions and my own were more than justified.

"If that is true, wouldn't they be in a better position to estimate the whole situation than you are here?" Standley followed up.

"That is the way the system is laid," I told him.

But before I could make reference to the efforts that Kimmel and I had made to get access to diplomatic intelligence, the chairman interrupted, "If you are an intelligence officer for the Commander of the Fleet of the United States, you did not expect that anything of value to you as to any important information would be withheld from you by the authorities?"

At that time I had no idea that we had been shortchanged, so could only reply, "No, sir."

"Then why did you say they did not?" Justice Roberts responded with more than a shade of hostility.

"I merely meant that as an answer to a specific question that we were receiving copies of reports."[33] That was the only way I felt able to reply. I did not know whether the commission members had been cleared to hear about our most secret intelligence.

But Roberts persisted. I felt that I could not disagree when asked, "Do you mean they have more incoming matter which they digest, and then send you the gist of it?"

Since I did not know the degree to which the navy department had let us down, I accepted the veracity of Standley's rhetorical question: "You felt sure you would receive all conclusions from naval intelligence that were of any importance to you?" But when General McCoy asked pointedly whether we had been given any warning of the attack, my response was a very definite "No, sir; not here in Hawaii; no, sir. There was no warning that the negotiations were breaking down."

Despite the conflict between my testimony and the repeated as-

surances Justice Roberts had been given by Admiral Wilkinson about
Kimmel's having access to all the intelligence available in Washington,
the commission made no effort to follow the points I had raised. Nor did
they pursue the further evidence of the discrepancy between the intelligence picture at Pearl Harbor and Washington that surfaced when Justice Roberts, accompanied by Admirals Reeves and Standley, went down
to see Rochefort's code-breaking setup and look at the Hypo records.
Lieutenant Jasper Holmes, in addition to showing them the reconstructed
track of the Japanese attack, also mentioned the messages decrypted
from the Honolulu consulate on 10 December. He indicated that if these
had been available to us in time, they might have prevented our being
taken by surprise.

The presidential commission of inquiry chose, nonetheless, to overlook or ignore the possibility that the navy department might have broken into the consular traffic. No attempt was made to look at the records,
or to reexamine Wilkinson under oath, in the two days of questioning
that the commission contented itself with after returning to Washington.
This may have been because after Roberts left Honolulu on 10 January,
he took advantage of the Pullman car that carried the commission members across country from San Francisco to begin writing up his report.

Friday, 23 January 1942, found Justice Roberts putting the finishing
touches to the report, after some late-night discussion of his findings
three days earlier with Secretary Stimson and Supreme Court Chief Justice Felix Frankfurter. The final draft was not agreed to without some
bitter debate between the two admirals on the commission. Reeves was
convinced that Kimmel was wholly to blame. Standley believed that this
view did not show the whole picture.

Standley admitted years later that he had only agreed not to submit a
minority report after being persuaded that such a divisive opinion would
threaten the war effort. "The findings as to sins of commission presented
true enough statements," he wrote, "but the many sins of omission in the
picture were omitted from our findings because the President in his executive order setting up the Commission had specifically limited its jurisdiction."[34]

The Roberts Commission report was written with the intention of
keeping Magic, a vital intelligence source, secret. It carefully omitted any
mention of Magic. While concealing Washington's sins of omission it exaggerated the errors of commission of the local commanders. So when
Roosevelt read through the long report on that Saturday, he was no
doubt reassured to find that by shifting the burden of responsibility from
the war and navy departments, the commission's findings had not damaged the credibility of key members of his administration. He summoned
Marvin O. Macintyre, the White House secretary. Tossing the report
onto his desk, he said, "Mac, give that to the Sunday papers in full."[35]

The newspapers drew the inevitable conclusions that Admiral Kimmel and General Short had been found almost entirely to blame. They could hardly do otherwise. The three-part report concluded that the secretaries of state, war, and navy had "fulfilled their obligations." So too, apparently, had the chief of naval operations and the chief of the army. They were credited with discharging their "command responsibility" by warning Oahu. The only criticism leveled at the Washington military establishment was that the war department had failed to "reply to the anti-sabotage measures instituted by the commanding general, Hawaiian Department."[36]

The blame for Japan's success in attacking Pearl Harbor could not have been more nastily or unfairly attributed. Admiral Kimmel and General Short "in the light of the warnings and directions to take appropriate action" were found "in dereliction of duty" for not conferring with each other "respecting the meaning and intent of the warnings and the appropriate means of defense required by the imminence of hostilities." They had demonstrated "a lack of appreciation of the responsibilities vested in them and inherent in their positions." The Japanese attack achieved its surprise because "they had failed to make suitable dispositions to meet such an attack." The Hawaiian commanders had, moreover, "failed properly to evaluate the seriousness of the situation" and it was these "errors of judgment" that "were the effective causes for the success of the attack."[37]

The press and all but a few of Roosevelt's diehard isolationist opponents on Capitol Hill welcomed the verdict. Without access to the secret intelligence record, there was little that Kimmel or Short could do to challenge the judgment or escape the pillory of public scorn to which they were now subjected. Hate mail poured in. There were the inevitable death threats and proposals that they should be executed for treason.

Short submitted his resignation almost immediately. Kimmel held out for the reassignment that he had been promised, but by 28 January, he, too, submitted a letter to the secretary of the navy offering to retire. The president directed that it should be announced that both officers had applied for retirement and that this had been granted "without condonation of any offense or prejudice to future disciplinary actions."[38]

The implicit threat of court-martial proceedings, when the demands of the war were less pressing, caused Kimmel to protest "my crucifixion before the public" to Stark. "I have kept my mouth shut and propose to do so as long as it is humanly possible," he wrote to the chief of naval operations. "But I think in all justice the department should do nothing further to inflame the public against me. I am entitled to some consideration even though you may consider I erred grievously."[39]

Many of his fellow admirals sympathized with Kimmel's plight. But as long as the demands of wartime required national unity and public confidence in the navy's ability to conduct a successful fight, they held their peace. After the war even the hard-bitten Admiral King would concede

that the Roberts Commission failed in its duty of fairly assigning responsibility for the disaster. Not a man to admit errors lightly, "Ernie" King's
epitaph on the injustices of the presidential commission might be applied
to some extent to all the subsequent inquiries that sought to fix the blame
for the Pearl Harbor debacle on the local commanders:

> It seems to me that this committee did not get into the real meat of
> the matter but merely selected a "scapegoat" to satisfy the popular
> demand for fixing the responsibility for the Pearl Harbor debacle.
> For instance, Admiral Kimmel was not asked the important ques-
> tions nor was he given the proper chance to speak for himself. In
> fact, he and General Short were "sold down the river" as a political
> expedient.[40]

Expedient or not, the war had to be fought. Until we were on the road to
final victory, Kimmel and Short had to endure in painful silence the op-
probrium that fate and political necessity had dealt them.

26

"Heaven's Admonition"

CHRISTMAS DAY, 1941. Despair filled Pacific Fleet headquarters. Following the debacle to relieve Wake, the atmosphere was made more gloomy by the presence of the Roberts Commission investigators, who had just begun their interrogations. It was raining that morning and the weather matched the mood of Admiral Pye and his staff as we waited for the arrival of the new commander in chief, Pacific Fleet, Rear Admiral Chester W. Nimitz. Most of us at what was now to be known as Cincpac headquarters expected to be relieved. We hoped for sea duty as our chance to hit back against the Japanese.

The Catalina flying boat roared in through the gray overcast at 0700 to land in the east loch, the wreckage-strewn waters made even more dismal by the sight of the upturned hulls of *Oklahoma* and *Utah*. The stench of fuel oil still permeated the air. Nimitz, wearing civilian clothes, was greeted by Admiral Bellinger and the chiefs of staff. The party had to remain standing on the way to shore, because the whaleboat was begrimed with oil.

"What news of the relief of Wake?" was Nimitz's first question.[1]

When told the island had surrendered and the relief expedition had been recalled, he fell silent. He stayed that way during most of the trip ashore, which was made more miserable by the bloated corpses that were still surfacing from submerged wrecks.

"This is a terrible sight, seeing all these ships down," Nimitz finally remarked to Poco Smith as the boat pulled into the landing. Admiral Pye, the acting commander in chief, and a somber Admiral Kimmel were waiting to greet him at the submarine base wharf. Nimitz was startled at Kimmel's appearance. "You have my sympathy," Nimitz assured his old friend, who joined them for a working breakfast.[2] Nimitz was to demonstrate the same consideration to Kimmel's staff during the detailed tours of inspection he made in the next few days. Any apprehensions we might

353

have had about him as the new commander in chief were dispelled by his warm manner.

A solemn, thoughtful face framed thin, pursed lips, but it was Nimitz's ready and infectious smile that offered us reassurance. The twinkling blue of his eyes was heightened by a ruddy complexion and boyish mop of sandy-colored hair. But it was his firm jaw line and the incisive thrust of his questions that made it clear that he was steeled for the tremendous task he was to assume.

On Wednesday, 31 December, at 1000, Admiral Nimitz was formally handed command of the Pacific Fleet in a ceremony held on the deck of a submarine. It was uncharitably suggested by some wag in the mess that *Grayling*'s was the only available deck left afloat. But the fact was that Nimitz, as a submariner, chose her to first break out his four-star flag and, throughout the war, the Pacific Fleet flagship was always a submarine.

"We have taken a tremendous wallop, but I have no doubt about the outcome," Nimitz said in a brief address to newsmen and photographers.[3] He spoke in the same spirit to his staff officers that afternoon. Expecting that we would all be reassigned, we were surprised when he told us that as chief of the Bureau of Navigation (the Bureau of Naval Personnel after 13 May 1942), he knew that we had been chosen for our competence and he wished to keep us on. Nevertheless, he promised a sympathetic hearing to any who wanted sea duty.

At first opportunity, I asked Admiral Nimitz to be detached, and have a relief assigned. I said that I wanted to go to sea in command of a destroyer. He smiled understandingly. "You can kill more Japs here than you could ever kill in command of a destroyer flotilla."

Flattered, I was not so sure about his conclusion. But my respect for his enthusiasm and determination to restore the reputation of the fleet was fired up. Morale at Pearl Harbor was at a low ebb. The American military situation across the Pacific was desperate. Two days after Nimitz assumed command, General MacArthur abandoned the Philippine capital city of Manila, and the Asiatic Fleet lost its naval base at Cavite. Within the week a Japanese amphibious force had landed in Borneo; our naval outpost on the island of Samoa was shelled; and Rabaul, Australia's base in New Britain Island, was bombed.

The only American naval power (excluding our submarines) remaining in the central Pacific were the torpedo planes and bombers of the carriers and the heavy cruisers of our three task forces. And they were outnumbered more than three to one by the Japanese. Nimitz's immediate task was to hold the line "at all costs."[4]

This directive had been laid down in one of the first dispatches sent out by Admiral King, who had assumed overall operational command of the navy on 30 December. He chose to be known as Cominch (commander in chief, U.S. Fleet), because he regarded the old Cincus (pronounced Sink us) to be a negative. King, who Roosevelt liked to quip "shaved with a blowtorch," was making a forceful impression at the first wartime Anglo-American staff conference. Churchill had arrived at the Washington meeting determined to ensure that the "Europe first" strategy should be the dominant Allied war priority.

Ernie King was no Anglophile. His prejudices against the overbearing British Admiralty had been forged during World War I when he was chief of staff to Admiral Henry T. Mayo, the commander of our Atlantic Fleet. So King was determined that Britain was not going to dictate the strategic terms of the alliance and promote the Atlantic at the expense of the war in the Pacific. King also realized that winning the war against Japan would depend primarily on naval operations, whereas the army, in its partisan way, believed that Japan could best be defeated *after* beating Hitler in a major land campaign in Europe. When he argued against making the war against Japan the subsidiary theater of operations, King found he was up against more than the British. Admiral Stark supported Marshall's view that "Germany is still the prime enemy, and her defeat is the key to victory."[5]

Even the president endorsed the decision that obliged the Pacific commanders to take second place when it came to allocations of men, ships, and matériel. But King's underlying commitment to the war against Japan was to be a powerful factor in ensuring that Nimitz's requirements were not forgotten. King was a realist. As the Japanese invasion rolled across the Philippines, he saw that MacArthur's predicament could not be resolved by a naval solution. The Pacific Fleet just did not have the strength to battle a relief convoy through to Manila. MacArthur and the army were to bear a bitter grudge against us for letting them down. In the first week of the war it was Marshall and Stimson who reluctantly agreed with Stark to redirect to Australia the convoy of reinforcements that was en route for the Philippines.

King did not enjoy being on the defensive, even though this clearly had to be our first priority in the Pacific theater. His first dispatch to Cincpac outlined Nimitz's twin tasks of "holding the Hawaii-Midway line," and keeping open the sea route to Australia by "covering, securing, and holding the Hawaii-Samoa line, which should be extended to include Fiji at the earliest practicable date."[6]

King's directive made it clear that this was to be no static defense. He instructed Nimitz to conduct raids against enemy forward bases in the Marshall and Gilbert islands besides reinforcing Samoa with a division of marines from the west coast. Implicit in all this was the urgent need to boost general morale.

In three days, thanks to the preparatory studies made for Admiral Kimmel, the Pacific Fleet staff presented Nimitz with detailed proposals for a series of carrier strikes against the Gilberts and Marshalls. These were to be coordinated with the movement of the troop convoys to reinforce Samoa, escorted by carrier *Yorktown,* which had been recalled from the Atlantic.

Nimitz immediately faced opposition from other flag officers at Pearl Harbor. They believed that it was trying to achieve too much with our limited forces. Admiral Bloch, whose responsibility for defending the Hawaiian sea frontier was an essential part of his duty as Fourteenth Naval District commander, argued that it was too risky to attack island bases with carriers whose loss would leave us wide open to a Japanese rampage. Fortunately, this defensive mind set was torpedoed by Admiral Halsey.

Still fuming at the failure of the relief operation of Wake Island, Halsey had returned to Pearl on 8 January. Two days later he arrived at the Cincpac conference to thump the table and call for an end to defeatism and the start of aggressive counterattacks against the enemy. He was the only man in the fleet who could get away with it. Halsey not only enjoyed the reputation of being the navy's leatherbusting carrier commander, but was Nimitz's close personal friend. Nimitz now had his champion. The very next day Halsey's *Enterprise* and Task Force 8 put to sea with orders to join up with *Yorktown.* After covering the Samoan reinforcement, they were to head northwest for strikes against the Gilberts and the Marshalls.

The second American offensive operation of the Pacific war, however, suffered a worse initial setback than the first. *Saratoga* was torpedoed five hundred miles south of Oahu, and the wisdom of Nimitz's decision was thrown open to question. The damaged carrier limped into Pearl, but had to return to the west coast for major repairs. At a single blow, the Japanese had cut our offensive strength by 25 percent. Nimitz demonstrated his mettle by refusing to recall Halsey and cancel the Gilberts raid. But he had to call off *Lexington*'s intended raid on Wake when Task Force 11's oiler, *Neches,* was sunk on 23 January by submarine *I-72.*

No replacement oiler was available. With the U-boats' decimation of our tanker fleet in the blitz on east coast shipping, the fuel situation was to become more critical. This is a measure of how precarious things were during the first months of the war—and it also suggests how much more Admiral Nagumo might have accomplished if he had destroyed Pearl Harbor's exposed oil tanks.

Nimitz's forces were now cut back so sharply that it became more important than ever to know what the Japanese were doing. It was also vital to prevent them from learning about our movements, and on 3 January, Cincpac alerted all commands not to use any codes and ciphers that the Japanese might have captured on Wake Island.

Tense as the war situation was, an easy and informal atmosphere soon prevailed in our daily 0800 intelligence briefing. In addition to the morning session, Nimitz encouraged me to go to his office at any time with new bits of information on a priority basis. Apart from his flag secretary,

I was the only one accorded this privilege. Nimitz clearly appreciated and understood that good intelligence is essential to sound strategic decisions.

"I want you to be the Admiral Nagumo of my staff," Nimitz had told me. "I want your every thought, every instinct as you believe Admiral Nagumo might have them. You are to see the war, their operations, their aims, from the Japanese viewpoint and keep me advised what you are thinking about, what you are doing, and what purpose, what strategy, motivates your operations. If you can do this, you will give me the kind of information needed to win this war."

It was a tall order. We were still breaking into the enemy's main operational code system. But Nimitz would constantly keep me on my toes with questions about possible Japanese reactions to events. My bridge sessions with Admiral Yamamoto and personal knowledge of his staff were useful background, but my main source of information came from Hypo's traffic analysts, who were beginning to get back into their stride with the help of call sign pads salvaged from the downed bombers. This tactical guessing game progressed hand in hand with the efforts that Rochefort and his crippies were making to crack the JN-25 "B" system. First odd words, then phrases, then sentences became intelligible as information was obtained first from the process of decryption of known values, then from cryptanalysis to recover the remaining unknown values. In the case of ciphers, new keys were constantly having to be recovered.

In preparation for the hit-and-run carrier strikes in the Marshalls and Gilberts, Nimitz listed his critical intelligence requirements. We had to track the deployment of enemy carriers and carrier strike forces, the disposition and strength of the Fourth Fleet in the mandates, plus its associated submarine force—the Sixth Fleet. Accurate information was needed on the deployment and strength of the Twenty-fourth Air Force, which was scattered through the Marshalls. Nimitz also wanted to be kept informed of the enemy reinforcements that were likely to reach the area by the end of January.

I was at least able to reassure Nimitz of indications that made another raid on Pearl Harbor seem unlikely. Japan's submarines were being withdrawn from their close-in surveillance and attack missions in Hawaiian waters, and pulled back to distant observation patrols. Our own submarine reconnaissance was producing results by providing some vital intelligence details, for example that there were land-based aircraft operating from Kwajalein's Roi airfield and the auxiliaries massed in the lagoon of the largest atoll in the Marshalls. The move of Vice Admiral Shigeyoshi Inouye's Fourth Fleet units into Truk, 450 miles to the west in the Carolines, was confirmed by radio bearings and traffic routing. Meanwhile, Station Cast reported that the enemy's naval strength in Philippine waters had been reorganized into eastern and western forces, and that a large enemy force was moving southward through the Sulu Sea toward Borneo.

It was inevitable, however, that alternative estimates were made by the three radio intelligence units. The first of these sharp differences of opinion came in January, when Pearl challenged the assumption made by Washington that carriers and battleships were guarding Japan's home islands. Our analysis in Hypo was that the duty had been assigned to vessels that were mostly auxiliaries and patrol craft. Eventually, Rochefort's forecast was proved correct, as was his prediction that the *Kido Butai* was moving in support of the operations in the Dutch East Indies, while the detached Carrier Division 2 was in the vicinity of Truk in support of Admiral Inouye's Fourth (mandates) Fleet.

Positive confirmation of Hypo's inspired traffic analysis came on 16 January when an Australian reconnaissance flight reported twenty naval vessels, mostly destroyers and only a few cruisers, in Truk harbor. Identification of the aerial photographs also provided verification of the specific warship designators in the intercepted radio call signs.

The penetration of the JN-25 code was threatened by the rapidity of the Japanese advances. The British crypto unit had to interrupt its operations briefly and transfer from Singapore to Ceylon to become Station Anderson at Colombo. Station Cast had moved to fortified Corregidor Island's Malinta tunnel before war broke out. By 17 January it circulated on the secure Copek channel some 1,700 new additives, 950 new code group values, and 650 additional indicators. During that week Cast had also been able to provide the outnumbered Asiatic Fleet a warning of the destination, course, speed, and time of arrival of two enemy invasion convoys.

Hypo's dedicated band of crippies, led by Tommy Dyer and Ham Wright, had to rely on the support of only seven language officers to perform the actual translation. The new year did bring additional hands from battleship *California*'s band. When their duty station was sunk, Rochefort and Dyer believed that their musical ability might be useful in working out the chords and syncopations of codes and ciphers.

The bandsmen soon became a vital adjunct of the code-breaking process, taking over the task of running the IBM tabulating machines and transferring the code groups from the intercepts onto punch cards. Their labor was considerable, since each Japanese message required anywhere from seventy-five to one hundred IBM cards, and within a few months they were processing millions of cards every week.

Rochefort sent me up a summary of his daily report, but if there was something of spot urgency or importance, a messenger would bring me a copy of the rough decrypt in its actual state of development with a lot of unfilled blanks. I would then call Joe on our secure telephone line to compare notes on what Japanese words might fit. Whenever possible I would go down to the heavily guarded basement that we called his dungeon to chew over the tidbits that often contributed to the solution of problems.

In mid-January, Hypo was still having to rely heavily on traffic analysis. This formed the basis of Station Hypo's first daily intelligence bulletin that summarized strategic radio intelligence items, and was distributed throughout the Allied commands in the Indian Ocean area. The first issue noted the increase in Truk area radio traffic, coupled with the simultaneous decrease in the Marshalls. This augured well for Halsey and Fletcher, whose task forces were heading for the Marshalls and the neighboring Gilberts. By 18 January, Rochefort estimated that the main strength of an enemy naval force assembling in Truk was preparing to support a movement southward that appeared to be heading toward New Guinea. This key piece of information was derived from a message to a Japanese air unit in the Marshalls—the half-burned call-sign card recovered from the crashed Japanese bomber was again paying handsome intelligence dividends.

At the beginning of the third week in January, Rochefort told me about fragments from three intercepted messages that contained a common code group recovered as *koryaku butai* ("occupation force"). In all three instances the group had been preceded by a code group tentatively identified as the letter *R,* making the fragment "R occupation force." Joe had a hunch that *R* stood for Rabaul, the fine natural harbor at the tip of New Britain. Since the *koryaku butai* code group had appeared previously in messages connected with the occupation of Guam and Wake, it appeared to indicate that the Japanese were about to move south to take over the large island off the southeast coast of New Guinea.

When I reported this to Admiral Nimitz, he realized that although we had no forces with which to frustrate Japan's occupation of Rabaul, neither would they be able to send strong forces in the Marshalls and Gilberts to oppose our carrier raids. Joe, moreover, was right about the *R* meaning Rabaul. On 20 January, the Australians informed us that the Bismarck Archipelago between New Britain and New Guinea was attacked by more than one hundred planes. Carrier Division 1 appeared to be involved, so when the Japanese landings began three days later, we were somewhat relieved to find that the Australian estimate of Japanese forces agreed with our estimates. Admiral King reminded Nimitz of the serious threat that a potential loss of Rabaul posed to our communication line with Australia. King sent a dispatch that urged Nimitz to make sure that the upcoming raid on the Marshalls and Gilberts was driven home hard.

Confidence that we could pull it off increased during the week. Station Cast began sending us the first partially completed JN-25 decrypts. These ordered Carrier Division 2 southwest from the mandates to cover operations off New Guinea.[7] Hypo's traffic analysis, to our relief and joy, also continued to reveal a steady decline in enemy activity in the Marshalls as reports came in from the southwest Pacific of the continued Japanese strikes on the islands off the coast of New Guinea.

Traffic analysis revealed that these operations were being given air support by Carrier Division 2, raising Nimitz's anticipation that the enemy's main striking forces were operating more than two thousand miles away from their bases in the Marshalls and Gilberts. It was even more gratifying to know that the Japanese were about to be caught facing in the wrong direction—just as we had been six weeks earlier at Pearl Harbor.

Japanese army leaders had insisted on carrier support to speed up the southern operations, which were to conclude with the occupation of Java. The generals then wanted to bring their troops north to prepare for a strike against Siberia, since they believed that the Soviet Union was to be defeated by Germany. The naval staff wanted to continue the southward advance by raiding the Australian rear base at Port Darwin so as to cut off the allied forces in Java and "prevent another Dunkirk." The Combined Fleet would then sortie into the Indian Ocean to "draw out, and destroy the British Eastern Fleet."[8]

According to Japan's estimates the attack on Pearl Harbor had forced us to suspend all carrier operations. They considered it safe to send Nagumo's carrier striking force to operate with the Second Fleet to reinforce the landings on the New Guinea coast in the first week of February.[9] Their succession of easy victories had so exceeded expectations that they dismissed the possibility of our undertaking major fleet offensives in less than six months—or even a year.

Because of the speed with which objectives had been achieved, Japanese naval planners were preparing to exploit their advantage by pushing southward toward Australia. The first step in Japan's mushrooming strategic mission was the capture of Rabaul, and the establishment of a base at Kavieng on the adjoining island of New Ireland. Controlling the Bismarck Archipelago would open a northern gateway to the Coral Sea and provide a springboard for the invasion of New Guinea and the Solomon Island chain to the west. Japan would then be in a position to threaten the continent of Australia. Rabaul was the linchpin of this strategy. To ensure its capture, the *Kido Butai* was to sail south to lend its air support to Admiral Inouye's Fourth Fleet, which would sally forth from his base at Truk.

The first symptom of what the Japanese themselves would come to call "victory disease" was their decision to reduce the submarine surveillance of Hawaii and the west coast in favor of attacking Allied shipping in the southwest Pacific. This forced them to rely on radio intelligence for information about our movements. Even with Japan's preponderance of naval strength in the Pacific, they still needed to know what we were doing while their own forces were being so widely spread.[10] Apart from a brief advantage that came from the discovery of some of our ciphers on board the gunboat *Wake*, which they had captured at Shanghai, they had not made any significant penetration of our code traffic.

Meanwhile, concern about the destination of one of our carrier task forces sighted by submarine *I-23* at the beginning of the first week of January had resulted in precautionary alerts to Wake and bases in the Marshalls. An inquiry from the emperor himself sent jitters running through the naval staff in Tokyo, which were increased when a floatplane from another submarine came snooping over Pearl that week to reveal another carrier in harbor.

The Japanese panic subsided somewhat after 12 January, when submarine *I-6* reported sinking *Lexington*. In reality it was the look-alike *Saratoga* that had been torpedoed, but not sunk. Naval intelligence headquarters in Tokyo, however, took the initial report at face value. They assumed we had been reduced to one operational carrier, because they had never discovered that *Saratoga* had been sent out from the west coast. In the absence of any other sightings, and because our two remaining task forces maintained radio silence, naval headquarters concluded that the loss of the carrier had stunned us into canceling all offensive operations!

Tokyo was soon to discover that this was wishful thinking! If Yamamoto had had an intelligence officer on his staff, instead of relying on estimates made by commanders on the spot, the forces under his control might not have succumbed to such a preposterous assumption. Not until after the lesson had been learned six months later at Midway was the first full-time intelligence specialist appointed to the Japanese Combined Fleet.

Around noon on 31 January, the 6th Communications Unit at Kwajalein transmitted a warning that in recent days there had been an increase of a dozen or so new American radio call signs, a sure indication that some kind of offensive action was imminent. But the naval staff in Tokyo did not believe that this report warranted any general alert. The same complacency evidently infected Rear Admiral Sukeyoshi Yatsushiro at his Marshalls Defense Force headquarters on Kwajalein. That evening he threw a large dinner party. The next day he died in the air raid.

Admiral Yatsushiro's failure to call an alert cost him his life—although he was posthumously promoted one rank, because he was the first Japanese flag officer to be killed in action in the Pacific war. Afterward, Yamamoto's staff claimed not to have received the warning. This was "horsefeathers" because superbattleship *Yamato* was moored to its buoy in the Hashirajima fleet anchorage, with direct cable, radio, and telephone connections to Tokyo.

Saké was flowing as Yatsushiro toasted his officers that evening and looked forward to his celebratory dinner and Halsey's task force was charging undetected toward the Marshalls at high speed. A unique experiment was also proving its worth. Flagship *Enterprise* carried a radio intelligence unit borrowed from Station Hypo for the occasion. The unit consisted of a language officer, Captain Bankson T. Holcomb, Jr., USMC, and three radio operators. Halsey had asked Admiral Nimitz for this special capability on the chance that they might overhear enemy transmissions helpful to his attack. Late that afternoon Holcomb heard a Japanese pilot from Taroa reporting that he had reached the end of his patrol sector, was heading back to base, and had "nothing to report."

This crucial piece of information, showing that his ships had not been detected, delighted Halsey. With gusto, he dictated a "Thank you for not spotting us" note and addressed it to the commanding officer of Marshall Islands forces.[11] He had Holcomb translate it into Japanese for mimeographed leaflets, which the attacking planes dropped next day, along with their bombs.

When Halsey flashed the news that morning to Nimitz that the attack had achieved complete surprise, it was clear that the Japanese had been caught more completely off guard than we had dared hope. But our intercept stations soon heard Japanese naval radios crackle into action as the American attack began and radio silence was broken. The Owada communications center tried to communicate direction-finding bearings from Japan, adding to the confusion and slowing up the reaction of the local commands.

For nine hours, starting at dawn, Halsey stretched his luck with a succession of air strikes that shuttled back and forth from *Enterprise* to strafe and bomb the Kwajalein anchorage. Transports were attacked, along with shore installations. The exuberance of the American pilots, taking advantage of their first opportunity to fight, was evident from their excited radio talk: "Ease off to the right. That big one's mine. . . . Get that cruiser heading off to the right! . . . Take 'em home, boys, take 'em home! . . . We sure got that big bastard, didn't we, sir?"[12]

The airwaves were alive with our pilots congratulating themselves. Meanwhile, Rear Admiral Raymond A. Spruance's cruisers *Northampton* and *Salt Lake City* hit Wotje, and Fletcher's *Yorktown* task force, to the south, struck at Makin, Mili, and Jaluit.

"Bingo! Bongo! I got one! . . . I'm all out of ammunition. . . . Who has lots of gas and ammo left? . . . Affirmative from Blue. . . . OK, I will go along. I will pick up that guy yet. . . . From Black—I'm out of ammo, request permission to get some more."[13]

Thirteen American planes were lost and Halsey was impressed by the ferocity and accuracy of the attacking enemy planes. A "Betty" twin-engine bomber tried to crash-dive flagship *Enterprise*. Quick helm action and alert machine-gunners foiled the first would-be kamikaze, which nicked the port edge of the flight deck and toppled into the sea. Heavy cruiser *Chester* took one bomb hit before the strike commander issued a characteristically earthy signal: "Haul ass with Halsey!"

During the long night of retirement, radar operators in *Enterprise* tracked enemy planes groping for contacts. Halsey took advantage of a northeast weather front by steering his force into the protection of its cloud cover and low visibility. American pilots celebrated, entertaining the messes with ebullient reports claiming a submarine, auxiliaries, and even a small carrier. None of this turned out to be true; no Japanese ships were sunk. But the psychological impact of the strikes on the Japanese was just as great as the loss of a capital ship might have been.

"This attack was Heaven's admonition for our shortcomings" was how Captain Yoshitake Miwa, Yamamoto's chief of operations, put it. "Our staff could only grit their teeth and jump up and down in frustration."[14] According to the diary of Chief of Staff Ugaki, who grieved the death of Admiral Yatsushiro, his Etajima classmate, their own "carelessness and stupidity" was to blame. "We were asleep at the switch," he lamented. "To be so completely surprised, long after the start of a war, is incredible."[15]

In a frantic bolting of the stable door after all the horses had fled, on 2 February every Japanese radio intelligence station from Tokyo to Jaluit tried to pinpoint Halsey's elusive task force. Heaping chagrin on mortification, Japanese radio operators heard only American commercial radio broadcasts, announcing somewhat exaggeratedly that Pearl Harbor had been avenged.

After such a debacle, the Combined Fleet staff had good reason to grow jittery about the future. "Now, having learned that the defenses of our advance bases are relatively weak, he will probably continue such attacks in the future," observed Admiral Miwa. "Whatever happens, we must absolutely prevent any air attack on Tokyo. . . . Against enemy aircraft carriers, the defensive is bad strategy, and worse tactics."[16]

The first full month of the war had concluded with a classic demonstration of American resiliency and a vindication of the strategy that Admiral Kimmel had shaped after Pearl Harbor. Nimitz had skillfully used our carriers and radio intelligence to deliver the first American counterpunch. At the same time our raids had exposed the inflexibility of our enemy and their failure to make proper use of intelligence to coordinate their far-flung and overambitious Pacific strategy.

27

Where and When?

IRENS SHRIEKED. Horns and whistles blew. Sailors manned the rail of every ship to welcome *Enterprise* back to Pearl Harbor on the morning of 5 February. Admiral Nimitz was so eager to congratulate his friend Bill Halsey that he did not even wait for a gangway to be secured. A bosun's chair hoisted the Pacific Fleet commander in chief to the hangar deck of the carrier.[1]

Nimitz hopped on board and pumped Halsey's hand, saying, "Bill, it was wonderful, a great job."

Halsey said, "I've got something for you, Chester," handing Nimitz a paper.

"What's this, Bill? It looks like Japanese writing."

Halsey chuckled. "You remember I asked for a language officer. Well, they gave me a marine, and I want you to meet him. Come over here, Captain Holcomb. Tell Admiral Nimitz about this paper."

Nimitz smiled at the account of Halsey's dictating a message to the Japanese commander at Kwajalein, and he doubled up with laughter when he heard how the message was translated, mimeographed, and scattered over the island by our pilots. "Wonderful," Nimitz exclaimed, "a great show all around."[2]

Photographers snapped Halsey's grizzled features, and the press reported his briny remarks. The American public needed a hero, and he was it. His bold strike provided relief from daily headlines, chronicling round after gloomy round of Allied defeat and retreat. Advancing Japanese troops had rolled MacArthur's weary army down the Bataan Peninsula, and invaded Singapore. American and Dutch naval forces were being driven out of the Dutch East Indies.

The morale boost from Halsey's raid was all to the good, but Nimitz knew—from our interception of Japan's own radio reports—that American headlines greatly exaggerated the results. Other advantages accrued

364

from the raid, however. It caused a surge of frantic Japanese radio messages. The increased volume of radio traffic provided our analysts with additional clues toward solving the all-important puzzle of the Japanese geographic designators. Partial recoveries suggested that "A" seemed to represent places in the Hawaiian chain, and "R" prefixed British islands in the South Pacific. The more deeply our naval code breakers unraveled the JN-25 fleet code, the more important became the first two letters when the emerging pattern confirmed that the first letter referred to the territorial area and the second to specific places—it was often the initial of the name or places which had no designators.

"M," from its frequent appearance in radio transmissions originating from units in the Philippines, clearly stood for the whole of that newly conquered territory. We were able to work out that "MM" represented Manila; "MD" appeared to be Davao. Similarly, "R" was Rabaul, "P" the mandated islands; and hence "PP" came out as Palau, "PT" Truk, and "PY" Jaluit. Throughout the spring of 1942 one or more of these geographic designators was being identified almost every day.

Radio intelligence was, of course, a game that two could play, and did. The more Japanese traffic we were able to read, the more we realized that they were making progress identifying our own call signs. This revelation caused a monumental flap. But our best information was that all the compromised calls belonged to shore-based commands, either naval or ones that used adjacent naval base facilities. Admiral Nimitz was particularly concerned about these Japanese recoveries. But I was able to assure him that, from all indications, the enemy had not identified the call signs of any of our seagoing commands. To make the task of Japanese traffic analysts harder, the order went out to cut down unnecessary radio traffic. Shore-based commands that had to issue a great amount of traffic were not to use the same encipherment that was used for highly classified operational traffic.

Nimitz continued to express concern about how much enemy radio intelligence was finding out about us. His questions were always searching, and often led to long discussion of radio communications and intelligence procedures. He insisted that the daily briefings should always tell "who, what, where, when, and why."

Radio intelligence, by its very nature, often led each of our intercept stations to reach differing conclusions. On 5 February, Admiral Stark, who remained chief of naval operations until 26 March, sent a dispatch warning us that Station Negat in Washington had intercepted signals that led the naval staff to believe Japan was planning to attack the New Hebrides, off the southeast coast of Australia.

But Rochefort could find no sign of the move predicted by Washington. My briefing for Nimitz on 6 February, based on the location and currently indicated activities of the major enemy forces, had the main thrust of the Japanese offensives moving toward occupation of Java and

Sumatra. In addition we had discovered a subsidiary operation code-named "MA" for the occupation of airfields and ports in eastern New Guinea and in the Solomons. Their westward shift of submarine forces and a stepping up of activities in the Indian Ocean from a new base at Penang on the northwest coast of Malaya did not suggest any immediate operations in the mid-Pacific.

When I finished this rundown, it came as a big surprise to read the dispatch that Nimitz handed me. Just in from the navy department, this time from Cominch—Admiral King—it confirmed the expectation of an offensive against the Dutch East Indies, but it also alerted us to "expedite dispositions and operations of war forces" to meet "raids against Midway, Oahu, New Hebrides, northeast Australia, and possibly the west coast or the canal."[3]

My reaction was that Washington's evaluation was way off. Perhaps it was prompted by the fear that some spectacular offensive would be launched on 11 February when Empire Day was celebrated to mark the founding of Japan by the Emperor Jimmu. We might anticipate that a few shells could be lobbed ashore from a submarine, but there were no signs of anything as spectacular as a major offense against Australia. King's attitude may well have been colored by the fact that the ANZAC (Australia–New Zealand) area command, established by the Allied chiefs of staff at the Arcadia conference, had been assigned directly to his control. He had activated it on 7 February, under Vice Admiral William F. Leary, after directing Nimitz to send out a heavy cruiser to join the Australian squadron of Rear Admiral John G. Crace, RN.

Nimitz had already sent heavy cruiser *Chicago* and two destroyers to join the Allied force, whose mission was to deter any Japanese moves into the waters west of Australia. But that was not the end of it. King continued to underline the "serious threat to lines of communication with Australia," and at the end of January he ordered Nimitz to send down a carrier task force. Since Halsey and Fletcher were occupied with the Marshalls raid, that left only Admiral Wilson Brown's *Lexington* group free. This move was opposed by most members of Nimitz's staff.

Still Admiral King pressed Nimitz for reinforcements. He sent two more messages on the sixth, warning of an imminent, stepped-up Japanese offensive in the southwest Pacific, accompanied probably by strong raids elsewhere, and calling for Cincpac to take "prompt action to check enemy advance."[4] Before replying to King, Nimitz called a staff conference, at which I repeated my summary of the intelligence situation. The dilemma he faced was how to tell Washington that their intelligence estimate was dead wrong.

The next day Nimitz sent off a tactful but oblique response that "such employment considered inadvisable at present" because our fleet was inferior in all ship types to the enemy and, except for hit-and-run operations, there was little that could be done to "check enemy advance" in the southwest Pacific. Two days later a blistering reply came stating that the "Pacific Fleet not, repeat *not* markedly inferior" because Japan was "committed to extensive operations in the southwest Pacific." Nimitz was ordered by King to review the situation and "consider active operations against Mandates and Wake."[5]

This blast from Washington left Nimitz with limited options. After considering whether to send Halsey's *Enterprise* task force to reinforce Brown's intended strike on Rabaul, he concluded it was tactically sounder to have Halsey join Fletcher's *Yorktown* task force to make another diversionary raid on the mandates. To explain the strategic rationale that prompted his decision and soothe King's ruffled feathers, Admiral Pye was sent posthaste to Washington by navy flying boat.

The spat over the evaluation of radio intelligence, as we were to discover, was the result of changes that were being made in the navy department. Although Stark was to remain as chief of naval operations in an uneasy partnership with King (until Stark's role was absorbed by Cominch at the end of March), King considered he had been given authority by the president and secretary of the navy to make a shake-up that would sweep out the men he considered to be defeatist and whose failures had contributed to the disaster at Pearl Harbor.

The first casualties were to be the directors of naval intelligence and naval communications, who were shortly to be assigned to sea duty. Their memoranda of self-vindication were challenged by Turner who saw eye to eye with King on the need for Cominch to centralize control of the intelligence and code-breaking operation in Washington.

The informal style in which Captain Safford had run the sixty-person OP-20-G organization may have worked in peacetime, but it was less appropriate for coping with the rapid expansion that was necessary in wartime. He wanted to assign even more independence to his friend Joe Rochefort in Station Hypo at Pearl, but this infuriated certain ambitious naval communications officers who, like King and Turner, wanted to keep control of the intercept work in Washington. Foremost among them was Noyes's deputy director of communications, Captain Joseph R. Redman. His brother, Commander John R. Redman, was then one of Safford's deputies in OP-20-G. Their views were shared by Commander Joseph N. Wenger, another high-flying naval communications officer who had been intelligence officer on the Asiatic Fleet staff.

The Redman brothers were adept politicians. They seized on King's arrival to ingratiate themselves by supporting his determination to be master of his own intelligence organization. Safford played into their hands on 23 January when he submitted his proposals to Noyes in response to a directive to all department directors to streamline their organizations. Safford's three-page memorandum, headed "Reorganization of OP-20-G Section," suggested separating responsibility for the security of our code systems from day-by-day cryptanalysis. He also suggested that "certain personnel will be transferred to the CI unit, Pearl Harbor, in accordance with present plans."[6]

Safford's intention to decentralize the intelligence function came under fire three days later. Commander Wenger was convinced that "while security activities can and should be separated from intelligence activities . . . breakup of the latter can only be seriously detrimental to results."[7] It was no accident that the thrust of his proposed reorganization coincided with the ambitions of the Redman brothers and Admiral King.

According to Wenger, the navy department must "assume *active* coordinating control . . . of all intercept stations, D/F nets, and decrypting units [emphasis added]." He proposed a drastic reorganization of OP-20-G, to ensure "a central coordinating authority for all communications intelligence activities," which would restrict Rochefort's Hypo unit in Hawaii. Henceforth, Hypo would "be concerned chiefly with combat intelligence, and . . . the research section in Washington should assist it as much as possible until we can begin to assume the offensive more definitely in the Pacific."[8] To achieve this end, OP-20-G would be reorganized into subsections: Commander John Redman would head a communications combat intelligence section; Wenger would be chief of a communications cryptanalytical section to handle decryption and translation; Safford was to be removed from the day-to-day intelligence process and shifted to an administrative support and cryptographic research role.

Deputy Naval Communications Director Joseph Redman reviewed the conflicting plans on 6 February and gave notice of "a conference on this subject" the following week. But that very day the Redman-Wenger plan was submitted to Admiral King who gave it his immediate approval. Outmaneuvered and outraged, Safford tried to salvage the outfit from dismemberment. In a memorandum eloquent with despair, he conceded the reorganization, but remained adamant in denying that "the senior officers concerned would be utilized to the best advantage."[9] He challenged John Redman's ability for duties beyond the field of his specialization, and proposed that he, not Wenger, be officer in charge of the OP-20-G section.

"I should be logically assigned to cryptological duties as long as I am on active duty," Safford protested, and "respectfully" requested a transfer if his appeal was turned down.[10] It was. Three days later Safford found himself bounced as head of the navy's cryptographic and radio intelligence section, a cause that had occupied most of his thoughts and energies for the past seventeen years.

The relationship of cozy confidence between Negat and Hypo, which depended on the longtime friendship of Safford and Rochefort, was terminated. As the Redman brothers and their supporters moved in to take over OP-20-G, their reorganization made administrative machinery hum more efficiently. But it also destroyed the personal loyalties and relationships that were essential to the creative effort of code breaking. At the same time, the determination of the new regime in Washington to dictate and control the intelligence function brought a clash of jurisdiction and personalities. The result was to exacerbate the inevitable differences in intelligence estimates that emerged with Rochefort at Hypo.

The Japanese were also facing command conflicts in reconciling wartime strategic decisions with intelligence, and were to be repeatedly panicked into wild-goose chases by false estimates they made of our movements. But the alerts ordered for 11 February in both Tokyo and Washington—out of fear that the enemy would make some dastardly attack on Japan's national holiday—proved unfounded. Empire Day passed without any attacks materializing. It was not until three days later that the Combined Fleet was told by Tokyo that the signals announcing the supposed enemy task forces that had brought the most recent panic had been ascertained to be routine radio exchanges between American commercial planes flying west coast routes. Nor was there yet any sign of Cominch's anticipated Japanese offensive in the southwest Pacific.

When Halsey's Task Force 8 sailed from Pearl on 14 February for another raiding operation, Nimitz was relieved to be told that King had finally been won over to our estimates of Japanese strategy. Within hours *Yorktown* was out of Pearl Harbor and setting course west for the Marshalls.

Radio intelligence has never been considered an exact science. Interpretations and deductions drawn from it are sometimes incorrect, tending to undermine its otherwise consistent reliability. As with the baseball player, it's the batting average that counts, and while our own was a long way from perfect, the Japanese average was in the cellar. On 14 February the increase in our voice communications from the Hawaii area prompted another Japanese alert. Three days later two American task forces were divined to be west of Midway and northwest of Jaluit, and the emperor was advised by a nervous navy chief that they might attack the Marshalls by the twentieth—or be off the Tokyo coast by the twenty-third.

One of the things that prompted the Japanese confusion was later discovered to be our profligate use of voice radio in the belief that the range of these high-frequency ship-to-air circuits was limited to the horizon. Only later was it discovered that these transmissions bounced up and down from the Heaviside layer and could skip across the breadth of the Pacific. The Japanese were inclined to jump to conclusions and order alerts too readily. Their radio intelligence center at Owada, however, achieved a good record in deducing whenever our task forces sortied from Pearl Harbor from the increased radio activity when they flew on board their complement of planes. Their conclusions were often reinforced by sightings of our submarines, which they correctly assumed were deployed ahead in target areas to provide weather reports, intelligence data, and "lifeguard services" during actual raids.

So while Tokyo was tracking a nonexistent American striking force heading for the Marshalls—or Tokyo—on 19 February, a sighting from Fourth Fleet headquarters in Truk reported that hostile destroyers had been spotted south of the Carolines. Air searches that afternoon and next morning found nothing. Another false alert had to be canceled. But as fate would have it, the Japanese long-range air patrol from New Britain had chanced upon a real carrier task force. Admiral Wilson Brown in *Lexington* was steaming on a northwesterly course to raid the Rabaul naval base. A Kawanishi "Mavis" flying boat reported at 0830, "Large enemy force sighted 460 miles bearing 76 from Rabaul on course 315."[11]

That sighting report—which was also picked up at Pearl Harbor—stirred up a hornet's nest of activity by the Fourth Fleet after Truk headquarters flashed out immediate orders. Surface ships and submarines were deployed across the line of the American advance, land-based bombers were summoned east from the Marshalls, and Mavis flying boats were ordered to coordinate dawn to dusk torpedo attacks. But because Rabaul's fighters lacked the range, Admiral Inouye had to order undefended bombers "to apprehend the attack and annihilate the enemy force."

That afternoon *Lexington*'s fighters and intense antiaircraft barrage from Brown's cruisers made short work of all but two of the Japanese bombers and three of the flying boats. No damage was inflicted on our ships. The action revealed that the large Mavis flying boats had a distressing tendency to burst into flames when hit. They were henceforth nicknamed by the Japanese as Type I "*Rai-Ta*"—roughly translated as "Zippo lighter."

Admiral Brown, however, had not won the victory, which he had been sent to achieve. Rabaul was now fully alerted. The surprise that was so essential to the success of his mission had been lost. After two fatally hit bombers had tried to crash-dive *Lexington,* he held course northward only until sunset and then ordered a withdrawal. His feint did succeed in a maximum diversionary impact because the Japanese spent two frantic days scouring the seas west of Rabaul for the enemy without result.

Naval intelligence in Tokyo, Admiral Yamamoto's staff, and the commander in chief of the Fourth Fleet were now in a state of confusion and uncertainty. Where might the next raid come? It was clear that the carrier force they had attacked southeast of Rabaul could not be the same one that the Owada radio intelligence center had reported as leaving Pearl Harbor only four days earlier. But by 22 February when extensive air patrols had failed to make any sightings, Admiral Inouye cautiously directed his forces to resume preparation for their southward offensive against Lae and Salamaua. The assault on these two ports on the northeast coast of New Guinea had originally been scheduled for 6 March, but now had to be postponed ten days because the Fourth fleet warships had exhausted so much fuel and time.

The Japanese garrison on Wake raised another false alarm that day. But it was forty-eight hours later, at dawn on 24 February, that the pilots of Halsey's task force delivered their bombs, while the guns of Admiral Spruance's heavy cruisers bombarded the sandy spits of what had recently been a United States outpost. The half-hour raid dazed the enemy and cost him a patrol craft and three flying boats, and damaged buildings. Halsey withdrew to the northeast, having lost just one plane. He was belatedly chased by a flock of Kwajalein-based bombers that failed to score a single hit.

Admiral Nimitz awoke that morning to the news of another Halsey success. He chided me for having overestimated the effectiveness of Japanese air searches. For the third time in less than a month, our surprise attacks had succeeded against an enemy base.

On board Yamamoto's flagship the same news produced a very different reaction. Had not Wake been alerted against just such an attack? Why had the enemy force not been sighted during its approach? Once again an enemy carrier raid had stirred a massive movement of planes from Truk to the Marshalls. Again the Japanese were caught off guard. Yamamoto's chief of staff once again bemoaned their unpreparedness and promised his diary, "Someday, when he has launched his planes and closed in for gun bombardment we'll get him—the golden opportunity to get him will surely come."[12]

A golden opportunity that Japan did not pass up came three days later when their Third Fleet heavy cruisers smashed the remnants of the joint ABDA (American, British, Dutch, Australian) naval force. The Japanese sent five of our cruisers—one American, one British, two Dutch, and one Australian—to the bottom of the Java Sea. A week later, in the mid-Pacific, Japan was going to be presented with another opportunity. This one, had they been more alert, might have had a devastating effect on our strategy.

When Admiral Nimitz signaled his congratulations to Halsey for the successful Wake strike, he added. "DESIRABLE TO HIT MARCUS IF YOU THINK IT POSSIBLE."[13] This was all the encouragement Bill Halsey needed to begin another charge. After refueling Task Force 8, he turned toward that lonely Japanese outpost, six hundred miles northwest of Wake. Marcus Island, only one thousand miles east of the Japanese home islands, was a forward Japanese base from which air patrols covered an important sector of her eastern early warning and defense perimeter.

Yet again there was no warning of Halsey's predawn attack on 4 March. The first *Enterprise* bombs that morning knocked out the island's radio transmitters and power supply. No report of the raid could be sent until makeshift transmitters were rigged. Once more the Japanese defenses had been caught napping. Yamamoto ordered Carrier Division 5 to join a chase that became even more confused and frantic the next day after a false sighting report that enemy ships were heading for Japan's coast. "Small errors cause big trouble," Ugaki observed. "At this pace, they will surely come to Tokyo Bay next."[14]

Meanwhile, we did not shine brightly in our handling of a Japanese move against Hawaii. It was an operation that was intended to bomb Pearl Harbor by using the new Kawanishi H8K long-range flying boats, which had been designed to make the round trip to Pearl from Japan's bases in the Marshalls. Unfortunately for the plan, however, test flights showed that "Emily," as we code-named the twenty-four-ton, four-engine monsters, could not meet its design range. This meant arranging for an operation of refueling from submarines at French Frigate Shoals, at the extreme western tip of the Hawaiian chain.[15]

We might never have learned of these plans if the Japanese had executed the change in their JN-25 additives that had been foreshadowed in a decrypt by Station Cast of 26 February. New tactical call signs came into effect on 1 March, but no changes were noted in the Japanese service call signs or the cipher system.

On 2 March I was able to give Nimitz the good news that not only was there no change, but that Hypo was able to isolate the two-kana designators for all the Japanese submarine tenders. This meant we had located the general operating areas of their submarines. Rochefort also noted that a movement was under way for a "pending offensive operation." What it was Joe could not yet predict, but his cryptanalysts had succeeded in breaking two intercepts. One, dated 12 February, from CinC Fourth Fleet, addressed to "AA" (which was presumed to be Wake Island), was a request to ascertain the number of ships in harbor in "AK." Wake's reply was also translated, leaving us in no doubt about the identity of these two most important geographic designators.

> Referring to Pearl Harbor, no repairs required. Aviation facilities repairs completed. Three battleships present at Pearl Harbor. Repairs impossible to [?, or, are being investigated with regard to ?] Other battleships have returned to the mainland for necessary repairs. [Midget?] submarine base now being established on land. Prisoner[s] to depart "AA" [Wake] on 3 March by air to Yokosuka.[16]

This Japanese signal confirmed Station Cast's previous identifications of "AA" as Wake and "AK" as Pearl Harbor. The prisoners referred to were two American fliers captured during *Enterprise*'s 24 February raid on Wake, information that was immediately relayed to Admiral Halsey.

Another clue that Japan had something afoot and directed toward Hawaii came from direction-finding bearings that placed two enemy submarines east of Midway. Then there was a reference in another signal to a "pending offensive" scheduled for 5 March, which was designated by "K." There seemed little doubt that the operation was to be directed against Pearl Harbor and this time it did not appear that enemy carriers were involved.

Nimitz remarked that intelligence had produced only the "when and where" portion of the problem. He asked my estimate of the "what." I said that since enemy submarines were still active in the Hawaii area, they might use their deck guns in a night shelling of Pearl's oil tanks and airfields. This would follow the pattern of the recent attack on the Ellwood oil fields at Goleta on the California coast on 23 February. I reminded him that Pearl Harbor had been reconnoitered three times in moonlight by small floatplanes from submarines.

Joe had a hunch about a floatplane raid on Pearl launched from *Chitose*-class seaplane carriers. He added that such planes could carry only a small bomb load at long range. Admiral Bloch accordingly put the Fourteenth Naval District air patrols on alert against the possibility of such raid, which would be made more for propaganda than for its military effect.

On 3 March there were no further clues as to the "what," but we received a dispatch from Cominch that "intercepts concerning these movements be most carefully watched and analyzed."[17] It left us wondering why Washington assumed we were *not* watching and analyzing all pieces of this (and every other) radio intelligence puzzle.

At 2100 that same day Station Cast, which was continuing its outstanding decryption work despite the miseries of the constant bombing of Corregidor, gave us more clues. A garbled intercept from Tokyo naval intelligence was readable enough for it to be seen as a reference to the forces in "AH, AFH, and AF areas" involved in the 5 March operation.[18] Rochefort and I agreed that "AH" stood for the Hawaiian Islands. But although "AF" had appeared before in a fragmentary intelligence-type message, this was the first appearance of "AFH." Since "A" appeared to be the prefix for American Pacific possessions, it seemed clear that "AFH" stood for islands in the Hawaiian group, but we had no clue as to which islands it represented.

Cast's message was studied carefully for new clues. Traffic analysis had shown that the association of a submarine force and air commands as addressees in the same message was not entirely unusual. But one of the two air groups in the Marshalls to which it was addressed was known to operate four-engine flying boats. But we blew it.

Neither Rochefort nor I had spotted the one clue that later seemed so obvious—that the "K" operation was derived from the newly proven designator, "AK," for Pearl Harbor. Hypo would also rework on 5 March a new translation of Cast's 3 March message that made it plain that it was referring to their decrypt of our weather forecast for Pearl Harbor.[19] But the revelation came a day and a half too late.

Operation K revealed itself at 0015 on 4 March. The army radar station on Kauai to the west of Oahu reported, "Aircraft bearing 290 true distant 204 miles from Oahu."[20] As the general alert was sounded, torpedo-laden PBYs took off to attack the ships suspected of launching the raiders. Pursuit planes were sent up to give chase but were foiled by a tropical rainstorm that blanked the harbor area. Just before 0200, the population of Honolulu was awakened by the air raid sirens and minutes later explosions were heard to the west of the city.

The intruders escaped undetected; however, there was no apparent damage except to a cluster of algaroba trees on the slope of Mount Tantalus. Fragments of bomb fins and fuses were later recovered and proved to be identical with those dropped in the raid of 7 December. Admiral Nimitz came to my office to see these exhibits. He was accompanied by his staff air officer, Captain Arthur Davis, who was busily explaining that the Japanese had no planes capable of making a roundtrip from Wake, their nearest base, to Oahu.

Nimitz examined the fragments and was told by the bomb-disposal chief that they were Japanese. When the admiral asked if I had any idea how this morning's bombing had been accomplished, I reminded him of the story "Rendezvous" written by Alec Hudson (the pen name of my friend and naval colleague Jasper Holmes who was then working in Hypo), which had appeared the previous August in *The Saturday Evening Post*. It concerned the refueling of American PBYs by submarine at an isolated atoll to increase their range for a special long-distance operation. I told Nimitz I believed that the Japanese had used this idea to get their flying boats in from Wotje in the Marshalls by landing to take on fuel from submarines at the French Frigate Shoals.

Recent direction-finding fixes had indicated that Japanese submarines were operating in the vicinity of the shoals to the northwest of the Hawaiian chain. That morning Nimitz directed Admiral Bloch to send seaplane tender *Ballard*, a converted destroyer, to the French Frigate Shoals under radio silence, to patrol there and deny their future use for such an operation. Later, he had a defensive minefield laid for the same purpose.[21]

The morning after the raid we were dumbfounded by a "Show immediately to Cincpac in person" message from Cominch. It had obviously been sent before King received our report of the attack. It revised Negat's forecast of Japan's possible 11 March raid. The Johnny-come-lately warning that indications of a raid by the Carrier Division 5 "have some foundation and cannot be ignored"[22] must have brought some red faces in Washington when the next batch of decrypts revealed that these carriers were heading southeast from Japan to chase Admiral Halsey, whose raid on Marcus had taken place that morning.

The next three days were to be filled with alarums and excursions for both sides. The final stage of Japan's takeover of the Dutch East Indies began with the invasion of Java. By 8 March the remnants of the Allied forces had surrendered in Bandung. At the same time our radio intelligence detected a growing concentration of naval forces off New Guinea. This pointed to a resumption of their southward move. Air reconnaissance patrols on 6 March confirmed that enemy invasion forces had sailed from Rabaul and appeared to be heading for the twin ports of Lae and Salamaua on New Guinea's southeastern bight, which borders the Solomon Sea. This appeared to be a first step toward the assault and capture of Port Moresby, the administrative capital of Papua, which was New Guinea's nearest point to Australia.

News that the actual landings were under way on 8 March found Admiral Wilson Brown within striking distance. Two days earlier he had joined up with Admiral Fletcher's *Yorktown* task force to make a second attempt to raid Rabaul. *Lexington*'s pilots were raring to have another crack at the Japanese. To Captain Turner Joy, Brown's operations officer, the opportunity to hit back and disrupt an enemy landing was an "answer to prayer."[23] An all-night conference in *Lexington* weighed the alternate risks of hazarding carriers in uncharted waters off western Papua or sending pilots over the fifteen-thousand-foot Owen Stanley mountain range. The latter option was decided on, and the pilots flew off on the tenth, armed with hastily gathered road maps with which to navigate the treacherous cloud-covered passes and peaks.

The raid was coordinated with an attack by Allied bombers from New Guinea land bases. Tropical rainstorms concealed the approach of our air strikes, which roared in just before 0730 to attack ships of the Japanese occupation force with bombs, torpedoes, and strafing runs. Of the eighteen ships present, four were sunk and thirteen damaged. The Japanese navy suffered its heaviest losses of the war, and the raid forced a badly shaken Admiral Inouye to postpone his assault on Port Moresby from early April to early May because of the need for repairs and for carrier support.[24]

The delay was to cause the first significant hesitation in Japan's southward march of triumph. When Inouye attempted to resume the advance two months later, our forces were in position to turn the hiccup of Lae and Salamaua into a full-blown case of strategic indigestion. Japan's progress toward Australia was halted.

The temporary setback to their New Guinea campaign was a shock to imperial general headquarters. Naval intelligence issued a dispatch that same afternoon forecasting that "in addition to offensive moves against Rabaul and Truk, the enemy plans surprise attack on Tokyo or the Bonin Islands."[25] To guard against this possibility, air and naval units were recalled to defend the approaches to Japan. It also brought a jittery series of alerts as the naval headquarters in Tokyo responded to fears of the national disgrace should American carrier planes manage to drop a single bomb on the sacred soil of the home islands.

Rochefort was soon reporting that radio intelligence showed that the Japanese were reacting to the increase in our patrol activity in the

Hawaiian area. Decrypts of the messages flashed out by their Owada center indicated their concern that "an enemy force has sortied," and the presence of our submarines in Japan's coastal waters suggested "that the enemy is planning something aggressive, possibly an air attack on Japan's home islands." Combined Fleet units raised steam "to take appropriate measures to cope with the situation."[26] Carrier Division 5 was recalled to assist.

The streams of such urgent anticipatory messages between Japanese naval commands were being intercepted by Station Hypo, decrypted, translated, encoded in our secure communications channels, and disseminated within six hours of Japanese transmission. It was a dramatic demonstration of the progress that Rochefort's team had made in penetrating the enemy's operational ciphers. We were puzzled by the flood of messages that showed the increase in Japan's air and submarine searches and the concentration of naval forces in the approaches to Tokyo Bay. Joe observed that this renewed concern with the defense of their home waters was "creating more panic than seems reasonable." Admiral Nimitz was intrigued by Rochefort's theory that our carrier raids were paying such unexpected dividends that the Japanese were redeploying their forces against a "nonexistent force."[27]

The diary of Yamamoto's chief of staff confirmed that Rochefort's analysis was correct. Ugaki was complaining that it was "irksome" to be on the defensive in the midst of victory. "Today Japan is celebrating the fall of the Netherlands East Indies," Ugaki wrote on 12 March while units of the Combined Fleet screening force sortied to defend Tokyo against another imaginary American raid. "I can't help but shudder at the thought of enemy aircraft attacking masses of our rejoicing people celebrating a great victory."[28]

The overreaction of the Japanese navy's radio intelligence center, and the consequent wild-goose chases by the Combined Fleet, wasted enormous reserves of fuel. It also caused unnecessary wear and tear to the machinery of their warships and to their morale and self-confidence. All this had been achieved at little cost to us. The damage we had inflicted may have been military pinpricks, but each attack put mounting pressure on the Japanese to turn the tables and "make face" for previous failures.

A major reason for the success of Nimitz's strategy was this: In just three months we had established a reliable basis for tactical and strategic intelligence to support the Allied war effort in the Pacific. It was our ability to intercept and break significant portions of the enemy's operational traffic that gave us the edge.

What was to turn out to be the most significant bit of intelligence of all—though we did not appreciate it at the time—was uncovered in a 9 March message from Tokyo addressed specifically to air group commanders in the mandates. It gave a two-day forecast of wind force and direction at "AF." Since the local submarine commander was not an addressee of this message as in the previous ones, Rochefort interpreted the intended targets of Japanese air attack as being our island bases within range of the Marshalls. It was our very first inkling that "AF" could be Midway.

28

"A Bungling Attack Is Better Than the Most Skillful Defense"

O N 11 MARCH 1942, the day after Halsey's task force had returned from the raids on Wake and Marcus islands, Admiral Nimitz received another alarm from Admiral King. A secret and personal dispatch warned "that recent enemy air and submarine activities may well indicate another full-scale effort against the Hawaii-Midway line with the likely principal objective of crippling or destroying our vital base at Pearl Harbor."

King's "strong" belief that an attack requiring Nimitz's "unremitting supervision of readiness" was the result of naval intelligence putting two and two together and making five—again.[1] It appears that Captain Redman and Commander Wenger had linked a decrypt about the intended changes in the JN-25 additives with a misreading of Rochefort's "AF" weather decrypt. The result was their belief that the Japanese were about to strike us once more in the mid-Pacific. King was especially concerned that "attempts at long-range bombing of the Hawaiian Islands may be planned."[2]

But our estimates of the same decrypts pointed to an opposite conclusion. Japan appeared committed to the southward movement through New Guinea and was sending her main striking forces into the Indian Ocean. Confirmation of this came on 12 March from the British at Station Anderson in Colombo. Their analysis had ascertained the arrival of a carrier at Singapore to cover the invasion of the Andaman Islands south of Burma. The analysis reported that Japanese "operations now appear a full-scale one, and possibly a prelude to further western advance."[3]

None of the Allied intercept stations, however, revealed the extent to which the Indian Ocean operation, originally scheduled to begin on 15 March, had been delayed by a month after the Combined Fleet sortied in response to the false report of American carriers off Wake. So the Cincpac intelligence bulletin that I issued the next day reported that Carrier Division 5 and two submarine squadrons were "expected to operate in Malay area and Indian Ocean."[4]

This was the first of the daily summaries of enemy movements that King had authorized Nimitz to issue. Other bulletins superseded the Hypo summary and they were radioed in code to all commands. They were intended to convey the gist of our latest radio intelligence estimates without making direct reference to the sources of the information. This information was confined to the exchanges among our stations in cipher on the Copek circuits; derivative information for other commands and task forces was confided to less secure ciphers without disclosing the source, as and when appropriate.

Guarding the security of our radio intelligence network now became a major concern. During the final stages of the battle for the Philippines, as the Japanese relentlessly drove MacArthur's forces down to the dead end of the Bataan Peninsula, Cominch ordered the evacuation of all members of Station Cast. If any one of these men fell into enemy hands he would be tortured to reveal details of American code breaking. King regarded the unit to be "of such importance to the successful prosecution of the war in the Far East" that "to preserve its continuity" advanced plans had been made for its safe withdrawal by "any means of transportation."[5] A three-stage evacuation by submarine was planned so that each unit—consisting of linguists, cryptanalysts, radiomen, and equipment—could continue to operate independently of the others.

The first group of four officers, thirteen enlisted men, and equipment left Corregidor on 5 February 1942 in submarine *Seadragon*. On 11 March thirty more left for Australia on board *Permit*. (This was five days after General Douglas MacArthur put to sea from embattled Corregidor to make his escape by PT boat.) Three officers and eighteen men remained working without respite in the Malinta Tunnel until the early hours of 8 April. Under merciless bombardment that caused the American forces on Bataan to surrender later that day, they were ferried out to *Seadragon* and survived a prolonged depth-charge attack en route to Fremantle on the west coast of Australia.

On 16 March, while the second group of cryptanalysts was awaiting its turn to be evacuated, Station Cast relayed a worrying decrypt indicating that Tokyo naval intelligence was disseminating the call signs of our units. The call signs were so accurate we feared that they might have captured one of our call-sign books. The following day Hypo confirmed the bad news that "enciphered calls as given by Tokyo for the 16th indicate he has a copy of our Call Sign Publication #1161."[6]

This dispatch caused a real flap. It reinforced the principle laid down by the office of naval operations of "maintaining maximum security by minimum distribution."[7] Postwar evidence confirmed that the Japanese had obtained a copy of one of our old communications manuals that spelled out the three-tier system of our letter-numeral-letter designators for commanders and the three-letter indicators for our principal shore bases. From the manual the Owada analysts had been able to work out the structure of our naval communications system and were almost as good at keeping track of our call signs as we had become at keeping up with theirs.

Call signs were one thing, but intensive checking at Hypo and Negat provided no evidence that they were breaking any substantive messages in our ciphers. We, however, were making steady progress penetrating theirs. That is why Nimitz was able to endorse my bulletin of 18 March dismissing Washington's week-old alert against Japanese attacks in the mid-Pacific. It stated, "No indication of immediate major offensive action except in Malaya area."[8]

While Nimitz's steadfast confidence in his intelligence outfit saved the fleet from dashing off in response to every one of Washington's nervous twitches, he could not ignore the strategic directions of Cominch. On 19 March he learned for the first time that he was expected to assign one third of our entire Pacific carrier forces to a risky operation that had been cooked up in the navy department. That Thursday, Captain Donald B. Duncan arrived at Pearl Harbor on a top-secret mission. King's air officer had come to tell Nimitz that he had been given charge of one of America's biggest gambles of the war—an operation to bomb Tokyo itself.

The plan to strike the Japanese homeland had its genesis in a discussion two months earlier in which Admiral King reviewed, with Duncan and his war plans officer, Captain Francis S. "Frog" Low, ways to hit back at the Japanese. Nimitz had been directed to make carrier strikes against Japan's forward island bases. But King wanted a more dramatic demonstration that the navy was able to counter Japan's cataract of victories. Something was needed to shake enemy morale and provide a boost for sagging American morale. The ideal thing, they agreed, would be some kind of attack on Japan's sacred home soil.

Radio intercepts and American submarine sightings had shown that Japan had land-based planes reconnoitering to seaward, and a string of picket boats on patrol, as much as five hundred miles off her southeastern coasts. Our navy Dauntless bombers lacked sufficient range for a seaborne launch, because the carriers would have to be brought so close that they ran the risk of being sunk, like *Repulse* and *Prince of Wales,* by a massive land-based air attack. The army's B-25 medium bombers had range enough, but could they be launched from carrier decks?

King directed Duncan and Lowe to look into the possibilities and discuss them with General Hap Arnold. Within a week they reported that B-25s could do it, and that Arnold was willing and eager to organize and equip the necessary planes and crews. Preparations of B-25s and crews from the 17th Bombardment Group, USAAF, were begun under Lieutenant Colonel James H. Doolittle at Eglin Field, Florida. Lieutenant Henry F. Miller, USN, instructed the pilots in short-takeoff techniques, using an airstrip on which the outline of a carrier flight deck was painted, somewhat elongated to allow for the wind generated by the forward motion of the ship.

Specially modified medium-range bombers would cross the Pacific by aircraft carrier to a point close enough for them to launch, strike targets in Japan, and cross the East China Sea to airfields in eastern China. While the crews trained, negotiations were carried on for Chiang Kai-shek's approval and cooperation. The secrecy of the mission was so tight that the Chinese were not given specific details and no part of the planning was committed to writing.

The B-25 crews were still in training at Eglin Field on 19 March when Captain Duncan arrived at Pearl Harbor to brief Nimitz on the plan, which had just been endorsed by the newly instituted Joint Chiefs of Staff, whose responsibility was the overall military direction of the war. With army bombers filling *Hornet*'s flight deck her own planes could not be used for air patrol, so Nimitz was directed to assign that job to carrier *Enterprise* of Halsey's Task Force 8.

When Duncan had completed his presentation, Nimitz spoke to Halsey. "Do you think it will work, Bill?"

"They'll need a lot of luck."

"Are you willing to take them out there?"

"Yes, I am."

"Good!" said Nimitz. "It's all yours,"[9]

Task Force 8 sailed from Pearl Harbor 8 April for an ocean rendezvous with *Hornet*, which had left San Francisco six days earlier, carrying sixteen B-25s lashed down on her deck. Code-named Task Force Mike, the combined group plowed through heavy North Pacific seas on the final leg to reduce the chance of detection. Once the carriers had rendezvoused without a hitch, Nimitz's enthusiasm for the operation increased, encouraged by intelligence intercepts that detected no signs of increased air activity off Japan's east coast.

The gamble of risking two precious carriers to this venture, at a time when we had so few, still made him uneasy. But his fears were lessened by Rochefort's radio intelligence briefs, which indicated that the Japanese were preparing to resume operations in the southwest Pacific for an "RZP" campaign. Rochefort tentatively identified the RZP target as being in the Port Moresby area at the southern tip of New Guinea. "Numerous indications which point to impending offensive from Rabaul Base," Joe reported on 3 April. Four days later we knew that repairs on *Kaga* were being rushed ahead so that the carrier could "participate in the RZP campaign."[10]

The locations of American and Japanese carriers were of critical importance in the strategic picture at this juncture. With two carriers in the North Pacific committed to the Tokyo raid, and *Lexington* in dry dock for overhaul at Pearl, Nimitz had only one carrier task force left, and it was cruising in the Coral Sea. Its mission was to prevent southward advances by the Japanese in that area. For the present there was no doubt that the main enemy naval power was being committed to the Indian Ocean. On 5 April the *Kido Butai* raided the British Far East naval base at Colombo, and Trincomalee four days later, sinking a carrier and cruiser. The Japanese occupation of the Andaman Islands and cruiser strikes against merchant shipping in the Bay of Bengal forced the numerically inferior British fleet to beat a strategic retreat from Ceylon to the African port of Mombasa. It left the Japanese in total control of the Indian Ocean.

The American army suffered the biggest defeat in its history when Bataan fell on 9 April. In the midst of these gloomy events, Nimitz's burdens were vastly increased in March by the Joint Chiefs' reorganization of the command structure in the Pacific, which divided responsibility between Nimitz and General Douglas MacArthur in Australia, who assumed the additional title of Commander in Chief of the Southwest Pacific Area (Cincsowespac). MacArthur was put on a par with Admiral Nimitz, whose official designation now was Commander in Chief Pacific Ocean Areas (Cincpoa) as well as Commander in Chief Pacific (Cincpac).

The 160th meridian marked the official dividing line between the two Allied commanders; accordingly, Cincpac was assigned the Allied naval forces in the eastern approaches to Australia, including the Coral Sea. On 14 April, Nimitz informed Admiral Fletcher that he had assumed command of the South Pacific area from King. Task Force 17 was to proceed to our Tongatabu base south of Samoa for replenishment in order to be back on station in the Coral Sea by the end of the month when the RZP operation against Port Moresby was anticipated to commence.

The need for haste was endorsed by the relay of a British decrypt on 15 April which indicated that the Japanese striking forces were leaving the Indian Ocean and that Carrier Division 5 was to be detached "proceeding to Truk, arriving about 28 April."[11] This message, and Rochefort's report of continual southward movement of Japanese air units and supplies, revealed to Nimitz that "an offensive in the southwest Pacific is shaping up."[12] At his 17 April staff conference, Nimitz reviewed the intelligence picture in great detail. What concerned him was when Japan's southward operation could be expected to resume, and how far it would extend. Station Belconnen, the code name assigned to the evacuated Cast cryptanalysts now in Melbourne where they had joined forces with the Australian navy's radio intelligence team, gave one estimate of 21 April. But we considered this to be too early, since we judged that the Japanese could not have all their forces in place until early May. Australian reports of intensifying air attacks on Port Moresby clearly showed that it was the main Japanese objective. Nimitz was determined to block them.

"We are trying to get together a force to oppose [it]," Nimitz reported to King. "Task Force 17 [Fletcher] will be ready; Task Force 11 [Fitch] and Task Force 8 [Halsey] are otherwise committed." With *Yorktown* in the Coral Sea vicinity; *Lexington* just two days out of Pearl, heading south; and *Hornet* and *Enterprise* on their way to raid Tokyo, Nimitz regarded it as essential to remind Cominch of the possibility that our carrier forces would find themselves outnumbered two to one. It was a measure of King's concern that he took the unusual step of directly requesting Station Hypo's analysis of the situation. King's request was unprecedented. It was the only time he ever went directly to Rochefort for information. "We were a little surprised," Joe was to recall, "that he would ask us what our views were. I personally felt that he was not even aware of our existence."[13] Rochefort later joked about King's having gone over my head.

Rochefort's reply was completed and on its way within six hours, with an information copy to Cincpac. The Hypo team consensus made five main points: (1) Indian Ocean operations by the Japanese were now concluded. (2 and 3) There were two other offensives planned for eastern New Guinea and the Coral Sea. (4) No evidence had emerged that Japan intended to invade Australia. (5) Another Pacific operation was being planned whose objective and details had yet to become clear. The same day Rochefort's team discovered that the light carrier whose name we were erroneously reading as *Ryukaku* (actually it was *Shoho*) was assigned, along with a cruiser division, to cover movements into the Rabaul area.[14] This further increased the tense atmosphere in Washington, and Nimitz warned King that "Cincpac will probably be unable to send enough force to be sure of stopping the Jap offensive."[15]

The enemy operation that was causing us so much concern marked the opening of the *second* phase of Japan's grand strategy. It was really a compromise that resulted from a long-running debate about how Japan was going to achieve her war objectives. The first phase, which had called for the surprise attack on Pearl Harbor as a diversion to the capture of the Philippines, Malaya, and the Dutch East Indies, was well on the way to being fulfilled. However, the American carrier strikes had demonstrated the fallacy of the hoped-for "invincible strategic position for Japan."

The original goal of the second phase had been the consolidation of Japan's island defense system in the Pacific for operations against the American fleet. After "a strategic situation of long-term invincibility" had been established according to the Japanese strategic master plan, the plan's ambitious third phase called for the "capture of Hawaii and the outlying islands, attack on the United States, Canada, Panama Canal, as well as against Central America until the United States loses its fighting spirit and the war can be brought to a conclusion."[16]

Yamamoto, who had always regarded the original war plan's "wait-in-ambush" policy for the American fleet as self-defeating, had wanted to cash in on the supposed success of Pearl Harbor by revising the second phase. He wanted to remove the threat posed by Allied bases in Australia. But in January the army staff had opposed the plan to invade the northern and eastern part of Australia because of the tremendous resources of shipping and troops this would demand. They compromised on a plan that was intended to achieve the same effect by strangling the lines of communication between Hawaii and Australia by seizing the islands of Fiji, Samoa, and New Caledonia.

Yamamoto and his Combined Fleet staff, after concluding that it was necessary to knock out only the Allied bases in the southwest Pacific islands, proposed opening the second phase with the capture of Ceylon, New Guinea, and Port Darwin in northern Australia. The army staff refused to yield on the Australian adventure and opposed the invasion of Ceylon as premature. But imperial general headquarters agreed to extend the first phase in their 29 January directive. It authorized the Combined Fleet to assault and occupy, as soon as feasible, the Lae and Salamaua bases in New Guinea, Tulagi in the Solomon Islands, to be followed by the capture of Port Moresby.

Yamamoto, however, refused to give up. He interpreted these operations as "preliminary moves to the invasion of Australia or interruption of communications between the United States and Australia."[17] The American carrier strikes of February and March burned the fingers, but not the ambitions, of the Combined Fleet staff. But the raids provided them with the rationale for a makeshift plan of attacking Midway: It would entice the American carriers out from Pearl Harbor to their destruction. Yamamoto's staff argued that such an operation would not only be feasible for the second phase but that a "continued initiative," including an assault on Hawaii, was now essential to ensure "a short decisive war."[18]

On 3 April Yamamoto sent Commander Yasuji Watanabe, his persuasive staff gunnery officer, to sell his draft to the naval staff in Tokyo. The war plans section charged that the Midway operation would be too dangerous. It might not succeed in luring out the American carriers. They insisted on the occupation of the southwest Pacific islands to cut Australia off from the United States. Commander Watanabe, seeing no hope of changing the mind set at headquarters, appealed over the heads of his opponents directly to Vice Admiral Seiichi Ito, the deputy chief of the naval staff. Yamamoto's former chief of staff agreed to intercede. The wrangling continued for three more days until Watanabe phoned his chief to report the impasse. Yamamoto's mind was "firmly made up," however, and there was no change in his views. Admiral Shigeru Fukudome took Yamamoto's implicit threat of resignation as the signal for him to capitulate. He turned to Ito. "Since the CinC is so set on it, shall we leave it to him?" The deputy chief nodded without speaking and a compromise was hammered out that same day.[19]

Yamamoto got his Midway operation, and Fukudome got his occupation of Fiji and New Caledonia, but only the destruction of facilities on Samoa. Japan's second operational phase was scheduled to begin on 7 May with the capture of Port Moresby. Midway and the Aleutians were slated for assault a month later. By the third week in July the operations to secure the southwest Pacific islands were to be completed. After reaching agreement with the Combined Fleet, the naval staff managed to persuade the initially reluctant army leaders that the Midway operation did not necessarily commit them to the occupation of the Hawaiian Islands. But the capture of the Aleutians was deemed essential to prevent their being used as bases for long-range air strikes against Tokyo.

Imperial general headquarters gave its final approval to the operational schedule on 15 April after the chief of the naval general staff, Admiral Nagano, obtained the emperor's sanction for the second-phase objectives. Any lingering dissension over the Midway operation was quelled three days later when, for the first time in her long history, an enemy force struck at the heart of Japan.

The Combined Fleet was now about to pay the price for its previous bouts of jumpiness. This time there was not even a false alarm that two American carriers were less than a thousand miles off the Japanese coast. And this time Japanese radio intelligence failed to appreciate evidence that *was* available.

On the day *Enterprise* set sail to rendezvous with *Hornet,* Tokyo radio intelligence reported, "Many patrol aircraft appeared in the Pearl Harbor area on 9 April." Nothing was made of this, nor was any increased alert ordered after analysis of patrol plane traffic indicated that "a strong enemy surface force" was apparently operating south of the Aleutians. Also overlooked or ignored was another radio intelligence warning that "there has been steadily increasing activity of enemy submarines off the approaches to our main islands."[20] Both Combined Fleet flagship and the headquarters of the Fifth Fleet, which had the prime responsibility for defending the home islands, received these reports. But after the recent siege of jitters neither command was ready to order another false alert on such slender evidence.

Nevertheless, Halsey's plan, to launch bombers on the afternoon of 18 April at a distance of five hundred miles from the coast, was knocked into a cocked hat when his radars pierced the early-morning blackness 700 miles off the Japanese coast to detect two vessels of the naval picket line. The task force altered course to avoid them, and launched scout planes at first light. Some 40 miles ahead of the task force they sighted a picket boat which, before being sunk, reported to Tokyo that she had spotted the planes.

Halsey knew that full surprise was probably lost but decided, with Doolittle's concurrence, to launch as soon as the B-25s could be readied. "Good luck and God bless you!" Halsey flashed to *Hornet,* just before Doolittle lifted his twin-engine bomber off the bucking carrier's flight deck at 0725. Within an hour the last of the sixteen planes were Tokyo-bound. Halsey hauled course 90 degrees and, still keeping radio silence, raced northeastward at twenty-five knots.

Our intercept stations heard a Japanese picket boat reporting, "THREE ENEMY PLANES, COURSE SOUTHWEST."[21] Four hours later, when Doolittle's bombers roared in over noontime Tokyo, our radio listening posts actually picked up the wail of air raid sirens on the civilian Radio Tokyo broadcast. The planes stirred up a hornet's nest of plain-language contact reports and a flurry of alert orders to warships. Cincpac informed Halsey of "considerable 5th Fleet activity," including Japanese warships ordered out in search of "three U.S. carriers and two cruisers."[22] Halsey's own radio intelligence unit in the flagship also kept him informed of Japanese stirrings, and he was able to show his furious pursuers a clean pair of heels.

"Abruptly the air became tense at headquarters," recorded Admiral Matome Ugaki with uncharacteristic understatement after the picket boats had raised the alarm.[23] Yamamoto immediately grasped the urgency of the situation and made the urgent signal, "ENEMY TASK FORCE CONTAINING THREE AIRCRAFT CARRIERS AS MAIN STRENGTH SIGHTED 0630 THIS MORNING 730 MILES EAST OF TOKYO. . . . OPERATE AGAINST AMERICAN FLEET."[24]

A submarine squadron en route to Truk was diverted to make a sweep to the north of the Bonin Islands. Another patrol five hundred miles out from Honshū was ordered to intercept and attack the enemy carriers. In the Combined Fleet home anchorage at Hashirajima, boiler-room gangs in battleships, cruisers, and destroyers labored to raise steam and head out through the Inland Sea to give chase. A thousand miles to the northwest, Admiral Nobutake Kondo ordered his cruiser force out of Yokosuka.

The nearest warships were two armed merchant cruisers. They raced out into the Pacific, but failed to make any contact, and poor visibility hampered the land bombers that by midmorning were scouring the seas hundreds of miles offshore. So great was Japanese optimism about this massive air search's making contact that the one flight of thirty bombers that took off shortly after midday was ordered "AT APPROXIMATELY 1600 . . . MAKE TORPEDO ATTACKS."[25]

Nerves at Japanese headquarters were frayed that evening after all planes returned to base without reporting any sightings. Six months earlier Admiral Yamamoto had written to the navy minister of his fears that a surprise air attack on Tokyo would turn public opinion against the navy. So the next day almost every warship that Japan could muster, from the home islands to the Marianas and the Marshalls, was committed to the hunt. It even included the carrier striking force returning from the Indian Ocean. Even Soviet freighters north of Japan were stopped and boarded in case they had picked up ditched American fliers. Not until darkness fell over the northern Pacific two days after the raid did Yamamoto issue the order, "CEASE OPERATIONS AGAINST AMERICAN FLEET."[26]

The effects of the raid were not momentous, nor commensurate with the American risk of two of our four precious aircraft carriers in the Pacific. Military and utility installations in four Japanese cities were targeted. But the modest load of four five-hundred-pound bombs carried by each of the thirteen B-25s assigned to Tokyo could not inflict any really significant damage. The other three planes assigned to Nagoya, Kobē, and Osaka carried only incendiary bombs.

A school had been inadvertently struck, and a total of twelve people killed, fifty houses and shops demolished, and the bow of a warship in dry dock damaged. There was no significant military damage. The real impact of the attack was psychological: to boost American morale and dent that of the Japanese. That it succeeded was indicated by such triumphant headlines in the United States as JAPAN BOMBED, DOOLITTLE DOOED IT and the outrage expressed in Japanese newspapers that innocent schoolchildren had been "murdered" by the enemy fliers. Four American airmen were killed in crash landings of our planes in China, and three who were captured were later tried and executed after a show trial in Tokyo.

The frantic air and sea searches had not produced so much as a single clue concerning the size of or the direction taken by the American carrier task force. The Japanese embarrassment was greatly enhanced and the cataclysmic emotional shock the raid inflicted on the naval staff was aggravated because, as Ugaki put it, "we were not able to strike one blow in retribution."

"Even though there wasn't much damage, it's a disgrace that the skies over the imperial capital should have been defiled without a single enemy plane shot down," Yamamoto wrote. "It provides a regrettably graphic illustration of the saying that a bungling attack is better than the most skillful defense."[27]

It was not only Yamamoto and his immediate Combined Fleet staff who were mortified by the raid. So were the upper echelons of the Japanese naval staff in Tokyo, who shared the sense of personal disgrace that resulted from the public having witnessed enemy planes winging over the imperial palace. Most important of all, the naval staff resolved that they must save face. First by tightening up defenses to prevent any repetition, but also by some retributive mission against the United States carrier task forces that had poked such a painful thorn in the national pride. As Ugaki saw it: "This brings up the necessity for fundamental changes, from now on, in our plans and countermeasures."[28]

Those fundamental changes were to have such a far-reaching impact on the future course of the Pacific war that the Halsey-Doolittle raid must never be dismissed as having been militarily useless. This is borne out by the official history published by the Japan Defense Agency that assigns the raid a far greater impact than any of us at Cincpac could have calculated. The record said the raid:

1. Caused great morale problems to the Japanese.
2. Caused the military to lose face, for they had said that Tokyo would *never* be bombed.
3. Caused diversions of Japanese forces—a fact that most historians overlook.
4. Caused the Japanese army to jump on the bandwagon for *Midway*.
5. Aligned the imperial general headquarters unreservedly behind Combined Fleet's Midway-Aleutian operation plan.

It was the eventual failure of Japan's Midway plan that put the Japanese navy on the strategic defensive (with the sinking of their four finest frontline carriers), and cost them the initiative in the war.

29

Fog of Battle

A S HALSEY WITHDREW from Japanese waters, we were able to follow the frantic air and sea search for his task force. Since we knew the Combined Fleet's objective, and because every available ship was pressed into the futile hunt, the radio traffic brought a bonus of intercepted messages that updated and confirmed the latest call signs of ships and shore stations.

Once we knew that Halsey's carriers were safe, Nimitz's staff conferences were occupied with considering how best to deploy our forces to meet the impending Japanese offensive in the southwest Pacific. One unexpected outcome of the Tokyo raid was that so many enemy units would have to return for replenishment after chasing Halsey that their next operation would be delayed.[1]

"We are taking steps to oppose Japan's expected move in the southwest Pacific," Nimitz recorded in the daily headquarters summary. His main worry was whether we would "be able to send enough forces to be *sure* of stopping the expected Jap offensive [emphasis added]."[2] The delay, however, brought our evaluation into line with Washington's estimate that the attack would commence in the first week in May. Admiral King was breathing down our necks. Hardly a day passed without some chivvying message.

On 20 April, Nimitz discussed "ways and means to deal with the expected Japanese offensive in the southwest Pacific." Australian naval intelligence had reported an intensification of air surveillance in the northern sector of the Coral Sea. Orders were flashed out to *Lexington* for Admiral Fitch's Task Force 11 to make for the southwest Pacific. That evening a dispatch from Washington informed us that a joint army-navy committee was studying Pacific logistics. "So are we," Nimitz noted laconically in his daily log.[3]

The next day the British reported that a cruiser division, and a carrier whose name ended in *kaku,* were scheduled to be in Truk by 25 April.[4] A Belconnen decrypt from Australia alerted us that the Japanese had scheduled 1 May for the introduction of a new operational cipher. This was sure evidence that major operations would soon follow.[5]

I summarized the intelligence picture on 22 April at one of the most critical Cincpac staff meetings of the war by saying: "There are many indications that the enemy will launch an offensive in the New Guinea-New Britain-Solomon area." All the signs showed that it would "start very soon."[6] I believed that our chance was coming to turn the tables on the enemy. As long as they were flushed with victory, their efficiency would remain high. But I predicted from my experience with the Japanese character that once they had suffered a major setback, they would be forced to improvise, and morale and fighting efficiency would fall.

According to my estimate, the enemy's plan was an amphibious operation to complete the takeover of New Guinea and the adjacent islands. I warned the staff not to underestimate what it would take to stop this offensive. Excellence of naval planning and training had been demonstrated in the attack on Pearl Harbor. Their army was no less effective. Their long war in China had shown that it had been trained to reach its objectives against fierce opposition, over impossible terrain. Their soldiers were able to survive on a few handfuls of rice a day. Malaya and the Philippines had shown that the Japanese were able to accept heavy losses from gunfire and drownings during an assault and still achieve their goals.[7]

Radio intelligence had as yet revealed only sketchy details of the impending operation. But I was able to tell Nimitz and his staff that they might deploy as many as 5 carriers, 1 battleship, 5 heavy cruisers, at least 4 light cruisers, 12 destroyers, and more than a dozen submarines. In addition, their air strength in the southwest Pacific might run to 135 land-based bombers, plus the same number of fighter planes and at least 100 reconnaissance aircraft. The springboard of the southward thrust appeared to be their heavily fortified base at Truk in the Carolines where I estimated that as many as twenty-thousand troops were ready to sail.

Against the Japanese advantages of superior carrier strength and land-based airpower, we could count on radio intelligence to reveal direction and deployment. This was the crucial factor that persuaded Nimitz to commit his outnumbered forces to stopping the Japanese advance toward Australia. But since his primary duty was to guard the Hawaiian Islands and protect the Pacific route to Australia, Nimitz needed to be certain about the direction and scale of the enemy offensive before deploying all of our task forces against it. Would they go for Port Moresby only, or would they go for Port Moresby and the Solomons at this time? There was also the possibility that they would ignore Port Moresby and the Solomons for a direct advance on New Caledonia and Fiji.[8]

Our intelligence could not provide a categorical answer at the time. It was clear, however, that there were no signs of Japanese movements toward the Hawaiian Islands. "Past performance indicates that the enemy much prefers to make his moves under protection of land-based aircraft," I told the conference that Wednesday. "Our immediate problem . . . being an attack for the capture of Moresby is correct."[9]

"To know your enemy's intentions is fine but such knowledge does not always mean you can stop him" was how naval historian Samuel Eliot Morison would sum up the dilemma that Nimitz faced. But like Kimmel three months earlier, Nimitz appreciated that carrier-borne airpower was the decisive naval weapon in the vast Pacific theater. He therefore concluded that the best chance of stemming the Japanese tide in the southwest was to concentrate all our available task forces against it.

Lexington with Fitch's Task Force 11 was ordered to rendezvous with *Yorktown,* which was then replenishing at Tongatabu in order to make the thousand-mile trip into the Coral Sea. There they would join Rear Admiral John Crace, RN, and his Anzac cruisers. *Enterprise* and *Hornet* were not due to return to Pearl until 25 April, so it was unlikely that Halsey could make the ten-day trip to the Coral Sea before the Japanese offensive began. But Fitch and Fletcher could count on the support of the land-based planes of MacArthur's forces in northeast Australia and New Guinea. We could only hope that our intelligence estimates were correct and that the Japanese would not consider it necessary at the last minute to commit more than three carriers to the Port Moresby operation.

Nimitz decided that "we should be able to accept odds in battle if necessary."[10] His belief was based on my prediction that the enemy would—contrary to Captain Mahan, the American naval strategist who had articulated the doctrine of the concentration of naval forces—divide their strength in an ambitious effort to cover both the Moresby landing and an occupation of the Solomon Islands. Nimitz was required, nonetheless, to embark on a colossal strategic gamble, the enormity of which justified his decision to fly to San Francisco on 25 April to brief Admiral King.

Somewhat to Nimitz's surprise, his "calculated risk" for meeting the Japanese in the Coral Sea proved less of a concern to King than the "desirability of ridding Pearl Harbor of pessimists and defeatists."[11] He was principally concerned that Frank Jack Fletcher had not shown himself aggressive enough to conduct operations until Halsey could arrive in the southwest Pacific in the second week of May. King was one of those who held the Task Force 17 commander partly to blame for the debacle that cost us Wake Island, an impression that had not been erased later when Fletcher failed to push home his carrier raids in the Marshalls with the resolution and tenacity demonstrated by Halsey.

Nimitz, who was known for his loyalty to subordinates, expressed his confidence in Fletcher's capability. After calling for precautionary reinforcement of the Midway garrison, King approved the overall Cincpac strategy. But he also required that a carrier task force was henceforth to remain in the southwest Pacific. King considered protecting our route to

Australia so strategically important that on 20 April a South Pacific Area had been established. Vice Admiral Robert L. Ghormley was designated its commander in chief, but until he could depart from Washington to set up his headquarters in New Zealand, it was agreed that Nimitz would maintain direct control of operations in the area.

Nimitz returned to Pearl Harbor on 28 April, and, the next day, issued "Cincpac Operation Plan No. 23-42," outlining our Coral Sea strategy. We still needed to fill in critical details of the Japanese plan and it was a blessed relief when Rochefort reported that the Japanese were not changing their JN-25 cipher as an earlier intercept had foreshadowed. Apparently the distribution and delivery of the new code books had been delayed and a decrypt revealed that the changeover was being postponed until 27 May.

We heaved a deep sigh of relief when we realized that the old version of the Japanese JN-25 naval cipher was to continue for another three and a half weeks. This was to prove to be one of the most critical periods of the war. Our ability to eavesdrop on the enemy's main operational traffic enabled us to discover the details of Yamamoto's Port Moresby operation. More important, it simultaneously made us aware that there was an even bigger offensive in the making: Midway.

Unknown to us, our hit-and-run carrier raids had forced the Japanese navy to recast their entire Pacific strategy. First, the raids had forced a delay in the enemy's southward advance to secure New Guinea until after the end of April, when carriers could be detached from Admiral Nagumo's striking force as it returned from raiding operations in the Indian Ocean. Second, Yamamoto was obliged to extend his palisade of island defenses by ordering the simultaneous capture and occupation of Nauru and Ocean to plug the gap between the Gilberts and Solomons. Third, the urgent need to protect the eastern flank of Japan's southward advance had been Yamamoto's principal justification for the Midway operation. But by scheduling it for the first week in June, he forced the naval staff to advance the date for completing the Port Morseby and Solomons operations.

At Fourth Fleet headquarters in Rabaul, Admiral Inouye was dismayed when he was told that he had only until the second week of May to secure Port Moresby. This was long before he was due to receive the land-based air cover in New Guinea he needed to ensure the success of the landing. Next he was informed that fleet carrier *Kaga* could not be repaired in time and that he would have to rely only on the planes from *Shokaku* and *Zuikaku*. The relatively inexperienced pilots of Rear Admiral Chuichi Hara's Carrier Division 5 were no substitute for the crack pilots of Carrier Division 2; nor was it much consolation that light carrier *Shoho* was assigned to operate as close escort for the four heavy cruisers of Rear Admiral Aritomo Goto's main force.

In addition to providing mobile cover for the Port Moresby invasion, Carrier Division 5 would also be overstretched. Its planes were scheduled to provide distant support for the assaults on Tulagi in the Solomons and the Deboynes—the group of small islands flanking the northern neck of the Coral Sea. Their capture was considered essential; they were needed for use as seaplane bases from which to fly patrols that could give early warning of any American task forces steaming to interdict the invasion as it threaded its way from Rabaul through the treacherous shoal waters of the Louisade Islands off New Guinea's southernmost tip.

In addition to these complex operations, Admiral Hara's carriers were also expected to carry out preliminary raids on the Allied airfields in northern Australia. So when Hara sailed into the imposing sweep of Truk lagoon on 25 April he was appalled to learn the potential for disaster in the number of tasks assigned him, and that he would be subordinate commander of the Port Moresby striking force. He appealed over the head of Vice Admiral Takeo Takagi, the cruiser force commander, objecting to Inouye's instructions ordering him to risk his carriers to make the Australian raid within range of Allied land-based bombers.[12]

Fourth Fleet headquarters dithered. Not until the eve of the intricately balanced operation was Hara given the discretion to abandon the Australian raids. But Inouye responded by adding yet another complication. He requested that Hara's carriers ferry additional Zeros to reinforce Rabaul during their run south. This was to prove the straw that broke the camel's back.

Unaware of these last-minute changes, our radio intelligence analysts were having difficulty unraveling the various objectives of the Japanese operation from the complex orders flying among the three forces involved. Less than 20 percent of the intercepted JN-25 traffic was eventually made readable, and Nimitz was also having to cope with King's second-guessing about Japan's real intentions. After a bombing raid on Port Darwin, these fears appeared to be confirmed on 25 April by a decrypted message requesting a thousand copies of maps of northern Australia.[13] Washington appears to have been panicked by the thought that the enemy would not stop at New Guinea.

Rochefort, however, was able to prove that these fears were exaggerated by an unfortunate error in decryption made by Belconnen and Negat. Their discovery of a new "RO" operation turned out to be a misreading of the "MO" for the Moresby campaign.[14] The same day—27 April—Hypo picked up an order for the so-called Mandates Force to sail from Truk to join with another group for "operations against an enemy in RX area."[15] It was Joe's belief that "RX" was an island in the western Solomons—probably Bougainville—and this was consistent with our prediction of Japan's forthcoming operations in the northern sector of the Coral Sea.

On 28 April, Rochefort found another indication that the Japanese plan involved the Solomons with the identification of "RXB" as the island of Tulagi, which lay in the northeasterly bight of Guadalcanal in the middle of the island chain. This was important. But Rochefort really struck paydirt the following day when Hypo decrypted a message from Tokyo that referred to the dispatch of maps covering the Aleutian Islands. This was the first hint we received that Yamamoto was contemplating another, more ambitious, operation.[16] The value of Hypo's product was now so essential to Nimitz that he made a request to Cominch that Rochefort's team concentrate on "reading today's traffic today while it is of value to forces afloat," while Washington's cryptanalysts "undertake code recovery on back traffic,"[17]

King gave immediate approval for this practical division of effort. Evidently he did so without asking the opinion of Commander John R. Redman, the head of OP-20-G, whose feathers were ruffled by the independence that Rochefort had achieved. This victory for Hypo made the Redman brothers more determined than ever to centralize the control of radio intelligence in their own hands. It was another score to be settled with Joe and myself in the long term. And it added fuel to the rivalry that was developing between Negat and Hypo over which unit best evaluated intelligence.

Fortunately for us, Nimitz's intervention with King made Hypo's supremacy a fait accompli. Washington accepted our broad estimate of both the timing and objective of the Japanese advance to Port Moresby and the Solomons. The opening moves were being made in what would become known as the Battle of the Coral Sea.

On 1 May local time, as the two Japanese covering forces headed south from Truk, *Yorktown* joined up with *Lexington* at Point Buttercup, some three hundred miles due south of the tiny island of Tulagi. Lying in the middle of the Solomons, it was the target of another enemy force that was bearing down from the northwest. Since all the warships involved were observing radio silence, they had not revealed themselves yet to the radio intelligence units (RIU) on board our carriers. (Each unit consisted of one of Hypo's Japanese language officers and two or three radiomen; their responsibility was to monitor local enemy broadcasts for tactical information.)

Halsey had been the first task force commander to profit from the RIU teams. But Fletcher, who had never been properly indoctrinated in radio intelligence, did not have much use for his RIU officer. For any admiral of the old school, it all came down to a question of prestige and the reluctance to take the word of a junior lieutenant on important tactical information. To build up the trust of an admiral often demanded considerable tact and diplomacy by the intelligence officer. But in Fletcher's case, establishing this mutual confidence, so essential for getting important tactical intelligence across during an action, had been prejudiced when he had tried to browbeat Lieutenant Forrest R. Biard over his strict security regulations.[18]

"I want you to tell me and my staff all about your communications intelligence organization and the code breaking it does," Fletcher demanded of Biard during a lunch in the wardroom. Aware that most of the admiral's staff had not been cleared, Biard flatly refused to explain the details of his work, thereby incurring his admiral's extreme displeasure.

But his regard for the value of *Yorktown*'s RIU nose-dived on 1 May when Biard could not confirm whether a Japanese submarine, which was depth-charged thirty miles north of the carrier, had radioed a sighting report.[19] Later that afternoon Fitch had been flown over to *Yorktown* for a conference with the news that *Lexington*'s RIU officer, Lieutenant Commander Ranson Fullinwider, had heard the submarine signaling.[20] Biard was hauled before the admiral and chewed out for his failure.

If such a signal was made, it evidently failed to reach Rabaul—and we did not pick it up at Pearl Harbor. But Fletcher and Fitch did not know that. They quite properly had to assume that the Japanese knew their position. It became an imperative factor governing their decision after they received our dispatch a few hours later alerting them that the enemy operation was "now under way" and that it "involves New Guinea and the Louisade Archipelago." The message summarized the air and sea forces involved and gave a general summary of objectives as we had been able to piece them together. Included was a reference to an intercept mentioning Townesville and advice that we "do not believe Australia involved in immediate future except for submarine operations."[21]

Fletcher evidently inferred that the Japanese carriers would make this northern Australian port one of their targets. He concluded that the main enemy force was, therefore, at least nine hundred miles away to the northwest. Despite the enemy submarine reports, refueling was conducted at a leisurely pace the next day. When Task Force 11 had still not finished with the oilers that afternoon, Fletcher—contrary to specific orders from Nimitz—split his forces and headed off west after instructing Task Force 11 to rendezvous forty-eight hours later after Crace's cruisers had topped up their fuel tanks.

The following morning the Japanese occupied Tulagi, but Fletcher and Fitch remained ignorant of the unopposed landing. Not until 1900 that day, when they were more than a hundred miles apart, did they receive a radio relay from MacArthur's headquarters informing them that troop transports and five or six enemy warships had been spotted in the sound between Guadalcanal and Tulagi.

To Fletcher the tempting target was less than five hundred miles away and "just the kind of opportunity we have been waiting two months to receive." He could not break radio silence and considered it too late to send a plane off to *Lexington*. So he dispatched a destroyer, *Sims,* and oiler, *Neosho,* to meet Fletcher and Crace the next morning to instruct

them to head for a new rendezvous point three hundred miles south of
Guadalcanal on 5 May. Then he ordered *Yorktown*'s task force to steam
north at twenty-four knots in order to be off Guadalcanal to launch a
dawn strike on Tulagi the next day.

As Fletcher raced north, through a night punctuated by tropical
squalls, he received a Cincpac intelligence dispatch that appeared to justify his risky decision to rush into the attack with only half his forces. This
was the impression conveyed by a mistranslated four-day-old decrypt suggesting that the Japanese carriers would divide their attention between
countering American naval forces and raids on the airfields of northern
Australia.

Fletcher was luckier than he knew. Only the bad weather preventing
Hara from flying off the Zero reinforcements to Rabaul had prevented
Carrier Division 5 from being within striking distance of Tulagi that afternoon. But for this two-day delay, *Yorktown*'s pilots would have taken off
the next morning into well-defended air space and Task Force 17 would
have found itself outnumbered two to one by enemy carrier planes.

Fortunately for us, when *Yorktown*'s dive bombers came screaming
down over Tulagi an hour after sunrise on 4 May, there was no resistance. The Japanese garrison commander radioed the alarm, but
Hara's carriers were out of air strike range, and refueling off Rabaul
some four hundred miles away. News of the attack brought a hasty dis-
connection of oiling hoses as Hara's two carriers charged southward off
the eastern Solomons. Admiral Goto detached light carrier *Shoho* from
escorting the Port Moresby invasion transports. But none of the Japanese
forces could get within striking distance of Tulagi before darkness
brought an end to the first day of action in the Coral Sea.

Round one of the battle had gone to Fletcher as Task Force 17 retreated undetected into the two-hundred-mile curtain of bad weather that
hung east to west across the Coral Sea. Three waves of planes had been
launched, but the strikes against Tulagi had not been well coordinated.
Although *Yorktown*'s exuberant pilots reported they had totally destroyed the enemy forces, only two minesweepers and a transport had
been sunk, a destroyer beached, and five floatplanes sent up in flames.
Fletcher was so fired up that afternoon that he ordered his two cruisers in
to polish off any survivors. But his innate sense of caution prevailed and
they were recalled before nightfall, saving them from what would have
been certain destruction from the bombs and torpedoes of the Japanese
carrier planes that arrived over Tulagi the next morning.

At 1945 on 5 May, *Yorktown*'s combat air patrol shot down a four-
engine Mavis flying boat that had been picked up by the carrier's radar
shortly before Fletcher reached the rendezvous point with Fitch and
Crace. A simultaneous submarine sighting by a scout plane convinced our
admirals that their positions were again known to the Japanese. But
Fletcher, on the basis of the intelligence he had received, had no reason

to believe that enemy carriers were only four hundred miles to the north, so he spent most of the day refueling on a southerly course.

That afternoon an Allied reconnaissance flight spotted a Japanese convoy steaming down the Louisades toward the Jomard Passage. This was the route through the shoals that the enemy was expected to take. The pilot mistakenly identified a heavy carrier escorting the transports, further reinforcing Fletcher's belief that the main Japanese force was at that moment heading for the archipelago that trailed from the southern tip of New Guinea.

At dusk on 5 May when Fletcher hauled his combined task force around to head for the Jomard Passage, he still believed that the enemy carriers were over 400 miles ahead. In fact, Carrier Division 5 had that day looped around the southern Solomons and was that evening just astern less than 250 miles off his starboard quarter. That night the wakes of the two protagonists carved phosphorescent tracks up the dark waters of the Coral Sea.

Fletcher was so certain that the enemy lay ahead of him that it prejudiced any chance of his making a correct reading of the situation from a Cincpac intelligence dispatch, which provided him with a partial decrypt of the 4 May order to Carrier Division 5. But at Hypo we had slipped up too. By mistranslating the word "pass"[22] as "proceed" in the instruction telling Hara to "pass north-northeast of Bougainville thence to southward" the impression given was that the two Japanese carriers immediately entered the Coral Sea.[23] As Fitch's action report makes only too plain, this was read as an indication that Carrier Division 5 "would run southward from the vicinity of Bougainville and might be within striking distance on the morning of 7 May."[24]

In making this assumption, however, both Fletcher and Fitch appear to have discounted the second part of the dispatch, which clearly ordered the Japanese carriers to "go to Tulagi." But this did not square with the information in the second dispatch he received during the night of 6 May. It referred to a three-day-old decrypt stating that the Japanese carriers "will launch attacks on Allied bases in the Port Moresby area."[25] This suggested that if the enemy force had indeed entered the Coral Sea on 5 May as the first dispatch indicated, they would already have hurried westward to support the invasion force.

Unaware that Hara's two carriers were to the northeast of Fletcher's task force and sending out air patrols in search of them, our task forces spent 6 May holding course on the Coral Sea heading up toward the Louisades. But Fletcher's hopes of surprising the enemy force vanished the next day when they were spotted by a Japanese flying boat.

"Discovered what appears to be a large enemy force bearing 190 degrees," the Tulagi-based "Emily" flashed out just after 1000.[26] The report caught Hara's carriers refueling south of New Georgia. Once again hose connections were broken as Takagi ordered Carrier Division 5 ahead of his cruisers to try for a strike that afternoon. But Hara's scouts, who headed south along the vector given by the flying boat, ran smack into the heavy weather and turned back. Had they been just a little more persistent they would have penetrated the southern curtain of squalls to discover our two carriers steaming serenely under clear skies.

When Hara decided late that afternoon to reverse course to rejoin Takagi's cruiser force to prepare for a dawn strike the next day, he did not know that less than a hundred miles separated his pilots from a stunning chance victory. Nor had Fletcher realized just how close to disaster he was sailing that afternoon when he completed another refueling of his destroyers before ordering oiler *Neosho* to fall back with an escorting destroyer to keep out of range of enemy bombers from Rabaul.

While our task forces were engaged in this deadly round of blind man's buff, Pacific Fleet plotting room at Pearl Harbor was also in the dark about the precise location of the opposing forces in the Coral Sea. Because Fletcher and Fitch were observing radio silence, our only clue to their whereabouts came from the decrypt of the seaplane sighting, which had been relayed by Jaluit radio. When no further action reports had been picked up by nightfall, we could only assume that Carrier Division 5 had given up its chase and was now heading for the Jomard Passage to cover the most critical phase of the Port Moresby operation. I put "Cardiv 5 and Crudiv 5 with enemy forces to south of Rabaul" in my daily intelligence bulletin. Nimitz and his staff retired early, anticipating an early start to the clash the next day, which we believed would be fought on relatively even terms.

Dawn on 7 May in the northern quarter of the Coral Sea was disturbed by ten scout planes roaring off from *Yorktown*. At 0618 they fanned out into gusty squalls, and a sky fluffy with cumulus clouds that obscured horizon visibility to the northeast where the Japanese were expected to appear. Fletcher, who could not count on the static weather front as an ally, decided to fight a carrier duel without Crace's cruisers. They were sent ahead to guard the southern exit of the Jomard Passage.

Confirmation that the Japanese were also out searching for our carriers came at 0815 when a *Yorktown* scout shot down an enemy floatplane some 250 miles away over Misima Island, which marked the northern side of the Jomard Passage. Within half an hour another scout radioed that two enemy carriers and two cruisers had been sighted off Misima, heading south.

Fletcher was so confident that this must be the main enemy force that, without awaiting confirmation, he ordered a full air attack launched from *Yorktown* and *Lexington*. At 1015 when the ninety-three-plane strike went roaring off to the northwest, Biard came to inform Fletcher that a Japanese carrier aircraft had been spotted nearby. He was still in the flagship plot when the *Yorktown* scout pilot came to report that he had made an unfortunate coding error. What he had actually sighted were not two carriers, but two heavy cruisers and two destroyers.

"Young man, do you know what you have done? You have just cost the United States two carriers!" roared Admiral Fletcher. Disaster loomed with the realization that our task forces had shot their bolt. The awful dimension of his mistake caused the admiral to lose control. According to Biard, "Here was the commander of a vital naval task force shouting in the presence of officers and several enlisted men that we had already lost a battle we were yet to fight!"[27]

Leaving Fletcher and his staff to debate whether to recall the air strike, Biard withdrew to the RIU shack behind flag plot. He was full of apprehension that any moment he would hear that a Japanese pilot was making a sighting report that could seal the fate of our task forces. But fate appeared to be forgiving of Fletcher that week. At 1022 MacArthur's headquarters in Brisbane relayed a B-17 pilot's report of a Japanese carrier north of Misima.

The roller-coaster emotion on *Yorktown*'s flag bridge hurtled up again as Fletcher ordered the strike redirected thirty miles to the north of its original target. Then hope plunged down minutes later when oiler *Neosho* radioed from three hundred miles astern that enemy bombs were raining down. Since the hapless tanker and her escorting destroyer were well out of range of any Japanese land base, Fletcher faced his moment of truth: His task force was boxed in by enemy carriers fore and aft.

Fortunately for Fletcher, his potentially disastrous error had been duplicated by his opponent. When Hara ordered his seventy-six-plane strike launched at 1015, after a reconnaissance patrol had spotted an enemy carrier force some 200 miles south of flagship *Zuikaku,* he was convinced that it was the quarry he had been hunting for the previous day. But less than five minutes after he had watched his aircraft disappearing over the southern horizon, Hara was informed that another Japanese patrol had sighted an American task force 350 miles to the west of him off Deboyne Island. Then came a report that there was another force on the same bearing less than 200 miles away heading for the Louisades.

"We will join battle with the enemy in the west after we have attacked to the south," Hara decided after a brief discussion with his staff.[28] Just after midday he found out how badly he had called his shots. The target of the air strike turned out to be nothing more substantial than an oiler and destroyer. While one bomber group bombed *Neosho* into a drifting wreck and sank destroyer *Sims,* the other planes responded to the urgent recall signal.

Hara hauled his carriers around 180 degrees after concluding that the "enemy in the west" must be the American flattops. But he had to let his returning planes know where to find their flight decks. In his cramped RIU space on board *Yorktown,* Biard picked up *Zuikaku*'s repeated homing signal giving course "280 degrees speed 20 knots." Fletcher was immediately informed that the enemy carrier force was closing from astern. But he dismissed Biard's intelligence. Fletcher preferred to believe the message flashed from Fitch. It interpreted the same signals as "enemy course and speed as 280 degrees 20 knots," because Fullinwider, the RIU officer on board *Lexington,* had mistranslated the Japanese. "The explanation was easy," Biard recalled having tried to point out to Fletcher. "We had not recently been on any course even approximating to 280 degrees, and our steaming speed was nothing like 20 knots."[29]

Fletcher, however, "just would not accept it." The admiral was soon diverted from the significance of what Biard was trying to tell him by reports that our air strike had finally connected with an enemy carrier northeast of Misima Island.

From ten thousand feet the American dive bombers dropped like hawks out of clear skies. Japan's light carrier struggled to launch additional fighters. In what one *Yorktown* pilot described as "a spectacular and convincing pageant of destruction," the defending Japanese Zeros were swept aside. Bombs plummeted through *Shoho*'s flight deck as torpedoes ripped into the small carrier's flanks. At 1210 *Lexington*'s air group leader sent the prearranged message that was cheered in the radio rooms of our ships as loudly as it was at Pearl: "Scratch one flattop!"[30]

The light carrier had been sunk against the loss of a single dive bomber—the same price paid by the Japanese for our oiler and destroyer. Fletcher and Fitch ended the second round of the Coral Sea battle ahead on points. The appearance of Admiral Crace's cruisers south of the Jomard Passage had succeeded in forcing Admiral Inouye to stand off the invasion transports to the north until the carrier duel had been decided. The Anzac cruisers, which had escaped two hours of continuous bombing by land-based aircraft by skillful helmsmanship, had also diverted attacks from the carrier task force. But no sooner had the enemy been beaten off than three American B-26s mistakenly made an attack run. "Fortunately," Crace sardonically reported, "their bombing, in comparison with that of the Japanese a few minutes earlier, was disgraceful."[31]

When the morning strike returned to report that they had sunk only a light carrier, Fletcher knew that his priority must be to locate Carrier Division 5. Shortly after 1400 Task Force 17's planes were again ranged on the flight decks, refueled, bombed up, and ready to take off. But although the attack on *Neosho* and *Sims* indicated that the enemy carriers were somewhere astern, the precise whereabouts were hidden by the curtain of heavy weather. Incredibly, considering his predicament, Fletcher turned a deaf ear to Biard who had been plotting the course of Hara's carriers from the radio transmissions until 1400.

Biard tried again to explain his intelligence to Fletcher and asked if a search-and-strike mission was planned on the two enemy carriers he and his radiomen "knew to be within fighting distance and looking for us."[32] But the admiral remained unconvinced. Chastened by his earlier miscalculation, Fletcher ruled out launching a search-and-destroy mission, to preserve maximum fighter cover against the Japanese attack that he anticipated would materialize at any moment. He was especially reluctant to risk losing planes in the heavy weather, preferring to "rely on shore-based aircraft to locate the enemy carriers."[33] He later attributed his lack of action that afternoon to "insufficient daylight for an attack following an extensive search."[34]

In a strikingly parallel predicament, Hara was also paralyzed by caution and hesitation. Long before the afternoon grew old, he had effectively given up the hunt because "there is no possibility for an attack today."[35] He changed his mind just after 1600, when a floatplane reported that the American carriers could be close to within striking distance before nightfall. The most experienced aircrews volunteered for a hazardous dusk raid and twelve bombers and fifteen torpedo planes took off from *Shokaku* and headed out through the squall line.

The sun was setting two hours later at 1830 when the Japanese strike ran into the combat air patrols guarding Task Force 17. Bombs and torpedoes were jettisoned in a fight that cost the enemy seven aircraft for three of our fighters. But in the twilight some of the Japanese pilots managed to get a close look at an American flattop for the first time in the war. As they buzzed low over *Yorktown* they were at first mistaken for our own planes coming in to land, until it was realized that they were circling counterclockwise which was contrary to our navy's flight routine.

Fletcher did not relish Biard's report that the enemy planes had radioed very precise reports of our task force's position before they headed off to the northeast into the gathering darkness. In his action report Fletcher stressed that the direction and distance of the Japanese carriers was still uncertain, even though he discussed with his staff whether to detach his cruisers for a night attack. He abandoned the idea when advised of the enemy's night-fighting capabilities, deciding to commit himself to the main engagement the following day.

Less than two hundred miles away to the northeast, Admiral Hara's staff was making the same preparations.

At first light on 8 May, round three of the battle opened with American and Japanese scouts probing for each other's carriers. Hara had the advantage of the weather. His ships remained under cover. Task Force 17, on the other hand, was steaming in near-perfect visibility on the south side of the squall line. But thanks to radar Fletcher avoided premature discovery around 0800 when *Lexington*'s combat patrol fighters chased off a Japanese scout before it sighted the American ships.

The first actual contact was made fifteen minutes later when the *Shokaku* and *Zuikaku* were spotted 175 miles east-northeast of Fletcher's force. Minutes later a Japanese plane was heard radioing, "Have sighted enemy carriers."[36]

The American first strike of seventy-five aircraft roared off to the northeast just after 0900, when sixty-nine Japanese planes started their flight southward. To reduce signaling between carriers, and to allow "complete freedom of action for his carriers and air groups," Fletcher handed over tactical command of the task force to Admiral Fitch, in recognition of his greater experience in handling air operations.[37]

Yorktown's dive bombers reached the target first. At 1100 they came hurtling through a clear patch in the overcast onto *Shokaku,* while *Zuikaku* dodged away into the cover of a convenient squall. Our first strike on a large, well-defended carrier task force lacked the necessary coordination between the dive bombers and the torpedo planes, which made their low-level run in without fighter protection.

The defending Zeros easily broke up the attack and torpedoes went splashing wide of *Shokaku.* Antiaircraft fire disrupted the bombers and three were downed. But fifteen of our pilots managed to fight their way through to score three hits. *Shokaku* was set ablaze and flight operations were interrupted for an hour. Undamaged below the waterline, the carrier withdrew northward, trailing a long column of smoke.

"When last seen, about fifteen minutes after the attack, fires were burning fiercely," one *Yorktown* pilot reported optimistically. "It is believed that this carrier was so badly damaged that it finally sank."[38] But it was not until our aircrew rendezvoused with Task Force 17 around 1300 that Friday that they discovered how much more accurately their Japanese opponents had executed their attack.

Two hours earlier, *Lexington*'s radar had picked up "bandits" seventy miles away to the northeast. Fitch had sufficient warning to send up the twenty-three remaining dive bombers to augment his weak fighter screen. But this was not enough to break up the well-coordinated Japanese attack that erupted twenty minutes later. With no squalls to dodge into, the two carriers and their escorts were forced to weave like skaters. *Yorktown* answered her helm more adroitly than the larger *Lexington.*

Like a stately dowager, "Lady Lex" turned ponderously until two torpedoes slammed into her port side, letting in thousands of tons of water that caused a dangerous list. Damage-control parties struggled to right *Lexington* by counterflooding, but without maneuverability the large carrier became an easy target for a series of bombs that set fires raging belowdecks. Meanwhile, *Yorktown* suffered a hit near her island, which caused a temporary shutdown of her boilers and loss of way. The confusion was compounded in the closing stages of the action when *Lexington*'s fighters, low on fuel, came in for pancake landings on her battered deck and several went skidding over the side.

In less than a quarter of an hour the Japanese departed, jubilantly radioing that the loss of *Shoho* the previous day had been avenged two to one. Accepting at face value their reports of sinking one large and one medium carrier, Admiral Hara believed that both American carriers had been sent to the bottom.

Fletcher's preliminary report was almost as optimistic as Hara's. "First enemy attack completed, no vital damage our force," he radioed

Nimitz. "*Yorktown* now making thirty knots. I propose retire tonight, fill *Yorktown* complement planes as far as possible from *Lexington,* and send that ship to Pearl."[39]

At Pacific Fleet headquarters Fletcher's early after-action report made it appear that we had indeed won a significant victory. "This was a red-letter day for our forces operating in the Coral Sea," Nimitz had already recorded in the official diary.[40] Later Fletcher's initial optimism evaporated.

"Congratulations on your glorious accomplishments" from Nimitz had already been handed to Fletcher when disaster struck *Lexington.* The wounded carrier's list had been corrected and her fires brought under control, enabling her to recover her returning strike aircraft. Then just after 1245 the carrier was riven by a tumultuous explosion set off by sparks from a generator that ignited fuel vapor escaping from damaged internal tanks. The resulting inferno was to defeat the fire-fighting parties belowdecks even as the aircraft controllers aloft were rounding up the tail-end Charlies.

At 1507 it was clear that "Lady Lex" was doomed. Her captain gave the order to abandon ship. Five hours later *Lexington* was still afloat, her hull plating glowing cherry red in places from fires raging inside. The miserable spectacle ended only when destroyer *Phelps* was ordered to finish her off with torpedoes. As the great warship slid hissing and roaring to her final berth on the bottom of the Coral Sea, Fletcher was now facing a tactical defeat. To add to his predicament, his air commander alerted him to the "strong indications that an additional carrier had joined the enemy forces."[41] Plans for a night destroyer attack on the retreating enemy were abandoned and the order was given for Task Force 17 to withdraw to the southeast.

Hara, who could have pursued his victory with his undamaged carrier, also decided to leave the field of battle. Lack of fuel and planes was the reason he would give for not following Combined Fleet orders "to extend the gains of the battle and destroy the remaining enemy forces."[42] Whatever the reason, his failure to follow orders turned a tactical victory for Japan into a strategic defeat.

Admiral Inouye was to blame Hara's retreat for his decision to recall the invasion force the next morning. His dispatch informed Yamamoto, "Port Moresby attack will be postponed to a later date. Your approval is requested. Nauru-Ocean operation, however, will most likely be carried out as scheduled."

Lexington's loss was a terrible blow to Nimitz. He was visibly jolted and muttered several times that they should have saved her. But he was always self-possessed when things looked bleakest. He immediately tried to buoy us. "Remember this," he told us that night. "We don't *know* how *badly* he's hurt. You can bet your boots he's hurt too! Remember this— the enemy has got to be hurt, his situation is not all a bed of roses."[43]

Nimitz's optimism was infectious—and was justified, as we soon learned. Rochefort that evening sent over the decryption of Hara's afternoon battle summary, and although we were disappointed that *Shokaku* had suffered only "slight damage" and was steaming to Truk, by the following morning we knew that the Port Moresby operation had been postponed. Nimitz might have lost one of our most valuable carriers, but Task Force 17 had succeeded in its objective of halting Japan's southward advance. If this delay proved permanent, Nimitz would indeed be justified in claiming the Coral Sea as "a victory with decisive and far reaching consequences."[44]

For the first time since Pearl Harbor an important psychological defeat had been inflicted on the previously invincible Japanese navy. According to General MacArthur, who was loath to praise the navy, the Battle of the Coral Sea was "the real safeguard of Australian independence."[45] It provided him with a timely measure of revenge for Bataan, which had fallen on 6 May.

If the Coral Sea action had not yet put Japan on the defensive, it served Admiral Yamamoto with notice that despite our numerical inferiority, the Pacific Fleet could muster its forces at long range to check the Combined Fleet. The battle also marked the first naval engagement in history to be fought without the rival warships ever catching sight of one another. Radio intelligence had proved itself a crucial factor in turning the strategic outcome in our favor. But the action had shown how a commander who was inexperienced in the use of tactical radio intelligence could make egregious errors. Nonetheless a secret wartime navy department assessment concluded: "It takes nothing from the achievements of the fleets of the U.S. Navy at Coral Sea to say that they had been brought to the right spot at exactly the right time by the work of radio intelligence."[46]

30

"Science and Skill"

I F IT HAD NOT BEEN FOR radio intelligence, the first we would have heard about the Coral Sea probably would have been a victory announcement by the Tokyo *Domei* news agency. Only Nimitz and a few close aides knew, however, that our strategic success in the action was largely the result of Joe Rochefort's unique abilities to smell out "something fishy" in the intercepts. He had demonstrated a sixth sense when it came to assembling seemingly unrelated information in partially decrypted enemy messages and turning the puzzle into an accurate picture of enemy plans and intentions.

The Coral Sea was an important victory for Hypo because it persuaded Nimitz to trust Rochefort over and above the often conflicting assessments being made by naval intelligence in Washington. Perhaps more important, as I have said earlier, Joe had smelled out indications that another and bigger Japanese offensive was in the making before the first shots were fired in Coral Sea. On 27 April he had revealed Tokyo's interest in maps of the Aleutians.[1] On 4 May he discovered that a battleship had signaled that a 21 May schedule for completion of her refit made it impossible "to accompany you in the campaign."[2] The next day Joe reported that Yamamoto's flagship had ordered Tokyo to "expedite delivery" of a large quantity of refueling hose because it was needed for "scheduled operations."[3]

Just what "the campaign" might be was still unclear, but it was evidently something much bigger than Admiral Inouye's declared intention to capture Ocean and Nauru islands. A strike against the Aleutians would account for the Combined Fleet requesting more hoses for seagoing refueling operations, but Rochefort had a hunch. Based on a subtle shift in radio traffic, he believed that the main Japanese objective was in the mid-Pacific. Specific ship-movement decrypts, while individually insignificant, were creating a pattern that pointed to an impending operation in the area. Units began exchanging messages with Saipan at an increasing rate, an indication that the ports in the Marianas were becoming the focus of a Combined Fleet movement unconnected with the current operation in the south.[4]

"While the Japanese offensive in the south Pacific continues, it is noted they now have sufficient forces in the central Pacific to raid in the central and north Pacific area," Nimitz logged on 6 May, reflecting Hypo's current intelligence estimates.[5] That Wednesday, Rochefort uncovered the first clue to one of the elements in the Japanese operation. A decrypted message from Sixth Fleet submarine force headquarters on Kwajalein requested a new set of transmitter crystals "for use in aircraft in the second K campaign." The crystals had to reach Sixth Fleet headquarters by 17 May.[6]

Since submarines at the French Frigate Shoals had refueled flying boats for the first "K" Operation, Joe believed that the Japanese intended to duplicate that 5 March flight over Oahu, because "AK" was their designator for Pearl. On the strength of this information Nimitz ordered that a minelayer be stationed at the French Frigate Shoals.

It had been the unexpected appearance of our second carrier task force in the Coral Sea that had prompted Yamamoto to order a second long-range reconnaissance of Pearl Harbor. It was necessary as a prelude to the Combined Fleet's big offensive to know where our fleet was. But by ordering the reconnaissance Yamamoto had unwittingly dealt himself a losing card. So far he had been on a hot roll, the dice had been falling his way. But when he drew up the final plans for his Midway strategy he unwisely relied too much on his lucky streak continuing. The Japanese, who are adept at turning an appropriate phrase to explain the tides of fate that govern human affairs, were to attribute their reverses after five months of triumph to shōribyō—"victory disease."

While the battle was being fought in the Coral Sea, Yamamoto and his staff appear to have been afflicted with a bad case of shōribyō during the tabletop maneuvers in which they rehearsed the Midway operation. The heat of battle was absent in the calculations that were made by the principal naval commanders of the Combined Fleet during their five-day conference in Hashirajima Bay.

"The Combined Fleet cannot assume a long drawn-out defense," Yamamoto told the conference, which assembled on 1 May in superbattleship Yamato's cavernous wardroom.[7] He outlined his grand design for a massive attack on Midway, and a diversionary assault on the Aleutians, which was intended to lure the Pacific Fleet carriers out to be smashed.

The trap was to be sprung by deploying every available warship in the Combined Fleet that could be spared. Operation MI—for Midway, as it had been code-named—was the most ambitious operation ever mounted by the Japanese navy. It was also one of the most complex naval operations ever planned, depending for its success on the simultaneous cooperation of five tactical groups.

Admiral Nagumo's carrier striking force was to play the key role. The *Kido Butai* was to support amphibious landings on Midway, while a northern force including two carriers covered the capture of Kiska and Attu at the western end of the Aleutian chain. An advance force of submarines was to interpose a patrol line west of the Hawaiian Islands to provide early warning and launch underwater attacks on the anticipated American sortie to defend Midway. Yamamoto himself would then lead the Combined Fleet's main force into the final action, springing the jaws of the gigantic trap shut, with the northern force advancing south from the Aleutians to cut off the Pacific Fleet's line of retreat.

For four days the Japanese admirals and captains rehearsed the complex operation that involved the interlocking moves of over seven hundred planes and two hundred ships—including eleven battleships, eight carriers, twenty-three cruisers, sixty-five destroyers, and twenty submarines. The objective of Operation MI was to eliminate the American carrier threat and advance Japan's defensive perimeter another two thousand miles eastward into the Pacific. This was the preliminary step prior to the third phase of Yamamoto's grand design: to invade Hawaii and force the United States to sue for peace.

The war games, however, did not always produce the desired result. Instead they exposed a disturbing number of flaws. The Combined Fleet staff had calculated that the American carriers could not reach Midway before it had been captured and a strong Japanese air umbrella established on the atoll. If this condition was not met, disastrous results were demonstrated. In one run-through, the attacking force suffered two carriers sunk, a third bombed into retreat, and a whole division of destroyers lost for lack of fuel, while the actual capture of Midway was delayed for more than a week. But "victory disease" had infected the umpires. They permitted all three of the supposedly "sunken" carriers to be miraculously refloated to participate in the next stage of the operations!

In the critique that followed the tabletop maneuvers, Yamamoto was taxed by some of his subordinate commanders. They were so concerned at the complexity of the operation that they wanted a postponement for more preparations and training. There was considerable worry about how the commander in chief was going to personally coordinate so many scattered forces when he intended to be at sea himself, and would be obliged to maintain radio silence until the fleet action began.

But Yamamoto would allow no alterations to the plan which would delay the launch of his mid-Pacific offensive. He was boxed in by imperial general headquarters' inflexible timetable of conquest and by immovable meteorological considerations. Midway could be invaded only during the first days of the month, when slack high water after dawn would allow the assault craft to get over the atoll's reef. The weather forecast for July predicted the Aleutians would be locked in by impenetrable fog banks. These two factors dictated that the twin phases of the MI operation had to be set for the first week in June.

To pull off his Midway strategy, Yamamoto needed luck. His intricate battle choreography also required that his opponents move according to predicted positions; one false step or foreknowledge of the plan could throw the entire operation into disarray.

Imperial general headquarters issued the final orders for the "occupation of Midway and strategic points in the western Aleutians" on the 5 May national festival known as Boys Day, celebrating future achievement. But an inauspicious prelude to his big campaign came within forty-eight hours when Yamamoto received news from the Coral Sea that cost his Midway operation the services of two carriers and many skilled aircrews. It was at this point that he unwittingly drew a second losing card by ordering the flying boat reconnaissance of Pearl Harbor.[8]

The plan for a second "K" operation was spotted almost at once by Rochefort. On 7 May he learned that many Combined Fleet commanders were being summoned to Kagoshima in Japan for a mid-month briefing.[9] The next day a destroyer division announced that it would be unable to "participate in your forthcoming campaign."[10] On 9 May a large number of destroyers that were to screen the carriers and battleships involved in "the forthcoming campaign" were ordered to "to depart Yokosuka on 17 May."[11]

Decrypt by decrypt, Rochefort began peeling away the cover to reveal the extent and direction of Yamamoto's grand design. Joe was the ideal combination of intelligence-officer-cum-cryptanalyst. But his idiosyncratic ways and fierce independence were already irritating the new regime running naval intelligence in Washington. They wanted everything cut and dried. They wanted everyone assigned to a particular section of analysis so that the end product could be fit into a neat picture of Japanese intentions. But Rochefort and his team did not work that way, and, during the month of May, their method produced the results that Washington failed to achieve. The record bears out that most of the significant decrypts were made by Hypo. This was galling to the Redman brothers in Washington, who wanted to prove to Admiral King how effectively they had shaken up and reorganized naval intelligence.

"The war actually was being fought out yonder," Captain McCollum was to admit later. The head of naval intelligence's Far East section was succinct in his comments. He went on to say: "Whatever we did around here in Washington would be more or less in the category of toting buckets of water out there. The strategic setup and concepts were discussed here, but on the plane of commanders-in-chief and their staffs. The actual concept of the operations was largely left in the hands of Admiral Nimitz."[12]

McCollum might have been content to leave Cincpac to evaluate the concept of enemy operations, but this did not square with the ideas of naval communications director Captain Joseph R. Redman, or his younger brother, Commander "Jack" Redman, who was head of the restructured OP-20-G. They also had the ear of Admiral King, who was fighting his own battle with the Joint Chiefs to restore the priority of the Pacific theater. On 5 May, King warned the Joint Chiefs of the "disastrous consequences if we are unable to hold the present position in the Pacific."[13] But General Marshall persuaded Roosevelt that "it was impossible to make every point in the island chain impregnable." King was told that he would have to fight the Japanese with the ships and planes already assigned to the Pacific.

Nimitz had already made a flying visit to Midway on 2 May. This was in response to King's mounting concern about the defense of our Pacific island outposts and not, as many historians have wrongly suggested, because of his anticipation of the Japanese attack, which had yet to be revealed. On Nimitz's return he ordered the atoll's reinforcement with more planes and ammunition. But his principal concern was how to "make our position secure and provide for an adequate striking force" to deal with the new Japanese offensive.[14] Although *Saratoga* would complete her refit by the beginning of June, the loss of *Lexington,* plus *Yorktown*'s estimated three months for repairs, left our carrier forces outnumbered nearly five to one.

Distance may lend enchantment, but in King's case it produced a bout of strategic jitters in terms of the Pacific defense. The sinking of *Lexington* had been an almost personal blow. The carrier had once been his flagship. He knew as well as Nimitz that the loss of another flattop would cripple our ability to hold advanced positions between Alaska and Australia. It was this concern that prompted him to place impossible restrictions on Nimitz.

Halsey's orders to foil the Japanese move to Ocean and Nauru were hamstrung when Nimitz received King's dispatch directing that "operations of Task Force 16 inadvisable in forward areas beyond shore-based air cover and within range enemy shore-based air." Cominch went even further, suggesting that to "preserve our carriers . . . it may be better to operate one or more carrier [air] groups from shore."[15]

This proposal from a former flattop skipper—that carrier aircraft should be operated from land bases at New Caledonia and Fiji—was as disturbing to Nimitz as the revelation that King apparently believed that Japan's next campaign would be against our island bases in the South Pacific. If Nimitz was going to regain control of the carriers, he would have first to convince King of the error in his potentially disastrous miscalculation about the direction the next enemy offensive would take.

"If we listen to Washington," one Hypo staff officer warned Rochefort, "we will all end up as Japanese POWs."[16]

Joe and I faced a difficult task. We had the confidence of Nimitz, but now we had to demonstrate beyond any doubt that the evaluations being made in Washington were wrong. And this had to be done at a time when we had only a vague notion of the Japanese intentions. Our problem was made more complex by Washington's deductions, which were based on the same decrypts we were using, that the enemy had begun a buildup at Truk and not Saipan. If this was true, it would indeed indicate a Japanese advance south into New Caledonia, Port Moresby, and Fiji. Washington was dismissing Rochefort's estimate of a movement to the Marianas (Midway) as a feint—like the Aleutians—and claiming instead that four carriers and seven battleships were about to head southward.

We tried to understand why Washington had come up with such a contradictory evaluation of similar intelligence. Joe and I could conclude only that being so distant from operational headquarters they were more concerned with "enemy capabilities," while we concentrated on what the Japanese *were doing,* could do, and would probably do. Then there was the question of King's domineering personality. Like Turner, he over-awed his subordinates. They tended to feed him information that rein-forced his convictions, and every officer in Washington knew that King was struggling to get more resources for the Pacific war. Raising the level of the alarm about the Japanese threat to our lifeline to Australia evi-dently was more likely to evoke the support of General Marshall than asking for reinforcements for Midway or the Aleutians.

The different priorities of Washington and Pearl Harbor inevitably colored the estimates that were made by the two intelligence staffs. But once positions are taken, they are difficult to reverse, especially at a time when the communications intelligence outfit in the navy department was fighting to reassert Washington's authority over Station Hypo. But none of us at Pearl Harbor had forgotten what had happened six months ear-lier. Rochefort and his team were determined never again to be suckered by complacent evaluations of the type that had contributed to disaster. Joe particularly resented any attempt to confine his activities to any one area of additive or code recoveries. He remembered all too well how Washington had denied him access to the vital intelligence in the Jap-anese consular traffic that had been totally ignored by the navy depart-ment.

What had happened was that Washington had combined three partial messages and misinterpreted the results. They had confused the Midway phase of Yamamoto's plan with the third phase, which did indeed include a strike to the south toward Fiji, Samoa, and New Caledonia. The three signals involved included a Belconnen decrypt of a 2 May signal directing that carrier *Kaga* "upon completion of repairs will depart Sasebo and anchor at _____ in Truk."[17] Washington read this in conjunction with another message that assigned berths in Truk to Battleship Division 3.[18] Then there was a third signal that placed the First Air Fleet commander on board *Kaga*. This final message was misinterpreted in Washington to mean that Nomura's striking force must be heading southward for Truk.

Rochefort, however, assembled the pieces differently. First, he said that the air commander on board *Kaga* was ordering the other air commanders of the carrier strike force to a 17 May conference aboard *Kaga* in Kagoshima, the southernmost harbor in Japan. Second, Rochefort saw that Washington had misread the additive group and misidentified Kagoshima as being Truk.[19] Furthermore, other decrypts suggested that intensive operational exercises were being conducted off the southern coast of Japan, and it was only logical that these exercises would be followed by a staff conference. After ten more days of working on the additives, Rochefort was able to circulate the correct decrypt of the original message intercepted by Belconnen. It directed that the "striking force may be in Truk for a period of about two weeks after ((94539)), please arrange for _____ and designate anchorages."[20]

The date represented by the numerals "94539" was superenciphered and although it could not be broken out—it was later discovered to be 20 June—the reference to a two-week stay suggested that the Combined Fleet's main force would reassemble at Truk *after* the mid-Pacific operation. But the analysts of OP-20-G stuck to their guns, trying to justify their contention that the main force was heading south on the basis of the recent increase in traffic to Rabaul. Although this traffic was unreadable, Rochefort was able to point out that it had the characteristics of administrative rather than operational traffic.

While the navy department analysts were busily trying to bolster their case, systematic analysis of traffic by Hypo revealed that virtually every destroyer command in the Combined Fleet had been assigned to the mid-Pacific operation. We were positive that wherever the Japanese might be heading, it was not south. (No new destroyer assignments had been detected on the Truk radio circuits by the end of the second week in May.) Yet what appeared obvious to us was ignored or dismissed in Washington.

Decrypts of 11 May assigning the Second Fleet anchorages at Saipan prompted Rochefort to remind Washington: "Do not believe Japanese are carrying out a drill in Saipan area at this time. Suggest possibility that this and preceding message all refer to campaign or operation."[21] Three days later Joe made the big break that Nimitz had been waiting for.

"I've got something so hot here it's burning the top of my desk" was how Joe told me about it that Thursday. When I asked what it was he said, "You'll have to come over and see it. It's not cut and dried, but it's hot! The man with the blue eyes will want to know your opinion of it."

When I reached his underground headquarters, Rochefort was ebullient as he showed me a partially decrypted message. It contained the words *"koryaku butai."* It was the proven value for "invasion force" and it was followed by the geographic designator "AF" in a signal referring to the "forthcoming campaign." The term *"koryaku butai,"* Joe pointed out, had been used during the invasions of Rabaul, Java, Sumatra, and Bali.[22]

Now we knew that the Japanese intended to invade "AF." By a brilliant piece of detective work, Rochefort then convinced me that the objective was Midway. The clinchers were two messages sent out by the Second Fleet command to its associated air units. The first went to the "AF occupation force," which was ordered to "proceed direct to the Saipan-Guam area and wait for the forthcoming campaign." The second one ordered another unit to "load its base equipment and ground crews and advance to AF . . . everything in the way of base equipment and military supplies which will be needed for the K campaign will be included."[23]

Joe was jubilant. He had finally tied the mysterious "K" operation to the Japanese forces concentrating at Saipan. From there his deduction that AF must be Midway was simple and convincing. We knew that AH was Oahu and that AK was probably the French Frigate Shoals. Now that the base supplies for an air unit were being readied for shipment into "AF" with the occupation forces, it had to be one of our island bases within striking distance of Pearl Harbor. Midway was the obvious target, since it was nearly 150 miles nearer the Japanese on Wake than the alternative, Johnston Island.

I immediately reported Rochefort's analysis to Nimitz. He asked Captain Lynde V. McCormick, his war plans chief, to go down to Hypo with me for confirmation. McCormick was quickly convinced. From that afternoon on, despite all that has been written, there was never any doubt in Nimitz's mind that Midway was the main objective of the Japanese operation. But Washington changed its mind about the identity of AF even though the "Decryption Intelligence Bulletin" circulated earlier by naval intelligence in Washington on 30 April had listed AF as being Midway.

"It required no exceptional stretch of intelligence to appreciate that AF would have to be Midway," Rochefort pointed out.[24] But it was not such a simple deduction for the analysts in the navy department.[24] They challenged Hypo's analysis.

"The amazing part of the whole thing was that many people could not accept this line of reasoning," Rochefort was to say later while reflecting on the bitter dispute that broke out over the secure Copek cable circuit. "We were quite impatient at Station Hypo that people in Washington could not agree with our rationale, because they had the same information and should, without any particular stress on their brain, have come up with the same answer."[25]

The issue was not simply the correct interpretation of the first and sixth letters of the alphabet, but the question of whether or not radio intelligence evaluations were to be made in Washington or Pearl Harbor. Since the whole course of the Pacific war turned on the correct evaluation—and Washington made the wrong deductions—it is significant to note that the daily records of Cominch's decryption intelligence are missing from 8 May 1942 onward at this point. Furthermore there are extensive deletions in the summaries that survive from the White House map room.

One of the last of the navy department evaluations that has been located reveals the bones of the dispute: "An actual landing may be attempted on Midway or possibly on Johnston Island. Every effort is being made to determine more exactly the reliability of this report and which of the two locations is correct."[26] The OP-20-G head, Commander John R. Redman, evidently chose to conclude that the Japanese were heading for Johnston Island. One factor that apparently influenced his decision was a refusal to believe that by the most incredible coincidence the Japanese should have selected the same two letters as our own code designator for Midway—AF.[27]

"There was no doubt that Washington was totally in error," recalled Tommy Dyer, Rochefort's chief cryptanalyst. "There was never a question in our minds about AF being Midway."[28] According to Hypo's analysis the Japanese designator for Johnston Island was AG, but Washington got around that by claiming that Rochefort's JN-25 additives were unreliable and that what we were reading as AF in the intercept should have been correctly decrypted as AG. The fight was therefore not about whether AF was Midway, but about whose additives were to be accepted. This went right to the heart of the competence issue.

"It was a mess" was how Ham Wright, Dyer's chief assistant, recalled the adversarial relationship. "We would fight with OP-20-G all the time; we could not get together."[29] Rochefort had little respect for the abilities of Jack Redman who was not a trained cryptanalyst. His experience had been less important than his brother's influence in his becoming head of OP-20-G and gaining control of the "correlation and interpretation of all radio intelligence."[30] The feud between the two men exacerbated the natural rivalry of the two intelligence outfits. It became a veritable war of words, which was carried on even in the "padding"—the junk sentences inserted by enciphering officers before and after the actual message text as an additional measure of security.[31]

"Some of it was not too polite," Wright observed laconically. "Washington wanted to take complete charge and tell us what to do in detail, but Rochefort would have no part of it."[32] To the members of Hypo it seemed that the Redman brothers were determined to impose their intelligence evaluations and recoveries of the JN-25 additives on Hypo regardless of whether they were right or wrong. Each combat intelligence unit had been assigned a particular area to concentrate on in the additive recoveries and their results were shared daily on the secure interstation Copek line. The Coral Sea estimates had proved the Hypo cryptanalysts had the edge. This further rankled the Redmans and their allies in Washington.

"It boiled down to who was going to do the work and who was going to get the credit," said Wright, who was later sent to Washington to negotiate a truce. "The Negat cryptanalysts did not want to trust our additives and would not use them. This attitude reached down to OP-20-G's radio operators and the lists we sent in would often wind up in the waste basket. It was very easy to get additives wrong. We were certainly most reluctant to trust theirs, so we worked out our own."[33]

When Rochefort challenged Washington's additives on the "AF" issue, Jack Redman accused him of being uncooperative and getting out of his assigned area of additive recovery. Joe replied by referring curtly to King's recent authorization that Hypo was to deal with all current decrypts. Admiral Nimitz, moreover, had directed him (through me) to try to break *any* messages concerning the air fleet on board the Japanese carriers.[34]

This implicit challenge to Jack Redman's authority infuriated him. He wanted to bring Hypo into his preserve. So instead of utilizing Rochefort's unique cryptanalytic abilities, Redman dug his heels in about his own estimates. He became more and more irritated by some of Joe's tart replies to the estimates from Washington that Japan was preparing to raid Panama or California.

"I was trying to see it from the point of view of the Japanese general staff and was not at all interested in what our own assessments were" was how Rochefort dismissed the fear that the enemy might also be planning to attack the west coast. "I have never been able to understand why Cominch gave any more than a couple of thoughts to the idea that this operation might be directed against the mainland, because it was simply beyond the capability of the Japanese transport and supply operation."[35]

Washington might have raised every conceivable objection to Rochefort's Midway analysis, but after carefully reviewing his conclusions with McCormick, on 14 May Nimitz was firmly convinced that Joe was right. Any doubts about the direction of Japan's offensive he might have had were dispelled later that same day when Hypo decrypted a message from Tokyo listing the American charts to be sent to Saipan. Of the seven reference numbers given, all but one were sections of the Hawaiian Islands.[36]

Although we still had no clear idea of just what forces were being committed to the invasion of Midway, one decrypt revealed that battleship *Hiei,* and Carrier Division 3, were sharing escorts and would depart from Sasebo to take part in the operation. When Nimitz reviewed the situation with me on the evening of Thursday, 14 May, he was in a strategic bind.

On the assumption that our estimates were correct, and that the Japanese would launch their mid-Pacific campaign in about two weeks, there was no time to be lost before retrieving Halsey's two carriers, so that every available task force could be concentrated off Midway. But this had to be effected against Admiral King's express instructions—and at a time that King was still being wrongly advised by his own intelligence staff that the enemy was going south instead of east.

"Evidently Cominch believes the enemy will strike at 'Poppy' and 'Roses' after 25 May" was how Nimitz reacted to King's blast that the

Japanese were intending to seize New Caledonia and Fiji.[37] Nimitz played a tactful devil's advocate by hinting that Japanese forces might even be heading as far east as the west coast. He reassured King that seaplane tender *Tangier* had been dispatched to Noumea, and was able to reject as unnecessary the idea of stranding *Lexington*'s surviving air groups down in New Caledonia. King was assured that Halsey would remain outside the range of land-based bombers but it would be difficult for him to keep his distance from long-range flying boat patrols. Nimitz stressed that Japan's precise plan was still uncertain so it was essential to maintain "our striking forces in a state of maximum mobility to act against advancing enemy forces or to conduct offensive operations as opportunity presents."[38]

The most difficult problem that Nimitz faced was how to free Halsey's two carriers from King's standing order that would keep them down in the southwest Pacific. He proposed that Task Force 16 "may be retained or moved in accordance with information received," and that if the "enemy drive to the southeast is not indicated," it should be recalled to the central Pacific area. A decision was needed because of the "time and distances involved."[39]

Time was indeed the most critical factor. Nimitz recognized this that Thursday evening by setting in motion a stratagem to force King's prompt agreement. He fell in with my suggestion for sending a personal private message to Halsey to let his force be sighted steaming north toward Ocean and Nauru.

Halsey, who was "mad as hell" at the Cincpac relay of King's instruction that it was "inadvisable" for Task Force 16 to operate within enemy air range, fully grasped the situation when he got the second, "eyes only" message. We knew we could count on him to make good use of his onboard radio intelligence unit to confirm he had been spotted before hightailing south under cover of darkness. Since Halsey was effectively being told to ignore Cominch orders to comply with his secret instructions from Cincpac, Nimitz wanted no copies of the dispatch filed.[40]

The next morning Halsey played his assigned role to perfection. Task Force 16 was spotted steaming north 450 miles due east of Tulagi at 1015 by a Japanese flying boat making its patrol report. By late that afternoon he was satisfied he had persuaded the Japanese that he was heading full tilt for the Phosphate Islands, some 700 miles to the north, but he waited until dusk before altering course to the east. Nimitz received almost instantaneous confirmation that our ruse had worked. Decrypts from Fourth Fleet headquarters on Rabaul revealed that Admiral Inouye had mobilized his warships to guard the invasion transports from anticipated attack the following day and orders were issued for "wiping out the enemy striking force."[41]

Halsey managed to slip away to the east, but his very appearance had the desired effect. On the evening of 15 May, I was able to hand to

Nimitz a decrypt reading, "Occupation of Ocean and Nauru postponed indefinitely."[42] Indications of future activities now all pointed to the mid-Pacific. My Enemy Activities File the next day concluded from the map information and a spate of sub sightings off Midway that the Japanese were preparing an "advance to Midway (AF) via Saipan." It predicted, "The occupation of Midway is a necessary step toward an assault on Oahu."[43]

That Friday evening, after reviewing his options, Nimitz issued two dispatches that were to have far-reaching strategic implications. "Desire you proceed to Hawaiian area," he signaled Halsey in the early hours of 16 May. At the same time he sent off a long message to Admiral King—with Halsey as information addressee—justifying his decision to recall Task Force 16 in defiance of the intelligence estimates in Washington.

While Nimitz conceded the possibility of another Japanese thrust in the southwest toward Port Moresby, as well as the probable diversionary raid on the Aleutians, he predicted that the main enemy offensive would be "against Midway-Oahu line, probably involving initially a major landing attack against Midway, for which it is believed the enemy's main striking force will be employed." The timing of these offensives was not yet clear, but Nimitz advised King that "sighting Halsey in south yesterday caused postponement of Ocean and Nauru operations and will expedite northern and central operation."[44]

Since the Pacific Fleet did not have the necessary strength to counter all three offensives, Nimitz believed it essential that Halsey be recalled to Pearl Harbor for the defense of "the most vital area." "Unless the enemy is using radio deception on a grand scale, we have a fairly good idea of his intentions," he concluded, adding that it was possible that Japan would "attack Midway and raid Oahu in the first part of June."[45]

While Joe and I were impressed by this vote of confidence in our estimates, we were aware that by challenging King and his intelligence staff head on, Nimitz had put himself out on a limb—and we were clinging onto it behind him. On the basis of another review the following day, Nimitz considered it advisable to send a follow-up cable to King that addressed the issue dividing Hypo and Negat.

"Considerable difference in estimates probably on the same data is noted," Nimitz admitted. But he insisted that his latest information "does not confirm future enemy concentration at Truk."[46] That Saturday the Cincpac staff met to discuss ways to match our thin offensive and defensive resources. Reassuring news was received from our New Caledonia naval base. After *Yorktown* limped into Noumea, Fletcher reported that a preliminary damage inspection indicated that his carrier could be patched up at Pearl Harbor without the need for dry-docking on the west coast.

Nimitz received his second and even more important break the next evening in an "urgent and confidential" cable in our most secret flag officers code. Washington had made a remarkable turnabout. It now accepted our strategic evaluation. "Differences in estimate due to earlier receipt by you of decryption intelligence" was the face-saving formula that King employed to agree with Nimitz's assessment of the Japanese plan. Evidently Jack Redman had been hauled over the coals and made to eat his previous predictions.[47] It must have been an uncomfortable twenty-four hours spent reviewing and revising intelligence estimates. King did not appreciate being made anyone's fall guy, but now he had admitted that Hypo had been right and his staff wrong. He did not have to, but he did. And that was a remarkable tribute to Hypo.

"I have somewhat revised my estimate and now generally agree with you," King informed Nimitz. Concerned that Memorial Day and the emperor's birthday coincided, he added the caveat "except I believe enemy attempt to capture Midway and Unalaska will occur about May 30th (note the double holiday [sic]) or shortly thereafter." Washington apparently had discovered how their estimates had gone astray, because King now accepted that "enemy south Pacific campaign will be started middle or later part of June and will be strong attempt to capture Moresby plus northeast Australia, or New Guinea and Fijis."[48]

Washington now agreed that Midway was Yamamoto's immediate objective, and that the "enemy intention included effort to trap and destroy a substantial portion of the Pacific Fleet." King concluded by laying down that the "appropriate strategy" for the Pacific Fleet would be "to make a strong concentration" in the Hawaiian areas and "employ strong attrition tactics and not repeat not allow our forces to accept such decisive action as would be likely to incur heavy losses."[49]

These were the guidelines that Nimitz set before his staff at his 18 May strategic review. While I still could not provide a firm timetable for the Japanese offensive, all the indications were that enemy units would be heading east from Saipan in the final days of May. So Nimitz set a 25 May deadline for completing the reinforcement of Midway with planes and submarines, and for sending a North Pacific force to Alaskan waters. Halsey was expected back in Pearl Harbor by 26 May, and Fletcher by 27 May. Nimitz announced that if we could expedite *Yorktown*'s repairs we would have three carriers on station in the critical area off Midway by the first of June.

It did not need any mathematical wizardry to know that even if this near miracle was achievable, our forces would still be perilously outnumbered. Everything now depended on Rochefort's being able to balance the odds by discovering the details of the Japanese battle plan.

31

"You Don't Have to Be Crazy to Work Here —But It Helps"

W E DID NOT KNOW it at the time, but our whole intelligence effort—and the course of the war itself—had been put in jeopardy. It was an incident that I logged in my Enemy Activities File as being "possible raider activity 10 May at 26-43 south, 89-56 west." This pinpointed the location of distress signals we had picked up from a British steamer in the Indian Ocean that had reported being attacked by a German surface raider.[1]

Forty years were to pass before I was to understand the significance of the capture of a five-thousand-ton freighter by the armed merchant cruiser *Thor*. The whole picture emerged from declassified German records and the wartime intelligence records released recently by the New Zealand government. The facts were simple, the results complex. The freighter *Nankin* was seized by the raider *Thor* two days out of Freemantle en route from Wellington to Ceylon. On board were top-secret Royal Navy mail bags.

Fortunately for us the mail bags were not properly examined until they reached Japan more than two months later. When *Thor*'s supply ship *Regensberg* docked at Yokohama on 18 July, the mail was sent to Tokyo where Admiral Wenneker, the German naval attaché, at once realized the importance of the documents. Of special interest were the weekly summaries of the Combined Operations Intelligence Center (COIC) of the New Zealand armed forces. After cabling details of them to Berlin, Wenneker received authority to pass the documents to the Japanese.[2]

Pearl Harbor had supplied COIC with a great amount of sensitive data. Some of it was even referred to as being from "Ultra" sources in "Most Secret" summaries that were circulated on an officers-only basis to twenty-two recipients—including Admiral Nimitz. The intelligence digests were a treasure trove of information for the enemy. They gave the

418

positions of all Allied warships as well as our best estimates of the Japanese dispositions throughout the Pacific, based on my own daily bulletins.

Any Japanese intelligence officer worth his salt would immediately be aware of the success of our radio intercept operation from reading these COIC summaries. They might have suspected that such details as the transfer of flags, and the location of individual seaplane units in the mandates, could have come only from code breaking.[3]

If the Germans had given the *Nankin*'s secret mail to the Japanese as promptly as they had communicated the minutes of the British war cabinet captured eighteen months earlier, it would have blown our intelligence advantage before the most critical battle of the Pacific war. For if the Japanese had changed their operational codes even a week earlier, we would have been deprived of date and final details of their deployment at Midway. Or if Yamamoto had been alerted to the accuracy and detail of the information we had obtained, he might well have reconsidered his strategy. At the very least the Japanese forces would have steamed out to battle on the alert. The surprise that was so essential to our ability to ambush superior forces would have been lost, and the Battle of Midway—if it had been fought at all—might have been the decisive naval victory for Japan that Yamamoto intended.

Years later, another aspect of the situation still gave me sleepless nights. If the Japanese had received the New Zealand summaries before the end of May, and if we were stripped of our intelligence advantage, we would never have been aware of the reasons for it. The British *never* warned us then, or later, that this freighter was carrying a consignment of secret mail to the Royal Navy's Station Anderson in Colombo. My daily bulletins had been sent to the Australian and New Zealand naval boards under strictest secrecy at the express direction of Admiral King. This was against the better judgment of Admiral Nimitz, who was increasingly disturbed about how they were being used by Australia's prime minister. The day after the Cincpac bulletin had reported that the Japanese had called off their Port Moresby operation, for example, reassuring reports appeared in every Australian newspaper to that effect. The prime minister had then announced that there would be plenty of warning of any invasion attempt.

"If I were you, I would not put anything in your intelligence bulletin about the possibility of an attack on Midway," Nimitz told me. "I think the thing to do is to hold this one really close, so there will be no leaks."

We could not afford to raise the enemy's suspicions about their communications. Their radio security was better than before the Coral Sea action. No intercepts were being made that contained complete operational orders. Rochefort was trying instead to put together an outline of their plan from seemingly unrelated instructions that were being issued to the different units. Orders involving Saipan, the Aleutians, the "K" operation, and "AF" were the only guidelines he had to work on in sifting through the decrypts. Another problem was that Hypo was intercepting less than 60 percent of the total Japanese traffic, and less than 40 percent of those messages could be broken. Many of them were only partial translations, so it was like trying to assemble a jigsaw puzzle with lots of missing pieces.[4]

After Rochefort had discovered the key "AF" piece, which locked Midway into the center of the picture, he began the search for leads to the other units that might be involved, and for the date the operation was to begin. The date was the most critical piece of intelligence, and Joe called me on 19 May with an important pointer. That Tuesday he had broken out from a dispatch, sent by a member of Admiral Nagumo's *Kido Butai* staff, references to the attacks "from a northwesterly direction from N-2 day inclusive until N day."[5] Since N minus two was clearly forty-eight hours before the N-date of the invasion—and it specified an indecipherable map reference "50 miles northwest of AF"—this message confirmed that Japan's main carrier striking force was to play a pivotal role in the capture of Midway. Now all we needed to know was what date N-day represented.

Rochefort's cryptanalyst team, led by Dyer and Wright, began a marathon review of every intercept. They carefully checked even unimportant routing instructions to transports for hints of the date. Nimitz, who could not afford to miss the boat on this one, had flashed Task Force 16 an "expedite return" dispatch on 18 May. "That could only mean one thing" was Halsey's reaction to such an urgent summons. "Trouble was brewing somewhere else in the Pacific."[6]

At the beginning of the third week in May, the current decrypts and traffic analysis indicated that the Combined Fleet was still on operational maneuvers south of Japan. But a 20 May decrypt contained instructions for the prebattle conference on Saipan for 26 May. And it contained the vitally important clue "to depart on 27th."[7] Saipan was 2,191 miles from Midway, or five days' steaming at twenty knots. This suggested that N-day could be 2 or 3 June. This was two weeks before the mid-June date that King had predicted, and nearly a week earlier than our original estimates.

Washington refused to buy this new date. And Rochefort just did not have enough of the current additives to break the date-time code out of the superenciphered groups in which the Japanese transmitted them for additional security. What was needed at this crucial juncture was an all-out cooperative effort. But the cryptanalysts at Negat in Washington were not only reluctant to supply the correct additives (which would have proved their estimates wrong), but naval intelligence dug up their own justifications for sticking with the mid-June date.

"All evidence indicates that the Midway attack plans have brought a number of problems which are giving responsible commanders considerable concern, and causing delays," McCollum reported to Admiral King on 23 May. "Although the so-called occupation force is now principally in the Saipan-Guam area, there are indications that the 2nd Fleet striking force may proceed to Truk for some two weeks . . . it is an indication that the main attack is now planned for about the middle of June."[8]

There were even those in Washington who suggested that their Hypo rivals had been taken in by an elaborate Japanese deception. They believed that the real Japanese objective was an attack on the west coast.[9] It was to silence the skeptics in Washington that Rochefort embarked on a brilliant piece of deception that has been celebrated and misinterpreted by every historian who has ever written about Midway.

When he cooked up the stratagem for sending a fake message about a water shortage on Midway, Joe's intention was *not* to persuade Nimitz he was *right*, but to prove Washington *wrong*. The idea came from one of Joe's assistants, Lieutenant Commander Jasper Holmes. He had studied the Midway Pan Am facility before the war when he was with the engineering school at the University of Hawaii, and he had been impressed that the island's entire freshwater supply was obtained from an evaporator plant. On 19 May, after receiving Admiral Bloch's preliminary approval Rochefort brought the scheme over to me.[10]

I took the proposal to Nimitz, who authorized the transmission by submarine cable to Midway of a dispatch that ordered the garrison commander to immediately radio a plain-language emergency request for water. At the same time the report was to be made by one of the strip-cipher code systems we knew the Japanese had captured on Wake. This would make a convincing detailed follow-up to the emergency first-flash report of an explosion in their water distillation system.

The instructions were duly sent out to the Midway commander that same Tuesday. Midway broadcast the messages soon afterward. They were picked up by the Japanese listening post at Kwajalein and flashed to the Owada headquarters of the Special Duty Radio Intelligence Group the same day.

The American emergency report electrified the Special Duty unit, to the surprise of Lieutenant Kenichi Nakumuta who had just joined the staff as a language student-reservist. "It was puzzling to me," he was later to recall, "knowing nothing of the impending assault on Midway, why such a 'shortage of fresh water' should be so important."[11] Later, he was "mortified" when he discovered how his superiors had fallen for the ruse and radioed the intelligence to the units involved. For within hours, the commander of the air unit destined for Midway was signaling headquarters to supply his force with emergency water supplies.

When that message was intercepted at Pearl, it surprised even Rochefort's second-in-command, who had not been let in on our secret. "I happened to read the Japanese interception of the water message," Captain Dyer recalled, "and I was so ignorant of the whole affair that I told Rochefort, 'Those stupid bastards on Midway. What do they ever mean by sending out a message like this in plain language.'"[12]

Tactfully, Rochefort decided to let Station Belconnen in Melbourne be the first to break the news to Washington. They obliged the next day with their translation: "The AF air unit sent following radio message to commandant 14th Naval district. AK (Pearl Harbor) of 20th. With reference to this unit's report dated 19th. At present time we have only enough water for two weeks. Please supply us immediately."[13]

To keep up the deception, Fourteenth Naval District headquarters at Pearl Harbor had also radioed the Midway garrison that barges of fresh water were on the way. It was essential that Washington did not suspect that they were the main objects of our little piece of deception. Belconnen stated, "This will confirm identity of AF." Rochefort tactfully waited until Friday morning to send his reminder: "As stated previously AF confirmed here as Midway."[14]

Our deception about water produced an unexpected bonus—and another black eye for Hypo's detractors in Negat. The Japanese air unit's request for a two-week water reserve revealed that the Japanese planned the Midway assault to be completed *before* Washington's predicted date of 15 June. Rochefort set about trying to pin down his hunch that N-day, when the Japanese carrier force would be northwest of the atoll, would be 2 or 3 June. With Midway being only three days of hard steaming away from Pearl, and with Halsey's task force due on 26 May, and Fletcher anticipated a day later, Nimitz had no margin for error if he was going to concentrate our forces for an ambush.

Rochefort now put his phenomenal power of recall, and all his cryptanalysts, to the test. With less than a week remaining before Nimitz had to issue his final orders, decrypts were being processed at the rate of five hundred to a thousand a day. Each one had to be scanned, although many of them were reports of transport movement. Others were so badly garbled, or incomplete, that valuable hours might be taken up trying to make sense of a word or two. Just processing the intercepts was a demanding physical effort, because each one had its five-digit groups punched into IBM cards. A single message might require anywhere from sixty to seventy of the slim, manila three-by-seven, eighty-column IBM cards. A lengthy signal could easily consume two hundred of them. Each one had to be hand-punched and sorted by the former band members of battleship *California,* who manned the IBM machines that they kept chattering around the clock.

In the frantic but meticulous search for the key that would unlock the final piece of the Midway puzzle, Hypo was consuming nearly three million punch cards a month. Just keeping Hypo supplied without arousing the suspicion of outsiders created a security risk. And storing all the cards in hundreds of open boxes for future reference created severe problems. For the printouts produced from the tabulating process, from which the

Japanese messages could be translated, were piled up on desks, floors, and every available space. Each analyst working on current decrypts needed his own stack of binders containing the printouts of past messages for reference.

"We didn't have time to cross-file or cross-index, and it was one reason why people thought we were crazy" was how Rochefort recalled that hectic week of effort. "You'd mention something and someone would recall a previous message and they'd look in this pile of junk—all the previous messages that had come in—and were able to locate it."[15]

To outsiders like myself, who had the necessary security clearance to get past the armed marine door guard, the Hypo "dungeon" was organized chaos. Over his desk the enigmatic Captain Dyer had hung a sign reading, YOU DON'T HAVE TO BE CRAZY TO WORK HERE—BUT IT HELPS! Under the glass on his desk resided what was reputed to be the best collection of pin-ups in the Pacific Fleet, which added its own touch to an unbelievably cluttered appearance. But Tommy Dyer knew exactly where everything was on it. A new yeoman once made the mistake of tidying up the legendary "Dyer's desk" and it brought down Dyer's wrath after he was unable to locate a critical decrypt.[16]

What saved the whole system from collapsing was the team's overall easygoing lack of hierarchy and its remarkable ability to recall and relate details of decrypts made months earlier. "People might not believe that this was how it was done, because we had no machinery other than the IBM punches, sorters, and tabulators," Joe later recalled, noting how he "kept everything in his head."[17]

"I would receive the decrypted messages, in Japanese but not in full," Rochefort explained. "They might say, 'From Commander in Chief Sixth Fleet to Commander in Chief Striking Force: You will . . .' and then a bunch of blanks. 'Upon completion of this, you will proceed . . .' and then some more blanks. My job was to fill it in. I could remember back three or four months when that command had sent a similar message."[18]

In this way Rochefort personally reviewed and filled in the blanks of some 140 messages a day. New decrypts often enabled him to make new connections and after as many gaps as possible had been filled in, the cryptanalysts' work sheets had to be collated. Donald M. Showers, who had joined the Hypo team as an ensign in February 1942, stayed with the unit until January of 1945 when I took him to Cincpac advance headquarters in Guam as my assistant. He eventually became a rear admiral and a chief of staff of the Defense Intelligence Agency.

"When we read a partially decrypted message we would always try to mentally fill in the blanks with the help of our accumulation of similar examples. Often the meaning of an unknown code group would then materialize."[19] Showers recalled the work he did as an assistant to Holmes. "We typed the translated decrypts onto a five-by-eight card, the entire message: call signs, date-time groups, frequency of transmission when known, and then the text," Showers recalled. "We underlined everything that was meaningful. Then we used a multilith duplicator to make twenty or thirty copies of each, depending on the number of underlined items. The cards were then placed in racks of open boxes in date sequence with a special set for each underlined item, such as all abbreviations and designators. When one of the cryptanalysts recalled some earlier decrypt, I would break out a stack of cards for the day in question and search through them by the underlinings. Each of our recoveries was valued from A to D, according to reliability."[20]

Much was to be written after the war about Rochefort's eccentric dress, because he wore a battered smoking jacket and slippers to combat the frigidity of the temperamental air-conditioning system. The pressure of work was so great during the first six months of the war that Joe went into Honolulu only twice. And during the critical weeks of May he virtually lived in the Hypo office. He had a cot installed so that he could be on call around the clock. The other members of the team also put in long hours, fighting mental and physical fatigue with Benzedrine tablets that were passed around like jellybeans.

Slowly but surely, the enormous effort inspired by Rochefort began to pay off. On 21 May, Hypo decrypted an order for a *maru* transport to load munitions and supplies for the Occupation Force and Striking Force and "June 2nd (or 3rd) depart Kure for Truk." This bracketed the possible dates for the Midway invasion, because it was an indication that the second phase of Yamamoto's campaign "starts from Truk about 15 June."[21]

In best crossword puzzle tradition, some of the clues were misleading. A partial translation of a 21 May message listed "small craft which are to proceed to Truk by unknown date." Hypo cryptanalysts failed to break out the superencipherment dates, so it was forwarded to Washington with the comment that the 34839 group was "the date the forthcoming campaign gets under way." Negat replied that additives made this 15 June. Rochefort then realized that the message referred to the planned movement *after* Midway had been captured. But Washington seized on it as further proof that Japan's campaign would not begin until 15 June![22]

Mid-June did not, however, square with Hypo's intercept of orders to an oiler, previously identified as being part of the Japanese carrier striking force, which was to carry out refueling on 30 May.[23] Nor did it fit a Belconnen decrypt of a revision in the instructions transmitted to the submarine force commander at Kwajalein that his patrol "prior to _____ will be 150 miles more or less to the westward of AI."[29] We knew that AI was the designator for the Hawaiian Islands, so this clearly referred to the line of submarines that were intended to give warning of our forces heading out from Pearl for Midway, and which were to be in place *before* the invasion was launched.

These and other decrypts were read in conjunction with more signals that detailed the time and place of the prebattle conference, like the one to be held on board flagship *Akagi* "at 0830 26 May, regarding air operations of Striking Force."[25] Another confirmation that the Midway occupation was set for 2 or 3 June came from a signal summoning the Aleutians task force for a 26 May conference, from which Rochefort concluded from fragments, "date departure Ominato commencement of operations is 27th at the earliest."[26]

While the Hypo team were laboring through the decrypts to fit together the precise time sequence of the complex Japanese operation, Nimitz was pressing me for information. I sensed from his controlled impatience that he was weighing the magnitude of the risk that he was willing to run against the pressure from King to accept the mid-June date for the Japanese operation. But I knew that he had faith in us and that he would probably back Rochefort's estimate against the conflicting information that he was receiving from Washington. Joe and I were acutely aware we had to be certain of the date of Japan's N-day. We used the secure line to discuss every new clue forty or more times a day.

When Nimitz called his staff together on 26 May, on the eve of Halsey's return to Pearl, I could still not name the day with absolute certainty. My best calculation was that one attacking force would depart for the Aleutians from Ominato in northern Japan on 25 or 26 May, and that the Midway invasion force would sail from the Saipan area a day or so later. If my assumptions were correct, this meant that our forces would have to be in position in the Alaskan sector by 1 June, and off Midway by 3 June at the very latest.

Reviewing the options open to him, Nimitz was under no illusions. As he put it: "Common sense dictates that we cannot now afford to slug it out with the probably superior approaching Japanese forces." He reminded his staff of King's directive "to employ strong attrition tactics and not allow our forces to accept such decisive action as would be likely to incur heavy losses in our carriers and cruisers."[27] On the assumption that *Yorktown* could be repaired and turned around in four days—and that was a capital "IF" until the carrier had been dry-docked—Nimitz hoped to be able to get three task forces to the waters off Midway by "about 1 June." Carrier *Saratoga* was not scheduled to leave San Diego until 5 June and so "could be in the critical area of the Central Pacific only if the Japanese are considerably later than now expected." Every plane that could be spared was being rushed to reinforce Midway. A northern Pacific force of heavy cruisers was being formed of "all the forces which can reach Alaskan waters during the first week in June." Our submarines would concentrate in the waters off Midway with orders to attack "with regard to assigned sectors."[28]

Attrition tactics, however, required detailed knowledge of "enemy intentions." So Nimitz announced that he was counting on our "ability to detect changes in enemy intentions." Everything had to be done to preserve our tactical advantage: "Extreme care will be used to prevent the enemy from gaining information of our deployment by radio or otherwise."[29] It was essential that the Japanese believe that Task Force 17's two carriers were still in the southwest Pacific, and he had already alerted them, "Do not break radio silence to report position." Their pilots were instructed not to use their radios at any time, even when coming in to land.[30] Halsey and Fletcher had been informed that a search plane would be sent out to meet them with harbor entry instructions.[31]

"More information of the enemy is expected," Nimitz told his staff, and that his operations plan would be issued "prior to the departure of major forces."[32] With the sailing of the Japanese invasion force less than two days away, it had already been drafted on the assumption that his own intelligence staff had correctly estimated the date when the enemy would commence operations. Nimitz reasoned that this was the most prudent course of action. If Washington was right and the Japanese did not invade Midway until two weeks later, our only loss would be fuel. Waiting, however, could lead to disaster. And Nimitz had no desire to suffer the fate of Admiral Kimmel, who had been made a scapegoat for the miscalculations of the navy department in Washington.

Nimitz was too much of a realist not to take very serious account that the Japanese might be deceiving us. He questioned me closely about the possibility after receiving a personal warning the previous day from the Hawaiian Army commander. General Delos C. Emmons had evidently been alerted to naval intelligence's concerns by Admiral King.

"Japs may be practicing deception with radio orders intercepted by us," Emmons had cautioned Nimitz. "Estimates should be directed at capabilities rather than probable intentions. Forces reported in Cominch dispatch 21st have sufficient strength to make damaging raid on Oahu with view to wrecking facilities Pearl Harbor and Honolulu."[33]

Although Emmons was principally alarmed at losing control of his B-17, long-range bombers that Nimitz was urging be sent to help defend Midway, it was galling that Washington had backhandedly enlisted the army's support to try to turn Nimitz against Hypo. Apparently they shared Marshall's uneasiness that "one Japanese unit gave Midway as its post office address, and that seemed a little bit too thick."[34]

"If it sounds too good to be true, it probably is." This old saying may have been one of the factors that caused the naval staff in Washington to continue in its attempts to cast doubts on Hypo's analysis of both the timing and the objective of the impending enemy operation. "While all available information indicates that attack and occupation of Midway is the objective of the force assembled at Saipan," the Cominch intelligence summary of 24 May stated, "attention is invited to the fact that from this base a force can move with almost equal facility southward in the direction of Australia."[35]

This astonishing volte-face by Washington defied the logic of their own analysis. That very day a Hypo decrypt referring to the transport of American weapons that had been captured on Wake in a *maru* that would depart from the atoll "on N-3 day for Midway"[36] was connected to an earlier message arranging to have the captured "terror guns" sent by tender "on 4 June to be transported to AF."[37] The OP-20-G analysts had therefore made the logical deduction that if these guns were the same ones, then "N-3 days is at the earliest June 4th."[38] Yet, the very same day, Captain McCollum was advising Admiral King and the president's map room that "the forces involved in the attack are still scattered and not ready to move."[39]

The inability of naval communications and naval intelligence to adjust their preconceptions to factual information had proved fatal before the Pearl Harbor attack. The same clouded evaluations were again being made in Washington. Fortunately for the navy, the Pacific Fleet was not going to be trapped a second time by such wooden thinking and complacency. That Monday, Rochefort called me with a partially decrypted message referring to "Occupation Force Operational Order No. 4." It directed a unit to "depart Kure on N-5," on a date that was given in the code group 74448, in order to "join main body of occupation force."[40] It was hardly necessary for Rochefort to advise Negat "this date important," because it was self-evident that adding five days would give the date of the Midway invasion.

The battle with Washington over Midway, and their insistence that the Japanese had delayed their operation until mid-June, persuaded Rochefort that Hypo must make an all-out effort to break the recalcitrant Japanese date-time groups—with or without Negat's help. Their objective was to break through to discover the key to unlock the superenciphement of the date-time information which had been preencoded before the message was put into the JN-25B cipher. The Hypo staff searched back through their memories and the stacks of printouts and punch cards for similar five-digit number sequences. They found that all possible ones were only of C and D grades, not the most reliable. But at least they now had a starting point. Next they had to unravel the cipher itself. It was Lieutenant Joseph Finnegan, a linguist-cryptanalyst, who finally hit upon the method that the Japanese had used to lock up their date-time groups.

It was a neat, simple substitution cipher, with garble check, involving a 12 × 31 (12 rows for months, 31 columns for days) garble table. The 31 kana of the first row were A, I, U, E, O, KA, KI . . . . HA, HI, FU, HE, HO. The second row was I, U, E, O, ... HE, HO, A; the third, U, E, O . . . . . HO, A, I, and so on, for 12 rows. At the left, representing the 12 months, was a column of 12 kana, different from those in the table—SA, SI, SU, SE, SO, TA, TI, TU, TE, TO, NA, NI (SA for January, NI for December). To encipher, for example, 27 May, one picked the 5th line (May=SO), ran across to the twenty-seventh column, HA, and recorded the kana at that intersection, HO. The encipherment, then, was SO HA HO, the third kana providing the garble check.[41]

This simple table allowed Rochefort to break out the dates from a Combined Fleet intercept of 26 May that contained the orders for two groups of destroyers escorting the invasion transports to Midway. This signal really clinched the pivotal date of the operation, because they were to leave Saipan on 28 May and proceed at eleven knots for a 1 June rendezvous at an indecipherable location, then "at 1900 6 June arrive at AF."[42] This meant that the actual attack would occur a day earlier at least. There could no longer be any doubt that N-day was to be either 4 or 5 June.

Joe kept me posted by telephone on the progress the Hypo team made throughout 26 May. I informed Nimitz, who needed the information for the staff conference he had called for the next day as a final review of what he called "the Midway problem." At this time it was originally intended that I should brief Admiral Halsey. But the previous day Nimitz had received a shock for which he was unprepared.

When Task Force 16 had docked, the commander we were counting on to lead our outnumbered forces in the most critical action of the war reported to headquarters. He was worn, haggard, and ready only for a hospital bed. Unknown to us, Halsey had been suffering for weeks from a progressive skin irritation that was to be diagnosed as dermatitis. He vigorously protested when Nimitz ordered him to the base medical facility. Halsey called it "the most grievous disappointment of my career." But he insisted that the man to take his place on *Enterprise*'s flag bridge was his cruiser commander, Rear Admiral Raymond A. Spruance.

Nimitz did not demur. Spruance's intellectual capacity and readiness to take advice were qualities that had already marked him out for a place at Cincpac headquarters. Although he had no experience as a carrier tactician, the cruiser admiral was familiar with Halsey's staff, and he had the quickness of mind essential for a task force commander. His lack of seniority, however, would require him to defer to Admiral Fletcher if *Yorktown* could be repaired in time to join the action. Meanwhile, Nimitz counted on Spruance's proven ability as an administrator to dispel friction between the two commands.

Any apprehension on Nimitz's part about Spruance not being the right choice was dispelled by the rapidity with which he set about briefing himself for the next day's staff discussion. General Emmons had also been invited to attend so as to calm the army's fears that our carriers were not chasing a wild goose to Midway. Also attending was General Robert C. Richardson, who had been sent out to Hawaii by Marshall. The conference, therefore, was an occasion at which Nimitz wanted to present the whole intelligence picture. It was one of the rare occasions when he summoned Rochefort to attend.

Joe naturally wanted to be as certain as he could of the accuracy of the information on which the Pacific Fleet would be sent out to do battle. He was fully aware that the Pacific war might be lost on a miscalculated code break. So when the staff assembled at the appointed hour and Rochefort had not appeared, I checked my watch and wondered what had happened to him.

Joe finally turned up half an hour late, looking disheveled and bleary-eyed from lack of sleep. Well aware that he had kept the commander in chief waiting, he could not escape the icy gaze that greeted his brief apology. He explained that he had been reviewing all the intelligence details that we had assembled on the Midway invasion and he handed Nimitz the information about the escort forces, with a brief comment about its significance.

"The atmosphere was very impersonal," Rochefort would later remember.

> Admiral Nimitz asked me a question, and I would look over there and see four stars. I would answer that to the best of my ability I was sure of my facts, but stressed that they were only deductions. I could not have blamed him if he had not accepted my estimates. I think, looking back, that it was obvious when Nimitz sent for me that he had already decided on his course of action. His operational orders were set and the matter closed. My appearance at this final staff meeting was to ensure that everyone was thinking alike.[43]

In a sense, Rochefort was correct. Nimitz had decided to put his own staff intelligence above the conflicting estimates being made in Washington. On the previous day I had spent many hours at the Cincpac plot, calculating and tracing the possible elements of the Japanese strategy as they were revealed by traffic analysis and the decrypts.

The latest Hypo information had enabled me to make a more precise estimate of the distance-time factors by applying the rule that when you don't know things, you had to try to see them as if you were a Jap. Working backward from the sailing dates, and the decrypted orders for the 6 June arrival of the invasion force transports, I reconstructed a tentative plot that was accurate enough to predict when and where the transports carrying the assault troops should be sighted by search planes from Midway.

This was relatively simple to calculate, because transports had to take a pretty direct route from Guam. When it came to the carrier striking force, which would set out from Saipan, I could not be so certain. They had the speed to make the kind of detour they had made to reach Oahu undetected. I estimated that they would probably do so again, but one thing was certain, they would have to be within air-strike distance of Midway on 3 or 4 June to carry out the scheduled softening-up raids set for N minus 2.

This was when Nimitz asked me for the all-important information: Name the dates and dispositions the enemy intends to take up around Midway. I told him that it was still very difficult for me to be specific.

"I want you to be specific," Nimitz said, fixing me with his cool blue eyes. "After all, this is the job I have given you—to be the admiral commanding the Japanese forces, and tell me what is going on."

It was a tall order, given that so much was speculation rather than hard fact. I knew that I would have to stick my neck out, but that was clearly what he wanted. Summarizing all my data, I told Nimitz that the carriers would probably attack on the morning of 4 June, from the northwest on a bearing of 325 degrees. They could be sighted at about 175 miles from Midway at around 0700 local time.

On the strength of this estimate Admiral Nimitz crossed his Rubicon on 27 May 1942. At the staff conference, which set the seal on our Midway defense plan, he gave the impression of being thoroughly confident that the Japanese would appear when and where I had predicted. But the next seven nights were sleepless ones for me. I knew very well the extent to which Nimitz had staked the fate of the Pacific Fleet on our estimates, and his own judgment, against those of Admiral King and his staff in Washington.

32

"A Glorious Page in Our History"

I T WOULD BE a week and a half before Nimitz received proof that the intelligence estimates on which he had staked the fate of the Pacific Fleet were correct. Those days seemed more like years to the staff. Rochefort, however, was relaxed and confident.

"If we get ready for this attack on June 3 and it does not come off, we may look silly," Joe was saying, "but there will be time for our ships to refuel and get back on station. If we are not prepared and the Japs strike, it will be a case of Pearl Harbor all over again—and the Navy will have no excuse."[1]

Nimitz was also quietly confident. After the crucial staff conference on 27 May, at which the plans for Midway had been approved, he visited carrier *Enterprise* and told one of the three pilots he decorated with the Distinguished Flying Cross, "I think you'll have a chance to win yourself another medal in the next few days."[2]

A few hours later *Yorktown* limped into Pearl, trailing a ten-mile-long oil slick from her leaking tanks. Tugs nudged the carrier through the open caisson gates of the flooded number 1 dry dock and powerful pumps roared into action. The last of the water was still being drained late that Wednesday afternoon when Nimitz donned waders to lead an inspection party of shipwrights and engineers under the dripping hull. After seeing for himself where the carrier's plates had been sprung by the near misses of Japanese bombs, he ordered the minimum repairs necessary to make her seaworthy. A giant steel patch was to be welded to the hull; weakened internal bulkheads were to be shored up with timber. Time did not permit anything fancier. All that mattered was that *Yorktown* be made ready for battle in the shortest possible time.

"We must have the ship back in three days," Nimitz told his engineers.[3] Within an hour the cranes were swinging the steel plates into position. As darkness fell, fifteen hundred dockyard workers were assembled from less-urgent tasks and lights were rigged for work to continue through the night in spite of the blackout.

When Nimitz returned to headquarters, he found Fletcher waiting in his office. He was prepared to make a preliminary oral report on the Coral Sea action. Reluctantly, Nimitz informed him that he needed to submit a detailed analysis by the next day to answer Admiral King's criticism of Task Force 17's tardy refueling and failure to conduct its operations with sufficient aggression. Admiral Spruance joined them briefly; then he and Fletcher got down to the afternoon's most important business. The conference included the task force's operational and intelligence staffs and Nimitz's own staff. It continued into the evening as we hammered out the final details of the battle plan.

"In carrying out the tasks assigned in OP Plan 29-42, you will be governed by the principle of calculated risk," read the ten-page-long Midway operational orders. Fletcher and Spruance's objective would be to "inflict maximum damage on the enemy by employing strong attrition tactics."[4] Our blueprint for the forthcoming action spelled out the estimated disposition of the Japanese. This included the mustering of their carrier striking force northwest of Midway for preliminary raids during the approach of their invasion force, while a diversionary attack was to be made on the Aleutians. Since not all of those attending had comint clearance, security considerations prevented me from revealing to the conference how we could be so certain of the enemy plans other than by stating that my confidence derived from information I had obtained from a "very reliable source."

"That man of ours in Tokyo is worth every cent we pay him," *Enterprise*'s navigating officer, Commander Richard Ruble, commented.[5] Like many of the other officers who were briefed on our plan, he assumed that our detailed knowledge of the enemy intentions must have come from espionage. I could only hope that our intelligence would not betray their confidence, because the following morning both Rochefort and I would have dearly loved it if we had our mythical man in Tokyo. During the night the Japanese put a new version of their naval code system into action, effectively blacking out our ability to detect last-minute changes in the enemy's battle plan.

Although we had been anticipating this revision in the JN-25 naval operational code (it had been postponed twice), the change from the B version of the cipher to the C version was a body blow. It meant that eighteen months of hard work had to be abandoned overnight, and the grueling labor of assembling additive groups had to begin all over again. It was some consolation to know that the blackout would have been even more disastrous had it occurred a few days earlier, for in the week prior to the forthcoming battle we decrypted only four enemy signals and none of these pertained to the Midway operation.

As the navy's top secret 1942 evaluation of our radio intelligence put it, in a report that remained classified for forty years: "It was all over but the shooting!"[6] We had certainly done our best. But we still had to wait and hope that our best was good enough for the sailors and airmen on whom everything now depended.

Even if we could no longer eavesdrop directly on the Japanese moves, we could fool Admiral Yamamoto into believing that our carriers were still in the South Pacific. So as Task Force 16 slipped out of Pearl Harbor on 28 May, and Spruance set course for the aptly named Point Luck some 350 miles northeast of Midway, we began an elaborate radio deception to disguise our own movements. At Efate, 1,500 miles to the southwest in the New Hebrides, seaplane tender *Tangier* pretended to be a full-fledged carrier making transmissions in a pattern similar to that of a task force flying routine air operations. The same ploy was used by heavy cruiser *Salt Lake City* on patrol in the Coral Sea. The idea was to persuade Japanese traffic analysts at the Owada intelligence center outside Tokyo that Halsey's two carriers were more than 1,000 miles away from Midway.[7]

The major units of the Japanese Combined Fleet began their eastward sorties the same day. First to sail was Admiral Nagumo's Striking Force, the *Kido Butai*. This time it was composed of Carrier Divisions 1 and 2, plus two battleships escorted by two heavy cruisers and a dozen destroyers, and accompanied by five oilers. Also, the main force of three battlewagons, a light carrier, two seaplane carriers, and nine destroyers left tranquil Hashirajima anchorage through the Bungo Strait. Our radio intelligence had not revealed this latter and vital part of Yamamoto's operation. Nor did we know that it would be led by the commander in chief himself in superbattleship *Yamato*.

According to the elaborate choreography of Yamamoto's plan, twelve *maru* transports, carrying the five-thousand-strong Midway occupation force, departed from Saipan the next morning. They were escorted by a light cruiser and ten destroyers. Also setting sail from nearby Guam were the two battleships, four heavy cruisers, one light cruiser, and seven destroyers of the Midway covering force, together with the four heavy cruisers and two destroyers of the support force.

As for the attack on the Aleutians, that striking force of two light cruisers, two heavy cruisers, two seaplane tenders, and four destroyers was already plowing its way across the northern Pacific when the eight transports carrying the Kiska and Attu invasion force sailed from Ominato in northern Japan on 29 May. Their close escort of two cruisers and six destroyers was to rendezvous with another cruiser squadron off the Kurile Islands.

By 30 May, 145 Japanese warships were at sea. Their boilers were devouring more fuel than the imperial navy had consumed during the previous year. The tiny patch of Pacific coral sand whose two thousand acres was the object for their invasion represented less dry land than the total deck area of the Japanese ships involved in the operation.

The thirty-five surface ships that Nimitz had mustered to oppose this armada were insignificant by comparison. Spruance's Task Force 16 included only five heavy cruisers, one light cruiser, and nine destroyers with carriers *Enterprise* and *Hornet*. That Saturday morning Fletcher sailed from Pearl to rendezvous with Spruance at Point Luck with *Yorktown* and the two heavy cruisers and six destroyers of Task Force 17.

A few hours later, Rear Admiral Robert A. Theobald headed north from Pearl in command of two heavy cruisers, three light cruisers, and four destroyers. Theobald had been briefed that our "reliable sources" indicated the enemy intended to capture Kiska and Attu and raid Dutch Harbor. But without telling us, he decided to ignore our intelligence estimate. He believed it was an enemy ruse. Instead he decided to follow his own hunch that the Japanese intended to attack Alaska. Accordingly he headed out to ambush them four hundred miles south of Kodiak Island. This blunder put Theobald's force a thousand miles east of the position we had anticipated for him. As a result, his force was helpless to intervene when the Japanese attacked three days later exactly where and when we had predicted.[8]

Fortunately, Fletcher and Spruance did not duplicate Theobald's total disregard of intelligence. If they had, Nimitz's strategy would have been in ruins. As it was, shortly after midday, 31 May, we sent out to all task force commanders our updated "Estimate of Midway Force Organization." This listed *Akagi, Kaga, Hiryu,* and *Soryu* as the four Japanese carriers in the striking force. We predicted they would be accompanied by two battleships, four heavy cruisers, and twelve destroyers. The support force would include one carrier, two battleships, four heavy cruisers, two light cruisers, and ten destroyers. We were less certain about the number and type of escorts for the four *maru* transports of the occupation force, but we predicted that at least fourteen enemy submarines would be on patrol off Midway.

Our final estimate omitted entirely Yamamoto's main force that was bringing up the rear. Therefore, it did not appear on the large-scale maps on which we laid out the courses of the opposing forces converging on Midway. At that time the Cincpac operation plotting room was a rather primitive affair that consisted of a large chart of the Pacific laid over plywood across a pair of sawhorses.[9] On top of the chart was tracing paper on which plotting officers laid down the movements of our ships in blue crayon, with the estimated tracks of the Japanese forces in orange. Every midnight we replaced the overlays with fresh ones, incorporating the latest intelligence data and predictions.

Apart from our serious omission of Yamamoto's main force, another bit of data that did not find its way onto the Midway plot was the presence of John Ford and his film crew on the atoll. At the time the Hollywood director was at Pearl Harbor on attachment as a lieutenant commander in the navy, and it seemed to me a good idea to get some morale-boosting footage of the upcoming action. I called Ford into my office and, without disclosing any details, asked if he was interested in a trip "somewhere in the Pacific" that might produce some interesting shots.

"Can you guarantee action?" Ford asked.

"As near as I can guarantee anything," I told him. Ford agreed and I went to see Nimitz. He approved the plan and asked me to have Ford and his cameraman flown out to Midway. He insisted on absolute secrecy, so I called Ford into my office after putting everyone else out.

"Where you are going, you won't know till you get there, and you won't be able to send any messages," I told him. "It's so secret and the United States is right on the line. If you want this assignment we'll put you on an airplane and fly you there this afternoon."

"You wouldn't kid me," Ford said.

I assured him I would not. He promised me honorary membership in the Hollywood drinking club he had formed with John Wayne, so I swore on my nomination that what I was telling him about a major battle was true. "It's a chance for a scoop that no one else is going to have and it may even get you an Oscar." He was finally convinced. By 1500 he and his cameraman reported to Kaneohe air station where two PBYs were waiting to take them to Midway.

When Ford returned two weeks later with his remarkable shots of Midway under attack, he thanked me. After the war he gave me a bit part in a movie called *Big Jim McClain*. Still, the fact remains that had it not been for three critical blunders by the Japanese during the last forty-eight hours of May, Ford might have become a prisoner of war. His film footage would then have ended up in a Japanese victory documentary celebrating their capture of the island "Minazuki"—the classical Japanese name for the month of June—the mailing address that they had overconfidently assigned to the Midway occupation force. (The characters for it translate "no water month," an interesting coincidence of our "AF" ruse.)

The first setback to Yamamoto's Midway campaign came with the cancellation of the 30 May reconnaissance flight over Pearl Harbor. This occurred when the submarines detailed to refuel the "K" operation seaplanes arrived off the French Frigate Shoals and found one of our patrol boats anchored in the lagoon. The next error was a two-day delay in getting all their submarines on station west of the Hawaiian Islands, which allowed our two task forces to slip by undetected. The third lapse was Yamamoto's decision not to break radio silence to ensure that Admiral Nagumo had picked up signals indicating that an American carrier task force might be in Hawaiian waters.

Three hundred miles ahead of the main force, the four carriers of the

Kido Butai continued steaming toward Midway ignorant of the possibility that the Americans might be within striking distance. *Akagi*'s radio operators had failed to pick up the suspicious radio transmissions that had alerted Yamamoto's communications officer, and Nagumo relied on the reassuring reports that were relayed from Tokyo reporting that the only two American carriers afloat were a thousand miles away in the South Pacific. It had apparently not occurred to the Japanese intelligence analyst that *Yorktown* might not only have survived the trip back from the Coral Sea, but that it would be possible for us to get her back into action in any less time than the three months needed to repair the damaged *Shokaku*.

The Japanese were completely taken in by our radio deception scheme. We, however, were not fooled by their elaborate efforts to divert our attention. They materialized on 1 June with reports of midget-submarine attacks on a British battleship at Madagascar, and the torpedoing of a ferryboat in Sydney Harbor. Although we had not picked up any advance warning of these diversions, they failed to arouse Washington's fears that Japan might be preparing to invade Australia.

We knew too much about Yamamoto's operation to be taken in on 3 June, when an urgent dispatch was received just after 0800 that Wednesday, informing us that Japanese carrier planes had just bombed Dutch Harbor on Unalaska Island off the western tip of Alaska. The message that really galvanized Pacific Fleet headquarters had come in a hour earlier. It was the electrifying sighting report of a Midway-based PBY reconnaissance plane: "Main Body . . . bearing 262, distance 700 miles. . . . Eleven ships, course 090, speed 19 knots."[10]

I happened to be in Nimitz's office when this message came in. His eyes lit up like searchlights.

"Layton," he said excitedly, "have you seen this?"

"What is it, sir?"

"The sighting of the Japanese forces," Nimitz replied, giving me a dazzling smile. "It ought to make your heart warm."

The admiral was positively beaming as he waved the PBY dispatch reporting the invasion force west of Midway. The Japanese were exactly where we had put them on our plot. "This will clear up the doubters now," Nimitz declared. "They just have to see this to know that what I told them is correct."

To avoid any chance that Fletcher and Spruance would be confused, Nimitz immediately sent them an urgent dispatch: "Main body . . . that is not, repeat not, the enemy striking force."[11]

The invasion force was attacked that afternoon from ten thousand feet by nineteen army B-17s flown from Midway. The unpracticed bombardiers failed to score a single hit, despite enthusiastic claims that they had sunk several "*Normandie*-type" transports. Later that evening, Navy PBY pilots swooped down on the convoy to make a low-level torpedo attack and managed to damage an oiler. But they failed to halt the convoy's eastward march toward Midway.

Admiral Yamamoto was apparently unconcerned about the reports of the two bombing attacks. According to the calculations made by his staff, our discovery of the intention to invade Midway would hasten any possible sortie from Pearl Harbor by only a few noncritical hours.

Confidence was building, too, at Pacific Fleet headquarters that evening. Nimitz flashed out an encouraging dispatch to the task force commanders. "The situation is developing as expected. Carriers, our most important objective, should soon be located. Tomorrow may be the day you can give them the works." That day's entry in the Cincpac Command Summary concluded with the prophetic words: "The whole course of the war in the Pacific may hinge on the developments of the next two or three days."[12]

That night our armed forces were on maximum alert on the west coast and in the Hawaiian Islands. California's radio stations closed down early to prevent enemy bombers from homing in on their transmitters. Standing out to sea from Seattle to San Diego, a long line of requisitioned motor yachts and fishing boats, manned by naval reservists, patrolled the dark waters to give early warning of any Japanese attempt to raid the mainland.

The defenders of Midway had no doubt that they were the objective of enemy forces bearing down on them. As the first gray streaks of light over the eastern horizon signaled the dawn of 4 June, the atoll was at the point of an invisible four-hundred-mile-long V, with the opposing fleets closing on each other as they advanced down its sides. Nagumo's carriers were off to the northwest. Our own task forces were four hundred miles away to the northeast. Unknown to the Japanese, the distance between them and three hostile carriers was steadily decreasing as the pilots, bombardiers, and navigators of both sides breakfasted, were briefed and clambered into their cockpits.

The opposing aircrews, awaiting signals to take off, had very different targets in mind. Shortly after dawn, the Japanese planes began taking off to raid Midway. They had been armed with high-explosive bombs. At their briefings the pilots of their seventy-six bombers and thirty-six escorting fighters had been reassured by the latest Tokyo intelligence estimate: "There is no evidence of an enemy task force in our vicinity."[13] Nagumo nonetheless prudently retained thirty-six Zeros to fly combat air patrol over his four carriers. He made the mistake, however, of not ordering out all of his ten floatplanes for a dawn reconnaissance. Only four were catapulted off the heavy cruisers, and fate decreed that the launch of the scout assigned to patrol the eastern sector was delayed a critical half hour by a faulty catapult.

Meanwhile, Fletcher's scouts flew off to the west at dawn, across the V, to concentrate their search for the Japanese in an area two hundred miles northwest of Midway whence Cincpac operation orders had predicted that the enemy carriers would be making their run in to Midway. The same patch of Pacific was also being scoured by PBY patrols from the atoll's airstrip, and it was one of the Catalinas that first sighted enemy planes flying south. Then, at 0545 local time, Lieutenant Howard Ady nosed his PBY through a cloud bank and saw "the curtain rise on the Biggest Show on Earth."[14]

"ENEMY CARRIERS" was all that Ady managed to get off before taking evasive action to avoid being jumped by a pair of Japanese fighters. Once inside the safety of some clouds, he completed the report that we had all been waiting for: "PLANE REPORTS TWO CARRIERS, TWO BATTLESHIPS, BEARING 320 DEGREES, DISTANT 180 MILES, COURSE 135 DEGREES, SPEED 25 KNOTS."[15]

It was shortly after 0600 at Pearl when we went to the Operations Room. The position of the enemy carrier force, which I was certain numbered at least four, was marked on the plot 180 miles northwest of Midway.

"Well, you were only five minutes, five degrees, and five miles out," Nimitz remarked to me with a smile.

The position of the striking force, and the report of enemy planes heading toward Midway, made it obvious that Nagumo must still be unaware that our carriers were in the vicinity. Otherwise, he would not have been holding steady to his course down the west leg of the V toward Midway. While Fletcher and Spruance might still be too far away to launch an air strike, we were confident that after receiving the PBY report they would be steaming hard to close the range.

We assumed that every land-based plane on Midway had been scrambled and was either preparing to beat off the raid or heading northwest to attack the Japanese carriers. Our task forces had been instructed to maintain radio silence to ensure that their ambush achieved the maximum element of surprise, so Nimitz relayed the latest reports out to them, the implication being that they were to launch a strike as soon as practical. Although he retained operational command, Nimitz had announced that he would not interfere with the conduct of the action unless he felt that the task force commanders were being led astray.

"AIR RAID MIDWAY" came by submarine cable from the garrison commander at 0625. While this informed us that the Japanese attack had begun, we were to learn nothing more until 0830 when Midway reported, "ONLY 3 FIGHTING PLANES REMAIN. NO CONTACT DIVE BOMBING PLANES."[16] Another two hours went by before the exaggerated reports of the returning Midway pilots were relayed to us. Based on their past performance, we were very skeptical of their claims to have hit several carriers, leaving one of them ablaze. Unfortunately, we could believe that the Japanese Zeros had taken a heavy toll of our planes, including all but one of the marines' slow torpedo bombers.

Still no word came from Fletcher and Spruance. This was a good sign, because we assumed that it meant that the enemy had yet to spot them. But this assumption did not reduce the tension. Nimitz had retreated to his office and I followed his example. There I could use my private telephone line to keep in touch with Rochefort. Hypo's main source of news came from the Japanese as its radio operators monitored the progress of the Japanese end of the battle, picking up the voice and Morse circuits being used by Nagumo's pilots.

Thanks to their reports I was able to tell Nimitz just after 0800 that a Japanese carrier scout plane had been heard radioing that it had spotted "TEN SURFACE SHIPS" 240 miles northeast of Midway heading south at twenty knots.[17] He took the message out to the plot to see whether it coincided with our estimated position for the task forces. When it agreed, he wanted to know if the pilot had sighted our carriers yet. I checked with Rochefort. Not yet. I was able to confirm that they were still undetected. But eleven minutes later Rochefort called me with the news that the Japanese plane had just made the signal, "Enemy is accompanied by what appears to be a carrier bringing up the rear."[18]

It was both bad and good news. Nagumo now knew about Yorktown, but he was still unaware of Spruance's two carriers. As we studied the operations plot, it was clear to us that the outcome of the impending clash depended on the urgent decision that was even then being made by Admiral Nagumo. The discovery of our carrier put him in a dilemma. Either he launched his remaining planes against this contact, or he waited until his planes returning from the Midway strike had been recovered to send off a full attack. Either way, a golden opportunity had opened up for Spruance and Fletcher to strike the first blow and catch the enemy carriers with their flight decks crowded with refueling aircraft.

We could only wait. But we need not have worried. As Nimitz predicted, Spruance had reacted to the news of the Midway raid by seizing the chance that fate handed him. Calculating that the enemy was just within reach of the two-hundred-mile range of his aircraft, he advanced by two hours the launch of his first strike.

Spruance had decided to risk his torpedo planes, which had a combat radius of only 175 miles and might not have enough gas to get back to the carriers. But Midway was an alternative landing site. Only thirty-six fighters were held back for combat air patrol when the strike headed off to the southwest just after 0730 local time. Spruance's caution was soon justified. Task Force 16's sixty-seven Dauntless dive bombers and twenty-seven Devastator torpedo bombers, escorted by twenty-seven Wildcats, were winging their way to their targets when a lone enemy floatplane appeared over the horizon. Enterprise's radio intelligence unit reported that the pilot could be heard radioing the task force's position.

Admiral Fletcher, following sixteen miles astern of Task Force 16, now decided that the time had come to launch seventeen Dauntlesses, sixteen Devastators, and six Wildcats. The memory of his near fatal error at the Coral Sea persuaded him to retain half his planes in case another Japanese force appeared.

Our strike of 155 planes was therefore well on its way across the open arms of the V before Admiral Nagumo began wrestling with his tactical problem. The shocking news that American carriers were within striking range of the *Kido Butai* also coincided with the arrival of our land-based bombers from Midway. These were easily beaten off, but the carriers had to weave and dodge. Adding to the problems on the flag bridge were additional evasive measures adopted to counter the attack made by submarine *Nautilus*. Although her torpedoes also failed to find a target, Nagumo's tight defensive formations were disrupted as the debate about what to do continued.

On the *Akagi*'s hangar deck, a second strike against Midway had been prepared. The planes, armed with high-explosive, impact-fused bombs, were already starting to be arranged on deck. To rearm the aircraft with armor-piercing bombs and torpedoes would require an extensive delay, and so Nagumo reluctantly complied with the impatient request flashed to *Akagi* from the Carrier Division 2 commander: "CONSIDER IT ADVISABLE TO LAUNCH ATTACK FORCE IMMEDIATELY."[19]

Assuming that only a single American carrier was in the area, and assured by Commander Genda and his air staff that refueling could be completed in less than an hour, Nagumo finally decided to give priority to landing and refueling the planes that had attacked Midway rather than hitting the opposing naval force. This meant removing those aircraft already on the flight deck. More valuable minutes were lost as they were shuttled below and disarmed, while the returning aircraft began circling overhead for permission to land.

Nagumo and his staff knew that they had made a fatal miscalculation when, half an hour later, a scouting Zero radioed "TEN ENEMY TORPEDO PLANES HEADING TOWARD YOU."[20] The decks of their carriers were covered with planes, snaking gasoline hoses, and trolley loads of bombs and ammunition. Belowdecks lay rows of torpedoes and high-explosive bombs, which, in the frenzy of rearming the second strike, had not been returned to the protected magazines.

The Japanese air commanders urgently signaled "SPEED PREPARATIONS FOR IMMEDIATE TAKEOFF," as a fierce antiaircraft barrage opened up against the *Hornet*'s torpedo bombers.[21] The slow and ungainly Devastators, led by Lieutenant Commander John C. Waldron, made a courageous attempt at low-level runs although they lacked the cover of their fighters. "He went straight for the Japanese fleet as if he had a string tied to them," reported Ensign George Gay, who was the sole survivor of the attack as every one of the torpedo bombers fell victim to gunfire and the forty Zeros flying protective cover for the *Kido Butai*.[22] Following hard on the tails of Waldron's gallant band, Lieutenant Commander Eugene

E. Lindsey lost nine of *Enterprise*'s fourteen Devastators without scoring a single hit. And only two of *Yorktown*'s twelve torpedo bombers managed to make it back after fighting through a curtain of antiaircraft fire. Out of those slow-running torpedoes dropped by the American planes, none found a target.

The slaughter of the first wave of the American attack gave Nagumo and his staff temporary respite. At Pearl, where we calculated that the climax of the battle must be fast approaching, tension was running high. We had heard nothing. Admiral Nimitz was frantic; I mean as frantic as I have ever seen him. He appeared agitated and called for his communications officer, Commander Curts, to know why we were not getting any messages or hearing something. Although they must have known by now that they could break radio silence, it seemed that our task force commanders were neglecting to keep Nimitz informed of what was going on. Germany Curts, however, advised against requesting information that might distract Fletcher and Fitch at what might be a critical juncture of the action.

Not until 1008 did the communications center at Pacific Fleet headquarters report hearing *Enterprise*'s air officer yelling, "Attack! Attack immediately!"[23] This frenzied order, and the tantalizing reply to it, only added to our apprehension.

"Wilco, as soon as I can find the bastards!" Lieutenant Commander Clarence W. McClusky[24] radioed *Enterprise*. Like the other leaders, he was unaware that the enemy carriers had swung about onto a more northerly course to recover their first strike. *Hornet*'s thirty-five dive bombers were to hunt for their quarry fruitlessly for more than an hour before giving up to refuel at Midway. Fortunately, Clarence McClusky followed his nose north and discovered the Japanese destroyer which had dropped behind to depth-charge *Nautilus,* and was now hightailing it to the northwest to rejoin the strike force.

The fortune that had deserted our torpedo bombers that morning now smiled on the dive bombers. McClusky sighted the four enemy carriers after all their patrolling fighters had been drawn to deck height to prepare to chase off the last of *Yorktown*'s torpedo planes. Not even the high-performing Zeros could climb back up to ten thousand feet in time to disrupt *Enterprise*'s sixty-seven Dauntlesses. Picking the two largest carriers, they came hurtling down in a 70-degree dive, their bombsights locked on the red deck roundels of *Akagi* and *Kaga.*

"Hell divers!" was how Captain Fuchida recalled that awful moment when the attack alarms sounded. The man who had led the attack on Pearl Harbor, who had risen to watch flight operations from his berth in sick bay after undergoing an appendectomy, was now forced to crawl for cover. "The terrifying scream of the dive bombers reached me first, followed by a direct hit," Fuchida wrote. "I was horrified at the destruction that had been wrought in a matter of seconds. There was a huge hole in the flight deck just abaft the amidships elevator. The elevator itself, twisted like molten glass, was drooping into the hangar. Deck plates reeled upward in grotesque configurations. Planes stood tail up belching livid flames and jet-black smoke."25

The flight deck was turned into an inferno by detonating torpedoes and bombs. Within the hour, Nagumo was forced to take refuge from the blazing *Akagi* and transfer his staff to a destroyer. Off the flag carrier's starboard quarter, four direct hits made short work of *Kaga*. Later that afternoon the blazing *Kaga* was the target of three *Nautilus* torpedoes, but they all missed. Then *Yorktown's* dive bombers arrived to concentrate their attack on *Soryu*. Two of their bombs hurled the elevator against the bridge, setting parked planes ablaze, as a third detonated in the hangar.

At the cost of forty-seven planes, we had wiped out, at a single blow, three quarters of the vaunted *Kido Butai*. All of *Yorktown's* dive bombers escaped unscathed. McClusky's flight was not so lucky. Sixteen of his planes were shot down by the pursuing Zeros and others had to ditch when they ran out of fuel looking for *Enterprise,* which had not updated her position by radio to avoid homing in a Japanese attack.

At Pacific Fleet headquarters, however, we still had no definite news of how the battle was going. I was in constant touch with Rochefort. He was making every effort to try to break into an action report that appeared to have been sent from Admiral Nagumo. But he could get nothing solid, except for an important clue that the flagship's call sign had been shifted from *Akagi* to a cruiser. I hoped this meant that *Akagi* had been hit, but I cautioned Nimitz that we could not yet be certain.

Then Hypo reported picking up a plain-language order made to a Japanese plane: "Inform us of position of enemy carriers." Another plane radioed a sighting report, and an air group commander gave them a "STAND BY," followed shortly by "ATTACK! ATTACK! ATTACK!"26 We did not know which of our task forces was being attacked, nor how many enemy carriers were still able to respond to Nagumo's desperate signal, "ATTACK ENEMY CARRIERS."27

Fortunately for us it turned out that Rear Admiral Tamon Yamaguchi of *Hiryu* was evidently under the impression that the earlier floatplane sighting represented the sum total of our task forces, because he sent only eighteen dive bombers and six fighters. Nor did he tell Nagumo how small a strike he had launched when he radioed confirmation that his planes had departed "for purpose of destroying enemy carrier."28

Yamamoto also believed that his operation was being opposed by a single carrier task force. After receiving the devastating report that Nagumo was retiring to the north leaving three of his carriers ablaze, he attempted to snatch a victory from the jaws of defeat. He began urgently summoning the carriers in the northern force back from the Aleutians. They were to join the Midway covering force while the main force raced in from the west. Too late, Yamamoto discovered the peril of ignoring

Mahan's dictum on the need to concentrate forces before a major battle. The overwhelmingly superior forces of the Combined Fleet, which might have proved decisive if they had been marshaled off Midway on that day, were scattered far and wide over the Pacific.

Yamamoto's hopes of winning a decisive surface engagement now depended entirely on *Hiryu*'s pilots. They found *Yorktown* around noon as she was recovering her dive bombers. Although Fletcher's position was now known to the enemy, he did not break radio silence until he received a reminder from Nimitz.

Only then did we learn that our task forces had successfully attacked two or three enemy carriers. But Fletcher reported, "NO INDICATION OF ADDITIONAL CARRIERS WHICH HAVE SIGHTED THIS FORCE."[29] Then twenty minutes after we had picked up the Japanese planes being vectored in by voice, Fletcher sent a further dispatch, "HAVE BEEN ATTACKED BY AIR 150 MILES NORTH MIDWAY."[30]

Three direct hits were scored, but the precautionary flooding of the gasoline refueling lines with inert carbon dioxide averted the conflagration that had doomed the three Japanese carriers. One bomb detonated in the smokestack and put five of *Yorktown*'s six boilers temporarily out of commission. It also swept away all the communications aerials, and Fletcher was obliged to transfer his flag to cruiser *Astoria* and turn over tactical command of our task forces to Spruance.

Before 1400 that day, damage-control parties succeeded in dousing the flames, and *Yorktown*'s engine room staff nursed the carrier's speed up so that she could recover her remaining planes. The Japanese strike leader, however, had radioed that they had left *Yorktown* a blazing wreck.

This report led Yamaguchi to believe that his strike had evened the score. Now Yamamoto's main force had a fighting chance of victory. Then a lone scouting plane, which had suffered a radio failure, landed on *Hiryu* shortly after 1300 to report the presence of at least one more carrier. Only ten torpedo planes and six fighters were available until the first strike returned, but Yamaguchi decided the situation demanded that he immediately send them on to hunt for the second American carrier.

An hour later the leader of *Hiryu*'s second strike reported that he had sighted the target. What he did not realize was that they had spotted the supposedly sunk *Yorktown*. The attack went in and the Japanese pilots skillfully sent two torpedoes into her port side, jamming the rudder and ripping open her patched-up hull. The list increased so alarmingly that *Yorktown*'s captain decided, prematurely as it turned out, to abandon ship. A destroyer was ordered alongside to take off the crew.

From Fletcher's urgent message requesting that tugs be sent out from Pearl, we knew that *Yorktown* had become a salvage operation at best. But the crippled carrier's Dauntless scouts, which had been sent off an hour earlier, now located *Hiryu* 110 miles to the northwest. Their urgent sighting reports were what Spruance had been waiting for. At 1530 he ordered *Enterprise* around into the wind to launch another strike of twenty-four dive bombers, including ten of *Yorktown*'s Dauntlesses, which had taken refuge on the flagship of Task Force 16 when their own flattop was being bombed.

Even with no Wildcat fighters for escorts, Lieutenant W. Earl Gallaher, who lead the strike, was eager to chalk up a second enemy carrier after his earlier successful attack on *Kaga*. An hour and a half later, he was able to claim that distinction as his bombs tore into the bowels of *Hiryu*. Yamaguchi's flagship was soon transformed into a floating torch. She was to burn through the night, long after the diminutive admiral had ordered his crew to abandon ship as he remained on board his doomed command.

That was a fate that some of Yamamoto's staff felt would have been appropriate for Admiral Nagumo when he radioed he was "retiring" in the face of at least five enemy carriers that were advancing westward. Nagumo's action was in direct defiance of Yamamoto's rallying order: "THE ENEMY FLEET HAS BEEN PRACTICALLY DESTROYED AND IS RETIR- ING TO THE EASTWARD."[31] Chief of Staff Ugaki took this to mean that Nagumo "has no stomach for a night action." He was therefore relieved of his command after being ordered to reverse course and prepare his battleships and cruisers to "PARTICIPATE IN THE NIGHT ENGAGEMENT."[32]

The night action that Yamamoto so desperately sought never took place. A reconnaissance at dusk by B-17s based at Midway reported being attacked by the Zeros that were buzzing around the blazing *Hiryu*. Spruance interpreted this as meaning there might yet be another Japanese carrier in the vicinity. Lacking a clear picture of the forces still opposing him, he decided not to risk our victory by making a stern chase through the hours of darkness.

Spruance then radioed his battle report, claiming a fourth enemy carrier had been sunk as well as hits on an escorting battleship and a heavy cruiser. Following reports by his pilots, he also informed us: "THREE SHIPS BELIEVED CARRIERS PREVIOUSLY ATTACKED WERE OBSERVED TO SOUTHEASTWARD STILL BURNING." On the strength of this Nimitz prepared a dispatch to be radioed to all units and Admiral King: "You who have participated in the battle of Midway today have written a glorious page in our history. I am proud to be associated with you. I estimate that another day of all-out effort on your part will complete the defeat of the enemy."[33]

When this victory message was flashed out on the early evening of 4 June, Nimitz still believed that the day's actions were "the start of what may be the greatest sea battle since Jutland."[34] Such hopes proved to be premature, because we had not yet discovered the presence of Admiral Yamamoto's powerful surface force. Also, as the night wore on, successive dispatches from Task Force 16 indicated that Spruance was not in hot pursuit, but was actually backing off to the east.

"I did not feel justified in risking a night encounter with possibly superior enemy forces," Spruance was to explain. "But on the other hand I did not wish to be too far away from Midway next morning."[35] It was not at first clear to us why Spruance had chosen to be so cautious. The Monday morning quarterbacks at Pacific Fleet headquarters thought that this was not the way to do it. But Nimitz was very reluctant to intervene, even when the issue was raised in his staff meeting during the early hours of Friday morning. "I am sure that Spruance has a better sense of what's going on there than we have here," he told us. "I'm sure he has a very good reason for this. You must remember that he's there and knows what's going on. From here we can't 'kibbitz' a commander on the field of action."

But it was already becoming apparent that Spruance had made the proper tactical decision. Late on Thursday evening, radio intelligence had come up with the ominous indications that Yamamoto in the Combined Fleet flagship was racing toward the action with two battleship divisions.

When Yamamoto finally broke radio silence and began rallying his scattered forces, Rochefort's On the Roof Gang was able to identify the unmistakable "fist" of Yamamoto's chief radioman tapping out messages from *Yamato*. This was so surprising to us that at first we thought the radio direction finder bearings, obtained from the same transmissions, were way off and that the fleet flagship could not be closer than the Bonin Islands south of Japan. But as Hypo obtained more fixes during the night, *Yamato* was confirmed heading into the western approaches to Midway.

"What do we make of that. How do you account for his getting here so suddenly?" Nimitz said to me. "I thought you said that they would remain as they did at Pearl Harbor, in home waters."

"Well, that's part of this radio intelligence game and I'm sorry," I had to admit.

"But they are apparently out there and they didn't show up previously."

Contrary to what some historians have written, and as I have said earlier, Yamamoto's main force was not part of our prebattle estimate of enemy forces engaged in the Midway operation. Rochefort had been able to make only one association of Yamamoto's call signs with the forces involved in the Midway operation. And we had dismissed it as being "accidental." In truth, it could have cost us the battle if Task Force 16 had ventured too far west, and had been lured under the guns of Yamamoto's battle fleet that Thursday night.

This was a chilling reminder that radio intelligence, which had provided us with the key to victory, could just as easily have been our undoing. If Spruance had not exercised the caution he did, our victory could have been shot to pieces before dawn. And Hypo and I would rightfully have been blamed for failing to identify two battleship divisions in the Japanese order of battle.[36]

The discovery that Yamamoto's battlewagons were bearing down on

Midway from the northwest raised Nimitz's concern that they intended to push ahead with the invasion. These fears became very real at 0130 on 5 June when the Midway garrison cabled that an enemy submarine was lobbing shells ashore.

""Do you think that the Japs still intend to land despite their damage?" Nimitz wanted to know.

"Well, they are pretty stubborn," I replied. "If they have plans, they always try to carry them out until it's obvious that they can't."

Nimitz was worried that the enemy's main forces had retired only temporarily. For a time, it looked as though he might be right. We knew that a bombardment by cruisers and submarines would be the preliminary to any assault on Midway, but as the night wore on without more shelling, I grew increasingly confident that the enemy had retreated. My estimate was that four carriers had been sunk, and because a large oil slick had been reported by our air patrols, that one was badly damaged and limping away.

During the small hours of 5 June, while Nimitz was concerned that the Japanese might still press on with their invasion, the feasibility of doing just that was being debated by staff of the Combined Fleet. Those who urged a face-saving occupation of Midway were finally silenced by Yamamoto's reminder: "In battle as in chess [shogi], it is the fool who lets himself be led into a reckless move through desperation."[37]

It was not until 0300, after Yamamoto had concluded that our surviving carriers were not going to be suckered into a night action, that he finally swallowed the bitter pill of defeat. "MIDWAY OPERATION CANCELED" was the signal that caused the transports to head back for Saipan. The covering force was ordered to join up with the remnants of Nagumo's Striking Force and rendezvous with the main force northwest of Midway. Only the invasion of the Aleutian Islands was to go ahead as scheduled.

It was not until late the next day, when Rochefort had been able to partially decrypt these messages, that Nimitz had confirmation that the Midway operation had been abandoned. Throughout the night of 5 June, however, plain-language Japanese messages continued to be picked up by Hypo that indicated that one of Yamamoto's battleships was damaged and sinking. This was deception pure and simple, aimed at luring our carrier force into a nighttime gunnery duel. "Keep an eye on this," Nimitz told me. "I may have to caution Spruance not to be drawn off in that direction."

A message to this effect was sent out to Spruance, warning him that while the Japanese were apparently retiring to the northwest, they were trying to draw him after them. Spruance didn't bite, but the deception continued. When I informed Nimitz of this he smiled. "Sometimes they can be quite transparent, can't they?"

I agreed. "Yes, and sometimes they can be pretty obtuse."

At 0300 we decided that the Japanese must be more obstinate than obtuse when we received a report from one of our submarines of "MANY UNIDENTIFIED SHIPS"[38] some ninety miles northwest of Midway. The four heavy cruisers of the close support were not preparing to invade, but responding to Yamamoto's orders to retreat when they spotted the unmistakably sinister profile of a submarine. In their hasty maneuvers to avoid any torpedoes as USS *Tambor* submerged, cruiser *Mogami* collided with cruiser *Mikuma*.

Two hours later *Tambor* surfaced to report that one of the heavy cruisers was damaged and leaking oil. But Nimitz was not taking any chances. He radioed all our submarines to gather west of Midway and be ready to disrupt any invasion attempt. He told his commanders, "There are strong indications the Japanese will attempt assault and occupation Midway regardless past losses."[39]

Early in the morning, search planes from Midway reported that the enemy was, in fact, retreating to the west. Dive bombers and B-17s managed to find the two damaged cruisers and reported two hits. After reversing course back to the east during the night, as the enemy activity appeared to increase around Midway, Spruance was also less than fifty miles north of the island when he radioed an alert to our submarines that Task Force 16 was resuming the westerly pursuit. But it was not until afternoon, after a report that the main Japanese force was still northwest of the island, that he launched a search-and-strike mission.

Spruance discovered that day, however, that there is truth in the old naval adage that "a stern chase is a long one." On the evening of 5 June, when his planes returned after failing to make any contact, he decided to give up trying to overtake the main enemy units. He was concerned that to do so would bring his task force within range of the Japanese land-based bombers at Wake. Instead, he decided to concentrate his efforts on locating the damaged cruisers.

When *Enterprise*'s dive bombers found the pair of cripples in the mid-morning on 6 June, it was like shooting fish in a barrel. After three successive strikes from Task Force 16, *Mikuma* sank. But *Mogami*, although ablaze and badly mauled, managed to limp away and make good an escape to Truk.

The final round of the epic battle of Midway, however, was not entirely ours. For a day and a half, the captain and volunteers from her crew had been struggling to save *Yorktown*. They had reboarded the ravaged carrier and brought her under tow with an accompanying destroyer supplying electric power for the pumps that kept her afloat. But one of the last acts of a floatplane from the retreating heavy cruisers had been to make a sighting report that brought a Japanese submarine stalking the crippled flattop.

On the afternoon of 6 June a salvo of torpedoes split destroyer *Hammann* in two, and opened up a new gash in *Yorktown*'s hull. As thousands of tons of green water poured in, for the second time in two days, the abandon-ship order was given. Without power to keep her pumps running, *Yorktown* succumbed, capsizing before making her death plunge shortly before dawn on 7 June.

While not unexpected, the news that *Yorktown* had foundered was made harder to bear by the reports that Sunday morning that the Japanese had landed on the westernmost Aleutian Islands of Attu and Kiska. Expectation that the American public would demand an immediate response prompted Nimitz to order Task Force 16 north to dislodge these embarrassing new outposts of the Japanese empire. But Spruance was relieved to be recalled the following day. This was after the Pacific Fleet staff had had time to reflect on the enormous risks involved in allowing our precious carriers to venture into the zone of northern storms where they would be easy prey to ambush by enemy battleships and submarines.

Despite Tokyo's crowing propaganda, the capture of the two barren outposts of the United States could not undo the ringing triumph that our carriers had won three days earlier. The eventual loss to Japan was to prove far greater than material casualties: four carriers, one cruiser, 2,500 men, and 322 aircraft. Although the Combined Fleet still outnumbered our Pacific Fleet, Yamamoto's grand strategic design for bringing about a quick Japanese victory through a decisive naval engagement had been wrecked. We had paid the considerable price of 347 lives, a carrier, a destroyer, and 147 aircraft. But during the months that followed, Midway proved to mark the beginning of the ebb tide for Japanese naval power in the Pacific.

"Pearl Harbor has now been partially avenged," Admiral Nimitz's communiqué of 6 June announced. "Vengeance will not be complete until Japanese seapower is reduced to impotence."[40]

Admiral King's congratulatory message and promise "to make the enemy realize that war is hell" was broadcast to the fleet in plain language to add to the discomfiture of the Japanese.

"The Battle of Midway was the first decisive defeat suffered by the Japanese Navy in 350 years," King was to write. "Furthermore it put an end to the long period of Japanese offensive action, and restored the balance of naval power in the Pacific."[41]

Admiral King's dispatch persuaded General Emmons to make a gracious gesture for having doubted our intelligence estimates. He arrived at Pacific Fleet headquarters that Sunday morning with a jeroboam of champagne, wrapped up navy-style in blue and gold ribbons. As glasses were handed around, Nimitz accepted Emmons's apologies. The admiral insisted on sending his car to fetch Commander Rochefort. But Joe took so long changing from his informal attire into uniform whites that the champagne had run dry by the time he arrived. Nimitz, nevertheless, magnanimously declared to his assembled staff, "This officer deserves a major share of the credit for the victory at Midway."[42]

It was typical of Joe that he waited another couple of days before giving his exhausted staff a two-day break so they could hold what can only be described as a great big drunken brawl.[43]

33

"One Unforgivable Sin"

I N THE MONTHS AFTER Midway, when the success of our intelligence operation at Pearl Harbor should have been recognized, you can imagine our dismay when Washington launched a bitter attack against us.

We knew that more fighting was about to break out in the southwest Pacific, and we knew how good our operation was with Rochefort running Station Hypo. There was no doubt in our minds that if Nimitz had listened to Washington's forecasts about Midway, there would have been no victory to celebrate.

As it turned out, Washington believed differently. Neither Captain Joseph Redman nor his younger brother, John, who was head of OP-20-G, was inclined to recognize that Hypo had made any contribution to the victory. They were determined to hide the facts about how badly they had blundered by predicting the wrong date and target of the Japanese operation.

The director of naval communications was also taking his share of the credit for the "remarkable intelligence work" that had ensured that our outnumbered forces had achieved tactical surprise. As he put it: "It is not believed that the enemy knew the whereabouts of our carriers until after radio silence was broken."[1] And the Redman brothers, thanks to their ready access to senior members of the naval staff in Washington, circulated the word that Midway was the result of their outfit's work, and not that of Rochefort's team. Furthermore, the Redmans claimed that their operation was the one that had broken out the 3 June date from the Japanese ciphers that allowed Nimitz to get his carriers on station. They were soon boasting that without the efforts of the Negat cryptanalysts in Washington, Midway and the Hawaiian Islands would have been captured by the Japanese. Their campaign of disinformation worked: Within two months the elder brother was promoted to rear admiral, while the younger brother was given a leg up to captain.

We knew something of what was going on, but not enough. Just how successful the Redmans were at perpetrating their fraud didn't come to light for more than a year, when Commander John S. Holtwick reported to Rear Admiral Joseph R. Redman in October 1943. Redman was six months into his second tour of duty as director of naval communications at the time—for which he was awarded the Distinguished Service Medal—and he remarked that "Pearl Harbor had missed the boat at the battle of Midway but the Navy Department had saved the day."[2]

The assuredness with which the lie was told "took the breath away" from Commander Holtwick. As one of Rochefort's traffic analysts, he had played a key role in providing the intelligence that proved OP-20-G wrong about Midway. Although "boiling mad," Holtwick managed to state that Admiral Nimitz believed the reverse was true. Redman dismissively insisted that he "must have been misinformed."[3] Then Holtwick respectfully pointed out that he had received a letter of commendation from the commander in chief of the Pacific Fleet for the part he had played in the Hypo intelligence breakthrough that had been instrumental in securing our victory on 4 June.

When he found that other members of the department appeared to have been taken in by the Redman version, Holtwick was determined to "tell the truth about the Midway tip-off."[4] But with the elder Redman so firmly entrenched in the hierarchy of the navy department, Holtwick's campaign resulted in an anonymous monograph that was written by another ranking officer in the naval intelligence community who, understandably, chose to remain anonymous.

The memo was headlined: *The Inside Story of Midway and the Ousting of Commander Rochefort,* and it set down in precise detail how a clique of officers in league with the Redman brothers had conspired to cast slurs on Rochefort to deny him and the Hypo team their proper credit. The memorandum also stated that there had been a move in Washington during the spring of that year to shift some of the blame for Pearl Harbor onto Hypo by falsely accusing Rochefort of allowing himself to become the victim of a nonexistent Japanese radio deception.

By the end of 1943, a number of copies of the memo appear to have been circulated in Washington confidentially and unofficially. Each of the twenty pages that exposed "the dirty work that went on in the Navy Department" was stamped SECRET. Although this was not an official stamp, because the monograph contained a classified listing of the sequential changes in the Japanese naval codes, it was to remain locked in the safes of the naval intelligence establishment for forty years. Another reason why it was quarantined and kept from declassification was the fact that it washed the navy department's dirty linen.

Although recently released records indicate that some of the memo's charges are overstated, the memo itself is a telling indictment of how self-serving officers advanced their careers and authority by distorting—and in some cases rewriting—the historical record. That the Redmans and their associates rose to the most senior rank in the naval establishment is perhaps another reason why their successors wanted to conceal this indictment. Fortunately, it was "officially" declassified and released in late 1984 after a navy security review determined that it contained "no currently classified information."[5]

The memo contains startling revelations that are supported by the most recently released radio intelligence records and copies of official reports discovered among the papers of Captain Rochefort. Statements made by Captain Dyer before his death have added to the revelations that demonstrate how the power play by the Redman brothers to further their own careers had an immediate and deleterious impact on the conduct and consequences of the war. The charge that they pursued a vendetta against Rochefort is confirmed by the recent declassification of two memoranda of 20 June 1942. These prove how the Redmans worked hand in glove to distort the facts, to ensure Rochefort's ouster from Hypo, and how they tried to bring the Pacific Fleet combat intelligence unit directly under their control.

These two memos were addressed to Vice Admiral Frederick J. Horne, King's deputy chief of naval operations, who appears to have been a willing assistant, if not an active promoter of the Redman cause. One memo is signed by Captain Joseph Redman, although it is clear that both were drafted so as to be mutually supportive, and it argued that "radio intelligence cannot thrive and function efficiently except under the direct control of naval communications."[6] To this end Joseph Redman charged that Hypo "has been, by virtue of seniority, in the hands of an ex-Japanese language student" who was "not technically trained in Naval Communications" and that the navy's own war effort against the Japanese was "suffering because the importance and possibilities of the phases of Radio Intelligence are not fully realized."[7]

This was an outrageous accusation. Rochefort not only had been present at the birth of the navy's radio intelligence effort, but he had demonstrated only three weeks earlier what it could achieve by setting the stage for our victory at Midway.

Captain Joseph Redman also complained that the "realization of combined radio intelligence unit objectives worked out more smoothly in the Melbourne unit [Belconnen] than in the Com 14 unit [Hypo]." He argued that this was because the officer in Belconnen was more experienced and attuned to the needs of naval intelligence in Washington! He further charged that "administration was weak" at Hypo, and he said that Rochefort should be replaced by "a senior officer trained in radio intelligence rather than one whose background is in Japanese language."[8] To support this charge, he enclosed a detailed list of Hypo's omissions and errors prepared by his younger brother, and he recommended that Commander John Redman "make a quick trip to Honolulu to get first hand information on which to base recommendation *for remedial action* [emphasis added]."[9]

The younger Redman's memorandum was an even more self-serving document. It implicitly accused Rochefort of insubordination and belittled his ability to achieve results. "Experience has indicated," Commander Redman disingenuously concluded, "that units in combat areas cannot be relied upon to accomplish more than the business of merely reading enemy messages and performing routine work necessary to keep abreast of minor changes in the cryptographic systems involved."[10]

Now that historians have access to the revealing record for the first time, it is extraordinary to find that immediately after Midway, the head of OP-20-G was asserting that only Washington had the "large numbers of skilled persons and expensive, complicated machinery" for the "extremely complex" task of "obtaining intelligence from enemy communications." Yet Redman, whose supposedly more talented and experienced team had got it so wrong, was able to get away with his claim that "a properly qualified officer" should be put in charge of Hypo "in order that proper relations between the intelligence activities and the operational staff may be maintained."[11]

The charges made by the Redmans were contradicted by reality. As Captain Dyer observed years later, the Redmans' "slur" against Hypo's achievements was "more than amply refuted by the record."[12] Rochefort's former deputy drew attention to some particular examples that give the lie to the Redmans' suggestion that Hypo had been incapable of serious cryptanalytic effort.

"In April 1942," Dyer pointed out, "it was suggested to Washington that a solution of JN-20 might be helpful. Their reply was, 'It cannot be done.' In May of same year Pearl did it! [And] the same month, Wright and Finnegan came up with a brilliant solution of the internal time-date code which was vitally important in determining when the attack on Midway should be expected."[13]

The Redmans' memoranda confirm what many of us have suspected for so long. The two brothers led a conspiracy, knowing that they could count on a receptive audience in Admiral King's staff for their contention that radio intelligence had "worked well," and that it should continue "under the control and administration of the Chief of Naval Operations" with the director of naval communications in immediate charge.[14] While we were busy fighting for our country out at Pearl, the Redmans were more concerned with winning bureaucratic turf.

"I have given a great deal of thought to the Rochefort affair, and I have been unwillingly forced to the conclusion that Rochefort committed the one unforgivable sin," Dyer wrote shortly before his death in 1985. "To certain individuals of small mind and overweening ambition, there is no greater insult than to be proved wrong. I have rather a bitter personal memory of having been threatened with reprisal for being right when Washington was wrong."[15]

It was especially ironic that Rochefort, who kept a notice on his desk saying "We can accomplish *anything* provided no one cares who gets the credit," found himself the target of the Redmans' campaign for self-aggrandizement. But we now know that they were prepared to stop at nothing to effect his recall as part of their plan to centralize control of radio intelligence in Washington. Yet this private war was also to lead to the Japanese being sent an alert about our code-breaking successes at one of the most critical junctures of the war.

The opportunity for that damaging betrayal surfaced with the headlines of the *Chicago Tribune* on Sunday, 7 June:

JAP FLEET SMASHED BY U.S.
2 CARRIERS SUNK AT MIDWAY. NAVY HAD WORD OF JAP PLAN TO STRIKE AT SEA
KNEW DUTCH HARBOR WAS A FEINT

The sensational story, which also appeared simultaneously in the *New York Daily News*, the *Washington Times-Herald,* and four other midwestern newspapers associated with the *Chicago Tribune,* was attributed to "reliable sources in the navy department."[16] While the story stopped short of saying that the information had been obtained by code breaking, it was clear that unless Admiral Nimitz had a personal spy in the enemy camp, there was no other way that he could have known the names of the four carriers, two battleships, two heavy cruisers, and twelve destroyers that were listed as part of the striking force. The article went on to name the classes of warships that made up support and occupation forces. And it detailed how we had worked out the broad objectives of Yamamoto's plan to invade Midway in order not to be taken in by the feint attack on Dutch Harbor.

Nimitz and I were dismayed when we learned about the newspaper articles in a dispatch from Washington on 8 June. My personal horror of the situation was greater, because it appeared that the information on which the story was based had been taken directly from our Cincpac bulletin, which had been sent to all task force commanders on 31 May. We launched an investigation and found that the fleet public relations officer had not insisted the *Tribune*'s Johnson sign a security pledge before he went on board *Lexington.*[17]

Admiral King was furious. He moved swiftly to have the office of naval censorship hush up the story. As a former newspaperman, Secretary of the Navy Knox pulled out all the stops to have the seven newspapers involved drop the coverage voluntarily. Even though characters in the comic strips would soon be portrayed busily stealing Japanese codes and solving ciphers, it was hoped that if Tokyo did pick up the story, the fact that it was a one-time item would persuade them that it was nothing more than sensationalistic speculation.

The Redmans, however, were determined to run the culprits to the ground. They may well have concluded that Rochefort or I must have been involved in the leak. Commander Redman knew as well as we did that the story could have been written only from the 31 May Cincpac intelligence bulletin and his suspicions were evidently aroused because the story carried the by-line of war correspondent Stanley Johnson, who had passed through Pearl Harbor a week earlier after his rescue from *Lexington* during the Coral Sea action.

For over a month Secretary Knox managed to prevent a full-scale investigation of Johnson, which, he predicted, would lead to more unfortunate publicity. Commander John Redman, however, refused to let the matter rest. Along with his brother he continued to urge that "something ought to be done about it."[18]

The chance to "do something" came after newspaper columnist Walter Winchell made a radio broadcast on 5 July in which he made reference to Coral Sea and Midway, asserting: "When the history of these times is written it will be revealed that *twice* the fate of the civilized world was changed by intercepted messages." Winchell claimed, moreover, that he "could not enlarge on that as it is military information."[19]

Two days later Winchell apparently abandoned any such scruples he might have had by dropping another juicy morsel in his "On Broadway" gossip column in the *New York Daily News.* In it he accused Colonel McCormick, the anti-Roosevelt proprietor of the *Chicago Tribune,* of having "tossed safety out of the windows" when he "allegedly printed the lowdown on why we won at Midway—claiming that the U.S. Navy decoded the Japs' secret messages." Winchell pointed out the irony that his "deadliest enemy in Chicago, publisher Frank Knox," had saved McCormick from being brought to account for his disregard for military secrecy.[20]

Commander Redman never raised any protest about who was leaking Winchell his inside information. But the columnist's revival of the issue gave Redman the excuse to send Admiral King a trenchant memorandum on "Security of Radio Intelligence Activities."

In it Redman charged, "Such statements are considered to be extremely prejudicial to our interests."[21] The memorandum was backed up by personal word of mouth when Captain Joseph Redman took up the campaign and succeeded in getting King and his staff so stirred up that they prevailed on Knox to reverse his decision not to move against the *Chicago Tribune.*

A naval investigation was launched. The managing editor of the *Chicago Tribune* was summoned to the navy department to testify to investigators on 9 July. He maintained that his correspondent Johnson had obtained the information legally from naval sources. But when Johnson was examined four days later he sought to protect the identity of the officer who had communicated the top-secret information. He claimed, moreover, that he had never been required to sign a written pledge agreeing to submit to strict security regulations and was therefore free to publish information freely volunteered to him.

Had the matter been allowed to rest there, the curse would have been taken off the whole incident. But the Redmans were out for blood. Evidently they smelled Rochefort's. They would not be stopped, even though the issue was now alarming the ranking officers of naval intelligence. Captain McCollum, who had by this time got wind of their vendetta, warned Admiral Wilkinson of the serious damage that the affair could do to our code-breaking effort if the Japanese got wind of it. But the Redmans had the bit between their teeth and were determined to resort to the public courts to force Johnson to reveal his sources. The Judge Advocate General's Office, which had investigated the case, informed Knox that there were some grounds for legal action.

On 29 July, the day after receiving the attorney general's express warning of "the possibility of disclosure of our naval code and the means by which the Navy obtains its information concerning the enemy,"[22] the secretary of the navy reluctantly asked the attorney general to prosecute Johnson and the *Chicago Tribune* under the 1917 Espionage Act.[23] The affair now became public property. A Chicago grand jury heard testimony from seven of *Lexington*'s officers, as well as Johnson and the newspaper's managing editor. It quickly emerged that the source of the story was our 31 May estimate. Johnson had been shown the copy addressed to Admiral Fitch by *Lexington*'s executive officer while the party was on board cruiser *Chester* en route to the west coast. This violated every security rule in the book, but the grand jury refused to return an indictment. The *Chicago Tribune* beat the rap because the intelligence estimate had been volunteered to Johnson without any injunction about its being secret.

Barrages of publicity surrounded the case. They could not possibly have escaped the watchful eyes and ears of Tokyo. Just as McCollum and Wilkinson had warned, the prosecution backfired and the welter of accusations and denials made good newspaper copy. Less than a week after the story broke on 8 August 1942, the Japanese adopted a brand-new version of the JN-25 code. All the progress we had made in breaking into the C version of the operational cipher was made worthless when the new D books came into use on 14 August.[24]

This was a double setback. Our cryptanalytic effort had to begin all over again. And it would take almost four months of grueling intellectual effort to rebuild the "dictionary" and recover sufficient additives and cipher keys before we could regain any real penetration of the Japanese navy's principal operational system. (Some of the minor administrative systems, such as the one used for weather reports, were not changed.) Hypo was forced to fall back on traffic analysis to keep Nimitz informed during the bitterly fought Solomons campaign, which involved some of the fiercest naval actions of the war.

Such a drastic revision of their main code only a week after the Midway publicity indicated that the Johnson affair must have triggered concerns in Tokyo about the security of their naval ciphers. What really upset Rochefort was that the change came just at the time he had his hands on a complete copy of the current JN-25 C code and additive books. These had been recovered from a cache of Japanese documents discovered by our marines after their landing in the Solomons on 6 August. (Many other cryptographic aids had also been discovered buried near the partially completed airstrip on Guadalcanal Island.)

The Japanese did not suspect that our invasion of Guadalcanal had prejudiced their security; this is clear from one of the last decrypts made in the old system, which revealed that the local Japanese commanders had radioed that all confidential material had been destroyed.[25] There were only two other reasons that could have led them to believe that a cipher had been prejudiced after being in use for less than two and a half months. One was the revelations, which I mentioned earlier, of the advanced state of our naval intelligence as betrayed by documents captured two months earlier on board *Nankin*. But according to German records these were not handed over to the Japanese until 29 August.[26] The other reason was the publicity resulting from the Johnson case.

Rochefort had suspected that the Johnson leak had something to do with the JN-25 code change on 8 August. But when the news reached him that the Redmans had been the prime instigators of the second round of undesirable publicity, the Hypo team was filled with a burning resentment. The blackout could not have come at a more unfortunate juncture for Nimitz, because we had gone onto the offensive despite our very limited resources of ships, men, and aircraft. The whole Guadalcanal campaign was to be bedeviled by our failure to get up-to-date radio intelligence.

34

Guadalcanal

A T THE JUNE SUMMIT in Washington between Roosevelt and Churchill, the Joint Chiefs of Staff blocked any increase in the forces assigned to the Pacific theater. Admiral King then conceived a campaign to seize control of the Solomons as the starting point for the navy's offensive against the Japanese. In the optimistic afterglow of Midway, he anticipated a rapid advance up the strategically placed chain of islands, which would lead to an early capture of Rabaul, followed by an advance to Truk, Guam, Saipan, and a smash up through the underbelly of the enemy's southern defensive perimeter.

At the same time, General MacArthur was to begin a northward drive up New Guinea from the Allied base at Port Moresby. To avert a dispute between MacArthur and Admiral Ghormley, who had assumed control of the South Pacific Area under Nimitz, the Joint Chiefs had shifted the Cincpac boundary of control west of Guadalcanal.

The Japanese were equally determined to consolidate their position and continue their advance. Although Yamamoto's defeat at Midway had forced imperial general headquarters to abandon their plan to seize American bases in Samoa and Fiji, they pressed on with the plan to capture Port Moresby. This time they would do it overland, with a punishing trek across the precipitous, jungle-clad peaks of the Owen Stanley mountain range. At the same time preparations were made to nail down their hold on the Solomons by building an airfield on Guadalcanal. This ominous development had been monitored earlier as intercepted signals of the C version of the JN-25 code began to yield up its additives.

This was the intelligence that Admiral Nimitz brought with him on 3 July to a strategic conference with King in San Francisco. The capture of the Santa Cruz Islands, south of the Solomons, had been the original objective of Operation Watchtower, as it had been code-named in deference to King's intention that it should be the curtain raiser to a full-scale naval campaign in the Pacific. But news of the progress of the airfields on Guadalcanal brought a major revision in the plan. It meant abandoning the Santa Cruz operation in favor of invading Guadalcanal, and the seaplane base at Tulagi, before the enemy could achieve air superiority over the Coral Sea, which, in turn, would threaten our bases in Fiji and New Caledonia.

Admiral Richmond Kelly Turner was to be in charge of the landing, exercising his new responsibility as commander of Amphibious Forces South Pacific. (He had been cooling his heels for six months following his replacement as war plans chief, because of his inability to work with army planners.) He and Admiral Ghormley therefore had less than five weeks to plan and execute our first major amphibious operation. Because of the demands of the Allied agreement to commit their major effort to the invasion of North Africa in the fall, King had been assigned only the 1st Marine Division for Watchtower—an operation whose commanders called it Shoestring because of its makeshift nature.

The first wave of our assault splashed ashore on the beaches of Tulagi and Guadalcanal shortly before dawn on 6 August. The Japanese were completely taken by surprise. After some sharp fighting the marines captured the seaplane base and took over the half-finished airfield. But it was not just the hostile reception that made these steamy jungle-clad islands very different from the tropical paradise which many of the leathernecks had been expecting.

In the six months that were to follow, a bitter campaign of attrition developed for control of the island that was the strategic key to the Solomons. Within forty-eight hours of the landings, Yamamoto issued urgent orders to the Fourth Fleet to intervene, and then erupted the first of six savage naval battles that were to cost us and the Japanese twenty-four warships apiece.

The enemy force of seven cruisers that came charging south from Rabaul was spotted by Australian coast watchers as it entered the northern Solomons on 7 August. An Allied air patrol was sent up to the Bougainville area, but when the Japanese ships knew they had been spotted they turned around to mislead our pilots. Hypo's ability to read the JN-25 C traffic was running a week or more behind current intercepts. Vice Admiral Gunichi Mikawa's heavy cruisers came rushing south in response to our landing. But because they kept radio silence their advance was not picked up from our traffic analysis.

Admiral Fletcher, who was in overall command of the naval forces, was determined not to lose any more carriers. Admiral Leigh Noyes, in immediate command of the air support force, which included carriers *Saratoga, Wasp,* and *Enterprise,* also favored an early withdrawal. His defenses had already been weakened by the loss of one fifth of his fighter aircraft in dogfights with Japanese land-based planes for control of the airspace over Guadalcanal. On the afternoon of 8 August, Fletcher made the independent decision to withdraw his task forces to the south for refueling.

Fletcher's decision to withdraw *all* our air cover simultaneously, instead of removing one carrier at a time, enormously increased the vulnerability of Turner's transports. They were still unloading supplies. Also jeopardized was the covering cruiser force. As usual, Turner had insisted, as he had before the attack on Pearl Harbor, that he would be his own intelligence officer. So while he protested Fletcher's decision, he nonetheless decided from his reading of the intelligence that no enemy surface force could arrive to interfere with his landing until late the following day.[1]

Given the information that he had received on enemy movements, Turner's error was understandable. But he might have saved himself and his ships if he had not refused to have one of Hypo's mobile radio intelligence units on board his headquarters ship. If he had not been so pigheaded, Turner could have received an early warning that enemy forces were approaching that evening when the Japanese cruisers sent a floatplane to radio a reconnaissance report. It succeeded in reporting the disposition of our transports off the beachhead, and that of the ships guarding the entrance to the sound between Tulagi and Guadalcanal.

As a result, Mikawa achieved total surprise when his force swept in from the darkness north of Savo Island and set the night ablaze in a twenty-minute gunnery duel that sank four Allied cruisers and a destroyer. Turner's transports were saved from complete destruction only by the Japanese decision to withdraw because they believed our carrier task force was still in the vicinity and might catch them in a dawn counterstrike.

After suffering one of the worst naval defeats in our history, Turner withdrew his transports and a surviving cruiser after the enemy stepped up their bombing raids from Rabaul the next morning. Major General Alexander Vandegrift's force of six thousand marines on Tulagi and ten thousand on Guadalcanal were then left stranded. They had lost their one-thousand-man reserve, and their heavy weapons. They had only a few entrenching tools and less than a months' rations and medical stores.

"It was as if the Marines held Jones Beach and the rest of Long Island were loosely dominated by the enemy" was how my old Annapolis classmate Hanson Baldwin summed it up for *The New York Times*.[2] But in a remarkable feat of bravery, and despite their lack of resources, the marines managed to complete the airstrip within a week using the single bulldozer that the Japanese had abandoned.

The arrival of marine fighter planes was the signal for the contest for Guadalcanal to begin in earnest. Now it was the Japanese who were faced with the strategic necessity for eliminating the airfield. On 20 August they made their first attempt to drive through the jungle to dislodge the marines who had dug themselves in around the airstrip perimeter. The attacks collapsed in a bloody series of banzai charges against machine guns. The Japanese then began a series of nighttime destroyer runs from Rabaul, which we dubbed "the Tokyo Express," to land troop reinforcements for a major offensive. Our fighters fought the enemy bombing raids as replacement aircraft were ferried in from our carrier task forces south of the Solomons.

As the level of attrition escalated, more and more units of the Combined Fleet were sucked into the struggle. This raised Yamamoto's hopes for a decisive naval engagement. Nimitz realized that with Fletcher's task forces outnumbered by more than two to one, we had to avoid a major confrontation at all costs, especially when the odds worsened after the 23 August carrier duel off the eastern Solomons. *Saratoga* was sent limping back to the west coast after a torpedo hit. Although his planes sank an enemy light carrier, Fletcher was forced to retreat southward when *Enterprise* was also damaged. It was another tactical defeat for the Pacific Fleet.

The naval setback in the Guadalcanal campaign was partially offset when MacArthur's tough Australian troops finally halted the stubborn Japanese assault on Port Moresby in the first week of September. The imperial general headquarters ordered the army to retreat from the Moresby front and concentrate all its efforts on regaining control of Guadalcanal. Fortunately, the Japanese were less effective at achieving results on land than they were at sea. On 13 September the marines beat off a second major attack on the airfield's perimeter, but enemy submarines torpedoed, in short order, a carrier, a destroyer, and a battleship.

Wasp and her destroyer escort foundered. *North Carolina* managed to make it back to Pearl with a thirty-foot gash in her hull. This was a major blow to Nimitz. He could not understand why Admiral Leigh Noyes had confined his task force to operating in a narrow patch of water south of the Solomons when our intelligence bulletin had warned that the area was heavily patrolled by enemy submarines. Later we found that Noyes had misinterpreted his operational orders. He had assumed that he was to confine his operations to the Cincpac area and that he was not allowed to stray into the waters that were technically under the command of MacArthur.

The next major clash came a month later. The Tokyo Express of 11 October was derailed south of Savo Island by Fletcher's heavy cruiser squadron, which sank an enemy cruiser and destroyer in what was the first-ever defeat of the Japanese navy in a night action. But Yamamoto promptly raised the stakes in the naval war of attrition. He sent down battleships to escort the nightly reinforcement runs and bombard our marine defenses with fourteen-inch shells. The climax was fast approaching. We estimated that much of the Combined Fleet had been sent south. Yamamoto had now concentrated four battleships, five carriers, ten cruisers, and twenty-nine destroyers in a massive blockade and bombardment operation.

"It now appears that we are unable to control the sea in the Guadalcanal area" was how Nimitz's headquarters diary summed up the grim situation. "Thus our supply of the position will only be done at great expense to us. The situation is not hopeless but it is certainly critical."[3] It was evident to all of us at Pearl that Commander in Chief South Pacific Admiral Ghormley was faltering. His actions—or lack of them—had abdicated command of the sea to the enemy. The marines were undersupplied and having a very hard time under the daily air raids and nighttime battleship bombardment. Their aviators were suffering from lack of fuel, from attrition, and fatigue as their planes were being shot out of the skies faster than our remaining carriers could ferry in replacements.

It was now clear to Nimitz that unless we could fight more reinforcements through, we were in danger of losing the campaign. During a full meeting of his staff, his eyes turned from sunny blue to a very grim gray. "I don't want to hear, or see, such gloom and such defeatism," he snapped. "Remember the enemy is hurt too, but our job here is to provide them with everything they need on Guadalcanal to fight this battle. We aren't going to do any good sitting here moaning or wailing or wringing our hands."

After the meeting was over, Nimitz kept a few of his staff, including myself, for a further review of the worsening situation. We sat around the admiral's desk. He asked each one of us for recommendations as to what we would do to improve the situation. His principal concern was that the navy was obviously not in control of the approaches to Guadalcanal. Although he did not say so directly, it was obvious that he felt that Ghormley had handed over command of the sea to the Japanese. We proposed that personalities should be set aside and that the commander South Pacific should be replaced by someone who could do a more effective job. Nimitz would not hear of it, saying that this was "mutiny."

After several more days, during which the situation on Guadalcanal grew even bleaker, a number of the staff, including me, got together one evening to chew over the matter. As a result of our discussion, we agreed that we should see Admiral Nimitz right away—it was then about 2200. We phoned his orderly, who told us that the admiral was ready to go to bed, but that he would give us five minutes. We arrived at his Makalapa quarters to find Nimitz in pajamas and dressing gown. We wasted no time spelling out what was on our minds. Halsey was on a tour of the South Pacific preparatory to relieving Fletcher as carrier task forces commander. Thus Halsey was on the spot to take over from Ghormley. We tried to assure the admiral that we were aware of his appreciation of personnel problems from his time spent at the Bureau of Navigation. In our view, however, the situation was so grave that he could not allow any thought of kindness or sympathy for a brother officer to stand in the way.

Nimitz thanked us. He said he understood entirely why we had spoken so frankly. There was no further discussion of the painful issue, which he resolved on 18 October by a dispatch sent out ordering Halsey to "take command of the South Pacific and South Pacific Forces immediately."[4] The news that America's preeminent fighting admiral was taking over command at this critical juncture in the campaign put new heart into the marines on Guadalcanal.

"One minute we were too limp with malaria to crawl from our foxholes, the next we were whooping it up like kids," General Vandegrift was to record. He flew to Halsey's New Caledonia headquarters for a straight-talking conference with the new commander South Pacific, who promised to do whatever was possible to get more supplies and reinforcements through. With only carrier *Hornet* available, Halsey admitted that the situation appeared "almost hopeless." Then on 23 October the patched-up *Enterprise* task force sailed back to Noumea accompanied by battleship *South Dakota*. Halsey was guardedly optimistic: "Now we had a fighting chance," he later recalled.[5]

The marines on Guadalcanal were battling off another attempt by the Japanese to break through their defenses on 26 October. Meanwhile, Admiral Thomas C. Kinkaid, with *Enterprise* and *Hornet* in his task force, was playing an equally desperate round of hide-and-seek with Admiral Kondo's Second Fleet south of Santa Cruz Island. During the night less than two hundred miles separated the opposing fleets. We knew that the Japanese battleships were out. So did Kinkaid.

Hypo was still lagging behind the current JN-25 decrypts, so we could not provide Kinkaid with an accurate intelligence picture. But that morning we had picked up and relayed to him the familiar "TE TE TE" used by Japanese carrier scouting planes when radioing a sighting report. We did not know that Kinkaid had already launched a strike against three enemy carriers to the north. Two of the enemy carriers were damaged in the duel. But the Japanese came out ahead. Their planes mauled *Hornet* so badly that Kinkaid ordered the carrier sunk rather than trying to save her and risking his task force to a superior enemy.

We knew from partial decryption of the intercepts that evening that Kondo was charging south with his battleships in hope of capturing the crippled carrier and engaging our task force in a night action. I think that Nimitz felt better when he realized this and appreciated that if *Hornet* had not been sunk and Kinkaid had not withdrawn, our forces might have been overwhelmed. But there was no getting away from the disappointment that the Battle of the Santa Cruz Islands, as the action was called, had been another tactical defeat. We could take some consolation that although he left Halsey with only *Enterprise* to keep on fighting supplies through to Guadalcanal, two of Japan's big carriers were now on their way home for repairs. The main question was how long Yamamoto would be willing to go on accepting this level of attrition to the Combined Fleet.

The answer came after a fierce three-day naval action fought in the narrow channel off Guadalcanal. Those waters had been dubbed Ironbottom Sound because they had become the graveyard of so much naval tonnage. Two of our cruisers were lost on 12 November in a head-on collision with a Tokyo Express that was escorted by two Japanese battleships. But the score was evened up when battleship *Hiei* was sunk the following morning as the retreating Japanese force was caught by dive bombers from Guadalcanal and *Enterprise*.

Halsey judged that the odds and time were now ripe for challenging the Tokyo Express with his battlewagons, despite the risks they would run maneuvering in such narrow waters. *Enterprise*'s aircraft smashed up a Japanese cruiser force the next day, and the night action fought on 14 November was to prove that our new radar and our big-gun superiority were decisive. When *Washington* and *South Dakota* came crashing up Ironbottom Sound to trade their sixteen-inch salvos with the fourteen-inch guns of *Kirishima* at close range, the enemy battleship was pounded into a blazing wreck.

The victory that our naval forces had won coincided with the failure of an all-out bid by the Japanese army to capture the Guadalcanal airstrip. This was the excuse Yamamoto used to withdraw the Combined Fleet the next day from its close support role. The loss of twenty-four warships, including a carrier and two battleships, had finally proved unacceptable to the imperial navy. This was the decisive turning point. Although destroyers continued to supply the remaining Japanese troops until they were evacuated three months later, the Guadalcanal campaign had, for all intents and purposes, been won. As Halsey was to observe of the enemy's crushing defeat: "Until then he had been advancing at his will. From then on he retreated at ours."[6]

35

"I'm Not Coming Back"

THE STRUGGLE FOR Guadalcanal was raging toward its climax at the same time that the feud between Hypo and Negat reached its unhappy conclusion. The bad blood between the two camps was made worse by the refusal of Admiral King to accept Nimitz's recommendation that Rochefort should receive the Distinguished Service Medal for Joe's contribution to the Midway victory. While Joe was flattered that his name had been put forward, he had advised Nimitz against it, saying that it would only aggravate the opposition of the Redmans. Joe was right. The Redmans were among those who strongly advised King against singling out Rochefort for the decoration. For him to have received it would have been a tacit admission that the principal intelligence breakthrough had been made by Hypo. Worse, it would not have squared with the Redmans' claims that their Negat team was responsible for the crucial cryptanalytic success. The 22 June memorandum to Admiral King advised that he "disapprove" Rochefort's recommended decoration because "equal credit is due to the Cominch planning section for the correct evaluation of enemy intelligence. . . ."[1]

Relations were further strained when Rochefort discovered that the Redman brothers had been instrumental in pressing the investigation of the Stanley Johnson case, and how they had caused the public discussion that had warned the Japanese that we had been reading their naval messages.

Joe held the Washington clique responsible for the arduous struggle that he and his cryptanalysts were waging to get back into the new D version of the JN-25 code. This in turn brought to a head the touchy debate about which station was producing the most accurate additive recoveries. There were some nasty exchanges, and Joe took increasing exception to what he described as "the bullying tactics to try to make us conform to their way of thinking."[2]

There was so much questioning and arguing going back and forth that it began to interfere with our efforts to get back into the Japanese operational traffic. Joe had also been warned by a friend in the navy department that a "special agent" was being sent out by an officer on King's staff to investigate us both. This would be done under a cover of making arrangements for a survey of the office equipment needed to set up a new interservice intelligence center.

The snooper, who turned out to be a chief yeoman who had been a mail orderly in *West Virginia* when I was on board the battleship in 1924, appeared less interested in the number of desks, chairs, and telephones the new facility needed than about how well I got on with Hypo. Thanks to Joe's alert we agreed to give the impression that our relationship was strictly professional and that we were not the best of friends. Even this was to be turned against Joe later with accusations that I found him difficult to work with. After the snooper had departed, Rochefort and I concluded that we were being targeted for removal by the Redmans and their allies in OP-20-G. We could assume only that they were determined to remove us before we again made them look like fools as we had over the "AF" issue before Midway. Then there was the matter of the new intelligence facility for which Nimitz had won King's approval, and which evidently appeared to Washington to be another bid for independence by Hypo.

The new operation, Intelligence Center Pacific Ocean Area, or Icpoa as it was to be known, had its origins in a proposal that I had made to Nimitz shortly after the Battle of Midway for increasing the size of our intelligence operation. Nimitz was adamantly opposed to expanding his own staff. Instead, he proposed to Washington that a new intelligence facility be attached to the Fourteenth Naval District as an adjunct to Rochefort's combat intelligence unit.

Captain Joseph Redman, anticipating that this was an attempt to carve off a piece from his naval communications empire, tried to pour cold water on the scheme in his June memorandum. But the scheme had been strongly supported by the director of naval intelligence, who saw it as an extension of his turf. Captain McCollum had also come out strongly in favor because he had observed firsthand how successfully the British had integrated their interservice intelligence operations. With King's blessing the new outfit was established on 24 June 1942 and Joe was appointed the first commanding officer of Icpoa.[3]

Although the duties that Rochefort shouldered in addition to Hypo were not onerous, his responsibility for Icpoa opened another front in his confrontation with the Redmans. They immediately renewed their efforts to bring Hypo under the direct control of OP-20-G. When the newly promoted Captain John Redman arrived to become Nimitz's communications officer on 15 September, Rochefort suspected that an attempt was being made to box him in. This appeared confirmed, because the younger

Redman's sudden transfer to Pearl came hard on the heels of his elder brother's promotion, which required that he perform six months' sea duty with a Pacific Fleet cruiser force before resuming his former post as director of naval communications.

The appointment of Captain William B. Goggins as OP-20-G in Washington on 3 September also made nonsense of John Redman's insistence two months earlier that only those "properly qualified" should command radio intelligence units. Although Goggins had been in the radio division of the Bureau of Engineering, the new head of Station Negat lacked any extensive experience in code breaking, traffic analysis, or intelligence evaluation. The principal factor behind his selection appears to have been that he was a close friend of the Redmans. And the fact that his appointment was approved was yet another indication of the lack of emphasis that the navy bureaucracy—even in wartime—placed on seeing that intelligence officers were properly qualified for their jobs.

When Captain John Redman arrived at fleet headquarters in mid-September, his first mission appears to have been to make good on the brothers' June promise to take "remedial action" as far as Hypo was concerned.[4] This translated into effecting the removal of Rochefort as rapidly as possible. There can be little doubt that this was a carefully planned conspiracy. Before John Redman left Washington for Pearl, he had arranged with Commander Wenger to open up a secret line of private communications by using a strip cipher and one of the navy radio circuits. Redman had not been at fleet headquarters for more than a couple of weeks before he was using this channel to report that Rochefort was uncooperative and that Wenger should arrange for his transfer to be requested.

Joe had already picked up what was in the wind: that Redman's arrival at Cincpac headquarters was another attempt to chip away at the measure of independence that Hypo had achieved from Washington with Nimitz's blessings. With the Guadalcanal campaign reaching its critical phase, he complained to Nimitz that the repeated petty disputes with Washington had become counterproductive to our intelligence effort.

The final straw came in the second week of October when Goggins arrived at Pearl Harbor. After less than seven weeks as OP-20-G, he had been replaced by Captain Earl E. Stone, another officer who was equally inexperienced in radio intelligence. Neither Cincpac nor the Fourteenth Naval District had been given any official or unofficial notice of Goggins's arrival. His orders merely indicated that he was taking up duties as "executive officer" of Icpoa. But it was soon evident that he had another mission, because of his insistence on advising Rochefort how to reorganize the combat intelligence unit. There was an embarrassing incident when Goggins made his first attempt to get past the armed guard and was denied admission to Hypo until he had established his identity and shown the proper written security clearance.

Rochefort, naturally, resented Goggins's intrusion. Joe suspected that the new arrival was really trying to undermine his position when he began to receive directions on how Hypo and Icpoa were to collaborate in radio intelligence work. One of Joe's team suggested that he should "just tell Washington to go to hell."[5] After seeking assurances from Nimitz's chief of staff, then Admiral Spruance, that is precisely what Joe tried to do. He drafted a cablegram to that effect. I showed it to Nimitz, who personally approved that it should be sent. Diplomatically but firmly it told Negat in effect, "I'm working for Admiral Nimitz so get off my back!"

Captain Redman evidently found out about Rochefort's protest, and that Nimitz was entirely sympathetic to it. He sent a second coded alert to Wenger: "Get rid of Rochefort at all costs."[6] Captain Stone of OP-20-G was shown this message. He tried to wash his hands of the affair, because he recognized the illegality of using navy cipher systems for private communications. Wenger was then obliged to take it up himself with Captain C. F. Holden, the new director of naval communications.

Holden's first action was to order his ambitious subordinate to destroy his private cipher and report the whole affair to Admiral Horne, who was King's deputy chief of naval operations. Horne, who already had been primed with misinformation by the Redmans' June memoranda, concluded that despite the questionable methods that Captain Redman had employed, he was right. The obstructive Rochefort must be removed. After obtaining King's authorization—but without consulting either the Fourteenth Naval District commandant, Cincpac, or the director of naval communications—the necessary arrangements were made with the Bureau of Personnel.[7]

Exactly a week after Goggins arrived at Pearl, Joe received orders on 22 October 1942 detaching him from Hypo for "temporary additional duty" in Washington. Admiral Nimitz immediately protested to King. Nimitz said that while he had nothing against Goggins, he did not want Joe detached. Nimitz's communication stressed that Rochefort had been instrumental in effecting the Pacific Fleet's Midway victory. "I will do all that I can," King cabled back in a "Personal" message that Nimitz showed me. King promised to intervene to get Rochefort's detachment order canceled.

King, however, was apparently caused to change his mind by those members of his staff, such as Admiral Horne who had been persuaded by the Redmans' memoranda that Rochefort was insubordinate and uncooperative and in need of direct supervision. Nimitz received a second message from King that said that Rochefort was to return to Washington for ten days of temporary duty. This made it appear that they wanted Joe's specialist advice on restructuring of Negat's radio intelligence organization. Nimitz could hardly refuse what, on the face of it, was a reasonable proposal.

Rochefort, however, realized that he had lost. "When I leave Pearl,

I'm not coming back," he told a number of us, and he sadly turned over a package of personal papers and the keys to his desk before leaving Pearl Harbor on 25 October.[8]

Two weeks after Joe's departure, Captain Goggins was introduced to the Hypo team as "your new boss."[9] This came as a surprise to his deputy, Captain Dyer, as it did to the other officers.

"It was another blow to our morale," wrote Lieutenant Jasper Holmes, who would shortly receive a melancholy letter from Rochefort. It conveyed his "sincere regrets on leaving under such circumstances" and thanked "the best damn intelligence organization the U.S. Navy or any other navy has seen."[10]

On 15 November Nimitz received notice that Rochefort's "temporary orders" had been "modified to permanent duty." Since this dispatch had been deliberately sent by surface mail rather than cable, it was too late for him to intervene. Nimitz was furious, and it was said that he refused to speak to John Redman for two weeks. His communications officer, however, was an adept politician who was able to mend his fences and remain on the Cincpac staff for the next two and a half years.

Rochefort arrived in Washington, exhausted, and justifiably resentful at the shabby treatment he had received. "I made several mistakes in a great big hurry, one of which compounded the other," he was to admit later. "And the net effect was that I flatly refused the offer of special work in Washington."[11] This confirmed rather than dispelled the slurs that the Redmans had spread about him. No consideration was given to making him head of OP-20-G, the one other post besides Hypo in which Rochefort's talents could have continued assisting our war effort.

Joe insisted on sea duty, although he knew that it was against standing regulations to send anyone with knowledge of our work on the Japanese codes into the war zone. After a series of minor intelligence postings on the west coast, Rochefort was finally granted his wish—in a backhanded way—when he was assigned the command of a floating dry dock at Tiburon, California. But it was conditional that he would not take it to sea, merely supervise its fitting out. Not until April 1944 were Rochefort's real talents again tapped when he returned to Washington to work on Pacific Fleet Strategic Intelligence studies and on plans for the anticipated invasion of Japan.[12]

It was very disturbing for me, his friend of many years, to see how Rochefort was speared like a frog and hung out to dry for the rest of the war when he could have done so much more to help us win it. When it was apparent that Joe had been spirited away over the personal protests of Nimitz, I tried to persuade the admiral to back up his request that Rochefort be awarded the Distinguished Service Medal.

"When the time comes, I hope to take this up," Nimitz promised. But he reminded me, "Layton, if you know anything about Admiral King, you know that when he has made his mind up, it is made up. I've got enough to do to fight this war right now." Unlike the Redmans, he was not one to elevate a personal feud above struggle with the enemy.

About ten days later Nimitz sent for me. He showed me a personal letter on Admiral King's hand-laid bond and told me to read the paragraph he pointed out. It began, "Now that I have taken care of Rochefort, I will leave it up to you to take care of Layton."

"Layton, you've got an enemy there in Washington," the admiral said. "Why do they want to get rid of you?" I was dumbfounded because I had not at the time appreciated the machinations of the Redman clique. I suggested that maybe he might like to find a nice destroyer for me to command.

"Go back to your office and don't think any more about it," Nimitz told me with a reassuring chuckle. With that he pulled from his desk a portrait photograph, which he signed then and there: "To Commander Edwin T. Layton. As my intelligence officer you are more valuable to me than any division of cruisers."

Epilogue: On to Tokyo Bay

"THE FATE OF THE NATION quite literally depended upon about a dozen men who had devoted their lives and their careers, in peace and war, to radio intelligence."[1] That was how Captain Jasper Holmes, then deputy director of Jicpoa, summed it up in a postwar assessment that Nimitz enthusiastically endorsed. Actually, the intelligence war had been won by the end of 1942, so you can imagine the blow to Hypo's morale, to say nothing of my own disappointment, when Rochefort left Pearl Harbor just before the tide turned in the campaign for Guadalcanal.

After Joe left, and the fleet shifted to the offensive in 1943, radio intelligence remained the cornerstone of our effort in the Pacific. The concepts remained the same. But it was inevitable that major changes would be made in our operations at Pearl. The Intelligence Center Pacific Ocean Area (Icpoa) increasingly acted as the middleman between fleet headquarters and Hypo, especially after Icpoa received its first large group of translators in February 1943. These twenty reserve officers were graduates of an eleven-month crash course in Japanese at the naval language school at the University of Colorado in Boulder. They were the first of a growing stream of linguists and analysts necessary to meet the demands of our expanding amphibious operations.[2]

A major reorganization of intelligence was made seven months later when Nimitz was named commander in chief Pacific Ocean Area. In September 1943, almost a year after Rochefort's replacement, Joe's plans for Hypo were finally vindicated. Its code-breaking and traffic analysis function was placed directly under Cincpac command as the Fleet Radio Unit Pacific Fleet or Frupac. The new Icpoa became Jicpoa, reflecting the "Joint" nature of Nimitz's command, and its staff continued to grow. By the final year of the war it was almost two thousand strong. Members of the army, navy, air force, marines, and coast guard all helped make it one of the most effective intelligence organizations in military history.

Jicpoa's task was to prepare strategic estimates for our major operations by drawing together information from every source of intelligence: from radio intercepts to prisoner of war interrogations. One new role was combat intelligence, which proved most effective. Intelligence teams would go ashore with the first wave of our landings to collect any documentation that would assist with the assault.

While Jicpoa provided the clearinghouse for assembling and disseminating other intelligence, our principal source throughout the war remained the radio intelligence units. Especially important was the Hypo team. Dyer, Wright, Finnegan, and the other men, who had been inspired by Rochefort, continued their brilliant work of penetrating the enemy code traffic. So well did their operation function that despite temporary setbacks as a result of the Japanese introducing new additives or code books, there was never a sustained period when we were not able to read communications in the principal JN-25 operational system.

"During the whole war the enemy's traffic was consistently read in detail and in great volume," stated an official wartime naval appraisal. "After the battle of the Coral Sea, most of his moves were disclosed through this source alone. Whenever the main code was not being read, a feeling of frustration and exasperation permeated the radio intelligence organization and spurred them on to each new success."[3]

The road to Tokyo was to be bitterly fought. Its route was to be disputed among our own commands, but the intelligence obtained from enemy radio traffic provided Admiral Nimitz with the tactical and strategic key to his Pacific campaign. Even General MacArthur was to concede that radio intelligence "saved us many thousands of lives and shortened the war by no less than two years."[4]

Twelve months of fighting on the defensive after Pearl Harbor had helped us forge radio intelligence into a potent, war-winning weapon. But the Japanese never remedied the fundamental flaws in their communications security, which should have been exposed by our success at Midway. They also failed to make any serious penetration of our own code systems, perhaps on the fatalistic assumption that our ciphers, like theirs, were too complex to admit any sustained eavesdropping. Fortunately for us, our enemy paid no heed to the injunction made a century earlier by Edgar Allan Poe: "It may be roundly asserted that human ingenuity cannot concoct a cipher which human ingenuity cannot resolve."

While the Japanese never read our ciphers, we were able to maintain our penetration of their principal naval operational ciphers from early 1943 onward. This included the four-digit code used by their merchant shipping. The breakthrough into the so-called *maru* cipher used by the Japanese transports was the product of five months' sustained effort by the Hypo team led by Captain Dyer and Commander Wright.[6] The Japanese modeled their merchant ship communications system on British "reporting and routing" practice. So our ability to read the *maru* code allowed us to plot the Japanese convoy routes from their daily noon position reports. Their merchant skippers obligingly and methodically transmitted reports at 0800 and 2000 each day. Our ability to know exactly where their convoys were heading was to become the vital factor in running our successful submarine war, which, by late 1944, had effectively severed the seaborne lifelines of Japan's scattered empire.

Only after the *maru* code had been broken early in 1943 was it possible for Nimitz to begin the undersea war in earnest. Until then we had tried to use radio intelligence to direct our submarines against enemy warships. It had been my duty to keep the commander of our submarine force posted with the movements of major Japanese warships. A simple code was used to disguise the source of the information by which our boats were directed to map references where they could expect "whales" (carriers) or "bears" (cruisers). Enemy carriers were given high priority, but at long distance it proved difficult to direct our submarines in attacking fast-moving and well-protected naval units.

Radio intelligence, however, did eventually provide an explanation of some of our more notable failures, such as the ten torpedoes that submarine *Tunny* successfully fired at close range into an enemy task force south of Truk on 10 April 1943. After her skipper's report, we had high hopes that two out of three Japanese carriers had been hit.[7] But within a few hours, I was reluctantly reporting to Nimitz that we had decrypted a message from Truk's port director reporting the safe arrival of all of the task force. Such disappointments were all too frequent. They culminated on 11 June in a string of failures by our submarines in Tokyo Bay to sink any fleet units, although *Trigger*'s skipper reported explosions after a full salvo successfully fired at carrier *Hiyo*.

Following my radio intelligence report that *Hiyo* had signaled that she was only slightly damaged, Nimitz summoned Rear Admiral Charles Lockwood, his submarine force commander, for an emergency conference on 23 June. After I had given my evidence to support the long list of our attack failures, they concluded that the magnetic detonators on our torpedoes were probably defective.

"I think that we ought to deactivate the magnetic exploders," Nimitz proposed.

"I can't order that," Lockwood said, "but I wish that you would."

"I can and will," Nimitz declared. He promptly ordered that the magnetic detonators on the torpedoes in all ships and airplanes under his command were to be deactivated.

The Bureau of Ordnance at first refused to believe that their torpedoes were at fault. But they could not argue with the submarine skippers' action reports, or my list of decrypts confirming the failure to inflict any major damage in most of their attacks despite some hits. An investigation revealed that there were indeed design faults with a poorly tested exploder, as well as other defects that caused our torpedoes to run deeper than their set depth. Until an improved design was manufactured, temporary measures were ordered to correct the defects, and the sinking of Japanese ships by our submarines increased through the summer of 1943 on a satisfyingly rising curve.[8]

While radio intelligence was helping to uncover the eccentricities of our torpedoes, the ability to read the *maru* code system enabled us to redirect our submarines economically and effectively against the slow-moving, poorly escorted enemy convoys. (As an old submariner, Nimitz was an enthusiastic advocate of unrestricted warfare against Japan's most vulnerable line of supply and communications.) Commander Jasper Holmes, who was later promoted to captain and made deputy director of Jicpoa, was chosen by Nimitz to mastermind this offensive. He soon established a routine that began at 0900 each day when he met with the operations officer of the Pacific Fleet submarine force to update their plot of Japanese convoys and decide which targets would be allocated to each submarine patrol.

Orders would be flashed out with up-to-date information on the courses of Japanese convoys. This made for a very efficient use of our forces, because it eliminated long and fruitless searches for likely targets. It was not unusual for all of our submarines on patrol in the central Pacific to be occupied simultaneously in an attack directed on the basis of information supplied by radio intelligence. Sometimes it was only a matter of hours between decryption of a *maru* message and one of our submarines reporting a sinking. A hand-powered telephone link with the commander of the submarine force and Jicpoa completed what Holmes described as "the basis of almost perfect coordination between operations and intelligence."[9]

The breaking of the *maru* code was a major factor in sending the annual sinking rates up by the end of 1943 to a million and a half tons. By January 1944 our submarines were sending enemy merchantmen to the bottom at the rate of almost a third of a million tons a month. There was no way for the Japanese shipbuilding industry to keep pace. Over eight and a half million tons of enemy shipping had been sunk by 1945, an attrition that made a significant strategic contribution to winning the war.

In the early months of 1943, Hypo also broke the Japanese navy's main weather code. Later, this played an important part in our strategic bombing offensive. But it was our ability to keep eavesdropping on the Japanese JN-25 fleet operations code which continued to make the biggest contribution of our war effort. Hypo's ability to keep track of the changed editions of the cipher's additive groups was greatly assisted by our salvage of confidential documents from Japanese submarine *I-23*, which had been sunk on 29 January in shallow water off Guadalcanal. Although the current JN-25 code book was buried when the crew escaped ashore, we recovered a red-covered code book, and additive tables from earlier versions, that yielded valuable intelligence data.[10]

The Japanese navy's main operational JN-25 D code system remained substantially unchanged except for the regular key changes until 31 May, when it was succeeded by the E version. By then it had been in use for over nine months, three months longer than the maximum prewar period. Their failure to change their main ciphers more frequently had permitted us to make the Midway code breaks a year earlier. In April 1943 a similar lapse of cryptographic security enabled us to strike another deadly blow. The target this time was not enemy ships or bases, but the irreplaceable commander in chief of the Combined Fleet.

We knew from the call sign intercepts that Admiral Yamamoto had arrived in Rabaul at the beginning of April to direct an all-out naval air offensive, code-named I-Go, against our bases in the lower Solomons and New Guinea. On 7 April, he had waved good luck to the first two hundred fighters and bombers that took off to blast Guadalcanal in the biggest air raid since Pearl Harbor. Four days later he decided to make a personal tour of the Japanese air bases in the northern Solomons. His staff gunnery officer, Captain Yasuji Watanabe, had planned Yamamoto's itinerary and ordered that it be transmitted only by naval communications because he did not trust the security of army codes. Contrary to his request it was sent by both systems and we picked up both of them. Major Alva B. Lasswell had the duty at Hypo that day and was first to break the message.

Ever since Combined Fleet headquarters had moved south, we were keeping a special watch on the Rabaul radio circuits. This attention paid off in the early hours of 14 April when a signal was intercepted. The partial decrypt was to prove to be Yamamoto's death warrant:

> On 18 April CinC Combined Fleet will visit RYZ, R—— and RXP in accordance with the following schedule:
>
> 1. Depart RR at 0600 in a medium attack plane escorted by 6 fighters. Arrive at RYZ at 0800. Proceed by minesweeper to R—— arriving at 0840.
>
> 2. At each of the above places commander in chief will make a tour of inspection and at —— he will visit the sick and wounded but current operations should continue.[11]

Although Tommy Dyer and Ham Wright had not been able to recover all of the area designator code groups, we knew that RR was Rabaul, RXZ was Ballale, and RXP was Buin on the southern tip of Bougainville. Since the message was addressed to the garrison commander at nearby Ballale island, it was clear that the first part of this trip would bring his plane within range of our fighters from Guadalcanal. The question that confronted me, when Jasper Holmes called me on our private telephone line that Wednesday morning, was what action to take. After he hand-carried the text of the message to Cincpac headquarters, I hurried down the corridor to consult with Nimitz.[12]

It was shortly after 0800 when Commander H. Arthur Lamar, Nimitz's flag secretary, told me, "Zero Zero is in and will see you now."[13] After the admiral had studied the message and checked his wall chart to confirm that Yamamoto's itinerary would bring him within range of our fighters, his question was: "Do we try to get him?"[14]

There was no doubt in my mind that shooting down Yamamoto would be a vital and serious blow to the Japanese. There was no one of the same stature to replace him. Admiral Yamaguchi had gone down with carrier *Hiryu* at the Battle of Midway, and during our review of who might succeed to the command of the Combined Fleet, Nimitz proved surprisingly well informed of the reputations and qualifications of the senior Japanese naval staff. In a final summary I assured him that there was indeed only one Yamamoto. "You know, Admiral Nimitz, it would be just as if they shot you down," I said. "There isn't anybody to replace you."

After our meeting Nimitz sent Admiral Halsey an "eyes only" message telling him that Yamamoto himself would arrive at Buin at 0600 on 18 April in two "Betty" bombers escorted by six Zeros. Halsey responded by confirming that the army air commander on Guadalcanal could arrange for his shootdown by long-range P-38 fighters. But he expressed his concern that such an operation might alert the Japanese that we were breaking their codes.

In anticipation of this reply I had already prepared a draft for Nimitz that "authorized and directed" them to go ahead "provided all personnel concerned, particularly the pilots, are briefed that the information comes from Australian Coastwatchers near Rabaul." Nimitz, who had already received the president's approval for the operation via the secretary of the navy, read my message carefully. He initialed it for release after adding "Best of luck and good hunting."

There were some qualms of conscience on my part. I was signing the death warrant of a man whom I knew personally. It was impossible for me not to feel for Admiral Yamamoto with a certain amount of fondness. It was not as though we were involved in the shooting of somebody whom I had never met. Although he had been my "official friend" four years ago, however, I could not dismiss the fact that he was now my sworn enemy. War, in essence, involves the destruction of your enemy. As the leader and inspiration for the Japanese navy, Yamamoto was an important foe whose death would benefit the Allied cause.

That was very much my reaction on the Sunday afternoon when Nimitz showed me the signal that Halsey had relayed to him:

P-38s led by Major John W. Mitchell, U.S.A., visited Kahili area about 0930. Shot down two bombers escorted by Zeros flying close formation. One shot believed to be test flight. Four Zeros added to score sum total six. One P-38 failed to return. April 18 seems to be our day.[15]

"Sounds as though one of the ducks in their bag was a peacock," Halsey added.

"It seems probable that CinC Combined Fleet was shot down in a plane over the Buin area today by Army P-38s" was the epitaph Nimitz accorded Yamamoto in the Cincpac war log.[16] Any public reaction had to wait another month until Tokyo Radio on 21 May announced that their fallen leader's ashes had been returned to Tokyo and that Yamamoto had been killed "while directing general strategy at the front line in April of this year, engaged in combat with the enemy and met a gallant death in a war plane."[17]

The shooting down of Yamamoto was a trauma for most Japanese. His death also struck at the fighting morale of their navy, not the least because Admiral Mineichi Koga, his chosen successor, was a conservative strategist who lacked flair and charisma. Yamamoto's distraught friend and gunnery chief, Watanabe, was mortified when he discovered that his chief's itinerary had also been broadcast in army cipher to the Buin garrison. Although Watanabe was never able to confirm his suspicions, he always remained convinced that we obtained our tip-off from army rather than from navy communications.[18] That was also the scuttlebutt opinion of our army pilots who had carried out the operation. But fortunately for us the newspapers back home did not pick up this story or Watanabe's suspicions might have prompted another major code change.

The impact of Yamamoto's death was intensified a month later when eleven hundred men of the Seventh U.S. Army landed on Attu on 11 May and recaptured our Aleutian island by the end of the month. The operation was not carried out without considerable difficulty. Surprising as it may seem, we lacked any detailed maps.

The assault had to be planned on the basis of aerial reconnaissance missions. The photographs provided the troops with accurate dispositions of the enemy's installations and order of battle. But they did not warn us how hard an enemy outnumbered five to one would fight. Instead of surrendering when their predicament became hopeless, they launched a suicidal banzai charge on 30 May, which left the slopes of Chicagof Harbor strewn with corpses. Only twenty-eight Japanese were left alive out of the garrison of nearly twenty-five hundred, and the recapture of this inhospitable scrap of rock and tundra cost us a thousand dead.[19]

It became clear that the only easy way to overcome the Japanese on neighboring Kiska Island was to kill as many of them as possible before our troops went in. But when our assault landed on 15 August after a two-day air-and-sea bombardment, there were no Japanese on the island. Undetected by our intelligence, they had executed a skillful evacuation operation three weeks earlier. Nimitz was greatly relieved at the lives saved, but there were some red faces in the Pearl Harbor intelligence organizations when an examination of photographic intelligence records showed that we had overlooked one picture on which the photo interpreter had noted "things strewn around beaches and other places as if the island had been abandoned."

While the Japanese were being dislodged from their toeholds in the Aleutians, Halsey's campaign was driving them back up the Solomons as he advanced from Guadalcanal to New Georgia at the end of June. Intelligence provided a timely alert that a big Tokyo Express was heading down from Rabaul to land enemy reinforcements behind our newly established beachhead.

Halsey promptly dispatched a task group of three light cruisers and four destroyers under Rear Admiral Walden L. "Pug" Ainsworth to guard the entrance to the Kula Gulf off the northern tip of New Georgia. Shortly after midnight on 5 July the Tokyo Express of ten destroyers collided with our force. The Japanese managed to land their reinforcements although they lost two destroyers, and our cruiser *Helena* was torpedoed and sunk. Admiral Ainsworth, however, reported that he had sunk two enemy cruisers and he claimed additional destroyers, which had "vanished" from his radar screens during the action.

On the day following the action, Nimitz asked for my assessment. A year earlier, after too many "sinkings" had turned up in our after-action radio reports, Nimitz had determined Cincpac would make no official action reports until they had been reviewed by fleet intelligence. Nimitz was very enthusiastic when he asked me to check up on how many cruisers Ainsworth had sunk at Kula Gulf.

"Admiral, we did not get any cruisers," I reported. "There were no Japanese cruisers within five hundred miles of the action." He was reluctant at first to believe that one of his admirals could have made such an exaggerated claim. The following day I was able to tell him that the Japanese decrypts indicated that only one destroyer had been sunk by naval gunfire; the other had run aground on a reef. When Ainsworth flew in to Pearl to make a personal report, Nimitz, very uncharacteristically for him, put me in the firing line by calling me in to confront Ainsworth with the facts.

"How can you sit here on your fat ass, thousands of miles from the action and make such a statement," a furious Ainsworth demanded. "How can you say this, it's absolutely preposterous!"

"All I can do is report what we get from radio intelligence," I tried to explain. "I have no stake in this matter personally, but I have a stake in the war."

Ainsworth continued to berate me after Nimitz had passed the matter to Soc McMorris, for arbitration. We went around and around on the issue but Ainsworth remained unconvinced. Twelve days later, I had hard evidence proving that my version was correct. It reached Halsey's headquarters from a Japanese survivor of another destroyer sinking. He was carrying a folder whose red border designated it a top-secret Japanese document. It was the Japanese action report for the Kula Gulf action.

The report was flown to Pearl, and I showed it to Nimitz to confirm that there had been no cruisers involved and that only two enemy destroyers had been lost. He ordered it translated immediately—and I assigned the task to Commander Alwin Kramer, who had just arrived to join the Cincpac intelligence staff. In checking on his progress with this urgent project, I discovered that Kramer had left it half translated and had gone off to Honolulu, where he was finally located in a pool hall. I did the translation myself, with my yeoman doing the tracing of the action chart.

Nimitz had already drafted a covering letter to convey the translation to Admiral Ainsworth, saying that it would be "grievous to you to hear that our intelligence was found to be more accurate than your report," but as commander in chief he had to rely on intelligence and "not be carried away by overoptimistic estimates of enemy losses." I heard no more from Ainsworth—and Kramer shortly found himself posted to Halsey's headquarters in the southwest Pacific.

While our admirals sometimes became carried away with their action reports, more often it was our carrier pilots. There was a spate of overestimates after the Bougainville landings in the first week of November. Radio intelligence had alerted us that major units of the Combined Fleet were being rushed to Rabaul to threaten our Empress Augusta Bay beachhead. Halsey decided to take a calculated risk by sending his carriers north to launch a series of raids against the enemy forces assembling in the heavily defended fleet base at Simpson Harbor. Starting on 11 November, five carrier air groups began a series of massive air strikes to "change the name from Rabaul to Rubble," as Halsey graphically put it.[20]

We knew from the radio decrypts that Admiral Koga had made the too-cautious decision not to challenge our cruiserless task forces, and had withdrawn the Combined Fleet units to Truk. Our fliers, nevertheless, were soon claiming to have sunk five or six Japanese carriers. Although there were no longer any large warships at Simpson Harbor, they were still reporting hits on battleships and carriers. Nimitz became very concerned.

"There is nothing that we can do about this," I told him, explaining that they were probably mistaking landing craft for capital ships. "It is my assessment that when these boys drop a bomb, they are under great mental stress. They see a big explosion and they figure they must have sunk a large warship."

Nimitz's concern was, however, justified. We could not afford to underestimate the enemy strength at this critical point of the war when the final phase of the Solomons campaign coincided with the launch of the navy's long-awaited central Pacific offensive. This offensive had originally been intended to follow the Rainbow war plan strategy for seizing a major base in the Marshalls. Our intelligence estimates, however, had revealed that enemy air strength was being built up in anticipation of our assault on the outer islands of their Pacific defense perimeter.

Nimitz was a careful strategist. He was able to convince Admiral King that we should advance into the heavily defended Marshalls by way of the island stepping-stones in the Gilberts. These were within bombing range of our air bases at Canton Island and Funafuti in the Ellice group. The northernmost atolls of Tarawa and Makin were selected for capture, after the Cincpac staff had ruled out Ocean and Nauru because their steep bluffs would make them difficult to assault. The capture of the enemy airfield at Betio, the largest of the pair of islands that composed Tarawa, along with that of the Makin airfield, would then afford us the land-based air cover for a northwest advance into the Marshalls.

Admiral Spruance was designated as the overall commander. Turner was in charge of the amphibious force with marine General Holland M. Smith commanding the actual landing. These two officers both held strong opinions about how to conduct such an operation. But the warfare that erupted during the planning sessions between Terrible Turner and Howlin' Mad Smith was only a foretaste of the reception awaiting their forces on the narrow beach at Tarawa.

Carrier raids the month before the scheduled landing date of 20 November had softened up the enemy defenses. But the strikes had also alerted the enemy. When the marines hit the beach at Betio on 20 November 1943, despite a heavy predawn bombardment from the battleships, the Japanese kept up a concentrated fire from their fortified bunkers. A tragic miscalculation from the tide tables stranded the second wave of amphibious tanks and landing craft hundreds of yards from the beach, forcing the marines to wade ashore under a murderous hail of gunfire.

Jicpoa intelligence estimates had put the Tarawa garrison at fewer than 4,000, but they had been reinforced by a contingent of Japanese marines of the Special Naval Landing Force who had been exhorted to fight to the last man. Only 150 Japanese and Korean noncombatant laborers survived the three-day battle for the 291 acres of battered palm and coral that cost the lives of 1,027 of our marines with 2,292 wounded. Makin was weakly garrisoned by comparison, and the army lost only 64 men, but it nevertheless took almost as long to secure as Tarawa.

Nimitz flew in to inspect the devastation at Tarawa. Deeply shocked, he compared it to the terrible slaughter at the Battle of Ypres in World War I. The gallantry and courage of the assault was in the finest tradition of the marine corps, but our commanders returned to Pearl determined to avoid such costly landings in the future. One of the "Lessons Learned at Tarawa," according to a special report prepared by Turner, was the

need for much heavier and more accurate bombardment of enemy for-
tifications.[21]

After "Bloody Tarawa," the task force commanders assumed that we
would crack the outer shell of the Marshalls first. But radio intelligence
revealed that this was precisely what the enemy anticipated. They were
moving army units and artillery from their Kwajalein headquarters to the
outer atolls. Nimitz instructed me to keep track of this movement and
draw up a new order of battle for each of the island groups. This was kept
up on a day-to-day basis and cross-checked against such intelligence as
the latest intercepted ration reports and the routine lists of sick and hospitalized personnel. By the end of the first week in December it was
indisputable that Jaluit, Wotje, Maloelap, and Mili had been heavily reinforced at the expense of the defenses of the inner islands.

"Are you sure of this information?" Nimitz asked me. To convince
him that our intelligence was right, I brought him actual decoded messages and showed him the traffic analysis. By this time the admiral was
familiar with all the technical data and the special language used in the
decrypts. After making a careful study of the raw decrypts, he called his
task force commanders to a conference at fleet headquarters on 14 December.

Admiral Spruance, General Smith, and Admiral Turner assembled,
along with their chiefs of staff and planning officers. Just before the meeting began, Nimitz again reviewed my order of battle. He told me to bring
along my intelligence summary to the meeting, and to be prepared to
answer any questions.

Carefully avoiding any revelation as to how we had obtained the details, Nimitz reviewed the new intelligence on the enemy order of battle
in the Marshalls. He then polled each of his commanders individually
in turn to determine whether they still thought it advisable to proceed
with their plans to assault the outer islands. Mili and Maloelap emerged
as their preferred targets. No one mentioned Kwajalein. Nimitz heard all
their discussion patiently, and then dropped his bombshell.

"No, gentlemen, we are not going to any of your islands," Nimitz
declared. "I have decided we are going to Kwajalein. The Japanese
aren't going to know this and they're going to be just as surprised as you
are."

The admirals and the general looked at him as if he had lost his mind.
They argued that all of their plans were complete, down to the details of
the landing areas, troop deployments, and resupply. They unanimously
favored the original objectives.

"I don't care what you've done; just go back and redo it for Kwajalein," Nimitz stated firmly. "That's the enemy's weakest point and they
won't expect us."

The point was then made that Japanese air strength, which was deployed along the outer perimeter, would make a penetration of their de-

fenses all the way to Kwajalein too hazardous. It seemed to me that since their original plans were practically complete, they did not want to change them, despite solid intelligence against them.

Some of the commanders wanted to know what would be done about the outer islands. "We're going to bypass them," Nimitz said, smiling benignly. "We'll just let them wither on the vine."

"I think we should go the other way," General Smith objected for a third time. But Nimitz was quite firm, telling them in effect, "We are going to take Kwajalein and if you don't want to, I'll just replace you."

Majuro was the only concession that Nimitz would make to seizing an atoll in the outer Marshalls—and that was only because radio intelligence and aerial reconnaissance showed that it was almost undefended. When he insisted that this island be captured by a single army battalion, General Smith protested that there must be "a couple of thousand Japs there."

"Layton, you tell General Smith how many Japs are there," Nimitz said, addressing me for the first time since our morning meeting.

"Six."

Smith jumped up and said, "*Six*! You mean six thousand, don't you?"

When I insisted that there were indeed six, according to their ration reports for the past few months, Howlin' Mad Smith growled, "I'll bet you the best bottle of bourbon there is in the Pacific against anything you name that there's at least six hundred on Majuro when we go ashore." Just before the operation I upped my predicted figure to a dozen, because a Japanese sub chaser had been sunk off the atoll and we had intercepted a radio message reporting that some of the crew had managed to get ashore. But I had no doubt about winning the bet.

When Majuro was captured on 31 January 1944, it turned out that there was only one Japanese on the island. He had been left as the so-called police chief when the others were taken off just before the start of Operation Flintlock, as our Marshalls campaign was code-named. The name was singularly inappropriate for an operation involving the largest amphibious force yet marshaled by the navy. Spruance's fleet consisted of 375 ships and 700 carrier aircraft. Their mission was to put ashore fifty-three thousand troops under the air umbrella of another 475 land-based planes from the Gilberts. Additional air and sea bombardment was to be supplied by Rear Admiral Marc Mitscher's task force of 12 carriers, 8 fast battleships, 6 cruisers, and 36 destroyers. This force was also to guard the two invading forces against any attempt by the enemy to send units east from Truk.

Yet even after three days of sustained battering from sea and air, Kwajalein resisted. It took four days of fierce skirmishing until the last of the garrison was overcome. Across the largest coral lagoon in the Pacific, the opposition on Roi and Namur islands was more quickly overcome. Overwhelming force might not have accelerated Kwajalein's capture, but it certainly saved the lives of our men. Fewer than four hundred were killed crushing the enemy defenders.[22]

A fortuitous minor error in the Flintlock plan produced an intelligence bonanza. It proved to be of inestimable value for the next stages in the so-called atoll war. One army raider unit missed its intended landing and went ashore on an islet too far to the west, off the southeast entrance to the Kwajalein lagoon. There a Japanese officer was captured who was carrying a roll of red-edged charts. Standing instructions identified all red-bordered documents as top-secret, so the haul was rushed to Turner's command ship. This windfall provided us with detailed charts of all the mandate islands, showing which areas were mined and which lagoons had been cleared of coral heads.

These charts proved to be invaluable aids in planning our future operations, and I was not the only one on Nimitz's staff to wonder if that army unit had not made their wrong landing as a result of some divine "misguidance." The chart for Kwajalein, for example, enabled us to quickly clear the lagoon of minefields, while possession of the details of the approach to Eniwetok was a great advantage when we put into effect stage two of Operation Flintlock.

Even before we received the captured charts, our intelligence estimates had assured Nimitz that our large troop reserves allocated to the Kwajalein and Majuro assaults would enable Turner to move on directly to capture Eniwetok, 360 miles to the northwest. The atoll was captured within forty-eight hours of our 18 February 1944 landing. But this was only after a last-minute revision of the assault plan, following the capture of yet another set of enemy documents, which indicated that the garrison was stronger than we had predicted. At the same time, Mitscher's carriers completed two and a half days of almost continuous raids on Truk and destroyed 275 Japanese planes and a quarter of a million tons of auxiliary shipping.

Admiral Koga had ordered all his warships west to the Palaus immediately after the Kwajalein attack. But the auxiliaries were scheduled to leave later, however, and the delay was fatal. When our pilots arrived over Truk, they were disappointed not to find the carriers, battleships, and cruisers that they had expected in Japan's "Gibraltar of the Pacific." They nevertheless sank many oilers, submarine tenders, and supply ships.

The destruction of the fleet supply train proved just as effective in curtailing Combined Fleet operations as would have the sinking of its capital ships. Without these support vessels, Japan's ability to mount offensive operations was ended. After the war, the Japanese admirals I talked to always referred to the raid on Truk as the one that broke their back. They had "endured" Midway and the loss of the carriers and their skilled aircrews, but our two-day air strike in the second week of February 1944 was the body blow that had caused them to abandon any hope of forward operations thereafter.

The evacuation of Truk meant that we had successfully cracked through the outer shell of Japan's defensive perimeter and that the enemy bases in the Carolines could be left to "wither on the vine." Truk was safe to bypass. The road to Tokyo could now be opened by breaking through the Marianas to the north, and Palaus to the west, and capturing Formosa as the springboard for an invasion of Japan.

While this was the strategic picture of operations that opened up for Nimitz and Admiral King, it did not agree with MacArthur's grand design. His forces were still battling up the northern coast of New Guinea. He had just secured a foothold in the Admiralty Islands as a prelude to capturing Rabaul, which would serve as a forward base for "a big piece of the fleet"[23] that he anticipated being put under his command. This would enable him to fulfill his promise to liberate the Philippines. MacArthur was determined that any road to Tokyo should pass through Manila. He saw the rapid progress of Nimitz's mid-Pacific campaign as a threat to his strategic concept, and he feared King would sabotage his plans if the navy succeeded in persuading the Joint Chiefs in Washington that the Philippines should be bypassed.

MacArthur and his supporters began a bitter campaign in Washington that lasted throughout the spring and summer of 1944. He was determined to persuade the president, and the Joint Chiefs, to agree to his commanding a single line of advance through the Philippines. Nimitz was under no illusions. The general had sent his key staff members to argue his case that spring at Pearl Harbor. But Nimitz knew that MacArthur could not make any large-scale amphibious assault without the Pacific Fleet. Nor would Admiral King ever agree to putting major naval forces under the control of any general. Although Halsey was technically subject to MacArthur's authority in the southwest Pacific area, he stoutly rejected the general's offer to make him "a greater man than Nelson ever dreamed of being."[24]

In March, however, the Joint Chiefs postponed a final decision on the route to Tokyo by authorizing MacArthur to begin preliminary planning for a fall invasion of the Philippines, while, at the same time, they endorsed Nimitz's plan for an assault on the Marianas (as a first step to a tentative Formosan invasion the following February). Much to his chagrin, MacArthur was denied Rabaul. But Nimitz was also directed to send the Fifth Fleet south. This was to support MacArthur's ambitious plan to bring the New Guinea campaign to a swift conclusion by leapfrogging assaults up the north coast toward the Philippines.

When members of MacArthur's staff arrived at Pearl shortly afterward with their concept of an eight-hundred-mile leapfrog to capture the strategic port of Hollandia, it was agreed the Fifth Fleet would be in support after its carrier task forces had been detached to launch strikes to keep enemy planes from interfering from their bases to the north in the Palaus. Tension between the two staffs was running high, because Mac-

Arthur's headquarters had bombarded Nimitz with a series of communications that should have been written on asbestos.

MacArthur told Nimitz later that his chief of staff had issued these dispatches without his knowledge. Even so, I always wondered why Nimitz kept a picture of the general prominently displayed in his office. It was an unsigned rotogravure clipped from a magazine. One day when I asked about the general's perpetual presence, Nimitz gave me one of his smiles: "Layton, I'll tell you. It's to remind me not to be a horse's ass."

For one of these March sessions with MacArthur's staff Nimitz asked me to play the role of the Japanese command and plot the expected movements of the Japanese land-based air forces in response to the reports of our operation that we assumed Combined Fleet headquarters would receive.

My principal observation was that most of their planes were now piloted by army fliers who lacked overwater navigational experience. Thus, they seldom ventured more than 150 miles to seaward. As a result our carrier task forces were directed to advance on a southerly route close to the New Guinea coast. This enabled them to reach their destination off Palau on 29 March undetected. Our carrier planes destroyed 150 enemy aircraft and sank 70 auxiliary vessels before heading south to cover the Hollandia landings.

The total surprise achieved by this tremendous leap forward encouraged MacArthur to advance, by almost a month, the capture of the Japanese bases at New Guinea's northern tip. The success of his leapfrogging strategy depended on our ability to read the Japanese army ciphers, which we had broken for the first time the previous year. As the army intelligence division put it: "Never has a commander gone into battle as did the Allied Commander Southwest Pacific, knowing so much about the enemy."[25]

After lending a helping hand to MacArthur in New Guinea, the Pacific Fleet staff turned their attention to the June assault on the Marianas. Like the Jicpoa analysts we were heavily dependent on the enemy radio traffic for intelligence, because Saipan, Guam, and Tinian were beyond the range of our reconnaissance flights. The Fifth Fleet was also sent up to make a preliminary raid and to obtain photographs of the Japanese defenses. But our biggest break came not from our reconnaissance flights or enemy radio transmissions, but from another batch of captured documents.

One unforeseen result of the Hollandia operation was that the carrier strikes on the Palaus forced Admiral Koga and his staff to abandon the islands as their fleet headquarters. It was the third time that the Combined Fleet staff had been forced into an evacuation in less than a year. This time the number one flying boat carrying the commander in chief vanished in a typhoon. The number two plane, carrying his chief of staff, Admiral Shigeru Fukudome, was forced down in the water off the island of Cebu in the southern Philippines. Fukudome was still clutching his waterlogged briefcase when he was rescued by Filipino guerrillas. Although he was later released after threats of reprisals, his documents were confiscated. Word was sent to MacArthur that important Japanese papers had been captured. A submarine was sent to collect them.

The Japanese linguists at MacArthur's headquarters were unfamiliar with naval terminology. From their gist translation, however, it was evident to me that the captured documents were the Combined Fleet's operational plans for concentrating its total sea and air strength against our next advance into their island defense system.

As our Fifth Fleet and the Marianas invasion forces were already assembling at Eniwetok, I urged Nimitz to get a photographic copy of this plan sent to Pearl as soon as possible. When it arrived we stayed up all night translating the enemy's so-called A-Go operational strategy. It was plain that their tactical effort to hurl everything they had against us would remain in effect. The next day, a flying boat rushed the copies of my translation of the A-Go plan with Nimitz's final instructions out to the task force at Eniwetok.

Spruance and Mitscher, who commanded the Fifth Fleet carrier task forces, were therefore well aware of the enemy strategy when they set course north across the Philippine Sea for the Marianas. The combined force of 535 ships and 127,571 troops made Operation Forager the largest amphibious assault yet mounted in the Pacific. It began with an air strike on Saipan on 15 June.

This attack caught the Combined Fleet completely off balance, with their battleships poorly disposed to intervene. This was because of faulty intelligence estimates. They had concluded from MacArthur's attack two weeks earlier on the island of Biak, off the northwest tip of New Guinea, that our next objective would be in the Palaus. At his Borneo headquarters, Admiral Soemu Toyoda, the new commander in chief, had to recast their A-Go strategy to deal with our attack on the Marianas. He had already sent superbattleships *Yamato* and *Musashi* charging south to Biak. Now they had to be turned around and redirected northeast into the Philippine Sea where Toyoda hoped that the decisive naval battle could be fought under skies controlled by his land-based aircraft.

Sighting reports from our submarines on patrol off Luzon on 16 June alerted Nimitz that two large naval forces were heading eastward from the Philippines. The frantic scale of enemy naval and air activity was confirmed by radio intelligence. Spruance was warned accordingly. That afternoon he cautioned his staff that the Fifth Fleet was to make ready for action because the Japanese were coming after them.

The Fifth Fleet could send nearly nine hundred planes up from its fifteen carriers. This outnumbered by more than two to one the air power that could be flown off the six Japanese carriers. But Toyoda intended to even up the odds by using the airfields on Tinian and Guam for shuttle bombing while he rushed in his reserve of land-based planes from Japan using the Bonin Islands as way stations.

An elaborate decoy operation was supposed to lure our forces westward, but Spruance did not take the bait on 17 June when our radio direction finding put the approaching Japanese warships some six hundred miles west of Guam. Spruance's primary task was to protect the Saipan beachhead. He also knew from the captured Japanese plan that if he went after them full tilt, the enemy carrier planes would be able to multiply their effectiveness by using the other airfields in the Marianas for shuttle-bombing runs. It would also expose him to attack from a stream of land-based planes flying south from Japan.

Spruance, therefore, did not give chase as the Japanese intended—he waited for the enemy to come for him. On 18 June Mitscher's fifteen carriers and light carriers gained the tactical advantage by whittling down the land-based air force in the Marianas before the main enemy air attack.

Then on 19 June when the Japanese carriers launched nearly three hundred planes against our forces from the southwest, Mitscher's radio intelligence unit came into its own by monitoring the voice circuit of the Japanese pilot who coordinated the strikes from high above the swirling air battles. The stream of orders issued by Coordinator "Jo," as he was dubbed by Mitscher's air commander, enabled our fighters to be vectored onto the incoming enemy attack waves long before they reached our task forces. When he was eventually heard radioing for his relief to take over, it was suggested that one of our fighters should be directed up to shoot down Coordinator Jo.

"No indeed," said Captain Arleigh A. Burke, who was then Mitscher's chief of staff. "He's done us too much good this day!"[26]

Mitscher concurred. Thanks to radio intelligence our pilots had won what they jubilantly dubbed the Great Marianas Turkey Shoot in which they had bagged 243 Japanese aircraft.

Toyoda's A-Go plan was already falling into a shambles that afternoon when our submarines torpedoed and sank carriers *Shokaku* and *Taiho.* Another carrier, *Hiyo,* was sunk and two more were badly damaged by a Fifth Fleet air strike late the following afternoon. Spruance was to be criticized by the Monday morning quarterbacks at Fleet headquarters for not keeping up his hot pursuit westward during that night. But his primary duty to guard the beachhead justified his reluctance to expose his carriers to a night action with the five enemy battleships.

Although he denied himself an overwhelming triumph at the Battle of the Philippine Sea, Spruance nevertheless had won one of the most decisive victories of the Pacific war. The Combined Fleet had lost three of its remaining carriers and *all but thirty-six of its aircraft.* While the enemy still maintained a powerful naval presence in theory, in practice Toyoda now commanded an enfeebled fleet. Without carrier air power for its protection, and lacking the auxiliaries to sustain itself for long-range sea-going operations, the Combined Fleet was never again to pose a threat to our command of the Pacific Ocean area.

The Philippine Sea battle also wiped out a large part of the Japanese land-based air power. It also ensured the success of the Saipan operation that followed. During the assault phase, a Jicpoa intelligence team discovered a hastily abandoned Japanese command post in a schoolhouse. After a night spent translating captured documents by flashlight, our forces possessed the enemy battle plan, including precise locations of their batteries and tanks, in time to thwart the counterattack when it came on the following evening.

Yet despite our early success, the battle for Saipan turned into a bloody slugging match. Three more weeks of fighting were required to bring the island under our control. When the firing ceased, three thousand Americans were dead in addition to the more than forty-five thousand enemy killed. Thousands of Japanese chose to commit suicide in the caves of their embattled redoubt, and on the northern peninsula of Saipan many others hurled themselves from cliffs rather than face the disgrace of surrendering.

The loss of Saipan, however, drained the fight from the less-determined defenders on Guam and Tinian. The islands were secured within three weeks of our landings. By the final week of July work was under way to extend their airfields for the launching of the strategic air offensive against Japan.

Meanwhile, Roosevelt journeyed to Pearl Harbor by sea on 26 July. In a well-publicized demonstration of his authority as commander in chief, carefully timed to kick off his bid for reelection to a fourth term in the White House, he was to adjudicate the strategic issue of the Philippines invasion. The army and navy staffs were still divided on whether bypassing or capturing the occupied commonwealth would accelerate the end of the war. While MacArthur had campaigned vigorously behind the scenes for the invasion, Admiral King was opposed to it. Nimitz was stranded somewhat uncomfortably between the two.

MacArthur had arrived on time at Oahu that Wednesday afternoon after his long flight from Australia, but somehow he contrived to be an hour late for his dockside rendezvous with heavy cruiser *Baltimore,* which had carried the president from the mainland. He finally rolled up in a presidential-style motorcade like a conquering hero, a gesture that was no doubt calculated to overawe his totally unflamboyant rival Pacific commander as much as to impress the assembled newsmen.

Nimitz knew that he was in for a tough battle. That evening the two Pacific commanders plunged right into the debate with presentations of their differing strategic views of the next phase of the Pacific war. We had prepared a battery of charts to support the Cincpac contention that it was necessary only to neutralize the Japanese air bases in the Philippines before moving to invade Formosa as the final springboard to Japan. By contrast MacArthur spoke without a map or a note, delivering an impassioned appeal intended to remind the president that any attempt to bypass the Philippines would be militarily and politically disastrous. "American public opinion will condemn you," he concluded. "And it will be justified."[27]

After the general's masterfully eloquent histrionics, Nimitz sensed that Roosevelt's mind had already been made up. When MacArthur left by air the next day for Australia he told his staff on board his plane that he had "sold it." The victory that he won owed more to the political realities of Roosevelt's reelection campaign than to sound military calculation—as evidenced by the fact that it took a month before Admiral King and the naval staff were persuaded to give their reluctant endorsement of the Philippine invasion. On 8 September the Joint Chiefs of Staff issued their directive for the campaign. It was to be launched Christmas week, with a major amphibious assault on the southern island of Mindanao.

At Pacific Fleet headquarters, preparations were already in their final stages for the occupation of Peleliu in the Palaus and the capture of Yap and Ulithi to the north to provide air cover and an advanced base for the fleet. After Nimitz's decision to rotate the fleet's commanders in chief to keep up the pace of our offensive, Admiral Halsey was to take charge of the next round of operations.

The Fifth Fleet was therefore renamed the Third Fleet on 11 September when Halsey arrived in battleship *New Jersey* to lead a series of carrier strikes on airfields in the Philippines. The raids had no sooner begun than the reports of his pilots prompted an enthusiastic dispatch advising Nimitz that enemy air strength on Mindanao had been wiped out. The Philippines defenses appeared to be wide open. Halsey therefore urged that his fleet's intended assault on the Palaus be abandoned in favor of advancing the Philippines invasion. This, he contended, should go in at Leyte. He claimed the change would shorten the war by "many months" by making our initial assault one step nearer the main island of Luzon.[28]

Our intelligence, however, did not make us quite so sanguine as Halsey about the weakness of Japanese air defenses in the Philippines. Nonetheless, Nimitz forwarded Halsey's proposal to the Joint Chiefs. When they approved the Leyte operation for the end of November, Nimitz dropped the Yap assault. But he held fast to the Palaus operation to provide nearby support and repair bases if enemy resistance proved more formidable than Halsey predicted.

A week later, while Third Fleet task forces stood guard, MacArthur's troops captured the island of Morotai off the northeastern extremity of New Guinea and the marines went into the Palaus. Ulithi fell within a matter of minutes; Angaur was in our hands in three days. But the struggle for the nearby island of "Bloody Peleliu," as it came to be called, raged on for over two months. The Japanese had dug themselves into well-fortified positions in the hilly interior of the island. They had to be fought out, cave by inaccessible cave, in hand-to-hand combat whose ferocity exceeded the worst days of the Guadalcanal campaign. Almost two thousand Americans died securing an island which, despite Nimitz's predictions, made little strategic contribution to the winning of the war itself. As one of Halsey's admirals was later to observe, "If military leaders were gifted with the same accuracy of foresight as they are with hindsight, undoubtedly the assault of the Palaus would never have been attempted."[29]

While the struggle for Peleliu was raging in its second month, a thousand fighters and bombers from Third Fleet carriers were carrying out raids on the Japanese airfields on Okinawa and the Ryukyu Islands. More than five hundred enemy planes were shot down, like "so many eggs thrown against the stone wall of indomitable enemy formations," as the now reinstated Admiral Fukudome reported.[30]

With the enemy now battering the inner ring of Japan's defenses, Admiral Toyoda decided that it was time for desperate measures. He submitted his Sho (victory) plan for the emperor's approval. It represented the navy's supreme and final strategic gamble to hurl the remaining strength of the Combined Fleet against the anticipated American assault on the Philippines. To bolster the efforts of the navy's 150 surviving carrier planes, pilots with only basic training had volunteered to make one-way suicide missions against the enemy. They had taken the name *kamikaze*, after the "divine wind" typhoon that had saved Japan in 1281 from invasion by the Mongol fleet.

Divine intervention of some kind was certainly going to be needed if the 7 battleships, 4 carriers, 2 hybrid battleship-carriers, 20 cruisers, and 29 destroyers remaining to the Combined Fleet were going to stop the invasion. Halsey now had the kind of overwhelming naval superiority that few admirals in history have commanded. He could muster 32 carriers, 12 battleships, 23 cruisers, 100 destroyers, and 1,400 planes in the Third Fleet's air umbrella. The Leyte operation was under the joint command of Halsey and MacArthur. Their 430 transports were to be covered by Admiral Kinkaid's Seventh Fleet. The scale of the invasion was such that it rivaled the armada that five months earlier had landed the Allied armies in Normandy.

The 20 October invasion date was designated "A-Day" by MacArthur to distinguish his triumphant return to the Philippines from "D-Day." The landings on Leyte were executed with clockwork precision against almost no enemy interference. By the evening of A-Day MacArthur's troops had secured a seventeen-mile front against little enemy ground resistance.

The real opposition came forty-eight hours later, when Toyoda's

Sho-1 started to roll and the surviving and still-formidable might of the Combined Fleet came steaming out of the Borneo port of Brunei. As they headed northeast, the main force led by five battleships set course for the San Bernardino Strait, which separates Luzon from Leyte. The second force, led by two battleships, headed for the Surigao Strait off the southern tip of Leyte. Their intention was to debouch north and south and smash our invasion beachhead in a pincer movement. They were counting on the main strength of our Third Fleet being lured away to the northeast of the Philippine Sea by a decoy force of aircraft carriers that was already heading toward Cape Engaño from the north.

A major change in the Japanese naval code and the observation by their forces of strict radio silence had denied us advance intelligence of the Sho-1 plan. But early on the morning of 23 November, we received some inkling of what was afoot. Two of our submarines sighted and attacked the main force, sinking two heavy cruisers and damaging a third.

The next day, the main force was subjected to heavy air attacks from Third Fleet planes as it headed northwest across the Sulu Sea toward the San Bernardino Strait. After superbattleship *Musashi* had been sunk and *Yamato* damaged, the force turned around to await the cover of night before attempting to force the straits. Halsey therefore assumed that the enemy battle force was in full retreat when he received reports late in the afternoon from his other scouting planes that enemy carriers had been spotted 190 miles northeast of Luzon's Cape Engaño.

"Central force heavily damaged according to strike report," Halsey radioed Cincpac headquarters that evening. "Am proceeding north with three groups to attack carrier force at dawn."[31] This dispatch, however, failed to make it clear to Nimitz, or any of our task force commanders, that the Third Fleet battleships were no longer standing guard off the San Bernardino Strait.

Admiral Kinkaid was also unaware that his force guarding the beachhead was now wide open to attack from the north. He naturally assumed that Halsey would have left at least some of his Task Force 34 battleships as a precaution against an enemy breakthrough. Kinkaid deployed his six old battlewagons off Surigao Strait that evening after sporadic air attacks had failed to halt the advance of the enemy's southern force. When the Japanese made a desperate attempt to fight their way through the Surigao Strait, they were wiped out in the only battleship action of the Pacific war.

An evening air patrol reported that the first Japanese force had reversed course and was again heading for the San Bernardino passage. But Halsey appears to have misread, or ignored, the danger during his dash to the north.

The magnitude of this blunder was not appreciated until the following morning when superbattleship *Yamato* was spotted leading the enemy force racing down the coast toward the beachhead. At Pearl we just could not understand how all these Japanese battleships and cruisers with their destroyer screen had broken through the San Bernardino Strait undetected and unmolested. They would have smashed the invasion beachhead, too, but for the stark heroism of Rear Admiral Clifton S. Sprague, the commander of a group of escorts. His "Jeep" carriers were all that stood between the wolves and the fold. For more than an hour Sprague's pilots fought off the enemy battleships. Such a fierce fight was put up by our planes that in the fog of battle the Japanese commander, believing that he was confronting the Third Fleet carriers, ordered a retreat. The action fought by the "Jeep" carriers that morning saved the invasion. It was one of the most magnificent displays of gallantry in the Pacific war.

Nimitz was pretty perturbed when he realized that Halsey had taken all his forces off to the north and left the gate open for the wolves to jump the sheep. After we had picked up Sprague's urgent report, followed by Kinkaid's plain-language call for Halsey to send back the fast battleships, Nimitz decided to intervene. But the Third Fleet commander in chief was racing full tilt to finish off the carriers, which were under attack from his air strikes, when the Cincpac dispatch reached him on the flag bridge of battleship *New Jersey*. Nimitz's message appeared even more of a rebuke than he intended, because Halsey's decipher had failed to strip off the padding at the end of the message.

"Where is repeat where is Task force 34? The world wonders"[32] was what Halsey read. Choking with rage at this apparent rebuff from Nimitz, the four-star admiral hurled his famous cap onto the deck and stomped on it. Then, after debating the tactical situation with his staff, Halsey turned flagship *New Jersey* about to lead his battleships back to Leyte, leaving his quarry to the mercies of Mitscher's air strikes. The planeless carriers were sunk, but two battered hybrid battleship-carriers, two cruisers, and six destroyers managed to get away. It added to Halsey's chagrin when he learned that the enemy's main force, including superbattleship *Yamato*, had also made good their escape through the San Bernardino Strait.

The Japanese never realized how close they had come to achieving a punishing victory as the three-day Battle of Leyte Gulf came to a close with the planes of the Special Attack Force making their fiery debut. The first group of kamikazes made their suicidal crashes on Sprague's unfortunate Jeep carriers, inflicting heavy damage and sinking *St. Lo*. But even if "rotten communications," as Halsey described them, had denied him the total naval victory he had anticipated, by disrupting the imperial navy's suicidal banzai charge, he and Kinkaid had inflicted a terrible defeat on the imperial navy. The largest naval battle in history, which had swirled around Leyte Gulf, cost the Japanese more than a hundred aircraft in addition to the sinking of four carriers, three battleships, six cruisers, and twelve destroyers. It had reduced the Combined Fleet to an impotent force; it was now too weak to defend the approaches to Japan.

The naval war in the Pacific effectively ended with the Battle of Leyte

Gulf. But there still remained nine more months of hard fighting for the Pacific Fleet. It had to battle against the growing menace of the kamikazes at Iwo Jima in February 1945, and the four-month-long struggle for Okinawa that began in April.

The only attempt that the Japanese made at another surface engagement was the suicidal death ride of *Yamato,* which ended on 7 April when the superbattleship was pounded beneath the waves off Okinawa by our carrier planes. Our marines and soldiers continued fighting the bloody battles ashore, while our submarines sank Japanese ships until no enemy merchantman dared venture to sea during daylight. By the late spring of 1945 our carrier air power was increasing and it turned to raiding mainland ports and defense installations. From the end of 1944, Japan had been blockaded by sea and air as swarms of B-29 Flying Fortresses from the airfields of Saipan and Tinian began a systematic destruction of Japan's centers of production and fire-bombed her major cities.

Yet the Japanese fought on with a fanatic zeal. For the majority at home and overseas there could be no question of surrender. The high casualty rates that we had suffered during the landing at Iwo Jima and during the grueling Okinawa campaign were terrible harbingers of the cost we would have to pay as we began planning an invasion of Japan proper.

Nimitz had moved the Cincpac advance headquarters to Guam at the end of January. It was there that I first learned of the weapon that promised hope for our deliverance. I was brought into the secret of the atomic bomb because Nimitz insisted that his intelligence officer be fully briefed as to what was going on. This occurred when Major General Leslie Groves, the Manhattan Project's director, arrived with representatives of the secretary of war's ad hoc committee shortly after the first atomic bomb had been exploded in Alamogordo, New Mexico, on 16 July.

After we had watched the movies of the Alamogordo test, I was convinced that if the bomb worked, it could give the Japanese a psychological "out" from the terrible dilemma they were facing. Although they were defeated and knew it, they just could not surrender. I told the team from Washington that it was my firm opinion that only a decisive intervention from the emperor would end the war. The atomic bomb represented a new kind of warfare. It would give the emperor the chance to "turn off the faucet" on the slaughter and end the war without loss of face. When I was asked my opinion of an appropriate target, I named Okura, an army arsenal city that had not yet been raided.

Hiroshima, however, was selected. When Nimitz was given the top-secret alert that the superfortress carrying the first atomic bomb would take off from Tinian in the early hours of 6 August, I called in Jasper Holmes and told him that we wanted all the army air force radio networks covered, even at the expense of the loss of fleet circuits. After we received the news that the B-29 named *Enola Gay* was airborne, I had nothing more to relay to Nimitz until we picked up the "Bombs away" message the next morning. Minutes later it was followed by the word "Bingo!"

I did not know that there was a second bomb ready to go, but I was disappointed when the Japanese did not accept our surrender ultimatum after Hiroshima. Four days later another atomic blast flattened Nagasaki. I was in my office on 15 August when my special cipher teletype sprang to life with a message from the chief of naval operations at 0720. It clattered away, typing out the actual decrypt of the Japanese acceptance of surrender message. I tore off the top sheet and dashed into Nimitz's outer office.

"This is the hottest thing we've had," I told his flag secretary and went directly in to see Nimitz.

"Here it is," I said, handing over the message.

He read it, beamed one of his searchlight smiles, and announced, "I've just got one from Admiral King."

That morning he issued a dispatch to all ships: "This is a peace warning." But not until the next day did Cincpac send the dispatch to "Suspend all operations," which ended the fighting in the Pacific.

When Nimitz told me two weeks later that I would be accompanying him as his guest to the formal surrender ceremony in Tokyo Bay, he wanted to know if he would face any trouble from right-wing extremists during his intended visit to the Yokosuka naval base. I told him that I did not think so. But I hoped that he would take a marine orderly who was a crack pistol shot "just in case."

"They wouldn't attack me," the admiral said with surprise. "They'd attack MacArthur."

"Not the Japanese," I replied. "MacArthur didn't win this war as far as the Japanese are concerned. It's been your carriers that have been attacking their port cities and it's been the B-29s based in your command area that have carried the bombs to Japan, including the two atomic bombs. They know that it was our naval power that has brought Japan to its knees because they have no shipping. You're the one they would kill, not MacArthur, if anyone were to try such a thing."

Nimitz then asked me if I was a good shot, since I was to accompany him, and there would be no marine orderly. To improve my skills, he took me down to the personal shooting range, which he had set up at Guam headquarters. There we practiced with Colt .45s every day until we left for Japan. So it was with a heavy pistol in a shoulder holster that I accompanied Nimitz when he went ashore at Yokosuka with Admiral Halsey. Fortunately, there were no incidents.

The afternoon of the surrender ceremony, Admiral Nimitz suggested that we take ashore the Chevrolet sedan we had brought with us, and I proposed a trip to Kamakura. This beautiful town had never been bombed. It was a historic enclave full of aged cryptomeria trees and ancient shrines, including the *daibutsu,* or great buddha, and the Tsurugaoka-hachimangu, which had been built by the first shōgun, Yoritomo Minamoto, in the twelfth century. It struck me as particularly appropriate, on the day that marked the formal beginning of peace, that Admiral Nimitz should see for himself the shrine which for so many Japanese had symbolized their god of war.

THE RAID ON PEARL HARBOR: 7 December 1941

The Attack on Oahu

The Strike on Battleship Row

JAPAN INVADES THE PHILIPPINES: December 1941–May 1942

The Luzon Campaign

THE BATTLE OF THE CORAL SEA: 3–7 May 1942

THE BATTLE OF MIDWAY: 3–5 June 1942

Admiral Yamamoto's Operational Plan

The U.S. Pacific Fleet's Victory

THE SOUTHWEST PACIFIC THEATER CAMPAIGNS: 1942–1944

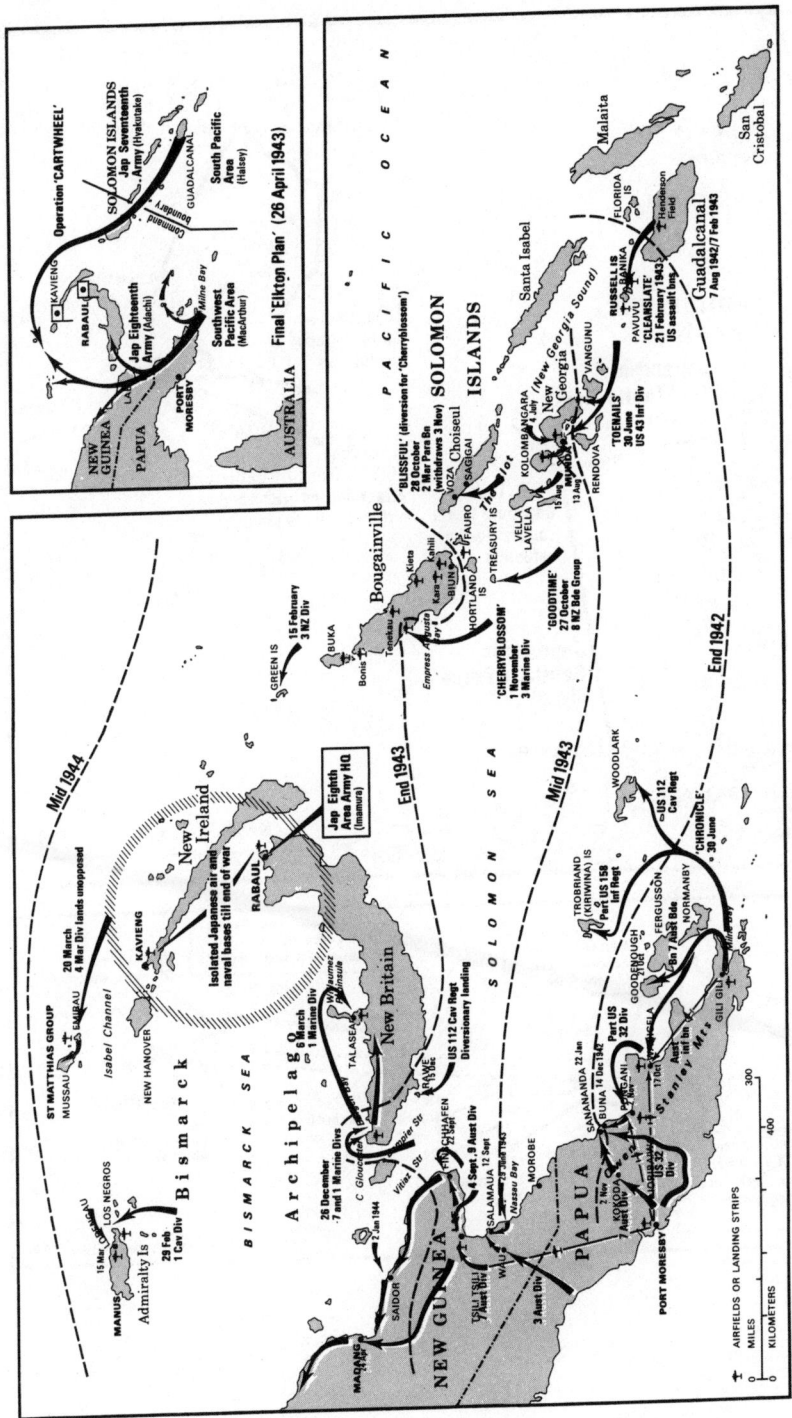

THE BATTLE OF THE PHILIPPINE SEA: 13–16 June 1944

Formosa

PHILIPPINE
ISLANDS

Luzon

**Japanese
1st Mobile Fleet**
(Ozawa)

NEGROS

PANAY

Mindanao

TAWITAWI

**Japanese
Southern Force**
(Ugaki)

HALMAHERA

BATJAN

Celebes

NEW GUINEA

IWO JIMA

16 June
TG 58.1 and 58.4
make air strikes

**Mariana
Islands**

1030, 18 June
All task groups
rendezvous

SAIPAN
TINIAN

12 June

GUAM

13/15 June
TG 58.2, 3 and 7 ('Battle Line')
attack Jap positions and
airfields prior to landings

Task Force 58
(Mitscher)

1700, 16 June
Japanese fleets
rendezvous for
refueling

YAP

PALAU

WOLEAI

TRUK

0   NAUTICAL MILES   600

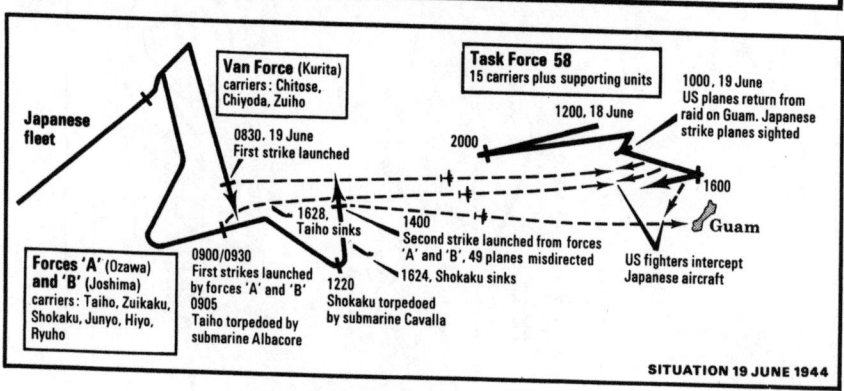

**Japanese
fleet**

Van Force (Kurita)
carriers: Chitose,
Chiyoda, Zuiho

Task Force 58
15 carriers plus supporting units

1000, 19 June
US planes return from
raid on Guam. Japanese
strike planes sighted

1200, 18 June

2000

0830, 19 June
First strike launched

Forces 'A' (Ozawa)
and 'B' (Joshima)
carriers: Taiho, Zuikaku,
Shokaku, Junyo, Hiyo,
Ryuho

0900/0930
First strikes launched
by forces 'A' and 'B'
0905
Taiho torpedoed by
submarine Albacore

1628,
Taiho sinks

1400

1220
Shokaku
torpedoed
by submarine Cavalla

Second strike launched from forces
'A' and 'B', 49 planes misdirected

1624, Shokaku sinks

1600

Guam

US fighters intercept
Japanese aircraft

SITUATION 19 JUNE 1944

THE BATTLE OF LEYTE GULF: 23–25 October 1945

POSITIONS OF US CARRIER TASK GROUPS, 0600, 24 OCTOBER
TIMES ARE THOSE FOR 24 OCTOBER UNLESS OTHERWISE INDICATED

0   NAUTICAL MILES   300

Carrier 'Decoy'
Force (Ozawa)   0100
0001, 25th
0600, 25th
1140
Group 'A'
(Matsuda)
2000
2241
0822, 25th

C. Engaño

Luzon

Second Striking Force
(Shima)

Task Force 38
(Halsey's Third Fleet)
steams north to engage
Ozawa's force

Clark
Field

TG 38.3
(Sherman)

2345

0935 Carrier Princeton hit,
sinks at 1630

Princeton

2000

PHILIPPINE
ISLANDS

MANILA

TG 38.2
(Bogan)

1200, 23 Oct

Mindoro

Sibuyan

San Bernardino Str

1026/1530
US air strikes. Battleship Musashi
sinks at 1935, cruiser Myoko
retires damaged

CALAMIAN
GROUP

1000
24 Oct

Sea
Masbate

Samar

0600, 25th

TG 38.4
(Davison)

1200, 23 Oct

Panay

0400,
25th

Leyte

US Seventh Fleet
(Kinkaid)

Force 'A'
(Kurita)

Negros

Cebu

0632, 23 Oct
US Submarines sink
cruisers Atago and Maya,
Takao retires damaged

1000
24 Oct

Bohol

Surigao Str

Palawan

0918
24 Oct

2000

2330

TG 38.1 (McCain)
to Ulithi

1000

Force 'C'
(Nishimura)

Mindanao

1200, 23 Oct

Sulu   Sea

First Striking
Force (Kurita)

BRITISH
NORTH BORNEO

Sails 22 Oct

BRUNEI

PUBLISHER'S NOTE

ADMIRAL CHESTER W. NIMITZ twice recommended Captain Joseph J. Rochefort for the Distinguished Service Medal because of Rochefort's singular contribution to the victory at Midway. The first recommendation was made in 1942; it received eleven endorsements within the Navy Department, but was rejected on Admiral King's recommendation. In 1958, Nimitz made a second plea in behalf of Rochefort. It, too, was rejected, this time on the basis that World War II awards had closed.

Meanwhile, Rochefort's wartime colleagues—including Layton—kept encouraging historians to set the record straight about the critical role that Rochefort and his team had played in turning the tide of war in the Pacific. Captain W. "Jaspar" Holmes published *Double Edged Secrets: U.S. Naval Intelligence Operations in the Pacific During World War II* in 1979 and while the book highlighted Rochefort's achievements, and some of the subsequent shabby treatment he received, it did not reach a wide audience. With the support of Holmes and others involved in the Pacific Fleet intelligence staff, Rear Admiral Donald "Mac" Showers then determined to make a final effort to fulfill Nimitz's recommendations of 1942 and 1958. While Layton was writing this book, Admiral Showers prepared a full dossier that included previously unknown documents the authors had just discovered in Rochefort's private files. By the fall of 1985, this persuasively documented recommendation had circulated within the Navy Department and gained endorsements of key department heads.

Only two months before the scheduled publication of *And I Was There,* Admiral Showers conceded that his effort "had come to naught." He was speaking to a standing-room-only audience at the Naval History Symposium that had come to hear a panel discussion on the battle of Midway based on Admiral Layton's forthcoming book. Showers commented sadly about the situation, because the recommendation that Rochefort should receive the DSM had been strengthened by the Director of Naval Intelligence. Showers also pointed out that it was further supported "by the director of Naval Security Group Command, with the help of the National Security Agency and many others."

The audience had already been aroused by Captain Pineau's account of Rochefort's performance at Midway as it was to be documented for the first time in Admiral Layton's book. Distinguished members of the audience rose to speak and demanded vigorously that the issue not be allowed to rest. The conviction of the audience, and their informed and impassioned support for Rochefort's cause, impressed a representative of the Secretary of the Navy's office who was present. He told the assembly in Annapolis that the background information that Admiral Showers had referred to had not been seen in the Secretary's office, but that he would make sure that the complete file was brought to the Secretary's attention, and that the case would be reexamined in the light of this new evidence.

Two weeks later, Secretary of the Navy John F. Lehman signed the authorization awarding to Rochefort the Distinguished Service Medal. Admiral Showers called Captain Holmes, who was critically ill in Hawaii, to report the news. Holmes brightened at the report, saying: "This is a promise fulfilled."

The Sunday New York Times of 17 November 1985 broke the news of the award on the front page, saying: "A spokesman for the Navy said the award to Captain Rochefort was based 'solely on the merits of the case.' But several Rochefort supporters said the award was being given because a new book, which gives details of Captain Rochefort's case and the machinations within the naval intelligence community, had already found its way into military circles."

The Baltimore *Sun* put it more bluntly, commenting: "Rarely has a book righted an old wrong even before it is published, but the memoirs of Adm. Edwin T. Layton have accomplished this remarkable feat. . . ."

Thus, the Distinguished Service Medal was presented to Rochefort's son and daughter at the White House on 30 May 1986 by President Ronald Reagan—on the eve of the forty-fourth anniversary of the Battle of Midway.

As for the new evidence about Pearl Harbor that Admiral Layton presented in this book: A public request to clear Admiral Husband E. Kimmel's name has been made by leading historians and members of the navy. This campaign—which was Admiral Layton's second goal in committing his story to print—continues. . . .

While Controversy Rages, Lessons to Be Learned

I. A CASE FOR REVISION

E DWIN THOMAS LAYTON was a naval intelligence officer who cared deeply about his craft and its application in defense of the United States. He saw a need to establish precisely what went wrong before the disaster of 7 December 1941, and to explain what happened in the following six months that enabled us to halt the Japanese at Midway and end any hope of their winning the Pacific war. He also believed that the nation needed a final explanation of the intelligence failures of 1941 to reduce the possibility of a nuclear Pearl Harbor in the 1980s and beyond.

When we first considered the possibility that Layton might agree, at the age of eighty, to undertake an account of his World War II experiences, we discussed the idea with Admiral Arleigh Burke. He said that he knew Layton to be a "one channel man, nicely stubborn, who realized the importance of a job to be done, and did not transfer that importance to himself." He added: "If Eddie Layton would publish his story, it could be one of the most important books to come out of the war in the Pacific."

A native of Nauvoo, Illinois, Layton was born in 1903 and after high school he entered the Naval Academy in 1920 and graduated and was commissioned an ensign in June 1924. After serving in battleship *West Virginia* and destroyer *Chase,* he went to Japan in June 1929 for three years of language study. In October 1932 he served in Peiping as assistant naval attaché at the American legation.

In February 1933 Lieutenant Layton returned to the United States for duty in the office of naval intelligence. He joined battleship *Pennsylvania* in June 1933 for a three-year stint as a main turret captain. He returned to ONI Washington in June 1936 and was shortly thereafter assigned as officer in charge of the Japanese translation section (OP-20-GZ) of the cryptanalytic section of naval communications.

Lieutenant Layton went to our embassy in Tokyo as assistant naval attaché in April 1937. Two years later, he was given command of de-stroyer-minesweeper *Boggs* based on the west coast and then Hawaii. On 7 December 1940 Lieutenant Commander Layton reported for duty as intelligence officer on the staff of commander in chief, U.S. Fleet (Cin-cus), Admiral James O. Richardson. Two months later he stayed on as intelligence officer to Admiral Husband E. Kimmel—a post in which Ad-miral Chester W. Nimitz retained him throughout the war.

Detached from Pacific Fleet duty in February 1946, Captain Layton next commanded the naval net depot at Tiburon, California, before re-turning to Washington in October 1948 and founding the naval intel-ligence school. He returned to Pearl Harbor, again as intelligence officer on the staff of the commandant Fourteenth Naval District, and also on the staff of commander naval forces Far East. In July 1953, Rear Admiral Layton was assigned to the office of the Joint Chiefs of Staff as assistant director for intelligence. He was assistant chief of staff to the commander in chief of the Pacific Fleet from September 1956 to April 1958. He then resumed duty as director of the naval intelligence school until his retire-ment on 1 November 1959. His decorations include the Distinguished Service Medal and the Navy Commendation Medal.

In 1959, Layton established Far East headquarters for the Northrop Corporation in Japan, and served as its director until 1963. He continued to write and lecture extensively on naval intelligence, World War II, and Japan.

Captain Roger Pineau was a Japanese linguist during World War II. As a junior officer he served with the code-breaking section of naval communi-cations at the Nebraska Avenue annex that is today the Washington, D.C., headquarters of the Naval Security Group Command. During the final year of the war he was an assistant to Captain Joseph J. Rochefort in Pacific Strategic Intelligence Studies. Immediately after the war, he had duty in Japan with the U.S. Strategic Bombing Survey interviewing Jap-anese leaders.

At that time Pineau made contacts that were to prove invaluable when he later became assistant to Admiral Samuel Eliot Morison, when the Harvard professor was preparing and writing much of his fifteen-vol-ume *History of United States Naval Operations in World War II*. During his ten years with Morison, Pineau had access both to the navy's opera-tional archives and to the captured records of Japan's naval headquarters.

The Japanese source material had never been properly studied by American historians, and except for the small fraction that Pineau did for Morison, was shipped back to Tokyo untranslated. This documentation forms the basis for the works of naval history in the hundred-volume

Senshi Sōsho—War History Series—published in the 1970s by the historical section of Japan's Self-defense Force. It has yet to be published in English.

Layton was initially helpful to Morison in his volumes III (*Rising Sun in the Pacific*) and IV (*Coral Sea, Midway, and Submarine Actions*). Throughout 1948, Pineau consulted frequently with Layton, who was director of the navy's intelligence school in Washington. Layton retained a vivid personal interest in, and memory of, his service as fleet intelligence officer to Admiral Kimmel and then Admiral Nimitz. Pineau found that Layton was especially intrigued by the new information that was revealed by the Japanese naval staff records. A warm personal friendship grew out of these meetings.

In 1949 Pineau made his second extended visit to Japan, this time to conduct interviews with Admiral Yamamoto's surviving naval commanders for Morison's volumes covering the battles of Coral Sea, Midway, and Guadalcanal. En route to Tokyo, he stopped off in Honolulu for research and consultation with officers including Layton, who was beginning yet another tour of duty as Pacific Fleet intelligence officer. The cooperation Pineau received at Pearl Harbor contrasted with the obstacles encountered when he reached Japan.

General MacArthur, the supreme commander for the Allies, had his intelligence chief, Major General Charles Willoughby, assembling material for a "definitive" history of the Pacific campaign. It was to be based not on the captured Japanese records, still in Washington, but on a series of monographs. These were generalized accounts prepared under U.S. Army direction.

Pineau had difficulty in getting Willoughby's historians to let him interview Japanese officers. Neither Pineau nor his mentor Morison agreed with what they termed MacArthur's "military approach to history." It was obviously aimed at emphasizing and enshrining the general's role as the American commander who had done the most to win the war in the Pacific.

The chief civilian historian attached to MacArthur's headquarters was Dr. Gordon W. Prange, who volunteered, "as one naval officer to another," that he would help Pineau all he could. But all interviews were to be conducted under his auspices. Prange, who neither spoke nor wrote Japanese, was following orders to restrict all questioning to the type of "intensive interrogations"[1] he conducted through army interpreters. These provided material for *The Reports of General MacArthur* and appear to form the basis for much of Prange's own writings on Pearl Harbor and Midway.

Pineau found this military historical procedure unsatisfactory. It blocked the easy flow of information, and he readily accepted the direct help of such Japanese as Captain Yasuji Watanabe (Yamamoto's friend and staff officer), headquarters planning officer Captain Toshikazu

Ohmae, and many others. They invited Pineau to their homes for relaxed interviews. Through them Pineau was able to meet informally with a range of Japanese: from kamikaze pilots to commanders in chief of the Combined Fleet, Soemu Toyada and Jisaburo Ozawa.

These sessions included Pineau's invitation to a select dinner party at the old navy club in Tokyo. Rear Admiral Sadatoshi Tomioka, who had been instrumental in the planning of the Pearl Harbor attack, was the host. On this occasion he questioned Pineau about Morison's judgment that "one can search military history in vain for an operation more fatal to the aggressor. On a tactical level, the Pearl Harbor attack was wrongly concentrated on ships rather than port installations and oil tanks. On a strategic level it was idiotic."[2] Tomioka said, "We thought we did a pretty good job."

Pineau thereupon asked Tomioka how long Yamamoto's staff had predicted it would take for the Pacific Fleet to recover and begin offensive operations after the Pearl Harbor raid.

"Twelve to eighteen months," Tomioka answered almost instantaneously.

"And how long was it before we did make an offensive move?"

There was a long pause as they sat cross-legged at the low dining table. Tomioka sucked in his breath, deep in thought. Simultaneously the others, captains and commanders, dutifully did the same, as though helping him to ponder the matter.

Tomioka eventually looked up and said, with a touch of astonishment, as though it were occurring to him for the first time: "The carrier strikes on the Gilberts and Marshalls at the beginning of February 1942."

Pineau then produced Morison's volume on the Pearl Harbor attack. The Japanese officers smiled when he pointed out the familiar photograph taken from one of their attacking planes over Ford Island. When he asked them to identify the small white circles in the corner of the picture, they all said confidently, "Fuel tanks."

"How many bombs had been dropped on them?" Pineau asked.

"None," said Tomioka. "Only your capital ships and airfields were assigned as targets."

Pineau then pointed out that since Japan wanted to immobilize our fleet, the surest way to have done this would have been to have bombed the fuel tanks. Every drop of fuel used by our warships at Pearl Harbor had to be brought from the west coast. If Japan had knocked out the oil farm, no ships could have moved until tankers arrived with more fuel. By stationing submarines east of Oahu the Japanese could have interdicted any attempt to resupply Pearl Harbor. Had Yamamoto's staff done this, then Tomioka's "twelve to eighteen months" would have been closer to reality.

The former staff officers sat in stunned silence. Pineau then diplomatically assured Tomioka that if he had promoted the bombing of the fuel tanks, he would have earned another star on his shoulder marks. The admiral said with a wry smile, "Pineau-san, you should have been in the Japanese navy."

Pineau's diplomatic skills and his oath of secrecy were to be tested later in his visit. Watanabe, with whom he by now had established a warm rapport, asked if it was because the U.S. Navy had intercepted the Japanese army's message about Yamamoto's itinerary that we had been able to shoot down his "chief." Pineau tactfully told him that Morison's historical research had not yet reached April 1943.

While Pineau was establishing his own contacts with the Japanese admirals, Willoughby's staff tried to prevent him from contacting the leaders held in Sugamo prison for war crimes. But thanks to a personal intervention of the prison commandant, Pineau managed to interview several of the key detainees, including Lord Keeper of the Privy Seal Koichi Kido and Mamoru Shigemitsu, the one-legged former foreign minister who had signed the formal surrender document on board battleship *Missouri.*

The following year Pineau returned to Japan with Morison. They conducted further interviews in Sugamo and also had a long session with MacArthur. During the course of this meeting, the general surprised them with his sincerity and conviction in assuring Morison that the strategy of bypassing Japanese strongholds and letting them wither on the vine had been his idea. MacArthur's claims certainly did not agree with the recent study Pineau had prepared. Wartime staff records showed how the general's representatives had argued for a frontal assault on Rabaul, and that it was Admiral Nimitz who had proposed bypassing the Japanese strongholds.

Morison and Pineau were also concerned to find that MacArthur was still unaware of the outcome of the March 1943 Battle of the Bismarck Sea. He assured Morison that the original claim that twenty or more destroyers and transports had been sunk by his bombers off the New Guinea coast was correct. Captured documents, however, translated soon after the action by Layton at Cincpac, had revealed that only eight destroyers and eight transports participated in the operation—and four destroyers survived. After seeing the evidence, Nimitz had sent a cautionary dispatch to MacArthur's headquarters about accepting air force claims at face value. The general had angrily fired back that such a remark impugned his integrity and should be resolved by court-martial if the official report was to be altered. Nimitz let the matter drop.

MacArthur, to assure Morison that there had been no mistake, summoned his intelligence chief for corroboration. Willoughby, as usual, agreed with the general, and promised Morison proof the following morning. When Pineau dropped into the history section that afternoon he found Prange in a conference with his staff. Willoughby had ordered them to substantiate MacArthur's point, but they were at a loss about how to do so. Pineau reminded Prange of the photostatic copies of the official Japanese record on the subject, which he had sent two months earlier. Prange then pulled the report from his office file, and he acknowledged that it was a sensitive point that he had not yet raised in preparing the manuscript of *MacArthur's War Against Japan.*

The challenge that this incident presented to the chief of MacArthur's history team evidently worried Prange. Shortly afterward Pineau was summoned to Willoughby's office. The general announced that Pineau's activities had "displeased many officers in the command" and he would have to leave Japan within forty-eight hours. When pressed, Willoughby conceded that Prange had complained to him that Pineau was "being a nuisance." By now it was clear to Pineau that MacArthur's historical team was anxious to limit "outsiders" in search of information in Japan. Thanks to Admiral C. Turner Joy, our commander of naval forces in Japan, Willoughby's whimsical order was nullified. Pineau stayed to complete his research. In 1952, Pineau returned to Japan to complete his work and discovered the conditions easier. MacArthur had returned to the United States, along with his historians Willoughby and Prange.

The Morison volumes were completed in 1962 and remain unchallenged for their narrative insight and accurate accounting of the naval war against Japan. But in one vitally important aspect they are lacking— *they include no mention of the key role played by radio intelligence.* The 1945 congressional investigation had produced sensational revelations about our ability to read Japan's secret diplomatic exchanges, but the extent to which we had penetrated the Japanese naval ciphers remained classified. Neither Pineau nor Layton—nor even Nimitz himself—was permitted to hint at the real source of the "various bits of information"[3] to which Morison attributed our success at Midway. Pineau eventually arranged officially for Morison to be let in on the secret—but he could never write about it.

Not until 1967 did the public begin to learn the extent to which code breaking contributed to the Battle of Midway in Walter Lord's stirring account *Incredible Victory,* and David Kahn's landmark study *The Codebreakers: The Story of Secret Writing.* The same year also saw the publication of *The Broken Seal: The Story of Operation Magic and the Pearl Harbor Disaster.* Written by Ladislas Farago, a former civilian employee of the office of naval intelligence, the book detailed some of the undocumented background that Roberta Wohlstetter had been unable to include in her scholarly study *Pearl Harbor: Warning and Decision.*

Published five years earlier, when it had been hailed as "the definitive book" on Pearl Harbor, Professor Wohlstetter's book was less concerned than other writers' with apportioning blame for the disaster. Relying principally on the evidence contained in the record of the 1945 congressional investigations, which Layton and McCollum helped her interpret, her scholarly account set out to show how "relevant signals, so clearly audible after the event, will be partially obscured before the event by surrounding noise. . . ."[4]

Prior to these works, the fifties had seen a spate of books by so-called revisionist historians. Their principal champions were Charles Callan Tansill in *Back Door to War: The Roosevelt Foreign Policy 1933–41* and by Rear Admiral Robert A. Theobald, *The Final Secret of Pearl Harbor: The Washington Contribution to the Japanese Attack*. As their titles suggest, these polemics sought to demonstrate that Roosevelt deliberately provoked Japan—then denied Pearl Harbor intelligence—so that the United States would have a *casus belli* for joining Britain's struggle against Hitler.

Wohlstetter's articulate reconstruction of the evidence then available revealed just how insubstantial was the foundation on which the revisionist edifice had been constructed. But reexamining Pearl Harbor, as Wohlstetter has acknowledged, had already become something of a preoccupation for historians. To date the Library of Congress computer lists over a hundred and two titles on the subject that have been published so far. The need to establish precisely what went wrong before 7 December 1941 clearly reflects the nervous uncertainty of an age that needs a final explanation to reassure the nation that the United States could not fall victim to a nuclear Pearl Harbor.

Layton had continued to keep up with the latest publications in the final years of his service career, during which he was a ranking intelligence officer to the Joint Chiefs of Staff. Pineau corresponded regularly with him, including the three years Layton spent in Japan as representative of the Northrop Corporation. It was during this time that Layton renewed his acquaintance with some of Yamamoto's staff officers with whom he had become acquainted as assistant naval attaché in Tokyo.

After his retirement in 1962 to the picturesque tranquillity of his home overlooking the restless Pacific at Carmel, Layton finally found the time to start assembling the full evidence about Pearl Harbor. He began to make meticulous handwritten translations of the *Senshi Sōsho* war histories in school exercise books. He also started the laborious task of reconstructing the Pacific Fleet's wartime radio intelligence communications from microfilmed message files he was able to study at the navy's language school in nearby Monterey.

Meanwhile, Pineau, encouraged by Layton, had begun his own retirement project: to compile a history of Japanese language officers in the U.S. Navy. The admiral's knowledge was so extensive that Pineau urged him to write his own story, but Layton always maintained that this would be impossible without the release of the wartime intelligence records. During the course of the sixties many historians such as Nimitz's biographer, Professor E. B. Potter, and Prange—then a professor at the University of Maryland—consulted Layton. But he was able to give them only general information, in keeping with the constraints imposed by the oath of secrecy he had taken as an intelligence officer. At the same time, Layton turned his hand to writing insightful articles and book reviews for *Proceedings,* the journal of the U.S. Naval Institute.

Layton was dismayed that his forays into print multiplied the number of inquiries he received soliciting information about Pearl Harbor, from naval cadets to distinguished historians from all over the world. If he had answered every one, it would have left him no time to pursue his other interests, which ranged from ship modeling and scrimshaw to bird and whale watching. But he would always find the time to encourage diligent young historians to take their research in fresh directions. One such was John B. Lundstrom, whose thesis *The First South Pacific Campaign* was the first published work on Midway and Coral Sea to make use of Cincpac's so-called Gray Book, the running estimate and summary kept at Nimitz's headquarters.

John Costello, a former BBC producer who had coauthored a best-selling book, *D Day,* first met Layton at the 1977 Naval History Symposium at the U.S. Naval Academy, Annapolis. Costello had just published *The Battle of the Atlantic,* and the admiral offered to help him on a comprehensive history of the Pacific war.

Three years later *The Pacific War* was in its final stages when a massive amount of hitherto classified naval records became available in the National Archives. President Jimmy Carter had effected the release of the World War II communications intelligence records, and it meant that all previous histories were to a degree rendered obsolete.

While Costello was completing his book, Layton was learning about the hundred thousand unindexed Japanese navy and diplomatic messages that were steadily building up in the National Archives. Costello could use only a small part of the documents to meet the publication schedule for *The Pacific War.* It was then that John Taylor of the National Archives introduced Costello to Pineau, who agreed to help with the interpretation of the new material.

Published simultaneously with *The Pacific War* in the fall of 1981 was Professor Gordon W. Prange's work *At Dawn We Slept.* The latter book drew heavily on the thirty years of interviewing effort that had commenced with Prange's "intensive interrogations" of the Japanese for MacArthur's history project. He illustrated with minute anecdotal detail Japan's massive expertise at planning the Pearl Harbor attack. But he devoted proportionally less effort to uncovering the underlying intelligence failure that ensured the success of the Japanese attack.

Although widely praised for its apparently exhaustive research, Prange's account did nothing to provide any new understanding of what had really gone wrong in Washington. *At Dawn We Slept* merely served to reinforce the politically loaded thirty-five-year-old report produced by the congressional investigating committee.

"One cannot fault the logic," Prange explained, of the majority report that had apportioned the major blame for the disaster on the Hawaiian commanders.[5] Kimmel and Short, according to Prange, were correctly charged with a "devastating list of failures." Principal among them was their failure "to discharge their responsibilities in the light of the warning received from Washington, other information possessed by them, and the principle of command by mutual cooperation."[6] Prange believed that Washington's miscalculations were insignificant compared to the failures of the Hawaiian commanders—although magnanimously agreeing that this constituted "errors of judgement and not dereliction of duty. . . ."[7] Prange therefore affirms that the "verdict of history" demands that we leave the inequitable judgments of 1946 undisturbed.

Layton, who had been one of Prange's interviewees, was particularly concerned by some of the erroneous charges made in *At Dawn We Slept*, but most especially with the renewed attack on his former commander in chief. Layton had always suspected that Kimmel had been given a "raw deal" by Washington, but it was not until after the war that he discovered just how Kimmel had been framed. Layton knew that the fundamental cause of the Pearl Harbor disaster was Washington's failure to properly evaluate and disseminate radio intelligence information. He was especially angered to read Prange's charge that when deciding in which sectors to send out long-range aerial patrols that Kimmel did not "seek the advice and professional judgment of . . . Layton, his Fleet intelligence officer."[8]

This was a distortion of the facts as they had been made available to Prange. But it was also evident to Layton that in spite of Prange's claims that "my scholarship and credibility are unimpeachable,"[9] that *At Dawn We Slept* took no account of new documentation from General Marshall's declassified files, which appeared to indicate that the Hawaiian commanders were made scapegoats not simply for Washington's intelligence failure, but also for the collapse of the entire American Pacific strategy.

The declassification of the most secret files of the U.S. Army chief of staff now reveals that the decision to switch the entire output of B-17 bomber production from England to the Philippines was a key factor in establishing an Anglo-American Far East deterrent force. We can now see that by November 1941 MacArthur was making preparations to threaten the Japanese with preemptive bombing raids. The Hawaiian commanders were not made aware of the extent to which our Pacific strategy had been dramatically revised in the fall of 1941. But MacArthur was—and he enthusiastically encouraged it. The need to get the bombers out to the Philippines explains why Washington so recklessly stripped Pearl Harbor's aerial defenses and long-range reconnaissance capabilities. The bomber strategy also explains why Washington was caught flat-footed on 7 December 1941. Not only was the attack being anticipated from the wrong direction, but the debacle that overtook the intended strategic bombing force in the Philippines the same day was a humiliating coup de grâce to Washington's ill-founded deterrent posture against Japan.

Worse, for reasons that have never been fully or properly examined or explained, MacArthur failed to respond to the Japanese threat facing him for nine hours after the attack on Pearl Harbor. And while Kimmel and Short were pilloried for a failure that was unfairly blamed on them, MacArthur was never called to account. The flamboyant general was not even hinted at as a target of blame when Washington had to produce scapegoats to cover its strategic and intelligence blunders to assuage an outraged American public.

Significantly, *At Dawn We Slept* makes no mention of the army chief of staff's reports that clearly demonstrate that MacArthur had received 250 maps of industrial targets in and around Tokyo in the final weeks before war broke out. Whether this was because Prange's researches were less exhaustive than he claimed or because he was unduly influenced by his five-year supervision of the MacArthur histories is a matter for speculation. But Prange's failure to take the intended role of the bomber force in the Philippines into account certainly contributes to his erroneous claims that "Kimmel's primary problem on December 2 continued to be the proposed moving of Marine Corps aircraft to outlying islands."[10] We now know that it was a direct request from General Marshall that resulted in Admiral Stark's 27 November order to Kimmel to use his two carriers to ferry fighter reinforcements to Wake and Midway. This was to cover the impending flight of forty-eight more B-17 bombers from the west coast to the Philippines.

Prange endorsed navy secretary Forrestal's 1945 charge that Kimmel's "most grievous failure was his failure to conduct long-range air reconnaissance in the more dangerous sectors from Oahu during the week preceding the attack."[11] He does not explain that Forrestal's endorsement was the result of a systematic effort by the administration to shift the blame for Pearl Harbor back onto the Hawaiian commands after the secret 1944 Navy Court of Inquiry had exonerated Kimmel of any failure. But then Prange errs in claiming that Kimmel failed "by rejecting long-distance aerial reconnaissance."[12]

Kimmel did *not* reject aerial reconnaissance. The record of the Pearl Harbor hearings shows that in the first week of December, as Layton has pointed out, extensive deep-ocean aerial reconnaissance *was* being conducted to the west and southwest of Oahu. This was the one sector—according to radio intelligence—from which the main danger threatened in the shape of a Japanese striking force sortie from the Marshalls.

Prange appears to have completely disregarded that the Pacific Fleet's war orders required an immediate advance to capture a forward base in the mandates. In spite of his misrepresentation that Kimmel did not take Layton's advice, his decision to concentrate available long-range reconnaissance west of Oahu was the result of his intelligence officer's detailed reports on the Japanese buildup in the Marshalls. Layton makes it clear that the "nearest snake" was a recurring subject of their daily briefing sessions.

By accepting Forrestal's politically motivated second-guessing of Kimmel, Prange condemned the admiral, showing none of the "special advantage" he professed to possess as a result of having been a naval officer. Had he done so, a few simple calculations with a protractor and chart would have shown him that Kimmel did all that he was told to do—and more. In the final week before the attack Kimmel even rotated some of his scarce long-range air capability to patrolling the northern approaches to Oahu. But since this was not possible on a daily basis, not even Forrestal—who *did* know the facts—went as far as to suggest that Kimmel should have sent patrols out to the north on Sunday.

In spite of what Prange and others have asserted, in the prewar American fleet exercises, strikes were launched from the *northwest* but not from due north, which leaves an awfully large expanse of ocean to be covered. But it stretches credulity to argue that Kimmel should have second-guessed both Washington's guidance and the Japanese threat from the Marshalls.

Another of Prange's conclusions is that Kimmel should have "taken the possibility of aerial torpedo strikes on his ships as seriously as the Japanese took the possibility of antitorpedo nets protecting the American vessels."[13]

Prange claims that if he had been Pacific Fleet commander, he would have spent 1941 "hounding the Navy Department" to provide the fleet with net defenses. But he neglects to inform us that this issue was thoroughly aired in the 1945 congressional hearings. The navy department, it emerged, had examined the question and had assured fleet headquarters that net defenses were unnecessary. Kimmel was reassured by the chief of naval operations that Pearl Harbor was too shallow for a successful Taranto-style raid. Until it was realized on 7 December that the Japanese had overcome this problem by boxing in the fins, it was assumed torpedoes dropped from aircraft would simply plunge harmlessly into the mud.

Another of Prange's confusions shows in his interpretation of the radio intelligence record. It is as faulty as his characterization of Kimmel as wandering "blindly as any dark-starred hero of Greek or Elizabethan drama."[14] Prange asserts that "blackout of the task force, the dummy message traffic, and American complacency effectively canceled out the possibility of locating Japan's First Air Fleet by this means."[15] But neither Layton, Rochefort, nor Kimmel was at all complacent about the lack of information they were receiving after the 1 December change in Japanese call signs. Nor, as the archival records now show, was there any concerted Japanese radio deception plan that led a "blindly" wandering Kimmel and his staff astray. It was the *absence of any radio messages* to

and from the First Air Fleet (the *Kido Butai*) that so successfully concealed their progress across the north Pacific toward Hawaii.

The facts are a matter of record. They negate Prange's allegations that
culminate with his assertion that Kimmel "lacked the perception to read
the meanings of the warnings and events of those last ten days before the
disaster." Ironically, as Layton has pointed out, this charge *would* have
been true *if* applied to the navy department rather than Kimmel.

"Mistakes at Washington level were many and varied, but it seems
most unlikely that any one of them in itself was a decisive factor."[16]
Prange's conclusion, as Layton has demonstrated, could not be more
wrong. How did the real explanation of the disaster evade one who asserts so confidently that he "burrowed more deeply into published and
unpublished materials on Pearl Harbor than anyone in the historical and
writing professions?"[17]

The simple answer is that Prange died before he had a chance to
examine the vast amount of newly declassified intelligence documentation. In that case the fault may lie with his collaborators, who prepared
the voluminous manuscripts for publication after his death. They declare
that in "a thorough search of more than thirty years, including all publications released up to May 1, 1981, we have not discovered one document or one word of testimony that substantiates the revisionist
position."[18]

Could they have repeated Prange's own mistake of confusing revisors
of history for revisionists? By doing so they evade the major flaw in his
researches. Neither he nor they take account of the vast new body of
documentary evidence that became available before the publication of *At
Dawn We Slept* and its sequel, *Miracle at Midway,* which relies so heavily
on the accounts of Fuchida, Lord, and Morison.

Significantly, while acknowledging his indebtedness to Captain Safford, Prange took little notice of his account. He wrote that Safford had
"something of a guilt complex about Kimmel and as a result became a
rabid revisionist, so I had to be cautious in evaluating his material."[19]
Like many historians who had studied Pearl Harbor, Prange felt obliged
to protect his "unimpeachable" scholarship from being tainted. In doing
so he failed to show the flexibility that conscientiously seeks to revise our
understanding of historical events as new facts become available. The
revisionist school of historians, championed by Harry Elmer Barnes, who
in his edition of *Perpetual War for Perpetual Peace* set out to "prove" that
Roosevelt goaded Japan into war and then denied Pearl Harbor access to
advance intelligence of the attack.

A more recent revisionist recruit, John Toland, charged that the navy
department in Washington actually plotted on a chart the course of the
Japanese carriers as they advanced toward Pearl Harbor. His "new" evidence was based on mysterious radio signals picked up northwest of
Hawaii that could have been made by a Russian freighter or Japanese

submarine. Toland supported his thesis by quoting an erroneous translation of an entry in the diary of the Dutch naval attaché in Washington. That material was withdrawn from subsequent editions of *Infamy* without explanation by the author.

Prange did not live to challenge the revisionist revival led by Toland. But by denying Safford's credibility and failing to research the collection of papers that the National Archives list as the "Navy Pearl Harbor Liaison Office" in record group 80, Prange missed important documentation that the former head of OP-20-G had been assembling from early 1943. These would have alerted him to the truth in Safford's charges of incompetence and conspiracy in the upper reaches of the navy department. Another important reason why Prange did not get to the real heart of the Pearl Harbor failure was that those who suspected, or knew, what had gone wrong in Washington—like Layton, Rochefort, and McCollum—did not feel free to talk.

Prange's reliance on the interviews and monographs he supervised while a member of MacArthur's headquarters historical section also suggests that an important caveat has to be applied when making a final evaluation of the conclusions reached in *At Dawn We Slept*. Prange himself admitted that he owed his "once in a lifetime opportunity" to his position on MacArthur's staff.[20]

New documentation has revealed the reason for the concentration of American strategic air power in the Philippines in the months before the Japanese attack. Given what we now know about his intention to make preemptive raids on Tokyo, MacArthur's failure to heed the clear warnings he received both before and after the attack on Pearl Harbor must raise questions about his own dereliction of duty. *At Dawn We Slept* devotes fewer than a dozen lines to what Prange terms the "undeniable irony which made a hero of one surprised and defeated commander and drove two others off active duty."

Yet MacArthur's culpability for the destruction of his air force and our military defeat in the Philippines is largely uncriticized by Prange. Compared to this strategic disaster, the damaging of the five battleships at Pearl Harbor had relatively little influence on the course of the war. The Japanese learned this when the Pacific Fleet was able to take the offensive almost immediately after Pearl Harbor and was able to win a major victory at Midway only six months later.

Prange's special pleading is evident in his unsupported assertion that "few Americans with the interests of their country at heart can regret that MacArthur remained on the job."[21] The convenient destruction of all but a few of MacArthur's headquarters files in the retreat to Bataan, and the carefully groomed accounts prepared by MacArthur's history section—eventually to be headed by Prange—have left us with a lopsided view of the American Caesar.

Layton certainly did not agree with Prange's adulation of Mac-

Arthur—nor would Admiral Nimitz, or any of the "Battling Bastards of Bataan" who composed the disparaging verses about "Dugout Doug." For years it has been known how MacArthur inflated his victories by means of self-laudatory communiqués, but only recently has a formerly secret wartime intelligence history revealed that MacArthur won battles because his advance knowledge of his enemy's intentions made him the "best informed general in history."[22]

As Layton shows, MacArthur's running feud with Nimitz brought the naval war against Japan to a dead stop in 1943. A year later, MacArthur employed political blackmail to pressure Roosevelt into overriding the navy department's strong recommendation that a Philippine invasion was unnecessary to secure the defeat of Japan. MacArthur's determination to vindicate his earlier defeat by fulfilling his pledge to return to Manila can now be seen to have been a costly diversion of naval and military resources that prolonged the war in the Pacific by as much as six months.

MacArthur never once—even after the war—raised his voice in defense of his fellow Pacific commanders Kimmel and Short, who were made the scapegoats for Pearl Harbor. This was presumably another one of those sensitive subjects like the glaring discrepancy over the results of the Battle of the Bismarck Sea. For any exoneration of Kimmel and Short would inevitably open the way to bring in a new verdict of history on MacArthur.

The willingness of the public to accept *At Dawn We Slept* as the definitive word on Pearl Harbor, followed by the sensational charges against the navy made by Toland in *Infamy*, persuaded Layton that there was an urgent need for a surviving insider to set the record straight before it was too late. But first he wanted to assure himself that the documentation he needed to prove his case was available. In the fall of 1982 Pineau, Costello, and Layton spent several days in the National Archives with John Taylor, examining the latest releases of wartime radio intelligence summaries and Japanese naval intercepts.

As a preliminary step, Layton decided to work up a paper on Admiral Halsey's early carrier raids for delivery to the 1983 Naval History Symposium. The Naval Academy had also invited Costello to give a paper on Pearl Harbor, so the admiral and he spent a March weekend comparing their documentation and research. It was then that the admiral decided to speak more frankly than he had ever done before. Layton's account of how an intelligence blunder by Washington similar to Pearl Harbor almost lost the Battle of Midway so impressed Costello that he contacted his publisher.

By coincidence, Costello's editor, Bruce Lee, had also been Prange's editor for *At Dawn We Slept*. Lee knew the strengths and weaknesses of the Prange book. Years earlier he recalled having been told by Admiral Thomas C. Kinkaid, a longtime friend of the family, that he should publish the full story of Pearl Harbor and that one day the documentation would be available to establish the true story. Accordingly, Lee went to the National Archives with Costello and wrote to Pineau to enlist his help in persuading Layton that the time was now ripe to write his book. "I am not interested in looking for scapegoats, nor in protecting the good name of various services," Lee declared. "I want a book that tells the facts within the limits of national security."[23]

So after Costello and Pineau had visited Layton at Carmel to assure him of their willingness to assist in the research and writing, the admiral finally agreed. Many hours of tape recordings resulted in an agreed outline; work began in the summer of 1983 to marry the information gathered by Layton in his collection of notebooks and in the translations he had made of Japanese publications. The object was to weave his personal narrative into the contemporary story of how radio intelligence was developed in the twenties and thirties, and how it was applied—and misapplied—during the Pacific war.

From the outset the project received the fullest cooperation from the history section of the National Security Agency thanks to the personal interest shown in the project by Rear Admiral Paul W. Dillingham. By September, when Layton and Costello presented their papers to the Naval History Symposium, the first chapters were already being drafted. Layton felt that the project was proceeding well enough to announce publicly that he was working on his memoir. The news was enthusiastically received and his surviving contemporaries volunteered their accounts, confident that the full story of Pearl Harbor and Midway was at last going to be told by someone from the inside who knew the truth.

The admiral prepared his longhand drafts, which were assembled and typed by Mrs. Layton. Between trips to Carmel, Pineau and Costello concentrated on excavating and assembling, at the admiral's direction, the new documentary material. This involved the preparation of a computer finding aide for the decrypts of more than a third of a million Japanese naval messages that are boxed in random order in the National Archives. Such was the progress made that by April 1984 when the admiral suffered his fatal stroke, the first draft of the manuscript up to the Battle of Midway was approaching completion.

Costello and Pineau were immediately invited by Mrs. Layton to come to Carmel to box up all the papers, notebooks, and memorabilia that the admiral had been working on the afternoon he was taken ill. They were shipped to Pineau's home in Bethesda and after a detailed review, the coauthors and their publisher were agreed that the project should be continued.

In the year that it has taken to complete and edit the manuscript, much new information has surfaced from declassified documentation and personal testimony. Where appropriate it has been incorporated to reinforce the narrative left by Layton. Bringing such a complex project to publication would not have been possible but for the support that Pineau and Costello have received from many of those who knew and worked alongside Layton during the war. In particular the late Captain Thomas Dyer, Captain Wesley A. "Ham" Wright, and Rear Admiral Donald M. Showers devoted generous amounts of time to answering many questions when it came to interpreting the details of Layton's voluminous notes. Captain Raymond P. Schmidt, U.S.N.R., formerly naval cryptologic historian and now serving on active duty, gave unstinting assistance with many details in the manuscript.

In completing the book, Pineau and Costello are confident that *And I Was There* tells Layton's story in the way that he began it. No reputations have been spared for the sake of modesty. The blame for Pearl Harbor and the credit for Midway are accordingly laid where he wanted them to be, wherever possible supported by new documentation and research. The same applies to the evidence of possible Soviet involvement in Pearl Harbor and the disastrous consequences of the code losses that the British have never officially admitted.

Layton's testimony and the declassified documents demonstrate the strength of his central assertion: that he and Kimmel were "short-changed" of intelligence information by Washington before the attack. It should now be indisputable that the information that might have averted the disaster *had been received* by the navy department by 6 December 1941. There is now convincing evidence that the bomb plot messages, or even the eleventh-hour "lights code" message, could have alerted Pearl Harbor to the threat.

Prange merely attributed "the gap between knowledge of possible danger and belief in its existence"[24] as the "root of the whole tragedy." But Layton's blow-by-blow account shows how the real cause of the tragedy was the internal feuding in the navy department that limited Washington's ability to evaluate and disseminate intelligence. Supported by documents never before made public, Layton reveals how this war within a war raged on through the first half of 1942 while the Pacific Fleet was locked in deadly struggle with the Japanese.

Layton breaks the forty-three-year-old silence on how Japan was really checked at Midway. He relates the never-before-told story of the fight that was waged between Pearl Harbor and Washington over Midway three weeks before the actual battle. The fight over who had made the right intelligence evaluation of Japanese objectives was every bit as fierce and vital as the battle itself was to prove. Layton reveals how Nimitz and he had to resort to subterfuge to get our carriers to Midway in time to fight, and how Pearl Harbor's code breakers were right and Washington was wrong about the date for the projected battle. For a week in May, the entire course of the war turned on the outcome of a struggle fought by cablegram and intercept within the navy department.

Layton tells how Washington then successfully covered up their second major intelligence blunder to take credit for the code breaks and intelligence evaluation that rightfully belonged to Commander Rochefort. A report that has until now remained locked in a navy safe details the shocking story of how a few ambitious officers in the navy department put their careers before their country to wage a vendetta against Rochefort. Their campaign succeeded, and in the fall of 1942, the fleet was denied the services of its most brilliant radio intelligence officer. One of its unintended results was the Japanese code change that brought a four-month blackout of our intelligence during the close-run Guadalcanal campaign.

Writing from his unique position, Layton reviews the major contributions that radio intelligence made to winning the war in the Pacific. He discusses the shootdown of his old bridge partner Admiral Yamamoto, "The Great Marianas Turkey" shoot during the Battle of the Philippine Sea, and the staggering success of our submarine war against Japan. Nimitz's ability to outmaneuver both Washington and MacArthur so that he could effectively deploy his forces made him one of the war's most effective commanders. Layton's account shows that while MacArthur was more adept at public relations, it was Nimitz's effective application of radio intelligence that made him the understated and unsung hero of the Pacific war.

Of this account we can be certain only that it will not be the last word. But while new information may surface to adjust the perspective, it is unlikely that there will be any dramatic alteration in the scene. Layton did not subscribe to Samuel Taylor Coleridge's view of history—that "the light which experience gives is a lantern at the stern which shines only on the ways behind." Layton's hope was that by shattering old myths, illumination might also be cast on the way ahead with its lurking peril of a nuclear Pearl Harbor.

—ROGER PINEAU
—JOHN COSTELLO

Bethesda, Maryland
July 1985

II. THE FLAWS IN THE OFFICIAL INVESTIGATIONS

1. The Roberts Commission

18 December 1941–23 January 1942

*Convened:*By presidential executive order to establish the facts relating to the Japanese attack on Pearl Harbor. The prime object was to determine whether any dereliction of duty or errors of judgment had contributed to the enemy success.

Members: Associate Justice Owen J. Roberts, U.S. Supreme Court, chairman; Admiral William H. Standley, U.S.N. (Ret.); Rear Admiral Joseph M. Reeves, U.S.N. (Ret.); Major General Frank R. Mc-Coy, U.S. Army (Ret.); Brigadier General Joseph T. McNarney, U.S. Army.

Proceedings: The first critical days of Washington testimony were unsworn and unrecorded. Magic was discussed, but who received it and what it contained were not detailed. No actual intercepts were introduced into evidence, but the impression was given by the senior officers of the war and navy departments that the Hawaiian commands *were* receiving *all* the intelligence available to Washington.

Findings: The secretaries of state, war, and navy as well as General Marshall and Admiral Stark had discharged their duties. Admiral Kimmel and General Short were severely censured for their failures to take appropriate action in light of the warnings they had received.

2. The Hart Inquiry

15 February 1944–June 15 1944

Convened: By order of the navy department to take evidence pertinent to the Pearl Harbor attack so that important testimony should not be lost by hazard of war.

Composition: A one-member inquiry conducted by Admiral Thomas C. Hart, U.S.N. (Ret.).

Proceedings: Collected statements of parties concerned. It did not consider Magic but Hart, who had been Asiatic Fleet commander at the outbreak of war, was fully aware of the extent of radio intelligence about Japanese naval and diplomatic activity.

Findings: Hart was not required to make specific recommendations since the purpose of this inquiry was ostensibly to forestall the statute of limitations that would prevent the trial by court-martial of officers considered to be guilty of serious derelictions of duty.

3. The Army Pearl Harbor Board

20 July 1944–20 October 1944

Convened: By the adjutant general in response to the Act of Congress 13 July 1944, which directed the secretaries of navy and war to investigate the Pearl Harbor catastrophe. Directed to ascertain and report the facts and make such recommendations as deemed proper.

Composition: Lieutenant General George Grunert, U.S. Army, president; Major General Henry D. Russell, U.S. Army; Major General Walter H. Frank, U.S. Army; Colonel Charles W. West, U.S. Army, recorder (without vote); Colonel Harry A. Toulmin, U.S. Army, executive officer (without vote); Major General Henry C. Clausen, U.S. Army, recorder (without vote).

Proceedings: The board heard evidence in Washington, San Francisco, and Hawaii from 151 witnesses. The voting members of the board were advised of the existence of the radio intelligence intercepts, but considered evidence of Magic only in the final week of testimony.

Findings: The report was published, without reference to Magic. It therefore appeared unduly critical of General Short, but General Marshall and the war department were also censured for the first time.

Marshall failed in his duty: (1) to keep Short fully advised of the worsening situation with Japan; (2) to reply to Short's "sabotage alert" report; (3) by not forwarding to Short on the evening of 6 December and the morning of 7 December the critical information; (4) by not determining the state of readiness of the Hawaiian command.

General Gerow, chief of war plans division, failed in his duty: (1) by not keeping the Hawaiian command informed with the substance of Magic; (2) by not making the 27 November warning a clear, concise directive and for approving the confusing dispatch that was sent; (3) by not taking steps to see that the joint plans agreed between the army and navy were properly effected.

General Short was held to have failed in his duties: (1) by not placing his command in a higher state of alert; (2) by not implementing the Joint Army-Navy Coastal Frontier Defense Plan; (3) by not informing himself of the partial effectiveness of the navy's aerial reconnaissance; (4) by not replacing inefficient staff officers.

4. The Naval Court of Inquiry

24 July 1944–19 October 1944

Convened: By the secretary of the navy in response to the same congressional act as the army board, and its hearings ran parallel to the other inquiry.

Composition: Admiral Orin G. Murfin, U.S.N. (Ret.), president; Admiral Edward C. Kalbfus, U.S.N. (Ret.); Vice Admiral Adolphus Andrews, U.S.N. (Ret.).

Proceedings: The naval court was the first inquiry to take full consideration and testimony on the role of radio intelligence and decryption.

All testimony on Magic was suppressed in its public report. Evidence was heard in Washington and at Pearl Harbor, but no account was taken—as the army board did—of the failures in the navy department to effect the Joint Army-Navy Coastal Frontier Defense Plans for all Pacific commands or send a precise, specific war warning to Pearl Harbor.

Findings: The report of the navy inquiry was a complete exoneration for Admiral Kimmel. It found that he had conferred adequately with Short and each "was informed of the measures being undertaken by the other in defense of the Base to a degree sufficient for all useful purposes."[25] Kimmel's plan of defense was held to be "sound" but it depended on "advance knowledge that an attack was to be expected." Kimmel was held to have conducted the proper long-range aerial reconnaissance appropriate to the intelligence he received and the planes available.

Admiral Stark, however, was severely criticized for the first time. He was censured for sending a war warning that "standing alone could not convey to the commanders in the field the picture as it was seen in Washington."[26] He was criticized for failing to relay to Kimmel information that had come into his possession, "especially on the morning of 7 December." No further proceedings, however, were recommended against any officer because the court concluded that the attack, "delivered under the circumstances then existing, was unpreventable. When it would take place was unpredictable."[27]

The secretaries of war and navy—and their departments—were understandably unhappy with the opinions of the Army Pearl Harbor Board and the Naval Court of Inquiry, which shifted the responsibility back to Washington. Stimson and Forrestal decided on the ploy of keeping the findings secret until additional investigations could be made to redirect the burden of failure back onto the Hawaiian commanders.

5. The Clausen Investigation

23 November 1944–12 September 1945

Convened: By the personal direction of the secretary of war to supplement the investigation of the Army Pearl Harbor Board.

Composition: A one-man inquiry by Major Henry C. Clausen, the assistant recorder of the Army Pearl Harbor Board.

Proceedings: This was a secret inquiry that relied on affidavits rather than direct testimony.

Findings: No public report, but Clausen later testified before the congressional investigating committee.

6. The Hewitt Inquiry

14 May 1945–11 July 1945

Convened: By the secretary of the navy to continue the investigation of the Navy Court of Inquiry.

Composition: Admiral K. Kent Hewitt, U.S.N., with John F. Sonnet, special assistant to the secretary of the navy as counsel.

Proceedings: Magic and radio intelligence were discussed in detail. Witnesses testified and were cross-examined in secret proceedings by Sonnet, whose conduct of the inquiry, especially in off-the-record questioning, was later to be criticized. Admiral Kimmel was denied the right of an interested party to be present and conduct his own cross-examination of witnesses.

Findings: No separate report was published. But as a result of Hewitt's findings and the Naval Court of Inquiry, the secretary of the navy, James P. Forrestal, issued an announcement on 29 August 1945 that "the Admiral Husband E. Kimmel and Admiral Harold R. Stark, particularly during the period 27 November to 7 December, 1941, failed to demonstrate the superior judgment necessary to exercising command commensurate with their rank and assigned duties."[28]

7. The Clarke Investigation

14–16 September 1944, and 13 July 1945–4 August 1945

Convened: Ordered by the war department to investigate the handling of top secret communications by the military intelligence division before the Pearl Harbor attack.

Composition: Conducted by Colonel Carter W. Clarke, then chief of the military intelligence division.

Proceedings: The top secret investigation was reconvened to investigate testimony given to the Hewitt inquiry by Safford and others to the effect that war department signal archives relating to the Winds code messages had to be destroyed on the orders of General Marshall.

Findings: No evidence was adduced to support the destruction of radio intelligence documents.

8. The Joint Congressional Committee

15 November 1945–31 May 1946

Convened: By a concurrent resolution of Congress to make a full investigation of the events and circumstances connected with the Japanese attack on Pearl Harbor and to report the results to Congress with such recommendations as deemed advisable.

Composition: Six Democrats and four Republicans: Senator Alben W. Barkley, (D) Kentucky, chairman; Representative Jere Cooper, (R) Tennessee; Senator Walter F. George, (D) Georgia; Senator Scott W. Lucas, (D) Illinois; Senator Owen Brewster, (R) Maine; Senator Homer Ferguson, (R) Michigan; Representative J. Bayard Clark, (D) North Carolina; Representative John W. Murphy, (D) Pennsylvania; Representative Bertrand W. Gearhart, (R) California; Representative Frank B. Keefe, (R) Wisconsin. The legal staff consisted of a general counsel and three assistants.

Proceedings: Witnesses were called and cross-examined, but the politics of the day inevitably intruded and the democratic majority effectively managed the course of the proceedings to divert criticism from the Roosevelt administration. The principal surviving participants were called and examined, except for the ailing Stimson. Magic was discussed exhaustively to the concern of the military intelligence officers. But any mention of the extent of the penetration of the Japanese naval code systems was severely restricted.

The evidence of the seven previous Pearl Harbor inquiries was not introduced until three months into the hearings. The findings of the earlier investigations also remained secret until the entire forty-volume congressional report with its eleven volumes of evidence, ten volumes of exhibits, seventeen volumes of hearings, and one-volume report was published.

Findings: A summary of the six-member majority concludes that:

(1) Japan's attack was unprovoked.
(2) the attack had been skillfully planned.
(3) American policies had provided no provocation for the attack.
(4) there was no evidence that Roosevelt's cabinet had provoked the attack to facilitate a declaration of war from Congress.
(5) the president had made every effort to avoid war with Japan.
(6) the disaster was due to the Hawaiian commanders' failure to effect adequate measures to detect the attack and to go to a state of readiness commensurate with the imminence of war.
(7) the Japanese attack was a total surprise although the possibility

of an air raid and the imminence of war was appreciated as a possibility at Pearl Harbor and Washington.

(8) the Hawaiian commanders failed to make disposition commensurate with the warnings and intelligence received, but the errors made by the Hawaiian commanders were of judgment, not derelictions of duty.

(10) the war department failed in its duty to warn Short that a sabotage was an inadequate state of alert.

(11) army and navy intelligence had failed to evaluate the significance of the bomb plot and 1 P.M. deadline messages and communicate them to the Pacific commands.

(12) during the final forty-eight hours before the attack, the war and navy departments were not sufficiently on alert to the imminence of war.

The two-member minority report also censured Roosevelt for not taking "quick and instant executive action on Saturday night, December 6th and Sunday morning."[29] Apart from the president they concluded that Secretary Stimson, Secretary Knox, General Marshall, Admiral Stark, General Gerow, as well as the two Hawaiian commanders, had failed to discharge their responsibilities.

III. THE EAST WINDS RAIN ENIGMA

Was a genuine winds alert message ever received? If so, when was it picked up? These questions became a *cause célèbre* of the 1945 congressional hearings when conflicting testimony denied admissions made in the secret wartime investigations. A furiously partisan public debate erupted that has smoldered ever since. Safford charged that a winds alert did come in, that it was later removed from the records, and that officers who had earlier claimed to have seen and handled it were pressured into changing their accounts.

The controversy refused to go away, because the postwar interrogations of Japanese officials failed to produce clear-cut answers on whether Tokyo had or had not transmitted a winds alert broadcast in the prescribed form. Many historians, such as Wohlstetter and Prange, have sidestepped the issue by pointing out that Japan's 2 December codes-destruct messages—which Kimmel had received—were a more accurate indication of Japan's intention of going to war.

The fact is, however, that Washington believed that the east winds rain message would be the ultimate signal that war would break out. They were the ones who considered it even more important after 2 December, when it was assumed that an "east winds rain" phrase in Tokyo radio's daily weather broadcast would be the final war warning. Safford's

1944 testimony, supported by Kramer and Sadtler until they modified their recollections in 1945, suggests that some message that was taken to be that warning was received toward the end of the first week of December. Safford claimed that when he tried to locate the "east winds rain" alert in the fall of 1943, it was missing from the OP-20-G files. Up till then he had been unable to understand why the Pacific Fleet commander had ignored the warning. When Safford discovered that none had been sent to Pearl Harbor as a result of this message, he began his campaign to "expose the people who had framed Admiral Kimmel and General Short."[30]

The navy department went to great lengths to contradict Safford's charges. Witnesses and affidavits were produced to deny that a "*Higashi No Kaze Ame*" ("East Winds Rain") message had ever been picked up. But the newly declassified records do show that Safford was correct in claiming that there is a suspiciously blank page in the OP-20-G Japanese diplomatic message file. Whether or not it contained a now-missing "east winds rain" intercept, the records show that a colossal amount of navy department bureaucratic effort was exerted in 1945 to proving that no such message had ever existed. The "no message, no case" argument certainly succeeded in drawing a very large red herring across the congressional hearings—to confuse the real issue of Washington's failure to pass on to the Hawaiian commanders other more important and specific intelligence such as the "bomb plot" and "lights" intercepts.

Certainly if an "east winds rain" message had been produced at the congressional hearing, it would have provided irrefutable indication of Washington's failure to communicate such a warning to Pearl Harbor. But as Safford discovered to his cost and credibility, trying to prove his case without that vital message challenged the institution and integrity of the navy department. It brought a collective closing of ranks in the navy that lasted for over forty years.

Safford's testimony rested largely on the blank page in the run of serial numbers in the running record by Kramer's translation section. As each decrypt of an intercepted Japanese diplomatic message was typed up, it was assigned a serial number—and after it had been circulated to naval intelligence, it was returned to be refiled.[31] The one that Safford claims was originally "east winds rain" is now a blank page with the notation "7001-Cancelled."[32] Safford repeatedly affirmed under cross-examination that the number had originally been assigned to a true winds-execute message that had been intercepted by Station M in Maryland, which had been relayed from the Cheltenham teleprinter to OP-20-G on the morning of either 4 or 5 December 1941.

Although Safford's case was not helped by his confusion over the date, his recollection of the intercept's appearance was impressively precise. He described it as "a teletype copy (typed on yellow paper) of the entire Japanese broadcast about 200 or 300 words long. Three significant words (*Kita, Higashi,* and *Nishi*) appeared and they were in Japanese. Kramer's translation appeared in pencil, or colored crayon, at the bottom of the sheet. There was very little chance of confusion."[33]

In a November 1943 letter to Safford from Kramer—which predates the first official inquiry—Kramer admitted that he had only "a hazy recollection of being called down to the office" because of the "arrangements to handle it expeditiously." But at the 1944 Navy Court of Inquiry Kramer unhesitatingly answered yes when asked whether he had seen Safford's teleprinter sheet with the winds message containing the Japanese code words indicating relations with the United States were in danger.

"'*Higashi no kaze ame*,' I am quite certain," Kramer testified: "The literal meaning of '*Higashi no kaze ame*' is 'East wind, rain.' That is plain Japanese language. The sense of that, however, meant strained relations or a break in relations, possibly even implying war with a nation to the eastward, the United States." But by April 1945, however, Kramer "was less positive" in his testimony before Admiral Hewitt's inquiry. Now he was "under the impression that the message referred to England and possibly the Dutch rather than the United States." By February 1945 when he came before the congressional hearings, Kramer's recollection was that there had been "a false alarm on the winds system," which he thought at the time was authentic and which referred to only one country: "To the best of my recollection, it was England."[34]

Kramer's contradictory evidence was the result of "being instructed on orders from above to deny delivering the message," according to Mrs. Eunice Willson Rice, longtime OP-20-G staff member who used to type up and file the Japanese diplomatic messages. She has recently confirmed that no copies were ever made, but the originals were kept in a sequentially numbered file.[35]

Although Mrs. Rice was away visiting her sister in Maine the week before the Pearl Harbor attack, she recalled that after her return she noticed that one message appeared to be missing from the numerical sequence. She asked Kramer about it. He said that it was one indicating that war was imminent and that he himself had turned it over to the duty officer in the chief of naval operations office and called attention to its importance. When it had not come back after the Japanese attack after the usual period of time, Kramer had asked about it, only to receive a noncommittal answer.[36]

Mrs. Rice was not the only one to claim she believed that considerable pressure was put on Kramer to change his testimony before the congressional investigating committee in 1945. His Arlington neighbor and friend at the time, Lieutenant Commander (now rear admiral retired) Robert H. Weeks, recalls Kramer's telling him that he had been directed to "speak right or undergo more mental treatment."[37]

This was a reference to the fact that Kramer had been in the neuropsychiatric ward of Bethesda Naval Hospital in November, two months before he was called to testify. The story made newspaper headlines after Representative Keefe, a member of the congressional investigating committee, had charged that Kramer was being held there "under orders" and that his uniform had been taken away. When he testified, Kramer denied that he had been "beset and beleaguered" or badgered in any way.[38]

Kramer did, however, make a substantial change in his story. Safford was in no doubt that it was a result of the strong pressure Kramer was under to support the navy department contention that no winds message had been received. According to his friend Weeks, Kramer was a man of character whose arm was twisted. On the eve of his appearance in the Capitol Hill committee room, Weeks recalled, "He said he would have to lay it on the line next day."[39]

One witness, who also claimed to have seen a winds alert, was apparently not allowed to give testimony in 1945. Ralph T. Briggs believed that he was deliberately prevented from appearing before the congressional hearings to corroborate Safford's story. In 1977 this former On-the-Roof Gang radioman asserted that he was the one who intercepted the actual message when he was on duty at the navy's Cheltenham Station M in Maryland in December 1941.

Briggs, experienced in taking kana Morse, went on to become a chief warrant officer with the staff of naval intelligence command. In 1960, Briggs made a thorough search of the wartime microfilm records. But like Safford and the 1945 team of navy investigators, Briggs found that all the Cheltenham station signal sheets for the first week in December 1941 were missing. Unable to locate the original "*Higashi no kaze ame*" intercept, he settled for writing on one of the original duty personnel log sheets that "all transmissions intercepted by me between 0500 thru 1300 on the above date are missing from these files and that these intercepts contained the 'Winds message warning code.'"[40]

Sixteen years later Briggs recounted his story to the Naval Security Group. Historian Raymond Schmidt, who took his deposition, recorded Briggs's statement that the winds alert, which Briggs claimed to have taken down on 4 December 1941, could not be picked up by any other overseas listening post because of atmospheric conditions. Briggs also told how Safford had contacted him in 1945 during the congressional hearings but that his commanding officer had ordered him not to give any testimony. Briggs regarded this as "a definite effort to cover up the truth of the matter" and put to rest what had happened to the missing winds execute message.[41]

A puzzling inconsistency, however, must be noted in Briggs's testimony. Apart from the length of time that elapsed before he decided to give his version of the story to posterity, Briggs claimed to have picked up the winds message on 4 December. But the duty log that bears his 1960 inscription is for 2 December.

If it was the intercept that Briggs made that set alarm bells ringing in OP-20-G, apart from the fact that there is no east winds rain message on the intercept file, his account further confuses the issue of when it was supposed to have been received. Much was made of this confusion to cast doubt on Safford's testimony and to suggest that he was confused by a number of false alarms.

According to Kramer, the watch officers were inundated by "reams, yards of teletype paper covering the plain-language broadcasts of the Japanese."[42] Every message from the navy's listening posts had to be translated and checked. More winds alerts arrived from the Federal Communications Commission whose monitoring stations had also been instructed to listen in to Tokyo radio weather reports. False alarms were raised, such as one on the afternoon of 4 December, by a weather report that stated:

> Tokyo today north wind, slightly stronger; may become cloudy tonight; tomorrow slightly cloudy and fine weather. Kanagawa prefecture today north wind cloudy from afternoon more clouds.
>
> Chiba prefecture today *north wind clear* may become slightly cloudy ocean surface calm.[43]

This particular message appeared so similar to one on the prompt cards that the Thursday cryptanalyst GY watch officer checked it with a translator before telephoning the director of naval communications the winds message was in.[44] By the time it had been realized that it was an innocent weather forecast, news of the alert had spread throughout the navy department. Turner, however, recalled how he had been able to discount the "north wind clear" phrase as "obviously not matching" the prearranged Japanese code words.[45]

Turner made a great point, during the congressional hearings, of dismissing this and other false winds alerts. Yet it's difficult to believe that Safford, with his long experience in radio intelligence, would have put his career on the line for a *deus ex machina* that was as obviously incorrect as the one Turner cited. But testimony volunteered in 1980 by another GY watch officer, George W. Linn, confirms that "this episode established that an execute had not been received prior to late on December 4."[46] Linn's 1983 deposition to the Navy Security Group historian asserts he did not see any genuine winds message. But it could have arrived when he was not on duty, the following morning—which is precisely when Sadtler, in his persuasive testimony to the 1944 army board of inquiry, claims that it did come in.[47]

Further corroboration that the Japanese transmitted a winds code message was provided by Brigadier General R. Thorpe, who in 1941 was lend-lease commissioner and military observer with the Dutch command on Java. Thorpe, who did not testify at any of the Pearl Harbor investigations, later claimed that the commander of the Dutch army in the East Indies—

General Hein ter Poorten—showed him a winds execute message. It was contained in a decrypt of "an intercepted and decoded dispatch from the Foreign Office in Tokyo addressed to the Japanese ambassador in Bangkok."[48] Thorpe took it to the American consul general in Batavia, who forwarded it to Washington—but with a comment to the effect that it was not to be taken seriously.[49] Not content with Dr. Walter Foote's assessment, Thorpe—whose own code books were a hundred miles away in his Bandoeng office— took his message to the senior naval attaché, Commander Paul S. Slawson, who sent it off in navy cipher.

When this message was produced for the 1945 congressional inquiry it contained only details of the winds code setup, but *not* the text of the actual Tokyo radio "east winds rain" execute phrase.[50] According to the written recollection of General ter Poorten, he had called in the American and British liaison officers and he also had sent a teletype of the winds message to the Dutch embassy in Washington.[51]

The Dutch consulate in Honolulu also received a copy of this same message warning of "an imminent attack somewhere in the Pacific." Ter Poorten notes, "I did not specifically mention Pearl Harbor."[52] He also reports that when the winds execute was hand-delivered by the Dutch military attaché in Washington to the war department, the only response from General Marshall was to ask for the source of the information.[53]

The Dutch intelligence records were all destroyed before their evacuation of Bandoeng. So Ter Poorten's written postwar confirmation of Thorpe's account—while convincing—still does not prove that an "east winds rain" alert was transmitted by Tokyo. But Thorpe also claimed that while stationed in Japan after the war he eventually located a Japanese who had actually transmitted the message. Thorpe's account is supported with information that has recently surfaced in the Royal Netherlands archives. Dutch army headquarters in Bandoeng, Java, maintained throughout 1941 a small but highly successful cryptanalytic unit that had succeeded in breaking into the Japanese diplomatic codes independently of the American or British efforts. Although they had not penetrated Purple, they were reading the messages in the Red machine cipher and also the J-19 consular traffic.

According to Captain J. W. Henning, then chief cryptanalyst of the so-called *Kamer 14* at Bandoeng, they were "doing business on a mutual basis" with their potential allies and "all Japanese coded telegrams, which were decoded by us, were subsequently passed to the British, Americans and Australians." Henning confirmed that Bandoeng headquarters had indeed been aware of the winds code setup and that an execute broadcast was intercepted. "From a deciphered teletype of the beginning of December 1941, we concluded that a Japanese attack was to be expected at short notice."[54]

In spite of what Toland has claimed in *Infamy* about Washington receiving a *specific* warning from the Dutch about Pearl Harbor, it is pertinent to note that Henning's evidence denies this completely. "When and where the first Japanese attack would explode could not be concluded from the telegram."[55]

Yet another piece of the "east winds rain" jigsaw puzzle was provided in the spring of 1985 by Lieutenant Commander Cedric Brown, a British naval officer who in 1941 was in charge of ciphers at R.N. headquarters in Hong Kong. After his capture by the Japanese, he encountered in a prisoner of war camp a New Zealand naval officer, Lieutenant H. C. Dixon. He had served at the Hong Kong naval base signal's intelligence intercept unit on Stonecutter's Island, known by its secret designation "Q." Dixon told Brown that he could not understand how the Americans had been caught so unprepared for the Japanese attack because, several weeks before war broke out, the Royal Navy cryptanalysts at "Q" had intercepted and decoded the preliminary winds alert setup and that they had subsequently picked up the Tokyo weather broadcast "a few days before the attack on Pearl Harbor."[56]

The new evidence must add to the presumption that the Japanese did send out the winds alert and that it was picked up by the British as well as the Dutch. Since such intelligence was being freely exchanged, it would indicate that Washington did receive the warning from two other sources besides the intercept that Safford claimed arrived through OP-20-G.

This may be another reason why the British are so reluctant to release any of their Japanese intercepts. Until an east winds rain message turns up, however, there can be no final proof that Safford and Sadtler were correct in asserting that one was received and that it was later removed by ranking officers in the Washington cover-up. The new evidence must tip the scale of probability to indicate that some alert was received on the morning of 5 December. The suspicious blank page in the Japanese diplomatic signal log, the large volume of paperwork generated to deny Safford's charge, and the pressure brought to bear on Kramer and others to amend their testimony are also factors that point toward this conclusion.

IV. THE COMINT FEUD

The peremptory ousting of Joe Rochefort in October 1942 from his position as officer in charge of Hypo caused strong feelings in the comint community. A harbinger of that action can now be seen in the lateral displacement of Laurence F. Safford, which took place the preceding February. Safford was shunted aside as head of OP-20-G to take charge of the less important OP-20-Q cryptography office. The other half of his former duties—cryptanalysis—was turned over to Commander John R. Redman, as OP-20-G, with Commander Joseph N. Wenger as his deputy.

Captain Joseph R. Redman, John's older brother, was then assistant director of naval communications and therefore largely instrumental in effecting these arrangements. Commander Wenger, who had been serving in Negat at the outbreak of war, was "directed by Captain Redman to make an investigation of OP-20-G and submit recommendations for any corrective measures considered advisable."[57] He spent "about a month" preparing his critique and "naturally consulted Safford with a view towards ascertaining if he had any special problems that needed attention or ideas that he had not been able to implement."[58]

According to Wenger, he "offered me no suggestions" but Safford, as we have seen, on 23 January 1943, submitted his memorandum urging that the status quo be maintained. Three days later Wenger put in his recommendations for a radical reorganization that separated the day-to-day operational effort from the administrative and code-security functions of OP-20-G. It appears that these were immediately approved, over Safford's head, by Admiral King as part of his administrative shake-up of the office of naval operations. By mid-February, John Redman, who was "regarded as a forceful administrator," had assumed full control of OP-20-G and Wenger was given authority to "reorganize it according to my proposals."[59] His task was facilitated because shortly afterward the elder Redman replaced Admiral Leigh Noyes as head of the office of naval communications.

Safford had been promoting a decentralized radio intelligence operation, based on a vertical division by tasks, with Negat assigned to a particular enemy cipher system, while Hypo specialized on another, and Cast on a third. By contrast, the so-called Redman-Wenger plan envisaged that Negat would manage the entire radio intercept and analysis operation centrally. A greatly expanded cyrptanalytic operation in Washington was intended to perform the basic solution and recovery in the whole range of enemy ciphers. This called for a horizontal division of functions by which Hypo would be directed in the exploitation of Negat's results to some of its own recoveries to provide the fleet with basic combat intelligence.

Views vary among the World War II veterans of the communications and intelligence service as to the proprieties of this reorganization. But there is general agreement that Safford would probably not have been the most effective of managers under wartime pressures. The organization that he founded in 1924, and directed for seventeen years except for two tours of sea duty, had grown up in response to a hit-or-miss, crisis-reaction style of operation that was a product of prewar budgetary constraints and the lack of understanding of the importance of the intelligence function by gunnery club admirals. In the wake of Pearl Harbor trauma Safford faced criticism for the intelligence failure and charges that his unmethodical ways might lead to future disasters.

With the advantage of 20/20 hindsight it can be argued that if the Redman-Wenger concept had been operative throughout 1941, the Pacific

Fleet might have received proper intelligence that would have warned of Japan's impending attack. But such a hypothesis does not take into consideration the extent to which Admiral Turner had imposed his own stranglehold on operational intelligence throughout 1941. Nor does it take into account the long-running feud for control of the OP-20-G between the offices of naval intelligence and communications.

Safford had also come under suspicion for drifting into increasing collaboration with ONI and the Redmans' perception of Rochefort's independence might well have been colored by his 1932 memorandum advocating "that the Cryptographic Section be removed from the Office of Naval Communications and placed under the Office of Naval Intelligence."[60]

Comint, as its name implies, combines elements of communications and intelligence in both staffing and end product. To give the entire operation to either specialization would have left the other in the lurch. In the navy department, as in any institution, sectional rivalry and personalities played a role in determining how intelligence was evaluated and disseminated. The events leading up to Pearl Harbor had underlined the importance of radio intelligence just as Midway demonstrated its war-winning potential. A stake in its operation was therefore regarded as a cap-feather for those officers who controlled the flow of information to the fleet.

So while Safford was a highly intelligent, if undisciplined prodigy, the Redman brothers were quick to spot the importance of the organization he had created. They were down-to-earth, practical, ambitious bureaucrats who seized the main chance. They enlisted an ally in Wenger, a communications officer of proven abilities who was also a farsighted opportunist. Although he lacked Safford's intuitive flair for code breaking, Wenger—perhaps more clearly than the Redmans—anticipated the importance that intelligence would play in military operations. His foresight led to the creation of the Navy Security Group, which he later ably commanded, and it presaged the postwar growth of comint at the National Security Agency.

It was Safford who singlehandedly had conceived, founded, and built the navy's comint entity. It was Wenger who harnessed the power and drive of the Redmans to organize radio intelligence for the navy's, and the nation's, long-term goals.

At the same time the Hypo team of Rochefort-Dyer-Wright was to prove the Redman-Wenger philosophy of a centrally controlled and directed radio intelligence operation was not applicable to a tactical command. The Hypo contribution was to show what could be achieved by an extremely competent, well-motivated team working in close liaison with the Pacific Fleet command. It was Rochefort who made one element of the organization work superbly at a crucial time in a crucial place, thereby justifying Safford's vision, regardless of any previous or subsequent performance. It was Layton who avoided direct involvement in the

Negat-Hypo feud to remain the conduit and analyst to Nimitz of comint. Captain Jasper Holmes, a member of the Cincpac-Hypo organization throughout the war, observed, "If Admiral Nimitz had not had Eddie Layton as his intelligence officer, he might not have had the confidence to risk everything on the conclusion of what many other senior officers considered to be a bunch of nuts, in a basement, dreaming up wild hallucinations." As Admiral Burke has said, "Layton, by keeping his job above his personality, contributed the necessary rapport that someone else might not have been able to provide."

Growth of United States Navy Radio Intelligence

		OFFICER	ENLISTED	CIVILIAN	TOTAL
	1924	1		1	2
	1925	1	2	4	7
	1936	11	88	10	109
June	1940	12	121	15	147
January	1941	44	489	10	543
December	1941	75	645	10	730*
July	1942	114	496	110	720
December	1942	234	784	170	1188
July	1943	365	2175	116	2656
December	1943	734	2622	96	3452
February	1944	780	2854	88	3722
October	1945	1499	6908	47	8454

Geographic Distribution, December 1941

	OFFICER	ENLISTED	CIVILIAN	TOTAL
Negat	52	351	10	413**
West Coast	3	99		102
Hypo	18	128		146
Cast	9	61		70
Port Darwin	1	8		9
	——	——	——	——
	83	647	10	740*

Officer in Charge, Research Desk (OP-20-G)

January 1924–February 1926	Lt. Laurence F. Safford
February 1926–September 1927	Lt. Joseph J. Rochefort
November 1927–March 1929	Lt. Bern Anderson
August 1929–April 1932	Lt. Cdr. Laurence F. Safford
April 1932–May 1933	Lt. Cdr. J. W. McClaran
May 1933–June 1935	Cdr. H. F. Kingman
September 1935–May 1936	Cdr. J. W. McClaran
May 1936–February 1942	Cdr./Capt. Laurence F. Safford
February 1942–	Capt. John R. Redman

*Discrepancy accountable to new arrivals and departures during December.
**Total does not include translators, who were furnished by ONI. These were Lt. Cdr. Alwin D. Kramer, U.S.N., and six civilians: Phillip H. Cate, B. T. Hoffman, Fred C. Woodrough, Jr., Ralph Cory, C. F. Thurston, and Dorothy Woodrough Edgers.

Officer in Charge, Translation Section (OP-20-GZ)

June 1934–mid-1936   Lt. Thomas D. Birtley
mid-1936   Lt. Edward S. Pearce
August 1936–February 1937   Lt. Edwin T. Layton
March 1937–February 1939   Lt. Redfield Mason
February 1939–May 1942   Lt./Lt. Cdr. Alwin D. Kramer
May 1942–December 1945   Lt. Cdr./Capt. Redfield Mason
December 1945–   Capt. John G. Roenigk

—SOURCE: SRH 355

528

TRANSLATION Date	By	JD#	SIS#	OTHER #		BRIEF
**Dec. 1	A	6943	(25552) (25553)	Tokyo	985	The conversations between Tokyo and Washington now stand ruptured - broken. Say very secretly to Hitler and Ribbentrop that there is extreme danger that war may suddenly break out between the Anglo-Saxon nations and Japan, and this war may come quicker than anyone dreams. Will not relax our pressure on the Soviet, but for the time being we would prefer to refrain from any direct moves in the north. Impress on the Germans and Italians how important secrecy is. (Nov. 30, 1941.) /Note: Coded message forwarded by Com 16 as GYRCF Ø1ØØ1, Ø1ØØ14, or Ø1ØØ27. Also forwarded from London as Admiralty #104 and #105. Admiralty Ø1153Ø advised "Tokyo to Berlin #985 of immediate interest."/
*Dec. 1	A	6944	(25554) (25555)	Tokyo	986	The Imperial Govt. can no longer continue negotiations with the U.S. The proposal presented by the U.S. on the 26th contains one insulting clause. It is clearly a trick. The U.S. has decided to regard Japan as an enemy. (Nov. 30, 1941.) /Forwarded by Com 16 as GYROF Ø1ØØ1, Ø1ØØ14, or Ø1ØØ29./
*Dec. 1	N	6983	-	Tokyo	865	To prevent the United States from becoming unduly suspicious we have been advising the press and others that the negotiations are continuing. The above is for only your information. (GY Log #6428.)
**Dec. 1	N	6984	-	Tokyo	2444	The four offices in London, Hongkong, Singapore, and Manila have been instructed to abandon the use of the code machines and to dispose of them. The machine in Batavia has been returned to Japan. (GY Log #6432.)
*Dec. 2	N	6985	25609	Tokyo	2409	Hidden Word Code (Nov. 27, 1941 - J19). For later additions see:

		JD#	SIS#	OTHER #
		7122	25830	Tokyo 2432
				Tokyo 2433 (?)
		7214	25943	Tokyo 2450
		7360		Tokyo 2431

TRANSLATION Date	By	JD#	SIS#	OTHER #		BRIEF
***Dec. 4	N	7001	-	-		JD #7001 is believed to be the (missing) translation of the Winds Message.
**Dec. 3	A	7017	25640	Tokyo	867	Washington burn all codes except one copy of "Oite" (Pa-K2) and "L" (LA). Stop using the code machine and destroy it completely. When you have finished this, wire back "HARUNA." Destroy all message files and other secret documents. (Dec. 2, 1941.)

1944 OP-20-G listing of Japanese diplomatic intercepts—asterisks indicated that this intelligence was of critical importance. ROCHEFORT PAPERS

SECRET

WDCSA/381 Philippines (12-4-41)

November 21, 1941.

MEMORANDUM FOR THE SECRETARY, GENERAL STAFF:
(For inclusion in special Philippine file)

Subject: Air Offensive Against Japan.

While talking informally on November 19, General Marshall directed that information be obtained referring to an air offensive against the Japanese Empire.

Specifically, he wanted answers to the questions--what General MacArthur would attack in Japan (from bases in the Vladivostok area) if war were declared December 1, 1941; what data we have assembled in Washington on the subject; what appears to us to be profitable systems of objectives, and how much of our data was presented to and was taken to the Philippines by General Brereton.

As of this date, the following data have been assembled:

1. Before General Brereton's departure for the Philippines, all of his discussions were based on the employment of the Philippine Air Force on the strategic defensive. With the very small offensive force projected for the Philippine Air Force (never over two heavy bombardment groups), a sustained air offensive against the Japanese Empire was never discussed. The conception of the employment of the offensive Air Force at that time was limited to operations against lines of communication from Japan proper. Specific objectives for this attack would obviously consist almost wholly of shipping in the northern approaches to the China seas. Japanese naval bases in the islands off Formosa and at the mandated islands (from bases in New Britain) were discussed, but no data are available as to the details of those naval bases.

2. General Brereton did take with him, however, separate Air Staff studies on the steel and petroleum industries and on the electric power establishment in Japan.

3. Shortly after General Brereton's arrival in the Philippines, G-2 received cable requests for data on objectives in Japan. In reply thereto there have been mailed to General MacArthur a series of maps showing the location of approximately 600 industrial objectives, in Japan proper. He has also been informed that objectives folder data to support these maps are in preparation and will be forwarded to him at the earliest possible date. The present status of this project (now under way in the Chief of Air Corps branch office at Bolling Field) indicates that about one-third of the total projected number of objective folders may be completed and prepared for shipment to the Philippines

SECRET

Map and memorandum detailing the extent of preparations for a strategic-bombing offensive against Japan. NATIONAL ARCHIVES, SECRETARY OF WAR SECRET FILE

November 25, 1941

MEMORANDUM FOR THE PRESIDENT:

Subject: Japanese Convoy Movement towards
Indo-China.

About a month and a half ago we learned through Magic
that the Japanese Government informed the Vichy Government that
they proposed to move approximately 50,000 troops into Indo-China
in addition to the 40,000 already there by previous agreement.

Today information has accumulated to the effect that a
convoy of from ten to thirty ships , some of 10,000 tons displacement, has been assembled near the mouth of the Yangtse River below
Shanghai. This could mean a force as great as 50,000, but more
probably a smaller number. Included in this ship concentration
was at least one landing-boat carrier. The deck-load of one vessel
contained heavy bridge equipment.

The officers concerned, in the Military Intelligence
Division, feel that unless we receive other information, this is
more or less a normal movement, that is, a logical follow-up of
their previous notification to the Vichy Government.

I will keep you informed of any other information in
this particular field.

Henry L. Stimson
Secretary of War.

November 27, 1941.

Dear Mr. Secretary:

I am sending herewith the
English estimate and the original of
your report sent to the President
Tuesday afternoon.

We found this in due course
in the inside pocket of the coat of a
very distinguished gentleman.

I am,

Very sincerely yours,

Pa" Watson
EDWIN M. WATSON.

Honorable Henry L. Stimson,
The Secretary of War.

The "missing" 25 November communication and covering note.   NATIONAL
ARCHIVES, SECRETARY OF WAR SECRET FILE

259

P.M. approved of draft of this telegram 8.30 p.m 7.12.41. Subsequently in view of news of Japanese commencement of hostilities instructions were given to cancel it. [initials] 7.12.41

Draft Telegram to Lord Halifax, Washington.

Most Immediate.   Most Secret.

1.   From your recent telegrams we understand we can rely on armed support of United States if we become involved in hostilities with Japan in the following circumstances:-

   (a)   Japanese invasion of Malaya or Netherlands East Indies.

   (b)   Action on our part in the Kra Isthmus to fore-stall or repel Japanese landing in that Isthmus.

   (c)   Action on our part in Kra Isthmus in event of Japanese encroachment on Thailand by force or threat of force (President's 3rd hypothesis in your Telegram No. 5519 of December 1).

2.   We read your Telegram 5653 (of December 6) as meaning that in President Roosevelt's view we should be justified in attacking at sea any Japanese expedition sailing in direction of Thailand or Malaya (and presumably East Indies).   We ourselves should desire to have this latitude.

Telegram drafted half an hour before the Pearl Harbor attack by Churchill confirming that Roosevelt *had* guaranteed U.S. armed support even if Britain made a preemptive attack on the Japanese. PUBLIC RECORDS OFFICE, PRIME MINISTER'S FILES

(ed)

U WO 2   All Fleets
DE
HA FU 6   TOKYO Radio
- SO U   W 90
- - - - - - - - - - - -

From: TU HI Ø17.   *Secty, COMBINED FLEET.*
Action: YA MI 9   ~~FROM~~ O N F/S COMBINED FLEET
Info: Missing.   (Probably Chief Tokyo Comm. Office)*

2300/24 November 1941   (TOI 11/2500ИG WE 4155A) H

████████ Serial   618И

          Additions to Call List "RY TO YO"

          1. Additions to the "surface force" section (pages 1 and 2).

          CALL   UNIT

SE TA to HI TE (6 calls)   E (British Malay) Force.
                             H (Dutch Indies) Force.
                             M (Philippine) Force.
                             N (Japan) Force.
                             AA (Wake) Occupation Force.
                             G (Guam) Occupation Force.

HI SE to WU FU   Main Force.

FO I to N RE   Flagship of Maru Force.

Z RO to HO A   Striking Force.

SE WI to WU HU   Flagship of Striking Force.

NI HI to WU KU   Air Force (Southern Force).

SI YO to RU RO   Ship-shore administrative offices of Commander
                           Air Force (Southern Force).

WI SO to KO WU   Advance Expeditionary Force.

EE WI to SI NU   Flagship of Advance Expeditionary Force.

HO RU to G NA   Submarine Force (Southern Force).

KI NU to HA SO   Flagship of Submarine Force (Southern Force).

FO WE to SE WU   Southern Force.

JN 5 0063 Z JWH   (crown) Navy Trans 11/29/45 ~~TOP SECRET ULTRA~~

(cb)

From: YO WI ∅∅   Combined Fleet, CinC.
Action: SE TU 7   Combined Fleet.

12/021500/I 1941   (TOI 12/022100 & XT 4155 A) - H

Serial 676

This despatch is Top Secret.

This order is effective at 1750 on 2 December:

Combined Fleet Serial) # 10.

Climb NIITAKAYAMA 1208, repeat 1208!

Comment: Interpreted freely, above means "Attack on 8 December". Explanation:
This was undoubtedly the prearranged signal for specifying the date for opening
hostilities. However, the significance of the phrase is interesting in that it
is so appropriately used in this connection.

NIITAKAYAMA is the highest mountain in the Japanese Empire. To
climb NIITAKAYAMA is to accomplish one of the greatest feats. In other words
undertake the task (of carrying out assigned operations). 1208 signifies the
12th month, 8th day, Itex time.

[handwritten] Comment: Intercepted 2100, 2?
Dec 1941,

[handwritten] 8H
F

(JAPANESE)

JN 5   0012 Z   (KK) Navy from TOP SECRET ULTRA

NAVAL MESSAGE   NAVY DEPARTMENT

PHONE EXTENSION NUMBER		ADDRESSEES	MESSAGE PRECEDENCE
FROM OPNAV	FOR ACTION	CINCAF CINCPAC	PRIORITY ROUTINE DEFERRED
RELEASED BY ADM INGERSOLL 27 NOV 1941 DATE			
TOR CODEROOM	INFORMATION	CINCLANT SPENAVO	PRIORITY ROUTINE DEFERRED
DECODED BY			
PARAPHRASED BY			

INDICATE BY ASTERISK ADDRESSEES FOR WHICH MAIL DELIVERY IS SATISFACTORY

262337   (CR0921)

UNLESS OTHERWISE DESIGNATED THIS DISPATCH WILL BE TRANSMITTED WITH DEFERRED PRECEDENCE.
ORIGINATOR FILL IN DATE AND TIME FOR DEFERRED AND MAIL DELIVERY

DATE   TIME   GCT

TEXT THIS DISPATCH IS TO BE CONSIDERED A WAR WARNING X NEGOTIATIONS WITH JAPAN LOOKING TOWARD STABILIZATION OF CONDITIONS IN THE

PACIFIC HAVE CEASED AND AN AGGRESSIVE MOVE BY JAPAN IS EXPECTED WITHIN THE NEXT FEW DAYS X THE NUMBER AND EQUIPMENT OF JAPANESE

TROOPS AND THE ORGANIZATION OF NAVAL TASK FORCES INDICATES AN AMPHIBIOUS EXPEDITION AGAINST EITHER THE PHILIPPINES THAI

OR KRA PENINSULA OR POSSIBLY BORNEO X EXECUTE AN APPROPRIATE DEFENSIVE DEPLOYMENT PREPARATORY TO CARRYING OUT THE TASKS ASSIG

ED IN WPL46X INFORM DISTRICT AND ARMY AUTHORITIES X A SIMILAR WARNING IS BEING SENT BY WAR DEPARTMENT X SPENAVO INFORM BRITISH

CONTINENTAL DISTRICTS GUAM SAMOA DIRECTED TAKE APPROPRIATE MEASURES AGAINST SABOTAGE

SEE ART 76(4)
NAV REGS

MAKE ORIGINAL ONLY, DELIVER TO COMMUNICATION WATCH OFFICER IN PERSON

The navy's 27 November 1941 alert that was phrased to warn both the Asiatic and Pacific fleet commanders of impending war, but clearly applied primarily to the former. NATIONAL ARCHIVES, PEARL HARBOR LIAISON OFFICE

INDICATE BY ASTERISK ADDRESSEES FOR WHICH MAIL DELIVERY IS SATISFACTORY

Ø12356CRØ313

UNLESS OTHERWISE DESIGNATED THIS DISPATCH WILL BE TRANSMITTED WITH DEFERRED PRECEDENC

ORIGINATOR FILL IN DATE AND TIME FOR DEFERRED AND MAIL DELIVERY

DATE   TIME   GCT

TEXT
PRESIDENT DIRECTS THAT THE FOLLOWING BE DONE AS SOON AS POSSIBLE

AND WITHIN TWO DAYS IF POSSIBLE AFTER RECEIPT THIS DESPATCH.
CHARTER 3 SMALL VESSELS TO FORM A "DEFENSIVE INFORMATION PATROL"
MINIMUM REQUIREMENTS TO ESTABLISH IDENTITY AS U.S. MEN-OF-WAR

ARE COMMANDED BY A NAVAL OFFICER AND TO MOUNT A SMALL GUN AND 1
MACHINE GUN WOULD SUFFICE. FILIPINO CREWS MAY BE EMPLOYED WITH
NUMBER
MINIMUM/NAVAL RATINGS TO ACCOMPLISH PURPOSE WHICH IS TO OBSERVE
AND REPORT BY RADIO JAPANESE MOVEMENTS IN WEST CHINA SEA AND GU

OF SIAM. 1 VESSEL TO BE STATIONED BETWEEN HAINAN AND HUE ONE
VESSEL OFF THE INDO-CHINA COAST BETWEEN CAMRANH BAY AND CAPE ST.

JAQUES AND ONE VESSEL OFF POINTE DE CAMAU. USE OF ISABEL AUTHOR
ED BY PRESIDENT AS ONE OF THE THREE BUT NOT OTHER NAVAL VESSELS.

REPORT MEASURES TAKEN TO CARRY OUT PRESIDENTS VIEWS. AT SAME TI
INFORM ME AS TO WHAT RECONNAISSANCE MEASURES ARE BEING REGULARLY

PERFORMED AT SEA BY BOTH ARMY AND NAVY WHETHER BY AIR SURFACE VE
SELS OR SUBMARINES AND YOUR OPINION AS TO THE EFFECTIVENESS OF

THESE LATTER MEASURES.   FILES...CNO..GENERAL..2Ø Ø
DISTRIBUTION...38...ORIGINATOR...RECORD COPY..12

MAKE ORIGINAL ONLY, DELIVER TO COMMUNICATION WATCH OFFICER IN PERSON

The president's order to the Asiatic Fleet to send out three expendable vessels on what appears to have been a "fishbait" mission. NATIONAL ARCHIVES, PEARL HARBOR LIAISON OFFICE

I KA MI (GUADALCANAL Oper. For.)
DE: SO SU FU (RABAUL Comm. Unit)
U TU 785 W 176
- - - . - - - - - - - - - - - - - -

From: 7
Action: RO HI 2 · | (SOLOMONS Defense Force)
             HO KO 8 · | ?
             KU TA 2 | (Air Group #204)
             YU YO 2 _ _ ____ | (Air Flotilla #26)

                 (Ballale Garrison Comdr.)
Info: NO KA 1   ?

4/131755/I ɓ943   (TCI 4/140009/I on 4990 A kcs) bt

#?   From: CinC Southeastern Air Fleet.

            On 18 April CinC Combined Fleet will visit
RXZ, R___ and RXT in accordance following schedule:

            1. Depart RR at 0600 in a medium attack
plane escorted by 6 fighters. Arrive RXZ at 0800.
Proceed by minesweeper to R___ arriving at 0840.
(___ have minesweeper ready at #1 Base). Depart R____
at 0945 in above minesweeper and arrive RXZ at 1030?
(- - - - - - -). Depart RXZ at 1100? ➤ in medium
attack plane and arrive RXF at 1110. ~xxxxx~
- - - - - - -. Depart RXP at 1400 in medium attack
plane and arrive RR at ~iss~ 1540.

            2. At each of the above places the Commander-
in-Chief will make short tour of inspection and at _____
he will visit the sick and wounded, but current
operations should continue. Each force commander - - - - ·

JN-3: 2825 (MR)   (Japanese)
                        (S) Navy Trans. 4/141705/Q(?)

The decrypted intercept of Admiral Yamamoto's scheduled tour of Bougainville bases that became his death warrant. Note five-minute disparity in minesweeper trip, because of tides. NATIONAL ARCHIVES, SRN SERIES

II

The Navy Department Decrypting Unit had been assisting Pearl Harbor in the solution of the Jap Naval Operations Code for about a year, and had handled solution single-handed before this "project" was assigned to Pearl Harbor in 1941. The British C.I. Unit in Singapore had been evacuated to Ceylon and then withdrawn to East Africa, so that it was temporarily in a state of "suspended animation" so far as its cryptanalytical efforts were concerned. The Asiatic C.I. Unit had been evacuated (by submarine) from Corregidor to Australia during March, April, and early May, 1942: there they joined the enthusiastic but inexperienced Australian C.I. Unit at Canberra and were just getting on their feet again when Midway was fought. So the whole burden of communication intelligence (in the Pacific) fell on Pearl Harbor and Washington. It is true that the Navy Department was turning out more "key recoveries" and "code values" than Pearl Harbor. (They had more personnel to assign to this project.) However, Pearl Harbor was always several days ahead in its information— because it was adjacent to the Intercept Station—and in this instance made a correct evaluation of available evidence while the Navy Department busted cold.'

Neither John Redman nor Wenger were inclined to share credit with anyone else, let alone admit a blunder, so they proceeded to bluff their way through. They told the Director of Naval Communications (Capt. Joseph R. Redman) that they had spotted the change of date, that Pearl Harbor had missed the boat on this occasion, and that without the warning from Washington, Midway and parts of the Hawaiian Islands would have been captured! It is presumed that Captain Redman told this to Vice Admiral Horne, to Vice Admiral Willson, and to Admiral King. This could be verified by questioning these Admirals - if they still remember the incident.

The exposure of the above-mentioned fraud did not come until October, 1943, when Commander J. S. Holtwick was ordered to the Navy Department for a short period of temporary duty prior to going to Chungking for liaison duty with the Chinese Government. Holtwick called on the D.N.C. (Rear Admiral Joseph R. Redman) to pay his respects. In the course of conversation, Admiral Redman casually remarked that Pearl Harbor had missed the boat at the Battle of Midway but the Navy Department had saved the day. This took Holtwick's breath away, but he managed to say that Admiral Nimitz thought the reverse was true. Admiral Redman then said that the Commander in Chief must have been misinformed, to which Holtwick replied:

> "Admiral Nimitz read the official dispatches and drew
> his own conclusions. Also, he has just given me a
> letter of commendation for my part in the work."

(Incidentally, Admiral Nimitz gave similar letters of commendation to Dyer, Wright, Rochefort (?), and others.)

A page from the anonymous wartime memorandum accusing certain members of the navy department of conspiring to sack Rochefort. ADMIRAL SHOWERS

UNITED STATES FLEET
HEADQUARTERS OF THE COMMANDER IN CHIEF
NAVY DEPARTMENT, WASHINGTON, D.C.

SECRET

June 22, 1942.

MEMORANDUM FOR: The Admiral.

Subject: Commander Rochefort Recommendation for Medal
            Award.

    1.   I do not concur in the recommendation that
Commander Rochefort be awarded a Distinguished Service
Medal.

    2.   This officer is not the originator of this
particular service, though he has been very active in it,
and, while he has apparently performed his present duties
in a highly successful manner, he has merely efficiently used
the tools previously prepared for his use.

    3.   Ground-work, prepared over a period of many
years, is the result of the efforts of many officers and
it would seem hardly befitting to award a medal only to
the officer who happens to be in a position to reap the
benefits, at a particular time, unless in actual combat
operation with the enemy.

    4.   The work of Corregidor, Belconnen and the
Navy Department has been, I think, of as high an order
as that done in Honolulu. However, these Officers in
Charge performed a more or less mechanical, technical job
in utilizing a tool already forged to their use.

    5.   I consider that equal credit is due to the
COMINCH Planning Section for the correct evaluation of enemy
intentions, based upon all sorts of intelligence, and
strategical application of that intelligence. In this particular case radio intelligence was invaluable.

OK   6.   I recommend that you disapprove this recommendation ation and other similar ones which may be received,
particularly at this time.

Done   7.   I do recommend, however, that a "Well Done" be
sent from COMINCH to the stations and units concerned in
their particular private cipher system. Despatch attached
for your release if you approve.

                                    Respectfully,

                                    RUSSELL WILLSON,
                                    Chief of Staff.

King rejected the recommended award to Rochefort. Notations indicate King's
acceptance of the advice of his chief of staff. ROCHEFORT PAPERS

Notes

Essentially this book is the autobiographic memoir of Admiral Edwin T. Layton. He determined with his coauthors that where his recollections were the primary source there was no need for references and footnotes. The basis for these recollections is derived from a wide variety of his writings contained in dozens of school exercise books and the notes with which he filled hundreds of pieces of paper. These include translations from Japanese books and documents, transcriptions from message file marginal notes, and the notations in the books from his personal library. Layton's correspondence files, his tape-recorded interviews and reminiscences conducted with his coauthors are primary sources. So too are the oral history produced by the United States Naval Institute in Annapolis and Professor E. B. Potter's detailed interview with Layton conducted for the biography of Admiral Nimitz. Among other important sources are Layton's published papers and writings, and his verbatim testimony and cross-examinations recorded in the following official hearings into the attack on Pearl Harbor:

Roberts Commission	Part 23	pages 657–672
Hart Inquiry	Part 26	pages 225–240
Army Board	Part 28	pages 1577–1595
Navy Inquiry	Part 33	pages 832–839
Clausen Investigation	Part 35	pages 49–51
Hewitt Inquiry	Part 36	pages 111–173
Joint Congressional	Part 10	pages 4829–4909

Detailed citations of the author's personal quotations and references are all incorporated in the Edwin T. Layton Collection held by the U.S. Naval War College, Newport, Rhode Island. This collection includes the original notebooks, pencil drafts, tape recordings, and correspondence as well as the admiral's own collection of documents and microfilms.

Chapter 1 (pages 17–22) "I Was There"

1. *Hearings Before the Joint Committee on the Investigation of the Pearl Harbor Attack, Congress of the United States, Seventy-ninth Congress* (Washington, 1946), Part 4, page 1976, (hereafter PHH 4/1976).

2. PHH 4/1975.

3. PHH 26/22; 28/1594.

4. PHH 23/663.

Chapter 2 (pages 23–37) The Undeclared War

1. Capt. Wesley A. Wright conversation, 9 January 1985.

2. Kenichi Nakamuta, *Joohoo shikan no kaisoo* (Reflections of an intelligence officer) (hereafter Nakamuta) (Tokyo: Daiya Mendosha, 1947), p. 74.

3. National Archives of the United States (Record Group 457, Modern Military Branch, Military Archives Division) SRH histories. SRH 355: "Naval Security Group History to World War II," compiled by Captain J. S. Holtwick, Jr., June 1971; Volume II as quoted on page 19 (hereafter SRH 355).

4. Laurence F. Safford, "History of Radio Intelligence: The Undeclared War," 15 November 1943, SRH 305, p. 11.

5. Laurence F. Safford, "A Brief History of Communications Intelligence in the United States," 21–27 March 1952, SRH 149, p. 1.

6. David Kahn, *The Codebreakers* (hereafter Kahn), pp. 352–54.

7. SRH 355, pp. 26–27.

8. Ibid., p. 28.

9. SRH 305, p. 1.

10. Henry L. Stimson and McGeorge Bundy, *On Active Service in Peace and War* (hereafter Bundy), p. 188.

11. SRH 305, p. 1.

12. Kanya Miyauchi *Niitakayama nobore 1208* (hereafter Miyauchi), p. 481.

13. Ibid.

14. SRH 355, p. 30.

15. Ibid., p. 23.

16. Mrs. Eunice Willson Rice letter to Pineau, 23 June 1985.

17. SRH 355, pp. 18–19, 29, 160, 341.

18. Rice letter.

19. SRH 305, p. 3.

20. SRH 355, p. 72, Capt. Raymond Schmidt interview, 1970.

21. SRH 305, p. 8.

22. SRH 149, p. 5.

23. SRH 305, p. 8.

24. Ibid.

25. Ibid.

26. Ibid.

27. Ibid., p. 10.

28. Ibid.

29. Ibid., pp. 4–6.

30. SRH 305, p. 5.

31. Private papers of Capt. J. J. Rochefort (hereafter Rochefort papers): "Memorandum for Captain Ogan [acting director of naval intelligence] re Cryptographic Section," dated 21 December 1932.

32. SRH 305, p. 6.

33. Rochefort memo, 21 December 1932.

34. Ibid.

35. Ibid.

36. SRH 305, p. 5.

Chapter 3 (pages 38–51)   Keep the Dogs Yapping

1. Herbert O. Yardley, *The American Black Chamber,* pp. 163–65, 187–211.(Republished by Ballantine Books.)
2. Japanese Foreign Ministry Files: Memorandum of 10 June 1931.
3. Elting E. Morison, *A Study of the Life and Times of Henry L. Stimson* (Boston, 1960), p. 382.
4. Grew to Stimson, 23 February 1933, *Foreign Relations of the United States, Diplomatic Papers* (hereafter FRUS-DP) (Department of State, 1949) Vol. 3, p. 195.
5. SRH 305, p. 4.
6. U.S. Naval Institute Oral History Program, transcript of 1969 interviews with Capt. J. J. Rochefort, p. 30 (hereafter Rochefort OH).
7. Dyer interview, 27 June 1984.
8. SRH 355, pp. 80, 88.
9. SRH 305, p. 12.
10. Nakamuta, pp. 83–84.
11. Rochefort papers: "Memorandum for Lieutenant Curts," 25 September 1934.
12. Toshiyuki Yokoi, *Nihon no kimitsu shitsu* ("The Japanese Version of the Black Chamber") (hereafter Yokoi), draft article, English translation 1953, p. 6.
13. Ibid., p. 7.
14. Ibid., p. 9.
15. Ibid., p. 12.
16. SRH 305, p. 14.
17. Rochefort papers, letter from Adm. J. M. Reeves dated 22 April 1935.
18. Ibid.
19. Wright interview, 24 May 1984.
20. Ibid.
21.Captain Forrest R. Biard letter to Pineau, 1 July 1984.

Chapter 4 (pages 52–69)   Codebreaking and Kabuki

1. Vice Admiral George C. Dyer, U.S.N. (Ret.), *On the Treadmill to Pearl Harbor: The Memoirs of Admiral James O. Richardson U.S.N. (Retired)* (hereafter Dyer, *Richardson),* p. 10.
2. Ibid., p. 320.
3. Ibid., p. 332.
4. Ibid.
5. Ibid., p. 435.
6. *Webster's Third New International Dictionary of the English Language* (Springfield, Mass.: G. & C. Merriam Co., 1964), p. 1174.
7. SRH 355, p. 40.
8. Ibid., p. 147.
9. Ibid., pp. 40–41.
10. SRH 305, p. 13.
11. Ibid.
12. SRH 355, p. 19.
13. Ibid., pp. 353–55.
14. Yokoi, p. 7.
15. SRH 355, pp. 115–16.
16. Yokoi, p. 7.
17. Ibid., p. 8.
18. PHH 7/3251.
19. Ibid., pp. 3355–58.
20. Ibid., p. 3356.

Chapter 5 (pages 70–81)   When We Fight

1. Shinsaku Hirata, *Warera moshi tatakawaba (When We Fight)* (Tokyo: Kodansha, 1933), Chapter I.

2. Shigeru Fukudome, *Shikan: Shinjuwan koogeki* (Tokyo: Jiyu Ajiya 1955), p. 137.

3. Dorothy Borg and Shumpei Okamoto, eds., *Pearl Harbor as History*, p. 167.

4. Hiroyuki Agawa, *The Reluctant Admiral: Yamamoto and the Imperial Navy* (hereafter Agawa), p. 158.

5. Ibid.

6. Ibid., p. 189.

7. Ibid., p. 219.

8. PHH 14/1402.

9. U.S. Navy Operational Archives, Strategic Plans Division Records (hereafter NWPD), secretary of navy to secretary of war, January 1941 [reference (SC) A7-2(2)/FF1]

10. Ibid.

11. PHH 22/330.

12. Ibid., p. 332.

13. Ibid., p. 334.

14. PHH 15/1437; and PHH 22/350.

15. Ibid.

16. PHH 22/351.

17. PHH 4/1941.

18. SRH 355, p. 395.

19. Ibid., p. 319*n*.

20. Ibid., p. 329.

21. Dyer interview, Rochefort papers "Top Secret Ultra" memorandum, dated 15 August 1944; and SRH 355, pp. 396–99.

22. Captain E.S.L. Goodwin letter, 1 April 1985.

23. Ibid.; and SRH 355, p. 398.

24. Ibid.

25. Ibid., p. 396.

26. SRH 355, pp. 161, 247–49, 401; and SRH 149, pp. 8–9.

27. SRH 355, p. 161.

28. Ibid.

29. Ibid., pp. 160–163.

30. Ibid., p. 159.

31. Ibid., p. 8.

32. SRH 159, "Preliminary Historical Report on the Solution of the 'B' Machine," William F. Friedman, December 1945; and Theodore M. Hannah, "Frank Rowlett," in *Cryptologic Spectrum,* Spring 1981, p. 16.

33. Ibid., p. 18.

34. Ibid., p. 15.

Chapter 6 (pages 82–91)   Pacific Overtures

1. FRUS-Japan, 1941, Vol. II, pp. 387–89.

2. FDR Lib., Hyde Park, New York, Complete Press Conferences #702, 17 December 1940.

3. NA/RG 457: SRA individual translations, Japanese military attaché messages, No. 1848, Washington-Tokyo, 16 April 1941, tr. 1945.

4. Ibid.

5. NA/RG 457: SRDJ individual translations, Japanese diplomatic messages. See in particular: SRNA 000001, Tokyo-Washington, 5 May 1940, concerning

meeting at Nipponese Club, New York, between agent Katoo and German agent Steamer (probably phonetic spelling of "Sthaemer"); and SRDJ 011811, JD-1 2360, Washington-Tokyo, 14 May 1941 re a request for half a million Yen for intelligence operations in the United States. It details the assistance given spy chief Terasaki by Senator "G" and his links with the America First Committee and Charles Lindbergh who "according to W [name deleted) has been cautioned by the German Embassy."

SRDJ 011769, JD-1 2598, Washington-Tokyo, 9 May 1941 (tr. 19 May 1941) re cultivation of contacts among "very influential Negro leaders" to stir racial discontent "to stall the program the US plans for national defense and the economy, as well as for sabotage." This report also referred to a network of informants among "our second generation workers in airplane plants."

SRDJ 16637, SIS 24538, Washington-Tokyo, 6 November 1941 (tr. 8 November 1941) reporting liaison with Lindbergh through C. K. Armstrong and the America First Committee.

6. Cordell Hull, *The Memoirs of Cordell Hull* (hereafter Hull *Memoirs*), p. 982.

7. Hajime Sugiyama, *Sugiyama Memo (Sugiyama's Memoranda)* (Tokyo: Hara Shebo, 1967) Vol. 1, p. 1201.

8. NA/RG:457 SRNA, individual translations, Japanese naval attaché messages, No. 0020, Berlin-Tokyo, 12 December 1940.

9. NA/RG 242: Collection of foreign records seized 1941: *Oberkommando der Kriegsmarine: Marine Attaché Gruppe: "Kriegstagebuch des Marinesattaches und des Militarischen Leiters der Gross-Etappe Japan/China,"* 28 August 1939–31 March 1943 (hereafter Wenneker diary), entry 3 July 1940.

10. Wenneker diary, 13 August 1940.

11. *Senshi Soosho* [War history series] (Tokyo: Defense Headquarters History Office) (hereafter SSS) Vol. 91, *Daihonei kaigun bu—rengokantai,* pp. 420–31.

12. Ibid.

13. SSS, Vol. 91, p. 496n.

14. Public Records Office, Kew, England, War Cabinet records 66/10 (hereafter PRO CAB), "Situation in the Far East in the Event of Japanese Intervention Against Us," Chiefs of Staff Committee (hereafter COS), 31 July 1940.

15. Wenneker diary, 7 December 1940, Telegram No. 209–212; SRNA 0020: "Forty Years On—The Imperial Japanese Navy, the European War and the Tripartite Pact," Professor J.M.W. Chapman in 1980 Proceedings of British American Japan Society, Vol. 1, Part 1; *see also* "The Sinking of The *Nankin* and the Capture of the *Aretimedon,"* James Rusbridger, *Encounter,* May 1985, Vol. LXIV, No. 5

16. CAB 66/10; COS "Appreciation" covering letter, 15 August 1940.

17. Wenneker diary, 12 December 1940.

18. Warren Kimball, *Churchill-Roosevelt: The Complete Correspondence* (Princeton, 1984), Vol. 1, "Alliance Emerging" (hereafter Kimball WSC/FDR), C-60X 15 February 1941, pp. 135–36.

19. Maurice Matloff and Edwin M. Snell, *Strategic Planning for Coalition Warfare: 1941–1942* (hereafter Matloff and Snell) (Washington, D.C.: Office of the Chief of Military History, U.S. Army, 1953), p. 75.

20. Ibid.

21. Kimball WSC/FDR, C Box, 5 February 1941, pp. 135–36.

22. PHH 16/2151.

23. Ibid., p. 2163.

24. Ibid., pp. 2164–65.

25. Knox-Stimson letter, 24 January 1941.

26. PHH 20/4300.

27. PHH 15/1635.

28. Ibid.
29. Henry L. Stimson diary, 24 April 1941 (manuscript in Stimson papers) (Yale) (hereafter Stimson diary).
30. PHH 16/2160–61.
31. Ibid., p. 2229.
32. Ibid., p. 2160.
33. PHH 10/4846.

Chapter 7 (pages 92–102)   On the Mat

1. Rochefort papers, "High Frequency Direction Finding in the Pacific Ocean Prior to December 7, 1941," 9 August 1944; "RI Activities, 14th Naval District," confidential memorandum of 14 August 1940; also SRH 355, pp. 343–47.
2. Rochefort papers, top secret Ultra memoranda, 5 August 1944 and 15 August 1944.
3. Ibid.
4. Ibid.
5. Ibid., and SRH 149, p. 14 and SRH 355, pp. 297–399, which state in general terms that JN-25 was being decrypted to some extent throughout 1941. The precise amount of JN-25 traffic which could be read in December 1941 is a matter of some debate—and considerable historical importance—which may be why no contemporary decrypts have yet been released either by American or British sources. Admiral Layton, despite repeated efforts, was unable to obtain any official records or specific examples of messages that would clarify the issue. The British foreign office, shortly before this manuscript went to press, again insisted that it was not its policy ever to release any documents that would indicate that Britain decrypted the communications of a foreign power which was officially at peace.

The anonymous and undated "secret" memorandum "The Inside Story of the Battle of Midway and the Ousting of Commander Rochefort" (hereafter A Memo) asserts that JN-25 was "50% readable" but provides no details. This was an exaggeration—at least as far as the U.S. navy was concerned—according to the postwar opinions of Captains Rochefort, Dyer, and Wright. They estimated that Washington's success at reading JN-25B in November was probably on the order of 10 to 15 percent. This would agree with Safford's 1945 assessment of the extent of JN-25 penetration given in a secret 17 May 1945 memorandum to the Hewitt investigation (RG 80, PHLO Box 49). For details of his discussion see Chapter 21, note 27.
6. PHH 15/1864.
7. Ibid.
8. Julius A. Furer, *Administration of the Navy Department in World War II* (hereafter Dyer, *Admin.*), p. 123.
9. Ibid.
10. A. A. Hoehling, *The Week Before Pearl Harbor* (hereafter Hoehling), p. 54.
11. Ibid., p. 56.
12. Dyer, *Admin.*, p. 129.
13. PHH 4/1915.
14. Robert Sherrod, *On to Westward*, p. 250.
15. PHH 4/1914.
16. U.S. Navy Operational Archives, General Board file 429.
17. PHH 4/1926.
18. "The Reminiscences of RADM Arthur H. McCollum USN (Ret.)," an oral history (hereafter McCollum OH) (Annapolis, 1973), p. 309.

19. Ibid., p. 310.
20. Ibid., p. 311.
21. Ibid., pp. 311–12.
22. Ibid., p. 311.
23. Hoehling, p. 56.
24. PHH 4/1926.
25. Ibid.
26. PHH 4/1926.
27. Stimson diary, 6 May 1941.
28. PHH 4/1926.
29. Dyer, *Admin.*, p. 186.
30. McCollum OH, p. 112.
31. Ibid., p. 312.
32. Ibid., p. 313.
33. Ibid., p. 314.
34. Ibid., pp. 324–25.
35. SRH 305, p. 15.
36. Yokoi, p. 10.
37. Ibid.

Chapter 8 (pages 103–111)   The Biggest Rattlesnake

1. Samuel I. Rosenman, ed., *The Public Papers and Addresses of Franklin Delano Roosevelt* (New York: Random House, 1938–1950), 4 Vols., year of 1941, pp. 181–94.
2. NA/RG: 181, Records of the 14th Naval District, "Investigation Report: Japanese Consulate, Honolulu—Espionage Activities," 6 and 9 February 1942 (hereafter Com-14-espionage report).
3. Ibid.
4. SRNA 000006, Tokyo-Washington, 29 September 1940, tr. 11 October 1945 arranging agents' meeting in New York; similarly SRNA 000010, Berlin-Washington, 10 October 1940; SRNA 000015, Berlin-Tokyo, 13 December 1940; SRNA 00078, Washington-Tokyo, 27 June 1940 reporting Okada-Tachibana operations; and SRNA 000083, Tokyo-Washington, 7 June 1940 on precautions for undercover operations.
5. J. F. Bratzel and L. B. Rout, Jr., "Pearl Harbor, Microdots, and J. Edgar Hoover," *The American Historical Review,* Vol. 87, No. 5, pp. 1342–48; also Dusko Popov, *Spy/Counterspy* (New York: G&D, 1974).
6. NA/State Department, RG 59, State Department Decimal Intelligence File: 862.20210 Engles, Albrecht Gustav/71.
7. FDR-Lib. letter, Hoover-Gen. Watson, 3 September 1941 plus enclosures.
8. FDR-Lib., Hoover-Gen. Watson, "Memorandum Re: Japanese Activities," 13 November 1941.
9. SRDJ 012780, JD-1 3490, Washington-Tokyo, 4 July 1941, Tr. 8 July 1941.
10. SRNA 00007 and 8, op. cit.
11. Sources for Blake Account: "Me, Jap Agent—for Uncle Sam" by Al Blake in *Official Detective Stories* February-June 1942 and *Honolulu Advertiser,* 1 May 1941, p. 1.
12. SRDJ 012485, SIS 18626, Hollywood-Washington, 10 June 1941, tr. 25 June 1941.
13. NA/RG 181, Records of the 14th Naval District, District Intelligence Office, Sumner Welles—secretary of navy, 7 July 1941; FDR-Lib. H. R. Stark letter to secretary of state, 23 June 1941, ser. no. 0498416.
14. *The "Magic" Background of Pearl Harbor* (hereafter *"Magic" Back-*

ground), Appx. II, (Washington, D.C.: Department of Defense, 1977), message No. 85, p. A-46.

15. SRH 255, "Interview with Robert D. Ogg," 14 November 1983, pp. 12–20; see also RG: 181, Records of 12th Naval District memo "Coordination of FBI, ONI and MID," 5 June 1940 and subject index to box 8, "Japanese Individuals—Investigation of Japanese Organizations in the United States," 1941.

16. Mrs. William L. Magistretti interview, 6 August 1984.

17. SRH 255, pp. 28–30.

18. PHH 35/84.

19. Com 14 espionage report.

20. SSS, Vol. 10, pp. 14–22; Agawa, p. 253.

Chapter 9 (pages 112–122)   Dropping the Ball

1. PHH 16/2237–38.

2. Ibid.

3. Edwin T. Layton Oral History (hereafter ETL OH), U.S. Naval Institute, p. 48.

4. Rochefort papers, reports on Orange Naval Maneuvers, August 1940; PHLO Box 40, Layton reports on Orange Naval Maneuvers in mandates, May 1941.

5. PHH 10/4829.

6. PHH 6/2502.

7. Ibid.

8. PHH 33/693.

9. PHH 11/5475.

10. SRDJ 011563, JD-09, Tokyo-Washington, 5 May 1941, Tr. 5 May 1941.

11. NA/RG 80: "Records of the Navy Liaison Office to the Joint Congressional Committee Investigating the Attack on Pearl Harbor" (PHLO), Box 62: Japanese diplomatic intercepts JD-1 2372, 2368, 2346, 2367—these are 1945 photocopies of the originals and unlike the SRDJ file, which deletes the cipher identifier, those called JD cite precisely the Purple code in which they were transmitted.

12. Ibid., p. 2636.

13. Dr. Ruth Harris, "The 'Magic' Leak of 1941 and Japanese-American Relations," *Pacific Quarterly,* Vol. LX1, February 1981, pp. 77–96.

14. SRH 154, pp. 31–32.

15. PHH 11/5476.

16. SRDJ 012722, SIS 19018, Tokyo-Berlin, 2 July 1941, tr. 3 July 1941.

17. Ibid.

18. SRDJ 012724, SIS 19033, Berlin-Tokyo, 2 July 1941, tr. 5 July 1941.

19. Harold L. Ickes, *The Secret Diary of Harold L. Ickes: The Lowering Clouds, 1939–1941,* (hereafter Ickes diary), pp. 552–60.

20. Ibid., pp. 564–68.

21. Ibid.

22. PHH 20/4018–19.

23. SRDJ 012722, op. cit., p. 204.

24. PHH 14/1398.

25. Ibid.

26. Ibid.

27. Ibid., p. 1399.

28. PHH 6/2512.

29. Ibid., p. 2513.

30. PHH 16/2173.

31. PHH 5/2384.

32. PHH 14/1399.
33. Ickes diary, pp. 583–84.

Chapter 10 (pages 123–130)   A Ridiculous Situation

1. PHH 14/1327.
2. McCollum OH, p. 321.
3. Ibid., p. 315.
4. Ibid., p. 320.
5. PHH 14/1398.
6. PHH 36/113–14.
7. PHH 16/2322, 36/116.
8. PHH 36/132.
9. PHH 16/2276–77.
10. Ibid.
11. PHH 7/3130.
12. PHH 16/2239.
13. Ibid., p. 2174.
14. Ibid.
15. Ibid., p. 2242.
16. Ibid., p. 2176.
17. FDR Lib.: Frankfurter papers, Box 98, 11 March 1943.
18. Public Record Office, Kew, England (hereafter PRO), Prime Minister's Files (hereafter PREM) 4, 27/9, 13 March 1941.
19. Kimball FDR/WSC R-52X, p. 229.
20. PHH 12/9.

Chapter 11 (pages 131–137)   Deceptive Deterrents

1. FRUS-DP 1941, Vol. 1, pp. 351–54.
2. NA/RG 18: Records of the Army Air Forces, entry 293, Series II classified files, 337 B Memo for Chief of Staff, "Notes on Staff Conference, 11–12 August 1941, on board *Prince of Wales*" (hereafter Argentia notes), p. 4.
3. Ibid.
4. Library of Congress, Manuscript Division, papers of General Henry H. "Hap" Arnold, transcribed diary notes (hereafter Arnold diary), 10 August 1941 entry, p. 9 and 14 August 1941 entry, p. 15.
5. Argentia notes, p. 4.
6. Arnold diary, entry 14 August 1941, p. 15.
7. FRUS-JAPAN 1941, Vol. II, p. 355.
8. NA/RG 225, records of Joint Army and Navy Boards and committees, 301 minutes (hereafter J-Bd. Min.), 4 September 1941.
9. Ibid., 13 November 1941.
10. Ibid., Statement of Admiral Ingersoll before Joint Board, November 3, 1941.
11. PRO F13114/86/32, Halifax-Foreign Secretary, 1 December 1941.
12. Hansard, 27 January 1941, p. 607.
13. Ibid.
14. FDR-Lib., Hopkins papers, Hopkins-FDR, 21 February 1942.
15. PHH 6/2513.
16. Ibid., p. 2503.

Chapter 12 (pages 138–145)   Shortchanged

1. SRDJ 014086, JD-1 21045, Washington-Tokyo, 7 August 1941, tr. 15 September 1941.

2. SRDJ 014134, SIS 2116, London-Tokyo, 8 August 1941, tr. 18 September 1941.
3. SRA 17353, Washington-Tokyo, 9 August 1941, tr. 4 May 1945.
4. SRDJ 013967, Washington-Tokyo, 9 August 1941, tr. 12 September 1941.
5. PHH 10/4832.
6. J-Bd. Min., 25 July 1941.
7. PHH 33/889.
8. PHH 9/4594.
9. PHH 3/1210.
10. PHH 5/2176.
11. Ibid., p. 2175.
12. PHH 33/883.
13. Hoehling, p. 54.
14. Ibid., p. 56.
15. PHH 33/897.
16. Ibid., p. 898.
17. PHH 4/1976.
18. Ibid., p. 1975.
19. Ibid., p. 1976.
20. Ibid.
21. Ibid.
22. McCollum OH, p. 311.
23. Ibid.
24. Ibid.

Chapter 13 (pages 146–160)   Waves of Strife

1. PHH 17/2870.
2. *Colliers,* 14 June 1941, pp. 11–78 passim.
3. Dyer papers, letter, 6 June 1983.
4. PHH 17/2874.
5. NWPD memo to Leahy, 10 August 1936, SPDR, Box 89.
6. *Washington Times-Herald,* 21 September 1941.
7. Congressional Record, Vol. 67, Pt. 7, 2 October 1941, p. 7592.
8. Carl J. Pritchard letter to Pineau, 12 January 1985.
9. PHH 16/2244.
10. PHH 14/1401.
11. NA/RG 18, Entry 293, Series II, Central Decimal Files 1939–1942, p. 281; D War Plans 1941 classified files.
12. PHH 14/1021–30.
13. Ibid., p. 1031.
14. Ibid.
15. NA/RG 18, Entry 293, Series II, WPD Classified 381.D, memorandum "Aircraft Requirements for Defense of the Western Hemisphere and American Interests in Asia," 26 August 1941.
16. PHH 3/1119.
17. Masanobu Tsuji, *Singapore: The Japanese Version* (New York: St. Martin's Press, 1960), p. 22.
18. SRDJ 014152, SIS 21151, Washington-Tokyo, 16 August 1941, tr. 19 August 1941.
19. FRUS-Japan, Vol. 1, pp. 559–65.
20. SRDJ 014203 JD-1 502, 26 August 1941, tr. 29 September 1941.
21. Takushiro Hattori, *Dai-Toa Senso Zenshi (A Complete History of the Greater East Asia War)* (hereafter Hattori), Vol. 1, pp. 178–82. This is a translation done for the U.S. Army military intelligence in 1953, Document 77510, 500th Military Intelligence Group, NA: AF-8-5.1, Vol. 1.

22. Ibid.
23. Nobutake Ike, ed., *Japan's Decision for War* (hereafter Ike), pp. 95–96.
24. Ibid., pp. 133–63.
25. PHH 20/4004.
26. Hattori, pp. 176–82.
27. PHH 20/4005.
28. Ibid.
29. Ibid.
30. Joseph C. Grew, *Ten Years in Japan* (hereafter Grew), p. 426.
31. Ibid.
32. PHH 20/4214.
33. PHH 16/2209.
34. SSS, Vol. 10, pp. 101–4.
35. Agawa, pp. 228–29.
36. Pineau interview with Fuchida, May 1950.
37. Agawa, p. 230.
38. Ibid., p. 229.
39. Hattori, Vol. 1, pp. 190–96, 281–82; and see also Robert J. C. Butow, *Tōjō and the Coming of the War* (hereafter Butow *Tōjō*), (Princeton, N.J.: Princeton University Press, 1961), p. 263.
40. SRDJ 015229, SIS 22819, Tokyo-Washington, 28 September 1941, tr. 29 September 1941.
41. SRDJ 015178, SIS 22753, Tokyo-Washington, 26 September 1941, tr. 26 November 1941.
42. SRDJ 015491, Washington-Tokyo, 3 October 1941, tr. 7 October 1941 following full report of Hull meeting in SRDJ 015436, SIS 301, 2 October 1941, tr. 6 October 1941 and Tokyo reply in SRDJ 015450, Tokyo-Washington, 3 October 1941, tr. 6 October 1941.
43. Hattori, p. 191.
44. Ibid.
45. Stimson diary, 6 October 1941.
46. SRDJ 01539, SIS 23384, Tokyo-Washington, 10 October 1941, tr. 13 October 1941.
47. Ibid.
48. Grew, p. 456.
49. SRDJ 01552 JD-1 5779, Tokyo-Washington, 13 October 1941, tr. 13 October 1941.
50. Hattori, p. 197.
51. PHH 14/1402.
52. PHH 16/2212.
53. Ibid., p. 2213.
54. PHH 32/191.
55. Ibid.
56. PHH 16/2249.
57. Ibid., p. 2219.

Chapter 14 (pages 161–168)   Affirmative Misrepresentation

1. Interview with Tachibana cited by Gordon W. Prange, *At Dawn We Slept* (hereafter Prange), p. 248.
2. PHH 12/261.
3. Ibid., p. 262.
4. SRH 012, "The Role of Communications Intelligence in the American Japanese Naval War," 4 Vols., Vol. 1, "Diplomatic Background to Pearl Harbor," 1 August 1942 (hereafter SRH 012), pp. 137–202.

5. SRDJ 014545, SIS 21769, Tokyo-Washington, 2 September 1941, tr. 4 September 1941.

6. SRH 012, p. 141.

7. SRDJ 015132, SIS 22697, Honolulu-Tokyo, 4 September 1941, tr. 26 September 1941.

8. PHH 9/4196.

9. Ibid.

10. PHH 2/795.

11. Ibid.

12. PHH 9/4534.

13. Ibid.

14. PHH 5/2175.

15. PHH 4/1922.

16. RADM Alan G. Kirk Oral History transcript, Columbia University (hereafter Kirk OH), p. 179.

17. Rochefort papers, Wilkinson-Rochefort, 14 November 1941.

18. Kimmel papers, "The Bomb Plot Revised," draft apparently prepared from Safford's information by Commander C. C. Hiles.

19. PHH 4/1747.

20. Ibid., p. 1749.

21. SRDJ 017188, JD-1 6991, Tokyo-Honolulu, 15 November 1941, tr. 3 December 1941.

22. SRDJ 017270, JD-1 7063, Tokyo-Honolulu, 18 November 1941, tr. 5 December 1941.

23. SRDJ 017331, JD-1 17086, Tokyo-Honolulu, 20 November 1941, tr. 5 December 1941; SRDJ 017311, JD-1 17086, Tokyo-Honolulu, 29 November 1941, tr. 5 December 1941.

24. J-Bd. Min., 12 July 1941; letter from secretary of war-president, 27 September 1941 endorsed "Not Used."

25. PHH 2/911.

26. PHH 34/59.

27. PHH 6/2543.

28. Ibid., p. 2540.

29. Ibid.

Chapter 15 (pages 169–180)   Imperfect Threats

1. PHH 16/2214.

2. PHH 12/76.

3. PHH 4/1946.

4. PHH 16/2216.

5. Ibid., pp. 2214–15.

6. PHH 3/1120.

7. J-Bd. Min., 19 September 1941.

8. PHH 3/1119.

9. Ibid., p. 1167.

10. NA/RG 107: Formerly top secret correspondence of Secretary of War Stimson ("Safe File") July 1940-September 1945; Folder: White House Correspondence, Stimson to president, 21 October 1941 (hereafter Stimson Safe File).

11. FDR-Lib., Private Secretary's File (hereafter PSF), Stimson file.

12. NA/RG 165: Army Chief of Staff, memorandum for secretary of war from acting assistant chief of staff, "Strategic Concept of the Philippine Islands," 8 October 1941.

13. Ibid., memorandum "Strategic Air Offensive Against Japan" for General Marshall, 19 November 1941 (hereafter SAO-Japan).

14. Stimson memo to president, 21 October 1941, op. cit.
15. PHH 3/1167.
16. Ibid.
17. Stimson memo to president, 21 October 1941, op. cit.
18. Agawa, p. 232.
19. Ibid., p. 235.
20. Ibid., p. 237.
21. Ibid.
22. SSS, Vol. 10, pp. 225–26.
23. PHH 35/63.
24. Ibid.
25. Com 14 Japan-espionage investigation.
26. Ibid.
27. SRDJ 016190, SIS 24292, Tokyo-Washington, 2 November 1941, tr. 3 November 1941.
28. PHH 14/1052.
29. J-Bd., Min., 3 November 1941.
30. Ibid.
31. Ibid.
32. Ibid.
33. PHH 16/2222.
34. Ibid.
35. SRDJ 015226, SIS 22814, Washington to San Francisco, Los Angeles, Seattle consulates, 4 September 1941, tr. 29 September 1941. For Tokyo's concern about American bombers see also SRDJ 016786, Washington-Tokyo, 19 October 1941, tr. 20 November 1941 querying bombers sent to Russia via Persia. SRDJ 016587, SIS 24850, Manila-Tokyo, 10 November 1941, tr. 17 November 1941 reporting the arrival of more four-engine bombers, and SRDJ 016890, Tokyo-Manila, 15 November 1941, tr. 24 November 1941 "ascertain what route large bombers went to Philippines."
36. SAO-Japan, op. cit.
37. PRO Prem 3, 183/2, memo first Sea Lord, 29 August 1941.
38. Kimball WSC/FDR, c-125X, p. 265.
39. Ibid.
40. PRO Prem 3, 163/3, prime minister South Africa to WSC, 16 November 1941.
41. PHH 12/97.
42. Ibid., p. 92.
43. Ibid., p. 94.
44. Ibid., p. 98.
45. Ibid., pp. 99–100.
46. Ibid., p. 100.
47. PHH 2/429.
48. PHH 16/2219.
49. PHH 14/1403.
50. PHH 16/2220.

Chapter 16 (pages 181–188) "What Will We Do?"

1. PHH 16/2251.
2. Ibid., p. 2252.
3. PHH 17/2607.
4. Ibid., p. 2606.
5. Ibid., pp. 2608, 2615.
6. Ibid., p. 2614.

7. Ibid., p. 2616.
8. Ibid., p. 2620.
9. Ibid., p. 2621.
10. NA/RG 80: PHLO, and originals of Layton intelligence summaries and original reports located in boxes 40, 41, 42, 48, 49, and 63 (hereafter PHLO-ETL).
11. Ibid., and PHH 10/4834.
12. Ibid.
13. Ibid., p. 4836.
14. Ibid.
15. PHH 10/4834–35.
16. Ibid.
17. Ibid., p. 4834.
18. PHH 17/2623.
19. PHLO-ETL, and PHH 17/2623.
20. PHH 10/4836.
21. PHH 16/2220.
22. Ibid., p. 2223.
23. Ibid., p. 2253.
24. Ibid., p. 2223.
25. PHH 10/4886.
26. PHH 14/1405.
27. PHH 36/144.
28. Ibid., p. 145.
29. PHH 14/1106.
30. PHH 5/2306, 2319.
31. PHH 16/2224–25.
32. Ibid.

Chapter 17 (pages 189–197)   Negotiations On

1. *The New York Times,* 10 November 1941.
2. SRDJ 016641, SIS 168, Tokyo-San Francisco, 10 November 1941, tr. 18 November 1941.
3. SRDJ 016514, JD-1 6417, Tokyo-Washington, 11 November 1941, tr. 12 November 1941.
4. SRDJ 016626, JD-1 6559, Washington-Tokyo, 13 November 1941, tr. 17 November 1941.
5. SRDJ 016772, JD-1 1106, Washington-Tokyo, 15 November 1941, tr. 19 November 1941.
6. SRDJ 016598, JD-1 6553, Washington-Tokyo, 14 November 1941, tr. 17 November 1941.
7. SRDJ 016576, JD-1 6254, Tokyo-Washington, 15 November 1941, tr. 15 November 1941.
8. SRDJ 016617, JD-1 6556, Tokyo-Washington, 15 November 1941, tr. 17 November 1941.
9. SRDJ 016844, JD-1 6721, Washington-Tokyo, 17 November 1941, tr. 22 November 1941.
10. Ibid.
11. FDR-Lib. PSF 141: COI, Donovan—Whitney-Donovan telegram 5392, 12 November 1941.
12. PRO Foreign Office 12475, 86/23, Halifax-foreign office, 17 November 1941.
13. FRUS-DP 1941, Vol. IV, pp. 606–13.
14. Ibid., Vol. II, p. 755*f.*

15. SRDJ 016777, SIS 25806, Washington-Tokyo, 18 November 1941, tr. 21 November 1941.

16. SRDJ 016823, JD-1 6735, Tokyo-Washington, 18 November 1941, tr. 22 November 1941, and SRDJ 016875 of 19 November 1941, tr. 24 November 1941.

17. PHH 12/155.

18. Ibid., p. 158.

19. SRDJ 016855, SIS 25716, Washington-Tokyo, 24 November 1941, tr. 24 November 1945.

20. Ibid.

21. SRDJ 016816, JD-1 6742, Tokyo-Washington, 22 November 1941, tr. 22 November 1941.

22. Ibid.

23. PHLO Hull written testimony, p. 114 Hull; and PHH 2/554.

24. FRUS-DP 1941, Vol. II, p. 755.

25. Kimmel papers, the text of Hornbeck-Hull and Hull-Hornbeck exchange given in letter to Joseph C. Grew, 14 October 1955 from Max Bishop (before he became U.S. ambassador to Thailand). He had been attached to U.S. embassy Tokyo and in 1941 was a State Department aide who "kept the files of all American-Japanese conversations during the summer and fall of 1941." Bishop records how he was "directed" to "return to Hornbeck his 'personal' memoranda. . . . These two were included in that category. However, because of their historical significance I felt they should not disappear into the incinerator. Virginia Collins, who you will recall used to be with us in Tokyo, was in the Department at the time and made copies for me. The original [sic] were given to Hornbeck and are either in his files or destroyed. They were seen by Max Hamilton, by Joe Ballantine and myself in addition to, of course, Hornbeck and Secretary Hull."

26. Ibid.

27. Ibid.

28. SRDJ 016851, SIS 25177, Tokyo-Washington, 24 November 1941, tr. 24 November 1941.

29. Kimball WSC/FDR, R-69X, pp. 275–76.

30. PHLO: Contains two typewritten drafts of the Stimson diary: (1) A running abbreviated version (hereafter PHLO-Stimson A) and (2) full version similar to the Yale collection (hereafter PHLO-Stimson B). Gist the same, although wording sometimes differ. (A) 25 November 1941, p. 46.

31. Ibid., p. 47.

32. Ibid.

33. PHLO-Stimson B, p. 15.

34. PHLO-Hull-Hornbeck memorandum of conversation 24 November 1941 dated 25 November 1941.

35. PHH 14/1194.

36. PHLO-Hull memo of conversations with Chinese ambassador, 25 November 1941.

37. Ibid.

38. Ibid.

Chapter 18 (pages 198–207)   Negotiations Off

1. SRDJ 017036, Washington-Tokyo, 26 November 1941, tr. 28 November 1941.

2. PHLO-Stimson A, 26 November 1941, p. 49.

3. PRO Prem 3, 156/6, Minute-Foreign Secretary, 23 November 1941.

4. Ibid.

5. PRO FO 371, file 35957, Sir Robert Craigie's report, file dockets 22 August 1943.

6. Ibid.; and WSC Secret Minute-Foreign Secretary, 19 September 1943.

7. Winston Churchill, *The Second World War: The Grand Alliance* (hereafter WSC-Vol. III), p. 502.

8. Kimmel papers: Bishop-Grew letter of 14 October 1955 quoting information given him "the other day" by Landreth Harrison (until July 1941, he was second secretary at U.S. embassy Berlin): "It was just a day or so before November 26 when Harrison was in Mr. Hull's office and Hull was summoned by private telephone to the White House. He asked Harrison to wait in the office for he, Secretary Hull, expected to return immediately. The Secretary was gone only 15 minutes or so and came back in a very agitated frame of mind. He said something like this:

> Those madmen over there (White House—he may have used the [sic] term "madmen" but Harrison doesn't want to go that far) do not believe me when I tell them that the Japs will attack us. . . . You cannot give an ultimatum to a powerful and proud people and not expect them to react violently.

For contemporary confirmation of Hull's determination to achieve a *modus vivendi* see Robert Sherwood, *Roosevelt and Hopkins,* p. 428 quoting Hopkins's memorandum of events: "It is true that Hull told the Secretaries of War and Navy that he believed Japan might attack at any moment. On the other hand, up to the very last day, he undoubtedly had hopes that something could be worked out at the last moment. Hull had always been willing to work out a deal with Japan. . . . Hull wanted peace above everything, because he had set his heart on making an adjustment with the Japanese and had worked on it night and day for weeks. There was no question that up until the last ten days prior to the outbreak of war he was in hopes that some adjustment could be worked out."

9. Kimmel papers: Bishop letter quoting Hull-Hornbeck exchange of 27 November 1941.

10. Ibid.

11. Ibid.

12. PHLO-Stimson A, 26 November 1941 entry, p. 49.

13. Ibid., p. 50.

14. Ibid.

15. Ibid., 25 November 1941, p. 48.

16. Ibid.

17. Stimson Safe File, 25 November 1941 letter to White House, Watson 27 November 1941 note, and British 21 November 1941 Joint Intelligence Committee enclosed with same fold creases in Philippines folder.

18. Ibid.

19. Ibid., and White House folder, copy marked "For complete file see White House" was "hand delivered by Sergeant Quick 1225 Nov 26 1941." Original in FDR-Lib. Stimson correspondence file.

20. Ibid.

21. Ibid.

22. PHH 3/1444.

23. PHH 32/732.

24. Ibid.

25. PHH 3/1404-14.

26. PHH 5/2304.

27. H. Montgomery Hyde, *Room 3603* (London, 1962), p. 293; and Sir W. Stephenson-Costello telegram, 28 February 1982.

28. PRO Prem 3/469, and WSC-FDR and covering letters.

29. PRO Prem 3/2526/6B, closed index note; correspondence: minister of state for defense-Anthony Grant MP, 7 December 1979; and Cabinet office-J. Costello, 1 and 29 September 1983.

30. SRA 17952, Tokyo-Bangkok, 25 November 1941, tr. 20 June 1945.

31. SRH 154: "Signal Intelligence Disclosures in the Pearl Harbor Investigation," p. 33, and PHH 11/5179.

32. Michael Montgomery, *Who Sank the Sydney* (London, 1982), *q.v.* details, accounts and references.

33. RAAF reports as cited p. 173.

34. SRN 115385, Tokyo-AU Fleets, 20 November 1941.

35. F. H. Hinsley et al., *British Intelligence in the Second World War* (hereafter Hinsley), Vol. 1, p. 53*n*.

36. Robert Haslach, *Nishi no Kaze Hare* (*West Wind Clear*) (Netherlands: Urieboek, 1985) for background on Dutch intelligence in Far East prior to World War II. Royal Netherlands Army Archives (hereafter NAA), Captain J. W. Henning, chief cryptanalyst, Kamer 14, Bandoeing (hereafter Henning report), dated 11 March 1965.

37. NAA Ter Poorten letter, 23 July 1960.

38. Dr. L.G.M. Jaquet, *Aflossing van de Wacht* (Rotterdam, 1980) and letter to James Rushbridger, 22 June 1985.

39. PHH 13/414–18.

40. Henning report.

Chapter 19 (pages 208–213) "Future Action Unpredictable"

1. FDR-Lib., Morgenthau diary, 26 November 1941, p. 1020 (hereafter Morgenthau diary).

2. PHH 5/2319–22.

3. NA/RG 165: WDCSA/381 minutes, "Conference in the Office of the Chief of Staff 10:40 am, November 29, 1941."

4. Ibid.

5. Ibid.

6. J-Bd.-Min., 26 November 1941.

7. Ibid.

8. Nav. Op. Archives: Hart papers—handwritten "Private Diary Dec. 29, 1940-Dec. 26, 1941":

> 25 November: Today, I learn from Washington—straight from the horse's mouth—that the tension between the Japanese and ourselves is very far from having eased up. It's quite the reverse and I'm told that the barometer is so very low that the storm pretty much *must* break, somewhere. . . .
>
> 27 November: The plot grows thicker and thicker—today our communication system brought Sayre *his* war warning right straight from the very biggest horse's mouth [Hart's testimony referred to Philippine Commissioner Francis Sayre's cable from Roosevelt warning "that this next Japanese aggression might cause an outbreak of hostilities between the United States and Japan" (PHH 11/5214)].

9. Opnav 271442 November 1941, PHLO box 45, and *Magic Background* A, p. 109.

10. Ibid.

11. PHLO Stimson diary A, 27 November 1941, p. 51.

12. PHH 14/1083.

13. Ibid.

14. PHLO Stimson diary A, 27 November 1941, p. 52.

15. Ibid.

16. PHH 14/1407.

17. PHH 32/234.

18. Ibid.

19. PHH 4/1916, 2001.

20. SRDJ 016976, JD-1 6843, transpacific telephone call transcript, 26 November 1941.

21. Ibid.

22. SSS, Vol. 10, p. 269, and Onishi diary, entry 28 November 1941.

23. Ibid., and Fujita diary, entry 28 November 1941.

24. Agawa, p. 244.

25. Ibid.

26. SSS, Vol. 10, p. 268.

Chapter 20 (pages 214–221)   Going to Be a Fight

1. PHH 6/2519.

2. William F. Halsey and Joseph Bryan III, *Admiral Halsey's Story* (hereafter *Halsey's Story*), pp. 73–75.

3. Opnav, 27 November 1941, PHLO box 45.

4. PHH 14/1407.

5. PHH 36/115.

6. PHH 7/2943.

7. Ibid., p. 3029.

8. PHH 10/4938.

9. PHH 14/1328.

10. PHH 11/5429.

11. PHH 14/1329.

12. Ibid.

13. PHH 3/1421.

14. PHH 14/1405.

15. PHH 26/280.

16. PHH 14/407.

17. PHH 16/2278.

18. PHH 14/1405.

19. PHH 6/2518.

20. PHH 32/234.

21. Ibid.

22. PHH 16/2223.

23. PHH 12/154.

24. Ibid., p. 155.

25. PHH 17/2659.

26. SRDJ 017048, JD-1 6895, Tokyo-Washington, 28 November 1941, tr. 28 November 1941.

27. PHLO-Stimson diary A, p. 53.

28. Ibid.

29. Ibid.

30. Ibid.

31. SSS, Vol. 10, p. 269.

32. Ibid.

33. Robert Haslach: Paper delivered to 1983 naval history symposium at Annapolis, citing research and information from Record Group 36: Bureau of Customs, Los Angeles Collection, International Port of Los Angeles, "Records of Entrances and Clearances of Vessels Engaged in Foreign Trade 1897–1957," box 67. See also evidence of Russian sailing from San Francisco in the transportation section of *The San Francisco Chronicle* for 26-28 November 1941 citing 27 November 1941 for mail for vessel departing Soviet Union.

34. SRH 012, p. 162.

Chapter 21 (pages 222–235) Self-Deception

1. *Halsey's Story,* pp. 75–76.
2. PHH 16/2276.
3. PHH 23/1137.
4. PHH 16/2276.
5. PHLO-ETL.
6. PHH 36/149; Com 14 260110 November 1941.
7. PHH 36/159–60.
8. PHH 6/2431.
9. Ibid., p. 2535.
10. PHH 33/709.
11. PHH 6/2535.
12. Ibid., pp. 2535–36.
13. PHH 17/2632.
14. PHH 36/126.
15. *The New York Times,* 13 March 1982: "We kept absolute radio silence," said the former Commander Genda who helped plan the attack. For about two weeks before the attack the thirty-one ships "used flag and light signals," Mr. Genda, seventy-seven, said in an interview. Former Lieutenant Commander Chuichi Yoshoka, seventy-three, who was the communications officer on the flagship *Akagi,* said he did not recall any ship dispatching a radio message before the attack.
16. PHH 17/2666.
17. Ibid., p. 2667.
18. PHH 36/37.
19. A memo, pp. 14–15, referring to Navy Department Secret Publication CSP 1494A, which appeared under signature of Vice-Admiral F. J. Horne, sponsored by the Redmans, dated 15 April 1942, especially pp. 6–8 captioned: "Did the Japanese Paint Us a 'Picture.'" According to the well-informed author of the A Memorandum:

> The main effect (if not the intended purpose) of this particular story was to make the service believe that the old lie was actually true—that Rochefort, Huckins and Williams had been sucked in by Japanese radio deception. . . . Rochefort and the other officers at Pearl Harbor took offense at the contemptible way in which their reputations had been smeared. . . . There were *no* dummy messages on Japanese naval radio circuits *at any time* during 1941. There was one "High Command Cipher" used throughout 1941 and most of 1942 that neither we nor the British ever succeeded in solving. (Otherwise Cincpac would have had a tipoff of the Pearl Harbor raid that *no one* in Washington would have blocked.) No responsible person in the C. I. Organization ever believed that the messages in this system were "dummies." A partial solution by the British confirmed our earlier estimate. The Japs sometimes sent test or drill messages (their alphabet, for instance) but these were readily identified by our intercept operations.

20. PHH 36/128.
21. PHLO-ETL papers, Radio Intelligence Summaries, p. 18.
22. Ibid.
23. W. J. Holmes, *Double-Edged Secrets* (hereafter Holmes), p. 18; Wright interview, 15 March 1985.
24. SSS, Vol. 10, p. 270.
25. SRN 115428, Com Fleet to all flagships, 17 November 1941.
26. Dundas P. Tucker, "Rhapsody in Purple," *Cryptologia,* July 1982, p. 223.
27. The A Memorandum indicates that 50 percent of JN-25 was being read in 1941, but both Dyer and Wright believed that their opposite numbers in Washington and Cavite could not decipher more than 15 percent of the traffic. In the

absence of any actual decrypts, the most accurate record is that of Safford himself, who in May 1945 (PHLO box 49) produced a memorandum for Lieutenant Commander John F. Sonnet, the investigator of Admiral Hewitt's inquiry: "Evaluation of Messages, 26 November 1941":

> Com 16's estimates were more reliable than Com 14's not only because of better radio interception but because *Com 16 was currently reading messages in the Japanese Fleet's Cryptographic System ("5 number code" or "JN-25") and was exchanging technical information and translations with the British CI Unit at Singapore.* . . . The major project of the 14th Naval District CI Unit in November 1941 was to attack the Japanese Flag Officers Cryptographic system (transposition cipher) superposed [sic] on a 4 character code—I think we called it "AD"—in which they were being backed up by a similar attack in the Navy Department. This system (its earlier editions) had been our main source of information on the Japanese navy from 1926–27 up until November 1940. It was the most difficult, as well as the most important, system the Japanese navy was using and our most skilled and most experienced officers and men were attempting its solution.
>
> If we could have solved the flag-officers' system, Admiral Kimmel would probably have known of the Japanese plans and the Pacific fleet would not have been surprised on 7 December 1941. Unfortunately, neither the US navy nor the British cryptanalysts ever succeeded in cracking this system. The "5 numeral" system yielded no information which would arouse even a suspicion of the Pearl Harbor raid, either before or afterward. The Japanese abandoned the "AD" system in 1942 or 1943, apparently because of extensive delays and unreadable messages. As regards the "JN-25" or "5-numeral" system, the current code (JN-25B) had been in effect since 1 December 1940, remaining in effect until 27–31 May 1942, and *was partly readable in November 1941.* A new system of keys was introduced on 4 December 1941 and reported by Com 16 041502, but the carry-over of the old code made their solution quite simple, and we were reading messages again by Christmas, Corregidor getting the actual break on 8 December 1941. The Hawaiian CI unit did not commence work on the Japanese navy's "5-digit" system until 10 December 1941, at which date they discontinued their attack on the "flag officers" system. (The Navy Department continued its attack on the flag officers system as long as it remained in use.) [Emphases added].

28. Goodwin letter, 22 May 1985.

29. SRN 115380, Min. Navy to All Ships, 14 November 1941.

30. SRN 115491, Tokyo to Section, 15 November 1941.

31. SRN 115468, Comb. Fleet Sec. to All Fleet Secs., 16 November 1941.

32. SRN 115478, Desdiv 34 Com to Comb. Fleet Sec., 19 November 1941.

33. SRN 115491, Cardivs. Comb. Fleet to Comb. Fleet COS, 19 November 1941.

34. SRN 115375, *Shiya* to COS Cardivs Comb. Fleet, 20 November 1941.

35. SRN 115438, Hainan Guard District to Takao (Formosa), report of "factual case of leakage of secret information," 20 November 1941.

36. SRN 115385, Comb. Fleet CinC to Cardivs and expeditionary fleets: "At 000 on 21 November, repeat 21 November, carry out second phase of preparations for opening hostilities," 20 November 1941.

37. SRN 115435, 4th Fleet CinC to Crudiv 6, 29 November 1941.

38. SRN 115404–5, 115419–20, 115428–34.

39. SRN 115561, Kita to Tokyo, 27 November 1941.

40. PHH 10/4885.

Chapter 22 (pages 236–298)   Countdown to War

1. SSS, Vol. 10, p. 269.
2. Ibid., p. 270.
3. Ibid.
4. Ibid.
5. PHH 17/2664.
6. SRDJ 017113, SIS 2553, Tokyo-Berlin, 30 November 1941, tr. 1 December 1941.
7. SRDJ 017159, JD-1 6903, Tokyo-Washington, 1 December 1941, tr. 1 December 1941.
8. PHH 12/266.
9. SRDJ 017106, JD-1 6939, Tokyo-Washington, 1 December 1941, tr. 1 December 1941.
10. PHH 15/1840.
11. Ibid., p. 1842.
12. PHH 8/3385.
13. FDR-Lib., Morgenthau diary, p. 1036.
14. PRO Prem 3, 156/5, London-Halifax, 29 November 1941.
15. Ibid.
16. Ibid., Halifax-London, 1 December 1941, F13114.
17. Sugiyama 1:539–44; Ike, pp. 162–268.
18. Ibid.
19. Hattori, p. 457.
20. SRN 115376, CinC Comb. Fleet to Comb. Fleet 12/021500 December 1941.
21. SSS, Vol. 10, p. 267.
22. Ibid., p. 272.
23. PHLO-ETL, RI summary, 2 December 1941.
24. Rochefort papers; handwritten letter, envelope marked "SECRET To be opened only by Lt. Commander Rochefort, District Communications Officer."
25. PHH 26/336.
26. Dyer letter was of 4 June 1983.
27. PHH 26/226.
28. PHH 35/206; and R. T. Crowley interview, 1984.
29. PHH 16/2255.
30. Ibid., p. 2256.
31. Ibid.
32. PHH 11/5427.
33. Hoehling, p. 101.
34. Gallup survey as quoted in Robert Dallek, *Franklin D. Roosevelt and American Foreign Policy* (hereafter Dallek), p. 310.
35. PHLO box 45: Dispatches: Opnav-Cincaf 2 December 1941.
36. Ibid.
37. PHLO box 45, Opnav-Cincaf, 300419 November 1941.
38. PHLO box 45, CNO, 012358 December 1941.
39. PHLO box 45, Cincaf, 021320 December 1941.
40. Kemp Tolley, *The Cruise of the Lanikai* (Annapolis, Md.: USNIP, 1973), pp. 268–80.
41. Ibid., p. 71.
42. PRO Prem 3,165/5, Halifax-London.
43. Ibid., mins. of War Cabinet Defense Committee (Operations), 3 December 1941.
44. Ibid., London-Halifax, 3 December 1941, FO 1316/56/23.
45. International Military Tribunal for the Far East, "Transcript of Proceedings," pp. 420–21 (hereafter IMTFE).

46. Ibid., pp. 10830–49.

47. SRN 116741, Navy min. to commanders, 2 December 1941.

48. PHLO box 45, Opnav 031855, which derived from Magics: SRDJ 017160, JD-1 6984, Tokyo-Washington, 1 December 1941, tr. 1 December 1941; SRDJ 017287, JD-1 7091, Tokyo-London, 1 December 1941, tr. 5 November 1941, and SRDJ 017184, JD-1 7017, Tokyo-Washington, 3 December 1941, tr. 3 December 1941.

49. PHH 36/137.

50. Ibid.

51. PHH 6/2764.

52. PHH 36/137.

53. PHH 22/379.

54. PHH 5/2131.

55. PHH 9/4233.

56. PHH 4/2002.

57. McCollum OH, p. 384; PHH 9/4240.

58. McCollum OH, p. 329.

59. PHH 26/3921.

60. Ibid.

61. PHH 36/283.

62. PHH 11/5284.

63. Ibid.

64. PRO F113114/86/23, 3 December 1941 telegram, Halifax-London.

65. FDR-Lib., Morgenthau diary, p. 1067.

66. Gwen Terasaki, *Bridge to the Sun*, pp. 66–69.

67. SRDJ 017324, JD-1 017324, Rome-Tokyo, 3 December 1941, tr. 6 December 1941.

68. SRDJ 01732, JD-1 017323, Berlin-Tokyo, 3 December 1941, tr. 6 December 1941.

69. Agawa, p. 246.

70. SSS, Vol. 10, p. 273.

71. Ibid.

72. Ibid., p. 274.

73. Rochefort papers: "Station H Chronology," dated 1 December 1943 [sic].

74. SRH 012, p. 184: Opnav-Cincpac, 042017.

75. PHH 6/2765.

76. PHH 8/3413.

77. McCollum OH, p. 335.

78. PHH 10/4637.

79. PRO Halifax to FO 4 December 1941, F13114/86/32.

80. Nav.Op. Archives, Hart papers, private diary, entry 26/27 November 1941.

81. Ibid.

82. PHH 10/5083.

83. Opnav 124.

84. PHH 10/4802.

85. Ibid.

86. PHH 10/4812.

87. SSS, Vol. 10, p. 275.

88. Agawa, p. 251.

89. Haslach op. cit.

90. Ibid.

91. Matson Navigation Company Collection: Leslie E. Grogan journal, and see also *Ships in Gray*, the story of the Matson Line in World War II *(Infamy,* p. 351).

92. SRH 255, interview with Robert D. Ogg.
93. Ibid., p. 54.
94. Ibid., pp. 35–36.
95. Ibid., p. 53.
96. Haslach op. cit.
97. PHH 36/139.
98. PHH 26/345.
99. SRH 210: "Collection of Papers Related to 'Winds Execute' Message, US Navy 1945," p. 65.
100. SRDJ 017025, JD-1 6875, Tokyo-Washington, 19 November 1941.
101. PHLO Safford/Kramer correspondence; letters dated 22 December 1943 and questionnaire of 22 December 1943 with Safford's comments, 22 January 1944.
102. Rochefort papers: carbon copy of "Streamlined Index of Translations and Memoranda Re Pearl Harbor (1941)," marked SECRET and evidently compiled from the existing OP-20-G diplomatic file in September 1944 when Rochefort, then attached to OP-20-G, made a personal search for this material at the orders of the Director of Naval Communications in compliance with a War Department request for "any written record of the winds execute message." (Memorandum prepared by Safford dated 1 February 1945 in PHLO: Safford file.) See also in PHLO Top Secret-Ultra memorandum, "JD-1: 7001, special studies concerning," dated 8 November 1941 and attachments. These detail conclusions of Lieutenant Sally T. Lightle to find the "missing" winds message at the behest of congressional investigators. "From this study it would appear that JD-1: 7001, if it was assigned to a translation, was for a message dated 28 November 1941, translated on either 2 December 1941 or 3 December 1941 by the Army." Her investigation supported the navy department's "official" contention that the number was not used, or if it was, could not have been assigned on 4 or 5 December 1941. The testimony of Mrs. Eunice Willson Rice, however, who was responsible for keeping the JD intercept file for Kramer (see Authors' Notes on east winds rain controversy), suggests it was.
103. SRH 081: "US Army Investigations into the Handling of Certain Communications Prior to the Attack on Pearl Harbor." See transcript of testimony of Colonel Otis K. Sadtler to Clarke Investigation, 15 September 1944, p. 2:

> The first information that I had regarding any new developments on that message [east wind rain] was on the morning of December 5, when Adm. Noyes called me and said, "Sadtler, the message is in" or words to that effect.

For more details see Authors' Notes on "east wind rain" controversy.
104. PHLO: Memorandum Safford to Admiral Hewitt, subject "Pearl Harbor Investigation—My testimony given this date" 22 June 1945:

> The winds "execute" message which passed through my hands on the morning of 4 December 1941 was a teletype copy (typed on yellow teletype paper) of the entire Japanese broadcast about 200 or 300 words long. Three significant words (Kita, Higashi, and Nishi) appeared and they were in Japanese. Kramer's translation appeared in pencil, or colored crayons, at the bottom of the sheet. There was very little chance of confusion.

See Authors' Notes on "east wind rain" and Sadtler's testimony for the rationale that Safford must have confused 4th and 5th.
105. PHLO-Safford: comment by Safford on Kramer questionnaire dated 22 January 1944, p. 10.
106. Ibid.
107. PHH 26/394.
108. PHH 33/905.
109. Ibid.

110. PHH 10/4629.

111. Ibid.

112. Ibid.

113. Ibid., p. 3646.

114. Ibid.

115. Ibid., p. 4630.

116. Ibid., p. 4635.

117. Ibid., p. 4637.

118. PHH 9/4347.

119. PHH Turner 4/1963.

120. PHH 9/4269.

121. Hoehling, pp. 106–7.

122. Ibid.

123. PHH 26/393.

124. Ibid.

125. Ibid.

126. PHLO-Kramer/Safford correspondence, letter dated 22 January 1941.

127. PHH 8/3390.

128. Hoehling, p. 107.

129. PHH 8/3388.

130. McCollum OH, p. 333.

131. PHH 8/3388.

132. PHH 4/1970.

133. Ibid., and Hoehling, p. 106.

134. PHH 8/3388.

135. PHLO east wind rain message investigation for answers given to navy investigators by radiomen in charge of the intercept stations when asked "Did you know anything about the "winds message?":

"No, I did not know anything about this message until I read about it in the newspapers": Truett C. Lusk, Port Blakely, Washington.

"No, not until I read about it in the newspapers": P. W. Wigle, Cheltenham, Maryland.

"I did not know about this 'winds' code until I read about it in the newspapers": Max C. Gunn, Winter Harbor, Maine.

"No, I did not know about this 'winds' code until I read about it in the newspapers": W. J. Edens, Jupiter, Florida.

"No, I did not know about this 'winds' code until I read about it in the newspapers": E. J. Fowles, Jupiter, Florida.

This surprisingly uniform ignorance of the "winds" code conflicts with the specific instructions that had been issued to all these radiomen in charge to listen out for all weather broadcasts.

136. PHLO Lieutenant Baecher to SecNav, 13 February 1946, SO/1083A.

137. SRDJ 017328, JD-1 7136, Washington-Tokyo, 5 December 1941, tr. 6 December 1941.

138. SRDJ 017332, JD-1 7141, Washington-Tokyo, 5 December 1941, tr. 6 December 1941 in reply to SRDJ 017331, JD-1 7140, Tokyo-Washington, 5 December 1941.

139. SRDJ 107355, SIS 25848, Washington-Tokyo, 3 December 1941.

140. Ibid.

141. Hoehling, p. 102.

142. SRDJ 017334, JD-1 7139, Washington-Tokyo, 5 December 1941, tr. 6 December 1941.

143. Ibid.

144. Hull memoirs, p. 1093.

145. University of Columbia Oral History Project, interview with Frances Perkins (hereafter Perkins OH).

146. Ibid.

147. NA/RG 59: State Department; secretary of state confidential file (711-94); typewritten draft of thirty pages, pencil note "About Dec 5, 1941," p. 14.

148. Ibid., p. 30.

149. Ibid., pp. 23, 24.

150. SRN 115371, CinC Comb. Fleet-Comb. Fleet, 7 December 1941.

151. SRN 115367, CinC 6th Fleet relayed from Submarine *I-72,* 12/07 1450.

152. SSS, Vol. 10, p. 277.

153. SRN 115377, Chief of Naval Section IHQ-Commands 12/07 1800.

154. PHH 36/141.

155. PHH 10/4896.

156. Ibid., and PHH 14/1409.

157. PHH 35/274–75.

158. PHH 29/1666.

159. PHH 31/3188–89.

160. PHH 28/1542, and PHH 27/738.

161. PHH 36/350.

162. PHH 23/674.

163. Capt. Wesley A. Wright interview, 20 April 1985.

164. SRH A 012, p. 1941 as noted against Tokyo-Honolulu, 2 December 1941 translated by army on 30 December 1941: "This message was received in Washington on December 23."

165. SRDJ 017616, JD-1 7370, Honolulu-Tokyo, 3 December 1941, tr. 11 December 1941.

166. SRDJ 017633, JD-1 7381, Tokyo-Honolulu, 6 December 1941, tr. 12 December 1941.

167. SRDJ 017383, JD-1 7179, Honolulu-Tokyo, 6 December 1941, tr. 8 December 1941.

168. SSRDJ 017305, JD-1 7062, Tokyo-Honolulu, 18 November 1941, tr. 6 December 1941.

169. SRDJ 017188, JD-1 6991, Honolulu-Tokyo, 15 November 1941, tr. 3 December 1941.

170. SRDJ 017270, JD-1 7063, Tokyo-Honolulu, 18 November 1941, tr. 5 December 1941.

171. SRDJ 017209, JD-1 7029, Tokyo-Honolulu, 20 November 1941, tr. 4 December 1941; and SRDJ 017311, JD-1 7086, Tokyo-Honolulu, 29 November 1941, tr. 29 November 1941.

172. SRH 012, pp. 186–87.

173. PHH 36/303–4.

174. Fred C. Woodrough, Jr., interview, 8 June 1984.

175. Ibid.

176. PHH 36/304.

177. Woodrough interview.

178. PHH 9/4171.

179. Ibid.

180. Woodrough interview.

181. Ibid.

182. Ibid.

183. PHLO-Kramer file, Kramer memo dated 16 January [1946] to "Baecher re my N.Y. activities"; and Rear Admiral Robert Weeks interview, June 1983.

184. Ibid.

185. Ibid.

186. SRDJ 017350, JD-1 7144, Tokyo-Washington, 6 December 1941, tr. 6 December 1941.

187. PHH 14/1413–15.

188. PHH 29/2399.

189. Hoehling, p. 130.

190. Vice Admiral Frank E. Beatty, "The Background of the Secret Report," *National Review,* 13 December 1966, p. 1261 (hereafter Beatty report); and Hoehling, p. 59.

191. PHH 29/2395–2400.

192. SRH 012, p. 185, Opnav-Cincpac 06 17.43., 4 December 1941.

193. PHH 36/356.

194. Hoehling, p. 130.

195. PRO Prem 3, 158/6, Halifax-Foreign Office #5653, 6 December 1941; prime minister's minute for foreign secretary and chiefs of staff, 7 December 1941, "Noon."

196. Ibid.

197. PHH 2/931.

198. PHLO-Stimson diary A, 6 December 1941, p. 58.

199. FDR-Lib., Harold D. Smith diary, 6 December 1941.

200. Sherwood, p. 427.

201. Ibid.

202. PHH 11/5166.

203. Ibid.

204. PHH 14/1243–45.

205. Ibid., p. 1238; and Joseph P. Lash, *Eleanor and Franklin* (New York: W. W. Norton, 1971), p. 646.

206. Hoehling, p. 148.

207. PHLO-Safford/Kramer correspondence, "Memorandum for Captain Safford" from Kramer, dated 28 December 1943 (hereafter Kramer memo).

208. SRDJ 017336, JD-1 7143, Tokyo-Washington, 6 December 1941, Navy tr. 6 December 1941.

209. Ibid.

210. Ibid.

211. PHH 10/4662.

212. Ibid., p. 4663.

213. Ibid., p. 4664.

214. Kramer memo.

215. PHH 8/3905.

216. Kramer memo.

217. PHH 8/3903.

218. Kramer memo.

219. PHH 11/5545.

220. PHH 4/4026–30.

221. PHH 9/4513–18.

222. PHH 10/4608.

223. Ibid., pp. 4608–9.

224. Ibid., p. 4612.

225. PHH 9/4473.

226. PHH 10/4611.

227. Ibid., p. 4616.

228. Ibid., p. 4612.

229. Kimmel papers: "George Marshall's Actions in the Pearl Harbor Attack December 7, 1941," signed "Certified a true copy of the original statement made by Colonel Raymond Orr, USAF (Ret)" and dated 17 October 1941. The authenticity of Orr's claim that Bratton had told him he had gone to Marshall's headquarters around nine o'clock in the evening on 6 December 1941 with the thirteen parts of the Japanese message only to be "ordered . . . from the house, and severely reprimanded . . . for such a rude intrusion on a private dinner party" conflicts with the *Washington Times Herald* report that the chief of the army was at a veterans reunion. Marshall himself testified that he spent all evening at Fort Myer with his wife. There also appears to be a serious flaw in Orr's secondhand retelling of Bratton's account that "early the next morning" Bratton had again made the trip to Fort Myer. When informed that the general was "horseback riding in Rock Creek Park" he drove there and "found Marshall on horseback, and in company with a woman."

In fact Marshall testified that he was riding along the Potomac on the Virginia shore and there has never been any other corroboration of his mysterious female companion.

More reliance, however, may be accorded Bratton's account of Marshall's attitude on the afternoon of 6 December 1941 because it offers a credible explanation for the army chief's admitted and surprising determination to remain aloof from the onrush of events:

> Colonel Bratton, as Marshall's G-2, had numerous messages, especially on December 5 and 6, all pointing to an early Japanese attack on Hawaii. All this information was quickly given Marshall along with reminders of General Short's unanswered request. Finally, about noon December 6, Colonel Bratton suggested to Marshall that General Short's request be answered, giving General Short permission to move his forces into a defensive position, and allow Admiral Kimmel permission to move his ships out of Pearl Harbor. Marshall promptly refused Colonel Bratton's suggestion. During the afternoon of Saturday, December 6, Marshal left his office, telling Colonel Bratton he was going to his quarters at Fort Myer, Virginia, and that he did not want to be disturbed.

According to a report in the next day's *Washington Herald Tribune,* Marshall had attended a reunion of World War I veterans who had "made a pilgrimage to Fort Myer, Va., scene of part of their training. . . . Later at a dinner in University Club, they honored their former 'CO,' Brig. Gen. Joseph A. Atkins, who came from San Antonio, Tex., for the celebration. *Gen. George C. Marshall, Chief of Staff, attended and was given a vote of confidence."* The reunion might explain why Marshall was so anxious to leave the war department early that afternoon— but it is surprising when he was cross-questioned at the 1945 congressional hearings that he could not recall attending the dinner in the University Club that evening.

230. PHH 2/968.

231. SRDJ 01726, SIS 25764, Manila-Tokyo, 28 November 1941, tr. 5 December 1941.

232. PHH 3/1429.

233. Ibid., p. 1430.

234. PHH 2/925.

235. Ibid.

236. Ibid., p. 926.

237. Ibid., p. 942.

238. Kimmel papers: James G. Stahlman to Professor Preston Slosson, Vanderbilt University, dated 28 April 1975. The credibility of this firsthand account is vouchsafed by his unique access and relationship to the secretary of the navy:

> I was on duty in the Navy from 20 January '41, eleven months before Pearl, until the war was practically over in 1945. I was in Naval Intelligence most of that time as Chief of the Navy Section of the Joint Intelligence Collection Agencies, embracing A-2, G-2, ONI, OSS, BEW and State Department Intelligence. . . . Frank Knox was my close personal friend, by reason of our long service together in the newspaper business. I had entree to his office as a junior reserve which irritated the hell out of some of the regular USN boys.

239. Sherwood, p. 428.
240. Ibid.
241. B. Berle and T. Jacobs, eds., *Navigating the Rapids* (hereafter Berle), p. 382.
242. Ibid.
243. Ibid.
244. PHH 2/942.
245. J-Bd. Min., 22 October 1941 op. cit.; see also PRO Prem 3,158/6, especially draft telegram to Halifax from Churchill 8:30 P.M. 7 December 1941: "From your recent telegrams we understand we can rely on armed support of United States if we become involved in hostilities with Japan. . . ."
246. PHH 3/1121.
247. Donald G. Brownlow, *The Accused*, p. 127.

Chapter 23 (pages 299–324)   Day of Infamy

1. 1st Destroyer Div. diary, as quoted in Prange, p. 776.
2. PHH 12/584.
3. PHH 8/3393.
4. Ibid.
5. McCollum OH, p. 411.
6. PHH 11/5274.
7. PHH 37/1299.
8. Ibid., p. 1283.
9. Mitsuo Fuchida, "I Led the Air Attack on Pearl Harbor" (hereafter Fuchida), *U.S. Naval Institute Proceedings* (hereafter *USNIP*), September 1952, Vol. 78, No. 9, p. 945.
10. SRDJ 017357, JD-1 7145, Tokyo-Washington, 7 December 1941, tr. 7 December 1941.
11. PHH 9/4527.
12. Ibid., p. 4571.
13. Ibid., p. 4539.
14. Butow, *Tōjō*, p. 392.
15. PHH 9/4524.
16. PHH 11/5175–76.
17. PHH 8/3910.
18. PHH 9/4048.
19. PHH 8/3909.
20. PHH 9/4043.
21. PHH 36/26.
22. Ibid.
23. Hoehling, p. 172; and McCollum OH, p. 411.
24. McCollum OH, p. 411.
25. PHH 33/859–60.
26. PHH 9/4518.
27. PHH 14/1410.
28. PHH 9/4518.
29. Ibid.
30. PHH 5/2132.
31. Ibid., p. 2184.
32. Ibid.
33. PHH 29/2313.
34. PHH 9/4519.
35. Ibid.
36. PHH 14/1334.

37. PHH 9/4519.
38. PHH 36/57.
39. PHH 32/444.
40. Hoehling, p. 178.
41. PHLO-Stimson diary A, 7 December 1941 entry, p. 59.
42. Ibid.
43. Ibid.
44. PHH 27/520.
45. Ibid., p. 531.
46. Ibid., p. 532.
47. Ibid.; and PHH 27/569.
48. Hoehling, p. 179.
49. J. Leasor, *Singapore, The Battle That Changed the World,* pp. 166–67.
50. Fuchida, p. 947.
51. Ibid., p. 949.
52. Ibid., p. 950.
53. PHLO box 45: Cincpac-Cinclant Cincaf Opnav (reference NPM 1516 1850), 7 December 1941.
54. Fuchida, p. 950.
55. Interview as quoted in Prange, p. 507.
56. Wright conversation, April 1985.
57. Fuchida, p. 949.
58. PHH 8/3829.
59. Ibid.
60. Sherwood, pp. 430–31.
61. Hull, p. 106.
62. Ibid.
63. Hull's oath quoted but unattributed by John Toland, *The Rising Sun,* p. 357.
64. Walter Karig and Wellborn Kelly, *Battle Report: Pearl Harbor to Coral Sea* (New York: Farrar and Rinehart, 1944), p. 79.
65. PHH 23/899.
66. PHH 32/426.
67. PHH 37/1250.
68. Samuel Eliot Morison, *History of United Sates Naval Operations to World War II,* Vol. III, *The Rising Sun in the Pacific* (hereafter SEM III), p. 215.
69. SEM III, p. 212.
70. Churchill, Vol. III, p. 510.
71. J. J. Beck, *MacArthur and Wainwright* (Albuquerque: University of New Mexico Press, 1974), p. 11; William Manchester, *American Caesar,* p. 205; and D. MacArthur, *Reminiscences,* p. 117.
72. D. Clayton James, *The Year of MacArthur, Vol. 11, 1941–45* (hereafter James, *MacArthur*) (Boston: Houghton-Mifflin, 1975), p. 10.
73. Fuchida, p. 971.
74. SEM III, p. 126.
75. Joseph K. Taussig, Jr., "I Remember Pearl Harbor," *USNIP,* December 1972, p. 20; Prange, p. 568; and PHH 35/212.
76. Fuchida, p. 952.
77. Prange, p. 546.
78. Matome Ugaki, *Sensōroku (War Diary)* (hereafter Ugaki diary), p. 34.
79. PHH 6/2812.
80. Perkins OH, Vol. 8, pp. 70, 87–88.
81. PHH 19/3503-4.
82. PHLO-Stimson diary A, p. 62; and Hull, Vol. II, pp. 199–1100.
83. Alexander Kendrick, *Prime Time: The Life of Edward R. Murrow* (Boston: Little, Brown, 1969), p. 239.

84. Edgar G. Whitcomb, *Escape from Corregidor* (Chicago: Regnery, 1958), p. 23.

Chapter 24 (pages 325–337)   Hard for Us to Take

1. Ernest Saftig letter, 1985.
2. The Congressional Record, Vol. 87, Pt. 9, p. 9504 for 8 December 1941.
3. Arthur Bryant, *The Turn of the Tide,* p. 282.
4. William L. Shirer, *Rise and Fall of the Third Reich* (New York: Simon and Schuster, 1960), p. 1173.
5. Samuel I. Rosenman, *Working with Roosevelt* (New York: Harper, 1952), p. 156.
6. Library of Congress, Knox papers, box 1, letter to Paul S. Mowrer, 18 December 1941.
7. Beatty report, p. 1262.
8. Ibid.
9. Nav.Op. Archives Cincpac message, file 1941: Opnav 09 1812, 1941.
10. Ibid.
11. University of Wyoming, papers of Harry E. Barnes, box 61, letter Safford-Barnes.
12. FDR Lib. Map Box, Box 31.
13. SEM III, p. 220.
14. Ibid.
15. SEM III, p. 222.
16. Beatty report, p. 1263.
17. Ibid.
18. Ibid.
19. Ibid.
20. Ibid.
21. Ibid.
22. Ibid.
23. Ibid.
24. Ibid.
25. Ibid.
26. Stimson diary, 11 December 1941.
27. SEM III, p. 232.
28. Paul S. Dull, *A Battle History of the Imperial Japanese Navy, 1941–1945,* p. 25.
29. SEM III, p. 235.
30. Beatty report, p. 1264.
31. Kimmel papers, Stahlman, op. cit.
32. FDR-Lib., Morgenthau diary, 15 December 1941.
33. PHH 6/2749–60.
34. E. B. Potter, *Nimitz* (hereafter Potter), p. 9.
35. Stimson diary, 15 December 1941.
36. *The New York Times,* 16 December 1941.
37. Ibid.
38. Ibid.
39. Stimson diary, 15 December 1941.
40. Potter, p. 9.
41. *The New York Times,* 18 December 1941.

Chapter 25 (pages 338–352)   Sold Down the River

1. Edwin P. Hoyt, *How They Won the War in the Pacific,* p. 15.
2. PHH 17/2733.

3. Hoehling, p. 211.
4. Ibid.
5. Kimmel papers: "Memorandum of Interview with Admiral King in Washington on Thursday, 7 December 1944," signed by Admiral Kimmel, p. 6.
6. SEM III, p. 250.
7. Rochefort papers: Opnav-Com 14, 17 December 1941.
8. Ibid.; and copy Copek Com 16-Opnav, 15 December 1941.
9. Nav.Op.Archives: NWPD, chief of war plans copy of "SECRET Memorandum for The Chief of Naval Operations, Subject: Proceedings of President's Investigating Committee, 1000 to 1200, December 19, 1941," signed T. S. Wilkinson, dated 19 December 1941 (hereafter Wilkinson report).
10. Ibid., p. 1.
11. Ibid.
12. Ibid.
13. Ibid., p. 2.
14. Ibid., p. 3.
15. Ibid., p. 4.
16. Ibid., p. 3.
17. PHH 7/3280.
18. SEM III, p. 240.
19. Ibid. (November 1960 reprint by Little, Brown), p. 243.
20. SEM III, p. 248.
21. Ibid., p. 252.
22. Ibid., p. 106.
23. Ibid., p. 253.
24. PHH 7/3155.
25. PHH 23/987.
26. Wilkinson report, p. 1.
27. Husband E. Kimmel, *Admiral Kimmel's Story*, p. 151.
28. Prange interview as quoted in *At Dawn We Slept*, p. 594.
29. PHH 7/3268.
30. Kimmel papers: William H. Standley and Arthur A. Ageton, "The Pearl Harbor Debacle," unpublished manuscript, p. 84 (hereafter Standley); and *Infamy*, pp. 33, 338n.
31. PHH 23/657.
32. PHH 23/663.
33. Ibid.
34. Standley ms., p. 88.
35. PHH 7/3266.
36. PHH 39/1–21.
37. Ibid.
38. Kimmel papers, letter of retirement dated 18 February 1942.
39. Ibid.
40. King papers, LoC.

Chapter 26 (pages 353–363)   Heaven's Admonition

1. Potter, p. 16.
2. Ibid., p. 17.
3. Ibid., p. 19.
4. SEM III, p. 257.
5. RG 165: Minutes of Arcadia ABC Conference, 24 December 1941–14 January 1942.
6. Ernest J. King and Walter M. Whitehill, *Fleet Admiral King: A Naval Record*, pp. 144–45.

7. Com 16, 190215 January 1942.

8. SSS, Vol. 80, *Dai honei kaigunbu-rengokantai* (Imperial naval general headquarters and Combined Fleet) (hereafter SSS, Vol. 80), Vol. 2, p. 176.

9. Ibid.

10. SSS, Vol. 38, *Chubu taiheiyo homen kaigun sakusen* (Central Pacific naval operations) (hereafter SSS, Vol. 38), Vol. 1, p. 486.

11. Brigadier General Bankson T. Holcomb interview, 8 May 1983 (hereafter Holcomb interview).

12. Com TF 8-Cincpac, 9 February 1942, "Report of Action in the Marshall Islands, 1 Febuary 1942."

13. Ibid.

14. SSS, Vol. 43, p. 25.

15. Ugaki diary, p. 75.

16. Ibid.

Chapter 27 (pages 364–377) Where and When?

1. Nav.Op. Archives: *Enterprise* log, 5 February 1942.

2. Holcomb interview.

3. Cominch-Cincpac, 061513 February 1942.

4. Potter, p. 41.

5. Cincpac-Cominch, 9 February 1942.

6. SRH 355: "Memorandum for Admiral Noyes," dated 23 January 1942, signed L. S. Safford, pp. 451–52.

7. Ibid., pp. 453–57, Memorandum for 20-A; Subject: Reorganization of Section 20-G, Reference (A) Captain Safford's memo of 23 January 1942, dated 26 Jan. 1942, signed J. N. Wenger.

8. Ibid.

9. SRH 279: "Communication Intelligence Organization, 1942–1946." See also John Redman memorandum in SRH 355, "Naval Security History," p. 458.

10. SRH 279, passim.

11. *Nanto homen kaigun sakusen* (*Southeast Asia Naval Operations*) (hereafter SSS, Vol. 49), pp. 88–89.

12. Ugaki diary, p. 87.

13. Ibid.

14. Ibid., p. 91.

15. SSS, Vol. 38, No. 1, p. 489.

16. Com 14, 021113 March 1942.

17. Cominch, 032230 March 1942.

18. Com 16, 040630 March 1942.

19. SSS, Vol. 38, p. 503, Layton, "Rendezvous in Reverse," *USNIP*, May 1953.

20. Ibid.

21. Cincpac-CTF 9, 05001 March 1942.

22. Cominch-Cincpac, 042227 March 1942.

23. SEM III, p. 388.

24. SSS, Vol. 38, p. 517.

25. SSS, Vol. 26, *Ranin-Bengare Wan homen kaigun shinko sakusen* (*Netherlands East Indies-Bengal Bay naval operations*) (hereafter SSS, Vol. 26), p. 123.

26. Ibid.

27. Ibid.

28. SSS, Vol 38, p. 93.

Chapter 28 (pages 378–388) A Bungling Attack

1. Cominch (AIDAC), 111620 March 1942.

2. Cominch, 102313 March 1942, Orange intelligence, Vol. 36.

3. SRH 209: "OP-20-G Traffic and Decryption Charts, Japanese Navy," p. 53.
4. Cincpac 160615 and Cominch 140815 March 1942.
5. Cominch-Cincaf 011500 February 1942 (signal to Cincpac).
6. Com 14, 180922 March 1942.
7. SRH 012: "Coral Sea, Midway Appendix" (hereafter SRH 012 (B)), pp. 209–10.
8. Cincpac, 182359 March 1941.
9. Potter, p. 66.
10. Com 14, 030217 April 1942.
11. Opnav to Cincpac, 152049 April 1942.
12. "Captain Steele's Running Estimate and Summary, 7 December 1941–31 August 1942" (hereafter Cincpac Gray Book), 15 April 1942.
13. Gray Book: 17 April 1942.
14. Com 14, 172343 April 1942.
15. Cincpac Gray Book, 18 April 1942.
16. SSS, Vol. 43, *Middue-kaissen (Midway Sea Battle)* (hereafter SSS, Vol. 43), p. 23.
17. SSS, Vol. 80, pp. 64–75.
18. SSS, Vol. 43, p. 40.
19. Ibid., p. 44.
20. SSS, Vol. 29, *Hokuto homen kaigun sakusen (Northeast area naval operations)* (hereafter SSS, Vol. 29), p. 155.
21. Com 14, 170305 April 1942; and SSS, Vol. 85, p. 82.
22. Cincpac to all TF commanders 181807, 181957, 181147 April 1942.
23. SSS, Vol. 29, p. 116.
24. SSS, Vol. 85, p. 82.
25. Ibid., pp. 85–86.
26. Ibid., p. 95.
27. Agawa, p. 300.
28. SSS, Vol. 85, p. 171.

Chapter 29 (pages 389–404) Fog of Battle

1. Gray Book, 18 April 1942; and Cincpac, 180153 April 1942.
2. Gray Book, pp. 371–442.
3. Ibid.
4. Admiralty, 211552 April 1942.
5. Melbourne, 211306 April 1942.
6. Cincpac, 220109 April 1942.
7. Gray Book, 22 April 1942.
8. Ibid.
9. Ibid.
10. Ibid.
11. John B. Lundstrom, *The First South Pacific Campaign: Pacific Fleet Strategy December 1941–June 1942* (hereafter Lundstrom, *South Pacific*), p. 87.
12. SSS, Vol. 1, p. 18.
13. Com 14, 260052 April 1942.
14. Belconnen, 250110 April 1942.
15. Com 14, 261208 April 1942.
16. Com 14, 271032 April 1942.
17. Com 14, 291010 April 1942.
18. When Captain Arleigh Burke joined Admiral Mark Mitscher in the spring of 1944 as chief of staff, he was surprised to find that a lieutenant jg—Charles A. Sandy Sims, U.S.N.R.—had access to the admiral at any hour, and often took him aside for discussions. Burke inquired of the young officer why he conferred with the admiral in private so frequently. Sims answered politely, but firmly, that

he was not free to divulge the subject of their talks. "I'm his chief of staff and I want to know what you tell him," he insisted. Sims referred him to the admiral. Mitscher agreed, but Sims had to check with his superior at Pearl. It was only after the necessary authority had been radioed from Frupac that Burke was initiated into the intricacies of comint [Burke interview, July 1985].

19. Forrest R. Biard, unpublished manuscript, "Some Notes on Radio Intercept Work in the Coral Sea Action," 20 June 1984, pp. 26–27 (hereafter Biard ms.).
20. Ibid., p. 27.
21. Com 14, 011145, 011138, 011108 May 1942.
22. SRH 012 (B), p. 243.
23. Cincpac, 052329 May 1942.
24. N-OpA: CTF 17, afteraction report.
25. Cincpac, 050345 May 1942.
26. SSS, Vol. 49, *Nanto homen kaigun sakusen* (Southern Area Naval Operations), Vol. 1 (Until Guadalcanal counteroffensive) (hereafter SSS, Vol. 49), p. 239.
27. Biard ms., p. 34.
28. SSS, Vol. 49, pp. 276–77.
29. Biard ms., p. 35.
30. Lundstrom, *The First Team*, p. 205.
31. James, *MacArthur*, p. 161.
32. Biard ms., p. 38.
33. N-OpA: CTF 17 report, action report (May 1942), p. 6.
34. Ibid.
35. SSS, Vol. 49, pp. 291–92.
36. CTF 17, p. 7.
37. Ibid.
38. Ibid.
39. Potter, p. 75.
40. Gray Book, p. 443.
41. CTF 17, p. 9.
42. SSS, Vol. 49, p.299.
43. Potter, p. 76.
44. Ibid., p. 77.
45. SRH 012(B), p. 254.

Chapter 30 (pages 405–417)   Science and Skill

1. Com 14, 271032 April 1942.
2. Com 14, 040816 May 1942.
3. Com 14, 051014 May 1942.
4. Rochefort OH, pp. 189–91.
5. Gray Book, 6 May 1942.
6. Com 14, 060526 May 1942.
7. SSS, Vol. 43, pp. 87–88.
8. Ibid., p. 96.
9. Com 14, 070205 May 1942.
10. Com 14, 092236 May 1942.
11. Com 14, 090114 May 1942.
12. McCollum OH, p. 484.
13. Lundstrum, *South Pacific*, p. 134.
14. Gray Book, 12 May 1942.
15. Cominch 121945, 121950 May 1942.
16. Dyer interview, 27 June 1984.
17. Belconnen, 050202 May 1942.

18. SRNM: "Miscellaneous Records Pertaining to Japanese Naval Communications 13 March–4 June 1942 OP-20-G," p. 778.

19. Com 14, 070205 May 1942.

20. Ibid., 170614 May 1942.

21. Com 14, 140945, 141020, 141022 May 1942.

22. ETL letter to RADM D. M. Showers, 5 November 1982, and see Com 14, 140945 May 1942.

23. SRH 012, pp. 271–72, and see Com 14, 140700 May 1942.

24. Rochefort OH, p. 203.

25. Ibid.

26. SRNS: "Japanese Naval Intelligence Summaries," p. 31, and SRNM 0697.

27. SRH 355, p. 432.

28. Dyer interview, June 1984.

29. Wright interview, July 1984.

30. SRH 279: "OP-20-G File Communication Intelligence Organization, 1942–1946," p. 1. Memorandum for Admiral Noyes via OP-20-A, "Reorganization of OP-20-G," dated 23 January 1942, signed L. Safford, and p. 4 memorandum on same subject dated 26 January 1942, signed J. N. Wenger.

31. Ibid.

32. Wright interview, July 1984.

33. Ibid.

34. Layton OH, p. 137.

35. Rochefort OH, pp. 190–93.

36. Com 14, 142136 May 1942.

37. Gray Book, 13 May 1942.

38. Cincpac, 140639 May 1942.

39. Gray Book, 14 May 1942.

40. Layton letter to Lundstrom, 12 June 1974.

41. Com 14, 160638 May 1942; SSS, Vol. 49, p. 255.

42. Cincpac, 161921 May 1942.

43. SRH 272: "CINPAC Enemy Activities File, April–May 1942," 15 May 1942, p. 66.

44. Cincpac, 160325 May 1942.

45. Ibid.

46. Cincpac, 170407 May 1942 and Gray Book p. 490.

47. Cominch, 172220 May 1942.

48. Ibid., and Gray Book, p. 489.

49. Ibid.

Chapter 31 (pages 418–430) You Don't Have to Be Crazy

1. SRH 272, p. 68.

2. Captain's loss report, Australian Naval Archives 2026/10/1854, MP 1185/8, and Wenneker diary op. cit.

3. New Zealand National Archives, Navy Series, List 11, Intelligence Summaries, 21–30 March, 6 April 1942.

4. PHH 10/4855.

5. Com 14, 161900 May 1942.

6. *Halsey's Story*, p. 106.

7. Opnav, 201630 May 1942.

8. SRNS 0062, 23 May 1942.

9. E. B. Potter interview of Admiral Layton (hereafter Layton/Potter OH), p. 49.

10. Layton letter to Showers, 5 November 1982.

11. Nakumuta, p. 23.

12. Dyer interview, 27 June 1984.
13. Belconnen, 212245 May 1942.
14. Com 14, 220732 May 1942.
15. Rochefort OH, p. 132.
16. Dyer interview, and Showers interview, June 1984.
17. Rochefort OH, p. 131, passim.
18. Ibid.
19. Showers interview.
20. Ibid.
21. Various decrypts, significantly *not* attributed to Com 14 (the *were* decrypted by Rochefort), cited pp. 293–95 SRH 012(B).
22. Com 14, 212245 May 1942.
23. SRH 012, p. 291.
24. Belconnen, 220238 May 1942.
25. SRH 012, p. 297.
26. Com 14, 23/1922 May 1942.
27. Cincpac, 172220 May 1942.
28. Ibid.
29. Ibid.
30. Cincpac, 220135 May 1942.
31. Gray Book, 26 May 1942, "Estimate of Situation."
32. Ibid., p. 521.
33. Cominch to Comgenhaw, 251930 May 1942.
34. PHH 3/1158.
35. SRNS, p. 64, 24 May 1942.
36. Com 14, 252140 May 1942.
37. Ibid., and Com 14, 222350 May 1942.
38. SRH 012, p. 303.
39. SRNS, p. 66, 25 May 1942.
40. Com 14, 252140 May 1942.
41. Ibid., Com 14, 272118, 272158 May 1942, and Goodwin letters.
42. Ibid., and Com 14, 272058 May 1942.
43. Rochefort OH, pp. 223–24; 230–31.

Chapter 32 (pages 431–448)   A Glorious Page in Our History

1. A memorandum, "The Inside Story of the Battle of Midway and the Ousting of Commander Rochefort," op. cit., p. 3.
2. Potter, *Nimitz*, p. 85.
3. Ibid.
4. Ibid., p. 87.
5. Ibid.
6. SRH 012, p. 320.
7. Lundstrom, *South Pacific*, p. 180.
8. SEM *Coral Sea, Midway, and Submarine Actions* (hereafter Vol. IV), pp. 170–72.
9. Potter, *Nimitz*, p. 70.
10. RG 181: Com 14 Midway Battle dispatches (hereafter Midway dispatches).
11. Ibid.
12. Ibid.
13. Fuchida and Okumiya, *Midway*, p. 144.
14. SEM IV, p. 103.
15. ETL-Potter OH, p. 45.
16. Midway dispatches.
17. Ibid.

18. Ibid.
19. Ibid.
20. Fuchida and Okumiya, *Midway,* pp. 170–73.
21. Ibid.
22. S. L. James and G. H. Gay, eds., "Torpedo Squadron 8: The Heroic Story of 30 Men Who Attacked the Japanese Fleet," *Life* magazine, 31 August 1942, pp. 70–72.
23. SEM IV, p. 122.
24. Ibid.
25. Fuchida and Okumiya, *Midway,* p. 177.
26. Potter-Layton OH, p. 41.
27. Fuchida, p. 178.
28. SEM IV, p. 132.
29. Potter, p. 97.
30. Ibid.
31. Fuchida and Okumiya, *Midway,* p. 213.
32. Ibid., p. 214.
33. Midway dispatches.
34. Potter, p. 98.
35. SEM IV, p. 142.
36. Potter, pp. 99–101.
37. Fuchida and Okumiya, *Midway,* p. 216.
38. Midway dispatches.
39. Ibid.
40. Potter, p. 107.
41. King and Whitehill, p. 171.
42. Rochefort OH, p. 234.
43. Ibid., p. 266.

Chapter 33 (pages 449–456)   One Unforgivable Sin

1. The A Memorandum, op. cit., p. 7.
2. Ibid.
3. Ibid.
4. Ibid.
5. Letter covering formal release of A Memorandum by Naval Security Group Command, 9 August 1984.
6. SRH 279: "OP-20-G File, Communications Intelligence Organization 1942–46," pp. 9–14.
7. Ibid.
8. Ibid.
9. Ibid.
10. Ibid.
11. Ibid.
12. Dyer letter, *Cryptalog,* Summer, 1984.
13. Ibid.
14. Ibid.
15. Ibid.
16. *The Chicago Tribune,* 7 June 1942.
17. Rochefort papers: memorandum for secretary of the navy signed by Lieutenant Waldo Drake, public relations officer, Cincpac, and dated 18 June 1942.
18. A Memo, p. 8.
19. *The New York Daily Mirror,* 7 July 1942.
20. A Memo, p. 8.
21. A Memo reproducing memorandum "Security of Radio Intelligence Ac-

tivities" for Admiral King, signed "Respectfully John R. Redman" 6 July 1942.

22. Rochefort papers: Copy of confidential letter from attorney general to secretary of the navy dated 28 July 1942.

23. Ibid.: Secretary of the navy to attorney general, 29 July 1942: "The Navy Department believes that the evidence in its possession is sufficient to convict. . . ."

24. A Memo, pp. 9–10.

25. Wenneker diary, op. cit.; and PRO: ADM 223/51 supplied by James Rusbridger.

Chapter 34 (pages 457–463)   Guadalcanal

1. SEM V, pp. 19–28.

2. Heinl, *Soldiers of the Sea* (Annapolis: USNIP, 1962) (hereafter Heinl), p. 353.

3. SEM V, p. 178.

4. James M. Merrill, *A Sailor's Admiral: A Biography of William F. Halsey* (New York: Crowell, 1976), p. 52.

5. Ibid., p. 120.

6. Ibid., p. 131.

Chapter 35 (pages 464–469)   "I'm Not Coming Back"

1. Rochefort OH, pp. 251–52.

2. Ibid., p. 52.

3. Rochefort papers: Bupers orders "Temporary additional duty" dated 24 June 1942.

4. SRH 268: "Advanced Intelligence Centers in the US Navy, 1942." Memoranda for Vice Admiral F. J. Horne: (1) "Establishment of advanced intelligence centers," signed John R. Redman, OP-20-G, dated 20 June 1942. (2) "Radio Intelligence Organization," signed Joseph R. Redman, dated 20 June 1942.

5. Rochefort OH, p. 136.

6. A Memo, pp. 19–21.

7. Ibid.

8. Rochefort OH, p. 258.

9. Holmes, p. 115.

10. A Memo, p. 21.

11. Rochefort OH, p. 158.

12. Ibid., p. 272.

Epilogue (pages 470–494)

1. SRH 306, "OP-20-G, Exploits and Commendations World War II, 1942–1948," p. 30; and JICPOA 8 November 1945.

2. Holmes, p. 125.

3. SRH 306, p. 30, DOIC JICPOA 8 November 1945.

4. Ibid.

5. As quoted SRH 213: "Office of Naval Operations Bulletins," p. 30.

6. Dyer, *Cryptalog* letter, op. cit.

7. Holmes, p. 134.

8. Clay Blair, *Silent Victory,* pp. 275–78.

9. Holmes, p. 126.

10. Ibid., p. 125.

11. SRN 006430 13 April 1941.

12. Holmes, p. 135.

13. Potter, p. 233.

14. Ibid.
15. Potter, p. 233.
16. Gray Book, 17 April 1943.
17. Potter, p. 234.
18. Pineau interview with Watanabe, 1950.
19. SEM VII, pp. 37–51.
20. Halsey, p. 183.
21. Potter, p. 262.
22. SEM VII, pp. 264–72.
23. Halsey, p. 186.
24. Ibid.
25. SRH 035: "History of the Special Branch, MIS, War Department, 1942–45."
26. Interview with Admiral Arleigh Burke, July 1985.
27. Potter, p. 318.
28. SEM XII, pp. 12–15.
29. Heinl, p. 473.
30. Shigeru Fukudome, "Strategic Aspects of the Battle off Formosa," in *USNIP,* December 1952.
31. Potter, p. 335.
32. Ibid., p. 340.

Authors' Notes (pages 495–529)

1. *Reports of General MacArthur—Japanese Operations in the South West Pacific Area,* compiled from Japanese Demobilization Bureau records, 2 Vols., 4 Pts. (Washington, D.C.: Department of the Army, GPO, 1966–67).
2. SEM III, p. 132.
3. SEM IV, pp. 79–80.
4. Roberta Wohlstetter, *Pearl Harbor—Warning and Decision,* p. 397.
5. Prange, p. 723.
6. PHH report of Joint Committee, p. 252.
7. Prange, p. 723.
8. Ibid., p. 733.
9. Ibid., p. 796.
10. Ibid., p. 443
11. Ibid., p. 733.
12. Ibid.
13. Ibid.
14. Ibid., p. 734.
15. Ibid.
16. Ibid.
17. Ibid., p. 802.
18. Ibid., p. 850.
19. Ibid., p. 799.
20. Ibid., p. 796.
21. Ibid., p. 591.
22. SRH 035: "History of the Special Branch, MIS, War Department, 1942–45."
23. Lee to Pineau, 10 March 1983.
24. Prange, p. 736.
25. PHH 39/299.
26. Ibid., p. 317.
27. Ibid., p. 308.
28. Robert A. Theobald, *The Final Secret of Pearl Harbor,* p. 166.

29. PHH report of Joint Committee.

30. PHLO-Safford/Kramer correspondence: Safford 26 November 1943.

31. Ibid.; and see official report, op. cit.

32. Eunice Willson Rice letter, op. cit., and Rochefort papers analysis of Japanese diplomatic messages, op. cit.

33. PHLO: Safford letter to Adm. Hewitt, 22 June 1945, op. cit.

34. PHH 9/3936.

35. Rice letter.

36. Ibid.

37. Admiral Weeks interview, op. cit.

38. PHH 9/4009.

39. Weeks interview.

40. Copy of Briggs entry provided by Navy Operational Archives.

41. SRH 051: "Interview with Mr. Ralph T. Briggs by the Historian of the Naval Security Group Command," 13 January 1977.

42. PHH 9/3934.

43. PHH 4/1960.

44. SRH 81: "Information from George W. Linn, Captain USNR (Ret.) 23/10/80" (hereafter Linn), pp. 1–3, "The Winds Message."

45. PHH 4/1969.

46. Linn, p. 3. In his epilogue, Linn's statement added yet another mystery to the whole winds controversy:

> Early in the afternoon [7 December] GZ [Kramer] came into the watch office and motioned me to one side. I was floored when he asked if we could encrypt a message in the Purple system for transmission. This was a requirement I had never even considered and had to do some fast thinking before saying we could but it would be a very slow process. Next, I can remember saying something along the following lines (probably needlessly): I hope that whatever this message is supposed to accomplish is of the highest importance. Ultimately, the Japanese will discover our ruse and certainly will re-evaluate all of their crypto-systems, including military. Years of work will go down the drain and we may not be reading Japanese traffic for months or years. GZ nodded and left, saying he would let me know. . . . I have no knowledge of the addressee or content of the contemplated message. I sensed it was not GZ's idea; it came from higher up. I did not question GZ about it then or later. I doubt that he would have told me—I had no need to know.

This astonishing revelation by Linn aroused Admiral Layton's intense curiosity. But after much discussion neither he nor his co-authors were able to come up with an explanation which satisfied him. The obvious deduction is that the director of war plans or communications, or intelligence, briefly considered a madcap scheme that involved sending some false message to Tokyo, perhaps purporting to come from their Washington envoys. If so, it was quickly realized that any such transmission would threaten the whole Allied comint operation. Given this, another hypothesis was that the "fake" Purple message was *never intended to be transmitted,* but merely to reside on the diplomatic files to cover up or confuse any investigation—but even this requires a farfetched conspiracy. The explanation—as Linn's testimony indicates—depended on who was the ranking officer who initiated the request?

47. PHH: Sadtler testimony, op. cit. Clarke.

48. Kimmel papers: Thorpe letter.

49. Ibid.

50. PHH 33/757.

51. Royal Netherlands Army Archives (hereafter RNAA), Thorpe-Long, 23 July 1960, File DC 40/8 (courtesy James Rusbridger).

52. Ibid.
53. Ibid.
54. RNAA 40/8, Henning letter, 11 May 65.
55. Ibid.
56. Rusbridger interview with Brown, 9 May 1985.

Radio Intelligence: Personalities and Principles

57. SRH 355: p. 460.
58. Ibid.
59. Ibid.

Selected Bibliography

Books

Agawa, Hiroyuki. *The Reluctant Admiral: Yamamoto and the Imperial Navy*. New York: Harper & Row, 1979.

Allen, Louis. *Singapore, 1941–1942*. Newark, Delaware: University of Delaware Press, 1979.

Army Times, eds. *Attack on Pearl Harbor,* Washington D.C., 1941.

Arnold, Henry H. *Global Mission*. New York: Harper, 1949.

Baker, Leonard. *Roosevelt and Pearl Harbor*. New York: Macmillan, 1970.

Baldwin, Hanson W. *Battles Lost and Won: Great Campaigns of World War II*. New York: 1966.

Bamford, James. *The Puzzle Palace*. Boston: Houghton Mifflin, 1982.

Barker, Arthur J. *Pearl Harbor*. New York: Ballantine Books, 1969.

———. *Midway: The Turning Point*. New York: Macmillan, 1971.

———. *Midway*. Englewood Cliffs, N.J.: Prentice-Hall, 1983.

Barkley, Alben W. *That Reminds Me*. Garden City, N.Y.: Doubleday, 1954.

Barnes, Harry E., ed. *Perpetual War for Perpetual Peace*. Caldwell, Idaho: The Caxton Printers Ltd., 1953.

———. *Pearl Harbor After a Quarter of a Century*. New York: Arno Press, 1972.

Bartlett, Bruce R. *Cover-up*. New Rochelle, N.Y.: Arlington House, 1978.

Beard, Charles A. *American Foreign Policy in the Making, 1932–1940*. New Haven, Conn.:Yale University Press, 1948.

———. *President Roosevelt and the Coming of the War*. New Haven, Conn.: Yale University Press, 1941.

Belote, James H., and William M. Belote. *Titans of the Seas: The Development and Operations of Japanese and American Carrier Task Forces During World War II*. New York: Harper and Row, 1975.

Bergamini, David. *Japan's Imperial Conspiracy*. New York: William Morrow, 1971.

Berle, Beatrice, and Travis Jacobs, eds. *Navigating the Rapids: From the Papers of Adolf A. Berle*. New York: Harcourt Brace, 1973.

Blair, Clay. *Silent Victory*. Philadelphia: J. B. Lippincott, 1975.

Blum, John M. *From the Morgenthau Diaries: Years of War, 1941–1945*. Boston: Houghton-Mifflin, 1959–1967.

———. *Roosevelt and Morgenthau*. Boston: Houghton-Mifflin, 1970.

———. *The Price of Vision: The Diary of Henry A. Wallace, 1942–1946*. Boston: Houghton-Mifflin, 1973.

Borg, Dorothy. *The United States and the Far Eastern Crisis of 1933–1938.* Cambridge, Mass.: Harvard University Press, 1964.

————, and Shumpei Okamoto, eds. *Pearl Harbor as History: Japanese-American Relations, 1931–1941.* New York: Columbia University Press, 1973.

Boyle, John H. *China and Japan at War 1937–1945.* Stanford, Calif.: Stanford University Press, 1972.

Braisted, William R. *The United States Navy in the Pacific, 1897–1909,* Vol. I., Austin, Tex.: University of Texas Press, 1958.

————. *The United States Navy in the Pacific, 1909–1922,* Vol. II., Austin, Tex.: University of Texas Press, 1971.

Brownlow, Donald G. *The Accused: The Ordeal of Rear Admiral Husband Edward Kimmel, U.S.N.* New York: Vantage, 1968.

Buell, Thomas B. *The Quiet Warrior: A Biography of Admiral Raymond A. Spruance.* Boston: Little, Brown, 1974.

Burns, James MacGregor. *Roosevelt, The Soldier of Freedom.* New York: Harcourt Brace, 1970.

Burtness, Paul S., and Warren U. Ober, eds. *The Puzzle of Pearl Harbor.* Evanston, Ill.: Row, Peterson, 1962.

Busch, Noel F. *The Emperor's Sword: Japan vs. Russia in the Battle of Tsushima.* New York: Funk & Wagnalls, 1969.

Butow, Robert J. C. *The John Doe Associates: Backdoor Diplomacy for Peace, 1941.* Stanford, Calif.: Stanford University Press, 1974.

————. *Tojo and the Coming of the War.* Princeton, N.J.: Princeton University Press, 1961.

————. *Japan's Decision to Surrender.* Stanford, Calif.: Stanford University Press, 1954.

Byas, Hugh. *Government by Assassination.* New York: Alfred A. Knopf, 1942.

Caffrey, Kate. *Out in the Midday Sun: Singapore 1941–1945.* New York: Stein & Day, 1973.

Calvocoressi, Peter, and Guy Wint. *Total War.* New York: Pantheon Books, 1972.

Carver, Michael, ed. *The War Lords: The Military Commanders of the Twentieth Century.* Boston: Little, Brown, 1976.

Castillo, Edmund L. *Midway: Battle for the Pacific.* New York: Random House, 1968.

Chihaya, Masataka. *Teikoku Rengo Kantai (Imperial Combined Fleet).* Tokyo: Kodansha, 1969.

————. *Nihon kaigun senryaku hassō (Strategic Concepts of the Japanese Navy).* Tokyo: Purejidento sha, 1985.

Churchill, Winston L. S. *The Second World War.* Vols. I–VI. Boston: Houghton-Mifflin, 1948–1953.

Clark, Blake. *Remember Pearl Harbor!* New York: Modern Age Books, 1942.

Clark, Ronald W. *The Man Who Broke Purple: The Life of the World's Greatest Cryptologist, Colonel William F. Friedman.* Boston: Little, Brown, 1977.

Coffey, Thomas M. *Imperial Tragedy: Japan in World War II, the First Days and the Last.* New York: World Publishers. 1970.

Coggins, Jack. *The Campaign for Guadalcanal: The Battle That Made History.* Garden City, New York: Doubleday, 1972.

Cole, Wayne S. *Charles A. Lindbergh and the Battle Against American Intervention in World War II.* New York: Harcourt Brace, 1974.

Collier, Basil. *The War in the Far East, 1941–1945.* New York: Morrow, 1969.

Collier, Richard. *The Road to Pearl Harbor—1941.* New York: Atheneum, 1981.

Corson, William R. *The Armies of Ignorance: The Rise of the American Intelligence Empire.* New York: Dial Press, 1977.

Costello, John. *The Pacific War.* New York: Rawson & Wade, 1981.

Craigie, Sir Robert Leslie. *Behind the Japanese Mask.* London: Hutchinson, 1945.

Craven, Wesley Frank, and James Lea Cate, eds. *The Army Air Forces in World War II, Vol. 1.* Chicago: University of Chicago Press, 1948.

Crowley, James B., ed. *Modern East Asia: Essays in Interpretation.* New York: Harcourt Brace, 1970.

Current, Richard N. *Secretary Stimson: A Study in Statecraft.* New Brunswick, N.J.: Rutgers University Press, 1954.

Dallek, Robert. *Franklin D. Roosevelt and American Foreign Policy, 1932–1945.* New York: Oxford University Press, 1979.

David, Jules. *America and the World of Our Time: U.S. Diplomacy in the Twentieth Century.* New York: Random House, 1960.

Davis, Kenneth Sydney. *Experience of War: The United States in World War II.* Garden City, N.Y.: Doubleday, 1965.

Deacon, Richard (aka Donald McCormack). *Kempeitai: A History of the Japanese Secret Police.* New York: Berkley Edition, 1985.

Deane, John R. *The Strange Alliance.* Toronto: Viking, 1947.

Dorwart, Jeffery M. *Conflict of Duty.* Annapolis, Md.: U.S. Naval Institute Press, 1983.

Drury, Allen. *A Senate Journal, 1943–1945.* New York: McGraw-Hill, 1961.

Dull, Paul S. *A Battle History of the Imperial Japanese Navy (1941–1945).* Annapolis, Md.: U.S. Naval Institute Press, 1978.

Dyer, VADM. George C. *On the Treadmill to Pearl Harbor: The Memoirs of Admiral James O. Richardson, U.S.N. (Retired).* Washington, D.C.: Naval History Division, Department of the Navy, 1973.

———. *The Amphibians Came to Conquer: The Story of Admiral Richmond Kelly Turner.* Washington, D.C.: Naval History Division, Department of the Navy, 1971.

Farago, Ladislas. *The Broken Seal: Operation Magic and the Pearl Harbor Disaster.* New York: Random House, 1967.

Feis, Herbert. *The Road to Pearl Harbor.* Princeton, N.J.: Princeton University Press, 1950.

Flynn, John T. *The Truth About Pearl Harbor.* New York: privately printed pamphlet, 1944.

Fuchida, Mitsuo, and Masatake Okumiya. Tr. Masataka Chihaya; Clarke H. Kawakami and Roger Pineau, eds. *Midway, The Battle That Doomed Japan.* Annapolis, Md.: U.S. Naval Institute Press, 1955.

Furer, RADM. Julius Augustus. *Administration of the Navy Department in World War II.* Washington, D.C.: Naval History Division, Department of the Navy, 1959.

Geneki kaigun shikan meibo [Directory of active duty naval officers]. 1939.

Goldston, Robert C. *Pearl Harbor: 7 December 1941.* New York: Watts, 1972.

Grenfell, Russell. *Main Fleet to Singapore.* London: Faber and Faber, 1951.

Grew, Joseph C. *Ten Years in Japan.* New York: Simon & Schuster, 1944.

———. *Turbulent Era: A Diplomatic Record of Forty Years, 1904–1945, Part II.* Walter Johnson, ed. Boston: Houghton-Mifflin, 1952.

Halsey, Fleet Adm. William F., U.S.N., and Lt. Cmdr. Joseph Bryan III, U.S.N.R., *Admiral Halsey's Story.* New York: McGraw-Hill, 1947.

Hara, Captain Tameichi, with Fred Saito and Roger Pineau. *Japanese Destroyer Captain.* New York: Ballantine Books, 1961.

Harada, Kumao. *Saionji Ko to Seiyoku.* Tokyo: Iwanami Shoten, 1950–56.

Hashimoto, Mochitsura. *Sunk: The Story of the Japanese Submarine Fleet.* Tr. Cmdr. E.H.M. Colegrave, RN (Ret.). New York: Henry Holt, 1954.

Hattori, Takushiro, *Dai-toa senso zenshi (A Complete History of the Greater East Asia War).* Tokyo: Hara Shobo, 1953.

Heinl, Lt. Col. Robert D., Jr. *The Defense of Wake.* Washington, D.C.: Historical Section, Division of Public Information, Headquarters U.S. Marine Corps, 1945.

————. *Marines at Midway*. Washington, D.C.: Historical Section, Division of Public Information, Headquarters U.S. Marine Corps, 1948.

Hinsley, Francis A., et al. *British Intelligence in the Second World War*, 3 Volumes. Cambridge, Eng.: Cambridge University Press, 1979–1983.

Hoehling, A. A. *The Week Before Pearl Harbor*. New York: W. W. Norton, 1963.

Holmes, Wilfred J. *Double-Edged Secrets*. Annapolis, Md.: U.S. Naval Institute Press, 1979.

————. *Undersea Victory*. Garden City, N.Y.: Doubleday, 1966.

Hough, Richard A. *The Battle of Midway*. New York: Macmillan, 1969.

Howarth, Stephen. *The Fighting Ships of the Rising Sun*. New York: Atheneum, 1983.

Hoyt, Edwin P. *How They Won the War in the Pacific: Nimitz and His Admirals*. New York: Weybright & Talley, 1970.

Huie, William B. *The Fight for Air Power*. New York: L. B. Fisher 1942.

Hull, Cordell. *The Memoirs of Cordell Hull*. New York: Macmillan, 1948.

Ickes, Harold L. *The Secret Diary of Harold L. Ickes, Vol. III, The Lowering Clouds 1939–1941*. New York: Simon & Schuster, 1954.

Ike, Nobutake, ed. *Japan's Decision for War: Records of the 1941 Policy Conferences*. Stanford, Calif.: Stanford University Press, 1967.

Ito, Masanori, with Roger Pineau and Andrew Y. Kuroda. *The End of the Imperial Japanese Navy*. New York: W. W. Norton, 1962.

Jones, Ken, and Hubert Kelley. *Admiral Arleigh ("31-Knot") Burke*. Radnor, Pa.: Chilton Book Co., 1962.

Kahn, David. *The Codebreakers*. New York: Macmillan, 1967.

Kaigun shikan meibo [Directory of naval officers]. 1 July 1944.

Kase, Toshikazu. *Journey to the "Missouri."* New Haven, Conn.: Yale University Press, 1950.

Kato, Masuo. *The Lost War*. New York: Alfred A. Knopf, 1946.

Kennett, Lee B. *For the Duration*. New York: Charles Scribner's Sons, 1985.

Kimball, Warren F. *Churchill and Roosevelt: The Complete Correspondence*. Princeton, N.J.: Princeton University Press, 1984.

Kimmell, Husband E. *Admiral Kimmel's Story*. Chicago: Henry Regnery Co., 1955.

King, Ernest J. *U.S. Navy at War, 1941–1945* (Official Report to the Secretary of the Navy). Washington, D.C.: Government Printing Office, 1946.

————, and Walter Muir Whitehead. *Fleet Admiral King: A Naval Record*. New York: W. W. Norton, 1952.

Langer, William L., and S. Everett Gleason. *The Undeclared War: 1940–1941*. New York: Harper & Brothers, 1953.

Lash, Joseph P. *Roosevelt and Churchill 1931–1941: The Partnership That Saved the West*. New York: W. W. Norton, 1976.

Leasor, James. *Singapore: The Battle That Changed the World*. Garden City, N.Y.: Doubleday, 1968.

Lewin, Ronald. *The American Magic*. New York: Farrar Straus Giroux, 1982.

Lord, Walter. *Day of Infamy*. New York: Holt, Rinehart & Co., 1957.

————. *Incredible Victory*. New York: Harper & Row, 1967.

Lundstrom, John B. *The First South Pacific Campaign: Pacific Fleet Strategy December 1941–June 1942*. Annapolis, Md.: U.S. Naval Institute Press, 1976.

————. *The First Team*. Annapolis, Md.: U.S. Naval Institute Press, 1984.

MacArthur, Douglas. *Reminiscences*. New York: McGraw-Hill, 1964.

McGowen, Tom. *Midway and Guadalcanal*. New York: F. Watts, 1984.

McIntire, VADM. Ross T. *White House Physician*. New York: G. P. Putnam's Sons, 1946.

Manchester, William. *American Caesar: Douglas MacArthur, 1880–1964*. Boston: Little, Brown, 1978.

Melosi, Martin V. *The Shadow of Pearl Harbor*. College Station, Tex.: Texas

A & M University Press, 1977.

Middleton, Drew. *Crossroads of Modern Warfare.* Garden City, N.Y.: Doubleday, 1983.

Millis, Walter. *This Is Pearl! The United States and Japan—1941.* New York: William Morrow, 1947.

Mitchell, Joseph B., and Sir Edward Creasy. *Twenty Decisive Battles of the World.* New York: Macmillan, 1964.

Miyauchi, Kanya. *Niitakayama nobore 1208 (Climb Mount Niitaka 8 December).* Tokyo: Rokko Shuppan, 1975.

Morgenstern, George E. *Pearl Harbor: The Story of the Secret War.* New York: Devin-Adair Co., 1947.

Morison, Samuel Eliot. *The Rising Sun in the Pacific.* Boston: Little, Brown, 1948.

———. *Coral Sea, Midway and Submarine Actions, May 1942–August 1942.* Boston: Little, Brown, 1950.

———. *The Struggle for Guadalcanal August 1942–February 1943.* Boston: Little, Brown, 1954.

Morton, Louis. *United States Army in World War II: The War in the Pacific: Strategy and Command: The First Two Years.* Washington, D.C.: Department of the Army, Office, Chief of Military History, 1962.

Mosley, Leonard. *Hirohito, Emperor of Japan.* Englewood Cliffs, N.J.: Prentice-Hall, 1966.

Nakamuta, Kenichi. *Jihō shikan no kaisu (Recollections of an Intelligence Officer).* Tokyo: Daiya Mendosha, 1947.

Nihon rikukaigun no seido, soshiki, jinji (The System, Organization, and Personnel of the Japanese Army and Navy). Tokyo: Tokyo daigaku shiryo kenkyuukai, 1971.

Okumiya, Masatake. *Nihon kaigun no senryaku hasso (Strategic Ideas of the Japanese Navy).* Tokyo, 1982.

———, and Jiro Horikoshi. *Zero!* New York: E. P. Dutton, 1956.

Pantzer, Eric F. *The Debacle at Pearl Harbor.* Indianapolis, Ind.: Thesis, Indiana University, 1965.

Perkins, Frances. *The Roosevelt I Knew.* New York: Viking Press, 1946.

Pogue, Forrest C. *George C. Marshall: Education of a General.* New York: Viking Press, 1963.

———. *George C. Marshall: Ordeal and Hope, 1939–1942.* New York: Viking Press, 1966.

———. *George C. Marshall, Organizer of Victory, 1943–1945.* New York: Viking Press, 1973.

Potter, Elmer B. *Nimitz.* Annapolis, Md.: U.S. Naval Institute Press, 1976.

———. *Bull Halsey.* Annapolis, Md.: Naval Institute Press, 1985.

Potter, John Deane. *Yamamoto, the Man Who Menaced America.* New York: Viking Press, 1965.

Prange, Gordon W. *Tora! Tora! Tora!* Tokyo: Reader's Digest (in Japanese), 1966.

———. *At Dawn We Slept.* New York: McGraw-Hill, 1981.

Reynolds, David. *The Creation of the Anglo-American Alliance 1937–41.* London: Europa, 1981.

Roscoe, Theodore. *United States Destroyer Operations in World War II.* Annapolis, Md.: U.S. Naval Institute Press, 1953.

———. *United States Submarine Operations in World War II.* Annapolis, Md.: U.S. Naval Institute Press, 1949.

Sakamaki, Kazuo. *I Attacked Pearl Harbor.* New York: Association Press, 1949.

Sanson, G. B. *The Western World and Japan.* New York: Alfred A. Knopf, 1950.

Schlesinger, Arthur M., Jr., and Roger Bruns, eds. *Congress Investigates: A Doc-*

umented History, 1792–1974, Vol. 5. New York: Chelsea House, 1975.

Sherrod, Robert. *Tarawa*. New York: Duell, Sloan and Pearce, 1944.

———. *On to Westward*. New York: Duell, Sloan, and Pearce, 1945.

———. *History of Marine Corps Aviation in World War II*. Washington, D.C.: Combat Forces Press, 1952.

Sherwood, Robert E. *Roosevelt and Hopkins*. New York: Harper & Brothers, 1948.

Smith, Chester L. *Midway, 4 June 1942*. London: Regency, 1962.

Smith, Peter C. *The Battle of Midway*. London: New English Library, 1976.

Smith, William W. *Midway, Turning Point of the Pacific*. New York: Crowell, 1966.

Sontag, Raymond Japme, and James Stuart Beddie, eds. *Nazi-Soviet Relations, 1939–1941*. Washington, D.C.: Department of State, 1948.

Spector, Ronald H. *The Eagle Against the Sun: The American War with Japan*. New York: The Free Press, 1985.

Standley, William H., and Arthur A. Ageton. *Admiral Ambassador to Russia*. Chicago: Henry Regnery Co., 1955.

Stillwell, Paul, ed. *Air Raid: Pearl Harbor!* Annapolis, Md.: U.S. Naval Institute Press, 1981.

Stimson, Henry L., and McGeorge Bundy. *On Active Service in Peace and War*. New York: Harper & Row, 1947.

Tansill, Charles C. *Back Door to War*. Chicago: Henry Regnery Co., 1952.

Taylor, Theodore. *Air Raid—Pearl Harbor*. New York: Crowell, 1971.

———. *The Magnificent Mitscher*. New York: W. W. Norton, 1954.

Terasaki, Gwen. *Bridge to the Sun*. Chapel Hill, N.C.: University of North Carolina Press, 1957.

Theobald, Robert A. *The Final Secret of Pearl Harbor*. New York: Devin-Adair Co., 1954.

Thorne, Christopher. *Allies of a Kind: The United States, Great Britain and the War Against Japan 1941–43*. New York: Oxford University Press, 1978.

Thorpe, Elliott R. *East Wind, Rain*. Boston: Gambit, Inc., 1969.

Togo, Shigenori. *The Cause of Japan*. New York: Simon & Schuster, 1956.

Toland, John. *The Rising Sun*. New York: Random House, 1970.

———. *Infamy*. Garden City, N.Y.: Doubleday, 1982.

Toyama, Isao. *Rikukaigun shookan jinji sookan* [A collection of army and naval officers]. Tokyo: Fuyo shobo, 1981.

Trefousse, Hans L. *What Happened at Pearl Harbor?* New York: Twayne Publishers, 1958.

———. *Pearl Harbor, the Continuing Controversy*. Malabar, Fla.: Krieger, 1982.

Tuleja, Thaddeus V. *Climax at Midway*. New York: W. W. Norton, 1960.

Tully, Grace. *F.D.R., My Boss*. New York: Charles Scribner's Sons, 1949.

Ugaki, Matome. *Sensōroku* [war record]. Tokyo: Nihon Shuppen Kyodo, 1952–1953.

United States Department of State. *Papers Relating to the Foreign Relations of the United States: Japan, 1931–1941*, 2 Volumes. Washington, D.C.: GPO, 1943.

United States Naval War College. *Battle of Midway Including the Aleutians Phase 3–14 June 1942: Strategic and Tactical Analysis* (NAVPERS 91067). Newport, R.I.: 1946.

———. *Battle of the Coral Sea 1–11 May 1942: Strategic and Tactical Analysis* (NAVPERS 91050). Newport, R.I.: 1947.

United States Office of Naval Intelligence. *The Japanese Story of the Battle of Midway*. Tr. Fred C. Woodrough. Washington, D.C.: Government Printing Office, 1947.

Van Der Rhoer, Edward. *Deadly Magic: A Personal Account of Communication*

Intelligence in World War II in the Pacific. New York: Charles Scribner's Sons, 1978.

Waller, George M. *Pearl Harbor: Roosevelt and the Coming of the War.* Boston: Heath, 1965.

——. *Pearl Harbor.* Lexington, Mass.: Heath, 1976.

Wallin, Homer N. *Pearl Harbor: Why, How, Fleet Salvage, and Final Appraisal.* Washington, D.C.: Naval History Division, 1968.

Whitehead, Don. *The FBI Story.* New York: Random House, 1956.

Wilson, Rose Page. *General Marshall Remembered.* Englewood Cliffs, N.J.: Prentice-Hall, 1968.

Willmott, H. P. *The Barrier and the Javelin.* Annapolis, Md.: U.S. Naval Institute Press, 1983.

Wohlstetter, Roberta. *Pearl Harbor—Warning and Decision.* Stanford, Calif.: Stanford University Press, 1962.

Yardley, Herbert O. *The American Black Chamber.* New York: Ballantine Books, 1981.

Yokoi, Toshiyuki. *Nihon no kimitsu shitsu [Japan's Secret Chamber].* Tokyo: Rokumaisha, 1951.

Zacharias, Ellis M. *Secret Missions.* New York: G. P. Putnam's Sons, 1946.

Series

"Magic" Background of Pearl Harbor. Washington, D.C.: Department of Defense, 1977.

    Vol. I, 14 February–12 May 1941.
    Vol. II, 12 May–6 August 1941.
    Vol. II, Appendix.
    Vol. III, 5 August–17 October 1941.
    Vol. III, Appendix.
    Vol. IV, 17 August–7 December 1941.
    Vol. IV, Appendix.
    Vol. V, Index.

Reports of General MacArthur. Washington, D.C.: Government Printing Office, 1966.

    Vol. I, *The Campaigns of MacArthur in the Pacific,* prepared by his general staff.
    Vol. II, parts I and II, *Japanese Operations in the Southwest Pacific Area,* compiled from Japanese Demobilization Bureau records.

Senshi Sōsho [War History series]. Tokyo: Defense Headquarters History Office. Dates indicated.

    Vol. 10, *Hawai sakusen [Hawaii operation],* 1967.
    Vol. 12, *Marianas oki kaisen [Sea Battles off the Marianas],* 1968.
    Vol. 24, *Philippines-Marei hoomen kaigun shinkoo sakusen [Philippines-Malay Area Naval Attack Operations],* 1969.
    Vol. 26, *N.E.I.-Bengaru wan hoomen kaigun shinkoo sakusen [N.E.I.-Bengal Bay Area Naval Attack Operations],* 1969.
    Vol. 29, *Hokutoo hoomen kaigun sakusen [Northeast Area Naval Operations],* 1969.
    Vol. 38, *Chuubu taiheiyoo hoomen kaigun sakusen [Central Pacific Naval Operations],* 1970.
    Vol. 39, *Daihonei kaigunbu-rengoo kantai (4) [Imperial General Headquarters–Combined Fleet],* 1970.
    Vol. 43, *Midooei kaisen [Midway Sea Battle],* 1971.
    Vol. 46, *Kaijō bōei sen [Surface Defensive Actions],* 1971.
    Vol. 49, *Nantoo hoomen kaigun sakusen [Southeast Area Naval Actions Until Guadalcanal Reinforcement],* 1971.

Vol. 62, *Chuubu taiheiyoo hoomen kaigun sakusen [Central Pacific Area Naval Operations* (after June 1942)], 1973.

Vol. 83, *Nantoo hoomen kaigun sakusen [Southeast Area Naval Operations Until Guadalcanal evacuation]*, 1975.

Magazine and Newspaper Articles

Adair, RADM. Charles, U.S.N. (Ret.), "As I Recall . . . End of Peace in the Philippines," *USNIP*, August 1985.

Costello, John E., "Remember Pearl Harbor," *USNIP*, September 1983.

Cressman, Robert J., "That Gallant Ship: A History of USS *Yorktown* (CV-5)," *The Hook*, Spring 1981, pp. 11–24.

D'Andrea, Thomas M., "Marines at Midway," *Marine Corps Gazette*, November 1964, pp. 27–31.

Davenport, Walter, "Impregnable Pearl Harbor," *Colliers*, 14 June 1941.

Forrest, Jerome, and Clarke H. Kawakami, "General MacArthur and His Vanishing War History," *The Reporter*, 14 October 1952, pp. 20–25.

Frank, Larry J., *"The United States Navy* v. *the Chicago Tribune," Historian*, February 1980, pp. 284–303.

Hannah, Theodore M., "Frank B. Rowlett—A Personal Profile," *Cryptologic Spectrum*, Spring 1981, pp. 4–22.

Harris, Dr. Ruth M., "The Purple Code," *Pacific Quarterly*, Vol. LXI, February 1981.

"Hawaii: Sugar-Coated Fort," *Fortune*, August 1940, pp. 30–82, passim.

Layton, RADM, Edwin T., "Rendezvous in Reverse," *USNIP*, May 1953.

———, "24th Sentai, Japan's Commerce Raiders," *USNIP*, June 1976.

———, "America Deciphered Our Code," *USNIP*, June 1979, pp. 98–100.

Meigs, LCOL Montgomery C., USA, "This Must Mean the Philippines," *USNIP*, August 1985.

Nagumo, Chuichi, "The Japanese Story of the Battle of Midway," tr. Fred C. Woodrough, Jr., *ONI Review*, May 1947, pp. 3–72.

Nubser, RADM. J.F.W., "A History of Adeling I (Intelligence) Naval Staff, Batana, NEI," *The Cryptogram*, Vol. XLVII, No. 2, Summer 1985.

Robinson, Walton L., *"Akagi*, Famous Japanese Carrier," *USNIP*, May 1948, pp. 578–95.

Rusbridger, James, "The Sinking of the *Nankin* and the Capture of the *Automedon*," *Encounter*, May 1985, Vol. LXIV, No. 5.

Tucker, Dundas P., "Rhapsody in Purple: A New History of Pearl Harbor," *Cryptologia*, July (pp. 193–229) and October (pp. 346–67), 1982.

Vogel, Bertram, "Japan's Navy and the Battle of Midway," *Marine Corps Gazette*, December 1947, pp. 36–41.

Unpublished Sources

Unlike previous analysts, Layton insisted, wherever possible, in returning to the actual message files for both signals and intercepts. Although this confronts the researcher with a daunting task of having to sift through thousands of randomly filed intercepts in the SRN and SRDJ records in addition to the Cincpac message files, it provides a unique access to primary sources.

Researchers are urged to resist the temptation of some recent writers to rely only upon the SRH histories. Although these provide a digest of radio intelligence materials, they are not primary sources. In the case of SRH 012, Layton was to demonstrate how its interpretation of the comint account of Pearl Harbor and Midway was slanted to reflect the bias of the navy department. It provides the historian only with Washington's view by omitting the errors of misevaluation made by OP-20-G while claiming the credit for the correct analyses.

So too does the interpretation so given the Purple intercepts in the so-called *Magic Background to Pearl Harbor*. Like the selected records presented in the congressional hearings, the decrypts are incomplete and presented out of context. In the SRDJ files, we now have the ability to analyze how the intercepts were perceived as they were actually decrypted. In the sequential pattern that emerges, it is evident that the "noise" of similar messages should have reinforced as much as some historians have argued that it confused the evaluations being made in 1941. As an anonymous wartime navy analyst pointed out, the concentration pattern of the Honolulu consulate traffic that was being decrypted in Washington ought to have triggered a special alarm to the fleet.

Even with an expert guide like Layton, who was familiar with many of the intercepts, his co-authors had to employ a computer data base to bring order to the chaos of the SRN files. After months of sifting through the intercepts they developed a finding aid that could locate individual Japanese intercepts by date-time group. This resulted in the discovery of two blocks of JN-25 intercepts that were received—but not decrypted—in the three months before Pearl Harbor. This finding aid will be made available to the National Archives to help researchers to tap more deeply into this rich lode of material on the intelligence war in the Pacific.

All of the following cryptologic documents are available in Record Group 457, Records of the National Security Agency, on file in the National Archives of the United States.

Japanese Military Attaché Messages (SRA)
  SRA 1 through 16401

Translations of Japanese Naval Messages (SRN)
  SRN   1–125,093   1942–1946
  SRN 125,094–129,615   1942–1946
  SRN 129,616–133,367 5 December 1941–25 March 1942
  SRN 133,368–165,038 19 December 1942–31 December 1943
                                     (Cincpac)

Translations of Japanese Naval Attaché Messages (SRNA)
      SRNA 1–5,308   1942–1946

Japanese Naval Radio Intelligence Summaries (SRNS)
      SRNS 1–1,289   1942–1946

Miscellaneous Records of Japanese Naval Communication (SRNM)
      SRNM 1–1,292   March–June 1942

Japanese Diplomatic Messages (SRDJ)
  SRDJ   1–2,204   (1940–March 1941)
  SRDJ   9,361–19,978   (April 1941–January 1942)
  SRDJ 19,979–32,199 (February 1942–February 1943)

SRDJ   32,201–43,166   (February 1943–September 1943)
SRDJ   43,167–113,784   (September 1943–March 1945)
SRDJ   113,785–114,197   (September 1940–April 1941)

Where cited, the chapter notes provide an SRDJ number, which in general represents when the intercept was decrypted, followed by the JD-1 number (Japanese diplomatic number according to the OP-20-G filing system—or the Army SIS number), from-to, date transmitted, and the date that the translation was made.

Example: SRDJ 012780, JD-1 3490, Washington-Tokyo, 4 July 1941, tr. 8 July 1941.

Cincpac Message File: The dispatches received and sent from Pacific Fleet headquarters have been assembled from the microfilm records of the navy's operational archives and the so-called Gray Book. They are cited in the following form:
    Cominch 092245 May 1942
    This indicates a dispatch from the commander in chief U.S. Fleet transmitted on 9 May at 2245 hours.

Histories (SRH)

SRH 012 Role of Radio Intelligence in the American-Japanese naval war. Four vols., August 1941–September 1942 (2,128 pages).
    Appendix II, Coral Sea.
    Appendix III, Midway.
SRH 029 A Brief History of the Signal Intelligence Service, by William F. Friedman 29 June 1942 (18 pages).
SRH 035 History of the Special Branch, MIS, war department 1942–1944 (63 pages).
SRH 036 Radio Intelligence in World War II Tactical Operations, Pacific Ocean Areas, January 1943 (688 pages).
    136 Pacific Ocean Areas, December 1942 (707 pages).
    144 Pacific Ocean Areas, Parts I & II, February 1943 (639 pages).
SRH 041 MIS Contribution to the War Effort, December 1945 (22 pages).
SRH 043 Comment on Marshall-Dewey exchange concerning Pearl Harbor, September 1944 (14 pages).
SRH 051 Interview with Mr. Ralph T. Briggs, January 1977 (17 pages).
SRH 081 Information from George W. Linn, Capt. U.S.N.R. (Ret.), October 1980 (15 pages).
SRH 106 Special Intelligence, Specific Instructions for Handling and Dissemination, 25 January 1941, G2, DA, DNI, USN.
SRH 115 U.S. Army Investigations into the Handling of Certain Communications Prior to the Attack on Pearl Harbor 1944–45 (387 pages).
SRH 125 Certain aspects of "Magic" in cryptological background of various investigations into Pearl Harbor attack, by William F. Friedman (74 pages).
SRH 128 Study of Pearl Harbor Hearings, MIS, 1947 (39 pages).
SRH 136 Radio Intelligence in World War II, Tactical Operations, Pacific Ocean Areas, December 1942 (707 pages).
SRH 149 Communications Intelligence in the United States, a brief history, by Laurence F. Safford, Captain U.S.N. (Ret.) (22 pages).
SRH 150 Birthday of Naval Security Group (6 pages).
SRH 152 History Review of OP-20-G (13 pages).

SRH 154 Signal Intelligence Disclosures in the Pearl Harbor Investigations (147 pages).

SRH 159 William F. Friedman preliminary Historical Report on the Solution of the "B" Machine (10 pages).

SRH 177 Interrogation of Japanese Concerning Possible Broadcast of the Winds Message, October–November 1945 (15 pages).

SRH 207 Evacuation of U.S.N. Comint Personnel from Corregidor in World War II (99 pages).

SRH 209 Decryption Intelligence Charts, OP-20-G, 20 January–May 1942 (250 pages).

SRH 210 Collection of papers relating to the "Winds Execute" Messages (80 pages).

SRH 211 Japanese Radio Communications and Radio Intelligence, Cincpac-poa Bull, May 1945 (34 pages).

SRH 222 Japanese grand fleet maneuvers, May–June 1930, OP-20 report (211 pages).

SRH 223 Japanese grand fleet maneuvers, June–August 1933, various reports (278 pages).

SRH 224 Japanese grand fleet maneuvers, August–October 1934 (119 pages).

SRH 225 Japanese grand fleet maneuvers, July–September 1935 (78 pages).

SRH 230 The Role of Comint in the Battle of Midway (9 pages).

SRH 231 Japanese reports on monitoring of Allied wireless communications in Philippines, January–December 1943 (113 pages).

SRH 235 Comint contributions, Submarine Warfare in World War II (4 pages).

SRH 239 Japanese army signal centers and officer lists, MIS, war department, 1 September 1945 (27 pages).

SRH 254 Japanese Intelligence System, MISWDGS, 4 September 1945 (171 pages).

SRH 255 Robert D. Ogg, history interview (82 pages).

SRH 268 Advance Intelligence Centers in U.S. Navy [Redman memos] (2 pages).

SRH 272 Cincpac enemy activities file, April–May 1942 (122 pages).

SRH 275 Fleet Radio Unit, Melbourne (Frumel), 28 June 1943–2 September 1945 (24 photos and 130 pages).

SRH 278 War diary, combat intelligence unit (Pacific), 1942 (190 pages).

SRH 279 Communications Intelligence Activities, OP-20-G, 1942–1946 [including reorganization memos] (82 pages).

SRH 287 Radio Intelligence in World War II, Tactical Operations in the Pacific Ocean Areas, March 1943 (444 pages).

SRH 289 Mobile radio intelligence units (RIU), by commands afloat in World War II (151 pages).

SRH 305 History of Radio Intelligence, the Undeclared War, Captain Laurence F. Safford (29 pages).

SRH 306 OP-20-G, Exploits and Commendations, World War II (82 pages).

SRH 309 Mobile RIU reports, Pacific, 1945, Pt. I (236 pages).
Mobile RIU reports, Pacific, 1945, Pt. II (274 pages).
Mobile RIU reports, Pacific, 1945, Pt. III (338 pages).

SRH 313 Mobile RIU reports, Pacific, 1942 (39 pages).

SRH 314 Mobile RIU reports, Pacific, 1944 (116 pages).

SRH 317 Mobile RIU reports, Pacific, 1943 (304 pages).

SRH 355 Naval Security Group History to World War II, prepared by Captain J. S. Holtwick, Jr., U.S.N. (Ret.), June 1971 (464 pages).

Among other collections in the National Archives, which include RG 165, RG 187 and RG 80 and which have yielded new primary source material, is the so-called Pearl Harbor Liaison Office File containing many thousands of documents pertaining to the navy's investigations for the congressional hearings in 1945. Its 136 boxes contain a trove of original documentation, from Layton's contemporary notes and reports to a complete set of Purple decrypts still bearing the code notations that have been sanitized from the SRDJ series.

Documents, statements, and memoranda collected by Admiral Kimmel during more than two decades are available in the University of Wyoming library. They provide some revealing insights into the character of the commander who was made a scapegoat by Washington and the methods of his accusers. Rochefort's papers, by contrast, are mainly copies of official documents, many of which are not readily accessible or have been destroyed.

The most intriguing document of all is the anonymous SECRET memorandum entitled "The Inside Story of the Battle of Midway and the Ousting of Commander Rochefort," which we had designated "A." While unable to establish its authorship, from the secrecy with which it has been accorded for nearly forty years and the information it contains—much confirmed by recently declassified documentation—must make it a significant primary source. Whoever wrote it appears to have been a ranking officer on the naval intelligence staff and it appears several copies were clandestinely circulated in the navy department sometime after 1943. It would be out of keeping for Rochefort himself to have been either the instigator or the author of the A Memorandum, but the marginal comments appear to be in his handwriting.

Copies of the memorandum and many of the other documents that have provided the authors with their primary sources will be incorporated into the Edwin T. Layton Collection and be available for research at the Naval War College.

Index

About the Authors

Rear Admiral Edwin T. Layton, U.S.N. (Ret.), was, from 7 December until the surrender of Japan, the staff officer who bore responsibility for keeping the Commander in Chief Pacific Fleet informed about Japan's strategic objectives, capabilities, and intended operations.

Captain Roger Pineau, U.S.N.R. (Ret.), an expert on the Japanese language, served in radio communications intelligence in World War II. He was assistant to Admiral Samuel Eliot Morison for his fifteen-volume history of U.S. Naval Operations.

John Costello is a Cambridge-educated historian. He is an authority on Allied intelligence, and the author of a number of books on World War II, including *The Pacific War*.

Introduction

On the final day of the 2011 season, two playoff races were still underway in four different cities. Just before 10:30 PM eastern the St. Louis Cardinals kept their season alive by defeating the Houston Astros. An hour later the Philadelphia Phillies eliminated the Atlanta Braves with a win in the 13th inning, sending St. Louis to the playoffs. Then just after midnight the Baltimore Orioles staged a ninth-inning comeback win over the Boston Red Sox. Moments later the season ended on an Evan Longoria home run, winning the wildcard for Tampa Bay.

It was a remarkable ending to a remarkable season. We saw Derek Jeter join the 3000 hit club. Jim Thome hit his 600th home run. Mariano Rivera became the all-time saves leader. Justin Verlander, Ervin Santana, and Francisco Liriano threw no-hitters. Vladimir Guerrero became the all-time hits leader among Dominican-born players. Matt Kemp nearly became the first Triple Crown winner since Carl Yastrzemski.

That only scratches the surface of the 2011 baseball season. The *Bill James Handbook* is here to celebrate and remember the entirety of the season that was. It is particularly special to me, because it is the first Handbook that I've been a part of.

In early April, I was at the Baltimore Orioles' first home game of the season. The next day I was interviewing at Baseball Info Solutions, and a month later I started working at this wonderful company. A few days ago a friend of mine asked me what makes *The Bill James Handbook* worthwhile, and I thought to myself that if I was asked that question back in April I would not have had a satisfying answer.

The effort that goes into making sure that this book is the most accurate and complete source of statistics for the 2011 baseball season is exceptional. There is no one place outside of this book to find all the information contained within. This book contains more information about the season than any other place. The Handbook is indispensible, and that is entirely owed to the tremendous work of the staff at BIS.

I couldn't be prouder to be a part of that team, and of this book.

Andrew Gibson
Baseball Info Solutions

2011 Team Statistics

We've made some updates to the Team Statistics section this year. The standings section and league stats pages haven't changed, but we're pleased to bring you a new Team Defense chart that summarizes Defensive Runs Saved by position and team. This chart will enable you to compare team defenders to their counterparts on other teams. You'll be able to look at Yankee shortstops and see that they're over 50 runs worse than the best shortstops in baseball, who play in Tampa Bay.

Another new addition is Team Pitching Staff Summary. For years, we've provided comprehensive data on starters and relief pitchers individually, but this table provides an overview of both starting pitchers and relievers on a team level.

2011 American League Standings

Overall

EAST							CENTRAL							WEST					
Team	W-L	Pct	GB	D1	LD1	LLd	Team	W-L	Pct	GB	D1	LD1	LLd	Team	W-L	Pct	GB	D1	LD1	LLd
New York Yankees	97-65	.599	0.0	98	9/28	8.0	Detroit Tigers	95-67	.586	0.0	83	9/28	15.0	Texas Rangers	96-66	.593	0.0	168	9/28	10.0
Tampa Bay Rays*	91-71	.562	6.0	9	5/20	3.0	Cleveland Indians	80-82	.494	15.0	95	7/20	7.0	Los Angeles Angels	86-76	.531	10.0	24	7/5	2.0
Boston Red Sox	90-72	.556	7.0	68	9/1	3.0	Chicago White Sox	79-83	.488	16.0	3	4/7	0.5	Oakland Athletics	74-88	.457	22.0	1	5/17	0.0
Toronto Blue Jays	81-81	.500	16.0	3	4/6	0.0	Kansas City Royals	71-91	.438	24.0	9	4/16	1.5	Seattle Mariners	67-95	.414	29.0	2	4/2	0.0
Baltimore Orioles	69-93	.426	28.0	13	4/13	1.0	Minnesota Twins	63-99	.389	32.0	0	-	0.0							

* Clinched Wild Card Berth on 9/28. Division Clinch Dates: Detroit 9/16, New York 9/21, Texas 9/23.

D1 = Number of days a team had at least a share of first place of their division; LD1 = Last date the team had at least a share of first place; LLd = The largest number of games that a team led their division by.

East Division

Tm	AT		VERSUS						CONDITIONS				GAME			MONTHLY						ALL-STAR	
	Home	Road	East	Cent	West	NL	LHS	RHS	Day	Night	Grass	Turf	1-Rn	5+Rn	XInn	April	May	June	July	Aug	Sept	Pre	Post
NYY	52-29	45-36	39-33	22-14	23-13	13-5	35-17	62-48	44-12	53-53	90-54	7-11	21-24	34-13	4-12	15-9	15-14	18-8	16-11	17-11	16-12	53-35	44-30
TB	47-34	44-37	42-30	21-17	16-18	12-6	31-19	60-52	34-24	57-47	38-34	53-37	26-18	24-18	9-5	15-12	14-13	16-11	11-15	18-10	17-10	49-41	42-30
Bos	45-36	45-36	38-34	21-16	21-14	10-8	33-22	57-50	20-20	60-52	82-62	8-10	19-19	32-17	6-5	11-15	19-10	16-9	20-6	17-12	7-20	55-35	35-37
Tor	42-39	39-42	33-39	18-15	22-17	8-10	23-19	58-62	26-34	55-47	36-36	45-45	29-28	19-17	13-4	13-14	15-13	12-15	15-11	13-15	13-13	45-47	36-34
Bal	39-42	30-51	28-44	22-20	12-18	7-11	20-27	49-66	20-28	49-65	60-84	9-9	22-22	17-28	8-8	12-13	12-16	11-14	7-20	12-17	15-13	36-52	33-41

Central Division

Tm	AT		VERSUS						CONDITIONS				GAME			MONTHLY						ALL-STAR	
	Home	Road	East	Cent	West	NL	LHS	RHS	Day	Night	Grass	Turf	1-Rn	5+Rn	XInn	April	May	June	July	Aug	Sept	Pre	Post
Det	50-31	45-36	20-16	50-22	18-18	7-11	31-20	64-47	38-23	57-44	89-65	6-2	29-17	24-18	6-2	12-15	16-11	16-13	18-10	20-6	19-6	49-43	46-24
Cle	44-37	36-45	19-18	36-36	14-21	11-7	23-26	57-56	21-31	59-51	77-79	3-3	30-26	14-25	6-8	18-8	14-12	10-17	11-15	15-13	12-17	47-42	33-40
CWS	36-45	43-38	17-20	32-40	19-16	11-7	24-22	55-61	28-27	51-56	77-77	2-6	24-25	19-21	7-11	10-18	16-13	14-11	12-12	16-12	11-17	44-48	35-35
KC	40-41	31-50	16-21	32-40	18-17	5-13	16-26	55-65	23-26	48-65	69-86	2-5	25-32	19-19	10-8	14-13	10-17	9-18	13-14	10-19	15-10	37-54	34-37
Min	33-48	30-51	10-29	30-42	15-18	8-10	21-26	42-73	24-36	39-63	61-94	2-5	27-32	15-30	6-4	9-17	8-19	17-9	16-13	7-21	6-20	41-48	22-51

West Division

Tm	AT		VERSUS						CONDITIONS				GAME			MONTHLY						ALL-STAR	
	Home	Road	East	Cent	West	NL	LHS	RHS	Day	Night	Grass	Turf	1-Rn	5+Rn	XInn	April	May	June	July	Aug	Sept	Pre	Post
Tex	52-29	44-37	22-22	25-18	40-17	9-9	26-21	70-45	26-22	70-44	92-61	4-5	19-24	34-21	4-5	16-11	13-15	14-13	18-9	16-12	19-6	50-42	36-34
LAA	45-36	41-40	21-23	25-18	27-30	13-5	32-28	54-48	28-21	58-55	79-71	7-5	27-31	22-18	8-13	15-12	14-16	13-12	17-10	14-13	13-13	39-53	35-35
Oak	43-38	31-50	20-23	20-24	26-31	8-10	25-29	49-59	32-31	42-57	69-84	5-4	20-25	20-20	8-11	13-14	14-15	9-17	13-13	11-17	14-12	43-48	24-47
Sea	39-45	28-50	17-26	20-24	21-36	9-9	13-28	54-67	17-32	50-63	67-89	0-6	26-28	11-24	6-5	13-15	15-11	11-16	6-20	13-15	9-18	43-48	24-47

Team vs. Team Breakdown

	EAST					CENTRAL					WEST			
	NYY	TB	Bos	Tor	Bal	Det	Cle	CWS	KC	Min	Tex	LAA	Oak	Sea
New York Yankees	-	9	6	11	13	3	4	6	3	6	7	5	6	5
Tampa Bay Rays	9	-	12	12	9	1	4	4	5	7	4	4	2	6
Boston Red Sox	12	6	-	10	10	5	4	2	5	5	4	6	6	5
Toronto Blue Jays	7	6	8	-	12	2	4	4	3	5	6	5	5	6
Baltimore Orioles	5	9	8	6	-	5	2	4	5	6	1	3	4	4
Detroit Tigers	4	6	1	4	5	-	12	13	11	14	6	3	5	4
Cleveland Indians	3	2	6	3	5	6	-	7	12	11	1	3	5	5
Chicago White Sox	2	4	4	3	4	5	11	-	7	9	4	2	6	7
Kansas City Royals	3	2	3	4	4	7	6	11	-	8	2	7	4	5
Minnesota Twins	2	3	2	1	2	4	7	9	10	-	4	3	4	3
Texas Rangers	2	5	6	4	5	3	9	4	6	3	-	12	13	15
Los Angeles Angels	4	4	2	5	6	4	6	6	3	6	7	-	8	12
Oakland Athletics	3	5	2	5	5	5	2	4	5	4	6	11	-	9
Seattle Mariners	4	4	4	3	2	6	4	2	3	5	4	7	10	-

2011 National League Standings

Overall

EAST

Team	W-L	Pct	GB	D1	LD1	LLd
Philadelphia Phillies	102-60	.630	0.0	180	9/28	13.0
Atlanta Braves	89-73	.549	13.0	2	4/1	1.0
Washington Nationals	80-81	.497	21.5	0	-	0.0
New York Mets	77-85	.475	25.0	1	4/5	0.0
Florida Marlins	72-90	.444	30.0	3	5/2	0.5

CENTRAL

Team	W-L	Pct	GB	D1	LD1	LLd
Milwaukee Brewers	96-66	.593	0.0	97	9/28	10.5
St Louis Cardinals*	90-72	.556	6.0	70	7/26	3.5
Cincinnati Reds	79-83	.488	17.0	28	5/18	2.5
Pittsburgh Pirates	72-90	.444	24.0	7	7/25	0.5
Chicago Cubs	71-91	.438	25.0	1	4/20	0.0
Houston Astros	56-106	.346	40.0	0	-	0.0

WEST

Team	W-L	Pct	GB	D1	LD1	LLd
Arizona Diamondbacks	94-68	.580	0.0	60	9/28	9.5
San Francisco Giants	86-76	.531	8.0	79	8/9	4.5
Los Angeles Dodgers	82-79	.509	11.5	4	4/4	0.5
Colorado Rockies	73-89	.451	21.0	38	5/17	4.5
San Diego Padres	71-91	.438	23.0	3	4/5	0.5

* Clinched Wild Card Berth on 9/28. Division Clinch Dates: Philadelphia 9/17, Milwaukee 9/23, Arizona 9/23.
D1 = Number of days a team had at least a share of first place of their division; LD1 = Last date the team had at least a share of first place; LLd = The largest number of games that a team led their division

East Division

Tm	AT Home	AT Road	VERSUS East	VERSUS Cent	VERSUS West	AL	LHS	RHS	CONDITIONS Day	CONDITIONS Night	Grass	Turf	GAME 1-Rn	GAME 5+Rn	XInn	MONTHLY April	May	June	July	Aug	Sept	ALL-STAR Pre	ALL-STAR Post
Phi	52-29	50-31	43-29	27-16	23-9	9-6	30-14	72-46	33-18	69-42	100-59	2-1	28-19	30-10	9-10	18-8	16-13	17-10	17-8	18-7	16-14	57-34	45-26
Atl	47-34	42-39	36-36	22-17	21-15	10-5	24-23	65-50	26-20	63-53	89-73	0-0	29-26	17-15	14-12	13-15	17-11	17-9	16-11	17-9	9-18	54-38	35-35
Was	44-36	36-45	36-36	20-19	16-19	8-7	19-17	61-64	27-28	53-53	80-81	0-0	27-27	12-15	12-8	12-14	11-17	17-10	11-15	12-15	17-10	46-46	34-35
NYM	34-47	43-38	33-39	19-20	16-17	9-9	18-22	59-63	24-26	53-59	77-85	0-0	21-28	15-20	7-7	11-16	14-13	16-11	14-13	10-16	12-16	46-45	31-40
Fla	31-47	41-43	32-40	20-20	12-20	8-10	23-23	49-67	15-24	57-66	72-87	0-3	27-32	11-15	9-13	16-9	15-13	5-23	17-10	7-20	12-15	43-48	29-42

Central Division

Tm	AT Home	AT Road	VERSUS East	VERSUS Cent	VERSUS West	AL	LHS	RHS	CONDITIONS Day	CONDITIONS Night	Grass	Turf	GAME 1-Rn	GAME 5+Rn	XInn	MONTHLY April	May	June	July	Aug	Sept	ALL-STAR Pre	ALL-STAR Post
Mil	57-24	39-42	20-14	51-29	19-14	6-9	18-18	78-48	30-20	66-46	96-66	0-0	30-18	23-16	7-7	13-13	17-12	14-13	16-11	21-7	15-10	49-43	47-23
StL	45-36	45-36	22-13	44-35	16-17	8-7	20-20	70-52	25-26	65-46	89-70	1-2	26-23	24-16	8-13	16-11	17-12	11-15	13-13	15-13	18-8	49-43	41-29
Cin	42-39	37-44	13-20	42-37	18-14	6-12	17-22	62-61	28-30	51-53	77-82	2-1	29-33	20-17	12-5	14-13	14-15	14-12	11-15	14-14	12-14	45-47	34-36
Pit	36-45	36-45	12-22	39-41	13-20	8-7	23-22	49-68	25-30	47-60	70-89	2-1	21-22	15-26	6-7	12-15	13-13	16-11	13-13	8-22	10-16	47-43	25-47
ChC	39-42	32-49	15-18	34-46	17-17	5-10	20-24	51-67	32-41	39-50	71-91	0-0	25-28	12-24	9-5	12-14	11-16	11-18	9-17	16-13	12-13	37-55	34-36
Hou	31-50	25-56	10-21	28-50	14-24	4-11	22-26	34-80	13-37	43-69	54-105	2-1	20-28	15-28	5-13	10-17	11-17	8-19	6-20	12-17	9-16	30-62	26-44

West Division

Tm	AT Home	AT Road	VERSUS East	VERSUS Cent	VERSUS West	AL	LHS	RHS	CONDITIONS Day	CONDITIONS Night	Grass	Turf	GAME 1-Rn	GAME 5+Rn	XInn	MONTHLY April	May	June	July	Aug	Sept	ALL-STAR Pre	ALL-STAR Post
Ari	51-30	43-38	18-14	23-17	43-29	10-8	24-24	70-44	23-20	71-48	94-68	0-0	28-16	19-16	9-4	11-15	19-10	14-13	15-11	19-10	16-9	49-43	45-25
SF	46-35	40-41	13-20	20-22	43-29	10-5	26-18	60-58	26-28	60-48	86-76	0-0	33-22	15-20	13-8	13-13	16-12	17-11	15-11	11-18	14-11	52-40	34-36
LAD	42-39	40-40	15-17	22-20	39-33	6-9	24-20	58-59	25-25	57-54	82-79	0-0	23-21	21-20	8-3	14-14	12-16	10-16	12-13	17-11	17-9	41-51	41-28
Col	38-43	35-46	15-18	22-20	28-44	8-7	25-23	48-66	20-31	53-58	73-89	0-0	21-27	18-24	4-8	17-8	8-21	14-13	12-15	13-16	9-16	43-48	30-41
SD	35-46	36-45	19-19	19-18	27-45	6-9	19-30	52-61	32-24	39-67	71-91	0-0	20-31	17-17	4-12	10-17	14-14	13-14	10-17	13-15	11-14	40-52	31-39

Team vs. Team Breakdown

	EAST Phi	Atl	Was	NYM	Fla	CENTRAL Mil	StL	Cin	Pit	ChC	Hou	WEST Ari	SF	LAD	Col	SD
Philadelphia Phillies	-	12	8	11	12	4	3	7	4	5	4	3	4	5	4	7
Atlanta Braves	6	-	9	9	12	5	1	3	4	4	5	3	6	2	6	4
Washington Nationals	10	9	-	10	7	3	4	2	4	4	3	3	4	2	3	4
New York Mets	7	9	8	-	9	2	3	5	4	2	3	3	2	5	2	4
Florida Marlins	6	6	11	9	-	0	2	3	6	3	6	2	4	3	3	0
Milwaukee Brewers	3	3	3	4	7	-	9	8	12	10	12	3	3	4	6	3
St Louis Cardinals	6	5	2	3	6	9	-	6	9	10	10	4	2	3	4	3
Cincinnati Reds	1	3	4	2	3	8	9	-	5	11	9	2	5	4	3	4
Pittsburgh Pirates	2	2	4	4	0	3	7	10	-	8	11	3	3	2	3	2
Chicago Cubs	2	3	3	4	3	6	5	7	8	-	8	4	5	4	2	3
Houston Astros	2	1	3	3	1	3	5	6	7	7	-	1	4	4	2	3
Arizona Diamondbacks	3	2	5	3	5	4	3	4	3	3	6	-	9	10	13	11
San Francisco Giants	3	1	3	4	2	3	5	2	3	4	3	9	-	9	13	12
Los Angeles Dodgers	1	5	4	2	3	2	4	2	6	3	5	8	9	-	9	13
Colorado Rockies	1	2	4	5	3	3	2	4	4	4	5	5	5	9	-	9
San Diego Padres	1	5	3	3	7	2	3	2	4	3	5	7	6	5	9	-

American League Batting

				BATTING																BASERUNNING					PERCENTAGES		
Tm	G	AB	H	2B	3B	HR	(Hm	Rd)	TB	R	RBI	TBB	IBB	SO	HBP	SH	SF	ShO	SB	CS	SB%	GDP	LOB	Avg	OBP	Slg
Bos	162	5710	1600	352	35	203	(91	112)	2631	875	842	578	52	1108	50	22	50	11	102	42	.71	136	1793	.280	.349	.461
NYY	162	5518	1452	267	33	222	(122	100)	2451	867	836	627	34	1138	74	36	51	8	147	46	.76	146	1709	.263	.343	.444
Tex	162	5659	1599	310	32	210	(126	84)	2603	855	807	475	35	930	39	39	49	8	143	45	.76	135	1748	.283	.340	.460
Det	162	5563	1540	297	34	169	(94	75)	2412	787	750	521	47	1143	39	50	58	5	49	20	.71	142	1750	.277	.340	.434
Tor	162	5559	1384	285	34	186	(103	83)	2295	743	704	525	41	1184	48	31	47	8	131	52	.72	108	1644	.249	.317	.413
KC	162	5672	1560	325	41	129	(53	76)	2354	730	705	442	37	1006	39	55	57	8	153	58	.73	122	1848	.275	.329	.415
Bal	162	5585	1434	273	13	191	(106	85)	2306	708	684	452	24	1120	52	24	43	7	81	25	.76	154	1642	.257	.316	.413
TB	162	5436	1324	273	37	172	(81	91)	2187	707	674	571	31	1193	73	37	35	15	155	62	.71	101	1696	.244	.322	.402
Cle	162	5509	1380	290	26	154	(89	65)	2184	704	671	494	30	1269	65	31	43	13	89	42	.68	111	1618	.250	.317	.396
LAA	162	5513	1394	289	34	155	(62	93)	2216	667	629	442	33	1086	51	50	32	11	135	52	.72	126	1638	.253	.313	.402
CWS	162	5502	1387	252	16	154	(86	68)	2133	654	625	475	31	989	84	52	46	10	81	53	.60	125	1742	.252	.319	.388
Oak	162	5452	1330	280	29	114	(50	64)	2010	645	612	509	20	1094	50	34	57	15	117	43	.73	119	1723	.244	.311	.369
Min	162	5487	1357	259	25	103	(46	57)	1975	619	572	440	24	1048	37	31	25	13	92	39	.70	115	1659	.247	.306	.360
Sea	162	5421	1263	253	22	109	(57	52)	1887	556	534	435	33	1280	37	38	41	16	125	40	.76	82	1621	.233	.292	.348
AL	1134	77586	20004	4005	411	2271	(1166	1105)	31644	10117	9645	6986	472	15588	738	530	634	148	1600	619	.72	1722	23831	.258	.323	.408

American League Pitching

HOW MUCH THEY PITCHED					WHAT THEY GAVE UP												THE RESULTS									
Tm	G	CG	Rel	IP	BFP	H	R	ER	HR	SH	SF	HB	TBB	IBB	SO	WP	Bk	W	L	Pct.	ShO	Sv-Op	Hld	OAvg	OOBP	OSlg	ERA
TB	162	15	438	1449.0	6010	1263	614	577	161	27	37	46	504	38	1143	45	3	91	71	.562	13	32-44	51	.234	.303	.383	3.58
LAA	162	12	386	1465.0	6124	1388	633	581	142	46	41	36	476	34	1058	55	4	86	76	.531	11	39-64	58	.251	.313	.388	3.57
NYY	162	5	465	1458.1	6216	1423	657	605	152	36	54	58	507	43	1222	67	3	97	65	.599	8	47-63	95	.256	.322	.399	3.73
Sea	162	12	351	1433.0	6014	1369	675	621	145	31	41	51	436	27	1088	68	6	67	95	.414	10	39-55	39	.251	.310	.386	3.90
Tex	162	10	417	1441.1	6021	1327	677	607	170	36	32	46	461	21	1179	43	6	96	66	.593	19	38-57	65	.244	.307	.392	3.79
Oak	162	6	460	1447.2	6159	1380	679	597	136	45	41	41	519	24	1160	53	3	74	88	.457	12	39-57	65	.250	.317	.378	3.71
CWS	162	6	410	1460.0	6188	1463	706	665	147	41	50	44	439	50	1220	55	4	79	83	.488	14	42-62	72	.261	.317	.397	4.10
Det	162	4	421	1440.0	6108	1406	711	647	149	36	50	52	492	34	1115	69	5	95	67	.586	14	52-62	60	.257	.321	.396	4.04
Bos	162	2	444	1457.1	6242	1366	737	680	156	40	43	90	540	11	1213	58	7	90	72	.556	13	36-52	75	.247	.322	.392	4.20
Cle	162	2	483	1453.1	6235	1482	760	683	153	35	49	60	463	34	1024	42	3	80	82	.494	4	38-54	78	.263	.323	.413	4.23
Tor	162	7	474	1458.2	6286	1433	761	700	179	34	44	77	540	28	1169	73	3	81	81	.500	10	33-58	52	.256	.328	.419	4.32
KC	162	2	420	1451.1	6280	1487	762	716	163	51	51	58	557	42	1080	69	7	71	91	.438	6	37-59	58	.267	.337	.425	4.44
Min	162	7	457	1421.2	6210	1564	804	724	161	43	62	54	480	37	940	47	5	63	99	.389	8	32-52	59	.281	.340	.435	4.58
Bal	162	3	478	1446.2	6332	1568	860	786	210	37	49	45	535	42	1044	32	4	69	93	.426	7	32-51	59	.277	.341	.460	4.89
AL	1134	93	6104	20283.1	86425	19919	10036	9189	2224	538	644	758	6949	465	15655	776	63	1139	1129	.502	149	536-790	884	.257	.322	.405	4.08

American League Fielding

						Fielding													
Team	G	Inn	PO	Ast	OFAst	E (Throw)	(Field)	TC	DP	GDP	SB	CS	SB%	CPkof	PPkof	PB	UER	UERA	FPct
Tampa Bay	162	1449.0	4347	1519	24	73	37	36	5939	138	111	104	33	.76	1	16	5	37	0.23	.988
Chicago	162	1460.0	4380	1667	16	79	37	42	6126	129	113	135	37	.78	1	7	10	41	0.25	.987
Los Angeles	162	1465.0	4395	1723	31	93	40	53	6211	157	140	126	40	.76	3	9	7	52	0.32	.985
Boston	162	1457.1	4372	1526	17	92	38	54	5990	149	99	156	50	.76	0	5	32	57	0.35	.985
Kansas City	162	1451.1	4354	1700	51	95	60	35	6149	149	117	115	49	.70	3	2	6	46	0.29	.985
New York	162	1458.1	4375	1569	28	102	48	54	6046	142	114	128	49	.72	0	4	7	52	0.32	.983
Detroit	162	1440.0	4320	1639	37	103	42	61	6062	149	120	119	49	.71	0	3	8	64	0.40	.983
Toronto	162	1458.2	4376	1703	29	110	51	59	6189	148	124	111	40	.74	3	6	20	61	0.38	.982
Cleveland	162	1453.1	4360	1689	22	110	45	65	6159	130	105	104	48	.68	1	5	9	77	0.48	.982
Seattle	162	1433.0	4299	1623	28	108	47	61	6030	152	124	110	46	.71	1	4	11	54	0.34	.982
Baltimore	162	1446.2	4340	1655	36	110	40	70	6105	159	135	83	42	.66	0	0	4	74	0.46	.982
Texas	162	1441.1	4324	1552	21	114	44	70	5990	165	142	85	46	.65	1	3	9	70	0.44	.981
Minnesota	162	1421.2	4265	1621	30	119	62	57	6005	153	128	96	44	.69	2	5	12	80	0.51	.980
Oakland	162	1447.2	4343	1529	21	124	67	57	5996	145	120	119	47	.72	1	2	6	82	0.51	.979
American League	1134	20283.1	60850	22715	391	1432	658	774	84997	2037	1692	1591	620	.70	17	71	148	847	0.38	.983

National League Batting

Tm	G	AB	H	2B	3B	HR	(Hm	Rd)	TB	R	RBI	TBB	IBB	SO	HBP	SH	SF	ShO	SB	CS	SB%	GDP	LOD	Avg	OBP	Slg
StL	162	5532	1513	308	22	162	(67	95)	2351	762	726	542	64	978	44	84	40	8	57	39	.59	169	1755	.273	.341	.425
Cin	162	5612	1438	264	19	183	(105	78)	2289	735	697	535	52	1250	63	78	40	9	97	50	.66	98	1753	.256	.326	.408
Col	162	5544	1429	274	40	163	(94	69)	2272	735	697	555	54	1201	57	75	44	8	118	42	.74	112	1742	.258	.329	.410
Ari	162	5421	1357	293	37	172	(93	79)	2240	731	702	531	55	1249	61	50	33	4	133	55	.71	82	1608	.250	.322	.413
Mil	162	5447	1422	276	31	185	(102	83)	2315	721	693	481	53	1083	56	85	44	12	94	31	.75	114	1675	.261	.325	.425
NYM	162	5600	1477	309	39	108	(50	58)	2188	718	676	571	56	1085	51	65	48	9	130	35	.79	112	1885	.264	.335	.391
Phi	162	5579	1409	258	38	153	(77	76)	2202	713	693	539	52	1024	56	65	38	7	96	24	.80	108	1778	.253	.323	.395
ChC	162	5549	1423	285	36	148	(73	75)	2224	654	610	425	35	1202	59	60	35	10	69	23	.75	123	1727	.256	.314	.401
LAD	161	5436	1395	237	28	117	(53	64)	2039	644	613	498	61	1087	45	71	43	13	126	40	.76	101	1770	.257	.322	.375
Atl	162	5528	1345	244	16	173	(90	83)	2140	641	606	504	45	1260	28	75	30	10	77	44	.64	113	1643	.243	.308	.387
Fla	162	5508	1358	274	30	149	(72	77)	2139	625	596	542	38	1244	51	89	42	12	95	41	.70	111	1785	.247	.318	.388
Was	161	5441	1319	257	22	154	(83	71)	2082	624	594	470	40	1323	65	82	32	14	106	38	.74	103	1641	.242	.309	.383
Hou	162	5598	1442	309	28	95	(46	49)	2092	615	579	401	34	1164	46	66	37	12	118	33	.78	111	1742	.258	.311	.374
Pit	162	5421	1325	277	35	107	(49	58)	1993	610	580	489	31	1308	34	75	44	14	108	52	.68	123	1630	.244	.309	.368
SD	162	5417	1284	247	42	91	(46	45)	1888	593	563	501	42	1320	48	55	47	19	170	44	.79	105	1656	.237	.305	.349
SF	162	5486	1327	282	24	121	(42	79)	2020	570	534	448	47	1122	52	62	43	14	85	51	.63	118	1740	.242	.303	.368
NL	1295	88119	22263	4394	487	2281	(1142	1139)	34474	10691	10159	8032	759	18900	816	1137	640	175	1679	642	.72	1803	27530	.253	.319	.391

National League Pitching

Tm	G	CG	Rel	IP	BFP	H	R	ER	HR	SH	SF	HB	TBB	IBB	SO	WP	Bk	W	L	Pct.	ShO	Sv-Op	Hld	OAvg	OOBP	OSlg	ERA
Phi	162	18	395	1477.0	6069	1320	529	495	120	83	33	47	404	41	1299	23	6	102	60	.630	21	47-55	56	.240	.296	.361	3.02
SF	162	3	480	1468.0	6130	1260	578	522	96	71	28	50	559	46	1316	42	4	86	76	.531	12	52-66	81	.232	.309	.346	3.20
Atl	162	3	510	1479.2	6220	1332	605	572	125	65	39	53	521	73	1332	61	5	89	73	.549	16	52-77	99	.240	.310	.361	3.48
SD	162	0	490	1449.1	6065	1324	611	551	125	68	30	37	521	56	1139	45	6	71	91	.438	10	44-62	82	.245	.314	.375	3.42
LAD	161	7	461	1432.0	5997	1287	612	563	132	69	33	43	507	48	1565	50	7	82	79	.509	17	40-53	63	.241	.310	.371	3.54
Mil	162	1	434	1441.2	6048	1348	638	582	147	57	35	33	440	16	1257	70	5	96	66	.593	13	47-66	74	.246	.304	.385	3.63
Was	161	3	503	1449.1	6141	1403	643	577	129	84	41	52	477	43	1049	49	6	80	81	.497	10	49-77	98	.256	.319	.382	3.58
Ari	162	5	463	1443.1	6102	1414	662	609	159	62	46	53	442	16	1058	39	7	94	68	.580	12	58-71	75	.257	.316	.409	3.80
StL	162	7	468	1462.0	6211	1461	692	608	136	73	36	44	448	44	1098	48	3	90	72	.556	9	47-73	68	.261	.319	.398	3.74
Fla	162	7	508	1459.2	6200	1403	702	640	149	69	40	37	500	72	1218	43	10	72	90	.444	11	40-59	69	.253	.316	.401	3.95
Pit	162	5	549	1449.1	6317	1513	712	650	152	69	53	62	535	65	1031	60	6	72	90	.444	11	43-65	92	.270	.338	.409	4.04
Cin	162	3	502	1467.2	6259	1414	720	678	185	60	52	59	539	47	1112	51	13	79	83	.488	5	39-61	73	.255	.325	.415	4.16
NYM	162	6	514	1448.0	6316	1482	742	674	147	95	42	70	514	48	1126	46	7	77	85	.475	9	43-67	75	.265	.332	.411	4.19
ChC	162	4	495	1434.1	6262	1439	756	690	162	81	44	53	580	45	1224	51	5	71	91	.438	5	40-64	86	.262	.335	.413	4.33
Col	162	5	517	1447.2	6215	1471	774	713	176	51	41	48	522	47	1118	65	7	73	89	.451	7	41-64	97	.265	.331	.431	4.43
Hou	162	2	503	1435.0	6268	1477	796	719	188	72	37	53	560	59	1191	39	9	56	106	.346	6	25-50	50	.266	.337	.432	4.51
NL	1295	80	7792	23244.0	98820	22348	10772	9843	2328	1129	630	796	8069	766	18833	782	106	1290	1300	.498	174	707-1030	1238	.253	.320	.394	3.81

National League Fielding

Team	G	Inn	PO	Ast	OFAst	E	(Throw	Field)	TC	DP	GDP	SB	CS	SB%	CPkof	PPkof	PB	UER	UERA	FPct
Philadelphia	162	1477.0	4431	1620	15	74	32	42	6125	136	122	106	29	.79	1	2	12	34	0.21	.988
Atlanta	162	1479.2	4439	1675	16	83	31	52	6197	131	110	128	41	.76	1	1	9	33	0.20	.987
Los Angeles	161	1432.0	4296	1511	36	85	45	40	5892	121	95	116	40	.74	5	3	8	49	0.31	.986
Cincinnati	162	1467.2	4403	1758	28	91	37	54	6252	146	121	81	44	.65	0	5	5	42	0.26	.985
Arizona	162	1443.1	4330	1604	24	90	42	48	6024	131	108	61	43	.59	2	3	9	53	0.33	.985
San Diego	162	1449.1	4348	1694	25	94	41	53	6136	139	117	141	60	.70	5	5	10	60	0.37	.985
Florida	162	1459.2	4379	1553	25	93	43	50	6025	126	102	103	24	.81	2	6	10	62	0.38	.985
Colorado	162	1447.2	4343	1758	32	98	44	54	6199	156	131	99	49	.67	1	6	17	61	0.38	.984
San Francisco	162	1468.0	4404	1657	38	104	40	64	6165	127	100	124	59	.68	2	3	14	56	0.34	.983
Washington	161	1449.1	4348	1691	38	104	43	61	6143	145	115	76	40	.66	0	3	8	66	0.41	.983
Pittsburgh	162	1449.1	4348	1771	25	112	53	59	6231	154	130	123	40	.75	2	6	13	62	0.39	.982
St Louis	162	1462.0	4386	1815	22	116	48	68	6317	167	144	64	25	.72	2	7	10	84	0.52	.982
Milwaukee	162	1441.2	4325	1587	25	111	45	66	6023	130	111	102	37	.73	0	2	4	56	0.35	.982
New York	162	1448.0	4344	1697	17	116	53	63	6157	128	111	121	33	.79	0	6	26	68	0.42	.981
Houston	162	1435.0	4305	1632	39	116	54	62	6053	142	113	131	31	.81	4	5	8	77	0.48	.981
Chicago	162	1434.1	4303	1558	31	134	71	63	5995	128	103	112	46	.71	0	6	7	66	0.41	.978
National League	1295	23244.0	69732	26581	446	1621	722	899	97934	2205	1833	1688	641	.72	27	69	170	929	0.36	.983

Team Pitching Staff Summary

Team	Starters				Bullpen				
	IP	ERA	ERA Rank	W-L	IP	ERA	ERA Rank	W-L	Sv-Opp
Arizona Diamondbacks	1004.0	3.84	13	71-54	439.1	3.71	14	23-14	58-71
Atlanta Braves	957.1	3.73	9	63-48	522.1	3.03	1	26-25	52-77
Baltimore Orioles	881.0	5.39	30	46-72	565.2	4.19	27	23-21	32-51
Boston Red Sox	940.0	4.49	22	64-50	517.1	3.67	13	26-22	36-52
Chicago Cubs	931.2	4.79	28	46-65	502.2	3.51	9	25-26	40-64
Chicago White Sox	1021.2	4.20	18	58-61	438.1	3.88	21	21-22	42-62
Cincinnati Reds	968.2	4.47	21	50-55	499.0	3.55	11	29-28	39-61
Cleveland Indians	961.1	4.51	23	53-61	492.0	3.71	14	27-21	38-54
Colorado Rockies	939.0	4.73	27	53-68	508.2	3.91	23	20-21	41-64
Detroit Tigers	991.0	4.10	16	72-47	449.0	3.93	25	23-20	52-62
Florida Marlins	944.1	4.23	20	42-60	515.1	3.44	7	30-30	40-59
Houston Astros	964.0	4.52	24	35-71	471.0	4.49	29	21-35	25-50
Kansas City Royals	943.0	4.82	29	45-65	508.1	3.76	19	26-26	37-60
Los Angeles Angels	1043.0	3.59	5	62-50	422.0	3.52	10	24-26	39-64
Los Angeles Dodgers	993.0	3.41	3	65-61	439.0	3.92	24	17-18	40-53
Milwaukee Brewers	992.0	3.78	10	73-43	449.2	3.33	6	23-23	47-66
Minnesota Twins	961.0	4.64	26	46-71	460.2	4.52	30	17-28	32-52
New York Mets	974.0	4.12	17	53-58	474.0	4.33	28	24-27	43-67
New York Yankees	979.1	4.04	14	71-45	479.0	3.12	4	26-20	47-63
Oakland Athletics	992.2	3.70	8	59-63	455.0	3.74	18	15-25	39-57
Philadelphia Phillies	1064.2	2.86	1	76-42	412.1	3.45	8	26-18	47-56
Pittsburgh Pirates	923.1	4.21	19	49-61	526.0	3.76	19	23-29	43-65
San Diego Padres	965.2	3.62	6	52-66	483.2	3.05	3	19-25	44-62
San Francisco Giants	997.2	3.29	2	60-58	470.1	3.04	2	26-18	52-66
Seattle Mariners	1021.1	4.04	14	49-75	411.2	3.61	12	18-20	39-55
St Louis Cardinals	999.0	3.81	12	62-42	463.0	3.73	16	28-30	47-73
Tampa Bay Rays	1058.0	3.53	4	67-56	391.0	3.73	16	24-15	32-44
Texas Rangers	994.1	3.65	7	74-40	447.0	4.11	26	22-26	38-57
Toronto Blue Jays	964.2	4.56	25	51-61	494.0	3.88	21	30-20	33-58
Washington Nationals	928.2	3.80	11	49-58	520.2	3.20	5	31-23	49-77

Team Defense
Defensive Runs Saved by Position and Team

Team	Pitcher	Catcher	First Base	Second Base	Third Base	Shortstop	Left Field	Center Field	Right Field	Total
Tampa Bay Rays	-2	1	2	21	11	20	15	-2	11	77
Los Angeles Angels	-6	0	9	8	10	0	5	23	10	59
Cincinnati Reds	12	-1	3	7	10	13	14	-3	-1	54
Texas Rangers	1	-1	-9	14	10	13	6	9	2	45
San Diego Padres	8	-2	11	-9	12	-6	0	10	12	36
Arizona Diamondbacks	10	7	-4	2	-4	1	9	6	6	33
Washington Nationals	-3	3	-6	3	0	1	14	13	8	33
San Francisco Giants	1	7	10	-14	27	3	6	1	-15	26
Atlanta Braves	1	-1	0	-11	3	12	10	-5	15	24
Toronto Blue Jays	3	-2	-6	12	27	9	-9	-12	-1	21
Milwaukee Brewers	7	-6	1	8	-2	-5	-7	20	3	19
Colorado Rockies	20	10	-4	-4	0	13	-8	-7	-3	17
Seattle Mariners	1	-3	-6	14	1	16	-6	-5	3	15
Cleveland Indians	11	2	-7	-8	8	-5	9	-5	3	8
Los Angeles Dodgers	6	-1	2	-13	8	-8	1	4	7	6
Kansas City Royals	0	4	-18	-2	-5	4	8	2	10	3
Boston Red Sox	-15	0	6	12	-8	-6	1	6	0	-4
Oakland Athletics	-5	0	0	4	-17	-2	5	-5	11	-9
Florida Marlins	2	-3	3	-3	-10	-16	1	1	15	-10
St Louis Cardinals	11	-7	0	-1	-4	-19	1	4	2	-13
Houston Astros	-6	-1	8	-13	-23	9	10	-7	9	-14
New York Yankees	-8	1	2	6	5	-31	22	-15	3	-15
Pittsburgh Pirates	-1	-3	-5	-6	1	-2	4	5	-11	-18
Detroit Tigers	-9	-1	-4	-9	-8	-2	3	21	-9	-18
Chicago White Sox	-7	-3	-12	0	-3	8	-2	-5	6	-18
Minnesota Twins	11	-1	7	-12	-13	-27	-1	11	-2	-27
Philadelphia Phillies	-7	-8	-11	0	12	0	-15	4	-7	-32
New York Mets	5	-8	13	-16	-7	-13	-4	1	-7	-36
Chicago Cubs	-6	-1	4	-6	-17	-15	-3	-4	11	-37
Baltimore Orioles	4	13	-4	-4	-37	6	-6	-13	-4	-45

2011 Team Efficiency Summary

Bill James

The concept of "efficiency", as we mean it here, asks the question "Does this team put together the elements of wins in combinations that work?" Given the number of singles, doubles, triples and whatnot that the team's hitters have, do they score the number of runs that they should score? Given the number of hits and walks and such like that the pitchers surrender, do they give up the number of runs that we would expect them to give up? And, given the number of runs that they score and allow, does this team win the number of games that they should win?

The Pittsburgh Pirates in 2011 had a better year than they have had recently in large part because they were super-efficient, the most efficient team in baseball. The Kansas City Royals—the Pittsburgh Pirates of the American League—showed much more progress than the Pirates did in terms of underlying skills, but finished with a worse record than the Pirates because they were very inefficient in terms of putting things together to make wins. If the Royals had been as efficient as the Pirates were the Royals would have made the playoffs; if the Pirates had been as inefficient as the Royals were they would have lost easily more than 100 games. Instead, the Pirates won 72 games, and the Royals 71.

2011 American League Team Efficiency Summary

	RC	Runs	Hit Eff	Exp RA	RA	Pit Eff	Exp Wins	Wins	Runs Eff	Eff Wins	Wins	Overall Eff
Minnesota Twins	600	619	103	796	804	99	60	63	104	59	63	107
Toronto Blue Jays	717	743	104	754	761	99	79	81	102	77	81	105
Cleveland Indians	683	704	103	723	760	95	75	80	107	76	80	105
Baltimore Orioles	702	708	101	840	860	98	65	69	105	67	69	104
New York Yankees	836	867	104	698	657	106	103	97	94	95	97	102
Detroit Tigers	804	787	98	686	711	96	89	95	107	94	95	101
Los Angeles Angels	673	667	99	639	633	101	85	86	101	85	86	101
Chicago White Sox	671	654	98	676	706	96	75	79	106	80	79	98
Oakland Athletics	629	645	103	668	679	98	77	74	96	76	74	97
Seattle Mariners	558	556	100	644	675	95	65	67	102	69	67	97
Tampa Bay Rays	705	707	100	595	614	97	92	91	99	95	91	96
Texas Rangers	864	855	99	640	677	94	100	96	96	105	96	92
Boston Red Sox	896	875	98	699	737	95	95	90	95	101	90	89
Kansas City Royals	764	730	96	764	762	100	78	71	92	81	71	88

2011 National League Team Efficiency Summary

	RC	Runs	Hit Eff	Exp RA	RA	Pit Eff	Exp Wins	Wins	Runs Eff	Eff Wins	Wins	Overall Eff
Pittsburgh Pirates	605	610	101	764	712	107	69	72	105	63	72	115
Arizona Diamondbacks	720	731	102	674	662	102	89	94	106	86	94	109
Atlanta Braves	645	641	99	607	605	100	86	89	104	86	89	104
Milwaukee Brewers	743	721	97	631	638	99	91	96	106	94	96	102
San Francisco Giants	597	570	95	571	578	99	80	86	108	85	86	102
Washington Nationals	639	624	98	653	643	101	78	80	102	79	80	102
Philadelphia Phillies	720	713	99	548	529	104	104	102	98	103	102	99
Chicago Cubs	684	654	96	766	756	101	69	71	102	72	71	99
St Louis Cardinals	770	762	99	673	692	97	89	90	101	92	90	98
Cincinnati Reds	744	735	99	723	720	100	83	79	96	83	79	95
New York Mets	749	718	96	746	742	100	78	77	98	81	77	95
Los Angeles Dodgers	671	644	96	601	612	98	85	82	97	89	82	92
San Diego Padres	591	593	100	613	611	100	79	71	90	78	71	91
Colorado Rockies	750	735	98	751	774	97	77	73	95	81	73	90
Florida Marlins	678	625	92	666	702	95	72	72	101	83	72	87
Houston Astros	647	615	95	788	796	99	61	56	92	65	56	86

Albert Pujols   Brett Gardner
Dustin Pedroia   Austin Jackson
Adrian Beltre   Justin Upton
Troy Tulowitzki   Matt Wieters
Mark Buehrle

THE FIELDING BIBLE AWARDS 2011

The Fielding Bible Awards 2011

John Dewan

Chase Utley, baseball's best baserunner, is on first base with nobody out in the top of the sixth in the 2011 NLDS. Utley and his fellow Phillies are one win away from advancing to the league championship series, leading the five-game series two games to one, but they are down in the game 3-2. If they can score, it's a tie game.

Hunter Pence hits a groundball to shortstop Rafael Furcal. Since Utley is running with the pitch there's no chance to get him on a force at second, so Furcal throws to first.

Utley knows baserunning, down to the split second. He has a full head of steam rounding second base and he knows that, as the Cards make the out at first, he'll have just enough time, even with a throw, to make it safely into third.

Except that Albert Pujols decides to skip the out at first. He comes off the bag early to intercept the throw. His momentum takes him about ten to fifteen feet closer to third base and his perfectly accurate throw nabs Utley despite his head-first slide. Instead of having the tying run on third with one out, there's just a runner on first.

A brilliant play by a brilliant defender taking out a brilliant baserunner in an extremely crucial situation. Plays like this are the reason that Albert Pujols has won his fifth Fielding Bible Award for defensive excellence in the six seasons that the award has been in existence.

Joining Pujols as repeat winners in 2011 are: Mark Buehrle (his third in a row), Troy Tulowitzki (three), Adrian Beltre (three), and Brett Gardner (two). First time Fielding Bible Award winners this year are Dustin Pedroia, Austin Jackson, Justin Upton and Matt Wieters.

Here's a short refresher course on how the awards are determined: We asked our panel of ten experts to rank 10 players at each position on a scale from one to ten. We then use the same voting technique as the Major League Baseball MVP voting. A first place vote gets 10 points, second place 9 points, third place 8 points, etc. Total up the points for each player and the player with the most points wins the award. A perfect score is 100.

One important distinction that differentiates our award from most other baseball awards, including the Gold Gloves, is that we only have one winner for all of Major League Baseball, instead of separate winners for each league. Our intention is to continue to stand up and say, "This is the best fielder at this position in the major leagues last season."

Oh, and one more distinction from the Gold Gloves that isn't a distinction anymore. They have finally agreed with us this year that separate awards should be given for left fielders, center fielders, and right fielders. They are different positions, folks, and now even the Gold Glove award establishment admits it.

Here are the Fielding Bible Awards for the 2011 season:

First Base – Albert Pujols, St. Louis

Albert Pujols reclaims his award after a one-year hiatus (Daric Barton). The Throw in the NLDS was no fluke. Since Baseball Info Solutions started tracking Good Fielding Plays (GFP) in 2004, Albert Pujols has 37 GFPs on throws. The next best first basemen are Todd Helton with 16, and three others with 15, Mark Teixeira, Prince Fielder and Lyle Overbay.

Previous Winners:

2010	Daric Barton
2009	Albert Pujols
2008	Albert Pujols
2007	Albert Pujols
2006	Albert Pujols

Second Base – Dustin Pedroia, Boston

Dustin Pedroia wins his first Fielding Bible Award with 97 of a possible 100 points. He took seven first place votes and was voted second by the other three panelists. Pedroia has done well in voting in each of the last four years. He lost in a tie-breaker to Aaron Hill in 2009 (each had 76 points), placed fourth in 2008 and seventh in 2010.

Previous Winners:

2010   Chase Utley
2009   Aaron Hill
2008   Brandon Phillips
2007   Aaron Hill
2006   Orlando Hudson

Third Base – Adrian Beltre, Texas

Adrian Beltre received eight first place votes beating last year's winner, Evan Longoria, 98 to 90. It doesn't matter where he plays. Los Angeles, Seattle, Boston and now Texas. Beltre excels year after year. He has saved an estimated 156 runs defensively for his teams since 2003, an average of 17 runs prevented per year. That was his exact total for the Rangers in 2011, which translates into about two extra wins per year for his clubs, just on defense.

Previous Winners:

2010   Evan Longoria
2009   Ryan Zimmerman
2008   Adrian Beltre
2007   Pedro Feliz
2006   Adrian Beltre

Shortstop – Troy Tulowitzki, Colorado

Troy Tulowitzki goes back-to-back, two Fielding Bible Awards in two years, and his third award of his five-year MLB career. Tulo is especially adept at making plays to his right. The Plus/Minus System credits him with 45 more plays in the shortstop hole compared to an average MLB shortstop over his five seasons. Tulowitzki also excels in another area. He had 67 Good Fielding Plays in 2011 compared to only 29 Defensive Misplays or Errors. That +38 figure was tops in baseball. (Alcides Escobar was second at shortstop with +30.) Dustin Pedroia was tops among second basemen in 2011 with +44, so he and Tulowitzki make a truly spectacular double play combination as Fielding Bible Award winners.

Previous Winners:

2010   Troy Tulowitzki
2009   Jack Wilson
2008   Jimmy Rollins
2007   Troy Tulowitzki
2006   Adam Everett

Left Field – Brett Gardner, New York Yankees

Brett Gardner is the new Carl Crawford. Gardner repeats as the Fielding Bible Award winner in left field after Crawford won three of the four previous years. It was nearly unanimous as Gardner took nine first-place votes and one second. Gardner's 22 Defensive Runs Saved tied him with center field winner Austin Jackson for the most runs saved by an outfielder in 2011. That's an extraordinary total for a left fielder. Normally the best center fielders save significantly more runs defensively than the best left fielders. For Gardner, having a center fielder's range gives him a tremendous advantage, but he has an excellent throwing arm as well. He has saved the Yankees 13 runs (out of his 35 total) with his arm over the last two years.

Previous Winners:

2010   Brett Gardner
2009   Carl Crawford
2008   Carl Crawford
2007   Eric Byrnes
2006   Carl Crawford

Center Field – Austin Jackson, Detroit

He topped all center fielders with 21 Runs Saved in 2010, but Austin Jackson had to do it even better (with 22 Runs Saved) in 2011 to earn his first Fielding Bible Award. Jackson has made 63 more plays than an average center fielder over the last two years. That's an incredible total. It's on the plays over his head that AJ really excels (43 of the 63). Making 43 more catches than an average center fielder on balls hit deep is where those lofty Runs Saved totals come in, as he is saving doubles and triples when he makes these catches.

Previous Winners:

2010   Michael Bourn
2009   Franklin Gutierrez

2008 Carlos Beltran
2007 Andruw Jones
2006 Carlos Beltran

Right Field – Justin Upton, Arizona

Justin Upton wins his first Fielding Bible Award in 2011, unseating three-time winner Ichiro Suzuki. With Ichiro's down year defensively (he finished tenth in the voting), panelists were divided in their balloting with seven different right fielders receiving first place votes. Upton received three first-place votes, Jason Heyward two, with one apiece for Mike Stanton, Torii Hunter, Andre Ethier, Jay Bruce and Nate Schierholtz. Like Austin Jackson in center field, Upton excels on deeply hit balls, where he fielded 18 more balls in 2011 than the average right fielder would have, based on the depth, angle and velocity of those hit to him.

Previous Winners:

2010 Ichiro Suzuki
2009 Ichiro Suzuki
2008 Franklin Gutierrez
2007 Alex Rios
2006 Ichiro Suzuki

Catcher – Matt Wieters, Baltimore

After Yadier Molina won the previous four Fielding Bible Awards, Matt Wieters wins his first. And it wasn't even close in the voting, Wieters 97 to Molina 74. When you look at the numbers, it wasn't close there either. Prior to 2011, Molina has thrown out 42% of baserunners. On top of that, he has picked off an average of six baserunners per year. In 2011, Yadier dropped to 25% caught stealing and only picked two runners off. Wieters threw out 36% of basestealers in 2011. But it was the pitcher handling department where Wieters really excelled. Nine of his 14 runs saved are estimated for his pitcher handling, while Molina also had a down year in this area, costing the Cardinals six runs.

Previous Winners:

2010 Yadier Molina
2009 Yadier Molina
2008 Yadier Molina
2007 Yadier Molina
2006 Ivan Rodriguez

Pitcher – Mark Buehrle, Chicago White Sox

It's a third consecutive Fielding Bible Award for Mark Buehrle. It is remarkable how Buehrle puts up excellent Defensive Runs Saved numbers year after year. He saved an estimated nine runs defensively for the White Sox in 2011, tops among all pitchers in baseball. He had eight saved runs in 2010, 11 in 2009, and has averaged about eight per year going back to 2004. His control of the running game is uncanny. Only three baserunners were successful stealing bases in 2011 with Buehrle on the mound, while nine of them were caught stealing or picked off by Buehrle. He covers his position as well, with 15 of his Runs Saved guarding the territory around the mound over the last three years.

Previous Winners:

2010	Mark Buehrle
2009	Mark Buehrle
2008	Kenny Rogers
2007	Johan Santana
2006	Greg Maddux

Background of the Fielding Bible Awards

While the first *The Fielding Bible* and *The Fielding Bible—Volume II* (and the upcoming *The Fielding Bible—Volume III*) put a lot of emphasis on the numbers, especially Defensive Runs Saved and the Plus-Minus system, I feel that visual observation and subjective judgment are still very important parts of determining the best defensive players. Also, I think people have a right to know who is voting and all the players they are voting for. Therefore, in setting up the Fielding Bible Awards, we took the following steps:

1. *We appointed a panel of experts to vote.* We have a panel of ten experts plus three "tie-breaker" ballots. (See below.)

2. *We rate everybody in one group.* The Gold Glove vote is divided into National League and American League. We make ours different by putting everybody together. Besides, is playing shortstop in the American League one thing and playing shortstop in the National League a different thing, or are they really very much the same thing? Two years ago we had a great example of this rule. Without the Fielding Bible Award, Jack Wilson wins nada, because he switched teams in mid-year. According to our panelists (and unlike the Gold Glove voters), Jack was the best fielding shortstop in baseball in 2009. Period. He deserved to be recognized for that.

3. *We use a ten-man ballot and a ten-point scale.* We use a ten-man ballot (I'm referring to the players listed, not the panel of experts). Then we give ten points for first place, nine

points for second place, etc, down to one point for tenth place. We feel strongly that a ten-man ballot with weighted positions leads to more accurate outcomes.

4. We defined the list of candidates. Only players who actually were regulars at the position are candidates. This eliminates the possibility of a vote going to somebody who wasn't really playing the position.

5. We are publishing the balloting. We summarize the voting at each position, clearly identifying whom everybody voted for. Publishing the actual vote totals encourages the voters to take their votes more seriously. Also, we feel the public will have more respect for the voting if they have more insight into the process.

There is something cool about having 10 experts and a 10-man ballot and a 10-point scale, because that gives each position 100 possible points. If all 10 voters place one player first on their ballot, he scores 100. This year it was close for Brett Gardner as he scored 99.

Here are the tie-breaker rules (which came into play in our very first year and did so again in 2010). They are applied one at a time until we have a winner:
   1. Most first-place votes wins.
   2. Count the tie-breaker ballots, highest point tally wins.
   3. Award goes to player with the higher plus/minus rating.

Ballots were due two days after the end of the regular season. Here is this year's panel:

Since you have this book, you probably know **Bill James**, a baseball writer and analyst published for more than thirty years. Bill is the Senior Baseball Operations Advisor for the Boston Red Sox.

The **BIS Video Scouts** at Baseball Info Solutions (BIS) study every game of the season, multiple times, charting a huge list of valuable game details.

The man who created Strat-O-Matic Baseball, **Hal Richman**, continues to lead his company's annual in-depth analysis of each player's season. Hal cautions SOM players that his voting on this ballot may or may not reflect the eventual fielding ratings for players in his game. Ballots were due prior to the completion of his annual research effort to evaluate player defense.

Named the best sports columnist in America by the Associated Press Sports Editors in 2003 and 2005, **Joe Posnanski** is a Senior Writer at Sports Illustrated and occasional columnist for the Kansas City Star. His website is joeposnanski.com

For over twenty-five years, BIS owner **John Dewan** has collected, analyzed, and published in-depth baseball statistics and analysis. He wrote *The Fielding Bible* in 2006 and *The Fielding Bible—Volume II* in 2009. *The Fielding Bible—Volume III* comes out this spring.

Peter Gammons serves as on-air and online analyst for MLB Network, MLB.com and NESN (New England Sports Network). He is the 56th recipient of the J. G. Taylor Spink Award for outstanding baseball writing given by the BBWAA (Baseball Writers Association of America).

Doug Glanville played nine seasons in Major League Baseball and was well known for his excellent outfield defense. Currently, he is a baseball analyst at ESPN, primarily on Baseball Tonight, ESPN.com and ESPN The Magazine.

After nearly fifteen years with ESPN.com, **Rob Neyer** joined SB Nation as National Baseball Editor in 2011. He has written six books about baseball.

Todd Radcliffe is Lead Video Scout at Baseball Info Solutions and brings 15 years of Major League Baseball scouting experience to the panel.

The **Tom Tango Fan Poll** represents the results of a poll taken at the website, Tango on Baseball (www.tangotiger.net). Besides hosting the website, Tom writes research articles devoted to sabermetrics.

Our three tie-breakers are **Steve Moyer**, president of Baseball Info Solutions, **Dan Casey**, veteran Video Scout at BIS, and **Dave Studenmund**, one of the founders of www.hardballtimes.com and The Hardball Times Baseball Annual.

The Fielding Bible Awards

Below we show the final point tally for The Fielding Bible Awards in the 2011 season. We asked a panel of experts to complete a ten-man ballot ranking players from 1 to 10 based on the defensive abilities. We show the ranks in the tables below. We then awarded points in the same way as Major League Baseball's MVP voting: ten points for a first place vote, nine for second, etc., down to one point for tenth place. We cover all nine positions, looking at only their fielding work for the 2011 season. Non-pitchers are only eligible if they played at least 500 innings. Pitchers require a minimum of 100 innings pitched.

First Basemen

First Basemen	Bill James	BIS Video Scouts	Doug Glanville	Hal Richman	Joe Posnanski	John Dewan	Peter Gammons	Rob Neyer	Tango Fan Poll	Todd Radcliffe	Total Points
Albert Pujols	1	4	2	4	1	2	8	1	1	4	82
Adrian Gonzalez	7	2	3	2	2	1	2	2	3	8	78
James Loney	3	3	1	8	6	3	3	3	9	1	70
Mark Teixeira	9	5	6	1	8	7	4	9	4	2	55
Todd Helton	6	6			10	5	5	4	2	10	40
Daric Barton	2	9	9	10	3	4			6	6	39
Mark Trumbo	4	1	8		4	8				5	36
Casey Kotchman	8	8		3	7			6	8	3	34
Carlos Pena		7	5	9		9	7	8		9	23
Daniel Murphy	5	10			5	6					18

Others receiving points: Joey Votto 17, Derrek Lee 16, Freddie Freeman 14, Eric Hosmer 10, Aubrey Huff 7, Gaby Sanchez 7, Adam Lind 4

Second Basemen

Second Basemen	Bill James	BIS Video Scouts	Doug Glanville	Hal Richman	Joe Posnanski	John Dewan	Peter Gammons	Rob Neyer	Tango Fan Poll	Todd Radcliffe	Total Points
Dustin Pedroia	1	1	1	2	1	2	2	1	1	1	97
Ben Zobrist	4	2	6	5	2	1	3	2	7	2	76
Brandon Phillips	8	5	5	1	4	5	5	8	2	3	64
Mark Ellis	6	6	3	7	8	4	4	5	8	5	54
Ian Kinsler	2	3	8	9	10	3	10	4	4	4	53
Chase Utley	9	9	10	6	5	6	1	3	5	6	50
Robinson Cano	3	7		3	3	8	6			7	40
Howie Kendrick	7	4	4		6	7	9	7	9	9	37
Gordon Beckham	10	8	2			9	7	6	10	10	26
Danny Espinosa			7	8					3		15
Omar Infante				4			8		6		15

Others receiving points: Dustin Ackley 8, Aaron Hill 6, Orlando Hudson 6, Chris Getz 2, Neil Walker 1

Third Basemen

Third Basemen	Bill James	BIS Video Scouts	Doug Glanville	Hal Richman	Joe Posnanski	John Dewan	Peter Gammons	Rob Neyer	Tango Fan Poll	Todd Radcliffe	Total Points
Adrian Beltre	2	1	2	1	1	1	1	1	1	1	98
Evan Longoria	1	2	1	2	2	3	3	2	2	2	90
Pablo Sandoval	9	3	3	7	4	2	2	4	10	3	63
Placido Polanco	3	4	9	4	6	4	5	3	6	7	59
Scott Rolen	4	8	10	5	5	5	7	7	5	6	48
Jack Hannahan		6	7	6	9	6	4	6	3	5	47
Ryan Zimmerman	6	7		3	3	7	6		4	8	44
Alex Rodriguez	8	5	8		7	9	8	5			27
Brent Morel	7	9	6	9			9	9	7		21
Miguel Tejada			5		8	10					10
Alberto Callaspo	5	10							10	9	10

Others receiving points: Chase Headley 8, Juan Uribe 8, Chone Figgins 7, Brandon Inge 6, Daniel Descalso 2, Mike Moustakas 1, Scott Sizemore 1

Shortstops

Shortstops	Bill James	BIS Video Scouts	Doug Glanville	Hal Richman	Joe Posnanski	John Dewan	Peter Gammons	Rob Neyer	Tango Fan Poll	Todd Radcliffe	Total Points
Troy Tulowitzki	3	1	1	1	1	2	1	3	1	2	94
Brendan Ryan	4	2	4	2	2	1		1	5	1	77
Alex Gonzalez	1	3	2	6	3	3	3	8	4	3	74
Alcides Escobar	5	5	3	4	5		7	2	3	4	61
Clint Barmes	2	6	5		4	7	4	4			45
Paul Janish	7			8	8	5	2	6	9	5	38
Elvis Andrus	6	4	9		6	4	6		6	9	38
Alexei Ramirez		7	8	3		6	10	5		7	31
Jimmy Rollins			6	7					2	6	23
Ronny Cedeno			10		7		5	7			15

Others receiving points: Yunel Escobar 13, Reid Brignac 12, Asdrubal Cabrera 10, J.J. Hardy 8, Jose Reyes 6, Erick Aybar 3, Cliff Pennington 2

Left Fielders

Left Fielders	Bill James	BIS Video Scouts	Doug Glanville	Hal Richman	Joe Posnanski	John Dewan	Peter Gammons	Rob Neyer	Tango Fan Poll	Todd Radcliffe	Total Points
Brett Gardner	1	1	1	1	1	1	1	1	2	1	99
Tony Gwynn	4	5	4	5	3	3	3	4	3	2	74
Gerardo Parra	5	3	2	4	4	7	4	2	4	3	72
Alex Gordon	2	2	7		2	6	7	3	8	5	57
Sam Fuld	3	4	3	7	5	5		5	6		50
Josh Hamilton		6	6	3		2	9	9	5	7	41
Carlos Gonzalez	10	7	5	2		4			1		37
Carl Crawford		10		6	6	10		6	7	6	26
Michael Brantley	9	8			7	8	5	7			22
Ryan Braun			10		10		2			4	18

Others receiving points: Jose Tabata 11, Matt Holliday 8, David Murphy 6, Corey Patterson 5, Jason Bay 5, Ryan Sweeney 5, Carlos Lee 3, Jonny Gomes 3, Vernon Wells 3, Brennan Boesch 2, Martin Prado 2, Juan Pierre 1

Center Fielders

Center Fielders	Bill James	BIS Video Scouts	Doug Glanville	Hal Richman	Joe Posnanski	John Dewan	Peter Gammons	Rob Neyer	Tango Fan Poll	Todd Radcliffe	Total Points
Austin Jackson	1	1	3	2	2	1	2	2	5	2	89
Chris Young	2	3	1	6	1	2	5	1	7	7	75
Franklin Gutierrez	5	7	2	4	4	4	8	5	2	1	68
Carlos Gomez	4	6	5	5	6	5	3	3	4	4	65
Peter Bourjos	8	2	4	1	8	3	9	7	1	9	58
Jacoby Ellsbury	6	5	6	10	7	7	4	4		3	47
Denard Span	3		7		5		1	9		6	35
Cameron Maybin	7	4	9	9	10	6	7	6	9	10	33
Michael Bourn				3	3	10			6	8	25
Shane Victorino				7		8			3	5	21

Others receiving points: Andrew McCutchen 12, Ben Revere 12, Andres Torres 4, Rick Ankiel 4, Adam Jones 1, Coco Crisp 1

Right Fielders

Right Fielders	Bill James	BIS Video Scouts	Doug Glanville	Hal Richman	Joe Posnanski	John Dewan	Peter Gammons	Rob Neyer	Tango Fan Poll	Todd Radcliffe	Total Points
Justin Upton	2	1	1	6	1	3	2	2	6	2	84
Jason Heyward	3	3	4		2	2	3	1	7	1	73
Mike Stanton	4	2	8	7	7	8	1	5	4		53
Torii Hunter	9	4	3	3	6	1	8	6		7	52
Andre Ethier	1	5	2		3		4	4		8	50
Jay Bruce	7			1		7	5		3	5	38
Nick Markakis	5	6	10	4	4	6	9		10		34
David DeJesus	8	7	5		10	9		3		3	32
Jeff Francoeur		8		2	8	5		7		9	27
Ichiro Suzuki		10		9		10	6		2	4	25

Others receiving points: Nate Schierholtz 16, Shin-Soo Choo 13, Will Venable 12, Josh Reddick 10, Hunter Pence 7, J.D. Drew 6, Seth Smith 5, Jayson Werth 3, Jose Bautista 3, Nick Swisher 3, Carlos Quentin 2, Nelson Cruz 2

Catchers

Catchers	Bill James	BIS Video Scouts	Doug Glanville	Hal Richman	Joe Posnanski	John Dewan	Peter Gammons	Rob Neyer	Tango Fan Poll	Todd Radcliffe	Total Points
Matt Wieters	1	1	1	3	1	1	1	2	1	1	97
Yadier Molina	4	2		1	2	6	3	3	2	2	74
Carlos Ruiz	3	9	3	2	4	5	4		3	7	59
Jeff Mathis	2	3	6	4	3	2		1			56
Russell Martin	7	7		6		3	9	5	4	4	43
Miguel Montero	9	5	5	8		9	2	4		5	41
Humberto Quintero	6	8			5	4			10	9	24
Alex Avila			2		7		6		7		22
Lou Marson			7	9	9		10		6	3	22
Chris Iannetta	5	4	8	7		10					21

Others receiving points: Joe Mauer 12, Kelly Shoppach 12, Wilson Ramos 12, Rod Barajas 11, Ryan Hanigan 11, Kurt Suzuki 8, Brayan Pena 7, J.P. Arencibia 5, Drew Butera 3, Jonathan Lucroy 3, Matt Treanor 3, Geovany Soto 2, Jarrod Saltalamacchia 1, Nick Hundley 1

Pitchers

Pitchers	Bill James	BIS Video Scouts	Doug Glanville	Hal Richman	Joe Posnanski	John Dewan	Peter Gammons	Rob Neyer	Tango Fan Poll	Todd Radcliffe	Total Points
Mark Buehrle	1	1	1	1	1	1	1	1		1	90
R.A. Dickey	8	2	2		4	3	4	2	6	7	61
Jake Westbrook		6	7	2	3	2	6	6	5	6	56
James Shields	3	3	4	4	5			3		3	52
Jhoulys Chacin	9	4	3	3	6	5		4			43
Hiroki Kuroda	7	5	5	5	8			5	4		38
Zack Greinke	2	10			2	4	10	7		8	34
Joe Saunders	4	8	6		7	8		8			25
Ricky Romero	6			10		7				5	16
Jeremy Guthrie						6	3	9			15

Others receiving points: Doug Fister 14, Clayton Kershaw 11, Cory Luebke 10, Bud Norris 9, Cole Hamels 9, Tim Stauffer 9, Livan Hernandez 7, Mike Leake 7, Ian Kennedy 6, John Lannan 6, Josh Tomlin 6, Chris Narveson 5, Kyle Lohse 3, Nick Blackburn 3, Shaun Marcum 3, Trevor Cahill 3, Chris Capuano 2, Cliff Lee 2, Jeff Francis 2, Tim Wakefield 2, Jair Jurrjens 1

Runs Saved and Plus/Minus Leaders

The Runs Saved and Plus/Minus leaders showcase baseball's best fielders from 2011 and over the past three years. The three-year leaders identify the best defensive players in baseball. Take a look at the top five at each position on the 3-Year Runs Saved and Plus/Minus Leaderboards and you get an excellent idea of the best defenders at each position.

The Plus/Minus System is a way to evaluate defensive range by measuring how often defenders turn grounders and fly balls into outs. A number greater than zero (plus "+") is above average. Below zero (minus "-") is below average. In 2011, Ben Zobrist had a plus/minus figure of +23, which means he made 23 more plays than an average second baseman would have made on the same types of batted balls. Runs Saved is an estimate of the number of runs each fielder saves with his defense. It combines Plus/Minus with our analysis of bunts, double plays, outfield arms, catchers' earned runs, catchers' stolen bases allowed, pitchers' stolen bases allowed, and home run saving catches to form a complete evaluation of a fielder.

Please see the Glossary for a more complete description of Plus/Minus and Runs Saved.

Infield Runs Saved Leaders

First Basemen 3-Year Leaders		Second Basemen 3-Year Leaders		Third Basemen 3-Year Leaders		Shortstops 3-Year Leaders	
Barton,Daric	26	Kinsler,Ian	46	Beltre,Adrian	48	Ryan,Brendan	65
Gonzalez,Adrian	18	Zobrist,Ben	43	Longoria,Evan	42	Escobar,Yunel	37
Pujols,Albert	15	Hill,Aaron	35	Zimmerman,Ryan	42	Tulowitzki,Troy	36
Youkilis,Kevin	15	Utley,Chase	31	Figgins,Chone	33	Wilson,Jack	34
Davis,Ike	15	Pedroia,Dustin	31	Rolen,Scott	24	Barmes,Clint	29
Morneau,Justin	13	Cano,Robinson	20	Hannahan,Jack	22	Andrus,Elvis	28
Branyan,Russell	10	Ellis,Mark	19	Blake,Casey	21	Gonzalez,Alex	26
Overbay,Lyle	9	Hudson,Orlando	12	Headley,Chase	21	Ramirez,Alexei	25
Trumbo,Mark	8	Polanco,Placido	12	Polanco,Placido	17	Janish,Paul	19
Loney,James	7	Kendrick,Howie	11	Sandoval,Pablo	16	Izturis,Cesar	18

First Basemen 3-Year Trailers		Second Basemen 3-Year Trailers		Third Basemen 3-Year Trailers		Shortstops 3-Year Trailers	
Dunn,Adam	-31	Uggla,Dan	-28	Reynolds,Mark	-38	Betancourt,Yuniesky	-46
Konerko,Paul	-25	Keppinger,Jeff	-21	Young,Michael	-37	Cabrera,Orlando	-35
Howard,Ryan	-24	Schumaker,Skip	-21	Johnson,Chris	-31	Jeter,Derek	-29
Cabrera,Miguel	-16	Walker,Neil	-14	Wright,David	-30	Ramirez,Hanley	-20
Fielder,Prince	-15	Getz,Chris	-9	Ramirez,Aramis	-26	Tejada,Miguel	-19
Butler,Billy	-13	Kennedy,Adam	-8	Teahen,Mark	-22	Castro,Starlin	-15

First Basemen 2011 Leaders		Second Basemen 2011 Leaders		Third Basemen 2011 Leaders		Shortstop 2011 Leaders	
Trumbo,Mark	7	Zobrist,Ben	17	Sandoval,Pablo	22	Ryan,Brendan	18
Gonzalez,Adrian	6	Kinsler,Ian	16	Beltre,Adrian	17	Gonzalez,Alex	15
Murphy,Daniel	6	Kendrick,Howie	15	Polanco,Placido	16	Andrus,Elvis	13
Lee,Carlos	5	Pedroia,Dustin	13	Longoria,Evan	12	Barmes,Clint	12
Votto,Joey	4	Ellis,Mark	10	Hannahan,Jack	9	Tulowitzki,Troy	11
Sanchez,Gaby	4	Ackley,Dustin	10	Rodriguez,Alex	9	Cedeno,Ronny	8
Loney,James	4	Phillips,Brandon	7	Rolen,Scott	7	Janish,Paul	8
Huff,Aubrey	4	Hill,Aaron	7	Uribe,Juan	5	Brignac,Reid	8
Barton,Daric	4	Cano,Robinson	6	Callaspo,Alberto	4	Ramirez,Alexei	7
Pujols,Albert	3	Espinosa,Danny	4	Chisenhall,Lonnie	3	Crawford,Brandon	6

First Basemen 2011 Trailers		Second Basemen 2011 Trailers		Third Basemen 2011 Trailers		Shortstops 2011 Trailers	
Hosmer,Eric	-16	Keppinger,Jeff	-12	Reynolds,Mark	-29	Jeter,Derek	-18
Howard,Ryan	-9	Turner,Justin	-11	Johnson,Chris	-16	Castro,Starlin	-16
Morse,Michael	-7	Carroll,Jamey	-9	Sizemore,Scott	-13	Theriot,Ryan	-12
LaPorta,Matt	-7	Hudson,Orlando	-9	Betemit,Wilson	-13	Reyes,Jose	-11
Konerko,Paul	-7	Uggla,Dan	-9	Valencia,Danny	-13	Nishioka,Tsuyoshi	-10
Cabrera,Miguel	-6	Izturis,Maicer	-6	Ramirez,Aramis	-12	Ramirez,Hanley	-8

Outfield Runs Saved Leaders

Left Fielders 3-Year Leaders		Center Fielders 3-Year Leaders		Right Fielders 3-Year Leaders	
Gardner,Brett	35	Gutierrez,Franklin	54	Stanton,Mike	28
Crawford,Carl	34	Jackson,Austin	43	Suzuki,Ichiro	25
Parra,Gerardo	28	Bourjos,Peter	36	Heyward,Jason	25
Holliday,Matt	24	Gomez,Carlos	32	Zobrist,Ben	25
Nix,Laynce	23	Bourn,Michael	27	Bruce,Jay	24
Rivera,Juan	18	Morgan,Nyjer	27	Cruz,Nelson	24
Raburn,Ryan	13	Gwynn,Tony	25	Pence,Hunter	23
Gordon,Alex	10	Young,Chris	20	Werth,Jayson	23
Lewis,Fred	9	Ankiel,Rick	18	Francoeur,Jeff	22
Saunders,Michael	9	Span,Denard	15	Upton,Justin	21

Left Fielders 3-Year Trailers		Center Fielders 3-Year Trailers		Right Fielders 3-Year Trailers	
Ibanez,Raul	-21	Fowler,Dexter	-18	Hawpe,Brad	-16
Young,Delmon	-20	Wells,Vernon	-17	Quentin,Carlos	-16
Braun,Ryan	-14	McLouth,Nate	-13	Cuddyer,Michael	-16
Soriano,Alfonso	-13	Cabrera,Melky	-12	Ethier,Andre	-11
Lee,Carlos	-12	Kemp,Matt	-12	Hart,Corey	-10
Gomes,Jonny	-9	McCutchen,Andrew	-11	Markakis,Nick	-10

Left Fielders 2011 Leaders		Center Fielders 2011 Leaders		Right Fielders 2011 Leaders	
Gardner,Brett	22	Jackson,Austin	22	Hunter,Torii	15
Parra,Gerardo	11	Bourjos,Peter	21	Heyward,Jason	15
Fuld,Sam	9	Ankiel,Rick	16	DeJesus,David	13
Wells,Vernon	6	Gomez,Carlos	16	Stanton,Mike	11
Lee,Carlos	6	Maybin,Cameron	12	Venable,Will	10
Brantley,Michael	5	Revere,Ben	8	Francoeur,Jeff	6
Nix,Laynce	5	Gutierrez,Franklin	8	Ethier,Andre	5
Presley,Alex	5	Jay,Jon	8	Reddick,Josh	5
Gordon,Alex	4	McCutchen,Andrew	7	Werth,Jayson	4
Hamilton,Josh	4	Morgan,Nyjer	7	Joyce,Matt	4

Left Fielders 2011 Trailers		Center Fielders 2011 Trailers		Right Fielders 2011 Trailers	
Ibanez,Raul	-16	Granderson,Curtis	-15	Berkman,Lance	-10
Thames,Eric	-6	Davis,Rajai	-13	Boesch,Brennan	-8
Ludwick,Ryan	-6	Jones,Adam	-9	Smith,Seth	-7
Soriano,Alfonso	-5	Rios,Alex	-7	Schierholtz,Nate	-5
Young,Delmon	-4	McLouth,Nate	-5	Pence,Hunter	-5
Crawford,Carl	-4	Coghlan,Chris	-5	Francisco,Ben	-4

Pitcher/Catcher Runs Saved Leaders

Pitchers 3-Year Leaders		Catchers 3-Year Leaders	
Buehrle,Mark	28	Wieters,Matt	18
Westbrook,Jake	15	Montero,Miguel	14
Romero,Ricky	14	Martin,Russell	11
Greinke,Zack	14	Olivo,Miguel	11
Bergesen,Brad	14	Quintero,Humberto	10
Cahill,Trevor	12	Molina,Yadier	10
Dickey,R.A.	12	Hanigan,Ryan	10
Arroyo,Bronson	12	Mathis,Jeff	9
Garland,Jon	12	Mauer,Joe	7
Guthrie,Jeremy	12	Johnson,Rob	7

Pitchers 3-Year Trailers		Catchers 3-Year Trailers	
Santana,Ervin	-14	Martinez,Victor	-21
Lackey,John	-11	Hernandez,Ramon	-16
Jackson,Edwin	-10	Buck,John	-15
Hanson,Tommy	-10	McCann,Brian	-11
Penny,Brad	-9	Napoli,Mike	-11
Wells,Randy	-9	Doumit,Ryan	-9

Pitcher 2011 Leaders		Catchers 2011 Leaders	
Chacin,Jhoulys	9	Wieters,Matt	14
Buehrle,Mark	9	Iannetta,Chris	7
Dickey,R.A.	8	Montero,Miguel	6
Shields,James	7	Mathis,Jeff	4
Westbrook,Jake	6	Shoppach,Kelly	3
Kuroda,Hiroki	6	Marson,Lou	3
Cook,Aaron	6	Hanigan,Ryan	3
Fister,Doug	5	4 tied with	2
Guthrie,Jeremy	5		
Saunders,Joe	5		

Pitchers 2011 Trailers		Catchers 2011 Trailers	
Morrow,Brandon	-6	Torrealba,Yorvit	-6
Hanson,Tommy	-5	Ruiz,Carlos	-6
Lackey,John	-5	Molina,Yadier	-6
Humber,Philip	-5	Thole,Josh	-5
Santana,Ervin	-5	McCann,Brian	-5
Sabathia,CC	-5	Pierzynski,A.J.	-5

Infield Plus/Minus Leaders

First Basemen 3-Year Leaders		Second Basemen 3-Year Leaders		Third Basemen 3-Year Leaders		Shortstops 3-Year Leaders	
Barton,Daric	+36	Zobrist,Ben	+56	Beltre,Adrian	+58	Ryan,Brendan	+78
Pujols,Albert	+25	Kinsler,Ian	+46	Longoria,Evan	+50	Escobar,Yunel	+47
Youkilis,Kevin	+22	Utley,Chase	+39	Zimmerman,Ryan	+48	Wilson,Jack	+43
Overbay,Lyle	+18	Hill,Aaron	+35	Figgins,Chone	+41	Tulowitzki,Troy	+37
Morneau,Justin	+16	Pedroia,Dustin	+34	Rolen,Scott	+35	Barmes,Clint	+33
Davis,Ike	+16	Cano,Robinson	+22	Hannahan,Jack	+32	Ramirez,Alexei	+30
Gonzalez,Adrian	+15	Hudson,Orlando	+22	Headley,Chase	+28	Andrus,Elvis	+30
Branyan,Russell	+13	Ellis,Mark	+20	Blake,Casey	+26	Gonzalez,Alex	+30
Trumbo,Mark	+13	Phillips,Brandon	+15	Lopez,Jose	+24	Janish,Paul	+26
Kotchman,Casey	+11	Kendrick,Howie	+9	Kouzmanoff,Kevin	+23	Izturis,Cesar	+22

First Basemen 3-Year Trailers		Second Basemen 3-Year Trailers		Third Basemen 3-Year Trailers		Shortstops 3-Year Trailers	
Dunn,Adam	-45	Schumaker,Skip	-31	Reynolds,Mark	-44	Betancourt,Yuniesky	-56
Howard,Ryan	-31	Uggla,Dan	-28	Johnson,Chris	-43	Cabrera,Orlando	-41
Konerko,Paul	-27	Keppinger,Jeff	-20	Ramirez,Aramis	-39	Jeter,Derek	-33
Fielder,Prince	-24	Walker,Neil	-18	Young,Michael	-39	Tejada,Miguel	-25
Butler,Billy	-16	Getz,Chris	-12	Wright,David	-34	Ramirez,Hanley	-25
Cabrera,Miguel	-15	Roberts,Brian	-11	McGehee,Casey	-30	Theriot,Ryan	-15

First Basemen 2011 Leaders		Second Basemen 2011 Leaders		Third Basemen 2011 Leaders		Shortstops 2011 Leaders	
Trumbo,Mark	+11	Zobrist,Ben	+23	Sandoval,Pablo	+26	Gonzalez,Alex	+22
Loney,James	+7	Kendrick,Howie	+19	Beltre,Adrian	+21	Ryan,Brendan	+22
Sanchez,Gaby	+6	Pedroia,Dustin	+18	Polanco,Placido	+20	Cedeno,Ronny	+15
Teixeira,Mark	+6	Kinsler,Ian	+13	Hannahan,Jack	+14	Andrus,Elvis	+14
Barton,Daric	+6	Phillips,Brandon	+13	Longoria,Evan	+12	Barmes,Clint	+14
Lee,Carlos	+6	Ellis,Mark	+12	Rodriguez,Alex	+12	Janish,Paul	+14
Murphy,Daniel	+6	Ackley,Dustin	+10	Rolen,Scott	+9	Escobar,Alcides	+12
Gonzalez,Adrian	+5	Utley,Chase	+9	Callaspo,Alberto	+7	Brignac,Reid	+11
Pujols,Albert	+5	Cano,Robinson	+7	Uribe,Juan	+5	Tulowitzki,Troy	+10
Votto,Joey	+4	Hill,Aaron	+7	Headley,Chase	+3	Escobar,Yunel	+8

First Basemen 2011 Trailers		Second Basemen 2011 Trailers		Third Basemen 2011 Trailers		Shortstops 2011 Trailers	
Hosmer,Eric	-19	Carroll,Jamey	-12	Reynolds,Mark	-33	Jeter,Derek	-22
Howard,Ryan	-12	Izturis,Maicer	-10	Johnson,Chris	-23	Theriot,Ryan	-15
Morse,Michael	-8	Keppinger,Jeff	-9	Ramirez,Aramis	-19	Castro,Starlin	-15
Cabrera,Miguel	-7	Turner,Justin	-8	Sizemore,Scott	-15	Reyes,Jose	-13
LaPorta,Matt	-6	Hudson,Orlando	-8	Betemit,Wilson	-15	Pennington,Cliff	-10
Konerko,Paul	-5	Sanchez,Freddy	-5	Valencia,Danny	-15	Bartlett,Jason	-10

Outfield Plus/Minus Leaders

Left Fielders 3-Year Leaders		Center Fielders 3-Year Leaders		Right Fielders 3-Year Leaders	
Crawford,Carl	+46	Gutierrez,Franklin	+72	Heyward,Jason	+53
Gardner,Brett	+40	Jackson,Austin	+63	Suzuki,Ichiro	+40
Parra,Gerardo	+38	Gwynn,Tony	+45	Upton,Justin	+34
Holliday,Matt	+37	Morgan,Nyjer	+41	Stanton,Mike	+32
Nix,Laynce	+23	Bourjos,Peter	+40	Cruz,Nelson	+26
Tabata,Jose	+20	Young,Chris	+35	Venable,Will	+26
Smith,Seth	+19	Span,Denard	+34	Zobrist,Ben	+25
Murphy,David	+16	Gomez,Carlos	+33	Bruce,Jay	+22
Saunders,Michael	+15	Bourn,Michael	+32	DeJesus,David	+19
Lewis,Fred	+14	Crisp,Coco	+27	Sweeney,Ryan	+14

Left Fielders 3-Year Trailers		Center Fielders 3-Year Trailers		Right Fielders 3-Year Trailers	
Ibanez,Raul	-43	Jones,Adam	-70	Markakis,Nick	-44
Young,Delmon	-38	Kemp,Matt	-42	Cuddyer,Michael	-41
Soriano,Alfonso	-29	Wells,Vernon	-40	Abreu,Bobby	-36
Lee,Carlos	-28	Fowler,Dexter	-31	Hawpe,Brad	-22
Gomes,Jonny	-25	Upton,B.J.	-30	Ordonez,Magglio	-22
Morrison,Logan	-22	McCutchen,Andrew	-27	Kubel,Jason	-18

Left Fielders 2011 Leaders		Center Fielders 2011 Leaders		Right Fielders 2011 Leaders	
Gardner,Brett	+31	Jackson,Austin	+30	Heyward,Jason	+30
Wells,Vernon	+15	Bourjos,Peter	+24	DeJesus,David	+21
Parra,Gerardo	+14	Revere,Ben	+20	Hunter,Torii	+15
Murphy,David	+11	Gomez,Carlos	+20	Venable,Will	+15
Tabata,Jose	+8	Maybin,Cameron	+19	Stanton,Mike	+12
Presley,Alex	+8	Morgan,Nyjer	+15	Quentin,Carlos	+10
Jennings,Desmond	+7	Ellsbury,Jacoby	+14	Reddick,Josh	+9
Fuld,Sam	+6	Young,Chris	+13	Ethier,Andre	+8
Holliday,Matt	+4	Jay,Jon	+13	Upton,Justin	+7
Hamilton,Josh	+4	Ankiel,Rick	+12	Suzuki,Ichiro	+3

Left Fielders 2011 Trailers		Center Fielders 2011 Trailers		Right Fielders 2011 Trailers	
Ibanez,Raul	-29	Jones,Adam	-35	Pence,Hunter	-19
Gordon,Alex	-14	Granderson,Curtis	-34	Markakis,Nick	-18
Soriano,Alfonso	-13	Davis,Rajai	-17	Berkman,Lance	-17
Bay,Jason	-11	Stubbs,Drew	-16	Kubel,Jason	-15
Ludwick,Ryan	-10	Rios,Alex	-13	Bautista,Jose	-13
Gonzalez,Carlos	-8	Upton,B.J.	-10	Boesch,Brennan	-12

Pitcher Plus/Minus Leaders

Pitchers
3-Year Leaders

Buehrle,Mark	+19
Westbrook,Jake	+19
Cahill,Trevor	+16
Bergesen,Brad	+15
Carmona,Fausto	+13
Garland,Jon	+13
Dickey,R.A.	+12
Arroyo,Bronson	+12
Romero,Ricky	+11
Wolf,Randy	+11

Pitchers
3-Year Trailers

Holland,Derek	-11
Wells,Randy	-10
Lee,Cliff	-10
Scherzer,Max	-9
Carpenter,Chris	-9
Paulino,Felipe	-8

Pitchers
2011 Leaders

Chacin,Jhoulys	+9
Westbrook,Jake	+7
Dickey,R.A.	+6
Buehrle,Mark	+6
Kuroda,Hiroki	+6
Fister,Doug	+5
Cook,Aaron	+5
Guthrie,Jeremy	+4
Hammel,Jason	+4
2 tied with	+4

Pitchers
2011 Trailers

Sabathia,CC	-8
Holland,Derek	-7
Scherzer,Max	-6
Morrow,Brandon	-6
Humber,Philip	-5
Carpenter,Chris	-5

Career Register

For players who have appeared in fewer than three major league seasons, we have included their full minor league statistics. For those players with three or more years in the big leagues who also spent time in the minor leagues in 2011 (for example, if they had a rehab assignment) we included only their 2011 minor league statistics—indicated by an asterisk. Those players who split time between the majors and the minors last season but have fewer than three years of major league experience will still have their full minor league stats included.

If a player led either the American or National League in a particular category, that number will appear in **boldface.**

Age is seasonal as of June 30, 2012.

For pitchers, BFP is Batters Facing Pitcher; TBB is Total Bases on Balls (or, Total Walks, intentional and unintentional); Op is Save Opportunities; Hld is Holds.

For the various levels of Class-A ball, we have used "A+" to indicate High A and "A-" to indicate Low A. To help readers decode our minor league team abbreviations, we added a legend in the back of the book. Thank you for the suggestion, David G. Barlow.

Regardless of whether their name at the time was Los Angeles, Anaheim, California, or Los Angeles of Anaheim, the abbreviation LAA denotes a reference to the Angels franchise.

Introduced in last year's book, a pronunciation guide is provided underneath the name of select players.

The Register also features Runs Created (RC) for hitters and Component ERA (ERC) for pitchers, in addition to the more traditional statistics. Developed by Bill James, Runs Created is a method of measuring every facet of a hitter's strengths and weaknesses, combining those factors into one number, indicative of a player's production. Component ERA estimates what a pitcher's ERA should have been based upon his raw pitching statistics and gives us a good indication of whether or not a pitcher actually deserved his ERA. An explanation of Bill's most-current formulas for both RC and ERC can be found in the Baseball Glossary at the end of the Handbook.

A player's total career numbers in the postseason appear on one line above his total regular season career numbers. Since we work hard to bring you this publication by November 1, 2011, postseason data from 2011 is not included.

David Aardsma

Pitches: R Bats: R Pos: P

ARDZ-muh

Ht: 6'3" Wt: 205 Born: 12/27/1981 Age: 30

Year	Team	Lg	HOW MUCH HE PITCHED						WHAT HE GAVE UP											THE RESULTS					
			G	GS	CG	GF	IP	BFP	H	R	ER	HR	SH	SF	HB	TBB	IBB	SO	WP	Bk	W	L	Pct	Sh	Sv-Op	Hld	ERC	ERA
2011	Tacom*	AAA	5	0	0	0	4.0	24	8	7	7	1	0	1	0	4	0	5	2	0	0	1	.000	0	0--	-	16.72	15.75
2004	SF	NL	11	0	0	5	10.2	61	20	8	8	1	0	1	2	10	0	5	0	0	1	0	1.000	0	0-1	-	13.38	6.75
2006	ChC	NL	45	0	0	9	53.0	225	41	25	24	9	1	3	1	28	0	49	1	0	3	0	1.000	0	0-0	5	3.88	4.08
2007	CWS	AL	25	0	0	7	32.1	151	39	24	23	4	2	1	1	17	3	36	2	0	2	1	.667	0	0-3	3	5.93	6.40
2008	Bos	AL	47	0	0	7	48.2	228	49	32	30	4	3	2	5	35	2	49	3	0	4	2	.667	0	0-1	4	5.63	5.55
2009	Sea	AL	73	0	0	53	71.1	296	49	23	20	4	2	1	0	34	3	80	2	0	3	6	.333	0	38-42	6	2.34	2.52
2010	Sea	AL	53	0	0	43	49.2	202	33	19	19	5	7	1	2	25	5	49	2	0	0	6	.000	0	31-36	0	2.74	3.44
	6 ML YEARS		254	0	0	124	265.2	1163	231	131	124	27	15	9	11	149	13	268	10	0	13	15	.464	0	69-83	19	4.07	4.20

Fernando Abad

Pitches: L Bats: L Pos: RP-29

ah-BAHD

Ht: 6'2" Wt: 207 Born: 12/17/1985 Age: 26

Year	Team	Lg	HOW MUCH HE PITCHED						WHAT HE GAVE UP											THE RESULTS					
			G	GS	CG	GF	IP	BFP	H	R	ER	HR	SH	SF	HB	TBB	IBB	SO	WP	Bk	W	L	Pct	Sh	Sv-Op	Hld	ERC	ERA
2007	Grnsvle	R+	17	4	0	6	50.0	210	47	29	23	6	3	2	2	12	0	54	2	3	6	4	.600	0	1--	-	3.36	4.14
2007	TriCity	A-	2	0	0	1	3.0	13	2	2	2	0	0	0	0	2	0	5	0	0	0	0	-	0	0--	-	2.54	6.00
2008	Lxngtn	A	45	0	0	27	76.1	325	78	31	28	9	4	3	4	13	3	94	1	2	2	7	.222	0	3--	-	3.47	3.30
2009	Lancst	A+	41	0	0	23	82.2	330	78	43	38	4	8	5	3	5	0	79	3	0	4	6	.400	0	6--	-	2.86	4.14
2009	CpChr	AA	3	3	0	0	14.0	57	12	7	5	1	0	0	0	3	0	13	1	0	0	1	.000	0	0--	-	2.41	3.21
2010	CpChr	AA	14	4	0	0	39.2	167	48	16	11	3	3	1	0	6	1	33	2	1	4	3	.571	0	0--	-	4.12	2.50
2010	RdRck	AAA	5	0	0	1	6.1	26	5	1	1	1	0	0	0	2	0	9	0	0	0	0	-	0	0--	-	2.94	1.42
2011	OKCity	AAA	29	0	0	11	30.0	127	32	16	16	4	3	0	0	6	2	31	1	0	2	3	.400	0	0--	-	3.73	4.80
2011	Astros	R	2	0	0	0	2.0	7	1	0	0	0	0	0	0	0	0	2	0	0	0	0	-	0	0--	-	0.54	0.00
2010	Hou	NL	22	0	0	6	19.0	76	14	6	6	3	0	1	0	5	0	12	0	0	0	1	.000	0	0-0	6	2.49	2.84
2011	Hou	NL	29	0	0	1	19.2	99	28	18	16	5	1	2	1	9	0	15	0	0	1	4	.200	0	0-2	7	8.06	7.32
	2 ML YEARS		51	0	0	7	38.2	175	42	24	22	8	1	3	1	14	0	27	0	0	1	5	.167	0	0-2	13	5.12	5.12

Bobby Abreu

Bats: L Throws: R Pos: DH-108; LF-18; RF-10; PH-7

Ht: 6'0" Wt: 220 Born: 3/11/1974 Age: 38

Year	Team	Lg	BATTING																			BASERUNNING				AVERAGES		
			G	AB	H	2B	3B	HR	(Hm	Rd)	TB	R	RBI	RC	TBB	IBB	SO	HBP	SH	SF	SB	CS	SB%	GDP	Avg	OBP	Slg
1996	Hou	NL	15	22	5	1	0	0	(0	0)	6	1	1	1	2	0	3	0	0	0	0	0	-	1	.227	.292	.273
1997	Hou	NL	59	188	47	10	2	3	(3	0)	70	22	26	25	21	0	48	1	0	0	7	2	.78	0	.250	.329	.372
1998	Phi	NL	151	497	155	29	6	17	(10	7)	247	68	74	101	84	14	133	0	4	4	19	10	.66	6	.312	.409	.497
1999	Phi	NL	152	546	183	35	11	20	(13	7)	300	118	93	131	109	8	113	3	0	4	27	9	.75	13	.335	.446	.549
2000	Phi	NL	154	576	182	42	10	25	(14	11)	319	103	79	130	100	9	116	1	0	3	28	8	.78	12	.316	.416	.554
2001	Phi	NL	162	588	170	48	4	31	(13	18)	319	118	110	125	106	11	137	1	0	9	36	14	.72	13	.289	.393	.543
2002	Phi	NL	157	572	176	50	6	20	(8	12)	298	102	85	112	104	9	117	3	0	6	31	12	.72	11	.308	.413	.521
2003	Phi	NL	158	577	173	35	1	20	(11	9)	270	99	101	120	109	13	126	2	0	7	22	9	.71	13	.300	.409	.468
2004	Phi	NL	159	574	173	47	1	30	(13	17)	312	118	105	139	127	10	116	5	0	7	40	5	.89	5	.301	.428	.544
2005	Phi	NL	162	588	168	37	1	24	(15	9)	279	104	102	116	117	15	134	6	0	8	31	9	.78	7	.286	.405	.474
2006	2 Tms		156	548	163	41	2	15	(8	7)	253	98	107	123	124	6	138	3	2	9	30	6	.83	13	.297	.424	.462
2007	NYY	AL	158	605	171	40	5	16	(10	6)	269	123	101	101	84	0	115	3	0	7	25	8	.76	11	.283	.369	.445
2008	NYY	AL	156	609	180	39	4	20	(14	6)	287	100	100	108	73	2	109	1	0	1	22	11	.67	14	.296	.371	.471
2009	LAA	AL	152	563	165	29	3	15	(7	8)	245	96	103	109	94	7	113	1	0	9	30	8	.79	15	.293	.390	.435
2010	LAA	AL	154	573	146	41	1	20	(11	9)	249	88	78	91	87	3	132	2	0	5	24	10	.71	13	.255	.352	.435
2011	LAA	AL	142	502	127	30	1	8	(3	5)	183	54	60	74	78	5	113	1	1	3	21	5	.81	8	.253	.353	.365
06	Phi	NL	98	339	94	25	2	8	(5	3)	147	61	65	76	91	5	86	2	0	6	20	4	.83	8	.277	.427	.434
06	NYY	AL	58	209	69	16	0	7	(3	4)	106	37	42	47	33	1	52	1	2	3	10	2	.83	5	.330	.419	.507
	Postseason		20	67	19	6	0	1	(1	0)	28	9	9	11	12	3	15	0	0	0	2	1	.67	0	.284	.392	.418
	16 ML YEARS		2247	8128	2384	554	58	284	(153	131)	3906	1412	1325	1606	1419	112	1763	33	7	82	393	126	.76	155	.293	.397	.481

Juan Abreu

Pitches: R Bats: R Pos: RP-7

Ht: 6'0" Wt: 170 Born: 4/8/1985 Age: 27

Year	Team	Lg	HOW MUCH HE PITCHED						WHAT HE GAVE UP											THE RESULTS					
			G	GS	CG	GF	IP	BFP	H	R	ER	HR	SH	SF	HB	TBB	IBB	SO	WP	Bk	W	L	Pct	Sh	Sv-Op	Hld	ERC	ERA
2005	Royals	R	14	13	0	0	52.1	259	72	49	40	4	2	4	6	27	0	52	10	0	2	5	.286	0	0--	-	7.02	6.88
2006	Idaho	R+	20	0	0	4	50.0	222	39	34	32	4	2	5	5	35	0	57	12	0	4	2	.667	0	2--	-	4.29	5.76
2008	Burlgtn	A	22	4	0	10	76.1	328	59	40	31	6	3	3	4	42	0	104	5	2	4	4	.500	0	7--	-	3.45	3.66
2009	Wilmg	A+	20	0	0	18	21.1	85	8	5	4	1	1	0	0	14	0	28	2	1	3	2	.600	0	12--	-	1.57	1.69
2009	NWArk	AA	16	0	0	11	20.1	103	19	15	13	3	2	0	1	22	3	25	2	0	2	2	.500	0	4--	-	6.61	5.75
2010	MrtlBh	A+	8	0	0	3	15.1	69	14	14	14	5	0	1	2	8	0	15	0	1	0	0	-	0	1--	-	6.27	8.22
2010	Missi	AA	39	0	0	32	44.2	194	41	18	15	2	1	1	1	22	0	47	6	0	4	2	.667	0	11--	-	3.67	3.02
2011	Gwnntt	AAA	41	0	0	14	48.0	209	34	18	12	5	1	3	2	27	1	68	4	0	4	2	.667	0	1--	-	3.16	2.25
2011	OKCity	AAA	7	0	0	3	9.2	44	8	3	2	0	1	0	0	7	3	9	0	0	1	0	1.000	0	3--	-	2.99	1.86
2011	Hou	NL	7	0	0	2	6.2	34	6	2	2	1	0	0	5	3	0	12	0	0	0	0	-	0	0-0	0	7.01	2.70

Jeremy Accardo

Pitches: R Bats: R Pos: RP-31

uh-CAR-doe

Ht: 6'1" Wt: 192 Born: 12/8/1981 Age: 30

Year	Team	Lg	HOW MUCH HE PITCHED						WHAT HE GAVE UP											THE RESULTS					
			G	GS	CG	GF	IP	BFP	H	R	ER	HR	SH	SF	HB	TBB	IBB	SO	WP	Bk	W	L	Pct	Sh	Sv-Op	Hld	ERC	ERA
2011	Norfolk*	AAA	26	0	0	9	33.1	134	26	9	8	1	5	0	1	11	1	27	1	0	1	1	.500	0	2--	-	2.32	2.16
2005	SF	NL	28	0	0	7	29.2	124	26	13	13	2	1	1	1	9	1	16	1	0	1	5	.167	0	0-1	4	2.87	3.94
2006	2 Tms		65	0	0	27	69.0	297	76	42	41	7	1	4	1	20	5	54	4	1	2	4	.333	0	3-8	10	4.17	5.35
2007	Tor	AL	64	0	0	48	67.1	275	51	19	16	4	0	1	2	24	2	57	0	1	4	4	.500	0	30-35	2	2.44	2.14

34

Year Team	Lg	G	GS	CG	GF	IP	BFP	H	R	ER	HR	SH	SF	HB	TBB	IBB	SO	WP	Bk	W	L	Pct	Sh	Sv-Op	Hld	ERC	ERA
2008 Tor	AL	16	0	0	6	12.1	56	15	10	9	1	0	1	1	4	2	5	1	0	0	3	.000	0	4-6	2	4.88	6.57
2009 Tor	AL	26	0	0	5	24.2	107	23	8	7	2	0	2	2	17	1	18	0	0	0	0	-	0	1-1	4	5.26	2.55
2010 Tor	AL	5	0	0	2	6.2	34	12	6	6	0	0	0	1	3	0	3	2	0	0	1	.000	0	0-0	0	9.38	8.10
2011 Bal	AL	31	0	0	7	37.2	167	43	24	24	5	2	0	1	18	4	23	0	0	3	3	.500	0	0-1	2	5.53	5.73
06 SF	NL	38	0	0	16	40.1	170	38	23	22	2	0	4	1	11	3	40	2	0	1	3	.250	0	3-6	8	2.88	4.91
06 Tor		27	0	0	11	28.2	127	38	19	19	5	1	0	0	9	2	14	2	1	1	1	.500	0	0-2	5	6.25	5.97
7 ML YEARS		235	0	0	102	247.1	1060	246	122	116	21	4	9	9	95	15	176	8	2	10	20	.333	0	38-52	24	3.96	4.22

Alfredo Aceves

ah-SEVV-us

Pitches: R Bats: R Pos: RP-51; SP-4   Ht: 6'3" Wt: 218 Born: 12/8/1981 Age: 30

Year Team	Lg	G	GS	CG	GF	IP	BFP	H	R	ER	HR	SH	SF	HB	TBB	IBB	SO	WP	Bk	W	L	Pct	Sh	Sv-Op	Hld	ERC	ERA
2011 Pwtckt*	AAA	2	2	0	0	8.0	33	6	6	5	0	0	3	1	4	0	6	0	0	0	1	.000	0	0- -	-	3.00	5.63
2008 NYY	AL	6	4	0	1	30.0	120	25	8	8	4	0	0	0	10	0	16	1	0	1	0	1.000	0	0-0	0	3.23	2.40
2009 NYY	AL	43	1	0	10	84.0	337	69	36	33	10	1	2	5	16	2	69	0	0	10	1	.909	0	1-2	5	2.65	3.54
2010 NYY	AL	10	0	0	2	12.0	53	10	5	4	1	0	0	1	4	1	2	0	0	3	0	1.000	0	1-1	1	2.80	3.00
2011 Bos	AL	55	4	0	15	114.0	474	84	37	33	8	3	3	15	42	1	80	1	2	10	2	.833	0	2-5	11	2.84	2.61
Postseason		4	0	0	1	4.1	20	5	2	2	0	1	0	0	3	1	2	0	0	0	1	.000	0	0-0	0	5.01	4.15
4 ML YEARS		114	9	0	28	240.0	984	188	86	78	23	4	5	21	72	4	167	2	2	24	3	.889	0	4-8	17	2.82	2.93

Dustin Ackley

Bats: L Throws: R Pos: 2B-86; PH-3; DH-2; 1B-1   Ht: 6'1" Wt: 185 Born: 2/26/1988 Age: 24

Year Team	Lg	G	AB	H	2B	3B	HR	(Hm	Rd)	TB	R	RBI	RC	TBB	IBB	SO	HBP	SH	SF	SB	CS	SB%	GDP	Avg	OBP	Slg
2010 WTenn	AA	82	289	76	21	4	2	(-	-)	111	42	28	49	55	0	41	5	0	1	8	2	.80	5	.263	.389	.384
2010 Tacom	AAA	52	212	58	12	4	5	(-	-)	93	37	23	32	20	1	38	2	0	3	2	1	.67	3	.274	.338	.439
2011 Tacom	AAA	66	271	82	17	3	9	(-	-)	132	57	35	58	55	2	38	1	3	1	7	3	.70	3	.303	.421	.487
2011 Sea	AL	90	333	91	16	7	6	(3	3)	139	39	36	53	40	1	79	0	0	3	6	0	1.00	3	.273	.348	.417

Manny Acosta

Pitches: R Bats: B Pos: RP-44   Ht: 6'4" Wt: 213 Born: 5/1/1981 Age: 31

Year Team	Lg	G	GS	CG	GF	IP	BFP	H	R	ER	HR	SH	SF	HB	TBB	IBB	SO	WP	Bk	W	L	Pct	Sh	Sv-Op	Hld	ERC	ERA
2011 Buffalo*	AAA	20	0	0	15	20.1	89	13	6	4	0	1	1	0	17	0	27	1	0	1	0	1.000	0	4- -	-	3.03	1.77
2007 Atl	NL	21	0	0	5	23.2	93	13	6	6	2	0	0	0	14	1	22	1	0	1	1	.500	0	0-0	4	2.39	2.28
2008 Atl	NL	46	0	0	22	53.0	226	48	25	21	7	4	1	1	26	5	31	5	0	3	5	.375	0	3-5	4	4.12	3.57
2009 Atl	NL	36	0	0	17	37.1	174	45	19	18	4	3	0	2	19	2	32	3	0	1	1	.500	0	0-2	5	5.90	4.34
2010 NYM	NL	41	0	0	12	39.2	157	30	13	13	4	1	1	0	18	1	42	3	0	3	2	.600	0	1-3	3	3.10	2.95
2011 NYM	NL	44	0	0	15	47.0	204	50	21	18	6	0	1	2	15	0	46	0	0	4	1	.800	0	4-7	7	4.47	3.45
5 ML YEARS		188	0	0	71	200.2	854	186	84	76	23	8	3	5	92	9	173	12	0	12	10	.545	0	8-15	19	4.10	3.41

Mike Adams

Pitches: R Bats: R Pos: RP-76   Ht: 6'5" Wt: 190 Born: 7/29/1978 Age: 33

Year Team	Lg	G	GS	CG	GF	IP	BFP	H	R	ER	HR	SH	SF	HB	TBB	IBB	SO	WP	Bk	W	L	Pct	Sh	Sv-Op	Hld	ERC	ERA
2004 Mil	NL	46	0	0	13	53.0	225	50	21	20	5	5	2	2	14	2	39	2	0	2	3	.400	0	0-5	12	3.22	3.40
2005 Mil	NL	13	0	0	5	13.1	61	12	4	4	2	0	0	0	10	1	14	1	0	0	1	.000	0	1-2	2	5.12	2.70
2006 Mil	NL	2	0	0	0	2.1	13	4	3	3	1	0	0	0	2	0	1	0	0	0	0	-	0	0-0	0	13.74	11.57
2008 SD	NL	54	0	0	11	65.1	259	49	18	18	7	2	3	0	19	2	74	0	0	2	3	.400	0	0-2	10	2.38	2.48
2009 SD	NL	37	0	0	5	37.0	136	14	9	3	1	2	0	0	8	1	45	1	0	0	0	-	0	0-1	15	0.65	0.73
2010 SD	NL	70	0	0	3	66.2	268	48	14	13	2	0	0	0	23	2	73	0	0	4	1	.800	0	0-4	38	1.95	1.76
2011 2 Tms		76	0	0	11	73.2	277	44	13	12	5	2	1	0	14	2	74	0	0	5	4	.556	0	2-5	32	1.31	1.47
11 SD	NL	49	0	0	6	48.0	179	26	7	6	2	1	1	0	9	1	49	0	0	3	1	.750	0	1-3	23	1.06	1.13
11 Tex	AL	27	0	0	5	25.2	98	18	6	6	3	1	0	0	5	1	25	0	0	2	3	.400	0	1-2	9	1.88	2.10
7 ML YEARS		298	0	0	50	311.1	1239	221	82	73	23	11	6	2	90	10	320	4	0	13	12	.520	0	3-19	109	1.99	2.11

Ryan Adams

Bats: R Throws: R Pos: 2B-26; PH-2; PR-1   Ht: 5'11" Wt: 185 Born: 4/21/1987 Age: 25

Year Team	Lg	G	AB	H	2B	3B	HR	(Hm	Rd)	TB	R	RBI	RC	TBB	IBB	SO	HBP	SH	SF	SB	CS	SB%	GDP	Avg	OBP	Slg
2006 Bluefld	R	34	133	34	8	1	2	(-	-)	50	24	7	19	19	1	32	3	1	0	2	2	.50	1	.256	.361	.376
2006 Abrdn	A-	6	19	6	3	0	1	(-	-)	12	2	5	5	4	0	7	1	0	0	0	0	-	0	.316	.458	.632
2007 Abrdn	A-	67	246	58	10	2	3	(-	-)	81	29	22	25	18	0	63	4	2	2	8	3	.73	1	.236	.296	.329
2008 Dlmrva	A	119	448	138	26	5	11	(-	-)	207	68	57	77	36	0	109	6	6	1	12	5	.71	10	.308	.367	.462
2009 Frdrck	A+	59	215	62	14	0	2	(-	-)	82	27	25	28	19	0	41	1	0	0	2	4	.33	6	.288	.349	.381
2010 Bowie	AA	134	530	158	43	0	15	(-	-)	246	81	68	91	47	4	121	12	0	5	2	3	.40	16	.298	.365	.464
2011 Norfolk	AAA	94	377	107	28	3	10	(-	-)	171	46	37	59	30	0	103	4	1	3	5	2	.71	12	.284	.341	.454
2011 Bal	AL	29	89	25	4	0	0	(0	0)	29	9	7	10	6	0	25	1	0	0	0	0	-	7	.281	.333	.326

Nathan Adcock

Pitches: R Bats: R Pos: RP-21; SP-3   Ht: 6'5" Wt: 220 Born: 2/25/1988 Age: 24

Year	Team	Lg	G	GS	CG	GF	IP	BFP	H	R	ER	HR	SH	SF	HB	TBB	IBB	SO	WP	Bk	W	L	Pct	Sh	Sv-Op	Hld	ERC	ERA
2006	Ms	R	10	6	0	0	35.1	159	33	21	13	1	2	0	5	16	0	31	5	0	0	2	.000	0	0--	-	3.86	3.31
2007	Wisc	A	17	16	0	0	87.2	392	85	60	36	7	1	4	5	38	0	66	13	0	2	8	.200	0	0--	-	4.00	3.70
2007	Hi Dsrt	A+	5	5	0	0	18.1	98	20	26	18	0	0	2	2	22	0	11	2	0	1	3	.250	0	0--	-	7.33	8.84
2008	Wisc	A	15	14	0	0	77.1	339	81	45	32	3	3	1	5	29	0	82	13	0	2	5	.286	0	0--	-	4.05	3.72
2009	Hi Dsrt	A+	21	19	1	0	102.0	457	103	72	60	10	5	4	6	54	0	71	6	0	5	7	.417	0	0--	-	4.89	5.29
2009	Lynbrg	A+	7	4	0	1	24.0	109	29	17	14	5	0	2	2	7	0	15	3	0	3	2	.600	0	0--	-	5.93	5.25
2010	Bradtn	A+	27	26	0	0	141.1	593	131	66	53	8	3	5	7	38	0	113	12	0	11	7	.611	0	0--	-	3.05	3.38
2011	KC	AL	24	3	0	5	60.1	265	63	34	31	5	3	1	3	26	3	36	4	1	1	1	.500	0	1-2	0	4.47	4.62

Jeremy Affeldt

Pitches: L Bats: L Pos: RP-67   Ht: 6'4" Wt: 220 Born: 6/6/1979 Age: 33

AFF-felt

Year	Team	Lg	G	GS	CG	GF	IP	BFP	H	R	ER	HR	SH	SF	HB	TBB	IBB	SO	WP	Bk	W	L	Pct	Sh	Sv-Op	Hld	ERC	ERA
2002	KC	AL	34	7	0	4	77.2	353	85	41	40	8	2	1	3	37	4	67	5	2	3	4	.429	0	0-1	1	4.97	4.64
2003	KC	AL	36	18	0	5	126.0	533	126	58	55	12	2	5	5	38	1	98	2	2	7	6	.538	0	4-4	3	3.82	3.93
2004	KC	AL	38	8	0	26	76.1	344	91	49	42	6	4	4	3	32	2	49	4	3	3	4	.429	0	13-17	0	5.26	4.95
2005	KC	AL	49	0	0	13	49.2	232	56	35	29	3	0	1	0	29	2	39	5	0	0	2	.000	0	0-0	12	5.08	5.26
2006	2 Tms		54	9	0	12	97.1	448	102	74	67	13	4	4	2	55	3	48	2	0	8	8	.500	0	1-3	5	5.21	6.20
2007	Col	NL	75	0	0	11	59.0	253	47	26	23	3	3	6	3	33	9	46	6	1	4	3	.571	0	0-4	9	3.19	3.51
2008	Cin	NL	74	0	0	20	78.1	335	78	36	29	9	7	0	3	25	0	80	6	1	1	1	.500	0	0-1	5	3.98	3.33
2009	SF	NL	74	0	0	8	62.1	248	42	14	12	3	0	1	3	31	3	55	5	0	2	2	.500	0	0-0	33	2.61	1.73
2010	SF	NL	53	0	0	14	50.0	228	56	25	23	4	7	1	3	24	5	44	4	0	4	3	.571	0	4-7	7	4.99	4.14
2011	SF	NL	67	0	0	12	61.2	259	47	22	18	5	4	0	4	24	3	54	4	0	3	2	.600	0	3-6	13	2.77	2.63
06	KC	AL	27	9	0	3	70.0	320	71	51	46	9	3	3	1	42	0	28	2	0	4	6	.400	0	0-0	2	5.18	5.91
06	Col	NL	27	0	0	9	27.1	128	31	23	21	4	1	1	1	13	3	20	0	0	4	2	.667	0	1-3	3	5.29	6.91
	Postseason		12	0	0	1	9.1	33	4	3	3	1	0	0	0	3	1	8	1	0	0	0	-	0	0-0	2	1.23	2.89
	10 ML YEARS		554	42	0	125	738.1	3233	730	380	338	66	33	23	29	328	32	580	43	8	35	35	.500	0	25-43	88	4.19	4.12

Matt Albers

Pitches: R Bats: L Pos: RP-56   Ht: 6'0" Wt: 230 Born: 1/20/1983 Age: 29

Year	Team	Lg	G	GS	CG	GF	IP	BFP	H	R	ER	HR	SH	SF	HB	TBB	IBB	SO	WP	Bk	W	L	Pct	Sh	Sv-Op	Hld	ERC	ERA
2011	Pwtckt*	AAA	2	0	0	0	3.0	10	1	0	0	0	0	0	0	0	0	2	0	0	0	0	-	0	0--	-	0.25	0.00
2006	Hou	NL	4	2	0	0	15.0	66	17	10	10	1	2	0	0	7	0	11	0	0	0	2	.000	0	0-0	0	4.97	6.00
2007	Hou	NL	31	18	0	2	110.2	508	127	77	72	18	6	8	7	50	6	71	7	0	4	11	.267	0	0-0	0	5.76	5.86
2008	Bal	AL	28	3	0	5	49.0	208	43	21	19	4	1	3	2	22	1	26	1	0	3	3	.500	0	0-2	6	3.62	3.49
2009	Bal	AL	56	0	0	13	67.0	309	80	43	41	3	5	2	2	36	3	49	3	0	3	6	.333	0	0-4	10	5.41	5.51
2010	Bal	AL	62	0	0	19	75.2	329	78	41	38	6	3	0	2	34	5	49	2	0	5	3	.625	0	0-2	7	4.35	4.52
2011	Bos	AL	56	0	0	14	64.2	289	62	35	34	7	4	2	5	31	1	68	2	0	4	4	.500	0	0-3	10	4.44	4.73
	6 ML YEARS		237	23	0	49	382.0	1709	407	227	214	39	21	15	18	180	16	274	15	0	19	29	.396	0	0-11	33	4.88	5.04

Al Alburquerque

Pitches: R Bats: R Pos: RP-41   Ht: 6'0" Wt: 195 Born: 6/10/1986 Age: 26

Year	Team	Lg	G	GS	CG	GF	IP	BFP	H	R	ER	HR	SH	SF	HB	TBB	IBB	SO	WP	Bk	W	L	Pct	Sh	Sv-Op	Hld	ERC	ERA
2006	Cubs	R	8	5	0	0	12.2	56	10	8	8	1	1	2	0	10	0	15	1	0	0	2	.000	0	0--	-	4.32	5.68
2007	Peoria	A	11	4	0	0	25.1	123	36	29	26	5	0	1	0	12	1	20	4	0	1	4	.200	0	0--	-	7.56	9.24
2007	Boise	A-	10	6	0	0	41.0	180	42	20	17	2	2	0	3	17	0	49	3	0	3	2	.600	0	1--	-	4.20	3.73
2009	Dytona	A	24	0	0	11	34.2	144	26	11	8	4	0	1	1	14	0	44	3	2	1	0	1.000	0	2--	-	2.93	2.08
2009	Tulsa	AA	23	0	0	7	26.1	113	23	13	11	0	2	0	2	13	0	31	1	0	1	3	.250	0	0--	-	3.36	3.76
2010	Tulsa	AA	25	0	0	0	34.1	149	32	23	19	1	4	0	2	19	0	32	4	4	2	4	.333	0	3--	-	4.10	4.98
2011	Toledo	AAA	4	0	0	3	4.2	22	5	1	1	0	0	1	0	2	0	10	0	0	0	0	-	0	0--	-	4.53	1.93
2011	Det	AL	41	0	0	11	43.1	182	21	9	9	0	2	1	2	29	4	67	4	0	6	1	.857	0	0-0	6	1.73	1.87

Eliezer Alfonzo

Bats: R Throws: R Pos: C-19; PH-6   Ht: 5'11" Wt: 220 Born: 2/7/1979 Age: 33

ell-ee-AY-zer

Year	Team	Lg	G	AB	H	2B	3B	HR	(Hm	Rd)	TB	R	RBI	RC	TBB	IBB	SO	HBP	SH	SF	SB	CS	SB%	GDP	Avg	OBP	Slg
2011	ColSpr*	AAA	31	94	30	7	0	12	(-	-)	73	21	37	24	2	0	16	3	0	2	2	1	.67	3	.319	.347	.777
2006	SF	NL	87	286	76	17	2	12	(3	9)	133	27	39	36	9	7	74	7	4	3	1	0	1.00	10	.266	.302	.465
2007	SF	NL	26	64	16	2	1	1	(1	0)	23	5	6	5	2	2	23	1	0	0	0	2	.00	2	.250	.284	.359
2008	SF	NL	5	11	1	0	0	0	(0	0)	1	0	1	0	0	0	4	0	0	0	0	0	-	2	.091	.091	.091
2009	SD	NL	37	114	20	3	0	2	(1	1)	29	6	8	4	3	0	34	0	0	0	0	0	-	2	.175	.197	.254
2010	Sea	AL	13	41	9	1	0	1	(0	1)	13	4	4	2	0	0	10	0	0	0	0	0	-	2	.220	.220	.317
2011	Col	NL	25	75	20	1	0	1	(0	1)	24	2	9	8	3	0	13	1	0	0	0	0	-	1	.267	.304	.320
	6 ML YEARS		193	591	142	24	3	17	(5	12)	223	44	67	55	17	9	158	9	4	3	1	2	.33	17	.240	.271	.377

Brandon Allen

Bats: L Throws: R Pos: 1B-51; PH-1
Ht: 6'2" Wt: 235 Born: 2/12/1986 Age: 26

Year	Team	Lg	G	AB	H	2B	3B	HR	(Hm	Rd)	TB	R	RBI	RC	TBB	IBB	SO	HBP	SH	SF	SB	CS	SB%	GDP	Avg	OBP	Slg
2011	Reno*	AAA	83	304	93	21	4	18	(-	-)	176	75	66	76	64	1	90	4	0	5	7	4	.64	6	.306	.427	.579
2011	Scrmto*	AAA	10	40	10	2	1	3	(-	-)	23	4	6	6	2	0	11	0	0	0	0	0	-	1	.250	.286	.575
2009	Ari	NL	32	104	21	7	0	4	(1	3)	40	13	14	12	12	2	40	0	0	0	0	0	-	4	.202	.284	.385
2010	Ari	NL	22	45	12	3	0	1	(1	0)	18	5	6	7	10	1	20	0	0	1	0	0	-	0	.267	.393	.400
2011	2 Tms		52	175	35	9	2	6	(2	4)	66	23	18	18	18	3	68	1	0	1	3	0	1.00	0	.200	.277	.377
11	Ari	NL	11	29	5	0	0	3	(2	1)	14	5	7	6	7	2	13	1	0	0	1	0	1.00	0	.172	.351	.483
11	Oak	AL	41	146	30	9	2	3	(0	3)	52	18	11	12	11	1	55	0	0	1	2	0	1.00	0	.205	.259	.356
	3 ML YEARS		106	324	68	19	2	11	(4	7)	124	41	38	37	40	6	128	1	0	2	3	0	1.00	4	.210	.297	.383

Erick Almonte

Bats: R Throws: R Pos: PH-8; RF-7; 1B-2
al-MONN-tay
Ht: 6'2" Wt: 245 Born: 2/1/1978 Age: 34

Year	Team	Lg	G	AB	H	2B	3B	HR	(Hm	Rd)	TB	R	RBI	RC	TBB	IBB	SO	HBP	SH	SF	SB	CS	SB%	GDP	Avg	OBP	Slg
2011	Nashv*	AAA	83	244	74	15	1	6	(-	-)	109	43	42	43	31	0	46	0	0	1	2	1	.67	8	.303	.380	.447
2001	NYY	AL	8	4	2	1	0	0	(0	0)	3	0	0	2	0	0	1	0	0	0	2	0	1.00	0	.500	.500	.750
2003	NYY	AL	31	100	26	6	0	1	(0	1)	35	17	11	11	8	0	24	1	2	0	1	0	1.00	3	.260	.321	.350
2011	Mil	NL	16	29	3	0	0	1	(0	1)	6	1	3	0	0	0	4	0	0	0	0	0	-	2	.103	.103	.207
	3 ML YEARS		55	133	31	7	0	2	(0	2)	44	18	14	13	8	0	29	1	2	0	3	0	1.00	5	.233	.282	.331

Yonder Alonso

Bats: L Throws: R Pos: PH-27; LF-16; 1B-3; 3B-1
Ht: 6'2" Wt: 241 Born: 4/8/1987 Age: 25

Year	Team	Lg	G	AB	H	2B	3B	HR	(Hm	Rd)	TB	R	RBI	RC	TBB	IBB	SO	HBP	SH	SF	SB	CS	SB%	GDP	Avg	OBP	Slg
2008	Srsota	A+	6	19	6	1	0	0	(-	-)	7	1	2	3	5	0	5	0	0	1	0	0	-	0	.316	.440	.368
2009	Srsota	A+	49	175	53	13	0	7	(-	-)	87	21	38	33	24	0	30	0	0	2	1	1	.00	6	.303	.383	.497
2009	Carlina	AA	29	105	31	11	0	2	(-	-)	48	12	14	19	14	0	15	0	0	2	1	0	1.00	1	.295	.372	.457
2009	Reds	R	6	15	2	0	0	0	(-	-)	2	0	0	0	3	1	1	0	0	0	0	0	-	0	.133	.278	.133
2010	Carlina	AA	31	101	27	5	0	3	(-	-)	41	19	13	17	19	2	16	1	0	0	4	2	.67	5	.267	.384	.406
2010	Lsvlle	AAA	101	406	120	31	2	12	(-	-)	191	50	56	70	37	2	76	1	0	1	9	1	.90	12	.296	.355	.470
2011	Lsvlle	AAA	91	358	106	24	4	12	(-	-)	174	46	56	66	46	6	60	1	0	4	6	5	.55	13	.296	.374	.486
2010	Cin	NL	22	29	6	2	0	0	(0	0)	8	2	3	0	0	0	10	0	0	0	0	0	-	1	.207	.207	.276
2011	Cin	NL	47	88	29	4	0	5	(2	3)	48	9	15	16	10	0	21	0	0	0	0	0	-	2	.330	.398	.545
	2 ML YEARS		69	117	35	6	0	5	(2	3)	56	11	18	16	10	0	31	0	0	0	0	0	-	3	.299	.354	.479

Jose Altuve

Bats: R Throws: R Pos: 2B-55; PH-2; PR-2
al-TOO-vay
Ht: 5'7" Wt: 170 Born: 5/6/1990 Age: 22

Year	Team	Lg	G	AB	H	2B	3B	HR	(Hm	Rd)	TB	R	RBI	RC	TBB	IBB	SO	HBP	SH	SF	SB	CS	SB%	GDP	Avg	OBP	Slg
2008	Grnville	R	40	141	40	9	3	2	(-	-)	61	26	21	20	8	0	26	0	2	1	8	2	.80	2	.284	.320	.433
2009	Grnville	R	45	179	58	20	2	3	(-	-)	91	45	18	40	26	0	16	0	2	1	21	4	.84	6	.324	.408	.508
2009	TriCity	A-	21	76	19	5	0	0	(-	-)	24	13	7	9	8	0	10	2	1	0	7	2	.78	0	.250	.337	.316
2010	Lxngtn	A	94	393	121	15	3	11	(-	-)	175	75	45	67	33	0	49	2	5	1	39	14	.74	7	.308	.364	.445
2011	Lancst	A+	52	213	87	13	7	5	(-	-)	129	38	34	54	19	1	26	0	3	3	19	9	.68	5	.408	.451	.606
2011	CpChr	AA	35	144	52	9	3	5	(-	-)	82	21	25	29	7	0	14	0	1	1	5	5	.50	5	.361	.388	.569
2011	Hou	NL	57	221	61	10	1	2	(2	0)	79	26	12	18	5	0	29	2	5	1	7	3	.70	5	.276	.297	.357

Henderson Alvarez

Pitches: R Bats: R Pos: SP-10
Ht: 6'1" Wt: 195 Born: 4/18/1990 Age: 22

Year	Team	Lg	G	GS	CG	GF	IP	BFP	H	R	ER	HR	SH	SF	HB	TBB	IBB	SO	WP	Bk	W	L	Pct	Sh	Sv-Op	Hld	ERC	ERA
2008	B Jays	R	12	11	0	0	46.1	218	63	41	29	3	0	3	6	6	0	34	3	1	1	4	.200	0	0- -		5.08	5.63
2009	Lnsng	A	23	23	1	0	124.1	515	121	54	48	1	2	4	6	19	0	92	4	3	9	6	.600	0	0- -		2.55	3.47
2010	Dnedin	A+	23	21	0	0	112.1	498	137	65	54	10	4	3	7	27	0	78	5	0	8	7	.533	0	0- -		4.85	4.33
2011	Dnedin	A+	2	2	0	0	8.1	39	11	9	6	0	0	0	2	1	0	4	1	0	0	1	.000	0	0- -		4.85	6.48
2011	NHam	AA	15	14	1	0	88.0	353	81	31	28	7	0	1	4	17	0	66	1	0	8	4	.667	0	0- -		2.97	2.86
2011	Tor	AL	10	10	0	0	63.2	259	64	26	25	8	1	2	4	8	0	40	2	0	1	3	.250	0	0-0	0	3.49	3.53

Pedro Alvarez

Bats: L Throws: R Pos: 3B-66; PH-10
Ht: 6'3" Wt: 235 Born: 2/6/1987 Age: 25

Year	Team	Lg	G	AB	H	2B	3B	HR	(Hm	Rd)	TB	R	RBI	RC	TBB	IBB	SO	HBP	SH	SF	SB	CS	SB%	GDP	Avg	OBP	Slg
2009	Lynbrg	A+	66	243	60	14	1	14	(-	-)	118	38	55	42	37	4	70	0	0	4	1	1	.50	3	.247	.342	.486
2009	Altna	AA	60	222	74	18	0	13	(-	-)	131	42	40	53	34	5	59	0	0	2	1	0	1.00	4	.333	.419	.590
2010	Indy	AAA	66	242	67	15	4	13	(-	-)	129	42	53	46	32	2	68	2	0	2	4	4	.50	4	.277	.363	.533
2011	Pirates	R	1	1	0	0	0	0	(-	-)	0	0	0	0	0	0	0	0	0	0	0	0	-	0	.000	.000	.000
2011	Bradtn	A+	6	16	3	0	0	1	(-	-)	6	2	2	2	3	0	5	2	0	0	0	0	-	0	.188	.381	.375
2011	Indy	AAA	35	125	32	5	1	5	(-	-)	54	16	19	20	22	3	42	0	0	1	1	0	.00	3	.256	.365	.432
2010	Pit	NL	95	347	89	21	1	16	(12	4)	160	42	64	50	37	1	119	0	0	2	0	0	-	8	.256	.326	.461
2011	Pit	NL	74	235	45	9	1	4	(0	4)	68	18	19	14	24	1	80	2	1	0	1	0	1.00	11	.191	.272	.289
	2 ML YEARS		169	582	134	30	2	20	(12	8)	228	60	83	64	61	2	199	2	1	2	1	0	1.00	19	.230	.304	.392

Alexi Amarista

Bats: L **Throws:** R **Pos:** 2B-14; LF-8; PH-3; SS-1; PR-1   ah-mah-REE-stah   **Ht:** 5'8" **Wt:** 150 **Born:** 4/6/1989 **Age:** 23

Year	Team	Lg	G	AB	H	2B	3B	HR	(Hm	Rd)	TB	R	RBI	RC	TBB	IBB	SO	HBP	SH	SF	SB	CS	SB%	GDP	Avg	OBP	Slg
2008	Angels	R	51	202	67	6	4	2	(-	-)	87	46	21	37	29	0	20	1	3	1	22	14	.61	3	.332	.416	.431
2008	CRpds	A	1	2	0	0	0	0	(-	-)	0	0	0	0	0	0	1	0	0	0	0	0	-	0	.000	.000	.000
2009	CRpds	A	125	477	152	39	10	4	(-	-)	223	84	49	89	50	0	61	8	18	4	38	20	.66	10	.319	.390	.468
2010	RCuca	A+	72	297	90	19	6	4	(-	-)	133	39	39	46	19	2	42	3	2	2	17	10	.63	1	.303	.349	.448
2010	Salt Lk	AAA	15	65	26	6	3	0	(-	-)	38	13	9	14	1	0	4	1	2	1	4	2	.67	1	.400	.412	.585
2010	Ark	AA	48	191	55	2	1	1	(-	-)	62	25	20	23	13	0	15	2	2	5	4	1	.80	8	.288	.332	.325
2011	Salt Lk	AAA	86	363	106	24	5	4	(-	-)	152	49	50	52	22	0	56	4	4	3	15	8	.65	4	.292	.337	.419
2011	LAA	AL	23	52	8	3	1	0	(0	0)	13	2	5	1	2	0	8	0	1	1	0	0	-	1	.154	.182	.250

Alfredo Amezaga

Bats: B **Throws:** R **Pos:** 2B-16; PH-14; LF-4; 3B-2; SS-2; RF-2; PR-1   ah-MEH-zah-gah   **Ht:** 5'11" **Wt:** 165 **Born:** 1/16/1978 **Age:** 34

Year	Team	Lg	G	AB	H	2B	3B	HR	(Hm	Rd)	TB	R	RBI	RC	TBB	IBB	SO	HBP	SH	SF	SB	CS	SB%	GDP	Avg	OBP	Slg
2011	ColSpr*	AAA	67	239	73	19	1	4	(-	-)	106	49	41	43	29	1	36	4	2	3	4	2	.67	1	.305	.385	.444
2002	LAA	AL	12	13	7	2	0	0	(0	0)	9	3	2	6	0	0	1	0	0	0	1	0	1.00	1	.538	.538	.692
2003	LAA	AL	37	105	22	3	2	2	(0	2)	35	15	7	7	9	0	23	1	5	0	2	2	.50	2	.210	.278	.333
2004	LAA	AL	73	93	15	2	0	2	(0	2)	23	12	11	5	3	0	24	3	6	0	3	2	.60	2	.161	.212	.247
2005	2 Tms	NL	5	6	1	0	0	0	(0	0)	1	2	0	0	1	0	0	0	0	0	1	0	1.00	0	.167	.286	.167
2006	Fla	NL	132	334	87	9	3	3	(0	3)	111	42	19	32	33	4	46	3	7	1	20	12	.63	5	.260	.332	.332
2007	Fla	NL	133	400	105	14	9	2	(1	1)	143	46	30	38	35	0	52	4	4	5	13	7	.65	4	.263	.324	.358
2008	Fla	NL	125	311	82	13	5	3	(2	1)	114	41	32	37	19	1	47	3	4	0	8	2	.80	6	.264	.312	.367
2009	Fla	NL	27	69	15	3	0	0	(0	0)	18	6	5	3	5	2	16	0	0	1	1	1	.50	0	.217	.267	.261
2011	2 Tms	NL	40	77	14	1	0	0	(0	0)	15	6	4	4	7	0	14	0	2	1	0	0	-	1	.182	.247	.195
05	Col	NL	2	3	1	0	0	0	(0	0)	1	1	0	0	0	0	0	0	0	0	0	0	-	0	.333	.333	.333
05	Pit	NL	3	3	0	0	0	0	(0	0)	0	1	0	0	1	0	0	0	0	0	1	0	1.00	0	.000	.250	.000
11	Col	NL	20	33	8	1	0	0	(0	0)	9	5	2	3	3	0	7	0	1	1	0	0	-	0	.242	.297	.273
11	Fla	NL	20	44	6	0	0	0	(0	0)	6	1	2	1	4	0	7	0	1	0	0	0	-	1	.136	.208	.136
	Postseason		2	2	0	0	0	0	(0	0)	0	0	0	0	0	0	2	1	0	0	0	0	-	0	.000	.000	.000
	9 ML YEARS		584	1408	348	47	19	12	(3	9)	469	173	110	132	112	7	223	14	28	8	49	26	.65	21	.247	.307	.333

Brett Anderson

Pitches: L **Bats:** L **Pos:** SP-13   **Ht:** 6'4" **Wt:** 235 **Born:** 2/1/1988 **Age:** 24

Year	Team	Lg	G	GS	CG	GF	IP	BFP	H	R	ER	SH	SF	HB	TBB	IBB	SO	WP	Bk	W	L	Pct	Sh	Sv-Op	Hld	ERC	ERA
2009	Oak	AL	30	30	1	0	175.1	735	180	94	79	20	4	4	3	45	1	150	0	1	11	11	.500	1	0-0	0	3.84	4.06
2010	Oak	AL	19	19	0	0	112.1	470	112	41	35	6	3	2	7	22	2	75	4	2	7	6	.538	0	0-0	0	3.16	2.80
2011	Oak	AL	13	13	1	0	83.1	356	86	40	37	8	4	1	7	25	1	61	0	1	3	6	.333	0	0-0	0	4.20	4.00
	3 ML YEARS		62	62	2	0	371.0	1561	378	175	151	34	11	7	17	92	4	286	4	4	21	23	.477	1	0-0		3.71	3.66

Lars Anderson

Bats: L **Throws:** L **Pos:** 1B-6; PR-3   **Ht:** 6'4" **Wt:** 215 **Born:** 9/25/1987 **Age:** 24

Year	Team	Lg	G	AB	H	2B	3B	HR	(Hm	Rd)	TB	R	RBI	RC	TBB	IBB	SO	HBP	SH	SF	SB	CS	SB%	GDP	Avg	OBP	Slg
2007	Grnville	A	124	458	132	35	3	10	(-	-)	203	69	69	81	71	1	112	2	0	2	2	4	.33	10	.288	.385	.443
2007	Lancst	A+	10	35	12	2	0	1	(-	-)	17	13	9	9	11	0	9	0	0	1	0	0	-	0	.343	.489	.486
2008	Lancst	A+	77	306	97	19	1	13	(-	-)	157	58	50	65	46	1	64	3	0	3	0	0	-	10	.317	.408	.513
2008	Portlnd	AA	41	133	42	13	0	5	(-	-)	70	27	30	31	29	1	43	0	0	1	1	0	1.00	6	.316	.436	.526
2009	Portlnd	AA	119	447	104	23	0	9	(-	-)	154	50	51	55	63	4	114	1	0	1	2	0	1.00	8	.233	.328	.345
2010	Portlnd	AA	17	62	22	5	0	5	(-	-)	42	13	16	16	7	0	16	0	0	2	1	1	.50	0	.355	.408	.677
2010	Pwtckt	AAA	113	409	107	32	3	10	(-	-)	175	49	53	62	44	2	109	6	0	3	2	2	.50	0	.262	.340	.428
2011	Pwtckt	AAA	136	491	130	31	2	14	(-	-)	207	65	78	83	80	2	120	3	0	3	5	0	1.00	12	.265	.369	.422
2010	Bos	AL	18	35	7	1	0	0	(0	0)	8	4	4	4	7	0	8	0	0	0	0	0	-	1	.200	.326	.229
2011	Bos	AL	6	5	0	0	0	0	(0	0)	0	2	0	0	0	0	3	0	0	0	0	0	-	0	.000	.000	.000
	2 ML YEARS		24	40	7	1	0	0	(0	0)	8	6	4	4	7	0	11	0	0	0	0	0	-	1	.175	.292	.200

Robert Andino

Bats: R **Throws:** R **Pos:** 2B-94; SS-30; 3B-22; PH-4; LF-3; PR-1   ann-DEE-no   **Ht:** 6'0" **Wt:** 195 **Born:** 4/25/1984 **Age:** 28

Year	Team	Lg	G	AB	H	2B	3B	HR	(Hm	Rd)	TB	R	RBI	RC	TBB	IBB	SO	HBP	SH	SF	SB	CS	SB%	GDP	Avg	OBP	Slg
2005	Fla	NL	17	44	7	4	0	0	(0	0)	11	4	1	1	5	1	8	0	1	0	1	0	1.00	2	.159	.245	.250
2006	Fla	NL	11	24	4	1	0	0	(0	0)	5	0	2	0	1	0	6	0	1	2	1	0	1.00	0	.167	.185	.208
2007	Fla	NL	7	13	5	1	0	0	(0	0)	6	0	0	1	0	0	2	0	0	0	0	0	-	0	.385	.385	.462
2008	Fla	NL	44	63	13	2	0	2	(1	1)	21	7	9	7	4	0	23	0	1	0	0	0	-	1	.206	.254	.333
2009	Bal	AL	78	198	44	7	0	2	(1	1)	57	31	10	11	15	1	47	0	0	2	3	3	.50	6	.222	.274	.288
2010	Bal	AL	16	61	18	4	0	2	(2	0)	28	6	6	4	3	0	13	1	0	1	1	1	.50	3	.295	.333	.459
2011	Bal	AL	139	457	120	22	0	5	(2	3)	157	63	36	52	41	0	83	3	9	1	13	3	.81	14	.263	.327	.344
	7 ML YEARS		312	860	211	41	0	11	(6	5)	285	111	64	76	69	2	182	4	12	6	19	7	.73	26	.245	.302	.331

Elvis Andrus

Bats: R Throws: R Pos: SS-147; PH-6; DH-1 AHN-drews Ht: 6'0" Wt: 200 Born: 8/26/1988 Age: 23

Year	Team	Lg	G	AB	H	2B	3B	HR	(Hm	Rd)	TB	R	RBI	RC	TBB	IBB	SO	HBP	SH	SF	SB	CS	SB%	GDP	Avg	OBP	Slg
2009	Tex	AL	145	480	128	17	8	6	(3	3)	179	72	40	65	40	0	77	6	12	3	33	6	.85	4	.267	.329	.373
2010	Tex	AL	148	588	156	15	3	0	(0	0)	177	88	35	79	64	0	96	5	17	0	32	15	.68	6	.265	.342	.301
2011	Tex	AL	150	587	164	27	3	5	(2	3)	212	96	60	76	56	0	74	5	16	1	37	12	.76	17	.279	.347	.361
	Postseason		16	68	20	3	0	0	(0	0)	23	8	4	8	5	0	8	0	1	1	8	1	.89	3	.294	.338	.338
	3 ML YEARS		443	1655	448	59	14	11	(5	6)	568	256	135	220	160	0	247	16	45	4	102	33	.76	27	.271	.340	.343

Matt Angle

Bats: L Throws: R Pos: CF-16; LF-14; PR-3; RF-2; PH-2 Ht: 5'10" Wt: 175 Born: 9/10/1985 Age: 26

Year	Team	Lg	G	AB	H	2B	3B	HR	(Hm	Rd)	TB	R	RBI	RC	TBB	IBB	SO	HBP	SH	SF	SB	CS	SB%	GDP	Avg	OBP	Slg
2007	Abrdn	A-	66	236	71	4	4	0	(-	-)	83	60	14	45	47	0	40	2	2	0	34	4	.89	3	.301	.421	.352
2008	Dlmrva	A	126	478	137	22	5	4	(-	-)	181	82	35	80	71	0	86	7	7	3	37	11	.77	3	.287	.385	.379
2009	Frdrck	A+	123	478	138	17	4	1	(-	-)	166	78	32	71	59	0	72	4	10	2	39	12	.76	2	.289	.370	.347
2009	Bowie	AA	8	28	10	1	0	0	(-	-)	11	6	1	5	4	0	5	0	0	0	2	0	1.00	0	.357	.438	.393
2010	Bowie	AA	14	60	23	2	0	1	(-	-)	28	11	9	12	6	0	5	0	3	1	5	2	.71	0	.383	.433	.467
2010	Norfolk	AAA	87	350	91	4	4	1	(-	-)	106	55	24	43	41	2	54	1	5	2	24	4	.86	4	.260	.338	.303
2011	Norfolk	AAA	108	424	115	13	3	4	(-	-)	146	67	33	60	47	1	88	5	8	5	27	3	.90	1	.271	.347	.344
2011	Bal	AL	31	79	14	4	0	1	(0	1)	21	12	7	9	12	0	13	1	3	0	11	1	.92	0	.177	.293	.266

Rick Ankiel

Bats: L Throws: L Pos: CF-105; PH-13; RF-9; PR-2 ANN-keel Ht: 6'2" Wt: 225 Born: 7/19/1979 Age: 32

Year	Team	Lg	G	AB	H	2B	3B	HR	(Hm	Rd)	TB	R	RBI	RC	TBB	IBB	SO	HBP	SH	SF	SB	CS	SB%	GDP	Avg	OBP	Slg
2011	Hrsbrg*	AA	1	4	0	0	0	0	(-	-)	0	0	0	0	0	0	4	0	0	0	0	0	-	0	.000	.000	.000
2011	Nats*	R	1	2	1	0	0	0	(-	-)	1	0	0	0	1	0	0	0	0	0	0	0	-	0	.500	.667	.500
2011	Syrcse*	AAA	2	7	1	1	0	0	(-	-)	2	2	0	0	1	0	2	0	0	0	1	0	1.00	0	.143	.250	.286
1999	StL	NL	9	10	1	0	0	0	(0	0)	1	0	0	0	0	0	3	0	1	0	0	0	-	0	.100	.100	.100
2000	StL	NL	33	68	17	1	1	2	(2	0)	26	8	9	4	4	0	20	0	1	0	0	0	-	1	.250	.292	.382
2001	StL	NL	6	8	0	0	0	0	(0	0)	0	1	0	0	1	0	5	0	1	0	0	0	-	0	.000	.111	.000
2004	StL	NL	5	1	0	0	0	0	(0	0)	0	0	0	0	0	1	0	1	0	0	0	0	-	0	.000	.500	.000
2007	StL	NL	47	172	49	8	1	11	(9	2)	92	31	39	32	13	0	41	0	1	4	1	0	1.00	3	.285	.328	.535
2008	StL	NL	120	413	109	21	2	25	(11	14)	209	65	71	60	42	3	100	5	0	3	2	1	.67	8	.264	.337	.506
2009	StL	NL	122	372	86	21	2	11	(4	7)	144	50	38	32	26	4	99	3	0	3	4	3	.57	5	.231	.285	.387
2010	2 Tms		74	211	49	13	1	6	(1	5)	82	31	24	22	26	2	71	2	0	1	3	1	.75	3	.232	.321	.389
2011	Was	NL	122	380	91	20	0	9	(8	1)	138	46	37	35	29	1	96	2	3	1	10	3	.77	7	.239	.296	.363
10	KC	AL	27	92	24	7	0	4	(1	3)	43	14	15	11	7	0	29	1	0	1	1	0	1.00	2	.261	.317	.467
10	Atl	NL	47	119	25	6	1	2	(0	2)	39	17	9	11	19	2	42	1	0	0	2	1	.67	1	.210	.324	.328
	Postseason		9	15	2	0	0	1	(0	1)	5	1	1	1	2	0	6	0	0	0	0	0	-	0	.133	.235	.333
	9 ML YEARS		538	1635	402	84	7	64	(35	29)	692	232	218	181	142	10	436	12	7	12	20	8	.71	27	.246	.309	.423

J.P. Arencibia

Bats: R Throws: R Pos: C-122; DH-4; PH-3 air-en-SEE-bee-uh Ht: 6'1" Wt: 210 Born: 1/5/1986 Age: 26

Year	Team	Lg	G	AB	H	2B	3B	HR	(Hm	Rd)	TB	R	RBI	RC	TBB	IBB	SO	HBP	SH	SF	SB	CS	SB%	GDP	Avg	OBP	Slg
2007	Auburn	A-	63	228	58	17	1	3	(-	-)	86	31	25	27	14	I	56	5	0	2	0	0	-	3	.254	.309	.377
2008	Dnedin	A+	59	248	78	22	0	13	(-	-)	139	38	62	47	11	2	46	1	0	2	0	0	-	9	.315	.344	.560
2008	NHam	AA	67	262	74	14	0	14	(-	-)	130	32	43	39	7	0	55	2	0	4	0	0	-	7	.202	.302	.496
2009	LsVgs	AAA	116	466	110	32	1	21	(-	-)	207	67	75	60	26	0	114	6	0	2	0	1	.00	11	.236	.284	.444
2010	LsVgs	AAA	104	412	124	36	1	32	(-	-)	258	76	85	91	38	1	85	3	0	6	0	0	-	13	.301	.359	.626
2010	Tor	AL	11	35	5	1	0	2	(2	0)	12	3	4	4	2	0	11	0	0	0	0	0	-	0	.143	.189	.343
2011	Tor	AL	129	443	97	20	4	23	(13	10)	194	47	78	58	36	3	133	4	0	3	1	1	.50	6	.219	.282	.438
	2 ML YEARS		140	478	102	21	4	25	(15	10)	206	50	82	62	38	3	144	4	0	3	1	1	.50	6	.213	.275	.431

Jose Arredondo

Pitches: R Bats: R Pos: RP-53 air-eh-DON-doe Ht: 6'0" Wt: 175 Born: 3/12/1984 Age: 28

Year	Team	Lg	G	GS	CG	GF	IP	BFP	H	R	ER	HR	SH	SF	HB	TBB	IBB	SO	WP	Bk	W	L	Pct	Sh	Sv-Op	Hld	ERC	ERA
2011	Carlina*	AA	6	0	0	2	7.2	29	4	2	2	0	0	0	0	4	0	11	0	0	1	0	1.000	0	0- -	-	1.63	2.35
2011	Lsvlle*	AAA	6	0	0	1	8.0	34	6	3	2	0	0	0	0	2	0	10	1	0	1	1	.500	0	0- -	-	1.55	2.25
2008	LAA	AL	52	0	0	10	61.0	244	42	15	11	3	0	0	1	22	0	55	1	0	10	2	.833	0	0-7	16	2.08	1.62
2009	LAA	AL	43	0	0	15	45.0	202	47	30	30	6	3	1	0	23	2	47	5	1	2	3	.400	0	0-1	16	4.91	6.00
2011	Cin	NL	53	0	0	10	53.0	226	43	21	19	5	3	0	2	31	5	48	4	2	4	4	.500	0	0-1	4	3.78	3.23
	Postseason		3	0	0	1	3.2	15	2	0	0	0	0	0	0	2	0	6	0	0	0	0	-	0	0-0	0	1.65	0.00
	3 ML YEARS		148	0	0	35	159.0	672	132	66	60	14	6	1	3	76	7	150	10	3	16	9	.640	0	0-9	36	3.38	3.40

Jake Arrieta

Pitches: R Bats: R Pos: SP-22   air-ee-ETT-uh   Ht: 6'4" Wt: 220 Born: 3/6/1986 Age: 26

Year	Team	Lg	G	GS	CG	GF	IP	BFP	H	R	ER	HR	SH	SF	HB	TBB	IBB	SO	WP	Bk	W	L	Pct	Sh	Sv-Op	Hld	ERC	ERA
2008	Frdrck	A+	20	20	0	0	113.0	463	80	44	36	7	2	2	6	51	0	120	3	1	6	5	.545	0	0- -	-	2.70	2.87
2009	Bowie	AA	11	11	2	0	59.0	244	45	21	17	4	0	1	4	23	0	70	2	0	6	3	.667	2	0- -	-	2.82	2.59
2009	Norfolk	AAA	17	17	0	0	91.2	401	97	46	40	9	6	2	9	33	0	78	4	0	5	8	.385	0	0- -	-	4.68	3.93
2010	Norfolk	AAA	12	11	0	0	73.0	293	48	18	15	3	3	0	2	34	0	64	1	0	6	2	.750	0	0- -	-	2.31	1.85
2010	Bal	AL	18	18	0	0	100.1	449	106	57	52	9	4	2	4	48	3	52	5	0	6	6	.500	0	0-0	0	4.74	4.66
2011	Bal	AL	22	22	0	0	119.1	523	115	70	67	21	3	2	4	59	2	93	0	0	10	8	.556	0	0-0	0	4.93	5.05
2 ML YEARS			40	40	0	0	219.2	972	221	127	119	30	7	4	8	107	5	145	5	0	16	14	.533	0	0-0	0	4.85	4.88

Bronson Arroyo

Pitches: R Bats: R Pos: SP-32   uh-ROY-oh   Ht: 6'4" Wt: 196 Born: 2/24/1977 Age: 35

Year	Team	Lg	G	GS	CG	GF	IP	BFP	H	R	ER	HR	SH	SF	HB	TBB	IBB	SO	WP	Bk	W	L	Pct	Sh	Sv-Op	Hld	ERC	ERA
2000	Pit	NL	20	12	0	1	71.2	338	88	61	51	10	5	2	4	36	6	50	3	1	2	6	.250	0	0-0	0	6.18	6.40
2001	Pit	NL	24	13	1	1	88.1	390	99	54	50	12	4	6	4	34	6	39	4	1	5	7	.417	0	0-0	2	5.09	5.09
2002	Pit	NL	9	4	0	1	27.0	123	30	14	12	1	1	1	0	15	3	22	0	0	2	1	.667	0	0-0	1	4.64	4.00
2003	Bos	AL	6	0	0	2	17.1	66	10	5	4	0	0	0	1	4	2	14	0	0	0	0	-	0	1-1	0	1.14	2.08
2004	Bos	AL	32	29	0	1	178.2	764	171	99	80	17	5	4	20	47	3	142	5	0	10	9	.526	0	0-0	0	3.65	4.03
2005	Bos	AL	35	32	0	1	205.1	878	213	116	103	22	4	4	14	54	3	100	5	1	14	10	.583	0	0-0	0	4.04	4.51
2006	Cin	NL	35	35	3	0	240.2	992	222	98	88	31	9	2	5	64	7	184	6	0	14	11	.560	1	0-0	0	3.37	3.29
2007	Cin	NL	34	34	1	0	210.2	921	232	109	99	28	10	7	13	63	6	156	4	0	9	15	.375	0	0-0	0	4.68	4.23
2008	Cin	NL	34	34	1	0	200.0	871	219	116	106	29	13	6	6	68	2	163	6	0	15	11	.577	0	0-0	0	4.83	4.77
2009	Cin	NL	33	33	3	0	220.1	923	214	101	94	31	9	5	9	65	6	127	1	0	15	13	.536	2	0-0	0	3.94	3.84
2010	Cin	NL	33	33	2	0	215.2	880	188	95	93	29	6	5	6	59	5	121	1	1	17	10	.630	0	0-0	0	3.21	3.88
2011	Cin	NL	32	32	1	0	199.0	855	227	119	112	46	6	5	6	45	5	108	0	0	9	12	.429	1	0-0	0	5.20	5.07
Postseason			11	3	0	3	22.1	104	23	17	15	5	0	0	2	12	0	22	0	0	0	0	-	0	0-0	2	6.00	6.04
12 ML YEARS			327	291	12	6	1874.2	8001	1913	987	892	256	72	47	88	554	54	1226	35	4	112	105	.516	4	1-1	3	4.18	4.28

Jose Ascanio

Pitches: R Bats: R Pos: RP-8   Ht: 5'11" Wt: 195 Born: 5/2/1985 Age: 27

Year	Team	Lg	G	GS	CG	GF	IP	BFP	H	R	ER	HR	SH	SF	HB	TBB	IBB	SO	WP	Bk	W	L	Pct	Sh	Sv-Op	Hld	ERC	ERA
2011	Bradtn*	A+	3	2	0	0	3.2	17	4	4	4	0	0	2	0	1	0	6	1	0	0	0	-	0	0- -	-	3.07	9.82
2011	Indy*	AAA	30	5	0	11	44.0	198	50	25	24	2	2	0	4	15	0	50	4	0	2	3	.400	0	1- -	-	4.53	4.91
2007	Atl	NL	13	0	0	6	16.0	74	17	11	9	3	1	0	0	6	2	13	0	0	1	1	.500	0	0-0	0	4.43	5.06
2008	ChC	NL	6	0	0	1	5.2	30	8	5	5	1	1	1	1	4	1	3	0	0	0	0	-	0	0-0	0	8.81	7.94
2009	2 Tms	NL	16	0	0	5	18.0	86	22	8	8	1	2	2	3	9	2	20	1	0	0	2	.000	0	0-0	1	5.89	4.00
2011	Pit	NL	8	0	0	4	6.1	31	10	5	5	2	0	0	0	2	0	5	0	0	0	0	-	0	0-0	0	8.89	7.11
09	ChC	NL	14	0	0	4	15.1	73	18	6	6	1	1	0	2	9	2	18	1	0	0	1	.000	0	0-0	1	5.87	3.52
09	Pit	NL	2	0	0	1	2.2	13	4	2	2	0	1	2	1	0	0	2	0	0	0	1	.000	0	0-0	0	5.97	6.75
4 ML YEARS			43	0	0	16	46.0	221	57	29	27	7	4	3	4	21	5	41	1	0	1	3	.250	0	0-0	1	6.12	5.28

Jairo Asencio

Pitches: R Bats: R Pos: RP-6   HIGH-row   Ht: 6'2" Wt: 180 Born: 5/5/1984 Age: 28

Year	Team	Lg	G	GS	CG	GF	IP	BFP	H	R	ER	HR	SH	SF	HB	TBB	IBB	SO	WP	Bk	W	L	Pct	Sh	Sv-Op	Hld	ERC	ERA
2004	Pirates	R	11	11	2	0	61.1	250	58	22	19	1	2	1	4	10	0	41	3	2	7	2	.778	1	0- -	-	2.61	2.79
2005	Hkry	A	7	2	0	1	18.0	87	24	19	15	1	1	1	1	9	0	9	2	0	0	2	.000	0	0- -	-	6.25	7.50
2005	Wmspt	A-	16	7	0	2	59.2	259	67	39	30	4	0	2	4	17	0	30	3	1	4	5	.444	0	0- -	-	4.38	4.53
2006	Hkry	A	22	22	2	0	122.0	521	131	73	58	20	5	3	7	26	0	71	8	0	7	8	.467	1	0- -	-	4.40	4.28
2006	Lynbrg	A+	1	1	0	0	3.2	22	7	6	6	0	0	0	0	5	0	1	0	0	0	0	-	0	0- -	-	13.66	14.73
2007	Lynbrg	A+	36	1	0	15	73.1	331	87	44	39	4	2	0	4	26	1	78	6	0	3	4	.429	0	5- -	-	4.78	4.79
2008	Missi	AA	55	0	0	45	65.1	282	48	30	20	3	4	3	4	36	3	77	4	0	4	3	.571	0	28- -	-	2.95	2.76
2009	Gwnntt	AAA	58	0	0	51	71.1	302	66	37	26	4	0	5	0	19	0	75	2	0	5	4	.556	0	27- -	-	2.78	3.28
2011	Gwnntt	AAA	47	0	0	42	54.2	222	39	14	11	3	0	1	0	22	0	70	4	0	3	2	.600	0	26- -	-	2.30	1.81
2009	Atl	NL	3	0	0	2	2.2	13	3	1	1	0	0	0	0	2	0	0	0	0	0	1	.000	0	0-0	0	5.24	3.38
2011	Atl	NL	6	0	0	3	10.1	52	16	11	8	1	0	0	0	5	2	8	0	0	0	0	-	0	0-1	0	7.18	6.97
2 ML YEARS			9	0	0	5	13.0	65	19	12	9	1	0	0	0	7	2	8	0	0	0	1	.000	0	0-1	0	6.77	6.23

Scott Atchison

Pitches: R Bats: R Pos: RP-17   Ht: 6'2" Wt: 200 Born: 3/29/1976 Age: 36

Year	Team	Lg	G	GS	CG	GF	IP	BFP	H	R	ER	HR	SH	SF	HB	TBB	IBB	SO	WP	Bk	W	L	Pct	Sh	Sv-Op	Hld	ERC	ERA
2011	Pwtckt*	AAA	36	1	0	10	61.1	245	50	20	18	5	4	2	4	9	1	72	5	0	6	2	.750	0	5- -	-	2.26	2.64
2004	Sea	AL	25	0	0	8	30.2	133	29	12	12	4	2	1	0	14	2	36	2	0	2	3	.400	0	0-0	2	4.08	3.52
2005	Sea	AL	6	0	0	2	6.2	27	7	5	5	1	0	0	0	1	0	9	0	0	0	0	-	0	0-0	0	3.77	6.75
2007	SF	NL	22	0	0	4	30.2	131	32	14	14	5	1	2	1	10	0	25	2	0	0	0	-	0	0-1	5	4.65	4.11
2010	Bos	AL	43	1	0	8	60.0	253	58	37	30	9	1	2	1	19	2	41	4	0	2	3	.400	0	0-0	7	3.92	4.50
2011	Bos	AL	17	0	0	4	30.1	122	31	11	11	0	1	2	2	6	0	17	2	0	1	0	1.000	0	1-1	0	3.15	3.26
5 ML YEARS			113	1	0	26	158.1	666	157	79	72	19	5	7	4	50	4	128	10	0	5	6	.455	0	1-2	14	3.94	4.09

Mitch Atkins

Pitches: R Bats: R Pos: SP-3   Ht: 6'3" Wt: 230 Born: 10/1/1985 Age: 26

Year	Team	Lg	G	GS	CG	GF	IP	BFP	H	R	ER	HR	SH	SF	HB	TBB	IBB	SO	WP	Bk	W	L	Pct	Sh	Sv-Op	Hld	ERC	ERA
2011	Frdrck*	A+	2	2	0	0	9.0	35	7	3	3	1	0	0	1	0	0	14	0	0	0	1	.000	0	0--	-	1.91	3.00
2011	Bowie*	AA	4	4	0	0	26.2	111	21	13	10	2	2	2	2	11	0	19	0	0	1	2	.333	0	0--	-	3.12	3.38
2011	Norfolk*	AAA	17	17	0	0	94.1	418	95	63	57	10	4	4	13	37	0	74	1	0	3	7	.300	0	0--	-	4.69	5.44
2009	ChC	NL	2	0	0	1	2.0	7	1	0	0	0	0	0	0	0	0	0	0	0	0	0	-	0	0-0	0	0.54	0.00
2010	ChC	NL	5	0	0	2	10.0	49	12	8	7	2	0	0	1	6	0	10	0	0	0	0	-	0	0-0	0	7.19	6.30
2011	Bal	AL	3	3	0	0	10.2	56	21	10	10	5	0	1	1	3	0	7	0	0	0	0	-	0	0-0	0	13.72	8.44
	3 ML YEARS		10	3	0	3	22.2	112	34	18	17	7	0	1	2	9	0	17	0	0	0	0	-	0	0-0	0	9.21	6.75

Bryan Augenstein

Pitches: R Bats: R Pos: RP-5   Ht: 6'6" Wt: 232 Born: 7/11/1986 Age: 25

Year	Team	Lg	G	GS	CG	GF	IP	BFP	H	R	ER	HR	SH	SF	HB	TBB	IBB	SO	WP	Bk	W	L	Pct	Sh	Sv-Op	Hld	ERC	ERA
2007	Msoula	R+	10	2	0	4	21.1	92	20	13	8	2	2	1	2	7	0	16	2	0	0	2	.000	0	0--	-	3.73	3.38
2008	Sbend	A	13	13	0	0	87.1	337	73	21	21	2	1	1	0	9	1	69	0	0	5	1	.833	0	0--	-	1.72	2.16
2008	Visalia	A+	9	9	0	0	44.0	188	57	26	19	5	2	1	1	5	0	30	1	0	2	4	.333	0	0--	-	4.87	3.89
2009	Mobile	AA	9	9	0	0	45.2	165	27	5	5	0	0	0	0	8	0	36	0	0	5	0	1.000	0	0--	-	1.09	0.99
2009	Reno	AAA	8	7	0	0	36.0	155	43	23	22	2	1	2	1	7	0	29	1	0	2	5	.286	0	0--	-	4.16	5.50
2010	Reno	AAA	22	22	0	0	120.2	558	162	95	88	12	6	4	7	35	0	101	5	2	6	8	.429	0	0--	-	5.81	6.56
2010	Mobile	AA	3	0	0	0	8.1	37	10	5	5	1	0	1	0	3	0	9	1	0	0	1	.000	0	0--	-	5.24	5.40
2011	PlmBh	A+	3	2	0	0	4.1	19	6	5	5	2	0	0	0	0	0	6	0	0	0	2	.000	0	0--	-	7.04	10.38
2011	Memp	AAA	26	1	0	6	35.2	158	36	18	16	5	0	1	1	12	1	35	0	0	3	0	1.000	0	0--	-	4.07	4.04
2009	Ari	NL	7	2	0	2	17.0	81	23	16	15	2	2	2	2	6	2	6	0	0	0	1	.000	0	0-0	0	6.32	7.94
2011	StL	NL	5	0	0	1	5.2	31	11	7	6	1	0	0	1	3	3	6	1	0	0	1	.000	0	0-0	0	11.19	9.53
	2 ML YEARS		12	2	0	3	22.2	112	34	23	21	3	2	2	3	9	5	12	1	0	0	2	.000	0	0-0	0	7.47	8.34

Alex Avila

Bats: L Throws: R Pos: C-133; DH-4; PH-4; 3B-1   ah-VEE-lah   Ht: 5'11" Wt: 210 Born: 1/29/1987 Age: 25

Year	Team	Lg	G	AB	H	2B	3B	HR	(Hm	Rd)	TB	R	RBI	RC	TBB	IBB	SO	HBP	SH	SF	SB	CS	SB%	GDP	Avg	OBP	Slg
2009	Det	AL	29	61	17	4	0	5	(4	1)	36	9	14	12	10	0	18	0	0	1	0	0	-	0	.279	.375	.590
2010	Det	AL	104	294	67	12	0	7	(4	3)	100	28	31	26	36	0	71	2	1	0	2	2	.50	12	.228	.316	.340
2011	Det	AL	141	464	137	33	4	19	(10	9)	235	63	82	86	73	9	131	3	3	8	3	1	.75	8	.295	.389	.506
	3 ML YEARS		274	819	221	49	4	31	(18	13)	371	100	127	124	119	9	220	5	4	9	5	3	.63	20	.270	.362	.453

Mike Aviles

Bats: R Throws: R Pos: 3B-46; 2B-27; SS-14; PR-8; PH-6; RF-4; DH-2; LF-1   uh-VEE-less   Ht: 5'10" Wt: 204 Born: 3/13/1981 Age: 31

Year	Team	Lg	G	AB	H	2B	3B	HR	(Hm	Rd)	TB	R	RBI	RC	TBB	IBB	SO	HBP	SH	SF	SB	CS	SB%	GDP	Avg	OBP	Slg
2011	Omha*	AAA	35	140	43	8	2	9	(-	-)	82	21	25	26	6	2	17	0	1	3	6	4	.60	10	.307	.329	.586
2008	KC	AL	102	419	136	27	4	10	(4	6)	201	68	51	62	18	4	58	2	0	2	8	3	.73	12	.325	.354	.480
2009	KC	AL	36	120	22	3	1	1	(1	0)	30	10	8	4	4	0	26	0	2	1	1	0	1.00	3	.183	.208	.250
2010	KC	AL	110	424	129	16	3	8	(4	4)	175	63	32	47	20	0	49	1	0	3	14	5	.74	13	.304	.335	.413
2011	2 Tms	AL	91	286	73	17	3	7	(4	3)	117	31	39	31	13	0	44	2	4	4	14	4	.78	8	.255	.289	.409
11	KC	AL	53	185	41	11	3	5	(2	3)	73	14	31	18	9	0	27	2	3	3	10	2	.83	5	.222	.261	.395
11	Bos	AL	38	101	32	6	0	2	(2	0)	44	17	8	13	4	0	17	0	1	1	4	2	.67	3	.317	.340	.436
	4 ML YEARS		339	1249	360	63	11	26	(13	13)	523	172	130	144	55	4	177	5	6	10	37	12	.76	36	.288	.318	.419

Dylan Axelrod

Pitches: R Bats: R Pos: SP-3; RP-1   Ht: 6'0" Wt: 195 Born: 7/30/1985 Age: 26

Year	Team	Lg	G	GS	CG	GF	IP	BFP	H	R	ER	HR	SH	SF	HB	TBB	IBB	SO	WP	Bk	W	L	Pct	Sh	Sv-Op	Hld	ERC	ERA
2007	Padres	R	11	0	0	9	11.2	55	15	11	7	0	0	0	0	4	0	15	1	0	0	2	.000	0	2--	-	4.50	5.40
2007	FtWyn	A	10	0	0	3	21.1	81	18	4	3	0	1	0	0	4	0	15	1	0	2	1	.667	0	0--	-	2.00	1.27
2008	Lk Els	A+	32	0	0	5	49.1	224	51	36	29	4	0	5	2	19	0	55	9	0	2	1	.667	0	0--	-	4.04	5.29
2008	FtWyn	A	23	0	0	8	27.1	115	26	12	11	2	1	1	0	7	0	25	4	0	1	1	.500	0	0--	-	3.02	3.62
2009	Lk Els	A+	11	0	0	4	12.0	54	12	6	6	0	0	0	0	5	0	6	0	0	0	0	-	0	0--	-	3.27	4.50
2009	Knapol	A	2	0	0	1	4.1	20	3	2	1	0	0	0	0	1	0	3	0	0	0	0	-	0	0--	-	1.22	2.08
2009	WinSa	AA	5	5	0	0	28.1	114	29	7	6	2	4	0	0	4	1	17	1	0	2	1	.667	0	0--	-	3.02	1.91
2010	WinSa	A+	23	13	1	2	99.1	397	95	30	22	2	3	3	2	12	0	84	5	0	8	3	.727	1	0--	-	2.40	1.99
2010	Brham	AA	2	2	0	0	10.0	41	8	3	3	0	0	1	0	3	0	8	0	0	0	1	.000	0	0--	-	2.00	2.70
2011	Brham	AA	11	9	0	0	59.1	238	52	23	22	1	2	0	3	14	0	57	4	1	3	2	.600	0	0--	-	2.52	3.34
2011	Charltt	AAA	15	15	0	0	91.1	367	74	27	23	2	1	4	4	21	0	75	0	0	6	1	.857	0	0--	-	2.14	2.27
2011	CWS	AL	4	3	0	1	18.2	82	18	6	6	1	0	2	1	9	2	19	0	0	1	0	1.000	0	0-0	0	3.89	2.89

John Axford

Pitches: R Bats: R Pos: RP-74   Ht: 6'5" Wt: 195 Born: 4/1/1983 Age: 29

Year	Team	Lg	G	GS	CG	GF	IP	BFP	H	R	ER	HR	SH	SF	HB	TBB	IBB	SO	WP	Bk	W	L	Pct	Sh	Sv-Op	Hld	ERC	ERA
2009	Mil	NL	7	0	0	6	7.2	34	5	3	3	0	0	0	0	6	1	9	1	0	0	0	-	0	1-1	0	2.62	3.52
2010	Mil	NL	50	0	0	43	58.0	238	42	17	16	1	2	2	1	27	3	76	4	0	8	2	.800	0	24-27	3	2.33	2.48
2011	Mil	NL	74	0	0	63	73.2	305	59	19	16	4	1	1	0	25	1	86	8	0	2	2	.500	0	**46-48**	2	2.44	1.95
	3 ML YEARS		131	0	0	112	139.1	577	106	39	35	5	3	3	1	58	5	171	13	0	10	4	.714	0	71-76	5	2.41	2.26

Luis Ayala

Pitches: R Bats: R Pos: RP-52 Ht: 6'2" Wt: 190 Born: 1/12/1978 Age: 34

			HOW MUCH HE PITCHED						WHAT HE GAVE UP										THE RESULTS						
Year	Team	Lg	G	GS	CG	GF	IP	BFP	H	R	ER	HR	SF	SF	HB	TBB	IBB	SO	WP	Bk	W	L	Pct	Sh	Sv-Op	Hld	ERC	ERA
2011	S-WB*	AAA	3	0	0	1	5.0	19	6	1	1	0	2	1	0	0	0	7	0	0	0	0	-	0	0- -	-	3.25	1.80
2003	Mon	NL	65	0	0	24	71.0	288	65	27	23	8	3	1	5	13	3	46	1	0	10	3	.769	0	5-8	19	3.11	2.92
2004	Mon	NL	81	0	0	28	90.1	367	92	30	27	6	2	5	2	15	2	63	3	1	6	12	.333	0	2-7	21	3.32	2.69
2005	Was	NL	68	0	0	18	71.0	293	75	23	21	7	8	3	6	14	4	40	0	0	8	7	.533	0	1-3	22	3.95	2.66
2007	Was	NL	44	0	0	11	42.1	181	43	16	15	5	3	4	1	12	0	28	1	0	2	2	.500	0	1-2	6	3.88	3.19
2008	2 Tms		81	0	0	25	75.2	335	86	53	48	9	4	3	4	24	4	50	1	0	2	10	.167	0	9-15	19	4.76	5.71
2009	2 Tms		38	0	0	13	40.0	180	50	28	25	5	3	2	4	14	3	28	0	0	1	5	.167	0	0-4	3	5.94	5.63
2011	NYY	AL	52	0	0	20	56.0	233	51	17	13	5	4	4	6	20	3	39	2	1	2	2	.500	0	0-1	4	3.80	2.09
08	Was	NL	62	0	0	12	57.2	257	63	41	37	6	4	2	4	22	4	36	1	0	1	8	.111	0	0-4	19	4.70	5.77
08	NYM	NL	19	0	0	13	18.0	78	23	12	11	3	0	1	0	2	0	14	0	0	1	2	.333	0	9-11	0	4.91	5.50
09	Min	AL	28	0	0	11	32.1	138	38	18	15	4	1	2	3	8	0	21	0	0	1	2	.333	0	0-3	1	5.21	4.18
09	Fla	NL	10	0	0	2	7.2	42	12	10	10	1	2	0	1	6	3	7	0	0	0	3	.000	0	0-1	2	9.04	11.74
	7 ML YEARS		429	0	0	139	446.1	1877	462	194	172	45	27	19	31	112	19	294	8	2	31	41	.431	0	18-40	94	3.96	3.47

Erick Aybar

Bats: B Throws: R Pos: SS-142; PR-1 EYE-barr Ht: 5'10" Wt: 180 Born: 1/14/1984 Age: 28

			BATTING																BASERUNNING				AVERAGES		
Year	Team	Lg	G	AB	H	2B	3B	HR	(Hm | Rd)	TB	R	RBI	RC	TBB	IBB	SO	HBP	SH	SF	SB	CS	SB%	GDP	Avg	OBP	Slg
2011	Salt Lk*	AAA	1	4	1	0	0	0	(- | -)	1	1	0	0	0	0	1	0	0	0	0	0	-	0	.250	.250	.250
2006	LAA	AL	34	40	10	1	1	0	(0 | 0)	13	5	2	4	0	0	8	0	0	0	1	0	1.00	1	.250	.250	.325
2007	LAA	AL	79	194	46	5	1	1	(0 | 1)	56	18	19	16	10	0	32	2	3	2	4	4	.50	8	.237	.279	.289
2008	LAA	AL	98	346	96	18	5	3	(2 | 1)	133	53	39	49	14	0	45	5	9	1	7	2	.78	2	.277	.314	.384
2009	LAA	AL	137	504	157	23	9	5	(2 | 3)	213	70	58	73	30	1	54	5	12	5	14	7	.67	9	.312	.353	.423
2010	LAA	AL	138	534	135	18	4	5	(3 | 2)	176	69	29	51	35	1	81	7	11	2	22	8	.73	7	.253	.306	.330
2011	LAA	AL	143	556	155	33	8	10	(2 | 8)	234	71	59	72	31	1	68	6	9	3	30	6	.83	13	.279	.322	.421
	Postseason		14	50	11	2	1	0	(0 | 0)	15	4	4	4	1	0	4	0	2	0	3	0	1.00	2	.220	.235	.300
	6 ML YEARS		629	2174	599	98	28	24	(9 | 15)	825	286	206	265	120	3	288	25	44	13	78	27	.74	40	.276	.319	.379

Burke Badenhop

Pitches: R Bats: R Pos: RP-50 BADE-en-hopp Ht: 6'5" Wt: 220 Born: 2/8/1983 Age: 29

			HOW MUCH HE PITCHED						WHAT HE GAVE UP										THE RESULTS						
Year	Team	Lg	G	GS	CG	GF	IP	BFP	H	R	ER	HR	SH	SF	HB	TBB	IBB	SO	WP	Bk	W	L	Pct	Sh	Sv-Op	Hld	ERC	ERA
2011	NewOr*	AAA	11	0	0	3	14.2	71	20	16	11	1	1	1	1	7	0	10	1	0	1	1	.500	0	1- -	-	6.52	6.75
2008	Fla	NL	13	8	0	2	47.1	218	55	34	32	7	2	2	3	21	1	35	2	0	2	3	.400	0	0-0	0	5.74	6.08
2009	Fla	NL	35	2	0	7	72.0	303	71	32	30	5	3	2	1	24	4	57	1	0	7	4	.636	0	0-1	3	3.53	3.75
2010	Fla	NL	53	0	0	16	67.2	281	62	33	30	5	5	1	2	21	5	47	1	0	2	5	.286	0	1-3	8	3.12	3.99
2011	Fla	NL	50	0	0	15	63.2	276	65	29	29	1	1	2	4	24	4	51	4	0	2	3	.400	0	1-1	5	3.65	4.10
	4 ML YEARS		151	10	0	40	250.2	1078	253	128	121	18	11	7	10	90	14	190	8	0	13	15	.464	0	2-5	15	3.85	4.34

Danys Baez

Pitches: R Bats: R Pos: RP-29 BYE-ezz Ht: 6'3" Wt: 225 Born: 9/10/1977 Age: 34

			HOW MUCH HE PITCHED						WHAT HE GAVE UP										THE RESULTS						
Year	Team	Lg	G	GS	CG	GF	IP	BFP	H	R	ER	HR	SH	SF	HB	TBB	IBB	SO	WP	Bk	W	L	Pct	Sh	Sv-Op	Hld	ERC	ERA
2001	Cle	AL	43	0	0	8	50.1	202	34	22	14	5	0	1	3	20	4	52	3	0	5	3	.625	0	0-1	14	2.51	2.50
2002	Cle	AL	39	26	1	9	165.1	726	160	84	81	14	2	8	9	82	5	130	6	1	10	11	.476	0	6-8	0	4.35	4.41
2003	Cle	AL	73	0	0	46	75.2	318	65	36	32	9	6	1	4	23	0	66	5	0	2	9	.182	0	25-35	5	3.22	3.81
2004	TB	AL	62	0	0	59	68.0	295	60	31	27	6	5	1	7	29	4	52	3	1	4	4	.500	0	30-33	1	3.73	3.57
2005	TB	AL	67	0	0	64	72.1	308	66	27	23	7	4	2	2	30	0	51	0	0	5	4	.556	0	41-49	3	3.74	2.86
2006	2 Tms	NL	57	0	0	28	59.2	257	60	35	30	3	4	5	7	17	3	39	3	0	5	6	.455	0	9-17	12	3.69	4.53
2007	Bal	AL	53	0	0	25	50.1	233	50	36	36	8	3	1	7	29	5	29	0	0	0	6	.000	0	3-5	14	5.56	6.44
2009	Bal	AL	59	0	0	9	71.2	295	59	36	32	8	0	2	5	22	3	40	2	1	4	6	.400	0	0-2	15	3.06	4.02
2010	Phi	NL	51	0	0	17	47.2	216	55	31	29	6	4	3	3	23	2	28	1	0	3	4	.429	0	0-2	6	5.78	5.48
2011	Phi	NL	29	0	0	14	36.0	163	43	28	25	5	0	0	3	13	2	18	1	0	2	4	.333	0	0-1	0	5.60	6.25
06	LAD	NL	46	0	0	27	49.2	213	53	29	24	3	4	5	6	11	2	29	3	0	5	5	.500	0	9-16	6	3.90	4.35
06	Atl	NL	11	0	0	1	10.0	44	7	6	6	0	0	0	1	6	1	10	0	0	0	1	.000	0	0-1	6	2.64	5.40
	Postseason		3	0	0	2	3.2	15	4	1	1	0	0	0	0	0	0	6	0	0	0	0	-	0	0-0	0	2.36	2.45
	10 ML YEARS		533	26	1	279	697.0	3013	652	366	329	71	28	24	50	288	28	505	24	3	40	57	.412	0	114-153	67	4.00	4.25

Andrew Bailey

Pitches: R Bats: R Pos: RP-42 Ht: 6'3" Wt: 243 Born: 5/31/1984 Age: 28

			HOW MUCH HE PITCHED						WHAT HE GAVE UP										THE RESULTS						
Year	Team	Lg	G	GS	CG	GF	IP	BFP	H	R	ER	HR	SH	SF	HB	TBB	IBB	SO	WP	Bk	W	L	Pct	Sh	Sv-Op	Hld	ERC	ERA
2011	Scrmto*	AAA	4	0	0	0	4.0	18	3	0	0	0	0	0	2	1	0	3	0	0	0	0	-	0	0- -	-	3.21	0.00
2009	Oak	AL	68	0	0	54	83.1	323	49	17	17	5	3	2	6	24	3	91	6	0	6	3	.667	0	26-30	2	1.44	1.84
2010	Oak	AL	47	0	0	42	49.0	189	34	8	8	3	2	3	0	13	1	42	0	0	1	3	.250	0	25-28	0	1.82	1.47
2011	Oak	AL	42	0	0	37	41.2	170	34	18	15	3	1	1	0	12	2	41	0	0	0	4	.000	0	24-26	1	2.42	3.24
	3 ML YEARS		157	0	0	133	174.0	682	117	43	40	11	6	6	0	49	6	174	6	0	7	10	.412	0	75-84	3	1.73	2.07

Homer Bailey

Pitches: R **Bats:** R **Pos:** SP-22   **Ht:** 6'3" **Wt:** 202 **Born:** 5/3/1986 **Age:** 26

Year	Team	Lg	G	GS	CG	GF	IP	BFP	H	R	ER	HR	SH	SF	HB	TBB	IBB	SO	WP	Bk	W	L	Pct	Sh	Sv-Op	Hld	ERC	ERA
2011	Lsvlle*	AAA	6	6	0	0	30.0	128	34	10	10	1	0	0	0	6	0	22	0	0	2	1	.667	0	0- -		3.54	3.00
2007	Cin	NL	9	9	0	0	45.1	205	43	32	29	3	1	6	3	28	1	28	1	1	4	2	.667	0	0-0	0	4.61	5.76
2008	Cin	NL	8	8	0	0	36.1	180	59	36	32	8	5	2	0	17	1	18	4	1	0	6	.000	0	0-0	0	9.31	7.93
2009	Cin	NL	20	20	0	0	113.1	496	115	61	57	12	4	4	3	52	1	86	6	0	8	5	.615	0	0-0	0	4.56	4.53
2010	Cin	NL	19	19	1	0	109.0	465	109	55	54	11	2	1	3	40	6	100	3	1	4	3	.571	1	0-0	0	4.01	4.46
2011	Cin	NL	22	22	0	0	132.0	561	136	68	65	18	4	4	5	33	2	106	4	0	9	7	.563	0	0-0	0	4.01	4.43
Postseason			1	0	0	0	2.0	8	2	0	0	0	0	0	0	0	0	2	0	0	0	0	-	0	0-0	0	1.95	0.00
5 ML YEARS			78	78	1	0	436.0	1907	462	252	237	52	16	17	14	170	11	338	18	3	25	23	.521	1	0-0	0	4.61	4.89

Jeff Baker

Bats: R **Throws:** R **Pos:** PH-30; 1B-19; 2B-18; 3B-11; RF-10; DH-3; LF-1   **Ht:** 6'2" **Wt:** 210 **Born:** 6/21/1981 **Age:** 31

Year	Team	Lg	G	AB	H	2B	3B	HR	(Hm	Rd)	TB	R	RBI	RC	TBB	IBB	SO	HBP	SH	SF	SB	CS	SB%	GDP	Avg	OBP	Slg
2011	Iowa*	AAA	3	10	3	1	1	0	(-	-)	6	1	1	1	0	0	1	0	0	0	0	0	-	0	.300	.300	.600
2005	Col	NL	12	38	8	4	0	1	(1	0)	15	6	4	4	5	0	12	0	0	0	0	0	-	1	.211	.302	.395
2006	Col	NL	18	57	21	7	2	5	(4	1)	47	13	21	17	1	0	14	0	0	0	2	0	1.00	0	.368	.379	.825
2007	Col	NL	85	144	32	2	2	4	(4	0)	50	17	12	8	13	1	40	2	0	0	0	0	-	7	.222	.296	.347
2008	Col	NL	104	299	80	22	1	12	(8	4)	140	55	48	40	26	2	85	1	1	6	4	1	1.00	5	.268	.322	.468
2009	2 Tms	NL	81	226	65	15	2	4	(3	1)	96	27	24	28	18	0	53	2	0	2	1	0	1.00	6	.288	.343	.425
2010	ChC	NL	79	206	56	13	2	4	(3	1)	85	29	21	21	16	0	50	1	0	1	1	0	1.00	6	.272	.326	.413
2011	ChC	NL	81	201	54	12	1	3	(1	2)	77	20	23	20	10	0	46	0	0	0	0	0	-	8	.269	.302	.383
09 Col		NL	12	23	3	0	1	0	(0	0)	5	0	3	0	1	0	7	0	0	0	1	0	1.00	3	.130	.167	.217
09 ChC		NL	69	203	62	15	1	4	(3	1)	91	27	21	28	17	0	46	2	0	2	0	0	-	5	.305	.362	.448
Postseason			4	4	2	0	0	0	(0	0)	2	0	1	1	0	0	1	0	0	0	0	0	-	0	.500	.500	.500
7 ML YEARS			460	1171	316	75	10	33	(24	9)	510	167	153	138	89	3	300	6	1	10	8	1	1.00	35	.270	.322	.436

John Baker

Bats: L **Throws:** R **Pos:** PH-15; C-1   **Ht:** 6'1" **Wt:** 220 **Born:** 1/20/1981 **Age:** 31

Year	Team	Lg	G	AB	H	2B	3B	HR	(Hm	Rd)	TB	R	RBI	RC	TBB	IBB	SO	HBP	SH	SF	SB	CS	SB%	GDP	Avg	OBP	Slg
2011	Jupiter*	A+	12	28	8	2	2	0	(-	-)	14	8	1	7	10	0	8	1	0	0	0	0	-	1	.286	.487	.500
2011	Jaxnvl*	AA	3	9	1	1	0	0	(-	-)	2	0	0	0	1	0	5	0	0	0	0	0	-	0	.111	.200	.222
2008	Fla	NL	61	197	59	14	0	5	(3	2)	88	32	32	36	30	4	48	2	1	3	0	0	-	6	.299	.392	.447
2009	Fla	NL	112	373	101	25	0	9	(3	6)	153	59	50	54	41	5	89	5	2	2	0	0	-	10	.271	.349	.410
2010	Fla	NL	23	78	17	3	1	0	(0	0)	22	7	6	4	9	1	18	1	0	0	0	0	-	5	.218	.307	.282
2011	Fla	NL	16	13	2	0	0	0	(0	0)	2	0	1	0	2	0	3	0	1	0	0	0	-	0	.154	.267	.154
4 ML YEARS			212	661	179	42	1	14	(6	8)	265	98	89	94	82	10	158	8	4	5	0	0	-	21	.271	.356	.401

Scott Baker

Pitches: R **Bats:** R **Pos:** SP-21; RP-2   **Ht:** 6'4" **Wt:** 220 **Born:** 9/19/1981 **Age:** 30

Year	Team	Lg	G	GS	CG	GF	IP	BFP	H	R	ER	HR	SH	SF	HB	TBB	IBB	SO	WP	Bk	W	L	Pct	Sh	Sv-Op	Hld	ERC	ERA
2005	Min	AL	10	9	0	0	53.2	217	48	21	20	5	2	2	0	14	0	32	0	0	3	3	.500	0	0-0	1	2.97	3.35
2006	Min	AL	16	16	0	0	83.1	377	114	63	59	17	2	4	3	16	1	62	0	0	5	8	.385	0	0-0	0	6.26	6.37
2007	Min	AL	24	23	2	0	143.2	606	162	70	68	15	6	2	5	29	4	102	0	0	9	9	.500	1	0-0	0	4.19	4.26
2008	Min	AL	28	28	0	0	172.1	703	161	66	66	20	2	3	3	42	2	141	6	0	11	4	.733	0	0-0	0	3.31	3.45
2009	Min	AL	33	33	1	0	200.0	828	190	99	97	28	1	6	4	48	1	162	4	0	15	9	.625	1	0-0	0	3.51	4.37
2010	Min	AL	29	29	0	0	170.1	725	186	87	85	23	1	4	6	43	0	148	7	0	12	9	.571	0	0-0	0	4.43	4.49
2011	Min	AL	23	21	1	2	134.2	548	126	50	47	15	1	2	4	32	2	123	4	0	8	6	.571	0	0-0	0	3.32	3.14
Postseason			1	0	0	0	2.1	10	3	1	1	1	0	0	0	0	0	2	0	0	0	0	-	0	0-0	0	6.14	3.86
7 ML YEARS			163	159	4	2	958.0	4004	987	456	442	123	15	23	25	224	10	770	21	0	63	48	.568	2	0-0	2	3.90	4.15

Collin Balester

Pitches: R **Bats:** R **Pos:** RP-23   BAL-iss-ster   **Ht:** 6'5" **Wt:** 199 **Born:** 6/6/1986 **Age:** 26

Year	Team	Lg	G	GS	CG	GF	IP	BFP	H	R	ER	HR	SH	SF	HB	TBB	IBB	SO	WP	Bk	W	L	Pct	Sh	Sv-Op	Hld	ERC	ERA
2011	Syrcse*	AAA	28	0	0	9	39.1	174	47	19	19	2	0	1	1	15	1	46	3	0	2	1	.667	0	1- -		4.89	4.35
2008	Was	NL	15	15	0	0	80.0	358	92	53	49	12	2	3	6	28	1	50	4	0	3	7	.300	0	0-0	0	5.40	5.51
2009	Was	NL	7	7	0	0	30.1	135	34	24	23	10	0	0	0	14	0	20	0	0	1	4	.200	0	0-0	0	6.85	6.82
2010	Was	NL	17	0	0	8	21.0	89	15	6	6	2	2	0	2	11	1	28	4	0	0	1	.000	0	0-0	0	3.26	2.57
2011	Was	NL	23	0	0	9	35.2	159	38	21	18	7	1	1	1	14	0	34	2	1	1	4	.200	0	0-1	2	5.16	4.54
4 ML YEARS			62	22	0	17	167.0	741	179	104	96	31	5	4	9	67	2	132	10	1	5	16	.238	0	0-1	2	5.32	5.17

Grant Balfour

Pitches: R **Bats:** R **Pos:** RP-62   BAL-fore   **Ht:** 6'2" **Wt:** 195 **Born:** 12/30/1977 **Age:** 34

Year	Team	Lg	G	GS	CG	GF	IP	BFP	H	R	ER	HR	SH	SF	HB	TBB	IBB	SO	WP	Bk	W	L	Pct	Sh	Sv-Op	Hld	ERC	ERA
2011	Scrmto*	AAA	1	0	0	0	1.0	6	2	1	1	0	0	0	0	1	0	0	0	0	0	0	-	0	0- -	0	12.01	9.00
2001	Min	AL	2	0	0	1	2.2	14	3	4	4	2	1	0	0	3	0	2	0	0	0	0	-	0	0-0	0	13.78	13.50
2003	Min	AL	17	1	0	6	26.0	115	23	12	12	4	2	1	0	14	2	30	0	0	1	0	1.000	0	0-1	1	4.14	4.15
2004	Min	AL	36	0	0	14	39.1	172	35	19	19	4	2	0	2	21	1	42	3	0	4	1	.800	0	0-1	4	4.16	4.35
2007	2 Tms		25	0	0	8	24.2	121	30	21	21	4	3	2	3	1	20	0	30	0	0	1	2	.333	0	0-0	1	7.15	7.66

(pitcher, continued)

Year Team	Lg	G	GS	CG	GF	IP	BFP	H	R	ER	HR	SH	SF	HB	TBB	IBB	SO	WP	Bk	W	L	Pct	Sh	Sv-Op	Hld	ERC	ERA
2008 TB	AL	51	0	0	12	58.1	224	28	10	10	3	1	3	0	24	1	82	2	0	6	2	.750	0	4-5	14	1.38	1.54
2009 TB	AL	73	0	0	15	67.1	289	59	38	36	6	1	2	2	33	0	69	1	0	5	4	.556	0	4-9	18	3.79	4.81
2010 TB	AL	57	0	0	15	55.1	222	43	16	14	3	2	4	0	17	2	56	4	1	2	1	.667	0	0-1	16	2.24	2.28
2011 Oak	AL	62	0	0	15	62.0	242	44	17	17	8	1	0	0	20	1	59	0	0	5	2	.714	0	2-7	26	2.49	2.47
07 Mil	NL	3	0	0	2	2.2	18	4	6	6	1	1	0	1	4	0	3	0	0	0	2	.000	0	0-0	0	15.83	20.25
07 TB	AL	22	0	0	6	22.0	103	26	15	15	1	1	3	0	16	0	27	0	0	1	0	1.000	0	0-0	1	6.19	6.14
Postseason		15	0	0	3	15.0	65	13	6	6	2	1	0	1	8	3	10	1	0	0	0	-	0	0-0	2	4.06	3.60
8 ML YEARS		323	1	0	79	335.2	1399	265	137	133	32	12	14	5	152	7	370	10	1	24	12	.667	0	10-24	80	3.15	3.57

Rod Barajas

Bats: R Throws: R Pos: C-88; PH-11 bah-RAH-hahss **Ht: 6'2" Wt: 245 Born: 9/5/1975 Age: 36**

Year Team	Lg	G	AB	H	2B	3B	HR	(Hm	Rd)	TB	R	RBI	RC	TBB	IBB	SO	HBP	SH	SF	SB	CS	SB%	GDP	Avg	OBP	Slg
2011 RCuca*	A+	4	18	7	2	0	1	(-	-)	12	4	2	4	1	0	2	0	0	0	0	0	-	1	.389	.421	.667
1999 Ari	NL	5	16	4	1	0	1	(1	0)	8	3	3	2	1	0	1	0	1	0	0	0	-	0	.250	.294	.500
2000 Ari	NL	5	13	3	0	0	1	(1	0)	6	1	3	1	0	0	4	0	0	0	0	0	-	0	.231	.231	.462
2001 Ari	NL	51	106	17	3	0	3	(2	1)	29	9	9	4	4	0	26	0	0	0	0	0	-	0	.160	.191	.274
2002 Ari	NL	70	154	36	10	0	3	(1	2)	55	12	23	15	10	4	25	3	2	3	1	0	1.00	4	.234	.288	.357
2003 Ari	NL	80	220	48	15	0	3	(3	0)	72	19	28	19	14	7	43	1	1	3	0	0	-	6	.218	.265	.327
2004 Tex	AL	108	358	89	26	1	15	(8	7)	162	50	58	43	13	0	63	3	8	7	0	1	.00	3	.249	.276	.453
2005 Tex	AL	120	410	104	24	0	21	(7	14)	191	53	60	56	26	0	70	6	4	3	0	0	-	6	.254	.306	.466
2006 Tex	AL	97	344	88	20	0	11	(6	5)	141	49	41	36	17	0	51	4	5	1	0	0	-	9	.256	.290	.410
2007 Phi	NL	48	122	28	8	0	4	(1	3)	48	16	10	12	21	3	24	2	1	0	0	1	.00	3	.230	.352	.393
2008 Tor	AL	104	349	87	23	0	11	(4	7)	143	44	49	37	17	0	61	7	0	4	0	0	-	9	.249	.294	.410
2009 Tor	AL	125	429	97	19	0	19	(8	11)	173	43	71	50	20	2	76	1	3	7	1	0	1.00	4	.226	.258	.403
2010 2 Tms	NL	99	313	75	14	0	17	(7	10)	140	39	47	42	13	6	54	8	1	4	0	0	-	5	.240	.284	.447
2011 LAD	NL	98	305	70	13	0	16	(3	13)	131	29	47	31	22	4	71	4	2	3	0	0	-	5	.230	.287	.430
10 NYM	NL	74	249	56	11	0	12	(5	7)	103	30	34	27	8	3	39	6	1	3	0	0	-	4	.225	.263	.414
10 LAD	NL	25	64	19	3	0	5	(2	3)	37	9	13	15	5	3	15	2	0	1	0	0	-	2	.297	.361	.578
Postseason		5	9	3	0	0	2	(0	2)	9	2	2	2	0	0	1	0	0	0	0	0	-	0	.333	.333	1.000
13 ML YEARS		1010	3139	746	176	1	125	(52	73)	1299	367	449	348	178	26	569	39	28	35	2	2	.50	57	.238	.284	.414

Daniel Bard

Pitches: R Bats: R Pos: RP-70 **Ht: 6'4" Wt: 215 Born: 6/25/1985 Age: 27**

Year Team	Lg	G	GS	CG	GF	IP	BFP	H	R	ER	HR	SH	SF	HB	TBB	IBB	SO	WP	Bk	W	L	Pct	Sh	Sv-Op	Hld	ERC	ERA
2009 Bos	AL	49	0	0	12	49.1	212	41	24	20	5	4	3	3	22	3	63	1	1	2	2	.500	0	1-4	13	3.43	3.65
2010 Bos	AL	73	0	0	12	74.2	295	45	18	16	6	2	5	2	30	3	76	2	0	1	2	.333	0	3-10	32	1.99	1.93
2011 Bos	AL	70	0	0	10	73.0	288	46	29	27	5	5	0	2	24	3	74	2	1	2	9	.182	0	1-6	34	1.80	3.33
Postseason		2	0	0	1	3.0	8	0	0	0	0	0	0	0	0	0	4	0	0	0	0	-	0	0-0	1	0.00	0.00
3 ML YEARS		192	0	0	34	197.0	795	132	71	63	16	11	8	7	76	9	213	5	2	5	13	.278	0	5-20	79	2.26	2.88

Josh Bard

Bats: B Throws: R Pos: C-25; DH-1 **Ht: 6'3" Wt: 225 Born: 3/30/1978 Age: 34**

Year Team	Lg	G	AB	H	2B	3B	HR	(Hm	Rd)	TB	R	RBI	RC	TBB	IBB	SO	HBP	SH	SF	SB	CS	SB%	GDP	Avg	OBP	Slg
2011 Tacom*	AAA	58	226	68	18	0	2	(-	-)	92	28	41	34	21	0	39	0	2	1	0	0	-	7	.301	.359	.407
2002 Cle	AL	24	90	20	5	0	3	(2	1)	34	9	12	7	4	0	13	0	1	0	0	0	-	6	.222	.255	.378
2003 Cle	AL	91	303	74	13	1	8	(5	3)	113	25	36	34	22	1	53	0	1	3	0	2	.00	9	.244	.293	.373
2004 Cle	AL	7	19	8	2	0	1	(1	0)	13	5	4	6	3	0	0	0	0	1	0	0	-	0	.421	.478	.684
2005 Cle	AL	34	83	16	4	0	1	(0	1)	23	6	9	8	9	0	11	0	1	2	0	0	-	2	.193	.266	.277
2006 2 Tms		100	249	83	20	0	9	(5	4)	130	30	40	44	30	1	42	1	2	2	1	0	1.00	9	.333	.404	.522
2007 SD	NL	118	389	111	27	2	5	(4	1)	157	42	51	65	50	7	58	0	1	3	0	1	.00	16	.285	.364	.404
2008 SD	NL	57	178	36	9	0	1	(0	1)	48	11	16	13	18	2	25	1	1	0	0	0	-	5	.202	.279	.270
2009 Was	NL	90	274	63	18	0	6	(4	2)	99	20	31	27	24	1	50	1	1	1	0	0	.00	5	.230	.293	.361
2010 Sea	AL	39	112	24	7	0	3	(1	2)	40	9	10	8	10	0	27	0	3	1	0	0	-	4	.214	.276	.357
2011 Sea	AL	26	81	17	4	0	2	(1	1)	27	5	11	9	5	0	20	0	0	1	0	0	-	2	.210	.256	.333
06 Bos	AL	7	18	5	1	0	0	(0	0)	6	2	0	2	3	0	3	0	0	0	0	0	-	0	.278	.381	.333
06 SD	NL	93	231	78	19	0	9	(5	4)	124	28	40	42	27	1	39	1	2	2	1	0	1.00	9	.338	.406	.537
Postseason		3	7	1	0	0	0	(0	0)	1	0	0	1	0	1	2	1	0	0	0	0	-	0	.143	.333	.143
10 ML YEARS		586	1778	452	109	3	39	(23	16)	684	162	220	221	175	12	299	3	11	13	1	4	.20	56	.254	.320	.385

Clint Barmes

Bats: R Throws: R Pos: SS-122; PH-1 BAR-mess **Ht: 6'1" Wt: 205 Born: 3/6/1979 Age: 33**

Year Team	Lg	G	AB	H	2B	3B	HR	(Hm	Rd)	TB	R	RBI	RC	TBB	IBB	SO	HBP	SH	SF	SB	CS	SB%	GDP	Avg	OBP	Slg
2011 OKCity*	AAA	2	6	2	1	0	0	(-	-)	3	2	1	1	1	0	0	0	0	0	0	0	-	1	.333	.429	.500
2011 CpChr*	AA	2	9	4	0	0	0	(-	-)	4	2	2	2	1	0	1	0	0	0	0	0	-	0	.444	.500	.444
2003 Col	NL	12	25	8	2	0	0	(0	0)	10	2	2	3	0	0	10	2	0	1	0	0	-	0	.320	.357	.400
2004 Col	NL	20	71	20	3	1	2	(0	2)	31	14	10	12	3	0	10	1	2	0	0	1	.00	2	.282	.320	.437
2005 Col	NL	81	350	101	19	1	10	(7	3)	152	55	46	49	16	1	36	6	4	1	6	4	.60	4	.289	.330	.434
2006 Col	NL	131	478	105	26	4	7	(4	3)	160	57	56	47	22	6	72	9	19	7	5	4	.56	2	.220	.264	.335
2007 Col	NL	27	37	8	3	0	0	(0	0)	11	5	1	1	1	1	13	0	1	0	0	0	-	1	.216	.237	.297
2008 Col	NL	107	393	114	25	6	11	(8	3)	184	47	44	54	17	0	69	2	4	1	13	4	.76	9	.290	.322	.468
2009 Col	NL	154	550	135	32	3	23	(13	10)	242	69	76	66	31	2	121	10	6	7	12	10	.55	6	.245	.294	.440

Year	Team	Lg	G	AB	H	2B	3B	HR	(Hm	Rd)	TB	R	RBI	RC	TBB	IBB	SO	HBP	SH	SF	SB	CS	SB%	GDP	Avg	OBP	Slg
									BATTING												BASERUNNING				AVERAGES		
2010	Col	NL	133	387	91	21	0	8	(4	4)	136	43	50	43	35	10	66	5	2	3	3	2	.60	5	.235	.305	.351
2011	Hou	NL	123	446	109	27	0	12	(5	7)	172	47	39	46	38	2	88	7	2	2	3	1	.75	9	.244	.312	.386
Postseason			4	14	0	0	0	0	(0	0)	0	0	0	0	0	0	2	0	1	0	0	0	-	0	.000	.000	.000
9 ML YEARS			788	2737	691	158	15	73	(40	33)	1098	339	324	318	163	22	485	42	40	22	42	26	.62	38	.252	.302	.401

Darwin Barney

Bats: R **Throws:** R **Pos:** 2B-135; PH-8; SS-5   **Ht:** 5'10" **Wt:** 179 **Born:** 11/8/1985 **Age:** 26

Year	Team	Lg	G	AB	H	2B	3B	HR	(Hm	Rd)	TB	R	RBI	RC	TBB	IBB	SO	HBP	SH	SF	SB	CS	SB%	GDP	Avg	OBP	Slg
									BATTING												BASERUNNING				AVERAGES		
2007	Cubs	R	5	18	8	3	0	0	(-	-)	11	6	2	5	4	1	0	0	0	0	0	0	-	0	.444	.545	.611
2007	Peoria	A	44	176	48	9	3	2	(-	-)	69	27	21	23	11	0	22	3	0	2	5	2	.71	5	.273	.323	.392
2008	Dytona	A+	123	409	107	22	4	3	(-	-)	146	46	51	51	38	2	58	3	4	5	8	3	.73	8	.262	.325	.357
2009	Tenn	AA	74	252	80	12	0	3	(-	-)	101	30	32	40	23	3	33	0	4	5	5	1	.83	5	.317	.368	.401
2009	Iowa	AAA	63	212	56	12	1	0	(-	-)	70	25	17	22	13	0	32	0	2	2	4	1	.80	7	.264	.304	.330
2010	Iowa	AAA	114	479	143	24	4	2	(-	-)	181	72	49	63	23	1	52	3	2	3	11	3	.79	12	.299	.333	.378
2011	Iowa	AAA	4	14	5	1	0	1	(-	-)	9	3	3	3	0	0	2	1	0	0	1	0	1.00	0	.357	.400	.643
2010	ChC	NL	30	79	19	4	0	0	(0	0)	23	12	2	6	6	0	12	0	0	0	0	0	-	0	.241	.294	.291
2011	ChC	NL	143	529	146	23	6	2	(2	0)	187	66	43	60	22	2	67	8	7	4	9	2	.82	14	.276	.313	.353
2 ML YEARS			173	608	165	27	6	2	(2	0)	210	78	45	66	28	2	79	8	7	4	9	2	.82	14	.271	.310	.345

Jason Bartlett

Bats: R **Throws:** R **Pos:** SS-138; PH-3   **Ht:** 6'0" **Wt:** 190 **Born:** 10/30/1979 **Age:** 32

Year	Team	Lg	G	AB	H	2B	3B	HR	(Hm	Rd)	TB	R	RBI	RC	TBB	IBB	SO	HBP	SH	SF	SB	CS	SB%	GDP	Avg	OBP	Slg
									BATTING												BASERUNNING				AVERAGES		
2004	Min	AL	8	12	1	0	0	0	(0	0)	1	2	1	1	1	0	1	0	1	0	2	0	1.00	0	.083	.154	.083
2005	Min	AL	74	224	54	10	1	3	(2	1)	75	33	16	22	21	0	37	4	2	1	4	0	1.00	6	.241	.316	.335
2006	Min	AL	99	333	103	18	2	2	(0	2)	131	44	32	50	22	1	46	11	1	5	10	5	.67	8	.309	.367	.393
2007	Min	AL	140	510	135	20	7	5	(2	3)	184	75	43	65	50	3	73	8	0	2	23	3	.88	8	.265	.339	.361
2008	TB	AL	128	454	130	25	3	1	(1	0)	164	48	37	56	22	1	69	9	5	4	20	6	.77	9	.286	.329	.361
2009	TB	AL	137	500	160	29	7	14	(3	11)	245	90	66	97	54	2	89	5	4	4	30	7	.81	5	.320	.389	.490
2010	TB	AL	135	468	119	27	3	4	(1	3)	164	71	47	62	45	1	83	5	11	3	11	6	.65	6	.254	.324	.350
2011	SD	NL	139	554	136	22	3	2	(1	1)	170	61	40	50	48	0	98	5	5	6	23	10	.70	13	.245	.308	.307
Postseason			24	77	21	3	1	1	(1	0)	29	8	3	6	5	0	13	3	1	0	2	0	1.00	2	.273	.341	.377
8 ML YEARS			860	3055	838	151	26	31	(10	21)	1134	424	282	403	263	8	496	47	29	25	123	37	.77	55	.274	.339	.371

Daric Barton

Bats: L **Throws:** R **Pos:** 1B-65; PH-3; PR-1   **Ht:** 6'0" **Wt:** 207 **Born:** 8/16/1985 **Age:** 26

Year	Team	Lg	G	AB	H	2B	3B	HR	(Hm	Rd)	TB	R	RBI	RC	TBB	IBB	SO	HBP	SH	SF	SB	CS	SB%	GDP	Avg	OBP	Slg
									BATTING												BASERUNNING				AVERAGES		
2011	Scrmto*	AAA	17	61	12	2	0	0	(-	-)	14	10	4	6	14	0	16	0	0	0	0	0	-	2	.197	.347	.230
2007	Oak	AL	18	72	25	9	0	4	(2	2)	46	16	8	14	10	0	11	1	0	1	1	0	1.00	6	.347	.429	.639
2008	Oak	AL	140	446	101	17	5	9	(1	8)	155	59	47	56	65	5	99	3	6	3	2	1	.67	6	.226	.327	.348
2009	Oak	AL	54	160	43	12	1	3	(2	1)	66	31	24	28	26	0	25	2	1	3	0	2	.00	1	.269	.372	.413
2010	Oak	AL	159	556	152	33	5	10	(1	9)	225	79	57	92	110	2	102	3	12	5	7	3	.70	8	.273	.393	.405
2011	Oak	AL	67	236	50	13	0	0	(0	0)	63	27	21	24	39	3	47	2	0	3	2	1	.67	6	.212	.325	.267
5 ML YEARS			438	1470	371	84	11	26	(6	20)	555	212	157	214	250	10	284	11	19	15	12	7	.63	23	.252	.362	.378

Anthony Bass

Pitches: R **Bats:** R **Pos:** RP-24; SP-3   **Ht:** 6'2" **Wt:** 190 **Born:** 11/1/1987 **Age:** 24

Year	Team	Lg	G	GS	CG	GF	IP	BFP	H	R	ER	HR	SH	SF	HB	TBB	IBB	SO	WP	Bk	W	L	Pct	Sh	Sv-Op	Hld	ERC	ERA
			HOW MUCH HE PITCHED						WHAT HE GAVE UP												THE RESULTS							
2008	Eugene	A-	25	0	0	21	34.1	145	25	12	8	3	2	1	1	14	0	41	6	0	2	2	.500	0	7--	-	2.60	2.10
2009	FtWyn	A	18	18	0	0	90.1	369	79	31	22	5	4	1	3	25	0	69	3	1	9	3	.750	0	0--	-	2.80	2.19
2009	Lk Els	A+	10	8	0	1	33.1	143	33	17	13	3	2	1	2	14	0	20	3	0	1	0	1.000	0	0--	-	4.36	3.51
2010	Lk Els	A+	27	27	0	0	132.1	528	124	59	46	9	3	3	1	20	0	109	3	0	8	7	.533	0	0--	-	2.66	3.13
2010	Portlnd	AAA	1	1	0	0	5.2	27	7	5	5	1	0	2	1	3	0	3	0	1	0	1	.000	0	0--	-	7.53	7.94
2011	SnAnt	AA	13	13	0	0	69.2	282	62	31	29	6	2	3	0	21	0	62	3	0	6	4	.600	0	0--	-	3.08	3.75
2011	Tucsn	AAA	1	1	0	0	5.0	21	6	1	1	0	0	0	1	0	0	3	1	0	1	0	1.000	0	0--	-	3.80	1.80
2011	SD	NL	27	3	0	6	48.1	198	41	9	9	3	2	0	1	21	1	24	1	0	2	0	1.000	0	0-0	4	3.28	1.68

Antonio Bastardo

Pitches: L **Bats:** R **Pos:** RP-64   **Ht:** 5'11" **Wt:** 193 **Born:** 9/21/1985 **Age:** 26

Year	Team	Lg	G	GS	CG	GF	IP	BFP	H	R	ER	HR	SH	SF	HB	TBB	IBB	SO	WP	Bk	W	L	Pct	Sh	Sv-Op	Hld	ERC	ERA
			HOW MUCH HE PITCHED						WHAT HE GAVE UP												THE RESULTS							
2009	Phi	NL	6	5	0	0	23.2	106	26	18	17	4	0	0	2	9	0	19	0	0	2	3	.400	0	0-0	0	5.41	6.46
2010	Phi	NL	25	0	0	2	18.2	86	19	9	9	1	0	0	2	9	0	26	0	0	2	0	1.000	0	0-1	2	4.46	4.34
2011	Phi	NL	64	0	0	15	58.0	225	28	17	17	6	2	2	0	26	0	70	4	0	6	1	.857	0	8-9	17	1.69	2.64
Postseason			3	0	0	0	0.2	4	2	0	0	0	0	0	0	0	0	1	0	0	0	0	-	0	0-0	0	14.52	0.00
3 ML YEARS			95	5	0	17	100.1	417	73	44	43	11	2	2	4	44	0	115	4	0	10	4	.714	0	8-10	19	2.96	3.86

Miguel Batista

Pitches: R Bats: R Pos: RP-30; SP-5   Ht: 6'1" Wt: 210 Born: 2/19/1971 Age: 41

Year	Team	Lg	G	GS	CG	GF	IP	BFP	H	R	ER	HR	SH	SF	HB	TBB	IBB	SO	WP	Bk	W	L	Pct	Sh	Sv-Op	Hld	ERC	ERA
2011	Buffalo*	AAA	10	8	0	1	46.2	206	46	25	22	4	1	2	2	25	0	36	3	1	3	0	1.000	0	0--	-	4.65	4.24
1992	Pit	NL	1	0	0	1	2.0	13	4	2	2	1	0	0	0	3	0	1	0	0	0	0	-	0	0-0	0	20.26	9.00
1996	Fla	NL	9	0	0	4	11.1	49	9	8	7	0	3	0	0	7	2	6	1	0	0	0	-	0	0-0	0	2.77	5.56
1997	ChC	NL	11	6	0	2	36.1	168	36	24	23	4	4	4	1	24	2	27	2	0	0	5	.000	0	0-0	0	5.09	5.70
1998	Mon	NL	56	13	0	12	135.0	598	141	66	57	12	7	5	6	65	7	92	6	1	3	5	.375	0	0-0	3	4.70	3.80
1999	Mon	NL	39	17	2	3	134.2	606	146	88	73	10	8	11	7	58	2	95	6	0	8	7	.533	1	1-1	0	4.62	4.88
2000	2 Tms		18	9	0	2	65.1	310	85	68	62	19	1	2	2	37	2	37	4	0	2	7	.222	0	0-2	0	8.37	8.54
2001	Ari	NL	48	18	0	6	139.1	581	113	57	52	13	9	3	10	60	2	90	6	0	11	8	.579	0	0-0	4	3.43	3.36
2002	Ari	NL	36	29	1	2	184.2	790	172	99	88	12	5	8	6	70	3	112	9	2	8	9	.471	0	0-0	0	3.45	4.29
2003	Ari	NL	36	29	2	5	193.1	822	197	85	76	13	10	6	8	60	3	142	7	0	10	9	.526	1	0-0	0	3.77	3.54
2004	Tor	AL	38	31	2	7	198.2	867	206	115	106	22	7	6	3	96	1	104	12	0	10	13	.435	1	5-5	0	4.84	4.80
2005	Tor	AL	71	0	0	62	74.2	331	80	39	34	9	2	2	2	27	5	54	3	0	5	8	.385	0	31-39	0	4.39	4.10
2006	Ari	NL	34	33	3	0	206.1	910	231	116	105	18	12	5	6	84	5	110	14	1	11	8	.579	1	0-0	0	4.82	4.58
2007	Sea	AL	33	32	0	0	193.0	860	209	101	92	18	5	5	8	85	3	133	15	2	16	11	.593	0	0-0	0	4.81	4.29
2008	Sea	AL	44	20	0	9	115.0	556	135	89	80	19	3	11	6	79	6	73	5	0	4	14	.222	0	1-4	4	6.92	6.26
2009	Sea	AL	56	0	0	18	71.1	326	79	37	32	7	4	1	2	39	1	52	4	0	7	4	.636	0	1-5	14	5.37	4.04
2010	Was	NL	58	1	0	18	82.2	350	71	36	34	9	1	2	5	39	8	55	4	0	1	2	.333	0	2-2	1	3.78	3.70
2011	2 Tms		35	5	1	2	60.0	262	49	29	24	2	4	1	6	33	5	31	3	0	5	2	.714	1	0-1	7	3.40	3.60
00	Mon	NL	4	0	0	0	8.1	49	19	14	13	2	1	1	2	3	0	7	0	0	0	1	.000	0	0-2	0	14.73	14.04
00	KC	AL	14	9	0	2	57.0	261	66	54	49	17	0	1	0	34	2	30	4	0	2	6	.250	0	0-0	0	7.50	7.74
11	StL	NL	26	1	0	2	29.1	137	27	20	15	2	2	0	4	19	4	16	2	0	3	2	.600	0	0-1	6	4.56	4.60
11	NYM	NL	9	4	1	0	30.2	125	22	9	9	0	2	1	2	14	1	15	1	0	2	0	1.000	1	0-0	1	2.38	2.64
	Postseason		7	4	0	1	25.1	104	18	10	10	3	3	0	1	11	0	14	1	0	1	2	.333	0	0-0	0	2.94	3.55
	17 ML YEARS		623	243	11	153	1903.2	8399	1963	1059	947	188	85	72	78	866	57	1214	101	6	101	112	.474	5	41-59	35	4.59	4.48

Jose Bautista

Bats: R Throws: R Pos: RF-116; 3B-25; DH-9   Ht: 6'0" Wt: 195 Born: 10/19/1980 Age: 31

Year	Team	Lg	G	AB	H	2B	3B	HR	(Hm	Rd)	TB	R	RBI	RC	TBB	IBB	SO	HBP	SH	SF	SB	CS	SB%	GDP	Avg	OBP	Slg
2004	4 Tms		64	88	18	3	0	0	(0	0)	21	6	2	2	7	0	40	0	1	0	0	1	.00	1	.205	.263	.239
2005	Pit	NL	11	28	4	1	0	0	(0	0)	5	3	1	0	3	0	7	0	0	0	1	0	1.00	2	.143	.226	.179
2006	Pit	NL	117	400	94	20	3	16	(11	5)	168	58	51	55	46	2	110	16	3	4	2	4	.33	12	.235	.335	.420
2007	Pit	NL	142	532	135	36	2	15	(8	7)	220	75	63	71	68	1	101	4	4	6	6	3	.67	16	.254	.339	.414
2008	2 Tms		128	370	88	17	0	15	(5	10)	150	45	54	43	40	5	91	2	8	4	1	1	.50	12	.238	.313	.405
2009	Tor	AL	113	336	79	13	3	13	(5	8)	137	54	40	42	56	1	85	4	6	2	4	0	1.00	9	.235	.349	.408
2010	Tor	AL	161	569	148	35	3	54	(33	21)	351	109	124	132	100	2	116	10	0	4	9	2	.82	10	.260	.378	.617
2011	Tor	AL	149	513	155	24	2	43	(20	23)	312	105	103	133	132	24	111	6	0	4	9	5	.64	8	.302	.447	.608
04	Bal	AL	16	11	3	0	0	0	(0	0)	3	3	0	1	1	0	3	0	0	0	0	0	-	0	.273	.333	.273
04	TB	AL	12	12	2	0	0	0	(0	0)	2	1	1	0	3	0	7	0	0	0	0	1	.00	0	.167	.333	.167
04	KC	AL	13	25	5	1	0	0	(0	0)	6	1	1	0	1	0	12	0	0	0	0	0	-	0	.200	.231	.240
04	Pit	NL	23	40	8	2	0	0	(0	0)	10	1	0	1	2	0	18	0	1	0	0	0	-	0	.200	.238	.250
08	Pit	NL	107	314	76	15	0	12	(3	9)	127	38	44	39	38	4	77	2	6	3	1	1	.50	10	.242	.325	.404
08	Tor	AL	21	56	12	2	0	3	(2	1)	23	7	10	4	2	1	14	0	2	1	0	0	-	2	.214	.237	.411
	8 ML YEARS		885	2836	721	149	13	156	(82	74)	1364	455	438	478	452	35	661	42	22	24	32	16	.67	70	.254	.362	.481

Mike Baxter

Bats: L Throws: R Pos: RF-10; PH-8; LF-3; PR-1   Ht: 6'0" Wt: 190 Born: 12/7/1984 Age: 27

Year	Team	Lg	G	AB	H	2B	3B	HR	(Hm	Rd)	TB	R	RBI	RC	TBB	IBB	SO	HBP	SH	SF	SB	CS	SB%	GDP	Avg	OBP	Slg
2005	FtWyn	A	45	183	40	12	1	1	(-	-)	57	11	17	15	12	0	29	0	0	0	4	1	.80	4	.219	.267	.311
2006	FtWyn	A	117	476	122	28	7	3	(-	-)	173	67	40	55	31	2	66	4	1	5	13	5	.72	7	.256	.304	.363
2007	Lk Els	A+	111	417	115	21	6	7	(-	-)	169	74	44	62	44	2	75	3	2	4	12	6	.67	14	.276	.346	.405
2007	Portlnd	AAA	10	29	6	2	1	0	(-	-)	10	1	7	2	1	0	8	0	0	0	1	0	1.00	0	.207	.233	.345
2008	Lk Els	A+	24	92	22	4	1	1	(-	-)	31	13	17	11	10	0	12	2	0	1	3	0	1.00	1	.239	.324	.337
2008	SnAnt	AA	100	324	88	18	4	8	(-	-)	138	41	48	51	39	5	41	2	2	3	2	2	.50	9	.272	.351	.426
2009	SnAnt	AA	51	202	76	23	1	4	(-	-)	113	38	45	48	23	1	42	2	0	1	5	2	.71	3	.376	.441	.559
2009	Portlnd	AAA	82	303	84	17	4	5	(-	-)	124	38	34	47	38	1	53	3	0	1	9	5	.64	10	.277	.362	.409
2010	Portlnd	AAA	136	482	145	30	10	18	(-	-)	249	89	72	97	58	1	78	8	0	4	22	10	.69	11	.301	.382	.517
2011	Lk Els	A+	11	36	10	1	0	0	(-	-)	11	5	2	5	9	0	8	0	0	1	0	1	.00	0	.278	.413	.306
2011	StLuci	A+	4	16	7	2	0	0	(-	-)	9	2	4	3	1	0	2	0	0	1	0	0	-	1	.438	.444	.563
2011	Buffalo	AAA	18	64	12	0	2	1	(-	-)	19	4	7	5	5	0	19	1	1	0	1	0	1.00	1	.188	.257	.297
2010	SD	NL	9	8	1	0	0	0	(0	0)	1	0	1	0	0	0	2	0	0	1	0	0	-	1	.125	.111	.125
2011	NYM	NL	22	34	8	2	1	1	(1	0)	15	6	4	5	5	0	9	1	0	0	0	0	-	1	.235	.350	.441
	2 ML YEARS		31	42	9	2	1	1	(1	0)	16	6	5	5	5	0	11	1	0	1	0	0	-	2	.214	.306	.381

Jason Bay

Bats: R Throws: R Pos: LF-122; PR-1   Ht: 6'2" Wt: 205 Born: 9/20/1978 Age: 33

Year	Team	Lg	G	AB	H	2B	3B	HR	(Hm	Rd)	TB	R	RBI	RC	TBB	IBB	SO	HBP	SH	SF	SB	CS	SB%	GDP	Avg	OBP	Slg
2011	StLuci*	A+	4	12	6	0	0	2	(-	-)	12	5	4	6	4	1	0	0	0	0	0	0	-	0	.500	.625	1.000
2003	2 Tms		30	87	25	7	1	4	(2	2)	46	15	14	19	19	0	29	1	0	0	3	1	.75	0	.287	.421	.529
2004	Pit	NL	120	411	116	24	4	26	(15	11)	226	61	82	75	41	2	129	10	5	5	4	6	.40	8	.282	.358	.550
2005	Pit	NL	162	599	183	44	6	32	(9	23)	335	110	101	128	95	9	142	6	0	7	21	1	.95	12	.306	.402	.559
2006	Pit	NL	159	570	163	29	3	35	(14	21)	303	101	109	103	102	9	156	8	0	9	11	2	.85	15	.286	.396	.532
2007	Pit	NL	145	538	133	25	2	21	(7	14)	225	78	84	74	59	3	141	9	0	8	4	1	.80	8	.247	.327	.418
2008	2 Tms		155	577	165	35	4	31	(18	13)	301	111	101	104	81	4	137	4	0	8	10	0	1.00	7	.286	.373	.522

			BATTING																	BASERUNNING				AVERAGES		
Year	Team	Lg	G	AB	H	2B	3B	HR	(Hm	Rd)	TB	R	RBI	RC	TBB	IBB	SO	HBP	SH	SF	SB	CS	SB%	GDP	Avg	OBP	Slg
2009	Bos	AL	151	531	142	29	3	36	(15	21)	285	103	119	122	94	4	162	9	0	4	13	3	.81	9	.267	.384	.537
2010	NYM	NL	95	348	90	20	6	6	(3	3)	140	48	47	50	44	3	91	5	0	4	10	0	1.00	7	.259	.347	.402
2011	NYM	NL	123	444	109	19	1	12	(6	6)	166	59	57	50	56	3	109	2	1	6	11	1	.92	8	.245	.329	.374
03	SD	NL	3	8	2	1	0	1	(0	1)	6	2	2	2	1	0	1	1	0	0	0	0	-	0	.250	.400	.750
03	Pit	NL	27	79	23	6	1	3	(2	1)	40	13	12	17	18	0	28	0	0	0	3	1	.75	0	.291	.423	.506
08	Pit	NL	106	393	111	23	2	22	(15	7)	204	72	64	73	59	2	86	2	0	5	7	0	1.00	3	.282	.375	.519
08	Bos	AL	49	184	54	12	2	9	(3	6)	97	39	37	31	22	2	51	2	0	3	0	0	1.00	4	.293	.370	.527
	Postseason		14	49	15	3	0	3	(0	3)	27	6	9	11	12	1	15	1	0	0	0	0	-	0	.306	.452	.551
	9 ML YEARS		1140	4105	1126	232	30	203	(88	115)	2027	686	714	725	591	37	1096	54	6	51	87	15	.85	75	.274	.369	.494

Brandon Beachy

Pitches: R **Bats:** R **Pos:** SP-25

Ht: 6'3" **Wt:** 210 **Born:** 9/3/1986 **Age:** 25

			HOW MUCH HE PITCHED					WHAT HE GAVE UP											THE RESULTS						
Year	Team	Lg	G	GS	CG	GF	IP	BFP	H	R	ER	HR	SH	SF	HB	TBB	IBB	SO	WP	Bk	W	L	Pct	Sh	Sv-Op Hld	ERC	ERA
2008	Danvle	R	6	0	0	1	12.0	51	12	5	3	1	1	1	1	2	0	16	2	0	2	0	1.000	0	0- -	3.31	2.25
2009	Rome	A	12	0	0	5	17.2	75	20	11	11	0	0	0	2	4	0	17	0	0	0	0	-	0	0- -	3.98	5.60
2009	Missi	AA	1	0	0	0	1.0	4	1	0	0	0	0	0	0	0	0	0	0	0	0	0	-	0	0- -	1.95	0.00
2009	MrtlBh	A+	22	8	0	8	58.0	248	59	31	22	2	1	2	8	15	1	47	5	0	4	3	.571	0	1- -	3.70	3.41
2010	Missi	AA	27	6	0	6	73.2	295	53	17	12	3	5	1	2	22	0	100	2	0	3	1	.750	0	1- -	1.99	1.47
2010	Gwnntt	AAA	8	7	0	1	45.2	187	40	17	11	2	2	2	2	6	0	48	1	0	2	0	1.000	0	1- -	2.17	2.17
2011	Gwnntt	AAA	1	1	0	0	5.0	21	4	1	1	1	0	0	0	2	0	8	0	0	1	0	1.000	0	0- -	3.57	1.80
2010	Atl	NL	3	3	0	0	15.0	67	16	9	5	0	0	0	0	7	3	15	1	0	0	2	.000	0	0-0	3.58	3.00
2011	Atl	NL	25	25	0	0	141.2	591	125	62	58	16	6	5	5	46	9	169	11	1	7	3	.700	0	0-0	3.27	3.68
	2 ML YEARS		28	28	0	0	156.2	658	141	71	63	16	6	5	5	53	12	184	12	1	7	5	.583	0	0-0	3.30	3.62

Pedro Beato

Pitches: R **Bats:** R **Pos:** RP-60

bay-AHH-toe

Ht: 6'4" **Wt:** 222 **Born:** 10/27/1986 **Age:** 25

			HOW MUCH HE PITCHED					WHAT HE GAVE UP											THE RESULTS						
Year	Team	Lg	G	GS	CG	GF	IP	BFP	H	R	ER	HR	SH	SF	HB	TBB	IBB	SO	WP	Bk	W	L	Pct	Sh	Sv-Op Hld	ERC	ERA
2006	Abrdn	A-	14	10	0	1	57.0	240	47	31	23	6	5	6	0	23	0	52	3	1	3	2	.600	0	0- -	3.13	3.63
2007	Dlmrva	A	27	27	0	0	142.1	620	139	75	64	10	6	8	3	59	0	106	12	1	7	8	.467	0	0- -	3.84	4.05
2008	Frdrck	A+	19	19	0	0	97.0	438	119	74	63	11	3	5	7	33	0	51	3	1	4	10	.286	0	0- -	5.58	5.85
2008	Orioles	R	2	2	0	0	10.2	44	10	3	3	1	1	0	1	1	0	3	1	0	0	0	-	0	0- -	2.83	2.53
2009	Frdrck	A+	20	20	1	0	105.1	475	125	60	53	12	2	3	9	40	0	70	6	1	5	7	.417	0	0- -	5.59	4.53
2009	Bowie	AA	6	5	0	0	32.0	133	33	16	16	6	2	1	0	7	0	18	1	0	1	3	.250	0	0- -	4.13	4.50
2010	Bowie	AA	43	0	0	33	59.2	242	49	14	14	4	2	0	3	19	0	50	4	0	4	0	1.000	0	16- -	2.84	2.11
2011	Buffalo	AAA	1	0	0	0	1.1	7	2	0	0	0	1	0	0	1	0	0	0	0	1	0	1.000	0	0- -	7.52	0.00
2011	NYM	NL	60	0	0	7	67.0	283	59	41	32	5	2	4	4	27	3	39	1	0	2	1	.667	0	0-1 11	3.45	4.30

Blake Beavan

Pitches: R **Bats:** R **Pos:** SP-15

BEV-uhn

Ht: 6'7" **Wt:** 240 **Born:** 1/17/1989 **Age:** 23

			HOW MUCH HE PITCHED					WHAT HE GAVE UP											THE RESULTS						
Year	Team	Lg	G	GS	CG	GF	IP	BFP	H	R	ER	HR	SH	SF	HB	TBB	IBB	SO	WP	Bk	W	L	Pct	Sh	Sv-Op Hld	ERC	ERA
2008	Clinton	A	23	23	0	0	121.2	479	105	42	32	12	1	5	4	20	0	73	2	0	10	6	.625	0	0- -	2.63	2.37
2009	Bkrsfld	A+	12	12	1	0	73.1	310	75	44	35	6	1	4	5	16	0	51	2	2	5	4	.556	0	0- -	3.63	4.30
2009	Frisco	AA	15	15	0	0	89.2	390	113	47	40	4	3	7	1	13	0	34	6	0	4	4	.500	0	0- -	4.14	4.01
2010	Frisco	AA	17	17	0	0	110.0	432	100	37	34	6	3	3	1	12	0	68	2	0	10	5	.667	0	0- -	2.30	2.78
2010	WTenn	AA	3	3	0	0	18.0	73	18	11	10	1	4	3	1	2	1	11	1	0	2	1	.667	0	0- -	2.92	5.00
2010	Tacom	AAA	7	7	0	0	40.1	180	56	31	29	6	1	0	2	8	0	22	3	0	2	2	.500	0	0- -	6.22	6.47
2011	Tacom	AAA	16	16	0	0	93.0	413	118	52	46	10	2	2	1	20	0	64	3	0	5	3	.625	0	0-0	4.91	4.45
2011	Sea	AL	15	15	0	0	97.0	405	106	46	46	13	1	5	3	15	0	42	4	0	5	6	.455	0	0-0	3.99	4.27

Chad Beck

Pitches: R **Bats:** R **Pos:** RP-3

Ht: 6'4" **Wt:** 245 **Born:** 1/17/1985 **Age:** 27

			HOW MUCH HE PITCHED					WHAT HE GAVE UP											THE RESULTS						
Year	Team	Lg	G	GS	CG	GF	IP	BFP	H	R	ER	HR	SH	SF	HB	TBB	IBB	SO	WP	Bk	W	L	Pct	Sh	Sv-Op Hld	ERC	ERA
2006	Yakima	A-	16	2	0	1	40.1	186	47	37	28	8	4	3	2	18	0	45	3	1	1	5	.167	0	0- -	6.13	6.25
2007	Sbend	A	31	0	0	14	52.0	227	53	27	25	5	3	0	3	20	1	48	5	0	1	2	.333	0	1- -	4.29	4.33
2008	Sbend	A	7	0	0	3	17.2	73	13	7	4	0	0	0	0	3	0	19	2	1	2	0	1.000	0	1- -	1.36	2.04
2008	Visalia	A+	25	15	0	8	95.0	392	86	45	42	8	1	1	5	25	0	89	10	0	6	5	.545	0	1- -	3.15	3.98
2009	Dnedin	A+	9	0	0	2	10.1	51	12	9	5	1	1	0	1	6	1	14	2	0	0	0	-	0	0- -	5.67	4.35
2009	Lnsng	A	20	20	1	0	110.2	501	135	78	73	10	4	5	9	29	0	85	7	1	6	8	.429	0	0- -	4.96	5.94
2010	Dnedin	A+	41	11	0	5	101.2	432	97	44	42	5	3	0	1	31	0	79	6	0	3	6	.333	0	0- -	3.10	3.72
2011	Dnedin	A+	1	1	0	0	5.1	20	4	1	1	1	0	0	1	1	0	7	0	0	0	0	-	0	0- -	3.51	1.69
2011	NHam	AA	22	14	0	0	95.0	393	92	41	39	7	1	4	3	26	0	70	2	0	7	4	.636	0	0- -	3.51	3.69
2011	LsVgs	AAA	8	8	0	0	41.2	209	61	36	31	7	0	2	2	26	0	23	3	0	2	4	.333	0	0- -	8.72	6.70
2011	Tor	AL	3	0	0	3	2.1	8	1	0	0	0	0	0	0	0	0	3	0	0	0	0	-	0	0-0	0.40	0.00

Josh Beckett

Pitches: R Bats: R Pos: SP-30   Ht: 6'5" Wt: 225 Born: 5/15/1980 Age: 32

Year	Team	Lg	G	GS	CG	GF	IP	BFP	H	R	ER	HR	SH	SF	HB	TBB	IBB	SO	WP	Bk	W	L	Pct	Sh	Sv-Op	Hld	ERC	ERA
2001	Fla	NL	4	4	0	0	24.0	99	14	9	4	3	0	0	1	11	0	24	1	0	2	2	.500	0	0-0	0	2.36	1.50
2002	Fla	NL	23	21	0	0	107.2	454	93	56	49	13	5	3	1	44	2	113	5	0	6	7	.462	0	0-0	0	3.50	4.10
2003	Fla	NL	24	23	0	1	142.0	601	132	54	48	9	5	1	2	56	4	152	6	1	9	8	.529	0	0-0	0	3.44	3.04
2004	Fla	NL	26	26	1	0	156.2	654	137	72	66	16	9	3	6	54	3	152	5	0	9	9	.500	1	0-0	0	3.32	3.79
2005	Fla	NL	29	29	2	0	178.2	728	153	75	67	14	8	2	7	58	2	166	5	0	15	8	.652	1	0-0	0	3.07	3.38
2006	Bos	AL	33	33	0	0	204.2	869	191	120	114	36	2	3	10	74	1	158	11	1	16	11	.593	0	0-0	0	4.28	5.01
2007	Bos	AL	30	30	1	0	200.2	822	189	76	73	17	3	2	5	40	0	194	3	0	20	7	.741	0	0-0	0	2.99	3.27
2008	Bos	AL	27	27	1	0	174.1	725	173	80	78	18	4	3	9	34	1	172	5	0	12	10	.545	0	0-0	0	3.45	4.03
2009	Bos	AL	32	32	4	0	212.1	883	198	99	91	25	5	5	7	55	1	199	3	1	17	6	.739	2	0-0	0	3.39	3.86
2010	Bos	AL	21	21	0	0	127.2	577	151	89	82	20	4	2	8	45	3	116	3	0	6	6	.500	0	0-0	0	5.56	5.78
2011	Bos	AL	30	30	1	0	193.0	767	146	65	62	21	8	5	9	52	1	175	6	0	13	7	.650	1	0-0	0	2.56	2.89
	Postseason		14	13	3	0	93.2	366	67	32	32	11	2	1	4	21	1	99	3	0	7	3	.700	3	0-0	0	2.22	3.07
11 ML YEARS			279	276	10	1	1721.2	7179	1577	795	734	192	53	29	65	523	18	1621	53	3	125	81	.607	5	0-0	0	3.46	3.84

Gordon Beckham

Bats: R Throws: R Pos: 2B-149; DH-1; PH-1; PR-1   Ht: 6'0" Wt: 185 Born: 9/16/1986 Age: 25

			BATTING																	BASERUNNING				AVERAGES		
Year	Team	Lg	G	AB	H	2B	3B	HR	(Hm | Rd)	TB	R	RBI	RC	TBB	IBB	SO	HBP	SH	SF	SB	CS	SB%	GDP	Avg	OBP	Slg
2009	CWS	AL	103	378	102	28	1	14	(4 | 10)	174	58	63	60	41	0	65	6	1	4	7	4	.64	10	.270	.347	.460
2010	CWS	AL	131	444	112	25	2	9	(7 | 2)	168	58	49	52	37	0	92	7	6	4	4	6	.40	9	.252	.317	.378
2011	CWS	AL	150	499	115	23	0	10	(7 | 3)	168	60	44	48	35	0	111	13	7	3	5	3	.63	6	.230	.296	.337
3 ML YEARS			384	1321	329	76	3	33	(18 | 15)	510	176	156	160	113	0	268	26	14	11	16	13	.55	25	.249	.318	.386

Erik Bedard

Pitches: L Bats: L Pos: SP-24   Ht: 6'1" Wt: 200 Born: 3/5/1979 Age: 33

Year	Team	Lg	G	GS	CG	GF	IP	BFP	H	R	ER	HR	SH	SF	HB	TBB	IBB	SO	WP	Bk	W	L	Pct	Sh	Sv-Op	Hld	ERC	ERA
2002	Bal	AL	2	0	0	0	0.2	4	2	1	1	0	0	0	0	0	0	1	0	0	0	0	-	0	0-0	0	14.52	13.50
2004	Bal	AL	27	26	0	0	137.1	633	149	83	70	13	0	4	7	71	1	121	7	2	6	10	.375	0	0-0	0	5.11	4.59
2005	Bal	AL	24	24	0	0	141.2	606	139	66	63	10	3	6	5	57	1	125	4	1	6	8	.429	0	0-0	0	3.95	4.00
2006	Bal	AL	33	33	0	0	196.1	844	196	92	82	16	6	4	5	69	0	171	6	0	15	11	.577	0	0-0	0	3.83	3.76
2007	Bal	AL	28	28	1	0	182.0	733	141	66	64	19	2	4	5	57	0	221	3	0	13	5	.722	1	0-0	0	2.71	3.16
2008	Sea	AL	15	15	0	0	81.0	347	70	38	33	9	1	2	4	37	0	72	3	0	6	4	.600	0	0-0	0	3.82	3.67
2009	Sea	AL	15	15	0	0	83.0	348	65	29	26	8	2	1	4	34	0	90	2	0	5	3	.625	0	0-0	0	3.08	2.82
2011	2 Tms	AL	24	24	0	0	129.1	541	118	63	52	14	1	1	1	48	0	125	5	0	5	9	.357	0	0-0	0	3.60	3.62
11	Sea	AL	16	16	0	0	91.1	373	77	41	35	11	1	0	1	30	0	87	5	0	4	7	.364	0	0-0	0	3.16	3.45
11	Bos	AL	8	8	0	0	38.0	168	41	22	17	3	0	1	0	18	0	38	0	0	1	2	.333	0	0-0	0	4.70	4.03
8 ML YEARS			168	165	1	0	951.1	4056	880	438	391	89	15	22	31	373	2	926	30	3	56	50	.528	1	0-0	0	3.71	3.70

Joe Beimel

Pitches: L Bats: L Pos: RP-35   BYE-mull   Ht: 6'3" Wt: 215 Born: 4/19/1977 Age: 35

Year	Team	Lg	G	GS	CG	GF	IP	BFP	H	R	ER	HR	SH	SF	HB	TBB	IBB	SO	WP	Bk	W	L	Pct	Sh	Sv-Op	Hld	ERC	ERA
2011	Bradtn*	A+	2	2	0	0	2.0	6	0	0	0	0	0	0	0	0	0	2	0	0	0	0	-	0	0- -	0	0.00	0.00
2011	Indy*	AAA	2	0	0	0	2.0	8	0	0	0	0	0	0	0	0	0	3	0	0	0	0	-	0	0- -	0	0.00	0.00
2011	Altna*	AA	4	2	0	0	3.1	12	2	0	0	0	0	0	0	1	0	1	0	0	0	0	-	0	0- -	0	1.41	0.00
2001	Pit	NL	42	15	0	9	115.1	511	131	72	67	12	3	1	6	49	4	58	3	0	7	11	.389	0	0-0	0	5.24	5.23
2002	Pit	NL	53	8	0	8	85.1	389	88	49	44	9	7	3	4	45	12	53	2	0	2	5	.286	0	0-1	5	4.68	4.64
2003	Pit	NL	69	0	0	11	62.1	276	69	35	35	7	3	5	4	33	6	42	0	1	1	3	.250	0	0-5	12	5.62	5.05
2004	Min	AL	3	0	0	1	1.2	15	8	8	8	1	0	0	0	2	0	2	1	0	0	0	-	0	0-0	0	44.44	43.20
2005	TB	AL	7	0	0	3	11.0	51	15	4	4	1	0	0	0	4	1	3	1	0	0	0	-	0	0-0	0	5.80	3.27
2006	LAD	NL	62	0	0	10	70.0	295	70	26	23	7	4	3	0	21	3	50	6	1	2	1	.667	0	2-2	10	3.62	2.96
2007	LAD	NL	83	0	0	10	67.1	281	63	30	29	1	5	2	1	24	6	39	3	2	4	2	.667	0	1-1	16	2.93	3.88
2008	LAD	NL	71	0	0	10	49.0	214	50	11	11	0	1	4	3	21	4	32	1	1	5	1	.833	0	0-0	12	3.70	2.02
2009	2 Tms	NL	71	0	0	26	55.1	240	57	24	22	5	4	6	1	19	5	35	4	1	1	6	.143	0	1-6	13	3.84	3.58
2010	Col	NL	71	0	0	11	45.0	188	46	18	17	5	1	1	0	15	3	21	2	1	1	2	.333	0	0-1	20	4.00	3.40
2011	Pit	NL	35	0	0	9	25.1	117	34	17	15	6	1	0	1	9	1	17	0	0	1	1	.500	0	0-2	7	7.15	5.33
09	Was	NL	45	0	0	19	39.2	172	38	17	15	3	2	4	1	15	4	24	2	1	1	5	.167	0	1-5	10	3.46	3.40
09	Col	NL	26	0	0	7	15.2	68	19	7	7	2	2	2	0	4	1	11	2	0	0	1	.000	0	0-1	3	4.84	4.02
	Postseason		6	0	0	1	1.1	7	1	0	0	0	0	0	0	2	0	0	0	0	0	0	-	0	0-0	0	5.91	0.00
11 ML YEARS			567	23	0	107	587.2	2577	631	294	275	54	29	25	20	242	45	332	22	7	24	32	.429	0	4-18	95	4.53	4.21

Matt Belisle

Pitches: R Bats: R Pos: RP-74   bell-EYE-el   Ht: 6'4" Wt: 225 Born: 6/6/1980 Age: 32

Year	Team	Lg	G	GS	CG	GF	IP	BFP	H	R	ER	HR	SH	SF	HB	TBB	IBB	SO	WP	Bk	W	L	Pct	Sh	Sv-Op	Hld	ERC	ERA
2003	Cin	NL	6	0	0	2	8.2	39	10	5	5	1	2	1	1	2	0	6	0	0	1	1	.500	0	0-1	0	4.73	5.19
2005	Cin	NL	60	5	0	17	85.2	382	101	49	42	11	4	2	6	26	6	59	3	0	4	8	.333	0	1-4	8	5.08	4.41
2006	Cin	NL	30	2	0	5	40.0	180	43	18	16	5	1	2	3	19	1	26	3	0	2	0	1.000	0	0-1	0	5.29	3.60
2007	Cin	NL	30	30	1	0	177.2	771	212	111	105	26	7	9	7	43	4	125	6	1	8	9	.471	0	0-0	0	5.05	5.32
2008	Cin	NL	6	6	0	0	29.2	142	47	27	24	4	1	2	0	6	0	14	2	0	1	4	.200	0	0-0	0	6.87	7.28
2009	Col	NL	24	0	0	6	31.0	133	35	21	19	6	0	2	1	5	1	22	1	0	3	1	.750	0	0-0	1	4.50	5.52

Year	Team	Lg	G	GS	CG	GF	IP	BFP	H	R	ER	HR	SH	SF	HB	TBB	IBB	SO	WP	Bk	W	L	Pct	Sh	Sv-Op	Hld	ERC	ERA
2010	Col	NL	76	0	0	11	92.0	365	84	34	30	7	4	2	4	16	5	91	3	1	7	5	.583	0	1-2	15	2.67	2.93
2011	Col	NL	74	0	0	10	72.0	301	77	33	26	5	4	0	4	14	3	58	2	0	10	4	.714	0	0-7	14	3.65	3.25
	Postseason		2	0	0	0	2.0	7	0	0	0	0	0	0	0	1	0	2	0	0	0	0	-	0	0-0	1	0.27	0.00
	8 ML YEARS		306	43	1	51	536.2	2313	609	298	267	65	23	20	24	131	20	401	20	2	36	32	.529	0	2-15	44	4.51	4.48

Heath Bell

Pitches: R **Bats:** R **Pos:** RP-64 **Ht:** 6'3" **Wt:** 259 **Born:** 9/29/1977 **Age:** 34

Year	Team	Lg	G	GS	CG	GF	IP	BFP	H	R	ER	HR	SH	SF	HB	TBB	IBB	SO	WP	Bk	W	L	Pct	Sh	Sv-Op	Hld	ERC	ERA
2004	NYM	NL	17	0	0	2	24.1	94	22	9	9	5	1	0	0	6	0	27	0	0	0	2	.000	0	0-1	1	3.86	3.33
2005	NYM	NL	42	0	0	12	46.2	206	56	30	29	3	4	0	1	13	3	43	0	1	1	3	.250	0	0-0	4	4.42	5.59
2006	NYM	NL	22	0	0	6	37.0	166	51	25	21	6	1	0	1	11	2	35	1	0	0	0	-	0	0-0	0	6.40	5.11
2007	SD	NL	81	0	0	16	93.2	363	60	21	21	3	4	1	2	30	1	102	4	0	6	4	.600	0	2-6	34	1.67	2.02
2008	SD	NL	74	0	0	8	78.0	324	66	31	31	5	3	2	3	28	4	71	2	0	6	6	.500	0	0-7	23	2.93	3.58
2009	SD	NL	68	0	0	59	69.2	278	54	21	21	3	0	0	0	24	1	79	4	0	6	4	.600	0	**42-48**	0	2.36	2.71
2010	SD	NL	67	0	0	57	70.0	287	56	17	15	1	4	1	1	28	3	86	1	0	6	1	.857	0	47-50	0	2.47	1.93
2011	SD	NL	64	0	0	54	62.2	256	51	20	17	4	5	1	0	21	2	51	8	0	3	4	.429	0	43-48	0	2.57	2.44
	8 ML YEARS		435	0	0	214	482.0	1974	416	174	164	30	22	5	7	161	16	494	20	1	28	24	.538	0	134-160	62	2.88	3.06

Josh Bell

Bats: B **Throws:** R **Pos:** 3B-21; DH-2; PH-2; LF-1; RF-1; PR-1 **Ht:** 6'3" **Wt:** 220 **Born:** 11/13/1986 **Age:** 25

Year	Team	Lg	G	AB	H	2B	3B	HR	(Hm	Rd)	TB	R	RBI	RC	TBB	IBB	SO	HBP	SH	SF	SB	CS	SB%	GDP	Avg	OBP	Slg
2005	Ddgrs	R	45	157	50	7	1	1	(-	-)	62	26	21	26	20	1	33	1	0	0	5	2	.71	2	.318	.399	.395
2006	Ogden	R+	64	250	77	17	3	12	(-	-)	136	45	53	50	23	3	72	1	1	1	4	0	1.00	5	.308	.367	.544
2007	Gt Lks	A	108	398	115	21	3	15	(-	-)	187	65	62	67	39	2	109	1	0	0	5	1	.83	11	.289	.354	.470
2007	InldEm	A+	20	75	13	2	1	2	(-	-)	23	4	9	4	3	0	19	0	0	1	0	0	-	4	.173	.203	.307
2008	InldEm	A+	51	187	51	12	2	6	(-	-)	85	34	21	33	31	1	56	0	0	2	4	2	.67	3	.273	.373	.455
2009	Chatt	AA	94	334	99	30	2	11	(-	-)	166	47	52	65	50	2	70	2	0	5	3	5	.38	7	.296	.386	.497
2009	Bowie	AA	33	114	34	5	0	9	(-	-)	66	18	24	23	11	0	28	0	0	0	0	0	-	4	.298	.354	.579
2010	Norfolk	AAA	81	316	88	25	0	13	(-	-)	152	43	50	49	23	3	79	2	0	3	2	4	.33	3	.278	.328	.481
2011	Norfolk	AAA	101	395	100	12	2	19	(-	-)	173	62	57	58	40	3	118	0	0	3	4	0	1.00	11	.253	.320	.438
2010	Bal	AL	53	159	34	5	0	3	(2	1)	48	15	12	10	2	0	53	0	0	0	0	1	.00	4	.214	.224	.302
2011	Bal	AL	26	61	10	0	0	0	(0	0)	10	6	6	4	4	0	25	0	0	0	0	0	-	1	.164	.215	.164
	2 ML YEARS		79	220	44	5	0	3	(2	1)	58	21	18	14	6	0	78	0	0	0	0	1	.00	5	.200	.221	.264

Trevor Bell

Pitches: R **Bats:** L **Pos:** RP-19 **Ht:** 6'2" **Wt:** 200 **Born:** 10/12/1986 **Age:** 25

Year	Team	Lg	G	GS	CG	GF	IP	BFP	H	R	ER	HR	SH	SF	HB	TBB	IBB	SO	WP	Bk	W	L	Pct	Sh	Sv-Op	Hld	ERC	ERA
2011	Salt Lk*	AAA	11	0	0	0	56.0	248	71	41	39	10	0	1	2	13	1	49	5	0	2	5	.286	0	0- -		5.66	6.27
2009	LAA	AL	8	4	0	1	20.1	110	40	25	22	3	0	2	0	11	2	14	1	0	1	2	.333	0	0-0	0	11.15	9.74
2010	LAA	AL	25	7	0	8	61.0	273	77	35	32	2	3	1	1	21	2	45	5	0	2	5	.286	0	0-0	1	4.90	4.72
2011	LAA	AL	19	0	0	14	34.1	146	39	14	13	2	0	1	1	10	1	17	2	0	1	1	.500	0	0-1	0	4.29	3.41
	3 ML YEARS		52	11	0	23	115.2	529	156	74	67	7	3	4	2	42	5	76	8	0	4	8	.333	0	0-1	1	5.71	5.21

Duane Below

Pitches: L **Bats:** L **Pos:** RP-12; SP-2 BEE-low **Ht:** 6'2" **Wt:** 218 **Born:** 11/15/1985 **Age:** 26

Year	Team	Lg	G	GS	CG	GF	IP	BFP	H	R	ER	HR	SH	SF	HB	TBB	IBB	SO	WP	Bk	W	L	Pct	Sh	Sv-Op	Hld	ERC	ERA
2006	Tigers	R	15	4	0	2	33.2	136	27	8	6	1	1	0	0	10	0	30	2	0	2	0	1.000	0	0- -		2.22	1.60
2006	Oneont	A-	2	2	0	0	9.1	44	11	6	4	0	0	0	0	5	0	8	0	0	0	0	-	0	0- -		4.73	3.86
2007	WMich	A	26	26	0	0	145.2	608	128	54	48	6	1	3	3	58	0	160	9	2	13	5	.722	0	0- -		3.12	2.97
2008	Lkland	A+	27	26	0	0	133.1	594	144	75	66	10	2	3	2	70	0	126	6	2	8	7	.533	0	0- -		4.98	4.46
2009	Lkland	A+	6	6	0	0	28.2	123	22	11	10	4	0	3	0	14	0	38	2	0	1	4	.200	0	0- -		3.32	3.14
2009	Erie	AA	2	2	0	0	11.1	48	7	4	2	1	1	1	0	6	0	7	1	0	1	0	1.000	0	0- -		2.37	1.59
2010	Erie	AA	28	28	0	0	126.0	544	137	78	69	17	1	4	3	37	0	103	6	2	7	12	.368	0	0- -		4.48	4.93
2011	Toledo	AAA	18	18	0	0	115.0	472	99	42	40	12	0	4	5	37	0	83	0	0	9	4	.692	0	0- -		3.26	3.13
2011	Det	AL	14	2	0	4	29.0	127	28	16	14	2	1	3	1	11	2	14	2	0	0	2	.000	0	0-0	0	3.52	4.34

Brandon Belt

Bats: L **Throws:** L **Pos:** 1B-31; LF-31; PH-8; PR-2; RF-1 **Ht:** 6'5" **Wt:** 219 **Born:** 4/20/1988 **Age:** 24

Year	Team	Lg	G	AB	H	2B	3B	HR	(Hm	Rd)	TB	R	RBI	RC	TBB	IBB	SO	HBP	SH	SF	SB	CS	SB%	GDP	Avg	OBP	Slg
2010	SnJos	A+	77	269	103	28	4	10	(-	-)	169	62	62	80	58	3	50	3	0	3	18	7	.72	1	.383	.492	.628
2010	Rchmd	AA	46	175	59	11	6	9	(-	-)	109	26	40	43	22	1	34	2	0	2	5	1	.67	1	.337	.413	.623
2010	Fresno	AAA	13	48	11	4	0	4	(-	-)	27	11	10	11	13	0	15	0	0	0	2	0	1.00	0	.229	.393	.563
2011	Fresno	AAA	49	165	51	12	0	8	(-	-)	87	32	32	40	42	2	47	2	0	3	4	4	.50	1	.309	.448	.527
2011	SnJos	A+	4	13	6	1	0	0	(-	-)	7	3	4	4	5	0	1	0	0	0	1	0	1.00	0	.462	.611	.538
2011	SF	NL	63	187	42	6	1	9	(2	7)	77	21	18	20	20	1	57	2	0	0	3	2	.60	3	.225	.306	.412

Carlos Beltran

Bats: B **Throws:** R **Pos:** RF-134; PH-5; DH-3 **Ht:** 6'1" **Wt:** 215 **Born:** 4/24/1977 **Age:** 35

									BATTING												BASERUNNING				AVERAGES		
Year Team	Lg	G	AB	H	2B	3B	HR	(Hm	Rd)	TB	R	RBI	RC	TBB	IBB	SO	HBP	SH	SF	SB	CS	SB%	GDP	Avg	OBP	Slg
1998 KC	AL	14	58	16	5	3	0	(0	0)	27	12	7	9	3	0	12	1	0	1	3	0	1.00	2	.276	.317	.466
1999 KC	AL	156	663	194	27	7	22	(12	10)	301	112	108	100	46	2	123	4	0	10	27	8	.77	17	.293	.337	.454
2000 KC	AL	98	372	92	15	4	7	(4	3)	136	49	44	43	35	2	69	0	2	4	13	0	1.00	12	.247	.309	.366
2001 KC	AL	155	617	189	32	12	24	(7	17)	317	106	101	118	52	2	120	5	1	5	31	1	.97	7	.306	.362	.514
2002 KC	AL	162	637	174	44	7	29	(19	10)	319	114	105	117	71	1	135	4	3	7	35	7	.83	12	.273	.346	.501
2003 KC	AL	141	521	160	14	10	26	(10	16)	272	102	100	117	72	4	81	2	0	7	41	4	.91	8	.307	.389	.522
2004 2 Tms		159	599	160	36	9	38	(15	23)	328	121	104	124	92	10	101	7	3	7	42	3	.93	8	.267	.367	.548
2005 NYM	NL	151	582	155	34	2	16	(6	10)	241	83	78	88	56	5	96	2	4	6	17	6	.74	9	.266	.330	.414
2006 NYM	NL	140	510	140	38	1	41	(15	26)	303	127	116	121	95	6	99	4	1	7	18	3	.86	6	.275	.388	.594
2007 NYM	NL	144	554	153	33	3	33	(11	22)	291	93	112	97	69	10	111	2	1	10	23	2	.92	8	.276	.353	.525
2008 NYM	NL	161	606	172	40	5	27	(14	13)	303	116	112	116	92	13	96	1	1	6	25	3	.89	11	.284	.376	.500
2009 NYM	NL	81	308	100	22	1	10	(3	7)	154	50	48	54	47	10	43	1	0	1	11	1	.92	9	.325	.415	.500
2010 NYM	NL	64	220	56	11	3	7	(3	4)	94	21	27	31	30	5	39	1	0	4	3	1	.75	4	.255	.341	.427
2011 2 Tms	NL	142	520	156	39	6	22	(14	8)	273	78	84	96	71	7	88	3	0	4	4	2	.67	18	.300	.385	.525
04 KC	AL	69	266	74	19	2	15	(8	7)	142	51	51	57	37	7	44	2	1	3	14	3	.82	4	.278	.367	.534
04 Hou	NL	90	333	86	17	7	23	(7	16)	186	70	53	67	55	3	57	5	2	4	28	0	1.00	4	.258	.368	.559
11 NYM	NL	98	353	102	30	2	15	(9	6)	181	61	66	72	60	6	61	2	0	4	3	0	1.00	9	.289	.391	.513
11 SF	NL	44	167	54	9	4	7	(5	2)	92	17	18	24	11	1	27	1	0	0	1	2	.33	9	.323	.369	.551
Postseason		22	82	30	4	0	11	(4	7)	67	31	19	26	18	1	13	1	0	0	8	0	1.00	1	.366	.485	.817
14 ML YEARS		1768	6767	1917	390	73	302	(133	169)	3359	1184	1146	1231	831	77	1213	37	16	79	293	41	.88	131	.283	.361	.496

Adrian Beltre

Bats: R **Throws:** R **Pos:** 3B-112; DH-11; PH-1 **Ht:** 5'11" **Wt:** 220 **Born:** 4/7/1979 **Age:** 33

									BATTING												BASERUNNING				AVERAGES		
Year Team	Lg	G	AB	H	2B	3B	HR	(Hm	Rd)	TB	R	RBI	RC	TBB	IBB	SO	HBP	SH	SF	SB	CS	SB%	GDP	Avg	OBP	Slg
2011 RdRck*	AAA	2	8	2	0	0	0	(-	-)	2	1	0	0	0	0	3	0	0	0	0	0	-	0	.250	.250	.250
1998 LAD	NL	77	195	42	9	0	7	(5	2)	72	18	22	20	14	0	37	3	2	0	3	1	.75	4	.215	.278	.369
1999 LAD	NL	152	538	148	27	5	15	(6	9)	230	84	67	84	61	12	105	6	4	5	18	7	.72	4	.275	.352	.428
2000 LAD	NL	138	510	148	30	2	20	(7	13)	242	71	85	85	56	2	80	2	3	4	12	5	.71	13	.290	.360	.475
2001 LAD	NL	126	475	126	22	4	13	(4	9)	195	59	60	60	28	1	82	5	2	5	13	4	.76	9	.265	.310	.411
2002 LAD	NL	159	587	151	26	5	21	(7	14)	250	70	75	74	37	4	96	4	1	6	7	5	.58	17	.257	.303	.426
2003 LAD	NL	158	559	134	30	2	23	(13	10)	237	50	80	64	37	4	103	5	1	6	2	2	.50	13	.240	.290	.424
2004 LAD	NL	156	598	200	32	0	48	(23	25)	376	104	121	120	53	9	87	2	0	4	7	2	.78	15	.334	.388	.629
2005 Sea	AL	156	603	154	36	1	19	(7	12)	249	69	87	75	38	6	108	5	0	4	3	1	.75	15	.255	.303	.413
2006 Sea	AL	156	620	166	39	4	25	(16	9)	288	88	89	85	47	4	118	10	1	3	11	5	.69	15	.268	.328	.465
2007 Sea	AL	149	595	164	41	2	26	(11	15)	287	87	99	79	38	2	104	2	0	4	14	2	.88	18	.276	.319	.482
2008 Sea	AL	143	556	148	29	1	25	(10	15)	254	74	77	71	50	10	90	2	0	4	8	2	.80	11	.266	.327	.457
2009 Sea	AL	111	449	119	27	0	8	(4	4)	170	54	44	48	19	1	74	7	0	2	13	2	.87	19	.265	.304	.379
2010 Bos	AL	154	589	189	49	2	28	(13	15)	326	84	102	103	40	10	82	5	0	7	2	1	.67	25	.321	.365	.553
2011 Tex	AL	124	487	144	33	0	32	(23	9)	273	82	105	80	25	0	53	5	0	5	1	1	.50	13	.296	.331	.561
Postseason		4	15	4	0	0	0	(0	0)	4	1	1	1	0	0	3	0	0	1	0	0	-	0	.267	.250	.267
14 ML YEARS		1959	7361	2033	430	28	310	(149	161)	3449	994	1113	1050	543	65	1219	63	14	62	114	40	.74	191	.276	.329	.469

Omar Beltre

Pitches: R **Bats:** R **Pos:** P **Ht:** 6'3" **Wt:** 190 **Born:** 8/24/1981 **Age:** 30

					HOW MUCH HE PITCHED					WHAT HE GAVE UP											THE RESULTS					
Year Team	Lg	G	GS	CG	GF	IP	BFP	H	R	ER	HR	SH	SF	HB	TBB	IBB	SO	WP	Bk	W	L	Pct	Sh	Sv-Op Hld	ERC	ERA
2000 Rngrs	R	13	13	0	0	61.0	251	54	30	24	2	1	2	6	15	0	44	2	2	5	4	.556	0	0- -	2.83	3.54
2001 Pulaski	R+	13	12	0	0	69.1	290	56	28	26	4	3	3	9	23	0	83	12	1	6	3	.667	0	0- -	2.99	3.38
2003 Clinton	A	16	5	0	7	49.0	198	46	19	13	4	1	1	1	11	0	27	5	1	3	3	.500	0	1- -	3.09	2.39
2004 Stcktn	A+	46	0	0	22	58.2	262	60	32	16	1	0	0	3	24	1	47	6	1	4	5	.444	0	6- -	3.72	2.45
2010 OKCity	AAA	24	14	0	6	85.0	348	69	35	25	2	3	4	2	38	1	85	9	0	3	9	.250	0	2- -	2.88	2.65
2011 Rngrs	R	2	2	0	0	2.0	9	2	0	0	0	0	0	0	2	0	4	0	0	0	0	-	0	0- -	6.15	0.00
2010 Tex	AL	2	2	0	0	7.0	38	9	7	7	3	1	0	2	7	0	9	0	0	0	1	.000	0	0-0 0	13.10	9.00

Joaquin Benoit

Pitches: R **Bats:** R **Pos:** RP-66 ben-WAH **Ht:** 6'3" **Wt:** 220 **Born:** 7/26/1977 **Age:** 34

					HOW MUCH HE PITCHED					WHAT HE GAVE UP											THE RESULTS					
Year Team	Lg	G	GS	CG	GF	IP	BFP	H	R	ER	HR	SH	SF	HB	TBB	IBB	SO	WP	Bk	W	L	Pct	Sh	Sv-Op Hld	ERC	ERA
2001 Tex	AL	1	1	0	0	5.0	26	8	6	6	3	0	1	0	3	0	4	0	0	0	0	-	0	0-0 0	13.11	10.80
2002 Tex	AL	17	13	0	0	84.2	405	91	51	50	6	4	3	5	58	2	59	7	0	4	5	.444	0	1-1 0	5.52	5.31
2003 Tex	AL	25	17	0	1	105.0	462	99	67	64	23	1	4	3	51	0	87	3	1	8	5	.615	0	0-0 0	5.03	5.49
2004 Tex	AL	28	15	0	2	103.0	456	113	67	65	19	2	10	8	31	0	95	3	0	3	5	.375	0	0-0 0	5.10	5.68
2005 Tex	AL	32	9	0	6	87.0	369	69	39	36	9	2	1	2	38	0	78	1	0	4	4	.500	0	0-0 5	3.15	3.72
2006 Tex	AL	56	0	0	7	79.2	347	68	49	44	5	0	3	3	38	4	85	3	0	1	1	.500	0	0-2 7	3.30	4.86
2007 Tex	AL	70	0	0	22	82.0	337	68	28	26	6	3	2	2	28	2	87	3	0	7	4	.636	0	6-13 19	2.83	2.85
2008 Tex	AL	44	0	0	8	45.0	209	40	28	25	6	2	0	0	35	2	43	3	0	3	2	.600	0	1-4 13	5.02	5.00
2010 TB	AL	63	0	0	16	60.1	217	30	10	9	6	0	2	0	11	1	75	1	0	1	2	.333	0	1-4 25	1.14	1.34
2011 Det	AL	66	0	0	13	61.0	241	47	22	20	5	1	5	2	17	1	63	3	0	4	3	.571	0	2-7 29	2.46	2.95
Postseason		3	0	0	0	3.2	11	0	0	0	0	0	0	0	0	0	3	0	0	1	0	1.000	0	0-0 1	0.00	0.00
10 ML YEARS		402	55	0	77	712.2	3069	633	367	344	88	15	31	25	310	12	676	27	1	35	31	.530	0	11-31 98	3.83	4.34

Joe Benson

Bats: R Throws: R Pos: LF-11; RF-7; CF-2; PH-1; PR-1
Ht: 6'2" Wt: 211 Born: 3/5/1988 Age: 24

								BATTING											BASERUNNING				AVERAGES		
Year	Team	Lg	G	AB	H	2B	3B	HR	(Hm | Rd)	TB	R	RBI	RC	TBB	IBB	SO	HBP	SH	SF	SB	CS	SB%	GDP	Avg	OBP	Slg
2006	Twins	R	52	196	51	11	5	5	(- | -)	87	30	28	28	21	0	41	2	0	2	9	10	.47	3	.260	.335	.444
2006	Beloit	A	8	19	5	0	0	0	(- | -)	5	2	1	1	0	0	6	0	0	0	1	0	1.00	1	.263	.263	.263
2007	Beloit	A	122	432	110	18	8	5	(- | -)	159	73	38	58	49	0	124	15	6	5	18	16	.53	3	.255	.347	.368
2008	Beloit	A	69	254	63	16	3	4	(- | -)	97	39	27	32	24	0	73	7	2	3	17	11	.61	5	.248	.326	.382
2009	FtMyrs	A+	80	263	75	10	3	5	(- | -)	106	46	29	49	46	3	74	13	3	2	14	7	.67	3	.285	.414	.403
2009	Twins	R	2	5	1	0	0	0	(- | -)	1	1	0	0	2	0	0	0	0	0	1	1	.50	0	.200	.429	.200
2010	NwBrit	AA	103	373	93	19	7	23	(- | -)	195	64	49	65	39	1	115	9	0	1	14	9	.61	4	.249	.334	.523
2010	FtMyrs	A+	21	85	25	11	4	4	(- | -)	50	16	13	19	8	0	21	3	0	0	5	0	1.00	1	.294	.375	.588
2011	NwBrit	AA	111	400	114	28	4	16	(- | -)	198	69	67	78	56	5	109	13	0	3	13	9	.59	16	.285	.388	.495
2011	Twins	R	3	9	2	1	0	0	(- | -)	3	2	0	1	2	0	2	0	0	0	1	1	.50	0	.222	.364	.333
2011	Min	AL	21	71	17	6	1	0	(0 | 0)	25	3	2	4	3	0	21	0	0	0	2	2	.50	1	.239	.270	.352

Justin Berg

Pitches: R Bats: R Pos: RP-8
Ht: 6'3" Wt: 230 Born: 6/7/1984 Age: 28

			HOW MUCH HE PITCHED						WHAT HE GAVE UP											THE RESULTS						
Year	Team	Lg	G	GS	CG	GF	IP	BFP	H	R	ER	HR	SH	SF	HB	TBB	IBB	SO	WP	Bk	W	L	Pct	Sh	Sv-Op	Hld	ERC	ERA
2011	Iowa*	AAA	27	0	0	12	29.2	132	29	18	17	4	2	0	5	17	0	17	1	0	4	1	.800	0	3- -	-	5.83	5.16
2009	ChC	NL	11	0	0	6	12.0	46	10	1	1	0	1	0	0	1	0	7	0	1	0	0	-	0	0-0	0	1.58	0.75
2010	ChC	NL	41	0	0	12	40.0	187	45	27	23	3	1	2	3	20	1	14	2	0	0	1	.000	0	0-0	5	5.16	5.18
2011	ChC	NL	8	0	0	0	12.0	52	11	5	5	1	0	0	2	6	1	6	0	0	0	0	-	0	0-0	0	4.55	3.75
	3 ML YEARS		60	0	0	18	64.0	285	66	33	29	4	2	2	5	27	2	27	2	1	0	1	.000	0	0-0	5	4.29	4.08

Brad Bergesen

BURR-guess-inn
Pitches: R Bats: L Pos: RP-22; SP-12
Ht: 6'3" Wt: 205 Born: 9/25/1985 Age: 26

			HOW MUCH HE PITCHED						WHAT HE GAVE UP											THE RESULTS						
Year	Team	Lg	G	GS	CG	GF	IP	BFP	H	R	ER	HR	SH	SF	HB	TBB	IBB	SO	WP	Bk	W	L	Pct	Sh	Sv-Op	Hld	ERC	ERA
2011	Norfolk*	AAA	3	3	1	0	22.0	88	14	4	4	1	0	1	0	8	0	18	0	0	2	1	.667	1	0- -	-	1.75	1.64
2009	Bal	AL	19	19	1	0	123.1	519	126	52	47	11	3	4	5	32	4	65	2	0	7	5	.583	0	0-0	0	3.70	3.43
2010	Bal	AL	30	28	2	1	170.0	746	193	104	94	26	5	5	7	51	4	81	0	3	8	12	.400	0	0-0	0	4.95	4.98
2011	Bal	AL	34	12	1	0	101.0	451	119	73	64	16	0	3	3	32	3	61	2	0	2	7	.222	0	0-0	5	5.22	5.70
	3 ML YEARS		83	59	4	4	394.1	1716	438	229	205	53	8	12	15	115	11	207	4	3	17	24	.415	1	0-0	5	4.62	4.68

Jason Berken

Pitches: R Bats: R Pos: RP-40
Ht: 6'0" Wt: 210 Born: 11/27/1983 Age: 28

			HOW MUCH HE PITCHED						WHAT HE GAVE UP											THE RESULTS						
Year	Team	Lg	G	GS	CG	GF	IP	BFP	H	R	ER	HR	SH	SF	HB	TBB	IBB	SO	WP	Bk	W	L	Pct	Sh	Sv-Op	Hld	ERC	ERA
2011	Norfolk*	AAA	5	4	0	0	18.0	80	20	7	7	1	3	2	1	7	0	16	1	0	0	1	.000	0	0- -	-	4.56	3.50
2009	Bal	AL	24	24	0	0	119.2	560	164	92	87	19	3	5	6	44	2	66	0	1	6	12	.333	0	0-0	0	6.81	6.54
2010	Bal	AL	41	0	0	8	62.1	262	64	24	21	5	4	1	0	19	3	45	3	0	3	3	.500	0	0-4	7	3.68	3.03
2011	Bal	AL	40	0	0	10	47.0	223	63	29	28	10	1	2	1	21	2	41	4	0	1	2	.333	0	0-3	4	7.18	5.36
	3 ML YEARS		105	24	0	18	229.0	1045	291	145	136	34	8	8	7	84	7	152	7	1	10	17	.370	0	0-7	11	5.98	5.34

Lance Berkman

Bats: B Throws: L Pos: RF-110; 1B-21; LF-16; PH-3; DH-2
Ht: 6'1" Wt: 229 Born: 2/10/1976 Age: 36

								BATTING											BASERUNNING				AVERAGES		
Year	Team	Lg	G	AB	H	2B	3B	HR	(Hm	Rd)	TB	R	RBI	RC	TBB	IBB	SO	HBP	SH	SF	SB	CS	SB%	GDP	Avg	OBP	Slg
1999	Hou	NL	34	93	22	2	0	4	(2	2)	36	10	15	12	12	0	21	0	0	1	5	1	.83	2	.237	.321	.387
2000	Hou	NL	114	353	105	28	1	21	(10	11)	198	76	67	76	56	1	73	1	0	7	6	2	.75	6	.297	.388	.561
2001	Hou	NL	156	577	191	55	5	34	(13	21)	358	110	126	144	92	5	121	13	0	6	7	9	.44	8	.331	.430	.620
2002	Hou	NL	158	578	169	35	2	42	(20	22)	334	106	128	130	107	20	118	4	0	3	5	3	.63	10	.292	.405	.578
2003	Hou	NL	153	538	155	35	6	25	(11	14)	277	110	93	115	107	13	108	9	1	3	7	5	.56	10	.288	.412	.515
2004	Hou	NL	160	544	172	40	3	30	(8	22)	308	104	106	126	127	14	101	10	0	6	4	1	.80	18	.316	.450	.566
2005	Hou	NL	132	468	137	34	1	24	(13	11)	245	76	82	88	91	12	72	4	0	2	3	2	.60	11	.293	.411	.524
2006	Hou	NL	152	536	169	29	0	45	(24	21)	333	95	136	138	98	22	106	4	0	8	3	2	.60	11	.315	.420	.621
2007	Hou	NL	153	561	156	24	2	34	(13	21)	286	95	102	105	94	11	125	8	0	5	7	3	.70	11	.278	.386	.510
2008	Hou	NL	159	554	173	46	4	29	(16	13)	314	114	106	129	99	18	108	9	0	5	18	4	.82	13	.312	.420	.567
2009	Hou	NL	136	460	126	31	1	25	(14	11)	234	73	80	83	97	14	98	1	0	4	7	4	.64	13	.274	.399	.509
2010	2 Tms		122	404	100	23	1	14	(10	4)	167	48	58	61	77	7	85	0	0	3	3	2	.60	18	.248	.368	.413
2011	StL	NL	145	488	147	23	2	31	(9	22)	267	90	94	107	92	17	93	3	0	4	2	6	.25	7	.301	.412	.547
10	Hou	NL	85	298	73	16	1	13	(9	4)	130	39	49	48	60	4	70	0	0	2	3	2	.60	12	.245	.372	.436
10	NYY	AL	37	106	27	7	0	1	(1	0)	37	9	9	13	17	3	15	0	0	1	0	0	-	6	.255	.358	.349
	Postseason		34	122	39	9	1	7	(4	3)	71	21	30	31	22	5	29	1	0	3	2	1	.67	4	.320	.419	.582
	13 ML YEARS		1774	6154	1822	405	28	358	(163	195)	3357	1107	1193	1314	1149	154	1229	64	1	54	84	48	.64	137	.296	.409	.545

Roger Bernadina

Bats: L Throws: L Pos: CF-56; LF-36; RF-10; PH-7; PR-4
burn-ah-DEEN-ah
Ht: 6'2" Wt: 198 Born: 6/12/1984 Age: 28

								BATTING											BASERUNNING				AVERAGES		
Year	Team	Lg	G	AB	H	2B	3B	HR	(Hm	Rd)	TB	R	RBI	RC	TBB	IBB	SO	HBP	SH	SF	SB	CS	SB%	GDP	Avg	OBP	Slg
2011	Syrcse*	AAA	46	164	41	9	0	6	(-	-)	68	26	14	25	18	1	47	4	2	0	14	5	.74	0	.250	.339	.415
2008	Was	NL	26	76	16	1	1	0	(0	0)	19	10	2	4	9	0	21	0	1	0	4	3	.57	3	.211	.294	.250

Year	Team	Lg	G	AB	H	2B	3B	HR	(Hm	Rd)	TB	R	RBI	RC	TBB	IBB	SO	HBP	SH	SF	SB	CS	SB%	GDP	Avg	OBP	Slg
2009	Was	NL	3	4	1	1	0	0	(0	0)	2	1	0	1	1	0	1	0	0	0	1	0	1.00	0	.250	.400	.500
2010	Was	NL	134	414	102	18	3	11	(3	8)	159	52	47	53	35	1	93	4	2	6	16	2	.89	3	.246	.307	.384
2011	Was	NL	91	309	75	12	2	7	(5	2)	112	40	27	34	22	1	63	4	2	0	17	3	.85	7	.243	.301	.362
4 ML YEARS			254	803	194	32	6	18	(8	10)	292	103	76	92	67	2	178	8	5	6	38	8	.83	13	.242	.304	.364

Dellin Betances

Pitches: R Bats: R Pos: SP-1; RP-1
DELL-inn buh-TAN-siss
Ht: 6'8" Wt: 260 Born: 3/23/1988 Age: 24

Year	Team	Lg	G	GS	CG	GF	IP	BFP	H	R	ER	HR	SH	SF	HB	TBB	IBB	SO	WP	Bk	W	L	Pct	Sh	Sv-Op	Hld	ERC	ERA
2006	Yanks	R	7	7	0	0	23.1	90	14	5	3	1	0	1	1	7	0	27	2	1	0	1	.000	0	0--	-	1.60	1.16
2007	StIsInd	A-	6	6	0	0	25.0	113	24	11	10	0	0	0	2	17	0	29	3	1	1	2	.333	0	0--	-	4.57	3.60
2008	CtnSC	A	22	22	0	0	115.1	494	87	57	47	9	1	4	11	59	0	135	9	3	9	4	.692	0	0--	-	3.37	3.67
2008	Yanks	R	3	2	0	0	6.1	35	13	7	6	0	0	0	3	0	6	2	0	0	1	.000	0	0--	-	9.96	8.53
2009	Tampa	A+	11	11	0	0	44.1	206	48	29	27	2	2	2	2	27	0	44	3	0	2	5	.286	0	0--	-	5.11	5.48
2010	Tampa	A+	14	14	0	0	71.0	278	43	18	14	1	1	1	3	19	0	88	3	0	8	1	.889	0	0--	-	1.40	1.77
2010	Trntn	AA	3	3	0	0	14.1	56	10	7	6	3	1	0	1	3	0	20	3	0	0	0	-	0	0--	-	2.75	3.77
2011	Trntn	AA	21	21	0	0	105.1	460	86	49	40	7	3	1	9	55	0	115	5	1	4	6	.400	0	0--	-	3.59	3.42
2011	S-WB	AAA	4	4	1	0	21.0	94	16	12	12	2	1	0	1	15	0	27	2	0	0	3	.000	0	0--	-	4.07	5.14
2011	NYY	AL	2	1	0	0	2.2	16	1	2	2	0	0	1		6	0	2	0	0	0	0	-	0	0-0	0	7.94	6.75

Rafael Betancourt

Pitches: R Bats: R Pos: RP-68
BETT-an-court
Ht: 6'2" Wt: 215 Born: 4/29/1975 Age: 37

Year	Team	Lg	G	GS	CG	GF	IP	BFP	H	R	ER	HR	SH	SF	HB	TBB	IBB	SO	WP	Bk	W	L	Pct	Sh	Sv-Op	Hld	ERC	ERA
2003	Cle	AL	33	0	0	13	38.0	154	27	11	9	5	1	1	1	13	2	36	1	0	2	2	.500	0	1-3	4	2.54	2.13
2004	Cle	AL	68	0	0	21	66.2	286	71	32	29	7	1	2	0	18	6	76	5	1	5	6	.455	0	4-11	12	3.77	3.92
2005	Cle	AL	54	0	0	12	67.2	272	57	23	21	5	1	0	0	17	2	73	0	0	4	3	.571	0	1-3	10	2.49	2.79
2006	Cle	AL	50	0	0	17	56.2	231	52	25	24	7	2	2	0	11	5	48	0	0	3	4	.429	0	3-6	7	2.84	3.81
2007	Cle	AL	68	0	0	15	79.1	289	51	13	13	4	0	2	0	9	3	80	0	0	5	1	.833	0	3-6	31	1.24	1.47
2008	Cle	AL	69	0	0	20	71.0	309	76	41	40	11	4	5	0	25	5	64	2	0	3	4	.429	0	4-8	12	4.53	5.07
2009	2 Tms		61	0	0	10	56.0	227	42	20	17	4	2	4	0	20	5	61	0	0	4	3	.571	0	2-6	20	2.30	2.73
2010	Col	NL	72	0	0	18	62.1	248	52	25	25	9	3	1	0	8	2	89	0	0	5	1	.833	0	1-5	23	2.35	3.61
2011	Col	NL	68	0	0	24	62.1	237	46	21	20	7	0	2	0	8	0	73	1	2	2	0	1.000	0	8-12	22	1.84	2.89
09	Cle	AL	29	0	0	7	30.2	129	25	15	12	3	1	2	0	15	4	32	0	0	1	2	.333	0	1-3	8	3.21	3.52
09	Col	NL	32	0	0	10	25.1	98	17	5	5	1	1	2	0	5	1	29	0	0	3	1	.750	0	1-3	12	1.42	1.78
Postseason			10	0	0	2	12.1	49	9	8	7	2	1	1	0	2	1	12	0	0	0	0	-	0	0-3	3	1.98	5.11
9 ML YEARS			543	0	0	150	560.0	2253	474	211	198	59	14	19	1	129	30	600	16	3	33	24	.579	0	27-60	141	2.58	3.18

Yuniesky Betancourt

Bats: R Throws: R Pos: SS-149; PH-4; PR-1
yoo-NESS-kee BETT-an-coor
Ht: 5'11" Wt: 210 Born: 1/31/1982 Age: 30

Year	Team	Lg	G	AB	H	2B	3B	HR	(Hm	Rd)	TB	R	RBI	RC	TBB	IBB	SO	HBP	SH	SF	SB	CS	SB%	GDP	Avg	OBP	Slg
2005	Sea	AL	60	211	54	11	5	1	(1	0)	78	24	15	21	11	0	24	2	2	2	1	3	.25	2	.256	.296	.370
2006	Sea	AL	157	558	161	28	6	8	(2	6)	225	68	47	60	17	0	54	1	7	1	11	8	.58	10	.289	.310	.403
2007	Sea	AL	155	536	155	38	2	9	(6	3)	224	72	67	73	15	3	48	1	3	4	4	4	.50	10	.289	.308	.418
2008	Sea	AL	153	559	156	36	3	7	(3	4)	219	66	51	53	17	0	42	2	6	6	4	4	.50	23	.279	.300	.392
2009	2 Tms	AL	134	470	115	20	6	6	(2	4)	165	40	49	41	21	0	44	0	11	6	3	3	.50	17	.245	.274	.351
2010	KC	AL	151	556	144	29	2	16	(8	8)	225	60	78	56	23	1	64	1	4	4	4	4	.50	17	.259	.288	.405
2011	Mil	NL	152	556	140	27	3	13	(8	5)	212	51	68	47	16	3	63	2	0	10	4	4	.50	16	.252	.271	.381
09	Sea	AL	63	224	56	10	1	2	(1	1)	74	15	22	19	10	0	18	0	8	3	3	1	.75	9	.250	.278	.330
09	KC	AL	71	246	59	10	5	4	(1	3)	91	25	27	22	11	0	26	0	3	3	2	2	.00	8	.240	.269	.370
7 ML YEARS			962	3446	925	189	27	60	(30	30)	1348	381	375	351	120	7	339	9	33	33	30	29	.51	91	.268	.292	.391

Wilson Betemit

Bats: B Throws: R Pos: 3B-87; PH-10; 1B-3; DH-3; 2B-1
BETT-uh-meet
Ht: 6'2" Wt: 222 Born: 11/2/1981 Age: 30

Year	Team	Lg	G	AB	H	2B	3B	HR	(Hm	Rd)	TB	R	RBI	RC	TBB	IBB	SO	HBP	SH	SF	SB	CS	SB%	GDP	Avg	OBP	Slg
2001	Atl	NL	8	3	0	0	0	0	(0	0)	0	1	0	0	2	0	3	0	0	0	1	0	1.00	0	.000	.400	.000
2004	Atl	NL	22	47	8	0	0	0	(0	0)	8	2	3	0	4	0	16	0	0	1	0	1	.00	0	.170	.231	.170
2005	Atl	NL	115	246	75	12	4	4	(0	4)	107	36	20	36	22	4	55	0	4	2	1	3	.25	5	.305	.359	.435
2006	2 Tms	NL	143	373	98	23	0	18	(7	11)	175	49	53	52	36	6	102	0	1	2	3	1	.75	11	.263	.326	.469
2007	2 Tms	NL	121	240	55	12	0	14	(8	6)	109	33	50	43	38	0	82	1	2	3	0	0	-	11	.229	.333	.454
2008	NYY	AL	87	189	50	13	0	6	(5	1)	81	24	25	17	6	0	56	1	1	1	0	0	-	2	.265	.289	.429
2009	CWS	AL	20	45	9	5	0	0	(0	0)	14	2	3	3	5	0	13	0	0	0	0	0	-	7	.200	.280	.311
2010	KC	AL	84	276	82	20	0	13	(7	6)	141	36	43	48	36	2	74	1	0	2	0	0	-	3	.297	.378	.511
2011	2 Tms	AL	97	323	92	22	4	8	(6	2)	146	40	46	50	31	6	105	0	0	5	4	1	.80	7	.285	.343	.452
06	Atl	NL	88	199	56	16	0	9	(3	6)	99	30	29	35	19	3	57	0	1	0	2	1	.67	4	.281	.344	.497
06	LAD	NL	55	174	42	7	0	9	(4	5)	76	19	24	17	17	3	45	0	0	2	1	0	1.00	7	.241	.306	.437
07	LAD	NL	84	156	36	8	0	10	(6	4)	74	22	26	26	32	0	49	1	0	3	0	0	-	1	.231	.359	.474
07	NYY	AL	37	84	19	4	0	4	(2	2)	35	11	24	17	6	0	33	0	2	0	0	0	-	1	.226	.278	.417
11	KC	AL	57	203	57	15	1	3	(2	1)	83	29	27	30	20	6	58	0	0	3	3	1	.75	6	.281	.341	.409
11	Det	AL	40	120	35	7	3	5	(4	1)	63	11	19	20	11	0	47	0	0	2	1	0	1.00	1	.292	.346	.525
Postseason			6	10	5	1	0	1	(0	1)	9	3	1	2	2	1	2	0	0	0	0	0	-	0	.500	.583	.900
9 ML YEARS			697	1742	469	107	8	63	(33	30)	781	223	243	248	180	18	506	3	8	16	9	7	.56	37	.269	.336	.448

Bruce Billings

Pitches: R Bats: R Pos: RP-4   Ht: 6'0" Wt: 200 Born: 11/18/1985 Age: 26

Year	Team	Lg	G	GS	CG	GF	IP	BFP	H	R	ER	HR	SH	SF	HB	TBB	IBB	SO	WP	Bk	W	L	Pct	Sh	Sv-Op	Hld	ERC	ERA
2007	TriCity	A-	15	15	0	0	78.2	311	59	30	26	8	2	2	7	16	0	89	2	0	4	2	.667	0	0--	-	2.41	2.97
2008	Ashvll	A	27	27	2	0	161.1	685	163	85	74	11	1	5	5	42	0	144	3	0	9	11	.450	1	0--	-	3.46	4.13
2009	Mdest	A+	21	20	0	0	99.1	432	91	60	46	10	3	2	6	38	0	122	3	0	6	10	.375	0	0--	-	3.71	4.17
2010	Tulsa	AA	34	14	0	5	109.2	453	86	40	40	6	4	2	6	44	0	101	3	0	11	6	.647	0	1--	-	2.86	3.28
2011	ColSpr	AAA	29	0	0	3	50.1	225	58	29	25	4	0	1	2	21	0	47	2	0	6	2	.750	0	1--	-	5.07	4.47
2011	Scrmto	AAA	15	2	0	0	26.1	114	22	15	13	1	3	2	1	13	0	25	1	0	1	0	1.000	0	0--	-	3.20	4.44
2011	2 Tms		4	0	0	1	7.0	38	13	10	8	1	0	0	0	6	0	7	1	0	0	0	-	0	0-0	0	12.51	10.29
11	Col	NL	1	0	0	1	2.0	9	5	1	1	0	0	0	0	0	0	1	1	0	0	0	-	0	0-0	0	13.40	4.50
11	Oak	AL	3	0	0	0	5.0	29	8	9	7	1	0	0	0	6	0	7	0	0	0	0	-	0	0-0	0	12.25	12.60

Chad Billingsley

Pitches: R Bats: R Pos: SP-32   Ht: 6'1" Wt: 240 Born: 7/29/1984 Age: 27

Year	Team	Lg	G	GS	CG	GF	IP	BFP	H	R	ER	HR	SH	SF	HB	TBB	IBB	SO	WP	Bk	W	L	Pct	Sh	Sv-Op	Hld	ERC	ERA
2006	LAD	NL	18	16	0	0	90.0	403	92	43	38	7	4	0	3	58	3	59	5	0	7	4	.636	0	0-0	-	5.22	3.80
2007	LAD	NL	43	20	1	6	147.0	623	131	56	54	15	9	3	3	64	3	141	5	0	12	5	.706	0	0-1	3	3.70	3.31
2008	LAD	NL	35	32	1	1	200.2	859	188	76	70	14	8	5	8	80	6	201	10	0	16	10	.615	1	0-0	1	3.62	3.14
2009	LAD	NL	33	32	0	0	196.1	823	173	94	88	17	9	11	7	86	7	179	14	0	12	11	.522	0	0-0	0	3.63	4.03
2010	LAD	NL	31	31	1	0	191.2	817	176	82	76	8	7	11	10	69	7	171	4	0	12	11	.522	1	0-0	0	3.20	3.57
2011	LAD	NL	32	32	1	0	188.0	829	189	98	88	14	13	8	7	84	4	152	5	0	11	11	.500	0	0-0	0	4.19	4.21
Postseason			6	3	0	0	17.0	78	20	14	13	1	0	0	0	10	2	22	2	0	1	2	.333	0	0-0	0	5.40	6.88
6 ML YEARS			192	163	4	7	1013.2	4354	949	449	414	75	50	38	38	441	30	903	43	0	70	52	.574	2	0-1	4	3.79	3.68

Brian Bixler

Bats: R Throws: R Pos: LF-27; PH-23; PR-21; 3B-14; RF-6; CF-4; 1B-2; SS-2; DH-1   Ht: 6'1" Wt: 195 Born: 10/22/1982 Age: 29

Year	Team	Lg	G	AB	H	2B	3B	HR	(Hm	Rd)	TB	R	RBI	RC	TBB	IBB	SO	HBP	SH	SF	SB	CS	SB%	GDP	Avg	OBP	Slg
2011	Syrcse*	AAA	25	86	27	5	0	1	(-	-)	35	17	6	17	16	1	30	4	1	1	4	1	1.00	1	.314	.439	.407
2008	Pit	NL	50	108	17	2	1	0	(0	0)	21	16	2	2	6	2	36	4	2	0	1	0	1.00	0	.157	.229	.194
2009	Pit	NL	18	44	10	5	0	0	(0	0)	15	5	3	3	2	0	26	0	0	0	1	0	1.00	0	.227	.261	.341
2011	Was	NL	79	83	17	1	2	0	(0	0)	22	9	2	5	7	3	19	0	4	0	4	3	.57	1	.205	.267	.265
3 ML YEARS			147	235	44	8	3	0	(0	0)	58	30	7	10	15	5	81	4	6	0	6	3	.67	2	.187	.248	.247

Nick Blackburn

Pitches: R Bats: R Pos: SP-26   Ht: 6'4" Wt: 240 Born: 2/24/1982 Age: 30

Year	Team	Lg	G	GS	CG	GF	IP	BFP	H	R	ER	HR	SH	SF	HB	TBB	IBB	SO	WP	Bk	W	L	Pct	Sh	Sv-Op	Hld	ERC	ERA
2007	Min	AL	6	0	0	3	11.2	54	19	12	10	2	0	0	0	2	0	8	0	0	0	2	.000	0	0-1	1	7.61	7.71
2008	Min	AL	33	33	0	0	193.1	823	224	102	87	23	5	4	7	39	4	96	2	0	11	11	.500	0	0-0	0	4.48	4.05
2009	Min	AL	33	33	3	0	205.2	882	240	103	92	25	5	5	3	41	1	98	2	0	11	11	.500	0	0-0	0	4.42	4.03
2010	Min	AL	28	26	1	2	161.0	692	194	100	97	25	2	3	4	40	1	68	3	1	10	12	.455	0	0-0	0	5.24	5.42
2011	Min	AL	26	26	1	0	148.1	670	183	91	74	19	7	5	4	54	5	76	5	0	7	10	.412	0	0-0	0	5.56	4.49
Postseason			1	1	0	0	5.2	22	3	1	1	0	0	0	0	2	0	3	0	0	0	0	-	0	0-0	0	1.21	1.59
5 ML YEARS			126	118	5	5	720.0	3121	860	409	360	94	19	17	18	176	11	346	12	1	39	46	.459	0	0-1	4	4.90	4.50

Charlie Blackmon

Bats: L Throws: L Pos: LF-25; CF-2; PH-2   Ht: 6'3" Wt: 200 Born: 7/1/1986 Age: 25

Year	Team	Lg	G	AB	H	2B	3B	HR	(Hm	Rd)	TB	R	RBI	RC	TBB	IBB	SO	HBP	SH	SF	SB	CS	SB%	GDP	Avg	OBP	Slg
2008	TriCity	A-	68	290	98	21	5	2	(-	-)	135	42	33	52	16	2	37	10	3	2	13	7	.65	2	.338	.390	.466
2009	Mdest	A+	133	550	169	34	7	7	(-	-)	238	87	69	92	39	1	83	19	3	5	30	13	.70	5	.307	.370	.433
2010	Tulsa	AA	86	337	100	22	4	11	(-	-)	163	53	55	61	32	2	43	4	3	5	19	7	.73	4	.297	.360	.484
2011	ColSpr	AAA	58	243	82	19	4	10	(-	-)	139	49	49	53	19	0	34	5	2	3	12	5	.71	2	.337	.393	.572
2011	Col	NL	27	98	25	1	0	1	(1	0)	29	9	8	10	3	1	8	0	1	0	5	1	.83	2	.255	.277	.296

Casey Blake

Bats: R Throws: R Pos: 3B-45; PH-12; 1B-8; LF-2   Ht: 6'2" Wt: 204 Born: 8/23/1973 Age: 38

Year	Team	Lg	G	AB	H	2B	3B	HR	(Hm	Rd)	TB	R	RBI	RC	TBB	IBB	SO	HBP	SH	SF	SB	CS	SB%	GDP	Avg	OBP	Slg
2011	Albq*	AAA	4	14	2	1	0	0	(-	-)	3	1	0	0	2	0	8	0	0	0	0	0	-	1	.143	.250	.214
2011	RCuca*	A+	2	8	3	1	0	0	(-	-)	4	2	1	1	0	0	2	0	0	0	0	0	-	0	.375	.375	.500
1999	Tor	AL	14	39	10	2	0	1	(0	1)	15	6	1	4	2	0	7	0	0	0	0	0	-	1	.256	.293	.385
2000	Min	AL	7	16	3	2	0	0	(0	0)	5	1	1	2	3	0	7	1	0	1	0	0	-	1	.188	.333	.313
2001	2 Tms	AL	19	37	9	1	0	1	(0	1)	13	3	4	5	4	1	12	0	0	1	3	0	1.00	0	.243	.317	.351
2002	Min	AL	9	20	4	1	0	0	(0	0)	5	2	1	1	2	0	7	0	0	0	0	0	-	0	.200	.273	.250
2003	Cle	AL	152	557	143	35	4	17	(2	15)	229	80	67	68	38	1	109	10	8	8	7	9	.44	11	.257	.312	.411
2004	Cle	AL	152	587	159	36	3	28	(13	15)	285	93	88	88	68	2	139	9	1	3	5	8	.38	19	.271	.354	.486
2005	Cle	AL	147	523	126	32	1	23	(7	16)	229	72	58	53	43	3	116	10	2	5	4	5	.44	9	.241	.308	.438
2006	Cle	AL	109	401	113	20	1	19	(9	10)	192	63	68	62	45	5	93	4	1	5	6	0	1.00	11	.282	.356	.479
2007	Cle	AL	156	588	159	36	4	18	(11	7)	257	81	78	69	54	2	123	10	5	5	4	5	.44	14	.270	.339	.437
2008	2 Tms	AL	152	536	147	36	1	21	(6	15)	248	71	81	85	49	11	120	11	1	4	3	0	1.00	12	.274	.345	.463
2009	LAD	NL	139	485	136	25	6	18	(7	11)	227	84	79	76	63	8	116	6	1	10	4		.43	12	.280	.363	.468

Year Team	Lg	G	AB	H	2B	3B	HR	(Hm Rd)	TB	R	RBI	RC	TBB	IBB	SO	HBP	SH	SF	SB	CS	SB%	GDP	Avg	OBP	Slg
2010 LAD	NL	146	509	126	28	1	17	(6 11)	207	56	64	60	48	3	138	8	3	3	0	4	.00	8	.248	.320	.407
2011 LAD	NL	63	202	51	10	1	4	(2 2)	75	32	26	26	26	1	50	3	5	3	1	2	.33	9	.252	.342	.371
01 Min	AL	13	22	7	1	0	0	(0 0)	8	1	2	4	3	1	8	0	0	0	1	0	1.00	0	.318	.400	.364
01 Bal	AL	6	15	2	0	0	1	(0 1)	5	2	2	1	1	0	4	0	0	0	2	0	1.00	0	.133	.188	.333
08 Cle	AL	94	325	94	24	0	11	(1 10)	151	46	58	64	33	6	68	7	1	2	2	0	1.00	0	.289	.365	.465
08 LAD	NL	58	211	53	12	1	10	(5 5)	97	25	23	21	16	5	52	4	0	2	1	0	1.00	9	.251	.313	.460
Postseason		27	103	24	3	0	2	(2 0)	33	10	10	9	5	1	23	1	1	0	1	0	1.00	2	.233	.275	.320
13 ML YEARS		1265	4500	1186	264	18	167	(63 104)	1987	644	616	599	445	37	1037	72	27	47	36	37	.49	107	.264	.336	.442

Andres Blanco

Bats: B **Throws:** R **Pos:** SS-23; 3B-6; 2B-5; PH-2; PR-2; RF-1

Ht: 5'10" **Wt:** 180 **Born:** 4/11/1984 **Age:** 28

Year Team	Lg	G	AB	H	2B	3B	HR	(Hm Rd)	TB	R	RBI	RC	TBB	IBB	SO	HBP	SH	SF	SB	CS	SB%	GDP	Avg	OBP	Slg
2011 RdRck*	AAA	6	22	5	3	0	0	(- -)	8	3	5	2	3	0	3	0	0	0	0	0	-	1	.227	.320	.364
2004 KC	AL	19	60	19	2	2	0	(0 0)	25	9	5	12	5	0	6	1	1	0	1	2	.33	0	.317	.379	.417
2005 KC	AL	26	79	17	0	1	0	(0 0)	19	6	5	3	5	0	5	1	4	2	0	1	.00	3	.215	.220	.241
2006 KC	AL	33	87	21	4	1	0	(0 0)	27	9	9	9	5	0	14	1	3	0	0	1	.00	2	.241	.290	.310
2009 ChC	NL	53	123	31	8	0	1	(1 0)	42	15	12	9	8	3	14	1	6	0	0	2	.00	4	.252	.303	.341
2010 Tex	AL	68	166	46	10	1	0	(0 0)	58	17	13	19	11	1	24	3	3	2	0	2	.00	4	.277	.330	.349
2011 Tex	AL	36	76	17	3	0	2	(2 0)	26	9	3	4	4	0	14	0	2	0	1	0	.00	1	.224	.263	.342
6 ML YEARS		235	591	151	27	5	3	(3 0)	197	65	47	56	33	4	77	7	19	4	1	9	.10	10	.255	.301	.333

Henry Blanco

Bats: R **Throws:** R **Pos:** C-37; PH-1

Ht: 5'11" **Wt:** 220 **Born:** 8/29/1971 **Age:** 40

Year Team	Lg	G	AB	H	2B	3B	HR	(Hm Rd)	TB	R	RBI	RC	TBB	IBB	SO	HBP	SH	SF	SB	CS	SB%	GDP	Avg	OBP	Slg
1997 LAD	NL	3	5	2	0	0	1	(0 1)	5	1	1	2	0	0	1	0	0	0	0	0	-	0	.400	.400	1.000
1999 Col	NL	88	263	61	12	3	6	(3 3)	97	30	28	32	34	1	38	1	3	2	1	1	.50	4	.232	.320	.369
2000 Mil	NL	93	284	67	24	0	7	(3 4)	112	29	31	33	36	6	60	0	0	4	0	3	.00	9	.236	.318	.394
2001 Mil	NL	104	314	66	18	3	6	(4 2)	108	33	31	30	34	6	72	2	5	2	3	1	.75	10	.210	.290	.344
2002 Atl	NL	81	221	45	9	1	6	(4 2)	74	17	22	15	20	5	51	1	2	5	0	2	.00	5	.204	.267	.335
2003 Atl	NL	55	151	30	8	0	1	(0 1)	41	11	13	13	10	2	21	1	3	1	0	0	-	3	.199	.252	.272
2004 Min	AL	114	315	65	19	1	10	(4 6)	116	36	37	25	21	0	56	3	11	3	0	3	.00	6	.206	.260	.368
2005 ChC	NL	54	161	39	6	0	6	(2 4)	63	16	25	17	11	1	24	0	4	2	0	0	-	6	.242	.287	.391
2006 ChC	NL	74	241	64	15	2	6	(2 4)	101	23	37	26	14	1	38	0	4	2	0	0	-	8	.266	.304	.419
2007 ChC	NL	22	54	9	3	0	0	(0 0)	12	3	4	2	2	0	12	0	1	1	0	0	-	0	.167	.193	.222
2008 ChC	NL	58	120	35	3	0	3	(2 1)	47	15	12	11	6	1	22	0	2	0	0	0	-	4	.292	.325	.392
2009 SD	NL	67	204	48	12	0	6	(4 2)	78	21	16	20	26	2	50	0	1	1	0	0	-	5	.235	.320	.382
2010 NYM	NL	50	130	28	5	0	2	(2 0)	39	10	8	7	11	2	26	0	0	3	1	0	1.00	2	.215	.271	.300
2011 Ari	NL	37	100	25	3	1	8	(6 2)	54	12	12	13	12	1	21	0	0	1	0	1	.00	2	.250	.330	.540
Postseason		6	14	3	0	0	1	(1 0)	6	1	2	0	0	0	4	0	1	1	0	0	-	1	.214	.200	.429
14 ML YEARS		900	2563	584	137	11	68	(36 32)	947	257	277	246	237	28	492	8	36	26	5	11	.31	65	.228	.293	.369

Kyle Blanks

Bats: R **Throws:** R **Pos:** LF-37; 1B-14; PH-10

Ht: 6'6" **Wt:** 270 **Born:** 9/11/1986 **Age:** 25

Year Team	Lg	G	AB	H	2B	3B	HR	(Hm Rd)	TB	R	RBI	RC	TBB	IBB	SO	HBP	SH	SF	SB	CS	SB%	GDP	Avg	OBP	Slg
2011 SnAnt*	AA	44	177	50	16	3	4	(- -)	84	33	27	31	17	3	41	4	0	3	3	0	1.00	3	.282	.353	.475
2011 Tucsn*	AAA	35	134	47	12	2	11	(- -)	96	36	35	36	16	1	37	1	0	1	0	1	.00	0	.351	.421	.716
2009 SD	NL	54	148	37	9	0	10	(6 4)	76	24	22	21	18	1	55	6	0	0	1	1	.50	4	.250	.355	.514
2010 SD	NL	33	102	16	6	1	3	(2 1)	33	14	15	10	15	0	46	3	0	0	1	0	1.00	3	.157	.283	.324
2011 SD	NL	55	170	39	7	1	7	(2 5)	69	21	26	16	16	0	51	2	0	2	2	0	1.00	3	.229	.300	.406
3 ML YEARS		142	420	92	22	2	20	(10 10)	178	59	63	47	49	1	152	11	0	2	4	1	.80	8	.219	.315	.424

Joe Blanton

Pitches: R **Bats:** R **Pos:** SP-8; RP-3

Ht: 6'3" **Wt:** 244 **Born:** 12/11/1980 **Age:** 31

	HOW MUCH HE PITCHED						WHAT HE GAVE UP											THE RESULTS							
Year Team	Lg	G	GS	CG	GF	IP	BFP	H	R	ER	HR	SH	SF	HB	TBB	IBB	SO	WP	Bk	W	L	Pct	Sh	Sv-Op Hld	ERC	ERA
2011 Lakwd*	A	1	1	0	0	1.0	3	0	0	0	0	0	0	0	0	0	0	0	0	0	0	-	0	0-- -	0.00	0.00
2004 Oak	AL	3	0	0	1	8.0	30	6	5	5	1	0	0	0	2	0	6	0	0	0	0	-	0	0-0 0	2.52	5.63
2005 Oak	AL	33	33	2	0	201.1	835	178	86	79	23	2	7	5	67	3	116	4	2	12	12	.500	1	0-0 0	3.37	3.53
2006 Oak	AL	32	31	1	0	194.1	856	241	111	104	17	3	9	5	58	4	107	3	0	16	12	.571	1	0-0 0	5.09	4.82
2007 Oak	AL	34	34	3	0	230.0	950	240	106	101	16	5	8	4	40	4	140	3	1	14	10	.583	1	0-0 0	3.30	3.95
2008 2 Tms		33	33	0	0	197.2	855	211	110	103	22	2	4	4	66	3	111	2	0	9	12	.429	0	0-0 0	4.33	4.69
2009 Phi	NL	31	31	0	0	195.1	837	198	89	88	30	11	4	8	59	4	163	7	0	12	8	.600	0	0-0 0	4.25	4.05
2010 Phi	NL	29	28	0	0	175.2	765	206	104	94	27	5	7	3	43	6	134	2	0	9	6	.600	0	0-0 0	4.81	4.82
2011 Phi	NL	11	8	0	1	41.1	180	52	23	23	5	5	2	1	9	0	35	0	0	1	2	.333	0	0-0 0	5.13	5.01
08 Oak	AL	20	20	0	0	127.0	550	145	74	70	12	1	2	1	35	3	62	1	0	5	12	.294	0	0-0 0	4.33	4.96
08 Phi	NL	13	13	0	0	70.2	305	66	36	33	10	1	2	3	31	0	49	1	0	4	0	1.000	0	0-0 0	4.33	4.20
Postseason		9	6	0	1	39.1	169	36	19	18	5	1	1	3	13	2	33	2	0	2	0	1.000	0	0-0 0	3.68	4.12
8 ML YEARS		206	198	6	2	1243.2	5308	1332	634	597	141	33	41	30	344	24	812	21	3	73	62	.541	2	0-0 0	4.16	4.32

Jerry Blevins

Pitches: L Bats: L Pos: RP-26 Ht: 6'6" Wt: 178 Born: 9/6/1983 Age: 28

			HOW MUCH HE PITCHED							WHAT HE GAVE UP										THE RESULTS							
Year	Team	Lg	G	GS	CG	GF	IP	BFP	H	R	ER	HR	SH	SF	HB	TBB	IBB	SO	WP	Bk	W	L	Pct	Sh	Sv-Op	Hld	ERC	ERA
2011	Scrmto*	AAA	27	0	0	6	29.2	121	25	16	16	3	2	1	1	7	0	35	1	0	2	0	1.000	0	0- -	-	2.73	4.85
2007	Oak	AL	6	0	0	1	4.2	25	8	6	5	1	0	0	0	2	0	3	0	0	0	1	.000	0	0-0	5	9.08	9.64
2008	Oak	AL	36	0	0	8	37.2	156	32	14	13	2	0	1	3	13	2	35	0	0	1	3	.250	0	0-1	5	3.09	3.11
2009	Oak	AL	20	0	0	5	22.1	90	19	12	12	2	0	1	0	6	1	23	0	0	0	0	-	0	0-0	0	2.68	4.84
2010	Oak	AL	63	0	0	9	48.2	220	54	20	20	7	3	1	1	18	1	46	0	0	2	1	.667	0	1-2	11	4.81	3.70
2011	Oak	AL	26	0	0	11	28.1	122	24	14	9	2	2	3	1	14	1	26	0	0	0	0	-	0	0-0	0	3.45	2.86
5 ML YEARS			151	0	0	34	141.2	613	137	66	59	14	5	6	5	53	5	133	0	0	3	5	.375	0	1-3	16	3.82	3.75

Willie Bloomquist

Bats: R Throws: R Pos: SS-59; LF-25; PH-16; 2B-1; PR-1 Ht: 5'11" Wt: 194 Born: 11/27/1977 Age: 34

							BATTING																BASERUNNING				AVERAGES		
Year	Team	Lg	G	AB	H	2B	3B	HR	(Hm	Rd)	TB	R	RBI	RC	TBB	IBB	SO	HBP	SH	SF	SB	CS	SB%	GDP	Avg	OBP	Slg
2002	Sea	AL	12	33	15	4	0	0	(0	0)	19	11	7	10	5	0	2	0	0	0	3	1	.75	0	.455	.526	.576
2003	Sea	AL	89	196	49	7	2	1	(1	0)	63	30	14	18	19	1	39	1	2	2	4	1	.80	6	.250	.317	.321
2004	Sea	AL	93	188	46	10	0	2	(0	2)	62	27	18	18	10	0	48	0	3	0	13	2	.87	2	.245	.283	.330
2005	Sea	AL	82	249	64	15	2	0	(0	0)	83	27	22	26	11	0	38	1	4	2	14	1	.93	5	.257	.289	.333
2006	Sea	AL	102	251	62	6	2	1	(0	1)	75	36	15	27	24	0	40	4	2	2	16	3	.84	3	.247	.320	.299
2007	Sea	AL	91	173	48	3	0	2	(1	1)	57	28	13	16	10	0	35	1	4	0	7	5	.58	7	.277	.321	.329
2008	Sea	AL	71	165	46	1	0	0	(0	0)	47	32	9	24	25	1	29	1	1	0	14	3	.82	1	.279	.377	.285
2009	KC	AL	125	434	115	11	8	4	(0	4)	154	52	29	45	27	1	73	1	4	2	25	6	.81	7	.265	.308	.355
2010	2 Tms		83	187	50	10	1	3	(2	1)	71	31	17	19	9	0	28	0	2	1	8	5	.62	4	.267	.299	.380
2011	Ari	NL	97	350	93	10	2	4	(2	2)	119	44	26	37	23	3	51	4	2	2	20	10	.67	3	.266	.317	.340
10	KC	AL	72	170	45	10	1	3	(2	1)	66	31	17	18	8	0	25	0	2	1	8	5	.62	4	.265	.296	.388
10	Cin	NL	11	17	5	0	0	0	(0	0)	5	0	0	1	1	0	3	0	0	0	0	0	-	0	.294	.333	.294
10 ML YEARS			845	2226	588	77	17	17	(6	11)	750	318	170	240	163	6	383	13	24	11	124	37	.77	38	.264	.317	.337

Geoff Blum

Bats: B Throws: R Pos: 3B-14; PH-11 Ht: 6'3" Wt: 221 Born: 4/26/1973 Age: 39

							BATTING																BASERUNNING				AVERAGES		
Year	Team	Lg	G	AB	H	2B	3B	HR	(Hm	Rd)	TB	R	RBI	RC	TBB	IBB	SO	HBP	SH	SF	SB	CS	SB%	GDP	Avg	OBP	Slg
2011	DBcks*	R	5	15	5	0	0	0	(-	-)	5	1	1	2	1	1	1	0	0	0	0	0	-	0	.333	.375	.333
2011	Reno*	AAA	4	14	6	1	0	0	(-	-)	7	2	1	3	2	0	0	0	0	0	0	0	-	0	.429	.500	.500
2011	Visalia*	A+	2	5	3	2	0	1	(-	-)	8	1	2	3	0	0	0	0	0	0	0	0	-	0	.600	.600	1.600
1999	Mon	NL	45	133	32	7	2	8	(0	8)	67	21	18	22	17	3	25	0	3	0	1	0	1.00	3	.241	.327	.504
2000	Mon	NL	124	343	97	20	2	11	(5	6)	154	40	45	50	26	2	60	3	3	4	1	4	.20	4	.283	.335	.449
2001	Mon	NL	148	453	107	25	4	5	(6	3)	159	57	50	49	43	8	94	10	3	5	9	5	.64	12	.236	.313	.351
2002	Hou	NL	130	368	104	20	4	10	(6	4)	162	45	52	62	49	5	70	1	1	2	2	0	1.00	8	.283	.367	.440
2003	Hou	NL	123	420	110	19	0	10	(6	4)	159	51	52	40	20	1	50	2	2	5	0	0	-	15	.262	.295	.379
2004	TB	AL	112	339	73	21	0	8	(2	6)	118	38	35	29	24	1	58	0	4	2	2	3	.40	4	.215	.266	.348
2005	2 Tms		109	319	73	15	2	6	(1	5)	110	32	25	27	28	0	43	3	0	1	3	3	.50	6	.229	.296	.345
2006	SD	NL	109	276	70	17	1	4	(0	4)	101	27	34	26	17	1	51	0	2	4	0	1	.00	5	.254	.293	.366
2007	SD	NL	122	330	83	21	1	5	(1	4)	121	34	33	38	32	4	52	2	3	3	0	0	-	10	.252	.319	.367
2008	Hou	NL	114	325	78	14	1	14	(6	8)	136	36	53	42	21	2	54	3	0	7	1	2	.33	5	.240	.287	.418
2009	Hou	NL	120	381	94	14	1	10	(4	6)	140	34	49	39	33	4	61	7	0	6	0	1	.00	9	.247	.314	.367
2010	Hou	NL	93	202	54	10	1	2	(1	1)	72	22	22	22	15	2	33	1	0	0	0	0	-	3	.267	.321	.356
2011	Ari	NL	23	49	11	3	0	2	(1	1)	20	8	10	3	5	1	9	1	0	0	0	0	-	0	.224	.309	.408
05	SD	NL	78	224	54	13	1	5	(1	4)	84	26	22	23	24	0	28	3	0	1	3	2	.60	5	.241	.321	.375
05	CWS	AL	31	95	19	2	1	1	(0	1)	26	6	3	4	4	0	15	0	0	0	0	1	.00	1	.200	.232	.274
Postseason			6	10	2	1	0	1	(0	1)	6	1	2	1	4	1	1	0	0	1	0	0	-	1	.200	.400	.600
13 ML YEARS			1372	3938	986	206	15	99	(39	60)	1519	445	478	455	330	34	660	33	21	39	19	19	.50	86	.250	.311	.386

Brennan Boesch

Bats: L Throws: L Pos: LF-57; RF-51; DH-10; PH-6; PR-1 BOSH Ht: 6'4" Wt: 235 Born: 4/12/1985 Age: 27

							BATTING																BASERUNNING				AVERAGES		
Year	Team	Lg	G	AB	H	2B	3B	HR	(Hm	Rd)	TB	R	RBI	RC	TBB	IBB	SO	HBP	SH	SF	SB	CS	SB%	GDP	Avg	OBP	Slg
2006	Oneont	A-	70	292	85	15	6	5	(-	-)	127	27	54	43	21	2	42	3	4	.43	4	.291	.344	.435		
2007	WMich	A	126	513	137	19	4	10	(-	-)	194	52	86	60	23	2	81	1	0	5	15	4	.79	16	.267	.297	.378
2008	Lkland	A+	111	417	104	17	8	7	(-	-)	158	46	64	50	36	6	90	3	0	5	3	5	.38	9	.249	.310	.379
2009	Erie	AA	131	527	145	26	7	28	(-	-)	269	89	93	88	33	6	127	3	1	7	11	2	.85	10	.275	.318	.510
2010	Toledo	AAA	15	58	22	3	1	3	(-	-)	36	6	17	15	4	0	17	4	0	0	2	1	.67	1	.379	.455	.621
2010	Det	AL	133	464	119	26	3	14	(7	7)	193	49	67	61	40	5	99	5	0	3	7	1	.88	5	.256	.320	.416
2011	Det	AL	115	428	121	25	1	16	(9	7)	196	75	54	56	35	2	83	5	0	4	5	3	.63	7	.283	.341	.458
2 ML YEARS			248	892	240	51	4	30	(16	14)	389	124	121	117	75	7	182	10	0	7	12	4	.75	12	.269	.330	.436

Brandon Boggs

Bats: B Throws: R Pos: PH-12; LF-2; RF-2; CF-1; PR-1 Ht: 5'10" Wt: 212 Born: 1/9/1983 Age: 29

							BATTING																BASERUNNING				AVERAGES		
Year	Team	Lg	G	AB	H	2B	3B	HR	(Hm	Rd)	TB	R	RBI	RC	TBB	IBB	SO	HBP	SH	SF	SB	CS	SB%	GDP	Avg	OBP	Slg
2011	Nashv*	AAA	94	270	65	19	1	9	(-	-)	113	45	38	46	53	3	82	8	2	0	3	5	.38	4	.241	.381	.419
2008	Tex	AL	101	283	64	17	4	8	(6	2)	113	30	41	37	44	1	93	3	1	3	3	2	.60	3	.226	.333	.399
2009	Tex	AL	9	17	1	1	0	0	(0	0)	2	0	0	0	1	0	8	0	0	0	0	0	-	0	.059	.111	.118
2010	Tex	AL	4	7	0	0	0	0	(0	0)	0	0	0	0	1	0	4	0	0	0	0	0	-	0	.000	.125	.000
2011	Mil	NL	16	19	3	0	0	2	(2	0)	9	4	2	0	3	2	8	0	0	0	1	0	1.00	0	.158	.273	.474
4 ML YEARS			130	326	68	18	4	10	(8	2)	124	34	43	37	49	3	113	3	1	3	4	2	.67	3	.209	.315	.380

Mitchell Boggs

Pitches: R **Bats:** R **Pos:** RP-51   **Ht:** 6'4" **Wt:** 215 **Born:** 2/15/1984 **Age:** 28

Year	Team	Lg	G	GS	CG	GF	IP	BFP	H	R	ER	HR	SH	SF	HB	TBB	IBB	SO	WP	Bk	W	L	Pct	Sh	Sv-Op	Hld	ERC	ERA
2011	Memp*	AAA	4	4	0	0	14.2	60	12	5	4	1	0	0	2	5	0	14	1	0	0	2	.000	0	0- -	-	3.28	2.45
2008	StL	NL	8	6	0	1	34.0	164	42	29	28	5	1	1	2	22	0	13	2	0	3	2	.600	0	0-0	0	7.17	7.41
2009	StL	NL	16	9	0	2	58.0	268	71	28	27	3	1	2	4	33	0	46	4	1	2	3	.400	0	0-0	1	6.15	4.19
2010	StL	NL	61	0	0	22	67.1	285	60	29	27	4	4	3	4	27	2	52	5	0	2	3	.400	0	0-0	6	3.51	3.61
2011	StL	NL	51	0	0	20	60.2	260	62	27	24	4	2	2	2	21	2	48	5	0	2	3	.400	0	4-8	8	3.84	3.56
	Postseason		1	0	0	1	1.0	5	0	0	0	0	0	0	0	2	0	1	0	0	0	0	-	0	0-0	0	3.47	0.00
	4 ML YEARS		136	15	0	45	220.0	977	235	113	106	17	8	8	12	103	4	159	16	1	9	11	.450	0	4-8	8	4.81	4.34

Brian Bogusevic

Bats: L **Throws:** L **Pos:** RF-40; PH-38; LF-13; PR-5   boe-gah-SEVV-ick   **Ht:** 6'3" **Wt:** 215 **Born:** 2/18/1984 **Age:** 28

Year	Team	Lg	G	AB	H	2B	3B	HR	(Hm	Rd)	TB	R	RBI	RC	TBB	IBB	SO	HBP	SH	SF	SB	CS	SB%	GDP	Avg	OBP	Slg
2007	CpChr	AA	7	2	1	0	0	0	(-	-)	1	0	0	0	0	0	0	0	0	0	0	0	-	0	.500	.500	.500
2008	CpChr	AA	51	124	46	10	2	3	(-	-)	69	21	20	31	16	1	24	1	4	0	8	1	.89	3	.371	.447	.556
2008	Salem	A+	8	53	5	2	0	1	(-	-)	10	4	6	4	4	1	1	1	0	0	1	0	1.00	2	.217	.357	.435
2009	RdRck	AAA	138	520	141	25	3	6	(-	-)	190	68	53	72	53	3	118	3	5	0	22	3	.88	11	.271	.342	.365
2010	RdRck	AAA	131	502	139	26	2	13	(-	-)	208	91	57	84	67	2	108	3	1	2	23	1	.96	13	.277	.364	.414
2011	OKCity	AAA	58	218	57	11	5	3	(-	-)	87	27	35	36	30	1	49	5	0	1	20	3	.87	8	.261	.362	.399
2010	Hou	NL	19	28	5	3	0	0	(0	0)	8	5	3	2	3	0	12	0	0	0	1	1	.50	2	.179	.258	.286
2011	Hou	NL	87	164	47	14	1	4	(2	2)	75	22	15	19	15	1	40	1	1	1	4	2	.67	8	.287	.348	.457
	2 ML YEARS		106	192	52	17	1	4	(2	2)	83	27	18	21	18	1	52	1	1	1	5	3	.63	10	.271	.335	.432

Emilio Bonifacio

Bats: B **Throws:** R **Pos:** SS-67; 3B-36; LF-32; CF-16; RF-15; PH-10; 2B-5   **Ht:** 5'11" **Wt:** 200 **Born:** 4/23/1985 **Age:** 27

Year	Team	Lg	G	AB	H	2B	3B	HR	(Hm	Rd)	TB	R	RBI	RC	TBB	IBB	SO	HBP	SH	SF	SB	CS	SB%	GDP	Avg	OBP	Slg
2007	Ari	NL	11	23	5	1	0	0	(0	0)	6	2	2	4	4	0	3	0	0	0	0	1	.00	0	.217	.333	.261
2008	2 Tms	NL	49	169	41	6	5	0	(0	0)	57	29	14	16	14	0	46	0	0	3	7	4	.64	2	.243	.296	.337
2009	Fla	NL	127	461	116	11	6	1	(1	0)	142	72	27	41	34	0	95	2	8	4	21	9	.70	5	.252	.303	.308
2010	Fla	NL	73	180	47	6	3	0	(0	0)	59	30	10	24	17	0	42	0	1	3	12	0	1.00	1	.261	.320	.328
2011	Fla	NL	152	565	167	26	7	5	(1	4)	222	78	36	83	59	1	129	1	11	5	40	11	.78	4	.296	.360	.393
08	Ari	NL	8	12	2	1	0	0	(0	0)	3	3	2	1	0	0	5	0	0	0	1	0	1.00	0	.167	.167	.250
08	Was	NL	41	157	39	5	5	0	(0	0)	54	26	12	15	14	0	41	0	0	3	6	4	.60	2	.248	.305	.344
	5 ML YEARS		412	1398	376	50	21	6	(2	4)	486	211	89	168	128	1	315	3	20	15	80	25	.76	12	.269	.328	.348

Julio Borbon

Bats: L **Throws:** L **Pos:** CF-32   **Ht:** 6'0" **Wt:** 195 **Born:** 2/20/1986 **Age:** 26

Year	Team	Lg	G	AB	H	2B	3B	HR	(Hm	Rd)	TB	R	RBI	RC	TBB	IBB	SO	HBP	SH	SF	SB	CS	SB%	GDP	Avg	OBP	Slg
2011	Frisco*	AA	1	4	0	0	0	0	(-	-)	0	0	0	0	0	0	1	0	0	0	0	0	-	0	.000	.000	.000
2011	RdRck*	AAA	32	131	39	10	4	0	(-	-)	57	27	14	24	14	0	22	3	4	1	16	4	.80	2	.298	.376	.435
2009	Tex	AL	46	157	49	4	0	4	(2	2)	65	30	20	27	15	0	28	1	6	0	19	4	.83	3	.312	.376	.414
2010	Tex	AL	137	438	121	14	4	3	(2	1)	149	60	42	48	19	0	59	2	8	1	15	7	.68	5	.276	.309	.340
2011	Tex	AL	32	89	24	1	3	0	(0	0)	31	10	11	14	3	0	9	2	3	1	6	2	.75	2	.270	.305	.348
	Postseason		8	9	1	0	0	0	(0	0)	1	4	0	1	0	0	3	0	0	0	0	0	-	0	.111	.111	.111
	3 ML YEARS		215	684	194	16	7	7	(4	3)	245	100	73	89	37	0	96	5	17	2	40	13	.75	10	.284	.324	.358

J.C. Boscan

Bats: R **Throws:** R **Pos:** C-3; PH-1   BAHS-cann   **Ht:** 6'2" **Wt:** 215 **Born:** 12/26/1979 **Age:** 32

Year	Team	Lg	G	AB	H	2B	3B	HR	(Hm	Rd)	TB	R	RBI	RC	TBB	IBB	SO	HBP	SH	SF	SB	CS	SB%	GDP	Avg	OBP	Slg
1997	Braves	R	36	104	21	5	0	1	(-	-)	29	7	12	10	16	0	21	2	0	1	0	1	.00	2	.202	.317	.279
1998	Danvle	R+	51	170	37	3	0	4	(-	-)	52	35	24	22	37	0	44	2	3	0	2	3	.40	4	.218	.362	.306
1999	Macon	A	105	368	83	17	0	4	(-	-)	112	40	38	31	26	0	94	2	2	3	2	4	.33	10	.226	.278	.304
2000	Macon	A	93	302	62	12	0	9	(-	-)	101	31	35	34	42	1	74	5	2	1	1	1	.50	6	.205	.311	.334
2001	MrtlBh	A+	18	54	9	2	0	0	(-	-)	11	3	6	1	3	0	25	1	1	1	0	1	.00	1	.167	.220	.204
2001	Braves	R	8	30	10	4	0	0	(-	-)	14	5	6	4	0	0	3	0	0	1	0	1	.00	1	.333	.323	.467
2001	Macon	A	35	124	35	7	0	4	(-	-)	54	16	22	20	14	0	27	1	2	1	2	0	1.00	1	.282	.357	.435
2002	MrtlBh	A+	86	276	60	19	0	2	(-	-)	85	21	27	27	28	1	71	3	4	2	3	1	.75	8	.217	.294	.308
2002	Grnville	AA	10	27	7	1	0	1	(-	-)	11	2	3	4	4	0	10	0	0	0	0	0	-	0	.259	.355	.407
2002	Rchmd	AAA	2	6	1	0	0	0	(-	-)	1	0	0	0	1	0	2	0	0	0	0	1	.00	1	.167	.286	.167
2003	MrtlBh	A+	28	87	18	4	0	1	(-	-)	25	9	11	8	11	0	33	0	2	0	2	0	1.00	1	.207	.296	.287
2003	Rchmd	AAA	3	12	3	2	0	0	(-	-)	5	0	1	1	1	0	4	0	0	0	0	0	-	1	.250	.308	.417
2003	Grnville	AA	41	130	24	5	0	2	(-	-)	35	13	15	9	14	0	35	0	1	0	0	0	-	2	.185	.259	.269
2004	Grnville	AA	53	163	36	10	0	1	(-	-)	49	15	15	18	25	1	40	1	4	1	1	1	.50	3	.221	.326	.301
2004	Rchmd	AAA	21	61	19	2	0	0	(-	-)	21	4	6	9	9	0	14	1	0	1	0	0	-	2	.311	.403	.344
2005	Rchmd	AAA	72	212	47	6	0	3	(-	-)	62	17	20	21	25	1	59	4	5	2	1	2	.33	8	.222	.313	.292
2006	Hntsvl	AA	43	124	24	7	0	0	(-	-)	31	7	14	7	11	1	38	1	1	3	0	1	.00	5	.194	.259	.250
2006	Nashv	AAA	2	8	2	1	0	0	(-	-)	3	0	1	0	0	0	3	0	0	0	0	0	-	0	.250	.250	.375
2007	Lsvlle	AAA	8	21	6	0	0	0	(-	-)	6	0	1	3	5	0	5	0	0	0	0	0	-	1	.286	.407	.286
2007	Chatt	AA	30	86	17	1	0	1	(-	-)	21	7	9	10	24	3	21	0	0	1	1	0	1.00	4	.198	.369	.244
2008	Missi	AA	79	255	60	13	0	2	(-	-)	79	26	29	29	34	3	49	4	4	0	0	0	-	5	.235	.334	.310
2009	Gwnntt	AAA	13	44	11	4	0	0	(-	-)	15	5	2	4	2	0	9	1	1	0	0	0	-	1	.250	.298	.341
2009	Missi	AA	73	250	65	12	0	0	(-	-)	77	20	30	30	33	0	50	2	2	2	1	1	.50	12	.260	.348	.308

Year	Team	Lg	G	AB	H	2B	3B	HR	(Hm	Rd)	TB	R	RBI	RC	TBB	IBB	SO	HBP	SH	SF	SB	CS	SB%	GDP	Avg	OBP	Slg
											BATTING										BASERUNNING				AVERAGES		
2010	Gwnntt	AAA	66	220	55	11	0	5	(-	-)	81	20	21	28	22	0	51	2	4	0	1	0	1.00	7	.250	.324	.368
2011	Gwnntt	AAA	61	203	37	8	0	0	(-	-)	45	12	8	8	12	0	41	2	1	0	0	2	.00	5	.182	.235	.222
2010	Atl	NL	1	0	0	0	0	0	(0	0)	0	1	0	1	1	0	0	0	0	0	0	0	-	0	-	1.000	-
2011	Atl	NL	4	9	3	0	0	0	(0	0)	3	0	0	0	0	0	5	0	0	0	0	0	-	0	.333	.333	.333
	2 ML YEARS		5	9	3	0	0	0	(0	0)	3	1	0	1	1	0	5	0	0	0	0	0	-	0	.333	.400	.333

Jason Bourgeois

Bats: R **Throws:** R **Pos:** LF-34; CF-34; PH-17; RF-13; PR-13; 2B-2   boosh-WAH   **Ht:** 5'9" **Wt:** 190 **Born:** 1/4/1982 **Age:** 30

Year	Team	Lg	G	AB	H	2B	3B	HR	(Hm	Rd)	TB	R	RBI	RC	TBB	IBB	SO	HBP	SH	SF	SB	CS	SB%	GDP	Avg	OBP	Slg
											BATTING										BASERUNNING				AVERAGES		
2011	OKCity*	AAA	4	18	8	3	1	0	(-	-)	13	4	1	4	1	0	1	0	0	0	0	1	.00	0	.444	.474	.722
2011	Astros*	R	3	10	3	0	0	0	(-	-)	3	1	4	1	0	0	2	0	0	0	0	0	-	0	.300	.364	.300
2011	CpChr*	AA	2	10	2	0	0	0	(-	-)	2	1	0	0	0	0	0	0	0	0	1	0	1.00	0	.200	.200	.200
2008	CWS	AL	6	3	1	1	0	0	(0	0)	2	0	0	0	0	0	0	0	0	0	0	0	-	0	.333	.333	.667
2009	Mil	NL	24	37	7	0	0	1	(1	0)	10	6	3	1	3	0	7	0	0	0	3	0	1.00	2	.189	.250	.270
2010	Hou	NL	69	123	27	4	1	0	(0	0)	33	16	3	8	13	0	16	0	0	0	12	4	.75	5	.220	.294	.268
2011	Hou	NL	93	238	70	8	2	1	(0	1)	85	30	16	31	10	0	24	0	4	0	31	6	.84	5	.294	.323	.357
	4 ML YEARS		192	401	105	13	3	2	(1	1)	130	52	22	40	26	0	47	0	4	0	46	10	.82	12	.262	.307	.324

Peter Bourjos

Bats: R **Throws:** R **Pos:** CF-147; PH-1   BORE-juss   **Ht:** 6'1" **Wt:** 180 **Born:** 3/31/1987 **Age:** 25

Year	Team	Lg	G	AB	H	2B	3B	HR	(Hm	Rd)	TB	R	RBI	RC	TBB	IBB	SO	HBP	SH	SF	SB	CS	SB%	GDP	Avg	OBP	Slg
											BATTING										BASERUNNING				AVERAGES		
2006	Orem	R+	65	250	73	16	7	5	(-	-)	118	42	28	42	22	1	67	2	5	0	13	5	.72	3	.292	.354	.472
2007	CRpds	A	63	237	65	9	6	5	(-	-)	101	37	29	36	20	0	53	4	4	5	19	9	.68	3	.274	.335	.426
2007	Angels	R	4	16	5	0	1	0	(-	-)	7	3	2	2	1	0	2	0	0	0	0	0	-	0	.313	.353	.438
2008	RCuca	A+	121	509	150	29	10	9	(-	-)	226	83	51	80	19	0	96	7	5	5	50	10	.83	5	.295	.326	.444
2009	Ark	AA	110	437	123	16	14	6	(-	-)	185	72	51	71	49	1	77	3	10	5	32	12	.73	8	.281	.354	.423
2010	Salt Lk	AAA	102	414	130	13	12	13	(-	-)	206	86	51	78	24	1	78	10	4	3	27	5	.84	5	.314	.364	.498
2010	LAA	AL	51	181	37	6	4	6	(1	5)	69	19	15	13	6	0	40	2	3	1	10	3	.77	2	.204	.237	.381
2011	LAA	AL	147	502	136	26	11	12	(7	5)	220	72	43	66	32	0	124	10	7	1	22	9	.71	7	.271	.327	.438
	2 ML YEARS		198	683	173	32	15	18	(8	10)	289	91	58	79	38	0	164	12	10	2	32	12	.73	9	.253	.303	.423

Michael Bourn

Bats: L **Throws:** R **Pos:** CF-156; PH-2; PR-1   BORN   **Ht:** 5'11" **Wt:** 180 **Born:** 12/27/1982 **Age:** 29

Year	Team	Lg	G	AB	H	2B	3B	HR	(Hm	Rd)	TB	R	RBI	RC	TBB	IBB	SO	HBP	SH	SF	SB	CS	SB%	GDP	Avg	OBP	Slg
											BATTING										BASERUNNING				AVERAGES		
2006	Phi	NL	17	8	1	0	0	0	(0	0)	1	2	0	0	1	0	3	0	2	0	1	2	.33	0	.125	.222	.125
2007	Phi	NL	105	119	33	3	3	1	(1	0)	45	29	6	19	13	2	21	0	1	0	18	1	.95	1	.277	.348	.378
2008	Hou	NL	138	467	107	10	4	5	(3	2)	140	57	29	43	37	0	111	2	7	1	41	10	.80	3	.229	.288	.300
2009	Hou	NL	157	606	173	27	12	3	(2	1)	233	97	35	94	63	1	140	2	5	2	61	12	.84	1	.285	.354	.384
2010	Hou	NL	141	535	142	25	6	2	(0	2)	185	84	38	74	59	5	109	3	6	2	52	12	.81	6	.265	.341	.346
2011	2 Tms	NL	158	656	193	34	10	2	(2	0)	253	94	50	92	53	3	140	4	5	4	61	14	.81	6	.294	.349	.386
11	Hou	NL	105	429	130	26	7	1	(1	0)	173	64	32	66	38	2	90	3	2	1	39	7	.85	5	.303	.363	.403
11	Atl	NL	53	227	63	8	3	1	(1	0)	80	30	18	26	15	1	50	1	3	3	22	7	.76	1	.278	.321	.352
	Postseason		2	1	0	0	0	0	(0	0)	0	0	0	0	0	0	0	0	0	0	0	0	-	0	.000	.000	.000
	6 ML YEARS		716	2391	649	99	35	13	(8	5)	857	363	158	322	226	11	524	11	26	9	234	51	.82	17	.271	.336	.358

Michael Bowden

Pitches: R **Bats:** R **Pos:** RP-14   BOE-din   **Ht:** 6'3" **Wt:** 215 **Born:** 9/9/1986 **Age:** 25

Year	Team	Lg	G	GS	CG	GF	IP	BFP	H	R	ER	HR	SH	SF	HB	TBB	IBB	SO	WP	Bk	W	L	Pct	Sh	Sv-Op Hld	ERC	ERA
			HOW MUCH HE PITCHED						WHAT HE GAVE UP												THE RESULTS						
2011	Pwtckt*	AAA	41	0	0	35	52.2	219	43	19	16	5	2	0	1	18	1	61	1	0	3	3	.500	0	16--	2.84	2.73
2008	Bos	AL	1	1	0	0	5.0	22	7	2	2	0	0	0	0	1	0	3	0	0	1	0	1.000	0	0-0	4.92	3.60
2009	Bos	AL	8	1	0	3	16.0	75	23	17	17	3	0	0	0	6	0	12	3	0	1	1	.500	0	0-0	1	7.35	9.56
2010	Bos	AL	14	0	0	7	15.1	66	20	8	8	2	0	0	0	4	0	13	2	0	0	1	.000	0	0-0	0	5.73	4.70
2011	Bos	AL	14	0	0	9	20.0	90	19	9	9	3	0	0	0	11	0	17	3	0	0	0	-	0	0-0	0	4.65	4.05
	4 ML YEARS		37	2	0	19	56.1	253	69	36	36	8	0	0	0	22	0	45	8	0	2	2	.500	0	0-0	1	5.70	5.75

John Bowker

Bats: L **Throws:** L **Pos:** PH-28; 1B-2; RF-2   BAU-ker   **Ht:** 6'1" **Wt:** 203 **Born:** 7/8/1983 **Age:** 28

Year	Team	Lg	G	AB	H	2B	3B	HR	(Hm	Rd)	TB	R	RBI	RC	TBB	IBB	SO	HBP	SH	SF	SB	CS	SB%	GDP	Avg	OBP	Slg
											BATTING										BASERUNNING				AVERAGES		
2011	Indy*	AAA	106	421	129	27	1	15	(-	-)	203	56	76	70	27	1	73	1	0	2	2	3	.40	10	.306	.348	.482
2008	SF	NL	111	326	83	14	3	10	(6	4)	133	31	43	41	19	1	74	3	0	2	1	1	.50	7	.255	.300	.408
2009	SF	NL	31	67	13	2	2	2	(2	0)	25	7	7	4	4	0	18	1	0	1	1	0	1.00	1	.194	.247	.373
2010	2 Tms	NL	67	151	33	8	0	5	(2	3)	56	16	21	12	14	2	33	0	0	0	0	4	.00	4	.219	.281	.371
2011	2 Tms	NL	31	30	4	1	0	0	(0	0)	5	0	2	0	2	1	11	0	0	0	0	1	.00	0	.133	.188	.167
10	SF	NL	41	82	17	3	0	3	(0	3)	29	9	8	5	6	1	23	0	0	0	0	0	-	3	.207	.256	.354
10	Pit	NL	26	69	16	5	0	2	(2	0)	27	7	13	7	8	1	10	0	0	0	0	1	.00	1	.232	.312	.391
11	Pit	NL	19	17	4	1	0	0	(0	0)	5	0	2	0	2	1	4	0	0	0	0	1	.00	0	.235	.316	.294
11	Phi	NL	12	13	0	0	0	0	(0	0)	0	0	0	0	0	0	7	0	0	0	0	0	-	0	.000	.000	.000
	4 ML YEARS		240	574	133	25	5	17	(10	7)	219	54	73	57	39	4	136	4	0	5	2	6	.40	11	.232	.283	.382

Blaine Boyer

Pitches: R Bats: R Pos: RP-5

Ht: 6'3" Wt: 245 Born: 7/11/1981 Age: 30

Year	Team	Lg	G	GS	CG	GF	IP	BFP	H	R	ER	HR	SH	SF	HB	TBB	IBB	SO	WP	Bk	W	L	Pct	Sh	Sv-Op	Hld	ERC	ERA
2011	Indy*	AAA	11	0	0	2	8.0	49	14	14	12	3	0	0	1	9	0	8	2	0	0	0	-	0	0--	-	15.18	13.50
2011	PlmBh*	A+	3	3	0	0	10.2	41	6	6	6	1	0	0	0	3	0	11	0	0	1	1	.500	0	0--	-	1.50	5.06
2011	Memp*	AAA	4	4	0	0	16.0	87	34	26	24	5	1	3	1	9	0	5	1	0	0	2	.000	0	0--	-	15.31	13.50
2005	Atl	NL	43	0	0	5	37.2	158	32	13	13	1	1	1	2	17	0	33	2	0	4	2	.667	0	0-2	9	3.21	3.11
2006	Atl	NL	2	0	0	0	0.2	7	4	3	3	0	0	0	0	1	0	0	0	0	0	0	-	0	0-0	1	47.92	40.50
2007	Atl	NL	5	0	0	2	5.1	26	10	3	2	0	1	0	0	1	1	3	2	0	0	0	-	0	0-0	1	7.41	3.38
2008	Atl	NL	76	0	0	18	72.0	313	73	51	47	10	3	4	2	25	4	67	2	0	2	6	.250	0	1-5	14	4.19	5.88
2009	3 Tms	NL	48	0	0	21	54.2	241	56	36	25	1	4	1	5	20	0	29	2	0	2	2	.000	0	0-0	4	3.81	4.12
2010	Ari	NL	54	0	0	11	57.0	251	59	32	27	3	3	2	1	29	1	29	2	0	3	2	.600	0	0-4	5	4.45	4.26
2011	NYM	NL	5	0	0	3	6.2	33	13	8	8	2	1	0	1	1	0	1	0	0	0	2	.000	0	1-1	0	12.04	10.80
09	Atl	NL	3	0	0	1	1.1	11	3	6	6	0	0	0	1	3	0	2	0	0	0	1	.000	0	0-0	0	23.46	40.50
09	StL	NL	15	0	0	4	16.1	70	14	10	8	1	3	0	1	5	0	9	0	0	0	0	-	0	0-0	2	2.82	4.41
09	Ari	NL	30	0	0	16	37.0	160	39	20	11	0	1	1	3	12	0	18	2	0	0	1	.000	0	0-0	2	3.71	2.68
7 ML YEARS			233	0	0	60	234.0	1029	247	146	125	17	13	8	11	94	6	162	10	0	9	14	.391	0	2-12	34	4.35	4.81

Brad Brach

Pitches: R Bats: R Pos: RP-9

BROCK

Ht: 6'6" Wt: 210 Born: 4/12/1986 Age: 26

Year	Team	Lg	G	GS	CG	GF	IP	BFP	H	R	ER	HR	SH	SF	HB	TBB	IBB	SO	WP	Bk	W	L	Pct	Sh	Sv-Op	Hld	ERC	ERA
2008	Padres	R	18	0	0	11	22.1	94	21	5	5	0	3	0	2	5	0	33	2	0	1	1	.500	0	4--	-	2.73	2.01
2009	FtWyn	A	60	0	0	57	63.2	235	36	10	9	1	0	4	4	11	0	82	3	0	3	3	.500	0	33--	-	1.17	1.27
2010	Lk Els	A+	62	0	0	60	65.2	255	50	20	18	6	2	0	0	11	0	74	2	1	5	2	.714	0	41--	-	1.95	2.47
2011	SnAnt	AA	42	0	0	40	44.0	169	32	11	11	3	0	0	2	5	1	64	3	0	2	2	.500	0	23--	-	1.64	2.25
2011	Tucsn	AAA	25	0	0	22	27.2	118	28	13	12	1	4	0	0	7	1	30	4	0	1	3	.250	0	11--	-	3.02	3.90
2011	SD	NL	9	0	0	4	7.0	38	9	5	4	0	0	0	1	7	4	11	1	0	0	2	.000	0	0-0	0	6.51	5.14

Andrew Brackman

Pitches: R Bats: R Pos: RP-3

Ht: 6'10" Wt: 230 Born: 12/4/1985 Age: 26

Year	Team	Lg	G	GS	CG	GF	IP	BFP	H	R	ER	HR	SH	SF	HB	TBB	IBB	SO	WP	Bk	W	L	Pct	Sh	Sv-Op	Hld	ERC	ERA
2009	CtnSC	A	29	19	0	1	106.2	499	106	79	70	8	5	9	10	76	0	103	26	0	2	12	.143	0	0--	-	5.48	5.91
2010	Tampa	A+	12	12	0	0	60.0	258	67	38	34	5	2	1	5	9	0	56	6	0	5	4	.556	0	0--	-	3.91	5.10
2010	Trntn	AA	15	14	0	0	80.2	346	77	38	27	3	2	2	7	30	0	70	6	0	5	7	.417	0	0--	-	3.63	3.01
2011	S-WB	AAA	33	13	0	7	96.0	446	82	65	64	10	4	5	14	75	0	74	19	0	3	6	.333	0	1--	-	5.40	6.00
2011	NYY	AL	3	0	0	1	2.1	13	1	0	0	0	0	0	0	3	0	0	0	0	0	0	-	0	0-0	0	2.76	0.00

Zach Braddock

Pitches: L Bats: L Pos: RP-25

Ht: 6'2" Wt: 233 Born: 8/23/1987 Age: 24

Year	Team	Lg	G	GS	CG	GF	IP	BFP	H	R	ER	HR	SH	SF	HB	TBB	IBB	SO	WP	Bk	W	L	Pct	Sh	Sv-Op	Hld	ERC	ERA
2006	Helena	R+	14	8	0	0	39.1	175	32	26	24	3	2	0	1	31	0	33	3	0	2	2	.500	0	0--	-	4.54	5.49
2007	WV	A	10	9	0	0	47.0	183	28	6	6	1	0	0	1	15	0	68	0	0	3	1	.750	0	0--	-	1.47	1.15
2008	WV	A	2	2	0	0	6.0	24	2	1	0	0	0	0	0	3	0	13	0	0	0	0	-	0	0--	-	0.92	0.00
2008	BrvdCt	A+	21	11	0	3	65.1	295	55	44	40	7	2	1	7	42	0	80	6	3	4	7	.364	0	0--	-	4.59	5.51
2009	BrvdCt	A+	14	0	0	2	24.2	92	12	3	3	2	2	0	2	4	1	40	2	0	1	1	.500	0	0--	-	1.13	1.09
2009	Hntsvl	AA	12	0	0	2	15.2	68	16	9	5	2	2	1	1	3	0	22	0	0	2	1	.667	0	0--	-	3.66	2.87
2010	Nashv	AAA	11	0	0	4	16.0	69	10	8	8	1	2	1	2	9	0	28	2	0	0	0	-	0	1--	-	2.82	4.50
2011	Wisc	A	2	2	0	0	4.2	15	0	0	0	0	0	0	0	1	0	7	0	0	0	0	-	0	0--	-	0.05	0.00
2011	Nashv	AAA	6	0	0	4	5.2	28	4	3	3	0	0	1	0	7	0	10	2	0	0	0	-	0	1--	-	4.67	4.76
2010	Mil	NL	46	0	0	4	33.2	151	29	11	11	1	1	2	2	19	0	41	2	0	1	2	.333	0	0-2	15	3.56	2.94
2011	Mil	NL	25	0	0	4	17.1	82	16	15	14	2	0	2	2	11	1	18	2	0	0	1	.000	0	0-1	3	4.85	7.27
2 ML YEARS			71	0	0	8	51.0	233	45	26	25	3	1	4	4	30	1	59	4	0	1	3	.250	0	0-3	18	3.99	4.41

Dallas Braden

Pitches: L Bats: L Pos: SP-3

Ht: 6'1" Wt: 184 Born: 8/13/1983 Age: 28

Year	Team	Lg	G	GS	CG	GF	IP	BFP	H	R	ER	HR	SH	SF	HB	TBB	IBB	SO	WP	Bk	W	L	Pct	Sh	Sv-Op	Hld	ERC	ERA
2007	Oak	AL	20	14	0	1	72.1	332	91	59	54	9	4	0	2	26	1	55	6	1	1	8	.111	0	0-0	1	5.63	6.72
2008	Oak	AL	19	10	0	7	71.2	301	77	36	33	8	1	2	2	25	2	41	0	1	5	4	.556	0	0-0	4	4.63	4.14
2009	Oak	AL	22	22	0	0	136.2	589	144	63	59	9	4	4	2	42	2	81	1	0	8	9	.471	0	0-0	0	3.78	3.89
2010	Oak	AL	30	30	5	0	192.2	781	180	83	75	17	6	4	5	43	0	113	2	1	11	14	.440	2	0-0	0	3.11	3.50
2011	Oak	AL	3	3	0	0	18.0	73	18	7	6	2	0	0	0	5	0	15	0	0	1	1	.500	0	0-0	0	3.82	3.00
5 ML YEARS			94	79	5	8	491.1	2076	510	248	227	45	15	10	11	141	5	305	9	3	26	36	.419	2	0-0	1	3.89	4.16

Milton Bradley

Bats: B Throws: R Pos: LF-26; DH-1; PH-1

Ht: 6'0" Wt: 215 Born: 4/15/1978 Age: 34

| | | | BATTING | | | | | | | | | | | | | | | | | BASERUNNING | | | | AVERAGES | | |
Year	Team	Lg	G	AB	H	2B	3B	HR	(Hm	Rd)	TB	R	RBI	RC	TBB	IBB	SO	HBP	SH	SF	SB	CS	SB%	GDP	Avg	OBP	Slg
2000	Mon	NL	42	154	34	8	1	2	(1	1)	50	20	15	14	14	0	32	1	1	1	2	1	.67	3	.221	.288	.325
2001	2 Tms		77	238	53	17	3	1	(0	1)	79	22	19	21	21	0	65	1	2	0	8	5	.62	7	.223	.288	.332
2002	Cle	AL	98	325	81	18	3	9	(4	5)	132	48	38	40	32	2	58	0	1	0	6	3	.67	12	.249	.317	.406
2003	Cle	AL	101	377	121	34	2	10	(4	6)	189	61	56	77	64	8	73	5	0	5	17	7	.71	10	.321	.421	.501

Year	Team	Lg	G	AB	H	2B	3B	HR	(Hm	Rd)	TB	R	RBI	RC	TBB	IBB	SO	HBP	SH	SF	SB	CS	SB%	GDP	Avg	OBP	Slg
2004	LAD	NL	141	516	138	24	0	19	(8	11)	219	72	67	70	71	3	123	6	3	1	15	11	.58	12	.267	.362	.424
2005	LAD	NL	75	283	82	14	1	13	(6	7)	137	49	38	40	25	1	47	2	4	1	6	1	.86	6	.290	.350	.484
2006	Oak	AL	96	351	97	14	2	14	(7	7)	157	53	52	60	51	1	65	2	0	1	10	2	.83	13	.276	.370	.447
2007	2 Tms		61	209	64	9	1	13	(7	6)	114	37	37	42	31	3	41	3	0	1	5	2	.71	5	.306	.402	.545
2008	Tex	AL	126	414	133	32	1	22	(16	6)	233	78	77	90	80	13	112	9	0	6	5	3	.63	10	.321	**.436**	.563
2009	ChC	NL	124	393	101	17	1	12	(9	3)	156	61	40	56	66	4	95	11	2	1	2	3	.40	10	.257	.378	.397
2010	Sea	AL	73	244	50	9	1	8	(2	6)	85	28	29	23	28	2	75	3	1	2	8	2	.80	2	.205	.292	.348
2011	Sea	AL	28	101	22	6	1	2	(2	0)	36	12	13	11	13	1	31	1	0	0	4	0	1.00	1	.218	.313	.356
01	Mon	NL	67	220	49	16	3	1	(0	1)	74	19	19	20	19	0	62	1	2	0	7	4	.64	6	.223	.288	.336
01	Cle	AL	10	18	4	1	0	0	(0	0)	5	3	0	1	2	0	3	0	0	0	1	1	.50	1	.222	.300	.278
07	Oak	AL	19	65	19	4	0	2	(1	1)	29	6	7	10	8	1	14	1	0	1	2	1	.67	2	.292	.373	.446
07	SD	NL	42	144	45	5	1	11	(6	5)	85	31	30	32	23	2	27	2	0	0	3	1	.75	3	.313	.414	.590
	Postseason		11	42	13	3	0	4	(3	1)	28	6	8	7	5	0	5	0	0	0	2	0	1.00	3	.310	.383	.667
	12 ML YEARS		1042	3605	976	202	17	125	(66	59)	1587	541	481	544	496	38	817	44	14	19	88	40	.69	91	.271	.364	.440

Michael Brantley

Bats: L Throws: L Pos: LF-66; CF-52; DH-3; PR-2; PH-1 Ht: 6'2" Wt: 200 Born: 5/15/1987 Age: 25

Year	Team	Lg	G	AB	H	2B	3B	HR	(Hm	Rd)	TB	R	RBI	RC	TBB	IBB	SO	HBP	SH	SF	SB	CS	SB%	GDP	Avg	OBP	Slg
2009	Cle	AL	28	112	35	4	0	0	(0	0)	39	10	11	16	8	0	19	0	1	0	4	4	.50	3	.313	.358	.348
2010	Cle	AL	72	297	73	9	3	3	(2	1)	97	38	22	32	22	0	38	0	4	2	10	2	.83	6	.246	.296	.327
2011	Cle	AL	114	451	120	24	4	7	(4	3)	173	63	46	56	34	2	76	3	3	5	13	5	.72	11	.266	.318	.384
	3 ML YEARS		214	860	228	37	7	10	(6	4)	309	111	79	104	64	2	133	3	8	7	27	11	.71	20	.265	.316	.359

Russell Branyan

Bats: L Throws: R Pos: PH-34; 1B-25; DH-13; 3B-2   BRAN-yenn Ht: 6'3" Wt: 230 Born: 12/19/1975 Age: 36

Year	Team	Lg	G	AB	H	2B	3B	HR	(Hm	Rd)	TB	R	RBI	RC	TBB	IBB	SO	HBP	SH	SF	SB	CS	SB%	GDP	Avg	OBP	Slg
1998	Cle	AL	1	4	0	0	0	0	(0	0)	0	0	0	0	0	0	2	0	0	0	0	0	-	0	.000	.000	.000
1999	Cle	AL	11	38	8	2	0	1	(0	1)	13	4	6	4	3	0	19	1	0	0	0	0	-	0	.211	.286	.342
2000	Cle	AL	67	193	46	7	2	16	(13	3)	105	32	38	34	22	1	76	4	0	1	0	0	-	2	.238	.327	.544
2001	Cle	AL	113	315	73	16	2	20	(11	9)	153	48	54	50	38	1	132	3	0	5	1	1	.50	2	.232	.316	.486
2002	2 Tms		134	378	86	13	1	24	(5	19)	173	50	56	49	51	3	151	2	0	4	4	3	.57	5	.228	.320	.458
2003	Cin	NL	74	176	38	12	0	9	(7	2)	77	22	26	23	27	0	69	1	0	1	0	0	-	1	.216	.322	.438
2004	Mil	NL	51	158	37	11	1	11	(8	3)	83	21	27	23	20	0	68	2	0	2	1	0	1.00	3	.234	.324	.525
2005	Mil	NL	85	202	52	11	0	12	(3	9)	99	23	31	38	39	10	80	0	1	0	1	0	1.00	1	.257	.378	.490
2006	2 Tms		91	241	55	11	0	18	(9	9)	120	37	36	34	34	1	89	3	1	3	2	0	1.00	3	.228	.327	.498
2007	3 Tms	NL	89	163	32	5	1	10	(6	4)	69	24	20	28	28	1	69	2	0	1	1	0	1.00	1	.196	.320	.423
2008	Mil	NL	50	132	33	8	0	12	(9	3)	77	24	20	22	19	4	42	0	0	1	1	0	1.00	0	.250	.342	.583
2009	Sea	AL	116	431	108	21	1	31	(16	15)	224	64	76	69	58	6	149	9	1	6	2	0	1.00	6	.251	.347	.520
2010	2 Tms	AL	109	376	89	19	0	25	(7	18)	183	47	57	45	46	3	131	3	1	2	1	0	1.00	5	.237	.323	.487
2011	2 Tms		68	127	25	7	0	5	(3	2)	47	11	14	13	18	0	41	0	0	1	2	0	1.00	1	.197	.295	.370
02	Cle	AL	50	161	33	4	0	8	(1	7)	61	16	17	14	17	0	65	0	0	2	1	2	.33	3	.205	.278	.379
02	Cin	NL	84	217	53	9	1	16	(4	12)	112	34	39	35	34	3	86	2	0	2	3	1	.75	2	.244	.349	.516
06	TB	AL	64	169	34	10	0	12	(7	5)	80	23	27	22	19	0	62	2	1	2	2	0	1.00	1	.201	.286	.473
06	SD	NL	27	72	21	1	0	6	(2	4)	40	14	9	12	15	1	27	1	0	1	0	0	-	0	.292	.416	.556
07	SD	NL	61	122	24	5	1	7	(5	2)	52	16	19	18	21	1	48	2	0	1	1	0	1.00	1	.197	.322	.426
07	Phi	NL	7	9	2	0	0	2	(0	2)	8	2	5	2	0	0	6	0	0	0	0	0	-	0	.222	.222	.889
07	StL	NL	21	32	6	0	0	1	(1	0)	9	4	2	3	7	0	15	0	0	1	0	0	-	1	.188	.333	.281
10	Cle	AL	52	171	45	9	0	10	(1	9)	84	24	24	23	16	1	49	1	1	1	0	0	-	2	.263	.328	.491
10	Sea	AL	57	205	44	10	0	15	(6	9)	99	23	33	22	30	2	82	2	0	1	1	0	1.00	3	.215	.319	.483
11	Ari	NL	31	62	13	5	0	1	(1	0)	21	4	2	7	7	0	20	0	0	0	0	0	-	0	.210	.290	.339
11	LAA	AL	37	65	12	2	0	4	(2	2)	26	7	12	10	11	0	21	0	0	1	2	0	1.00	2	.185	.299	.400
	Postseason		6	16	4	1	1	0	(0	0)	7	2	3	1	1	0	6	0	0	0	0	0	-	0	.250	.294	.438
	14 ML YEARS		1059	2934	682	143	8	194	(97	97)	1423	405	467	427	403	30	1118	30	4	27	16	4	.80	31	.232	.329	.485

Ryan Braun

Bats: R Throws: R Pos: LF-147; PH-3; DH-1 Ht: 6'1" Wt: 210 Born: 11/17/1983 Age: 28

Year	Team	Lg	G	AB	H	2B	3B	HR	(Hm	Rd)	TB	R	RBI	RC	TBB	IBB	SO	HBP	SH	SF	SB	CS	SB%	GDP	Avg	OBP	Slg
2007	Mil	NL	113	451	146	26	6	34	(17	17)	286	91	97	94	29	1	112	7	0	5	15	5	.75	13	.324	.370	**.634**
2008	Mil	NL	151	611	174	39	7	37	(23	14)	338	92	106	100	42	4	129	6	0	4	14	4	.78	13	.285	.335	.553
2009	Mil	NL	158	635	**203**	39	6	32	(15	17)	350	113	114	133	57	1	121	13	0	3	20	6	.77	7	.320	.386	.551
2010	Mil	NL	157	619	188	45	6	25	(13	12)	310	101	103	104	56	1	105	6	0	3	14	3	.82	17	.304	.365	.501
2011	Mil	NL	150	563	187	38	6	33	(16	17)	336	109	111	124	58	2	93	5	0	3	33	6	.85	9	.332	.397	**.597**
	Postseason		4	16	5	2	0	0	(0	0)	7	0	2	2	0	0	4	0	0	1	0	0	-	0	.313	.294	.438
	5 ML YEARS		729	2879	898	187	26	161	(84	77)	1620	506	531	555	242	9	560	37	0	18	96	24	.80	59	.312	.371	.563

Bill Bray

Pitches: L Bats: L Pos: RP-79 Ht: 6'3" Wt: 226 Born: 6/5/1983 Age: 29

			HOW MUCH HE PITCHED						WHAT HE GAVE UP												THE RESULTS						
Year	Team	Lg	G	GS	CG	GF	IP	BFP	H	R	ER	HR	SH	SF	HB	TBB	IBB	SO	WP	Bk	W	L	Pct	Sh	Sv-Op	Hld	ERC	ERA
2006	2 Tms	NL	48	0	0	10	50.2	223	57	27	26	5	2	1	1	18	3	39	0	0	3	2	.600	0	2-3	3	4.58	4.09
2007	Cin	NL	19	0	0	5	14.1	63	16	10	10	1	0	1	0	5	1	14	0	0	3	3	.500	0	1-1	3	4.16	6.28
2008	Cin	NL	63	0	0	6	47.0	215	50	19	15	4	3	1	1	24	5	54	2	0	2	2	.500	0	0-4	9	4.57	2.87
2010	Cin	NL	35	0	0	4	28.1	117	21	13	13	4	1	0	0	10	1	30	2	0	2	0	.000	0	0-0	2	2.66	4.13
2011	Cin	NL	79	0	0	11	48.1	196	35	16	16	3	1	3	2	17	3	44	1	0	5	3	.625	0	0-3	20	2.28	2.98

Year	Team	Lg	G	GS	CG	GF	IP	BFP	H	R	ER	HR	SH	SF	HB	TBB	IBB	SO	WP	Bk	W	L	Pct	Sh	Sv-Op	Hld	ERC	ERA
06	Was	NL	19	0	0	4	23.0	100	24	11	10	2	1	1	1	9	2	16	0	0	1	1	.500	0	0-0	1	4.25	3.91
06	Cin	NL	29	0	0	6	27.2	123	33	16	13	3	1	0	0	9	1	23	0	0	2	1	.667	0	2-3	2	4.85	4.23
	Postseason		2	0	0	1	1.2	5	0	0	0	0	0	0	0	0	0	2	0	0	0	0	-	0	0-0	0	0.00	0.00
5 ML YEARS			244	0	0	41	188.2	814	179	85	77	17	7	6	4	74	13	181	5	0	13	12	.520	0	3-11	37	3.62	3.67

Yhency Brazoban

Pitches: R **Bats:** R **Pos:** RP-6

YEN-see BRAZ-ah-bonn　　　　　**Ht:** 6'1" **Wt:** 250 **Born:** 11/6/1980 **Age:** 31

Year	Team	Lg	G	GS	CG	GF	IP	BFP	H	R	ER	HR	SH	SF	HB	TBB	IBB	SO	WP	Bk	W	L	Pct	Sh	Sv-Op	Hld	ERC	ERA
2011	RdRck*	AAA	15	0	0	4	26.1	114	23	12	10	5	2	1	0	11	0	31	2	1	3	0	1.000	0	1- -	-	3.93	3.42
2011	Reno*	AAA	8	0	0	5	10.0	40	8	3	3	1	0	0	0	3	0	11	0	0	1	1	.500	0	1- -	-	2.67	2.70
2004	LAD	NL	31	0	0	10	32.2	133	25	9	9	2	4	0	0	15	2	27	1	0	6	2	.750	0	0-0	5	2.76	2.48
2005	LAD	NL	74	0	0	44	72.2	317	70	46	43	11	7	2	5	32	4	61	1	0	4	10	.286	0	21-27	8	4.60	5.33
2006	LAD	NL	5	0	0	2	5.0	23	7	3	3	0	0	1	0	2	0	4	1	0	0	0	-	0	0-1	0	5.74	5.40
2007	LAD	NL	4	0	0	1	1.2	12	3	4	3	0	0	0	0	3	1	5	0	0	0	0	-	0	0-0	0	11.51	16.20
2008	LAD	NL	2	0	0	1	3.0	16	4	2	2	0	0	0	0	3	0	3	1	0	0	0	-	0	0-0	0	7.51	6.00
2011	Ari	NL	6	0	0	1	6.0	31	8	4	4	1	0	0	1	4	1	8	0	1	0	0	-	0	0-1	2	8.01	6.00
	Postseason		2	0	0	1	3.0	13	1	1	1	0	0	0	1	2	0	2	0	0	0	0	-	0	0-0	0	2.02	3.00
6 ML YEARS			122	0	0	59	121.0	532	117	68	64	14	11	3	6	59	8	108	4	1	10	12	.455	0	21-29	15	4.45	4.76

Craig Breslow

Pitches: L **Bats:** L **Pos:** RP-67

　　　　　Ht: 5'11" **Wt:** 190 **Born:** 8/8/1980 **Age:** 31

Year	Team	Lg	G	GS	CG	GF	IP	BFP	H	R	ER	HR	SH	SF	HB	TBB	IBB	SO	WP	Bk	W	L	Pct	Sh	Sv-Op	Hld	ERC	ERA
2005	SD	NL	14	0	0	3	16.1	78	15	6	4	1	0	1	1	13	0	14	1	0	0	0	-	0	0-0	1	4.98	2.20
2006	Bos	AL	13	0	0	3	12.0	55	12	5	5	0	0	2	1	6	1	12	2	1	0	2	.000	0	0-0	3	3.78	3.75
2008	2 Tms	AL	49	0	0	13	47.0	189	34	12	10	1	2	0	0	19	2	39	4	1	0	2	.000	0	1-2	5	2.12	1.91
2009	2 Tms	AL	77	0	0	9	69.2	281	48	31	26	8	4	1	3	29	0	55	3	1	8	7	.533	0	0-2	15	2.79	3.36
2010	Oak	AL	75	0	0	23	74.2	304	53	26	25	9	2	0	0	29	4	71	0	1	4	4	.500	0	5-7	16	2.53	3.01
2011	Oak	AL	67	0	0	10	59.1	261	69	29	25	4	3	2	2	21	1	44	3	0	0	2	.000	0	0-3	8	4.74	3.79
08	Cle	AL	7	0	0	3	8.1	40	10	3	3	1	0	0	0	5	0	7	0	0	0	0	-	0	0-0	0	6.09	3.24
08	Min	AL	42	0	0	10	38.2	149	24	9	7	0	2	0	0	14	2	32	4	1	0	2	.000	0	1-2	5	1.49	1.63
09	Min	AL	17	0	0	5	14.1	64	11	11	10	3	2	0	1	11	0	11	3	0	1	2	.333	0	0-0	2	5.38	6.28
09	Oak	AL	60	0	0	4	55.1	217	37	20	16	5	2	1	2	18	0	44	0	1	7	5	.583	0	0-2	13	2.21	2.60
6 ML YEARS			295	0	0	61	279.0	1168	231	109	95	23	11	6	7	117	8	235	13	4	12	17	.414	0	6-14	48	3.16	3.06

Reid Brignac

Bats: L **Throws:** R **Pos:** SS-91; PR-1

BRINN-yak　　　　　**Ht:** 6'3" **Wt:** 195 **Born:** 1/16/1986 **Age:** 26

Year	Team	Lg	G	AB	H	2B	3B	HR	(Hm	Rd)	TB	R	RBI	RC	TBB	IBB	SO	HBP	SH	SF	SB	CS	SB%	GDP	Avg	OBP	Slg
2011	Drhm*	AAA	11	39	9	2	1	1	(-	-)	16	7	4	5	7	0	6	0	2	0	0	1	.00	0	.231	.348	.410
2008	TB	AL	4	10	0	0	0	0	(0	0)	0	1	0	0	1	0	5	0	0	0	0	0	-	0	.000	.091	.000
2009	TB	AL	31	90	25	8	2	1	(0	1)	40	10	6	10	3	0	20	0	0	0	2	2	.50	1	.278	.301	.444
2010	TB	AL	113	301	77	13	1	8	(3	5)	116	39	45	38	20	3	75	3	0	2	3	3	.50	6	.256	.307	.385
2011	TB	AL	92	249	48	4	0	1	(0	1)	55	18	15	8	10	1	63	1	4	0	3	1	.75	2	.193	.227	.221
	Postseason		2	3	0	0	0	0	(0	0)	0	0	0	0	0	0	3	0	0	0	0	0	-	0	.000	.000	.000
4 ML YEARS			240	650	150	25	3	10	(3	7)	211	68	66	56	34	4	165	4	4	2	8	6	.57	9	.231	.272	.325

Zach Britton

Pitches: L **Bats:** L **Pos:** SP-28

　　　　　Ht: 6'3" **Wt:** 195 **Born:** 12/22/1987 **Age:** 24

Year	Team	Lg	G	GS	CG	GF	IP	BFP	H	R	ER	HR	SH	SF	HB	TBB	IBB	SO	WP	Bk	W	L	Pct	Sh	Sv-Op	Hld	ERC	ERA
2006	Bluefld	R	11	11	0	0	34.0	153	35	22	20	4	1	1	2	20	0	21	5	0	0	4	.000	0	0- -	-	5.47	5.29
2007	Abrdn	A-	15	15	0	0	63.2	278	64	33	26	1	0	1	5	22	0	45	4	0	6	4	.600	0	0- -	-	3.56	3.68
2008	Dlmrva	A	27	27	1	0	147.1	605	118	68	51	9	6	4	6	49	0	114	13	0	12	7	.632	0	0- -	-	2.66	3.12
2009	Frdrck	A+	25	24	0	0	140.0	599	123	64	42	6	3	1	9	55	0	131	21	0	9	6	.600	0	0- -	-	3.21	2.70
2010	Bowie	AA	15	14	0	0	87.0	363	76	33	24	4	3	0	1	28	1	68	10	0	7	3	.700	0	0- -	-	2.84	2.48
2010	Norfolk	AAA	12	12	0	0	66.1	281	63	31	22	3	0	0	1	23	0	56	8	0	3	4	.429	0	0- -	-	3.27	2.98
2011	Bowie	AA	3	3	0	0	11.2	52	14	11	7	3	0	0	1	2	0	15	1	1	0	2	.000	0	0- -	-	5.66	5.40
2011	Norfolk	AAA	1	1	0	0	5.0	18	3	1	1	0	0	0	0	1	0	3	0	0	1	0	1.000	0	0- -	-	1.17	1.80
2011	Bal	AL	28	28	0	0	154.1	666	162	93	79	12	8	7	1	62	3	97	7	0	11	11	.500	0	0-0	0	4.24	4.61

Brian Broderick

Pitches: R **Bats:** R **Pos:** RP-11

　　　　　Ht: 6'6" **Wt:** 205 **Born:** 9/1/1986 **Age:** 25

Year	Team	Lg	G	GS	CG	GF	IP	BFP	H	R	ER	HR	SH	SF	HB	TBB	IBB	SO	WP	Bk	W	L	Pct	Sh	Sv-Op	Hld	ERC	ERA
2007	JhsCty	R+	8	5	0	1	36.0	145	31	12	7	3	1	0	2	4	0	23	0	0	2	2	.500	0	0- -	-	2.33	1.75
2007	Batvia	A-	8	4	0	1	31.0	126	31	13	12	5	0	0	0	3	0	30	1	0	1	1	.500	0	0- -	-	3.24	3.48
2008	QuadC	A	19	12	0	4	81.0	347	98	45	42	5	2	5	1	12	0	38	2	0	3	6	.333	0	3- -	-	4.02	4.67
2009	PlmBh	A+	21	19	0	1	109.1	473	136	62	56	4	2	2	6	17	0	64	1	0	9	7	.563	0	0- -	-	4.27	4.61
2009	Sprgfld	AA	7	5	0	0	29.0	135	43	27	19	4	2	1	0	8	0	12	1	0	0	5	.000	0	0- -	-	6.74	5.90
2010	PlmBh	A+	9	9	0	0	49.1	223	63	32	30	3	1	2	5	11	0	37	3	0	3	5	.375	0	0- -	-	5.04	5.47
2010	Sprgfld	AA	17	15	2	0	100.2	410	96	42	31	6	3	2	5	14	0	55	0	0	11	2	.846	1	0- -	-	2.76	2.77
2011	Memp	AAA	22	15	0	2	91.0	408	121	56	51	11	4	6	3	21	1	45	2	0	7	7	.500	0	0- -	-	5.59	5.04
2011	Was	NL	11	0	0	3	12.1	57	16	9	9	0	4	1	1	2	0	4	1	1	0	1	.000	0	0-0	0	5.00	6.57

Rex Brothers

Pitches: L Bats: L Pos: RP-48   Ht: 6'0" Wt: 205 Born: 12/18/1987 Age: 24

		HOW MUCH HE PITCHED							WHAT HE GAVE UP											THE RESULTS							
Year	Team	Lg	G	GS	CG	GF	IP	BFP	H	R	ER	HR	SH	SF	HB	TBB	IBB	SO	WP	Bk	W	L	Pct	Sh	Sv-Op	Hld	ERC	ERA
2009	TriCity	A-	8	0	0	2	10.2	44	10	4	4	0	0	0	0	5	0	18	0	0	2	0	1.000	0	0- -	-	3.46	3.38
2009	Ashvll	A	9	0	0	2	10.2	41	6	4	4	1	0	0	2	3	0	10	0	0	0	0	-	0	0- -	-	2.14	3.38
2010	Mdest	A+	33	0	0	12	37.0	147	20	14	11	0	4	3	0	19	1	43	8	1	0	2	.000	0	3- -	-	1.57	2.68
2010	Tulsa	AA	24	0	0	8	23.0	101	14	13	10	2	2	1	1	18	1	27	2	0	2	1	.667	0	4- -	-	3.35	3.91
2011	ColSpr	AAA	25	0	0	9	28.0	126	29	10	9	2	1	1	0	15	1	45	2	0	3	2	.600	0	0- -	-	4.50	2.89
2011	Col	NL	48	0	0	6	40.2	172	33	14	13	4	0	0	0	20	2	59	2	0	1	2	.333	0	1-3	16	3.31	2.88

Andrew Brown

Bats: R Throws: R Pos: RF-7; PH-5   Ht: 6'0" Wt: 185 Born: 9/10/1984 Age: 27

								BATTING													BASERUNNING				AVERAGES		
Year	Team	Lg	G	AB	H	2B	3B	HR	(Hm	Rd)	TB	R	RBI	RC	TBB	IBB	SO	HBP	SH	SF	SB	CS	SB%	GDP	Avg	OBP	Slg
2007	Batvia	A-	66	239	57	14	7	7	(-	-)	106	34	40	36	31	1	52	3	0	3	1	2	.33	6	.238	.330	.444
2008	QuadC	A	34	117	32	10	0	5	(-	-)	57	18	23	21	17	0	30	1	0	1	0	1	.00	3	.274	.368	.487
2008	PlmBh	A+	24	88	29	8	0	4	(-	-)	49	14	15	19	11	0	25	1	0	0	0	0	-	2	.330	.410	.557
2008	Sprgfld	AA	68	247	62	14	0	12	(-	-)	112	36	38	39	30	1	81	4	0	1	1	0	1.00	11	.251	.340	.453
2009	Sprgfld	AA	74	263	75	11	2	13	(-	-)	129	40	42	49	31	2	49	6	0	2	1	0	1.00	5	.285	.371	.490
2009	Cards	R	1	3	2	0	0	0	(-	-)	2	1	0	1	0	0	0	0	0	0	0	0	-	0	.667	.667	.667
2009	PlmBh	A+	4	11	2	1	1	0	(-	-)	5	1	2	1	2	0	4	1	0	0	0	0	-	0	.182	.357	.455
2010	Sprgfld	AA	98	361	105	17	1	22	(-	-)	190	65	63	70	41	3	98	5	0	0	1	2	.33	11	.291	.371	.526
2011	Memp	AAA	107	359	102	12	3	20	(-	-)	180	67	73	71	56	1	105	5	1	7	4	4	.50	6	.284	.382	.501
2011	StL	NL	11	22	4	1	0	0	(0	0)	5	1	3	1	0	0	8	0	0	0	0	0	-	1	.182	.182	.227

Corey Brown

Bats: L Throws: L Pos: PH-3   Ht: 6'2" Wt: 210 Born: 11/26/1985 Age: 26

								BATTING													BASERUNNING				AVERAGES		
Year	Team	Lg	G	AB	H	2B	3B	HR	(Hm	Rd)	TB	R	RBI	RC	TBB	IBB	SO	HBP	SH	SF	SB	CS	SB%	GDP	Avg	OBP	Slg
2007	Vancvr	A-	59	213	57	18	4	11	(-	-)	116	31	48	45	37	0	77	3	0	3	5	3	.63	2	.268	.379	.545
2008	Kane	A	85	300	81	18	2	14	(-	-)	145	44	49	56	41	1	96	3	3	4	12	0	1.00	0	.270	.359	.483
2008	Stcktn	AA	49	196	51	9	0	16	(-	-)	108	34	34	35	17	0	72	1	0	0	4	1	.80	1	.260	.322	.551
2009	Mdland	AA	66	250	67	20	4	9	(-	-)	122	46	43	43	27	0	69	4	0	0	5	2	.71	5	.268	.349	.488
2010	Scrmto	AAA	41	135	26	4	3	5	(-	-)	51	21	20	20	11	1	36	0	2	0	3	1	.75	1	.193	.253	.378
2010	Mdland	AA	90	331	106	14	8	10	(-	-)	166	63	49	73	52	1	93	2	0	1	19	1	.95	5	.320	.415	.502
2011	Syrcse	AAA	124	396	93	18	3	14	(-	-)	159	50	39	53	47	1	134	7	11	1	4	7	.36	1	.235	.326	.402
2011	Was	NL	3	3	0	0	0	0	(0	0)	0	0	0	0	0	0	2	0	0	0	0	0	-	0	.000	.000	.000

Domonic Brown

Bats: L Throws: L Pos: RF-52; PH-5; PR-1   Ht: 6'5" Wt: 200 Born: 9/3/1987 Age: 24

								BATTING													BASERUNNING				AVERAGES		
Year	Team	Lg	G	AB	H	2B	3B	HR	(Hm	Rd)	TB	R	RBI	RC	TBB	IBB	SO	HBP	SH	SF	SB	CS	SB%	GDP	Avg	OBP	Slg
2006	Phillies	R	34	117	25	3	0	1	(-	-)	31	13	7	10	12	0	30	1	1	0	13	3	.81	2	.214	.292	.265
2007	Clrwtr	A+	3	9	4	1	0	1	(-	-)	8	2	7	3	2	0	0	0	0	0	0	0	-	0	.444	.545	.889
2007	Wmspt	A-	74	285	84	11	5	3	(-	-)	114	43	32	43	27	0	49	2	0	3	14	7	.67	1	.295	.356	.400
2008	Lakwd	A	114	444	129	23	3	9	(-	-)	185	77	54	76	64	4	72	4	0	4	22	7	.76	11	.291	.382	.417
2009	Clrwtr	A+	66	238	72	12	3	11	(-	-)	123	41	44	48	34	3	48	2	0	6	15	8	.65	3	.303	.386	.517
2009	Phillies	R	3	10	5	0	2	0	(-	-)	9	4	0	3	1	0	1	1	0	0	0	1	.00	0	.500	.583	.900
2009	Rdng	AA	37	147	41	9	4	3	(-	-)	67	20	20	24	14	3	37	1	0	0	8	1	.89	3	.279	.346	.456
2010	Rdng	AA	65	236	75	16	3	15	(-	-)	142	50	47	54	29	2	51	2	0	4	12	6	.67	2	.318	.391	.602
2010	LV	AAA	28	107	37	6	1	5	(-	-)	60	15	21	23	8	0	23	1	0	2	5	1	.83	4	.346	.390	.561
2011	Clrwtr	A+	5	19	7	1	0	2	(-	-)	14	4	4	5	2	1	3	0	0	0	0	0	-	1	.368	.429	.737
2011	LV	AAA	41	138	36	6	0	3	(-	-)	51	22	15	24	28	0	33	4	0	4	12	4	.75	3	.261	.391	.370
2010	Phi	NL	35	62	13	3	0	2	(2	0)	22	8	13	5	5	1	24	0	0	3	2	1	.67	1	.210	.257	.355
2011	Phi	NL	56	184	45	10	1	5	(4	1)	72	28	19	21	25	1	35	0	0	1	3	1	.75	2	.245	.333	.391
	Postseason		3	3	0	0	0	0	(0	0)	0	1	0	0	0	0	0	0	0	0	0	0	-	0	.000	.000	.000
	2 ML YEARS		91	246	58	13	1	7	(6	1)	94	36	32	26	30	2	59	0	0	4	5	2	.71	3	.236	.314	.382

Dusty Brown

Bats: R Throws: R Pos: C-10; PH-1   Ht: 6'0" Wt: 180 Born: 6/19/1982 Age: 30

								BATTING													BASERUNNING				AVERAGES		
Year	Team	Lg	G	AB	H	2B	3B	HR	(Hm	Rd)	TB	R	RBI	RC	TBB	IBB	SO	HBP	SH	SF	SB	CS	SB%	GDP	Avg	OBP	Slg
2011	Indy*	AAA	55	172	49	17	0	7	(-	-)	87	18	28	32	22	2	35	2	0	3	0	2	.00	4	.285	.367	.506
2009	Bos	AL	7	3	1	0	0	1	(1	0)	4	1	1	1	1	0	0	0	0	0	0	0	-	0	.333	.500	1.333
2010	Bos	AL	7	12	3	1	0	0	(0	0)	4	0	2	1	0	0	2	0	0	0	0	0	-	1	.250	.250	.333
2011	Pit	NL	11	28	3	0	0	0	(0	0)	3	2	0	0	1	0	10	0	1	0	1	0	1.00	0	.107	.138	.107
	3 ML YEARS		25	43	7	1	0	1	(1	0)	11	3	3	2	2	0	12	0	1	0	1	0	1.00	1	.163	.200	.256

Jonathan Broxton

Pitches: R **Bats:** R **Pos:** RP-14 **Ht:** 6'4" **Wt:** 300 **Born:** 6/16/1984 **Age:** 28

				HOW MUCH HE PITCHED				WHAT HE GAVE UP											THE RESULTS					
Year	Team	Lg	G	GS	CG	GF	IP	BFP	H	R	ER	HR	SH	SF	HB	TBB	IBB	SO	WP	Bk	W	L	Pct	Sh	Sv-Op Hld	ERC	ERA
2011	Albq*	AAA	2	2	0	0	2.0	9	2	1	1	0	0	0	0	1	0	5	0	0	0	0	-	0	0- -	3.63	4.50
2005	LAD	NL	14	0	0	5	13.2	68	13	11	9	0	0	2	1	12	2	22	2	0	1	0	1.000	0	0-1 1	4.65	5.93
2006	LAD	NL	68	0	0	20	76.1	320	61	25	22	7	3	1	1	33	6	97	7	0	4	1	.800	0	3-7 12	2.97	2.59
2007	LAD	NL	83	0	0	18	82.0	334	69	30	26	6	0	1	1	25	3	99	4	0	4	4	.500	0	2-8 32	2.71	2.85
2008	LAD	NL	70	0	0	32	69.0	285	54	29	24	2	3	3	3	27	5	88	3	0	3	5	.375	0	14-22 13	2.48	3.13
2009	LAD	NL	73	0	0	58	76.0	300	44	24	22	4	0	3	1	29	1	114	2	0	7	2	.778	0	36-42 1	1.65	2.61
2010	LAD	NL	64	0	0	46	62.1	271	64	30	28	4	3	1	2	28	5	73	1	0	5	6	.455	0	22-29 3	4.21	4.04
2011	LAD	NL	14	0	0	12	12.2	62	15	10	8	2	0	0	0	9	2	10	0	0	1	2	.333	0	7-8 0	6.47	5.68
	Postseason		13	0	0	10	14.1	64	14	7	7	1	0	0	1	6	0	15	0	0	0	2	.000	0	3-5 0	3.97	4.40
	7 ML YEARS		386	0	0	191	392.0	1640	320	159	139	25	9	11	9	163	24	503	19	0	25	20	.556	0	84-117 62	2.89	3.19

Jay Bruce

Bats: L **Throws:** L **Pos:** RF-155; PH-4 **Ht:** 6'3" **Wt:** 226 **Born:** 4/3/1987 **Age:** 25

							BATTING													BASERUNNING				AVERAGES		
Year	Team	Lg	G	AB	H	2B	3B	HR	(Hm	Rd)	TB	R	RBI	RC	TBB	IBB	SO	HBP	SH	SF	SB	CS	SB%	GDP	Avg	OBP	Slg
2008	Cin	NL	108	413	105	17	1	21	(13	8)	187	63	52	49	33	1	110	4	0	2	4	6	.40	8	.254	.314	.453
2009	Cin	NL	101	345	77	15	2	22	(13	9)	162	47	58	47	38	2	75	2	1	1	3	3	.50	5	.223	.303	.470
2010	Cin	NL	148	509	143	23	5	25	(19	6)	251	80	70	71	58	5	136	1	0	5	5	4	.56	12	.281	.353	.493
2011	Cin	NL	157	585	150	27	2	32	(16	16)	277	84	97	96	71	14	158	5	1	2	8	7	.53	8	.256	.341	.474
	Postseason		3	8	2	0	0	1	(0	1)	5	1	1	1	2	0	0	0	0	0	0	0	-	0	.250	.400	.625
	4 ML YEARS		514	1852	475	82	10	100	(61	39)	877	274	277	263	200	22	479	12	2	10	20	20	.50	33	.256	.331	.474

Brian Bruney

Pitches: R **Bats:** R **Pos:** RP-23 BRUE-nee **Ht:** 6'3" **Wt:** 235 **Born:** 2/17/1982 **Age:** 30

						HOW MUCH HE PITCHED				WHAT HE GAVE UP									THE RESULTS						
Year	Team	Lg	G	GS	CG	GF	IP	BFP	H	R	ER	HR	SH	SF	HB	TBB	IBB	SO	WP	Bk	W	L	Pct	Sh	Sv-Op Hld	ERC	ERA
2011	Charltt*	AAA	19	0	0	18	20.2	84	12	3	3	0	0	0	1	9	0	30	0	0	1	0	1.000	0	7- -	1.63	1.31
2004	Ari	NL	30	0	0	14	31.1	135	20	16	15	2	1	0	1	27	5	34	2	0	3	4	.429	0	0-1 3	3.54	4.31
2005	Ari	NL	47	0	0	21	46.0	230	56	39	38	6	2	1	5	35	2	51	2	0	1	3	.250	0	12-16 4	7.48	7.43
2006	NYY	AL	19	0	0	2	20.2	90	14	2	2	1	0	0	1	15	0	25	2	0	1	1	.500	0	0-0 4	3.37	0.87
2007	NYY	AL	58	0	0	16	50.0	228	44	28	26	5	1	6	3	37	2	39	4	0	3	2	.600	0	0-2 6	4.92	4.68
2008	NYY	AL	32	1	0	5	34.1	137	18	7	7	2	0	2	1	16	0	33	1	0	3	0	1.000	0	1-2 12	1.75	1.83
2009	NYY	AL	44	0	0	6	39.0	175	36	17	17	6	2	1	1	23	3	36	2	0	5	0	1.000	0	0-1 14	4.71	3.92
2010	Was	NL	19	0	0	6	17.2	93	21	18	15	1	3	2	0	20	1	16	1	0	1	2	.333	0	0-0 3	7.65	7.64
2011	CWS	AL	23	0	0	6	19.2	93	26	15	15	4	3	1	0	12	0	16	0	0	1	0	1.000	0	0-0 5	7.95	6.86
	Postseason		4	0	0	1	3.0	18	4	3	3	1	0	0	1	0	0	4	0	0	0	0	-	0	0-0 0	5.82	9.00
	8 ML YEARS		272	1	0	76	258.2	1181	235	142	135	27	12	13	12	185	13	250	14	0	18	12	.600	0	13-22 49	4.93	4.70

Clay Buchholz

Pitches: R **Bats:** L **Pos:** SP-14 BUCK-holtz **Ht:** 6'3" **Wt:** 190 **Born:** 8/14/1984 **Age:** 27

						HOW MUCH HE PITCHED				WHAT HE GAVE UP									THE RESULTS						
Year	Team	Lg	G	GS	CG	GF	IP	BFP	H	R	ER	HR	SH	SF	HB	TBB	IBB	SO	WP	Bk	W	L	Pct	Sh	Sv-Op Hld	ERC	ERA
2007	Bos	AL	4	3	1	0	22.2	88	14	6	4	0	1	1	1	10	0	22	0	0	3	1	.750	1	0-0 0	1.90	1.59
2008	Bos	AL	16	15	1	0	76.0	357	93	63	57	11	0	3	2	41	1	72	2	1	2	9	.182	0	0-0 0	6.40	6.75
2009	Bos	AL	16	16	0	0	92.0	399	91	44	43	13	2	3	2	36	1	68	1	0	7	4	.636	0	0-0 0	4.31	4.21
2010	Bos	AL	28	28	1	0	173.2	711	142	55	45	9	5	5	5	67	1	120	7	1	17	7	.708	1	0-0 0	2.88	2.33
2011	Bos	AL	14	14	0	0	82.2	353	76	34	32	10	1	4	2	31	1	60	3	0	6	3	.667	0	0-0 0	3.72	3.48
	Postseason		1	1	0	0	5.0	23	6	2	2	1	0	0	1	1	0	3	0	1	0	0	-	0	0-0 0	5.87	3.60
	5 ML YEARS		78	76	3	0	447.0	1908	416	202	181	43	8	16	12	185	4	342	13	2	35	24	.593	2	0-0 0	3.82	3.64

Taylor Buchholz

Pitches: R **Bats:** R **Pos:** RP-23 BUCK-holtz **Ht:** 6'4" **Wt:** 220 **Born:** 10/13/1981 **Age:** 30

						HOW MUCH HE PITCHED				WHAT HE GAVE UP									THE RESULTS						
Year	Team	Lg	G	GS	CG	GF	IP	BFP	H	R	ER	HR	SH	SF	HB	TBB	IBB	SO	WP	Bk	W	L	Pct	Sh	Sv-Op Hld	ERC	ERA
2006	Hou	NL	22	19	1	1	113.0	479	107	80	74	21	5	6	3	34	4	77	5	0	6	10	.375	1	0-0 1	3.97	5.89
2007	Col	NL	41	8	0	6	93.2	396	105	47	44	8	5	5	2	20	4	61	3	1	6	5	.545	0	0-0 1	3.97	4.23
2008	Col	NL	63	0	0	19	66.1	263	45	23	16	5	2	2	2	18	2	56	5	1	6	6	.500	0	1-3 21	1.87	2.17
2010	2 Tms		9	0	0	4	12.0	49	10	5	5	2	1	0	0	6	0	9	0	0	1	0	1.000	0	0-0 0	4.19	3.75
2011	NYM	NL	23	0	0	8	26.0	107	22	10	9	5	2	3	1	7	0	26	0	0	1	1	.500	0	0-0 5	3.45	3.12
	10 Col	NL	7	0	0	2	10.0	43	10	5	5	2	1	0	0	6	0	9	0	0	1	0	1.000	0	0-0 0	5.94	4.50
	10 Tor	AL	2	0	0	2	2.0	6	0	0	0	0	0	0	0	0	0	0	0	0	0	0	-	0	0-0 0	0.00	0.00
	5 ML YEARS		158	27	1	38	311.0	1294	289	165	148	41	15	16	8	85	10	229	13	2	20	22	.476	1	1-3 27	3.45	4.28

John Buck

Bats: R **Throws:** R **Pos:** C-135; PH-9 **Ht:** 6'3" **Wt:** 230 **Born:** 7/7/1980 **Age:** 31

							BATTING												BASERUNNING				AVERAGES		
Year	Team	Lg	G	AB	H	2B	3B	HR	(Hm | Rd)	TB	R	RBI	RC	TBB	IBB	SO	HBP	SH	SF	SB	CS	SB%	GDP	Avg	OBP	Slg
2004	KC	AL	71	238	56	9	0	12	(6 | 6)	101	36	30	26	15	0	79	0	4	1	1	1	.50	6	.235	.280	.424
2005	KC	AL	118	401	97	21	1	12	(3 | 9)	156	40	47	43	23	2	94	3	1	2	2	2	.50	9	.242	.287	.389
2006	KC	AL	114	371	91	21	1	11	(6 | 5)	147	37	50	43	26	2	84	7	4	1	0	2	.00	7	.245	.306	.396
2007	KC	AL	113	347	77	18	0	18	(6 | 12)	149	41	48	37	36	0	92	10	0	6	0	1	.00	11	.222	.308	.429
2008	KC	AL	109	370	83	23	1	9	(4 | 5)	135	48	48	42	38	2	96	6	0	4	0	3	.00	12	.224	.304	.365

Year	Team	Lg	G	AB	H	2B	3B	HR	(Hm	Rd)	TB	R	RBI	RC	TBB	IBB	SO	HBP	SH	SF	SB	CS	SB%	GDP	Avg	OBP	Slg
2009	KC	AL	59	186	46	12	4	8	(3	5)	90	16	36	30	13	0	55	1	1	1	1	1	.50	2	.247	.299	.484
2010	Tor	AL	118	409	115	25	0	20	(9	11)	200	53	66	61	16	1	111	6	0	6	0	0	-	6	.281	.314	.489
2011	Fla	NL	140	466	106	15	1	16	(7	9)	171	41	57	55	54	7	115	7	2	1	0	1	.00	11	.227	.316	.367
8 ML YEARS			842	2788	671	144	8	106	(44	62)	1149	312	382	337	221	14	726	40	12	22	4	11	.27	64	.241	.303	.412

Travis Buck

Bats: L Throws: R Pos: LF-25; RF-14; PH-7; DH-6; PR-2; CF-1　　　　Ht: 6'2" Wt: 232 Born: 11/18/1983 Age: 28

Year	Team	Lg	G	AB	H	2B	3B	HR	(Hm	Rd)	TB	R	RBI	RC	TBB	IBB	SO	HBP	SH	SF	SB	CS	SB%	GDP	Avg	OBP	Slg
2011	Clmbs*	AAA	36	121	31	6	1	4	(-	-)	51	21	25	20	19	2	26	3	1	2	1	1	.50	5	.256	.366	.421
2007	Oak	AL	82	285	82	22	5	7	(3	4)	135	41	34	48	39	2	66	4	2	4	4	1	.80	9	.288	.377	.474
2008	Oak	AL	38	155	35	9	1	7	(3	4)	67	16	25	22	11	0	38	4	0	2	1	0	1.00	2	.226	.291	.432
2009	Oak	AL	36	105	23	3	0	3	(2	1)	35	11	10	10	10	0	20	0	0	0	1	1	.50	0	.219	.287	.333
2010	Oak	AL	14	42	7	2	0	1	(1	0)	12	6	2	2	4	0	14	1	1	0	1	0	1.00	0	.167	.255	.286
2011	Cle	AL	50	149	34	11	0	2	(2	0)	51	18	18	17	8	0	30	2	0	1	1	1	.50	3	.228	.275	.342
5 ML YEARS			220	736	181	47	6	20	(11	9)	300	92	89	99	72	2	168	11	3	7	8	3	.73	14	.246	.320	.408

Mark Buehrle

Pitches: L Bats: L Pos: SP-31　　　　BURR-lee　　　　Ht: 6'2" Wt: 230 Born: 3/23/1979 Age: 33

			HOW MUCH HE PITCHED					WHAT HE GAVE UP										THE RESULTS						
Year	Team	Lg	G	GS	CG	GF	IP	BFP	H	R	ER	HR	SH	SF	HB	TBB	IBB	SO	WP	Bk	W	L	Pct	Sh	Sv-Op	Hld	ERC	ERA
2000	CWS	AL	28	3	0	6	51.1	225	55	27	24	5	1	0	3	19	1	37	0	0	4	1	.800	0	0-2	3	4.56	4.21
2001	CWS	AL	32	32	4	0	221.1	885	188	89	81	24	9	4	8	48	2	126	1	5	16	8	.667	2	0-0	0	2.79	3.29
2002	CWS	AL	34	34	5	0	239.0	984	236	102	95	25	9	3	3	61	7	134	6	1	19	12	.613	2	0-0	0	3.53	3.58
2003	CWS	AL	35	35	2	0	230.1	978	250	124	106	22	7	7	5	61	2	119	1	0	14	14	.500	0	0-0	0	4.10	4.14
2004	CWS	AL	35	35	4	0	245.1	1016	257	119	106	33	4	6	8	51	2	165	0	0	16	10	.615	1	0-0	0	4.00	3.89
2005	CWS	AL	33	33	3	0	236.2	971	240	99	82	20	7	4	4	40	4	149	2	2	16	8	.667	1	0-0	0	3.21	3.12
2006	CWS	AL	32	32	1	0	204.0	876	247	124	113	36	6	7	6	48	5	98	0	1	12	13	.480	1	0-0	0	5.37	4.99
2007	CWS	AL	30	30	3	0	201.0	835	208	86	81	22	7	5	5	45	5	115	1	0	10	9	.526	1	0-0	0	3.75	3.63
2008	CWS	AL	34	34	1	0	218.2	918	240	106	92	22	2	6	5	52	4	140	4	0	15	12	.556	0	0-0	0	4.12	3.79
2009	CWS	AL	33	33	1	0	213.1	874	222	97	91	27	11	7	5	45	3	105	2	1	13	10	.565	1	0-0	0	3.91	3.84
2010	CWS	AL	33	33	3	0	210.1	897	246	105	100	17	6	7	1	49	1	99	3	5	13	13	.500	0	0-0	0	4.29	4.28
2011	CWS	AL	31	31	0	0	205.1	858	221	93	82	21	6	7	2	45	3	109	1	0	13	9	.591	0	0-0	0	3.86	3.59
Postseason			6	4	1	2	30.2	124	32	14	14	3	2	1	1	1	1	16	0	0	2	1	.667	0	1-1	0	2.95	4.11
12 ML YEARS			390	365	27	6	2476.2	10317	2610	1171	1053	274	75	63	55	564	39	1396	21	15	161	119	.575	8	0-2	3	3.89	3.83

Jay Buente

Pitches: R Bats: R Pos: SP-1; RP-1　　　　BENN-tay　　　　Ht: 6'2" Wt: 187 Born: 9/28/1983 Age: 28

			HOW MUCH HE PITCHED					WHAT HE GAVE UP										THE RESULTS						
Year	Team	Lg	G	GS	CG	GF	IP	BFP	H	R	ER	HR	SH	SF	HB	TBB	IBB	SO	WP	Bk	W	L	Pct	Sh	Sv-Op	Hld	ERC	ERA
2006	Jmstwn	A-	22	3	0	5	43.2	182	40	17	15	2	1	1	2	13	0	41	3	0	2	3	.400	0	1--	-	3.05	3.09
2007	Grnsbr	A	42	0	0	18	60.0	261	58	36	25	6	1	1	3	19	2	71	11	0	5	2	.714	0	2--	-	3.61	3.75
2008	Jupiter	A+	40	0	0	9	60.0	258	49	22	20	4	4	1	3	27	0	63	10	1	5	1	.833	0	1--	-	3.17	3.00
2009	Jaxnvl	AA	16	0	0	7	22.0	91	17	6	6	1	0	1	0	11	0	23	2	0	0	1	.000	0	1--	-	2.91	2.45
2009	NewOr	AAA	35	0	0	14	61.0	270	59	24	23	6	4	0	1	32	5	56	5	0	5	1	.833	0	1--	-	4.28	3.39
2010	NewOr	AAA	20	0	0	8	30.1	130	22	13	9	3	2	0	0	18	0	38	2	0	0	1	.000	0	0--	-	3.27	2.67
2010	Jaxnvl	AA	10	1	0	3	13.1	55	13	6	6	1	0	0	0	5	0	12	0	0	1	0	1.000	0	1--	-	3.81	4.05
2010	Mrlns	R	4	0	0	1	5.0	19	5	2	2	0	0	0	0	1	0	4	0	0	1	0	1.000	0	0--	-	2.93	3.60
2011	NewOr	AAA	10	5	1	0	41.2	156	23	9	9	1	1	2	2	10	0	44	4	1	3	0	1.000	0	0--	-	1.27	1.94
2011	Drhm	AAA	24	4	1	7	42.2	192	48	31	27	4	2	1	4	17	1	43	2	1	1	3	.250	0	1--	-	5.09	5.70
2010	Fla	NL	8	0	0	2	11.0	59	16	8	8	0	1	0	0	11	2	9	1	0	0	0	-	0	0-0	0	8.02	6.55
2011	2 Tms		2	1	0	1	5.0	28	7	6	5	0	0	0	1	5	0	2	0	0	0	1	.000	0	0-0	0	8.78	9.00
11	Fla	NL	1	1	0	0	3.0	18	5	4	3	0	0	0	1	3	0	1	0	0	0	1	.000	0	0-0	0	11.18	9.00
11	TB	AL	1	0	0	1	2.0	10	2	2	2	0	0	0	0	2	0	1	0	0	0	0	-	0	0-0	0	5.48	9.00
2 ML YEARS			10	1	0	3	16.0	87	23	14	13	0	1	0	1	16	2	11	1	0	0	1	.000	0	0-0	0	8.26	7.31

Jason Bulger

Pitches: R Bats: R Pos: RP-5　　　　BULL-jerr　　　　Ht: 6'4" Wt: 210 Born: 12/6/1978 Age: 33

			HOW MUCH HE PITCHED					WHAT HE GAVE UP										THE RESULTS						
Year	Team	Lg	G	GS	CG	GF	IP	BFP	H	R	ER	HR	SH	SF	HB	TBB	IBB	SO	WP	Bk	W	L	Pct	Sh	Sv-Op	Hld	ERC	ERA
2011	Salt Lk*	AAA	35	0	0	10	38.0	155	31	17	17	7	1	1	1	17	0	49	1	0	1	0	1.000	0	1--	-	4.07	4.03
2005	Ari	NL	9	0	0	5	10.0	48	14	6	6	1	1	0	0	5	1	9	0	0	1	0	1.000	0	0-0	0	6.68	5.40
2006	LAA	AL	2	0	0	1	1.2	9	1	3	3	0	0	0	0	3	0	1	1	0	0	0	-	0	0-0	0	6.15	16.20
2007	LAA	AL	6	0	0	4	6.1	25	5	2	2	0	0	0	0	3	0	8	1	0	0	0	-	0	0-0	0	2.74	2.84
2008	LAA	AL	14	0	0	7	16.0	73	15	13	13	3	0	0	2	9	0	20	0	0	0	0	-	0	0-0	0	5.50	7.31
2009	LAA	AL	64	0	0	20	65.2	262	46	26	26	7	5	4	1	30	1	68	5	0	6	1	.857	0	1-4	9	2.88	3.56
2010	LAA	AL	25	0	0	5	24.0	111	25	14	13	3	1	0	2	15	0	25	1	0	0	0	-	0	0-0	2	5.79	4.88
2011	LAA	AL	5	0	0	4	9.1	43	6	4	1	2	0	0	0	10	1	7	0	0	1	0	1.000	0	0-0	0	5.41	0.96
Postseason			4	0	0	0	3.1	16	1	1	1	1	0	0	1	4	0	5	1	0	0	0	-	0	0-0	0	5.88	2.70
7 ML YEARS			125	0	0	46	133.0	571	112	68	64	16	7	4	5	75	3	138	8	0	7	2	.778	0	1-4	11	4.16	4.33

Madison Bumgarner

Pitches: L Bats: R Pos: SP-33 Ht: 6'5" Wt: 227 Born: 8/1/1989 Age: 22

		HOW MUCH HE PITCHED						WHAT HE GAVE UP											THE RESULTS						
Year Team	Lg	G	GS	CG	GF	IP	BFP	H	R	ER	HR	SH	SF	HB	TBB	IBB	SO	WP	Bk	W	L	Pct	Sh	Sv-Op	Hld	ERC	ERA
2009 SF	NL	4	1	0	1	10.0	40	8	2	2	2	1	1	0	3	1	10	0	0	0	0	-	0	0-0	0	3.14	1.80
2010 SF	NL	18	18	0	0	111.0	472	119	40	37	11	0	4	5	26	2	86	1	1	7	6	.538	0	0-0	0	3.98	3.00
2011 SF	NL	33	33	0	0	204.2	844	202	82	73	12	12	4	5	46	5	191	0	1	13	13	.500	0	0-0	0	3.14	3.21
Postseason		4	3	0	0	20.2	83	18	5	5	1	2	1	1	5	1	18	0	0	2	0	1.000	0	0-0	0	2.63	2.18
3 ML YEARS		55	52	0	1	325.2	1356	329	124	112	25	13	9	10	75	8	287	1	2	20	19	.513	0	0-0	0	3.42	3.10

A.J. Burnett

Pitches: R Bats: R Pos: SP-32; RP-1 Ht: 6'4" Wt: 230 Born: 1/3/1977 Age: 35

		HOW MUCH HE PITCHED						WHAT HE GAVE UP											THE RESULTS						
Year Team	Lg	G	GS	CG	GF	IP	BFP	H	R	ER	HR	SH	SF	HB	TBB	IBB	SO	WP	Bk	W	L	Pct	Sh	Sv-Op	Hld	ERC	ERA
1999 Fla	NL	7	7	0	0	41.1	182	37	23	16	3	1	3	0	25	2	33	0	0	4	2	.667	0	0-0	0	4.00	3.48
2000 Fla	NL	13	13	0	0	82.2	364	80	46	44	8	6	3	2	44	3	57	2	0	3	7	.300	0	0-0	0	4.45	4.79
2001 Fla	NL	27	27	2	0	173.1	733	145	82	78	20	6	8	7	83	3	128	7	1	11	12	.478	1	0-0	0	3.76	4.05
2002 Fla	NL	31	29	7	0	204.1	844	153	84	75	12	9	4	9	90	5	203	14	0	12	9	.571	5	0-1	0	2.77	3.30
2003 Fla	NL	4	4	0	0	23.0	106	18	13	12	2	2	1	2	18	2	21	2	0	0	2	.000	0	0-0	0	4.36	4.70
2004 Fla	NL	20	19	1	0	120.0	490	102	50	49	9	3	3	4	38	0	113	7	0	7	6	.538	0	0-0	0	2.95	3.68
2005 Fla	NL	32	32	4	0	209.0	873	184	97	80	12	7	5	7	79	1	198	12	0	12	12	.500	0	0-0	0	3.20	3.44
2006 Tor	AL	21	21	2	0	135.2	577	138	67	60	14	4	3	8	39	3	118	6	1	10	8	.556	1	0-0	0	3.97	3.98
2007 Tor	AL	25	25	2	0	165.2	691	131	74	69	23	0	2	12	66	2	176	5	0	10	8	.556	0	0-0	0	3.47	3.75
2008 Tor	AL	35	34	1	1	221.1	957	211	109	100	19	8	5	9	86	2	231	11	2	18	10	.643	0	0-0	0	3.78	4.07
2009 NYY	AL	33	33	1	0	207.0	896	193	99	93	25	2	5	10	97	0	195	17	1	13	9	.591	0	0-0	0	4.34	4.04
2010 NYY	AL	33	33	1	0	186.2	829	204	118	109	25	7	10	19	78	2	145	16	0	10	15	.400	0	0-0	0	5.43	5.26
2011 NYY	AL	33	32	0	0	190.1	837	190	115	109	31	4	10	9	83	2	173	25	0	11	11	.500	0	0-0	0	4.83	5.15
Postseason		6	6	0	0	33.1	149	28	21	21	2	1	0	6	19	2	28	3	0	1	2	.333	0	0-0	0	4.15	5.67
13 ML YEARS		314	309	21	1	1960.1	8379	1786	977	894	203	59	62	98	826	27	1791	124	5	121	111	.522	9	0-1	0	3.88	4.10

Alex Burnett

Pitches: R Bats: R Pos: RP-66 Ht: 6'0" Wt: 221 Born: 7/26/1987 Age: 24

		HOW MUCH HE PITCHED						WHAT HE GAVE UP											THE RESULTS						
Year Team	Lg	G	GS	CG	GF	IP	BFP	H	R	ER	HR	SH	SF	HB	TBB	IBB	SO	WP	Bk	W	L	Pct	Sh	Sv-Op	Hld	ERC	ERA
2005 Twins	R	13	8	0	2	48.1	212	50	25	22	6	1	3	7	14	0	33	1	0	4	2	.667	0	0- -		4.57	4.10
2006 Elizab	R+	13	13	1	0	71.1	294	66	41	32	6	0	2	6	13	0	71	1	1	4	3	.571	1	0- -		3.05	4.04
2007 Beloit	A	27	27	1	0	155.0	640	140	60	52	9	3	4	10	38	1	117	6	1	9	8	.529	0	0- -		2.93	3.02
2008 FtMyrs	A+	28	25	0	0	143.2	608	151	72	60	12	2	3	5	36	0	84	7	0	8	6	.571	0	0- -		3.81	3.76
2009 FtMyrs	A+	18	0	0	16	22.2	91	14	6	5	0	2	1	1	7	0	26	0	0	2	1	.667	0	4- -		1.45	1.99
2009 NwBrit	AA	40	0	0	19	55.1	217	37	14	14	2	1	1	3	19	4	52	1	0	1	2	.333	0	9- -		1.93	2.28
2010 Roch	AAA	14	0	0	7	19.2	91	26	12	12	1	1	3	0	8	2	18	2	0	2	2	.000	0	2- -		5.40	5.49
2011 Roch	AAA	4	0	0	3	3.2	16	5	3	3	1	0	0	0	1	0	3	0	0	0	0	-	0	1- -		7.34	7.36
2010 Min	AL	41	0	0	11	47.2	211	52	28	28	6	4	1	2	23	3	37	2	2	2	2	.500	0	0-0	2	5.30	5.29
2011 Min	AL	66	0	0	12	50.2	225	50	32	31	4	2	4	8	21	1	33	2	0	2	5	.286	0	0-2	10	4.51	5.51
2 ML YEARS		107	0	0	23	98.1	436	102	60	59	10	6	5	10	44	4	70	4	2	4	7	.364	0	0-2	12	4.89	5.40

Sean Burnett

Pitches: L Bats: L Pos: RP-69 Ht: 6'1" Wt: 200 Born: 9/17/1982 Age: 29

		HOW MUCH HE PITCHED						WHAT HE GAVE UP											THE RESULTS						
Year Team	Lg	G	GS	CG	GF	IP	BFP	H	R	ER	HR	SH	SF	HB	TBB	IBB	SO	WP	Bk	W	L	Pct	Sh	Sv-Op	Hld	ERC	ERA
2004 Pit	NL	13	13	1	0	71.2	318	86	41	40	9	2	1	1	28	2	30	2	0	5	5	.500	1	0-0	0	5.49	5.02
2008 Pit	NL	58	0	0	16	56.2	253	57	31	30	7	4	3	2	34	3	42	4	0	1	1	.500	0	0-0	8	5.23	4.76
2009 2 Tms	NL	71	0	0	8	57.2	237	36	21	20	6	6	1	3	28	8	43	4	0	2	3	.400	0	1-3	11	2.43	3.12
2010 Was	NL	73	0	0	10	63.0	261	52	17	15	3	4	0	1	20	4	62	2	0	1	7	.125	0	3-4	20	2.43	2.14
2011 Was	NL	69	0	0	17	56.2	242	54	24	24	6	3	2	3	21	4	33	2	0	5	5	.500	0	4-11	15	3.85	3.81
09 Pit	NL	38	0	0	7	32.1	133	22	12	11	3	4	1	3	15	4	23	2	0	1	2	.333	0	1-2	6	2.77	3.06
09 Was	NL	33	0	0	1	25.1	104	14	9	9	3	2	0	0	13	4	20	2	0	1	1	.500	0	0-1	5	2.02	3.20
5 ML YEARS		284	13	1	51	305.2	1311	285	134	129	31	19	7	10	131	21	210	14	0	14	21	.400	1	8-18	54	3.85	3.80

Pat Burrell

Bats: R Throws: R Pos: LF-54; PH-41 BURL Ht: 6'4" Wt: 235 Born: 10/10/1976 Age: 35

		BATTING																			BASERUNNING				AVERAGES		
Year Team	Lg	G	AB	H	2B	3B	HR	(Hm	Rd)	TB	R	RBI	RC	TBB	IBB	SO	HBP	SH	SF	SB	CS	SB%	GDP	Avg	OBP	Slg
2011 SnJos*	A+	2	8	3	0	0	0	(-	-)	3	0	2	1	0	0	1	0	0	0	0	0	-	0	.375	.375	.375
2011 Fresno*	AAA	2	5	0	0	0	0	(-	-)	0	0	0	0	0	0	2	0	0	0	0	0	-	0	.000	.000	.000
2000 Phi	NL	111	408	106	27	1	18	(7	11)	189	57	79	69	63	2	139	1	0	2	0	0	-	5	.260	.359	.463
2001 Phi	NL	155	539	139	29	2	27	(10	17)	253	70	89	86	70	7	162	5	0	4	2	1	.67	12	.258	.346	.469
2002 Phi	NL	157	586	165	39	2	37	(18	19)	319	96	116	104	89	9	153	3	0	6	1	0	1.00	16	.282	.376	.544
2003 Phi	NL	146	522	109	31	4	21	(9	12)	211	57	64	57	72	2	142	4	0	1	0	0	-	18	.209	.309	.404
2004 Phi	NL	127	448	115	17	0	24	(14	10)	204	66	84	72	78	7	130	2	0	6	2	0	1.00	10	.257	.365	.455
2005 Phi	NL	154	562	158	27	1	32	(20	12)	283	78	117	109	99	6	160	3	0	5	0	0	-	12	.281	.389	.504
2006 Phi	NL	144	462	119	24	1	29	(12	17)	232	80	95	81	98	5	131	4	0	4	0	0	-	11	.258	.388	.502
2007 Phi	NL	155	472	121	26	0	30	(16	14)	237	77	97	96	114	1	120	4	0	8	0	0	-	10	.256	.400	.502
2008 Phi	NL	157	536	134	33	3	33	(12	21)	272	74	86	93	102	8	136	1	0	6	0	0	-	10	.250	.367	.507
2009 TB	AL	122	412	91	16	1	14	(8	6)	151	45	64	52	57	2	119	2	0	5	2	0	1.00	6	.221	.315	.367
2010 2 Tms	NL	120	373	94	21	0	20	(10	10)	175	50	64	63	57	4	105	1	0	6	0	2	.00	7	.252	.348	.469
2011 SF	NL	92	183	42	9	1	7	(3	4)	74	17	21	25	33	0	67	2	0	1	0	0	-	2	.230	.352	.404

Year	Team	Lg	G	AB	H	2B	3B	HR	(Hm	Rd)	TB	R	RBI	RC	TBB	IBB	SO	HBP	SH	SF	SB	CS	SB%	GDP	Avg	OBP	Slg
10	TB	AL	24	84	17	5	0	2	(1	1)	28	9	13	9	10	0	28	1	0	1	0	0	-	2	.202	.292	.333
10	SF	NL	96	289	77	16	0	18	(9	9)	147	41	51	54	47	4	77	0	0	5	0	2	.00	5	.266	.364	.509
	Postseason		31	97	18	4	0	5	(3	2)	37	9	13	10	17	0	38	0	0	0	0	0	-	2	.186	.307	.381
	12 ML YEARS		1640	5503	1393	299	16	292	(139	153)	2600	767	976	909	932	53	1564	31	0	54	7	3	.70	119	.253	.361	.472

Brian Burres

Pitches: L Bats: L Pos: RP-3; SP-2   BURR-iss   Ht: 6'2" Wt: 188 Born: 4/8/1981 Age: 31

			HOW MUCH HE PITCHED						WHAT HE GAVE UP										THE RESULTS						
Year	Team	Lg	G	GS	CG	GF	IP	BFP	H	R	ER	HR	SH	SF	HB	TBB	IBB	SO	WP	Bk	W	L	Pct	Sh	Sv-Op Hld	ERC	ERA
2011	Indy*	AAA	25	23	0	0	129.1	561	140	71	67	18	6	1	7	45	1	95	4	0	5	9	.357	0	0- - -	4.89	4.66
2006	Bal	AL	11	0	0	2	8.0	31	6	2	2	1	0	0	0	1	0	6	0	0	0	0	-	0	0-0 4	1.91	2.25
2007	Bal	AL	37	17	0	9	121.0	559	140	81	80	14	2	0	5	66	1	96	8	0	6	8	.429	0	0-0 0	5.89	5.95
2008	Bal	AL	31	22	0	1	129.2	596	165	90	87	17	1	8	6	50	2	63	3	1	7	10	.412	0	0-1 0	6.03	6.04
2009	Tor	AL	2	2	0	0	6.1	37	12	12	10	0	0	0	0	5	0	4	0	0	0	2	.000	0	0-0 0	10.02	14.21
2010	Pit	NL	20	13	0	1	79.1	362	87	48	44	9	3	3	6	34	4	45	3	0	4	5	.444	0	0-0 0	4.99	4.99
2011	Pit	NL	5	2	0	0	14.0	60	12	6	6	4	2	1	0	4	0	10	2	0	1	0	1.000	0	0-0 0	3.80	3.86
	6 ML YEARS		106	56	0	15	358.1	1645	422	239	229	45	8	12	17	160	7	224	16	1	18	25	.419	0	0-1 4	5.63	5.75

Manny Burriss

Bats: B Throws: R Pos: 2B-39; PR-15; SS-9; PH-8; 1B-2; 3B-2; LF-2   Ht: 6'0" Wt: 203 Born: 1/17/1985 Age: 27

			BATTING																		BASERUNNING				AVERAGES		
Year	Team	Lg	G	AB	H	2B	3B	HR	(Hm	Rd)	TB	R	RBI	RC	TBB	IBB	SO	HBP	SH	SF	SB	CS	SB%	GDP	Avg	OBP	Slg
2011	Fresno*	AAA	45	175	52	8	1	2	(-	-)	68	31	10	31	22	1	19	4	4	1	24	5	.83	2	.297	.386	.389
2008	SF	NL	95	240	68	6	1	1	(0	1)	79	37	18	22	23	1	24	5	5	1	13	5	.72	7	.283	.357	.329
2009	SF	NL	61	202	48	6	0	0	(0	0)	54	18	13	15	14	1	34	2	1	1	11	4	.73	3	.238	.292	.267
2010	SF	NL	7	5	2	0	0	0	(0	0)	2	3	0	1	0	0	1	0	0	0	0	0	-	0	.400	.400	.400
2011	SF	NL	59	137	28	1	0	0	(0	0)	29	14	4	6	6	0	17	3	6	0	11	3	.79	2	.204	.253	.212
	4 ML YEARS		222	584	146	13	1	1	(0	1)	164	72	35	44	43	2	76	10	12	2	35	12	.74	12	.250	.311	.281

Sean Burroughs

Bats: L Throws: R Pos: PH-60; 3B-20   Ht: 6'2" Wt: 180 Born: 9/12/1980 Age: 31

			BATTING																		BASERUNNING				AVERAGES		
Year	Team	Lg	G	AB	H	2B	3B	HR	(Hm	Rd)	TB	R	RBI	RC	TBB	IBB	SO	HBP	SH	SF	SB	CS	SB%	GDP	Avg	OBP	Slg
2011	Reno*	AAA	34	102	42	11	2	2	(-	-)	63	19	25	25	7	0	8	0	1	0	2	0	.00	3	.412	.450	.618
2002	SD	NL	63	192	52	5	1	1	(0	1)	62	18	11	15	12	1	30	1	1	0	2	0	1.00	6	.271	.317	.323
2003	SD	NL	146	517	148	27	6	7	(2	5)	208	62	58	68	44	4	75	11	2	4	7	2	.78	13	.286	.352	.402
2004	SD	NL	130	523	156	23	3	2	(0	2)	191	76	47	70	31	4	52	9	1	0	5	4	.56	6	.298	.348	.365
2005	SD	NL	93	284	71	7	2	1	(1	0)	85	20	17	24	24	4	41	5	3	1	4	0	1.00	7	.250	.318	.299
2006	TB	AL	8	21	4	1	0	0	(0	0)	5	3	1	2	4	0	7	0	0	0	1	0	1.00	1	.190	.320	.238
2011	Ari	NL	78	110	30	4	0	1	(0	1)	37	8	8	10	3	0	15	0	1	1	1	0	1.00	4	.273	.289	.336
	Postseason		2	1	0	0	0	0	(0	0)	0	0	0	0	0	0	0	0	0	0	0	0	-	0	.000	.000	.000
	6 ML YEARS		518	1647	461	67	12	12	(3	9)	588	187	142	189	118	13	220	26	8	6	20	6	.77	37	.280	.337	.357

Jared Burton

Pitches: R Bats: R Pos: RP-6   Ht: 6'5" Wt: 228 Born: 6/2/1981 Age: 31

			HOW MUCH HE PITCHED						WHAT HE GAVE UP										THE RESULTS						
Year	Team	Lg	G	GS	CG	GF	IP	BFP	H	R	ER	HR	SH	SF	HB	TBB	IBB	SO	WP	Bk	W	L	Pct	Sh	Sv-Op Hld	ERC	ERA
2011	Reds*	R	3	3	0	0	4.0	19	7	5	4	1	1	0	0	0	0	6	0	0	0	1	.000	0	0- - -	7.95	9.00
2011	Lsvlle*	AAA	11	0	0	3	13.0	57	12	6	6	1	1	0	3	5	0	11	0	0	2	0	1.000	0	0- - -	4.38	4.15
2007	Cin	NL	47	0	0	12	43.0	176	28	15	12	2	1	1	2	22	4	36	3	1	4	2	.667	0	0-3 11	2.37	2.51
2008	Cin	NL	54	0	0	12	58.2	257	56	24	21	6	2	3	2	25	3	58	2	1	5	1	.833	0	0-2 11	3.93	3.22
2009	Cin	NL	53	0	0	13	59.1	265	61	30	29	5	3	1	4	23	6	45	2	0	1	0	1.000	0	0-0 7	4.08	4.40
2010	Cin	NL	4	0	0	2	3.1	10	0	0	0	0	0	0	0	0	0	1	0	0	0	0	-	0	0-0 1	0.00	0.00
2011	Cin	NL	6	0	0	1	4.2	23	6	2	2	1	1	0	0	3	0	3	0	0	0	0	-	0	0-0 1	7.61	3.86
	5 ML YEARS		164	0	0	40	169.0	731	151	71	64	14	7	5	8	73	13	143	7	2	10	3	.769	0	0-5 31	3.51	3.41

Dave Bush

Pitches: R Bats: R Pos: RP-14; SP-3   Ht: 6'2" Wt: 204 Born: 11/9/1979 Age: 32

			HOW MUCH HE PITCHED						WHAT HE GAVE UP										THE RESULTS						
Year	Team	Lg	G	GS	CG	GF	IP	BFP	H	R	ER	HR	SH	SF	HB	TBB	IBB	SO	WP	Bk	W	L	Pct	Sh	Sv-Op Hld	ERC	ERA
2011	Iowa*	AAA	5	5	0	0	22.0	102	28	15	15	3	0	1	4	9	0	12	0	0	1	2	.333	0	0- - -	6.99	6.14
2011	LV*	AAA	4	4	0	0	23.0	97	20	10	10	3	0	3	2	6	0	16	0	0	1	2	.333	0	0- - -	3.30	3.91
2004	Tor	AL	16	16	1	0	97.2	412	95	47	40	11	4	4	6	25	2	64	3	0	5	4	.556	1	0-0 0	3.65	3.69
2005	Tor	AL	25	24	2	1	136.1	575	142	73	68	20	3	2	13	29	3	75	2	0	5	11	.313	0	0-0 0	4.28	4.49
2006	Mil	NL	34	32	3	0	210.0	869	201	111	103	26	6	8	11	38	2	166	6	0	12	11	.522	2	0-0 0	3.47	4.41
2007	Mil	NL	33	31	0	0	186.1	810	217	110	106	27	6	2	11	44	1	134	3	0	12	10	.545	0	0-0 0	4.93	5.12
2008	Mil	NL	31	29	0	0	185.0	763	163	92	86	29	4	3	10	48	3	109	2	1	9	10	.474	0	0-0 0	3.44	4.18
2009	Mil	NL	22	21	0	0	114.1	508	131	84	81	19	6	15	5	37	2	89	2	0	5	9	.357	0	0-0 0	5.70	6.38
2010	Mil	NL	32	31	0	0	174.1	781	198	108	88	28	9	10	4	65	6	107	1	1	8	13	.381	0	0-0 0	5.17	4.54
2011	Tex	AL	17	3	0	7	37.1	166	47	27	24	6	2	0	3	9	2	23	2	0	0	1	.000	0	0-0 0	5.67	5.79
	Postseason		1	1	0	0	5.1	21	5	1	1	0	0	0	0	0	0	3	0	0	1	0	1.000	0	0-0 0	1.68	1.69
	8 ML YEARS		210	187	6	10	1141.1	4884	1194	652	596	166	43	32	80	295	21	767	21	2	56	69	.448	3	0-0 3	4.35	4.70

Drew Butera

Bats: R Throws: R Pos: C-93; PH-1; PR-1   bue-TARE-ah   Ht: 6'1" Wt: 195 Born: 8/9/1983 Age: 28

Year	Team	Lg	G	AB	H	2B	3B	HR	(Hm	Rd)	TB	R	RBI	RC	TBB	IBB	SO	HBP	SH	SF	SB	CS	SB%	GDP	Avg	OBP	Slg
2005	Bklyn	A-	55	175	38	9	1	1	(-	-)	52	13	23	18	22	0	33	2	1	4	1	0	1.00	7	.217	.305	.297
2006	Hgrstn	A	95	295	55	13	0	5	(-	-)	83	24	38	28	42	1	72	7	5	6	1	0	1.00	5	.186	.297	.281
2007	StLuci	A+	52	182	47	14	0	5	(-	-)	76	22	22	28	24	0	28	2	0	2	0	1	.00	5	.258	.348	.418
2007	Bnghtn	AA	30	117	22	2	0	1	(-	-)	27	7	4	4	2	0	22	1	1	0	0	0	-	4	.188	.208	.231
2007	NwBrit	AA	17	50	13	3	1	0	(-	-)	18	3	3	6	5	0	5	0	1	0	0	0	-	1	.260	.327	.360
2008	NwBrit	AA	96	302	66	18	1	7	(-	-)	107	39	39	36	35	0	55	6	4	4	0	1	.00	7	.219	.308	.354
2009	Roch	AAA	99	298	63	16	1	2	(-	-)	87	23	25	23	22	0	49	2	8	3	0	1	.00	9	.211	.268	.292
2010	Min	AL	49	142	28	6	1	2	(0	2)	42	12	13	7	4	0	25	4	3	2	0	0	-	5	.197	.237	.296
2011	Min	AL	93	234	39	9	1	2	(1	1)	56	19	23	11	11	0	42	2	6	1	0	0	-	7	.167	.210	.239
2 ML YEARS			142	376	67	15	2	4	(1	3)	98	31	36	18	15	0	67	6	9	3	0	0	-	12	.178	.220	.261

Billy Butler

Bats: R Throws: R Pos: DH-142; 1B-11; PH-6   Ht: 6'1" Wt: 240 Born: 4/18/1986 Age: 26

Year	Team	Lg	G	AB	H	2B	3B	HR	(Hm	Rd)	TB	R	RBI	RC	TBB	IBB	SO	HBP	SH	SF	SB	CS	SB%	GDP	Avg	OBP	Slg
2007	KC	AL	92	329	96	23	2	8	(5	3)	147	38	52	50	27	5	55	2	0	2	0	0	-	8	.292	.347	.447
2008	KC	AL	124	443	122	22	0	11	(4	7)	177	44	55	57	33	0	57	0	0	2	0	1	.00	23	.275	.324	.400
2009	KC	AL	159	608	183	51	1	21	(16	5)	299	78	93	99	58	3	103	2	0	4	1	0	1.00	20	.301	.362	.492
2010	KC	AL	158	595	189	45	0	15	(9	6)	279	77	78	91	69	8	78	5	0	9	0	0	-	32	.318	.388	.469
2011	KC	AL	159	597	174	44	0	19	(9	10)	275	74	95	94	66	15	95	3	0	7	2	1	.67	16	.291	.361	.461
5 ML YEARS			692	2572	764	185	3	74	(43	31)	1177	311	373	391	253	31	388	12	0	24	3	2	.60	99	.297	.360	.458

Marlon Byrd

Bats: R Throws: R Pos: CF-118; PH-1   Ht: 6'0" Wt: 245 Born: 8/30/1977 Age: 34

Year	Team	Lg	G	AB	H	2B	3B	HR	(Hm	Rd)	TB	R	RBI	RC	TBB	IBB	SO	HBP	SH	SF	SB	CS	SB%	GDP	Avg	OBP	Slg
2011	Iowa*	AAA	4	15	4	1	0	1	(-	-)	8	4	3	3	2	0	2	2	0	0	1	0	1.00	0	.267	.421	.533
2002	Phi	NL	10	35	8	2	0	1	(1	0)	13	2	1	0	1	0	8	0	0	0	0	2	.00	0	.229	.250	.371
2003	Phi	NL	135	495	150	28	4	7	(3	4)	207	86	45	72	44	3	94	7	4	3	11	1	.92	8	.303	.366	.418
2004	Phi	NL	106	346	79	13	2	5	(3	2)	111	48	33	35	22	1	68	7	2	1	2	2	.50	10	.228	.287	.321
2005	2 Tms	NL	79	229	61	15	2	2	(0	2)	86	20	26	30	19	1	50	2	5	4	5	1	.83	5	.266	.323	.376
2006	Was	NL	78	197	44	8	1	5	(1	4)	69	28	18	18	22	1	47	6	1	2	3	3	.50	6	.223	.317	.350
2007	Tex	AL	109	414	127	17	8	10	(4	6)	190	60	70	70	29	3	88	5	0	6	5	3	.63	9	.307	.355	.459
2008	Tex	AL	122	403	120	28	4	10	(7	3)	186	70	53	63	46	3	62	9	2	2	7	2	.78	10	.298	.380	.462
2009	Tex	AL	146	547	155	43	2	20	(14	6)	262	66	89	91	32	2	98	10	0	10	8	4	.67	11	.283	.329	.479
2010	ChC	NL	152	580	170	39	2	12	(6	6)	249	84	66	80	31	1	98	17	0	2	5	1	.83	12	.293	.346	.429
2011	ChC	NL	119	446	123	22	2	9	(4	5)	176	51	35	43	25	2	78	8	1	2	3	2	.60	13	.276	.324	.395
05	Phi	NL	5	13	4	0	0	0	(0	0)	4	0	0	2	1	0	3	1	0	0	0	0	-	0	.308	.400	.308
05	Was	NL	74	216	57	15	2	2	(0	2)	82	20	26	28	18	1	47	1	5	4	5	1	.83	5	.264	.318	.380
10 ML YEARS			1056	3692	1037	215	27	81	(43	38)	1549	515	436	500	271	17	691	71	15	32	49	21	.70	84	.281	.339	.420

Tim Byrdak

Pitches: L Bats: L Pos: RP-72   BURR-dack   Ht: 5'11" Wt: 190 Born: 10/31/1973 Age: 38

Year	Team	Lg	G	GS	CG	GF	IP	BFP	H	R	ER	HR	SH	SF	HB	TBB	IBB	SO	WP	Bk	W	L	Pct	Sh	Sv-Op	Hld	ERC	ERA
1998	KC	AL	3	0	0	0	1.2	9	5	1	1	1	0	0	0	0	0	1	0	0	0	0	-	0	0-0	0	23.52	5.40
1999	KC	AL	33	0	0	5	24.2	128	32	24	21	5	3	0	1	20	2	17	3	1	0	3	.000	0	1-4	10	8.29	7.66
2000	KC	AL	12	0	0	1	6.1	34	11	8	8	3	0	0	0	4	0	8	1	0	0	1	.000	0	0-2	3	13.14	11.37
2005	Bal	AL	41	0	0	3	26.2	131	27	14	12	1	2	1	1	21	1	31	5	0	0	1	.000	0	1-1	11	5.04	4.05
2006	Bal	AL	16	0	0	2	7.0	42	14	10	10	2	2	0	0	8	1	2	1	0	1	0	1.000	0	0-0	3	15.90	12.86
2007	Det	AL	39	0	0	3	45.0	199	38	23	16	3	2	5	1	26	4	49	3	0	3	0	1.000	0	1-2	8	3.53	3.20
2008	Hou	NL	59	0	0	9	55.1	237	45	24	24	10	2	1	2	29	2	47	0	0	2	1	.667	0	0-0	8	4.18	3.90
2009	Hou	NL	76	0	0	8	61.1	261	39	23	22	10	0	3	3	36	0	58	2	0	1	2	.333	0	0-2	9	3.38	3.23
2010	Hou	NL	64	0	0	9	38.2	170	40	15	15	4	0	2	3	20	0	29	2	0	2	2	.500	0	0-0	11	4.83	3.49
2011	NYM	NL	72	0	0	10	37.2	168	34	20	16	3	4	2	1	19	4	47	1	0	2	1	.667	0	1-4	8	3.61	3.82
10 ML YEARS			415	0	0	50	304.1	1379	285	162	145	42	15	15	9	183	14	289	18	1	11	11	.500	0	4-15	71	4.77	4.29

Asdrubal Cabrera

Bats: B Throws: R Pos: SS-151   azz-DRUE-bull   Ht: 6'0" Wt: 180 Born: 11/13/1985 Age: 26

Year	Team	Lg	G	AB	H	2B	3B	HR	(Hm	Rd)	TB	R	RBI	RC	TBB	IBB	SO	HBP	SH	SF	SB	CS	SB%	GDP	Avg	OBP	Slg
2007	Cle	AL	45	159	45	9	2	3	(1	2)	67	30	22	27	17	0	29	2	5	3	0	0	-	7	.283	.354	.421
2008	Cle	AL	114	352	91	20	0	6	(5	1)	129	48	47	48	46	2	77	4	11	5	4	4	.50	8	.259	.346	.366
2009	Cle	AL	131	523	161	42	4	6	(4	2)	229	81	68	81	44	1	89	1	10	3	17	4	.81	13	.308	.361	.438
2010	Cle	AL	97	381	105	16	1	3	(2	1)	132	39	29	46	25	0	60	5	11	3	6	4	.60	10	.276	.326	.346
2011	Cle	AL	151	604	165	32	3	25	(13	12)	278	87	92	100	44	5	119	11	4	4	17	5	.77	10	.273	.332	.460
Postseason			11	46	10	0	0	1	(1	0)	13	5	6	5	2	0	12	0	3	1	0	0	-	2	.217	.245	.283
5 ML YEARS			538	2019	567	119	10	43	(25	18)	835	285	258	302	176	8	374	23	41	18	44	17	.72	48	.281	.343	.414

Everth Cabrera

Bats: B Throws: R Pos: SS-2   Ht: 5'10" Wt: 176 Born: 11/17/1986 Age: 25

Year	Team	Lg	G	AB	H	2B	3B	HR	(Hm	Rd)	TB	R	RBI	RC	TBB	IBB	SO	HBP	SH	SF	SB	CS	SB%	GDP	Avg	OBP	Slg
2011	Tucsn*	AAA	58	246	73	12	4	2	(-	-)	99	52	15	41	29	0	40	0	2	1	29	8	.78	4	.297	.370	.402
2009	SD	NL	103	377	96	18	8	2	(1	1)	136	59	31	48	46	5	88	5	8	2	25	8	.76	3	.255	.342	.361
2010	SD	NL	76	212	44	6	3	1	(0	1)	59	22	22	15	19	3	54	2	8	0	10	6	.63	8	.208	.279	.278
2011	SD	NL	2	8	1	0	0	0	(0	0)	1	1	0	1	1	0	3	0	0	0	2	0	1.00	0	.125	.222	.125
	3 ML YEARS		181	597	141	24	11	3	(1	2)	196	82	53	64	66	8	145	7	16	2	37	14	.73	11	.236	.318	.328

Melky Cabrera

Bats: B Throws: L Pos: CF-144; LF-12; RF-2; DH-2; PH-1   Ht: 6'0" Wt: 200 Born: 8/11/1984 Age: 27

Year	Team	Lg	G	AB	H	2B	3B	HR	(Hm	Rd)	TB	R	RBI	RC	TBB	IBB	SO	HBP	SH	SF	SB	CS	SB%	GDP	Avg	OBP	Slg
2005	NYY	AL	6	19	4	0	0	0	(0	0)	4	1	0	0	0	0	2	0	0	0	0	0	-	0	.211	.211	.211
2006	NYY	AL	130	460	129	26	2	7	(3	4)	180	75	50	68	56	3	59	2	5	1	12	5	.71	9	.280	.360	.391
2007	NYY	AL	150	545	149	24	8	8	(4	4)	213	66	73	70	43	0	68	5	10	9	13	5	.72	14	.273	.327	.391
2008	NYY	AL	129	414	103	12	1	8	(4	4)	141	42	37	37	29	5	58	3	4	4	9	2	.82	11	.249	.301	.341
2009	NYY	AL	154	485	133	28	1	13	(9	4)	202	66	68	69	43	4	59	4	4	4	10	2	.83	15	.274	.336	.416
2010	Atl	NL	147	458	117	27	3	4	(1	3)	162	50	42	45	42	11	64	1	5	3	7	1	.88	8	.255	.317	.354
2011	KC	AL	155	658	201	44	5	18	(6	12)	309	102	87	92	35	3	94	1	7	5	20	10	.67	13	.305	.339	.470
	Postseason		22	75	16	2	0	1	(0	1)	21	8	7	5	3	0	16	0	2	0	0	0	-	0	.213	.244	.280
	7 ML YEARS		871	3039	836	161	20	58	(27	31)	1211	402	357	381	248	26	404	16	35	25	71	25	.74	70	.275	.331	.398

Miguel Cabrera

Bats: R Throws: R Pos: 1B-152; DH-7; PH-2   Ht: 6'4" Wt: 240 Born: 4/18/1983 Age: 29

Year	Team	Lg	G	AB	H	2B	3B	HR	(Hm	Rd)	TB	R	RBI	RC	TBB	IBB	SO	HBP	SH	SF	SB	CS	SB%	GDP	Avg	OBP	Slg
2003	Fla	NL	87	314	84	21	3	12	(7	5)	147	39	62	51	25	3	84	2	4	1	0	2	.00	12	.268	.325	.468
2004	Fla	NL	160	603	177	31	1	33	(14	19)	309	101	112	92	68	5	148	6	0	4	5	2	.71	20	.294	.366	.512
2005	Fla	NL	158	613	198	43	2	33	(11	22)	344	106	116	108	64	12	125	2	0	6	1	0	1.00	20	.323	.385	.561
2006	Fla	NL	158	576	195	50	2	26	(15	11)	327	112	114	132	86	27	108	10	0	4	9	6	.60	18	.339	.430	.568
2007	Fla	NL	157	588	188	38	2	34	(19	15)	332	91	119	122	79	23	127	5	1	7	2	1	.67	17	.320	.401	.565
2008	Det	AL	160	616	180	36	2	37	(19	18)	331	85	127	109	56	6	126	3	0	9	1	0	1.00	16	.292	.349	.537
2009	Det	AL	160	611	198	34	0	34	(19	15)	334	96	103	114	68	14	107	5	0	1	6	2	.75	22	.324	.396	.547
2010	Det	AL	150	548	180	45	1	38	(17	21)	341	111	126	122	89	32	95	3	0	5	3	3	.50	17	.328	.420	.622
2011	Det	AL	161	572	197	48	0	30	(15	15)	335	111	105	141	108	22	89	3	0	5	2	1	.67	24	.344	.448	.586
	Postseason		17	68	18	2	0	4	(1	3)	32	11	12	9	4	0	19	1	1	0	0	0	-	2	.265	.315	.471
	9 ML YEARS		1351	5041	1597	346	13	277	(136	141)	2800	852	984	991	643	144	1009	39	5	49	29	17	.63	166	.317	.395	.555

Orlando Cabrera

Bats: R Throws: R Pos: 2B-85; SS-39; 3B-5; PH-4; PR-4   Ht: 5'10" Wt: 194 Born: 11/2/1974 Age: 37

Year	Team	Lg	G	AB	H	2B	3B	HR	(Hm	Rd)	TB	R	RBI	RC	TBB	IBB	SO	HBP	SH	SF	SB	CS	SB%	GDP	Avg	OBP	Slg
1997	Mon	NL	16	18	4	0	0	0	(0	0)	4	4	2	0	1	0	3	0	1	0	1	2	.33	1	.222	.263	.222
1998	Mon	NL	79	261	73	16	5	3	(2	1)	108	44	22	34	18	1	27	0	5	1	6	2	.75	6	.280	.325	.414
1999	Mon	NL	104	382	97	23	5	8	(6	2)	154	48	39	42	18	4	38	3	4	0	2	2	.50	9	.254	.293	.403
2000	Mon	NL	125	422	100	25	1	13	(7	6)	166	47	55	43	25	3	28	1	3	3	4	4	.50	12	.237	.279	.393
2001	Mon	NL	162	626	173	41	6	14	(7	7)	268	64	96	85	43	5	54	4	4	7	19	7	.73	15	.276	.324	.428
2002	Mon	NL	153	563	148	43	1	7	(3	4)	214	64	56	61	48	4	53	2	9	4	25	7	.78	16	.263	.321	.380
2003	Mon	NL	162	626	186	47	2	17	(8	9)	288	95	80	92	52	3	64	1	3	9	24	2	.92	18	.297	.347	.460
2004	2 Tms		161	618	163	38	3	10	(2	8)	237	74	62	67	39	0	54	3	3	10	16	4	.80	16	.264	.306	.383
2005	LAA	AL	141	540	139	28	3	8	(2	6)	197	70	57	61	38	4	50	3	4	2	21	2	.91	10	.257	.309	.365
2006	LAA	AL	153	607	171	45	1	9	(3	6)	245	95	72	77	51	0	58	3	3	11	27	3	.90	12	.282	.335	.404
2007	LAA	AL	155	638	192	35	1	8	(3	5)	253	101	86	95	44	0	64	5	3	11	20	4	.83	12	.301	.345	.397
2008	CWS	AL	161	661	186	33	1	8	(5	3)	245	93	57	83	56	1	71	1	3	9	19	6	.76	16	.281	.334	.371
2009	2 Tms		160	656	186	36	3	9	(3	6)	255	83	77	74	36	1	71	0	6	10	13	4	.76	22	.284	.316	.389
2010	Cin	NL	123	494	130	33	0	4	(3	1)	175	64	42	49	28	0	53	3	5	7	11	4	.73	11	.263	.303	.354
2011	2 Tms		130	450	107	16	0	5	(3	2)	138	39	51	34	17	0	57	3	1	6	8	4	.67	12	.238	.267	.307
04	Mon	NL	103	390	96	19	2	4	(1	3)	131	41	31	37	28	0	31	2	2	3	12	3	.80	12	.246	.298	.336
04	Bos	AL	58	228	67	19	1	6	(1	5)	106	33	31	30	11	0	23	1	1	7	4	1	.80	4	.294	.320	.465
09	Oak	AL	101	414	116	23	0	4	(0	4)	151	41	41	48	25	1	39	0	5	4	11	4	.73	13	.280	.318	.365
09	Min	AL	59	242	70	13	3	5	(3	2)	104	42	36	26	11	0	32	0	1	6	2	0	1.00	9	.289	.313	.430
11	Cle	AL	91	324	79	13	0	4	(3	1)	104	35	38	26	13	0	40	3	1	3	6	2	.75	10	.244	.277	.321
11	SF	NL	39	126	28	3	0	1	(0	1)	34	4	13	8	4	0	17	0	0	3	2	2	.50	2	.222	.241	.270
	Postseason		37	149	34	8	0	1	(1	0)	45	15	18	15	11	0	20	2	0	1	2	0	1.00	1	.228	.288	.302
	15 ML YEARS		1985	7562	2055	459	32	123	(57	66)	2947	985	854	897	514	26	745	32	57	90	216	57	.79	188	.272	.317	.390

Trevor Cahill

Pitches: R Bats: R Pos: SP-34   KAY-hill   Ht: 6'4" Wt: 222 Born: 3/1/1988 Age: 24

| | HOW MUCH HE PITCHED | | | | | | WHAT HE GAVE UP | | | | | | | | | | THE RESULTS | | | | | | |
Year	Team	Lg	G	GS	CG	GF	IP	BFP	H	R	ER	HR	SH	SF	HB	TBB	IBB	SO	WP	Bk	W	L	Pct	Sh	Sv-Op	Hld	ERC	ERA
2009	Oak	AL	32	32	0	0	178.2	773	185	99	92	27	4	7	4	72	1	90	5	0	10	13	.435	0	0-0	0	4.79	4.63
2010	Oak	AL	30	30	1	0	196.2	783	155	73	65	19	3	6	6	63	1	118	2	2	18	8	.692	1	0-0	0	2.81	2.97
2011	Oak	AL	34	34	0	0	207.2	901	214	102	96	19	8	6	8	82	1	147	15	0	12	14	.462	0	0-0	0	4.34	4.16
	3 ML YEARS		96	96	1	0	583.0	2457	554	274	253	65	15	19	18	217	3	355	22	2	40	35	.533	1	0-0	0	3.94	3.91

Lorenzo Cain

Bats: R **Throws:** R **Pos:** RF-4; CF-2   **Ht:** 6'2" **Wt:** 192 **Born:** 4/13/1986 **Age:** 26

								BATTING												BASERUNNING				AVERAGES		
Year	Team	Lg	G	AB	H	2B	3B	HR	(Hm Rd)	TB	R	RBI	RC	TBB	IBB	SO	HBP	SH	SF	SB	CS	SB%	GDP	Avg	OBP	Slg
2005	Brewrs	R	50	205	73	18	5	5	(- -)	116	45	37	48	20	0	32	4	0	3	12	3	.80	7	.356	.418	.566
2005	Helena	R+	6	24	5	0	0	0	(- -)	5	4	1	1	1	0	6	3	0	0	0	0	-	1	.208	.321	.208
2006	WV	A	132	527	162	36	4	6	(- -)	224	91	60	93	58	1	104	11	2	5	34	11	.76	12	.307	.384	.425
2007	BrvdCt	A+	126	482	133	21	3	2	(- -)	166	67	44	61	37	0	97	9	4	1	24	9	.73	9	.276	.338	.344
2008	BrvdCt	A+	80	317	91	22	4	7	(- -)	142	50	41	54	29	1	68	7	1	2	19	4	.83	7	.287	.358	.448
2008	Nashv	AAA	6	19	3	0	0	0	(- -)	3	0	2	0	3	1	6	0	0	0	0	0	-	1	.158	.273	.158
2008	Hntsvl	AA	40	148	41	9	5	4	(- -)	72	21	17	27	19	1	41	2	1	2	6	2	.75	3	.277	.363	.486
2009	Hntsvl	AA	42	145	31	6	0	4	(- -)	49	17	15	13	10	0	35	3	1	1	3	3	.50	2	.214	.277	.338
2009	Brewrs	R	3	9	4	1	0	0	(- -)	5	1	1	2	1	0	0	0	0	1	0	0	-	0	.444	.455	.556
2009	Wisc	A	15	52	10	4	0	0	(- -)	14	3	3	4	9	0	15	0	0	0	0	0	-	1	.192	.311	.269
2010	Hntsvl	AA	62	244	79	6	6	3	(- -)	106	45	18	48	34	2	52	1	1	0	21	2	.91	4	.324	.409	.434
2010	Nashv	AAA	22	87	26	5	3	0	(- -)	37	13	9	15	11	0	17	1	1	0	5	1	.83	5	.299	.384	.425
2011	Omha	AAA	128	487	152	28	7	16	(- -)	242	84	81	93	40	0	102	15	4	3	16	6	.73	9	.312	.380	.497
2010	Mil	NL	43	147	45	11	1	1	(1 0)	61	17	13	23	9	0	28	1	0	1	7	1	.88	1	.306	.348	.415
2011	KC	AL	6	22	6	1	0	0	(0 0)	7	4	1	2	1	0	4	0	0	0	0	0	-	0	.273	.304	.318
2 ML YEARS			49	169	51	12	1	1	(1 0)	68	21	14	25	10	0	32	1	0	1	7	1	.88	1	.302	.343	.402

Matt Cain

Pitches: R **Bats:** R **Pos:** SP-33   **Ht:** 6'3" **Wt:** 230 **Born:** 10/1/1984 **Age:** 27

			HOW MUCH HE PITCHED						WHAT HE GAVE UP											THE RESULTS							
Year	Team	Lg	G	GS	CG	GF	IP	BFP	H	R	ER	HR	SH	SF	HB	TBB	IBB	SO	WP	Bk	W	L	Pct	Sh	Sv-Op Hld	ERC	ERA
2005	SF	NL	7	7	1	0	46.1	181	24	12	12	4	2	1	0	19	1	30	1	0	2	1	.667	0	0-0 0	1.61	2.33
2006	SF	NL	32	31	1	1	190.2	818	157	93	88	18	11	6	6	87	1	179	9	2	13	12	.520	1	0-0 0	3.35	4.15
2007	SF	NL	32	32	1	0	200.0	832	173	84	81	14	8	5	5	79	3	163	12	0	7	16	.304	0	0-0 0	3.23	3.65
2008	SF	NL	34	34	1	0	217.2	933	206	95	91	19	7	7	7	91	9	186	7	2	8	14	.364	1	0-0 0	3.84	3.76
2009	SF	NL	33	33	4	0	217.2	886	184	73	70	22	10	6	3	73	6	171	9	0	14	8	.636	0	0-0 0	3.06	2.89
2010	SF	NL	33	33	4	0	223.1	896	181	84	78	22	6	7	4	61	4	177	8	0	13	11	.542	2	0-0 0	2.65	3.14
2011	SF	NL	33	33	1	0	221.2	907	177	82	71	9	11	6	9	63	5	179	4	0	12	11	.522	0	0-0 0	2.31	2.88
Postseason			3	3	0	0	21.1	85	13	1	0	0	1	0	2	7	1	13	1	0	2	0	1.000	0	0-0 0	1.56	0.00
7 ML YEARS			204	203	13	1	1317.1	5453	1102	523	491	108	55	38	34	473	29	1085	50	4	69	73	.486	4	0-0 0	2.99	3.35

Miguel Cairo

Bats: R **Throws:** R **Pos:** 3B-58; PH-34; 2B-13; 1B-5; PR-1   **Ht:** 6'1" **Wt:** 222 **Born:** 5/4/1974 **Age:** 38

								BATTING												BASERUNNING				AVERAGES		
Year	Team	Lg	G	AB	H	2B	3B	HR	(Hm Rd)	TB	R	RBI	RC	TBB	IBB	SO	HBP	SH	SF	SB	CS	SB%	GDP	Avg	OBP	Slg
1996	Tor	AL	9	27	6	2	0	0	(0 0)	8	5	1	2	2	0	9	1	0	0	0	0	-	1	.222	.300	.296
1997	ChC	NL	16	29	7	1	0	0	(0 0)	8	7	1	3	2	0	3	1	0	0	0	0	-	0	.241	.313	.276
1998	TB	AL	150	515	138	26	5	5	(3 2)	189	49	46	58	24	0	44	6	11	2	19	8	.70	9	.268	.307	.367
1999	TB	AL	120	465	137	15	5	3	(1 2)	171	61	36	57	24	0	46	7	7	5	22	7	.76	13	.295	.335	.368
2000	TB	AL	119	375	98	18	2	1	(0 1)	123	49	34	42	29	0	34	2	6	5	28	7	.80	7	.261	.314	.328
2001	2 Tms	NL	93	156	46	8	1	3	(2 1)	65	25	16	23	18	1	23	0	7	1	2	1	.67	4	.295	.366	.417
2002	StL	NL	108	184	46	9	2	2	(1 1)	65	28	23	19	13	2	36	3	6	2	1	1	.50	5	.250	.307	.353
2003	StL	NL	92	261	64	15	2	5	(2 3)	98	41	32	25	13	1	30	6	3	7	4	1	.80	6	.245	.289	.375
2004	NYY	AL	122	360	105	17	5	6	(4 2)	150	48	42	50	18	1	49	14	12	4	11	3	.79	7	.292	.346	.417
2005	NYM	NL	100	327	82	18	0	2	(1 1)	106	31	19	29	19	2	31	4	12	5	13	3	.81	5	.251	.296	.324
2006	NYY	AL	81	222	53	12	3	0	(0 0)	71	28	30	26	13	0	31	1	5	3	13	1	.93	4	.239	.280	.320
2007	2 Tms		82	174	44	9	2	0	(0 0)	57	20	15	21	11	1	24	2	5	1	10	2	.83	3	.253	.303	.328
2008	Sea	AL	108	221	55	14	2	0	(0 0)	73	34	23	26	18	0	32	4	6	1	5	2	.71	6	.249	.316	.330
2009	Phi	NL	27	45	12	2	1	1	(1 0)	19	6	2	2	0	0	4	1	1	0	0	0	-	1	.267	.283	.422
2010	Cin	NL	91	200	58	12	0	4	(4 0)	82	30	28	27	17	0	30	4	2	3	4	0	1.00	4	.290	.353	.410
2011	Cin	NL	102	245	65	8	2	8	(8 0)	101	33	33	37	18	1	36	7	3	3	3	4	.43	3	.265	.330	.412
01	ChC	NL	66	123	35	3	1	2	(1 1)	46	20	9	17	16	1	21	0	7	1	2	1	.67	3	.285	.364	.374
01	StL	NL	27	33	11	5	0	1	(1 0)	19	5	7	6	2	0	2	0	0	0	0	0	-	1	.333	.371	.576
07	NYY	AL	54	107	27	7	0	0	(0 0)	34	12	10	12	8	1	19	1	4	1	8	1	.89	3	.252	.308	.318
07	StL	NL	28	67	17	2	2	0	(0 0)	23	8	5	9	3	0	5	1	1	0	2	1	.67	0	.254	.296	.343
Postseason			26	69	20	5	0	1	(1 0)	28	11	6	9	4	0	14	5	2	0	2	1	.67	0	.290	.372	.406
16 ML YEARS			1420	3806	1016	186	32	40	(27 13)	1386	495	381	447	239	9	462	63	86	42	135	40	.77	78	.267	.318	.364

Alberto Callaspo

Bats: B **Throws:** R **Pos:** 3B-129; PH-13; PR-1   ky-AHS-po   **Ht:** 5'9" **Wt:** 195 **Born:** 4/19/1983 **Age:** 29

								BATTING												BASERUNNING				AVERAGES		
Year	Team	Lg	G	AB	H	2B	3B	HR	(Hm Rd)	TB	R	RBI	RC	TBB	IBB	SO	HBP	SH	SF	SB	CS	SB%	GDP	Avg	OBP	Slg
2006	Ari	NL	23	42	10	1	1	0	(0 0)	13	2	6	5	4	0	6	0	0	1	0	1	.00	0	.238	.298	.310
2007	Ari	NL	56	144	31	8	0	0	(0 0)	39	10	7	7	9	0	14	1	1	1	1	1	.50	8	.215	.265	.271
2008	KC	AL	74	213	65	8	3	0	(0 0)	79	21	16	25	19	0	14	0	1	1	2	1	.67	6	.305	.361	.371
2009	KC	AL	155	576	173	41	8	11	(6 5)	263	79	73	90	52	4	51	1	0	5	2	1	.67	15	.300	.356	.457
2010	2 Tms	AL	146	562	149	27	2	10	(2 8)	210	61	56	54	31	3	42	1	1	6	5	3	.63	22	.265	.302	.374
2011	LAA	AL	141	475	137	23	0	6	(1 5)	178	54	46	66	58	8	48	1	0	2	8	1	.89	11	.288	.366	.375
10	KC	AL	88	349	96	19	2	8	(2 6)	143	40	43	38	19	2	29	0	0	5	3	1	.75	14	.275	.308	.410
10	LAA	AL	58	213	53	8	0	2	(0 2)	67	21	13	16	12	1	13	1	1	1	2	2	.50	8	.249	.291	.315
Postseason			2	2	0	0	0	0	(0 0)	0	0	0	0	0	0	0	0	0	0	0	0	-	0	.000	.000	.000
6 ML YEARS			595	2012	565	108	14	27	(9 18)	782	227	204	247	173	15	175	4	3	16	18	8	.69	62	.281	.337	.389

Mike Cameron

Bats: R Throws: R Pos: CF-42; RF-25; PH-12; LF-4; DH-2   Ht: 6'2" Wt: 210 Born: 1/8/1973 Age: 39

Year	Team	Lg	G	AB	H	2B	3B	HR	(Hm	Rd)	TB	R	RBI	RC	TBB	IBB	SO	HBP	SH	SF	SB	CS	SB%	GDP	Avg	OBP	Slg
1995	CWS	AL	28	38	7	2	0	1	(0	1)	12	4	2	3	3	0	15	0	3	0	0	0	-	0	.184	.244	.316
1996	CWS	AL	11	11	1	0	0	0	(0	0)	1	1	0	0	1	0	3	0	0	0	0	1	.00	0	.091	.167	.091
1997	CWS	AL	116	379	98	18	3	14	(10	4)	164	63	55	63	55	1	105	5	2	5	23	2	.92	8	.259	.356	.433
1998	CWS	AL	141	396	83	16	5	8	(5	3)	133	53	43	39	37	0	101	6	1	3	27	11	.71	6	.210	.285	.336
1999	Cin	NL	146	542	139	34	9	21	(12	9)	254	93	66	96	80	2	145	6	5	3	38	12	.76	4	.256	.357	.469
2000	Sea	AL	155	543	145	28	4	19	(5	14)	238	96	78	91	78	0	133	9	7	6	24	7	.77	10	.267	.365	.438
2001	Sea	AL	150	540	144	30	5	25	(7	18)	259	99	110	96	69	3	155	10	1	13	34	5	.87	13	.267	.353	.480
2002	Sea	AL	158	545	130	26	5	25	(7	18)	241	84	80	78	79	3	176	7	4	5	31	8	.79	8	.239	.340	.442
2003	Sea	AL	147	534	135	31	5	18	(11	7)	230	74	76	80	70	1	137	5	1	2	17	7	.71	13	.253	.344	.431
2004	NYM	NL	140	493	114	30	1	30	(11	19)	236	76	76	70	57	2	143	8	1	3	22	6	.79	5	.231	.319	.479
2005	NYM	NL	76	308	84	23	2	12	(7	5)	147	47	39	52	29	0	85	4	1	1	13	1	.93	5	.273	.342	.477
2006	SD	NL	141	552	148	34	9	22	(11	11)	266	88	83	98	71	2	142	6	0	5	25	9	.74	8	.268	.355	.482
2007	SD	NL	151	571	138	33	6	21	(10	11)	246	88	78	83	67	1	160	8	2	3	18	5	.78	9	.242	.328	.431
2008	Mil	NL	120	444	108	25	2	25	(11	18)	212	69	70	70	54	1	142	6	1	3	17	5	.77	4	.243	.331	.477
2009	Mil	NL	149	544	136	32	3	24	(14	10)	246	78	70	75	75	3	156	4	0	5	7	3	.70	12	.250	.342	.452
2010	Bos	AL	48	162	42	11	0	4	(1	3)	65	24	15	17	14	0	44	3	0	1	0	1	.00	3	.259	.328	.401
2011	2 Tms		78	237	48	10	0	9	(5	4)	85	27	27	19	28	0	59	0	2	2	1	0	1.00	3	.203	.285	.359
11	Bos	AL	33	94	14	2	0	3	(2	1)	25	9	9	2	8	0	25	0	1	2	0	0	-	3	.149	.212	.266
11	Fla	NL	45	143	34	8	0	6	(3	3)	60	18	18	17	20	0	34	0	1	0	1	0	1.00	0	.238	.331	.420
	Postseason		27	92	16	6	0	1	(1	0)	25	14	7	7	14	0	29	4	2	0	3	1	.75	2	.174	.309	.272
17 ML YEARS			1955	6839	1700	383	59	278	(123	155)	3035	1064	968	1030	867	19	1901	87	31	60	297	83	.78	114	.249	.338	.444

Shawn Camp

Pitches: R Bats: R Pos: RP-67   Ht: 6'0" Wt: 204 Born: 11/18/1975 Age: 36

			HOW MUCH HE PITCHED					WHAT HE GAVE UP											THE RESULTS						
Year	Team	Lg	G	GS	CG	GF	IP	BFP	H	R	ER	HR	SH	SF	HB	TBB	IBB	SO	WP	Bk	W	L	Pct	Sh	Sv-Op	Hld	ERC	ERA
2004	KC	AL	42	0	0	12	66.2	286	74	37	29	10	2	3	5	16	1	51	2	1	2	2	.500	0	2-3	5	4.74	3.92
2005	KC	AL	29	0	0	7	49.0	228	69	40	35	4	0	3	4	13	3	28	3	0	1	4	.200	0	0-2	0	6.00	6.43
2006	TB	AL	75	0	0	15	75.0	328	93	43	39	9	2	3	7	19	3	53	4	0	7	4	.636	0	4-6	12	5.48	4.68
2007	TB	AL	50	0	0	8	40.0	198	63	33	32	7	5	1	3	18	6	36	2	0	0	3	.000	0	0-2	11	8.59	7.20
2008	Tor	AL	40	0	0	16	39.1	166	40	18	18	2	0	1	2	11	3	31	0	0	3	1	.750	0	0-0	7	3.47	4.12
2009	Tor	AL	59	0	0	17	79.2	333	73	36	31	7	1	1	4	29	4	58	0	0	2	6	.250	0	1-1	6	3.57	3.50
2010	Tor	AL	70	0	0	13	72.1	298	71	26	24	8	0	2	4	18	5	46	2	0	4	3	.571	0	2-4	13	3.65	2.99
2011	Tor	AL	67	0	0	23	66.1	292	79	36	31	3	2	1	6	22	9	32	0	0	6	3	.667	0	1-4	5	4.72	4.21
8 ML YEARS			432	0	0	111	488.1	2129	562	269	239	50	12	15	35	146	34	335	13	1	25	26	.490	0	10-22	59	4.79	4.40

Tony Campana

Bats: L Throws: L Pos: LF-35; CF-29; PH-28; PR-17; RF-5   Ht: 5'8" Wt: 165 Born: 5/30/1986 Age: 26

Year	Team	Lg	G	AB	H	2B	3B	HR	(Hm	Rd)	TB	R	RBI	RC	TBB	IBB	SO	HBP	SH	SF	SB	CS	SB%	GDP	Avg	OBP	Slg
2008	Boise	A-	1	3	0	0	0	0	(-	-)	0	0	0	0	1	0	1	0	0	0	0	1	.00	1	.000	.400	.000
2008	Cubs	R	24	83	23	0	0	0	(-	-)	23	17	10	10	8	0	14	0	1	1	22	2	.92	2	.277	.337	.277
2009	Peoria	A	18	53	15	1	1	0	(-	-)	18	14	5	7	5	0	6	0	0	0	11	2	.85	0	.283	.345	.340
2009	Dytona	A+	108	430	122	8	2	0	(-	-)	134	56	25	52	34	0	78	0	7	2	55	16	.77	2	.284	.335	.312
2010	Tenn	AA	131	489	156	22	5	0	(-	-)	188	76	39	77	44	1	82	5	8	4	47	20	.70	2	.319	.378	.384
2011	Iowa	AAA	30	120	41	8	2	0	(-	-)	53	27	9	21	6	0	23	2	1	0	8	1	.89	0	.342	.383	.442
2011	ChC	NL	95	143	37	3	0	1	(1	0)	43	24	6	17	8	1	30	1	3	0	24	2	.92	1	.259	.303	.301

Robinson Cancel

Bats: R Throws: R Pos: C-2   cann-SELL   Ht: 6'0" Wt: 239 Born: 5/4/1976 Age: 36

Year	Team	Lg	G	AB	H	2B	3B	HR	(Hm	Rd)	TB	R	RBI	RC	TBB	IBB	SO	HBP	SH	SF	SB	CS	SB%	GDP	Avg	OBP	Slg
2011	OKCity*	AAA	94	318	95	19	0	4	(-	-)	126	37	50	50	37	0	59	2	0	1	10	3	.77	9	.299	.374	.396
1999	Mil	NL	15	44	8	2	0	0	(	)	10	5	5	2	2	0	12	1	1	0	0	0	-	0	.182	.234	.227
2008	NYM	NL	27	49	12	2	0	1	(1	0)	17	5	5	3	3	0	6	0	1	0	1	2	.33	0	.245	.288	.347
2009	NYM	NL	1	1	0	0	0	0	(0	0)	0	0	0	0	0	0	0	0	0	0	0	0	-	0	.000	.000	.000
2011	Hou	NL	2	6	0	0	0	0	(0	0)	0	0	0	0	1	1	4	0	0	0	0	0	-	0	.000	.143	.000
4 ML YEARS			45	100	20	4	0	1	(1	0)	27	10	10	5	6	1	22	1	2	0	1	2	.33	0	.200	.252	.270

Robinson Cano

Bats: L Throws: R Pos: 2B-157; DH-7; PH-2   kuh-NOE   Ht: 6'0" Wt: 205 Born: 10/22/1982 Age: 29

Year	Team	Lg	G	AB	H	2B	3B	HR	(Hm	Rd)	TB	R	RBI	RC	TBB	IBB	SO	HBP	SH	SF	SB	CS	SB%	GDP	Avg	OBP	Slg
2005	NYY	AL	132	522	155	34	4	14	(5	9)	239	78	62	59	16	1	68	3	7	3	1	3	.25	16	.297	.320	.458
2006	NYY	AL	122	482	165	41	1	15	(9	6)	253	62	78	74	18	3	54	2	1	5	5	2	.71	19	.342	.365	.525
2007	NYY	AL	160	617	189	41	7	19	(10	9)	301	93	97	94	39	5	85	8	1	4	4	5	.44	19	.306	.353	.488
2008	NYY	AL	159	597	162	35	3	14	(7	7)	245	70	72	64	26	3	65	5	1	5	2	4	.33	18	.271	.305	.410
2009	NYY	AL	161	637	204	48	2	25	(14	11)	331	103	85	79	30	2	63	3	0	4	5	7	.42	22	.320	.352	.520
2010	NYY	AL	160	626	200	41	3	29	(16	13)	334	103	109	118	57	14	77	8	0	5	3	2	.60	19	.319	.381	.534
2011	NYY	AL	159	623	188	46	7	28	(16	12)	332	104	118	111	38	11	96	12	0	8	8	2	.80	18	.302	.349	.533
	Postseason		37	141	35	6	3	6	(3	3)	65	19	20	16	8	1	18	2	0	1	0	2	.00	6	.248	.296	.461
7 ML YEARS			1053	4104	1263	286	27	144	(77	67)	2035	613	621	599	224	39	508	41	10	34	28	25	.53	131	.308	.347	.496

Jorge Cantu

Bats: R Throws: R Pos: 1B-26; PH-25; 3B-10; 2B-1   Ht: 6'3" Wt: 205 Born: 1/30/1982 Age: 30

Year	Team	Lg	G	AB	H	2B	3B	HR	(Hm	Rd)	TB	R	RBI	RC	TBB	IBB	SO	HBP	SH	SF	SB	CS	SB%	GDP	Avg	OBP	Slg
2011	ColSpr*	AAA	30	118	33	6	0	5	(-	-)	54	16	18	17	6	0	16	1	0	0	0	0	-	7	.280	.320	.458
2004	TB	AL	50	173	52	20	1	2	(0	2)	80	25	17	22	9	0	44	2	0	1	0	0	-	5	.301	.341	.462
2005	TB	AL	150	598	171	40	1	28	(16	12)	297	73	117	88	19	1	83	6	0	7	1	0	1.00	24	.286	.311	.497
2006	TB	AL	107	413	103	18	2	14	(7	7)	167	40	62	42	26	2	91	3	0	6	1	1	.50	16	.249	.295	.404
2007	2 Tms		52	115	29	9	0	1	(0	1)	41	12	13	12	12	0	26	3	0	3	0	0	-	6	.252	.331	.357
2008	Fla	NL	155	628	174	41	0	29	(18	11)	302	92	95	89	40	6	111	10	0	7	6	2	.75	15	.277	.327	.481
2009	Fla	NL	149	585	169	42	0	16	(8	8)	259	67	100	85	47	4	81	6	0	5	3	1	.75	15	.289	.345	.443
2010	2 Tms		127	472	121	29	1	11	(4	7)	185	50	56	52	29	1	95	6	1	7	0	0	-	15	.256	.304	.392
2011	SD	NL	57	144	28	4	0	3	(2	1)	41	8	16	8	7	1	28	1	0	3	0	0	-	6	.194	.232	.285
07	TB	AL	25	58	12	1	0	0	(0	0)	13	4	4	3	5	0	16	1	0	1	0	0	-	3	.207	.277	.224
07	Cin		27	57	17	8	0	1	(0	1)	28	8	9	9	7	0	10	2	0	2	0	0	-	3	.298	.382	.491
10	Fla	NL	97	374	98	25	0	10	(4	6)	153	41	54	47	23	1	76	6	0	7	0	0	-	11	.262	.310	.409
10	Tex	AL	30	98	23	4	1	1	(0	1)	32	9	2	5	6	0	19	0	1	0	0	0	-	4	.235	.279	.327
	Postseason		3	8	0	0	0	0	(0	0)	0	0	0	0	0	0	3	0	0	0	0	0	-	0	.000	.000	.000
	8 ML YEARS		847	3128	847	203	5	104	(55	49)	1372	367	476	398	189	15	559	37	1	39	11	4	.73	102	.271	.316	.439

Russ Canzler

Bats: R Throws: R Pos: PH-3; DH-2   Ht: 6'2" Wt: 215 Born: 4/11/1986 Age: 26

Year	Team	Lg	G	AB	H	2B	3B	HR	(Hm	Rd)	TB	R	RBI	RC	TBB	IBB	SO	HBP	SH	SF	SB	CS	SB%	GDP	Avg	OBP	Slg
2004	Cubs	R	32	105	26	2	3	1	(-	-)	37	12	13	11	9	0	35	1	3	1	0	1	.00	2	.248	.310	.352
2005	Cubs	R	49	157	47	11	3	1	(-	-)	67	22	20	26	24	1	41	1	2	4	1	5	.17	4	.299	.387	.427
2006	Boise	A-	73	280	74	22	4	16	(-	-)	152	49	61	49	22	0	70	3	1	5	7	4	.64	10	.264	.319	.543
2007	Peoria	A	125	460	124	24	2	7	(-	-)	173	60	54	57	35	2	88	2	1	5	12	8	.60	11	.270	.321	.376
2008	Dytona	A+	98	326	89	22	2	12	(-	-)	151	47	59	50	27	1	70	1	3	4	7	4	.64	12	.273	.327	.463
2009	Dytona	A+	28	100	27	8	1	2	(-	-)	43	14	14	14	7	0	24	0	0	1	2	0	1.00	1	.270	.315	.430
2009	Tenn	AA	91	233	60	15	0	6	(-	-)	93	27	36	33	31	1	41	1	1	1	2	5	.29	6	.258	.346	.399
2010	Tenn	AA	113	356	102	28	4	21	(-	-)	201	68	66	74	46	1	95	5	0	5	5	4	.56	5	.287	.371	.565
2011	Drham	AAA	131	474	149	40	4	18	(-	-)	251	78	83	101	67	0	129	4	0	4	5	2	.71	10	.314	.401	.530
2011	TB	AL	3	3	1	0	0	0	(0	0)	1	0	1	1	1	0	1	0	0	1	0	0	-	0	.333	.400	.333

Matt Capps

Pitches: R Bats: R Pos: RP-69   Ht: 6'2" Wt: 245 Born: 9/3/1983 Age: 28

Year	Team	Lg	G	GS	CG	GF	IP	BFP	H	R	ER	HR	SH	SF	HB	TBB	IBB	SO	WP	Bk	W	L	Pct	Sh	Sv-Op	Hld	ERC	ERA
2005	Pit	NL	4	0	0	0	4.0	16	5	2	2	0	0	0	0	0	0	3	0	0	0	0	-	0	0-0	0	4.62	4.50
2006	Pit	NL	85	0	0	15	80.2	329	81	37	34	12	8	2	3	12	5	56	4	0	9	1	.900	0	1-10	13	3.52	3.79
2007	Pit	NL	76	0	0	47	79.0	315	64	22	20	5	3	2	3	16	10	64	1	0	4	7	.364	0	18-21	15	2.10	2.28
2008	Pit	NL	49	0	0	39	53.2	211	47	20	18	5	2	0	2	5	0	39	0	0	2	3	.400	0	21-26	0	2.39	3.02
2009	Pit	NL	57	0	0	50	54.1	251	73	36	35	10	2	4	3	17	3	46	0	0	4	8	.333	0	27-32	1	6.53	5.80
2010	2 Tms		74	0	0	66	73.0	305	75	27	20	6	5	0	0	17	4	59	1	0	5	3	.625	0	42-48	3	3.37	2.47
2011	Min	AL	69	0	0	35	65.2	274	66	31	31	10	2	3	4	13	1	34	1	0	4	7	.364	0	15-24	7	3.89	4.25
10	Was	NL	47	0	0	43	46.0	199	51	20	14	5	4	0	0	9	3	38	0	0	3	3	.500	0	26-30	3	3.72	2.74
10	Min	AL	27	0	0	23	27.0	106	24	7	6	1	1	0	0	8	1	21	1	0	2	0	1.000	0	16-18	0	2.78	2.00
	Postseason		1	0	0	1	1.0	5	2	1	1	0	0	0	0	0	0	0	0	0	0	0	-	0	0-0	0	7.48	9.00
	7 ML YEARS		414	0	0	252	410.1	1701	411	175	160	48	22	11	16	80	23	301	7	0	28	29	.491	0	124-161	36	3.48	3.51

Chris Capuano

Pitches: L Bats: L Pos: SP-31; RP-2   capp-ue-AHH-noe   Ht: 6'3" Wt: 224 Born: 8/19/1978 Age: 33

Year	Team	Lg	G	GS	CG	GF	IP	BFP	H	R	ER	HR	SH	SF	HB	TBB	IBB	SO	WP	Bk	W	L	Pct	Sh	Sv-Op	Hld	ERC	ERA
2003	Ari	NL	9	5	0	2	33.0	139	27	19	17	3	4	1	6	11	1	23	3	0	2	4	.333	0	0-0	1	3.45	4.64
2004	Mil	NL	17	17	0	0	88.1	385	91	55	49	18	4	1	5	37	1	80	3	1	6	8	.429	0	0-0	0	5.37	4.99
2005	Mil	NL	35	35	0	0	219.0	949	212	105	97	31	14	5	12	91	6	176	3	4	18	12	.600	0	0-0	0	4.44	3.99
2006	Mil	NL	34	34	3	0	221.1	936	229	108	99	29	9	8	8	47	4	174	7	0	11	12	.478	2	0-0	0	3.84	4.03
2007	Mil	NL	29	25	0	1	150.0	669	170	93	85	20	10	3	8	54	2	132	10	0	5	12	.294	0	0-0	0	5.11	5.10
2010	Mil	NL	24	9	0	5	66.0	278	65	29	29	9	3	2	1	21	1	54	5	0	4	4	.500	0	0-0	1	3.98	3.95
2011	NYM	NL	33	31	1	0	186.0	802	198	99	94	27	9	1	5	53	5	168	4	0	11	12	.478	1	0-0	1	4.33	4.55
	7 ML YEARS		181	156	4	7	963.2	4158	992	508	470	137	53	21	46	314	20	807	35	5	57	64	.471	3	0-0	3	4.40	4.39

Andrew Carignan

Pitches: R Bats: R Pos: RP-6   CARE-uh-gun   Ht: 5'11" Wt: 205 Born: 7/23/1986 Age: 25

Year	Team	Lg	G	GS	CG	GF	IP	BFP	H	R	ER	HR	SH	SF	HB	TBB	IBB	SO	WP	Bk	W	L	Pct	Sh	Sv-Op	Hld	ERC	ERA
2007	Kane	A	12	0	0	10	13.1	57	6	7	3	0	1	1	0	11	1	19	4	0	1	1	.500	0	4- -		1.92	2.03
2008	Stcktn	A+	9	0	0	9	10.0	40	5	1	1	0	0	0	1	5	0	17	1	0	1	1	.500	0	4- -		1.66	0.90
2008	Mdland	AA	46	0	0	42	52.2	230	36	15	13	4	4	0	3	39	1	67	4	0	3	3	.500	0	24- -		3.67	2.22
2009	Stcktn	A+	2	0	0	0	2.0	10	1	1	1	0	0	1	0	3	0	2	0	0	0	0	-	0	0- -		4.47	4.50
2010	Stcktn	A+	30	0	0	10	33.0	163	28	31	23	2	1	0	5	34	0	44	7	0	3	3	.500	0	0- -		5.94	6.27
2011	Scrmto	AAA	13	0	0	5	16.2	68	11	5	4	1	0	1	0	7	0	19	0	0	0	0	-	0	0- -		2.34	2.16
2011	Stcktn	A+	9	0	0	7	11.0	40	4	1	0	0	0	0	1	2	0	12	1	0	1	0	1.000	0	5- -		0.66	0.00
2011	Mdland	AA	11	0	0	8	11.1	46	10	4	4	1	0	0	1	3	0	15	0	0	0	0	-	0	3- -		3.27	3.18
2011	Oak	AL	6	0	0	3	6.1	31	8	4	3	1	0	0	0	2	0	5	1	0	0	0	-	0	0-0	0	5.17	4.26

Buddy Carlyle

Pitches: R Bats: L Pos: RP-8 Ht: 6'3" Wt: 210 Born: 12/21/1977 Age: 34

Year	Team	Lg	G	GS	CG	GF	IP	BFP	H	R	ER	HR	SH	SF	HB	TBB	IBB	SO	WP	Bk	W	L	Pct	Sh	Sv-Op	Hld	ERC	ERA
2011	S-WB*	AAA	27	2	0	8	43.0	175	35	19	19	5	1	0	1	16	0	31	4	0	2	2	.500	0	1- -	-	3.22	3.98
1999	SD	NL	7	7	0	0	37.2	162	36	28	25	7	1	2	2	17	0	29	1	0	1	3	.250	0	0-0	0	4.95	5.97
2000	SD	NL	4	0	0	2	3.0	18	6	7	7	0	0	0	0	3	0	2	0	0	0	0	-	0	0-0	0	12.01	21.00
2005	LAD	NL	10	0	0	2	14.0	62	16	13	13	4	2	0	1	4	0	13	0	0	0	0	-	0	0-1	0	6.07	8.36
2007	Atl	NL	22	20	0	1	107.0	462	117	67	62	19	11	5	2	32	8	74	3	0	8	7	.533	0	0-0	0	4.71	5.21
2008	Atl	NL	45	0	0	5	62.2	259	52	26	25	5	4	0	1	26	6	59	4	1	2	0	1.000	0	0-0	0	3.03	3.59
2009	Atl	NL	16	0	0	7	21.1	107	35	23	21	5	2	1	0	12	4	12	2	0	0	1	.000	0	0-0	2	9.78	8.86
2011	NYY	AL	8	0	0	6	7.2	34	5	4	4	1	0	0	0	7	1	9	2	0	0	1	.000	0	0-0	0	4.16	4.70
	7 ML YEARS		112	27	0	23	253.1	1104	267	168	157	41	20	8	6	101	19	198	12	1	11	12	.478	0	0-1	2	4.83	5.58

Fausto Carmona

Pitches: R Bats: R Pos: SP-32 FAHW-sto Ht: 6'4" Wt: 230 Born: 12/7/1983 Age: 28

Year	Team	Lg	G	GS	CG	GF	IP	BFP	H	R	ER	HR	SH	SF	HB	TBB	IBB	SO	WP	Bk	W	L	Pct	Sh	Sv-Op	Hld	ERC	ERA
2006	Cle	AL	38	7	0	12	74.2	340	88	46	45	9	2	4	7	31	3	58	3	1	1	10	.091	0	0-3	10	5.69	5.42
2007	Cle	AL	32	32	2	0	215.0	879	199	78	73	16	2	4	11	61	2	137	5	1	19	8	.704	1	0-0	0	3.32	3.06
2008	Cle	AL	22	22	1	0	120.2	549	126	80	73	7	1	4	9	70	0	58	8	1	8	7	.533	1	0-0	0	5.07	5.44
2009	Cle	AL	24	24	0	0	125.1	596	151	97	88	16	4	2	8	70	0	79	5	1	5	12	.294	0	0-0	0	6.38	6.32
2010	Cle	AL	33	33	4	0	210.1	880	203	98	88	17	2	10	9	72	0	124	3	0	13	14	.481	1	0-0	0	3.77	3.77
2011	Cle	AL	32	32	0	0	188.2	833	205	125	110	22	9	7	14	60	3	109	3	1	7	15	.318	0	0-0	0	4.59	5.25
	Postseason		3	3	0	0	15.0	66	13	12	12	2	0	0	0	11	0	12	0	0	0	1	.000	0	0-0	0	5.02	7.20
	6 ML YEARS		181	150	7	12	934.2	4077	972	524	477	87	20	31	58	364	8	565	27	5	53	66	.445	3	0-3	10	4.48	4.59

Mike Carp

Bats: L Throws: R Pos: 1B-34; LF-27; DH-19; PH-4; RF-1 Ht: 6'2" Wt: 210 Born: 6/30/1986 Age: 26

Year	Team	Lg	G	AB	H	2B	3B	HR	(Hm	Rd)	TB	R	RBI	RC	TBB	IBB	SO	HBP	SH	SF	SB	CS	SB%	GDP	Avg	OBP	Slg
2011	Tacom*	AAA	66	251	86	14	0	21	(-	-)	163	55	64	64	28	1	50	3	1	3	6	2	.75	6	.343	.411	.649
2009	Sea	AL	21	54	17	3	1	1	(1	0)	25	7	5	8	8	0	10	2	0	1	0	0	-	1	.315	.415	.463
2010	Sea	AL	14	37	7	2	0	0	(0	0)	9	1	0	2	4	0	8	0	0	0	0	0	-	0	.189	.268	.243
2011	Sea	AL	79	290	80	17	1	12	(5	7)	135	27	46	39	19	0	81	3	0	1	0	2	.00	10	.276	.326	.466
	3 ML YEARS		114	381	104	22	2	13	(6	7)	169	35	51	49	31	0	99	5	0	2	0	2	.00	11	.273	.334	.444

Chris Carpenter

Pitches: R Bats: R Pos: SP-34 Ht: 6'6" Wt: 230 Born: 4/27/1975 Age: 37

Year	Team	Lg	G	GS	CG	GF	IP	BFP	H	R	ER	HR	SH	SF	HB	TBB	IBB	SO	WP	Bk	W	L	Pct	Sh	Sv-Op	Hld	ERC	ERA
1997	Tor	AL	14	13	1	1	81.1	374	108	55	46	7	1	2	2	37	0	55	7	1	3	7	.300	1	0-0	0	6.38	5.09
1998	Tor	AL	33	24	1	4	175.0	742	177	97	85	18	4	5	5	61	1	136	5	0	12	7	.632	1	0-0	0	4.12	4.37
1999	Tor	AL	24	24	4	0	150.0	663	177	81	73	16	4	6	3	48	1	106	9	1	9	8	.529	1	0-0	0	4.90	4.38
2000	Tor	AL	34	27	2	1	175.1	795	204	130	122	30	3	1	5	83	1	113	3	0	10	12	.455	0	0-0	0	6.04	6.26
2001	Tor	AL	34	34	3	0	215.2	930	229	112	98	29	3	1	16	75	5	157	5	0	11	11	.500	2	0-0	0	4.82	4.09
2002	Tor	AL	13	13	1	0	73.1	327	89	45	43	11	1	4	2	27	0	45	3	0	4	5	.444	0	0-0	0	5.91	5.28
2004	StL	NL	28	28	1	0	182.0	746	169	75	70	24	6	3	8	38	2	152	4	0	15	5	.750	0	0-0	0	3.32	3.46
2005	StL	NL	33	33	7	0	241.2	953	204	82	76	18	7	7	3	51	0	213	5	0	21	5	.808	4	0-0	0	2.75	2.83
2006	StL	NL	32	32	5	0	221.2	896	194	81	76	21	12	4	10	43	3	184	3	0	15	8	.652	3	0-0	0	5.80	7.50
2007	StL	NL	1	1	0	0	6.0	29	9	5	5	0	1	0	1	1	0	3	0	0	0	1	.000	0	0-0	0	3.19	1.76
2008	StL	NL	4	3	0	0	15.1	63	16	5	3	0	2	1	0	4	0	7	0	0	0	1	.000	0	0-0	0	3.19	1.76
2009	StL	NL	28	28	3	0	192.2	750	156	49	48	7	10	4	7	38	1	144	1	0	17	4	.810	1	0-0	0	2.14	2.24
2010	StL	NL	35	35	1	0	235.0	969	214	99	84	21	9	7	13	63	4	179	3	0	16	9	.640	0	0-0	0	3.23	3.22
2011	StL	NL	34	34	4	0	237.1	996	243	98	91	16	11	3	6	55	5	191	3	1	11	9	.550	2	0-0	0	3.40	3.45
	Postseason		9	9	0	0	58.1	244	54	20	19	6	7	2	3	19	0	38	1	0	5	2	.714	0	0-0	0	3.63	2.93
	14 ML YEARS		347	329	33	6	2202.1	9233	2189	1014	920	218	74	48	83	624	23	1685	51	3	144	92	.610	15	0-0	0	3.75	3.76

Chris Carpenter

Pitches: R Bats: R Pos: RP-10 Ht: 6'4" Wt: 220 Born: 12/26/1985 Age: 26

Year	Team	Lg	G	GS	CG	GF	IP	BFP	H	R	ER	HR	SH	SF	HB	TBB	IBB	SO	WP	Bk	W	L	Pct	Sh	Sv-Op	Hld	ERC	ERA
2008	Cubs	R	1	1	0	0	1.0	5	2	2	2	0	0	0	0	1	0	1	0	0	0	0	-	0	0- -	-	14.53	18.00
2008	Boise	A-	10	6	0	0	32.0	150	32	21	15	2	1	1	2	22	0	24	2	0	4	2	.667	0	0- -	-	5.12	4.22
2009	Peoria	A	15	15	1	0	73.2	301	55	23	20	4	2	3	1	33	1	60	0	1	4	3	.571	1	0- -	-	2.68	2.44
2009	Dytona	A+	5	5	0	0	25.0	101	15	7	4	1	0	0	1	8	0	33	3	0	2	1	.667	0	0- -	-	1.56	1.44
2009	Tenn	AA	7	7	0	0	32.0	138	30	20	17	0	1	0	4	11	0	25	2	0	0	3	.000	0	0- -	-	3.28	4.78
2010	Tenn	AA	23	23	0	0	119.2	514	117	56	42	5	7	2	7	48	2	100	11	0	8	6	.571	0	0- -	-	3.78	3.16
2010	Iowa	AAA	3	3	0	0	15.0	70	19	9	9	3	0	1	0	9	0	12	1	0	0	0	-	0	0- -	-	7.50	5.40
2011	Iowa	AAA	22	0	0	8	30.1	145	32	25	22	3	4	3	3	23	1	28	6	0	2	3	.400	0	1- -	-	6.21	6.53
2011	Tenn	AA	10	0	0	6	12.1	50	10	6	6	2	1	0	1	4	0	6	1	0	1	1	.500	0	1- -	-	3.57	4.38
2011	ChC	NL	10	0	0	1	9.2	47	12	3	3	1	0	0	0	7	1	8	2	0	0	0	-	0	0-0	0	6.67	2.79

David Carpenter

Pitches: R **Bats:** R **Pos:** RP-34   **Ht:** 6'2" **Wt:** 210 **Born:** 7/15/1985 **Age:** 26

		HOW MUCH HE PITCHED						WHAT HE GAVE UP											THE RESULTS						
Year Team	Lg	G	GS	CG	GF	IP	BFP	H	R	ER	HR	SH	SF	HB	TBB	IBB	SO	WP	Bk	W	L	Pct	Sh	Sv-Op Hld	ERC	ERA
2008 Cards	R	9	0	0	6	8.2	41	9	6	1	0	2	0	1	6	0	9	1	0	0	0	-	0	3- --	5.10	1.04
2008 JhsCty	R	6	0	0	2	6.0	28	7	3	2	1	1	0	1	1	0	8	0	0	0	0	-	0	0- --	4.93	3.00
2009 QuadC	A	52	0	0	32	67.1	302	61	34	32	2	1	5	10	36	0	77	1	1	5	3	.625	0	12- --	4.12	4.28
2010 PlmBh	A+	49	0	0	44	53.1	219	45	16	14	3	1	1	3	15	1	50	3	0	5	3	.625	0	20- --	2.70	2.36
2010 Lancst	A+	6	0	0	5	7.2	34	8	4	3	0	0	0	0	4	2	8	1	0	1	1	.500	0	0- --	3.61	3.52
2011 CpChr	AA	14	0	0	14	14.0	59	14	7	7	4	0	0	2	3	1	17	0	0	0	1	.000	0	5- --	5.16	4.50
2011 OKCity	AAA	19	0	0	15	19.0	76	15	0	0	0	0	2	0	6	0	21	3	0	0	0	-	0	9- --	2.07	0.00
2011 Hou	NL	34	0	0	12	27.2	125	28	9	9	3	4	1	4	13	7	29	2	1	1	3	.250	0	1-2 3	4.62	2.93

Drew Carpenter

Pitches: R **Bats:** R **Pos:** RP-12   **Ht:** 6'3" **Wt:** 238 **Born:** 5/18/1985 **Age:** 27

		HOW MUCH HE PITCHED						WHAT HE GAVE UP											THE RESULTS						
Year Team	Lg	G	GS	CG	GF	IP	BFP	H	R	ER	HR	SH	SF	HB	TBB	IBB	SO	WP	Bk	W	L	Pct	Sh	Sv-Op Hld	ERC	ERA
2011 LV*	AAA	34	1	0	3	60.1	238	48	13	12	2	1	1	0	11	0	65	4	1	5	1	.833	0	0- --	1.83	1.79
2008 Phi	NL	1	0	0	1	1.0	5	1	0	0	0	1	0	0	1	1	1	0	0	0	0	-	0	0-0 0	3.46	0.00
2009 Phi	NL	3	1	0	0	5.2	32	11	7	7	1	1	0	1	4	0	5	0	0	1	0	1.000	0	0-0 0	13.36	11.12
2010 Phi	NL	1	0	0	0	3.0	14	5	3	3	1	1	0	0	0	0	2	1	0	1	0	1.000	0	0-0 0	8.04	9.00
2011 2 Tms	NL	12	0	0	3	14.2	68	19	13	13	3	2	0	0	7	1	16	3	0	0	0	-	0	0-1 0	6.93	7.98
11 Phi	NL	6	0	0	1	9.1	44	13	8	8	2	1	0	0	4	0	10	0	0	0	0	-	0	0-1 0	7.50	7.71
11 SD	NL	6	0	0	2	5.1	24	6	5	5	1	1	0	0	3	1	6	3	0	0	0	-	0	0-0 0	5.94	8.44
4 ML YEARS		17	1	0	4	24.1	119	36	23	23	5	5	0	1	12	2	24	4	0	1	1	.500	0	0-1 0	8.36	8.51

Matt Carpenter

Bats: L **Throws:** R **Pos:** 3B-5; PH-2   **Ht:** 6'3" **Wt:** 200 **Born:** 11/26/1985 **Age:** 26

		BATTING																		BASERUNNING				AVERAGES		
Year Team	Lg	G	AB	H	2B	3B	HR	(Hm	Rd)	TB	R	RBI	RC	TBB	IBB	SO	HBP	SH	SF	SB	CS	SB%	GDP	Avg	OBP	Slg
2009 Batvia	A-	9	32	15	3	0	0	(-	-)	18	9	3	8	4	0	2	1	0	0	0	1	.00	0	.469	.541	.563
2009 QuadC	A	29	105	31	6	2	0	(-	-)	41	11	10	19	17	0	13	3	0	1	2	0	1.00	3	.295	.405	.390
2009 PlmBh	A+	32	114	25	6	1	2	(-	-)	39	13	9	12	10	0	24	1	2	1	1	0	1.00	1	.219	.286	.342
2010 PlmBh	A+	28	99	28	5	2	1	(-	-)	40	17	16	20	26	0	14	2	1	0	0	1	.00	1	.283	.441	.404
2010 Sprgfld	AA	105	396	125	26	3	12	(-	-)	193	76	53	84	64	4	88	4	4	4	11	2	.85	12	.316	.412	.487
2011 Memp	AAA	130	434	130	29	3	12	(-	-)	201	61	70	90	84	6	68	8	3	6	5	4	.56	12	.300	.417	.463
2011 StL	NL	7	15	1	1	0	0	(0	0)	2	0	0	0	4	0	4	0	0	0	0	0	-	0	.067	.263	.133

Carlos Carrasco

Pitches: R **Bats:** R **Pos:** SP-21   **Ht:** 6'3" **Wt:** 215 **Born:** 3/21/1987 **Age:** 25

		HOW MUCH HE PITCHED						WHAT HE GAVE UP											THE RESULTS						
Year Team	Lg	G	GS	CG	GF	IP	BFP	H	R	ER	HR	SH	SF	HB	TBB	IBB	SO	WP	Bk	W	L	Pct	Sh	Sv-Op Hld	ERC	ERA
2011 Akron*	AA	1	1	0	0	3.2	19	4	4	4	1	0	0	1	3	0	3	1	0	0	0	-	0	0- --	8.90	9.82
2009 Cle	AL	5	5	0	0	22.1	112	40	23	22	6	0	1	0	11	1	11	0	1	0	4	.000	0	0-0 0	11.36	8.87
2010 Cle	AL	7	7	1	0	44.2	188	47	20	19	6	2	1	4	14	1	38	1	0	2	2	.500	0	0-0 0	4.42	3.83
2011 Cle	AL	21	21	1	0	124.2	536	130	68	64	15	3	7	4	40	3	85	3	0	8	9	.471	0	0-0 0	4.24	4.62
3 ML YEARS		33	33	2	0	191.2	836	217	111	105	27	5	9	5	65	5	134	4	1	10	15	.400	0	0-0 0	5.00	4.93

D.J. Carrasco

Pitches: R **Bats:** R **Pos:** RP-41; SP-1   **Ht:** 6'4" **Wt:** 215 **Born:** 4/12/1977 **Age:** 35

		HOW MUCH HE PITCHED						WHAT HE GAVE UP											THE RESULTS						
Year Team	Lg	G	GS	CG	GF	IP	BFP	H	R	ER	HR	SH	SF	HB	TBB	IBB	SO	WP	Bk	W	L	Pct	Sh	Sv-Op Hld	ERC	ERA
2011 Buffalo*	AAA	9	8	0	0	46.2	199	46	23	18	4	1	1	4	17	0	37	2	0	2	3	.400	0	0- --	4.17	3.47
2003 KC	AL	50	0	0	21	80.1	355	82	44	43	8	1	4	7	40	4	57	6	0	6	5	.545	0	2-5 6	4.94	4.82
2004 KC	AL	30	0	0	11	35.1	163	41	22	19	5	1	1	3	15	3	22	2	0	2	2	.500	0	0-3 4	5.56	4.84
2005 KC	AL	21	20	1	0	114.2	511	129	67	61	11	3	5	6	51	2	49	7	3	6	8	.429	0	0-0 0	5.20	4.79
2008 CWS	AL	31	0	0	6	38.2	158	30	17	17	2	1	1	5	14	1	30	0	0	1	0	1.000	0	0-1 7	2.94	3.96
2009 CWS	AL	49	1	0	11	93.1	405	103	42	39	5	2	4	2	29	4	62	3	0	5	1	.833	0	0-1 7	3.98	3.76
2010 2 Tms	NL	63	0	0	8	78.1	330	68	39	32	5	3	3	5	34	3	65	6	0	3	2	.600	0	0-1 7	3.48	3.68
2011 NYM	NL	42	1	0	15	49.1	225	67	35	33	7	4	0	6	16	4	27	3	1	1	3	.250	0	0-1 2	6.80	6.02
10 Pit	NL	45	0	0	6	55.2	232	50	24	24	4	3	1	4	22	1	45	4	0	2	2	.500	0	3-6 3	3.66	3.88
10 Ari	NL	18	0	0	2	22.2	98	18	15	8	1	0	2	1	12	2	20	2	0	1	0	1.000	0	0-1 3	3.05	3.18
7 ML YEARS		286	24	1	72	490.0	2147	520	266	244	43	15	18	34	199	21	312	27	4	24	21	.533	0	2-12 26	4.62	4.48

Joel Carreno

Pitches: R **Bats:** R **Pos:** RP-11   jo-ELL kuh-RAIN-yo   **Ht:** 6'0" **Wt:** 190 **Born:** 3/7/1987 **Age:** 25

		HOW MUCH HE PITCHED						WHAT HE GAVE UP											THE RESULTS						
Year Team	Lg	G	GS	CG	GF	IP	BFP	H	R	ER	HR	SH	SF	HB	TBB	IBB	SO	WP	Bk	W	L	Pct	Sh	Sv-Op Hld	ERC	ERA
2007 B Jays	R	12	12	0	0	65.1	274	60	27	19	4	2	3	9	13	0	64	3	0	6	4	.600	0	0- --	3.11	2.62
2008 Auburn	A-	15	13	0	0	76.1	318	74	32	29	6	3	1	5	19	0	85	4	0	5	5	.500	0	0- --	3.46	3.42
2009 Auburn	A-	2	2	0	0	11.0	42	6	2	1	0	0	0	1	3	0	12	0	0	1	0	1.000	0	0- --	1.31	0.82
2009 Lnsng	A	14	14	0	0	79.2	333	76	36	32	5	0	4	4	29	0	62	3	1	2	4	.333	0	0- --	3.54	3.62
2010 Dnedin	A+	27	25	1	1	137.2	588	147	65	57	8	6	6	12	30	0	173	6	3	9	6	.600	0	0- --	3.80	3.73
2011 NHam	AA	24	23	0	0	134.2	563	100	56	51	12	2	1	12	68	0	152	16	3	7	9	.438	0	0- --	3.41	3.41
2011 Tor	AL	11	0	0	3	15.2	59	11	2	2	1	0	0	0	4	0	14	0	0	1	0	1.000	0	0-0 0	1.92	1.15

Ezequiel Carrera

Bats: L Throws: L Pos: CF-55; LF-9; RF-6; PH-5; PR-4; DH-3   ee-ZEEK-ee-ull   **Ht: 5'10" Wt: 185 Born: 6/11/1987 Age: 25**

Year	Team	Lg	G	AB	H	2B	3B	HR	(Hm	Rd)	TB	R	RBI	RC	TBB	IBB	SO	HBP	SH	SF	SB	CS	SB%	GDP	Avg	OBP	Slg
2007	Mets	R	45	179	61	8	3	1	(-	-)	78	41	26	36	26	0	29	2	2	0	16	5	.76	0	.341	.430	.436
2007	Bklyn	A-	20	70	21	2	0	0	(-	-)	23	11	6	9	4	0	13	1	2	0	6	1	.86	0	.300	.347	.329
2008	StLuci	A+	114	430	113	11	12	7	(-	-)	169	61	29	63	46	1	86	9	6	3	28	9	.76	6	.263	.344	.393
2009	WTenn	AA	91	329	111	12	4	2	(-	-)	137	68	38	67	59	1	62	4	10	3	27	13	.68	4	.337	.441	.416
2010	Tacoma	AAA	64	213	57	6	2	0	(-	-)	67	24	18	24	20	0	32	3	7	0	9	5	.64	2	.268	.339	.315
2010	Clmbs	AAA	41	161	46	7	3	1	(-	-)	62	19	16	23	12	0	34	1	8	1	11	3	.79	5	.286	.337	.385
2010	Indns	R	4	14	6	1	0	0	(-	-)	7	2	4	3	1	0	2	0	0	0	0	0	-	0	.429	.467	.500
2011	Clmbs	AAA	82	328	94	8	3	2	(-	-)	114	63	25	52	39	0	53	5	5	0	35	4	.90	4	.287	.371	.348
2011	Cle	AL	68	202	49	8	3	0	(0	0)	63	27	14	25	16	0	35	1	7	0	10	5	.67	4	.243	.301	.312

Brett Carroll

Bats: R Throws: R Pos: CF-1; PH-1   **Ht: 6'0" Wt: 210 Born: 10/3/1982 Age: 29**

Year	Team	Lg	G	AB	H	2B	3B	HR	(Hm	Rd)	TB	R	RBI	RC	TBB	IBB	SO	HBP	SH	SF	SB	CS	SB%	GDP	Avg	OBP	Slg
2011	Nashv*	AAA	93	335	94	14	2	15	(-	-)	157	66	51	58	34	2	73	7	2	3	9	3	.75	8	.281	.356	.469
2011	Pwtckt*	AAA	24	83	19	6	1	1	(-	-)	30	10	12	10	8	0	20	1	0	2	2	0	1.00	3	.229	.298	.361
2007	Fla	NL	23	49	9	1	0	0	(0	0)	10	10	2	0	3	0	15	0	1	0	0	0	-	1	.184	.231	.204
2008	Fla	NL	26	17	1	0	1	0	(0	0)	3	5	1	0	1	0	6	0	0	0	0	0	-	0	.059	.111	.176
2009	Fla	NL	92	141	33	8	2	3	(1	2)	54	18	18	20	11	1	33	4	1	1	0	0	-	2	.234	.306	.383
2010	Fla	NL	32	76	15	4	0	2	(1	1)	25	13	7	5	6	3	29	7	0	1	2	1	.67	2	.197	.311	.329
2011	Mil	NL	2	3	0	0	0	0	(0	0)	0	0	0	0	0	0	1	0	0	0	0	0	-	0	.000	.000	.000
5 ML YEARS			175	286	58	13	3	5	(2	3)	92	46	28	25	21	4	84	11	2	2	2	1	.67	5	.203	.281	.322

Jamey Carroll

Bats: R Throws: R Pos: 2B-81; SS-66; PH-13; PR-2   **Ht: 5'9" Wt: 168 Born: 2/18/1974 Age: 38**

Year	Team	Lg	G	AB	H	2B	3B	HR	(Hm	Rd)	TB	R	RBI	RC	TBB	IBB	SO	HBP	SH	SF	SB	CS	SB%	GDP	Avg	OBP	Slg
2002	Mon	NL	16	71	22	5	3	1	(1	0)	36	16	6	12	4	0	12	0	4	0	1	0	1.00	1	.310	.347	.507
2003	Mon	NL	105	227	59	10	1	1	(1	0)	74	31	10	18	19	0	39	3	9	2	5	2	.71	10	.260	.323	.326
2004	Mon	NL	102	218	63	14	2	0	(0	0)	81	36	16	28	32	1	21	1	2	3	5	1	.83	3	.289	.378	.372
2005	Was	NL	113	303	76	8	1	0	(0	0)	86	44	22	38	34	1	55	5	13	3	3	4	.43	2	.251	.333	.284
2006	Col	NL	136	463	139	23	5	5	(2	3)	187	84	36	65	56	1	66	3	9	3	10	12	.45	10	.300	.377	.404
2007	Col	NL	108	227	51	9	1	2	(1	1)	68	45	22	24	28	1	34	4	6	3	6	2	.75	2	.225	.317	.300
2008	Cle	AL	113	347	96	13	4	1	(0	1)	120	60	36	48	34	0	65	9	10	2	7	3	.70	2	.277	.355	.346
2009	Cle	AL	93	315	87	10	2	2	(0	2)	107	53	26	43	36	0	63	3	3	1	4	2	.67	8	.276	.355	.340
2010	LAD	NL	133	351	102	15	1	0	(0	0)	119	48	23	48	51	3	64	2	5	5	12	4	.75	8	.291	.379	.339
2011	LAD	NL	146	452	131	14	6	0	(0	0)	157	52	17	55	47	3	58	2	8	1	10	0	1.00	3	.290	.359	.347
Postseason			4	2	0	0	0	0	(0	0)	0	0	0	0	1	0	0	0	0	0	0	0	-	0	.000	.333	.000
10 ML YEARS			1065	2974	826	121	26	12	(5	7)	1035	469	214	379	341	10	477	32	69	23	63	30	.68	49	.278	.356	.348

Chris Carter

Bats: R Throws: R Pos: 1B-11; DH-4; PH-1   **Ht: 6'4" Wt: 245 Born: 12/18/1986 Age: 25**

Year	Team	Lg	G	AB	H	2B	3B	HR	(Hm	Rd)	TB	R	RBI	RC	TBB	IBB	SO	HBP	SH	SF	SB	CS	SB%	GDP	Avg	OBP	Slg
2005	Bristol	R+	65	233	66	17	0	10	(-	-)	113	33	37	40	17	0	64	8	2	2	2	1	.67	4	.283	.350	.485
2006	Knapol	A	13	46	6	3	0	1	(-	-)	12	4	5	2	5	0	17	1	0	0	0	0	-	1	.130	.231	.261
2006	Gr Falls	R+	69	251	75	21	1	15	(-	-)	143	37	59	55	34	5	70	8	0	1	4	4	.50	3	.299	.398	.570
2007	Knapol	A	126	467	136	27	3	25	(-	-)	244	84	93	95	67	3	112	6	0	5	3	2	.60	6	.291	.383	.522
2008	Stcktn	A+	137	506	131	32	4	39	(-	-)	288	101	104	106	77	2	156	7	0	6	4	0	1.00	7	.259	.361	.569
2009	Mdland	AA	125	490	165	41	2	24	(-	-)	282	108	101	123	82	2	119	11	0	10	13	5	.72	11	.337	.435	.576
2009	Scrmto	AAA	13	54	14	2	0	4	(-	-)	28	7	14	8	3	0	14	0	0	1	0	1	.00	1	.259	.293	.519
2010	Scrmto	AAA	125	465	120	29	2	31	(-	-)	246	92	94	92	73	1	138	6	0	8	1	1	.50	8	.258	.365	.529
2011	Scrmto	AAA	75	296	81	18	2	18	(-	-)	157	55	72	59	42	0	85	3	0	3	5	1	.83	9	.274	.366	.530
2011	Stcktn	A+	6	24	8	0	0	3	(-	-)	17	3	7	6	4	0	8	0	0	0	0	0	-	0	.333	.429	.708
2010	Oak	AL	24	70	13	1	0	3	(1	2)	23	8	7	5	7	0	21	0	0	1	1	0	1.00	3	.186	.256	.329
2011	Oak	AL	15	44	6	0	0	0	(0	0)	6	2	0	0	2	0	20	0	0	0	0	0	-	1	.136	.174	.136
2 ML YEARS			39	114	19	1	0	3	(1	2)	29	10	7	5	9	0	41	0	0	1	1	0	1.00	4	.167	.226	.254

Andrew Cashner

Pitches: R Bats: R Pos: RP-6; SP-1   **Ht: 6'6" Wt: 200 Born: 9/11/1986 Age: 25**

	HOW MUCH HE PITCHED						WHAT HE GAVE UP												THE RESULTS						
Year	Team	Lg	G	GS	CG	GF	IP	BFP	H	R	ER	HR	SH	SF	HB	TBB	IBB	SO	WP	Bk	W	L	Pct	Sh	Sv-Op	Hld	ERC	ERA
2008	Cubs	R	1	1	0	0	1.0	4	1	1	0	0	0	0	0	0	0	2	0	0	0	0	-	0	0--	-	1.95	0.00
2008	Boise	A-	6	4	0	0	16.1	85	19	12	9	1	0	2	1	19	0	16	1	0	1	1	.500	0	0--	-	8.25	4.96
2008	Dytona	A+	1	1	0	0	2.2	16	4	4	4	0	1	0	0	4	0	1	0	1	0	1	.000	0	0--	-	10.76	13.50
2009	Dytona	A+	12	12	0	0	42.0	173	31	8	7	1	0	1	3	15	0	34	1	1	0	0	-	0	0--	-	2.30	1.50
2009	Tenn	AA	12	12	0	0	58.1	248	45	30	22	0	1	4	2	27	0	41	1	0	3	4	.429	0	0--	-	2.50	3.39
2010	Tenn	AA	6	6	1	0	36.0	139	22	12	11	1	1	0	0	13	0	42	1	0	3	1	.750	0	0--	-	1.62	2.75
2010	Iowa	AAA	5	3	0	0	21.0	80	17	3	2	0	0	0	1	2	0	17	1	0	3	0	1.000	0	0--	-	1.66	0.86
2011	Tenn	AA	3	3	0	0	2.2	11	3	2	2	0	0	0	0	6	0	6	0	0	0	1	.000	0	0--	-	2.52	6.75
2011	Iowa	AAA	2	0	0	0	2.0	6	0	0	0	0	0	0	0	0	0	2	0	0	0	0	-	0	0--	-	0.00	0.00
2010	ChC	NL	53	0	0	9	54.1	248	55	31	29	8	6	2	4	30	5	50	4	1	2	6	.250	0	0-1	16	5.22	4.80
2011	ChC	NL	7	1	0	0	10.2	39	3	2	1	0	0	0	0	4	0	8	0	0	0	0	-	0	0-0	1	0.91	1.69
2 ML YEARS			60	1	0	9	65.0	287	58	33	31	9	6	2	4	34	5	58	4	1	2	6	.250	0	0-1	17	4.31	4.29

Alexi Casilla

Bats: B Throws: R Pos: 2B-56; SS-36; PR-5; DH-3; PH-1   cuh-SEE-ya   Ht: 5'9" Wt: 185 Born: 7/20/1984 Age: 27

									BATTING													BASERUNNING				AVERAGES		
Year	Team	Lg	G	AB	H	2B	3B	HR	(Hm	Rd)	TB	R	RBI	RC	TBB	IBB	SO	HBP	SH	SF	SB	CS	SB%	GDP	Avg	OBP	Slg
2011	FtMyrs*	A+	1	2	0	0	0	0	(-	-)	0	0	0	0	0	0	0	0	0	0	0	0	-	0	.000	.000	.000
2006	Min	AL	9	4	1	0	0	0	(0	0)	1	1	0	1	2	0	1	0	0	0	0	0	-	0	.250	.500	.250
2007	Min	AL	56	189	42	5	1	0	(0	0)	49	15	9	11	9	0	29	0	5	1	11	1	.92	5	.222	.256	.259
2008	Min	AL	98	385	108	15	0	7	(2	5)	144	58	50	50	31	0	45	2	13	6	7	2	.78	8	.281	.333	.374
2009	Min	AL	80	228	46	7	3	0	(0	0)	59	25	17	20	22	0	36	3	2	1	11	0	1.00	6	.202	.280	.259
2010	Min	AL	69	152	42	7	4	1	(1	0)	60	26	20	23	13	0	17	0	4	1	6	1	.86	5	.276	.331	.395
2011	Min	AL	97	323	84	21	4	2	(1	1)	119	52	21	33	28	0	45	3	8	3	15	4	.79	4	.260	.322	.368
	6 ML YEARS		409	1281	323	55	12	10	(4	6)	432	177	117	138	105	0	173	8	32	12	50	8	.86	28	.252	.310	.337

Santiago Casilla

Pitches: R Bats: R Pos: RP-49   cuh-SEE-ya   Ht: 6'0" Wt: 220 Born: 7/25/1980 Age: 31

			HOW MUCH HE PITCHED						WHAT HE GAVE UP												THE RESULTS							
Year	Team	Lg	G	GS	CG	GF	IP	BFP	H	R	ER	HR	SH	SF	HB	TBB	IBB	SO	WP	Bk	W	L	Pct	Sh	Sv-Op	Hld	ERC	ERA
2011	SnJos*	A+	2	2	0	0	3.0	13	3	0	0	0	0	0	0	2	0	1	0	0	0	0	-	0	0--	-	4.60	0.00
2011	Fresno*	AAA	4	0	0	1	5.0	18	3	1	1	1	0	0	1	1	0	4	0	0	0	0	-	0	0--	-	2.90	1.80
2004	Oak	AL	4	0	0	2	5.2	32	5	8	8	3	0	0	1	9	0	5	0	0	0	0	-	0	0-0	0	13.22	12.71
2005	Oak	AL	3	0	0	3	3.0	12	2	1	1	0	0	0	0	1	0	1	1	0	0	0	-	0	0-0	0	1.57	3.00
2006	Oak	AL	2	0	0	1	2.1	10	2	3	3	0	0	0	0	2	0	2	0	0	0	0	-	0	0-0	0	4.61	11.57
2007	Oak	AL	46	0	0	10	50.2	219	43	25	25	6	0	3	1	23	6	52	5	0	3	1	.750	0	2-5	12	3.39	4.44
2008	Oak	AL	51	0	0	9	50.1	229	60	22	22	5	3	2	3	20	2	43	6	0	2	1	.667	0	2-3	7	5.34	3.93
2009	Oak	AL	46	0	0	15	48.1	233	61	36	32	6	1	3	3	25	3	35	5	0	1	2	.333	0	0-0	5	6.32	5.96
2010	SF	NL	52	0	0	13	55.1	225	40	14	12	2	2	1	4	26	4	56	10	0	7	2	.778	0	2-3	11	2.68	1.95
2011	SF	NL	49	0	0	20	51.2	211	33	11	10	1	4	0	2	25	1	45	5	0	2	2	.500	0	6-7	6	2.11	1.74
	Postseason		4	0	0	0	4.2	20	3	1	1	0	0	0	1	1	1	5	1	0	0	0	-	0	0-0	2	1.41	1.93
	8 ML YEARS		253	0	0	73	267.1	1171	246	120	113	23	10	9	14	131	16	239	32	0	15	8	.652	0	12-18	41	3.97	3.80

Bobby Cassevah

Pitches: R Bats: R Pos: RP-30   CASS-eh-vah   Ht: 6'3" Wt: 220 Born: 9/11/1985 Age: 26

			HOW MUCH HE PITCHED						WHAT HE GAVE UP												THE RESULTS							
Year	Team	Lg	G	GS	CG	GF	IP	BFP	H	R	ER	HR	SH	SF	HB	TBB	IBB	SO	WP	Bk	W	L	Pct	Sh	Sv-Op	Hld	ERC	ERA
2005	Angels	R	15	4	0	2	45.0	204	57	28	27	2	3	1	7	14	0	27	2	0	2	5	.286	0	0--	-	5.58	5.40
2006	Orem	R+	16	10	0	0	41.0	214	57	40	31	1	3	2	2	38	0	32	0	0	2	5	.286	0	0--	-	8.25	6.80
2007	CRpds	A	18	0	0	10	31.0	132	25	9	8	0	3	1	5	13	1	25	1	0	2	1	.667	0	1--	-	2.98	2.32
2007	Orem	R+	6	0	0	3	8.1	40	9	6	4	0	0	0	4	5	1	9	3	0	0	0	-	0	0--	-	6.50	4.32
2008	RCuca	A+	44	0	0	10	71.1	318	67	33	30	1	2	2	5	40	2	52	8	0	2	3	.400	0	1--	-	3.94	3.79
2009	Ark	AA	57	0	0	27	73.2	315	64	40	31	2	1	3	4	37	6	45	3	0	3	7	.300	0	4--	-	3.35	3.79
2010	Salt Lk	AAA	45	0	0	21	59.0	269	69	32	28	7	2	0	4	25	3	38	2	0	3	4	.429	0	5--	-	5.48	4.27
2011	Salt Lk	AAA	18	0	0	5	21.1	98	23	13	11	2	1	0	0	10	0	12	1	0	1	3	.250	0	0--	-	4.58	4.64
2010	LAA	AL	16	0	0	9	20.0	94	23	11	7	0	1	1	1	8	2	8	0	0	1	2	.333	0	0-0	0	3.98	3.15
2011	LAA	AL	30	0	0	6	39.2	157	28	12	12	1	1	1	1	19	2	24	3	0	1	1	.500	0	0-1	6	2.48	2.72
	2 ML YEARS		46	0	0	15	59.2	251	51	23	19	1	2	2	2	27	4	32	4	0	2	3	.400	0	0-1	6	2.97	2.87

Alberto Castillo

Pitches: L Bats: L Pos: RP-17   Ht: 6'3" Wt: 220 Born: 7/5/1975 Age: 36

			HOW MUCH HE PITCHED						WHAT HE GAVE UP												THE RESULTS							
Year	Team	Lg	G	GS	CG	GF	IP	BFP	H	R	ER	HR	SH	SF	HB	TBB	IBB	SO	WP	Bk	W	L	Pct	Sh	Sv-Op	Hld	ERC	ERA
2011	Norfolk*	AAA	20	0	0	14	33.1	128	24	8	7	1	3	3	3	8	2	26	1	0	2	4	.333	0	1--	-	1.97	1.89
2011	Reno*	AAA	8	0	0	1	9.0	36	5	2	2	0	1	0	0	5	0	12	0	0	0	0	-	0	0--	-	1.77	2.00
2008	Bal	AL	28	0	0	5	26.0	121	27	11	11	3	0	0	7	10	0	23	1	0	1	0	1.000	0	0-1	0	5.36	3.81
2009	Bal	AL	20	0	0	4	12.0	49	12	4	3	0	1	0	1	4	1	8	0	0	0	0	-	0	0-0	5	3.51	2.25
2010	Bal	AL	14	0	0	6	10.2	51	16	12	12	5	0	0	0	6	0	11	1	0	1	0	1.000	0	0-0	1	11.61	10.13
2011	Ari	NL	17	0	0	4	11.2	50	10	3	3	0	0	1	1	7	0	6	0	0	1	0	1.000	0	0-0	3	3.79	2.31
	4 ML YEARS		79	0	0	19	60.1	271	65	30	29	8	1	1	9	27	1	48	2	0	3	0	1.000	0	0-1	9	5.65	4.33

Welington Castillo

Bats: R Throws: R Pos: C-4   Ht: 5'10" Wt: 210 Born: 4/24/1987 Age: 25

									BATTING													BASERUNNING				AVERAGES		
Year	Team	Lg	G	AB	H	2B	3B	HR	(Hm	Rd)	TB	R	RBI	RC	TBB	IBB	SO	HBP	SH	SF	SB	CS	SB%	GDP	Avg	OBP	Slg
2006	Boise	A-	3	6	1	0	0	0	(-	-)	1	1	0	0	1	0	0	0	1	0	0	0	-	0	.167	.286	.167
2006	Cubs	R	7	26	5	0	0	0	(-	-)	5	4	0	1	1	0	6	1	0	0	0	0	-	2	.192	.250	.192
2007	Peoria	A	98	317	86	11	2	11	(-	-)	134	41	44	46	23	1	77	8	3	2	1	3	.25	9	.271	.334	.423
2008	Dytona	A+	33	121	33	8	0	0	(-	-)	41	15	12	13	4	0	23	1	0	1	1	0	1.00	3	.273	.299	.339
2008	Tenn	AA	57	198	59	11	0	4	(-	-)	82	25	24	30	14	2	50	6	2	0	0	0	-	11	.298	.362	.414
2008	Iowa	AAA	1	5	1	0	0	0	(-	-)	1	0	1	0	0	0	1	0	0	0	0	0	-	0	.200	.200	.200
2009	Tenn	AA	95	319	74	16	0	11	(-	-)	123	27	38	34	15	2	71	4	1	0	1	0	1.00	8	.232	.275	.386
2010	Iowa	AAA	69	239	61	17	1	13	(-	-)	119	35	59	39	19	1	58	6	1	7	0	2	.00	11	.255	.317	.498
2011	Dytona	A+	12	42	10	3	0	1	(-	-)	16	6	7	5	6	0	9	0	0	0	0	0	-	2	.238	.327	.381
2011	Iowa	AAA	61	227	65	9	0	15	(-	-)	119	38	35	41	20	1	57	3	0	1	0	0	-	6	.286	.351	.524
2011	Cubs	R	2	6	4	3	0	0	(-	-)	7	2	0	1	3	0	0	0	0	0	0	0	-	0	.667	.778	1.167
2010	ChC	NL	7	20	6	4	0	1	(0	1)	13	3	5	3	1	0	7	0	0	0	0	0	-	0	.300	.333	.650
2011	ChC	NL	4	13	2	0	0	0	(0	0)	2	0	0	0	0	0	4	0	0	0	0	0	-	1	.154	.154	.154
	2 ML YEARS		11	33	8	4	0	1	(0	1)	15	3	5	3	1	0	11	0	0	0	0	0	-	1	.242	.265	.455

Jason Castro

Bats: L Throws: R Pos: C Ht: 6'3" Wt: 200 Born: 6/18/1987 Age: 25

Year	Team	Lg	G	AB	H	2B	3B	HR	Hm	Rd	TB	R	RBI	RC	TBB	IBB	SO	HBP	SH	SF	SB	CS	SB%	GDP	Avg	OBP	Slg
2008	TriCity	A-	39	138	38	9	0	2	(-	-)	53	10	12	22	22	2	32	2	6	0	0	2	.00	1	.275	.383	.384
2009	Lancst	A+	56	207	64	20	1	7	(-	-)	107	27	44	43	30	2	41	3	3	3	1	1	.50	5	.309	.399	.517
2009	CpChr	AA	63	239	70	11	1	3	(-	-)	92	38	29	35	25	0	35	2	0	2	2	1	.67	5	.293	.362	.385
2010	RdRck	AAA	57	211	56	7	0	4	(-	-)	75	31	26	30	32	0	34	1	0	0	1	1	.50	5	.265	.365	.355
2010	Hou	NL	67	195	40	8	1	2	(1	1)	56	26	8	12	22	2	41	0	0	0	0	0	-	4	.205	.286	.287

Juan Castro

Bats: R Throws: R Pos: 2B-4; PH-2; 3B-1 Ht: 5'11" Wt: 190 Born: 6/20/1972 Age: 40

Year	Team	Lg	G	AB	H	2B	3B	HR	Hm	Rd	TB	R	RBI	RC	TBB	IBB	SO	HBP	SH	SF	SB	CS	SB%	GDP	Avg	OBP	Slg
2011	Albq*	AAA	9	25	11	2	1	0	(-	-)	15	6	3	6	2	0	5	0	0	0	0	0	-	1	.440	.481	.600
1995	LAD	NL	11	4	1	0	0	0	(0	0)	1	0	0	1	1	0	1	0	0	0	0	0	-	0	.250	.400	.250
1996	LAD	NL	70	132	26	5	3	0	(0	0)	37	16	5	8	10	0	27	0	4	0	1	0	1.00	3	.197	.254	.280
1997	LAD	NL	40	75	11	3	1	0	(0	0)	16	3	4	2	7	1	20	0	2	0	0	0	-	2	.147	.220	.213
1998	LAD	NL	89	220	43	7	0	2	(0	2)	56	25	14	12	15	0	37	0	9	2	0	0	-	5	.195	.245	.255
1999	LAD	NL	2	1	0	0	0	0	(0	0)	0	0	0	0	0	0	1	0	0	0	0	0	-	0	.000	.000	.000
2000	Cin	NL	82	224	54	12	2	4	(1	3)	82	20	23	20	14	1	33	0	4	2	0	2	.00	9	.241	.283	.366
2001	Cin	NL	96	242	54	10	0	3	(0	3)	73	27	13	16	13	2	50	0	4	2	0	0	-	9	.223	.261	.302
2002	Cin	NL	54	82	18	3	0	2	(0	2)	27	5	11	11	7	0	18	0	1	1	0	0	-	0	.220	.278	.329
2003	Cin	NL	113	320	81	14	1	9	(4	5)	124	28	33	36	18	1	58	0	7	3	2	3	.40	7	.253	.290	.388
2004	Cin	NL	111	299	73	21	2	5	(3	2)	113	36	26	26	14	1	51	0	2	1	1	0	1.00	11	.244	.277	.378
2005	Min	AL	97	272	70	18	1	5	(2	3)	105	27	33	28	9	1	39	0	9	2	0	1	.00	8	.257	.279	.386
2006	2 Tms		104	251	63	10	3	3	(3	0)	88	18	28	26	11	0	36	0	1	1	1	2	.33	9	.251	.281	.351
2007	Cin	NL	54	89	16	5	0	0	(0	0)	21	5	5	2	4	0	21	0	3	2	0	0	-	2	.180	.211	.236
2008	2 Tms		61	161	31	6	0	2	(0	2)	43	16	16	7	11	0	26	1	2	2	0	0	-	9	.193	.246	.267
2009	LAD	NL	57	112	31	4	0	1	(0	1)	38	18	9	11	6	1	25	0	2	1	0	0	-	1	.277	.311	.339
2010	2 Tms		55	129	25	5	0	0	(0	0)	30	7	13	9	8	0	25	0	1	2	0	1	.00	1	.194	.237	.233
2011	LAD	NL	7	14	4	0	0	0	(0	0)	4	2	1	1	1	0	4	0	0	0	0	0	-	0	.286	.333	.286
06	Min	AL	50	156	36	5	2	1	(1	0)	48	10	14	11	6	0	23	0	1	1	1	1	.50	6	.231	.258	.308
06	Cin	NL	54	95	27	5	1	2	(2	0)	40	8	14	15	5	0	13	0	0	0	0	1	.00	3	.284	.320	.421
08	Cin	NL	7	10	0	0	0	0	(0	0)	0	1	0	0	1	0	0	0	0	0	0	0	-	0	.000	.091	.000
08	Bal	AL	54	151	31	6	0	2	(0	2)	43	15	16	7	10	0	26	1	2	2	0	0	-	9	.205	.256	.285
10	Phi	NL	54	126	25	5	0	0	(0	0)	30	7	13	9	7	0	23	0	1	2	0	1	.00	1	.198	.237	.238
10	LAD	NL	1	3	0	0	0	0	(0	0)	0	0	0	0	1	0	2	0	0	0	0	0	-	0	.000	.250	.000
	Postseason		3	5	1	1	0	0	(0	0)	2	0	1	0	1	0	1	0	0	0	0	0	-	0	.200	.333	.400
17 ML YEARS			1103	2627	601	123	13	36	(13	23)	858	253	234	216	149	8	472	1	51	21	5	9	.36	73	.229	.268	.327

Ramon Castro

Bats: R Throws: R Pos: C-21; PH-2; DH-1 Ht: 6'3" Wt: 240 Born: 3/1/1976 Age: 36

Year	Team	Lg	G	AB	H	2B	3B	HR	Hm	Rd	TB	R	RBI	RC	TBB	IBB	SO	HBP	SH	SF	SB	CS	SB%	GDP	Avg	OBP	Slg
1999	Fla	NL	24	67	12	4	0	2	(0	2)	22	4	4	6	10	3	14	0	0	1	0	0	-	1	.179	.282	.328
2000	Fla	NL	50	138	33	4	0	2	(0	2)	43	10	14	14	16	7	36	1	0	2	0	0	-	0	.239	.318	.312
2001	Fla	NL	7	11	2	0	0	0	(0	0)	2	0	1	0	1	0	1	0	0	0	0	0	-	0	.182	.250	.182
2002	Fla	NL	54	101	24	4	0	6	(4	2)	46	11	18	14	14	3	24	0	1	3	0	0	-	4	.238	.322	.455
2003	Fla	NL	40	53	15	2	0	5	(4	1)	32	6	8	8	4	0	11	0	0	0	0	0	-	0	.135	.231	.260
2004	Fla	NL	32	96	13	3	0	3	(0	3)	25	9	8	4	11	2	30	1	0	0	0	0	-	0	.244	.321	.435
2005	NYM	NL	99	299	51	16	0	8	(5	3)	91	26	41	30	25	2	58	0	3	3	1	0	1.00	7	.238	.322	.389
2006	NYM	NL	40	126	30	7	0	4	(1	3)	49	13	12	11	15	2	40	1	1	1	0	0	-	2	.285	.331	.556
2007	NYM	NL	52	144	41	6	0	11	(3	8)	80	24	31	23	10	0	39	1	0	2	0	0	-	2	.245	.312	.441
2008	NYM	NL	52	143	35	7	0	7	(5	2)	63	15	24	23	13	2	34	1	0	0	0	0	-	4	.219	.292	.406
2009	2 Tms		57	155	34	8	0	7	(2	5)	63	13	25	18	16	1	39	0	0	0	0	0	-	4	.219	.292	.406
2010	CWS	AL	37	115	32	2	0	8	(3	5)	58	18	21	20	9	0	26	0	3	1	1	0	1.00	3	.278	.328	.504
2011	CWS	AL	23	68	16	3	0	4	(2	2)	31	6	10	9	7	0	23	0	0	0	0	0	-	0	.235	.307	.456
09	NYM	NL	26	79	20	5	0	3	(1	2)	34	5	13	9	8	1	16	0	0	0	0	0	-	3	.253	.322	.430
09	CWS	AL	31	76	14	3	0	4	(1	3)	29	8	12	9	8	0	23	0	0	0	0	0	-	1	.184	.262	.382
13 ML YEARS			567	1426	338	66	0	67	(29	38)	605	155	217	180	151	22	375	5	8	13	2	0	1.00	26	.237	.310	.424

Starlin Castro

Bats: R Throws: R Pos: SS-158 Ht: 6'0" Wt: 190 Born: 3/24/1990 Age: 22

Year	Team	Lg	G	AB	H	2B	3B	HR	Hm	Rd	TB	R	RBI	RC	TBB	IBB	SO	HBP	SH	SF	SB	CS	SB%	GDP	Avg	OBP	Slg
2008	Cubs	R	51	196	61	11	5	3	(-	-)	91	33	22	30	14	0	33	3	1	5	6	5	.55	4	.311	.364	.464
2009	Dytona	A+	96	358	108	17	3	3	(-	-)	140	45	35	49	19	1	41	3	5	2	22	11	.67	4	.302	.340	.391
2009	Tenn	AA	31	111	32	6	3	0	(-	-)	44	11	14	17	10	0	12	1	0	1	6	0	1.00	2	.288	.347	.396
2010	Tenn	AA	26	109	41	8	5	1	(-	-)	62	20	20	24	9	0	11	1	0	2	4	5	.44	3	.376	.421	.569
2010	ChC	NL	125	463	139	31	5	3	(1	2)	189	53	41	56	29	7	71	6	4	4	10	8	.56	14	.300	.347	.408
2011	ChC	NL	158	674	207	36	9	10	(4	6)	291	91	66	93	35	2	96	2	0	4	22	9	.71	20	.307	.341	.432
2 ML YEARS			283	1137	346	67	14	13	(5	8)	480	144	107	149	64	9	167	8	4	8	32	17	.65	34	.304	.343	.422

Brett Cecil

Pitches: L **Bats:** R **Pos:** SP-20   **Ht:** 6'1" **Wt:** 235 **Born:** 7/2/1986 **Age:** 25

Year	Team	Lg	G	GS	CG	GF	IP	BFP	H	R	ER	HR	SH	SF	HB	TBB	IBB	SO	WP	Bk	W	L	Pct	Sh	Sv-Op	Hld	ERC	ERA
2011	LsVgs*	AAA	12	12	2	0	78.2	345	89	51	46	15	3	3	0	24	0	63	1	0	8	2	.800	1	0- -	-	5.04	5.26
2009	Tor	AL	18	17	0	1	93.1	422	116	59	55	17	0	2	5	38	0	69	0	0	7	4	.636	0	0-0	0	6.53	5.30
2010	Tor	AL	28	28	0	0	172.2	726	175	87	81	18	1	6	1	54	2	117	7	1	15	7	.682	0	0-0	0	3.88	4.22
2011	Tor	AL	20	20	2	0	123.2	532	122	68	65	22	3	5	6	42	1	87	1	0	4	11	.267	1	0-0	0	4.47	4.73
	3 ML YEARS		66	65	2	1	389.2	1680	413	214	201	57	4	13	12	134	3	273	8	1	26	22	.542	1	0-0	0	4.67	4.64

Jose Ceda

Pitches: R **Bats:** R **Pos:** RP-17   SAY-dah   **Ht:** 6'4" **Wt:** 275 **Born:** 1/28/1987 **Age:** 25

Year	Team	Lg	G	GS	CG	GF	IP	BFP	H	R	ER	HR	SH	SF	HB	TBB	IBB	SO	WP	Bk	W	L	Pct	Sh	Sv-Op	Hld	ERC	ERA
2006	Padres	R	8	4	0	0	23.0	100	20	14	13	1	0	1	1	13	0	31	0	0	2	0	1.000	0	0- -	-	3.78	5.09
2006	Cubs	R	5	3	0	0	12.0	47	6	2	1	0	0	1	1	7	0	21	1	0	0	0	-	0	0- -	-	1.65	0.75
2006	Boise	A-	3	3	0	0	11.0	41	5	4	4	1	0	0	3	2	0	11	2	0	1	0	1.000	0	0- -	-	1.62	3.27
2007	Peoria	A	21	6	0	5	46.1	186	14	18	16	1	0	0	2	31	0	66	8	0	2	2	.500	0	0- -	-	1.35	3.11
2007	Cubs	R	2	1	0	0	3.2	15	2	1	1	0	0	1	0	3	0	3	0	0	0	0	-	0	0- -	-	2.64	2.45
2008	Dytona	A+	15	12	0	1	54.1	229	41	29	29	4	0	4	4	28	0	53	3	1	2	2	.500	0	0- -	-	3.32	4.80
2008	Tenn	AA	22	0	0	19	30.1	129	26	8	8	2	3	0	1	14	1	42	3	0	2	1	.667	0	9- -	-	3.38	2.37
2010	Grnsbr	A	7	0	0	0	8.0	33	7	4	4	2	0	0	1	1	0	5	0	0	0	0	-	0	0- -	-	3.68	4.50
2010	Jaxnvl	AA	27	0	0	18	32.1	134	18	5	5	2	3	1	3	20	2	45	0	0	4	1	.800	0	6- -	-	2.57	1.39
2011	NewOr	AAA	36	0	0	34	39.2	165	30	14	6	1	1	1	1	13	0	53	6	1	3	1	.750	0	24- -	-	2.09	1.36
2010	Fla	NL	8	0	0	1	8.2	45	8	5	5	1	0	0	0	11	1	9	0	1	0	0	-	0	0-0	0	7.53	5.19
2011	Fla	NL	17	0	0	9	20.1	88	16	11	10	1	0	0	0	12	0	21	1	0	0	1	.000	0	0-0	0	3.25	4.43
	2 ML YEARS		25	0	0	10	29.0	133	24	16	15	2	0	0	1	23	1	30	1	1	0	1	.000	0	0-0	0	4.43	4.66

Ronny Cedeno

Bats: R **Throws:** R **Pos:** SS-125; PH-2; PR-2; 2B-1   **Ht:** 6'0" **Wt:** 190 **Born:** 2/2/1983 **Age:** 29

Year	Team	Lg	G	AB	H	2B	3B	HR	(Hm	Rd)	TB	R	RBI	RC	TBB	IBB	SO	HBP	SH	SF	SB	CS	SB%	GDP	Avg	OBP	Slg
2011	Indy*	AAA	4	15	4	1	1	0	(-	-)	7	2	1	2	1	0	5	0	0	0	0	0	-	0	.267	.313	.467
2005	ChC	NL	41	80	24	3	0	1	(0	1)	30	13	6	11	5	1	11	2	2	0	1	0	1.00	4	.300	.356	.375
2006	ChC	NL	151	534	131	18	7	6	(4	2)	181	51	41	41	17	4	109	3	15	3	8	8	.50	10	.245	.271	.339
2007	ChC	NL	38	74	15	2	0	4	(2	2)	29	6	13	8	3	0	18	0	2	1	2	1	.67	0	.203	.231	.392
2008	ChC	NL	99	216	58	12	0	2	(2	0)	76	36	28	23	18	2	41	1	1	0	4	1	.80	6	.269	.328	.352
2009	2 Tms		105	341	71	8	3	10	(7	3)	115	32	38	29	19	3	79	3	13	0	5	2	.71	9	.208	.256	.337
2010	Pit	NL	139	468	120	29	3	8	(4	4)	179	42	38	46	23	4	106	2	7	2	12	3	.80	10	.256	.293	.382
2011	Pit	NL	128	413	103	25	3	2	(0	2)	140	43	32	36	30	7	93	0	6	5	2	5	.29	11	.249	.297	.339
09	Sea	AL	59	186	31	4	2	5	(2	3)	54	15	17	7	10	1	50	1	9	0	3	2	.60	6	.167	.213	.290
09	Pit	NL	46	155	40	4	1	5	(5	0)	61	17	21	22	9	2	29	2	4	0	2	0	1.00	3	.258	.307	.394
	Postseason		3	0	0	0	0	0	(0	0)	0	0	0	0	0	0	0	0	0	0	1	0	1.00	0	-	-	-
	7 ML YEARS		701	2126	522	97	16	33	(19	14)	750	223	196	194	115	21	457	11	46	11	34	20	.63	50	.246	.286	.353

Xavier Cedeno

Pitches: L **Bats:** L **Pos:** RP-3   **Ht:** 6'1" **Wt:** 165 **Born:** 8/26/1986 **Age:** 25

Year	Team	Lg	G	GS	CG	GF	IP	BFP	H	R	ER	HR	SH	SF	HB	TBB	IBB	SO	WP	Bk	W	L	Pct	Sh	Sv-Op	Hld	ERC	ERA
2005	Casper	R+	12	12	0	0	53.0	236	62	36	32	4	3	1	8	17	0	47	3	0	1	3	.250	0	0- -	-	5.26	5.43
2006	Ashvll	A	27	27	0	0	138.0	615	144	79	62	8	9	4	5	63	0	99	14	0	8	9	.471	0	0- -	-	4.35	4.04
2007	Mdest	A+	23	23	0	0	116.2	530	121	78	66	6	2	7	5	61	0	83	12	0	6	8	.429	0	0- -	-	4.52	5.09
2008	Tulsa	AA	19	19	0	0	102.2	473	126	66	47	10	10	3	3	37	0	52	8	0	7	7	.500	0	0- -	-	5.21	4.12
2009	Tulsa	AA	28	0	0	7	47.0	212	46	30	25	6	1	3	3	22	1	25	2	0	3	2	.600	0	0- -	-	4.54	4.79
2009	Mdest	A+	16	0	0	4	16.2	78	15	10	8	0	1	0	0	9	0	21	1	0	1	2	.333	0	0- -	-	3.06	4.32
2011	CpChr	AA	23	19	0	1	111.2	478	98	59	49	8	6	5	5	45	5	110	7	0	5	6	.455	0	0- -	-	3.29	3.95
2011	OKCity	AAA	12	3	0	2	26.0	117	32	20	18	2	1	1	0	8	0	27	1	1	2	3	.400	0	0- -	-	4.78	6.23
2011	Hou	NL	3	0	0	0	1.2	11	7	5	5	2	0	0	0	0	0	0	0	0	0	0	-	0	0-0	0	43.10	27.00

Francisco Cervelli

Bats: R **Throws:** R **Pos:** C-41; 3B-2; PH-2; 2B-1; PR-1   serr-VELL-ee   **Ht:** 6'1" **Wt:** 210 **Born:** 3/6/1986 **Age:** 26

Year	Team	Lg	G	AB	H	2B	3B	HR	(Hm	Rd)	TB	R	RBI	RC	TBB	IBB	SO	HBP	SH	SF	SB	CS	SB%	GDP	Avg	OBP	Slg
2011	Tampa*	A+	3	10	3	0	0	0	(-	-)	3	0	1	0	0	0	2	0	0	0	0	0	-	0	.300	.300	.300
2011	S-WB*	AAA	3	13	2	0	0	0	(-	-)	2	2	1	0	1	0	5	1	0	0	0	0	-	1	.154	.267	.154
2008	NYY	AL	3	5	0	0	0	0	(0	0)	0	0	0	0	0	0	3	0	0	0	0	0	-	1	.000	.000	.000
2009	NYY	AL	42	94	28	4	0	1	(0	1)	35	13	11	11	2	0	11	0	4	1	0	1	.00	1	.298	.309	.372
2010	NYY	AL	93	266	72	11	3	0	(0	0)	89	27	38	40	33	1	42	6	8	4	1	1	.50	7	.271	.359	.335
2011	NYY	AL	43	124	33	4	0	4	(2	2)	49	17	22	17	9	0	29	2	1	1	4	1	.80	4	.266	.324	.395
	Postseason		3	3	0	0	0	0	(0	0)	0	0	0	0	0	0	2	0	0	0	0	0	-	0	.000	.000	.000
	4 ML YEARS		181	489	133	19	3	5	(2	3)	173	57	71	68	44	1	85	8	13	6	5	5	.50	13	.272	.338	.354

Jhoulys Chacin

Pitches: R **Bats:** R **Pos:** SP-31

yo-LEASE cha-SHEEN

Ht: 6'3" **Wt:** 215 **Born:** 1/7/1988 **Age:** 24

Year Team	Lg	G	GS	CG	GF	IP	BFP	H	R	ER	HR	SH	SF	HB	TBB	IBB	SO	WP	Bk	W	L	Pct	Sh	Sv-Op	Hld	ERC	ERA
2009 Col	NL	9	1	0	3	11.0	48	6	6	6	1	1	0	0	11	0	13	2	0	0	1	.000	0	0-0	0	3.87	4.91
2010 Col	NL	28	21	0	2	137.1	583	114	64	50	10	6	5	9	61	5	138	4	0	9	11	.450	0	0-0	0	3.33	3.28
2011 Col	NL	31	31	2	0	194.0	827	168	87	78	20	5	3	4	87	1	150	7	0	11	14	.440	1	0-0	0	3.61	3.62
3 ML YEARS		68	53	2	5	342.1	1458	288	157	134	31	12	8	13	159	6	301	13	0	20	26	.435	1	0-0	0	3.51	3.52

Joba Chamberlain

Pitches: R **Bats:** R **Pos:** RP-27

JOBB-ah CHAME-berr-linn

Ht: 6'2" **Wt:** 240 **Born:** 9/23/1985 **Age:** 26

Year Team	Lg	G	GS	CG	GF	IP	BFP	H	R	ER	HR	SH	SF	HB	TBB	IBB	SO	WP	Bk	W	L	Pct	Sh	Sv-Op	Hld	ERC	ERA
2007 NYY	AL	19	0	0	3	24.0	91	12	2	1	1	1	0	1	6	0	34	1	0	2	0	1.000	0	1-1	8	1.16	0.38
2008 NYY	AL	42	12	0	5	100.1	417	87	32	29	5	2	1	2	39	3	118	4	2	4	3	.571	0	0-1	19	3.04	2.60
2009 NYY	AL	32	31	0	0	157.1	709	167	94	83	21	6	5	12	76	2	133	5	2	9	6	.600	0	0-0	0	5.32	4.75
2010 NYY	AL	73	0	0	18	71.2	305	71	37	35	6	0	1	1	22	2	77	5	1	3	4	.429	0	3-7	26	3.53	4.40
2011 NYY	AL	27	0	0	3	28.2	110	23	10	9	3	0	1	1	7	0	24	1	0	2	0	1.000	0	0-1	12	2.76	2.83
Postseason		15	0	0	0	13.1	62	16	5	5	1	1	1	1	6	0	14	2	0	1	0	1.000	0	0-2	3	5.51	3.38
5 ML YEARS		193	43	0	29	382.0	1632	360	175	157	36	9	8	17	150	7	386	16	5	20	13	.606	0	4-10	65	3.85	3.70

Adron Chambers

Bats: L **Throws:** L **Pos:** LF-6; PR-6; CF-5; PH-5; RF-1

AID-run

Ht: 5'10" **Wt:** 185 **Born:** 10/8/1986 **Age:** 25

Year Team	Lg	G	AB	H	2B	3B	HR	Hm	Rd	TB	R	RBI	RC	TBB	IBB	SO	HBP	SH	SF	SB	CS	SB%	GDP	Avg	OBP	Slg
2007 JhsCty	R	36	111	31	7	1	0	(-	-)	40	16	10	15	10	0	21	5	2	1	6	5	.55	1	.279	.362	.360
2008 QuadC	A	95	336	80	13	7	3	(-	-)	116	56	25	41	33	0	66	10	2	3	13	8	.62	2	.238	.322	.345
2009 PlmBh	A+	122	448	127	17	16	1	(-	-)	179	66	46	69	47	0	96	16	4	2	21	12	.64	7	.283	.370	.400
2010 Sprgfld	AA	75	252	71	9	5	5	(-	-)	105	52	27	42	31	0	50	7	2	0	8	4	.67	2	.282	.376	.417
2010 Memp	AAA	37	69	20	0	1	1	(-	-)	25	11	8	11	9	0	18	3	1	1	6	1	.86	0	.290	.390	.362
2011 Memp	AAA	128	426	118	19	5	10	(-	-)	177	73	44	69	53	0	90	10	9	3	22	13	.63	9	.277	.368	.415
2011 StL	NL	18	8	3	0	1	0	(0	0)	5	2	4	3	0	0	1	0	0	0	0	0	-	0	.375	.375	.625

Aroldis Chapman

Pitches: L **Bats:** L **Pos:** RP-54

ah-ROLL-diss

Ht: 6'4" **Wt:** 196 **Born:** 2/28/1988 **Age:** 24

Year Team	Lg	G	GS	CG	GF	IP	BFP	H	R	ER	HR	SH	SF	HB	TBB	IBB	SO	WP	Bk	W	L	Pct	Sh	Sv-Op	Hld	ERC	ERA
2010 Lsvlle	AAA	39	13	1	12	95.2	412	77	46	38	7	1	1	5	52	0	125	14	0	9	6	.600	0	8--	-	3.57	3.57
2011 Lsvlle	AAA	4	1	0	1	5.2	29	9	7	7	0	0	0	0	2	0	9	2	1	0	1	.000	0	0--	-	6.17	11.12
2011 Carlina	AA	5	2	0	0	7.1	31	5	5	5	1	0	0	0	8	0	11	2	0	1	1	.500	0	0--	-	4.40	6.14
2010 Cin	NL	15	0	0	3	13.1	51	9	4	3	0	0	0	0	5	0	19	2	0	2	2	.500	0	0-1	4	1.82	2.03
2011 Cin	NL	54	0	0	13	50.0	207	24	21	20	2	1	0	2	41	0	71	4	0	4	1	.800	0	1-3	13	2.69	3.60
Postseason		2	0	0	1	1.2	11	3	3	0	0	0	0	0	1	0	1	0	0	0	0	1.000	0	0-1	0	7.12	0.00
2 ML YEARS		69	0	0	16	63.1	258	33	25	23	2	1	0	2	46	0	90	6	0	6	3	.667	0	1-4	17	2.50	3.27

Tyler Chatwood

Pitches: R **Bats:** R **Pos:** SP-25; RP-2

Ht: 6'0" **Wt:** 185 **Born:** 12/16/1989 **Age:** 22

Year Team	Lg	G	GS	CG	GF	IP	BFP	H	R	ER	HR	SH	SF	HB	TBB	IBB	SO	WP	Bk	W	L	Pct	Sh	Sv-Op	Hld	ERC	ERA
2008 Angels	R	11	11	0	0	38.0	166	25	15	13	1	1	1	0	36	0	48	7	0	1	2	.333	0	0--	-	3.84	3.08
2009 CRpds	A	24	24	0	0	116.1	492	99	60	52	8	2	3	3	66	0	106	11	0	8	7	.533	0	0--	-	3.58	4.02
2010 RCuca	A+	14	13	0	0	81.1	335	71	18	16	6	1	1	2	36	0	70	5	0	8	3	.727	0	0--	-	3.59	1.77
2010 Ark	AA	12	12	1	0	68.1	296	72	38	29	3	2	1	2	27	0	36	7	0	4	6	.400	1	0--	-	4.11	3.82
2011 Salt Lk	AAA	1	1	0	0	5.2	26	9	4	4	1	0	0	0	0	0	3	0	0	1	0	1.000	0	0--	-	6.31	6.35
2011 Salt Lk	AAA	4	4	0	0	16.0	79	21	11	9	2	1	0	2	11	0	11	1	0	1	2	.333	0	0--	-	8.06	5.06
2011 LAA	AL	27	25	0	0	142.0	633	166	81	75	14	6	3	6	71	4	74	3	1	6	11	.353	0	0-0	0	5.78	4.75

Endy Chavez

Bats: L **Throws:** L **Pos:** CF-66; LF-12; PH-11; RF-6; PR-3

EN-dee SHAH-vezz

Ht: 6'0" **Wt:** 170 **Born:** 2/7/1978 **Age:** 34

Year Team	Lg	G	AB	H	2B	3B	HR	Hm	Rd	TB	R	RBI	RC	TBB	IBB	SO	HBP	SH	SF	SB	CS	SB%	GDP	Avg	OBP	Slg
2011 RdRck*	AAA	30	128	39	8	2	2	(-	-)	57	16	17	21	10	0	6	0	3	1	6	0	1.00	3	.305	.353	.445
2001 KC	AL	29	77	16	2	0	0	(0	0)	18	4	5	2	3	0	8	0	0	0	0	2	.00	1	.208	.238	.234
2002 Mon	NL	36	125	37	8	5	1	(0	1)	58	20	9	14	5	0	16	0	7	1	3	5	.38	0	.296	.321	.464
2003 Mon	NL	141	483	121	25	5	5	(4	1)	171	66	47	56	31	3	59	0	9	3	18	7	.72	7	.251	.294	.354
2004 Mon	NL	132	502	139	20	6	5	(4	1)	186	65	34	56	30	0	40	1	12	2	32	7	.82	6	.277	.318	.371
2005 2 Tms	NL	98	116	25	4	3	0	(0	0)	35	19	11	8	7	0	14	0	7	0	2	2	.50	3	.216	.260	.302
2006 NYM	NL	133	353	108	22	5	4	(2	2)	152	48	42	54	24	3	44	0	11	2	12	3	.80	7	.306	.348	.431
2007 NYM	NL	71	150	43	7	2	1	(1	0)	57	20	17	20	9	0	16	0	5	1	5	2	.71	5	.287	.325	.380
2008 NYM	NL	133	270	72	10	2	1	(1	0)	89	30	12	21	17	3	22	0	9	2	6	1	.86	6	.267	.308	.330
2009 Sea	AL	54	161	44	3	1	2	(1	1)	55	17	13	15	14	1	22	0	5	2	9	1	.90	4	.273	.328	.342
2011 Tex	AL	83	256	77	11	3	5	(3	2)	109	37	27	32	10	0	30	0	4	1	10	5	.67	7	.301	.323	.426
05 Was	NL	7	9	2	1	0	0	(0	0)	3	2	1	1	3	0	1	0	0	0	0	0	.00	1	.222	.417	.333
05 Phi	NL	91	107	23	3	3	0	(0	0)	32	17	10	7	4	0	13	0	7	0	2	1	.67	2	.215	.243	.299
Postseason		10	35	8	2	0	0	(0	0)	10	2	0	0	0	0	1	0	0	0	0	0	-	1	.229	.229	.286
10 ML YEARS		910	2493	682	112	32	24	(16	8)	930	326	217	278	150	10	271	1	70	16	97	35	.73	48	.274	.313	.373

Eric Chavez

Bats: L **Throws:** R **Pos:** 3B-42; PH-12; DH-7; 1B-3   shah-VEZZ   **Ht:** 6'1" **Wt:** 215 **Born:** 12/7/1977 **Age:** 34

Year	Team	Lg	G	AB	H	2B	3B	HR	(Hm	Rd)	TB	R	RBI	RC	TBB	IBB	SO	HBP	SH	SF	SB	CS	SB%	GDP	Avg	OBP	Slg
2011	Tampa*	A+	6	21	7	2	0	1	(-	-)	12	4	3	4	2	0	4	0	0	0	0	0	-	0	.333	.391	.571
1998	Oak	AL	16	45	14	4	1	0	(0	0)	20	6	6	7	3	1	5	0	0	0	1	1	.50	1	.311	.354	.444
1999	Oak	AL	115	356	88	21	2	13	(8	5)	152	47	50	50	46	4	56	0	0	0	1	1	.50	7	.247	.333	.427
2000	Oak	AL	153	501	139	23	4	26	(15	11)	248	89	86	86	62	8	94	1	0	5	2	2	.50	9	.277	.355	.495
2001	Oak	AL	151	552	159	43	0	32	(14	18)	298	91	114	99	41	9	99	4	0	7	8	2	.80	9	.288	.338	.540
2002	Oak	AL	153	585	161	31	3	34	(17	17)	300	87	109	103	65	13	119	1	0	2	8	3	.73	8	.275	.348	.513
2003	Oak	AL	156	588	166	39	5	29	(12	17)	302	94	101	97	62	10	89	1	0	3	8	3	.73	14	.282	.350	.514
2004	Oak	AL	125	475	131	20	0	29	(15	14)	238	87	77	84	95	10	99	3	0	4	6	3	.67	21	.276	.397	.501
2005	Oak	AL	160	625	168	40	1	27	(15	12)	291	92	101	95	58	4	129	2	0	9	6	0	1.00	9	.269	.329	.466
2006	Oak	AL	137	485	117	24	2	22	(8	14)	211	74	72	70	84	6	100	1	0	6	3	0	1.00	19	.241	.351	.435
2007	Oak	AL	90	341	82	21	2	15	(10	5)	152	43	46	38	34	2	76	0	0	4	4	2	.67	9	.240	.306	.446
2008	Oak	AL	23	89	22	7	0	2	(1	1)	35	10	14	14	6	0	18	0	0	0	0	0	-	2	.247	.295	.393
2009	Oak	AL	8	30	3	1	0	0	(0	0)	4	0	1	0	1	0	7	0	0	0	0	0	-	0	.100	.129	.133
2010	Oak	AL	33	111	26	8	0	1	(0	1)	37	10	10	7	8	0	31	0	0	4	0	0	-	3	.234	.276	.333
2011	NYY	AL	58	160	42	7	1	2	(0	2)	57	16	26	26	14	3	34	0	0	1	0	0	-	4	.263	.320	.356
	Postseason		27	108	24	7	0	3	(3	0)	40	11	12	12	7	2	22	0	0	0	1	0	1.00	0	.222	.270	.370
	14 ML YEARS		1378	4943	1318	289	21	232	(115	117)	2345	746	813	776	579	70	956	13	0	45	47	17	.73	113	.267	.342	.474

Jesse Chavez

Pitches: R **Bats:** R **Pos:** RP-4   CHAH-vezz   **Ht:** 6'2" **Wt:** 170 **Born:** 8/21/1983 **Age:** 28

Year	Team	Lg	G	GS	CG	GF	IP	BFP	H	R	ER	HR	SH	SF	HB	TBB	IBB	SO	WP	Bk	W	L	Pct	Sh	Sv-Op	Hld	ERC	ERA
2011	Omha*	AAA	45	0	0	30	57.2	249	63	30	24	6	6	3	0	16	3	54	4	0	2	4	.333	0	16- -	-	4.01	3.75
2008	Pit	NL	15	0	0	6	15.0	74	20	11	11	2	3	1	0	9	2	16	2	0	0	1	.000	0	0-2	0	6.76	6.60
2009	Pit	NL	73	0	0	24	67.1	286	69	33	30	11	1	1	1	22	3	47	5	0	1	4	.200	0	0-4	15	4.39	4.01
2010	2 Tms		51	0	0	26	62.2	280	69	44	41	11	5	3	1	23	7	45	2	0	5	5	.500	0	0-1	6	4.85	5.89
2011	KC	AL	4	0	0	3	7.2	39	12	9	9	3	0	0	0	5	0	8	0	0	0	0	-	0	0-0	0	11.48	10.57
10	Atl	NL	28	0	0	16	36.2	162	40	24	24	6	3	2	1	12	3	29	0	0	3	2	.600	0	0-0	0	4.65	5.89
10	KC	AL	23	0	0	10	26.0	118	29	20	17	5	2	1	0	11	4	16	2	0	2	3	.400	0	0-1	6	5.13	5.88
	4 ML YEARS		143	0	0	59	152.2	679	170	97	91	27	9	5	2	59	12	116	9	0	6	10	.375	0	0-7	21	5.12	5.36

Bruce Chen

Pitches: L **Bats:** L **Pos:** SP-25   **Ht:** 6'1" **Wt:** 215 **Born:** 6/19/1977 **Age:** 35

Year	Team	Lg	G	GS	CG	GF	IP	BFP	H	R	ER	HR	SH	SF	HB	TBB	IBB	SO	WP	Bk	W	L	Pct	Sh	Sv-Op	Hld	ERC	ERA
2011	NWArk*	AA	1	1	0	0	2.0	11	5	4	4	0	0	1	0	0	0	2	0	0	0	1	.000	0	0- -	-	10.86	18.00
2011	Omha*	AAA	2	2	0	0	9.0	40	11	6	6	3	0	1	1	1	0	8	0	0	0	0	-	0	0- -	-	6.18	6.00
1998	Atl	NL	4	4	0	0	20.1	91	23	9	9	3	1	0	1	9	1	17	0	0	2	0	1.000	0	0-0	0	5.55	3.98
1999	Atl	NL	16	7	0	3	51.0	214	38	32	31	11	1	1	2	27	3	45	0	0	2	2	.500	0	0-0	0	4.07	5.47
2000	2 Tms	NL	37	15	0	4	134.0	559	116	54	49	18	8	3	2	46	4	112	4	1	7	4	.636	0	0-0	0	3.35	3.29
2001	2 Tms	NL	27	27	0	0	146.0	634	146	90	79	29	4	7	1	59	4	126	5	0	7	7	.500	0	0-0	0	4.75	4.87
2002	3 Tms	NL	55	6	0	9	77.2	360	85	53	48	16	2	3	2	43	5	80	4	0	2	5	.286	0	0-0	4	5.99	5.56
2003	2 Tms	NL	16	2	0	4	24.1	110	26	16	15	6	3	3	2	10	1	20	0	0	1	0	1.000	0	0-0	1	5.81	5.55
2004	Bal	AL	8	7	1	0	47.2	196	39	19	16	7	2	1	0	16	0	32	0	0	2	1	.667	0	0-0	0	3.13	3.02
2005	Bal	AL	34	32	1	0	197.1	832	187	94	84	33	3	3	9	63	0	133	2	1	13	10	.565	0	0-0	0	4.12	3.83
2006	Bal	AL	40	12	0	16	98.2	453	137	81	76	28	3	5	0	35	3	70	1	0	0	7	.000	0	0-0	1	7.73	6.93
2007	Tex	AL	5	0	0	3	10.0	46	11	11	8	3	0	0	0	6	1	7	0	0	0	0	-	0	0-0	0	6.90	7.20
2009	KC	AL	17	9	0	4	62.1	279	74	44	40	12	2	2	4	25	3	45	4	0	1	6	.143	0	0-0	0	6.18	5.78
2010	KC	AL	33	23	1	4	140.1	608	136	68	65	17	6	7	3	57	4	98	3	0	12	7	.632	1	1-1	0	4.09	4.17
2011	KC	AL	25	25	1	0	155.0	654	152	71	65	18	3	5	7	50	2	97	2	0	12	8	.600	0	0-0	0	3.98	3.77
00	Atl	NL	22	0	0	4	39.2	176	35	11	11	4	3	2	1	19	2	32	0	1	4	0	1.000	0	0-0	0	3.62	2.50
00	Phi	NL	15	15	0	0	94.1	383	81	39	38	14	5	1	1	27	2	80	4	0	3	4	.429	0	0-0	0	3.22	3.63
01	Phi	NL	16	16	0	0	86.1	381	90	53	48	19	2	4	1	31	4	79	2	0	4	5	.444	0	0-0	0	4.87	5.00
01	NYM	NL	11	11	0	0	59.2	253	56	37	31	10	2	3	0	28	0	47	3	0	3	2	.600	0	0-0	0	4.58	4.68
02	NYM	NL	1	0	0	0	0.2	3	1	0	0	0	0	0	0	0	0	0	0	0	0	0	-	0	0-0	0	4.47	0.00
02	Mon	NL	15	5	0	4	37.1	179	47	29	29	9	0	0	1	23	3	43	3	0	2	3	.400	0	0-0	1	7.69	6.99
02	Cin	NL	39	1	0	5	39.2	178	37	24	19	7	2	3	1	20	2	37	1	0	0	2	.000	0	0-0	3	4.55	4.31
03	Hou	NL	11	0	0	2	12.0	60	14	8	8	2	3	2	2	8	1	8	0	0	0	0	-	0	0-0	1	7.11	6.00
03	Bos	AL	5	2	0	2	12.1	50	12	8	7	4	0	1	0	2	0	12	0	0	1	0	1.000	0	0-0	0	4.40	5.11
	13 ML YEARS		317	169	4	47	1164.2	5036	1170	640	585	201	38	40	33	446	31	882	25	2	60	58	.508	1	1-1	6	4.62	4.52

Robinson Chirinos

Bats: R **Throws:** R **Pos:** C-19; PH-2; 1B-1   chee-REE-nos   **Ht:** 6'1" **Wt:** 195 **Born:** 6/5/1984 **Age:** 28

Year	Team	Lg	G	AB	H	2B	3B	HR	(Hm	Rd)	TB	R	RBI	RC	TBB	IBB	SO	HBP	SH	SF	SB	CS	SB%	GDP	Avg	OBP	Slg
2001	Cubs	R	47	154	36	12	0	2	(-	-)	54	15	15	16	10	0	42	4	6	3	4	3	.57	0	.234	.292	.351
2002	Boise	A-	62	231	57	15	2	8	(-	-)	100	35	38	32	16	0	66	6	1	1	5	2	.71	2	.247	.311	.433
2003	Lansng	A	108	362	84	27	1	7	(-	-)	134	51	39	43	28	0	82	7	4	2	10	2	.83	11	.232	.298	.370
2004	Lansng	A	84	319	77	18	6	7	(-	-)	128	56	39	42	25	1	70	8	3	0	7	2	.78	4	.241	.313	.401
2005	Dytona	A+	73	227	62	6	0	7	(-	-)	89	29	27	29	16	0	41	3	1	2	3	4	.43	5	.273	.327	.392
2006	Peoria	A	126	433	105	30	2	9	(-	-)	166	74	47	67	69	0	79	14	7	6	19	10	.66	7	.242	.360	.383
2007	Dytona	A+	79	239	62	14	2	3	(-	-)	89	35	20	38	37	0	48	12	5	0	8	5	.62	5	.259	.385	.372
2007	Tenn	AA	42	127	28	4	2	2	(-	-)	42	11	16	13	13	2	31	1	5	0	1	1	.50	1	.220	.298	.331
2008	Tenn	AA	38	103	25	7	3	0	(-	-)	38	12	8	12	10	0	18	0	2	2	0	0	-	3	.243	.304	.369
2008	Cubs	R	4	13	6	1	1	0	(-	-)	9	5	4	5	0	0	2	0	0	0	1	0	1.00	0	.462	.632	.692
2008	Dytona	A+	37	120	34	4	2	5	(-	-)	57	22	18	27	26	0	21	6	3	1	3	1	.75	2	.283	.431	.475

78

		BATTING																		BASERUNNING				AVERAGES		
Year Team	Lg	G	AB	H	2B	3B	HR	(Hm Rd)	TB	R	RBI	RC	TBB	IBB	SO	HBP	SH	SF	SB	CS	SB%	GDP	Avg	OBP	Slg
2009 Dytona	A+	69	227	68	13	5	11	(- -)	124	40	47	49	35	0	40	5	0	3	1	1	.50	4	.300	.400	.546
2009 Tenn	AA	12	35	9	3	0	0	(- -)	12	4	5	4	7	0	4	0	0	1	0	1	1.00	1	.257	.372	.343
2010 Tenn	AA	77	264	84	24	0	15	(- -)	153	53	64	62	42	4	35	5	0	7	1	5	.17	6	.318	.412	.580
2010 Iowa	AAA	15	55	20	4	0	3	(- -)	33	10	10	13	2	0	8	5	0	0	0	0	-	3	.364	.435	.600
2011 Drham	AAA	78	282	73	13	1	6	(- -)	106	24	24	38	29	0	69	7	1	0	1	1	.50	9	.259	.343	.376
2011 TB	AL	20	55	12	2	0	1	(1 0)	17	4	7	5	5	0	13	0	0	0	0	0	-	0	.218	.283	.309

Lonnie Chisenhall

Bats: L **Throws:** R **Pos:** 3B-58; PH-7; DH-4; PR-2; LF-1   CHIZZ-en-hall   **Ht:** 6'1" **Wt:** 200 **Born:** 10/4/1988 **Age:** 23

		BATTING																		BASERUNNING				AVERAGES		
Year Team	Lg	G	AB	H	2B	3B	HR	(Hm Rd)	TB	R	RBI	RC	TBB	IBB	SO	HBP	SH	SF	SB	CS	SB%	GDP	Avg	OBP	Slg
2008 MhVlly	A-	68	276	80	20	3	5	(- -)	121	38	45	45	24	2	32	4	1	0	7	2	.78	6	.290	.355	.438
2009 Knstn	A+	99	388	107	26	2	18	(- -)	191	59	79	67	37	1	80	5	1	1	2	1	.67	15	.276	.346	.492
2009 Akron	AA	24	93	17	5	1	4	(- -)	36	13	13	9	7	1	16	0	0	1	1	0	1.00	2	.183	.238	.387
2010 Akron	AA	117	460	128	22	3	17	(- -)	207	81	84	77	46	1	77	10	0	8	3	0	1.00	12	.278	.351	.450
2011 Clmbs	AAA	66	255	68	16	3	7	(- -)	111	45	45	41	28	2	47	7	0	2	0	1	.00	9	.267	.353	.435
2011 Cle	AL	66	212	54	13	0	7	(2 5)	88	27	22	24	8	1	49	1	1	1	1	0	1.00	3	.255	.284	.415

Randy Choate

Pitches: L **Bats:** L **Pos:** RP-54   CHOTE   **Ht:** 6'1" **Wt:** 200 **Born:** 9/5/1975 **Age:** 36

		HOW MUCH HE PITCHED						WHAT HE GAVE UP											THE RESULTS						
Year Team	Lg	G	GS	CG	GF	IP	BFP	H	R	ER	HR	SH	SF	HB	TBB	IBB	SO	WP	Bk	W	L	Pct	Sh	Sv-Op Hld	ERC	ERA
2000 NYY	AL	22	0	0	6	17.0	75	14	10	9	3	0	1	1	8	0	12	1	0	0	1	.000	0	0-0 2	3.99	4.76
2001 NYY	AL	37	0	0	13	48.1	207	34	21	18	0	2	1	9	27	2	35	3	0	3	1	.750	0	0-0 3	3.03	3.35
2002 NYY	AL	18	0	0	11	22.1	101	18	18	15	1	0	0	3	15	0	17	3	0	0	0	-	0	0-0 0	4.13	6.04
2003 NYY	AL	5	0	0	2	3.2	16	7	3	3	0	0	0	0	1	0	0	0	0	0	0	-	0	0-0 0	9.72	7.36
2004 Ari	NL	74	0	0	17	50.2	232	52	26	26	1	0	4	5	28	11	49	1	1	2	4	.333	0	0-2 11	4.18	4.62
2005 Ari	NL	8	0	0	0	7.0	35	8	7	7	0	0	0	1	5	1	4	1	0	0	0	-	0	0-0 2	5.48	9.00
2006 Ari	NL	30	0	0	3	16.0	75	21	9	7	0	0	0	0	3	0	12	0	0	0	1	.000	0	0-0 5	4.87	3.94
2007 Ari	NL	2	0	0	0	0.0	3	3	0	0	0	0	0	0	0	0	0	0	0	0	0	-	0	0-0 0		
2009 TB	AL	61	0	0	13	36.1	142	28	15	14	4	0	0	0	11	3	28	0	0	1	0	1.000	0	5-5 9	2.54	3.47
2010 TB	AL	85	0	0	8	44.2	187	41	23	21	3	2	2	3	17	5	40	4	0	4	3	.571	0	0-2 18	3.48	4.23
2011 Fla	NL	54	0	0	6	24.2	103	13	7	5	3	1	0	2	13	5	31	0	0	1	1	.500	0	0-0 14	2.16	1.82
Postseason		7	0	0	0	6.1	30	7	5	2	0	0	0	0	2	1	4	0	0	0	0	-	0	0-0 0	3.01	2.84
11 ML YEARS		396	0	0	79	270.2	1176	239	139	125	15	5	8	27	128	27	228	13	1	11	11	.500	0	5-9 64	3.62	4.16

Shin-Soo Choo

Bats: L **Throws:** L **Pos:** RF-85   **Ht:** 5'11" **Wt:** 200 **Born:** 7/13/1982 **Age:** 29

		BATTING																		BASERUNNING				AVERAGES		
Year Team	Lg	G	AB	H	2B	3B	HR	(Hm Rd)	TB	R	RBI	RC	TBB	IBB	SO	HBP	SH	SF	SB	CS	SB%	GDP	Avg	OBP	Slg
2011 Lk Cty*	A	3	8	0	0	0	0	(- -)	0	0	1	0	0	0	2	0	0	0	0	0	-	0	.000	.000	.000
2005 Sea	AL	10	18	1	0	0	0	(0 0)	1	1	1	0	3	0	4	0	0	0	5	3	.63	3	.056	.190	.056
2006 2 Tms	AL	49	157	44	12	3	3	(2 1)	71	23	22	24	18	2	50	2	1	1	5	3	.63	3	.280	.360	.452
2007 Cle	AL	6	17	5	0	0	0	(0 0)	5	5	5	3	2	1	5	0	0	1	0	1	.00	3	.294	.350	.294
2008 Cle	AL	94	317	98	28	3	14	(10 4)	174	68	66	72	44	4	78	5	0	4	4	3	.57	5	.309	.397	.549
2009 Cle	AL	156	583	175	38	6	20	(11 9)	285	87	86	111	78	5	151	17	0	7	21	2	.91	9	.300	.394	.489
2010 Cle	AL	144	550	165	31	2	22	(8 14)	266	81	90	106	83	11	118	11	0	2	22	7	.76	11	.300	.401	.484
2011 Cle	AL	85	313	81	11	3	8	(7 1)	122	37	36	38	36	3	78	6	0	3	12	5	.71	7	.259	.344	.390
06 Sea	AL	4	11	1	1	0	0	(0 0)	2	0	0	0	0	0	4	1	0	0	0	0	-	1	.091	.167	.182
06 Cle	AL	45	146	43	11	3	3	(2 1)	69	23	22	24	18	2	46	1	1	1	5	3	.63	2	.295	.373	.473
7 ML YEARS		544	1955	569	120	17	67	(38 29)	924	302	306	354	264	26	484	41	1	18	64	21	.75	35	.291	.384	.473

Justin Christian

Bats: R **Throws:** R **Pos:** CF-10; LF-6; RF-3; PR-2   **Ht:** 6'1" **Wt:** 188 **Born:** 4/30/1980 **Age:** 32

		BATTING																		BASERUNNING				AVERAGES		
Year Team	Lg	G	AB	H	2B	3B	HR	(Hm Rd)	TB	R	RBI	RC	TBB	IBB	SO	HBP	SH	SF	SB	CS	SB%	GDP	Avg	OBP	Slg
2004 Yanks	R	3	7	4	3	0	0	(- -)	7	1	4	4	4	0	0	0	0	0	0	0	-	0	.571	.727	1.000
2004 StlsInd	A-	50	208	57	9	2	7	(- -)	91	29	33	33	19	0	39	2	0	3	14	4	.78	2	.274	.336	.438
2005 CtnSC	A	29	100	29	5	0	3	(- -)	43	31	10	20	14	0	12	3	1	0	17	2	.89	2	.290	.393	.430
2005 Tampa	A+	95	372	114	27	6	8	(- -)	177	52	37	72	33	0	47	6	4	1	38	5	.88	2	.306	.371	.476
2005 Clmbs	AAA	1	0	0	0	0	0	(- -)	0	0	0	0	0	0	0	0	0	0	0	0	-	0	-	-	-
2006 Trntn	AA	129	467	129	19	9	6	(- -)	184	76	43	73	43	1	73	3	3	0	68	13	.84	8	.276	.341	.394
2007 Trntn	AA	65	255	60	8	3	3	(- -)	83	25	32	26	16	2	43	2	2	3	18	4	.82	9	.235	.283	.325
2007 S-WB	AAA	40	169	55	8	4	1	(- -)	74	32	16	30	10	0	19	2	2	0	17	2	.89	5	.325	.370	.438
2008 S-WB	AAA	74	268	82	17	1	6	(- -)	119	48	45	46	20	0	34	4	0	5	22	4	.85	10	.306	.357	.444
2009 Norfolk	AAA	88	356	96	18	5	3	(- -)	133	54	25	46	20	0	51	2	5	3	25	6	.80	11	.270	.310	.374
2010 Trntn	AA	87	343	102	21	6	9	(- -)	162	65	51	65	40	0	47	5	1	5	18	2	.90	5	.297	.374	.472
2010 S-WB	AAA	16	66	16	0	0	0	(- -)	16	9	4	6	8	1	9	0	0	0	2	0	1.00	2	.242	.324	.242
2011 Rchmd	AA	73	273	70	12	2	4	(- -)	98	46	32	37	23	1	31	7	4	2	36	3	.92	5	.256	.320	.359
2011 Fresno	AAA	64	237	80	20	3	10	(- -)	136	57	41	63	35	0	31	4	2	2	33	3	.92	5	.338	.428	.574
2008 NYY	AL	24	40	10	3	0	0	(0 0)	13	6	6	7	3	0	4	0	0	0	7	1	.88	1	.250	.302	.325
2011 SF	NL	18	47	12	5	0	0	(0 0)	17	6	4	5	2	0	8	0	2	0	3	2	.60	0	.255	.286	.362
2 ML YEARS		42	87	22	8	0	0	(0 0)	30	12	10	12	5	0	12	0	2	0	10	3	.77	1	.253	.293	.345

Pedro Ciriaco

Bats: R **Throws:** R **Pos:** PH-10; SS-7; PR-4; 3B-2; LF-2   see-ree-AH-koe   **Ht:** 6'0" **Wt:** 172 **Born:** 9/27/1985 **Age:** 26

Year	Team	Lg	G	AB	H	2B	3B	HR	(Hm	Rd)	TB	R	RBI	RC	TBB	IBB	SO	HBP	SH	SF	SB	CS	SB%	GDP	Avg	OBP	Slg
2005	Msoula	R+	69	254	61	9	4	2	(-	-)	84	28	31	22	7	0	50	2	3	2	7	2	.78	3	.240	.264	.331
2006	Sbend	A	128	550	145	15	5	2	(-	-)	176	77	32	57	32	0	96	5	10	3	19	8	.70	8	.264	.308	.320
2007	Visalia	A+	119	463	116	14	5	3	(-	-)	149	61	39	43	20	1	81	4	5	3	20	11	.65	12	.251	.286	.322
2008	Visalia	A+	124	520	161	26	5	5	(-	-)	212	85	61	77	18	0	89	6	7	11	40	9	.82	9	.310	.333	.408
2009	Mobile	AA	121	469	139	15	3	4	(-	-)	172	56	54	60	16	2	71	2	5	5	39	10	.80	10	.296	.319	.367
2010	Reno	AAA	87	355	92	15	7	6	(-	-)	139	44	51	41	10	1	53	1	6	4	14	3	.82	7	.259	.278	.392
2010	Indy	AAA	32	121	34	9	1	0	(-	-)	45	19	6	13	2	0	21	0	1	2	5	1	.83	1	.281	.288	.372
2011	Indy	AAA	71	277	64	7	3	2	(-	-)	83	31	24	19	5	0	49	0	5	2	13	7	.65	7	.231	.243	.300
2010	Pit	NL	8	6	3	1	1	0	(0	0)	6	3	1	3	0	0	3	0	0	0	0	0	-	0	.500	.500	1.000
2011	Pit	NL	23	33	10	2	1	0	(0	0)	14	4	6	5	1	0	6	0	0	0	2	1	.67	0	.303	.324	.424
	2 ML YEARS		31	39	13	3	2	0	(0	0)	20	7	7	8	1	0	9	0	0	0	2	1	.67	1	.333	.350	.513

Steve Cishek

Pitches: R **Bats:** R **Pos:** RP-45   SEE-sheck   **Ht:** 6'6" **Wt:** 200 **Born:** 6/18/1986 **Age:** 26

Year	Team	Lg	G	GS	CG	GF	IP	BFP	H	R	ER	HR	SH	SF	HB	TBB	IBB	SO	WP	Bk	W	L	Pct	Sh	Sv-Op	Hld	ERC	ERA
2007	Jmstwn	A-	25	0	0	19	32.1	137	20	13	7	1	2	0	2	19	0	30	3	0	1	2	.333	0	9--	-	2.48	1.95
2008	Grnsbr	A	50	0	0	23	75.1	329	69	40	39	8	4	3	10	34	3	75	6	0	3	5	.375	0	2--	-	4.35	4.66
2009	Jupiter	A+	37	0	0	11	57.0	230	36	23	18	2	6	1	9	16	1	45	6	2	3	4	.429	0	2--	-	1.89	2.84
2010	Jupiter	A+	26	0	0	11	35.0	157	29	15	11	0	1	1	6	19	3	28	2	0	0	6	.000	0	4--	-	3.39	2.83
2010	Jaxnvl	AA	22	0	0	5	31.1	135	30	16	15	0	4	0	5	10	2	34	6	0	3	1	.750	0	2--	-	3.35	4.31
2011	NewOr	AAA	15	0	0	6	23.0	99	18	7	6	1	1	1	2	12	2	19	2	0	1	1	.500	0	0--	-	3.14	2.35
2010	Fla	NL	3	0	0	2	4.1	15	1	0	0	0	0	0	0	1	0	3	0	0	0	0	-	0	0-0	0	0.35	0.00
2011	Fla	NL	45	0	0	21	54.2	229	45	18	16	1	3	0	3	19	7	55	5	0	2	1	.667	0	3-3	2	2.38	2.63
	2 ML YEARS		48	0	0	23	59.0	244	46	18	16	1	3	0	3	20	7	58	5	0	2	1	.667	0	3-3	2	2.15	2.44

Maikel Cleto

Pitches: R **Bats:** R **Pos:** RP-3   MY-kel CLAY-toe   **Ht:** 6'3" **Wt:** 235 **Born:** 5/1/1989 **Age:** 23

Year	Team	Lg	G	GS	CG	GF	IP	BFP	H	R	ER	HR	SH	SF	HB	TBB	IBB	SO	WP	Bk	W	L	Pct	Sh	Sv-Op	Hld	ERC	ERA
2007	Mets	R	11	4	0	2	34.0	157	34	21	19	2	2	2	2	25	0	28	8	0	1	2	.333	0	1--	-	5.40	5.03
2008	Savann	A	25	22	1	0	135.2	577	140	78	64	8	5	9	7	34	0	81	25	1	5	11	.313	1	0--	-	3.58	4.25
2008	StLuci	A+	1	1	0	0	5.0	21	5	5	5	1	1	0	0	2	0	1	0	0	0	1	.000	0	0--	-	4.93	9.00
2009	Ms	R	1	0	0	0	0.2	8	3	6	1	0	0	0	1	1	0	1	0	0	0	1	.000	0	0--	-	37.16	13.50
2009	Clinton	A	8	8	0	0	25.1	123	35	20	15	4	0	1	2	11	0	24	2	0	0	3	.000	0	0--	-	7.22	5.33
2010	Hi Dsrt	A+	23	21	0	0	102.1	466	125	81	70	10	4	1	7	44	0	83	19	1	4	9	.308	0	0--	-	5.84	6.16
2011	PlmBh	A+	5	5	0	0	29.0	119	20	10	8	2	1	1	2	10	0	33	2	0	1	1	.500	0	0--	-	2.27	2.48
2011	Sprgfld	AA	7	6	0	0	34.1	154	40	19	15	2	3	1	5	12	1	36	1	0	2	2	.500	0	0--	-	5.12	3.93
2011	Memp	AAA	13	13	0	0	71.1	311	57	37	34	6	2	2	3	43	0	66	4	1	5	3	.625	0	0--	-	3.79	4.29
2011	StL	NL	3	0	0	2	4.1	25	7	6	6	2	0	0	0	4	0	6	0	0	0	0	-	0	0-0	0	13.10	12.46

Steve Clevenger

Bats: L **Throws:** R **Pos:** C-2; PH-1   **Ht:** 6'0" **Wt:** 185 **Born:** 4/5/1986 **Age:** 26

Year	Team	Lg	G	AB	H	2B	3B	HR	(Hm	Rd)	TB	R	RBI	RC	TBB	IBB	SO	HBP	SH	SF	SB	CS	SB%	GDP	Avg	OBP	Slg
2006	Boise	A-	63	220	63	8	1	2	(-	-)	79	35	21	31	26	0	28	1	1	1	5	2	.71	7	.286	.363	.359
2007	Boise	A-	22	83	31	9	0	0	(-	-)	40	10	18	15	4	0	6	0	0	1	0	0	-	6	.373	.398	.482
2007	Dytona	A+	43	164	53	8	1	2	(-	-)	69	21	24	26	13	0	5	1	1	4	0	0	-	7	.323	.368	.421
2008	Dytona	A+	84	284	89	20	0	2	(-	-)	115	36	39	49	39	3	41	1	1	4	7	3	.70	9	.313	.393	.405
2008	Tenn	AA	29	89	22	5	1	1	(-	-)	32	5	15	11	10	1	10	0	2	3	0	0	-	4	.247	.314	.360
2009	Tenn	AA	26	77	28	4	3	1	(-	-)	41	12	10	17	10	1	8	1	1	0	0	0	-	3	.364	.443	.532
2009	Iowa	AAA	68	230	61	12	1	0	(-	-)	75	21	26	24	15	0	31	1	2	3	4	3	.57	7	.265	.309	.326
2010	Tenn	AA	88	271	86	24	0	5	(-	-)	125	37	47	60	20	4	28	2	0	1	0	6	.00	11	.317	.367	.461
2011	Tenn	AA	95	312	92	27	3	5	(-	-)	140	42	39	53	35	2	39	0	1	3	1	0	1.00	8	.295	.363	.449
2011	Iowa	AAA	25	86	35	3	1	3	(-	-)	49	9	15	21	9	0	7	0	0	2	1	0	1.00	8	.407	.454	.570
2011	ChC	NL	2	4	1	1	0	0	(0	0)	2	1	0	0	0	0	0	1	0	0	0	0	-	0	.250	.400	.500

Tyler Clippard

Pitches: R **Bats:** R **Pos:** RP-72   **Ht:** 6'3" **Wt:** 200 **Born:** 2/14/1985 **Age:** 27

Year	Team	Lg	G	GS	CG	GF	IP	BFP	H	R	ER	HR	SH	SF	HB	TBB	IBB	SO	WP	Bk	W	L	Pct	Sh	Sv-Op	Hld	ERC	ERA
2007	NYY	AL	6	6	0	0	27.0	124	29	19	19	6	0	0	0	17	1	18	2	1	3	1	.750	0	0-0	0	6.37	6.33
2008	Was	NL	2	2	0	0	10.1	48	12	5	5	2	0	0	0	7	1	8	1	0	1	1	.500	0	0-0	0	6.90	4.35
2009	Was	NL	41	0	0	8	60.1	246	36	20	18	9	3	1	1	32	1	67	1	1	4	2	.667	0	0-1	3	2.79	2.69
2010	Was	NL	78	0	0	18	91.0	378	69	33	31	8	3	7	2	41	4	112	1	1	11	8	.579	0	1-11	23	2.91	3.07
2011	Was	NL	72	0	0	8	88.1	329	48	18	18	11	4	3	0	26	2	104	1	0	3	0	1.000	0	0-7	38	1.61	1.83
	5 ML YEARS		199	8	0	34	277.0	1125	194	95	91	36	10	11	3	123	9	309	6	3	22	12	.647	0	1-19	64	2.86	2.96

Alex Cobb

Pitches: R Bats: R Pos: SP-9   Ht: 6'1" Wt: 195 Born: 10/7/1987 Age: 24

				HOW MUCH HE PITCHED						WHAT HE GAVE UP										THE RESULTS						
Year Team	Lg	G	GS	CG	GF	IP	BFP	H	R	ER	HR	SH	SF	HB	TBB	IBB	SO	WP	Bk	W	L	Pct	Sh	Sv-Op	Hld	ERC	ERA
2006 Princtn	R	6	1	0	1	8.2	38	9	7	5	3	0	1	0	3	0	8	1	0	0	0	-	0	0- -	-	5.69	5.19
2007 HudVal	A-	16	16	0	0	81.1	345	78	36	32	4	5	4	4	31	0	62	2	1	5	6	.455	0	0- -	-	3.66	3.54
2008 Clmbs	A	25	25	0	0	139.2	560	113	59	51	16	2	3	16	35	0	97	3	2	9	7	.563	0	0- -	-	3.10	3.29
2009 Charltt	A+	24	23	0	0	124.2	515	116	49	42	6	3	6	9	31	1	107	8	2	8	5	.615	0	0- -	-	3.07	3.03
2010 Mont	AA	23	22	0	0	119.2	503	119	46	35	7	2	5	4	35	1	128	5	0	7	5	.583	0	0- -	-	3.49	2.63
2011 Drham	AAA	12	12	0	0	67.1	264	61	19	14	4	2	1	2	16	0	70	1	0	5	1	.833	0	0- -	-	2.96	1.87
2011 TB	AL	9	9	0	0	52.2	224	49	21	20	3	0	1	1	21	1	37	2	0	3	2	.600	0	0-0	-	3.44	3.42

Todd Coffey

Pitches: R Bats: R Pos: RP-69   Ht: 6'4" Wt: 241 Born: 9/9/1980 Age: 31

				HOW MUCH HE PITCHED						WHAT HE GAVE UP										THE RESULTS						
Year Team	Lg	G	GS	CG	GF	IP	BFP	H	R	ER	HR	SH	SF	HB	TBB	IBB	SO	WP	Bk	W	L	Pct	Sh	Sv-Op	Hld	ERC	ERA
2005 Cin	NL	57	0	0	14	58.0	265	84	33	29	5	3	2	5	11	2	26	1	0	4	1	.800	0	1-2	3	6.11	4.50
2006 Cin	NL	81	0	0	28	78.0	340	85	34	31	7	0	1	2	27	5	60	4	0	6	7	.462	0	8-12	15	4.29	3.58
2007 Cin	NL	58	0	0	8	51.0	242	70	36	33	12	1	0	5	19	4	43	4	0	2	1	.667	0	0-3	7	7.58	5.82
2008 2 Tms	NL	26	0	0	9	26.2	116	31	13	13	4	2	1	1	8	0	15	0	0	1	0	1.000	0	0-0	-	5.19	4.39
2009 Mil	NL	78	0	0	17	83.2	336	76	28	27	8	2	2	3	21	3	65	1	0	4	4	.500	0	2-6	27	3.16	2.90
2010 Mil	NL	69	0	0	12	62.1	274	65	40	33	8	2	5	3	23	5	56	6	0	2	4	.333	0	0-2	13	4.42	4.76
2011 Was	NL	69	0	0	15	59.2	254	55	25	24	4	5	3	1	20	3	46	1	0	5	1	.833	0	0-2	10	3.11	3.62
08 Cin	NL	17	0	0	6	19.1	87	25	13	13	4	1	1	1	6	0	8	0	0	0	0	-	0	0-0	-	6.57	6.05
08 Mil	NL	9	0	0	3	7.1	29	6	0	0	1	0	0	2	2	0	7	0	0	1	0	1.000	0	0-0	1	2.09	0.00
7 ML YEARS		438	0	0	103	419.1	1827	466	209	190	48	15	14	20	129	22	311	17	0	24	18	.571	0	11-27	76	4.56	4.08

Chris Coghlan

Bats: L Throws: R Pos: CF-65   COGG-lan   Ht: 6'0" Wt: 204 Born: 6/18/1985 Age: 27

					BATTING																	BASERUNNING				AVERAGES		
Year Team	Lg	G	AB	H	2B	3B	HR	(Hm	Rd)	TB	R	RBI	RC	TBB	IBB	SO	HBP	SH	SF		SB	CS	SB%	GDP	Avg	OBP	Slg
2011 Jupiter*	A+	10	35	12	1	0	0	(-	-)	13	4	2	5	5	0	5	0	0	1		1	1	.50	0	.343	.415	.371
2011 Jaxnvl*	AA	5	19	4	1	0	0	(-	-)	5	3	0	2	4	0	1	0	0	0		0	0	-	0	.211	.348	.263
2011 NewOr*	AAA	15	53	13	4	0	1	(-	-)	20	11	7	8	8	0	5	3	1	3		3	1	.75	5	.245	.358	.377
2009 Fla	NL	128	504	162	31	6	9	(5	4)	232	84	47	91	53	2	77	4	3	1		8	5	.62	3	.321	.390	.460
2010 Fla	NL	91	358	96	20	3	5	(5	0)	137	60	28	43	33	1	84	4	3	2		10	3	.77	3	.268	.335	.383
2011 Fla	NL	65	269	62	20	1	5	(4	1)	99	33	22	23	22	3	49	4	1	2		7	6	.54	3	.230	.296	.368
3 ML YEARS		284	1131	320	71	10	19	(14	5)	468	177	97	157	108	6	210	12	7	5		25	14	.64	9	.283	.350	.414

Phil Coke

Pitches: L Bats: L Pos: RP-34; SP-14   Ht: 6'1" Wt: 210 Born: 7/19/1982 Age: 29

				HOW MUCH HE PITCHED						WHAT HE GAVE UP										THE RESULTS						
Year Team	Lg	G	GS	CG	GF	IP	BFP	H	R	ER	HR	SH	SF	HB	TBB	IBB	SO	WP	Bk	W	L	Pct	Sh	Sv-Op	Hld	ERC	ERA
2011 Toledo*	AAA	1	1	0	0	5.1	25	8	3	3	0	0	0	0	2	0	6	0	0	0	0	-	0	0- -	-	6.23	5.06
2008 NYY	AL	12	0	0	0	14.2	52	8	1	1	0	0	0	0	2	0	14	1	0	1	0	1.000	0	0-0	5	0.89	0.61
2009 NYY	AL	72	0	0	13	60.0	238	44	34	30	10	1	5	1	20	4	49	7	0	4	3	.571	0	2-7	21	2.84	4.50
2010 Det	AL	74	1	0	18	64.2	279	67	29	27	2	2	3	4	26	4	53	3	0	7	5	.583	0	2-4	17	4.00	3.76
2011 Det	AL	48	14	0	6	108.2	474	118	64	54	5	4	3	4	40	5	69	4	0	3	9	.250	0	1-2	8	4.13	4.47
Postseason		6	0	0	1	2.2	11	4	2	2	2	0	0	0	1	0	3	0	0	0	0	-	0	0-0	0	14.65	6.75
4 ML YEARS		206	15	0	37	248.0	1043	237	128	112	17	7	11	9	88	13	185	15	0	15	17	.469	0	5-13	51	3.55	4.06

Casey Coleman

Pitches: R Bats: L Pos: SP-17; RP-2   Ht: 6'0" Wt: 180 Born: 7/3/1987 Age: 24

				HOW MUCH HE PITCHED						WHAT HE GAVE UP										THE RESULTS						
Year Team	Lg	G	GS	CG	GF	IP	BFP	H	R	ER	HR	SH	SF	HB	TBB	IBB	SO	WP	Bk	W	L	Pct	Sh	Sv-Op	Hld	ERC	ERA
2008 Boise	A-	7	4	0	0	26.2	115	27	13	12	4	1	1	1	7	0	24	2	0	1	1	.500	0	0- -	-	4.00	4.05
2008 Peoria	A	5	5	0	0	23.1	96	25	11	7	1	0	0	0	4	0	18	0	0	2	2	.500	0	0- -	-	3.24	2.70
2008 Dytona	A+	1	1	0	0	5.0	21	4	1	0	0	1	0	0	2	0	2	0	0	1	0	1.000	0	0- -	-	2.31	0.00
2009 Tenn	AA	27	27	1	0	149.0	633	142	63	61	8	10	4	5	58	0	84	2	1	14	6	.700	0	0- -	-	3.62	3.68
2010 Iowa	AAA	21	21	2	0	117.1	481	106	58	53	10	3	5	2	35	0	59	4	0	10	7	.588	0	0- -	-	3.17	4.07
2011 Iowa	AAA	12	12	0	0	74.0	299	69	32	30	11	5	0	0	22	1	54	0	0	5	2	.714	0	0- -	-	3.72	3.65
2010 ChC	NL	12	8	0	0	57.0	248	56	27	26	3	2	4	2	25	2	27	3	0	4	2	.667	0	0-0	-	3.87	4.11
2011 ChC	NL	19	17	0	1	84.1	398	102	62	60	10	6	2	4	46	3	75	3	1	3	9	.250	0	0-0	-	6.15	6.40
2 ML YEARS		31	25	0	1	141.1	646	158	89	86	13	8	6	6	71	5	102	6	1	7	11	.389	0	0-0	-	5.20	5.48

Louis Coleman

Pitches: R Bats: R Pos: RP-48   Ht: 6'4" Wt: 195 Born: 4/4/1986 Age: 26

				HOW MUCH HE PITCHED						WHAT HE GAVE UP										THE RESULTS						
Year Team	Lg	G	GS	CG	GF	IP	BFP	H	R	ER	HR	SH	SF	HB	TBB	IBB	SO	WP	Bk	W	L	Pct	Sh	Sv-Op	Hld	ERC	ERA
2009 Burlgtn	A	4	0	0	2	7.1	24	2	2	2	0	0	0	1	1	0	6	0	0	1	0	1.000	0	1- -	-	0.51	2.45
2009 Wilmg	A+	10	0	0	4	14.1	54	8	3	2	0	0	0	0	3	0	16	1	0	3	1	.750	0	1- -	-	1.02	1.26
2010 NWArk	AA	21	1	0	13	51.2	198	31	13	12	5	1	0	2	14	1	55	4	0	2	1	.667	0	6- -	-	1.72	2.09
2010 Omha	AAA	21	0	0	5	40.1	164	31	11	10	2	2	2	5	11	1	48	1	0	5	2	.714	0	1- -	-	2.50	2.23
2011 Omha	AAA	6	0	0	5	7.0	30	4	4	3	0	0	1	0	4	0	16	1	0	1	0	1.000	0	2- -	-	1.74	3.86
2011 KC	AL	48	0	0	11	59.2	244	44	20	19	9	1	1	3	26	6	64	4	0	1	4	.200	0	1-2	11	3.23	2.87

Tim Collins

Pitches: L Bats: L Pos: RP-68

Ht: 5'7" Wt: 163 Born: 8/29/1989 Age: 22

Year	Team	Lg	G	GS	CG	GF	IP	BFP	H	R	ER	HR	SH	SF	HB	TBB	IBB	SO	WP	Bk	W	L	Pct	Sh	Sv-Op Hld	ERC	ERA
2007	B Jays	R	7	0	0	1	6.0	24	6	3	3	0	0	0	0	2	0	7	0	0	0	0	-	0	0- -	3.35	4.50
2008	Lnsng	A	39	0	0	28	68.1	267	36	13	12	3	1	1	2	32	1	98	5	2	4	2	.667	0	14- -	1.72	1.58
2009	Dnedin	A+	40	0	0	15	64.2	270	47	21	17	2	2	1	3	28	1	99	2	0	7	4	.636	0	3- -	2.42	2.37
2009	NHam	AA	9	0	0	2	12.2	56	12	9	8	1	2	0	0	7	0	17	2	0	2	3	.400	0	0- -	4.21	5.68
2010	NHam	AA	35	0	0	18	43.0	171	27	12	12	4	0	0	0	16	0	73	2	1	1	0	1.000	0	9- -	2.01	2.51
2010	Missi	AA	6	0	0	4	8.0	29	4	1	1	1	0	0	0	3	0	14	0	0	0	0	-	0	2- -	1.77	1.13
2010	Omha	AAA	15	0	0	8	20.1	79	9	3	3	0	0	0	0	8	0	21	0	0	2	1	.667	0	4- -	1.04	1.33
2011	KC	AL	68	0	0	18	67.0	295	52	28	27	5	3	1	2	48	2	60	3	0	4	4	.500	0	0-1 11	3.95	3.63

Josh Collmenter

Pitches: R Bats: R Pos: SP-24; RP-7

COLE-men-ter

Ht: 6'2" Wt: 235 Born: 2/7/1986 Age: 26

Year	Team	Lg	G	GS	CG	GF	IP	BFP	H	R	ER	HR	SH	SF	HB	TBB	IBB	SO	WP	Bk	W	L	Pct	Sh	Sv-Op Hld	ERC	ERA
2007	Yakima	A-	14	12	0	1	66.1	275	60	22	20	4	2	4	2	21	0	57	2	1	6	3	.667	0	0- -	3.11	2.71
2008	Sbend	A	27	27	0	0	145.1	606	126	62	55	8	2	4	6	47	0	123	3	0	12	8	.600	0	0- -	2.91	3.41
2009	Visalia	A+	27	27	1	0	145.1	612	127	76	67	9	6	8	8	55	0	152	9	0	8	10	.444	0	0- -	3.22	4.15
2010	Visalia	A+	3	3	0	0	15.0	59	11	4	4	2	1	0	1	3	0	21	0	0	2	0	1.000	0	0- -	2.40	2.40
2010	Reno	AAA	10	10	0	0	57.2	258	64	40	37	8	2	1	1	26	1	39	3	0	4	3	.571	0	0- -	5.25	5.77
2010	Mobile	AA	12	12	2	0	79.1	315	61	18	16	3	3	2	1	22	0	73	4	0	8	3	.727	1	0- -	2.11	1.82
2011	Reno	AAA	1	1	0	0	6.0	21	2	2	1	1	0	0	0	2	0	7	1	0	1	0	1.000	0	0- -	1.24	1.50
2011	Ari	NL	31	24	0	3	154.1	621	137	61	58	17	9	2	5	28	2	100	1	1	10	10	.500	0	0-0 0	2.82	3.38

Bartolo Colon

Pitches: R Bats: R Pos: SP-26; RP-3

Ht: 5'11" Wt: 267 Born: 5/24/1973 Age: 39

Year	Team	Lg	G	GS	CG	GF	IP	BFP	H	R	ER	HR	SH	SF	HB	TBB	IBB	SO	WP	Bk	W	L	Pct	Sh	Sv-Op Hld	ERC	ERA
1997	Cle	AL	19	17	1	0	94.0	427	107	66	59	12	4	1	3	45	1	66	5	0	4	7	.364	0	0-0 0	5.53	5.65
1998	Cle	AL	31	31	6	0	204.0	883	205	91	84	15	10	2	3	79	5	158	4	0	14	9	.609	2	0-0 0	3.87	3.71
1999	Cle	AL	32	32	1	0	205.0	858	185	97	90	24	5	4	7	76	5	161	4	0	18	5	.783	1	0-0 0	3.68	3.95
2000	Cle	AL	30	30	2	0	188.0	807	163	86	81	21	2	3	4	98	4	212	4	0	15	8	.652	1	0-0 0	3.97	3.88
2001	Cle	AL	34	34	1	0	222.1	947	220	106	101	26	8	4	2	90	2	201	4	1	14	12	.538	0	0-0 0	4.24	4.09
2002	2 Tms		33	33	8	0	233.1	966	219	85	76	20	19	6	2	70	5	149	4	0	20	8	.714	3	0-0 0	3.29	2.93
2003	CWS	AL	34	34	9	0	242.0	984	223	107	104	30	5	8	5	67	3	173	8	3	15	13	.536	0	0-0 0	3.47	3.87
2004	LAA	AL	34	34	0	0	208.1	897	215	122	116	38	5	8	3	71	1	158	1	0	18	12	.600	0	0-0 0	4.64	5.01
2005	LAA	AL	33	33	2	0	222.2	906	215	93	86	26	9	4	3	43	0	157	2	1	21	8	.724	0	0-0 0	3.28	3.48
2006	LAA	AL	10	10	1	0	56.1	251	71	39	32	11	4	1	3	29	1	31	1	0	1	5	.167	1	0-0 0	5.61	5.11
2007	LAA	AL	19	18	0	0	99.1	453	132	74	70	15	4	3	5	29	1	76	1	0	6	8	.429	0	0-0 1	6.17	6.34
2008	Bos	AL	7	7	0	0	39.0	173	44	23	17	5	3	2	2	10	0	27	0	0	4	2	.667	0	0-0 0	4.53	3.92
2009	CWS	AL	12	12	0	0	62.1	276	69	42	29	13	4	3	2	21	3	38	1	0	3	6	.333	0	0-0 0	5.22	4.19
2011	NYY	AL	29	26	1	0	164.1	694	172	85	73	21	2	6	3	40	3	135	0	0	8	10	.444	1	0-0 0	3.95	4.00
02	Cle	AL	16	16	4	0	116.1	467	104	37	33	11	6	3	2	31	1	75	3	0	10	4	.714	2	0-0 0	3.09	2.55
02	Mon	NL	17	17	4	0	117.0	499	115	48	43	9	13	3	0	39	4	74	1	0	10	4	.714	1	0-0 0	3.48	3.31
	Postseason		9	9	1	0	52.1	215	49	21	21	5	1	1	1	22	1	41	0	0	2	3	.400	0	0-0 0	4.01	3.61
14 ML YEARS			357	351	32	0	2241.0	9522	2240	1116	1018	277	84	55	47	750	33	1742	39	5	161	113	.588	9	0-0 1	4.06	4.09

Tyler Colvin

Bats: L Throws: L Pos: RF-44; PH-21; LF-10; CF-8; 1B-4; PR-2

Ht: 6'3" Wt: 210 Born: 9/5/1985 Age: 26

Year	Team	Lg	G	AB	H	2B	3B	HR	(Hm	Rd)	TB	R	RBI	RC	TBB	IBB	SO	HBP	SH	SF	SB	CS	SB%	GDP	Avg	OBP	Slg
2011	Iowa*	AAA	50	203	52	12	6	7	(-	-)	97	32	32	26	5	0	55	0	1	3	1	1	.50	6	.256	.270	.478
2009	ChC	NL	6	17	3	0	0	0	(0	0)	3	1	2	1	2	0	5	0	0	1	0	0	-	0	.176	.250	.176
2010	ChC	NL	135	358	91	18	5	20	(9	11)	179	60	56	46	30	2	100	3	1	2	6	1	.86	6	.254	.316	.500
2011	ChC	NL	80	206	31	8	3	6	(2	4)	63	17	20	9	14	3	58	0	1	1	0	0	-	2	.150	.204	.306
3 ML YEARS			221	581	125	26	8	26	(11	15)	245	78	78	56	46	5	163	3	2	4	6	1	.86	8	.215	.274	.422

Hank Conger

Bats: B Throws: R Pos: C-56; PH-7; DH-1

KONG-gerr

Ht: 6'1" Wt: 220 Born: 1/29/1988 Age: 24

Year	Team	Lg	G	AB	H	2B	3B	HR	(Hm	Rd)	TB	R	RBI	RC	TBB	IBB	SO	HBP	SH	SF	SB	CS	SB%	GDP	Avg	OBP	Slg
2006	Angels	R	19	69	22	3	4	1	(-	-)	36	11	11	13	7	0	11	0	0	0	1	0	1.00	0	.319	.382	.522
2007	CRpds	A	84	290	84	20	1	7	(-	-)	137	33	48	47	21	0	48	2	2	5	9	4	.69	9	.290	.336	.472
2007	Angels	R	3	15	4	1	0	0	(-	-)	5	2	3	1	0	0	3	0	0	0	0	0	-	1	.267	.267	.333
2008	RCuca	A+	73	294	89	20	2	13	(-	-)	152	47	75	51	14	1	55	3	0	7	2	1	.67	3	.303	.333	.517
2009	Ark	AA	123	459	135	20	3	11	(-	-)	194	61	56	75	55	5	68	2	3	6	3	2	.60	19	.294	.368	.423
2010	Salt Lk	AAA	108	387	116	26	2	11	(-	-)	179	56	49	71	55	1	58	1	5	4	0	2	.00	5	.300	.385	.463
2011	Salt Lk	AAA	27	100	30	4	0	5	(-	-)	49	14	26	18	12	3	18	0	2	0	0	0	-	2	.300	.375	.490
2010	LAA	AL	13	29	5	1	1	0	(0	0)	8	2	5	3	5	0	9	0	0	0	0	0	-	1	.172	.294	.276
2011	LAA	AL	59	177	37	8	0	6	(2	4)	63	14	19	18	17	2	37	1	2	0	0	0	-	2	.209	.282	.356
2 ML YEARS			72	206	42	9	1	6	(2	4)	71	16	24	21	22	2	46	1	2	0	0	0	-	3	.204	.284	.345

Brooks Conrad

Bats: B **Throws:** R **Pos:** PH-75; 2B-10; 3B-8; 1B-1   **Ht:** 5'11" **Wt:** 190 **Born:** 1/16/1980 **Age:** 32

						BATTING															BASERUNNING				AVERAGES		
Year	Team	Lg	G	AB	H	2B	3B	HR	(Hm	Rd)	TB	R	RBI	RC	TBB	IBB	SO	HBP	SH	SF	SB	CS	SB%	GDP	Avg	OBP	Slg
2008	Oak	AL	6	19	3	1	0	0	(0	0)	4	0	2	1	0	0	9	0	0	0	0	0	-	1	.158	.158	.211
2009	Atl	NL	30	54	11	1	2	2	(0	2)	22	7	8	6	3	1	14	1	0	0	0	0	-	1	.204	.259	.407
2010	Atl	NL	103	156	39	11	1	8	(4	4)	76	31	33	32	16	0	45	1	4	0	5	1	.83	0	.250	.324	.487
2011	Atl	NL	92	103	23	5	0	4	(2	2)	40	11	13	12	15	2	41	1	2	1	2	0	1.00	0	.223	.325	.388
	Postseason		4	11	1	0	0	0	(0	0)	1	0	0	0	0	0	4	0	1	0	0	0	-	0	.091	.091	.091
	4 ML YEARS		231	332	76	18	3	14	(6	8)	142	49	56	51	34	3	109	3	6	1	7	1	.88	2	.229	.305	.428

Jose Constanza

Bats: L **Throws:** L **Pos:** LF-17; RF-16; PH-8; CF-4; PR-4   **Ht:** 5'9" **Wt:** 150 **Born:** 9/1/1983 **Age:** 28

						BATTING															BASERUNNING				AVERAGES		
Year	Team	Lg	G	AB	H	2B	3B	HR	(Hm	Rd)	TB	R	RBI	RC	TBB	IBB	SO	HBP	SH	SF	SB	CS	SB%	GDP	Avg	OBP	Slg
2005	Lk Cty	A	23	72	17	0	0	0	(-	-)	17	9	4	8	15	0	13	0	1	0	2	1	.67	2	.236	.368	.236
2005	MhVlly	A-	64	270	71	5	5	0	(-	-)	86	30	20	34	28	1	39	4	1	1	24	6	.80	6	.263	.340	.319
2006	Lk Cty	A	44	159	44	5	3	1	(-	-)	58	31	9	28	30	0	30	1	1	0	19	4	.83	1	.277	.395	.365
2006	Knstn	A+	76	275	90	15	6	1	(-	-)	120	55	27	55	42	0	50	2	1	1	20	4	.83	5	.327	.419	.436
2007	Knstn	A+	112	445	122	13	4	2	(-	-)	149	71	34	57	39	0	80	2	10	2	39	9	.81	1	.274	.334	.335
2008	Akron	AA	95	338	94	12	6	0	(-	-)	118	44	34	44	28	1	42	2	5	3	24	6	.80	7	.278	.334	.349
2009	Akron	AA	130	486	137	15	7	0	(-	-)	166	98	46	75	75	1	65	1	11	2	49	14	.78	3	.282	.378	.342
2010	Clmbs	AAA	113	404	129	11	8	1	(-	-)	159	69	32	66	35	1	54	0	8	1	34	6	.85	7	.319	.373	.394
2011	Gwnntt	AAA	86	333	104	2	4	1	(-	-)	117	47	25	46	25	3	41	1	3	1	23	8	.74	7	.312	.361	.351
2011	Atl	NL	42	109	33	1	1	2	(1	1)	42	21	10	12	6	0	14	0	4	0	7	4	.64	1	.303	.339	.385

Jose Contreras

Pitches: R **Bats:** R **Pos:** RP-17   conn-TRAIR-us   **Ht:** 6'4" **Wt:** 255 **Born:** 12/6/1971 **Age:** 40

			HOW MUCH HE PITCHED					WHAT HE GAVE UP											THE RESULTS						
Year	Team	Lg	G	GS	CG	GF	IP	BFP	H	R	ER	HR	SH	SF	HB	TBB	IBB	SO	WP	Bk	W	L	Pct	Sh	Sv-Op Hld	ERC	ERA
2011	Clrwtr*	A+	1	1	0	0	0.2	6	4	3	3	0	0	0	0	0	0	0	0	0	0	1	.000	0	0- -	39.65	40.50
2011	Rdng*	AA	1	0	0	0	1.0	6	2	0	0	0	0	0	0	1	0	1	0	0	0	0	-	0	0- -	12.01	0.00
2011	LV*	AAA	1	0	0	1	2.0	7	2	0	0	0	0	0	0	0	0	0	0	0	0	0	-	0	0- -	2.31	0.00
2003	NYY	AL	18	9	0	2	71.0	293	52	27	26	4	0	1	5	30	1	72	2	0	7	2	.778	0	0-1 1	2.71	3.30
2004	2 Tms	AL	31	31	0	0	170.1	758	166	114	104	31	3	6	8	84	1	150	17	0	13	9	.591	0	0-0 0	5.05	5.50
2005	CWS	AL	32	32	1	0	204.2	857	177	91	82	23	7	2	9	75	2	154	20	2	15	7	.682	0	0-0 0	3.46	3.61
2006	CWS	AL	30	30	1	0	196.0	833	194	101	93	20	2	8	10	55	4	134	16	0	13	9	.591	1	0-0 0	3.72	4.27
2007	CWS	AL	32	30	2	2	189.0	858	232	134	117	21	8	10	15	62	1	113	3	0	10	17	.370	2	0-0 0	5.49	5.57
2008	CWS	AL	20	20	1	0	121.0	522	130	64	61	12	4	2	3	35	0	70	6	0	7	6	.538	0	0-0 0	4.13	4.54
2009	2 Tms		28	23	0	0	131.2	589	141	86	72	13	10	2	6	53	4	106	8	0	6	13	.316	0	0-1 1	4.55	4.92
2010	Phi	NL	67	0	0	21	56.2	233	53	22	21	5	4	1	4	16	2	57	0	0	4	6	.600	0	4-5 13	3.50	3.34
2011	Phi	NL	17	0	0	8	14.0	60	11	6	6	0	1	0	1	8	0	13	0	0	0	0	-	0	5-5 4	3.15	3.86
04	NYY	AL	18	18	0	0	95.2	425	93	66	60	22	1	4	6	42	1	82	10	0	8	5	.615	0	0-0 0	5.18	5.64
04	CWS	AL	13	13	0	0	74.2	333	73	48	44	9	2	2	2	42	0	68	7	0	4	4	.556	0	0-0 0	4.87	5.30
09	CWS	AL	21	21	0	0	114.2	513	121	83	69	11	7	2	6	45	3	89	8	0	5	13	.278	0	0-0 0	4.41	5.42
09	Col	NL	7	2	0	0	17.0	76	20	3	3	2	3	0	0	8	1	17	0	0	1	0	1.000	0	0-1 1	5.51	1.59
	Postseason		18	4	1	4	49.0	199	41	19	19	2	5	1	3	11	0	38	3	0	4	3	.571	0	0-1 4	2.41	3.49
	9 ML YEARS		275	175	5	33	1154.1	5003	1156	645	582	129	39	32	61	418	15	869	72	2	77	67	.535	3	9-12 19	4.20	4.54

Aaron Cook

Pitches: R **Bats:** R **Pos:** SP-17; RP-1   **Ht:** 6'3" **Wt:** 215 **Born:** 2/8/1979 **Age:** 33

			HOW MUCH HE PITCHED					WHAT HE GAVE UP											THE RESULTS						
Year	Team	Lg	G	GS	CG	GF	IP	BFP	H	R	ER	HR	SH	SF	HB	TBB	IBB	SO	WP	Bk	W	L	Pct	Sh	Sv-Op Hld	ERC	ERA
2011	Tulsa*	AA	3	3	0	0	14.0	58	16	9	9	1	0	0	0	3	0	13	1	0	0	1	.000	0	0- -	4.07	5.79
2011	ColSpr*	AAA	2	2	0	0	14.2	57	13	9	9	2	0	0	0	2	0	5	1	0	1	0	1.000	0	0- -	2.75	5.52
2002	Col	NL	9	5	0	1	35.2	154	41	18	18	4	0	0	0	13	0	14	0	0	2	1	.667	0	0-0 1	5.31	4.54
2003	Col	NL	43	16	1	4	124.0	579	160	89	83	8	4	6	8	57	7	43	10	0	4	6	.400	0	0-0 1	5.95	6.02
2004	Col	NL	16	16	1	0	96.2	433	112	47	46	7	5	1	7	39	5	40	6	1	6	4	.600	0	0-0 0	5.05	4.28
2005	Col	NL	13	13	2	0	83.1	357	101	38	34	8	1	3	2	16	2	24	3	0	7	2	.778	0	0-0 0	4.53	3.67
2006	Col	NL	32	32	0	0	212.2	915	242	107	100	18	8	5	7	55	11	92	2	0	9	15	.375	0	0-0 0	4.23	4.23
2007	Col	NL	25	25	2	0	166.0	698	178	87	76	15	6	3	6	44	6	61	0	0	8	7	.533	0	0-0 0	4.05	4.12
2008	Col	NL	32	32	2	0	211.1	886	236	102	93	13	9	4	4	48	2	96	6	0	16	9	.640	1	0-0 0	3.92	3.96
2009	Col	NL	27	27	1	0	158.0	675	175	76	73	19	3	6	2	47	2	78	2	0	11	6	.647	1	0-0 0	4.51	4.16
2010	Col	NL	23	23	2	0	127.2	572	147	77	72	11	3	6	4	52	4	62	3	1	6	8	.429	0	0-0 0	4.95	5.08
2011	Col	NL	18	17	0	0	97.0	441	127	67	65	9	1	8	5	37	5	48	3	0	3	10	.231	0	0-0 0	6.00	6.03
	Postseason		2	2	0	0	11.0	45	13	6	6	1	0	0	0	2	0	6	0	0	1	1	.500	0	0-0 0	4.37	4.91
	10 ML YEARS		238	206	11	5	1312.1	5710	1519	708	660	111	40	42	47	408	44	558	35	2	72	68	.514	2	0-0 2	4.65	4.53

Ryan Cook

Pitches: R **Bats:** R **Pos:** RP-12   **Ht:** 6'3" **Wt:** 200 **Born:** 6/30/1987 **Age:** 25

			HOW MUCH HE PITCHED					WHAT HE GAVE UP											THE RESULTS						
Year	Team	Lg	G	GS	CG	GF	IP	BFP	H	R	ER	HR	SH	SF	HB	TBB	IBB	SO	WP	Bk	W	L	Pct	Sh	Sv-Op Hld	ERC	ERA
2008	Yakima	A-	7	7	0	0	33.0	152	37	25	17	4	0	5	1	11	0	23	1	0	2	2	.500	0	0- -	5.15	4.64
2009	Sbend	A	25	25	0	0	142.2	590	140	71	58	5	2	6	10	44	0	103	7	1	11	11	.500	0	0- -	3.56	3.66
2010	Visalia	A+	20	20	0	0	108.1	475	110	62	51	3	3	4	13	36	0	100	8	1	4	7	.364	0	0- -	3.82	4.24
2010	Reno	AAA	1	1	0	0	5.0	25	7	6	6	1	0	0	2	2	0	5	0	1	0	0	-	0	0- -	9.34	10.80

Year	Team	Lg	G	GS	CG	GF	IP	BFP	H	R	ER	HR	SH	SF	HB	TBB	IBB	SO	WP	Bk	W	L	Pct	Sh	Sv-Op	Hld	ERC	ERA
2010	Mobile	AA	3	3	0	0	18.2	77	13	7	6	1	1	0	1	10	0	12	1	0	1	1	.500	0	0--	-	2.91	2.89
2011	Mobile	AA	34	0	0	21	44.0	174	28	12	11	2	1	1	2	14	2	50	3	0	1	4	.200	0	13--	-	1.72	2.25
2011	Reno	AAA	14	0	0	9	17.0	67	13	6	4	0	0	0	1	8	1	12	4	0	0	1	.000	0	6--	-	2.74	2.12
2011	Ari	NL	12	0	0	5	7.2	41	11	6	6	0	0	0	0	8	0	7	1	1	0	1	.000	0	0-0	1	8.56	7.04

David Cooper

Bats: L Throws: L Pos: 1B-15; DH-9; PH-4; PR-1   **Ht: 6'0" Wt: 200 Born: 2/12/1987 Age: 25**

Year	Team	Lg	G	AB	H	2B	3B	HR	(Hm	Rd)	TB	R	RBI	RC	TBB	IBB	SO	HBP	SH	SF	SB	CS	SB%	GDP	Avg	OBP	Slg
2008	Auburn	A-	21	85	29	10	1	2	(-	-)	47	10	21	18	10	2	16	0	0	0	0	1	.00	5	.341	.411	.553
2008	Lnsng	A	24	96	34	10	0	2	(-	-)	50	15	17	20	10	0	14	0	0	0	0	0	-	0	.354	.415	.521
2008	Dnedin	A+	24	92	28	9	0	1	(-	-)	40	10	13	15	10	1	16	0	0	0	0	0	-	3	.304	.373	.435
2009	NHam	AA	128	473	122	32	0	10	(-	-)	184	62	66	67	59	3	92	2	0	4	0	0	-	17	.258	.340	.389
2010	NHam	AA	132	498	128	30	1	20	(-	-)	220	59	78	75	52	1	74	1	0	2	0	0	-	9	.257	.327	.442
2011	LsVgs	AAA	120	467	170	51	1	9	(-	-)	250	77	96	109	67	6	43	2	0	9	1	3	.25	14	.364	.439	.535
2011	Tor	AL	27	71	15	7	0	2	(2	0)	28	9	12	10	7	0	14	1	0	2	0	0	-	2	.211	.284	.394

Alex Cora

Bats: L Throws: R Pos: PH-37; 3B-31; SS-16; 1B-9; 2B-5; PR-4   **Ht: 6'0" Wt: 200 Born: 10/18/1975 Age: 36**

Year	Team	Lg	G	AB	H	2B	3B	HR	(Hm	Rd)	TB	R	RBI	RC	TBB	IBB	SO	HBP	SH	SF	SB	CS	SB%	GDP	Avg	OBP	Slg
1998	LAD	NL	29	33	4	0	1	0	(0	0)	6	1	0	1	2	0	8	1	2	0	0	0	-	0	.121	.194	.182
1999	LAD	NL	11	30	5	1	0	0	(0	0)	6	2	3	0	0	0	4	1	0	0	0	0	-	1	.167	.194	.200
2000	LAD	NL	109	353	84	18	6	4	(2	2)	126	39	32	38	26	4	53	7	6	2	4	1	.80	6	.238	.302	.357
2001	LAD	NL	134	405	88	18	3	4	(2	2)	124	38	29	30	31	6	58	8	3	2	0	2	.00	16	.217	.285	.306
2002	LAD	NL	115	258	75	14	4	5	(4	1)	112	37	28	46	26	4	38	7	2	0	7	2	.78	3	.291	.371	.434
2003	LAD	NL	148	477	119	24	3	4	(3	1)	161	39	34	46	16	3	59	10	9	2	4	2	.67	5	.249	.287	.338
2004	LAD	NL	138	405	107	9	4	10	(4	6)	154	47	47	63	47	10	41	18	12	2	3	4	.43	6	.264	.364	.380
2005	2 Tms	AL	96	250	58	4	3	1	(1	2)	83	25	24	21	11	0	30	5	4	3	7	2	.78	6	.232	.275	.332
2006	Bos	AL	96	235	56	7	2	1	(1	0)	70	31	18	24	19	1	29	6	4	0	2	6	.75	4	.238	.312	.298
2007	Bos	AL	83	207	51	10	5	3	(0	3)	80	30	18	19	7	2	23	9	7	2	1	1	.50	5	.246	.298	.386
2008	Bos	AL	75	152	41	8	2	0	(0	0)	53	14	9	19	16	1	13	9	1	1	1	1	.50	3	.270	.371	.349
2009	NYM	NL	82	271	68	11	1	1	(0	1)	84	31	18	26	25	1	28	3	8	1	8	3	.73	2	.251	.320	.310
2010	2 Tms		66	176	37	6	3	0	(0	0)	49	14	20	17	10	1	16	4	2	2	4	1	.80	4	.210	.266	.278
2011	Was	NL	91	156	35	6	1	0	(0	0)	43	12	6	12	12	0	23	2	1	1	2	0	1.00	4	.224	.287	.276
05	Cle	AL	49	146	30	5	2	1	(1	0)	42	11	8	9	5	0	18	4	1	1	6	0	1.00	3	.205	.250	.288
05	Bos	AL	47	104	28	3	2	2	(0	2)	41	14	16	12	6	0	12	1	3	2	1	2	.33	3	.269	.310	.394
10	NYM	NL	62	169	35	6	3	0	(0	0)	47	14	20	16	10	1	16	4	2	2	4	1	.80	4	.207	.265	.278
10	Tex	AL	4	7	2	0	0	0	(0	0)	2	0	0	1	0	0	0	0	0	0	0	0	-	0	.286	.286	.286
	Postseason		13	26	4	1	1	0	(0	0)	7	2	1	1	1	0	5	1	1	0	0	0	-	2	.154	.214	.269
14 ML YEARS			1273	3408	828	140	39	35	(17	18)	1151	360	286	362	248	33	423	90	61	18	47	21	.69	68	.243	.310	.338

Francisco Cordero

Pitches: R Bats: R Pos: RP-68   **Ht: 6'3" Wt: 245 Born: 5/11/1975 Age: 37**

Year	Team	Lg	G	GS	CG	GF	IP	BFP	H	R	ER	HR	SH	SF	HB	TBB	IBB	SO	WP	Bk	W	L	Pct	Sh	Sv-Op	Hld	ERC	ERA
1999	Det	AL	20	0	0	4	19.0	91	19	7	7	2	2	4	0	18	2	19	1	0	2	2	.500	0	0-0	6	6.19	3.32
2000	Tex	AL	56	0	0	13	77.1	365	87	51	46	11	2	6	4	48	3	49	7	0	1	2	.333	0	0-3	4	6.15	5.35
2001	Tex	AL	3	0	0	2	2.1	12	3	1	1	0	0	0	0	2	1	1	1	0	0	1	.000	0	0-0	1	5.73	3.86
2002	Tex	AL	39	0	0	25	45.1	177	33	12	9	2	0	0	2	13	1	41	1	0	2	0	1.000	0	10-12	5	2.11	1.79
2003	Tex	AL	73	0	0	36	82.2	352	70	33	27	4	3	4	2	38	6	90	1	0	5	8	.385	0	15-25	18	3.08	2.94
2004	Tex	AL	67	0	0	63	71.2	304	60	19	17	1	5	1	1	32	2	79	3	2	3	4	.429	0	49-54	0	2.78	2.13
2005	Tex	AL	69	0	0	60	69.0	302	61	28	26	5	4	3	4	30	2	79	0	0	3	1	.750	0	37-45	0	3.47	3.39
2006	2 Tms		77	0	0	47	75.1	322	69	32	31	7	3	5	3	32	2	84	4	0	10	5	.667	0	22-33	16	3.79	3.70
2007	Mil	NL	66	0	0	58	63.1	261	52	23	21	4	2	1	1	18	1	86	2	0	0	4	.000	0	44-51	0	2.45	2.98
2008	Cin	NL	72	0	0	63	70.1	307	61	28	26	6	3	3	3	38	5	78	3	0	5	4	.556	0	34-40	0	3.86	3.33
2009	Cin	NL	68	0	0	59	66.2	276	58	21	16	2	3	4	0	30	2	58	3	0	2	6	.250	0	39-43	0	3.11	2.16
2010	Cin	NL	75	0	0	64	72.2	316	68	32	31	5	1	1	2	36	1	59	2	0	6	5	.545	0	40-48	1	3.96	3.84
2011	Cin	NL	68	0	0	63	69.2	274	49	20	19	6	1	1	3	22	0	42	4	1	5	3	.625	0	37-43	0	2.35	2.45
06	Tex	AL	49	0	0	21	48.2	210	49	27	26	5	1	5	3	16	1	54	3	0	7	4	.636	0	6-15	15	4.05	4.81
06	Mil	NL	28	0	0	26	26.2	112	20	5	5	2	2	0	0	16	1	30	1	0	3	1	.750	0	16-18	1	3.30	1.69
13 ML YEARS			753	0	0	557	785.1	3359	690	307	277	55	29	33	25	357	26	765	32	3	44	45	.494	0	327-397	47	3.48	3.17

Lance Cormier

Pitches: R Bats: R Pos: RP-9   CORE-mee-ay   **Ht: 6'1" Wt: 200 Born: 8/19/1980 Age: 31**

Year	Team	Lg	G	GS	CG	GF	IP	BFP	H	R	ER	HR	SH	SF	HB	TBB	IBB	SO	WP	Bk	W	L	Pct	Sh	Sv-Op	Hld	ERC	ERA
2011	Drham*	AAA	20	4	0	1	47.1	214	62	34	29	8	0	1	0	18	0	25	5	2	4	3	.571	0	0--	-	6.47	5.51
2004	Ari	NL	17	5	0	3	45.1	218	62	42	41	13	2	3	2	25	2	24	2	1	1	4	.200	0	0-0	2	8.76	8.14
2005	Ari	NL	67	0	0	13	79.1	356	86	50	45	7	4	1	5	43	5	63	6	0	7	3	.700	0	0-1	13	5.30	5.11
2006	Atl	NL	29	9	0	5	73.2	333	90	44	40	8	1	4	2	39	7	43	3	0	4	5	.444	0	0-0	2	6.13	4.89
2007	Atl	NL	10	9	0	1	45.2	210	56	38	36	16	3	0	0	23	3	27	4	0	2	6	.250	0	0-0	0	7.66	7.09
2008	Bal	AL	45	1	0	10	71.2	319	78	36	32	4	1	3	1	34	3	46	2	1	3	3	.500	0	1-3	0	4.55	4.02
2009	TB	AL	53	0	0	11	77.1	331	75	31	28	6	2	2	1	25	2	36	3	1	3	3	.500	0	2-2	6	3.41	3.26
2010	TB	AL	60	0	0	17	62.0	279	68	28	27	7	2	1	0	34	3	30	3	1	4	3	.571	0	0-0	4	5.30	3.92
2011	LAD	NL	9	0	0	8	13.2	70	22	17	15	4	0	0	0	5	0	7	2	0	1	0	1.000	0	0-0	0	8.88	9.88
8 ML YEARS			290	24	0	68	468.2	2116	537	286	264	65	15	14	11	227	25	276	24	4	24	28	.462	0	3-6	27	5.61	5.07

Carlos Corporan

Bats: B Throws: R Pos: C-50; PH-4 Ht: 6'2" Wt: 218 Born: 1/7/1984 Age: 28

Year	Team	Lg	G	AB	H	2B	3B	HR	Hm	Rd	TB	R	RBI	RC	TBB	IBB	SO	HBP	SH	SF	SB	CS	SB%	GDP	Avg	OBP	Slg
2003	Brewrs	R	34	120	30	6	0	2	-	-	42	13	9	11	3	0	22	2	0	1	0	1	.00	5	.250	.278	.350
2003	Helena	R+	10	27	6	1	0	0	-	-	7	4	4	3	4	0	7	2	0	1	0	0	-	2	.222	.353	.259
2004	Beloit	A	63	197	45	7	2	1	-	-	59	20	16	14	7	0	65	3	3	4	1	3	.25	1	.228	.261	.299
2005	WV	A-	99	343	82	15	2	9	-	-	128	46	38	41	28	3	97	7	9	3	0	0	-	10	.239	.307	.373
2006	BrvdCt	A+	86	282	76	14	0	3	-	-	99	29	38	33	13	1	45	10	5	3	0	2	.00	8	.270	.321	.351
2006	Hntsvl	AA	3	9	3	0	0	0	-	-	3	2	1	0	0	0	3	0	0	0	0	0	-	1	.333	.333	.333
2007	BrvdCt	A+	23	80	29	8	0	3	-	-	46	11	19	17	2	0	9	3	3	0	0	1	.00	1	.363	.400	.575
2007	Hntsvl	AA	56	179	36	14	0	2	-	-	56	18	24	15	8	0	48	8	8	2	1	0	1.00	1	.201	.264	.313
2008	Hntsvl	AA	34	113	30	8	0	3	-	-	47	14	15	18	14	1	15	3	5	0	1	1	.50	0	.265	.362	.416
2008	Nashv	AAA	25	87	20	6	1	3	-	-	37	8	12	9	1	0	24	1	2	1	0	1	.00	6	.230	.244	.425
2009	Nashv	AAA	57	179	36	9	1	1	-	-	50	9	18	13	9	1	43	5	2	7	0	0	-	2	.201	.250	.279
2009	BrvdCt	A+	14	46	12	1	0	0	-	-	13	1	6	3	1	0	10	1	0	0	0	0	-	2	.261	.292	.283
2010	Reno	AAA	87	286	83	20	4	12	-	-	147	38	50	53	24	2	63	8	3	5	4	2	.67	8	.290	.356	.514
2011	OKCity	AAA	22	80	20	4	0	3	-	-	33	9	12	11	8	0	16	2	1	1	0	1	.00	5	.250	.330	.413
2009	Mil	NL	1	1	1	0	0	0	0	0	1	1	0	1	0	0	0	0	0	0	0	0	-	0	1.000	1.000	1.000
2011	Hou	NL	52	154	29	8	1	0	0	0	39	9	11	11	10	4	49	4	3	2	0	0	-	5	.188	.253	.253
2 ML YEARS			53	155	30	8	1	0	0	0	40	10	11	12	10	4	49	4	3	2	0	0	-	5	.194	.257	.258

Kevin Correia

kore-AY-ah

Pitches: R Bats: R Pos: SP-26; RP-1 Ht: 6'3" Wt: 200 Born: 8/24/1980 Age: 31

Year	Team	Lg	G	GS	CG	GF	IP	BFP	H	R	ER	HR	SH	SF	HB	TBB	IBB	SO	WP	Bk	W	L	Pct	Sh	Sv-Op	Hld	ERC	ERA
2003	SF	NL	10	7	0	1	39.1	173	41	16	16	6	1	1	4	18	1	28	2	0	3	1	.750	0	0-0	0	5.46	3.66
2004	SF	NL	12	1	0	5	19.0	92	25	20	17	3	3	3	1	10	0	14	0	0	0	1	.000	0	0-0	0	7.12	8.05
2005	SF	NL	16	11	0	1	58.1	264	61	31	30	12	5	1	4	31	2	44	2	0	2	5	.286	0	0-1	10	5.94	4.63
2006	SF	NL	48	0	0	9	69.2	295	64	27	27	5	4	3	2	22	0	57	0	0	2	0	1.000	0	0-3	12	3.25	3.49
2007	SF	NL	59	8	0	9	101.2	437	94	39	39	9	4	3	2	40	7	80	1	1	4	7	.364	0	0-3	12	3.48	3.45
2008	SF	NL	25	19	0	2	110.0	514	141	80	74	15	3	5	4	47	3	66	5	0	3	8	.273	0	0-0	0	6.19	6.05
2009	SD	NL	33	33	1	0	198.0	830	194	92	86	17	9	3	4	64	6	142	5	1	12	11	.522	1	0-0	0	4.87	5.40
2010	SD	NL	28	26	0	0	145.0	641	152	89	87	20	6	5	5	64	6	115	3	0	10	10	.500	0	0-0	0	4.74	4.79
2011	Pit	NL	27	26	1	1	154.0	660	175	90	82	24	7	2	2	39	0	77	3	1	12	11	.522	0	0-0	0	4.57	4.61
9 ML YEARS			258	131	2	28	895.0	3906	947	484	458	111	39	27	29	335	25	623	21	3	48	54	.471	1	0-4	22	4.57	4.61

Dan Cortes

core-TESS

Pitches: R Bats: R Pos: RP-10 Ht: 6'6" Wt: 230 Born: 3/4/1987 Age: 25

Year	Team	Lg	G	GS	CG	GF	IP	BFP	H	R	ER	HR	SH	SF	HB	TBB	IBB	SO	WP	Bk	W	L	Pct	Sh	Sv-Op	Hld	ERC	ERA
2005	Bristol	R+	15	7	0	3	38.1	171	44	23	22	2	0	2	4	13	0	38	3	0	1	4	.200	0	0- -	-	4.76	5.17
2006	Knapol	A	20	19	0	0	107.2	470	109	61	48	6	5	2	5	38	0	96	12	0	3	9	.250	0	0- -	-	3.78	4.01
2006	Burlgtn	A	7	7	0	0	35.0	165	40	27	26	7	2	2	3	17	0	30	2	0	1	2	.333	0	0- -	-	6.26	6.69
2007	Wilmg	A+	24	24	0	0	123.0	513	102	50	42	7	4	5	8	45	0	120	11	0	8	8	.500	0	0- -	-	2.99	3.07
2008	NWArk	AA	23	23	0	0	116.2	497	103	51	49	13	3	3	8	55	0	109	3	0	10	4	.714	0	0- -	-	4.13	3.78
2009	NWArk	AA	16	15	0	0	80.1	360	77	43	35	3	2	5	4	50	0	57	6	0	6	6	.500	0	0- -	-	4.48	3.92
2009	WTenn	AA	10	10	0	0	54.2	244	51	33	30	4	0	2	1	35	1	55	6	0	1	5	.167	0	0- -	-	4.51	4.94
2010	WTenn	AA	25	16	0	7	83.2	383	77	54	49	4	2	2	4	53	1	85	19	0	6	4	.600	0	1- -	-	4.22	5.27
2010	Tacom	AAA	9	0	0	7	12.2	54	13	8	7	1	1	2	0	4	0	13	2	0	1	2	.333	0	1- -	-	4.52	4.97
2011	Tacom	AAA	32	0	0	17	39.0	182	43	25	22	3	3	0	1	29	1	46	9	0	1	2	.333	0	3- -	-	6.07	5.08
2010	Sea	AL	4	0	0	2	5.1	23	3	3	2	0	0	1	0	3	0	6	2	0	0	1	.000	0	0-0	-	1.66	3.38
2011	Sea	AL	10	0	0	3	10.2	50	13	7	7	1	0	1	1	6	0	9	1	0	0	2	.000	0	0-1	-	6.49	5.91
2 ML YEARS			14	0	0	5	16.0	73	16	10	9	1	0	1	1	9	0	9	3	0	0	3	.000	0	0-1	-	4.63	5.06

Craig Counsell

Bats: L Throws: R Pos: PH-54; 2B-25; SS-23; 3B-14; PR-5; LF-1 Ht: 6'0" Wt: 179 Born: 8/21/1970 Age: 41

Year	Team	Lg	G	AB	H	2B	3B	HR	Hm	Rd	TB	R	RBI	RC	TBB	IBB	SO	HBP	SH	SF	SB	CS	SB%	GDP	Avg	OBP	Slg
1995	Col	NL	3	1	0	0	0	0	0	0	0	0	0	0	1	0	0	0	0	0	0	0	-	0	.000	.500	.000
1997	2 Tms	NL	52	164	49	9	2	1	1	0	65	20	16	24	18	2	17	3	3	1	1	1	.50	5	.299	.376	.396
1998	Fla	NL	107	335	84	19	5	4	2	2	125	43	40	48	51	7	47	4	8	1	3	0	1.00	5	.251	.355	.373
1999	2 Tms	NL	87	174	38	7	0	0	0	0	45	24	11	12	14	0	24	0	5	2	3	3	.50	2	.218	.274	.259
2000	Ari	NL	67	152	48	8	1	2	0	2	64	23	11	25	20	0	18	2	1	1	3	3	.50	4	.316	.400	.421
2001	Ari	NL	141	458	126	22	3	4	4	0	166	76	38	61	61	3	76	2	6	6	6	8	.43	9	.275	.359	.362
2002	Ari	NL	112	436	123	22	1	2	0	2	153	63	51	65	45	3	52	1	4	3	7	5	.58	10	.282	.348	.351
2003	Ari	NL	89	303	71	6	3	3	3	0	92	40	21	29	41	0	32	2	3	2	11	4	.73	4	.234	.328	.304
2004	Mil	NL	140	473	114	19	5	2	1	1	149	59	23	48	59	9	88	5	3	5	17	4	.81	5	.241	.350	.315
2005	Ari	NL	150	578	148	34	4	9	5	4	217	85	42	80	78	4	69	8	2	4	26	7	.79	8	.256	.350	.375
2006	Ari	NL	105	372	95	14	4	4	3	1	129	56	30	45	31	0	47	3	6	2	4	2	.67	7	.255	.323	.347
2007	Mil	NL	122	282	62	12	2	3	0	3	87	31	24	29	41	4	47	3	6	2	3	1	.75	5	.220	.323	.309
2008	Mil	NL	110	248	56	14	1	1	1	0	75	31	14	26	46	1	42	5	1	2	3	4	.43	12	.226	.355	.302
2009	Mil	NL	130	404	115	22	8	4	2	2	165	61	39	57	42	0	54	6	3	4	1	1	.50	1	.285	.357	.408
2010	Mil	NL	102	204	51	8	0	2	1	1	65	16	21	27	20	2	21	3	5	2	2	1	.67	1	.250	.322	.319
2011	Mil	NL	107	157	28	2	1	1	0	1	35	19	9	13	20	2	21	3	5	2	0	0	-	0	.178	.280	.223
97	Col	NL	1	0	0	0	0	0	0	0	0	0	0	0	0	0	0	0	0	0	0	0	-	0	-	-	-
97	Fla	NL	51	164	49	9	2	1	1	0	65	20	16	24	18	2	17	3	3	1	1	1	.50	5	.299	.376	.396

Year	Team	Lg		G	AB	H	2B	3B	HR	(Hm	Rd)	TB	R	RBI	RC	TBB	IBB	SO	HBP	SH	SF		SB	CS	SB%	GDP		Avg	OBP	Slg
			BATTING																				**BASERUNNING**				**AVERAGES**			
99	Fla	NL		37	66	10	1	0	0	(0	0)	11	4	2	1	5	0	10	0	2	0		0	0	-	1		.152	.211	.167
99	LAD	NL		50	108	28	6	0	0	(0	0)	34	20	9	11	9	0	14	0	3	2		0	0	-	1		.259	.311	.315
	Postseason			35	114	27	5	0	2	(1	1)	38	12	14	11	12	3	23	1	7	1		2	0	1.00	1		.237	.313	.333
16	ML YEARS			1624	4741	1208	218	40	42	(23	19)	1632	647	390	589	589	35	663	54	57	35		103	49	.68	78		.255	.342	.344

Scott Cousins

Bats: L **Throws:** L **Pos:** PH-30; RF-12; CF-5; LF-4; PR-4   **Ht:** 6'2" **Wt:** 190 **Born:** 1/22/1985 **Age:** 27

Year	Team	Lg		G	AB	H	2B	3B	HR	(Hm	Rd)	TB	R	RBI	RC	TBB	IBB	SO	HBP	SH	SF		SB	CS	SB%	GDP		Avg	OBP	Slg
			BATTING																				**BASERUNNING**				**AVERAGES**			
2006	Jmstwn	A-		21	90	19	1	0	1	(-	-)	23	11	6	5	4	0	17	1	2	0		3	1	.75	2		.211	.253	.256
2007	Grnsbr	A		110	421	123	25	6	18	(-	-)	202	69	74	74	38	3	92	7	3	3		16	7	.70	8		.292	.358	.480
2008	Jupiter	A+		49	191	58	9	2	9	(-	-)	98	35	29	37	20	2	47	0	0	0		11	3	.79	4		.304	.370	.513
2008	Mrlns	R		2	6	0	0	0	0	(-	-)	0	0	0	0	0	0	5	0	0	0		0	0	-	0		.000	.000	.000
2008	Carlina	AA		27	91	24	7	1	1	(-	-)	36	15	9	13	10	1	28	2	0	0		4	1	.80	1		.264	.350	.396
2009	Jaxnvl	AA		130	482	127	31	11	12	(-	-)	216	60	74	74	42	1	107	3	1	5		27	9	.75	6		.263	.323	.448
2010	NewOr	AAA		118	410	117	20	5	14	(-	-)	189	74	49	66	32	3	78	2	1	6		12	4	.75	2		.285	.336	.461
2011	Jupiter	A+		5	13	4	0	0	0	(-	-)	4	2	2	2	3	0	4	0	0	0		0	0	-	0		.308	.438	.308
2011	NewOr	AAA		2	9	2	0	0	0	(-	-)	2	1	1	0	1	0	3	0	0	0		0	0	-	0		.222	.300	.222
2010	Fla	NL		27	37	11	2	0	0	(0	0)	17	2	2	4	1	0	13	0	0	0		0	0	-	0		.297	.316	.459
2011	Fla	NL		48	52	7	1	0	1	(1	0)	11	5	4	2	6	0	21	0	0	0		1	1	.50	0		.135	.224	.212
2	ML YEARS			75	89	18	3	2	1	(1	0)	28	7	6	6	7	0	34	0	0	0		1	1	.50	0		.202	.260	.315

Collin Cowgill

Bats: R **Throws:** L **Pos:** LF-18; CF-10; PH-10; PR-3   **Ht:** 5'9" **Wt:** 185 **Born:** 5/22/1986 **Age:** 26

Year	Team	Lg		G	AB	H	2B	3B	HR	(Hm	Rd)	TB	R	RBI	RC	TBB	IBB	SO	HBP	SH	SF		SB	CS	SB%	GDP		Avg	OBP	Slg
			BATTING																				**BASERUNNING**				**AVERAGES**			
2008	Yakima	A-		20	79	24	3	1	11	(-	-)	62	21	28	24	12	0	17	3	1	0		5	0	1.00	2		.304	.415	.785
2008	Sbend	A		50	201	50	13	3	1	(-	-)	72	31	17	27	25	0	61	5	0	0		1	0	1.00	2		.249	.346	.358
2009	Visalia	A+		61	220	61	9	5	6	(-	-)	98	39	36	39	29	3	49	7	0	4		11	4	.73	6		.277	.373	.445
2010	Mobile	AA		131	502	143	34	4	16	(-	-)	233	89	83	90	57	1	73	8	0	10		25	9	.74	23		.285	.360	.464
2011	Reno	AAA		98	395	140	24	8	13	(-	-)	219	95	70	96	51	0	63	2	7	1		30	3	.91	9		.354	.430	.554
2011	Ari	NL		37	92	22	3	0	1	(1	0)	28	8	9	8	8	1	28	0	0	0		4	2	.67	0		.239	.300	.304

Zack Cozart

COE-zart   **Ht:** 6'0" **Wt:** 196 **Born:** 8/12/1985 **Age:** 26

Bats: R **Throws:** R **Pos:** SS-11; PH-1

Year	Team	Lg		G	AB	H	2B	3B	HR	(Hm	Rd)	TB	R	RBI	RC	TBB	IBB	SO	HBP	SH	SF		SB	CS	SB%	GDP		Avg	OBP	Slg
			BATTING																				**BASERUNNING**				**AVERAGES**			
2007	Dayton	A		53	184	44	7	2	2	(-	-)	61	28	18	18	11	0	36	2	3	1		3	1	.75	3		.239	.288	.332
2008	Dayton	A		109	418	117	20	6	14	(-	-)	191	57	49	64	24	0	77	10	6	6		3	3	.50	6		.280	.330	.457
2009	Carlina	AA		131	463	121	29	2	10	(-	-)	184	72	59	73	63	2	88	10	2	4		10	2	.83	8		.261	.359	.397
2010	Lsvlle	AAA		136	553	141	30	4	17	(-	-)	230	91	67	78	40	0	107	6	6	5		30	4	.88	15		.255	.310	.416
2011	Lsvlle	AAA		77	323	100	26	2	7	(-	-)	151	57	32	55	23	2	51	2	0	2		9	2	.82	4		.310	.357	.467
2011	Cin	NL		11	37	12	0	0	2	(2	0)	18	6	3	3	0	0	6	0	1	0		0	0	-	2		.324	.324	.486

Allen Craig

Bats: R **Throws:** R **Pos:** LF-26; PH-23; RF-18; 2B-8; CF-5; 1B-2; 3B-2   **Ht:** 6'2" **Wt:** 210 **Born:** 7/18/1984 **Age:** 27

Year	Team	Lg		G	AB	H	2B	3B	HR	(Hm	Rd)	TB	R	RBI	RC	TBB	IBB	SO	HBP	SH	SF		SB	CS	SB%	GDP		Avg	OBP	Slg
			BATTING																				**BASERUNNING**				**AVERAGES**			
2006	StCol	A-		48	175	45	13	0	4	(-	-)	70	21	29	24	13	0	28	7	1	5		0	0	-	1		.257	.325	.400
2007	PlmBh	A+		112	423	132	25	2	21	(-	-)	224	77	77	83	35	4	79	6	0	4		8	3	.73	10		.312	.370	.530
2007	Sprgfld	AA		7	24	7	2	0	3	(-	-)	18	5	3	5	1	0	6	0	0	0		0	0	-	1		.292	.320	.750
2008	Sprgfld	AA		129	506	154	30	0	22	(-	-)	250	84	86	94	48	1	87	10	0	4		2	1	.67	16		.304	.373	.494
2009	Memp	AAA		126	472	152	26	1	26	(-	-)	258	78	83	96	37	1	95	6	0	6		1	0	1.00	12		.322	.374	.547
2010	Memp	AAA		83	306	98	24	2	14	(-	-)	168	57	81	65	34	0	59	4	0	6		1	0	1.00	0		.320	.389	.549
2011	Sprgfld	AA		2	6	0	0	0	0	(-	-)	0	0	1	0	1	0	1	0	0	0		0	0	-	1		.000	.125	.000
2011	Memp	AAA		10	35	10	2	1	1	(-	-)	17	9	5	6	3	0	3	1	0	0		0	0	-	0		.286	.359	.486
2010	StL	NL		44	114	28	7	0	4	(3	1)	47	12	18	14	9	1	26	0	0	1		0	1	.00	1		.246	.298	.412
2011	StL	NL		75	200	63	15	0	11	(3	8)	111	33	40	37	15	0	40	1	1	2		5	0	1.00	7		.315	.362	.555
2	ML YEARS			119	314	91	22	0	15	(6	9)	158	45	58	51	24	1	66	1	1	3		5	1	.83	8		.290	.339	.503

Jesse Crain

Pitches: R **Bats:** R **Pos:** RP-67   **Ht:** 6'1" **Wt:** 215 **Born:** 7/5/1981 **Age:** 30

Year	Team	Lg		G	GS	CG	GF	IP	BFP		H	R	ER	HR	SH	SF	HB	TBB	IBB	SO	WP	Bk		W	L	Pct	Sh	Sv-Op	Hld	ERC	ERA
			HOW MUCH HE PITCHED							**WHAT HE GAVE UP**														**THE RESULTS**							
2004	Min	AL		22	0	0	3	27.0	109		17	6	6	2	1	0	1	12	1	14	1	0		3	0	1.000	0	0-1	2	2.25	2.00
2005	Min	AL		75	0	0	17	79.2	326		61	28	24	6	9	3	5	29	7	25	2	0		12	5	.706	0	1-4	11	2.66	2.71
2006	Min	AL		68	0	0	24	76.2	325		79	31	30	6	1	2	2	18	2	60	1	0		4	5	.444	0	1-4	10	3.48	3.52
2007	Min	AL		18	0	0	5	16.1	71		19	16	10	4	0	1	1	4	0	10	0	1		1	2	.333	0	0-0	6	5.73	5.51
2008	Min	AL		66	0	0	14	62.2	268		62	29	25	6	2	1	4	24	3	50	2	0		3	4	.556	0	0-3	17	3.93	3.59
2009	Min	AL		56	0	0	15	51.2	230		48	28	27	3	3	3	5	27	3	43	1	1		7	4	.636	0	0-4	12	4.12	4.70
2010	Min	AL		71	0	0	16	68.0	278		53	27	23	5	3	0	1	27	4	62	3	0		1	1	.500	0	1-4	21	2.71	3.04
2011	CWS	AL		67	0	0	11	65.1	268		50	20	19	7	1	3	0	31	5	70	0	1		8	3	.727	0	1-7	24	3.08	2.62
	Postseason			4	0	0	0	1.2	14		7	5	3	2	0	0	0	1	0	1	0	0		0	1	.000	0	0-0	0	40.37	16.20
8	ML YEARS			443	0	0	105	447.1	1875		389	185	164	39	18	14	16	172	25	334	10	3		41	24	.631	0	4-23	95	3.29	3.30

Bobby Cramer

Pitches: L **Bats:** L **Pos:** RP-5 **Ht:** 6'1" **Wt:** 205 **Born:** 10/28/1979 **Age:** 32

Year	Team	Lg	G	GS	CG	GF	IP	BFP	H	R	ER	HR	SH	SF	HB	TBB	IBB	SO	WP	Bk	W	L	Pct	Sh	Sv-Op	Hld	ERC	ERA
2003	HudVal	A-	5	2	0	2	10.2	41	9	2	2	1	1	0	0	1	0	6	0	0	0	1	.000	0	1- -	-	2.13	1.69
2003	Bkrsfld	A+	5	0	0	0	12.2	52	10	6	5	1	1	0	0	5	0	10	0	0	0	0	-	0	0- -	-	2.80	3.55
2004	CtnSC	A	35	0	0	12	62.1	254	52	27	23	4	0	0	4	12	0	48	6	1	6	4	.600	0	4- -	-	2.41	3.32
2007	Stcktn	A+	9	8	0	0	45.0	192	45	23	19	1	0	1	5	10	1	41	4	0	4	1	.800	0	0- -	-	3.22	3.80
2007	Mdland	AA	12	7	0	0	52.1	213	45	17	11	3	2	0	1	10	0	50	5	0	5	1	.833	0	0- -	-	2.32	1.89
2009	Scrmto	AAA	6	1	0	2	14.0	73	24	11	10	0	1	2	0	8	2	14	0	0	1	1	.500	0	0- -	-	7.94	6.43
2009	Stcktn	A+	2	0	0	1	5.2	24	4	1	1	1	0	0	1	2	0	6	0	0	1	0	1.000	0	0- -	-	3.42	1.59
2009	Mdland	AA	12	8	0	0	43.0	194	48	29	16	1	3	1	2	13	0	39	3	0	3	4	.429	0	0- -	-	3.82	3.35
2010	Scrmto	AAA	7	7	0	0	41.2	174	41	10	9	0	0	0	3	11	0	35	3	0	2	2	.500	0	0- -	-	2.79	1.94
2011	Scrmto	AAA	6	6	0	0	22.1	103	22	11	10	3	1	0	3	12	0	26	0	0	0	0	-	0	0- -	-	5.27	4.03
2010	Oak	AL	4	4	0	0	23.2	93	20	8	8	5	1	0	0	6	0	13	0	0	2	1	.667	0	0-0	0	3.47	3.04
2011	Oak	AL	5	0	0	3	8.1	31	6	1	1	1	0	0	0	1	0	6	0	0	0	1	.000	0	0-0	0	1.81	1.08
	2 ML YEARS		9	4	0	3	32.0	124	26	9	9	6	1	0	0	7	0	19	0	0	2	2	.500	0	0-0	0	3.00	2.53

Brandon Crawford

Bats: L **Throws:** R **Pos:** SS-65; PR-1 **Ht:** 6'2" **Wt:** 215 **Born:** 1/21/1987 **Age:** 25

Year	Team	Lg	G	AB	H	2B	3B	HR	(Hm	Rd)	TB	R	RBI	RC	TBB	IBB	SO	HBP	SH	SF	SB	CS	SB%	GDP	Avg	OBP	Slg
2008	Giants	R	4	14	6	1	1	0	(-	-)	9	3	3	2	0	0	3	0	0	0	0	1	.00	1	.429	.429	.643
2008	SlmKzr	A-	1	2	0	0	0	0	(-	-)	0	0	0	0	0	0	0	0	0	0	0	0	-	0	.000	.000	.000
2009	SnJos	A+	25	105	39	2	2	6	(-	-)	63	21	17	25	10	0	32	4	0	0	2	4	.33	1	.371	.445	.600
2009	Conn	AA	108	392	101	25	2	4	(-	-)	142	38	31	42	20	0	100	1	8	2	12	7	.63	8	.258	.294	.362
2010	Rchmd	AA	79	291	70	12	3	7	(-	-)	109	43	22	41	39	0	77	6	1	5	4	1	.80	8	.241	.337	.375
2010	SnJos	A+	5	18	3	1	0	0	(-	-)	4	4	1	0	2	0	5	0	0	0	0	0	-	0	.167	.250	.222
2011	SnJos	A+	14	59	19	5	1	3	(-	-)	35	14	15	14	9	0	13	0	0	0	0	0	-	1	.322	.412	.593
2011	Fresno	AAA	29	107	25	5	1	1	(-	-)	35	13	9	10	9	1	20	0	1	1	5	2	.71	2	.234	.291	.327
2011	SF	NL	66	196	40	5	2	3	(0	3)	58	22	21	20	23	1	31	0	1	0	1	3	.25	4	.204	.288	.296

Carl Crawford

Bats: L **Throws:** L **Pos:** LF-127; DH-2; PH-2 **Ht:** 6'2" **Wt:** 215 **Born:** 8/5/1981 **Age:** 30

Year	Team	Lg	G	AB	H	2B	3B	HR	(Hm	Rd)	TB	R	RBI	RC	TBB	IBB	SO	HBP	SH	SF	SB	CS	SB%	GDP	Avg	OBP	Slg
2011	Pwtckt*	AAA	2	5	1	0	0	0	(-	-)	1	1	1	0	1	0	1	0	0	0	0	0	-	0	.200	.333	.200
2002	TB	AL	63	259	67	11	6	2	(1	1)	96	23	30	34	9	0	41	3	6	1	9	5	.64	0	.259	.290	.371
2003	TB	AL	151	630	177	18	9	5	(5	0)	228	80	54	80	26	4	102	1	1	3	55	10	.85	5	.281	.309	.362
2004	TB	AL	152	626	185	26	**19**	11	(6	5)	282	104	55	96	35	2	81	1	4	6	**59**	15	.80	2	.296	.331	.450
2005	TB	AL	156	644	194	33	**15**	15	(5	10)	302	101	81	102	27	1	84	5	5	6	46	8	.85	11	.301	.331	.469
2006	TB	AL	151	600	183	20	**16**	18	(7	11)	289	89	77	113	37	3	85	4	9	2	**58**	9	.87	8	.305	.348	.482
2007	TB	AL	143	584	184	37	9	11	(6	5)	272	93	80	97	32	5	112	5	1	2	**50**	10	.83	11	.315	.355	.466
2008	TB	AL	109	443	121	12	10	8	(3	5)	177	69	57	57	30	1	60	2	0	5	25	7	.78	10	.273	.319	.400
2009	TB	AL	156	606	185	28	8	15	(9	6)	274	96	68	91	51	1	99	8	2	5	60	16	.79	7	.305	.364	.452
2010	TB	AL	154	600	184	30	**13**	19	(11	8)	297	110	90	120	46	3	104	3	3	5	47	10	.82	2	.307	.356	.495
2011	Bos	AL	130	506	129	29	7	11	(4	7)	205	65	56	54	23	1	104	3	2	4	18	6	.75	7	.255	.289	.405
	Postseason		21	83	21	3	1	3	(1	2)	35	10	9	11	3	0	14	1	0	0	8	0	1.00	1	.253	.287	.422
	10 ML YEARS		1365	5498	1609	244	112	115	(57	58)	2422	830	648	844	316	21	872	35	33	39	427	96	.82	63	.293	.333	.441

Coco Crisp

Bats: B **Throws:** R **Pos:** CF-133; PR-3; DH-2; PH-2 **Ht:** 5'10" **Wt:** 185 **Born:** 11/1/1979 **Age:** 32

Year	Team	Lg	G	AB	H	2B	3B	HR	(Hm	Rd)	TB	R	RBI	RC	TBB	IBB	SO	HBP	SH	SF	SB	CS	SB%	GDP	Avg	OBP	Slg
2002	Cle	AL	32	127	33	9	2	1	(1	0)	49	16	9	19	11	0	19	0	3	2	4	1	.80	0	.260	.314	.386
2003	Cle	AL	99	414	110	15	6	3	(3	0)	146	55	27	48	23	1	51	0	7	3	15	9	.63	4	.266	.302	.353
2004	Cle	AL	139	491	146	24	2	15	(8	7)	219	78	71	72	36	4	69	0	9	2	20	13	.61	8	.297	.344	.446
2005	Cle	AL	145	594	178	42	4	16	(4	12)	276	86	69	92	44	1	81	0	**13**	5	15	6	.71	7	.300	.345	.465
2006	Bos	AL	105	413	109	22	2	8	(4	4)	159	58	36	51	31	1	67	1	7	0	22	4	.85	5	.264	.317	.385
2007	Bos	AL	145	526	141	28	7	6	(1	5)	201	85	60	68	50	1	84	1	9	5	28	6	.82	12	.268	.330	.382
2008	Bos	AL	118	361	102	18	3	7	(1	6)	147	55	41	49	35	0	59	1	8	4	20	7	.74	6	.283	.344	.407
2009	KC	AL	49	180	41	8	5	3	(0	3)	68	30	14	25	29	1	23	1	4	1	13	2	.87	4	.228	.336	.378
2010	Oak	AL	75	290	81	14	4	8	(6	2)	127	51	38	49	30	0	49	0	3	5	32	3	**.91**	6	.279	.342	.438
2011	Oak	AL	136	531	140	27	5	8	(4	4)	201	69	54	69	41	2	65	1	4	6	**49**	9	.84	11	.264	.314	.379
	Postseason		20	57	16	3	0	0	(0	0)	19	7	3	6	6	0	12	0	0	0	3	0	1.00	3	.281	.349	.333
	10 ML YEARS		1043	3927	1081	207	40	75	(32	43)	1593	583	419	542	330	11	567	5	67	33	218	60	.78	63	.275	.330	.406

Mike Crotta

Pitches: R **Bats:** R **Pos:** RP-15 CRAW-tah **Ht:** 6'6" **Wt:** 235 **Born:** 9/24/1984 **Age:** 27

Year	Team	Lg	G	GS	CG	GF	IP	BFP	H	R	ER	HR	SH	SF	HB	TBB	IBB	SO	WP	Bk	W	L	Pct	Sh	Sv-Op	Hld	ERC	ERA
2006	Wmspt	A-	11	7	0	1	43.2	170	43	14	13	1	1	1	0	4	0	28	0	0	1	3	.250	0	0- -	-	2.44	2.68
2006	Hkry	A	4	4	0	0	17.1	88	36	20	20	1	0	1	2	2	0	7	0	0	1	2	.333	0	0- -	-	9.64	10.38
2007	Hkry	A	26	25	1	1	137.1	595	169	82	67	10	1	3	3	28	0	74	2	0	10	5	.667	0	0- -	-	4.52	4.39
2007	Altna	AA	1	1	0	0	2.2	17	5	7	3	0	0	0	0	2	0	0	0	0	0	1	.000	0	0- -	-	8.76	10.13
2008	Lynbrg	A+	28	28	0	0	146.1	641	171	94	76	8	5	3	4	25	1	97	9	1	9	10	.474	0	0- -	-	3.78	4.67
2009	Altna	AA	27	27	0	0	143.2	647	181	90	76	7	6	6	6	33	1	98	6	0	7	8	.467	0	0- -	-	4.56	4.76
2010	Altna	AA	4	4	0	0	25.1	93	14	5	5	0	0	0	0	3	0	16	0	0	2	0	1.000	0	0- -	-	0.84	1.78

			HOW MUCH HE PITCHED						WHAT HE GAVE UP												THE RESULTS							
Year	Team	Lg	G	GS	CG	GF	IP	BFP	H	R	ER	HR	SH	SF	HB	TBB	IBB	SO	WP	Bk	W	L	Pct	Sh	Sv-Op Hld	ERC	ERA
2010	Indy	AAA	24	24	0	0	131.1	570	160	76	72	10	4	1	3	37	1	89	1	0	5	10	.333	0	0- -	-	4.85	4.93
2011	Altna	AA	1	0	0	0	1.0	4	1	0	0	0	0	0	0	0	0	1	0	0	0	0	-	0	0- -	-	1.95	0.00
2011	Indy	AAA	11	0	0	1	10.2	45	11	7	7	2	0	0	0	2	0	5	0	0	0	0	-	0	0- -	-	3.90	5.91
2011	Pit	NL	15	0	0	1	10.2	56	20	11	11	2	0	0	0	5	0	7	1	0	0	1	.000	0	0-1	2	10.75	9.28

Aaron Crow

Pitches: R Bats: R Pos: RP-57

Ht: 6'3" Wt: 190 Born: 11/11/1986 Age: 25

			HOW MUCH HE PITCHED						WHAT HE GAVE UP												THE RESULTS							
Year	Team	Lg	G	GS	CG	GF	IP	BFP	H	R	ER	HR	SH	SF	HB	TBB	IBB	SO	WP	Bk	W	L	Pct	Sh	Sv-Op Hld	ERC	ERA
2010	NWArk	AA	22	22	0	0	119.1	539	130	86	75	13	4	4	6	59	1	90	8	1	7	7	.500	0	0- -	-	5.25	5.66
2010	Wilmg	A+	7	7	0	0	44.0	185	51	32	29	6	2	0	1	6	0	53	6	0	2	3	.400	0	0- -	-	4.28	5.93
2011	KC	AL	57	0	0	19	62.0	266	55	20	19	8	3	0	0	31	2	65	9	1	4	4	.500	0	0-7	8	4.00	2.76

Trevor Crowe

Bats: B Throws: R Pos: LF-10; CF-7; PH-1   CROW

Ht: 6'0" Wt: 190 Born: 11/17/1983 Age: 28

			BATTING																		BASERUNNING				AVERAGES		
Year	Team	Lg	G	AB	H	2B	3B	HR	(Hm	Rd)	TB	R	RBI	RC	TBB	IBB	SO	HBP	SH	SF		SB	CS	SB%	GDP	Avg	OBP	Slg
2011	Indns*	R	6	18	8	3	1	2	(-	-)	19	9	8	8	6	0	4	0	0	0		2	1	.67	0	.444	.583	1.056
2011	Clmbs*	AAA	5	20	2	0	0	0	(-	-)	2	1	1	0	1	0	3	0	0	0		2	0	1.00	1	.100	.143	.100
2009	Cle	AL	68	183	43	9	3	1	(0	1)	61	22	17	18	11	0	39	1	4	3		6	0	1.00	7	.235	.278	.333
2010	Cle	AL	122	442	111	24	3	2	(1	1)	147	48	36	43	29	1	73	3	5	0		20	7	.74	13	.251	.302	.333
2011	Cle	AL	15	28	6	1	0	0	(0	0)	7	6	2	4	4	0	9	0	0	0		3	0	1.00	1	.214	.313	.250
3 ML YEARS			205	653	160	34	6	3	(1	2)	215	76	55	65	44	1	121	4	9	3		29	7	.81	21	.245	.295	.329

Juan Cruz

Pitches: R Bats: R Pos: RP-56

Ht: 6'2" Wt: 165 Born: 10/15/1978 Age: 33

			HOW MUCH HE PITCHED						WHAT HE GAVE UP												THE RESULTS							
Year	Team	Lg	G	GS	CG	GF	IP	BFP	H	R	ER	HR	SH	SF	HB	TBB	IBB	SO	WP	Bk	W	L	Pct	Sh	Sv-Op Hld	ERC	ERA
2011	Charltt*	A+	1	1	0	0	1.0	6	2	0	0	0	0	1	0	0	0	2	0	0	0	0	-	0	0- -	-	12.01	0.00
2001	ChC	NL	8	8	0	0	44.2	185	40	16	16	4	2	0	2	17	1	39	0	0	3	1	.750	0	0-0	0	3.59	3.22
2002	ChC	NL	45	9	0	14	97.1	431	84	56	43	11	7	8	8	59	4	81	1	0	3	11	.214	0	1-4	3	4.49	3.98
2003	ChC	NL	25	6	0	3	61.0	284	66	44	41	7	7	2	7	28	0	65	4	0	2	7	.222	0	0-1	1	5.23	6.05
2004	Atl	NL	50	0	0	22	72.0	300	59	24	22	7	4	1	2	30	1	70	1	0	6	2	.750	0	0-0	2	3.25	2.75
2005	Oak	AL	28	0	0	14	32.2	159	38	33	27	5	0	2	4	22	4	34	3	0	0	3	.000	0	0-0	1	6.87	7.44
2006	Ari	NL	31	15	0	5	94.2	413	80	45	44	7	5	2	11	47	2	88	2	0	5	6	.455	0	0-0	4	3.82	4.18
2007	Ari	NL	53	0	0	15	61.0	262	45	28	21	7	2	2	5	32	3	87	1	2	6	1	.857	0	0-0	4	3.43	3.10
2008	Ari	NL	57	0	0	10	51.2	215	34	17	15	5	2	2	3	31	0	71	1	0	4	0	1.000	0	0-2	8	3.25	2.61
2009	KC	AL	46	0	0	18	50.1	219	46	34	32	6	1	1	1	29	1	38	6	0	3	4	.429	0	2-6	7	4.55	5.72
2010	KC	AL	5	0	0	1	5.1	28	9	2	2	0	1	0	0	4	0	7	0	0	0	0	-	0	0-1	0	9.07	3.38
2011	TB	AL	56	0	0	9	48.2	200	36	21	21	5	2	2	3	28	2	46	3	0	5	0	1.000	0	0-1	6	3.40	3.88
Postseason			8	0	0	2	9.0	44	7	5	4	0	1	0	1	8	0	15	1	0	0	0	-	0	0-0	0	4.12	4.00
11 ML YEARS			404	38	0	111	619.1	2696	537	320	284	64	31	21	43	327	18	626	22	2	37	35	.514	0	3-15	31	4.10	4.13

Nelson Cruz

Bats: R Throws: R Pos: RF-109; LF-18; DH-8; PH-2

Ht: 6'2" Wt: 240 Born: 7/1/1980 Age: 31

			BATTING																		BASERUNNING				AVERAGES		
Year	Team	Lg	G	AB	H	2B	3B	HR	(Hm	Rd)	TB	R	RBI	RC	TBB	IBB	SO	HBP	SH	SF		SB	CS	SB%	GDP	Avg	OBP	Slg
2011	Frisco*	AA	3	11	2	1	0	0	(-	-)	3	1	1	0	1	0	0	0	0	0		0	0	-	1	.182	.250	.273
2011	RdRck*	AAA	3	11	5	0	0	3	(-	-)	14	3	4	5	2	1	1	0	0	0		0	0	-	0	.455	.538	1.273
2005	Mil	NL	8	5	1	1	0	0	(0	0)	2	1	0	1	2	0	0	0	0	0		0	0	-	0	.200	.429	.400
2006	Tex	AL	41	130	29	3	0	6	(3	3)	50	15	22	18	7	0	32	0	0	1		1	0	1.00	1	.223	.261	.385
2007	Tex	AL	96	307	72	15	2	9	(4	5)	118	35	34	32	21	1	87	2	1	1		2	4	.33	5	.235	.287	.384
2008	Tex	AL	31	115	38	9	1	7	(4	3)	70	19	26	30	17	2	28	1	0	0		3	1	.75	1	.330	.421	.609
2009	Tex	AL	128	462	120	21	1	33	(18	15)	242	75	76	72	49	6	118	2	0	2		20	4	.83	9	.260	.332	.524
2010	Tex	AL	108	399	127	31	3	22	(13	9)	230	60	78	77	38	5	81	1	1	6		17	4	.81	12	.318	.374	.576
2011	Tex	AL	124	475	125	28	1	29	(19	10)	242	64	87	79	33	1	116	2	0	3		9	5	.64	8	.263	.312	.509
Postseason			16	60	19	7	0	6	(4	2)	44	13	11	13	3	1	17	0	0	1		1	0	1.00	1	.317	.349	.733
7 ML YEARS			536	1893	512	108	8	106	(61	45)	954	269	323	309	167	15	462	8	2	13		52	18	.74	36	.270	.330	.504

Tony Cruz

Bats: R Throws: R Pos: C-20; PH-18; 3B-3; 1B-2; RF-2; 2B-1; PR-1

Ht: 5'11" Wt: 205 Born: 8/18/1986 Age: 25

			BATTING																		BASERUNNING				AVERAGES		
Year	Team	Lg	G	AB	H	2B	3B	HR	(Hm	Rd)	TB	R	RBI	RC	TBB	IBB	SO	HBP	SH	SF		SB	CS	SB%	GDP	Avg	OBP	Slg
2007	Cards	R	7	32	12	5	0	0	(-	-)	17	8	4	6	1	0	7	0	0	1		1	0	1.00	0	.375	.382	.531
2007	JhsCty	R+	6	25	7	2	0	2	(-	-)	15	2	2	5	2	1	2	0	0	0		1	0	1.00	0	.280	.333	.600
2007	Batvia	A-	4	16	6	1	0	0	(-	-)	7	2	4	2	0	0	5	0	0	0		0	0	-	0	.375	.412	.438
2007	QuadC	A	49	195	55	10	1	5	(-	-)	82	26	34	29	17	0	25	1	0	3		3	1	.75	10	.282	.338	.421
2008	PlmBh	A+	89	351	98	22	3	8	(-	-)	150	41	58	49	19	0	50	2	1	5		1	0	1.00	17	.279	.316	.427
2009	Sprgfld	AA	111	405	89	25	2	10	(-	-)	148	44	48	43	34	2	85	1	2	3		1	0	1.00	16	.220	.280	.365
2010	PlmBh	A+	46	181	51	16	1	1	(-	-)	72	21	25	26	19	0	33	0	1	1		0	0	-	5	.282	.348	.398
2010	Sprgfld	AA	40	149	43	10	0	6	(-	-)	71	26	20	26	17	3	30	1	1	1		0	0	-	5	.289	.363	.477
2010	Memp	AAA	4	14	3	0	0	1	(-	-)	6	2	1	1	1	0	1	0	0	0		0	0	-	1	.214	.267	.429
2011	Memp	AAA	45	149	39	5	1	4	(-	-)	58	13	25	18	11	0	31	1	2	1		0	1	.00	7	.262	.315	.389
2011	StL	NL	38	65	17	5	0	0	(0	0)	22	8	6	7	6	1	13	1	0	0		0	1	.00	1	.262	.333	.338

Michael Cuddyer

Bats: R **Throws:** R **Pos:** RF-77; 1B-46; 2B-17; DH-8   cuh-DYE-err   **Ht:** 6'2" **Wt:** 225 **Born:** 3/27/1979 **Age:** 33

Year	Team	Lg	G	AB	H	2B	3B	HR	(Hm	Rd)	TB	R	RBI	RC	TBB	IBB	SO	HBP	SH	SF	SB	CS	SB%	GDP	Avg	OBP	Slg
2001	Min	AL	8	18	4	2	0	0	(0	0)	6	1	1	2	2	0	6	0	0	0	1	0	1.00	1	.222	.300	.333
2002	Min	AL	41	112	29	7	0	4	(2	2)	48	12	13	14	8	0	30	1	1	1	2	0	1.00	3	.259	.311	.429
2003	Min	AL	35	102	25	1	3	4	(1	3)	44	14	8	10	12	0	19	0	0	0	1	1	.50	6	.245	.325	.431
2004	Min	AL	115	339	89	22	1	12	(8	4)	149	49	45	51	37	2	74	3	2	1	5	5	.50	8	.263	.339	.440
2005	Min	AL	126	422	111	25	3	12	(8	4)	178	55	42	43	41	5	93	3	1	3	3	4	.43	19	.263	.330	.422
2006	Min	AL	150	557	158	41	5	24	(15	9)	281	102	109	101	62	5	130	10	0	6	6	0	1.00	11	.284	.362	.504
2007	Min	AL	144	547	151	28	5	16	(8	8)	237	87	81	82	64	1	107	7	0	5	5	0	1.00	19	.276	.356	.433
2008	Min	AL	71	249	62	13	4	3	(1	2)	92	30	36	37	25	4	40	5	0	0	5	1	.83	7	.249	.330	.369
2009	Min	AL	153	588	162	34	7	32	(18	14)	306	93	94	89	54	3	118	6	0	2	6	1	.86	22	.276	.342	.520
2010	Min	AL	157	609	165	37	5	14	(7	7)	254	93	81	77	58	7	93	4	0	4	7	3	.70	26	.271	.336	.417
2011	Min	AL	139	529	150	29	2	20	(10	10)	243	70	70	75	48	3	95	4	0	3	11	1	.92	18	.284	.346	.459
	Postseason		22	74	25	2	1	2	(2	0)	35	5	8	4	4	1	18	0	0	0	0	2	.00	1	.338	.372	.473
11 ML YEARS			1139	4072	1106	239	35	141	(78	63)	1838	606	580	581	411	30	805	43	4	25	52	16	.76	140	.272	.343	.451

Johnny Cueto

Pitches: R **Bats:** R **Pos:** SP-24   KWAY-toe   **Ht:** 5'10" **Wt:** 220 **Born:** 2/15/1986 **Age:** 26

			HOW MUCH HE PITCHED						WHAT HE GAVE UP											THE RESULTS						
Year	Team	Lg	G	GS	CG	GF	IP	BFP	H	R	ER	HR	SH	SF	HB	TBB	IBB	SO	WP	Bk	W	L	Pct	Sh	Sv-Op Hld	ERC	ERA
2011	Lsvlle*	AAA	4	4	0	0	14.1	68	19	12	10	1	1	0	0	6	0	13	1	0	0	2	.000	0	0- - -	5.68	6.28
2008	Cin	NL	31	31	0	0	174.0	769	178	101	93	29	9	5	14	68	1	158	6	1	9	14	.391	0	0-0 0	4.95	4.81
2009	Cin	NL	30	30	0	0	171.1	740	172	90	84	24	5	3	14	61	0	132	4	0	11	11	.500	0	0-0 0	4.57	4.41
2010	Cin	NL	31	31	1	0	185.2	780	181	79	75	19	9	3	9	56	5	138	5	2	12	7	.632	1	0-0 0	3.75	3.64
2011	Cin	NL	24	24	3	0	156.0	631	123	51	40	8	10	4	10	47	0	104	5	1	9	5	.643	1	0-0 0	2.55	2.31
	Postseason		1	1	0	0	5.0	22	5	2	1	1	1	0	0	1	0	2	0	0	0	1	.000	0	0-0 0	3.66	1.80
4 ML YEARS			116	116	4	0	687.0	2920	654	321	292	80	33	15	47	232	6	532	20	4	41	37	.526	2	0-0 0	3.96	3.83

Aaron Cunningham

Bats: R **Throws:** R **Pos:** PH-28; RF-18; LF-13; PR-2   **Ht:** 5'11" **Wt:** 203 **Born:** 4/24/1986 **Age:** 26

Year	Team	Lg	G	AB	H	2B	3B	HR	(Hm	Rd)	TB	R	RBI	RC	TBB	IBB	SO	HBP	SH	SF	SB	CS	SB%	GDP	Avg	OBP	Slg
2011	Tucsn*	AAA	87	340	112	34	4	9	(-	-)	181	65	63	71	38	0	54	3	0	3	4	4	.50	5	.329	.398	.532
2008	Oak	AL	22	80	20	7	1	1	(1	0)	32	7	14	12	6	1	24	1	0	0	2	0	1.00	1	.250	.310	.400
2009	Oak	AL	23	53	8	2	0	1	(0	1)	13	6	6	3	3	0	16	1	0	0	0	0	-	3	.151	.211	.245
2010	SD	NL	53	132	38	12	1	1	(1	0)	55	17	15	16	7	1	28	3	2	3	1	3	.25	3	.288	.331	.417
2011	SD	NL	52	90	16	6	1	3	(1	2)	33	12	9	6	9	0	17	1	0	1	1	0	1.00	2	.178	.257	.367
4 ML YEARS			150	355	82	27	3	6	(3	3)	133	42	44	37	25	2	85	6	2	4	4	3	.57	9	.231	.290	.375

Jack Cust

Bats: L **Throws:** R **Pos:** DH-63; PH-4   **Ht:** 6'1" **Wt:** 247 **Born:** 1/7/1979 **Age:** 33

Year	Team	Lg	G	AB	H	2B	3B	HR	(Hm	Rd)	TB	R	RBI	RC	TBB	IBB	SO	HBP	SH	SF	SB	CS	SB%	GDP	Avg	OBP	Slg
2011	LV*	AAA	6	20	5	2	0	1	(-	-)	10	3	2	3	3	0	3	0	0	0	0	0	-	3	.250	.348	.500
2001	Ari	NL	3	2	1	0	0	0	(0	0)	1	0	0	1	1	0	0	0	0	0	0	0	-	0	.500	.667	.500
2002	Col	NL	35	65	11	2	0	1	(0	1)	16	8	8	6	12	0	32	0	0	1	0	1	.00	3	.169	.295	.246
2003	Bal	AL	27	73	19	7	0	4	(2	2)	38	7	11	17	10	0	25	1	0	0	0	0	-	0	.260	.357	.521
2004	Bal	AL	1	1	0	0	0	0	(0	0)	0	0	0	0	0	0	1	0	0	0	0	0	-	0	.000	.000	.000
2006	SD	NL	4	3	1	0	0	0	(0	0)	1	1	0	0	0	0	1	0	0	0	0	0	-	0	.333	.333	.333
2007	Oak	AL	124	395	101	18	1	26	(14	12)	199	61	82	87	105	2	164	1	0	6	0	2	.00	6	.256	.408	.504
2008	Oak	AL	148	481	111	19	0	33	(20	13)	229	77	77	84	111	3	197	2	0	4	0	0	-	7	.231	.375	.476
2009	Oak	AL	149	513	123	16	0	25	(14	11)	214	88	70	83	93	5	185	2	0	4	4	1	.80	7	.240	.356	.417
2010	Oak	AL	112	349	95	19	0	13	(7	6)	153	50	52	58	68	0	127	5	0	3	2	2	.50	6	.272	.395	.438
2011	Sea	AL	67	225	48	15	1	3	(2	1)	74	19	23	28	44	2	87	1	0	0	0	0	-	3	.213	.344	.329
10 ML YEARS			670	2107	510	96	2	105	(59	46)	925	311	323	364	444	12	819	12	0	18	6	6	.50	32	.242	.374	.439

Matt Daley

Pitches: R **Bats:** R **Pos:** RP-7   **Ht:** 6'2" **Wt:** 180 **Born:** 6/23/1982 **Age:** 30

			HOW MUCH HE PITCHED						WHAT HE GAVE UP											THE RESULTS						
Year	Team	Lg	G	GS	CG	GF	IP	BFP	H	R	ER	HR	SH	SF	HB	TBB	IBB	SO	WP	Bk	W	L	Pct	Sh	Sv-Op Hld	ERC	ERA
2011	ColSpr*	AAA	17	0	0	2	14.1	61	20	12	10	2	0	0	0	3	0	15	1	0	0	2	.000	0	0- - -	6.28	6.28
2009	Col	NL	57	0	0	15	51.0	211	43	24	24	6	2	3	2	18	2	55	0	0	1	1	.500	0	0-3 12	3.27	4.24
2010	Col	NL	28	0	0	4	23.1	108	27	11	11	2	2	1	3	10	1	18	1	0	0	1	.000	0	0-0 6	5.41	4.24
2011	Col	NL	7	0	0	0	6.0	27	8	7	7	1	0	1	0	2	0	7	0	0	0	0	-	0	0-0 0	6.38	10.50
	Postseason		1	0	0	0	1.0	5	1	0	0	0	1	0	0	1	0	1	0	0	0	0	-	0	0-0 0	5.48	0.00
3 ML YEARS			92	0	0	19	80.1	346	78	42	42	9	4	5	5	30	3	80	1	0	1	2	.333	0	0-3 18	4.09	4.71

Johnny Damon

Bats: L **Throws:** L **Pos:** DH-135; LF-16; PH-6; 1B-1   **Ht:** 6'2" **Wt:** 205 **Born:** 11/5/1973 **Age:** 38

Year	Team	Lg	G	AB	H	2B	3B	HR	(Hm	Rd)	TB	R	RBI	RC	TBB	IBB	SO	HBP	SH	SF	SB	CS	SB%	GDP	Avg	OBP	Slg
1995	KC	AL	47	188	53	11	5	3	(1	2)	83	32	23	29	12	0	22	1	2	3	7	0	1.00	2	.282	.324	.441
1996	KC	AL	145	517	140	22	5	6	(3	3)	190	61	50	64	31	3	64	3	10	5	25	5	.83	4	.271	.313	.368
1997	KC	AL	146	472	130	12	8	8	(3	5)	182	70	48	63	42	2	70	3	6	1	16	10	.62	3	.275	.338	.386
1998	KC	AL	161	642	178	30	10	18	(11	7)	282	104	66	98	58	4	84	4	3	3	26	12	.68	4	.277	.339	.439
1999	KC	AL	145	583	179	39	9	14	(5	9)	278	101	77	108	67	5	50	3	3	4	36	6	.86	13	.307	.379	.477
2000	KC	AL	159	655	214	42	10	16	(10	6)	324	136	88	129	65	4	60	1	8	12	46	9	.84	7	.327	.382	.495
2001	Oak	AL	155	644	165	34	4	9	(2	7)	234	108	49	79	61	1	70	5	5	4	27	12	.69	7	.256	.324	.363
2002	Bos	AL	154	623	178	34	11	14	(5	9)	276	118	63	101	65	5	70	6	3	5	31	6	.84	4	.286	.356	.443
2003	Bos	AL	145	608	166	32	6	12	(5	7)	246	103	67	92	68	4	74	2	6	6	30	6	.83	5	.273	.345	.405
2004	Bos	AL	150	621	189	35	6	20	(9	11)	296	123	94	115	76	1	71	2	0	3	19	8	.70	8	.304	.380	.477
2005	Bos	AL	148	624	197	35	6	10	(3	7)	274	117	75	105	53	3	69	2	0	9	18	1	.95	5	.316	.366	.439
2006	NYY	AL	149	593	169	35	5	24	(13	11)	286	115	80	99	67	1	85	4	2	5	25	10	.71	4	.285	.359	.482
2007	NYY	AL	141	533	144	27	2	12	(5	7)	211	93	63	84	66	1	79	2	1	3	27	3	.90	4	.270	.351	.396
2008	NYY	AL	143	555	168	27	5	17	(7	10)	256	95	71	109	64	0	82	1	2	1	29	8	.78	6	.303	.375	.461
2009	NYY	AL	143	550	155	36	3	24	(17	7)	269	107	82	97	71	1	98	2	2	1	12	0	1.00	9	.282	.365	.489
2010	Det	AL	145	539	146	36	5	8	(7	1)	216	81	51	73	69	2	90	2	2	1	11	1	.92	5	.271	.355	.401
2011	TB	AL	150	582	152	29	7	16	(6	10)	243	79	73	81	51	1	92	7	2	5	19	6	.76	4	.261	.326	.418
	Postseason		55	244	68	12	2	9	(3	6)	111	36	30	36	17	0	36	1	0	0	13	1	.93	5	.279	.328	.455
17 ML YEARS			2426	9529	2723	516	107	231	(112	119)	4146	1643	1120	1526	986	38	1230	50	57	71	404	103	.80	94	.286	.353	.435

John Danks

Pitches: L **Bats:** L **Pos:** SP-27   **Ht:** 6'2" **Wt:** 210 **Born:** 4/15/1985 **Age:** 27

Year	Team	Lg	G	GS	CG	GF	IP	BFP	H	R	ER	HR	SH	SF	HB	TBB	IBB	SO	WP	Bk	W	L	Pct	Sh	Sv-Op	Hld	ERC	ERA
2011	Charltt*	AAA	2	2	0	0	9.0	36	9	2	2	0	0	0	0	2	0	6	0	0	1	0	1.000	0	0--	-	4.35	2.00
2007	CWS	AL	26	26	0	0	139.0	622	160	92	85	28	7	4	4	54	4	109	3	0	6	13	.316	0	0-0	0	5.73	5.50
2008	CWS	AL	33	33	0	0	195.0	804	182	74	72	15	2	2	4	57	1	159	7	0	12	9	.571	0	0-0	0	3.26	3.32
2009	CWS	AL	32	32	1	0	200.1	839	184	89	84	28	5	6	5	73	1	149	1	0	13	11	.542	0	0-0	0	3.89	3.77
2010	CWS	AL	32	32	1	0	213.0	878	189	93	88	18	5	0	4	70	2	162	2	1	15	11	.577	1	0-0	0	3.18	3.72
2011	CWS	AL	27	27	2	0	170.1	728	182	89	82	19	4	6	7	46	5	135	6	0	8	12	.400	1	0-0	0	4.16	4.33
	Postseason		1	1	0	0	6.2	30	7	3	3	1	0	0	0	3	0	7	0	0	1	0	1.000	0	0-0	0	4.81	4.05
5 ML YEARS			150	150	4	0	917.2	3871	897	437	411	108	23	18	24	300	13	714	19	1	54	56	.491	2	0-0	0	3.89	4.03

Chase d'Arnaud

Bats: R **Throws:** R **Pos:** SS-29; 3B-12; PR-6; PH-3; 2B-1   dar-NO   **Ht:** 6'1" **Wt:** 200 **Born:** 1/21/1987 **Age:** 25

Year	Team	Lg	G	AB	H	2B	3B	HR	(Hm	Rd)	TB	R	RBI	RC	TBB	IBB	SO	HBP	SH	SF	SB	CS	SB%	GDP	Avg	OBP	Slg
2008	StCol	A-	43	168	48	10	5	1	(-	-)	71	26	21	23	11	0	30	2	0	2	14	2	.88	4	.286	.333	.423
2009	WV	A	62	213	62	14	3	3	(-	-)	91	32	31	36	30	1	31	8	1	3	17	3	.85	2	.291	.394	.427
2009	Lynbrg	A+	54	210	62	19	4	4	(-	-)	101	45	26	39	30	0	41	9	2	2	14	5	.74	0	.295	.402	.481
2010	Altna	AA	132	530	131	33	9	6	(-	-)	200	91	48	75	56	0	102	12	5	4	33	7	.83	5	.247	.331	.377
2011	Indy	AAA	74	288	76	12	6	4	(-	-)	112	43	37	41	23	0	53	5	4	1	20	4	.83	2	.264	.328	.389
2011	Bradtn	A+	4	12	4	1	0	1	(-	-)	8	3	3	1	1	0	0	0	0	0	2	0	1.00	0	.333	.385	.667
2011	Pit	NL	48	143	31	6	2	0	(0	0)	41	17	6	8	4	0	36	1	2	1	12	2	.86	3	.217	.242	.287

James Darnell

Bats: R **Throws:** R **Pos:** 3B-12; PH-4; LF-3   **Ht:** 6'2" **Wt:** 195 **Born:** 1/19/1987 **Age:** 25

Year	Team	Lg	G	AB	H	2B	3B	HR	(Hm	Rd)	TB	R	RBI	RC	TBB	IBB	SO	HBP	SH	SF	SB	CS	SB%	GDP	Avg	OBP	Slg
2008	Eugene	A-	16	67	25	6	1	2	(-	-)	39	9	15	17	11	1	12	0	0	0	1	1	.50	3	.373	.462	.582
2009	FtWyn	A	66	222	73	17	2	7	(-	-)	115	40	38	55	57	0	51	0	1	1	5	5	.50	5	.329	.468	.518
2009	Lk Els	A+	60	235	69	18	2	13	(-	-)	130	40	43	49	30	0	38	2	1	1	3	1	.75	2	.294	.377	.553
2010	SnAnt	AA	101	373	99	21	1	10	(-	-)	152	46	50	57	44	0	64	5	1	3	2	0	1.00	11	.265	.348	.408
2010	FtWyn	A	7	25	9	4	0	1	(-	-)	16	5	8	7	5	0	4	2	0	0	0	0	-	0	.360	.500	.640
2011	SnAnt	AA	76	288	96	25	1	17	(-	-)	174	62	62	74	52	4	48	2	0	4	2	1	.67	10	.333	.434	.604
2011	Tucsn	AAA	35	134	35	4	0	6	(-	-)	57	20	17	21	16	0	30	2	1	2	0	0	-	3	.261	.344	.425
2011	SD	NL	18	45	10	2	0	1	(0	1)	15	2	7	4	5	0	7	0	1	1	1	0	1.00	6	.222	.294	.333

Yu Darvish

Pitches: R **Bats:** R **Pos:** P   **Ht:** 6'5" **Wt:** 198 **Born:** 8/16/1986 **Age:** 25

Year	Team	Lg	G	GS	CG	GF	IP	BFP	H	R	ER	HR	SH	SF	HB	TBB	IBB	SO	WP	Bk	W	L	Pct	Sh	Sv-Op	Hld	ERC	ERA
2005	HNHF	Jap	14	-	2	-	94.1	410	97	37	37	7	-	-	3	48	-	52	2	0	5	5	.500	1	0--	-	4.74	3.53
2006	HNHF	Jap	25	-	3	-	149.2	627	128	55	48	12	-	-	6	64	-	115	5	1	12	5	.706	2	0--	-	3.46	2.89
2007	HNHF	Jap	26	-	12	-	207.2	790	123	48	42	9	-	13	49	-	210	4	0	15	5	.750	3	0--	-	1.48	1.82
2008	HNHF	Jap	25	-	10	-	200.2	764	136	44	42	11	-	-	9	44	-	208	4	1	16	4	.800	2	0--	-	1.75	1.88
2009	HNHF	Jap	23	-	8	-	182.0	701	118	36	35	9	-	-	6	45	-	167	5	0	15	5	.750	2	0--	-	1.63	1.73
2010	HNHF	Jap	26	-	10	-	202.0	805	158	48	40	5	-	-	7	47	-	222	6	0	12	8	.600	2	0--	-	2.01	1.78
2011	HNHF	Jap	28	-	10	-	232.0	885	156	42	37	5	-	-	6	36	-	276	10	1	18	6	.750	6	0--	-	1.37	1.44

Kyle Davies

Pitches: R Bats: R Pos: SP-13   DAY-vees   Ht: 6'1" Wt: 211 Born: 9/9/1983 Age: 28

			HOW MUCH HE PITCHED						WHAT HE GAVE UP											THE RESULTS						
Year	Team	Lg	G	GS	CG	GF	IP	BFP	H	R	ER	HR	SH	SF	HB	TBB	IBB	SO	WP	Bk	W	L	Pct	Sh	Sv-Op	Hld	ERC	ERA
2011	NWArk*	AA	2	2	0	0	8.0	36	10	7	5	0	1	2	0	0	0	7	0	0	0	2	.000	0	0- -	-	2.93	5.63
2011	Omha*	AAA	2	1	0	1	12.0	45	8	3	1	0	1	0	0	0	0	14	1	0	1	1	.500	0	0- -	-	0.89	0.75
2011	LsVgs*	AAA	6	0	0	2	8.0	31	3	3	3	1	0	0	1	3	0	8	1	0	0	0	-	0	0- -	-	1.53	3.38
2005	Atl	NL	21	14	0	2	87.2	403	98	51	48	8	3	0	1	49	5	62	4	0	7	6	.538	0	0-1	2	5.25	4.93
2006	Atl	NL	14	14	1	0	63.1	312	90	60	59	14	3	2	3	33	0	51	3	0	3	7	.300	0	0-0	0	8.33	8.38
2007	2 Tms		28	28	0	0	136.0	628	155	102	92	22	5	3	5	70	4	99	8	1	7	15	.318	0	0-0	0	5.90	6.09
2008	KC	AL	21	21	0	0	113.0	487	121	57	51	10	1	3	2	43	0	71	8	1	9	7	.563	0	0-0	0	4.46	4.06
2009	KC	AL	22	22	1	0	123.0	538	122	76	72	18	3	4	4	66	1	86	10	0	8	9	.471	0	0-0	0	5.16	5.27
2010	KC	AL	32	32	1	0	183.2	817	206	114	109	20	3	5	2	80	1	126	5	1	8	12	.400	0	0-0	0	5.04	5.34
2011	KC	AL	13	13	0	0	61.1	293	84	52	46	7	3	5	2	26	2	50	4	0	1	9	.100	0	0-0	0	6.76	6.75
07	Atl	NL	17	17	0	0	86.0	389	92	61	55	12	3	2	2	44	3	59	1	1	4	8	.333	0	0-0	0	5.24	5.76
07	KC	AL	11	11	0	0	50.0	239	63	41	37	10	2	1	3	26	1	40	7	0	3	7	.300	0	0-0	0	7.09	6.66
	7 ML YEARS		151	144	3	2	768.0	3478	876	512	477	99	21	23	22	367	13	545	42	3	43	65	.398	0	0-1	2	5.54	5.59

Blake Davis

Bats: L Throws: R Pos: 2B-18; PH-3; SS-2; 3B-1; PR-1   Ht: 5'11" Wt: 170 Born: 12/22/1983 Age: 28

			BATTING																			BASERUNNING				AVERAGES		
Year	Team	Lg	G	AB	H	2B	3B	HR	(Hm	Rd)	TB	R	RBI	RC	TBB	IBB	SO	HBP	SH	SF	SB	CS	SB%	GDP	Avg	OBP	Slg
2006	Dlmrva	A	50	199	54	8	2	3	(-	-)	75	30	20	26	15	1	28	2	4	0	9	2	.82	4	.271	.329	.377
2007	Frdrck	A+	93	357	104	24	3	4	(-	-)	146	49	28	52	35	0	71	5	8	1	11	13	.46	6	.291	.362	.409
2007	Bowie	AA	35	115	24	7	0	0	(-	-)	31	12	10	8	9	0	25	0	4	1	1	1	.50	2	.209	.264	.270
2008	Bowie	AA	132	457	130	22	7	4	(-	-)	178	57	53	58	26	0	80	3	7	4	8	7	.53	10	.284	.324	.389
2009	Abrdn	A-	13	50	16	2	0	1	(-	-)	21	6	5	8	4	0	7	0	0	3	2	0	-	3	.320	.357	.420
2009	Norfolk	AAA	55	180	38	4	2	1	(-	-)	49	21	14	13	14	0	40	1	1	1	3	2	.60	4	.211	.270	.272
2010	Bowie	AA	7	21	4	1	0	0	(-	-)	5	1	2	1	3	0	2	0	0	1	0	0	-	2	.190	.280	.238
2010	Norfolk	AAA	75	244	60	14	2	4	(-	-)	90	32	23	26	17	0	43	0	6	1	3	4	.43	8	.246	.294	.369
2011	Norfolk	AAA	62	232	65	3	3	5	(-	-)	89	28	27	29	15	1	46	1	1	3	6	5	.55	4	.280	.323	.384
2011	Bal	AL	25	59	15	3	1	1	(1	0)	23	6	6	7	6	0	13	0	0	0	1	1	.50	1	.254	.323	.390

Chris Davis

Bats: L Throws: R Pos: 1B-31; 3B-26; PH-3; DH-2   Ht: 6'3" Wt: 232 Born: 3/17/1986 Age: 26

			BATTING																			BASERUNNING				AVERAGES		
Year	Team	Lg	G	AB	H	2B	3B	HR	(Hm	Rd)	TB	R	RBI	RC	TBB	IBB	SO	HBP	SH	SF	SB	CS	SB%	GDP	Avg	OBP	Slg
2011	RdRck*	AAA	48	193	71	14	1	24	(-	-)	159	39	66	58	11	2	58	3	0	3	1	0	1.00	6	.368	.405	.824
2011	Bowie*	AA	2	6	3	1	0	0	(-	-)	4	2	0	2	1	0	2	1	0	0	0	0	-	0	.500	.625	.667
2008	Tex	AL	80	295	84	23	2	17	(8	9)	162	51	55	44	20	1	88	1	0	1	1	2	.33	5	.285	.331	.549
2009	Tex	AL	113	391	93	15	1	21	(11	10)	173	48	59	50	24	2	150	2	0	2	0	0	-	6	.238	.284	.442
2010	Tex	AL	45	120	23	9	0	1	(0	1)	35	7	4	5	15	3	40	0	0	1	3	0	1.00	3	.192	.279	.292
2011	2 Tms		59	199	53	12	0	5	(2	3)	80	25	19	23	11	1	63	0	0	0	1	0	1.00	4	.266	.305	.402
11	Tex	AL	28	76	19	3	0	3	(1	2)	31	9	6	7	5	0	24	0	0	0	0	0	-	2	.250	.296	.408
11	Bal	AL	31	123	34	9	0	2	(1	1)	49	16	13	16	6	1	39	0	0	0	1	0	1.00	2	.276	.310	.398
	4 ML YEARS		297	1005	253	59	3	44	(21	23)	450	131	137	122	70	7	341	3	0	4	5	2	.71	18	.252	.301	.448

Doug Davis

Pitches: L Bats: R Pos: SP-9   Ht: 6'4" Wt: 213 Born: 9/21/1975 Age: 36

			HOW MUCH HE PITCHED						WHAT HE GAVE UP											THE RESULTS						
Year	Team	Lg	G	GS	CG	GF	IP	BFP	H	R	ER	HR	SH	SF	HB	TBB	IBB	SO	WP	Bk	W	L	Pct	Sh	Sv-Op	Hld	ERC	ERA
2011	Dytona*	A+	1	1	0	0	6.2	23	2	0	0	0	0	0	0	2	0	7	0	0	1	0	1.000	0	0- -	-	0.59	0.00
2011	Iowa*	AAA	1	1	0	0	3.2	15	4	2	2	0	0	0	0	0	0	5	0	0	0	0	-	0	0- -	-	2.36	4.91
2011	Charltt*	AAA	9	9	0	0	52.0	213	51	20	15	2	1	2	1	12	0	46	5	1	2	5	.286	0	0- -	-	3.04	2.60
1999	Tex	AL	2	0	0	0	2.2	20	12	10	10	3	0	0	0	0	0	3	0	0	0	0	-	0	0-0	0	41.42	33.75
2000	Tex	AL	30	13	1	4	98.2	450	109	61	59	14	6	4	3	58	3	66	5	1	7	6	.538	0	0-3	2	5.93	5.38
2001	Tex	AL	30	30	1	0	186.0	828	220	103	92	14	4	6	3	69	1	115	7	2	11	10	.524	0	0-0	0	4.90	4.45
2002	Tex	AL	10	10	1	0	59.2	262	67	36	33	7	3	3	3	22	0	28	2	2	3	5	.375	1	0-0	0	5.05	4.98
2003	3 Tms		21	20	1	0	109.1	491	123	55	49	16	6	2	1	51	1	62	7	0	7	8	.467	0	0-0	0	5.46	4.03
2004	Mil	NL	34	34	0	0	207.1	880	192	84	78	14	11	5	7	79	3	166	4	1	12	12	.500	1	0-0	0	3.49	3.39
2005	Mil	NL	35	35	2	0	222.2	946	196	103	95	26	12	2	4	93	5	208	3	2	11	11	.500	1	0-0	0	3.62	3.84
2006	Mil	NL	34	34	1	0	203.1	904	206	118	111	19	16	8	5	102	1	159	3	0	11	11	.500	1	0-0	0	4.59	4.91
2007	Ari	NL	33	33	0	0	192.2	862	211	100	91	21	10	2	5	95	7	144	10	1	13	12	.520	0	0-0	0	5.15	4.25
2008	Ari	NL	26	26	0	0	146.0	650	160	76	70	13	10	4	4	64	4	112	7	0	6	8	.429	0	0-0	0	4.77	4.32
2009	Ari	NL	34	34	0	0	203.1	889	203	101	93	25	15	6	4	103	1	146	12	1	9	14	.391	0	0-0	0	4.80	4.12
2010	Mil	NL	8	8	0	0	38.1	191	55	36	32	6	2	4	0	21	1	34	3	0	1	4	.200	0	0-0	0	8.08	7.51
2011	ChC	NL	9	9	0	0	45.2	224	59	38	33	2	5	3	2	26	1	36	0	1	1	7	.125	0	0-0	0	6.02	6.50
03	Tex	AL	1	1	0	0	3.0	17	4	4	4	2	0	0	0	4	0	2	0	0	0	0	-	0	0-0	0	15.81	12.00
03	Tor	AL	12	11	0	0	54.0	250	70	33	30	9	4	1	1	26	1	25	6	0	4	6	.400	0	0-0	0	6.39	5.00
03	Mil	NL	8	8	1	0	52.1	224	49	18	15	5	2	1	0	21	0	35	1	0	3	2	.600	0	0-0	0	4.06	2.58
	Postseason		2	2	0	0	10.2	50	10	6	5	1	1	1	0	8	0	13	0	0	1	0	1.000	0	0-0	0	4.94	4.22
	13 ML YEARS		306	286	7	4	1715.2	7597	1813	921	846	180	100	45	44	783	28	1279	63	10	92	108	.460	3	0-3	2	4.75	4.44

Ike Davis

Bats: L **Throws:** L **Pos:** 1B-36　　　　　　　　　　　　**Ht:** 6'4" **Wt:** 231 **Born:** 3/22/1987 **Age:** 25

Year	Team	Lg	G	AB	H	2B	3B	HR	(Hm	Rd)	TB	R	RBI	RC	TBB	IBB	SO	HBP	SH	SF	SB	CS	SB%	GDP	Avg	OBP	Slg
2008	Bklyn	A-	58	215	55	15	0	0	(-	-)	70	17	17	24	23	2	43	0	0	1	0	0	-	8	.256	.326	.326
2009	StLuci	A+	59	222	64	17	3	7	(-	-)	108	28	28	41	31	3	52	1	0	1	0	2	.00	2	.288	.376	.486
2009	Bnghtn	AA	55	207	64	14	0	13	(-	-)	117	30	43	44	26	0	60	0	0	0	0	0	-	1	.309	.386	.565
2010	Buffalo	AAA	10	33	12	3	0	2	(-	-)	21	8	4	10	9	0	5	0	0	0	0	0	-	0	.364	.500	.636
2010	NYM	NL	147	523	138	33	1	19	(8	11)	230	73	71	75	72	6	138	1	0	5	3	2	.60	13	.264	.351	.440
2011	NYM	NL	36	129	39	8	1	7	(5	2)	70	20	25	22	17	3	31	1	0	2	0	0	-	5	.302	.383	.543
	2 ML YEARS		183	652	177	41	2	26	(13	13)	300	93	96	97	89	9	169	2	0	7	3	2	.60	18	.271	.357	.460

Rajai Davis

Bats: R **Throws:** R **Pos:** CF-79; RF-8; PR-5; LF-4; PH-4; DH-1　　　RAHJ-ay　　　**Ht:** 5'10" **Wt:** 195 **Born:** 10/19/1980 **Age:** 31

Year	Team	Lg	G	AB	H	2B	3B	HR	(Hm	Rd)	TB	R	RBI	RC	TBB	IBB	SO	HBP	SH	SF	SB	CS	SB%	GDP	Avg	OBP	Slg
2011	NHam*	AA	4	10	3	1	0	0	(-	-)	4	1	0	1	2	0	2	2	0	0	0	2	.00	0	.300	.500	.400
2011	Dnedin*	A+	2	5	2	0	0	1	(-	-)	5	1	1	1	0	0	1	0	0	0	0	0	-	0	.400	.400	1.000
2006	Pit	NL	20	14	2	1	0	0	(0	0)	3	1	0	0	2	0	3	0	1	0	1	3	.25	0	.143	.250	.214
2007	2 Tms	NL	75	190	53	11	2	1	(0	1)	71	32	9	26	21	1	28	4	3	1	22	6	.79	1	.279	.361	.374
2008	2 Tms		113	214	52	5	4	3	(0	3)	74	30	19	24	8	0	40	1	2	1	29	6	.83	1	.243	.272	.346
2009	Oak	AL	125	390	119	27	5	3	(1	2)	165	65	48	63	29	0	70	7	4	1	41	12	.77	12	.305	.360	.423
2010	Oak	AL	143	525	149	28	3	5	(5	0)	198	66	52	62	26	0	78	4	1	5	50	11	.82	10	.284	.320	.377
2011	Tor	AL	95	320	76	21	6	1	(1	0)	112	44	29	32	15	0	63	1	1	1	34	11	.76	4	.238	.273	.350
	07 Pit	NL	24	48	13	2	1	0	(0	0)	17	6	2	6	7	0	7	0	1	1	5	2	.71	1	.271	.357	.354
	07 SF	NL	51	142	40	9	1	1	(0	1)	54	26	7	20	14	1	25	4	2	0	17	4	.81	0	.282	.363	.380
	08 SF	NL	12	18	1	0	0	0	(0	0)	1	2	0	0	1	0	6	0	0	0	4	0	1.00	0	.056	.105	.056
	08 Oak	AL	101	196	51	5	4	3	(0	3)	73	28	19	24	7	0	34	1	2	1	25	6	.81	1	.260	.288	.372
	6 ML YEARS		571	1653	451	93	20	13	(7	6)	623	238	157	207	101	1	282	17	10	12	177	49	.78	28	.273	.319	.377

Wade Davis

Pitches: R **Bats:** R **Pos:** SP-29　　　　　　　　　　　　**Ht:** 6'5" **Wt:** 220 **Born:** 9/7/1985 **Age:** 26

			HOW MUCH HE PITCHED					WHAT HE GAVE UP											THE RESULTS						
Year	Team	Lg	G	GS	CG	GF	IP	BFP	H	R	ER	HR	SH	SF	HB	TBB	IBB	SO	WP	Bk	W	L	Pct	Sh	Sv-Op	Hld	ERC	ERA
2009	TB	AL	6	6	1	0	36.1	150	33	19	15	2	0	0	0	13	1	36	1	0	2	2	.500	1	0-0	0	3.12	3.72
2010	TB	AL	29	29	0	0	168.0	722	165	77	76	24	3	6	5	62	2	113	4	0	12	10	.545	0	0-0	0	4.25	4.07
2011	TB	AL	29	29	1	0	184.0	795	190	96	91	23	5	7	8	63	1	105	6	0	11	10	.524	0	0-0	0	4.38	4.45
	Postseason		1	1	0	0	5.0	24	7	2	2	1	0	0	0	3	0	7	0	0	1	0	1.000	0	0-0	0	8.40	3.60
	3 ML YEARS		64	64	2	0	388.1	1667	388	192	182	49	8	13	13	138	4	254	11	0	25	22	.532	1	0-0	0	4.20	4.22

Alejandro De Aza

Bats: L **Throws:** L **Pos:** RF-31; CF-19; LF-4; PH-4; PR-4; DH-3　　　day-AH-zah　　　**Ht:** 5'11" **Wt:** 189 **Born:** 4/11/1984 **Age:** 28

Year	Team	Lg	G	AB	H	2B	3B	HR	(Hm	Rd)	TB	R	RBI	RC	TBB	IBB	SO	HBP	SH	SF	SB	CS	SB%	GDP	Avg	OBP	Slg
2011	Charltt*	AAA	99	385	124	29	5	9	(-	-)	190	64	37	72	33	2	72	4	9	4	22	11	.67	8	.322	.378	.494
2007	Fla	NL	45	144	33	8	2	0	(0	0)	45	14	8	11	6	1	37	1	5	2	2	0	1.00	2	.229	.261	.313
2009	Fla	NL	22	20	5	1	0	0	(0	0)	6	6	3	4	5	0	5	0	1	1	0	0	-	0	.250	.385	.300
2010	CWS	AL	19	30	9	3	0	0	(0	0)	12	7	2	4	1	0	4	0	1	0	2	1	.67	0	.300	.323	.400
2011	CWS	AL	54	152	50	11	3	4	(2	2)	79	29	23	34	17	1	34	1	1	0	12	5	.71	2	.329	.400	.520
	4 ML YEARS		140	346	97	23	5	4	(2	2)	142	56	36	53	29	2	80	2	8	3	16	6	.73	4	.280	.337	.410

Justin De Fratus

Pitches: R **Bats:** B **Pos:** RP-5　　　duh-FRAY-tiss　　　**Ht:** 6'4" **Wt:** 215 **Born:** 10/21/1987 **Age:** 24

			HOW MUCH HE PITCHED					WHAT HE GAVE UP											THE RESULTS						
Year	Team	Lg	G	GS	CG	GF	IP	BFP	H	R	ER	HR	SH	SF	HB	TBB	IBB	SO	WP	Bk	W	L	Pct	Sh	Sv-Op	Hld	ERC	ERA
2007	Phillies	R	10	8	0	0	46.0	194	51	25	22	1	1	1	2	3	0	34	1	0	2	3	.400	0	0--	-	2.95	4.30
2008	Wmspt	A-	14	14	1	0	83.1	367	87	39	34	1	4	1	2	25	0	74	5	0	6	5	.545	0	0--	-	3.29	3.67
2009	Lakwd	A	36	12	0	5	110.0	454	108	44	39	3	5	4	10	16	1	101	4	0	5	6	.455	0	3--	-	2.87	3.19
2010	Clrwtr	A+	29	0	0	28	40.1	159	31	9	8	1	1	2	2	11	0	43	3	0	2	0	1.000	0	15--	-	2.18	1.79
2010	Rdng	AA	20	0	0	17	24.2	94	17	6	6	2	1	1	0	5	1	28	0	0	1	0	1.000	0	6--	-	1.67	2.19
2011	Rdng	AA	23	0	0	21	34.1	148	28	11	8	1	4	2	3	14	2	43	2	0	4	0	1.000	0	8--	-	2.80	2.10
2011	LV	AAA	28	0	0	18	41.0	170	35	19	17	3	3	1	3	11	1	56	5	0	2	3	.400	0	7--	-	2.84	3.73
2011	Phi	NL	5	0	0	2	4.0	17	1	2	1	0	1	0	1	3	1	3	1	0	1	0	1.000	0	0-0	0	1.39	2.25

Ivan De Jesus

Bats: R **Throws:** R **Pos:** 2B-11; PH-7; PR-1　　　　　　　　　　　　**Ht:** 5'11" **Wt:** 199 **Born:** 5/1/1987 **Age:** 25

Year	Team	Lg	G	AB	H	2B	3B	HR	(Hm	Rd)	TB	R	RBI	RC	TBB	IBB	SO	HBP	SH	SF	SB	CS	SB%	GDP	Avg	OBP	Slg
2005	Ddgrs	R	33	121	41	5	0	0	(-	-)	46	18	11	19	10	0	22	0	1	0	8	2	.80	2	.339	.389	.380
2005	Ogden	R+	20	72	15	1	0	0	(-	-)	16	4	3	4	6	0	18	3	0	0	3	3	.50	1	.208	.296	.222
2006	Clmbs	A	126	483	134	17	2	1	(-	-)	158	65	44	66	63	0	85	4	6	7	16	5	.76	13	.277	.361	.327
2007	InldEm	A+	121	428	123	22	3	4	(-	-)	163	69	52	66	57	1	64	3	9	5	11	6	.65	20	.287	.371	.381
2008	Jaxnvl	AA	128	463	150	22	2	7	(-	-)	197	91	58	93	76	3	81	5	9	7	18	2	.90	18	.324	.419	.425

					BATTING																	BASERUNNING				AVERAGES		
Year	Team	Lg	G	AB	H	2B	3B	HR	(Hm	Rd)	TB	R	RBI	RC	TBB	IBB	SO	HBP	SH	SF		SB	CS	SB%	GDP	Avg	OBP	Slg
2009	Ddgrs	R	4	10	2	1	0	0	(-	-)	3	1	3	1	1	0	6	1	0	1		0	0	-	0	.200	.308	.300
2010	Albq	AAA	130	533	158	33	2	7	(-	-)	216	89	70	76	32	0	81	2	7	6		6	1	.86	14	.296	.335	.405
2011	Albq	AAA	100	387	120	19	2	8	(-	-)	167	61	59	68	45	0	68	6	3	2		4	1	.80	19	.310	.389	.432
2011	LAD	NL	17	32	6	0	0	0	(0	0)	6	2	1	1	2	0	11	0	1	0		0	0	-	1	.188	.235	.188

Frankie de la Cruz

Pitches: R **Bats:** R **Pos:** RP-11

Ht: 5'10" **Wt:** 215 **Born:** 3/12/1984 **Age:** 28

			HOW MUCH HE PITCHED						WHAT HE GAVE UP										THE RESULTS							
Year	Team	Lg	G	GS	CG	GF	IP	BFP	H	R	ER	HR	SH	SF	HB	TBB	IBB	SO	WP	Bk	W	L	Pct	Sh	Sv-Op Hld	ERC	ERA
2011	Nashv*	AAA	25	23	0	2	137.0	598	130	67	59	14	6	2	4	63	0	126	13	1	7	6	.538	0	0- -	-	4.13	3.88
2007	Det	AL	6	0	0	4	6.2	32	10	8	5	1	0	0	0	4	1	5	3	0	0	0	-	0	0-0	0	8.47	6.75
2008	Fla	NL	6	1	0	1	9.0	53	15	20	18	2	1	1	0	11	0	4	1	0	0	0	-	0	0-0	0	13.08	18.00
2009	SD	NL	3	0	0	2	3.1	17	2	2	2	0	0	1	0	6	0	2	0	0	0	0	-	0	0-0	0	6.55	5.40
2011	Mil	NL	11	0	0	9	13.0	55	10	4	4	0	0	1	2	5	0	9	3	0	0	0	-	0	0-0	0	2.67	2.77
	4 ML YEARS		26	1	0	16	32.0	157	37	34	29	3	1	3	2	26	1	20	7	0	0	0	-	0	0-0	0	6.87	8.16

Dane de la Rosa

Pitches: R **Bats:** R **Pos:** RP-7

Ht: 6'6" **Wt:** 245 **Born:** 2/1/1983 **Age:** 29

			HOW MUCH HE PITCHED						WHAT HE GAVE UP										THE RESULTS							
Year	Team	Lg	G	GS	CG	GF	IP	BFP	H	R	ER	HR	SH	SF	HB	TBB	IBB	SO	WP	Bk	W	L	Pct	Sh	Sv-Op Hld	ERC	ERA
2003	Yanks	R	5	1	0	2	9.0	37	5	3	3	0	0	0	0	6	0	12	3	1	0	0	-	0	0- -	-	2.10	3.00
2004	Yanks	R	14	1	0	5	34.1	149	25	13	11	1	0	1	5	12	0	32	2	0	2	0	1.000	0	1- -	-	2.39	2.88
2004	StlsInd	A-	1	0	0	1	1.2	8	1	2	0	0	0	0	0	2	0	1	0	0	0	0	-	0	0- -	-	3.97	0.00
2007	Helena	R+	1	0	0	0	2.0	8	1	0	0	0	0	0	0	1	0	3	2	0	0	0	-	0	0- -	-	1.41	0.00
2010	Charltt	A+	2	0	0	0	3.0	13	4	1	1	0	0	0	0	0	0	5	2	0	0	0	-	0	0- -	-	3.56	3.00
2010	Mont	AA	47	0	0	16	73.0	301	66	20	16	3	6	3	1	26	5	75	8	0	9	3	.750	0	4- -	-	3.00	1.97
2011	Drham	AAA	52	0	0	20	70.1	296	63	26	25	8	5	3	4	26	1	84	3	0	6	5	.545	0	6- -	-	3.71	3.20
2011	TB	AL	7	0	0	2	7.1	34	10	8	8	1	0	0	0	3	0	8	1	0	0	0	-	0	0-0	0	6.62	9.82

Jorge de la Rosa

Pitches: L **Bats:** L **Pos:** SP-10

Ht: 6'1" **Wt:** 215 **Born:** 4/5/1981 **Age:** 31

			HOW MUCH HE PITCHED						WHAT HE GAVE UP										THE RESULTS							
Year	Team	Lg	G	GS	CG	GF	IP	BFP	H	R	ER	HR	SH	SF	HB	TBB	IBB	SO	WP	Bk	W	L	Pct	Sh	Sv-Op Hld	ERC	ERA
2004	Mil	NL	5	5	0	0	22.2	113	29	20	16	1	1	3	1	14	0	5	3	0	0	3	.000	0	0-0	-	6.12	6.35
2005	Mil	NL	38	0	0	13	42.1	208	48	23	21	1	2	2	0	38	4	42	6	0	2	2	.500	0	0-2	5	6.04	4.46
2006	2 Tms		28	13	0	4	79.0	367	81	59	57	14	2	4	2	54	1	67	6	1	5	6	.455	0	0-0	1	6.05	6.49
2007	KC	AL	26	23	0	1	130.0	589	160	88	84	20	2	4	3	53	6	82	4	1	8	12	.400	0	0-0	0	5.93	5.82
2008	Col	NL	28	23	0	0	130.0	571	128	77	71	13	6	7	7	62	3	128	14	1	10	8	.556	0	0-0	0	4.50	4.92
2009	Col	NL	33	32	0	0	185.0	799	172	95	90	20	1	6	9	83	3	193	12	1	16	9	.640	0	0-0	0	4.11	4.38
2010	Col	NL	20	20	0	0	121.2	512	105	62	57	15	3	3	5	55	4	113	9	1	8	7	.533	0	0-0	0	3.86	4.22
2011	Col	NL	10	10	1	0	59.0	245	48	25	23	4	4	1	2	22	0	52	6	1	5	2	.714	0	0-0	0	2.88	3.51
06	Mil	NL	18	3	0	4	30.1	146	32	30	29	4	1	3	1	22	1	31	4	0	2	2	.500	0	0-0	1	5.90	8.60
06	KC	AL	10	10	0	0	48.2	221	49	29	28	10	1	1	1	32	0	36	2	1	3	4	.429	0	0-0	0	6.14	5.18
	8 ML YEARS		188	126	1	18	769.2	3404	771	449	419	88	31	30	29	381	21	682	60	6	54	49	.524	0	0-2	6	4.69	4.90

Rubby de la Rosa

Pitches: R **Bats:** R **Pos:** SP-10; RP-3

ROO-bee

Ht: 6'1" **Wt:** 185 **Born:** 3/4/1989 **Age:** 23

			HOW MUCH HE PITCHED						WHAT HE GAVE UP										THE RESULTS							
Year	Team	Lg	G	GS	CG	GF	IP	BFP	H	R	ER	HR	SH	SF	HB	TBB	IBB	SO	WP	Bk	W	L	Pct	Sh	Sv-Op Hld	ERC	ERA
2009	Ddgrs	R	5	2	0	0	16.1	77	17	12	11	0	0	0	2	11	0	22	5	1	0	1	.000	0	0- -	-	5.08	6.06
2010	Gt Lks	A	14	5	0	8	59.1	242	49	23	21	3	0	0	5	17	0	55	7	0	4	1	.800	0	6- -	-	2.75	3.19
2010	Chatt	AA	8	8	0	0	51.0	202	38	12	8	1	3	0	1	21	0	39	2	1	3	1	.750	0	0- -	-	2.44	1.41
2011	Chatt	AA	8	8	0	0	40.0	174	30	19	12	1	1	1	2	19	0	52	1	0	2	2	.500	0	0- -	-	2.59	2.70
2011	LAD	NL	13	10	0	2	60.2	254	54	26	25	6	2	0	0	31	3	60	3	0	4	5	.444	0	0-1	1	3.94	3.71

Fautino De Los Santos

Pitches: R **Bats:** R **Pos:** RP-34

faw-TEE-no

Ht: 6'2" **Wt:** 220 **Born:** 2/15/1986 **Age:** 26

			HOW MUCH HE PITCHED						WHAT HE GAVE UP										THE RESULTS							
Year	Team	Lg	G	GS	CG	GF	IP	BFP	H	R	ER	HR	SH	SF	HB	TBB	IBB	SO	WP	Bk	W	L	Pct	Sh	Sv-Op Hld	ERC	ERA
2007	Knapol	A	21	15	0	1	97.2	384	49	33	26	5	2	6	8	36	1	121	18	3	9	4	.692	0	0- -	-	1.52	2.40
2007	WinSa	A+	5	5	0	0	24.2	99	20	12	10	3	0	0	1	7	0	32	1	0	1	1	.500	0	0- -	-	2.96	3.65
2008	Stcktn	A+	5	5	0	0	23.0	109	29	17	15	3	2	1	1	11	0	26	5	1	2	2	.500	0	0- -	-	6.28	5.87
2009	As	R	7	7	0	0	11.2	48	12	6	5	0	0	0	1	4	0	16	4	1	0	1	.000	0	0- -	-	3.87	3.86
2010	Stcktn	A+	12	0	0	7	15.2	61	13	4	4	0	0	0	0	3	0	22	0	0	1	0	1.000	0	1- -	-	1.88	2.30
2010	Mdland	AA	25	0	0	10	31.2	144	31	26	23	1	2	0	2	16	1	51	5	0	1	5	.167	0	0- -	-	3.95	6.54
2011	Mdland	AA	8	0	0	6	9.1	40	8	3	3	1	0	0	0	4	1	15	0	0	0	0	-	0	3- -	-	3.22	2.89
2011	Scrmto	AAA	15	0	0	1	19.2	86	18	4	4	0	1	0	0	12	0	21	3	0	0	0	-	0	0- -	-	3.72	1.83
2011	Oak	AL	34	0	0	8	33.1	143	27	19	16	4	2	1	0	17	1	43	9	0	3	2	.600	0	0-2	3	3.50	4.32

Sam Deduno

Pitches: R Bats: R Pos: RP-2
deh-DUE-noh
Ht: 6'3" Wt: 190 Born: 7/2/1983 Age: 28

Year	Team	Lg	G	GS	CG	GF	IP	BFP	H	R	ER	HR	SH	SF	HB	TBB	IBB	SO	WP	Bk	W	L	Pct	Sh	Sv-Op	Hld	ERC	ERA
2004	Casper	R+	15	15	0	0	76.1	331	62	40	27	3	4	3	10	32	0	118	14	0	6	4	.600	0	0--	-	3.15	3.18
2005	Ashvll	A	20	20	1	0	89.2	410	82	67	56	9	3	1	11	65	0	110	13	1	8	8	.500	0	0--	-	5.48	5.62
2006	Mdest	A+	27	26	0	0	146.1	670	121	88	78	3	4	7	22	92	0	167	34	1	5	8	.385	0	0--	-	3.89	4.80
2007	Mdest	A+	2	2	0	0	11.0	51	9	8	8	1	0	0	2	7	0	8	2	0	1	1	.500	0	0--	-	4.50	6.55
2007	Tulsa	AA	21	21	1	0	124.0	564	120	90	74	13	7	1	11	66	1	122	11	0	5	8	.385	0	0--	-	4.72	5.37
2009	Tulsa	AA	24	24	1	0	133.0	551	94	48	38	3	3	2	8	72	0	123	9	1	12	4	.750	1	0--	-	2.80	2.57
2009	ColSpr	AAA	1	1	0	0	5.2	25	5	4	4	0	0	1	0	4	0	8	1	0	0	1	.000	0	0--	-	3.91	6.35
2010	ColSpr	AAA	6	6	0	0	30.2	133	20	12	10	3	3	2	5	18	0	29	4	0	3	1	.750	0	0--	-	3.48	2.93
2010	TriCity	A-	4	4	0	0	16.1	70	18	11	10	0	1	1	1	5	0	20	0	0	0	2	.000	0	0--	-	3.87	5.51
2011	Tucsn	AAA	40	12	0	1	105.1	471	101	58	46	2	2	4	7	58	1	85	17	2	4	6	.400	0	0--	-	4.06	3.93
2010	Col	NL	4	0	0	3	2.2	12	3	1	1	1	0	0	0	1	0	3	0	0	0	0	-	0	0-0	1	6.59	3.38
2011	SD	NL	2	0	0	0	3.0	17	5	1	1	0	0	0	0	3	1	4	1	0	0	0	-	0	0-0	0	8.91	3.00
2 ML YEARS			6	0	0	3	5.2	29	8	2	2	1	0	0	0	4	1	7	1	0	0	0	-	0	0-0	1	8.02	3.18

David DeJesus

Bats: L Throws: L Pos: RF-116; CF-8; PH-5; DH-3; PR-2
Ht: 5'11" Wt: 192 Born: 12/20/1979 Age: 32

Year	Team	Lg	G	AB	H	2B	3B	HR	(Hm	Rd)	TB	R	RBI	RC	TBB	IBB	SO	HBP	SH	SF	SB	CS	SB%	GDP	Avg	OBP	Slg
2003	KC	AL	12	7	2	0	0	0	(0	0)	4	0	0	2	1	0	2	1	1	0	0	0	-	0	.286	.444	.571
2004	KC	AL	96	363	104	15	3	7	(2	5)	146	58	39	53	33	0	53	9	8	0	8	11	.42	6	.287	.360	.402
2005	KC	AL	122	461	135	31	6	9	(6	3)	205	69	56	77	42	1	76	9	5	6	5	5	.50	6	.293	.359	.445
2006	KC	AL	119	491	145	36	7	4	(4	4)	219	83	56	76	43	4	70	12	2	4	6	3	.67	10	.295	.364	.446
2007	KC	AL	157	605	157	29	9	7	(3	4)	225	101	58	87	64	7	83	**23**	7	4	10	4	.71	10	.260	.351	.372
2008	KC	AL	135	518	159	25	7	12	(6	6)	234	70	73	93	46	3	71	5	4	4	11	8	.58	10	.307	.366	.452
2009	KC	AL	144	558	157	28	9	13	(4	9)	242	74	71	83	51	0	87	8	5	5	4	9	.31	10	.281	.347	.434
2010	KC	AL	91	352	112	23	3	5	(2	3)	156	46	37	50	34	2	47	4	3	1	3	3	.50	10	.318	.384	.443
2011	Oak	AL	131	442	106	20	5	10	(4	6)	166	60	46	49	45	1	86	11	4	4	4	3	.57	14	.240	.323	.376
9 ML YEARS			1007	3797	1077	207	50	71	(31	40)	1597	561	436	570	359	18	575	82	39	28	51	46	.53	76	.284	.356	.421

Enerio Del Rosario

Pitches: R Bats: R Pos: RP-54
en-AIR-ee-oh
Ht: 6'2" Wt: 181 Born: 10/16/1985 Age: 26

Year	Team	Lg	G	GS	CG	GF	IP	BFP	H	R	ER	HR	SH	SF	HB	TBB	IBB	SO	WP	Bk	W	L	Pct	Sh	Sv-Op	Hld	ERC	ERA
2007	Billings	R+	15	15	0	0	70.1	305	77	40	31	6	4	3	1	30	0	40	6	2	5	4	.556	0	0--	-	4.79	3.97
2008	Dayton	A	19	9	1	8	70.0	269	52	19	9	3	5	1	0	11	0	49	0	1	5	2	.714	1	5--	-	1.62	1.16
2008	Srsota	A+	13	6	0	1	44.1	205	57	31	30	2	0	2	1	23	0	32	2	0	1	4	.200	0	0--	-	6.02	6.09
2009	Srsota	A+	31	0	0	17	50.0	200	40	14	11	2	2	1	5	6	0	33	1	0	2	1	.667	0	7--	-	2.00	1.98
2009	Carlina	AA	4	0	0	2	5.2	21	2	1	1	0	0	0	0	0	0	9	0	0	0	0	-	0	1--	-	0.76	1.59
2009	Lsvlle	AAA	15	0	0	7	24.2	99	24	6	3	1	0	0	0	6	0	12	2	0	1	0	1.000	0	4--	-	3.05	1.09
2010	Lsvlle	AAA	50	0	0	14	64.0	264	61	22	22	7	0	0	3	17	0	34	5	0	4	4	.500	0	4--	-	3.60	3.09
2011	OKCity	AAA	3	0	0	0	3.0	10	3	0	0	0	0	0	0	0	0	0	0	0	0	0	-	0	0--	-	2.46	0.00
2010	2 Tms	NL	11	0	0	3	10.0	51	17	7	5	0	3	1	1	4	0	4	0	0	1	1	.500	0	0-2	0	7.90	4.50
2011	Hou	NL	54	0	0	13	53.0	250	59	30	27	3	3	1	3	31	3	31	2	1	0	3	.000	0	0-2	2	5.16	4.58
10	Cin	NL	9	0	0	2	8.2	42	13	4	2	0	3	0	1	4	0	3	0	0	1	1	.500	0	0-2	0	6.48	2.08
10	Hou	NL	2	0	0	1	1.1	9	4	3	3	0	0	0	0	0	0	1	0	0	0	0	-	0	0-0	0	18.29	20.25
2 ML YEARS			65	0	0	16	63.0	301	76	37	32	3	6	2	4	35	3	35	2	1	1	4	.200	0	0-4	2	5.57	4.57

Steve Delabar

Pitches: R Bats: R Pos: RP-6
DELL-uh-bar
Ht: 6'5" Wt: 220 Born: 7/17/1983 Age: 28

Year	Team	Lg	G	GS	CG	GF	IP	BFP	H	R	ER	HR	SH	SF	HB	TBB	IBB	SO	WP	Bk	W	L	Pct	Sh	Sv-Op	Hld	ERC	ERA
2004	Casper	R	14	6	0	1	45.1	204	51	32	22	1	3	2	6	21	0	39	2	1	3	4	.429	0	0--	-	5.21	4.37
2004	Eugene	A-	3	3	0	0	17.0	69	13	7	5	1	0	1	1	3	0	11	0	0	1	1	.500	0	0--	-	1.94	2.65
2005	Eugene	A-	16	16	0	0	75.2	340	84	45	40	7	2	4	15	18	0	59	4	0	4	6	.400	0	0--	-	4.74	4.76
2006	FtWyn	A	27	27	1	0	145.0	613	129	66	55	8	1	6	7	65	0	118	12	1	8	9	.471	0	0--	-	3.59	3.41
2007	Lk Els	A+	20	0	0	5	29.0	131	26	21	18	5	0	3	2	16	1	33	3	1	2	6	.250	0	0--	-	4.73	5.59
2007	FtWyn	A	21	12	0	1	68.0	318	63	49	45	8	0	5	13	46	0	48	6	0	2	5	.286	0	0--	-	5.68	5.96
2008	FtWyn	A	11	0	0	4	13.2	59	17	8	8	0	0	0	1	5	1	12	0	0	2	1	.667	0	0--	-	5.03	5.27
2011	Hi Dsrt	A+	7	0	0	4	12.1	59	12	6	6	0	0	0	2	8	0	20	3	0	1	1	.500	0	3--	-	4.61	4.38
2011	Jacksn	AA	23	0	0	17	30.2	139	23	10	7	0	2	0	1	26	3	30	0	1	1	3	.250	0	12--	-	3.57	2.05
2011	Tacom	AAA	10	0	0	7	13.0	58	11	1	1	0	1	0	2	6	1	18	2	0	1	1	.500	0	0--	-	3.12	0.69
2011	Sea	AL	6	0	0	4	7.0	28	5	2	2	1	0	0	0	4	1	7	0	0	1	1	.500	0	0-0	0	4.15	2.57

Rob Delaney

Pitches: R Bats: L Pos: RP-4
Ht: 6'3" Wt: 220 Born: 9/8/1984 Age: 27

Year	Team	Lg	G	GS	CG	GF	IP	BFP	H	R	ER	HR	SH	SF	HB	TBB	IBB	SO	WP	Bk	W	L	Pct	Sh	Sv-Op	Hld	ERC	ERA
2006	Twins	R+	17	0	0	7	33.0	142	37	23	17	4	3	1	4	1	0	27	1	0	1	3	.250	0	2--	-	3.79	4.64
2006	FtMyrs	A+	3	0	0	2	5.0	21	7	3	3	1	0	0	0	0	0	3	0	0	0	0	-	0	0--	-	5.60	5.40
2007	Beloit	A	36	0	0	32	46.2	172	25	8	4	1	0	0	0	6	1	56	1	0	1	0	1.000	0	28--	-	0.95	0.77
2007	FtMyrs	A+	17	0	0	15	23.1	98	19	4	4	1	1	1	0	10	2	27	2	0	2	0	1.000	0	7--	-	2.65	1.54
2008	FtMyrs	A+	23	0	0	18	31.2	121	24	6	5	1	1	0	1	4	1	34	2	0	1	2	.333	0	13--	-	1.53	1.42
2008	NwBrit	AA	24	0	0	16	34.1	126	20	6	4	2	0	0	2	7	0	38	1	0	2	1	.667	0	5--	-	1.46	1.05
2009	NwBrit	AA	26	0	0	4	36.0	143	33	12	9	1	2	1	1	6	0	40	2	0	1	1	.500	0	2--	-	2.46	2.25

Year	Team	Lg	G	GS	CG	GF	IP	BFP	H	R	ER	HR	SH	SF	HB	TBB	IBB	SO	WP	Bk	W	L	Pct	Sh	Sv-Op	Hld	ERC	ERA
2009	Roch	AAA	36	0	0	23	47.2	199	43	25	24	5	2	3	0	15	2	38	2	0	7	3	.700	0	7- -	-	3.16	4.53
2010	Roch	AAA	61	0	0	31	80.0	343	82	48	42	12	5	2	1	23	5	92	4	1	7	9	.438	0	4- -	-	4.01	4.73
2011	Drham	AAA	51	0	0	27	67.2	265	51	15	14	3	3	5	0	17	2	57	1	0	4	2	.667	0	13- -	-	1.92	1.86
2010	Min	AL	1	0	0	1	1.0	5	2	1	1	1	0	0	0	1	0	0	0	0	0	0	-	0	0-0	0	27.72	9.00
2011	TB	AL	4	0	0	1	5.0	25	4	6	6	0	0	1	0	7	1	3	0	0	0	0	-	0	0-0	1	5.64	10.80
2 ML YEARS			5	0	0	2	6.0	30	6	7	7	1	0	1	0	8	1	3	0	0	0	0	-	0	0-0	1	8.59	10.50

Randall Delgado

Pitches: R **Bats:** R **Pos:** SP-7 **Ht:** 6'3" **Wt:** 200 **Born:** 2/9/1990 **Age:** 22

Year	Team	Lg	G	GS	CG	GF	IP	BFP	H	R	ER	HR	SH	SF	HB	TBB	IBB	SO	WP	Bk	W	L	Pct	Sh	Sv-Op	Hld	ERC	ERA
2008	Danvle	R	14	14	0	0	69.0	292	63	32	24	5	2	2	5	30	1	81	9	2	3	8	.273	0	0- -	-	3.89	3.13
2009	Rome	A	25	25	1	0	124.0	542	123	70	60	9	2	4	6	49	0	141	7	2	5	10	.333	0	0- -	-	3.97	4.35
2010	MrtlBh	A+	20	20	0	0	117.1	469	89	46	36	7	6	1	7	32	1	120	6	0	4	7	.364	0	0- -	-	2.32	2.76
2010	Missi	AA	8	8	0	0	43.2	190	36	26	23	2	3	3	2	20	0	42	2	0	3	5	.375	0	0- -	-	3.05	4.74
2011	Missi	AA	21	21	2	0	117.1	508	116	58	50	11	5	3	4	46	1	110	5	3	5	5	.500	0	0- -	-	4.05	3.84
2011	Gwnntt	AAA	4	4	0	0	21.2	92	19	10	10	4	0	1	0	11	0	25	2	1	2	2	.500	0	0- -	-	4.47	4.15
2011	Atl	NL	7	7	0	0	35.0	147	29	12	11	5	0	0	1	14	1	18	2	0	1	1	.500	0	0-0	0	3.48	2.83

Sam Demel

Pitches: R **Bats:** R **Pos:** RP-34   DEMM-ell   **Ht:** 6'0" **Wt:** 215 **Born:** 10/23/1985 **Age:** 26

Year	Team	Lg	G	GS	CG	GF	IP	BFP	H	R	ER	HR	SH	SF	HB	TBB	IBB	SO	WP	Bk	W	L	Pct	Sh	Sv-Op	Hld	ERC	ERA
2007	Stcktn	A+	11	0	0	2	14.0	72	16	16	11	2	1	1	2	15	1	13	4	0	0	0	-	0	0- -	-	8.79	7.07
2007	Kane	A	9	0	0	8	9.1	34	3	2	1	0	2	0	0	4	1	10	2	0	0	1	.000	0	4- -	-	0.75	0.96
2008	Stcktn	A+	54	0	0	35	67.0	307	61	31	25	1	1	2	3	32	1	90	10	0	5	2	.714	0	18- -	-	3.61	3.36
2009	Mdland	AA	27	0	0	23	29.1	121	23	5	2	1	2	0	0	9	1	26	1	0	0	2	.000	0	11- -	-	2.09	0.61
2009	Scrmto	AAA	28	0	0	10	32.1	146	27	14	13	1	3	1	1	21	4	33	5	0	2	3	.400	0	3- -	-	3.43	3.62
2010	Scrmto	AAA	22	0	0	11	28.2	116	22	6	4	1	0	2	1	9	0	28	1	0	2	0	1.000	0	6- -	-	2.26	1.26
2011	Reno	AAA	11	0	0	6	10.2	49	11	6	6	1	1	0	1	5	1	9	0	0	2	0	.000	0	1- -	-	4.57	5.06
2010	Ari	NL	37	0	0	10	37.0	165	42	27	22	5	0	1	1	12	2	33	5	0	2	1	.667	0	2-2	4	4.73	5.35
2011	Ari	NL	34	0	0	7	25.2	117	31	13	12	4	0	0	2	13	1	15	0	0	2	2	.500	0	0-1	6	6.64	4.21
2 ML YEARS			71	0	0	17	62.2	282	73	40	34	9	0	1	3	25	3	48	5	0	4	3	.571	0	2-3	10	5.49	4.88

Ryan Dempster

Pitches: R **Bats:** R **Pos:** SP-34 **Ht:** 6'2" **Wt:** 215 **Born:** 5/3/1977 **Age:** 35

Year	Team	Lg	G	GS	CG	GF	IP	BFP	H	R	ER	HR	SH	SF	HB	TBB	IBB	SO	WP	Bk	W	L	Pct	Sh	Sv-Op	Hld	ERC	ERA
1998	Fla	NL	14	11	0	1	54.2	272	72	47	43	6	5	6	9	38	1	35	5	0	1	5	.167	0	0-1	0	8.14	7.08
1999	Fla	NL	25	25	0	0	147.0	666	146	77	77	21	3	6	6	93	2	126	8	0	7	8	.467	0	0-0	0	5.49	4.71
2000	Fla	NL	33	33	2	0	226.1	974	210	102	92	30	4	5	5	97	7	209	4	0	14	10	.583	1	0-0	0	4.04	3.66
2001	Fla	NL	34	34	2	0	211.1	954	218	123	116	21	15	7	10	112	5	171	5	0	15	12	.556	1	0-0	0	4.91	4.94
2002	2 Tms	NL	33	33	4	0	209.0	915	228	127	125	28	9	6	10	93	2	153	2	0	10	13	.435	0	0-0	0	5.35	5.38
2003	Cin	NL	22	20	0	1	115.2	545	134	89	84	14	9	4	5	70	4	84	3	0	3	7	.300	0	0-0	0	6.11	6.54
2004	ChC	NL	23	0	0	8	20.2	93	16	9	9	1	1	0	2	13	0	18	1	0	1	1	.500	0	2-3	3	3.61	3.92
2005	ChC	NL	63	6	0	53	92.0	401	83	35	32	4	5	0	4	49	7	89	4	0	5	3	.625	0	33-35	0	3.69	3.13
2006	ChC	NL	74	0	0	64	75.0	342	77	47	40	5	5	4	3	36	3	67	6	0	1	9	.100	0	24-33	2	4.26	4.80
2007	ChC	NL	66	0	0	58	66.2	282	59	36	35	8	3	2	1	30	4	55	2	1	2	7	.222	0	28-31	5	3.77	4.73
2008	ChC	NL	33	33	1	0	206.2	856	174	75	68	14	4	3	7	76	1	187	5	0	17	6	.739	0	0-0	0	3.03	2.96
2009	ChC	NL	31	31	1	0	200.0	842	196	94	81	22	10	8	6	65	4	172	11	0	11	9	.550	1	0-0	0	3.87	3.65
2010	ChC	NL	34	34	1	0	215.1	918	198	110	92	25	9	2	10	86	4	208	6	0	15	12	.556	0	0-0	0	3.91	3.85
2011	ChC	NL	34	34	0	0	202.1	881	211	111	108	23	12	3	5	82	2	191	7	0	10	14	.417	0	0-0	0	4.55	4.80
02	Fla	NL	18	18	3	0	120.1	521	126	66	64	12	7	3	7	55	1	87	0	0	5	8	.385	0	0-0	0	4.95	4.79
02	Cin	NL	15	15	1	0	88.2	394	102	61	61	16	2	3	3	38	1	66	2	0	5	5	.500	0	0-0	0	5.90	6.19
Postseason			2	1	0	1	5.2	27	4	4	4	1	0	0	0	7	0	4	0	0	0	1	.000	0	0-0	0	6.45	6.35
14 ML YEARS			519	294	11	185	2042.2	8941	2022	1082	1002	222	94	56	83	940	46	1765	69	1	112	116	.491	3	87-102	5	4.46	4.41

Chris Denorfia

Bats: R **Throws:** R **Pos:** RF-62; LF-34; PH-25; CF-15; PR-4   denn-ORE-fee-ah   **Ht:** 6'0" **Wt:** 204 **Born:** 7/15/1980 **Age:** 31

Year	Team	Lg	G	AB	H	2B	3B	HR	(Hm	Rd)	TB	R	RBI	RC	TBB	IBB	SO	HBP	SH	SF	SB	CS	SB%	GDP	Avg	OBP	Slg
2011	Tucsn*	AAA	7	17	2	1	0	0	(-	-)	3	0	0	0	3	0	4	0	0	0	0	0	-	0	.118	.250	.176
2011	Lk Els*	A+	2	6	4	1	0	0	(-	-)	5	1	2	2	0	0	1	0	0	0	0	0	-	0	.667	.667	.833
2005	Cin	NL	18	38	10	3	0	1	(1	0)	16	8	2	6	6	0	9	0	0	0	1	0	1.00	1	.263	.364	.421
2006	Cin	NL	49	106	30	6	0	1	(0	1)	39	14	7	13	11	1	21	1	2	0	1	1	.50	1	.283	.356	.368
2008	Oak	AL	29	62	18	3	0	1	(0	1)	24	10	9	9	6	0	16	1	2	0	2	0	1.00	3	.290	.362	.387
2009	Oak	AL	4	2	0	0	0	0	(0	0)	0	1	1	0	0	0	0	0	0	0	0	0	-	0	.000	.000	.000
2010	SD	NL	99	284	77	15	2	9	(3	6)	123	41	36	37	22	3	51	1	3	2	8	4	.67	5	.271	.335	.433
2011	SD	NL	111	307	85	13	2	5	(4	1)	117	38	19	34	28	1	49	1	2	2	11	6	.65	10	.277	.337	.381
6 ML YEARS			310	799	220	40	4	17	(5	12)	319	112	74	96	78	5	146	5	7	5	23	11	.68	20	.275	.342	.399

Mark DeRosa

Bats: R **Throws:** R **Pos:** PH-22; 3B-16; 1B-10; 2B-2   **Ht:** 6'0" **Wt:** 211 **Born:** 2/26/1975 **Age:** 37

Year	Team	Lg	G	AB	H	2B	3B	HR	(Hm	Rd)	TB	R	RBI	RC	TBB	IBB	SO	HBP	SH	SF	SB	CS	SB%	GDP	Avg	OBP	Slg
2011	Fresno*	AAA	11	42	13	1	0	0	(-	-)	14	6	3	4	0	0	8	0	1	0	0	0	-	2	.310	.310	.333
2011	SnJos*	A+	2	5	2	1	0	0	(-	-)	3	2	0	1	1	0	1	0	0	0	0	0	-	0	.400	.500	.600
1998	Atl	NL	5	3	1	0	0	0	(0	0)	1	2	0	0	0	0	1	0	0	0	0	0	-	0	.333	.333	.333
1999	Atl	NL	7	8	0	0	0	0	(0	0)	0	0	0	0	0	0	2	0	0	0	0	0	-	0	.000	.000	.000
2000	Atl	NL	22	13	4	1	0	0	(0	0)	5	9	3	2	2	0	1	0	0	0	0	0	-	0	.308	.400	.385
2001	Atl	NL	66	164	47	8	0	3	(3	0)	64	27	20	22	12	6	19	5	1	2	2	1	.67	3	.287	.350	.390
2002	Atl	NL	72	212	63	9	2	5	(3	2)	91	24	23	27	12	3	24	3	2	3	2	3	.40	5	.297	.339	.429
2003	Atl	NL	103	266	70	14	0	6	(3	3)	102	40	22	28	16	0	49	5	0	1	1	0	1.00	5	.263	.316	.383
2004	Atl	NL	118	309	74	16	0	3	(0	3)	99	33	31	24	23	3	53	3	4	6	1	3	.25	6	.239	.293	.320
2005	Tex	AL	66	148	36	5	0	8	(7	1)	65	26	20	20	16	0	35	2	0	0	1	0	1.00	5	.243	.325	.439
2006	Tex	AL	136	520	154	40	2	13	(5	8)	237	78	74	78	44	1	102	6	0	2	4	4	.50	13	.296	.357	.456
2007	ChC	NL	149	502	147	28	3	10	(5	5)	211	64	72	76	58	2	93	7	3	4	1	2	.33	17	.293	.371	.420
2008	ChC	NL	149	505	144	30	3	21	(11	10)	243	103	87	95	69	0	106	9	2	8	6	0	1.00	9	.285	.376	.481
2009	2 Tms		139	515	129	23	1	23	(11	12)	223	78	78	68	47	1	121	7	2	5	3	2	.60	11	.250	.319	.433
2010	SF	NL	26	93	18	3	0	1	(0	1)	24	9	10	6	9	0	16	2	0	0	0	2	.00	6	.194	.279	.258
2011	SF	NL	47	86	24	2	0	0	(0	0)	26	9	12	10	8	0	18	2	0	1	1	1	.50	4	.279	.351	.302
09	Cle	AL	71	278	75	13	0	13	(8	5)	127	47	50	45	29	1	63	3	1	3	1	1	.50	6	.270	.342	.457
09	StL	NL	68	237	54	10	1	10	(3	7)	96	31	28	23	18	0	58	4	1	2	2	1	.67	5	.228	.291	.405
	Postseason		22	53	19	6	1	1	(1	0)	30	8	10	7	4	0	8	1	0	0	0	0	-	2	.358	.414	.566
14 ML YEARS			1105	3344	911	179	11	93	(48	45)	1391	502	452	456	316	16	640	51	14	32	22	18	.55	85	.272	.341	.416

Daniel Descalso

Bats: L **Throws:** R **Pos:** 3B-117; PH-26; 2B-18; SS-13; PR-8   dess-CAL-so   **Ht:** 5'10" **Wt:** 190 **Born:** 10/19/1986 **Age:** 25

Year	Team	Lg	G	AB	H	2B	3B	HR	(Hm	Rd)	TB	R	RBI	RC	TBB	IBB	SO	HBP	SH	SF	SB	CS	SB%	GDP	Avg	OBP	Slg
2007	Batvia	A-	66	250	67	7	5	0	(-	-)	84	29	31	33	26	0	37	5	0	2	12	3	.80	6	.268	.346	.336
2008	PlmBh	A+	115	403	98	24	2	8	(-	-)	150	57	50	49	33	3	53	10	5	5	7	7	.50	11	.243	.313	.372
2008	Sprgfld	AA	9	37	13	1	1	0	(-	-)	16	6	4	6	3	1	3	1	0	1	1	1	.50	1	.351	.405	.432
2009	Sprgfld	AA	73	288	93	26	5	8	(-	-)	153	46	51	59	31	1	41	4	1	0	0	1	.00	7	.323	.396	.531
2009	Memp	AAA	46	150	38	4	0	2	(-	-)	48	23	17	17	16	0	21	1	4	1	3	0	1.00	3	.253	.327	.320
2010	Memp	AAA	116	468	132	32	3	9	(-	-)	197	86	71	73	47	1	48	5	5	6	8	4	.67	13	.282	.350	.421
2010	StL	NL	11	34	9	2	0	0	(0	0)	11	6	4	5	2	0	6	1	0	0	1	0	1.00	1	.265	.324	.324
2011	StL	NL	148	326	86	20	3	1	(1	0)	115	35	28	40	33	9	65	3	10	3	2	2	.50	3	.264	.334	.353
2 ML YEARS			159	360	95	22	3	1	(1	0)	126	41	32	45	35	9	71	4	10	3	3	2	.60	3	.264	.333	.350

Ian Desmond

Bats: R **Throws:** R **Pos:** SS-152; PH-4; PR-1   **Ht:** 6'2" **Wt:** 210 **Born:** 9/20/1985 **Age:** 26

Year	Team	Lg	G	AB	H	2B	3B	HR	(Hm	Rd)	TB	R	RBI	RC	TBB	IBB	SO	HBP	SH	SF	SB	CS	SB%	GDP	Avg	OBP	Slg
2009	Was	NL	21	82	23	7	2	4	(2	2)	46	9	12	10	5	0	14	0	1	1	1	0	1.00	2	.280	.318	.561
2010	Was	NL	154	525	141	27	4	10	(8	2)	206	59	65	58	28	3	109	5	9	7	17	5	.77	9	.269	.308	.392
2011	Was	NL	154	584	148	27	5	8	(7	1)	209	65	49	65	35	2	139	4	11	5	25	10	.71	9	.253	.298	.358
3 ML YEARS			329	1191	312	61	11	22	(17	5)	461	133	126	133	68	5	262	9	21	13	43	15	.74	20	.262	.304	.387

Ross Detwiler

Pitches: L **Bats:** R **Pos:** SP-10; RP-5   DETT-why-lerr   **Ht:** 6'5" **Wt:** 174 **Born:** 3/6/1986 **Age:** 26

			HOW MUCH HE PITCHED					WHAT HE GAVE UP										THE RESULTS						
Year	Team	Lg	G	GS	CG	GF	IP	BFP	H	R	ER	HR	SH	SF	HB	TBB	IBB	SO	WP	Bk	W	L	Pct	Sh	Sv-Op Hld	ERC	ERA
2011	Syrcse*		16	16	0	0	87.1	380	98	48	44	4	1	2	1	32	1	63	2	0	6	6	.500	0	0- - -	4.31	4.53
2007	Was	NL	1	0	0	1	1.0	4	0	0	0	0	0	0	0	0	0	1	0	0	0	0	-	0	0-0 0	0.00	0.00
2009	Was	NL	15	14	1	0	75.2	341	87	43	42	3	4	1	2	33	3	43	4	0	1	6	.143	0	0-0 0	4.65	5.00
2010	Was	NL	8	5	0	1	29.2	135	34	22	14	5	2	0	1	14	1	17	1	0	1	3	.250	0	0-0 0	5.83	4.25
2011	Was	NL	15	10	0	1	66.0	277	63	26	22	7	7	3	3	20	2	41	2	0	4	5	.444	0	0-0 1	3.64	3.00
4 ML YEARS			39	29	1	2	172.1	757	184	91	78	15	13	4	6	67	6	102	7	0	6	14	.300	0	0-0 1	4.40	4.07

Joey Devine

Pitches: R **Bats:** R **Pos:** RP-26   **Ht:** 6'0" **Wt:** 235 **Born:** 9/19/1983 **Age:** 28

			HOW MUCH HE PITCHED					WHAT HE GAVE UP										THE RESULTS						
Year	Team	Lg	G	GS	CG	GF	IP	BFP	H	R	ER	HR	SH	SF	HB	TBB	IBB	SO	WP	Bk	W	L	Pct	Sh	Sv-Op Hld	ERC	ERA
2011	Scrmto*	AAA	23	0	0	6	23.1	98	15	12	11	2	1	1	5	9	0	35	3	0	4	0	1.000	0	3- - -	2.80	4.24
2005	Atl	NL	5	0	0	1	5.0	26	6	7	7	2	0	0	0	5	1	3	0	0	0	1	.000	0	0-0 1	9.97	12.60
2006	Atl	NL	10	0	0	1	6.1	36	8	7	7	1	0	0	1	9	1	10	4	1	0	0	-	0	0-1 0	11.11	9.95
2007	Atl	NL	10	0	0	5	8.1	39	7	1	1	0	1	1	0	8	2	7	1	0	1	0	1.000	0	0-0 0	4.08	1.08
2008	Oak	AL	42	0	0	10	45.2	170	23	7	3	0	1	1	0	15	2	49	0	0	6	1	.857	0	1-2 11	1.09	0.59
2011	Oak	AL	26	0	0	3	23.0	100	18	9	9	0	1	2	2	11	0	20	0	0	1	1	.500	0	0-1 7	2.76	2.35
	Postseason		3	0	0	1	1.2	10	3	2	2	1	0	0	1	1	1	3	0	0	0	1	.000	0	0-0 0	16.60	10.80
5 ML YEARS			93	0	0	20	88.1	371	62	31	27	3	3	4	3	48	6	89	5	1	8	3	.727	0	1-4 19	2.60	2.75

Blake DeWitt

Bats: L Throws: R Pos: PH-71; LF-23; 2B-19; 3B-14   Ht: 5'11" Wt: 199 Born: 8/20/1985 Age: 26

Year	Team	Lg	G	AB	H	2B	3B	HR	(Hm	Rd)	TB	R	RBI	RC	TBB	IBB	SO	HBP	SH	SF	SB	CS	SB%	GDP	Avg	OBP	Slg
2008	LAD	NL	117	368	97	13	2	9	(5	4)	141	45	52	51	45	9	68	3	0	5	3	0	1.00	6	.264	.344	.383
2009	LAD	NL	31	49	10	3	0	2	(1	1)	19	4	4	1	3	0	7	0	0	1	0	0	-	2	.204	.245	.388
2010	2 Tms	NL	135	440	115	24	5	5	(4	1)	164	47	52	62	47	8	86	4	2	3	3	2	.60	5	.261	.336	.373
2011	ChC	NL	121	230	61	11	4	5	(2	3)	95	21	26	25	12	1	31	1	0	0	1	0	1.00	6	.265	.305	.413
10	LAD	NL	82	256	69	15	4	1	(1	0)	95	29	30	36	30	4	49	3	2	1	2	2	.50	4	.270	.352	.371
10	ChC	NL	53	184	46	9	1	4	(3	1)	69	18	22	26	17	4	37	1	0	2	1	0	1.00	1	.250	.314	.375
Postseason			8	24	4	2	1	0	(0	0)	8	2	6	0	1	0	6	0	0	1	0	0	-	3	.167	.192	.333
4 ML YEARS			404	1087	283	51	11	21	(12	9)	419	117	134	139	107	18	192	8	2	9	7	2	.78	19	.260	.329	.385

Scott Diamond

Pitches: L Bats: L Pos: SP-7   Ht: 6'3" Wt: 215 Born: 7/30/1986 Age: 25

Year	Team	Lg	G	GS	CG	GF	IP	BFP	H	R	ER	HR	SH	SF	HB	TBB	IBB	SO	WP	Bk	W	L	Pct	Sh	Sv-Op	Hld	ERC	ERA
2008	Rome	A	9	9	0	0	52.2	210	47	20	18	2	0	2	1	11	0	38	1	0	3	1	.750	0	0- -	-	2.52	3.08
2008	MrtlBh	A+	17	15	1	0	100.0	425	95	42	31	6	4	2	4	28	0	85	6	0	12	2	.857	1	0- -	-	3.17	2.79
2009	Missi	AA	23	23	0	0	131.0	583	152	68	54	5	6	5	2	53	0	111	4	0	5	10	.333	0	0- -	-	4.63	3.50
2010	Missi	AA	17	17	0	0	102.1	442	113	45	40	4	4	4	2	40	1	89	5	0	4	6	.400	0	0- -	-	4.34	3.52
2010	Gwnntt	AAA	10	10	1	0	56.1	226	53	25	21	2	3	3	1	15	0	33	4	0	4	1	.800	1	0- -	-	3.00	3.36
2011	Roch	AAA	23	23	2	0	123.0	553	158	85	76	11	2	6	1	36	2	90	4	1	4	14	.222	0	0- -	-	5.19	5.56
2011	Min	AL	7	7	0	0	39.0	181	51	25	22	3	2	1	0	17	3	19	3	0	1	5	.167	0	0-0	0	5.69	5.08

Matt Diaz

Bats: R Throws: R Pos: RF-54; PH-54; LF-18; DH-2   DYE-azz   Ht: 6'1" Wt: 215 Born: 3/3/1978 Age: 34

Year	Team	Lg	G	AB	H	2B	3B	HR	(Hm	Rd)	TB	R	RBI	RC	TBB	IBB	SO	HBP	SH	SF	SB	CS	SB%	GDP	Avg	OBP	Slg
2003	TB	AL	4	9	1	0	0	0	(0	0)	1	2	0	0	1	0	3	0	0	0	0	0	-	0	.111	.200	.111
2004	TB	AL	10	21	4	1	1	1	(1	0)	10	3	3	2	1	0	6	2	0	0	0	0	-	0	.190	.292	.476
2005	KC	AL	34	89	25	4	2	1	(0	1)	36	7	9	11	4	0	15	2	1	1	0	1	.00	3	.281	.323	.404
2006	Atl	NL	124	297	97	15	4	7	(3	4)	141	37	32	40	11	3	49	9	1	4	5	5	.50	9	.327	.364	.475
2007	Atl	NL	135	358	121	21	0	12	(5	7)	178	44	45	53	16	3	63	4	1	5	4	0	1.00	8	.338	.368	.497
2008	Atl	NL	43	135	33	2	0	2	(2	0)	41	9	14	10	3	0	32	1	0	1	4	2	.67	4	.244	.264	.304
2009	Atl	NL	125	371	116	18	4	13	(4	9)	181	56	58	67	35	2	90	13	5	1	12	5	.71	14	.313	.390	.488
2010	Atl	NL	84	224	56	17	2	7	(5	2)	98	27	31	30	13	3	44	4	2	1	3	1	.75	6	.250	.302	.438
2011	2 Tms	NL	116	251	66	13	1	0	(0	0)	81	16	20	20	12	0	52	3	0	2	5	2	.71	11	.263	.302	.323
11	Pit	NL	100	216	56	12	1	0	(0	0)	70	14	19	19	11	0	44	3	0	1	4	2	.67	8	.259	.303	.324
11	Atl	NL	16	35	10	1	0	0	(0	0)	11	2	1	1	1	0	8	0	0	1	1	0	1.00	3	.286	.297	.314
Postseason			4	10	1	0	0	0	(0	0)	1	0	0	0	0	0	2	0	0	0	0	0	-	0	.100	.100	.100
9 ML YEARS			675	1755	519	91	14	43	(20	23)	767	201	212	233	96	11	354	38	10	15	33	16	.67	55	.296	.343	.437

Chris Dickerson

Bats: L Throws: L Pos: RF-42; LF-14; PR-9; PH-4; DH-1   Ht: 6'3" Wt: 228 Born: 4/10/1982 Age: 30

Year	Team	Lg	G	AB	H	2B	3B	HR	(Hm	Rd)	TB	R	RBI	RC	TBB	IBB	SO	HBP	SH	SF	SB	CS	SB%	GDP	Avg	OBP	Slg
2011	S-WB*	AAA	57	212	51	10	1	2	(-	-)	69	33	16	28	30	1	63	3	1	1	18	4	.82	1	.241	.341	.325
2008	Cin	NL	31	102	31	9	2	6	(4	2)	62	20	15	22	17	0	35	2	1	0	5	3	.63	0	.304	.413	.608
2009	Cin	NL	97	255	70	13	3	2	(0	2)	95	31	15	34	39	1	66	1	2	2	11	3	.79	3	.275	.370	.373
2010	2 Tms	NL	45	97	20	2	2	0	(0	0)	26	11	5	6	6	0	34	0	2	1	4	0	1.00	1	.206	.250	.268
2011	NYY	AL	60	50	13	2	0	1	(0	1)	18	9	7	6	2	0	17	1	1	1	4	0	1.00	1	.260	.296	.360
10	Cin	NL	20	44	9	1	1	0	(0	0)	12	9	0	3	1	0	19	0	0	0	3	0	1.00	0	.205	.222	.273
10	Mil	NL	25	53	11	1	1	0	(0	0)	14	2	5	3	5	0	15	0	2	1	1	0	1.00	0	.208	.271	.264
4 ML YEARS			233	504	134	26	7	9	(4	5)	201	71	42	68	64	1	152	4	6	4	24	6	.80	5	.266	.351	.399

R.A. Dickey

Pitches: R Bats: R Pos: SP-32; RP-1   Ht: 6'2" Wt: 216 Born: 10/29/1974 Age: 37

Year	Team	Lg	G	GS	CG	GF	IP	BFP	H	R	ER	HR	SH	SF	HB	TBB	IBB	SO	WP	Bk	W	L	Pct	Sh	Sv-Op	Hld	ERC	ERA
2001	Tex	AL	4	0	0	1	12.0	53	13	9	9	3	0	0	0	7	1	4	1	0	0	1	.000	0	0-0	0	6.57	6.75
2003	Tex	AL	38	13	1	6	116.2	513	135	68	66	16	4	3	5	38	5	94	5	2	9	8	.529	1	1-1	3	5.09	5.09
2004	Tex	AL	25	15	0	2	104.1	480	136	77	65	17	3	3	4	33	1	57	5	1	6	7	.462	0	1-1	0	6.08	5.61
2005	Tex	AL	9	4	0	0	29.2	134	29	23	22	4	0	1	2	17	0	15	2	0	1	2	.333	0	0-0	0	5.18	6.67
2006	Tex	AL	1	1	0	0	3.1	18	8	7	7	6	0	0	0	1	0	1	0	0	1	0	1.000	0	0-0	0	32.05	18.90
2008	Sea	AL	32	14	0	9	112.1	500	124	66	65	15	4	6	2	51	4	58	11	1	5	8	.385	0	0-0	0	5.19	5.21
2009	Min	AL	35	1	0	13	64.1	293	74	34	33	8	2	2	4	30	1	42	4	0	1	1	.500	0	0-0	1	5.66	4.62
2010	NYM	NL	27	26	2	0	174.1	713	165	62	55	13	7	3	4	42	3	104	11	0	11	9	.550	1	0-0	1	3.11	2.84
2011	NYM	NL	33	32	1	0	208.2	876	202	85	76	18	**16**	7	9	54	2	134	9	1	8	13	.381	0	0-0	1	3.40	3.28
9 ML YEARS			204	106	4	33	825.2	3580	886	430	398	100	36	25	30	273	17	509	48	5	41	50	.451	2	2-2	6	4.49	4.34

Brandon Dickson

Pitches: R Bats: R Pos: RP-3; SP-1   Ht: 6'5" Wt: 190 Born: 11/3/1984 Age: 27

Year	Team	Lg	G	GS	CG	GF	IP	BFP	H	R	ER	HR	SH	SF	HB	TBB	IBB	SO	WP	Bk	W	L	Pct	Sh	Sv-Op	Hld	ERC	ERA
2006	JhsCty	R+	9	0	0	1	11.1	56	16	11	8	1	0	0	0	6	0	15	0	0	1	0	1.000	0	1--	-	6.83	6.35
2007	QuadC	A	31	23	0	4	144.0	626	148	74	56	9	2	2	12	41	1	84	11	0	11	7	.611	0	1--	-	3.78	3.50
2008	PlmBh	A+	23	17	1	1	115.1	488	119	49	45	7	3	3	2	37	0	66	5	0	7	8	.467	0	1--	-	3.78	3.51
2008	Sprgfld	AA	6	6	0	0	29.1	141	42	23	22	3	0	2	2	16	0	21	0	0	3	2	.600	0	0--	-	7.84	6.75
2009	Sprgfld	AA	28	20	1	2	147.2	637	160	75	62	12	6	3	7	50	3	112	9	0	8	10	.444	1	0--	-	4.39	3.78
2010	Memp	AAA	28	27	0	1	167.0	721	180	77	60	11	5	3	9	53	1	137	7	0	11	8	.579	0	0--	-	4.18	3.23
2011	Memp	AAA	26	25	1	0	157.1	656	169	75	69	22	5	4	4	32	1	124	5	1	8	9	.471	0	0--	-	4.13	3.95
2011	StL	NL	4	1	0	0	8.1	34	9	3	3	2	0	0	0	3	0	7	0	0	0	0	-	0	0-0	0	5.77	3.24

Mark DiFelice

Pitches: R Bats: R Pos: RP-3   Ht: 6'2" Wt: 181 Born: 8/23/1976 Age: 35

Year	Team	Lg	G	GS	CG	GF	IP	BFP	H	R	ER	HR	SH	SF	HB	TBB	IBB	SO	WP	Bk	W	L	Pct	Sh	Sv-Op	Hld	ERC	ERA
2011	Nashv*	AAA	17	3	0	10	29.0	117	25	7	7	3	0	0	1	6	1	31	1	0	2	1	.667	0	6--	-	2.72	2.17
2008	Mil	NL	15	0	0	5	19.0	78	17	7	6	4	0	0	0	4	0	20	1	0	1	0	1.000	0	0-0	1	3.39	2.84
2009	Mil	NL	59	0	0	9	51.2	219	49	21	21	6	3	0	1	15	6	48	1	0	4	1	.800	0	0-1	9	3.63	3.66
2011	Mil	NL	3	0	0	1	3.0	14	3	4	4	1	0	0	0	2	0	3	0	0	0	0	-	0	0-0	0	6.85	12.00
	3 ML YEARS		77	0	0	15	73.2	311	69	32	31	11	3	0	1	21	6	71	2	0	5	1	.833	0	0-1	10	3.48	3.79

Tim Dillard

Pitches: R Bats: R Pos: RP-24   Ht: 6'4" Wt: 223 Born: 7/19/1983 Age: 28

Year	Team	Lg	G	GS	CG	GF	IP	BFP	H	R	ER	HR	SH	SF	HB	TBB	IBB	SO	WP	Bk	W	L	Pct	Sh	Sv-Op	Hld	ERC	ERA
2011	Nashv*	AAA	17	0	0	3	37.2	152	31	19	15	3	1	0	2	13	1	30	0	0	4	2	.667	0	1--	-	3.04	3.58
2008	Mil	NL	13	0	0	5	14.1	65	17	12	7	2	0	1	0	6	2	5	1	0	0	0	-	0	0-0	1	5.24	4.40
2009	Mil	NL	2	0	0	0	4.1	23	7	6	6	1	0	1	0	5	1	1	0	0	0	1	.000	0	0-1	0	12.99	12.46
2011	Mil	NL	24	0	0	11	28.2	117	26	13	13	3	2	1	2	4	0	27	2	0	1	1	.500	0	0-0	1	2.85	4.08
	3 ML YEARS		39	0	0	16	47.1	205	50	31	26	6	2	3	2	15	3	33	3	0	1	2	.333	0	0-1	2	4.31	4.94

Brian Dinkelman

Bats: L Throws: R Pos: 2B-11; LF-5; RF-5; DH-2; PH-2   Ht: 5'11" Wt: 195 Born: 11/10/1983 Age: 28

Year	Team	Lg	G	AB	H	2B	3B	HR	(Hm	Rd)	TB	R	RBI	RC	TBB	IBB	SO	HBP	SH	SF	SB	CS	SB%	GDP	Avg	OBP	Slg
2006	Elizab	R+	46	188	56	11	0	4	(-	-)	79	24	32	27	10	0	29	2	2	1	2	1	.67	3	.298	.338	.420
2007	Beloit	A	67	240	68	16	6	7	(-	-)	117	48	21	47	30	2	34	5	2	1	10	0	1.00	4	.283	.373	.488
2007	FtMyrs	A+	64	247	63	7	4	6	(-	-)	96	56	21	38	36	0	43	5	4	0	8	3	.73	7	.255	.361	.389
2008	FtMyrs	A+	63	232	68	18	2	2	(-	-)	96	44	19	43	33	4	28	8	1	0	10	1	.91	1	.293	.399	.414
2008	NwBrit	AA	52	198	49	14	2	2	(-	-)	73	26	21	22	10	1	24	5	2	1	2	2	.50	3	.247	.299	.369
2009	NwBrit	AA	129	459	136	38	2	8	(-	-)	202	62	65	81	55	1	73	13	10	5	5	6	.45	11	.296	.383	.440
2010	Roch	AAA	137	525	139	32	2	8	(-	-)	199	58	54	71	52	6	99	6	6	3	9	4	.69	10	.265	.336	.379
2011	Roch	AAA	127	469	114	27	1	3	(-	-)	152	54	41	52	45	4	92	7	1	4	7	2	.78	8	.243	.316	.324
2011	Min	AL	23	73	22	1	0	0	(0	0)	23	5	4	8	4	2	14	1	0	0	2	0	1.00	0	.301	.346	.315

Andy Dirks

Bats: L Throws: L Pos: LF-38; RF-22; CF-16; PH-10; PR-4; DH-2   Ht: 6'0" Wt: 195 Born: 1/24/1986 Age: 26

Year	Team	Lg	G	AB	H	2B	3B	HR	(Hm	Rd)	TB	R	RBI	RC	TBB	IBB	SO	HBP	SH	SF	SB	CS	SB%	GDP	Avg	OBP	Slg
2008	WMich	A	3	10	1	0	0	0	(-	-)	1	0	2	0	1	0	2	0	0	0	0	0	-	0	.100	.182	.100
2008	Tigers	R	10	34	14	3	2	0	(-	-)	21	10	7	9	3	1	6	0	0	1	2	0	1.00	0	.412	.447	.618
2009	Lkland	A+	27	103	34	5	0	0	(-	-)	39	11	18	18	13	0	11	1	0	0	10	2	.83	2	.330	.410	.379
2009	Erie	AA	98	361	92	14	1	6	(-	-)	126	46	44	44	36	2	61	3	2	6	11	5	.69	2	.255	.323	.349
2010	Erie	AA	98	388	108	20	2	11	(-	-)	165	64	46	61	35	2	59	5	1	5	19	4	.83	8	.278	.342	.425
2010	Toledo	AAA	22	88	33	10	1	4	(-	-)	57	14	17	21	3	0	12	1	0	1	3	0	1.00	1	.375	.398	.648
2011	Toledo	AAA	41	157	51	8	1	7	(-	-)	82	30	24	31	12	0	28	0	1	2	12	2	.86	1	.325	.368	.522
2011	Det	AL	78	219	55	13	0	7	(6	1)	89	34	28	27	11	1	36	3	2	0	5	2	.71	3	.251	.296	.406

Greg Dobbs

Bats: L Throws: R Pos: 3B-100; PH-30; 1B-4; RF-4; LF-3; DH-2   Ht: 6'1" Wt: 207 Born: 7/2/1978 Age: 33

Year	Team	Lg	G	AB	H	2B	3B	HR	(Hm	Rd)	TB	R	RBI	RC	TBB	IBB	SO	HBP	SH	SF	SB	CS	SB%	GDP	Avg	OBP	Slg
2004	Sea	AL	18	53	12	1	0	1	(1	0)	16	4	9	5	1	0	14	1	0	1	0	0	-	0	.226	.250	.302
2005	Sea	AL	59	142	35	7	1	1	(0	1)	47	8	20	16	9	3	25	0	1	2	1	0	1.00	4	.246	.288	.331
2006	Sea	AL	23	27	10	3	1	0	(0	0)	15	4	3	5	0	0	4	1	0	0	0	1	.00	0	.370	.393	.556
2007	Phi	NL	142	324	88	20	4	10	(5	5)	146	45	55	42	29	4	67	1	0	4	3	0	1.00	7	.272	.330	.451
2008	Phi	NL	128	226	68	14	1	9	(3	6)	111	30	40	38	11	1	40	1	0	2	3	1	.75	4	.301	.333	.491
2009	Phi	NL	97	154	38	6	0	5	(3	2)	59	15	20	15	11	1	29	1	0	3	1	0	1.00	2	.247	.296	.383
2010	Phi	NL	88	163	32	7	0	5	(2	3)	54	13	15	14	12	1	39	0	1	0	1	1	.50	2	.196	.251	.331
2011	Fla	NL	134	411	113	20	0	8	(2	6)	160	38	49	40	22	3	83	1	2	3	0	0	-	12	.275	.311	.389
	Postseason		16	21	7	1	0	0	(0	0)	8	2	0	2	3	2	6	0	0	0	0	0	-	0	.333	.417	.381
	8 ML YEARS		689	1500	396	81	7	39	(16	23)	608	157	211	175	95	13	301	6	4	15	9	3	.75	31	.264	.308	.405

Rafael Dolis

Pitches: R **Bats:** R **Pos:** RP-1   DOE-leese   **Ht:** 6'4" **Wt:** 215 **Born:** 1/10/1988 **Age:** 24

			HOW	MUCH	HE	PITCHED			WHAT	HE	GAVE	UP								THE	RESULTS					
Year	Team	Lg	G	GS	CG	GF	IP	BFP	H	R	ER	HR	SH	SF	HB	TBB	IBB	SO	WP	Bk	W	L	Pct	Sh	Sv-Op	Hld	ERC	ERA
2006	Cubs	R	13	3	0	1	25.0	125	30	27	23	1	1	1	4	16	0	33	4	0	0	2	.000	0	0- -	-	6.23	8.28
2007	Peoria	A	6	6	0	0	30.0	121	23	7	6	1	1	1	4	16	0	24	3	0	3	1	.750	0	0- -	-	3.03	1.80
2009	Dytona	A+	27	25	0	0	99.2	420	78	46	42	4	4	3	7	53	0	75	8	1	3	9	.250	0	0- -	-	3.31	3.79
2010	Dytona	A+	14	13	0	1	71.0	299	63	31	23	3	4	3	2	30	0	48	3	1	4	5	.444	0	0- -	-	3.29	2.92
2010	Tenn	AA	12	12	0	0	55.1	251	65	32	25	3	1	2	1	27	0	45	7	0	5	4	.556	0	0- -	-	5.20	4.07
2011	Tenn	AA	51	4	0	36	72.2	313	61	36	26	2	5	1	3	35	1	48	6	0	8	5	.615	0	17- -	-	3.11	3.22
2011	ChC	NL	1	0	0	0	1.1	4	0	0	0	0	0	0	0	1	0	1	0	0	0	0	-	0	0-0	0	0.71	0.00

Matt Dominguez

Bats: R **Throws:** R **Pos:** 3B-16; PH-1   **Ht:** 6'1" **Wt:** 205 **Born:** 8/28/1989 **Age:** 22

							BATTING																BASERUNNING				AVERAGES		
Year	Team	Lg	G	AB	H	2B	3B	HR	(Hm	Rd)	TB	R	RBI	RC	TBB	IBB	SO	HBP	SH	SF	SB	CS	SB%	GDP	Avg	OBP	Slg
2007	Mrlns	R	5	20	2	0	0	0	(-	-)	2	0	2	0	1	0	2	0	0	1	0	0	-	0	.100	.136	.100
2007	Jmstwn	A-	10	37	7	2	0	1	(-	-)	12	3	4	2	1	0	12	0	0	0	0	0	-	0	.189	.211	.324
2008	Grnsbr	A	88	345	102	16	0	18	(-	-)	172	59	70	61	28	0	68	5	0	3	0	1	.00	13	.296	.354	.499
2009	Jupiter	A+	103	381	100	25	1	11	(-	-)	160	49	53	56	38	2	68	5	0	5	1	0	1.00	9	.262	.333	.420
2009	Jaxnvl	AA	31	97	18	7	0	2	(-	-)	31	10	9	10	14	0	24	1	1	1	0	0	-	3	.186	.292	.320
2010	Jaxnvl	AA	138	504	127	34	2	14	(-	-)	207	61	81	73	56	3	96	9	1	7	0	2	.00	13	.252	.333	.411
2011	Jupiter	A+	4	18	3	0	0	0	(-	-)	3	0	2	0	1	0	3	1	0	0	0	0	-	0	.167	.250	.167
2011	Jaxnvl	AA	4	15	2	0	0	0	(-	-)	2	1	1	0	3	0	2	1	0	0	0	0	-	0	.133	.316	.133
2011	NewOr	AAA	87	325	84	18	1	12	(-	-)	140	47	55	45	24	0	50	3	0	4	0	1	.00	11	.258	.312	.431
2011	Fla	NL	17	45	11	4	0	0	(0	0)	15	2	2	3	2	0	8	1	0	0	0	0	-	2	.244	.292	.333

Jason Donald

Bats: R **Throws:** R **Pos:** 2B-19; SS-16; 3B-4; PH-3   **Ht:** 6'1" **Wt:** 190 **Born:** 9/4/1984 **Age:** 27

							BATTING																BASERUNNING				AVERAGES		
Year	Team	Lg	G	AB	H	2B	3B	HR	(Hm	Rd)	TB	R	RBI	RC	TBB	IBB	SO	HBP	SH	SF	SB	CS	SB%	GDP	Avg	OBP	Slg
2006	Batvia	A-	63	213	56	14	2	1	(-	-)	77	33	24	31	23	0	42	5	1	1	12	1	.92	5	.263	.347	.362
2007	Lakwd	A	51	197	61	9	3	4	(-	-)	88	41	30	37	29	0	39	6	3	3	2	5	.29	6	.310	.409	.447
2007	Clrwtr	A+	83	293	88	22	5	8	(-	-)	144	48	41	56	35	0	70	6	2	0	3	2	.60	8	.300	.386	.491
2008	Rdng	AA	92	362	111	19	4	14	(-	-)	180	57	54	72	47	1	86	4	0	1	11	2	.85	9	.307	.391	.497
2009	LV	AAA	51	208	49	15	1	1	(-	-)	69	26	16	22	14	1	53	5	1	2	6	0	1.00	4	.236	.297	.332
2009	Phillies	R	9	26	6	1	1	0	(-	-)	9	4	1	2	2	0	5	0	0	0	1	0	1.00	1	.231	.286	.346
2009	Clmbs	AAA	10	35	9	2	0	1	(-	-)	14	10	1	5	3	0	11	2	0	0	1	0	1.00	0	.257	.350	.400
2010	Clmbs	AAA	37	137	38	10	2	2	(-	-)	58	27	17	26	21	0	33	6	1	0	10	2	.83	3	.277	.396	.423
2011	Akron	AA	9	29	7	0	0	0	(-	-)	7	4	2	2	2	0	6	0	0	0	1	0	1.00	2	.241	.290	.241
2011	Clmbs	AAA	47	174	54	12	0	4	(-	-)	78	32	15	32	19	0	33	6	2	0	7	3	.70	5	.310	.397	.448
2010	Cle	AL	88	296	75	19	3	4	(2	2)	112	39	24	29	22	2	70	3	4	0	5	1	.83	3	.253	.312	.378
2011	Cle	AL	39	132	42	6	1	1	(0	1)	53	13	8	18	7	0	35	3	0	1	3	2	.60	2	.318	.364	.402
	2 ML YEARS		127	428	117	25	4	5	(2	3)	165	52	32	47	29	2	105	6	4	1	8	3	.73	5	.273	.328	.386

Octavio Dotel

Pitches: R **Bats:** R **Pos:** RP-65   **Ht:** 6'0" **Wt:** 220 **Born:** 11/25/1973 **Age:** 38

			HOW	MUCH	HE	PITCHED			WHAT	HE	GAVE	UP								THE	RESULTS					
Year	Team	Lg	G	GS	CG	GF	IP	BFP	H	R	ER	HR	SH	SF	HB	TBB	IBB	SO	WP	Bk	W	L	Pct	Sh	Sv-Op	Hld	ERC	ERA
1999	NYM	NL	19	14	0	1	85.1	368	69	52	51	12	3	5	6	49	1	85	3	2	8	3	.727	0	0-0	0	4.30	5.38
2000	Hou	NL	50	16	0	25	125.0	563	127	80	75	26	7	8	7	61	3	142	6	0	3	7	.300	0	16-23	6	5.47	5.40
2001	Hou	NL	61	4	0	20	105.0	438	79	35	31	5	2	2	2	47	2	145	4	0	7	5	.583	0	2-4	14	2.62	2.66
2002	Hou	NL	83	0	0	22	97.1	376	58	21	20	7	3	7	4	27	2	118	2	0	6	4	.600	0	6-10	31	1.61	1.85
2003	Hou	NL	76	0	0	13	87.0	346	53	25	24	9	2	1	3	31	2	97	2	0	6	4	.600	0	4-6	33	2.02	2.48
2004	2 Tms		77	0	0	70	85.1	356	68	38	35	13	4	2	4	33	7	122	4	1	6	6	.500	0	36-45	0	3.31	3.69
2005	Oak	AL	15	0	0	13	15.1	65	10	6	6	2	0	0	0	11	2	16	1	0	1	2	.333	0	7-11	0	3.44	3.52
2006	NYY	AL	14	0	0	7	10.0	59	18	13	12	2	0	1	0	11	1	7	3	0	0	0	-	0	0-0	1	12.97	10.80
2007	2 Tms		33	0	0	25	30.2	138	29	16	14	4	1	0	4	12	4	41	2	0	2	1	.667	0	11-15	1	4.12	4.11
2008	CWS	AL	72	0	0	10	67.0	288	52	34	28	12	4	0	5	29	3	92	4	0	4	4	.500	0	1-5	21	3.44	3.76
2009	CWS	AL	62	0	0	12	62.1	268	54	26	23	7	3	3	0	36	1	75	4	1	3	3	.500	0	0-3	16	4.14	3.32
2010	3 Tms	NL	68	0	0	50	64.0	279	52	32	29	9	2	4	3	32	5	75	8	0	3	4	.429	0	22-28	4	3.69	4.08
2011	2 Tms		65	0	0	21	54.0	218	36	23	21	6	3	1	3	17	2	62	1	0	5	4	.556	0	3-3	9	2.15	3.50
04	Hou	NL	32	0	0	29	34.2	146	27	15	12	4	2	1	1	15	4	50	3	1	0	4	.000	0	14-17	0	3.01	3.12
04	Oak	AL	45	0	0	41	50.2	210	41	23	23	9	2	1	3	18	3	72	1	0	6	2	.750	0	22-28	0	3.52	4.09
07	KC	AL	24	0	0	22	23.0	108	24	11	10	3	1	0	4	11	4	29	2	0	2	1	.667	0	11-14	0	5.13	3.91
07	Atl	NL	9	0	0	3	7.2	30	5	5	4	1	0	0	0	1	0	12	0	0	0	0	-	0	0-1	1	1.51	4.70
10	Pit	NL	41	0	0	37	40.0	173	35	21	19	5	2	3	3	17	2	48	2	0	2	2	.500	0	21-26	3	3.83	4.28
10	LAD	NL	19	0	0	12	18.2	78	11	7	7	3	0	1	0	11	3	21	3	0	1	1	.500	0	1-2	3	2.72	3.38
10	Col	NL	8	0	0	1	5.1	28	6	4	3	1	0	0	0	4	0	6	3	0	0	1	.000	0	0-0	1	6.30	5.06
11	Tor	AL	36	0	0	11	29.1	122	20	13	12	5	1	0	2	12	2	30	0	0	2	1	.667	0	1-1	4	2.97	3.68
11	StL	NL	29	0	0	10	24.2	96	16	10	9	1	2	1	1	5	0	32	1	0	3	3	.500	0	2-2	5	1.38	3.28
	Postseason		8	0	0	2	8.0	40	12	7	7	1	0	0	1	4	1	13	1	0	1	0	1.000	0	0-0	1	8.09	7.88
	13 ML YEARS		695	34	0	289	888.1	3762	705	401	369	114	34	34	40	396	35	1077	44	4	54	47	.535	0	108-153	130	3.41	3.74

Felix Doubront

Pitches: L **Bats:** L **Pos:** RP-11   due-BRAWNDT   **Ht:** 6'2" **Wt:** 165 **Born:** 10/23/1987 **Age:** 24

		HOW MUCH HE PITCHED						WHAT HE GAVE UP													THE RESULTS							
Year	Team	Lg	G	GS	CG	GF	IP	BFP	H	R	ER	HR	SH	SF	HB	TBB	IBB	SO	WP	Bk	W	L	Pct	Sh	Sv-Op	Hld	ERC	ERA
2006	RedSx	R	11	11	0	0	53.2	212	41	17	15	6	1	2	3	13	0	36	1	0	2	3	.400	0	0- -	-	2.57	2.52
2006	Lowell	A-	2	2	0	0	11.0	43	7	6	6	1	0	0	1	3	0	7	1	0	2	0	1.000	0	0- -	-	2.06	4.91
2007	Grnville	A	11	11	0	0	42.1	206	63	49	42	8	0	1	1	17	0	22	4	0	3	7	.300	0	0- -	-	7.80	8.93
2007	Lowell	A-	8	8	0	0	35.0	160	41	24	22	2	1	1	2	11	0	25	2	0	1	3	.250	0	0- -	-	4.47	5.66
2008	Grnville	A	23	23	0	0	115.1	475	115	53	47	9	3	2	4	24	0	118	5	0	12	8	.600	0	0- -	-	3.34	3.67
2008	Lancst	A+	3	3	0	0	14.0	59	15	6	6	1	0	1	0	4	0	20	0	0	1	1	.500	0	0- -	-	3.88	3.86
2009	Portlnd	AA	26	26	1	0	121.0	536	119	59	45	8	1	7	9	52	0	101	3	1	8	6	.571	1	0- -	-	4.10	3.35
2010	Portlnd	AA	8	8	0	0	43.0	177	39	13	12	0	1	1	2	17	0	38	1	2	4	0	1.000	0	0- -	-	3.16	2.51
2010	Pwtckt	AAA	9	8	0	0	37.0	158	36	13	13	1	0	0	4	16	0	34	2	1	4	3	.571	0	0- -	-	4.08	3.16
2011	Pwtckt	AAA	18	16	0	1	70.1	301	65	37	33	10	3	0	2	26	0	61	1	0	2	5	.286	0	0- -	-	3.90	4.22
2011	Portlnd	AA	1	1	0	0	5.0	19	4	1	1	0	0	0	0	0	0	9	0	0	1	0	1.000	0	0- -	-	1.27	1.80
2011	Lowell	A-	1	1	0	0	2.0	6	0	0	0	0	0	0	0	0	0	4	0	0	0	0	-	0	0- -	-	0.00	0.00
2010	Bos	AL	12	3	0	5	25.0	113	27	16	12	3	1	1	1	10	0	23	3	0	2	2	.500	0	2-3	1	4.72	4.32
2011	Bos	AL	11	0	0	1	10.1	47	12	7	7	1	0	1	0	8	0	6	0	0	0	0	-	0	1-1	0	6.97	6.10
	2 ML YEARS		23	3	0	6	35.1	160	39	23	19	4	1	2	1	18	0	29	3	0	2	2	.500	0	3-4	1	5.35	4.84

Ryan Doumit

Bats: B **Throws:** R **Pos:** C-60; PH-20   DOE-mitt   **Ht:** 6'1" **Wt:** 210 **Born:** 4/3/1981 **Age:** 31

						BATTING																BASERUNNING				AVERAGES		
Year	Team	Lg	G	AB	H	2B	3B	HR	(Hm	Rd)	TB	R	RBI	RC	TBB	IBB	SO	HBP	SH	SF	SB	CS	SB%	GDP	Avg	OBP	Slg
2011	Bradtn*	A+	5	14	2	0	0	0	(-	-)	2	1	1	0	2	0	3	0	0	0	0	0	-	0	.143	.250	.143
2011	Indy*	AAA	8	26	6	1	1	0	(-	-)	9	4	3	3	4	1	4	1	0	0	0	0	-	1	.231	.355	.346
2005	Pit	NL	75	231	59	13	1	6	(4	2)	92	25	35	32	11	1	48	13	1	1	2	1	.67	5	.255	.324	.398
2006	Pit	NL	61	149	31	9	0	6	(3	3)	58	15	17	17	15	1	42	11	1	2	0	0	-	3	.208	.322	.389
2007	Pit	NL	83	252	69	19	2	9	(7	2)	119	33	32	34	22	2	59	4	0	1	1	2	.33	5	.274	.341	.472
2008	Pit	NL	116	431	137	34	0	15	(8	7)	216	71	69	79	23	4	55	6	0	5	2	2	.50	10	.318	.357	.501
2009	Pit	NL	75	280	70	16	0	10	(6	4)	116	31	38	26	20	6	49	1	0	3	4	0	1.00	12	.250	.299	.414
2010	Pit	NL	124	406	102	22	1	13	(7	6)	165	42	45	47	41	4	87	8	0	1	1	0	1.00	18	.251	.331	.406
2011	Pit	NL	77	218	66	12	1	8	(6	2)	104	17	30	36	16	0	35	1	1	0	0	1	.00	5	.303	.353	.477
	7 ML YEARS		611	1967	534	125	5	67	(41	26)	870	234	266	271	148	18	375	44	3	13	10	6	.63	58	.271	.334	.442

Matt Downs

Bats: R **Throws:** R **Pos:** PH-52; 2B-27; 3B-19; 1B-13; RF-3; SS-2; PR-2   **Ht:** 6'1" **Wt:** 184 **Born:** 3/19/1984 **Age:** 28

						BATTING																BASERUNNING				AVERAGES		
Year	Team	Lg	G	AB	H	2B	3B	HR	(Hm	Rd)	TB	R	RBI	RC	TBB	IBB	SO	HBP	SH	SF	SB	CS	SB%	GDP	Avg	OBP	Slg
2009	SF	NL	17	53	9	2	0	1	(0	1)	14	6	2	1	6	1	13	0	0	1	1	0	1.00	2	.170	.250	.264
2010	2 Tms	NL	40	97	21	7	0	1	(1	0)	31	8	7	9	9	0	20	2	0	1	0	0	-	1	.216	.294	.320
2011	Hou	NL	106	199	55	18	0	10	(5	5)	103	29	41	37	17	0	47	5	0	1	0	0	-	3	.276	.347	.518
10	SF	NL	29	78	19	7	0	1	(1	0)	29	6	7	9	8	0	18	1	0	1	0	0	-	1	.244	.318	.372
10	Hou	NL	11	19	2	0	0	0	(0	0)	2	2	0	0	1	0	2	1	0	0	0	0	-	0	.105	.190	.105
	3 ML YEARS		163	349	85	27	0	12	(6	6)	148	43	50	47	32	1	80	7	0	3	1	0	1.00	6	.244	.317	.424

Scott Downs

Pitches: L **Bats:** L **Pos:** RP-60   **Ht:** 6'2" **Wt:** 209 **Born:** 3/17/1976 **Age:** 36

			HOW MUCH HE PITCHED						WHAT HE GAVE UP												THE RESULTS							
Year	Team	Lg	G	GS	CG	GF	IP	BFP	H	R	ER	HR	SH	SF	HB	TBB	IBB	SO	WP	Bk	W	L	Pct	Sh	Sv-Op	Hld	ERC	ERA
2011	InldEm*	A+	2	1	0	0	2.0	12	5	2	2	0	0	0	0	1	0	1	0	0	1	1	.500	0	0- -	-	13.27	9.00
2000	2 Tms	NL	19	19	0	0	97.0	442	122	62	57	13	2	4	5	40	1	63	1	0	4	3	.571	0	0-0	0	6.19	5.29
2003	Mon	NL	1	1	0	0	3.0	17	5	5	5	2	0	0	0	3	2	4	0	1	0	1	.000	0	0-0	0	15.01	15.00
2004	Mon	NL	12	12	1	0	63.0	284	79	47	36	9	2	1	3	23	2	38	2	0	3	6	.333	1	0-0	0	5.97	5.14
2005	Tor	AL	26	13	0	0	94.0	407	93	49	45	12	0	1	5	34	0	75	3	0	4	3	.571	0	0-0	0	4.25	4.31
2006	Tor	AL	59	5	0	13	77.0	327	73	38	35	9	1	1	2	30	6	61	7	0	6	2	.750	0	1-4	6	3.87	4.09
2007	Tor	AL	81	0	0	13	58.0	239	47	15	14	3	1	2	1	24	3	57	2	1	4	2	.667	0	1-4	24	2.81	2.17
2008	Tor	AL	66	0	0	14	70.2	290	54	15	14	3	5	0	4	27	7	57	3	0	0	3	.000	0	5-9	24	2.47	1.78
2009	Tor	AL	48	0	0	24	46.2	200	46	18	16	4	0	2	2	13	1	43	1	0	1	3	.250	0	9-13	10	3.50	3.09
2010	Tor	AL	67	0	0	14	61.1	241	47	19	18	3	0	0	4	14	3	48	1	0	5	5	.500	0	0-2	26	2.14	2.64
2011	LAA	AL	60	0	0	10	53.2	218	39	11	8	3	5	2	0	15	3	35	2	0	6	3	.667	0	1-4	26	1.83	1.34
00	ChC	NL	18	18	0	0	94.0	426	117	59	54	13	2	4	5	37	1	63	1	0	4	3	.571	0	0-0	0	6.07	5.17
00	Mon	NL	1	1	0	0	3.0	16	5	3	3	0	0	0	0	3	0	0	0	0	0	0	-	0	0-0	0	10.34	9.00
	10 ML YEARS		439	50	1	88	624.1	2665	605	279	248	61	16	13	26	223	28	481	22	2	33	31	.516	1	17-36	116	3.82	3.58

Kyle Drabek

Pitches: R **Bats:** R **Pos:** SP-14; RP-4   **Ht:** 6'1" **Wt:** 219 **Born:** 12/8/1987 **Age:** 24

			HOW MUCH HE PITCHED						WHAT HE GAVE UP												THE RESULTS							
Year	Team	Lg	G	GS	CG	GF	IP	BFP	H	R	ER	HR	SH	SF	HB	TBB	IBB	SO	WP	Bk	W	L	Pct	Sh	Sv-Op	Hld	ERC	ERA
2006	Phillies	R	6	6	0	0	23.1	112	33	24	20	2	0	2	3	11	0	14	0	1	1	3	.250	0	0- -	-	7.21	7.71
2007	Lakwd	A	11	10	0	0	54.0	236	50	29	26	9	1	1	2	23	0	46	1	0	5	1	.833	0	0- -	-	4.30	4.33
2008	Phillies	R	4	4	0	0	12.0	47	6	3	3	0	0	0	1	6	0	6	2	0	1	0	1.000	0	0- -	-	1.65	2.25
2008	Wmspt	A-	4	4	0	0	20.1	78	11	6	5	1	1	1	1	6	0	10	3	0	1	2	.333	0	0- -	-	1.43	2.21
2009	Clrwtr	A+	10	9	1	0	61.2	249	49	19	17	0	3	0	2	19	0	74	2	1	4	1	.800	1	0- -	-	2.17	2.48
2009	Rdng	AA	15	14	0	0	96.1	405	92	40	39	9	5	3	1	31	2	76	2	3	8	2	.800	0	0- -	-	3.49	3.64
2010	NHam	AA	27	27	1	0	162.0	663	126	67	53	12	2	2	4	68	0	132	5	2	14	9	.609	1	0- -	-	2.93	2.94

			HOW MUCH HE PITCHED						WHAT HE GAVE UP										THE RESULTS					
Year	Team	Lg	G	GS	CG	GF	IP	BFP	H	R	ER	HR	SH	SF	HB	TBB	IBB	SO	WP	Bk	W	L	Pct	Sh	Sv-Op Hld	ERC	ERA
2011	LsVgs	AAA	15	15	1	0	75.0	362	111	70	62	12	2	4	2	41	0	45	9	2	5	4	.556	0	0- -	8.50	7.44
2010	Tor	AL	3	3	0	0	17.0	69	18	9	9	2	1	2	0	5	0	12	2	0	0	3	.000	0	0-0	4.34	4.76
2011	Tor	AL	18	14	0	2	78.2	365	87	54	53	10	3	5	1	55	0	51	11	0	4	5	.444	0	0-0	6.30	6.06
	2 ML YEARS		21	17	0	2	95.2	434	105	63	62	12	4	7	1	60	0	63	13	0	4	8	.333	0	0-0	5.94	5.83

J.D. Drew

Bats: L Throws: R Pos: RF-76; PH-16   Ht: 6'1" Wt: 200 Born: 11/20/1975 Age: 36

			BATTING																		BASERUNNING				AVERAGES		
Year	Team	Lg	G	AB	H	2B	3B	HR	(Hm	Rd)	TB	R	RBI	RC	TBB	IBB	SO	HBP	SH	SF	SB	CS	SB%	GDP	Avg	OBP	Slg
2011	Lowell*	A-	1	2	0	0	0	0	(-	-)	0	1	0	0	1	0	1	1	0	0	0	0	-	0	.000	.500	.000
2011	Pwtckt*	AAA	1	3	3	0	0	0	(-	-)	3	1	0	1	0	0	0	0	0	0	0	0	-	0	1.000	1.000	1.000
1998	StL	NL	14	36	15	3	1	5	(4	1)	35	9	13	12	4	0	10	0	0	1	0	0	-	4	.417	.463	.972
1999	StL	NL	104	368	89	16	6	13	(5	8)	156	72	39	58	50	0	77	6	3	3	19	3	.86	4	.242	.340	.424
2000	StL	NL	135	407	120	17	2	18	(11	7)	195	73	57	80	67	4	99	6	5	1	17	9	.65	3	.295	.401	.479
2001	StL	NL	109	375	121	18	5	27	(15	12)	230	80	73	92	57	4	75	4	3	4	13	3	.81	6	.323	.414	.613
2002	StL	NL	135	424	107	19	1	18	(9	9)	182	61	56	65	57	4	104	8	3	4	8	2	.80	4	.252	.349	.429
2003	StL	NL	100	287	83	13	3	15	(7	8)	147	60	42	58	36	0	48	3	2	0	2	2	.50	6	.289	.374	.512
2004	Atl	NL	145	518	158	28	4	31	(14	17)	295	118	93	121	118	2	116	5	1	3	12	3	.80	7	.305	.436	.569
2005	LAD	NL	72	252	72	12	1	15	(10	5)	131	48	36	49	51	3	50	5	0	3	1	1	.50	3	.286	.412	.520
2006	LAD	NL	146	494	140	34	6	20	(12	8)	246	84	100	92	89	8	106	4	1	6	2	3	.40	4	.283	.393	.498
2007	Bos	AL	140	466	126	30	4	11	(4	7)	197	84	64	68	79	10	100	1	0	6	4	2	.67	12	.270	.373	.423
2008	Bos	AL	109	368	103	23	4	19	(10	9)	191	79	64	72	79	5	80	4	0	5	4	1	.80	11	.280	.408	.519
2009	Bos	AL	137	452	126	30	4	24	(11	13)	236	84	68	81	82	5	109	3	1	1	2	6	.25	6	.279	.392	.522
2010	Bos	AL	139	478	122	24	2	22	(9	13)	216	69	68	67	60	3	105	4	0	4	3	1	.75	12	.255	.341	.452
2011	Bos	AL	81	248	55	6	1	4	(2	2)	75	23	22	24	33	4	58	2	0	3	1	0	1.00	2	.222	.315	.302
	Postseason		55	184	48	6	0	7	(4	3)	75	19	25	22	18	0	36	2	2	0	3	1	.75	4	.261	.333	.408
	14 ML YEARS		1566	5173	1437	273	48	242	(123	119)	2532	944	795	939	862	52	1137	55	19	44	87	37	.70	84	.278	.384	.489

Stephen Drew

Bats: L Throws: R Pos: SS-84; PH-3   Ht: 6'0" Wt: 185 Born: 3/16/1983 Age: 29

			BATTING																		BASERUNNING				AVERAGES		
Year	Team	Lg	G	AB	H	2B	3B	HR	(Hm	Rd)	TB	R	RBI	RC	TBB	IBB	SO	HBP	SH	SF	SB	CS	SB%	GDP	Avg	OBP	Slg
2006	Ari	NL	59	209	66	13	7	5	(3	2)	108	27	23	31	14	4	50	0	2	1	2	0	1.00	1	.316	.357	.517
2007	Ari	NL	150	543	129	28	4	12	(6	6)	201	60	60	71	60	5	100	3	5	8	9	0	1.00	4	.238	.313	.370
2008	Ari	NL	152	611	178	44	11	21	(9	12)	307	91	67	97	41	6	109	1	3	7	3	3	.50	5	.291	.333	.502
2009	Ari	NL	135	533	139	29	12	12	(4	8)	228	71	65	76	49	7	87	1	4	5	5	1	.83	5	.261	.320	.428
2010	Ari	NL	151	565	157	33	12	15	(5	10)	259	83	61	84	62	2	108	3	2	1	10	5	.67	8	.278	.352	.458
2011	Ari	NL	86	321	81	21	5	5	(3	2)	127	44	45	41	30	0	74	1	1	1	4	4	.50	3	.252	.317	.396
	Postseason		7	31	12	1	1	2	(1	1)	21	6	4	5	1	0	7	0	0	0	1	0	1.00	1	.387	.406	.677
	6 ML YEARS		733	2782	750	168	51	70	(30	40)	1230	376	321	400	256	24	528	9	18	25	33	13	.72	26	.270	.330	.442

Lucas Duda

Bats: L Throws: R Pos: 1B-43; RF-42; PH-19; LF-4; DH-1   Ht: 6'4" Wt: 254 Born: 2/3/1986 Age: 26

			BATTING																		BASERUNNING				AVERAGES		
Year	Team	Lg	G	AB	H	2B	3B	HR	(Hm	Rd)	TB	R	RBI	RC	TBB	IBB	SO	HBP	SH	SF	SB	CS	SB%	GDP	Avg	OBP	Slg
2007	Bklyn	A-	67	234	70	20	3	4	(-	-)	108	32	32	43	34	3	45	5	0	1	3	5	.38	2	.299	.398	.462
2008	StLuci	A+	133	483	127	26	3	11	(-	-)	192	58	66	71	66	3	129	7	0	3	2	7	.22	15	.263	.358	.398
2009	Bnghtn	AA	110	395	111	29	1	9	(-	-)	169	49	53	69	61	5	91	5	1	5	2	2	.50	10	.281	.380	.428
2010	Bnghtn	AA	45	161	46	17	0	6	(-	-)	81	30	34	34	29	1	27	6	0	1	1	0	1.00	2	.286	.411	.503
2010	Buffalo	AAA	70	264	83	23	2	17	(-	-)	161	44	53	60	31	3	57	2	0	1	0	0	-	4	.314	.389	.610
2011	Buffalo	AAA	38	129	39	8	0	10	(-	-)	77	22	24	32	23	1	27	3	0	2	0	0	-	2	.302	.414	.597
2010	NYM	NL	29	84	17	6	0	4	(3	1)	35	11	13	5	6	0	22	1	0	1	0	0	-	2	.202	.261	.417
2011	NYM	NL	100	301	88	21	3	10	(2	8)	145	38	50	44	33	3	57	7	1	5	1	0	1.00	5	.292	.370	.482
	2 ML YEARS		129	385	105	27	3	14	(5	9)	180	49	63	49	39	3	79	8	1	6	1	0	1.00	7	.273	.347	.468

Brian Duensing

Pitches: L Bats: L Pos: SP-28; RP-4   DUNN-sing   Ht: 5'11" Wt: 205 Born: 2/22/1983 Age: 29

			HOW MUCH HE PITCHED						WHAT HE GAVE UP										THE RESULTS					
Year	Team	Lg	G	GS	CG	GF	IP	BFP	H	R	ER	HR	SH	SF	HB	TBB	IBB	SO	WP	Bk	W	L	Pct	Sh	Sv-Op Hld	ERC	ERA
2009	Min	AL	24	9	0	3	84.0	359	84	37	34	7	3	2	3	31	1	53	1	0	5	2	.714	0	0-0	4.00	3.64
2010	Min	AL	53	13	1	11	130.2	535	122	42	38	11	4	0	3	35	5	78	1	0	10	3	.769	1	0-0 9	3.18	2.62
2011	Min	AL	32	28	1	0	161.2	711	193	102	94	21	7	6	1	52	3	115	3	0	9	14	.391	1	0-0 0	5.12	5.23
	Postseason		2	0	0	0	8.0	39	14	10	10	2	0	0	0	2	0	4	1	0	0	2	.000	0	0-0	9.43	11.25
	3 ML YEARS		109	50	2	14	376.1	1605	399	181	166	39	14	8	7	118	9	246	5	0	24	19	.558	2	0-0 10	4.17	3.97

Danny Duffy

Pitches: L Bats: L Pos: SP-20   Ht: 6'3" Wt: 195 Born: 12/21/1988 Age: 23

			HOW MUCH HE PITCHED						WHAT HE GAVE UP										THE RESULTS					
Year	Team	Lg	G	GS	CG	GF	IP	BFP	H	R	ER	HR	SH	SF	HB	TBB	IBB	SO	WP	Bk	W	L	Pct	Sh	Sv-Op Hld	ERC	ERA
2007	Royals	R	11	9	0	0	37.1	157	24	14	6	0	1	1	3	17	0	63	5	0	2	3	.400	0	0- -	2.01	1.45
2008	Burlgtn	A	17	17	0	0	81.2	325	56	26	20	4	3	3	4	25	0	102	10	0	8	4	.667	0	0- -	1.99	2.20
2009	Wilmg	A+	24	24	1	0	126.2	516	108	49	42	6	2	2	1	41	0	125	8	1	9	3	.750	0	0- -	2.72	2.98
2010	Royals	R	2	2	0	0	2.2	10	2	1	1	0	0	0	0	1	0	4	1	0	0	0	-	0	0- -	2.27	3.38
2010	Idaho	R+	2	2	0	0	6.0	23	4	1	1	0	0	0	0	6	1	0	1	0	0	1	.000	0	0- -	1.23	1.50

Year	Team	Lg	G	GS	CG	GF	IP	BFP	H	R	ER	HR	SH	SF	HB	TBB	IBB	SO	WP	Bk	W	L	Pct	Sh	Sv-Op	Hld	ERC	ERA
			HOW MUCH HE PITCHED						WHAT HE GAVE UP												THE RESULTS							
2010	Wilmg*	A+	3	3	0	0	14.0	56	8	6	4	2	1	0	1	7	0	18	1	0	0	0	-	0	0- -	-	2.80	2.57
2010	NWArk	AA	7	7	1	0	39.2	160	38	17	13	3	0	1	0	9	0	41	4	0	5	2	.714	1	0- -	-	3.09	2.95
2011	Omha	AAA	8	8	0	0	42.0	171	37	17	16	5	1	1	3	10	0	48	1	0	3	1	.750	0	0- -	-	3.25	3.43
2011	KC	AL	20	20	0	0	105.1	474	119	66	66	15	2	2	5	51	1	87	4	1	4	8	.333	0	0-0	0	5.76	5.64

Zach Duke

Pitches: L Bats: L Pos: RP-12; SP-9   Ht: 6'2" Wt: 205 Born: 4/19/1983 Age: 29

Year	Team	Lg	G	GS	CG	GF	IP	BFP	H	R	ER	HR	SH	SF	HB	TBB	IBB	SO	WP	Bk	W	L	Pct	Sh	Sv-Op	Hld	ERC	ERA
			HOW MUCH HE PITCHED						WHAT HE GAVE UP												THE RESULTS							
2011	Visalia*	A+	1	1	0	0	5.0	19	5	1	1	0	0	0	0	0	0	4	0	0	1	0	1.000	0	0- -	-	2.09	1.80
2011	Reno*	AAA	1	1	0	0	5.1	24	7	5	5	2	0	0	0	1	0	2	0	0	1	0	1.000	0	0- -	-	6.90	8.44
2005	Pit	NL	14	14	0	0	84.2	341	79	20	17	3	3	1	2	23	2	58	1	0	8	2	.800	0	0-0	0	2.96	1.81
2006	Pit	NL	34	34	2	0	215.1	935	255	116	107	17	13	4	7	68	6	117	8	1	10	15	.400	1	0-0	0	4.82	4.47
2007	Pit	NL	20	19	0	0	107.1	482	161	74	66	14	2	4	3	25	2	41	0	1	3	8	.273	0	0-0	0	6.96	5.53
2008	Pit	NL	31	31	1	0	185.0	829	230	111	99	19	14	4	7	47	1	87	2	2	5	14	.263	1	0-0	0	4.99	4.82
2009	Pit	NL	32	32	3	0	213.0	891	231	101	96	23	18	10	3	49	0	106	2	1	11	16	.407	1	0-0	0	4.05	4.06
2010	Pit	NL	29	29	0	0	159.0	730	212	115	101	25	9	6	4	51	2	96	4	3	8	15	.348	0	0-0	0	6.22	5.72
2011	Ari	NL	21	9	0	5	76.2	338	101	42	42	6	3	3	1	19	0	32	1	0	3	4	.429	0	1-1	0	5.27	4.93
7 ML YEARS			181	168	6	5	1041.0	4546	1269	579	528	107	62	32	27	282	13	537	18	8	48	74	.393	3	1-1	0	4.98	4.56

Phil Dumatrait

Pitches: L Bats: R Pos: RP-45   doo-MAH-tray   Ht: 6'2" Wt: 210 Born: 7/12/1981 Age: 30

Year	Team	Lg	G	GS	CG	GF	IP	BFP	H	R	ER	HR	SH	SF	HB	TBB	IBB	SO	WP	Bk	W	L	Pct	Sh	Sv-Op	Hld	ERC	ERA
			HOW MUCH HE PITCHED						WHAT HE GAVE UP												THE RESULTS							
2011	Roch*	AAA	15	0	0	8	15.2	68	10	4	2	1	0	0	1	11	1	12	0	0	0	1	.000	0	4- -	-	3.11	1.15
2007	Cin	NL	6	6	0	0	18.0	104	39	30	30	6	1	2	1	12	0	9	0	0	0	4	.000	0	0-0	0	15.81	15.00
2008	Pit	NL	21	11	0	4	78.2	351	82	48	46	7	1	3	2	42	2	52	1	0	3	4	.429	0	0-0	0	4.87	5.26
2009	Pit	NL	15	0	0	2	13.0	64	13	11	10	4	0	1	0	11	0	7	0	0	0	2	.000	0	0-1	1	7.35	6.92
2011	Min	AL	45	0	0	14	41.1	196	45	22	18	7	3	4	1	25	5	29	2	0	1	3	.250	0	1-1	4	5.68	3.92
4 ML YEARS			87	17	0	20	151.0	715	179	111	104	24	6	10	4	90	7	97	3	0	4	13	.235	0	1-2	5	6.43	6.20

Shelley Duncan

Bats: R Throws: R Pos: LF-37; DH-23; PH-10; 1B-7; RF-2; PR-1   Ht: 6'5" Wt: 225 Born: 9/29/1979 Age: 32

Year	Team	Lg	G	AB	H	2B	3B	HR	(Hm	Rd)	TB	R	RBI	RC	TBB	IBB	SO	HBP	SH	SF	SB	CS	SB%	GDP	Avg	OBP	Slg
			BATTING																		BASERUNNING				AVERAGES		
2011	Clmbs*	AAA	33	109	22	3	0	5	(-	-)	40	20	19	16	24	1	24	2	0	2	1	0	1.00	6	.202	.350	.367
2007	NYY	AL	34	74	19	1	0	7	(6	1)	41	16	17	14	8	0	20	0	1	0	0	0	-	2	.257	.329	.554
2008	NYY	AL	23	57	10	3	0	1	(1	0)	16	7	6	4	7	0	13	0	0	1	0	0	-	1	.175	.262	.281
2009	NYY	AL	11	15	3	0	0	0	(0	0)	3	1	1	1	0	0	5	0	0	0	0	0	-	1	.200	.200	.200
2010	Cle	AL	85	229	53	10	0	11	(9	2)	96	29	36	30	26	2	76	3	0	1	1	0	1.00	4	.231	.317	.419
2011	Cle	AL	76	223	58	17	0	11	(4	7)	108	29	47	38	19	1	56	3	0	2	0	1	.00	7	.260	.324	.484
Postseason			3	4	2	0	0	0	(0	0)	2	1	0	1	0	0	1	0	0	0	0	0	-	0	.500	.500	.500
5 ML YEARS			229	598	143	31	0	30	(20	10)	264	82	107	87	60	3	170	6	1	4	1	1	.50	15	.239	.313	.441

Adam Dunn

Bats: L Throws: R Pos: DH-81; 1B-35; PH-5; RF-2   Ht: 6'6" Wt: 287 Born: 11/9/1979 Age: 32

Year	Team	Lg	G	AB	H	2B	3B	HR	(Hm	Rd)	TB	R	RBI	RC	TBB	IBB	SO	HBP	SH	SF	SB	CS	SB%	GDP	Avg	OBP	Slg
			BATTING																		BASERUNNING				AVERAGES		
2001	Cin	NL	66	244	64	18	1	19	(8	11)	141	54	43	51	38	2	74	4	0	0	4	2	.67	4	.262	.371	.578
2002	Cin	NL	158	535	133	28	2	26	(13	13)	243	84	71	96	128	13	170	9	1	3	19	9	.68	8	.249	.400	.454
2003	Cin	NL	116	381	82	12	1	27	(16	11)	177	70	57	61	74	8	126	10	0	4	8	2	.80	4	.215	.354	.465
2004	Cin	NL	161	568	151	34	0	46	(25	21)	323	105	102	108	108	11	195	5	0	0	6	1	.86	8	.266	.388	.569
2005	Cin	NL	160	543	134	35	2	40	(26	14)	293	107	101	112	114	14	168	12	0	2	4	2	.67	6	.247	.387	.540
2006	Cin	NL	160	561	131	24	0	40	(22	18)	275	99	92	96	112	12	194	6	1	3	7	0	1.00	8	.234	.365	.490
2007	Cin	NL	152	522	138	27	2	40	(19	21)	289	101	106	103	101	8	165	5	0	4	9	2	.82	12	.264	.386	.554
2008	2 Tms	NL	158	517	122	23	0	40	(21	19)	265	79	100	101	122	13	164	7	0	5	2	1	.67	7	.236	.386	.513
2009	Was	NL	159	546	146	29	0	38	(19	19)	289	81	105	109	116	16	177	4	0	2	0	1	.00	8	.267	.398	.529
2010	Was	NL	158	558	145	36	2	38	(20	18)	299	85	103	88	77	10	199	9	0	4	0	1	.00	10	.260	.356	.536
2011	CWS	AL	122	415	66	16	0	11	(8	3)	115	36	42	34	75	0	177	4	0	2	0	1	.00	10	.159	.292	.277
08 Cin		NL	114	373	87	14	0	32	(16	16)	197	58	74	74	80	6	120	6	0	5	1	1	.50	4	.233	.373	.528
08 Ari		NL	44	144	35	9	0	8	(5	3)	68	21	26	27	42	7	44	1	0	0	1	0	1.00	3	.243	.417	.472
11 ML YEARS			1570	5390	1312	282	10	365	(197	168)	2709	901	922	959	1065	107	1809	75	2	29	59	22	.73	85	.243	.374	.503

Mike Dunn

Pitches: L Bats: L Pos: RP-72   Ht: 6'1" Wt: 195 Born: 5/23/1985 Age: 27

Year	Team	Lg	G	GS	CG	GF	IP	BFP	H	R	ER	HR	SH	SF	HB	TBB	IBB	SO	WP	Bk	W	L	Pct	Sh	Sv-Op	Hld	ERC	ERA
			HOW MUCH HE PITCHED						WHAT HE GAVE UP												THE RESULTS							
2009	NYY	AL	4	0	0	3	4.0	20	3	3	3	1	0	0	0	5	0	5	1	0	0	0	-	0	0-0	0	7.17	6.75
2010	Atl	NL	25	0	0	5	19.0	88	15	4	4	1	0	0	0	17	2	27	2	0	2	0	1.000	0	0-0	1	4.19	1.89
2011	Fla	NL	72	0	0	11	63.0	267	51	28	24	9	4	2	2	31	2	68	3	0	5	6	.455	0	0-4	15	3.77	3.43
Postseason			3	0	0	2	1.1	6	2	0	0	0	0	0	0	0	0	2	0	0	0	0	-	0	0-1	0	4.47	0.00
3 ML YEARS			101	0	0	19	86.0	375	69	35	31	11	4	2	2	53	4	100	6	0	7	6	.538	0	0-4	16	4.03	3.24

Luis Durango

Bats: B Throws: R Pos: CF-2   Ht: 5'9" Wt: 158 Born: 4/23/1986 Age: 26

								BATTING												BASERUNNING				AVERAGES		
Year	Team	Lg	G	AB	H	2B	3B	HR	(Hm | Rd)	TB	R	RBI	RC	TBB	IBB	SO	HBP	SH	SF	SB	CS	SB%	GDP	Avg	OBP	Slg
2011	Tucsn*	AAA	61	177	43	3	3	0	(- | -)	52	36	15	19	19	0	31	4	6	1	10	5	.67	3	.243	.328	.294
2011	OKCity*	AAA	47	154	42	2	1	0	(- | -)	46	33	9	19	22	0	23	0	3	1	18	9	.67	2	.273	.362	.299
2009	SD	NL	9	11	6	0	0	0	(0 | 0)	6	3	0	3	2	0	2	0	1	0	2	1	.67	0	.545	.615	.545
2010	SD	NL	28	48	12	0	0	0	(0 | 0)	12	8	4	3	4	0	7	0	1	0	5	0	1.00	3	.250	.308	.250
2011	Hou	NL	2	6	1	0	0	0	(0 | 0)	1	0	1	1	1	0	1	0	0	0	0	0	-	0	.167	.286	.167
	3 ML YEARS		39	65	19	0	0	0	(0 | 0)	19	11	5	7	7	0	10	0	2	0	7	1	.88	3	.292	.361	.292

Chad Durbin

Pitches: R Bats: R Pos: RP-56   DURR-binn   Ht: 6'2" Wt: 224 Born: 12/3/1977 Age: 34

			HOW MUCH HE PITCHED						WHAT HE GAVE UP											THE RESULTS						
Year	Team	Lg	G	GS	CG	GF	IP	BFP	H	R	ER	HR	SH	SF	HB	TBB	IBB	SO	WP	Bk	W	L	Pct	Sh	Sv-Op	Hld	ERC	ERA
1999	KC	AL	1	0	0	0	2.1	9	1	0	0	0	0	0	1	0	3	1	0	0	0		0	0-0	0	1.08	0.00
2000	KC	AL	16	16	0	0	72.1	349	91	71	66	14	1	3	0	43	1	37	7	0	2	5	.286	0	0-0	0	7.05	8.21
2001	KC	AL	29	29	2	0	179.0	777	201	109	98	26	2	7	11	58	0	95	6	0	9	16	.360	0	0-0	0	5.15	4.93
2002	KC	AL	2	2	0	0	8.1	43	13	11	11	3	0	0	1	4	0	5	0	0	0	1	.000	0	0-0	0	10.58	11.88
2003	Cle	AL	3	1	0	0	8.2	45	18	12	7	2	0	0	0	3	0	8	2	0	0	1	.000	0	0-0	0	12.37	7.27
2004	2 Tms		24	8	1	5	60.2	291	72	50	47	11	2	2	5	35	3	48	5	0	6	7	.462	0	0-0	0	6.75	6.97
2006	Det	AL	3	0	0	1	6.0	24	6	1	1	1	0	0	0	0	0	3	0	0	0	0		0	0-0	0	2.87	1.50
2007	Det	AL	36	19	0	7	127.2	561	133	71	67	21	1	7	8	49	4	66	2	0	8	7	.533	0	1-2	3	4.92	4.72
2008	Phi	NL	71	0	0	12	87.2	365	81	33	28	5	4	2	4	35	7	63	3	0	5	4	.556	0	1-7	17	3.51	2.87
2009	Phi	NL	59	0	0	15	69.2	314	56	38	34	8	3	3	7	47	2	62	2	0	2	2	.500	0	2-3	8	4.47	4.39
2010	Phi	NL	64	0	0	9	68.2	291	63	29	29	7	1	2	5	27	2	63	0	0	4	1	.800	0	0-1	15	3.70	3.80
2011	Cle	AL	56	0	0	11	68.1	318	86	45	42	12	1	7	3	26	3	59	6	0	2	2	.500	0	0-1	3	6.11	5.53
	04 Cle	AL	17	8	1	5	51.1	239	63	40	38	10	0	2	4	24	3	38	3	0	5	6	.455	0	0-0	0	6.70	6.66
	04 Ari	NL	7	0	0	0	9.1	52	9	10	9	1	2	0	1	11	0	10	2	0	1	1	.500	0	0-0	1	6.92	8.68
	Postseason		15	0	0	2	10.0	51	12	8	7	1	1	0	2	8	0	7	0	0	2	0	1.000	0	0-1	3	7.77	6.30
	12 ML YEARS		364	75	3	60	759.1	3387	821	470	430	110	15	33	44	328	22	512	34	0	38	46	.452	0	4-14	47	5.21	5.10

Jarrod Dyson

Bats: L Throws: R Pos: CF-17; PR-12; PH-2; DH-1   juh-ROD   Ht: 5'9" Wt: 161 Born: 8/15/1984 Age: 27

								BATTING												BASERUNNING				AVERAGES		
Year	Team	Lg	G	AB	H	2B	3B	HR	(Hm	Rd)	TB	R	RBI	RC	TBB	IBB	SO	HBP	SH	SF	SB	CS	SB%	GDP	Avg	OBP	Slg
2006	Royals	R	51	161	44	4	6	0	(-	-)	60	40	19	26	18	1	30	5	2	3	19	4	.83	0	.273	.358	.373
2007	Burlgtn	A	10	37	10	1	0	0	(-	-)	11	6	0	3	2	0	12	0	0	0	3	1	.75	0	.270	.308	.297
2008	Wilmg	A+	93	288	75	8	0	0	(-	-)	83	40	24	35	32	0	60	2	8	1	39	9	.81	1	.260	.337	.288
2009	Burlgtn	A	17	67	23	2	1	0	(-	-)	27	14	5	11	5	0	14	1	2	0	9	4	.69	0	.343	.397	.403
2009	NWArk	AA	63	248	64	7	4	0	(-	-)	79	38	14	33	27	0	54	0	8	0	37	6	.86	4	.258	.331	.319
2010	Royals	R	6	25	13	1	1	0	(-	-)	16	4	6	6	0	0	3	0	0	0	3	1	.75	0	.520	.520	.640
2010	Wilmg	A+	12	49	16	6	2	0	(-	-)	26	7	9	9	1	0	9	0	0	2	5	1	.83	0	.327	.327	.531
2010	NWArk	AA	7	25	6	0	0	0	(-	-)	6	6	2	2	5	0	2	1	0	1	3	3	.50	2	.240	.375	.240
2010	Omha	AAA	46	195	53	10	1	1	(-	-)	68	33	19	25	16	0	32	1	5	2	13	3	.81	6	.272	.327	.349
2011	Omha	AAA	83	319	89	10	3	3	(-	-)	114	69	26	50	35	1	47	3	12	0	38	2	.95	4	.279	.356	.357
2010	KC	AL	18	57	12	4	2	1	(1	0)	23	11	5	9	6	0	16	0	2	0	9	1	.90	2	.211	.286	.404
2011	KC	AL	26	44	9	1	0	0	(0	0)	10	8	3	7	7	0	14	0	1	1	11	1	.92	0	.205	.308	.227
	2 ML YEARS		44	101	21	5	2	1	(1	0)	33	19	8	16	13	0	30	0	3	1	20	2	.91	2	.208	.296	.327

Steve Edlefsen

Pitches: R Bats: B Pos: RP-13   ED-leff-sen   Ht: 6'2" Wt: 180 Born: 6/27/1985 Age: 27

			HOW MUCH HE PITCHED						WHAT HE GAVE UP											THE RESULTS						
Year	Team	Lg	G	GS	CG	GF	IP	BFP	H	R	ER	HR	SH	SF	HB	TBB	IBB	SO	WP	Bk	W	L	Pct	Sh	Sv-Op	Hld	ERC	ERA
2007	Salem	A+	18	0	0	6	33.1	127	14	8	6	0	0	0	3	16	1	26	2	0	2	0	1.000	0	2- -	-	1.35	1.62
2008	SnJos	A+	40	0	0	10	77.2	330	71	34	29	5	0	1	7	38	1	77	7	0	8	5	.615	0	0- -	-	4.17	3.36
2009	Conn	AA	6	0	0	2	11.1	50	10	4	4	1	0	0	2	8	1	8	2	0	2	0	1.000	0	0- -	-	5.36	3.18
2009	SnJos	A+	21	0	0	16	28.0	114	15	4	3	1	0	0	0	13	1	40	1	0	1	1	.500	0	7- -	-	1.53	0.96
2009	Fresno	AAA	22	0	0	8	30.0	129	23	9	8	2	0	0	3	16	2	24	2	1	5	0	1.000	0	2- -	-	3.36	2.40
2010	Fresno	AAA	49	0	0	13	64.1	273	55	22	17	6	5	1	6	34	1	50	3	0	7	2	.778	0	6- -	-	3.98	2.38
2011	Fresno	AAA	32	0	0	6	41.1	183	50	28	26	2	2	0	2	19	0	29	3	0	2	4	.333	0	1- -	-	5.56	5.66
2011	Giants	R	4	0	0	0	3.1	20	4	4	1	0	0	0	0	4	1	6	1	0	0	0	-	0	0- -	-	6.08	2.70
2011	SF	NL	13	0	0	2	11.1	60	17	12	12	2	0	0	1	10	0	6	0	0	0	0	-	0	0-0	1	10.57	9.53

Mike Ekstrom

Pitches: R Bats: R Pos: RP-1   Ht: 6'0" Wt: 190 Born: 8/30/1983 Age: 28

			HOW MUCH HE PITCHED						WHAT HE GAVE UP											THE RESULTS						
Year	Team	Lg	G	GS	CG	GF	IP	BFP	H	R	ER	HR	SH	SF	HB	TBB	IBB	SO	WP	Bk	W	L	Pct	Sh	Sv-Op	Hld	ERC	ERA
2011	Drham*	AAA	46	1	0	20	68.1	302	75	37	33	5	2	2	1	29	2	65	4	0	6	4	.600	0	5- -	-	4.55	4.35
2008	SD	NL	8	0	0	3	9.2	47	14	8	8	2	0	0	0	7	1	6	0	0	0	2	.000	0	0-0	0	9.38	7.45
2009	SD	NL	12	0	0	5	18.1	83	21	14	13	3	0	2	1	8	0	19	2	0	0	0	-	0	0-0	0	5.80	6.38
2010	TB	AL	15	0	0	10	16.1	68	12	6	6	0	0	1	2	9	1	10	1	0	0	1	.000	0	0-0	0	2.98	3.31
2011	TB	AL	1	0	0	1	1.0	4	1	0	0	0	0	0	0	0	0	1	0	0	0	0	-	0	0-0	0	1.95	0.00
	4 ML YEARS		36	0	0	17	45.1	202	48	28	27	5	0	3	3	24	2	36	3	0	0	3	.000	0	0-0	0	5.32	5.36

Scott Elbert

Pitches: L Bats: L Pos: RP-47   Ht: 6'1" Wt: 210 Born: 8/13/1985 Age: 26

Year	Team	Lg	G	GS	CG	GF	IP	BFP	H	R	ER	HR	SH	SF	HB	TBB	IBB	SO	WP	Bk	W	L	Pct	Sh	Sv-Op	Hld	ERC	ERA
2011	Albq*	AAA	13	0	0	4	14.1	65	13	9	8	1	0	0	1	9	1	16	1	0	2	0	1.000	0	3- -		4.33	5.02
2008	LAD	NL	10	0	0	1	6.0	31	9	8	8	2	0	0	1	4	0	8	0	0	0	0	.000	0	0-0	2	11.46	12.00
2009	LAD	NL	19	0	0	3	19.2	83	19	11	11	4	1	0	0	7	0	21	1	0	2	0	1.000	0	0-0	3	4.45	5.03
2010	LAD	NL	1	0	0	0	0.2	6	1	1	1	0	0	0	0	3	0	0	0	0	0	0	-	0	0-0	0	24.61	13.50
2011	LAD	NL	47	0	0	11	33.1	139	27	9	9	1	0	1	1	14	4	34	2	0	0	1	.000	0	2-2	7	2.60	2.43
	Postseason		1	0	0	0	0.1	3	0	0	0	0	0	0	0	2	0	0	1	0	0	0	-	0	0-0	0	19.60	0.00
	4 ML YEARS		77	0	0	15	59.2	259	56	29	29	7	1	1	2	28	4	63	3	0	2	2	.500	0	2-2	12	4.16	4.37

A.J. Ellis

Bats: R Throws: R Pos: C-29; PH-2   Ht: 6'2" Wt: 224 Born: 4/9/1981 Age: 31

Year	Team	Lg	G	AB	H	2B	3B	HR	(Hm	Rd)	TB	R	RBI	RC	TBB	IBB	SO	HBP	SH	SF	SB	CS	SB%	GDP	Avg	OBP	Slg
2011	Albq*	AAA	59	184	56	15	0	2	(-	-)	77	36	28	42	50	1	23	7	6	1	0	1	.00	5	.304	.467	.418
2008	LAD	NL	4	3	0	0	0	0	(0	0)	0	1	0	0	0	0	2	0	0	0	0	0	-	0	.000	.000	.000
2009	LAD	NL	8	10	1	0	0	0	(0	0)	1	0	1	0	0	0	1	0	0	0	0	0	-	0	.100	.100	.100
2010	LAD	NL	44	108	30	5	0	0	(0	0)	35	6	16	16	14	1	18	1	4	1	0	0	-	5	.278	.363	.324
2011	LAD	NL	31	85	23	1	1	2	(0	2)	32	8	11	11	14	0	16	3	1	0	0	1	.00	2	.271	.392	.376
	4 ML YEARS		87	206	54	6	1	2	(0	2)	68	15	28	27	28	1	37	4	5	1	0	1	.00	7	.262	.360	.330

Mark Ellis

Bats: R Throws: R Pos: 2B-123; PH-7; 1B-2   Ht: 5'10" Wt: 185 Born: 6/6/1977 Age: 35

Year	Team	Lg	G	AB	H	2B	3B	HR	(Hm	Rd)	TB	R	RBI	RC	TBB	IBB	SO	HBP	SH	SF	SB	CS	SB%	GDP	Avg	OBP	Slg
2011	Scrmto*	AAA	3	10	2	1	0	0	(-	-)	3	0	1	0	1	0	0	0	0	0	0	0	-	1	.200	.273	.300
2002	Oak	AL	98	345	94	16	4	6	(6	0)	136	58	35	55	44	1	54	4	8	3	4	2	.67	3	.272	.359	.394
2003	Oak	AL	154	553	137	31	5	9	(7	2)	205	78	52	69	48	4	94	7	9	5	6	2	.75	7	.248	.313	.371
2005	Oak	AL	122	434	137	21	5	13	(5	8)	207	76	52	78	44	1	51	4	4	0	1	3	.25	10	.316	.384	.477
2006	Oak	AL	124	441	110	25	1	11	(4	7)	170	64	52	53	40	1	76	8	4	7	4	0	1.00	13	.249	.319	.385
2007	Oak	AL	150	583	161	33	3	19	(10	9)	257	84	76	76	44	1	94	10	2	3	9	4	.69	10	.276	.336	.441
2008	Oak	AL	117	442	103	20	3	12	(7	5)	165	55	41	54	53	2	65	5	5	2	14	2	.88	11	.233	.321	.373
2009	Oak	AL	105	377	99	23	0	10	(4	6)	152	52	61	54	23	1	54	2	3	5	10	3	.77	10	.263	.305	.403
2010	Oak	AL	124	436	127	24	0	5	(0	5)	166	45	49	66	40	4	56	8	3	5	7	6	.54	7	.291	.358	.381
2011	2 Tms		132	480	119	24	1	7	(6	1)	166	55	41	40	22	0	75	6	9	2	14	5	.74	8	.248	.288	.346
11	Oak	AL	62	217	47	11	1	1	(1	0)	63	21	16	10	8	0	32	3	4	1	7	2	.78	3	.217	.253	.290
11	Col	NL	70	263	72	13	0	6	(5	1)	103	34	25	30	14	0	43	3	5	1	7	3	.70	5	.274	.317	.392
	Postseason		12	43	11	2	0	1	(1	0)	16	3	4	6	5	0	11	1	0	0	0	0	-	0	.256	.347	.372
	9 ML YEARS		1126	4091	1087	217	22	92	(52	40)	1624	567	459	545	358	15	619	54	47	32	69	27	.72	79	.266	.331	.397

Jacoby Ellsbury

Bats: L Throws: L Pos: CF-154; DH-3; PH-3; PR-2   Ht: 6'1" Wt: 185 Born: 9/11/1983 Age: 28

Year	Team	Lg	G	AB	H	2B	3B	HR	(Hm	Rd)	TB	R	RBI	RC	TBB	IBB	SO	HBP	SH	SF	SB	CS	SB%	GDP	Avg	OBP	Slg
2007	Bos	AL	33	116	41	7	1	3	(3	0)	59	20	18	26	8	0	15	1	0	2	9	0	1.00	2	.353	.394	.509
2008	Bos	AL	145	554	155	22	7	9	(4	5)	218	98	47	71	41	2	80	7	4	3	50	11	.82	10	.280	.336	.394
2009	Bos	AL	153	624	188	27	10	8	(4	4)	259	94	60	97	49	3	74	6	6	6	70	12	.85	13	.301	.355	.415
2010	Bos	AL	18	78	15	4	0	0	(0	0)	19	10	5	4	4	0	9	1	0	0	7	1	.88	0	.192	.241	.244
2011	Bos	AL	158	660	212	46	5	32	(15	17)	364	119	105	134	52	1	98	9	3	5	39	15	.72	8	.321	.376	.552
	Postseason		22	69	18	7	1	0	(0	0)	27	12	11	11	6	1	10	0	0	1	5	1	.83	2	.261	.316	.391
	5 ML YEARS		507	2032	611	106	23	52	(26	26)	919	341	235	332	154	6	276	24	13	16	175	39	.82	33	.301	.354	.452

John Ely

Pitches: R Bats: R Pos: RP-4; SP-1   Ht: 6'2" Wt: 200 Born: 5/13/1986 Age: 26

Year	Team	Lg	G	GS	CG	GF	IP	BFP	H	R	ER	HR	SH	SF	HB	TBB	IBB	SO	WP	Bk	W	L	Pct	Sh	Sv-Op	Hld	ERC	ERA
2007	Gr Falls	R+	13	12	0	0	56.0	230	55	26	24	6	1	0	3	14	0	56	1	0	6	1	.857	0	0- -	-	3.75	3.86
2008	WinSa	A+	27	27	0	0	145.1	610	142	83	76	18	3	5	5	46	0	134	6	3	10	12	.455	0	0- -	-	3.97	4.71
2009	Brham	AA	27	27	1	0	156.1	638	140	63	49	9	5	2	1	50	0	125	6	0	14	2	.875	0	0- -	-	3.01	2.82
2010	Albq	AAA	13	13	1	0	68.0	299	70	48	47	10	6	1	3	29	0	56	3	1	5	4	.556	0	0- -	-	4.88	6.22
2011	Albq	AAA	25	25	2	0	144.1	652	178	109	96	21	4	5	7	44	0	99	7	2	7	8	.467	1	0- -	-	5.54	5.99
2010	LAD	NL	18	18	0	0	100.0	430	105	63	61	12	4	4	2	40	2	76	4	0	4	10	.286	0	0-0	0	4.64	5.49
2011	LAD	NL	5	1	0	1	12.2	56	12	6	6	2	0	0	0	7	1	13	0	0	0	1	.000	0	0-0	0	4.66	4.26
	2 ML YEARS		23	19	0	1	112.2	486	117	69	67	14	4	4	2	47	3	89	4	0	4	11	.267	0	0-0	0	4.64	5.35

Brad Emaus

Bats: R Throws: R Pos: 2B-11; PH-3   EE-muss   Ht: 5'11" Wt: 210 Born: 3/28/1986 Age: 26

Year	Team	Lg	G	AB	H	2B	3B	HR	(Hm	Rd)	TB	R	RBI	RC	TBB	IBB	SO	HBP	SH	SF	SB	CS	SB%	GDP	Avg	OBP	Slg
2007	Auburn	A-	39	136	31	6	0	2	(-	-)	43	21	14	14	12	0	26	2	1	1	2	0	1.00	2	.228	.298	.316
2008	Dnedin	A+	124	473	143	34	3	12	(-	-)	219	87	71	87	60	1	56	2	0	3	12	4	.75	6	.302	.380	.463
2009	NHam	AA	137	505	128	28	2	10	(-	-)	190	67	67	71	59	4	69	8	0	9	10	3	.77	15	.253	.336	.376

			BATTING																		BASERUNNING				AVERAGES		
Year	Team	Lg	G	AB	H	2B	3B	HR	(Hm	Rd)	TB	R	RBI	RC	TBB	IBB	SO	HBP	SH	SF	SB	CS	SB%	GDP	Avg	OBP	Slg
2010	NHam	AA	38	136	37	7	0	5	(-	-)	59	21	26	27	31	2	19	0	1	2	5	0	1.00	4	.272	.402	.434
2010	LsVgs	AAA	87	309	92	25	3	10	(-	-)	153	58	49	63	50	1	50	1	2	2	8	2	.80	7	.298	.395	.495
2011	ColSpr	AAA	45	163	51	10	2	9	(-	-)	92	37	28	34	20	0	24	1	1	1	3	3	.50	3	.313	.389	.564
2011	NYM	NL	14	37	6	0	0	0	(0	0)	6	2	1	0	4	1	9	1	0	0	0	0	-	3	.162	.262	.162

Edwin Encarnacion

Bats: R Throws: R Pos: DH-70; 3B-36; 1B-25; PH-11

Ht: 6'2" Wt: 231 Born: 1/7/1983 Age: 29

			BATTING																		BASERUNNING				AVERAGES		
Year	Team	Lg	G	AB	H	2B	3B	HR	(Hm	Rd)	TB	R	RBI	RC	TBB	IBB	SO	HBP	SH	SF	SB	CS	SB%	GDP	Avg	OBP	Slg
2005	Cin	NL	69	211	49	16	0	9	(3	6)	92	25	31	24	20	2	60	3	0	0	3	0	1.00	8	.232	.308	.436
2006	Cin	NL	117	406	112	33	1	15	(7	8)	192	60	72	66	41	3	78	13	0	3	6	3	.67	9	.276	.359	.473
2007	Cin	NL	139	502	145	25	1	16	(10	6)	220	66	76	86	39	4	86	14	0	1	8	1	.89	5	.289	.356	.438
2008	Cin	NL	146	506	127	29	1	26	(15	11)	236	75	68	72	61	1	102	10	0	5	1	0	1.00	13	.251	.340	.466
2009	2 Tms		85	293	66	11	2	13	(5	8)	120	35	39	37	37	0	67	5	0	3	2	1	.67	5	.225	.320	.410
2010	Tor	AL	96	332	81	16	0	21	(7	14)	160	47	51	41	29	1	60	2	0	4	1	0	1.00	9	.244	.305	.482
2011	Tor	AL	134	481	131	36	2	17	(14	3)	218	70	55	67	43	2	77	3	0	3	8	2	.80	17	.272	.334	.453
09	Cin	NL	43	139	29	6	1	5	(3	2)	52	10	16	19	24	0	38	2	0	0	1	1	.50	3	.209	.333	.374
09	Tor	AL	42	154	37	5	1	8	(2	6)	68	25	23	18	13	0	29	3	0	3	1	0	1.00	2	.240	.306	.442
7 ML YEARS			786	2731	711	166	5	117	(61	56)	1238	378	392	393	270	13	530	50	0	19	29	7	.81	66	.260	.336	.453

Barry Enright

Pitches: R Bats: R Pos: SP-7

Ht: 6'3" Wt: 220 Born: 3/30/1986 Age: 26

			HOW MUCH HE PITCHED						WHAT HE GAVE UP											THE RESULTS						
Year	Team	Lg	G	GS	CG	GF	IP	BFP	H	R	ER	HR	SH	SF	HB	TBB	IBB	SO	WP	Bk	W	L	Pct	Sh	Sv-Op	Hld	ERC	ERA
2007	Yakima	A-	5	0	0	2	8.0	30	4	0	0	0	0	0	0	3	0	12	0	0	0	0	-	0	0--	-	1.21	0.00
2007	Sbend	A	1	0	0	1	2.0	6	1	0	0	0	0	0	0	2	0	1	0	0	0	0	-	0	1--	-	0.63	0.00
2007	Visalia	A+	4	0	0	2	5.0	20	3	1	0	0	0	0	0	2	1	4	0	0	0	0	-	0	1--	-	1.32	0.00
2008	Visalia	A+	29	29	0	0	164.1	705	185	88	81	17	2	5	4	35	1	143	7	2	12	8	.600	0	0--	-	4.13	4.44
2009	Mobile	AA	27	27	0	0	156.0	661	171	73	69	16	10	8	4	37	1	103	1	0	10	9	.526	0	0--	-	4.11	3.98
2010	Mobile	AA	14	14	1	0	93.2	368	81	34	30	9	5	3	5	15	0	83	7	0	4	1	.800	0	0--	-	2.70	2.88
2011	Reno	AAA	21	21	0	0	122.2	521	127	71	71	20	5	9	5	42	1	86	2	3	9	5	.643	0	0--	-	4.74	5.21
2010	Ari	NL	17	17	0	0	99.0	410	97	43	43	20	8	1	1	29	0	49	0	0	6	7	.462	0	0-0	0	4.34	3.91
2011	Ari	NL	7	7	0	0	37.2	175	50	31	31	11	3	2	1	15	1	21	2	0	1	4	.200	0	0-0	0	7.65	7.41
2 ML YEARS			24	24	0	0	136.2	585	147	74	74	31	11	3	2	44	1	70	2	0	7	11	.389	0	0-0	0	5.20	4.87

Nathan Eovaldi

Pitches: R Bats: R Pos: SP-6; RP-4

eh-VOLL-dee

Ht: 6'3" Wt: 195 Born: 2/13/1990 Age: 22

			HOW MUCH HE PITCHED						WHAT HE GAVE UP											THE RESULTS						
Year	Team	Lg	G	GS	CG	GF	IP	BFP	H	R	ER	HR	SH	SF	HB	TBB	IBB	SO	WP	Bk	W	L	Pct	Sh	Sv-Op	Hld	ERC	ERA
2008	Ddgrs	R	6	0	0	4	8.0	33	6	1	1	0	1	0	0	3	0	9	2	0	0	1	.000	0	1--	-	2.01	1.13
2008	Ogden	R+	1	0	0	0	2.2	8	1	0	0	0	0	0	0	0	0	2	0	0	0	0	-	0	0--	-	0.35	0.00
2009	Gt Lks	A	26	16	0	4	96.1	417	95	48	35	2	1	10	6	41	0	71	5	1	3	5	.375	0	1--	-	3.81	3.27
2010	InldEm	A+	16	14	2	0	85.0	369	99	46	42	3	3	1	4	33	0	58	6	0	3	5	.375	2	0--	-	2.76	4.45
2010	Ddgrs	R	3	3	0	0	8.1	34	6	4	4	0	1	0	1	4	0	10	1	0	0	1	.000	0	0--	-	2.76	4.32
2010	Ogden	R+	1	1	0	0	5.0	19	3	2	1	0	0	0	0	1	0	4	1	0	1	0	1.000	0	0--	-	1.11	1.80
2011	Chatt	AA	20	19	0	0	103.0	427	76	41	30	3	1	4	2	46	2	99	6	0	6	5	.545	0	0--	-	2.43	2.62
2011	LAD	NL	10	6	0	1	34.2	146	28	14	14	2	2	0	2	20	0	23	0	0	1	2	.333	0	0-0	1	3.75	3.63

Cody Eppley

Pitches: R Bats: R Pos: RP-10

Ht: 6'5" Wt: 205 Born: 10/8/1985 Age: 26

			HOW MUCH HE PITCHED						WHAT HE GAVE UP											THE RESULTS						
Year	Team	Lg	G	GS	CG	GF	IP	BFP	H	R	ER	HR	SH	SF	HB	TBB	IBB	SO	WP	Bk	W	L	Pct	Sh	Sv-Op	Hld	ERC	ERA
2008	Rngrs	R	19	0	0	15	25.2	104	19	12	6	1	0	0	6	5	0	34	5	0	2	2	.500	0	7--	-	1.61	2.10
2008	Clinton	A	2	0	0	0	2.0	9	2	2	2	0	0	0	1	0	0	3	1	0	0	0	-	0	0--	-	3.63	9.00
2009	Hkry	A	37	0	0	21	67.2	278	65	31	22	4	1	2	3	6	0	76	5	0	1	3	.250	0	6--	-	2.53	2.93
2010	Bkrsfld	A+	14	0	0	7	18.0	65	9	0	0	0	0	0	1	1	0	24	4	0	2	0	1.000	0	6--	-	0.71	0.00
2010	Frisco	AA	19	0	0	16	22.2	88	12	3	3	0	1	0	9	1	0	27	0	0	1	1	.500	0	9--	-	1.27	1.19
2010	OKCity	AAA	18	0	0	10	28.2	128	32	13	13	3	0	0	13	0	0	31	0	0	2	1	.667	0	1--	-	5.00	4.08
2011	RdRck	AAA	43	0	0	29	55.1	250	51	27	24	3	0	1	1	34	4	55	7	0	4	2	.667	0	10--	-	4.01	3.90
2011	Tex	AL	10	0	0	1	9.0	43	11	8	8	3	1	0	1	5	1	6	1	0	1	1	.500	0	0-1	2	8.30	8.00

Edgmer Escalona

Pitches: R Bats: R Pos: RP-14

EGG-merr

Ht: 6'4" Wt: 215 Born: 10/6/1986 Age: 25

			HOW MUCH HE PITCHED						WHAT HE GAVE UP											THE RESULTS						
Year	Team	Lg	G	GS	CG	GF	IP	BFP	H	R	ER	HR	SH	SF	HB	TBB	IBB	SO	WP	Bk	W	L	Pct	Sh	Sv-Op	Hld	ERC	ERA
2007	Casper	R+	18	0	0	8	26.2	118	22	17	12	1	0	0	1	13	1	20	3	0	1	1	.500	0	1--	-	2.97	4.05
2008	Ashvll	A	44	0	0	17	78.1	320	71	32	28	9	2	1	6	18	0	79	5	1	6	2	.750	0	1--	-	3.35	3.22
2009	Mdest	A+	28	0	0	7	32.2	130	25	10	9	3	0	0	2	7	0	34	3	0	2	0	1.000	0	0--	-	2.34	2.48
2009	Tulsa	AA	31	0	0	15	36.2	158	33	12	10	5	2	0	3	11	0	32	1	0	1	2	.333	0	4--	-	3.60	2.45
2010	ColSpr	AAA	57	0	0	18	69.0	306	66	47	46	17	3	6	4	32	3	74	6	4	3	5	.375	0	1--	-	5.25	6.00
2011	ColSpr	AAA	34	0	0	11	39.2	162	35	14	14	4	2	1	3	11	1	40	5	1	3	1	.750	0	1--	-	3.29	3.18
2010	Col	NL	5	0	0	2	6.0	26	4	1	1	0	0	1	0	4	2	2	1	0	0	0	-	0	0-0	0	2.02	1.50
2011	Col	NL	14	0	0	5	25.2	99	17	5	5	3	1	0	0	7	2	14	0	0	0	0	-	0	0-0	0	1.92	1.75
2 ML YEARS			19	0	0	7	31.2	125	21	6	6	3	1	0	0	11	4	16	1	0	0	0	-	0	0-0	0	1.97	1.71

Sergio Escalona

Pitches: L **Bats:** L **Pos:** RP-49

Ht: 6'0" **Wt:** 210 **Born:** 8/3/1984 **Age:** 27

Year	Team	Lg	G	GS	CG	GF	IP	BFP	H	R	ER	HR	SH	SF	HB	TBB	IBB	SO	WP	Bk	W	L	Pct	Sh	Sv-Op	Hld	ERC	ERA
2007	Clrwtr	A+	1	1	0	0	4.0	21	8	1	1	0	1	0	0	2	0	4	0	0	0	0	-	0	0- -	-	10.21	2.25
2007	Wmspt	A-	7	7	0	0	27.1	128	32	26	23	2	0	1	2	19	0	26	2	0	2	2	.500	0	0- -	-	6.58	7.57
2007	Lakwd	A	7	7	0	0	39.0	177	51	25	18	4	2	4	1	11	0	32	1	0	1	4	.200	0	0- -	-	5.47	4.15
2008	Lakwd	A	28	0	0	8	44.2	181	36	18	17	1	1	1	0	18	1	60	1	0	5	1	.833	0	2- -	-	2.58	3.43
2008	Rdng	AA	15	0	0	5	24.1	112	27	12	6	3	1	0	1	14	0	29	0	0	0	1	.000	0	1- -	-	5.80	2.22
2009	Rdng	AA	32	0	0	22	40.2	168	31	12	8	1	2	0	3	14	1	38	3	0	2	1	.667	0	12- -	-	2.35	1.77
2009	LV	AAA	15	1	0	9	19.2	89	21	15	13	4	0	1	1	8	1	15	3	1	0	2	.000	0	2- -	-	5.26	5.95
2010	Rdng	AA	50	0	0	25	54.1	229	46	25	23	6	2	2	0	22	0	53	0	0	4	8	.333	0	10- -	-	3.29	3.81
2011	OKCity	AAA	14	0	0	10	17.0	70	13	6	6	1	2	1	1	5	0	18	2	0	1	0	1.000	0	3- -	-	2.36	3.18
2009	Phi	NL	14	0	0	4	13.2	60	12	7	7	0	0	2	3	5	1	10	1	0	1	0	1.000	0	0-0	2	3.24	4.61
2011	Hou	NL	49	0	0	5	27.2	115	24	10	9	3	2	0	2	11	1	25	2	0	2	1	.667	0	0-1	6	3.72	2.93
	2 ML YEARS		63	0	0	9	41.1	175	36	17	16	3	2	2	5	16	2	35	3	0	3	1	.750	0	0-1	8	3.57	3.48

Alcides Escobar

Bats: R **Throws:** R **Pos:** SS-158; PR-1

al-SEE-dess

Ht: 6'1" **Wt:** 182 **Born:** 12/16/1986 **Age:** 25

Year	Team	Lg	G	AB	H	2B	3B	HR	(Hm	Rd)	TB	R	RBI	RC	TBB	IBB	SO	HBP	SH	SF	SB	CS	SB%	GDP	Avg	OBP	Slg
2008	Mil	NL	9	4	2	0	0	0	(0	0)	2	2	0	0	0	0	1	0	0	0	0	0	-	0	.500	.500	.500
2009	Mil	NL	38	125	38	5	1	0	(0	1)	46	20	11	16	4	0	18	2	2	1	4	2	.67	0	.304	.333	.368
2010	Mil	NL	145	506	119	14	10	4	(3	1)	165	57	41	51	36	7	70	4	3	4	10	4	.71	8	.235	.288	.326
2011	KC	AL	158	548	139	21	8	4	(0	4)	188	69	46	46	25	1	73	4	18	3	26	9	.74	10	.254	.290	.343
	4 ML YEARS		350	1183	298	38	19	9	(3	6)	401	148	98	113	65	8	162	9	24	7	40	15	.73	18	.252	.294	.339

Eduardo Escobar

Bats: B **Throws:** R **Pos:** SS-3; PH-3; PR-3; 2B-2; DH-1

Ht: 5'10" **Wt:** 150 **Born:** 1/5/1989 **Age:** 23

Year	Team	Lg	G	AB	H	2B	3B	HR	(Hm	Rd)	TB	R	RBI	RC	TBB	IBB	SO	HBP	SH	SF	SB	CS	SB%	GDP	Avg	OBP	Slg
2008	Gr Falls	R+	6	24	10	2	1	1	(-	-)	17	6	4	7	2	0	3	1	0	1	1	1	.50	0	.417	.464	.708
2008	Knapol	A	60	243	65	6	1	0	(-	-)	73	37	22	22	13	0	65	0	8	2	4	3	.57	1	.267	.302	.300
2009	Knapol	A	128	464	119	10	7	3	(-	-)	152	64	41	49	29	1	91	1	17	3	20	6	.77	9	.256	.300	.328
2010	WinSa	A+	87	368	105	18	8	3	(-	-)	148	57	39	50	23	2	76	1	11	4	8	5	.62	9	.285	.327	.402
2010	Brham	AA	49	202	53	8	3	3	(-	-)	76	22	22	23	9	0	35	0	5	0	3	0	1.00	5	.262	.294	.376
2011	Charltt	AAA	137	489	130	23	4	4	(-	-)	173	55	49	54	27	0	104	1	15	4	13	8	.62	6	.266	.303	.354
2011	CWS	AL	9	7	2	0	0	0	(0	0)	2	0	0	1	0	0	1	0	0	0	0	0	-	0	.286	.286	.286

Yunel Escobar

Bats: R **Throws:** R **Pos:** SS-132; PH-2; DH-1

you-NELL

Ht: 6'2" **Wt:** 200 **Born:** 11/2/1982 **Age:** 29

Year	Team	Lg	G	AB	H	2B	3B	HR	(Hm	Rd)	TB	R	RBI	RC	TBB	IBB	SO	HBP	SH	SF	SB	CS	SB%	GDP	Avg	OBP	Slg
2007	Atl	NL	94	319	104	25	0	5	(3	2)	144	54	28	52	27	1	44	5	2	2	5	3	.63	6	.326	.385	.451
2008	Atl	NL	136	514	148	24	2	10	(5	5)	206	71	60	70	59	4	62	5	7	2	2	5	.29	24	.288	.366	.401
2009	Atl	NL	141	528	158	26	2	14	(7	7)	230	89	76	90	57	3	62	10	7	2	5	4	.56	21	.299	.377	.436
2010	2 Tms		135	497	127	19	0	4	(2	2)	158	60	35	53	56	1	57	5	9	0	6	2	.75	18	.256	.337	.318
2011	Tor	AL	133	513	149	24	3	11	(8	3)	212	77	48	84	61	1	70	6	5	5	3	3	.50	14	.290	.369	.413
10	Atl	NL	75	261	62	12	0	0	(0	0)	74	28	19	25	37	1	31	1	2	0	5	1	.83	9	.238	.334	.284
10	Tor	AL	60	236	65	7	0	4	(2	2)	84	32	16	29	19	0	26	4	7	0	1	1	.50	9	.275	.340	.356
	5 ML YEARS		639	2371	686	118	7	44	(25	19)	950	351	247	349	260	10	295	31	30	11	21	17	.55	83	.289	.366	.401

Danny Espinosa

Bats: B **Throws:** R **Pos:** 2B-158; PH-1

Ht: 6'0" **Wt:** 190 **Born:** 4/25/1987 **Age:** 25

Year	Team	Lg	G	AB	H	2B	3B	HR	(Hm	Rd)	TB	R	RBI	RC	TBB	IBB	SO	HBP	SH	SF	SB	CS	SB%	GDP	Avg	OBP	Slg
2008	Vrmnt	A-	19	64	21	2	0	0	(-	-)	23	8	4	13	17	1	17	2	3	1	2	2	.50	1	.328	.476	.359
2009	Ptomc	A+	133	474	125	31	4	18	(-	-)	218	90	72	88	74	2	129	13	10	5	29	11	.73	8	.264	.375	.460
2010	Hrsbrg	AA	99	386	101	16	4	18	(-	-)	179	66	54	62	33	0	94	10	3	2	20	8	.71	9	.262	.334	.464
2010	Syrcse	AAA	24	95	28	2	1	4	(-	-)	44	14	15	15	8	2	22	1	2	2	5	3	.63	2	.295	.349	.463
2010	Was	NL	28	103	22	4	1	6	(4	2)	46	16	15	15	9	1	30	0	0	0	2	0	.00	4	.214	.277	.447
2011	Was	NL	158	573	135	29	5	21	(11	10)	237	72	66	83	57	4	166	19	5	4	17	6	.74	6	.236	.323	.414
	2 ML YEARS		186	676	157	33	6	27	(15	12)	283	88	81	98	66	5	196	19	5	4	17	8	.68	6	.232	.316	.419

Marco Estrada

Pitches: R **Bats:** R **Pos:** RP-36; SP-7

Ht: 6'0" **Wt:** 180 **Born:** 7/5/1983 **Age:** 28

Year	Team	Lg	G	GS	CG	GF	IP	BFP	H	R	ER	HR	SH	SF	HB	TBB	IBB	SO	WP	Bk	W	L	Pct	Sh	Sv-Op	Hld	ERC	ERA
2008	Was	NL	11	0	0	3	12.2	63	17	13	11	4	0	0	2	5	1	10	0	0	0	0	-	0	0-1	3	8.13	7.82
2009	Was	NL	4	1	0	1	7.1	33	6	6	5	1	1	0	1	4	0	9	1	0	0	1	.000	0	0-0	0	3.67	6.14
2010	Mil	NL	7	1	0	0	11.1	58	14	13	12	3	1	0	1	6	0	13	2	0	0	0	-	0	0-0	0	7.17	9.53
2011	Mil	NL	43	7	0	12	92.2	381	83	45	42	11	7	1	2	29	2	88	4	2	4	8	.333	0	0-3	4	3.39	4.08
	4 ML YEARS		65	9	0	16	124.0	535	120	77	70	19	9	1	5	44	3	120	7	2	4	9	.308	0	0-4	7	4.17	5.08

Andre Ethier

Bats: L **Throws:** L **Pos:** RF-126; PH-8; DH-2 **Ht:** 6'2" **Wt:** 205 **Born:** 4/10/1982 **Age:** 30

Year	Team	Lg	G	AB	H	2B	3B	HR	(Hm	Rd)	TB	R	RBI	RC	TBB	IBB	SO	HBP	SH	SF	SB	CS	SB%	GDP	Avg	OBP	Slg
2006	LAD	NL	126	396	122	20	7	11	(9	2)	189	50	55	62	34	2	77	5	0	6	5	5	.50	11	.308	.365	.477
2007	LAD	NL	153	447	127	32	2	13	(8	5)	202	50	64	65	46	12	68	4	0	8	0	4	.00	10	.284	.350	.452
2008	LAD	NL	141	525	160	38	5	20	(10	10)	268	90	77	99	59	0	88	4	1	7	6	3	.67	6	.305	.375	.510
2009	LAD	NL	160	596	162	42	3	31	(22	9)	303	92	106	94	72	10	116	13	0	4	6	4	.60	19	.272	.361	.508
2010	LAD	NL	139	517	151	33	1	23	(14	9)	255	71	82	89	59	11	102	3	0	6	2	1	.67	11	.292	.364	.493
2011	LAD	NL	135	487	142	30	0	11	(8	3)	205	67	62	73	58	9	103	3	0	3	0	1	.00	8	.292	.368	.421
	Postseason		18	64	17	4	1	3	(1	2)	32	13	6	8	8	0	16	1	0	0	0	1	.00	1	.266	.356	.500
6 ML YEARS			854	2968	864	195	18	109	(71	38)	1422	420	446	482	328	44	554	32	1	34	19	18	.51	65	.291	.364	.479

Nick Evans

Bats: R **Throws:** R **Pos:** 1B-45; PH-14; RF-8; 3B-2; LF-1 **Ht:** 6'2" **Wt:** 219 **Born:** 1/30/1986 **Age:** 26

Year	Team	Lg	G	AB	H	2B	3B	HR	(Hm	Rd)	TB	R	RBI	RC	TBB	IBB	SO	HBP	SH	SF	SB	CS	SB%	GDP	Avg	OBP	Slg
2011	Buffalo*	AAA	64	249	78	13	6	8	(-	-)	115	31	32	44	26	2	50	0	0	2	3	0	1.00	9	.313	.375	.462
2008	NYM	NL	50	109	28	10	0	2	(0	2)	44	18	9	10	7	2	24	1	0	2	0	0	-	1	.257	.303	.404
2009	NYM	NL	30	65	15	5	1	1	(1	0)	25	5	7	8	4	0	20	0	0	0	0	0	-	4	.231	.275	.385
2010	NYM	NL	20	36	11	3	0	1	(1	0)	17	5	5	5	1	0	10	0	0	0	0	0	-	1	.306	.324	.472
2011	NYM	NL	59	176	45	10	2	4	(0	4)	71	26	25	21	15	0	48	1	0	2	0	1	.00	6	.256	.314	.403
4 ML YEARS			159	386	99	28	3	8	(2	6)	157	54	46	44	27	2	102	2	0	4	0	1	.00	12	.256	.305	.407

Dana Eveland

Pitches: L **Bats:** L **Pos:** SP-5 EVE-land **Ht:** 6'1" **Wt:** 235 **Born:** 10/29/1983 **Age:** 28

			HOW MUCH HE PITCHED					WHAT HE GAVE UP											THE RESULTS						
Year	Team	Lg	G	GS	CG	GF	IP	BFP	H	R	ER	HR	SH	SF	HB	TBB	IBB	SO	WP	Bk	W	L	Pct	Sh	Sv-Op	Hld	ERC	ERA
2011	Albq*	AAA	25	25	2	0	154.0	666	151	83	75	11	7	6	11	60	0	107	8	0	12	8	.600	1	0- -	-	4.06	4.38
2005	Mil	NL	27	0	0	3	31.2	146	40	21	21	2	0	1	1	18	3	23	1	0	1	1	.500	0	1-2	7	6.16	5.97
2006	Mil	NL	9	5	0	1	27.2	141	39	25	25	4	1	1	5	16	2	32	2	0	0	3	.000	0	0-1	0	8.30	8.13
2007	Ari	NL	5	1	0	0	5.0	28	8	8	8	0	0	1	0	5	0	3	1	0	1	0	1.000	0	0-0	0	9.25	14.40
2008	Oak	AL	29	29	1	0	168.0	737	172	82	81	10	2	5	12	77	2	118	6	1	9	9	.500	0	0-0	0	4.47	4.34
2009	Oak	AL	13	9	0	2	44.0	221	70	39	35	4	1	2	0	26	1	22	2	0	2	4	.333	0	0-0	0	8.50	7.16
2010	2 Tms		12	10	0	1	54.1	262	72	44	41	4	0	4	4	32	2	24	4	0	3	5	.375	0	0-0	0	6.90	6.79
2011	LAD	NL	5	5	0	0	29.2	118	28	10	10	1	1	0	2	6	0	16	0	0	3	2	.600	0	0-0	0	2.98	3.03
10	Tor	AL	9	9	0	0	44.2	213	57	35	32	4	0	2	2	27	1	21	3	0	3	4	.429	0	0-0	0	6.69	6.45
10	Pit	NL	3	1	0	1	9.2	49	15	9	9	0	0	2	2	5	1	3	1	0	0	1	.000	0	0-0	0	7.85	8.38
7 ML YEARS			100	59	1	7	360.1	1653	429	229	221	25	5	14	24	180	10	238	16	1	19	24	.442	0	1-3	7	5.65	5.52

Adam Everett

Bats: R **Throws:** R **Pos:** 3B-16; PR-9; 2B-8; DH-5; SS-4; PH-3 **Ht:** 6'0" **Wt:** 178 **Born:** 2/5/1977 **Age:** 35

Year	Team	Lg	G	AB	H	2B	3B	HR	(Hm	Rd)	TB	R	RBI	RC	TBB	IBB	SO	HBP	SH	SF	SB	CS	SB%	GDP	Avg	OBP	Slg
2001	Hou	NL	9	3	0	0	0	0	(0	0)	0	1	0	0	0	0	1	0	0	0	1	0	1.00	0	.000	.000	.000
2002	Hou	NL	40	88	17	3	0	0	(0	0)	20	11	4	6	12	1	19	1	2	0	3	0	1.00	1	.193	.297	.227
2003	Hou	NL	128	387	99	18	3	8	(5	3)	147	51	51	50	28	6	66	9	11	7	8	1	.89	7	.256	.320	.380
2004	Hou	NL	104	384	105	15	2	8	(5	3)	148	66	31	51	17	0	56	9	22	3	13	2	.87	6	.273	.317	.385
2005	Hou	NL	152	549	136	27	4	11	(7	4)	200	58	54	61	26	1	103	8	8	4	21	7	.75	5	.248	.290	.364
2006	Hou	NL	150	514	123	28	6	6	(2	4)	181	52	59	50	34	5	71	4	10	4	9	6	.60	5	.239	.290	.352
2007	Hou	NL	66	220	51	11	1	2	(1	1)	70	18	15	21	14	0	31	1	1	0	4	2	.67	3	.232	.281	.318
2008	Min	AL	48	127	27	6	1	2	(2	0)	41	19	20	15	12	1	15	1	6	4	0	0	-	0	.213	.278	.323
2009	Det	AL	118	345	82	21	0	3	(1	2)	112	43	44	34	22	0	61	4	15	4	5	2	.71	9	.238	.288	.325
2010	Det	AL	31	81	15	5	0	0	(0	0)	20	6	4	1	4	0	18	0	3	1	2	1	.67	1	.185	.221	.247
2011	Cle	AL	34	60	13	1	0	0	(0	0)	14	9	1	2	5	0	14	0	2	0	1	0	1.00	0	.217	.277	.233
	Postseason		19	53	11	1	1	0	(0	0)	14	5	3	1	2	0	9	0	2	1	0	1	.00	2	.208	.232	.264
11 ML YEARS			880	2758	668	135	15	40	(23	17)	953	334	283	291	174	14	455	37	80	21	67	21	.76	35	.242	.294	.346

Willie Eyre

Pitches: R **Bats:** R **Pos:** RP-19 AIR **Ht:** 6'2" **Wt:** 205 **Born:** 7/21/1978 **Age:** 33

			HOW MUCH HE PITCHED					WHAT HE GAVE UP											THE RESULTS						
Year	Team	Lg	G	GS	CG	GF	IP	BFP	H	R	ER	HR	SH	SF	HB	TBB	IBB	SO	WP	Bk	W	L	Pct	Sh	Sv-Op	Hld	ERC	ERA
2011	Scrmto*	AAA	39	2	0	23	62.0	268	63	29	24	5	3	2	1	28	2	45	10	0	4	1	.444	0	9- -	-	4.31	3.48
2011	Norfolk*	AAA	3	0	0	1	3.1	12	1	0	0	0	0	0	1	1	1	1	0	0	1	0	1.000	0	0- -	-	0.85	0.00
2006	Min	AL	42	0	0	20	59.1	275	75	36	35	8	1	3	6	22	4	26	4	0	1	0	1.000	0	0-0	1	6.07	5.31
2007	Tex	AL	33	2	0	10	68.0	307	78	42	39	8	5	1	1	32	4	42	5	0	4	6	.400	0	1-1	1	5.32	5.16
2009	Tex	AL	17	0	0	6	18.0	72	18	9	9	0	2	0	0	6	2	8	0	0	0	0	-	0	0-0	0	3.16	4.50
2011	Bal	AL	19	0	0	4	18.1	72	12	7	7	2	1	2	0	5	0	10	1	0	2	2	.500	0	0-0	3	1.88	3.44
4 ML YEARS			111	2	0	40	163.2	726	183	94	90	18	9	6	7	65	10	86	10	0	7	8	.467	0	1-1	4	4.91	4.95

Kyle Farnsworth

Pitches: R Bats: R Pos: RP-63   Ht: 6'4" Wt: 230 Born: 4/14/1976 Age: 36

Year	Team	Lg	G	GS	CG	GF	IP	BFP	H	R	ER	HR	SH	SF	HB	TBB	IBB	SO	WP	Bk	W	L	Pct	Sh	Sv-Op	Hld	ERC	ERA
1999	ChC	NL	27	21	1	1	130.0	579	140	80	73	28	6	2	3	52	1	70	7	1	5	9	.357	1	0-0	0	5.39	5.05
2000	ChC	NL	46	5	0	8	77.0	371	90	58	55	14	4	4	4	50	8	74	3	0	2	9	.182	0	1-6	6	6.72	6.43
2001	ChC	NL	76	0	0	24	82.0	339	65	26	25	8	2	2	1	29	2	107	2	2	4	6	.400	0	2-3	24	2.76	2.74
2002	ChC	NL	45	0	0	17	46.2	213	53	47	38	9	2	5	1	24	7	46	1	0	4	6	.400	0	1-7	6	5.89	7.33
2003	ChC	NL	77	0	0	13	76.1	312	53	31	28	6	4	1	0	36	1	92	6	0	3	2	.600	0	0-3	19	2.58	3.30
2004	ChC	NL	72	0	0	25	66.2	298	67	39	35	10	5	0	2	33	1	78	1	0	4	5	.444	0	0-4	18	4.91	4.73
2005	2 Tms		72	0	0	34	70.0	277	44	18	17	5	2	1	3	27	0	87	3	1	1	1	.500	0	16-18	19	2.12	2.19
2006	NYY	AL	72	0	0	24	66.0	289	62	34	32	8	3	2	1	28	3	75	5	1	3	6	.333	0	6-10	19	3.88	4.36
2007	NYY	AL	64	0	0	11	60.0	266	60	35	32	9	1	2	2	27	2	48	4	2	2	1	.667	0	0-3	15	4.67	4.80
2008	2 Tms		61	0	0	11	60.1	261	70	32	30	15	3	1	1	22	4	61	1	1	2	3	.400	0	1-4	14	6.11	4.48
2009	KC	AL	41	0	0	18	37.1	168	43	22	19	3	1	2	1	14	2	42	2	1	1	5	.167	0	0-2	5	4.65	4.58
2010	2 Tms		60	0	0	15	64.2	267	55	25	24	4	3	2	4	19	1	61	3	0	3	2	.600	0	0-3	9	2.84	3.34
2011	TB	AL	63	0	0	51	57.2	231	45	15	14	5	1	2	3	12	1	51	2	0	5	1	.833	0	25-31	0	2.29	2.18
05	Det	AL	46	0	0	16	42.2	174	29	12	11	1	1	1	1	20	0	55	2	0	1	1	.500	0	6-8	15	2.26	2.32
05	Atl	NL	26	0	0	18	27.1	103	15	6	6	4	1	0	2	7	0	32	1	1	0	0	-	0	10-10	4	1.86	1.98
08	NYY	AL	45	0	0	6	44.1	185	43	18	18	11	3	1	1	17	3	43	1	1	1	2	.333	0	1-1	11	5.02	3.65
08	Det	AL	16	0	0	5	16.0	76	27	14	12	4	0	0	0	5	1	18	0	0	1	1	.500	0	0-3	3	9.43	6.75
10	KC	AL	37	0	0	9	44.2	185	40	13	12	2	1	1	4	12	0	36	2	0	3	0	1.000	0	0-2	7	3.01	2.42
10	Atl	NL	23	0	0	6	20.0	82	15	12	12	2	2	1	0	7	1	25	1	0	0	2	.000	0	0-1	2	2.46	5.40
	Postseason		15	0	0	5	16.0	66	12	9	9	2	1	1	1	6	2	17	0	0	1	0	1.000	0	0-0	2	2.86	5.06
	13 ML YEARS		776	26	1	252	894.2	3871	847	462	422	124	37	26	26	373	33	892	40	9	39	56	.411	1	52-94	154	4.15	4.25

Danny Farquhar

Pitches: R Bats: R Pos: RP-3   FARK-war   Ht: 5'10" Wt: 170 Born: 2/17/1987 Age: 25

Year	Team	Lg	G	GS	CG	GF	IP	BFP	H	R	ER	HR	SH	SF	HB	TBB	IBB	SO	WP	Bk	W	L	Pct	Sh	Sv-Op	Hld	ERC	ERA
2008	Auburn	A-	12	0	0	4	26.1	105	20	10	7	1	3	0	3	6	0	27	2	0	2	2	.500	0	0- -	-	2.26	2.39
2008	Lnsng	A	3	0	0	0	6.0	21	0	1	0	0	0	0	1	2	0	4	1	0	0	0	-	0	0- -	-	0.27	0.00
2009	Dnedin	A+	17	0	0	15	17.0	73	10	4	1	0	0	0	1	11	0	23	2	0	1	0	1.000	0	7- -	-	2.29	0.53
2009	NHam	AA	37	0	0	27	45.2	199	31	15	12	1	1	2	5	30	3	51	4	0	1	4	.200	0	15- -	-	3.03	2.36
2010	NHam	AA	53	0	0	35	76.2	322	50	32	30	7	5	2	8	42	3	79	3	0	4	3	.571	0	17- -	-	3.06	3.52
2011	Scrmto	AAA	4	0	0	1	8.0	36	7	1	0	0	1	0	2	3	1	9	0	0	0	0	-	0	1- -	-	3.21	0.00
2011	LsVgs	AAA	50	0	0	40	51.2	234	63	32	27	4	1	1	4	18	0	43	2	0	4	5	.444	0	14- -	-	5.29	4.70
2011	Tor	AL	3	0	0	2	2.0	11	4	4	3	0	0	1	0	2	0	1	0	0	0	0	-	0	0-0	-	13.16	13.50

Eric Farris

Bats: R Throws: R Pos: PH-1   Ht: 5'9" Wt: 180 Born: 3/3/1986 Age: 26

Year	Team	Lg	G	AB	H	2B	3B	HR	(Hm	Rd)	TB	R	RBI	RC	TBB	IBB	SO	HBP	SH	SF	SB	CS	SB%	GDP	Avg	OBP	Slg
2007	Helena	R+	63	239	78	16	2	1	(-	-)	101	34	34	41	16	0	22	2	9	3	21	5	.81	3	.326	.369	.423
2008	WV	A	103	454	133	21	4	3	(-	-)	171	73	54	61	24	0	50	5	4	5	32	10	.76	11	.293	.332	.377
2009	BrvdCt	A+	124	473	141	18	1	7	(-	-)	182	68	49	76	29	1	46	3	26	3	70	6	.92	10	.298	.341	.385
2010	Nashv	AAA	60	230	63	9	1	2	(-	-)	80	28	15	27	9	0	25	4	5	1	14	2	.88	8	.274	.311	.348
2010	Brewrs	R	10	32	8	5	0	1	(-	-)	16	4	8	4	1	0	4	0	0	2	1	0	1.00	0	.250	.257	.500
2011	Nashv	AAA	134	538	146	26	5	6	(-	-)	200	70	55	68	32	0	70	6	14	4	21	7	.75	17	.271	.317	.372
2011	Mil	NL	1	1	0	0	0	0	(0	0)	0	0	0	0	0	0	0	0	0	0	0	0	-	0	.000	.000	.000

Tim Federowicz

Bats: R Throws: R Pos: C-7; PH-1   fed-ur-OWE-vitch   Ht: 5'11" Wt: 200 Born: 8/5/1987 Age: 24

Year	Team	Lg	G	AB	H	2B	3B	HR	(Hm	Rd)	TB	R	RBI	RC	TBB	IBB	SO	HBP	SH	SF	SB	CS	SB%	GDP	Avg	OBP	Slg
2008	Lowell	A-	36	127	31	6	0	1	(-	-)	40	14	15	16	19	0	24	0	0	2	2	0	1.00	2	.244	.338	.315
2009	Grnville	A	55	226	78	19	0	10	(-	-)	127	34	34	48	15	1	42	4	0	2	1	0	1.00	2	.345	.393	.562
2009	Salem	A+	51	187	48	13	0	4	(-	-)	73	18	24	20	5	0	22	1	1	3	0	0	-	8	.257	.276	.390
2010	Salem	A+	109	407	103	34	1	4	(-	-)	151	47	61	51	43	1	86	2	0	5	1	1	.50	17	.253	.324	.371
2011	Portlnd	AA	90	339	94	20	0	8	(-	-)	138	46	52	50	32	1	63	3	0	8	1	0	1.00	14	.277	.338	.407
2011	Albq	AAA	25	83	27	7	0	6	(-	-)	52	17	17	22	15	0	20	2	0	2	0	0	-	4	.325	.431	.627
2011	LAD	NL	7	13	2	0	0	0	(0	0)	2	0	1	1	2	0	4	1	0	0	0	0	-	0	.154	.313	.154

Scott Feldman

Pitches: R Bats: L Pos: RP-9; SP-2   Ht: 6'7" Wt: 230 Born: 2/7/1983 Age: 29

Year	Team	Lg	G	GS	CG	GF	IP	BFP	H	R	ER	HR	SH	SF	HB	TBB	IBB	SO	WP	Bk	W	L	Pct	Sh	Sv-Op	Hld	ERC	ERA
2011	Frisco*	AA	2	2	0	0	9.0	34	5	3	3	0	0	0	0	2	0	8	0	0	1	0	1.000	0	0- -	-	1.04	3.00
2011	RdRck*	AAA	8	8	0	0	40.2	175	48	24	20	5	3	1	1	9	0	24	1	0	2	1	.667	0	0- -	-	4.68	4.43
2005	Tex	AL	8	0	0	3	9.1	37	9	1	1	0	0	0	0	2	1	4	0	0	0	1	.000	0	0-0	1	2.48	0.96
2006	Tex	AL	36	0	0	5	41.1	175	42	19	18	4	2	1	4	10	0	30	0	0	0	2	.000	0	0-1	7	3.94	3.92
2007	Tex	AL	29	0	0	10	39.0	192	44	26	25	3	0	2	3	32	5	19	2	2	1	2	.333	0	0-0	0	6.40	5.77
2008	Tex	AL	28	25	0	2	151.1	651	161	103	89	22	1	9	10	56	2	74	4	2	6	8	.429	0	0-0	0	5.03	5.29
2009	Tex	AL	34	31	0	0	189.2	791	178	87	86	18	1	3	9	65	0	113	5	2	17	8	.680	0	0-0	0	3.74	4.08
2010	Tex	AL	29	22	0	6	141.1	641	181	98	86	18	5	8	5	45	2	75	11	0	7	11	.389	0	0-0	0	5.71	5.48
2011	Tex	AL	11	2	0	5	32.0	129	25	14	14	3	0	1	2	10	0	22	2	0	2	1	.667	0	0-0	1	2.83	3.94
	7 ML YEARS		175	80	0	27	604.0	2616	640	348	319	68	9	24	33	220	10	337	24	6	33	33	.500	0	0-1	8	4.61	4.75

Neftali Feliz

Pitches: R **Bats:** R **Pos:** RP-64 — neff-TAH-lee — **Ht:** 6'3" **Wt:** 215 **Born:** 5/2/1988 **Age:** 24

		HOW MUCH HE PITCHED			WHAT HE GAVE UP											THE RESULTS						
Year Team	Lg	G GS CG GF	IP	BFP	H	R	ER	HR SH SF HB	TBB IBB	SO	WP Bk	W	L	Pct	Sh	Sv-Op	Hld	ERC	ERA
2011 Frisco*	AA	1 1 0 0	1.0	4	1	0	0	0 0 0 0	0 0	3	0 0	0	0	-	0	0--	-	1.95	0.00
2009 Tex	AL	20 0 0 3	31.0	117	13	6	6	2 1 0 3	8 0	39	0 0	1	0	1.000	0	2-3	9	1.14	1.74
2010 Tex	AL	70 0 0 59	69.1	269	43	21	21	5 1 0 5	18 1	71	5 0	4	3	.571	0	40-43	3	1.75	2.73
2011 Tex	AL	64 0 0 56	62.1	252	42	22	19	4 3 2 0	30 1	54	2 1	2	3	.400	0	32-38	0	2.45	2.74
Postseason		7 0 0 6	7.1	30	3	1	1	1 0 0 0	5 0	11	0 0	0	0	-	0	1-1	0	2.25	1.23
3 ML YEARS		154 0 0 118	162.2	638	98	49	46	11 5 2 8	56 2	164	7 1	7	6	.538	0	74-84	12	1.84	2.55

Tommy Field

Bats: R **Throws:** R **Pos:** SS-15; RF-1; PH-1 — **Ht:** 5'9" **Wt:** 175 **Born:** 2/22/1987 **Age:** 25

								BATTING											BASERUNNING				AVERAGES		
Year Team	Lg	G	AB	H	2B	3B	HR	(Hm Rd)	TB	R	RBI	RC	TBB IBB	SO	HBP SH SF		SB	CS	SB%	GDP	Avg	OBP	Slg
2008 TriCity	A-	56	182	45	8	2	5	(- -)	72	34	32	33	42 0	34	6 1 1		10	6	.63	3	.247	.403	.396
2009 Ashvll	A	89	304	78	17	0	2	(- -)	101	42	32	37	26 2	58	11 5 2		8	3	.73	3	.257	.335	.332
2010 Mdest	A+	124	440	125	21	7	15	(- -)	205	84	72	88	66 2	114	21 9 7		16	5	.76	5	.284	.397	.466
2011 Tulsa	AA	134	472	128	22	3	17	(- -)	207	77	61	78	53 1	108	12 3 4		9	4	.69	7	.271	.357	.439
2011 Col	NL	16	48	13	0	0	0	(0 0)	13	4	3	4	3 0	14	0 0 0		0	0	-	1	.271	.314	.271

Prince Fielder

Bats: L **Throws:** R **Pos:** 1B-159; DH-3 — **Ht:** 5'11" **Wt:** 268 **Born:** 5/9/1984 **Age:** 28

								BATTING											BASERUNNING				AVERAGES		
Year Team	Lg	G	AB	H	2B	3B	HR	(Hm Rd)	TB	R	RBI	RC	TBB IBB	SO	HBP SH SF		SB	CS	SB%	GDP	Avg	OBP	Slg
2005 Mil	NL	39	59	17	4	0	2	(2 0)	27	2	10	10	2 0	17	0 0 1		0	0	-	0	.288	.306	.458
2006 Mil	NL	157	569	154	35	1	28	(11 17)	275	82	81	84	59 5	125	12 0 8		7	2	.78	17	.271	.347	.483
2007 Mil	NL	158	573	165	35	2	50	(27 23)	354	109	119	125	90 21	121	14 0 4		2	2	.50	9	.288	.395	.618
2008 Mil	NL	159	588	162	30	2	34	(18 16)	298	86	102	105	84 19	134	12 0 10		3	2	.60	12	.276	.372	.507
2009 Mil	NL	162	591	177	35	3	46	(23 23)	356	103	141	134	110 21	138	9 0 9		2	3	.40	14	.299	.412	.602
2010 Mil	NL	161	578	151	25	0	32	(18 14)	272	94	83	94	114 17	138	21 0 1		1	0	1.00	12	.261	.401	.471
2011 Mil	NL	162	569	170	36	1	38	(24 14)	322	95	120	120	107 32	106	10 0 6		1	1	.50	17	.299	.415	.566
Postseason		4	14	1	0	0	1	(1 0)	4	1	2	0	2 2	5	0 0 1		0	0	-	0	.071	.176	.286
7 ML YEARS		998	3527	996	200	9	230	(123 107)	1904	571	656	672	566 115	779	78 0 39		16	10	.62	81	.282	.390	.540

Michael Fiers

Pitches: R **Bats:** R **Pos:** RP-2 — FIRES — **Ht:** 6'3" **Wt:** 205 **Born:** 6/15/1985 **Age:** 27

		HOW MUCH HE PITCHED			WHAT HE GAVE UP											THE RESULTS						
Year Team	Lg	G GS CG GF	IP	BFP	H	R	ER	HR SH SF HB	TBB IBB	SO	WP Bk	W	L	Pct	Sh	Sv-Op	Hld	ERC	ERA
2009 Helena	R+	13 0 0 12	21.0	77	10	3	3	2 2 0 1	1 0	35	2 0	1	0	1.000	0	8--	-	0.86	1.29
2009 Wisc	A	3 0 0 3	6.0	24	4	0	0	0 0 0 1	2 0	8	0 0	0	0	-	0	1--	-	2.13	0.00
2009 BrvdCt	A+	6 0 0 5	13.2	51	10	3	3	2 0 0 0	2 0	16	0 0	1	0	1.000	0	2--	-	2.10	1.98
2010 BrvdCt	A+	17 15 0 1	93.1	378	78	37	36	6 1 2 11	23 0	94	5 0	4	8	.333	0	0--	-	2.89	3.47
2010 Hntsvl	AA	10 4 0 4	31.2	133	27	13	13	3 0 0 3	9 0	36	1 0	1	1	.500	0	1--	-	3.12	3.69
2011 Hntsvl	AA	22 8 0 10	61.1	241	42	21	18	7 2 1 2	14 0	63	1 2	5	3	.625	0	5--	-	2.02	2.64
2011 Nashv	AAA	12 10 1 1	64.2	263	41	18	8	4 3 0 3	22 0	69	1 0	8	0	1.000	1	0--	-	1.87	1.11
2011 Mil	NL	2 0 0 2	2.0	10	2	0	0	0 0 0 0	3 0	2	0 0	0	0	-	0	0-0	0	8.25	0.00

Chone Figgins

Bats: B **Throws:** R **Pos:** 3B-80; PR-3; LF-2 — SHAWN — **Ht:** 5'8" **Wt:** 180 **Born:** 1/22/1978 **Age:** 34

								BATTING											BASERUNNING				AVERAGES		
Year Team	Lg	G	AB	H	2B	3B	HR	(Hm Rd)	TB	R	RBI	RC	TBB IBB	SO	HBP SH SF		SB	CS	SB%	GDP	Avg	OBP	Slg
2002 LAA	AL	15	12	2	1	0	0	(0 0)	3	6	1	0	0 0	5	0 0 0		2	1	.67	1	.167	.167	.250
2003 LAA	AL	71	240	71	9	4	0	(0 0)	88	34	27	39	20 0	38	0 6 4		13	7	.65	1	.296	.345	.367
2004 LAA	AL	148	577	171	22	17	5	(3 2)	242	83	60	93	49 0	94	0 10 2		34	13	.72	6	.296	.350	.419
2005 LAA	AL	158	642	186	25	10	8	(2 6)	255	113	57	94	64 1	101	0 9 5		62	17	.78	9	.290	.352	.397
2006 LAA	AL	155	604	161	23	8	9	(2 7)	227	93	62	84	65 1	100	2 5 7		52	16	.76	6	.267	.336	.376
2007 LAA	AL	115	442	146	24	6	3	(1 2)	191	81	58	88	51 0	81	0 2 8		41	12	.77	7	.330	.393	.432
2008 LAA	AL	116	453	125	14	1	1	(0 1)	144	72	22	59	62 3	80	3 2 0		34	13	.72	7	.276	.367	.318
2009 LAA	AL	158	615	183	30	7	5	(2 3)	242	114	54	110	101 1	114	1 8 4		42	17	.71	8	.298	.395	.393
2010 Sea	AL	161	602	156	21	2	1	(0 1)	184	62	35	66	74 0	114	3 17 6		42	15	.74	20	.259	.340	.306
2011 Sea	AL	81	288	54	11	1	1	(0 1)	70	24	15	10	21 1	42	0 2 2		11	6	.65	6	.188	.241	.243
Postseason		35	122	21	5	2	0	(0 0)	30	13	6	6	6 0	35	2 5 0		4	1	.80	1	.172	.223	.246
10 ML YEARS		1178	4475	1255	180	56	33	(10 23)	1646	682	391	643	507 6	769	9 61 38		333	117	.74	71	.280	.352	.368

Nelson Figueroa

Pitches: R **Bats:** R **Pos:** SP-5; RP-3 — figg-uh-ROE-ah — **Ht:** 6'1" **Wt:** 180 **Born:** 5/18/1974 **Age:** 38

		HOW MUCH HE PITCHED			WHAT HE GAVE UP											THE RESULTS						
Year Team	Lg	G GS CG GF	IP	BFP	H	R	ER	HR SH SF HB	TBB IBB	SO	WP Bk	W	L	Pct	Sh	Sv-Op	Hld	ERC	ERA
2011 OKCity*	AAA	16 15 0 0	81.2	380	113	63	59	14 4 2 6	30 0	52	3 0	6	7	.462	0	0--	-	7.24	6.50
2011 Indy*	AAA	3 3 1 0	18.0	78	20	8	8	0 0 2 1	4 0	14	2 0	1	1	.500	0	0--	-	3.47	4.00
2000 Ari	NL	3 3 0 0	15.2	68	17	13	13	4 1 2 0	5 0	7	2 0	1	0	1.000	0	0-0	0	5.31	7.47
2001 Phi	NL	19 13 0 1	89.0	393	95	40	39	8 4 0 7	37 3	61	2 0	4	5	.444	0	0-0	0	4.76	3.94
2002 Mil	NL	30 11 0 4	93.0	412	96	59	52	18 11 5 4	37 6	51	5 0	1	7	.125	0	0-0	1	4.94	5.03
2003 Pit	NL	12 3 0 1	35.1	146	28	13	13	8 2 4 2	13 2	23	2 0	2	1	.667	0	0-0	0	3.80	3.31
2004 Pit	NL	10 3 0 0	28.1	121	32	18	18	4 4 0 0	11 1	10	3 0	0	3	.000	0	0-0	0	5.21	5.72

Year	Team	Lg	G	GS	CG	GF	IP	BFP	H	R	ER	HR	SH	SF	HB	TBB	IBB	SO	WP	Bk	W	L	Pct	Sh	Sv-Op	Hld	ERC	ERA
2008	NYM	NL	16	6	0	2	45.1	211	48	26	23	3	2	1	2	26	1	40	0	0	3	3	.500	0	0-1	0	4.88	4.57
2009	NYM	NL	16	10	1	2	70.1	320	80	33	32	8	3	4	9	24	4	59	1	0	3	8	.273	1	0-0	0	5.09	4.09
2010	2 Tms	NL	31	11	0	6	93.0	390	84	38	34	10	5	3	2	34	4	73	6	0	7	4	.636	0	1-1	0	3.49	3.29
2011	Hou	NL	8	5	0	2	29.0	146	45	33	28	3	1	1	0	16	0	17	1	0	0	3	.000	0	0-0	0	8.07	8.69
10	Phi	NL	13	1	0	5	26.0	104	20	10	10	1	4	0	0	9	2	15	2	0	2	1	.667	0	1-1	0	2.21	3.46
10	Hou	NL	18	10	0	1	67.0	286	64	28	24	9	1	3	2	25	2	58	4	0	5	3	.625	0	0-0	0	4.03	3.22
9 ML YEARS			145	65	1	18	499.0	2207	525	273	252	66	33	18	26	203	21	337	22	0	20	35	.364	1	1-2	1	4.76	4.55

Carlos Fisher

Pitches: R **Bats:** R **Pos:** RP-17   **Ht:** 6'4" **Wt:** 225 **Born:** 2/22/1983 **Age:** 29

Year	Team	Lg	G	GS	CG	GF	IP	BFP	H	R	ER	HR	SH	SF	HB	TBB	IBB	SO	WP	Bk	W	L	Pct	Sh	Sv-Op	Hld	ERC	ERA
2011	Lsvlle*	AAA	32	0	0	13	40.1	167	31	17	15	4	2	0	1	18	1	40	2	0	4	1	.800	0	6- -	-	3.08	3.35
2009	Cin	NL	39	0	0	17	52.1	226	50	26	26	4	2	1	1	31	2	48	6	0	1	1	.500	0	0-1	2	4.58	4.47
2010	Cin	NL	18	0	0	5	22.1	100	22	14	14	1	0	0	1	13	2	21	2	0	1	1	.500	0	0-0	0	4.33	5.64
2011	Cin	NL	17	0	0	8	24.0	110	25	15	12	3	2	1	1	11	1	17	1	0	0	3	.000	0	0-0	0	4.66	4.50
3 ML YEARS			74	0	0	30	98.2	436	97	55	52	8	4	2	3	55	5	86	9	0	2	5	.286	0	0-1	2	4.55	4.74

Doug Fister

Pitches: R **Bats:** L **Pos:** SP-31; RP-1   **Ht:** 6'8" **Wt:** 195 **Born:** 2/4/1984 **Age:** 28

Year	Team	Lg	G	GS	CG	GF	IP	BFP	H	R	ER	HR	SH	SF	HB	TBB	IBB	SO	WP	Bk	W	L	Pct	Sh	Sv-Op	Hld	ERC	ERA
2009	Sea	AL	11	10	0	1	61.0	256	63	29	28	11	0	0	2	15	0	36	1	0	3	4	.429	0	0-0	0	4.36	4.13
2010	Sea	AL	28	28	0	0	171.0	720	187	85	78	13	2	4	6	32	2	93	8	3	6	14	.300	0	0-0	0	3.73	4.11
2011	2 Tms	AL	32	31	3	0	216.1	875	193	76	68	11	4	9	12	37	2	146	3	1	11	13	.458	0	0-0	0	2.53	2.83
11	Sea	AL	21	21	3	0	146.0	602	139	57	54	7	3	7	9	32	2	89	3	1	3	12	.200	0	0-0	0	3.02	3.33
11	Det	AL	11	10	0	0	70.1	273	54	19	14	4	1	2	3	5	0	57	0	0	8	1	.889	0	0-0	0	1.63	1.79
3 ML YEARS			71	69	3	1	448.1	1851	443	190	174	35	6	13	20	84	4	275	12	4	20	31	.392	0	0-0	0	3.21	3.49

Jesus Flores

Bats: R **Throws:** R **Pos:** C-22; PH-8   **Ht:** 6'1" **Wt:** 229 **Born:** 10/26/1984 **Age:** 27

Year	Team	Lg	G	AB	H	2B	3B	HR	(Hm	Rd)	TB	R	RBI	RC	TBB	IBB	SO	HBP	SH	SF	SB	CS	SB%	GDP	Avg	OBP	Slg
2011	Syrcse*	AAA	56	209	49	15	0	5	(-	-)	79	17	30	20	5	0	54	1	0	3	0	0	-	7	.234	.252	.378
2007	Was	NL	79	180	44	9	0	4	(1	3)	65	21	25	19	14	0	48	3	0	0	0	1	.00	7	.244	.310	.361
2008	Was	NL	90	301	77	18	1	8	(2	6)	121	23	59	45	15	1	78	4	0	4	0	1	.00	7	.256	.296	.402
2009	Was	NL	29	93	28	3	2	4	(0	4)	47	13	15	14	11	1	26	0	1	1	0	0	-	1	.301	.371	.505
2011	Was	NL	30	86	18	6	0	1	(1	0)	27	5	2	3	5	2	27	0	0	0	0	0	-	1	.209	.253	.314
4 ML YEARS			228	660	167	36	3	17	(4	13)	260	62	101	81	45	4	179	7	1	5	0	2	.00	14	.253	.305	.394

Pedro Florimon

Bats: B **Throws:** R **Pos:** SS-4; PH-1   **Ht:** 6'2" **Wt:** 165 **Born:** 12/10/1986 **Age:** 25

Year	Team	Lg	G	AB	H	2B	3B	HR	(Hm	Rd)	TB	R	RBI	RC	TBB	IBB	SO	HBP	SH	SF	SB	CS	SB%	GDP	Avg	OBP	Slg
2006	Bluefld	R+	33	120	40	6	1	1	(-	-)	51	23	8	25	28	0	29	0	1	1	7	6	.54	0	.333	.456	.425
2006	Abrdn	A-	26	105	26	4	1	0	(-	-)	32	13	5	11	13	1	26	1	0	0	0	0	-	2	.248	.336	.305
2007	Dlmrva	A	111	371	73	14	1	4	(-	-)	101	50	34	26	28	0	107	3	13	3	16	6	.73	8	.197	.257	.272
2008	Dlmrva	A	81	269	60	18	1	0	(-	-)	80	28	19	27	27	0	97	3	3	3	13	2	.87	3	.223	.298	.297
2009	Frdrck	A+	115	430	115	32	5	9	(-	-)	184	76	68	66	42	1	107	5	4	5	26	9	.74	10	.267	.336	.428
2009	Bowie	AA	7	22	2	0	0	0	(-	-)	2	0	1	0	1	0	9	0	1	0	0	0	-	1	.091	.130	.091
2010	Bowie	AA	37	120	22	3	0	1	(-	-)	28	16	12	7	11	0	31	0	2	1	4	1	.80	3	.183	.250	.233
2010	Abrdn	A-	5	19	3	0	0	0	(-	-)	3	1	0	0	1	0	6	0	0	0	0	1	.00	0	.158	.200	.158
2010	Frdrck	A+	62	222	64	10	4	4	(-	-)	94	32	33	35	20	1	52	7	0	3	8	5	.62	4	.288	.361	.423
2011	Bowie	AA	133	454	121	27	4	8	(-	-)	180	53	60	64	51	5	114	5	6	4	15	12	.56	5	.267	.344	.396
2011	Bal	AL	4	8	1	1	0	0	(0	0)	2	1	2	1	1	0	6	0	1	0	0	0	-	0	.125	.222	.250

Tyler Flowers

Bats: R **Throws:** R **Pos:** C-31; 1B-3; PH-3; DH-1   **Ht:** 6'4" **Wt:** 245 **Born:** 1/24/1986 **Age:** 26

Year	Team	Lg	G	AB	H	2B	3B	HR	(Hm	Rd)	TB	R	RBI	RC	TBB	IBB	SO	HBP	SH	SF	SB	CS	SB%	GDP	Avg	OBP	Slg
2011	Charltt*	AAA	65	222	58	8	0	15	(-	-)	111	36	32	45	39	1	85	8	1	0	2	0	1.00	5	.261	.390	.500
2009	CWS	AL	10	16	3	1	0	0	(0	0)	4	3	0	2	3	0	8	1	0	0	0	0	-	1	.188	.350	.250
2010	CWS	AL	8	11	1	0	0	0	(0	0)	1	2	0	1	4	0	5	0	0	0	0	0	-	0	.091	.333	.091
2011	CWS	AL	38	110	23	5	1	5	(3	2)	45	13	16	13	14	0	38	3	0	2	0	1	.00	2	.209	.310	.409
3 ML YEARS			56	137	27	6	1	5	(3	2)	50	18	16	16	21	0	51	4	0	2	0	1	.00	3	.197	.317	.365

Gavin Floyd

Pitches: R **Bats:** R **Pos:** SP-30; RP-1   **Ht:** 6'6" **Wt:** 235 **Born:** 1/27/1983 **Age:** 29

		HOW MUCH HE PITCHED						WHAT HE GAVE UP											THE RESULTS						
Year	Team	Lg	G	GS	CG	GF	IP	BFP	H	R	ER	HR	SH	SF	HB	TBB	IBB	SO	WP	Bk	W	L	Pct	Sh	Sv-Op	Hld	ERC	ERA
2004	Phi	NL	6	4	0	0	28.1	126	25	11	11	1	1	0	5	16	0	24	1	1	2	0	1.000	0	0-0	0	4.33	3.49
2005	Phi	NL	7	4	0	0	26.0	127	30	31	29	5	1	1	3	16	2	17	2	0	1	2	.333	0	0-0	0	6.82	10.04
2006	Phi	NL	11	11	1	0	54.1	264	70	48	44	14	2	5	3	32	3	34	2	0	4	3	.571	1	0-0	0	8.02	7.29
2007	CWS	AL	16	10	0	4	70.0	314	85	45	41	17	3	2	6	19	0	49	1	0	1	5	.167	0	0-0	0	6.22	5.27
2008	CWS	AL	33	33	1	0	206.1	878	190	107	88	30	7	5	9	70	6	145	9	0	17	8	.680	0	0-0	0	3.80	3.84
2009	CWS	AL	30	30	1	0	193.0	797	178	93	87	21	2	3	2	59	4	163	8	0	11	11	.500	0	0-0	0	3.38	4.06
2010	CWS	AL	31	31	1	0	187.1	798	199	92	85	14	3	4	6	58	4	151	9	1	10	13	.435	0	0-0	0	4.03	4.08
2011	CWS	AL	31	30	1	1	193.2	798	180	97	94	22	4	8	11	45	2	151	12	1	12	13	.480	0	0-0	0	3.36	4.37
Postseason			1	1	0	0	3.0	16	5	4	4	2	0	0	0	2	0	4	0	0	0	1	.000	0	0-0	0	14.65	12.00
8 ML YEARS			165	153	5	5	959.0	4102	957	524	479	124	23	28	45	315	21	734	44	3	58	55	.513	1	0-0	0	4.15	4.50

Mike Fontenot

Bats: L **Throws:** R **Pos:** SS-37; PH-28; 2B-23; 3B-8   FONT-uh-no   **Ht:** 5'8" **Wt:** 170 **Born:** 6/9/1980 **Age:** 32

			BATTING																	BASERUNNING				AVERAGES		
Year	Team	Lg	G	AB	H	2B	3B	HR	(Hm	Rd)	TB	R	RBI	RC	TBB	IBB	SO	HBP	SH	SF	SB	CS	SB%	GDP	Avg	OBP	Slg
2011	Fresno*	AAA	10	32	7	0	0	1	(-	-)	10	5	3	3	5	0	4	0	0	0	0	0	-	2	.219	.324	.313
2005	ChC	NL	7	2	0	0	0	0	(0	0)	0	4	0	1	2	0	1	0	0	0	0	0	-	0	.000	.600	.000
2007	ChC	NL	86	234	65	12	4	3	(2	1)	94	32	29	26	22	0	43	0	1	3	5	4	.56	5	.278	.336	.402
2008	ChC	NL	119	243	74	22	1	9	(4	5)	125	42	40	49	34	2	51	3	3	1	2	0	1.00	1	.305	.395	.514
2009	ChC	NL	135	377	89	22	2	9	(3	6)	142	38	43	37	35	4	83	2	0	5	4	1	.80	7	.236	.301	.377
2010	2 Tms	NL	103	240	68	13	3	1	(0	1)	90	24	25	32	15	0	41	3	1	2	1	4	.20	3	.283	.331	.375
2011	SF	NL	85	220	50	15	3	4	(1	3)	83	22	21	22	25	3	48	1	2	4	5	1	.83	3	.227	.304	.377
10	ChC	NL	75	169	48	11	3	1	(0	1)	68	14	20	25	10	0	28	3	1	2	1	2	.33	3	.284	.332	.402
10	SF	NL	28	71	20	2	0	0	(0	0)	22	10	5	7	5	0	13	0	0	0	0	2	.00	0	.282	.329	.310
Postseason			13	22	5	0	1	0	(0	0)	7	1	0	1	1	0	5	0	0	0	1	0	1.00	0	.227	.261	.318
6 ML YEARS			535	1316	346	84	13	26	(10	16)	534	162	158	167	133	9	266	10	7	15	17	10	.63	19	.263	.332	.406

Darren Ford

Bats: R **Throws:** R **Pos:** CF-15; PR-14; PH-2   **Ht:** 5'9" **Wt:** 188 **Born:** 10/1/1985 **Age:** 26

			BATTING																	BASERUNNING				AVERAGES		
Year	Team	Lg	G	AB	H	2B	3B	HR	(Hm	Rd)	TB	R	RBI	RC	TBB	IBB	SO	HBP	SH	SF	SB	CS	SB%	GDP	Avg	OBP	Slg
2005	Helena	R+	61	236	64	4	3	1	(-	-)	77	57	24	33	33	0	70	3	3	2	18	4	.82	1	.271	.365	.326
2006	WV	A	125	491	139	24	3	7	(-	-)	190	93	54	79	56	1	133	4	14	1	69	15	.82	4	.283	.361	.387
2007	WV	A	51	224	75	15	4	5	(-	-)	113	48	33	46	23	1	56	1	5	1	31	10	.76	2	.335	.398	.504
2007	BrvdCt	A+	72	273	63	7	1	4	(-	-)	84	46	27	34	35	0	67	1	5	3	36	6	.86	1	.231	.317	.308
2008	BrvdCt	A+	91	343	79	13	3	2	(-	-)	104	57	27	42	46	1	88	2	7	3	48	11	.81	4	.230	.322	.303
2008	SnJos	A+	38	128	28	4	1	0	(-	-)	34	21	7	16	23	1	42	1	3	2	14	1	.93	1	.219	.346	.266
2009	SnJos	A+	101	380	114	17	9	9	(-	-)	176	81	50	72	49	1	97	6	3	3	35	12	.74	4	.300	.386	.463
2010	Rchmd	AA	113	463	116	20	9	5	(-	-)	169	64	40	57	39	0	106	5	8	1	37	15	.71	6	.251	.315	.365
2011	Fresno	AAA	18	71	15	2	0	2	(-	-)	23	10	7	7	4	0	23	1	0	0	10	0	1.00	2	.211	.263	.324
2011	Giants	R	8	24	9	0	1	2	(-	-)	17	9	6	8	6	0	4	1	0	1	2	1	.67	0	.375	.500	.708
2011	Rchmd	AA	23	86	24	3	0	0	(-	-)	27	11	2	10	9	0	24	0	2	0	6	3	.67	3	.279	.347	.314
2010	SF	NL	7	0	0	0	0	0	(0	0)	0	1	0	0	0	0	0	0	0	0	2	1	.67	0	-	-	-
2011	SF	NL	26	14	4	0	0	0	(0	0)	4	7	0	2	1	0	5	1	0	0	7	5	.58	0	.286	.375	.286
2 ML YEARS			33	14	4	0	0	0	(0	0)	4	8	0	2	1	0	5	1	0	0	9	6	.60	0	.286	.375	.286

Logan Forsythe

Bats: R **Throws:** R **Pos:** 3B-26; 2B-23; PH-20; SS-1; PR-1   **Ht:** 6'1" **Wt:** 206 **Born:** 1/14/1987 **Age:** 25

			BATTING																	BASERUNNING				AVERAGES		
Year	Team	Lg	G	AB	H	2B	3B	HR	(Hm	Rd)	TB	R	RBI	RC	TBB	IBB	SO	HBP	SH	SF	SB	CS	SB%	GDP	Avg	OBP	Slg
2008	Eugene	A-	3	9	3	1	0	0	(-	-)	4	2	0	1	1	0	3	1	0	0	0	0	-	0	.333	.455	.444
2008	Padres	R	9	26	6	0	0	0	(-	-)	6	2	0	3	5	0	8	4	0	0	0	0	-	0	.231	.429	.231
2009	Lk Els	A+	66	236	76	13	3	8	(-	-)	119	46	30	60	61	3	48	7	0	1	6	2	.75	9	.322	.472	.504
2009	SnAnt	AA	66	244	68	9	3	3	(-	-)	92	37	31	40	41	0	63	2	1	2	5	0	1.00	5	.279	.384	.377
2010	SnAnt	AA	107	392	99	22	1	3	(-	-)	132	66	38	59	75	2	95	4	0	1	17	5	.77	2	.253	.377	.337
2011	Tucsn	AAA	46	178	58	12	0	8	(-	-)	94	41	34	42	33	0	50	6	0	1	8	4	.67	0	.326	.445	.528
2011	SD	NL	62	150	32	9	1	0	(0	0)	43	12	12	15	12	3	33	3	2	2	3	1	.75	3	.213	.281	.287

Dexter Fowler

Bats: B **Throws:** R **Pos:** CF-122; PH-5   **Ht:** 6'4" **Wt:** 190 **Born:** 3/22/1986 **Age:** 26

			BATTING																	BASERUNNING				AVERAGES		
Year	Team	Lg	G	AB	H	2B	3B	HR	(Hm	Rd)	TB	R	RBI	RC	TBB	IBB	SO	HBP	SH	SF	SB	CS	SB%	GDP	Avg	OBP	Slg
2011	ColSpr*	AAA	24	97	23	6	1	2	(-	-)	37	17	9	13	15	0	24	1	1	0	2	1	.67	2	.237	.345	.381
2008	Col	NL	13	26	4	0	0	0	(0	0)	4	3	0	0	0	0	5	1	0	0	0	1	.00	0	.154	.185	.154
2009	Col	NL	135	433	115	29	10	4	(2	2)	176	73	34	68	67	1	116	1	14	3	27	10	.73	4	.266	.363	.406
2010	Col	NL	132	439	114	20	**14**	6	(5	1)	180	73	36	68	57	0	104	2	7	0	13	8	.62	5	.260	.347	.410
2011	Col	NL	125	481	128	35	15	5	(3	2)	208	84	45	79	68	3	130	6	7	1	12	9	.57	6	.266	.363	.432
Postseason			4	14	3	0	0	0	(0	0)	3	1	2	1	1	0	3	0	1	2	0	0	-	1	.214	.235	.214
4 ML YEARS			405	1379	361	84	39	15	(10	5)	568	233	115	215	192	4	355	10	28	4	52	28	.65	15	.262	.355	.412

Jake Fox

Bats: R Throws: R Pos: C-10; PH-8; 1B-6; LF-5; DH-2; PR-1   Ht: 6'0" Wt: 220 Born: 7/20/1982 Age: 29

Year	Team	Lg	G	AB	H	2B	3B	HR	(Hm	Rd)	TB	R	RBI	RC	TBB	IBB	SO	HBP	SH	SF	SB	CS	SB%	GDP	Avg	OBP	Slg
2011	Norfolk*	AAA	68	265	73	19	1	12	(-	-)	130	38	58	47	22	1	52	10	0	2	0	0	-	6	.275	.351	.491
2007	ChC	NL	7	14	2	2	0	0	(0	0)	4	3	1	1	1	0	2	0	0	0	0	0	-	1	.143	.200	.286
2009	ChC	NL	82	216	56	12	0	11	(4	7)	101	23	44	32	14	1	47	5	0	6	0	0	-	5	.259	.311	.468
2010	2 Tms	AL	77	198	43	10	1	7	(1	6)	76	21	22	15	8	0	49	4	0	1	0	0	-	7	.217	.261	.384
2011	Bal	AL	27	61	15	4	1	2	(0	2)	27	8	6	7	4	0	8	2	0	0	0	0	-	4	.246	.313	.443
10	Oak	AL	39	98	21	5	0	2	(1	1)	32	11	12	7	5	0	26	2	0	1	0	0	-	6	.214	.264	.327
10	Bal	AL	38	100	22	5	1	5	(0	5)	44	10	10	8	3	0	23	2	0	0	0	0	-	1	.220	.257	.440
	4 ML YEARS		193	489	116	28	2	20	(5	15)	208	55	73	55	27	1	106	11	0	7	0	0	-	17	.237	.288	.425

Jeff Francis

Pitches: L Bats: L Pos: SP-31   Ht: 6'5" Wt: 220 Born: 1/8/1981 Age: 31

Year	Team	Lg	G	GS	CG	GF	IP	BFP	H	R	ER	HR	SH	SF	HB	TBB	IBB	SO	WP	Bk	W	L	Pct	Sh	Sv-Op	Hld	ERC	ERA
2004	Col	NL	7	7	0	0	36.2	164	42	22	21	8	2	1	1	13	1	32	2	0	3	2	.600	0	0-0	0	5.62	5.15
2005	Col	NL	33	33	0	0	183.2	828	228	119	116	26	6	10	8	70	5	128	2	0	14	12	.538	0	0-0	0	5.94	5.68
2006	Col	NL	32	32	1	0	199.0	843	187	101	92	18	7	7	13	69	15	117	0	0	13	11	.542	1	0-0	0	3.63	4.16
2007	Col	NL	34	34	1	0	215.1	922	234	103	101	25	7	4	7	63	7	165	1	1	17	9	.654	1	0-0	0	4.37	4.22
2008	Col	NL	24	24	0	0	143.2	636	164	84	80	21	6	4	3	49	4	94	0	0	4	10	.286	0	0-0	0	5.00	5.01
2010	Col	NL	20	19	0	0	104.1	441	119	61	58	11	6	4	2	23	3	67	1	0	4	6	.400	0	0-0	0	4.29	5.00
2011	KC	AL	31	31	1	0	183.0	803	224	102	98	19	7	8	5	39	5	91	5	1	6	16	.273	0	0-0	0	4.67	4.82
	Postseason		3	3	0	0	16.2	75	21	9	9	3	0	0	2	6	2	15	0	0	2	1	.667	0	0-0	0	6.57	4.86
	7 ML YEARS		181	180	3	0	1065.2	4637	1198	592	566	128	41	38	39	326	40	694	11	2	61	66	.480	2	0-0	0	4.66	4.78

Ben Francisco

Bats: R Throws: R Pos: RF-55; PH-33; LF-14; DH-1   Ht: 6'1" Wt: 190 Born: 10/23/1981 Age: 30

Year	Team	Lg	G	AB	H	2B	3B	HR	(Hm	Rd)	TB	R	RBI	RC	TBB	IBB	SO	HBP	SH	SF	SB	CS	SB%	GDP	Avg	OBP	Slg
2007	Cle	AL	25	62	17	5	0	3	(2	1)	31	10	12	6	3	0	19	0	0	1	0	2	.00	2	.274	.303	.500
2008	Cle	AL	121	447	119	32	0	15	(7	8)	196	65	54	57	40	0	86	6	2	4	4	3	.57	10	.266	.332	.438
2009	2 Tms	AL	126	405	104	30	1	15	(6	9)	181	58	46	56	38	0	83	9	4	3	14	7	.67	12	.257	.332	.447
2010	Phi	NL	88	179	48	13	0	6	(1	5)	79	24	28	26	14	1	35	2	1	1	8	0	1.00	6	.268	.327	.441
2011	Phi	NL	100	250	61	10	1	6	(4	2)	91	24	34	32	33	1	42	5	2	3	4	4	.50	5	.244	.340	.364
09	Cle	AL	89	308	77	21	1	10	(4	6)	130	48	33	43	33	0	59	8	4	2	13	3	.81	11	.250	.336	.422
09	Phi	NL	37	97	27	9	0	5	(2	3)	51	10	13	13	5	0	24	1	0	1	1	4	.20	1	.278	.317	.526
	Postseason		15	17	1	0	0	0	(0	0)	1	1	0	0	1	0	5	1	0	0	0	0	-	1	.059	.158	.059
	5 ML YEARS		460	1343	349	90	2	45	(20	25)	578	181	174	177	128	2	265	22	9	12	30	16	.65	35	.260	.332	.430

Frank Francisco

Pitches: R Bats: R Pos: RP-54   Ht: 6'2" Wt: 250 Born: 9/11/1979 Age: 32

Year	Team	Lg	G	GS	CG	GF	IP	BFP	H	R	ER	HR	SH	SF	HB	TBB	IBB	SO	WP	Bk	W	L	Pct	Sh	Sv-Op	Hld	ERC	ERA
2011	Dnedin*	A+	5	0	0	0	5.0	24	6	7	6	2	0	0	0	4	0	6	0	0	0	1	.000	0	0- -	-	9.81	10.80
2004	Tex	AL	45	0	0	7	51.1	216	36	19	19	4	2	1	3	28	2	60	4	1	5	1	.833	0	0-3	10	3.04	3.33
2006	Tex	AL	8	0	0	2	7.1	32	8	4	4	2	0	0	0	2	0	6	1	0	0	1	.000	0	0-0	2	5.17	4.91
2007	Tex	AL	59	0	0	16	59.1	268	57	33	30	3	6	1	2	38	4	49	8	0	1	1	.500	0	0-0	21	4.44	4.55
2008	Tex	AL	58	0	0	18	63.1	264	47	24	22	7	0	3	0	26	2	83	5	0	3	5	.375	0	5-11	12	2.70	3.13
2009	Tex	AL	51	0	0	42	49.1	203	40	21	21	6	0	0	1	15	1	57	3	0	2	3	.400	0	25-29	4	2.85	3.83
2010	Tex	AL	56	0	0	20	52.2	221	49	23	22	5	3	1	1	18	2	60	2	1	6	4	.600	0	2-6	15	3.46	3.76
2011	Tor	AL	54	0	0	38	50.2	218	49	21	20	7	1	0	0	18	2	53	2	0	1	4	.200	0	17-21	2	3.85	3.55
	7 ML YEARS		331	0	0	143	334.0	1422	286	145	138	34	12	6	7	145	13	368	25	2	18	19	.486	0	49-70	66	3.43	3.72

Juan Francisco

Bats: L Throws: R Pos: 3B-24; PH-11   Ht: 6'2" Wt: 238 Born: 6/24/1987 Age: 25

Year	Team	Lg	G	AB	H	2B	3B	HR	(Hm	Rd)	TB	R	RBI	RC	TBB	IBB	SO	HBP	SH	SF	SB	CS	SB%	GDP	Avg	OBP	Slg
2011	Lsville*	AAA	74	300	92	23	1	15	(-	-)	162	46	50	53	10	0	65	3	0	1	0	0	-	4	.307	.334	.540
2011	Reds*	R	5	18	9	3	0	1	(-	-)	15	3	3	6	1	0	3	0	0	0	0	0	-	0	.500	.526	.833
2009	Cin	NL	14	21	9	1	0	1	(1	0)	13	4	7	6	3	0	7	1	0	0	0	0	-	0	.429	.520	.619
2010	Cin	NL	36	55	15	3	0	1	(1	0)	21	3	7	3	4	0	20	0	0	0	0	1	.00	2	.273	.322	.382
2011	Cin	NL	31	93	24	7	1	3	(1	2)	42	10	15	12	4	1	24	0	0	0	1	0	1.00	1	.258	.289	.452
	Postseason		1	1	0	0	0	0	(0	0)	0	0	0	0	0	0	0	0	0	0	0	0	-	0	.000	.000	.000
	3 ML YEARS		81	169	48	11	1	5	(3	2)	76	17	29	21	11	1	51	1	0	0	1	1	.50	3	.284	.331	.450

Jeff Francoeur

Bats: R Throws: R Pos: RF-153; PH-1   frann-COOR   Ht: 6'5" Wt: 220 Born: 1/8/1984 Age: 28

Year	Team	Lg	G	AB	H	2B	3B	HR	(Hm	Rd)	TB	R	RBI	RC	TBB	IBB	SO	HBP	SH	SF	SB	CS	SB%	GDP	Avg	OBP	Slg
2005	Atl	NL	70	257	77	20	1	14	(11	3)	141	41	45	50	11	3	58	4	0	2	3	2	.60	4	.300	.336	.549
2006	Atl	NL	162	651	169	24	6	29	(19	10)	292	83	103	91	23	6	132	3	0	5	1	6	.14	15	.260	.293	.449
2007	Atl	NL	162	642	188	40	0	19	(7	12)	285	84	105	97	42	5	129	5	0	7	5	2	.71	14	.293	.338	.444
2008	Atl	NL	155	599	143	33	3	11	(5	6)	215	70	71	49	39	5	111	10	0	4	0	1	.00	18	.239	.294	.359
2009	2 Tms	NL	157	593	166	32	4	15	(7	8)	251	72	76	59	23	5	92	6	1	9	6	4	.60	13	.280	.309	.423

112

Year	Team	Lg	G	AB	H	2B	3B	HR	(Hm	Rd)	TB	R	RBI	RC	TBB	IBB	SO	HBP	SH	SF	SB	CS	SB%	GDP	Avg	OBP	Slg
2010	2 Tms		139	454	113	18	2	13	(5	8)	174	52	65	46	30	8	81	8	0	11	8	3	.73	9	.249	.305	.383
2011	KC	AL	153	601	171	47	4	20	(10	10)	286	77	87	83	37	3	123	8	0	10	22	10	.69	17	.285	.329	.476
09	Atl	NL	82	304	76	12	2	5	(3	2)	107	32	35	25	12	2	46	3	1	4	5	1	.83	10	.250	.282	.352
09	NYM	NL	75	289	90	20	2	10	(4	6)	144	40	41	34	11	3	46	3	0	5	1	3	.25	3	.311	.338	.498
10	NYM	NL	124	401	95	16	2	11	(5	6)	148	43	54	39	29	8	76	7	0	10	8	2	.80	7	.237	.293	.369
10	Tex	AL	15	53	18	2	0	2	(0	2)	26	9	11	7	1	0	5	1	0	1	0	1	.00	2	.340	.357	.491
	Postseason		13	41	7	2	1	0	(0	0)	11	3	2	3	3	1	7	1	1	0	0	0	-	2	.171	.244	.268
	7 ML YEARS		998	3797	1027	214	20	121	(64	57)	1644	479	552	475	205	35	726	50	1	46	45	28	.62	90	.270	.313	.433

Ryan Franklin

Pitches: R **Bats:** R **Pos:** RP-21 **Ht:** 6'3" **Wt:** 190 **Born:** 3/5/1973 **Age:** 39

Year	Team	Lg	G	GS	CG	GF	IP	BFP	H	R	ER	HR	SH	SF	HB	TBB	IBB	SO	WP	Bk	W	L	Pct	Sh	Sv-Op Hld	ERC	ERA
1999	Sea	AL	6	0	0	2	11.1	51	10	6	6	2	0	0	1	8	1	6	0	0	0	0	-	0	0-1 1	5.52	4.76
2001	Sea	AL	38	0	0	14	78.1	335	76	32	31	13	1	2	4	24	4	60	2	0	5	1	.833	0	0-1 5	4.08	3.56
2002	Sea	AL	41	12	0	10	118.2	495	117	62	53	14	5	5	5	22	1	65	0	0	7	5	.583	0	0-1 3	3.40	4.02
2003	Sea	AL	32	32	2	0	212.0	877	199	93	84	34	8	5	9	61	3	99	1	2	11	13	.458	1	0-0 0	3.90	3.57
2004	Sea	AL	32	32	0	0	200.1	870	224	116	109	33	2	11	10	61	1	104	0	3	4	16	.200	1	0-0 0	5.08	4.90
2005	Sea	AL	32	30	2	0	190.2	832	212	110	108	28	3	3	7	62	4	93	3	1	8	15	.348	1	0-0 0	4.89	5.10
2006	2 Tms	NL	66	0	0	19	77.1	343	86	42	39	13	2	2	4	33	10	43	2	0	6	7	.462	0	0-3 8	5.41	4.54
2007	StL	NL	69	0	0	8	80.0	317	70	28	27	8	2	2	3	11	0	44	2	0	4	4	.500	0	1-6 25	2.59	3.04
2008	StL	NL	74	0	0	39	78.2	346	86	34	31	10	2	2	3	30	4	51	3	0	6	6	.500	0	17-25 13	4.82	3.55
2009	StL	NL	62	0	0	54	61.0	250	49	13	13	2	0	1	1	24	3	44	1	0	4	3	.571	0	38-43 1	2.58	1.92
2010	StL	NL	59	0	0	51	65.0	264	57	25	25	7	1	1	4	10	1	42	5	0	6	2	.750	0	27-29 0	2.72	3.46
2011	StL	NL	21	0	0	9	27.2	133	44	27	26	9	4	1	1	7	2	17	1	0	1	4	.200	0	1-5 0	8.91	8.46
06	Phi	NL	46	0	0	13	53.0	233	59	28	27	10	0	1	4	17	4	25	1	0	1	5	.167	0	0-1 8	5.26	4.58
06	Cin	NL	20	0	0	6	24.1	110	27	14	12	3	2	1	0	16	6	18	1	0	5	2	.714	0	0-2 0	5.67	4.44
	Postseason		2	0	0	2	1.1	10	3	2	0	0	0	0	0	2	0	1	0	0	0	1	.000	0	0-1 0	14.53	0.00
	12 ML YEARS		532	106	6	206	1201.0	5113	1230	588	552	173	30	36	52	353	34	668	20	6	62	76	.449	3	84-113 56	4.24	4.14

Jason Frasor

Pitches: R **Bats:** R **Pos:** RP-64 FRAY-zer **Ht:** 5'10" **Wt:** 175 **Born:** 8/9/1977 **Age:** 34

Year	Team	Lg	G	GS	CG	GF	IP	BFP	H	R	ER	HR	SH	SF	HB	TBB	IBB	SO	WP	Bk	W	L	Pct	Sh	Sv-Op Hld	ERC	ERA
2004	Tor	AL	63	0	0	37	68.1	299	64	31	31	4	3	3	2	36	3	54	4	2	4	6	.400	0	17-19 8	3.97	4.08
2005	Tor	AL	67	0	0	12	74.2	305	67	31	27	8	2	1	3	28	2	61	2	1	3	5	.375	0	1-3 15	3.72	3.25
2006	Tor	AL	51	0	0	12	50.0	215	47	24	24	8	0	3	2	17	1	51	3	0	3	2	.600	0	0-1 12	3.98	4.32
2007	Tor	AL	51	0	0	18	57.0	242	47	29	29	3	1	2	2	23	1	59	2	1	1	5	.167	0	3-6 4	2.88	4.58
2008	Tor	AL	49	0	0	21	47.1	208	36	23	22	4	0	2	1	32	4	42	6	0	1	2	.333	0	0-1 4	3.62	4.18
2009	Tor	AL	61	0	0	36	57.2	227	43	17	16	4	1	2	2	16	3	56	2	0	7	3	.700	0	11-14 4	2.22	2.50
2010	Tor	AL	69	0	0	18	63.2	279	61	30	26	6	1	0	4	27	6	65	5	0	3	4	.429	0	4-8 14	3.72	3.68
2011	2 Tms	AL	64	0	0	10	60.0	261	58	25	24	7	2	4	3	26	3	57	3	0	3	3	.500	0	0-2 24	4.26	3.60
11	Tor	AL	44	0	0	6	42.1	178	38	15	14	4	2	3	2	15	1	37	2	0	2	1	.667	0	0-2 10	3.46	2.98
11	CWS	AL	20	0	0	4	17.2	83	20	10	10	3	0	1	1	11	2	20	1	0	1	2	.333	0	0-0 4	6.37	5.09
	8 ML YEARS		475	0	0	164	478.2	2036	423	210	199	42	10	17	19	205	23	446	26	3	25	30	.455	0	36-54 75	3.55	3.74

Todd Frazier

Bats: R **Throws:** R **Pos:** 3B-27; PH-12; LF-4; 2B-2; SS-2; 1B-1 **Ht:** 6'3" **Wt:** 220 **Born:** 2/12/1986 **Age:** 26

Year	Team	Lg	G	AB	H	2B	3B	HR	(Hm	Rd)	TB	R	RBI	RC	TBB	IBB	SO	HBP	SH	SF	SB	CS	SB%	GDP	Avg	OBP	Slg
2007	Billings	R+	41	160	51	6	5	5	(-	-)	82	29	25	33	18	0	22	7	0	1	3	3	.50	2	.319	.409	.513
2007	Dayton	A	6	22	7	3	0	2	(-	-)	16	4	5	5	2	0	4	0	0	0	0	0	-	0	.318	.375	.727
2008	Dayton	A	30	112	36	10	0	7	(-	-)	67	25	20	25	15	0	28	0	0	0	4	2	.67	2	.321	.402	.598
2008	Srsota	A+	100	366	103	20	3	12	(-	-)	165	62	54	61	41	3	84	4	0	3	8	4	.67	9	.281	.357	.451
2009	Carlina	AA	119	451	131	40	2	14	(-	-)	217	59	67	76	42	1	67	2	0	5	7	8	.47	9	.290	.350	.481
2009	Lsvlle	AAA	16	63	19	5	0	2	(-	-)	30	9	9	11	6	0	12	0	0	0	2	0	1.00	0	.302	.362	.476
2010	Lsvlle	AAA	130	480	124	32	4	17	(-	-)	215	71	66	75	45	6	127	10	1	2	14	4	.78	11	.258	.333	.448
2011	Lsvlle	AAA	90	315	82	18	1	15	(-	-)	147	47	46	53	34	3	82	6	0	4	17	4	.81	7	.260	.340	.467
2011	Cin	NL	41	112	26	5	0	6	(2	4)	49	17	15	13	7	0	27	2	0	0	1	0	1.00	2	.232	.289	.438

Freddie Freeman

Bats: L **Throws:** R **Pos:** 1B-156; PH-1 **Ht:** 6'5" **Wt:** 220 **Born:** 9/12/1989 **Age:** 22

Year	Team	Lg	G	AB	H	2B	3B	HR	(Hm	Rd)	TB	R	RBI	RC	TBB	IBB	SO	HBP	SH	SF	SB	CS	SB%	GDP	Avg	OBP	Slg
2007	Braves	R	59	224	60	7	0	6	(-	-)	85	24	30	24	7	0	33	2	0	1	1	2	.33	3	.268	.295	.379
2008	Rome	A	130	491	155	33	7	18	(-	-)	256	70	95	94	46	1	84	3	0	0	5	5	.50	9	.316	.378	.521
2009	MrtlBh	A+	70	255	77	19	0	6	(-	-)	114	43	34	46	26	0	41	14	0	2	1	4	.20	8	.302	.394	.447
2009	Missi	AA	41	149	37	8	0	2	(-	-)	51	15	24	17	11	1	19	4	0	5	0	0	-	5	.248	.308	.342
2010	Gwnntt	AAA	124	461	147	35	2	18	(-	-)	240	73	87	92	43	3	84	6	0	9	6	2	.75	14	.319	.378	.521
2010	Atl	NL	20	24	4	1	0	1	(0	1)	8	3	1	0	0	0	8	0	0	0	0	0	-	1	.167	.167	.333
2011	Atl	NL	157	571	161	32	0	21	(9	12)	256	67	76	79	53	3	142	6	0	5	4	4	.50	15	.282	.346	.448
	2 ML YEARS		177	595	165	33	0	22	(9	13)	264	70	77	79	53	3	150	6	0	5	4	4	.50	16	.277	.340	.444

David Freese

Bats: R Throws: R Pos: 3B-88; PH-9; 1B-5   FREEZE   Ht: 6'2" Wt: 220 Born: 4/28/1983 Age: 29

Year	Team	Lg	G	AB	H	2B	3B	HR	(Hm	Rd)	TB	R	RBI	RC	TBB	IBB	SO	HBP	SH	SF	SB	CS	SB%	GDP	Avg	OBP	Slg
2011	Memp*	AAA	4	13	3	1	0	0	(-	-)	4	1	1	1	1	0	3	0	0	0	0	0	-	0	.231	.286	.308
2009	StL	NL	17	31	10	2	0	1	(0	1)	15	3	7	4	2	0	7	0	0	1	0	0	-	1	.323	.353	.484
2010	StL	NL	70	240	71	12	1	4	(3	1)	97	28	36	36	21	0	59	4	4	1	1	1	.50	7	.296	.361	.404
2011	StL	NL	97	333	99	16	1	10	(6	4)	147	41	55	50	24	0	75	4	0	2	1	0	1.00	18	.297	.350	.441
	3 ML YEARS		184	604	180	30	2	15	(9	6)	259	72	98	90	47	0	141	8	4	4	2	1	.67	26	.298	.354	.429

Ernesto Frieri

Pitches: R Bats: R Pos: RP-59   free-AIR-ee   Ht: 6'2" Wt: 200 Born: 7/19/1985 Age: 26

			HOW MUCH HE PITCHED						WHAT HE GAVE UP											THE RESULTS						
Year	Team	Lg	G	GS	CG	GF	IP	BFP	H	R	ER	HR	SH	SF	HB	TBB	IBB	SO	WP	Bk	W	L	Pct	Sh	Sv-Op	Hld	ERC	ERA
2011	Tucsn*	AAA	4	0	0	0	3.1	15	3	1	1	0	0	0	0	2	0	5	0	0	1	0	1.000	0	0- -	-	3.46	2.70
2009	SD	NL	2	0	0	2	2.0	7	0	0	0	0	0	0	0	1	0	2	0	0	0	0	-	0	0-0	0	0.27	0.00
2010	SD	NL	33	0	0	12	31.2	128	18	7	6	2	0	0	0	17	3	41	2	0	1	1	.500	0	0-0	7	1.99	1.71
2011	SD	NL	59	0	0	19	63.0	276	51	21	19	3	1	1	9	34	5	76	1	1	1	2	.333	0	0-0	4	3.60	2.71
	3 ML YEARS		94	0	0	33	96.2	411	69	28	25	5	1	1	9	52	8	119	3	1	2	3	.400	0	0-0	11	2.94	2.33

Eric Fryer

Bats: R Throws: R Pos: C-8; PH-2   Ht: 6'2" Wt: 215 Born: 8/26/1985 Age: 26

Year	Team	Lg	G	AB	H	2B	3B	HR	(Hm	Rd)	TB	R	RBI	RC	TBB	IBB	SO	HBP	SH	SF	SB	CS	SB%	GDP	Avg	OBP	Slg
2007	Helena	R+	43	139	29	7	0	3	(-	-)	45	25	19	14	14	0	28	2	1	1	4	3	.57	5	.209	.288	.324
2008	WV	A	104	385	129	26	5	10	(-	-)	195	76	63	81	43	1	74	6	0	3	15	3	.83	3	.335	.407	.506
2009	Tampa	A+	59	224	56	11	2	2	(-	-)	77	34	24	27	27	0	43	2	0	2	11	5	.69	11	.250	.333	.344
2009	Lynbrg	A+	47	157	38	11	0	3	(-	-)	58	22	14	23	22	1	25	7	1	0	0	0	-	6	.242	.360	.369
2010	Bradtn	A+	83	287	86	16	5	8	(-	-)	136	53	48	55	37	0	64	8	2	3	10	1	.91	6	.300	.391	.474
2010	Pirates	R	3	7	1	0	0	0	(-	-)	1	1	0	1	5	0	0	1	0	0	1	0	1.00	3	.143	.500	.143
2011	Altna	AA	37	113	39	4	2	5	(-	-)	62	24	16	26	16	0	21	1	3	1	1	0	1.00	2	.345	.427	.549
2011	Indy	AAA	38	118	24	5	1	2	(-	-)	37	16	11	14	21	0	30	2	2	0	3	0	1.00	2	.203	.333	.314
2011	Pit	NL	10	26	7	0	0	0	(0	0)	7	5	0	2	3	1	7	0	0	0	1	1	.50	0	.269	.345	.269

Brian Fuentes

Pitches: L Bats: L Pos: RP-67   Ht: 6'4" Wt: 230 Born: 8/9/1975 Age: 36

			HOW MUCH HE PITCHED						WHAT HE GAVE UP											THE RESULTS						
Year	Team	Lg	G	GS	CG	GF	IP	BFP	H	R	ER	HR	SH	SF	HB	TBB	IBB	SO	WP	Bk	W	L	Pct	Sh	Sv-Op	Hld	ERC	ERA
2001	Sea	AL	10	0	0	3	11.2	47	6	6	6	2	0	1	3	8	0	10	1	0	1	1	.500	0	0-1	1	4.39	4.63
2002	Col	NL	31	0	0	9	26.2	118	25	14	14	4	0	2	3	13	0	38	1	0	2	0	1.000	0	0-0	0	4.91	4.73
2003	Col	NL	75	0	0	23	75.1	320	64	24	23	7	0	3	6	34	2	82	2	1	3	3	.500	0	4-6	19	3.71	2.75
2004	Col	NL	47	0	0	12	44.2	201	46	30	28	5	7	0	4	19	6	48	3	0	2	4	.333	0	0-1	13	4.50	5.64
2005	Col	NL	78	0	0	55	74.1	321	59	25	24	6	5	1	10	34	4	91	8	0	2	5	.286	0	31-34	6	3.44	2.91
2006	Col	NL	66	0	0	58	65.1	274	50	25	25	8	2	1	6	26	4	73	6	0	3	4	.429	0	30-36	3	3.19	3.44
2007	Col	NL	64	0	0	38	61.1	255	46	26	21	6	1	1	7	23	0	56	2	0	3	5	.375	0	20-27	8	3.06	3.08
2008	Col	NL	67	0	0	48	62.2	256	47	22	19	3	3	1	1	22	1	82	1	0	1	5	.167	0	30-34	6	2.27	2.73
2009	LAA	AL	65	0	0	57	55.0	242	53	24	24	6	2	2	5	24	2	46	1	0	1	5	.167	0	48-55	0	4.37	3.93
2010	2 Tms	AL	48	0	0	35	48.0	196	31	17	15	5	2	1	2	20	1	47	3	1	4	1	.800	0	24-28	3	2.41	2.81
2011	Oak	AL	67	0	0	29	58.1	250	52	30	24	6	4	3	4	20	5	42	2	0	2	8	.200	0	12-15	9	3.35	3.70
	10 LAA	AL	39	0	0	33	38.1	161	28	17	15	5	2	1	1	18	1	39	2	1	4	1	.800	0	23-27	0	3.11	3.52
	10 Min	AL	9	0	0	2	9.2	35	3	0	0	0	0	0	1	2	0	8	1	0	0	0	-	0	1-1	3	0.60	0.00
	Postseason		17	0	0	4	17.0	76	16	8	8	3	0	0	1	9	2	16	1	0	1	0	1.000	0	3-4	3	4.82	4.24
	11 ML YEARS		618	0	0	367	583.1	2480	479	243	223	58	26	16	51	243	25	615	30	2	24	41	.369	0	199-237	65	3.42	3.44

Kosuke Fukudome

Bats: L Throws: R Pos: RF-131; CF-13; PH-11; DH-1   KOE-skay foo-koo-DOE-may   Ht: 6'0" Wt: 200 Born: 4/26/1977 Age: 35

Year	Team	Lg	G	AB	H	2B	3B	HR	(Hm	Rd)	TB	R	RBI	RC	TBB	IBB	SO	HBP	SH	SF	SB	CS	SB%	GDP	Avg	OBP	Slg
2008	ChC	NL	150	501	129	25	3	10	(6	4)	190	79	58	77	81	9	104	1	2	5	12	4	.75	7	.257	.359	.379
2009	ChC	NL	146	499	129	38	5	11	(4	7)	210	79	54	76	93	3	112	3	3	5	6	10	.38	15	.259	.375	.421
2010	ChC	NL	130	358	94	20	2	13	(4	9)	157	45	44	59	64	1	67	0	3	4	7	8	.47	5	.263	.371	.439
2011	2 Tms	NL	146	530	139	27	3	8	(8	0)	196	59	35	65	61	4	110	4	6	2	4	6	.40	8	.262	.342	.370
	11 ChC	NL	87	293	80	15	2	3	(3	0)	108	33	13	46	46	1	57	1	5	0	2	2	.50	2	.273	.374	.369
	11 Cle	AL	59	237	59	12	1	5	(5	0)	88	26	22	19	15	3	53	3	1	2	2	4	.33	6	.249	.300	.371
	Postseason		3	10	1	0	0	0	(0	0)	1	0	0	0	0	0	4	0	0	0	0	0	-	0	.100	.100	.100
	4 ML YEARS		572	1888	491	110	13	42	(22	20)	753	262	191	277	299	17	393	8	14	16	29	28	.51	35	.260	.361	.399

Jeff Fulchino

Pitches: R Bats: R Pos: RP-39   full-CHEE-no   Ht: 6'5" Wt: 286 Born: 11/26/1979 Age: 32

			HOW MUCH HE PITCHED						WHAT HE GAVE UP											THE RESULTS						
Year	Team	Lg	G	GS	CG	GF	IP	BFP	H	R	ER	HR	SH	SF	HB	TBB	IBB	SO	WP	Bk	W	L	Pct	Sh	Sv-Op	Hld	ERC	ERA
2011	OKCity*	AAA	17	0	0	11	16.0	58	11	1	1	0	0	0	0	3	0	15	1	0	1	0	1.000	0	3- -	-	1.42	0.56
2006	Fla	NL	1	0	0	0	0.1	2	0	0	0	0	0	0	0	1	0	0	0	0	0	0	-	0	0-0	0	7.00	0.00
2008	KC	AL	12	0	0	7	14.0	72	21	15	14	2	0	1	1	8	0	12	1	0	0	1	.000	0	0-0	0	8.38	9.00
2009	Hou	NL	61	0	0	18	82.0	336	70	33	31	7	4	1	3	27	3	71	2	1	6	4	.600	0	0-3	12	3.05	3.40
2010	Hou	NL	50	0	0	16	47.1	217	53	30	29	7	1	1	3	22	2	46	2	0	2	1	.667	0	0-1	5	5.54	5.51

Year Team	Lg	G	GS	CG	GF	IP	BFP	H	R	ER	HR	SH	SF	HB	TBB	IBB	SO	WP	Bk	W	L	Pct	Sh	Sv-Op	Hld	ERC	ERA
2011 2 Tms	NL	39	0	0	10	34.2	162	37	22	22	5	2	2	0	22	4	33	1	0	1	4	.200	0	0-3	4	5.46	5.71
11 Hou	NL	36	0	0	9	33.0	150	34	19	19	5	2	2	0	18	3	31	0	0	1	4	.200	0	0-3	4	4.98	5.18
11 SD	NL	3	0	0	1	1.2	12	3	3	3	0	0	0	0	4	1	2	1	0	0	0	-	0	0-0	0	15.29	16.20
5 ML YEARS		163	0	0	51	178.1	789	181	100	96	21	7	5	7	80	9	162	6	1	9	10	.474	0	0-7	21	4.53	4.84

Sam Fuld

Bats: L **Throws:** L **Pos:** LF-75; PH-21; RF-9; CF-7; DH-2; PR-1   **Ht:** 5'10" **Wt:** 180 **Born:** 11/20/1981 **Age:** 30

Year Team	Lg	G	AB	H	2B	3B	HR	(Hm	Rd)	TB	R	RBI	RC	TBB	IBB	SO	HBP	SH	SF	SB	CS	SB%	GDP	Avg	OBP	Slg
2007 ChC	NL	14	6	0	0	0	0	(0	0)	0	3	0	0	3	0	3	0	0	0	0	0	-	0	.000	.333	.000
2009 ChC	NL	65	97	29	6	1	1	(1	0)	40	17	2	15	17	1	10	1	0	0	2	1	.67	1	.299	.409	.412
2010 ChC	NL	19	28	4	1	0	0	(0	0)	5	3	3	1	3	0	5	0	0	0	0	0	-	2	.143	.226	.179
2011 TB	AL	105	308	74	18	5	3	(2	1)	111	41	27	37	32	0	49	1	4	1	20	8	.71	3	.240	.313	.360
4 ML YEARS		203	439	107	25	6	4	(3	1)	156	64	32	53	55	1	67	2	4	1	22	9	.71	6	.244	.330	.355

Charlie Furbush

Pitches: L **Bats:** L **Pos:** RP-16; SP-12   FUR-bush   **Ht:** 6'5" **Wt:** 215 **Born:** 4/11/1986 **Age:** 26

Year Team	Lg	G	GS	CG	GF	IP	BFP	H	R	ER	HR	SH	SF	HB	TBB	IBB	SO	WP	Bk	W	L	Pct	Sh	Sv-Op	Hld	ERC	ERA
2007 Tigers	R	4	3	0	1	16.0	62	11	5	5	2	0	0	0	3	0	23	1	0	2	0	1.000	0	0- -	-	1.83	2.81
2007 WMich	A	8	7	0	0	45.2	185	40	14	11	2	1	2	2	11	0	46	3	0	4	1	.800	0	0- -	-	2.65	2.17
2009 Lkland	A+	24	23	0	0	111.1	474	111	59	49	10	1	3	6	32	1	93	5	0	6	7	.462	0	0- -	-	3.74	3.96
2010 Lkland	A+	13	13	0	0	77.0	317	68	35	29	7	3	1	2	14	1	109	4	1	4	5	.444	0	0- -	-	2.58	3.39
2010 Erie	AA	5	5	0	0	33.1	138	31	12	12	5	1	1	1	10	1	37	0	0	1	0	1.000	0	0- -	-	3.75	3.24
2010 Toledo	AAA	9	9	0	0	48.2	212	59	37	34	9	3	3	0	16	0	37	2	1	3	4	.429	0	0- -	-	5.78	6.29
2011 Toledo	AAA	10	9	2	0	54.0	212	35	21	19	7	1	0	1	16	0	61	4	0	5	3	.625	1	0- -	-	2.13	3.17
2011 2 Tms	AL	28	12	0	1	85.1	372	97	59	52	16	2	4	6	30	2	67	2	1	4	10	.286	0	0-0	1	5.72	5.48
11 Det	AL	17	2	0	1	32.1	139	36	18	13	5	2	1	3	14	1	26	0	1	1	3	.250	0	0-0	1	5.96	3.62
11 Sea	AL	11	10	0	0	53.0	233	61	41	39	11	0	3	3	16	1	41	2	0	3	7	.300	0	0-0	0	5.57	6.62

Rafael Furcal

Bats: B **Throws:** R **Pos:** SS-85; PH-2   furr-CALL   **Ht:** 5'8" **Wt:** 187 **Born:** 10/24/1977 **Age:** 34

Year Team	Lg	G	AB	H	2B	3B	HR	(Hm	Rd)	TB	R	RBI	RC	TBB	IBB	SO	HBP	SH	SF	SB	CS	SB%	GDP	Avg	OBP	Slg
2011 Albq*	AAA	4	13	5	1	0	1	(-	-)	9	2	6	4	3	0	1	0	0	0	0	0	-	0	.385	.500	.692
2011 RCuca*	A+	6	22	7	0	0	0	(-	-)	7	10	1	3	3	0	3	0	0	0	1	0	1.00	0	.318	.400	.318
2000 Atl	NL	131	455	134	20	4	4	(1	3)	174	87	37	78	73	0	80	3	9	2	40	14	.74	2	.295	.394	.382
2001 Atl	NL	79	324	89	19	0	4	(3	1)	120	39	30	41	24	1	56	1	4	6	22	6	.79	5	.275	.323	.370
2002 Atl	NL	154	636	175	31	8	8	(4	4)	246	95	47	80	43	0	114	3	9	2	27	15	.64	8	.275	.323	.387
2003 Atl	NL	156	664	194	35	10	15	(4	11)	294	130	61	107	60	2	76	3	3	4	25	2	**.93**	1	.292	.352	.443
2004 Atl	NL	143	563	157	24	5	14	(5	9)	233	103	59	82	58	4	71	1	5	5	29	6	.83	9	.279	.344	.414
2005 Atl	NL	154	616	175	31	11	12	(9	3)	264	100	58	98	62	3	78	1	5	3	46	10	.82	11	.284	.348	.429
2006 LAD	NL	159	654	196	32	9	15	(12	3)	291	113	63	110	73	0	98	1	5	3	37	13	.74	7	.300	.369	.445
2007 LAD	NL	138	581	157	23	4	6	(4	2)	206	87	47	65	55	3	68	1	2	3	25	6	.81	11	.270	.333	.355
2008 LAD	NL	36	143	51	12	2	5	(3	2)	82	34	16	33	20	0	17	1	0	0	8	3	.73	3	.357	.439	.573
2009 LAD	NL	150	613	165	28	5	9	(5	4)	230	92	47	73	61	2	89	1	3	2	12	6	.67	11	.269	.335	.375
2010 LAD	NL	97	383	115	23	7	8	(5	3)	176	66	43	66	40	5	60	1	2	2	22	4	.85	5	.300	.366	.460
2011 2 Tms		87	333	77	15	0	8	(5	3)	116	44	28	31	28	0	39	4	3	1	9	5	.64	3	.231	.298	.348
11 LAD	NL	37	137	27	4	0	1	(1	0)	34	15	12	12	11	0	21	3	1	0	5	3	.63	0	.197	.272	.248
11 StL	NL	50	196	50	11	0	7	(4	3)	82	29	16	19	17	0	18	1	2	1	4	2	.67	3	.255	.316	.418
Postseason		41	170	41	2	3	3	(3	0)	58	25	13	22	23	1	25	1	4	2	12	2	.86	1	.241	.332	.341
12 ML YEARS		1484	5965	1685	293	65	108	(60	48)	2432	990	536	864	597	23	846	21	50	35	302	90	.77	76	.282	.348	.408

Armando Galarraga

Pitches: R **Bats:** R **Pos:** SP-8   **Ht:** 6'4" **Wt:** 235 **Born:** 1/15/1982 **Age:** 30

Year Team	Lg	G	GS	CG	GF	IP	BFP	H	R	ER	HR	SH	SF	HB	TBB	IBB	SO	WP	Bk	W	L	Pct	Sh	Sv-Op	Hld	ERC	ERA
2011 Reno*	AAA	5	5	0	0	23.1	120	30	24	24	9	0	0	3	17	0	16	1	0	1	2	.333	0	0- -	-	10.16	9.26
2007 Tex	AL	3	1	0	2	8.2	40	8	6	6	2	0	1	0	7	0	6	0	0	0	0	-	0	0-0	0	6.35	6.23
2008 Det	AL	30	28	0	0	178.2	746	152	83	74	28	2	4	6	61	2	126	6	0	13	7	.650	0	0-1	0	3.50	3.73
2009 Det	AL	29	25	0	1	143.2	642	158	93	90	24	1	11	6	67	1	95	1	0	6	10	.375	0	0-0	0	5.65	5.64
2010 Det	AL	25	24	2	0	144.1	617	143	75	72	21	1	7	4	51	1	74	4	3	4	9	.308	1	0-0	0	4.27	4.49
2011 Ari	NL	8	8	0	0	42.2	198	47	36	28	13	3	5	1	22	2	28	1	1	3	4	.429	0	0-0	0	6.60	5.91
5 ML YEARS		95	86	2	3	518.0	2243	508	293	270	88	7	28	17	208	6	329	12	4	26	30	.464	1	0-1	0	4.58	4.69

Yovani Gallardo

Pitches: R **Bats:** R **Pos:** SP-33   guy-YARR-doe   **Ht:** 6'2" **Wt:** 210 **Born:** 2/27/1986 **Age:** 26

Year Team	Lg	G	GS	CG	GF	IP	BFP	H	R	ER	HR	SH	SF	HB	TBB	IBB	SO	WP	Bk	W	L	Pct	Sh	Sv-Op	Hld	ERC	ERA
2007 Mil	NL	20	17	0	1	110.1	466	103	48	45	8	4	3	2	37	2	101	3	0	9	5	.643	0	0-0	0	3.30	3.67
2008 Mil	NL	4	4	0	0	24.0	97	22	5	5	3	2	1	0	8	0	20	0	0	0	0	-	0	0-0	0	3.66	1.88
2009 Mil	NL	30	30	1	0	185.2	793	150	78	77	21	5	3	5	94	5	204	9	0	13	12	.520	0	0-0	0	3.57	3.73

Year Team	Lg	G	GS	CG	GF	IP	BFP	H	R	ER	HR	SH	SF	HB	TBB	IBB	SO	WP	Bk	W	L	Pct	Sh	Sv-Op	Hld	ERC	ERA
2010 Mil	NL	31	31	2	0	185.0	803	178	89	79	12	11	4	3	75	5	200	7	1	14	7	.667	2	0-0	0	3.61	3.84
2011 Mil	NL	33	33	1	0	207.1	865	193	92	81	27	10	7	1	59	1	207	12	0	17	10	.630	1	0-0	0	3.43	3.52
Postseason		2	1	0	0	7.0	30	4	3	0	0	1	0	0	5	1	4	0	0	0	1	.000	0	0-0	0	2.03	0.00
5 ML YEARS		118	115	4	1	712.1	3024	646	312	287	71	32	18	11	273	13	732	31	1	53	34	.609	3	0-0	0	3.51	3.63

Mat Gamel

Bats: L **Throws:** R **Pos:** 3B-3; 1B-2; LF-2; DH-2; PH-1   GAMM-ell   **Ht:** 6'0" **Wt:** 215 **Born:** 7/26/1985 **Age:** 26

Year Team	Lg	G	AB	H	2B	3B	HR	(Hm	Rd)	TB	R	RBI	RC	TBB	IBB	SO	IBP	SH	SF	SB	CS	SB%	GDP	Avg	OBP	Slg
2011 Nashv*	AAA	128	493	153	29	0	28	(-	-)	266	90	96	98	46	6	84	4	0	2	2	0	1.00	16	.310	.372	.540
2008 Mil	NL	2	2	1	0	0	0	(0	0)	2	0	0	1	0	0	1	0	0	0	0	0	-	0	.500	.500	1.000
2009 Mil	NL	61	128	31	6	1	5	(4	1)	54	11	20	20	18	2	54	1	0	1	1	0	1.00	1	.242	.338	.422
2010 Mil	NL	12	15	3	1	0	0	(0	0)	4	1	1	1	1	0	8	1	0	0	0	0	-	1	.200	.294	.267
2011 Mil	NL	10	26	3	1	0	0	(0	0)	4	1	2	2	1	0	4	0	0	0	0	0	-	1	.115	.148	.154
4 ML YEARS		85	171	38	9	1	5	(4	1)	64	13	23	24	20	2	67	2	0	1	1	0	1.00	3	.222	.309	.374

Freddy Garcia

Pitches: R **Bats:** R **Pos:** SP-25; RP-1   **Ht:** 6'4" **Wt:** 250 **Born:** 10/6/1976 **Age:** 35

Year Team	Lg	G	GS	CG	GF	IP	BFP	H	R	ER	HR	SH	SF	HB	TBB	IBB	SO	WP	Bk	W	L	Pct	Sh	Sv-Op	Hld	ERC	ERA
2011 S-WB*	AAA	1	0	0	0	4.0	19	8	2	2	1	0	0	0	1	0	0	0	0	1	0	1.000	0	0- -	-	12.16	4.50
1999 Sea	AL	33	33	2	0	201.1	888	205	96	91	18	3	6	10	90	4	170	12	3	17	8	.680	1	0-0	0	4.46	4.07
2000 Sea	AL	21	20	0	0	124.1	538	112	62	54	16	6	1	2	64	4	79	4	2	9	5	.643	0	0-0	0	4.20	3.91
2001 Sea	AL	34	34	4	0	238.2	971	199	88	81	16	8	5	5	69	6	163	3	1	18	6	.750	3	0-0	0	2.61	3.05
2002 Sea	AL	34	34	1	0	223.2	955	227	110	109	30	4	8	6	63	3	181	7	1	16	10	.615	0	0-0	0	3.98	4.39
2003 Sea	AL	33	33	1	0	201.1	862	196	109	101	31	2	8	11	71	2	144	11	0	12	14	.462	0	0-0	0	4.33	4.51
2004 2 Tms	AL	31	31	1	0	210.0	878	192	92	89	22	8	3	7	64	3	184	8	0	13	11	.542	0	0-0	0	3.37	3.81
2005 CWS	AL	33	33	2	0	228.0	943	225	102	98	26	5	5	3	60	2	146	20	1	14	8	.636	0	0-0	0	3.65	3.87
2006 CWS	AL	33	33	1	0	216.1	917	228	116	109	32	1	6	7	48	3	135	4	0	17	9	.654	0	0-0	0	4.09	4.53
2007 Phi	NL	11	11	0	0	58.0	264	74	39	38	12	4	3	5	19	3	50	5	0	1	5	.167	0	0-0	0	6.57	5.90
2008 Det	AL	3	3	0	0	15.0	61	11	8	7	3	0	0	1	6	0	12	0	0	1	1	.500	0	0-0	0	3.61	4.20
2009 CWS	AL	9	9	0	0	56.0	229	56	27	27	4	0	1	0	12	0	37	2	0	3	4	.429	0	0-0	0	3.21	4.34
2010 CWS	AL	28	28	0	0	157.0	671	171	85	81	23	5	4	3	45	5	89	4	0	12	6	.667	0	0-0	0	4.52	4.64
2011 NYY	AL	26	25	0	1	146.2	626	152	63	59	16	4	7	3	45	5	96	4	0	12	8	.600	0	0-0	0	4.01	3.62
04 Sea	AL	15	15	1	0	107.0	446	96	39	38	8	4	1	2	32	1	82	5	0	4	7	.364	0	0-0	0	3.00	3.20
04 CWS	AL	16	16	0	0	103.0	432	96	53	51	14	4	2	5	32	2	102	3	0	9	4	.692	0	0-0	0	3.77	4.46
Postseason		9	9	1	0	55.0	230	51	20	19	5	2	0	2	22	1	45	1	0	6	2	.750	0	0-0	0	3.82	3.11
13 ML YEARS		329	327	12	1	2076.1	8803	2048	997	944	249	50	57	63	656	40	1486	84	8	145	95	.604	4	0-0	0	3.90	4.09

Jaime Garcia

Pitches: L **Bats:** L **Pos:** SP-32   HY-may   **Ht:** 6'2" **Wt:** 215 **Born:** 7/8/1986 **Age:** 25

Year Team	Lg	G	GS	CG	GF	IP	BFP	H	R	ER	HR	SH	SF	HB	TBB	IBB	SO	WP	Bk	W	L	Pct	Sh	Sv-Op	Hld	ERC	ERA
2008 StL	NL	10	1	0	4	16.0	69	14	10	10	4	0	0	1	8	0	8	3	0	1	1	.500	0	0-0	3	5.15	5.63
2010 StL	NL	28	28	1	0	163.1	695	151	64	49	9	3	3	3	64	4	132	4	1	13	8	.619	1	0-0	0	3.34	2.70
2011 StL	NL	32	32	2	0	194.2	826	207	100	77	15	10	5	2	50	2	156	12	1	13	7	.650	2	0-0	0	3.73	3.56
3 ML YEARS		70	61	3	4	374.0	1590	372	174	136	28	13	8	6	122	6	296	19	2	27	16	.628	3	0-0	3	3.62	3.27

Brett Gardner

Bats: L **Throws:** L **Pos:** LF-149; CF-18; PR-5; PH-2   **Ht:** 5'10" **Wt:** 183 **Born:** 8/24/1983 **Age:** 28

Year Team	Lg	G	AB	H	2B	3B	HR	(Hm	Rd)	TB	R	RBI	RC	TBB	IBB	SO	HBP	SH	SF	SB	CS	SB%	GDP	Avg	OBP	Slg
2008 NYY	AL	42	127	29	5	2	0	(0	0)	38	18	16	17	8	0	30	2	3	1	13	1	.93	0	.228	.283	.299
2009 NYY	AL	108	248	67	6	6	3	(1	2)	94	48	23	38	26	0	40	3	6	1	26	5	.84	3	.270	.345	.379
2010 NYY	AL	150	477	132	20	7	5	(5	0)	181	97	47	77	79	1	101	5	5	3	47	9	.84	6	.277	.383	.379
2011 NYY	AL	159	510	132	19	8	7	(4	3)	188	87	36	77	60	1	93	8	8	2	49	13	.79	5	.259	.345	.369
Postseason		23	40	7	0	0	0	(0	0)	7	5	2	1	3	0	12	0	2	1	3	2	.60	0	.175	.227	.175
4 ML YEARS		459	1362	360	50	23	15	(10	5)	501	250	122	209	173	2	264	18	22	7	135	28	.83	14	.264	.353	.368

Jon Garland

Pitches: R **Bats:** R **Pos:** SP-9   **Ht:** 6'6" **Wt:** 210 **Born:** 9/27/1979 **Age:** 32

Year Team	Lg	G	GS	CG	GF	IP	BFP	H	R	ER	HR	SH	SF	HB	TBB	IBB	SO	WP	Bk	W	L	Pct	Sh	Sv-Op	Hld	ERC	ERA
2011 RCuca*	A+	1	1	0	0	4.2	20	6	3	3	0	0	0	0	0	0	3	0	0	0	0	-	0	0- -	-	3.32	5.79
2000 CWS	AL	15	13	0	1	69.2	324	82	55	50	10	0	2	1	40	0	42	4	0	4	8	.333	0	0-0	1	6.26	6.46
2001 CWS	AL	35	16	0	8	117.0	510	123	59	48	16	2	5	4	55	2	61	3	0	6	7	.462	0	1-1	2	5.16	3.69
2002 CWS	AL	33	33	1	0	192.2	827	188	109	98	23	3	4	9	83	2	112	5	0	12	12	.500	1	0-0	0	4.46	4.58
2003 CWS	AL	32	32	0	0	191.2	813	188	100	96	28	4	8	4	74	1	108	8	0	12	13	.480	0	0-0	0	4.38	4.51
2004 CWS	AL	34	33	1	0	217.0	923	223	125	118	34	9	5	4	76	2	113	3	0	12	11	.522	0	0-0	0	4.56	4.89
2005 CWS	AL	32	32	3	0	221.0	901	212	93	86	26	9	8	7	47	3	115	2	0	18	10	.643	3	0-0	0	3.39	3.50
2006 CWS	AL	33	32	1	0	211.1	900	247	112	106	26	5	8	6	41	4	112	4	0	18	7	.720	1	0-0	0	4.50	4.51
2007 CWS	AL	32	32	2	0	208.1	883	219	114	98	19	3	7	4	57	3	98	1	0	10	13	.435	1	0-0	0	3.87	4.23
2008 LAA	AL	32	32	1	0	196.2	864	237	116	107	23	8	8	8	59	4	90	4	0	14	8	.636	0	0-0	0	5.18	4.90
2009 2 Tms	NL	33	33	0	0	204.0	882	225	106	91	23	11	6	6	61	7	109	6	0	11	13	.458	0	0-0	0	4.42	4.01
2010 SD	NL	33	33	0	0	200.0	837	176	86	77	20	5	6	6	87	9	136	6	0	14	12	.538	0	0-0	0	3.67	3.47

Year	Team	Lg	G	GS	CG	GF	IP	BFP	H	R	ER	HR	SH	SF	HB	TBB	IBB	SO	WP	Bk	W	L	Pct	Sh	Sv-Op	Hld	ERC	ERA
			HOW MUCH HE PITCHED						WHAT HE GAVE UP												THE RESULTS							
2011	LAD	NL	9	9	1	0	54.0	230	55	26	26	6	5	4	2	20	0	28	0	1	1	5	.167	0	0-0	0	4.37	4.33
09	Ari	NL	27	27	1	0	167.2	728	188	90	80	19	9	4	6	52	5	83	5	0	8	11	.421	0	0-0	0	4.63	4.29
09	LAD	NL	6	6	0	0	36.1	154	37	16	11	4	2	2	0	9	2	26	1	0	3	2	.600	0	0-0	0	3.51	2.72
Postseason			2	2	1	0	16.0	58	11	6	4	2	2	0	0	3	0	11	0	0	1	0	1.000	0	0-0	0	2.00	2.25
12 ML YEARS			353	330	11	9	2083.1	8894	2175	1104	1001	254	64	70	61	700	36	1124	46	1	132	119	.526	6	1-1	3	4.37	4.32

Cole Garner

Bats: R **Throws:** R **Pos:** LF-2; PH-2; RF-1   **Ht:** 6'2" **Wt:** 210 **Born:** 12/15/1984 **Age:** 27

Year	Team	Lg	G	AB	H	2B	3B	HR	(Hm	Rd)	TB	R	RBI	RC	TBB	IBB	SO	HBP	SH	SF	SB	CS	SB%	GDP	Avg	OBP	Slg
			BATTING																		BASERUNNING				AVERAGES		
2005	Casper	R+	66	265	69	21	1	10	(-	-)	122	34	48	34	9	1	105	8	0	2	2	8	.20	3	.260	.303	.460
2006	Ashvll	A	120	464	140	40	2	19	(-	-)	241	100	88	87	25	0	127	15	2	6	35	13	.73	6	.302	.353	.519
2007	Mdest	A+	96	319	68	18	4	8	(-	-)	118	39	33	32	20	0	115	7	5	1	7	5	.58	11	.213	.274	.370
2008	Mdest	A+	50	192	61	14	2	2	(-	-)	85	27	17	29	9	0	51	4	1	0	7	5	.58	5	.318	.361	.443
2009	Tulsa	AA	112	396	114	25	4	16	(-	-)	195	65	64	68	23	2	78	12	4	5	13	5	.72	11	.288	.342	.492
2010	ColSpr	AAA	111	415	126	31	10	13	(-	-)	216	81	61	80	39	2	89	8	6	1	8	5	.62	7	.304	.374	.520
2011	ColSpr	AAA	46	185	61	8	5	8	(-	-)	103	38	35	37	10	0	47	3	1	4	4	2	.67	1	.330	.366	.557
2011	Col	NL	4	9	2	0	0	0	(0	0)	2	1	3	2	1	0	6	0	0	0	0	0	-	0	.222	.300	.222

Steve Garrison

Pitches: L **Bats:** B **Pos:** RP-1   **Ht:** 6'1" **Wt:** 195 **Born:** 9/12/1986 **Age:** 25

Year	Team	Lg	G	GS	CG	GF	IP	BFP	H	R	ER	HR	SH	SF	HB	TBB	IBB	SO	WP	Bk	W	L	Pct	Sh	Sv-Op	Hld	ERC	ERA
			HOW MUCH HE PITCHED						WHAT HE GAVE UP												THE RESULTS							
2005	Brewrs	R	11	4	0	2	34.2	138	39	13	11	0	2	1	0	5	0	28	5	0	2	2	.500	0	2--	-	3.28	2.86
2006	WV	A-	17	16	0	0	88.2	372	86	38	34	10	4	3	3	22	0	77	1	1	7	6	.538	0	0--	-	3.51	3.45
2007	BrvdCt	A+	20	20	1	0	104.2	451	105	58	40	6	3	4	1	28	0	74	2	0	8	4	.667	1	0--	-	3.23	3.44
2007	Lk Els	A+	7	7	0	0	42.0	166	32	15	13	2	0	3	1	6	0	28	1	1	2	3	.400	0	0--	-	1.68	2.79
2008	SnAnt	AA	24	24	0	0	129.2	542	123	59	55	13	4	5	2	37	1	108	5	0	7	7	.500	0	0--	-	3.39	3.82
2009	Padres	R	9	9	0	0	20.1	94	22	14	14	1	0	0	2	5	0	22	3	0	0	2	.000	0	0--	-	3.80	6.20
2009	Lk Els	A+	2	1	0	1	7.2	30	5	2	1	0	0	0	1	2	0	7	0	0	0	0	-	0	1--	-	1.71	1.17
2009	SnAnt	AA	2	2	0	0	6.0	26	9	6	6	2	1	1	0	1	0	3	0	0	1	0	1.000	0	0--	-	8.38	9.00
2010	Lk Els	A+	9	3	0	0	28.2	119	28	13	10	1	3	0	1	10	1	13	0	1	1	1	.500	0	0--	-	3.49	3.14
2010	Portlnd	AAA	5	5	0	0	22.1	106	34	22	22	5	0	2	1	7	0	17	0	0	1	3	.250	0	0--	-	8.17	8.87
2010	Padres	R	3	3	0	0	6.0	22	5	2	2	0	0	0	0	1	0	8	0	0	0	0	-	0	0--	-	1.95	3.00
2011	Trntn	AA	17	16	0	0	75.2	348	102	58	50	12	1	2	3	20	0	46	3	0	4	8	.333	0	0--	-	6.11	5.95
2011	StIsInd	A-	1	1	0	0	5.0	18	4	0	0	0	0	0	0	1	0	4	0	0	0	0	-	0	0--	-	1.95	0.00
2011	NYY	AL	1	0	0	1	0.2	2	0	0	0	0	0	0	0	0	0	0	0	0	0	0	-	0	0-0	0	0.00	0.00

Matt Garza

Pitches: R **Bats:** R **Pos:** SP-31   **Ht:** 6'4" **Wt:** 215 **Born:** 11/26/1983 **Age:** 28

Year	Team	Lg	G	GS	CG	GF	IP	BFP	H	R	ER	HR	SH	SF	HB	TBB	IBB	SO	WP	Bk	W	L	Pct	Sh	Sv-Op	Hld	ERC	ERA
			HOW MUCH HE PITCHED						WHAT HE GAVE UP												THE RESULTS							
2006	Min	AL	10	9	0	0	50.0	232	62	33	32	6	0	3	0	23	0	38	1	0	3	6	.333	0	0-0	0	5.82	5.76
2007	Min	AL	16	15	0	0	83.0	367	96	44	34	8	1	4	4	32	4	67	4	0	5	7	.417	0	0-0	0	5.08	3.69
2008	TB	AL	30	30	3	0	184.2	772	170	83	76	19	3	9	6	59	2	128	3	2	11	9	.550	2	0-0	0	3.47	3.70
2009	TB	AL	32	32	0	0	203.0	861	177	93	89	25	2	8	11	79	0	189	3	0	8	12	.400	0	0-0	0	3.69	3.95
2010	TB	AL	33	32	1	0	204.2	855	193	94	89	28	1	6	7	63	2	150	12	2	15	10	.600	1	1-1	0	3.80	3.91
2011	ChC	NL	31	31	2	0	198.0	839	186	90	73	14	11	2	3	63	5	197	6	0	10	10	.500	0	0-0	0	3.21	3.32
Postseason			5	5	0	0	31.0	131	26	13	12	5	0	1	1	14	0	29	2	0	2	1	.667	0	0-0	0	3.95	3.48
6 ML YEARS			152	149	8	2	923.1	3926	884	437	393	100	18	32	31	319	13	769	29	4	52	54	.491	3	1-1	0	3.79	3.83

Joey Gathright

Bats: L **Throws:** R **Pos:** LF-4; PR-4; DH-1   **Ht:** 5'10" **Wt:** 185 **Born:** 4/27/1981 **Age:** 31

Year	Team	Lg	G	AB	H	2B	3B	HR	(Hm	Rd)	TB	R	RBI	RC	TBB	IBB	SO	HBP	SH	SF	SB	CS	SB%	GDP	Avg	OBP	Slg
			BATTING																		BASERUNNING				AVERAGES		
2011	Pwtckt*	AAA	4	8	3	0	0	0	(-	-)	3	3	2	1	1	0	1	0	1	0	1	0	1.00	0	.375	.444	.375
2004	TB	AL	19	52	13	0	0	0	(0	0)	13	11	1	4	2	0	14	3	0	0	6	1	.86	2	.250	.316	.250
2005	TB	AL	76	203	56	7	3	0	(0	0)	69	29	13	22	10	0	39	2	3	0	20	5	.80	5	.276	.316	.340
2006	2 Tms	AL	134	383	91	12	3	1	(1	0)	112	59	41	46	42	0	75	7	9	4	22	9	.71	3	.238	.321	.292
2007	KC	AL	74	228	70	8	0	0	(0	0)	78	28	19	31	20	0	36	3	10	0	9	8	.53	3	.307	.371	.342
2008	KC	AL	105	279	71	3	1	0	(0	0)	76	41	22	31	20	0	40	4	10	2	21	4	.84	3	.254	.311	.272
2009	2 Tms	AL	37	30	8	0	0	0	(0	0)	8	9	1	2	2	0	8	0	0	0	2	2	.50	2	.267	.313	.267
2011	Bos	AL	7	0	0	0	0	0	(0	0)	0	1	0	0	1	0	0	0	0	0	1	1	.50	0	-	1.000	
06	TB	AL	55	154	31	6	0	0	(0	0)	37	25	13	15	20	0	30	3	5	0	12	3	.80	1	.201	.305	.240
06	KC	AL	79	229	60	6	3	1	(1	0)	75	34	28	31	22	0	45	4	4	4	10	6	.63	2	.262	.332	.292
09	ChC	NL	20	14	3	0	0	0	(0	0)	3	2	0	1	1	0	6	0	0	0	1	2	.33	0	.214	.267	.214
09	Bos	AL	17	16	5	0	0	0	(0	0)	5	7	1	1	1	0	2	0	0	0	1	0	1.00	2	.313	.353	.313
Postseason			1	0	0	0	0	0	(0	0)	0	1	0	0	0	0	0	0	0	0	1	0	1.00		-	-	
7 ML YEARS			452	1175	309	30	7	1	(1	0)	356	178	96	136	97	0	212	19	32	6	81	30	.73	17	.263	.328	.303

John Gaub

Pitches: L Bats: R Pos: RP-4 GOB Ht: 6'2" Wt: 200 Born: 4/28/1985 Age: 27

		HOW MUCH HE PITCHED				WHAT HE GAVE UP											THE RESULTS						
Year Team	Lg	G	GS	CG	GF	IP	BFP	H	R	ER	HR	SH	SF	HB	TBB	IBB	SO	WP	Bk	W	L	Pct	Sh	Sv-Op Hld	ERC	ERA
2007 Indns	R	4	0	0	1	4.0	17	4	1	1	0	0	0	0	4	0	4	0	0	0	0	-	0	0- -	6.54	2.25
2008 Lk Cty	A	34	0	0	6	64.0	266	44	30	24	3	4	3	1	32	0	100	9	0	1	1	.500	0	2- -	2.49	3.38
2009 Tenn	AA	26	0	0	9	28.2	122	19	12	9	3	1	2	1	17	0	40	2	0	3	1	.750	0	4- -	3.12	2.83
2009 Iowa	AAA	26	0	0	8	31.1	126	17	6	6	1	1	0	0	16	2	40	0	0	1	1	.500	0	1- -	1.65	1.72
2010 Iowa	AAA	30	0	0	13	29.0	139	27	21	21	1	3	0	2	25	1	38	6	1	3	4	.429	0	3- -	5.13	6.52
2010 Cubs	R	1	1	0	0	0.1	15	1	4	3	0	0	0	0	2	0	1	0	0	0	1	.000	0	0- -	35.68	81.00
2011 Iowa	AAA	50	0	0	22	55.1	247	42	24	21	6	4	1	1	40	3	75	5	0	4	4	.500	0	7- -	3.97	3.42
2011 ChC	NL	4	0	0	0	2.2	12	2	2	2	0	0	0	0	2	0	3	1	0	0	0	-	0	0-0 0	3.21	6.75

Chad Gaudin

Pitches: R Bats: R Pos: RP-10 goe-DANN Ht: 5'10" Wt: 188 Born: 3/24/1983 Age: 29

		HOW MUCH HE PITCHED				WHAT HE GAVE UP											THE RESULTS						
Year Team	Lg	G	GS	CG	GF	IP	BFP	H	R	ER	HR	SH	SF	HB	TBB	IBB	SO	WP	Bk	W	L	Pct	Sh	Sv-Op Hld	ERC	ERA
2011 Ptomc*	A+	1	1	0	0	1.0	3	0	0	0	0	0	0	0	0	0	0	0	0	0	0	-	0	0- -	0.00	0.00
2011 Hgrstn*	A	1	0	0	0	2.0	8	2	0	0	0	0	0	0	0	0	0	0	0	0	0	-	0	0- -	1.95	0.00
2011 Syrcse*	AAA	6	2	0	2	12.1	56	17	9	6	0	0	1	1	3	0	14	1	0	0	2	.000	0	0- -	5.25	4.38
2011 LsVgs*	AAA	6	6	0	0	29.1	129	37	21	20	2	0	0	4	9	0	13	1	0	2	3	.400	0	0- -	5.80	6.14
2003 TB	AL	15	3	0	5	40.0	173	37	18	16	4	0	2	1	16	0	23	1	0	2	0	1.000	0	0-0	3.70	3.60
2004 TB	AL	26	4	0	5	42.2	201	59	27	23	4	2	4	4	16	4	30	0	0	1	2	.333	0	0-1 5	6.46	4.85
2005 Tor	AL	5	3	0	0	13.0	74	31	19	19	6	0	1	1	6	0	12	0	0	1	3	.250	0	0-0	18.35	13.15
2006 Oak	AL	55	0	0	13	64.0	276	51	24	22	3	0	3	1	42	2	36	2	2	4	2	.667	0	2-3 11	3.62	3.09
2007 Oak	AL	34	34	1	0	199.1	886	205	108	98	21	3	6	8	100	8	154	3	1	11	13	.458	0	0-0	4.80	4.42
2008 2 Tms		50	6	0	14	90.0	382	92	50	44	11	2	2	3	27	3	71	2	2	9	5	.643	0	0-1 4	4.06	4.40
2009 2 Tms		31	25	0	4	147.1	664	146	85	76	14	7	8	8	76	4	139	7	1	6	10	.375	0	0-0	4.56	4.64
2010 2 Tms		42	0	0	23	65.1	295	73	45	41	16	4	2	8	25	0	53	3	0	1	4	.200	0	0-1 6	6.33	5.65
2011 Was	NL	10	0	0	0	8.1	45	12	10	6	1	1	0	0	8	0	10	0	0	1	1	.500	0	0-0	9.20	6.48
08 Oak	AL	26	6	0	9	62.2	263	63	29	25	6	2	1	3	17	1	44	2	1	5	3	.625	0	0-0 2	3.78	3.59
08 ChC	NL	24	0	0	5	27.1	119	29	21	19	5	0	1	0	10	2	27	0	1	4	2	.667	0	0-1 2	4.74	6.26
09 SD	NL	20	19	0	0	105.1	476	105	69	60	7	7	6	5	56	3	105	4	1	4	10	.286	0	0-0	4.41	5.13
09 NYY	AL	11	6	0	4	42.0	188	41	16	16	7	0	2	3	20	1	34	3	0	2	0	1.000	0	0-0	4.93	3.43
10 Oak	AL	12	0	0	6	17.1	86	27	18	17	5	2	1	3	5	0	20	0	0	0	2	.000	0	0-0 1	9.34	8.83
10 NYY	AL	30	0	0	17	48.0	209	46	27	24	11	2	1	5	20	0	33	3	0	1	2	.333	0	0-1 5	5.32	4.50
Postseason		4	0	0	1	4.1	18	2	0	0	0	1	0	0	3	1	1	0	0	0	0	-	0	0-0	1.45	0.00
9 ML YEARS		268	75	1	65	670.0	2996	706	386	345	80	19	28	34	316	21	528	18	6	36	40	.474	0	2-6 23	4.97	4.63

Cory Gearrin

Pitches: R Bats: R Pos: RP-18 GARE-inn Ht: 6'3" Wt: 200 Born: 4/14/1986 Age: 26

		HOW MUCH HE PITCHED				WHAT HE GAVE UP											THE RESULTS						
Year Team	Lg	G	GS	CG	GF	IP	BFP	H	R	ER	HR	SH	SF	HB	TBB	IBB	SO	WP	Bk	W	L	Pct	Sh	Sv-Op Hld	ERC	ERA
2007 Danvle	R+	18	0	0	10	26.1	122	21	14	13	1	1	1	6	16	3	37	7	0	1	1	.500	0	0- -	3.84	4.44
2008 Rome	A	19	0	0	15	22.1	105	19	11	7	1	2	1	0	15	0	36	4	0	3	2	.600	0	1- -	3.62	2.82
2008 MrtlBh	A+	17	0	0	9	23.2	115	19	14	14	2	1	1	4	21	2	36	2	0	3	1	.750	0	0- -	5.11	5.32
2009 MrtlBh	A+	27	0	0	24	29.1	115	22	6	6	2	0	0	1	3	0	32	0	0	0	2	.000	0	17- -	1.65	1.84
2009 Missi	AA	20	0	0	10	25.1	102	19	9	8	2	2	0	3	8	1	20	1	0	1	2	.333	0	2- -	2.75	2.84
2010 Gwnntt	AAA	52	0	0	15	80.1	339	72	32	30	6	2	3	9	32	1	66	12	0	3	5	.375	0	0- -	3.83	3.36
2011 Gwnntt	AAA	35	0	0	17	50.0	211	42	11	10	0	1	1	3	20	1	60	4	0	4	1	.800	0	4- -	2.72	1.80
2011 Atl	NL	18	0	0	4	18.1	85	17	16	16	0	2	1	2	12	4	25	1	0	1	1	.500	0	0-1 3	3.84	7.85

Dillon Gee

Pitches: R Bats: R Pos: SP-27; RP-3 JEE Ht: 6'1" Wt: 205 Born: 4/28/1986 Age: 26

		HOW MUCH HE PITCHED				WHAT HE GAVE UP											THE RESULTS						
Year Team	Lg	G	GS	CG	GF	IP	BFP	H	R	ER	HR	SH	SF	HB	TBB	IBB	SO	WP	Bk	W	L	Pct	Sh	Sv-Op Hld	ERC	ERA
2007 Bklyn	A-	14	11	0	0	62.0	250	57	17	17	1	3	3	6	9	1	56	0	0	3	1	.750	0	0- -	2.53	2.47
2008 StLuci	A+	21	21	0	0	127.1	510	117	49	46	6	2	3	9	19	0	94	3	0	8	6	.571	0	0- -	2.68	3.25
2008 Bnghtn	AA	4	4	0	0	27.0	101	18	4	4	1	1	1	1	5	0	20	0	0	2	0	1.000	0	0- -	1.54	1.33
2009 Buffalo	AAA	9	9	1	0	48.1	209	47	22	22	5	0	2	5	16	0	42	1	0	1	3	.250	0	0- -	4.07	4.10
2010 Buffalo	AAA	28	28	0	0	161.1	697	174	96	89	23	3	7	13	41	1	165	3	0	13	8	.619	0	0- -	4.55	4.96
2011 Buffalo	AAA	2	2	0	0	11.2	47	7	8	6	1	0	0	1	5	0	8	0	0	1	1	.500	0	0- -	2.35	4.63
2010 NYM	NL	5	5	0	0	33.0	136	25	10	8	2	3	0	0	15	2	17	0	0	2	2	.500	0	0-0	2.66	2.18
2011 NYM	NL	30	27	1	1	160.2	706	150	85	79	18	10	5	14	71	4	114	6	1	13	6	.684	0	0-0	4.23	4.43
2 ML YEARS		35	32	1	1	193.2	842	175	95	87	20	13	5	14	86	6	131	6	1	15	8	.652	0	0-0	3.95	4.04

Craig Gentry

Bats: R Throws: R Pos: CF-55; PR-8; RF-7; PH-5; LF-2 Ht: 6'2" Wt: 190 Born: 11/29/1983 Age: 28

		BATTING																			BASERUNNING				AVERAGES		
Year Team	Lg	G	AB	H	2B	3B	HR	(Hm	Rd)	TB	R	RBI	RC	TBB	IBB	SO	HBP	SH	SF	SB	CS	SB%	GDP	Avg	OBP	Slg
2011 RdRck*	AAA	30	110	27	5	1	1	(-	-)	37	21	10	13	11	0	17	2	0	0	5	1	.83	2	.245	.325	.336
2009 Tex	AL	11	17	2	1	0	0	(0	0)	3	4	1	1	2	0	5	0	0	0	0	0	-	0	.118	.211	.176
2010 Tex	AL	20	33	7	0	0	0	(0	0)	7	4	3	1	1	0	11	0	0	1	1	0	1.00	1	.212	.229	.212
2011 Tex	AL	64	133	36	5	1	1	(1	0)	46	26	13	21	10	1	27	6	3	1	18	0	1.00	2	.271	.347	.346
3 ML YEARS		95	183	45	6	1	1	(1	0)	56	34	17	23	13	1	43	6	3	2	19	0	1.00	3	.246	.314	.306

Esteban German

Bats: R **Throws:** R **Pos:** 3B-4; PH-3; PR-3; 2B-2; DH-2 her-MAHN **Ht:** 5'9" **Wt:** 195 **Born:** 1/26/1978 **Age:** 34

										BATTING												BASERUNNING				AVERAGES		
Year	Team	Lg	G	AB	H	2B	3B	HR	(Hm	Rd)	TB	R	RBI	RC	TBB	IBB	SO	HBP	SH	SF	SB	CS	SB%	GDP	Avg	OBP	Slg
2011	RdRck*	AAA	123	508	153	29	3	7	(-	-)	209	94	56	92	72	0	58	1	3	2	44	9	.83	16	.301	.388	.411
2002	Oak	AL	9	35	7	0	0	0	(0	0)	7	4	0	2	4	0	11	1	0	0	1	0	1.00	0	.200	.300	.200
2003	Oak	AL	5	4	1	0	0	0	(0	0)	1	0	1	1	0	0	1	0	0	0	0	0	-	1	.250	.250	.250
2004	Oak	AL	31	60	15	1	1	0	(0	0)	18	9	7	8	4	0	13	0	1	0	0	1	.00	1	.250	.297	.300
2005	Tex	AL	5	4	3	1	0	0	(0	0)	4	3	1	2	0	0	1	0	0	0	2	0	1.00	0	.750	.750	1.000
2006	KC	AL	106	279	91	18	5	3	(2	1)	128	44	34	55	40	0	49	6	6	0	7	3	.70	8	.326	.422	.459
2007	KC	AL	121	348	92	15	6	4	(3	1)	131	49	37	48	43	0	60	5	6	3	11	7	.61	11	.264	.351	.376
2008	KC	AL	89	216	53	14	3	0	(0	0)	73	30	22	26	18	1	42	1	4	3	7	3	.70	5	.245	.303	.338
2009	Tex	AL	19	46	14	4	0	0	(0	0)	18	9	4	7	4	0	7	0	0	0	1	0	1.00	0	.304	.360	.391
2010	Tex	AL	13	13	3	0	0	0	(0	0)	3	5	1	3	3	0	2	0	0	0	4	1	.80	0	.231	.375	.231
2011	Tex	AL	11	11	5	1	0	1	(0	1)	9	6	4	4	1	0	1	0	0	1	1	0	1.00	0	.455	.462	.818
	10 ML YEARS		409	1016	284	54	15	8	(5	3)	392	159	111	156	117	1	187	13	17	7	34	15	.69	26	.280	.359	.386

Justin Germano

Pitches: R **Bats:** R **Pos:** RP-9 jerr-MAHN-oh **Ht:** 6'2" **Wt:** 210 **Born:** 8/6/1982 **Age:** 29

			HOW MUCH HE PITCHED						WHAT HE GAVE UP										THE RESULTS						
Year	Team	Lg	G	GS	CG	GF	IP	BFP	H	R	ER	HR	SH	SF	HB	TBB	IBB	SO	WP	Bk	W	L	Pct	Sh	Sv-Op Hld	ERC	ERA
2011	Clmbs*	AAA	16	6	1	8	49.0	194	50	23	23	5	2	1	3	4	1	39	0	1	1	2	.333	1	3- - -	3.29	4.22
2004	SD	NL	7	5	0	0	21.1	109	31	24	21	7	2	3	1	14	0	16	0	0	1	2	.333	0	0-0	7.69	8.86
2006	Cin	NL	2	1	0	0	6.2	31	8	4	4	1	0	0	1	3	1	8	0	0	0	1	.000	0	0-0	6.26	5.40
2007	SD	NL	26	23	0	3	133.1	566	133	72	66	14	4	0	8	40	3	78	1	0	7	10	.412	0	0-0	3.93	4.46
2008	SD	NL	12	6	0	4	43.2	194	54	31	29	8	2	1	1	13	2	17	4	0	0	3	.000	0	0-0	5.69	5.98
2010	Cle	AL	23	1	0	4	35.1	146	27	15	13	6	1	0	6	8	1	29	0	0	0	3	.000	0	0-1	3.17	3.31
2011	Cle	AL	9	0	0	5	12.2	60	15	8	8	1	1	0	2	5	0	5	0	0	0	1	.000	0	0-0	5.46	5.68
	6 ML YEARS		79	36	0	16	253.0	1106	268	154	141	32	11	2	18	83	7	153	5	0	8	20	.286	0	0-1	4.55	5.02

Chris Getz

Bats: L **Throws:** R **Pos:** 2B-110; PR-5; SS-4; DH-3; PH-2 **Ht:** 5'11" **Wt:** 181 **Born:** 8/30/1983 **Age:** 28

										BATTING												BASERUNNING				AVERAGES		
Year	Team	Lg	G	AB	H	2B	3B	HR	(Hm	Rd)	TB	R	RBI	RC	TBB	IBB	SO	HBP	SH	SF	SB	CS	SB%	GDP	Avg	OBP	Slg
2008	CWS	AL	10	7	2	0	0	0	(0	0)	2	2	1	1	0	0	1	0	0	0	1	1	.50	0	.286	.286	.286
2009	CWS	AL	107	375	98	18	4	2	(1	1)	130	49	31	47	30	1	54	6	1	3	25	2	.93	4	.261	.324	.347
2010	KC	AL	72	224	53	9	0	0	(0	0)	62	23	18	21	19	1	28	2	3	0	15	2	.88	3	.237	.302	.277
2011	KC	AL	118	380	97	6	3	0	(0	0)	109	50	26	43	30	0	45	3	14	2	21	7	.75	5	.255	.313	.287
	4 ML YEARS		307	986	250	33	7	2	(1	1)	303	124	76	112	79	2	128	11	18	5	62	12	.84	12	.254	.315	.307

Jason Giambi

Bats: L **Throws:** R **Pos:** PH-35; 1B-23; DH-6 **Ht:** 6'3" **Wt:** 240 **Born:** 1/8/1971 **Age:** 41

										BATTING												BASERUNNING				AVERAGES		
Year	Team	Lg	G	AB	H	2B	3B	HR	(Hm	Rd)	TB	R	RBI	RC	TBB	IBB	SO	HBP	SH	SF	SB	CS	SB%	GDP	Avg	OBP	Slg
2011	ColSpr*	AAA	3	7	3	0	0	0	(-	-)	3	2	3	1	0	0	2	1	0	0	0	0	-	0	.429	.500	.429
1995	Oak	AL	54	176	45	7	0	6	(3	3)	70	27	25	27	28	0	31	3	1	2	2	1	.67	4	.256	.364	.398
1996	Oak	AL	140	536	156	40	1	20	(6	14)	258	84	79	88	51	3	95	5	1	5	0	1	.00	15	.291	.355	.481
1997	Oak	AL	142	519	152	41	2	20	(14	6)	257	66	81	91	55	3	89	6	0	8	0	0	-	11	.293	.362	.495
1998	Oak	AL	153	562	166	28	0	27	(12	15)	275	92	110	103	81	7	102	5	0	9	2	2	.50	16	.295	.384	.489
1999	Oak	AL	158	575	181	36	1	33	(17	16)	318	115	123	132	105	6	106	7	0	8	1	1	.50	11	.315	.422	.553
2000	Oak	AL	152	510	170	29	1	43	(23	20)	330	108	137	152	137	6	96	9	0	8	2	0	1.00	9	.333	.476	.647
2001	Oak	AL	154	520	178	47	2	38	(27	11)	343	109	120	153	129	24	83	13	0	9	2	0	1.00	17	.342	.477	.660
2002	NYY	AL	155	560	176	34	1	41	(19	22)	335	120	122	139	109	4	112	15	0	5	2	2	.50	18	.314	.435	.598
2003	NYY	AL	156	535	134	25	0	41	(12	29)	282	97	107	120	129	9	140	21	0	6	2	1	.67	9	.250	.412	.527
2004	NYY	AL	80	264	55	9	0	12	(5	7)	100	33	40	42	47	1	62	8	0	3	0	1	.00	5	.208	.342	.379
2005	NYY	AL	139	417	113	14	0	32	(16	16)	223	74	87	102	108	5	109	19	0	1	0	0	-	7	.271	.440	.535
2006	NYY	AL	139	446	113	25	0	37	(20	17)	249	92	113	104	110	12	106	10	0	7	2	0	1.00	10	.253	.413	.558
2007	NYY	AL	83	254	60	8	0	14	(6	8)	110	31	39	41	40	2	66	8	0	1	1	0	1.00	1	.236	.356	.433
2008	NYY	AL	145	458	113	19	1	32	(16	16)	230	68	96	79	76	5	111	22	0	9	2	1	.67	6	.247	.373	.502
2009	2 Tms		102	293	59	14	0	13	(7	6)	112	43	51	44	57	1	80	7	0	2	0	0	-	6	.201	.343	.382
2010	Col	NL	87	176	43	9	0	6	(4	2)	70	17	35	35	35	5	47	6	0	1	2	0	1.00	6	.244	.378	.398
2011	Col	NL	64	131	34	6	0	13	(6	7)	79	20	32	26	17	0	45	3	0	1	0	0	-	1	.260	.355	.603
09 Oak		AL	83	269	52	13	0	11	(7	4)	98	39	40	36	50	1	72	7	0	2	0	0	-	5	.193	.332	.364
09 Col		NL	19	24	7	1	0	2	(0	2)	14	4	11	8	7	0	8	0	0	0	0	0	-	1	.292	.452	.583
	Postseason		45	138	40	6	0	7	(5	2)	67	19	19	25	30	2	30	4	0	2	2	0	1.00	3	.290	.425	.486
	17 ML YEARS		2103	6932	1948	391	9	428	(213	215)	3641	1196	1397	1480	1314	93	1480	173	2	88	20	11	.65	151	.281	.404	.525

Johnny Giavotella

Bats: R **Throws:** R **Pos:** 2B-46 gee-uh-vo-TELL-uh **Ht:** 5'8" **Wt:** 185 **Born:** 7/10/1987 **Age:** 24

										BATTING												BASERUNNING				AVERAGES		
Year	Team	Lg	G	AB	H	2B	3B	HR	(Hm	Rd)	TB	R	RBI	RC	TBB	IBB	SO	HBP	SH	SF	SB	CS	SB%	GDP	Avg	OBP	Slg
2008	Burlgtn	A	68	278	83	18	2	4	(-	-)	117	50	26	42	25	0	34	1	3	3	10	7	.59	10	.299	.355	.421
2009	Wilmg	A+	133	476	123	24	8	6	(-	-)	181	84	52	71	66	0	54	4	11	4	26	9	.74	7	.258	.351	.380
2010	NWArk	AA	134	522	168	35	5	9	(-	-)	240	92	65	97	61	1	67	4	7	3	13	7	.65	17	.322	.395	.460
2011	Omha	AAA	110	453	153	34	2	9	(-	-)	218	67	72	85	40	1	57	2	3	5	9	5	.64	8	.338	.390	.481
2011	KC	AL	46	178	44	9	4	2	(2	0)	67	20	21	15	6	0	32	1	0	2	5	2	.71	4	.247	.273	.376

Jay Gibbons

Bats: L **Throws:** L **Pos:** LF-10; PH-9; RF-4; DH-1   **Ht:** 6'0" **Wt:** 195 **Born:** 3/2/1977 **Age:** 35

Year Team	Lg	G	AB	H	2B	3B	HR	(Hm Rd)	TB	R	RBI	RC	TBB	IBB	SO	HBP	SH	SF	SB	CS	SB%	GDP	Avg	OBP	Slg
2011 Albq*	AAA	76	263	79	12	1	9	(- -)	120	38	46	51	44	3	44	2	0	1	1	0	1.00	7	.300	.403	.456
2011 Ddgrs*	R	2	7	2	0	0	0	(- -)	2	1	2	0	0	0	3	0	0	1	0	0	-	0	.286	.250	.286
2001 Bal	AL	73	225	53	10	0	15	(9 6)	108	27	36	31	17	0	39	4	0	0	0	1	.00	7	.236	.301	.480
2002 Bal	AL	136	490	121	29	1	28	(17 11)	236	71	69	71	45	3	66	2	0	4	1	3	.25	9	.247	.311	.482
2003 Bal	AL	160	625	173	39	2	23	(12 11)	285	80	100	94	49	11	89	3	0	5	0	1	.00	12	.277	.330	.456
2004 Bal	AL	97	346	85	14	1	10	(4 6)	131	36	47	38	29	0	64	1	1	3	1	1	.50	11	.246	.303	.379
2005 Bal	AL	139	488	135	33	3	26	(13 13)	252	72	79	73	28	3	56	1	0	1	0	0	-	15	.277	.317	.516
2006 Bal	AL	90	343	95	23	0	13	(8 5)	157	34	46	50	32	2	48	2	0	1	0	0	-	12	.277	.341	.458
2007 Bal	AL	84	270	62	14	0	6	(1 5)	94	28	28	23	15	1	52	2	0	3	0	0	-	5	.230	.272	.348
2010 LAD	NL	37	75	21	2	0	5	(2 3)	38	11	17	13	4	0	14	0	0	1	0	1	.00	2	.280	.313	.507
2011 LAD	NL	24	55	14	2	0	1	(0 1)	19	5	5	5	5	1	14	1	0	1	0	0	-	0	.255	.323	.345
9 ML YEARS		840	2917	759	166	7	127	(66 61)	1320	364	427	398	224	21	442	16	1	19	2	7	.22	73	.260	.315	.453

Conor Gillaspie

Bats: L **Throws:** R **Pos:** PH-12; 3B-4   **Ht:** 6'1" **Wt:** 200 **Born:** 7/18/1987 **Age:** 24

Year Team	Lg	G	AB	H	2B	3B	HR	(Hm Rd)	TB	R	RBI	RC	TBB	IBB	SO	HBP	SH	SF	SB	CS	SB%	GDP	Avg	OBP	Slg
2008 Giants	R	6	22	6	3	0	0	(- -)	9	2	7	3	3	0	1	0	0	0	0	1	.00	2	.273	.360	.409
2008 SlmKzr	A+	18	71	19	4	0	0	(- -)	23	4	8	9	9	0	13	0	0	0	2	0	1.00	2	.268	.350	.324
2009 SnJos	A+	126	469	134	31	2	4	(- -)	181	62	67	69	55	2	68	3	2	1	2	3	.40	6	.286	.364	.386
2010 Rchmd	AA	132	491	141	25	8	8	(- -)	206	57	67	70	37	4	67	2	2	8	4		.00	6	.287	.335	.420
2011 Fresno	AAA	124	428	127	22	6	11	(- -)	194	63	61	78	66	0	79	1	4	4	9	9	.50	11	.297	.389	.453
2008 SF	NL	8	5	1	0	0	0	(0 0)	1	1	0	1	2	0	0	0	0	0	0	0	-	0	.200	.429	.200
2011 SF	NL	15	19	5	0	0	1	(1 0)	8	2	2	4	2	0	1	0	0	0	0	0	-	0	.263	.333	.421
2 ML YEARS		23	24	6	0	0	1	(1 0)	9	3	2	5	4	0	1	0	0	0	0	0	-	0	.250	.357	.375

Cole Gillespie

Bats: R **Throws:** R **Pos:** LF-2; RF-2; PH-1; PR-1   **Ht:** 6'1" **Wt:** 205 **Born:** 6/20/1984 **Age:** 28

Year Team	Lg	G	AB	H	2B	3B	HR	(Hm Rd)	TB	R	RBI	RC	TBB	IBB	SO	HBP	SH	SF	SB	CS	SB%	GDP	Avg	OBP	Slg
2006 Helena	R+	51	186	64	12	1	8	(- -)	102	49	31	50	40	1	34	4	0	3	18	4	.82	4	.344	.464	.548
2007 BrvdCt	A+	129	438	117	25	3	12	(- -)	184	75	62	75	72	1	95	8	1	3	16	8	.67	9	.267	.378	.420
2008 Hntsvl	AA	131	462	130	38	4	14	(- -)	218	73	79	91	74	1	102	7	3	4	17	1	.94	10	.281	.386	.472
2009 BrvdCt	A+	12	43	15	2	3	1	(- -)	26	10	9	11	7	1	11	0	0	1	4	0	1.00	1	.349	.431	.605
2009 Nashv	AAA	75	236	57	12	5	7	(- -)	100	29	27	35	31	1	56	3	3	4	6	5	.55	5	.242	.332	.424
2009 Reno	AAA	42	138	42	6	4	5	(- -)	71	33	27	32	27	0	31	2	0	3	8	0	1.00	6	.304	.418	.514
2010 Reno	AAA	69	264	76	14	6	8	(- -)	126	54	49	51	44	1	49	3	0	1	8	5	.62	11	.288	.394	.477
2011 Reno	AAA	137	484	145	19	16	12	(- -)	232	100	79	102	81	2	91	10	0	7	24	5	.83	14	.300	.405	.479
2010 Ari	NL	45	104	24	8	0	2	(2 0)	38	11	12	10	7	1	29	1	0	1	1	1	.50	2	.231	.283	.365
2011 Ari	NL	5	6	2	0	0	1	(1 0)	5	2	4	3	1	0	1	0	0	0	0	0	-	0	.333	.429	.833
2 ML YEARS		50	110	26	8	0	3	(3 0)	43	13	16	13	8	1	30	1	0	1	1	1	.50	2	.236	.292	.391

Chris Gimenez

Bats: R **Throws:** R **Pos:** C-20; LF-3; 1B-2   JIMM-inn-ezz   **Ht:** 6'2" **Wt:** 215 **Born:** 12/27/1982 **Age:** 29

Year Team	Lg	G	AB	H	2B	3B	HR	(Hm Rd)	TB	R	RBI	RC	TBB	IBB	SO	HBP	SH	SF	SB	CS	SB%	GDP	Avg	OBP	Slg
2011 Tacom*	AAA	13	49	13	1	0	1	(- -)	17	8	4	6	7	0	13	0	0	0	1	1	.00	2	.265	.357	.347
2009 Cle	AL	45	111	16	2	0	3	(0 3)	27	12	7	3	17	0	36	0	1	1	1	1	.50	3	.144	.256	.243
2010 Cle	AL	28	58	11	5	0	1	(1 0)	19	6	8	5	8	0	22	0	1	0	0	0	-	1	.190	.288	.328
2011 Sea	AL	24	59	12	1	0	1	(0 1)	16	6	6	5	10	0	13	0	0	1	0	1	.00	1	.203	.314	.271
3 ML YEARS		97	228	39	8	0	5	(1 4)	62	24	21	13	35	0	71	0	2	2	1	2	.33	5	.171	.279	.272

Hector Gimenez

Bats: B **Throws:** R **Pos:** PH-3; C-1   hee-MEN-ezz   **Ht:** 5'10" **Wt:** 225 **Born:** 9/28/1982 **Age:** 29

Year Team	Lg	G	AB	H	2B	3B	HR	(Hm Rd)	TB	R	RBI	RC	TBB	IBB	SO	HBP	SH	SF	SB	CS	SB%	GDP	Avg	OBP	Slg
2002 Lxngtn	A	85	297	78	16	1	11	(- -)	129	41	42	41	25	1	78	0	1	0	2	3	.40	4	.263	.320	.434
2003 Salem	A+	109	381	94	17	1	7	(- -)	134	41	54	43	29	1	75	4	1	4	2	0	1.00	7	.247	.304	.352
2004 RdRck	AA	97	331	81	16	3	6	(- -)	121	38	46	36	18	0	64	2	3	5	2	0	1.00	3	.245	.284	.366
2005 CpChr	AA	121	454	124	19	1	12	(- -)	181	47	58	59	32	2	88	2	7	3	2	3	.40	8	.273	.322	.399
2006 RdRck	AAA	76	275	75	8	0	8	(- -)	107	31	37	36	24	3	42	1	0	2	2	3	.40	8	.273	.331	.389
2008 Drham	AA	43	146	33	8	2	2	(- -)	51	11	16	14	8	1	36	1	1	1	0	0	-	3	.226	.269	.349
2008 VeroB	A+	38	134	26	2	1	4	(- -)	42	11	21	12	15	1	32	0	1	2	0	0	-	0	.194	.272	.313
2009 Altna	AA	41	133	38	6	1	6	(- -)	64	16	18	20	6	0	22	0	1	1	2	1	.67	1	.286	.314	.481
2009 Indy	AA	48	168	45	12	0	2	(- -)	63	16	20	20	13	1	35	0	1	0	1		.00	6	.268	.319	.375
2010 Altna	AA	94	338	103	29	0	16	(- -)	180	49	72	71	46	7	72	1	1	6	6	1	.86	9	.305	.384	.533
2011 Chatt	AA	66	231	66	21	0	11	(- -)	120	44	54	42	23	0	46	1	0	5	0	0	-	6	.286	.346	.519
2006 Hou	NL	2	2	0	0	0	0	(0 0)	0	0	0	0	0	0	0	1	0	0	0	0	-	0	.000	.000	.000
2011 LAD	NL	4	7	1	0	0	0	(0 0)	1	0	0	0	0	0	3	0	0	0	0	0	-	0	.143	.143	.143
2 ML YEARS		6	9	1	0	0	0	(0 0)	1	0	0	0	0	0	4	0	0	0	0	0	-	0	.111	.111	.111

Ross Gload

Bats: L Throws: L Pos: PH-79; 1B-10; RF-3; DH-1   Ht: 6'1" Wt: 190 Born: 4/5/1976 Age: 36

Year	Team	Lg	G	AB	H	2B	3B	HR	(Hm	Rd)	TB	R	RBI	RC	TBB	IBB	SO	HBP	SH	SF	SB	CS	SB%	GDP	Avg	OBP	Slg
2000	ChC	NL	18	31	6	0	1	1	(0	1)	11	4	3	3	3	0	10	0	0	1	0	0	-	1	.194	.257	.355
2002	Col	NL	26	31	8	1	0	1	(1	0)	12	4	4	3	3	0	7	0	0	0	0	0	-	0	.258	.324	.387
2004	CWS	AL	110	234	75	16	0	7	(3	4)	112	28	44	41	20	1	37	2	1	3	0	3	.00	11	.321	.375	.479
2005	CWS	AL	28	42	7	2	0	0	(0	0)	9	2	5	2	2	0	9	0	0	0	0	0	-	1	.167	.205	.214
2006	CWS	AL	77	156	51	8	2	3	(1	2)	72	22	18	24	6	0	15	1	3	1	6	0	1.00	3	.327	.354	.462
2007	KC	AL	102	320	92	22	3	7	(2	5)	141	37	51	45	16	2	39	2	0	8	2	2	.50	13	.288	.318	.441
2008	KC	AL	122	388	106	18	1	3	(2	1)	135	46	37	41	23	4	39	3	1	3	3	4	.43	12	.273	.317	.348
2009	Fla	NL	125	230	60	10	2	6	(3	3)	92	33	30	26	23	4	30	2	1	3	0	0	-	3	.261	.329	.400
2010	Phi	NL	94	128	36	8	0	6	(5	1)	62	16	22	22	8	3	15	1	1	0	1	0	1.00	1	.281	.328	.484
2011	Phi	NL	93	113	29	8	0	0	(0	0)	37	3	8	5	3	0	23	0	0	0	0	0	-	2	.257	.276	.327
	Postseason		6	5	0	0	0	0	(0	0)	0	0	0	0	1	0	1	0	0	0	0	0	-	0	.000	.167	.000
	10 ML YEARS		795	1673	470	93	9	34	(17	17)	683	195	222	212	107	14	224	11	7	19	12	9	.57	47	.281	.325	.408

Graham Godfrey

Pitches: R Bats: R Pos: SP-4; RP-1   Ht: 6'3" Wt: 215 Born: 8/9/1984 Age: 27

	HOW MUCH HE PITCHED							WHAT HE GAVE UP											THE RESULTS						
Year	Team	Lg	G	GS	CG	GF	IP	BFP	H	R	ER	HR	SH	SF	HB	TBB	IBB	SO	WP	Bk	W	L	Pct	Sh	Sv-Op	Hld	ERC	ERA
2007	Lansng	A	21	21	0	0	110.2	481	132	63	49	8	2	3	3	36	1	74	5	0	6	7	.462	0	0--	-	4.88	3.98
2008	Stcktn	A+	29	24	0	1	134.0	597	157	90	76	14	6	4	14	37	2	119	2	0	5	8	.385	0	0--	-	4.99	5.10
2008	Scrmto	AAA	2	0	0	0	6.2	26	6	3	3	1	1	0	0	2	0	4	0	0	0	0	-	0	0--	-	3.70	4.05
2009	Mdland	AA	28	28	1	0	159.1	686	153	70	62	8	4	7	7	51	0	110	5	0	11	8	.579	0	0--	-	3.31	3.50
2010	Scrmto	AAA	24	16	0	4	106.1	479	108	76	66	9	5	7	8	53	3	87	4	0	4	7	.364	0	0--	-	4.67	5.59
2010	Mdland	AA	5	4	0	0	18.2	84	22	9	8	0	1	0	1	9	1	16	1	0	0	1	.000	0	0--	-	4.88	3.86
2011	Mdland	AA	1	1	0	0	4.0	17	3	2	0	0	0	1	0	1	0	6	0	0	0	0	-	0	0--	-	1.55	0.00
2011	Scrmto	AAA	19	18	0	0	107.1	446	92	38	32	6	1	2	7	30	0	89	1	0	14	3	.824	0	0--	-	2.79	2.68
2011	Oak	AL	5	4	0	0	25.0	112	32	14	11	3	1	0	1	5	0	13	0	0	1	2	.333	0	0-0	0	5.11	3.96

Paul Goldschmidt

Bats: R Throws: R Pos: 1B-43; PH-6   Ht: 6'3" Wt: 245 Born: 9/10/1987 Age: 24

	BATTING																				BASERUNNING				AVERAGES		
Year	Team	Lg	G	AB	H	2B	3B	HR	(Hm	Rd)	TB	R	RBI	RC	TBB	IBB	SO	HBP	SH	SF	SB	CS	SB%	GDP	Avg	OBP	Slg
2009	Msoula	R+	74	287	96	27	3	18	(-	-)	183	51	62	71	36	0	74	3	0	5	4	3	.57	6	.334	.408	.638
2010	Visalia	A+	138	525	165	42	3	35	(-	-)	318	102	108	120	57	0	161	8	0	9	5	1	.83	9	.314	.384	.606
2011	Mobile	AA	103	366	112	21	3	30	(-	-)	229	84	94	99	82	12	92	5	0	4	8	3	.73	5	.306	.435	.626
2011	Ari	NL	48	156	39	9	1	8	(2	6)	74	28	26	26	20	0	53	0	0	1	4	0	1.00	4	.250	.333	.474

Greg Golson

Bats: R Throws: R Pos: LF-4; CF-3; RF-3; PR-2; PH-1   GOLE-sun   Ht: 6'0" Wt: 190 Born: 9/17/1985 Age: 26

	BATTING																				BASERUNNING				AVERAGES		
Year	Team	Lg	G	AB	H	2B	3B	HR	(Hm	Rd)	TB	R	RBI	RC	TBB	IBB	SO	HBP	SH	SF	SB	CS	SB%	GDP	Avg	OBP	Slg
2011	S-WB*	AAA	105	384	101	9	7	8	(-	-)	148	55	34	52	30	0	105	9	5	1	15	5	.75	7	.263	.330	.385
2008	Phi	NL	6	6	0	0	0	0	(0	0)	0	2	0	0	0	0	4	0	0	0	1	0	1.00	0	.000	.000	.000
2009	Tex	AL	1	1	0	0	0	0	(0	0)	0	0	0	0	0	0	1	0	0	0	0	0	-	0	.000	.000	.000
2010	NYY	AL	24	23	6	2	0	0	(0	0)	8	3	2	1	0	0	3	0	0	0	0	2	.00	0	.261	.261	.348
2011	NYY	AL	9	11	2	0	0	0	(0	0)	2	1	0	0	1	0	2	0	0	0	1	0	1.00	0	.182	.250	.182
	Postseason		3	0	0	0	0	0	(0	0)	0	0	0	0	0	0	0	0	0	0	0	0	-	0	-	-	-
	4 ML YEARS		40	41	8	2	0	0	(0	0)	10	6	2	1	1	0	10	0	0	0	2	2	.50	0	.195	.214	.244

Brandon Gomes

Pitches: R Bats: R Pos: RP-40   Ht: 5'11" Wt: 175 Born: 7/15/1984 Age: 27

	HOW MUCH HE PITCHED							WHAT HE GAVE UP											THE RESULTS						
Year	Team	Lg	G	GS	CG	GF	IP	BFP	H	R	ER	HR	SH	SF	HB	TBB	IBB	SO	WP	Bk	W	L	Pct	Sh	Sv-Op	Hld	ERC	ERA
2007	Eugene	A-	4	0	0	2	6.1	20	1	0	0	0	0	0	1	0	6	0	0	1	0	1.000	0	0--	-	0.18	0.00
2007	FtWyn	A	14	11	0	2	59.2	261	65	41	31	3	2	0	6	11	0	44	6	2	1	4	.200	0	0--	-	3.68	4.68
2008	FtWyn	A	29	2	0	3	56.2	242	63	24	22	5	1	5	3	19	1	45	1	0	4	2	.667	0	0--	-	4.70	3.49
2008	Lk Els	A+	22	0	0	7	28.0	120	27	13	9	3	0	1	1	6	0	36	0	0	2	1	.667	0	0--	-	3.21	2.89
2009	SnAnt	AA	65	0	0	22	72.0	294	54	27	21	4	1	1	2	28	2	100	5	0	4	1	.800	0	3--	-	2.50	2.63
2010	SnAnt	AA	51	0	0	9	72.1	291	52	19	15	2	1	1	1	25	1	93	8	0	7	2	.778	0	1--	-	2.01	1.87
2011	Drham	AAA	20	0	0	12	25.1	101	17	4	3	1	1	1	1	7	0	40	3	0	0	1	.000	0	7--	-	1.72	1.07
2011	TB	AL	40	0	0	17	37.0	160	34	15	12	3	1	3	1	16	0	32	1	0	2	1	.667	0	0-0	5	3.69	2.92

Jonny Gomes

Bats: R Throws: R Pos: LF-73; PH-34; RF-11; DH-8; PR-1   Ht: 6'1" Wt: 223 Born: 11/22/1980 Age: 31

	BATTING																				BASERUNNING				AVERAGES		
Year	Team	Lg	G	AB	H	2B	3B	HR	(Hm	Rd)	TB	R	RBI	RC	TBB	IBB	SO	HBP	SH	SF	SB	CS	SB%	GDP	Avg	OBP	Slg
2003	TB	AL	8	15	2	1	0	0	(0	0)	3	1	0	0	0	0	6	1	0	0	0	0	-	0	.133	.188	.200
2004	TB	AL	5	14	1	0	0	0	(0	0)	1	0	1	0	1	0	6	0	0	0	0	0	-	0	.071	.133	.071
2005	TB	AL	101	348	98	13	6	21	(11	10)	186	61	54	62	39	1	113	14	1	5	9	5	.64	6	.282	.372	.534
2006	TB	AL	117	385	83	21	1	20	(7	13)	166	53	59	53	61	2	116	6	0	9	1	5	.17	10	.216	.325	.431
2007	TB	AL	107	348	85	20	2	17	(10	7)	160	48	49	47	35	1	126	7	0	4	12	4	.75	1	.244	.322	.460
2008	TB	AL	77	154	28	5	1	8	(2	6)	59	23	21	18	15	1	46	7	0	1	8	1	.89	1	.182	.282	.383
2009	Cin	NL	98	281	75	17	0	20	(11	9)	152	39	51	46	26	2	85	5	0	2	3	1	.75	8	.267	.338	.541

Year	Team	Lg	G	AB	H	2B	3B	HR	(Hm	Rd)	TB	R	RBI	RC	TBB	IBB	SO	HBP	SH	SF	SB	CS	SB%	GDP	Avg	OBP	Slg
							BATTING														BASERUNNING				AVERAGES		
2010	Cin	NL	148	511	136	24	3	18	(11	7)	220	77	86	83	39	3	123	12	0	9	5	3	.63	4	.266	.327	.431
2011	2 Tms	NL	120	311	65	12	1	14	(8	6)	121	41	43	36	48	1	105	8	0	5	7	3	.70	2	.209	.325	.389
11	Cin	NL	77	218	46	8	0	11	(7	4)	87	30	31	28	38	1	74	5	0	4	5	3	.63	1	.211	.336	.399
11	Was	NL	43	93	19	4	1	3	(1	2)	34	11	12	8	10	0	31	3	0	1	2	0	1.00	1	.204	.299	.366
	Postseason		2	6	0	0	0	0	(0	0)	0	0	0	0	0	0	3	0	0	0	0	0	-	0	.000	.000	.000
9 ML YEARS			781	2367	573	113	14	118	(60	58)	1068	343	364	345	264	11	726	60	1	35	45	22	.67	32	.242	.329	.451

Carlos Gomez

Bats: R **Throws:** R **Pos:** CF-87; PR-11; PH-5   **Ht:** 6'4" **Wt:** 215 **Born:** 12/4/1985 **Age:** 26

Year	Team	Lg	G	AB	H	2B	3B	HR	(Hm	Rd)	TB	R	RBI	RC	TBB	IBB	SO	HBP	SH	SF	SB	CS	SB%	GDP	Avg	OBP	Slg
							BATTING														BASERUNNING				AVERAGES		
2011	Wisc*	A	4	12	4	0	0	0	(-	-)	4	3	0	1	1	0	0	0	0	0	3	1	.75	1	.333	.385	.333
2007	NYM	NL	58	125	29	3	0	2	(1	1)	38	14	12	11	8	2	27	3	0	3	12	3	.80	0	.232	.288	.304
2008	Min	AL	153	577	149	24	7	7	(3	4)	208	79	59	66	25	0	142	7	3	2	33	11	.75	7	.258	.296	.360
2009	Min	AL	137	315	72	15	5	3	(1	2)	106	51	28	33	22	0	72	4	7	1	14	7	.67	1	.229	.287	.337
2010	Mil	NL	97	291	72	11	3	5	(3	2)	104	38	24	28	17	1	72	4	6	0	18	3	.86	10	.247	.298	.357
2011	Mil	NL	94	231	52	11	3	8	(4	4)	93	37	24	25	15	0	64	2	8	2	16	2	.89	2	.225	.276	.403
	Postseason		1	4	0	0	0	0	(0	0)	0	1	0	0	1	0	2	1	0	0	0	0	-	0	.000	.333	.000
5 ML YEARS			539	1539	374	64	18	25	(12	13)	549	219	147	163	87	3	377	20	24	8	93	26	.78	20	.243	.291	.357

Hector Gomez

Bats: R **Throws:** R **Pos:** SS-2; PH-1   **Ht:** 6'2" **Wt:** 180 **Born:** 3/5/1988 **Age:** 24

Year	Team	Lg	G	AB	H	2B	3B	HR	(Hm	Rd)	TB	R	RBI	RC	TBB	IBB	SO	HBP	SH	SF	SB	CS	SB%	GDP	Avg	OBP	Slg
							BATTING														BASERUNNING				AVERAGES		
2006	Casper	R+	50	202	66	9	4	5	(-	-)	98	24	35	35	11	1	26	3	1	4	5	3	.63	5	.327	.364	.485
2006	TriCity	A-	12	45	11	3	0	0	(-	-)	14	4	6	3	0	0	14	1	1	1	0	1	.00	0	.244	.255	.311
2007	Ashvll	A	124	534	142	34	8	11	(-	-)	225	89	61	71	29	0	120	5	6	2	20	10	.67	4	.266	.309	.421
2008	Mdest	A+	1	3	1	0	0	0	(-	-)	1	0	0	0	0	0	0	0	2	0	0	0	-	0	.333	.333	.333
2009	Mdest	A+	83	338	93	21	4	7	(-	-)	143	39	46	46	15	1	68	5	4	6	10	4	.71	4	.275	.310	.423
2010	Tulsa	AA	9	35	11	4	0	0	(-	-)	15	6	3	4	0	0	8	0	0	0	0	0	-	0	.314	.314	.429
2010	TriCity	A-	18	69	17	2	1	2	(-	-)	27	8	7	7	5	0	15	0	0	1	0	3	.00	2	.246	.293	.391
2011	Tulsa	AA	102	425	100	23	6	14	(-	-)	177	46	50	50	19	1	94	3	5	1	16	4	.80	9	.235	.272	.416
2011	Col	NL	2	6	2	0	0	0	(0	0)	2	1	0	1	1	1	2	0	0	0	0	0	-	0	.333	.429	.333

Jeanmar Gomez

Pitches: R **Bats:** R **Pos:** SP-10; RP-1   JENN-marr   **Ht:** 6'3" **Wt:** 170 **Born:** 2/10/1988 **Age:** 24

Year	Team	Lg	G	GS	CG	GF	IP	BFP	H	R	ER	HR	SH	SF	HB	TBB	IBB	SO	WP	Bk	W	L	Pct	Sh	Sv-Op	Hld	ERC	ERA
				HOW MUCH HE PITCHED						WHAT HE GAVE UP											THE RESULTS						
2006	Indns	R	11	9	0	0	54.1	231	50	24	15	2	1	2	6	12	0	34	2	1	4	3	.571	0	0- -		2.89	2.48
2007	Lk Cty	A	27	27	1	0	140.2	609	152	84	75	19	3	6	8	46	0	94	10	0	11	7	.611	0	0- -		4.77	4.80
2008	Knstn	A+	27	27	0	0	138.1	609	154	76	70	14	3	4	12	46	0	110	3	1	5	9	.357	0	0- -		4.85	4.55
2009	Knstn	A+	4	4	0	0	24.0	92	17	8	7	2	1	1	1	5	0	15	1	0	2	2	.500	0	0- -		1.99	2.63
2009	Akron	AA	22	22	1	0	123.1	521	117	56	47	11	4	5	3	40	0	109	3	0	10	4	.714	1	0- -		3.51	3.43
2010	Clmbs	AAA	20	20	1	0	116.0	504	129	74	67	16	1	5	1	42	0	78	8	1	8	8	.500	0	0- -		4.93	5.20
2011	Clmbs	AAA	21	21	2	0	137.2	569	123	54	39	8	4	3	5	49	0	107	0	0	10	7	.588	1	0- -		3.25	2.55
2011	MhVlly	A-	1	1	0	0	4.0	17	5	1	1	0	0	0	0	0	0	3	0	0	0	0	-	0	0- -		3.14	2.25
2010	Cle	AL	11	11	0	0	57.2	265	73	36	30	7	0	3	2	22	3	34	1	0	4	5	.444	0	0-0	0	5.75	4.68
2011	Cle	AL	11	10	0	0	58.1	259	73	31	29	6	0	2	1	15	1	31	2	0	5	3	.625	0	0-0	0	4.99	4.47
2 ML YEARS			22	21	0	0	116.0	524	146	67	59	13	0	5	3	37	4	65	3	0	9	8	.529	0	0-0	0	5.36	4.58

Adrian Gonzalez

Bats: L **Throws:** L **Pos:** 1B-156; RF-2; DH-2   **Ht:** 6'2" **Wt:** 225 **Born:** 5/8/1982 **Age:** 30

Year	Team	Lg	G	AB	H	2B	3B	HR	(Hm	Rd)	TB	R	RBI	RC	TBB	IBB	SO	HBP	SH	SF	SB	CS	SB%	GDP	Avg	OBP	Slg
							BATTING														BASERUNNING				AVERAGES		
2004	Tex	AL	16	42	10	3	0	1	(1	0)	16	7	7	7	2	0	6	0	0	0	0	0	-	0	.238	.273	.381
2005	Tex	AL	43	150	34	7	1	6	(3	3)	61	17	17	13	10	2	37	0	0	2	0	0	-	3	.227	.272	.407
2006	SD	NL	156	570	173	38	1	24	(10	14)	285	83	82	82	52	9	113	3	1	5	0	1	.00	24	.304	.362	.500
2007	SD	NL	161	646	182	46	3	30	(10	20)	324	101	100	108	65	9	140	3	0	6	0	0	-	6	.282	.347	.502
2008	SD	NL	162	616	172	32	1	36	(14	22)	314	103	119	107	74	18	142	7	0	3	0	0	-	24	.279	.361	.510
2009	SD	NL	160	552	153	27	2	40	(12	28)	304	90	99	109	119	22	109	5	1	4	1	1	.50	23	.277	.407	.551
2010	SD	NL	160	591	176	33	0	31	(11	20)	302	87	101	122	93	35	114	2	2	4	0	0	-	15	.298	.393	.511
2011	Bos	AL	159	630	213	45	3	27	(10	17)	345	108	117	121	74	20	119	6	0	5	1	0	1.00	28	.338	.410	.548
	Postseason		4	14	5	0	0	0	(0	0)	5	2	0	1	3	0	3	0	0	0	0	0	-	0	.357	.471	.357
8 ML YEARS			1017	3797	1113	231	11	195	(71	124)	1951	596	642	669	489	115	780	26	4	29	2	2	.50	123	.293	.375	.514

Alberto Gonzalez

Bats: R **Throws:** R **Pos:** 2B-41; SS-30; 3B-21; PH-19; 1B-4; PR-2   **Ht:** 5'10" **Wt:** 194 **Born:** 4/18/1983 **Age:** 29

Year	Team	Lg	G	AB	H	2B	3B	HR	(Hm	Rd)	TB	R	RBI	RC	TBB	IBB	SO	HBP	SH	SF	SB	CS	SB%	GDP	Avg	OBP	Slg
							BATTING														BASERUNNING				AVERAGES		
2007	NYY	AL	12	14	1	0	0	0	(0	0)	1	3	1	0	1	0	1	0	0	0	0	1	.00	1	.071	.133	.071
2008	2 Tms	NL	45	101	26	8	0	1	(0	1)	37	13	10	11	8	0	14	1	2	0	0	1	.00	6	.257	.318	.366
2009	Was	NL	105	291	77	16	3	1	(1	0)	102	31	33	30	14	1	27	3	2	6	1	1	.50	8	.265	.299	.351
2010	Was	NL	115	186	46	8	1	0	(0	0)	56	19	5	9	7	0	30	1	3	1	0	0	-	8	.247	.277	.301

Year	Team	Lg	G	AB	H	2B	3B	HR	(Hm	Rd)	TB	R	RBI	RC	TBB	IBB	SO	HBP	SH	SF	SB	CS	SB%	GDP	Avg	OBP	Slg
									BATTING												**BASERUNNING**				**AVERAGES**		
2011	SD	NL	102	247	53	10	2	1	(1	0)	70	18	32	20	13	3	37	2	1	4	1	2	.33	5	.215	.256	.283
08	NYY	AL	28	52	9	2	0	0	(0	0)	11	4	1	0	4	0	8	0	2	0	0	0	-	4	.173	.232	.212
08	Was	NL	17	49	17	6	0	1	(0	1)	26	9	9	11	4	0	6	1	0	0	0	1	.00	2	.347	.407	.531
5 ML YEARS			379	839	203	42	6	3	(2	1)	266	84	81	70	43	4	109	7	8	11	2	5	.29	28	.242	.281	.317

Alex Gonzalez

Bats: R **Throws:** R **Pos:** SS-149; PH-2   **Ht:** 5'11" **Wt:** 216 **Born:** 2/15/1977 **Age:** 35

Year	Team	Lg	G	AB	H	2B	3B	HR	(Hm	Rd)	TB	R	RBI	RC	TBB	IBB	SO	HBP	SH	SF	SB	CS	SB%	GDP	Avg	OBP	Slg
									BATTING												**BASERUNNING**				**AVERAGES**		
1998	Fla	NL	25	86	13	2	0	3	(1	2)	24	11	7	5	9	0	30	1	2	0	0	0	-	2	.151	.240	.279
1999	Fla	NL	136	560	155	28	8	14	(7	7)	241	81	59	69	15	0	113	12	1	3	3	5	.38	13	.277	.308	.430
2000	Fla	NL	109	385	77	17	4	7	(5	2)	123	35	42	26	13	0	77	2	5	2	7	1	.88	7	.200	.229	.319
2001	Fla	NL	145	515	129	36	1	9	(5	4)	194	57	48	56	30	6	107	10	3	3	2	2	.50	13	.250	.303	.377
2002	Fla	NL	42	151	34	7	1	2	(1	1)	49	15	18	14	12	1	32	4	3	2	3	1	.75	2	.225	.296	.325
2003	Fla	NL	150	528	135	33	6	18	(7	11)	234	52	77	67	33	13	106	13	3	5	0	4	.00	8	.256	.313	.443
2004	Fla	NL	159	561	130	30	3	23	(13	10)	235	67	79	58	27	9	126	4	3	4	3	1	.75	17	.232	.270	.419
2005	Fla	NL	130	435	115	30	0	5	(2	3)	160	45	45	47	31	10	81	5	4	3	5	3	.63	11	.264	.319	.368
2006	Bos	AL	111	388	99	24	2	9	(4	5)	154	48	50	40	22	1	67	5	7	7	1	0	1.00	6	.255	.299	.397
2007	Cin	NL	110	393	107	27	1	16	(8	8)	184	55	55	51	24	1	75	8	2	3	0	1	.00	13	.272	.325	.468
2009	2 Tms		112	391	93	22	0	8	(7	1)	139	42	41	40	20	4	65	4	10	4	2	1	.67	7	.238	.279	.355
2010	2 Tms		157	595	149	42	3	23	(11	12)	266	74	88	75	31	2	118	7	3	4	1	2	.33	16	.250	.294	.447
2011	Atl	NL	149	564	136	27	1	15	(7	8)	210	59	56	50	22	1	126	1	4	2	2	0	1.00	19	.241	.270	.372
09	Cin	NL	68	243	51	12	0	3	(2	1)	72	16	26	25	15	4	36	2	6	4	0	1	.00	3	.210	.258	.296
09	Bos	AL	44	148	42	10	0	5	(5	0)	67	26	15	15	5	0	29	2	4	0	2	0	1.00	4	.284	.316	.453
10	Tor	NL	85	328	85	25	1	17	(8	9)	163	47	50	47	17	0	65	1	0	2	1	0	1.00	9	.259	.296	.497
10	Atl	NL	72	267	64	17	2	6	(3	3)	103	27	38	28	14	2	53	6	3	2	0	2	.00	7	.240	.291	.386
Postseason			24	83	14	5	0	1	(1	0)	22	8	8	3	2	0	22	0	1	0	0	1	.00	2	.169	.188	.265
13 ML YEARS			1535	5552	1372	325	30	152	(78	74)	2213	641	665	598	289	48	1123	76	50	42	29	21	.58	134	.247	.291	.399

Carlos Gonzalez

Bats: L **Throws:** L **Pos:** LF-61; RF-34; CF-30; PH-2   **Ht:** 6'1" **Wt:** 205 **Born:** 10/17/1985 **Age:** 26

Year	Team	Lg	G	AB	H	2B	3B	HR	(Hm	Rd)	TB	R	RBI	RC	TBB	IBB	SO	HBP	SH	SF	SB	CS	SB%	GDP	Avg	OBP	Slg
									BATTING												**BASERUNNING**				**AVERAGES**		
2011	ColSpr*	AAA	3	10	3	0	0	0	(-	-)	3	1	0	0	0	0	0	0	0	0	0	0	-	0	.300	.300	.300
2008	Oak	AL	85	302	73	22	1	4	(3	1)	109	31	26	30	13	1	81	0	1	0	4	1	.80	7	.242	.273	.361
2009	Col	NL	89	278	79	14	7	13	(7	6)	146	53	29	42	28	3	70	3	5	3	16	4	.80	3	.284	.353	.525
2010	Col	NL	145	587	197	34	9	34	(18	16)	351	111	117	118	40	8	135	2	0	7	26	8	.76	9	.336	.376	.598
2011	Col	NL	127	481	142	27	3	26	(16	10)	253	92	92	95	48	8	105	7	0	6	20	5	.80	11	.295	.363	.526
Postseason			4	17	10	2	0	1	(1	0)	15	5	1	5	2	0	1	0	0	0	2	1	.67	0	.588	.632	.882
4 ML YEARS			446	1648	491	97	20	77	(52	25)	859	287	264	285	129	20	391	12	6	16	66	18	.79	30	.298	.350	.521

Edgar Gonzalez

Pitches: R **Bats:** R **Pos:** RP-1   **Ht:** 6'2" **Wt:** 210 **Born:** 2/23/1983 **Age:** 29

Year	Team	Lg	G	GS	CG	GF	IP	BFP	H	R	ER	HR	SH	SF	HB	TBB	IBB	SO	WP	Bk	W	L	Pct	Sh	Sv-Op	Hld	ERC	ERA
							HOW MUCH HE PITCHED					**WHAT HE GAVE UP**												**THE RESULTS**				
2011	Drham*	AAA	11	11	0	0	53.1	239	62	32	27	4	3	3	0	17	0	34	1	0	3	3	.500	0	0--	-	4.38	4.56
2011	ColSpr*	AAA	15	14	0	0	80.0	353	93	56	47	9	2	3	4	24	0	53	6	0	5	3	.625	0	0--	-	4.90	5.29
2003	Ari	NL	9	2	0	1	18.1	85	28	10	10	3	1	1	0	7	2	14	2	0	2	1	.667	0	0-1	0	7.81	4.91
2004	Ari	NL	10	10	0	0	46.1	228	72	49	48	15	5	1	5	18	4	31	3	1	0	9	.000	0	0-0	0	9.78	9.32
2005	Ari	NL	1	0	0	0	0.1	5	2	4	4	1	0	0	0	2	0	1	1	0	0	0	-	0	0-0	0	124.7	108.00
2006	Ari	NL	11	5	0	1	42.2	182	45	20	20	7	4	1	3	9	0	28	2	0	3	4	.429	0	0-0	1	4.33	4.22
2007	Ari	NL	32	12	0	5	102.0	437	110	61	57	18	2	3	4	28	4	62	5	1	8	4	.667	0	0-0	0	4.67	5.03
2008	Ari	NL	17	6	0	3	48.0	221	58	34	32	8	4	1	3	21	2	32	4	0	1	3	.250	0	0-0	0	6.16	6.00
2009	Oak	AL	26	6	0	10	65.1	299	76	41	40	4	2	3	6	28	4	39	4	0	0	4	.000	0	0-0	0	5.09	5.51
2011	Col	NL	1	0	0	1	2.0	11	5	2	2	0	0	0	0	1	0	1	0	0	0	0	-	0	0-0	0	14.52	9.00
8 ML YEARS			107	41	0	21	325.0	1468	396	221	213	56	18	10	21	114	16	208	21	2	14	25	.359	0	0-1	1	5.91	5.90

Enrique Gonzalez

Pitches: R **Bats:** R **Pos:** RP-8   **Ht:** 5'10" **Wt:** 224 **Born:** 7/14/1982 **Age:** 29

Year	Team	Lg	G	GS	CG	GF	IP	BFP	H	R	ER	HR	SH	SF	HB	TBB	IBB	SO	WP	Bk	W	L	Pct	Sh	Sv-Op	Hld	ERC	ERA
							HOW MUCH HE PITCHED					**WHAT HE GAVE UP**												**THE RESULTS**				
2011	Toledo*	AAA	35	3	0	25	47.2	209	52	30	29	7	1	3	1	21	3	60	2	0	4	6	.400	0	13- -	-	5.18	5.48
2006	Ari	NL	22	18	0	1	106.1	462	114	71	67	14	7	3	4	34	0	66	1	0	3	7	.300	0	0-0	0	4.53	5.67
2007	Ari	NL	1	0	0	1	2.0	11	4	4	3	0	0	0	0	1	0	0	0	0	0	0	-	0	0-0	0	9.72	13.50
2008	SD	NL	4	0	0	3	3.1	15	4	4	4	0	0	0	0	2	0	1	0	0	1	0	1.000	0	0-1	0	5.47	10.80
2009	Bos	AL	2	0	0	2	3.2	18	5	2	2	1	0	0	0	2	0	1	0	0	0	0	-	0	0-0	0	8.17	4.91
2010	Det	AL	18	0	0	13	26.0	107	21	11	11	4	0	1	0	17	0	13	1	0	0	1	.000	0	0-0	4	4.70	3.81
2011	Det	AL	8	0	0	5	9.0	44	12	10	10	1	0	2	0	7	2	3	0	0	0	0	-	0	0-1	0	7.49	10.00
6 ML YEARS			55	18	0	25	150.1	657	160	102	97	20	7	6	4	63	2	84	2	0	4	8	.333	0	0-2	0	4.90	5.81

Gio Gonzalez

Pitches: L **Bats:** R **Pos:** SP-32 **Ht:** 5'11" **Wt:** 205 **Born:** 9/19/1985 **Age:** 26

Year	Team	Lg	G	GS	CG	GF	IP	BFP	H	R	ER	HR	SH	SF	HB	TBB	IBB	SO	WP	Bk	W	L	Pct	Sh	Sv-Op	Hld	ERC	ERA
2008	Oak	AL	10	7	0	3	34.0	163	32	34	29	9	2	1	3	25	1	34	1	0	1	4	.200	0	0-0	0	6.54	7.68
2009	Oak	AL	20	17	0	0	98.2	455	113	68	63	14	2	3	1	56	2	109	2	0	6	7	.462	0	0-0	0	5.96	5.75
2010	Oak	AL	33	33	1	0	200.2	851	171	75	72	15	5	2	4	92	1	171	4	1	15	9	.625	0	0-0	0	3.39	3.23
2011	Oak	AL	32	32	0	0	202.0	864	175	81	70	17	3	2	8	91	1	197	6	1	16	12	.571	0	0-0	0	3.56	3.12
4 ML YEARS			95	89	1	3	535.1	2333	491	258	234	55	12	8	16	264	5	511	13	2	38	32	.543	0	0-0	0	4.09	3.93

Mike Gonzalez

Pitches: L **Bats:** R **Pos:** RP-56 **Ht:** 6'2" **Wt:** 215 **Born:** 5/23/1978 **Age:** 34

Year	Team	Lg	G	GS	CG	GF	IP	BFP	H	R	ER	HR	SH	SF	HB	TBB	IBB	SO	WP	Bk	W	L	Pct	Sh	Sv-Op	Hld	ERC	ERA
2003	Pit	NL	16	0	0	2	8.1	38	7	7	7	4	1	1	0	6	0	6	1	0	0	1	.000	0	0-0	3	7.18	7.56
2004	Pit	NL	47	0	0	12	43.1	169	32	7	6	2	3	0	1	6	0	55	0	0	3	1	.750	0	1-4	13	1.60	1.25
2005	Pit	NL	51	0	0	15	50.0	212	35	15	15	2	0	1	1	31	2	58	3	0	1	3	.250	0	3-3	15	2.90	2.70
2006	Pit	NL	54	0	0	47	54.0	234	42	13	13	1	3	1	2	31	2	64	0	0	3	4	.429	0	24-24	3	3.00	2.17
2007	Atl	NL	18	0	0	5	17.0	70	15	3	3	0	0	1	0	8	0	13	0	0	2	0	1.000	0	2-2	5	3.13	1.59
2008	Atl	NL	36	0	0	29	33.2	142	26	21	16	6	1	2	1	14	3	44	0	0	0	3	.000	0	14-16	3	3.33	4.28
2009	Atl	NL	80	0	0	29	74.1	315	56	28	20	7	6	1	7	33	8	90	5	0	5	4	.556	0	10-17	17	3.04	2.42
2010	Bal	AL	29	0	0	7	24.2	106	18	11	11	1	3	1	0	14	4	31	3	0	1	3	.250	0	1-3	10	2.54	4.01
2011	2 Tms	AL	56	0	0	15	53.1	230	51	30	26	7	0	3	2	21	1	51	5	0	2	2	.500	0	1-2	8	4.13	4.39
11	Bal	AL	49	0	0	14	46.1	202	46	26	22	7	0	2	2	18	1	46	4	0	2	2	.500	0	1-2	6	4.46	4.27
11	Tex	AL	7	0	0	1	7.0	28	5	4	4	0	0	1	0	3	0	5	1	0	0	0	—	0	0-0	2	2.11	5.14
9 ML YEARS			387	0	0	161	358.2	1516	282	135	117	30	17	12	14	164	20	412	21	0	17	21	.447	0	56-71	74	3.07	2.94

Alex Gordon

Bats: L **Throws:** R **Pos:** LF-148; 1B-7; PH-1 **Ht:** 6'2" **Wt:** 220 **Born:** 2/10/1984 **Age:** 28

Year	Team	Lg	G	AB	H	2B	3B	HR	(Hm	Rd)	TB	R	RBI	RC	TBB	IBB	SO	HBP	SH	SF	SB	CS	SB%	GDP	Avg	OBP	Slg
2007	KC	AL	151	543	134	36	4	15	(8	7)	223	60	60	69	41	4	137	13	1	2	14	4	.78	12	.247	.314	.411
2008	KC	AL	134	493	128	35	1	16	(9	7)	213	72	59	71	66	5	120	6	1	5	9	2	.82	8	.260	.351	.432
2009	KC	AL	49	164	38	6	0	6	(2	4)	62	28	22	16	21	0	43	2	1	1	5	0	1.00	5	.232	.324	.378
2010	KC	AL	74	242	52	10	0	8	(5	3)	86	34	20	23	34	1	62	2	2	1	1	5	.17	9	.215	.315	.355
2011	KC	AL	151	611	185	45	4	23	(12	11)	307	101	87	103	67	2	139	7	0	3	17	8	.68	9	.303	.376	.502
5 ML YEARS			559	2053	537	132	9	68	(36	32)	891	295	248	282	229	12	501	30	5	12	46	19	.71	43	.262	.343	.434

Brian Gordon

Pitches: R **Bats:** L **Pos:** SP-2 **Ht:** 6'0" **Wt:** 190 **Born:** 8/16/1978 **Age:** 33

Year	Team	Lg	G	GS	CG	GF	IP	BFP	H	R	ER	HR	SH	SF	HB	TBB	IBB	SO	WP	Bk	W	L	Pct	Sh	Sv-Op	Hld	ERC	ERA
2007	CpChr	AA	30	0	0	13	50.1	215	44	17	16	3	1	1	2	19	6	43	0	1	5	1	.833	0	1--	-	2.95	2.86
2007	RdRck	AAA	9	0	0	5	11.0	45	14	7	6	1	0	3	0	1	0	8	0	0	1	1	.500	0	0--	-	4.52	4.91
2008	CpChr	AA	1	0	0	0	2.0	8	2	1	1	1	0	0	0	1	0	1	0	0	0	0	—	0	0--	-	8.28	4.50
2008	Frisco	AA	15	0	0	9	22.0	79	9	1	0	1	0	0	0	4	0	18	2	1	2	0	1.000	0	3--	-	0.62	0.00
2008	Okla	AAA	18	11	0	1	71.0	304	85	43	36	14	1	2	2	15	0	51	2	1	4	5	.444	0	0--	-	5.34	4.56
2009	Okla	AAA	43	2	0	19	77.1	320	72	32	30	5	2	6	0	20	3	51	2	0	7	3	.700	0	2--	-	2.86	3.49
2010	LV	AAA	40	0	0	12	78.0	320	73	33	30	2	1	3	1	19	1	86	5	0	1	3	.250	0	0--	-	2.69	3.46
2011	LV	AAA	12	9	0	2	55.1	208	39	11	7	4	1	1	1	7	0	56	1	0	5	0	1.000	0	0--	-	1.59	1.14
2011	S-WB	AAA	1	1	0	0	5.0	18	4	0	0	0	0	0	0	0	0	7	0	0	0	0	—	0	0--	-	1.34	0.00
2008	Tex	AL	3	0	0	0	4.0	16	4	1	1	0	0	0	0	0	0	1	0	0	0	0	—	0	0-0	0	1.95	2.25
2011	NYY	AL	2	2	0	0	10.1	46	12	6	6	3	1	0	2	3	1	4	0	0	0	1	.000	0	0-0	0	6.83	5.23
2 ML YEARS			5	2	0	0	14.1	62	16	7	7	3	1	0	2	3	1	5	0	0	0	1	.000	0	0-0	0	5.28	4.40

Dee Gordon

Bats: L **Throws:** R **Pos:** SS-54; PR-3; PH-1 **Ht:** 5'11" **Wt:** 150 **Born:** 4/22/1988 **Age:** 24

Year	Team	Lg	G	AB	H	2B	3B	HR	(Hm	Rd)	TB	R	RBI	RC	TBB	IBB	SO	HBP	SH	SF	SB	CS	SB%	GDP	Avg	OBP	Slg
2008	Ogden	R+	60	251	83	13	3	2	(-	-)	108	45	27	42	16	0	29	2	2	3	18	5	.78	3	.331	.371	.430
2009	Gt Lks	A	131	538	162	17	12	3	(-	-)	212	96	35	85	43	3	90	10	7	3	73	25	.74	7	.301	.362	.394
2010	Chatt	AA	133	555	154	17	10	2	(-	-)	197	86	39	72	40	1	89	7	9	3	53	20	.73	3	.277	.332	.355
2011	RCuca	A+	3	11	3	0	0	0	(-	-)	3	4	0	1	1	0	1	0	0	0	2	1	.67	1	.273	.333	.273
2011	Albq	AAA	70	288	96	10	6	0	(-	-)	118	51	24	49	18	1	40	2	2	3	30	4	.88	1	.333	.373	.410
2011	LAD	NL	56	224	68	9	2	0	(0	0)	81	34	11	25	7	0	27	0	2	0	24	7	.77	1	.304	.325	.362

Tom Gorzelanny

Pitches: L **Bats:** B **Pos:** SP-15; RP-15
gore-zah-LAWN-ee **Ht:** 6'2" **Wt:** 205 **Born:** 7/12/1982 **Age:** 29

Year	Team	Lg	G	GS	CG	GF	IP	BFP	H	R	ER	HR	SH	SF	HB	TBB	IBB	SO	WP	Bk	W	L	Pct	Sh	Sv-Op	Hld	ERC	ERA
2011	Syrcse*	AAA	1	1	0	0	4.0	18	5	4	4	1	0	0	1	1	0	3	0	0	0	1	.000	0	0--	-	7.44	9.00
2005	Pit	NL	3	1	0	0	6.0	32	10	8	8	1	1	0	0	3	0	3	0	0	0	1	.000	0	0-0	0	8.76	12.00
2006	Pit	NL	11	11	0	0	61.2	267	50	29	26	3	7	4	4	31	2	40	3	0	2	5	.286	0	0-0	0	3.23	3.79
2007	Pit	NL	32	32	1	0	201.2	874	214	90	87	18	3	9	11	68	3	135	5	1	14	10	.583	1	0-0	0	4.63	3.88
2008	Pit	NL	21	21	0	0	105.1	490	120	79	78	20	8	9	1	70	0	67	5	1	6	9	.400	0	0-0	0	6.86	6.66
2009	2 Tms	NL	22	7	0	2	47.0	204	45	30	29	6	3	3	1	17	0	47	1	0	7	3	.700	0	0-1	2	3.88	5.55

	HOW MUCH HE PITCHED						WHAT HE GAVE UP										THE RESULTS						
Year Team	Lg	G	GS	CG	GF	IP	BFP	H	R	ER	HR	SH	SF	HB	TBB	IBB	SO	WP	Bk	W	L	Pct	Sh	Sv-Op Hld	ERC	ERA
2010 ChC	NL	29	23	0	3	136.1	604	136	70	62	11	4	6	2	68	4	119	0	0	7	9	.438	0	1-1 1	4.30	4.09
2011 Was	NL	30	15	0	1	105.0	447	102	50	47	15	8	4	6	33	5	95	5	1	4	6	.400	0	0-1 4	4.03	4.03
09 Pit	NL	9	0	0	2	8.2	36	6	5	5	0	1	0	0	4	0	7	0	0	3	1	.750	0	0-1 1	2.02	5.19
09 ChC	NL	13	7	0	0	38.1	168	39	25	24	6	2	3	1	13	0	40	1	0	4	2	.667	0	0-0 1	4.33	5.63
7 ML YEARS		148	110	1	6	663.0	2918	677	356	337	74	29	32	25	290	14	506	19	3	40	43	.482	1	1-3 7	4.54	4.57

John Grabow

Pitches: L Bats: L Pos: RP-58   GRAE-boe   **Ht:** 6'2" **Wt:** 205 **Born:** 11/4/1978 **Age:** 33

	HOW MUCH HE PITCHED						WHAT HE GAVE UP										THE RESULTS						
Year Team	Lg	G	GS	CG	GF	IP	BFP	H	R	ER	HR	SH	SF	HB	TBB	IBB	SO	WP	Bk	W	L	Pct	Sh	Sv-Op Hld	ERC	ERA
2003 Pit	NL	5	0	0	1	5.0	22	6	3	2	0	0	0	0	0	0	9	0	0	0	0	-	0	0-0 0	2.73	3.60
2004 Pit	NL	68	0	0	10	61.2	286	81	39	35	8	6	1	0	28	7	64	5	0	2	5	.286	0	1-7 11	6.21	5.11
2005 Pit	NL	63	0	0	8	52.0	222	46	31	28	6	2	0	2	25	2	42	1	0	2	3	.400	0	0-1 14	4.00	4.85
2006 Pit	NL	72	0	0	17	69.2	303	68	34	32	7	5	3	3	30	3	66	0	0	4	2	.667	0	0-2 11	4.17	4.13
2007 Pit	NL	63	0	0	14	51.2	228	56	27	26	6	4	2	1	19	2	62	3	0	3	2	.600	0	1-2 8	4.51	4.53
2008 Pit	NL	74	0	0	18	76.0	322	60	25	24	9	3	2	1	37	2	62	4	2	6	3	.667	0	4-8 16	3.37	2.84
2009 2 Tms	NL	75	0	0	12	72.1	314	62	28	27	5	1	4	3	40	3	57	1	0	3	0	1.000	0	0-2 23	3.76	3.36
2010 ChC	NL	28	0	0	9	25.2	126	35	24	21	5	3	0	1	13	0	20	1	0	1	3	.250	0	0-1 7	7.51	7.36
2011 ChC	NL	58	0	0	22	62.1	282	67	39	33	9	4	2	1	28	4	38	3	3	3	1	.750	0	0-0 5	4.89	4.76
09 Pit	NL	45	0	0	4	47.1	209	43	19	18	4	1	3	2	28	2	41	0	0	3	0	1.000	0	0-2 16	4.32	3.42
09 ChC	NL	30	0	0	8	25.0	105	19	9	9	1	0	1	1	12	1	16	1	0	0	0	-	0	0-0 7	2.77	3.24
9 ML YEARS		506	0	0	111	476.1	2105	481	250	228	55	28	14	12	220	23	400	18	5	24	19	.558	0	6-23 95	4.49	4.31

Curtis Granderson

Bats: L Throws: R Pos: CF-155; PH-4; DH-1   **Ht:** 6'1" **Wt:** 185 **Born:** 3/16/1981 **Age:** 31

	BATTING																	BASERUNNING				AVERAGES		
Year Team	Lg	G	AB	H	2B	3B	HR	(Hm | Rd)	TB	R	RBI	RC	TBB	IBB	SO	HBP	SH	SF	SB	CS	SB%	GDP	Avg	OBP	Slg
2004 Det	AL	9	25	6	1	0	0	(0 | 0)	9	2	0	2	3	0	8	0	0	0	0	0	-	1	.240	.321	.360
2005 Det	AL	47	162	44	6	3	8	(5 | 3)	80	18	20	26	10	0	43	0	2	0	1	1	.50	2	.272	.314	.494
2006 Det	AL	159	596	155	31	9	19	(7 | 12)	261	90	68	89	66	0	174	4	7	6	8	5	.62	4	.260	.335	.438
2007 Det	AL	158	612	185	38	23	23	(10 | 13)	338	122	74	106	52	3	141	5	5	2	26	1	.96	3	.302	.361	.552
2008 Det	AL	141	553	155	26	13	22	(11 | 11)	273	112	66	100	71	1	111	3	1	1	12	4	.75	7	.280	.365	.494
2009 Det	AL	160	631	157	23	8	30	(10 | 20)	286	91	71	92	72	4	141	2	3	2	20	6	.77	1	.249	.327	.453
2010 NYY	AL	136	466	115	17	7	24	(14 | 10)	218	76	67	71	53	3	116	2	4	3	12	2	.86	3	.247	.324	.468
2011 NYY	AL	156	583	153	26	10	41	(21 | 20)	322	136	119	113	85	0	169	12	4	7	25	10	.71	12	.262	.364	.552
Postseason		22	81	22	5	2	4	(2 | 2)	43	11	13	16	13	0	15	1	1	1	3	1	.75	2	.272	.375	.531
8 ML YEARS		966	3628	970	168	74	167	(78 | 89)	1787	647	485	599	412	11	903	28	26	21	104	29	.78	33	.267	.345	.493

Jeff Gray

Pitches: R Bats: R Pos: RP-30   **Ht:** 6'3" **Wt:** 196 **Born:** 11/19/1981 **Age:** 30

	HOW MUCH HE PITCHED						WHAT HE GAVE UP										THE RESULTS						
Year Team	Lg	G	GS	CG	GF	IP	BFP	H	R	ER	HR	SH	SF	HB	TBB	IBB	SO	WP	Bk	W	L	Pct	Sh	Sv-Op Hld	ERC	ERA
2008 Oak	AL	5	0	0	2	4.2	24	8	4	4	1	0	0	1	1	0	4	0	0	0	0	-	0	0-0 0	9.48	7.71
2009 Oak	AL	24	0	0	11	26.1	116	30	12	11	3	2	0	2	4	1	19	0	0	0	1	.000	0	0-0 1	4.07	3.76
2010 ChC	NL	7	0	0	0	9.1	45	12	9	7	1	1	0	1	5	0	4	1	0	1	0	1.000	0	0-0 0	6.85	6.75
2011 2 Tms	AL	30	0	0	11	48.1	215	52	23	23	4	1	3	1	21	2	23	2	0	0	1	.000	0	1-4 2	4.51	4.28
11 CWS	AL	6	0	0	5	13.1	57	13	4	4	1	0	1	0	4	0	7	1	0	0	0	-	0	0-0 0	3.65	2.70
11 Sea	AL	24	0	0	6	35.0	158	39	19	19	3	1	2	0	17	2	16	1	0	0	1	.000	0	1-4 2	4.84	4.89
4 ML YEARS		66	0	0	24	88.2	400	102	48	45	9	4	3	5	31	3	50	3	0	1	2	.333	0	1-4 3	4.85	4.57

Sean Green

Pitches: R Bats: R Pos: RP-14   **Ht:** 6'6" **Wt:** 227 **Born:** 4/20/1979 **Age:** 33

	HOW MUCH HE PITCHED						WHAT HE GAVE UP										THE RESULTS						
Year Team	Lg	G	GS	CG	GF	IP	BFP	H	R	ER	HR	SH	SF	HB	TBB	IBB	SO	WP	Bk	W	L	Pct	Sh	Sv-Op Hld	ERC	ERA
2011 Nashv*	AAA	33	0	0	20	46.0	201	41	22	20	3	5	1	5	27	4	40	6	0	1	5	.167	0	6- -	4.33	3.91
2006 Sea	AL	24	0	0	11	32.0	139	34	16	16	2	1	1	2	13	1	15	2	0	0	0	-	0	0-1 3	4.47	4.50
2007 Sea	AL	64	0	0	10	68.0	304	77	31	29	2	4	5	3	34	6	53	2	0	5	2	.714	0	0-3 13	4.81	3.84
2008 Sea	AL	72	0	0	13	79.0	358	80	47	41	3	3	7	6	36	1	62	5	1	4	5	.444	0	1-4 17	4.09	4.67
2009 NYM	NL	79	0	0	19	69.2	316	64	37	35	5	4	0	9	36	5	54	8	1	1	4	.200	0	1-3 14	4.17	4.52
2010 NYM	NL	11	0	0	0	9.1	48	7	6	4	1	1	0	4	8	3	12	0	0	0	0	-	0	0-0 2	5.28	3.86
2011 Mil	NL	14	0	0	3	11.2	56	14	8	7	0	0	0	0	6	1	7	1	0	0	1	.000	0	0-0 1	4.52	5.40
6 ML YEARS		264	0	0	56	269.2	1221	276	145	132	13	13	13	24	133	17	203	18	2	10	12	.455	0	2-11 50	4.39	4.41

Taylor Green

Bats: L Throws: R Pos: PH-12; 2B-7; 3B-5   **Ht:** 5'10" **Wt:** 195 **Born:** 11/2/1986 **Age:** 25

	BATTING																	BASERUNNING				AVERAGES		
Year Team	Lg	G	AB	H	2B	3B	HR	(Hm	Rd)	TB	R	RBI	RC	TBB	IBB	SO	HBP	SH	SF	SB	CS	SB%	GDP	Avg	OBP	Slg
2006 Helena	R+	62	221	51	12	1	1	(-	-)	68	36	23	25	29	0	35	4	4	2	0	1	.00	4	.231	.328	.308
2007 WV	A-	111	397	130	29	2	14	(-	-)	205	68	86	82	51	1	65	5	2	5	0	5	.00	6	.327	.406	.516
2008 BrvdCt	A+	114	418	121	19	0	15	(-	-)	185	46	73	75	61	7	59	4	3	4	2	1	.67	8	.289	.382	.443
2009 Wisc	A	6	20	8	1	0	1	(-	-)	12	6	5	6	4	0	4	2	0	0	0	0	-	1	.400	.538	.600
2009 Hntsvl	AA	87	306	79	15	0	5	(-	-)	109	34	43	39	33	1	37	2	0	4	0	1	.00	4	.258	.330	.356

			BATTING																				BASERUNNING				AVERAGES		
Year	Team	Lg	G	AB	H	2B	3B	HR	(Hm	Rd)	TB	R	RBI	RC	TBB	IBB	SO	HBP	SH	SF		SB	CS	SB%	GDP		Avg	OBP	Slg
2010	Hntsvl	AA	113	393	102	29	1	13	(-	-)	172	51	81	61	45	6	67	4	1	8		0	2	.00	10		.260	.336	.438
2011	Hntsvl	AA	3	11	4	1	0	0	(-	-)	5	2	3	2	0	0	3	1	0	1		0	0	-	0		.364	.385	.455
2011	Nashv	AAA	120	420	141	36	1	22	(-	-)	245	74	88	99	55	2	72	4	3	5		1	0	1.00	11		.336	.413	.583
2011	Mil	NL	20	37	10	3	0	0	(0	0)	13	2	1	3	0	0	6	0	0	0		0	0	-	1		.270	.270	.351

Tyler Greene

Bats: R **Throws:** R **Pos:** 2B-25; SS-20; PH-13; PR-9; RF-8; LF-2   **Ht:** 6'2" **Wt:** 190 **Born:** 8/17/1983 **Age:** 28

			BATTING																				BASERUNNING				AVERAGES		
Year	Team	Lg	G	AB	H	2B	3B	HR	(Hm	Rd)	TB	R	RBI	RC	TBB	IBB	SO	HBP	SH	SF		SB	CS	SB%	GDP		Avg	OBP	Slg
2011	Memp*	AAA	66	254	81	18	2	14	(-	-)	145	53	43	63	37	1	75	8	2	2		19	2	.90	3		.319	.419	.571
2009	StL	NL	48	108	24	5	0	2	(1	1)	35	9	7	6	4	0	32	3	1	0		3	0	1.00	2		.222	.270	.324
2010	StL	NL	44	104	23	3	1	2	(2	0)	34	14	10	10	13	4	24	4	0	1		2	0	1.00	1		.221	.328	.327
2011	StL	NL	58	104	22	5	0	1	(0	1)	30	22	11	12	13	2	31	4	0	0		11	0	1.00	3		.212	.322	.288
3 ML YEARS			150	316	69	13	1	5	(3	2)	99	45	28	28	30	6	87	11	1	1		16	0	1.00	6		.218	.307	.313

Luke Gregerson

Pitches: R **Bats:** L **Pos:** RP-61   **Ht:** 6'3" **Wt:** 200 **Born:** 5/14/1984 **Age:** 28

			HOW MUCH HE PITCHED						WHAT HE GAVE UP												THE RESULTS						
Year	Team	Lg	G	GS	CG	GF	IP	BFP	H	R	ER	HR	SH	SF	HB	TBB	IBB	SO	WP	Bk		W	L	Pct	Sh	Sv-Op	Hld	ERC	ERA
2011	Tucsn*	AAA	2	0	0	0	1.1	9	3	3	3	0	0	0	0	2	0	2	0	0		0	0	-	0	0- -	-	16.21	20.25
2009	SD	NL	72	0	0	7	75.0	318	62	29	27	3	3	1	3	31	9	93	4	0		2	4	.333	0	1-7	27	2.72	3.24
2010	SD	NL	80	0	0	9	78.1	297	47	30	28	8	1	1	1	18	2	89	0	0		4	7	.364	0	2-7	40	1.56	3.22
2011	SD	NL	61	0	0	11	55.2	241	57	23	17	2	5	1	2	19	3	34	2	0		3	3	.500	0	0-4	16	3.55	2.75
3 ML YEARS			213	0	0	27	209.0	856	166	82	72	13	9	3	6	68	14	216	6	0		9	14	.391	0	3-18	83	2.47	3.10

Kevin Gregg

Pitches: R **Bats:** R **Pos:** RP-63   **Ht:** 6'6" **Wt:** 230 **Born:** 6/20/1978 **Age:** 34

			HOW MUCH HE PITCHED						WHAT HE GAVE UP												THE RESULTS						
Year	Team	Lg	G	GS	CG	GF	IP	BFP	H	R	ER	HR	SH	SF	HB	TBB	IBB	SO	WP	Bk		W	L	Pct	Sh	Sv-Op	Hld	ERC	ERA
2003	LAA	AL	5	3	0	0	24.2	97	18	9	9	3	0	0	1	8	0	14	0	0		2	0	1.000	0	0-0	0	2.74	3.28
2004	LAA	AL	55	0	0	23	87.2	377	86	43	41	6	4	5	3	28	3	84	13	1		5	2	.714	0	1-2	3	3.47	4.21
2005	LAA	AL	33	2	0	9	64.1	290	70	37	36	8	1	1	3	29	2	52	5	0		1	2	.333	0	0-1	1	5.08	5.04
2006	LAA	AL	32	3	0	12	78.1	341	88	41	36	10	0	3	2	21	0	71	6	0		3	4	.429	0	0-0	0	4.51	4.14
2007	Fla	NL	74	0	0	55	84.0	355	63	34	33	7	3	0	6	40	1	87	6	0		0	5	.000	0	32-36	6	3.15	3.54
2008	Fla	NL	72	0	0	59	68.2	296	51	30	26	3	3	1	4	37	4	58	7	0		7	8	.467	0	29-38	4	2.90	3.41
2009	ChC	NL	72	0	0	51	68.2	298	60	38	36	13	0	3	3	30	2	71	7	0		5	6	.455	0	23-30	1	4.19	4.72
2010	Tor	AL	63	0	0	56	59.0	254	52	24	23	4	1	3	1	30	1	58	3	0		2	6	.250	0	37-43	3	3.66	3.51
2011	Bal	AL	63	0	0	48	59.2	275	58	35	29	7	4	1	2	40	4	53	2	0		0	3	.000	0	22-29	0	5.10	4.37
Postseason			2	0	0	0	4.0	18	4	0	0	0	0	0	0	2	0	3	1	0		0	0	-	0	0-0	0	3.63	0.00
9 ML YEARS			469	8	0	313	595.0	2583	546	291	269	61	16	17	25	263	17	548	49	1		25	36	.410	0	144-179	18	3.89	4.07

Zack Greinke

Pitches: R **Bats:** R **Pos:** SP-28   GRAIN-key   **Ht:** 6'2" **Wt:** 190 **Born:** 10/21/1983 **Age:** 28

			HOW MUCH HE PITCHED						WHAT HE GAVE UP												THE RESULTS						
Year	Team	Lg	G	GS	CG	GF	IP	BFP	H	R	ER	HR	SH	SF	HB	TBB	IBB	SO	WP	Bk		W	L	Pct	Sh	Sv-Op	Hld	ERC	ERA
2011	BrvdCt*	A+	1	1	0	0	3.0	10	1	0	0	0	0	0	0	0	0	4	0	0		0	0	-	0	0- -	-	0.25	0.00
2011	Nashv*	AAA	2	2	0	0	7.2	33	10	4	4	1	0	1	0	2	0	9	0	0		0	1	.000	0	0- -	-	5.73	4.70
2004	KC	AL	24	24	0	0	145.0	599	143	64	64	26	3	2	8	26	3	100	1	1		8	11	.421	0	0-0	0	3.85	3.97
2005	KC	AL	33	33	2	0	183.0	829	233	125	118	23	4	4	13	53	0	114	4	2		5	17	.227	0	0-0	0	5.71	5.80
2006	KC	AL	3	0	0	1	6.1	28	7	3	3	1	0	0	0	3	2	5	0	0		1	0	1.000	0	0-0	0	4.93	4.26
2007	KC	AL	52	14	0	7	122.0	507	122	52	50	12	3	4	3	36	5	106	3	1		7	7	.500	0	1-1	12	3.77	3.69
2008	KC	AL	32	32	1	0	202.1	851	202	87	78	21	2	4	4	56	1	183	8	1		13	10	.565	0	0-0	0	3.68	3.47
2009	KC	AL	33	33	6	0	229.1	915	195	64	55	11	8	3	4	51	0	242	5	0		16	8	.667	3	0-0	0	2.39	2.16
2010	KC	AL	33	33	3	0	220.0	919	219	114	102	18	6	7	7	55	1	181	4	0		10	14	.417	0	0-0	0	3.48	4.17
2011	Mil	NL	28	28	0	0	171.2	715	161	82	73	19	6	1	4	45	0	201	10	0		16	6	.727	0	0-0	0	3.35	3.83
8 ML YEARS			238	197	12	8	1279.2	5363	1282	591	543	131	32	25	43	325	12	1132	35	5		76	73	.510	3	1-1	12	3.66	3.82

Jason Grilli

Pitches: R **Bats:** R **Pos:** RP-28   **Ht:** 6'5" **Wt:** 225 **Born:** 11/11/1976 **Age:** 35

			HOW MUCH HE PITCHED						WHAT HE GAVE UP												THE RESULTS						
Year	Team	Lg	G	GS	CG	GF	IP	BFP	H	R	ER	HR	SH	SF	HB	TBB	IBB	SO	WP	Bk		W	L	Pct	Sh	Sv-Op	Hld	ERC	ERA
2011	LV*	AAA	28	0	0	12	32.2	136	26	8	7	2	2	1	1	12	0	43	1	1		4	1	.800	0	3- -	-	2.70	1.93
2000	Fla	NL	1	1	0	0	6.2	35	11	4	4	0	2	0	2	2	0	3	0	0		1	0	1.000	0	0-0	0	7.84	5.40
2001	Fla	NL	6	5	0	1	26.2	115	30	18	18	6	1	0	2	11	0	17	0	0		2	2	.500	0	0-0	0	6.44	6.08
2004	CWS	AL	8	8	1	0	45.0	203	52	38	37	11	2	1	3	20	0	26	0	0		2	3	.400	0	0-0	0	6.67	7.40
2005	Det	AL	3	2	0	0	16.0	63	14	6	6	1	1	1	0	6	0	5	0	0		1	1	.500	0	0-0	0	3.27	3.38
2006	Det	AL	51	0	0	18	60.0	270	61	31	29	6	2	4	5	25	3	31	5	0		2	3	.400	0	0-0	9	4.23	4.21
2007	Det	AL	57	0	0	13	79.2	352	81	46	42	5	1	4	5	32	1	62	5	0		5	3	.625	0	0-2	11	4.09	4.74
2008	2 Tms		60	0	0	16	75.0	323	67	27	25	2	1	3	2	38	7	69	4	0		3	3	.500	0	1-2	5	3.34	3.00
2009	2 Tms		52	0	0	11	45.2	212	50	27	27	4	2	1	1	27	2	49	2	0		2	3	.400	0	1-1	7	5.25	5.32
2011	Pit	NL	28	0	0	4	32.2	140	24	10	9	2	1	0	4	15	5	37	3	0		2	1	.667	0	1-1	9	2.79	2.48
08	Det	AL	9	0	0	4	13.2	59	12	5	5	1	0	0	1	7	1	10	1	0		0	1	.000	0	0-1	0	3.85	3.29
08	Col	NL	51	0	0	12	61.1	264	55	22	20	1	1	3	1	31	6	59	3	0		3	2	.600	0	1-1	4	3.23	2.93

Year	Team	Lg	HOW MUCH HE PITCHED						WHAT HE GAVE UP												THE RESULTS							
			G	GS	CG	GF	IP	BFP	H	R	ER	HR	SH	SF	HB	TBB	IBB	SO	WP	Bk	W	L	Pct	Sh	Sv-Op	Hld	ERC	ERA
09	Col	NL	22	0	0	6	19.1	99	29	13	13	2	1	1	0	13	2	22	2	0	0	1	.000	0	1-1	3	8.02	6.05
09	Tex	AL	30	0	0	5	26.1	113	21	14	14	2	1	0	1	14	0	27	0	0	2	2	.500	0	0-0	4	3.44	4.78
	Postseason		5	0	0	0	3.0	14	1	0	0	0	0	0	0	4	1	1	0	0	0	0	-	0	0-0	1	2.44	0.00
	9 ML YEARS		266	16	1	63	389.1	1713	390	207	197	37	13	15	24	176	18	299	21	0	20	19	.513	0	3-6	40	4.44	4.55

Javy Guerra

Pitches: R **Bats:** R **Pos:** RP-47   GEHR-uh   **Ht:** 6'0" **Wt:** 205 **Born:** 10/31/1985 **Age:** 26

Year	Team	Lg	HOW MUCH HE PITCHED						WHAT HE GAVE UP												THE RESULTS							
			G	GS	CG	GF	IP	BFP	H	R	ER	HR	SH	SF	HB	TBB	IBB	SO	WP	Bk	W	L	Pct	Sh	Sv-Op	Hld	ERC	ERA
2004	Ddgrs	R	11	9	0	0	40.0	168	31	18	15	3	1	0	3	19	0	36	9	0	4	1	.800	0	0- -		3.29	3.38
2005	Clmbs	A-	11	11	0	0	52.2	242	51	35	29	3	0	3	10	23	0	40	2	1	2	5	.286	0	0- -		4.35	4.96
2006	Ogden	R+	7	7	0	0	28.0	140	37	18	15	1	3	1	4	20	0	22	6	0	1	3	.250	0	0- -		7.45	4.82
2007	InldEm	A+	27	24	0	1	117.2	572	139	98	82	10	2	6	14	80	0	121	16	0	6	9	.400	0	1- -		6.68	6.27
2008	InldEm	A+	31	3	0	10	66.1	317	68	34	30	0	3	6	4	44	0	63	5	0	5	4	.556	0	2- -		4.55	4.07
2009	Gt Lks	A	28	0	0	23	41.0	162	23	7	7	1	2	1	1	15	3	55	8	0	3	1	.750	0	16- -		1.40	1.54
2009	Chatt	AA	23	0	0	8	28.1	129	32	15	13	2	2	1	0	16	0	29	2	0	3	1	.750	0	0- -		5.30	4.13
2010	Chatt	AA	28	0	0	10	27.0	125	24	12	7	1	2	0	1	22	2	27	5	0	2	0	1.000	0	5- -		4.58	2.33
2010	Ddgrs	R	2	0	0	0	2.0	9	2	1	1	1	0	0	0	0	0	3	0	0	0	1	.000	0	0- -		7.30	4.50
2011	Chatt	AA	14	0	0	9	17.0	61	8	2	2	1	0	1	0	5	0	15	3	0	1	0	1.000	0	3- -		1.20	1.06
2011	LAD	NL	47	0	0	38	46.2	195	37	12	12	2	3	1	3	18	1	38	2	0	2	2	.500	0	21-23	0	2.73	2.31

Vladimir Guerrero

Bats: R **Throws:** R **Pos:** DH-137; PH-8   **Ht:** 6'3" **Wt:** 235 **Born:** 2/9/1975 **Age:** 37

Year	Team	Lg	BATTING																					BASERUNNING				AVERAGES		
			G	AB	H	2B	3B	HR	(Hm	Rd)	TB	R	RBI	RC	TBB	IBB	SO	HBP	SH	SF				SB	CS	SB%	GDP	Avg	OBP	Slg
2011	Bowie*	AA	1	4	1	0	0	0	(-	-)	1	1	0	0	0	0	0	0	0	0				0	0	-	0	.250	.250	.250
1996	Mon	NL	9	27	5	0	0	1	(0	1)	8	2	1	1	0	0	3	0	0	0				0	0	-	1	.185	.185	.296
1997	Mon	NL	90	325	98	22	2	11	(5	6)	157	44	40	51	19	2	39	7	0	3				3	4	.43	11	.302	.350	.483
1998	Mon	NL	159	623	202	37	7	38	(19	19)	367	108	109	124	42	13	95	7	0	5				11	9	.55	15	.324	.371	.589
1999	Mon	NL	160	610	193	37	5	42	(23	19)	366	102	131	127	55	14	62	7	0	2				14	7	.67	18	.316	.378	.600
2000	Mon	NL	154	571	197	28	11	44	(25	19)	379	101	123	137	58	23	74	8	0	4				9	10	.47	15	.345	.410	.664
2001	Mon	NL	159	599	184	45	4	34	(21	13)	339	107	108	116	60	24	88	9	0	3				37	16	.70	24	.307	.377	.566
2002	Mon	NL	161	614	206	37	2	39	(20	19)	364	106	111	123	84	32	70	6	0	5				40	20	.67	20	.336	.417	.593
2003	Mon	NL	112	394	130	20	3	25	(15	10)	231	71	79	83	63	22	53	6	0	4				9	5	.64	18	.330	.426	.586
2004	LAA	AL	156	612	206	39	2	39	(19	20)	366	124	126	122	52	14	74	8	0	8				15	3	.83	19	.337	.391	.598
2005	LAA	AL	141	520	165	29	2	32	(19	13)	294	95	108	108	61	26	48	8	0	5				13	1	.93	16	.317	.394	.565
2006	LAA	AL	156	607	200	34	1	33	(14	19)	335	92	116	109	50	25	68	4	0	4				15	5	.75	16	.329	.382	.552
2007	LAA	AL	150	574	186	45	1	27	(13	14)	314	89	125	127	71	28	62	9	0	6				2	3	.40	19	.324	.403	.547
2008	LAA	AL	143	541	164	31	3	27	(13	14)	282	85	91	96	51	16	77	4	0	4				5	3	.63	27	.303	.365	.521
2009	LAA	AL	100	383	113	16	1	15	(7	8)	176	59	50	51	19	3	56	4	0	1				2	1	.67	16	.295	.334	.460
2010	Tex	AL	152	593	178	27	1	29	(16	13)	294	83	115	97	35	5	60	9	0	6				4	5	.44	19	.300	.345	.496
2011	Bal	AL	145	562	163	30	1	13	(10	3)	234	60	63	55	17	3	56	7	0	4				2	2	.50	23	.290	.317	.416
	Postseason		44	171	45	7	0	2	(1	1)	58	17	20	19	14	2	30	2	0	1				2	2	.50	4	.263	.324	.339
	16 ML YEARS		2147	8155	2590	477	46	449	(239	210)	4506	1328	1496	1527	737	250	985	103	0	64				181	94	.66	277	.318	.379	.553

Matt Guerrier

Pitches: R **Bats:** R **Pos:** RP-70   gurr-REAR   **Ht:** 6'3" **Wt:** 195 **Born:** 8/2/1978 **Age:** 33

Year	Team	Lg	HOW MUCH HE PITCHED						WHAT HE GAVE UP												THE RESULTS							
			G	GS	CG	GF	IP	BFP	H	R	ER	HR	SH	SF	HB	TBB	IBB	SO	WP	Bk	W	L	Pct	Sh	Sv-Op	Hld	ERC	ERA
2004	Min	AL	9	2	0	5	19.0	84	22	13	12	5	2	0	1	6	0	11	0	0	0	1	.000	0	0-0	0	6.10	5.68
2005	Min	AL	43	0	0	14	71.2	306	71	29	27	6	4	1	3	24	5	46	3	0	0	3	.000	0	0-0	1	3.71	3.39
2006	Min	AL	39	1	0	13	69.2	300	78	29	26	9	3	4	0	21	0	37	6	0	1	0	1.000	0	1-1	2	4.59	3.36
2007	Min	AL	73	0	0	16	88.0	351	71	23	23	9	0	3	5	21	1	68	6	0	2	4	.333	0	1-4	14	2.70	2.35
2008	Min	AL	76	0	0	15	76.1	344	84	47	44	12	1	1	0	37	9	59	2	0	6	9	.400	0	1-5	20	5.23	5.19
2009	Min	AL	79	0	0	15	76.1	304	58	23	20	10	3	1	4	16	2	47	6	0	5	1	.833	0	1-4	33	2.44	2.36
2010	Min	AL	74	0	0	13	71.0	286	56	28	25	7	2	3	3	22	1	42	2	0	5	7	.417	0	1-7	23	2.78	3.17
2011	LAD	NL	70	0	0	12	66.1	282	59	31	30	4	3	1	0	25	5	50	2	0	4	3	.571	0	1-4	13	2.95	4.07
	Postseason		5	0	0	4	4.2	16	1	0	0	0	0	0	0	1	0	4	0	0	0	0	-	0	0-0	1	0.30	0.00
	8 ML YEARS		463	3	0	103	538.1	2257	499	223	207	62	18	14	16	172	23	360	27	0	23	28	.451	0	6-25	106	3.52	3.46

Carlos Guillen

Bats: B **Throws:** R **Pos:** 2B-25; PH-2; 1B-1; DH-1   **Ht:** 6'1" **Wt:** 213 **Born:** 9/30/1975 **Age:** 36

Year	Team	Lg	BATTING																					BASERUNNING				AVERAGES		
			G	AB	H	2B	3B	HR	(Hm	Rd)	TB	R	RBI	RC	TBB	IBB	SO	HBP	SH	SF				SB	CS	SB%	GDP	Avg	OBP	Slg
2011	Lkland*	A+	4	15	3	2	0	0	(-	-)	5	1	2	1	1	0	2	0	0	0				0	0	-	0	.200	.250	.333
2011	Toledo*	AAA	14	49	17	6	0	1	(-	-)	26	9	9	10	6	0	10	0	0	0				1	0	1.00	1	.347	.418	.531
2011	Erie*	AA	4	4	1	0	0	0	(-	-)	1	0	0	0	0	0	2	0	0	0				0	0	-	0	.250	.250	.250
1998	Sea	AL	10	39	13	1	1	0	(0	0)	16	9	5	7	3	0	9	0	0	0				2	0	1.00	0	.333	.381	.410
1999	Sea	AL	5	19	3	0	0	1	(1	0)	6	2	3	1	1	0	6	0	1	0				0	0	-	1	.158	.190	.316
2000	Sea	AL	90	288	74	15	2	7	(3	4)	114	45	42	36	28	0	53	2	7	3				1	3	.25	6	.257	.324	.396
2001	Sea	AL	140	456	118	21	4	5	(2	3)	162	72	53	56	53	0	89	1	7	6				4	1	.80	9	.259	.333	.355
2002	Sea	AL	134	475	124	24	6	9	(4	5)	187	73	56	58	46	4	91	1	3	3				4	5	.44	8	.261	.326	.394
2003	Sea	AL	109	388	107	19	3	7	(4	3)	153	63	52	53	52	2	64	1	5	5				4	4	.50	12	.276	.359	.394
2004	Det	AL	136	522	166	37	10	20	(7	13)	283	97	97	98	52	3	87	2	3	4				12	5	.71	12	.318	.379	.542
2005	Det	AL	87	334	107	15	4	5	(3	2)	145	48	23	39	24	3	45	2	0	1				2	3	.40	9	.320	.368	.434
2006	Det	AL	153	543	174	41	5	19	(10	9)	282	100	85	106	71	10	87	4	0	4				20	9	.69	16	.320	.400	.519
2007	Det	AL	151	564	167	35	9	21	(12	9)	283	86	102	94	55	10	93	4	0	4				13	8	.62	14	.296	.357	.502

Year	Team	Lg	G	AB	H	2B	3B	HR	(Hm	Rd)	TB	R	RBI	RC	TBB	IBB	SO	HBP	SH	SF	SB	CS	SB%	GDP	Avg	OBP	Slg
2008	Det	AL	113	420	120	29	2	10	(8	2)	183	68	54	65	60	3	67	3	2	4	9	3	.75	11	.286	.376	.436
2009	Det	AL	81	277	67	10	3	11	(6	5)	116	36	41	38	39	2	56	3	0	3	1	3	.25	7	.242	.339	.419
2010	Det	AL	68	253	69	17	1	6	(4	2)	106	26	34	29	21	2	41	0	0	1	1	2	.33	10	.273	.327	.419
2011	Det	AL	28	95	22	2	1	3	(2	1)	35	8	13	9	5	0	16	0	0	2	1	1	.50	4	.232	.265	.368
Postseason			19	61	21	5	1	2	(0	2)	34	8	7	10	8	0	12	0	0	0	1	1	.50	2	.344	.420	.557
14 ML YEARS			1305	4673	1331	266	51	124	(66	58)	2071	733	660	689	510	39	804	22	28	44	74	47	.61	119	.285	.355	.443

Jeremy Guthrie

Pitches: R **Bats:** R **Pos:** SP-32; RP-2 **Ht:** 6'1" **Wt:** 205 **Born:** 4/8/1979 **Age:** 33

			HOW MUCH HE PITCHED					WHAT HE GAVE UP										THE RESULTS						
Year	Team	Lg	G	GS	CG	GF	IP	BFP	H	R	ER	HR	SH	SF	HB	TBB	IBB	SO	WP	Bk	W	L	Pct	Sh	Sv-Op	Hld	ERC	ERA
2004	Cle	AL	6	0	0	2	11.2	49	9	6	6	1	0	0	1	6	0	7	1	0	0	0	-	0	0-0	0	3.58	4.63
2005	Cle	AL	1	0	0	1	6.0	29	9	4	4	2	1	1	0	2	0	3	0	0	0	0	-	0	0-0	0	8.58	6.00
2006	Cle	AL	9	1	0	1	19.1	93	24	15	15	2	0	0	2	15	1	14	3	0	0	0	-	0	0-0	0	7.78	6.98
2007	Bal	AL	32	26	0	3	175.1	723	165	78	72	23	4	6	4	47	2	123	8	1	7	5	.583	0	0-1	0	3.55	3.70
2008	Bal	AL	30	30	1	0	190.2	796	176	82	77	24	2	2	7	58	2	120	3	0	10	12	.455	0	0-0	0	3.59	3.63
2009	Bal	AL	33	33	1	0	200.0	874	224	120	112	35	1	8	9	60	1	110	1	1	10	17	.370	0	0-0	0	5.08	5.04
2010	Bal	AL	32	32	0	0	209.1	872	193	93	89	25	3	9	16	50	1	119	1	1	11	14	.440	0	0-0	0	3.44	3.83
2011	Bal	AL	34	32	2	1	208.0	889	213	113	100	26	5	10	9	66	5	130	1	0	9	17	.346	0	0-0	0	4.21	4.33
8 ML YEARS			177	154	4	8	1020.1	4325	1013	511	475	138	16	36	48	304	12	626	17	3	47	65	.420	0	0-1	0	4.06	4.19

Franklin Gutierrez

Bats: R **Throws:** R **Pos:** CF-92; PH-2 **Ht:** 6'2" **Wt:** 190 **Born:** 2/21/1983 **Age:** 29

			BATTING																		BASERUNNING				AVERAGES		
Year	Team	Lg	G	AB	H	2B	3B	HR	(Hm	Rd)	TB	R	RBI	RC	TBB	IBB	SO	HBP	SH	SF	SB	CS	SB%	GDP	Avg	OBP	Slg
2011	Tacom*	AAA	11	40	11	2	2	0	(-	-)	17	7	6	6	6	0	7	0	0	1	0	0	-	0	.275	.362	.425
2005	Cle	AL	7	1	0	0	0	0	(0	0)	0	2	0	0	1	0	0	0	0	0	0	0	-	0	.000	.500	.000
2006	Cle	AL	43	136	37	9	0	1	(1	0)	49	21	8	12	3	0	28	0	2	0	0	0	-	0	.272	.288	.360
2007	Cle	AL	100	271	72	13	2	13	(10	3)	128	41	36	36	21	1	77	1	5	3	8	3	.73	7	.266	.318	.472
2008	Cle	AL	134	399	99	26	2	8	(6	2)	153	54	41	37	27	1	87	8	4	2	9	3	.75	10	.248	.307	.383
2009	Sea	AL	153	565	160	24	1	18	(7	11)	240	85	70	80	46	3	122	3	13	2	16	5	.76	14	.283	.339	.425
2010	Sea	AL	152	568	139	25	3	12	(6	6)	206	61	64	61	50	5	137	1	2	8	25	3	.89	10	.245	.303	.363
2011	Sea	AL	92	322	72	13	0	1	(0	1)	88	26	19	25	16	1	56	1	3	2	13	2	.87	6	.224	.261	.273
Postseason			10	29	6	0	0	1	(0	1)	9	5	4	3	5	0	11	0	0	0	0	-	-	1	.207	.324	.310
7 ML YEARS			681	2262	579	110	8	53	(30	23)	864	290	238	251	164	11	507	14	29	17	71	16	.82	51	.256	.308	.382

Juan Gutierrez

Pitches: R **Bats:** R **Pos:** RP-20 **Ht:** 6'3" **Wt:** 260 **Born:** 7/14/1983 **Age:** 28

			HOW MUCH HE PITCHED					WHAT HE GAVE UP										THE RESULTS						
Year	Team	Lg	G	GS	CG	GF	IP	BFP	H	R	ER	HR	SH	SF	HB	TBB	IBB	SO	WP	Bk	W	L	Pct	Sh	Sv-Op	Hld	ERC	ERA
2007	Hou	NL	7	3	0	1	21.1	93	25	14	14	3	0	3	0	6	2	16	1	0	1	1	.500	0	0-0	0	4.71	5.91
2009	Ari	NL	65	0	0	21	71.0	307	67	33	32	2	2	4	3	30	5	66	5	0	4	3	.571	0	9-10	7	3.38	4.06
2010	Ari	NL	58	0	0	35	56.2	247	55	33	32	13	1	1	4	23	5	47	1	0	0	6	.000	0	15-17	8	5.00	5.08
2011	Ari	NL	20	0	0	3	18.1	90	22	16	11	3	0	0	1	9	0	23	0	0	0	0	-	0	0-1	2	5.99	5.40
4 ML YEARS			150	3	0	60	167.1	737	169	96	89	21	3	8	8	68	12	152	7	0	5	10	.333	0	24-28	17	4.37	4.79

Brandon Guyer

Bats: R **Throws:** R **Pos:** RF-11; LF-3; DH-1; PH-1 GYE-er **Ht:** 6'1" **Wt:** 210 **Born:** 1/28/1986 **Age:** 26

			BATTING																		BASERUNNING				AVERAGES		
Year	Team	Lg	G	AB	H	2B	3B	HR	(Hm	Rd)	TB	R	RBI	RC	TBB	IBB	SO	HBP	SH	SF	SB	CS	SB%	GDP	Avg	OBP	Slg
2007	Cubs	R	17	72	16	4	1	1	(-	-)	25	10	5	8	5	0	16	4	0	0	6	2	.75	0	.222	.309	.347
2007	Boise	A-	19	71	19	1	0	0	(-	-)	20	9	14	9	6	0	9	3	7	1	5	0	1.00	6	.268	.346	.282
2008	Peoria	A	88	327	88	27	3	14	(-	-)	163	55	38	56	19	0	63	13	1	3	22	7	.76	8	.269	.331	.498
2009	Tenn	AA	57	189	36	12	2	1	(-	-)	55	22	14	12	10	1	33	2	2	2	7	5	.58	3	.190	.236	.291
2009	Dytona	A+	73	265	92	16	3	2	(-	-)	120	40	32	55	24	1	34	8	0	8	23	2	.92	3	.347	.407	.453
2010	Tenn	AA	102	369	127	39	6	13	(-	-)	217	76	58	87	27	1	51	7	5	2	30	3	.91	6	.344	.398	.588
2011	Drham	AAA	107	388	121	29	5	14	(-	-)	202	78	61	78	35	1	79	12	6	2	16	6	.73	8	.312	.384	.521
2011	TB	AL	15	41	8	1	0	2	(1	1)	15	7	3	2	1	0	9	0	1	0	0	0	-	1	.195	.214	.366

Jesus Guzman

Bats: R **Throws:** R **Pos:** 1B-53; PH-14; LF-6; DH-4; RF-1 **Ht:** 5'10" **Wt:** 190 **Born:** 6/14/1984 **Age:** 28

			BATTING																		BASERUNNING				AVERAGES		
Year	Team	Lg	G	AB	H	2B	3B	HR	(Hm	Rd)	TB	R	RBI	RC	TBB	IBB	SO	HBP	SH	SF	SB	CS	SB%	GDP	Avg	OBP	Slg
2004	InldEm	A+	114	442	137	35	3	6	(-	-)	196	80	71	79	57	0	105	6	3	4	9	8	.53	6	.310	.393	.443
2005	SnAnt	AA	119	453	117	18	5	9	(-	-)	178	61	53	59	45	0	101	4	11	1	6	11	.35	10	.258	.330	.393
2006	SnAnt	AA	115	408	105	18	3	9	(-	-)	156	57	55	56	46	0	74	4	9	4	7	3	.70	12	.257	.335	.382
2007	Hi Dsrt	A+	130	518	156	38	5	25	(-	-)	279	102	112	102	50	1	85	8	6	3	3	3	.50	14	.301	.370	.539
2008	Mdland	AA	80	341	124	21	2	14	(-	-)	191	57	76	76	33	4	56	0	1	1	5	2	.71	6	.364	.419	.560
2008	Scrmto	AAA	15	59	14	2	0	2	(-	-)	22	5	9	5	4	0	13	0	1	1	0	2	.00	2	.237	.281	.373
2008	As	R	5	15	7	3	0	1	(-	-)	13	2	3	5	0	0	1	2	0	0	1	0	1.00	0	.467	.529	.867
2009	Fresno	AAA	116	452	145	26	5	16	(-	-)	229	75	71	86	37	2	82	7	1	3	0	2	.00	9	.321	.379	.507
2010	Fresno	AAA	125	445	143	28	1	18	(-	-)	227	66	72	85	38	1	68	3	3	3	6	4	.60	12	.321	.376	.510

			BATTING																							BASERUNNING				AVERAGES		
Year	Team	Lg	G	AB	H	2B	3B	HR	(Hm	Rd)	TB	R	RBI	RC	TBB	IBB	SO	HBP	SH	SF		SB	CS	SB%	GDP		Avg	OBP	Slg
2011	Tucsn	AAA	63	244	81	22	1	8	(-	-)	129	40	57	54	34	1	42	5	2	1		4	4	.50	7		.332	.423	.529
2009	SF	NL	12	20	5	0	0	0	(0	0)	5	0	0	0	0	0	3	0	0	0		0	0	-	2		.250	.250	.250
2011	SD	NL	76	247	77	22	2	5	(4	1)	118	33	44	49	22	2	43	1	0	1		9	2	.82	6		.312	.369	.478
	2 ML YEARS		88	267	82	22	2	5	(4	1)	123	33	44	49	22	2	46	1	0	1		9	2	.82	8		.307	.361	.461

Tony Gwynn

Bats: L **Throws:** R **Pos:** LF-110; PH-27; CF-12; PR-8; RF-2   **Ht:** 5'11" **Wt:** 193 **Born:** 10/4/1982 **Age:** 29

			BATTING																							BASERUNNING				AVERAGES		
Year	Team	Lg	G	AB	H	2B	3B	HR	(Hm	Rd)	TB	R	RBI	RC	TBB	IBB	SO	HBP	SH	SF		SB	CS	SB%	GDP		Avg	OBP	Slg
2006	Mil	NL	32	77	20	2	1	0	(0	0)	24	5	4	5	2	0	15	0	0	1		3	1	.75	2		.260	.275	.312
2007	Mil	NL	69	123	32	3	2	0	(0	0)	39	13	10	16	12	1	24	0	0	0		8	1	.89	0		.260	.326	.317
2008	Mil	NL	29	42	8	1	0	0	(0	0)	9	5	1	2	4	0	7	1	1	1		3	1	.75	1		.190	.271	.214
2009	SD	NL	119	393	106	11	6	2	(1	1)	135	59	21	48	48	2	65	2	5	3		11	7	.61	2		.270	.350	.344
2010	SD	NL	117	289	59	9	3	3	(2	1)	83	30	20	31	41	4	50	1	7	1		17	4	.81	3		.204	.304	.287
2011	LAD	NL	136	312	80	12	6	2	(0	2)	110	37	22	35	23	1	61	1	2	2		22	6	.79	2		.256	.308	.353
	Postseason		3	3	1	0	0	0	(0	0)	1	0	0	0	0	0	1	0	0	0		0	0	-	0		.333	.333	.333
	6 ML YEARS		502	1236	305	38	18	7	(3	4)	400	149	78	137	130	8	222	5	15	8		64	20	.76	10		.247	.319	.324

Eric Hacker

Pitches: R **Bats:** B **Pos:** RP-2   **Ht:** 6'1" **Wt:** 230 **Born:** 3/26/1983 **Age:** 29

			HOW MUCH HE PITCHED						WHAT HE GAVE UP												THE RESULTS							
Year	Team	Lg	G	GS	CG	GF	IP	BFP	H	R	ER	HR	SH	SF	HB	TBB	IBB	SO	WP	Bk		W	L	Pct	Sh	Sv-Op Hld		ERC	ERA
2002	Yanks	R	3	0	0	0	3.2	15	2	0	0	0	1	0	1	1	0	2	0	0		0	0	-	0	0- - -		1.65	0.00
2003	Yanks	R	7	5	0	1	28.1	114	25	9	9	1	0	0	0	7	0	26	1	0		3	2	.600	0	0- - -		2.50	2.86
2003	StlsInd	A-	2	2	0	0	9.0	40	10	2	1	0	0	0	1	1	0	5	0	0		0	0	-	0	0- - -		3.13	1.00
2005	CtnSC	A	10	10	1	0	62.0	238	49	14	11	0	0	0	0	14	0	40	0	0		5	2	.714	0	0- - -		1.84	1.60
2007	CtnSC	A	17	17	0	0	95.0	379	89	34	27	5	1	2	7	18	0	54	4	1		9	2	.818	0	0- - -		3.02	2.56
2007	Tampa	A+	9	7	0	0	38.1	178	52	28	26	3	2	1	3	14	1	22	0	0		3	3	.500	0	0- - -		6.21	6.10
2007	S-WB	AAA	1	0	0	0	2.2	15	5	2	2	0	0	1	1	1	0	3	0	0		1	0	1.000	0	0- - -		10.00	6.75
2008	Tampa	A+	9	9	0	0	53.0	197	38	14	11	1	0	1	2	9	1	31	0	1		2	2	.500	0	0- - -		1.60	1.87
2008	Trntn	AA	17	17	0	0	91.1	375	83	33	28	3	3	4	5	28	1	84	4	1		7	4	.636	0	0- - -		3.04	2.76
2009	Trntn	AA	3	3	0	0	15.1	67	16	10	7	0	1	1	0	7	0	8	2	1		1	1	.500	0	0- - -		3.83	4.11
2009	S-WB	AAA	3	3	0	0	16.0	70	19	14	14	3	1	2	2	4	0	12	0	1		0	1	.000	0	0- - -		5.85	7.88
2009	Indy	AAA	21	21	0	0	116.1	516	135	57	52	6	5	5	8	46	2	82	4	1		5	5	.500	0	0- - -		4.95	4.02
2010	Fresno	AAA	29	29	0	0	165.2	734	181	93	83	21	5	6	14	62	0	129	2	4		16	8	.667	0	0- - -		5.07	4.51
2011	Roch	AAA	26	25	0	0	135.2	616	161	103	92	18	2	4	12	50	0	98	7	0		7	14	.333	0	0- - -		5.65	6.10
2009	Pit	NL	3	0	0	2	3.0	14	4	2	2	0	0	0	0	2	0	1	0	0		0	0	-	0	0-0 -		6.62	6.00
2011	Min	AL	2	0	0	0	5.1	22	4	1	0	0	0	1	0	4	0	2	0	0		0	0	-	0	0-0 -		3.56	0.00
	2 ML YEARS		5	0	0	2	8.1	36	8	3	2	0	0	1	0	6	0	3	0	0		0	0	-	0	0-0 -		4.60	2.16

Travis Hafner

Bats: L **Throws:** R **Pos:** DH-85; PH-10   HAFF-nerr   **Ht:** 6'3" **Wt:** 240 **Born:** 6/3/1977 **Age:** 35

			BATTING																							BASERUNNING				AVERAGES		
Year	Team	Lg	G	AB	H	2B	3B	HR	(Hm	Rd)	TB	R	RBI	RC	TBB	IBB	SO	HBP	SH	SF		SB	CS	SB%	GDP		Avg	OBP	Slg
2011	Akron*	AA	2	6	3	1	0	0	(-	-)	4	2	0	2	1	0	1	0	0	0		0	0	-	0		.500	.571	.667
2002	Tex	AL	23	62	15	4	1	1	(0	1)	24	6	6	7	8	1	15	0	0	0		0	1	.00	0		.242	.329	.387
2003	Cle	AL	91	291	74	19	3	14	(7	7)	141	35	40	42	22	2	81	10	0	1		2	1	.67	7		.254	.327	.485
2004	Cle	AL	140	482	150	41	3	28	(7	21)	281	96	109	103	68	7	111	17	0	6		3	2	.60	11		.311	.410	.583
2005	Cle	AL	137	486	148	42	0	33	(14	19)	289	94	108	115	79	7	123	9	0	4		0	0	-	9		.305	.408	.595
2006	Cle	AL	129	454	140	31	1	42	(21	21)	299	100	117	118	100	16	111	7	0	2		0	0	-	10		.308	**.439**	**.659**
2007	Cle	AL	152	545	145	25	2	24	(12	12)	246	80	100	94	102	17	115	7	0	5		1	1	.50	15		.266	.385	.451
2008	Cle	AL	57	198	39	10	0	5	(2	3)	64	21	24	21	27	6	55	5	0	3		1	1	.50	4		.197	.305	.323
2009	Cle	AL	94	338	92	19	0	16	(9	7)	159	46	49	49	41	6	67	3	0	1		0	0	-	7		.272	.355	.470
2010	Cle	AL	118	396	110	29	0	13	(10	3)	178	46	50	57	51	10	94	12	0	3		2	1	.67	2		.278	.374	.449
2011	Cle	AL	94	325	91	16	0	13	(9	4)	146	41	57	61	36	5	78	6	0	1		0	0	-	7		.280	.361	.449
	Postseason		11	43	8	1	0	2	(1	1)	15	6	4	3	7	1	15	0	0	0		0	0	-	1		.186	.300	.349
	10 ML YEARS		1035	3577	1004	236	10	189	(91	98)	1827	565	660	667	534	77	850	76	0	26		9	7	.56	72		.281	.383	.511

Nick Hagadone

Pitches: L **Bats:** L **Pos:** RP-9   HAGG-uh-donn   **Ht:** 6'5" **Wt:** 230 **Born:** 1/1/1986 **Age:** 26

			HOW MUCH HE PITCHED						WHAT HE GAVE UP												THE RESULTS							
Year	Team	Lg	G	GS	CG	GF	IP	BFP	H	R	ER	HR	SH	SF	HB	TBB	IBB	SO	WP	Bk		W	L	Pct	Sh	Sv-Op Hld		ERC	ERA
2007	Lowell	A-	10	10	0	0	24.1	94	14	5	5	1	0	0	0	8	0	33	1	0		1	0	1.000	0	0- - -		1.46	1.85
2008	Grnville	A	3	3	0	0	10.0	43	5	3	0	0	0	0	0	6	0	12	2	0		1	1	.500	0	0- - -		1.54	0.00
2009	Grnville	A	10	10	0	0	25.0	105	13	8	7	0	0	0	4	14	0	32	1	0		2	0	.000	0	0- - -		2.05	2.52
2009	Lk Cty	A	5	5	0	0	14.2	55	8	4	4	0	0	0	1	5	0	21	3	0		0	1	.000	0	0- - -		1.44	2.45
2009	Knstn	A+	2	2	0	0	5.1	25	5	3	3	0	0	0	0	5	0	6	1	0		0	0	-	0	0- - -		5.10	5.06
2010	Knstn	A+	10	10	0	0	37.2	167	28	11	10	2	2	0	0	29	0	45	2	0		1	3	.250	0	0- - -		3.71	2.39
2010	Akron	AA	19	7	0	3	48.0	218	44	27	24	5	1	0	1	34	0	44	7	0		2	2	.500	0	1- - -		4.94	4.50
2011	Akron	AA	12	0	0	1	22.2	88	14	4	4	0	1	0	0	7	0	24	1	0		2	1	.667	0	0- - -		1.39	1.59
2011	Clmbs	AAA	34	0	0	14	48.1	204	42	27	18	5	2	3	0	15	2	53	1	2		4	3	.571	0	4- - -		2.90	3.35
2011	Cle	AL	9	0	0	3	11.0	42	4	6	5	0	0	1	1	6	0	11	2	0		1	0	1.000	0	0-0 0		1.35	4.09

Jerry Hairston

Bats: R Throws: R Pos: 3B-49; 2B-30; LF-23; CF-20; PH-13; PR-4; SS-2   Ht: 5'10" Wt: 190 Born: 5/29/1976 Age: 36

Year	Team	Lg	G	AB	H	2B	3B	HR	(Hm	Rd)	TB	R	RBI	RC	TBB	IBB	SO	HBP	SH	SF	SB	CS	SB%	GDP	Avg	OBP	Slg
2011	Hrsbrg*	AA	2	6	1	0	0	0	(-	-)	1	1	0	0	2	0	0	0	0	0	0	0	-	0	.167	.375	.167
1998	Bal	AL	6	7	0	0	0	0	(0	0)	0	2	0	0	0	0	1	0	0	0	0	0	-	0	.000	.000	.000
1999	Bal	AL	50	175	47	12	1	4	(1	3)	73	26	17	24	11	0	24	3	4	0	9	4	.69	2	.269	.323	.417
2000	Bal	AL	49	180	46	5	0	5	(2	3)	66	27	19	22	21	0	22	6	5	0	8	5	.62	8	.256	.353	.367
2001	Bal	AL	159	532	124	25	5	8	(5	3)	183	63	47	57	44	0	73	13	9	4	29	11	.73	12	.233	.305	.344
2002	Bal	AL	122	426	114	25	3	5	(2	3)	160	55	32	55	34	0	55	7	8	4	21	6	.78	5	.268	.329	.376
2003	Bal	AL	58	218	59	12	2	2	(1	1)	81	25	21	32	23	0	25	6	10	2	14	5	.74	8	.271	.353	.372
2004	Bal	AL	86	287	87	19	1	2	(0	2)	114	43	24	45	29	1	29	8	6	4	13	8	.62	3	.303	.384	.397
2005	ChC	NL	114	380	99	25	4	4	(3	1)	140	51	30	46	31	0	46	12	7	0	8	9	.47	5	.261	.336	.368
2006	2 Tms		101	170	35	6	1	0	(0	0)	43	25	10	9	13	2	34	2	7	0	5	2	.71	5	.206	.270	.253
2007	Tex	AL	73	159	30	7	0	3	(1	2)	46	22	16	12	11	0	24	3	7	4	5	1	.83	5	.189	.249	.289
2008	Cin	NL	80	261	85	20	2	6	(3	3)	127	47	36	52	23	0	36	3	8	2	15	3	.83	0	.326	.384	.487
2009	2 Tms		131	383	96	23	1	10	(8	2)	151	62	39	42	32	0	54	6	8	4	7	4	.64	3	.251	.315	.394
2010	SD	NL	119	430	105	13	2	10	(7	3)	152	53	50	47	31	2	54	5	4	6	9	6	.60	5	.244	.299	.353
2011	2 Tms		120	337	91	21	1	5	(2	3)	129	43	31	41	33	1	46	5	1	0	3	2	.60	7	.270	.344	.383
06	ChC	NL	38	82	17	3	0	0	(0	0)	20	8	4	5	4	2	14	1	5	0	3	0	1.00	1	.207	.253	.244
06	Tex	AL	63	88	18	3	1	0	(0	0)	23	17	6	4	9	0	20	1	2	0	2	2	.50	4	.205	.286	.261
09	Cin	NL	86	307	78	18	1	8	(6	2)	122	47	27	30	21	0	46	3	6	3	7	3	.70	2	.254	.305	.397
09	NYY	AL	45	76	18	5	0	2	(2	0)	29	15	12	12	11	0	8	3	2	1	0	1	.00	1	.237	.352	.382
11	Was	NL	75	213	57	11	1	4	(2	2)	82	25	24	28	22	1	30	2	1	0	2	2	.50	3	.268	.342	.385
11	Mil	NL	45	124	34	10	0	1	(0	1)	47	18	7	13	11	0	16	3	0	0	1	0	1.00	4	.274	.348	.379
	Postseason		6	8	2	0	0	0	(0	0)	2	1	0	0	0	0	2	0	1	0	0	0	-	0	.250	.250	.250
14 ML YEARS			1268	3945	1018	213	21	64	(35	29)	1465	544	372	484	336	6	523	79	84	30	146	66	.69	68	.258	.326	.371

Scott Hairston

Bats: R Throws: R Pos: PH-49; RF-15; LF-10; CF-10; DH-3; 2B-1   Ht: 6'0" Wt: 204 Born: 5/25/1980 Age: 32

Year	Team	Lg	G	AB	H	2B	3B	HR	(Hm	Rd)	TB	R	RBI	RC	TBB	IBB	SO	HBP	SH	SF	SB	CS	SB%	GDP	Avg	OBP	Slg
2004	Ari	NL	101	339	84	15	6	13	(6	7)	150	39	29	32	21	0	88	1	2	1	3	3	.50	4	.248	.293	.442
2005	Ari	NL	15	20	2	1	0	0	(0	0)	3	0	0	0	0	0	6	0	0	0	0	0	-	1	.100	.100	.150
2006	Ari	NL	9	15	6	2	0	0	(0	0)	8	2	2	2	1	0	5	0	0	0	0	0	-	1	.400	.438	.533
2007	2 Tms	NL	107	263	64	18	2	11	(6	5)	119	37	36	36	26	0	55	1	3	1	2	0	1.00	4	.243	.313	.452
2008	SD	NL	112	326	81	18	3	17	(9	8)	156	42	31	43	28	2	84	3	0	2	3	1	.75	2	.248	.312	.479
2009	2 Tms	NL	116	430	114	27	2	17	(9	8)	196	50	64	60	25	0	83	3	1	5	11	3	.79	9	.265	.307	.456
2010	SD	NL	104	295	62	10	0	10	(5	5)	102	34	36	28	31	1	69	6	0	4	6	1	.86	3	.210	.295	.346
2011	NYM	NL	79	132	31	8	1	7	(2	5)	62	20	24	16	11	2	34	2	0	0	1	1	.50	2	.235	.303	.470
07	Ari	NL	76	176	39	13	1	3	(1	2)	63	21	16	19	19	0	37	1	3	0	2	0	1.00	4	.222	.301	.358
07	SD	NL	31	87	25	5	1	8	(5	3)	56	16	20	17	7	0	18	0	0	1	0	0	-	0	.287	.337	.644
09	SD	NL	56	197	59	14	1	10	(5	5)	105	26	29	35	17	0	45	1	1	0	8	1	.89	4	.299	.358	.533
09	Oak	AL	60	233	55	13	1	7	(4	3)	91	24	35	25	8	0	38	2	0	5	3	2	.60	5	.236	.262	.391
8 ML YEARS			643	1820	444	99	14	75	(37	38)	796	224	222	217	143	5	424	16	9	13	26	9	.74	26	.244	.303	.437

Bill Hall

Bats: R Throws: R Pos: 2B-51; PH-8; PR-4; LF-1; DH-1   Ht: 6'0" Wt: 210 Born: 12/28/1979 Age: 32

Year	Team	Lg	G	AB	H	2B	3B	HR	(Hm	Rd)	TB	R	RBI	RC	TBB	IBB	SO	HBP	SH	SF	SB	CS	SB%	GDP	Avg	OBP	Slg
2011	Fresno*	AAA	31	113	31	9	0	7	(-	-)	61	17	20	20	9	1	36	1	0	2	0	0	-	3	.274	.328	.540
2002	Mil	NL	19	36	7	1	1	1	(0	1)	13	3	5	3	3	0	13	0	0	0	0	1	.00	1	.194	.256	.361
2003	Mil	NL	52	142	37	9	2	5	(2	3)	65	23	20	18	7	0	28	1	4	1	1	2	.33	5	.261	.298	.458
2004	Mil	NL	126	390	93	20	3	9	(5	4)	146	43	53	41	20	1	119	1	2	2	12	6	.67	4	.238	.276	.374
2005	Mil	NL	146	501	146	39	6	17	(12	5)	248	69	62	73	39	2	103	1	2	3	18	6	.75	11	.291	.342	.495
2006	Mil	NL	148	537	145	39	4	35	(18	17)	297	101	85	87	63	6	162	1	3	4	8	9	.47	12	.270	.345	.553
2007	Mil	NL	136	452	115	35	0	14	(10	4)	192	59	63	59	40	1	128	3	1	7	4	5	.44	9	.254	.315	.425
2008	Mil	NL	128	404	91	22	1	15	(10	5)	160	50	55	43	37	2	124	3	1	3	6	5	.45	4	.225	.293	.396
2009	2 Tms		110	334	67	20	1	8	(4	4)	113	32	36	23	27	0	120	0	0	4	2	2	.50	11	.201	.258	.338
2010	Bos	AL	120	344	85	16	1	18	(8	10)	157	44	46	51	34	0	104	1	2	1	9	1	.90	4	.247	.316	.456
2011	2 Tms	NL	62	185	39	9	2	2	(2	0)	58	24	14	11	11	1	63	2	0	1	3	2	.60	3	.211	.261	.314
09	Mil	NL	76	214	43	12	0	6	(3	3)	73	22	24	15	19	0	72	0	0	1	1	0	1.00	10	.201	.265	.341
09	Sea	AL	34	120	24	8	1	2	(1	1)	40	10	12	8	8	0	48	0	0	3	1	2	.33	1	.200	.244	.333
11	Hou	NL	46	147	33	7	2	2	(2	0)	50	18	13	11	8	1	55	2	0	1	1	1	.50	1	.224	.272	.340
11	SF	NL	16	38	6	2	0	0	(0	0)	8	6	1	0	3	0	8	0	0	0	2	1	.67	2	.158	.220	.211
	Postseason		3	8	2	0	0	0	(0	0)	2	1	0	1	1	0	3	0	0	0	0	0	-	0	.250	.333	.250
10 ML YEARS			1047	3325	825	210	21	124	(71	53)	1449	448	439	409	281	13	964	13	15	26	62	40	.61	64	.248	.307	.436

Roy Halladay

Pitches: R Bats: R Pos: SP-32   Ht: 6'6" Wt: 230 Born: 5/14/1977 Age: 35

			HOW MUCH HE PITCHED						WHAT HE GAVE UP											THE RESULTS						
Year	Team	Lg	G	GS	CG	GF	IP	BFP	H	R	ER	HR	SH	SF	HB	TBB	IBB	SO	WP	Bk	W	L	Pct	Sh	Sv-Op	Hld	ERC	ERA
1998	Tor	AL	2	2	1	0	14.0	53	9	4	3	2	0	0	0	2	0	13	0	0	1	0	1.000	0	0-0	0	1.61	1.93
1999	Tor	AL	36	18	1	2	149.1	668	156	76	65	19	3	4	4	79	1	82	6	0	8	7	.533	1	1-1	2	5.19	3.92
2000	Tor	AL	19	13	0	4	67.2	349	107	87	80	14	2	3	2	42	0	44	6	1	4	7	.364	0	0-0	0	9.70	10.64
2001	Tor	AL	17	16	1	0	105.1	432	97	41	37	3	3	1	1	25	0	96	4	1	5	3	.625	1	0-0	0	2.61	3.16
2002	Tor	AL	34	34	2	0	239.1	993	223	93	78	10	9	2	7	62	6	168	4	1	19	7	.731	1	0-0	0	2.85	2.93
2003	Tor	AL	36	36	9	0	266.0	1071	253	111	96	26	3	2	9	32	1	204	6	1	22	7	.759	2	0-0	0	2.86	3.25
2004	Tor	AL	21	21	1	0	133.0	561	140	66	62	13	4	3	1	39	1	95	2	2	8	8	.500	1	0-0	0	4.00	4.20
2005	Tor	AL	19	19	5	0	141.2	553	118	39	38	11	2	1	7	18	2	108	2	1	12	4	.750	2	0-0	0	2.26	2.41

130

Year Team	Lg	G	GS	CG	GF	IP	BFP	H	R	ER	HR	SH	SF	HB	TBB	IBB	SO	WP	Bk	W	L	Pct	Sh	Sv-Op	Hld	ERC	ERA
2006 Tor	AL	32	32	4	0	220.0	876	208	82	78	19	3	5	5	34	5	132	3	0	16	5	.762	0	0-0	0	2.87	3.19
2007 Tor	AL	31	31	7	0	225.1	927	232	101	93	15	2	7	3	48	3	139	4	0	16	7	.696	1	0-0	0	3.37	3.71
2008 Tor	AL	34	33	9	0	246.0	987	220	88	76	18	5	4	12	39	3	206	4	0	20	11	.645	2	0-0	1	2.62	2.78
2009 Tor	AL	32	32	9	0	239.0	963	234	82	74	22	1	9	5	35	0	208	2	0	17	10	.630	4	0-0	0	3.06	2.79
2010 Phi	NL	33	33	9	0	250.2	993	231	74	68	24	9	5	6	30	1	219	5	1	21	10	.677	4	0-0	0	2.69	2.44
2011 Phi	NL	32	32	8	0	233.2	933	208	65	61	10	15	7	4	35	4	220	2	1	19	6	.760	1	0-0	0	2.26	2.35
Postseason		3	3	1	0	22.0	83	14	6	6	2	0	0	0	3	0	20	0	0	2	1	.667	1	0-0	0	1.40	2.45
14 ML YEARS		378	352	66	6	2531.0	10359	2436	1009	909	206	61	53	66	520	27	1934	50	9	188	92	.671	20	1-1	3	3.11	3.23

Greg Halman

Bats: R **Throws:** R **Pos:** LF-29; CF-8; RF-2; PR-2; PH-1   HALL-min

Ht: 6'4" **Wt:** 192 **Born:** 8/26/1987 **Age:** 24

Year Team	Lg	G	AB	H	2B	3B	HR	(Hm	Rd)	TB	R	RBI	RC	TBB	IBB	SO	HBP	SH	SF	SB	CS	SB%	GDP	Avg	OBP	Slg
2005 Ms	R	26	89	23	2	3	3	(-	-)	40	17	11	13	10	0	19	3	0	1	1	3	.25	5	.258	.350	.449
2006 Everett	A-	28	116	30	6	4	5	(-	-)	59	19	15	17	3	1	32	3	1	0	10	4	.71	2	.259	.295	.509
2007 Wisc	A	52	187	34	5	0	4	(-	-)	51	26	15	11	8	0	77	5	1	1	15	7	.68	1	.182	.234	.273
2007 Everett	A-	62	238	73	19	1	16	(-	-)	142	37	37	51	21	4	85	4	1	1	16	8	.67	2	.307	.371	.597
2008 Hi Dsrt	A+	67	257	69	15	3	19	(-	-)	147	52	53	51	16	1	76	5	1	3	23	1	.96	6	.268	.331	.572
2008 WTenn	AA	62	236	65	14	2	10	(-	-)	113	43	30	37	16	2	67	4	0	1	8	6	.57	6	.275	.331	.479
2009 WTenn	AA	121	457	96	17	2	25	(-	-)	192	64	72	54	29	1	183	15	2	3	9	7	.56	9	.210	.278	.420
2009 Ms	R	3	11	2	0	1	0	(-	-)	4	1	2	1	2	0	8	0	0	0	0	0	-	0	.182	.308	.364
2010 Tacom	AAA	112	424	103	21	4	33	(-	-)	231	82	80	73	37	0	169	4	0	0	15	4	.79	8	.243	.310	.545
2011 Tacom	AAA	40	177	53	14	1	3	(-	-)	78	35	15	30	13	0	53	3	1	0	11	1	.92	4	.299	.358	.441
2010 Sea	AL	9	29	4	1	0	0	(0	0)	5	1	3	1	1	0	11	0	0	0	1	0	1.00	0	.138	.167	.172
2011 Sea	AL	35	87	20	2	1	2	(1	1)	30	7	6	8	2	0	32	1	1	0	5	1	.83	2	.230	.256	.345
2 ML YEARS		44	116	24	3	1	2	(1	1)	35	8	9	9	3	0	43	1	1	0	6	1	.86	2	.207	.233	.302

Mark Hamburger

Pitches: R **Bats:** R **Pos:** RP-5

Ht: 6'4" **Wt:** 195 **Born:** 2/5/1987 **Age:** 25

Year Team	Lg	G	GS	CG	GF	IP	BFP	H	R	ER	HR	SH	SF	HB	TBB	IBB	SO	WP	Bk	W	L	Pct	Sh	Sv-Op	Hld	ERC	ERA
2007 Twins	R	8	0	0	2	15.0	63	12	4	2	0	0	0	0	4	0	12	1	1	2	1	.667	0	0- -	-	1.82	1.20
2008 Elizab	R	27	0	0	25	36.2	155	35	19	17	2	1	1	0	13	0	40	6	0	1	2	.333	0	13- -	-	3.34	4.17
2008 Clinton	A	4	0	0	4	4.0	18	5	1	1	0	0	0	0	2	0	0	0	0	0	0	-	0	3- -	-	5.31	2.25
2009 Hkry	A	41	0	0	25	66.1	315	79	49	35	8	4	3	3	25	0	55	9	0	2	9	.182	0	1- -	-	5.13	4.75
2010 Bkrsfld	A+	37	0	0	28	45.2	191	38	12	9	3	1	0	0	18	3	49	3	0	3	2	.600	0	18- -	-	2.80	1.77
2010 Frisco	AA	13	0	0	10	19.2	84	20	7	7	1	1	0	0	8	0	20	0	0	1	0	1.000	0	3- -	-	3.90	3.20
2011 Frisco	AA	11	0	0	7	19.2	74	11	4	4	3	1	0	0	5	2	22	2	0	1	0	1.000	0	4- -	-	1.58	1.83
2011 RdRck	AAA	31	4	0	4	62.2	257	54	27	27	5	1	1	3	20	0	48	2	0	7	4	.636	0	0- -	-	3.12	3.88
2011 Tex	AL	5	0	0	1	8.0	31	5	4	4	0	0	0	0	3	0	6	1	0	0	1	1.000	0	0-0	0	1.58	4.50

Cole Hamels

Pitches: L **Bats:** L **Pos:** SP-31; RP-1

Ht: 6'3" **Wt:** 192 **Born:** 12/27/1983 **Age:** 28

Year Team	Lg	G	GS	CG	GF	IP	BFP	H	R	ER	HR	SH	SF	HB	TBB	IBB	SO	WP	Bk	W	L	Pct	Sh	Sv-Op	Hld	ERC	ERA
2006 Phi	NL	23	23	0	0	132.1	558	117	66	60	19	6	8	3	48	4	145	5	0	9	8	.529	0	0-0	0	3.61	4.08
2007 Phi	NL	28	28	2	0	183.1	743	163	72	69	25	5	5	3	43	4	177	5	0	15	5	.750	0	0-0	0	3.12	3.39
2008 Phi	NL	33	33	2	0	227.1	914	193	89	78	28	6	2	1	53	7	196	0	0	14	10	.583	2	0-0	0	2.76	3.09
2009 Phi	NL	32	32	2	0	193.2	814	206	95	93	24	7	5	5	43	4	168	1	0	10	11	.476	2	0-0	0	3.98	4.32
2010 Phi	NL	33	33	1	0	208.2	856	185	74	71	26	7	0	8	61	5	211	3	0	12	11	.522	0	0-0	0	3.36	3.06
2011 Phi	NL	32	31	3	0	216.0	850	169	68	67	19	9	3	5	44	2	194	3	3	14	9	.609	0	0-0	0	2.23	2.79
Postseason		12	12	1	0	75.2	299	60	29	28	9	3	2	1	18	0	69	0	0	6	4	.600	1	0-0	0	2.57	3.33
6 ML YEARS		181	180	10	0	1161.1	4735	1033	464	438	141	40	23	25	292	26	1091	17	3	74	54	.578	4	0-0	0	3.11	3.39

Josh Hamilton

Bats: L **Throws:** L **Pos:** LF-85; CF-35; DH-9

Ht: 6'4" **Wt:** 240 **Born:** 5/21/1981 **Age:** 31

Year Team	Lg	G	AB	H	2B	3B	HR	(Hm	Rd)	TB	R	RBI	RC	TBB	IBB	SO	HBP	SH	SF	SB	CS	SB%	GDP	Avg	OBP	Slg
2011 Frisco*	AA	2	7	2	0	0	1	(-	-)	5	3	3	1	1	0	1	0	0	0	0	0	-	0	.286	.375	.714
2011 RdRck*	AAA	3	11	2	1	0	1	(-	-)	6	2	3	1	2	1	4	0	0	0	0	0	-	0	.182	.308	.545
2007 Cin	NL	90	298	87	17	2	19	(11	8)	165	52	47	58	33	4	65	4	0	2	3	3	.50	6	.292	.368	.554
2008 Tex	AL	156	624	190	35	5	32	(19	13)	331	98	130	119	64	9	126	7	0	9	9	1	.90	8	.304	.371	.530
2009 Tex	AL	89	336	90	19	2	10	(6	4)	143	43	54	51	24	2	79	1	0	4	8	3	.73	5	.268	.315	.426
2010 Tex	AL	133	518	186	40	3	32	(22	10)	328	95	100	121	43	13	95	5	1	4	8	1	.89	11	.359	.411	.633
2011 Tex	AL	121	487	145	31	5	25	(14	11)	261	80	94	78	39	13	93	2	0	10	8	1	.89	8	.298	.346	.536
Postseason		16	58	11	1	0	5	(2	3)	27	9	9	7	11	5	13	0	0	0	4	1	.80	2	.190	.319	.466
5 ML YEARS		589	2263	698	142	17	118	(72	46)	1228	368	425	427	203	33	458	19	1	29	36	9	.80	38	.308	.366	.543

Mark Hamilton

Bats: L **Throws:** L **Pos:** PH-30; 1B-8; LF-2; DH-2   **Ht:** 6'3" **Wt:** 220 **Born:** 7/29/1984 **Age:** 27

Year	Team	Lg	G	AB	H	2B	3B	HR	(Hm	Rd)	TB	R	RBI	RC	TBB	IBB	SO	HBP	SH	SF	SB	CS	SB%	GDP	Avg	OBP	Slg
2006	StCol	A-	30	106	28	3	1	8	(-	-)	57	18	24	20	13	2	24	1	0	1	1	1	.50	1	.264	.347	.538
2006	QuadC	A	38	142	36	8	0	3	(-	-)	53	16	25	16	10	0	32	1	0	0	0	0	-	5	.254	.307	.373
2007	PlmBh	A+	60	221	64	12	0	13	(-	-)	115	31	49	40	20	0	48	1	0	2	1	0	1.00	5	.290	.348	.520
2007	Sprgfld	AA	68	248	62	15	0	6	(-	-)	95	32	41	31	24	2	55	1	2	1	1	1	.50	4	.250	.318	.383
2008	Sprgfld	AA	70	245	59	11	0	8	(-	-)	94	27	29	34	35	2	67	1	0	0	0	0	-	7	.241	.338	.384
2009	Sprgfld	AA	48	163	50	11	0	8	(-	-)	85	26	28	36	28	3	46	4	0	0	0	1	.00	6	.307	.421	.521
2009	Memp	AAA	46	130	40	11	0	6	(-	-)	69	22	19	25	13	0	34	1	0	0	0	0	-	3	.308	.375	.531
2010	Memp	AAA	72	258	77	20	0	18	(-	-)	151	53	60	59	35	1	70	7	0	6	0	0	-	2	.298	.389	.585
2010	Cards	R	9	27	8	1	0	2	(-	-)	15	2	2	6	4	0	9	1	0	0	0	0	-	0	.296	.406	.556
2011	Memp	AAA	69	252	87	26	0	2	(-	-)	119	46	39	55	42	1	44	4	0	5	0	0	-	8	.345	.439	.472
2010	StL	NL	9	14	2	0	0	0	(0	0)	2	0	0	0	1	0	5	0	0	0	0	0	-	0	.143	.200	.143
2011	StL	NL	38	47	10	3	0	0	(0	0)	13	5	4	4	4	0	16	0	0	0	0	0	-	1	.213	.275	.277
2 ML YEARS			47	61	12	3	0	0	(0	0)	15	5	4	4	5	0	21	0	0	0	0	0	-	1	.197	.258	.246

Jason Hammel

Pitches: R **Bats:** R **Pos:** SP-27; RP-5   **Ht:** 6'6" **Wt:** 215 **Born:** 9/2/1982 **Age:** 29

Year	Team	Lg	G	GS	CG	GF	IP	BFP	H	R	ER	HR	SH	SF	HB	TBB	IBB	SO	WP	Bk	W	L	Pct	Sh	Sv-Op	Hld	ERC	ERA
2006	TB	AL	9	9	0	0	44.0	208	61	38	38	7	0	3	1	21	0	32	3	2	0	6	.000	0	0-0	0	7.40	7.77
2007	TB	AL	24	14	0	2	85.0	384	100	58	58	12	2	0	2	40	1	64	3	0	3	5	.375	0	0-0	0	5.86	6.14
2008	TB	AL	40	5	0	21	78.1	346	83	45	40	11	2	2	2	35	4	44	7	0	4	4	.500	0	2-2	1	4.94	4.60
2009	Col	NL	34	30	1	0	176.2	771	203	94	85	17	10	9	9	42	6	133	4	0	10	8	.556	0	0-0	0	4.37	4.33
2010	Col	NL	30	30	0	0	177.2	770	201	97	95	18	11	6	6	47	1	141	13	2	10	9	.526	0	0-0	0	4.41	4.81
2011	Col	NL	32	27	0	2	170.1	739	175	100	90	21	11	6	6	68	3	94	8	1	7	13	.350	0	1-1	0	4.54	4.76
Postseason			1	1	0	0	3.2	17	4	4	4	1	0	0	0	3	0	5	0	0	0	0	-	0	0-0	0	8.12	9.82
6 ML YEARS			169	115	1	25	732.0	3218	823	432	406	86	36	26	26	253	15	508	38	5	34	45	.430	0	3-3	1	4.82	4.99

Robby Hammock

Bats: R **Throws:** R **Pos:** LF-1; PH-1   **Ht:** 5'10" **Wt:** 187 **Born:** 5/13/1977 **Age:** 35

Year	Team	Lg	G	AB	H	2B	3B	HR	(Hm	Rd)	TB	R	RBI	RC	TBB	IBB	SO	HBP	SH	SF	SB	CS	SB%	GDP	Avg	OBP	Slg
2011	Reno*	AAA	37	101	26	7	1	5	(-	-)	50	18	21	18	15	0	17	1	1	2	0	0	-	4	.257	.353	.495
2003	Ari	NL	65	195	55	10	2	8	(5	3)	93	30	28	28	17	3	44	2	0	2	3	2	.60	5	.282	.343	.477
2004	Ari	NL	62	195	47	16	2	4	(1	3)	79	22	18	14	13	6	39	0	1	1	3	3	.50	9	.241	.287	.405
2006	Ari	NL	1	2	1	1	0	0	(0	0)	2	1	0	0	0	0	0	0	0	0	0	0	-	0	.500	.500	1.000
2007	Ari	NL	34	45	11	2	0	0	(0	0)	13	5	0	4	3	0	7	1	0	0	0	0	-	3	.244	.306	.289
2008	Ari	NL	18	42	8	1	0	0	(0	0)	9	4	2	3	5	1	9	1	0	0	0	0	-	3	.190	.292	.214
2011	Ari	NL	2	2	0	0	0	0	(0	0)	0	0	0	0	0	0	0	0	0	0	0	0	-	0	.000	.000	.000
6 ML YEARS			182	481	122	30	4	12	(6	6)	196	62	48	49	38	10	99	4	1	3	6	5	.55	17	.254	.312	.407

Erik Hamren

Pitches: R **Bats:** R **Pos:** RP-14   **Ht:** 6'1" **Wt:** 195 **Born:** 8/21/1986 **Age:** 25

Year	Team	Lg	G	GS	CG	GF	IP	BFP	H	R	ER	HR	SH	SF	HB	TBB	IBB	SO	WP	Bk	W	L	Pct	Sh	Sv-Op	Hld	ERC	ERA
2008	Cubs	R	7	2	0	2	7.2	32	8	5	5	0	0	0	1	4	0	5	0	0	1	1	.500	0	2- -	-	5.04	5.87
2008	Boise	A-	6	0	0	2	8.1	46	16	5	4	0	0	1	1	6	0	6	2	0	1	0	1.000	0	0- -	-	11.21	4.32
2009	Peoria	A	38	0	0	19	58.2	275	64	43	39	3	4	3	7	32	4	42	14	3	3	4	.429	0	7- -	-	5.09	5.98
2011	Lk Els	A+	15	0	0	8	16.2	61	12	2	2	0	1	0	1	2	0	21	2	1	2	0	1.000	0	1- -	-	1.50	1.08
2011	SnAnt	AA	33	0	0	16	49.0	192	34	7	5	0	4	2	6	12	2	48	3	0	3	0	1.000	0	1- -	-	1.77	0.92
2011	Tucsn	AAA	2	0	0	1	3.0	16	3	1	1	1	1	0	1	3	2	2	0	0	0	0	-	0	1- -	-	8.51	3.00
2011	SD	NL	14	0	0	5	12.1	55	10	7	6	2	2	1	2	9	1	10	0	0	1	0	1.000	0	0-0	1	5.47	4.38

Brad Hand

Pitches: L **Bats:** L **Pos:** SP-12   **Ht:** 6'3" **Wt:** 200 **Born:** 3/20/1990 **Age:** 22

Year	Team	Lg	G	GS	CG	GF	IP	BFP	H	R	ER	HR	SH	SF	HB	TBB	IBB	SO	WP	Bk	W	L	Pct	Sh	Sv-Op	Hld	ERC	ERA
2008	Mrlns	R	9	7	0	0	32.2	132	25	16	9	0	1	0	2	11	0	34	4	0	2	0	1.000	0	0- -	-	2.23	2.48
2008	Jmstwn	A-	3	3	0	0	15.0	64	11	6	5	0	0	0	1	10	0	12	2	0	1	2	.333	0	0- -	-	3.24	3.00
2009	Grnsbr	A	26	26	0	0	127.2	571	130	83	69	12	2	4	7	66	2	122	22	2	7	13	.350	0	0- -	-	4.81	4.86
2010	Jupiter	A+	26	26	2	0	140.2	609	153	68	52	10	1	3	5	49	2	134	3	3	8	8	.500	2	0- -	-	4.32	3.33
2010	Jaxnvl	AA	1	1	0	0	6.0	24	3	2	2	0	0	0	0	3	0	4	0	0	1	0	1.000	0	0- -	-	1.41	3.00
2011	Jaxnvl	AA	19	18	0	1	108.2	447	90	42	41	11	5	2	1	50	0	71	0	2	11	4	.733	0	0- -	-	3.51	3.40
2011	Jupiter	A+	1	1	0	0	5.0	24	5	5	4	1	0	1	0	5	0	4	0	0	0	1	.000	0	0- -	-	7.56	7.20
2011	Fla	NL	12	12	0	0	60.0	263	53	32	28	10	4	3	1	35	1	38	0	1	1	8	.111	0	0-0	0	4.68	4.20

Ryan Hanigan

HANN-eh-gann

Bats: R **Throws:** R **Pos:** C-89; PH-3   **Ht:** 6'0" **Wt:** 207 **Born:** 8/16/1980 **Age:** 31

Year	Team	Lg	G	AB	H	2B	3B	HR	(Hm	Rd)	TB	R	RBI	RC	TBB	IBB	SO	HBP	SH	SF	SB	CS	SB%	GDP	Avg	OBP	Slg
2007	Cin	NL	5	10	3	1	0	0	(0	0)	4	3	2	2	1	1	2	0	0	0	0	0	-	0	.300	.364	.400
2008	Cin	NL	31	85	23	2	0	2	(1	1)	31	9	9	12	10	1	9	3	0	0	0	0	-	2	.271	.367	.365
2009	Cin	NL	90	251	66	6	1	3	(3	0)	83	22	11	25	37	7	31	2	2	1	0	0	-	9	.263	.361	.331
2010	Cin	NL	70	203	61	11	0	5	(2	3)	87	25	40	41	33	4	21	4	1	2	0	0	-	6	.300	.405	.429
2011	Cin	NL	91	266	71	6	0	6	(4	2)	95	27	31	38	35	3	32	2	1	0	0	0	-	3	.267	.356	.357
	Postseason		2	4	0	0	0	0	(0	0)	0	0	0	0	0	0	0	0	0	0	0	0	-	0	.000	.000	.000
	5 ML YEARS		287	815	224	26	1	16	(10	6)	300	86	93	118	116	16	95	11	4	3	0	0	-	20	.275	.371	.368

Jack Hannahan

Bats: L **Throws:** R **Pos:** 3B-104; 1B-8; PH-2; PR-1   **Ht:** 6'2" **Wt:** 210 **Born:** 3/4/1980 **Age:** 32

Year	Team	Lg	G	AB	H	2B	3B	HR	(Hm	Rd)	TB	R	RBI	RC	TBB	IBB	SO	HBP	SH	SF	SB	CS	SB%	GDP	Avg	OBP	Slg
2006	Det	AL	3	9	0	0	0	0	(0	0)	0	0	0	0	1	0	1	0	0	0	0	0	-	0	.000	.100	.000
2007	Oak	AL	41	144	40	12	0	3	(1	2)	61	16	24	23	21	0	39	1	1	2	1	0	1.00	6	.278	.369	.424
2008	Oak	AL	143	436	95	27	0	9	(4	5)	149	48	47	38	55	4	131	2	3	5	2	0	1.00	5	.218	.305	.342
2009	2 Tms	AL	103	267	57	14	2	4	(2	2)	87	27	19	20	30	0	71	2	1	1	1	1	.50	4	.213	.297	.326
2011	Cle	AL	110	320	80	16	2	8	(7	1)	124	38	40	47	38	0	80	2	4	2	2	1	.67	7	.250	.331	.388
09	Oak	AL	52	119	23	6	2	1	(1	0)	36	12	8	7	13	0	36	1	1	0	0	0	-	2	.193	.278	.303
09	Sea	AL	51	148	34	8	0	3	(1	2)	51	15	11	13	17	0	35	1	0	1	1	1	.50	2	.230	.311	.345
	5 ML YEARS		400	1176	272	69	4	24	(14	10)	421	129	130	128	145	4	322	7	9	10	6	2	.75	22	.231	.317	.358

Joel Hanrahan

Pitches: R **Bats:** R **Pos:** RP-70   **Ht:** 6'4" **Wt:** 245 **Born:** 10/6/1981 **Age:** 30

Year	Team	Lg	G	GS	CG	GF	IP	BFP	H	R	ER	HR	SH	SF	HB	TBB	IBB	SO	WP	Bk	W	L	Pct	Sh	Sv-Op	Hld	ERC	ERA
2007	Was	NL	12	11	0	0	51.0	247	59	35	34	9	2	1	0	38	0	43	3	0	5	3	.625	0	0-0	0	7.01	6.00
2008	Was	NL	69	0	0	34	84.1	364	73	40	37	9	2	6	1	42	7	93	6	0	6	3	.667	0	9-13	5	3.65	3.95
2009	2 Tms	NL	67	0	0	30	64.0	297	73	40	34	3	0	1	3	34	1	72	11	1	1	4	.200	0	5-10	9	5.12	4.78
2010	Pit	NL	72	0	0	27	69.2	294	58	28	28	6	0	1	4	26	0	100	5	0	4	1	.800	0	6-10	18	3.16	3.62
2011	Pit	NL	70	0	0	59	68.2	274	56	17	14	1	1	2	1	16	2	61	6	0	1	4	.200	0	40-44	0	2.00	1.83
09	Was	NL	34	0	0	23	32.2	163	50	28	28	3	0	1	2	14	0	35	6	1	1	3	.250	0	5-10	2	7.49	7.71
09	Pit	NL	33	0	0	7	31.1	134	23	12	6	0	0	0	1	20	1	37	5	0	0	1	.000	0	0-0	7	2.92	1.72
	5 ML YEARS		290	11	0	150	337.2	1476	319	160	147	28	5	11	9	156	10	369	31	1	17	15	.531	0	60-77	30	3.91	3.92

Tommy Hanson

Pitches: R **Bats:** R **Pos:** SP-22   **Ht:** 6'6" **Wt:** 220 **Born:** 8/28/1986 **Age:** 25

Year	Team	Lg	G	GS	CG	GF	IP	BFP	H	R	ER	HR	SH	SF	HB	TBB	IBB	SO	WP	Bk	W	L	Pct	Sh	Sv-Op	Hld	ERC	ERA
2009	Atl	NL	21	21	0	0	127.2	522	105	42	41	10	4	1	5	46	1	116	2	0	11	4	.733	0	0-0	0	3.02	2.89
2010	Atl	NL	34	34	1	0	202.2	845	182	86	75	14	9	5	14	56	3	173	3	0	10	11	.476	0	0-0	0	3.08	3.33
2011	Atl	NL	22	22	0	0	130.0	540	106	55	52	17	4	3	3	46	3	142	5	0	11	7	.611	0	0-0	0	3.13	3.60
	Postseason		1	1	0	0	4.0	17	5	4	4	1	0	0	0	1	0	5	0	0	0	0	-	0	0-0	0	6.26	9.00
	3 ML YEARS		77	77	1	0	460.1	1907	393	183	168	41	17	9	22	148	7	431	10	0	32	22	.593	0	0-0	0	3.08	3.28

J.A. Happ

JAY

Pitches: L **Bats:** L **Pos:** SP-28   **Ht:** 6'6" **Wt:** 200 **Born:** 10/19/1982 **Age:** 29

Year	Team	Lg	G	GS	CG	GF	IP	BFP	H	R	ER	HR	SH	SF	HB	TBB	IBB	SO	WP	Bk	W	L	Pct	Sh	Sv-Op	Hld	ERC	ERA
2011	OKCity*	AAA	3	3	0	0	18.0	71	11	5	3	0	0	0	0	9	0	16	0	0	1	0	1.000	0	0- -	-	1.88	1.50
2007	Phi	NL	1	1	0	0	4.0	21	7	5	5	3	0	0	0	2	0	5	0	0	0	1	.000	0	0-0	0	15.13	11.25
2008	Phi	NL	8	4	0	1	31.2	138	28	13	13	3	2	1	1	14	1	26	1	0	1	0	1.000	0	0-0	1	3.55	3.69
2009	Phi	NL	35	23	0	4	166.0	685	149	55	54	20	7	6	5	56	2	119	2	0	12	4	.750	2	0-0	1	3.57	2.93
2010	2 Tms	NL	16	16	1	0	87.1	374	73	37	33	8	5	4	1	47	1	70	4	0	6	4	.600	1	0-0	0	3.69	3.40
2011	Hou	NL	28	28	0	0	156.1	698	157	103	93	21	12	8	2	83	5	134	3	2	6	15	.286	0	0-0	0	4.86	5.35
10	Phi	NL	3	3	0	0	15.1	70	13	4	3	1	1	1	0	12	0	9	1	0	1	0	1.000	0	0-0	0	4.40	1.76
10	Hou	NL	13	13	1	0	72.0	304	60	33	30	7	4	3	1	35	1	61	3	0	5	4	.556	1	0-0	0	3.53	3.75
	Postseason		8	1	0	0	9.1	46	12	5	5	1	0	0	0	8	0	10	0	0	0	0	-	0	0-0	1	7.96	4.82
	5 ML YEARS		88	72	4	5	445.1	1916	414	213	198	55	26	19	9	202	9	354	10	2	25	24	.510	3	0-0	1	4.12	4.00

Aaron Harang

huh-RANG

Pitches: R **Bats:** R **Pos:** SP-28   **Ht:** 6'7" **Wt:** 261 **Born:** 5/9/1978 **Age:** 34

Year	Team	Lg	G	GS	CG	GF	IP	BFP	H	R	ER	HR	SH	SF	HB	TBB	IBB	SO	WP	Bk	W	L	Pct	Sh	Sv-Op	Hld	ERC	ERA
2011	Lk Els*	A+	1	1	0	0	4.0	17	5	3	3	0	0	0	0	1	0	7	0	0	0	1	.000	0	0- -	-	4.32	6.75
2002	Oak	AL	16	15	0	0	78.1	354	78	44	42	7	3	4	3	45	2	64	1	0	5	4	.556	0	0-0	0	4.76	4.83
2003	2 Tms		16	15	0	1	76.1	327	89	47	45	11	5	1	1	19	0	42	3	1	5	6	.455	0	0-0	0	4.84	5.31
2004	Cin	NL	28	28	1	0	161.0	711	177	90	87	26	13	6	5	53	5	125	7	0	10	9	.526	1	0-0	0	4.81	4.86
2005	Cin	NL	32	32	1	0	211.2	887	217	93	90	22	11	5	8	51	3	163	6	0	11	13	.458	0	0-0	0	3.77	3.83
2006	Cin	NL	36	35	6	0	234.1	993	242	109	98	28	21	8	8	56	8	216	6	1	16	11	.593	2	0-0	0	3.82	3.76
2007	Cin	NL	34	34	2	0	231.2	948	213	100	96	28	4	5	8	52	3	218	12	1	16	6	.727	1	0-0	0	3.22	3.73
2008	Cin	NL	30	29	1	0	184.1	793	205	104	98	35	11	7	2	50	5	153	2	0	6	17	.261	1	0-0	0	4.83	4.78
2009	Cin	NL	26	26	2	0	162.1	703	186	82	76	24	6	4	3	43	6	142	6	0	6	14	.300	1	0-0	0	4.76	4.21

Year	Team	Lg	G	GS	CG	GF	IP	BFP	H	R	ER	HR	SH	SF	HB	TBB	IBB	SO	WP	Bk	W	L	Pct	Sh	Sv-Op	Hld	ERC	ERA
2010	Cin	NL	22	20	0	1	111.2	504	139	71	66	16	4	3	4	38	0	82	9	0	6	7	.462	0	0-0	0	5.75	5.32
2011	SD	NL	28	28	0	0	170.2	719	175	73	69	20	5	2	3	58	4	124	3	0	14	7	.667	0	0-0	0	4.22	3.64
03	Oak	AL	7	6	0	1	30.1	136	41	19	18	5	2	1	0	9	0	16	0	1	1	3	.250	0	0-0	0	6.32	5.34
03	Cin	NL	9	9	0	0	46.0	191	48	28	27	6	3	0	1	10	0	26	3	0	4	3	.571	0	0-0	0	3.94	5.28
10 ML YEARS			268	262	13	2	1622.1	6939	1721	813	767	217	83	43	46	465	36	1329	55	3	95	94	.503	6	0-0	0	4.29	4.25

Rich Harden

Pitches: R Bats: L Pos: SP-15

Ht: 6'1" Wt: 195 Born: 11/30/1981 Age: 30

Year	Team	Lg	G	GS	CG	GF	IP	BFP	H	R	ER	HR	SH	SF	HB	TBB	IBB	SO	WP	Bk	W	L	Pct	Sh	Sv-Op	Hld	ERC	ERA
2011	Scrmto*	AAA	2	2	0	0	7.2	29	3	3	3	1	0	0	0	3	0	12	0	0	0	0	-	0	0--	-	1.36	3.52
2003	Oak	AL	15	13	0	0	74.2	324	72	38	37	5	2	3	1	40	1	67	6	0	5	4	.556	0	0-0	0	4.28	4.46
2004	Oak	AL	31	31	0	0	189.2	803	171	90	84	16	5	6	3	81	6	167	4	1	11	7	.611	0	0-0	0	3.57	3.99
2005	Oak	AL	22	19	2	0	128.0	514	93	42	36	7	4	2	2	43	0	121	6	0	10	5	.667	1	0-0	0	2.20	2.53
2006	Oak	AL	9	9	0	0	46.2	191	31	22	22	5	0	2	1	26	0	49	0	0	4	0	1.000	0	0-0	0	3.07	4.24
2007	Oak	AL	7	4	0	2	25.2	100	18	7	7	3	0	0	0	11	1	27	0	0	1	2	.333	0	0-0	0	2.80	2.45
2008	2 Tms		25	25	0	0	148.0	595	96	38	34	11	2	3	3	61	2	181	3	0	10	2	.833	0	0-0	0	2.20	2.07
2009	ChC	NL	26	26	0	0	141.0	609	122	74	64	23	12	3	6	67	5	171	7	0	9	9	.500	0	0-0	0	4.15	4.09
2010	Tex	AL	20	18	0	0	92.0	430	91	61	57	18	0	4	9	62	0	75	4	0	5	5	.500	0	0-0	0	6.27	5.58
2011	Oak	AL	15	15	0	0	82.2	363	87	48	47	17	1	3	2	31	0	91	4	0	4	4	.500	0	0-0	0	5.10	5.12
08	Oak	AL	13	13	0	0	77.0	311	57	21	20	5	0	2	1	31	1	92	1	0	5	1	.833	0	0-0	0	2.56	2.34
08	ChC	NL	12	12	0	0	71.0	284	39	17	14	6	2	1	2	30	1	89	2	0	5	1	.833	0	0-0	0	1.84	1.77
Postseason			4	2	0	2	11.1	55	12	8	8	2	0	0	0	10	3	9	1	0	1	3	.250	0	0-0	0	6.49	6.35
9 ML YEARS			170	160	2	2	928.1	3929	781	420	388	105	26	26	27	422	15	949	34	1	59	38	.608	1	0-0	1	3.60	3.76

J.J. Hardy

Bats: R Throws: R Pos: SS-129

Ht: 6'2" Wt: 202 Born: 8/19/1982 Age: 29

Year	Team	Lg	G	AB	H	2B	3B	HR	(Hm	Rd)	TB	R	RBI	RC	TBB	IBB	SO	HBP	SH	SF	SB	CS	SB%	GDP	Avg	OBP	Slg
2011	Norfolk*	AAA	3	9	2	0	0	0	(-	-)	2	2	0	1	3	0	1	0	0	0	0	0	-	0	.222	.417	.222
2005	Mil	NL	124	372	92	22	1	9	(6	3)	143	46	50	49	44	7	48	1	8	2	0	0	-	10	.247	.327	.384
2006	Mil	NL	35	128	31	5	0	5	(4	1)	51	13	14	13	10	0	23	0	0	1	1	1	.50	4	.242	.295	.398
2007	Mil	NL	151	592	164	30	1	26	(15	11)	274	89	80	84	40	1	73	1	4	1	2	3	.40	13	.277	.323	.463
2008	Mil	NL	146	569	161	31	4	24	(14	10)	272	78	74	78	52	3	98	1	5	2	2	1	.67	18	.283	.343	.478
2009	Mil	NL	115	414	95	16	2	11	(6	5)	148	53	47	32	43	0	85	2	1	5	0	1	.00	14	.229	.302	.357
2010	Min	AL	101	340	91	19	3	6	(1	5)	134	44	38	41	28	1	54	0	3	4	1	1	.50	8	.268	.320	.394
2011	Bal	AL	129	527	142	27	0	30	(15	15)	259	76	80	78	31	3	92	2	2	5	0	0	-	10	.269	.310	.491
Postseason			7	24	7	2	0	0	(0	0)	9	2	2	3	2	0	2	0	0	0	0	0	-	0	.292	.346	.375
7 ML YEARS			801	2942	776	150	11	111	(61	50)	1281	399	383	375	248	15	473	7	23	20	6	7	.46	77	.264	.320	.435

Dan Haren

Pitches: R Bats: R Pos: SP-34; RP-1

Ht: 6'5" Wt: 215 Born: 9/17/1980 Age: 31

Year	Team	Lg	G	GS	CG	GF	IP	BFP	H	R	ER	HR	SH	SF	HB	TBB	IBB	SO	WP	Bk	W	L	Pct	Sh	Sv-Op	Hld	ERC	ERA
2003	StL	NL	14	14	0	0	72.2	320	84	44	41	9	4	2	5	22	0	43	3	0	3	7	.300	0	0-0	0	5.07	5.08
2004	StL	NL	14	5	0	2	46.0	195	45	23	23	4	4	2	2	17	2	32	1	0	3	3	.500	0	0-0	0	3.91	4.50
2005	Oak	AL	34	34	3	0	217.0	897	212	101	90	26	3	5	6	53	5	163	6	0	14	12	.538	0	0-0	0	3.58	3.73
2006	Oak	AL	34	34	2	0	223.0	930	224	109	102	31	3	3	10	45	6	176	10	0	14	13	.519	0	0-0	0	3.72	4.12
2007	Oak	AL	34	34	0	0	222.2	935	214	91	76	24	2	8	3	55	1	192	10	0	15	9	.625	0	0-0	0	3.32	3.07
2008	Ari	NL	33	33	1	0	216.0	881	204	86	80	19	7	3	6	40	4	206	11	0	16	8	.667	1	0-0	0	2.96	3.33
2009	Ari	NL	33	33	3	0	229.1	909	192	83	80	27	8	3	4	38	2	223	13	0	14	10	.583	1	0-0	0	2.50	3.14
2010	2 Tms		35	35	2	0	235.0	994	245	110	102	31	6	10	5	54	6	216	12	2	12	12	.500	0	0-0	0	3.88	3.91
2011	LAA	AL	35	34	4	1	238.1	953	211	91	84	20	**12**	5	5	33	1	192	6	0	16	10	.615	3	0-0	0	2.45	3.17
10	Ari	NL	21	21	1	0	141.0	607	161	79	72	23	6	4	3	29	4	141	8	1	7	8	.467	0	0-0	0	4.55	4.60
10	LAA	AL	14	14	1	0	94.0	387	84	31	30	8	0	6	2	25	2	75	4	1	5	4	.556	0	0-0	0	2.94	2.87
Postseason			7	2	0	0	19.1	86	24	7	7	3	1	0	0	7	0	16	2	0	2	0	1.000	0	0-0	0	5.83	3.26
9 ML YEARS			266	256	15	3	1700.0	7014	1631	738	678	191	49	41	46	357	27	1443	72	2	107	84	.560	5	0-0	0	3.28	3.59

Lucas Harrell

Pitches: R Bats: B Pos: RP-7; SP-2

HAH-rell

Ht: 6'2" Wt: 210 Born: 6/3/1985 Age: 27

Year	Team	Lg	G	GS	CG	GF	IP	BFP	H	R	ER	HR	SH	SF	HB	TBB	IBB	SO	WP	Bk	W	L	Pct	Sh	Sv-Op	Hld	ERC	ERA
2004	Bristol	R+	13	9	0	1	48.1	230	53	39	30	5	3	3	4	32	1	33	2	0	3	5	.375	0	0--	-	6.00	5.59
2005	Knapol	A-	26	26	0	0	133.1	607	128	86	54	8	2	7	11	71	0	85	13	4	7	11	.389	0	0--	-	4.31	3.65
2006	WinSa	A+	17	17	0	0	91.2	374	58	29	25	3	2	2	7	44	0	70	3	0	7	2	.778	0	0--	-	2.32	2.45
2006	Brham	AA	3	3	0	0	9.2	52	12	12	11	1	0	1	0	14	0	4	2	1	0	2	.000	0	0--	-	10.47	10.24
2008	Brham	AA	11	10	0	0	54.2	231	56	30	21	3	3	1	2	19	0	34	3	0	3	3	.500	0	0--	-	3.92	3.46
2008	Bristol	R+	1	1	0	0	3.0	12	3	1	1	0	0	0	0	1	0	5	0	0	0	0	-	0	0--	-	3.35	3.00
2008	Knapol	A	3	3	0	0	10.2	49	13	7	7	0	1	0	1	4	0	7	0	0	1	1	.500	0	0--	-	4.81	5.91
2009	Brham	AA	14	14	0	0	80.1	334	78	38	29	4	1	3	2	32	0	51	5	0	8	3	.727	0	0--	-	3.80	3.25
2009	Charltt	AAA	11	11	0	0	65.2	280	58	26	24	3	2	1	3	37	0	42	3	1	4	1	.800	0	0--	-	3.97	3.29
2010	Charltt	AAA	26	26	0	0	137.2	602	141	79	70	11	3	6	5	61	1	84	4	1	10	10	.500	0	0--	-	4.40	4.58
2011	Charltt	AAA	13	12	0	1	74.1	305	67	28	27	6	0	3	1	26	0	56	5	0	7	3	.700	0	0--	-	3.34	3.27
2011	OKCity	AAA	9	9	0	0	52.1	221	42	12	10	0	4	0	2	24	3	38	1	0	5	2	.714	0	0--	-	2.60	1.72
2010	CWS	AL	8	3	0	3	24.0	119	34	18	13	2	1	0	0	17	1	15	1	0	1	0	1.000	0	0-0	0	7.77	4.88

Year Team	Lg	HOW MUCH HE PITCHED						WHAT HE GAVE UP													THE RESULTS							
		G	GS	CG	GF	IP	BFP	H	R	ER	HR	SH	SF	HB	TBB	IBB	SO	WP	Bk	W	L	Pct	Sh	Sv-Op	Hld	ERC	ERA
2011 2 Tms		9	2	0	2	18.0	86	23	12	9	0	1	1	1	8	0	15	1	1	0	2	.000	0	0-0	0	5.16	4.50
11 CWS	AL	3	0	0	2	5.0	26	11	4	4	0	0	0	0	1	0	5	0	0	0	0	-	0	0-0	0	10.11	7.20
11 Hou	NL	6	2	0	0	13.0	60	12	8	5	0	1	1	1	7	0	10	1	1	0	2	.000	0	0-0	0	3.57	3.46
2 ML YEARS		17	5	0	5	42.0	205	57	30	22	2	2	1	1	25	1	30	2	1	1	2	.333	0	0-0	0	6.60	4.71

Willie Harris

Bats: L Throws: R Pos: PH-72; LF-33; 2B-10; 3B-7; CF-7; RF-6; DH-2; PR-1 Ht: 5'9" Wt: 191 Born: 6/22/1978 Age: 34

Year Team	Lg	BATTING																		BASERUNNING				AVERAGES		
		G	AB	H	2B	3B	HR	(Hm Rd)	TB	R	RBI	RC	TBB	IBB	SO	HBP	SH	SF	SB	CS	SB%	GDP	Avg	OBP	Slg
2001 Bal	AL	9	24	3	1	0	0	(0 0)	4	3	0	0	7	0	1	0	1	0	0	0	-	0	.125	.125	.167
2002 CWS	AL	49	163	38	4	0	2	(2 0)	48	14	12	15	9	0	21	0	3	2	8	1	1.00	3	.233	.270	.294
2003 CWS	AL	79	137	28	3	1	0	(0 0)	33	19	5	11	10	0	28	0	3	0	12	2	.86	1	.204	.259	.241
2004 CWS	AL	129	409	107	15	2	2	(2 0)	132	68	27	53	51	1	79	1	7	3	19	7	.73	4	.262	.343	.323
2005 CWS	AL	56	121	31	2	1	1	(1 0)	38	17	8	15	13	0	25	1	4	0	10	3	.77	1	.256	.333	.314
2006 Bos	AL	47	45	7	2	0	0	(0 0)	9	17	1	1	4	0	11	2	0	1	6	3	.67	0	.156	.250	.200
2007 Atl	NL	117	344	93	20	8	2	(1 1)	135	56	32	47	40	0	71	3	1	3	17	11	.61	3	.270	.349	.392
2008 Was	NL	140	367	92	14	4	13	(4 9)	153	58	43	50	50	2	66	3	3	1	13	3	.81	8	.251	.344	.417
2009 Was	NL	137	323	76	18	6	7	(6 1)	127	47	27	47	57	1	62	9	3	1	11	4	.73	4	.235	.364	.393
2010 Was	NL	132	224	41	6	2	10	(7 3)	81	25	32	25	33	0	60	2	1	2	5	2	.71	3	.183	.291	.362
2011 NYM	NL	126	240	59	11	0	2	(0 2)	76	36	23	26	36	3	62	4	1	2	5	4	.56	6	.246	.351	.317
Postseason		3	2	2	0	0	0	(0 0)	2	1	1	2	0	0	0	0	0	0	1	0	1.00	0	1.000	1.000	1.000
11 ML YEARS		1021	2397	575	96	24	39	(23 16)	836	360	210	290	303	6	492	25	27	15	106	39	.73	33	.240	.330	.349

Josh Harrison

Bats: R Throws: R Pos: 3B-50; PH-9; 2B-6; PR-4 Ht: 5'8" Wt: 185 Born: 7/8/1987 Age: 24

Year Team	Lg	BATTING																		BASERUNNING				AVERAGES		
		G	AB	H	2B	3B	HR	(Hm Rd)	TB	R	RBI	RC	TBB	IBB	SO	HBP	SH	SF	SB	CS	SB%	GDP	Avg	OBP	Slg
2008 Boise	A-	33	114	40	11	2	1	(- -)	58	27	25	28	23	1	12	3	1	3	12	6	.67	1	.351	.462	.509
2008 Peoria	A	31	122	32	4	1	1	(- -)	41	15	4	12	3	0	11	1	0	0	6	2	.75	1	.262	.286	.336
2009 Peoria	A	79	303	102	17	7	4	(- -)	145	51	33	54	16	2	25	5	9	2	16	9	.64	5	.337	.377	.479
2009 Dytona	A+	18	70	20	3	1	1	(- -)	28	10	9	11	6	0	7	1	1	0	10	1	.91	1	.286	.351	.400
2009 Lynbrg	A+	34	141	38	8	1	1	(- -)	51	15	13	15	1	0	19	4	6	3	4	1	.80	1	.270	.289	.362
2010 Altna	AA	135	520	156	33	3	4	(- -)	207	74	74	77	32	2	52	9	14	10	19	7	.73	15	.300	.345	.398
2011 Indy	AAA	62	226	70	15	2	5	(- -)	104	35	23	39	15	0	28	6	5	2	13	5	.72	2	.310	.365	.460
2011 Pit	NL	65	195	53	13	2	1	(1 0)	73	21	16	19	3	0	24	0	5	1	4	1	.80	6	.272	.281	.374

Matt Harrison

Pitches: L Bats: L Pos: SP-30; RP-1 Ht: 6'4" Wt: 240 Born: 9/16/1985 Age: 26

Year Team	Lg	HOW MUCH HE PITCHED						WHAT HE GAVE UP													THE RESULTS							
		G	GS	CG	GF	IP	BFP	H	R	ER	HR	SH	SF	HB	TBB	IBB	SO	WP	Bk	W	L	Pct	Sh	Sv-Op	Hld	ERC	ERA
2008 Tex	AL	15	15	1	0	83.2	372	100	57	51	12	1	5	2	31	2	42	2	2	9	3	.750	1	0-0	0	5.53	5.49
2009 Tex	AL	11	11	2	0	63.1	283	81	43	43	9	1	1	2	23	0	34	0	0	4	5	.444	1	0-0	0	6.17	6.11
2010 Tex	AL	37	6	0	9	78.1	356	80	45	41	10	2	8	2	39	0	46	4	0	3	2	.600	0	2-3	3	4.71	4.71
2011 Tex	AL	31	30	0	0	185.2	772	180	79	70	13	8	5	1	57	1	126	6	1	14	9	.609	0	0-0	0	3.40	3.39
4 ML YEARS		94	62	3	9	411.0	1783	441	224	205	44	12	19	7	150	6	248	12	3	30	19	.612	2	2-3	3	4.47	4.49

Corey Hart

Bats: R Throws: R Pos: RF-126; PH-7 Ht: 6'6" Wt: 229 Born: 3/24/1982 Age: 30

Year Team	Lg	BATTING																		BASERUNNING				AVERAGES		
		G	AB	H	2B	3B	HR	(Hm Rd)	TB	R	RBI	RC	TBB	IBB	SO	HBP	SH	SF	SB	CS	SB%	GDP	Avg	OBP	Slg
2011 Nashv*	AAA	5	15	2	2	0	0	(- -)	4	1	1	0	0	0	3	0	0	0	0	0	-	1	.133	.133	.267
2004 Mil	NL	1	1	0	0	0	0	(0 0)	0	0	0	0	0	0	1	0	0	0	0	0	-	0	.000	.000	.000
2005 Mil	NL	21	57	11	2	1	2	(2 0)	21	9	7	4	6	0	11	0	0	0	2	0	1.00	6	.193	.270	.368
2006 Mil	NL	87	237	67	13	2	9	(6 3)	111	32	33	30	17	1	58	0	0	2	5	8	.38	7	.283	.328	.468
2007 Mil	NL	140	505	149	33	9	24	(15 9)	272	86	81	94	36	3	99	13	5	7	23	7	.77	6	.295	.353	.539
2008 Mil	NL	157	612	164	45	6	20	(7 13)	281	76	91	81	27	2	109	5	4	9	23	7	.77	17	.268	.300	.459
2009 Mil	NL	115	419	109	24	3	12	(9 3)	175	64	48	51	43	0	92	6	1	3	11	6	.65	9	.260	.335	.418
2010 Mil	NL	145	558	158	34	4	31	(16 15)	293	91	102	83	45	2	140	6	0	5	7	6	.54	14	.283	.340	.525
2011 Mil	NL	130	492	140	26	4	26	(17 9)	251	80	63	79	51	1	114	4	3	1	7	6	.54	12	.285	.356	.510
Postseason		4	13	3	0	0	0	(0 0)	3	0	0	0	1	0	3	1	1	0	0	0	-	1	.231	.333	.231
8 ML YEARS		796	2881	798	176	29	124	(72 52)	1404	438	425	422	225	9	624	34	13	27	78	40	.66	71	.277	.334	.487

Chris Hatcher

Pitches: R Bats: B Pos: RP-11 Ht: 6'2" Wt: 205 Born: 1/12/1985 Age: 27

Year Team	Lg	HOW MUCH HE PITCHED						WHAT HE GAVE UP													THE RESULTS							
		G	GS	CG	GF	IP	BFP	H	R	ER	HR	SH	SF	HB	TBB	IBB	SO	WP	Bk	W	L	Pct	Sh	Sv-Op	Hld	ERC	ERA
2009 Jaxnvl	AA	1	0	0	1	0.1	1	0	0	0	0	0	0	0	0	0	0	0	0	0	0	-	0	0--	-	0.00	0.00
2010 Jaxnvl	AA	1	0	0	1	1.0	3	0	0	0	0	0	0	0	0	0	1	0	0	1	0	1.000	0	0--	-	0.00	0.00
2011 Jaxnvl	AA	42	0	0	12	47.1	189	32	11	10	2	1	2	0	19	0	57	9	1	2	2	.500	0	6--	-	2.07	1.90
2011 Fla	NL	11	0	0	4	10.1	48	14	8	8	2	0	3	0	4	1	8	2	0	0	0	-	0	0-0	0	6.69	6.97

LaTroy Hawkins

Pitches: R Bats: R Pos: RP-52

Ht: 6'5" Wt: 219 Born: 12/21/1972 Age: 39

Year	Team	Lg	G	GS	CG	GF	IP	BFP	H	R	ER	HR	SH	SF	HB	TBB	IBB	SO	WP	Bk	W	L	Pct	Sh	Sv-Op	Hld	ERC	ERA
2011	BrvdCt*	A+	3	0	0	0	3.2	16	6	3	2	1	0	0	0	0	0	5	0	0	0	0	-	0	0- -	-	7.86	4.91
2011	Nashv*	AAA	2	0	0	1	1.1	6	1	0	0	0	0	0	0	2	0	1	0	0	0	0	-	0	0- -	-	6.99	0.00
1995	Min	AL	6	6	1	0	27.0	131	39	29	26	3	0	3	1	12	0	9	1	1	2	3	.400	0	0-0	-	7.14	8.67
1996	Min	AL	7	6	0	1	26.1	124	42	24	24	8	1	1	0	9	0	24	1	1	1	1	.500	0	0-0	-	9.49	8.20
1997	Min	AL	20	20	0	0	103.1	478	134	71	67	19	2	2	4	47	0	58	6	3	6	12	.333	0	0-0	-	7.01	5.84
1998	Min	AL	33	33	0	0	190.1	840	227	126	111	27	4	10	5	61	1	105	10	2	7	14	.333	0	0-0	-	5.31	5.25
1999	Min	AL	33	33	1	0	174.1	803	238	136	129	29	1	5	1	60	2	103	9	0	10	14	.417	0	0-0	-	6.55	6.66
2000	Min	AL	66	0	0	38	87.2	370	85	34	33	7	4	1	1	32	1	59	6	0	2	5	.286	0	14-14	7	3.70	3.39
2001	Min	AL	62	0	0	51	51.1	248	59	34	34	3	1	4	1	39	3	36	7	0	1	5	.167	0	28-37	1	6.02	5.96
2002	Min	AL	65	0	0	15	80.1	310	63	23	19	5	2	3	0	15	1	63	5	0	6	0	1.000	0	0-3	13	1.99	2.13
2003	Min	AL	74	0	0	12	77.1	310	69	20	16	4	4	1	1	15	1	75	5	0	9	3	.750	0	2-8	28	2.48	1.86
2004	ChC	NL	77	0	0	50	82.0	333	72	27	24	10	6	2	2	14	5	69	2	0	5	4	.556	0	25-34	4	2.66	2.63
2005	2 Tms	NL	66	0	0	21	56.1	247	58	27	24	7	3	1	0	24	3	43	1	0	2	8	.200	0	6-15	15	4.41	3.83
2006	Bal	AL	60	0	0	12	60.1	261	73	30	30	4	1	2	2	15	3	27	2	0	3	2	.600	0	0-4	16	4.37	4.48
2007	Col	NL	62	0	0	10	55.1	225	52	21	21	6	2	1	0	16	1	29	2	0	2	5	.286	0	0-5	18	3.43	3.42
2008	2 Tms	NL	57	0	0	15	62.0	252	53	29	27	3	1	3	0	22	4	48	3	0	3	1	.750	0	1-2	13	2.75	3.92
2009	Hou	NL	65	0	0	34	63.1	259	60	16	15	7	2	2	2	16	2	45	2	0	1	4	.200	0	11-15	19	3.42	2.13
2010	Mil	NL	18	0	0	5	16.0	74	21	15	15	2	1	0	2	6	1	18	1	0	0	3	.000	0	0-2	6	6.55	8.44
2011	Mil	NL	52	0	0	10	48.1	204	50	15	13	1	1	1	0	10	1	28	2	0	3	1	.750	0	0-0	20	2.91	2.42
05	ChC	NL	21	0	0	12	19.0	80	18	9	7	4	1	0	0	7	0	13	0	0	1	4	.200	0	4-8	0	4.44	3.32
05	SF	NL	45	0	0	9	37.1	167	40	18	17	3	2	1	0	17	3	30	1	0	1	4	.200	0	2-7	15	4.36	4.10
08	NYY	AL	33	0	0	11	41.0	173	42	26	26	3	1	2	0	17	3	23	2	0	1	1	.500	0	0-1	1	4.09	5.71
08	Hou	NL	24	0	0	4	21.0	79	11	3	1	0	0	1	0	5	1	25	1	0	2	0	1.000	0	1-1	12	0.95	0.43
	Postseason		15	0	0	4	11.2	48	11	7	6	0	2	1	0	2	0	14	0	0	1	0	1.000	0	0-0	4	2.24	4.63
17 ML YEARS			823	98	2	274	1261.2	5469	1395	677	628	145	36	42	20	413	29	839	65	7	63	85	.426	0	87-139	160	4.54	4.48

Blake Hawksworth

Pitches: R Bats: R Pos: RP-49

Ht: 6'3" Wt: 195 Born: 3/1/1983 Age: 29

Year	Team	Lg	G	GS	CG	GF	IP	BFP	H	R	ER	HR	SH	SF	HB	TBB	IBB	SO	WP	Bk	W	L	Pct	Sh	Sv-Op	Hld	ERC	ERA
2011	RCuca*	A+	4	4	0	0	4.0	15	2	1	1	0	0	1	0	1	0	5	0	0	0	0	-	0	0- -	-	0.94	2.25
2009	StL	NL	30	0	0	10	40.0	160	29	10	9	2	4	1	1	15	3	20	0	0	4	0	1.000	0	0-0	2	2.26	2.03
2010	StL	NL	45	8	0	9	90.1	409	113	56	50	15	4	4	2	35	0	61	1	3	4	8	.333	0	0-0	4	6.15	4.98
2011	LAD	NL	49	0	0	12	53.0	219	45	29	24	6	2	0	0	17	3	43	1	0	2	5	.286	0	0-1	7	2.94	4.08
	Postseason		1	0	0	0	1.0	4	1	0	0	0	0	0	0	1	0	1	0	0	0	0	-	0	0-0	0	6.99	0.00
3 ML YEARS			124	8	0	31	183.1	788	187	95	83	23	10	5	3	67	6	124	6	3	10	13	.435	0	0-1	13	4.26	4.07

Brad Hawpe

Bats: L Throws: L Pos: 1B-44; PH-11; RF-7; DH-1

Ht: 6'3" Wt: 210 Born: 6/22/1979 Age: 33

Year	Team	Lg	G	AB	H	2B	3B	HR	(Hm	Rd)	TB	R	RBI	RC	TBB	IBB	SO	HBP	SH	SF	SB	CS	SB%	GDP	Avg	OBP	Slg
2004	Col	NL	42	105	26	3	2	3	(1	2)	42	12	9	11	11	3	34	1	0	1	1	1	.50	4	.248	.322	.400
2005	Col	NL	101	305	80	10	3	9	(5	4)	123	38	47	44	43	7	70	0	0	3	2	2	.50	5	.262	.350	.403
2006	Col	NL	150	499	146	33	6	22	(6	16)	257	67	84	85	74	11	123	0	0	2	5	5	.50	8	.293	.383	.515
2007	Col	NL	152	516	150	33	4	29	(19	10)	278	80	116	103	81	11	137	3	1	5	0	2	.00	13	.291	.387	.539
2008	Col	NL	138	488	138	24	4	25	(14	11)	243	69	85	86	76	6	134	3	0	2	2	2	.50	7	.283	.381	.498
2009	Col	NL	145	501	143	42	3	23	(9	14)	260	82	86	91	79	7	145	4	0	4	1	3	.25	18	.285	.384	.519
2010	2 Tms		103	298	73	21	2	9	(6	3)	125	31	44	35	42	4	85	2	0	4	2	1	.67	5	.245	.338	.419
2011	SD	NL	62	195	45	10	0	4	(3	1)	67	19	19	16	19	2	68	1	0	1	0	0	-	7	.231	.301	.344
10	Col	NL	88	259	66	21	2	7	(6	1)	112	24	37	30	36	4	68	1	0	4	2	1	.67	4	.255	.343	.432
10	TB	AL	15	39	7	0	0	2	(0	2)	13	7	7	5	6	0	17	1	0	0	0	0	-	1	.179	.304	.333
	Postseason		13	43	11	0	1	1	(1	0)	16	4	4	6	8	0	17	0	0	0	0	0	-	0	.256	.373	.372
8 ML YEARS			893	2907	801	176	23	124	(63	61)	1395	398	490	471	425	47	796	14	1	22	13	16	.45	67	.276	.368	.480

Brett Hayes

Bats: R Throws: R Pos: C-50; PH-11; PR-11; 1B-1; LF-1; RF-1

Ht: 6'1" Wt: 205 Born: 2/13/1984 Age: 28

Year	Team	Lg	G	AB	H	2B	3B	HR	(Hm	Rd)	TB	R	RBI	RC	TBB	IBB	SO	HBP	SH	SF	SB	CS	SB%	GDP	Avg	OBP	Slg
2009	Fla	NL	14	11	3	1	0	1	(0	1)	7	5	2	1	0	0	4	1	0	0	0	0	-	1	.273	.333	.636
2010	Fla	NL	26	77	16	6	1	2	(1	1)	30	6	6	7	6	1	26	0	0	0	0	0	-	1	.208	.265	.390
2011	Fla	NL	64	130	30	9	0	5	(3	2)	54	19	16	13	11	2	39	1	0	3	0	0	-	0	.231	.291	.415
3 ML YEARS			104	218	49	16	1	8	(4	4)	91	30	24	21	17	3	69	1	3	0	0	0	-	2	.225	.284	.417

Jerad Head

JERR-edd

Bats: R Throws: R Pos: LF-9; PH-1; PR-1

Ht: 6'1" Wt: 205 Born: 11/15/1982 Age: 29

Year	Team	Lg	G	AB	H	2B	3B	HR	(Hm	Rd)	TB	R	RBI	RC	TBB	IBB	SO	HBP	SH	SF	SB	CS	SB%	GDP	Avg	OBP	Slg
2006	Lk Cty	A	1	4	0	0	0	0	(-	-)	0	1	0	0	0	0	1	0	0	0	0	0	-	0	.000	.000	.000
2006	Burlgtn	A	59	240	59	12	5	10	(-	-)	111	44	52	36	16	3	41	6	0	1	7	2	.78	4	.246	.308	.463
2007	Knstn	A+	83	252	67	17	3	5	(-	-)	105	39	32	43	19	1	56	17	2	1	7	3	.70	5	.266	.378	.417
2008	Knstn	A+	92	307	73	17	4	11	(-	-)	131	53	46	44	25	1	58	12	2	2	14	6	.70	5	.238	.318	.427
2008	Buffalo	AAA	3	7	2	1	0	1	(-	-)	6	1	2	2	1	0	1	0	0	0	0	0	-	0	.286	.375	.857
2008	Akron	AA	2	7	1	0	0	0	(-	-)	1	0	1	0	1	0	1	0	0	0	0	0	-	0	.143	.250	.143
2009	Akron	AA	98	327	92	23	4	6	(-	-)	141	49	47	51	23	1	72	12	4	0	6	2	.75	4	.281	.349	.431

Year	Team	Lg	G	AB	H	2B	3B	HR	(Hm	Rd)	TB	R	RBI	RC	TBB	IBB	SO	HBP	SH	SF	SB	CS	SB%	GDP	Avg	OBP	Slg
2010	Clmbs	AAA	21	74	19	9	0	2	(-	-)	34	12	15	11	5	0	20	3	0	1	0	0	-	4	.257	.325	.459
2010	Akron	AA	65	237	74	18	0	15	(-	-)	137	47	51	49	18	0	46	4	1	3	2	1	.67	11	.312	.366	.578
2011	Clmbs	AAA	114	422	120	28	1	24	(-	-)	222	67	70	75	25	2	99	11	1	4	3	1	.75	11	.284	.338	.526
2011	Cle	AL	10	24	3	1	0	0	(0	0)	4	2	1	1	0	0	5	1	0	0	1	0	1.00	0	.125	.160	.167

Chase Headley

Bats: B **Throws:** R **Pos:** 3B-107; PH-7; PR-1   HEDD-lee   **Ht:** 6'2" **Wt:** 202 **Born:** 5/9/1984 **Age:** 28

Year	Team	Lg	G	AB	H	2B	3B	HR	(Hm	Rd)	TB	R	RBI	RC	TBB	IBB	SO	HBP	SH	SF	SB	CS	SB%	GDP	Avg	OBP	Slg
2007	SD	NL	8	18	4	1	0	0	(0	0)	5	1	0	1	2	0	4	1	0	0	0	0	-	2	.222	.333	.278
2008	SD	NL	91	331	89	19	2	9	(4	5)	139	34	38	42	30	1	104	5	0	2	4	1	.80	5	.269	.337	.420
2009	SD	NL	156	543	142	31	2	12	(7	5)	213	62	64	68	62	3	133	5	0	2	10	2	.83	19	.262	.342	.392
2010	SD	NL	161	610	161	29	3	11	(3	8)	229	77	58	70	56	3	139	3	1	4	17	5	.77	11	.264	.327	.375
2011	SD	NL	113	381	110	28	1	4	(1	3)	152	43	44	61	52	8	92	2	1	3	13	2	.87	6	.289	.374	.399
5 ML YEARS			529	1883	506	108	8	36	(15	21)	738	217	204	242	202	15	472	16	2	11	44	10	.81	43	.269	.343	.392

Aaron Heilman

Pitches: R **Bats:** R **Pos:** RP-32   HYLE-man   **Ht:** 6'5" **Wt:** 225 **Born:** 11/11/1978 **Age:** 33

Year	Team	Lg	G	GS	CG	GF	IP	BFP	H	R	ER	HR	SH	SF	HB	TBB	IBB	SO	WP	Bk	W	L	Pct	Sh	Sv-Op Hld	ERC	ERA
2011	LV*	AAA	9	0	0	2	9.2	48	14	9	9	1	2	0	0	6	0	8	1	0	0	0	-	0	0- -	7.76	8.38
2011	Indy*	AAA	7	0	0	2	8.2	31	3	0	0	0	0	0	0	3	0	6	0	0	2	0	1.000	0	1- -	0.76	0.00
2003	NYM	NL	14	13	0	0	65.1	315	79	53	49	13	5	3	3	41	2	51	5	0	2	7	.222	0	0-0 0	7.16	6.75
2004	NYM	NL	5	5	0	0	28.0	119	27	17	17	4	1	0	0	13	0	22	0	0	1	3	.250	0	0-0 0	4.54	5.46
2005	NYM	NL	53	7	1	20	108.0	439	87	40	38	6	4	1	6	37	4	106	1	1	5	3	.625	1	5-6 5	2.74	3.17
2006	NYM	NL	74	0	0	14	87.0	356	73	37	35	5	7	2	3	28	2	73	5	0	4	5	.444	0	0-5 27	2.76	3.62
2007	NYM	NL	81	0	0	28	86.0	352	72	36	29	8	4	2	5	20	1	63	2	0	7	7	.500	0	1-6 22	2.71	3.03
2008	NYM	NL	78	0	0	23	76.0	356	75	48	44	10	8	2	9	46	8	80	2	0	3	8	.273	0	3-8 15	5.26	5.21
2009	ChC	NL	70	0	0	11	72.1	313	68	34	33	9	9	4	1	34	4	65	4	0	4	4	.500	0	1-7 10	4.16	4.11
2010	Ari	NL	70	0	0	26	72.0	316	73	37	36	9	2	2	5	26	4	55	8	0	5	8	.385	0	6-14 12	4.32	4.50
2011	Ari	NL	32	0	0	10	35.1	164	48	28	27	8	1	0	1	11	0	33	0	0	4	1	.800	0	0-1 5	6.88	6.88
Postseason			6	0	0	1	7.1	30	7	3	3	2	0	0	0	1	1	6	1	0	0	1	.000	0	0-0 1	3.60	3.68
9 ML YEARS			477	25	1	132	630.0	2730	602	330	308	72	41	16	33	256	25	548	27	1	35	46	.432	1	16-47 96	4.08	4.40

Chris Heisey

Bats: R **Throws:** R **Pos:** LF-88; PH-36; CF-18; RF-10; PR-1   HY-zee   **Ht:** 6'0" **Wt:** 224 **Born:** 12/14/1984 **Age:** 27

Year	Team	Lg	G	AB	H	2B	3B	HR	(Hm	Rd)	TB	R	RBI	RC	TBB	IBB	SO	HBP	SH	SF	SB	CS	SB%	GDP	Avg	OBP	Slg
2006	Billings	R+	70	245	70	10	0	6	(-	-)	98	46	37	38	28	0	33	2	9	1	11	5	.69	4	.286	.362	.400
2007	Dayton	A	104	374	108	24	2	9	(-	-)	163	60	46	60	25	0	57	10	5	0	19	5	.79	5	.289	.350	.436
2007	Srsota	A+	12	43	15	1	0	1	(-	-)	19	6	5	8	4	0	6	0	1	1	3	1	.75	1	.349	.396	.442
2008	Srsota	A+	117	436	125	31	7	7	(-	-)	191	77	51	82	57	2	69	11	8	3	27	2	.93	2	.287	.381	.438
2008	Chatt	AA	19	79	25	6	1	2	(-	-)	39	11	10	14	3	0	15	0	0	0	5	0	1.00	1	.316	.341	.494
2009	Carlina	AA	71	271	94	18	2	13	(-	-)	155	54	40	66	34	1	34	5	2	2	13	1	.93	3	.347	.426	.572
2009	Lsvlle	AAA	63	245	68	17	1	9	(-	-)	114	37	33	39	14	0	43	5	2	5	8	2	.80	1	.278	.323	.465
2010	Lsvlle	AAA	20	79	19	3	0	4	(-	-)	34	6	13	11	7	0	23	1	1	1	2	0	1.00	1	.241	.307	.430
2011	Lsvlle	AAA	4	12	1	0	0	1	(-	-)	4	1	2	0	0	0	5	0	0	1	0	0	-	0	.083	.077	.333
2010	Cin	NL	97	201	51	10	1	8	(2	6)	87	33	21	22	16	1	57	6	1	2	1	2	.33	3	.254	.324	.433
2011	Cin	NL	120	279	71	9	1	18	(11	7)	136	44	50	40	19	3	78	5	1	4	6	1	.86	1	.254	.309	.487
Postseason			1	2	0	0	0	0	(0	0)	0	0	0	0	0	0	1	0	0	0	0	0	-	0	.000	.000	.000
2 ML YEARS			217	480	122	19	2	26	(13	13)	223	77	71	62	35	4	135	11	2	6	7	3	.70	4	.254	.316	.465

Jeremy Hellickson

Pitches: R **Bats:** R **Pos:** SP-29   **Ht:** 6'1" **Wt:** 185 **Born:** 4/8/1987 **Age:** 25

Year	Team	Lg	G	GS	CG	GF	IP	BFP	H	R	ER	HR	SH	SF	HB	TBB	IBB	SO	WP	Bk	W	L	Pct	Sh	Sv-Op Hld	ERC	ERA
2005	Princtn	R+	4	0	0	1	6.0	27	6	4	4	1	0	0	1	1	0	11	0	0	0	0	-	0	0- -	4.00	6.00
2006	HudVal	A-	15	14	0	0	77.2	309	55	24	21	3	1	0	6	16	0	96	4	0	4	3	.571	0	0- -	1.78	2.43
2007	Clmbs	A	21	21	1	0	111.1	446	87	36	33	7	1	2	3	34	0	106	4	0	13	3	.813	0	0- -	2.47	2.67
2008	VeroB	A+	14	14	0	0	76.2	296	64	19	17	7	0	1	4	5	0	83	3	1	7	1	.875	0	0- -	2.15	2.00
2008	Mont	AA	13	13	0	0	75.1	308	84	36	33	15	3	0	2	15	1	79	1	0	4	4	.500	0	0- -	4.90	3.94
2009	Mont	AA	11	11	0	0	56.2	226	41	16	15	4	0	1	4	14	0	62	1	0	3	1	.750	0	0- -	2.16	2.38
2009	Drhm	AAA	9	9	0	0	57.1	220	31	19	16	4	2	2	4	15	0	70	2	0	6	1	.857	0	0- -	1.47	2.51
2010	Drhm	AAA	21	21	0	0	117.2	483	103	35	32	5	5	3	7	35	0	123	0	0	12	3	.800	0	0- -	2.90	2.45
2010	Charltt	A+	1	0	0	0	1.2	11	4	4	4	0	0	0	0	2	0	4	0	0	0	0	-	0	0- -	15.90	21.60
2010	TB	AL	10	4	0	0	36.1	149	32	14	14	5	0	1	2	8	2	33	2	0	4	0	1.000	0	0-1 0	3.10	3.47
2011	TB	AL	29	29	2	0	189.0	774	146	64	62	21	1	2	4	72	8	117	8	1	13	10	.565	1	0-0 0	2.89	2.95
2 ML YEARS			39	33	2	0	225.1	923	178	78	76	26	1	3	6	80	10	150	10	1	17	10	.630	1	0-1 0	2.92	3.04

Wes Helms

Bats: R **Throws:** R **Pos:** PH-39; 3B-33; 1B-5; 2B-2   **Ht:** 6'4" **Wt:** 227 **Born:** 5/12/1976 **Age:** 36

Year	Team	Lg	G	AB	H	2B	3B	HR	(Hm	Rd)	TB	R	RBI	RC	TBB	IBB	SO	HBP	SH	SF	SB	CS	SB%	GDP	Avg	OBP	Slg
2011	Gwnntt*	AAA	9	34	6	0	0	0	(-	-)	6	2	3	1	3	0	9	2	0	1	0	0	-	0	.176	.275	.176
1998	Atl	NL	7	13	4	1	0	1	(0	1)	8	2	2	2	0	0	4	0	0	0	0	0	-	0	.308	.308	.615
2000	Atl	NL	6	5	1	0	0	0	(0	0)	1	0	0	0	0	0	2	0	0	0	0	0	-	0	.200	.200	.200
2001	Atl	NL	100	216	48	10	3	10	(6	4)	94	28	36	27	21	2	56	1	0	1	1	1	.50	3	.222	.293	.435
2002	Atl	NL	85	210	51	16	0	6	(4	2)	85	20	22	15	11	2	57	3	1	6	1	1	.50	5	.243	.283	.405
2003	Mil	NL	134	476	124	21	0	23	(16	7)	214	56	67	66	43	3	131	10	0	7	0	1	.00	10	.261	.330	.450
2004	Mil	NL	92	274	72	13	1	4	(3	1)	99	24	28	28	24	1	60	5	1	2	0	1	.00	10	263	.331	.361
2005	Mil	NL	95	168	50	13	1	4	(2	2)	77	18	24	26	14	0	30	3	0	3	0	1	.00	7	.298	.356	.458
2006	Fla	NL	140	240	79	19	5	10	(4	6)	138	30	47	45	21	1	55	6	6	5	0	4	.00	7	.329	.390	.575
2007	Phi	NL	112	280	69	19	0	5	(3	2)	103	21	39	24	19	2	62	3	2	4	0	0	-	10	.246	.297	.368
2008	Fla	NL	132	251	61	11	0	5	(1	4)	87	28	31	29	17	0	65	5	0	5	0	0	-	6	.243	.299	.347
2009	Fla	NL	113	214	58	11	0	3	(1	2)	78	18	33	26	13	1	54	3	1	3	1	1	.50	10	.271	.318	.364
2010	Fla	NL	127	254	56	12	4	4	(1	3)	88	25	39	35	26	1	76	4	0	3	0	2	.00	7	.220	.300	.346
2011	Fla	NL	69	110	21	5	0	0	(0	0)	26	10	6	6	11	1	35	2	1	0	0	0	-	2	.191	.276	.236
Postseason			3	2	0	0	0	0	(0	0)	0	1	0	0	1	0	0	0	0	0	0	0	-	0	.000	.333	.000
13 ML YEARS			1212	2711	694	151	14	75	(41	34)	1098	280	374	329	220	14	687	45	12	39	3	12	.20	77	.256	.318	.405

Todd Helton

Bats: L **Throws:** L **Pos:** 1B-119; PH-5   **Ht:** 6'2" **Wt:** 215 **Born:** 8/20/1973 **Age:** 38

Year	Team	Lg	G	AB	H	2B	3B	HR	(Hm	Rd)	TB	R	RBI	RC	TBB	IBB	SO	HBP	SH	SF	SB	CS	SB%	GDP	Avg	OBP	Slg
1997	Col	NL	35	93	26	2	1	5	(3	2)	45	13	11	15	8	0	11	0	0	0	0	1	.00	1	.280	.337	.484
1998	Col	NL	152	530	167	37	1	25	(13	12)	281	78	97	101	53	5	54	6	1	5	3	3	.50	15	.315	.380	.530
1999	Col	NL	159	578	185	39	5	35	(23	12)	339	114	113	124	68	6	77	6	0	4	7	6	.54	14	.320	.395	.587
2000	Col	NL	160	580	216	59	2	42	(27	15)	405	138	147	169	103	22	61	4	0	10	5	3	.63	12	.372	.463	.698
2001	Col	NL	159	587	197	54	2	49	(27	22)	402	132	146	157	98	15	104	5	1	5	7	5	.58	14	.336	.432	.685
2002	Col	NL	156	553	182	39	4	30	(18	12)	319	107	109	127	99	21	91	5	0	10	5	1	.83	10	.329	.429	.577
2003	Col	NL	160	583	209	49	5	33	(23	10)	367	135	117	160	111	21	72	2	0	7	0	4	.00	19	.358	.458	.630
2004	Col	NL	154	547	190	49	2	32	(21	11)	339	115	96	143	127	19	72	3	0	6	3	0	1.00	14	.347	.469	.620
2005	Col	NL	144	509	163	45	2	20	(13	7)	272	92	79	114	106	22	80	9	1	1	3	0	1.00	14	.320	.445	.534
2006	Col	NL	145	546	165	40	5	15	(8	7)	260	94	81	118	91	15	64	6	0	6	3	2	.60	10	.302	.404	.476
2007	Col	NL	154	557	178	42	2	17	(9	8)	275	86	91	115	116	16	74	2	0	7	0	1	.00	15	.320	.434	.494
2008	Col	NL	83	299	79	16	0	7	(5	2)	116	39	29	45	61	8	50	1	0	0	0	0	-	9	.264	.391	.388
2009	Col	NL	151	544	177	38	3	15	(10	5)	266	79	86	108	89	5	73	2	0	10	0	1	.00	15	.325	.416	.489
2010	Col	NL	118	398	102	18	1	8	(4	4)	146	48	37	51	67	3	90	2	0	6	0	0	-	10	.256	.362	.367
2011	Col	NL	124	421	127	27	0	14	(8	6)	196	59	69	68	59	5	71	3	0	8	0	1	.00	6	.302	.385	.466
Postseason			15	57	12	2	1	0	(0	0)	16	11	4	2	8	0	11	0	0	0	0	0	-	0	.211	.303	.281
15 ML YEARS			2054	7325	2363	554	35	347	(212	135)	4028	1329	1308	1615	1256	183	1044	56	3	85	36	28	.56	176	.323	.421	.550

Mark Hendrickson

Pitches: L **Bats:** L **Pos:** RP-8   **Ht:** 6'9" **Wt:** 240 **Born:** 6/23/1974 **Age:** 38

Year	Team	Lg	G	GS	CG	GF	IP	BFP	H	R	ER	HR	SH	SF	HB	TBB	IBB	SO	WP	Bk	W	L	Pct	Sh	Sv-Op	Hld	ERC	ERA
2011	Norfolk*	AAA	24	0	0	5	59.2	243	52	22	19	9	2	0	0	16	1	29	1	0	2	4	.333	0	0- -	1	3.17	2.87
2002	Tor	AL	16	4	0	0	36.2	142	25	11	10	1	2	2	2	12	3	21	0	0	3	0	1.000	0	0-1	1	1.90	2.45
2003	Tor	AL	30	30	1	0	158.1	703	207	111	97	24	1	8	0	40	3	76	4	0	9	9	.500	1	0-0	0	5.64	5.51
2004	TB	AL	32	30	2	1	183.1	803	211	113	98	21	4	5	7	46	5	87	5	2	10	15	.400	0	0-0	0	4.51	4.81
2005	TB	AL	31	31	1	0	178.1	796	227	126	117	24	8	7	2	49	1	89	4	1	11	8	.579	0	0-0	0	5.44	5.90
2006	2 Tms		31	25	1	0	164.2	719	173	87	77	17	5	4	4	62	0	99	6	1	6	15	.286	1	0-0	1	4.38	4.21
2007	LAD	NL	39	15	0	4	122.2	532	142	75	71	15	12	4	1	29	4	92	4	0	4	8	.333	0	0-1	2	4.42	5.21
2008	Fla	NL	36	19	0	4	133.2	590	148	87	81	17	9	5	5	48	7	81	4	0	7	8	.467	0	0-3	3	4.78	5.45
2009	Bal	AL	53	11	0	12	105.0	457	116	59	51	16	2	5	2	33	4	61	2	1	6	5	.545	0	1-3	2	4.71	4.37
2010	Bal	AL	52	1	0	6	75.1	339	97	47	44	9	3	3	3	20	4	55	2	0	1	6	.143	0	0-2	8	5.40	5.26
2011	Bal	AL	8	0	0	1	11.0	51	15	7	7	1	1	1	0	6	1	5	0	0	1	0	1.000	0	0-0	0	6.85	5.73
06	TB	AL	13	13	1	0	89.2	377	81	42	38	10	2	3	2	34	0	51	4	0	4	8	.333	1	0-0	0	3.65	3.81
06	LAD	NL	18	12	0	0	75.0	342	92	45	39	7	3	1	2	28	0	48	2	1	2	7	.222	0	0-0	1	5.29	4.68
Postseason			3	0	0	0	2.2	10	1	0	0	0	0	0	1	1	0	1	0	0	0	0	-	0	0-0	0	1.70	0.00
10 ML YEARS			328	166	5	28	1169.0	5132	1361	723	653	145	47	44	26	345	32	666	31	5	58	74	.439	2	1-7	17	4.80	5.03

Liam Hendriks

Pitches: R **Bats:** R **Pos:** SP-4   **Ht:** 6'1" **Wt:** 190 **Born:** 2/10/1989 **Age:** 23

Year	Team	Lg	G	GS	CG	GF	IP	BFP	H	R	ER	HR	SH	SF	HB	TBB	IBB	SO	WP	Bk	W	L	Pct	Sh	Sv-Op Hld	ERC	ERA
2007	Twins	R	10	10	0	0	44.0	182	41	14	10	2	0	0	1	11	0	52	0	0	4	2	.667	0	0- -	2.86	2.05
2009	Elizab	R	3	3	0	0	17.0	71	19	8	7	0	0	0	0	1	0	13	0	0	2	0	1.000	0	0- -	2.69	3.71
2009	Beloit	A	11	11	0	0	66.2	284	73	34	26	3	3	1	2	15	0	62	5	1	3	5	.375	0	0- -	3.65	3.51
2010	Beloit	A	6	6	0	0	34.0	123	16	6	5	0	1	1	4	4	0	39	2	0	2	1	.667	0	0- -	0.70	1.32
2010	FtMyrs	A+	13	12	1	0	74.2	292	63	20	16	2	2	1	1	8	0	66	3	0	6	3	.667	0	0- -	1.83	1.93
2011	NwBrit	AA	16	15	2	0	90.0	365	85	30	27	5	0	1	3	18	1	81	0	0	8	2	.800	0	0- -	2.88	2.70
2011	Roch	AAA	9	9	0	0	49.1	199	52	26	25	0	2	4	2	3	0	30	1	1	4	4	.500	0	0- -	2.62	4.56
2011	Min	AL	4	4	0	0	23.1	100	29	16	16	3	0	1	0	6	0	16	1	0	0	2	.000	0	0-0	5.26	6.17

Clay Hensley

Pitches: R Bats: R Pos: RP-28; SP-9   Ht: 5'11" Wt: 188 Born: 8/31/1979 Age: 32

			HOW MUCH HE PITCHED					WHAT HE GAVE UP										THE RESULTS						
Year	Team	Lg	G	GS	CG	GF	IP	BFP	H	R	ER	HR	SH	SF	HB	TBB	IBB	SO	WP	Bk	W	L	Pct	Sh	Sv-Op Hld	ERC	ERA
2011	Mrlns*	R	1	0	0	0	3.1	12	2	1	1	0	0	0	0	0	0	6	0	0	0	0	-	0	0- - -	0.75	2.70
2011	Jupiter*	A+	1	1	0	0	4.0	14	2	2	2	1	0	0	0	0	0	2	0	0	0	1	.000	0	0- - -	1.13	4.50
2011	Jaxnvl*	AA	1	1	0	0	4.1	19	5	1	1	0	0	0	0	1	0	7	0	0	0	0	-	0	0- - -	3.47	2.08
2005	SD	NL	24	1	0	5	47.2	189	33	12	9	0	1	2	0	17	2	28	2	0	1	1	.500	0	0-0 2	1.70	1.70
2006	SD	NL	37	29	1	2	187.0	787	174	82	77	15	10	3	3	76	7	122	3	0	11	12	.478	1	0-1 1	3.64	3.71
2007	SD	NL	13	9	0	1	50.0	238	62	40	38	5	2	1	1	32	2	30	4	1	2	3	.400	0	0-0 0	6.54	6.84
2008	SD	NL	32	1	0	8	39.0	173	36	27	23	2	1	3	1	25	3	26	1	0	1	2	.333	0	0-1 3	4.23	5.31
2010	Fla	NL	68	0	0	23	75.0	307	54	20	18	3	3	1	4	29	4	77	2	0	3	4	.429	0	7-10 22	2.29	2.16
2011	Fla	NL	37	9	0	7	67.2	297	62	41	39	9	2	1	4	30	1	46	0	0	6	7	.462	0	0-2 8	4.16	5.19
	Postseason		5	0	0	1	7.1	32	6	2	2	0	1	0	0	4	0	1	0	0	0	0	-	0	0-0 0	2.87	2.45
	6 ML YEARS		211	49	1	46	466.1	1991	421	222	204	34	19	11	13	209	19	329	12	1	24	29	.453	1	7-14 36	3.60	3.94

Jeremy Hermida

Bats: L Throws: R Pos: RF-14; PH-13; LF-3   her-MEE-dah   Ht: 6'3" Wt: 222 Born: 1/30/1984 Age: 28

									BATTING											BASERUNNING				AVERAGES		
Year	Team	Lg	G	AB	H	2B	3B	HR	(Hm	Rd)	TB	R	RBI	RC	TBB	IBB	SO	HBP	SH	SF	SB	CS	SB%	GDP	Avg	OBP	Slg
2011	Lsvlle*	AAA	105	395	126	28	1	17	(-	-)	207	67	55	83	46	3	97	8	0	1	3	0	1.00	3	.319	.400	.524
2005	Fla	NL	23	41	12	2	0	4	(4	0)	26	9	11	10	6	1	12	0	0	0	0	1	1.00	1	.293	.383	.634
2006	Fla	NL	99	307	77	19	1	5	(3	2)	113	37	28	38	33	3	70	5	2	1	4	1	.80	6	.251	.332	.368
2007	Fla	NL	123	429	127	32	1	18	(8	10)	215	54	63	69	47	2	105	4	1	3	3	4	.43	10	.296	.369	.501
2008	Fla	NL	142	502	125	22	3	17	(4	13)	204	74	61	65	48	5	138	7	1	1	6	1	.86	12	.249	.323	.406
2009	Fla	NL	129	429	111	14	2	13	(4	9)	168	48	47	57	56	4	101	4	0	2	5	2	.71	6	.259	.348	.392
2010	2 Tms	AL	73	222	48	12	0	6	(4	2)	78	19	29	20	16	0	58	0	0	1	1	0	1.00	6	.216	.268	.351
2011	2 Tms	NL	30	58	11	2	1	2	(2	0)	21	5	9	8	7	0	26	1	0	0	0	0	-	0	.190	.288	.362
10	Bos	AL	52	158	32	8	0	5	(4	1)	55	14	27	17	12	0	45	0	0	1	1	0	1.00	1	.203	.257	.348
10	Oak	AL	21	64	16	4	0	1	(0	1)	23	5	2	3	4	0	13	0	0	0	0	0	-	5	.250	.294	.359
11	Cin	NL	10	18	2	0	0	0	(1	0)	5	2	3	1	0	0	7	0	0	0	0	0	-	0	.111	.111	.278
11	SD	NL	20	40	9	2	1	1	(1	0)	16	3	6	7	7	0	19	1	0	0	0	0	-	0	.225	.354	.400
	7 ML YEARS		619	1988	511	103	8	65	(29	36)	825	246	248	267	213	15	510	21	4	8	21	8	.72	41	.257	.334	.415

David Hernandez

Pitches: R Bats: R Pos: RP-74   Ht: 6'2" Wt: 250 Born: 5/13/1985 Age: 27

			HOW MUCH HE PITCHED					WHAT HE GAVE UP										THE RESULTS						
Year	Team	Lg	G	GS	CG	GF	IP	BFP	H	R	ER	HR	SH	SF	HB	TBB	IBB	SO	WP	Bk	W	L	Pct	Sh	Sv-Op Hld	ERC	ERA
2009	Bal	AL	20	19	0	0	101.1	462	118	62	61	27	2	3	1	46	0	68	3	0	4	10	.286	0	0-0 0	6.55	5.42
2010	Bal	AL	41	8	0	16	79.1	348	72	40	38	9	1	3	4	42	4	72	9	0	8	8	.500	0	2-6 2	4.28	4.31
2011	Ari	NL	74	0	0	28	69.1	291	49	27	26	4	3	2	2	30	1	77	7	1	5	3	.625	0	11-14 23	2.40	3.38
	3 ML YEARS		135	27	0	44	250.0	1101	239	129	125	40	6	8	7	118	5	217	19	1	17	21	.447	0	13-20 25	4.58	4.50

Diory Hernandez

Bats: R Throws: R Pos: PH-15; 3B-6; SS-3; 1B-1   dee-OR-ee   Ht: 6'0" Wt: 185 Born: 4/8/1984 Age: 28

									BATTING											BASERUNNING				AVERAGES		
Year	Team	Lg	G	AB	H	2B	3B	HR	(Hm	Rd)	TB	R	RBI	RC	TBB	IBB	SO	HBP	SH	SF	SB	CS	SB%	GDP	Avg	OBP	Slg
2011	Gwnntt*	AAA	79	273	55	12	1	5	(-	-)	84	19	26	18	7	0	46	3	5	1	2	2	.50	10	.201	.229	.308
2009	Atl	NL	33	85	12	3	0	1	(1	0)	18	6	6	6	3	3	22	0	2	0	0	1	.00	4	.141	.198	.212
2010	Atl	NL	20	9	1	0	0	0	(1	0)	4	5	1	0	0	0	4	0	1	0	0	0	-	0	.111	.111	.444
2011	Atl	NL	22	33	7	1	0	1	(0	1)	11	4	4	3	0	0	5	0	2	0	0	0	-	0	.212	.212	.333
	Postseason		2	1	0	0	0	0	(0	0)	0	0	0	0	0	0	1	0	0	0	0	0	-	0	.000	.000	.000
	3 ML YEARS		75	127	20	4	0	3	(2	1)	33	15	11	3	6	3	31	0	5	0	0	1	.00	4	.157	.195	.260

Felix Hernandez

Pitches: R Bats: R Pos: SP-33   Ht: 6'3" Wt: 225 Born: 4/8/1986 Age: 26

			HOW MUCH HE PITCHED					WHAT HE GAVE UP										THE RESULTS						
Year	Team	Lg	G	GS	CG	GF	IP	BFP	H	R	ER	HR	SH	SF	HB	TBB	IBB	SO	WP	Bk	W	L	Pct	Sh	Sv-Op Hld	ERC	ERA
2005	Sea	AL	12	12	0	0	84.1	328	61	26	25	5	1	2	2	23	0	77	3	0	4	4	.500	0	0-0 0	2.08	2.67
2006	Sea	AL	31	31	2	0	191.0	816	195	105	96	23	2	3	6	60	2	176	11	0	12	14	.462	1	0-0 0	4.11	4.52
2007	Sea	AL	30	30	1	0	190.1	808	209	88	83	20	6	1	3	53	4	165	7	1	14	7	.667	1	0-0 0	4.27	3.92
2008	Sea	AL	31	31	2	0	200.2	857	198	85	77	17	4	6	8	80	7	175	8	1	9	11	.450	0	0-0 0	4.05	3.45
2009	Sea	AL	34	34	2	0	238.2	977	200	81	66	15	6	11	8	71	0	217	17	1	19	5	.792	1	0-0 0	2.72	2.49
2010	Sea	AL	34	34	6	0	249.2	1001	194	80	63	17	6	3	6	70	1	232	14	1	13	12	.520	1	0-0 0	2.39	2.27
2011	Sea	AL	33	33	5	0	233.2	964	218	99	90	19	3	7	7	67	0	222	12	1	14	14	.500	1	0-0 0	3.31	3.47
	7 ML YEARS		205	205	18	0	1388.1	5751	1275	564	500	116	28	33	42	424	14	1264	72	5	85	67	.559	4	0-0 0	3.29	3.24

Livan Hernandez

Pitches: R Bats: R Pos: SP-29   lee-VAHN   Ht: 6'2" Wt: 245 Born: 2/20/1975 Age: 37

			HOW MUCH HE PITCHED					WHAT HE GAVE UP										THE RESULTS						
Year	Team	Lg	G	GS	CG	GF	IP	BFP	H	R	ER	HR	SH	SF	HB	TBB	IBB	SO	WP	Bk	W	L	Pct	Sh	Sv-Op Hld	ERC	ERA
1996	Fla	NL	1	0	0	0	3.0	13	3	0	0	0	0	0	0	2	0	2	0	0	0	0	-	0	0-0 0	4.60	0.00
1997	Fla	NL	17	17	0	0	96.1	405	81	39	34	5	4	7	3	38	1	72	0	0	9	3	.750	0	0-0 0	2.96	3.18
1998	Fla	NL	33	33	9	0	234.1	1040	265	133	123	37	8	5	6	104	8	162	4	3	10	12	.455	0	0-0 0	5.58	4.72
1999	2 Tms	NL	30	30	2	0	199.2	886	227	110	103	23	7	6	2	76	5	144	2	2	8	12	.400	0	0-0 0	4.88	4.64
2000	SF	NL	33	33	5	0	240.0	1030	254	114	100	22	12	9	4	73	3	165	3	0	17	11	.607	2	0-0 0	4.01	3.75

Year	Team	Lg	G	GS	CG	GF	IP	BFP	H	R	ER	HR	SH	SF	HB	TBB	IBB	SO	WP	Bk	W	L	Pct	Sh	Sv-Op	Hld	ERC	ERA
2001	SF	NL	34	34	2	0	226.2	1008	266	143	132	24	12	12	3	85	7	138	7	0	13	15	.464	0	0-0	0	5.03	5.24
2002	SF	NL	33	33	5	0	216.0	921	233	113	105	19	14	8	4	71	5	134	1	1	12	16	.429	3	0-0	0	4.26	4.38
2003	Mon	NL	33	33	8	0	233.1	967	225	92	83	27	6	4	10	57	3	178	6	1	15	10	.600	0	0-0	0	3.55	3.20
2004	Mon	NL	35	35	9	0	255.0	1053	234	105	102	26	11	4	10	83	9	186	1	0	11	15	.423	2	0-0	0	3.52	3.60
2005	Was	NL	35	35	2	0	246.1	1065	268	116	109	25	15	9	13	84	14	147	3	2	15	10	.600	0	0-0	0	4.54	3.98
2006	2 Tms	NL	34	34	0	0	216.0	959	246	125	116	29	16	8	4	78	6	128	1	0	13	13	.500	0	0-0	0	4.97	4.83
2007	Ari	NL	33	33	1	0	204.1	913	247	116	112	34	17	8	6	79	1	90	3	2	11	11	.500	0	0-0	0	5.94	4.93
2008	2 Tms	NL	31	31	2	0	180.0	811	257	129	121	25	5	9	2	43	4	67	3	1	13	11	.542	0	0-0	0	6.35	6.05
2009	2 Tms	NL	31	31	2	0	183.2	806	220	112	111	19	13	10	1	67	5	102	1	0	9	12	.429	0	0-0	0	5.17	5.44
2010	Was	NL	33	33	2	0	211.2	896	216	93	86	16	17	10	4	64	5	114	1	1	10	12	.455	1	0-0	0	3.69	3.66
2011	Was	NL	29	29	1	0	175.1	751	199	98	87	16	10	6	5	46	6	99	3	0	8	13	.381	1	0-0	0	4.34	4.47
99	Fla	NL	20	20	2	0	136.0	612	161	78	72	17	3	4	2	55	3	97	2	1	5	9	.357	0	0-0	0	5.37	4.76
99	SF	NL	10	10	0	0	63.2	274	66	32	31	6	4	2	0	21	2	47	0	1	3	3	.500	0	0-0	0	3.88	4.38
06	Was	NL	24	24	0	0	146.2	661	176	94	87	22	10	7	2	52	4	89	0	0	9	8	.529	0	0-0	0	5.38	5.34
06	Ari	NL	10	10	0	0	69.1	298	70	31	29	7	6	1	2	26	2	39	1	0	4	5	.444	0	0-0	0	4.13	3.76
08	Min	AL	23	23	2	0	139.2	627	199	93	85	18	4	9	1	29	3	54	2	1	10	8	.556	0	0-0	0	6.06	5.48
08	Col	NL	8	8	0	0	40.1	184	58	36	36	7	1	0	1	14	1	13	1	0	3	3	.500	0	0-0	0	7.38	8.03
09	NYM	NL	23	23	1	0	135.0	593	164	83	82	16	8	8	1	51	3	75	1	0	7	8	.467	0	0-0	0	5.50	5.47
09	Was	NL	8	8	1	0	48.2	213	56	29	29	3	5	2	0	16	2	27	0	0	2	4	.333	0	0-0	0	4.30	5.36
	Postseason		12	10	1	0	68.0	305	67	32	30	6	5	2	4	36	3	47	1	0	7	3	.700	0	0-0	0	4.56	3.97
	16 ML YEARS		475	474	50	0	3121.2	13524	3441	1638	1524	347	167	115	77	1050	82	1928	39	13	174	176	.497	9	0-0	0	4.58	4.39

Ramon Hernandez

Bats: R Throws: R Pos: C-82; PH-10; 1B-1
Ht: 6'0" Wt: 222 Born: 5/20/1976 Age: 36

Year	Team	Lg	G	AB	H	2B	3B	HR	(Hm	Rd)	TB	R	RBI	RC	TBB	IBB	SO	HBP	SH	SF	SB	CS	SB%	GDP	Avg	OBP	Slg
1999	Oak	AL	40	136	38	7	0	3	(1	2)	54	13	21	20	18	0	11	1	1	2	1	0	1.00	5	.279	.363	.397
2000	Oak	AL	143	419	101	19	0	14	(7	7)	162	52	62	49	38	1	64	7	10	5	1	0	1.00	14	.241	.311	.387
2001	Oak	AL	136	453	115	25	0	15	(5	10)	185	55	60	58	37	3	68	6	9	4	1	1	.50	10	.254	.316	.408
2002	Oak	AL	136	403	94	20	0	7	(3	4)	135	51	42	41	43	1	64	5	3	3	0	0	-	11	.233	.313	.335
2003	Oak	AL	140	483	132	24	1	21	(9	12)	221	70	78	69	33	2	79	12	2	6	0	0	-	14	.273	.331	.458
2004	SD	NL	111	384	106	23	0	18	(10	8)	183	45	63	50	35	0	45	5	4	4	1	0	1.00	16	.276	.341	.477
2005	SD	NL	99	369	107	19	2	12	(5	7)	166	36	58	44	18	0	40	1	1	3	1	0	1.00	14	.290	.322	.450
2006	Bal	AL	144	501	138	29	2	23	(17	6)	240	66	91	82	43	2	79	11	0	5	1	0	1.00	13	.275	.343	.479
2007	Bal	AL	106	364	94	18	0	9	(4	5)	139	40	62	56	36	1	59	6	0	3	1	3	.25	9	.258	.331	.382
2008	Bal	AL	133	463	119	22	1	15	(10	5)	188	49	65	59	32	3	62	5	1	6	0	0	-	9	.257	.308	.406
2009	Cin	NL	81	287	74	13	1	5	(2	3)	104	25	37	42	33	2	34	3	4	4	1	0	1.00	7	.258	.336	.362
2010	Cin	NL	97	313	93	18	1	7	(3	4)	134	30	48	49	29	1	49	5	3	2	0	0	-	8	.297	.364	.428
2011	Cin	NL	91	298	84	13	0	12	(6	6)	133	28	36	36	23	6	41	5	0	2	0	0	-	11	.282	.341	.446
	Postseason		25	76	16	3	0	1	(1	0)	22	6	6	7	5	0	13	3	2	0	0	0	-	2	.211	.286	.289
	13 ML YEARS		1457	4873	1295	250	8	161	(82	79)	2044	560	723	655	418	22	695	72	38	49	8	4	.67	141	.266	.330	.419

David Herndon

Pitches: R Bats: R Pos: RP-45
Ht: 6'5" Wt: 230 Born: 9/4/1985 Age: 26

Year	Team	Lg	G	GS	CG	GF	IP	BFP	H	R	ER	HR	SH	SF	HB	TBB	IBB	SO	WP	Bk	W	L	Pct	Sh	Sv-Op	Hld	ERC	ERA
2006	Orem	R+	14	14	0	0	69.1	283	65	25	17	6	2	0	2	10	0	36	2	0	5	2	.714	0	0- -	-	2.76	2.21
2007	CRpds	A	25	24	2	1	152.1	640	175	80	68	10	4	7	6	20	0	83	2	0	13	8	.619	0	0- -	-	3.79	4.02
2008	RCuca	A+	43	12	0	30	100.2	426	120	58	56	10	4	5	3	16	1	70	0	0	3	7	.300	0	17- -	-	4.36	5.01
2009	Ark	AA	50	0	0	30	65.1	271	70	25	22	9	7	0	2	14	3	35	0	0	5	6	.455	0	11- -	-	4.14	3.03
2011	LV	AAA	8	0	0	3	14.2	60	15	4	4	1	1	0	0	2	0	14	0	0	2	0	1.000	0	1- -	-	2.97	2.45
2010	Phi	NL	47	0	0	14	52.1	232	67	27	25	2	2	2	2	17	4	29	1	0	1	3	.250	0	0-1	1	5.06	4.30
2011	Phi	NL	45	0	0	22	57.0	243	54	26	21	9	7	1	2	24	7	39	3	0	1	4	.200	0	1-2	4	4.27	3.32
	2 ML YEARS		92	0	0	36	109.1	475	121	53	46	11	9	3	4	41	11	68	4	0	2	7	.222	0	1-3	5	4.65	3.79

Daniel Herrera

Pitches: L Bats: L Pos: RP-18
Ht: 5'6" Wt: 165 Born: 10/21/1984 Age: 27

Year	Team	Lg	G	GS	CG	GF	IP	BFP	H	R	ER	HR	SH	SF	HB	TBB	IBB	SO	WP	Bk	W	L	Pct	Sh	Sv-Op	Hld	ERC	ERA
2011	Lsvlle*	AAA	17	0	0	6	18.2	84	20	11	8	1	2	1	1	7	0	15	0	0	0	4	.000	0	1- -	-	4.14	3.86
2011	Nashv*	AAA	29	0	0	10	42.2	169	32	8	7	2	1	1	1	8	0	39	4	0	1	0	1.000	0	2- -	-	1.78	1.48
2008	Cin	NL	7	0	0	0	7.1	37	10	7	6	1	2	0	2	3	2	8	0	0	0	0	-	0	0-0	0	7.05	7.36
2009	Cin	NL	70	0	0	13	61.2	262	63	30	21	5	3	5	2	24	2	44	1	0	4	4	.500	0	0-0	9	4.20	3.06
2010	Cin	NL	36	0	0	8	23.0	104	31	10	10	2	0	2	0	6	0	14	0	0	1	3	.250	0	0-1	9	5.41	3.91
2011	2 Tms	NL	18	0	0	2	9.2	44	13	6	5	1	2	1	0	3	0	5	1	1	0	1	.000	0	0-0	1	5.75	4.66
11	Mil	NL	2	0	0	0	1.2	11	6	5	4	1	0	0	0	1	0	0	0	0	0	0	-	0	0-0	0	32.79	21.60
11	NYM	NL	16	0	0	2	8.0	33	7	1	1	0	2	1	0	2	0	5	1	1	0	1	.000	0	0-0	1	2.18	1.13
	4 ML YEARS		131	0	0	18	101.2	447	117	53	42	9	7	8	4	36	4	71	2	1	5	8	.385	0	0-1	19	4.81	3.72

Jonathan Herrera

Bats: B Throws: R Pos: 2B-62; PH-23; SS-21; 3B-9; PR-1
Ht: 5'9" Wt: 150 Born: 11/3/1984 Age: 27

Year	Team	Lg	G	AB	H	2B	3B	HR	(Hm	Rd)	TB	R	RBI	RC	TBB	IBB	SO	HBP	SH	SF	SB	CS	SB%	GDP	Avg	OBP	Slg
2008	Col	NL	28	61	14	1	1	0	(0	0)	17	5	3	6	4	0	10	0	1	0	1	1	.50	0	.230	.277	.279
2010	Col	NL	76	222	63	6	2	1	(0	1)	76	34	21	29	25	1	36	0	7	3	2	2	.50	2	.284	.352	.342
2011	Col	NL	104	281	68	5	1	3	(2	1)	84	28	14	24	28	0	40	1	10	0	4	4	.50	7	.242	.313	.299
	3 ML YEARS		208	564	145	12	4	4	(2	2)	177	67	38	59	57	1	86	1	18	3	7	7	.50	9	.257	.325	.314

Kelvin Herrera

Pitches: R Bats: R Pos: RP-2   Ht: 5'10" Wt: 188 Born: 12/31/1989 Age: 22

Year	Team	Lg	G	GS	CG	GF	IP	BFP	H	R	ER	HR	SH	SF	HB	TBB	IBB	SO	WP	Bk	W	L	Pct	Sh	Sv-Op	Hld	ERC	ERA
2008	Burlgtn	R	11	8	0	0	50.2	198	48	17	8	0	1	0	3	5	0	45	2	1	2	2	.500	0	0- -	-	2.36	1.42
2008	Burlgtn	A	3	1	0	1	12.2	53	13	4	3	0	0	1	1	2	0	7	1	0	2	0	1.000	0	0- -	-	2.91	2.13
2009	Burlgtn	A	1	1	0	0	5.0	17	3	0	0	0	0	0	0	0	0	1	0	0	1	0	1.000	0	0- -	-	0.80	0.00
2010	Burlgtn	A	8	8	0	0	41.1	173	38	20	20	2	2	2	4	15	0	40	1	0	2	3	.400	0	0- -	-	3.60	4.35
2011	Wilmg	A+	8	0	0	6	14.2	53	8	1	1	1	0	0	0	2	0	12	0	0	2	1	.667	0	1- -	-	1.09	0.61
2011	NWArk	AA	23	0	0	17	36.0	138	22	9	7	4	3	3	1	6	2	40	0	1	4	0	1.000	0	7- -	-	1.46	1.75
2011	Omha	AAA	14	0	0	10	17.0	70	12	5	4	1	0	0	0	7	0	18	0	0	1	0	1.000	0	6- -	-	2.28	2.12
2011	KC	AL	2	0	0	0	2.0	9	2	3	3	1	1	0	1	0	0	0	0	0	0	1	.000	0	0-0	1	7.30	13.50

Frank Herrmann

Pitches: R Bats: L Pos: RP-40   Ht: 6'4" Wt: 220 Born: 5/30/1984 Age: 28

Year	Team	Lg	G	GS	CG	GF	IP	BFP	H	R	ER	HR	SH	SF	HB	TBB	IBB	SO	WP	Bk	W	L	Pct	Sh	Sv-Op	Hld	ERC	ERA
2006	Lk Cty	A	26	26	0	0	122.1	540	122	61	53	8	7	1	17	47	0	89	5	0	4	6	.400	0	0- -	-	4.30	3.90
2007	Knstn	A+	26	26	3	0	146.0	623	163	75	65	15	5	7	11	28	1	88	2	1	11	5	.688	0	0- -	-	4.24	4.01
2008	Akron	AA	23	23	0	0	131.2	563	142	70	60	9	1	7	3	36	0	86	6	0	11	6	.647	0	0- -	-	3.89	4.10
2008	Knstn	A+	1	1	0	0	5.1	25	8	7	7	1	0	0	0	1	0	4	1	0	0	0	-	0	0- -	-	6.69	11.81
2008	Buffalo	AAA	2	2	0	0	13.0	55	11	3	2	1	3	0	0	6	0	14	0	0	0	2	.000	0	0- -	-	3.31	1.38
2009	Akron	AA	5	5	0	0	30.2	119	27	11	10	4	1	2	0	5	0	12	2	0	2	1	.667	0	0- -	-	2.81	2.93
2009	Clmbs	AAA	44	0	0	9	76.0	319	83	33	25	3	4	2	2	13	3	50	4	0	3	3	.000	0	2- -	-	3.32	2.96
2010	Clmbs	AAA	19	0	0	4	28.2	105	15	1	1	0	1	0	0	8	1	22	1	0	3	0	1.000	0	2- -	-	1.07	0.31
2011	Clmbs	AAA	9	0	0	1	10.2	48	13	7	7	1	0	2	0	4	0	12	1	0	0	0	-	0	0- -	-	5.18	5.91
2010	Cle	AL	40	0	0	8	44.2	189	48	22	20	6	1	2	2	9	0	24	2	0	0	1	.000	0	1-2	7	4.12	4.03
2011	Cle	AL	40	0	0	17	56.1	253	71	35	32	7	2	0	0	16	1	34	1	0	4	0	1.000	0	0-0	0	5.20	5.11
	2 ML YEARS		80	0	0	25	101.0	442	119	57	52	13	3	2	2	25	1	58	3	0	4	1	.800	0	1-2	7	4.72	4.63

Jason Heyward

Bats: L Throws: L Pos: RF-122; PH-7; PR-6   Ht: 6'5" Wt: 240 Born: 8/9/1989 Age: 22

Year	Team	Lg	G	AB	H	2B	3B	HR	(Hm	Rd)	TB	R	RBI	RC	TBB	IBB	SO	HBP	SH	SF	SB	CS	SB%	GDP	Avg	OBP	Slg
2007	Braves	R	8	27	8	4	0	1	(-	-)	15	1	5	5	2	0	4	1	0	1	1	1	.50	1	.296	.355	.556
2007	Danvle	R+	4	16	5	1	0	0	(-	-)	6	3	1	2	1	0	5	0	0	0	0	0	-	1	.313	.353	.375
2008	Rome	A	120	449	145	27	6	11	(-	-)	217	88	52	87	49	3	74	3	0	7	15	3	.83	4	.323	.388	.483
2008	MrtlBh	A+	7	22	4	2	0	0	(-	-)	6	3	4	1	2	0	4	0	0	1	0	0	-	1	.182	.240	.273
2009	MrtlBh	A+	49	189	56	12	0	10	(-	-)	98	34	31	37	21	1	30	2	0	2	4	0	1.00	2	.296	.369	.519
2009	Missi	AA	47	162	57	13	4	7	(-	-)	99	32	30	43	28	4	19	2	0	3	5	1	.83	1	.352	.446	.611
2009	Gwnntt	AAA	3	11	4	0	0	0	(-	-)	4	3	2	2	2	0	2	0	0	0	1	0	1.00	0	.364	.462	.364
2011	Gwnntt	AAA	2	6	1	1	0	0	(-	-)	2	1	0	0	1	0	1	0	0	0	0	0	-	0	.167	.286	.333
2010	Atl	NL	142	520	144	29	5	18	(9	9)	237	83	72	96	91	2	128	10	0	2	11	6	.65	13	.277	.393	.456
2011	Atl	NL	128	396	90	18	2	14	(5	9)	154	50	42	49	51	4	93	4	0	3	9	2	.82	7	.227	.319	.389
	Postseason		4	16	2	0	0	0	(0	0)	2	0	0	0	1	0	8	0	0	1	0	0	-	1	.125	.176	.125
	2 ML YEARS		270	916	234	47	7	32	(14	18)	391	133	114	145	142	6	221	14	0	5	20	8	.71	20	.255	.362	.427

Brandon Hicks

Bats: R Throws: R Pos: PH-9; 3B-6; SS-3; PR-1   Ht: 6'2" Wt: 200 Born: 9/14/1985 Age: 26

Year	Team	Lg	G	AB	H	2B	3B	HR	(Hm	Rd)	TB	R	RBI	RC	TBB	IBB	SO	HBP	SH	SF	SB	CS	SB%	GDP	Avg	OBP	Slg
2007	Danvle	R+	18	58	13	3	1	3	(-	-)	27	14	13	10	12	0	18	2	1	1	1	2	.33	1	.224	.370	.466
2007	Rome	A	37	128	40	11	0	4	(-	-)	63	26	15	28	27	2	26	1	0	1	5	3	.63	2	.313	.433	.492
2008	MrtlBh	A+	93	342	80	23	2	19	(-	-)	164	68	56	59	45	1	122	8	3	2	14	3	.82	9	.234	.335	.480
2008	Missi	AA	16	54	13	3	1	1	(-	-)	21	9	7	7	7	0	17	1	1	1	0	0	-	1	.241	.333	.389
2009	Missi	AA	128	464	110	25	4	10	(-	-)	173	63	48	62	53	1	131	5	8	4	17	1	.94	5	.237	.319	.373
2010	Gwnntt	AAA	77	261	55	9	1	7	(-	-)	87	27	22	24	20	1	74	5	1	0	10	6	.63	6	.211	.280	.333
2011	Gwnntt	AAA	104	361	91	14	1	18	(-	-)	161	52	50	55	41	0	137	3	2	0	8	3	.73	7	.252	.333	.446
2010	Atl	NL	16	5	0	0	0	0	(0	0)	0	7	0	0	1	0	2	0	0	0	0	0	-	0	.000	.167	.000
2011	Atl	NL	17	21	1	0	0	0	(0	0)	1	1	1	0	1	0	9	0	0	0	0	0	-	0	.048	.091	.048
	2 ML YEARS		33	26	1	0	0	0	(0	0)	1	8	1	0	2	0	11	0	0	0	0	0	-	0	.038	.107	.038

Aaron Hill

Bats: R Throws: R Pos: 2B-137; PH-2; PR-1   Ht: 5'11" Wt: 205 Born: 3/21/1982 Age: 30

Year	Team	Lg	G	AB	H	2B	3B	HR	(Hm	Rd)	TB	R	RBI	RC	TBB	IBB	SO	HBP	SH	SF	SB	CS	SB%	GDP	Avg	OBP	Slg
2011	Dnedin*	A+	2	6	1	0	0	0	(-	-)	1	2	1	0	1	0	1	1	0	0	0	0	-	0	.167	.375	.167
2005	Tor	AL	105	361	99	25	3	3	(3	0)	139	49	40	50	34	0	41	5	3	4	2	1	.67	5	.274	.342	.385
2006	Tor	AL	155	546	159	28	3	6	(4	2)	211	70	50	68	42	5	66	9	4	5	5	2	.71	15	.291	.349	.386
2007	Tor	AL	160	608	177	47	2	17	(8	9)	279	87	78	88	41	1	102	0	3	5	4	3	.57	21	.291	.333	.459
2008	Tor	AL	55	205	54	14	0	2	(1	1)	74	19	20	24	16	0	31	3	4	1	4	2	.67	4	.263	.324	.361
2009	Tor	AL	158	682	195	37	0	36	(21	15)	340	103	108	110	42	1	98	5	1	4	6	2	.75	17	.286	.330	.499
2010	Tor	AL	138	528	108	22	0	26	(15	11)	208	70	68	57	41	2	85	8	1	2	2	2	.50	8	.205	.271	.394
2011	2 Tms		137	520	128	27	3	8	(4	4)	185	61	61	61	35	1	72	7	2	7	21	7	.75	10	.246	.299	.356
11	Tor	AL	104	396	89	15	1	6	(3	3)	124	38	45	38	23	1	53	4	0	6	16	3	.84	8	.225	.270	.313
11	Ari	NL	33	124	39	12	2	2	(1	1)	61	23	16	23	12	0	19	3	2	1	5	4	.56	2	.315	.386	.492
	7 ML YEARS		908	3450	920	200	11	98	(56	42)	1436	459	425	458	251	10	495	37	18	28	44	19	.70	80	.267	.321	.416

Koyie Hill

Bats: B **Throws:** R **Pos:** C-45; PH-2
COY
Ht: 6'1" **Wt:** 210 **Born:** 3/9/1979 **Age:** 33

Year	Team	Lg	G	AB	H	2B	3B	HR	(Hm	Rd)	TB	R	RBI	RC	TBB	IBB	SO	HBP	SH	SF	SB	CS	SB%	GDP	Avg	OBP	Slg
2003	LAD	NL	3	3	1	1	0	0	(0	0)	2	0	0	0	0	0	2	0	0	0	0	0	-	0	.333	.333	.667
2004	Ari	NL	13	36	9	1	0	1	(1	0)	13	3	6	5	2	1	6	0	0	0	1	0	1.00	1	.250	.289	.361
2005	Ari	NL	34	78	17	5	0	0	(0	0)	22	6	6	6	11	0	27	0	0	2	0	1	.00	0	.218	.308	.282
2007	ChC	NL	36	93	15	4	0	2	(1	1)	25	7	12	3	8	0	18	1	1	2	0	0	-	4	.161	.231	.269
2008	ChC	NL	10	21	2	1	0	0	(0	0)	3	0	1	0	0	0	12	0	1	0	0	0	-	0	.095	.095	.143
2009	ChC	NL	83	253	60	12	2	2	(1	1)	82	26	24	23	27	6	78	1	2	1	0	0	-	9	.237	.312	.324
2010	ChC	NL	77	215	46	13	1	1	(1	0)	64	18	17	17	12	3	61	0	3	1	1	0	1.00	5	.214	.254	.298
2011	ChC	NL	46	134	26	3	1	2	(1	1)	37	15	9	2	14	3	40	0	4	1	1	0	1.00	3	.194	.268	.276
	8 ML YEARS		302	833	176	40	4	8	(5	3)	248	75	75	56	74	13	244	2	11	7	3	1	.75	22	.211	.275	.298

Rich Hill

Pitches: L **Bats:** L **Pos:** RP-9
Ht: 6'5" **Wt:** 220 **Born:** 3/11/1980 **Age:** 32

			HOW MUCH HE PITCHED						WHAT HE GAVE UP											THE RESULTS						
Year	Team	Lg	G	GS	CG	GF	IP	BFP	H	R	ER	HR	SH	SF	HB	TBB	IBB	SO	WP	Bk	W	L	Pct	Sh	Sv-Op	Hld	ERC	ERA
2011	Pwtckt*	AAA	10	0	0	4	16.0	62	8	3	2	1	0	0	1	5	0	18	0	0	1	0	1.000	0	1--	-	1.40	1.13
2005	ChC	NL	10	4	0	1	23.2	115	25	24	24	3	1	0	1	17	1	21	0	0	0	2	.000	0	0-0	0	5.81	9.13
2006	ChC	NL	17	16	2	1	99.1	417	83	51	46	16	8	3	2	39	1	90	3	0	6	7	.462	1	0-0	0	3.59	4.17
2007	ChC	NL	32	32	0	0	195.0	812	170	89	85	27	9	4	12	63	3	183	1	1	11	8	.579	2	0-0	0	3.56	3.92
2008	ChC	NL	5	5	0	0	19.2	89	13	9	9	2	0	2	1	18	0	15	1	0	1	0	1.000	0	0-0	0	4.38	4.12
2009	Bal	AL	14	13	0	0	57.2	275	68	53	50	7	2	2	1	40	2	46	1	1	3	3	.500	0	0-0	1	6.55	7.80
2010	Bos	AL	6	0	0	0	4.0	18	5	0	0	0	0	0	0	1	0	3	0	0	1	0	1.000	0	0-0	1	4.05	0.00
2011	Bos	AL	9	0	0	3	8.0	30	3	0	0	0	0	0	1	3	0	12	1	0	0	0	-	0	0-0	3	1.10	0.00
	Postseason		1	1	0	0	3.0	18	6	3	3	1	0	0	1	2	0	3	0	0	0	1	.000	0	0-0	0	15.68	9.00
	7 ML YEARS		93	70	2	5	407.1	1756	367	226	214	55	20	11	18	181	7	370	7	2	22	20	.524	1	0-0	4	4.08	4.73

Eric Hinske

Bats: L **Throws:** R **Pos:** PH-64; LF-33; RF-16; 1B-13; DH-1
Ht: 6'2" **Wt:** 235 **Born:** 8/5/1977 **Age:** 34

Year	Team	Lg	G	AB	H	2B	3B	HR	(Hm	Rd)	TB	R	RBI	RC	TBB	IBB	SO	HBP	SH	SF	SB	CS	SB%	GDP	Avg	OBP	Slg
2002	Tor	AL	151	566	158	38	2	24	(15	9)	272	99	84	103	77	5	138	2	0	5	13	1	.93	12	.279	.365	.481
2003	Tor	AL	124	449	109	45	3	12	(4	8)	196	74	63	66	59	1	104	1	0	5	12	2	.86	11	.243	.329	.437
2004	Tor	AL	155	570	140	23	3	15	(6	9)	214	66	69	60	54	2	109	4	0	6	12	8	.60	14	.246	.312	.375
2005	Tor	AL	147	477	125	31	4	15	(7	8)	205	79	68	74	46	4	121	8	0	6	8	4	.67	8	.262	.333	.430
2006	2 Tms	AL	109	277	75	17	2	13	(7	6)	135	43	34	39	35	2	79	0	0	0	2	2	.50	8	.271	.353	.487
2007	Bos	AL	84	186	38	12	3	6	(4	2)	74	25	21	22	28	2	54	3	0	1	3	0	1.00	7	.204	.317	.398
2008	TB	AL	133	381	94	21	1	20	(8	12)	177	59	60	53	47	4	88	3	0	1	10	3	.77	13	.247	.333	.465
2009	2 Tms		93	190	46	12	0	8	(2	6)	82	31	25	27	27	1	52	5	0	2	1	0	1.00	2	.242	.348	.432
2010	Atl	NL	131	281	72	21	1	11	(4	7)	128	38	51	40	33	5	75	0	0	3	0	0	-	4	.256	.338	.456
2011	Atl	NL	117	236	55	10	0	10	(3	7)	95	24	28	26	26	1	71	1	0	1	0	1	.00	5	.233	.311	.403
06	Tor	AL	78	197	52	9	2	12	(6	6)	101	35	29	29	27	2	49	0	0	0	1	1	.50	6	.264	.353	.513
06	Bos	AL	31	80	23	8	0	1	(1	0)	34	8	5	10	8	0	30	0	0	0	1	1	.50	2	.288	.352	.425
09	Pit	NL	54	106	27	9	0	1	(0	1)	39	18	11	16	17	0	27	3	0	0	0	0	-	0	.255	.373	.368
09	NYY	AL	39	84	19	3	0	7	(2	5)	43	13	14	11	10	1	25	2	0	2	1	0	1.00	2	.226	.316	.512
	Postseason		10	7	2	0	0	2	(1	1)	8	4	3	2	2	0	4	0	0	0	0	0	-	0	.286	.444	1.143
	10 ML YEARS		1244	3613	912	230	17	134	(63	71)	1578	538	503	507	432	27	891	30	0	30	61	21	.74	84	.252	.335	.437

Luke Hochevar

Pitches: R **Bats:** R **Pos:** SP-31
HOE-chay-vur
Ht: 6'5" **Wt:** 218 **Born:** 9/15/1983 **Age:** 28

			HOW MUCH HE PITCHED						WHAT HE GAVE UP											THE RESULTS						
Year	Team	Lg	G	GS	CG	GF	IP	BFP	H	R	ER	HR	SH	SF	HB	TBB	IBB	SO	WP	Bk	W	L	Pct	Sh	Sv-Op	Hld	ERC	ERA
2007	KC	AL	4	1	0	1	12.2	54	11	4	3	1	1	0	3	4	0	5	1	0	0	1	.000	0	0-0	0	3.86	2.13
2008	KC	AL	22	22	0	0	129.0	566	143	84	79	12	1	2	5	47	1	72	7	0	6	12	.333	0	0-0	0	4.67	5.51
2009	KC	AL	25	25	2	0	143.0	631	167	104	104	23	2	0	8	46	0	106	9	0	7	13	.350	1	0-0	0	5.46	6.55
2010	KC	AL	18	17	1	0	103.0	450	110	61	55	9	2	4	2	37	1	76	2	1	6	6	.500	0	0-0	0	4.34	4.81
2011	KC	AL	31	31	0	0	198.0	835	192	110	103	23	2	2	7	62	4	128	7	2	11	11	.500	1	0-0	0	3.80	4.68
	5 ML YEARS		100	96	3	1	585.2	2536	623	368	344	68	8	6	27	196	6	387	26	3	30	43	.411	1	0-0	0	4.48	5.29

Jim Hoey

Pitches: R **Bats:** R **Pos:** RP-26
HOE-ee
Ht: 6'6" **Wt:** 210 **Born:** 12/30/1982 **Age:** 29

			HOW MUCH HE PITCHED						WHAT HE GAVE UP											THE RESULTS						
Year	Team	Lg	G	GS	CG	GF	IP	BFP	H	R	ER	HR	SH	SF	HB	TBB	IBB	SO	WP	Bk	W	L	Pct	Sh	Sv-Op	Hld	ERC	ERA
2011	Roch*	AAA	33	0	0	25	42.1	176	32	20	18	6	2	0	1	21	2	38	5	0	1	3	.250	0	9--	-	3.46	3.83
2006	Bal	AL	12	0	0	2	9.2	49	14	11	11	1	1	2	2	5	0	6	0	0	0	1	.000	0	0-1	4	8.22	10.24
2007	Bal	AL	23	0	0	1	24.2	115	25	21	20	2	0	4	1	18	1	18	1	0	3	4	.429	0	0-3	4	5.43	7.30
2011	Min	AL	26	0	0	11	24.2	118	34	20	15	4	0	2	0	13	0	14	1	0	1	2	.333	0	0-1	2	7.44	5.47
	3 ML YEARS		61	0	0	14	59.0	282	73	52	46	7	1	8	3	36	1	38	2	1	4	7	.364	0	0-5	10	6.71	7.02

Jamie Hoffmann

Bats: R Throws: R Pos: LF-1; PH-1 Ht: 6'3" Wt: 235 Born: 8/20/1984 Age: 27

Year	Team	Lg	G	AB	H	2B	3B	HR	(Hm	Rd)	TB	R	RBI	RC	TBB	IBB	SO	HBP	SH	SF	SB	CS	SB%	GDP	Avg	OBP	Slg
2005	Clmbs	A	79	321	99	13	9	1	(-	-)	133	53	24	54	39	1	73	1	5	2	10	4	.71	6	.308	.383	.414
2005	VeroB	A+	46	166	40	6	2	1	(-	-)	53	26	10	15	10	0	45	1	0	1	3	1	.75	5	.241	.287	.319
2006	VeroB	A+	121	433	109	16	0	5	(-	-)	140	50	29	44	35	0	94	2	7	2	15	11	.58	9	.252	.309	.323
2006	LsVgs	AAA	4	10	3	0	0	0	(-	-)	3	0	0	1	1	0	3	1	1	0	1	0	1.00	0	.300	.417	.300
2007	InldEm	A+	116	433	134	22	7	9	(-	-)	197	67	81	78	47	3	70	4	5	6	19	7	.73	5	.309	.378	.455
2008	Jaxnvl	AA	133	478	133	20	3	10	(-	-)	189	64	71	73	54	3	72	2	4	6	29	9	.76	9	.278	.350	.395
2009	Chatt	AA	29	101	31	9	2	2	(-	-)	50	25	16	24	22	0	18	6	0	0	5	3	.63	4	.307	.457	.495
2009	Albq	AAA	68	257	73	14	3	8	(-	-)	117	44	48	43	32	2	37	0	1	3	10	8	.56	6	.284	.360	.455
2010	Albq	AAA	139	545	169	36	3	8	(-	-)	235	91	74	90	43	3	98	11	4	5	17	7	.71	6	.310	.369	.431
2011	Albq	AAA	133	475	141	23	3	22	(-	-)	236	91	84	87	44	1	102	5	0	9	14	4	.78	11	.297	.356	.497
2009	LAD	NL	14	22	4	2	0	1	(1	0)	9	2	7	2	0	0	5	0	0	2	0	0	-	2	.182	.167	.409
2011	LAD	NL	2	4	0	0	0	0	(0	0)	0	0	0	0	0	0	1	0	0	0	0	0	-	0	.000	.000	.000
	2 ML YEARS		16	26	4	2	0	1	(1	0)	9	2	7	2	0	0	6	0	0	2	0	0	-	2	.154	.143	.346

Derek Holland

Pitches: L Bats: B Pos: SP-32 Ht: 6'2" Wt: 193 Born: 10/9/1986 Age: 25

			HOW MUCH HE PITCHED						WHAT HE GAVE UP										THE RESULTS							
Year	Team	Lg	G	GS	CG	GF	IP	BFP	H	R	ER	HR	SH	SF	HB	TBB	IBB	SO	WP	Bk	W	L	Pct	Sh	Sv-Op	Hld	ERC	ERA
2009	Tex	AL	33	21	1	0	138.1	611	160	98	94	26	2	3	4	47	0	107	3	3	8	13	.381	1	0-1	2	5.52	6.12
2010	Tex	AL	14	10	0	2	57.1	253	55	30	26	6	0	2	4	24	0	54	0	1	3	4	.429	0	0-0	1	4.17	4.08
2011	Tex	AL	32	32	4	0	198.0	843	201	97	87	22	1	3	6	67	1	162	2	1	16	5	.762	4	0-0	0	4.15	3.95
	Postseason		6	0	0	2	11.1	47	9	6	6	1	0	0	0	7	0	9	0	0	1	0	1.000	0	0-0	0	3.88	4.76
	3 ML YEARS		79	63	5	2	393.2	1707	416	225	207	54	3	8	14	138	1	323	5	5	27	22	.551	5	0-1	3	4.62	4.73

Greg Holland

Pitches: R Bats: R Pos: RP-46 Ht: 5'11" Wt: 189 Born: 11/20/1985 Age: 26

			HOW MUCH HE PITCHED						WHAT HE GAVE UP										THE RESULTS							
Year	Team	Lg	G	GS	CG	GF	IP	BFP	H	R	ER	HR	SH	SF	HB	TBB	IBB	SO	WP	Bk	W	L	Pct	Sh	Sv-Op	Hld	ERC	ERA
2007	Idaho	R+	22	0	0	18	33.2	143	28	16	13	1	1	0	1	15	0	37	3	1	6	1	.857	0	6- -		2.95	3.48
2008	Wilmg	A+	32	7	0	8	84.1	355	70	37	32	4	3	6	1	35	2	96	8	0	4	5	.444	0	4- -		2.85	3.42
2009	NWArk	AA	29	0	0	19	45.1	194	46	16	16	2	0	1	0	19	0	49	6	0	3	2	.600	0	8- -		3.89	3.18
2009	Omha	AAA	6	0	0	3	9.0	42	12	7	7	2	0	1	1	5	0	1	0	0	1	1	.500	0	2- -		8.72	7.00
2010	Omha	AAA	36	0	0	16	56.2	235	40	26	24	3	2	2	0	30	1	60	4	0	3	3	.500	0	3- -		2.67	3.81
2011	Omha	AAA	13	0	0	6	21.2	86	13	5	5	1	0	1	0	11	0	27	2	0	2	0	1.000	0	2- -		2.12	2.08
2010	KC	AL	15	0	0	10	18.2	87	23	15	14	3	1	0	0	8	0	23	2	0	0	1	.000	0	0-0	0	5.88	6.75
2011	KC	AL	46	0	0	15	60.0	233	37	13	12	3	1	1	1	19	3	74	7	0	5	1	.833	0	4-6	18	1.60	1.80
	2 ML YEARS		61	0	0	25	78.2	320	60	28	26	6	2	1	1	27	3	97	9	0	5	2	.714	0	4-6	18	2.45	2.97

Matt Holliday

Bats: R Throws: R Pos: LF-115; DH-5; PH-5 Ht: 6'4" Wt: 235 Born: 1/15/1980 Age: 32

Year	Team	Lg	G	AB	H	2B	3B	HR	(Hm	Rd)	TB	R	RBI	RC	TBB	IBB	SO	HBP	SH	SF	SB	CS	SB%	GDP	Avg	OBP	Slg
2004	Col	NL	121	400	116	31	3	14	(10	4)	195	65	57	61	31	0	86	6	1	1	3	3	.50	9	.290	.349	.488
2005	Col	NL	125	479	147	24	7	19	(12	7)	242	68	87	88	36	1	79	7	0	4	14	3	.82	11	.307	.361	.505
2006	Col	NL	155	602	196	45	5	34	(22	12)	353	119	114	112	47	3	110	15	0	3	10	5	.67	22	.326	.387	.586
2007	Col	NL	158	636	216	50	6	36	(25	11)	386	120	137	134	63	7	126	10	0	4	11	4	.73	23	.340	.405	.607
2008	Col	NL	139	539	173	38	2	25	(15	10)	290	107	88	104	74	6	104	8	0	2	28	2	.93	9	.321	.409	.538
2009	2 Tms		156	581	182	39	3	24	(16	8)	299	94	109	112	72	8	101	10	0	7	14	7	.67	13	.313	.394	.515
2010	StL	NL	158	596	186	45	1	28	(13	15)	317	95	103	107	69	10	93	8	0	2	9	5	.64	13	.312	.390	.532
2011	StL	NL	124	446	132	36	0	22	(12	10)	234	83	75	81	60	4	93	8	0	2	2	1	.67	21	.296	.388	.525
09	Oak	AL	93	346	99	23	1	11	(7	4)	157	52	54	62	46	3	58	6	0	2	12	3	.80	8	.286	.378	.454
09	StL	NL	63	235	83	16	2	13	(9	4)	142	42	55	50	26	5	43	4	0	5	2	4	.33	5	.353	.419	.604
	Postseason		14	57	15	0	0	6	(3	3)	33	7	11	7	1	0	14	2	0	0	0	0	-	1	.263	.300	.579
	8 ML YEARS		1136	4279	1348	308	27	202	(125	77)	2316	751	770	799	452	39	792	72	1	25	91	30	.75	121	.315	.388	.541

Steve Holm

Bats: R Throws: R Pos: C-6 Ht: 6'0" Wt: 210 Born: 10/21/1979 Age: 32

Year	Team	Lg	G	AB	H	2B	3B	HR	(Hm	Rd)	TB	R	RBI	RC	TBB	IBB	SO	HBP	SH	SF	SB	CS	SB%	GDP	Avg	OBP	Slg
2011	Roch*	AAA	47	151	27	6	0	1	(-	-)	36	13	13	10	17	0	38	2	2	2	0	0	-	3	.179	.267	.238
2008	SF	NL	49	84	22	9	0	1	(1	0)	34	10	6	8	10	1	16	3	0	1	0	0	-	3	.262	.357	.405
2009	SF	NL	4	7	2	0	0	0	(0	0)	2	1	0	2	2	0	0	0	0	0	0	0	-	0	.286	.444	.286
2011	Min	AL	6	17	2	1	0	0	(0	0)	3	1	0	0	1	0	4	0	0	0	0	1	.00	0	.118	.167	.176
	3 ML YEARS		59	108	26	10	0	1	(1	0)	39	12	6	10	13	1	20	3	0	1	0	1	.00	3	.241	.336	.361

Jeremy Horst

Pitches: L Bats: L Pos: RP-12   Ht: 6'3" Wt: 217 Born: 10/1/1985 Age: 26

			HOW MUCH HE PITCHED						WHAT HE GAVE UP												THE RESULTS							
Year	Team	Lg	G	GS	CG	GF	IP	BFP	H	R	ER	HR	SH	SF	HB	TBB	IBB	SO	WP	Bk	W	L	Pct	Sh	Sv-Op	Hld	ERC	ERA
2007	Reds	R	1	0	0	0	2.0	12	3	4	1	0	0	0	0	2	0	4	1	0	0	0	.-	0	0- -	-	7.82	4.50
2007	Billings	R+	16	0	0	4	39.2	168	34	15	14	2	0	0	1	22	0	51	3	2	3	2	.600	0	2- -	-	3.73	3.18
2008	Dayton	A	36	10	0	9	102.0	410	74	30	27	3	3	4	3	33	1	110	2	1	8	2	.800	0	4- -	-	2.03	2.38
2009	Srsota	A+	23	23	1	0	133.0	569	136	61	48	15	4	7	9	41	0	101	2	1	6	13	.316	0	0- -	-	4.23	3.25
2009	Carlina	AA	5	5	0	0	29.0	123	35	20	20	7	0	0	0	10	0	21	2	0	1	4	.200	0	0- -	-	6.46	6.21
2010	Lynbrg	A+	11	0	0	4	14.2	67	17	8	7	1	1	1	1	4	1	17	1	0	0	2	.000	0	0- -	-	4.21	4.30
2010	Carlina	AA	27	0	0	8	43.0	173	35	13	10	1	2	1	0	9	2	46	2	0	3	2	.600	0	0- -	-	1.86	2.09
2010	Lsvlle	AAA	6	2	0	0	14.1	64	17	5	4	0	3	0	1	5	0	12	0	0	1	0	1.000	0	0- -	-	4.48	2.51
2011	Lsvlle	AAA	36	0	0	9	51.1	210	41	18	16	2	4	3	2	14	0	42	1	0	1	4	.200	0	0- -	-	2.28	2.81
2011	Cin	NL	12	0	0	4	15.1	69	18	6	5	2	0	1	0	6	1	9	0	1	0	0	-	0	0-0	0	5.11	2.93

Eric Hosmer

Bats: L Throws: L Pos: 1B-127; PH-1   HOZZ-mer   Ht: 6'4" Wt: 229 Born: 10/24/1989 Age: 22

			BATTING																				BASERUNNING				AVERAGES		
Year	Team	Lg	G	AB	H	2B	3B	HR	(Hm	Rd)	TB	R	RBI	RC	TBB	IBB	SO	HBP	SH	SF	SB	CS	SB%	GDP	Avg	OBP	Slg
2008	Idaho	R+	3	11	4	2	0	0	(-	-)	6	2	2	3	3	0	2	1	0	0	0	0	.-	0	.364	.533	.545
2009	Burlgtn	A	79	280	71	17	2	5	(-	-)	107	31	49	41	44	3	68	0	0	3	3	2	.60	10	.254	.352	.382
2009	Wilmg	A+	27	97	20	2	2	1	(-	-)	29	9	10	8	9	0	22	1	0	0	0	0	.-	1	.206	.280	.299
2010	Wilmg	A+	87	325	115	29	6	7	(-	-)	177	48	51	77	44	6	39	2	0	4	11	1	.92	12	.354	.429	.545
2010	NWArk	AA	50	195	61	14	3	13	(-	-)	120	39	35	42	15	2	27	1	0	0	3	1	.75	11	.313	.365	.615
2011	Omha	AAA	26	98	43	5	0	3	(-	-)	57	21	15	29	19	0	16	0	0	1	3	0	1.00	1	.439	.525	.582
2011	KC	AL	128	523	153	27	3	19	(3	16)	243	66	78	71	34	7	82	1	0	5	11	5	.69	13	.293	.334	.465

Tommy Hottovy

Pitches: L Bats: L Pos: RP-8   HAWT-uh-vee   Ht: 6'1" Wt: 195 Born: 7/9/1981 Age: 30

			HOW MUCH HE PITCHED						WHAT HE GAVE UP												THE RESULTS							
Year	Team	Lg	G	GS	CG	GF	IP	BFP	H	R	ER	HR	SH	SF	HB	TBB	IBB	SO	WP	Bk	W	L	Pct	Sh	Sv-Op	Hld	ERC	ERA
2004	Lowell	A-	14	14	0	0	30.1	121	24	5	3	0	0	0	3	4	0	39	2	0	0	1	.000	0	0- -	-	1.78	0.89
2005	Wilmg	A+	25	23	0	0	104.0	467	116	74	63	18	6	5	7	37	0	82	8	0	3	12	.200	0	0- -	-	5.32	5.45
2006	Wilmg	A+	21	21	2	0	122.0	506	109	49	38	3	2	5	5	35	0	91	6	0	8	6	.571	0	0- -	-	2.73	2.80
2006	Portlnd	AA	7	7	0	0	41.0	166	28	20	19	1	0	1	3	15	2	31	2	0	2	4	.333	0	0- -	-	2.04	4.17
2007	Portlnd	AA	24	23	0	0	120.1	540	144	78	75	17	6	9	3	49	0	69	6	1	4	10	.286	0	0- -	-	5.72	5.61
2008	Portlnd	AA	2	2	0	0	9.0	39	9	7	5	2	0	0	1	2	0	4	0	0	0	1	1.000	0	0- -	-	4.55	5.00
2009	Lowell	A-	5	0	0	0	8.0	31	4	2	2	1	1	0	0	3	0	12	0	0	1	0	1.000	0	0- -	-	1.64	2.25
2009	Portlnd	AA	16	0	0	5	26.0	115	26	12	10	2	2	2	2	10	0	29	3	0	0	2	.000	0	0- -	-	4.09	3.46
2010	Portlnd	AA	15	0	0	6	39.2	182	49	25	23	6	0	0	0	20	1	34	5	1	3	2	.600	0	0- -	-	6.32	5.22
2010	Pwtckt	AAA	26	0	0	6	35.2	169	37	19	18	5	0	2	4	23	2	22	5	0	0	1	.000	0	0- -	-	5.89	4.54
2011	Portlnd	AA	8	0	0	2	18.2	70	12	4	4	0	1	0	0	4	0	18	0	0	0	0	.-	0	0- -	-	1.29	1.93
2011	Pwtckt	AAA	24	0	0	6	36.0	138	23	13	11	8	1	0	1	9	0	29	0	0	2	0	1.000	0	1- -	-	2.48	2.75
2011	Bos	AL	8	0	0	1	4.0	19	4	3	3	0	0	0	1	3	0	2	0	0	0	0	-	0	0-0	2	5.79	6.75

Ryan Howard

Bats: L Throws: L Pos: 1B-149; PH-4; DH-1; PR-1   Ht: 6'4" Wt: 242 Born: 11/19/1979 Age: 32

			BATTING																				BASERUNNING				AVERAGES		
Year	Team	Lg	G	AB	H	2B	3B	HR	(Hm	Rd)	TB	R	RBI	RC	TBB	IBB	SO	HBP	SH	SF	SB	CS	SB%	GDP	Avg	OBP	Slg
2004	Phi	NL	19	39	11	5	0	2	(1	1)	22	5	5	7	2	0	13	1	0	0	0	0	.-	2	.282	.333	.564
2005	Phi	NL	88	312	90	17	2	22	(11	11)	177	52	63	50	33	8	100	1	0	2	0	1	.00	6	.288	.356	.567
2006	Phi	NL	159	581	182	25	1	58	(29	29)	383	104	149	138	108	37	181	9	0	6	0	0	.-	7	.313	.425	.659
2007	Phi	NL	144	529	142	26	0	47	(23	24)	309	94	136	119	107	35	199	5	0	7	1	0	1.00	13	.268	.392	.584
2008	Phi	NL	162	610	153	26	4	48	(26	22)	331	105	146	117	81	17	199	3	0	6	1	1	.50	11	.251	.339	.543
2009	Phi	NL	160	616	172	37	4	45	(18	27)	352	105	141	117	75	8	186	6	0	6	8	1	.89	11	.279	.360	.571
2010	Phi	NL	143	550	152	23	5	31	(16	15)	278	87	108	92	59	11	157	8	0	3	1	1	.50	14	.276	.353	.505
2011	Phi	NL	152	557	141	30	1	33	(17	16)	272	81	116	91	75	16	172	7	0	5	1	0	1.00	10	.253	.346	.488
	Postseason		41	151	42	13	1	7	(5	2)	78	21	27	26	25	7	61	1	0	1	1	1	.50	1	.278	.382	.517
	8 ML YEARS		1027	3794	1043	189	17	286	(141	145)	2124	633	864	733	540	132	1207	40	0	35	12	4	.75	74	.275	.368	.560

J.P. Howell

Pitches: L Bats: L Pos: RP-46   Ht: 6'0" Wt: 195 Born: 4/25/1983 Age: 29

			HOW MUCH HE PITCHED						WHAT HE GAVE UP												THE RESULTS							
Year	Team	Lg	G	GS	CG	GF	IP	BFP	H	R	ER	HR	SH	SF	HB	TBB	IBB	SO	WP	Bk	W	L	Pct	Sh	Sv-Op	Hld	ERC	ERA
2011	Charltt*	A+	3	3	0	0	3.1	14	3	1	1	0	0	0	0	1	0	4	0	0	0	1	.000	0	0- -	-	2.46	2.70
2011	Drham*	AAA	4	0	0	0	3.2	16	5	4	0	0	0	0	0	1	0	5	1	0	0	0	-	0	0- -	-	5.10	0.00
2005	KC	AL	15	15	0	0	72.2	328	73	55	50	9	3	3	6	39	0	54	7	0	3	5	.375	0	0-0	0	5.18	6.19
2006	TB	AL	8	8	0	0	42.1	187	52	25	24	4	0	2	3	14	0	33	1	0	1	3	.250	0	0-0	0	5.51	5.10
2007	TB	AL	10	10	0	0	51.0	244	69	45	43	8	2	1	3	21	0	49	3	0	1	6	.143	0	0-0	0	6.84	7.59
2008	TB	AL	64	0	0	9	89.1	370	62	29	22	6	6	1	4	39	1	92	6	0	6	1	.857	0	3-5	14	2.51	2.22
2009	TB	AL	69	0	0	41	66.2	278	47	22	21	7	2	1	3	33	3	79	3	1	7	5	.583	0	17-25	4	2.99	2.84
2011	TB	AL	46	0	0	5	30.2	138	30	24	21	5	1	1	2	18	1	26	2	2	2	3	.400	0	1-2	10	5.43	6.16
	Postseason		12	0	0	1	12.0	50	9	4	4	0	0	1	2	4	1	17	1	0	0	3	.000	0	0-0	4	2.33	3.00
	6 ML YEARS		212	33	0	55	352.2	1545	333	200	181	39	14	9	21	164	5	333	21	3	20	23	.465	0	21-32	28	4.30	4.62

Chin-lung Hu

Bats: R Throws: R Pos: PH-12; 2B-10; PR-3; SS-1   Ht: 5'11" Wt: 188 Born: 2/2/1984 Age: 28

									BATTING											BASERUNNING				AVERAGES		
Year	Team	Lg	G	AB	H	2B	3B	HR	(Hm	Rd)	TB	R	RBI	RC	TBB	IBB	SO	HBP	SH	SF	SB	CS	SB%	GDP	Avg	OBP	Slg
2011	Buffalo*	AAA	13	31	6	2	0	0	(-	-)	8	3	1	1	0	0	11	1	0	0	0	0	-	0	.194	.219	.258
2011	Mets*	R	13	49	9	0	0	0	(-	-)	9	8	1	4	8	0	7	0	0	0	2	1	.67	1	.184	.298	.184
2007	LAD	NL	12	29	7	0	1	2	(2	0)	15	5	5	5	0	0	8	0	2	0	0	0	-	0	.241	.241	.517
2008	LAD	NL	65	116	21	2	2	0	(0	0)	27	16	9	5	11	4	23	0	2	0	2	0	1.00	5	.181	.252	.233
2009	LAD	NL	5	5	2	1	0	0	(0	0)	3	2	2	1	0	0	2	0	0	1	0	0	-	1	.400	.333	.600
2010	LAD	NL	14	23	3	1	0	0	(0	0)	4	2	1	0	0	0	5	1	0	1	1	0	1.00	1	.130	.160	.174
2011	NYM	NL	22	20	1	0	0	0	(0	0)	1	2	1	0	1	0	11	0	1	1	1	0	1.00	0	.050	.091	.050
	5 ML YEARS		118	193	34	4	3	2	(2	0)	50	27	18	11	12	4	49	1	5	3	4	0	1.00	7	.176	.225	.259

Daniel Hudson

Pitches: R Bats: R Pos: SP-33   Ht: 6'3" Wt: 225 Born: 3/9/1987 Age: 25

			HOW MUCH HE PITCHED					WHAT HE GAVE UP									THE RESULTS							
Year	Team	Lg	G	GS	CG	GF	IP	BFP	H	R	ER	HR	SH	SF	HB	TBB	IBB	SO	WP	Bk	W	L	Pct	Sh	Sv-Op	Hld	ERC	ERA
2009	CWS	AL	6	2	0	1	18.2	82	16	9	7	3	0	1	1	9	0	14	1	0	1	1	.500	0	0-0	0	4.15	3.38
2010	2 Tms		14	14	0	0	95.1	372	68	26	26	8	2	2	4	27	1	84	5	0	8	2	.800	0	0-0	0	2.26	2.45
2011	Ari	NL	33	33	3	0	222.0	921	217	98	86	17	6	6	8	50	1	169	4	1	16	12	.571	0	0-0	0	3.26	3.49
	10 CWS	AL	3	3	0	0	15.2	71	17	11	11	1	1	0	1	11	0	14	2	0	1	1	.500	0	0-0	0	5.69	6.32
	10 Ari	NL	11	11	0	0	79.2	301	51	15	15	7	1	1	4	16	1	70	3	0	7	1	.875	0	0-0	0	1.70	1.69
	3 ML YEARS		53	49	3	1	336.0	1375	301	133	119	28	8	9	13	86	2	267	10	1	25	15	.625	0	0-0	0	3.02	3.19

Kyle Hudson

Bats: L Throws: L Pos: LF-8; PR-4; CF-2; DH-1   Ht: 5'11" Wt: 175 Born: 1/7/1987 Age: 25

									BATTING											BASERUNNING				AVERAGES		
Year	Team	Lg	G	AB	H	2B	3B	HR	(Hm	Rd)	TB	R	RBI	RC	TBB	IBB	SO	HBP	SH	SF	SB	CS	SB%	GDP	Avg	OBP	Slg
2008	Abrdn	A-	11	37	8	1	0	0	(-	-)	9	5	5	3	8	1	12	0	1	0	4	3	.57	0	.216	.356	.243
2009	Dlmrva	A	117	398	113	8	2	0	(-	-)	125	61	21	51	49	0	85	2	7	0	31	16	.66	2	.284	.365	.314
2009	Frdrck	A+	6	20	5	0	0	0	(-	-)	5	4	0	3	4	0	6	1	1	0	3	0	1.00	0	.250	.400	.250
2010	Frdrck	A+	136	516	134	17	3	0	(-	-)	157	83	28	63	62	0	129	8	11	1	40	15	.73	2	.260	.348	.304
2011	Frdrck	A+	23	86	24	3	0	0	(-	-)	27	12	2	9	10	0	16	0	2	0	8	6	.57	1	.279	.354	.314
2011	Bowie	AA	28	91	28	3	1	0	(-	-)	33	9	10	13	10	0	24	0	2	0	7	2	.78	0	.308	.376	.363
2011	Norfolk	AAA	68	246	73	7	1	0	(-	-)	82	39	11	37	33	1	55	1	4	0	26	8	.76	3	.297	.382	.333
2011	Bal	AL	14	28	4	0	0	0	(0	0)	4	3	2	0	0	0	6	0	1	0	2	0	1.00	3	.143	.143	.143

Orlando Hudson

Bats: B Throws: R Pos: 2B-114; PH-7   Ht: 6'0" Wt: 190 Born: 12/12/1977 Age: 34

									BATTING											BASERUNNING				AVERAGES		
Year	Team	Lg	G	AB	H	2B	3B	HR	(Hm	Rd)	TB	R	RBI	RC	TBB	IBB	SO	HBP	SH	SF	SB	CS	SB%	GDP	Avg	OBP	Slg
2011	Tucsn*	AAA	2	4	3	2	0	0	(-	-)	5	4	1	3	3	0	0	0	0	0	0	0	-	0	.750	.857	1.250
2011	Lk Els*	A+	4	7	4	0	0	1	(-	-)	7	6	3	5	6	0	0	0	0	0	2	0	1.00	0	.571	.769	1.000
2002	Tor	AL	54	192	53	10	5	4	(2	2)	85	20	23	30	11	0	27	2	0	2	0	1	.00	6	.276	.319	.443
2003	Tor	AL	142	474	127	21	6	9	(5	4)	187	54	57	64	39	1	87	5	0	3	5	4	.56	13	.268	.328	.395
2004	Tor	AL	135	489	132	32	7	12	(5	7)	214	73	58	71	51	0	98	4	3	4	7	3	.70	12	.270	.341	.438
2005	Tor	AL	131	461	125	25	5	10	(4	6)	190	62	63	59	30	1	65	3	0	7	7	1	.88	10	.271	.315	.412
2006	Ari	NL	157	579	166	34	9	15	(7	8)	263	87	67	89	61	5	78	2	4	4	9	6	.60	17	.287	.354	.454
2007	Ari	NL	139	517	152	28	9	10	(7	3)	228	69	63	82	70	1	87	2	5	7	10	2	.83	21	.294	.376	.441
2008	Ari	NL	107	407	124	29	3	8	(6	2)	183	54	41	66	40	2	62	2	3	3	4	1	.80	18	.305	.367	.450
2009	LAD	NL	149	551	156	35	6	9	(4	5)	230	74	62	78	62	4	99	4	9	5	8	1	.89	16	.283	.357	.417
2010	Min	AL	126	497	133	24	5	6	(3	3)	185	80	37	56	50	0	87	4	5	3	10	3	.77	14	.268	.338	.372
2011	SD	NL	119	398	98	15	3	7	(4	3)	140	54	43	52	49	6	84	2	1	4	19	3	.86	5	.246	.329	.352
	Postseason		11	16	5	0	0	2	(1	1)	11	3	3	2	0	0	3	0	1	0	0	0	-	2	.313	.313	.688
	10 ML YEARS		1259	4565	1266	253	58	90	(47	43)	1905	627	514	647	463	20	774	30	30	42	79	25	.76	132	.277	.345	.417

Tim Hudson

Pitches: R Bats: R Pos: SP-33   Ht: 6'1" Wt: 174 Born: 7/14/1975 Age: 36

			HOW MUCH HE PITCHED					WHAT HE GAVE UP									THE RESULTS							
Year	Team	Lg	G	GS	CG	GF	IP	BFP	H	R	ER	HR	SH	SF	HB	TBB	IBB	SO	WP	Bk	W	L	Pct	Sh	Sv-Op	Hld	ERC	ERA
1999	Oak	AL	21	21	1	0	136.1	580	121	56	49	8	1	2	4	62	2	132	6	0	11	2	.846	0	0-0	0	3.50	3.23
2000	Oak	AL	32	32	2	0	202.1	847	169	100	93	24	5	7	7	82	5	169	7	0	20	6	.769	2	0-0	0	3.43	4.14
2001	Oak	AL	35	35	3	0	235.0	980	216	100	88	20	12	8	6	71	5	181	9	1	18	9	.667	0	0-0	0	3.22	3.37
2002	Oak	AL	34	34	4	0	238.1	983	237	87	79	19	6	5	8	62	9	152	7	1	15	9	.625	2	0-0	0	3.51	2.98
2003	Oak	AL	34	34	3	0	240.0	967	197	84	72	15	11	2	10	61	9	162	6	0	16	7	.696	2	0-0	0	2.47	2.70
2004	Oak	AL	27	27	3	0	188.2	793	194	82	74	8	7	4	12	44	3	103	4	1	12	6	.667	2	0-0	0	3.44	3.53
2005	Atl	NL	29	29	2	0	192.0	817	194	79	75	20	9	1	9	65	5	115	4	0	14	9	.609	0	0-0	0	4.12	3.52
2006	Atl	NL	35	35	2	0	218.1	959	235	129	118	25	8	3	9	79	10	141	7	0	13	12	.520	1	0-0	0	4.54	4.86
2007	Atl	NL	34	34	1	0	224.1	925	221	87	83	10	11	6	8	53	8	132	5	2	16	10	.615	1	0-0	0	3.12	3.33
2008	Atl	NL	23	22	1	0	142.0	573	125	53	50	11	5	4	2	40	5	85	3	1	11	7	.611	1	0-0	0	2.90	3.17
2009	Atl	NL	7	7	0	0	42.1	180	49	17	17	4	1	0	0	13	0	30	0	0	2	1	.667	0	0-0	0	4.70	3.61
2010	Atl	NL	34	34	1	0	228.2	920	189	74	72	20	9	2	9	74	8	139	5	0	17	9	.654	0	0-0	0	2.95	2.83
2011	Atl	NL	33	33	1	0	215.0	884	189	86	77	14	6	7	15	56	6	158	10	0	16	10	.615	1	0-0	0	2.91	3.22
	Postseason		10	9	1	0	54.2	236	54	28	21	5	4	2	2	20	1	37	1	0	1	3	.250	0	0-0	0	3.91	3.46
	13 ML YEARS		378	377	24	0	2503.1	10408	2336	1034	947	198	91	51	99	762	75	1699	73	6	181	97	.651	12	0-0	0	3.34	3.40

Aubrey Huff

Bats: L Throws: R Pos: 1B-120; RF-13; PH-13; LF-9; DH-2   Ht: 6'4" Wt: 217 Born: 12/20/1976 Age: 35

						BATTING																			BASERUNNING				AVERAGES		
Year	Team	Lg	G	AB	H	2B	3B	HR	(Hm	Rd)	TB	R	RBI	RC	TBB	IBB	SO	HBP	SH	SF	SB	CS	SB%	GDP	Avg	OBP	Slg
2000	TB	AL	39	122	35	7	0	4	(3	1)	54	12	14	15	5	1	18	1	0	1	0	0	-	6	.287	.318	.443
2001	TB	AL	111	411	102	25	1	8	(5	3)	153	42	45	37	23	2	72	0	0	0	1	3	.25	18	.248	.288	.372
2002	TB	AL	113	454	142	25	0	23	(17	6)	236	67	59	66	37	7	55	1	0	2	4	1	.80	17	.313	.364	.520
2003	TB	AL	162	636	198	47	3	34	(15	19)	353	91	107	112	53	17	80	8	0	9	2	3	.40	19	.311	.367	.555
2004	TB	AL	157	600	178	27	2	29	(16	13)	296	92	104	96	56	6	74	6	0	5	5	1	.83	9	.297	.360	.493
2005	TB	AL	154	575	150	26	2	22	(9	13)	246	70	92	77	49	13	88	5	0	7	8	7	.53	12	.261	.321	.428
2006	2 Tms		131	454	121	25	2	21	(9	12)	213	57	66	55	50	6	64	7	0	6	0	0	-	11	.267	.344	.469
2007	Bal	AL	151	550	154	34	5	15	(8	7)	243	68	72	79	48	2	87	1	0	4	1	1	.50	13	.280	.337	.442
2008	Bal	AL	154	598	182	48	2	32	(18	14)	330	96	108	111	53	7	89	3	0	7	4	0	1.00	9	.304	.360	.552
2009	2 Tms		150	536	129	30	1	15	(11	4)	206	59	85	67	51	7	87	5	0	5	0	6	.00	15	.241	.310	.384
2010	SF	NL	157	569	165	35	5	26	(12	14)	288	100	86	108	83	5	91	9	0	7	7	0	1.00	17	.290	.385	.506
2011	SF	NL	150	521	128	27	1	12	(3	9)	193	45	59	54	47	6	90	2	0	9	5	3	.63	11	.246	.306	.370
06	TB	AL	63	230	65	15	1	8	(4	4)	106	26	28	28	24	3	25	0	0	2	0	0	-	4	.283	.348	.461
06	Hou	NL	68	224	56	10	1	13	(5	8)	107	31	38	27	26	3	39	7	0	4	0	0	-	7	.250	.341	.478
09	Bal	AL	110	430	109	24	1	13	(10	3)	174	51	72	58	41	7	74	4	0	5	0	6	.00	12	.253	.321	.405
09	Det	AL	40	106	20	6	0	2	(1	1)	32	8	13	9	10	0	13	1	0	0	0	0	-	3	.189	.265	.302
	Postseason		15	56	15	2	0	1	(0	1)	20	7	8	7	5	1	10	1	1	0	0	2	.00	0	.268	.339	.357
	12 ML YEARS		1629	6026	1684	356	24	241	(126	115)	2811	799	897	877	555	79	895	48	0	62	37	25	.60	157	.279	.342	.466

David Huff

Pitches: L Bats: B Pos: SP-10; RP-1   Ht: 6'2" Wt: 215 Born: 8/22/1984 Age: 27

			HOW MUCH HE PITCHED					WHAT HE GAVE UP											THE RESULTS							
Year	Team	Lg	G	GS	CG	GF	IP	BFP	H	R	ER	HR	SH	SF	HB	TBB	IBB	SO	WP	Bk	W	L	Pct	Sh	Sv-Op Hld	ERC	ERA
2011	Clmbs*	AAA	18	18	0	0	107.0	454	111	52	46	10	1	0	2	30	0	66	2	0	9	3	.750	0	0-- -	3.85	3.87
2009	Cle	AL	23	23	0	0	128.1	574	159	82	80	16	2	2	1	41	1	65	1	0	11	8	.579	0	0-0 0	5.33	5.61
2010	Cle	AL	15	15	1	0	79.2	369	101	61	55	14	3	3	3	34	1	37	2	0	2	11	.154	0	0-0 0	6.50	6.21
2011	Cle	AL	11	10	0	1	50.2	227	55	35	23	6	0	3	0	17	1	36	4	0	2	6	.250	0	0-0 0	4.23	4.09
	3 ML YEARS		49	48	1	1	258.2	1170	315	178	158	36	5	8	4	92	3	138	7	0	15	25	.375	0	0-0 0	5.45	5.50

Dusty Hughes

Pitches: L Bats: L Pos: RP-15   Ht: 5'10" Wt: 186 Born: 6/29/1982 Age: 30

			HOW MUCH HE PITCHED					WHAT HE GAVE UP											THE RESULTS							
Year	Team	Lg	G	GS	CG	GF	IP	BFP	H	R	ER	HR	SH	SF	HB	TBB	IBB	SO	WP	Bk	W	L	Pct	Sh	Sv-Op Hld	ERC	ERA
2011	Roch*	AAA	43	2	0	11	56.2	251	55	32	27	6	2	4	2	24	2	68	1	0	3	1	.750	0	1-- -	4.03	4.29
2009	KC	AL	8	1	0	0	14.0	63	13	9	8	2	0	0	2	8	0	15	1	0	0	2	.000	0	0-0 2	5.31	5.14
2010	KC	AL	57	0	0	19	56.1	252	59	28	24	3	1	6	5	24	0	34	1	0	1	3	.250	0	0-0 7	4.43	3.83
2011	Min	AL	15	0	0	6	12.2	62	19	14	14	4	0	1	1	8	2	11	0	0	1	0	1.000	0	0-0 0	10.64	9.95
	3 ML YEARS		80	1	0	25	83.0	377	91	51	46	9	1	7	8	40	2	60	2	0	2	5	.286	0	0-0 9	5.41	4.99

Jared Hughes

Pitches: R Bats: R Pos: RP-12   Ht: 6'7" Wt: 220 Born: 7/4/1985 Age: 26

			HOW MUCH HE PITCHED					WHAT HE GAVE UP											THE RESULTS							
Year	Team	Lg	G	GS	CG	GF	IP	BFP	H	R	ER	HR	SH	SF	HB	TBB	IBB	SO	WP	Bk	W	L	Pct	Sh	Sv-Op Hld	ERC	ERA
2006	Wmspt	A-	5	5	0	0	23.0	88	14	7	7	2	0	0	3	7	0	11	3	0	1	2	.333	0	0-- -	2.23	2.74
2006	Hkry	A	10	10	0	0	48.1	226	46	38	31	6	3	2	6	31	0	25	8	0	5	4	.556	0	0-- -	5.37	5.77
2007	Hkry	A	27	27	0	0	145.1	659	162	94	75	11	10	8	10	54	2	109	27	0	8	9	.471	0	0-- -	4.59	4.64
2008	Lynbrg	A+	21	21	0	0	105.2	466	108	73	54	7	1	5	8	50	0	54	17	0	3	9	.250	0	0-- -	4.60	4.60
2008	Altna	AA	6	6	0	0	31.0	146	35	19	17	4	1	2	1	16	1	18	1	0	2	2	.500	0	0-- -	5.42	4.94
2009	Altna	AA	17	7	0	4	46.1	209	55	31	20	1	3	0	4	16	0	36	7	0	1	6	.143	0	3-- -	4.67	3.88
2009	Pirates	R	3	3	0	0	6.0	21	3	1	1	0	0	0	1	1	0	5	0	0	0	0	-	0	0-- -	1.20	1.50
2010	Altna	AA	30	23	0	2	150.2	656	166	93	74	15	4	8	11	41	0	120	15	0	12	8	.600	0	0-- -	4.43	4.42
2011	Altna	AA	13	11	0	0	61.2	270	62	31	28	2	4	1	8	18	0	33	3	0	3	4	.429	0	0-- -	3.66	4.09
2011	Indy	AAA	35	0	0	8	42.2	177	35	10	10	1	3	2	3	18	4	45	3	0	3	1	.750	0	0-- -	2.85	2.11
2011	Pit	NL	12	0	0	1	11.0	46	9	5	5	1	1	0	0	4	0	10	0	0	0	1	.000	0	0-0 2	2.85	4.09

Luke Hughes

Bats: R Throws: R Pos: 2B-37; 1B-36; 3B-13; PH-10; PR-7; DH-3   Ht: 5'11" Wt: 205 Born: 8/2/1984 Age: 27

							BATTING														BASERUNNING				AVERAGES		
Year	Team	Lg	G	AB	H	2B	3B	HR	(Hm	Rd)	TB	R	RBI	RC	TBB	IBB	SO	HBP	SH	SF	SB	CS	SB%	GDP	Avg	OBP	Slg
2003	Twins	R	54	190	58	9	4	2	(-	-)	81	22	25	29	15	1	22	2	4	1	5	5	.50	5	.305	.361	.426
2004	Elizab	R+	44	141	40	8	1	3	(-	-)	59	20	19	20	9	0	30	4	2	3	1	3	.25	1	.284	.338	.418
2005	Beloit	A	72	292	75	14	2	7	(-	-)	114	42	42	38	21	0	63	7	2	3	4	2	.67	6	.257	.319	.390
2005	FtMyrs	A+	23	84	17	3	1	0	(-	-)	22	9	7	4	2	0	15	1	3	2	0	0	-	3	.202	.222	.262
2006	FtMyrs	A+	95	333	77	15	0	4	(-	-)	104	31	37	32	23	1	72	5	2	5	6	2	.75	8	.231	.287	.312
2007	NwBrit	AA	92	315	89	18	2	9	(-	-)	138	56	43	52	34	2	68	4	5	4	4	1	.80	5	.283	.356	.438
2008	NwBrit	AA	70	285	91	15	3	15	(-	-)	157	53	40	59	28	0	70	3	2	1	4	1	.80	3	.319	.385	.551
2008	Roch	AAA	29	106	30	7	1	3	(-	-)	48	17	21	16	7	0	30	1	0	3	2	0	1.00	2	.283	.325	.453
2009	Roch	AAA	37	135	35	8	2	6	(-	-)	65	19	28	23	18	0	38	1	0	3	2	0	1.00	1	.259	.344	.481
2009	Twins	R	4	11	3	0	0	0	(-	-)	3	0	0	2	4	0	1	0	0	0	0	0	-	0	.273	.467	.273
2009	NwBrit	AA	56	200	50	15	3	6	(-	-)	89	22	36	30	19	2	38	4	1	5	1	1	.50	6	.250	.320	.445
2010	Roch	AAA	22	74	19	8	0	1	(-	-)	30	12	7	10	5	0	18	1	1	0	2	0	1.00	3	.257	.313	.405

							BATTING													BASERUNNING					AVERAGES		
Year	Team	Lg	G	AB	H	2B	3B	HR	(Hm	Rd)	TB	R	RBI	RC	TBB	IBB	SO	HBP	SH	SF	SB	CS	SB%	GDP	Avg	OBP	Slg
2011	Roch	AAA	30	117	27	6	1	4	(-	-)	47	16	11	14	10	0	18	0	0	2	2	0	1.00	1	.231	.287	.402
2010	Min	AL	2	7	2	0	0	1	(0	1)	5	1	1	0	0	0	3	0	0	0	0	1	.00	0	.286	.286	.714
2011	Min	AL	96	287	64	12	0	7	(4	3)	97	31	30	29	24	0	79	3	2	1	3	2	.60	2	.223	.289	.338
	2 ML YEARS		98	294	66	12	0	8	(4	4)	102	32	31	29	24	0	82	3	2	1	3	3	.50	2	.224	.289	.347

Phil Hughes

Pitches: R Bats: R Pos: SP-14; RP-3   **Ht: 6'5" Wt: 240 Born: 6/24/1986 Age: 26**

			HOW MUCH HE PITCHED						WHAT HE GAVE UP										THE RESULTS						
Year	Team	Lg	G	GS	CG	GF	IP	BFP	H	R	ER	HR	SH	SF	HB	TBB	IBB	SO	WP	Bk	W	L	Pct	Sh	Sv-Op Hld	ERC	ERA
2011	StlsInd*	A-	1	1	0	0	4.1	17	3	1	1	1	0	0	0	1	0	7	0	0	0	0	-	0	0- -	2.55	2.08
2011	Trntn*	AA	2	2	0	0	9.2	38	6	2	2	0	0	0	0	4	0	11	0	0	1	0	1.000	0	0- -	1.64	1.86
2007	NYY	AL	13	13	0	0	72.2	306	64	39	36	8	2	1	2	29	0	58	4	0	5	3	.625	0	0-0 0	3.61	4.46
2008	NYY	AL	8	8	0	0	34.0	157	43	26	25	3	1	3	1	15	0	23	2	0	0	4	.000	0	0-0 0	5.84	6.62
2009	NYY	AL	51	7	0	6	86.0	351	68	31	29	8	0	4	5	28	1	96	4	2	8	3	.727	0	3-6 18	2.86	3.03
2010	NYY	AL	31	29	0	0	176.1	730	162	83	82	25	2	5	0	58	1	146	9	1	18	8	.692	0	0-0 0	3.65	4.19
2011	NYY	AL	17	14	1	1	74.2	334	84	48	48	9	3	3	4	27	2	47	3	0	5	5	.500	1	0-0 0	4.92	5.79
	Postseason		14	3	0	2	27.2	125	32	18	18	3	1	0	0	12	3	25	3	0	2	3	.400	0	0-1 2	4.95	5.86
	5 ML YEARS		120	71	1	7	443.2	1878	421	227	220	53	8	16	12	157	4	370	22	3	36	23	.610	1	3-6 18	3.85	4.46

Philip Humber

Pitches: R Bats: R Pos: SP-26; RP-2   UMM-burr   **Ht: 6'3" Wt: 209 Born: 12/21/1982 Age: 29**

			HOW MUCH HE PITCHED						WHAT HE GAVE UP										THE RESULTS						
Year	Team	Lg	G	GS	CG	GF	IP	BFP	H	R	ER	HR	SH	SF	HB	TBB	IBB	SO	WP	Bk	W	L	Pct	Sh	Sv-Op Hld	ERC	ERA
2011	Charltt*	AAA	1	1	0	0	5.0	23	7	4	4	1	0	0	0	1	0	5	0	0	0	0	-	0	0- -	6.22	7.20
2006	NYM	NL	2	0	0	1	2.0	7	0	0	0	0	0	0	0	1	0	2	0	0	0	0	-	0	0-0 0	0.27	0.00
2007	NYM	NL	3	1	0	2	7.0	32	9	6	6	1	0	0	0	2	0	2	0	0	0	0	-	0	0-0 0	5.46	7.71
2008	Min	AL	5	0	0	2	11.2	50	11	6	6	4	0	0	1	5	0	6	0	0	0	0	-	0	0-0 0	6.11	4.63
2009	Min	AL	8	0	0	3	9.0	50	17	8	8	1	0	0	0	9	2	9	1	0	0	0	-	0	0-0 0	12.62	8.00
2010	KC	AL	8	1	0	1	21.2	94	22	10	10	1	0	1	1	7	2	16	2	0	2	1	.667	0	0-0 0	3.47	4.15
2011	CWS	AL	28	26	0	0	163.0	676	151	71	68	14	2	5	6	41	2	116	9	1	9	9	.500	0	0-0 0	3.13	3.75
	6 ML YEARS		54	28	0	9	214.1	909	210	101	98	21	2	6	8	65	6	151	12	1	11	10	.524	0	0-0 1	3.67	4.12

Nick Hundley

Bats: R Throws: R Pos: C-76; PH-9   **Ht: 6'1" Wt: 205 Born: 9/8/1983 Age: 28**

							BATTING													BASERUNNING					AVERAGES		
Year	Team	Lg	G	AB	H	2B	3B	HR	(Hm	Rd)	TB	R	RBI	RC	TBB	IBB	SO	HBP	SH	SF	SB	CS	SB%	GDP	Avg	OBP	Slg
2011	Tucsn*	AAA	4	11	3	2	0	1	(-	-)	8	3	5	2	2	0	2	0	0	0	0	0	-	0	.273	.385	.727
2011	SnAnt*	AA	7	23	4	0	0	0	(-	-)	4	1	1	2	6	0	10	0	0	0	0	0	-	0	.174	.345	.174
2008	SD	NL	60	198	47	7	1	5	(4	1)	71	21	24	17	11	0	52	2	0	5	0	0	-	1	.237	.278	.359
2009	SD	NL	78	256	61	15	2	8	(4	4)	104	23	30	33	28	1	76	1	1	3	5	1	.83	2	.238	.313	.406
2010	SD	NL	85	273	68	18	2	8	(7	1)	114	33	43	37	25	0	66	1	2	6	0	5	.00	8	.249	.308	.418
2011	SD	NL	82	281	81	16	5	9	(6	3)	134	34	29	40	22	3	74	4	0	1	1	1	.50	3	.288	.347	.477
	4 ML YEARS		305	1008	257	56	10	30	(21	9)	423	111	126	127	86	4	268	8	3	15	6	7	.46	14	.255	.314	.420

Cedric Hunter

Bats: L Throws: L Pos: PH-4; CF-2; PR-1   **Ht: 6'0" Wt: 185 Born: 3/10/1988 Age: 24**

							BATTING													BASERUNNING					AVERAGES		
Year	Team	Lg	G	AB	H	2B	3B	HR	(Hm	Rd)	TB	R	RBI	RC	TBB	IBB	SO	HBP	SH	SF	SB	CS	SB%	GDP	Avg	OBP	Slg
2006	Padres	R	52	213	79	13	4	1	(-	-)	103	46	44	52	40	1	22	3	1	5	17	5	.77	3	.371	.467	.484
2006	Eugene	A-	5	15	4	0	0	0	(-	-)	4	0	0	0	1	0	3	0	0	0	0	1	.00	1	.267	.313	.267
2007	FtWyn	A	129	496	140	20	2	7	(-	-)	185	53	58	66	47	4	78	2	0	4	8	9	.47	7	.282	.344	.373
2007	Portlnd	AAA	3	4	2	0	0	1	(-	-)	5	1	3	2	1	0	1	0	0	0	0	0	-	0	.500	.600	1.250
2008	Lk Els	A+	134	584	186	33	3	11	(-	-)	258	98	84	96	42	0	47	4	0	11	12	6	.67	12	.318	.362	.442
2009	SnAnt	AA	131	541	141	20	6	2	(-	-)	179	71	54	56	25	1	43	3	2	6	13	3	.81	8	.261	.294	.331
2010	SnAnt	AA	71	279	86	14	3	4	(-	-)	118	34	38	46	31	6	23	2	0	5	9	7	.56	10	.308	.375	.423
2010	Portlnd	AAA	65	262	69	13	3	3	(-	-)	97	42	26	31	16	0	22	0	6	1	5	1	.83	2	.263	.305	.370
2011	Tucsn	AAA	81	282	72	17	3	2	(-	-)	101	44	33	35	28	1	24	1	2	3	9	4	.69	5	.255	.322	.358
2011	SD	NL	6	4	1	0	0	0	(0	0)	1	1	0	0	1	0	0	0	0	0	0	1	.00	0	.250	.400	.250

Tommy Hunter

Pitches: R Bats: R Pos: SP-11; RP-9   **Ht: 6'3" Wt: 280 Born: 7/3/1986 Age: 25**

			HOW MUCH HE PITCHED						WHAT HE GAVE UP										THE RESULTS						
Year	Team	Lg	G	GS	CG	GF	IP	BFP	H	R	ER	HR	SH	SF	HB	TBB	IBB	SO	WP	Bk	W	L	Pct	Sh	Sv-Op Hld	ERC	ERA
2011	Frisco*	AA	1	0	0	0	4.0	16	3	2	2	1	0	1	1	1	0	5	0	0	0	0	-	0	0- -	4.30	4.50
2011	RdRck*	AAA	8	5	0	1	26.2	119	37	17	15	2	0	0	1	3	0	16	0	0	2	2	.500	0	1- -	5.07	5.06
2008	Tex	AL	3	3	0	0	11.0	63	23	20	20	4	0	0	1	3	0	9	0	0	0	2	.000	0	0-0 0	12.66	16.36
2009	Tex	AL	19	19	1	0	112.0	475	113	55	51	18	2	1	2	33	2	64	6	1	9	6	.600	0	0-0 0	3.86	4.10
2010	Tex	AL	23	22	1	0	128.0	536	126	55	53	21	3	2	3	33	0	68	1	0	13	4	**.765**	0	0-0 0	3.95	3.73
2011	2 Tms	AL	20	11	0	2	84.2	367	100	50	44	12	2	2	4	15	1	45	0	0	4	4	.500	0	0-1 1	4.65	4.68
11	Tex	AL	8	0	0	2	15.1	62	12	6	5	1	1	1	0	5	0	10	0	0	1	1	.500	0	0-1 0	2.44	2.93
11	Bal	AL	12	11	0	0	69.1	305	88	44	39	11	1	1	4	10	1	35	0	0	3	3	.500	0	0-0 1	5.19	5.06
	Postseason		3	3	0	0	11.1	52	16	8	7	2	0	0	1	1	0	13	0	1	0	2	.000	0	0-0 0	6.00	5.56
	4 ML YEARS		65	55	2	2	335.2	1441	362	180	168	50	7	5	10	84	3	186	7	1	26	16	.619	0	0-1 1	4.34	4.50

Torii Hunter

Bats: R **Throws:** R **Pos:** RF-136; DH-19; CF-1   **Ht:** 6'2" **Wt:** 225 **Born:** 7/18/1975 **Age:** 36

Year	Team	Lg	G	AB	H	2B	3B	HR	(Hm	Rd)	TB	R	RBI	RC	TBB	IBB	SO	HBP	SH	SF	SB	CS	SB%	GDP	Avg	OBP	Slg
1997	Min	AL	1	0	0	0	0	0	(0	0)	0	0	0	0	0	0	0	0	0	0	0	0	-	0	-	-	-
1998	Min	AL	6	17	4	1	0	0	(0	0)	5	0	2	1	2	0	6	0	0	0	0	1	.00	1	.235	.316	.294
1999	Min	AL	135	384	98	17	2	9	(2	7)	146	52	35	44	26	1	72	6	1	5	10	6	.63	9	.255	.309	.380
2000	Min	AL	99	336	94	14	7	5	(4	1)	137	44	44	39	18	2	68	2	0	2	4	3	.57	13	.280	.318	.408
2001	Min	AL	148	564	147	32	5	27	(13	14)	270	82	92	79	29	0	125	8	1	1	9	6	.60	12	.261	.306	.479
2002	Min	AL	148	561	162	37	4	29	(13	16)	294	89	94	85	35	3	118	5	0	3	23	8	.74	17	.289	.334	.524
2003	Min	AL	154	581	145	31	4	26	(12	14)	262	83	102	76	50	7	106	5	0	6	6	7	.46	15	.250	.312	.451
2004	Min	AL	138	520	141	37	0	23	(9	14)	247	79	81	09	40	4	101	7	0	2	21	7	.75	23	.271	.330	.475
2005	Min	Al	98	372	100	24	1	14	(6	8)	168	63	56	53	34	3	65	6	0	4	23	7	.77	8	.269	.337	.452
2006	Min	AL	147	557	155	21	2	31	(15	16)	273	86	98	81	45	2	108	5	0	4	12	6	.67	19	.278	.336	.490
2007	Min	AL	160	600	172	45	1	28	(11	17)	303	94	107	99	40	10	101	5	0	5	18	9	.67	17	.287	.334	.505
2008	LAA	AL	146	551	153	37	2	21	(10	11)	257	85	78	80	50	6	108	6	0	1	19	5	.79	15	.278	.344	.466
2009	LAA	AL	119	451	135	26	1	22	(15	7)	229	74	90	84	47	4	92	3	0	5	18	4	.82	9	.299	.366	.508
2010	LAA	AL	152	573	161	36	0	23	(8	15)	266	76	90	93	61	6	106	7	0	5	9	12	.43	22	.281	.354	.464
2011	LAA	AL	156	580	152	24	2	23	(15	8)	249	80	82	79	62	2	125	4	0	3	5	7	.42	24	.262	.336	.429
	Postseason		34	131	40	10	1	4	(1	3)	64	19	18	18	13	2	19	1	2	1	3	1	.75	4	.305	.370	.489
	15 ML YEARS		1807	6647	1819	382	31	281	(133	148)	3106	987	1051	962	539	50	1301	69	2	46	177	88	.67	204	.274	.332	.467

Chris Iannetta

Bats: R **Throws:** R **Pos:** C-105; PH-6; 1B-2; 3B-1   eye-ah-NETT-ah   **Ht:** 6'0" **Wt:** 230 **Born:** 4/8/1983 **Age:** 29

Year	Team	Lg	G	AB	H	2B	3B	HR	(Hm	Rd)	TB	R	RBI	RC	TBB	IBB	SO	HBP	SH	SF	SB	CS	SB%	GDP	Avg	OBP	Slg
2006	Col	NL	21	77	20	4	0	2	(0	2)	30	12	10	9	13	2	17	1	1	1	0	1	.00	1	.260	.370	.390
2007	Col	NL	67	197	43	8	3	4	(1	3)	69	22	27	27	29	3	58	5	1	2	0	0	-	3	.218	.330	.350
2008	Col	NL	104	333	88	22	2	18	(11	7)	168	50	65	65	56	0	92	14	2	2	0	0	-	6	.264	.390	.505
2009	Col	NL	93	289	66	15	2	16	(8	8)	133	41	52	47	43	3	75	11	1	6	0	1	.00	4	.228	.344	.460
2010	Col	NL	61	188	37	6	1	9	(7	2)	72	20	27	21	30	2	48	4	0	1	1	0	1.00	4	.197	.318	.383
2011	Col	NL	112	345	82	17	1	14	(10	4)	143	51	55	62	70	5	89	5	2	4	6	3	.67	10	.238	.370	.414
	6 ML YEARS		458	1429	336	72	9	63	(37	26)	615	196	236	231	241	15	379	40	7	16	7	5	.58	28	.235	.357	.430

Raul Ibanez

Bats: L **Throws:** R **Pos:** LF-134; PH-11; DH-1   ee-BAHN-yezz   **Ht:** 6'2" **Wt:** 227 **Born:** 6/2/1972 **Age:** 40

Year	Team	Lg	G	AB	H	2B	3B	HR	(Hm	Rd)	TB	R	RBI	RC	TBB	IBB	SO	HBP	SH	SF	SB	CS	SB%	GDP	Avg	OBP	Slg
1996	Sea	AL	4	5	0	0	0	0	(0	0)	0	0	0	0	0	0	1	1	0	0	0	0	-	0	.000	.167	.000
1997	Sea	AL	11	26	4	0	1	1	(1	0)	9	3	4	1	0	0	6	0	0	0	0	0	-	4	.154	.154	.346
1998	Sea	AL	37	98	25	7	1	2	(1	1)	40	12	12	10	5	0	22	0	0	0	0	0	-	4	.255	.291	.408
1999	Sea	AL	87	209	54	7	0	9	(3	6)	88	23	27	28	17	1	32	0	0	1	5	1	.83	4	.258	.313	.421
2000	Sea	AL	92	140	32	8	0	2	(2	0)	46	21	15	15	14	1	25	1	0	1	2	0	1.00	1	.229	.301	.329
2001	KC	AL	104	279	78	11	5	13	(5	8)	138	44	54	46	32	2	51	0	0	1	0	2	.00	6	.280	.353	.495
2002	KC	AL	137	497	146	37	6	24	(14	10)	267	70	103	89	40	5	76	2	1	4	5	3	.63	11	.294	.346	.537
2003	KC	AL	157	608	179	33	5	18	(8	10)	276	95	90	91	49	5	81	3	1	10	4	4	.67	10	.294	.345	.454
2004	Sea	AL	123	481	146	31	1	16	(9	7)	227	67	62	67	36	5	72	3	0	4	1	2	.33	10	.304	.353	.472
2005	Sea	AL	162	614	172	32	2	20	(9	11)	268	92	89	99	71	6	99	2	0	3	9	4	.69	12	.280	.355	.436
2006	Sea	AL	159	626	181	33	5	33	(17	16)	323	103	123	114	65	15	115	1	0	7	2	4	.33	13	.289	.353	.516
2007	Sea	AL	149	573	167	35	5	21	(7	14)	275	80	105	101	53	4	97	3	0	7	0	0	-	14	.291	.351	.480
2008	Sea	AL	162	635	186	43	3	23	(14	9)	304	85	110	107	64	11	110	3	0	5	2	4	.33	13	.293	.358	.479
2009	Phi	NL	134	500	136	32	3	34	(13	21)	276	93	93	80	56	8	119	4	0	5	4	0	1.00	16	.272	.347	.552
2010	Phi	NL	155	561	154	37	5	16	(9	7)	249	75	83	86	68	11	108	0	0	7	4	3	.57	15	.275	.349	.444
2011	Phi	NL	144	535	131	31	1	20	(15	5)	224	65	84	64	33	3	106	2	0	5	2	0	1.00	13	.245	.289	.419
	Postseason		32	102	24	8	0	2	(1	1)	38	11	13	12	8	1	27	0	0	0	0	0	-	2	.235	.291	.373
	16 ML YEARS		1817	6387	1791	377	43	252	(127	125)	3010	928	1054	998	603	77	1120	25	2	60	44	27	.62	142	.280	.342	.471

Ryota Igarashi

Pitches: R **Bats:** R **Pos:** RP-45   ree-OH-tah ig-ah-RAH-she   **Ht:** 5'11" **Wt:** 198 **Born:** 5/28/1979 **Age:** 33

			HOW MUCH HE PITCHED						WHAT HE GAVE UP											THE RESULTS						
Year	Team	Lg	G	GS	CG	GF	IP	BFP	H	R	ER	HR	SH	SF	HB	TBB	IBB	SO	WP	Bk	W	L	Pct	Sh	Sv-Op	Hld	ERC	ERA
1999	Yakult	Jap	36	0	0	-	47.2	206	34	27	26	4	-	-	1	29	-	59	3	1	6	4	.600	0	1- -	-	3.23	4.91
2000	Yakult	Jap	56	0	0	-	75.1	301	42	28	26	11	-	-	1	33	-	90	6	0	11	4	.733	0	1- -	-	2.24	3.11
2001	Yakult	Jap	41	0	0	-	41.2	178	25	13	12	2	-	-	2	28	-	51	1	0	2	3	.400	0	0- -	-	2.75	2.59
2002	Yakult	Jap	64	0	0	-	78.0	301	49	19	18	8	-	-	3	18	-	97	8	0	8	2	.800	0	4- -	-	1.75	2.08
2003	Yakult	Jap	66	0	0	-	74.0	315	60	33	32	9	-	-	1	33	-	83	7	1	5	5	.500	0	0- -	-	3.36	3.89
2004	Yakult	Jap	66	0	0	-	74.1	316	57	24	22	9	-	-	1	36	-	86	4	0	5	3	.625	0	37- -	-	3.27	2.66
2005	Yakult	Jap	49	0	0	-	56.2	249	52	24	22	6	-	-	1	27	-	60	6	0	3	2	.600	0	4- -	-	3.95	3.49
2006	Yakult	Jap	29	0	0	-	25.0	119	33	20	17	3	-	-	2	11	-	18	4	0	1	2	.333	0	1- -	-	6.60	6.12
2008	Yakult	Jap	44	0	0	-	43.2	171	35	13	12	3	-	-	1	6	0	42	3	0	3	2	.600	0	3- -	-	2.08	2.47
2009	Yakult	Jap	56	0	0	-	53.2	221	42	19	19	3	-	-	1	20	1	44	1	0	3	2	.600	0	3- -	-	2.72	3.19
2010	StLuci	A+	5	2	0	1	7.2	34	10	2	2	0	0	1	0	1	0	11	1	0	1	0	1.000	0	0- -	-	3.89	2.35
2010	Buffalo	AAA	15	0	0	9	16.1	73	18	8	6	2	2	0	0	6	0	16	3	0	2	1	.667	0	2- -	-	4.58	3.31
2011	Buffalo	AAA	21	0	0	13	31.0	117	15	7	3	2	1	0	0	9	0	34	2	2	0	1	.000	0	5- -	-	1.19	0.87
2010	NYM	NL	34	0	0	11	50.0	135	29	24	24	4	0	3	0	18	1	25	3	0	1	1	.500	0	0-0	2	4.78	7.12
2011	NYM	NL	45	0	0	9	38.2	190	43	20	20	2	2	0	4	28	2	42	3	0	4	1	.800	0	0-1	2	5.85	4.66
	2 ML YEARS		79	0	0	20	69.0	325	72	44	44	6	2	3	4	46	3	67	6	0	5	2	.714	0	0-1	4	5.38	5.74

Jose Iglesias

Bats: R Throws: R Pos: SS-8; PR-5   EE-glay-see-us   Ht: 5'11" Wt: 175 Born: 1/5/1990 Age: 22

Year	Team	Lg	G	AB	H	2B	3B	HR	(Hm	Rd)	TB	R	RBI	RC	TBB	IBB	SO	HBP	SH	SF	SB	CS	SB%	GDP	Avg	OBP	Slg
2010	Portlnd	AA	57	221	63	10	3	0	(-	-)	79	29	13	26	8	1	49	3	1	3	5	2	.71	6	.285	.315	.357
2010	Lowell	A-	13	40	14	2	2	0	(-	-)	20	8	7	9	7	0	8	1	0	0	2	1	.67	0	.350	.458	.500
2011	Pwtckt	AAA	101	357	84	9	0	1	(-	-)	96	35	31	29	21	0	58	4	5	0	12	4	.75	18	.235	.285	.269
2011	Bos	AL	10	6	2	0	0	0	(0	0)	2	3	0	0	0	0	2	0	0	0	0	0	-	0	.333	.333	.333

Omar Infante

Bats: R Throws: R Pos: 2B-146; PH-2   in-FAHN-tay   Ht: 6'0" Wt: 180 Born: 12/26/1981 Age: 30

Year	Team	Lg	G	AB	H	2B	3B	HR	(Hm	Rd)	TB	R	RBI	RC	TBB	IBB	SO	HBP	SH	SF	SB	CS	SB%	GDP	Avg	OBP	Slg
2011	Jupiter*	A+	1	5	3	0	0	0	(-	-)	3	0	0	1	0	0	0	0	0	0	0	0	-	0	.600	.600	.600
2002	Det	AL	18	72	24	3	0	1	(0	1)	30	4	6	12	3	0	10	0	0	0	1	0	1.00	0	.333	.360	.417
2003	Det	AL	69	221	49	6	1	0	(0	0)	57	24	8	16	18	0	37	0	3	2	6	3	.67	1	.222	.278	.258
2004	Det	AL	142	503	133	27	9	16	(7	9)	226	69	55	69	40	3	112	1	7	5	13	7	.65	4	.264	.317	.449
2005	Det	AL	121	406	90	28	2	9	(3	6)	149	36	43	38	16	0	73	2	8	2	8	0	1.00	5	.222	.254	.367
2006	Det	AL	78	224	62	11	4	4	(0	4)	93	35	25	26	14	0	45	3	2	2	3	2	.60	5	.277	.325	.415
2007	Det	AL	66	166	45	6	1	2	(0	2)	59	24	17	23	9	0	29	0	2	1	4	1	.80	4	.271	.307	.355
2008	Atl	NL	96	317	93	24	3	3	(1	2)	132	45	40	45	22	2	44	2	2	5	0	1	.00	4	.293	.338	.416
2009	Atl	NL	70	203	62	9	1	2	(1	1)	79	24	27	29	19	0	28	1	2	4	2	0	1.00	5	.305	.361	.389
2010	Atl	NL	134	471	151	15	3	8	(1	7)	196	65	47	70	29	1	62	0	4	2	7	6	.54	14	.321	.359	.416
2011	Fla	NL	148	579	160	24	8	7	(2	5)	221	55	49	66	34	1	67	2	17	8	7	4	.64	12	.276	.315	.382
	Postseason		6	21	5	1	0	0	(0	0)	6	1	0	2	2	0	6	0	0	0	1	0	1.00	0	.238	.304	.286
10 ML YEARS			942	3162	869	153	32	52	(15	37)	1242	381	317	394	204	7	507	11	47	31	47	23	.67	54	.275	.318	.393

Brandon Inge

Bats: R Throws: R Pos: 3B-99; PH-3; PR-2; DH-1   Ht: 5'11" Wt: 188 Born: 5/19/1977 Age: 35

Year	Team	Lg	G	AB	H	2B	3B	HR	(Hm	Rd)	TB	R	RBI	RC	TBB	IBB	SO	HBP	SH	SF	SB	CS	SB%	GDP	Avg	OBP	Slg
2011	Toledo*	AAA	29	108	31	4	0	7	(-	-)	56	18	19	22	17	0	30	1	0	0	0	0	-	0	.287	.389	.519
2001	Det	AL	79	189	34	11	0	0	(0	0)	45	13	15	6	9	0	41	0	2	2	1	4	.20	2	.180	.215	.238
2002	Det	AL	95	321	65	15	3	7	(3	4)	107	27	24	24	24	0	101	4	1	1	1	3	.25	7	.202	.266	.333
2003	Det	AL	104	330	67	15	3	8	(4	4)	112	32	30	23	24	0	79	5	4	3	4	4	.50	8	.203	.265	.339
2004	Det	AL	131	408	117	15	7	13	(9	4)	185	43	64	63	32	0	72	4	8	6	5	4	.56	4	.287	.340	.453
2005	Det	AL	160	616	161	31	9	16	(10	6)	258	75	72	82	63	1	140	3	6	6	7	6	.54	14	.261	.330	.419
2006	Det	AL	159	542	137	29	2	27	(12	15)	251	83	83	79	43	2	128	7	4	5	7	4	.64	12	.253	.313	.463
2007	Det	AL	151	508	120	25	2	14	(9	5)	191	64	71	65	47	5	150	11	7	4	9	2	.82	8	.236	.312	.376
2008	Det	AL	113	347	71	16	4	11	(8	3)	128	41	51	44	43	2	94	8	5	4	4	3	.57	4	.205	.303	.369
2009	Det	AL	161	562	129	16	1	27	(14	13)	228	71	84	70	54	1	170	17	1	3	2	5	.29	12	.230	.314	.406
2010	Det	AL	144	514	127	28	5	13	(4	9)	204	47	70	64	54	4	134	5	0	7	4	3	.57	12	.247	.321	.397
2011	Det	AL	102	269	53	10	2	3	(3	0)	76	29	23	12	24	0	74	2	5	3	1	1	.50	9	.197	.265	.283
	Postseason		13	44	12	3	0	1	(0	1)	18	4	4	5	4	2	15	0	1	1	0	0	-	1	.273	.327	.409
11 ML YEARS			1399	4606	1081	211	38	139	(76	63)	1785	525	587	532	417	15	1183	66	43	44	45	39	.54	92	.235	.305	.388

Joe Inglett

Bats: L Throws: R Pos: PH-18; 2B-3; 3B-2   Ht: 5'9" Wt: 177 Born: 6/29/1978 Age: 34

Year	Team	Lg	G	AB	H	2B	3B	HR	(Hm	Rd)	TB	R	RBI	RC	TBB	IBB	SO	HBP	SH	SF	SB	CS	SB%	GDP	Avg	OBP	Slg
2011	OKCity*	AAA	11	28	2	0	0	0	(-	-)	2	1	0	1	8	0	9	0	1	0	2	0	1.00	1	.071	.278	.071
2006	Cle	AL	64	201	57	8	3	2	(1	1)	77	26	21	28	14	0	39	1	5	1	5	1	.83	1	.284	.332	.383
2007	Tor	AL	2	5	3	0	1	0	(0	0)	5	0	2	3	0	0	0	0	0	0	1	0	1.00	0	.600	.600	1.000
2008	Tor	AL	109	344	102	15	7	3	(2	1)	140	45	39	52	28	0	43	4	8	1	9	2	.82	5	.297	.355	.407
2009	Tor	AL	36	89	25	4	1	0	(0	0)	31	11	6	14	8	0	21	1	1	0	3	1	.75	0	.281	.347	.348
2010	Mil	NL	102	142	36	8	5	1	(1	0)	57	15	8	19	15	0	34	2	0	1	1	0	1.00	1	.254	.331	.401
2011	Hou	NL	20	27	6	1	0	0	(0	0)	7	3	1	1	0	0	7	0	0	0	0	0	-	0	.222	.222	.259
6 ML YEARS			333	808	229	36	17	6	(4	2)	317	100	77	117	65	0	144	8	14	3	19	4	.83	7	.283	.342	.392

Jason Isringhausen

Pitches: R Bats: R Pos: RP-53   Ht: 6'3" Wt: 230 Born: 9/7/1972 Age: 39

			HOW MUCH HE PITCHED						WHAT HE GAVE UP											THE RESULTS					
Year	Team	Lg	G	GS	CG	GF	IP	BFP	H	R	ER	HR	SH	SF	HB	TBB	IBB	SO	WP	Bk	W	L	Pct	Sh	Sv-Op Hld	ERC	ERA
1995	NYM	NL	14	14	1	0	93.0	385	88	29	29	6	3	3	2	31	2	55	4	1	9	2	.818	0	0-0	3.40	2.81
1996	NYM	NL	27	27	2	0	171.2	766	190	103	91	13	7	9	8	73	5	114	14	0	6	14	.300	1	0-0	4.75	4.77
1997	NYM	NL	6	6	0	0	29.2	145	40	27	25	3	1	2	1	22	0	25	3	0	2	2	.500	0	0-0	7.99	7.58
1999	2 Tms		33	5	0	20	64.2	286	64	35	34	9	0	1	3	34	4	51	4	0	1	4	.200	0	9-9	4.94	4.73
2000	Oak		66	0	0	57	69.0	304	67	34	29	6	2	1	3	32	5	57	5	1	6	4	.600	0	33-40	4.09	3.78
2001	Oak	AL	65	0	0	54	71.1	293	54	24	21	5	3	1	0	23	5	74	2	0	4	3	.571	0	34-43	2.18	2.65
2002	StL	NL	60	0	0	51	65.1	257	46	22	18	0	4	3	1	18	1	68	0	0	3	2	.600	0	32-37	1.61	2.48
2003	StL	NL	40	0	0	31	42.0	174	31	14	11	2	1	0	1	18	1	41	6	0	0	1	.000	0	22-25	2.40	2.36
2004	StL	NL	74	0	0	66	75.1	308	55	27	24	5	6	1	2	23	4	71	1	0	4	2	.667	0	47-54	2.09	2.87
2005	StL	NL	63	0	0	52	59.0	245	43	14	14	4	3	1	1	27	5	51	2	0	1	2	.333	0	39-43	2.56	2.14
2006	StL	NL	59	0	0	51	58.1	257	47	25	23	10	1	3	3	38	3	52	3	0	4	8	.333	0	33-43	4.63	3.55
2007	StL	NL	63	0	0	54	65.1	267	42	21	18	4	1	1	2	28	3	54	3	0	4	0	1.000	0	32-34	2.11	2.48
2008	StL	NL	42	0	0	27	42.2	200	48	28	27	5	0	1	5	22	0	36	1	0	1	5	.167	0	12-19	5.84	5.70
2009	TB	AL	9	0	0	4	8.0	37	6	2	2	0	4	2	0	5	0	6	1	0	1	0	1.000	0	0-1	3.64	2.25
2011	NYM	NL	53	0	0	15	46.2	200	36	23	21	6	2	1	2	24	2	44	1	0	3	3	.500	0	7-11 19	3.43	4.05

Year	Team	Lg	G	GS	CG	GF	IP	BFP	H	R	ER	HR	SH	SF	HB	TBB	IBB	SO	WP	Bk	W	L	Pct	Sh	Sv-Op	Hld	ERC	ERA
99	NYM	NL	13	5	0	2	39.1	179	43	29	28	7	0	1	2	22	2	31	2	0	1	3	.250	0	1-1	0	6.07	6.41
99	Oak	AL	20	0	0	18	25.1	107	21	6	6	2	0	0	1	12	2	20	2	0	0	1	1.000	0	8-8	0	3.33	2.13
	Postseason		23	0	0	22	26.2	110	17	8	7	2	2	1	1	12	4	23	0	0	1	1	.500	0	11-12	0	2.10	2.36
15 ML YEARS			674	52	3	482	962.0	4124	857	428	387	78	34	29	34	418	40	799	50	2	48	53	.475	1	300-359	23	3.53	3.62

Hisashi Iwakuma

Pitches: R Bats: R Pos: P hee-SAH-shee ee-wah-KOOM-ah **Ht: 6'3" Wt: 170 Born: 4/12/1981 Age: 31**

Year	Team	Lg	G	GS	CG	GF	IP	BFP	H	R	ER	HR	SH	SF	HB	TBB	IBB	SO	WP	Bk	W	L	Pct	Sh	Sv-Op	Hld	ERC	ERA
2001	Kintets	Jap	9	-	1	-	43.2	192	46	28	22	3	-	-	3	13	-	25	1	0	4	2	.667	1	0- -	-	3.94	4.53
2002	Kintets	Jap	23	-	2	-	141.1	594	132	62	58	10	-	-	8	42	-	131	4	1	8	7	.533	0	0- -	-	3.34	3.69
2003	Kintets	Jap	27	-	11	-	195.2	809	201	85	75	19	-	-	3	48	-	149	2	0	15	10	.600	0	0- -	-	3.73	3.45
2004	Kintets	Jap	21	-	7	-	158.2	647	149	57	53	13	-	-	8	30	-	123	0	0	15	2	.882	1	0- -	-	3.04	3.01
2005	Tohoku	Jap	27	-	9	-	182.1	796	218	113	101	19	-	-	6	40	-	124	7	0	9	15	.375	0	0- -	-	4.61	4.99
2006	Tohoku	Jap	6	-	2	-	38.2	169	43	18	16	4	-	1	1	12	-	16	0	0	1	2	.333	0	0- -	-	4.46	3.72
2007	Tohoku	Jap	16	-	0	-	90.0	388	95	47	34	6	-	-	2	23	-	84	0	1	5	5	.500	0	0- -	-	3.61	3.40
2008	Tohoku	Jap	28	-	5	-	201.2	787	161	48	42	3	-	-	4	36	-	159	4	0	21	4	.840	2	0- -	-	1.83	1.87
2009	Tohoku	Jap	24	-	5	-	169.0	710	179	62	61	15	-	-	6	43	-	121	3	0	13	6	.684	0	0- -	-	3.96	3.25
2010	Tohoku	Jap	28	-	4	-	201.0	821	184	68	63	11	-	-	12	36	-	153	1	1	10	9	.526	1	0- -	-	2.72	2.82
2011	Tohoku	Jap	17	-	2	-	119.0	471	106	34	32	6	-	-	5	19	-	90	1	0	6	7	.462	1	0- -	-	2.50	2.42

Cesar Izturis

Bats: B Throws: R Pos: SS-12; 2B-3; PR-3; 3B-1; DH-1 izz-TOUR-iss **Ht: 5'9" Wt: 180 Born: 2/10/1980 Age: 32**

Year	Team	Lg	G	AB	H	2B	3B	HR	(Hm	Rd)	TB	R	RBI	RC	TBB	IBB	SO	HBP	SH	SF	SB	CS	SB%	GDP	Avg	OBP	Slg
2011	Orioles*	R	1	2	0	0	0	0	(-	-)	0	0	0	0	0	0	1	0	0	0	0	0	-	0	.000	.000	.000
2011	Bowie*	AA	7	25	6	1	0	0	(-	-)	7	3	3	1	2	0	5	0	1	1	1	0	1.00	0	.240	.286	.280
2001	Tor	AL	46	134	36	6	2	2	(1	1)	52	19	9	16	2	0	15	0	4	0	8	1	.89	0	.269	.279	.388
2002	LAD	NL	135	439	102	24	2	1	(0	1)	133	43	31	26	14	1	39	0	10	5	7	7	.50	12	.232	.253	.303
2003	LAD	NL	158	558	140	21	6	1	(0	1)	176	47	40	42	25	8	70	0	7	3	10	5	.67	8	.251	.282	.315
2004	LAD	NL	159	670	193	32	9	4	(1	3)	255	90	62	95	43	2	70	0	12	3	25	9	.74	6	.288	.330	.381
2005	LAD	NL	106	444	114	19	2	2	(1	1)	143	48	31	37	25	1	51	4	4	1	8	8	.50	11	.257	.302	.322
2006	2 Tms	NL	54	192	47	9	1	1	(1	0)	61	14	18	14	12	3	14	2	1	1	1	4	.20	4	.245	.295	.318
2007	2 Tms	NL	110	314	81	14	2	0	(0	0)	99	31	16	27	19	2	19	1	3	0	3	3	.50	7	.258	.302	.315
2008	StL	NL	135	414	109	10	3	1	(0	1)	128	50	24	39	29	1	26	6	3	2	24	6	.80	6	.263	.319	.309
2009	Bal	AL	114	387	99	14	4	2	(1	1)	127	34	30	37	18	0	38	3	4	0	12	4	.75	11	.256	.294	.328
2010	Bal	AL	150	473	109	13	1	1	(0	1)	127	42	28	32	25	1	53	6	7	2	11	5	.69	11	.230	.277	.268
2011	Bal	AL	18	30	6	0	0	0	(0	0)	6	4	1	2	2	0	10	0	1	0	0	0	-	0	.200	.250	.200
06	LAD	NL	32	119	30	7	1	1	(1	0)	42	10	12	10	7	3	6	2	0	1	1	3	.25	1	.252	.302	.353
06	ChC	NL	22	73	17	2	0	0	(0	0)	19	4	6	4	5	0	8	0	1	0	0	1	.00	3	.233	.282	.260
07	ChC	NL	65	191	47	11	0	0	(0	0)	58	15	8	13	13	2	16	1	2	0	3	0	1.00	6	.246	.298	.304
07	Pit	NL	45	123	34	3	2	0	(0	0)	41	16	8	14	6	0	3	0	1	0	0	3	.00	1	.276	.310	.333
	Postseason		4	17	3	1	0	0	(0	0)	4	1	0	0	1	0	2	0	0	0	0	0	-	0	.176	.222	.235
11 ML YEARS			1185	4055	1036	162	32	15	(5	10)	1307	422	290	367	214	19	405	22	56	17	109	52	.68	76	.255	.295	.322

Maicer Izturis

Bats: B Throws: R Pos: 2B-49; 3B-37; PH-17; SS-16; DH-12 MY-sare izz-TOUR-iss **Ht: 5'8" Wt: 170 Born: 9/12/1980 Age: 31**

Year	Team	Lg	G	AB	H	2B	3B	HR	(Hm	Rd)	TB	R	RBI	RC	TBB	IBB	SO	HBP	SH	SF	SB	CS	SB%	GDP	Avg	OBP	Slg
2004	Mon	NL	32	107	22	5	2	1	(1	0)	34	10	4	8	10	1	20	2	2	0	4	0	1.00	1	.206	.286	.318
2005	LAA	AL	77	191	47	8	4	1	(0	1)	66	18	15	25	17	2	21	0	1	1	9	3	.75	5	.246	.306	.346
2006	LAA	AL	104	352	103	21	3	5	(1	4)	145	64	44	56	38	1	35	3	5	1	14	6	.70	7	.293	.365	.412
2007	LAA	AL	102	336	97	17	2	6	(4	2)	136	47	51	65	33	2	39	0	1	4	7	1	.88	4	.289	.349	.405
2008	LAA	AL	79	290	78	14	2	3	(1	2)	105	44	37	39	26	0	27	1	2	2	11	2	.85	9	.269	.329	.362
2009	LAA	AL	114	387	116	22	3	8	(3	5)	168	74	65	66	35	2	41	5	3	7	13	5	.72	7	.300	.359	.434
2010	LAA	AL	61	212	53	13	1	3	(0	3)	77	27	27	30	21	0	27	2	1	2	7	3	.70	1	.250	.321	.363
2011	LAA	AL	122	449	124	35	0	5	(1	4)	174	51	38	53	33	3	65	8	0	4	9	6	.60	6	.276	.334	.388
	Postseason		10	29	6	3	0	0	(0	0)	9	3	2	2	1	1	5	0	0	1	3	0	1.00	0	.207	.226	.310
8 ML YEARS			691	2324	640	135	17	32	(11	21)	905	335	281	342	213	11	275	21	15	21	74	26	.74	40	.275	.339	.389

Austin Jackson

Bats: R Throws: R Pos: CF-152; PR-3; PH-2; DH-1 **Ht: 6'1" Wt: 185 Born: 2/1/1987 Age: 25**

Year	Team	Lg	G	AB	H	2B	3B	HR	(Hm	Rd)	TB	R	RBI	RC	TBB	IBB	SO	HBP	SH	SF	SB	CS	SB%	GDP	Avg	OBP	Slg
2005	Yanks	R	40	148	45	11	2	0	(-	-)	60	32	14	25	18	0	26	1	0	4	11	2	.85	4	.304	.374	.405
2006	CtnSC	A	134	535	139	24	5	4	(-	-)	185	90	47	71	61	0	151	6	5	4	37	12	.76	7	.260	.340	.346
2007	CtnSC	A	60	235	61	16	1	3	(-	-)	88	33	25	33	24	0	59	4	1	2	19	6	.76	1	.260	.336	.374
2007	Tampa	A+	67	258	89	15	6	10	(-	-)	146	53	34	56	22	0	48	2	0	2	13	5	.72	9	.345	.398	.566
2007	S-WB	AAA	1	3	1	0	0	0	(-	-)	2	2	0	1	2	0	2	0	0	0	1	0	1.00	0	.333	.600	.667
2008	Trntn	AA	131	520	148	33	5	9	(-	-)	218	75	69	82	56	3	113	2	2	4	19	6	.76	9	.285	.354	.419
2009	S-WB	AAA	132	504	151	23	9	4	(-	-)	204	67	65	78	40	1	123	6	1	6	24	4	.86	10	.300	.354	.405
2010	Det	AL	151	618	181	34	10	4	(0	4)	247	103	41	84	47	4	170	4	3	3	27	6	.82	5	.293	.345	.400
2011	Det	AL	153	591	147	22	11	10	(5	5)	221	90	45	67	56	3	181	4	14	3	22	5	.81	11	.249	.317	.374
2 ML YEARS			304	1209	328	56	21	14	(5	9)	468	193	86	151	103	7	351	8	17	6	49	11	.82	16	.271	.331	.387

Conor Jackson

Bats: R **Throws:** R **Pos:** 1B-53; RF-31; LF-23; PH-20; 3B-7; DH-1 **Ht:** 6'2" **Wt:** 215 **Born:** 5/7/1982 **Age:** 30

Year	Team	Lg	G	AB	H	2B	3B	HR	(Hm	Rd)	TB	R	RBI	RC	TBB	IBB	SO	HBP	SH	SF	SB	CS	SB%	GDP	Avg	OBP	Slg
2005	Ari	NL	40	85	17	3	0	2	(2	0)	26	8	8	6	12	0	11	1	0	1	0	0	-	6	.200	.303	.306
2006	Ari	NL	140	485	141	26	1	15	(8	7)	214	75	79	77	54	2	73	9	1	7	1	0	1.00	18	.291	.368	.441
2007	Ari	NL	130	415	118	29	1	15	(8	7)	194	56	60	67	53	2	50	4	2	3	2	2	.50	8	.284	.368	.467
2008	Ari	NL	144	540	162	31	6	12	(6	6)	241	87	75	88	59	3	61	9	1	3	10	2	.83	14	.300	.376	.446
2009	Ari	NL	30	99	18	4	0	1	(1	0)	25	8	14	10	11	0	16	0	0	0	5	0	1.00	1	.182	.264	.253
2010	2 Tms		60	208	49	13	0	2	(2	0)	68	25	16	24	31	3	27	1	0	1	6	1	.86	6	.236	.336	.327
2011	2 Tms	AL	114	352	86	17	1	5	(4	1)	120	32	43	35	32	0	53	3	0	3	3	1	.75	13	.244	.310	.341
10	Ari	NL	42	151	36	11	0	1	(1	0)	50	19	11	19	20	2	18	0	0	1	4	1	.80	4	.238	.326	.331
10	Oak	AL	18	57	13	2	0	1	(1	0)	18	6	5	5	11	1	9	1	0	0	2	0	1.00	2	.228	.362	.316
11	Oak	AL	102	333	83	17	1	4	(3	1)	114	30	38	33	30	0	50	3	0	2	3	1	.75	12	.249	.315	.342
11	Bos	AL	12	19	3	0	0	1	(1	0)	6	2	5	2	2	0	3	0	0	1	0	0	-	1	.158	.227	.316
Postseason			6	17	4	1	0	0	(0	0)	5	1	2	1	0	0	3	0	0	1	0	0	-	1	.235	.222	.294
7 ML YEARS			658	2184	591	123	9	52	(31	21)	888	291	295	307	252	10	291	27	4	18	27	6	.82	66	.271	.351	.407

Edwin Jackson

Pitches: R **Bats:** R **Pos:** SP-31; RP-1 **Ht:** 6'3" **Wt:** 210 **Born:** 9/9/1983 **Age:** 28

Year	Team	Lg	G	GS	CG	GF	IP	BFP	H	R	ER	HR	SH	SF	HB	TBB	IBB	SO	WP	Bk	W	L	Pct	Sh	Sv-Op	Hld	ERC	ERA
2003	LAD	NL	4	3	0	0	22.0	91	17	6	6	2	1	1	1	11	1	19	3	0	2	1	.667	0	0-0	0	3.36	2.45
2004	LAD	NL	8	5	0	1	24.2	113	31	20	20	7	1	0	0	11	1	16	0	0	2	1	.667	0	0-0	0	7.21	7.30
2005	LAD	NL	7	6	0	0	28.2	134	31	22	20	2	0	2	1	17	0	13	2	1	2	2	.500	0	0-0	0	5.13	6.28
2006	TB	AL	23	1	0	7	36.1	174	42	27	22	2	2	2	1	25	0	27	3	1	0	0	-	0	0-0	0	5.86	5.45
2007	TB	AL	32	31	1	0	161.0	755	195	116	103	19	5	6	4	88	3	128	7	1	5	15	.250	1	0-0	0	6.11	5.76
2008	TB	AL	32	31	1	0	183.1	792	199	91	90	23	3	3	2	77	1	108	7	1	14	11	.560	0	0-1	0	4.99	4.42
2009	Det	AL	33	33	1	0	214.0	890	200	93	86	27	4	2	5	70	3	161	6	0	13	9	.591	0	0-0	0	3.72	3.62
2010	2 Tms		32	32	1	0	209.1	902	214	111	104	21	6	4	6	78	4	181	20	0	10	12	.455	1	0-0	0	4.20	4.47
2011	2 Tms		32	31	1	1	199.2	861	225	92	84	16	15	6	2	62	4	148	9	2	12	9	.571	1	0-0	0	4.34	3.79
10	Ari	NL	21	21	1	0	134.1	587	141	80	77	13	6	2	5	60	2	104	13	0	6	10	.375	1	0-0	0	4.72	5.16
10	CWS	AL	11	11	0	0	75.0	315	73	31	27	8	0	2	1	18	2	77	7	0	4	2	.667	0	0-0	0	3.32	3.24
11	CWS	AL	19	19	1	0	121.2	522	134	55	53	8	6	4	0	39	2	97	7	1	7	7	.500	1	0-0	0	4.10	3.92
11	StL	NL	13	12	0	1	78.0	339	91	37	31	8	9	2	2	23	2	51	2	1	5	2	.714	0	0-0	0	4.73	3.58
Postseason			3	0	0	2	4.1	17	2	1	1	1	0	0	0	3	1	5	0	0	0	0	-	0	0-0	0	2.98	2.08
9 ML YEARS			203	173	4	9	1079.0	4712	1154	578	535	119	37	26	22	439	17	801	57	6	60	60	.500	3	0-1	0	4.67	4.46

Chris Jakubauskas

Pitches: R **Bats:** L **Pos:** RP-27; SP-6 jack-uh-BAU-skiss **Ht:** 6'2" **Wt:** 215 **Born:** 12/22/1978 **Age:** 33

Year	Team	Lg	G	GS	CG	GF	IP	BFP	H	R	ER	HR	SH	SF	HB	TBB	IBB	SO	WP	Bk	W	L	Pct	Sh	Sv-Op	Hld	ERC	ERA
2011	Norfolk*	AAA	5	5	0	0	20.0	85	23	9	9	3	0	0	0	7	0	14	1	1	0	1	.000	0	0--	1	5.31	4.05
2009	Sea	AL	35	8	1	6	93.0	390	91	60	55	15	0	3	2	27	3	47	8	1	6	7	.462	0	0-1	3	3.99	5.32
2010	Pit	NL	1	1	0	0	0.2	4	2	2	2	0	0	0	0	0	0	0	0	0	0	1	.000	0	0-0	0	14.52	27.00
2011	Bal	AL	33	6	0	11	72.1	331	93	46	46	11	1	4	3	29	3	52	5	0	2	2	.500	0	0-1	1	6.35	5.72
3 ML YEARS			69	15	1	17	166.0	725	186	108	103	26	1	7	5	56	6	99	13	1	8	10	.444	0	0-1	4	5.02	5.58

Chuck James

Pitches: L **Bats:** L **Pos:** RP-8 **Ht:** 6'0" **Wt:** 190 **Born:** 11/9/1981 **Age:** 30

Year	Team	Lg	G	GS	CG	GF	IP	BFP	H	R	ER	HR	SH	SF	HB	TBB	IBB	SO	WP	Bk	W	L	Pct	Sh	Sv-Op	Hld	ERC	ERA
2011	Roch*	AAA	38	0	0	14	62.2	261	49	16	16	4	0	3	1	27	1	67	6	0	3	2	.600	0	1--	-	2.81	2.30
2005	Atl	NL	2	0	0	0	5.2	23	4	1	1	0	0	0	0	3	0	5	1	0	0	0	-	0	0-0	0	2.41	1.59
2006	Atl	NL	25	18	0	0	119.0	504	101	54	50	20	8	7	6	47	2	91	2	0	11	4	.733	0	0-0	0	3.84	3.78
2007	Atl	NL	30	30	0	0	161.1	691	164	77	76	32	9	4	1	58	5	116	1	1	11	10	.524	0	0-0	0	4.69	4.24
2008	Atl	NL	7	7	0	0	29.2	146	36	30	30	10	4	3	3	20	2	22	1	1	2	5	.286	0	0-0	0	8.81	9.10
2011	Min	AL	8	0	0	3	10.1	46	12	7	7	1	0	1	0	4	0	8	0	2	0	0	-	0	0-0	0	4.92	6.10
5 ML YEARS			72	55	0	3	326.0	1410	317	169	164	63	21	15	10	132	9	242	5	4	24	19	.558	0	0-0	0	4.67	4.53

Paul Janish

Bats: R **Throws:** R **Pos:** SS-103; 3B-8; 2B-5; PH-2; PR-1 YONN-ish **Ht:** 6'2" **Wt:** 200 **Born:** 10/12/1982 **Age:** 29

Year	Team	Lg	G	AB	H	2B	3B	HR	(Hm	Rd)	TB	R	RBI	RC	TBB	IBB	SO	HBP	SH	SF	SB	CS	SB%	GDP	Avg	OBP	Slg
2011	Lsvlle*	AAA	13	43	11	2	0	1	(-	-)	16	9	3	7	7	0	4	2	0	1	1	0	1.00	1	.256	.377	.372
2008	Cin	NL	38	80	15	2	0	1	(1	0)	20	5	6	5	7	0	18	2	0	0	0	0	-	2	.188	.270	.250
2009	Cin	NL	90	256	54	21	0	1	(1	0)	78	36	16	18	26	1	40	5	5	0	2	0	1.00	8	.211	.296	.305
2010	Cin	NL	82	200	52	10	0	5	(0	5)	77	23	25	31	22	2	30	2	3	1	1	3	.25	4	.260	.338	.385
2011	Cin	NL	114	336	72	14	1	0	(0	0)	88	27	23	21	18	1	46	4	3	5	3	2	.60	7	.214	.259	.262
Postseason			1	1	0	0	0	0	(0	0)	0	0	0	0	0	0	0	0	1	0	0	0	-	0	.000	.000	.000
4 ML YEARS			324	872	193	47	1	7	(2	5)	263	91	70	75	73	4	134	13	11	6	6	5	.55	21	.221	.289	.302

Kenley Jansen

Pitches: R Bats: B Pos: RP-51
Ht: 6'5" Wt: 257 Born: 9/30/1987 Age: 24

Year	Team	Lg	G	GS	CG	GF	IP	BFP	H	R	ER	HR	SH	SF	HB	TBB	IBB	SO	WP	Bk	W	L	Pct	Sh	Sv-Op	Hld	ERC	ERA
2009	InldEm	A+	12	0	0	4	11.2	58	14	6	6	1	0	0	0	11	0	19	1	1	0	0	-	0	0--	-	7.50	4.63
2010	InldEm	A+	11	0	0	4	18.0	73	15	3	3	0	2	0	0	6	1	28	1	0	1	1	.500	0	0--	-	2.25	1.50
2010	Chatt	AA	22	0	0	13	27.0	111	14	6	5	0	1	0	0	17	0	50	3	0	4	0	1.000	0	8--	-	1.78	1.67
2011	Chatt	AA	5	0	0	1	6.0	22	2	3	3	1	1	0	0	3	1	9	0	0	1	0	1.000	0	0--	-	1.48	4.50
2011	RCuca	AA	2	2	0	0	2.0	6	0	0	0	0	0	0	0	0	0	4	0	0	0	0	-	0	0--	-	0.00	0.00
2010	LAD	NL	25	0	0	8	27.0	109	12	2	2	0	1	0	1	15	1	41	1	0	1	0	1.000	0	4-4	4	1.40	0.67
2011	LAD	NL	51	0	0	13	53.2	218	30	17	17	3	0	1	2	26	0	96	0	2	2	1	.667	0	5-6	9	1.96	2.85
	2 ML YEARS		76	0	0	21	80.2	327	42	19	19	3	1	1	3	41	1	137	1	2	3	1	.750	0	9-10	13	1.74	2.12

Casey Janssen

Pitches: R Bats: R Pos: RP-55
JANN-sen
Ht: 6'4" Wt: 210 Born: 9/17/1981 Age: 30

Year	Team	Lg	G	GS	CG	GF	IP	BFP	H	R	ER	HR	SH	SF	HB	TBB	IBB	SO	WP	Bk	W	L	Pct	Sh	Sv-Op	Hld	ERC	ERA
2011	LsVgs*	AAA	1	0	0	0	2.0	7	1	0	0	0	0	0	0	0	0	3	0	0	0	0	-	0	0--	-	0.54	0.00
2011	NHam*	AA	5	0	0	0	5.0	17	1	0	0	0	0	0	0	1	0	7	0	0	0	0	-	0	0--	-	0.27	0.00
2006	Tor	AL	19	17	0	1	94.0	407	103	58	53	12	2	2	7	21	3	44	3	2	6	10	.375	0	0-0	0	4.32	5.07
2007	Tor	AL	70	0	0	21	72.2	297	67	22	19	4	0	3	3	20	2	39	4	0	2	3	.400	0	6-11	24	3.06	2.35
2009	Tor	AL	21	5	0	5	40.0	192	59	29	26	5	1	2	2	14	1	24	1	0	2	4	.333	0	1-1	2	7.04	5.85
2010	Tor	AL	56	0	0	16	68.2	298	74	29	28	8	0	1	4	21	1	63	3	0	5	2	.714	0	0-0	7	4.48	3.67
2011	Tor	AL	55	0	0	11	55.2	223	47	14	14	2	1	0	2	14	1	53	2	0	6	0	1.000	0	2-4	7	2.44	2.26
	5 ML YEARS		221	22	0	54	331.0	1417	350	152	140	31	4	8	18	90	8	223	13	2	21	19	.525	0	9-16	35	4.03	3.81

Jason Jaramillo

Bats: B Throws: R Pos: C-14; PH-13
HARE-ah-mee-yoh
Ht: 6'0" Wt: 209 Born: 10/9/1982 Age: 29

Year	Team	Lg	G	AB	H	2B	3B	HR	(Hm	Rd)	TB	R	RBI	RC	TBB	IBB	SO	HBP	SH	SF	SB	CS	SB%	GDP	Avg	OBP	Slg
2011	Indy*	AAA	46	134	37	7	0	2	(-	-)	50	13	23	20	17	2	22	3	0	1	1	1	.50	1	.276	.368	.373
2011	Pirates*	R	7	26	5	3	0	0	(-	-)	8	6	4	2	4	0	8	1	0	0	0	0	-	0	.192	.323	.308
2009	Pit	NL	63	206	52	14	0	3	(3	0)	75	20	26	18	17	2	33	0	1	0	1	0	1.00	11	.252	.309	.364
2010	Pit	NL	33	87	13	2	0	1	(0	1)	18	2	6	6	8	1	14	1	0	1	0	0	-	7	.149	.227	.207
2011	Pit	NL	23	43	14	3	0	0	(0	0)	17	1	6	7	2	0	12	0	0	0	1	0	1.00	1	.326	.356	.395
	3 ML YEARS		119	336	79	19	0	4	(3	1)	110	23	38	25	27	3	59	1	1	1	2	0	1.00	19	.235	.293	.327

John Jaso

Bats: L Throws: R Pos: C-82; PH-18; PR-2
JAY-soe
Ht: 6'2" Wt: 205 Born: 9/19/1983 Age: 28

Year	Team	Lg	G	AB	H	2B	3B	HR	(Hm	Rd)	TB	R	RBI	RC	TBB	IBB	SO	HBP	SH	SF	SB	CS	SB%	GDP	Avg	OBP	Slg
2011	Drham*	AAA	6	20	6	2	0	0	(-	-)	8	2	4	3	2	0	3	0	0	0	0	0	-	1	.300	.364	.400
2008	TB	AL	5	10	2	0	0	0	(0	0)	2	2	0	0	0	0	2	0	0	0	0	0	-	1	.200	.200	.200
2010	TB	AL	109	339	89	18	3	5	(1	4)	128	57	44	57	59	1	39	2	1	3	4	0	1.00	8	.263	.372	.378
2011	TB	AL	89	246	55	15	1	5	(3	2)	87	26	27	20	25	0	36	1	1	0	1	2	.33	9	.224	.298	.354
	Postseason		3	10	3	0	0	0	(0	0)	3	0	1	1	1	0	2	0	0	0	0	0	-	0	.300	.364	.300
	3 ML YEARS		203	595	146	33	4	10	(4	6)	217	85	71	77	84	1	77	3	2	3	5	2	.71	18	.245	.340	.365

Jon Jay

Bats: L Throws: L Pos: CF-75; RF-56; PH-29; LF-19; PR-2
Ht: 5'11" Wt: 200 Born: 3/15/1985 Age: 27

Year	Team	Lg	G	AB	H	2B	3B	HR	(Hm	Rd)	TB	R	RBI	RC	TBB	IBB	SO	HBP	SH	SF	SB	CS	SB%	GDP	Avg	OBP	Slg
2006	QuadC	A	60	234	80	13	3	3	(-	-)	108	42	45	46	28	3	27	3	1	2	9	4	.69	3	.342	.416	.462
2007	Sprgfld	AA	26	102	24	4	2	2	(-	-)	38	17	11	14	11	0	19	4	0	0	4	1	.80	0	.235	.333	.373
2007	Cards	R	1	2	1	0	0	0	(-	-)	1	0	0	0	0	0	1	0	0	0	0	0	-	0	.500	.500	.500
2007	PlmBh	A+	32	126	36	8	0	2	(-	-)	50	19	10	16	5	0	25	2	0	1	5	2	.71	1	.286	.321	.397
2008	Sprgfld	AA	96	372	114	17	3	11	(-	-)	170	57	47	66	39	2	46	6	7	3	10	7	.59	5	.306	.379	.457
2008	Memp	AAA	16	58	20	4	1	1	(-	-)	29	8	10	11	6	0	10	0	0	0	0	1	.00	0	.345	.406	.500
2009	Memp	AAA	136	505	142	23	2	10	(-	-)	199	72	54	72	34	3	64	12	8	5	20	8	.71	6	.281	.338	.394
2010	Memp	AAA	42	165	53	16	0	4	(-	-)	81	31	32	35	17	0	22	4	3	2	13	0	1.00	3	.321	.394	.491
2010	StL	NL	105	287	86	19	2	4	(2	2)	121	47	27	40	24	0	50	3	8	1	2	4	.33	5	.300	.359	.422
2011	StL	NL	159	455	135	24	2	10	(5	5)	193	56	37	56	28	1	81	7	9	4	6	7	.46	11	.297	.344	.424
	2 ML YEARS		264	742	221	43	4	14	(7	7)	314	103	64	96	52	1	131	10	17	5	8	11	.42	16	.298	.350	.423

Jeremy Jeffress

Pitches: R Bats: R Pos: RP-14
Ht: 6'0" Wt: 197 Born: 9/21/1987 Age: 24

Year	Team	Lg	G	GS	CG	GF	IP	BFP	H	R	ER	HR	SH	SF	HB	TBB	IBB	SO	WP	Bk	W	L	Pct	Sh	Sv-Op	Hld	ERC	ERA
2006	Brewrs	R	13	4	0	2	33.2	168	30	26	22	0	2	3	6	25	0	37	13	0	2	5	.286	0	0--	-	4.38	5.88
2007	WV	A	18	18	0	0	86.1	366	62	43	30	8	2	5	7	44	0	95	13	5	9	5	.643	0	0--	-	3.22	3.13
2008	BrvdCt	A+	15	14	1	0	79.1	339	65	39	36	5	5	1	5	41	0	102	5	1	4	6	.400	1	0--	-	3.55	4.08
2008	Hntsvl	AA	4	4	0	0	14.2	71	17	9	9	2	0	1	2	11	0	13	0	1	2	1	.667	0	0--	-	7.52	5.52
2009	Hntsvl	AA	8	8	0	0	27.1	138	26	29	23	1	1	1	1	33	0	34	3	0	1	3	.250	0	0--	-	6.67	7.57
2009	BrvdCt	A+	6	5	1	0	33.0	137	16	13	8	2	1	1	3	22	0	36	5	0	2	1	.667	0	0--	-	2.44	2.18
2010	Wisc	A	5	0	0	0	8.0	28	0	0	0	0	0	0	1	3	0	14	0	0	0	0	-	0	0--	-	0.27	0.00
2010	BrvdCt	A+	8	0	0	4	10.0	48	10	8	6	0	0	0	0	7	0	14	5	0	0	0	-	0	1--	-	4.25	5.40

Year	Team	Lg	G	GS	CG	GF	IP	BFP	H	R	ER	HR	SH	SF	HB	TBB	IBB	SO	WP	Bk	W	L	Pct	Sh	Sv-Op	Hld	ERC	ERA
			HOW MUCH HE PITCHED						WHAT HE GAVE UP												THE RESULTS							
2010	Hntsvl	AA	11	0	0	9	14.1	53	8	3	2	0	0	0	1	2	0	15	1	0	1	1	.500	0	3- -	-	1.04	1.26
2011	Omha	AAA	16	3	0	9	24.0	114	27	20	19	5	3	0	1	18	1	24	4	0	2	3	.400	0	3- -	-	7.38	7.13
2011	NWArk	AA	9	8	0	0	31.2	142	32	17	15	2	0	0	2	22	0	20	7	0	1	3	.250	0	0- -	-	5.50	4.26
2010	Mil	NL	10	0	0	5	10.0	42	8	4	3	0	0	1	0	6	1	8	1	0	1	0	1.000	0	0-0	-	2.96	2.70
2011	KC	AL	14	0	0	6	15.1	67	12	8	8	1	2	0	0	11	0	13	1	0	1	1	.500	0	1-2	0	3.87	4.70
	2 ML YEARS		24	0	0	11	25.1	109	20	12	11	1	2	1	0	17	1	21	2	0	2	1	.667	0	1-2	0	3.51	3.91

Bobby Jenks

Pitches: R Bats: R Pos: RP-19 Ht: 6'4" Wt: 275 Born: 3/14/1981 Age: 31

Year	Team	Lg	G	GS	CG	GF	IP	BFP	H	R	ER	HR	SH	SF	HB	TBB	IBB	SO	WP	Bk	W	L	Pct	Sh	Sv-Op	Hld	ERC	ERA
			HOW MUCH HE PITCHED						WHAT HE GAVE UP												THE RESULTS							
2011	Pwtckt*	AAA	2	2	0	0	2.0	9	2	1	1	0	0	0	0	1	0	2	0	0	0	0	-	0	0- -	-	3.63	4.50
2011	Portlnd*	AA	1	1	0	0	1.0	3	1	0	0	0	0	0	0	0	0	1	0	0	0	0	-	0	0- -	-	2.79	0.00
2005	CWS	AL	32	0	0	18	39.1	168	34	15	12	3	1	0	1	15	3	50	4	0	1	1	.500	0	6-8	3	3.02	2.75
2006	CWS	AL	67	0	0	58	69.2	300	66	32	31	5	4	2	2	31	10	80	3	0	3	4	.429	0	41-45	0	3.65	4.00
2007	CWS	AL	66	0	0	62	65.0	249	45	20	20	2	5	3	1	13	4	56	4	0	3	5	.375	0	40-46	0	1.49	2.77
2008	CWS	AL	57	0	0	52	61.2	243	51	18	18	3	2	1	1	17	4	38	3	0	3	1	.750	0	30-34	0	2.43	2.63
2009	CWS	AL	52	0	0	46	53.1	228	52	24	22	9	0	2	2	16	1	49	0	0	3	4	.429	0	29-35	0	4.08	3.71
2010	CWS	AL	55	0	0	46	52.2	231	54	28	26	3	4	0	1	18	1	61	2	0	1	3	.250	0	27-31	0	3.64	4.44
2011	Bos	AL	19	0	0	4	15.2	80	22	12	11	1	0	0	0	13	0	17	3	1	2	2	.500	0	0-2	2	8.06	6.32
	Postseason		7	0	0	5	9.0	36	5	2	2	0	1	0	1	3	0	9	0	0	0	0	-	0	5-6	0	1.47	2.00
	7 ML YEARS		348	0	0	286	357.1	1499	324	149	140	26	16	8	8	123	23	351	19	1	16	20	.444	0	173-201	5	3.15	3.53

Desmond Jennings

Bats: R Throws: R Pos: LF-53; CF-8; PH-2; RF-1; DH-1 Ht: 6'2" Wt: 200 Born: 10/30/1986 Age: 25

Year	Team	Lg	G	AB	H	2B	3B	HR	(Hm	Rd)	TB	R	RBI	RC	TBB	IBB	SO	HBP	SH	SF	SB	CS	SB%	GDP	Avg	OBP	Slg
			BATTING																		BASERUNNING				AVERAGES		
2006	Princtn	R+	56	213	59	10	1	4	(-	-)	83	48	20	36	22	0	39	6	4	1	32	5	.86	3	.277	.360	.390
2007	Clmbs	A	99	387	122	21	5	9	(-	-)	180	75	37	78	45	1	53	12	2	2	45	15	.75	1	.315	.401	.465
2008	VeroB	A+	24	85	22	5	1	2	(-	-)	35	17	6	14	14	0	16	0	2	1	5	2	.71	0	.259	.360	.412
2009	Mont	AA	100	383	120	25	8	8	(-	-)	185	69	45	80	48	2	52	5	0	4	37	5	.88	4	.313	.393	.483
2009	Drham	AAA	32	114	37	6	2	3	(-	-)	56	23	17	26	19	0	15	1	1	2	15	2	.88	3	.325	.419	.491
2010	Drham	AAA	109	399	111	25	6	3	(-	-)	157	82	36	66	47	1	67	6	5	1	37	4	.90	8	.278	.362	.393
2011	Drham	AAA	89	338	93	19	3	12	(-	-)	154	68	39	63	45	3	78	9	4	1	17	1	.94	4	.275	.374	.456
2010	TB	AL	17	21	4	1	1	0	(0	0)	7	5	2	2	2	0	4	1	0	0	2	2	.50	0	.190	.292	.333
2011	TB	AL	63	247	64	9	4	10	(3	7)	111	44	25	45	31	1	59	6	3	0	20	6	.77	1	.259	.356	.449
	Postseason		2	2	0	0	0	0	(0	0)	0	1	0	0	0	0	1	0	0	0	0	0	-	0	.000	.000	.000
	2 ML YEARS		80	268	68	10	5	10	(3	7)	118	49	27	47	33	1	63	7	3	0	22	8	.73	1	.254	.351	.440

Kevin Jepsen

Pitches: R Bats: R Pos: RP-16 Ht: 6'3" Wt: 230 Born: 7/26/1984 Age: 27

Year	Team	Lg	G	GS	CG	GF	IP	BFP	H	R	ER	HR	SH	SF	HB	TBB	IBB	SO	WP	Bk	W	L	Pct	Sh	Sv-Op	Hld	ERC	ERA
			HOW MUCH HE PITCHED						WHAT HE GAVE UP												THE RESULTS							
2011	Salt Lk*	AAA	24	0	0	20	28.1	119	32	14	14	4	1	0	0	8	1	20	4	0	1	3	.250	0	7- -	-	4.72	4.45
2008	LAA	AL	9	0	0	0	8.1	36	8	5	4	0	0	0	0	4	0	7	1	0	0	1	.000	0	0-0	3	3.46	4.32
2009	LAA	AL	54	0	0	13	54.2	237	63	33	30	2	0	2	0	19	2	48	6	0	6	4	.600	0	1-2	17	4.27	4.94
2010	LAA	AL	68	0	0	4	59.0	253	54	26	26	2	4	2	2	29	5	61	8	0	2	4	.333	0	0-4	27	3.53	3.97
2011	LAA	AL	16	0	0	5	13.0	68	21	11	11	2	1	1	1	9	4	6	5	0	1	2	.333	0	0-1	2	9.45	7.62
	Postseason		5	0	0	0	5.0	24	8	2	2	1	0	0	0	2	0	3	0	0	1	0	1.000	0	0-0	1	8.81	3.60
	4 ML YEARS		147	0	0	22	135.0	594	146	75	71	6	5	5	3	61	11	122	20	0	9	11	.450	0	1-7	49	4.33	4.73

Derek Jeter

Bats: R Throws: R Pos: SS-122; DH-10 Ht: 6'3" Wt: 195 Born: 6/26/1974 Age: 38

Year	Team	Lg	G	AB	H	2B	3B	HR	(Hm	Rd)	TB	R	RBI	RC	TBB	IBB	SO	HBP	SH	SF	SB	CS	SB%	GDP	Avg	OBP	Slg
			BATTING																		BASERUNNING				AVERAGES		
2011	Trntn*	AA	2	4	2	0	0	0	(-	-)	2	1	0	1	2	0	1	0	0	0	0	0	-	0	.500	.667	.500
1995	NYY	AL	15	48	12	4	1	0	(0	0)	18	5	7	5	3	0	11	0	0	0	0	0	-	0	.250	.294	.375
1996	NYY	AL	157	582	183	25	6	10	(3	7)	250	104	78	92	48	1	102	9	6	9	14	7	.67	13	.314	.370	.430
1997	NYY	AL	159	654	190	31	7	10	(5	5)	265	116	70	99	74	0	125	10	8	2	23	12	.66	14	.291	.370	.405
1998	NYY	AL	149	626	203	25	8	19	(9	10)	301	127	84	115	57	1	119	5	3	3	30	6	.83	13	.324	.384	.481
1999	NYY	AL	158	627	219	37	9	24	(15	9)	346	134	102	146	91	5	116	12	3	6	19	8	.70	12	.349	.438	.552
2000	NYY	AL	148	593	201	31	4	15	(8	7)	285	119	73	118	68	4	99	12	3	3	22	4	.85	14	.339	.416	.481
2001	NYY	AL	150	614	191	35	3	21	(13	8)	295	110	74	112	56	3	99	10	5	1	27	3	.90	13	.311	.377	.480
2002	NYY	AL	157	644	191	26	0	18	(8	10)	271	124	75	108	73	2	114	7	3	3	32	3	.91	10	.297	.373	.421
2003	NYY	AL	119	482	156	25	3	10	(7	3)	217	87	52	86	43	2	88	13	3	1	11	5	.69	10	.324	.393	.450
2004	NYY	AL	154	643	188	44	1	23	(11	12)	303	111	78	100	46	1	99	14	16	2	23	4	.85	19	.292	.352	.471
2005	NYY	AL	159	654	202	25	5	19	(12	7)	294	122	70	105	77	3	117	11	7	3	14	5	.74	15	.309	.389	.450
2006	NYY	AL	154	623	214	39	3	14	(8	6)	301	118	97	132	69	4	102	12	7	4	34	5	.87	13	.343	.417	.483
2007	NYY	AL	156	639	206	39	4	12	(4	8)	289	102	73	112	56	3	100	14	3	3	15	8	.65	21	.322	.388	.452
2008	NYY	AL	150	596	179	25	3	11	(3	8)	243	88	69	88	52	0	85	9	7	4	11	5	.69	24	.300	.363	.408
2009	NYY	AL	153	634	212	27	1	18	(13	5)	295	107	66	109	72	4	90	7	4	4	30	5	.86	18	.334	.406	.465
2010	NYY	AL	157	663	179	30	3	10	(7	3)	245	111	67	86	63	4	106	9	1	5	18	5	.78	22	.270	.340	.370
2011	NYY	AL	131	546	162	24	4	6	(4	2)	212	84	61	75	46	0	81	6	4	5	16	6	.73	10	.297	.355	.388
	Postseason		147	599	185	30	4	20	(12	8)	283	101	57	94	63	3	117	5	8	4	17	5	.77	13	.309	.377	.472
	17 ML YEARS		2426	9868	3088	492	65	240	(130	110)	4430	1769	1196	1688	994	37	1653	158	83	52	339	91	.79	245	.313	.383	.449

Cesar Jimenez

Pitches: L **Bats:** L **Pos:** RP-8 **Ht:** 5'11" **Wt:** 215 **Born:** 11/12/1984 **Age:** 27

Year	Team	Lg	G	GS	CG	GF	IP	BFP	H	R	ER	HR	SH	SF	HB	TBB	IBB	SO	WP	Bk	W	L	Pct	Sh	Sv-Op	Hld	ERC	ERA
2011	Tacom*	AAA	43	0	0	9	71.0	310	71	33	32	3	1	0	0	35	3	81	6	0	5	4	.556	0	1--	-	3.97	4.06
2006	Sea	AL	4	1	0	1	7.1	38	13	12	12	4	0	0	0	4	0	3	2	0	0	0	-	0	0-0	0	14.01	14.73
2008	Sea	AL	31	2	0	8	34.1	141	32	13	13	2	2	1	1	13	0	26	2	0	0	2	.000	0	0-4	4	3.59	3.41
2011	Sea	AL	8	0	0	1	6.2	30	6	4	4	0	0	0	0	3	0	7	2	0	1	0	1.000	0	0-0	0	2.83	5.40
	3 ML YEARS		43	3	0	10	48.1	209	51	29	29	6	2	1	1	20	0	36	6	0	1	2	.333	0	0-4	4	4.79	5.40

Ubaldo Jimenez

Pitches: R **Bats:** R **Pos:** SP-32 · ooh-BALL-doh · **Ht:** 6'4" **Wt:** 210 **Born:** 1/22/1984 **Age:** 28

Year	Team	Lg	G	GS	CG	GF	IP	BFP	H	R	ER	HR	SH	SF	HB	TBB	IBB	SO	WP	Bk	W	L	Pct	Sh	Sv-Op	Hld	ERC	ERA
2006	Col	NL	2	1	0	0	7.2	30	5	4	3	1	0	0	0	3	0	3	0	0	0	0	-	0	0-0	0	2.48	3.52
2007	Col	NL	15	15	0	0	82.0	354	70	46	39	10	3	1	6	37	4	68	3	0	4	4	.500	0	0-0	0	3.80	4.28
2008	Col	NL	34	34	1	0	198.2	868	182	97	88	11	7	4	10	103	4	172	16	0	12	12	.500	0	0-0	0	3.92	3.99
2009	Col	NL	33	33	1	0	218.0	914	183	87	84	13	15	6	10	85	6	198	8	3	15	12	.556	0	0-0	0	3.03	3.47
2010	Col	NL	33	33	4	0	221.2	894	164	73	71	10	7	1	9	92	7	214	16	1	19	8	.704	2	0-0	0	2.57	2.88
2011	2 Tms		32	32	2	0	188.1	822	186	111	98	17	2	2	9	78	5	180	8	0	10	13	.435	1	0-0	0	4.13	4.68
11	Col	NL	21	21	2	0	123.0	532	118	68	61	10	2	2	7	51	5	118	6	0	6	9	.400	1	0-0	0	3.94	4.46
11	Cle	AL	11	11	0	0	65.1	290	68	43	37	7	0	0	2	27	0	62	2	0	4	4	.500	0	0-0	0	4.48	5.10
	Postseason		5	5	0	0	28.0	123	26	11	11	3	0	1	1	16	2	24	1	0	0	2	.000	0	0-0	0	4.47	3.54
	6 ML YEARS		149	148	8	0	916.1	3882	790	418	383	62	34	14	44	398	26	835	51	4	60	49	.550	3	0-0	0	3.39	3.76

Waldis Joaquin

Pitches: R **Bats:** R **Pos:** RP-5 · WALL-diss wah-KEEN · **Ht:** 6'0" **Wt:** 238 **Born:** 12/25/1986 **Age:** 25

Year	Team	Lg	G	GS	CG	GF	IP	BFP	H	R	ER	HR	SH	SF	HB	TBB	IBB	SO	WP	Bk	W	L	Pct	Sh	Sv-Op	Hld	ERC	ERA
2011	Fresno*	AAA	35	0	0	7	49.2	219	53	26	19	5	1	1	4	23	1	27	5	0	2	2	.500	0	1--	-	5.13	3.44
2009	SF	NL	10	0	0	4	10.2	51	10	5	5	1	0	0	2	7	0	12	3	0	0	0	-	0	0-0	0	5.30	4.22
2010	SF	NL	4	0	0	0	4.2	27	6	6	5	0	1	0	1	7	0	2	2	1	0	0	-	0	0-0	1	10.62	9.64
2011	SF	NL	5	0	0	1	6.1	27	6	3	3	0	0	1	0	3	0	3	2	0	1	0	1.000	0	0-0	0	3.41	4.26
	3 ML YEARS		19	0	0	5	21.2	105	22	14	13	1	1	1	3	17	0	17	7	1	1	0	1.000	0	0-0	1	5.79	5.40

Alan Johnson

Pitches: R **Bats:** R **Pos:** SP-1 · **Ht:** 6'1" **Wt:** 180 **Born:** 8/24/1983 **Age:** 28

Year	Team	Lg	G	GS	CG	GF	IP	BFP	H	R	ER	HR	SH	SF	HB	TBB	IBB	SO	WP	Bk	W	L	Pct	Sh	Sv-Op	Hld	ERC	ERA
2005	Casper	R+	15	15	0	0	79.1	349	90	44	35	1	1	2	2	24	0	78	4	0	3	2	.600	0	0--	-	3.87	3.97
2006	Ashvll	A	27	27	0	0	160.1	685	171	82	72	11	4	4	13	40	0	123	8	1	13	5	.722	0	0--	-	3.98	4.04
2007	Mdest	A+	26	26	1	0	168.2	703	162	69	56	9	3	5	9	47	1	119	2	1	14	7	.667	0	0--	-	3.31	2.99
2007	Tulsa	AA	2	2	0	0	13.0	47	7	0	0	0	1	0	0	2	0	7	0	0	2	0	1.000	0	0--	-	0.89	0.00
2008	Tulsa	AA	28	28	0	0	175.2	782	217	121	102	19	9	14	9	54	1	92	9	0	4	14	.222	0	0--	-	5.37	5.23
2009	ColSpr	AAA	26	24	0	0	143.0	648	169	105	90	22	8	4	6	53	3	76	7	0	10	6	.625	0	0--	-	5.50	5.66
2010	ColSpr	AAA	28	25	1	1	141.2	631	189	106	93	14	3	7	6	43	1	100	5	0	10	8	.556	0	0--	-	5.89	5.91
2011	ColSpr	AAA	26	23	0	0	132.0	631	201	118	109	13	6	6	2	60	0	85	0	0	5	11	.313	0	0--	-	7.71	7.43
2011	Col	NL	1	1	0	0	4.0	20	6	5	4	0	1	0	0	3	0	3	1	0	0	0	-	0	0-0	0	7.93	9.00

Chris Johnson

Bats: R **Throws:** R **Pos:** 3B-101; PH-7; PR-1 · **Ht:** 6'3" **Wt:** 220 **Born:** 10/1/1984 **Age:** 27

Year	Team	Lg	G	AB	H	2B	3B	HR	(Hm	Rd)	TB	R	RBI	RC	TBB	IBB	SO	HBP	SH	SF	SB	CS	SB%	GDP	Avg	OBP	Slg
2011	OKCity*	AAA	21	81	22	7	0	4	(-	-)	41	18	15	15	10	1	25	3	0	0	1	1	.50	3	.272	.372	.506
2009	Hou	NL	11	22	2	0	0	0	(0	0)	2	1	1	0	1	0	6	0	0	0	0	0	-	0	.091	.130	.091
2010	Hou	NL	94	341	105	22	2	11	(6	5)	164	40	52	55	15	2	91	2	0	4	3	0	1.00	8	.308	.337	.481
2011	Hou	NL	107	378	95	21	3	7	(2	5)	143	32	42	42	16	3	97	7	0	4	2	2	.50	2	.251	.291	.378
	3 ML YEARS		212	741	202	43	5	18	(8	10)	309	73	95	97	32	5	194	9	0	8	5	2	.71	10	.273	.308	.417

Dan Johnson

Bats: L **Throws:** R **Pos:** 1B-21; PH-7; 3B-3; DH-3 · **Ht:** 6'2" **Wt:** 210 **Born:** 8/10/1979 **Age:** 32

Year	Team	Lg	G	AB	H	2B	3B	HR	(Hm	Rd)	TB	R	RBI	RC	TBB	IBB	SO	HBP	SH	SF	SB	CS	SB%	GDP	Avg	OBP	Slg
2011	Drham*	AAA	93	333	91	23	0	13	(-	-)	153	52	52	61	58	2	65	2	0	2	0	1	.00	5	.273	.382	.459
2005	Oak	AL	109	375	103	21	0	15	(2	13)	169	54	58	56	50	1	52	1	0	8	0	1	.00	11	.275	.355	.451
2006	Oak	AL	91	286	67	13	1	9	(4	5)	109	30	37	33	40	2	45	0	0	5	0	0	-	6	.234	.323	.381
2007	Oak	AL	117	416	98	20	1	18	(4	14)	174	53	62	58	72	4	77	0	0	4	0	0	-	12	.236	.349	.418
2008	2 Tms	AL	11	26	5	0	0	2	(1	1)	11	3	4	3	3	0	7	0	0	0	0	0	-	0	.192	.276	.423
2010	TB	AL	40	111	22	3	0	7	(4	3)	46	15	23	20	25	0	27	1	0	3	1	0	1.00	1	.198	.343	.414
2011	TB	AL	31	84	10	1	0	2	(1	1)	17	7	4	0	6	0	18	1	0	0	0	0	-	3	.119	.187	.202
08	Oak	AL	1	1	0	0	0	0	(0	0)	0	0	0	0	0	0	0	0	0	0	0	0	-	0	.000	.000	.000
08	TB	AL	10	25	5	0	0	2	(1	1)	11	3	4	3	3	0	7	0	0	0	0	0	-	0	.200	.286	.440
	Postseason		5	9	2	1	0	0	(0	0)	3	1	0	0	3	0	4	0	0	0	0	0	-	1	.222	.417	.333
	6 ML YEARS		399	1298	305	58	2	53	(21	32)	526	162	188	170	196	7	226	6	0	20	1	1	.50	33	.235	.334	.405

Elliot Johnson

Bats: B **Throws:** R **Pos:** SS-52; PH-16; 2B-9; PR-6; 1B-2; LF-1; CF-1   **Ht:** 6'0" **Wt:** 190 **Born:** 3/9/1984 **Age:** 28

									BATTING													BASERUNNING				AVERAGES		
Year	Team	Lg	G	AB	H	2B	3B	HR	(Hm	Rd)	TB	R	RBI	RC	TBB	IBB	SO	HBP	SH	SF	SB	CS	SB%	GDP	Avg	OBP	Slg
2002	Princtn	R+	42	152	40	10	1	1	(-	-)	55	21	13	22	18	0	48	1	1	0	14	2	.88	2	.263	.345	.362
2003	CtnSC	A	54	151	32	4	0	0	(-	-)	36	22	15	17	38	0	32	0	0	0	8	5	.62	2	.212	.370	.238
2004	CtnSC	A	126	503	132	22	7	6	(-	-)	186	92	41	70	54	1	91	5	10	2	43	15	.74	2	.262	.339	.370
2005	Visalia	A+	56	227	62	10	3	8	(-	-)	102	42	33	40	24	1	49	3	2	0	28	5	.85	2	.273	.350	.449
2005	Mont	AA	63	264	69	9	6	3	(-	-)	99	31	22	32	13	0	68	4	1	1	14	4	.78	3	.261	.305	.375
2006	Mont	AA	122	494	139	21	10	15	(-	-)	225	69	50	74	39	1	121	2	4	3	21	18	.54	6	.281	.335	.455
2007	Drham	AAA	129	463	96	17	6	11	(-	-)	158	56	45	48	43	2	139	8	9	1	16	6	.73	1	.207	.285	.341
2008	Drham	AAA	107	387	101	26	5	9	(-	-)	164	49	50	56	33	1	104	2	5	1	15	3	.83	6	.261	.322	.424
2009	Drham	AAA	63	233	61	9	1	11	(-	-)	105	31	35	35	17	0	56	3	6	1	7	2	.78	1	.262	.319	.451
2009	Rays	R	5	16	5	2	0	0	(-	-)	7	2	2	2	2	0	1	0	0	0	0	0	-	0	.313	.389	.438
2010	Drham	AAA	109	427	136	24	5	11	(-	-)	203	72	56	80	37	2	92	3	12	2	30	6	.83	7	.319	.375	.475
2011	Drham	AAA	2	9	2	0	0	0	(-	-)	2	1	0	0	0	0	3	0	0	0	0	0	-	0	.222	.222	.222
2008	TB	AL	7	19	3	0	0	0	(0	0)	3	0	0	0	0	0	7	0	0	0	0	1	.00	0	.158	.158	.158
2011	TB	AL	70	160	31	7	2	4	(2	2)	54	20	17	10	14	0	53	0	6	1	6	7	.46	3	.194	.257	.338
2 ML YEARS			77	179	34	7	2	4	(2	2)	57	20	17	10	14	0	60	0	6	1	6	8	.43	3	.190	.247	.318

Jim Johnson

Pitches: R **Bats:** R **Pos:** RP-69   **Ht:** 6'6" **Wt:** 230 **Born:** 6/27/1983 **Age:** 29

			HOW MUCH HE PITCHED						WHAT HE GAVE UP											THE RESULTS						
Year	Team	Lg	G	GS	CG	GF	IP	BFP	H	R	ER	HR	SH	SF	HB	TBB	IBB	SO	WP	Bk	W	L	Pct	Sh	Sv-Op	Hld	ERC	ERA
2006	Bal	AL	1	1	0	0	3.0	21	9	8	8	1	0	1	1	3	0	0	0	0	0	1	.000	0	0-0	0	26.81	24.00
2007	Bal	AL	1	0	0	1	2.0	11	3	2	2	0	0	1	0	2	0	1	0	0	0	0	-	0	0-0	0	8.58	9.00
2008	Bal	AL	54	0	0	18	68.2	281	54	18	17	0	2	1	3	28	3	38	1	1	2	4	.333	0	1-1	19	2.45	2.23
2009	Bal	AL	64	0	0	29	70.0	300	73	32	32	8	2	3	3	23	3	49	2	1	4	6	.400	0	10-16	14	4.28	4.11
2010	Bal	AL	26	0	0	6	26.1	117	32	11	10	2	3	0	1	5	1	22	4	0	1	1	.500	0	1-6	11	4.26	3.42
2011	Bal	AL	69	0	0	20	91.0	366	80	30	27	5	4	2	2	21	3	58	2	1	6	5	.545	0	9-14	18	2.58	2.67
6 ML YEARS			215	1	0	74	261.0	1096	251	101	96	16	11	7	10	82	10	168	9	3	13	17	.433	0	21-37	62	3.38	3.31

Josh Johnson

Pitches: R **Bats:** L **Pos:** SP-9   **Ht:** 6'7" **Wt:** 249 **Born:** 1/31/1984 **Age:** 28

			HOW MUCH HE PITCHED						WHAT HE GAVE UP											THE RESULTS						
Year	Team	Lg	G	GS	CG	GF	IP	BFP	H	R	ER	HR	SH	SF	HB	TBB	IBB	SO	WP	Bk	W	L	Pct	Sh	Sv-Op	Hld	ERC	ERA
2005	Fla	NL	4	1	0	0	12.1	55	11	5	5	0	1	0	1	10	0	10	0	0	0	0	-	0	0-0	0	4.82	3.65
2006	Fla	NL	31	24	0	1	157.0	659	136	63	54	14	11	0	4	68	6	133	3	1	12	7	.632	0	0-1	0	3.48	3.10
2007	Fla	NL	4	4	0	0	15.2	82	26	17	13	1	2	1	0	12	3	14	1	0	0	3	.000	0	0-0	0	9.16	7.47
2008	Fla	NL	14	14	1	0	87.1	365	91	36	35	7	5	1	1	27	1	77	4	0	7	1	.875	0	0-0	0	3.94	3.61
2009	Fla	NL	33	33	2	0	209.0	855	184	77	75	14	11	4	6	58	6	191	10	0	15	5	.750	0	0-0	0	2.84	3.23
2010	Fla	NL	28	28	1	0	183.2	744	155	51	47	7	5	8	5	48	2	186	4	0	11	6	.647	0	0-0	0	2.44	**2.30**
2011	Fla	NL	9	9	0	0	60.1	234	39	13	11	2	1	1	1	20	2	56	2	1	3	1	.750	0	0-0	0	1.70	1.64
7 ML YEARS			123	113	4	1	725.1	2994	642	262	240	45	36	15	18	243	20	667	24	2	48	23	.676	0	0-1	0	3.04	2.98

Kelly Johnson

Bats: L **Throws:** R **Pos:** 2B-141; PH-8   **Ht:** 6'1" **Wt:** 195 **Born:** 2/22/1982 **Age:** 30

									BATTING													BASERUNNING				AVERAGES		
Year	Team	Lg	G	AB	H	2B	3B	HR	(Hm	Rd)	TB	R	RBI	RC	TBB	IBB	SO	HBP	SH	SF	SB	CS	SB%	GDP	Avg	OBP	Slg
2005	Atl	NL	87	290	70	12	3	9	(2	7)	115	46	40	41	40	1	75	1	2	1	2	1	.67	11	.241	.334	.397
2007	Atl	NL	147	521	144	26	10	16	(5	11)	238	91	68	87	79	3	117	4	2	2	9	5	.64	8	.276	.375	.457
2008	Atl	NL	150	547	157	39	6	12	(5	7)	244	86	69	87	52	2	113	2	9	4	11	6	.65	3	.287	.349	.446
2009	Atl	NL	106	303	68	20	3	8	(4	4)	118	47	29	31	32	1	54	3	6	2	7	2	.78	4	.224	.303	.389
2010	Ari	NL	154	585	166	36	5	26	(16	10)	290	93	71	92	79	1	148	2	3	2	13	7	.65	12	.284	.370	.496
2011	2 Tms	NL	147	545	121	27	7	21	(10	11)	225	75	58	70	60	2	163	4	4	0	16	6	.73	3	.222	.304	.413
11	Ari	NL	114	430	90	23	5	18	(10	8)	177	59	49	53	44	2	132	3	4	0	13	3	.81	3	.209	.287	.412
11	Tor	AL	33	115	31	4	2	3	(0	3)	48	16	9	17	16	0	31	1	0	0	3	3	.50	0	.270	.364	.417
Postseason			4	2	0	0	0	0	(0	0)	0	0	0	0	1	0	0	0	0	0	0	0	-	0	.000	.333	.000
6 ML YEARS			791	2791	726	160	34	92	(42	50)	1230	438	335	408	342	10	670	16	26	11	58	27	.68	41	.260	.343	.441

Reed Johnson

Bats: R **Throws:** R **Pos:** RF-44; PH-33; LF-27; CF-24; PR-1   **Ht:** 5'10" **Wt:** 185 **Born:** 12/8/1976 **Age:** 35

									BATTING													BASERUNNING				AVERAGES		
Year	Team	Lg	G	AB	H	2B	3B	HR	(Hm	Rd)	TB	R	RBI	RC	TBB	IBB	SO	HBP	SH	SF	SB	CS	SB%	GDP	Avg	OBP	Slg
2011	Iowa*	AAA	3	6	0	0	0	0	(-	-)	0	0	0	0	1	0	3	2	0	0	0	0	-	0	.000	.333	.000
2003	Tor	AL	114	412	121	21	2	10	(6	4)	176	79	52	64	20	1	67	20	1	4	5	3	.63	10	.294	.353	.427
2004	Tor	AL	141	537	145	25	2	10	(8	2)	204	68	61	65	28	2	98	12	3	2	6	3	.67	17	.270	.320	.380
2005	Tor	AL	142	398	107	21	6	8	(4	4)	164	55	58	57	22	1	82	16	2	1	5	6	.45	8	.269	.332	.412
2006	Tor	AL	134	461	147	34	2	12	(4	8)	221	86	49	76	33	4	81	21	1	1	8	2	.80	9	.319	.390	.479
2007	Tor	AL	79	275	65	13	2	2	(1	1)	88	31	14	24	16	0	56	11	5	0	4	2	.67	7	.236	.305	.320
2008	ChC	NL	109	333	101	21	0	6	(3	3)	140	52	50	57	19	1	68	12	5	5	5	6	.45	3	.303	.358	.420
2009	ChC	NL	65	165	42	10	2	4	(3	1)	68	23	22	19	13	0	27	6	1	1	2	1	.67	5	.255	.330	.412
2010	LAD	NL	102	202	53	11	2	2	(1	1)	74	24	15	18	5	0	50	4	2	2	2	2	.50	3	.262	.291	.366
2011	ChC	NL	111	246	76	22	1	5	(4	1)	115	33	28	35	5	1	63	11	2	2	2	1	.67	4	.309	.348	.467
9 ML YEARS			997	3029	857	178	19	59	(34	25)	1250	451	349	415	161	10	592	113	22	18	39	26	.60	66	.283	.341	.413

Rob Johnson

Bats: R **Throws:** R **Pos:** C-63; PH-7; PR-2   **Ht:** 6'1" **Wt:** 215 **Born:** 7/22/1982 **Age:** 29

Year	Team	Lg	G	AB	H	2B	3B	HR	(Hm	Rd)	TB	R	RBI	RC	TBB	IBB	SO	HBP	SH	SF	SB	CS	SB%	GDP	Avg	OBP	Slg
2007	Sea	AL	6	3	1	0	0	0	(0	0)	1	1	0	0	0	0	0	0	0	0	1	0	1.00	0	.333	.333	.333
2008	Sea	AL	14	31	4	0	0	1	(1	0)	7	2	2	0	0	0	6	0	1	0	0	0	-	1	.129	.129	.226
2009	Sea	AL	80	258	55	19	2	2	(2	0)	84	21	27	22	26	1	60	2	3	1	1	1	.50	11	.213	.289	.326
2010	Sea	AL	61	178	34	10	0	2	(0	2)	50	24	13	12	25	2	46	2	1	3	1	1	.50	5	.191	.293	.281
2011	SD	NL	67	179	34	6	1	3	(1	2)	51	9	16	12	14	1	58	3	2	1	3	0	1.00	3	.190	.259	.285
5 ML YEARS			228	649	128	35	3	8	(4	4)	193	57	58	46	65	4	170	7	7	5	6	2	.75	20	.197	.275	.297

Adam Jones

Bats: R **Throws:** R **Pos:** CF-148; PR-3; DH-2   **Ht:** 6'2" **Wt:** 215 **Born:** 8/1/1985 **Age:** 26

Year	Team	Lg	G	AB	H	2B	3B	HR	(Hm	Rd)	TB	R	RBI	RC	TBB	IBB	SO	HBP	SH	SF	SB	CS	SB%	GDP	Avg	OBP	Slg
2006	Sea	AL	32	74	16	4	0	1	(0	1)	23	6	8	4	2	0	22	0	0	0	3	1	.75	3	.216	.237	.311
2007	Sea	AL	41	65	16	2	1	2	(1	1)	26	16	4	5	4	0	21	1	1	0	2	1	.67	0	.246	.300	.400
2008	Bal	AL	132	477	129	21	7	9	(4	5)	191	61	57	56	23	0	108	7	2	5	10	3	.77	12	.270	.311	.400
2009	Bal	AL	119	473	131	22	3	19	(11	8)	216	83	70	71	36	3	93	7	0	3	10	4	.71	13	.277	.335	.457
2010	Bal	AL	149	581	165	25	5	19	(9	10)	257	76	69	72	23	1	119	13	2	2	7	7	.50	17	.284	.325	.442
2011	Bal	AL	151	567	159	26	2	25	(19	6)	264	68	83	77	29	2	113	9	1	**12**	12	4	.75	16	.280	.319	.466
6 ML YEARS			624	2237	616	100	18	75	(44	31)	977	310	291	285	117	6	476	37	6	22	44	20	.69	61	.275	.319	.437

Andruw Jones

Bats: R **Throws:** R **Pos:** LF-39; RF-19; DH-16; PH-12; PR-1   **Ht:** 6'1" **Wt:** 230 **Born:** 4/23/1977 **Age:** 35

Year	Team	Lg	G	AB	H	2B	3B	HR	(Hm	Rd)	TB	R	RBI	RC	TBB	IBB	SO	HBP	SH	SF	SB	CS	SB%	GDP	Avg	OBP	Slg
1996	Atl	NL	31	106	23	7	1	5	(3	2)	47	11	13	13	7	0	29	0	0	0	3	0	1.00	1	.217	.265	.443
1997	Atl	NL	153	399	92	18	1	18	(5	13)	166	60	70	54	56	2	107	4	5	3	20	11	.65	11	.231	.329	.416
1998	Atl	NL	159	582	158	33	8	31	(16	15)	300	89	90	97	40	8	129	4	1	4	27	4	.87	10	.271	.321	.515
1999	Atl	NL	162	592	163	35	5	26	(10	16)	286	97	84	103	76	11	103	9	0	2	24	12	.67	12	.275	.365	.483
2000	Atl	NL	161	**656**	199	36	6	36	(15	21)	355	122	104	127	59	0	100	9	0	5	21	6	.78	12	.303	.366	.541
2001	Atl	NL	161	625	157	25	2	34	(16	18)	288	104	104	90	56	3	142	3	0	9	11	4	.73	10	.251	.312	.461
2002	Atl	NL	154	560	148	34	0	35	(18	17)	287	91	94	94	83	4	135	10	0	6	8	3	.73	14	.264	.366	.513
2003	Atl	NL	156	595	165	28	2	36	(16	20)	305	101	116	92	53	2	125	5	0	6	4	3	.57	18	.277	.338	.513
2004	Atl	NL	154	570	149	34	4	29	(13	16)	278	85	91	75	71	9	147	3	0	2	6	6	.50	24	.261	.345	.488
2005	Atl	NL	160	586	154	24	3	51	(21	30)	337	95	**128**	91	64	13	112	15	0	7	5	3	.63	19	.263	.347	.575
2006	Atl	NL	156	565	148	29	0	41	(19	22)	300	107	129	108	82	9	127	13	0	9	4	1	.80	13	.262	.363	.531
2007	Atl	NL	154	572	127	27	2	26	(10	16)	236	83	94	71	70	4	138	8	0	9	5	2	.71	16	.222	.311	.413
2008	LAD	NL	75	209	33	8	1	3	(0	3)	52	21	14	6	27	0	76	1	0	1	0	1	.00	5	.158	.256	.249
2009	Tex	AL	82	281	60	18	0	17	(9	8)	129	43	43	42	45	3	72	2	0	3	5	1	.83	7	.214	.323	.459
2010	CWS	AL	107	278	64	12	1	19	(12	7)	135	41	48	45	45	0	73	3	0	2	9	2	.82	15	.230	.341	.486
2011	NYY	AL	77	190	47	8	1	13	(7	6)	94	27	33	36	29	0	62	3	0	0	0	0	-	3	.247	.356	.495
Postseason			75	238	65	8	0	10	(5	5)	103	43	33	34	34	2	50	2	1	3	5	5	.50	5	.273	.365	.433
16 ML YEARS			2102	7366	1887	376	36	420	(196	224)	3595	1177	1255	1144	863	68	1677	92	6	68	152	59	.72	190	.256	.339	.488

Chipper Jones

Bats: B **Throws:** R **Pos:** 3B-116; PH-11; DH-3   **Ht:** 6'4" **Wt:** 210 **Born:** 4/24/1972 **Age:** 40

Year	Team	Lg	G	AB	H	2B	3B	HR	(Hm	Rd)	TB	R	RBI	RC	TBB	IBB	SO	HBP	SH	SF	SB	CS	SB%	GDP	Avg	OBP	Slg
2011	Rome*	A	2	3	1	0	0	0	(-	-)	1	0	1	1	2	0	1	0	0	1	0	0	-	0	.333	.500	.333
1993	Atl	NL	8	3	2	1	0	0	(0	0)	3	2	0	2	1	0	1	0	0	0	0	0	-	0	.667	.750	1.000
1995	Atl	NL	140	524	139	22	3	23	(15	8)	236	87	86	84	73	1	99	0	1	4	8	4	.67	10	.265	.353	.450
1996	Atl	NL	157	598	185	32	5	30	(18	12)	317	114	110	123	87	0	88	0	1	7	14	1	.93	14	.309	.393	.530
1997	Atl	NL	157	597	176	41	3	21	(7	14)	286	100	111	104	76	8	88	0	0	6	20	5	.80	19	.295	.371	.479
1998	Atl	NL	160	601	188	29	5	34	(17	17)	329	123	107	129	96	1	93	1	1	8	16	6	.73	17	.313	.404	.547
1999	Atl	NL	157	567	181	41	1	45	(25	20)	359	116	110	150	126	18	94	2	0	6	25	3	.89	20	.319	.441	.633
2000	Atl	NL	156	579	180	38	1	36	(18	18)	328	118	111	128	95	10	64	2	0	10	14	7	.67	14	.311	.404	.566
2001	Atl	NL	159	572	189	33	5	38	(19	19)	346	113	102	136	98	20	82	2	0	5	9	10	.47	13	.330	.427	.605
2002	Atl	NL	158	548	179	35	1	26	(17	9)	294	90	100	119	107	23	89	2	0	5	8	2	.80	18	.327	.435	.536
2003	Atl	NL	153	555	169	33	2	27	(16	11)	287	103	106	110	94	13	83	1	0	6	2	2	.50	10	.305	.402	.517
2004	Atl	NL	137	472	117	20	1	30	(19	11)	229	69	96	82	84	8	96	4	0	7	2	0	1.00	14	.248	.362	.485
2005	Atl	NL	109	358	106	30	0	21	(9	12)	199	66	72	78	72	5	56	0	0	2	5	1	.83	9	.296	.412	.556
2006	Atl	NL	110	411	133	28	3	26	(12	14)	245	87	86	94	61	4	73	1	0	4	6	1	.86	12	.324	.409	.596
2007	Atl	NL	134	513	173	42	4	29	(14	15)	310	108	102	110	82	10	75	0	0	5	5	1	.83	21	.337	.425	.604
2008	Atl	NL	128	439	160	24	1	22	(10	12)	252	82	75	98	90	16	61	1	0	4	4	0	1.00	13	**.364**	**.470**	.574
2009	Atl	NL	143	488	129	23	2	18	(10	8)	210	80	71	85	101	18	89	1	0	6	4	1	.80	14	.264	.388	.430
2010	Atl	NL	95	317	84	21	0	10	(9	1)	135	47	46	53	61	6	47	0	0	3	5	0	1.00	14	.265	.381	.426
2011	Atl	NL	126	455	125	33	1	18	(12	6)	214	56	70	72	51	10	80	0	0	6	2	2	.50	10	.275	.344	.470
Postseason			92	333	96	18	0	13	(7	6)	153	58	47	60	72	11	60	1	1	5	8	3	.73	10	.288	.411	.459
18 ML YEARS			2387	8597	2615	526	38	454	(249	205)	4579	1561	1561	1757	1455	171	1358	17	3	94	149	46	.76	238	.304	.402	.533

Garrett Jones

Bats: L Throws: L Pos: RF-90; 1B-34; PH-33; DH-2; PR-1   Ht: 6'4" Wt: 240 Born: 6/21/1981 Age: 31

Year	Team	Lg	G	AB	H	2B	3B	HR	(Hm	Rd)	TB	R	RBI	RC	TBB	IBB	SO	HBP	SH	SF	SB	CS	SB%	GDP	Avg	OBP	Slg
2007	Min	AL	31	77	16	2	1	2	(1	1)	26	7	5	3	6	0	20	0	0	1	1	1	.50	2	.208	.262	.338
2009	Pit	NL	82	314	92	21	1	21	(13	8)	178	45	44	47	40	8	76	1	0	3	10	2	.83	6	.293	.372	.567
2010	Pit	NL	158	592	146	34	1	21	(11	10)	245	64	86	69	53	2	123	1	0	8	7	3	.70	18	.247	.306	.414
2011	Pit	NL	148	423	103	30	1	16	(8	8)	183	51	58	57	48	2	104	2	0	4	6	3	.67	7	.243	.321	.433
	4 ML YEARS		419	1406	357	87	4	60	(33	27)	632	167	193	176	147	12	323	4	0	16	24	9	.73	33	.254	.323	.450

Matt Joyce

Bats: L Throws: R Pos: RF-126; PH-16; LF-15; DH-1   Ht: 6'2" Wt: 205 Born: 8/3/1984 Age: 27

Year	Team	Lg	G	AB	H	2B	3B	HR	(Hm	Rd)	TB	R	RBI	RC	TBB	IBB	SO	HBP	SH	SF	SB	CS	SB%	GDP	Avg	OBP	Slg
2008	Det	AL	92	242	61	16	3	12	(6	6)	119	40	33	36	31	0	65	2	0	2	0	2	.00	3	.252	.339	.492
2009	TB	AL	11	32	6	1	0	3	(2	1)	16	3	7	5	3	0	7	1	0	1	1	0	1.00	0	.188	.270	.500
2010	TB	AL	77	216	52	15	3	10	(4	6)	103	30	40	41	40	2	55	2	0	3	2	2	.50	2	.241	.360	.477
2011	TB	AL	141	462	128	32	2	19	(11	8)	221	69	75	77	49	9	106	4	0	7	13	1	.93	7	.277	.347	.478
	Postseason		4	9	2	0	0	0	(0	0)	2	0	0	0	0	0	4	0	0	0	1	0	1.00	0	.222	.222	.222
	4 ML YEARS		321	952	247	64	8	44	(23	21)	459	142	155	159	123	11	233	9	0	13	16	5	.76	12	.259	.345	.482

Josh Judy

Pitches: R Bats: R Pos: RP-12   Ht: 6'4" Wt: 200 Born: 2/9/1986 Age: 26

Year	Team	Lg	G	GS	CG	GF	IP	BFP	H	R	ER	HR	SH	SF	HB	TBB	IBB	SO	WP	Bk	W	L	Pct	Sh	Sv-Op	Hld	ERC	ERA
2007	Indns	R	9	0	0	4	14.1	65	11	4	1	0	1	0	2	8	1	14	0	0	1	2	.333	0	0- -	-	2.95	0.63
2007	MhVlly	A-	4	1	0	2	11.0	40	7	0	0	0	0	0	1	3	0	7	0	0	0	0	-	0	1- -	-	1.70	0.00
2008	Lk Cty	A	35	0	0	6	74.1	310	60	38	29	6	7	3	6	25	2	80	4	0	12	1	.923	0	1- -	-	2.92	3.51
2008	Knstn	A+	7	0	0	2	14.0	56	12	3	3	0	0	2	0	1	0	17	0	0	0	0	-	0	0- -	-	1.56	1.93
2009	Knstn	A+	5	0	0	5	4.2	17	4	0	0	0	0	0	0	0	0	7	0	0	0	0	-	0	3- -	-	1.52	0.00
2009	Akron	AA	36	1	0	23	49.1	201	35	19	17	2	3	0	3	18	0	63	2	0	4	3	.571	0	11- -	-	2.27	3.10
2010	Akron	AA	2	0	0	1	2.0	11	6	2	2	0	0	0	0	0	0	2	1	0	0	0	-	0	0- -	-	15.89	9.00
2010	Clmbs	AAA	38	0	0	14	47.0	199	48	18	14	5	1	1	0	14	0	55	1	0	3	0	1.000	0	2- -	-	3.84	2.68
2011	Clmbs	AAA	50	0	0	45	52.0	223	44	23	18	5	4	2	1	25	2	60	1	0	6	2	.750	0	23- -	-	3.50	3.12
2011	Cle	AL	12	0	0	4	14.0	66	18	11	11	4	1	1	4	4	0	10	0	0	0	0	-	0	0-0	0	8.14	7.07

Jair Jurrjens

Pitches: R Bats: R Pos: SP-23   jye-AIR JURR-jens   Ht: 6'1" Wt: 200 Born: 1/29/1986 Age: 26

Year	Team	Lg	G	GS	CG	GF	IP	BFP	H	R	ER	HR	SH	SF	HB	TBB	IBB	SO	WP	Bk	W	L	Pct	Sh	Sv-Op	Hld	ERC	ERA
2011	Gwnntt*	AAA	1	1	0	0	6.0	23	4	2	2	1	0	0	0	2	0	3	0	0	1	0	1.000	0	0- -	-	2.58	3.00
2007	Det	AL	7	7	0	0	30.2	122	24	16	16	4	0	1	1	11	0	13	2	0	3	1	.750	0	0-0	0	3.19	4.70
2008	Atl	NL	31	31	0	0	188.1	813	188	87	77	11	12	5	4	70	9	139	3	0	13	10	.565	0	0-0	0	3.65	3.68
2009	Atl	NL	34	34	0	0	215.0	884	186	71	62	15	16	4	3	75	1	152	3	2	14	10	.583	0	0-0	0	3.03	2.60
2010	Atl	NL	20	20	0	0	116.1	500	120	63	60	13	7	4	2	42	5	86	2	0	7	6	.538	0	0-0	0	4.20	4.64
2011	Atl	NL	23	23	2	0	152.0	627	142	52	50	14	6	3	4	44	5	90	4	2	13	6	.684	1	0-0	0	3.33	2.96
	5 ML YEARS		115	115	2	0	702.1	2946	660	289	265	57	41	17	14	242	20	480	14	4	50	33	.602	1	0-0	0	3.46	3.40

Kila Ka'aihue

Bats: L Throws: R Pos: 1B-19; DH-4   KEY-luh kuh-eye-HOO-ah   Ht: 6'4" Wt: 235 Born: 3/29/1984 Age: 28

Year	Team	Lg	G	AB	H	2B	3B	HR	(Hm	Rd)	TB	R	RBI	RC	TBB	IBB	SO	HBP	SH	SF	SB	CS	SB%	GDP	Avg	OBP	Slg
2011	Omha*	AAA	95	323	88	19	0	11	(-	-)	140	43	65	57	57	3	81	2	0	6	1	1	.50	8	.272	.379	.433
2008	KC	AL	12	21	6	0	0	1	(1	0)	9	4	1	3	3	0	2	0	0	0	0	0	-	0	.286	.375	.429
2010	KC	AL	52	180	39	6	1	8	(5	3)	71	22	25	15	24	2	39	0	1	0	0	1	.00	5	.217	.307	.394
2011	KC	AL	23	82	16	4	0	2	(1	1)	26	6	6	5	12	0	26	0	1	1	0	0	-	3	.195	.295	.317
	3 ML YEARS		87	283	61	10	1	11	(7	4)	106	32	32	23	39	2	67	0	2	2	0	1	.00	8	.216	.309	.375

Jeff Karstens

Pitches: R Bats: R Pos: SP-26; RP-4   Ht: 6'3" Wt: 185 Born: 9/24/1982 Age: 29

Year	Team	Lg	G	GS	CG	GF	IP	BFP	H	R	ER	HR	SH	SF	HB	TBB	IBB	SO	WP	Bk	W	L	Pct	Sh	Sv-Op	Hld	ERC	ERA
2006	NYY	AL	8	6	0	2	42.2	179	40	20	18	6	0	2	1	11	2	16	3	1	2	1	.667	0	0-0	0	3.42	3.80
2007	NYY	AL	7	3	0	2	14.2	80	27	21	18	4	2	1	0	9	0	5	2	0	1	4	.200	0	0-0	0	11.86	11.05
2008	Pit	NL	9	9	1	0	51.1	220	56	32	23	7	2	4	0	13	0	23	1	0	2	6	.250	1	0-0	0	4.22	4.03
2009	Pit	NL	39	13	0	8	108.0	471	115	66	65	12	6	6	2	45	5	52	1	0	4	6	.400	0	0-0	1	4.64	5.42
2010	Pit	NL	26	19	0	1	122.2	525	146	72	67	21	2	9	1	27	5	72	0	1	3	10	.231	0	0-0	0	4.97	4.92
2011	Pit	NL	30	26	1	1	162.1	668	163	69	61	22	6	5	4	33	6	96	4	1	9	9	.500	1	0-0	0	3.64	3.38
	6 ML YEARS		119	76	2	14	501.2	2143	547	280	252	72	18	27	8	138	18	264	11	3	21	36	.368	2	0-0	1	4.42	4.52

Scott Kazmir

Pitches: L **Bats:** L **Pos:** SP-1 **Ht:** 6'0" **Wt:** 195 **Born:** 1/24/1984 **Age:** 28

Year	Team	Lg	G	GS	CG	GF	IP	BFP	H	R	ER	HR	SH	SF	HB	TBB	IBB	SO	WP	Bk	W	L	Pct	Sh	Sv-Op Hld	ERC	ERA
2011	Salt Lk*	AAA	5	5	0	0	15.1	94	22	30	29	0	2	4	6	20	0	14	5	0	0	5	.000	0	0- - -	11.17	17.02
2004	TB	AL	8	7	0	0	33.1	152	33	22	21	4	0	0	2	21	0	41	3	0	2	3	.400	0	0-0	5.36	5.67
2005	TB	AL	32	32	0	0	186.0	818	172	90	78	12	6	9	10	100	3	174	7	1	10	9	.526	0	0-0	4.13	3.77
2006	TB	AL	24	24	1	0	144.2	610	132	59	52	15	0	5	2	52	3	163	6	0	10	8	.556	1	0-0	3.47	3.24
2007	TB	AL	34	34	0	0	206.2	887	196	91	80	18	6	3	7	89	1	239	10	0	13	9	.591	0	0-0	3.97	3.48
2008	TB	AL	27	27	0	0	152.1	641	123	61	59	23	4	5	4	70	2	166	5	0	12	8	.600	0	0-0	3.69	3.49
2009	2 Tms	AL	26	26	0	0	147.1	647	149	85	80	16	1	4	6	60	0	117	13	0	10	9	.526	0	0-0	4.36	4.89
2010	LAA	AL	28	28	0	0	150.0	682	158	103	99	25	3	6	12	79	2	93	6	0	9	15	.375	0	0-0	5.74	5.94
2011	LAA	AL	1	1	0	0	1.2	14	5	5	5	1	0	0	2	2	0	0	0	1	0	0	-	0	0-0	35.08	27.00
09	TB	AL	20	20	0	0	111.0	504	121	77	73	15	1	4	5	50	0	91	10	0	8	7	.533	0	0-0	5.18	5.92
09	LAA	AL	6	6	0	0	36.1	143	28	8	7	1	0	0	1	10	0	26	3	0	2	2	.500	0	0-0	2.13	1.73
	Postseason		8	7	0	0	36.1	176	37	22	21	5	3	2	3	26	0	26	2	0	1	2	.333	0	0-0	5.92	5.20
8 ML YEARS			180	179	1	0	1022.0	4451	968	516	474	114	20	32	45	473	11	993	50	2	66	61	.520	1	0-0	4.27	4.17

Austin Kearns

Bats: R **Throws:** R **Pos:** LF-36; RF-19; PH-3; PR-3; DH-1 **Ht:** 6'3" **Wt:** 240 **Born:** 5/20/1980 **Age:** 32

Year	Team	Lg	G	AB	H	2B	3B	HR	(Hm	Rd)	TB	R	RBI	RC	TBB	IBB	SO	HBP	SH	SF	SB	CS	SB%	GDP	Avg	OBP	Slg
2002	Cin	NL	107	372	117	24	3	13	(7	6)	186	66	56	70	54	3	81	6	0	3	6	3	.67	11	.315	.407	.500
2003	Cin	NL	82	292	77	11	0	15	(8	7)	133	39	58	52	41	1	68	5	0	0	5	2	.71	7	.264	.364	.455
2004	Cin	NL	64	217	50	10	2	9	(3	6)	91	28	32	26	28	0	71	1	0	0	1	.67	8	.230	.321	.419
2005	Cin	NL	112	387	93	26	1	18	(9	9)	175	62	67	55	48	2	107	8	0	5	0	0	-	8	.240	.333	.452
2006	2 Tms	NL	150	537	142	33	2	24	(12	12)	251	86	86	81	76	4	135	10	1	5	9	4	.69	18	.264	.363	.467
2007	Was	NL	161	587	156	35	1	16	(8	8)	241	84	74	87	71	5	106	12	0	4	2	2	.50	13	.266	.355	.411
2008	Was	NL	86	313	68	10	0	7	(1	6)	99	40	32	28	35	0	63	8	0	1	2	2	.50	11	.217	.311	.316
2009	Was	NL	80	174	34	6	2	3	(1	2)	53	20	17	17	32	1	51	5	0	0	1	1	.50	12	.195	.336	.305
2010	2 Tms	AL	120	403	106	21	1	10	(5	5)	159	55	49	51	46	2	116	10	0	2	4	1	.80	16	.263	.351	.395
2011	Cle	AL	57	150	30	5	1	2	(1	1)	43	18	7	11	18	0	48	4	2	0	0	4	.00	2	.200	.302	.287
06	Cin	NL	87	325	89	21	1	16	(8	8)	160	53	50	46	35	2	85	5	0	3	7	1	.88	14	.274	.351	.492
06	Was	NL	63	212	53	12	1	8	(4	4)	91	33	36	35	41	2	50	5	1	2	2	3	.40	4	.250	.381	.429
10	Cle	AL	84	301	82	18	1	8	(4	4)	126	42	42	43	34	2	78	5	0	2	4	1	.80	12	.272	.354	.419
10	NYY	AL	36	102	24	3	0	2	(1	1)	33	13	7	8	12	0	38	5	0	0	0	0	-	4	.235	.345	.324
10 ML YEARS			1019	3432	873	181	13	117	(55	62)	1431	498	478	478	449	18	846	69	3	20	31	20	.61	106	.254	.350	.417

Shawn Kelley

Pitches: R **Bats:** R **Pos:** RP-10 **Ht:** 6'2" **Wt:** 215 **Born:** 4/26/1984 **Age:** 28

Year	Team	Lg	G	GS	CG	GF	IP	BFP	H	R	ER	HR	SH	SF	HB	TBB	IBB	SO	WP	Bk	W	L	Pct	Sh	Sv-Op Hld	ERC	ERA
2011	Jacksn*	AA	3	2	0	0	3.0	14	4	3	0	0	1	1	0	0	3	1	0	0	1	.000	0	0- - -	4.83	0.00
2011	Tacom*	AAA	12	0	0	4	14.2	60	11	3	3	3	1	0	0	6	1	15	0	0	1	0	1.000	0	0- - -	3.34	1.84
2009	Sea	AL	41	0	0	12	46.0	191	45	23	23	9	2	2	3	9	1	41	2	1	5	4	.556	0	0-4 9	4.02	4.50
2010	Sea	AL	22	0	0	7	25.0	112	26	11	11	5	0	0	1	12	2	26	0	0	3	1	.750	0	0-0 3	5.38	3.96
2011	Sea	AL	10	0	0	2	12.2	47	7	0	0	0	0	0	0	3	1	10	0	0	0	0	-	0	0-0 1	1.01	0.00
3 ML YEARS			73	0	0	21	83.2	350	78	34	34	14	2	2	4	24	4	77	2	1	8	5	.615	0	0-4 13	3.83	3.66

Don Kelly

Bats: L **Throws:** R **Pos:** 3B-45; RF-39; LF-17; 1B-15; PH-9; PR-9; CF-4; DH-2; C-1 **Ht:** 6'4" **Wt:** 190 **Born:** 2/15/1980 **Age:** 32

Year	Team	Lg	G	AB	H	2B	3B	HR	(Hm	Rd)	TB	R	RBI	RC	TBB	IBB	SO	HBP	SH	SF	SB	CS	SB%	GDP	Avg	OBP	Slg
2007	Pit	NL	25	27	4	0	0	0	(0	0)	4	2	0	1	3	0	3	2	0	0	0	0	-	1	.148	.281	.148
2009	Det	AL	31	56	14	3	1	0	(0	0)	19	8	3	7	4	0	10	1	1	0	1	0	1.00	0	.250	.311	.339
2010	Det	AL	119	238	58	4	0	9	(4	5)	89	30	27	26	8	0	42	2	1	2	3	0	1.00	1	.244	.272	.374
2011	Det	AL	113	257	63	8	3	7	(1	6)	98	35	28	27	14	0	32	3	6	1	2	1	.67	8	.245	.291	.381
4 ML YEARS			288	578	139	15	4	16	(5	11)	210	75	58	61	29	0	87	8	8	3	6	1	.86	10	.240	.285	.363

Matt Kemp

Bats: R **Throws:** R **Pos:** CF-159; DH-2; PH-1 **Ht:** 6'3" **Wt:** 220 **Born:** 9/23/1984 **Age:** 27

Year	Team	Lg	G	AB	H	2B	3B	HR	(Hm	Rd)	TB	R	RBI	RC	TBB	IBB	SO	HBP	SH	SF	SB	CS	SB%	GDP	Avg	OBP	Slg
2006	LAD	NL	52	154	39	7	0	7	(4	3)	69	30	23	20	9	1	53	0	0	3	6	0	1.00	6	.253	.289	.448
2007	LAD	NL	98	292	100	12	5	10	(9	1)	152	47	42	49	16	0	66	0	0	3	10	5	.67	6	.342	.373	.521
2008	LAD	NL	155	606	176	38	5	18	(14	4)	278	93	76	86	46	6	153	1	1	3	35	11	.76	11	.290	.340	.459
2009	LAD	NL	159	606	180	25	7	26	(13	13)	297	97	101	100	52	6	139	3	0	6	34	8	.81	14	.297	.352	.490
2010	LAD	NL	162	602	150	25	6	28	(15	13)	271	82	89	74	53	4	170	4	0	9	19	15	.56	14	.249	.310	.450
2011	LAD	NL	161	602	195	33	4	39	(19	20)	353	115	126	129	74	24	159	6	0	7	40	11	.78	16	.324	.399	.586
	Postseason		16	62	14	3	0	2	(1	1)	23	5	5	1	5	0	25	0	0	0	0	2	.00	2	.226	.284	.371
6 ML YEARS			787	2862	840	140	28	128	(74	54)	1420	464	457	458	250	41	740	14	1	31	144	50	.74	62	.294	.350	.496

Howie Kendrick

Bats: R **Throws:** R **Pos:** 2B-108; LF-23; 1B-17; PH-3   **Ht:** 5'10" **Wt:** 215 **Born:** 7/12/1983 **Age:** 28

											BATTING												BASERUNNING				AVERAGES		
Year	Team	Lg	G	AB	H	2B	3B	HR	(Hm	Rd)	TB	R	RBI	RC	TBB	IBB	SO	HBP	SH	SF	SB	CS	SB%	GDP	Avg	OBP	Slg
2006	LAA	AL	72	267	76	21	1	4	(2	2)	111	25	30	32	9	2	44	4	0	3	6	0	1.00	5	.285	.314	.416
2007	LAA	AL	88	338	109	24	2	5	(3	2)	152	55	39	41	9	2	61	4	1	1	5	4	.56	15	.322	.347	.450
2008	LAA	AL	92	340	104	26	2	3	(1	2)	143	43	37	50	12	3	58	4	1	4	11	4	.73	8	.306	.333	.421
2009	LAA	AL	105	374	109	21	3	10	(5	5)	166	61	61	58	20	1	71	4	2	0	11	4	.73	8	.291	.334	.444
2010	LAA	AL	158	616	172	41	4	10	(4	6)	251	67	75	81	28	2	94	5	4	5	14	4	.78	16	.279	.313	.407
2011	LAA	AL	140	537	153	30	6	18	(5	13)	249	86	63	69	33	3	119	10	3	0	14	6	.70	18	.285	.338	.464
	Postseason		13	46	9	0	1	1	(1	0)	14	4	2	3	1	0	11	0	2	1	3	0	1.00	1	.196	.208	.304
	6 ML YEARS		655	2472	723	163	18	50	(20	30)	1072	337	305	331	111	13	447	31	11	13	61	22	.73	70	.292	.329	.434

Kyle Kendrick

Pitches: R **Bats:** R **Pos:** RP-19; SP-15   **Ht:** 6'3" **Wt:** 213 **Born:** 8/26/1984 **Age:** 27

			HOW MUCH HE PITCHED					WHAT HE GAVE UP											THE RESULTS						
Year	Team	Lg	G	GS	CG	GF	IP	BFP	H	R	ER	HR	SH	SF	HB	TBB	IBB	SO	WP	Bk	W	L	Pct	Sh	Sv-Op	Hld	ERC	ERA
2007	Phi	NL	20	20	0	0	121.0	499	129	63	52	16	4	2	7	25	3	49	0	0	10	4	.714	0	0-0	0	4.23	3.87
2008	Phi	NL	31	30	0	1	155.2	722	194	103	95	23	8	4	14	57	2	68	4	1	11	9	.550	0	0-0	0	6.05	5.49
2009	Phi	NL	9	2	0	2	26.1	112	27	11	10	1	1	2	1	9	0	15	0	1	3	1	.750	0	0-0	0	3.75	3.42
2010	Phi	NL	33	31	1	1	180.2	771	199	103	95	26	9	6	3	49	4	84	1	2	11	10	.524	0	0-0	0	4.51	4.73
2011	Phi	NL	34	15	0	5	114.2	478	110	50	41	14	6	3	7	30	5	59	1	1	8	6	.571	0	0-1	0	3.66	3.22
	Postseason		1	1	0	0	3.2	18	5	5	5	2	0	0	0	2	1	2	0	0	0	1	.000	0	0-0	0	9.97	12.27
	5 ML YEARS		127	98	1	9	598.1	2582	659	320	293	80	28	17	32	170	14	275	6	5	43	30	.589	0	0-1	0	4.64	4.41

Adam Kennedy

Bats: L **Throws:** R **Pos:** 1B-36; 2B-34; 3B-27; DH-17; PH-12; PR-4   **Ht:** 6'1" **Wt:** 195 **Born:** 1/10/1976 **Age:** 36

											BATTING												BASERUNNING				AVERAGES		
Year	Team	Lg	G	AB	H	2B	3B	HR	(Hm	Rd)	TB	R	RBI	RC	TBB	IBB	SO	HBP	SH	SF	SB	CS	SB%	GDP	Avg	OBP	Slg
1999	StL	NL	33	102	26	10	1	1	(1	0)	41	12	16	12	3	0	8	2	1	2	0	1	.00	1	.255	.284	.402
2000	LAA	AL	156	598	159	33	11	9	(7	2)	241	82	72	72	28	5	73	3	8	4	22	8	.73	10	.266	.300	.403
2001	LAA	AL	137	478	129	25	3	6	(4	2)	178	48	40	57	27	3	71	11	7	9	12	7	.63	7	.270	.318	.372
2002	LAA	AL	144	474	148	32	6	7	(6	1)	213	65	52	70	19	1	80	7	5	4	17	4	.81	5	.312	.345	.449
2003	LAA	AL	143	449	121	17	1	13	(8	5)	179	71	49	61	45	4	73	9	2	5	22	9	.71	7	.269	.344	.399
2004	LAA	AL	144	468	130	20	5	10	(5	5)	190	70	48	60	41	7	92	13	9	2	15	5	.75	10	.278	.351	.406
2005	LAA	AL	129	416	125	23	0	2	(1	1)	154	49	37	62	29	1	64	7	5	3	19	4	.83	5	.300	.354	.370
2006	LAA	AL	139	451	123	26	4	4	(3	1)	173	50	55	62	39	5	72	5	3	5	16	10	.62	15	.273	.334	.384
2007	StL	NL	87	279	61	9	1	3	(0	3)	81	27	18	19	22	6	33	3	1	1	6	2	.75	9	.219	.282	.290
2008	StL	NL	115	339	95	17	4	2	(1	1)	126	42	36	39	21	4	43	1	0	4	7	1	.88	13	.280	.321	.372
2009	Oak	AL	129	529	153	29	1	11	(4	7)	217	65	63	88	45	2	86	4	5	3	20	6	.77	8	.289	.348	.410
2010	Was	NL	135	342	85	16	1	3	(0	3)	112	43	31	37	37	1	44	5	1	4	14	2	.88	10	.249	.327	.327
2011	Sea	AL	114	380	89	23	1	7	(5	2)	135	36	38	35	22	3	67	1	4	2	8	2	.80	3	.234	.277	.355
	Postseason		25	78	24	3	1	4	(4	0)	41	13	13	11	1	0	15	1	3	2	1	2	.33	1	.308	.317	.526
	13 ML YEARS		1605	5305	1444	280	41	78	(45	33)	2040	660	555	674	378	42	806	71	51	48	178	61	.74	103	.272	.326	.385

Ian Kennedy

Pitches: R **Bats:** R **Pos:** SP-33   **Ht:** 6'0" **Wt:** 195 **Born:** 12/19/1984 **Age:** 27

			HOW MUCH HE PITCHED					WHAT HE GAVE UP											THE RESULTS						
Year	Team	Lg	G	GS	CG	GF	IP	BFP	H	R	ER	HR	SH	SF	HB	TBB	IBB	SO	WP	Bk	W	L	Pct	Sh	Sv-Op	Hld	ERC	ERA
2007	NYY	AL	3	3	0	0	19.0	77	13	6	4	1	0	0	0	9	0	15	0	0	1	0	1.000	0	0-0	0	2.42	1.89
2008	NYY	AL	10	9	0	1	39.2	194	50	37	36	5	1	4	1	26	0	27	3	0	0	4	.000	0	0-0	0	6.93	8.17
2009	NYY	AL	1	0	0	0	1.0	6	0	0	0	0	0	0	0	2	0	1	0	0	0	0	-	0	0-0	1	7.00	0.00
2010	Ari	NL	32	32	0	0	194.0	810	163	87	82	26	11	5	10	70	2	168	16	0	9	10	.474	0	0-0	0	3.47	3.80
2011	Ari	NL	33	33	1	0	222.0	900	186	73	71	19	9	9	9	55	0	198	11	1	21	4	.840	1	0-0	0	2.71	2.88
	5 ML YEARS		79	77	1	1	475.2	1987	412	203	193	51	21	18	21	162	2	409	30	1	31	18	.633	1	0-0	1	3.33	3.65

Jeff Keppinger

Bats: R **Throws:** R **Pos:** 2B-93; PH-7   **Ht:** 6'0" **Wt:** 187 **Born:** 4/21/1980 **Age:** 32

											BATTING												BASERUNNING				AVERAGES		
Year	Team	Lg	G	AB	H	2B	3B	HR	(Hm	Rd)	TB	R	RBI	RC	TBB	IBB	SO	HBP	SH	SF	SB	CS	SB%	GDP	Avg	OBP	Slg
2011	CpChr*	AA	4	16	7	1	0	1	(-	-)	11	4	2	5	3	1	1	0	0	0	0	0	-	0	.438	.526	.688
2011	OKCity*	AAA	7	28	7	0	0	0	(-	-)	7	2	1	1	0	0	0	0	1	1	0	0	-	0	.250	.241	.250
2004	NYM	NL	33	116	33	2	0	3	(3	0)	44	9	9	12	6	0	7	0	0	1	2	1	.67	6	.284	.317	.379
2006	KC	AL	22	60	16	2	0	2	(0	2)	24	11	8	8	5	1	6	0	2	0	0	0	-	2	.267	.323	.400
2007	Cin	NL	67	241	80	16	2	5	(2	3)	115	39	32	42	24	0	12	4	6	1	2	1	.67	11	.332	.400	.477
2008	Cin	NL	121	459	122	24	2	3	(3	0)	159	45	43	52	30	3	24	2	6	5	3	1	.75	14	.266	.310	.346
2009	Hou	NL	107	305	78	13	3	7	(1	6)	118	35	29	28	27	3	33	3	7	2	0	2	.00	13	.256	.320	.387
2010	Hou	NL	137	514	148	34	1	6	(4	2)	202	62	59	72	51	1	36	1	5	4	4	1	.80	15	.288	.351	.393
2011	2 Tms	NL	99	379	105	20	0	6	(4	2)	143	39	35	38	12	0	24	2	2	4	0	1	.00	5	.277	.300	.377
11	Hou	NL	43	163	50	9	0	4	(3	1)	71	22	20	18	4	0	7	0	0	2	0	1	.00	5	.307	.320	.436
11	SF	NL	56	216	55	11	0	2	(1	1)	72	17	15	20	8	0	17	2	2	2	0	0	-	6	.255	.285	.333
	7 ML YEARS		586	2074	582	111	8	32	(17	15)	805	240	215	252	155	8	142	12	28	17	11	7	.61	72	.281	.332	.388

Clayton Kershaw

Pitches: L **Bats:** L **Pos:** SP-33 **Ht:** 6'3" **Wt:** 217 **Born:** 3/19/1988 **Age:** 24

Year	Team	Lg		HOW MUCH HE PITCHED						WHAT HE GAVE UP											THE RESULTS						
			G	GS	CG	GF	IP	BFP	H	R	ER	HR	SH	SF	HB	TBB	IBB	SO	WP	Bk	W	L	Pct	Sh	Sv-Op	Hld	ERC	ERA
2008	LAD	NL	22	21	0	0	107.2	470	109	51	51	11	3	3	1	52	3	100	7	0	5	5	.500	0	0-0	1	4.53	4.26
2009	LAD	NL	31	30	0	1	171.0	701	119	55	53	7	11	2	1	91	4	185	11	2	8	8	.500	0	0-0	0	2.60	2.79
2010	LAD	NL	32	32	1	0	204.1	848	160	73	66	13	8	4	7	81	9	212	5	2	13	10	.565	1	0-0	0	2.72	2.91
2011	LAD	NL	33	33	5	0	233.1	912	174	66	59	15	11	2	3	54	2	248	5	1	21	5	.808	2	0-0	0	2.00	2.28
	Postseason		5	2	0	0	15.1	68	15	10	10	3	3	0	1	9	1	11	4	0	0	1	.000	0	0-0	1	5.72	5.87
	4 ML YEARS		118	116	6	1	716.1	2931	562	245	229	46	33	11	12	278	18	745	28	5	47	28	.627	3	0-0	1	2.70	2.88

Cole Kimball

Pitches: R **Bats:** R **Pos:** RP-12 **Ht:** 6'3" **Wt:** 225 **Born:** 8/1/1985 **Age:** 26

Year	Team	Lg		HOW MUCH HE PITCHED						WHAT HE GAVE UP											THE RESULTS						
			G	GS	CG	GF	IP	BFP	H	R	ER	HR	SH	SF	HB	TBB	IBB	SO	WP	Bk	W	L	Pct	Sh	Sv-Op	Hld	ERC	ERA
2006	Vrmnt	A-	16	5	0	3	34.0	169	43	26	22	3	0	2	3	24	0	28	6	0	1	4	.200	0	0- -	-	7.17	5.82
2007	Vrmnt	A-	14	13	0	1	64.1	282	52	35	30	4	2	3	4	40	1	72	13	0	3	6	.333	0	1- -	-	3.82	4.20
2008	Hgrstn	A	28	27	1	0	128.1	564	103	75	72	5	3	6	17	83	0	122	16	1	6	8	.429	1	0- -	-	4.07	5.05
2009	Ptomc	A+	39	0	0	23	46.2	219	49	37	33	4	3	4	2	28	2	52	11	1	4	5	.444	0	9- -	-	5.02	6.36
2010	Ptomc	A+	19	0	0	17	24.2	97	17	5	5	0	3	3	2	8	1	27	1	0	3	0	1.000	0	6- -	-	1.88	1.82
2010	Hrsbrg	AA	38	0	0	24	54.0	235	33	21	14	4	2	4	5	31	2	74	14	3	5	1	.833	0	12- -	-	2.65	2.33
2011	Syrcse	AAA	12	0	0	11	13.2	57	8	0	0	0	0	0	0	8	1	14	1	0	1	0	1.000	0	5- -	-	1.82	0.00
2011	Was	NL	12	0	0	4	14.0	59	8	3	3	0	0	1	1	11	0	11	2	0	1	0	1.000	0	0-1	0	2.85	1.93

Craig Kimbrel

Pitches: R **Bats:** R **Pos:** RP-79 **Ht:** 5'11" **Wt:** 205 **Born:** 5/28/1988 **Age:** 24

Year	Team	Lg		HOW MUCH HE PITCHED						WHAT HE GAVE UP											THE RESULTS						
			G	GS	CG	GF	IP	BFP	H	R	ER	HR	SH	SF	HB	TBB	IBB	SO	WP	Bk	W	L	Pct	Sh	Sv-Op	Hld	ERC	ERA
2008	Danvle	R	12	0	0	11	19.0	81	5	4	1	0	1	1	3	10	1	27	4	0	1	2	.333	0	6- -	-	0.97	0.47
2008	Rome	A	10	0	0	9	12.2	48	6	1	1	0	1	0	0	4	0	26	0	0	2	0	1.000	0	4- -	-	0.99	0.71
2008	MrtlBh	A+	2	0	0	0	3.2	14	5	0	0	0	0	0	0	1	0	3	0	0	0	0	-	0	0- -	-	5.90	0.00
2009	MrtlBh	A+	19	0	0	8	26.1	123	18	19	16	2	2	2	1	28	1	45	8	1	0	2	.000	0	2- -	-	4.75	5.47
2009	Rome	A	16	0	0	14	20.0	76	9	2	2	0	1	0	1	6	0	38	0	0	0	0	-	0	10- -	-	0.99	0.90
2009	Missi	AA	12	0	0	12	11.2	45	3	1	1	0	0	1	0	7	0	17	1	0	2	1	.667	0	6- -	-	1.11	0.77
2009	Gwnntt	AAA	2	0	0	1	2.0	10	0	0	0	0	0	0	0	4	0	3	1	0	0	0	-	0	0- -	-	3.47	0.00
2010	Gwnntt	AAA	48	0	0	43	55.2	230	28	13	10	3	2	0	4	35	0	83	8	1	3	2	.600	0	23- -	-	2.29	1.62
2010	Atl	NL	21	0	0	7	20.2	88	9	2	1	0	0	0	0	16	1	40	4	0	4	0	1.000	0	1-1	2	1.72	0.44
2011	Atl	NL	79	0	0	64	77.0	306	48	19	18	3	1	2	1	32	1	127	4	0	4	3	.571	0	46-54	0	1.88	2.10
	Postseason		4	0	0	2	4.1	13	1	2	1	0	0	0	0	1	0	7	0	0	0	1	.000	0	0-0	1	0.40	2.08
	2 ML YEARS		100	0	0	71	97.2	394	57	21	19	3	1	2	1	48	2	167	8	0	8	3	.727	0	47-55	2	1.85	1.75

Josh Kinney

Pitches: R **Bats:** R **Pos:** RP-13 **Ht:** 6'1" **Wt:** 214 **Born:** 3/31/1979 **Age:** 33

Year	Team	Lg		HOW MUCH HE PITCHED						WHAT HE GAVE UP											THE RESULTS						
			G	GS	CG	GF	IP	BFP	H	R	ER	HR	SH	SF	HB	TBB	IBB	SO	WP	Bk	W	L	Pct	Sh	Sv-Op	Hld	ERC	ERA
2011	Charltt*	AAA	49	0	0	39	61.2	250	49	22	19	2	3	3	5	17	0	66	6	1	6	3	.667	0	14- -	-	2.42	2.77
2006	StL	NL	21	0	0	4	25.0	99	17	9	9	3	0	0	1	8	0	22	0	0	0	0	-	0	0-0	2	2.40	3.24
2008	StL	NL	7	0	0	1	7.0	25	3	0	0	0	0	0	0	1	0	8	0	0	0	0	-	0	0-0	0	0.60	0.00
2009	StL	NL	17	0	0	3	15.1	81	23	15	15	2	1	0	2	11	1	8	0	0	1	0	1.000	0	0-1	2	9.17	8.80
2011	CWS	AL	13	0	0	8	17.2	81	23	13	13	1	0	0	2	7	1	20	1	0	0	0	-	0	0-0	0	6.00	6.62
	Postseason		7	0	0	1	6.1	25	3	0	0	0	0	0	1	4	0	6	0	0	1	0	1.000	0	0-0	3	2.24	0.00
	4 ML YEARS		58	0	0	16	65.0	286	66	37	37	6	1	0	5	27	2	58	1	0	1	0	1.000	0	0-1	4	4.43	5.12

Ian Kinsler

Bats: R **Throws:** R **Pos:** 2B-144; DH-11; PH-1 **Ht:** 6'0" **Wt:** 200 **Born:** 6/22/1982 **Age:** 30

Year	Team	Lg						BATTING														BASERUNNING				AVERAGES		
			G	AB	H	2B	3B	HR	(Hm	Rd)	TB	R	RBI	RC	TBB	IBB	SO	HBP	SH	SF	SB	CS	SB%	GDP	Avg	OBP	Slg
2006	Tex	AL	120	423	121	27	1	14	(10	4)	192	65	55	65	40	1	64	3	1	7	11	4	.73	12	.286	.347	.454
2007	Tex	AL	130	483	127	22	2	20	(12	8)	213	96	61	79	62	2	83	9	8	4	23	2	.92	14	.263	.355	.441
2008	Tex	AL	121	518	165	41	4	18	(4	14)	268	102	71	106	45	1	67	6	7	7	26	2	.93	12	.319	.375	.517
2009	Tex	AL	144	566	143	32	4	31	(20	11)	276	101	86	99	59	0	77	6	3	6	31	5	.86	9	.253	.327	.488
2010	Tex	AL	103	391	112	20	1	9	(4	5)	161	73	45	59	56	2	57	7	2	4	15	5	.75	11	.286	.382	.412
2011	Tex	AL	155	620	158	34	4	32	(16	16)	296	121	77	100	89	2	71	8	4	2	30	4	.88	17	.255	.355	.477
	Postseason		16	54	16	2	1	3	(1	2)	29	7	9	11	8	0	7	0	1	1	3	1	.75	1	.296	.381	.537
	6 ML YEARS		773	3001	826	176	16	124	(66	58)	1406	558	395	508	351	8	419	39	25	30	136	22	.86	75	.275	.355	.469

Brandon Kintzler

Pitches: R **Bats:** R **Pos:** RP-9 **Ht:** 5'10" **Wt:** 180 **Born:** 8/1/1984 **Age:** 27

Year	Team	Lg		HOW MUCH HE PITCHED						WHAT HE GAVE UP											THE RESULTS						
			G	GS	CG	GF	IP	BFP	H	R	ER	HR	SH	SF	HB	TBB	IBB	SO	WP	Bk	W	L	Pct	Sh	Sv-Op	Hld	ERC	ERA
2004	Padres	R	21	0	0	12	34.0	140	36	12	9	0	1	0	0	9	4	38	3	0	3	2	.600	0	6- -	-	3.10	2.38
2004	Eugene	A-	3	0	0	3	3.0	12	3	0	0	0	0	0	0	0	0	4	0	0	0	0	-	0	3- -	-	1.95	0.00
2005	Padres	R	8	0	0	6	11.0	54	15	5	5	2	1	0	0	4	0	17	1	0	2	0	1.000	0	1- -	-	6.31	4.09
2005	Eugene	A-	3	0	0	0	3.1	12	3	0	0	0	1	0	0	1	0	6	0	0	0	0	-	0	0- -	-	1.70	0.00
2005	FtWyn	A	19	0	0	9	23.1	97	20	12	8	2	1	0	2	7	0	19	0	0	1	2	.333	0	0- -	-	3.16	3.09
2009	Hntsvl	AA	9	6	0	0	35.2	154	41	21	18	5	0	0	1	9	0	32	1	0	1	2	.333	0	0- -	-	4.76	4.54

160

Year	Team	Lg	G	GS	CG	GF	IP	BFP	H	R	ER	HR	SH	SF	HB	TBB	IBB	SO	WP	Bk	W	L	Pct	Sh	Sv-Op	Hld	ERC	ERA
2010	Hntsvl	AA	20	0	0	19	22.1	80	11	2	1	0	0	0	1	1	0	23	0	0	1	0	1.000	0	10--	-	0.66	0.40
2010	Nashv	AAA	22	0	0	13	26.2	105	19	7	7	1	1	0	1	6	1	21	1	0	3	0	1.000	0	6--	-	1.70	2.36
2011	Nashv	AAA	1	0	0	0	1.0	3	0	0	0	0	0	0	0	0	0	2	0	0	0	0	-	0	0--	-	0.00	0.00
2010	Mil	NL	7	0	0	2	7.1	33	10	6	6	2	1	0	0	4	1	9	1	0	0	1	.000	0	0-0	0	8.67	7.36
2011	Mil	NL	9	0	0	3	14.2	61	14	9	6	3	0	2	0	3	0	15	0	1	1	1	.500	0	0-0	0	3.65	3.68
	2 ML YEARS		16	0	0	5	22.0	94	24	15	12	5	1	2	0	7	1	24	1	1	1	2	.333	0	0-0	0	5.16	4.91

Jason Kipnis

KIP-niss

Bats: L **Throws:** R **Pos:** 2B-36; PH-1   **Ht:** 5'11" **Wt:** 185 **Born:** 4/3/1987 **Age:** 25

						BATTING													BASERUNNING				AVERAGES		
Year	Team	Lg	G	AB	H	2B	3B	HR	(Hm | Rd)	TB	R	RBI	RC	TBB	IBB	SO	HBP	SH	SF	SB	CS	SB%	GDP	Avg	OBP	Slg
2009	MhVlly	A-	29	111	34	8	3	1	(- | -)	51	19	19	20	15	1	18	1	0	2	3	3	.50	1	.306	.388	.459
2010	Knstn	A+	54	203	61	12	3	6	(- | -)	97	33	31	38	24	1	46	6	2	2	2	3	.40	5	.300	.387	.478
2010	Akron	AA	79	315	98	20	5	10	(- | -)	158	63	43	62	31	1	61	7	2	0	7	1	.88	15	.311	.385	.502
2011	Clmbs	AAA	92	343	96	16	9	12	(- | -)	166	65	55	64	44	1	72	3	5	5	12	1	.92	5	.280	.362	.484
2011	Cle	AL	36	136	37	9	1	7	(3 | 4)	69	24	19	22	11	0	34	2	0	1	5	0	1.00	5	.272	.333	.507

Michael Kirkman

Pitches: L **Bats:** L **Pos:** RP-15   **Ht:** 6'4" **Wt:** 195 **Born:** 9/18/1986 **Age:** 25

				HOW MUCH HE PITCHED						WHAT HE GAVE UP									THE RESULTS								
Year	Team	Lg	G	GS	CG	GF	IP	BFP	H	R	ER	HR	SH	SF	HB	TBB	IBB	SO	WP	Bk	W	L	Pct	Sh	Sv-Op	Hld	ERC	ERA
2005	Rngrs	R	14	9	0	1	52.1	227	51	28	20	0	1	1	1	19	0	58	3	0	3	1	.750	0	0--	-	3.11	3.44
2006	Clinton	A	6	6	0	0	19.1	103	23	17	15	0	2	0	1	24	0	22	5	0	0	3	.000	0	0--	-	8.05	6.98
2006	Rngrs	R	8	4	0	2	15.0	97	21	27	22	0	0	2	5	27	0	8	9	0	1	2	.333	0	0--	-	13.00	13.20
2007	Spkane	A-	9	6	0	0	27.0	140	33	30	21	2	2	3	2	25	0	24	7	0	1	4	.200	0	0--	-	7.56	7.00
2007	Clinton	A	5	2	0	1	13.1	69	17	12	11	1	1	0	0	12	0	12	1	0	0	1	.000	0	0--	-	7.43	7.43
2008	Clinton	A	15	14	0	0	74.1	321	78	43	36	8	2	3	3	23	0	58	6	1	4	3	.571	0	0--	-	4.20	4.36
2008	Spkane	A-	2	2	0	0	10.0	41	7	4	0	0	0	0	1	2	0	9	0	0	1	1	.500	0	0--	-	1.56	0.00
2009	Bkrsfld	A+	8	7	0	0	48.0	202	43	16	11	1	1	3	4	18	0	54	3	0	4	1	.800	0	0--	-	3.23	2.06
2009	Frisco	AA	18	18	0	0	96.2	418	93	54	45	9	3	2	4	43	0	64	5	0	5	7	.417	0	0--	-	4.19	4.19
2010	OKCity	AAA	24	22	0	0	131.0	571	115	52	45	8	4	7	3	68	0	130	9	0	13	3	.813	0	0--	-	3.64	3.09
2011	RdRck	AAA	27	7	0	2	73.0	339	87	45	41	6	2	2	3	37	0	84	3	1	3	3	.500	0	1--	-	5.64	5.05
2010	Tex	AL	14	0	0	2	16.1	68	9	3	3	0	0	2	0	10	1	16	0	0	0	0	-	0	0-1	2	1.76	1.65
2011	Tex	AL	15	0	0	7	27.1	122	26	22	20	5	1	2	3	12	2	21	2	0	1	1	.500	0	0-0	1	4.81	6.59
	Postseason		3	0	0	2	2.2	13	4	1	1	0	1	0	0	2	0	2	0	0	0	0	-	0	0-0	0	8.14	3.38
	2 ML YEARS		29	0	0	9	43.2	190	35	25	23	5	1	4	3	22	3	37	2	0	1	1	.500	0	0-1	3	3.58	4.74

Corey Kluber

Pitches: R **Bats:** R **Pos:** RP-3   **Ht:** 6'4" **Wt:** 215 **Born:** 4/10/1986 **Age:** 26

				HOW MUCH HE PITCHED						WHAT HE GAVE UP									THE RESULTS								
Year	Team	Lg	G	GS	CG	GF	IP	BFP	H	R	ER	HR	SH	SF	HB	TBB	IBB	SO	WP	Bk	W	L	Pct	Sh	Sv-Op	Hld	ERC	ERA
2007	Eugene	A-	10	7	0	0	33.1	143	28	16	13	1	2	2	2	15	0	33	0	0	1	1	.500	0	0--	-	3.11	3.51
2008	Lk Els	A+	19	16	0	0	85.1	377	93	62	57	9	5	4	2	34	1	75	5	0	2	5	.286	0	0--	-	4.69	6.01
2008	FtWyn	A	10	10	0	0	56.0	234	49	25	20	8	0	1	6	13	0	72	4	0	4	3	.571	0	0--	-	3.41	3.21
2009	Lk Els	A+	19	19	0	0	109.0	469	110	65	55	9	5	1	6	36	0	124	8	0	7	9	.438	0	0--	-	3.95	4.54
2009	SnAnt	AA	9	9	0	0	45.0	210	45	25	23	5	2	3	2	34	0	35	1	1	2	4	.333	0	0--	-	5.81	4.60
2010	SnAnt	AA	22	21	0	0	122.2	525	121	59	47	7	5	4	9	40	0	136	5	0	6	6	.500	0	0--	-	3.71	3.45
2010	Akron	AA	5	5	0	0	26.1	124	38	12	11	0	1	1	2	10	0	21	1	0	2	2	.500	0	0--	-	6.22	3.76
2010	Clmbs	AAA	2	2	0	0	11.0	47	10	4	4	1	0	0	2	6	0	8	0	0	1	1	.500	0	0--	-	5.11	3.27
2011	Clmbs	AAA	27	27	0	0	150.2	667	153	101	93	19	6	2	8	70	0	143	12	0	7	11	.389	0	0--	-	4.84	5.56
2011	Cle	AL	3	0	0	2	4.1	25	6	4	4	0	0	0	2	3	0	5	1	0	0	0	-	0	0-0	0	8.12	8.31

Michael Kohn

KAHN

Pitches: R **Bats:** R **Pos:** RP-14   **Ht:** 6'0" **Wt:** 200 **Born:** 6/26/1986 **Age:** 26

				HOW MUCH HE PITCHED						WHAT HE GAVE UP									THE RESULTS								
Year	Team	Lg	G	GS	CG	GF	IP	BFP	H	R	ER	HR	SH	SF	HB	TBB	IBB	SO	WP	Bk	W	L	Pct	Sh	Sv-Op	Hld	ERC	ERA
2008	Orem	R+	16	0	0	4	23.1	93	11	5	5	1	0	0	0	11	0	44	3	0	2	0	1.000	0	0--	-	1.43	1.93
2009	CRpds	A	28	0	0	11	37.0	140	20	9	9	1	0	1	2	12	0	60	1	1	4	1	.800	0	6--	-	1.45	2.19
2009	RCuca	A+	22	0	0	14	28.2	108	13	3	3	0	1	1	1	14	0	43	2	0	2	0	1.000	0	3--	-	1.32	0.94
2010	Ark	AA	15	0	0	13	18.1	72	12	5	5	0	1	0	1	8	1	25	2	0	2	2	.500	0	8--	-	2.00	2.45
2010	Salt Lk	AAA	26	0	0	23	27.2	115	16	7	6	3	3	0	1	17	2	32	0	0	3	2	.600	0	8--	-	2.73	1.95
2011	Salt Lk	AAA	46	0	0	34	48.1	212	47	27	22	5	1	2	3	20	0	64	0	0	1	3	.250	0	12--	-	4.21	4.10
2010	LAA	AL	24	0	0	8	21.1	95	17	5	5	4	0	0	0	16	1	20	0	0	2	0	1.000	0	1-1	1	3.45	2.11
2011	LAA	AL	14	0	0	7	12.1	60	14	10	10	6	0	0	1	9	0	9	1	0	0	1	.000	0	1-2	1	9.92	7.30
	2 ML YEARS		38	0	0	15	33.2	155	31	15	15	6	4	0	1	25	1	29	1	0	2	1	.667	0	2-3	2	5.66	4.01

Paul Konerko

Bats: R **Throws:** R **Pos:** 1B-111; DH-37; PH-2   **Ht:** 6'2" **Wt:** 220 **Born:** 3/5/1976 **Age:** 36

						BATTING													BASERUNNING				AVERAGES		
Year	Team	Lg	G	AB	H	2B	3B	HR	(Hm	Rd)	TB	R	RBI	RC	TBB	IBB	SO	HBP	SH	SF	SB	CS	SB%	GDP	Avg	OBP	Slg
1997	LAD	NL	6	7	1	0	0	0	(0	0)	1	0	0	0	1	0	2	0	0	0	0	0	-	1	.143	.250	.143
1998	2 Tms	NL	75	217	47	4	0	7	(2	5)	72	21	29	17	16	0	40	3	0	3	0	1	.00	10	.217	.276	.332
1999	CWS	AL	142	513	151	31	4	24	(16	8)	262	71	81	86	45	0	68	2	1	3	1	0	1.00	19	.294	.352	.511
2000	CWS	AL	143	524	156	31	1	21	(10	11)	252	84	97	86	47	0	72	10	0	5	1	0	1.00	22	.298	.363	.481
2001	CWS	AL	156	582	164	35	0	32	(19	13)	295	92	99	99	54	6	89	9	0	5	1	0	1.00	17	.282	.349	.507

BATTING

Year	Team	Lg	G	AB	H	2B	3B	HR	(Hm	Rd)	TB	R	RBI	RC	TBB	IBB	SO	HBP	SH	SF	SB	CS	SB%	GDP	Avg	OBP	Slg
2002	CWS	AL	151	570	173	30	0	27	(13	14)	284	81	104	96	44	2	72	9	0	7	0	0	-	17	.304	.359	.498
2003	CWS	AL	137	444	104	19	0	18	(9	9)	177	49	65	42	43	7	50	4	0	4	0	0	-	28	.234	.305	.399
2004	CWS	AL	155	563	156	22	0	41	(29	12)	301	84	117	106	69	5	107	6	0	5	1	0	1.00	23	.277	.359	.535
2005	CWS	AL	158	575	163	24	0	40	(23	17)	307	98	100	106	81	10	109	5	0	3	0	0	-	9	.283	.375	.534
2006	CWS	AL	152	566	177	30	0	35	(21	14)	312	97	113	110	60	3	104	8	0	9	1	0	1.00	25	.313	.381	.551
2007	CWS	AL	151	549	142	34	0	31	(17	14)	269	71	90	88	78	9	102	3	0	6	0	1	.00	21	.259	.351	.490
2008	CWS	AL	122	438	105	19	1	22	(15	7)	192	59	62	60	65	4	80	7	0	4	2	0	1.00	17	.240	.344	.438
2009	CWS	AL	152	546	151	30	1	28	(18	10)	267	75	88	91	58	4	89	10	0	7	1	0	1.00	15	.277	.353	.489
2010	CWS	AL	149	548	171	30	0	39	(26	13)	320	89	111	118	72	7	110	5	0	6	0	1	.00	9	.312	.393	.584
2011	CWS	AL	149	543	163	25	0	31	(19	12)	281	69	105	100	77	17	89	8	0	11	1	1	.50	14	.300	.388	.517
98	LAD	NL	49	144	31	1	0	4	(2	2)	44	14	16	10	10	0	30	2	0	2	0	1	.00	5	.215	.272	.306
98	Cin	NL	26	73	16	3	0	3	(0	3)	28	7	13	7	6	0	10	1	0	1	0	0	-	5	.219	.284	.384
	Postseason		19	74	18	2	0	7	(3	4)	41	10	17	12	5	2	10	1	0	0	0	0	-	4	.243	.300	.554
	15 ML YEARS		1998	7185	2024	364	8	396	(237	159)	3592	1040	1261	1205	810	74	1183	89	1	78	9	4	.69	247	.282	.358	.500

George Kontos

Pitches: R **Bats:** R **Pos:** RP-7
CON-toes
Ht: 6'3" **Wt:** 215 **Born:** 6/12/1985 **Age:** 27

			HOW MUCH HE PITCHED					WHAT HE GAVE UP											THE RESULTS						
Year	Team	Lg	G	GS	CG	GF	IP	BFP	H	R	ER	HR	SH	SF	HB	TBB	IBB	SO	WP	Bk	W	L	Pct	Sh	Sv-Op	Hld	ERC	ERA
2006	StlsInd	A-	14	14	0	0	78.1	313	64	25	23	3	4	6	2	19	0	82	3	0	7	3	.700	0	0--	-	2.27	2.64
2007	Tampa	A+	19	17	0	0	94.0	397	95	51	42	15	1	1	0	30	0	101	6	0	4	6	.400	0	0--	-	4.25	4.02
2008	Trntn	AA	27	27	0	0	151.2	635	134	76	62	14	4	8	4	57	1	152	2	0	6	11	.353	0	0--	-	3.40	3.68
2009	Trntn	AA	4	4	0	0	20.1	95	19	7	6	0	0	2	2	9	0	24	5	0	1	1	.500	0	0--	-	3.27	2.66
2009	S-WB	AAA	9	9	1	0	51.0	218	44	24	19	6	2	1	2	21	0	39	2	0	3	4	.429	0	0--	-	3.60	3.35
2010	Tampa	A+	5	2	0	2	10.1	40	7	3	3	0	0	1	0	3	0	8	0	0	0	1	.000	0	0--	-	1.55	2.61
2010	Trntn	AA	17	0	0	3	32.0	130	30	13	12	2	0	1	0	11	0	28	0	0	0	2	.000	0	0--	-	3.39	3.38
2010	S-WB	AAA	2	0	0	2	2.2	14	5	3	3	1	0	0	0	1	0	2	0	0	0	1	.000	0	0--	-	11.86	10.13
2011	S-WB	AAA	40	4	0	11	89.1	359	72	27	26	12	4	1	2	26	1	91	3	0	4	4	.500	0	2--	-	2.94	2.62
2011	NYY	AL	7	0	0	4	6.0	24	4	2	2	1	0	0	0	3	0	6	0	0	0	0	-	0	0-0	0	3.20	3.00

Casey Kotchman

Bats: L **Throws:** L **Pos:** 1B-146; PH-1
Ht: 6'3" **Wt:** 220 **Born:** 2/22/1983 **Age:** 29

BATTING

Year	Team	Lg	G	AB	H	2B	3B	HR	(Hm	Rd)	TB	R	RBI	RC	TBB	IBB	SO	HBP	SH	SF	SB	CS	SB%	GDP	Avg	OBP	Slg
2011	Drham*	AAA	1	4	1	0	0	0	(-	-)	1	0	0	0	1	0	0	0	0	0	0	0	-	0	.250	.400	.250
2004	LAA	AL	38	116	26	6	0	0	(0	0)	32	7	15	14	7	3	11	4	0	1	3	0	1.00	3	.224	.289	.276
2005	LAA	AL	47	126	35	5	0	7	(5	2)	61	16	22	21	15	0	18	0	1	1	1	1	.50	3	.278	.352	.484
2006	LAA	AL	29	79	12	2	0	1	(0	1)	17	6	6	1	7	0	13	0	2	0	0	1	.00	2	.152	.221	.215
2007	LAA	AL	137	443	131	37	3	11	(5	6)	207	64	68	74	53	1	43	4	3	5	2	4	.33	17	.296	.372	.467
2008	2 Tms		143	525	143	28	1	14	(3	11)	215	65	74	70	36	5	39	9	0	3	2	1	.67	18	.272	.328	.410
2009	2 Tms		126	385	103	23	0	7	(1	6)	147	37	48	49	39	6	42	4	0	3	1	0	1.00	11	.268	.339	.382
2010	Sea	AL	125	414	90	20	1	9	(5	4)	139	37	51	40	35	6	57	3	0	5	0	0	-	15	.217	.280	.336
2011	TB	AL	146	500	153	24	2	10	(7	3)	211	44	48	74	48	5	66	12	0	3	2	2	.50	13	.306	.378	.422
08	LAA	AL	100	373	107	24	0	12	(2	10)	167	47	54	53	18	3	23	5	0	2	2	1	.67	14	.287	.327	.448
08	Atl	NL	43	152	36	4	1	2	(1	1)	48	18	20	17	18	2	16	4	0	1	0	0	-	4	.237	.331	.316
09	Atl	NL	87	298	84	20	0	6	(1	5)	122	28	41	43	32	6	28	3	0	3	0	0	-	7	.282	.354	.409
09	Bos	AL	39	87	19	3	0	1	(0	1)	25	9	7	6	7	0	14	1	0	0	1	0	1.00	4	.218	.284	.287
	Postseason		11	16	2	1	0	0	(0	0)	3	1	1	1	3	0	2	0	0	0	0	0	-	0	.125	.263	.188
	8 ML YEARS		791	2588	693	145	7	59	(26	33)	1029	276	332	343	240	26	289	36	6	21	11	9	.55	82	.268	.336	.398

Mark Kotsay

Bats: L **Throws:** L **Pos:** PH-45; RF-30; LF-19; 1B-11; CF-10
Ht: 6'0" **Wt:** 210 **Born:** 12/2/1975 **Age:** 36

BATTING

Year	Team	Lg	G	AB	H	2B	3B	HR	(Hm	Rd)	TB	R	RBI	RC	TBB	IBB	SO	HBP	SH	SF	SB	CS	SB%	GDP	Avg	OBP	Slg
1997	Fla	NL	14	52	10	1	1	0	(0	0)	13	5	4	3	4	0	7	0	1	0	3	0	1.00	1	.192	.250	.250
1998	Fla	NL	154	578	161	25	7	11	(5	6)	233	72	68	70	34	2	61	1	7	3	10	5	.67	17	.279	.318	.403
1999	Fla	NL	148	495	134	23	9	8	(5	3)	199	57	50	58	29	5	50	0	2	9	7	6	.54	11	.271	.306	.402
2000	Fla	NL	152	530	158	31	5	12	(5	7)	235	87	57	78	42	2	46	0	2	4	19	9	.68	17	.298	.347	.443
2001	SD	NL	119	406	118	29	1	10	(3	7)	179	67	58	65	48	1	58	2	1	3	13	5	.72	11	.291	.366	.441
2002	SD	NL	153	578	169	27	7	17	(11	6)	261	82	61	92	59	0	89	3	2	4	11	9	.55	10	.292	.359	.452
2003	SD	NL	128	482	128	28	4	7	(1	6)	185	64	38	59	56	3	82	0	3	4	6	3	.67	8	.266	.343	.384
2004	Oak	AL	148	606	190	37	3	15	(9	6)	278	78	63	94	55	5	70	2	4	3	8	5	.62	6	.314	.370	.459
2005	Oak	AL	139	582	163	35	1	15	(4	11)	245	75	82	86	40	4	51	1	2	4	5	5	.50	13	.280	.325	.421
2006	Oak	AL	129	502	138	29	3	7	(1	6)	194	57	59	63	44	1	55	2	4	6	6	3	.67	18	.275	.332	.386
2007	Oak	AL	56	206	44	14	0	1	(0	1)	61	20	20	19	19	3	20	0	1	1	1	1	.50	4	.214	.279	.296
2008	2 Tms		110	402	111	25	4	6	(4	2)	162	45	49	49	32	3	45	0	1	1	2	4	.33	14	.276	.329	.403
2009	2 Tms	AL	67	187	52	9	0	4	(4	0)	73	16	23	22	15	3	21	0	1	3	2	2	.50	7	.278	.327	.390
2010	CWS	AL	107	327	78	17	2	8	(4	4)	123	30	31	33	32	3	36	0	0	0	1	3	.25	9	.239	.306	.376
2011	Mil	AL	104	233	63	13	1	3	(1	2)	87	18	31	31	21	3	27	0	0	0	3	0	1.00	4	.270	.329	.373
08	Atl	NL	88	318	92	17	3	6	(4	2)	133	39	37	37	25	2	34	0	1	1	2	3	.40	13	.289	.340	.418
08	Bos	AL	22	84	19	8	1	0	(0	0)	29	6	12	12	7	1	11	0	0	0	0	1	.00	1	.226	.286	.345
09	Bos	AL	27	74	19	2	0	1	(1	0)	24	4	5	6	4	1	12	0	0	0	2	1	.67	1	.257	.291	.324
09	CWS	AL	40	113	33	7	0	3	(3	0)	49	12	18	16	11	2	9	0	1	2	1	1	.50	5	.292	.349	.434
	Postseason		17	70	16	5	0	1	(0	1)	24	7	2	3	2	0	10	0	0	0	0	0	-	4	.229	.250	.343
	15 ML YEARS		1728	6166	1717	343	48	124	(57	67)	2528	773	694	822	530	37	718	12	29	45	98	60	.62	149	.278	.335	.410

George Kottaras

Bats: L Throws: R Pos: C-36; PH-14   kah-TARR-iss   Ht: 6'0" Wt: 185 Born: 5/10/1983 Age: 29

Year	Team	Lg	G	AB	H	2B	3B	HR	(Hm	Rd)	TB	R	RBI	RC	TBB	IBB	SO	HBP	SH	SF	SB	CS	SB%	GDP	Avg	OBP	Slg
2011	Nashv*	AAA	29	102	35	8	1	4	(-	-)	57	19	21	23	16	0	29	0	0	0	0	1	.00	4	.343	.432	.559
2008	Bos	AL	3	5	1	1	0	0	(0	0)	2	1	0	0	0	0	2	0	0	0	0	0	-	0	.200	.200	.400
2009	Bos	AL	45	93	22	11	0	1	(1	0)	36	15	10	10	11	0	25	0	0	3	0	0	-	1	.237	.308	.387
2010	Mil	NL	67	212	43	12	1	9	(5	4)	84	24	26	22	33	1	44	0	1	1	2	0	1.00	5	.203	.305	.396
2011	Mil	NL	49	111	28	6	1	5	(1	4)	51	15	17	15	10	0	26	0	1	1	0	1	.00	2	.252	.311	.459
4 ML YEARS			164	421	94	30	2	15	(7	8)	173	55	53	47	54	1	97	0	2	8	2	1	.67	8	.223	.306	.411

Kevin Kouzmanoff

Bats: R Throws: R Pos: 3B-71; PH-4   KOOZ-man-off   Ht: 6'1" Wt: 210 Born: 7/25/1981 Age: 30

Year	Team	Lg	G	AB	H	2B	3B	HR	(Hm	Rd)	TB	R	RBI	RC	TBB	IBB	SO	HBP	SH	SF	SB	CS	SB%	GDP	Avg	OBP	Slg
2011	Scrmto*	AAA	61	262	79	24	1	13	(-	-)	144	41	58	48	11	0	36	5	0	1	1	1	.50	7	.302	.341	.550
2006	Cle	AL	16	56	12	2	0	3	(0	3)	23	4	11	7	5	0	12	0	0	0	0	0	-	3	.214	.279	.411
2007	SD	NL	145	484	133	30	2	18	(5	13)	221	57	74	69	32	2	94	10	2	6	1	0	1.00	9	.275	.329	.457
2008	SD	NL	154	624	162	31	4	23	(11	12)	270	71	84	70	23	3	139	15	0	6	0	0	-	14	.260	.299	.433
2009	SD	NL	141	529	135	31	1	18	(9	9)	222	50	88	64	27	3	106	11	0	6	1	0	1.00	25	.255	.302	.420
2010	Oak	AL	143	551	136	32	1	16	(5	11)	218	59	71	49	24	2	96	6	0	5	2	1	.67	20	.247	.283	.396
2011	2 Tms		73	234	55	11	0	7	(0	7)	87	24	33	26	12	1	46	6	0	5	2	0	1.00	4	.235	.284	.372
11	Oak	AL	46	136	30	6	0	4	(0	4)	48	13	17	13	8	0	27	1	0	4	2	0	1.00	2	.221	.262	.353
11	Col	NL	27	98	25	5	0	3	(0	3)	39	11	16	13	4	1	19	5	0	1	0	0	-	2	.255	.315	.398
6 ML YEARS			672	2478	633	137	8	85	(30	55)	1041	265	361	285	123	11	493	48	2	28	6	1	.86	75	.255	.300	.420

Pete Kozma

Bats: R Throws: R Pos: 2B-10; PH-5; SS-3; PR-2; 3B-1   KAHZ-muh   Ht: 6'0" Wt: 170 Born: 4/11/1988 Age: 24

Year	Team	Lg	G	AB	H	2B	3B	HR	(Hm	Rd)	TB	R	RBI	RC	TBB	IBB	SO	HBP	SH	SF	SB	CS	SB%	GDP	Avg	OBP	Slg
2007	JhsCty	R+	30	106	28	8	0	2	(-	-)	42	16	9	15	12	0	21	2	0	0	3	2	.60	1	.264	.350	.396
2007	Cards	R	4	13	2	0	0	0	(-	-)	2	4	0	0	2	0	2	0	0	0	0	0	-	0	.154	.267	.154
2007	Batvia	A-	8	27	4	0	1	0	(-	-)	6	1	2	0	1	0	7	0	0	0	1	1	.50	0	.148	.179	.222
2008	QuadC	A	99	377	107	20	4	5	(-	-)	150	58	40	59	45	0	69	5	1	6	12	5	.71	7	.284	.363	.398
2008	PlmBh	A+	24	77	10	4	0	0	(-	-)	14	4	10	2	10	0	27	1	3	3	0	1	.00	6	.130	.231	.182
2009	PlmBh	A+	18	73	23	5	0	0	(-	-)	28	8	8	11	8	0	16	1	0	2	1	0	1.00	1	.315	.381	.384
2009	Sprgfld	AA	113	407	88	15	3	6	(-	-)	127	52	37	39	42	0	88	1	4	5	4	2	.67	6	.216	.288	.312
2010	Sprgfld	AA	132	503	122	28	2	13	(-	-)	193	69	72	67	56	2	111	1	7	3	13	2	.87	9	.243	.318	.384
2011	Memp	AAA	112	398	85	17	2	3	(-	-)	115	48	47	33	36	3	91	3	5	6	2	2	.50	7	.214	.280	.289
2011	StL	NL	16	17	3	1	0	0	(0	0)	4	2	1	2	4	0	4	0	1	0	0	0	-	0	.176	.333	.235

Erik Kratz

Bats: R Throws: R Pos: C-1; PH-1   Ht: 6'4" Wt: 255 Born: 6/15/1980 Age: 32

Year	Team	Lg	G	AB	H	2B	3B	HR	(Hm	Rd)	TB	R	RBI	RC	TBB	IBB	SO	HBP	SH	SF	SB	CS	SB%	GDP	Avg	OBP	Slg
2002	MdHat	R+	44	142	39	5	0	4	(-	-)	56	20	11	17	6	1	32	3	0	1	0	1	.00	4	.275	.318	.394
2003	CtnWV	A	8	19	6	3	0	0	(-	-)	9	0	2	3	1	0	7	2	0	0	0	0	-	1	.316	.409	.474
2003	Auburn	A-	49	157	49	15	0	5	(-	-)	79	25	26	33	21	0	31	6	0	1	0	1	.00	2	.312	.411	.503
2003	NwHav	AA	1	4	0	0	0	0	(-	-)	0	0	0	0	0	0	1	0	0	0	0	0	-	0	.000	.000	.000
2004	Dnedin	A+	15	49	14	4	0	1	(-	-)	21	6	6	6	2	0	16	1	0	0	0	0	-	2	.286	.327	.429
2004	NHam	AA	4	9	3	1	0	0	(-	-)	4	1	0	2	2	0	2	1	0	0	0	0	-	0	.333	.500	.444
2004	Auburn	A-	10	39	12	6	0	0	(-	-)	18	5	10	5	1	0	8	0	0	1	0	0	-	2	.308	.317	.462
2005	NHam	AA	91	293	60	10	0	11	(-	-)	103	27	33	31	27	1	86	6	3	3	2	0	1.00	7	.205	.283	.352
2006	NHam	AA	72	258	58	10	0	6	(-	-)	86	34	27	26	16	0	54	8	1	1	1	0	1.00	6	.225	.290	.333
2006	Syrcse	AAA	12	40	10	2	0	1	(-	-)	15	12	7	5	5	0	4	0	0	2	0	0	-	0	.250	.319	.375
2007	NHam	AA	49	160	40	15	1	8	(-	-)	81	22	30	33	12	1	33	5	2	3	0	0	-	3	.250	.317	.506
2007	Syrcse	AAA	35	112	24	2	0	5	(-	-)	41	10	19	11	8	0	28	1	3	0	0	1	.00	2	.214	.273	.366
2008	NHam	AA	33	102	25	5	0	7	(-	-)	51	15	19	19	13	2	26	4	0	2	2	0	1.00	3	.245	.347	.500
2008	Syrcse	AAA	40	145	34	11	1	9	(-	-)	74	20	24	22	9	0	33	2	1	1	1	0	1.00	4	.234	.287	.510
2009	Indy	AAA	93	319	87	30	0	11	(-	-)	150	45	43	53	31	2	72	1	0	2	1	0	1.00	7	.273	.337	.470
2010	Indy	AAA	70	230	63	22	1	9	(-	-)	114	30	41	44	32	0	54	9	0	3	1	2	.33	9	.274	.380	.496
2011	LV	AAA	103	358	103	19	0	15	(-	-)	167	56	53	64	38	5	72	11	0	2	2	0	1.00	7	.288	.372	.466
2010	Pit	NL	9	34	4	0	0	0	(0	0)	4	2	1	0	2	0	9	0	0	0	0	0	-	0	.118	.167	.118
2011	Phi	NL	2	6	2	1	0	0	(0	0)	3	0	0	1	0	0	1	0	0	0	0	0	-	0	.333	.333	.500
2 ML YEARS			11	40	6	1	0	0	(0	0)	7	2	1	1	2	0	10	0	0	0	0	0	-	0	.150	.190	.175

Zach Kroenke

Pitches: L Bats: R Pos: RP-4   KRONN-neck-ee   Ht: 6'3" Wt: 210 Born: 4/21/1984 Age: 28

Year	Team	Lg	G	GS	CG	GF	IP	BFP	H	R	ER	HR	SH	SF	HB	TBB	IBB	SO	WP	Bk	W	L	Pct	Sh	Sv-Op Hld	ERC	ERA
2005	Yanks	R	1	1	0	0	2.0	10	4	2	1	0	0	0	0	0	0	2	1	0	0	1	.000	0	0- --	7.48	4.50
2005	StIsInd	A-	11	5	0	3	39.0	159	30	14	11	2	1	3	3	15	0	28	2	0	1	1	.500	0	2- --	2.82	2.54
2006	Tampa	A+	4	4	0	0	14.0	74	23	19	13	0	0	1	0	8	0	8	0	0	0	3	.000	0	0- --	7.56	8.36
2006	CtnSC	A	25	20	0	5	113.0	502	124	65	45	9	5	3	5	41	0	86	11	0	8	6	.571	0	0- --	4.46	3.58
2007	Tampa	A+	29	0	0	9	43.2	188	34	16	11	2	3	2	1	19	3	33	2	0	2	2	.500	0	2- --	2.54	2.27
2007	Trntn	AA	15	0	0	5	14.1	73	21	16	15	5	0	0	0	12	0	12	2	0	0	1	.000	0	2- --	11.47	9.42
2008	Trntn	AA	36	0	0	9	42.2	182	28	16	15	4	5	3	1	26	0	42	3	0	6	0	1.000	0	1- --	3.02	3.16
2008	S-WB	AAA	4	0	0	1	10.0	38	7	3	2	0	1	0	0	2	0	10	1	0	1	0	1.000	0	0- --	1.69	1.80

			HOW MUCH HE PITCHED						WHAT HE GAVE UP												THE RESULTS							
Year	Team	Lg	G	GS	CG	GF	IP	BFP	H	R	ER	HR	SH	SF	HB	TBB	IBB	SO	WP	Bk	W	L	Pct	Sh	Sv-Op	Hld	ERC	ERA
2009	S-WB	AAA	36	2	0	8	72.1	292	54	24	16	4	4	4	0	30	1	55	3	0	7	1	.875	0	4- -	-	2.53	1.99
2010	Reno	AAA	40	9	0	12	97.1	416	94	41	38	5	6	2	1	39	2	69	11	1	7	3	.700	0	2- -	-	3.56	3.51
2011	Reno	AAA	23	23	0	0	128.1	594	173	88	84	14	4	3	5	50	1	73	9	0	10	3	.769	0	0- -	-	6.38	5.89
2010	Ari	NL	3	1	0	0	6.2	32	9	5	5	2	1	0	0	4	0	2	0	0	1	0	1.000	0	0-0	0	8.86	6.75
2011	Ari	NL	4	0	0	3	4.0	19	6	4	4	1	0	0	0	1	0	3	0	0	0	1	.000	0	0-0	0	7.48	9.00
2 ML YEARS			7	1	0	3	10.2	51	15	9	9	3	1	0	0	5	0	5	0	0	1	1	.500	0	0-0	0	8.34	7.59

Jason Kubel

Bats: L **Throws:** R **Pos:** RF-50; DH-37; LF-9; PH-5 KOO-bull **Ht:** 6'0" **Wt:** 220 **Born:** 5/25/1982 **Age:** 30

			BATTING																		BASERUNNING				AVERAGES		
Year	Team	Lg	G	AB	H	2B	3B	HR	(Hm	Rd)	TB	R	RBI	RC	TBB	IBB	SO	HBP	SH	SF	SB	CS	SB%	GDP	Avg	OBP	Slg
2011	FtMyrs*	A+	2	3	0	0	0	0	(-	-)	0	0	1	0	3	0	0	0	0	0	0	0	-	0	.000	.500	.000
2011	Roch*	AAA	5	18	6	1	0	1	(-	-)	10	3	2	4	3	0	4	0	0	0	0	0	-	0	.333	.429	.556
2004	Min	AL	23	60	18	2	0	2	(0	2)	26	10	7	13	6	0	9	0	0	1	1	1	.50	0	.300	.358	.433
2006	Min	AL	73	220	53	8	0	8	(3	5)	85	23	26	20	12	0	45	0	2	1	2	0	1.00	6	.241	.279	.386
2007	Min	AL	128	418	114	31	2	13	(6	7)	188	49	65	64	41	2	79	1	1	5	5	0	1.00	9	.273	.335	.450
2008	Min	AL	141	463	126	22	5	20	(9	11)	218	74	78	66	47	2	91	0	0	7	0	1	.00	12	.272	.335	.471
2009	Min	AL	146	514	154	35	2	28	(15	13)	277	73	103	95	56	9	106	3	0	5	1	1	.50	13	.300	.369	.539
2010	Min	AL	143	518	129	23	3	21	(8	13)	221	68	92	65	56	5	116	3	0	5	0	1	.00	16	.249	.323	.427
2011	Min	AL	99	366	100	21	1	12	(4	8)	159	37	58	59	32	2	86	1	0	2	1	1	.50	8	.273	.332	.434
Postseason			8	29	2	1	0	0	(0	0)	3	0	0	0	3	0	13	0	0	0	0	0	-	0	.069	.156	.103
7 ML YEARS			753	2559	694	142	13	104	(45	59)	1174	334	429	382	250	20	532	8	3	26	10	5	.67	71	.271	.335	.459

Hong-Chih Kuo

Pitches: L **Bats:** L **Pos:** RP-40 KWO **Ht:** 6'2" **Wt:** 241 **Born:** 7/23/1981 **Age:** 30

			HOW MUCH HE PITCHED						WHAT HE GAVE UP												THE RESULTS							
Year	Team	Lg	G	GS	CG	GF	IP	BFP	H	R	ER	HR	SH	SF	HB	TBB	IBB	SO	WP	Bk	W	L	Pct	Sh	Sv-Op	Hld	ERC	ERA
2011	RCuca*	A+	5	1	0	0	4.1	21	7	3	3	0	0	0	0	1	0	7	0	0	0	1	.000	0	0- -	-	6.07	6.23
2011	Albq*	AAA	2	0	0	0	1.2	7	0	0	0	0	1	0	0	1	0	3	0	0	0	0	-	0	0- -	-	0.32	0.00
2005	LAD	NL	9	0	0	0	5.1	26	5	4	4	1	0	0	0	5	1	10	0	1	0	1	.000	0	0-1	3	6.10	6.75
2006	LAD	NL	28	5	0	6	59.2	258	54	30	28	3	2	1	1	33	5	71	2	0	1	5	.167	0	0-0	2	3.76	4.22
2007	LAD	NL	8	6	0	1	30.1	140	35	26	25	3	1	1	1	14	0	27	1	0	1	4	.200	0	0-0	0	5.25	7.42
2008	LAD	NL	42	3	0	10	80.0	323	60	21	19	4	4	1	3	21	2	96	1	1	5	3	.625	0	1-3	12	2.05	2.14
2009	LAD	NL	35	0	0	2	30.0	124	21	10	10	2	3	0	2	13	2	32	5	0	2	0	1.000	0	0-1	14	2.54	3.00
2010	LAD	NL	56	0	0	16	60.0	229	29	8	8	1	1	1	1	18	0	73	3	1	3	2	.600	0	12-13	21	1.07	1.20
2011	LAD	NL	40	0	0	5	27.0	127	24	29	27	4	3	0	2	23	2	36	2	0	1	2	.333	0	0-2	3	5.80	9.00
Postseason			9	1	0	2	12.1	47	10	4	4	1	1	0	0	2	1	15	1	0	1	1	.500	0	0-0	3	2.08	2.92
7 ML YEARS			218	14	0	40	292.1	1227	228	128	121	18	14	4	10	127	12	345	14	3	13	17	.433	0	13-20	55	2.82	3.73

Hiroki Kuroda

Pitches: R **Bats:** R **Pos:** SP-32 hih-ROE-kee kuh-ROE-duh **Ht:** 6'1" **Wt:** 190 **Born:** 2/10/1975 **Age:** 37

			HOW MUCH HE PITCHED						WHAT HE GAVE UP												THE RESULTS							
Year	Team	Lg	G	GS	CG	GF	IP	BFP	H	R	ER	HR	SH	SF	HB	TBB	IBB	SO	WP	Bk	W	L	Pct	Sh	Sv-Op	Hld	ERC	ERA
2008	LAD	NL	31	31	2	0	183.1	776	181	85	76	13	7	5	7	42	8	116	5	0	9	10	.474	2	0-0	0	3.18	3.73
2009	LAD	NL	21	20	0	0	117.1	485	110	59	49	12	7	1	1	24	1	87	5	0	8	7	.533	0	0-0	0	2.98	3.76
2010	LAD	NL	31	31	0	0	196.1	810	180	87	74	15	9	7	5	48	13	159	12	0	11	13	.458	0	0-0	0	2.87	3.39
2011	LAD	NL	32	32	0	0	202.0	838	196	77	69	24	6	5	5	49	6	161	12	1	13	16	.448	0	0-0	0	3.49	3.07
Postseason			3	3	0	0	13.2	60	17	8	8	1	1	0	0	3	1	8	0	0	2	1	.667	0	0-0	0	4.39	5.27
4 ML YEARS			115	114	2	0	699.0	2909	667	308	268	64	29	18	18	163	28	523	34	1	41	46	.471	2	0-0	0	3.14	3.45

John Lackey

Pitches: R **Bats:** R **Pos:** SP-28 **Ht:** 6'6" **Wt:** 245 **Born:** 10/23/1978 **Age:** 33

			HOW MUCH HE PITCHED						WHAT HE GAVE UP												THE RESULTS							
Year	Team	Lg	G	GS	CG	GF	IP	BFP	H	R	ER	HR	SH	SF	HB	TBB	IBB	SO	WP	Bk	W	L	Pct	Sh	Sv-Op	Hld	ERC	ERA
2011	Pwtckt*	AAA	1	1	0	0	5.2	20	3	1	1	1	0	0	0	0	0	4	0	0	0	0	-	0	0- -	-	1.04	1.59
2002	LAA	AL	18	18	1	0	108.1	465	113	52	44	10	0	4	4	33	0	69	7	2	9	4	.692	0	0-0	0	4.03	3.66
2003	LAA	AL	33	33	2	0	204.0	895	223	117	105	31	2	6	10	66	4	151	11	1	10	16	.385	2	0-0	0	4.88	4.63
2004	LAA	AL	33	32	1	0	198.1	855	215	108	103	22	9	4	8	60	4	144	11	1	14	13	.519	1	0-0	0	4.39	4.67
2005	LAA	AL	33	33	1	0	209.0	892	208	85	80	13	1	2	11	71	3	199	18	0	14	5	.737	0	0-0	0	3.76	3.44
2006	LAA	AL	33	33	3	0	217.2	922	203	98	86	14	8	6	9	72	4	190	16	0	13	11	.542	2	0-0	0	3.31	3.56
2007	LAA	AL	33	33	2	0	224.0	929	219	87	75	18	1	1	12	52	2	179	9	1	19	9	.679	2	0-0	0	3.40	**3.01**
2008	LAA	AL	24	24	3	0	163.1	675	161	71	68	26	5	1	10	40	1	130	5	0	12	5	.706	0	0-0	0	4.10	3.75
2009	LAA	AL	27	27	1	0	176.1	748	177	84	75	17	9	10	9	47	1	139	6	0	11	8	.579	1	0-0	0	3.73	3.83
2010	Bos	AL	33	33	0	0	215.0	930	233	114	105	18	4	5	9	72	2	156	3	0	14	11	.560	0	0-0	0	4.37	4.40
2011	Bos	AL	28	28	0	0	160.0	743	203	119	**114**	20	2	6	**19**	56	1	108	11	0	12	12	.500	0	0-0	0	6.11	6.41
Postseason			14	12	0	0	78.0	328	75	29	27	4	2	3	1	29	4	53	4	0	3	4	.429	0	0-0	0	3.43	3.12
10 ML YEARS			295	294	14	0	1876.0	8044	1955	935	855	189	41	45	101	569	22	1465	97	5	128	94	.577	8	0-0	0	4.15	4.10

Aaron Laffey

Pitches: L Bats: L Pos: RP-47   LAFF-ee   Ht: 6'0" Wt: 200 Born: 4/15/1985 Age: 27

Year	Team	Lg	G	GS	CG	GF	IP	BFP	H	R	ER	HR	SH	SF	HB	TBB	IBB	SO	WP	Bk	W	L	Pct	Sh	Sv-Op Hld	ERC	ERA
2011	S-WB*	AAA	2	1	0	0	3.2	18	5	5	3	0	0	0	1	2	0	1	0	0	0	1	.000	0	0- -	7.37	7.36
2007	Cle	AL	9	9	0	0	49.1	207	54	26	25	2	1	2	4	12	0	25	2	1	4	2	.667	0	0-0 0	4.02	4.56
2008	Cle	AL	16	16	0	0	93.2	409	103	52	44	10	2	0	9	31	1	43	5	1	5	7	.417	0	0-0 0	4.86	4.23
2009	Cle	AL	25	19	0	3	121.2	539	140	69	60	9	0	4	2	57	1	59	1	1	7	9	.438	0	1-1 0	5.20	4.44
2010	Cle	AL	29	5	0	1	55.2	253	62	30	28	1	0	3	2	28	1	28	1	0	2	3	.400	0	0-0 5	4.61	4.53
2011	2 Tms	AL	47	0	0	7	53.1	247	67	24	23	7	2	2	3	21	3	30	2	1	3	2	.600	0	0-1 5	5.89	3.88
11	Sea	AL	36	0	0	7	42.2	197	54	20	19	7	2	1	1	16	3	24	2	1	1	1	.500	0	0-1 5	5.92	4.01
11	NYY	AL	11	0	0	0	10.2	50	13	4	4	0	0	1	2	5	0	6	0	0	2	1	.667	0	0-0 0	5.66	3.38
	Postseason		1	0	0	0	4.2	16	1	0	0	0	0	0	0	1	0	3	0	0	0	0	-	0	0-0 0	0.30	0.00
5 ML YEARS			126	49	0	11	373.2	1655	426	201	180	29	5	11	20	149	6	185	11	4	21	23	.477	0	1-2 10	4.96	4.34

Bryan LaHair

Bats: L Throws: R Pos: RF-9; LF-5; 1B-4; PH-3   Ht: 6'5" Wt: 240 Born: 11/5/1982 Age: 29

Year	Team	Lg	G	AB	H	2B	3B	HR	(Hm	Rd)	TB	R	RBI	RC	TBB	IBB	SO	HBP	SH	SF	SB	CS	SB%	GDP	Avg	OBP	Slg
2003	Everett	A-	57	201	49	14	0	2	(-	-)	69	26	20	19	11	1	40	1	0	0	4	3	.57	3	.244	.286	.343
2004	Everett	A-	7	25	11	6	0	1	(-	-)	20	5	7	8	1	0	3	1	0	1	0	0	-	1	.440	.464	.800
2004	Wisc	A	67	262	73	24	0	5	(-	-)	112	30	28	34	16	1	66	1	1	0	0	6	.00	5	.279	.323	.427
2005	InldEm	A+	126	509	158	28	2	22	(-	-)	256	81	113	96	51	4	125	3	0	6	0	1	.00	19	.310	.373	.503
2006	SnAnt	AA	60	222	65	12	0	6	(-	-)	95	22	30	36	24	3	52	4	1	1	0	0	-	3	.293	.371	.428
2006	Tacom	AAA	54	202	66	10	0	10	(-	-)	106	36	44	42	23	0	49	1	1	3	3	0	1.00	4	.327	.393	.525
2007	Tacom	AAA	138	552	152	46	2	12	(-	-)	238	79	81	81	49	1	126	0	1	4	1	1	.00	10	.275	.332	.431
2008	Tacom	AAA	86	316	83	26	1	12	(-	-)	147	39	53	54	45	4	87	1	0	0	1	1	.50	5	.263	.356	.465
2009	Tacom	AAA	121	457	132	28	2	26	(-	-)	242	72	85	84	45	3	116	3	1	4	0	5	.00	18	.289	.354	.530
2010	Iowa	AAA	125	422	130	30	0	25	(-	-)	235	71	81	89	51	9	94	3	0	2	3	1	.75	14	.308	.385	.557
2011	Iowa	AAA	129	456	151	38	0	38	(-	-)	303	91	109	117	60	9	111	1	0	6	2	0	1.00	14	.331	.405	.664
2008	Sea	AL	45	136	34	4	0	3	(0	3)	47	15	10	14	13	1	40	0	1	0	0	1	.00	4	.250	.315	.346
2011	ChC	NL	20	59	17	5	1	2	(2	0)	30	9	6	9	9	0	18	0	0	1	0	0	-	1	.288	.377	.508
2 ML YEARS			65	195	51	9	1	5	(2	3)	77	24	16	23	22	1	58	0	1	1	0	1	.00	5	.262	.335	.395

Brandon Laird

Bats: R Throws: R Pos: 3B-9; 1B-3; PH-1   Ht: 6'1" Wt: 215 Born: 9/11/1987 Age: 24

Year	Team	Lg	G	AB	H	2B	3B	HR	(Hm	Rd)	TB	R	RBI	RC	TBB	IBB	SO	HBP	SH	SF	SB	CS	SB%	GDP	Avg	OBP	Slg
2007	Yanks	AAA	45	168	57	14	1	8	(-	-)	97	27	29	34	6	0	26	2	1	1	0	0	-	4	.339	.367	.577
2008	CtnSC	A	122	454	124	31	1	23	(-	-)	226	71	86	78	40	4	86	5	0	7	1	0	1.00	15	.273	.334	.498
2009	Tampa	A+	124	451	120	20	4	13	(-	-)	187	53	75	64	39	3	75	6	0	5	1	1	.50	19	.266	.329	.415
2010	Trntn	AA	107	409	119	22	2	23	(-	-)	214	73	90	76	38	3	84	4	0	3	2	2	.50	14	.291	.355	.523
2010	S-WB	AAA	31	122	30	6	0	2	(-	-)	42	13	12	11	4	0	27	0	0	1	0	0	-	6	.246	.268	.344
2011	S-WB	AAA	123	462	120	27	0	16	(-	-)	195	51	69	57	17	1	84	4	0	6	0	0	-	14	.260	.288	.422
2011	NYY	AL	11	21	4	0	0	0	(0	0)	4	3	1	2	3	0	4	0	1	0	0	0	-	1	.190	.292	.190

Gerald Laird

Bats: R Throws: R Pos: C-31; PH-7; 1B-1; DH-1; PR-1   Ht: 6'1" Wt: 225 Born: 11/13/1979 Age: 32

Year	Team	Lg	G	AB	H	2B	3B	HR	(Hm	Rd)	TB	R	RBI	RC	TBB	IBB	SO	HBP	SH	SF	SB	CS	SB%	GDP	Avg	OBP	Slg
2011	Memp*	AAA	2	7	3	1	0	0	(-	-)	4	2	1	2	2	0	1	0	0	0	0	0	-	0	.429	.556	.571
2003	Tex	AL	19	44	12	2	1	1	(0	1)	19	9	4	5	5	0	11	1	0	0	0	0	-	2	.273	.360	.432
2004	Tex	AL	49	147	33	6	0	1	(1	0)	42	20	16	11	12	0	35	2	4	3	0	1	.00	5	.224	.287	.286
2005	Tex	AL	13	40	9	2	0	1	(0	1)	14	7	4	4	2	0	7	0	0	0	0	0	-	1	.225	.262	.350
2006	Tex	AL	78	243	72	20	1	7	(3	4)	115	46	22	24	12	0	54	2	1	2	3	1	.75	7	.296	.332	.473
2007	Tex	AL	120	407	91	18	3	9	(6	3)	142	48	47	45	30	1	103	2	5	4	6	2	.75	3	.224	.278	.349
2008	Tex	AL	95	344	95	24	0	6	(3	3)	137	54	41	46	23	2	63	6	4	4	2	4	.33	5	.276	.329	.398
2009	Det	AL	135	413	93	23	2	4	(1	3)	132	49	33	41	40	0	68	10	10	4	5	0	1.00	11	.225	.306	.320
2010	Det	AL	89	270	56	11	0	5	(2	3)	82	22	25	22	18	0	57	3	6	2	3	1	.75	7	.207	.263	.304
2011	StL	NL	37	95	22	7	1	1	(1	0)	34	11	12	10	9	3	19	1	2	1	1	1	.50	3	.232	.302	.358
9 ML YEARS			635	2003	483	113	8	35	(17	18)	717	266	204	208	151	6	417	27	32	20	20	10	.67	44	.241	.300	.358

Ryan Langerhans

Bats: L Throws: L Pos: CF-12; LF-5; PR-2; RF-1; DH-1; PH-1   LANG-err-hans   Ht: 6'3" Wt: 220 Born: 2/20/1980 Age: 32

Year	Team	Lg	G	AB	H	2B	3B	HR	(Hm	Rd)	TB	R	RBI	RC	TBB	IBB	SO	HBP	SH	SF	SB	CS	SB%	GDP	Avg	OBP	Slg
2011	Tacom*	AAA	57	214	67	10	0	16	(-	-)	125	46	37	49	37	1	63	2	0	2	3	6	.33	4	.313	.416	.584
2011	Reno*	AAA	38	130	40	10	2	6	(-	-)	72	23	23	36	39	2	31	1	0	1	8	1	.89	2	.308	.468	.554
2002	Atl	NL	1	1	0	0	0	0	(0	0)	0	0	0	0	0	0	0	0	0	0	0	0	-	0	.000	.000	.000
2003	Atl	NL	16	15	4	0	0	0	(0	0)	4	2	0	1	0	0	6	0	0	0	0	0	-	1	.267	.267	.267
2005	Atl	NL	128	326	87	22	3	8	(3	5)	139	48	42	49	37	3	75	5	2	3	0	2	.00	2	.267	.348	.426
2006	Atl	NL	131	315	76	16	3	7	(3	4)	119	46	28	45	50	8	91	3	0	1	1	2	.33	9	.241	.350	.378
2007	3 Tms	NL	125	210	35	7	2	6	(1	5)	64	27	23	22	29	2	81	2	1	2	3	1	.75	4	.167	.272	.305
2008	Was	NL	73	111	26	5	2	3	(1	2)	44	17	12	14	25	1	31	1	2	0	2	0	1.00	1	.234	.380	.396
2009	Sea	AL	38	101	22	6	1	3	(2	1)	39	12	10	11	14	1	28	1	3	3	1	0	.00	2	.218	.311	.386
2010	Sea	AL	60	107	21	2	1	3	(1	2)	34	16	4	11	24	1	51	0	1	0	4	1	.80	0	.196	.344	.318
2011	Sea	AL	19	52	9	0	0	3	(2	1)	18	6	6	5	11	0	22	0	1	0	0	0	-	0	.173	.317	.346
07	Atl	NL	20	44	3	1	0	0	(0	0)	4	3	1	0	6	1	16	1	0	1	0	1	.00	0	.068	.192	.091

Year Team	Lg	G	AB	H	2B	3B	HR	(Hm	Rd)	TB	R	RBI	RC	TBB	IBB	SO	HBP	SH	SF	SB	CS	SB%	GDP	Avg	OBP	Slg
								BATTING												BASERUNNING				AVERAGES		
07 Oak	AL	2	4	0	0	0	0	(0	0)	0	0	0	0	1	0	2	0	0	0	0	0	-	0	.000	.200	.000
07 Was	NL	103	162	32	6	2	6	(1	5)	60	24	22	22	22	1	63	1	1	1	3	0	1.00	1	.198	.296	.370
Postseason		4	12	4	1	0	0	(0	0)	5	1	0	2	3	1	3	1	0	0	1	0	1.00		.333	.500	.417
9 ML YEARS		591	1238	280	58	12	33	(13	20)	461	174	125	166	190	16	385	12	10	9	10	8	.56	17	.226	.333	.372

John Lannan

Pitches: L Bats: L Pos: SP-33 Ht: 6'4" Wt: 215 Born: 9/27/1984 Age: 27

Year Team	Lg	G	GS	CG	GF	IP	BFP	H	R	ER	HR	SH	SF	HB	TBB	IBB	SO	WP	Bk	W	L	Pct	Sh	Sv-Op	Hld	ERC	ERA
		HOW MUCH HE PITCHED						WHAT HE GAVE UP												THE RESULTS							
2007 Was	NL	6	6	0	0	34.2	153	36	17	16	3	2	0	2	17	1	10	1	0	2	2	.500	0	0-0	0	4.82	4.15
2008 Was	NL	31	31	0	0	182.0	779	172	89	79	23	13	5	7	72	1	117	6	2	9	15	.375	0	0-0	0	4.09	3.91
2009 Was	NL	33	33	2	0	206.1	875	210	100	89	22	12	1	6	68	5	89	3	0	9	13	.409	1	0-0	0	4.07	3.88
2010 Was	NL	25	25	0	0	143.1	643	175	82	74	14	5	5	4	49	3	71	1	0	8	8	.500	0	0-0	0	5.18	4.65
2011 Was	NL	33	33	0	0	184.2	808	194	90	76	15	10	1	7	76	3	106	4	0	10	13	.435	0	0-0	0	4.42	3.70
5 ML YEARS		128	128	2	0	751.0	3258	787	378	334	77	42	12	26	282	13	393	15	2	38	51	.427	1	0-0	0	4.40	4.00

Matt LaPorta

Bats: R Throws: R Pos: 1B-97; DH-8; PH-6 lah-POR-tah Ht: 6'2" Wt: 210 Born: 1/8/1985 Age: 27

Year Team	Lg	G	AB	H	2B	3B	HR	(Hm	Rd)	TB	R	RBI	RC	TBB	IBB	SO	HBP	SH	SF	SB	CS	SB%	GDP	Avg	OBP	Slg
								BATTING												BASERUNNING				AVERAGES		
2011 Clmbs*	AAA	2	9	4	0	0	1	(-	-)	7	2	3	2	0	0	1	0	0	0	0	0	-	1	.444	.444	.778
2009 Cle	AL	52	181	46	13	0	7	(2	5)	80	29	21	22	12	0	37	3	0	2	2	0	1.00	6	.254	.308	.442
2010 Cle	AL	110	376	83	15	1	12	(9	3)	136	41	41	41	46	1	82	1	0	2	0	0	-	12	.221	.306	.362
2011 Cle	AL	107	352	87	23	1	11	(6	5)	145	34	53	46	23	1	87	5	0	5	1	0	1.00	2	.247	.299	.412
3 ML YEARS		269	909	216	51	2	30	(17	13)	361	104	115	109	81	2	206	9	0	9	3	0	1.00	20	.238	.304	.397

Adam LaRoche

Bats: L Throws: L Pos: 1B-43 Ht: 6'3" Wt: 205 Born: 11/6/1979 Age: 32

Year Team	Lg	G	AB	H	2B	3B	HR	(Hm	Rd)	TB	R	RBI	RC	TBB	IBB	SO	HBP	SH	SF	SB	CS	SB%	GDP	Avg	OBP	Slg
								BATTING												BASERUNNING				AVERAGES		
2004 Atl	NL	110	324	90	27	1	13	(7	6)	158	45	45	43	27	1	78	1	2	2	0	0	-	10	.278	.333	.488
2005 Atl	NL	141	451	117	28	0	20	(11	9)	205	53	78	63	39	7	87	4	2	6	0	2	.00	15	.259	.320	.455
2006 Atl	NL	149	492	140	38	1	32	(11	21)	276	89	90	83	55	5	128	2	1	7	0	2	.00	9	.285	.354	.561
2007 Pit	NL	152	563	153	42	0	21	(10	11)	258	71	88	84	62	5	131	3	0	4	1	1	.50	18	.272	.345	.458
2008 Pit	NL	136	492	133	32	3	25	(14	11)	246	66	85	76	54	7	122	2	0	6	1	1	.50	9	.270	.341	.500
2009 3 Tms	NL	150	555	154	38	2	25	(15	10)	271	78	83	84	69	12	142	0	0	5	2	2	.50	11	.277	.355	.488
2010 Ari	NL	151	560	146	37	4	25	(13	12)	262	75	100	84	48	4	172	3	0	4	0	1	.00	8	.261	.320	.468
2011 Was	NL	43	151	26	4	0	3	(1	2)	39	15	15	11	25	0	37	0	0	1	1	0	1.00	2	.172	.288	.258
09 Pit	NL	87	324	80	25	1	12	(7	5)	143	46	40	38	41	6	81	0	0	3	2	2	.50	9	.247	.329	.441
09 Bos	AL	6	19	5	2	0	1	(1	0)	10	2	3	3	0	0	2	0	0	0	0	0	-	0	.263	.263	.526
09 Atl	NL	57	212	69	11	1	12	(7	5)	118	30	40	43	28	6	59	0	0	2	0	0	-	1	.325	.401	.557
Postseason		8	25	8	2	0	2	(0	2)	16	3	10	6	5	1	6	0	1	0	0	0	-	1	.320	.433	.640
8 ML YEARS		1032	3588	959	246	9	164	(82	82)	1715	492	584	528	379	41	897	15	5	35	5	9	.36	82	.267	.337	.478

Andy LaRoche

Bats: R Throws: R Pos: 3B-27; SS-9; 2B-8; 1B-1 Ht: 6'1" Wt: 195 Born: 9/13/1983 Age: 28

Year Team	Lg	G	AB	H	2B	3B	HR	(Hm	Rd)	TB	R	RBI	RC	TBB	IBB	SO	HBP	SH	SF	SB	CS	SB%	GDP	Avg	OBP	Slg
								BATTING												BASERUNNING				AVERAGES		
2011 Scrmto*	AAA	54	197	50	12	0	4	(-	-)	74	24	27	26	19	0	24	6	0	2	3	2	.60	10	.254	.335	.376
2007 LAD	NL	35	93	21	5	0	1	(0	1)	29	16	10	12	20	5	24	1	0	1	2	1	.67	1	.226	.365	.312
2008 2 Tms	NL	76	223	37	5	0	5	(1	4)	57	17	18	10	24	1	37	2	2	1	2	0	1.00	8	.166	.252	.256
2009 Pit	NL	150	524	135	29	5	12	(7	5)	210	64	64	64	50	1	84	8	6	2	3	1	.75	16	.258	.330	.401
2010 Pit	NL	102	247	51	8	0	4	(2	2)	71	26	16	17	19	0	43	2	2	1	1	1	.50	7	.206	.268	.287
2011 Oak	AL	40	93	23	6	1	0	(0	0)	31	10	5	8	8	1	19	2	1	0	0	0	-	6	.247	.320	.333
08 LAD	NL	27	59	12	1	0	2	(0	2)	19	6	6	3	10	0	7	0	0	0	0	0	-	5	.203	.319	.322
08 Pit	NL	49	164	25	4	0	3	(1	2)	38	11	12	7	14	1	30	2	2	1	2	0	1.00	3	.152	.227	.232
5 ML YEARS		403	1180	267	53	6	22	(10	12)	398	133	113	111	121	8	207	15	11	5	8	3	.73	38	.226	.305	.337

Mat Latos

Pitches: R Bats: R Pos: SP-31 LAY-tos Ht: 6'6" Wt: 225 Born: 12/9/1987 Age: 24

Year Team	Lg	G	GS	CG	GF	IP	BFP	H	R	ER	HR	SH	SF	HB	TBB	IBB	SO	WP	Bk	W	L	Pct	Sh	Sv-Op	Hld	ERC	ERA
		HOW MUCH HE PITCHED						WHAT HE GAVE UP												THE RESULTS							
2009 SD	NL	10	10	0	0	50.2	212	43	29	26	7	3	1	0	23	1	39	0	2	4	5	.444	0	0-0	0	3.72	4.62
2010 SD	NL	31	31	1	0	184.2	748	150	63	60	16	4	1	2	50	3	189	5	1	14	10	.583	1	0-0	0	2.52	2.92
2011 SD	NL	31	31	0	0	194.1	799	168	82	75	16	8	7	1	62	3	185	5	0	9	14	.391	0	0-0	0	2.93	3.47
3 ML YEARS		72	72	1	0	429.2	1759	361	174	161	39	15	9	3	135	7	413	10	3	27	29	.482	1	0-0	0	2.84	3.37

Ryan Lavarnway

Bats: R Throws: R Pos: C-8; DH-8; PH-2 Ht: 6'4" Wt: 225 Born: 8/7/1987 Age: 24

							BATTING															BASERUNNING				AVERAGES		
Year	Team	Lg	G	AB	H	2B	3B	HR	(Hm	Rd)	TB	R	RBI	RC	TBB	IBB	SO	HBP	SH	SF	SB	CS	SB%	GDP	Avg	OBP	Slg
2008	Lowell	A-	22	71	15	5	0	2	(-	-)	26	10	9	8	8	0	18	3	0	0	0	0	-	1	.211	.317	.366
2009	Grnville	A	106	404	115	36	2	21	(-	-)	218	60	87	81	50	2	113	6	0	6	1	2	.33	7	.285	.367	.540
2010	Salem	A+	82	304	88	18	0	14	(-	-)	148	66	63	61	44	1	62	9	0	3	1	0	1.00	9	.289	.392	.487
2010	Portlnd	AA	44	158	45	9	0	8	(-	-)	78	25	39	32	26	2	42	4	0	2	0	0	-	2	.285	.395	.494
2011	Portlnd	AA	55	208	59	5	0	14	(-	-)	106	35	38	39	25	0	47	2	0	4	0	0	-	11	.284	.360	.510
2011	Pwtckt	AAA	61	227	67	18	0	18	(-	-)	139	40	55	53	32	2	60	4	0	1	1	1	.50	10	.295	.390	.612
2011	Bos	AL	17	39	9	2	0	2	(0	2)	17	5	8	4	4	0	10	0	0	0	0	0	-	1	.231	.302	.436

Brett Lawrie

Bats: R Throws: R Pos: 3B-43 LORI Ht: 6'0" Wt: 213 Born: 1/18/1990 Age: 22

							BATTING															BASERUNNING				AVERAGES		
Year	Team	Lg	G	AB	H	2B	3B	HR	(Hm	Rd)	TB	R	RBI	RC	TBB	IBB	SO	HBP	SH	SF	SB	CS	SB%	GDP	Avg	OBP	Slg
2009	Wisc	A	105	372	102	18	5	13	(-	-)	169	48	65	61	41	1	70	4	0	6	19	11	.63	6	.274	.348	.454
2009	Hntsvl	AA	13	52	14	0	1	0	(-	-)	16	6	0	3	0	0	14	1	0	0	0	2	.00	0	.269	.283	.308
2010	Hntsvl	AA	135	554	158	36	16	8	(-	-)	250	90	63	89	47	3	118	5	2	1	30	13	.70	6	.285	.346	.451
2011	LsVgs	AAA	69	292	103	24	6	18	(-	-)	193	64	61	76	26	0	53	6	4	1	13	2	.87	3	.353	.415	.661
2011	Dnedin	A+	4	8	1	0	0	0	(-	-)	1	0	1	0	0	0	1	0	0	0	0	0	-	0	.125	.364	.125
2011	Tor	AL	43	150	44	8	4	9	(5	4)	87	26	25	33	16	1	31	3	2	0	7	1	.88	0	.293	.373	.580

Brandon League

Pitches: R Bats: R Pos: RP-65 Ht: 6'2" Wt: 205 Born: 3/16/1983 Age: 29

			HOW MUCH HE PITCHED					WHAT HE GAVE UP											THE RESULTS					
Year	Team	Lg	G	GS	CG	GF	IP	BFP	H	R	ER	HR	SH	SF	HB	TBB	IBB	SO	WP	Bk	W	L	Pct	Sh	Sv-Op Hld	ERC	ERA
2004	Tor	AL	3	0	0	0	4.2	18	3	0	0	0	0	0	0	1	0	2	0	0	1	0	1.000	0	0-0 1	1.26	0.00
2005	Tor	AL	20	0	0	4	35.2	162	42	27	26	8	0	1	2	20	1	17	5	0	1	0	1.000	0	0-0 1	7.24	6.56
2006	Tor	AL	33	0	0	8	42.2	173	34	17	12	3	2	0	3	9	2	29	0	0	1	2	.333	0	1-4 12	2.30	2.53
2007	Tor	AL	14	0	0	2	11.2	58	19	8	8	1	0	1	0	7	0	7	3	0	0	0	-	0	0-1 0	8.98	6.17
2008	Tor	AL	31	0	0	8	33.0	141	28	9	8	2	1	0	3	15	2	23	2	0	1	2	.333	0	1-1 5	3.45	2.18
2009	Tor	AL	67	0	0	18	74.2	313	72	40	38	8	5	0	7	21	2	76	9	0	3	6	.333	0	0-3 9	3.85	4.58
2010	Sea	AL	70	0	0	30	79.0	326	67	38	30	7	4	1	2	27	6	56	7	0	9	7	.563	0	6-12 13	2.96	3.42
2011	Sea	AL	65	0	0	60	61.1	250	56	25	19	3	4	0	2	10	2	45	4	0	1	5	.167	0	37-42 0	2.45	2.79
	8 ML YEARS		303	0	0	130	342.2	1441	321	164	141	32	16	3	19	110	15	255	30	0	17	22	.436	0	45-63 41	3.55	3.70

Mike Leake

Pitches: R Bats: R Pos: SP-26; RP-3 LEEK Ht: 6'1" Wt: 186 Born: 11/12/1987 Age: 24

			HOW MUCH HE PITCHED					WHAT HE GAVE UP											THE RESULTS					
Year	Team	Lg	G	GS	CG	GF	IP	BFP	H	R	ER	HR	SH	SF	HB	TBB	IBB	SO	WP	Bk	W	L	Pct	Sh	Sv-Op Hld	ERC	ERA
2011	Lsvlle	AAA	2	1	0	0	7.1	35	12	8	8	3	0	0	0	5	0	0	0	0	0	1	.000	0	0- - -	8.16	9.82
2010	Cin	NL	24	22	0	0	138.1	604	158	77	65	19	7	3	3	49	2	91	2	0	8	4	.667	0	0-0 0	5.12	4.23
2011	Cin	NL	29	26	0	2	167.2	693	159	74	72	23	3	6	8	38	3	118	2	1	12	9	.571	0	0-0 0	3.53	3.86
	2 ML YEARS		53	48	0	2	306.0	1297	317	151	137	42	10	9	11	87	5	209	4	1	20	13	.606	0	0-0 0	4.23	4.03

Wade LeBlanc

Pitches: L Bats: L Pos: SP-14 lah-BLAHNK Ht: 6'3" Wt: 214 Born: 8/7/1984 Age: 27

			HOW MUCH HE PITCHED					WHAT HE GAVE UP											THE RESULTS					
Year	Team	Lg	G	GS	CG	GF	IP	BFP	H	R	ER	HR	SH	SF	HB	TBB	IBB	SO	WP	Bk	W	L	Pct	Sh	Sv-Op Hld	ERC	ERA
2011	Tucsn*	AAA	17	17	0	0	106.2	445	108	54	51	8	2	3	1	28	0	92	1	0	9	1	.900	0	0- - -	3.50	4.30
2008	SD	NL	5	4	0	0	21.1	104	29	19	19	7	1	0	0	15	2	14	0	0	1	3	.250	0	0-0 0	9.57	8.02
2009	SD	NL	9	9	0	0	46.1	194	35	19	19	6	3	1	4	19	1	30	0	0	3	1	.750	0	0-0 0	3.28	3.69
2010	SD	NL	26	25	0	0	146.0	625	157	69	69	24	7	2	2	51	5	110	2	0	8	12	.400	0	0-0 0	4.84	4.25
2011	SD	NL	14	14	0	0	79.2	339	84	42	41	7	3	3	1	28	1	51	1	1	5	6	.455	0	0-0 0	4.21	4.63
	4 ML YEARS		54	52	0	0	293.1	1262	305	149	148	44	14	6	7	113	9	205	3	1	17	22	.436	0	0-0 0	4.71	4.54

Sam LeCure

Pitches: R Bats: R Pos: RP-39; SP-4 leh-CURE Ht: 6'1" Wt: 207 Born: 5/4/1984 Age: 28

			HOW MUCH HE PITCHED					WHAT HE GAVE UP											THE RESULTS					
Year	Team	Lg	G	GS	CG	GF	IP	BFP	H	R	ER	HR	SH	SF	HB	TBB	IBB	SO	WP	Bk	W	L	Pct	Sh	Sv-Op Hld	ERC	ERA
2005	Billings	R+	13	6	0	0	41.1	176	43	18	15	2	1	0	2	15	0	44	2	1	5	1	.833	0	0- - -	4.07	3.27
2006	Srsota	A+	27	27	0	0	141.2	592	130	63	54	12	2	4	6	46	3	115	7	0	7	12	.368	0	0- - -	3.38	3.43
2007	Chatt	AA	21	21	0	0	110.0	482	119	55	51	12	3	5	4	46	0	104	1	0	7	5	.583	0	0- - -	4.90	4.17
2007	Srsota	A+	1	1	0	0	5.0	17	2	1	1	0	0	1	0	0	0	8	0	0	1	0	1.000	0	0- - -	0.35	1.80
2008	Chatt	AA	27	27	0	0	155.1	660	146	61	59	12	6	3	8	58	2	128	3	0	9	7	.563	0	0- - -	3.69	3.42
2009	Lsvlle	AAA	25	25	0	0	143.1	605	143	76	71	17	6	6	7	44	0	125	4	0	10	8	.556	0	0- - -	4.07	4.46
2010	Lsvlle	AAA	15	15	1	0	98.0	403	98	40	40	8	0	0	6	23	0	87	3	0	8	3	.727	1	0- - -	3.64	3.67
2011	Lsvlle	AAA	4	0	0	1	6.2	25	5	1	1	0	0	0	0	2	0	6	0	0	0	1	.000	0	1- - -	2.90	1.35
2010	Cin	NL	15	6	0	0	48.0	217	50	24	24	6	1	2	5	25	3	37	1	0	2	5	.286	0	0-0 0	5.36	4.50
2011	Cin	NL	43	4	0	7	77.2	307	57	33	32	10	4	0	4	21	3	73	0	0	2	1	.667	0	0-0 5	2.55	3.71
	2 ML YEARS		58	10	0	11	125.2	524	107	57	56	16	5	2	9	46	6	110	1	0	4	6	.400	0	0-0 5	3.56	4.01

Wil Ledezma

Pitches: L **Bats:** L **Pos:** RP-5   **Ht:** 6'4" **Wt:** 227 **Born:** 1/21/1981 **Age:** 31

Year	Team	Lg	G	GS	CG	GF	IP	BFP	H	R	ER	HR	SH	SF	HB	TBB	IBB	SO	WP	Bk	W	L	Pct	Sh	Sv-Op	Hld	ERC	ERA
2011	LsVgs*	AAA	36	0	0	9	48.0	220	49	32	24	6	1	1	2	19	0	64	7	0	1	1	.500	0	3- -	-	4.28	4.50
2003	Det	AL	34	8	0	13	84.0	376	99	55	54	12	1	4	3	35	3	49	2	0	3	7	.300	0	0-1	1	5.67	5.79
2004	Det	AL	15	8	0	1	53.1	225	55	28	26	3	0	3	2	18	0	29	3	1	4	3	.571	0	0-1	0	3.94	4.39
2005	Det	AL	10	10	0	0	49.2	234	61	46	39	10	3	4	2	24	0	30	2	2	2	4	.333	0	0-0	0	6.66	7.07
2006	Det	AL	24	7	0	2	60.1	264	60	28	24	5	2	1	2	23	0	39	2	0	3	3	.500	0	0-1	2	3.92	3.58
2007	3 Tms		44	1	0	13	59.1	280	70	42	37	7	2	3	0	38	4	47	3	2	3	3	.500	0	0-2	4	6.13	5.61
2008	2 Tms	NL	28	6	0	8	58.1	266	51	29	27	4	4	4	3	41	2	53	4	0	0	2	.000	0	0-0	0	4.41	4.17
2009	Was	NL	5	0	0	2	5.2	30	8	7	6	1	0	2	0	4	0	8	1	0	0	0	-	0	0-0	0	8.09	9.53
2010	Pit	NL	27	0	0	4	19.2	92	25	16	15	2	0	0	1	6	0	22	1	0	0	3	.000	0	0-0	3	5.29	6.86
2011	Tor	AL	5	0	0	2	6.0	36	11	10	10	1	1	0	1	7	0	6	2	0	0	0	-	0	0-0	0	13.43	15.00
07	Det	AL	23	0	0	5	35.2	166	38	21	19	4	2	1	0	26	2	24	3	2	3	1	.750	0	0-2	2	5.83	4.79
07	Atl	NL	12	0	0	4	9.1	45	12	10	8	1	0	1	0	4	0	7	0	0	0	2	.000	0	0-0	2	5.64	7.71
07	SD	NL	9	1	0	4	14.1	69	20	11	10	2	0	1	0	8	2	16	0	0	0	0	-	0	0-0	0	7.23	6.28
08	SD	NL	25	6	0	6	54.1	249	49	29	27	4	4	4	3	38	2	49	4	0	0	2	.000	0	0-0	0	4.61	4.47
08	Ari	NL	3	0	0	2	4.0	17	2	0	0	0	0	0	0	3	0	4	0	0	0	0	-	0	0-0	0	2.03	0.00
	Postseason		4	0	0	1	4.0	17	4	1	1	1	0	0	0	1	0	2	0	0	1	0	1.000	0	0-0	0	4.38	2.25
	9 ML YEARS		192	40	0	45	396.1	1803	440	261	238	45	12	22	13	196	9	283	20	5	15	25	.375	0	0-5	10	5.27	5.40

Carlos Lee

Bats: R **Throws:** R **Pos:** LF-80; 1B-79; DH-6; PH-1   **Ht:** 6'2" **Wt:** 266 **Born:** 6/20/1976 **Age:** 36

Year	Team	Lg	G	AB	H	2B	3B	HR	(Hm	Rd)	TB	R	RBI	RC	TBB	IBB	SO	HBP	SH	SF	SB	CS	SB%	GDP	Avg	OBP	Slg
1999	CWS	AL	127	492	144	32	2	16	(10	6)	228	66	84	68	13	0	72	4	1	7	4	2	.67	11	.293	.312	.463
2000	CWS	AL	152	572	172	29	2	24	(12	12)	277	107	92	91	38	1	94	3	1	5	13	4	.76	17	.301	.345	.484
2001	CWS	AL	150	558	150	33	3	24	(12	12)	261	75	84	81	38	2	85	6	1	2	17	7	.71	15	.269	.321	.468
2002	CWS	AL	140	492	130	26	2	26	(14	12)	238	82	80	86	75	4	73	2	0	7	1	4	.20	5	.264	.359	.484
2003	CWS	AL	158	623	181	35	1	31	(18	13)	311	100	113	105	37	2	91	4	0	7	18	4	.82	20	.291	.331	.499
2004	CWS	AL	153	591	180	37	0	31	(17	14)	310	103	99	112	54	3	86	7	0	6	11	5	.69	10	.305	.366	.525
2005	Mil		162	618	164	41	0	32	(15	17)	301	85	114	98	57	7	87	2	0	11	13	4	.76	8	.265	.324	.487
2006	2 Tms		161	624	187	37	1	37	(15	22)	337	102	116	113	58	6	65	2	0	11	19	2	.90	22	.300	.355	.540
2007	Hou	NL	162	627	190	43	1	32	(15	17)	331	93	119	104	53	10	63	4	0	13	10	5	.67	27	.303	.354	.528
2008	Hou	NL	115	436	137	27	0	28	(11	17)	248	61	100	85	37	7	49	3	0	5	4	1	.80	8	.314	.368	.569
2009	Hou	NL	160	610	183	35	1	26	(16	10)	298	65	102	96	41	5	51	3	0	8	5	3	.63	21	.300	.343	.489
2010	Hou	NL	157	605	149	29	1	24	(16	8)	252	67	89	75	37	1	59	3	0	4	3	3	.50	20	.246	.291	.417
2011	Hou	NL	155	585	161	38	4	18	(9	9)	261	66	94	83	59	8	60	3	0	6	4	3	.57	9	.275	.342	.446
06	Mil	NL	102	388	111	18	0	28	(10	18)	213	60	81	75	38	4	39	2	0	7	12	6	.86	13	.286	.347	.549
06	Tex	NL	59	236	76	19	1	9	(5	4)	124	42	35	38	20	2	26	0	0	4	7	0	1.00	9	.322	.369	.525
	Postseason		3	11	1	1	0	0	(0	0)	2	0	1	0	0	0	2	0	0	1	0	0	-	0	.091	.083	.182
	13 ML YEARS		1952	7433	2128	442	18	349	(182	167)	3653	1072	1286	1186	597	56	935	46	3	92	122	47	.72	193	.286	.339	.491

Cliff Lee

Pitches: L **Bats:** L **Pos:** SP-32   **Ht:** 6'3" **Wt:** 190 **Born:** 8/30/1978 **Age:** 33

Year	Team	Lg	G	GS	CG	GF	IP	BFP	H	R	ER	HR	SH	SF	HB	TBB	IBB	SO	WP	Bk	W	L	Pct	Sh	Sv-Op	Hld	ERC	ERA
2002	Cle	AL	2	2	0	0	10.1	44	6	2	2	0	1	0	0	8	1	6	0	1	0	1	.000	0	0-0	0	2.38	1.74
2003	Cle	AL	9	9	0	0	52.1	210	41	28	21	7	1	1	2	20	1	44	3	0	3	3	.500	0	0-0	0	3.29	3.61
2004	Cle	AL	33	33	0	0	179.0	802	188	113	108	30	2	6	11	81	1	161	6	0	14	8	.636	0	0-0	0	5.31	5.43
2005	Cle	AL	32	32	1	0	202.0	838	194	91	85	22	5	7	0	52	1	143	4	0	18	5	.783	0	0-0	0	3.35	3.79
2006	Cle	AL	33	33	1	0	200.2	882	224	114	98	29	3	6	8	58	3	129	3	0	14	11	.560	0	0-0	0	4.69	4.40
2007	Cle	AL	20	16	1	1	97.1	443	112	73	68	17	3	2	7	36	1	66	5	0	5	8	.385	0	0-0	0	5.59	6.29
2008	Cle	AL	31	31	4	0	223.1	891	214	68	63	12	2	3	5	34	1	170	4	0	22	3	.880	2	0-0	0	2.75	2.54
2009	2 Tms		34	34	6	0	231.2	969	245	88	83	17	11	9	5	43	1	181	7	0	14	13	.519	2	0-0	0	3.45	3.22
2010	2 Tms		28	28	7	0	212.1	843	195	84	75	16	4	6	1	18	2	185	3	1	12	9	.571	1	0-0	0	2.31	3.18
2011	Phi	NL	32	32	6	0	232.2	920	197	66	62	18	6	4	6	42	0	238	0	0	17	8	.680	6	0-0	0	2.44	2.40
09	Cle	AL	22	22	3	0	152.0	641	165	53	53	10	6	5	3	33	1	107	6	0	7	9	.438	1	0-0	0	3.68	3.14
09	Phi	NL	12	12	3	0	79.2	328	80	35	30	7	5	4	2	10	0	74	1	0	7	4	.636	1	0-0	0	3.03	3.39
10	Sea	AL	13	13	5	0	103.2	408	92	31	27	5	0	3	0	6	0	89	2	1	8	3	.727	1	0-0	0	1.91	2.34
10	Tex	AL	15	15	2	0	108.2	435	103	53	48	11	4	3	1	12	2	96	1	0	4	6	.400	0	0-0	0	2.71	3.98
	Postseason		10	10	3	0	76.0	289	54	22	18	2	1	0	1	8	0	80	2	0	7	2	.778	0	0-0	0	1.36	2.13
	10 ML YEARS		254	250	26	1	1641.2	6842	1616	727	665	168	38	44	45	392	12	1323	35	2	119	69	.633	11	0-0	0	3.48	3.65

Derrek Lee

Bats: R **Throws:** R **Pos:** 1B-113   **Ht:** 6'5" **Wt:** 245 **Born:** 9/6/1975 **Age:** 36

Year	Team	Lg	G	AB	H	2B	3B	HR	(Hm	Rd)	TB	R	RBI	RC	TBB	IBB	SO	HBP	SH	SF	SB	CS	SB%	GDP	Avg	OBP	Slg
2011	Bowie*	AA	1	3	2	0	0	0	(-	-)	2	0	0	1	1	0	0	0	0	0	0	0	-	0	.667	.750	.667
1997	SD	NL	22	54	14	3	0	1	(0	1)	20	9	4	8	9	0	24	0	0	0	0	0	-	1	.259	.365	.370
1998	Fla	NL	141	454	106	29	1	17	(4	13)	188	62	74	59	47	1	120	10	0	2	5	2	.71	12	.233	.318	.414
1999	Fla	NL	70	218	45	9	1	5	(0	5)	71	21	20	18	17	1	70	0	0	1	2	1	.67	3	.206	.263	.326
2000	Fla	NL	158	477	134	18	3	28	(9	19)	242	70	70	84	63	6	123	4	0	2	3	0	.00	14	.281	.368	.507
2001	Fla	NL	158	561	158	37	4	21	(8	13)	266	83	75	88	50	1	126	8	0	6	4	2	.67	18	.282	.346	.474
2002	Fla	NL	162	581	157	35	7	27	(9	18)	287	95	86	96	98	8	164	5	0	4	19	9	.68	14	.270	.378	.494
2003	Fla	NL	155	539	146	31	2	31	(11	20)	274	91	92	99	88	7	131	10	0	6	21	8	.72	9	.271	.379	.508
2004	ChC	NL	161	603	168	39	1	32	(18	14)	305	90	98	101	68	4	128	8	2	5	12	5	.71	14	.278	.356	.504
2005	ChC	NL	158	594	199	50	3	46	(24	22)	393	120	107	135	85	23	109	5	0	7	15	3	.83	12	.335	.418	.662
2006	ChC	NL	50	175	50	9	0	8	(5	3)	83	30	30	27	25	1	41	0	0	4	8	4	.67	11	.286	.368	.474

168

Year	Team	Lg	G	AB	H	2B	3B	HR	(Hm	Rd)	TB	R	RBI	RC	TBB	IBB	SO	HBP	SH	SF	SB	CS	SB%	GDP	Avg	OBP	Slg
2007	ChC	NL	150	567	180	43	1	22	(16	6)	291	91	82	108	71	8	114	9	0	3	6	5	.55	15	.317	.400	.513
2008	ChC	NL	155	623	181	41	3	20	(15	5)	288	93	90	93	71	3	119	0	0	4	8	2	.80	27	.291	.361	.462
2009	ChC	NL	141	532	163	36	2	35	(20	15)	308	91	111	112	76	6	109	3	0	4	1	0	1.00	12	.306	.393	.579
2010	2 Tms	NL	148	547	142	35	0	19	(9	10)	234	80	80	71	73	1	134	2	0	4	1	3	.25	23	.260	.347	.428
2011	2 Tms		113	435	116	17	2	19	(10	9)	194	55	59	54	33	2	110	6	0	3	2	1	.67	14	.267	.325	.446
10	ChC	NL	109	418	105	21	0	16	(7	9)	174	63	56	49	52	1	101	2	0	3	1	3	.25	16	.251	.335	.416
10	Atl	NL	39	129	37	14	0	3	(2	1)	60	17	24	22	21	0	33	0	0	1	0	0	-	7	.287	.384	.465
11	Bal	AL	85	334	82	15	1	12	(6	6)	135	39	41	34	25	2	83	3	0	2	2	1	.67	13	.246	.302	.404
11	Pit	NL	28	101	34	2	1	7	(4	3)	59	16	18	20	8	0	27	3	0	1	0	0	-	1	.337	.398	.584
	Postseason		27	111	27	6	0	1	(0	1)	36	11	8	6	6	0	29	3	0	0	2	0	1.00	5	.243	.300	.324
15 ML YEARS			1942	6962	1959	432	30	331	(158	173)	3444	1081	1078	1153	874	72	1622	70	2	55	104	48	.68	199	.281	.365	.495

DJ LeMahieu

Bats: R **Throws:** R **Pos:** 2B-15; 3B-11; PH-8; PR-4; 1B-1   la-MAY-hugh   **Ht:** 6'4" **Wt:** 205 **Born:** 7/13/1988 **Age:** 23

Year	Team	Lg	G	AB	H	2B	3B	HR	(Hm	Rd)	TB	R	RBI	RC	TBB	IBB	SO	HBP	SH	SF	SB	CS	SB%	GDP	Avg	OBP	Slg
2009	Cubs	R	3	12	5	0	1	0	(-	-)	7	2	4	3	1	0	3	0	0	1	1	0	1.00	0	.417	.429	.583
2009	Peoria	A	38	152	48	4	2	0	(-	-)	56	19	30	21	12	1	22	2	1	1	2	2	.50	11	.316	.371	.368
2010	Dytona	A+	135	554	174	24	5	2	(-	-)	214	63	73	75	29	0	61	1	10	6	15	7	.68	18	.314	.346	.386
2011	Tenn	AA	50	187	67	15	2	2	(-	-)	92	32	27	35	11	0	22	0	0	4	4	3	.57	4	.358	.386	.492
2011	Iowa	AAA	58	227	65	7	1	3	(-	-)	83	23	23	28	14	0	27	2	0	4	5	5	.50	10	.286	.328	.366
2011	ChC	NL	37	60	15	2	0	0	(0	0)	17	3	4	3	1	0	12	0	1	0	0	0	-	2	.250	.262	.283

Chris Leroux

Pitches: R **Bats:** L **Pos:** RP-23   leh-RUE   **Ht:** 6'6" **Wt:** 226 **Born:** 4/14/1984 **Age:** 28

			HOW MUCH HE PITCHED					WHAT HE GAVE UP									THE RESULTS							
Year	Team	Lg	G	GS	CG	GF	IP	BFP	H	R	ER	HR	SH	SF	HB	TBB	IBB	SO	WP	Bk	W	L	Pct	Sh	Sv-Op Hld	ERC	ERA
2011	Indy*	AAA	32	0	0	7	61.0	253	48	20	19	1	3	1	6	21	1	57	4	0	6	3	.667	0	1- - -	2.53	2.80
2011	Altna*	AA	5	0	0	2	7.0	33	9	5	2	2	1	1	1	0	0	6	1	0	1	2	.333	0	0- - -	5.48	2.57
2009	Fla	NL	5	0	0	3	6.2	35	11	8	8	0	0	0	0	4	0	2	0	0	0	0	-	0	0-0 0	7.84	10.80
2010	2 Tms	NL	23	0	0	7	22.2	105	28	18	17	1	0	3	0	14	2	22	1	0	0	1	.000	0	0-2 3	5.86	6.75
2011	Pit	NL	23	0	0	5	25.0	110	26	9	8	0	1	0	1	7	2	24	2	0	1	1	.500	0	0-1 2	3.05	2.88
10	Fla	NL	17	0	0	5	18.0	84	24	15	14	1	0	3	0	11	2	18	0	0	0	0	-	0	0-1 3	6.58	7.00
10	Pit	NL	6	0	0	2	4.2	21	4	3	3	0	0	0	0	3	0	4	1	0	0	1	.000	0	0-1 0	3.39	5.79
3 ML YEARS			51	0	0	15	54.1	250	65	35	33	1	1	3	1	25	4	48	3	0	1	2	.333	0	0-3 5	4.71	5.47

Jon Lester

Pitches: L **Bats:** L **Pos:** SP-31   **Ht:** 6'4" **Wt:** 240 **Born:** 1/7/1984 **Age:** 28

			HOW MUCH HE PITCHED					WHAT HE GAVE UP									THE RESULTS							
Year	Team	Lg	G	GS	CG	GF	IP	BFP	H	R	ER	HR	SH	SF	HB	TBB	IBB	SO	WP	Bk	W	L	Pct	Sh	Sv-Op Hld	ERC	ERA
2006	Bos	AL	15	15	0	0	81.1	367	91	43	43	7	2	8	5	43	1	60	5	0	7	2	.778	0	0-0 0	5.52	4.76
2007	Bos	AL	12	11	0	0	63.0	275	61	33	32	10	1	5	1	31	0	50	1	0	4	0	1.000	0	0-0 0	4.78	4.57
2008	Bos	AL	33	33	2	0	210.1	874	202	78	75	14	6	3	10	66	1	152	3	1	16	6	.727	2	0-0 0	3.55	3.21
2009	Bos	AL	32	32	2	0	203.1	843	186	80	77	20	2	6	3	64	0	225	6	0	15	8	.652	0	0-0 0	3.35	3.41
2010	Bos	AL	32	32	2	0	208.0	861	167	81	75	14	4	6	10	83	0	225	6	0	19	9	.679	0	0-0 0	3.00	3.25
2011	Bos	AL	31	31	0	0	191.2	799	166	77	74	20	2	2	11	75	0	182	4	0	15	9	.625	0	0-0 0	3.62	3.47
	Postseason		8	6	0	2	42.0	175	34	14	12	5	2	0	0	13	0	39	0	0	2	3	.400	0	0-0 0	2.75	2.57
6 ML YEARS			155	154	6	0	957.2	4019	873	392	376	85	17	30	40	362	2	894	25	1	76	34	.691	2	0-0 0	3.63	3.53

Colby Lewis

Pitches: R **Bats:** R **Pos:** SP-32   **Ht:** 6'4" **Wt:** 230 **Born:** 8/2/1979 **Age:** 32

			HOW MUCH HE PITCHED					WHAT HE GAVE UP									THE RESULTS							
Year	Team	Lg	G	GS	CG	GF	IP	BFP	H	R	ER	HR	SH	SF	HB	TBB	IBB	SO	WP	Bk	W	L	Pct	Sh	Sv-Op Hld	ERC	ERA
2002	Tex	AL	15	4	0	4	34.1	168	42	26	24	4	2	0	2	26	2	28	3	1	1	3	.250	0	0-2 1	7.22	6.29
2003	Tex	AL	26	26	0	0	127.0	594	163	104	103	23	2	2	5	70	1	88	5	0	10	9	.526	0	0-0 0	7.38	7.30
2004	Tex	AL	3	3	0	0	15.1	71	13	7	7	1	0	0	1	13	0	11	0	0	1	1	.500	0	0-0 0	4.98	4.11
2006	Det	AL	2	0	0	1	3.0	18	8	1	1	1	0	0	0	1	0	5	0	0	0	0	-	0	0-0 0	17.35	3.00
2007	Oak	AL	26	1	0	8	37.2	170	44	28	27	7	1	2	3	14	3	23	1	1	0	2	.000	0	0-1 3	5.79	6.45
2010	Tex	AL	32	32	1	0	201.0	844	174	90	83	21	4	4	6	65	0	196	9	0	12	13	.480	0	0-0 0	3.15	3.72
2011	Tex	AL	32	32	2	0	200.1	839	187	103	98	35	4	5	6	56	1	169	4	0	14	10	.583	1	0-0 0	3.82	4.40
	Postseason		4	4	0	0	26.1	106	16	5	5	3	0	0	2	13	0	24	2	0	3	0	1.000	0	0-0 0	2.80	1.71
7 ML YEARS			136	98	3	13	618.2	2704	631	359	343	92	13	13	23	245	7	520	22	2	38	38	.500	1	0-3 4	4.64	4.99

Fred Lewis

Bats: L **Throws:** R **Pos:** LF-45; PH-33; RF-4; DH-1; PR-1   **Ht:** 6'2" **Wt:** 200 **Born:** 12/9/1980 **Age:** 31

Year	Team	Lg	G	AB	H	2B	3B	HR	(Hm	Rd)	TB	R	RBI	RC	TBB	IBB	SO	HBP	SH	SF	SB	CS	SB%	GDP	Avg	OBP	Slg
2011	Lsvlle*	AAA	8	20	6	1	1	1	(-	-)	12	6	3	6	8	0	5	0	0	0	1	0	1.00	0	.300	.500	.600
2011	Carlina*	AA	7	23	6	3	0	0	(-	-)	9	3	1	3	4	0	4	0	0	0	1	0	1.00	0	.261	.370	.391
2006	SF	NL	13	11	5	1	0	0	(0	0)	6	5	2	4	0	0	3	0	0	0	0	0	-	0	.455	.455	.545
2007	SF	NL	58	157	45	6	2	3	(0	3)	64	34	19	27	19	0	32	3	1	0	5	1	.83	4	.287	.374	.408
2008	SF	NL	133	468	132	25	11	9	(4	5)	206	81	40	67	51	3	124	0	0	2	21	7	.75	5	.282	.351	.440

			BATTING																					BASERUNNING				AVERAGES		
Year	Team	Lg	G	AB	H	2B	3B	HR	(Hm	Rd)	TB	R	RBI	RC	TBB	IBB	SO	HBP	SH	SF	SB	CS	SB%	GDP	Avg	OBP	Slg
2009	SF	NL	122	295	76	21	3	4	(2	2)	115	49	20	37	36	3	84	5	0	0	8	4	.67	4	.258	.348	.390
2010	Tor	AL	110	428	112	31	5	8	(4	4)	177	70	36	56	38	1	104	9	1	4	17	6	.74	9	.262	.332	.414
2011	Cin	NL	81	183	42	7	0	3	(2	1)	58	20	19	17	22	2	38	3	1	1	2	5	.29	1	.230	.321	.317
6 ML YEARS			517	1542	412	91	21	27	(12	15)	626	259	136	208	166	9	385	20	3	7	53	23	.70	23	.267	.345	.406

Rommie Lewis

Pitches: L Bats: L Pos: RP-6

Ht: 6'6" Wt: 230 Born: 9/2/1982 Age: 29

			HOW MUCH HE PITCHED						WHAT HE GAVE UP												THE RESULTS							
Year	Team	Lg	G	GS	CG	GF	IP	BFP	H	R	ER	HR	SH	SF	HB	TBB	IBB	SO	WP	Bk	W	L	Pct	Sh	Sv-Op Hld	ERC	ERA
2001	Orioles	R	10	7	0	1	33.2	144	37	16	8	3	1	1	2	6	0	27	2	1	1	1	.500	0	0- - -	3.88	2.14
2001	Frdrck	A+	1	0	0	0	4.0	22	8	7	4	1	1	0	0	1	0	2	0	0	0	1	.000	0	0- - -	10.43	9.00
2002	Dlmrva	A	53	0	0	36	71.0	282	50	19	17	1	4	1	4	20	1	77	5	0	1	2	.333	0	25- - -	1.81	2.15
2003	Frdrck	A+	26	20	1	2	113.1	503	108	54	42	9	2	4	6	60	1	69	6	0	4	9	.308	0	0- - -	4.36	3.34
2004	Frdrck	A+	47	4	0	14	86.2	395	92	67	54	4	4	1	7	41	3	52	5	0	1	7	.125	0	0- - -	4.51	5.61
2006	Frdrck	A+	31	0	0	15	51.2	213	46	16	12	3	1	0	4	11	2	36	6	0	5	3	.625	0	6- - -	2.73	2.09
2007	Bowie	AA	47	1	0	12	69.0	312	80	44	41	10	6	3	2	29	2	64	2	1	5	5	.500	0	1- - -	5.47	5.35
2008	Bowie	AA	38	5	0	12	66.0	295	81	29	25	4	3	0	3	26	3	63	3	0	1	6	.143	0	1- - -	5.28	3.41
2009	NHam	AA	26	0	0	5	42.0	179	35	12	12	2	2	0	2	22	0	45	0	0	2	4	.333	0	1- - -	3.50	2.57
2009	LsVgs	AAA	19	0	0	3	24.0	105	23	10	9	1	1	2	2	9	1	20	1	0	2	3	.400	0	0- - -	3.54	3.38
2010	LsVgs	AAA	24	8	0	9	53.1	249	72	51	45	7	1	2	1	22	0	41	5	0	1	5	.167	0	5- - -	6.55	7.59
2011	LsVgs	AAA	42	0	0	19	58.2	273	71	47	43	10	1	3	0	29	0	50	7	0	3	3	.500	0	4- - -	6.18	6.60
2010	Tor	AL	14	0	0	4	18.2	82	20	14	14	4	0	0	0	8	0	15	0	0	0	0	-	0	0-0 - -	5.46	6.75
2011	Tor	AL	6	0	0	3	5.0	31	12	8	5	1	0	0	2	2	0	5	0	0	0	0	-	0	0-0 - -	16.24	9.00
2 ML YEARS			20	0	0	7	23.2	113	32	22	19	5	0	0	2	10	0	20	0	0	0	0	-	0	0-0 - -	7.54	7.23

Alex Liddi

Bats: R Throws: R Pos: 3B-14; PH-1

LID-ee

Ht: 6'4" Wt: 230 Born: 8/14/1988 Age: 23

			BATTING																			BASERUNNING				AVERAGES		
Year	Team	Lg	G	AB	H	2B	3B	HR	(Hm	Rd)	TB	R	RBI	RC	TBB	IBB	SO	HBP	SH	SF	SB	CS	SB%	GDP	Avg	OBP	Slg
2006	Ms	R	47	182	57	13	6	3	(-	-)	91	31	25	33	12	0	48	1	0	2	9	2	.82	2	.313	.355	.500
2006	Wisc	A	11	38	7	1	0	0	(-	-)	8	4	2	0	1	0	8	0	0	1	0	1	.00	2	.184	.200	.211
2007	Wisc	A	113	400	96	28	3	8	(-	-)	154	41	52	49	36	1	123	6	5	4	5	4	.56	4	.240	.308	.385
2008	Wisc	A	125	447	109	26	4	6	(-	-)	161	65	53	54	42	3	115	4	1	2	17	5	.77	9	.244	.313	.360
2009	Hi Dsrt	A+	129	493	170	44	5	23	(-	-)	293	97	104	116	53	5	122	8	3	8	10	6	.63	11	.345	.411	.594
2010	WTenn	AA	134	502	141	37	8	15	(-	-)	239	78	92	84	50	4	145	7	4	2	5	7	.42	17	.281	.353	.476
2011	Tacom	AAA	138	559	145	32	3	30	(-	-)	273	121	104	95	61	0	170	5	2	10	5	1	.83	14	.259	.332	.488
2011	Sea	AL	15	40	9	3	0	3	(0	3)	21	7	6	8	3	0	17	1	0	0	1	0	1.00	1	.225	.295	.525

Brad Lidge

Pitches: R Bats: R Pos: RP-25

Ht: 6'5" Wt: 210 Born: 12/23/1976 Age: 35

			HOW MUCH HE PITCHED						WHAT HE GAVE UP												THE RESULTS							
Year	Team	Lg	G	GS	CG	GF	IP	BFP	H	R	ER	HR	SH	SF	HB	TBB	IBB	SO	WP	Bk	W	L	Pct	Sh	Sv-Op Hld	ERC	ERA
2011	Lakwd*	A	4	0	0	0	4.0	16	5	1	1	0	0	0	0	0	0	5	0	0	0	0	-	0	0- - -	3.37	2.25
2011	Rdng*	AA	4	0	0	0	3.2	17	3	2	2	0	0	0	2	1	0	5	3	0	0	0	-	0	0- - -	3.80	4.91
2002	Hou	NL	6	1	0	2	8.2	48	12	6	6	0	1	0	2	9	1	12	0	0	1	0	1.000	0	0-0 - 0	8.90	6.23
2003	Hou	NL	78	0	0	9	85.0	349	60	36	34	6	2	3	5	42	7	97	4	1	6	3	.667	0	1-6 28	2.82	3.60
2004	Hou	NL	80	0	0	44	94.2	369	57	21	20	8	3	2	6	30	5	157	3	1	6	5	.545	0	29-33 17	1.85	1.90
2005	Hou	NL	70	0	0	65	70.2	291	58	21	18	5	4	1	3	23	1	103	8	0	4	4	.500	0	42-46 0	2.79	2.29
2006	Hou	NL	78	0	0	52	75.0	340	69	47	44	10	6	2	6	36	4	104	11	0	1	5	.167	0	32-38 4	4.25	5.28
2007	Hou	NL	66	0	0	34	67.0	287	54	29	25	9	5	1	4	30	4	88	6	0	5	3	.625	0	19-27 7	3.52	3.36
2008	Phi	NL	72	0	0	61	69.1	292	50	17	15	2	2	1	1	35	4	92	5	0	2	0	1.000	0	41-41 0	2.45	1.95
2009	Phi	NL	67	0	0	55	58.2	283	72	51	47	11	4	1	5	34	3	61	4	0	0	8	.000	0	31-42 1	7.11	7.21
2010	Phi	NL	50	0	0	38	45.2	193	32	16	15	5	3	0	1	24	4	52	3	1	1	1	.500	0	27-32 0	2.92	2.96
2011	Phi	NL	25	0	0	19	19.1	86	16	3	3	0	1	0	1	13	3	23	2	0	0	2	.000	0	1-1 8	3.34	1.40
Postseason			36	0	0	31	43.1	177	30	11	11	2	2	0	3	18	1	61	3	0	2	4	.333	0	18-20 0	2.41	2.28
10 ML YEARS			592	1	0	364	594.0	2538	480	247	227	56	31	11	34	276	36	789	46	3	26	31	.456	0	223-266 67	3.34	3.44

Brent Lillibridge

Bats: R Throws: R Pos: RF-43; PR-24; 1B-22; CF-11; LF-9; PH-9; 2B-6; DH-6

Ht: 5'11" Wt: 185 Born: 9/18/1983 Age: 28

			BATTING																			BASERUNNING				AVERAGES		
Year	Team	Lg	G	AB	H	2B	3B	HR	(Hm	Rd)	TB	R	RBI	RC	TBB	IBB	SO	HBP	SH	SF	SB	CS	SB%	GDP	Avg	OBP	Slg
2008	Atl	NL	29	80	16	6	1	1	(0	1)	27	9	8	6	3	0	23	1	1	0	2	0	1.00	0	.200	.238	.338
2009	CWS	AL	46	95	15	2	0	0	(0	0)	17	9	3	5	14	0	26	1	2	0	6	3	.67	2	.158	.273	.179
2010	CWS	AL	64	98	22	5	2	2	(1	1)	37	19	16	11	3	0	36	0	0	0	5	3	.63	2	.224	.248	.378
2011	CWS	AL	97	186	48	5	1	13	(8	5)	94	38	29	30	17	1	62	7	4	2	10	6	.63	2	.258	.340	.505
4 ML YEARS			236	459	101	18	4	16	(9	7)	175	75	56	52	37	1	147	9	7	2	23	12	.66	6	.220	.290	.381

Ted Lilly

Pitches: L Bats: L Pos: SP-33

Ht: 6'1" Wt: 195 Born: 1/4/1976 Age: 36

			HOW MUCH HE PITCHED						WHAT HE GAVE UP												THE RESULTS							
Year	Team	Lg	G	GS	CG	GF	IP	BFP	H	R	ER	HR	SH	SF	HB	TBB	IBB	SO	WP	Bk	W	L	Pct	Sh	Sv-Op Hld	ERC	ERA
1999	Mon	NL	9	3	0	1	23.2	110	30	20	20	7	0	1	3	9	0	28	1	0	0	1	.000	0	0-0 - -	7.76	7.61
2000	NYY	AL	7	0	0	1	8.0	39	8	6	5	1	0	0	0	5	0	11	1	1	0	0	-	0	0-0 - -	4.76	5.63
2001	NYY	AL	26	21	0	2	120.2	537	126	81	72	20	2	5	7	51	1	112	9	2	5	6	.455	0	0-0 - -	5.10	5.37
2002	2 Tms	AL	22	16	2	1	100.0	413	80	43	41	15	0	3	6	31	3	77	6	1	5	7	.417	1	0-0 - -	3.14	3.69

Year Team	Lg	G	GS	CG	GF	IP	BFP	H	R	ER	HR	SH	SF	HB	TBB	IBB	SO	WP	Bk	W	L	Pct	Sh	Sv-Op	Hld	ERC	ERA
		HOW MUCH HE PITCHED						**WHAT HE GAVE UP**												**THE RESULTS**							
2003 Oak	AL	32	31	0	0	178.1	773	179	92	86	24	3	4	5	58	3	147	5	4	12	10	.545	0	0-0	0	4.06	4.34
2004 Tor	AL	32	32	2	0	197.1	845	171	92	89	26	3	3	6	89	2	168	6	4	12	10	.545	1	0-0	0	3.84	4.06
2005 Tor	AL	25	25	0	0	126.1	566	135	79	78	23	3	5	3	58	1	96	2	2	10	11	.476	0	0-0	0	5.38	5.56
2006 Tor	AL	32	32	0	0	181.2	797	179	98	87	28	4	2	4	81	6	160	7	4	15	13	.536	0	0-0	0	4.57	4.31
2007 ChC	NL	34	34	0	0	207.0	847	181	91	88	28	11	9	3	55	2	174	7	0	15	8	.652	0	0-0	0	3.14	3.83
2008 ChC	NL	34	**34**	0	0	204.2	861	187	96	93	32	5	3	7	64	2	184	4	4	17	9	.654	0	0-0	0	3.73	4.09
2009 ChC	NL	27	27	0	0	177.0	706	151	66	61	22	9	3	2	36	2	151	3	3	12	9	.571	0	0-0	0	2.74	3.10
2010 2 Tms	NL	30	30	1	0	193.2	785	165	83	78	32	14	2	5	44	4	166	2	2	10	12	.455	1	0-0	0	3.08	3.62
2011 LAD	NL	33	33	0	0	192.2	800	172	88	85	28	12	5	9	51	8	158	2	2	12	14	.462	0	0-0	0	3.36	3.97
02 NYY	AL	16	11	2	1	76.2	314	57	31	29	10	0	3	5	24	3	59	6	0	3	6	.333	1	0-0	0	2.74	3.40
02 Oak	AL	6	5	0	0	23.1	99	23	12	12	5	0	0	1	7	0	18	0	1	2	1	.667	0	0-0	0	4.56	4.63
10 ChC	NL	18	18	0	0	117.0	480	104	53	48	19	8	1	2	29	3	89	2	2	3	8	.273	0	0-0	0	3.30	3.69
10 LAD	NL	12	12	1	0	76.2	305	61	30	30	13	6	1	3	15	1	77	0	0	7	4	.636	1	0-0	0	2.77	3.52
Postseason		5	2	0	0	16.1	76	19	13	12	2	1	0	1	7	0	14	1	0	0	2	.000	0	0-1	0	5.43	6.61
13 ML YEARS		343	318	5	5	1911.0	8079	1764	935	883	286	66	45	60	632	34	1632	55	29	125	110	.532	3	0-0	0	3.79	4.16

Tim Lincecum

Pitches: R Bats: L Pos: SP-33   Ht: 5'11" Wt: 163 Born: 6/15/1984 Age: 28

Year Team	Lg	G	GS	CG	GF	IP	BFP	H	R	ER	HR	SH	SF	HB	TBB	IBB	SO	WP	Bk	W	L	Pct	Sh	Sv-Op	Hld	ERC	ERA
		HOW MUCH HE PITCHED						**WHAT HE GAVE UP**												**THE RESULTS**							
2007 SF	NL	24	24	0	0	146.1	618	122	70	65	12	5	7	2	65	5	150	10	0	7	5	.583	0	0-0	0	3.21	4.00
2008 SF	NL	34	33	2	0	227.0	928	182	72	66	11	11	3	6	84	1	**265**	**17**	2	18	5	**.783**	1	0-0	0	**2.69**	2.62
2009 SF	NL	32	32	4	0	225.1	905	168	69	62	10	12	5	6	68	2	**261**	11	0	15	7	.682	**2**	0-0	0	**2.14**	2.48
2010 SF	NL	33	33	1	0	212.1	900	194	84	81	18	9	5	5	76	7	**231**	9	0	16	10	.615	1	0-0	0	3.37	3.43
2011 SF	NL	33	33	1	0	217.0	900	176	74	66	15	13	1	6	86	5	220	9	0	13	14	.481	1	0-0	0	2.92	2.74
Postseason		6	5	1	0	37.0	145	25	11	10	3	1	1	1	9	0	43	0	0	4	1	.800	1	0-0	1	1.84	2.43
5 ML YEARS		156	155	8	0	1028.0	4248	842	369	340	66	50	21	25	379	20	1127	56	2	69	41	.627	5	0-0	0	2.82	2.98

Brad Lincoln

Pitches: R Bats: L Pos: SP-8; RP-4   Ht: 6'0" Wt: 210 Born: 5/25/1985 Age: 27

Year Team	Lg	G	GS	CG	GF	IP	BFP	H	R	ER	HR	SH	SF	HB	TBB	IBB	SO	WP	Bk	W	L	Pct	Sh	Sv-Op	Hld	ERC	ERA
		HOW MUCH HE PITCHED						**WHAT HE GAVE UP**												**THE RESULTS**							
2006 Pirates	R	2	2	0	0	7.2	29	6	1	0	0	1	0	1	0	0	9	0	0	0	0	-	0	0- -	-	1.54	0.00
2006 Hkry	A	4	4	0	0	16.0	76	25	15	12	2	1	0	1	6	0	10	1	0	1	2	.333	0	0- -	-	8.14	6.75
2008 Hkry	A	11	11	0	0	62.0	260	72	34	32	8	2	0	2	6	0	46	1	2	5	5	.500	0	0- -	-	4.11	4.65
2008 Lynbrg	A+	8	8	1	0	41.2	176	42	24	22	5	1	1	1	11	0	29	0	0	1	5	.167	0	0- -	-	3.80	4.75
2009 Altna	AA	13	13	1	0	75.0	298	63	22	19	4	1	1	2	18	0	65	3	0	1	5	.167	1	0- -	-	2.49	2.28
2009 Indy	AAA	12	12	0	0	61.1	257	72	37	32	7	1	5	1	10	1	42	2	1	6	2	.750	0	0- -	-	4.33	4.70
2010 Indy	AAA	17	17	0	0	94.0	388	83	47	43	9	2	2	7	24	0	84	4	0	7	5	.583	0	0- -	-	3.15	4.12
2011 Indy	AAA	19	19	0	0	111.2	464	115	55	52	6	3	5	9	21	0	94	3	0	7	8	.467	0	0- -	-	3.47	4.19
2010 Pit	NL	11	9	0	0	52.2	240	66	42	39	9	3	4	5	15	0	25	1	0	1	4	.200	0	0-0	0	5.99	6.66
2011 Pit	NL	12	8	0	0	47.2	211	54	27	25	4	2	2	2	16	4	29	0	0	2	3	.400	0	0-0	0	4.46	4.72
2 ML YEARS		23	17	0	0	100.1	451	120	69	64	13	5	6	7	31	4	54	1	0	3	7	.300	0	0-0	0	5.25	5.74

Adam Lind

Bats: L Throws: L Pos: 1B-109; DH-16   Ht: 6'1" Wt: 215 Born: 7/17/1983 Age: 28

Year Team	Lg	G	AB	H	2B	3B	HR	(Hm	Rd)	TB	R	RBI	RC	TBB	IBB	SO	HBP	SH	SF	SB	CS	SB%	GDP	Avg	OBP	Slg
		BATTING																		**BASERUNNING**				**AVERAGES**		
2011 Dnedin*	A+	3	10	6	3	0	0	(-	-)	9	2	4	5	2	0	1	0	0	0	2	0	1.00	0	.600	.667	.900
2006 Tor	AL	18	60	22	8	0	2	(0	2)	36	8	8	13	5	0	12	0	0	0	0	0	-	0	.367	.415	.600
2007 Tor	AL	89	290	69	14	0	11	(10	1)	116	34	46	38	16	0	65	1	2	2	1	2	.33	7	.238	.278	.400
2008 Tor	AL	88	326	92	16	4	9	(2	7)	143	48	40	39	16	3	59	2	1	4	2	0	1.00	8	.282	.316	.439
2009 Tor	AL	151	587	179	46	0	35	(14	21)	330	93	114	114	58	7	110	5	0	4	1	1	.50	15	.305	.370	.562
2010 Tor	AL	150	569	135	32	3	23	(15	8)	242	57	72	65	38	3	144	3	0	3	0	0	-	10	.237	.287	.425
2011 Tor	AL	125	499	125	16	0	26	(12	14)	219	56	87	67	32	4	107	3	0	8	1	1	.50	12	.251	.295	.439
6 ML YEARS		621	2331	622	132	7	106	(53	53)	1086	296	367	336	165	17	497	14	3	21	5	4	.56	52	.267	.316	.466

Josh Lindblom

Pitches: R Bats: R Pos: RP-27   Ht: 6'4" Wt: 239 Born: 6/15/1987 Age: 25

LIN-bloom

Year Team	Lg	G	GS	CG	GF	IP	BFP	H	R	ER	HR	SH	SF	HB	TBB	IBB	SO	WP	Bk	W	L	Pct	Sh	Sv-Op	Hld	ERC	ERA
		HOW MUCH HE PITCHED						**WHAT HE GAVE UP**												**THE RESULTS**							
2008 Gt Lks	A	8	8	0	0	29.0	107	14	6	6	2	0	0	1	4	0	33	0	0	0	0	-	0	0- -	-	0.96	1.86
2008 Jaxnvl	AA	1	1	0	0	5.0	20	5	2	2	0	0	0	0	1	0	4	1	0	0	0	-	0	0- -	-	2.76	3.60
2009 Chatt	AA	14	11	0	1	57.1	243	55	35	30	4	1	3	5	14	2	46	3	0	3	5	.375	0	0- -	-	3.30	4.71
2009 Albq	AAA	20	3	0	3	39.0	163	34	11	11	3	4	0	3	12	0	36	1	0	3	0	1.000	0	1- -	-	3.17	2.54
2010 Albq	AAA	40	10	0	3	95.0	463	143	79	69	12	1	1	7	32	3	84	6	1	3	2	.600	0	0- -	-	7.23	6.54
2011 Chatt	AA	34	0	0	27	42.1	167	30	10	10	3	2	1	4	14	3	54	2	0	1	3	.250	0	17- -	-	2.45	2.13
2011 LAD	NL	27	0	0	8	29.2	116	21	9	9	0	2	3	2	10	3	28	3	0	1	0	1.000	0	0-1	3	1.90	2.73

Shane Lindsay

Pitches: R **Bats:** R **Pos:** RP-4 **Ht:** 6'1" **Wt:** 205 **Born:** 1/25/1985 **Age:** 27

			HOW MUCH HE PITCHED					WHAT HE GAVE UP											THE RESULTS						
Year	Team	Lg	G	GS	CG	GF	IP	BFP	H	R	ER	HR	SH	SF	HB	TBB	IBB	SO	WP	Bk	W	L	Pct	Sh	Sv-Op Hld	ERC	ERA
2004	Casper	R+	17	0	0	7	21.1	107	22	24	16	1	0	0	2	19	0	31	4	0	1	1	.500	0	0- - -	6.01	6.75
2005	TriCity	A-	13	13	0	0	66.2	269	37	21	14	1	1	1	6	34	0	107	12	1	6	1	.857	0	0- - -	2.00	1.89
2006	TriCity	A-	6	5	0	1	29.0	121	18	10	9	0	0	0	1	17	0	48	7	0	2	2	.500	0	0- - -	2.23	2.79
2006	Ashvll	A	7	7	0	0	33.2	154	26	15	10	2	2	1	1	27	0	43	7	0	2	1	.667	0	0- - -	4.09	2.67
2008	Mdest	A+	10	10	0	0	47.1	210	33	29	21	1	0	2	4	34	0	56	5	0	2	3	.400	0	0- - -	3.33	3.99
2008	Ashvll	A	6	6	0	0	24.1	112	30	16	15	1	0	1	1	12	0	26	1	0	1	2	.333	0	0- - -	5.58	5.55
2009	Tulsa	AA	22	0	0	5	27.2	117	12	8	8	0	2	1	2	19	0	36	3	0	3	1	.750	0	1- - -	1.75	2.60
2009	Ashvll	A	5	0	0	1	5.2	25	4	1	1	0	0	1	1	4	0	7	2	0	1	1	.500	0	0- - -	3.60	1.59
2010	ColSpr	AAA	14	0	0	1	13.2	72	15	10	10	0	0	1	2	17	0	19	4	0	0	1	.000	0	0- - -	7.96	6.59
2010	Akron	AA	12	1	0	5	15.2	77	7	8	6	0	0	0	5	17	0	23	3	0	1	0	1.000	0	1- - -	3.80	3.45
2010	Clmbs	AAA	7	0	0	2	11.0	64	13	11	10	1	1	1	2	16	0	12	4	0	0	1	.000	0	0- - -	10.16	8.18
2011	Brham	AAA	5	0	0	3	6.2	32	4	3	3	0	1	1	0	8	0	12	2	0	1	1	.500	0	0- - -	3.97	4.05
2011	Charltt	AAA	45	0	0	24	63.2	275	28	15	14	2	2	1	9	51	0	78	8	0	2	2	.500	0	4- - -	2.60	1.98
2011	CWS	AL	4	0	0	2	6.0	34	11	8	8	1	0	0	0	5	0	6	1	0	0	0	-	0	0-0 0	11.81	12.00

Matt Lindstrom

Pitches: R **Bats:** R **Pos:** RP-63 **Ht:** 6'3" **Wt:** 218 **Born:** 2/11/1980 **Age:** 32

			HOW MUCH HE PITCHED					WHAT HE GAVE UP											THE RESULTS						
Year	Team	Lg	G	GS	CG	GF	IP	BFP	H	R	ER	HR	SH	SF	HB	TBB	IBB	SO	WP	Bk	W	L	Pct	Sh	Sv-Op Hld	ERC	ERA
2011	ColSpr*	AAA	2	0	0	0	2.0	10	4	3	3	1	0	0	0	0	0	4	0	0	0	0	-	0	0- - -	11.88	13.50
2007	Fla	NL	71	0	0	11	67.0	284	66	27	23	2	3	1	3	21	4	62	5	0	3	4	.429	0	0-2 19	3.26	3.09
2008	Fla	NL	66	0	0	27	57.1	245	57	21	20	1	6	1	1	26	4	43	4	0	3	3	.500	0	5-6 14	3.69	3.14
2009	Hou	NL	54	0	0	32	47.1	219	54	35	31	5	1	0	2	24	2	39	0	1	2	1	.667	0	15-17 8	5.41	5.89
2010	Hou	NL	58	0	0	41	53.1	244	68	26	26	5	2	0	0	20	1	43	8	0	2	5	.286	0	23-29 4	5.45	4.39
2011	Col	NL	63	0	0	16	54.0	226	52	21	18	3	3	3	2	14	4	36	2	0	2	2	.500	0	2-5 15	3.06	3.00
	5 ML YEARS		312	0	0	127	279.0	1218	297	130	118	16	15	5	8	105	15	223	19	1	12	15	.444	0	45-59 60	4.06	3.81

Scott Linebrink

Pitches: R **Bats:** R **Pos:** RP-64 LYNE-brink **Ht:** 6'3" **Wt:** 220 **Born:** 8/4/1976 **Age:** 35

			HOW MUCH HE PITCHED					WHAT HE GAVE UP											THE RESULTS						
Year	Team	Lg	G	GS	CG	GF	IP	BFP	H	R	ER	HR	SH	SF	HB	TBB	IBB	SO	WP	Bk	W	L	Pct	Sh	Sv-Op Hld	ERC	ERA
2000	2 Tms	NL	11	0	0	4	12.0	63	18	8	8	4	0	0	3	8	0	6	0	0	0	0	-	0	0-0 0	11.88	6.00
2001	Hou	NL	9	0	0	2	10.1	44	6	4	3	0	1	1	2	6	0	9	1	0	0	0	-	0	0-0 0	2.54	2.61
2002	Hou	NL	22	0	0	4	24.1	120	31	21	19	2	0	2	1	13	4	24	0	0	0	0	-	0	0-0 1	5.70	7.03
2003	2 Tms	NL	52	6	0	8	92.1	397	93	37	34	9	4	6	6	36	4	68	11	0	3	2	.600	0	0-0 6	4.32	3.31
2004	SD	NL	73	0	0	7	84.0	326	61	22	20	8	2	3	3	26	2	83	3	0	7	3	.700	0	0-5 28	2.48	2.14
2005	SD	NL	73	0	0	17	73.2	288	55	17	15	4	2	0	0	23	4	70	3	0	8	1	.889	0	1-6 26	2.15	1.83
2006	SD	NL	73	0	0	11	75.2	314	70	31	30	9	1	2	1	22	3	68	2	0	7	4	.636	0	2-11 36	3.36	3.57
2007	2 Tms	NL	71	0	0	11	70.1	295	68	33	29	12	0	0	1	25	3	50	6	0	5	6	.455	0	1-8 21	4.26	3.71
2008	CWS	AL	50	0	0	13	46.1	186	41	20	19	8	2	0	0	9	1	40	3	0	2	2	.500	0	1-4 19	3.09	3.69
2009	CWS	AL	57	0	0	24	56.0	259	70	34	29	9	0	3	3	23	6	55	5	0	3	7	.300	0	2-4 7	6.07	4.66
2010	CWS	AL	52	0	0	28	57.1	249	59	31	28	11	4	0	3	17	0	52	7	0	3	2	.600	0	0-1 4	4.62	4.40
2011	Atl	NL	64	0	0	27	54.1	237	58	22	22	6	2	4	4	21	6	42	3	0	4	4	.500	0	1-2 7	4.67	3.64
00	SF	NL	3	0	0	1	2.1	16	7	3	3	1	0	0	0	2	0	0	0	0	0	0	-	0	0-0 0	24.13	11.57
00	Hou	NL	8	0	0	3	9.2	47	11	5	5	3	0	0	3	6	0	6	0	0	0	0	-	0	0-0 0	9.21	4.66
03	Hou	NL	9	6	0	2	31.2	140	38	15	15	4	2	1	3	14	1	17	5	0	1	1	.500	0	0-0 0	6.27	4.26
03	SD	NL	43	0	0	6	60.2	257	55	22	19	5	2	5	3	22	3	51	6	0	2	1	.667	0	0-0 6	3.41	2.82
07	SD	NL	44	0	0	7	45.0	186	41	19	19	9	0	0	1	14	1	25	4	0	3	3	.500	0	1-7 15	3.99	3.80
07	Mil	NL	27	0	0	4	25.1	109	27	14	10	3	0	0	0	11	2	25	2	0	2	3	.400	0	0-1 6	4.71	3.55
	Postseason		4	0	0	3	3.1	15	4	1	1	1	0	0	0	2	1	2	0	0	0	0	-	0	0-0 1	7.51	2.70
	12 ML YEARS		607	6	0	156	656.2	2778	630	280	256	82	18	21	27	229	33	567	44	0	42	31	.575	0	8-41 155	3.94	3.51

Francisco Liriano

Pitches: L **Bats:** L **Pos:** SP-24; RP-2 **Ht:** 6'2" **Wt:** 215 **Born:** 10/26/1983 **Age:** 28

			HOW MUCH HE PITCHED					WHAT HE GAVE UP											THE RESULTS						
Year	Team	Lg	G	GS	CG	GF	IP	BFP	H	R	ER	HR	SH	SF	HB	TBB	IBB	SO	WP	Bk	W	L	Pct	Sh	Sv-Op Hld	ERC	ERA
2005	Min	AL	6	4	0	2	23.2	93	19	15	15	4	0	0	0	7	0	33	0	0	1	2	.333	0	0-0 0	3.15	5.70
2006	Min	AL	28	16	0	2	121.0	473	89	31	29	9	4	2	1	32	0	144	9	1	12	3	.800	0	1-1 0	2.12	2.16
2008	Min	AL	14	14	0	0	76.0	329	74	40	33	7	2	3	1	32	1	67	3	0	6	4	.600	0	0-0 0	3.97	3.91
2009	Min	AL	29	24	0	2	136.2	609	147	93	88	21	5	6	6	65	0	122	5	1	5	13	.278	0	0-0 0	5.46	5.80
2010	Min	AL	31	31	0	0	191.2	806	184	77	77	9	6	2	10	58	0	201	10	1	14	10	.583	0	0-0 0	3.34	3.62
2011	Min	AL	26	24	1	0	134.1	591	125	81	76	14	0	6	7	75	1	112	9	0	9	10	.474	1	0-0 0	4.58	5.09
	Postseason		2	1	0	0	7.2	34	7	6	5	1	0	0	0	4	0	8	1	0	0	0	-	0	0-0 0	4.19	5.87
	6 ML YEARS		134	113	1	6	683.1	2901	638	337	318	64	17	19	25	269	2	679	36	3	47	42	.528	1	1-1 1	3.81	4.19

Jesse Litsch

Pitches: R **Bats:** R **Pos:** RP-20; SP-8 **Ht:** 6'1" **Wt:** 225 **Born:** 3/9/1985 **Age:** 27

			HOW MUCH HE PITCHED					WHAT HE GAVE UP											THE RESULTS						
Year	Team	Lg	G	GS	CG	GF	IP	BFP	H	R	ER	HR	SH	SF	HB	TBB	IBB	SO	WP	Bk	W	L	Pct	Sh	Sv-Op Hld	ERC	ERA
2011	LsVgs*	AAA	6	6	0	0	28.2	137	41	26	26	5	0	0	3	11	0	27	4	3	1	2	.333	0	0- - -	7.74	8.16
2011	Lnsng*	A	1	1	0	0	2.0	11	3	3	2	0	0	0	1	0	3	1	0	0	0	0	-	0	0- - -	5.84	9.00
2011	NHam*	AA	2	2	0	0	8.2	32	6	1	1	0	0	0	1	0	0	9	1	0	0	0	-	0	0- - -	1.24	1.04
2007	Tor	AL	20	20	0	0	111.0	478	116	56	47	14	3	3	7	36	2	50	2	0	7	9	.438	0	0-0 0	4.48	3.81
2008	Tor	AL	29	28	2	0	176.0	735	178	79	70	20	1	4	8	39	2	99	4	0	13	9	.591	2	0-0 0	3.71	3.58

Year	Team	Lg	G	GS	CG	GF	IP	BFP	H	R	ER	HR	SH	SF	HB	TBB	IBB	SO	WP	Bk	W	L	Pct	Sh	Sv-Op	Hld	ERC	ERA
2009	Tor	AL	2	2	0	0	9.0	42	14	9	9	4	0	0	1	1	0	8	0	0	0	1	.000	0	0-0	0	9.55	9.00
2010	Tor	AL	9	9	0	0	46.2	202	53	30	30	7	0	0	2	15	0	16	1	0	1	5	.167	0	0-0	0	5.18	5.79
2011	Tor	AL	28	8	0	4	75.0	317	69	40	37	10	2	2	3	28	2	66	3	0	6	3	.667	0	1-2	3	3.90	4.44
	5 ML YEARS		88	67	2	4	417.2	1774	430	214	193	55	6	9	21	119	6	239	10	0	27	27	.500	2	1-2	3	4.22	4.16

Jose Lobaton

Bats: B Throws: R Pos: C-14; PH-3   LOE-bah-tone   Ht: 6'0" Wt: 195 Born: 10/21/1984 Age: 27

Year	Team	Lg	G	AB	H	2B	3B	HR	(Hm	Rd)	TB	R	RBI	RC	TBB	IBB	SO	HBP	SH	SF	SB	CS	SB%	GDP	Avg	OBP	Slg
2003	Idaho	R+	56	191	52	15	0	1	(-	-)	70	22	32	26	22	2	50	2	1	1	0	1	.00	4	.272	.352	.366
2004	Eugene	A-	44	151	33	12	0	7	(-	-)	66	13	23	20	17	0	35	0	1	0	0	0	-	3	.219	.298	.437
2005	Padres	R	5	14	5	2	0	0	(-	-)	7	2	2	4	6	0	4	0	0	0	1	0	1.00	0	.357	.550	.500
2005	FtWyn	A	9	34	6	1	0	0	(-	-)	7	2	1	1	2	0	5	0	1	0	0	0	-	2	.176	.222	.206
2005	Eugene	A-	11	32	9	2	0	0	(-	-)	11	4	3	5	6	0	8	1	3	0	0	0	-	0	.281	.410	.344
2006	Lk Els	A+	42	122	26	7	0	4	(-	-)	45	12	15	15	20	0	42	1	1	1	0	2	.00	3	.213	.326	.369
2006	FtWyn	A	20	61	17	3	1	1	(-	-)	25	15	11	11	12	0	12	2	1	1	0	0	-	2	.279	.408	.410
2007	Lk Els	A+	90	304	79	15	3	10	(-	-)	130	50	47	48	41	1	79	3	2	7	0	0	-	2	.260	.346	.428
2008	SnAnt	AA	92	294	76	21	0	9	(-	-)	124	35	45	45	39	1	75	0	2	7	1	1	.50	8	.259	.338	.422
2009	Portlnd	AAA	39	133	32	6	0	3	(-	-)	47	14	8	14	10	0	35	0	4	1	0	0	-	2	.241	.292	.353
2009	Mont	AA	26	84	22	7	0	3	(-	-)	38	13	11	15	15	1	19	1	1	1	0	0	-	3	.262	.376	.452
2010	Mont	AA	7	24	6	1	0	0	(-	-)	7	3	2	2	4	0	5	0	0	0	0	0	-	1	.250	.357	.292
2010	Drham	AAA	72	241	63	11	0	7	(-	-)	95	26	33	34	27	1	52	1	1	1	1	0	1.00	10	.261	.337	.394
2011	Drham	AAA	54	184	54	10	1	8	(-	-)	90	24	31	38	37	2	50	0	2	1	0	0	-	5	.293	.410	.489
2011	Charltt	A+	6	18	8	4	0	0	(-	-)	12	0	2	5	2	0	5	0	0	0	0	0	-	0	.444	.500	.667
2009	SD	NL	7	17	3	0	0	0	(0	0)	3	0	0	0	0	0	5	0	0	0	0	0	-	1	.176	.176	.176
2011	TB	AL	15	34	4	1	0	0	(0	0)	5	2	0	0	4	0	8	1	0	0	0	0	-	2	.118	.231	.147
	2 ML YEARS		22	51	7	1	0	0	(0	0)	8	2	0	0	4	0	13	1	0	0	0	0	-	3	.137	.214	.157

Jeff Locke

Pitches: L Bats: L Pos: SP-4   Ht: 6'2" Wt: 215 Born: 11/20/1987 Age: 24

Year	Team	Lg	G	GS	CG	GF	IP	BFP	H	R	ER	HR	SH	SF	HB	TBB	IBB	SO	WP	Bk	W	L	Pct	Sh	Sv-Op	Hld	ERC	ERA
2006	Braves	R	10	5	0	1	32.0	135	38	18	15	4	0	1	1	5	0	38	1	1	4	3	.571	0	0--	-	4.53	4.22
2007	Danvle	R+	13	11	0	1	61.0	237	48	23	18	2	0	1	3	8	0	74	7	0	7	1	.875	0	1--	-	1.81	2.66
2008	Rome	A	25	24	1	1	139.2	610	150	75	63	6	3	7	4	38	0	113	8	1	5	12	.294	0	0--	-	3.61	4.06
2009	MrtlBh	A+	10	10	0	0	45.2	208	47	31	28	1	2	2	5	26	0	43	6	0	1	4	.200	0	0--	-	4.78	5.52
2009	Lynbrg	A+	17	17	0	0	81.2	348	98	44	37	4	6	2	1	18	0	56	0	0	4	4	.500	0	0--	-	4.25	4.08
2010	Bradtn	A+	17	17	0	0	86.1	353	82	42	34	6	0	1	7	14	0	83	0	0	9	3	.750	0	0--	-	3.03	3.54
2011	Altna	AA	10	10	0	0	57.2	243	57	24	23	5	2	2	4	12	0	56	3	1	3	2	.600	0	0--	-	3.42	3.59
2011	Altna	AA	23	22	0	0	125.0	535	118	68	56	9	5	5	8	46	0	114	10	1	7	8	.467	0	0--	-	3.70	4.03
2011	Indy	AAA	5	5	0	0	28.1	114	25	8	7	1	1	0	0	9	1	25	0	0	1	2	.333	0	0--	-	2.74	2.22
2011	Pit	NL	4	4	0	0	16.2	78	21	12	12	3	1	1	1	10	0	5	0	0	0	3	.000	0	0-0	0	7.62	6.48

Kameron Loe

Pitches: R Bats: R Pos: RP-72   Ht: 6'8" Wt: 240 Born: 9/10/1981 Age: 30

Year	Team	Lg	G	GS	CG	GF	IP	BFP	H	R	ER	HR	SH	SF	HB	TBB	IBB	SO	WP	Bk	W	L	Pct	Sh	Sv-Op	Hld	ERC	ERA
2004	Tex	AL	2	1	0	0	6.2	29	6	5	4	0	0	0	1	6	0	3	0	0	0	0	-	0	0-0	0	5.87	5.40
2005	Tex	AL	48	8	0	13	92.0	392	89	43	35	7	5	1	2	31	6	45	2	0	9	6	.600	0	1-4	4	3.45	3.42
2006	Tex	AL	15	15	1	0	78.1	358	105	54	51	10	1	3	1	22	0	34	3	0	3	6	.333	1	0-0	0	5.79	5.86
2007	Tex	AL	28	23	0	0	136.0	615	162	96	81	13	1	5	4	56	6	78	6	0	6	11	.353	0	0-0	0	5.24	5.36
2008	Tex	AL	14	0	0	4	30.2	134	36	18	11	3	0	1	0	8	1	20	0	0	1	0	1.000	0	0-1	2	4.40	3.23
2010	Mil	NL	53	0	0	9	58.1	240	54	23	18	6	1	2	2	15	1	46	4	0	3	5	.375	0	0-2	22	3.27	2.78
2011	Mil	NL	72	0	0	19	72.0	291	65	30	28	4	2	0	2	16	2	61	5	0	4	7	.364	0	1-8	16	2.70	3.50
	7 ML YEARS		232	47	1	45	474.0	2059	517	269	228	43	10	12	12	154	16	287	20	0	26	35	.426	1	2-15	44	4.27	4.33

Adam Loewen

Bats: L Throws: L Pos: RF-4; CF-3; DH-3; PR-2; LF-1; PH-1   LOW-en   Ht: 6'5" Wt: 235 Born: 4/9/1984 Age: 28

Year	Team	Lg	G	AB	H	2B	3B	HR	(Hm	Rd)	TB	R	RBI	RC	TBB	IBB	SO	HBP	SH	SF	SB	CS	SB%	GDP	Avg	OBP	Slg
2011	LsVgs*	AAA	134	520	159	46	4	17	(-	-)	264	83	85	99	61	2	136	0	1	3	11	7	.61	10	.306	.377	.508
2006	Bal	AL	22	2	0	0	0	0	(0	0)	0	0	0	0	0	0	0	0	0	0	0	0	-	0	.000	.000	.000
2007	Bal	AL	6	0	0	0	0	0	(0	0)	0	0	0	0	0	0	0	0	0	0	0	0	-	0	-	-	-
2008	Bal	AL	7	0	0	0	0	0	(0	0)	0	0	0	0	0	0	0	0	0	0	0	0	-	0	-	-	-
2011	Tor	AL	14	32	6	1	0	1	(1	0)	10	4	4	2	3	0	13	2	0	0	0	0	-	0	.188	.297	.313
	4 ML YEARS		49	34	6	1	0	1	(1	0)	10	4	4	2	3	0	13	2	0	0	0	0	-	0	.176	.282	.294

Boone Logan

Pitches: L Bats: R Pos: RP-64   Ht: 6'5" Wt: 225 Born: 8/13/1984 Age: 27

Year	Team	Lg	G	GS	CG	GF	IP	BFP	H	R	ER	HR	SH	SF	HB	TBB	IBB	SO	WP	Bk	W	L	Pct	Sh	Sv-Op	Hld	ERC	ERA
2006	CWS	AL	21	0	0	4	17.1	93	21	18	16	2	1	1	3	15	2	15	1	0	0	0	-	0	1-2	2	7.56	8.31
2007	CWS	AL	68	0	0	13	50.2	226	59	30	28	7	2	6	0	20	3	35	2	0	2	1	.667	0	0-2	11	5.18	4.97
2008	CWS	AL	55	0	0	12	42.1	197	57	31	28	7	2	0	1	14	3	42	1	0	2	3	.400	0	0-1	3	6.24	5.95
2009	Atl	NL	20	0	0	7	17.1	82	21	12	10	2	2	0	0	9	3	10	0	0	1	1	.500	0	0-0	1	5.29	5.19

Year	Team	Lg	G	GS	CG	GF	IP	BFP	H	R	ER	HR	SH	SF	HB	TBB	IBB	SO	WP	Bk	W	L	Pct	Sh	Sv-Op	Hld	ERC	ERA
			HOW MUCH HE PITCHED						**WHAT HE GAVE UP**												**THE RESULTS**							
2010	NYY	AL	51	0	0	8	40.0	169	34	13	13	3	0	1	1	20	3	38	1	0	2	0	1.000	0	0-0	13	3.50	2.93
2011	NYY	AL	64	0	0	6	41.2	185	43	20	16	4	2	1	4	13	3	46	1	0	5	3	.625	0	0-2	10	4.04	3.46
	Postseason		5	0	0	0	1.2	9	3	2	2	1	0	0	0	1	0	1	0	0	0	0	-	0	0-0	2	14.69	10.80
	6 ML YEARS		279	0	0	50	209.1	952	235	124	111	24	7	9	10	91	17	186	6	0	12	8	.600	0	1-7	40	5.03	4.77

Kyle Lohse

Pitches: R **Bats:** R **Pos:** SP-30
LOESH
Ht: 6'2" **Wt:** 210 **Born:** 10/4/1978 **Age:** 33

Year	Team	Lg	G	GS	CG	GF	IP	BFP	H	R	ER	HR	SH	SF	HB	TBB	IBB	SO	WP	Bk	W	L	Pct	Sh	Sv-Op	Hld	ERC	ERA
			HOW MUCH HE PITCHED						**WHAT HE GAVE UP**												**THE RESULTS**							
2001	Min	AL	19	16	0	2	90.1	402	102	60	57	16	1	5	8	29	0	64	5	0	4	7	.364	0	0-0	0	5.43	5.68
2002	Min	AL	32	31	1	0	180.2	783	181	92	85	26	3	3	9	70	2	124	8	0	13	8	.619	1	0-1	0	4.55	4.23
2003	Min	AL	33	33	2	0	201.0	850	211	107	103	28	8	5	5	45	1	130	10	1	14	11	.560	1	0-0	0	4.00	4.61
2004	Min	AL	35	34	1	1	194.0	883	240	128	115	28	5	7	7	76	5	111	6	0	9	13	.409	1	0-0	0	5.89	5.34
2005	Min	AL	31	30	0	1	178.2	769	211	85	83	22	3	7	9	44	5	86	4	1	9	13	.409	0	0-0	0	4.91	4.18
2006	2 Tms		34	19	0	6	126.2	566	150	83	82	15	8	5	6	44	4	97	3	1	5	10	.333	0	0-0	0	5.21	5.83
2007	2 Tms	NL	34	32	2	0	192.2	829	207	109	99	22	14	4	12	57	3	122	3	0	9	12	.429	1	0-0	0	4.45	4.62
2008	StL	NL	33	33	0	0	200.0	839	211	88	84	18	6	4	3	49	3	119	5	0	15	6	.714	0	0-0	0	3.77	3.78
2009	StL	NL	23	22	1	0	117.2	512	125	69	62	16	3	5	3	36	2	77	3	1	6	10	.375	1	0-0	0	4.33	4.74
2010	StL	NL	18	18	0	0	92.0	431	129	75	67	9	5	4	3	35	2	54	1	0	4	8	.333	0	0-0	0	6.50	6.55
2011	StL	NL	30	30	1	0	188.1	775	178	80	71	16	8	6	3	42	1	111	1	0	14	8	.636	1	0-0	0	3.05	3.39
06	Min	AL	22	8	0	5	63.2	295	80	50	50	8	1	3	6	25	2	46	1	1	2	5	.286	0	0-0	0	6.10	7.07
06	Cin	NL	12	11	0	1	63.0	271	70	33	32	7	7	2	0	19	2	51	2	0	3	5	.375	0	0-0	0	4.36	4.57
07	Cin	NL	21	21	2	0	131.2	561	143	76	67	16	8	4	6	33	1	80	3	0	6	12	.333	1	0-0	0	4.32	4.58
07	Phi	NL	13	11	0	0	61.0	268	64	33	32	6	6	0	6	24	2	42	0	0	3	0	1.000	0	0-0	0	4.71	4.72
	Postseason		6	1	0	3	13.1	52	10	5	5	2	0	0	0	2	0	15	1	0	0	2	.000	0	0-0	0	2.12	3.38
	11 ML YEARS		322	298	8	10	1762.0	7639	1945	976	908	216	64	55	68	527	28	1095	49	4	102	106	.490	6	0-1	0	4.57	4.64

Steve Lombardozzi

Bats: B **Throws:** R **Pos:** PH-7; 2B-3; 3B-3; SS-1
Ht: 6'0" **Wt:** 170 **Born:** 9/20/1988 **Age:** 23

Year	Team	Lg	G	AB	H	2B	3B	HR	(Hm	Rd)	TB	R	RBI	RC	TBB	IBB	SO	HBP	SH	SF	SB	CS	SB%	GDP	Avg	OBP	Slg
							BATTING														**BASERUNNING**				**AVERAGES**		
2008	Nats	R	48	152	43	4	1	0	(-	-)	49	23	24	22	21	0	32	2	6	3	4	1	.80	1	.283	.371	.322
2009	Hgrstn	A	128	496	147	26	7	3	(-	-)	196	90	58	80	62	0	80	5	6	7	16	7	.70	3	.296	.375	.395
2010	Ptomc	A+	110	440	129	30	9	1	(-	-)	180	71	38	72	49	1	60	6	10	2	20	10	.67	11	.293	.370	.409
2010	Hrsbrg	AA	27	105	31	5	2	5	(-	-)	55	19	12	20	12	0	15	1	0	0	4	2	.67	2	.295	.373	.524
2011	Hrsbrg	AA	65	262	81	12	7	4	(-	-)	119	40	23	46	18	0	38	6	4	1	16	3	.84	3	.309	.366	.454
2011	Syrcse	AAA	69	294	91	13	2	4	(-	-)	120	46	29	45	21	2	40	1	6	3	14	5	.74	4	.310	.354	.408
2011	Was	NL	13	31	6	1	0	0	(0	0)	7	3	1	2	1	0	4	0	0	0	0	0	-	0	.194	.219	.226

James Loney

Bats: L **Throws:** L **Pos:** 1B-150; PH-14; DH-1
Ht: 6'2" **Wt:** 204 **Born:** 5/7/1984 **Age:** 28

Year	Team	Lg	G	AB	H	2B	3B	HR	(Hm	Rd)	TB	R	RBI	RC	TBB	IBB	SO	HBP	SH	SF	SB	CS	SB%	GDP	Avg	OBP	Slg
							BATTING														**BASERUNNING**				**AVERAGES**		
2006	LAD	NL	48	102	29	6	5	4	(3	3)	57	20	18	17	8	1	10	1	0	0	1	0	1.00	8	.284	.342	.559
2007	LAD	NL	96	344	114	18	4	15	(5	10)	185	41	67	71	28	5	48	1	0	2	0	1	.00	6	.331	.381	.538
2008	LAD	NL	161	595	172	35	6	13	(5	8)	258	66	90	79	45	6	85	3	1	7	7	4	.64	25	.289	.338	.434
2009	LAD	NL	158	576	162	25	2	13	(1	12)	230	73	90	84	70	10	68	0	1	4	7	3	.70	16	.281	.357	.399
2010	LAD	NL	161	588	157	41	2	10	(6	4)	232	67	88	81	52	9	95	4	0	4	10	5	.67	14	.267	.329	.395
2011	LAD	NL	158	531	153	30	1	12	(7	5)	221	56	65	71	42	7	67	1	3	5	4	0	1.00	8	.288	.339	.416
	Postseason		17	63	22	3	0	3	(1	2)	34	5	14	13	7	1	10	0	0	0	0	0	-	2	.349	.414	.540
	6 ML YEARS		782	2736	787	155	20	67	(25	42)	1183	323	418	403	245	38	373	10	5	22	29	13	.69	77	.288	.346	.432

Evan Longoria

Bats: R **Throws:** R **Pos:** 3B-130; DH-3; PH-2
Ht: 6'2" **Wt:** 210 **Born:** 10/7/1985 **Age:** 26

Year	Team	Lg	G	AB	H	2B	3B	HR	(Hm	Rd)	TB	R	RBI	RC	TBB	IBB	SO	HBP	SH	SF	SB	CS	SB%	GDP	Avg	OBP	Slg
							BATTING														**BASERUNNING**				**AVERAGES**		
2011	Mont*	AA	4	15	4	0	0	3	(-	-)	13	5	3	4	1	0	2	1	0	0	0	0	-	0	.267	.353	.867
2008	TB	AL	122	448	122	31	2	27	(18	9)	238	67	85	72	46	4	122	6	0	8	7	0	1.00	8	.272	.343	.531
2009	TB	AL	157	584	164	44	0	33	(16	17)	307	100	113	102	72	11	140	8	0	7	9	0	1.00	27	.281	.364	.526
2010	TB	AL	151	574	169	46	5	22	(10	12)	291	96	104	99	72	12	124	5	0	10	15	5	.75	15	.294	.372	.507
2011	TB	AL	133	483	118	26	1	31	(14	17)	239	78	99	91	80	6	93	6	0	5	3	2	.60	11	.244	.355	.495
	Postseason		21	82	16	5	0	7	(3	4)	42	12	15	9	6	0	24	0	0	0	1	0	1.00	3	.195	.250	.512
	4 ML YEARS		563	2089	573	147	8	113	(58	55)	1075	341	401	364	270	33	479	25	0	30	34	7	.83	61	.274	.360	.515

Felipe Lopez

Bats: B **Throws:** R **Pos:** 3B-24; 2B-11; PH-10; 1B-6; DH-2
Ht: 6'0" **Wt:** 205 **Born:** 5/12/1980 **Age:** 32

Year	Team	Lg	G	AB	H	2B	3B	HR	(Hm	Rd)	TB	R	RBI	RC	TBB	IBB	SO	HBP	SH	SF	SB	CS	SB%	GDP	Avg	OBP	Slg
							BATTING														**BASERUNNING**				**AVERAGES**		
2011	Drham*	AAA	48	190	58	11	0	7	(-	-)	90	25	37	32	14	1	41	2	0	1	1	0	1.00	9	.305	.357	.474
2011	Nashv*	AAA	4	12	3	0	0	0	(-	-)	3	1	1	2	4	0	1	1	0	0	0	0	-	0	.250	.471	.250
2001	Tor	AL	49	177	46	5	4	5	(3	2)	74	21	23	22	12	1	39	0	1	2	4	3	.57	2	.260	.304	.418
2002	Tor	AL	85	282	64	15	3	8	(5	3)	109	35	34	32	23	1	90	1	2	1	5	4	.56	4	.227	.287	.387
2003	Cin	NL	59	197	42	7	2	2	(-	-)	59	28	13	21	28	1	59	1	2	1	8	5	.62	2	.213	.313	.299
2004	Cin	NL	79	264	64	18	2	7	(3	4)	107	35	31	34	25	0	81	3	2	1	1	1	.50	1	.242	.314	.405
2005	Cin	NL	148	580	169	34	5	23	(16	7)	282	97	85	95	57	2	111	1	3	7	15	7	.68	8	.291	.352	.486

Year	Team	Lg	G	AB	H	2B	3B	HR	(Hm	Rd)	TB	R	RBI	RC	TBB	IBB	SO	HBP	SH	SF	SB	CS	SB%	GDP	Avg	OBP	Slg
															BATTING						BASERUNNING				AVERAGES		
2006	2 Tms	NL	156	617	169	27	3	11	(5	6)	235	98	52	84	81	1	126	2	11	3	44	12	.79	9	.274	.358	.381
2007	Was	NL	154	603	148	25	6	9	(2	7)	212	70	50	63	53	1	109	4	5	6	24	9	.73	11	.245	.308	.352
2008	2 Tms	NL	143	481	136	28	2	6	(2	4)	186	64	46	56	43	2	82	3	2	3	8	8	.50	13	.283	.343	.387
2009	2 Tms	NL	151	604	187	38	3	9	(8	1)	258	88	57	98	71	4	100	2	1	2	6	6	.50	5	.310	.383	.427
2010	2 Tms		113	391	91	18	1	8	(4	4)	135	52	37	46	44	1	81	1	3	2	8	2	.80	7	.233	.311	.345
2011	2 Tms		48	141	29	4	0	2	(1	1)	39	12	11	7	8	1	35	0	3	1	1	1	.50	4	.206	.247	.277
06	Cin	NL	85	343	92	14	1	9	(5	4)	135	55	30	48	47	1	66	0	3	1	23	6	.79	6	.268	.355	.394
06	Was	NL	71	274	77	13	2	2	(0	2)	100	43	22	36	34	0	60	2	8	2	21	6	.78	3	.281	.362	.365
08	Was	NL	100	325	76	20	0	2	(1	1)	102	34	25	25	32	1	54	2	2	2	4	5	.44	13	.234	.305	.314
08	StL	NL	43	156	60	8	2	4	(1	3)	84	30	21	31	11	1	28	1	0	1	4	3	.57	0	.385	.426	.538
09	Ari	NL	85	345	104	18	1	6	(5	1)	142	44	25	49	34	3	59	1	1	2	6	3	.67	2	.301	.364	.412
09	Mil	NL	66	259	83	20	2	3	(3	0)	116	44	32	49	37	1	41	1	0	0	0	3	.00	3	.320	.407	.448
10	StL	NL	109	376	87	18	1	7	(3	4)	128	50	36	45	43	1	77	1	3	2	8	2	.80	7	.231	.310	.340
10	Bos	AL	4	15	4	0	0	1	(1	0)	7	2	1	1	1	0	4	0	0	0	0	0	-	0	.267	.313	.467
11	TB	AL	32	97	21	4	0	2	(1	1)	31	8	8	6	4	1	28	0	1	0	1	1	.50	2	.216	.248	.320
11	Mil	NL	16	44	8	0	0	0	(0	0)	8	4	3	1	4	0	7	0	2	1	0	0	-	2	.182	.245	.182
11 ML YEARS			1185	4337	1145	219	31	90	(49	41)	1696	600	439	558	445	15	913	18	35	29	124	58	.68	66	.264	.333	.391

Javier Lopez

Pitches: L Bats: L Pos: RP-70

Ht: 6'4" Wt: 220 Born: 7/11/1977 Age: 34

Year	Team	Lg	G	GS	CG	GF	IP	BFP	H	R	ER	HR	SH	SF	HB	TBB	IBB	SO	WP	Bk	W	L	Pct	Sh	Sv-Op	Hld	ERC	ERA
			HOW MUCH HE PITCHED						WHAT HE GAVE UP												THE RESULTS							
2003	Col	NL	75	0	0	11	58.1	242	58	25	24	5	1	0	4	12	2	40	1	3	4	1	.800	0	1-2	15	3.44	3.70
2004	Col	NL	64	0	0	10	40.2	187	45	34	34	1	1	0	3	26	4	20	3	0	1	2	.333	0	0-1	12	5.28	7.52
2005	2 Tms	NL	32	0	0	6	16.1	87	26	20	20	2	1	0	1	11	3	12	0	0	1	1	.500	0	2-4	6	8.82	11.02
2006	Bos	AL	27	0	0	8	16.2	69	13	10	5	1	0	1	2	10	1	11	0	0	1	0	1.000	0	1-1	6	3.96	2.70
2007	Bos	AL	61	0	0	11	40.2	174	36	16	14	2	1	1	4	18	2	26	1	0	2	1	.667	0	0-2	13	3.59	3.10
2008	Bos	AL	70	0	0	10	59.1	247	53	18	16	4	1	1	2	27	0	38	1	0	2	0	1.000	0	0-1	10	3.73	2.43
2009	Bos	AL	14	0	0	5	11.2	64	20	13	12	1	1	1	2	9	0	5	1	0	0	2	.000	0	0-0	0	11.00	9.26
2010	2 Tms	NL	77	0	0	18	57.2	235	50	17	15	2	1	2	2	20	3	38	3	0	4	2	.667	0	0-0	0	2.85	2.34
2011	SF	NL	70	0	0	17	53.0	222	42	16	16	0	3	0	3	26	6	40	1	0	5	2	.714	0	1-3	20	2.69	2.72
05	Col	NL	3	0	0	1	2.0	13	7	5	5	0	0	0	0	0	1	1	0	0	0	0	-	0	0-1	0	18.39	22.50
05	Ari	NL	29	0	0	5	14.1	74	19	15	15	2	1	0	1	11	3	11	0	0	1	1	.500	0	2-3	6	7.63	9.42
10	Pit	NL	50	0	0	14	38.2	166	39	14	12	2	1	2	2	18	3	22	3	0	2	2	.500	0	0-0	6	4.24	2.79
10	SF	NL	27	0	0	4	19.0	69	11	3	3	0	0	0	0	2	0	16	0	0	2	0	1.000	0	0-0	5	0.90	1.42
Postseason			17	0	0	1	10.2	46	12	6	6	0	1	1	0	3	1	7	1	0	1	1	.500	0	0-0	6	3.44	5.06
9 ML YEARS			490	0	0	96	354.1	1527	343	169	156	18	10	6	23	159	21	230	11	3	20	11	.645	0	5-14	93	3.96	3.96

Jose Lopez

Bats: R Throws: R Pos: 3B-39; PH-24; 2B-20; 1B-8; DH-2

Ht: 6'0" Wt: 205 Born: 11/24/1983 Age: 28

Year	Team	Lg	G	AB	H	2B	3B	HR	(Hm	Rd)	TB	R	RBI	RC	TBB	IBB	SO	HBP	SH	SF	SB	CS	SB%	GDP	Avg	OBP	Slg
															BATTING						BASERUNNING				AVERAGES		
2011	NewOr*	AAA	32	125	50	9	0	9	(-	-)	86	24	30	34	6	0	12	2	0	2	2	0	1.00	5	.400	.430	.688
2004	Sea	AL	57	207	48	13	0	5	(4	1)	76	28	22	20	8	0	31	1	1	1	0	1	.00	1	.232	.263	.367
2005	Sea	AL	54	190	47	19	0	2	(1	1)	72	18	25	24	6	0	25	4	1	2	4	2	.67	5	.247	.282	.379
2006	Sea	AL	151	603	170	28	8	10	(4	6)	244	78	79	84	26	1	80	9	12	5	5	2	.71	17	.282	.319	.405
2007	Sea	AL	149	524	132	17	2	11	(5	6)	186	58	62	52	20	0	64	5	9	3	2	3	.40	16	.252	.284	.355
2008	Sea	AL	159	644	191	41	1	17	(13	4)	285	80	89	83	27	5	67	1	6	9	6	3	.67	14	.297	.322	.443
2009	Sea	AL	153	613	167	42	0	25	(8	17)	284	69	96	71	24	5	69	6	3	7	3	3	.50	25	.272	.303	.463
2010	Sea	AL	150	593	142	29	0	10	(3	7)	201	49	58	42	23	1	66	3	0	3	3	2	.60	20	.239	.270	.339
2011	2 Tms	NL	82	231	50	12	0	8	(4	4)	86	23	21	17	7	1	28	2	1	1	2	0	1.00	6	.216	.245	.372
11	Col	NL	38	125	26	4	0	2	(1	1)	36	10	8	7	3	0	15	1	0	0	2	0	1.00	2	.208	.233	.288
11	Fla	NL	44	106	24	8	0	6	(3	3)	50	13	13	10	4	1	13	1	1	1	0	0	-	4	.226	.259	.472
8 ML YEARS			955	3605	947	201	11	88	(42	46)	1434	403	452	393	141	13	430	31	33	31	25	16	.61	104	.263	.294	.398

Rodrigo Lopez

Pitches: R Bats: R Pos: SP-16; RP-10

Ht: 6'1" Wt: 185 Born: 12/14/1975 Age: 36

Year	Team	Lg	G	GS	CG	GF	IP	BFP	H	R	ER	HR	SH	SF	HB	TBB	IBB	SO	WP	Bk	W	L	Pct	Sh	Sv-Op	Hld	ERC	ERA
			HOW MUCH HE PITCHED						WHAT HE GAVE UP												THE RESULTS							
2011	Gwnntt*	AAA	9	9	0	0	59.0	246	59	19	17	2	0	3	2	14	0	44	2	0	6	1	.857	0	0--	-	3.15	2.59
2000	SD	NL	6	6	0	0	24.2	120	40	24	24	5	1	0	1	13	0	17	0	0	0	3	.000	0	0-0	0	9.78	8.76
2002	Bal	AL	33	28	1	0	196.2	809	172	83	78	24	2	4	5	62	4	136	2	1	15	9	.625	0	0-0	0	3.27	3.57
2003	Bal	AL	26	26	3	0	147.0	663	188	101	95	24	3	7	10	43	6	103	2	1	7	10	.412	1	0-0	0	6.00	5.82
2004	Bal	AL	37	23	1	3	170.2	714	164	71	68	21	5	2	2	54	2	121	4	1	14	9	.609	1	0-1	4	3.74	3.59
2005	Bal	AL	35	35	0	0	209.1	918	232	126	114	28	3	5	7	63	1	118	5	1	15	12	.556	0	0-0	0	4.62	4.90
2006	Bal	AL	36	29	0	2	189.0	847	234	129	124	32	5	5	4	59	2	136	6	1	9	18	.333	0	0-0	0	5.68	5.90
2007	Col	NL	14	14	0	0	79.1	333	83	43	39	11	3	5	0	21	6	43	0	0	5	4	.556	0	0-0	0	3.97	4.42
2009	Phi	NL	7	5	0	0	30.0	137	42	24	19	3	0	2	0	11	1	19	0	0	3	1	.750	0	0-0	0	6.39	5.70
2010	Ari	NL	33	33	0	0	200.0	874	227	126	111	37	14	7	3	56	1	116	2	0	7	16	.304	0	0-0	0	4.98	5.00
2011	ChC	NL	26	16	0	3	97.2	430	116	56	48	18	6	2	5	29	3	54	0	0	6	6	.500	0	0-0	0	5.58	4.42
10 ML YEARS			253	215	5	8	1344.1	5845	1498	783	720	202	41	40	36	411	26	863	21	5	81	88	.479	0	0-1	4	4.79	4.82

Wilton Lopez

Pitches: R Bats: R Pos: RP-73
Ht: 6'0" Wt: 199 Born: 7/19/1983 Age: 28

Year	Team	Lg	HOW MUCH HE PITCHED						WHAT HE GAVE UP													THE RESULTS						
			G	GS	CG	GF	IP	BFP	H	R	ER	HR	SH	SF	HB	TBB	IBB	SO	WP	Bk	W	L	Pct	Sh	Sv-Op Hld	ERC	ERA
2009	Hou	NL	8	2	0	0	19.1	97	32	21	18	4	3	2	1	8	0	9	1	0	0	2	.000	0	0-1 0	9.39	8.38
2010	Hou	NL	68	0	0	14	67.0	262	66	23	22	4	2	2	0	5	1	50	2	2	5	2	.714	0	1-3 14	2.56	2.96
2011	Hou	NL	73	0	0	13	71.0	298	72	26	22	6	4	0	3	18	3	56	1	1	2	6	.250	0	0-6 14	3.60	2.79
3 ML YEARS			149	2	0	27	157.1	657	170	70	62	14	9	4	4	31	4	115	4	3	7	10	.412	0	1-10 28	3.75	3.55

Derek Lowe

Pitches: R Bats: R Pos: SP-34
Ht: 6'6" Wt: 230 Born: 6/1/1973 Age: 39

Year	Team	Lg	HOW MUCH HE PITCHED						WHAT HE GAVE UP													THE RESULTS						
			G	GS	CG	GF	IP	BFP	H	R	ER	HR	SH	SF	HB	TBB	IBB	SO	WP	Bk	W	L	Pct	Sh	Sv-Op Hld	ERC	ERA
1997	2 Tms	AL	20	9	0	1	69.0	298	74	49	47	11	4	2	4	23	3	52	2	0	2	6	.250	0	0-2 1	4.88	6.13
1998	Bos	AL	63	10	0	8	123.0	527	126	65	55	5	4	5	4	42	5	77	8	0	3	9	.250	0	4-9 12	3.64	4.02
1999	Bos	AL	74	0	0	32	109.1	436	84	35	32	7	1	2	4	25	1	80	1	0	6	3	.667	0	15-20 22	2.14	2.63
2000	Bos	AL	74	0	0	64	91.1	379	90	27	26	6	4	1	2	22	5	79	2	1	4	4	.500	0	42-47 0	3.17	2.56
2001	Bos	AL	67	3	0	50	91.2	404	103	39	36	7	5	1	5	29	9	82	4	0	5	10	.333	0	24-30 4	4.31	3.53
2002	Bos	AL	32	32	1	0	219.2	854	166	65	63	12	5	2	12	48	0	127	5	0	21	8	.724	1	0-0 0	2.13	2.58
2003	Bos	AL	33	33	1	0	203.1	886	216	113	101	17	3	5	11	72	4	110	3	0	17	7	.708	0	0-0 0	4.32	4.47
2004	Bos	AL	33	33	0	0	182.2	839	224	138	110	15	8	4	8	71	2	105	3	0	14	12	.538	0	0-0 0	5.31	5.42
2005	LAD	NL	35	35	2	0	222.0	934	223	113	89	28	12	5	5	55	1	146	3	2	12	15	.444	2	0-0 0	3.75	3.61
2006	LAD	NL	35	34	1	1	218.0	913	221	97	88	14	7	2	5	55	2	123	3	2	16	8	.667	0	0-0 0	3.42	3.63
2007	LAD	NL	33	32	3	0	199.1	831	194	100	86	20	6	2	1	59	2	147	3	1	12	14	.462	0	0-0 0	3.55	3.88
2008	LAD	NL	34	34	1	0	211.0	851	194	84	76	14	8	7	1	45	7	147	2	0	14	11	.560	0	0-0 0	2.72	3.24
2009	Atl	NL	34	34	0	0	194.2	855	232	109	101	16	11	6	4	63	7	111	4	2	15	10	.600	0	0-0 0	4.80	4.67
2010	Atl	NL	33	33	0	0	193.2	824	204	88	86	18	10	2	4	61	10	136	4	2	16	12	.571	0	0-0 0	4.03	4.00
2011	Atl	NL	34	34	0	0	187.0	830	212	110	105	14	9	5	3	70	4	137	1	2	9	17	.346	0	0-0 0	4.56	5.05
97	Sea	AL	12	9	0	1	53.0	234	59	43	41	11	2	1	2	20	2	39	2	0	2	4	.333	0	0-0 0	5.55	6.96
97	Bos	AL	8	0	0	0	16.0	64	15	6	6	0	2	1	2	3	1	13	0	0	0	2	.000	0	0-2 1	2.78	3.38
Postseason			23	12	0	3	95.1	399	78	42	34	10	6	0	4	32	6	69	1	0	5	7	.417	0	1-2 1	2.90	3.21
15 ML YEARS			634	356	9	156	2515.2	10661	2563	1232	1101	204	97	51	73	740	62	1659	48	12	166	146	.532	3	85-108 40	3.72	3.94

Mark Lowe

Pitches: R Bats: L Pos: RP-52
Ht: 6'3" Wt: 210 Born: 6/7/1983 Age: 29

Year	Team	Lg	HOW MUCH HE PITCHED						WHAT HE GAVE UP													THE RESULTS						
			G	GS	CG	GF	IP	BFP	H	R	ER	HR	SH	SF	HB	TBB	IBB	SO	WP	Bk	W	L	Pct	Sh	Sv-Op Hld	ERC	ERA
2011	RdRck*	AAA	6	0	0	3	9.1	39	7	3	3	0	0	0	0	4	0	13	0	0	1	0	1.000	0	0- - 1	2.18	2.89
2006	Sea	AL	15	0	0	3	18.2	75	12	4	4	1	1	0	2	9	1	20	1	0	1	0	1.000	0	0-0 6	2.61	1.93
2007	Sea	AL	4	0	0	1	2.2	13	2	2	2	1	0	0	0	3	0	3	0	0	0	0	-	0	0-0 2	7.69	6.75
2008	Sea	AL	57	0	0	19	63.2	303	78	44	38	6	3	3	4	34	0	55	2	0	1	5	.167	0	1-5 1	6.10	5.37
2009	Sea	AL	75	0	0	18	80.0	339	71	39	29	7	0	4	0	29	1	69	4	0	2	7	.222	0	3-13 26	3.16	3.26
2010	2 Tms	AL	14	0	0	5	13.1	61	18	9	8	2	0	1	0	6	1	12	1	0	1	3	.250	0	0-0 4	6.82	5.40
2011	Tex	AL	52	0	0	10	45.0	196	46	26	19	6	1	1	0	19	4	42	3	0	2	3	.400	0	1-3 11	4.38	3.80
10	Sea	AL	11	0	0	4	10.1	45	11	5	4	1	0	1	0	5	1	7	1	0	1	3	.250	0	0-0 4	4.70	3.48
10	Tex	AL	3	0	0	1	3.0	16	7	4	4	1	0	0	0	1	0	5	0	0	0	0	-	0	0-0 0	15.67	12.00
Postseason			2	0	0	0	0.2	7	4	5	5	0	0	0	0	1	0	0	0	0	0	0	-	0	0-0 0	47.92	67.50
6 ML YEARS			217	0	0	56	223.1	987	227	124	100	23	5	9	6	100	7	201	11	0	7	18	.280	0	5-21 50	4.41	4.03

Jed Lowrie

Bats: B Throws: R Pos: SS-50; 3B-33; PH-7; 1B-4; DH-2; 2B-1
LAU-ree
Ht: 6'0" Wt: 180 Born: 4/17/1984 Age: 28

Year	Team	Lg	BATTING																BASERUNNING				AVERAGES		
			G	AB	H	2B	3B	HR	(Hm | Rd)	TB	R	RBI	RC	TBB	IBB	SO	HBP	SH	SF	SB	CS	SB%	GDP	Avg	OBP	Slg
2011	Pwtckt*	AAA	5	17	7	4	0	0	(- | -)	11	2	5	4	2	0	1	0	0	0	0	0	-	0	.412	.474	.647
2008	Bos	AL	81	260	67	25	3	2	(0 | 2)	104	34	46	35	35	0	68	1	2	8	1	0	1.00	8	.258	.339	.400
2009	Bos	AL	32	68	10	2	0	2	(1 | 1)	18	5	11	5	6	0	20	0	0	2	0	0	-	0	.147	.211	.265
2010	Bos	AL	55	171	49	14	0	9	(3 | 6)	90	31	24	32	25	0	25	1	0	1	1	1	.50	2	.287	.381	.526
2011	Bos	AL	88	309	78	14	4	6	(3 | 3)	118	40	36	33	23	2	60	2	1	6	1	1	.50	6	.252	.303	.382
Postseason			12	31	6	1	0	0	(0 | 0)	7	4	2	2	5	0	8	1	0	1	0	0	-	0	.194	.316	.226
4 ML YEARS			256	808	204	55	7	19	(7 | 12)	330	110	117	105	89	2	173	4	3	16	3	2	.60	16	.252	.324	.408

Jonathan Lucroy

Bats: R Throws: R Pos: C-132; PH-14
LOO-croy
Ht: 6'0" Wt: 185 Born: 6/13/1986 Age: 26

Year	Team	Lg	BATTING																BASERUNNING				AVERAGES		
			G	AB	H	2B	3B	HR	(Hm | Rd)	TB	R	RBI	RC	TBB	IBB	SO	HBP	SH	SF	SB	CS	SB%	GDP	Avg	OBP	Slg
2007	Helena	R+	61	234	80	18	2	4	(- | -)	114	35	39	42	16	0	37	1	0	2	0	3	.00	8	.342	.383	.487
2008	WV	A	65	239	74	16	1	10	(- | -)	122	45	33	48	30	1	39	3	0	2	8	1	.89	2	.310	.391	.510
2008	BrvdCt	A+	64	236	69	12	1	10	(- | -)	113	31	44	43	28	0	45	2	0	6	1	2	.33	5	.292	.364	.479
2009	Hntsvl	AA	125	419	112	32	2	9	(- | -)	175	61	66	73	78	1	66	2	1	6	1	1	.50	14	.267	.380	.418
2010	Hntsvl	AA	10	42	19	3	0	0	(- | -)	22	8	5	10	4	0	3	0	1	0	0	0	-	0	.452	.500	.524
2010	Nashv	AAA	21	80	19	4	0	2	(- | -)	29	8	11	7	3	0	14	0	0	0	0	0	-	4	.238	.265	.363
2011	Hntsvl	AA	4	11	3	1	0	0	(- | -)	4	3	4	3	6	0	1	0	0	0	1	0	1.00	0	.273	.529	.364
2010	Mil	NL	75	277	70	9	0	4	(4 | 0)	91	24	26	23	18	1	44	1	0	1	4	2	.67	9	.253	.300	.329
2011	Mil	NL	136	430	114	16	1	12	(8 | 4)	168	45	59	50	29	0	99	2	4	3	2	1	.67	7	.265	.313	.391
2 ML YEARS			211	707	184	25	1	16	(12 | 4)	259	69	85	73	47	1	143	3	4	4	6	3	.67	16	.260	.307	.366

Donny Lucy

Bats: R Throws: R Pos: C-3; PH-3; DH-1   Ht: 6'2" Wt: 205 Born: 8/8/1982 Age: 29

Year Team	Lg	G	AB	H	2B	3B	HR	(Hm	Rd)	TB	R	RBI	RC	TBB	IBB	SO	HBP	SH	SF	SB	CS	SB%	GDP	Avg	OBP	Slg
2011 Charltt*	AAA	40	133	21	1	0	4	(-	-)	34	11	9	7	10	0	35	3	1	0	0	0	-	0	.158	.233	.256
2007 CWS	AL	8	15	3	0	0	0	(0	0)	3	0	0	0	0	0	6	0	0	0	0	0	-	0	.200	.200	.200
2010 CWS	AL	7	15	5	3	0	1	(0	1)	11	2	2	4	2	0	3	1	0	0	1	0	1.00	0	.333	.444	.733
2011 CWS	AL	6	10	2	1	0	0	(0	0)	3	1	1	1	1	0	5	1	0	0	0	0	-	0	.200	.273	.300
3 ML YEARS		21	40	10	4	0	1	(0	1)	17	3	3	5	3	0	14	1	0	0	1	0	1.00	0	.250	.318	.425

Ryan Ludwick

Bats: R Throws: L Pos: LF-117; RF-14; PH-5; DH-4   Ht: 6'3" Wt: 218 Born: 7/13/1978 Age: 33

Year Team	Lg	G	AB	H	2B	3B	HR	(Hm	Rd)	TB	R	RBI	RC	TBB	IBB	SO	HBP	SH	SF	SB	CS	SB%	GDP	Avg	OBP	Slg
2011 Indy*	AAA	4	13	5	1	0	1	(-	-)	9	3	5	4	3	0	2	0	0	0	0	0	-	0	.385	.500	.692
2002 Tex	AL	23	81	19	6	0	1	(1	0)	28	10	9	6	7	0	24	0	0	0	2	1	.67	4	.235	.295	.346
2003 2 Tms	AL	47	162	40	8	1	7	(2	5)	71	17	26	28	12	1	48	0	1	0	2	0	1.00	1	.247	.299	.438
2004 Cle	AL	15	50	11	2	0	2	(0	2)	19	3	4	4	2	0	14	2	0	0	0	0	-	0	.220	.278	.380
2005 Cle	AL	19	41	9	0	0	4	(3	1)	21	8	5	3	7	0	13	0	0	0	0	1	.00	1	.220	.333	.512
2007 StL	NL	120	303	81	22	0	14	(7	7)	145	42	52	45	26	1	72	7	3	0	4	4	.50	1	.267	.339	.479
2008 StL	NL	152	538	161	40	3	37	(18	19)	318	104	113	100	62	3	146	8	1	8	4	4	.50	9	.299	.375	.591
2009 StL	NL	139	486	129	20	1	22	(4	18)	217	63	97	82	41	3	106	7	1	4	4	2	.67	6	.265	.329	.447
2010 2 Tms	NL	136	490	123	27	2	17	(8	9)	205	63	69	76	48	0	121	6	3	0	0	4	.00	13	.251	.325	.418
2011 2 Tms	NL	139	490	116	23	0	13	(6	7)	178	56	75	59	51	4	124	4	2	6	1	1	.50	9	.237	.310	.363
03 Tex	AL	8	26	4	1	0	0	(0	0)	5	3	0	1	4	0	9	0	0	0	0	0	-	0	.154	.267	.192
03 Cle	AL	39	136	36	7	1	7	(2	5)	66	14	26	27	8	1	39	0	1	0	2	0	1.00	1	.265	.306	.485
10 StL	NL	77	281	79	20	2	11	(4	7)	136	44	43	55	24	0	64	4	0	3	0	3	.00	4	.281	.343	.484
10 SD	NL	59	209	44	7	0	6	(4	2)	69	19	26	21	24	0	57	4	0	2	0	1	.00	9	.211	.301	.330
11 SD	NL	101	378	90	18	0	11	(5	6)	141	42	64	44	32	1	87	4	1	5	1	1	.50	8	.238	.301	.373
11 Pit	NL	38	112	26	5	0	2	(1	1)	37	14	11	15	19	3	37	0	1	1	0	0	-	1	.232	.341	.330
Postseason		3	12	4	0	0	0	(0	0)	4	1	1	1	1	0	0	0	0	0	0	0	-	0	.333	.385	.333
9 ML YEARS		790	2641	689	148	7	117	(49	68)	1202	366	450	403	256	12	668	36	8	23	17	17	.50	44	.261	.332	.455

Cory Luebke

Pitches: L Bats: R Pos: RP-29; SP-17   LUBE-kee   Ht: 6'4" Wt: 200 Born: 3/4/1985 Age: 27

Year Team	Lg	G	GS	CG	GF	IP	BFP	H	R	ER	HR	SH	SF	HB	TBB	IBB	SO	WP	Bk	W	L	Pct	Sh	Sv-Op	Hld	ERC	ERA
2007 Eugene	A-	8	3	0	0	24.2	95	18	6	4	2	0	0	0	2	0	26	0	0	3	0	1.000	0	0- -	-	1.50	1.46
2007 FtWyn	A	5	5	0	0	27.0	118	29	13	10	2	1	2	2	5	0	30	0	0	1	2	.333	0	0- -	-	3.63	3.33
2007 Lk Els	A+	2	1	0	0	7.0	31	10	6	6	1	0	1	1	1	0	5	0	0	1	1	.500	0	0- -	-	6.77	7.71
2008 Lk Els	A+	17	15	0	0	72.1	329	97	61	55	8	2	4	0	23	0	60	2	0	3	6	.333	0	0- -	-	5.83	6.84
2008 FtWyn	A	10	10	0	0	56.0	216	52	19	18	6	6	2	3	9	0	40	2	0	3	3	.500	0	0- -	-	3.22	2.89
2009 Lk Els	A+	14	14	1	0	88.1	347	73	24	23	3	2	1	5	17	1	80	2	1	8	2	.800	0	0- -	-	2.25	2.34
2009 SnAnt	AA	9	9	0	0	41.1	179	38	21	17	3	3	1	2	15	0	32	2	0	3	2	.600	0	0- -	-	3.41	3.70
2010 SnAnt	AA	10	8	1	0	56.1	227	41	18	15	2	6	2	2	12	0	44	2	1	5	1	.833	0	0- -	-	1.71	2.40
2010 Portlnd	AAA	9	9	0	0	57.2	227	42	22	19	6	0	1	0	17	0	44	0	0	5	0	1.000	0	0- -	-	2.32	2.97
2010 SD	NL	4	3	0	1	17.2	76	17	8	8	3	0	0	1	6	0	18	0	0	1	1	.500	0	0-0	-	4.30	4.08
2011 SD	NL	46	17	0	3	139.2	555	105	54	51	12	3	4	2	44	3	154	5	2	6	10	.375	0	0-0	3	2.43	3.29
2 ML YEARS		50	20	0	4	157.1	631	122	62	59	15	3	4	3	50	3	172	5	2	7	11	.389	0	0-0	3	2.63	3.38

Josh Lueke

Pitches: R Bats: R Pos: RP-25   LOO-kee   Ht: 6'5" Wt: 220 Born: 12/5/1984 Age: 27

Year Team	Lg	G	GS	CG	GF	IP	BFP	H	R	ER	HR	SH	SF	HB	TBB	IBB	SO	WP	Bk	W	L	Pct	Sh	Sv-Op	Hld	ERC	ERA
2007 Spkane	A-	2	0	0	0	2.2	11	2	0	0	0	0	0	1	0	0	6	0	0	0	0	-	0	0- -	-	2.01	0.00
2007 Clinton	A	20	0	0	8	35.0	145	29	19	13	4	3	0	3	10	0	31	3	0	0	3	.000	0	6- -	-	3.12	3.34
2008 Clinton	A	8	0	0	5	10.1	44	10	3	3	0	0	0	1	2	0	12	1	0	1	1	.500	0	2- -	-	2.75	2.61
2008 Bkrsfld	A+	35	0	0	22	59.0	266	65	39	33	6	1	4	4	16	0	72	3	0	2	6	.250	0	1- -	-	4.24	5.03
2009 Bkrsfld	A+	4	0	0	2	7.2	29	5	2	1	0	0	0	0	1	0	11	1	0	0	1	.000	0	1- -	-	1.12	1.17
2010 Hkry	A	17	0	0	17	19.2	80	12	4	1	0	0	1	2	5	1	36	3	1	2	1	.667	0	10- -	-	1.37	0.46
2010 Frisco	AA	15	0	0	5	18.2	77	18	9	8	2	1	0	0	5	0	26	2	0	1	1	.500	0	2- -	-	3.44	3.86
2010 WTenn	AA	6	0	0	6	7.1	27	4	0	0	0	0	0	0	0	0	14	0	0	1	0	1.000	0	3- -	-	0.61	0.00
2010 Tacom	AAA	12	0	0	10	17.1	71	14	5	4	0	1	0	0	5	0	18	1	0	1	0	1.000	0	2- -	-	2.00	2.08
2011 Tacom	AAA	30	0	0	26	42.1	176	34	17	13	1	1	1	5	12	1	35	1	0	2	4	.333	0	11- -	-	2.48	2.76
2011 Sea	AL	25	0	0	8	32.2	142	34	22	22	2	2	1	0	13	1	29	5	0	1	1	.500	0	0-0	2	3.96	6.06

Julio Lugo

Bats: R Throws: R Pos: 3B-8; PH-8; SS-5; 2B-2; PR-2   Ht: 6'1" Wt: 175 Born: 11/16/1975 Age: 36

Year Team	Lg	G	AB	H	2B	3B	HR	(Hm	Rd)	TB	R	RBI	RC	TBB	IBB	SO	HBP	SH	SF	SB	CS	SB%	GDP	Avg	OBP	Slg
2011 Gwnntt*	AAA	13	52	12	4	0	1	(-	-)	19	9	7	5	4	0	8	0	2	0	1	0	1.00	1	.231	.286	.365
2000 Hou	NL	116	420	119	22	5	10	(6	4)	181	78	40	62	37	0	93	4	3	1	22	9	.71	9	.283	.346	.431
2001 Hou	NL	140	513	135	20	3	10	(6	4)	191	93	37	63	46	0	116	5	15	5	12	11	.52	7	.263	.326	.372
2002 Hou	NL	88	322	84	15	1	8	(6	2)	125	45	35	43	28	3	74	2	4	2	9	3	.75	6	.261	.322	.388
2003 2 Tms		139	498	135	16	4	15	(5	10)	204	64	55	68	44	1	100	4	7	1	12	4	.75	7	.271	.333	.410
2004 TB	AL	157	581	160	41	4	7	(3	4)	230	83	75	86	54	0	106	5	7	8	21	5	.81	8	.275	.338	.396
2005 TB	AL	158	616	182	36	6	6	(0	6)	248	89	57	94	61	0	72	6	3	4	39	11	.78	7	.295	.362	.403
2006 2 Tms		122	435	121	22	2	12	(7	5)	183	69	37	61	39	0	76	4	5	3	24	9	.73	9	.278	.341	.421

					BATTING																BASERUNNING				AVERAGES		
Year	Team	Lg	G	AB	H	2B	3B	HR	(Hm	Rd)	TB	R	RBI	RC	TBB	IBB	SO	HBP	SH	SF	SB	CS	SB%	GDP	Avg	OBP	Slg
2007	Bos	AL	147	570	135	36	2	8	(2	6)	199	71	73	65	48	0	82	0	8	4	33	6	.85	9	.237	.294	.349
2008	Bos	AL	82	261	70	13	0	1	(1	0)	86	27	22	20	34	0	51	4	3	5	12	4	.75	13	.268	.355	.330
2009	2 Tms		88	257	72	13	5	3	(2	1)	104	40	21	37	29	0	45	1	3	3	9	0	1.00	3	.280	.352	.405
2010	Bal	AL	93	241	60	4	2	0	(0	0)	68	26	20	20	15	0	50	2	6	0	5	7	.42	6	.249	.298	.282
2011	Atl	NL	22	44	6	0	0	0	(0	0)	6	3	3	0	4	0	11	0	0	0	0	0	-	0	.136	.208	.136
03	Hou	NL	22	65	16	3	0	0	(0	0)	19	6	2	7	9	1	12	0	0	0	2	1	.67	2	.246	.338	.292
03	TB	AL	117	433	119	13	4	15	(5	10)	185	58	53	61	35	0	88	4	7	3	10	3	.77	5	.275	.333	.427
06	TB	AL	73	289	89	17	1	12	(7	5)	144	53	27	52	27	0	47	3	3	0	18	4	.82	7	.308	.373	.498
06	LAD	NL	49	146	32	5	1	0	(0	0)	39	16	10	9	12	0	29	1	2	3	6	5	.55	2	.219	.278	.267
09	Bos	AL	37	109	31	4	1	1	(1	0)	40	16	8	15	12	0	18	0	1	1	3	0	1.00	0	.284	.352	.367
09	StL	NL	51	148	41	9	4	2	(1	1)	64	24	13	22	17	0	27	1	2	2	6	0	1.00	3	.277	.351	.432
	Postseason		22	65	16	5	0	0	(0	0)	21	9	3	4	7	0	13	0	2	0	3	1	.75	6	.246	.319	.323
12	ML YEARS		1352	4758	1279	238	34	80	(38	42)	1825	688	475	619	439	4	876	37	64	40	198	69	.74	82	.269	.333	.384

Jordan Lyles

Pitches: R Bats: R Pos: SP-15; RP-5   Ht: 6'4" Wt: 212 Born: 10/19/1990 Age: 21

			HOW MUCH HE PITCHED						WHAT HE GAVE UP										THE RESULTS						
Year	Team	Lg	G	GS	CG	GF	IP	BFP	H	R	ER	HR	SH	SF	HB	TBB	IBB	SO	WP	Bk	W	L	Pct	Sh	Sv-Op Hld	ERC	ERA
2008	Grnville	R	13	13	0	0	49.2	208	44	26	22	4	0	2	3	10	0	64	1	0	3	3	.500	0	0-- -	2.73	3.99
2008	TriCity	A-	2	2	0	0	5.2	31	7	5	4	2	0	0	0	7	0	4	1	0	0	0	-	0	0-- -	11.36	6.35
2009	Lxngtn	A	26	26	0	0	144.2	601	134	56	52	5	1	5	14	38	1	167	6	0	7	11	.389	0	0-- -	3.11	3.24
2010	CpChr	AA	21	20	1	0	127.0	541	133	54	44	10	1	2	5	35	2	115	3	1	7	9	.438	0	0-- -	3.84	3.12
2010	RdRck	AAA	6	6	1	0	31.2	153	48	21	19	2	1	1	2	11	0	22	0	0	3	0	.000	0	0-- -	6.89	5.40
2011	OKCity	AAA	12	10	0	0	62.1	257	64	25	25	4	2	2	5	17	2	42	0	0	3	3	.500	0	0-- -	3.91	3.61
2011	Hou	NL	20	15	0	2	94.0	415	107	61	56	14	7	1	5	26	1	67	0	0	2	8	.200	0	0-0 -	4.87	5.36

Lance Lynn

Pitches: R Bats: R Pos: RP-16; SP-2   Ht: 6'5" Wt: 250 Born: 5/12/1987 Age: 25

			HOW MUCH HE PITCHED						WHAT HE GAVE UP										THE RESULTS						
Year	Team	Lg	G	GS	CG	GF	IP	BFP	H	R	ER	HR	SH	SF	HB	TBB	IBB	SO	WP	Bk	W	L	Pct	Sh	Sv-Op Hld	ERC	ERA
2008	Batvia	A-	6	4	0	1	18.2	73	12	5	2	0	1	0	1	4	0	22	1	0	1	0	1.000	0	0-- -	1.36	0.96
2008	QuadC	A	2	2	0	0	8.0	34	8	2	2	2	0	0	1	2	0	7	0	0	0	1	.000	0	0-- -	5.08	2.25
2009	PlmBh	A+	5	2	0	0	15.2	64	16	4	4	0	1	2	0	3	0	17	0	0	0	0	-	0	0-- -	2.77	2.30
2009	Sprgfld	AA	22	22	0	0	126.1	532	117	51	41	5	5	5	4	51	0	98	5	0	11	4	.733	0	0-- -	3.44	2.92
2009	Memp	AAA	1	1	0	0	6.2	28	5	2	2	0	0	0	0	3	0	9	1	0	0	0	-	0	0-- -	2.24	2.70
2010	Memp	AAA	29	29	0	0	164.0	709	164	96	87	21	4	3	8	62	0	141	2	2	13	10	.565	0	0-- -	4.40	4.77
2011	Memp	AAA	12	12	0	0	75.0	317	79	33	32	2	4	3	2	25	0	64	2	0	7	3	.700	0	0-- -	3.78	3.84
2011	StL	NL	18	2	0	2	34.2	136	25	12	12	3	1	0	1	11	1	40	1	0	1	1	.500	0	1-2 3	2.37	3.12

Brandon Lyon

Pitches: R Bats: R Pos: RP-15   Ht: 6'1" Wt: 195 Born: 8/10/1979 Age: 32

			HOW MUCH HE PITCHED						WHAT HE GAVE UP										THE RESULTS						
Year	Team	Lg	G	GS	CG	GF	IP	BFP	H	R	ER	HR	SH	SF	HB	TBB	IBB	SO	WP	Bk	W	L	Pct	Sh	Sv-Op Hld	ERC	ERA
2011	OKCity*	AAA	2	0	0	0	2.0	7	2	0	0	0	0	0	0	0	0	0	0	0	0	0	-	0	0-- -	2.31	0.00
2001	Tor	AL	11	11	0	0	63.0	261	63	31	30	6	2	6	1	15	0	35	0	1	5	4	.556	0	0-0 -	3.50	4.29
2002	Tor	AL	15	10	0	0	62.0	279	78	47	45	14	3	2	2	19	2	30	2	0	1	4	.200	0	0-1 0	6.24	6.53
2003	Bos	AL	49	0	0	31	59.0	273	73	33	27	6	1	4	2	19	5	50	0	0	4	6	.400	0	9-12 2	4.96	4.12
2005	Ari	NL	32	0	0	22	29.1	144	44	25	21	6	2	1	2	10	2	17	1	1	2	2	.000	0	14-15 1	7.72	6.44
2006	Ari	NL	68	0	0	22	69.1	293	68	32	30	7	3	4	0	22	7	46	1	0	2	4	.333	0	0-7 23	3.49	3.89
2007	Ari	NL	73	0	0	20	74.0	307	70	25	22	2	3	2	1	22	2	40	3	1	6	4	.600	0	2-5 35	2.93	2.68
2008	Ari	NL	61	0	0	50	59.1	265	75	34	31	7	2	1	0	13	1	44	1	0	3	5	.375	0	26-31 3	4.86	4.70
2009	Det	AL	65	0	0	27	78.2	314	56	25	25	7	5	3	2	31	9	57	3	0	6	5	.545	0	3-6 15	2.46	2.86
2010	Hou	NL	79	0	0	28	78.0	333	68	28	27	2	4	0	3	31	12	54	3	0	6	6	.500	0	20-22 19	2.73	3.12
2011	Hou	NL	15	0	0	13	13.1	71	27	17	17	4	0	0	0	5	1	6	1	0	3	3	.500	0	4-8 6	12.27	11.48
	Postseason		5	0	0	1	6.0	20	1	0	0	0	0	0	0	1	0	5	0	0	0	0	-	0	0-0 2	0.19	0.00
10	ML YEARS		468	21	0	213	586.0	2540	622	297	275	61	25	23	13	187	41	379	15	3	36	43	.456	0	78-107 98	4.08	4.22

Mike MacDougal

Pitches: R Bats: B Pos: RP-69   Ht: 6'4" Wt: 185 Born: 3/5/1977 Age: 35

			HOW MUCH HE PITCHED						WHAT HE GAVE UP										THE RESULTS						
Year	Team	Lg	G	GS	CG	GF	IP	BFP	H	R	ER	HR	SH	SF	HB	TBB	IBB	SO	WP	Bk	W	L	Pct	Sh	Sv-Op Hld	ERC	ERA
2001	KC	AL	3	3	0	0	15.1	67	18	10	8	2	0	0	1	4	0	7	3	0	1	1	.500	0	0-0 0	5.04	4.70
2002	KC	AL	6	0	0	1	9.0	38	5	5	5	0	0	0	0	7	1	10	1	0	0	1	.000	0	0-0 0	2.26	5.00
2003	KC	AL	68	0	0	61	64.0	285	64	36	29	4	3	2	8	32	0	57	6	0	3	5	.375	0	27-35 1	4.76	4.08
2004	KC	AL	13	0	0	8	11.1	61	16	8	7	2	0	0	1	9	0	14	2	0	1	1	.500	0	1-3 0	9.04	5.56
2005	KC	AL	68	0	0	53	70.1	298	69	32	26	6	1	1	3	24	2	72	6	1	5	6	.455	0	21-25 0	3.80	3.33
2006	2 Tms	AL	29	0	0	29	29.0	110	21	5	5	1	1	0	1	6	0	21	1	1	1	1	.500	0	1-2 11	1.80	1.55
2007	CWS	AL	54	0	0	8	42.1	208	50	37	32	3	0	1	2	33	3	39	8	0	2	5	.286	0	0-3 19	6.49	6.80
2008	CWS	AL	16	0	0	8	17.0	78	16	4	4	0	0	0	2	12	2	12	4	1	0	0	-	0	0-0 4	4.45	2.12
2009	2 Tms		57	0	0	41	54.1	246	52	31	26	3	2	3	3	38	3	34	10	0	1	1	.500	0	20-21 0	4.87	4.31
2010	StL	NL	17	0	0	7	18.2	92	23	15	15	1	1	0	1	12	2	14	1	0	0	1	.500	0	0-1 0	5.91	7.23
2011	LAD	NL	69	0	0	14	57.0	247	54	16	13	3	3	2	3	29	3	41	3	0	3	1	.750	0	1-2 14	4.05	2.05
06	KC	AL	4	0	0	3	4.0	13	2	0	0	0	0	0	0	0	0	2	0	0	0	0	-	0	1-1 0	0.58	0.00
06	CWS	AL	25	0	0	4	25.0	97	19	5	5	1	1	0	1	6	0	19	1	0	1	1	.500	0	0-1 11	2.10	1.80
09	CWS	AL	5	0	0	1	4.1	25	7	6	6	0	0	0	0	7	0	3	3	0	0	0	-	0	0-0 0	13.09	12.46
09	Was	NL	52	0	0	40	50.0	221	45	25	20	3	2	3	3	31	3	31	7	0	1	1	.500	0	20-21 0	4.26	3.60
11	ML YEARS		400	3	0	208	388.1	1730	388	199	170	25	11	9	25	206	16	321	45	2	18	23	.439	0	71-92 45	4.54	3.94

Ryan Madson

Pitches: R Bats: L Pos: RP-62   Ht: 6'6" Wt: 202 Born: 8/28/1980 Age: 31

Year	Team	Lg	G	GS	CG	GF	IP	BFP	H	R	ER	HR	SH	SF	HB	TBB	IBB	SO	WP	Bk	W	L	Pct	Sh	Sv-Op	Hld	ERC	ERA
2011	Clrwtr*	A+	1	1	0	0	1.0	4	0	0	0	0	0	0	1	0	0	1	0	0	0	0	-	0	0- -		0.95	0.00
2003	Phi	NL	1	0	0	0	2.0	6	0	0	0	0	0	0	0	0	0	0	0	0	0	0	-	0	0-0	0	0.00	0.00
2004	Phi	NL	52	1	0	14	77.0	312	68	23	20	6	1	1	5	19	4	55	7	0	9	3	.750	0	1-2	7	2.95	2.34
2005	Phi	NL	78	0	0	10	87.0	365	84	44	40	11	5	5	6	25	6	79	6	1	6	5	.545	0	0-7	32	3.83	4.14
2006	Phi	NL	50	17	0	8	134.1	620	176	92	85	20	9	3	10	50	4	99	12	0	11	9	.550	0	2-4	6	6.50	5.69
2007	Phi	NL	38	0	0	9	56.0	237	48	19	19	5	2	2	2	23	4	43	2	2	2	2	.500	0	1-2	7	3.28	3.05
2008	Phi	NL	76	0	0	14	82.2	340	79	29	28	6	3	2	1	23	4	67	2	1	4	2	.667	0	1-3	17	3.20	3.05
2009	Phi	NL	79	0	0	28	77.1	320	73	29	28	7	3	1	3	22	3	78	1	0	5	5	.500	0	10-16	26	3.39	3.26
2010	Phi	NL	55	0	0	21	53.0	217	42	16	15	4	2	0	4	13	3	64	2	0	6	2	.750	0	5-10	15	2.42	2.55
2011	Phi	NL	62	0	0	46	60.2	246	54	16	16	2	6	1	1	16	8	62	0	0	4	2	.667	0	32-34	3	2.45	2.37
	Postseason		29	0	0	7	30.2	130	29	8	8	2	2	2	1	10	2	37	2	0	2	1	.667	0	1-5	7	3.26	2.35
	9 ML YEARS		491	18	0	150	630.0	2663	624	268	251	61	31	15	32	191	36	547	32	4	47	30	.610	0	52-78	113	3.76	3.59

Trystan Magnuson

Pitches: R Bats: L Pos: RP-9   Ht: 6'8" Wt: 210 Born: 6/6/1985 Age: 27

Year	Team	Lg	G	GS	CG	GF	IP	BFP	H	R	ER	HR	SH	SF	HB	TBB	IBB	SO	WP	Bk	W	L	Pct	Sh	Sv-Op	Hld	ERC	ERA
2008	Lnsng	A	24	24	0	0	81.2	372	91	57	49	6	2	5	7	35	0	49	8	0	0	9	.000	0	0- -		4.95	5.40
2009	Dnedin	A+	38	0	0	12	61.2	264	56	23	19	2	4	3	4	27	1	45	3	0	4	1	.800	0	1- -		3.49	2.77
2009	NHam	AA	5	0	0	2	10.0	35	4	0	0	0	0	0	0	1	0	7	0	0	1	0	1.000	0	0- -		0.48	0.00
2010	NHam	AA	46	0	0	17	73.1	288	70	22	21	1	1	2	2	10	0	63	2	1	3	0	1.000	0	5- -		2.49	2.58
2011	Scrmto	AAA	30	0	0	14	45.1	187	34	20	15	4	2	2	2	19	3	46	3	0	4	2	.667	0	5- -		2.82	2.98
2011	Oak	AL	9	0	0	3	14.2	65	15	11	10	3	0	0	0	5	0	11	3	0	0	0	-	0	0-0	0	4.52	6.14

Paul Maholm

Pitches: L Bats: L Pos: SP-26   mah-HALL-uhm   Ht: 6'2" Wt: 224 Born: 6/25/1982 Age: 30

Year	Team	Lg	G	GS	CG	GF	IP	BFP	H	R	ER	HR	SH	SF	HB	TBB	IBB	SO	WP	Bk	W	L	Pct	Sh	Sv-Op	Hld	ERC	ERA
2005	Pit	NL	6	6	0	0	41.1	168	31	10	10	2	0	0	3	17	0	26	0	0	3	1	.750	0	0-0	0	2.79	2.18
2006	Pit	NL	30	30	0	0	176.0	788	202	98	93	19	7	4	12	81	6	117	3	1	8	10	.444	0	0-0	0	5.58	4.76
2007	Pit	NL	29	29	2	0	177.2	765	204	110	99	22	13	6	6	49	3	105	5	0	10	15	.400	1	0-0	0	4.77	5.02
2008	Pit	NL	31	31	1	0	206.1	853	201	89	85	21	8	8	9	63	2	139	2	1	9	9	.500	0	0-0	0	3.84	3.71
2009	Pit	NL	31	31	0	0	194.2	836	221	102	96	14	7	1	6	60	4	119	11	1	8	9	.471	0	0-0	0	4.45	4.44
2010	Pit	NL	32	32	1	0	185.1	840	228	119	105	15	6	6	9	62	2	102	2	0	9	15	.375	1	0-0	0	5.14	5.10
2011	Pit	NL	26	26	1	0	162.1	687	160	72	66	11	8	**10**	8	50	6	97	3	0	6	14	.300	1	0-0	0	3.57	3.66
	7 ML YEARS		185	185	5	0	1143.2	4937	1247	600	554	104	53	35	53	382	23	705	26	3	53	73	.421	3	0-0	0	4.47	4.36

Mitch Maier

Bats: L Throws: R Pos: PH-12; LF-11; RF-10; CF-9; PR-6; DH-3   MY-err   Ht: 6'2" Wt: 213 Born: 6/30/1982 Age: 30

Year	Team	Lg	G	AB	H	2B	3B	HR	(Hm	Rd)	TB	R	RBI	RC	TBB	IBB	SO	HBP	SH	SF	SB	CS	SB%	GDP	Avg	OBP	Slg
2006	KC	AL	5	13	2	0	0	0	(0	0)	2	3	0	0	2	0	4	0	0	0	0	0	-	1	.154	.267	.154
2008	KC	AL	34	91	26	1	1	0	(0	0)	29	9	9	7	2	0	18	2	2	0	0	2	.00	3	.286	.316	.319
2009	KC	AL	127	341	83	15	3	3	(1	2)	113	42	31	42	43	2	76	4	7	2	9	2	.82	6	.243	.333	.331
2010	KC	AL	117	373	98	15	6	5	(1	4)	140	41	39	49	41	2	68	0	4	3	3	2	.60	3	.263	.333	.375
2011	KC	AL	45	95	22	4	3	0	(0	0)	32	19	7	11	16	0	32	1	0	1	1	0	1.00	1	.232	.345	.337
	5 ML YEARS		328	913	231	35	13	8	(2	6)	316	114	86	109	104	4	198	7	13	6	13	6	.68	14	.253	.332	.346

Scott Maine

Pitches: L Bats: L Pos: RP-7   Ht: 6'3" Wt: 210 Born: 2/2/1985 Age: 27

Year	Team	Lg	G	GS	CG	GF	IP	BFP	H	R	ER	HR	SH	SF	HB	TBB	IBB	SO	WP	Bk	W	L	Pct	Sh	Sv-Op	Hld	ERC	ERA
2007	Yakima	A-	8	0	0	3	10.1	52	6	9	7	0	0	0	1	12	0	20	3	0	1	0	1.000	0	1- -		3.89	6.10
2008	Visalia	A+	32	0	0	16	48.0	211	48	20	17	4	2	1	4	21	1	53	10	0	3	2	.600	0	5- -		4.42	3.19
2009	Mobile	AA	36	0	0	22	47.1	206	56	16	14	2	1	0	2	15	2	46	5	0	3	3	.500	0	5- -		4.55	2.66
2009	Reno	AAA	12	0	0	4	14.2	65	13	7	6	0	0	1	0	7	0	15	0	0	1	2	.333	0	2- -		2.92	3.68
2010	Iowa	AAA	33	0	0	12	41.0	180	33	17	16	4	2	0	2	21	3	47	1	0	3	1	.750	0	5- -		3.39	3.51
2010	Tenn	AA	12	0	0	8	16.1	66	12	8	4	1	1	0	1	4	1	15	0	0	1	1	.500	0	5- -		2.01	2.20
2011	Iowa	AAA	38	0	0	30	51.1	221	38	22	21	3	4	0	5	25	2	72	3	0	3	4	.429	0	12- -		2.97	3.68
2010	ChC	NL	13	0	0	4	13.0	54	9	4	3	1	0	1	0	5	1	11	0	0	0	0	-	0	0-0	2	2.08	2.08
2011	ChC	NL	7	0	0	3	7.0	37	11	8	8	4	0	0	0	5	0	5	0	0	0	0	-	0	0-0	1	13.26	10.29
	2 ML YEARS		20	0	0	7	20.0	91	20	12	11	5	0	1	0	10	1	16	0	0	0	0	-	0	0-0	3	5.31	4.95

Martin Maldonado

Bats: R Throws: R Pos: C-3; PH-1   Ht: 6'1" Wt: 225 Born: 8/16/1986 Age: 25

Year	Team	Lg	G	AB	H	2B	3B	HR	(Hm	Rd)	TB	R	RBI	RC	TBB	IBB	SO	HBP	SH	SF	SB	CS	SB%	GDP	Avg	OBP	Slg
2004	Angels	R	25	60	13	1	0	0	(-	-)	14	5	4	3	3	0	13	2	0	0	2	1	.67	4	.217	.277	.233
2005	Angels	R	27	86	22	2	0	0	(-	-)	24	6	10	6	2	0	9	1	1	1	0	0	-	3	.256	.278	.279
2005	Orem	R+	9	32	8	0	0	1	(-	-)	11	4	2	3	2	0	6	0	0	0	0	0	-	1	.250	.294	.344
2006	Angels	R	21	63	14	1	1	0	(-	-)	17	9	6	5	7	0	12	3	3	0	0	2	.00	3	.222	.329	.270
2007	WV	A-	66	208	46	8	0	2	(-	-)	60	20	22	21	14	0	36	13	6	1	2	0	1.00	6	.221	.309	.288

(Batting — top table)

Year	Team	Lg	G	AB	H	2B	3B	HR	(Hm	Rd)	TB	R	RBI	RC	TBB	IBB	SO	HBP	SH	SF	SB	CS	SB%	GDP	Avg	OBP	Slg
2008	BrvdCt	A+	34	94	25	8	0	0	(-	-)	33	8	9	13	8	0	17	5	2	1	3	1	.75	4	.266	.352	.351
2008	Hntsvl	AA	31	98	19	2	0	2	(-	-)	27	4	8	5	4	0	24	0	4	0	0	0	-	5	.194	.225	.276
2009	BrvdCt	A+	81	251	50	9	0	2	(-	-)	65	25	21	22	30	0	51	7	9	2	2	1	.67	6	.199	.300	.259
2009	Nashv	AAA	7	18	6	1	0	0	(-	-)	7	1	3	2	1	0	2	0	0	1	0	0	-	0	.333	.350	.389
2009	Wisc	A	7	19	2	0	0	0	(-	-)	2	1	2	0	2	0	7	0	0	1	1	0	1.00	1	.105	.182	.105
2010	BrvdCt	A+	10	33	4	0	0	0	(-	-)	4	1	3	0	1	0	8	2	0	1	1	0	1.00	1	.121	.189	.121
2010	Hntsvl	AA	34	103	26	6	0	2	(-	-)	38	9	12	14	9	0	24	7	2	2	1	2	.33	5	.252	.347	.369
2010	Nashv	AAA	52	174	44	9	0	7	(-	-)	74	19	26	24	14	2	45	2	7	4	0	1	.00	6	.253	.309	.425
2011	Nashv	AAA	39	134	43	5	0	8	(-	-)	72	23	25	29	16	0	21	5	4	1	0	0	-	6	.321	.410	.537
2011	Hntsvl	AA	64	208	55	13	0	3	(-	-)	77	24	34	29	19	0	56	9	3	2	2	1	.67	6	.264	.349	.370
2011	Mil	NL	3	1	0	0	0	0	(0	0)	0	0	0	0	0	0	1	0	0	0	0	0	-	0	.000	.000	.000

Matt Maloney

Pitches: L Bats: L Pos: RP-6; SP-2 **Ht: 6'4" Wt: 212 Born: 1/16/1984 Age: 28**

Year	Team	Lg	G	GS	CG	GF	IP	BFP	H	R	ER	HR	SH	SF	HB	TBB	IBB	SO	WP	Bk	W	L	Pct	Sh	Sv-Op	Hld	ERC	ERA
2011	Lsvlle*	AAA	14	13	0	1	81.1	323	77	29	27	8	3	0	6	11	0	51	0	0	7	1	.875	0	0--	-	3.15	2.99
2011	Reds*	R	1	1	0	0	2.0	8	2	0	0	0	1	0	0	0	0	2	0	0	0	0	-	0	0--	-	1.95	0.00
2009	Cin	NL	7	7	0	0	40.2	170	43	22	22	9	2	4	3	8	1	28	0	0	2	4	.333	0	0-0	0	4.76	4.87
2010	Cin	NL	7	2	0	0	20.2	86	20	7	7	2	2	0	1	5	1	13	0	0	2	2	.500	0	0-0	0	3.39	3.05
2011	Cin	NL	8	2	0	1	18.2	96	36	21	19	7	1	2	1	4	0	13	0	0	0	3	.000	0	0-0	0	11.82	9.16
	3 ML YEARS		22	11	0	1	80.0	352	99	50	48	18	5	6	5	17	2	54	0	0	4	9	.308	0	0-0	0	5.85	5.40

Jeff Manship

Pitches: R Bats: R Pos: RP-5 **Ht: 6'2" Wt: 210 Born: 1/16/1985 Age: 27**

Year	Team	Lg	G	GS	CG	GF	IP	BFP	H	R	ER	HR	SH	SF	HB	TBB	IBB	SO	WP	Bk	W	L	Pct	Sh	Sv-Op	Hld	ERC	ERA
2011	Roch*	AAA	11	3	0	2	25.0	102	24	12	12	4	0	0	0	4	0	21	1	0	1	2	.333	0	0--	-	3.28	4.32
2011	Twins*	R	2	2	0	0	6.0	22	5	1	1	0	0	0	0	0	0	5	0	0	0	0	-	0	0--	-	1.43	1.50
2009	Min	AL	11	5	0	1	31.2	146	39	21	20	4	1	3	1	15	0	21	2	0	1	1	.500	0	0-0	0	6.11	5.68
2010	Min	AL	13	1	0	1	29.0	124	34	20	17	3	1	1	0	6	0	21	0	0	2	1	.667	0	0-0	0	4.31	5.28
2011	Min	AL	5	0	0	1	3.1	19	5	3	3	0	0	2	0	4	1	2	0	0	0	0	-	0	0-0	0	8.73	8.10
	3 ML YEARS		29	6	0	3	64.0	289	78	44	40	7	2	6	1	25	1	44	2	0	3	2	.600	0	0-0	0	5.42	5.63

Shaun Marcum

Pitches: R Bats: R Pos: SP-33 **Ht: 6'0" Wt: 197 Born: 12/14/1981 Age: 30**

Year	Team	Lg	G	GS	CG	GF	IP	BFP	H	R	ER	HR	SH	SF	HB	TBB	IBB	SO	WP	Bk	W	L	Pct	Sh	Sv-Op	Hld	ERC	ERA
2005	Tor	AL	5	0	0	3	8.0	32	6	0	0	0	0	0	0	4	0	4	0	0	0	0	-	0	0-0	0	2.58	0.00
2006	Tor	AL	21	14	0	3	78.1	357	87	44	44	14	1	2	4	38	3	65	1	0	3	4	.429	0	0-0	0	5.80	5.06
2007	Tor	AL	38	25	0	6	159.0	660	149	76	73	27	3	3	5	49	1	122	1	0	12	6	.667	0	1-2	1	4.00	4.13
2008	Tor	AL	25	25	0	0	151.1	630	126	60	57	21	1	3	8	50	2	123	3	0	7	7	.563	0	0-0	0	3.32	3.39
2010	Tor	AL	31	31	1	0	195.1	800	181	84	79	24	1	3	6	43	3	165	3	0	13	8	.619	0	0-0	0	3.24	3.64
2011	Mil	NL	33	33	0	0	200.2	823	175	84	79	22	6	6	0	57	3	158	6	0	13	7	.650	0	0-0	0	2.97	3.54
	6 ML YEARS		153	128	1	12	792.2	3302	724	348	332	108	12	17	23	241	12	637	14	0	50	32	.610	0	1-2	1	3.56	3.77

Nick Markakis

Bats: L Throws: L Pos: RF-157; 1B-3; DH-1 mar-KAY-kiss **Ht: 6'1" Wt: 200 Born: 11/17/1983 Age: 28**

Year	Team	Lg	G	AB	H	2B	3B	HR	(Hm	Rd)	TB	R	RBI	RC	TBB	IBB	SO	HBP	SH	SF	SB	CS	SB%	GDP	Avg	OBP	Slg
2006	Bal	AL	147	491	143	25	2	16	(9	7)	220	72	62	67	43	3	72	3	3	2	2	0	1.00	15	.291	.351	.448
2007	Bal	AL	161	637	191	43	3	23	(15	8)	309	97	112	103	61	5	112	5	1	6	18	6	.75	22	.300	.362	.485
2008	Bal	AL	157	595	182	48	1	20	(11	9)	292	106	87	113	99	7	113	2	0	1	10	7	.59	10	.306	.406	.491
2009	Bal	AL	161	642	188	45	2	18	(8	10)	291	94	101	97	56	0	98	3	0	10	6	2	.75	12	.293	.347	.453
2010	Bal	AL	160	629	187	45	3	12	(8	4)	274	79	60	99	73	9	93	2	0	5	7	2	.78	18	.297	.370	.436
2011	Bal	AL	160	641	182	31	1	15	(8	7)	260	72	73	90	62	6	75	7	0	6	12	3	.80	16	.284	.351	.406
	6 ML YEARS		946	3635	1073	237	12	104	(59	45)	1646	520	495	569	394	30	563	22	4	30	55	20	.73	93	.295	.365	.453

Carlos Marmol

Pitches: R Bats: R Pos: RP-75 **Ht: 6'2" Wt: 215 Born: 10/14/1982 Age: 29**

Year	Team	Lg	G	GS	CG	GF	IP	BFP	H	R	ER	HR	SH	SF	HB	TBB	IBB	SO	WP	Bk	W	L	Pct	Sh	Sv-Op	Hld	ERC	ERA
2006	ChC	NL	19	13	0	1	77.0	356	71	54	52	14	6	2	13	59	2	59	3	1	5	7	.417	0	0-0	0	6.01	6.08
2007	ChC	NL	59	0	0	6	69.1	285	41	11	11	3	1	2	4	35	3	96	5	1	5	1	.833	0	1-2	16	2.11	1.43
2008	ChC	NL	82	0	0	22	87.1	348	40	30	26	10	2	3	6	41	3	114	6	1	2	4	.333	0	7-9	30	1.86	2.68
2009	ChC	NL	79	0	0	29	74.0	335	43	29	28	2	4	1	12	65	3	93	6	1	2	4	.333	0	15-19	27	3.55	3.41
2010	ChC	NL	77	0	0	70	77.2	332	40	23	22	1	0	0	8	52	2	138	2	2	2	3	.400	0	38-43	6	2.18	2.55
2011	ChC	NL	75	0	0	61	74.0	327	54	33	33	5	4	2	9	48	2	99	4	0	2	6	.250	0	34-44	2	3.71	4.01
	Postseason		4	0	0	0	5.2	26	6	5	5	2	1	1	0	3	0	9	0	0	0	1	.000	0	0-0	0	6.73	7.94
	6 ML YEARS		391	13	0	189	459.1	1983	289	180	172	35	17	10	44	300	17	599	26	6	18	25	.419	0	95-117	75	3.14	3.37

Jeff Marquez

Pitches: R **Bats:** R **Pos:** RP-3
marr-KEZZ
Ht: 6'2" **Wt:** 190 **Born:** 8/10/1984 **Age:** 27

Year	Team	Lg	G	GS	CG	GF	IP	BFP	H	R	ER	HR	SH	SF	HB	TBB	IBB	SO	WP	Bk	W	L	Pct	Sh	Sv-Op	Hld	ERC	ERA
2004	Yanks	R	4	2	0	0	14.1	58	10	1	1	0	0	0	1	4	0	18	0	1	2	0	1.000	0	0- -	-	1.71	0.63
2004	StlsInd	A-	11	11	0	0	50.2	222	51	26	17	2	3	3	5	20	0	36	2	1	2	4	.333	0	0- -	-	4.05	3.02
2005	CtnSC	A	27	27	1	0	139.2	604	138	64	53	4	1	3	3	61	0	107	10	0	9	13	.409	0	0- -	-	3.74	3.42
2006	Tampa	A+	18	17	0	0	92.1	401	102	56	37	4	2	2	3	29	0	82	2	0	7	5	.583	0	0- -	-	4.05	3.61
2006	Yanks	R	2	2	0	0	5.2	24	7	2	2	1	0	0	0	1	0	8	0	0	0	1	.000	0	0- -	-	5.17	3.18
2007	Trntn	AA	27	27	2	0	155.1	673	166	80	63	11	1	5	8	44	0	94	9	1	15	9	.625	0	0- -	-	3.97	3.65
2008	S-WB	AAA	14	14	1	0	80.2	349	93	51	42	12	7	4	4	24	1	33	1	0	6	7	.462	0	0- -	-	5.18	4.69
2008	Yanks	R	2	1	0	0	6.2	33	10	4	4	0	0	1	1	1	0	6	1	0	1	0	1.000	0	0- -	-	5.47	5.40
2008	Trntn	AA	3	3	0	0	15.1	63	12	5	5	0	0	0	1	7	0	12	0	0	1	1	.500	0	0- -	-	2.77	2.93
2009	Charltt	AAA	11	11	0	0	45.2	227	72	51	50	12	1	3	2	22	0	27	5	0	2	8	.200	0	0- -	-	9.71	9.85
2010	Charltt	AAA	27	26	0	0	144.2	623	160	79	72	14	2	1	3	49	1	89	4	1	8	9	.471	0	0- -	-	4.55	4.48
2011	Charltt	AAA	9	9	1	0	47.2	213	53	27	21	5	3	3	6	15	0	36	1	0	3	4	.429	1	0- -	-	4.90	3.97
2011	Yanks	R	2	2	0	0	4.0	16	1	0	0	0	0	0	0	2	0	5	0	0	0	0	-	0	0- -	-	0.71	0.00
2011	Tampa	A+	4	4	0	0	13.1	58	17	9	9	2	0	0	3	4	0	7	2	0	1	1	.500	0	0- -	-	7.20	6.08
2011	Trntn	AA	3	3	0	0	20.0	72	9	7	5	2	1	1	2	3	0	11	1	0	2	0	1.000	0	0- -	-	1.16	2.25
2010	CWS	AL	1	0	0	1	1.0	5	2	2	2	1	0	0	0	0	0	0	0	0	0	0	-	0	0-0	0	16.28	18.00
2011	NYY	AL	3	0	0	3	4.0	18	5	1	1	0	0	0	0	0	0	2	0	0	0	0	-	0	0-0	0	2.93	2.25
2 ML YEARS			4	0	0	4	5.0	23	7	3	3	1	0	0	0	0	0	2	0	0	0	0	-	0	0-0	0	5.06	5.40

Jason Marquis

Pitches: R **Bats:** L **Pos:** SP-23
marr-KEE
Ht: 6'1" **Wt:** 210 **Born:** 8/21/1978 **Age:** 33

Year	Team	Lg	G	GS	CG	GF	IP	BFP	H	R	ER	HR	SH	SF	HB	TBB	IBB	SO	WP	Bk	W	L	Pct	Sh	Sv-Op	Hld	ERC	ERA
2000	Atl	NL	15	0	0	7	23.1	103	23	16	13	4	1	1	1	12	1	17	1	0	1	0	1.000	0	0-1	1	5.13	5.01
2001	Atl	NL	38	16	0	9	129.1	556	113	62	50	14	6	5	4	59	4	98	1	2	5	6	.455	0	0-2	2	3.70	3.48
2002	Atl	NL	22	22	0	0	114.1	507	127	66	64	19	4	3	3	49	3	84	4	0	8	9	.471	0	0-0	0	5.43	5.04
2003	Atl	NL	21	2	0	10	40.2	182	43	27	25	3	0	3	2	18	2	19	2	0	0	0	-	0	1-1	0	4.69	5.53
2004	StL	NL	32	32	0	0	201.1	874	215	90	83	26	5	6	10	70	1	138	6	0	15	7	.682	0	0-0	0	4.69	3.71
2005	StL	NL	33	32	3	0	207.0	868	206	110	95	29	4	3	5	69	2	100	10	3	13	14	.481	1	0-0	0	4.23	4.13
2006	StL	NL	33	33	0	0	194.1	870	221	136	130	35	12	3	16	75	2	96	2	1	14	16	.467	0	0-0	0	4.28	4.60
2007	ChC	NL	34	33	1	0	191.2	846	190	111	98	22	13	1	13	76	6	109	3	0	12	9	.571	1	0-0	0	4.35	4.53
2008	ChC	NL	29	28	0	0	167.0	738	172	87	84	15	10	7	8	70	6	91	8	1	11	9	.550	0	0-0	0	3.86	4.04
2009	Col	NL	33	33	2	0	216.0	921	218	104	97	15	10	10	4	80	6	115	6	1	15	13	.536	1	0-0	0	6.93	6.60
2010	Was	NL	13	13	0	0	58.2	276	76	47	49	9	3	0	8	24	0	31	1	1	2	9	.182	0	0-0	0	4.72	4.43
2011	2 Tms	NL	23	23	1	0	132.0	587	154	74	65	11	9	5	5	43	1	76	1	0	8	6	.571	0	0-0	0	4.19	3.95
11	Was	NL	20	20	1	0	120.2	524	132	58	53	8	8	5	4	39	1	71	1	0	8	5	.615	1	0-0	0	11.25	9.53
11	Ari	NL	3	3	0	0	11.1	63	22	16	12	3	1	0	1	4	0	5	0	0	0	2	.000	0	0-0	0	6.85	4.56
Postseason			11	3	0	6	23.2	115	25	17	12	6	4	1	0	18	1	14	0	0	0	0	-	0	0-0	0		
12 ML YEARS			326	267	7	26	1675.2	7328	1758	930	847	202	77	47	79	645	34	974	45	9	104	98	.515	4	1-4	4	4.61	4.55

Chris Marrero

Bats: R **Throws:** R **Pos:** 1B-31; PH-1
Ht: 6'3" **Wt:** 210 **Born:** 7/2/1988 **Age:** 23

Year	Team	Lg	G	AB	H	2B	3B	HR	(Hm	Rd)	TB	R	RBI	RC	TBB	IBB	SO	HBP	SH	SF	SB	CS	SB%	GDP	Avg	OBP	Slg
2006	Nats	R	22	81	25	9	0	0	(-	-)	34	10	16	13	8	1	19	1	0	1	0	0	-	0	.309	.374	.420
2007	Hgrstn	A	57	222	65	14	0	14	(-	-)	121	31	53	39	14	3	39	3	0	4	0	4	.00	5	.293	.337	.545
2007	Ptomc	A+	68	255	66	11	3	9	(-	-)	110	40	35	39	32	3	63	0	0	3	0	0	-	6	.259	.338	.431
2008	Ptomc	A+	70	256	64	15	2	11	(-	-)	116	40	38	39	25	1	55	5	0	5	2	3	.40	9	.250	.325	.453
2009	Ptomc	A+	112	414	119	21	2	16	(-	-)	192	58	65	64	42	0	97	8	0	5	0	1	.00	2	.287	.360	.464
2009	Hrsbrg	AA	23	75	20	6	0	1	(-	-)	29	9	11	10	8	0	18	1	0	0	0	1	.00	2	.267	.345	.387
2010	Hrsbrg	AA	141	524	154	28	0	18	(-	-)	236	73	82	84	43	2	102	5	0	5	1	3	.25	16	.294	.350	.450
2011	Syrcse	AAA	127	483	145	30	0	14	(-	-)	217	59	69	84	58	2	97	2	0	3	3	2	.60	14	.300	.375	.449
2011	Was	NL	31	109	27	5	0	0	(0	0)	32	6	10	7	4	0	27	1	0	3	0	0	-	1	.248	.274	.294

Sean Marshall

Pitches: L **Bats:** L **Pos:** RP-78
Ht: 6'7" **Wt:** 220 **Born:** 8/30/1982 **Age:** 29

Year	Team	Lg	G	GS	CG	GF	IP	BFP	H	R	ER	HR	SH	SF	HB	TBB	IBB	SO	WP	Bk	W	L	Pct	Sh	Sv-Op	Hld	ERC	ERA
2006	ChC	NL	24	24	0	0	125.2	563	132	85	78	20	7	1	7	59	3	77	6	0	6	9	.400	0	0-0	0	5.27	5.59
2007	ChC	NL	21	19	0	0	103.1	446	107	52	45	13	7	2	1	35	3	67	4	0	7	8	.467	0	0-0	0	4.18	3.92
2008	ChC	NL	34	7	0	6	65.1	279	60	28	28	9	4	3	4	23	4	58	3	0	3	5	.375	0	1-2	3	4.43	4.32
2009	ChC	NL	55	9	1	10	85.1	373	91	43	41	10	7	1	5	32	4	68	2	0	7	5	.583	0	0-0	7	2.26	2.65
2010	ChC	NL	80	0	0	16	74.2	307	58	25	22	3	2	2	2	25	5	90	1	0	7	8	.467	0	5-9	34	2.22	2.65
2011	ChC	NL	78	0	0	18	75.2	307	66	21	19	1	6	0	2	17	4	79	0	1	6	6	.500	0	0-0	0	2.70	2.70
Postseason			2	0	0	0	3.1	13	2	1	1	1	0	0	0	1	0	5	0	0	0	0	-	0	0-0	0		
6 ML YEARS			292	59	1	50	530.0	2275	514	254	233	56	33	9	17	191	23	439	16	1	32	40	.444	0	7-14	66	3.83	3.96

Lou Marson

Bats: R Throws: R Pos: C-78; DH-1; PH-1
MARR-son
Ht: 6'1" Wt: 200 Born: 6/26/1986 Age: 26

Year	Team	Lg	G	AB	H	2B	3B	HR	(Hm	Rd)	TB	R	RBI	RC	TBB	IBB	SO	HBP	SH	SF	SB	CS	SB%	GDP	Avg	OBP	Slg
2008	Phi	NL	1	4	2	0	0	1	(1	0)	5	2	2	2	0	0	2	0	0	0	0	0	-	0	.500	.500	1.250
2009	2 Tms		21	61	15	7	0	0	(0	0)	22	9	4	7	10	0	21	0	0	1	0	0	-	3	.246	.347	.361
2010	Cle	AL	87	262	51	15	0	3	(0	3)	75	29	22	17	26	0	55	3	2	1	8	1	.89	7	.195	.274	.286
2011	Cle	AL	79	243	56	9	2	1	(0	1)	72	26	19	19	24	0	68	1	2	2	4	2	.67	7	.230	.300	.296
09	Phi	NL	7	17	4	1	0	0	(0	0)	5	3	0	1	3	0	1	0	0	0	0	0	-	1	.235	.350	.294
09	Cle	AL	14	44	11	6	0	0	(0	0)	17	6	4	6	7	0	14	0	0	1	0	0	-	2	.250	.346	.386
4 ML YEARS			188	570	124	31	2	5	(1	4)	174	66	47	45	60	0	146	4	4	4	12	3	.80	17	.218	.295	.305

Luis Marte

Pitches: R Bats: R Pos: RP-4
Ht: 5'11" Wt: 200 Born: 8/26/1986 Age: 25

Year	Team	Lg	G	GS	CG	GF	IP	BFP	H	R	ER	HR	SH	SF	HB	TBB	IBB	SO	WP	Bk	W	L	Pct	Sh	Sv-Op Hld	ERC	ERA
2007	Tigers	R	2	2	1	0	12.0	45	8	1	1	0	0	0	1	1	0	12	1	0	2	0	1.000	1	0- - -	1.26	0.75
2007	WMich	A	15	2	0	6	35.0	140	28	13	11	2	2	0	0	11	1	36	1	0	1	2	.333	0	3- - -	2.43	2.83
2008	Lkland	A+	7	7	0	0	41.0	161	29	11	9	1	0	0	2	11	0	41	3	1	3	2	.600	0	0- - -	1.85	1.98
2008	Erie	AA	10	10	0	0	57.0	247	57	35	32	8	1	3	1	26	0	32	5	0	4	4	.500	0	0- - -	4.72	5.05
2008	Tigers	R	1	0	0	0	5.0	21	5	2	2	0	0	0	0	0	0	5	0	0	0	1	.000	0	0- - -	1.83	3.60
2009	Erie	AA	19	17	0	1	105.1	445	106	57	47	18	3	3	2	28	1	84	4	0	5	8	.385	0	0- - -	4.10	4.02
2010	Erie	AA	38	0	0	24	48.0	216	44	31	27	5	4	2	4	26	4	53	3	0	2	2	.500	0	7- - -	4.32	5.06
2010	Toledo	AAA	1	0	0	1	1.0	5	1	1	0	0	0	0	0	1	0	0	0	0	0	0	-	0	0- - -	5.48	0.00
2011	Erie	AA	23	1	0	13	53.0	204	29	10	10	3	1	1	1	18	0	68	3	1	3	0	1.000	0	3- - -	1.51	1.70
2011	Toledo	AAA	2	0	0	1	3.1	18	3	2	2	0	0	0	0	4	1	2	0	0	1	0	1.000	0	0- - -	6.15	5.40
2011	Det	AL	4	0	0	2	3.2	17	6	1	1	0	0	0	0	1	0	3	1	0	1	0	1.000	0	0-0 0	6.78	2.45

Leonys Martin

Bats: L Throws: R Pos: CF-8; PH-3
lee-OH-niss
Ht: 6'1" Wt: 180 Born: 3/6/1988 Age: 24

Year	Team	Lg	G	AB	H	2B	3B	HR	(Hm	Rd)	TB	R	RBI	RC	TBB	IBB	SO	HBP	SH	SF	SB	CS	SB%	GDP	Avg	OBP	Slg
2011	Frisco	AA	29	112	39	9	2	4	(-	-)	64	24	24	26	15	1	8	3	4	1	10	8	.56	3	.348	.435	.571
2011	Rngrs	R	4	15	4	0	2	0	(-	-)	8	2	1	2	1	0	6	0	0	0	0	1	.00	0	.267	.313	.533
2011	RdRck	AAA	40	175	46	7	1	0	(-	-)	55	27	17	19	11	0	24	3	2	1	9	2	.82	4	.263	.316	.314
2011	Tex	AL	8	8	3	1	0	0	(0	0)	4	2	0	1	0	0	1	0	0	0	0	0	-	0	.375	.375	.500

Russell Martin

Bats: R Throws: R Pos: C-125; 3B-3; PH-3; 2B-1; PR-1
Ht: 5'10" Wt: 231 Born: 2/15/1983 Age: 29

Year	Team	Lg	G	AB	H	2B	3B	HR	(Hm	Rd)	TB	R	RBI	RC	TBB	IBB	SO	HBP	SH	SF	SB	CS	SB%	GDP	Avg	OBP	Slg
2006	LAD	NL	121	415	117	26	4	10	(8	2)	181	65	65	58	45	8	57	4	1	3	10	5	.67	17	.282	.355	.436
2007	LAD	NL	151	540	158	32	3	19	(8	11)	253	87	87	84	67	1	89	7	0	6	21	9	.70	16	.293	.374	.469
2008	LAD	NL	155	553	155	25	0	13	(6	7)	219	87	69	89	90	8	83	5	0	2	18	6	.75	16	.280	.385	.396
2009	LAD	NL	143	505	126	19	0	7	(3	4)	166	63	53	62	69	9	80	11	2	1	11	6	.65	18	.250	.352	.329
2010	LAD	NL	97	331	82	13	0	5	(2	3)	110	45	26	40	48	7	61	4	1	3	6	2	.75	7	.248	.347	.332
2011	NYY	AL	125	417	99	17	0	18	(8	10)	170	57	65	56	50	1	81	5	1	3	8	2	.80	19	.237	.324	.408
Postseason			19	67	15	4	0	1	(0	1)	22	9	9	6	9	0	16	4	0	0	1	0	1.00	1	.224	.350	.328
6 ML YEARS			792	2761	737	132	7	72	(35	37)	1099	404	365	389	369	34	451	36	5	18	74	30	.71	93	.267	.359	.398

Cristhian Martinez

Pitches: R Bats: R Pos: RP-46
KRISS-jen
Ht: 6'1" Wt: 185 Born: 3/6/1982 Age: 30

Year	Team	Lg	G	GS	CG	GF	IP	BFP	H	R	ER	HR	SH	SF	HB	TBB	IBB	SO	WP	Bk	W	L	Pct	Sh	Sv-Op Hld	ERC	ERA
2011	Gwnntt	AAA	4	4	0	0	22.0	95	26	9	7	2	1	2	0	2	0	18	2	0	2	1	.667	0	0- - -	3.67	2.86
2009	Fla	NL	15	0	0	4	26.1	112	27	16	15	2	1	0	0	8	1	18	1	0	1	1	.500	0	0-1 0	3.60	5.13
2010	Atl	NL	18	0	0	8	26.0	110	28	14	14	3	0	1	0	6	1	22	1	0	0	0	-	0	0-0 0	3.87	4.85
2011	Atl	NL	46	0	0	12	77.2	308	56	30	29	8	2	0	3	19	2	58	3	0	1	3	.250	0	0-0 3	2.18	3.36
3 ML YEARS			79	0	0	24	130.0	530	111	60	58	13	3	1	3	33	4	98	5	0	2	4	.333	0	0-1 3	2.77	4.02

Fernando Martinez

Bats: L Throws: R Pos: PH-6; RF-3; DH-2; LF-1
Ht: 6'1" Wt: 200 Born: 10/10/1988 Age: 23

Year	Team	Lg	G	AB	H	2B	3B	HR	(Hm	Rd)	TB	R	RBI	RC	TBB	IBB	SO	HBP	SH	SF	SB	CS	SB%	GDP	Avg	OBP	Slg
2011	Buffalo*	AAA	63	223	58	11	0	8	(-	-)	93	29	30	32	18	0	60	1	0	1	0	0	-	10	.260	.329	.417
2009	NYM	NL	29	91	16	6	0	1	(0	1)	25	11	8	5	5	0	14	3	1	0	2	0	1.00	0	.176	.242	.275
2010	NYM	NL	7	18	3	0	0	0	(0	0)	3	1	2	1	1	0	5	2	0	1	0	1	.00	0	.167	.273	.167
2011	NYM	NL	11	22	5	2	0	1	(0	1)	10	3	2	1	1	0	7	0	0	0	0	0	-	0	.227	.261	.455
3 ML YEARS			47	131	24	8	0	2	(0	2)	38	15	12	7	7	0	26	5	1	1	2	1	.67	0	.183	.250	.290

J.D. Martinez

Bats: R Throws: R Pos: LF-51; RF-1; PH-1 Ht: 6'3" Wt: 200 Born: 8/21/1987 Age: 24

Year	Team	Lg	G	AB	H	2B	3B	HR	Hm	Rd	TB	R	RBI	RC	TBB	IBB	SO	HBP	SH	SF	SB	CS	SB%	GDP	Avg	OBP	Slg
2009	Grnville	R	19	77	31	9	1	5	-	-	57	17	23	22	5	1	14	1	0	0	0	0	-	1	.403	.446	.740
2009	TriCity	A-	53	187	61	15	2	7	-	-	101	25	33	38	15	2	30	3	0	1	1	0	1.00	8	.326	.380	.540
2010	Lxngtn	A	88	348	126	31	3	15	-	-	208	83	64	86	33	2	55	11	0	1	3	0	1.00	7	.362	.433	.598
2010	CpChr	AA	50	189	57	9	1	3	-	-	77	24	25	28	15	0	42	2	0	1	2	2	.50	9	.302	.357	.407
2011	CpChr	AA	88	317	107	25	1	13	-	-	173	50	72	72	42	2	55	4	0	7	1	0	1.00	6	.338	.414	.546
2011	Hou	NL	53	208	57	13	0	6	3	3	88	29	35	30	13	1	48	2	0	3	0	1	.00	4	.274	.319	.423

Luis Martinez

Bats: R Throws: R Pos: C-19; PH-4 Ht: 6'0" Wt: 210 Born: 4/3/1985 Age: 27

Year	Team	Lg	G	AB	H	2B	3B	HR	Hm	Rd	TB	R	RBI	RC	TBB	IBB	SO	HBP	SH	SF	SB	CS	SB%	GDP	Avg	OBP	Slg
2007	FtWyn	A	24	78	18	3	0	1	-	-	24	12	6	7	8	0	23	0	1	1	0	0	-	2	.231	.299	.308
2008	FtWyn	A	94	305	68	12	1	3	-	-	91	30	19	35	51	0	66	2	6	0	3	1	.75	13	.223	.338	.298
2009	Lk Els	A+	83	280	84	20	0	4	-	-	116	39	41	48	34	0	58	7	0	0	2	1	.67	12	.300	.389	.414
2009	Portlnd	AAA	11	35	6	0	0	0	-	-	6	3	0	1	4	1	7	0	0	0	0	0	-	3	.171	.256	.171
2010	SnAnt	AA	106	358	101	16	1	2	-	-	125	48	31	51	49	1	59	1	0	2	3	2	.60	8	.282	.368	.349
2011	Tucsn	AAA	58	198	64	17	1	1	-	-	86	24	27	33	17	1	46	2	0	2	2	0	1.00	9	.323	.379	.434
2011	SD	NL	22	59	12	1	1	1	1	0	18	7	10	9	8	2	14	1	0	0	1	0	1.00	0	.203	.309	.305

Michael Martinez

Bats: B Throws: R Pos: 3B-26; PH-20; 2B-19; SS-13; CF-12; PR-8; LF-2 Ht: 5'9" Wt: 145 Born: 9/16/1982 Age: 29

Year	Team	Lg	G	AB	H	2B	3B	HR	Hm	Rd	TB	R	RBI	RC	TBB	IBB	SO	HBP	SH	SF	SB	CS	SB%	GDP	Avg	OBP	Slg
2006	Savann	A	30	87	15	0	0	0	-	-	15	9	4	2	7	0	10	0	6	0	4	3	.57	2	.172	.234	.172
2006	Vrmnt	A-	45	159	51	5	2	1	-	-	63	26	19	22	9	0	28	2	8	1	6	8	.43	2	.321	.363	.396
2006	Ptomc	A+	7	23	5	2	0	0	-	-	7	1	2	2	1	0	1	1	0	0	1	0	1.00	1	.217	.280	.304
2007	Hgrstn	A	115	404	101	21	1	0	-	-	132	54	32	43	27	0	68	4	11	4	13	3	.81	9	.250	.301	.327
2008	Ptomc	A+	104	417	111	25	6	3	-	-	157	63	58	55	27	0	49	7	20	2	25	7	.78	7	.266	.320	.376
2009	Hrsbrg	AA	65	188	42	7	2	1	-	-	56	22	8	18	20	1	34	5	5	1	0	3	.00	5	.223	.313	.298
2009	Ptomc	A+	49	198	58	14	5	4	-	-	94	40	29	32	16	0	31	1	2	0	10	6	.63	4	.293	.347	.475
2010	Hrsbrg	AA	100	359	91	14	6	8	-	-	141	41	37	42	20	0	54	3	4	1	15	9	.63	4	.253	.298	.393
2010	Syrcse	AAA	33	126	41	7	0	3	-	-	57	16	19	20	3	1	20	3	2	1	8	3	.73	2	.325	.353	.452
2011	Phi	NL	88	209	41	5	2	3	1	2	59	25	24	20	18	0	35	0	5	2	3	0	1.00	2	.196	.258	.282

Osvaldo Martinez

Bats: R Throws: R Pos: PH-13; SS-6; PR-3; 3B-1 Ht: 5'10" Wt: 190 Born: 5/7/1988 Age: 24

Year	Team	Lg	G	AB	H	2B	3B	HR	Hm	Rd	TB	R	RBI	RC	TBB	IBB	SO	HBP	SH	SF	SB	CS	SB%	GDP	Avg	OBP	Slg
2006	Mrlns	R	49	171	45	4	1	1	-	-	54	21	21	19	19	0	21	0	3	1	7	4	.64	4	.263	.335	.316
2007	Jupiter	A+	1	0	0	0	0	0	-	-	0	0	0	0	1	0	0	0	0	0	0	0	-	0	-	1.000	-
2007	Jmstwn	A-	38	114	21	5	0	0	-	-	26	8	6	7	11	0	25	1	4	0	8	2	.80	3	.184	.262	.228
2008	Grnsbr	A	85	304	90	11	3	6	-	-	125	44	29	41	13	0	46	4	8	2	5	5	.50	12	.296	.331	.411
2009	Jupiter	A+	130	433	110	16	5	1	-	-	139	54	45	50	41	0	51	4	5	2	16	4	.80	15	.254	.323	.321
2010	Jaxnvl	AA	130	516	156	28	4	5	-	-	207	90	54	80	49	0	64	9	11	2	13	9	.59	10	.302	.372	.401
2011	NewOr	AAA	88	339	83	15	1	3	-	-	109	43	26	34	21	0	57	5	3	3	11	4	.73	9	.245	.296	.322
2010	Fla	NL	14	43	14	4	1	0	0	0	20	8	2	7	4	0	6	0	0	0	1	0	1.00	1	.326	.383	.465
2011	Fla	NL	20	23	3	0	0	0	0	0	3	0	1	0	0	0	9	0	0	0	0	0	-	1	.130	.130	.130
2 ML YEARS			34	66	17	4	1	0	0	0	23	8	3	7	4	0	15	0	1	0	1	0	1.00		.258	.300	.348

Victor Martinez

Bats: B Throws: R Pos: DH-112; C-26; 1B-6; PH-1 Ht: 6'2" Wt: 210 Born: 12/23/1978 Age: 33

Year	Team	Lg	G	AB	H	2B	3B	HR	Hm	Rd	TB	R	RBI	RC	TBB	IBB	SO	HBP	SH	SF	SB	CS	SB%	GDP	Avg	OBP	Slg
2011	Toledo*	AAA	2	6	3	1	0	0	-	-	4	1	2	2	1	0	1	0	0	1	0	0	-	1	.500	.500	.667
2002	Cle	AL	12	32	9	1	0	1	1	0	13	2	5	5	3	0	2	1	0	1	0	0	-	1	.281	.333	.406
2003	Cle	AL	49	159	46	4	0	1	0	1	53	15	16	17	13	0	21	1	0	1	0	1	.00	16	.289	.345	.333
2004	Cle	AL	141	520	147	38	1	23	8	15	256	77	108	90	63	11	69	5	0	7	0	0	-	16	.283	.359	.492
2005	Cle	AL	147	547	167	33	0	20	10	10	260	73	80	90	63	9	78	3	0	6	0	0	-	27	.305	.378	.475
2006	Cle	AL	153	572	181	37	0	16	4	12	266	82	93	96	71	8	78	3	0	11	0	0	-	19	.316	.391	.465
2007	Cle	AL	147	562	169	40	0	25	12	13	284	78	114	108	62	12	76	10	0	3	0	0	-	12	.301	.374	.505
2008	Cle	AL	73	266	74	17	0	2	2	0	97	30	35	36	24	4	32	1	0	3	0	0	-	17	.278	.337	.365
2009	2 Tms	AL	155	588	178	33	1	23	7	16	282	88	108	101	75	3	74	3	0	6	1	0	1.00	17	.303	.368	.480
2010	Bos	AL	127	493	149	32	1	20	10	10	243	64	79	74	40	5	52	2	0	7	1	0	1.00	20	.302	.351	.493
2011	Det	AL	145	540	178	40	1	12	5	7	254	76	103	103	46	6	51	2	0	5	1	0	1.00	11	.330	.380	.470
09	Cle	AL	99	377	107	21	1	15	6	9	175	56	67	64	51	3	51	2	0	5	1	0	1.00	6	.284	.368	.464
09	Bos	AL	56	211	71	12	0	8	1	7	107	32	41	37	24	0	23	1	0	0	0	0	-	0	.336	.405	.507
Postseason			14	55	16	2	0	2	1	1	24	6	9	10	5	3	10	1	0	0	0	0	-	0	.291	.361	.436
10 ML YEARS			1149	4279	1298	275	3	143	59	84	2008	585	741	720	457	58	533	30	0	53	4	3	.57	153	.303	.370	.469

Nick Masset

Pitches: R Bats: R Pos: RP-75

MASS-it

Ht: 6'4" Wt: 238 Born: 5/17/1982 Age: 30

Year	Team	Lg	G	GS	CG	GF	IP	BFP	H	R	ER	HR	SH	SF	HB	TBB	IBB	SO	WP	Bk	W	L	Pct	Sh	Sv-Op	Hld	ERC	ERA
2006	Tex	AL	8	0	0	7	8.2	36	9	4	4	0	0	2	2	2	0	4	0	0	0	0	-	0	0-0	0	4.05	4.15
2007	CWS	AL	27	1	0	4	39.1	193	52	33	31	2	1	3	2	26	5	21	4	0	2	3	.400	0	0-1	2	6.63	7.09
2008	2 Tms		42	1	0	12	62.0	271	71	32	27	7	3	1	2	26	4	43	3	1	2	0	1.000	0	1-3	2	5.27	3.92
2009	Cin	NL	74	0	0	15	76.0	292	54	22	20	6	1	1	0	24	0	70	6	0	5	1	.833	0	0-2	20	2.24	2.37
2010	Cin	NL	82	0	0	22	76.2	322	64	31	29	7	3	2	1	33	3	85	8	0	4	4	.500	0	2-5	20	3.23	3.40
2011	Cin	NL	75	0	0	21	70.1	313	76	30	29	5	2	1	1	31	6	62	2	4	3	6	.333	0	1-7	14	4.37	3.71
08	CWS	AL	32	1	0	11	44.2	203	55	26	23	4	3	1	2	21	4	32	2	1	1	0	1.000	0	1-1	2	5.78	4.63
08	Cin	NL	10	0	0	1	17.1	68	16	6	4	3	0	0	0	5	0	11	1	0	1	0	1.000	0	0-2	1	3.93	2.08
	Postseason		2	0	0	1	2.0	10	2	1	1	0	0	0	0	2	2	1	0	0	0	0	-	0	0-0	0	3.46	4.50
6 ML YEARS			308	2	0	81	333.0	1427	326	152	140	27	10	10	8	142	18	285	23	5	16	14	.533	0	4-18	58	3.98	3.78

Justin Masterson

Pitches: R Bats: R Pos: SP-33; RP-1

Ht: 6'6" Wt: 250 Born: 3/22/1985 Age: 27

Year	Team	Lg	G	GS	CG	GF	IP	BFP	H	R	ER	HR	SH	SF	HB	TBB	IBB	SO	WP	Bk	W	L	Pct	Sh	Sv-Op	Hld	ERC	ERA
2008	Bos	AL	36	9	0	6	88.1	365	68	31	31	10	1	1	8	40	3	68	1	0	6	5	.545	0	0-1	3	3.51	3.16
2009	2 Tms	AL	42	16	1	4	129.1	568	128	73	65	12	10	7	8	60	3	119	5	0	4	10	.286	0	0-1	6	4.45	4.52
2010	Cle	AL	34	29	1	0	180.0	802	197	107	94	14	5	4	11	73	4	140	12	0	6	13	.316	1	0-0	2	4.68	4.70
2011	Cle	AL	34	33	1	0	216.0	908	211	89	77	11	5	5	11	65	4	158	5	0	12	10	.545	0	0-0	3	3.43	3.21
09	Bos	AL	31	6	0	4	72.0	312	72	38	36	7	9	6	6	25	2	67	3	0	3	3	.500	0	0-1	6	4.13	4.50
09	Cle	AL	11	10	1	0	57.1	256	56	35	29	5	1	1	2	35	1	52	2	0	1	7	.125	0	0-0	0	4.85	4.55
	Postseason		9	0	0	1	9.2	40	10	3	2	0	1	0	1	5	0	9	0	0	1	0	1.000	0	0-1	4	4.85	1.86
4 ML YEARS			146	87	3	10	613.2	2643	604	300	267	47	21	17	38	238	14	485	23	0	28	38	.424	1	0-2	11	4.01	3.92

Darin Mastroianni

Bats: R Throws: R Pos: CF-1

mass-tree-AH-nee

Ht: 5'11" Wt: 190 Born: 8/26/1985 Age: 26

Year	Team	Lg	G	AB	H	2B	3B	HR	(Hm	Rd)	TB	R	RBI	RC	TBB	IBB	SO	HBP	SH	SF	SB	CS	SB%	GDP	Avg	OBP	Slg
2007	Auburn	A-	68	230	66	11	4	3	(-	-)	94	50	26	40	36	1	42	5	0	3	20	10	.67	4	.287	.391	.409
2008	Lnsng	A	95	325	74	10	4	3	(-	-)	101	51	25	38	31	0	77	4	8	1	30	1	.97	9	.228	.302	.311
2009	Dnedin	A+	61	231	75	11	2	0	(-	-)	90	55	26	46	37	0	38	4	2	0	32	7	.82	1	.325	.426	.390
2009	NHam	AA	70	247	67	10	2	1	(-	-)	84	39	25	39	39	0	45	1	4	1	38	8	.83	3	.271	.372	.340
2010	NHam	AA	132	525	158	25	7	4	(-	-)	209	101	46	94	77	0	96	3	7	5	46	10	.82	10	.301	.390	.398
2011	LsVgs	AAA	79	319	88	18	6	2	(-	-)	124	63	23	48	40	0	54	1	4	0	20	7	.74	6	.276	.358	.389
2011	NHam	AA	44	169	43	8	3	1	(-	-)	60	29	13	24	22	2	24	2	2	3	14	3	.82	1	.254	.342	.355
2011	Tor	AL	1	2	0	0	0	0	(0	0)	0	0	0	0	0	0	1	0	1	0	0	0	-	0	.000	.000	.000

Marcos Mateo

Pitches: R Bats: R Pos: RP-23

Ht: 6'1" Wt: 220 Born: 4/18/1984 Age: 28

Year	Team	Lg	G	GS	CG	GF	IP	BFP	H	R	ER	HR	SH	SF	HB	TBB	IBB	SO	WP	Bk	W	L	Pct	Sh	Sv-Op	Hld	ERC	ERA
2005	Reds	R	13	4	0	6	44.0	192	54	26	21	2	3	1	3	10	0	20	3	0	2	3	.400	0	0--	-	4.61	4.30
2006	Billings	R+	18	0	0	1	45.0	191	43	17	16	2	1	3	3	20	0	30	5	0	5	1	.833	0	1--	-	3.99	3.20
2007	Dayton	A	41	0	0	22	72.0	300	68	29	28	2	7	4	3	24	3	63	8	0	2	4	.333	0	6--	-	3.17	3.50
2008	Peoria	A	8	0	0	6	15.0	54	4	3	2	1	0	0	0	7	0	20	1	0	1	0	1.000	0	1--	-	0.99	1.20
2008	Dytona	A+	25	16	0	3	88.1	380	87	42	35	6	2	3	7	29	0	65	10	2	4	3	.571	0	0--	-	3.79	3.57
2009	Dytona	A+	3	0	0	0	9.0	32	4	0	0	0	1	0	1	2	0	7	0	0	0	0	-	0	0--	-	1.01	0.00
2009	Tenn	AA	34	14	0	0	97.1	435	97	47	44	9	6	0	10	43	0	70	1	1	3	6	.333	0	0--	-	4.54	4.07
2010	Tenn	AA	17	1	0	9	20.2	92	23	8	5	2	0	0	0	3	0	29	0	0	0	0	-	0	4--	-	3.41	2.18
2010	Iowa	AAA	8	0	0	6	12.2	55	12	8	7	0	0	0	0	4	0	15	0	0	0	0	-	0	0--	-	2.67	4.97
2010	Cubs	R	1	0	0	0	1.0	0	0	0	0	0	0	0	0	0	0	1	0	0	0	1	.000	0	0--	-	0.00	0.00
2011	Iowa	AAA	16	0	0	11	18.1	85	20	14	14	3	0	2	2	10	2	18	2	0	1	3	.250	0	2--	-	5.96	6.87
2010	ChC	NL	21	0	0	5	21.2	93	20	15	14	6	0	2	1	9	1	26	1	0	0	1	.000	0	0-0	1	5.07	5.82
2011	ChC	NL	23	0	0	8	23.0	98	24	11	11	2	1	0	0	10	0	25	1	0	1	2	.333	0	0-0	2	4.50	4.30
2 ML YEARS			44	0	0	13	44.2	191	44	26	25	8	1	2	1	19	1	51	2	0	1	3	.250	0	0-0	3	4.80	5.04

Joe Mather

Bats: R Throws: R Pos: RF-22; PH-13; LF-4; CF-3; PR-2; 1B-1; 3B-1

Ht: 6'4" Wt: 215 Born: 7/23/1982 Age: 29

Year	Team	Lg	G	AB	H	2B	3B	HR	(Hm	Rd)	TB	R	RBI	RC	TBB	IBB	SO	HBP	SH	SF	SB	CS	SB%	GDP	Avg	OBP	Slg
2011	Gwnntt*	AAA	18	62	16	5	0	1	(-	-)	24	13	4	8	8	0	14	0	0	0	2	1	.67	4	.258	.343	.387
2011	ColSpr*	AAA	55	209	67	14	1	6	(-	-)	101	36	31	38	18	0	39	0	0	7	3	0	1.00	8	.321	.363	.483
2008	StL	NL	54	133	32	7	0	8	(2	6)	63	20	18	18	12	1	32	1	0	1	1	0	1.00	2	.241	.306	.474
2010	StL	NL	36	60	13	4	0	0	(0	0)	17	7	3	1	2	0	11	0	2	0	1	1	.50	2	.217	.242	.283
2011	Atl	NL	36	75	16	4	0	1	(0	1)	23	4	9	8	6	2	23	0	2	0	0	1	.00	1	.213	.272	.307
3 ML YEARS			126	268	61	15	0	9	(2	7)	103	31	30	27	20	3	66	1	4	1	2	2	.50	5	.228	.283	.384

Scott Mathieson

Pitches: R Bats: R Pos: RP-4   MATH-ih-sun   Ht: 6'3" Wt: 230 Born: 2/27/1984 Age: 28

		HOW MUCH HE PITCHED						WHAT HE GAVE UP												THE RESULTS							
Year Team	Lg	G	GS	CG	GF	IP	BFP	H	R	ER	HR	SH	SF	HB	TBB	IBB	SO	WP	Bk	W	L	Pct	Sh	Sv-Op	Hld	ERC	ERA
2011 LV*	AAA	30	12	0	10	82.1	360	71	31	30	9	0	0	1	50	0	83	2	0	2	2	.500	0	5--	-	4.25	3.28
2006 Phi	NL	9	8	0	0	37.1	177	48	36	31	8	5	1	1	16	1	28	2	1	1	4	.200	0	0-0	0	6.71	7.47
2010 Phi	NL	2	0	0	0	1.2	12	5	3	2	0	1	0	0	2	0	1	1	0	0	0	-	0	0-0	0	20.56	10.80
2011 Phi	NL	4	0	0	2	5.0	28	9	0	0	0	1	0	2	3	0	5	0	0	0	0	-	0	0-0	0	11.01	0.00
3 ML YEARS		15	8	0	2	44.0	217	62	39	33	8	7	1	3	21	1	34	3	1	1	4	.200	0	0-0	0	7.68	6.75

Jeff Mathis

Bats: R Throws: R Pos: C-91; DH-2; PH-2   Ht: 6'0" Wt: 200 Born: 3/31/1983 Age: 29

		BATTING																		BASERUNNING				AVERAGES		
Year Team	Lg	G	AB	H	2B	3B	HR	(Hm	Rd)	TB	R	RBI	RC	TBB	IBB	SO	HBP	SH	SF	SB	CS	SB%	GDP	Avg	OBP	Slg
2005 LAA	AL	5	3	1	0	0	0	(0	0)	1	1	0	0	0	0	1	0	0	0	0	0	-	0	.333	.333	.333
2006 LAA	AL	23	55	8	2	0	2	(1	1)	16	9	6	4	7	1	14	0	0	1	0	0	-	0	.145	.238	.291
2007 LAA	AL	59	171	36	12	0	4	(3	1)	60	24	23	13	15	0	49	2	3	4	0	1	.00	1	.211	.276	.351
2008 LAA	AL	94	283	55	8	0	9	(4	5)	90	35	42	33	30	4	90	3	8	4	2	2	.50	1	.194	.275	.318
2009 LAA	AL	84	237	50	8	0	5	(3	2)	73	26	28	24	22	0	73	4	8	1	2	3	.40	2	.211	.288	.308
2010 LAA	AL	68	205	40	6	1	3	(2	1)	57	19	18	10	6	0	59	1	3	3	3	0	1.00	3	.195	.219	.278
2011 LAA	AL	93	247	43	12	0	3	(1	2)	64	18	22	12	15	2	75	2	14	3	1	2	.33	3	.174	.225	.259
Postseason		10	20	9	5	0	0	(0	0)	14	2	2	3	0	0	5	0	1	0	0	0	-	0	.450	.450	.700
7 ML YEARS		426	1201	233	48	1	26	(14	12)	361	132	139	96	95	7	361	12	36	16	8	8	.50	12	.194	.257	.301

Hideki Matsui

Bats: L Throws: R Pos: DH-109; LF-27; PH-6   Ht: 6'2" Wt: 210 Born: 6/12/1974 Age: 38

		BATTING																		BASERUNNING				AVERAGES		
Year Team	Lg	G	AB	H	2B	3B	HR	(Hm	Rd)	TB	R	RBI	RC	TBB	IBB	SO	HBP	SH	SF	SB	CS	SB%	GDP	Avg	OBP	Slg
2003 NYY	AL	163	623	179	42	1	16	(9	7)	271	82	106	96	63	5	86	3	0	6	2	2	.50	25	.287	.353	.435
2004 NYY	AL	162	584	174	34	2	31	(18	13)	305	109	108	117	88	2	103	3	0	5	3	0	1.00	11	.298	.390	.522
2005 NYY	AL	162	629	192	45	3	23	(15	8)	312	108	116	109	63	7	78	3	0	16	2	2	.50	16	.305	.367	.496
2006 NYY	AL	51	172	52	9	0	8	(1	7)	85	32	29	30	27	2	23	0	0	2	1	0	1.00	6	.302	.393	.494
2007 NYY	AL	143	547	156	28	4	25	(16	9)	267	100	103	91	73	2	73	3	0	10	4	2	.67	9	.285	.367	.488
2008 NYY	AL	93	337	99	17	0	9	(3	6)	143	43	45	56	38	6	47	3	0	0	0	0	-	10	.294	.370	.424
2009 NYY	AL	142	456	125	21	1	28	(13	15)	232	62	90	84	64	1	75	4	0	2	0	1	.00	4	.274	.367	.509
2010 LAA	AL	145	482	132	24	1	21	(10	11)	221	55	84	89	67	6	98	1	0	4	0	1	.00	10	.274	.361	.459
2011 Oak	AL	141	517	130	28	0	12	(4	8)	194	58	72	65	56	3	84	1	0	1	1	1	.50	10	.251	.321	.375
Postseason		56	205	64	15	1	10	(5	5)	111	32	39	40	27	2	33	1	0	2	0	0	-	5	.312	.391	.541
9 ML YEARS		1202	4347	1239	248	12	173	(89	84)	2030	649	753	741	539	34	667	21	0	46	13	9	.59	101	.285	.363	.467

Daisuke Matsuzaka

Pitches: R Bats: R Pos: SP-7; RP-1   DICE-kay maht-soo-ZAH-kah   Ht: 6'0" Wt: 185 Born: 9/13/1980 Age: 31

		HOW MUCH HE PITCHED						WHAT HE GAVE UP												THE RESULTS							
Year Team	Lg	G	GS	CG	GF	IP	BFP	H	R	ER	HR	SH	SF	HB	TBB	IBB	SO	WP	Bk	W	L	Pct	Sh	Sv-Op	Hld	ERC	ERA
2007 Bos	AL	32	32	1	0	204.2	874	191	100	100	25	3	2	13	80	1	201	5	0	15	12	.556	0	0-0	0	4.10	4.40
2008 Bos	AL	29	29	0	0	167.2	716	128	58	54	12	3	4	7	94	1	154	5	0	18	3	.857	0	0-0	0	3.36	2.90
2009 Bos	AL	12	12	0	0	59.1	283	81	38	38	10	1	1	2	30	1	54	8	0	4	6	.400	0	0-0	0	7.45	5.76
2010 Bos	AL	25	25	0	0	153.2	664	137	84	80	13	3	8	8	74	1	133	4	0	9	6	.600	0	0-0	0	3.89	4.69
2011 Bos	AL	8	7	0	1	37.1	167	32	24	22	4	0	0	1	23	0	26	0	0	3	3	.500	0	0-0	0	4.21	5.30
Postseason		7	7	0	0	35.2	163	39	19	19	4	0	1	1	17	0	33	4	0	3	1	.750	0	0-0	0	5.04	4.79
5 ML YEARS		106	105	1	1	622.2	2704	569	304	294	64	10	15	31	301	4	568	22	0	49	30	.620	0	0-0	0	4.14	4.25

Ryan Mattheus

Pitches: R Bats: R Pos: RP-35   MATH-uze   Ht: 6'3" Wt: 215 Born: 11/10/1983 Age: 28

		HOW MUCH HE PITCHED						WHAT HE GAVE UP												THE RESULTS							
Year Team	Lg	G	GS	CG	GF	IP	BFP	H	R	ER	HR	SH	SF	HB	TBB	IBB	SO	WP	Bk	W	L	Pct	Sh	Sv-Op	Hld	ERC	ERA
2004 Casper	R+	7	7	0	0	27.1	125	27	16	15	2	2	1	5	14	0	16	7	0	3	3	.500	0	0--	-	4.98	4.94
2005 Ashvll	A	23	23	0	0	128.1	581	142	90	83	16	3	3	12	52	0	102	14	0	7	6	.538	0	0--	-	5.25	5.82
2006 Mdest	A+	28	28	1	0	156.0	718	198	103	90	5	2	8	11	65	0	131	6	1	7	12	.368	1	0--	-	5.51	5.19
2007 Tulsa	AA	26	26	1	0	158.2	704	182	100	98	13	12	5	14	55	2	102	5	0	9	11	.450	0	0--	-	4.95	5.56
2008 Tulsa	AA	58	0	0	40	57.2	244	50	27	21	5	10	2	1	27	2	56	6	0	2	5	.286	0	17--	-	3.56	3.28
2009 Mdest	A+	3	0	0	2	4.1	18	2	1	1	0	0	0	1	2	1	2	0	0	0	1	.000	0	0--	-	1.45	2.08
2009 Tulsa	AA	3	0	0	1	5.0	17	3	2	2	0	1	0	0	1	0	5	0	0	0	1	.000	0	0--	-	1.24	3.60
2009 ColSpr	AAA	13	0	0	6	16.2	75	19	8	8	3	1	0	0	8	2	20	0	0	1	1	.500	0	0--	-	5.64	4.32
2010 Nats	R	6	3	0	0	6.0	24	5	2	1	0	0	1	0	1	0	6	1	0	0	1	.000	0	0--	-	1.74	1.50
2010 Vrmnt	A-	4	1	0	1	5.1	22	3	1	0	0	0	0	0	2	0	5	0	0	1	0	1.000	0	0--	-	1.29	0.00
2011 Hrsbrg	AA	13	0	0	12	14.2	58	9	4	4	1	0	0	1	5	2	18	1	0	2	1	.667	0	4--	-	1.78	2.45
2011 Syrcse	AAA	9	0	0	7	10.0	35	3	0	0	0	0	0	0	3	0	10	0	0	0	0	-	0	2--	-	0.58	0.00
2011 Was	NL	35	0	0	12	32.0	136	26	11	10	1	4	1	2	15	3	12	1	1	2	2	.500	0	0-0	8	2.94	2.81

Brian Matusz

Pitches: L Bats: L Pos: SP-12   MATT-uss   Ht: 6'4" Wt: 190 Born: 2/11/1987 Age: 25

Year	Team	Lg	G	GS	CG	GF	IP	BFP	H	R	ER	HR	SH	SF	HB	TBB	IBB	SO	WP	Bk	W	L	Pct	Sh	Sv-Op	Hld	ERC	ERA
2011	Frdrck*	A+	1	1	0	0	4.0	16	2	1	1	0	0	0	0	2	0	2	0	0	0	0	-	0	0--	-	1.41	2.25
2011	Bowie*	AA	1	1	0	0	6.0	22	3	0	0	0	0	0	0	1	0	1	0	0	0	0	-	0	0--	-	0.80	0.00
2011	Norfolk*	AAA	9	9	1	0	54.2	228	51	23	21	4	5	3	2	19	0	41	2	1	2	3	.400	1	0--	-	3.52	3.46
2009	Bal	AL	8	8	0	0	44.2	196	52	24	23	6	2	2	0	14	0	38	0	0	5	2	.714	0	0-0	0	4.91	4.63
2010	Bal	AL	32	32	0	0	175.2	760	173	88	84	19	6	6	7	63	3	143	1	0	10	12	.455	0	0-0	0	3.98	4.30
2011	Bal	AL	12	12	0	0	49.2	245	81	60	59	18	1	2	0	24	1	38	0	0	1	9	.100	0	0-0	0	10.88	10.69
3 ML YEARS			52	52	0	0	270.0	1201	306	172	166	43	9	10	7	101	4	219	1	0	16	23	.410	0	0-0	0	5.24	5.53

Joe Mauer

Bats: L Throws: R Pos: C-52; 1B-18; DH-14; PH-4; RF-1   Ht: 6'5" Wt: 230 Born: 4/19/1983 Age: 29

Year	Team	Lg	G	AB	H	2B	3B	HR	(Hm	Rd)	TB	R	RBI	RC	TBB	IBB	SO	HBP	SH	SF	SB	CS	SB%	GDP	Avg	OBP	Slg
2011	FtMyrs*	A+	7	23	6	2	0	1	(-	-)	11	3	6	4	3	0	1	1	0	0	0	0	-	2	.261	.370	.478
2004	Min	AL	35	107	33	8	1	6	(4	2)	61	18	17	21	11	0	14	1	0	3	1	0	1.00	1	.308	.369	.570
2005	Min	AL	131	489	144	26	2	9	(4	5)	201	61	55	78	61	12	64	1	0	3	13	1	.93	9	.294	.372	.411
2006	Min	AL	140	521	181	36	4	13	(3	10)	264	86	84	103	79	21	54	1	0	7	8	3	.73	24	.347	.429	.507
2007	Min	AL	109	406	119	27	3	7	(2	5)	173	62	60	69	57	10	51	3	2	3	7	1	.88	11	.293	.382	.426
2008	Min	AL	146	536	176	31	4	9	(7	2)	242	98	85	103	84	8	50	1	1	11	1	1	.50	21	.328	.413	.451
2009	Min	AL	138	523	191	30	1	28	(16	12)	307	94	96	123	76	14	63	2	0	5	4	1	.80	13	.365	.444	.587
2010	Min	AL	137	510	167	43	1	9	(1	8)	239	88	75	91	65	14	53	3	0	6	1	4	.20	19	.327	.402	.469
2011	Min	AL	82	296	85	15	0	3	(0	3)	109	38	30	39	32	7	38	3	0	2	0	0	-	9	.287	.360	.368
Postseason			9	35	10	1	0	0	(0	0)	11	1	1	2	4	0	7	0	0	0	0	0	-	0	.286	.359	.314
8 ML YEARS			918	3388	1096	216	16	84	(37	47)	1596	545	502	627	465	86	387	15	3	40	35	11	.76	107	.323	.403	.471

Yunesky Maya

Pitches: R Bats: R Pos: SP-5; RP-5   yoo-NESS-key MY-uh   Ht: 5'11" Wt: 170 Born: 8/28/1981 Age: 30

Year	Team	Lg	G	GS	CG	GF	IP	BFP	H	R	ER	HR	SH	SF	HB	TBB	IBB	SO	WP	Bk	W	L	Pct	Sh	Sv-Op	Hld	ERC	ERA
2010	Nats	R	2	2	0	0	7.0	27	3	2	1	0	0	0	1	2	0	5	0	0	0	0	-	0	0--	-	1.08	1.29
2010	Ptomc	A+	1	1	0	0	4.0	23	7	6	6	1	0	1	1	3	0	4	1	0	0	1	.000	0	0--	-	12.89	13.50
2010	Syrcse	AAA	2	2	0	0	10.1	44	8	2	1	0	1	0	0	5	0	9	2	1	1	1	.500	0	0--	-	2.46	0.87
2011	Syrcse	AAA	22	22	1	0	129.2	542	133	73	72	14	5	2	5	28	1	98	2	3	4	9	.308	0	0--	-	3.71	5.00
2010	Was	NL	5	5	0	0	26.0	118	30	18	17	3	2	1	2	11	1	12	2	3	0	3	.000	0	0-0	0	5.44	5.88
2011	Was	NL	10	5	0	2	32.2	142	40	19	19	3	5	1	2	10	2	15	1	0	1	1	.500	0	0-0	0	5.25	5.23
2 ML YEARS			15	10	0	2	58.2	260	70	37	36	6	7	2	4	21	3	27	3	3	1	4	.200	0	0-0	0	5.33	5.52

John Mayberry

Bats: R Throws: R Pos: PH-35; CF-32; LF-21; 1B-18; RF-10; PR-4   Ht: 6'6" Wt: 234 Born: 12/21/1983 Age: 28

Year	Team	Lg	G	AB	H	2B	3B	HR	(Hm	Rd)	TB	R	RBI	RC	TBB	IBB	SO	HBP	SH	SF	SB	CS	SB%	GDP	Avg	OBP	Slg
2011	LV*	AAA	28	113	30	8	0	4	(-	-)	50	16	15	15	5	0	23	0	0	4	2	0	1.00	2	.265	.287	.442
2009	Phi	NL	39	57	12	3	0	4	(1	3)	27	8	8	5	2	0	23	1	0	0	0	0	-	2	.211	.250	.474
2010	Phi	NL	11	12	4	0	0	2	(0	2)	10	4	6	4	1	0	4	0	0	0	0	1	.00	0	.333	.385	.833
2011	Phi	NL	104	267	73	17	1	15	(7	8)	137	37	49	44	26	2	55	2	0	1	8	3	.73	6	.273	.341	.513
3 ML YEARS			154	336	89	20	1	21	(8	13)	174	49	63	53	29	2	82	3	0	1	8	4	.67	8	.265	.328	.518

Cameron Maybin

Bats: R Throws: R Pos: CF-136; PH-2; PR-1   Ht: 6'3" Wt: 210 Born: 4/4/1987 Age: 25

Year	Team	Lg	G	AB	H	2B	3B	HR	(Hm	Rd)	TB	R	RBI	RC	TBB	IBB	SO	HBP	SH	SF	SB	CS	SB%	GDP	Avg	OBP	Slg
2011	Tucsn*	AAA	3	10	2	1	0	0	(-	-)	3	1	1	1	0	0	2	0	0	0	1	0	1.00	0	.200	.273	.300
2007	Det	AL	24	49	7	3	0	1	(0	1)	13	8	2	2	3	0	21	1	0	0	5	0	1.00	0	.143	.208	.265
2008	Fla	NL	8	32	16	2	0	0	(0	0)	18	9	2	8	3	0	8	0	1	0	4	0	1.00	0	.500	.543	.563
2009	Fla	NL	54	176	44	12	2	4	(1	3)	72	30	13	15	17	1	51	1	4	1	3	.25	2	.250	.318	.409
2010	Fla	NL	82	291	68	7	3	8	(5	3)	105	46	28	37	24	1	92	5	1	1	9	2	.82	4	.234	.302	.361
2011	SD	NL	137	516	136	24	8	9	(2	7)	203	82	40	69	44	2	125	2	4	2	40	8	.83	6	.264	.323	.393
5 ML YEARS			305	1064	271	48	13	22	(8	14)	411	175	85	131	91	4	297	9	10	4	59	13	.82	12	.255	.318	.386

Vin Mazzaro

Pitches: R Bats: R Pos: SP-4; RP-3   muh-ZAIR-oh   Ht: 6'2" Wt: 210 Born: 9/27/1986 Age: 25

Year	Team	Lg	G	GS	CG	GF	IP	BFP	H	R	ER	HR	SH	SF	HB	TBB	IBB	SO	WP	Bk	W	L	Pct	Sh	Sv-Op	Hld	ERC	ERA
2011	Omha*	AAA	22	22	0	0	123.2	563	140	63	59	9	3	2	8	60	1	107	9	0	7	2	.778	0	0--	-	5.24	4.29
2009	Oak	AL	17	17	0	0	91.1	423	120	61	54	12	1	3	4	39	3	59	5	0	4	9	.308	0	0-0	0	6.49	5.32
2010	Oak	AL	24	18	0	4	122.1	537	127	70	58	19	4	4	4	50	0	79	5	0	6	8	.429	0	0-0	0	4.86	4.27
2011	KC	AL	7	4	0	2	28.1	131	39	26	26	4	3	3	1	15	1	10	2	0	1	1	.500	0	0-0	0	7.67	8.26
3 ML YEARS			48	39	0	6	242.0	1091	286	157	138	35	8	10	9	104	4	148	12	0	11	18	.379	0	0-0	0	5.78	5.13

Zach McAllister

Pitches: R Bats: R Pos: SP-4 **Ht: 6'6" Wt: 230 Born: 12/8/1987 Age: 24**

				HOW	MUCH	HE	PITCHED			WHAT	HE	GAVE	UP											THE	RESULTS				
Year	Team	Lg	G	GS	CG	GF	IP	BFP	H	R	ER	HR	SH	SF	HB	TBB	IBB	SO	WP	Bk	W	L	Pct	Sh	Sv-Op Hld		ERC	ERA
2006	Yanks	R	11	1	0	6	35.0	148	35	14	12	1	0	0	1	12	0	28	3	0	5	2	.714	0	0- -	-	3.51	3.09
2007	StIsInd	A-	16	15	0	0	71.1	316	80	42	41	3	3	3	2	28	2	75	2	0	4	6	.400	0	0- -	-	4.38	5.17
2008	CtnSC	A	10	10	0	0	62.1	253	59	28	17	3	1	1	2	8	0	53	3	0	6	3	.667	0	0- -	-	2.54	2.45
2008	Tampa	A+	15	14	1	1	88.2	348	74	24	18	6	0	2	4	13	1	62	2	0	8	6	.571	1	1- -	-	2.26	1.83
2009	Trntn	AA	22	22	0	0	121.0	493	98	39	30	4	3	3	7	33	0	96	0	1	7	5	.583	0	0- -	-	2.39	2.23
2010	S-WB	AAA	24	24	1	0	132.2	591	166	82	78	20	3	7	6	38	0	88	7	0	8	10	.444	0	0- -	-	5.68	5.29
2010	Clmbs	AAA	3	3	0	0	17.0	78	20	13	13	1	0	4	1	7	0	11	0	0	1	2	.333	0	0- -	-	5.00	6.88
2011	Clmbs	AAA	25	25	3	0	154.2	644	155	61	57	11	6	7	6	31	0	128	1	0	12	3	.800	1	0- -	-	3.27	3.32
2011	Cle	AL	4	4	0	0	17.2	84	26	16	12	1	0	0	0	7	1	14	0	0	0	1	.000	0	0-0	0	6.41	6.11

Brian McCann

Bats: L Throws: R Pos: C-126; PH-6; DH-2 **Ht: 6'3" Wt: 230 Born: 2/20/1984 Age: 28**

						BATTING																BASERUNNING				AVERAGES		
Year	Team	Lg	G	AB	H	2B	3B	HR	(Hm	Rd)	TB	R	RBI	RC	TBB	IBB	SO	HBP	SH	SF	SB	CS	SB%	GDP	Avg	OBP	Slg
2011	Gwnntt*	AAA	2	6	2	0	0	1	(-	-)	5	1	2	1	0	0	1	0	0	0	0	0	-	1	.333	.333	.833
2005	Atl	NL	59	180	50	7	0	5	(2	3)	72	20	23	25	18	5	26	1	4	1	1	1	.50	5	.278	.345	.400
2006	Atl	NL	130	442	147	34	0	24	(10	14)	253	61	93	94	41	8	54	3	0	6	2	0	1.00	12	.333	.388	.572
2007	Atl	NL	139	504	136	38	0	18	(6	12)	228	51	92	68	35	7	74	5	2	6	0	1	.00	19	.270	.320	.452
2008	Atl	NL	145	509	153	42	1	23	(10	13)	266	68	87	84	57	4	64	4	0	3	5	0	1.00	17	.301	.373	.523
2009	Atl	NL	138	488	137	35	1	21	(12	9)	237	63	94	83	49	3	83	5	3	6	4	1	.80	17	.281	.349	.486
2010	Atl	NL	143	479	129	25	0	21	(13	8)	217	63	77	76	74	10	98	9	0	4	5	2	.71	12	.269	.375	.453
2011	Atl	NL	128	466	126	19	0	24	(15	9)	217	51	71	76	57	14	89	2	0	2	3	2	.60	10	.270	.351	.466
	Postseason		7	30	9	1	0	3	(2	1)	19	4	8	5	1	0	10	0	0	1	0	0	-	0	.300	.313	.633
	7 ML YEARS		882	3068	878	200	2	136	(68	68)	1490	377	537	506	331	51	488	29	9	28	20	7	.74	92	.286	.358	.486

Brandon McCarthy

Pitches: R Bats: R Pos: SP-25 **Ht: 6'7" Wt: 200 Born: 7/7/1983 Age: 28**

				HOW	MUCH	HE	PITCHED			WHAT	HE	GAVE	UP											THE	RESULTS				
Year	Team	Lg	G	GS	CG	GF	IP	BFP	H	R	ER	HR	SH	SF	HB	TBB	IBB	SO	WP	Bk	W	L	Pct	Sh	Sv-Op Hld		ERC	ERA
2011	Stcktn*	A+	2	2	0	0	10.0	36	7	2	0	0	0	0	0	0	0	8	0	0	1	0	1.000	0	0- -	-	1.03	0.00
2005	CWS	AL	12	10	0	0	67.0	277	62	30	30	13	1	1	2	17	0	48	1	1	3	2	.600	0	0-0	0	3.83	4.03
2006	CWS	AL	53	2	0	13	84.2	354	77	44	44	17	3	1	0	33	9	69	5	0	4	7	.364	0	0-1	11	4.10	4.68
2007	Tex	AL	23	22	0	0	101.2	459	111	62	55	9	3	5	3	48	0	59	4	1	5	10	.333	0	0-0	0	4.89	4.87
2008	Tex	AL	5	5	0	0	22.0	93	20	11	10	3	0	2	1	8	0	10	0	0	1	1	.500	0	0-0	0	3.87	4.09
2009	Tex	AL	17	17	1	0	97.1	420	96	55	50	13	0	5	3	36	0	65	0	0	7	4	.636	1	0-0	0	4.22	4.62
2011	Oak	AL	25	25	5	0	170.2	690	168	73	63	11	4	9	0	25	1	123	3	0	9	9	.500	1	0-0	0	2.80	3.32
	6 ML YEARS		135	81	6	13	543.1	2293	534	275	252	66	11	23	9	167	10	374	13	2	29	33	.468	2	0-1	11	3.80	4.17

Kyle McClellan

Pitches: R Bats: R Pos: RP-26; SP-17 **Ht: 6'2" Wt: 215 Born: 6/12/1984 Age: 28**

				HOW	MUCH	HE	PITCHED			WHAT	HE	GAVE	UP											THE	RESULTS				
Year	Team	Lg	G	GS	CG	GF	IP	BFP	H	R	ER	HR	SH	SF	HB	TBB	IBB	SO	WP	Bk	W	L	Pct	Sh	Sv-Op Hld		ERC	ERA
2008	StL	NL	68	0	0	7	75.2	327	79	37	34	7	2	1	4	26	2	59	6	0	2	7	.222	0	1-6	30	4.24	4.04
2009	StL	NL	66	0	0	14	66.2	288	56	27	25	4	5	2	2	34	2	51	4	0	4	4	.500	0	3-6	15	3.38	3.38
2010	StL	NL	68	0	0	18	75.1	307	58	20	19	9	4	1	3	23	3	60	2	0	1	4	.200	0	2-3	19	2.70	2.27
2011	StL	NL	43	17	0	5	141.2	607	143	71	66	21	6	2	6	43	3	76	6	0	12	7	.632	0	0-1	4	4.20	4.19
	Postseason		1	0	0	0	0.2	5	1	0	0	0	0	0	1	1	0	0	0	0	0	0	-	0	0-0	0	17.56	0.00
	4 ML YEARS		245	17	0	44	359.1	1529	336	155	144	41	17	6	15	126	10	246	18	0	19	22	.463	0	6-16	68	3.73	3.61

Mike McClendon

Pitches: R Bats: R Pos: RP-9 **Ht: 6'5" Wt: 215 Born: 4/3/1985 Age: 27**

				HOW	MUCH	HE	PITCHED			WHAT	HE	GAVE	UP											THE	RESULTS				
Year	Team	Lg	G	GS	CG	GF	IP	BFP	H	R	ER	HR	SH	SF	HB	TBB	IBB	SO	WP	Bk	W	L	Pct	Sh	Sv-Op Hld		ERC	ERA
2006	Helena	R+	18	4	0	6	44.2	191	54	23	21	4	0	1	0	8	0	34	3	0	3	2	.600	0	0- -	-	4.32	4.23
2007	WV	A	11	11	0	0	62.2	246	46	22	20	6	1	0	1	12	0	47	1	0	5	2	.714	0	0- -	-	1.97	2.87
2007	BrvdCt	A+	16	14	2	1	89.1	398	108	52	42	6	3	3	4	19	0	46	5	1	5	6	.455	1	1- -	-	4.35	4.23
2008	BrvdCt	A+	46	5	0	29	88.0	386	103	50	41	6	1	5	5	15	4	61	5	0	7	6	.538	0	10- -	-	3.96	4.19
2009	Hntsvl	AA	41	2	0	8	84.2	354	86	40	31	4	5	4	3	20	4	57	3	0	4	3	.571	0	3- -	-	3.25	3.30
2010	Nashv	AAA	25	3	0	9	55.1	225	53	16	15	1	2	1	3	14	0	44	2	1	4	3	.571	0	2- -	-	3.04	2.44
2010	Hntsvl	AA	7	0	0	2	14.2	52	7	1	1	0	0	1	1	1	0	15	0	0	1	1	.500	0	0- -	-	0.71	0.61
2011	Nashv	AAA	38	0	0	20	58.2	258	61	28	22	2	4	2	2	19	2	48	4	0	5	6	.455	0	8- -	-	3.52	3.38
2010	Mil	NL	17	0	0	3	21.0	84	15	7	7	2	0	0	0	7	0	21	1	0	2	0	1.000	0	0-1	3	2.31	3.00
2011	Mil	NL	9	0	0	7	13.2	59	15	5	4	1	0	0	1	3	0	10	2	0	3	0	1.000	0	0-0	0	3.99	2.63
	2 ML YEARS		26	0	0	10	34.2	143	30	12	11	3	0	0	1	10	0	31	3	0	5	0	1.000	0	0-1	3	2.94	2.86

Mike McCoy

Bats: R **Throws:** R **Pos:** SS-26; 3B-16; CF-16; PR-11; 2B-10; RF-5; DH-5; PH-3 　　　**Ht:** 5'9" **Wt:** 175 **Born:** 4/2/1981 **Age:** 31

							BATTING													BASERUNNING				AVERAGES		
Year	Team	Lg	G	AB	H	2B	3B	HR	(Hm | Rd)	TB	R	RBI	RC	TBB	IBB	SO	HBP	SH	SF	SB	CS	SB%	GDP	Avg	OBP	Slg
2011	LsVgs*	AAA	38	148	46	6	0	2	(- | -)	58	34	20	30	33	0	23	1	4	0	14	5	.74	3	.311	.440	.392
2009	Col	NL	12	5	0	0	0	0	(0 | 0)	0	1	0	0	0	0	2	0	1	0	2	0	1.00	0	.000	.000	.000
2010	Tor	AL	46	82	16	4	0	0	(0 | 0)	20	9	3	5	8	0	20	0	0	0	5	1	.83	0	.195	.267	.244
2011	Tor	AL	80	197	39	8	0	2	(0 | 2)	53	26	10	17	25	1	41	1	5	0	12	2	.86	0	.198	.291	.269
	3 ML YEARS		138	284	55	12	0	2	(0 | 2)	73	36	13	22	33	1	63	1	6	0	19	3	.86	0	.194	.280	.257

Andrew McCutchen

Bats: R **Throws:** R **Pos:** CF-155; PH-2; DH-1 　　　**Ht:** 5'10" **Wt:** 188 **Born:** 10/10/1986 **Age:** 25

							BATTING													BASERUNNING				AVERAGES		
Year	Team	Lg	G	AB	H	2B	3B	HR	(Hm | Rd)	TB	R	RBI	RC	TBB	IBB	SO	HBP	SH	SF	SB	CS	SB%	GDP	Avg	OBP	Slg
2009	Pit	NL	108	433	124	26	9	12	(8 | 4)	204	74	54	78	54	2	83	2	0	4	22	5	.81	3	.286	.365	.471
2010	Pit	NL	154	570	163	35	5	16	(8 | 8)	256	94	56	86	70	1	89	5	1	7	33	10	.77	6	.286	.365	.449
2011	Pit	NL	158	572	148	34	5	23	(10 | 13)	261	87	89	102	89	3	126	9	2	6	23	10	.70	7	.259	.364	.456
	3 ML YEARS		420	1575	435	95	19	51	(26 | 25)	721	255	199	266	213	6	298	16	3	17	78	25	.76	16	.276	.365	.458

Daniel McCutchen

Pitches: R **Bats:** R **Pos:** RP-73 　　　**Ht:** 6'2" **Wt:** 210 **Born:** 9/26/1982 **Age:** 29

			HOW MUCH HE PITCHED						WHAT HE GAVE UP												THE RESULTS					
Year	Team	Lg	G	GS	CG	GF	IP	BFP	H	R	ER	HR	SH	SF	HB	TBB	IBB	SO	WP	Bk	W	L	Pct	Sh	Sv-Op	Hld	ERC	ERA
2009	Pit	NL	6	6	0	0	36.1	155	38	17	17	6	3	0	1	11	2	19	0	0	1	2	.333	0	0-0	0	4.45	4.21
2010	Pit	NL	28	9	0	4	67.2	316	83	48	46	13	4	4	2	28	0	38	2	0	2	5	.286	0	0-0	0	6.16	6.12
2011	Pit	NL	73	0	0	15	84.2	364	87	38	35	7	4	3	4	33	5	47	7	0	5	3	.625	0	0-0	10	4.23	3.72
	3 ML YEARS		107	15	0	19	188.2	835	208	103	98	26	11	7	7	72	7	104	9	0	8	10	.444	0	0-0	10	4.95	4.67

Darnell McDonald

Bats: R **Throws:** R **Pos:** RF-37; LF-23; CF-13; PR-13; PH-9; DH-5 　　　**Ht:** 5'11" **Wt:** 205 **Born:** 11/17/1978 **Age:** 33

							BATTING													BASERUNNING				AVERAGES		
Year	Team	Lg	G	AB	H	2B	3B	HR	(Hm	Rd)	TB	R	RBI	RC	TBB	IBB	SO	HBP	SH	SF	SB	CS	SB%	GDP	Avg	OBP	Slg
2011	Pwtckt*	AAA	9	29	10	3	0	2	(-	-)	19	6	11	7	5	0	6	1	0	0	1	2	.33	0	.345	.457	.655
2004	Bal	AL	17	32	5	1	0	0	(0	0)	6	3	1	2	2	0	6	0	0	0	1	0	1.00	0	.156	.206	.188
2007	Min	AL	4	10	1	0	0	0	(0	0)	1	0	0	0	1	0	3	0	0	0	0	0	-	0	.100	.182	.100
2009	Cin	NL	47	105	28	6	1	2	(2	0)	42	12	10	10	5	0	31	1	0	0	1	0	1.00	4	.267	.306	.400
2010	Bos	AL	117	319	86	18	3	9	(5	4)	137	40	34	46	30	1	85	2	12	0	9	1	.90	5	.270	.336	.429
2011	Bos	AL	79	157	37	6	1	6	(2	4)	63	26	24	19	14	0	33	2	0	2	2	3	.40	3	.236	.303	.401
	5 ML YEARS		264	623	157	31	5	17	(9	8)	249	81	69	77	52	1	158	5	12	2	13	4	.76	12	.252	.314	.400

James McDonald

Pitches: R **Bats:** L **Pos:** SP-31 　　　**Ht:** 6'4" **Wt:** 200 **Born:** 10/19/1984 **Age:** 27

			HOW MUCH HE PITCHED						WHAT HE GAVE UP												THE RESULTS					
Year	Team	Lg	G	GS	CG	GF	IP	BFP	H	R	ER	HR	SH	SF	HB	TBB	IBB	SO	WP	Bk	W	L	Pct	Sh	Sv-Op	Hld	ERC	ERA
2008	LAD	NL	4	0	0	1	6.0	24	5	0	0	0	1	0	0	1	0	2	0	0	0	0	-	0	0-0	0	1.74	0.00
2009	LAD	NL	45	4	0	10	63.0	280	60	34	28	6	2	3	5	34	5	54	4	0	5	5	.500	0	0-0	5	4.53	4.00
2010	2 Tms	NL	15	12	0	0	71.2	306	70	32	32	4	5	3	0	29	5	68	5	0	4	6	.400	0	0-0	1	3.56	4.02
2011	Pit	NL	31	31	0	0	171.0	754	176	86	80	24	6	5	7	78	4	142	5	1	9	9	.500	0	0-0	0	4.92	4.21
	10 LAD	NL	4	1	0	0	7.2	38	11	7	7	1	0	1	0	5	1	7	0	0	0	1	.000	0	0-0	1	7.83	8.22
	10 Pit	NL	11	11	0	0	64.0	268	59	25	25	3	5	2	0	24	4	61	5	0	4	5	.444	0	0-0	0	3.12	3.52
	Postseason		2	0	0	0	5.1	21	3	0	0	0	0	0	0	2	0	7	0	0	0	0	-	0	0-0	0	1.35	0.00
	4 ML YEARS		95	47	0	11	311.2	1364	311	152	140	34	14	11	12	142	14	266	14	1	18	20	.474	0	0-0	6	4.45	4.04

John McDonald

Bats: R **Throws:** R **Pos:** SS-38; 3B-26; 2B-21; PR-5; PH-3 　　　**Ht:** 5'9" **Wt:** 180 **Born:** 9/24/1974 **Age:** 37

							BATTING													BASERUNNING				AVERAGES		
Year	Team	Lg	G	AB	H	2B	3B	HR	(Hm	Rd)	TB	R	RBI	RC	TBB	IBB	SO	HBP	SH	SF	SB	CS	SB%	GDP	Avg	OBP	Slg
2011	Dnedin*	A+	1	4	1	0	0	0	(-	-)	1	0	0	0	0	0	0	0	0	0	0	0	-	0	.250	.250	.250
1999	Cle	AL	18	21	7	0	0	0	(0	0)	7	2	0	1	0	0	3	0	0	0	0	1	.00	2	.333	.333	.333
2000	Cle	AL	9	9	4	0	0	0	(0	0)	4	0	0	2	0	0	1	0	0	0	0	0	-	0	.444	.444	.444
2001	Cle	AL	17	22	2	1	0	0	(0	0)	3	1	0	0	1	0	7	1	1	0	0	0	-	0	.091	.167	.136
2002	Cle	AL	93	264	66	11	3	1	(0	1)	86	35	12	24	10	0	50	5	7	2	3	0	1.00	4	.250	.288	.326
2003	Cle	AL	82	214	46	9	1	1	(0	1)	60	21	14	18	11	0	31	2	4	2	3	3	.50	4	.215	.258	.280
2004	Cle	AL	66	93	19	5	1	2	(0	2)	32	17	7	6	4	0	11	0	3	0	0	0	-	2	.204	.237	.344
2005	2 Tms	AL	68	166	46	6	1	0	(0	0)	54	18	16	19	11	0	24	2	3	2	6	1	.86	6	.277	.326	.325
2006	Tor	AL	104	260	58	7	3	3	(1	2)	80	35	23	20	16	0	41	2	6	2	7	2	.78	8	.223	.271	.308
2007	Tor	AL	123	327	82	20	2	1	(1	0)	109	32	31	35	11	0	48	2	12	1	7	2	.78	4	.251	.279	.333
2008	Tor	AL	84	186	39	8	0	1	(1	0)	50	21	18	11	10	0	25	2	7	1	3	1	.75	2	.210	.255	.269
2009	Tor	AL	73	151	39	7	0	4	(2	2)	58	18	13	16	1	0	18	0	1	1	0	2	.00	1	.258	.271	.384
2010	Tor	AL	63	152	38	9	2	6	(3	3)	69	27	23	20	6	0	26	0	2	3	2	1	.67	5	.250	.273	.454
2011	2 Tms	AL	84	227	52	10	1	2	(2	0)	70	21	22	23	12	0	27	1	3	2	2	4	.33	1	.229	.269	.308
	05 Tor	AL	37	93	27	3	0	0	(0	0)	30	8	12	13	6	0	12	2	3	2	5	0	1.00	3	.290	.340	.323
	05 Det	AL	31	73	19	3	1	0	(0	0)	24	10	4	6	5	0	12	0	0	0	1	1	.50	3	.260	.308	.329
	11 Tor	AL	65	168	42	8	1	2	(2	0)	58	19	20	21	8	0	18	1	3	2	2	4	.33	1	.250	.285	.345
	11 Ari	NL	19	59	10	2	0	0	(0	0)	12	2	2	2	4	0	9	0	0	0	0	0	-	0	.169	.222	.203
	13 ML YEARS		884	2092	498	93	14	21	(10	11)	682	248	179	195	93	0	312	19	49	17	33	17	.66	40	.238	.275	.326

Jake McGee

Pitches: L Bats: L Pos: RP-37   Ht: 6'3" Wt: 230 Born: 8/6/1986 Age: 25

			HOW MUCH HE PITCHED						WHAT HE GAVE UP										THE RESULTS							
Year	Team	Lg	G	GS	CG	GF	IP	BFP	H	R	ER	HR	SH	SF	HB	TBB	IBB	SO	WP	Bk	W	L	Pct	Sh	Sv-Op Hld	ERC	ERA
2004	Princtn	R+	12	12	0	0	56.2	233	49	30	25	5	3	4	0	25	1	53	5	0	4	1	.800	0	0- - -	3.49	3.97
2005	HudVal	A-	15	14	0	0	76.2	309	64	32	31	4	1	1	1	23	0	89	5	0	5	4	.556	0	0- - -	2.61	3.64
2006	SWMch	A	26	26	0	0	134.0	561	103	54	44	7	3	2	3	65	0	171	13	0	7	9	.438	0	0- - -	2.92	2.96
2007	VeroB	A+	21	21	0	0	116.2	470	86	45	38	8	2	3	3	39	0	145	5	0	5	4	.556	0	0- - -	2.36	2.93
2007	Mont	AA	5	5	0	0	23.1	99	19	11	11	1	2	1	0	13	0	30	1	0	3	2	.600	0	0- - -	3.60	4.24
2008	Mont	AA	15	15	0	0	77.2	325	65	38	34	6	2	1	1	37	0	65	3	0	6	4	.600	0	0- - -	3.43	3.94
2009	Rays	R	5	5	0	0	7.2	32	5	4	3	0	0	0	0	3	0	14	2	0	0	2	.000	0	0- - -	1.60	3.52
2009	Charltt	A+	11	11	0	0	22.1	97	26	16	16	2	1	0	0	9	0	26	4	0	2	0	.000	0	0- - -	5.11	6.45
2010	Mont	AA	19	19	0	0	88.1	375	81	42	35	3	7	4	1	33	0	100	7	0	3	7	.300	0	0- - -	3.09	3.57
2010	Drham	AAA	11	1	0	1	17.1	64	9	1	1	0	0	0	0	3	0	27	2	0	1	1	.500	0	1- - -	0.86	0.52
2011	Drham	AAA	24	0	0	13	33.1	139	30	10	10	4	3	1	1	8	0	38	2	0	4	2	.667	0	9- - -	3.10	2.70
2010	TB	AL	8	0	0	3	5.0	20	2	1	1	0	0	0	0	3	0	6	0	0	0	0	-	0	0-0 0	1.32	1.80
2011	TB	AL	37	0	0	9	28.0	124	30	14	14	5	1	0	0	12	1	27	0	0	5	2	.714	0	0-0 4	5.09	4.50
	2 ML YEARS		45	0	0	12	33.0	144	32	15	15	5	1	0	0	15	1	33	0	0	5	2	.714	0	0-0 4	4.41	4.09

Casey McGehee

Bats: R Throws: R Pos: 3B-147; PH-9; 1B-5; DH-1   McGEE   Ht: 6'1" Wt: 220 Born: 10/12/1982 Age: 29

							BATTING															BASERUNNING				AVERAGES		
Year	Team	Lg	G	AB	H	2B	3B	HR	(Hm	Rd)	TB	R	RBI	RC	TBB	IBB	SO	HBP	SH	SF	SB	CS	SB%	GDP	Avg	OBP	Slg
2008	ChC	NL	9	24	4	1	0	0	(0	0)	5	1	5	0	0	0	8	0	0	1	0	0	-	1	.167	.160	.208
2009	Mil	NL	116	355	107	20	1	16	(6	10)	177	58	66	65	34	2	67	1	0	4	0	2	.00	13	.301	.360	.499
2010	Mil	NL	157	610	174	38	1	23	(13	10)	283	70	104	93	50	5	102	2	0	8	1	1	.50	18	.285	.337	.464
2011	Mil	NL	155	546	122	24	2	13	(8	5)	189	46	67	50	45	4	104	1	0	8	0	3	.00	19	.223	.280	.346
	4 ML YEARS		437	1535	407	83	4	52	(27	25)	654	175	242	208	129	11	281	4	0	21	1	6	.14	51	.265	.320	.426

Dustin McGowan

Pitches: R Bats: R Pos: SP-4; RP-1   Ht: 6'3" Wt: 220 Born: 3/24/1982 Age: 30

			HOW MUCH HE PITCHED						WHAT HE GAVE UP										THE RESULTS							
Year	Team	Lg	G	GS	CG	GF	IP	BFP	H	R	ER	HR	SH	SF	HB	TBB	IBB	SO	WP	Bk	W	L	Pct	Sh	Sv-Op Hld	ERC	ERA
2011	Dnedin*	A+	7	7	0	0	15.2	66	13	5	5	0	0	2	0	7	0	17	0	0	0	2	.000	0	0- - -	2.65	2.87
2011	NHam*	AA	5	5	0	0	19.2	80	18	7	6	2	0	0	0	7	0	18	0	0	0	2	.000	0	0- - -	3.57	2.75
2005	Tor	AL	13	7	0	2	45.1	205	49	34	32	7	0	4	7	17	0	34	7	0	1	3	.250	0	0-0 1	5.47	6.35
2006	Tor	AL	16	3	0	3	27.1	143	35	27	22	2	0	1	2	25	2	22	3	1	1	2	.333	0	0-1 1	7.72	7.24
2007	Tor	AL	27	27	2	0	169.2	705	146	80	77	14	0	6	2	61	3	144	13	0	12	10	.545	1	0-0 0	3.07	4.08
2008	Tor	AL	19	19	1	0	111.1	474	115	60	54	9	2	8	5	38	1	85	5	0	6	7	.462	0	0-0 0	4.13	4.37
2011	Tor	AL	5	4	0	0	21.0	96	20	15	15	4	0	1	1	13	0	20	3	0	0	2	.000	0	0-0 0	5.50	6.43
	5 ML YEARS		80	60	3	5	374.2	1623	365	216	200	36	2	20	17	154	6	305	31	1	20	24	.455	1	0-1 2	4.10	4.80

Michael McKenry

Bats: R Throws: R Pos: C-58; 3B-1   Ht: 5'10" Wt: 200 Born: 3/4/1985 Age: 27

							BATTING															BASERUNNING				AVERAGES		
Year	Team	Lg	G	AB	H	2B	3B	HR	(Hm	Rd)	TB	R	RBI	RC	TBB	IBB	SO	HBP	SH	SF	SB	CS	SB%	GDP	Avg	OBP	Slg
2006	TriCity	A-	66	245	53	16	1	4	(-	-)	83	28	23	27	22	0	49	11	6	6	3	3	.50	1	.216	.303	.339
2007	Ashvll	A	113	408	117	35	1	22	(-	-)	220	79	90	86	66	0	84	6	3	2	8	9	.47	4	.287	.392	.539
2008	Mdest	A+	111	400	103	28	1	18	(-	-)	187	59	75	71	55	0	101	10	5	2	2	4	.33	8	.258	.360	.468
2009	Tulsa	AA	102	358	100	25	1	12	(-	-)	163	52	50	64	54	2	69	2	2	1	2	2	.50	12	.279	.376	.455
2010	ColSpr	AAA	99	347	92	23	1	10	(-	-)	147	44	49	50	32	1	77	2	0	3	1	1	.50	8	.265	.328	.424
2011	Pwtckt	AAA	29	95	26	5	0	3	(-	-)	40	10	12	16	14	0	24	1	0	1	1	0	1.00	0	.274	.369	.421
2010	Col	NL	6	8	0	0	0	0	(0	0)	0	0	0	0	1	0	5	0	0	0	0	0	-	0	.000	.111	.000
2011	Pit	NL	58	180	40	12	0	2	(1	1)	58	17	11	12	14	2	49	0	5	2	0	1	.00	3	.222	.276	.322
	2 ML YEARS		64	188	40	12	0	2	(1	1)	58	17	11	12	15	2	54	0	5	2	0	1	.00	3	.213	.268	.309

Nate McLouth

Bats: L Throws: R Pos: CF-55; LF-26; RF-3; PH-1   mc-CLOWTH   Ht: 5'11" Wt: 180 Born: 10/28/1981 Age: 30

							BATTING															BASERUNNING				AVERAGES		
Year	Team	Lg	G	AB	H	2B	3B	HR	(Hm	Rd)	TB	R	RBI	RC	TBB	IBB	SO	HBP	SH	SF	SB	CS	SB%	GDP	Avg	OBP	Slg
2011	Gwnntt*	AAA	3	6	3	0	0	0	(-	-)	3	2	1	2	2	0	2	1	0	0	0	0	-	0	.500	.667	.500
2005	Pit	NL	41	109	28	6	0	5	(2	3)	49	20	12	9	3	0	20	5	2	1	2	0	1.00	3	.257	.305	.450
2006	Pit	NL	106	270	63	16	2	7	(3	4)	104	50	16	25	18	0	59	5	3	1	10	1	.91	7	.233	.293	.385
2007	Pit	NL	137	329	85	21	3	13	(5	8)	151	62	38	52	39	2	77	9	3	2	22	1	.96	2	.258	.351	.459
2008	Pit	NL	152	597	165	46	4	26	(15	11)	297	113	94	105	65	11	93	12	5	6	23	3	.88	5	.276	.356	.497
2009	2 Tms	NL	129	507	130	27	2	20	(9	11)	221	86	70	85	68	1	99	9	3	4	19	6	.76	8	.256	.352	.436
2010	Atl	NL	85	242	46	12	1	6	(5	1)	78	30	24	23	33	2	57	5	6	2	7	2	.78	3	.190	.298	.322
2011	Atl	NL	81	267	61	12	2	4	(4	0)	89	35	16	36	44	4	52	3	7	0	4	2	.67	4	.228	.344	.333
09	Pit	NL	45	168	43	7	1	9	(5	4)	79	27	34	33	21	0	29	4	0	2	7	0	1.00	2	.256	.349	.470
09	Atl	NL	84	339	87	20	1	11	(4	7)	142	59	36	52	47	1	70	5	3	2	12	6	.67	6	.257	.354	.419
	Postseason		3	2	1	0	0	0	(0	0)	1	0	0	0	0	0	0	0	0	0	0	0	-	0	.500	.500	.500
	7 ML YEARS		731	2321	578	140	14	81	(43	38)	989	396	270	335	270	20	457	48	29	16	87	15	.85	32	.249	.337	.426

Dallas McPherson

Bats: L Throws: R Pos: 1B-6; 3B-5; PH-2; PR-2   Ht: 6'4" Wt: 225 Born: 7/23/1980 Age: 31

							BATTING														BASERUNNING				AVERAGES		
Year	Team	Lg	G	AB	H	2B	3B	HR	(Hm	Rd)	TB	R	RBI	RC	TBB	IBB	SO	HBP	SH	SF	SB	CS	SB%	GDP	Avg	OBP	Slg
2011	Charltt*	AAA	101	392	111	27	0	20	(-	-)	198	54	69	65	31	1	126	0	1	2	1	2	.33	9	.283	.334	.505
2004	LAA	AL	16	40	9	1	0	3	(2	1)	19	5	6	5	3	0	17	0	0	0	1	0	1.00	0	.225	.279	.475
2005	LAA	AL	61	205	50	14	2	8	(6	2)	92	29	26	28	14	0	64	1	0	0	3	3	.50	5	.244	.295	.449
2006	LAA	AL	40	115	30	4	0	7	(3	4)	55	16	13	16	6	0	40	0	0	0	1	0	1.00	3	.261	.298	.478
2008	Fla	NL	11	11	2	2	0	0	(0	0)	4	3	0	1	4	1	5	0	0	0	0	0	-	0	.182	.400	.364
2011	CWS	AL	11	15	2	0	0	0	(0	0)	2	1	0	0	0	0	7	0	0	0	0	0	-	0	.133	.133	.133
	Postseason		3	9	1	0	0	0	(0	0)	1	0	1	0	0	0	4	0	0	0	0	0	-	0	.111	.111	.111
	5 ML YEARS		139	386	93	21	2	18	(11	7)	172	54	45	50	27	1	133	1	0	0	5	3	.63	8	.241	.292	.446

Kris Medlen

Pitches: R Bats: B Pos: RP-2   Ht: 5'10" Wt: 190 Born: 10/7/1985 Age: 26

				HOW MUCH HE PITCHED				WHAT HE GAVE UP											THE RESULTS						
Year	Team	Lg	G	GS	CG	GF	IP	BFP	H	R	ER	HR	SH	SF	HB	TBB	IBB	SO	WP	Bk	W	L	Pct	Sh	Sv-Op	Hld	ERC	ERA
2009	Atl	NL	37	4	0	10	67.2	294	65	34	32	5	6	2	2	30	2	72	3	1	3	5	.375	0	0-2	1	3.90	4.26
2010	Atl	NL	31	14	0	5	107.2	438	108	48	44	13	7	3	3	21	1	83	1	1	6	2	.750	0	0-0	1	3.60	3.68
2011	Atl	NL	2	0	0	1	2.1	8	1	0	0	0	0	0	0	0	0	2	0	0	0	0	-	0	0-0	0	0.40	0.00
	3 ML YEARS		70	18	0	16	177.2	740	174	82	76	18	13	5	5	51	3	157	4	2	9	7	.563	0	0-2	2	3.66	3.85

Evan Meek

Pitches: R Bats: R Pos: RP-24   Ht: 6'0" Wt: 220 Born: 5/12/1983 Age: 29

				HOW MUCH HE PITCHED				WHAT HE GAVE UP											THE RESULTS						
Year	Team	Lg	G	GS	CG	GF	IP	BFP	H	R	ER	HR	SH	SF	HB	TBB	IBB	SO	WP	Bk	W	L	Pct	Sh	Sv-Op	Hld	ERC	ERA
2011	Indy*	AAA	8	0	0	1	8.0	31	6	2	2	0	2	0	0	1	0	8	0	0	0	0	-	0	1--	1	1.38	2.25
2011	Bradtn*	A+	2	1	0	0	2.0	7	1	0	0	0	0	0	0	0	0	2	0	0	0	0	-	0	0--	0	0.54	0.00
2008	Pit	NL	9	0	0	7	13.0	61	11	11	10	3	1	1	1	12	2	7	3	0	0	1	.000	0	0-0	0	6.46	6.92
2009	Pit	NL	41	0	0	14	47.0	195	34	18	18	2	2	1	0	29	2	42	5	0	1	1	.500	0	0-1	4	3.03	3.45
2010	Pit	NL	70	0	0	16	80.0	324	53	25	19	5	2	1	4	31	4	70	2	0	5	4	.556	0	4-10	15	2.15	2.14
2011	Pit	NL	24	0	0	6	20.2	100	27	11	8	1	1	0	0	12	0	17	2	0	1	1	.500	0	0-1	4	6.12	3.48
	4 ML YEARS		144	0	0	43	160.2	680	125	65	55	11	6	3	5	84	8	136	12	0	7	7	.500	0	4-12	23	3.17	3.08

Mark Melancon

Pitches: R Bats: R Pos: RP-71   muh-LANN-sun   Ht: 6'2" Wt: 215 Born: 3/28/1985 Age: 27

				HOW MUCH HE PITCHED				WHAT HE GAVE UP											THE RESULTS						
Year	Team	Lg	G	GS	CG	GF	IP	BFP	H	R	ER	HR	SH	SF	HB	TBB	IBB	SO	WP	Bk	W	L	Pct	Sh	Sv-Op	Hld	ERC	ERA
2009	NYY	AL	13	0	0	4	16.1	74	13	8	7	0	0	0	4	10	0	10	3	0	0	1	.000	0	0-1	0	3.94	3.86
2010	2 Tms		22	0	0	4	21.1	90	19	13	10	2	0	1	1	8	0	22	2	0	2	0	1.000	0	0-1	8	3.53	4.22
2011	Hou	NL	71	0	0	47	74.1	309	65	28	23	5	2	0	2	26	6	66	1	0	8	4	.667	0	20-25	3	2.98	2.78
	10 NYY	AL	2	0	0	2	4.0	19	7	5	4	1	0	1	0	0	0	3	0	0	-		-	0	0-0	0	7.95	9.00
	10 Hou	NL	20	0	0	2	17.1	71	12	8	6	1	0	0	1	8	0	19	2	0	2	0	1.000	0	0-1	8	2.65	3.12
	3 ML YEARS		106	0	0	55	112.0	473	97	49	40	7	2	1	7	44	6	98	6	0	10	5	.667	0	20-27	11	3.23	3.21

Luis Mendoza

Pitches: R Bats: R Pos: SP-2   Ht: 6'3" Wt: 235 Born: 10/31/1983 Age: 28

				HOW MUCH HE PITCHED				WHAT HE GAVE UP											THE RESULTS						
Year	Team	Lg	G	GS	CG	GF	IP	BFP	H	R	ER	HR	SH	SF	HB	TBB	IBB	SO	WP	Bk	W	L	Pct	Sh	Sv-Op	Hld	ERC	ERA
2011	Omha*	AAA	33	18	1	8	144.1	598	125	52	35	5	6	1	7	54	4	81	10	0	12	5	.706	1	2--	-	3.00	2.18
2007	Tex	AL	6	3	0	2	16.0	64	13	4	4	1	0	2	2	4	0	7	0	0	1	0	1.000	0	0-0	0	2.83	2.25
2008	Tex	AL	25	11	0	6	63.1	316	97	74	61	7	0	2	6	25	4	35	5	0	3	8	.273	0	1-2	0	7.53	8.67
2009	Tex	AL	1	0	0	0	1.0	7	2	4	4	1	0	0	1	1	0	0	0	0	0	0	-	0	0-0	0	29.25	36.00
2010	KC	AL	4	0	0	1	4.0	25	10	10	10	4	0	0	2	3	0	1	0	0	2	1	.000	0	0-1	0	25.91	22.50
2011	KC	AL	2	2	0	0	14.2	60	11	3	2	0	0	1	2	5	0	7	0	0	2	0	1.000	0	0-0	0	2.42	1.23
	5 ML YEARS		38	16	0	9	99.0	472	133	95	81	13	0	5	11	38	4	50	5	0	6	9	.400	0	1-3	0	6.64	7.36

Devin Mesoraco

Bats: R Throws: R Pos: C-16; PH-3   Ht: 6'1" Wt: 220 Born: 6/19/1988 Age: 24

							BATTING														BASERUNNING				AVERAGES		
Year	Team	Lg	G	AB	H	2B	3B	HR	(Hm	Rd)	TB	R	RBI	RC	TBB	IBB	SO	HBP	SH	SF	SB	CS	SB%	GDP	Avg	OBP	Slg
2007	Reds	R	40	137	30	4	0	1	(-	-)	37	16	8	13	15	0	26	3	0	0	2	0	1.00	7	.219	.310	.270
2008	Dayton	A	83	306	80	13	1	9	(-	-)	122	29	42	40	20	0	64	4	0	4	2	3	.40	8	.261	.311	.399
2009	Srsota	A+	92	312	71	22	1	8	(-	-)	119	32	37	40	35	0	76	4	3	3	0	1	.00	11	.228	.311	.381
2010	Lynbrg	A+	43	158	53	11	2	10	(-	-)	98	24	31	39	19	1	29	3	0	1	2	2	.50	4	.335	.414	.620
2010	Carlina	AA	56	187	55	11	3	13	(-	-)	111	42	31	40	18	0	37	4	0	3	1	0	1.00	0	.294	.363	.594
2010	Lsvlle	AAA	14	52	12	3	0	3	(-	-)	24	5	13	7	6	0	14	0	0	2	0	1	.00	2	.231	.310	.462
2011	Lsvlle	AAA	120	436	126	36	2	15	(-	-)	211	60	71	80	52	6	83	7	0	4	1	1	.50	9	.289	.371	.484
2011	Cin	NL	18	50	9	3	0	2	(2	0)	18	5	6	5	3	1	10	0	0	0	0	0	-	1	.180	.226	.360

Jason Michaels

Bats: R Throws: R Pos: PH-51; LF-26; RF-16; PR-1   Ht: 6'0" Wt: 210 Born: 5/4/1976 Age: 36

Year	Team	Lg	G	AB	H	2B	3B	HR	(Hm	Rd)	TB	R	RBI	RC	TBB	IBB	SO	HBP	SH	SF	SB	CS	SB%	GDP	Avg	OBP	Slg
2011	OKCity*	AAA	5	20	6	2	0	0	(-	-)	8	0	2	3	2	0	5	0	0	0	0	0	-	0	.300	.364	.400
2001	Phi	NL	6	6	1	0	0	0	(0	0)	1	0	1	0	0	0	2	0	0	0	0	0	-	0	.167	.167	.167
2002	Phi	NL	81	105	28	10	3	2	(0	2)	50	16	11	14	13	1	33	1	0	2	1	1	.50	1	.267	.347	.476
2003	Phi	NL	76	109	36	11	0	5	(1	4)	62	20	17	19	15	1	22	1	0	0	0	0	-	3	.330	.416	.569
2004	Phi	NL	115	299	82	12	0	10	(5	5)	124	44	40	47	42	1	80	2	0	3	2	2	.50	3	.274	.364	.415
2005	Phi	NL	105	289	88	16	2	4	(1	3)	120	54	31	47	44	1	45	4	2	4	3	3	.50	3	.304	.399	.415
2006	Cle	AL	123	494	132	32	1	9	(4	5)	193	77	55	62	43	0	101	3	2	6	9	5	.64	6	.267	.326	.391
2007	Cle	AL	105	267	72	11	1	7	(5	2)	106	43	39	37	20	1	50	3	2	3	3	4	.43	3	.270	.324	.397
2008	2 Tms		123	286	64	13	1	8	(4	4)	103	28	53	37	27	0	65	2	2	4	2	1	.67	9	.224	.292	.360
2009	Hou	NL	102	135	32	12	1	4	(3	1)	58	17	16	15	16	0	38	1	0	0	1	2	.33	2	.237	.322	.430
2010	Hou	NL	106	186	47	14	1	8	(4	4)	87	23	26	28	12	1	29	4	0	1	0	0	-	3	.253	.310	.468
2011	Hou	NL	89	156	31	9	0	2	(1	1)	46	10	10	9	11	1	31	1	1	0	1	0	1.00	5	.199	.256	.295
08	Cle	AL	21	58	12	4	0	0	(0	0)	16	3	9	5	4	0	13	1	1	3	1	1	.50	0	.207	.258	.276
08	Pit	NL	102	228	52	9	1	8	(4	4)	87	25	44	32	23	0	52	1	1	1	1	0	1.00	9	.228	.300	.382
	Postseason		2	1	1	1	0	0	(0	0)	2	1	0	1	0	0	0	0	1	0	0	0	-	0	1.000	1.000	2.000
11 ML YEARS			1031	2332	613	140	10	59	(28	31)	950	332	299	315	243	7	496	22	9	23	22	18	.55	38	.263	.335	.407

Kam Mickolio

Pitches: R Bats: R Pos: RP-6   mick-oh-LYE-oh   Ht: 6'9" Wt: 255 Born: 5/10/1984 Age: 28

Year	Team	Lg	G	GS	CG	GF	IP	BFP	H	R	ER	HR	SH	SF	HB	TBB	IBB	SO	WP	Bk	W	L	Pct	Sh	Sv-Op	Hld	ERC	ERA
2011	Reno*	AAA	48	0	0	23	58.0	258	58	34	32	4	2	1	0	25	2	63	4	0	3	4	.429	0	6- -	-	3.80	4.97
2008	Bal	AL	9	0	0	5	7.2	36	8	5	5	0	1	1	0	4	0	8	2	0	0	1	.000	0	0-1	0	3.81	5.87
2009	Bal	AL	11	0	0	7	13.2	59	11	4	4	0	0	2	0	7	1	14	0	0	0	2	.000	0	0-0	2	2.58	2.63
2010	Bal	AL	3	0	0	2	3.2	19	5	3	3	1	0	0	0	3	0	4	0	0	0	0	-	0	0-0	0	9.47	7.36
2011	Ari	NL	6	0	0	0	6.2	32	10	5	5	0	0	1	0	3	0	7	0	0	0	0	-	0	0-0	1	6.49	6.75
4 ML YEARS			29	0	0	14	31.2	146	34	17	17	1	1	4	0	17	1	33	2	0	0	3	.000	0	0-1	3	4.34	4.83

Jose Mijares

Pitches: L Bats: L Pos: RP-58   mee-HAHR-ess   Ht: 6'0" Wt: 230 Born: 10/29/1984 Age: 27

Year	Team	Lg	G	GS	CG	GF	IP	BFP	H	R	ER	HR	SH	SF	HB	TBB	IBB	SO	WP	Bk	W	L	Pct	Sh	Sv-Op	Hld	ERC	ERA
2008	Min	AL	10	0	0	3	10.1	34	3	1	1	0	0	0	0	5	1	0	1	0	0	1	.000	0	0-0	2	0.19	0.87
2009	Min	AL	71	0	0	12	61.2	253	50	17	16	7	2	3	2	23	1	55	0	0	2	2	.500	0	0-1	27	3.18	2.34
2010	Min	AL	47	0	0	10	32.2	139	34	14	12	4	1	1	1	9	1	28	1	0	1	1	.500	0	0-0	9	4.04	3.31
2011	Min	AL	58	0	0	13	49.0	228	53	31	25	4	0	2	3	30	2	30	1	0	0	2	.000	0	0-2	10	5.42	4.59
	Postseason		5	0	0	1	2.0	7	1	1	1	1	1	0	0	2	1	0	0	0	0	1	.000	0	0-0	0	7.39	4.50
4 ML YEARS			186	0	0	38	153.2	654	140	63	54	15	3	6	6	62	4	118	3	0	3	6	.333	0	0-3	48	3.70	3.16

Aaron Miles

Bats: B Throws: R Pos: 2B-72; 3B-61; PH-18; SS-1   Ht: 5'9" Wt: 180 Born: 12/15/1976 Age: 35

Year	Team	Lg	G	AB	H	2B	3B	HR	(Hm	Rd)	TB	R	RBI	RC	TBB	IBB	SO	HBP	SH	SF	SB	CS	SB%	GDP	Avg	OBP	Slg
2003	CWS	AL	8	12	4	3	0	0	(0	0)	7	3	2	3	0	0	0	0	0	0	0	0	-	0	.333	.333	.583
2004	Col	NL	134	522	153	15	3	6	(4	2)	192	75	47	70	29	0	53	2	7	6	12	7	.63	12	.293	.329	.368
2005	Col	NL	99	324	91	12	3	2	(0	2)	115	37	28	42	8	1	38	4	10	1	4	2	.67	6	.281	.306	.355
2006	StL	NL	135	426	112	20	5	2	(1	1)	148	48	30	49	38	9	42	2	2	3	2	1	.67	8	.263	.324	.347
2007	StL	NL	133	414	120	16	1	2	(0	2)	144	55	32	49	25	1	40	1	4	5	2	1	.67	11	.290	.328	.348
2008	StL	NL	134	379	120	15	2	4	(1	3)	151	49	31	44	23	2	37	0	5	1	3	3	.50	13	.317	.355	.398
2009	ChC	NL	74	157	29	7	1	0	(0	0)	38	17	5	3	8	1	21	0	5	0	3	0	1.00	4	.185	.224	.242
2010	StL	NL	79	139	39	5	0	0	(0	0)	44	14	9	13	6	1	14	1	3	2	0	1	.00	1	.281	.311	.317
2011	LAD	NL	136	454	125	17	3	3	(0	3)	157	49	45	51	25	1	49	3	3	5	4	3	.57	11	.275	.314	.346
	Postseason		7	11	4	0	1	0	(0	0)	6	2	0	2	1	1	2	0	0	0	1	0	1.00	0	.364	.417	.545
9 ML YEARS			932	2827	793	110	18	19	(6	13)	996	347	229	324	162	16	294	13	39	23	30	18	.63	66	.281	.320	.352

Wade Miley

Pitches: L Bats: L Pos: SP-7; RP-1   Ht: 6'2" Wt: 190 Born: 11/13/1986 Age: 25

Year	Team	Lg	G	GS	CG	GF	IP	BFP	H	R	ER	HR	SH	SF	HB	TBB	IBB	SO	WP	Bk	W	L	Pct	Sh	Sv-Op	Hld	ERC	ERA
2008	Yakima	A-	7	0	0	0	11.0	49	11	6	6	0	0	0	0	5	0	11	0	0	1	1	.500	0	0- -	-	3.47	4.91
2009	Sbend	A	21	21	0	0	113.2	480	127	60	52	8	1	4	4	29	0	91	7	0	5	9	.357	0	0- -	-	4.19	4.12
2009	Visalia	A+	3	3	0	0	15.0	65	18	10	8	0	0	0	0	4	0	11	0	0	1	1	.500	0	0- -	-	3.98	4.80
2010	Visalia	A+	14	14	0	0	80.1	345	81	36	29	1	2	0	1	37	0	50	10	0	4	5	.444	0	0- -	-	3.85	3.25
2010	Mobile	AA	13	13	1	0	72.2	292	60	26	16	5	4	0	1	28	2	63	2	3	5	2	.714	0	0- -	-	3.00	1.98
2011	Mobile	AA	14	14	0	0	75.1	322	74	49	40	6	1	2	3	28	0	46	3	2	4	2	.667	0	0- -	-	3.91	4.78
2011	Reno	AAA	8	8	1	0	54.1	226	53	23	22	4	2	0	0	16	0	56	3	2	4	1	.800	0	0- -	-	3.38	3.64
2011	Ari	NL	8	7	0	0	40.0	180	48	20	20	6	3	1	0	18	0	25	1	0	4	2	.667	0	0-0	0	5.90	4.50

Lastings Milledge

Bats: R Throws: R Pos: LF-2　　　　　　　　　　　　　　　　　　　Ht: 5'11" Wt: 210 Born: 4/5/1985 Age: 27

Year	Team	Lg	G	AB	H	2B	3B	HR	(Hm	Rd)	TB	R	RBI	RC	TBB	IBB	SO	HBP	SH	SF	SB	CS	SB%	GDP	Avg	OBP	Slg
2011	Charltt*	AAA	123	444	131	23	3	12	(-	-)	196	61	47	77	43	1	63	6	10	2	27	6	.82	15	.295	.364	.441
2006	NYM	NL	56	166	40	7	2	4	(2	2)	63	14	22	21	12	4	39	5	1	1	1	2	.33	4	.241	.310	.380
2007	NYM	NL	59	184	50	9	1	7	(6	1)	82	27	29	27	13	2	42	7	1	1	3	2	.60	5	.272	.341	.446
2008	Was	NL	138	523	140	24	2	14	(7	7)	210	65	61	60	38	1	96	14	5	7	24	9	.73	19	.268	.330	.402
2009	2 Tms	NL	65	244	68	11	0	4	(3	1)	91	21	21	24	13	0	47	4	2	2	7	4	.64	5	.279	.323	.373
2010	Pit	NL	113	379	105	21	3	4	(1	3)	144	38	34	48	28	3	62	3	2	0	5	3	.63	7	.277	.332	.380
2011	CWS	AL	2	4	1	1	0	0	(0	0)	2	1	0	0	0	0	1	0	0	0	0	0	-	0	.250	.250	.500
09	Was	NL	7	24	4	0	0	0	(0	0)	4	1	1	1	1	0	10	1	0	0	1	0	1.00	1	.167	.231	.167
09	Pit	NL	58	220	64	11	0	4	(3	1)	87	20	20	23	12	0	37	3	2	2	6	4	.60	4	.291	.333	.395
	6 ML YEARS		433	1500	404	73	8	33	(19	14)	592	166	167	180	104	10	287	33	11	11	40	20	.67	40	.269	.328	.395

Andrew Miller

Pitches: L Bats: L Pos: SP-12; RP-5　　　　　　　　　　　　　　　　　Ht: 6'7" Wt: 210 Born: 5/21/1985 Age: 27

Year	Team	Lg	G	GS	CG	GF	IP	BFP	H	R	ER	HR	SH	SF	HB	TBB	IBB	SO	WP	Bk	W	L	Pct	Sh	Sv-Op	Hld	ERC	ERA
2011	Pwtckt*	AAA	13	12	0	0	65.2	271	42	22	18	2	1	0	3	35	0	61	1	0	3	3	.500	0	0- -	-	2.40	2.47
2006	Det	AL	8	0	0	3	10.1	51	8	9	7	0	0	0	2	10	0	6	1	0	0	1	.000	0	0-0	1	4.79	6.10
2007	Det	AL	13	13	0	0	64.0	309	73	43	40	8	3	1	7	39	0	56	4	1	5	5	.500	0	0-0	0	6.31	5.63
2008	Fla	NL	29	20	0	1	107.1	492	120	78	70	7	10	7	4	56	4	89	4	0	6	10	.375	0	0-0	2	5.04	5.87
2009	Fla	NL	20	14	0	1	80.0	366	85	52	43	7	6	4	2	43	1	59	10	0	3	5	.375	0	0-0	1	4.90	4.84
2010	Fla	NL	9	7	0	1	32.2	171	51	34	31	6	5	2	1	26	2	28	5	0	1	5	.167	0	0-0	0	10.20	8.54
2011	Bos	AL	17	12	0	2	65.0	310	77	43	40	8	6	5	3	41	0	50	2	1	6	3	.667	0	0-0	0	6.48	5.54
	6 ML YEARS		96	66	0	8	359.1	1699	414	259	231	36	30	19	19	215	7	288	26	2	21	29	.420	0	0-0	4	5.91	5.79

Jai Miller

Bats: R Throws: R Pos: CF-3; PH-3; RF-2; PR-1　　JAY　　　　　　　　Ht: 6'3" Wt: 205 Born: 1/17/1985 Age: 27

Year	Team	Lg	G	AB	H	2B	3B	HR	(Hm	Rd)	TB	R	RBI	RC	TBB	IBB	SO	HBP	SH	SF	SB	CS	SB%	GDP	Avg	OBP	Slg
2011	Scrmto*	AAA	110	410	113	24	4	32	(-	-)	241	81	88	91	54	1	179	8	0	3	16	0	1.00	4	.276	.368	.588
2008	Fla	NL	1	1	0	0	0	0	(0	0)	0	0	0	0	0	0	1	0	0	0	0	0	-	0	.000	.000	.000
2010	KC	AL	20	55	13	3	0	1	(1	0)	19	5	4	4	4	0	23	1	0	0	1	0	1.00	0	.236	.300	.345
2011	Oak	AL	7	12	3	0	0	1	(0	1)	6	2	2	2	0	0	5	0	0	0	0	0	-	0	.250	.250	.500
	3 ML YEARS		28	68	16	3	0	2	(1	1)	25	7	6	6	4	0	29	1	0	0	1	0	1.00	0	.235	.288	.368

Jim Miller

Pitches: R Bats: R Pos: RP-6　　　　　　　　　　　　　　　　　　　Ht: 6'1" Wt: 200 Born: 4/28/1982 Age: 30

Year	Team	Lg	G	GS	CG	GF	IP	BFP	H	R	ER	HR	SH	SF	HB	TBB	IBB	SO	WP	Bk	W	L	Pct	Sh	Sv-Op	Hld	ERC	ERA
2004	TriCity	A-	34	0	0	32	37.0	145	21	6	4	1	0	0	2	11	0	65	1	0	1	1	.500	0	17- -	-	1.42	0.97
2005	Mdest	A+	48	0	0	44	47.2	201	39	22	20	3	0	0	1	17	0	68	3	0	1	3	.250	0	25- -	-	2.70	3.78
2005	Tulsa	AA	16	0	0	13	15.0	61	6	5	1	2	0	0	2	8	0	19	2	0	1	1	.500	0	9- -	-	2.14	0.60
2006	Tulsa	AA	45	0	0	27	44.1	205	50	23	19	10	1	3	5	14	2	41	1	1	0	3	.000	0	12- -	-	5.58	3.86
2007	Bowie	AA	30	0	0	13	38.2	167	26	13	12	0	0	1	3	25	0	49	3	0	2	3	.400	0	4- -	-	2.81	2.79
2007	Norfolk	AAA	22	0	0	13	27.2	126	25	13	13	3	2	0	1	16	0	30	2	0	1	2	.333	0	3- -	-	4.29	4.23
2008	Bowie	AA	7	0	0	2	13.0	57	11	5	5	1	0	1	0	5	0	17	0	0	0	1	.000	0	0- -	-	3.87	3.46
2008	Norfolk	AAA	49	0	0	29	67.0	271	50	26	23	4	4	1	0	22	1	79	1	1	3	5	.375	0	10- -	-	2.20	3.09
2009	Norfolk	AAA	54	0	0	39	64.2	272	64	20	19	3	1	1	1	19	3	59	0	0	4	4	.500	0	17- -	-	3.24	2.64
2010	Norfolk	AAA	33	0	0	11	57.2	243	60	33	31	9	2	2	0	18	2	53	3	0	1	0	1.000	0	0- -	-	4.35	4.84
2011	ColSpr	AAA	65	0	0	51	72.0	325	93	48	42	7	2	1	5	21	4	73	3	0	8	5	.615	0	24- -	-	5.54	5.25
2008	Bal	AL	8	0	0	5	7.2	39	9	3	1	0	1	1	1	5	2	8	1	0	0	2	.000	0	1-2	0	4.99	1.17
2011	Col	NL	6	0	0	4	7.0	29	3	2	2	0	2	0	0	4	0	5	0	0	0	0	-	0	0-0	0	1.30	2.57
	2 ML YEARS		14	0	0	9	14.2	68	12	5	3	0	3	1	1	9	2	13	1	0	0	2	.000	0	1-2	0	2.99	1.84

Trever Miller

Pitches: L Bats: R Pos: RP-48　　　　　　　　　　　　　　　　　　Ht: 6'3" Wt: 200 Born: 5/29/1973 Age: 39

Year	Team	Lg	G	GS	CG	GF	IP	BFP	H	R	ER	HR	SH	SF	HB	TBB	IBB	SO	WP	Bk	W	L	Pct	Sh	Sv-Op	Hld	ERC	ERA
2011	Pwtckt*	AAA	3	0	0	1	3.1	12	2	1	1	0	0	0	0	0	0	2	0	0	0	0	-	0	0- -	-	0.75	2.70
1996	Det	AL	5	4	0	0	16.2	88	28	17	17	3	2	2	2	9	0	8	0	0	0	4	.000	0	0-0	0	10.15	9.18
1998	Hou	NL	37	1	0	15	53.1	235	57	21	18	4	0	0	1	20	1	30	1	0	2	0	1.000	0	1-2	1	4.18	3.04
1999	Hou	NL	47	0	0	11	49.2	232	58	29	28	6	2	2	5	29	1	37	4	0	3	2	.600	0	1-1	4	6.48	5.07
2000	2 Tms	NL	16	0	0	2	16.1	90	27	22	19	3	1	1	2	12	1	11	1	0	0	0	-	0	0-0	0	10.68	10.47
2003	Tor	AL	79	0	0	18	52.2	233	46	30	27	7	1	0	5	28	3	44	2	0	2	2	.500	0	3-4	16	4.38	4.61
2004	TB	AL	60	0	0	15	49.0	208	48	21	17	3	3	0	3	15	4	43	2	0	1	1	.500	0	1-3	9	3.45	3.12
2005	TB	AL	61	0	0	13	44.1	206	45	23	20	4	3	5	7	29	6	35	2	0	2	2	.500	0	0-3	11	5.57	4.06
2006	Hou	NL	70	0	0	14	50.2	207	42	17	17	7	1	2	4	13	2	56	1	0	2	3	.400	0	1-3	12	3.11	3.02
2007	Hou	NL	76	0	0	12	46.1	211	45	26	25	6	3	0	4	23	6	46	1	0	0	0	-	0	1-3	12	4.52	4.86
2008	TB	AL	68	0	0	16	43.1	187	39	21	20	2	1	1	4	20	1	44	1	0	2	0	1.000	0	2-3	11	3.73	4.15
2009	StL	NL	70	0	0	9	43.2	173	31	11	10	5	2	1	2	11	1	46	1	0	4	1	.800	0	0-1	13	3.25	2.06
2010	StL	NL	57	0	0	3	36.0	151	30	17	16	2	2	2	2	16	0	22	4	0	0	1	.000	0	0-1	11	3.29	4.00
2011	3 Tms	NL	48	0	0	5	21.1	101	25	9	9	2	1	2	1	12	2	12	2	0	1	0	.000	0	1-4	5	5.88	3.80
00	Phi	NL	14	0	0	2	14.0	72	19	16	13	3	1	1	1	9	1	10	1	0	0	0	-	0	0-0	0	8.14	8.36
00	LAD	NL	2	0	0	0	2.1	18	8	6	6	0	0	0	1	3	0	1	0	0	0	0	-	0	0-0	0	28.18	23.14
11	StL	NL	39	0	0	4	15.2	77	19	7	7	1	1	2	2	10	2	9	1	0	0	1	.000	0	1-3	4	6.21	4.02

	HOW MUCH HE PITCHED						WHAT HE GAVE UP										THE RESULTS						
Year Team Lg	G	GS	CG	GF	IP	BFP	H	R	ER	HR	SH	SF	HB	TBB	IBB	SO	WP	Bk	W	L	Pct	Sh	Sv-Op	Hld	ERC	ERA
11 Tor AL	6	0	0	0	3.2	18	6	2	2	1	0	0	0	2	0	2	1	0	0	0	-	0	0-1	1	10.64	4.91
11 Bos AL	3	0	0	1	2.0	6	0	0	0	0	0	0	0	0	0	1	0	0	0	0	-	0	0-0	0	0.00	0.00
Postseason	11	0	0	2	3.2	18	3	2	2	1	0	0	0	4	0	5	1	0	0	0	-	0	0-0	2	7.11	4.91
13 ML YEARS	694	5	0	133	523.1	2322	521	264	243	54	22	18	43	237	28	434	22	0	18	17	.514	0	11-28	105	4.51	4.18

Brad Mills

Pitches: L **Bats:** R **Pos:** SP-4; RP-1   **Ht:** 5'11" **Wt:** 185 **Born:** 3/5/1985 **Age:** 27

	HOW MUCH HE PITCHED						WHAT HE GAVE UP										THE RESULTS						
Year Team Lg	G	GS	CG	GF	IP	BFP	H	R	ER	HR	SH	SF	HB	TBB	IBB	SO	WP	Bk	W	L	Pct	Sh	Sv-Op	Hld	ERC	ERA
2011 LsVgs* AAA	24	24	1	0	157.1	657	161	73	70	20	4	6	5	39	0	136	6	1	11	9	.550	0	0- -	-	3.96	4.00
2009 Tor AL	2	2	0	0	7.2	42	14	12	12	4	0	1	0	6	0	9	0	0	0	1	.000	0	0-0	0	15.52	14.09
2010 Tor AL	7	3	0	0	22.1	98	20	14	14	2	0	1	1	13	1	18	1	0	1	0	1.000	0	0-0	1	4.26	5.64
2011 Tor AL	5	4	0	0	18.1	91	23	20	20	4	0	0	2	12	1	18	1	0	1	2	.333	0	0-0	0	7.97	9.82
3 ML YEARS	14	9	0	0	48.1	231	57	46	46	10	0	2	3	31	2	45	2	0	2	3	.400	0	0-0	1	7.22	8.57

Kevin Millwood

Pitches: R **Bats:** R **Pos:** SP-9   **Ht:** 6'4" **Wt:** 235 **Born:** 12/24/1974 **Age:** 37

	HOW MUCH HE PITCHED						WHAT HE GAVE UP										THE RESULTS						
Year Team Lg	G	GS	CG	GF	IP	BFP	H	R	ER	HR	SH	SF	HB	TBB	IBB	SO	WP	Bk	W	L	Pct	Sh	Sv-Op	Hld	ERC	ERA
2011 Trntn* AA	1	1	1	0	7.0	26	1	0	0	0	1	0	0	4	0	3	0	0	1	0	1.000	1	0- -	-	0.62	0.00
2011 S-WB* AAA	2	2	1	0	9.0	41	14	8	8	3	0	0	0	2	0	7	0	0	1	1	.500	0	0- -	-	8.84	8.00
2011 Pwtckt* AAA	13	13	0	0	73.2	313	79	36	35	7	2	1	1	25	0	66	5	0	5	1	.833	0	0- -	-	4.35	4.28
1997 Atl NL	12	8	0	2	51.1	227	55	26	23	1	3	5	2	21	1	42	1	0	5	3	.625	0	0-0	0	4.03	4.03
1998 Atl NL	31	29	3	1	174.1	748	175	86	79	18	8	3	3	56	3	163	6	1	17	8	.680	1	0-0	1	3.81	4.08
1999 Atl NL	33	33	2	0	228.0	906	168	80	68	24	9	3	4	59	2	205	5	0	18	7	.720	0	0-0	0	2.26	2.68
2000 Atl NL	36	35	0	0	212.2	903	213	115	110	26	8	5	3	62	2	168	4	0	10	13	.435	0	0-0	0	3.83	4.66
2001 Atl NL	21	21	0	0	121.0	515	121	66	58	20	7	2	1	40	6	84	5	1	7	7	.500	0	0-0	0	4.20	4.31
2002 Atl NL	35	34	1	0	217.0	895	186	83	78	16	9	4	8	65	7	178	4	0	18	8	.692	1	0-0	0	2.85	3.24
2003 Phi NL	35	35	5	0	222.0	930	210	103	99	19	12	5	4	68	6	169	2	0	14	12	.538	3	0-0	0	3.35	4.01
2004 Phi NL	25	25	0	0	141.0	628	155	81	76	14	11	2	7	51	5	125	4	0	9	6	.600	0	0-0	0	4.57	4.85
2005 Cle AL	30	30	1	0	192.0	799	182	72	61	20	6	4	4	52	0	146	2	0	9	11	.450	0	0-0	0	3.40	2.86
2006 Tex AL	34	34	2	0	215.0	907	228	114	108	23	8	3	4	53	4	157	6	0	16	12	.571	0	0-0	0	3.92	4.52
2007 Tex AL	31	31	0	0	172.2	788	213	111	99	19	1	4	8	67	2	123	4	0	10	14	.417	0	0-0	0	5.64	5.16
2008 Tex AL	29	29	3	0	168.2	767	220	104	95	18	5	2	6	49	3	125	2	1	9	10	.474	0	0-0	0	5.54	5.07
2009 Tex AL	31	31	3	0	198.2	850	195	88	81	26	4	5	11	71	0	123	8	0	13	10	.565	0	0-0	0	4.27	3.67
2010 Bal AL	31	31	1	0	190.2	842	223	116	108	30	6	2	6	65	2	132	7	1	4	16	.200	0	0-0	0	5.39	5.10
2011 Col NL	9	9	0	0	54.1	222	58	26	24	9	2	0	0	8	0	36	2	0	4	3	.571	0	0-0	0	3.93	3.98
Postseason	9	7	1	1	41.1	164	33	20	18	7	1	1	0	6	0	38	1	1	3	3	.500	0	1-1	0	2.41	3.92
15 ML YEARS	423	415	21	3	2559.1	10927	2602	1271	1167	283	99	49	71	787	43	1976	62	4	163	140	.538	5	0-0	1	3.95	4.10

Tom Milone

Pitches: L **Bats:** L **Pos:** SP-5   mah-LONE   **Ht:** 6'1" **Wt:** 205 **Born:** 2/16/1987 **Age:** 25

	HOW MUCH HE PITCHED						WHAT HE GAVE UP										THE RESULTS						
Year Team Lg	G	GS	CG	GF	IP	BFP	H	R	ER	HR	SH	SF	HB	TBB	IBB	SO	WP	Bk	W	L	Pct	Sh	Sv-Op	Hld	ERC	ERA
2008 Vrmnt A-	6	3	0	0	21.2	91	27	12	11	4	0	0	0	3	0	22	0	0	1	3	.250	0	0- -	-	5.14	4.57
2008 Hgrstn A	7	7	0	0	37.1	150	36	16	12	0	3	1	0	6	0	27	0	0	3	0	.000	0	0- -	-	2.38	2.89
2009 Ptomc A+	27	25	0	0	151.1	611	144	57	49	9	5	4	5	36	2	106	8	1	12	5	.706	0	0- -	-	3.13	2.91
2010 Hrsbrg AA	27	27	2	0	158.0	650	161	57	50	10	3	3	4	23	0	155	7	2	12	5	.706	0	0- -	-	3.05	2.85
2011 Syrcse AAA	24	24	0	0	148.1	588	137	55	53	9	2	1	1	16	0	155	3	2	12	6	.667	0	0- -	-	2.37	3.22
2011 Was NL	5	5	0	0	26.0	110	28	11	11	2	3	2	2	4	2	15	0	0	1	0	1.000	0	0-0	0	3.55	3.81

Mike Minor

Pitches: L **Bats:** R **Pos:** SP-15   **Ht:** 6'4" **Wt:** 205 **Born:** 12/26/1987 **Age:** 24

	HOW MUCH HE PITCHED						WHAT HE GAVE UP										THE RESULTS						
Year Team Lg	G	GS	CG	GF	IP	BFP	H	R	ER	HR	SH	SF	HB	TBB	IBB	SO	WP	Bk	W	L	Pct	Sh	Sv-Op	Hld	ERC	ERA
2009 Rome A	4	4	0	0	14.0	48	10	1	1	0	0	0	0	0	0	17	0	0	0	1	.000	0	0- -	-	1.12	0.64
2010 Missi AA	15	15	0	0	87.0	360	74	48	39	8	5	3	1	34	1	109	2	1	2	6	.250	0	0- -	-	3.24	4.03
2010 Gwnntt AAA	6	6	0	0	33.1	127	19	7	7	1	1	3	0	12	0	37	0	0	4	1	.800	0	0- -	-	1.50	1.89
2011 Gwnntt AAA	16	16	0	0	100.2	415	93	43	35	12	4	4	2	27	2	99	1	0	4	5	.444	0	0- -	-	3.34	3.13
2010 Atl NL	9	8	0	1	40.2	185	53	28	27	6	1	3	1	11	0	43	0	0	3	2	.600	0	0-0	0	5.71	5.98
2011 Atl NL	15	15	0	0	82.2	361	93	39	38	7	3	1	1	30	5	77	2	0	5	3	.625	0	0-0	0	4.51	4.14
2 ML YEARS	24	23	0	1	123.1	546	146	67	65	13	4	4	2	41	5	120	2	0	8	5	.615	0	0-0	0	4.90	4.74

Juan Miranda

Bats: L **Throws:** L **Pos:** 1B-46; PH-19   **Ht:** 6'0" **Wt:** 220 **Born:** 4/25/1983 **Age:** 29

	BATTING																	BASERUNNING				AVERAGES		
Year Team Lg	G	AB	H	2B	3B	HR	(Hm	Rd)	TB	R	RBI	RC	TBB	IBB	SO	HBP	SH	SF	SB	CS	SB%	GDP	Avg	OBP	Slg
2011 Reno* AAA	34	105	24	4	1	5	(-	-)	45	17	24	17	20	1	36	1	0	0	0	1	.00	4	.229	.357	.429
2008 NYY AL	5	10	4	1	0	0	(0	0)	5	2	1	3	2	0	4	1	0	1	0	0	-	0	.400	.500	.500
2009 NYY AL	8	9	3	0	0	1	(0	1)	6	2	3	2	0	0	4	0	0	0	0	0	-	0	.333	.333	.667
2010 NYY AL	33	64	14	2	1	3	(3	0)	27	7	10	8	7	0	12	0	0	0	0	0	-	1	.219	.296	.422
2011 Ari NL	65	174	37	8	2	7	(3	4)	70	18	23	20	23	1	48	3	2	0	0	1	.00	1	.213	.315	.402
4 ML YEARS	111	257	58	11	3	11	(6	5)	108	29	37	33	32	1	68	4	2	1	0	1	.00	2	.226	.320	.420

Pat Misch

Pitches: L Bats: R Pos: RP-6   MISHH   Ht: 6'2" Wt: 190 Born: 8/18/1981 Age: 30

Year	Team	Lg	G	GS	CG	GF	IP	BFP	H	R	ER	HR	SH	SF	HB	TBB	IBB	SO	WP	Bk	W	L	Pct	Sh	Sv-Op	Hld	ERC	ERA
2011	Buffalo*	AAA	22	22	1	0	141.2	601	142	71	63	18	0	5	8	41	1	94	2	0	8	9	.471	0	0- -	-	4.07	4.00
2006	SF	NL	1	0	0	0	1.0	5	2	0	0	0	0	0	0	0	1	0	0	0	0	0	-	0	0-0	0	7.48	0.00
2007	SF	NL	18	4	0	2	40.1	176	47	21	19	3	1	2	2	12	2	26	0	0	0	4	.000	0	0-0	2	4.59	4.24
2008	SF	NL	15	7	0	6	52.1	230	56	34	33	11	3	4	3	15	2	38	1	1	0	3	.000	0	0-0	0	4.88	5.68
2009	2 Tms	NL	26	7	1	2	62.1	270	68	31	31	9	6	1	2	22	2	23	1	0	3	4	.429	1	0-1	0	4.86	4.48
2010	NYM	NL	12	6	0	2	37.2	159	43	20	16	4	0	2	1	4	1	23	0	0	0	4	.000	0	0-0	0	3.77	3.82
2011	NYM	NL	6	0	0	2	7.0	37	11	8	8	1	0	0	1	4	0	5	0	0	1	0	1.000	0	0-0	0	9.19	10.29
09	SF	NL	4	0	0	2	3.1	19	6	4	4	0	0	0	0	3	0	0	0	0	0	0	-	0	0-0	0	10.16	10.80
09	NYM	NL	22	7	1	0	59.0	251	62	27	27	9	6	1	2	19	2	23	1	0	3	4	.429	1	0-1	0	4.58	4.12
6 ML YEARS			78	24	1	14	200.2	877	227	114	107	28	10	9	9	57	7	116	2	1	4	15	.211	1	0-1	2	4.76	4.80

Russ Mitchell

Bats: R Throws: R Pos: 3B-11; PH-8; 1B-6; RF-1; PR-1   Ht: 6'1" Wt: 210 Born: 2/15/1985 Age: 27

Year	Team	Lg	G	AB	H	2B	3B	HR	(Hm	Rd)	TB	R	RBI	RC	TBB	IBB	SO	HBP	SH	SF	SB	CS	SB%	GDP	Avg	OBP	Slg
2003	Ddgrs	R	26	77	26	8	1	1	(-	-)	39	13	9	17	12	0	5	3	1	1	2	1	.67	1	.338	.441	.506
2004	VeroB	A+	46	169	42	8	1	0	(-	-)	52	12	17	14	4	0	32	3	5	0	1	1	.50	7	.249	.278	.308
2004	Clmbs	A	63	209	42	12	1	0	(-	-)	56	24	14	13	10	0	49	6	5	1	2	4	.33	4	.201	.257	.268
2005	VeroB	A+	13	33	10	1	0	1	(-	-)	14	5	4	4	2	0	6	0	1	1	0	0	-	2	.303	.333	.424
2005	Jaxnvl	AA	3	5	1	1	0	0	(-	-)	2	1	3	0	0	0	4	0	0	0	0	0	-	0	.200	.200	.400
2005	Ogden	R+	69	270	78	19	1	13	(-	-)	138	54	54	49	26	1	52	4	1	2	3	3	.50	14	.289	.358	.511
2006	Clmbs	A	105	435	104	32	2	15	(-	-)	185	71	75	56	29	2	83	3	1	5	3	0	1.00	13	.239	.288	.425
2006	VeroB	A+	22	83	23	8	0	4	(-	-)	43	12	16	13	4	0	14	1	2	1	1	1	.50	1	.277	.315	.518
2007	InldEm	A+	126	488	132	32	4	22	(-	-)	238	81	82	78	31	0	126	10	3	5	5	5	.50	9	.270	.324	.488
2008	Jaxnvl	AA	133	485	128	22	4	16	(-	-)	206	65	75	70	43	4	95	3	3	8	8	4	.67	16	.264	.323	.425
2009	Chatt	AA	131	456	110	30	3	13	(-	-)	185	63	63	58	36	2	84	2	4	3	4	1	.80	11	.241	.298	.406
2010	Albq	AAA	127	505	159	38	2	23	(-	-)	270	97	87	97	38	2	78	4	4	6	1	3	.25	7	.315	.363	.535
2011	Albq	AAA	93	336	95	22	2	16	(-	-)	169	66	69	65	46	0	62	5	0	5	1	1	.50	8	.283	.372	.503
2010	LAD	NL	15	42	6	0	0	2	(1	1)	12	3	4	0	0	0	8	0	0	1	0	0	-	1	.143	.140	.286
2011	LAD	NL	25	51	8	1	0	2	(1	1)	15	5	3	0	7	3	10	0	0	0	0	0	-	3	.157	.259	.294
2 ML YEARS			40	93	14	1	0	4	(2	2)	27	8	7	0	7	3	18	0	0	1	0	0	-	4	.151	.208	.290

Sergio Mitre

Pitches: R Bats: R Pos: RP-26   MEE-tray   Ht: 6'3" Wt: 225 Born: 2/16/1981 Age: 31

Year	Team	Lg	G	GS	CG	GF	IP	BFP	H	R	ER	HR	SH	SF	HB	TBB	IBB	SO	WP	Bk	W	L	Pct	Sh	Sv-Op	Hld	ERC	ERA
2003	ChC	NL	3	2	0	1	8.2	43	15	8	8	1	0	1	0	4	1	3	0	0	0	1	.000	0	0-0	0	9.02	8.31
2004	ChC	NL	12	9	0	2	51.2	244	71	38	38	6	3	0	4	20	1	37	5	1	2	4	.333	0	0-0	0	6.69	6.62
2005	ChC	NL	21	7	1	7	60.1	268	62	37	36	11	1	3	3	23	2	37	5	0	2	5	.286	1	0-0	0	4.81	5.37
2006	Fla	NL	15	7	0	3	41.0	189	44	28	26	7	2	1	6	20	3	31	1	0	1	5	.167	0	0-1	2	5.87	5.71
2007	Fla	NL	27	27	0	0	149.0	662	180	88	77	9	6	10	10	41	3	80	6	0	5	8	.385	0	0-0	0	4.71	4.65
2009	NYY	AL	12	9	0	2	51.2	241	71	45	39	10	0	4	3	13	0	32	3	0	3	3	.500	0	0-0	0	6.53	6.79
2010	NYY	AL	27	3	0	13	54.0	213	43	23	20	7	1	1	2	16	0	29	1	0	0	3	.000	0	1-1	1	3.03	3.33
2011	2 Tms	AL	26	0	0	12	38.1	168	39	23	19	3	1	2	2	14	0	16	1	0	0	1	.000	0	0-1	1	4.04	4.46
11	Mil	AL	22	0	0	8	33.0	138	30	14	12	3	1	1	1	10	0	14	0	0	0	1	.000	0	0-1	1	3.25	3.27
11	NYY	AL	4	0	0	4	5.1	30	9	9	7	0	0	1	1	4	0	2	1	0	0	0	-	0	0-0	0	9.56	11.81
Postseason			3	0	0	3	2.2	12	3	3	3	2	0	0	0	3	1	1	1	0	0	0	-	0	0-0	0	15.23	10.13
8 ML YEARS			143	64	1	40	454.2	2028	525	290	263	54	14	22	30	151	10	265	22	1	13	30	.302	1	1-3	4	5.05	5.21

Gustavo Molina

Bats: R Throws: R Pos: C-3   Ht: 6'1" Wt: 245 Born: 2/24/1982 Age: 30

Year	Team	Lg	G	AB	H	2B	3B	HR	(Hm	Rd)	TB	R	RBI	RC	TBB	IBB	SO	HBP	SH	SF	SB	CS	SB%	GDP	Avg	OBP	Slg
2011	S-WB*	AAA	47	162	41	6	0	4	(-	-)	59	9	21	17	7	0	37	1	2	1	0	0	-	1	.253	.287	.364
2007	2 Tms	AL	17	27	3	1	0	0	(0	0)	4	1	1	1	1	0	7	0	1	1	0	0	-	1	.111	.138	.148
2008	NYM	NL	2	7	1	0	0	0	(0	0)	1	0	0	0	1	0	1	0	0	0	0	0	-	0	.143	.250	.143
2010	Bos	AL	4	7	1	0	0	0	(0	0)	1	1	0	0	0	0	2	0	0	0	0	0	-	0	.143	.143	.143
2011	NYY	AL	3	6	1	1	0	0	(0	0)	2	0	0	0	0	0	0	0	0	0	0	0	-	0	.167	.167	.333
07	CWS	AL	10	18	1	0	0	0	(0	0)	1	0	1	0	1	0	4	0	1	1	0	0	-	0	.056	.100	.056
07	Bal	AL	7	9	2	1	0	0	(0	0)	3	1	0	1	0	0	3	0	0	0	0	0	-	1	.222	.222	.333
4 ML YEARS			26	47	6	2	0	0	(0	0)	8	2	1	1	2	0	10	0	1	1	0	0	-	0	.128	.160	.170

Jose Molina

Bats: R Throws: R Pos: C-48; DH-4; PH-3   Ht: 6'2" Wt: 250 Born: 6/3/1975 Age: 37

Year	Team	Lg	G	AB	H	2B	3B	HR	(Hm	Rd)	TB	R	RBI	RC	TBB	IBB	SO	HBP	SH	SF	SB	CS	SB%	GDP	Avg	OBP	Slg
1999	ChC	NL	10	19	5	1	0	0	(0	0)	6	3	1	2	2	1	4	0	0	0	0	0	-	0	.263	.333	.316
2001	LAA	AL	15	37	10	3	0	2	(0	2)	19	8	4	6	3	0	8	0	2	0	0	0	-	2	.270	.325	.514
2002	LAA	AL	29	70	19	3	0	0	(0	0)	22	5	5	4	5	0	15	0	4	2	0	2	.00	2	.271	.312	.314
2003	LAA	AL	53	114	21	4	0	0	(0	0)	25	12	6	5	1	0	26	3	4	1	0	0	-	1	.184	.210	.219
2004	LAA	AL	73	203	53	10	2	3	(1	2)	76	26	25	19	10	0	52	0	5	0	4	1	.80	6	.261	.296	.374
2005	LAA	AL	75	184	42	4	0	6	(2	4)	64	14	25	19	13	0	41	2	4	0	2	0	1.00	5	.228	.285	.348
2006	LAA	AL	78	225	54	17	0	4	(0	4)	83	18	22	21	9	0	49	2	7	2	1	0	1.00	6	.240	.273	.369
2007	2 Tms	AL	69	191	49	13	0	1	(1	0)	65	18	19	20	5	0	43	0	5	1	2	1	.67	4	.257	.274	.340

Year Team	Lg	G	AB	H	2B	3B	HR	(Hm Rd)	TB	R	RBI	RC	TBB	IBB	SO	HBP	SH	SF	SB	CS	SB%	GDP	Avg	OBP	Slg
2008 NYY	AL	100	268	58	17	0	3	(2 1)	84	32	18	15	12	0	52	6	8	3	0	0	-	9	.216	.263	.313
2009 NYY	AL	52	138	30	4	0	1	(0 1)	37	15	11	12	14	0	28	1	1	1	0	0	-	6	.217	.292	.268
2010 Tor	AL	57	167	41	4	0	6	(4 2)	63	13	12	12	9	1	36	5	2	0	1	0	1.00	7	.246	.304	.377
2011 Tor	AL	55	171	48	12	1	3	(1 2)	71	19	15	25	15	0	44	1	4	0	2	1	.67	2	.281	.342	.415
07 LAA	AL	40	125	28	8	0	0	(0 0)	36	9	10	9	3	0	30	0	3	0	2	1	.67	3	.224	.242	.288
07 NYY	AL	29	66	21	5	0	1	(1 0)	29	9	9	11	2	0	13	0	2	1	0	0	-	1	.318	.333	.439
Postseason		15	14	4	0	0	0	(0 0)	4	3	1	2	3	0	1	0	1	0	0	0	-	0	.286	.412	.286
12 ML YEARS		666	1787	430	92	3	29	(11 18)	615	183	163	160	98	2	398	20	46	10	12	5	.71	50	.241	.286	.344

Yadier Molina

Bats: R **Throws:** R **Pos:** C-138; 1B-2; PH-2   YAH-dee-air   **Ht:** 5'11" **Wt:** 230 **Born:** 7/13/1982 **Age:** 29

Year Team	Lg	G	AB	H	2B	3B	HR	(Hm Rd)	TB	R	RBI	RC	TBB	IBB	SO	HBP	SH	SF	SB	CS	SB%	GDP	Avg	OBP	Slg
2004 StL	NL	51	135	36	6	0	2	(1 1)	48	12	15	15	13	3	20	0	2	1	0	1	.00	4	.267	.329	.356
2005 StL	NL	114	385	97	15	1	8	(6 2)	138	36	49	46	23	3	30	2	8	3	2	3	.40	10	.252	.295	.358
2006 StL	NL	129	417	90	26	0	6	(2 4)	134	29	49	35	26	2	41	8	8	2	1	2	.33	15	.216	.274	.321
2007 StL	NL	111	353	97	15	0	6	(4 2)	130	30	40	38	34	5	43	3	2	4	1	1	.50	18	.275	.340	.368
2008 StL	NL	124	444	135	18	0	7	(2 5)	174	37	56	57	32	4	29	1	3	5	0	2	.00	21	.304	.349	.392
2009 StL	NL	140	481	141	23	1	6	(5 1)	184	45	54	64	50	2	39	6	6	1	9	3	.75	27	.293	.366	.383
2010 StL	NL	136	465	122	19	0	6	(1 5)	159	34	62	55	42	6	51	7	2	5	8	4	.67	19	.262	.329	.342
2011 StL	NL	139	475	145	32	1	14	(5 9)	221	55	65	64	33	4	44	1	5	4	4	5	.44	21	.305	.349	.465
Postseason		32	108	34	8	0	2	(1 1)	48	7	11	12	6	1	10	0	0	0	0	1	.00	4	.315	.351	.444
8 ML YEARS		944	3155	863	154	3	55	(26 29)	1188	278	390	374	253	29	297	28	36	25	25	21	.54	135	.274	.331	.377

Lou Montanez

Bats: R **Throws:** R **Pos:** RF-14; PH-12; LF-10; PR-3; CF-1   MONN-tah-nezz   **Ht:** 6'1" **Wt:** 195 **Born:** 12/15/1981 **Age:** 30

Year Team	Lg	G	AB	H	2B	3B	HR	(Hm Rd)	TB	R	RBI	RC	TBB	IBB	SO	HBP	SH	SF	SB	CS	SB%	GDP	Avg	OBP	Slg
2011 Iowa*	AAA	92	333	107	22	7	7	(- -)	164	52	69	64	38	1	47	5	3	3	4	6	.40	7	.321	.396	.492
2008 Bal	AL	38	112	33	6	1	3	(2 1)	50	18	14	17	4	0	20	0	0	1	0	0	-	0	.295	.316	.446
2009 Bal	AL	29	82	15	5	0	1	(1 0)	23	5	6	8	5	0	16	2	1	1	0	1	.00	0	.183	.244	.280
2010 Bal	AL	26	57	8	0	0	0	(0 0)	8	2	3	0	1	0	9	0	0	0	1	0	1.00	3	.140	.155	.140
2011 ChC	NL	36	54	12	4	0	1	(1 0)	19	6	9	8	2	0	9	1	0	0	0	1	.00	0	.222	.263	.352
4 ML YEARS		129	305	68	15	1	5	(4 1)	100	31	32	33	12	0	54	3	1	2	1	2	.33	3	.223	.258	.328

Jesus Montero

Bats: R **Throws:** R **Pos:** DH-14; C-3; PH-1   **Ht:** 6'4" **Wt:** 225 **Born:** 11/28/1989 **Age:** 22

Year Team	Lg	G	AB	H	2B	3B	HR	(Hm Rd)	TB	R	RBI	RC	TBB	IBB	SO	HBP	SH	SF	SB	CS	SB%	GDP	Avg	OBP	Slg
2007 Yanks	R	33	107	30	6	0	3	(- -)	45	13	19	17	12	0	18	3	0	1	0	0	-	7	.280	.366	.421
2008 CtnSC	A	132	525	171	34	1	17	(- -)	258	86	87	96	37	2	83	6	0	1	2	1	.67	16	.326	.376	.491
2009 Tampa	A+	48	180	64	15	1	8	(- -)	105	26	37	40	14	1	26	2	1	1	0	0	-	3	.356	.406	.583
2009 Trntn	AA	44	167	53	10	0	9	(- -)	90	19	33	32	14	1	21	0	0	0	0	0	-	10	.317	.370	.539
2010 S-WB	AAA	123	453	131	34	3	21	(- -)	234	66	75	83	46	2	91	1	0	4	0	0	-	14	.289	.353	.517
2011 S-WB	AAA	109	420	121	19	1	18	(- -)	196	52	66	69	36	6	98	4	0	3	0	0	-	16	.288	.348	.467
2011 NYY	AL	18	61	20	4	0	4	(3 1)	36	9	12	12	7	2	17	1	0	0	0	0	-	2	.328	.406	.590

Miguel Montero

Bats: L **Throws:** R **Pos:** C-134; PH-9   **Ht:** 5'11" **Wt:** 215 **Born:** 7/9/1983 **Age:** 28

Year Team	Lg	G	AB	H	2B	3B	HR	(Hm Rd)	TB	R	RBI	RC	TBB	IBB	SO	HBP	SH	SF	SB	CS	SB%	GDP	Avg	OBP	Slg
2006 Ari	NL	6	16	4	1	0	0	(0 0)	5	0	3	2	1	0	3	0	0	0	0	0	-	0	.250	.294	.313
2007 Ari	NL	84	214	48	7	0	10	(7 3)	85	30	37	19	20	2	35	3	1	6	0	0	-	7	.224	.292	.397
2008 Ari	NL	70	184	47	16	1	5	(1 4)	80	24	18	21	19	3	49	2	1	1	0	0	-	1	.255	.330	.435
2009 Ari	NL	128	425	125	30	0	16	(5 11)	203	61	59	65	38	5	78	3	2	2	1	2	.33	6	.294	.355	.478
2010 Ari	NL	85	297	79	20	2	9	(0 9)	130	36	43	38	29	3	71	2	0	3	0	1	.00	10	.266	.332	.438
2011 Ari	NL	140	493	139	36	1	18	(8 10)	231	65	86	84	47	10	97	8	1	4	1	1	.50	14	.282	.351	.469
Postseason		4	7	2	0	0	0	(0 0)	2	1	0	0	1	0	0	0	0	0	0	0	-	0	.286	.375	.286
6 ML YEARS		513	1629	442	110	4	58	(21 37)	734	216	246	229	154	23	333	18	5	16	2	4	.33	38	.271	.338	.451

Adam Moore

Bats: R **Throws:** R **Pos:** C-2   **Ht:** 6'3" **Wt:** 220 **Born:** 5/8/1984 **Age:** 28

Year Team	Lg	G	AB	H	2B	3B	HR	(Hm Rd)	TB	R	RBI	RC	TBB	IBB	SO	HBP	SH	SF	SB	CS	SB%	GDP	Avg	OBP	Slg
2009 Sea	AL	6	23	5	1	0	1	(1 0)	9	4	2	2	0	0	7	1	0	0	1	0	1.00	1	.217	.250	.391
2010 Sea	AL	60	205	40	6	0	4	(1 3)	58	12	15	9	8	1	63	2	1	2	0	1	.00	3	.195	.230	.283
2011 Sea	AL	2	6	1	1	0	0	(0 0)	2	0	0	0	0	0	2	0	0	0	0	0	-	0	.167	.167	.333
3 ML YEARS		68	234	46	8	0	5	(2 3)	69	16	17	11	8	1	72	3	1	2	1	1	.50	4	.197	.231	.295

Jeremy Moore

Bats: L **Throws:** R **Pos:** RF-3; PR-3; LF-2; PH-1   **Ht:** 6'1" **Wt:** 190 **Born:** 6/29/1987 **Age:** 25

Year	Team	Lg	G	AB	H	2B	3B	HR	(Hm	Rd)	TB	R	RBI	RC	TBB	IBB	SO	HBP	SH	SF	SB	CS	SB%	GDP	Avg	OBP	Slg
2005	Angels	R	34	110	25	3	1	0	(-	-)	30	15	11	9	11	0	46	1	2	0	12	6	.67	3	.227	.303	.273
2006	Angels	R	41	142	36	7	2	3	(-	-)	56	25	19	18	18	0	37	3	1	1	4	8	.33	4	.254	.348	.394
2007	Orem	R+	68	254	69	13	6	14	(-	-)	136	50	54	46	19	2	68	3	4	1	17	5	.77	5	.272	.329	.535
2008	CRpds	A	96	362	87	11	12	17	(-	-)	173	47	48	51	21	0	125	2	2	2	28	10	.74	1	.240	.284	.478
2009	RCuca	A+	124	470	131	20	12	11	(-	-)	208	61	58	68	34	2	144	4	4	4	17	13	.57	6	.279	.330	.443
2009	Ark	AA	7	21	7	0	1	2	(-	-)	15	5	10	5	3	0	7	1	0	1	1	1	.50	0	.333	.423	.714
2010	Ark	AA	128	456	138	14	10	13	(-	-)	211	72	61	77	39	2	122	3	5	5	24	10	.71	7	.303	.358	.463
2011	Salt Lk	AAA	113	426	127	24	18	15	(-	-)	232	76	66	76	21	0	114	3	4	6	21	10	.68	6	.298	.331	.545
2011	LAA	AL	8	8	1	0	0	0	(0	0)	1	3	0	0	0	0	2	0	0	0	0	0	-	0	.125	.125	.125

Matt Moore

Pitches: L **Bats:** L **Pos:** RP-2; SP-1   **Ht:** 6'2" **Wt:** 205 **Born:** 6/18/1989 **Age:** 23

Year	Team	Lg	G	GS	CG	GF	IP	BFP	H	R	ER	HR	SH	SF	HB	TBB	IBB	SO	WP	Bk	W	L	Pct	Sh	Sv-Op	Hld	ERC	ERA
2007	Princtn	R	8	3	0	0	20.1	93	12	6	6	1	0	0	2	16	0	29	2	0	0	0	-	0	0- -	-	3.14	2.66
2008	Princtn	R	12	12	0	0	54.1	221	30	22	10	0	2	1	4	19	0	77	4	0	2	2	.500	0	0- -	-	1.38	1.66
2009	BG	A	26	26	0	0	123.0	522	86	51	43	6	4	0	6	70	0	176	13	0	8	5	.615	0	0- -	-	2.92	3.15
2010	Charltt	A+	26	26	0	0	144.2	598	109	62	54	7	6	4	8	61	0	208	10	2	6	11	.353	0	0- -	-	2.73	3.36
2011	Mont	AA	18	18	1	0	102.1	400	68	31	25	8	2	1	5	28	0	131	3	1	8	3	.727	1	0- -	-	1.97	2.20
2011	Drham	AAA	9	9	0	0	52.2	204	33	8	8	3	1	0	1	18	0	79	4	0	4	0	1.000	0	0- -	-	1.83	1.37
2011	TB	AL	3	1	0	0	9.1	40	9	3	3	1	0	0	0	3	0	15	2	0	1	0	1.000	0	0-0	-	3.54	2.89

Melvin Mora

Bats: R **Throws:** R **Pos:** 3B-31; PH-11; 1B-1   **Ht:** 5'11" **Wt:** 200 **Born:** 2/7/1972 **Age:** 40

Year	Team	Lg	G	AB	H	2B	3B	HR	(Hm	Rd)	TB	R	RBI	RC	TBB	IBB	SO	HBP	SH	SF	SB	CS	SB%	GDP	Avg	OBP	Slg
1999	NYM	NL	66	31	5	0	0	0	(0	0)	5	6	1	2	4	0	7	1	3	0	2	1	.67	0	.161	.278	.161
2000	2 Tms		132	414	114	22	5	8	(5	3)	170	60	47	56	35	3	80	6	4	5	12	11	.52	5	.275	.337	.411
2001	Bal	AL	128	436	109	28	0	7	(6	1)	158	49	48	55	41	2	91	14	5	7	11	4	.73	6	.250	.329	.362
2002	Bal	AL	149	557	130	30	4	19	(8	11)	225	86	64	78	70	2	108	20	1	4	16	10	.62	7	.233	.388	.404
2003	Bal	AL	96	344	109	17	1	15	(8	7)	173	68	48	67	49	0	71	12	6	2	6	3	.67	3	.317	.418	.503
2004	Bal	AL	140	550	187	41	0	27	(15	12)	309	111	104	115	66	0	95	11	6	3	11	6	.65	10	.340	.419	.562
2005	Bal	AL	149	593	168	30	1	27	(13	14)	281	86	88	88	50	0	112	10	8	3	7	4	.64	9	.283	.348	.474
2006	Bal	AL	155	624	171	25	0	16	(8	8)	244	96	83	93	54	1	99	14	6	7	11	1	.92	9	.274	.342	.391
2007	Bal	AL	126	467	128	23	1	14	(7	7)	195	67	58	61	47	3	83	3	5	5	9	3	.75	22	.274	.341	.418
2008	Bal	AL	135	513	146	29	2	23	(15	8)	248	77	104	88	37	3	70	11	3	6	3	7	.30	14	.285	.342	.483
2009	Bal	AL	125	450	117	20	0	8	(8	0)	161	44	48	48	34	1	60	8	1	3	3	3	.50	13	.260	.321	.358
2010	Col	NL	113	316	90	12	5	7	(2	5)	133	39	45	49	31	2	53	5	2	0	2	1	.67	9	.285	.358	.421
2011	Ari	NL	42	127	29	6	0	0	(0	0)	35	5	16	10	2	1	24	2	0	4	1	0	.00	5	.228	.244	.276
00	NYM	NL	79	215	56	13	2	6	(4	2)	91	35	30	29	18	3	48	2	2	5	7	3	.70	3	.260	.317	.423
00	Bal	AL	53	199	58	9	3	2	(1	1)	79	25	17	27	17	0	32	4	2	0	5	8	.38	2	.291	.359	.397
	Postseason		9	15	6	0	0	1	(0	1)	9	4	2	4	3	0	2	0	1	0	2	0	1.00	0	.400	.500	.600
	13 ML YEARS		1556	5422	1503	283	19	171	(95	76)	2337	794	754	810	520	18	953	117	50	49	93	55	.63	112	.277	.350	.431

Franklin Morales

Pitches: L **Bats:** L **Pos:** RP-50   **Ht:** 6'0" **Wt:** 210 **Born:** 1/24/1986 **Age:** 26

Year	Team	Lg	G	GS	CG	GF	IP	BFP	H	R	ER	HR	SH	SF	HB	TBB	IBB	SO	WP	Bk	W	L	Pct	Sh	Sv-Op	Hld	ERC	ERA
2011	Pwtckt*	AAA	6	0	0	0	6.1	28	3	3	1	1	0	0	1	3	0	6	0	0	0	0	-	0	0- -	-	2.29	1.42
2007	Col	NL	8	8	0	0	39.1	163	34	15	15	2	4	2	2	14	1	26	0	0	3	2	.600	0	0-0	0	3.04	3.43
2008	Col	NL	5	5	0	0	25.1	120	28	18	18	2	2	2	1	17	2	9	1	3	1	2	.333	0	0-0	0	5.58	6.39
2009	Col	NL	40	2	0	14	40.0	179	38	22	20	4	3	0	1	23	4	41	2	0	3	2	.600	0	7-8	7	4.38	4.50
2010	Col	NL	35	0	0	15	28.2	140	28	22	20	5	1	2	3	24	2	27	3	2	0	4	.000	0	3-6	1	6.53	6.28
2011	2 Tms		50	0	0	13	46.1	193	40	21	19	6	2	1	2	19	1	42	2	1	1	2	.333	0	0-0	10	3.77	3.69
11	Col	NL	14	0	0	4	14.0	59	10	6	6	2	1	1	0	8	1	11	1	0	0	1	.000	0	0-0	2	3.36	3.86
11	Bos	AL	36	0	0	9	32.1	134	30	15	13	4	1	0	2	11	0	31	1	1	1	1	.500	0	0-0	8	3.96	3.62
	Postseason		8	2	0	0	12.2	59	15	11	11	1	0	0	2	7	1	7	1	0	0	0	-	0	0-0	1	6.28	7.82
	5 ML YEARS		138	15	0	42	179.2	795	168	98	92	19	12	7	9	97	10	145	8	6	8	12	.400	0	10-14	18	4.41	4.61

Jose Morales

Bats: B **Throws:** R **Pos:** C-17; PH-4; 2B-2   **Ht:** 5'11" **Wt:** 202 **Born:** 2/20/1983 **Age:** 29

Year	Team	Lg	G	AB	H	2B	3B	HR	(Hm	Rd)	TB	R	RBI	RC	TBB	IBB	SO	HBP	SH	SF	SB	CS	SB%	GDP	Avg	OBP	Slg
2007	Min	AL	1	3	3	1	0	0	(0	0)	4	1	0	2	0	0	0	0	0	0	0	0	-	0	1.000	1.000	1.333
2009	Min	AL	54	119	37	6	0	0	(0	0)	43	14	7	19	14	1	22	0	0	1	0	0	-	4	.311	.381	.361
2010	Min	AL	19	36	7	2	0	0	(0	0)	9	4	7	4	6	0	14	0	0	2	0	0	-	2	.194	.295	.250
2011	Col	NL	22	60	16	3	0	0	(0	0)	19	6	7	6	9	4	12	0	0	2	0	1	.00	1	.267	.352	.317
	Postseason		1	3	0	0	0	0	(0	0)	0	0	0	0	0	0	2	0	0	0	0	0	-	0	.000	.000	.000
	4 ML YEARS		96	218	63	12	0	0	(0	0)	75	25	21	31	29	5	48	0	0	5	0	1	.00	7	.289	.365	.344

Kendrys Morales

Bats: B **Throws:** R **Pos:** 1B   KEN-dreez   **Ht:** 6'1" **Wt:** 225 **Born:** 6/20/1983 **Age:** 29

Year	Team	Lg	G	AB	H	2B	3B	HR	(Hm	Rd)	TB	R	RBI	RC	TBB	IBB	SO	HBP	SH	SF	SB	CS	SB%	GDP	Avg	OBP	Slg
2006	LAA	AL	57	197	46	10	1	5	(1	4)	73	21	22	19	17	1	28	0	0	1	1	1	.50	11	.234	.293	.371
2007	LAA	AL	43	119	35	10	0	4	(2	2)	57	12	15	15	6	2	21	1	0	0	0	1	.00	5	.294	.333	.479
2008	LAA	AL	27	61	13	2	0	3	(0	3)	24	7	8	3	4	0	7	1	0	0	0	1	.00	3	.213	.273	.393
2009	LAA	AL	152	566	173	43	2	34	(21	13)	322	86	108	105	46	10	117	2	0	8	3	7	.30	15	.306	.355	.569
2010	LAA	AL	51	193	56	5	0	11	(7	4)	94	29	39	34	12	3	31	5	0	1	0	1	.00	5	.290	.346	.487
	Postseason		16	47	9	1	0	2	(1	1)	16	3	7	3	2	0	8	1	0	1	0	0	-	1	.191	.235	.340
	5 ML YEARS		330	1136	323	70	3	57	(31	26)	570	155	192	176	85	16	204	9	0	10	4	11	.27	39	.284	.336	.502

Brent Morel

Bats: R **Throws:** R **Pos:** 3B-125; PH-1   more-ELL   **Ht:** 6'2" **Wt:** 220 **Born:** 4/21/1987 **Age:** 25

Year	Team	Lg	G	AB	H	2B	3B	HR	(Hm	Rd)	TB	R	RBI	RC	TBB	IBB	SO	HBP	SH	SF	SB	CS	SB%	GDP	Avg	OBP	Slg
2008	Gr Falls	R+	15	64	24	0	2	0	(-	-)	28	11	3	13	6	0	7	1	0	0	7	0	1.00	0	.375	.437	.438
2008	Knapol	A	45	172	51	6	2	6	(-	-)	79	26	24	29	16	0	28	2	0	2	5	2	.71	2	.297	.359	.459
2009	WinSa	A+	128	481	135	33	1	16	(-	-)	218	82	79	76	38	2	66	3	1	3	25	9	.74	14	.281	.335	.453
2010	Brham	AA	49	184	60	13	1	2	(-	-)	81	25	30	30	14	0	36	2	1	2	5	5	.50	2	.326	.376	.440
2010	Charltt	AAA	81	306	98	24	4	8	(-	-)	154	40	34	53	13	0	50	0	5	0	3	0	1.00	6	.320	.348	.503
2010	CWS	AL	21	65	15	3	0	3	(3	0)	27	9	7	4	4	0	17	0	0	1	2	0	1.00	1	.231	.271	.415
2011	CWS	AL	126	413	101	18	1	10	(6	4)	151	44	41	36	22	0	57	3	5	1	5	4	.56	8	.245	.287	.366
	2 ML YEARS		147	478	116	21	1	13	(9	4)	178	53	48	40	26	0	74	3	5	2	7	4	.64	10	.243	.285	.372

Mitch Moreland

Bats: L **Throws:** L **Pos:** 1B-99; RF-34; DH-8; PH-6   **Ht:** 6'2" **Wt:** 230 **Born:** 9/6/1985 **Age:** 26

Year	Team	Lg	G	AB	H	2B	3B	HR	(Hm	Rd)	TB	R	RBI	RC	TBB	IBB	SO	HBP	SH	SF	SB	CS	SB%	GDP	Avg	OBP	Slg
2007	Spkane	A-	27	108	28	7	1	2	(-	-)	43	10	15	13	8	0	25	0	1	1	1	0	1.00	4	.259	.308	.398
2008	Clinton	A	123	466	151	37	4	18	(-	-)	250	64	99	99	60	3	67	2	0	5	2	4	.33	15	.324	.400	.536
2009	Bkrsfld	A+	43	170	58	19	0	8	(-	-)	101	34	26	41	21	1	26	4	0	2	1	0	1.00	4	.341	.421	.594
2009	Frisco	AA	73	301	98	19	3	8	(-	-)	147	51	59	54	23	1	42	1	0	2	1	1	.50	17	.326	.373	.488
2010	OKCity	AAA	95	353	102	29	2	12	(-	-)	171	52	65	66	47	2	63	3	2	7	2	1	.67	15	.289	.371	.484
2010	Tex	AL	47	145	37	4	0	9	(3	6)	68	20	25	27	25	5	36	1	0	2	3	1	.75	3	.255	.364	.469
2011	Tex	AL	134	464	120	22	1	16	(7	9)	192	60	51	56	39	6	92	4	2	3	2	2	.50	9	.259	.320	.414
	Postseason		15	46	16	4	0	1	(1	0)	23	5	7	12	4	1	9	0	1	0	0	0	-	1	.348	.400	.500
	2 ML YEARS		181	609	157	26	1	25	(10	15)	260	80	76	83	64	11	128	5	2	5	5	3	.63	12	.258	.331	.427

Nyjer Morgan

Bats: L **Throws:** L **Pos:** CF-95; RF-20; PH-18; LF-17; PR-2   NYE-jerr   **Ht:** 6'0" **Wt:** 175 **Born:** 7/2/1980 **Age:** 31

Year	Team	Lg	G	AB	H	2B	3B	HR	(Hm	Rd)	TB	R	RBI	RC	TBB	IBB	SO	HBP	SH	SF	SB	CS	SB%	GDP	Avg	OBP	Slg
2011	Nashv*	AAA	2	4	2	0	0	0	(-	-)	2	1	0	1	2	0	1	0	0	0	1	0	1.00	0	.500	.667	.500
2007	Pit	NL	28	107	32	3	4	1	(1	0)	46	15	7	18	9	0	19	1	1	0	7	3	.70	0	.299	.359	.430
2008	Pit	NL	58	160	47	13	0	0	(0	0)	60	26	7	18	10	0	32	3	1	1	9	5	.64	0	.294	.345	.375
2009	2 Tms	NL	120	469	144	15	7	3	(1	2)	182	74	39	69	40	2	74	9	10	5	42	17	.71	9	.307	.369	.388
2010	Was	NL	136	509	129	11	7	0	(0	0)	160	60	24	53	40	1	88	10	15	3	34	17	.67	2	.253	.319	.314
2011	Mil	NL	119	378	115	20	6	4	(0	4)	159	61	37	58	19	0	70	14	15	3	13	4	.76	6	.304	.357	.421
09	Pit	NL	71	278	77	6	5	2	(1	1)	99	39	27	37	29	2	49	5	5	4	18	10	.64	6	.277	.351	.356
09	Was	NL	49	191	67	9	2	1	(0	1)	83	35	12	32	11	0	25	4	5	1	24	7	.77	3	.351	.396	.435
	5 ML YEARS		461	1623	467	68	24	8	(2	6)	607	236	114	216	118	3	283	37	42	12	105	46	.70	17	.288	.347	.374

Justin Morneau

Bats: L **Throws:** R **Pos:** 1B-56; DH-13; PH-1   MORE-no   **Ht:** 6'4" **Wt:** 233 **Born:** 5/15/1981 **Age:** 31

Year	Team	Lg	G	AB	H	2B	3B	HR	(Hm	Rd)	TB	R	RBI	RC	TBB	IBB	SO	HBP	SH	SF	SB	CS	SB%	GDP	Avg	OBP	Slg
2011	Roch*	AAA	7	30	11	4	0	1	(-	-)	18	8	8	6	1	0	2	0	0	0	0	0	-	1	.367	.387	.600
2003	Min	AL	40	106	24	4	0	4	(1	3)	40	14	16	11	9	1	30	0	0	0	0	0	-	4	.226	.287	.377
2004	Min	AL	74	280	76	17	0	19	(9	10)	150	39	58	48	28	8	54	2	0	2	0	0	-	4	.271	.340	.536
2005	Min	AL	141	490	117	23	4	22	(9	13)	214	62	79	58	44	8	94	4	0	5	0	2	.00	12	.239	.304	.437
2006	Min	AL	157	592	190	37	1	34	(17	17)	331	97	130	118	53	9	93	5	0	11	3	3	.50	10	.321	.375	.559
2007	Min	AL	157	590	160	31	3	31	(15	16)	290	84	111	95	64	11	91	5	0	9	1	1	.50	17	.271	.343	.492
2008	Min	AL	163	623	187	47	4	23	(12	11)	311	97	129	122	76	16	85	3	0	10	0	1	.00	20	.300	.374	.499
2009	Min	AL	135	508	139	31	1	30	(14	16)	262	85	100	91	72	12	86	3	0	7	0	0	-	12	.274	.363	.516
2010	Min	AL	81	296	102	25	1	18	(4	14)	183	53	56	65	50	7	62	0	0	2	0	0	-	6	.345	.437	.618
2011	Min	AL	69	264	60	16	0	4	(0	4)	88	19	30	28	19	1	44	3	0	2	0	0	-	8	.227	.285	.333
	Postseason		7	29	9	3	0	2	(1	1)	18	4	4	3	0	0	3	0	0	0	0	0	-	0	.310	.310	.621
	9 ML YEARS		1017	3749	1055	231	14	185	(81	104)	1869	550	709	636	415	73	639	25	0	48	4	7	.36	93	.281	.353	.499

Logan Morrison

Bats: L Throws: L Pos: LF-119; PH-3; 1B-1; DH-1   Ht: 6'3" Wt: 237 Born: 8/25/1987 Age: 24

							BATTING													BASERUNNING				AVERAGES		
Year	Team	Lg	G	AB	H	2B	3B	HR	(Hm	Rd)	TB	R	RBI	RC	TBB	IBB	SO	HBP	SH	SF	SB	CS	SB%	GDP	Avg	OBP	Slg
2006	Mrlns	R	26	89	24	4	0	1	(-	-)	31	10	7	11	10	0	12	0	0	0	1	0	1.00	3	.270	.343	.348
2006	Jmstwn	A-	23	74	15	3	0	1	(-	-)	21	6	11	7	11	0	17	0	0	3	0	0	-	1	.203	.295	.284
2007	Grnsbr	A	128	453	121	22	2	24	(-	-)	219	71	86	77	48	5	96	7	0	5	2	2	.50	8	.267	.343	.483
2008	Jupiter	A+	130	488	162	38	1	13	(-	-)	241	71	74	99	57	6	80	4	0	6	9	3	.75	11	.332	.402	.494
2009	Jaxnvl	AA	79	278	77	18	2	8	(-	-)	123	48	47	55	63	5	46	1	0	1	9	4	.69	5	.277	.411	.442
2009	Jupiter	A+	3	11	3	1	0	0	(-	-)	4	0	2	1	1	0	2	0	0	0	0	1	.00	2	.273	.333	.364
2010	NewOr	AAA	68	238	73	17	4	6	(-	-)	116	36	45	52	48	4	35	4	0	3	1	2	.33	5	.307	.427	.487
2010	Jupiter	A+	5	21	8	2	2	0	(-	-)	14	3	2	4	0	0	3	0	0	0	0	0	-	1	.381	.381	.667
2011	Jupiter	A+	3	10	2	0	0	1	(-	-)	5	2	3	2	3	0	4	0	0	0	0	0	-	1	.200	.385	.500
2011	NewOr	AAA	6	24	4	2	0	1	(-	-)	9	3	5	2	2	0	4	0	0	1	0	0	-	0	.167	.222	.375
2010	Fla	NL	62	244	69	20	7	2	(1	1)	109	43	18	41	41	0	51	2	0	0	0	1	.00	4	.283	.390	.447
2011	Fla	NL	123	462	114	25	4	23	(12	11)	216	54	72	55	54	3	99	5	0	4	2	1	.67	9	.247	.330	.468
	2 ML YEARS		185	706	183	45	11	25	(13	12)	325	97	90	96	95	3	150	7	0	4	2	2	.50	13	.259	.351	.460

Brandon Morrow

Pitches: R Bats: R Pos: SP-30   Ht: 6'3" Wt: 195 Born: 7/26/1984 Age: 27

			HOW MUCH HE PITCHED						WHAT HE GAVE UP										THE RESULTS						
Year	Team	Lg	G	GS	CG	GF	IP	BFP	H	R	ER	HR	SH	SF	HB	TBB	IBB	SO	WP	Bk	W	L	Pct	Sh	Sv-Op Hld	ERC	ERA
2011	Dnedin*	A+	3	3	0	0	9.1	48	13	9	8	0	0	0	0	6	0	11	3	0	0	2	.000	0	0- - -	6.26	7.71
2007	Sea	AL	60	0	0	18	63.1	289	56	29	29	3	4	4	1	50	5	66	4	0	3	4	.429	0	0-2 18	4.47	4.12
2008	Sea	AL	45	5	0	24	64.2	265	40	26	24	10	1	0	0	34	1	75	5	0	3	4	.429	0	10-12 3	2.84	3.34
2009	Sea	AL	26	10	0	9	69.2	313	66	38	34	10	1	2	0	44	1	63	3	0	2	4	.333	0	6-8 1	4.99	4.39
2010	Tor	AL	26	26	1	0	146.1	629	136	76	73	11	2	4	9	66	0	178	8	0	10	7	.588	1	0-0 0	3.99	4.49
2011	Tor	AL	30	30	0	0	179.1	777	162	103	94	21	4	9	12	69	1	203	12	1	11	11	.500	0	0-0 0	3.79	4.72
	5 ML YEARS		187	71	1	51	523.1	2273	460	272	254	55	12	19	22	263	8	585	32	1	29	30	.492	1	16-22 22	3.97	4.37

Michael Morse

Bats: R Throws: R Pos: 1B-85; LF-55; PH-12; DH-1   Ht: 6'5" Wt: 230 Born: 3/22/1982 Age: 30

							BATTING													BASERUNNING				AVERAGES		
Year	Team	Lg	G	AB	H	2B	3B	HR	(Hm	Rd)	TB	R	RBI	RC	TBB	IBB	SO	HBP	SH	SF	SB	CS	SB%	GDP	Avg	OBP	Slg
2005	Sea	AL	72	230	64	10	1	3	(3	0)	85	27	23	28	18	0	50	8	0	2	3	1	.75	9	.278	.349	.370
2006	Sea	AL	21	43	16	5	0	0	(0	0)	21	5	11	9	3	0	7	0	0	2	1	0	1.00	2	.372	.396	.488
2007	Sea	AL	9	18	8	2	0	0	(0	0)	10	1	3	6	1	0	4	1	0	0	0	0	-	0	.444	.500	.556
2008	Sea	AL	5	9	2	1	0	0	(0	0)	3	0	0	1	1	0	4	1	0	0	0	0	-	0	.222	.364	.333
2009	Was	NL	32	52	13	3	0	3	(3	0)	25	4	10	8	3	0	16	0	0	0	0	0	-	1	.250	.291	.481
2010	Was	NL	98	266	77	12	2	15	(6	9)	138	36	41	42	22	1	64	4	0	1	0	1	.00	6	.289	.352	.519
2011	Was	NL	146	522	158	36	0	31	(11	20)	287	73	95	96	36	5	126	13	0	4	2	3	.40	9	.303	.360	.550
	7 ML YEARS		383	1140	338	69	3	52	(23	29)	569	146	183	190	84	6	271	27	0	9	6	5	.55	27	.296	.356	.499

Clayton Mortensen

Pitches: R Bats: R Pos: RP-10; SP-6   Ht: 6'4" Wt: 185 Born: 4/10/1985 Age: 27

			HOW MUCH HE PITCHED						WHAT HE GAVE UP										THE RESULTS						
Year	Team	Lg	G	GS	CG	GF	IP	BFP	H	R	ER	HR	SH	SF	HB	TBB	IBB	SO	WP	Bk	W	L	Pct	Sh	Sv-Op Hld	ERC	ERA
2011	ColSpr*	AAA	15	15	0	0	64.0	317	104	71	67	13	1	4	2	29	1	54	6	0	2	8	.200	0	0- - -	9.30	9.42
2009	2 Tms		7	6	0	1	30.2	149	42	34	26	6	1	4	3	13	0	13	1	0	2	4	.333	0	0-0 0	7.50	7.63
2010	Oak	AL	1	1	0	0	6.0	26	6	4	3	1	0	0	0	2	0	7	0	0	0	0	-	0	0-0 0	4.18	4.50
2011	Col	NL	16	6	0	6	58.1	244	55	30	25	9	4	0	2	24	2	30	3	0	2	4	.333	0	0-0 0	4.40	3.86
09	StL	NL	1	0	0	1	3.0	16	5	6	2	1	1	1	1	1	0	2	0	0	0	0	-	0	0-0 0	11.45	6.00
09	Oak	AL	6	6	0	0	27.2	133	37	28	24	5	0	3	2	12	0	11	1	0	2	4	.333	0	0-0 0	7.10	7.81
	3 ML YEARS		24	13	0	7	95.0	419	103	68	54	16	5	4	5	39	2	50	4	0	4	8	.333	0	0-0 0	5.34	5.12

Charlie Morton

Pitches: R Bats: R Pos: SP-29   Ht: 6'5" Wt: 230 Born: 11/12/1983 Age: 28

			HOW MUCH HE PITCHED						WHAT HE GAVE UP										THE RESULTS						
Year	Team	Lg	G	GS	CG	GF	IP	BFP	H	R	ER	HR	SH	SF	HB	TBB	IBB	SO	WP	Bk	W	L	Pct	Sh	Sv-Op Hld	ERC	ERA
2008	Atl	NL	16	15	0	0	74.2	345	80	56	51	9	5	4	2	41	2	48	2	0	4	8	.333	0	0-0 0	5.21	6.15
2009	Pit	NL	18	18	1	0	97.0	416	102	49	49	7	1	1	5	40	0	62	4	0	5	9	.357	1	0-0 0	4.56	4.55
2010	Pit	NL	17	17	0	0	79.2	382	112	79	67	15	6	6	7	26	3	59	5	1	2	12	.143	0	0-0 0	7.10	7.57
2011	Pit	NL	29	29	2	0	171.2	769	186	82	73	6	12	6	13	77	5	110	9	1	10	10	.500	1	0-0 0	4.52	3.83
	4 ML YEARS		80	79	3	0	423.0	1912	480	266	240	37	24	17	27	184	10	279	20	2	21	39	.350	2	0-0 0	5.12	5.11

Guillermo Moscoso

Pitches: R Bats: R Pos: SP-21; RP-2   mahs-KOE-soe   Ht: 6'1" Wt: 200 Born: 11/14/1983 Age: 28

			HOW MUCH HE PITCHED						WHAT HE GAVE UP										THE RESULTS						
Year	Team	Lg	G	GS	CG	GF	IP	BFP	H	R	ER	HR	SH	SF	HB	TBB	IBB	SO	WP	Bk	W	L	Pct	Sh	Sv-Op Hld	ERC	ERA
2011	Scrmto*	AAA	9	8	0	0	46.1	194	41	22	20	3	0	0	0	16	0	52	3	1	3	3	.500	0	0- - -	2.98	3.88
2009	Tex	AL	10	0	0	0	14.0	64	15	7	5	1	0	1	1	6	0	12	4	0	0	0	-	0	0-0 0	4.55	3.21
2010	Tex	AL	1	0	0	0	0.2	7	2	2	2	0	0	0	1	2	0	2	0	0	0	0	-	0	0-0 0	37.18	27.00
2011	Oak	AL	23	21	0	1	128.0	526	102	59	48	14	1	3	2	38	1	74	0	1	8	10	.444	0	0-0 0	2.67	3.38
	3 ML YEARS		34	21	0	1	142.2	597	119	68	55	15	1	4	4	46	1	88	4	1	8	10	.444	0	0-0 0	2.96	3.47

Dustin Moseley

Pitches: R Bats: R Pos: SP-20   MOZE-lee   Ht: 6'4" Wt: 215 Born: 12/26/1981 Age: 30

Year	Team	Lg	G	GS	CG	GF	IP	BFP	H	R	ER	HR	SH	SF	HB	TBB	IBB	SO	WP	Bk	W	L	Pct	Sh	Sv-Op	Hld	ERC	ERA
2006	LAA	AL	3	2	0	1	11.0	54	22	11	11	3	0	1	0	2	0	3	0	0	1	0	1.000	0	0-0	0	11.45	9.00
2007	LAA	AL	46	8	0	13	92.0	383	97	45	45	7	1	2	3	27	3	50	6	1	4	3	.571	0	0-0	4	4.00	4.40
2008	LAA	AL	12	10	0	1	50.1	237	70	38	38	6	1	3	2	20	0	37	3	1	2	4	.333	0	0-0	0	6.74	6.79
2009	LAA	AL	3	3	0	0	14.2	65	20	8	7	3	0	0	0	3	1	8	0	0	1	0	1.000	0	0-0	0	6.13	4.30
2010	NYY	AL	16	9	0	2	65.1	278	66	36	36	13	0	4	2	27	0	33	0	0	4	4	.500	0	0-0	0	5.17	4.96
2011	SD	NL	20	20	0	0	120.0	504	117	59	44	10	5	3	2	36	6	64	1	0	3	10	.231	0	0-0	0	3.43	3.30
	Postseason		2	0	0	1	3.0	10	1	0	0	0	0	0	0	0	0	5	0	0	1	0	1.000	0	0-0	0	0.25	0.00
	6 ML YEARS		100	52	0	17	353.1	1521	392	197	181	42	7	13	9	115	10	195	10	2	15	21	.417	0	0-0	4	4.66	4.61

Daniel Moskos

Pitches: L Bats: R Pos: RP-31   MOSS-kose   Ht: 6'1" Wt: 210 Born: 4/28/1986 Age: 26

Year	Team	Lg	G	GS	CG	GF	IP	BFP	H	R	ER	HR	SH	SF	HB	TBB	IBB	SO	WP	Bk	W	L	Pct	Sh	Sv-Op	Hld	ERC	ERA
2007	Pirates	R	2	0	0	0	3.0	12	4	0	0	0	0	0	0	0	0	3	0	0	0	0	-	0	0- -	-	3.91	0.00
2007	StCol	A-	11	0	0	2	30.0	126	19	8	6	1	0	0	2	6	0	13	0	0	1	1	-	0	1- -	1	7.62	4.26
2008	Lynbrg	A+	29	20	0	3	110.1	492	124	83	73	8	1	6	6	43	0	78	11	0	7	7	.500	0	0- -	0	4.76	5.95
2009	Altna	AA	27	25	1	0	149.0	643	159	75	62	11	8	2	6	58	1	77	6	1	11	10	.524	0	0- -	0	4.46	3.74
2010	Altna	AA	37	0	0	34	41.1	167	26	10	7	0	2	1	3	16	0	43	1	0	3	1	.750	0	21- -	1	1.77	1.52
2010	Indy	AAA	19	0	0	4	17.1	98	26	20	20	3	2	1	1	20	2	18	2	1	0	5	.000	0	1- -	0	11.15	10.38
2011	Indy	AAA	30	0	0	10	42.0	177	40	17	16	2	7	3	1	11	2	29	1	0	1	1	.500	0	3- -	0	2.91	3.43
2011	Pit	NL	31	0	0	6	24.1	110	29	11	8	0	4	1	0	9	3	11	0	0	1	1	.500	0	0-0	4	4.01	2.96

Brandon Moss

Bats: L Throws: R Pos: PH-4; RF-1; PR-1   Ht: 6'0" Wt: 205 Born: 9/16/1983 Age: 28

Year	Team	Lg	G	AB	H	2B	3B	HR	(Hm	Rd)	TB	R	RBI	RC	TBB	IBB	SO	HBP	SH	SF	SB	CS	SB%	GDP	Avg	OBP	Slg
2011	LV*	AAA	124	436	120	31	1	23	(-	-)	222	66	80	82	62	3	127	4	0	4	4	6	.40	3	.275	.368	.509
2007	Bos	AL	15	25	7	2	1	0	(0	0)	11	6	1	3	4	0	6	0	0	0	0	0	-	1	.280	.379	.440
2008	2 Tms		79	236	58	15	3	8	(4	4)	103	19	34	30	21	1	70	1	0	5	1	2	.33	2	.246	.304	.436
2009	Pit	NL	133	385	91	20	4	7	(4	3)	140	47	41	37	34	3	84	4	0	1	1	5	.17	7	.236	.304	.364
2010	Pit	NL	17	26	4	1	0	0	(0	0)	5	2	2	2	1	0	6	0	0	0	0	0	-	1	.154	.185	.192
2011	Phi	NL	5	6	0	0	0	0	(0	0)	0	0	0	0	0	0	2	0	0	0	0	0	-	1	.000	.000	.000
08	Bos	AL	34	78	23	5	1	2	(1	1)	36	7	11	11	6	0	25	0	0	2	1	1	.50	0	.295	.337	.462
08	Pit	NL	45	158	35	10	2	6	(3	3)	67	12	23	19	15	1	45	1	0	3	0	1	.00	2	.222	.288	.424
	5 ML YEARS		249	678	160	38	8	15	(8	7)	259	74	78	72	60	4	168	5	0	6	2	7	.22	12	.236	.300	.382

Guillermo Mota

Pitches: R Bats: R Pos: RP-52   Ht: 6'6" Wt: 240 Born: 7/25/1973 Age: 38

Year	Team	Lg	G	GS	CG	GF	IP	BFP	H	R	ER	HR	SH	SF	HB	TBB	IBB	SO	WP	Bk	W	L	Pct	Sh	Sv-Op	Hld	ERC	ERA
1999	Mon	NL	51	0	0	18	55.1	243	54	24	18	5	3	3	2	25	3	27	1	1	2	4	.333	0	0-1	3	4.10	2.93
2000	Mon	NL	29	0	0	7	30.0	126	27	21	20	3	1	1	2	12	0	24	1	1	1	1	.500	0	0-0	5	3.86	6.00
2001	Mon	NL	53	0	0	12	49.2	212	51	30	29	9	3	2	1	18	1	31	1	0	1	3	.250	0	0-3	12	4.77	5.26
2002	LAD	NL	43	0	0	11	60.2	256	45	30	28	4	3	1	2	27	6	49	3	0	1	3	.250	0	0-1	4	2.57	4.15
2003	LAD	NL	76	0	0	18	105.0	410	78	23	23	7	3	1	1	26	4	99	0	0	6	3	.667	0	1-3	13	2.01	1.97
2004	2 Tms		78	0	0	18	96.2	393	75	33	33	8	5	3	4	37	6	85	5	0	9	8	.529	0	4-8	30	2.82	3.07
2005	Fla	NL	56	0	0	24	67.0	293	65	38	35	5	1	3	1	32	7	60	4	0	2	2	.500	0	2-4	14	3.90	4.70
2006	2 Tms		52	0	0	17	55.2	241	55	29	28	11	0	3	0	24	4	46	2	0	4	3	.571	0	0-0	9	4.71	4.53
2007	NYM	NL	52	0	0	10	59.1	261	63	39	38	8	2	0	2	18	2	47	2	0	2	2	.500	0	0-3	6	4.26	5.76
2008	Mil	NL	58	0	0	18	57.0	244	52	28	26	7	1	3	0	28	0	50	4	1	5	6	.455	0	1-4	11	4.44	4.11
2009	LAD	NL	61	0	0	27	65.1	273	53	25	25	6	3	4	5	24	8	39	3	0	3	4	.429	0	0-2	2	2.98	3.44
2010	SF	NL	56	0	0	17	54.0	228	49	29	26	4	0	4	0	22	5	38	5	0	1	3	.250	0	1-3	8	3.28	4.33
2011	SF	NL	52	0	0	11	80.1	333	71	34	34	10	3	2	4	30	4	77	1	1	2	2	.500	0	1-2	4	3.58	3.81
04	LAD	NL	52	0	0	11	63.0	259	51	15	15	4	4	2	2	27	5	52	5	0	8	4	.667	0	1-1	17	2.98	2.14
04	Fla	NL	26	0	0	7	33.2	134	24	18	18	4	1	1	2	10	1	33	0	0	1	4	.200	0	3-7	13	2.51	4.81
06	Cle	AL	34	0	0	13	37.2	173	45	27	26	9	0	3	0	19	3	27	2	0	1	3	.250	0	0-0	5	6.62	6.21
06	NYM	NL	18	0	0	4	18.0	68	10	2	2	2	0	0	0	5	1	19	0	0	3	0	1.000	0	0-0	4	1.51	1.00
	Postseason		11	0	0	5	12.1	50	13	6	6	1	0	0	0	4	0	7	0	0	1	0	1.000	0	0-2	3	4.20	4.38
	13 ML YEARS		717	0	0	208	836.0	3513	738	383	363	87	28	30	22	323	50	672	32	4	39	44	.470	0	10-34	121	3.43	3.91

Jason Motte

Pitches: R Bats: R Pos: RP-78   MOTT   Ht: 6'0" Wt: 200 Born: 6/22/1982 Age: 30

Year	Team	Lg	G	GS	CG	GF	IP	BFP	H	R	ER	HR	SH	SF	HB	TBB	IBB	SO	WP	Bk	W	L	Pct	Sh	Sv-Op	Hld	ERC	ERA
2008	StL	NL	12	0	0	4	11.0	40	5	2	1	0	1	0	0	3	0	16	0	0	0	0	-	0	1-1	4	0.89	0.82
2009	StL	NL	69	0	0	14	56.2	244	57	32	30	10	0	3	2	23	1	54	2	1	4	4	.500	0	0-3	15	4.86	4.76
2010	StL	NL	56	0	0	13	52.1	208	41	13	13	5	1	3	0	18	3	54	1	0	4	2	.667	0	2-3	12	2.68	2.24
2011	StL	NL	78	0	0	27	68.0	268	49	22	17	2	1	3	5	16	2	63	1	0	5	2	.714	0	9-13	18	1.87	2.25
	Postseason		1	0	0	0	1.0	3	0	0	0	0	0	0	0	0	0	0	0	0	0	0	-	0	0-0	0	0.00	0.00
	4 ML YEARS		215	0	0	58	188.0	760	152	69	61	17	3	9	7	60	6	187	4	1	13	8	.619	0	12-20	49	2.83	2.92

Mike Moustakas

Bats: L Throws: R Pos: 3B-89   moo-STOCK-us   Ht: 5'11" Wt: 230 Born: 9/11/1988 Age: 23

									BATTING													BASERUNNING				AVERAGES		
Year	Team	Lg	G	AB	H	2B	3B	HR	(Hm	Rd)	TB	R	RBI	RC	TBB	IBB	SO	HBP	SH	SF	SB	CS	SB%	GDP	Avg	OBP	Slg
2007	Idaho	R+	11	41	12	4	1	0	(-	-)	18	6	10	7	4	0	8	2	0	0	0	0	-	1	.293	.383	.439
2008	Burlgtn	A	126	496	135	25	3	22	(-	-)	232	77	71	80	43	4	86	7	0	3	8	4	.67	5	.272	.337	.468
2009	Wilmg	A+	129	492	123	32	2	16	(-	-)	207	66	86	63	32	5	90	2	1	3	10	6	.63	10	.250	.297	.421
2010	NWArk	AA	66	259	90	25	0	21	(-	-)	178	58	76	69	26	9	42	7	0	6	0	1	.00	7	.347	.413	.687
2010	Omha	AAA	52	225	66	16	0	15	(-	-)	127	36	48	40	8	1	25	0	0	3	2	0	1.00	8	.293	.314	.564
2011	Omha	AAA	55	223	64	15	1	10	(-	-)	111	38	44	39	19	0	44	3	2	3	1	1	.50	3	.287	.347	.498
2011	KC	AL	89	338	89	18	1	5	(3	2)	124	26	30	31	22	0	51	1	2	2	2	0	1.00	5	.263	.309	.367

Peter Moylan

Pitches: R Bats: R Pos: RP-13   Ht: 6'2" Wt: 225 Born: 12/2/1978 Age: 33

			HOW MUCH HE PITCHED						WHAT HE GAVE UP											THE RESULTS						
Year	Team	Lg	G	GS	CG	GF	IP	BFP	H	R	ER	HR	SH	SF	HB	TBB	IBB	SO	WP	Bk	W	L	Pct	Sh	Sv-Op Hld	ERC	ERA
2011	Gwnntt*	AAA	6	1	0	0	6.0	29	5	1	0	0	0	0	0	4	0	10	1	0	0	1	.000	0	0- - -	3.08	0.00
2006	Atl	NL	15	0	0	5	15.0	68	18	8	8	1	1	0	0	5	1	14	0	0	0	0	-	0	0-0 0	4.47	4.80
2007	Atl	NL	80	0	0	16	90.0	359	65	27	18	6	4	4	7	31	12	63	2	0	5	3	.625	0	1-2 8	2.36	1.80
2008	Atl	NL	7	0	0	2	5.2	25	5	1	1	1	0	0	1	1	0	5	0	0	0	1	.000	0	1-2 4	3.51	1.59
2009	Atl	NL	87	0	0	6	73.0	309	65	29	23	0	4	3	2	35	8	61	1	0	6	2	.750	0	0-5 25	3.06	2.84
2010	Atl	NL	85	0	0	7	63.2	271	53	24	21	5	5	2	2	37	6	52	3	0	6	2	.750	0	1-4 21	3.75	2.97
2011	Atl	NL	13	0	0	2	8.1	38	12	3	3	0	0	0	0	3	0	10	0	0	2	1	.667	0	0-0 2	5.87	3.24
	Postseason		4	0	0	0	1.0	6	1	0	0	0	0	0	0	0	0	1	0	0	0	0	-	0	0-1 0	1.26	0.00
	6 ML YEARS		287	0	0	38	255.2	1070	218	92	74	13	14	9	12	112	27	205	6	0	19	9	.679	0	3-13 60	3.15	2.60

Edward Mujica

Pitches: R Bats: R Pos: RP-67   moo-HEE-kah   Ht: 6'2" Wt: 215 Born: 5/10/1984 Age: 28

			HOW MUCH HE PITCHED						WHAT HE GAVE UP											THE RESULTS						
Year	Team	Lg	G	GS	CG	GF	IP	BFP	H	R	ER	HR	SH	SF	HB	TBB	IBB	SO	WP	Bk	W	L	Pct	Sh	Sv-Op Hld	ERC	ERA
2006	Cle	AL	10	0	0	2	18.1	78	25	6	6	1	0	2	1	0	0	12	0	0	0	1	.000	0	0-0 0	4.50	2.95
2007	Cle	AL	10	0	0	5	13.0	60	19	12	12	3	0	1	0	2	0	7	0	0	0	0	-	0	0-0 0	6.63	8.31
2008	Cle	AL	33	0	0	13	38.2	168	46	29	29	5	0	4	1	10	3	27	1	0	3	2	.600	0	0-2 1	4.82	6.75
2009	SD	NL	67	4	0	15	93.2	393	101	47	41	14	1	3	0	19	4	76	3	1	3	5	.375	0	2-3 11	4.00	3.94
2010	SD	NL	59	0	0	24	69.2	268	59	29	28	14	1	0	0	6	0	72	1	0	2	1	.667	0	0-1 4	2.68	3.62
2011	Fla	NL	67	0	0	11	76.0	297	64	27	25	7	5	1	2	14	5	63	1	0	9	6	.600	0	0-3 17	2.46	2.96
	6 ML YEARS		246	4	0	70	309.1	1264	314	150	141	44	7	11	4	51	12	257	6	1	17	15	.531	0	2-9 33	3.54	4.10

Daniel Murphy

Bats: L Throws: R Pos: 1B-52; 3B-28; 2B-24; PH-19; LF-1   Ht: 6'2" Wt: 205 Born: 4/1/1985 Age: 27

									BATTING													BASERUNNING				AVERAGES		
Year	Team	Lg	G	AB	H	2B	3B	HR	(Hm	Rd)	TB	R	RBI	RC	TBB	IBB	SO	HBP	SH	SF	SB	CS	SB%	GDP	Avg	OBP	Slg
2008	NYM	NL	49	131	41	9	3	2	(1	1)	62	24	17	26	18	1	28	1	0	1	0	2	.00	4	.313	.397	.473
2009	NYM	NL	155	508	135	38	4	12	(7	5)	217	60	63	60	38	4	69	0	4	6	4	2	.67	13	.266	.313	.427
2011	NYM	NL	109	391	125	28	2	6	(2	4)	175	49	49	57	24	2	42	3	3	2	5	5	.50	14	.320	.362	.448
	3 ML YEARS		313	1030	301	75	9	20	(10	10)	454	133	129	143	80	7	139	4	7	9	9	9	.50	31	.292	.343	.441

David Murphy

Bats: L Throws: L Pos: LF-78; RF-32; CF-13; PH-10; DH-9; PR-1   Ht: 6'4" Wt: 205 Born: 10/18/1981 Age: 30

									BATTING													BASERUNNING				AVERAGES		
Year	Team	Lg	G	AB	H	2B	3B	HR	(Hm	Rd)	TB	R	RBI	RC	TBB	IBB	SO	HBP	SH	SF	SB	CS	SB%	GDP	Avg	OBP	Slg
2006	Bos	AL	20	22	5	1	0	1	(0	1)	9	4	2	2	4	0	4	0	0	0	0	0	-	1	.227	.346	.409
2007	2 Tms	AL	46	105	36	12	2	2	(1	1)	58	17	14	23	7	0	20	0	0	0	0	0	-	1	.343	.384	.552
2008	Tex	AL	108	415	114	28	3	15	(8	7)	193	64	74	62	31	3	70	0	2	6	7	2	.78	7	.275	.321	.465
2009	Tex	AL	128	432	116	24	1	17	(8	9)	193	61	57	60	49	3	106	1	2	9	9	4	.69	5	.269	.338	.447
2010	Tex	AL	138	419	122	26	2	12	(7	5)	188	54	65	68	45	2	71	0	0	3	14	2	.88	6	.291	.358	.449
2011	Tex	AL	120	404	111	14	2	11	(8	3)	162	46	46	52	33	3	61	0	1	2	11	6	.65	11	.275	.328	.401
07	Bos	AL	3	2	1	0	0	0	(0	0)	3	1	0	1	0	0	1	0	0	0	0	0	-	0	.500	.500	1.500
07	Tex	AL	43	103	35	12	1	2	(1	1)	55	16	14	22	7	0	19	0	0	0	0	0	-	1	.340	.382	.534
	Postseason		11	27	5	1	0	1	(1	0)	9	6	3	3	5	2	8	0	0	0	0	0	-	0	.185	.313	.333
	6 ML YEARS		560	1797	504	105	10	58	(32	26)	803	246	258	267	169	11	332	1	5	20	41	14	.75	31	.280	.339	.447

Donnie Murphy

Bats: R Throws: R Pos: SS-18; 3B-15; PH-7; PR-2; 2B-1   Ht: 5'10" Wt: 195 Born: 3/10/1983 Age: 29

									BATTING													BASERUNNING				AVERAGES		
Year	Team	Lg	G	AB	H	2B	3B	HR	(Hm	Rd)	TB	R	RBI	RC	TBB	IBB	SO	HBP	SH	SF	SB	CS	SB%	GDP	Avg	OBP	Slg
2011	Jupiter*	A+	8	23	3	0	1	0	(-	-)	5	4	2	2	5	0	6	2	0	0	0	0	-	0	.130	.333	.217
2011	NewOr*	AAA	6	23	2	2	0	0	(-	-)	4	3	2	0	3	0	4	0	0	0	0	0	-	0	.087	.192	.174
2004	KC	AL	7	27	5	3	0	0	(0	0)	8	1	3	2	0	0	7	0	0	0	1	0	1.00	1	.185	.185	.296
2005	KC	AL	32	77	12	5	0	1	(0	1)	20	4	8	1	9	0	23	0	1	1	0	1	.00	3	.156	.241	.260
2007	Oak	AL	42	118	26	8	0	6	(2	4)	52	21	21	16	10	0	35	2	1	1	2	1	.67	1	.220	.290	.441
2008	Oak	AL	46	103	19	3	0	3	(2	1)	31	10	13	6	11	0	38	2	0	1	0	0	-	0	.184	.274	.301
2010	Fla	NL	29	44	14	6	1	3	(2	1)	31	9	16	12	2	0	19	0	1	0	0	0	-	0	.318	.348	.705
2011	Fla	NL	36	92	17	4	1	2	(0	2)	29	10	9	5	4	1	21	3	0	1	0	0	-	2	.185	.240	.315
	6 ML YEARS		192	461	93	29	2	15	(6	9)	171	55	70	42	36	1	143	7	3	4	4	2	.67	8	.202	.268	.371

Brett Myers

Pitches: R **Bats:** R **Pos:** SP-33; RP-1   **Ht:** 6'4" **Wt:** 240 **Born:** 8/17/1980 **Age:** 31

Year	Team	Lg	G	GS	CG	GF	IP	BFP	H	R	ER	HR	SH	SF	HB	TBB	IBB	SO	WP	Bk	W	L	Pct	Sh	Sv-Op	Hld	ERC	ERA
2002	Phi	NL	12	12	1	0	72.0	307	73	38	34	11	6	2	6	29	1	34	2	1	4	5	.444	0	0-0	0	5.04	4.25
2003	Phi	NL	32	32	1	0	193.0	848	205	99	95	20	6	3	9	76	8	143	9	0	14	9	.609	1	0-0	0	4.56	4.43
2004	Phi	NL	32	31	1	1	176.0	778	196	113	108	31	9	3	6	62	4	116	5	0	11	11	.500	1	0-0	0	5.17	5.52
2005	Phi	NL	34	34	2	0	215.1	905	193	94	89	31	9	3	11	68	2	208	4	4	13	8	.619	0	0-0	0	3.64	3.72
2006	Phi	NL	31	31	1	0	198.0	833	194	93	86	29	7	4	3	63	3	189	3	0	12	7	.632	0	0-0	0	4.02	3.91
2007	Phi	NL	51	3	0	37	68.2	293	61	33	33	9	3	1	1	27	1	83	5	0	5	7	.417	0	21-24	3	3.63	4.33
2008	Phi	NL	30	30	2	0	190.0	817	197	103	96	29	4	3	6	65	6	163	2	0	10	13	.435	1	0-0	0	4.53	4.55
2009	Phi	NL	18	10	0	1	70.2	304	74	38	38	18	3	2	4	23	1	50	1	0	4	3	.571	0	0-0	3	5.41	4.84
2010	Hou	NL	33	33	2	0	223.2	936	212	88	78	20	9	4	3	66	3	180	2	0	14	8	.636	0	0-0	0	3.34	3.14
2011	Hou	NL	34	33	2	1	216.0	917	226	116	107	31	5	6	4	57	5	160	7	0	7	14	.333	0	0-0	0	4.13	4.46
Postseason			7	3	0	2	22.0	96	18	12	11	2	2	0	2	12	3	17	1	0	2	1	.667	0	0-0	0	3.69	4.50
10 ML YEARS			307	249	12	40	1623.1	6938	1631	815	764	229	61	31	53	536	34	1326	40	5	94	85	.525	3	21-24	6	4.22	4.24

Xavier Nady

Bats: R **Throws:** R **Pos:** 1B-52; PH-29; LF-10   **Ht:** 6'2" **Wt:** 215 **Born:** 11/14/1978 **Age:** 33

Year	Team	Lg	G	AB	H	2B	3B	HR	(Hm	Rd)	TB	R	RBI	RC	TBB	IBB	SO	HBP	SH	SF	SB	CS	SB%	GDP	Avg	OBP	Slg
2000	SD	NL	1	1	1	0	0	0	(0	0)	1	1	0	1	0	0	0	0	0	0	0	0	-	0	1.000	1.000	1.000
2003	SD	NL	110	371	99	17	1	9	(5	4)	145	50	39	39	24	0	74	6	2	1	6	2	.75	14	.267	.321	.391
2004	SD	NL	34	77	19	4	0	3	(1	2)	32	7	9	8	5	0	13	1	1	0	0	0	-	4	.247	.301	.416
2005	SD	NL	124	326	85	15	2	13	(5	8)	143	40	43	37	22	1	67	7	1	0	2	1	.67	5	.261	.321	.439
2006	2 Tms	NL	130	468	131	28	1	17	(10	7)	212	57	63	62	30	7	85	11	2	1	3	3	.50	12	.280	.337	.453
2007	Pit	NL	125	431	120	23	1	20	(7	13)	205	55	72	60	23	2	101	12	0	4	3	1	.75	16	.278	.330	.476
2008	2 Tms	NL	148	555	169	37	1	25	(11	14)	283	76	97	93	39	2	103	9	0	4	2	1	.67	14	.305	.357	.510
2009	NYY	AL	7	28	8	4	0	0	(0	0)	12	4	2	2	1	0	6	0	0	0	0	0	-	2	.286	.310	.429
2010	ChC	NL	119	317	81	13	0	6	(2	4)	112	33	33	33	17	0	85	8	1	4	0	0	-	12	.256	.306	.353
2011	Ari	NL	82	206	51	11	0	4	(1	3)	74	26	35	22	10	1	46	3	0	4	2	0	1.00	4	.248	.287	.359
06	NYM	NL	75	265	70	15	1	14	(10	4)	129	37	40	35	19	4	51	6	1	1	2	1	.67	7	.264	.326	.487
06	Pit	NL	55	203	61	13	0	3	(0	3)	83	20	23	27	11	3	34	5	1	0	1	2	.33	5	.300	.352	.409
08	Pit	NL	89	327	108	26	1	13	(6	7)	175	50	57	59	25	1	55	5	0	3	1	0	1.00	9	.330	.383	.535
08	NYY	AL	59	228	61	11	0	12	(5	7)	108	26	40	34	14	1	48	4	0	1	1	1	.50	5	.268	.320	.474
Postseason			2	3	1	0	0	0	(0	0)	1	0	2	1	0	0	1	2	0	0	0	0	-	0	.333	.600	.333
10 ML YEARS			880	2780	764	152	6	97	(42	55)	1219	349	393	357	171	13	580	57	7	18	18	8	.69	83	.275	.328	.438

Mike Napoli

Bats: R **Throws:** R **Pos:** C-61; 1B-35; DH-19; PH-7   NAPP-uh-lee   **Ht:** 6'0" **Wt:** 215 **Born:** 10/31/1981 **Age:** 30

Year	Team	Lg	G	AB	H	2B	3B	HR	(Hm	Rd)	TB	R	RBI	RC	TBB	IBB	SO	HBP	SH	SF	SB	CS	SB%	GDP	Avg	OBP	Slg
2011	RdRck*	AAA	4	15	4	1	0	3	(-	-)	14	3	9	4	2	0	4	0	0	1	0	0	-	1	.267	.333	.933
2006	LAA	AL	99	268	61	13	0	16	(10	6)	122	47	42	40	51	0	90	5	0	1	2	3	.40	2	.228	.360	.455
2007	LAA	AL	75	219	54	11	1	10	(5	5)	97	40	34	35	33	2	63	5	1	5	5	2	.71	5	.247	.351	.443
2008	LAA	AL	78	227	62	9	1	20	(10	10)	133	39	49	46	35	5	70	5	1	6	7	3	.70	3	.273	.374	.586
2009	LAA	AL	114	382	104	22	1	20	(10	10)	188	60	56	52	40	1	103	7	0	3	3	3	.50	6	.272	.350	.492
2010	LAA	AL	140	453	108	24	1	26	(13	13)	212	60	68	60	42	2	137	11	0	4	4	2	.67	15	.238	.316	.468
2011	Tex	AL	113	369	118	25	0	30	(13	17)	233	72	75	90	58	2	85	3	0	2	4	2	.67	10	.320	.414	.631
Postseason			14	31	6	1	0	2	(0	2)	13	4	4	4	2	0	10	3	0	0	0	0	-	0	.194	.306	.419
6 ML YEARS			619	1918	507	104	4	122	(61	61)	985	318	324	323	259	12	548	36	2	21	25	15	.63	41	.264	.359	.514

Chris Narveson

Pitches: L **Bats:** L **Pos:** SP-28; RP-2   NARR-vih-son   **Ht:** 6'3" **Wt:** 205 **Born:** 12/20/1981 **Age:** 30

Year	Team	Lg	G	GS	CG	GF	IP	BFP	H	R	ER	HR	SH	SF	HB	TBB	IBB	SO	WP	Bk	W	L	Pct	Sh	Sv-Op	Hld	ERC	ERA
2006	StL	NL	5	1	0	1	9.1	40	6	5	5	1	0	0	1	5	0	12	1	1	0	0	-	0	0-0	0	3.06	4.82
2009	Mil	NL	21	4	0	5	47.0	205	45	22	20	7	2	3	2	16	1	46	4	0	2	0	1.000	0	0-0	1	3.96	3.83
2010	Mil	NL	37	28	0	2	167.2	724	172	96	93	21	8	5	5	59	3	137	6	0	12	9	.571	0	0-1	3	4.30	4.99
2011	Mil	NL	30	28	0	0	161.2	699	160	82	80	17	6	4	1	65	1	126	4	1	11	8	.579	0	0-0	0	4.06	4.45
4 ML YEARS			93	61	0	8	385.2	1668	383	205	198	46	16	12	9	145	5	321	15	2	25	17	.595	0	0-1	4	4.13	4.62

Joe Nathan

Pitches: R **Bats:** R **Pos:** RP-48   **Ht:** 6'4" **Wt:** 225 **Born:** 11/22/1974 **Age:** 37

Year	Team	Lg	G	GS	CG	GF	IP	BFP	H	R	ER	HR	SH	SF	HB	TBB	IBB	SO	WP	Bk	W	L	Pct	Sh	Sv-Op	Hld	ERC	ERA
2011	Roch*	AAA	3	1	0	0	3.0	12	2	1	0	0	1	0	0	1	0	5	0	0	0	0	-	0	0--	1	1.57	0.00
1999	SF	NL	19	14	0	2	90.1	395	84	45	42	17	2	0	1	46	0	54	2	0	7	4	.636	0	1-1	0	4.78	4.18
2000	SF	NL	20	15	0	0	93.1	426	89	63	54	12	5	5	4	63	4	61	5	0	5	2	.714	0	0-1	0	5.23	5.21
2002	SF	NL	4	0	0	3	3.2	12	1	0	0	0	0	0	0	0	0	2	0	0	0	0	-	0	0-0	0	0.17	0.00
2003	SF	NL	78	0	0	9	79.0	316	51	26	26	7	2	4	3	33	3	83	4	1	12	4	.750	0	0-3	20	2.34	2.96
2004	Min	AL	73	0	0	63	72.1	284	48	14	13	3	2	0	2	23	3	89	5	0	1	2	.333	0	44-47	0	1.78	1.62
2005	Min	AL	69	0	0	58	70.0	276	46	22	21	5	1	2	0	22	1	94	2	0	7	4	.636	0	43-48	0	1.83	2.70
2006	Min	AL	64	0	0	61	68.1	262	38	12	12	3	2	1	1	16	4	95	3	0	7	0	1.000	0	36-38	0	1.18	1.58
2007	Min	AL	68	0	0	60	71.2	282	54	15	15	4	2	2	1	19	2	77	3	0	4	2	.667	0	37-41	0	2.08	1.88
2008	Min	AL	68	0	0	57	67.2	261	43	13	10	5	1	0	2	18	4	74	2	0	1	2	.333	0	39-45	0	1.67	1.33

	HOW MUCH HE PITCHED								WHAT HE GAVE UP											THE RESULTS						
Year	Team	Lg	G	GS	CG	GF	IP	BFP	H	R	ER	HR	SH	SF	HB	TBB	IBB	SO	WP	Bk	W	L	Pct	Sh	Sv-Op	Hld	ERC	ERA
2009	Min	AL	70	0	0	62	68.2	271	42	16	16	7	1	0	2	22	1	89	4	0	2	2	.500	0	47-52	0	1.89	2.10
2011	Min	AL	48	0	0	33	44.2	191	38	26	24	7	1	2	3	14	2	43	3	0	2	1	.667	0	14-17	8	3.38	4.84
	Postseason		8	0	0	3	8.0	43	12	7	7	2	0	0	0	7	3	10	1	0	0	2	.000	0	1-3	0	9.65	7.88
11 ML YEARS			581	29	0	408	729.2	2976	534	252	233	70	20	17	19	276	24	761	33	1	48	23	.676	0	261-293	28	2.60	2.87

Dioner Navarro

Bats: B **Throws:** R **Pos:** C-54; PH-11; DH-1   dee-AHN-err   **Ht:** 5'9" **Wt:** 205 **Born:** 2/9/1984 **Age:** 28

						BATTING															BASERUNNING				AVERAGES		
Year	Team	Lg	G	AB	H	2B	3B	HR	(Hm	Rd)	TB	R	RBI	RC	TBB	IBB	SO	HBP	SH	SF	SB	CS	SB%	GDP	Avg	OBP	Slg
2011	Chatt*	AA	5	14	2	0	0	0	(-	-)	2	0	1	1	3	0	1	0	0	0	2	0	1.00	0	.143	.294	.143
2004	NYY	AL	5	7	3	0	0	0	(0	0)	3	2	1	1	0	0	0	0	0	0	0	0	-	1	.429	.429	.429
2005	LAD	NL	50	176	48	9	0	3	(3	0)	66	21	14	18	20	1	21	2	1	0	0	0	-	3	.273	.354	.375
2006	2 Tms		81	268	68	9	0	6	(4	2)	95	28	28	27	31	6	51	1	1	1	2	1	.67	7	.254	.332	.354
2007	TB	AL	119	388	88	19	2	9	(5	4)	138	46	44	35	33	3	67	1	7	5	3	1	.75	11	.227	.286	.356
2008	TB	AL	120	427	126	27	0	7	(4	3)	174	43	54	59	34	1	49	3	3	3	0	4	.00	16	.295	.349	.407
2009	TB	AL	115	376	82	15	0	8	(4	4)	121	38	32	22	18	1	51	5	8	3	5	2	.71	14	.218	.261	.322
2010	TB	AL	48	124	24	5	0	1	(1	0)	32	11	7	4	12	0	20	1	5	0	0	1	.00	3	.194	.270	.258
2011	LAD	AL	64	176	34	6	1	5	(3	2)	57	13	17	14	20	4	35	1	3	2	0	0	-	3	.193	.276	.324
06	LAD	NL	25	75	21	2	0	2	(1	1)	29	5	8	8	11	4	18	0	0	0	1	0	1.00	1	.280	.372	.387
06	TB	AL	56	193	47	7	0	4	(3	1)	66	23	20	19	20	2	33	1	1	1	1	1	.50	6	.244	.316	.342
	Postseason		16	58	17	4	0	0	(0	0)	21	4	5	6	4	0	11	0	0	0	1	0	.00	2	.293	.339	.362
8 ML YEARS			602	1942	473	90	3	39	(24	15)	686	202	197	180	168	16	294	14	28	14	10	9	.53	58	.244	.306	.353

Efren Navarro

Bats: L **Throws:** L **Pos:** 1B-8; PH-2   **Ht:** 6'0" **Wt:** 200 **Born:** 5/14/1986 **Age:** 26

						BATTING															BASERUNNING				AVERAGES		
Year	Team	Lg	G	AB	H	2B	3B	HR	(Hm	Rd)	TB	R	RBI	RC	TBB	IBB	SO	HBP	SH	SF	SB	CS	SB%	GDP	Avg	OBP	Slg
2007	Angels	R	5	17	6	3	0	0	(-	-)	9	4	3	3	3	0	2	0	0	1	0	1	.00	1	.353	.429	.529
2007	Orem	R+	40	113	24	4	0	1	(-	-)	31	16	11	9	11	1	21	2	2	1	1	1	.50	6	.212	.291	.274
2008	CRpds	A	94	331	89	18	0	2	(-	-)	113	37	45	43	42	1	66	4	2	6	7	7	.50	2	.269	.352	.341
2008	RCuca	A+	35	129	45	9	0	2	(-	-)	60	13	18	25	19	2	20	0	0	3	0	3	.00	2	.349	.427	.465
2009	RCuca	A+	130	481	138	32	3	5	(-	-)	191	64	61	72	53	2	72	3	1	2	3	2	.60	13	.287	.360	.397
2010	Ark	AA	128	453	121	25	2	6	(-	-)	168	46	50	55	31	2	47	3	4	3	6	4	.60	10	.267	.316	.371
2011	Salt Lk	AAA	133	492	156	36	6	12	(-	-)	240	76	73	88	42	1	78	2	4	7	5	5	.50	10	.317	.368	.488
2011	LAA	AL	8	10	2	1	0	0	(0	0)	3	1	0	0	1	0	1	0	1	0	0	0	-	1	.200	.273	.300

Yamaico Navarro

Bats: R **Throws:** R **Pos:** 3B-16; SS-4; LF-3; PH-2; PR-1   ya-MIKE-oh   **Ht:** 5'11" **Wt:** 170 **Born:** 10/31/1987 **Age:** 24

						BATTING															BASERUNNING				AVERAGES		
Year	Team	Lg	G	AB	H	2B	3B	HR	(Hm	Rd)	TB	R	RBI	RC	TBB	IBB	SO	HBP	SH	SF	SB	CS	SB%	GDP	Avg	OBP	Slg
2007	Lowell	A-	62	225	65	10	1	5	(-	-)	92	36	37	34	22	0	52	3	1	2	12	6	.67	9	.289	.357	.409
2008	Grnville	A	83	325	91	14	4	7	(-	-)	134	46	54	47	29	0	73	3	0	4	3	2	.60	16	.280	.341	.412
2008	Lancst	A+	42	181	63	13	2	4	(-	-)	92	33	23	34	12	0	30	2	0	1	3	2	.60	2	.348	.393	.508
2009	Salem	A+	23	94	30	9	0	4	(-	-)	51	10	17	17	6	0	12	2	0	0	2	2	.50	6	.319	.373	.543
2009	Lowell	A-	5	21	5	1	0	0	(-	-)	6	1	2	1	2	0	3	0	0	0	2	0	.00	0	.238	.304	.286
2009	Portlnd	AA	39	135	25	6	2	2	(-	-)	41	16	11	12	14	0	28	2	0	1	5	1	.83	7	.185	.270	.304
2010	Portlnd	AAA	88	329	90	19	3	8	(-	-)	139	49	55	54	42	0	53	3	1	3	16	5	.76	9	.274	.358	.422
2010	Pwtckt	AAA	16	53	15	4	0	3	(-	-)	28	8	6	9	5	0	6	0	0	1	2	1	.67	2	.283	.339	.528
2011	Pwtckt	AAA	34	128	33	8	2	5	(-	-)	60	25	13	22	17	0	25	4	0	0	3	2	.60	2	.258	.362	.469
2011	Omha	AAA	25	92	25	3	1	2	(-	-)	36	11	9	11	7	0	18	0	0	2	3	4	.43	2	.272	.317	.391
2010	Bos	AL	20	42	6	0	0	0	(0	0)	6	4	5	1	2	1	17	0	0	2	0	0	-	0	.143	.174	.143
2011	2 Tms	AL	22	60	15	3	0	1	(0	1)	21	8	9	8	5	0	14	0	0	1	0	0	-	0	.250	.303	.350
11	Bos	AL	16	37	8	2	0	1	(0	1)	13	6	3	4	3	0	9	0	0	0	0	0	-	0	.216	.275	.351
11	KC	AL	6	23	7	1	0	0	(0	0)	8	2	6	4	2	0	5	0	0	1	0	0	-	0	.304	.346	.348
2 ML YEARS			42	102	21	3	0	1	(0	1)	27	12	14	9	7	1	31	0	0	3	0	0	-	0	.206	.250	.265

Chris Nelson

Bats: R **Throws:** R **Pos:** 2B-29; 3B-24; PH-11; SS-2; PR-2   **Ht:** 5'11" **Wt:** 175 **Born:** 9/3/1985 **Age:** 26

						BATTING															BASERUNNING				AVERAGES		
Year	Team	Lg	G	AB	H	2B	3B	HR	(Hm	Rd)	TB	R	RBI	RC	TBB	IBB	SO	HBP	SH	SF	SB	CS	SB%	GDP	Avg	OBP	Slg
2004	Casper	R+	38	147	51	6	3	4	(-	-)	75	36	20	31	20	0	42	2	0	0	6	5	.55	2	.347	.432	.510
2005	Ashvll	A	79	315	76	13	3	3	(-	-)	104	51	38	33	25	0	88	5	0	4	7	4	.64	2	.241	.304	.330
2006	Ashvll	A	118	466	121	38	1	11	(-	-)	194	69	76	65	32	0	101	7	5	7	14	2	.88	9	.260	.313	.416
2007	Mdest	A+	133	529	153	42	7	19	(-	-)	266	97	99	101	55	2	92	7	0	9	27	5	.84	11	.289	.358	.503
2008	Tulsa	AA	73	283	67	18	2	3	(-	-)	98	38	42	36	35	1	69	4	2	5	6	1	.86	10	.237	.324	.346
2008	Mdest	A+	8	30	5	1	0	1	(-	-)	9	2	5	1	2	0	8	0	0	0	0	2	.00	0	.167	.219	.300
2009	Tulsa	AA	29	107	30	5	2	4	(-	-)	51	21	17	18	12	1	21	1	1	1	5	2	.71	1	.280	.355	.477
2010	ColSpr	AAA	85	319	100	15	3	12	(-	-)	157	60	55	59	29	1	53	4	2	2	7	3	.70	8	.313	.376	.492
2011	ColSpr	AAA	73	289	95	20	5	11	(-	-)	158	52	65	56	17	0	48	3	1	5	3	3	.50	17	.329	.366	.547
2010	Col	NL	17	25	7	1	0	0	(0	0)	8	7	0	1	1	0	4	0	1	0	1	0	1.00	1	.280	.308	.320
2011	Col	NL	63	180	45	10	1	4	(3	1)	69	20	16	15	7	1	35	1	0	1	3	1	.75	5	.250	.280	.383
2 ML YEARS			80	205	52	11	1	4	(3	1)	77	27	16	16	8	1	39	1	1	1	4	1	.80	6	.254	.284	.376

Pat Neshek

Pitches: R Bats: B Pos: RP-25   NEE-sheck   Ht: 6'3" Wt: 210 Born: 9/4/1980 Age: 31

Year Team	Lg	G	GS	CG	GF	IP	BFP	H	R	ER	HR	SH	SF	HB	TBB	IBB	SO	WP	Bk	W	L	Pct	Sh	Sv-Op	Hld	ERC	ERA
2011 Tucsn*	AAA	24	0	0	7	26.1	113	29	12	12	5	2	2	0	10	1	13	0	0	1	2	.333	0	3- -	-	5.30	4.10
2006 Min	AL	32	0	0	3	37.0	138	23	9	9	6	0	1	0	6	0	53	0	0	4	2	.667	0	0-2	10	1.68	2.19
2007 Min	AL	74	0	0	20	70.1	278	44	25	23	7	4	5	2	27	5	74	2	0	7	2	.778	0	0-3	15	2.12	2.94
2008 Min	AL	15	0	0	3	13.1	56	12	7	7	2	1	1	0	4	1	15	0	0	0	1	.000	0	0-2	6	3.29	4.73
2010 Min	AL	11	0	0	3	9.0	43	7	5	5	1	0	0	1	8	0	9	0	0	0	1	.000	0	0-1	1	5.13	5.00
2011 SD	NL	25	0	0	13	24.2	112	19	12	11	4	1	0	1	22	1	20	1	0	1	1	.500	0	0-0	0	5.37	4.01
Postseason		2	0	0	1	1.0	4	1	1	1	0	0	0	0	0	0	1	0	0	0	1	.000	0	0-0	0	1.95	9.00
5 ML YEARS		157	0	0	42	154.1	627	105	58	55	20	6	7	4	67	7	171	3	0	12	7	.632	0	0-8	32	2.75	3.21

Juan Nicasio

Pitches: R Bats: R Pos: SP-13   nih-COSS-ee-oh   Ht: 6'3" Wt: 200 Born: 8/31/1986 Age: 25

Year Team	Lg	G	GS	CG	GF	IP	BFP	H	R	ER	HR	SH	SF	HB	TBB	IBB	SO	WP	Bk	W	L	Pct	Sh	Sv-Op	Hld	ERC	ERA
2007 Casper	R+	13	8	0	1	43.1	193	48	32	21	3	1	1	4	13	0	33	5	1	0	3	.000	0	0- -	-	4.37	4.36
2008 TriCity	A-	12	12	0	0	54.0	226	46	30	27	1	1	1	3	19	0	61	4	1	2	4	.333	0	0- -	-	2.76	4.50
2009 Ashvll	A-	18	18	1	0	112.0	468	110	44	30	6	4	1	4	23	0	115	5	0	9	3	.750	1	0- -	-	3.03	2.41
2010 Mdest	A+	28	28	1	0	177.1	744	186	91	77	14	2	8	4	31	0	171	7	1	12	10	.545	0	0- -	-	3.38	3.91
2011 Tulsa	AA	9	9	1	0	56.2	219	48	15	14	3	3	0	0	10	1	63	3	2	5	1	.833	1	0- -	-	2.22	2.22
2011 Col	NL	13	13	0	0	71.2	299	73	35	33	8	1	0	1	18	3	58	1	0	4	4	.500	0	0-0	0	3.69	4.14

Mike Nickeas

Bats: R Throws: R Pos: C-20; PH-2   NICK-ee-us   Ht: 6'0" Wt: 220 Born: 2/13/1983 Age: 29

Year Team	Lg	G	AB	H	2B	3B	HR	(Hm	Rd)	TB	R	RBI	RC	TBB	IBB	SO	HBP	SH	SF	SB	CS	SB%	GDP	Avg	OBP	Slg
2004 Spkane	A-	62	233	67	18	0	10	(-	-)	115	42	55	46	33	0	53	4	2	1	2	0	1.00	4	.288	.384	.494
2005 Frisco	AA	68	242	49	7	1	5	(-	-)	73	22	24	19	20	0	43	1	2	3	1	1	.50	6	.202	.263	.302
2005 Rngrs	R	6	21	6	1	0	1	(-	-)	10	2	6	4	3	0	4	1	0	0	0	0	-	1	.286	.400	.476
2006 Bkrsfld	A+	17	64	19	4	0	0	(-	-)	23	6	6	10	6	0	17	5	0	1	0	0	-	1	.297	.395	.359
2006 Frisco	AA	39	113	28	7	0	2	(-	-)	41	15	15	18	21	0	22	6	3	4	1	1	.50	3	.248	.382	.363
2006 Bnghtn	AA	4	12	2	0	0	0	(-	-)	2	1	3	0	1	0	4	1	0	1	0	0	-	0	.167	.267	.167
2007 Bnghtn	AA	65	212	46	10	0	1	(-	-)	59	26	15	16	18	0	37	2	2	3	2	3	.40	12	.217	.281	.278
2007 StLuci	A+	26	77	16	7	0	0	(-	-)	23	6	4	11	17	1	20	4	0	0	0	0	-	0	.208	.378	.299
2008 NewOr	AAA	54	163	35	9	0	2	(-	-)	50	16	17	14	14	1	42	1	2	4	0	1	.00	7	.215	.275	.307
2008 Bnghtn	AA	17	51	10	1	0	1	(-	-)	14	2	4	4	7	1	7	0	0	1	0	0	-	3	.196	.288	.275
2009 Bnghtn	AA	18	55	10	1	0	0	(-	-)	11	3	7	3	9	0	9	0	2	1	0	0	-	0	.182	.292	.200
2009 Buffalo	AAA	2	6	0	0	0	0	(-	-)	0	0	0	0	1	0	3	0	0	0	0	0	-	0	.000	.143	.000
2010 Bnghtn	AA	82	265	75	15	0	5	(-	-)	105	27	33	46	49	0	43	4	0	0	1	1	.50	8	.283	.403	.396
2010 Buffalo	AAA	7	28	6	1	0	0	(-	-)	7	1	0	1	1	0	7	0	0	0	0	0	-	0	.214	.241	.250
2011 Buffalo	AAA	60	168	36	9	0	2	(-	-)	51	15	15	15	16	1	27	2	3	3	0	0	-	8	.214	.286	.304
2010 NYM	NL	5	10	2	0	0	0	(0	0)	2	0	0	0	0	0	5	0	0	0	0	0	-	1	.200	.200	.200
2011 NYM	NL	21	53	10	1	0	1	(1	0)	14	4	6	3	4	0	11	0	2	0	0	1	.00	1	.189	.246	.264
2 ML YEARS		26	63	12	1	0	1	(1	0)	16	4	6	3	4	0	16	0	2	0	0	1	.00	2	.190	.239	.254

Jeff Niemann

Pitches: R Bats: R Pos: SP-23   NEE-min   Ht: 6'9" Wt: 260 Born: 2/28/1983 Age: 29

Year Team	Lg	G	GS	CG	GF	IP	BFP	H	R	ER	HR	SH	SF	HB	TBB	IBB	SO	WP	Bk	W	L	Pct	Sh	Sv-Op	Hld	ERC	ERA
2011 Charltt*	A+	1	1	0	0	4.0	12	1	0	0	0	0	0	0	0	0	2	0	0	0	0	-	0	0- -	-	0.16	0.00
2011 Drham*	AAA	2	2	0	0	9.1	41	10	4	4	0	1	0	0	3	0	8	2	0	1	1	.500	0	0- -	-	3.37	3.86
2008 TB	AL	5	2	0	2	16.0	76	18	12	9	3	2	0	1	8	0	14	0	0	2	2	.500	0	0-0	0	5.93	5.06
2009 TB	AL	31	30	2	1	180.2	769	185	84	79	17	2	4	9	59	1	125	6	0	13	6	.684	2	0-0	0	4.12	3.94
2010 TB	AL	30	29	1	0	174.1	733	159	86	85	25	5	2	7	61	6	131	4	0	12	8	.600	1	0-0	0	3.81	4.39
2011 TB	AL	23	23	1	0	135.1	572	131	65	61	18	2	4	5	37	1	105	7	0	11	7	.611	0	0-0	0	3.73	4.06
Postseason		1	0	0	1	3.0	13	1	0	0	0	0	0	0	1	0	4	0	0	0	0	-	0	0-0	0	0.84	0.00
4 ML YEARS		89	84	4	3	506.1	2150	493	247	234	63	11	10	22	165	8	375	17	0	38	23	.623	3	0-0	0	3.96	4.16

Jonathon Niese

Pitches: L Bats: L Pos: SP-26; RP-1   NEESS   Ht: 6'4" Wt: 215 Born: 10/27/1986 Age: 25

Year Team	Lg	G	GS	CG	GF	IP	BFP	H	R	ER	HR	SH	SF	HB	TBB	IBB	SO	WP	Bk	W	L	Pct	Sh	Sv-Op	Hld	ERC	ERA
2008 NYM	NL	3	3	0	0	14.0	69	20	11	11	2	1	0	0	8	0	11	0	0	1	1	.500	0	0-0	0	7.71	7.07
2009 NYM	NL	5	5	0	0	25.2	110	27	12	12	1	2	1	0	9	0	18	1	0	1	1	.500	0	0-0	0	3.76	4.21
2010 NYM	NL	30	30	2	0	173.2	770	192	97	81	20	9	4	9	62	3	148	5	0	9	10	.474	1	0-0	0	4.77	4.20
2011 NYM	NL	27	26	0	0	157.1	694	178	88	77	14	16	2	5	44	4	138	3	0	11	11	.500	0	0-0	0	4.27	4.40
4 ML YEARS		65	64	2	0	370.2	1643	417	208	181	37	28	7	14	123	7	315	9	0	22	23	.489	1	0-0	0	4.59	4.39

Wil Nieves

Bats: R **Throws:** R **Pos:** C-17; PH-3; PR-1   **Ht:** 5'11" **Wt:** 182 **Born:** 9/25/1977 **Age:** 34

Year	Team	Lg	G	AB	H	2B	3B	HR	(Hm	Rd)	TB	R	RBI	RC	TBB	IBB	SO	HBP	SH	SF	SB	CS	SB%	GDP	Avg	OBP	Slg
2011	Nashv*	AAA	23	88	15	2	0	1	(-	-)	20	3	6	3	4	0	11	1	1	1	0	0	-	9	.170	.213	.227
2011	Gwnntt*	AAA	21	71	20	2	0	1	(-	-)	25	8	6	9	6	0	11	0	1	1	1	0	1.00	2	.282	.333	.352
2002	SD	NL	28	72	13	3	1	0	(0	0)	18	2	3	4	4	4	15	0	0	0	1	0	1.00	1	.181	.224	.250
2005	NYY	AL	3	4	0	0	0	0	(0	0)	0	0	0	0	0	0	1	0	0	0	0	0	-	0	.000	.000	.000
2006	NYY	AL	6	6	0	0	0	0	(0	0)	0	0	0	0	0	0	1	0	0	0	0	0	-	0	.000	.000	.000
2007	NYY	AL	26	61	10	4	0	0	(0	0)	14	6	8	4	2	0	9	0	3	0	0	0	-	3	.164	.190	.230
2008	Was	NL	68	176	46	9	1	1	(1	0)	60	15	20	20	13	1	29	0	5	2	0	1	.00	7	.261	.309	.341
2009	Was	NL	72	224	58	6	0	1	(0	1)	67	20	26	21	17	1	45	3	0	5	1	0	1.00	5	.259	.313	.299
2010	Was	NL	59	158	32	8	0	3	(1	2)	49	10	16	9	8	2	29	1	4	1	0	0	-	6	.203	.244	.310
2011	Mil	NL	20	50	7	2	0	0	(0	0)	9	2	0	0	3	1	12	0	1	0	0	0	-	3	.140	.189	.180
	8 ML YEARS		282	751	166	32	2	5	(2	3)	217	55	73	58	47	9	141	4	13	8	2	1	.67	27	.221	.268	.289

Tsuyoshi Nishioka

Bats: B **Throws:** R **Pos:** SS-60; 2B-6; PR-2; DH-1; PH-1   soo-YO-shee nee-shee-OH-kah   **Ht:** 6'0" **Wt:** 176 **Born:** 7/27/1984 **Age:** 27

Year	Team	Lg	G	AB	H	2B	3B	HR	(Hm	Rd)	TB	R	RBI	RC	TBB	IBB	SO	HBP	SH	SF	SB	CS	SB%	GDP	Avg	OBP	Slg
2003	Chiba	Jap	7	9	3	2	0	0	(-	-)	5	3	1	2	2	-	1	0	0	0	0	0	-	0	.333	.455	.556
2004	Chiba	Jap	63	212	54	8	2	6	(-	-)	84	32	35	27	14	-	37	2	2	2	8	2	.80	2	.255	.304	.396
2005	Chiba	Jap	122	447	120	22	11	4	(-	-)	176	80	48	63	31	-	51	5	6	4	41	9	.82	6	.268	.320	.394
2006	Chiba	Jap	115	426	120	20	7	4	(-	-)	166	58	27	66	49	-	61	3	4	3	33	17	.66	6	.282	.358	.390
2007	Chiba	Jap	130	494	148	31	3	3	(-	-)	194	76	40	78	50	-	73	4	7	4	27	13	.68	3	.300	.366	.393
2008	Chiba	Jap	116	473	142	26	6	13	(-	-)	219	78	49	79	36	-	68	7	4	2	18	11	.62	3	.300	.357	.463
2009	Chiba	Jap	120	454	118	24	5	14	(-	-)	194	70	41	76	67	-	76	5	3	2	26	10	.72	6	.260	.360	.427
2010	Chiba	Jap	144	596	206	32	8	11	(-	-)	287	121	59	124	79	-	96	4	8	5	22	11	.67	8	.346	.423	.482
2011	FtMyrs	A+	4	12	4	1	0	0	(-	-)	5	4	1	2	2	0	2	1	0	0	1	0	1.00	0	.333	.467	.417
2011	Roch	AAA	3	12	4	1	0	0	(-	-)	5	0	1	2	2	0	1	0	0	0	0	0	-	0	.333	.429	.417
2011	Min	AL	68	221	50	5	0	0	(0	0)	55	14	19	16	15	1	43	1	3	0	2	4	.33	1	.226	.278	.249

Jayson Nix

Bats: R **Throws:** R **Pos:** 3B-41; 2B-4; PR-2; LF-1; DH-1   **Ht:** 5'11" **Wt:** 195 **Born:** 8/26/1982 **Age:** 29

Year	Team	Lg	G	AB	H	2B	3B	HR	(Hm	Rd)	TB	R	RBI	RC	TBB	IBB	SO	HBP	SH	SF	SB	CS	SB%	GDP	Avg	OBP	Slg
2011	Dnedin*	A+	3	12	1	0	0	0	(-	-)	1	0	2	0	1	0	3	0	0	0	0	0	-	0	.083	.154	.083
2011	LsVgs*	AAA	41	163	44	12	2	8	(-	-)	84	30	29	29	14	0	38	4	0	1	3	0	1.00	6	.270	.341	.515
2008	Col	NL	22	56	7	2	0	0	(0	0)	9	2	2	0	7	2	17	1	1	0	1	0	1.00	1	.125	.234	.161
2009	CWS	AL	94	255	57	11	0	12	(4	8)	104	36	32	31	28	1	64	4	1	2	10	2	.83	5	.224	.308	.408
2010	2 Tms	AL	102	331	74	15	0	14	(7	7)	131	32	34	35	20	2	87	7	3	2	1	2	.33	6	.224	.281	.396
2011	Tor	AL	46	136	23	5	1	4	(2	2)	42	15	16	12	12	1	42	2	0	1	4	1	.80	2	.169	.245	.309
10	CWS	AL	24	49	8	1	0	1	(0	1)	12	3	5	4	7	2	12	0	1	0	0	0	-	1	.163	.268	.245
10	Cle	AL	78	282	66	14	0	13	(7	6)	119	29	29	31	13	0	75	7	2	2	1	2	.33	5	.234	.283	.422
	4 ML YEARS		264	778	161	33	1	30	(13	17)	286	85	84	78	67	6	210	14	5	5	16	5	.76	14	.207	.280	.368

Laynce Nix

Bats: L **Throws:** L **Pos:** LF-73; PH-36; RF-12; 1B-9; CF-4; PR-3; DH-2   **Ht:** 6'1" **Wt:** 220 **Born:** 10/30/1980 **Age:** 31

Year	Team	Lg	G	AB	H	2B	3B	HR	(Hm	Rd)	TB	R	RBI	RC	TBB	IBB	SO	HBP	SH	SF	SB	CS	SB%	GDP	Avg	OBP	Slg
2003	Tex	AL	53	184	47	10	0	8	(7	1)	81	25	30	25	9	0	53	0	1	1	3	0	1.00	1	.255	.289	.440
2004	Tex	AL	115	371	92	20	4	14	(9	5)	162	58	46	44	23	4	113	2	1	3	1	1	.50	6	.248	.293	.437
2005	Tex	AL	63	229	55	12	3	6	(3	3)	91	28	32	26	9	3	45	0	0	2	2	0	1.00	3	.240	.267	.397
2006	2 Tms		19	67	11	2	0	1	(1	0)	16	3	10	3	0	0	28	2	0	1	0	0	-	1	.164	.186	.239
2007	Mil	NL	10	12	0	0	0	0	(0	0)	0	0	0	0	0	0	4	0	0	0	0	0	-	0	.000	.000	.000
2008	Mil	NL	10	12	1	0	0	0	(0	0)	1	1	0	0	1	0	3	0	0	0	0	0	-	0	.083	.154	.083
2009	Cin	NL	116	309	74	26	1	15	(5	10)	147	42	46	35	22	3	81	2	0	4	0	1	.00	5	.239	.291	.476
2010	Cin	NL	97	165	48	11	2	4	(1	3)	75	16	18	21	15	4	39	0	2	0	0	1	.00	5	.291	.350	.455
2011	Was	NL	124	324	81	15	1	16	(9	7)	146	38	44	37	23	2	82	1	0	3	2	2	.50	1	.250	.299	.451
06	Tex	AL	9	32	3	1	0	0	(0	0)	4	1	4	0	0	0	17	1	0	1	0	0	-	0	.094	.118	.125
06	Mil	NL	10	35	8	1	0	1	(1	0)	12	2	6	3	0	0	11	1	0	0	0	0	-	1	.229	.250	.343
	Postseason		1	3	0	0	0	0	(0	0)	0	1	0	0	0	0	1	0	0	0	0	0	-	0	.000	.000	.000
	9 ML YEARS		607	1673	409	96	11	64	(35	29)	719	211	226	191	102	16	448	7	4	14	8	5	.62	22	.244	.288	.430

Hector Noesi

Pitches: R **Bats:** R **Pos:** RP-28; SP-2   NO-ess-ee   **Ht:** 6'3" **Wt:** 200 **Born:** 1/26/1987 **Age:** 25

			HOW MUCH HE PITCHED					WHAT HE GAVE UP												THE RESULTS						
Year	Team	Lg	G	GS	CG	GF	IP	BFP	H	R	ER	HR	SH	SF	HB	TBB	IBB	SO	WP	Bk	W	L	Pct	Sh	Sv-Op Hld	ERC	ERA
2006	Yanks	R	5	0	0	2	7.0	27	5	1	1	0	0	0	0	1	0	11	0	0	0	0	-	0	1- -	1.32	1.29
2007	CtnSC	A	5	5	0	0	20.0	91	25	10	10	2	1	1	0	8	0	11	2	0	1	1	.500	0	0- -	5.53	4.50
2008	Yanks	R	9	2	0	1	24.2	98	23	11	10	2	2	1	1	3	1	24	1	0	2	1	.667	0	0- -	2.68	3.65
2008	StsIsnd	A-	5	5	0	0	24.0	99	20	12	8	5	2	0	1	7	0	31	3	1	1	1	.500	0	0- -	3.58	3.00
2009	CtnSC	A	17	11	0	0	75.2	297	62	24	20	3	2	0	0	11	0	78	0	1	3	4	.429	0	0- -	1.86	2.38
2009	Tampa	A+	9	9	0	0	41.1	161	34	18	18	3	0	3	1	4	0	40	2	0	3	0	1.000	0	0- -	1.98	3.92
2010	Tampa	A+	8	8	0	0	43.0	174	35	14	13	3	1	0	2	6	0	53	5	1	5	2	.714	0	0- -	2.07	2.72

Year Team	Lg	G	GS	CG	GF	IP	BFP	H	R	ER	HR	SH	SF	HB	TBB	IBB	SO	WP	Bk	W	L	Pct	Sh	Sv-Op	Hld	ERC	ERA
2010 Trntn	AA	17	16	2	1	98.2	395	90	37	34	7	1	3	2	18	1	86	5	0	8	4	.667	1	0--	-	2.70	3.10
2010 S-WB	AAA	3	3	1	0	18.2	81	23	10	10	1	0	2	1	4	0	14	1	0	1	1	.500	0	0--	-	4.60	4.82
2011 S-WB	AAA	6	5	0	0	24.2	111	28	11	9	0	0	0	2	9	0	17	2	1	1	1	.500	0	0--	-	4.24	3.28
2011 NYY	AL	30	2	0	14	56.1	247	63	29	28	6	1	2	2	22	4	45	4	0	2	2	.500	0	0-0	4	4.85	4.47

Ricky Nolasco

Pitches: R Bats: R Pos: SP-33 Ht: 6'2" Wt: 230 Born: 12/13/1982 Age: 29

Year Team	Lg	G	GS	CG	GF	IP	BFP	H	R	ER	HR	SH	SF	HB	TBB	IBB	SO	WP	Bk	W	L	Pct	Sh	Sv-Op	Hld	ERC	ERA
2006 Fla	NL	35	22	0	0	140.0	613	157	86	75	20	8	6	10	41	5	99	7	0	11	11	.500	0	0-0	2	4.89	4.82
2007 Fla	NL	5	4	0	0	21.1	99	26	16	13	3	3	5	1	9	2	11	1	0	1	2	.333	0	0-0	0	5.71	5.48
2008 Fla	NL	34	32	1	0	212.1	868	192	88	83	28	6	9	6	42	6	186	1	3	15	8	.652	1	0-0	0	3.03	3.52
2009 Fla	NL	31	31	2	0	185.0	785	188	111	104	23	8	5	2	44	7	195	2	0	13	9	.591	0	0-0	0	3.62	5.06
2010 Fla	NL	26	26	1	0	157.2	665	169	82	79	24	5	5	2	33	1	147	5	0	14	9	.609	0	0-0	0	4.11	4.51
2011 Fla	NL	33	33	2	0	206.0	891	244	117	107	20	11	5	3	44	8	148	6	0	10	12	.455	1	0-0	0	4.34	4.67
6 ML YEARS		164	148	6	0	922.1	3921	976	500	461	118	41	35	24	213	29	786	22	3	64	51	.557	2	0-0	2	3.95	4.50

Jordan Norberto

Pitches: L Bats: L Pos: RP-6 Ht: 6'0" Wt: 195 Born: 12/8/1986 Age: 25

Year Team	Lg	G	GS	CG	GF	IP	BFP	H	R	ER	HR	SH	SF	HB	TBB	IBB	SO	WP	Bk	W	L	Pct	Sh	Sv-Op	Hld	ERC	ERA
2006 Msoula	R+	16	16	0	0	75.2	326	59	30	26	4	8	1	4	40	0	64	6	3	3	2	.600	0	0--	-	3.21	3.09
2007 Sbend	A	21	21	0	0	102.1	443	102	67	60	10	2	9	2	46	0	111	6	0	6	7	.462	0	0--	-	4.36	5.28
2008 Sbend	A	31	18	0	3	101.2	460	108	72	60	15	2	6	5	56	1	109	4	6	5	7	.417	0	0--	-	5.65	5.31
2009 Visalia	A+	29	0	0	8	44.2	185	36	9	8	1	2	1	0	22	1	59	4	0	4	1	.800	0	2--	-	2.88	1.61
2009 Mobile	AA	19	0	0	11	23.2	119	29	23	21	4	0	3	2	18	0	30	8	0	0	2	.000	0	2--	-	7.80	7.99
2010 Reno	AAA	21	0	0	7	29.1	131	25	12	10	2	2	0	0	19	1	38	5	1	3	0	1.000	0	4--	-	3.86	3.07
2011 Reno	AAA	41	0	0	9	48.2	216	46	26	23	1	1	1	3	26	1	54	6	1	2	2	.750	0	1--	-	3.90	4.25
2011 Scrmto	AAA	6	0	0	1	8.1	34	6	1	1	1	1	0	0	4	0	10	0	0	0	0	-	0	1--	-	3.06	1.08
2010 Ari	NL	33	0	0	5	20.0	94	16	13	13	3	1	0	0	22	1	15	2	0	0	2	.000	0	0-1	3	6.16	5.85
2010 Oak	AL	6	0	0	3	6.2	35	8	6	6	0	0	1	1	7	0	4	1	0	0	0	-	0	0-0	0	7.72	8.10
2 ML YEARS		39	0	0	8	26.2	129	24	19	19	3	1	1	1	29	1	19	3	0	0	2	.000	0	0-1	3	6.56	6.41

Bud Norris

Pitches: R Bats: R Pos: SP-31 Ht: 6'0" Wt: 220 Born: 3/2/1985 Age: 27

Year Team	Lg	G	GS	CG	GF	IP	BFP	H	R	ER	HR	SH	SF	HB	TBB	IBB	SO	WP	Bk	W	L	Pct	Sh	Sv-Op	Hld	ERC	ERA
2009 Hou	NL	11	10	0	0	55.2	249	59	29	28	9	1	3	3	25	1	54	3	0	6	3	.667	0	0-0	0	5.26	4.53
2010 Hou	NL	27	27	0	0	153.2	683	151	94	84	18	6	4	6	77	3	158	5	2	9	10	.474	0	0-0	0	4.61	4.92
2011 Hou	NL	31	31	0	0	186.0	795	177	93	78	24	9	4	5	70	7	176	3	2	6	11	.353	0	0-0	0	3.96	3.77
3 ML YEARS		69	68	0	0	395.1	1727	387	216	190	51	16	11	14	172	11	388	11	4	21	24	.467	0	0-0	0	4.39	4.33

Ivan Nova

Pitches: R Bats: R Pos: SP-27; RP-1 ee-VAHN Ht: 6'4" Wt: 225 Born: 1/12/1987 Age: 25

Year Team	Lg	G	GS	CG	GF	IP	BFP	H	R	ER	HR	SH	SF	HB	TBB	IBB	SO	WP	Bk	W	L	Pct	Sh	Sv-Op	Hld	ERC	ERA
2006 Yanks	R	10	5	0	2	43.0	167	36	13	13	5	0	0	3	7	0	36	3	0	3	0	1.000	0	1--	-	2.79	2.72
2007 CtnSC	A	21	21	0	0	99.1	440	121	64	55	8	4	3	6	31	0	54	4	0	6	8	.429	0	0--	-	5.15	4.98
2008 Tampa	A+	26	24	0	1	148.2	637	168	81	72	6	6	4	9	46	2	109	12	1	8	13	.381	0	0--	-	4.36	4.36
2009 Trntn	AA	12	12	0	0	72.1	305	65	27	19	3	3	3	2	31	0	47	5	3	5	4	.556	0	0--	-	3.37	2.36
2009 S-WB	AAA	12	12	1	0	67.0	292	72	39	38	4	2	6	3	28	0	43	4	0	1	4	.200	0	0--	-	4.54	5.10
2010 S-WB	AAA	23	23	0	0	145.0	595	135	50	46	10	3	3	2	48	1	115	4	1	12	3	.800	0	0--	-	3.35	2.86
2011 S-WB	AAA	3	3	0	0	16.0	65	16	6	6	3	0	1	0	2	0	18	6	0	1	2	.333	0	0--	-	3.54	3.38
2010 NYY	AL	10	7	0	3	42.0	185	44	22	21	4	1	1	1	17	2	26	2	0	1	2	.333	0	0-1	0	4.31	4.50
2011 NYY	AL	28	27	0	0	165.1	704	163	74	68	13	2	6	6	57	3	98	11	0	16	4	.800	0	0-0	0	3.76	3.70
2 ML YEARS		38	34	0	4	207.1	889	207	96	89	17	3	7	7	74	5	124	13	0	17	6	.739	0	0-1	0	3.87	3.86

Eduardo Nunez

Bats: R Throws: R Pos: SS-50; 3B-40; 2B-16; PR-15; DH-8; PH-4; RF-3; LF-1 Ht: 6'0" Wt: 155 Born: 6/15/1987 Age: 25

Year Team	Lg	G	AB	H	2B	3B	HR	(Hm	Rd)	TB	R	RBI	RC	TBB	IBB	SO	HBP	SH	SF	SB	CS	SB%	GDP	Avg	OBP	Slg
2005 StIsInd	A-	73	281	88	11	6	3	(-	-)	120	37	46	44	20	1	43	3	6	0	6	3	.67	2	.313	.365	.427
2006 Tampa	A+	37	147	27	5	3	4	(-	-)	50	17	26	12	8	0	28	0	4	2	6	1	.86	3	.184	.223	.340
2006 CtnSC	A	90	344	78	11	3	2	(-	-)	101	36	40	30	23	1	48	2	0	2	16	5	.76	6	.227	.278	.294
2007 CtnSC	A	91	328	78	10	2	1	(-	-)	95	36	28	30	25	0	42	2	2	3	20	8	.71	16	.238	.293	.290
2007 Tampa	A+	30	123	35	5	0	1	(-	-)	43	16	13	17	7	0	18	3	0	1	9	0	1.00	1	.285	.336	.350
2008 Tampa	A+	94	373	101	18	3	6	(-	-)	143	45	42	44	19	1	48	1	5	4	14	10	.58	9	.271	.305	.383
2009 Trntn	AA	123	497	160	26	1	9	(-	-)	215	70	55	77	22	3	63	1	4	4	19	7	.73	19	.322	.349	.433
2010 S-WB	AAA	118	464	134	25	3	4	(-	-)	177	55	50	65	32	1	60	5	3	2	23	5	.82	10	.289	.340	.381
2010 NYY	AL	30	50	14	1	0	1	(0	1)	18	7	8	8	3	0	2	0	0	0	5	0	1.00	4	.280	.321	.360
2011 NYY	AL	112	309	82	18	2	5	(2	3)	119	38	30	42	22	2	37	0	6	1	22	6	.79	7	.265	.313	.385
2 ML YEARS		142	359	96	19	2	6	(2	4)	137	50	37	50	25	2	39	0	6	1	27	6	.82	10	.267	.314	.382

Leo Nunez

Pitches: R Bats: R Pos: RP-68

Ht: 6'2" Wt: 190 Born: 8/14/1983 Age: 28

				HOW MUCH HE PITCHED				WHAT HE GAVE UP										THE RESULTS						
Year	Team	Lg	G	GS	CG	GF	IP	BFP	H	R	ER	HR	SH	SF	HB	TBB	IBB	SO	WP	Bk	W	L	Pct	Sh	Sv-Op	Hld	ERC	ERA
2005	KC	AL	41	0	0	10	53.2	246	73	45	45	9	1	2	3	18	2	32	1	0	3	2	.600	0	0-1	2	6.76	7.55
2006	KC	AL	7	0	0	5	13.1	58	15	7	7	2	0	1	2	5	0	7	0	0	0	0	-	0	0-0	0	5.98	4.73
2007	KC	AL	13	6	0	2	43.2	182	44	21	19	8	0	2	0	10	0	37	1	0	2	4	.333	0	0-0	1	3.98	3.92
2008	KC	AL	45	0	0	12	48.1	205	45	19	16	2	3	2	4	15	2	26	3	0	4	1	.800	0	0-3	7	3.20	2.98
2009	Fla	NL	75	0	0	41	68.2	293	59	33	31	13	4	2	4	27	5	60	1	1	4	6	.400	0	26-33	14	3.96	4.06
2010	Fla	NL	68	0	0	50	65.0	270	62	27	25	5	1	0	0	21	2	71	1	1	4	3	.571	0	30-38	5	3.36	3.46
2011	Fla	NL	68	0	0	51	64.1	268	57	30	29	8	1	2	1	21	2	55	1	0	1	4	.200	0	36-42	0	3.33	4.06
7 ML YEARS			317	6	0	171	357.0	1522	355	182	172	47	10	11	14	117	13	288	8	2	18	20	.474	0	92-117	29	4.09	4.34

Mike O'Connor

Pitches: L Bats: L Pos: RP-9

Ht: 6'3" Wt: 186 Born: 8/17/1980 Age: 31

				HOW MUCH HE PITCHED				WHAT HE GAVE UP										THE RESULTS						
Year	Team	Lg	G	GS	CG	GF	IP	BFP	H	R	ER	HR	SH	SF	HB	TBB	IBB	SO	WP	Bk	W	L	Pct	Sh	Sv-Op	Hld	ERC	ERA
2011	Buffalo*	AAA	39	4	0	0	60.1	265	69	36	35	7	3	3	0	19	1	66	6	0	5	5	.500	0	0- -	-	4.60	5.22
2006	Was	NL	21	20	0	0	105.0	455	96	61	56	15	6	4	7	45	5	59	8	0	3	8	.273	0	0-0	0	4.19	4.80
2008	Was	NL	5	1	0	0	9.0	48	11	13	13	3	2	1	0	11	0	4	2	0	1	1	.500	0	0-1	0	11.25	13.00
2011	NYM	NL	9	0	0	2	6.2	29	5	2	2	0	0	0	1	3	0	8	0	0	0	1	.000	0	0-1	2	2.72	2.70
3 ML YEARS			35	21	0	2	120.2	532	112	76	71	18	8	5	8	59	5	71	10	0	4	10	.286	0	0-2	2	4.55	5.30

Darren O'Day

Pitches: R Bats: R Pos: RP-16

Ht: 6'4" Wt: 220 Born: 10/22/1982 Age: 29

				HOW MUCH HE PITCHED				WHAT HE GAVE UP										THE RESULTS						
Year	Team	Lg	G	GS	CG	GF	IP	BFP	H	R	ER	HR	SH	SF	HB	TBB	IBB	SO	WP	Bk	W	L	Pct	Sh	Sv-Op	Hld	ERC	ERA
2011	Frisco*	AA	1	1	0	0	1.0	4	1	1	1	1	0	0	0	0	0	1	0	0	0	0	-	0	0- -	-	7.45	9.00
2011	RdRck*	AAA	17	1	0	4	20.1	83	16	6	5	2	1	0	2	4	0	26	0	0	1	0	1.000	0	1- -	-	2.50	2.21
2008	LAA	AL	30	0	0	17	43.1	194	49	24	22	2	2	1	4	14	6	29	1	0	0	1	.000	0	0-0	1	4.20	4.57
2009	2 Tms		68	0	0	15	58.2	233	41	14	12	3	1	3	5	18	1	56	1	0	2	1	.667	0	2-2	20	2.20	1.84
2010	Tex	AL	72	0	0	14	62.0	240	43	15	14	5	1	3	5	12	2	45	0	0	6	2	.750	0	0-2	22	1.93	2.03
2011	Tex	AL	16	0	0	7	16.2	74	17	10	10	7	1	1	2	5	0	18	0	0	0	1	.000	0	0-0	3	6.45	5.40
09	NYM	NL	4	0	0	1	3.0	17	5	2	0	0	0	1	1	1	0	2	0	0	0	0	-	0	0-0	0	7.72	0.00
09	Tex	AL	64	0	0	14	55.2	216	36	12	12	3	1	2	4	17	1	54	1	0	2	1	.667	0	2-2	20	1.95	1.94
Postseason			11	0	0	1	4.2	23	6	4	4	2	0	0	1	1	0	8	0	0	0	1	.000	0	0-0	1	7.96	7.71
4 ML YEARS			186	0	0	53	180.2	741	150	63	58	17	5	8	16	49	9	148	2	0	8	5	.615	0	2-4	46	2.92	2.89

Trent Oeltjen

Bats: L Throws: L Pos: PH-31; LF-13; RF-11; PR-5; DH-2; CF-1   OLT-jenn

Ht: 6'1" Wt: 190 Born: 2/28/1983 Age: 29

				BATTING																	BASERUNNING				AVERAGES		
Year	Team	Lg	G	AB	H	2B	3B	HR	(Hm	Rd)	TB	R	RBI	RC	TBB	IBB	SO	HBP	SH	SF		SB	CS	SB%	GDP	Avg	OBP	Slg
2011	Albq*	AAA	56	180	61	14	3	8	(-	-)	105	33	34	43	25	5	50	4	2	1		7	4	.64	2	.339	.429	.583
2009	Ari	NL	24	70	17	4	1	3	(1	2)	32	11	4	4	1	0	13	0	1	1		3	1	.75	0	.243	.250	.457
2010	LAD	NL	15	23	5	1	1	0	(0	0)	8	5	1	2	4	0	8	1	2	0		0	0	-	1	.217	.357	.348
2011	LAD	NL	61	71	14	1	1	2	(0	2)	23	10	6	6	13	1	30	1	4	2		6	0	1.00	1	.197	.322	.324
3 ML YEARS			100	164	36	6	3	5	(1	4)	63	26	11	12	18	1	51	2	7	3		9	1	.90	2	.220	.299	.384

Eric O'Flaherty

Pitches: L Bats: L Pos: RP-78

Ht: 6'2" Wt: 220 Born: 2/5/1985 Age: 27

				HOW MUCH HE PITCHED				WHAT HE GAVE UP										THE RESULTS						
Year	Team	Lg	G	GS	CG	GF	IP	BFP	H	R	ER	HR	SH	SF	HB	TBB	IBB	SO	WP	Bk	W	L	Pct	Sh	Sv-Op	Hld	ERC	ERA
2006	Sea	AL	15	0	0	5	11.0	57	18	9	5	2	1	0	0	6	3	6	2	0	0	0	-	0	0-0	1	8.63	4.09
2007	Sea	AL	56	0	0	9	52.1	221	45	26	26	1	0	2	5	20	1	36	4	1	7	1	.875	0	0-1	4	3.04	4.47
2008	Sea	AL	7	0	0	1	6.2	42	16	15	15	2	0	1	2	4	2	4	0	0	0	1	.000	0	0-0	2	17.12	20.25
2009	Atl	NL	78	0	0	8	56.1	236	52	23	19	2	1	1	6	18	4	39	2	0	2	1	.667	0	0-2	15	3.26	3.04
2010	Atl	NL	56	0	0	7	44.0	181	37	14	12	2	1	0	2	18	2	36	3	0	3	2	.600	0	0-1	9	2.97	2.45
2011	Atl	NL	78	0	0	8	73.2	301	59	9	8	2	7	2	3	21	8	67	1	0	2	4	.333	0	0-4	32	2.13	0.98
6 ML YEARS			290	0	0	35	244.0	1038	227	96	85	11	10	6	17	87	20	188	12	1	14	9	.609	0	0-8	63	3.29	3.14

Alexi Ogando

Pitches: R Bats: R Pos: SP-29; RP-2   oh-GONN-doh

Ht: 6'4" Wt: 195 Born: 10/5/1983 Age: 28

				HOW MUCH HE PITCHED				WHAT HE GAVE UP										THE RESULTS						
Year	Team	Lg	G	GS	CG	GF	IP	BFP	H	R	ER	HR	SH	SF	HB	TBB	IBB	SO	WP	Bk	W	L	Pct	Sh	Sv-Op	Hld	ERC	ERA
2010	Frisco	AA	7	3	0	1	15.2	56	4	2	2	1	0	0	0	5	0	21	0	0	0	0	-	0	0- -	-	0.67	1.15
2010	OKCity	AAA	11	0	0	4	15.0	63	10	7	5	0	0	0	0	6	1	21	0	0	0	0	-	0	1- -	-	1.60	3.00
2010	Tex	AL	44	0	0	12	41.2	171	31	6	6	2	3	2	1	16	2	39	3	0	4	1	.800	0	0-2	7	2.34	1.30
2011	Tex	AL	31	29	1	2	169.0	693	149	73	66	16	2	3	7	43	0	126	5	0	13	8	.619	1	0-0	0	3.01	3.51
Postseason			5	0	0	1	6.0	23	5	1	1	1	0	0	0	1	0	8	0	0	0	0	-	0	0-1	0	2.80	1.50
2 ML YEARS			75	29	1	14	210.2	864	180	79	72	18	5	5	8	59	2	165	8	0	17	9	.654	1	0-2	7	2.88	3.08

Ross Ohlendorf

OH-lenn-dorf

Pitches: R **Bats:** R **Pos:** SP-9 **Ht:** 6'4" **Wt:** 245 **Born:** 8/8/1982 **Age:** 29

Year Team	Lg	G	GS	CG	GF	IP	BFP	H	R	ER	HR	SH	SF	HB	TBB	IBB	SO	WP	Bk	W	L	Pct	Sh	Sv-Op Hld	ERC	ERA
2011 Bradtn*	A+	2	2	0	0	8.0	35	10	4	4	0	0	0	1	1	0	6	0	0	0	0	-	0	0- -	4.18	4.50
2011 Altna*	AA	1	1	0	0	4.2	21	5	2	2	1	0	0	0	1	0	3	0	0	0	0	-	0	0- -	4.17	3.86
2011 Indy*	AAA	4	4	0	0	24.1	102	22	10	9	2	3	1	1	8	0	12	1	1	1	1	.500	0	0-0 1	2.94	2.84
2007 NYY	AL	6	0	0	3	6.1	26	5	2	2	1	0	0	0	2	0	9	0	0	0	0	-	0	0-0 1	7.16	6.46
2008 2 Tms		30	5	0	3	62.2	300	86	49	45	10	1	1	1	31	3	49	10	1	1	4	.200	0	0-0 4	3.84	3.92
2009 Pit	NL	29	29	0	0	176.2	725	165	80	77	25	11	8	7	53	1	109	2	1	11	10	.524	0	0-0 0	4.20	4.07
2010 Pit	NL	21	21	0	0	108.1	475	106	54	49	12	9	8	6	44	2	79	5	0	1	11	.083	0	0-0 0	9.12	8.15
2011 Pit	NL	9	9	0	0	38.2	194	60	38	35	9	5	3	6	15	2	27	2	0	1	3	.250	0	0-0 0	6.39	6.53
08 NYY	AL	25	0	0	3	40.0	187	50	31	29	7	0	0	1	19	3	36	6	0	1	1	.500	0	0-0 0	6.39	6.35
08 Pit	NL	5	5	0	0	22.2	113	36	18	16	3	1	1	0	12	0	13	4	1	0	3	.000	0	0-0 0	47.63	27.00
Postseason		1	0	0	0	1.0	9	4	3	3	1	0	0	1	1	0	0	0	0	0	0	-	0	0-0 0	4.90	4.77
5 ML YEARS		95	64	0	6	392.2	1720	422	223	208	57	26	20	20	145	8	273	19	2	14	28	.333	0	0-0 5	4.90	4.77

Will Ohman

OH-min

Pitches: L **Bats:** L **Pos:** RP-59 **Ht:** 6'2" **Wt:** 225 **Born:** 8/13/1977 **Age:** 34

Year Team	Lg	G	GS	CG	GF	IP	BFP	H	R	ER	HR	SH	SF	HB	TBB	IBB	SO	WP	Bk	W	L	Pct	Sh	Sv-Op Hld	ERC	ERA
2000 ChC	NL	6	0	0	2	3.1	17	4	3	3	0	0	0	0	4	1	2	1	0	1	0	1.000	0	0-0 1	7.25	8.10
2001 ChC	NL	11	0	0	0	11.2	54	14	10	10	2	0	0	0	6	0	12	2	0	0	1	.000	0	0-0 1	6.26	7.71
2005 ChC	NL	69	0	0	13	43.1	187	32	14	14	6	1	0	3	24	3	45	6	1	2	2	.500	0	0-3 13	3.62	2.91
2006 ChC	NL	78	0	0	14	65.1	286	51	30	30	6	0	2	5	34	2	74	4	0	1	1	.500	0	0-0 9	3.44	4.13
2007 ChC	NL	56	0	0	11	36.1	168	42	20	20	3	2	0	1	16	4	33	2	0	2	4	.333	0	1-1 12	4.79	4.95
2008 Atl	NL	83	0	0	16	58.2	248	51	27	24	3	3	0	1	22	4	53	2	0	4	1	.800	0	1-4 23	2.87	3.68
2009 LAD	NL	21	0	0	5	12.1	54	12	8	8	4	0	0	0	8	1	7	0	0	1	0	1.000	0	0-1 18	4.24	3.21
2010 2 Tms		68	0	0	12	42.0	186	40	18	15	4	2	4	1	23	5	43	3	0	0	2	.000	0	0-1 3	4.16	4.22
2011 CWS	AL	59	0	0	15	53.1	232	53	26	25	8	2	1	4	17	5	54	1	0	1	3	.250	0	0-1 15	4.80	3.30
10 Bal	AL	51	0	0	9	30.0	135	30	12	11	3	2	3	1	18	4	29	2	0	0	0	-	0	0-1 15	2.94	3.00
10 Fla	NL	17	0	0	3	12.0	51	10	6	4	1	0	1	0	5	1	14	1	0	0	2	.000	0	0-0 3	3.97	4.11
9 ML YEARS		451	0	0	88	326.1	1432	299	156	149	36	10	7	15	154	25	323	21	1	12	14	.462	0	3-12 84	3.97	4.11

Hideki Okajima

oh-kuh-JEE-muh

Pitches: L **Bats:** L **Pos:** RP-7 **Ht:** 6'1" **Wt:** 195 **Born:** 12/25/1975 **Age:** 36

Year Team	Lg	G	GS	CG	GF	IP	BFP	H	R	ER	HR	SH	SF	HB	TBB	IBB	SO	WP	Bk	W	L	Pct	Sh	Sv-Op Hld	ERC	ERA
2011 Pwtckt*	AAA	34	0	0	8	51.0	199	39	13	13	3	2	3	0	9	1	48	2	0	8	1	.889	0	- -	1.80	2.29
2007 Bos	AL	66	0	0	13	69.0	272	50	17	17	6	5	1	1	17	2	63	0	0	3	2	.600	0	5-7 27	2.03	2.22
2008 Bos	AL	64	0	0	11	62.0	258	49	18	18	6	0	3	1	23	1	60	0	0	3	2	.600	0	1-9 23	2.82	2.61
2009 Bos	AL	68	0	0	6	61.0	258	56	23	23	8	3	1	2	21	3	53	0	0	6	0	1.000	0	0-2 23	3.65	3.39
2010 Bos	AL	56	0	0	12	46.0	213	59	24	23	6	4	1	0	20	5	33	2	0	4	4	.500	0	0-4 11	5.90	4.50
2011 Bos	AL	7	0	0	2	8.1	36	7	4	4	1	0	0	0	5	0	6	0	0	0	0	-	0	0-0 8	1.50	4.32
Postseason		17	0	0	2	21.1	82	13	5	5	2	0	0	0	5	1	16	0	0	0	0	-	0	0-0 8	1.50	2.11
5 ML YEARS		261	0	0	44	246.1	1037	221	86	85	26	13	6	4	86	11	215	4	0	17	8	.680	0	6-22 84	3.33	3.11

Andrew Oliver

Pitches: L **Bats:** L **Pos:** SP-2 **Ht:** 6'3" **Wt:** 210 **Born:** 12/3/1987 **Age:** 24

Year Team	Lg	G	GS	CG	GF	IP	BFP	H	R	ER	HR	SH	SF	HB	TBB	IBB	SO	WP	Bk	W	L	Pct	Sh	Sv-Op Hld	ERC	ERA
2010 Erie	AA	14	14	0	0	77.1	322	74	35	31	7	2	1	2	25	0	70	7	0	6	4	.600	0	0- - -	3.57	3.61
2010 Toledo	AAA	9	9	0	0	53.0	220	43	23	19	6	2	2	1	25	0	49	1	0	3	4	.429	0	0- - -	3.55	3.23
2011 Toledo	AAA	26	26	0	0	147.0	646	149	83	77	15	5	9	4	80	0	143	13	1	8	12	.400	0	0- - -	4.96	4.71
2010 Det	AL	5	5	0	0	22.0	102	26	22	18	3	2	1	2	13	2	18	3	0	0	4	.000	0	0-0 0	6.62	7.36
2011 Det	AL	2	2	0	0	9.2	49	11	7	7	3	0	1	2	8	0	5	1	0	0	1	.000	0	0-0 0	9.50	6.52
2 ML YEARS		7	7	0	0	31.2	151	37	29	25	6	2	2	4	21	2	23	4	0	0	5	.000	0	0-0 0	7.48	7.11

Darren Oliver

Pitches: L **Bats:** R **Pos:** RP-61 **Ht:** 6'2" **Wt:** 200 **Born:** 10/6/1970 **Age:** 41

Year Team	Lg	G	GS	CG	GF	IP	BFP	H	R	ER	HR	SH	SF	HB	TBB	IBB	SO	WP	Bk	W	L	Pct	Sh	Sv-Op Hld	ERC	ERA
1993 Tex	AL	2	0	0	0	3.1	14	2	1	1	1	0	0	0	1	1	4	0	0	0	0	-	0	0-0 0	2.15	2.70
1994 Tex	AL	43	0	0	10	50.0	226	40	24	19	4	6	0	6	35	4	50	2	2	4	0	1.000	0	2-3 9	4.29	3.42
1995 Tex	AL	17	7	0	2	49.0	222	47	25	23	3	5	1	1	32	1	39	4	0	4	2	.667	0	0-0 0	5.10	4.66
1996 Tex	AL	30	30	1	0	173.2	777	190	97	90	20	2	7	10	76	3	112	5	1	14	6	.700	1	0-0 0	4.98	4.20
1997 Tex	AL	32	32	3	0	201.1	887	213	111	94	29	2	5	11	82	3	104	7	0	13	12	.520	1	0-0 0	6.01	5.73
1998 2 Tms		29	29	2	0	160.1	749	204	115	102	18	8	8	10	66	2	87	7	4	9	9	.500	1	0-0 0	4.11	4.26
1999 StL	NL	30	30	2	0	196.1	842	197	96	93	16	11	4	11	74	4	119	6	2	2	9	.182	0	0-0 0	7.04	7.42
2000 Tex	AL	21	21	0	0	108.0	501	151	95	89	16	5	4	4	42	3	49	4	1	11	11	.500	0	0-0 0	6.14	6.02
2001 Tex	AL	28	28	1	0	154.0	696	189	109	103	23	1	5	6	65	0	104	8	2	4	5	.444	1	0-0 0	6.49	4.66
2002 Bos	AL	14	9	1	0	58.0	258	70	30	30	7	1	3	6	27	0	32	1	0	4	5	.444	0	0-0 0	4.80	5.04
2003 Col	NL	33	32	1	0	180.1	786	201	108	101	21	4	5	8	61	3	88	0	0	13	11	.542	0	0-0 0	5.59	5.94
2004 2 Tms		27	10	0	5	72.2	314	87	50	48	14	4	3	1	21	1	46	1	0	4	1	.800	0	0-0 3	3.27	3.44
2006 NYM	AL	45	0	0	10	81.0	333	70	33	31	4	8	2	4	23	2	51	1	1	3	1	.750	0	0-0 8	3.19	3.78
2007 LAA	AL	61	0	0	20	64.1	273	58	31	27	5	2	4	1	23	2	51	1	1	7	1	.875	0	0-2 12	3.07	2.88
2008 LAA	AL	54	0	0	9	72.0	291	67	24	23	4	3	4	4	16	2	48	3	0	7	1	.833	0	0-1 20	2.81	2.71
2009 LAA	AL	63	1	0	9	73.0	293	61	22	22	5	4	5	2	22	8	65	1	0	5	1	.833	0	0-0 0	2.81	2.71

(continued)

Year	Team	Lg	G	GS	CG	GF	IP	BFP	H	R	ER	HR	SH	SF	HB	TBB	IBB	SO	WP	Bk	W	L	Pct	Sh	Sv-Op	Hld	ERC	ERA
2010	Tex	AL	64	0	0	7	61.2	244	53	20	17	4	5	3	2	15	4	65	0	0	1	2	.333	0	1-4	14	2.63	2.48
2011	Tex	AL	61	0	0	17	51.0	215	47	17	13	3	4	0	1	11	1	44	0	1	5	5	.500	0	2-6	16	2.64	2.29
98	Tex	AL	19	19	2	0	103.1	493	140	84	75	11	3	6	10	43	1	58	6	1	6	7	.462	0	0-0	0	6.68	6.53
98	StL	NL	10	10	0	0	57.0	256	64	31	27	7	5	2	0	23	1	29	1	3	4	4	.500	0	0-0	0	4.85	4.26
04	Fla	NL	18	8	0	3	58.2	260	75	44	42	13	4	3	1	17	1	33	1	0	2	3	.400	0	0-0	0	6.30	6.44
04	Hou	NL	9	2	0	2	14.0	54	12	6	6	1	0	0	0	4	0	13	0	0	1	0	1.000	0	0-0	0	2.89	3.86
Postseason			22	1	0	3	35.1	140	28	16	16	2	0	1		12	2	25	1	0	1	2	.333	0	1-2	1	2.60	4.08
18 ML YEARS			654	229	11	89	1810.0	7921	1947	1008	926	207	70	64	90	090	44	1167	57	14	112	90	.554	4	5-16	82	4.73	4.60

Lester Oliveros

Pitches: R Bats: R Pos: RP-19

Ht: 6'0" Wt: 225 Born: 5/28/1988 Age: 24

Year	Team	Lg	G	GS	CG	GF	IP	BFP	H	R	ER	HR	SH	SF	HB	TBB	IBB	SO	WP	Bk	W	L	Pct	Sh	Sv-Op	Hld	ERC	ERA
2008	Oneont	A-	15	0	0	9	20.2	83	15	4	4	1	1	0	0	6	1	34	0	0	1	2	.333	0	4--	-	1.86	1.74
2008	Lkland	A+	5	0	0	1	10.2	55	12	8	5	0	0	1	4	9	0	3	0	0	1	1	.500	0	0--	-	7.37	4.22
2009	Lkland	A+	34	0	0	14	54.0	235	53	27	25	5	1	1	4	16	1	58	2	1	4	2	.667	0	2--	-	3.69	4.17
2009	Toledo	AAA	1	0	0	0	2.0	9	2	0	0	0	0	0	1	1	0	3	0	0	0	0	-	0	0--	-	3.63	0.00
2010	Lkland	A+	20	0	0	13	19.0	76	13	5	4	0	0	1	2	6	0	24	2	0	0	1	.000	0	0--	-	1.93	1.89
2010	Erie	AA	24	0	0	20	25.1	117	20	14	14	3	2	0	2	21	4	36	0	1	0	1	.000	0	9--	-	4.70	4.97
2011	Erie	AA	10	0	0	6	17.0	63	11	1	1	0	1	0	0	4	1	28	1	0	1	2	.333	0	14--	-	1.46	0.53
2011	Toledo	AAA	22	0	0	16	28.0	136	37	20	20	7	2	0	0	17	3	26	1	0	2	0	1.000	0	0--	-	7.90	6.43
2011	Roch	AAA	2	0	0	0	3.0	11	2	1	1	1	0	0	0	0	0	4	0	0	1	3	.250	0	5--	-	1.99	3.00
2011	2 Tms		19	0	0	6	21.1	91	21	11	11	0	0	2	0	11	2	13	1	0	0	0	-	0	0--	-	3.75	4.05
11	Det	AL	9	0	0	3	8.0	35	8	5	5	0	0	0	0	4	1	4	1	0	0	0	-	0	0-0	1	3.67	4.64
11	Min	AL	10	0	0	3	13.1	56	13	6	6	0	0	2	0	7	1	9	0	0	0	0	-	0	0-0	1	3.53	5.63

Miguel Olivo

Bats: R Throws: R Pos: C-127; PH-5; DH-2

oh-LEEV-oh

Ht: 6'0" Wt: 229 Born: 7/15/1978 Age: 33

Year	Team	Lg	G	AB	H	2B	3B	HR	(Hm	Rd)	TB	R	RBI	RC	TBB	IBB	SO	HBP	SH	SF	SB	CS	SB%	GDP	Avg	OBP	Slg
2002	CWS	AL	6	19	4	1	0	1	(0	1)	8	2	5	4	2	0	5	0	0	0	0	0	-	1	.211	.286	.421
2003	CWS	AL	114	317	75	19	1	6	(4	2)	114	37	27	32	19	0	80	4	4	2	6	4	.60	3	.237	.287	.360
2004	2 Tms	AL	96	301	70	15	4	13	(8	5)	132	46	40	33	20	2	84	3	4	1	7	6	.54	4	.233	.286	.439
2005	2 Tms		91	267	58	11	4	9	(5	4)	98	30	34	23	8	2	80	3	1	2	7	2	.78	7	.217	.246	.367
2006	Fla	NL	127	430	113	22	3	16	(7	9)	189	52	58	49	9	4	103	3	7	3	2	3	.40	9	.263	.287	.440
2007	Fla	NL	122	452	107	20	4	16	(11	5)	183	43	60	43	14	2	123	2	0	1	3	2	.60	13	.237	.262	.405
2008	KC	AL	84	306	78	22	0	12	(3	9)	136	29	41	35	7	2	82	3	0	1	3	2	.60	13	.255	.278	.444
2009	KC	AL	114	390	97	15	5	23	(10	13)	191	51	65	47	19	0	126	5	1	1	5	2	.71	10	.249	.292	.490
2010	Col	NL	112	394	106	17	6	14	(10	4)	177	55	58	49	27	5	117	2	1	3	7	4	.64	6	.269	.315	.449
2011	Sea	AL	130	477	107	19	1	19	(10	9)	185	54	62	44	20	2	140	1	2	3	7	4	.64	6	.224	.253	.388
04	CWS	AL	46	141	38	7	2	7	(4	3)	70	21	26	21	10	1	29	0	4	1	6	5	.55	7	.270	.316	.496
04	Sea	AL	50	160	32	8	2	6	(4	2)	62	25	14	12	10	1	55	3	0	0	2	2	.50	2	.200	.260	.388
05	Sea	AL	54	152	23	4	0	5	(4	1)	42	14	18	6	4	0	49	0	0	1	1	1	.50	3	.151	.172	.276
05	SD	AL	37	115	35	7	1	4	(1	3)	56	16	16	17	4	2	31	3	1	1	6	1	.86	4	.304	.341	.487
Postseason			1	1	1	0	0	0	(0	0)	0	0	0	0	0	0	0	0	0	0	0	0	-	1	.000	.000	.000
10 ML YEARS			996	3353	815	161	25	129	(68	61)	1413	399	450	359	145	19	940	29	16	22	50	28	.64	66	.243	.279	.421

Garrett Olson

Pitches: L Bats: R Pos: RP-4

Ht: 6'1" Wt: 205 Born: 10/18/1983 Age: 28

Year	Team	Lg	G	GS	CG	GF	IP	BFP	H	R	ER	HR	SH	SF	HB	TBB	IBB	SO	WP	Bk	W	L	Pct	Sh	Sv-Op	Hld	ERC	ERA
2011	Indy*	AAA	24	15	0	1	85.2	361	63	35	29	7	2	6	3	47	1	61	3	1	4	3	.571	0	0--	-	3.22	3.05
2007	Bal	AL	7	7	0	0	32.1	162	42	28	28	4	0	3	2	28	1	28	1	1	1	3	.250	0	0-0	0	8.46	7.79
2008	Bal	AL	26	26	0	0	132.2	621	168	100	98	17	4	4	8	62	1	83	6	0	9	10	.474	0	0-0	0	6.40	6.65
2009	Sea	AL	31	11	0	5	80.1	347	79	54	50	19	1	2	4	34	0	47	2	0	3	5	.375	0	0-0	5	5.33	5.60
2010	Sea	AL	35	0	0	11	37.2	172	42	20	19	6	1	1	0	15	1	31	4	0	0	3	.000	0	1-1	4	4.94	4.54
2011	Pit	NL	4	0	0	1	4.1	21	2	1	1	0	1	1	0	3	1	4	1	0	1	1	.500	0	0-0	0	1.24	2.08
5 ML YEARS			103	44	0	17	287.1	1323	333	201	196	46	7	11	14	142	4	193	14	1	14	22	.389	0	1-1	6	6.03	6.14

Logan Ondrusek

Pitches: R Bats: R Pos: RP-66

ahn-DREW-seck

Ht: 6'8" Wt: 228 Born: 2/13/1985 Age: 27

Year	Team	Lg	G	GS	CG	GF	IP	BFP	H	R	ER	HR	SH	SF	HB	TBB	IBB	SO	WP	Bk	W	L	Pct	Sh	Sv-Op	Hld	ERC	ERA
2005	Billings	R+	15	9	0	1	55.1	257	72	49	37	9	2	1	6	19	0	46	10	0	1	6	.143	0	0--	-	6.59	6.02
2006	Dayton	A	27	0	0	6	52.2	226	48	24	20	2	3	1	3	19	0	47	4	0	4	5	.444	0	0--	-	3.19	3.42
2006	Billings	R+	1	0	0	1	1.0	8	4	3	3	0	0	0	0	1	0	3	1	0	0	1	.000	0	0--	-	27.72	27.00
2006	Chatt	AA	1	0	0	0	4.0	13	0	0	0	0	0	1	0	0	0	3	1	0	0	0	-	0	0--	-	0.65	0.00
2007	Srsota	A+	31	22	0	3	124.0	538	131	72	61	4	3	7	8	48	0	86	6	0	7	10	.412	0	0--	-	4.17	4.43
2008	Srsota	A+	40	3	0	6	79.2	367	93	47	44	5	1	1	6	32	2	58	3	0	1	7	.125	0	1--	-	4.93	4.97
2008	Lsvlle	AAA	1	0	0	0	1.1	7	1	0	0	0	0	0	0	2	0	5	0	0	0	0	-	0	1--	-	6.99	0.00
2009	Srsota	A+	13	0	0	7	18.2	71	7	4	2	0	0	0	0	2	0	11	1	0	0	0	-	0	0--	-	1.05	0.96
2009	Carlina	AA	24	0	0	15	32.2	128	21	7	6	0	2	0	2	7	0	12	0	0	2	0	1.000	0	1--	-	1.55	1.65
2009	Lsvlle	AAA	19	0	0	3	20.2	77	16	4	4	0	1	0	1	2	0	24	3	0	2	1	.667	0	7--	-	1.80	1.74
2010	Lsvlle	AAA	14	0	0	2	19.2	79	21	9	9	0	1	0	1	2	0	14	2	0	0	1	.000	0	1--	-	3.39	4.12

Year	Team	Lg	G	GS	CG	GF	IP	BFP	H	R	ER	HR	SH	SF	HB	TBB	IBB	SO	WP	Bk	W	L	Pct	Sh	Sv-Op	Hld	ERC	ERA
2010	Cin	NL	60	0	0	11	58.2	240	49	25	24	7	1	1	0	20	1	39	2	0	5	0	1.000	0	0-2	6	3.08	3.68
2011	Cin	NL	66	0	0	14	61.1	268	55	25	22	6	3	4	2	28	7	41	6	0	5	5	.500	0	0-3	14	3.58	3.23
	Postseason		2	0	0	0	2.0	9	0	0	0	0	0	0	1	1	0	0	0	0	0	0	-	0	0-0	1	0.84	0.00
	2 ML YEARS		126	0	0	25	120.0	508	104	50	46	13	4	5	2	48	8	80	8	0	10	5	.667	0	0-5	20	3.34	3.45

Magglio Ordonez

Bats: R **Throws:** R **Pos:** RF-69; DH-21; PH-3 **Ht:** 6'0" **Wt:** 215 **Born:** 1/28/1974 **Age:** 38

Year	Team	Lg	G	AB	H	2B	3B	HR	(Hm	Rd)	TB	R	RBI	RC	TBB	IBB	SO	HBP	SH	SF	SB	CS	SB%	GDP	Avg	OBP	Slg
2011	Toledo*	AAA	9	37	11	1	0	2	(-	-)	18	3	6	5	2	0	9	0	0	0	0	0	-	2	.297	.333	.486
1997	CWS	AL	21	69	22	6	0	4	(2	2)	40	12	11	12	2	0	8	0	1	0	1	2	.33	1	.319	.338	.580
1998	CWS	AL	145	535	151	25	2	14	(8	6)	222	70	65	67	28	1	53	9	2	4	9	7	.56	19	.282	.326	.415
1999	CWS	AL	157	624	188	34	3	30	(16	14)	318	100	117	102	47	4	64	1	0	5	13	6	.68	24	.301	.349	.510
2000	CWS	AL	153	588	185	34	3	32	(21	11)	321	102	126	112	60	3	64	2	0	15	18	4	.82	28	.315	.371	.546
2001	CWS	AL	160	593	181	40	1	31	(17	14)	316	97	113	117	70	7	70	5	0	3	25	7	.78	14	.305	.382	.533
2002	CWS	AL	153	590	189	47	1	38	(24	14)	352	116	135	119	53	2	77	7	0	3	7	5	.58	21	.320	.381	.597
2003	CWS	AL	160	606	192	46	3	29	(17	12)	331	95	99	109	57	1	73	7	0	4	9	5	.64	20	.317	.380	.546
2004	CWS	AL	52	202	59	8	2	9	(4	5)	98	32	37	39	16	2	22	3	0	1	0	2	.00	4	.292	.351	.485
2005	Det	AL	82	305	92	17	0	8	(2	6)	133	38	46	51	30	1	35	1	0	7	0	0	-	8	.302	.359	.436
2006	Det	AL	155	593	177	32	1	24	(8	16)	283	82	104	97	45	3	87	4	0	4	1	4	.20	13	.298	.350	.477
2007	Det	AL	157	595	216	54	0	28	(17	11)	354	117	139	146	76	8	79	2	0	5	4	1	.80	20	.363	.434	.595
2008	Det	AL	146	561	178	32	2	21	(13	8)	277	72	103	92	53	2	76	3	0	6	1	5	.17	27	.317	.376	.494
2009	Det	AL	131	465	144	24	2	9	(6	3)	199	54	50	69	51	2	65	0	0	2	3	1	.75	19	.310	.376	.428
2010	Det	AL	84	323	98	17	1	12	(7	5)	153	56	59	53	40	0	38	0	0	2	1	0	1.00	14	.303	.378	.474
2011	Det	AL	92	329	84	10	0	5	(3	2)	109	33	32	29	23	0	41	1	0	4	2	1	.67	10	.255	.303	.331
	Postseason		16	62	12	1	1	3	(3	0)	24	8	9	4	6	0	10	0	0	0	1	1	.50	3	.194	.265	.387
	15 ML YEARS		1848	6978	2156	426	21	294	(165	129)	3506	1076	1236	1214	651	36	852	45	3	65	94	50	.65	242	.309	.369	.502

Pete Orr

Bats: L **Throws:** R **Pos:** 2B-29; PH-17; 3B-3; PR-3 **Ht:** 6'1" **Wt:** 194 **Born:** 6/8/1979 **Age:** 33

Year	Team	Lg	G	AB	H	2B	3B	HR	(Hm	Rd)	TB	R	RBI	RC	TBB	IBB	SO	HBP	SH	SF	SB	CS	SB%	GDP	Avg	OBP	Slg
2011	LV*	AAA	75	281	75	16	2	5	(-	-)	110	40	26	38	17	0	56	7	3	1	15	5	.75	3	.267	.324	.391
2005	Atl	NL	112	150	45	8	1	1	(0	1)	58	32	8	18	6	0	23	1	5	0	7	1	.88	2	.300	.331	.387
2006	Atl	NL	102	154	39	3	4	1	(1	0)	53	22	8	16	5	1	30	0	5	0	2	4	.33	1	.253	.277	.344
2007	Atl	NL	57	65	13	1	0	0	(0	0)	14	11	2	3	3	0	14	0	1	0	1	0	1.00	1	.200	.235	.215
2008	Was	NL	49	75	19	2	1	0	(0	0)	23	10	7	6	2	0	16	1	1	0	1	0	1.00	0	.253	.282	.307
2009	Was	NL	27	75	19	2	1	1	(0	1)	26	5	10	8	3	0	15	0	0	3	2	1	.67	0	.253	.282	.347
2011	Phi	NL	46	96	21	3	0	0	(0	0)	24	7	4	8	6	2	19	2	0	0	3	0	1.00	0	.219	.279	.250
	Postseason		3	2	0	0	0	0	(0	0)	0	0	0	0	0	0	0	0	0	0	0	0	-	0	.000	.000	.000
	6 ML YEARS		393	615	156	19	7	3	(1	2)	198	87	39	59	25	3	117	4	12	3	16	6	.73	4	.254	.286	.322

David Ortiz

Bats: L **Throws:** L **Pos:** DH-136; PH-8; 1B-2 **Ht:** 6'4" **Wt:** 230 **Born:** 11/18/1975 **Age:** 36

Year	Team	Lg	G	AB	H	2B	3B	HR	(Hm	Rd)	TB	R	RBI	RC	TBB	IBB	SO	HBP	SH	SF	SB	CS	SB%	GDP	Avg	OBP	Slg
1997	Min	AL	15	49	16	3	0	1	(0	1)	22	10	6	7	2	0	19	0	0	0	0	0	-	1	.327	.353	.449
1998	Min	AL	86	278	77	20	0	9	(2	7)	124	47	46	46	39	3	72	5	0	4	1	0	1.00	8	.277	.371	.446
1999	Min	AL	10	20	0	0	0	0	(0	0)	0	1	0	0	5	0	12	0	0	0	0	0	-	2	.000	.200	.000
2000	Min	AL	130	415	117	36	1	10	(7	3)	185	59	63	66	57	2	81	0	0	6	1	0	1.00	13	.282	.364	.446
2001	Min	AL	89	303	71	17	1	18	(6	12)	144	46	48	48	40	8	68	1	1	2	1	0	1.00	6	.234	.324	.475
2002	Min	AL	125	412	112	32	1	20	(5	15)	206	52	75	62	43	0	87	3	0	8	1	2	.33	5	.272	.339	.500
2003	Bos	AL	128	448	129	39	2	31	(17	14)	265	79	101	80	58	8	83	1	0	2	0	0	-	9	.288	.369	.592
2004	Bos	AL	150	582	175	47	3	41	(17	24)	351	94	139	127	75	8	133	4	0	8	0	0	-	12	.301	.380	.603
2005	Bos	AL	159	601	180	40	1	47	(20	27)	363	119	148	137	102	9	124	1	0	9	1	0	1.00	13	.300	.397	.604
2006	Bos	AL	151	558	160	29	2	54	(22	32)	355	115	137	129	119	23	117	4	0	5	1	0	1.00	12	.287	.413	.636
2007	Bos	AL	149	549	182	52	1	35	(16	19)	341	116	117	138	111	12	103	4	0	3	3	1	.75	16	.332	.445	.621
2008	Bos	AL	109	416	110	30	1	23	(12	11)	211	74	89	82	70	12	74	1	1	3	1	0	1.00	11	.264	.369	.507
2009	Bos	AL	150	541	129	35	1	28	(18	10)	250	77	99	79	74	5	134	5	0	7	0	2	.00	9	.238	.332	.462
2010	Bos	AL	145	518	140	36	1	32	(15	17)	274	86	102	94	82	14	145	2	0	4	0	1	.00	12	.270	.370	.529
2011	Bos	AL	146	525	162	40	1	29	(13	16)	291	84	96	97	78	12	83	1	0	1	1	1	.50	24	.309	.398	.554
	Postseason		66	244	69	18	2	12	(7	5)	127	39	47	51	41	7	64	2	0	2	0	1	.00	3	.283	.388	.520
	15 ML YEARS		1742	6215	1760	456	16	378	(170	208)	3382	1059	1266	1190	955	116	1335	32	2	62	11	7	.61	153	.283	.378	.544

Ramon Ortiz

Pitches: R **Bats:** R **Pos:** RP-20; SP-2 **Ht:** 6'0" **Wt:** 175 **Born:** 5/23/1973 **Age:** 39

Year	Team	Lg	G	GS	CG	GF	IP	BFP	H	R	ER	HR	SH	SF	HB	TBB	IBB	SO	WP	Bk	W	L	Pct	Sh	Sv-Op	Hld	ERC	ERA
2011	Iowa*	AAA	16	16	0	0	99.1	427	115	53	47	12	5	5	3	20	0	81	4	1	6	3	.667	0	0- -		4.44	4.26
1999	LAA	AL	9	9	0	0	48.1	218	50	35	35	7	0	2	2	25	0	44	2	2	2	3	.400	0	0-0		5.23	6.52
2000	LAA	AL	18	18	2	0	111.1	472	96	69	63	18	4	4	2	55	0	73	7	4	8	6	.571	0	0-0		4.24	5.09
2001	LAA	AL	32	32	2	0	208.2	916	223	114	101	25	9	6	12	76	6	135	7	0	13	11	.542	0	0-0		4.65	4.36
2002	LAA	AL	32	32	4	0	217.1	896	188	97	91	40	2	5	5	68	0	162	7	3	15	9	.625	1	0-0		3.64	3.77
2003	LAA	AL	32	32	1	0	180.0	814	209	121	104	28	3	7	12	63	0	94	4	0	16	13	.552	0	0-0		5.44	5.20
2004	LAA	AL	34	14	0	13	128.0	543	139	64	63	18	2	3	4	38	4	82	5	3	5	7	.417	0	0-0		4.61	4.43
2005	Cin	NL	30	30	0	0	171.1	755	206	110	102	34	7	8	7	51	1	96	4	1	9	11	.450	0	0-0		5.78	5.36
2006	Was	NL	33	33	0	0	190.2	871	230	127	118	31	10	4	18	64	14	104	4	3	11	16	.407	0	0-0		5.71	5.57

(continued)

Year Team	Lg	G	GS	CG	GF	IP	BFP	H	R	ER	HR	SH	SF	HB	TBB	IBB	SO	WP	Bk	W	L	Pct	Sh	Sv-Op	Hld	ERC	ERA
2007 2 Tms		38	10	0	15	104.0	459	127	65	63	16	1	5	6	22	1	51	2	1	5	4	.556	0	0-0	0	5.17	5.45
2010 LAD	NL	16	2	0	3	30.0	135	33	22	21	5	3	1	0	16	2	21	1	1	1	2	.333	0	0-0	1	5.64	6.30
2011 ChC	NL	22	2	0	5	33.1	141	31	20	18	6	1	2	0	11	2	25	1	0	1	2	.333	0	0-0	1	3.81	4.86
07 Min	AL	28	10	0	11	91.0	400	112	54	52	12	0	4	5	15	1	44	2	1	4	4	.500	0	0-0	0	4.83	5.14
07 Col	NL	10	0	0	4	13.0	59	15	11	11	4	1	1	1	7	0	7	0	0	1	0	1.000	0	0-0	0	7.81	7.62
Postseason		4	3	0	1	15.0	73	20	14	14	2	1	2	1	10	2	7	1	0	2	0	1.000	0	0-0	0	7.66	8.40
11 ML YEARS		296	214	10	36	1423.0	6220	1532	844	779	228	42	47	68	489	30	887	44	18	86	84	.506	1	0-0	2	4.88	4.93

Sean O'Sullivan

Pitches: R Bats: R Pos: SP-10; RP-2
Ht: 6'2" Wt: 230 Born: 9/1/1987 Age: 24

Year Team	Lg	G	GS	CG	GF	IP	BFP	H	R	ER	HR	SH	SF	HB	TBB	IBB	SO	WP	Bk	W	L	Pct	Sh	Sv-Op	Hld	ERC	ERA
2011 Omha*	AAA	14	14	0	0	74.2	324	85	37	35	6	3	4	4	16	0	55	4	0	8	2	.800	0	0- -	-	4.16	4.22
2009 LAA	AL	12	10	0	1	51.2	227	60	34	34	12	2	4	1	16	1	29	1	0	4	2	.667	0	0-0	0	5.66	5.92
2010 2 Tms	AL	19	14	0	3	83.2	368	90	53	51	15	0	3	1	31	2	43	4	2	4	6	.400	0	0-0	0	4.93	5.49
2011 KC	AL	12	10	0	1	58.1	273	78	52	47	10	3	4	2	26	1	19	3	0	2	6	.250	0	0-1	0	7.03	7.25
10 LAA	AL	5	1	0	2	13.0	49	7	3	3	1	0	0	0	4	2	6	0	0	1	0	1.000	0	0-0	0	1.33	2.08
10 KC	AL	14	13	0	1	70.2	319	83	50	48	14	0	3	1	27	0	37	4	2	3	6	.333	0	0-0	0	5.76	6.11
3 ML YEARS		43	34	0	5	193.2	868	228	139	132	37	5	11	4	73	4	91	8	2	10	14	.417	0	0-1	0	5.74	6.13

Roy Oswalt

Pitches: R Bats: R Pos: SP-23
OWES-walt
Ht: 6'0" Wt: 192 Born: 8/29/1977 Age: 34

Year Team	Lg	G	GS	CG	GF	IP	BFP	H	R	ER	HR	SH	SF	HB	TBB	IBB	SO	WP	Bk	W	L	Pct	Sh	Sv-Op	Hld	ERC	ERA
2011 Clrwtr*	A+	1	1	0	0	5.0	23	7	3	3	0	0	0	0	1	0	5	0	0	0	0		0	0- -	-	4.69	5.40
2011 LV*	AAA	2	2	0	0	10.0	40	8	3	3	1	0	0	0	4	0	8	0	0	0	0		0	0- -	-	3.12	2.70
2001 Hou	NL	28	20	3	4	141.2	575	126	48	43	13	4	4	6	24	2	144	0	0	14	3	.824	1	0-0	0	2.68	2.73
2002 Hou	NL	35	34	0	0	233.0	956	215	86	78	17	12	7	5	62	4	208	3	0	19	9	.679	0	0-0	0	3.05	3.01
2003 Hou	NL	21	21	0	0	127.1	514	116	48	42	15	7	1	5	29	0	108	1	0	10	5	.667	0	0-0	0	3.26	2.97
2004 Hou	NL	36	35	2	0	237.0	983	233	100	92	17	11	4	11	62	5	206	5	1	20	10	.667	2	0-0	0	3.46	3.49
2005 Hou	NL	35	35	4	0	241.2	1002	243	85	79	18	12	7	8	48	3	184	5	1	20	12	.625	1	0-0	0	3.27	2.94
2006 Hou	NL	33	32	2	1	220.2	896	220	76	73	18	12	4	6	38	4	166	1	1	15	8	.652	0	0-0	0	3.19	2.98
2007 Hou	NL	33	32	1	0	212.0	910	221	80	75	14	6	4	5	60	6	154	1	1	14	7	.667	0	0-0	1	3.68	3.18
2008 Hou	NL	32	32	1	0	208.2	862	199	89	82	23	8	9	10	47	2	165	1	0	17	10	.630	2	0-0	0	3.40	3.54
2009 Hou	NL	30	30	3	0	181.1	757	183	83	83	19	12	5	6	42	4	138	4	0	8	6	.571	0	0-0	0	3.67	4.12
2010 2 Tms	NL	33	32	2	0	211.2	837	162	70	65	19	10	6	5	55	2	193	2	1	13	13	.500	2	0-0	0	2.37	2.76
2011 Phi	NL	23	23	0	0	139.0	594	153	60	57	10	7	3	5	33	2	93	3	0	9	10	.474	0	0-0	0	3.93	3.69
10 NL	NL	20	20	1	0	129.0	521	109	52	49	13	4	5	2	34	2	120	2	1	6	12	.333	1	0-0	0	2.79	3.42
10 Phi	NL	13	12	1	0	82.2	316	53	18	16	6	4	1	3	21	0	73	0	0	7	1	.875	1	0-0	0	1.76	1.74
Postseason		12	10	0	2	66.1	288	67	27	25	8	4	4	5	23	0	51	1	0	5	1	.833	0	0-0	1	4.37	3.39
11 ML YEARS		339	326	20	5	2154.0	8886	2071	825	769	183	101	54	76	500	34	1759	26	5	159	93	.631	8	0-0	1	3.25	3.21

Josh Outman

Pitches: L Bats: L Pos: SP-9; RP-4
Ht: 6'1" Wt: 186 Born: 9/14/1984 Age: 27

Year Team	Lg	G	GS	CG	GF	IP	BFP	H	R	ER	HR	SH	SF	HB	TBB	IBB	SO	WP	Bk	W	L	Pct	Sh	Sv-Op	Hld	ERC	ERA
2011 Scrmto*	AAA	17	17	0	0	78.1	354	77	47	34	7	3	1	2	47	0	72	7	0	8	3	.727	0	0- -	-	4.78	3.91
2008 Oak	AL	6	4	0	0	25.2	116	34	14	13	1	0	2	2	8	1	19	1	0	1	2	.333	0	0-0	0	5.49	4.56
2009 Oak	AL	14	12	0	1	67.1	276	53	30	26	9	1	0	0	25	0	53	1	0	4	1	.800	0	0-0	0	3.04	3.48
2011 Oak	AL	13	9	0	2	58.1	254	62	27	24	4	4	3	0	23	0	35	3	0	3	5	.375	0	0-0	0	4.19	3.70
3 ML YEARS		33	25	0	3	151.1	646	149	71	63	14	5	5	2	56	1	107	5	0	8	8	.500	0	0-0	1	3.87	3.75

Lyle Overbay

Bats: L Throws: L Pos: 1B-109; PH-14
Ht: 6'2" Wt: 220 Born: 1/28/1977 Age: 35

Year Team	Lg	G	AB	H	2B	3B	HR	(Hm	Rd)	TB	R	RBI	RC	TBB	IBB	SO	HBP	SH	SF	SB	CS	SB%	GDP	Avg	OBP	Slg
2001 Ari	NL	2	2	1	0	0	0	(0	0)	1	0	0	0	0	0	1	0	0	0	0	0	-	0	.500	.500	.500
2002 Ari	NL	10	10	1	0	0	0	(0	0)	1	0	1	0	0	0	5	0	0	0	0	0	-	0	.100	.100	.100
2003 Ari	NL	86	254	70	20	0	4	(2	2)	102	23	28	34	35	7	67	2	0	2	1	0	1.00	8	.276	.365	.402
2004 Mil	NL	159	579	174	53	1	16	(6	10)	277	83	87	94	81	9	128	2	0	6	2	1	.67	11	.301	.385	.478
2005 Mil	NL	158	537	148	34	1	19	(10	9)	241	80	72	84	78	8	98	2	1	4	1	0	1.00	19	.276	.367	.449
2006 Tor	AL	157	581	181	46	1	22	(17	5)	295	82	92	89	55	7	96	2	0	2	5	3	.63	19	.312	.372	.508
2007 Tor	AL	122	425	102	30	2	10	(6	4)	166	49	44	45	47	4	78	1	0	3	2	0	1.00	12	.240	.315	.391
2008 Tor	AL	158	544	147	32	2	15	(7	8)	228	74	69	73	74	3	116	3	1	5	1	2	.33	24	.270	.358	.419
2009 Tor	AL	132	423	112	35	1	16	(6	10)	197	57	64	64	74	6	95	0	0	3	0	0	-	8	.265	.372	.466
2010 Tor	AL	154	534	130	37	2	20	(13	7)	261	75	67	75	67	7	131	3	0	3	1	0	1.00	19	.243	.329	.433
2011 2 Tms	NL	121	394	92	21	1	9	(4	5)	142	43	47	41	42	2	88	2	1	1	2	1	.67	13	.234	.310	.360
11 Pit	NL	103	352	80	17	1	8	(3	5)	123	40	37	33	36	1	77	1	1	1	1	1	.50	12	.227	.300	.349
11 Ari	NL	18	42	12	4	0	1	(1	0)	19	3	10	8	6	1	11	1	0	0	1	0	1.00	1	.286	.388	.452
11 ML YEARS		1259	4283	1158	308	11	131	(71	60)	1881	566	571	599	553	53	903	17	3	29	15	7	.68	121	.270	.354	.439

Micah Owings

Pitches: R **Bats:** R **Pos:** RP-29; SP-4 **Ht:** 6'5" **Wt:** 220 **Born:** 9/28/1982 **Age:** 29

			HOW MUCH HE PITCHED						WHAT HE GAVE UP										THE RESULTS							
Year	Team	Lg	G	GS	CG	GF	IP	BFP	H	R	ER	HR	SH	SF	HB	TBB	IBB	SO	WP	Bk	W	L	Pct	Sh	Sv-Op	Hld	ERC	ERA
2011	Reno*	AAA	7	7	0	0	39.0	167	41	23	21	5	2	0	2	9	0	27	0	0	3	1	.750	0	0- -	-	4.05	4.85
2007	Ari	NL	29	27	2	0	152.2	651	146	81	73	20	7	3	14	50	2	106	5	0	8	8	.500	1	0-0	0	4.13	4.30
2008	2 Tms	NL	22	18	0	2	104.2	466	104	73	69	14	2	4	12	41	0	87	4	0	6	9	.400	0	0-0	1	4.66	5.93
2009	Cin	NL	26	19	0	4	119.2	542	126	75	71	18	3	5	6	64	3	68	1	0	7	12	.368	0	1-1	0	5.48	5.34
2010	Cin	NL	22	0	0	9	33.1	153	28	20	20	3	2	1	3	25	0	35	1	1	3	2	.600	0	0-0	0	4.80	5.40
2011	Ari	NL	33	4	0	2	63.0	263	56	27	25	8	4	1	2	23	0	44	3	0	8	0	1.000	0	0-0	3	3.67	3.57
	Postseason		1	1	0	0	3.2	21	6	6	2	1	0	0	1	2	0	2	0	0	0	1	.000	0	0-0	0	10.83	4.91
	5 ML YEARS		132	68	2	17	473.1	2075	460	276	258	63	18	14	37	203	5	340	14	1	32	31	.508	1	1-1	4	4.57	4.91

Jordan Pacheco

Bats: R **Throws:** R **Pos:** 1B-13; 3B-7; C-2; 2B-2; PH-1 puh-CHECK-oh **Ht:** 6'1" **Wt:** 190 **Born:** 1/30/1986 **Age:** 26

						BATTING															BASERUNNING				AVERAGES		
Year	Team	Lg	G	AB	H	2B	3B	HR	(Hm	Rd)	TB	R	RBI	RC	TBB	IBB	SO	HBP	SH	SF	SB	CS	SB%	GDP	Avg	OBP	Slg
2007	Casper	R+	55	192	56	10	2	3	(-	-)	79	27	29	32	21	0	36	7	3	1	3	1	.75	5	.292	.380	.411
2007	TriCity	A-	8	31	8	2	0	0	(-	-)	10	5	3	3	1	0	6	2	0	0	0	0	-	0	.258	.324	.323
2008	TriCity	A-	54	214	60	8	3	1	(-	-)	77	25	35	33	26	1	20	6	1	4	3	3	.50	8	.280	.368	.360
2009	Ashvll	A	117	451	145	30	4	13	(-	-)	222	67	79	87	38	2	44	8	3	7	12	2	.86	7	.322	.379	.492
2010	Mdest	A+	104	390	125	27	3	5	(-	-)	173	59	70	75	54	2	36	8	1	7	5	6	.45	10	.321	.407	.444
2010	Tulsa	AA	21	78	26	5	0	1	(-	-)	34	11	19	14	6	0	6	4	0	3	1	1	.50	3	.333	.396	.436
2011	ColSpr	AAA	97	363	101	21	3	3	(-	-)	137	57	50	50	30	0	48	9	3	6	2	2	.50	15	.278	.343	.377
2011	Col	NL	21	84	24	1	0	2	(2	0)	31	5	14	12	3	0	9	1	0	0	0	0	-	2	.286	.318	.369

Vicente Padilla

Pitches: R **Bats:** R **Pos:** RP-9 pah-DEE-ah **Ht:** 6'0" **Wt:** 232 **Born:** 9/27/1977 **Age:** 34

			HOW MUCH HE PITCHED						WHAT HE GAVE UP										THE RESULTS							
Year	Team	Lg	G	GS	CG	GF	IP	BFP	H	R	ER	HR	SH	SF	HB	TBB	IBB	SO	WP	Bk	W	L	Pct	Sh	Sv-Op	Hld	ERC	ERA
2011	RCuca*	A+	4	4	0	0	6.1	24	4	1	1	0	0	0	1	1	0	5	0	0	0	0	-	0	0- -	-	1.49	1.42
1999	Ari	NL	5	0	0	2	2.2	19	7	5	5	1	1	0	0	3	0	0	0	0	0	1	.000	0	0-1	1	20.65	16.88
2000	2 Tms	NL	55	0	0	16	65.1	291	72	33	27	3	5	3	1	28	7	51	1	0	4	7	.364	0	2-7	15	4.22	3.72
2001	Phi	NL	23	0	0	5	34.0	144	36	18	16	1	0	0	0	12	0	29	1	0	3	1	.750	0	0-3	1	3.80	4.24
2002	Phi	NL	32	32	1	0	206.0	862	198	83	75	16	10	3	15	53	5	128	6	2	14	11	.560	1	0-0	0	3.42	3.28
2003	Phi	NL	32	32	1	0	208.2	876	196	94	84	22	11	7	16	62	4	133	3	2	14	12	.538	1	0-0	0	3.68	3.62
2004	Phi	NL	20	20	0	0	115.1	503	119	63	58	16	7	5	10	36	6	82	2	0	7	7	.500	0	0-0	0	4.42	4.53
2005	Phi	NL	27	27	0	0	147.0	654	146	79	77	22	7	3	8	74	9	103	1	0	9	12	.429	0	0-0	0	4.94	4.71
2006	Tex	AL	33	33	0	0	200.0	872	206	108	100	21	6	6	17	70	2	156	4	2	15	10	.600	0	0-0	0	4.41	4.50
2007	Tex	AL	23	23	0	0	120.1	553	146	88	77	16	3	2	9	50	1	71	2	0	6	10	.375	0	0-0	0	5.95	5.76
2008	Tex	AL	29	29	1	0	171.0	757	185	100	90	26	1	3	15	65	4	127	12	3	14	8	.636	1	0-0	0	5.20	4.74
2009	2 Tms		26	25	0	0	147.1	634	156	76	73	16	6	3	8	54	0	97	5	2	12	6	.667	0	0-0	0	4.65	4.46
2010	LAD	NL	16	16	1	0	95.0	389	79	46	43	14	5	3	7	24	4	84	0	1	6	5	.545	1	0-0	0	3.13	4.07
2011	LAD	NL	9	0	0	4	8.2	36	7	4	4	0	0	0	0	5	0	9	0	0	0	0	-	0	3-3	5	3.12	4.15
00	Ari	NL	27	0	0	12	35.0	143	32	10	9	0	0	1	0	10	2	30	0	0	2	1	.667	0	0-1	7	2.48	2.31
00	Phi	NL	28	0	0	4	30.1	148	40	23	18	3	5	2	1	18	5	21	1	0	2	6	.250	0	2-6	8	6.52	5.34
09	Tex	AL	18	18	0	0	108.0	475	120	61	59	12	3	2	8	42	0	59	4	2	8	6	.571	0	0-0	0	5.15	4.92
09	LAD	NL	8	7	0	0	39.1	159	36	15	14	4	3	1	0	12	0	38	1	0	4	0	1.000	0	0-0	0	3.36	3.20
	Postseason		3	3	0	0	17.1	67	12	7	7	3	0	0	0	4	0	13	0	0	1	1	.500	0	0-0	0	2.29	3.63
	13 ML YEARS		330	237	4	27	1521.1	6590	1553	797	729	174	62	38	106	536	42	1070	37	12	104	90	.536	4	5-14	22	4.36	4.31

Angel Pagan

Bats: B **Throws:** R **Pos:** CF-121; PH-3 ANE-gell pah-GONN **Ht:** 6'2" **Wt:** 195 **Born:** 7/2/1981 **Age:** 30

						BATTING															BASERUNNING				AVERAGES		
Year	Team	Lg	G	AB	H	2B	3B	HR	(Hm	Rd)	TB	R	RBI	RC	TBB	IBB	SO	HBP	SH	SF	SB	CS	SB%	GDP	Avg	OBP	Slg
2011	StLuci*	A+	8	31	7	1	1	1	(-	-)	13	6	2	3	4	0	5	1	0	0	0	2	.00	0	.226	.333	.419
2006	ChC	NL	77	170	42	6	2	5	(4	1)	67	28	18	21	15	0	28	0	1	1	4	2	.67	3	.247	.306	.394
2007	ChC	NL	71	148	39	10	2	4	(3	1)	65	21	21	23	10	0	32	0	1	2	4	1	.80	0	.264	.306	.439
2008	NYM	NL	31	91	25	7	1	0	(0	0)	34	12	13	15	11	0	18	0	1	2	4	0	1.00	1	.275	.346	.374
2009	NYM	NL	88	343	105	22	11	6	(5	1)	167	54	32	53	25	2	56	0	5	3	14	7	.67	3	.306	.350	.487
2010	NYM	NL	151	579	168	31	7	11	(6	5)	246	80	69	90	44	5	97	1	6	3	37	9	.80	9	.290	.340	.425
2011	NYM	NL	123	478	125	24	4	7	(4	3)	178	68	56	64	44	4	62	1	4	5	32	7	.82	4	.262	.322	.372
	6 ML YEARS		541	1809	504	100	27	33	(22	11)	757	263	209	266	149	11	293	2	18	16	95	26	.79	19	.279	.331	.418

Matt Pagnozzi

Bats: R **Throws:** R **Pos:** C-9; PH-3 **Ht:** 6'2" **Wt:** 205 **Born:** 11/10/1982 **Age:** 29

						BATTING															BASERUNNING				AVERAGES		
Year	Team	Lg	G	AB	H	2B	3B	HR	(Hm	Rd)	TB	R	RBI	RC	TBB	IBB	SO	HBP	SH	SF	SB	CS	SB%	GDP	Avg	OBP	Slg
2011	ColSpr*	AAA	54	178	49	13	2	3	(-	-)	75	26	29	25	16	0	40	1	2	1	0	2	.00	4	.275	.342	.421
2009	StL	NL	6	3	0	0	0	0	(0	0)	0	1	0	0	1	0	1	0	0	0	0	0	-	1	.000	.250	.000
2010	StL	NL	15	39	14	2	0	1	(1	0)	19	4	10	7	2	0	8	1	2	0	0	0	-	1	.359	.405	.487
2011	2 Tms	NL	12	29	8	0	0	0	(0	0)	8	2	3	4	1	0	10	1	3	0	0	0	-	0	.276	.323	.276
11	Col	NL	7	21	6	0	0	0	(0	0)	6	2	2	3	1	0	8	1	2	0	0	0	-	0	.286	.348	.286
11	Pit	NL	5	8	2	0	0	0	(0	0)	2	0	1	1	0	0	2	0	1	0	0	0	-	0	.250	.250	.250
	3 ML YEARS		33	71	22	2	0	1	(1	0)	27	7	13	11	4	0	18	2	6	0	0	0	-	2	.310	.364	.380

Matt Palmer

Pitches: R **Bats:** R **Pos:** SP-3   **Ht:** 6'2" **Wt:** 235 **Born:** 3/21/1979 **Age:** 33

Year Team	Lg	G	GS	CG	GF	IP	BFP	H	R	ER	HR	SH	SF	HB	TBB	IBB	SO	WP	Bk	W	L	Pct	Sh	Sv-Op	Hld	ERC	ERA
2011 Salt Lk*	AAA	24	24	0	0	137.0	637	170	105	98	14	3	9	16	65	0	109	18	0	9	11	.450	0	0- -	-	6.41	6.44
2008 SF	NL	3	3	0	0	12.2	67	17	13	12	1	1	0	2	13	1	3	0	0	0	2	.000	0	0-0	0	9.37	8.53
2009 LAA	AL	40	13	1	10	121.1	505	105	55	53	12	6	3	4	55	2	69	5	0	11	2	.846	0	0-0	0	3.74	3.93
2010 LAA	AL	14	1	0	3	33.2	157	38	20	17	1	1	0	1	20	1	17	2	0	1	2	.333	0	0-0	1	5.07	4.54
2011 LAA	AL	3	3	0	0	15.2	69	19	11	10	0	0	2	1	4	0	7	0	0	1	1	.500	0	0-0	0	4.24	5.74
Postseason		2	0	0	2	2.2	14	5	4	4	1	0	0	0	1	0	2	0	0	0	0	-	0	0-0	0	11.86	13.50
4 ML YEARS		60	20	1	13	183.1	798	179	99	92	14	8	5	8	92	4	96	7	0	13	7	.650	0	0-0	1	4.38	4.52

Jonathan Papelbon

Pitches: R **Bats:** R **Pos:** RP-63   PAHP-ill-bonn   **Ht:** 6'4" **Wt:** 225 **Born:** 11/23/1980 **Age:** 31

Year Team	Lg	G	GS	CG	GF	IP	BFP	H	R	ER	HR	SH	SF	HB	TBB	IBB	SO	WP	Bk	W	L	Pct	Sh	Sv-Op	Hld	ERC	ERA
2005 Bos	AL	17	3	0	4	34.0	148	33	11	10	4	1	0	3	17	2	34	1	0	3	1	.750	0	0-1	4	4.82	2.65
2006 Bos	AL	59	0	0	49	68.1	257	40	8	7	3	1	2	1	13	2	75	2	0	4	2	.667	0	35-41	0	1.22	0.92
2007 Bos	AL	59	0	0	53	58.1	224	30	12	12	5	0	0	4	15	0	84	0	0	1	3	.250	0	37-40	2	1.43	1.85
2008 Bos	AL	67	0	0	62	69.1	273	58	24	18	4	4	1	0	8	0	77	2	0	5	4	.556	0	41-46	0	1.92	2.34
2009 Bos	AL	66	0	0	59	68.0	285	54	15	14	5	1	2	4	24	1	76	0	0	1	1	.500	0	38-41	0	2.78	1.85
2010 Bos	AL	65	0	0	53	67.0	287	57	34	29	7	5	0	2	28	4	76	4	0	5	7	.417	0	37-45	0	3.32	3.90
2011 Bos	AL	63	0	0	54	64.1	255	50	22	21	3	0	1	3	10	1	87	1	0	4	1	.800	0	31-34	0	1.86	2.94
Postseason		18	0	0	12	27.0	100	14	3	3	0	0	1	0	8	3	23	0	0	2	1	.667	0	7-9	0	1.01	1.00
7 ML YEARS		396	3	0	334	429.1	1729	322	126	111	31	12	6	17	115	10	509	10	0	23	19	.548	0	219-248	7	2.21	2.33

Jimmy Paredes

Bats: B **Throws:** R **Pos:** 3B-46; PR-1   pah-REY-dez   **Ht:** 6'1" **Wt:** 200 **Born:** 11/25/1988 **Age:** 23

Year Team	Lg	G	AB	H	2B	3B	HR	(Hm	Rd)	TB	R	RBI	RC	TBB	IBB	SO	HBP	SH	SF	SB	CS	SB%	GDP	Avg	OBP	Slg
2008 Yanks	R	47	161	45	9	2	1	(-	-)	61	23	15	22	8	1	20	4	1	1	6	0	1.00	4	.280	.328	.379
2009 StlsInd	A-	54	205	62	8	4	2	(-	-)	84	36	17	30	10	1	30	2	1	3	23	9	.72	5	.302	.336	.410
2010 CtnSC	A	99	404	114	24	6	5	(-	-)	165	59	48	54	18	1	82	2	5	5	36	10	.78	3	.282	.312	.408
2010 Lxngtn	A	34	147	44	10	1	3	(-	-)	65	24	17	23	7	0	25	0	0	0	14	1	.93	1	.299	.331	.442
2011 CpChr	AA	93	385	104	22	4	10	(-	-)	164	69	41	50	15	0	84	2	4	1	29	12	.71	8	.270	.300	.426
2011 Hou	NL	46	168	48	8	2	2	(0	2)	66	16	18	23	9	0	47	0	1	1	5	4	.56	3	.286	.320	.393

Jarrod Parker

Pitches: R **Bats:** R **Pos:** SP-1   **Ht:** 6'1" **Wt:** 195 **Born:** 11/24/1988 **Age:** 23

Year Team	Lg	G	GS	CG	GF	IP	BFP	H	R	ER	HR	SH	SF	HB	TBB	IBB	SO	WP	Bk	W	L	Pct	Sh	Sv-Op	Hld	ERC	ERA
2008 Sbend	A	24	24	0	0	117.2	502	113	56	44	8	4	8	7	33	0	117	8	0	12	5	.706	0	0- -	-	3.36	3.44
2009 Visalia	A+	4	4	0	0	19.0	72	12	2	2	0	1	0	0	4	0	21	4	0	1	0	1.000	0	0- -	-	1.24	0.95
2009 Mobile	AA	16	16	0	0	78.1	345	82	35	33	2	1	1	7	34	0	74	9	0	4	6	.400	0	0- -	-	4.33	3.79
2011 Mobile	AA	26	26	0	0	130.2	550	112	61	55	7	5	5	11	55	0	112	8	3	11	8	.579	0	0- -	-	3.43	3.79
2011 Ari	NL	1	1	0	0	5.2	22	4	0	0	0	2	0	0	1	0	1	0	0	0	0	-	0	0-0	0	1.36	0.00

Chris Parmelee

Bats: L **Throws:** L **Pos:** 1B-20; PH-1   PAR-muh-lee   **Ht:** 6'1" **Wt:** 230 **Born:** 2/24/1988 **Age:** 24

Year Team	Lg	G	AB	H	2B	3B	HR	(Hm	Rd)	TB	R	RBI	RC	TBB	IBB	SO	HBP	SH	SF	SB	CS	SB%	GDP	Avg	OBP	Slg
2006 Twins	R	45	154	43	7	4	8	(-	-)	82	29	32	30	23	1	47	0	0	2	0	3	.50	5	.279	.369	.532
2006 Beloit	A	11	22	5	1	0	0	(-	-)	6	2	2	2	5	0	9	0	0	0	0	2	.00	0	.227	.370	.273
2007 Beloit	A	128	447	107	23	5	15	(-	-)	185	56	70	60	46	1	137	4	0	4	8	4	.67	8	.239	.313	.414
2008 Beloit	A	68	226	54	10	3	14	(-	-)	112	41	49	47	52	1	83	5	1	5	3	1	.75	2	.239	.385	.496
2009 FtMyrs	A+	123	422	109	27	1	16	(-	-)	186	51	73	71	65	5	109	6	0	8	2	2	.50	4	.258	.359	.441
2010 NwBrit	AA	111	411	113	25	2	6	(-	-)	160	51	44	58	43	2	70	2	0	7	3	2	.60	12	.275	.341	.389
2010 FtMyrs	A+	22	80	27	2	1	2	(-	-)	37	9	17	16	13	0	11	0	1	.00	1	.338	.430	.463
2011 NwBrit	AA	142	530	152	30	5	13	(-	-)	231	76	83	89	68	4	94	3	0	9	0	1	.00	6	.287	.366	.436
2011 Min	AL	21	76	27	6	0	4	(2	2)	45	8	14	19	12	0	13	0	0	0	0	0	-	3	.355	.443	.592

Bobby Parnell

Pitches: R **Bats:** R **Pos:** RP-60   **Ht:** 6'4" **Wt:** 200 **Born:** 9/8/1984 **Age:** 27

Year Team	Lg	G	GS	CG	GF	IP	BFP	H	R	ER	HR	SH	SF	HB	TBB	IBB	SO	WP	Bk	W	L	Pct	Sh	Sv-Op	Hld	ERC	ERA
2011 StLuci*	A+	1	1	0	0	1.0	3	0	0	0	0	0	0	0	1	0	0	0	0	0	0	-	0	0- -	-	1.26	0.00
2011 Buffalo*	AAA	8	0	0	2	8.0	33	7	3	3	1	0	1	0	2	0	11	0	0	0	0	-	0	1- -	-	2.93	3.38
2008 NYM	NL	6	0	0	3	5.0	19	3	3	3	0	0	0	0	2	0	3	1	0	0	0	-	0	0-0	0	1.59	5.40
2009 NYM	NL	68	8	0	14	88.1	413	101	56	52	8	3	1	4	46	2	74	6	1	4	8	.333	0	1-5	16	5.37	5.30
2010 NYM	NL	41	0	0	10	35.0	149	41	13	11	1	2	0	0	8	2	33	0	0	0	1	.000	0	0-2	9	3.80	2.83
2011 NYM	NL	60	0	0	23	59.1	268	60	29	24	4	6	0	2	27	4	64	8	1	4	6	.400	0	6-12	11	4.01	3.64
4 ML YEARS		175	8	0	50	187.2	849	205	101	90	13	11	1	6	83	8	174	15	2	8	15	.348	0	7-19	36	4.52	4.32

Gerardo Parra

Bats: L Throws: L Pos: LF-125; RF-14; PH-9; PR-3; CF-2   PAH-ruh   Ht: 5'11" Wt: 195 Born: 5/6/1987 Age: 25

								BATTING												BASERUNNING				AVERAGES		
Year	Team	Lg	G	AB	H	2B	3B	HR	(Hm | Rd)	TB	R	RBI	RC	TBB	IBB	SO	HBP	SH	SF	SB	CS	SB%	GDP	Avg	OBP	Slg
2009	Ari	NL	120	455	132	21	8	5	(4 | 1)	184	59	60	58	25	1	89	1	4	6	5	7	.42	18	.290	.324	.404
2010	Ari	NL	133	364	95	19	6	3	(1 | 2)	135	31	30	38	23	10	76	2	3	1	1	0	1.00	8	.261	.308	.371
2011	Ari	NL	141	445	130	20	8	8	(3 | 5)	190	55	46	71	43	16	82	3	0	2	15	1	.94	8	.292	.357	.427
3 ML YEARS			394	1264	357	60	22	16	(8 | 8)	509	145	136	167	91	27	247	6	7	9	21	8	.72	34	.282	.331	.403

Andy Parrino

Bats: B Throws: R Pos: 3B-11; SS-4; RF-4; PH-4; 2B-3; LF-1   Ht: 6'0" Wt: 185 Born: 10/31/1985 Age: 26

								BATTING												BASERUNNING				AVERAGES		
Year	Team	Lg	G	AB	H	2B	3B	HR	(Hm | Rd)	TB	R	RBI	RC	TBB	IBB	SO	HBP	SH	SF	SB	CS	SB%	GDP	Avg	OBP	Slg
2007	Eugene	A-	69	251	68	20	1	3	(- | -)	99	32	38	38	30	0	73	7	1	0	2	2	.50	7	.271	.365	.394
2008	FtWyn	A	120	405	102	20	0	7	(- | -)	143	67	43	59	71	0	127	4	4	3	8	5	.62	7	.252	.366	.353
2009	Lk Els	A+	95	311	73	16	1	2	(- | -)	97	52	29	39	51	1	85	4	1	4	8	2	.80	3	.235	.346	.312
2009	FtWyn	A	5	18	9	2	0	0	(- | -)	11	3	3	5	3	0	3	0	0	0	0	0	-	0	.500	.571	.611
2010	SnAnt	AA	125	410	101	28	4	11	(- | -)	170	70	49	67	68	8	115	8	4	2	4	2	.67	9	.246	.363	.415
2011	Tucsn	AAA	48	153	50	13	1	3	(- | -)	74	26	24	30	16	0	25	5	0	4	2	1	.67	2	.327	.399	.484
2011	SnAnt	AA	40	152	46	7	1	9	(- | -)	82	28	32	32	22	1	40	1	1	3	3	1	.75	1	.303	.388	.539
2011	SD	NL	24	44	8	1	0	0	(0 | 0)	9	3	4	4	9	1	17	1	0	1	1	0	1.00	1	.182	.327	.205

Val Pascucci

Bats: R Throws: R Pos: PH-9; 1B-1   Ht: 6'6" Wt: 268 Born: 11/17/1978 Age: 33

								BATTING												BASERUNNING				AVERAGES		
Year	Team	Lg	G	AB	H	2B	3B	HR	(Hm | Rd)	TB	R	RBI	RC	TBB	IBB	SO	HBP	SH	SF	SB	CS	SB%	GDP	Avg	OBP	Slg
1999	Vrmnt	A-	72	259	91	26	1	7	(- | -)	140	62	48	69	53	3	46	14	0	2	17	2	.89	5	.351	.485	.541
2000	CapeF	A	20	69	22	4	0	3	(- | -)	35	17	10	16	16	0	15	0	0	1	5	0	1.00	3	.319	.442	.507
2000	Jupiter	A+	113	405	115	30	2	14	(- | -)	191	70	66	76	66	0	98	11	0	5	14	6	.70	9	.284	.394	.472
2001	Hrsbrg	AA	138	476	116	17	1	21	(- | -)	198	79	67	65	65	1	114	11	1	6	8	8	.50	8	.244	.344	.416
2002	Hrsbrg	AA	137	459	108	14	1	27	(- | -)	205	73	82	86	93	3	115	13	0	7	2	0	1.00	13	.235	.374	.447
2003	Edmtn	AAA	138	459	129	29	1	15	(- | -)	205	80	85	90	101	1	132	9	1	2	3	2	.60	11	.281	.419	.447
2004	Edmtn	AAA	109	392	117	32	1	25	(- | -)	226	83	92	90	78	4	95	8	0	2	9	2	.82	11	.298	.423	.577
2007	Albq	AAA	132	447	127	21	1	34	(- | -)	258	93	98	102	67	2	123	12	0	3	9	1	.90	14	.284	.389	.577
2008	LV	AAA	25	82	19	2	0	1	(- | -)	24	4	7	10	18	0	25	0	0	0	0	1	.00	2	.232	.370	.293
2008	NewOr	AAA	113	392	112	23	0	26	(- | -)	213	71	77	89	76	0	109	5	0	3	4	1	.80	9	.286	.405	.543
2009	Albq	AAA	61	194	41	8	1	8	(- | -)	75	31	29	27	34	1	55	2	0	1	2	0	1.00	4	.211	.333	.387
2009	Portlnd	AAA	65	242	67	17	1	11	(- | -)	119	31	48	44	32	2	64	2	0	4	1	0	1.00	7	.277	.361	.492
2010	Buffalo	AAA	72	190	49	10	0	17	(- | -)	110	40	38	44	44	0	65	1	0	1	0	0	-	5	.258	.398	.579
2011	Buffalo	AAA	130	443	117	29	1	21	(- | -)	211	58	91	82	76	2	149	3	0	1	1	2	.33	7	.264	.375	.476
2004	Mon	NL	32	62	11	1	0	2	(0 | 2)	18	6	6	5	10	1	22	1	0	1	1	0	1.00	3	.177	.297	.290
2011	NYM	NL	10	11	3	0	0	1	(1 | 0)	6	1	2	1	0	0	3	0	0	0	0	0	-	0	.273	.273	.545
2 ML YEARS			42	73	14	1	0	3	(1 | 2)	24	7	8	6	10	1	25	1	0	1	1	0	1.00	3	.192	.294	.329

Joe Paterson

Pitches: L Bats: R Pos: RP-62   Ht: 6'1" Wt: 210 Born: 5/19/1986 Age: 26

						HOW MUCH HE PITCHED				WHAT HE GAVE UP												THE RESULTS					
Year	Team	Lg	G	GS	CG	GF	IP	BFP	H	R	ER	HR	SH	SF	HB	TBB	IBB	SO	WP	Bk	W	L	Pct	Sh	Sv-Op	Hld	ERC	ERA
2007	Giants	R	4	0	0	2	5.0	16	1	1	0	0	0	0	0	0	0	8	0	0	1	0	1.000	0	0- -	-	0.09	0.00
2007	SlmKzr	A+	9	0	0	3	9.2	47	15	6	6	0	1	0	1	2	0	13	1	0	1	0	1.000	0	0- -	-	6.01	5.59
2008	Augsta	A	20	0	0	8	31.1	130	23	11	8	2	1	1	2	13	0	37	0	0	5	1	.833	0	1- -	-	2.71	2.30
2008	SnJos	A+	34	0	0	11	37.2	158	28	22	13	1	2	0	1	15	6	41	0	1	3	2	.600	0	7- -	-	2.06	3.11
2009	Conn	AA	55	0	0	26	69.0	274	47	18	15	3	5	3	3	24	3	69	1	3	5	6	.455	0	10- -	-	2.02	1.96
2010	Fresno	AAA	46	0	0	10	54.1	242	55	28	21	2	3	2	3	24	2	49	3	1	4	3	.571	0	2- -	-	3.95	3.48
2010	SnJos	A+	7	0	0	4	11.0	44	9	2	1	0	0	1	0	2	1	15	1	0	1	0	1.000	0	1- -	-	1.63	0.82
2011	Ari	NL	62	0	0	17	34.0	150	28	11	11	1	4	2	4	15	0	28	1	0	0	3	.000	0	1-1	10	3.12	2.91

Corey Patterson

Bats: L Throws: R Pos: LF-56; CF-40; RF-25; PH-24; PR-6; DH-2   Ht: 5'10" Wt: 180 Born: 8/13/1979 Age: 32

								BATTING												BASERUNNING				AVERAGES		
Year	Team	Lg	G	AB	H	2B	3B	HR	(Hm | Rd)	TB	R	RBI	RC	TBB	IBB	SO	HBP	SH	SF	SB	CS	SB%	GDP	Avg	OBP	Slg
2011	Dnedin*	A+	4	15	5	0	0	0	(- | -)	5	1	0	2	1	0	4	0	0	0	3	0	1.00	0	.333	.375	.333
2000	ChC	NL	11	42	7	1	0	2	(1 | 1)	14	9	2	3	3	0	14	1	1	0	1	1	.50	0	.167	.239	.333
2001	ChC	NL	59	131	29	3	0	4	(1 | 3)	44	26	14	13	6	0	33	3	2	3	4	0	1.00	3	.221	.266	.336
2002	ChC	NL	153	592	150	30	5	14	(7 | 7)	232	71	54	61	19	1	142	8	4	5	18	3	.86	8	.253	.284	.392
2003	ChC	NL	83	329	98	17	7	13	(7 | 6)	168	49	55	55	15	2	77	1	0	2	16	5	.76	5	.298	.329	.511
2004	ChC	NL	157	631	168	33	6	24	(14 | 10)	285	91	72	87	45	7	168	5	5	1	32	9	.78	7	.266	.320	.452
2005	ChC	NL	126	451	97	15	3	13	(9 | 4)	157	47	34	32	23	3	118	1	5	1	15	5	.75	5	.215	.254	.348
2006	Bal	AL	135	463	128	19	5	16	(9 | 7)	205	75	53	66	21	5	94	5	8	1	45	9	.83	3	.276	.314	.443
2007	Bal	AL	132	461	124	26	2	8	(5 | 3)	178	65	45	51	21	1	65	4	13	4	37	9	.80	3	.269	.304	.386
2008	Cin	NL	135	366	75	17	2	10	(2 | 8)	126	46	34	23	16	0	57	1	9	1	14	9	.61	3	.205	.238	.344
2009	2 Tms	NL	16	29	3	0	0	0	(0 | 0)	3	0	0	0	0	0	13	0	1	0	2	1	.67	1	.103	.103	.103
2010	Bal	AL	90	308	83	16	1	8	(4 | 4)	125	43	32	41	20	2	77	1	10	1	21	4	.84	3	.269	.315	.406
2011	2 Tms	NL	133	368	88	20	3	6	(3 | 3)	132	49	36	34	17	1	77	1	9	2	13	9	.59	8	.239	.273	.359
09	Was	NL	5	15	2	0	0	0	(0 | 0)	2	0	0	0	0	0	6	0	0	0	2	0	1.00	0	.133	.133	.133

Year Team	Lg	G	AB	H	2B	3B	HR	(Hm Rd)	TB	R	RBI	RC	TBB	IBB	SO	HBP	SH	SF	SB	CS	SB%	GDP	Avg	OBP	Slg
								BATTING													**BASERUNNING**			**AVERAGES**		
09 Mil	NL	11	14	1	0	0	0	(0 0)	1	0	0	0	0	0	7	0	1	0	0	1	.00	1	.071	.071	.071
11 Tor	AL	89	317	80	16	3	6	(3 3)	120	44	33	32	15	1	65	1	6	2	13	8	.62	7	.252	.287	.379
11 StL	NL	44	51	8	4	0	0	(0 0)	12	5	3	2	2	0	12	0	3	0	0	1	.00	1	.157	.189	.235
12 ML YEARS		1230	4171	1050	197	34	118	(62 56)	1669	571	431	466	206	22	933	31	63	24	218	64	.77	44	.252	.290	.400

Eric Patterson

Bats: L **Throws:** R **Pos:** PH-22; 2B-10; CF-7; RF-6; LF-4; PR-2   **Ht:** 6'0" **Wt:** 170 **Born:** 4/8/1983 **Age:** 29

Year Team	Lg	G	AB	H	2B	3B	HR	(Hm Rd)	TB	R	RBI	RC	TBB	IBB	SO	HBP	SH	SF	SB	CS	SB%	GDP	Avg	OBP	Slg
								BATTING													**BASERUNNING**			**AVERAGES**		
2011 Lk Els*	A+	2	4	0	0	0	0	(- -)	0	0	0	0	2	0	1	0	0	0	1	0	1.00	0	.000	.333	.000
2011 Tucsn*	AAA	51	190	48	12	4	3	(- -)	77	31	14	22	9	1	29	1	1	2	3	3	.50	2	.253	.287	.405
2007 ChC	NL	7	8	2	1	0	0	(0 0)	3	0	0	0	0	0	3	0	1	0	0	0	-	0	.250	.250	.375
2008 2 Tms		43	130	25	4	0	1	(1 0)	32	16	15	11	17	0	36	0	0	1	10	1	.91	1	.192	.284	.246
2009 Oak	AL	39	94	27	5	1	1	(1 0)	37	15	11	14	14	0	25	0	0	2	6	1	.86	0	.287	.373	.394
2010 2 Tms		90	187	40	8	5	6	(2 4)	76	26	16	20	14	0	62	1	2	0	11	1	.92	2	.214	.272	.406
2011 SD	NL	47	89	16	2	1	2	(2 0)	26	8	8	6	12	0	22	0	0	1	8	2	.80	1	.180	.272	.292
08 ChC	NL	13	38	9	1	0	1	(1 0)	13	5	7	5	5	0	12	0	0	1	2	1	.67	1	.237	.318	.342
08 Oak	AL	30	92	16	3	0	0	(0 0)	19	11	8	6	12	0	24	0	0	0	8	0	1.00	0	.174	.269	.207
10 Oak	AL	45	103	21	5	2	4	(2 2)	42	13	9	9	7	0	31	0	1	0	6	0	1.00	1	.204	.255	.408
10 Bos	AL	45	84	19	3	3	2	(0 2)	34	13	7	11	7	0	31	1	1	0	5	1	.83	1	.226	.293	.405
5 ML YEARS		226	508	110	20	7	10	(6 4)	174	65	50	51	57	0	148	1	3	5	35	5	.88	4	.217	.294	.343

Troy Patton

Pitches: L **Bats:** B **Pos:** RP-20   **Ht:** 6'1" **Wt:** 185 **Born:** 9/3/1985 **Age:** 26

Year Team	Lg	G	GS	CG	GF	IP	BFP	H	R	ER	HR	SH	SF	HB	TBB	IBB	SO	WP	Bk	W	L	Pct	Sh	Sv-Op	Hld	ERC	ERA
			HOW MUCH HE PITCHED							**WHAT HE GAVE UP**												**THE RESULTS**				
2011 Norfolk*	AAA	17	2	0	5	44.1	187	44	9	9	0	1	1	2	12	2	30	1	0	4	1	.800	0	0- -	-	2.96	1.83
2007 Hou	NL	3	2	0	1	12.2	54	10	6	5	3	1	0	2	4	0	8	0	0	0	2	.000	0	0-0	0	4.04	3.55
2010 Bal	AL	1	0	0	0	0.2	4	1	0	0	0	0	0	0	1	0	1	0	0	0	0	-	0	0-0	0	10.76	0.00
2011 Bal	AL	20	0	0	4	30.0	119	25	10	10	2	1	1	0	5	1	22	0	0	2	1	.667	0	0-0	2	2.09	3.00
3 ML YEARS		24	2	0	5	43.1	177	36	16	15	5	2	1	2	10	1	31	0	0	2	3	.400	0	0-0	2	2.74	3.12

Xavier Paul

Bats: L **Throws:** R **Pos:** RF-72; PH-46; LF-27; CF-9; PR-8   **Ht:** 5'9" **Wt:** 206 **Born:** 2/25/1985 **Age:** 27

Year Team	Lg	G	AB	H	2B	3B	HR	(Hm Rd)	TB	R	RBI	RC	TBB	IBB	SO	HBP	SH	SF	SB	CS	SB%	GDP	Avg	OBP	Slg
								BATTING													**BASERUNNING**			**AVERAGES**		
2009 LAD	NL	11	14	3	1	0	1	(0 1)	7	3	1	0	2	0	4	0	0	0	1	0	1.00	1	.214	.313	.500
2010 LAD	NL	44	121	28	8	1	0	(0 0)	38	16	11	8	8	0	24	0	3	1	3	1	.75	3	.231	.277	.314
2011 2 Tms		128	243	62	6	5	2	(1 1)	84	30	20	24	13	1	62	0	5	1	16	6	.73	2	.255	.292	.346
11 LAD	NL	7	11	3	0	0	0	(0 0)	3	0	0	1	0	0	5	0	0	0	0	0	-	0	.273	.273	.273
11 Pit	NL	121	232	59	6	5	2	(1 1)	81	30	20	23	13	1	57	0	5	1	16	6	.73	2	.254	.293	.349
3 ML YEARS		183	378	93	15	6	3	(1 2)	129	49	32	32	23	1	90	0	8	2	19	8	.70	6	.246	.288	.341

David Pauley

Pitches: R **Bats:** R **Pos:** RP-53   **Ht:** 6'2" **Wt:** 210 **Born:** 6/17/1983 **Age:** 29

Year Team	Lg	G	GS	CG	GF	IP	BFP	H	R	ER	HR	SH	SF	HB	TBB	IBB	SO	WP	Bk	W	L	Pct	Sh	Sv-Op	Hld	ERC	ERA
			HOW MUCH HE PITCHED							**WHAT HE GAVE UP**												**THE RESULTS**				
2006 Bos	AL	3	3	0	0	16.0	82	31	14	14	1	0	0	2	6	1	10	0	0	0	2	.000	0	0-0	0	10.41	7.88
2008 Bos	AL	6	2	0	3	12.1	67	23	17	16	2	0	1	1	5	0	11	0	0	0	1	.000	0	0-0	0	10.16	11.68
2010 Sea	AL	19	15	0	2	90.2	390	89	44	41	13	2	3	4	30	2	51	4	0	4	9	.308	0	0-0	0	4.11	4.07
2011 2 Tms		53	0	0	17	74.0	302	64	27	26	6	3	2	5	22	5	44	0	0	5	6	.455	0	0-2	8	3.05	3.16
11 Sea	AL	39	0	0	13	54.1	213	38	13	13	2	2	1	4	16	4	34	0	0	5	4	.556	0	0-1	7	1.98	2.15
11 Det	AL	14	0	0	4	19.2	89	26	14	13	4	1	1	1	6	1	10	0	0	0	2	.000	0	0-1	1	6.60	5.95
4 ML YEARS		81	20	0	22	193.0	841	207	102	97	22	5	6	12	63	8	116	4	0	9	18	.333	0	0-2	8	4.48	4.52

Felipe Paulino

Pitches: R **Bats:** R **Pos:** SP-20; RP-19   **Ht:** 6'2" **Wt:** 270 **Born:** 10/5/1983 **Age:** 28

Year Team	Lg	G	GS	CG	GF	IP	BFP	H	R	ER	HR	SH	SF	HB	TBB	IBB	SO	WP	Bk	W	L	Pct	Sh	Sv-Op	Hld	ERC	ERA
			HOW MUCH HE PITCHED							**WHAT HE GAVE UP**												**THE RESULTS**				
2007 Hou	NL	5	3	0	0	19.0	85	22	15	15	5	2	0	0	7	1	11	1	0	2	1	.667	0	0-0	1	5.93	7.11
2009 Hou	NL	23	17	0	0	97.2	448	126	73	68	20	8	1	4	37	2	93	5	0	3	11	.214	0	0-1	0	6.70	6.27
2010 Hou	NL	19	14	0	0	91.2	411	95	63	52	4	6	3	3	46	4	83	6	1	1	9	.100	0	0-1	1	4.29	5.11
2011 2 Tms		39	20	0	8	139.1	599	146	74	69	13	5	7	8	55	2	133	7	1	4	10	.286	0	0-1	2	4.60	4.46
11 Col	NL	18	0	0	8	14.2	68	23	12	12	3	0	1	0	7	0	14	1	0	0	4	.000	0	0-1	2	9.44	7.36
11 KC	AL	21	20	0	0	124.2	531	123	62	57	10	5	6	8	48	2	119	6	1	4	6	.400	0	0-0	0	4.11	4.11
4 ML YEARS		86	54	0	8	347.2	1543	389	225	204	42	21	11	15	145	9	320	19	2	10	31	.244	0	0-3	4	5.17	5.28

Ronny Paulino

Bats: R Throws: R Pos: C-68; PH-19

Ht: 6'3" Wt: 250 Born: 4/21/1981 Age: 31

									BATTING												BASERUNNING				AVERAGES		
Year	Team	Lg	G	AB	H	2B	3B	HR	(Hm	Rd)	TB	R	RBI	RC	TBB	IBB	SO	HBP	SH	SF		SB	CS	SB%	GDP	Avg	OBP	Slg
2011	StLuci*	A+	5	17	3	1	0	0	(-	-)	4	1	2	0	0	0	4	0	0	0		0	0	-	0	.176	.176	.235
2011	Buffalo*	AAA	7	25	5	1	0	0	(-	-)	6	2	2	1	1	0	4	0	0	0		0	0	-	0	.200	.231	.240
2005	Pit	NL	2	4	2	0	0	0	(0	0)	2	1	0	1	1	0	0	0	0	0		0	0	-	17	.310	.360	.394
2006	Pit	NL	129	442	137	19	0	6	(2	4)	174	37	55	60	34	5	79	2	1	2		0	0	-	14	.263	.314	.389
2007	Pit	NL	133	457	120	25	0	11	(7	4)	178	56	55	49	33	0	79	2	0	2		2	2	.50	4	.212	.277	.305
2008	Pit	NL	40	118	25	5	0	2	(0	2)	36	8	18	14	11	1	24	0	0	1		1	0	1.00	8	.272	.340	.432
2009	Fla	NL	80	239	65	10	1	8	(4	4)	101	24	27	31	25	2	48	0	1	1		1	0	1.00	11	.259	.311	.354
2010	Fla	NL	91	316	82	18	0	4	(0	4)	112	31	37	32	25	4	51	0	0	3		0	0	-	11	.268	.312	.354
2011	NYM	NL	78	228	61	13	0	2	(1	1)	80	19	19	20	15	3	38	1	1	3		0	0	-	9	.268	.312	.351
	7 ML YEARS		553	1804	492	90	1	33	(14	19)	683	176	211	207	144	15	319	5	3	12		4	2	.67	63	.273	.326	.379

Carl Pavano

pah-VAH-no

Pitches: R Bats: R Pos: SP-33

Ht: 6'5" Wt: 250 Born: 1/8/1976 Age: 36

			HOW MUCH HE PITCHED						WHAT HE GAVE UP										THE RESULTS							
Year	Team	Lg	G	GS	CG	GF	IP	BFP	H	R	ER	HR	SH	SF	HB	TBB	IBB	SO	WP	Bk	W	L	Pct	Sh	Sv-Op	Hld	ERC	ERA
1998	Mon	NL	24	23	0	0	134.2	580	130	70	63	18	5	6	8	43	1	83	1	0	6	9	.400	0	0-0	0	3.97	4.21
1999	Mon	NL	19	18	1	0	104.0	457	117	66	65	8	5	2	4	35	1	70	1	3	6	8	.429	1	0-0	0	4.51	5.63
2000	Mon	NL	15	15	0	0	97.0	408	89	40	33	8	4	3	8	34	1	64	1	1	8	4	.667	0	0-0	0	3.67	3.06
2001	Mon	NL	8	8	0	0	42.2	199	59	33	30	7	2	1	2	16	1	36	0	1	1	6	.143	0	0-0	0	6.99	6.33
2002	2 Tms	NL	37	22	0	2	136.0	619	174	88	78	19	4	4	10	45	8	92	3	2	6	10	.375	0	0-0	0	5.98	5.16
2003	Fla	NL	33	32	2	1	201.0	846	204	99	96	19	9	10	7	49	10	133	3	2	12	13	.480	0	0-0	0	3.57	4.30
2004	Fla	NL	31	31	2	0	222.1	909	212	80	74	16	7	4	11	49	13	139	2	3	18	8	.692	2	0-0	0	3.10	3.00
2005	NYY	AL	17	17	1	0	100.0	442	129	66	53	17	4	3	8	18	1	56	2	1	4	6	.400	1	0-0	0	5.74	4.77
2007	NYY	AL	2	2	0	0	11.1	46	12	7	6	1	0	0	0	2	0	4	0	0	1	0	1.000	0	0-0	0	3.54	4.76
2008	NYY	AL	7	7	0	0	34.1	154	41	23	22	5	3	3	4	10	0	15	0	1	4	2	.667	0	0-0	0	5.60	5.77
2009	2 Tms	AL	33	33	1	0	199.1	854	235	119	113	28	2	7	6	39	1	147	5	0	14	12	.538	1	0-0	0	4.63	5.10
2010	Min	AL	32	32	7	0	221.0	906	227	95	92	24	5	5	6	37	2	117	4	0	17	11	.607	2	0-0	0	3.51	3.75
2011	Min	AL	33	33	3	0	222.0	955	262	123	106	23	7	9	8	40	0	102	4	2	9	13	.409	1	0-0	0	4.38	4.30
02	Mon	NL	15	14	0	0	74.1	350	98	55	52	14	2	2	7	31	5	51	2	1	3	8	.273	0	0-0	0	7.07	6.30
02	Fla	NL	22	8	0	2	61.2	269	76	33	26	5	2	2	3	14	3	41	1	1	3	2	.600	0	0-0	0	4.74	3.79
09	Cle	AL	21	21	1	0	125.2	534	150	80	75	19	1	6	3	23	0	88	4	0	9	8	.529	1	0-0	0	4.83	5.37
09	Min	AL	12	12	0	0	73.2	320	85	39	38	7	1	1	3	16	1	59	1	0	5	4	.556	0	0-0	0	4.29	4.64
	Postseason		10	4	0	1	32.1	128	32	9	9	3	1	2	1	4	1	27	0	0	2	2	.500	0	0-0	0	3.09	2.51
	13 ML YEARS		291	273	17	3	1725.2	7375	1891	909	831	191	57	57	82	417	39	1058	26	16	106	102	.510	8	0-0	3	4.23	4.33

Brad Peacock

Pitches: R Bats: R Pos: SP-2; RP-1

Ht: 6'1" Wt: 175 Born: 2/2/1988 Age: 24

			HOW MUCH HE PITCHED						WHAT HE GAVE UP										THE RESULTS							
Year	Team	Lg	G	GS	CG	GF	IP	BFP	H	R	ER	HR	SH	SF	HB	TBB	IBB	SO	WP	Bk	W	L	Pct	Sh	Sv-Op	Hld	ERC	ERA
2007	Nats	R	13	7	0	2	39.1	176	38	23	17	1	0	2	2	15	0	34	5	0	1	1	.500	0	0- -	-	3.33	3.89
2008	Hgrstn	A	8	8	0	0	33.2	167	38	38	34	8	0	4	8	21	0	23	4	0	0	5	.000	0	0- -	-	7.83	9.09
2008	Vrmnt	A-	14	14	2	0	75.0	321	67	38	26	3	2	4	3	27	1	54	4	1	4	7	.364	0	0- -	-	3.01	3.12
2009	Hgrstn	A	19	17	0	1	100.0	429	104	49	45	10	4	2	8	32	0	77	5	0	5	8	.385	0	0- -	-	4.36	4.05
2009	Ptomc	A+	8	7	0	0	47.2	199	46	26	23	4	3	1	3	10	0	27	1	0	3	3	.500	0	0- -	-	3.27	4.34
2010	Ptomc	A+	19	18	1	1	103.1	444	109	59	51	11	5	3	4	25	0	118	10	2	4	9	.308	1	0- -	-	3.90	4.44
2010	Hrsbrg	AA	7	7	0	0	38.2	166	33	21	20	5	2	1	0	22	1	30	0	0	2	2	.500	0	0- -	-	4.13	4.66
2011	Hrsbrg	AA	16	13	1	0	98.2	376	62	25	22	4	2	3	2	23	1	129	4	0	10	2	.833	1	0- -	-	1.46	2.01
2011	Syrcse	AAA	9	9	0	0	48.0	204	36	18	17	5	1	1	2	24	0	48	4	0	5	1	.833	0	0- -	-	3.26	3.19
2011	Was	NL	3	2	0	0	12.0	48	7	1	1	0	0	0	0	6	0	4	1	0	2	0	1.000	0	0-1	0	1.71	0.75

Steve Pearce

Bats: R Throws: R Pos: PH-26; 1B-16; 3B-10; RF-5

Ht: 5'11" Wt: 210 Born: 4/13/1983 Age: 29

									BATTING												BASERUNNING				AVERAGES		
Year	Team	Lg	G	AB	H	2B	3B	HR	(Hm	Rd)	TB	R	RBI	RC	TBB	IBB	SO	HBP	SH	SF		SB	CS	SB%	GDP	Avg	OBP	Slg
2011	Bradtn*	A+	3	6	0	0	0	0	(-	-)	0	2	0	0	4	0	2	0	0	0		0	0	-	0	.000	.400	.000
2011	Pirates*	R	1	3	2	0	0	0	(-	-)	2	0	2	1	1	0	1	0	0	0		0	0	-	1	.667	.750	.667
2011	Indy*	AAA	7	30	8	2	0	3	(-	-)	19	5	6	5	0	0	9	0	0	0		0	0	-	1	.267	.267	.633
2007	Pit	NL	23	68	20	5	1	0	(0	0)	27	13	6	9	5	0	12	0	0	0		2	1	.67	2	.294	.342	.397
2008	Pit	NL	37	109	27	7	0	4	(0	4)	46	6	15	13	5	0	22	3	0	2		2	0	1.00	1	.248	.294	.422
2009	Pit	NL	60	165	34	13	1	4	(3	1)	61	19	16	17	21	0	43	0	0	0		0	0	-	6	.206	.296	.370
2010	Pit	NL	15	29	8	2	1	0	(0	0)	12	4	5	5	7	0	6	0	0	2		0	0	-	6	.276	.395	.414
2011	Pit	NL	50	94	19	2	0	1	(1	0)	24	8	10	5	7	0	21	1	1	2		0	0	-	6	.202	.260	.255
	5 ML YEARS		185	465	108	29	3	9	(4	5)	170	50	52	49	45	0	104	4	1	6		5	1	.83	11	.232	.302	.366

Jake Peavy

Pitches: R Bats: R Pos: SP-18; RP-1

Ht: 6'1" Wt: 195 Born: 5/31/1981 Age: 31

			HOW MUCH HE PITCHED						WHAT HE GAVE UP										THE RESULTS							
Year	Team	Lg	G	GS	CG	GF	IP	BFP	H	R	ER	HR	SH	SF	HB	TBB	IBB	SO	WP	Bk	W	L	Pct	Sh	Sv-Op	Hld	ERC	ERA
2011	Brham*	AA	2	2	0	0	4.1	23	9	5	3	0	0	0	0	1	0	4	1	0	0	0		0	0- -	-	9.02	6.23
2011	Charltt*	AAA	4	4	0	0	24.2	93	21	10	10	3	0	1	0	1	0	26	1	0	1	1	.500	0	0- -	-	2.15	3.65
2002	SD	NL	17	17	0	0	97.2	430	106	54	49	11	5	2	3	33	4	90	4	1	6	7	.462	0	0-0	0	4.41	4.52
2003	SD	NL	32	32	0	0	194.2	827	173	94	89	33	7	5	6	82	3	156	2	0	12	11	.522	0	0-0	0	4.13	4.11
2004	SD	NL	27	27	0	0	166.1	694	146	49	42	13	5	6	11	53	4	173	1	1	15	6	.714	1	0-0	0	3.18	2.27
2005	SD	NL	30	30	3	0	203.0	812	162	70	65	18	4	5	7	50	3	216	3	1	13	7	.650	3	0-0	0	2.49	2.88

(pitcher, continued)

Year	Team	Lg	G	GS	CG	GF	IP	BFP	H	R	ER	HR	SH	SF	HB	TBB	IBB	SO	WP	Bk	W	L	Pct	Sh	Sv-Op	Hld	ERC	ERA
2006	SD	NL	32	32	2	0	202.1	846	187	93	92	23	5	1	6	62	11	215	4	0	11	14	.440	0	0-0	0	3.42	4.09
2007	SD	NL	34	34	0	0	223.1	898	169	67	63	13	5	7	6	68	5	**240**	4	0	**19**	6	.760	0	0-0	0	**2.27**	2.54
2008	SD	NL	27	27	1	0	173.2	709	146	57	55	17	7	1	5	59	1	166	6	0	10	11	.476	0	0-0	0	3.12	2.85
2009	2 Tms		16	16	1	0	101.2	410	80	41	39	8	3	2	1	34	0	110	2	2	9	6	.600	0	0-0	0	2.63	3.45
2010	CWS	AL	17	17	1	0	107.0	450	98	55	55	13	1	5	5	34	2	93	2	1	7	6	.538	1	0-0	0	3.59	4.63
2011	CWS	AL	19	18	1	0	111.2	470	117	61	61	10	1	5	3	24	4	95	4	0	7	7	.500	1	0-0	0	3.59	4.92
09	SD	NL	13	13	1	0	81.2	335	69	38	36	7	2	2	1	28	0	92	2	1	6	6	.500	0	0-0	0	3.00	3.97
09	CWS	AL	3	3	0	0	20.0	75	11	3	3	1	1	0	0	6	0	18	0	1	3	0	1.000	0	0-0	0	1.38	1.35
Postseason			2	2	0	0	9.2	49	13	13	13	3	1	1	0	4	3	5	1	0	0	2	.000	0	0-0	0	12.16	12.10
10 ML YEARS			251	250	9	0	1581.1	6546	1384	641	610	159	43	39	53	499	37	1554	32	6	109	81	.574	5	0-0	0	3.18	3.47

Dustin Pedroia

Bats: R Throws: R Pos: 2B-159; PH-1
peh-DROY-uh
Ht: 5'9" Wt: 180 Born: 8/17/1983 Age: 28

Year	Team	Lg	G	AB	H	2B	3B	HR	(Hm	Rd)	TB	R	RBI	RC	TBB	IBB	SO	HBP	SH	SF	SB	CS	SB%	GDP	Avg	OBP	Slg
2006	Bos	AL	31	89	17	4	0	2	(1	1)	27	5	7	3	7	0	7	1	1	0	0	1	.00	1	.191	.258	.303
2007	Bos	AL	139	520	165	39	1	8	(5	3)	230	86	50	79	47	1	42	1	5	2	7	1	.88	8	.317	.380	.442
2008	Bos	AL	157	653	**213**	54	2	17	(7	10)	322	**118**	83	107	50	1	52	1	0	9	20	1	**.95**	17	.326	.376	.493
2009	Bos	AL	154	626	185	48	1	15	(10	5)	280	**115**	72	104	74	3	45	5	3	6	20	8	.71	19	.296	.371	.447
2010	Bos	AL	75	302	87	24	1	12	(4	8)	149	53	41	52	37	1	38	4	2	6	9	1	.90	7	.288	.367	.493
2011	Bos	AL	159	635	195	37	3	21	(13	8)	301	102	91	114	86	6	85	1	2	7	26	8	.76	12	.307	.387	.474
Postseason			28	115	29	9	0	5	(2	3)	53	22	18	18	14	0	12	2	1	0	2	1	.67	3	.252	.344	.461
6 ML YEARS			715	2825	862	206	8	75	(40	35)	1309	479	344	459	301	12	269	25	20	30	82	20	.80	64	.305	.373	.463

Carlos Peguero

Bats: L Throws: L Pos: LF-40; RF-3; DH-2; PH-1
peh-GEHR-oh
Ht: 6'5" Wt: 245 Born: 2/22/1987 Age: 25

Year	Team	Lg	G	AB	H	2B	3B	HR	(Hm	Rd)	TB	R	RBI	RC	TBB	IBB	SO	HBP	SH	SF	SB	CS	SB%	GDP	Avg	OBP	Slg
2006	Ms	R	34	134	42	10	7	7	(-	-)	87	27	30	31	13	0	49	2	0	1	3	2	.60	1	.313	.380	.649
2006	Everett	A-	25	93	19	4	1	2	(-	-)	31	7	9	5	2	1	34	0	0	1	3	2	.60		.204	.221	.333
2007	Wisc	A	79	297	78	21	6	9	(-	-)	138	35	50	43	16	0	97	7	0	1	4	3	.57	4	.263	.315	.465
2008	Hi Dsrt	A+	92	371	111	25	3	12	(-	-)	178	47	74	55	10	0	96	1	0	3	4	6	.60	4	.299	.317	.480
2009	Hi Dsrt	A+	126	491	133	21	14	31	(-	-)	275	92	98	91	42	2	172	1	1	3	4	6	.60	5	.271	.335	.560
2010	WTenn	AA	130	488	124	23	5	23	(-	-)	226	86	73	77	56	3	178	8	0	1	7	9	.44	8	.254	.340	.463
2011	Tacom	AAA	57	240	76	15	2	13	(-	-)	134	44	47	48	15	1	82	3	0	0	1	0	1.00	3	.317	.364	.558
2011	Sea	AL	46	143	28	3	2	6	(4	2)	53	14	19	12	8	2	54	3	0	1	0	1	.00	0	.196	.252	.371

Mike Pelfrey

Pitches: R Bats: R Pos: SP-33; RP-1
PELL-free
Ht: 6'7" Wt: 250 Born: 1/14/1984 Age: 28

Year	Team	Lg	G	GS	CG	GF	IP	BFP	H	R	ER	HR	SH	SF	HB	TBB	IBB	SO	WP	Bk	W	L	Pct	Sh	Sv-Op	Hld	ERC	ERA
2006	NYM	NL	4	4	0	0	21.1	99	25	14	13	1	1	1	3	12	0	13	2	0	2	1	.667	0	0-0	0	6.05	5.48
2007	NYM	NL	15	13	0	0	72.2	342	85	47	45	6	6	3	9	39	1	45	3	0	3	8	.273	0	0-0	0	5.99	5.57
2008	NYM	NL	32	32	2	0	200.2	851	209	86	83	12	11	5	13	64	1	110	2	0	13	11	.542	0	0-0	0	4.04	3.72
2009	NYM	NL	31	31	0	0	184.1	824	213	112	103	18	8	5	7	66	8	107	1	**6**	10	12	.455	0	0-0	0	4.83	5.03
2010	NYM	NL	34	33	0	1	204.0	870	213	88	83	12	**17**	4	6	68	5	113	1	1	15	9	.625	0	1-1	0	3.89	3.66
2011	NYM	NL	34	33	2	0	193.2	860	220	111	102	21	10	8	7	65	7	105	2	2	7	13	.350	0	0-0	0	4.70	4.74
6 ML YEARS			150	146	4	1	876.2	3846	965	458	429	70	53	26	45	314	22	493	11	9	50	54	.481	0	1-1	0	4.52	4.40

Brayan Pena

Bats: B Throws: R Pos: C-69; PH-4
BRIAN
Ht: 5'11" Wt: 234 Born: 1/7/1982 Age: 30

Year	Team	Lg	G	AB	H	2B	3B	HR	(Hm	Rd)	TB	R	RBI	RC	TBB	IBB	SO	HBP	SH	SF	SB	CS	SB%	GDP	Avg	OBP	Slg
2005	Atl	NL	18	39	7	2	0	0	(0	0)	9	2	4	0	1	1	7	0	0	0	0	0	-	1	.179	.200	.231
2006	Atl	NL	23	41	11	2	0	1	(0	1)	16	9	5	4	2	0	5	0	0	0	0	0	-	2	.268	.302	.390
2007	Atl	NL	16	33	7	0	0	1	(1	0)	10	2	3	0	1	0	3	0	0	0	0	0	-	2	.212	.212	.303
2008	Atl	NL	14	14	4	1	0	0	(0	0)	5	3	0	0	1	0	2	0	0	0	0	1	.00	2	.286	.333	.357
2009	KC	AL	64	165	45	10	0	6	(3	3)	73	17	18	18	12	2	18	0	4	2	0	0	-	5	.273	.318	.442
2010	KC	AL	60	158	40	10	0	1	(0	1)	53	11	19	16	12	0	27	1	1	2	2	0	1.00	6	.253	.306	.335
2011	KC	AL	72	222	55	11	0	3	(0	3)	75	17	24	23	12	0	24	2	0	4	0	0	-	6	.248	.288	.338
7 ML YEARS			267	672	169	36	0	12	(4	8)	241	61	73	61	40	3	86	3	5	8	2	1	.67	24	.251	.293	.359

Carlos Pena

Bats: L Throws: L Pos: 1B-153; PH-6; PR-1
Ht: 6'2" Wt: 225 Born: 5/17/1978 Age: 34

Year	Team	Lg	G	AB	H	2B	3B	HR	(Hm	Rd)	TB	R	RBI	RC	TBB	IBB	SO	HBP	SH	SF	SB	CS	SB%	GDP	Avg	OBP	Slg
2001	Tex	AL	22	62	16	4	1	3	(2	1)	31	6	12	11	10	0	17	0	0	0	0	0	-	1	.258	.361	.500
2002	2 Tms	AL	115	397	96	17	4	19	(10	9)	178	43	52	56	41	0	111	3	0	2	2	2	.50	7	.242	.316	.448
2003	Det	AL	131	452	112	21	6	18	(8	10)	199	51	50	61	53	1	123	6	1	4	4	5	.44	2	.248	.332	.440
2004	Det	AL	142	481	116	22	4	27	(10	17)	227	89	82	73	70	2	146	3	2	5	7	1	.88	11	.241	.338	.472
2005	Det	AL	79	260	61	9	0	18	(14	4)	124	37	44	40	31	2	95	4	0	0	1	0	1.00	3	.235	.325	.472
2006	Bos	AL	18	33	9	2	0	1	(1	0)	14	3	3	3	4	0	10	0	0	0	0	0	-	3	.273	.351	.424
2007	TB	AL	148	490	138	29	1	46	(23	23)	307	99	121	114	103	10	142	10	1	8	1	0	1.00	7	.282	.411	.627
2008	TB	AL	139	490	121	24	2	31	(14	17)	242	76	102	92	96	7	166	12	0	9	1	1	.50	6	.247	.377	.494
2009	TB	AL	135	471	107	25	2	**39**	(19	20)	253	91	100	88	87	11	163	9	0	3	3	3	.50	5	.227	.356	.537

Year	Team	Lg	G	AB	H	2B	3B	HR	(Hm	Rd)	TB	R	RBI	RC	TBB	IBB	SO	HBP	SH	SF	SB	CS	SB%	GDP	Avg	OBP	Slg
2010 TB		AL	144	484	95	18	0	28	(18	10)	197	64	84	73	87	4	158	7	0	4	5	1	.83	2	.196	.325	.407
2011 ChC		NL	153	493	111	27	3	28	(12	16)	228	72	80	79	101	7	161	4	1	7	2	2	.50	6	.225	.357	.462
02 Oak		AL	40	124	27	4	0	7	(5	2)	52	12	16	17	15	0	38	1	0	1	0	0	-	2	.218	.305	.419
02 Det		AL	75	273	69	13	4	12	(5	7)	126	31	36	39	26	0	73	2	0	1	2	2	.50	5	.253	.321	.462
Postseason			19	67	18	3	1	4	(0	4)	35	13	14	14	13	2	24	0	0	0	3	2	.60	1	.269	.388	.522
11 ML YEARS			1226	4113	982	198	23	258	(131	127)	2000	631	730	690	683	44	1292	58	5	42	25	16	.61	55	.239	.352	.486

Ramiro Pena

Bats: B **Throws:** R **Pos:** 3B-13; 2B-7; SS-4; PR-4; PH-1   **Ht:** 5'11" **Wt:** 175 **Born:** 7/18/1985 **Age:** 26

Year	Team	Lg	G	AB	H	2B	3B	HR	(Hm	Rd)	TB	R	RBI	RC	TBB	IBB	SO	HBP	SH	SF	SB	CS	SB%	GDP	Avg	OBP	Slg
2011 S-WB*		AAA	55	209	57	12	1	4	(-	-)	83	27	18	29	20	1	35	1	1	0	3	2	.60	1	.273	.339	.397
2011 Trntn*		AA	2	7	3	0	0	0	(-	-)	3	1	2	1	0	0	1	0	0	0	0	0	-	1	.429	.429	.429
2009 NYY		AL	69	115	33	6	1	1	(1	0)	44	17	10	15	5	0	20	0	1	0	4	1	.80	2	.287	.317	.383
2010 NYY		AL	85	154	35	1	1	0	(0	0)	38	18	18	10	6	0	27	1	4	2	7	1	.88	4	.227	.258	.247
2011 NYY		AL	23	40	4	0	0	1	(1	0)	7	5	4	0	2	0	11	1	2	1	0	0	-	0	.100	.159	.175
3 ML YEARS			177	309	72	7	2	2	(2	0)	89	40	32	25	13	0	58	2	7	3	11	2	.85	7	.233	.266	.288

Tony Pena

Pitches: R **Bats:** R **Pos:** RP-17   **Ht:** 6'2" **Wt:** 240 **Born:** 1/9/1982 **Age:** 30

			HOW MUCH HE PITCHED						WHAT HE GAVE UP										THE RESULTS						
Year	Team	Lg	G	GS	CG	GF	IP	BFP	H	R	ER	HR	SH	SF	HB	TBB	IBB	SO	WP	Bk	W	L	Pct	Sh	Sv-Op Hld	ERC	ERA
2011 Charltt*		AAA	5	0	0	0	5.1	20	3	1	1	1	0	0	0	2	0	6	0	0	0	0	-	0	0- - -	2.36	1.69
2006 Ari		NL	25	0	0	6	30.2	135	36	21	19	6	2	1	0	8	0	21	1	0	3	4	.429	0	1-1 2	5.12	5.58
2007 Ari		NL	75	0	0	13	85.1	344	63	36	31	8	1	3	5	31	4	63	3	1	5	4	.556	0	2-5 30	2.71	3.27
2008 Ari		NL	72	0	0	20	72.2	313	80	38	35	5	4	4	3	17	5	52	4	0	3	2	.600	0	3-8 23	3.79	4.33
2009 2 Tms			72	0	0	28	70.0	312	81	37	31	7	2	2	2	20	3	55	3	0	6	5	.545	0	2-4 13	4.46	3.99
2010 CWS		AL	52	3	0	10	100.2	444	108	63	57	10	4	6	1	45	6	56	6	1	5	3	.625	0	0-0 1	4.63	5.10
2011 CWS		AL	17	0	0	10	20.1	97	25	15	14	2	3	1	0	10	2	17	0	0	1	1	.500	0	0-1 0	5.40	6.20
09 Ari		NL	37	0	0	13	34.0	153	41	20	16	3	1	1	1	11	0	26	2	0	5	3	.625	0	1-2 8	4.93	4.24
09 CWS		AL	35	0	0	15	36.0	159	40	17	15	4	1	1	1	9	3	29	1	0	1	2	.333	0	1-2 5	4.03	3.75
Postseason			5	0	0	1	5.1	17	3	0	0	0	0	0	0	0	0	7	0	0	0	0	-	0	0-0 1	0.75	0.00
6 ML YEARS			313	3	0	96	379.2	1645	393	210	187	38	16	17	11	131	20	264	17	2	23	19	.548	0	8-19 69	4.07	4.43

Wily Mo Pena

Bats: R **Throws:** R **Pos:** DH-29; PH-9; PR-3; LF-1   **Ht:** 6'3" **Wt:** 268 **Born:** 1/23/1982 **Age:** 30

Year	Team	Lg	G	AB	H	2B	3B	HR	(Hm	Rd)	TB	R	RBI	RC	TBB	IBB	SO	HBP	SH	SF	SB	CS	SB%	GDP	Avg	OBP	Slg
2011 Reno*		AAA	63	237	86	17	3	21	(-	-)	172	52	63	69	25	3	48	8	0	1	5	2	.71	6	.363	.439	.726
2011 Tacom*		AAA	13	51	17	4	0	4	(-	-)	33	11	14	13	9	0	13	1	0	0	0	0	-	1	.333	.443	.647
2002 Cin		NL	13	18	4	0	0	1	(1	0)	7	1	1	1	0	0	11	0	0	0	0	0	-	0	.222	.222	.389
2003 Cin		NL	80	165	36	6	1	5	(1	4)	59	20	16	14	12	2	53	3	1	0	3	2	.60	2	.218	.283	.358
2004 Cin		NL	110	336	87	10	1	26	(13	13)	177	45	66	54	22	1	108	6	0	4	5	2	.71	9	.259	.316	.527
2005 Cin		NL	99	311	79	17	0	19	(11	8)	153	42	51	40	20	0	116	3	0	1	2	1	.67	7	.254	.304	.492
2006 Bos		AL	84	276	83	15	2	11	(5	6)	135	36	42	39	20	0	90	3	0	5	0	1	.00	7	.301	.349	.489
2007 2 Tms			110	289	73	13	1	13	(3	10)	127	42	39	31	22	2	94	6	0	1	2	1	.67	7	.253	.319	.439
2008 Was			64	195	40	6	0	2	(2	0)	52	10	10	9	10	0	48	0	0	1	0	1	.00	5	.205	.243	.267
2011 2 Tms			39	113	23	3	0	7	(1	6)	47	15	15	9	5	0	39	2	0	0	0	0	-	2	.204	.250	.416
07 Bos		AL	73	156	34	9	1	5	(1	4)	60	18	17	11	14	0	58	2	0	0	0	1	.00	5	.218	.291	.385
07 Was		NL	37	133	39	4	0	8	(2	6)	67	24	22	20	8	2	36	4	0	0	2	0	1.00	2	.293	.352	.504
11 Ari		NL	17	46	9	0	0	5	(1	4)	24	7	7	3	0	0	19	0	0	0	0	0	-	1	.196	.196	.522
11 Sea		AL	22	67	14	3	0	2	(0	2)	23	8	8	6	5	0	20	2	0	0	0	0	-	1	.209	.284	.343
8 ML YEARS			599	1703	425	70	5	84	(37	47)	757	211	240	197	111	5	559	23	1	7	12	8	.60	37	.250	.303	.445

Hunter Pence

Bats: R **Throws:** R **Pos:** RF-153; PH-2   **Ht:** 6'4" **Wt:** 218 **Born:** 4/13/1983 **Age:** 29

Year	Team	Lg	G	AB	H	2B	3B	HR	(Hm	Rd)	TB	R	RBI	RC	TBB	IBB	SO	HBP	SH	SF	SB	CS	SB%	GDP	Avg	OBP	Slg
2007 Hou		NL	108	456	147	30	9	17	(7	10)	246	57	69	77	26	0	95	1	0	1	11	5	.69	10	.322	.360	.539
2008 Hou		NL	157	595	160	34	4	25	(14	11)	277	78	83	82	40	2	124	4	0	3	11	10	.52	14	.269	.318	.466
2009 Hou		NL	159	585	165	26	5	25	(14	11)	276	76	72	80	58	1	109	1	0	3	14	11	.56	25	.282	.346	.472
2010 Hou		NL	156	614	173	29	5	25	(14	11)	283	93	91	89	41	2	105	0	0	3	18	9	.67	11	.282	.325	.461
2011 2 Tms		NL	154	606	190	38	5	22	(5	17)	304	84	97	102	56	3	124	1	0	5	8	2	.80	15	.314	.370	.502
11 Hou		NL	100	399	123	26	3	11	(4	7)	188	49	62	63	30	1	86	1	0	2	7	1	.88	7	.308	.356	.471
11 Phi		NL	54	207	67	12	2	11	(1	10)	116	35	35	39	26	2	38	0	0	3	1	1	.50	8	.324	.394	.560
5 ML YEARS			734	2856	835	157	26	114	(54	60)	1386	388	412	430	221	8	557	7	0	15	62	37	.63	75	.292	.343	.485

Lance Pendleton

Pitches: R **Bats:** L **Pos:** RP-15   **Ht:** 6'3" **Wt:** 195 **Born:** 9/10/1983 **Age:** 28

			HOW MUCH HE PITCHED						WHAT HE GAVE UP										THE RESULTS						
Year	Team	Lg	G	GS	CG	GF	IP	BFP	H	R	ER	HR	SH	SF	HB	TBB	IBB	SO	WP	Bk	W	L	Pct	Sh	Sv-Op Hld	ERC	ERA
2005 StlsInd		A-	9	6	0	0	27.0	124	27	11	7	1	1	0	1	13	0	23	2	1	1	0	1.000	0	0- - -	3.90	2.33
2007 Yanks		R	8	6	0	0	13.2	63	14	7	7	1	0	1	1	6	0	16	2	0	0	0	-	0	0- - -	4.27	4.61
2008 CtnSC		A	28	23	0	2	128.0	563	136	62	50	3	5	2	6	46	0	119	15	1	7	9	.438	0	0- - -	3.86	3.52
2009 Tampa		A+	20	18	0	0	104.2	442	101	43	30	1	1	8	5	31	1	87	3	1	11	5	.688	0	0- - -	3.03	2.58

Year	Team	Lg	G	GS	CG	GF	IP	BFP	H	R	ER	HR	SH	SF	HB	TBB	IBB	SO	WP	Bk	W	L	Pct	Sh	Sv-Op	Hld	ERC	ERA
2009	Trntn	AA	8	8	0	0	44.1	189	40	25	22	4	3	3	2	15	1	43	1	0	1	3	.250	0	0--	-	3.32	4.47
2010	Trntn	AA	23	22	0	0	120.2	491	95	50	46	9	0	1	4	45	0	111	4	0	10	4	.714	0	0--	-	2.84	3.43
2010	S-WB	AAA	6	5	0	0	34.0	141	29	17	16	6	0	0	0	12	0	22	1	0	2	1	.667	0	0--	-	3.58	4.24
2011	S-WB	AAA	18	10	0	3	66.2	274	58	23	23	7	1	0	2	24	0	45	3	1	3	4	.429	0	1--	-	3.43	3.11
2011	2 Tms		15	0	0	10	18.2	89	20	14	14	6	0	3	2	11	0	13	0	0	0	0	-	0	0-0	0	7.36	6.75
11	NYY	AL	11	0	0	9	14.0	62	10	5	5	2	0	2	0	10	0	8	0	0	0	0	-	0	0-0	0	3.93	3.21
11	Hou	NL	4	0	0	1	4.2	27	10	9	9	4	0	1	2	1	0	5	0	0	0	0	-	0	0-0	0	20.45	17.36

Cliff Pennington

Bats: B Throws: R Pos: SS-147; PR-2　　　　　　　　　　**Ht: 5'10" Wt: 213 Born: 6/15/1984 Age: 28**

Year	Team	Lg	G	AB	H	2B	3B	HR	(Hm	Rd)	TB	R	RBI	RC	TBB	IBB	SO	HBP	SH	SF	SB	CS	SB%	GDP	Avg	OBP	Slg
2008	Oak	AL	36	99	24	5	0	0	(0	0)	29	14	9	12	13	0	18	2	2	1	4	1	.80	1	.242	.339	.293
2009	Oak	AL	60	208	58	11	3	4	(3	1)	87	27	21	29	19	0	46	1	1	0	7	5	.58	5	.279	.342	.418
2010	Oak	AL	156	508	127	26	8	6	(2	4)	187	64	46	66	50	0	96	3	12	3	29	5	.85	7	.250	.319	.368
2011	Oak	AL	148	515	136	26	2	8	(3	5)	190	57	58	73	42	1	104	1	8	4	14	9	.61	5	.264	.319	.369
	4 ML YEARS		400	1330	345	68	13	18	(8	10)	493	162	134	180	124	1	264	7	23	8	54	20	.73	18	.259	.324	.371

Brad Penny

Pitches: R Bats: R Pos: SP-31　　　　　　　　　　**Ht: 6'4" Wt: 230 Born: 5/24/1978 Age: 34**

Year	Team	Lg	G	GS	CG	GF	IP	BFP	H	R	ER	HR	SH	SF	HB	TBB	IBB	SO	WP	Bk	W	L	Pct	Sh	Sv-Op	Hld	ERC	ERA
2000	Fla	NL	23	22	0	0	119.2	529	120	70	64	13	6	2	5	60	4	80	4	1	8	7	.533	0	0-0	0	4.70	4.81
2001	Fla	NL	31	31	1	0	205.0	833	183	92	84	15	8	2	7	54	3	154	2	0	10	10	.500	1	0-0	0	2.96	3.69
2002	Fla	NL	24	24	1	0	129.1	574	148	76	67	18	6	4	1	50	7	93	4	0	8	7	.533	1	0-0	0	5.08	4.66
2003	Fla	NL	32	32	0	0	196.1	811	195	96	90	21	7	5	3	56	6	138	3	4	14	10	.583	0	0-0	0	3.73	4.13
2004	2 Tms		24	24	0	0	143.0	590	130	55	50	12	3	3	3	45	6	111	5	0	9	10	.474	0	0-0	0	3.20	3.15
2005	LAD	NL	29	29	1	0	175.1	738	185	78	76	17	7	1	3	41	2	122	3	0	7	9	.438	0	0-0	0	3.77	3.90
2006	LAD	NL	34	33	0	0	189.0	813	206	94	91	19	8	3	9	54	4	148	6	0	16	9	.640	0	0-0	1	4.32	4.33
2007	LAD	NL	33	33	0	0	208.0	865	199	75	70	9	13	9	5	73	2	135	6	0	16	4	.800	0	0-0	0	3.41	3.03
2008	LAD	NL	19	17	0	1	94.2	426	112	68	66	13	10	2	3	42	0	51	1	1	6	9	.400	0	0-0	0	5.82	6.27
2009	2 Tms		30	30	1	0	173.1	751	191	102	94	22	0	7	5	51	0	109	6	0	11	9	.550	0	0-0	0	4.54	4.88
2010	StL	NL	9	9	0	0	55.2	232	63	25	20	4	2	3	3	9	1	35	1	0	3	4	.429	0	0-0	0	3.95	3.23
2011	Det	AL	31	31	0	0	181.2	803	222	117	107	24	5	6	4	62	1	74	9	0	11	11	.500	0	0-0	0	5.53	5.30
04	Fla	NL	21	21	0	0	131.1	545	124	50	46	10	3	3	3	39	6	105	5	0	8	8	.500	0	0-0	0	3.26	3.15
04	LAD	NL	3	3	0	0	11.2	45	6	5	4	2	0	0	0	6	0	6	0	0	1	2	.333	0	0-0	0	2.51	3.09
09	Bos	AL	24	24	0	0	131.2	590	160	89	82	17	0	7	5	42	0	89	4	0	7	8	.467	0	0-0	0	5.35	5.61
09	SF	NL	6	6	1	0	41.2	161	31	13	12	5	0	0	0	9	0	20	2	0	4	1	.800	0	0-0	0	2.22	2.59
	Postseason		8	4	0	0	23.0	106	31	17	16	3	2	1	0	11	1	14	0	0	3	2	.600	0	0-1	0	6.81	6.26
	12 ML YEARS		319	315	4	1	1871.0	7965	1954	948	879	187	75	47	51	597	36	1250	50	6	119	99	.546	2	0-0	1	4.13	4.23

Jhonny Peralta

Bats: R Throws: R Pos: SS-145; PH-6; 1B-1　　　pah-RALL-tah　　　**Ht: 6'2" Wt: 215 Born: 5/28/1982 Age: 30**

Year	Team	Lg	G	AB	H	2B	3B	HR	(Hm	Rd)	TB	R	RBI	RC	TBB	IBB	SO	HBP	SH	SF	SB	CS	SB%	GDP	Avg	OBP	Slg
2003	Cle	AL	77	242	55	10	1	4	(3	1)	79	24	21	24	20	0	65	4	2	2	1	3	.25	5	.227	.295	.326
2004	Cle	AL	8	25	6	1	0	0	(0	0)	7	2	2	2	3	0	6	0	0	0	0	1	.00	0	.240	.321	.280
2005	Cle	AL	141	504	147	35	4	24	(14	10)	262	82	78	87	58	3	128	3	1	4	0	2	.00	12	.292	.366	.520
2006	Cle	AL	149	569	146	28	3	13	(7	6)	219	84	68	66	56	0	152	1	3	3	0	1	.00	19	.257	.323	.385
2007	Cle	AL	152	574	155	27	1	21	(16	5)	247	87	72	85	61	2	146	4	1	7	4	4	.50	12	.270	.341	.430
2008	Cle	AL	154	605	167	42	4	23	(11	12)	286	104	89	84	48	2	126	4	2	5	3	1	.75	26	.276	.331	.473
2009	Cle	AL	151	582	148	35	1	11	(2	9)	218	57	83	63	51	0	134	4	2	6	0	2	.00	20	.254	.316	.375
2010	2 Tms	AL	148	551	137	30	2	15	(4	11)	216	60	81	71	53	2	103	1	0	10	1	0	1.00	11	.249	.311	.392
2011	Det	AL	146	525	157	25	3	21	(13	8)	251	68	86	77	40	2	95	2	0	9	0	2	.00	17	.299	.345	.478
10	Cle	AL	91	334	82	23	2	7	(3	4)	130	37	43	41	32	1	69	1	0	6	1	0	1.00	7	.246	.308	.389
10	Det	AL	57	217	55	7	0	8	(1	7)	86	23	38	30	21	1	34	0	0	4	0	0	-	4	.253	.314	.396
	Postseason		11	42	14	5	0	2	(1	1)	25	6	10	9	5	0	11	0	0	1	1	0	1.00	2	.333	.396	.595
	9 ML YEARS		1126	4177	1118	233	19	132	(70	62)	1785	568	580	559	390	11	955	23	11	46	9	16	.36	122	.268	.330	.427

Joel Peralta

Pitches: R Bats: R Pos: RP-71　　　joe-ELL pah-RALL-tah　　　**Ht: 5'11" Wt: 195 Born: 3/23/1976 Age: 36**

Year	Team	Lg	G	GS	CG	GF	IP	BFP	H	R	ER	HR	SH	SF	HB	TBB	IBB	SO	WP	Bk	W	L	Pct	Sh	Sv-Op	Hld	ERC	ERA
2005	LAA	AL	28	0	0	0	34.2	145	28	15	15	6	2	1	0	14	2	30	2	0	1	1.000		0	0-0	0	3.40	3.89
2006	KC	AL	64	0	0	21	73.2	304	74	37	36	10	1	3	2	17	2	57	5	0	1	3	.250	0	1-3	17	3.80	4.40
2007	KC	AL	62	0	0	18	87.2	366	93	39	37	9	2	4	2	19	5	66	2	0	1	3	.250	0	1-5	7	3.75	3.80
2008	KC	AL	40	0	0	12	52.2	224	56	37	35	15	1	3	2	14	0	38	1	0	1	2	.333	0	0-1	1	5.38	5.98
2009	Col	NL	27	0	0	6	24.2	113	27	17	17	3	0	1	3	12	2	22	0	0	0	3	.000	0	0-1	6	5.51	6.20
2010	Was	NL	39	0	0	10	49.0	189	30	12	11	5	2	1	1	9	4	49	0	0	1	0	1.000	0	0-2	9	1.43	2.02
2011	TB	AL	71	0	0	18	67.2	256	44	23	22	7	2	2	0	18	3	61	3	0	3	4	.429	0	6-8	19	1.84	2.93
	7 ML YEARS		331	0	0	95	390.0	1597	352	180	173	55	10	15	10	103	18	323	13	0	8	15	.348	0	8-20	59	3.34	3.99

Chris Perez

Pitches: R Bats: R Pos: RP-64   Ht: 6'4" Wt: 230 Born: 7/1/1985 Age: 26

			HOW MUCH HE PITCHED					WHAT HE GAVE UP										THE RESULTS					
Year	Team	Lg	G	GS	CG	GF	IP	BFP	H	R	ER	HR	SH	SF	HB	TBB	IBB	SO	WP	Bk	W	L	Pct	Sh	Sv-Op Hld	ERC	ERA
2008	StL	NL	41	0	0	23	41.2	177	34	18	16	5	1	3	1	22	0	42	2	0	3	3	.500	0	7-11 6	3.83	3.46
2009	2 Tms		61	0	0	16	57.0	239	41	28	27	8	0	2	6	27	0	68	8	0	1	2	.333	0	2-5 7	3.54	4.26
2010	Cle	AL	63	0	0	37	63.0	260	40	15	12	4	6	1	5	28	3	61	4	0	2	2	.500	0	23-27 9	2.30	1.71
2011	Cle	AL	64	0	0	57	59.2	248	46	24	22	5	4	1	3	26	4	39	1	0	4	7	.364	0	36-40 0	2.98	3.32
09	StL	NL	29	0	0	8	23.2	106	17	12	11	3	0	1	3	15	0	30	4	0	1	1	.500	0	1-2 3	4.01	4.18
09	Cle	AL	32	0	0	8	33.1	133	24	16	16	5	0	1	3	12	0	38	4	0	0	1	.000	0	1-3 4	3.19	4.32
4 ML YEARS			229	0	0	133	221.1	924	161	85	77	22	11	7	15	103	7	210	15	0	10	14	.417	0	68-83 22	3.07	3.13

Juan Perez

Pitches: L Bats: R Pos: RP-8   Ht: 6'0" Wt: 175 Born: 9/3/1978 Age: 33

			HOW MUCH HE PITCHED					WHAT HE GAVE UP										THE RESULTS					
Year	Team	Lg	G	GS	CG	GF	IP	BFP	H	R	ER	HR	SH	SF	HB	TBB	IBB	SO	WP	Bk	W	L	Pct	Sh	Sv-Op Hld	ERC	ERA
2011	LV*	AAA	36	0	0	13	36.1	167	37	24	24	5	1	0	0	25	1	53	4	0	0	5	.000	0	4- --	5.60	5.94
2006	Pit	NL	7	0	0	0	3.1	17	5	3	3	1	0	1	2	1	0	3	0	0	0	1	.000	0	0-0 0	11.77	8.10
2007	Pit	NL	17	0	0	4	12.1	57	14	7	6	2	0	0	0	8	0	10	1	0	0	0	-	0	0-0 0	6.48	4.38
2011	Phi	NL	8	0	0	1	5.0	21	1	2	2	0	0	0	0	5	0	8	1	0	1	0	1.000	0	0-0 1	1.51	3.60
3 ML YEARS			32	0	0	5	20.2	95	20	12	11	3	0	1	2	14	0	21	2	0	1	1	.500	0	0-0 1	5.81	4.79

Luis Perez

Pitches: L Bats: L Pos: RP-33; SP-4   Ht: 6'0" Wt: 160 Born: 1/20/1985 Age: 27

			HOW MUCH HE PITCHED					WHAT HE GAVE UP										THE RESULTS					
Year	Team	Lg	G	GS	CG	GF	IP	BFP	H	R	ER	HR	SH	SF	HB	TBB	IBB	SO	WP	Bk	W	L	Pct	Sh	Sv-Op Hld	ERC	ERA
2007	Auburn	A-	16	16	0	0	75.1	343	73	37	31	1	3	3	9	38	0	71	4	1	3	3	.500	0	0- -	4.05	3.70
2008	Lnsng	A	28	23	0	1	137.1	595	136	68	55	4	8	4	16	51	0	137	6	7	5	12	.294	0	0- -	3.89	3.60
2009	NHam	AA	28	27	2	0	162.1	693	145	78	64	11	3	3	13	67	2	112	6	0	9	11	.450	0	0- -	3.63	3.55
2010	NHam	AA	13	12	1	0	73.1	314	67	43	37	6	0	1	4	37	0	49	5	1	5	6	.455	0	0- -	4.19	4.54
2010	LsVgs	AAA	15	15	1	0	86.2	416	107	66	59	5	3	3	12	47	0	56	7	3	5	5	.500	0	0- -	6.27	6.13
2011	LsVgs	AAA	8	8	0	0	45.0	189	37	23	23	5	2	0	3	23	0	43	3	0	2	2	.500	0	0- -	3.98	4.60
2011	Tor	AL	37	4	0	7	65.0	294	74	40	37	9	1	3	5	27	1	54	4	0	3	3	.500	0	0-2 4	5.53	5.12

Rafael Perez

Pitches: L Bats: L Pos: RP-71   Ht: 6'3" Wt: 195 Born: 5/15/1982 Age: 30

			HOW MUCH HE PITCHED					WHAT HE GAVE UP										THE RESULTS					
Year	Team	Lg	G	GS	CG	GF	IP	BFP	H	R	ER	HR	SH	SF	HB	TBB	IBB	SO	WP	Bk	W	L	Pct	Sh	Sv-Op Hld	ERC	ERA
2006	Cle	AL	18	0	0	5	12.1	56	10	6	6	2	1	0	0	6	1	15	4	1	0	0	-	0	0-1 1	3.37	4.38
2007	Cle	AL	44	0	0	11	60.2	236	41	15	12	5	1	1	0	15	2	62	4	0	1	2	.333	0	1-2 12	1.74	1.78
2008	Cle	AL	73	0	0	14	76.1	313	67	32	30	8	2	0	2	23	3	86	3	0	4	4	.500	0	2-7 25	3.14	3.54
2009	Cle	AL	54	0	0	12	48.0	230	66	41	39	5	4	2	2	25	6	32	1	2	4	3	.571	0	0-1 6	6.85	7.31
2010	Cle	AL	70	0	0	13	61.0	272	72	23	22	3	6	1	0	25	4	36	6	0	6	1	.857	0	0-4 13	4.68	3.25
2011	Cle	AL	71	0	0	7	63.0	257	59	27	21	2	3	2	0	19	0	33	3	1	5	2	.714	0	0-2 12	2.97	3.00
Postseason			6	0	0	1	7.0	34	10	9	6	3	0	0	0	3	0	6	0	0	1	0	1.000	0	0-0 0	9.36	7.71
6 ML YEARS			330	0	0	62	321.1	1364	315	144	130	25	17	6	4	113	16	264	21	4	20	12	.625	0	3-17 69	3.60	3.64

Salvador Perez

Bats: R Throws: R Pos: C-39   Ht: 6'3" Wt: 230 Born: 5/10/1990 Age: 22

			BATTING																		BASERUNNING				AVERAGES		
Year	Team	Lg	G	AB	H	2B	3B	HR	(Hm	Rd)	TB	R	RBI	RC	TBB	IBB	SO	HBP	SH	SF	SB	CS	SB%	GDP	Avg	OBP	Slg
2007	Royals	R	30	86	21	3	0	0	(-	-)	24	10	10	9	5	0	10	5	2	1	1	1	.50	1	.244	.320	.279
2008	Burlgtn	R+	13	40	13	0	1	0	(-	-)	15	4	10	7	5	0	5	1	2	1	0	0	-	0	.325	.404	.375
2008	Idaho	R+	12	43	17	3	1	1	(-	-)	25	7	6	9	2	0	5	0	0	1	0	1	.00	0	.395	.413	.581
2009	Burlgtn	R+	36	127	24	6	0	0	(-	-)	30	10	7	5	6	0	15	1	2	1	0	1	.00	3	.189	.230	.236
2009	Idaho	R+	59	233	72	14	3	2	(-	-)	98	35	38	37	19	0	25	1	1	5	0	1	.00	6	.309	.357	.421
2010	Wilmg	A	99	365	106	21	1	7	(-	-)	150	35	53	50	18	1	38	3	1	9	1	1	.50	13	.290	.322	.411
2011	NWArk	AA	79	286	81	14	0	9	(-	-)	122	35	43	40	16	0	30	4	2	1	0	1	.00	12	.283	.329	.427
2011	Omha	AAA	12	48	16	5	0	1	(-	-)	24	5	10	8	0	0	6	1	0	0	0	0	-	1	.333	.347	.500
2011	KC	AL	39	148	49	8	2	3	(1	2)	70	20	21	26	7	0	20	1	0	2	0	0	-	5	.331	.361	.473

Glen Perkins

Pitches: L Bats: L Pos: RP-65   Ht: 6'0" Wt: 208 Born: 3/2/1983 Age: 29

			HOW MUCH HE PITCHED					WHAT HE GAVE UP										THE RESULTS					
Year	Team	Lg	G	GS	CG	GF	IP	BFP	H	R	ER	HR	SH	SF	HB	TBB	IBB	SO	WP	Bk	W	L	Pct	Sh	Sv-Op Hld	ERC	ERA
2011	Roch*	AAA	2	1	0	0	3.0	12	4	0	0	0	0	0	0	0	0	2	0	0	0	0	-	0	0- -	3.91	0.00
2006	Min	AL	4	0	0	1	5.2	20	3	1	1	0	0	0	0	0	0	6	0	0	0	0	-	0	0-0 1	0.60	1.59
2007	Min	AL	19	0	0	3	28.2	115	23	10	10	2	1	1	2	12	0	20	2	0	0	0	-	0	0-0 3	3.32	3.14
2008	Min	AL	26	26	0	0	151.0	661	183	81	74	25	7	4	3	39	0	74	2	1	12	4	.750	0	0-0 0	5.30	4.41
2009	Min	AL	18	17	0	1	96.1	423	120	64	63	13	1	3	1	23	0	45	2	1	6	7	.462	0	0-0 0	5.14	5.89
2010	Min	AL	13	1	0	5	21.2	98	29	16	14	3	1	2	4	5	1	14	0	0	1	1	.500	0	0-0 0	6.56	5.82
2011	Min	AL	65	0	0	17	61.2	253	55	19	17	2	5	1	1	21	5	65	3	0	4	4	.500	0	2-5 17	2.81	2.48
Postseason			1	0	0	0	0.1	3	2	0	0	0	0	0	0	0	0	0	0	0	0	0	-	0	0-0 0	39.65	0.00
6 ML YEARS			145	44	0	27	365.0	1570	413	191	179	45	15	11	11	100	6	224	9	2	23	16	.590	0	2-5 21	4.62	4.41

Ryan Perry

Pitches: R **Bats:** R **Pos:** RP-36　　　　　　　　**Ht:** 6'4" **Wt:** 200 **Born:** 2/13/1987 **Age:** 25

Year	Team	Lg	G	GS	CG	GF	IP	BFP	H	R	ER	HR	SH	SF	HB	TBB	IBB	SO	WP	Bk	W	L	Pct	Sh	Sv-Op	Hld	ERC	ERA
2011	Toledo*	AAA	20	0	0	12	32.2	127	24	12	11	1	0	1	1	9	1	30	2	0	3	0	1.000	0	7- -	-	1.97	3.03
2009	Det	AL	53	0	0	12	61.2	273	56	30	26	7	3	3	1	38	5	60	6	1	0	1	.000	0	0-3	6	4.45	3.79
2010	Det	AL	60	0	0	21	62.2	261	55	26	25	6	4	3	5	23	1	45	3	0	3	5	.375	0	2-5	19	3.61	3.59
2011	Det	AL	36	0	0	6	37.0	168	39	25	22	1	1	3	2	21	3	24	3	1	2	0	1.000	0	0-1	4	4.58	5.35
	3 ML YEARS		149	0	0	39	161.1	702	150	81	73	14	8	9	8	82	9	129	12	2	5	6	.455	0	2-9	29	4.15	4.07

Vinnie Pestano

Pitches: R **Bats:** R **Pos:** RP-68　　　　peh-STAH-no　　　　**Ht:** 6'0" **Wt:** 200 **Born:** 2/20/1985 **Age:** 27

Year	Team	Lg	G	GS	CG	GF	IP	BFP	H	R	ER	HR	SH	SF	HB	TBB	IBB	SO	WP	Bk	W	L	Pct	Sh	Sv-Op	Hld	ERC	ERA
2007	MhVlly	A-	21	0	0	17	22.2	95	17	9	9	5	0	0	2	7	0	27	1	0	1	1	.500	0	6- -	-	3.38	3.57
2008	Lk Cty	A	29	0	0	26	29.0	125	25	10	5	1	2	0	2	13	0	23	2	1	1	1	.500	0	15- -	-	3.29	1.55
2008	Knstn	A+	25	0	0	20	27.0	120	23	13	12	1	2	0	2	11	1	27	2	0	1	2	.333	0	9- -	-	2.93	4.00
2009	Akron	AA	34	0	0	31	34.2	147	30	11	11	2	4	0	2	13	3	31	0	0	2	3	.400	0	24- -	-	3.03	2.86
2010	Akron	AA	14	0	0	12	13.1	54	12	6	4	1	0	1	0	2	0	18	1	0	1	1	.500	0	3- -	-	2.41	2.70
2010	Clmbs	AAA	43	0	0	30	46.1	188	35	10	8	1	0	0	1	14	0	59	1	0	1	2	.333	0	14- -	-	2.02	1.55
2010	Cle	AL	5	0	0	5	5.0	23	4	2	2	0	0	0	0	5	0	8	0	0	0	0	-	0	1-1	0	4.56	3.60
2011	Cle	AL	68	0	0	20	62.0	250	41	16	16	5	0	0	3	24	3	84	0	0	1	2	.333	0	2-6	23	2.26	2.32
	2 ML YEARS		73	0	0	25	67.0	273	45	18	18	5	0	0	3	29	3	92	0	0	1	2	.333	0	3-7	23	2.42	2.42

Bryan Petersen

Bats: L **Throws:** R **Pos:** CF-42; LF-22; PH-16; RF-10; PR-1　　　　**Ht:** 6'0" **Wt:** 205 **Born:** 4/9/1986 **Age:** 26

Year	Team	Lg	G	AB	H	2B	3B	HR	(Hm	Rd)	TB	R	RBI	RC	TBB	IBB	SO	HBP	SH	SF	SB	CS	SB%	GDP	Avg	OBP	Slg
2007	Jmstwn	A-	57	216	54	13	1	5	(-	-)	84	27	24	29	18	0	53	4	1	1	11	2	.85	3	.250	.318	.389
2008	Grnsbr	A	79	296	89	10	2	19	(-	-)	160	60	58	62	38	0	74	4	1	6	15	6	.71	5	.301	.381	.541
2008	Jupiter	A+	40	155	41	5	0	3	(-	-)	55	23	12	21	15	1	29	3	1	1	7	1	.88	1	.265	.339	.355
2008	Carlina	AA	12	37	13	2	0	1	(-	-)	18	5	10	7	5	1	6	0	0	2	1	2	.33	0	.351	.409	.486
2009	Jaxnvl	AA	121	431	128	15	7	7	(-	-)	178	64	49	68	50	3	66	4	0	9	13	12	.52	4	.297	.368	.413
2010	NewOr	AAA	91	322	82	13	2	5	(-	-)	114	47	27	40	34	5	63	5	4	3	6	4	.56	4	.255	.332	.354
2011	NewOr	AAA	67	248	87	21	0	11	(-	-)	141	47	26	58	36	4	41	1	0	1	6	5	.55	5	.351	.434	.569
2010	Fla	NL	23	24	2	0	0	0	(0	0)	2	1	2	0	1	0	6	0	0	0	0	0	-	0	.083	.120	.083
2011	Fla	NL	74	204	54	13	3	2	(2	0)	79	18	10	27	26	2	49	5	3	3	7	1	.88	4	.265	.357	.387
	2 ML YEARS		97	228	56	13	3	2	(2	0)	81	19	12	27	27	2	55	5	3	3	7	1	.88	4	.246	.335	.355

Chris Pettit

Bats: R **Throws:** R **Pos:** PR-1　　　　PET-it　　　　**Ht:** 6'0" **Wt:** 200 **Born:** 8/15/1984 **Age:** 27

Year	Team	Lg	G	AB	H	2B	3B	HR	(Hm	Rd)	TB	R	RBI	RC	TBB	IBB	SO	HBP	SH	SF	SB	CS	SB%	GDP	Avg	OBP	Slg
2006	Orem	R+	68	226	76	25	3	7	(-	-)	128	41	54	57	31	1	48	14	0	1	5	1	.83	5	.336	.445	.566
2007	CRpds	A	64	228	79	24	1	9	(-	-)	132	47	41	57	23	3	41	12	0	3	17	4	.81	4	.346	.429	.579
2007	RCuca	A+	69	265	82	20	2	9	(-	-)	133	54	54	55	36	1	48	3	1	2	13	3	.81	5	.309	.395	.502
2008	Ark	AA	61	222	55	12	2	6	(-	-)	89	27	26	30	16	0	39	4	1	1	5	2	.71	4	.248	.320	.401
2008	Angels	R	3	13	3	1	0	0	(-	-)	4	3	2	1	2	0	2	0	0	0	0	0	-	0	.231	.333	.308
2009	Salt Lk	AAA	96	371	120	30	3	8	(-	-)	180	70	59	72	31	0	62	8	1	3	18	2	.90	9	.323	.385	.485
2009	Angels	R	4	14	5	1	0	0	(-	-)	6	2	1	3	3	0	6	0	0	0	1	0	1.00	0	.357	.471	.429
2011	Salt Lk	AAA	59	209	35	8	2	3	(-	-)	56	23	33	14	23	0	51	5	3	3	3	4	.43	5	.167	.263	.268
2011	Ark	AA	65	246	48	13	1	7	(-	-)	84	40	34	29	29	0	74	7	3	4	15	2	.88	5	.195	.294	.341
2009	LAA	AL	10	7	2	0	0	0	(0	0)	2	2	0	0	0	0	1	0	0	0	0	0	-	1	.286	.286	.286
2011	LAA	AL	1	0	0	0	0	0	(0	0)	0	0	0	0	0	0	0	0	0	0	0	0	-	0	-	-	-
	2 ML YEARS		11	7	2	0	0	0	(0	0)	2	2	0	0	0	0	1	0	0	0	0	0	-	1	.286	.286	.286

Cord Phelps

Bats: B **Throws:** R **Pos:** 2B-20; PR-11; DH-8; PH-3　　　　**Ht:** 6'2" **Wt:** 200 **Born:** 1/23/1987 **Age:** 25

Year	Team	Lg	G	AB	H	2B	3B	HR	(Hm	Rd)	TB	R	RBI	RC	TBB	IBB	SO	HBP	SH	SF	SB	CS	SB%	GDP	Avg	OBP	Slg
2008	Indns	R	1	3	0	0	0	0	(-	-)	0	0	1	0	0	0	2	0	0	1	0	0	-	0	.000	.000	.000
2008	MhVlly	A-	35	141	44	10	2	2	(-	-)	64	24	21	24	15	0	22	0	0	1	4	3	.57	3	.312	.376	.454
2009	Knstn	A+	130	479	125	27	5	4	(-	-)	174	72	53	75	93	1	97	6	2	2	17	14	.55	18	.261	.386	.363
2010	Akron	AA	53	199	59	8	3	2	(-	-)	79	25	23	27	15	0	29	1	1	2	1	4	.20	10	.296	.346	.397
2010	Clmbs	AAA	66	243	77	20	4	6	(-	-)	123	41	31	47	24	1	39	4	1	1	3	2	.60	3	.317	.386	.506
2011	Clmbs	AAA	97	378	111	25	4	14	(-	-)	186	51	63	70	51	2	89	1	0	4	3	6	.33	10	.294	.376	.492
2011	Cle	AL	35	71	11	2	1	1	(1	0)	18	10	6	3	8	0	17	0	1	0	1	0	1.00	2	.155	.241	.254

Brandon Phillips

Bats: R **Throws:** R **Pos:** 2B-148; PH-1; PR-1　　　　**Ht:** 6'0" **Wt:** 203 **Born:** 6/28/1981 **Age:** 31

Year	Team	Lg	G	AB	H	2B	3B	HR	(Hm	Rd)	TB	R	RBI	RC	TBB	IBB	SO	HBP	SH	SF	SB	CS	SB%	GDP	Avg	OBP	Slg
2002	Cle	AL	11	31	8	3	1	0	(0	0)	13	5	4	5	3	0	6	1	1	0	0	0	-	0	.258	.343	.419
2003	Cle	AL	112	370	77	18	1	6	(3	3)	115	36	33	22	14	0	77	3	5	1	4	5	.44	12	.208	.242	.311
2004	Cle	AL	6	22	4	2	0	0	(0	0)	6	1	1	0	2	0	5	0	0	0	0	2	.00	1	.182	.250	.273
2005	Cle	AL	6	9	0	0	0	0	(0	0)	0	1	0	0	0	0	4	0	0	0	0	0	-	0	.000	.000	.000

Year	Team	Lg	G	AB	H	2B	3B	HR	(Hm	Rd)	TB	R	RBI	RC	TBB	IBB	SO	HBP	SH	SF	SB	CS	SB%	GDP	Avg	OBP	Slg
									BATTING												**BASERUNNING**				**AVERAGES**		
2006	Cin	NL	149	536	148	28	1	17	(9	8)	229	65	75	74	35	3	88	6	4	6	25	2	.93	19	.276	.324	.427
2007	Cin	NL	158	650	187	26	6	30	(17	13)	315	107	94	88	33	4	109	12	2	5	32	8	.80	26	.288	.331	.485
2008	Cin	NL	141	559	146	24	7	21	(13	8)	247	80	78	74	39	6	93	5	0	6	23	10	.70	13	.261	.312	.442
2009	Cin	NL	153	584	161	30	5	20	(10	10)	261	78	98	80	44	3	75	6	2	8	25	9	.74	21	.276	.329	.447
2010	Cin	NL	155	626	172	33	5	18	(10	8)	269	100	59	77	46	1	83	8	6	1	16	12	.57	14	.275	.332	.430
2011	Cin	NL	150	610	183	38	2	18	(14	4)	279	94	82	92	44	3	85	9	5	6	14	9	.61	15	.300	.353	.457
Postseason			3	12	4	1	0	1	(0	1)	8	2	1	2	0	0	1	0	0	0	0	0	-	0	.333	.333	.667
10 ML YEARS			1041	3997	1086	202	28	130	(76	54)	1734	567	524	512	260	20	625	50	25	33	139	57	.71	121	.272	.322	.434

Kyle Phillips

Bats: L Throws: R Pos: C-24; PH-14   Ht: 6'2" Wt: 210 Born: 4/3/1984 Age: 28

Year	Team	Lg	G	AB	H	2B	3B	HR	(Hm	Rd)	TB	R	RBI	RC	TBB	IBB	SO	HBP	SH	SF	SB	CS	SB%	GDP	Avg	OBP	Slg
									BATTING												**BASERUNNING**				**AVERAGES**		
2002	Twins	R	35	101	20	4	1	1	(-	-)	29	10	12	9	14	0	18	0	0	1	0	0	-	0	.198	.293	.287
2003	Elizab	R+	63	246	71	12	0	8	(-	-)	107	36	49	40	26	2	34	3	0	4	1	0	1.00	4	.289	.358	.435
2003	FtMyrs	A+	1	2	1	0	0	0	(-	-)	1	0	0	0	0	0	0	0	0	0	0	0	-	0	.500	.500	.500
2004	QuadC	A	97	347	79	16	0	11	(-	-)	128	49	44	42	38	4	69	3	0	7	1	0	1.00	11	.228	.304	.369
2005	FtMyrs	A+	83	278	64	12	1	2	(-	-)	84	20	32	29	31	2	47	2	1	3	2	0	1.00	8	.230	.309	.302
2005	NwBrit	AA	22	67	14	1	0	2	(-	-)	21	6	8	6	6	2	17	0	1	3	0	0	-	0	.209	.263	.313
2006	BrvdCt	A+	58	216	51	4	0	3	(-	-)	64	13	35	20	21	2	40	1	2	2	1	1	.50	9	.236	.304	.296
2007	Dnedin	A+	104	389	119	19	0	10	(-	-)	168	44	62	62	35	1	51	0	0	4	0	0	-	4	.306	.360	.432
2008	NHam	AA	78	268	82	16	0	8	(-	-)	122	33	34	45	27	2	41	1	4	1	0	2	.00	3	.306	.370	.455
2009	NHam	AA	12	40	7	0	0	1	(-	-)	10	1	1	2	3	0	8	0	0	0	0	0	-	0	.175	.233	.250
2009	LsVgs	AAA	76	277	83	13	0	8	(-	-)	120	37	29	46	29	2	53	4	4	2	0	0	-	7	.300	.372	.433
2010	LsVgs	AAA	19	66	17	5	0	0	(-	-)	22	9	8	7	5	0	8	0	0	0	0	0	-	2	.258	.310	.333
2010	Portlnd	AAA	55	176	57	6	2	3	(-	-)	76	19	28	28	13	0	28	0	0	3	0	0	-	1	.324	.365	.432
2011	SnAnt	AA	19	76	24	4	0	2	(-	-)	34	10	15	12	4	0	1	0	0	2	0	0	-	1	.316	.341	.447
2011	Tucsn	AAA	35	95	17	2	0	2	(-	-)	25	9	9	5	8	0	10	0	0	1	0	0	-	6	.179	.240	.263
2009	Tor	AL	5	18	5	3	0	0	(0	0)	8	1	2	1	0	0	4	0	0	0	0	0	-	1	.278	.278	.444
2011	SD	NL	36	76	13	3	0	2	(0	2)	22	9	10	4	8	1	19	1	0	0	0	0	-	2	.171	.259	.289
2 ML YEARS			41	94	18	6	0	2	(0	2)	30	10	12	5	8	1	23	1	0	0	0	0	-	3	.191	.262	.319

Zach Phillips

Pitches: L Bats: L Pos: RP-10   Ht: 6'1" Wt: 225 Born: 9/21/1986 Age: 25

Year	Team	Lg	G	GS	CG	GF	IP	BFP	H	R	ER	HR	SH	SF	HB	TBB	IBB	SO	WP	Bk	W	L	Pct	Sh	Sv-Op	Hld	ERC	ERA
					HOW MUCH HE PITCHED						**WHAT HE GAVE UP**											**THE RESULTS**					
2005	Rngrs	R	14	11	0	0	50.1	216	52	26	22	3	0	0	3	13	0	73	2	0	1	3	.250	0	0--	-	3.63	3.93
2005	Clinton	A	2	0	0	0	4.0	19	7	3	3	0	1	0	0	4	0	4	0	0	0	0	-	0	0--	-	5.92	6.75
2006	Clinton	A	28	28	0	0	142.0	648	178	106	94	5	7	4	6	66	0	126	16	3	5	12	.294	0	0--	-	5.59	5.96
2007	Clinton	A	27	27	0	0	151.2	618	139	56	49	6	3	3	5	43	0	157	8	1	11	7	.611	0	0--	-	2.97	2.91
2008	Bkrsfld	A+	28	28	1	0	144.2	661	161	102	89	10	4	4	7	73	0	117	6	1	8	9	.471	0	0--	-	5.09	5.54
2009	Bkrsfld	A+	16	3	0	3	44.0	168	19	7	6	1	1	1	0	11	0	46	4	0	2	3	.400	0	2--	-	0.82	1.23
2009	Frisco	AA	20	0	0	4	33.2	152	27	11	6	1	3	1	1	19	0	29	1	0	0	0	-	0	2--	-	3.06	1.60
2010	Frisco	AA	12	0	0	9	16.2	63	9	2	2	0	0	0	0	5	0	23	1	1	0	0	-	0	4--	-	1.16	1.08
2010	OKCity	AAA	33	1	0	9	50.1	225	50	22	18	1	7	1	1	29	2	40	2	0	3	2	.600	0	1--	-	4.14	3.22
2011	RdRck	AAA	33	0	0	14	44.2	204	50	26	22	3	4	1	1	21	2	38	3	0	1	3	.250	0	3--	-	4.73	4.43
2011	Norfolk	AAA	14	0	0	8	13.2	57	12	5	4	0	0	1	0	7	1	7	1	0	1	1	.500	0	1--	-	3.12	2.63
2011	Bal	AL	10	0	0	2	8.0	33	6	1	1	1	0	0	0	2	0	8	0	0	0	0	-	0	0-0	0	2.24	1.13

Felix Pie

Bats: L Throws: L Pos: LF-67; PR-16; PH-11; CF-6; RF-3; DH-3   pee-YAY   Ht: 6'2" Wt: 190 Born: 2/8/1985 Age: 27

Year	Team	Lg	G	AB	H	2B	3B	HR	(Hm	Rd)	TB	R	RBI	RC	TBB	IBB	SO	HBP	SH	SF	SB	CS	SB%	GDP	Avg	OBP	Slg
									BATTING												**BASERUNNING**				**AVERAGES**		
2011	Norfolk*	AAA	7	24	6	2	1	0	(-	-)	10	6	1	4	3	0	4	0	0	0	3	0	1.00	0	.250	.333	.417
2007	ChC	NL	87	177	38	9	3	2	(1	1)	59	26	20	21	14	0	43	0	2	1	8	1	.89	0	.215	.271	.333
2008	ChC	NL	43	83	20	2	1	1	(1	0)	27	9	10	9	7	0	29	2	0	1	3	0	1.00	3	.241	.312	.325
2009	Bal	AL	101	252	67	10	3	9	(6	3)	110	38	29	30	24	1	58	0	2	3	1	3	.25	6	.266	.326	.437
2010	Bal	AL	82	288	79	15	5	5	(3	2)	119	39	31	34	13	0	52	1	3	3	5	2	.71	10	.274	.305	.413
2011	Bal	AL	85	164	36	8	1	0	(0	0)	46	15	7	14	10	0	32	0	1	0	3	2	.60	0	.220	.264	.280
Postseason			2	1	0	0	0	0	(0	0)	0	0	0	0	1	0	1	0	0	0	0	0	-	0	.000	.500	.000
5 ML YEARS			398	964	240	44	13	17	(10	7)	361	127	97	108	68	1	214	3	8	8	20	8	.71	19	.249	.298	.374

Juan Pierre

Bats: L Throws: L Pos: LF-155; DH-2; PR-2; PH-1   Ht: 5'11" Wt: 175 Born: 8/14/1977 Age: 34

Year	Team	Lg	G	AB	H	2B	3B	HR	(Hm	Rd)	TB	R	RBI	RC	TBB	IBB	SO	HBP	SH	SF	SB	CS	SB%	GDP	Avg	OBP	Slg
									BATTING												**BASERUNNING**				**AVERAGES**		
2000	Col	NL	51	200	62	2	0	0	(0	0)	64	26	20	23	13	0	15	1	4	1	7	6	.54	2	.310	.353	.320
2001	Col	NL	156	617	202	26	11	2	(0	2)	256	108	55	101	41	1	29	10	14	1	46	17	.73	6	.327	.378	.415
2002	Col	NL	152	592	170	20	5	1	(0	1)	203	90	35	79	31	0	52	9	8	0	47	12	.80	7	.287	.332	.343
2003	Fla	NL	162	668	204	28	7	1	(1	0)	249	100	41	92	55	1	35	5	15	3	65	20	.76	9	.305	.361	.373
2004	Fla	NL	162	678	221	22	12	3	(1	2)	276	100	49	101	45	1	35	8	15	2	45	24	.65	8	.326	.374	.407
2005	Fla	NL	162	656	181	19	13	2	(1	1)	232	96	47	76	41	1	45	9	10	2	57	17	.77	10	.276	.326	.354
2006	ChC	NL	162	699	204	32	13	3	(1	2)	271	87	40	84	32	0	38	8	10	1	58	20	.74	6	.292	.330	.388
2007	LAD	NL	162	668	196	24	8	0	(0	0)	236	96	41	75	33	0	37	6	20	2	64	15	.81	10	.293	.331	.353
2008	LAD	NL	119	375	106	10	2	1	(0	1)	123	44	28	48	22	1	24	3	5	1	40	12	.77	3	.283	.327	.328
2009	LAD	NL	145	380	117	16	8	0	(0	0)	149	57	31	58	27	3	27	6	3	1	30	12	.71	7	.308	.365	.392

					BATTING																BASERUNNING				AVERAGES		
Year Team	Lg	G	AB	H	2B	3B	HR	(Hm Rd)	TB	R	RBI	RC	TBB	IBB	SO	HBP	SH	SF		SB	CS	SB%	GDP		Avg	OBP	Slg
2010 CWS	AL	160	651	179	18	3	1	(0 1)	206	96	47	84	45	0	47	21	15	2		68	18	.79	8		.275	.341	.316
2011 CWS	AL	158	639	178	17	4	2	(2 0)	209	80	50	80	43	0	41	7	19	3		27	17	.61	7		.279	.329	.327
Postseason		26	79	24	5	2	0	(0 0)	33	16	7	14	8	2	4	1	2	0		3	5	.38	0		.304	.375	.418
12 ML YEARS		1751	6823	2020	234	86	16	(6 10)	2474	980	484	901	428	8	425	95	144	19		554	190	.74	84		.296	.345	.363

A.J. Pierzynski

Bats: L **Throws:** R **Pos:** C-120; PH-8; DH-7   perr-ZINN-ski   **Ht:** 6'3" **Wt:** 225 **Born:** 12/30/1976 **Age:** 35

					BATTING																BASERUNNING				AVERAGES		
Year Team	Lg	G	AB	H	2B	3B	HR	(Hm Rd)	TB	R	RBI	RC	TBB	IBB	SO	HBP	SH	SF		SB	CS	SB%	GDP		Avg	OBP	Slg
2011 Charltt*	AAA	3	10	2	0	0	0	(- -)	2	2	1	0	0	0	2	1	0	0		0	0	-	0		.200	.273	.200
1998 Min	AL	7	10	3	0	0	0	(0 0)	3	1	1	2	1	0	2	1	0	1		0	0	-	0		.300	.385	.300
1999 Min	AL	9	22	6	2	0	0	(0 0)	8	3	3	3	1	0	4	1	0	0		0	0	-	0		.273	.333	.364
2000 Min	AL	33	88	27	5	1	2	(1 1)	40	12	11	14	5	0	14	2	0	1		1	0	1.00	1		.307	.354	.455
2001 Min	AL	114	381	110	33	2	7	(3 4)	168	51	55	50	16	4	57	4	1	3		1	7	.13	7		.289	.322	.441
2002 Min	AL	130	440	132	31	6	6	(2 4)	193	54	49	60	13	1	61	11	2	3		1	2	.33	14		.300	.334	.439
2003 Min	AL	137	487	152	35	3	11	(6 5)	226	63	74	80	24	12	55	15	2	5		3	1	.75	13		.312	.360	.464
2004 SF	NL	131	471	128	28	2	11	(3 8)	193	45	77	58	19	4	27	15	2	3		0	1	.00	27		.272	.319	.410
2005 CWS	AL	128	460	118	21	0	18	(12 6)	193	61	56	55	23	5	68	12	1	1		0	2	.00	13		.257	.308	.420
2006 CWS	AL	140	509	150	24	0	16	(9 7)	222	65	64	68	22	6	72	8	3	1		1	0	1.00	13		.295	.333	.436
2007 CWS	AL	136	472	124	24	0	14	(8 6)	190	54	50	49	25	5	66	8	1	3		1	1	.50	21		.263	.309	.403
2008 CWS	AL	134	534	150	31	1	13	(7 6)	222	66	60	64	19	5	71	8	3	6		1	0	1.00	14		.281	.312	.416
2009 CWS	AL	138	504	151	22	1	13	(8 5)	214	57	49	59	24	6	52	1	3	3		1	1	.50	18		.300	.331	.425
2010 CWS	AL	128	474	128	29	0	9	(7 2)	184	43	56	51	15	2	39	6	6	2		3	4	.43	17		.270	.300	.388
2011 CWS	AL	129	464	133	29	1	8	(5 3)	188	38	48	53	23	6	33	5	2	6		0	0	-	19		.287	.323	.405
Postseason		30	100	30	5	1	5	(3 2)	52	16	17	19	10	1	13	2	1	1		2	3	.40	2		.300	.372	.520
14 ML YEARS		1494	5316	1512	314	17	128	(71 57)	2244	613	653	666	230	56	621	97	26	38		13	19	.41	174		.284	.324	.422

Brett Pill

Bats: R **Throws:** R **Pos:** 1B-14; PH-2   **Ht:** 6'4" **Wt:** 211 **Born:** 9/9/1984 **Age:** 27

					BATTING																BASERUNNING				AVERAGES		
Year Team	Lg	G	AB	H	2B	3B	HR	(Hm Rd)	TB	R	RBI	RC	TBB	IBB	SO	HBP	SH	SF		SB	CS	SB%	GDP		Avg	OBP	Slg
2006 SlmKzr	A-	60	223	49	16	0	5	(- -)	80	37	35	25	22	1	39	3	0	2		3	2	.60	10		.220	.296	.359
2007 Augsta	A	137	536	144	47	1	10	(- -)	223	72	91	75	38	2	81	7	1	7		4	2	.67	17		.269	.321	.416
2008 SnJos	A+	131	458	122	32	0	9	(- -)	181	73	65	62	33	1	85	8	0	9		5	2	.71	13		.266	.321	.395
2009 Conn	AA	139	527	157	37	1	19	(- -)	253	71	109	90	37	7	72	8	0	9		6	3	.67	13		.298	.348	.480
2010 Fresno	AAA	140	520	143	34	0	16	(- -)	225	63	84	75	30	2	65	8	0	9		7	2	.78	21		.275	.319	.433
2011 Fresno	AAA	133	536	167	36	3	25	(- -)	284	82	107	96	25	1	54	4	2	9		6	6	.50	16		.312	.341	.530
2011 SF	NL	15	50	15	3	2	2	(0 2)	28	7	9	6	2	0	8	0	0	1		0	1	.00	2		.300	.321	.560

Manny Pina

Bats: R **Throws:** R **Pos:** C-4   PEEN-yah   **Ht:** 6'0" **Wt:** 230 **Born:** 6/5/1987 **Age:** 25

					BATTING																BASERUNNING				AVERAGES		
Year Team	Lg	G	AB	H	2B	3B	HR	(Hm Rd)	TB	R	RBI	RC	TBB	IBB	SO	HBP	SH	SF		SB	CS	SB%	GDP		Avg	OBP	Slg
2005 Rngrs	R	27	85	21	3	1	0	(- -)	26	13	10	11	7	1	12	8	0	1		2	0	1.00	4		.247	.356	.306
2006 Rngrs	R	14	45	11	4	0	0	(- -)	15	1	3	4	2	0	4	2	0	1		0	0	-	0		.244	.300	.333
2007 Clinton	A	86	281	64	13	0	1	(- -)	80	20	23	23	15	0	28	6	0	4		0	0	-	4		.228	.278	.285
2008 Bkrsfld	A+	61	223	59	10	1	3	(- -)	80	31	24	26	14	0	22	3	1	3		1	0	1.00	7		.265	.313	.359
2008 Frisco	AA	23	80	22	7	0	0	(- -)	29	7	9	10	5	0	12	2	1	1		1	0	1.00	4		.275	.330	.363
2009 Frisco	AA	86	321	83	17	1	8	(- -)	126	36	42	41	19	1	58	8	3	4		1	0	1.00	9		.259	.313	.393
2010 NWArk	AA	74	266	69	16	0	7	(- -)	106	39	44	36	24	0	37	2	4	6		0	0	-	9		.259	.319	.398
2010 Omha	AAA	17	55	12	2	0	2	(- -)	20	5	5	5	3	0	7	1	0	1		0	0	-	4		.218	.267	.364
2011 Omha	AAA	68	210	50	13	0	5	(- -)	78	34	25	32	34	0	37	8	6	1		0	0	-	6		.238	.364	.371
2011 NWArk	AA	3	8	2	1	0	0	(- -)	3	0	3	1	2	0	3	0	0	0		0	0	-	0		.250	.400	.375
2011 KC	AL	4	14	3	2	0	0	(0 0)	5	2	0	1	1	0	2	0	0	0		0	0	-	1		.214	.267	.357

Michael Pineda

Pitches: R **Bats:** R **Pos:** SP-28   pih-NAY-duh   **Ht:** 6'5" **Wt:** 260 **Born:** 1/18/1989 **Age:** 23

			HOW MUCH HE PITCHED					WHAT HE GAVE UP											THE RESULTS							
Year Team	Lg	G GS CG GF				IP	BFP	H	R	ER	HR	SH	SF	HB	TBB	IBB	SO	WP	Bk	W	L	Pct	Sh	Sv-Op	Hld	ERC	ERA
2008 Wisc	A	26 21 1 0				138.1	551	109	38	30	7	3	4	5	35	0	128	6	3	8	6	.571	1	0- -	-	2.28	1.95
2009 Hi Dsrt	A+	10 8 0 0				44.1	168	29	16	14	3	1	2	6	6	0	48	2	0	4	2	.667	0	0- -	-	1.74	2.84
2009 Ms	R	2 2 0 0				3.0	10	2	0	0	0	0	0	0	0	0	4	0	0	0	0	-	0	0- -	-	1.01	0.00
2010 WTenn	AA	13 13 0 0				77.0	316	67	23	19	1	1	0	4	17	1	78	2	0	8	1	.889	0	0- -	-	2.32	2.22
2010 Tacom	AAA	12 12 0 0				62.1	260	54	33	33	9	2	0	3	17	0	76	0	3	3	3	.500	0	0- -	-	3.28	4.76
2011 Sea	AL	28 28 0 0				171.0	696	133	76	71	18	4	3	5	55	1	173	9	0	9	10	.474	0	0-0	-	2.73	3.74

Joel Pineiro

Pitches: R **Bats:** R **Pos:** SP-24; RP-3   jo-ELL pinn-YAIR-oh   **Ht:** 6'0" **Wt:** 200 **Born:** 9/25/1978 **Age:** 33

			HOW MUCH HE PITCHED					WHAT HE GAVE UP											THE RESULTS							
Year Team	Lg	G GS CG GF				IP	BFP	H	R	ER	HR	SH	SF	HB	TBB	IBB	SO	WP	Bk	W	L	Pct	Sh	Sv-Op	Hld	ERC	ERA
2011 InldEm*	A+	1 1 0 0				5.2	24	6	3	0	0	1	0	0	2	0	2	0	0	0	0	-	0	0- -	-	3.58	0.00
2000 Sea	AL	8 1 0 5				19.1	94	25	13	12	3	0	2	0	13	0	10	0	0	1	0	1.000	0	0-0	0	7.44	5.59
2001 Sea	AL	17 11 0 1				75.1	289	50	24	17	2	1	2	3	21	0	56	2	0	6	2	.750	0	0-0	1	1.71	2.03
2002 Sea	AL	37 28 2 4				194.1	812	189	75	70	24	5	7	7	54	1	136	8	0	14	7	.667	1	0-0	3	3.77	3.24
2003 Sea	AL	32 32 3 0				211.2	890	192	94	89	19	3	9	6	76	3	151	5	0	16	11	.593	2	0-0	0	3.43	3.78

Year	Team	Lg	G	GS	CG	GF	IP	BFP	H	R	ER	HR	SH	SF	HB	TBB	IBB	SO	WP	Bk	W	L	Pct	Sh	Sv-Op	Hld	ERC	ERA
			HOW MUCH HE PITCHED						**WHAT HE GAVE UP**												**THE RESULTS**							
2004	Sea	AL	21	21	1	0	140.2	596	144	77	73	21	1	5	4	43	1	111	4	0	6	11	.353	0	0-0	0	4.32	4.67
2005	Sea	AL	30	30	2	0	189.0	822	224	118	118	23	5	7	6	56	4	107	7	1	7	11	.389	0	0-0	0	5.05	5.62
2006	Sea	AL	40	25	1	6	165.2	753	209	123	117	23	1	6	10	64	13	87	4	1	8	13	.381	0	1-2	4	6.05	6.36
2007	2 Tms		42	11	0	15	97.2	419	110	49	47	14	3	1	2	26	0	60	3	0	7	5	.583	0	0-0	1	4.68	4.33
2008	StL	NL	26	25	0	1	148.2	645	180	89	85	22	7	3	2	35	0	81	1	0	7	7	.500	0	1-1	0	5.05	5.15
2009	StL	NL	32	32	3	0	214.0	865	218	94	83	11	12	6	8	27	1	105	4	0	15	12	.556	2	0-0	0	3.00	3.49
2010	LAA	AL	23	23	3	0	152.1	634	155	66	65	15	2	3	1	34	6	92	4	0	10	7	.588	1	0-0	0	3.44	3.84
2011	LAA	AL	27	24	0	2	145.2	631	182	90	83	16	1	5	2	38	3	62	2	0	7	7	.500	0	0-0	0	5.16	5.13
07	Bos	AL	31	0	0	15	34.0	157	41	20	19	3	1	1	1	14	0	20	3	0	1	1	.500	0	0-0	1	5.25	5.03
07	StL	NL	11	11	0	0	63.2	262	69	29	28	11	2	0	1	12	0	40	0	0	6	4	.600	0	0-0	0	4.36	3.96
	Postseason		2	1	0	0	6.0	32	11	5	5	1	0	0	0	2	0	8	1	0	0	1	.000	0	0-0	0	9.10	7.50
12 ML YEARS			335	263	15	34	1754.1	7450	1878	912	859	193	41	56	51	487	32	1058	44	2	104	93	.528	6	2-3	9	4.19	4.41

Trevor Plouffe

Bats: R Throws: R Pos: SS-45; 2B-17; RF-11; PH-6; DH-4; LF-3; PR-3; 1B-1   PLOOF   Ht: 6'2" Wt: 200 Born: 6/15/1986 Age: 26

Year	Team	Lg	G	AB	H	2B	3B	HR	(Hm	Rd)	TB	R	RBI	RC	TBB	IBB	SO	HBP	SH	SF	SB	CS	SB%	GDP	Avg	OBP	Slg
			BATTING																		**BASERUNNING**				**AVERAGES**		
2004	Elizab	R+	60	237	67	7	2	4	(-	-)	90	29	28	32	19	1	34	3	2	3	2	1	.67	4	.283	.340	.380
2005	Beloit	A	127	466	104	18	0	13	(-	-)	161	58	60	52	50	0	78	4	5	7	8	4	.67	7	.223	.300	.345
2006	FtMyrs	A+	125	455	112	26	4	4	(-	-)	158	60	45	57	58	1	93	4	2	5	8	5	.62	10	.246	.333	.347
2007	NwBrit	AA	126	497	136	37	2	9	(-	-)	204	75	50	69	38	0	89	2	15	3	12	7	.63	11	.274	.326	.410
2008	NwBrit	AA	58	227	61	17	3	3	(-	-)	93	32	21	31	16	2	43	3	3	0	4	2	.67	4	.269	.325	.410
2008	Roch	AAA	66	250	64	17	3	6	(-	-)	105	34	39	31	14	0	47	0	5	3	1	1	.50	2	.256	.292	.420
2009	Roch	AAA	118	430	112	23	5	10	(-	-)	175	53	60	56	34	1	68	2	4	7	3	6	.33	11	.260	.313	.407
2010	Roch	AAA	102	402	98	22	4	15	(-	-)	173	53	49	53	27	0	90	6	8	2	5	5	.50	8	.244	.300	.430
2011	Roch	AAA	51	192	60	11	3	15	(-	-)	122	33	33	45	21	0	39	3	1	3	3	1	.75	2	.313	.384	.635
2010	Min	AL	22	41	6	1	0	2	(1	1)	13	7	6	2	0	0	14	0	2	1	0	0	-	0	.146	.143	.317
2011	Min	AL	81	286	68	18	1	8	(3	5)	112	47	31	31	25	0	71	4	2	3	3	3	.50	6	.238	.305	.392
2 ML YEARS			103	327	74	19	1	10	(4	6)	125	54	37	33	25	0	85	4	4	4	3	3	.50	6	.226	.286	.382

Placido Polanco

Bats: R Throws: R Pos: 3B-118; PH-5; 2B-1; DH-1   PLAH-si-doh puh-LAHN-ko   Ht: 5'10" Wt: 189 Born: 10/10/1975 Age: 36

Year	Team	Lg	G	AB	H	2B	3B	HR	(Hm	Rd)	TB	R	RBI	RC	TBB	IBB	SO	HBP	SH	SF	SB	CS	SB%	GDP	Avg	OBP	Slg
			BATTING																		**BASERUNNING**				**AVERAGES**		
2011	LV*	AAA	2	6	0	0	0	0	(-	-)	0	0	0	0	1	0	1	0	0	0	0	0	-	0	.000	.143	.000
1998	StL	NL	45	114	29	3	2	1	(1	0)	39	10	11	12	5	0	9	1	2	0	2	0	1.00	1	.254	.292	.342
1999	StL	NL	88	220	61	9	3	1	(0	1)	79	24	19	23	15	1	24	0	3	2	1	3	.25	7	.277	.321	.359
2000	StL	NL	118	323	102	12	3	5	(2	3)	135	50	39	44	16	0	26	1	7	3	4	4	.50	8	.316	.347	.418
2001	StL	NL	144	564	173	26	4	3	(1	2)	216	87	38	70	25	0	43	6	14	1	12	3	.80	22	.307	.342	.383
2002	2 Tms	NL	147	548	158	32	2	9	(8	1)	221	75	49	64	26	1	41	8	13	0	5	3	.63	15	.288	.330	.403
2003	Phi	NL	122	492	142	30	3	14	(7	7)	220	87	63	74	42	1	38	8	8	4	14	2	.88	16	.289	.352	.447
2004	Phi	NL	126	503	150	21	0	17	(10	7)	222	74	55	71	27	0	39	12	7	6	7	4	.64	13	.298	.345	.441
2005	2 Tms	NL	129	501	166	27	2	9	(6	3)	224	84	56	56	33	0	25	11	2	4	4	3	.57	12	.331	.383	.447
2006	Det	AL	110	461	136	18	1	4	(2	2)	168	58	52	65	17	0	27	7	8	2	1	2	.33	18	.295	.329	.364
2007	Det	AL	142	587	200	36	3	9	(7	2)	269	105	67	100	37	3	30	11	2	4	7	3	.70	9	.341	.388	.458
2008	Det	AL	141	580	178	34	3	8	(2	6)	242	90	58	58	35	2	43	6	4	4	7	1	.88	14	.307	.350	.417
2009	Det	AL	153	618	176	31	4	10	(5	5)	245	82	72	84	36	2	46	9	7	5	7	2	.78	15	.285	.331	.396
2010	Phi	NL	132	554	165	27	2	6	(4	2)	214	76	52	68	32	1	47	7	1	8	5	0	1.00	14	.298	.339	.386
2011	Phi	NL	122	469	130	14	0	5	(4	1)	159	46	50	62	42	0	44	3	1	9	3	0	1.00	15	.277	.335	.339
02	StL	NL	94	342	97	19	1	5	(5	0)	133	47	27	38	12	1	27	4	9	0	3	1	.75	12	.284	.316	.389
02	Phi	NL	53	206	61	13	1	4	(3	1)	88	28	22	26	14	0	14	4	4	0	2	2	.50	3	.296	.353	.427
05	Phi	NL	43	158	50	7	0	3	(2	1)	66	26	20	26	12	0	9	3	0	0	0	0	-	3	.316	.376	.418
05	Det	AL	86	343	116	20	2	6	(4	2)	158	58	36	60	21	0	16	8	2	4	4	3	.57	9	.338	.386	.461
	Postseason		33	110	30	4	0	0	(0	0)	34	11	13	13	11	2	6	2	3	2	3	1	.75	5	.273	.344	.309
14 ML YEARS			1719	6534	1966	320	32	101	(59	42)	2653	948	681	898	388	11	482	90	79	51	79	30	.72	179	.301	.346	.406

Drew Pomeranz

Pitches: L Bats: R Pos: SP-4   Ht: 6'5" Wt: 230 Born: 11/22/1988 Age: 23

Year	Team	Lg	G	GS	CG	GF	IP	BFP	H	R	ER	HR	SH	SF	HB	TBB	IBB	SO	WP	Bk	W	L	Pct	Sh	Sv-Op	Hld	ERC	ERA
			HOW MUCH HE PITCHED						**WHAT HE GAVE UP**												**THE RESULTS**							
2011	Knstn	A+	15	15	0	0	77.0	313	56	22	16	2	2	1	1	32	0	95	6	0	3	2	.600	0	0--	-	2.30	1.87
2011	Akron	AA	3	3	0	0	14.0	57	10	4	4	1	0	1	0	6	0	17	0	0	0	1	.000	0	0--	-	2.50	2.57
2011	Tulsa	AA	2	2	0	0	10.0	32	2	0	0	0	0	0	0	0	0	7	0	0	1	0	1.000	0	0--	-	0.09	0.00
2011	Col	NL	4	4	0	0	18.1	77	19	11	11	0	1	0	1	5	0	13	1	0	2	1	.667	0	0-0	0	3.36	5.40

Rick Porcello

Pitches: R Bats: R Pos: SP-31   pore-SELL-oh   Ht: 6'5" Wt: 200 Born: 12/27/1988 Age: 23

Year	Team	Lg	G	GS	CG	GF	IP	BFP	H	R	ER	HR	SH	SF	HB	TBB	IBB	SO	WP	Bk	W	L	Pct	Sh	Sv-Op	Hld	ERC	ERA
			HOW MUCH HE PITCHED						**WHAT HE GAVE UP**												**THE RESULTS**							
2009	Det	AL	31	31	0	0	170.2	720	176	81	75	23	4	2	3	52	0	89	6	1	14	9	.609	0	0-0	0	4.24	3.96
2010	Det	AL	27	27	0	0	162.2	700	188	96	89	18	1	2	7	38	2	84	11	3	10	12	.455	0	0-0	0	4.56	4.92
2011	Det	AL	31	31	0	0	182.0	784	210	103	96	18	5	5	8	46	1	104	12	0	14	9	.609	0	0-0	0	4.57	4.75
3 ML YEARS			89	89	0	0	515.1	2204	574	280	260	59	10	9	18	136	3	277	29	4	38	30	.559	0	0-0	0	4.46	4.54

Jorge Posada

Bats: B **Throws:** R **Pos:** DH-90; PH-18; 1B-14; C-1; 2B-1; PR-1 **Ht:** 6'2" **Wt:** 215 **Born:** 8/17/1971 **Age:** 40

Year	Team	Lg	G	AB	H	2B	3B	HR	(Hm Rd)	TB	R	RBI	RC	TBB	IBB	SO	HBP	SH	SF	SB	CS	SB%	GDP	Avg	OBP	Slg
1995	NYY	AL	1	1	0	0	0	0	(0 0)	0	0	0	0	0	0	0	0	0	0	0	0	-	0	-	-	-
1996	NYY	AL	8	14	1	0	0	0	(0 0)	1	1	0	0	1	0	6	0	0	0	0	0	-	1	.071	.133	.071
1997	NYY	AL	60	188	47	12	0	6	(2 4)	77	29	25	29	30	2	33	3	1	2	1	2	.33	2	.250	.359	.410
1998	NYY	AL	111	358	96	23	0	17	(6 11)	170	56	63	56	47	7	92	0	0	4	0	1	.00	14	.268	.350	.475
1999	NYY	AL	112	379	93	19	2	12	(4 8)	152	50	57	52	53	2	91	3	0	2	1	0	1.00	9	.245	.341	.401
2000	NYY	AL	151	505	145	35	1	28	(18 10)	266	92	86	110	107	10	151	8	0	4	2	2	.50	11	.287	.417	.527
2001	NYY	AL	138	484	134	28	1	22	(14 8)	230	59	95	80	62	10	132	6	0	5	2	6	.25	10	.277	.363	.475
2002	NYY	AL	143	511	137	40	1	20	(12 8)	239	79	99	92	81	9	143	3	0	3	1	0	1.00	23	.268	.370	.468
2003	NYY	AL	142	481	135	24	0	30	(15 15)	249	83	101	98	93	6	110	10	0	4	2	4	.33	13	.281	.405	.518
2004	NYY	AL	137	449	122	31	0	21	(11 10)	216	72	81	78	88	5	92	9	0	1	1	3	.25	24	.272	.400	.481
2005	NYY	AL	142	474	124	23	0	19	(11 8)	204	67	71	71	66	5	94	2	0	4	1	0	1.00	8	.262	.352	.430
2006	NYY	AL	143	465	129	27	2	23	(11 12)	229	65	93	89	64	1	97	11	0	5	3	0	1.00	10	.277	.374	.492
2007	NYY	AL	144	506	171	42	1	20	(11 9)	275	91	90	99	74	7	98	6	0	3	2	0	1.00	18	.338	.426	.543
2008	NYY	AL	51	168	45	13	1	3	(1 2)	69	18	22	23	24	3	38	2	0	1	0	0	-	7	.268	.364	.411
2009	NYY	AL	111	383	109	25	0	22	(14 8)	200	55	81	73	48	4	101	2	0	5	1	0	1.00	13	.285	.363	.522
2010	NYY	AL	120	383	95	23	1	18	(11 7)	174	49	57	57	59	3	99	7	0	2	3	1	.75	6	.248	.357	.454
2011	NYY	AL	115	344	81	14	0	14	(11 3)	137	34	44	36	39	4	76	2	0	2	0	2	.00	17	.235	.315	.398
	Postseason		120	402	97	23	0	11	(4 7)	153	49	42	45	66	9	103	2	0	3	3	3	.50	15	.241	.349	.381
17 ML YEARS			1829	6092	1664	379	10	275	(152 123)	2888	900	1065	1043	936	78	1453	74	1	47	20	21	.49	186	.273	.374	.474

Buster Posey

Bats: R **Throws:** R **Pos:** C-41; 1B-2; PH-2 **Ht:** 6'1" **Wt:** 219 **Born:** 3/27/1987 **Age:** 25

Year	Team	Lg	G	AB	H	2B	3B	HR	(Hm Rd)	TB	R	RBI	RC	TBB	IBB	SO	HBP	SH	SF	SB	CS	SB%	GDP	Avg	OBP	Slg
2009	SF	NL	7	17	2	0	0	0	(0 0)	2	1	0	0	0	0	4	0	0	0	0	0	-	0	.118	.118	.118
2010	SF	NL	108	406	124	23	2	18	(6 12)	205	58	67	70	30	5	55	4	0	3	0	2	.00	12	.305	.357	.505
2011	SF	NL	45	162	46	5	0	4	(1 3)	63	17	21	26	18	3	30	4	0	1	3	0	1.00	4	.284	.368	.389
	Postseason		15	59	17	3	0	1	(0 1)	23	6	5	6	6	1	18	0	0	0	1	0	1.00	1	.288	.354	.390
3 ML YEARS			160	585	172	28	2	22	(7 15)	270	76	88	96	48	8	89	8	0	4	3	2	.60	16	.294	.353	.462

Landon Powell

Bats: B **Throws:** R **Pos:** C-33; PH-2; 1B-1 **Ht:** 6'3" **Wt:** 265 **Born:** 3/19/1982 **Age:** 30

Year	Team	Lg	G	AB	H	2B	3B	HR	(Hm Rd)	TB	R	RBI	RC	TBB	IBB	SO	HBP	SH	SF	SB	CS	SB%	GDP	Avg	OBP	Slg
2011	Scrmto*	AAA	12	46	13	0	0	1	(- -)	16	6	5	6	7	0	9	0	0	0	0	0	-	1	.283	.377	.348
2009	Oak	AL	46	140	32	7	0	7	(4 3)	60	19	30	22	14	0	36	0	0	1	0	0	-	3	.229	.297	.429
2010	Oak	AL	41	112	24	4	0	2	(0 2)	34	13	11	12	15	0	29	0	1	1	1	0	1.00	2	.214	.305	.304
2011	Oak	AL	36	111	19	3	0	1	(1 0)	25	10	4	2	11	0	32	0	0	0	0	0	-	4	.171	.246	.225
3 ML YEARS			123	363	75	14	0	10	(5 5)	119	42	45	36	40	0	97	0	1	2	1	0	1.00	9	.207	.284	.328

Martin Prado

Bats: R **Throws:** R **Pos:** LF-100; 3B-42; 1B-2; PH-1 mar-TEEN PRAH-doe **Ht:** 6'1" **Wt:** 190 **Born:** 10/27/1983 **Age:** 28

Year	Team	Lg	G	AB	H	2B	3B	HR	(Hm Rd)	TB	R	RBI	RC	TBB	IBB	SO	HBP	SH	SF	SB	CS	SB%	GDP	Avg	OBP	Slg
2011	Gwnntt*	AAA	6	17	3	0	0	0	(- -)	3	2	1	1	3	0	5	0	0	0	0	0	-	0	.176	.300	.176
2011	Missi*	AA	2	9	2	0	0	0	(- -)	2	2	2	0	1	0	1	0	0	0	0	0	-	0	.222	.300	.222
2006	Atl	NL	24	42	11	1	1	1	(1 0)	17	3	9	9	5	0	7	0	2	0	0	0	-	2	.262	.340	.405
2007	Atl	NL	28	59	17	3	0	0	(0 0)	20	5	2	6	3	0	6	0	0	0	0	0	-	0	.288	.323	.339
2008	Atl	NL	78	228	73	18	4	2	(1 1)	105	36	33	39	21	0	29	1	2	2	3	1	.75	3	.320	.377	.461
2009	Atl	NL	128	450	138	38	0	11	(4 7)	209	64	49	57	36	1	59	2	11	4	1	3	.25	17	.307	.358	.464
2010	Atl	NL	140	599	184	40	3	15	(4 11)	275	100	66	86	40	2	86	3	3	6	5	3	.63	13	.307	.350	.459
2011	Atl	NL	129	551	143	26	2	13	(9 4)	212	66	57	57	34	1	52	1	1	3	4	8	.33	16	.260	.302	.385
6 ML YEARS			527	1929	566	126	10	42	(19 23)	838	274	216	254	139	4	239	7	19	15	13	15	.46	51	.293	.341	.434

Alex Presley

Bats: L **Throws:** L **Pos:** LF-48; CF-5; PH-1 **Ht:** 5'9" **Wt:** 188 **Born:** 7/25/1985 **Age:** 26

Year	Team	Lg	G	AB	H	2B	3B	HR	(Hm Rd)	TB	R	RBI	RC	TBB	IBB	SO	HBP	SH	SF	SB	CS	SB%	GDP	Avg	OBP	Slg
2006	Wmspt	A-	61	223	58	7	8	3	(- -)	90	26	23	28	17	2	55	1	1	2	3	3	.50	1	.260	.313	.404
2007	Hkry	A	121	495	145	22	8	11	(- -)	216	79	63	77	45	2	108	0	7	6	18	10	.64	2	.293	.348	.436
2008	Lynbrg	A+	82	287	74	15	1	6	(- -)	109	39	35	38	29	0	50	1	5	3	13	6	.68	1	.258	.325	.380
2009	Lynbrg	A+	115	417	107	17	11	4	(- -)	158	51	37	49	30	0	87	0	7	2	9	5	.64	1	.257	.305	.379
2010	Altna	AA	67	246	86	13	7	6	(- -)	131	42	47	51	19	2	33	2	1	1	5	1	.83	6	.350	.399	.533
2010	Indy	AAA	69	272	80	15	6	6	(- -)	125	44	38	43	22	1	42	1	1	0	8	7	.53	4	.294	.349	.460
2011	Indy	AAA	87	342	114	18	5	8	(- -)	166	58	41	65	28	0	54	4	0	2	22	8	.73	4	.333	.388	.485
2011	Bradtn	A+	2	6	1	0	0	0	(- -)	1	2	0	0	1	0	0	0	0	0	0	0	-	0	.167	.286	.167
2010	Pit	NL	19	23	6	1	0	0	(0 0)	7	2	0	1	1	0	8	0	1	0	1	1	.50	0	.261	.292	.304
2011	Pit	NL	52	215	64	12	6	4	(1 3)	100	27	20	35	13	1	40	1	1	1	9	3	.75	1	.298	.339	.465
2 ML YEARS			71	238	70	13	6	4	(1 3)	107	29	20	36	14	1	48	1	2	1	10	4	.71	1	.294	.335	.450

David Price

Pitches: L Bats: L Pos: SP-34   Ht: 6'6" Wt: 225 Born: 8/26/1985 Age: 26

			HOW MUCH HE PITCHED						WHAT HE GAVE UP											THE RESULTS						
Year	Team	Lg	G	GS	CG	GF	IP	BFP	H	R	ER	HR	SH	SF	HB	TBB	IBB	SO	WP	Bk	W	L	Pct	Sh	Sv-Op	Hld	ERC	ERA
2008	TB	AL	5	1	0	0	14.0	57	9	4	3	1	0	1	1	4	0	12	0	0	0	0		0	0-0	1	1.86	1.93
2009	TB	AL	23	23	0	0	128.1	557	119	72	63	17	3	2	4	54	0	102	2	0	10	7	.588	0	0-0	0	4.05	4.42
2010	TB	AL	32	31	2	0	208.2	861	170	71	63	15	4	3	5	79	1	188	5	3	19	6	.760	1	0-0	0	2.91	2.72
2011	TB	AL	34	34	0	0	224.1	918	192	93	87	22	4	7	9	63	5	218	2	0	12	13	.480	0	0-0	0	2.97	3.49
	Postseason		7	2	0	5	18.1	79	19	10	8	3	0	0	0	4	0	22	0	0	1	2	.333	0	1-1	0	3.84	3.93
	4 ML YEARS		94	89	2	0	575.1	2393	490	240	216	55	11	13	19	200	6	520	9	3	41	26	.612	1	0-0	1	3.15	3.38

Jason Pridie

Bats: L Throws: R Pos: CF-43; PH-29; RF-21; LF-13; PR-6   PRY-dee   Ht: 6'1" Wt: 205 Born: 10/9/1983 Age: 28

						BATTING															BASERUNNING				AVERAGES		
Year	Team	Lg	G	AB	H	2B	3B	HR	(Hm	Rd)	TB	R	RBI	RC	TBB	IBB	SO	HBP	SH	SF	SB	CS	SB%	GDP	Avg	OBP	Slg
2011	Buffalo*	AAA	14	59	11	1	0	3	(-	-)	21	8	6	4	3	0	12	0	0	0	1	0	1.00	1	.186	.226	.356
2008	Min	AL	10	4	0	0	0	0	(0	0)	0	3	0	0	1	0	1	0	1	0	0	0	-	0	.000	.200	.000
2009	Min	AL	1	0	0	0	0	0	(0	0)	0	0	0	0	0	0	0	0	0	0	0	0	-	0	-	-	-
2011	NYM	NL	101	208	48	11	3	4	(3	1)	77	28	20	22	24	2	64	0	3	1	7	1	.88	2	.231	.309	.370
	3 ML YEARS		112	212	48	11	3	4	(3	1)	77	31	20	22	25	2	65	0	4	1	7	1	.88	2	.226	.307	.363

Scott Proctor

Pitches: R Bats: R Pos: RP-39   Ht: 6'1" Wt: 195 Born: 1/2/1977 Age: 35

						HOW MUCH HE PITCHED						WHAT HE GAVE UP											THE RESULTS						
Year	Team	Lg	G	GS	CG	GF	IP	BFP	H	R	ER	HR	SH	SF	HB	TBB	IBB	SO	WP	Bk	W	L	Pct	Sh	Sv-Op	Hld	ERC	ERA
2011	Gwnntt*	AAA	14	0	0	5	17.0	67	10	3	2	1	0	1	0	5	0	24	1	0	1	0	1.000	0	3- -	-	1.46	1.06
2011	S-WB*	AAA	6	0	0	0	7.0	31	8	2	2	0	0	0	0	2	0	8	0	0	0	0		0	0- -	-	3.61	2.57
2004	NYY	AL	26	0	0	12	25.0	118	29	18	15	5	0	2	0	14	0	21	1	1	2	1	.667	0	0-0	2	6.32	5.40
2005	NYY	AL	29	1	0	11	44.2	199	46	32	30	10	0	1	2	17	4	36	4	1	1	0	1.000	0	0-0	0	4.98	6.04
2006	NYY	AL	83	0	0	12	102.1	426	89	41	40	12	2	6	2	33	6	89	2	0	6	4	.600	0	1-8	26	3.15	3.52
2007	2 Tms		83	0	0	14	86.1	382	78	41	35	12	3	7	6	44	4	64	5	1	5	5	.500	0	0-6	18	4.41	3.65
2008	LAD	NL	41	0	0	11	38.2	184	41	30	26	7	1	2	0	24	1	46	6	0	2	0	1.000	0	0-1	2	5.67	6.05
2010	Atl	NL	6	0	0	2	5.2	24	4	4	4	1	0	0	0	4	1	6	0	0	0	0		0	0-0	0	3.99	6.35
2011	2 Tms		39	0	0	14	40.1	201	50	34	32	11	7	2	1	31	5	29	4	0	2	6	.250	0	0-2	4	8.35	7.14
07	NYY	AL	52	0	0	10	54.1	245	53	27	23	8	1	6	3	29	3	37	3	0	2	5	.286	0	0-4	11	4.90	3.81
07	LAD	NL	31	0	0	4	32.0	137	25	14	12	4	2	1	3	15	1	27	2	1	3	0	1.000	0	0-2	7	3.61	3.38
11	Atl	NL	31	0	0	11	29.1	139	31	21	21	5	6	2	1	19	4	18	2	0	2	3	.400	0	0-2	4	5.72	6.44
11	NYY	AL	8	0	0	3	11.0	62	19	13	11	6	1	0	0	12	1	11	2	0	0	3	.000	0	0-0	0	16.64	9.00
	Postseason		5	0	0	2	6.0	26	8	1	1	0	0	0	0	1	0	2	1	0	0	0		0	0-0	1	4.37	1.50
	7 ML YEARS		307	1	0	76	343.0	1534	337	200	182	58	13	20	11	167	21	291	22	3	18	16	.529	0	1-17	52	4.78	4.78

Albert Pujols

Bats: R Throws: R Pos: 1B-146; 3B-7; PH-2   Ht: 6'3" Wt: 230 Born: 1/16/1980 Age: 32

						BATTING															BASERUNNING				AVERAGES		
Year	Team	Lg	G	AB	H	2B	3B	HR	(Hm	Rd)	TB	R	RBI	RC	TBB	IBB	SO	HBP	SH	SF	SB	CS	SB%	GDP	Avg	OBP	Slg
2001	StL	NL	161	590	194	47	4	37	(18	19)	360	112	130	132	69	6	93	9	1	7	1	3	.25	21	.329	.403	.610
2002	StL	NL	157	590	185	40	2	34	(14	20)	331	118	127	121	72	13	69	9	0	4	2	4	.33	20	.314	.394	.561
2003	StL	NL	157	591	212	51	1	43	(21	22)	394	137	124	160	79	12	65	10	0	5	5	1	.83	13	.359	.439	.667
2004	StL	NL	154	592	196	51	2	46	(18	28)	389	133	123	143	84	12	52	7	0	9	5	5	.50	21	.331	.415	.657
2005	StL	NL	161	591	195	38	2	41	(23	18)	360	129	117	139	97	27	65	9	0	3	16	2	.89	19	.330	.430	.609
2006	StL	NL	143	535	177	33	1	49	(24	25)	359	119	137	146	92	28	50	4	0	3	7	2	.78	20	.331	.431	.671
2007	StL	NL	158	565	185	38	1	32	(12	20)	321	99	103	118	99	22	58	7	0	8	2	6	.25	27	.327	.429	.568
2008	StL	NL	148	524	187	44	0	37	(19	18)	342	100	116	130	104	34	54	5	0	7	7	3	.70	16	.357	.462	.653
2009	StL	NL	160	568	186	45	1	47	(22	25)	374	124	135	145	115	44	64	9	0	8	16	4	.80	23	.327	.443	.658
2010	StL	NL	159	587	183	39	1	42	(17	25)	350	115	118	131	103	38	76	4	0	6	14	4	.78	23	.312	.414	.596
2011	StL	NL	147	579	173	29	0	37	(16	21)	313	105	99	100	61	15	58	4	0	7	9	1	.90	29	.299	.366	.541
	Postseason		56	199	64	10	1	13	(7	6)	115	39	36	44	36	12	28	3	0	1	0	1	.00	5	.322	.431	.578
	11 ML YEARS		1705	6312	2073	455	15	445	(204	241)	3893	1291	1329	1465	975	251	704	77	1	68	84	35	.71	232	.328	.420	.617

Nick Punto

Bats: B Throws: R Pos: 2B-45; PH-15; SS-8; 3B-7; PR-1   POON-toh   Ht: 5'9" Wt: 190 Born: 11/8/1977 Age: 34

						BATTING															BASERUNNING				AVERAGES		
Year	Team	Lg	G	AB	H	2B	3B	HR	(Hm	Rd)	TB	R	RBI	RC	TBB	IBB	SO	HBP	SH	SF	SB	CS	SB%	GDP	Avg	OBP	Slg
2011	Sprgfld*	AA	7	24	8	1	0	0	(-	-)	9	3	2	3	2	0	3	0	0	0	1	0	1.00	0	.333	.385	.375
2011	Memp*	AAA	5	15	3	0	0	0	(-	-)	3	2	0	1	3	0	1	0	0	0	0	0	-	0	.200	.333	.200
2001	Phi	NL	4	5	2	0	0	0	(0	0)	2	0	1	0	1	0	0	0	0	0	0	0	-	0	.400	.400	.400
2002	Phi	NL	9	6	1	0	0	0	(0	0)	1	0	0	0	0	0	3	0	1	0	0	0	-	0	.167	.167	.167
2003	Phi	NL	64	92	20	2	0	1	(0	1)	25	14	4	7	7	1	22	0	1	0	2	1	.67	0	.217	.273	.272
2004	Min	AL	38	91	23	0	0	2	(2	0)	29	17	12	15	12	0	19	0	0	0	6	0	1.00	0	.253	.340	.319
2005	Min	AL	112	394	94	18	4	4	(3	1)	132	45	26	35	36	0	86	0	7	2	13	8	.62	9	.239	.301	.335
2006	Min	AL	135	459	133	21	7	1	(0	1)	171	73	45	59	47	0	68	1	10	7	17	5	.77	8	.290	.352	.373
2007	Min	AL	150	472	99	18	4	1	(0	1)	128	53	25	37	55	1	90	0	6	3	16	6	.73	7	.210	.291	.271
2008	Min	AL	99	338	96	19	4	2	(1	1)	129	43	28	42	32	1	57	0	5	2	15	6	.71	10	.284	.344	.382
2009	Min	AL	125	359	82	15	1	1	(0	1)	102	56	38	46	61	1	70	1	13	6	16	3	.84	5	.228	.337	.284
2010	Min	AL	88	252	60	11	1	1	(0	1)	76	24	20	25	28	2	50	1	4	3	3	1	.75	3	.238	.313	.302
2011	StL	NL	63	133	37	8	4	1	(0	1)	56	20	25	25	23	3	21	0	6	2	1	1	.50	3	.278	.388	.421
	Postseason		6	21	6	1	0	0	(0	0)	7	0	1	1	3	0	2	0	1	0	0	0	-	0	.286	.375	.333
	11 ML YEARS		887	2601	647	112	25	14	(6	8)	851	346	218	292	303	9	486	3	52	25	92	32	.74	49	.249	.325	.327

David Purcey

Pitches: L **Bats:** L **Pos:** RP-33 **Ht:** 6'4" **Wt:** 242 **Born:** 4/22/1982 **Age:** 30

			HOW MUCH HE PITCHED						WHAT HE GAVE UP												THE RESULTS							
Year	Team	Lg	G	GS	CG	GF	IP	BFP	H	R	ER	HR	SH	SF	HB	TBB	IBB	SO	WP	Bk	W	L	Pct	Sh	Sv-Op	Hld	ERC	ERA
2011	Toledo*	AAA	8	0	0	0	11.1	48	10	3	2	0	0	0	1	5	0	7	0	0	0	0	-	0	0--	-	3.29	1.59
2008	Tor	AL	12	12	0	0	65.0	289	67	41	40	9	2	3	4	29	0	58	3	0	3	6	.333	0	0-0	0	4.96	5.54
2009	Tor	AL	9	9	0	0	48.0	223	54	35	33	6	3	1	1	30	1	39	3	0	1	3	.250	0	0-0	0	6.00	6.19
2010	Tor	AL	33	0	0	18	34.0	143	26	16	14	3	2	2	0	15	1	32	3	0	1	1	.500	0	1-1	3	2.80	3.71
2011	3 Tms	AL	33	0	0	9	33.2	157	33	21	21	2	2	0	0	27	2	22	0	0	1	2	.333	0	0-0	3	5.14	5.61
11	Tor	AL	5	0	0	0	2.1	14	3	3	3	0	0	0	0	4	0	3	0	0	0	0	-	0	0-0	0	10.22	11.57
11	Oak	AL	9	0	0	3	12.2	50	9	3	3	1	0	0	0	3	0	7	0	0	0	0	-	0	0-0	1	1.86	2.13
11	Det	AL	19	0	0	6	18.2	93	21	15	15	1	2	0	0	20	2	12	0	0	1	2	.333	0	0-0	2	7.09	7.23
	4 ML YEARS		87	21	1	27	180.2	812	180	113	108	20	9	6	5	101	4	151	9	0	6	12	.333	0	1-1	6	4.83	5.38

Zach Putnam

Pitches: R **Bats:** R **Pos:** RP-8 **Ht:** 6'2" **Wt:** 225 **Born:** 7/3/1987 **Age:** 24

			HOW MUCH HE PITCHED						WHAT HE GAVE UP												THE RESULTS							
Year	Team	Lg	G	GS	CG	GF	IP	BFP	H	R	ER	HR	SH	SF	HB	TBB	IBB	SO	WP	Bk	W	L	Pct	Sh	Sv-Op	Hld	ERC	ERA
2008	MhVlly	A-	3	3	0	0	9.2	40	7	5	4	0	0	1	0	5	0	8	0	0	0	1	.000	0	0--	-	2.41	3.72
2009	Knstn	A+	5	5	0	0	24.0	96	22	12	11	1	1	1	0	5	0	23	0	0	2	0	1.000	0	0--	-	2.58	4.13
2009	Akron	AA	33	0	0	9	56.2	245	59	29	26	2	0	0	1	18	3	57	1	0	4	2	.667	0	2--	-	3.47	4.13
2010	Akron	AA	20	7	0	0	51.1	217	58	25	22	2	3	2	0	9	0	41	1	0	4	1	.800	0	3--	-	3.48	3.86
2010	Clmbs	AAA	17	0	0	5	24.1	99	20	10	9	2	1	1	0	7	0	24	1	0	0	1	.000	0	0--	-	2.58	3.33
2011	Clmbs	AAA	44	0	0	16	69.0	292	61	30	28	6	4	2	1	23	1	68	6	0	6	3	.667	0	9--	-	3.07	3.65
2011	Cle	AL	8	0	0	3	7.1	34	10	5	5	1	0	0	2	0	0	9	1	0	1	1	.500	0	0-1	0	5.82	6.14

J.J. Putz

Pitches: R **Bats:** R **Pos:** RP-60 PUTS **Ht:** 6'5" **Wt:** 250 **Born:** 2/22/1977 **Age:** 35

			HOW MUCH HE PITCHED						WHAT HE GAVE UP												THE RESULTS							
Year	Team	Lg	G	GS	CG	GF	IP	BFP	H	R	ER	HR	SH	SF	HB	TBB	IBB	SO	WP	Bk	W	L	Pct	Sh	Sv-Op	Hld	ERC	ERA
2011	DBcks*	R	2	2	0	0	2.0	7	1	0	0	0	0	0	0	0	0	0	0	0	0	0	-	0	0--	-	0.54	0.00
2011	Reno*	AAA	2	0	0	0	2.0	7	1	0	0	0	0	0	0	0	0	3	0	0	0	0	-	0	0--	-	0.54	0.00
2003	Sea	AL	3	0	0	0	3.2	18	4	2	2	0	0	0	0	3	0	3	0	0	0	0	-	0	0-0	0	5.31	4.91
2004	Sea	AL	54	0	0	30	63.0	275	66	35	33	10	3	2	5	24	4	47	1	0	0	3	.000	0	9-13	5	4.97	4.71
2005	Sea	AL	64	0	0	20	60.0	259	58	27	24	8	3	3	2	23	2	45	2	0	6	5	.545	0	1-4	21	4.11	3.60
2006	Sea	AL	72	0	0	57	78.1	303	59	20	20	4	1	2	2	13	1	104	1	0	4	1	.800	0	36-43	5	1.78	2.30
2007	Sea	AL	68	0	0	65	71.2	260	37	11	11	6	2	1	2	13	0	82	3	0	6	1	.857	0	40-42	0	1.21	1.38
2008	Sea	AL	47	0	0	35	46.1	211	46	20	20	4	0	1	2	28	2	56	2	0	6	5	.545	0	15-23	0	4.82	3.88
2009	NYM	NL	29	0	0	6	29.1	135	29	18	17	1	1	2	0	19	4	19	1	0	1	4	.200	0	2-4	10	4.16	5.22
2010	CWS	AL	60	0	0	16	54.0	219	41	18	17	4	1	1	1	15	2	65	4	0	7	5	.583	0	3-7	14	2.19	2.83
2011	Ari	NL	60	0	0	52	58.0	229	41	15	14	4	2	3	2	12	0	61	2	0	2	2	.500	0	45-49	0	1.80	2.17
	9 ML YEARS		457	0	0	281	464.1	1909	381	166	158	41	13	15	16	150	15	482	16	0	32	26	.552	0	151-185	53	2.83	3.06

Chad Qualls

Pitches: R **Bats:** R **Pos:** RP-77 **Ht:** 6'5" **Wt:** 220 **Born:** 8/17/1978 **Age:** 33

			HOW MUCH HE PITCHED						WHAT HE GAVE UP												THE RESULTS							
Year	Team	Lg	G	GS	CG	GF	IP	BFP	H	R	ER	HR	SH	SF	HB	TBB	IBB	SO	WP	Bk	W	L	Pct	Sh	Sv-Op	Hld	ERC	ERA
2004	Hou	NL	25	0	0	4	33.0	141	34	13	13	3	0	1	4	8	1	24	0	0	4	0	1.000	0	1-2	9	4.02	3.55
2005	Hou	NL	77	0	0	19	79.2	329	73	33	29	7	4	3	6	23	2	60	1	0	6	4	.600	0	0-0	22	3.42	3.28
2006	Hou	NL	81	0	0	13	88.2	356	76	38	37	10	4	4	6	28	6	56	0	0	7	3	.700	0	0-6	23	3.36	3.76
2007	Hou	NL	79	0	0	16	82.2	345	84	29	28	10	6	2	3	25	5	78	2	0	6	5	.545	0	5-10	21	4.07	3.05
2008	Ari	NL	77	0	0	21	73.2	300	61	29	23	4	4	3	3	18	2	71	6	0	4	8	.333	0	9-17	22	2.40	2.81
2009	Ari	NL	51	0	0	44	52.0	217	53	23	21	5	1	0	2	7	2	45	2	0	2	2	.500	0	24-29	0	3.17	3.63
2010	2 Tms	NL	70	0	0	29	59.0	281	85	56	48	7	4	4	2	21	4	49	4	0	3	4	.429	0	12-19	11	6.63	7.32
2011	SD	NL	77	0	0	20	74.1	306	73	30	29	7	7	1	0	20	5	43	4	0	6	8	.429	0	0-5	22	3.38	3.51
10	Ari	NL	43	0	0	28	38.0	190	61	41	35	5	4	2	1	15	4	34	3	0	1	4	.200	0	12-16	3	7.80	8.29
10	TB	NL	27	0	0	1	21.0	91	24	15	13	2	0	2	1	6	0	15	1	0	2	0	1.000	0	0-3	8	4.64	5.57
	Postseason		17	0	0	0	22.2	94	24	13	13	3	1	0	0	7	3	17	0	0	1	1	.500	0	0-2	4	4.20	5.16
	8 ML YEARS		537	0	0	166	543.0	2275	539	251	228	53	30	18	26	150	27	426	19	0	38	34	.528	0	51-88	130	3.69	3.78

Carlos Quentin

Bats: R **Throws:** R **Pos:** RF-102; DH-15; PH-4 **Ht:** 6'2" **Wt:** 235 **Born:** 8/28/1982 **Age:** 29

			BATTING																				BASERUNNING				AVERAGES		
Year	Team	Lg	G	AB	H	2B	3B	HR	(Hm	Rd)	TB	R	RBI	RC	TBB	IBB	SO	HBP	SH	SF			SB	CS	SB%	GDP	Avg	OBP	Slg
2006	Ari	NL	57	166	42	13	3	9	(3	6)	88	23	32	29	15	2	34	8	1	1			1	0	1.00	6	.253	.342	.530
2007	Ari	NL	81	229	49	16	0	5	(5	0)	80	29	31	27	18	1	54	11	1	4			2	2	.50	5	.214	.298	.349
2008	CWS	AL	130	480	138	26	1	36	(21	15)	274	96	100	104	66	0	80	20	0	3			7	3	.70	16	.288	.394	.571
2009	CWS	AL	99	351	83	14	0	21	(12	9)	160	47	56	47	31	2	52	15	0	2			3	0	1.00	11	.236	.323	.456
2010	CWS	AL	131	453	110	25	2	26	(19	7)	217	73	87	78	50	3	83	20	0	4			2	2	.50	16	.243	.342	.479
2011	CWS	AL	118	421	107	31	0	24	(7	17)	210	53	77	72	34	0	84	**23**	0	5			1	1	.50	7	.254	.340	.499
	6 ML YEARS		616	2100	529	125	6	121	(67	54)	1029	321	383	357	214	8	387	97	2	19			16	8	.67	61	.252	.346	.490

Omar Quintanilla

Bats: L **Throws:** R **Pos:** 2B-5; 3B-3; SS-3; PR-1   keen-tah-NEE-yah   **Ht:** 5'9" **Wt:** 190 **Born:** 10/24/1981 **Age:** 30

Year	Team	Lg	G	AB	H	2B	3B	HR	(Hm	Rd)	TB	R	RBI	RC	TBB	IBB	SO	HBP	SH	SF	SB	CS	SB%	GDP	Avg	OBP	Slg
2011	RdRck*	AAA	51	208	62	9	4	5	(-	-)	94	46	25	36	23	0	33	1	1	1	3	1	.75	4	.298	.369	.452
2005	Col	NL	39	128	28	1	1	0	(0	0)	31	16	7	9	9	0	15	0	6	0	2	1	.67	3	.219	.270	.242
2006	Col	NL	11	34	6	1	1	0	(0	0)	9	3	3	2	3	1	9	0	1	0	1	1	.50	1	.176	.243	.265
2007	Col	NL	27	70	16	4	0	0	(0	0)	20	6	5	6	5	0	15	0	0	0	0	0	-	3	.229	.280	.286
2008	Col	NL	81	210	50	17	0	2	(1	1)	73	28	15	18	15	3	46	0	8	1	0	0	-	3	.238	.288	.348
2009	Col	NL	58	58	10	2	0	0	(0	0)	12	7	2	4	8	0	27	0	3	0	0	0	-	0	.172	.273	.207
2011	Tex	AL	11	22	1	0	1	0	(0	0)	3	3	2	0	0	0	9	0	1	0	0	0	-	0	.045	.045	.136
6 ML YEARS			227	522	111	25	3	2	(1	1)	148	63	34	39	40	4	121	0	19	1	3	2	.60	10	.213	.268	.284

Humberto Quintero

Bats: R **Throws:** R **Pos:** C-77; PH-1; PR-1   oom-BARE-toe keen-TARE-oh   **Ht:** 5'9" **Wt:** 216 **Born:** 8/2/1979 **Age:** 32

Year	Team	Lg	G	AB	H	2B	3B	HR	(Hm	Rd)	TB	R	RBI	RC	TBB	IBB	SO	HBP	SH	SF	SB	CS	SB%	GDP	Avg	OBP	Slg
2011	OKCity*	AAA	4	14	4	1	0	0	(-	-)	5	1	0	1	0	0	5	1	0	0	0	0	-	0	.286	.333	.357
2003	SD	NL	12	23	5	0	0	0	(0	0)	5	1	2	2	1	1	6	0	0	0	0	0	-	0	.217	.250	.217
2004	SD	NL	23	72	18	3	0	2	(1	1)	27	7	10	6	5	0	16	0	0	1	0	2	.00	5	.250	.295	.375
2005	Hou	NL	18	54	10	1	0	1	(1	0)	14	6	8	2	1	1	10	0	2	0	0	0	-	3	.185	.200	.259
2006	Hou	NL	11	21	7	2	0	0	(0	0)	9	2	2	1	1	0	3	0	0	0	0	0	-	2	.333	.364	.429
2007	Hou	NL	29	53	12	2	0	0	(0	0)	14	2	1	3	2	1	13	2	0	0	0	0	-	2	.226	.281	.264
2008	Hou	NL	59	168	38	6	0	2	(1	1)	50	16	12	10	6	0	34	4	5	0	0	0	-	5	.226	.270	.298
2009	Hou	NL	60	157	37	8	1	4	(3	1)	59	11	14	13	7	1	41	4	0	0	0	0	-	8	.236	.286	.376
2010	Hou	NL	88	265	62	10	0	4	(2	2)	84	13	20	20	8	2	59	2	1	0	1	0	1.00	10	.234	.262	.317
2011	Hou	NL	79	262	63	12	1	2	(2	0)	83	22	25	14	6	2	53	1	1	2	0	0	-	5	.240	.258	.317
9 ML YEARS			379	1075	252	44	2	15	(10	5)	345	80	94	71	37	8	235	13	9	3	1	2	.33	40	.234	.268	.321

Ryan Raburn

Bats: R **Throws:** R **Pos:** 2B-56; LF-52; RF-20; PH-11; 3B-4; PR-3; 1B-2; CF-2; DH-2   **Ht:** 6'0" **Wt:** 185 **Born:** 4/17/1981 **Age:** 31

Year	Team	Lg	G	AB	H	2B	3B	HR	(Hm	Rd)	TB	R	RBI	RC	TBB	IBB	SO	HBP	SH	SF	SB	CS	SB%	GDP	Avg	OBP	Slg
2004	Det	AL	12	29	4	1	0	0	(0	0)	5	4	1	1	2	0	15	0	0	0	1	0	1.00	0	.138	.194	.172
2007	Det	AL	49	138	42	12	2	4	(2	2)	70	28	27	21	8	1	33	0	1	1	3	0	1.00	7	.304	.340	.507
2008	Det	AL	92	182	43	10	1	4	(2	2)	67	26	20	20	16	1	49	0	1	0	3	1	.75	2	.236	.298	.368
2009	Det	AL	113	261	76	11	2	16	(9	7)	139	44	45	42	26	2	60	2	1	1	5	4	.56	6	.291	.359	.533
2010	Det	AL	113	371	104	25	1	15	(5	10)	176	54	62	54	27	0	92	8	1	3	2	2	.50	8	.280	.340	.474
2011	Det	AL	121	387	99	22	2	14	(7	7)	167	53	49	48	21	2	114	3	4	3	1	1	.50	4	.256	.297	.432
6 ML YEARS			500	1368	368	81	8	53	(25	28)	624	209	204	186	100	6	363	13	8	8	15	8	.65	27	.269	.323	.456

Alexei Ramirez

Bats: R **Throws:** R **Pos:** SS-155; PH-2; DH-1   ah-lexx-AY   **Ht:** 6'2" **Wt:** 175 **Born:** 9/22/1981 **Age:** 30

Year	Team	Lg	G	AB	H	2B	3B	HR	(Hm	Rd)	TB	R	RBI	RC	TBB	IBB	SO	HBP	SH	SF	SB	CS	SB%	GDP	Avg	OBP	Slg
2008	CWS	AL	136	480	139	22	2	21	(13	8)	228	65	77	78	18	3	61	3	4	4	13	9	.59	14	.290	.317	.475
2009	CWS	AL	148	542	150	14	1	15	(9	6)	211	71	68	74	49	3	66	1	6	8	14	5	.74	15	.277	.333	.389
2010	CWS	AL	156	585	165	29	2	18	(11	7)	252	83	70	72	27	2	82	2	7	5	13	8	.62	12	.282	.313	.431
2011	CWS	AL	158	614	165	31	2	15	(7	8)	245	81	70	74	51	1	84	6	8	5	7	5	.58	19	.269	.328	.399
Postseason			4	12	3	0	0	0	(0	0)	3	1	2	1	1	0	1	0	0	2	0	0	-	0	.250	.267	.250
4 ML YEARS			598	2221	619	96	7	69	(40	29)	936	300	285	298	145	9	293	12	25	22	47	27	.64	60	.279	.323	.421

Aramis Ramirez

Bats: R **Throws:** R **Pos:** 3B-145; DH-3; PH-3   ah-RAH-miss   **Ht:** 6'1" **Wt:** 205 **Born:** 6/25/1978 **Age:** 34

Year	Team	Lg	G	AB	H	2B	3B	HR	(Hm	Rd)	TB	R	RBI	RC	TBB	IBB	SO	HBP	SH	SF	SB	CS	SB%	GDP	Avg	OBP	Slg
1998	Pit	NL	72	251	59	9	1	6	(3	3)	88	23	24	26	18	0	72	4	1	1	0	1	.00	3	.235	.296	.351
1999	Pit	NL	18	56	10	2	1	0	(0	0)	14	2	7	4	6	0	9	0	1	0	0	0	-	9	.179	.254	.250
2000	Pit	NL	73	254	65	15	2	6	(4	2)	102	19	35	28	10	0	36	5	1	4	0	0	-	9	.256	.293	.402
2001	Pit	NL	158	603	181	40	0	34	(16	18)	323	83	112	108	40	4	100	8	0	4	2	5	.29	17	.300	.350	.536
2002	Pit	NL	142	522	122	26	0	18	(7	11)	202	51	71	49	29	3	95	8	0	11	2	0	1.00	17	.234	.279	.387
2003	2 Tms	NL	159	607	165	32	2	27	(10	17)	282	75	106	88	42	3	99	10	0	11	2	2	.50	21	.272	.324	.465
2004	ChC	NL	145	547	174	32	1	36	(22	14)	316	99	103	100	49	6	62	3	0	7	0	2	.00	25	.318	.373	.578
2005	ChC	NL	123	463	140	30	0	31	(20	11)	263	72	92	79	35	4	60	6	0	2	0	1	.00	15	.302	.358	.568
2006	ChC	NL	157	594	173	38	4	38	(14	24)	333	93	119	109	50	4	63	9	0	7	2	1	.67	15	.291	.352	.561
2007	ChC	NL	132	506	157	35	4	26	(17	9)	278	72	101	95	43	8	66	4	0	5	0	0	-	13	.310	.366	.549
2008	ChC	NL	149	554	160	44	1	27	(17	10)	287	97	111	108	74	7	94	11	0	6	2	2	.50	13	.289	.380	.518
2009	ChC	NL	82	306	97	14	1	15	(7	8)	158	46	65	66	28	3	43	8	0	5	2	1	.67	8	.317	.389	.516
2010	ChC	NL	124	465	112	21	1	25	(14	11)	210	61	83	64	34	3	90	3	0	5	0	0	-	10	.241	.294	.452
2011	ChC	NL	149	565	173	35	1	26	(14	12)	288	80	93	96	43	5	69	10	0	8	1	1	.50	12	.306	.361	.510
03	Pit	NL	96	375	105	25	1	12	(6	6)	168	44	67	49	25	3	68	7	0	8	1	1	.50	17	.280	.330	.448
03	ChC	NL	63	232	60	7	1	15	(4	11)	114	31	39	39	17	0	31	3	0	3	1	1	.50	4	.259	.314	.491
Postseason			18	67	13	2	1	4	(1	3)	29	7	10	8	9	0	15	1	0	0	0	0	-	5	.194	.299	.433
14 ML YEARS			1683	6293	1788	373	19	315	(156	159)	3144	873	1122	1020	501	50	958	89	3	72	16	15	.52	170	.284	.342	.500

Hanley Ramirez

Bats: R Throws: R Pos: SS-86; DH-3; PH-3   Ht: 6'3" Wt: 229 Born: 12/23/1983 Age: 28

Year	Team	Lg	G	AB	H	2B	3B	HR	(Hm	Rd)	TB	R	RBI	RC	TBB	IBB	SO	HBP	SH	SF	SB	CS	SB%	GDP	Avg	OBP	Slg
2011	Jupiter*	A+	6	21	10	1	1	0	(-	-)	13	6	4	5	1	0	2	0	0	0	1	0	1.00	2	.476	.500	.619
2005	Bos	AL	2	2	0	0	0	0	(0	0)	0	0	0	0	0	0	2	0	0	0	0	0	-	0	.000	.000	.000
2006	Fla	NL	158	633	185	46	11	17	(9	8)	304	119	59	101	56	0	128	4	5	2	51	15	.77	7	.292	.353	.480
2007	Fla	NL	154	639	212	48	6	29	(15	14)	359	125	81	115	52	3	95	7	4	4	51	14	.78	10	.332	.386	.562
2008	Fla	NL	153	589	177	34	4	33	(17	16)	318	125	67	116	92	9	122	8	0	4	35	12	.74	5	.301	.400	.540
2009	Fla	NL	151	576	197	42	1	24	(17	7)	313	101	106	122	61	14	101	9	1	5	27	8	.77	9	.342	.410	.543
2010	Fla	NL	142	543	163	28	2	21	(12	9)	258	92	76	90	64	12	93	7	0	5	32	10	.76	14	.300	.378	.475
2011	Fla	NL	92	338	82	16	0	10	(5	5)	128	55	45	46	44	3	66	2	1	0	20	10	.67	6	.243	.333	.379
	7 ML YEARS		852	3320	1016	214	24	134	(75	59)	1680	617	434	590	369	41	607	37	11	20	216	69	.76	51	.306	.380	.506

Horacio Ramirez

hore-AH-see-oh

Pitches: L Bats: L Pos: RP-12   Ht: 6'1" Wt: 221 Born: 11/24/1979 Age: 32

Year	Team	Lg	G	GS	CG	GF	IP	BFP	H	R	ER	HR	SH	SF	HB	TBB	IBB	SO	WP	Bk	W	L	Pct	Sh	Sv-Op	Hld	ERC	ERA
2011	Salt Lk*	AAA	45	1	0	14	52.1	214	52	23	23	8	4	2	1	15	0	21	1	2	3	2	.600	0	6-	-	4.17	3.96
2003	Atl	NL	29	29	1	0	182.1	781	181	91	81	21	12	3	6	72	10	100	5	1	12	4	.750	0	0-0	0	4.21	4.00
2004	Atl	NL	10	9	1	0	60.1	259	51	24	16	7	2	1	0	30	5	31	0	2	2	4	.333	0	0-0	0	3.55	2.39
2005	Atl	NL	33	32	1	0	202.1	847	214	108	104	31	13	5	2	67	4	80	4	1	11	9	.550	1	0-0	0	4.66	4.63
2006	Atl	NL	14	14	0	0	76.1	337	85	42	38	6	3	3	4	31	2	37	0	1	5	5	.500	0	0-0	0	4.82	4.48
2007	Sea	AL	20	20	0	0	98.0	459	139	86	78	13	1	1	2	42	1	40	1	0	8	7	.533	0	0-0	0	7.17	7.16
2008	2 Tms	AL	32	0	0	7	37.1	168	45	20	18	1	3	1	2	9	1	13	2	0	1	4	.200	0	0-0	0	4.13	4.34
2009	KC	AL	19	1	0	1	22.2	104	27	16	15	3	1	0	0	11	3	13	1	0	0	2	.000	0	0-1	2	5.53	5.96
2011	LAA	AL	12	0	0	1	9.0	40	16	7	6	1	0	1	0	2	0	4	1	0	1	0	1.000	0	0-0	0	9.09	6.00
	08 CWS	AL	17	0	0	3	13.0	72	24	11	11	0	3	0	0	8	1	2	1	0	0	3	.000	0	0-0	1	8.89	7.62
	08 KC	AL	15	0	0	4	24.1	96	21	9	7	1	0	1	2	1	0	11	1	0	1	1	.500	0	0-0	1	1.99	2.59
	8 ML YEARS		169	105	3	11	688.1	2995	758	394	356	83	35	15	16	264	26	318	14	5	40	35	.533	1	0-1	4	4.84	4.65

Manny Ramirez

Bats: R Throws: R Pos: DH-4; PH-1   Ht: 6'0" Wt: 225 Born: 5/30/1972 Age: 40

Year	Team	Lg	G	AB	H	2B	3B	HR	(Hm	Rd)	TB	R	RBI	RC	TBB	IBB	SO	HBP	SH	SF	SB	CS	SB%	GDP	Avg	OBP	Slg
1993	Cle	AL	22	53	9	1	0	2	(0	2)	16	5	5	2	2	0	8	0	0	0	0	0	-	3	.170	.200	.302
1994	Cle	AL	91	290	78	22	0	17	(9	8)	151	51	60	53	42	4	72	0	0	4	4	2	.67	6	.269	.357	.521
1995	Cle	AL	137	484	149	26	1	31	(12	19)	270	85	107	103	75	6	112	5	2	5	6	6	.50	13	.308	.402	.558
1996	Cle	AL	152	550	170	45	3	33	(19	14)	320	94	112	120	85	8	104	3	0	9	8	5	.62	18	.309	.399	.582
1997	Cle	AL	150	561	184	40	0	26	(14	12)	302	99	88	117	79	5	115	7	0	4	2	3	.40	19	.328	.415	.538
1998	Cle	AL	150	571	168	35	2	45	(25	20)	342	108	145	121	76	6	121	6	0	10	5	3	.63	18	.294	.377	.599
1999	Cle	AL	147	522	174	34	3	44	(21	23)	346	131	165	141	96	9	131	13	0	9	2	4	.33	12	.333	.442	.663
2000	Cle	AL	118	439	154	34	2	38	(22	16)	306	92	122	127	86	9	117	3	0	4	1	1	.50	9	.351	.457	.697
2001	Bos	AL	142	529	162	33	2	41	(21	20)	322	93	125	122	81	25	147	8	0	9	0	1	.00	9	.306	.405	.609
2002	Bos	AL	120	436	152	31	0	33	(18	15)	282	84	107	125	73	14	85	8	0	1	0	0	-	3	.349	.450	.647
2003	Bos	AL	154	569	185	36	1	37	(18	19)	334	117	104	128	97	28	94	8	0	5	3	1	.75	22	.325	.427	.587
2004	Bos	AL	152	568	175	44	0	43	(23	20)	348	108	130	124	82	15	124	6	0	7	2	4	.33	17	.308	.397	.613
2005	Bos	AL	152	554	162	30	1	45	(22	23)	329	112	144	134	80	9	119	10	0	6	1	0	1.00	6	.292	.388	.594
2006	Bos	AL	130	449	144	27	1	35	(16	19)	278	79	102	114	100	16	102	1	0	8	0	1	.00	13	.321	.439	.619
2007	Bos	AL	133	483	143	33	1	20	(10	10)	238	84	88	78	71	13	92	7	0	8	0	0	-	21	.296	.388	.493
2008	2 Tms		153	552	183	36	1	37	(17	20)	332	102	121	133	87	24	124	11	0	4	3	0	1.00	17	.332	.430	.601
2009	LAD	NL	104	352	102	24	2	19	(10	9)	187	62	63	73	71	21	81	7	0	1	1	1	.50	7	.290	.418	.531
2010	2 Tms		90	265	79	16	0	9	(5	4)	122	38	42	50	46	4	61	6	0	3	1	1	.50	6	.298	.409	.460
2011	TB	AL	5	17	1	0	0	0	(0	0)	1	0	1	0	0	0	4	0	0	0	0	0	-	0	.059	.059	.059
	08 Bos	AL	100	365	109	22	1	20	(8	12)	193	66	68	69	52	8	86	8	0	0	1	0	1.00	12	.299	.398	.529
	08 LAD	NL	53	187	74	14	0	17	(9	8)	139	36	53	64	35	16	38	3	0	4	2	0	1.00	5	.396	.489	.743
	10 LAD	NL	66	196	61	15	0	8	(4	4)	100	32	40	41	32	4	38	1	0	3	1	1	.50	4	.311	.405	.510
	10 CWS	AL	24	69	18	1	0	1	(1	0)	22	6	2	9	14	0	23	5	0	0	0	0	-	2	.261	.420	.319
	Postseason		111	410	117	19	0	29	(12	17)	223	67	78	84	72	12	91	5	0	6	1	1	.50	17	.285	.394	.544
	19 ML YEARS		2302	8244	2574	547	20	555	(282	273)	4826	1544	1831	1865	1329	216	1813	109	2	90	38	33	.54	243	.312	.411	.585

Ramon Ramirez

Pitches: R Bats: R Pos: RP-66   Ht: 5'11" Wt: 199 Born: 8/31/1981 Age: 30

Year	Team	Lg	G	GS	CG	GF	IP	BFP	H	R	ER	HR	SH	SF	HB	TBB	IBB	SO	WP	Bk	W	L	Pct	Sh	Sv-Op	Hld	ERC	ERA
2006	Col	NL	61	0	0	14	67.2	285	58	28	26	5	2	3	1	27	3	61	2	0	4	3	.571	0	0-2	10	3.09	3.46
2007	Col	NL	22	0	0	5	17.1	78	21	16	16	2	2	1	2	6	2	15	2	0	2	2	.500	0	0-0	3	5.24	8.31
2008	KC	AL	71	0	0	15	71.2	295	57	23	21	2	4	3	0	31	6	70	6	1	3	2	.600	0	1-5	21	2.53	2.64
2009	Bos	AL	70	0	0	16	69.2	301	61	26	22	7	3	0	4	32	4	52	2	2	7	4	.636	0	0-4	12	3.73	2.84
2010	2 Tms		69	0	0	23	69.1	284	52	24	23	7	2	4	0	27	3	46	5	2	1	3	.250	0	0-4	14	2.64	2.99
2011	SF	NL	66	0	0	22	68.2	282	54	24	20	3	2	1	3	26	5	66	6	1	3	3	.500	0	4-5	11	2.57	2.62
	10 Bos	AL	44	0	0	17	42.1	178	39	21	21	6	2	4	0	16	2	31	4	1	0	3	.000	0	2-2	2	3.78	4.46
	10 SF	NL	25	0	0	6	27.0	106	13	3	2	1	0	0	0	11	1	15	1	1	1	0	1.000	0	1-1	4	1.28	0.67
	Postseason		6	0	0	2	4.0	24	6	8	8	2	1	0	1	3	1	2	0	0	0	1	.000	0	0-0	0	11.88	18.00
	6 ML YEARS		359	0	0	95	364.1	1525	303	141	128	26	15	13	9	149	23	310	23	6	20	17	.541	0	8-19	63	3.01	3.16

Wilkin Ramirez

Bats: R Throws: R Pos: PH-10; LF-5; PR-3; RF-2; DH-1   Ht: 6'2" Wt: 190 Born: 10/25/1985 Age: 26

Year	Team	Lg	G	AB	H	2B	3B	HR	(Hm	Rd)	TB	R	RBI	RC	TBB	IBB	SO	HBP	SH	SF	SB	CS	SB%	GDP	Avg	OBP	Slg
2003	Tigers	R	54	200	55	6	7	5	(-	-)	90	34	35	30	13	2	51	1	1	1	6	1	.86	4	.275	.321	.450
2005	WMich	A	131	493	129	21	2	16	(-	-)	202	69	65	67	35	1	143	7	1	5	21	8	.72	9	.262	.317	.410
2006	Lkland	A+	66	249	56	10	4	8	(-	-)	98	31	33	26	10	0	69	2	0	2	8	2	.80	8	.225	.259	.394
2007	Lkland	A+	88	319	87	7	4	10	(-	-)	132	48	41	45	20	0	86	1	0	3	28	6	.82	4	.273	.315	.414
2007	Erie	AA	34	121	26	3	1	2	(-	-)	37	15	14	10	8	0	38	2	1	1	6	2	.75	3	.215	.273	.306
2008	Erie	AA	110	433	131	24	7	19	(-	-)	226	74	73	83	43	1	138	5	0	1	26	12	.68	3	.303	.371	.522
2008	Toledo	AAA	11	36	3	1	0	0	(-	-)	4	2	0	0	1	0	11	1	0	0	1	0	1.00	1	.083	.132	.111
2009	Toledo	AAA	113	434	112	18	6	17	(-	-)	193	69	51	67	41	0	143	4	0	2	34	10	.77	6	.258	.326	.445
2010	Erie	AA	56	212	51	10	4	15	(-	-)	114	34	42	34	22	1	84	0	0	1	5	6	.45	0	.241	.311	.538
2010	Toledo	AAA	41	153	33	4	2	4	(-	-)	53	15	14	15	10	0	60	2	0	0	7	2	.78	0	.216	.273	.346
2010	Gwnntt	AAA	24	83	21	3	1	4	(-	-)	38	16	14	14	10	0	22	3	0	1	2	0	1.00	1	.253	.351	.458
2011	Gwnntt	AAA	81	288	77	16	3	11	(-	-)	132	40	36	42	17	0	70	1	4	3	19	6	.76	4	.267	.307	.458
2009	Det	AL	15	11	4	0	1	1	(1	0)	9	6	3	3	1	0	3	0	0	1	0	0	-	1	.364	.385	.818
2011	Atl	NL	20	26	6	2	0	0	(0	0)	8	5	2	1	4	0	11	0	0	0	0	2	.00	0	.231	.333	.308
	2 ML YEARS		35	37	10	2	1	1	(1	0)	17	11	5	4	5	0	14	0	0	1	0	2	.00	1	.270	.349	.459

Cesar Ramos

Pitches: L Bats: L Pos: RP-59   Ht: 6'2" Wt: 205 Born: 6/22/1984 Age: 28

Year	Team	Lg	G	GS	CG	GF	IP	BFP	H	R	ER	HR	SH	SF	HB	TBB	IBB	SO	WP	Bk	W	L	Pct	Sh	Sv-Op	Hld	ERC	ERA
2011	Drham*	AAA	4	0	0	1	4.0	19	5	2	2	1	0	1	0	2	0	1	0	0	2	0	1.000	0	0- -	-	7.02	4.50
2009	SD	NL	5	2	0	0	14.2	62	19	5	5	0	0	0	0	4	0	10	0	0	0	1	.000	0	0-0	0	4.78	3.07
2010	SD	NL	14	0	0	4	8.1	47	18	11	11	1	0	0	0	4	0	9	1	1	0	1	.000	0	0-0	2	11.97	11.88
2011	TB	AL	59	0	0	9	43.2	192	36	22	19	4	1	2	3	25	8	31	1	0	0	1	.000	0	0-2	3	3.64	3.92
	3 ML YEARS		78	2	0	13	66.2	301	73	38	35	5	1	2	3	33	8	50	2	1	0	3	.000	0	0-2	5	4.79	4.73

Wilson Ramos

Bats: R Throws: R Pos: C-108; PH-4; DH-1; PR-1   Ht: 6'0" Wt: 221 Born: 8/10/1987 Age: 24

Year	Team	Lg	G	AB	H	2B	3B	HR	(Hm	Rd)	TB	R	RBI	RC	TBB	IBB	SO	HBP	SH	SF	SB	CS	SB%	GDP	Avg	OBP	Slg
2006	Twins	R	46	154	44	12	1	3	(-	-)	67	18	26	24	12	0	14	2	1	3	4	2	.67	5	.286	.339	.435
2007	Beloit	A	73	292	85	17	1	8	(-	-)	128	40	42	44	19	2	61	5	0	0	1	1	.50	9	.291	.346	.438
2008	FtMyrs	A+	126	452	130	23	2	13	(-	-)	196	50	78	70	37	0	103	6	0	5	0	1	.00	23	.288	.346	.434
2009	NwBrit	AA	54	205	65	16	0	4	(-	-)	93	31	29	31	6	0	23	2	0	1	0	0	-	1	.317	.341	.454
2009	Twins	R	5	19	6	1	1	3	(-	-)	18	4	6	5	0	0	0	0	0	0	0	0	-	1	.316	.316	.947
2010	Roch	AAA	71	278	67	14	0	5	(-	-)	96	25	30	26	12	0	49	3	2	0	1	2	.33	8	.241	.280	.345
2010	Syrcse	AAA	20	79	25	3	1	3	(-	-)	39	14	8	13	3	2	12	0	0	0	0	0	-	2	.316	.341	.494
2010	2 Tms		79	22	7	0	1	1	(1	0)	32	5	5	10	2	0	12	1	0	0	0	0	-	2	.278	.305	.405
2011	Was	NL	113	389	104	22	1	15	(8	7)	173	48	52	43	38	8	76	2	4	2	0	2	.00	19	.267	.334	.445
10	Min	AL	7	27	8	3	0	0	(0	0)	11	2	1	3	0	0	3	1	0	0	0	0	-	1	.296	.321	.407
10	Was	NL	15	52	14	4	0	1	(1	0)	21	3	4	7	2	0	9	0	0	0	0	0	-	1	.269	.296	.404
	2 ML YEARS		135	468	126	29	1	16	(9	7)	205	53	57	53	40	8	88	3	4	2	0	2	.00	21	.269	.329	.438

Cody Ransom

Bats: R Throws: R Pos: SS-8; 3B-6; PH-1   Ht: 6'2" Wt: 190 Born: 2/17/1976 Age: 36

Year	Team	Lg	G	AB	H	2B	3B	HR	(Hm	Rd)	TB	R	RBI	RC	TBB	IBB	SO	HBP	SH	SF	SB	CS	SB%	GDP	Avg	OBP	Slg
2011	Reno*	AAA	101	372	118	29	3	27	(-	-)	234	86	92	92	55	1	94	2	0	3	10	3	.77	7	.317	.405	.629
2001	SF	NL	9	7	0	0	0	0	(0	0)	0	1	0	0	0	0	5	0	0	0	0	0	-	0	.000	.000	.000
2002	SF	NL	7	3	2	0	0	0	(0	0)	2	2	1	1	1	1	1	0	0	0	0	0	-	0	.667	.750	.667
2003	SF	NL	20	27	6	1	0	1	(1	0)	10	7	1	1	1	0	11	0	0	0	0	0	-	0	.222	.250	.370
2004	SF	NL	78	68	17	6	0	1	(0	1)	26	13	11	9	6	0	20	1	3	0	2	2	.50	2	.250	.320	.382
2007	Hou	NL	19	35	8	2	0	1	(1	0)	13	9	3	6	9	1	9	2	0	0	0	0	-	0	.229	.413	.371
2008	NYY	AL	33	43	13	3	0	4	(1	3)	28	9	8	10	6	0	12	1	1	0	0	0	-	0	.302	.400	.651
2009	NYY	AL	31	79	15	9	1	0	(0	0)	26	11	10	5	7	0	25	0	0	0	2	0	1.00	3	.190	.256	.329
2010	Phi	NL	22	42	8	0	0	2	(2	0)	14	6	5	5	3	0	11	0	1	0	1	0	1.00	3	.190	.244	.333
2011	Ari	NL	12	33	5	2	0	1	(1	0)	10	3	4	2	3	0	9	1	0	0	1	0	1.00	3	.152	.243	.303
	9 ML YEARS		231	337	74	23	1	10	(6	4)	129	61	43	39	36	2	103	5	5	0	6	2	.75	9	.220	.304	.383

Clay Rapada

Pitches: L Bats: R Pos: RP-32   Ht: 6'5" Wt: 200 Born: 3/9/1981 Age: 31

Year	Team	Lg	G	GS	CG	GF	IP	BFP	H	R	ER	HR	SH	SF	HB	TBB	IBB	SO	WP	Bk	W	L	Pct	Sh	Sv-Op	Hld	ERC	ERA
2011	Norfolk*	AAA	26	0	0	8	20.2	89	24	10	9	1	1	1	2	4	2	20	1	0	0	1	.000	0	1- -	-	4.06	3.92
2007	2 Tms		5	0	0	2	2.2	13	3	3	3	2	0	0	0	2	0	4	2	0	0	0	-	0	0-0	0	11.59	10.13
2008	Det	AL	25	0	0	4	21.1	94	19	11	10	0	1	0	1	14	1	15	1	0	3	0	1.000	0	0-0	2	3.87	4.22
2009	Det	AL	3	0	0	1	3.1	16	4	2	2	1	0	0	0	2	1	2	0	0	0	0	-	0	0-0	1	7.00	5.40
2010	Tex	AL	13	0	0	2	9.0	39	6	4	4	2	0	0	0	7	1	5	0	0	0	0	-	0	0-1	3	4.42	4.00
2011	Bal	AL	32	0	0	4	16.1	69	14	11	11	3	0	1	0	7	0	18	0	0	2	0	1.000	0	0-0	5	3.95	6.06
07	ChC	NL	1	0	0	0	0.1	1	0	0	0	0	0	0	0	0	0	0	0	0	0	0	-	0	0-0	0	0.00	0.00
07	Det	AL	4	0	0	2	2.1	12	3	3	3	2	0	0	0	2	0	4	2	0	0	0	-	0	0-0	0	14.48	11.57
	Postseason		3	0	0	0	0.1	3	1	0	0	0	0	0	0	1	0	1	0	0	0	0	-	0	0-1	0	29.63	0.00
	5 ML YEARS		78	0	0	12	52.2	231	46	31	30	8	1	1	1	32	3	44	3	0	5	0	1.000	0	0-1	10	4.57	5.13

Colby Rasmus

Bats: L Throws: L Pos: CF-127; PH-5   Ht: 6'2" Wt: 200 Born: 8/11/1986 Age: 25

Year	Team	Lg	G	AB	H	2B	3B	HR	(Hm	Rd)	TB	R	RBI	RC	TBB	IBB	SO	HBP	SH	SF	SB	CS	SB%	GDP	Avg	OBP	Slg
2009	StL	NL	147	474	119	22	2	16	(7	9)	193	72	52	60	36	3	95	3	5	2	3	1	.75	5	.251	.307	.407
2010	StL	NL	144	464	128	28	3	23	(11	12)	231	85	66	76	63	9	148	1	2	4	12	8	.60	5	.276	.361	.498
2011	2 Tms		129	471	106	24	6	14	(4	10)	184	75	53	50	50	2	116	0	2	3	5	2	.71	10	.225	.298	.391
11	StL	NL	94	338	83	14	6	11	(4	7)	142	61	40	43	45	2	77	0	1	2	5	2	.71	8	.246	.332	.420
11	Tor	AL	35	133	23	10	0	3	(0	3)	42	14	13	7	5	0	39	0	1	1	0	0	-	2	.173	.201	.316
	Postseason		3	9	4	3	0	0	(0	0)	7	1	1	1	2	0	1	0	0	0	0	0	-	1	.444	.545	.778
	3 ML YEARS		420	1409	353	74	11	53	(22	31)	608	232	171	186	149	14	359	4	9	9	20	11	.65	20	.251	.322	.432

Jon Rauch

Pitches: R Bats: R Pos: RP-53   RAUSH   Ht: 6'10" Wt: 290 Born: 9/27/1978 Age: 33

Year	Team	Lg	G	GS	CG	GF	IP	BFP	H	R	ER	HR	SH	SF	HB	TBB	IBB	SO	WP	Bk	W	L	Pct	Sh	Sv-Op	Hld	ERC	ERA
2002	CWS	AL	8	6	0	1	28.2	130	28	26	21	7	0	1	2	14	2	19	1	1	2	1	.667	0	0-0	0	5.41	6.59
2004	2 Tms		11	4	0	1	32.0	131	30	10	10	1	2	1	0	11	2	22	2	0	4	1	.800	0	0-0	0	3.05	2.81
2005	Was	NL	15	1	0	4	30.0	124	24	12	12	3	1	1	1	11	2	23	2	0	2	4	.333	0	0-0	0	2.90	3.60
2006	Was	NL	85	0	0	19	91.1	383	78	37	34	13	1	6	2	36	6	86	4	1	4	5	.444	0	2-5	18	3.52	3.35
2007	Was	NL	88	0	0	26	87.1	354	75	37	35	7	2	5	0	21	4	71	2	0	8	4	.667	0	4-10	33	2.53	3.61
2008	2 Tms	NL	74	0	0	51	71.2	295	69	36	33	11	6	3	0	16	2	66	1	0	4	8	.333	0	18-24	6	3.48	4.14
2009	2 Tms		75	0	0	15	70.0	299	70	30	28	6	3	4	2	23	1	49	6	0	7	3	.700	0	2-5	17	3.78	3.60
2010	Min	AL	59	0	0	41	57.2	245	61	20	20	3	1	1	1	14	0	46	1	0	3	1	.750	0	21-25	2	3.50	3.12
2011	Tor	AL	53	0	0	28	52.0	225	56	28	28	11	2	0	1	14	1	36	2	0	5	4	.556	0	11-16	4	4.75	4.85
04	CWS	AL	2	2	0	0	8.2	43	16	6	6	0	1	1	0	4	0	4	1	0	1	1	.500	0	0-0	0	9.15	6.23
04	Mon	NL	9	2	0	1	23.1	88	14	4	4	1	1	0	0	7	2	18	1	0	3	0	1.000	0	0-0	0	1.44	1.54
08	Was	NL	48	0	0	41	48.1	192	42	18	16	5	3	1	0	7	1	44	0	0	4	2	.667	0	17-22	6	2.41	2.98
08	Ari	NL	26	0	0	10	23.1	103	27	18	17	6	3	2	0	9	1	22	1	0	0	6	.000	0	1-2	6	6.09	6.56
09	Ari	NL	58	0	0	13	54.1	235	57	27	25	5	1	2	1	17	0	35	6	0	2	2	.500	0	2-3	12	3.98	4.14
09	Min	AL	17	0	0	2	15.2	64	13	3	3	1	2	2	1	6	1	14	0	0	5	1	.833	0	0-2	5	3.09	1.72
	Postseason		5	0	0	1	3.0	12	1	1	1	0	0	0	0	2	0	1	0	0	0	0	-	0	0-0	0	1.26	3.00
	9 ML YEARS		468	11	0	186	520.2	2186	491	236	221	62	18	22	9	160	20	418	21	2	39	31	.557	0	58-85	80	3.53	3.82

Chris Ray

Pitches: R Bats: R Pos: RP-29   Ht: 6'3" Wt: 210 Born: 1/12/1982 Age: 30

Year	Team	Lg	G	GS	CG	GF	IP	BFP	H	R	ER	HR	SH	SF	HB	TBB	IBB	SO	WP	Bk	W	L	Pct	Sh	Sv-Op	Hld	ERC	ERA
2005	Bal	AL	41	0	0	8	40.2	174	34	15	12	5	1	1	1	18	3	43	0	1	1	3	.250	0	0-4	8	3.43	2.66
2006	Bal	AL	61	0	0	56	66.0	267	45	22	20	10	2	4	1	27	2	51	2	0	4	4	.500	0	33-38	0	2.77	2.73
2007	Bal	AL	43	0	0	37	42.2	179	35	22	21	5	0	1	2	18	2	44	1	0	5	6	.455	0	16-20	0	3.42	4.43
2009	Bal	AL	46	0	0	12	43.1	214	64	36	35	8	4	4	1	23	7	39	0	0	0	4	.000	0	0-3	6	8.03	7.27
2010	2 Tms		63	0	0	13	55.2	234	48	23	23	5	5	0	0	25	2	31	1	0	5	0	1.000	0	2-4	9	3.41	3.72
2011	Sea	AL	29	0	0	15	32.2	139	33	18	17	2	2	3	0	12	2	22	4	1	3	2	.600	0	0-2	1	3.66	4.68
10	Tex	AL	35	0	0	6	31.2	133	24	12	12	4	0	0	0	16	1	16	1	0	2	0	1.000	0	1-3	7	3.28	3.41
10	SF	NL	28	0	0	7	24.0	101	24	11	11	1	5	0	0	9	1	15	0	0	3	0	1.000	0	1-1	2	3.57	4.13
	6 ML YEARS		283	0	0	141	281.0	1207	259	136	128	35	14	13	5	123	18	230	8	2	18	19	.486	0	51-71	24	3.92	4.10

Anthony Recker

Bats: R Throws: R Pos: C-5   Ht: 6'2" Wt: 240 Born: 8/29/1983 Age: 28

Year	Team	Lg	G	AB	H	2B	3B	HR	(Hm	Rd)	TB	R	RBI	RC	TBB	IBB	SO	HBP	SH	SF	SB	CS	SB%	GDP	Avg	OBP	Slg
2005	Vancvr	A-	43	150	35	8	0	5	(-	-)	58	16	18	19	16	0	40	2	1	0	0	0	-	5	.233	.315	.387
2006	Kane	A	109	407	117	24	3	14	(-	-)	189	52	57	68	42	2	115	3	0	1	5	5	.50	10	.287	.358	.464
2007	Stcktn	A+	56	207	66	17	2	13	(-	-)	126	39	47	50	27	0	48	5	0	5	2	0	1.00	5	.319	.402	.609
2007	Mdland	AA	58	201	41	12	0	4	(-	-)	65	16	20	17	17	0	63	1	0	0	0	1	.00	8	.204	.269	.323
2008	Mdland	AA	118	433	120	30	4	11	(-	-)	191	58	65	68	44	0	140	5	2	2	1	2	.33	11	.277	.349	.441
2009	Scrmto	AAA	78	272	71	11	2	12	(-	-)	122	30	45	42	28	0	80	2	3	1	2	0	1.00	6	.261	.333	.449
2010	Mdland	AA	16	57	17	4	0	3	(-	-)	30	11	9	11	8	0	22	0	0	0	0	0	-	1	.298	.385	.526
2010	Scrmto	AAA	11	38	8	1	0	1	(-	-)	12	8	3	5	7	0	12	2	0	0	1	0	1.00	0	.211	.362	.316
2010	Scrmto	AAA	80	250	72	18	2	10	(-	-)	124	36	42	42	22	1	62	0	0	5	0	1	.00	5	.288	.341	.496
2011	Scrmto	AAA	99	345	99	24	1	16	(-	-)	173	61	48	69	56	2	81	4	2	5	7	5	.58	6	.287	.388	.501
2011	Oak	AL	5	17	3	1	0	0	(0	0)	4	3	0	0	4	0	7	0	0	0	0	0	-	0	.176	.333	.235

Josh Reddick

Bats: L Throws: R Pos: RF-56; LF-21; PH-11; CF-3; DH-2; PR-2   Ht: 6'2" Wt: 180 Born: 2/19/1987 Age: 25

Year	Team	Lg	G	AB	H	2B	3B	HR	(Hm	Rd)	TB	R	RBI	RC	TBB	IBB	SO	HBP	SH	SF	SB	CS	SB%	GDP	Avg	OBP	Slg
2011	Pwtckt*	AAA	52	191	44	9	1	14	(-	-)	97	37	36	35	33	0	39	0	0	7	4	1	.80	8	.230	.333	.508
2009	Bos	AL	27	59	10	4	0	2	(0	2)	20	5	4	4	2	0	17	1	0	0	0	0	-	0	.169	.210	.339
2010	Bos	AL	29	62	12	3	1	1	(1	0)	20	5	5	1	1	0	15	0	0	0	1	0	1.00	1	.194	.206	.323
2011	Bos	AL	87	254	71	18	3	7	(2	5)	116	41	28	33	19	1	50	1	0	4	1	2	.33	1	.280	.327	.457
	3 ML YEARS		143	375	93	25	4	10	(3	7)	156	51	37	38	22	1	82	2	0	4	2	2	.50	2	.248	.290	.416

Addison Reed

Pitches: R Bats: L Pos: RP-6   Ht: 6'4" Wt: 215 Born: 12/27/1988 Age: 23

Year	Team	Lg	G	GS	CG	GF	IP	BFP	H	R	ER	HR	SH	SF	HB	TBB	IBB	SO	WP	Bk	W	L	Pct	Sh	Sv-Op	Hld	ERC	ERA
2010	Gr Falls	R+	13	2	0	3	30.0	115	17	7	6	1	1	1	2	6	0	44	1	0	1	0	1.000	0	1- -	-	1.27	1.80
2011	Knapol	A	4	0	0	1	8.0	29	4	1	1	0	1	0	0	1	0	11	1	0	0	0	-	0	0- -	-	0.73	1.13
2011	WinSa	A+	15	0	0	4	28.1	114	21	8	5	1	1	0	2	4	0	39	3	0	2	0	1.000	0	1- -	-	1.65	1.59
2011	Brham	AA	13	0	0	7	20.2	77	10	2	2	0	0	0	1	6	0	33	0	0	0	1	.000	0	2- -	-	1.09	0.87
2011	Charltt	AAA	11	0	0	3	21.1	73	8	3	3	2	0	0	0	3	0	28	2	0	0	0	-	0	2- -	-	0.74	1.27
2011	CWS	AL	6	0	0	2	7.1	33	10	3	3	1	0	0	0	1	0	12	0	0	0	0	-	0	0-0	0	5.24	3.68

Jeremy Reed

Bats: L Throws: L Pos: PH-7   Ht: 6'0" Wt: 193 Born: 6/15/1981 Age: 31

Year	Team	Lg	G	AB	H	2B	3B	HR	(Hm	Rd)	TB	R	RBI	RC	TBB	IBB	SO	HBP	SH	SF	SB	CS	SB%	GDP	Avg	OBP	Slg
2011	Nashv*	AAA	36	103	24	5	2	1	(-	-)	36	7	6	12	11	0	15	1	2	1	4	1	.80	3	.233	.310	.350
2011	Roch*	AAA	4	15	0	0	0	0	(-	-)	0	0	0	0	1	0	2	0	2	0	0	0	-	0	.000	.063	.000
2004	Sea	AL	18	58	23	4	0	0	(0	0)	27	11	5	11	7	1	4	1	0	0	3	1	.75	2	.397	.470	.466
2005	Sea	AL	141	488	124	33	3	3	(0	3)	172	61	45	49	48	1	74	2	4	2	12	11	.52	10	.254	.322	.352
2006	Sea	AL	67	212	46	6	5	6	(1	5)	80	27	17	13	11	1	31	2	2	2	2	3	.40	5	.217	.260	.377
2007	Sea	AL	13	17	3	0	1	0	(0	0)	5	2	0	0	0	0	3	0	0	0	0	0	-	0	.176	.176	.294
2008	Sea	AL	97	286	77	18	1	2	(1	1)	103	30	31	31	18	0	38	2	3	3	2	3	.40	5	.269	.314	.360
2009	NYM	NL	126	161	39	6	2	0	(0	0)	49	9	9	12	14	1	36	0	1	1	0	3	.00	4	.242	.301	.304
2010	Tor	AL	14	21	3	0	0	1	(0	1)	6	1	3	1	2	0	8	0	0	0	1	0	1.00	0	.143	.217	.286
2011	Mil	NL	7	7	0	0	0	0	(0	0)	0	0	0	0	0	0	2	0	0	0	0	0	-	0	.000	.000	.000
	8 ML YEARS		483	1250	315	67	12	12	(2	10)	442	141	110	117	100	4	196	7	10	8	20	21	.49	26	.252	.309	.354

Nolan Reimold

Bats: R Throws: R Pos: LF-73; RF-8; DH-6; PH-6; PR-2   RYE-mold   Ht: 6'4" Wt: 215 Born: 10/12/1983 Age: 28

Year	Team	Lg	G	AB	H	2B	3B	HR	(Hm	Rd)	TB	R	RBI	RC	TBB	IBB	SO	HBP	SH	SF	SB	CS	SB%	GDP	Avg	OBP	Slg
2011	Norfolk*	AAA	39	139	33	6	0	6	(-	-)	57	16	22	20	18	0	43	2	0	2	2	1	.67	1	.237	.365	.410
2009	Bal	AL	104	358	100	18	2	15	(8	7)	167	49	45	57	47	1	77	3	0	3	8	2	.80	8	.279	.365	.466
2010	Bal	AL	39	116	24	5	0	3	(0	3)	38	9	14	6	12	0	26	1	0	2	0	0	-	6	.207	.282	.328
2011	Bal	AL	87	267	66	10	3	13	(8	5)	121	40	45	48	28	1	57	6	0	4	7	2	.78	4	.247	.328	.453
	3 ML YEARS		230	741	190	33	5	31	(16	15)	326	98	104	111	87	2	160	10	0	9	15	4	.79	18	.256	.339	.440

Chad Reineke

Pitches: R Bats: R Pos: SP-1; RP-1   RHINE-eh-key   Ht: 6'6" Wt: 210 Born: 4/9/1982 Age: 30

Year	Team	Lg	G	GS	CG	GF	IP	BFP	H	R	ER	HR	SH	SF	HB	TBB	IBB	SO	WP	Bk	W	L	Pct	Sh	Sv-Op	Hld	ERC	ERA
2011	Lsvlle*	AAA	20	20	0	1	126.2	558	143	65	54	13	9	6	4	39	0	77	5	0	9	7	.563	0	1- -	-	4.55	3.84
2008	SD	NL	4	3	0	1	18.0	78	14	10	10	1	1	1	0	12	1	13	0	0	2	1	.667	0	0-0	0	3.48	5.00
2009	Oak	AL	1	1	0	0	5.0	22	7	4	4	2	0	0	1	0	0	1	0	0	0	0	-	0	0-0	0	8.12	7.20
2011	Cin	NL	2	1	0	0	6.2	30	5	6	5	2	0	1	0	6	0	3	1	0	0	1	.000	0	0-0	0	7.21	6.75
	3 ML YEARS		7	5	0	1	29.2	130	26	20	19	5	1	2	1	18	1	17	1	0	2	2	.500	0	0-0	0	5.01	5.76

Edgar Renteria

Bats: R Throws: R Pos: SS-86; PH-15; 2B-4; PR-1   Ht: 6'1" Wt: 200 Born: 8/7/1975 Age: 36

Year	Team	Lg	G	AB	H	2B	3B	HR	(Hm	Rd)	TB	R	RBI	RC	TBB	IBB	SO	HBP	SH	SF	SB	CS	SB%	GDP	Avg	OBP	Slg
1996	Fla	NL	106	431	133	18	3	5	(2	3)	172	68	31	62	33	0	68	2	2	3	16	2	.89	12	.309	.358	.399
1997	Fla	NL	154	617	171	21	3	4	(3	1)	210	90	52	68	45	1	108	4	19	6	32	15	.68	17	.277	.327	.340
1998	Fla	NL	133	517	146	18	2	3	(2	1)	177	79	31	61	48	1	78	4	9	2	41	22	.65	13	.282	.347	.342
1999	StL	NL	154	585	161	36	2	11	(6	5)	234	92	63	81	53	0	82	2	6	7	37	8	.82	16	.275	.334	.400
2000	StL	NL	150	562	156	32	1	16	(4	12)	238	94	76	80	63	3	77	1	8	9	21	13	.62	19	.278	.346	.423
2001	StL	NL	141	493	128	19	3	10	(3	7)	183	54	57	57	39	4	73	3	8	6	17	4	.81	15	.260	.314	.371
2002	StL	NL	152	544	166	36	2	11	(4	7)	239	77	83	94	49	7	57	4	7	5	22	7	.76	17	.305	.364	.439
2003	StL	NL	157	587	194	47	1	13	(4	9)	282	96	100	103	65	12	54	1	3	7	34	7	.83	21	.330	.394	.480
2004	StL	NL	149	586	168	37	0	10	(7	3)	235	84	72	74	39	5	78	1	6	10	17	11	.61	14	.287	.327	.401
2005	Bos	AL	153	623	172	36	4	8	(3	5)	240	100	70	82	55	0	100	3	6	5	9	4	.69	15	.276	.335	.385
2006	Atl	NL	149	598	175	40	2	14	(4	10)	261	100	70	89	62	0	89	3	8	2	17	6	.74	17	.293	.361	.436
2007	Atl	NL	124	494	164	30	1	12	(5	7)	232	87	57	82	46	0	77	1	2	0	11	2	.85	14	.332	.390	.470
2008	Det	AL	138	503	136	22	2	10	(5	5)	192	69	55	61	37	1	64	0	2	5	6	3	.67	19	.270	.317	.382
2009	SF	NL	124	460	115	19	1	5	(3	2)	151	50	48	50	39	5	69	1	5	5	7	2	.78	17	.250	.307	.328
2010	SF	NL	72	243	67	11	2	3	(2	1)	91	26	22	27	21	3	43	0	2	1	3	0	1.00	8	.276	.332	.374
2011	Cin	NL	96	299	75	14	0	5	(2	3)	104	34	36	35	24	0	65	1	6	3	4	2	.67	7	.251	.306	.348
	Postseason		66	242	61	12	0	3	(2	1)	82	37	23	29	24	1	39	4	6	2	9	1	.90	8	.252	.327	.339
	16 ML YEARS		2152	8142	2327	436	29	140	(59	81)	3241	1200	923	1106	718	42	1182	31	99	76	294	108	.73	241	.286	.343	.398

Jason Repko

Bats: R **Throws:** R **Pos:** RF-27; LF-24; PR-15; PH-7; CF-5; DH-3   **Ht:** 5'11" **Wt:** 198 **Born:** 12/27/1980 **Age:** 31

Year	Team	Lg	G	AB	H	2B	3B	HR	(Hm	Rd)	TB	R	RBI	RC	TBB	IBB	SO	HBP	SH	SF	SB	CS	SB%	GDP	Avg	OBP	Slg
2011	Roch*	AAA	10	37	8	1	0	2	(-	-)	15	4	5	5	6	0	11	0	0	1	2	0	1.00	0	.216	.318	.405
2005	LAD	NL	129	276	61	15	3	8	(4	4)	106	43	30	28	16	1	80	7	2	0	5	0	1.00	7	.221	.281	.384
2006	LAD	NL	69	130	33	5	1	3	(1	2)	49	21	16	21	15	1	24	3	2	0	10	4	.71	2	.254	.345	.377
2008	LAD	NL	22	18	3	1	0	0	(0	0)	4	0	0	0	2	0	9	0	0	0	1	0	1.00	0	.167	.250	.222
2009	LAD	NL	10	5	0	0	0	0	(0	0)	0	1	1	0	0	0	2	1	0	1	1	0	1.00	0	.000	.143	.000
2010	Min	AL	58	127	29	6	0	3	(0	3)	44	19	9	12	13	0	38	5	1	0	3	2	.60	2	.228	.324	.346
2011	Min	AL	67	133	30	2	0	2	(1	1)	38	21	11	14	6	0	38	2	3	0	7	2	.78	0	.226	.270	.286
	Postseason		2	0	0	0	0	0	(0	0)	0	0	0	0	0	0	0	0	0	0	0	0	-	0	-	-	-
	6 ML YEARS		355	689	156	29	4	16	(6	10)	241	105	67	75	52	2	191	18	8	1	27	8	.77	11	.226	.297	.350

Chris Resop

Pitches: R **Bats:** R **Pos:** RP-76   REE-sawp   **Ht:** 6'3" **Wt:** 222 **Born:** 11/4/1982 **Age:** 29

Year	Team	Lg	G	GS	CG	GF	IP	BFP	H	R	ER	HR	SH	SF	HB	TBB	IBB	SO	WP	Bk	W	L	Pct	Sh	Sv-Op	Hld	ERC	ERA
2005	Fla	NL	15	0	0	6	17.0	80	22	16	16	1	0	2	1	9	0	15	3	0	2	0	1.000	0	0-0	0	6.35	8.47
2006	Fla	NL	22	0	0	10	21.1	101	26	9	8	1	0	0	1	16	5	10	0	0	1	2	.333	0	0-1	2	6.30	3.38
2007	LAA	AL	4	0	0	3	4.1	17	4	2	2	1	2	1	0	1	0	2	0	0	0	0	-	0	0-0	0	4.00	4.15
2008	Atl	NL	16	0	0	9	18.1	82	16	12	12	2	2	1	2	10	2	13	0	0	0	1	.000	0	0-0	2	4.19	5.89
2010	2 Tms	NL	23	0	0	5	21.0	91	15	9	9	1	1	2	0	13	0	26	0	1	0	0	-	0	0-0	0	2.93	3.86
2011	Pit	NL	76	0	0	12	69.2	309	73	34	34	8	0	5	3	30	9	79	4	1	5	4	.556	0	1-6	15	4.52	4.39
10	Atl	NL	1	0	0	0	2.0	14	5	5	5	0	0	0	0	3	0	2	0	0	0	0	-	0	0-0	0	18.12	22.50
10	Pit	NL	22	0	0	5	19.0	77	10	4	4	1	1	2	0	10	0	24	0	1	0	0	-	0	0-0	5	1.80	1.89
	6 ML YEARS		156	0	0	45	151.2	680	156	82	81	14	5	11	7	79	16	145	7	2	8	7	.533	0	1-7	24	4.67	4.81

Ben Revere

Bats: L **Throws:** R **Pos:** CF-89; LF-13; PH-11; RF-5; DH-1; PR-1   **Ht:** 5'9" **Wt:** 175 **Born:** 5/3/1988 **Age:** 24

Year	Team	Lg	G	AB	H	2B	3B	HR	(Hm	Rd)	TB	R	RBI	RC	TBB	IBB	SO	HBP	SH	SF	SB	CS	SB%	GDP	Avg	OBP	Slg
2007	Twins	R	50	191	62	6	10	0	(-	-)	88	46	29	35	13	0	20	8	2	2	21	9	.70	1	.325	.388	.461
2008	Beloit	A	83	340	129	17	10	1	(-	-)	169	51	43	75	27	2	31	5	2	0	44	13	.77	1	.379	.433	.497
2009	FtMyrs	A+	121	466	145	13	4	2	(-	-)	172	75	48	70	40	0	34	7	1	3	45	17	.73	6	.311	.372	.369
2010	NwBrit	AA	94	361	110	10	4	1	(-	-)	131	44	23	55	32	1	41	8	2	3	36	13	.73	2	.305	.371	.363
2011	Roch	AAA	32	132	40	3	1	1	(-	-)	48	15	9	17	6	0	11	1	2	0	8	2	.80	4	.303	.338	.364
2010	Min	AL	13	28	5	0	0	0	(0	0)	5	1	2	2	0	0	5	0	0	0	0	1	.00	1	.179	.233	.179
2011	Min	AL	117	450	120	9	5	0	(0	0)	139	56	30	51	26	1	41	2	3	0	34	9	.79	7	.267	.310	.309
	2 ML YEARS		130	478	125	9	5	0	(0	0)	144	57	32	51	28	1	46	2	3	0	34	10	.77	8	.262	.305	.301

Dennys Reyes

Pitches: L **Bats:** R **Pos:** RP-4   DENN-eese   **Ht:** 6'3" **Wt:** 250 **Born:** 4/19/1977 **Age:** 35

Year	Team	Lg	G	GS	CG	GF	IP	BFP	H	R	ER	HR	SH	SF	HB	TBB	IBB	SO	WP	Bk	W	L	Pct	Sh	Sv-Op	Hld	ERC	ERA
2011	RedSx*	R	2	2	0	0	2.0	10	3	2	2	0	1	0	0	1	0	1	1	1	0	1	.000	0	0- -	-	6.48	9.00
1997	LAD	NL	14	5	0	0	47.0	207	51	21	20	4	5	1	1	18	3	36	2	1	2	3	.400	0	0-0	0	4.34	3.83
1998	2 Tms	NL	19	10	0	4	67.1	300	62	36	34	3	7	2	1	47	5	77	6	1	3	5	.375	0	0-0	0	4.37	4.54
1999	Cin	NL	65	1	0	12	61.2	277	53	30	26	5	4	3	3	39	1	72	5	1	2	2	.500	0	2-3	14	4.16	3.79
2000	Cin	NL	62	0	0	15	43.2	200	43	31	22	5	3	3	1	29	0	36	6	0	2	1	.667	0	0-1	10	5.24	4.53
2001	Cin	NL	35	6	0	8	53.0	246	51	35	29	5	2	2	1	35	1	52	5	0	2	6	.250	0	0-0	6	4.77	4.92
2002	2 Tms	NL	58	5	0	15	82.2	378	98	52	49	10	3	2	0	45	4	59	10	1	4	4	.500	0	0-0	6	5.90	5.33
2003	2 Tms	NL	15	0	0	4	12.2	63	15	16	15	2	1	2	0	10	1	16	5	0	0	0	-	0	0-0	2	6.96	10.66
2004	KC	AL	40	12	0	5	108.0	483	114	64	57	12	7	5	4	50	3	91	6	2	4	8	.333	0	0-1	5	4.81	4.75
2005	SD	NL	36	1	0	9	43.2	215	57	30	25	3	1	0	1	32	2	35	3	1	3	2	.600	0	0-1	0	7.06	5.15
2006	Min	AL	66	0	0	8	50.2	194	35	8	5	3	1	0	0	15	2	49	4	0	5	0	1.000	0	0-1	16	1.90	0.89
2007	Min	AL	50	0	0	7	29.1	139	34	14	13	1	3	3	2	21	1	21	4	0	2	1	.667	0	0-0	8	6.08	3.99
2008	Min	AL	75	0	0	16	46.1	188	40	12	12	4	1	0	2	15	2	39	5	0	3	0	1.000	0	0-3	17	3.14	2.33
2009	StL	NL	75	0	0	10	41.0	180	35	17	15	2	5	1	3	21	1	33	5	1	0	2	.000	0	1-1	18	3.53	3.29
2010	StL	NL	59	0	0	13	38.0	163	34	15	15	2	2	1	2	23	3	25	4	0	3	1	.750	0	1-4	6	3.92	3.55
2011	Bos	AL	4	0	0	0	1.2	10	2	3	3	0	0	0	0	2	0	1	0	0	0	0	-	0	0-0	0	13.94	16.20
98	LAD	NL	11	3	0	4	28.2	130	27	17	15	1	3	1	0	20	4	33	1	1	0	4	.000	0	0-0	0	4.16	4.71
98	Cin	NL	8	7	0	0	38.2	170	35	19	19	2	4	1	1	27	1	44	5	0	3	1	.750	0	0-0	0	4.54	4.42
02	Col	NL	43	0	0	13	40.1	182	43	19	19	1	2	2	0	24	3	30	4	0	0	1	.000	0	0-0	4	4.55	4.24
02	Tex	AL	15	5	0	2	42.1	196	55	33	30	9	1	0	0	21	1	29	6	1	4	3	.571	0	0-0	2	7.24	6.38
03	Pit	NL	12	0	0	4	10.1	50	10	13	12	1	1	2	0	9	1	11	5	0	0	0	-	0	0-0	2	5.43	10.45
03	Ari	NL	3	0	0	0	2.1	13	5	3	3	1	0	0	0	1	0	5	0	0	0	0	-	0	0-0	0	14.73	11.57
	Postseason		4	0	0	0	2.0	10	2	4	2	1	0	0	0	2	1	2	0	0	0	0	-	0	0-0	0	8.87	9.00
	15 ML YEARS		673	40	0	120	726.2	3243	724	384	340	61	45	25	23	400	29	642	70	8	35	35	.500	0	4-15	106	4.60	4.21

Jo-Jo Reyes

Pitches: L **Bats:** L **Pos:** SP-25; RP-4   **Ht:** 6'2" **Wt:** 230 **Born:** 11/20/1984 **Age:** 27

Year	Team	Lg	G	GS	CG	GF	IP	BFP	H	R	ER	HR	SH	SF	HB	TBB	IBB	SO	WP	Bk	W	L	Pct	Sh	Sv-Op	Hld	ERC	ERA
2007	Atl	NL	11	10	0	0	50.2	230	55	39	35	9	5	2	1	30	2	27	1	0	2	2	.500	0	0-0	0	6.06	6.22
2008	Atl	NL	23	22	0	0	113.0	512	134	77	73	18	9	3	3	52	4	78	2	0	3	11	.214	0	0-0	0	5.97	5.81
2009	Atl	NL	6	5	0	0	27.0	119	27	25	21	4	1	1	1	13	3	21	0	0	0	2	.000	0	0-0	0	4.73	7.00
2010	Atl	NL	1	0	0	0	3.1	23	10	9	9	2	0	0	0	3	0	2	0	0	0	0	-	0	0-0	0	26.51	24.30

		HOW MUCH HE PITCHED						WHAT HE GAVE UP											THE RESULTS							
Year	Team	Lg	G	GS	CG	GF	IP	BFP	H	R	ER	HR	SH	SF	HB	TBB	IBB	SO	WP	Bk	W	L	Pct	Sh	Sv-Op	Hld	ERC	ERA
2011	2 Tms	AL	29	25	1	1	140.2	641	176	99	87	21	3	3	7	48	0	87	7	0	7	11	.389	0	0-0	0	5.87	5.57
11	Tor	AL	20	20	1	0	110.0	504	140	78	66	14	3	3	6	35	0	64	6	0	5	8	.385	0	0-0	0	5.71	5.40
11	Bal	AL	9	5	0	1	30.2	137	36	21	21	7	0	0	1	13	0	23	1	0	2	3	.400	0	0-0	0	6.42	6.16
	5 ML YEARS		70	62	1	1	334.2	1525	402	249	225	54	18	9	12	146	9	215	10	0	12	26	.316	0	0-0	0	6.00	6.05

Jose Reyes

Bats: B Throws: R Pos: SS-124; PH-2   Ht: 6'1" Wt: 200 Born: 6/11/1983 Age: 29

								BATTING														BASERUNNING				AVERAGES		
Year	Team	Lg	G	AB	H	2B	3B	HR	(Hm	Rd)	TB	R	RBI	RC	TBB	IBB	SO	HBP	SH	SF		SB	CS	SB%	GDP	Avg	OBP	Slg
2011	Bklyn*	A-	1	3	1	1	0	0	(-	-)	2	1	0	0	0	0	0	0	0	0		0	0	-	0	.333	.333	.667
2011	Bnghtn*	AA	3	9	3	0	0	1	(-	-)	6	3	1	2	1	0	0	0	0	0		0	0	-	0	.333	.400	.667
2003	NYM	NL	69	274	84	12	4	5	(1	4)	119	47	32	46	13	0	36	0	2	3		13	3	.81	1	.307	.334	.434
2004	NYM	NL	53	220	56	16	2	2	(1	1)	82	33	14	25	5	0	31	0	4	0		19	2	.90	1	.255	.271	.373
2005	NYM	NL	161	696	190	24	17	7	(2	5)	269	99	58	84	27	0	78	2	4	4		60	15	.80	7	.273	.300	.386
2006	NYM	NL	153	647	194	30	17	19	(9	10)	315	122	81	121	53	6	81	1	2	0		64	17	.79	6	.300	.354	.487
2007	NYM	NL	160	681	191	36	12	12	(7	5)	287	119	57	99	77	13	78	1	5	1		78	21	.79	6	.280	.354	.421
2008	NYM	NL	159	688	204	37	19	16	(9	7)	327	113	68	117	66	8	82	1	5	3		56	15	.79	9	.297	.358	.475
2009	NYM	NL	36	147	41	7	2	2	(1	1)	58	18	15	20	18	1	19	0	0	1		11	2	.85	2	.279	.355	.395
2010	NYM	NL	133	563	159	29	10	11	(8	3)	241	83	54	76	31	4	63	2	4	3		30	10	.75	8	.282	.321	.428
2011	NYM	NL	126	537	181	31	16	7	(4	3)	265	101	44	90	43	9	41	0	2	4		39	7	.85	5	.337	.384	.493
	Postseason		10	44	11	1	1	1	(1	0)	17	7	5	6	3	1	5	0	0	0		3	1	.75	0	.250	.298	.386
	9 ML YEARS		1050	4453	1300	222	99	81	(42	39)	1963	735	423	678	333	41	509	7	28	19		370	92	.80	45	.292	.341	.441

Greg Reynolds

Pitches: R Bats: R Pos: RP-10; SP-3   Ht: 6'7" Wt: 225 Born: 7/3/1985 Age: 26

			HOW MUCH HE PITCHED						WHAT HE GAVE UP											THE RESULTS							
Year	Team	Lg	G	GS	CG	GF	IP	BFP	H	R	ER	HR	SH	SF	HB	TBB	IBB	SO	WP	Bk	W	L	Pct	Sh	Sv-Op	Hld	ERC	ERA
2006	Mdest	A+	11	11	0	0	48.2	205	51	22	18	1	0	0	3	14	0	29	3	0	2	1	.667	0	0- -	-	3.67	3.33
2007	Tulsa	AA	8	8	0	0	50.2	190	32	10	8	2	1	0	2	9	0	35	0	0	4	1	.800	0	0- -	-	1.41	1.42
2008	ColSpr	AAA	13	13	0	0	63.1	286	84	38	30	4	2	3	3	22	0	37	0	0	1	3	.250	0	0- -	-	5.81	4.26
2009	ColSpr	AAA	1	1	0	0	4.1	24	6	5	5	0	0	2	0	3	0	3	0	0	0	0	-	0	0- -	-	5.97	10.38
2010	Mdest	A+	2	2	0	0	11.0	52	13	4	1	1	0	0	0	2	0	6	1	0	1	0	1.000	0	0- -	-	3.71	0.82
2010	Tulsa	AA	17	17	0	0	89.2	384	105	55	52	10	1	2	4	15	0	45	3	0	7	6	.538	0	0- -	-	4.38	5.22
2011	ColSpr	AAA	19	19	0	0	109.2	511	160	88	83	10	5	6	2	32	1	65	0	0	6	7	.462	0	0- -	-	6.34	6.81
2008	Col	NL	14	13	0	0	62.0	294	83	58	56	14	4	2	4	26	3	22	2	0	2	8	.200	0	0-0	0	7.36	8.13
2011	Col	NL	13	3	0	3	32.0	144	40	22	22	6	0	1	1	10	2	18	1	0	3	0	1.000	0	0-0	0	5.85	6.19
	2 ML YEARS		27	16	0	3	94.0	438	123	80	78	20	4	3	5	36	5	40	3	0	5	8	.385	0	0-0	0	6.84	7.47

Mark Reynolds

Bats: R Throws: R Pos: 3B-114; 1B-44; PH-1   Ht: 6'2" Wt: 220 Born: 8/3/1983 Age: 28

								BATTING														BASERUNNING				AVERAGES		
Year	Team	Lg	G	AB	H	2B	3B	HR	(Hm	Rd)	TB	R	RBI	RC	TBB	IBB	SO	HBP	SH	SF		SB	CS	SB%	GDP	Avg	OBP	Slg
2007	Ari	NL	111	366	102	20	4	17	(7	10)	181	62	62	62	37	4	129	5	1	5		0	1	.00	5	.279	.349	.495
2008	Ari	NL	152	539	129	28	3	28	(13	15)	247	87	97	82	64	0	204	3	1	6		11	2	.85	10	.239	.320	.458
2009	Ari	NL	155	578	150	30	1	44	(19	25)	314	98	102	94	76	3	223	5	0	3		24	9	.73	8	.260	.349	.543
2010	Ari	NL	145	499	99	17	2	32	(21	11)	216	79	85	77	83	7	211	9	0	5		7	4	.64	8	.198	.320	.433
2011	Bal	AL	155	534	118	27	1	37	(17	20)	258	84	86	77	75	2	196	7	0	4		6	4	.60	11	.221	.323	.483
	Postseason		7	26	4	0	0	2	(1	1)	10	3	2	1	2	0	9	1	0	0		0	0	-	0	.154	.241	.385
	5 ML YEARS		718	2516	598	122	11	158	(77	81)	1216	410	432	392	335	16	963	29	2	23		48	20	.71	42	.238	.331	.483

Matt Reynolds

Pitches: L Bats: L Pos: RP-73   Ht: 6'5" Wt: 240 Born: 10/2/1984 Age: 27

			HOW MUCH HE PITCHED						WHAT HE GAVE UP											THE RESULTS							
Year	Team	Lg	G	GS	CG	GF	IP	BFP	H	R	ER	HR	SH	SF	HB	TBB	IBB	SO	WP	Bk	W	L	Pct	Sh	Sv-Op	Hld	ERC	ERA
2007	TriCity	A-	20	0	0	5	35.0	148	37	21	14	4	2	1	4	4	0	27	0	0	1	4	.200	0	0- -	-	3.37	3.60
2008	Ashvll	A	42	0	0	14	57.0	237	49	19	16	4	3	2	1	14	0	53	7	0	6	2	.750	0	2- -	-	2.55	2.53
2009	Mdest	A+	39	0	0	14	49.0	178	32	8	7	2	2	0	0	8	0	58	2	0	5	3	.625	0	3- -	-	1.40	1.29
2009	Tulsa	AA	21	0	0	9	25.2	108	23	12	12	3	1	0	1	9	0	29	2	0	1	2	.333	0	1- -	-	3.58	4.21
2010	ColSpr	AAA	50	0	0	31	55.0	227	49	18	16	2	2	0	1	16	0	67	2	0	1	3	.250	0	7- -	-	2.73	2.62
2010	Col	NL	21	0	0	2	18.0	70	10	4	4	2	1	2	1	5	0	17	1	0	1	0	1.000	0	0-0	2	1.87	2.00
2011	Col	NL	73	0	0	9	50.2	211	48	24	23	10	1	4	2	18	5	50	5	2	1	2	.333	0	0-2	18	4.18	4.09
	2 ML YEARS		94	0	0	11	68.2	281	58	28	27	12	2	5	2	23	5	67	6	2	2	2	.500	0	0-2	20	3.52	3.54

Arthur Rhodes

Pitches: L Bats: L Pos: RP-51   Ht: 6'2" Wt: 220 Born: 10/24/1969 Age: 42

			HOW MUCH HE PITCHED						WHAT HE GAVE UP											THE RESULTS							
Year	Team	Lg	G	GS	CG	GF	IP	BFP	H	R	ER	HR	SH	SF	HB	TBB	IBB	SO	WP	Bk	W	L	Pct	Sh	Sv-Op	Hld	ERC	ERA
1991	Bal	AL	8	8	0	0	36.0	174	47	35	32	4	1	3	0	23	0	23	2	0	0	3	.000	0	0-0	0	7.00	8.00
1992	Bal	AL	15	15	2	0	94.1	394	87	39	38	6	5	1	1	38	2	77	2	1	7	5	.583	1	0-0	0	3.48	3.63
1993	Bal	AL	17	17	0	0	85.2	387	91	62	62	16	2	3	1	49	1	49	2	0	5	6	.455	0	0-0	0	5.88	6.51
1994	Bal	AL	10	10	3	0	52.2	238	51	34	34	8	2	3	2	30	1	47	3	0	3	5	.375	2	0-0	0	5.03	5.81
1995	Bal	AL	19	9	0	3	75.1	336	68	53	52	13	4	0	0	48	1	77	3	1	2	5	.286	0	0-1	0	4.97	6.21
1996	Bal	AL	28	2	0	5	53.0	224	48	28	24	6	1	1	0	23	3	62	0	0	9	1	.900	0	1-1	2	3.72	4.08
1997	Bal	AL	53	0	0	6	95.1	378	75	32	32	9	0	4	4	26	5	102	2	0	10	3	.769	0	1-2	9	2.58	3.02
1998	Bal	AL	45	0	0	10	77.0	321	65	30	30	8	2	5	1	34	2	83	1	1	4	4	.500	0	4-8	10	3.47	3.51

(pitcher, continued)

Year	Team	Lg	G	GS	CG	GF	IP	BFP	H	R	ER	HR	SH	SF	HB	TBB	IBB	SO	WP	Bk	W	L	Pct	Sh	Sv-Op	Hld	ERC	ERA
1999	Bal	AL	43	0	0	11	53.0	244	43	37	32	9	2	2	0	45	6	59	4	0	3	4	.429	0	3-5	5	5.07	5.43
2000	Sea	AL	72	0	0	9	69.1	281	51	34	33	6	1	2	0	29	3	77	4	0	5	8	.385	0	0-7	24	2.62	4.28
2001	Sea	AL	71	0	0	16	68.0	258	46	14	13	5	1	0	1	12	0	83	3	0	8	0	1.000	0	3-7	31	1.61	1.72
2002	Sea	AL	66	0	0	9	69.2	257	45	18	18	4	2	1	0	13	1	81	2	0	10	4	.714	0	2-7	27	1.46	2.33
2003	Sea	AL	67	0	0	14	54.0	228	53	25	25	4	2	0	1	18	2	48	2	0	3	3	.500	0	3-6	18	3.57	4.17
2004	Oak	AL	37	0	0	25	38.2	182	46	23	22	9	3	1	0	21	4	34	2	0	3	3	.500	0	9-14	3	6.54	5.12
2005	Cle	AL	47	0	0	8	43.1	175	33	13	10	2	0	2	1	12	2	43	0	0	3	1	.750	0	0-3	16	2.06	2.08
2006	Phi	NL	55	0	0	10	45.2	214	47	27	27	2	1	0	2	30	7	48	7	0	0	5	.000	0	4-7	23	4.63	5.32
2008	2 Tms		61	0	0	6	35.1	146	28	9	8	0	4	1	0	16	4	40	1	0	4	1	.800	0	2-3	24	2.36	2.04
2009	Cin	NL	66	0	0	10	53.1	215	37	16	15	3	5	2	1	20	3	48	1	0	1	1	.500	0	0-2	25	2.11	2.53
2010	Cin	NL	70	0	0	8	55.0	217	38	14	14	4	2	2	1	18	0	50	1	0	4	4	.500	0	0-2	26	2.14	2.29
2011	2 Tms		51	0	0	11	33.0	138	34	17	17	8	0	1	0	11	1	21	1	0	3	4	.429	0	1-3	11	5.05	4.64
08	Sea	AL	36	0	0	4	22.0	92	17	8	7	0	3	1	0	13	2	26	1	0	2	1	.667	0	1-2	13	2.79	2.86
08	Fla	NL	25	0	0	2	13.1	54	11	1	1	0	1	0	0	3	2	14	0	0	2	0	1.000	0	1-1	11	1.69	0.68
11	Tex	AL	32	0	0	10	24.1	105	28	13	13	6	0	0	0	8	1	15	1	0	3	3	.500	0	1-3	7	5.76	4.81
11	StL	NL	19	0	0	1	8.2	33	6	4	4	2	0	1	0	3	0	6	0	0	0	1	.000	0	0-0	4	3.20	4.15
	Postseason		21	0	0	0	17.1	77	16	9	9	2	2	1	1	10	2	20	4	0	0	1	.000	0	0-3	5	4.50	4.67
20 ML YEARS			901	61	5	161	1187.2	5007	1033	560	538	126	40	34	16	516	48	1152	43	3	87	70	.554	3	33-78	254	3.54	4.08

Will Rhymes

Bats: L **Throws:** R **Pos:** 2B-24; DH-4; PH-4; PR-3 **Ht:** 5'9" **Wt:** 155 **Born:** 4/1/1983 **Age:** 29

Year	Team	Lg	G	AB	H	2B	3B	HR	(Hm	Rd)	TB	R	RBI	RC	TBB	IBB	SO	HBP	SH	SF	SB	CS	SB%	GDP	Avg	OBP	Slg
2005	Oneont	A-	61	250	82	11	3	2	(-	-)	105	49	27	44	25	0	15	1	3	0	14	3	.82	1	.328	.391	.420
2006	WMich	A	126	506	132	19	2	3	(-	-)	164	80	39	62	53	0	53	3	12	4	23	6	.79	4	.261	.332	.324
2007	Lkland	A+	88	326	99	12	2	4	(-	-)	127	43	35	57	44	0	38	2	12	1	24	3	.89	2	.304	.389	.390
2007	Erie	AA	39	155	41	6	0	1	(-	-)	50	21	21	16	6	0	20	2	6	2	5	1	.83	2	.265	.297	.323
2008	Erie	AA	131	516	158	21	7	3	(-	-)	202	76	60	78	44	2	66	3	10	3	17	6	.74	5	.306	.362	.391
2008	Toledo	AAA	6	25	8	0	1	0	(-	-)	10	5	2	3	2	0	4	0	0	0	0	0	-	0	.320	.370	.400
2009	Toledo	AAA	109	404	105	17	6	3	(-	-)	143	48	41	50	36	0	58	3	10	2	20	8	.71	5	.260	.324	.354
2010	Toledo	AAA	95	364	111	20	7	2	(-	-)	151	59	36	62	36	1	35	4	13	4	22	5	.81	2	.305	.370	.415
2011	Toledo	AAA	104	405	124	17	4	3	(-	-)	158	57	24	63	46	1	46	2	8	3	13	8	.62	7	.306	.377	.390
2010	Det	AL	54	191	58	12	3	1	(1	0)	79	30	19	27	14	0	16	0	7	1	0	3	.00	1	.304	.350	.414
2011	Det	AL	29	85	20	3	0	0	(0	0)	23	13	2	8	11	0	12	0	3	0	1	0	1.00	2	.235	.323	.271
2 ML YEARS			83	276	78	15	3	1	(1	0)	102	43	21	35	25	0	28	0	10	1	1	3	.25	3	.283	.341	.370

Clayton Richard

Pitches: L **Bats:** L **Pos:** SP-18 **Ht:** 6'5" **Wt:** 240 **Born:** 9/12/1983 **Age:** 28

Year	Team	Lg	G	GS	CG	GF	IP	BFP	H	R	ER	HR	SH	SF	HB	TBB	IBB	SO	WP	Bk	W	L	Pct	Sh	Sv-Op	Hld	ERC	ERA
2008	CWS	AL	13	8	0	3	47.2	215	61	37	32	5	0	1	0	13	2	29	1	1	2	5	.286	0	0-0	0	5.06	6.04
2009	2 Tms		38	26	1	3	153.0	663	154	81	75	17	8	5	3	71	0	114	7	3	9	5	.643	0	0-0	0	4.60	4.41
2010	SD	NL	33	33	1	0	201.2	861	206	89	84	16	6	2	4	78	6	153	4	2	14	9	.609	1	0-0	0	4.09	3.75
2011	SD	NL	18	18	0	0	99.2	427	104	52	43	8	4	1	2	38	2	53	3	1	5	9	.357	0	0-0	0	4.22	3.88
09	CWS	AL	26	14	1	3	89.0	387	94	50	46	10	3	4	3	37	0	66	5	2	4	3	.571	0	0-0	0	4.76	4.65
09	SD	NL	12	12	0	0	64.0	276	60	31	29	7	5	1	0	34	0	48	2	1	5	2	.714	0	0-0	0	4.38	4.08
	Postseason		2	0	0	0	6.1	25	5	1	1	0	0	0	0	3	0	6	0	0	0	0	-	0	0-0	0	2.74	1.42
4 ML YEARS			102	85	2	6	502.0	2166	525	259	234	46	18	9	9	200	10	349	15	7	30	28	.517	1	0-0	0	4.36	4.20

Garrett Richards

Pitches: R **Bats:** R **Pos:** RP-4; SP-3 **Ht:** 6'3" **Wt:** 215 **Born:** 5/27/1988 **Age:** 24

Year	Team	Lg	G	GS	CG	GF	IP	BFP	H	R	ER	HR	SH	SF	HB	TBB	IBB	SO	WP	Bk	W	L	Pct	Sh	Sv-Op	Hld	ERC	ERA
2009	Orem	R+	8	8	0	0	35.1	141	37	6	6	0	2	2		4	0	30	4	0	3	1	.750	0	0--	0	2.91	1.53
2010	CRpds	A	19	19	2	0	108.1	443	92	48	41	6	3	1	3	34	0	108	1	1	8	4	.667	0	0--	0	2.78	3.41
2010	RCuca	A+	7	7	0	0	34.2	147	38	17	15	4	0	2	1	9	0	41	4	1	4	1	.800	0	0--	0	4.34	3.89
2011	Ark	AA	22	21	3	0	143.0	579	123	58	50	10	3	1	8	40	0	103	7	0	12	2	.857	0	0--	0	2.95	3.15
2011	LAA	AL	7	3	0	2	14.0	62	16	11	9	0				7	0	9	2	0	0	2	.000	0	0-0	0	6.97	5.79

Antoan Richardson

Bats: B **Throws:** R **Pos:** PR-5; PH-4 ANN-twaan **Ht:** 5'8" **Wt:** 165 **Born:** 10/8/1983 **Age:** 28

Year	Team	Lg	G	AB	H	2B	3B	HR	(Hm	Rd)	TB	R	RBI	RC	TBB	IBB	SO	HBP	SH	SF	SB	CS	SB%	GDP	Avg	OBP	Slg
2005	Giants	R	53	193	62	4	2	1	(-	-)	73	45	10	46	44	1	43	8	7	0	40	6	.87	1	.321	.465	.378
2006	Augsta	A	124	418	122	17	4	2	(-	-)	153	78	28	74	54	0	73	9	7	5	66	9	.88	4	.292	.381	.366
2007	SnJos	A+	107	384	107	12	7	2	(-	-)	139	85	29	68	67	0	94	11	5	2	43	11	.80	2	.279	.399	.362
2008	Conn	AA	123	365	88	5	6	5	(-	-)	120	63	31	53	55	0	81	12	10	3	33	6	.85	3	.241	.356	.329
2009	Conn	AA	50	87	18	3	2	0	(-	-)	25	13	6	18	11	0	31	4	3	1	6	5	.55	0	.207	.320	.287
2010	Missi	AA	74	272	76	8	1	0	(-	-)	86	60	20	44	41	0	47	12	3	3	24	3	.89	4	.279	.393	.316
2010	Gwnntt	AAA	7	25	7	0	0	0	(-	-)	7	1	2	4	5	0	9	1	0	1	3	0	1.00	0	.280	.406	.280
2011	Missi	AA	91	272	77	9	0	1	(-	-)	89	64	21	49	60	1	66	11	9	1	17	5	.77	1	.283	.430	.327
2011	Gwnntt	AAA	2	3	1	0	0	0	(-	-)	1	1	0	0	1	0	1	0	0	0	0	0	-	0	.333	.500	.333
2011	Atl	NL	9	4	2	0	0	0	(0	0)	2	1	0	0	0	0	0	0	0	0	1	0	1.00	0	.500	.500	.500

Scott Richmond

Pitches: R **Bats:** R **Pos:** RP-1
Ht: 6'5" **Wt:** 215 **Born:** 8/30/1979 **Age:** 32

				HOW MUCH HE PITCHED						WHAT HE GAVE UP												THE RESULTS							
Year	Team	Lg	G	GS	CG	GF	IP	BFP	H	R	ER	HR	SH	SF	HB	TBB	IBB	SO	WP	Bk	W	L	Pct	Sh	Sv-Op	Hld	ERC	ERA
2011	LsVgs*	AAA	26	20	0	3	113.0	533	149	98	92	24	2	8	3	56	0	87	8	1	6	9	.400	-	0- -	-	7.46	7.33
2008	Tor	AL	5	5	1	0	27.0	113	32	12	12	2	0	1	2	2	0	20	0	0	1	3	.250	1	0-0	0	3.99	4.00
2009	Tor	AL	27	24	1	1	138.2	610	147	90	85	27	1	2	0	59	1	117	5	1	8	11	.421	0	0-0	0	5.20	5.52
2011	Tor	AL	1	0	0	1	0.1	1	0	0	0	0	0	0	0	0	0	0	0	0	0	0	-	0	0-0	0	0.00	0.00
	3 ML YEARS		33	29	2	2	166.0	724	179	102	97	29	1	3	2	61	1	137	5	1	9	14	.391	1	0-0	0	4.98	5.26

Alex Rios

Bats: R **Throws:** R **Pos:** CF-143; PR-3; DH-2
Ht: 6'5" **Wt:** 205 **Born:** 2/18/1981 **Age:** 31

									BATTING														BASERUNNING				AVERAGES		
Year	Team	Lg	G	AB	H	2B	3B	HR	(Hm	Rd)	TB	R	RBI	RC	TBB	IBB	SO	HBP	SH	SF	SB	CS	SB%	GDP	Avg	OBP	Slg
2004	Tor	AL	111	426	122	24	7	1	(0	1)	163	55	28	49	31	0	84	2	1	0	15	3	.83	14	.286	.338	.383
2005	Tor	AL	146	481	126	23	6	10	(5	5)	191	71	59	56	28	1	101	5	0	5	14	9	.61	14	.262	.306	.397
2006	Tor	AL	128	450	136	33	6	17	(12	5)	232	68	82	83	35	1	89	3	0	10	15	6	.71	10	.302	.349	.516
2007	Tor	AL	161	643	191	43	7	24	(13	11)	320	114	85	105	55	3	103	6	0	7	17	4	.81	9	.297	.354	.498
2008	Tor	AL	155	635	185	47	8	15	(9	6)	293	91	79	92	44	2	112	2	0	5	32	8	.80	20	.291	.337	.461
2009	2 Tms	AL	149	582	144	31	2	17	(15	2)	230	63	71	64	37	1	107	6	1	7	24	5	.83	21	.247	.296	.395
2010	CWS	AL	147	567	161	29	3	21	(10	11)	259	89	88	84	38	4	93	7	0	5	34	14	.71	21	.284	.334	.457
2011	CWS	AL	145	537	122	22	2	13	(7	6)	187	64	44	35	27	4	68	2	0	4	11	6	.65	20	.227	.265	.348
09	Tor	AL	108	436	115	25	2	14	(12	2)	186	52	62	60	31	1	78	6	0	6	19	3	.86	14	.264	.317	.427
09	CWS	AL	41	146	29	6	0	3	(3	0)	44	11	9	4	6	0	29	0	1	1	5	2	.71	7	.199	.229	.301
	8 ML YEARS		1142	4321	1187	252	41	118	(71	47)	1875	615	536	568	295	16	757	33	2	43	162	55	.75	129	.275	.323	.434

Juan Rivera

Bats: R **Throws:** R **Pos:** LF-56; 1B-38; DH-19; RF-17; PH-10
Ht: 6'2" **Wt:** 230 **Born:** 7/3/1978 **Age:** 33

									BATTING														BASERUNNING				AVERAGES		
Year	Team	Lg	G	AB	H	2B	3B	HR	(Hm	Rd)	TB	R	RBI	RC	TBB	IBB	SO	HBP	SH	SF	SB	CS	SB%	GDP	Avg	OBP	Slg
2001	NYY	AL	3	4	0	0	0	0	(0	0)	0	0	0	0	0	0	0	0	0	0	0	0	-	0	.000	.000	.000
2002	NYY	AL	28	83	22	5	0	1	(0	1)	30	9	6	8	6	0	10	0	1	1	1	1	.50	4	.265	.311	.361
2003	NYY	AL	57	173	46	14	0	7	(4	3)	81	22	26	23	10	1	27	0	1	1	0	0	-	8	.266	.304	.468
2004	Mon	NL	134	391	120	24	1	12	(6	6)	182	48	49	60	34	7	45	1	0	0	6	2	.75	11	.307	.364	.465
2005	LAA	AL	106	350	95	17	1	15	(8	7)	159	46	59	49	23	0	44	0	2	1	1	9	.10	15	.271	.316	.454
2006	LAA	AL	124	448	139	27	0	23	(12	11)	235	65	85	80	33	0	59	7	0	6	0	4	.00	14	.310	.362	.525
2007	LAA	AL	14	43	12	1	0	2	(1	1)	19	3	8	5	1	0	4	0	0	0	0	0	-	5	.279	.295	.442
2008	LAA	AL	89	256	63	13	0	12	(5	7)	112	31	45	28	16	0	33	0	0	8	1	1	.50	10	.246	.282	.438
2009	LAA	AL	138	529	152	24	1	25	(11	14)	253	72	88	82	36	1	57	2	0	5	0	1	.00	19	.287	.332	.478
2010	LAA	AL	124	416	105	20	0	15	(4	11)	170	53	52	50	33	4	58	4	0	2	2	2	.50	10	.252	.312	.409
2011	2 Tms	AL	132	466	120	23	1	11	(6	5)	178	46	74	58	43	1	76	3	0	9	5	3	.63	16	.258	.319	.382
11	Tor	AL	70	247	60	11	0	6	(3	3)	89	22	28	23	22	1	41	2	0	4	3	2	.60	11	.243	.305	.360
11	LAD	NL	62	219	60	12	1	5	(3	2)	89	24	46	35	21	0	35	1	0	5	2	1	.67	5	.274	.333	.406
	Postseason		36	105	25	5	0	1	(1	0)	33	10	8	5	8	2	14	0	1	0	1	0	1.00	5	.238	.292	.314
	11 ML YEARS		949	3159	874	168	4	123	(57	66)	1419	395	492	443	235	14	413	17	4	33	16	23	.41	112	.277	.327	.449

Mariano Rivera

Pitches: R **Bats:** R **Pos:** RP-64
Ht: 6'2" **Wt:** 185 **Born:** 11/29/1969 **Age:** 42

								HOW MUCH HE PITCHED								WHAT HE GAVE UP									THE RESULTS						
Year	Team	Lg	G	GS	CG	GF	IP	BFP	H	R	ER	HR	SH	SF	HB	TBB	IBB	SO	WP	Bk	W	L	Pct	Sh	Sv-Op	Hld	ERC	ERA
1995	NYY	AL	19	10	0	2	67.0	301	71	43	41	11	0	2	2	30	0	51	0	1	5	3	.625	0	0-1	0	5.14	5.51
1996	NYY	AL	61	0	0	14	107.2	425	73	25	25	1	2	1	2	34	3	130	1	0	8	3	.727	0	5-8	27	1.65	2.09
1997	NYY	AL	66	0	0	56	71.2	301	65	17	15	5	3	4	0	20	6	68	2	0	6	4	.600	0	43-52	0	2.73	1.88
1998	NYY	AL	54	0	0	49	61.1	246	48	13	13	3	2	3	1	17	1	36	0	0	3	0	1.000	0	36-41	0	2.21	1.91
1999	NYY	AL	66	0	0	63	69.0	268	43	15	14	2	0	2	3	18	3	52	2	1	4	3	.571	0	45-49	0	1.47	1.83
2000	NYY	AL	66	0	0	61	75.2	311	58	26	24	4	5	2	0	25	3	58	2	0	7	4	.636	0	36-41	0	2.20	2.85
2001	NYY	AL	71	0	0	66	80.2	310	61	24	21	5	4	1	1	12	2	83	1	0	4	6	.400	0	50-57	0	1.74	2.34
2002	NYY	AL	45	0	0	36	46.0	187	35	16	14	3	2	0	2	11	2	41	1	1	1	4	.200	0	28-32	2	2.08	2.74
2003	NYY	AL	64	0	0	57	70.2	277	61	15	13	3	1	2	4	10	1	63	0	0	5	2	.714	0	53-57	0	2.45	1.94
2004	NYY	AL	74	0	0	69	78.2	316	65	17	17	3	2	0	5	20	3	66	0	0	4	2	.667	0	43-47	0	1.48	1.38
2005	NYY	AL	71	0	0	67	78.1	306	50	18	12	2	0	1	4	18	0	80	0	0	7	4	.636	0	43-47	0	2.03	1.80
2006	NYY	AL	63	0	0	59	75.0	293	61	16	15	3	1	2	5	11	4	55	0	0	5	5	.500	0	34-37	0	2.92	3.15
2007	NYY	AL	67	0	0	59	71.1	295	68	25	25	4	1	1	6	12	2	74	1	0	3	4	.429	0	30-34	0	1.09	1.40
2008	NYY	AL	64	0	0	60	70.2	259	41	11	11	4	1	1	2	6	0	77	1	0	6	5	.545	0	39-40	0	1.93	1.76
2009	NYY	AL	66	0	0	55	66.1	257	48	14	13	7	0	0	1	12	1	72	1	0	3	3	.500	0	44-46	0	1.50	1.80
2010	NYY	AL	61	0	0	55	60.0	230	39	14	12	2	0	1	5	8	2	45	0	0	3	3	.500	0	33-38	0	1.75	1.80
2011	NYY	AL	64	0	0	54	61.1	233	47	13	13	3	2	2	2	8	2	60	1	0	1	2	.333	0	44-49	0	1.75	1.91
	Postseason		94	0	0	76	139.2	523	86	13	11	2	7	3	3	21	4	109	3	0	8	1	.889	0	42-47	4	1.14	0.71
	17 ML YEARS		1042	10	0	882	1211.1	4815	934	322	298	65	26	25	45	275	36	1111	13	3	75	57	.568	0	603-675	29	2.07	2.21

Mike Rivera

Bats: R **Throws:** R **Pos:** C-1
Ht: 6'1" **Wt:** 236 **Born:** 9/8/1976 **Age:** 35

									BATTING														BASERUNNING				AVERAGES		
Year	Team	Lg	G	AB	H	2B	3B	HR	(Hm	Rd)	TB	R	RBI	RC	TBB	IBB	SO	HBP	SH	SF	SB	CS	SB%	GDP	Avg	OBP	Slg
2011	Nashv*	AAA	61	193	46	10	0	7	(-	-)	77	16	31	25	19	1	55	3	2	1	2	1	.67	7	.238	.315	.399
2001	Det	AL	4	12	4	2	0	0	(0	0)	6	2	1	2	0	0	2	0	0	0	0	0	-	0	.333	.333	.500
2002	Det	AL	39	132	30	8	1	1	(0	1)	43	11	11	8	4	0	35	1	0	1	0	0	-	5	.227	.254	.326
2003	SD	NL	19	53	9	1	0	1	(0	1)	13	2	2	0	5	0	11	0	0	0	0	0	-	4	.170	.241	.245

(continued)

Year	Team	Lg	G	AB	H	2B	3B	HR	(Hm	Rd)	TB	R	RBI	RC	TBB	IBB	SO	HBP	SH	SF	SB	CS	SB%	GDP	Avg	OBP	Slg
2006	Mil	NL	46	142	38	9	0	6	(3	3)	65	16	24	19	10	5	21	3	1	2	0	0	-	3	.268	.325	.458
2007	Mil	NL	11	13	3	0	0	2	(1	1)	9	2	3	2	1	0	3	0	1	0	0	0	-	0	.231	.286	.692
2008	Mil	NL	21	62	19	5	0	1	(0	1)	27	8	14	13	6	0	10	1	0	0	0	0	-	0	.306	.377	.435
2009	Mil	NL	41	114	26	7	0	2	(2	0)	39	10	14	15	15	3	32	2	0	1	2	0	1.00	2	.228	.326	.342
2010	Fla	NL	7	14	0	0	0	0	(0	0)	0	0	0	0	2	0	3	1	0	0	0	0	-	0	.000	.176	.000
2011	Mil	NL	1	6	2	0	0	0	(0	0)	2	0	0	1	0	0	1	0	0	0	0	0	-	0	.333	.333	.333
9 ML YEARS			189	548	131	32	1	13	(6	7)	204	51	69	60	43	8	118	8	2	4	3	0	1.00	20	.239	.302	.372

Rene Rivera

Bats: R **Throws:** R **Pos:** C-44; PH-1
Ht: 5'10" **Wt:** 230 **Born:** 7/31/1983 **Age:** 28

Year	Team	Lg	G	AB	H	2B	3B	HR	(Hm	Rd)	TB	R	RBI	RC	TBB	IBB	SO	HBP	SH	SF	SB	CS	SB%	GDP	Avg	OBP	Slg
2011	Roch*	AAA	43	149	40	12	0	5	(-	-)	67	15	24	22	11	0	27	2	3	1	0	0	-	5	.268	.325	.450
2004	Sea	AL	2	3	0	0	0	0	(0	0)	0	0	0	0	0	0	1	0	0	0	0	0	-	0	.000	.000	.000
2005	Sea	AL	16	48	19	3	0	1	(0	1)	25	3	6	8	1	0	11	0	0	0	0	0	-	0	.396	.408	.521
2006	Sea	AL	35	99	15	4	0	2	(1	1)	25	8	4	4	3	0	29	1	3	0	1	0	1.00	2	.152	.184	.253
2011	Min	AL	45	104	15	3	0	1	(0	1)	21	9	5	3	8	0	32	1	0	1	0	0	-	2	.144	.211	.202
4 ML YEARS			98	254	49	10	0	4	(1	3)	71	20	15	15	12	0	73	2	4	1	1	0	1.00	4	.193	.234	.280

Anthony Rizzo

Bats: L **Throws:** L **Pos:** 1B-45; PH-6
Ht: 6'3" **Wt:** 220 **Born:** 8/8/1989 **Age:** 22

Year	Team	Lg	G	AB	H	2B	3B	HR	(Hm	Rd)	TB	R	RBI	RC	TBB	IBB	SO	HBP	SH	SF	SB	CS	SB%	GDP	Avg	OBP	Slg
2007	RedSx	R	6	21	6	0	0	1	(-	-)	9	6	3	3	1	0	2	2	0	0	0	0	-	1	.286	.375	.429
2008	Grnville	A	21	83	31	6	0	0	(-	-)	37	9	11	14	3	0	15	1	0	0	0	0	-	1	.373	.402	.446
2009	Grnville	A	64	245	73	21	0	9	(-	-)	121	40	42	44	25	0	60	2	0	2	2	1	.67	5	.298	.365	.494
2009	Salem	A+	55	200	59	16	0	3	(-	-)	84	23	24	33	25	5	39	1	0	3	2	0	1.00	4	.295	.371	.420
2010	Salem	A+	29	117	29	12	0	5	(-	-)	56	26	20	20	16	2	32	0	0	2	3	0	1.00	4	.248	.333	.479
2010	Portlnd	AA	107	414	109	30	0	20	(-	-)	199	66	80	70	45	3	100	2	0	6	7	1	.88	6	.263	.334	.481
2011	Tucsn	AAA	93	356	118	34	1	26	(-	-)	232	64	101	89	43	5	89	6	0	8	7	6	.54	4	.331	.404	.652
2011	SD	NL	49	128	18	8	1	1	(1	0)	31	9	9	7	21	1	46	4	0	0	2	1	.67	2	.141	.281	.242

Brian Roberts

Bats: B **Throws:** R **Pos:** 2B-39
Ht: 5'9" **Wt:** 175 **Born:** 10/9/1977 **Age:** 34

Year	Team	Lg	G	AB	H	2B	3B	HR	(Hm	Rd)	TB	R	RBI	RC	TBB	IBB	SO	HBP	SH	SF	SB	CS	SB%	GDP	Avg	OBP	Slg
2001	Bal	AL	75	273	69	12	3	2	(0	2)	93	42	17	27	13	0	36	0	3	3	12	3	.80	3	.253	.284	.341
2002	Bal	AL	38	128	29	6	0	1	(1	0)	38	18	11	12	15	0	21	1	3	2	9	2	.82	3	.227	.308	.297
2003	Bal	AL	112	460	124	22	4	5	(3	2)	169	65	41	62	46	1	58	1	4	1	23	6	.79	9	.270	.337	.367
2004	Bal	AL	159	641	175	50	2	4	(0	4)	241	107	53	91	71	1	95	1	15	6	29	12	.71	3	.273	.344	.376
2005	Bal	AL	143	561	176	45	7	18	(9	9)	289	92	73	106	67	5	83	3	5	4	27	10	.73	6	.314	.387	.515
2006	Bal	AL	138	563	161	34	3	10	(6	4)	231	85	55	74	55	4	66	0	6	5	36	7	.84	16	.286	.347	.410
2007	Bal	AL	156	621	180	42	5	12	(6	6)	268	103	57	89	89	6	99	0	2	4	50	7	.88	8	.290	.377	.432
2008	Bal	AL	155	611	181	51	8	9	(6	3)	275	107	57	101	82	3	104	2	3	6	40	10	.80	8	.296	.378	.450
2009	Bal	AL	159	632	179	56	1	16	(4	12)	285	110	79	106	74	3	112	2	1	8	30	7	.81	7	.283	.356	.451
2010	Bal	AL	59	230	64	14	0	4	(2	2)	90	28	15	31	26	1	40	2	1	2	12	2	.86	2	.278	.354	.391
2011	Bal	AL	39	163	36	7	1	3	(1	2)	54	18	19	18	12	0	21	0	2	1	6	1	.86	4	.221	.273	.331
11 ML YEARS			1233	4883	1374	339	34	84	(38	46)	2033	775	477	733	550	24	735	12	45	42	274	67	.80	69	.281	.353	.416

Ryan Roberts

Bats: R **Throws:** R **Pos:** 3B-107; 2B-28; PH-15; LF-3; SS-1
Ht: 5'11" **Wt:** 195 **Born:** 9/19/1980 **Age:** 31

Year	Team	Lg	G	AB	H	2B	3B	HR	(Hm	Rd)	TB	R	RBI	RC	TBB	IBB	SO	HBP	SH	SF	SB	CS	SB%	GDP	Avg	OBP	Slg
2006	Tor	AL	9	13	1	0	0	1	(0	1)	4	1	1	0	1	0	4	0	0	0	0	0	-	1	.077	.143	.308
2007	Tor	AL	8	13	1	0	0	0	(0	0)	1	2	0	0	2	0	7	1	0	0	0	0	-	0	.077	.250	.077
2008	Tex	AL	1	1	0	0	0	0	(0	0)	0	0	0	0	0	0	1	0	0	0	0	0	-	0	.000	.000	.000
2009	Ari	NL	110	305	85	17	2	7	(3	4)	127	45	25	41	40	1	55	3	2	1	7	3	.70	2	.279	.367	.416
2010	Ari	NL	36	66	13	4	0	2	(1	1)	23	8	9	7	3	1	17	0	1	1	0	0	-	0	.197	.229	.348
2011	Ari	NL	143	482	120	25	2	19	(9	10)	206	86	65	75	66	2	98	2	3	2	18	9	.67	6	.249	.341	.427
6 ML YEARS			307	880	220	46	4	29	(13	16)	361	138	100	123	112	4	182	6	6	4	25	12	.68	9	.250	.337	.410

David Robertson

Pitches: R **Bats:** R **Pos:** RP-70
Ht: 5'11" **Wt:** 190 **Born:** 4/9/1985 **Age:** 27

Year	Team	Lg	HOW MUCH HE PITCHED						WHAT HE GAVE UP												THE RESULTS							
			G	GS	CG	GF	IP	BFP	H	R	ER	HR	SH	SF	HB	TBB	IBB	SO	WP	Bk	W	L	Pct	Sh	Sv-Op	Hld	ERC	ERA
2008	NYY	AL	25	0	0	8	30.1	131	29	18	18	3	0	3	0	15	2	36	6	0	4	0	1.000	0	0-0	0	4.12	5.34
2009	NYY	AL	45	0	0	20	43.2	191	36	19	16	4	0	1	2	23	1	63	6	0	2	1	.667	0	1-1	5	3.51	3.30
2010	NYY	AL	64	0	0	10	61.1	273	59	26	26	5	5	3	3	33	6	71	7	2	4	5	.444	0	1-3	14	4.29	3.82
2011	NYY	AL	70	0	0	6	66.2	272	40	9	8	1	1	0	1	35	6	100	6	1	4	0	1.000	0	1-4	34	1.85	1.08
Postseason			11	0	0	2	8.2	44	12	6	6	1	1	0	0	1	0	8	1	0	2	0	1.000	0	0-0	2	6.25	6.23
4 ML YEARS			204	0	0	46	202.0	867	164	72	68	13	6	5	5	106	15	270	25	3	14	6	.700	0	3-8	53	3.24	3.03

Shane Robinson

Bats: R **Throws:** R **Pos:** CF-5; RF-3; PH-3; LF-1 **Ht:** 5'9" **Wt:** 160 **Born:** 10/30/1984 **Age:** 27

Year	Team	Lg	G	AB	H	2B	3B	HR	(Hm	Rd)	TB	R	RBI	RC	TBB	IBB	SO	HBP	SH	SF	SB	CS	SB%	GDP	Avg	OBP	Slg
2006	QuadC	A	63	252	71	9	2	0	(-	-)	84	41	21	33	20	1	20	6	1	2	13	3	.81	9	.282	.346	.333
2007	PlmBh	A+	43	166	42	6	1	3	(-	-)	59	22	13	21	16	0	16	2	3	3	14	4	.78	4	.253	.321	.355
2007	Cards	R	4	11	2	0	0	0	(-	-)	2	1	1	0	2	0	1	0	0	1	0	0	-	0	.182	.286	.182
2008	Sprgfld	AA	63	244	86	17	3	4	(-	-)	121	46	32	48	17	0	34	3	3	4	13	5	.72	4	.352	.396	.496
2008	Memp	AAA	42	141	31	4	1	1	(-	-)	40	10	10	9	5	0	24	1	2	2	2	3	.40	3	.220	.248	.284
2009	Memp	AAA	100	345	82	18	3	5	(-	-)	121	46	40	42	28	0	42	8	8	4	16	3	.84	14	.238	.306	.351
2010	Memp	AAA	26	86	24	5	0	2	(-	-)	35	9	13	11	7	0	13	0	3	1	3	3	.50	5	.279	.330	.407
2011	Memp	AAA	43	167	50	8	3	4	(-	-)	76	35	23	30	19	0	16	1	2	4	9	1	.90	5	.299	.366	.455
2011	Cards	R	6	22	3	2	1	0	(-	-)	7	4	0	1	0	0	1	1	0	0	0	0	-	0	.136	.174	.318
2011	Sprgfld	AA	7	31	15	2	0	3	(-	-)	26	8	8	11	4	0	1	2	0	0	0	1	.00	0	.484	.568	.839
2009	StL	NL	11	25	6	1	0	0	(0	0)	7	1	1	1	0	0	2	0	0	1	1	0	1.00	1	.240	.231	.280
2011	StL	NL	9	7	0	0	0	0	(0	0)	0	0	0	0	1	0	2	0	0	0	0	0	-	1	.000	.125	.000
	2 ML YEARS		20	32	6	1	0	0	(0	0)	7	1	1	1	1	0	4	0	0	1	1	0	1.00	2	.188	.206	.219

Trayvon Robinson

Bats: B **Throws:** R **Pos:** LF-30; CF-16; PH-2; DH-1; PR-1   trey-VONN **Ht:** 5'10" **Wt:** 201 **Born:** 9/1/1987 **Age:** 24

Year	Team	Lg	G	AB	H	2B	3B	HR	(Hm	Rd)	TB	R	RBI	RC	TBB	IBB	SO	HBP	SH	SF	SB	CS	SB%	GDP	Avg	OBP	Slg
2005	Ddgrs	R	40	115	34	7	2	3	(-	-)	54	19	15	19	8	0	25	3	0	0	6	4	.60	2	.296	.357	.470
2005	Ogden	R+	8	23	5	0	0	1	(-	-)	8	2	2	1	0	0	9	0	0	0	0	0	-	0	.217	.217	.348
2006	Ddgrs	R	39	134	34	7	2	2	(-	-)	51	24	20	19	16	0	48	2	2	1	5	1	.83	0	.254	.340	.381
2006	VeroB	A+	3	5	2	0	0	0	(-	-)	2	1	1	0	0	0	2	0	0	0	1	0	1.00	0	.400	.400	.400
2007	Gt Lks	A	110	396	100	9	4	2	(-	-)	123	50	31	41	32	0	119	4	10	1	22	9	.71	6	.253	.314	.311
2008	InldEm	A+	112	439	121	20	8	4	(-	-)	169	67	42	58	33	0	104	4	8	5	22	12	.65	5	.276	.328	.385
2009	InldEm	A+	117	470	144	28	9	15	(-	-)	235	82	54	90	50	4	125	4	1	4	43	18	.70	8	.306	.375	.500
2009	Chatt	AA	19	57	14	1	2	2	(-	-)	25	8	10	9	10	0	18	0	3	0	4	2	.67	3	.246	.358	.439
2010	Chatt	AA	120	434	129	23	5	9	(-	-)	189	80	57	83	73	2	125	5	8	3	38	15	.72	5	.297	.402	.435
2011	Albq	AAA	100	368	108	9	6	26	(-	-)	207	70	71	75	45	2	122	3	0	0	8	6	.57	4	.293	.375	.563
2011	Tacom	AAA	3	9	1	0	0	0	(-	-)	1	1	0	0	3	0	4	0	0	0	1	0	1.00	0	.111	.333	.111
2011	Sea	AL	44	143	30	12	0	2	(0	2)	48	12	14	10	8	0	61	0	3	1	1	0	1.00	1	.210	.250	.336

Fernando Rodney

Pitches: R **Bats:** R **Pos:** RP-39 **Ht:** 5'11" **Wt:** 215 **Born:** 3/18/1977 **Age:** 35

Year	Team	Lg	G	GS	CG	GF	IP	BFP	H	R	ER	HR	SH	SF	HB	TBB	IBB	SO	WP	Bk	W	L	Pct	Sh	Sv-Op	Hld	ERC	ERA
2011	InldEm*	A+	2	1	0	0	2.0	9	2	2	2	0	0	0	0	1	0	3	0	0	0	0	-	0	0- -	-	3.63	9.00
2002	Det	AL	20	0	0	10	18.0	89	25	15	12	2	2	1	0	12	2	10	0	1	1	3	.250	0	0-4	6	6.77	6.00
2003	Det	AL	27	0	0	11	29.2	143	35	20	20	2	3	3	1	17	1	33	0	1	1	3	.250	0	3-6	3	5.46	6.07
2005	Det	AL	39	0	0	26	44.0	185	39	14	14	5	2	0	2	17	3	42	2	0	2	3	.400	0	9-15	3	3.59	2.86
2006	Det	AL	63	0	0	30	71.2	304	51	36	28	6	2	0	8	34	4	65	3	0	7	4	.636	0	7-11	18	3.01	3.52
2007	Det	AL	48	0	0	12	50.2	223	46	27	24	5	4	2	3	21	0	54	4	0	2	6	.250	0	1-3	12	3.74	4.26
2008	Det	AL	38	0	0	25	40.1	188	34	22	22	3	1	2	3	30	5	49	3	0	0	6	.000	0	13-19	5	4.29	4.91
2009	Det	AL	73	0	0	65	75.2	330	70	38	37	8	4	2	2	41	4	61	5	0	5	4	.286	0	37-38	0	4.31	4.40
2010	LAA	AL	72	0	0	30	68.0	308	70	33	32	4	1	0	5	35	1	53	4	0	4	3	.571	0	14-21	21	4.63	4.24
2011	LAA	AL	39	0	0	15	32.0	150	26	18	16	1	3	0	3	28	0	26	2	0	3	5	.375	0	3-7	10	4.66	4.50
	Postseason		7	0	0	0	7.2	33	6	4	2	0	2	0	0	5	1	9	0	0	0	0	-	0	0-1	2	2.94	2.35
	9 ML YEARS		419	0	0	224	430.0	1920	396	223	205	36	22	10	27	233	20	393	23	1	22	38	.367	0	87-124	72	4.19	4.29

Alex Rodriguez

Bats: R **Throws:** R **Pos:** 3B-89; DH-10; PH-1; PR-1 **Ht:** 6'3" **Wt:** 228 **Born:** 7/27/1975 **Age:** 36

Year	Team	Lg	G	AB	H	2B	3B	HR	(Hm	Rd)	TB	R	RBI	RC	TBB	IBB	SO	HBP	SH	SF	SB	CS	SB%	GDP	Avg	OBP	Slg
2011	Tampa*	A+	2	6	2	1	0	1	(-	-)	6	2	2	2	1	0	3	0	0	0	0	0	-	0	.333	.429	1.000
2011	S-WB*	AAA	2	5	2	0	0	0	(-	-)	2	0	1	1	2	0	1	0	0	0	0	0	-	0	.400	.571	.400
1994	Sea	AL	17	54	11	0	0	0	(0	0)	11	4	2	3	3	0	20	0	1	1	3	0	1.00	0	.204	.241	.204
1995	Sea	AL	48	142	33	6	2	5	(1	4)	58	15	19	15	6	0	42	0	1	0	4	2	.67	0	.232	.264	.408
1996	Sea	AL	146	601	215	54	1	36	(18	18)	379	141	123	144	59	1	104	4	6	7	15	4	.79	15	.358	.414	.631
1997	Sea	AL	141	587	176	40	3	23	(16	7)	291	100	84	100	41	1	99	5	4	1	29	6	.83	14	.300	.350	.496
1998	Sea	AL	161	686	213	35	5	42	(18	24)	384	123	124	135	45	0	121	10	3	4	46	13	.78	12	.310	.360	.560
1999	Sea	AL	129	502	143	25	0	42	(20	22)	294	110	111	102	56	2	109	5	1	8	21	7	.75	12	.285	.357	.586
2000	Sea	AL	148	554	175	34	2	41	(13	28)	336	134	132	138	100	5	121	7	0	11	15	4	.79	10	.316	.420	.606
2001	Tex	AL	162	632	201	34	1	52	(26	26)	393	133	135	148	75	6	131	16	0	9	18	3	.86	17	.318	.399	.622
2002	Tex	AL	162	624	187	27	2	57	(34	23)	389	125	142	152	87	12	122	10	0	4	9	4	.69	14	.300	.392	.623
2003	Tex	AL	161	607	181	30	6	47	(26	21)	364	124	118	131	87	10	126	15	0	6	17	3	.85	16	.298	.396	.600
2004	NYY	AL	155	601	172	24	2	36	(17	19)	308	112	106	112	80	6	131	10	0	7	28	4	.88	18	.286	.375	.512
2005	NYY	AL	162	605	194	29	1	48	(26	22)	369	124	130	137	91	8	139	16	0	3	21	6	.78	8	.321	.421	.610
2006	NYY	AL	154	572	166	26	1	35	(20	15)	299	113	121	112	90	8	139	8	0	4	15	4	.79	22	.290	.392	.523
2007	NYY	AL	158	583	183	31	0	54	(26	28)	376	143	156	159	95	11	120	21	0	9	24	4	.86	15	.314	.422	.645
2008	NYY	AL	138	510	154	33	0	35	(21	14)	292	104	103	97	65	9	117	14	0	5	18	3	.86	16	.302	.392	.573
2009	NYY	AL	124	444	127	17	1	30	(17	13)	236	78	100	89	80	7	97	8	0	3	14	2	.88	13	.286	.402	.532
2010	NYY	AL	137	522	141	29	2	30	(15	15)	264	74	125	93	59	1	98	3	0	11	4	3	.57	7	.270	.341	.506
2011	NYY	AL	99	373	103	21	0	16	(9	7)	172	67	62	61	47	1	80	6	0	3	4	1	.80	13	.276	.362	.461
	Postseason		63	231	67	16	0	13	(5	8)	122	41	38	43	33	4	57	9	1	2	8	3	.73	5	.290	.396	.528
	18 ML YEARS		2402	9199	2775	495	29	629	(324	305)	5215	1824	1893	1928	1166	88	1916	157	16	96	305	73	.81	222	.302	.386	.567

237

Aneury Rodriguez

Pitches: R Bats: R Pos: RP-35; SP-8 — uh-NURR-ee — Ht: 6'4" Wt: 199 Born: 12/13/1987 Age: 24

Year	Team	Lg	G	GS	CG	GF	IP	BFP	H	R	ER	HR	SH	SF	HB	TBB	IBB	SO	WP	Bk	W	L	Pct	Sh	Sv-Op	Hld	ERC	ERA
2005	Casper	R+	15	15	0	0	62.0	285	77	54	52	7	2	1	7	26	0	47	11	1	3	4	.429	0	0- -	-	6.25	7.55
2006	TriCity	A-	15	15	1	0	76.0	337	78	42	35	2	2	0	6	30	0	69	6	0	4	4	.500	0	0- -	-	3.93	4.14
2007	Ashvll	A	28	28	1	0	152.0	675	182	105	87	19	1	5	10	48	1	160	14	2	9	9	.500	1	0- -	-	5.37	5.15
2008	Mdest	A+	27	27	2	0	156.1	650	148	78	65	12	3	6	10	40	2	139	7	3	9	10	.474	2	0- -	-	3.32	3.74
2009	Mont	AA	27	27	1	0	142.0	606	122	78	71	17	4	4	12	59	0	111	6	0	9	11	.450	1	0- -	-	3.83	4.50
2010	Mont	AA	2	2	0	0	10.0	41	9	6	3	0	0	2	0	2	0	6	2	0	1	0	1.000	0	0- -	-	2.14	2.70
2010	Drham	AAA	27	17	0	7	113.2	490	104	52	48	10	1	4	2	49	2	94	7	0	6	5	.545	0	0- -	-	3.65	3.80
2011	Hou	NL	43	8	0	16	85.1	369	83	57	50	13	3	3	2	32	3	64	3	0	1	6	.143	0	0-0	-	4.18	5.27

Fernando Rodriguez

Pitches: R Bats: R Pos: RP-47 — Ht: 6'3" Wt: 215 Born: 6/18/1984 Age: 28

Year	Team	Lg	G	GS	CG	GF	IP	BFP	H	R	ER	HR	SH	SF	HB	TBB	IBB	SO	WP	Bk	W	L	Pct	Sh	Sv-Op	Hld	ERC	ERA
2003	Angels	R	15	0	0	5	25.0	121	29	24	18	2	2	1	2	14	1	27	1	1	0	2	.000	0	0- -	-	5.56	6.48
2003	Provo	R+	4	0	0	3	6.0	28	9	4	1	1	0	0	0	1	0	9	1	0	0	0	-	0	1- -	-	6.43	1.50
2004	Provo	R+	14	12	0	1	58.2	238	64	35	27	7	1	4	2	18	0	54	5	0	4	3	.571	0	0- -	-	4.84	4.14
2005	CRpds	A	28	28	4	0	157.1	675	161	87	73	8	2	3	13	49	1	128	2	1	8	10	.444	0	0- -	-	3.85	4.18
2006	RCuca	A+	28	27	1	1	163.1	706	188	92	83	15	3	5	7	49	0	112	10	0	11	8	.579	0	0- -	-	4.73	4.57
2007	Ark	AA	22	22	1	0	125.1	547	138	71	63	14	5	7	5	46	2	61	3	0	8	4	.667	0	0- -	-	4.79	4.52
2008	Ark	AA	33	22	1	2	136.2	617	153	96	84	10	7	8	10	62	1	85	6	0	7	11	.389	1	0- -	-	5.09	5.53
2009	Salt Lk	AAA	23	0	0	5	37.0	172	44	33	31	5	2	4	2	23	0	25	3	0	1	1	.500	0	0- -	-	6.79	7.54
2009	Ark	AA	26	0	0	12	42.1	173	20	7	6	0	3	1	1	22	2	52	3	0	3	1	.750	0	4- -	-	1.35	1.28
2010	Salt Lk	AAA	31	17	0	5	97.1	462	134	78	64	12	5	1	6	42	0	84	4	0	4	6	.400	0	0- -	-	6.94	5.92
2011	OKCity	AAA	16	0	0	7	24.0	97	16	5	4	2	1	0	1	11	2	33	5	0	2	3	.400	0	2- -	-	2.51	1.50
2009	LAA	AL	1	0	0	0	0.2	6	1	3	2	1	0	0	0	2	0	1	1	0	0	0	-	0	0-0	0	31.03	27.00
2011	Hou	NL	47	0	0	11	52.1	231	51	24	23	6	5	0	3	30	5	57	2	0	2	3	.400	0	0-0	6	4.90	3.96
	2 ML YEARS		48	0	0	11	53.0	237	52	27	25	7	5	0	3	32	5	58	3	0	2	3	.400	0	0-0	6	5.17	4.25

Francisco Rodriguez

Pitches: R Bats: R Pos: RP-73 — Ht: 6'0" Wt: 195 Born: 1/7/1982 Age: 30

Year	Team	Lg	G	GS	CG	GF	IP	BFP	H	R	ER	HR	SH	SF	HB	TBB	IBB	SO	WP	Bk	W	L	Pct	Sh	Sv-Op	Hld	ERC	ERA
2002	LAA	AL	5	0	0	4	5.2	21	3	0	0	0	0	0	1	2	1	13	0	0	0	0	-	0	0-0	0	1.52	0.00
2003	LAA	AL	59	0	0	23	86.0	334	50	30	29	12	2	4	2	35	5	95	7	0	8	3	.727	0	2-6	7	2.25	3.03
2004	LAA	AL	69	0	0	29	84.0	335	51	21	17	2	2	1	1	33	1	123	5	0	4	1	.800	0	12-19	27	1.64	1.82
2005	LAA	AL	66	0	0	58	67.1	279	45	20	20	7	1	1	0	32	3	91	8	0	2	5	.286	0	45-50	0	2.52	2.67
2006	LAA	AL	69	0	0	58	73.0	296	52	16	14	6	3	0	1	28	5	98	10	0	2	3	.400	0	47-51	0	2.35	1.73
2007	LAA	AL	64	0	0	56	67.1	285	50	22	21	3	1	4	1	34	0	90	7	1	5	2	.714	0	40-46	0	2.74	2.81
2008	LAA	AL	76	0	0	69	68.1	288	54	21	17	4	1	1	2	34	4	77	6	0	2	3	.400	0	62-69	0	3.06	2.24
2009	NYM	NL	70	0	0	66	68.0	295	51	34	28	7	4	1	1	38	6	73	1	0	3	6	.333	0	35-42	0	3.18	3.71
2010	NYM	NL	53	0	0	46	57.1	236	45	14	14	3	1	1	2	21	4	67	3	1	4	2	.667	0	25-30	0	2.53	2.20
2011	2 Tms	NL	73	0	0	36	71.2	307	67	22	21	4	2	1	2	26	4	79	4	0	6	2	.750	0	23-29	17	3.25	2.64
11	NYM	NL	42	0	0	34	42.2	187	44	15	15	3	2	1	2	16	4	46	2	0	2	2	.500	0	23-26	0	3.94	3.16
11	Mil	NL	31	0	0	2	29.0	120	23	7	6	1	0	0	0	10	0	33	2	0	4	0	1.000	0	0-3	17	2.32	1.86
	Postseason		21	0	0	8	31.2	134	27	14	11	5	0	3	1	14	2	41	5	0	5	4	.556	0	3-5	3	3.86	3.13
	10 ML YEARS		604	0	0	445	648.2	2676	468	200	181	48	17	14	13	283	33	806	51	2	36	27	.571	0	291-342	51	2.56	2.51

Francisco Rodriguez

Pitches: R Bats: R Pos: RP-10 — Ht: 6'1" Wt: 220 Born: 2/26/1983 Age: 29

Year	Team	Lg	G	GS	CG	GF	IP	BFP	H	R	ER	HR	SH	SF	HB	TBB	IBB	SO	WP	Bk	W	L	Pct	Sh	Sv-Op	Hld	ERC	ERA
2006	RCuca	A+	26	25	1	0	133.1	617	158	95	81	11	6	4	13	68	0	83	10	0	5	13	.278	1	0- -	-	5.94	5.47
2007	RCuca	A+	39	8	0	9	105.2	476	117	76	70	11	2	5	6	53	0	70	12	0	4	8	.333	0	2- -	-	5.44	5.96
2008	Ark	AA	50	0	0	17	75.1	339	76	41	32	9	4	7	5	33	1	69	7	0	5	5	.500	0	2- -	-	4.57	3.82
2009	Salt Lk	AAA	44	1	0	6	77.1	331	67	35	34	8	8	6	2	40	1	60	4	1	5	4	.556	0	0- -	-	3.94	3.96
2010	Salt Lk	AAA	13	0	0	4	22.1	90	19	9	9	0	0	0	0	6	0	19	0	0	2	1	.667	0	0- -	-	2.19	3.63
2011	Angels	R	4	2	0	0	5.1	24	5	5	5	2	0	0	1	4	0	5	0	0	0	1	.000	0	0- -	-	8.77	8.44
2011	Salt Lk	AAA	6	1	0	0	4.2	36	12	16	14	1	2	0	1	8	0	5	1	0	0	1	.000	0	0- -	-	22.94	27.00
2010	LAA	AL	43	0	0	14	47.1	209	46	23	23	5	1	0	1	26	3	36	8	1	1	3	.250	0	0-1	2	4.56	4.37
2011	LAA	AL	10	0	0	4	13.2	59	13	7	7	2	0	0	0	5	0	7	0	0	0	0	-	0	0-0	1	3.90	4.61
	2 ML YEARS		53	0	0	18	61.0	268	59	30	30	7	1	0	1	31	3	43	8	1	1	3	.250	0	0-1	3	4.41	4.43

Henry Rodriguez

Pitches: R Bats: R Pos: RP-59 — Ht: 6'0" Wt: 219 Born: 2/25/1987 Age: 25

Year	Team	Lg	G	GS	CG	GF	IP	BFP	H	R	ER	HR	SH	SF	HB	TBB	IBB	SO	WP	Bk	W	L	Pct	Sh	Sv-Op	Hld	ERC	ERA
2011	Hrsbrg*	AA	3	1	0	0	4.0	15	3	0	0	0	0	0	0	0	0	7	1	0	0	0	-	0	0- -	-	1.13	0.00
2011	Syrcse*	AAA	6	0	0	1	8.1	34	5	2	1	0	1	0	0	6	0	9	1	0	0	0	-	0	0- -	-	2.57	1.08
2009	Oak	AL	3	0	0	1	4.0	20	4	2	1	0	0	1	0	2	0	4	3	0	0	0	-	0	0-0	0	4.28	2.25
2010	Oak	AL	29	0	0	4	27.2	121	25	16	14	2	2	1	1	13	0	33	7	0	1	0	1.000	0	0-1	3	3.70	4.55
2011	Was	NL	59	0	0	21	65.2	295	54	30	26	1	1	1	2	45	1	70	14	1	3	3	.500	0	2-5	10	3.59	3.56
	3 ML YEARS		91	0	0	30	97.1	436	83	48	41	3	3	2	4	60	1	107	24	1	4	3	.571	0	2-6	13	3.66	3.79

Ivan Rodriguez

Bats: R **Throws:** R **Pos:** C-37; PH-8; 1B-1   ee-VAHN   **Ht:** 5'11" **Wt:** 190 **Born:** 11/30/1971 **Age:** 40

Year	Team	Lg	G	AB	H	2B	3B	HR	(Hm	Rd)	TB	R	RBI	RC	TBB	IBB	SO	HBP	SH	SF	SB	CS	SB%	GDP	Avg	OBP	Slg
2011	Ptomc*	A+	1	3	1	0	0	1	(-	-)	4	1	1	1	0	0	0	0	0	0	0	0	-	0	.333	.333	1.333
2011	Hrsbrg*	AA	3	9	2	1	0	0	(-	-)	3	2	0	0	1	0	1	0	0	0	0	0	-	0	.222	.300	.333
1991	Tex	AL	88	280	74	16	0	3	(3	0)	99	24	27	23	5	0	42	0	2	1	0	1	.00	10	.264	.276	.354
1992	Tex	AL	123	420	109	16	1	8	(4	4)	151	39	37	41	24	2	73	1	7	2	0	0	-	15	.260	.300	.360
1993	Tex	AL	137	473	129	28	4	10	(7	3)	195	56	66	57	29	3	70	4	5	8	8	7	.53	16	.273	.315	.412
1994	Tex	AL	99	363	108	19	1	16	(7	9)	177	56	57	61	31	5	42	7	0	4	6	3	.67	10	.298	.360	.488
1995	Tex	AL	130	492	149	32	2	12	(5	7)	221	56	67	68	16	2	48	4	0	5	0	2	.00	11	.303	.327	.449
1996	Tex	AL	153	639	192	47	3	19	(10	9)	302	116	86	99	38	7	55	4	0	4	5	0	1.00	15	.300	.342	.473
1997	Tex	AL	150	597	187	34	4	20	(12	8)	289	98	77	98	38	7	89	8	1	4	7	3	.70	18	.313	.360	.484
1998	Tex	AL	145	579	186	40	4	21	(12	9)	297	88	91	100	32	4	88	3	0	3	9	0	1.00	18	.321	.358	.513
1999	Tex	AL	144	600	199	29	1	35	(12	23)	335	116	113	104	24	2	64	1	0	5	25	12	.68	31	.332	.356	.558
2000	Tex	AL	91	363	126	27	4	27	(16	11)	242	66	83	78	19	5	48	1	0	6	5	5	.50	17	.347	.375	.667
2001	Tex	AL	111	442	136	24	2	25	(16	9)	239	70	65	77	23	3	73	4	0	1	10	3	.77	13	.308	.347	.541
2002	Tex	AL	108	408	128	32	2	19	(15	4)	221	67	60	63	25	2	71	2	1	4	5	4	.56	13	.314	.353	.542
2003	Fla	NL	144	511	152	36	3	16	(8	8)	242	90	85	91	55	6	92	6	1	5	10	6	.63	18	.297	.369	.474
2004	Det	AL	135	527	176	32	2	19	(7	12)	269	72	86	98	41	6	91	3	0	4	7	4	.64	15	.334	.383	.510
2005	Det	AL	129	504	139	33	5	14	(8	6)	224	71	50	44	11	2	93	2	1	7	7	3	.70	19	.276	.290	.444
2006	Det	AL	136	547	164	28	4	13	(5	8)	239	74	69	82	26	4	86	1	4	2	8	3	.73	16	.300	.332	.437
2007	Det	AL	129	502	141	31	3	11	(4	7)	211	50	63	55	9	1	96	1	1	2	2	2	.50	16	.281	.294	.420
2008	2 Tms	AL	115	398	110	20	3	7	(5	2)	157	44	35	40	23	2	67	3	3	2	10	1	.91	15	.276	.319	.394
2009	2 Tms		121	425	106	23	2	10	(3	7)	163	55	47	30	18	0	92	1	1	3	1	2	.33	20	.249	.280	.384
2010	Was	NL	111	398	106	18	1	4	(2	2)	138	32	49	37	16	2	66	1	2	4	2	3	.40	25	.266	.294	.347
2011	Was	NL	44	124	27	7	0	2	(1	1)	40	14	19	11	10	2	28	1	2	0	0	0	-	6	.218	.281	.323
08	Det	AL	82	302	89	16	3	5	(3	2)	126	33	32	36	19	1	52	2	3	2	6	1	.86	9	.295	.338	.417
08	NYY	AL	33	96	21	4	0	2	(2	0)	31	11	3	4	4	1	15	1	0	0	4	0	1.00	6	.219	.257	.323
09	Hou	NL	93	327	82	15	2	8	(3	5)	125	41	34	21	13	0	74	1	1	2	0	2	.00	13	.251	.280	.382
09	Tex	AL	28	98	24	8	0	2	(0	2)	38	14	13	9	5	0	18	0	0	1	1	0	1.00	7	.245	.279	.388
	Postseason		40	153	39	9	0	4	(2	2)	60	17	25	22	14	3	32	0	1	2	1	0	1.00	3	.255	.314	.392
21 ML YEARS			2543	9592	2844	572	51	311	(162	149)	4451	1354	1332	1357	513	67	1474	58	31	76	127	64	.66	337	.296	.334	.464

Josh Rodriguez

Bats: R **Throws:** R **Pos:** SS-4; 2B-1; PH-1; PR-1   **Ht:** 6'0" **Wt:** 185 **Born:** 12/18/1984 **Age:** 27

Year	Team	Lg	G	AB	H	2B	3B	HR	(Hm	Rd)	TB	R	RBI	RC	TBB	IBB	SO	HBP	SH	SF	SB	CS	SB%	GDP	Avg	OBP	Slg
2006	MhVlly	A-	45	157	42	11	4	4	(-	-)	73	26	24	25	14	0	33	3	0	1	2	0	1.00	4	.268	.337	.465
2007	Knstn	A+	133	493	129	20	9	20	(-	-)	227	84	82	84	68	0	95	2	1	4	21	8	.72	11	.262	.351	.460
2008	Akron	AA	137	532	128	22	10	7	(-	-)	191	75	49	70	77	1	122	0	9	3	12	6	.67	9	.241	.335	.359
2009	Akron	AA	33	105	31	4	0	0	(-	-)	35	18	12	17	23	0	30	1	2	0	2	3	.40	1	.295	.426	.333
2010	Akron	AA	21	63	20	7	0	1	(-	-)	30	11	11	12	11	0	10	1	0	4	0	2	.00	3	.317	.405	.476
2010	Clmbs	AAA	86	317	93	23	1	12	(-	-)	154	49	46	59	40	1	75	1	4	2	6	2	.75	16	.293	.372	.486
2011	Clmbs	AAA	18	57	11	1	0	2	(-	-)	18	6	5	5	6	0	22	0	2	0	1	0	1.00	0	.193	.270	.316
2011	Indy	AAA	6	13	5	2	0	0	(-	-)	7	3	6	4	5	0	2	0	0	1	0	0	-	0	.385	.526	.538
2011	Altna	AA	57	225	60	3	0	5	(-	-)	78	24	19	26	18	1	41	1	0	2	3	1	.75	5	.267	.321	.347
2011	Pit	NL	7	12	1	0	0	0	(0	0)	1	1	1	1	1	0	8	1	0	0	0	0	-	0	.083	.214	.083

Luis Rodriguez

Bats: B **Throws:** R **Pos:** SS-23; 3B-11; 2B-7; PH-5; 1B-1; PR-1   **Ht:** 5'9" **Wt:** 188 **Born:** 6/27/1980 **Age:** 32

Year	Team	Lg	G	AB	H	2B	3B	HR	(Hm	Rd)	TB	R	RBI	RC	TBB	IBB	SO	HBP	SH	SF	SB	CS	SB%	GDP	Avg	OBP	Slg
2011	Tacom*	AAA	7	31	9	1	0	1	(-	-)	13	3	3	4	2	0	4	0	0	0	0	1	.00	3	.290	.333	.419
2011	Everett*	A-	3	9	3	1	0	0	(-	-)	4	2	2	1	2	0	1	0	0	0	0	1	.00	0	.333	.455	.444
2005	Min	AL	79	175	47	10	2	2	(1	1)	67	21	20	27	18	0	23	1	6	3	2	2	.50	4	.269	.335	.383
2006	Min	AL	59	115	27	4	0	2	(1	1)	37	11	6	8	14	1	16	0	2	1	0	0	-	3	.235	.315	.322
2007	Min	AL	68	155	34	5	1	2	(1	1)	47	18	12	11	12	0	14	2	2	2	1	0	1.00	8	.219	.281	.303
2008	SD	NL	64	202	58	11	1	0	(0	0)	71	22	12	19	13	0	13	0	7	3	1	1	.50	9	.287	.326	.351
2009	SD	NL	93	208	42	6	0	2	(0	2)	54	18	16	19	37	4	23	0	3	3	1	0	1.00	5	.202	.319	.260
2011	Sea	AL	44	117	23	10	0	2	(1	1)	39	10	14	14	16	0	21	2	2	2	1	2	.33	0	.197	.299	.333
6 ML YEARS			407	972	231	46	4	10	(4	6)	315	100	80	98	110	5	110	5	22	14	6	5	.55	29	.238	.314	.324

Sean Rodriguez

Bats: R **Throws:** R **Pos:** SS-60; 2B-48; 3B-30; PH-10; 1B-5; LF-2; PR-2   **Ht:** 6'0" **Wt:** 195 **Born:** 4/26/1985 **Age:** 27

Year	Team	Lg	G	AB	H	2B	3B	HR	(Hm	Rd)	TB	R	RBI	RC	TBB	IBB	SO	HBP	SH	SF	SB	CS	SB%	GDP	Avg	OBP	Slg
2008	LAA	AL	59	167	34	8	1	3	(2	1)	53	18	10	12	14	0	55	3	2	1	3	1	.75	3	.204	.276	.317
2009	LAA	AL	12	25	5	0	0	2	(0	2)	11	4	4	2	3	0	7	0	0	1	0	0	-	2	.200	.276	.440
2010	TB	AL	118	343	86	19	2	9	(5	4)	136	53	40	38	21	1	97	8	5	1	13	3	.81	10	.251	.308	.397
2011	TB	AL	131	373	83	20	3	8	(4	4)	133	45	36	41	38	2	87	18	5	2	11	7	.61	8	.223	.323	.357
	Postseason		4	10	2	0	0	0	(0	0)	2	2	0	0	0	0	5	0	0	0	0	0	-	0	.200	.200	.200
4 ML YEARS			320	908	208	47	6	22	(11	11)	333	120	90	93	76	3	246	29	12	5	27	11	.71	23	.229	.307	.367

Wandy Rodriguez

Pitches: L Bats: B Pos: SP-30

WONN-dee

Ht: 5'11" Wt: 193 Born: 1/18/1979 Age: 33

Year	Team	Lg	G	GS	CG	GF	IP	BFP	H	R	ER	HR	SH	SF	HB	TBB	IBB	SO	WP	Bk	W	L	Pct	Sh	Sv-Op	Hld	ERC	ERA
2011	CpChr*	AA	1	1	0	0	4.0	17	6	1	1	0	0	0	1	0	2	0	0	0			-	0	0- -	-	8.43	2.25
2005	Hou	NL	25	22	0	0	128.2	560	135	82	79	19	3	3	8	53	2	80	3	3	10	10	.500	0	0-0	0	5.08	5.53
2006	Hou	NL	30	24	0	1	135.2	611	154	96	85	17	7	4	6	63	7	98	6	0	9	10	.474	0	0-0	0	5.45	5.64
2007	Hou	NL	31	31	1	0	182.2	782	179	102	93	22	6	4	5	62	2	158	3	0	9	13	.409	1	0-0	0	3.94	4.58
2008	Hou	NL	25	25	0	0	137.1	587	136	65	54	14	2	5	5	44	3	131	2	3	9	7	.563	0	0-0	0	3.82	3.54
2009	Hou	NL	33	33	1	0	205.2	849	192	77	69	21	8	4	5	63	5	193	2	1	14	12	.538	1	0-0	0	3.47	3.02
2010	Hou	NL	32	32	0	0	195.0	822	183	95	78	16	6	5	9	68	3	178	8	0	11	12	.478	0	0-0	0	3.60	3.60
2011	Hou	NL	30	30	0	0	191.0	808	182	81	74	25	7	3	5	69	7	166	5	0	11	11	.500	0	0-0	0	3.95	3.49
	Postseason		3	0	0	1	4.2	22	5	2	2	2	1	0	0	5	1	4	0	0	0	1	.000	0	0-0	0	10.58	3.86
7 ML YEARS			206	197	2	1	1176.0	5019	1161	598	532	134	39	28	43	422	29	1004	29	7	73	75	.493	2	0-0	0	4.07	4.07

Josh Roenicke

Pitches: R Bats: H Pos: RP-19

RENN-ick-kee

Ht: 6'3" Wt: 195 Born: 8/4/1982 Age: 29

Year	Team	Lg	G	GS	CG	GF	IP	BFP	H	R	ER	HR	SH	SF	HB	TBB	IBB	SO	WP	Bk	W	L	Pct	Sh	Sv-Op	Hld	ERC	ERA
2011	LsVgs*	AAA	16	0	0	3	22.1	109	25	21	15	3	1	2	2	15	0	20	3	0	1	3	.250	0	0- -	-	6.39	6.04
2011	ColSpr*	AAA	23	0	0	5	30.2	126	30	14	12	3	1	3	1	7	0	22	0	1	0	1	.000	0	0- -	-	3.45	3.52
2008	Cin	NL	5	0	0	0	3.0	18	6	3	3	0	0	0	1	2	0	6	0	0	0	0	-	0	0-0	0	12.01	9.00
2009	2 Tms		24	0	0	5	31.0	138	32	19	18	2	0	1	1	16	1	33	2	0	0	0	-	0	0-0	1	4.55	5.23
2010	Tor	AL	16	0	0	3	19.0	91	18	15	12	1	0	0	2	13	0	18	1	0	1	0	1.000	0	0-0	2	4.76	5.68
2011	Col	NL	19	0	0	6	16.2	68	14	7	7	1	0	0	1	7	1	12	1	0	0	0	-	0	0-0	4	3.28	3.78
09	Cin	NL	11	0	0	2	13.1	54	13	4	4	0	0	0	0	4	0	14	1	0	0	0	-	0	0-0	0	3.00	2.70
09	Tor	AL	13	0	0	3	17.2	84	19	15	14	2	0	1	1	12	1	19	1	0	0	0	-	0	0-0	1	5.81	7.13
4 ML YEARS			64	0	0	14	69.2	315	70	44	40	4	0	1	5	38	2	69	4	0	1	0	1.000	0	0-0	7	4.58	5.17

Esmil Rogers

Pitches: R Bats: R Pos: SP-13; RP-5

ESS-mill

Ht: 6'1" Wt: 190 Born: 8/14/1985 Age: 26

Year	Team	Lg	G	GS	CG	GF	IP	BFP	H	R	ER	HR	SH	SF	HB	TBB	IBB	SO	WP	Bk	W	L	Pct	Sh	Sv-Op	Hld	ERC	ERA
2011	ColSpr*	AAA	5	5	0	0	23.0	108	36	16	16	3	1	1	2	5	0	15	3	0	1	2	.333	0	0- -	-	7.46	6.26
2011	Tulsa*	AA	1	1	0	0	4.0	19	5	3	1	1	0	0	0	1	0	2	0	1	0	1	.000	0	0- -	-	5.54	2.25
2009	Col	NL	1	1	0	0	4.0	16	3	2	2	0	0	0	0	2	0	3	0	0	0	0	-	0	0-0	0	2.58	4.50
2010	Col	NL	28	8	0	5	72.0	333	94	59	49	5	3	3	5	26	2	66	5	2	2	3	.400	0	0-1	5	5.70	6.13
2011	Col	NL	18	13	0	1	83.0	404	110	65	65	14	4	3	6	47	5	63	5	1	6	6	.500	0	0-0	2	7.49	7.05
3 ML YEARS			47	22	0	6	159.0	753	207	126	116	19	7	7	11	75	7	132	10	3	8	9	.471	0	0-1	6	6.53	6.57

Ryan Rohlinger

Bats: R Throws: R Pos: PH-1

ROE-ling-er

Ht: 6'0" Wt: 193 Born: 10/7/1983 Age: 28

Year	Team	Lg	G	AB	H	2B	3B	HR	(Hm	Rd)	TB	R	RBI	RC	TBB	IBB	SO	HBP	SH	SF	SB	CS	SB%	GDP	Avg	OBP	Slg
2011	Fresno*	AAA	33	121	21	4	0	4	(-	-)	40	22	16	13	19	1	14	2	1	1	2	1	.67	3	.174	.294	.331
2011	ColSpr*	AAA	70	243	69	15	5	5	(-	-)	109	49	35	43	37	1	43	3	1	2	0	2	.00	2	.284	.382	.449
2008	SF	NL	21	32	3	1	1	0	(0	0)	6	2	2	0	1	0	8	0	0	0	0	1	.00	2	.094	.121	.188
2009	SF	NL	12	19	3	1	0	0	(0	0)	4	0	4	1	1	0	6	0	0	0	0	0	-	1	.158	.200	.211
2010	SF	NL	12	15	3	0	0	0	(0	0)	3	1	1	0	2	0	5	0	1	0	0	0	-	1	.200	.294	.200
2011	SF	NL	1	1	0	0	0	0	(0	0)	0	0	0	0	0	0	1	0	0	0	0	0	-	0	.000	.000	.000
4 ML YEARS			46	67	9	2	1	0	(0	0)	13	3	7	1	4	0	20	0	1	0	0	1	.00	4	.134	.183	.194

Scott Rolen

Bats: R Throws: R Pos: 3B-63; PH-3

Ht: 6'4" Wt: 245 Born: 4/4/1975 Age: 37

Year	Team	Lg	G	AB	H	2B	3B	HR	(Hm	Rd)	TB	R	RBI	RC	TBB	IBB	SO	HBP	SH	SF	SB	CS	SB%	GDP	Avg	OBP	Slg
1996	Phi	NL	37	130	33	7	0	4	(2	2)	52	10	18	16	13	0	27	1	0	2	0	2	.00	4	.254	.322	.400
1997	Phi	NL	156	561	159	35	3	21	(11	10)	263	93	92	103	76	4	138	13	0	7	16	6	.73	6	.283	.377	.469
1998	Phi	NL	160	601	174	45	4	31	(19	12)	320	120	110	124	93	6	141	11	0	6	14	7	.67	10	.290	.391	.532
1999	Phi	NL	112	421	113	28	1	26	(9	17)	221	74	77	83	67	2	114	3	0	6	12	2	.86	8	.268	.368	.525
2000	Phi	NL	128	483	144	32	6	26	(12	14)	266	88	89	97	51	9	99	5	0	2	8	1	.89	4	.298	.370	.551
2001	Phi	NL	151	554	160	39	1	25	(12	13)	276	96	107	107	74	6	127	13	0	12	16	5	.76	6	.289	.378	.498
2002	2 Tms		155	580	154	29	8	31	(14	17)	292	89	110	98	72	4	102	12	0	3	8	4	.67	22	.266	.357	.503
2003	StL	NL	154	559	160	49	1	28	(12	16)	295	98	104	104	82	5	104	9	0	7	13	3	.81	19	.286	.382	.528
2004	StL	NL	142	500	157	32	4	34	(10	24)	299	109	124	124	72	5	92	13	1	7	4	3	.57	8	.314	.409	.598
2005	StL	NL	56	196	46	12	1	5	(2	3)	75	28	28	22	25	1	28	1	0	1	1	2	.33	3	.235	.323	.383
2006	StL	NL	142	521	154	48	1	22	(12	10)	270	94	95	89	56	7	69	9	0	8	7	4	.64	10	.296	.369	.518
2007	StL	NL	112	392	104	24	2	8	(4	4)	156	55	58	47	37	2	56	5	0	7	5	3	.63	13	.265	.331	.398
2008	Tor	AL	115	408	107	30	3	11	(6	5)	176	58	50	57	46	2	71	10	0	3	5	0	1.00	12	.262	.349	.431
2009	2 Tms		128	475	145	36	1	11	(8	3)	216	76	67	82	45	1	62	7	0	8	5	4	.56	4	.305	.368	.455
2010	Cin	NL	133	471	134	34	3	20	(10	10)	234	66	83	76	50	3	82	8	0	8	1	2	.33	12	.285	.358	.497
2011	Cin	NL	65	252	61	20	2	5	(3	2)	100	31	36	26	10	0	36	4	0	3	1	0	1.00	4	.242	.279	.397
02	Phi	NL	100	375	97	21	4	17	(8	9)	177	52	66	60	52	2	68	8	0	2	5	2	.71	12	.259	.358	.472
02	StL	NL	55	205	57	8	4	14	(6	8)	115	37	44	38	20	2	34	4	0	0	3	2	.60	10	.278	.354	.561
09	Tor	AL	88	338	108	29	0	8	(6	2)	161	52	43	60	26	1	42	4	0	5	4	2	.67	2	.320	.367	.476
09	Cin	NL	40	137	37	7	1	3	(2	1)	55	24	24	22	19	0	20	3	0	3	1	2	.33	2	.270	.364	.401
	Postseason		35	125	27	7	0	5	(3	2)	49	17	11	14	14	0	30	2	0	1	0	1	.00	5	.216	.303	.392
16 ML YEARS			1946	7104	2005	500	41	308	(146	162)	3511	1185	1248	1253	869	57	1348	124	1	90	116	48	.71	145	.282	.366	.494

Jimmy Rollins

Bats: B Throws: R Pos: SS-138; PH-5; DH-1 Ht: 5'8" Wt: 170 Born: 11/27/1978 Age: 33

										BATTING												BASERUNNING				AVERAGES		
Year	Team	Lg	G	AB	H	2B	3B	HR	(Hm	Rd)	TB	R	RBI	RC	TBB	IBB	SO	HBP	SH	SF		SB	CS	SB%	GDP	Avg	OBP	Slg
2000	Phi	NL	14	53	17	1	1	0	(0	0)	20	5	5	8	2	0	7	0	0	0		3	0	1.00	0	.321	.345	.377
2001	Phi	NL	158	656	180	29	12	14	(8	6)	275	97	54	96	48	2	108	2	9	5		46	8	.85	5	.274	.323	.419
2002	Phi	NL	154	637	156	33	10	11	(3	8)	242	82	60	72	54	3	103	4	6	4		31	13	.70	14	.245	.306	.380
2003	Phi	NL	156	628	165	42	6	8	(5	3)	243	85	62	76	54	4	113	0	5	2		20	12	.63	9	.263	.320	.387
2004	Phi	NL	154	657	190	43	12	14	(8	6)	299	119	73	108	57	3	73	3	6	2		30	9	.77	4	.289	.348	.455
2005	Phi	NL	158	677	196	38	11	12	(5	7)	292	115	54	100	47	8	71	4	2	2		41	6	.87	9	.290	.338	.431
2006	Phi	NL	158	689	191	45	9	25	(15	10)	329	127	83	114	57	2	80	5	0	7		36	4	.90	12	.277	.334	.478
2007	Phi	NL	162	716	212	38	20	30	(18	12)	380	139	94	124	49	5	85	7	0	6		41	6	.87	11	.296	.344	.531
2008	Phi	NL	137	556	154	38	9	11	(5	6)	243	76	59	95	58	7	55	5	3	3		47	3	.94	11	.277	.349	.437
2009	Phi	NL	155	672	168	43	5	21	(10	11)	284	100	77	88	44	1	70	2	2	5		31	8	.79	7	.250	.296	.423
2010	Phi	NL	88	350	85	16	3	8	(4	4)	131	48	41	54	40	2	32	1	0	3		17	1	.94	4	.243	.320	.374
2011	Phi	NL	142	567	152	22	2	16	(7	9)	226	87	63	82	58	5	39	3	0	3		30	8	.79	9	.268	.338	.399
Postseason			41	168	38	8	1	3	(1	2)	57	21	15	12	15	0	33	2	1	1		9	3	.75	5	.226	.296	.339
12 ML YEARS			1636	6858	1866	388	100	170	(88	82)	2964	1080	725	1017	568	42	856	36	33	42		373	78	.83	95	.272	.329	.432

J.C. Romero

Pitches: L Bats: B Pos: RP-36 Ht: 5'11" Wt: 205 Born: 6/4/1976 Age: 36

			HOW MUCH HE PITCHED					WHAT HE GAVE UP												THE RESULTS							
Year	Team	Lg	G	GS	CG	GF	IP	BFP	H	R	ER	HR	SH	SF	HB	TBB	IBB	SO	WP	Bk	W	L	Pct	Sh	Sv-Op	Hld	ERC	ERA
2011	Lakwd*	A	1	0	0	0	1.0	3	0	0	0	0	0	0	0	1	0	1	0	0	0	0	-	0	0- -	-	1.26	0.00
2011	Syrcse*	AAA	5	0	0	1	7.0	24	3	1	1	0	0	0	0	1	0	5	1	0	0	0	-	0	0- -	-	0.63	1.29
2011	S-WB*	AAA	11	0	0	3	12.1	55	11	5	4	0	0	0	3	5	1	10	1	0	1	0	1.000	0	0- -	-	3.53	2.92
2011	ColSpr*	AAA	3	0	0	0	2.2	13	2	1	1	0	0	0	0	3	0	3	0	0	0	0	-	0	0- -	-	4.52	3.38
1999	Min	AL	5	0	0	3	9.2	39	13	4	4	0	0	0	0	0	0	4	0	0	0	0	-	0	0-0	-	3.95	3.72
2000	Min	AL	12	11	0	0	57.2	268	72	51	45	8	4	2	1	30	0	50	2	1	2	7	.222	0	0-0	-	6.48	7.02
2001	Min	AL	14	11	0	0	65.0	286	71	48	45	10	3	2	1	24	1	39	1	0	1	4	.200	0	0-0	-	4.89	6.23
2002	Min	AL	81	0	0	15	81.0	332	62	17	17	3	1	0	4	36	4	76	9	0	9	2	.818	0	1-5	33	2.74	1.89
2003	Min	AL	73	0	0	17	63.0	295	66	37	35	7	4	0	6	42	7	50	9	2	2	0	1.000	0	0-4	22	5.72	5.00
2004	Min	AL	74	0	0	12	74.1	319	61	32	29	4	3	1	5	38	6	69	5	0	7	4	.636	0	1-8	16	3.33	3.51
2005	Min	AL	68	0	0	11	57.0	264	50	26	22	6	5	1	6	39	8	48	1	1	4	3	.571	0	0-1	11	4.62	3.47
2006	LAA	AL	65	0	0	16	48.1	226	57	40	36	3	1	5	1	28	2	31	1	0	1	2	.333	0	0-1	7	5.54	6.70
2007	2 Tms		74	0	0	10	56.1	237	39	12	12	3	1	1	2	40	5	42	4	0	2	2	.500	0	1-2	24	3.35	1.92
2008	Phi	NL	81	0	0	14	59.0	255	41	18	18	5	4	0	5	38	5	52	2	1	4	4	.500	0	1-5	24	3.42	2.75
2009	Phi	NL	21	0	0	5	16.2	73	13	6	5	2	0	0	2	13	0	12	0	0	1	0	1.000	0	0-1	6	5.20	2.70
2010	Phi	NL	60	0	0	14	36.2	171	30	17	15	3	2	0	5	29	7	28	0	1	1	0	1.000	0	3-6	9	4.58	3.68
2011	2 Tms	NL	36	0	0	6	24.2	116	28	14	11	1	2	0	1	15	2	19	0	0	1	0	1.000	0	0-0	3	5.19	4.01
07	Bos	AL	23	0	0	5	20.0	94	24	7	7	2	0	1	0	15	3	11	0	0	1	0	1.000	0	0-1	2	6.61	3.15
07	Phi	NL	51	0	0	5	36.1	143	15	5	5	1	1	0	2	25	2	31	4	0	1	2	.333	0	0-1	22	1.86	1.24
11	Phi	NL	24	0	0	4	16.1	75	16	7	7	0	1	0	1	12	2	10	0	0	0	0	-	0	0-0	3	4.56	3.86
11	Col	NL	12	0	0	2	8.1	41	12	7	4	1	1	0	0	3	0	9	0	0	1	0	1.000	0	0-0	0	6.37	4.32
Postseason			25	0	0	7	20.0	82	15	7	7	1	2	1	0	9	1	15	1	0	2	2	.500	0	0-0	6	2.56	3.15
13 ML YEARS			664	22	0	124	649.1	2881	603	322	294	55	30	12	39	372	47	520	34	6	34	28	.548	0	7-33	155	4.38	4.07

Ricky Romero

Pitches: L Bats: R Pos: SP-32 Ht: 6'0" Wt: 210 Born: 11/6/1984 Age: 27

			HOW MUCH HE PITCHED					WHAT HE GAVE UP												THE RESULTS							
Year	Team	Lg	G	GS	CG	GF	IP	BFP	H	R	ER	HR	SH	SF	HB	TBB	IBB	SO	WP	Bk	W	L	Pct	Sh	Sv-Op	Hld	ERC	ERA
2009	Tor	AL	29	29	0	0	178.0	771	192	88	85	18	3	3	10	79	0	141	6	1	13	9	.591	0	0-0	-	5.12	4.30
2010	Tor	AL	32	32	3	0	210.0	882	189	98	87	15	9	3	8	82	3	174	18	1	14	9	.609	1	0-0	-	3.46	3.73
2011	Tor	AL	32	32	4	0	225.0	917	176	85	73	26	6	1	14	80	2	178	9	1	15	11	.577	2	0-0	-	3.11	2.92
3 ML YEARS			93	93	7	0	613.0	2570	557	271	245	59	18	7	32	241	5	493	33	3	42	29	.592	3	0-0	-	3.79	3.60

Andrew Romine

Bats: B Throws: R Pos: SS-7; 3B-3 ROW-mine Ht: 6'1" Wt: 190 Born: 12/24/1985 Age: 26

										BATTING												BASERUNNING				AVERAGES		
Year	Team	Lg	G	AB	H	2B	3B	HR	(Hm	Rd)	TB	R	RBI	RC	TBB	IBB	SO	HBP	SH	SF		SB	CS	SB%	GDP	Avg	OBP	Slg
2007	Orem	R+	56	231	66	6	6	5	(-	-)	99	38	35	34	16	0	38	2	0	0		12	4	.75	3	.286	.337	.429
2008	CRpds	A	126	461	120	21	4	2	(-	-)	155	79	34	65	55	2	76	9	12	6		62	18	.78	5	.260	.347	.336
2009	RCuca	A+	131	479	133	13	9	1	(-	-)	167	68	36	65	51	1	83	5	16	4		26	11	.70	7	.278	.351	.349
2010	Ark	AA	106	383	108	15	4	3	(-	-)	140	55	34	58	50	1	66	5	13	2		21	9	.70	4	.282	.370	.366
2011	Salt Lk	AAA	105	381	107	9	2	4	(-	-)	132	67	35	54	45	0	87	4	8	0		23	6	.79	4	.281	.363	.346
2010	LAA	AL	5	11	1	0	0	0	(0	0)	1	0	0	0	0	0	4	0	1	0		0	0	-	0	.091	.091	.091
2011	LAA	AL	10	16	2	0	0	0	(0	0)	2	2	0	0	1	0	6	0	1	0		1	0	1.00	0	.125	.176	.125
2 ML YEARS			15	27	3	0	0	0	(0	0)	3	2	0	0	1	0	10	0	2	0		1	0	1.00	0	.111	.143	.111

Austin Romine

Bats: R Throws: R Pos: C-8; DH-1; PH-1 ROW-mine Ht: 6'1" Wt: 195 Born: 11/22/1988 Age: 23

										BATTING												BASERUNNING				AVERAGES		
Year	Team	Lg	G	AB	H	2B	3B	HR	(Hm	Rd)	TB	R	RBI	RC	TBB	IBB	SO	HBP	SH	SF		SB	CS	SB%	GDP	Avg	OBP	Slg
2007	Yanks	R	1	2	1	1	0	0	(-	-)	2	2	1	1	0	1	0	0	0	0		0	0	-	0	.500	.667	1.000
2008	CtnSC	A	104	407	122	24	1	10	(-	-)	178	66	49	63	25	0	56	3	0	1		3	0	1.00	8	.300	.344	.437
2009	Tampa	A+	118	442	122	28	3	13	(-	-)	195	61	72	66	29	2	78	4	0	6		11	5	.69	13	.276	.322	.441

Year	Team	Lg	G	AB	H	2B	3B	HR	(Hm	Rd)	TB	R	RBI	RC	TBB	IBB	SO	HBP	SH	SF	SB	CS	SB%	GDP	Avg	OBP	Slg
2010	Trntn	AA	115	455	122	31	0	10	(-	-)	183	61	69	62	37	1	94	2	0	3	2	0	1.00	13	.268	.324	.402
2011	Trntn	AA	85	336	96	13	0	6	(-	-)	127	43	47	47	32	1	60	3	0	2	2	2	.50	5	.286	.351	.378
2011	S-WB	AAA	4	15	2	0	0	0	(-	-)	2	1	1	0	0	0	3	0	0	0	0	0	-	2	.133	.133	.133
2011	NYY	AL	9	19	3	0	0	0	(0	0)	3	2	0	0	1	0	5	0	0	0	0	0	-	0	.158	.200	.158

Sergio Romo

Pitches: R **Bats:** R **Pos:** RP-65 **Ht:** 5'10" **Wt:** 185 **Born:** 3/4/1983 **Age:** 29

Year	Team	Lg	G	GS	CG	GF	IP	BFP	H	R	ER	HR	SH	SF	HB	TBB	IBB	SO	WP	Bk	W	L	Pct	Sh	Sv-Op	Hld	ERC	ERA
2011	Giants*	R	1	1	0	0	1.0	4	1	0	0	0	0	0	0	0	0	3	0	0	0	0	-	0	0- -	-	1.95	0.00
2008	SF	NL	29	0	0	8	34.0	130	16	13	8	3	2	1	3	8	1	33	0	0	3	1	.750	0	0-0	5	1.27	2.12
2009	SF	NL	45	0	0	9	34.0	143	30	15	15	1	2	0	1	11	0	41	2	0	5	2	.714	0	2-2	10	2.76	3.97
2010	SF	NL	68	0	0	13	62.0	247	46	16	15	6	2	2	4	14	2	70	0	0	5	3	.625	0	0-4	21	2.26	2.18
2011	SF	NL	65	0	0	16	48.0	175	29	8	8	2	2	0	0	5	1	70	0	0	3	1	.750	0	1-2	23	1.08	1.50
	Postseason		6	0	0		3.2	17	6	3	3	1	0	0	0	1	0	4	0	0	1	0	1.000	0	0-2	0	9.25	7.36
	4 ML YEARS		207	0	0	46	178.0	695	121	52	46	12	8	3	8	38	4	214	2	0	16	7	.696	0	3-8	59	1.72	2.33

Adam Rosales

Bats: R **Throws:** R **Pos:** SS-7; 3B-6; 1B-5; 2B-3; LF-2; PH-1; PR-1 **Ht:** 6'2" **Wt:** 195 **Born:** 5/20/1983 **Age:** 29

Year	Team	Lg	G	AB	H	2B	3B	HR	(Hm	Rd)	TB	R	RBI	RC	TBB	IBB	SO	HBP	SH	SF	SB	CS	SB%	GDP	Avg	OBP	Slg
2011	Scrmto*	AAA	40	147	39	5	1	3	(-	-)	55	23	22	18	13	0	32	1	0	3	1	1	.50	3	.265	.323	.374
2008	Cin	NL	18	29	6	1	0	0	(0	0)	7	0	2	2	1	0	4	0	0	0	1	0	1.00	0	.207	.233	.241
2009	Cin	NL	87	230	49	10	1	4	(2	2)	73	23	19	22	26	0	46	5	2	3	1	2	.33	2	.213	.303	.317
2010	Oak	AL	80	255	69	8	2	7	(1	6)	102	31	31	31	19	0	65	1	2	2	2	2	.50	1	.271	.321	.400
2011	Oak	AL	24	61	6	0	0	2	(0	2)	12	5	8	0	4	0	13	1	0	2	0	0	-	4	.098	.162	.197
	4 ML YEARS		209	575	130	19	3	13	(3	10)	194	59	60	55	50	0	128	7	4	7	4	4	.50	7	.226	.293	.337

Sandy Rosario

Pitches: R **Bats:** R **Pos:** RP-4 roh-SORRY-oh **Ht:** 6'1" **Wt:** 170 **Born:** 8/22/1985 **Age:** 26

Year	Team	Lg	G	GS	CG	GF	IP	BFP	H	R	ER	HR	SH	SF	HB	TBB	IBB	SO	WP	Bk	W	L	Pct	Sh	Sv-Op	Hld	ERC	ERA
2006	Mrlns	R	10	6	0	0	40.0	176	41	20	10	0	6	0	0	10	0	27	3	1	3	2	.600	0	0- -	-	2.79	2.25
2007	Grnsbr	A	2	2	0	0	7.1	33	11	8	8	1	0	0	0	2	0	7	2	0	0	1	.000	0	0- -	-	7.10	9.82
2008	Grnsbr	A	1	1	0	0	2.0	12	3	4	3	0	0	1	0	3	0	4	1	0	0	0	-	0	0- -	-	10.76	13.50
2009	Jmstwn	A-	9	9	0	0	42.1	186	48	12	8	1	0	0	5	8	0	41	1	0	4	2	.667	0	0- -	-	3.86	1.70
2009	Grnsbr	A	7	7	0	0	40.1	185	57	28	23	4	1	0	1	6	0	36	2	0	3	2	.600	0	0- -	-	5.41	5.13
2010	Grnsbr	A	43	0	0	16	90.0	377	92	47	36	9	5	2	3	17	1	122	4	0	7	2	.778	0	3- -	-	3.46	3.60
2010	Jaxnvl	AA	1	0	0	0	2.0	6	0	0	0	0	0	0	0	0	0	3	0	0	1	0	1.000	0	0- -	-	0.00	0.00
2011	Jaxnvl	AA	46	0	0	39	47.2	213	52	31	22	4	5	1	0	17	0	46	4	1	3	2	.600	0	23- -	-	4.17	4.15
2011	NewOr	AAA	7	0	0	6	6.2	28	5	4	3	0	0	0	0	5	0	4	1	0	0	1	.000	0	4- -	-	3.48	4.05
2010	Fla	NL	2	0	0	0	1.0	12	9	6	6	2	0	0	0	1	0	0	0	0	0	0	-	0	0-0	0	115.7	54.00
2011	Fla	NL	4	0	0	1	3.2	18	5	1	1	0	0	0	0	2	0	2	0	0	0	0	-	0	0-0	0	5.84	2.45
	2 ML YEARS		6	0	0	1	4.2	30	14	7	7	2	0	0	0	3	0	2	0	0	0	0	-	0	0-0	0	23.71	13.50

Wilin Rosario

Bats: R **Throws:** R **Pos:** C-14; PH-2 wih-LEAN roh-SORRY-oh **Ht:** 5'11" **Wt:** 190 **Born:** 2/23/1989 **Age:** 23

Year	Team	Lg	G	AB	H	2B	3B	HR	(Hm	Rd)	TB	R	RBI	RC	TBB	IBB	SO	HBP	SH	SF	SB	CS	SB%	GDP	Avg	OBP	Slg
2007	Casper	R+	34	115	24	4	0	2	(-	-)	34	11	9	9	11	0	38	1	0	0	2	2	.50	3	.209	.283	.296
2008	Casper	R+	66	263	83	15	3	12	(-	-)	140	48	49	52	24	0	57	1	0	3	4	3	.57	3	.316	.371	.532
2009	Mdest	A+	58	203	54	12	2	4	(-	-)	82	17	33	25	10	0	55	1	3	5	2	1	.67	4	.266	.297	.404
2010	Tulsa	AA	73	270	77	13	1	19	(-	-)	149	42	52	51	21	2	57	3	2	1	1	0	1.00	9	.285	.342	.552
2011	Tulsa	AA	102	405	101	15	3	21	(-	-)	185	52	48	53	19	0	91	1	0	1	1	2	.33	15	.249	.284	.457
2011	Col	NL	16	54	11	3	1	3	(1	2)	25	6	8	4	2	0	20	0	0	0	0	0	-	1	.204	.228	.463

Cody Ross

Bats: R **Throws:** L **Pos:** LF-83; RF-35; CF-22; PH-8 **Ht:** 5'10" **Wt:** 194 **Born:** 12/20/1980 **Age:** 31

Year	Team	Lg	G	AB	H	2B	3B	HR	(Hm	Rd)	TB	R	RBI	RC	TBB	IBB	SO	HBP	SH	SF	SB	CS	SB%	GDP	Avg	OBP	Slg
2011	Fresno*	AAA	2	6	3	1	0	0	(-	-)	4	1	2	2	2	0	1	0	0	0	0	0	-	0	.500	.625	.667
2003	Det	AL	6	19	4	1	0	1	(1	0)	8	1	5	4	1	0	3	1	1	0	0	0	-	0	.211	.286	.421
2005	LAD	NL	14	25	4	1	0	0	(0	0)	5	1	1	0	1	0	10	0	0	0	0	0	-	0	.160	.192	.200
2006	3 Tms	NL	101	269	61	12	2	13	(6	7)	116	34	46	36	22	0	65	4	1	2	1	1	.50	8	.227	.293	.431
2007	Fla	NL	66	173	58	19	0	12	(8	4)	113	35	39	42	20	3	38	3	0	1	2	0	1.00	2	.335	.411	.653
2008	Fla	NL	145	461	120	29	5	22	(7	15)	225	59	73	68	37	5	116	9	0	5	6	1	.86	5	.260	.316	.488
2009	Fla	NL	151	559	151	37	1	24	(13	11)	262	73	90	75	34	1	122	9	0	5	5	2	.71	18	.270	.321	.469
2010	2 Tms	NL	153	525	141	28	3	14	(5	9)	217	71	65	68	37	4	121	5	0	2	9	2	.82	9	.269	.322	.413
2011	SF	NL	121	405	97	25	0	14	(6	8)	164	54	52	53	49	4	96	4	0	3	5	2	.71	10	.240	.325	.405
06	LAD	NL	8	14	7	1	1	2	(0	2)	16	4	9	6	0	0	2	0	0	0	1	0	1.00	0	.500	.500	1.143
06	Cin	NL	2	5	1	0	0	0	(0	0)	1	0	0	1	0	0	2	0	0	0	0	0	-	0	.200	.200	.200
06	Fla	NL	91	250	53	11	1	11	(6	5)	99	30	37	29	22	0	61	4	1	2	0	1	.00	8	.212	.284	.396

							BATTING														BASERUNNING				AVERAGES		
Year	Team	Lg	G	AB	H	2B	3B	HR	(Hm	Rd)	TB	R	RBI	RC	TBB	IBB	SO	HBP	SH	SF	SB	CS	SB%	GDP	Avg	OBP	Slg
10	Fla	NL	120	452	120	24	3	11	(5	6)	183	60	58	58	30	4	100	4	0	1	9	1	.90	7	.265	.316	.405
10	SF	NL	33	73	21	4	0	3	(0	3)	34	11	7	10	7	0	21	1	0	1	0	1	.00	2	.288	.354	.466
	Postseason		15	51	15	5	0	5	(0	5)	35	11	10	12	7	0	11	1	0	0	0	0	-	1	.294	.390	.686
8 ML YEARS			757	2436	636	152	11	100	(46	54)	1110	328	371	346	197	14	571	33	2	15	28	8	.78	53	.261	.323	.456

David Ross

Bats: R Throws: R Pos: C-49; PH-5
Ht: 6'2" Wt: 205 Born: 3/19/1977 Age: 35

							BATTING														BASERUNNING				AVERAGES		
Year	Team	Lg	G	AB	H	2B	3B	HR	(Hm	Rd)	TB	R	RBI	RC	TBB	IBB	SO	HBP	SH	SF	SB	CS	SB%	GDP	Avg	OBP	Slg
2002	LAD	NL	8	10	2	1	0	1	(0	1)	6	2	2	2	2	0	4	1	0	0	0	0	-	0	.200	.385	.600
2003	LAD	NL	40	124	32	7	0	10	(5	5)	69	19	18	18	13	0	42	2	0	1	0	0	-	4	.258	.336	.556
2004	LAD	NL	70	165	28	3	1	5	(2	3)	48	13	15	11	15	1	62	5	0	5	0	0	-	3	.170	.253	.291
2005	2 Tms	NL	51	125	30	8	1	3	(2	1)	49	11	15	13	6	0	28	2	2	3	0	0	-	3	.240	.279	.392
2006	Cin	NL	90	247	63	15	1	21	(13	8)	143	37	52	43	37	7	75	3	4	5	0	0	-	9	.255	.353	.579
2007	Cin	NL	112	311	63	10	0	17	(12	5)	124	32	39	27	30	4	92	0	5	2	0	0	-	3	.203	.271	.399
2008	2 Tms	NL	60	142	32	9	0	3	(1	2)	50	18	13	19	32	4	39	1	6	1	0	1	.00	3	.225	.369	.352
2009	Atl	NL	54	128	35	9	0	7	(2	5)	65	18	20	20	21	0	39	1	1	0	0	1	.00	1	.273	.380	.508
2010	Atl	NL	59	121	35	13	2	2	(2	0)	58	15	28	22	20	0	28	1	2	1	0	1	.00	4	.289	.392	.479
2011	Atl	NL	52	152	40	7	0	6	(2	4)	65	14	23	22	16	0	51	0	2	0	0	1	.00	4	.263	.333	.428
05	Pit	NL	40	108	24	8	0	3	(2	1)	41	9	15	9	6	0	24	1	1	3	0	0	-	3	.222	.263	.380
05	SD	NL	11	17	6	0	1	0	(0	0)	8	2	0	4	0	0	4	1	1	0	0	0	-	0	.353	.389	.471
08	Cin	NL	52	134	31	9	0	3	(1	2)	49	17	13	19	32	4	36	1	5	1	0	1	.00	3	.231	.381	.366
08	Bos	AL	8	8	1	0	0	0	(0	0)	1	1	0	0	0	0	3	0	1	0	0	0	-	0	.125	.125	.125
	Postseason		5	3	0	0	0	0	(0	0)	0	0	0	0	1	0	0	0	0	0	0	0	-	0	.000	.250	.000
10 ML YEARS			596	1525	360	82	5	75	(41	34)	677	179	225	197	192	16	460	16	22	18	0	3	.00	36	.236	.324	.444

Tyson Ross

Pitches: R Bats: R Pos: SP-6; RP-3
Ht: 6'6" Wt: 225 Born: 4/22/1987 Age: 25

			HOW MUCH HE PITCHED						WHAT HE GAVE UP											THE RESULTS							
Year	Team	Lg	G	GS	CG	GF	IP	BFP	H	R	ER	HR	SH	SF	HB	TBB	IBB	SO	WP	Bk	W	L	Pct	Sh	Sv-Op	Hld	ERC	ERA
2008	Kane	A	6	4	0	0	19.1	80	16	11	10	1	0	2	5	0	16	1	0	0	1	.000	0	0- -	-	2.68	4.66
2009	Stcktn	A+	18	18	0	0	86.1	378	78	49	40	10	4	4	8	33	1	82	5	0	5	6	.455	0	0- -	-	3.84	4.17
2009	Mdland	AA	9	9	1	0	50.0	203	40	22	22	3	1	3	1	20	0	31	4	0	5	4	.556	0	0- -	-	2.89	3.96
2010	Scrmto	AAA	6	6	0	0	25.1	100	22	10	10	1	2	0	4	13	0	30	1	0	2	1	.667	0	0- -	-	4.22	3.55
2011	Scrmto	AAA	9	9	0	0	36.2	183	52	34	31	5	0	1	0	22	0	34	3	0	3	2	.600	0	0- -	-	12.01	9.00
2011	Stcktn	A+	1	1	0	0	1.0	6	2	1	1	0	0	0	0	1	0	1	0	0	0	0	-	0	0- -	-	12.01	9.00
2010	Oak	AL	26	2	0	9	39.1	169	39	24	24	4	1	4	0	20	0	32	5	0	1	4	.200	0	1-2	2	4.60	5.49
2011	Oak	AL	9	6	0	1	36.0	145	33	12	11	1	1	0	0	13	1	24	2	0	3	3	.500	0	0-0	0	3.09	2.75
2 ML YEARS			35	8	0	10	75.1	314	72	36	35	5	2	4	0	33	1	56	7	0	4	7	.364	0	1-2	2	3.86	4.18

Vinny Rottino

Bats: R Throws: R Pos: PH-5; RF-2; LF-1
row-TEEN-oh
Ht: 6'1" Wt: 206 Born: 4/7/1980 Age: 32

							BATTING														BASERUNNING				AVERAGES		
Year	Team	Lg	G	AB	H	2B	3B	HR	(Hm	Rd)	TB	R	RBI	RC	TBB	IBB	SO	HBP	SH	SF	SB	CS	SB%	GDP	Avg	OBP	Slg
2011	NewOr*	AAA	119	467	142	31	2	10	(-	-)	207	81	59	80	50	2	62	3	3	1	17	9	.65	14	.304	.374	.443
2006	Mil	NL	9	14	3	1	0	0	(0	0)	4	1	1	1	1	0	2	0	0	0	1	0	1.00	0	.214	.267	.286
2007	Mil	NL	8	9	2	1	0	0	(0	0)	3	0	3	2	0	0	1	0	0	0	0	0	-	0	.222	.222	.333
2008	Mil	NL	1	1	0	0	0	0	(0	0)	0	0	0	0	0	0	0	0	0	0	0	0	-	0	.000	.000	.000
2011	Fla	NL	8	12	2	0	0	0	(0	0)	2	1	0	0	2	0	4	0	0	0	0	0	-	0	.167	.286	.167
4 ML YEARS			26	36	7	2	0	0	(0	0)	9	2	4	3	3	0	7	0	0	0	1	0	1.00	0	.194	.256	.250

Aaron Rowand

Bats: R Throws: R Pos: CF-60; LF-46; PH-26; RF-3; DH-2
ROW-and
Ht: 6'0" Wt: 213 Born: 8/29/1977 Age: 34

							BATTING														BASERUNNING				AVERAGES		
Year	Team	Lg	G	AB	H	2B	3B	HR	(Hm	Rd)	TB	R	RBI	RC	TBB	IBB	SO	HBP	SH	SF	SB	CS	SB%	GDP	Avg	OBP	Slg
2001	CWS	AL	63	123	36	5	0	4	(3	1)	53	21	20	22	15	0	28	4	5	1	5	1	.83	2	.293	.385	.431
2002	CWS	AL	126	302	78	16	2	7	(5	2)	119	41	29	37	12	1	54	6	9	2	0	1	.00	8	.258	.296	.394
2003	CWS	AL	93	157	45	8	0	6	(5	1)	71	22	24	28	7	0	21	3	2	1	0	0	-	1	.287	.327	.452
2004	CWS	AL	140	487	151	38	2	24	(12	12)	265	94	69	92	30	1	91	10	5	2	17	5	.77	5	.310	.361	.544
2005	CWS	AL	157	578	156	30	5	13	(8	5)	235	77	69	78	32	3	116	21	5	4	16	5	.76	17	.270	.329	.407
2006	Phi	NL	109	405	106	24	3	12	(6	6)	172	59	47	47	18	2	76	18	2	2	6	3	.67	18	.309	.374	.425
2007	Phi	NL	161	612	189	45	2	27	(17	10)	315	105	89	100	47	3	119	19	2	4	4	4	.33	21	.309	.374	.515
2008	SF	NL	152	549	149	37	0	13	(6	7)	225	57	70	67	44	7	126	14	0	3	2	1	.80	12	.271	.339	.410
2009	SF	NL	144	499	130	30	2	15	(10	5)	209	61	64	63	30	2	125	14	0	3	4	1	.80	12	.261	.319	.419
2010	SF	NL	105	331	76	12	2	11	(6	5)	125	42	34	33	16	3	74	8	1	1	3	2	.60	11	.230	.281	.378
2011	SF	NL	108	331	77	22	2	4	(2	2)	115	34	21	23	10	1	84	9	0	1	1	0	1.00	3	.233	.274	.347
	Postseason		22	68	16	7	1	1	(1	0)	28	11	6	4	4	1	18	1	0	1	0	0	-	3	.235	.284	.412
11 ML YEARS			1358	4374	1193	267	18	136	(75	61)	1904	613	536	590	261	23	914	126	31	25	67	30	.69	114	.273	.330	.435

Chance Ruffin

Pitches: R Bats: R Pos: RP-15

Ht: 6'0" **Wt:** 185 **Born:** 9/8/1988 **Age:** 23

Year	Team	Lg	G	GS	CG	GF	IP	BFP	H	R	ER	HR	SH	SF	HB	TBB	IBB	SO	WP	Bk	W	L	Pct	Sh	Sv-Op	Hld	ERC	ERA
2011	Erie	AA	31	0	0	28	34.0	139	23	9	8	2	1	0	1	16	2	43	2	0	3	3	.500	0	10--	-	2.41	2.12
2011	Toledo	AAA	13	0	0	9	14.2	65	14	4	3	1	1	0	0	6	0	17	1	0	0	0	-	0	9--	-	3.49	1.84
2011	2 Tms	AL	15	0	0	2	17.2	78	18	8	8	4	0	0	0	9	0	18	1	0	1	0	1.000	0	0-0	1	5.60	4.08
11	Det	AL	2	0	0	0	3.2	16	5	2	2	2	0	0	0	0	0	3	0	0	0	0	-	0	0-0	0	7.47	4.91
11	Sea	AL	13	0	0	2	14.0	62	13	6	6	2	0	0	0	9	0	15	1	0	1	0	1.000	0	0-0	1	5.02	3.86

Justin Ruggiano

Bats: R Throws: R Pos: LF-27; PH-12; RF-6; CF-4; DH-3; PR-3   rouge-ee-AH-no

Ht: 6'2" **Wt:** 205 **Born:** 4/12/1982 **Age:** 30

Year	Team	Lg	G	AB	H	2B	3B	HR	(Hm	Rd)	TB	R	RBI	RC	TBB	IBB	SO	HBP	SH	SF	SB	CS	SB%	GDP	Avg	OBP	Slg
2011	Drham*	AAA	43	168	51	11	1	7	(-	-)	87	29	34	34	20	0	42	0	2	0	12	2	.86	4	.304	.378	.518
2007	TB	AL	7	14	3	0	0	0	(0	0)	3	2	3	1	0	0	5	0	0	0	0	0	-	0	.214	.267	.214
2008	TB	AL	45	76	15	4	0	2	(2	0)	25	9	7	4	1	0	27	1	0	0	2	0	1.00	2	.197	.247	.329
2011	TB	AL	46	105	26	4	0	4	(3	1)	42	11	13	16	4	0	26	0	1	1	1	1	.50	2	.248	.273	.400
	3 ML YEARS		98	195	44	8	0	6	(5	1)	70	22	23	21	9	0	58	1	1	1	3	1	.75	4	.226	.262	.359

Carlos Ruiz

Bats: R Throws: R Pos: C-128; PH-13; 3B-1

Ht: 5'10" **Wt:** 206 **Born:** 1/22/1979 **Age:** 33

Year	Team	Lg	G	AB	H	2B	3B	HR	(Hm	Rd)	TB	R	RBI	RC	TBB	IBB	SO	HBP	SH	SF	SB	CS	SB%	GDP	Avg	OBP	Slg
2011	Clrwtr*	A+	1	3	1	0	0	0	(-	-)	1	1	0	0	0	0	0	0	0	0	0	0	-	0	.333	.333	.333
2006	Phi	NL	27	69	18	1	1	3	(2	1)	30	5	10	10	5	2	8	1	2	1	0	0	-	3	.261	.316	.435
2007	Phi	NL	115	374	97	29	2	6	(4	2)	148	42	54	49	42	10	49	5	5	3	6	1	.86	17	.259	.340	.396
2008	Phi	NL	117	320	70	14	0	4	(2	2)	96	47	31	28	44	6	38	4	4	1	1	2	.33	14	.219	.320	.300
2009	Phi	NL	107	322	82	26	1	9	(5	4)	137	32	43	49	47	8	39	4	4	2	3	2	.60	8	.255	.355	.425
2010	Phi	NL	121	371	112	28	1	8	(3	5)	166	43	53	62	55	13	54	6	0	1	0	1	.00	8	.302	.400	.447
2011	Phi	NL	132	410	116	23	0	6	(1	5)	157	49	40	59	48	10	48	10	3	1	1	0	1.00	7	.283	.371	.383
	Postseason		41	125	35	8	1	4	(3	1)	57	18	15	24	23	2	13	5	1	0	3	0	1.00	3	.280	.412	.456
	6 ML YEARS		619	1866	495	121	5	36	(17	19)	734	218	231	257	241	49	236	30	18	9	11	6	.65	57	.265	.357	.393

Dan Runzler

Pitches: L Bats: L Pos: RP-30; SP-1

Ht: 6'4" **Wt:** 233 **Born:** 3/30/1985 **Age:** 27

Year	Team	Lg	G	GS	CG	GF	IP	BFP	H	R	ER	HR	SH	SF	HB	TBB	IBB	SO	WP	Bk	W	L	Pct	Sh	Sv-Op	Hld	ERC	ERA
2011	Fresno*	AAA	17	10	0	0	52.0	235	47	32	23	2	0	2	3	32	0	59	2	0	2	3	.400	0	0--	-	4.09	3.98
2009	SF	NL	11	0	0	0	8.2	38	6	1	1	0	0	0	1	5	0	11	0	0	0	0	-	0	0-0	2	3.54	1.04
2010	SF	NL	41	0	0	7	32.2	144	29	12	11	1	4	0	1	20	3	37	2	0	3	0	1.000	0	0-0	5	3.74	3.03
2011	SF	NL	31	1	0	9	27.1	120	29	21	19	0	0	1	0	16	1	25	1	0	1	2	.333	0	0-0	3	4.48	6.26
	3 ML YEARS		83	1	0	16	68.2	302	64	34	31	2	4	1	2	41	4	73	3	0	4	2	.667	0	0-0	10	4.00	4.06

Josh Rupe

Pitches: R Bats: R Pos: RP-9

ROOP

Ht: 6'2" **Wt:** 215 **Born:** 8/18/1982 **Age:** 29

Year	Team	Lg	G	GS	CG	GF	IP	BFP	H	R	ER	HR	SH	SF	HB	TBB	IBB	SO	WP	Bk	W	L	Pct	Sh	Sv-Op	Hld	ERC	ERA
2011	Norfolk*	AAA	30	0	0	12	42.0	195	50	37	33	5	6	2	1	21	4	29	6	0	2	5	.286	0	0--	-	5.62	7.07
2005	Tex	AL	4	1	0	1	9.2	39	7	4	3	0	1	0	2	4	0	6	1	0	1	0	1.000	0	0-0	0	2.91	2.79
2006	Tex	AL	16	0	0	3	29.0	126	33	11	11	2	1	0	1	9	0	14	2	0	0	0	1.000	0	0-1	4	4.45	3.41
2008	Tex	AL	46	0	0	10	89.1	392	93	52	51	8	2	7	10	46	3	53	3	0	3	1	.750	0	0-2	2	5.30	5.14
2009	Tex	AL	4	0	0	2	4.2	31	12	8	8	2	0	0	0	5	0	2	0	0	0	0	-	0	0-0	0	21.74	15.43
2010	KC	AL	11	0	0	1	9.2	49	14	6	6	1	1	0	0	7	0	8	1	0	1	1	.500	0	0-0	0	8.22	5.59
2011	Bal	AL	9	0	0	5	14.1	66	16	9	9	5	0	0	2	6	0	7	1	0	0	0	-	0	0-0	0	7.33	5.65
	6 ML YEARS		90	1	0	22	156.2	703	175	90	88	18	5	7	15	77	3	90	8	0	5	3	.625	0	0-3	8	5.75	5.06

Adam Russell

Pitches: R Bats: R Pos: RP-36

Ht: 6'8" **Wt:** 255 **Born:** 4/14/1983 **Age:** 29

Year	Team	Lg	G	GS	CG	GF	IP	BFP	H	R	ER	HR	SH	SF	HB	TBB	IBB	SO	WP	Bk	W	L	Pct	Sh	Sv-Op	Hld	ERC	ERA
2011	Drham*	AAA	15	0	0	5	17.0	76	14	8	8	2	2	0	0	12	0	14	0	0	0	1	.000	0	1--	-	4.37	4.24
2008	CWS	AL	22	0	0	16	26.0	118	30	15	15	1	2	1	2	10	1	22	3	0	4	0	1.000	0	0-0	4	4.63	5.19
2009	SD	NL	15	0	0	1	12.1	61	13	6	5	0	0	0	0	11	0	14	0	0	3	1	.750	0	0-0	4	5.38	3.65
2010	SD	NL	12	0	0	3	15.2	63	14	8	7	0	2	1	0	5	0	18	1	0	0	0	-	0	0-0	0	2.63	4.02
2011	TB	AL	36	0	0	14	32.2	147	31	13	11	2	2	0	3	20	1	13	1	0	1	2	.333	0	0-0	2	4.69	3.03
	4 ML YEARS		85	0	0	34	86.2	389	88	42	38	3	6	2	5	46	2	67	5	0	8	3	.727	0	0-0	6	4.38	3.95

James Russell

Pitches: L Bats: L Pos: RP-59; SP-5 Ht: 6'4" Wt: 200 Born: 1/8/1986 Age: 26

| | | | HOW MUCH HE PITCHED | | | | | | | WHAT HE GAVE UP | | | | | | | | | | THE RESULTS | | | | | | |
Year	Team	Lg	G	GS	CG	GF	IP	BFP	H	R	ER	HR	SH	SF	HB	TBB	IBB	SO	WP	Bk	W	L	Pct	Sh	Sv-Op Hld	ERC	ERA
2007	Cubs	R	1	1	0	0	2.0	6	0	0	0	0	0	0	0	0	0	2	0	0	0	0	-	0	0- -	0.00	0.00
2007	Peoria	A	2	2	0	0	7.0	26	3	0	0	0	0	0	0	4	0	9	0	0	0	0	-	0	0- -	1.45	0.00
2008	Dytona	A+	8	8	0	0	41.0	163	36	18	16	4	1	1	0	13	0	24	0	0	2	2	.500	0	0- -	3.22	3.51
2008	Tenn	AA	18	17	0	0	86.1	390	111	64	61	18	2	5	6	25	0	62	4	0	4	8	.333	0	0- -	6.47	6.36
2009	Tenn	AA	11	5	0	0	37.0	161	45	24	21	5	1	0	1	9	0	26	3	0	2	3	.400	0	0- -	5.10	5.11
2009	Iowa	AAA	26	7	0	3	65.2	287	71	25	25	6	3	1	0	19	1	46	2	0	3	3	.500	0	0- -	3.91	3.43
2010	Iowa	AAA	5	0	0	0	11.0	47	11	7	7	5	0	0	1	4	0	10	0	0	0	0	-	0	0- -	7.04	5.73
2010	ChC	NL	57	0	0	11	49.0	219	55	37	27	11	3	4	4	11	0	42	2	0	1	1	.500	0	0-2 6	5.12	4.96
2011	ChC	NL	64	5	0	10	67.2	292	76	37	31	12	4	6	2	14	4	43	1	0	1	6	.143	0	0-2 6	4.51	4.12
2 ML YEARS			121	5	0	21	116.2	511	131	74	58	23	7	10	6	25	4	85	3	0	2	7	.222	0	0-4 12	4.76	4.47

Brendan Ryan

Bats: R Throws: R Pos: SS-123; PR-2 Ht: 6'2" Wt: 195 Born: 3/26/1982 Age: 30

| | | | BATTING | | | | | | | | | | | | | | | | BASERUNNING | | | | AVERAGES | | |
Year	Team	Lg	G	AB	H	2B	3B	HR	(Hm	Rd)	TB	R	RBI	RC	TBB	IBB	SO	HBP	SH	SF	SB	CS	SB%	GDP	Avg	OBP	Slg
2007	StL	NL	67	180	52	9	0	4	(2	2)	73	30	12	21	15	0	19	1	3	0	7	0	1.00	3	.289	.347	.406
2008	StL	NL	80	197	48	9	0	0	(0	0)	57	30	10	12	16	0	31	2	3	0	7	2	.78	4	.244	.307	.289
2009	StL	NL	129	390	114	19	7	3	(1	2)	156	55	37	48	24	3	56	6	6	3	14	7	.67	9	.292	.340	.400
2010	StL	NL	139	439	98	19	3	2	(0	2)	129	50	36	37	33	5	60	2	9	3	11	4	.73	6	.223	.279	.294
2011	Sea	AL	123	436	108	19	3	3	(0	3)	142	51	39	46	34	0	87	10	9	5	13	3	.81	7	.248	.313	.326
Postseason			3	12	1	1	0	0	(0	0)	2	0	0	0	0	0	2	0	0	0	0	0	-	0	.083	.083	.167
5 ML YEARS			538	1642	420	75	13	12	(3	9)	557	216	134	164	122	8	253	21	30	11	52	16	.76	29	.256	.313	.339

Marc Rzepczynski

Pitches: L Bats: L Pos: RP-71 zepp-CHINN-ski Ht: 6'1" Wt: 205 Born: 8/29/1985 Age: 26

| | | | HOW MUCH HE PITCHED | | | | | | | WHAT HE GAVE UP | | | | | | | | | | THE RESULTS | | | | | | |
Year	Team	Lg	G	GS	CG	GF	IP	BFP	H	R	ER	HR	SH	SF	HB	TBB	IBB	SO	WP	Bk	W	L	Pct	Sh	Sv-Op Hld	ERC	ERA
2009	Tor	AL	11	11	0	0	61.1	261	51	27	25	7	2	1	1	30	0	60	4	1	2	4	.333	0	0-0 0	3.85	3.67
2010	Tor	AL	14	12	0	0	63.2	287	72	37	35	8	1	2	5	30	1	57	4	1	4	4	.500	0	0-0 2	5.71	4.95
2011	2 Tms		71	0	0	7	62.0	256	50	27	23	3	2	0	4	26	1	61	6	0	2	6	.250	0	0-4 18	3.04	3.34
11	Tor	AL	43	0	0	6	39.1	158	28	16	13	2	1	0	3	15	0	33	5	0	2	3	.400	0	0-3 10	2.52	2.97
11	StL	NL	28	0	0	1	22.2	98	22	11	10	1	1	0	1	11	1	28	1	0	0	3	.000	0	0-1 8	4.01	3.97
3 ML YEARS			96	23	0	7	187.0	804	173	91	83	18	5	3	10	86	2	178	14	2	8	14	.364	0	0-4 20	4.11	3.99

CC Sabathia

Pitches: L Bats: L Pos: SP-33 Ht: 6'7" Wt: 290 Born: 7/21/1980 Age: 31

| | | | HOW MUCH HE PITCHED | | | | | | | WHAT HE GAVE UP | | | | | | | | | | THE RESULTS | | | | | | |
Year	Team	Lg	G	GS	CG	GF	IP	BFP	H	R	ER	HR	SH	SF	HB	TBB	IBB	SO	WP	Bk	W	L	Pct	Sh	Sv-Op Hld	ERC	ERA
2001	Cle	AL	33	33	0	0	180.1	763	149	93	88	19	3	5	7	95	1	171	7	3	17	5	.773	0	0-0 0	3.86	4.39
2002	Cle	AL	33	33	2	0	210.0	891	198	109	102	17	5	10	1	88	2	149	6	3	13	11	.542	0	0-0 0	3.74	4.37
2003	Cle	AL	30	30	2	0	197.2	832	190	85	79	19	10	4	6	66	3	141	4	2	13	9	.591	1	0-0 0	3.70	3.60
2004	Cle	AL	30	30	1	0	188.0	787	176	90	86	20	3	6	7	72	3	139	1	1	11	10	.524	1	0-0 0	3.91	4.12
2005	Cle	AL	31	31	1	0	196.2	823	185	92	88	19	6	3	7	62	1	161	7	0	15	10	.600	0	0-0 0	3.55	4.03
2006	Cle	AL	28	28	6	0	192.2	802	182	83	69	17	8	5	7	44	3	172	3	0	12	11	.522	2	0-0 0	3.13	3.22
2007	Cle	AL	34	34	4	0	241.0	975	238	94	86	20	6	6	8	37	1	209	1	0	19	7	.731	1	0-0 0	3.12	3.21
2008	2 Tms		35	35	10	0	253.0	1023	223	85	76	19	9	6	7	59	1	251	2	2	17	10	.630	5	0-0 0	2.78	2.70
2009	NYY	AL	34	34	2	0	230.0	938	197	96	86	18	4	9	6	67	7	197	5	0	19	8	.704	1	0-0 0	2.89	3.37
2010	NYY	AL	34	34	2	0	237.2	970	209	92	84	20	5	8	7	74	6	197	8	1	21	7	.750	1	0-0 0	3.11	3.18
2011	NYY	AL	33	33	3	0	237.1	985	230	87	79	17	8	7	7	61	4	230	2	1	19	8	.704	1	0-0 0	3.27	3.00
08	Cle	AL	18	18	3	0	122.1	507	117	54	52	13	3	3	3	34	1	123	1	2	6	8	.429	2	0-0 0	3.52	3.83
08	Mil	NL	17	17	7	0	130.2	516	106	31	24	6	6	3	4	25	0	128	1	0	11	2	.846	3	0-0 0	2.13	1.65
Postseason			13	13	0	0	77.1	345	83	42	40	11	2	0	5	38	6	71	3	1	7	4	.636	0	0-0 0	5.40	4.66
11 ML YEARS			355	355	33	0	2364.1	9789	2177	1006	923	205	67	69	73	725	32	2017	46	13	176	96	.647	12	0-0 0	3.33	3.51

Takashi Saito

Pitches: R Bats: R Pos: RP-30 SYE-toe Ht: 6'2" Wt: 200 Born: 2/14/1970 Age: 42

| | | | HOW MUCH HE PITCHED | | | | | | | WHAT HE GAVE UP | | | | | | | | | | THE RESULTS | | | | | | |
Year	Team	Lg	G	GS	CG	GF	IP	BFP	H	R	ER	HR	SH	SF	HB	TBB	IBB	SO	WP	Bk	W	L	Pct	Sh	Sv-Op Hld	ERC	ERA
2011	Nashv*	AAA	6	0	0	0	5.2	19	3	0	0	0	0	0	0	0	0	7	0	0	0	0	-	0	0- -	0.63	0.00
2006	LAD	NL	72	0	0	48	78.1	303	48	19	18	3	3	4	2	23	3	107	2	0	6	2	.750	0	24-26 7	1.52	2.07
2007	LAD	NL	63	0	0	55	64.1	234	33	10	10	5	0	0	3	13	0	78	0	0	2	1	.667	0	39-43 1	1.28	1.40
2008	LAD	NL	45	0	0	35	47.0	191	40	14	13	1	0	2	2	16	3	60	1	0	4	4	.500	0	18-22 0	2.57	2.49
2009	Bos	AL	56	0	0	30	55.2	240	50	16	15	6	1	4	5	25	2	52	1	0	3	3	.500	0	2-4 3	4.08	2.43
2010	Atl	NL	56	0	0	14	54.0	221	41	20	17	4	2	0	0	17	2	69	2	0	2	3	.400	0	1-2 17	2.24	2.83
2011	Mil	NL	30	0	0	5	26.2	108	21	6	6	2	1	0	1	9	2	23	2	0	4	2	.667	0	0-2 10	2.62	2.03
Postseason			4	0	0	2	3.2	15	5	2	2	0	0	0	0	0	0	4	0	0	0	0	-	0	0-0 0	4.01	4.91
6 ML YEARS			322	0	0	187	326.0	1303	233	85	79	21	7	10	13	103	12	389	8	0	21	15	.583	0	84-99 38	2.17	2.18

245

Fernando Salas

Pitches: R Bats: R Pos: RP-68   SAH-lahss   Ht: 6'2" Wt: 200 Born: 5/30/1985 Age: 27

		HOW MUCH HE PITCHED					WHAT HE GAVE UP										THE RESULTS						
Year Team	Lg	G	GS	CG	GF	IP	BFP	H	R	ER	HR	SH	SF	HB	TBB	IBB	SO	WP	Bk	W	L	Pct	Sh	Sv-Op Hld	ERC	ERA
2007 PlmBh	A+	16	4	0	2	39.1	166	39	25	23	12	1	2	3	10	1	25	2	0	2	3	.400	0	0- - -	5.15	5.26
2008 Sprgfld	AA	60	0	0	37	74.0	300	65	31	30	12	4	2	2	16	2	100	2	2	7	3	.700	0	25- - -	3.17	3.65
2009 Memp	AAA	24	0	0	10	27.0	113	22	12	11	4	1	1	1	10	0	24	3	0	3	2	.600	0	0- - -	3.38	3.67
2009 Cards	R	1	0	0	0	1.0	3	0	0	0	0	0	0	0	0	0	1	0	0	0	0	-	0	0- - -	0.00	0.00
2009 Sprgfld	AA	10	0	0	1	11.1	45	10	5	4	0	0	2	0	2	0	7	1	0	1	0	1.000	0	0- - -	2.04	3.18
2010 Memp	AAA	34	0	0	24	35.2	137	26	15	15	2	1	1	1	9	0	44	2	0	1	0	1.000	0	19- - -	2.06	3.79
2011 Memp	AAA	3	0	0	3	3.0	12	2	0	0	0	1	0	2	0	0	4	0	0	0	0	-	0	2- - -	2.79	0.00
2010 StL	NL	27	0	0	11	30.2	133	28	13	12	4	1	1	0	15	2	29	2	0	0	0	-	0	0-1 1	4.03	3.52
2011 StL	NL	68	0	0	46	75.0	295	50	20	19	7	3	0	2	21	3	75	2	0	5	6	.455	0	24-30 6	1.94	2.28
2 ML YEARS		95	0	0	57	105.2	428	78	33	31	11	4	1	2	36	5	104	4	0	5	6	.455	0	24-31 7	2.50	2.64

Chris Sale

Pitches: L Bats: L Pos: RP-58   SAIL   Ht: 6'5" Wt: 170 Born: 3/30/1989 Age: 23

		HOW MUCH HE PITCHED					WHAT HE GAVE UP										THE RESULTS						
Year Team	Lg	G	GS	CG	GF	IP	BFP	H	R	ER	HR	SH	SF	HB	TBB	IBB	SO	WP	Bk	W	L	Pct	Sh	Sv-Op Hld	ERC	ERA
2010 WinSa	A+	4	0	0	0	4.0	17	3	2	1	0	0	0	0	2	0	4	0	0	0	0	-	0	0- - -	2.40	2.25
2010 Charltt	AAA	7	0	0	1	6.1	26	3	2	2	2	0	0	0	4	0	15	0	0	0	0	-	0	0- - -	3.45	2.84
2010 CWS	AL	21	0	0	8	23.1	92	15	5	5	2	1	0	0	10	0	32	1	0	2	1	.667	0	4-4 2	2.30	1.93
2011 CWS	AL	58	0	0	17	71.0	288	52	22	22	6	3	0	2	27	3	79	2	0	2	2	.500	0	8-10 16	2.55	2.79
2 ML YEARS		79	0	0	25	94.1	380	67	27	27	8	4	0	2	37	3	111	3	0	4	3	.571	0	12-14 18	2.49	2.58

Jarrod Saltalamacchia

Bats: B Throws: R Pos: C-101; PH-2; PR-1   salt-ah-luh-MOCK-ee-ah   Ht: 6'4" Wt: 235 Born: 5/2/1985 Age: 27

		BATTING																	BASERUNNING				AVERAGES		
Year Team	Lg	G	AB	H	2B	3B	HR	(Hm	Rd)	TB	R	RBI	RC	TBB	IBB	SO	HBP	SH	SF	SB	CS	SB%	GDP	Avg	OBP	Slg
2007 2 Tms		93	308	82	13	1	11	(6	5)	130	39	33	32	19	1	75	1	0	1	0	0	-	8	.266	.310	.422
2008 Tex	AL	61	198	50	13	0	3	(2	1)	72	27	26	29	31	1	74	0	0	1	0	2	.00	1	.253	.352	.364
2009 Tex	AL	84	283	66	12	0	9	(6	3)	105	34	34	30	22	1	97	1	3	1	0	2	.00	3	.233	.290	.371
2010 2 Tms	AL	12	24	4	3	0	0	(0	0)	7	2	2	3	6	0	5	0	0	0	0	0	-	0	.167	.333	.292
2011 Bos	AL	103	358	84	23	3	16	(6	10)	161	52	56	43	24	1	119	3	0	1	1	0	1.00	7	.235	.288	.450
07 Atl	NL	47	141	40	6	0	4	(4	0)	58	11	12	13	10	1	28	1	0	1	0	0	-	4	.284	.333	.411
07 Tex	AL	46	167	42	7	1	7	(2	5)	72	28	21	19	9	0	47	0	0	0	0	0	-	4	.251	.290	.431
10 Tex	AL	2	5	1	0	0	0	(0	0)	1	0	1	1	0	0	1	0	0	0	0	0	-	0	.200	.200	.200
10 Bos	AL	10	19	3	3	0	0	(0	0)	6	2	1	2	6	0	4	0	0	0	0	0	-	0	.158	.360	.316
5 ML YEARS		353	1171	286	64	4	39	(20	19)	475	154	151	137	102	4	370	5	3	4	1	4	.20	19	.244	.307	.406

Jeff Samardzija

Pitches: R Bats: R Pos: RP-75   suh-MAHR-jah   Ht: 6'5" Wt: 225 Born: 1/23/1985 Age: 27

		HOW MUCH HE PITCHED					WHAT HE GAVE UP										THE RESULTS						
Year Team	Lg	G	GS	CG	GF	IP	BFP	H	R	ER	HR	SH	SF	HB	TBB	IBB	SO	WP	Bk	W	L	Pct	Sh	Sv-Op Hld	ERC	ERA
2008 ChC	NL	26	0	0	6	27.2	124	24	12	7	0	1	1	1	15	2	25	2	0	1	0	1.000	0	1-4 3	3.08	2.28
2009 ChC	NL	20	2	0	7	34.2	161	46	29	29	7	4	1	1	15	1	21	2	0	1	3	.250	0	0-0 0	7.13	7.53
2010 ChC	NL	7	3	0	0	19.1	90	21	22	18	4	0	0	2	20	1	9	1	0	2	2	.500	0	0-0 0	8.45	8.38
2011 ChC	NL	75	0	0	18	88.0	380	64	35	29	5	3	2	5	50	3	87	8	0	8	4	.667	0	0-2 13	3.05	2.97
Postseason		1	0	0	0	1.0	4	2	1	1	0	0	0	0	0	0	0	0	0	0	0	-	0	0-0 0	9.49	9.00
4 ML YEARS		128	5	0	31	169.2	765	155	98	83	16	8	4	9	100	7	142	13	0	12	9	.571	0	1-6 16	4.37	4.40

Alex Sanabia

Pitches: R Bats: R Pos: SP-2; RP-1   suh-NAH-bee-ah   Ht: 6'2" Wt: 165 Born: 9/8/1988 Age: 23

		HOW MUCH HE PITCHED					WHAT HE GAVE UP										THE RESULTS						
Year Team	Lg	G	GS	CG	GF	IP	BFP	H	R	ER	HR	SH	SF	HB	TBB	IBB	SO	WP	Bk	W	L	Pct	Sh	Sv-Op Hld	ERC	ERA
2006 Mrlns	R	11	0	0	0	16.2	70	10	7	6	0	3	0	1	7	0	16	4	0	3	1	.750	0	0- - -	1.63	3.24
2007 Jmstwn	A-	15	15	1	0	66.2	296	73	45	38	5	2	1	7	17	0	69	13	2	2	6	.250	0	0- - -	4.18	5.13
2008 Grnsbr	A	19	19	0	0	96.2	420	106	60	53	11	1	3	2	25	0	75	6	1	5	5	.500	0	0- - -	4.17	4.93
2009 Jupiter	A+	19	18	0	0	104.1	434	89	45	40	6	2	3	7	36	0	68	7	0	9	5	.643	0	0- - -	3.06	3.45
2010 Jaxnvl	AA	14	14	0	0	84.1	325	59	22	19	2	1	4	3	16	0	65	2	0	5	1	.833	0	0- - -	1.56	2.03
2010 NewOr	AAA	2	2	0	0	14.0	52	9	2	2	0	0	0	0	3	0	5	0	0	1	0	1.000	0	0- - -	1.31	1.29
2011 Mrlns	R	3	3	0	0	8.0	31	5	1	0	0	0	1	1	0	0	5	0	0	0	0	-	0	0- - -	1.00	0.00
2011 Jupiter	A+	2	2	0	0	11.0	49	13	8	7	2	1	0	0	0	0	1	0	0	0	2	.000	0	0- - -	4.11	5.73
2011 NewOr	AAA	4	4	0	0	21.2	102	35	21	19	4	1	2	2	3	0	13	1	0	0	3	.000	0	0- - -	7.86	7.89
2010 Fla	NL	15	12	0	0	72.1	307	74	32	30	6	3	1	3	16	2	47	0	0	5	3	.625	0	0-0 0	3.47	3.73
2011 Fla	NL	3	2	0	0	11.0	48	13	4	4	2	0	0	0	3	0	8	2	0	0	0	-	0	0-0 0	5.19	3.27
2 ML YEARS		18	14	0	0	83.1	355	87	36	34	8	3	1	3	19	2	55	2	0	5	3	.625	0	0-0 0	3.68	3.67

Brian Sanches

Pitches: R Bats: R Pos: RP-37; SP-2   Ht: 6'0" Wt: 189 Born: 8/8/1978 Age: 33

		HOW MUCH HE PITCHED					WHAT HE GAVE UP										THE RESULTS						
Year Team	Lg	G	GS	CG	GF	IP	BFP	H	R	ER	HR	SH	SF	HB	TBB	IBB	SO	WP	Bk	W	L	Pct	Sh	Sv-Op Hld	ERC	ERA
2011 Jupiter*	A+	1	1	0	0	2.2	10	2	2	2	1	0	0	0	0	0	1	0	0	0	1	.000	0	0- - -	2.60	6.75
2006 Phi	NL	18	0	0	5	21.1	98	23	14	14	5	0	0	0	13	3	22	0	1	0	0	-	0	0-0 0	6.18	5.91
2007 Phi	NL	12	0	0	4	14.2	68	13	11	9	6	1	0	1	12	2	9	1	0	1	1	.500	0	0-0 1	7.73	5.52
2008 Was	NL	12	0	0	2	11.0	54	16	10	9	2	0	0	1	5	0	10	0	0	0	2	1.000	0	0-1 0	8.15	7.36

Year Team	Lg	G	GS	CG	GF	IP	BFP	H	R	ER	HR	SH	SF	HB	TBB	IBB	SO	WP	Bk	W	L	Pct	Sh	Sv-Op	Hld	ERC	ERA
		HOW MUCH HE PITCHED						**WHAT HE GAVE UP**												**THE RESULTS**							
2009 Fla	NL	47	0	0	7	56.1	248	50	18	16	5	3	0	6	26	8	51	5	0	4	2	.667	0	0-3	9	3.75	2.56
2010 Fla	NL	61	0	0	14	63.2	254	43	20	16	7	1	0	4	27	0	54	5	0	2	2	.500	0	0-1	12	2.63	2.26
2011 Fla	NL	39	0	2	8	61.2	270	52	32	27	7	1	2	2	36	6	53	4	1	4	1	.800	0	0-0	0	3.97	3.94
6 ML YEARS		189	2	0	40	228.2	992	197	105	91	32	6	6	11	119	19	199	15	2	13	6	.684	0	0-5	22	4.12	3.58

Angel Sanchez

Bats: R **Throws:** R **Pos:** SS-46; PH-37; 2B-19; 3B-10 — ahn-HELL — **Ht:** 6'2" **Wt:** 190 **Born:** 9/20/1983 **Age:** 28

Year Team	Lg	G	AB	H	2B	3B	HR	(Hm	Rd)	TB	R	RBI	RC	TBB	IBB	SO	HBP	SH	SF	SB	CS	SB%	GDP	Avg	OBP	Slg
		BATTING																		**BASERUNNING**				**AVERAGES**		
2006 KC	AL	8	27	6	0	0	0	(0	0)	6	2	1	0	0	0	4	0	0	1	0	0	-	0	.222	.214	.222
2010 2 Tms		66	253	70	9	4	0	(0	0)	87	30	25	29	11	0	45	2	6	0	0	1	.00	8	.277	.312	.344
2011 Hou	NL	100	288	69	10	0	1	(1	0)	82	35	28	27	27	1	44	1	10	2	3	0	1.00	3	.240	.305	.285
10 Bos	AL	1	3	0	0	0	0	(0	0)	0	0	0	0	0	0	0	0	0	0	0	0	-	0	.000	.000	.000
10 Hou	NL	65	250	70	9	4	0	(0	0)	87	30	25	29	11	0	45	2	6	0	0	1	.00	8	.280	.316	.348
3 ML YEARS		184	568	145	19	4	1	(1	0)	175	67	54	56	38	1	93	3	16	3	3	1	.75	11	.255	.304	.308

Anibal Sanchez

Pitches: R **Bats:** R **Pos:** SP-32 — ah-NEE-bahl — **Ht:** 6'0" **Wt:** 207 **Born:** 2/27/1984 **Age:** 28

Year Team	Lg	G	GS	CG	GF	IP	BFP	H	R	ER	HR	SH	SF	HB	TBB	IBB	SO	WP	Bk	W	L	Pct	Sh	Sv-Op	Hld	ERC	ERA
		HOW MUCH HE PITCHED						**WHAT HE GAVE UP**												**THE RESULTS**							
2006 Fla	NL	18	17	2	0	114.1	469	90	39	36	7	3	1	4	46	1	72	4	1	10	3	.769	1	0-0	0	2.96	2.83
2007 Fla	NL	6	6	0	0	30.0	151	43	17	16	3	2	2	2	19	1	14	3	0	2	1	.667	0	0-0	0	7.90	4.80
2008 Fla	NL	10	10	0	0	51.2	241	54	35	32	7	4	2	6	27	2	50	1	0	2	5	.286	0	0-0	0	5.40	5.57
2009 Fla	NL	16	16	0	0	86.0	383	84	39	37	10	2	2	1	46	5	71	0	1	4	8	.333	0	0-0	0	4.51	3.87
2010 Fla	NL	32	32	1	0	195.0	841	192	89	77	10	13	3	7	70	5	157	7	0	13	12	.520	1	0-0	0	3.56	3.55
2011 Fla	NL	32	32	3	0	196.1	830	187	85	80	20	12	1	5	64	8	202	4	**5**	8	9	.471	2	0-0	0	3.57	3.67
6 ML YEARS		114	113	6	0	673.1	2915	650	304	278	59	36	11	25	272	22	566	19	7	39	38	.506	4	0-0	0	3.89	3.72

Eduardo Sanchez

Pitches: R **Bats:** R **Pos:** RP-26 — **Ht:** 5'11" **Wt:** 170 **Born:** 2/16/1989 **Age:** 23

Year Team	Lg	G	GS	CG	GF	IP	BFP	H	R	ER	HR	SH	SF	HB	TBB	IBB	SO	WP	Bk	W	L	Pct	Sh	Sv-Op	Hld	ERC	ERA
		HOW MUCH HE PITCHED						**WHAT HE GAVE UP**												**THE RESULTS**							
2007 Cards	R	7	0	0	6	6.0	26	2	2	1	0	0	0	0	6	0	7	0	0	0	1	.000	0	3- -		2.02	1.50
2007 JhsCty	R+	12	0	0	9	15.1	57	8	2	2	0	2	0	0	3	0	22	3	1	2	1	.667	0	5- -		0.90	1.17
2008 QuadC	A	24	5	0	9	56.2	233	40	23	18	1	5	4	8	25	0	55	3	0	5	1	.833	0	1- -		2.70	2.86
2009 PlmBh	A+	19	0	0	9	25.0	93	12	4	4	2	2	1	3	5	0	26	1	0	0	1	.000	0	3- -		1.32	1.44
2009 Sprgfld	AA	41	0	0	19	50.0	197	32	16	15	4	0	1	4	20	0	56	4	1	2	0	1.000	0	10- -		2.46	2.70
2010 Sprgfld	AA	24	0	0	19	26.0	106	22	13	9	2	0	1	2	8	0	27	2	0	1	1	.500	0	11- -		3.10	3.12
2010 Memp	AAA	26	0	0	10	27.0	110	19	7	5	2	1	0	2	12	1	31	8	0	0	0	-	0	3- -		2.78	1.67
2011 Memp	AAA	2	0	0	1	3.0	9	0	0	0	0	0	0	0	0	0	3	0	0	1	0	1.000	0	0- -		0.00	0.00
2011 Sprgfld	AA	3	0	0	0	4.1	20	3	3	2	0	1	0	2	2	0	3	2	0	1	0	1.000	0	0- -		3.50	4.15
2011 StL	NL	26	0	0	11	30.0	118	14	6	6	1	0	2	3	16	0	35	5	0	3	1	.750	0	5-7	7	1.85	1.80

Freddy Sanchez

Bats: R **Throws:** R **Pos:** 2B-58; PH-2 — **Ht:** 6'0" **Wt:** 200 **Born:** 12/21/1977 **Age:** 34

Year Team	Lg	G	AB	H	2B	3B	HR	(Hm	Rd)	TB	R	RBI	RC	TBB	IBB	SO	HBP	SH	SF	SB	CS	SB%	GDP	Avg	OBP	Slg
		BATTING																		**BASERUNNING**				**AVERAGES**		
2002 Bos	AL	12	16	3	0	0	0	(0	0)	3	3	2	1	2	0	3	0	0	0	0	0	-	0	.188	.278	.188
2003 Bos	AL	20	34	8	2	0	0	(0	0)	10	6	2	1	0	0	8	0	0	0	0	0	-	0	.235	.235	.294
2004 Pit	NL	9	19	3	0	0	0	(0	0)	3	2	2	2	0	0	3	0	1	0	0	0	-	0	.158	.158	.158
2005 Pit	NL	132	453	132	26	4	5	(3	2)	181	54	35	57	27	1	36	5	4	3	2	2	.50	6	.291	.336	.400
2006 Pit	NL	157	582	200	53	2	6	(2	4)	275	85	85	101	31	6	52	7	3	9	3	2	.60	12	**.344**	.378	.473
2007 Pit	NL	147	602	183	42	4	11	(5	6)	266	77	81	94	32	2	76	8	2	9	0	1	.00	13	.304	.343	.442
2008 Pit	NL	145	569	154	26	2	9	(1	8)	211	75	52	61	21	1	63	4	8	6	0	1	.00	13	.271	.298	.371
2009 2 Tms		111	457	134	29	3	7	(3	4)	190	56	41	59	22	4	76	4	2	4	5	1	.83	12	.293	.326	.416
2010 SF	NL	111	431	126	22	1	7	(1	6)	171	55	47	59	32	1	68	3	8	5	3	1	.75	9	.292	.342	.397
2011 SF	NL	60	239	69	15	1	3	(0	3)	95	21	24	30	13	3	35	3	5	1	0	1	.00	2	.289	.332	.397
09 Pit	NL	86	355	105	28	3	6	(3	3)	157	45	34	49	20	4	60	2	2	3	5	1	.83	9	.296	.334	.442
09 SF	NL	25	102	29	1	0	1	(0	1)	33	11	7	10	2	0	16	0	2	1	0	0	-	3	.284	.295	.324
Postseason		15	63	16	4	0	0	(0	0)	20	5	3	5	1	0	8	1	2	0	0	0	-	2	.254	.277	.317
10 ML YEARS		904	3402	1012	215	17	48	(15	33)	1405	434	371	465	180	18	420	32	35	37	13	9	.59	67	.297	.335	.413

Gaby Sanchez

Bats: R **Throws:** R **Pos:** 1B-153; PH-6; DH-1; PR-1 — GABB-ee — **Ht:** 6'1" **Wt:** 216 **Born:** 9/2/1983 **Age:** 28

Year Team	Lg	G	AB	H	2B	3B	HR	(Hm	Rd)	TB	R	RBI	RC	TBB	IBB	SO	HBP	SH	SF	SB	CS	SB%	GDP	Avg	OBP	Slg
		BATTING																		**BASERUNNING**				**AVERAGES**		
2008 Fla	NL	5	8	3	2	0	0	(0	0)	5	0	1	2	0	0	2	0	0	0	0	0	-	0	.375	.375	.625
2009 Fla	NL	21	21	5	0	0	2	(2	0)	11	2	3	3	2	0	3	0	0	0	0	0	-	1	.238	.304	.524
2010 Fla	NL	151	572	156	37	3	19	(7	12)	256	72	85	88	57	2	101	5	3	6	5	0	1.00	14	.273	.341	.448
2011 Fla	NL	159	572	152	35	0	19	(11	8)	244	72	78	77	74	4	97	6	2	7	3	1	.75	18	.266	.352	.427
4 ML YEARS		336	1173	316	74	3	40	(20	20)	516	146	167	170	133	6	203	11	5	13	8	1	.89	33	.269	.346	.440

Hector Sanchez

Bats: B **Throws:** R **Pos:** C-11; PH-6   **Ht:** 5'11" **Wt:** 235 **Born:** 11/17/1989 **Age:** 22

								BATTING												BASERUNNING				AVERAGES		
Year Team	Lg	G	AB	H	2B	3B	HR	(Hm Rd)	TB	R	RBI	RC	TBB	IBB	SO	HBP	SH	SF	SB	CS	SB%	GDP	Avg	OBP	Slg
2009 Giants	R	33	117	35	8	1	1	(- -)	48	13	22	21	16	0	21	5	0	1	0	0	-	1	.299	.403	.410
2010 Augsta	A	89	310	85	20	1	5	(- -)	122	29	31	41	28	2	50	1	2	0	0	2	.00	14	.274	.336	.394
2011 SnJos	A+	52	212	64	14	1	11	(- -)	113	31	58	38	11	1	49	2	0	3	0	1	.00	3	.302	.338	.533
2011 Fresno	AAA	46	153	40	9	0	1	(- -)	52	15	26	17	13	2	22	0	0	2	0	1	.00	6	.261	.315	.340
2011 SF	NL	13	31	8	2	0	0	(0 0)	10	0	1	2	3	0	6	0	0	0	0	0	-	1	.258	.324	.323

Jonathan Sanchez

Pitches: L **Bats:** L **Pos:** SP-19   **Ht:** 6'0" **Wt:** 194 **Born:** 11/19/1982 **Age:** 29

		HOW MUCH HE PITCHED						WHAT HE GAVE UP											THE RESULTS							
Year Team	Lg	G	GS	CG	GF	IP	BFP	H	R	ER	HR	SH	SF	HB	TBB	IBB	SO	WP	Bk	W	L	Pct	Sh	Sv-Op	Hld	ERC	ERA
2011 SnJos*	A+	1	1	0	0	2.2	16	6	6	6	1	0	0	0	2	0	3	0	0	0	0	-	0	0- -		16.76	20.25
2011 Fresno*	AAA	2	2	0	0	11.0	44	10	4	4	1	0	0	0	5	0	13	1	0	1	0	1.000	0	0- -		4.02	3.27
2006 SF	NL	27	4	0	4	40.0	185	39	26	22	2	0	2	4	23	0	33	2	0	3	1	.750	0	0-0	5	4.54	4.95
2007 SF	NL	33	4	0	8	52.0	238	57	34	34	8	2	2	5	28	1	62	4	0	1	5	.167	0	0-0	2	6.06	5.88
2008 SF	NL	29	29	0	0	158.0	695	154	90	88	14	9	5	7	75	1	157	7	0	9	12	.429	0	0-0	4	4.31	5.01
2009 SF	NL	32	29	1	2	163.1	710	135	82	77	19	3	1	6	88	5	177	11	0	8	12	.400	1	0-0	1	3.83	4.24
2010 SF	NL	34	33	0	0	193.1	812	142	74	66	21	7	4	9	96	4	205	15	1	13	9	.591	0	0-0	1	3.21	3.07
2011 SF	NL	19	19	0	0	101.1	444	80	54	48	9	4	4	6	66	2	102	5	0	4	7	.364	0	0-0	1	4.02	4.26
Postseason		4	4	0	0	20.0	86	16	10	9	2	0	2	1	9	0	22	1	0	0	2	.000	0	0-0	3	3.30	4.05
6 ML YEARS		174	118	1	14	708.0	3084	607	360	335	73	25	18	37	376	13	736	44	1	38	46	.452	1	0-0	9	3.98	4.26

Pablo Sandoval

Bats: B **Throws:** R **Pos:** 3B-106; PH-7; 1B-6; DH-1   **Ht:** 5'11" **Wt:** 242 **Born:** 8/11/1986 **Age:** 25

								BATTING												BASERUNNING				AVERAGES		
Year Team	Lg	G	AB	H	2B	3B	HR	(Hm Rd)	TB	R	RBI	RC	TBB	IBB	SO	HBP	SH	SF	SB	CS	SB%	GDP	Avg	OBP	Slg
2011 SnJos*	A+	1	3	0	0	0	0	(- -)	0	1	0	0	0	0	1	0	0	0	0	0	-	0	.000	.000	.000
2011 Fresno*	AAA	5	18	5	0	0	2	(- -)	11	4	7	3	2	0	0	0	0	2	0	0	-	0	.278	.318	.611
2008 SF	NL	41	145	50	10	1	3	(1 2)	71	24	24	24	4	1	14	1	0	4	0	0	-	6	.345	.357	.490
2009 SF	NL	153	572	189	44	5	25	(13 12)	318	79	90	113	52	13	83	4	0	5	5	5	.50	10	.330	.387	.556
2010 SF	NL	152	563	151	34	3	13	(9 4)	230	61	63	55	47	12	81	1	0	5	3	2	.60	26	.268	.323	.409
2011 SF	NL	117	426	134	26	3	23	(7 16)	235	55	70	72	32	9	63	0	1	7	2	4	.33	12	.315	.357	.552
Postseason		6	17	3	1	0	0	(0 0)	4	0	2	1	2	1	3	0	0	0	0	0	-	3	.176	.263	.235
4 ML YEARS		463	1706	524	114	12	64	(30 34)	854	219	247	264	135	35	241	6	1	21	10	11	.48	54	.307	.356	.501

Jerry Sands

Bats: R **Throws:** R **Pos:** LF-41; RF-22; 1B-6; PH-5; CF-1   **Ht:** 6'4" **Wt:** 225 **Born:** 9/28/1987 **Age:** 24

								BATTING												BASERUNNING				AVERAGES		
Year Team	Lg	G	AB	H	2B	3B	HR	(Hm Rd)	TB	R	RBI	RC	TBB	IBB	SO	HBP	SH	SF	SB	CS	SB%	GDP	Avg	OBP	Slg
2008 Ddgrs	R	46	146	30	4	0	10	(- -)	64	29	33	25	29	0	43	5	0	5	5	0	1.00	4	.205	.346	.438
2009 Gt Lks	A	32	104	27	7	2	5	(- -)	53	22	19	20	15	0	32	2	1	1	1	0	1.00	2	.260	.361	.510
2009 Ogden	R+	41	163	57	9	2	14	(- -)	112	41	39	44	22	1	28	0	0	0	0	1	.00	1	.350	.427	.687
2010 Gt Lks	A	69	243	81	16	3	18	(- -)	157	48	46	66	40	6	61	3	0	1	14	2	.88	5	.333	.432	.646
2010 Chatt	AA	68	259	70	12	2	17	(- -)	137	54	47	51	33	2	62	6	0	5	4	0	1.00	9	.270	.360	.529
2011 Albq	AAA	94	370	103	21	3	29	(- -)	217	78	88	75	38	2	86	3	0	7	3	1	.75	11	.278	.344	.586
2011 LAD	NL	61	198	50	15	0	4	(2 2)	77	20	26	25	25	0	51	1	2	1	3	3	.50	5	.253	.338	.389

Amauri Sanit

Pitches: R **Bats:** R **Pos:** RP-4   uh-MORE-ee suh-NEET   **Ht:** 5'9" **Wt:** 205 **Born:** 7/4/1979 **Age:** 32

		HOW MUCH HE PITCHED						WHAT HE GAVE UP											THE RESULTS							
Year Team	Lg	G	GS	CG	GF	IP	BFP	H	R	ER	HR	SH	SF	HB	TBB	IBB	SO	WP	Bk	W	L	Pct	Sh	Sv-Op	Hld	ERC	ERA
2009 Tampa	A+	4	0	0	2	6.0	24	5	0	0	0	0	0	0	0	0	5	0	0	0	0	-	0	0- -		1.31	0.00
2009 Trntn	AA	21	0	0	19	21.1	83	13	7	7	1	4	1	0	8	0	18	2	0	1	2	.333	0	10- -		1.73	2.95
2009 S-WB	AAA	19	0	0	11	24.0	103	27	12	11	2	1	1	1	7	0	13	1	0	0	3	.000	0	0- -		4.48	4.13
2010 S-WB	AAA	21	1	0	7	33.2	156	47	29	29	7	0	0	0	15	0	22	5	1	3	2	.600	0	0- -		7.73	7.75
2010 Yanks	R	3	3	0	0	6.2	24	4	2	2	0	0	0	1	0	0	10	0	0	0	0	-	0	0- -		1.06	2.70
2010 Tampa	A+	3	0	0	0	5.0	16	0	1	1	0	0	0	0	2	0	6	0	0	0	0	-	0	0- -		0.19	1.80
2011 S-WB	AAA	10	2	0	3	19.0	89	24	11	11	4	1	0	2	7	0	25	4	0	2	1	.667	0	0- -		6.75	5.21
2011 NYY	AL	4	0	0	1	7.0	40	12	10	10	0	0	0	3	3	1	4	1	0	0	0	-	0	0-0	0	8.81	12.86

Carlos Santana

Bats: B **Throws:** R **Pos:** C-95; 1B-66; PH-3; DH-1   **Ht:** 5'11" **Wt:** 190 **Born:** 4/8/1986 **Age:** 26

								BATTING												BASERUNNING				AVERAGES		
Year Team	Lg	G	AB	H	2B	3B	HR	(Hm Rd)	TB	R	RBI	RC	TBB	IBB	SO	HBP	SH	SF	SB	CS	SB%	GDP	Avg	OBP	Slg
2005 Ddgrs	R	32	78	23	4	1	1	(- -)	32	14	14	14	16	1	8	1	0	2	0	2	.00	2	.295	.412	.410
2006 VeroB	A+	54	198	53	10	2	3	(- -)	76	16	18	26	23	0	43	1	0	1	0	3	.00	6	.268	.345	.384
2006 Ogden	R+	37	132	40	5	1	7	(- -)	68	31	27	31	30	0	19	1	0	5	4	0	1.00	5	.303	.423	.515
2007 Gt Lks	A	86	292	65	20	1	7	(- -)	108	32	36	37	40	0	45	1	1	0	5	3	.63	9	.223	.318	.370
2008 InldEm	A+	99	350	113	34	4	14	(- -)	197	88	96	86	69	4	59	4	2	9	7	4	.64	7	.323	.431	.563
2008 Knstn	A+	29	105	37	5	1	6	(- -)	62	34	19	28	20	0	24	0	0	1	3	0	1.00	1	.352	.452	.590
2008 Akron	AA	2	8	1	0	0	1	(- -)	4	3	2	0	0	0	2	0	0	0	0	0	-	0	.125	.125	.500
2009 Akron	AA	131	429	124	30	2	23	(- -)	227	91	97	98	90	7	84	7	0	10	2	2	.50	10	.289	.412	.529

Year	Team	Lg	G	AB	H	2B	3B	HR	(Hm	Rd)	TB	R	RBI	RC	TBB	IBB	SO	HBP	SH	SF	SB	CS	SB%	GDP	Avg	OBP	Slg
2010	Clmbs	AAA	57	196	62	14	1	13	(-	-)	117	39	51	53	45	4	39	3	0	2	6	0	1.00	5	.316	.447	.597
2010	Cle	AL	46	150	39	13	0	6	(2	4)	70	23	22	25	37	2	29	1	0	4	3	0	1.00	3	.260	.401	.467
2011	Cle	AL	155	552	132	35	2	27	(14	13)	252	84	79	81	97	7	133	2	0	7	5	3	.63	15	.239	.351	.457
2 ML YEARS			201	702	171	48	2	33	(16	17)	322	107	101	106	134	9	162	3	0	11	8	3	.73	18	.244	.362	.459

Ervin Santana

Pitches: R Bats: R Pos: SP-33   Ht: 6'2" Wt: 185 Born: 12/12/1982 Age: 29

Year	Team	Lg	G	GS	CG	GF	IP	BFP	H	R	ER	HR	SH	SF	HB	TBB	IBB	SO	WP	Bk	W	L	Pct	Sh	Sv-Op	Hld	ERC	ERA
2005	LAA	AL	23	23	1	0	133.2	583	139	73	69	17	1	4	8	47	2	99	4	0	12	8	.600	1	0-0	0	4.51	4.65
2006	LAA	AL	33	33	0	0	204.0	846	181	106	97	21	4	10	11	70	2	141	10	2	16	8	.667	0	0-0	0	3.51	4.28
2007	LAA	AL	28	26	0	1	150.0	675	174	103	96	26	3	2	8	58	3	126	7	0	7	14	.333	0	0-0	0	5.69	5.76
2008	LAA	AL	32	32	2	0	219.0	897	198	89	85	23	3	5	8	47	2	214	5	1	16	7	.696	1	0-0	0	3.00	3.49
2009	LAA	AL	24	23	2	0	139.2	614	159	83	78	24	2	1	10	47	4	107	4	0	8	8	.500	2	0-0	1	5.47	5.03
2010	LAA	AL	33	33	4	0	222.2	954	221	104	97	27	8	8	12	73	2	169	11	1	17	10	.630	1	0-0	0	4.10	3.92
2011	LAA	AL	33	33	4	0	228.2	949	207	95	86	26	4	7	8	72	4	178	10	1	11	12	.478	1	0-0	0	3.45	3.38
Postseason			8	2	0	3	22.2	101	21	17	14	4	1	1	3	9	1	14	0	0	2	2	.500	0	0-0	0	4.55	5.56
7 ML YEARS			206	203	13	1	1297.2	5518	1279	653	608	164	25	37	65	414	19	1034	51	5	87	67	.565	6	0-0	1	4.05	4.22

Johan Santana

Pitches: L Bats: L Pos: P   YOE-hahn   Ht: 6'0" Wt: 208 Born: 3/13/1979 Age: 33

Year	Team	Lg	G	GS	CG	GF	IP	BFP	H	R	ER	HR	SH	SF	HB	TBB	IBB	SO	WP	Bk	W	L	Pct	Sh	Sv-Op	Hld	ERC	ERA
2011	StLuci*	A+	2	2	0	0	5.0	20	5	1	1	0	0	0	0	0	0	5	0	0	0	0	-	0	0--	-	2.76	1.80
2000	Min	AL	30	5	0	9	86.0	398	102	64	62	11	1	3	2	54	0	64	5	2	2	3	.400	0	0-0	0	6.59	6.49
2001	Min	AL	15	4	0	5	43.2	195	50	25	23	6	2	3	3	16	0	28	3	0	1	0	1.000	0	0-0	0	5.36	4.74
2002	Min	AL	27	14	0	2	108.1	452	84	41	36	7	3	3	1	49	0	137	15	2	8	6	.571	0	1-1	3	2.86	2.99
2003	Min	AL	45	18	0	7	158.1	644	127	56	54	17	2	4	3	47	1	169	6	2	12	3	.800	0	0-0	5	2.73	3.07
2004	Min	AL	34	34	1	0	228.0	881	156	70	66	24	3	3	9	54	0	265	7	0	20	6	.769	1	0-0	0	2.07	2.61
2005	Min	AL	33	33	3	0	231.2	910	180	77	74	22	6	2	1	45	1	238	8	0	16	7	.696	2	0-0	0	2.14	2.87
2006	Min	AL	34	34	1	0	233.2	923	186	79	72	24	6	4	4	47	0	245	4	1	19	6	.760	0	0-0	0	2.36	2.77
2007	Min	AL	33	33	1	0	219.0	878	183	88	81	33	4	4	4	52	0	235	7	1	15	13	.536	1	0-0	0	2.98	3.33
2008	NYM	NL	34	34	3	0	234.1	964	206	74	66	23	9	1	4	63	5	206	9	2	16	7	.696	2	0-0	0	2.93	2.53
2009	NYM	NL	25	25	0	0	166.2	701	156	67	58	20	8	3	3	46	3	146	1	0	13	9	.591	0	0-0	0	3.37	3.13
2010	NYM	NL	29	29	4	0	199.0	817	179	67	66	16	10	5	2	55	2	144	2	2	11	9	.550	2	0-0	0	2.96	2.98
Postseason			11	5	0	0	34.0	143	35	15	15	2	0	0	1	10	1	32	2	0	1	3	.250	0	0-0	1	3.66	3.97
11 ML YEARS			339	263	13	23	1908.2	7763	1609	708	658	203	54	35	36	528	12	1877	67	12	133	69	.658	8	1-1	8	2.87	3.10

Hector Santiago

Pitches: L Bats: R Pos: RP-2   Ht: 6'0" Wt: 210 Born: 12/16/1987 Age: 24

Year	Team	Lg	G	GS	CG	GF	IP	BFP	H	R	ER	HR	SH	SF	HB	TBB	IBB	SO	WP	Bk	W	L	Pct	Sh	Sv-Op	Hld	ERC	ERA
2007	Bristol	R	17	0	0	4	32.2	129	19	7	6	1	4	0	1	16	0	38	1	0	1	1	.500	0	0--	-	1.99	1.65
2008	Knapol	A	38	0	0	12	64.1	291	57	37	29	1	6	1	3	44	0	83	8	2	5	1	.833	0	1--	-	4.06	4.06
2009	WinSa	A+	38	0	0	15	58.0	248	54	34	25	5	3	3	3	25	3	66	3	1	4	4	.500	0	1--	-	3.88	3.88
2010	WinSa	A+	37	1	0	9	60.2	269	63	29	28	4	3	7	3	19	1	61	1	1	4	5	.444	0	2--	-	3.75	4.15
2011	WinSa	A+	8	8	0	0	44.0	181	38	18	18	7	2	1	3	14	0	43	3	0	2	3	.400	0	0--	-	3.73	3.68
2011	Brham	AA	15	15	0	0	83.1	350	71	34	33	4	3	2	4	39	1	74	6	3	7	5	.583	0	0--	-	3.40	3.56
2011	CWS	AL	2	0	0	1	5.1	18	1	0	0	0	0	0	0	1	1	2	1	0	0	0	-	0	0-0	0	0.16	0.00

Ramon Santiago

Bats: B Throws: R Pos: 2B-75; SS-27; PH-7; PR-6; 3B-5   Ht: 5'11" Wt: 175 Born: 8/31/1979 Age: 32

Year	Team	Lg	G	AB	H	2B	3B	HR	(Hm	Rd)	TB	R	RBI	RC	TBB	IBB	SO	HBP	SH	SF	SB	CS	SB%	GDP	Avg	OBP	Slg
2002	Det	AL	65	222	54	5	5	4	(3	1)	81	33	20	23	13	0	48	8	4	2	8	5	.62	2	.243	.306	.365
2003	Det	AL	141	444	100	18	1	2	(1	1)	126	41	29	38	33	0	66	10	18	2	10	4	.71	9	.225	.292	.284
2004	Sea	AL	19	39	7	1	0	0	(0	0)	8	8	2	1	3	0	3	1	2	0	0	0	-	1	.179	.256	.205
2005	Sea	AL	8	8	1	0	0	0	(0	0)	1	2	0	1	1	0	2	3	1	0	0	0	-	0	.125	.417	.125
2006	Det	AL	43	80	18	1	1	0	(0	0)	21	9	3	3	1	0	14	1	4	0	2	0	1.00	1	.225	.244	.263
2007	Det	AL	32	67	19	5	1	0	(0	0)	26	10	7	11	1	0	10	3	3	0	3	0	1.00	0	.284	.324	.388
2008	Det	AL	58	124	35	6	2	4	(4	0)	57	30	18	26	22	0	17	5	5	0	1	0	1.00	1	.282	.411	.460
2009	Det	AL	93	262	70	6	2	7	(4	3)	101	29	35	35	17	1	57	4	10	3	1	2	.33	3	.267	.318	.385
2010	Det	AL	112	320	84	9	1	3	(3	0)	104	38	22	37	30	0	56	7	8	2	2	2	.50	6	.263	.337	.325
2011	Det	AL	101	258	67	11	3	5	(3	2)	99	29	30	25	17	0	38	4	11	4	0	0	-	5	.260	.311	.384
Postseason			6	12	1	0	0	0	(0	0)	1	0	0	0	1	0	2	0	1	0	0	0	-	0	.083	.154	.083
10 ML YEARS			672	1824	455	62	16	25	(18	7)	624	229	166	198	138	1	311	46	66	13	27	13	.68	28	.249	.316	.342

Omir Santos

Bats: R Throws: R Pos: C-10; PH-2; PR-1   OH-meer   Ht: 6'0" Wt: 213 Born: 4/29/1981 Age: 31

Year	Team	Lg	G	AB	H	2B	3B	HR	(Hm	Rd)	TB	R	RBI	RC	TBB	IBB	SO	HBP	SH	SF	SB	CS	SB%	GDP	Avg	OBP	Slg
2011	Toledo*	AAA	49	151	37	5	0	2	(-	-)	48	12	16	12	3	0	29	1	5	3	0	0	-	2	.245	.259	.318
2011	Tigers*	R	2	2	0	0	0	0	(-	-)	0	0	0	0	0	0	1	1	0	0	0	0	-	0	.000	.333	.000

			BATTING																				BASERUNNING				AVERAGES		
Year	Team	Lg	G	AB	H	2B	3B	HR	(Hm	Rd)	TB	R	RBI	RC	TBB	IBB	SO	HBP	SH	SF	SB	CS	SB%	GDP	Avg	OBP	Slg
2008	Bal	AL	11	10	1	0	0	0	(0	0)	1	0	0	0	0	0	2	0	0	0	0	0	-	0	.100	.100	.100
2009	NYM	NL	96	281	73	14	1	7	(2	5)	110	28	40	29	15	1	44	2	2	6	0	0	-	9	.260	.296	.391
2011	Det	AL	11	22	5	0	0	0	(0	0)	5	1	0	0	0	0	4	0	0	0	0	0	-	0	.227	.227	.227
	3 ML YEARS		118	313	79	14	1	7	(2	5)	116	29	40	29	15	1	50	2	2	6	0	0	-	9	.252	.286	.371

Sergio Santos

Pitches: R Bats: R Pos: RP-63

Ht: 6'2" Wt: 230 Born: 7/4/1983 Age: 28

			HOW MUCH HE PITCHED						WHAT HE GAVE UP												THE RESULTS							
Year	Team	Lg	G	GS	CG	GF	IP	BFP	H	R	ER	HR	SH	SF	HB	TBB	IBB	SO	WP	Bk	W	L	Pct	Sh	Sv-Op	Hld	ERC	ERA
2009	Knapol	A	8	0	0	3	7.1	31	8	6	6	0	0	0	0	3	0	10	2	0	0	1	.000	0	0- -	-	4.06	7.36
2009	WinSa	A+	8	0	0	0	7.2	35	9	5	5	2	0	0	1	3	0	7	2	0	0	0		0	0- -	-	6.93	5.87
2009	Brham	AA	7	0	0	0	8.2	51	15	10	10	0	0	1	3	7	0	6	1	0	0	1	.000	0	0- -	-	10.82	10.38
2009	Charltt	AAA	3	0	0	0	5.0	27	5	5	5	0	1	0	0	7	0	7	1	0	0	1	.000	0	0- -	-	7.04	9.00
2010	CWS	AL	56	0	0	13	51.2	235	53	18	17	2	2	1	3	26	3	56	8	0	2	2	.500	0	1-3	14	4.22	2.96
2011	CWS	AL	63	0	0	50	63.1	260	41	25	25	6	1	1	3	29	5	92	5	0	4	5	.444	0	30-36	2	2.46	3.55
	2 ML YEARS		119	0	0	63	115.0	495	94	43	42	8	3	2	6	55	8	148	13	0	6	7	.462	0	31-39	16	3.22	3.29

Dave Sappelt

Bats: R Throws: R Pos: LF-31; PH-9; CF-4; PR-3   sap-PELT   Ht: 5'9" Wt: 193 Born: 1/2/1987 Age: 25

			BATTING																				BASERUNNING				AVERAGES		
Year	Team	Lg	G	AB	H	2B	3B	HR	(Hm	Rd)	TB	R	RBI	RC	TBB	IBB	SO	HBP	SH	SF	SB	CS	SB%	GDP	Avg	OBP	Slg
2008	Billings	R+	62	254	76	19	5	7	(-	-)	126	47	35	44	21	0	45	1	2	1	6	3	.67	5	.299	.354	.496
2009	Dayton	A	74	301	81	14	7	3	(-	-)	118	44	25	40	23	1	46	2	2	3	26	11	.70	4	.269	.322	.392
2009	Srsota	A+	62	251	74	10	3	4	(-	-)	102	27	21	34	13	0	29	2	4	1	21	11	.66	2	.295	.333	.406
2010	Lynbrg	A+	19	71	20	5	0	0	(-	-)	25	7	4	8	5	0	15	1	0	0	6	4	.60	1	.282	.338	.352
2010	Carlina	AA	89	330	119	19	8	9	(-	-)	181	53	62	71	31	3	46	3	4	4	15	13	.54	4	.361	.416	.548
2010	Lsvlle	AAA	25	108	35	8	3	1	(-	-)	52	12	8	19	6	0	13	1	0	0	4	1	.80	0	.324	.365	.481
2011	Lsvlle	AAA	74	297	93	16	3	7	(-	-)	136	40	29	52	30	2	39	2	4	3	4	4	.50	5	.313	.377	.458
2011	Cin	NL	38	107	26	8	0	0	(0	0)	34	14	5	9	7	0	17	0	4	0	1	1	.50	1	.243	.289	.318

Dane Sardinha

Bats: R Throws: R Pos: C-15; PH-1; PR-1   sar-DEEN-yah   Ht: 6'0" Wt: 215 Born: 4/8/1979 Age: 33

			BATTING																				BASERUNNING				AVERAGES		
Year	Team	Lg	G	AB	H	2B	3B	HR	(Hm	Rd)	TB	R	RBI	RC	TBB	IBB	SO	HBP	SH	SF	SB	CS	SB%	GDP	Avg	OBP	Slg
2011	LV*	AAA	29	93	13	3	0	0	(-	-)	16	6	1	3	10	0	32	2	1	0	0	0	-	1	.140	.238	.172
2003	Cin	NL	1	2	0	0	0	0	(0	0)	0	0	0	0	0	0	1	0	0	0	0	0	-	0	.000	.000	.000
2005	Cin	NL	1	3	0	0	0	0	(0	0)	0	0	0	0	0	0	1	0	0	0	0	0	-	0	.000	.000	.000
2008	Det	AL	17	44	7	0	1	0	(0	0)	9	2	3	3	0	0	11	0	1	0	0	0	-	1	.159	.229	.205
2009	Det	AL	12	31	3	1	0	0	(0	0)	4	1	3	0	0	0	16	0	1	2	0	0	-	1	.097	.091	.129
2010	Phi	NL	13	39	8	2	0	3	(1	2)	19	5	8	3	1	0	13	0	0	0	0	0	-	1	.205	.225	.487
2011	Phi	NL	15	32	7	1	0	0	(0	0)	8	8	1	3	10	1	13	1	0	0	0	0	-	0	.219	.419	.250
	6 ML YEARS		59	151	25	4	1	3	(1	2)	40	16	15	9	15	1	55	1	2	2	0	0	-	3	.166	.243	.265

Josh Satin

Bats: R Throws: R Pos: PH-9; 1B-8; 3B-1; PR-1   Ht: 6'2" Wt: 200 Born: 12/23/1984 Age: 27

			BATTING																				BASERUNNING				AVERAGES		
Year	Team	Lg	G	AB	H	2B	3B	HR	(Hm	Rd)	TB	R	RBI	RC	TBB	IBB	SO	HBP	SH	SF	SB	CS	SB%	GDP	Avg	OBP	Slg
2008	Bklyn	A-	45	143	40	10	2	4	(-	-)	66	21	13	23	16	0	28	0	4	1	0	1	.00	4	.280	.350	.462
2008	Kngspt	R	3	12	7	2	0	1	(-	-)	12	3	2	5	1	0	2	0	0	0	0	0	-	0	.583	.615	1.000
2009	Savann	A	125	440	125	38	0	7	(-	-)	184	62	60	75	73	1	103	2	0	5	0	3	.00	6	.284	.385	.418
2009	StLuci	A+	7	22	8	2	0	1	(-	-)	13	6	5	6	5	0	7	0	0	1	0	0	-	0	.364	.464	.591
2010	StLuci	A+	58	209	66	15	0	5	(-	-)	96	27	35	39	30	0	50	3	1	2	1	5	.17	6	.316	.406	.459
2010	Bnghtn	AA	79	286	88	24	1	7	(-	-)	135	49	39	55	36	0	71	7	0	3	1	0	1.00	8	.308	.395	.472
2011	Bnghtn	AA	94	338	110	35	2	11	(-	-)	182	60	60	77	57	0	91	4	0	5	2	2	.50	6	.325	.423	.538
2011	Buffalo	AAA	38	145	46	8	0	1	(-	-)	57	17	16	22	14	0	33	1	0	0	1	2	.33	4	.317	.381	.393
2011	NYM	NL	15	25	5	1	0	0	(0	0)	6	3	2	1	1	0	11	1	0	0	0	0	-	1	.200	.259	.240

Joe Saunders

Pitches: L Bats: L Pos: SP-33   Ht: 6'3" Wt: 210 Born: 6/16/1981 Age: 31

			HOW MUCH HE PITCHED						WHAT HE GAVE UP												THE RESULTS							
Year	Team	Lg	G	GS	CG	GF	IP	BFP	H	R	ER	HR	SH	SF	HB	TBB	IBB	SO	WP	Bk	W	L	Pct	Sh	Sv-Op	Hld	ERC	ERA
2005	LAA	AL	2	2	0	0	9.1	41	10	8	8	3	0	0	0	4	0	4	1	0	0	0	-	0	0-0	0	6.27	7.71
2006	LAA	AL	13	13	0	0	70.2	302	71	42	37	6	1	2	1	29	1	51	2	1	7	3	.700	0	0-0	0	4.13	4.71
2007	LAA	AL	18	18	0	0	107.1	473	129	56	53	11	0	5	1	34	1	69	3	0	8	5	.615	0	0-0	0	4.96	4.44
2008	LAA	AL	31	31	1	0	198.0	807	187	82	75	21	5	2	6	53	2	103	3	0	17	7	.708	0	0-0	0	3.49	3.41
2009	LAA	AL	31	31	1	0	186.0	805	202	102	95	29	6	4	6	64	2	101	5	1	16	7	.696	1	0-0	0	4.91	4.60
2010	2 Tms		33	33	3	0	203.1	880	232	120	101	25	6	8	5	64	1	114	6	0	9	17	.346	1	0-0	0	4.86	4.47
2011	Ari	NL	33	33	1	0	212.0	874	210	94	87	29	9	5	3	67	4	108	3	0	12	13	.480	1	0-0	0	4.10	3.69
	10	LAA	AL	20	20	2	0	120.2	522	135	70	62	14	5	5	1	45	1	64	3	0	6	10	.375	1	0-0	0	4.88	4.62
	10	Ari	NL	13	13	1	0	82.2	358	97	50	39	11	1	3	4	19	0	50	3	0	3	7	.300	0	0-0	0	4.84	4.25
	Postseason		3	3	0	0	15.0	71	18	9	9	1	1	0	1	10	0	7	0	0	0	1	.000	0	0-0	0	6.48	5.40
	7 ML YEARS		161	161	6	0	986.2	4182	1041	504	456	124	27	26	22	315	11	550	23	2	69	52	.570	2	0-0	0	4.39	4.16

Michael Saunders

Bats: L Throws: R Pos: CF-46; LF-12; PR-4   Ht: 6'4" Wt: 225 Born: 11/19/1986 Age: 25

Year	Team	Lg	G	AB	H	2B	3B	HR	(Hm	Rd)	TB	R	RBI	RC	TBB	IBB	SO	HBP	SH	SF	SB	CS	SB%	GDP	Avg	OBP	Slg
2011	Tacom*	AAA	64	236	68	11	3	7	(-	-)	106	51	38	48	50	2	71	2	2	1	10	3	.77	1	.288	.415	.449
2009	Sea	AL	46	122	27	1	3	0	(0	0)	34	13	4	8	6	0	40	0	1	0	4	1	.80	1	.221	.258	.279
2010	Sea	AL	100	289	61	11	2	10	(5	5)	106	29	33	31	35	0	84	0	2	1	6	3	.67	1	.211	.295	.367
2011	Sea	AL	58	161	24	5	0	2	(1	1)	35	16	8	2	12	1	56	0	5	1	6	2	.75	1	.149	.207	.217
	3 ML YEARS		204	572	112	17	5	12	(6	6)	175	58	45	41	53	1	180	0	8	2	16	6	.73	3	.196	.263	.306

Joe Savery

Pitches: L Bats: L Pos: RP-4   SAVE-uh-ree   Ht: 6'3" Wt: 215 Born: 11/4/1985 Age: 26

Year	Team	Lg	G	GS	CG	GF	IP	BFP	H	R	ER	HR	SH	SF	HB	TBB	IBB	SO	WP	Bk	W	L	Pct	Sh	Sv-Op	Hld	ERC	ERA
2007	Wmspt	A-	7	7	0	0	26.1	116	22	9	8	0	0	0	0	13	0	22	1	0	2	3	.400	0	0- -	-	2.72	2.73
2008	Clrwtr	A+	27	24	0	0	150.1	667	171	84	69	10	1	3	6	60	1	122	6	0	9	10	.474	0	0- -	-	4.80	4.13
2009	Rdng	AA	21	20	1	0	112.1	488	111	55	55	13	7	4	1	53	1	77	6	0	12	4	.750	0	0- -	-	4.46	4.41
2009	LV	AAA	7	7	1	0	39.0	180	42	23	19	0	3	4	1	24	0	19	2	0	4	2	.667	0	0- -	-	4.67	4.38
2010	LV	AAA	28	19	0	3	127.1	578	154	78	66	13	3	12	4	51	1	67	1	1	1	12	.077	0	0- -	-	5.42	4.66
2011	Clrwtr	A+	1	0	0	0	2.0	8	2	0	0	0	0	0	0	0	0	1	0	0	0	0	-	0	0- -	-	1.95	0.00
2011	Rdng	AA	6	0	0	0	9.0	33	7	1	1	0	0	0	0	0	0	14	0	0	1	0	1.000	0	0- -	-	1.24	1.00
2011	LV	AAA	18	0	0	3	25.0	100	23	6	5	0	3	2	0	6	0	26	1	0	4	0	1.000	0	2- -	-	2.47	1.80
2011	Phi	NL	4	0	0	1	2.2	9	1	0	0	0	1	0	0	0	0	2	0	0	0	0	-	0	0-0	1	0.31	0.00

Jordan Schafer

Bats: L Throws: L Pos: CF-79; PH-3; PR-1   Ht: 6'1" Wt: 200 Born: 9/4/1986 Age: 25

Year	Team	Lg	G	AB	H	2B	3B	HR	(Hm	Rd)	TB	R	RBI	RC	TBB	IBB	SO	HBP	SH	SF	SB	CS	SB%	GDP	Avg	OBP	Slg
2005	Braves	R	49	182	37	12	3	3	(-	-)	64	18	19	17	13	0	49	1	1	3	13	6	.68	4	.203	.256	.352
2006	Rome	A	114	388	93	15	7	8	(-	-)	146	49	60	43	28	0	95	1	5	0	15	9	.63	4	.240	.293	.376
2007	Rome	A	30	129	48	15	2	5	(-	-)	82	16	20	32	16	0	31	0	0	0	4	4	.50	1	.372	.441	.636
2007	MrtlBh	A+	106	436	128	34	8	10	(-	-)	208	70	43	73	40	4	95	1	3	1	19	11	.63	7	.294	.354	.477
2008	Missi	AA	84	297	80	18	6	10	(-	-)	140	46	51	55	49	2	88	3	0	0	12	5	.71	6	.269	.378	.471
2009	Gwnntt	AAA	9	35	8	0	0	2	(-	-)	14	6	3	4	2	0	10	0	0	0	3	1	.75	0	.229	.263	.400
2010	Rome	A	6	22	6	2	0	0	(-	-)	8	4	1	3	4	0	5	0	0	0	2	1	.67	0	.273	.385	.364
2010	Gwnntt	AAA	52	189	38	5	1	1	(-	-)	48	16	8	10	14	0	47	0	5	1	9	8	.53	1	.201	.255	.254
2010	Missi	AA	18	63	11	3	0	0	(-	-)	14	7	5	3	8	0	12	0	0	1	1	1	.50	1	.175	.264	.222
2011	Gwnntt	AAA	42	164	42	8	0	1	(-	-)	53	21	21	17	14	0	28	0	5	3	6	3	.67	2	.256	.309	.323
2011	OKCity	AAA	5	20	10	2	0	0	(-	-)	12	4	3	6	2	0	5	0	0	0	3	1	.75	0	.500	.545	.600
2009	Atl	NL	50	167	34	8	0	2	(0	2)	48	18	8	11	27	3	63	0	0	1	2	1	.67	2	.204	.313	.287
2011	2 Tms	NL	82	302	73	10	3	2	(0	2)	95	46	13	34	28	0	70	2	4	1	22	4	.85	4	.242	.309	.315
11	Atl	NL	52	196	47	6	3	1	(0	1)	62	32	7	22	18	0	42	1	4	0	15	4	.79	3	.240	.307	.316
11	Hou	NL	30	106	26	4	0	1	(0	1)	33	14	6	12	10	0	28	1	0	1	7	0	1.00	1	.245	.314	.311
	2 ML YEARS		132	469	107	18	3	4	(0	4)	143	64	21	45	55	3	133	2	4	2	24	5	.83	6	.228	.311	.305

Logan Schafer

Bats: L Throws: L Pos: PH-4; PR-3; CF-1; RF-1   Ht: 6'1" Wt: 180 Born: 9/8/1986 Age: 25

Year	Team	Lg	G	AB	H	2B	3B	HR	(Hm	Rd)	TB	R	RBI	RC	TBB	IBB	SO	HBP	SH	SF	SB	CS	SB%	GDP	Avg	OBP	Slg
2008	Helena	R+	8	25	6	0	1	2	(-	-)	14	4	8	5	5	0	4	0	0	1	1	0	1.00	1	.240	.355	.560
2008	WV	A	43	181	50	13	2	0	(-	-)	67	25	20	18	8	0	42	1	3	3	3	8	.27	1	.276	.306	.370
2009	BrvdCt	A+	113	457	143	31	6	6	(-	-)	204	76	58	77	38	1	53	5	1	4	16	8	.67	5	.313	.369	.446
2009	Hntsvl	AA	7	23	5	0	1	0	(-	-)	7	4	0	3	4	0	3	2	1	0	1	0	1.00	0	.217	.379	.304
2010	Hntsvl	AA	7	23	4	2	0	0	(-	-)	6	7	1	2	4	0	6	0	0	1	0	0	-	1	.174	.286	.261
2011	BrvdCt	A+	9	36	11	0	0	0	(-	-)	11	4	1	4	5	0	4	0	0	0	1	1	.50	0	.306	.390	.306
2011	Hntsvl	AA	51	190	57	9	4	0	(-	-)	74	32	19	28	17	0	25	3	2	0	10	5	.67	0	.300	.367	.389
2011	Nashv	AAA	40	169	56	13	2	5	(-	-)	88	31	23	35	17	0	18	4	2	2	5	3	.63	1	.331	.401	.521
2011	Mil	NL	8	3	1	0	0	0	(0	0)	1	1	0	1	1	0	1	0	1	0	0	0	-	0	.333	.500	.333

Max Scherzer

Pitches: R Bats: R Pos: SP-33   SHERR-zer   Ht: 6'3" Wt: 220 Born: 7/27/1984 Age: 27

Year	Team	Lg	G	GS	CG	GF	IP	BFP	H	R	ER	HR	SH	SF	HB	TBB	IBB	SO	WP	Bk	W	L	Pct	Sh	Sv-Op	Hld	ERC	ERA
2008	Ari	NL	16	7	0	2	56.0	237	48	24	19	5	4	2	5	21	1	66	2	0	0	4	.000	0	0-0	0	3.45	3.05
2009	Ari	NL	30	30	0	0	170.1	741	166	94	78	20	5	6	10	63	1	174	5	1	9	11	.450	0	0-0	0	4.12	4.12
2010	Det	AL	31	31	0	0	195.2	800	174	84	76	20	5	5	7	70	1	184	8	0	12	11	.522	0	0-0	0	3.56	3.50
2011	Det	AL	33	33	0	0	195.0	833	207	101	96	29	3	7	7	56	1	174	12	0	15	9	.625	0	0-0	0	4.48	4.43
	4 ML YEARS		110	101	0	2	617.0	2611	595	303	269	74	17	20	29	210	4	598	27	1	36	35	.507	0	0-0	0	3.99	3.92

Nate Schierholtz

Bats: L **Throws:** R **Pos:** RF-96; PH-22; LF-8; PR-3 SHEER-holtz **Ht:** 6'1" **Wt:** 205 **Born:** 2/15/1984 **Age:** 28

Year Team	Lg	G	AB	H	2B	3B	HR	Hm	Rd	TB	R	RBI	RC	TBB	IBB	SO	HBP	SH	SF	SB	CS	SB%	GDP	Avg	OBP	Slg
2007 SF	NL	39	112	34	5	3	0	(0	0)	45	9	10	14	2	0	19	1	0	2	3	1	.75	0	.304	.316	.402
2008 SF	NL	19	75	24	8	1	1	(1	0)	37	12	5	12	3	0	8	3	0	0	0	1	.00	1	.320	.370	.493
2009 SF	NL	116	285	76	19	2	5	(1	4)	114	33	29	35	16	3	58	1	0	6	3	1	.75	5	.267	.302	.400
2010 SF	NL	137	227	55	13	3	3	(0	3)	83	34	17	26	20	5	38	3	1	1	4	5	.44	3	.242	.311	.366
2011 SF	NL	115	335	93	22	1	9	(4	5)	144	42	41	46	21	3	61	4	0	2	7	4	.64	5	.278	.326	.430
Postseason		11	12	2	0	0	0	(0	0)	2	2	1	1	1	0	5	0	0	0	0	0	-	0	.167	.231	.167
5 ML YEARS		426	1034	282	67	10	18	(6	12)	423	130	102	133	62	11	184	12	1	11	17	12	.59	14	.273	.318	.409

Daniel Schlereth

Pitches: L **Bats:** L **Pos:** RP-49 SHLARE-ith **Ht:** 6'0" **Wt:** 198 **Born:** 5/9/1986 **Age:** 26

Year Team	Lg	G	GS	CG	GF	IP	BFP	H	R	ER	HR	SH	SF	HB	TBB	IBB	SO	WP	Bk	W	L	Pct	Sh	Sv-Op	Hld	ERC	ERA
2011 Toledo*	AAA	8	0	0	1	11.2	45	6	1	1	0	1	0	0	5	1	18	1	0	1	0	1.000	0	0--	-	1.26	0.77
2009 Ari	NL	21	0	0	4	18.1	86	15	13	12	1	2	0	1	15	1	22	4	0	1	4	.200	0	0-3	0	4.32	5.89
2010 Det	AL	18	0	0	6	18.2	87	20	7	6	2	1	1	1	10	3	19	1	0	2	0	1.000	0	1-2	1	4.89	2.89
2011 Det	AL	49	0	0	16	49.0	212	36	20	19	6	3	1	5	31	3	44	6	0	2	2	.500	0	0-1	7	4.02	3.49
3 ML YEARS		88	0	0	26	86.0	385	71	40	37	9	6	2	7	56	7	85	11	0	5	6	.455	0	1-6	8	4.27	3.87

Brian Schneider

Bats: L **Throws:** R **Pos:** C-40; PH-3 SHNY-derr **Ht:** 6'1" **Wt:** 210 **Born:** 11/26/1976 **Age:** 35

Year Team	Lg	G	AB	H	2B	3B	HR	Hm	Rd	TB	R	RBI	RC	TBB	IBB	SO	HBP	SH	SF	SB	CS	SB%	GDP	Avg	OBP	Slg
2011 Rdng*	AA	7	24	6	1	0	0	(-	-)	7	2	1	2	3	1	4	0	0	0	0	0	-	1	.250	.333	.292
2000 Mon	NL	45	115	27	6	0	0	(0	0)	33	6	11	8	7	2	24	0	0	1	0	1	.00	1	.235	.276	.287
2001 Mon	NL	27	41	13	3	0	1	(1	0)	19	4	6	8	6	1	3	0	0	1	0	0	-	0	.317	.396	.463
2002 Mon	NL	73	207	57	19	2	5	(3	2)	95	21	29	29	21	8	41	0	2	2	1	2	.33	7	.275	.339	.459
2003 Mon	NL	108	335	77	26	1	9	(9	0)	132	34	46	36	37	8	75	2	1	2	0	2	.00	12	.230	.309	.394
2004 Mon	NL	135	436	112	20	3	12	(5	7)	174	40	49	52	42	10	63	3	5	2	0	1	.00	8	.257	.325	.399
2005 Was	NL	116	369	99	20	1	10	(5	5)	151	38	44	48	29	7	48	6	2	2	1	0	1.00	14	.268	.330	.409
2006 Was	NL	124	410	105	18	0	4	(3	1)	135	30	55	45	38	10	67	2	2	3	2	2	.50	14	.256	.320	.329
2007 Was	NL	129	408	96	21	1	6	(2	4)	137	33	54	41	56	7	56	2	4	7	0	0	-	15	.235	.326	.336
2008 NYM	NL	110	335	86	10	0	9	(4	5)	123	30	38	36	42	9	53	1	4	2	0	0	-	11	.257	.339	.367
2009 NYM	NL	59	170	37	11	0	3	(3	0)	57	11	24	16	18	1	21	1	2	3	0	0	-	5	.218	.292	.335
2010 Phi	NL	47	125	30	4	1	4	(2	2)	48	17	15	17	19	2	25	1	2	0	0	0	-	3	.240	.345	.384
2011 Phi	NL	41	125	22	4	0	2	(0	2)	32	11	9	7	11	1	35	1	1	1	0	0	-	3	.176	.246	.256
12 ML YEARS		1014	3076	761	162	9	65	(37	28)	1136	275	380	343	326	66	511	19	25	26	4	8	.33	89	.247	.321	.369

Skip Schumaker

Bats: L **Throws:** R **Pos:** 2B-95; RF-31; PH-15; LF-6; CF-5 **Ht:** 5'10" **Wt:** 195 **Born:** 2/3/1980 **Age:** 32

Year Team	Lg	G	AB	H	2B	3B	HR	Hm	Rd	TB	R	RBI	RC	TBB	IBB	SO	HBP	SH	SF	SB	CS	SB%	GDP	Avg	OBP	Slg
2005 StL	NL	27	24	6	1	0	0	(0	0)	7	9	1	2	2	0	2	0	0	0	1	0	1.00	0	.250	.308	.292
2006 StL	NL	28	54	10	1	0	1	(0	1)	14	3	2	2	5	1	6	0	1	0	2	1	.67	1	.185	.254	.259
2007 StL	NL	88	177	59	12	2	2	(1	1)	81	19	19	30	8	0	20	1	2	1	1	1	.50	5	.333	.358	.458
2008 StL	NL	153	540	163	22	5	8	(4	4)	219	87	46	74	47	2	60	2	4	1	8	2	.80	19	.302	.359	.406
2009 StL	NL	153	532	161	34	1	4	(2	2)	209	85	35	74	52	2	69	0	1	1	2	2	.50	4	.303	.364	.393
2010 StL	NL	137	476	126	19	1	5	(1	4)	161	66	42	61	43	2	64	4	2	4	5	3	.63	7	.265	.328	.338
2011 StL	NL	117	367	104	19	0	2	(1	1)	129	34	38	43	27	3	50	2	1	3	0	2	.00	10	.283	.333	.351
Postseason		2	6	2	1	0	0	(0	0)	3	1	1	1	1	0	0	1	0	0	0	0	-	0	.333	.500	.500
7 ML YEARS		703	2170	629	107	9	22	(9	13)	820	303	183	286	184	10	271	8	10	11	19	11	.63	46	.290	.346	.378

Michael Schwimer

Pitches: R **Bats:** R **Pos:** RP-12 SHWIMM-ur **Ht:** 6'8" **Wt:** 246 **Born:** 2/19/1986 **Age:** 26

Year Team	Lg	G	GS	CG	GF	IP	BFP	H	R	ER	HR	SH	SF	HB	TBB	IBB	SO	WP	Bk	W	L	Pct	Sh	Sv-Op	Hld	ERC	ERA
2008 Wmspt	A-	22	0	0	19	41.1	173	33	12	9	0	3	0	3	15	2	62	3	0	0	2	.000	0	8--	-	2.38	1.96
2009 Clrwtr	A+	48	0	0	36	60.0	239	44	21	19	2	1	1	2	19	0	82	2	1	1	1	.667	0	20--	-	2.12	2.85
2009 Rdng	AA	5	0	0	3	4.2	23	7	4	4	0	0	1	0	2	0	7	1	0	2	1	.667	0	0--	-	6.19	7.71
2010 Rdng	AA	32	0	0	27	40.0	170	34	16	16	5	3	0	2	14	1	58	1	1	5	3	.625	0	11--	-	3.32	3.60
2010 LV	AAA	16	0	0	7	20.0	85	16	6	3	1	2	0	1	7	1	18	1	0	2	2	.500	0	0--	-	2.52	1.35
2011 LV	AAA	47	0	0	29	68.0	277	51	15	14	4	2	1	1	22	1	86	4	0	9	1	.900	0	10--	-	2.24	1.85
2011 Phi	NL	12	0	0	5	14.1	64	15	8	8	2	2	0	1	7	1	16	0	0	1	1	.500	0	0-2	0	5.21	5.02

Chris Schwinden

Pitches: R **Bats:** R **Pos:** SP-4 **Ht:** 6'3" **Wt:** 215 **Born:** 9/22/1986 **Age:** 25

Year Team	Lg	G	GS	CG	GF	IP	BFP	H	R	ER	HR	SH	SF	HB	TBB	IBB	SO	WP	Bk	W	L	Pct	Sh	Sv-Op	Hld	ERC	ERA
2008 Bklyn	A-	14	8	0	2	62.2	245	53	21	14	3	1	3	2	12	1	70	2	0	4	1	.800	0	0--	-	2.34	2.01
2009 Savnnh	A	21	17	0	2	115.1	476	126	51	42	6	2	2	5	15	0	88	6	0	9	6	.600	0	0--	-	3.43	3.28
2009 StLuci	A+	2	2	0	0	11.1	48	12	5	5	0	0	0	2	3	0	4	1	0	1	0	1.000	0	0--	-	4.00	3.97
2010 StLuci	A+	7	2	0	2	34.1	139	34	8	7	2	1	0	1	5	0	23	1	0	3	0	1.000	0	0--	-	2.93	1.83

	HOW MUCH HE PITCHED							WHAT HE GAVE UP												THE RESULTS							
Year	Team	Lg	G	GS	CG	GF	IP	BFP	H	R	ER	HR	SH	SF	HB	TBB	IBB	SO	WP	Bk	W	L	Pct	Sh	Sv-Op	Hld	ERC	ERA
2010	Bnghtn	AA	17	14	1	0	79.1	352	100	53	49	8	0	2	4	19	1	69	3	0	4	7	.364	1	0--	-	5.13	5.56
2011	Bnghtn	AA	2	0	0	0	3.0	10	2	0	0	0	0	0	0	0	0	5	0	0	0	0	-	0	0--	-	1.01	0.00
2011	Buffalo	AAA	26	26	0	0	145.2	615	138	71	64	14	4	1	10	48	2	134	6	0	8	8	.500	0	0--	-	3.77	3.95
2011	NYM	NL	4	4	0	0	21.0	95	23	13	11	1	2	2	1	6	2	17	1	0	0	2	.000	0	0-0	0	3.63	4.71

Luke Scott

Bats: L **Throws:** R **Pos:** LF-45; 1B-12; PH-7; DH-4 **Ht:** 6'0" **Wt:** 205 **Born:** 6/25/1978 **Age:** 34

	BATTING																		BASERUNNING				AVERAGES		
Year	Team	Lg	G	AB	H	2B	3B	HR	(Hm | Rd)	TB	R	RBI	RC	TBB	IBB	SO	HBP	SH	SF	SB	CS	SB%	GDP	Avg	OBP	Slg
2011	Bowie*	AA	3	10	5	1	0	3	(- | -)	15	5	7	6	2	0	2	0	0	0	0	0	-	0	.500	.583	1.500
2005	Hou	NL	34	80	15	4	2	0	(0 | 0)	23	6	4	6	9	1	23	0	0	0	1	1	.50	0	.188	.270	.288
2006	Hou	NL	65	214	72	19	6	10	(8 | 2)	133	31	37	48	30	4	43	4	0	1	2	1	.67	2	.336	.426	.621
2007	Hou	NL	132	369	94	28	5	18	(8 | 10)	186	49	64	55	53	4	95	2	0	1	3	1	.75	8	.255	.351	.504
2008	Bal	AL	148	475	122	29	2	23	(11 | 12)	224	67	65	68	53	10	102	5	0	3	2	2	.50	7	.257	.336	.472
2009	Bal	AL	128	449	116	26	1	25	(18 | 7)	219	61	77	69	55	5	104	1	0	1	0	0	-	9	.258	.340	.488
2010	Bal	AL	131	447	127	29	1	27	(19 | 8)	239	70	72	71	59	4	98	4	0	7	2	0	1.00	9	.284	.368	.535
2011	Bal	AL	64	209	46	11	0	9	(5 | 4)	84	24	22	24	24	1	54	1	0	2	1	1	.50	2	.220	.301	.402
	Postseason		2	2	0	0	0	0	(0 | 0)	0	1	0	0	1	0	1	0	0	0	0	0	-	0	.000	.333	.000
7 ML YEARS			702	2243	592	146	17	112	(69 | 43)	1108	308	341	341	283	29	519	17	0	15	11	6	.65	32	.264	.349	.494

Evan Scribner

Pitches: R **Bats:** R **Pos:** RP-10 **Ht:** 6'3" **Wt:** 190 **Born:** 7/19/1985 **Age:** 26

	HOW MUCH HE PITCHED							WHAT HE GAVE UP												THE RESULTS							
Year	Team	Lg	G	GS	CG	GF	IP	BFP	H	R	ER	HR	SH	SF	HB	TBB	IBB	SO	WP	Bk	W	L	Pct	Sh	Sv-Op	Hld	ERC	ERA
2007	Msoula	R+	18	0	0	10	37.0	158	35	13	12	1	0	2	3	9	0	48	3	0	0	1	.000	0	2--	-	2.93	2.92
2007	Sbend	A	5	0	0	2	10.1	43	7	3	3	1	0	0	0	5	0	13	0	0	1	0	1.000	0	0--	-	2.61	2.61
2008	Sbend	A	23	0	0	22	34.1	136	23	7	6	0	1	0	3	8	2	52	1	0	2	3	.400	0	8--	-	1.51	1.57
2008	Visalia	A+	5	0	0	3	9.2	36	5	2	2	1	0	0	0	2	0	10	1	0	1	0	.000	0	1--	-	1.24	1.86
2008	Lk Els	A+	20	0	0	8	23.1	90	14	7	7	3	1	0	2	3	0	31	0	0	2	1	.667	0	1--	-	1.57	2.70
2009	SnAnt	AA	58	0	0	51	70.1	294	60	27	24	4	5	1	0	20	3	77	2	0	8	4	.667	0	21--	-	2.45	3.07
2010	SnAnt	AA	57	0	0	36	66.0	263	51	22	19	6	2	1	5	15	2	81	1	0	4	5	.444	0	16--	-	2.45	2.59
2011	Tucsn	AAA	28	0	0	20	28.2	123	27	15	15	2	2	3	0	12	1	27	1	0	2	3	.400	0	10--	-	3.54	4.71
2011	SD	NL	10	0	0	5	14.0	64	18	11	11	1	0	0	0	4	0	10	0	0	0	0	-	0	0-0	0	4.92	7.07

Marco Scutaro

Bats: R **Throws:** R **Pos:** SS-109; 2B-2; PH-2; PR-2 SKOO-tah-row **Ht:** 5'10" **Wt:** 185 **Born:** 10/30/1975 **Age:** 36

	BATTING																		BASERUNNING				AVERAGES		
Year	Team	Lg	G	AB	H	2B	3B	HR	(Hm | Rd)	TB	R	RBI	RC	TBB	IBB	SO	HBP	SH	SF	SB	CS	SB%	GDP	Avg	OBP	Slg
2011	Pwtckt*	AAA	3	11	5	1	0	0	(- | -)	6	4	0	2	1	0	0	0	0	0	0	0	-	1	.455	.500	.545
2002	NYM	NL	27	36	8	0	1	1	(1 | 0)	13	2	6	2	0	0	11	0	1	1	0	1	.00	1	.222	.216	.361
2003	NYM	NL	48	75	16	4	0	2	(0 | 2)	26	10	6	10	13	2	14	1	1	1	2	0	1.00	1	.213	.333	.347
2004	Oak	AL	137	455	124	32	1	7	(6 | 1)	179	50	43	48	16	1	58	0	5	1	0	0	-	9	.273	.297	.393
2005	Oak	AL	118	381	94	22	3	9	(5 | 4)	149	48	37	45	36	1	48	0	4	2	5	2	.71	6	.247	.310	.391
2006	Oak	AL	117	365	97	21	6	5	(1 | 4)	145	52	41	47	50	0	66	0	3	5	5	1	.83	16	.266	.350	.397
2007	Oak	AL	104	338	88	13	0	7	(2 | 5)	122	49	41	42	35	1	40	2	2	2	2	1	.67	13	.260	.332	.361
2008	Tor	AL	145	517	138	23	1	7	(5 | 2)	184	76	60	72	57	0	65	5	6	7	7	2	.78	8	.267	.341	.356
2009	Tor	AL	144	574	162	35	1	12	(7 | 5)	235	100	60	97	90	0	75	4	5	7	14	5	.74	12	.282	.379	.409
2010	Bos	AL	150	632	174	38	0	11	(6 | 5)	245	92	56	81	53	1	71	3	4	3	5	4	.56	13	.275	.333	.388
2011	Bos	AL	113	395	118	26	1	7	(3 | 4)	167	59	54	56	38	1	36	1	7	4	4	2	.67	12	.299	.358	.423
	Postseason		7	27	5	4	0	0	(0 | 0)	9	1	6	3	0	0	4	0	0	0	0	0	-	1	.185	.185	.333
10 ML YEARS			1103	3768	1019	214	14	68	(36 | 32)	1465	538	404	500	388	7	484	16	38	33	44	18	.71	91	.270	.338	.389

Kyle Seager

Bats: L **Throws:** R **Pos:** 3B-42; SS-10; 2B-3; PH-3 SEE-gurr **Ht:** 5'10" **Wt:** 175 **Born:** 11/3/1987 **Age:** 24

	BATTING																		BASERUNNING				AVERAGES		
Year	Team	Lg	G	AB	H	2B	3B	HR	(Hm | Rd)	TB	R	RBI	RC	TBB	IBB	SO	HBP	SH	SF	SB	CS	SB%	GDP	Avg	OBP	Slg
2009	Ms	R	1	3	0	0	0	0	(- | -)	0	0	0	0	0	0	1	0	0	0	0	0	-	0	.000	.000	.000
2009	Clinton	A	41	153	42	8	0	1	(- | -)	53	17	22	21	22	1	20	0	0	3	4	2	.67	0	.275	.360	.346
2009	Hi Dsrt	A+	2	5	0	0	0	0	(- | -)	0	1	0	0	0	0	0	0	0	0	0	0	-	0	.000	.000	.000
2010	Hi Dsrt	A+	135	557	192	40	3	14	(- | -)	280	126	74	117	71	0	94	5	3	7	13	12	.52	5	.345	.419	.503
2011	Jacksn	AA	66	266	83	25	1	4	(- | -)	122	33	37	47	26	1	38	5	0	2	8	5	.62	5	.312	.381	.459
2011	Tacom	AAA	24	106	41	8	2	3	(- | -)	62	24	17	26	11	0	12	0	0	0	3	1	.75	6	.387	.444	.585
2011	Sea	AL	53	182	47	13	0	3	(0 | 3)	69	22	13	16	13	0	36	2	2	2	3	1	.75	4	.258	.312	.379

Justin Sellers

Bats: R **Throws:** R **Pos:** SS-19; 2B-12; 3B-5; PH-3; PR-1 **Ht:** 5'10" **Wt:** 160 **Born:** 2/1/1986 **Age:** 26

	BATTING																		BASERUNNING				AVERAGES		
Year	Team	Lg	G	AB	H	2B	3B	HR	(Hm | Rd)	TB	R	RBI	RC	TBB	IBB	SO	HBP	SH	SF	SB	CS	SB%	GDP	Avg	OBP	Slg
2005	Vancvr	A-	47	175	48	8	1	0	(- | -)	58	31	13	25	19	0	24	8	4	1	8	3	.73	0	.274	.369	.331
2006	Kane	A	119	411	99	21	2	5	(- | -)	139	75	46	56	58	0	65	11	10	5	17	5	.77	7	.241	.346	.338
2007	Stcktn	A+	114	434	119	25	4	4	(- | -)	164	72	37	63	46	0	69	8	1	6	11	4	.73	11	.274	.350	.378
2007	Mdland	AA	14	45	7	1	0	0	(- | -)	8	2	3	1	3	0	10	1	2	0	2	0	1.00	1	.156	.224	.178
2008	Mdland	AA	124	442	112	15	8	6	(- | -)	161	72	46	58	48	0	77	7	9	5	10	6	.63	11	.253	.333	.364
2009	Chatt	AA	116	393	110	27	1	2	(- | -)	145	44	33	59	50	1	70	10	6	5	10	8	.56	12	.280	.371	.369

			BATTING																	BASERUNNING				AVERAGES		
Year	Team	Lg	G	AB	H	2B	3B	HR	(Hm	Rd)	TB	R	RBI	RC	TBB	IBB	SO	HBP	SH	SF	SB	CS	SB%	GDP	Avg	OBP	Slg
2010	InldEm	A+	24	96	25	7	0	0	(-	-)	32	15	12	11	9	0	16	1	1	2	2	0	1.00	0	.260	.324	.333
2010	Albq	AAA	90	288	82	17	1	14	(-	-)	143	51	56	55	40	0	49	3	7	6	5	3	.63	6	.285	.371	.497
2011	Albq	AAA	89	270	82	17	2	14	(-	-)	145	57	49	58	41	2	57	5	2	4	3	3	.50	6	.304	.400	.537
2011	LAD	NL	36	123	25	9	0	1	(1	0)	37	20	13	15	12	0	21	2	1	1	1	0	1.00	1	.203	.283	.301

Atahualpa Severino

Pitches: L **Bats:** L **Pos:** RP-6   ah-tah-WALL-pah sev-ur-EE-no   **Ht:** 5'9" **Wt:** 170 **Born:** 11/6/1984 **Age:** 27

			HOW MUCH HE PITCHED					WHAT HE GAVE UP											THE RESULTS						
Year	Team	Lg	G	GS	CG	GF	IP	BFP	H	R	ER	HR	SH	SF	HB	TBB	IBB	SO	WP	Bk	W	L	Pct	Sh	Sv-Op Hld	ERC	ERA
2007	Nats	R	13	5	0	1	33.2	137	25	12	11	3	2	1	4	10	0	28	0	0	1	0	1.000	0	0- - -	2.72	2.94
2008	Hgrstn	A	15	0	0	3	33.1	145	28	17	15	2	5	0	4	17	1	34	2	0	4	2	.667	0	1- - -	3.76	4.05
2008	Ptomc	A+	26	0	0	12	38.2	164	31	18	17	2	1	2	1	20	1	31	4	0	4	0	.000	0	0- - -	3.18	3.96
2009	Ptomc	A+	29	0	0	17	46.0	189	35	14	13	4	6	0	3	14	1	39	7	0	4	0	1.000	0	13- - -	2.55	2.54
2009	Hrsbrg	AA	15	0	0	6	22.2	101	19	8	7	1	3	0	3	14	3	27	2	1	6	0	1.000	0	2- - -	3.90	2.78
2010	Syrcse	AAA	54	0	0	15	67.1	292	60	27	25	5	5	0	5	29	2	46	1	1	6	3	.667	0	1- - -	3.62	3.34
2011	Syrcse	AAA	35	0	0	9	32.0	158	37	17	16	2	0	1	2	23	3	38	1	1	1	2	.333	0	1- - -	5.90	4.50
2011	Was	NL	6	0	0	0	4.2	19	5	2	2	1	0	0	0	1	0	7	0	0	1	0	1.000	0	0-0 1	4.67	3.86

Bryan Shaw

Pitches: R **Bats:** B **Pos:** RP-33   **Ht:** 6'1" **Wt:** 210 **Born:** 11/8/1987 **Age:** 24

			HOW MUCH HE PITCHED					WHAT HE GAVE UP											THE RESULTS						
Year	Team	Lg	G	GS	CG	GF	IP	BFP	H	R	ER	HR	SH	SF	HB	TBB	IBB	SO	WP	Bk	W	L	Pct	Sh	Sv-Op Hld	ERC	ERA
2008	Msoula	R+	10	0	0	5	17.1	87	24	19	13	2	0	0	4	7	0	17	4	0	0	1	.000	0	2- - -	7.35	6.75
2008	Sbend	A	11	0	0	4	22.1	90	18	12	10	0	0	0	1	6	0	16	1	0	0	1	.000	0	0- - -	2.13	4.03
2009	Visalia	A+	30	19	0	2	107.1	461	96	65	56	7	2	2	11	40	1	95	11	0	3	7	.300	0	0- - -	3.51	4.70
2010	Mobile	AA	33	13	0	9	101.1	447	102	57	48	4	7	3	10	43	3	75	11	0	4	9	.308	0	2- - -	4.11	4.26
2011	Mobile	AA	15	0	0	14	20.2	84	15	5	2	1	1	0	0	8	0	15	0	0	3	1	.750	0	7- - -	2.26	0.87
2011	Reno	AAA	16	0	0	12	17.2	70	14	9	9	4	1	0	2	4	0	15	2	0	1	0	1.000	0	9- - -	3.63	4.58
2011	Ari	NL	33	0	0	8	28.1	122	30	9	8	2	0	0	4	8	1	24	1	0	1	0	1.000	0	0-0 9	4.31	2.54

George Sherrill

Pitches: L **Bats:** L **Pos:** RP-51   **Ht:** 5'11" **Wt:** 237 **Born:** 4/19/1977 **Age:** 35

			HOW MUCH HE PITCHED					WHAT HE GAVE UP											THE RESULTS						
Year	Team	Lg	G	GS	CG	GF	IP	BFP	H	R	ER	HR	SH	SF	HB	TBB	IBB	SO	WP	Bk	W	L	Pct	Sh	Sv-Op Hld	ERC	ERA
2004	Sea	AL	21	0	0	4	23.2	104	24	12	10	3	0	1	1	9	1	16	4	1	2	1	.667	0	0-0 3	4.31	3.80
2005	Sea	AL	29	0	0	2	19.0	77	13	12	11	3	1	1	1	7	2	24	0	0	4	3	.571	0	0-0 9	2.70	5.21
2006	Sea	AL	72	0	0	6	40.0	174	30	19	19	0	4	2	0	27	4	42	0	0	2	4	.333	0	1-1 17	2.86	4.28
2007	Sea	AL	73	0	0	16	45.2	182	28	12	12	4	4	4	1	17	1	56	1	1	2	0	1.000	0	3-7 22	1.96	2.36
2008	Bal	AL	57	0	0	49	53.1	239	47	28	28	6	1	3	1	35	6	58	1	0	3	5	.375	0	31-37 0	4.18	4.73
2009	2 Tms		72	0	0	39	69.0	282	53	13	13	4	1	1	2	24	4	61	1	0	1	1	.500	0	21-26 11	2.41	1.70
2010	LAD	NL	65	0	0	12	36.1	180	46	28	27	4	5	2	1	24	4	25	1	0	2	2	.500	0	0-4 7	6.56	6.69
2011	Atl	NL	51	0	0	9	36.0	149	33	12	12	3	2	1	1	12	1	38	1	0	3	1	.750	0	0-1 7	3.37	3.00
09	Bal	AL	42	0	0	38	41.1	171	34	11	11	3	0	1	2	13	2	39	0	0	1	0	1.000	0	20-23 0	2.72	2.40
09	LAD	NL	30	0	0	1	27.2	111	19	2	2	1	1	0	0	11	2	22	1	0	1	0	1.000	0	1-3 11	1.96	0.65
	Postseason		6	0	0	1	4.1	22	3	4	4	1	0	0	3	4	0	2	1	0	1	0	1.000	0	0-0 2	8.61	8.31
	8 ML YEARS		440	0	0	137	323.0	1387	274	136	132	27	18	15	8	153	23	320	9	2	19	17	.528	0	56-76 76	3.37	3.68

James Shields

Pitches: R **Bats:** R **Pos:** SP-33   **Ht:** 6'4" **Wt:** 220 **Born:** 12/20/1981 **Age:** 30

			HOW MUCH HE PITCHED					WHAT HE GAVE UP											THE RESULTS						
Year	Team	Lg	G	GS	CG	GF	IP	BFP	H	R	ER	HR	SH	SF	HB	TBB	IBB	SO	WP	Bk	W	L	Pct	Sh	Sv-Op Hld	ERC	ERA
2006	TB	AL	21	21	1	0	124.2	540	141	69	67	18	4	3	5	38	5	104	9	0	6	8	.429	0	0-0 0	4.92	4.84
2007	TB	AL	31	31	1	0	215.0	874	202	98	92	28	4	5	10	36	0	184	9	0	12	8	.600	0	0-0 0	3.24	3.85
2008	TB	AL	33	33	3	0	215.0	877	208	94	85	24	6	0	12	40	0	160	6	0	14	8	.636	2	0-0 0	3.41	3.56
2009	TB	AL	33	33	0	0	219.2	930	239	113	101	29	6	3	1	52	1	167	3	1	11	12	.478	0	0-0 0	4.16	4.14
2010	TB	AL	34	33	0	0	203.1	899	246	128	117	34	5	2	5	51	2	187	13	2	13	15	.464	0	0-0 0	5.21	5.18
2011	TB	AL	33	33	11	0	249.1	975	195	83	78	26	5	3	5	65	1	225	4	0	16	12	.571	4	0-0 0	2.58	2.82
	Postseason		5	5	0	0	29.1	127	32	13	12	4	1	1	3	8	0	19	1	0	2	3	.400	0	0-0 0	4.81	3.68
	6 ML YEARS		185	184	16	0	1227.0	5095	1231	585	540	159	30	16	38	282	9	1027	44	3	72	63	.533	6	0-0 0	3.77	3.96

Kelly Shoppach

Bats: R **Throws:** R **Pos:** C-86; PH-5   **Ht:** 6'0" **Wt:** 220 **Born:** 4/29/1980 **Age:** 32

			BATTING																	BASERUNNING				AVERAGES		
Year	Team	Lg	G	AB	H	2B	3B	HR	(Hm	Rd)	TB	R	RBI	RC	TBB	IBB	SO	HBP	SH	SF	SB	CS	SB%	GDP	Avg	OBP	Slg
2005	Bos	AL	9	15	0	0	0	0	(0	0)	0	1	0	0	0	0	7	1	0	0	0	0	-	0	.000	.063	.000
2006	Cle	AL	41	110	27	6	0	3	(2	1)	42	7	16	13	8	0	45	0	2	0	0	0	-	2	.245	.297	.382
2007	Cle	AL	59	161	42	13	0	7	(4	3)	76	26	30	24	11	0	56	1	3	1	0	0	-	2	.261	.310	.472
2008	Cle	AL	112	352	92	27	0	21	(9	12)	182	67	55	58	36	3	133	11	3	1	0	0	-	7	.261	.348	.517
2009	Cle	AL	89	271	58	14	0	12	(5	7)	108	33	40	32	33	0	98	18	2	3	0	0	-	8	.214	.335	.399
2010	TB	AL	63	158	31	8	0	5	(4	1)	54	17	17	18	20	0	71	3	0	0	0	0	-	5	.196	.308	.342
2011	TB	AL	87	221	39	3	0	11	(4	7)	75	23	22	15	19	0	79	9	3	1	0	0	-	5	.176	.268	.339
	Postseason		5	15	3	2	0	0	(0	0)	5	1	0	2	1	0	5	2	0	0	0	0	-	0	.200	.333	.333
	7 ML YEARS		460	1288	289	71	0	59	(28	31)	537	174	180	160	127	3	489	46	15	7	0	0	-	26	.224	.315	.417

J.B. Shuck

Bats: L Throws: L Pos: RF-16; PH-14; CF-9; LF-6   Ht: 5'11" Wt: 185 Born: 6/18/1987 Age: 25

						BATTING												BASERUNNING				AVERAGES		
Year	Team	Lg	G	AB	H	2B	3B	HR	(Hm | Rd)	TB	R	RBI	RC	TBB	IBB	SO	HBP	SH	SF	SB	CS	SB%	GDP	Avg	OBP	Slg
2008	TriCity	A-	65	263	79	12	5	4	(- | -)	113	51	24	45	35	2	34	2	2	1	8	6	.57	0	.300	.385	.430
2009	Lancst	A+	133	556	175	30	11	1	(- | -)	230	98	36	94	64	5	55	4	4	0	18	9	.67	10	.315	.389	.414
2010	CpChr	AA	101	389	116	14	2	2	(- | -)	140	52	28	54	46	1	56	0	0	0	9	9	.50	3	.298	.372	.360
2010	RdRck	AAA	36	139	38	2	2	0	(- | -)	44	15	7	17	16	1	15	0	1	0	7	3	.70	4	.273	.348	.317
2011	OKCity	AAA	108	354	105	11	7	0	(- | -)	130	60	30	58	56	1	30	4	4	1	20	11	.65	6	.297	.398	.367
2011	Hou	NL	37	81	22	2	1	0	(0 | 0)	26	9	3	9	11	1	7	0	0	0	2	0	1.00	3	.272	.359	.321

Alfredo Simon

Pitches: R Bats: R Pos: SP-16; RP-7   si-MOHN   Ht: 6'6" Wt: 230 Born: 5/8/1981 Age: 31

			HOW MUCH HE PITCHED					WHAT HE GAVE UP											THE RESULTS						
Year	Team	Lg	G	GS	CG	GF	IP	BFP	H	R	ER	HR	SH	SF	HB	TBB	IBB	SO	WP	Bk	W	L	Pct	Sh	Sv-Op Hld	ERC	ERA
2011	Bowie*	AA	4	4	0	0	18.0	76	15	7	6	1	1	0	1	6	0	20	2	0	1	0	1.000	0	0- - -	2.79	3.00
2008	Bal	AL	4	1	0	0	13.0	59	16	10	9	4	0	1	2	2	0	8	2	0	0	0	-	0	0-0	6.45	6.23
2009	Bal	AL	2	2	0	0	6.1	28	8	7	7	5	0	0	0	2	0	3	0	0	0	1	.000	0	0-0	10.74	9.95
2010	Bal	AL	49	0	0	35	49.1	222	54	30	27	10	1	2	2	22	2	37	1	0	4	2	.667	0	17-21	5.66	4.93
2011	Bal	AL	23	16	0	1	115.2	499	128	69	63	15	1	4	4	40	6	83	2	2	4	9	.308	0	0-0	4.83	4.90
4 ML YEARS			78	19	0	36	184.1	808	206	116	106	34	2	7	8	66	8	131	5	2	8	12	.400	0	17-21	5.36	5.18

Tony Sipp

Pitches: L Bats: L Pos: RP-69   Ht: 6'0" Wt: 190 Born: 7/12/1983 Age: 28

			HOW MUCH HE PITCHED					WHAT HE GAVE UP											THE RESULTS						
Year	Team	Lg	G	GS	CG	GF	IP	BFP	H	R	ER	HR	SH	SF	HB	TBB	IBB	SO	WP	Bk	W	L	Pct	Sh	Sv-Op Hld	ERC	ERA
2009	Cle	AL	46	0	0	8	40.0	168	27	16	13	5	3	1	0	25	2	48	3	0	2	0	1.000	0	0-0 9	3.29	2.93
2010	Cle	AL	70	0	0	16	63.0	266	48	30	29	12	3	2	2	39	3	69	4	0	2	2	.500	0	1-3 15	4.42	4.14
2011	Cle	AL	69	0	0	17	62.1	251	45	22	21	10	1	2	0	24	3	57	2	1	6	3	.667	0	0-1 24	2.87	3.03
3 ML YEARS			185	0	0	41	165.1	685	120	68	63	27	7	5	2	88	8	174	9	1	10	5	.667	0	1-4 48	3.54	3.43

Grady Sizemore

Bats: L Throws: L Pos: CF-56; DH-11; PH-4   Ht: 6'2" Wt: 200 Born: 8/2/1982 Age: 29

						BATTING												BASERUNNING				AVERAGES		
Year	Team	Lg	G	AB	H	2B	3B	HR	(Hm | Rd)	TB	R	RBI	RC	TBB	IBB	SO	HBP	SH	SF	SB	CS	SB%	GDP	Avg	OBP	Slg
2011	Akron*	AA	6	20	8	3	0	0	(- | -)	11	3	4	3	2	0	2	0	0	0	0	0	-	1	.400	.455	.550
2011	Clmbs*	AAA	2	8	2	0	0	1	(- | -)	5	1	2	2	2	0	3	0	0	0	0	0	-	1	.250	.400	.625
2004	Cle	AL	43	138	34	6	2	4	(2 | 2)	56	15	24	21	14	0	34	5	0	2	2	0	1.00	0	.246	.333	.406
2005	Cle	AL	158	640	185	37	11	22	(10 | 12)	310	111	81	101	52	1	132	7	5	2	22	10	.69	17	.289	.348	.484
2006	Cle	AL	162	655	190	53	11	28	(14 | 14)	349	134	76	121	78	8	153	13	1	4	22	6	.79	2	.290	.375	.533
2007	Cle	AL	162	628	174	34	5	24	(11 | 13)	290	118	78	123	101	9	155	17	0	2	33	10	.77	3	.277	.390	.462
2008	Cle	AL	157	634	170	39	5	33	(21 | 12)	318	101	90	121	98	14	130	11	0	2	38	5	.88	5	.268	.374	.502
2009	Cle	AL	106	436	108	20	6	18	(5 | 13)	194	73	64	68	60	1	92	4	2	1	13	8	.62	4	.248	.343	.445
2011	Cle	AL	71	268	60	21	1	10	(6 | 4)	113	34	32	28	18	1	85	6	0	3	0	2	.00	4	.224	.285	.422
Postseason			11	43	12	2	1	2	(0 | 2)	22	9	3	5	8	3	9	1	0	1	2	1	.67	2	.279	.396	.512
8 ML YEARS			892	3527	948	216	43	139	(69 | 70)	1667	601	458	594	430	34	816	65	8	17	134	43	.76	36	.269	.357	.473

Scott Sizemore

Bats: R Throws: R Pos: 3B-91; 2B-18; PH-4   Ht: 6'0" Wt: 185 Born: 1/4/1985 Age: 27

						BATTING												BASERUNNING				AVERAGES		
Year	Team	Lg	G	AB	H	2B	3B	HR	(Hm | Rd)	TB	R	RBI	RC	TBB	IBB	SO	HBP	SH	SF	SB	CS	SB%	GDP	Avg	OBP	Slg
2006	Oneont	A-	70	294	96	15	4	3	(- | -)	128	49	37	52	32	2	47	2	3	2	7	5	.58	4	.327	.394	.435
2007	WMich	A	125	438	116	33	5	4	(- | -)	171	78	48	72	73	1	60	9	4	6	16	10	.62	11	.265	.376	.390
2008	Lkland	A+	53	203	58	11	4	1	(- | -)	83	32	20	34	24	1	44	3	1	3	14	3	.82	2	.286	.365	.409
2009	Erie	AA	59	228	70	17	4	9	(- | -)	122	39	33	49	35	0	46	2	3	1	7	3	.70	5	.307	.402	.535
2009	Toledo	AAA	71	292	90	22	1	8	(- | -)	138	49	33	55	29	0	49	4	5	0	14	1	.93	6	.308	.378	.473
2010	Toledo	AAA	76	299	89	23	1	9	(- | -)	141	49	37	54	31	0	77	9	1	2	2	2	.50	3	.298	.378	.472
2011	Toledo	AAA	23	76	31	7	1	2	(- | -)	46	17	15	21	12	0	19	2	1	1	3	1	.75	1	.408	.495	.605
2011	Scrmto	AAA	9	30	8	2	0	1	(- | -)	13	11	3	7	12	0	4	0	0	1	2	1	.67	2	.267	.465	.433
2010	Det	AL	48	143	32	7	0	3	(1 | 2)	48	19	14	13	15	0	40	0	4	1	0	0	-	4	.224	.296	.336
2011	2 Tms	AL	110	368	90	22	1	11	(4 | 7)	147	50	56	60	53	0	112	2	5	1	5	3	.63	8	.245	.342	.399
11	Det	AL	17	63	14	1	0	0	(0 | 0)	15	8	4	8	10	0	19	0	1	0	1	1	.50	0	.222	.329	.238
11	Oak	AL	93	305	76	21	1	11	(4 | 7)	132	42	52	52	43	0	93	2	4	1	4	2	.67	8	.249	.345	.433
2 ML YEARS			158	511	122	29	1	14	(5 | 9)	195	69	70	73	68	0	152	2	9	2	5	3	.63	12	.239	.329	.382

Anthony Slama

Pitches: R Bats: R Pos: RP-2   SLAMM-ah   Ht: 6'3" Wt: 204 Born: 1/6/1984 Age: 28

			HOW MUCH HE PITCHED					WHAT HE GAVE UP											THE RESULTS						
Year	Team	Lg	G	GS	CG	GF	IP	BFP	H	R	ER	HR	SH	SF	HB	TBB	IBB	SO	WP	Bk	W	L	Pct	Sh	Sv-Op Hld	ERC	ERA
2007	Elizab	R+	6	0	0	6	7.1	24	2	2	2	0	0	1	0	1	0	10	2	0	0	0	-	0	4- -	0.32	2.45
2007	Beloit	A	21	0	0	19	24.1	98	15	4	4	0	1	0	1	9	0	39	3	0	1	1	.500	0	10- -	1.58	1.48
2008	FtMyrs	A+	51	0	0	39	71.0	280	43	12	8	0	2	3	2	24	1	110	3	0	4	1	.800	0	25- -	1.49	1.01
2009	NwBrit	AA	51	0	0	43	65.1	270	46	18	18	5	3	4	2	32	6	93	3	1	4	2	.667	0	25- -	2.68	2.48
2009	Roch	AAA	11	0	0	10	15.2	63	11	6	6	0	2	1	0	8	3	19	2	0	0	2	.000	0	4- -	2.05	3.45
2010	Roch	AAA	54	0	0	41	65.1	265	41	16	16	7	4	1	1	32	3	74	2	0	2	2	.500	0	17- -	2.32	2.20

Year	Team	Lg	G	GS	CG	GF	IP	BFP	H	R	ER	HR	SH	SF	HB	TBB	IBB	SO	WP	Bk	W	L	Pct	Sh	Sv-Op	Hld	ERC	ERA
2011	Roch	AAA	27	0	0	16	37.0	155	27	15	12	4	2	0	3	16	4	42	3	0	3	2	.600	0	1--	-	2.93	2.92
2010	Min	AL	5	0	0	2	4.2	25	6	4	4	1	0	0	0	5	0	5	1	0	0	1	.000	0	0-1	-	9.58	7.71
2011	Min	AL	2	0	0	0	2.1	9	0	0	0	0	0	0	0	2	0	3	1	0	0	0	-	0	0-0	1	0.72	0.00
	2 ML YEARS		7	0	0	2	7.0	34	6	4	4	1	0	0	0	7	0	8	2	0	0	1	.000	0	0-1	1	5.86	5.14

Doug Slaten

Pitches: L Bats: L Pos: RP-31   Ht: 6'5" Wt: 215 Born: 2/4/1980 Age: 32

Year	Team	Lg	G	GS	CG	GF	IP	BFP	H	R	ER	HR	SH	SF	HB	TBB	IBB	SO	WP	Bk	W	L	Pct	Sh	Sv-Op	Hld	ERC	ERA
2011	Nats*	R	1	1	0	0	2.0	6	0	0	0	0	0	0	0	0	0	1	0	0	0	0	-	0	0--	-	0.00	0.00
2011	Hgrstn*	A	4	2	0	0	3.2	16	5	2	2	0	0	0	0	0	0	3	0	0	0	0	-	0	0--	-	3.72	4.91
2011	Hrsbrg*	AA	1	1	0	0	2.0	8	2	0	0	0	0	0	0	0	0	2	0	0	0	0	-	0	0--	-	1.95	0.00
2011	Syrcse*	AAA	3	0	0	1	2.2	9	2	0	0	0	1	0	0	0	0	5	0	0	0	0	-	0	0--	-	1.26	0.00
2006	Ari	NL	9	0	0	0	5.2	21	3	0	0	0	1	0	0	2	1	3	0	0	0	0	-	0	0-0	2	1.11	0.00
2007	Ari	NL	61	0	0	13	36.1	163	41	15	11	4	0	0	0	14	0	28	3	0	3	2	.600	0	0-1	7	4.74	2.72
2008	Ari	NL	45	0	0	13	32.1	147	33	20	17	4	1	1	4	14	1	20	0	0	0	3	.000	0	0-0	4	4.86	4.73
2009	Ari	NL	11	0	0	1	6.1	30	10	5	5	1	0	0	0	1	0	4	0	0	0	0	-	0	0-0	0	6.82	7.11
2010	Was	NL	49	0	0	13	40.2	174	34	18	14	2	0	0	4	19	2	36	2	0	4	1	.800	0	0-0	4	3.40	3.10
2011	Was	NL	31	0	0	11	16.1	84	26	10	8	3	1	0	1	9	3	13	0	0	0	2	.000	0	0-0	3	8.95	4.41
	Postseason		3	0	0	1	1.1	7	1	0	0	0	0	0	0	2	1	1	1	0	0	0	-	0	0-0	0	4.29	0.00
	6 ML YEARS		206	0	0	51	137.2	619	147	68	55	14	3	1	9	59	7	104	5	0	7	8	.467	0	0-1	20	4.72	3.60

Kevin Slowey

Pitches: R Bats: R Pos: SP-8; RP-6   Ht: 6'3" Wt: 205 Born: 5/4/1984 Age: 28

Year	Team	Lg	G	GS	CG	GF	IP	BFP	H	R	ER	HR	SH	SF	HB	TBB	IBB	SO	WP	Bk	W	L	Pct	Sh	Sv-Op	Hld	ERC	ERA
2011	FtMyrs*	A+	4	4	0	0	12.0	45	9	5	5	1	0	0	0	1	0	9	0	0	0	1	.000	0	0--	-	1.63	3.75
2011	Roch*	AAA	7	7	0	0	38.0	167	44	16	15	3	2	2	5	5	0	29	1	0	1	2	.333	0	0--	-	4.19	3.55
2007	Min	AL	13	11	0	0	66.2	297	82	39	35	16	0	1	0	11	0	47	3	0	4	1	.800	0	0-0	0	5.22	4.73
2008	Min	AL	27	27	3	0	160.1	653	161	74	71	22	1	5	4	24	1	123	1	0	12	11	.522	2	0-0	0	3.48	3.99
2009	Min	AL	16	16	0	0	90.2	394	113	50	49	15	3	5	4	15	1	75	3	0	10	3	.769	0	0-0	0	5.25	4.86
2010	Min	AL	30	28	0	0	155.2	662	172	80	77	21	2	11	4	29	0	116	3	0	13	6	.684	0	0-0	0	4.13	4.45
2011	Min	AL	14	8	0	1	59.1	258	78	44	44	10	3	4	3	5	0	34	0	0	0	8	.000	0	0-0	0	5.31	6.67
	5 ML YEARS		100	90	3	1	532.2	2264	606	287	276	84	9	26	16	84	2	395	10	0	39	29	.574	2	0-0	0	4.38	4.66

Joe Smith

Pitches: R Bats: R Pos: RP-71   Ht: 6'2" Wt: 205 Born: 3/22/1984 Age: 28

Year	Team	Lg	G	GS	CG	GF	IP	BFP	H	R	ER	HR	SH	SF	HB	TBB	IBB	SO	WP	Bk	W	L	Pct	Sh	Sv-Op	Hld	ERC	ERA
2011	Akron*	AA	4	0	0	0	3.2	14	1	1	1	0	0	0	0	2	0	7	0	0	0	0	-	0	0--	-	0.88	2.45
2007	NYM	NL	54	0	0	14	44.1	205	48	18	17	3	2	0	7	21	4	45	2	0	3	2	.600	0	0-0	10	5.04	3.45
2008	NYM	NL	82	0	0	12	63.1	271	51	28	25	4	4	0	4	31	4	52	1	0	6	3	.667	0	0-3	18	3.23	3.55
2009	Cle	AL	37	0	0	5	34.0	142	30	16	13	4	1	1	0	13	0	30	2	0	0	0	-	0	0-1	10	3.49	3.44
2010	Cle	AL	53	0	0	7	40.0	170	30	18	17	4	1	0	1	24	2	32	0	1	2	2	.500	0	0-1	17	3.53	3.83
2011	Cle	AL	71	0	0	13	67.0	267	52	16	15	1	2	2	2	21	1	45	2	0	3	3	.500	0	0-3	16	2.19	2.01
	5 ML YEARS		297	0	0	51	248.2	1055	211	96	87	16	10	3	14	110	11	204	7	1	14	10	.583	0	0-8	71	3.33	3.15

Jordan Smith

Pitches: R Bats: R Pos: RP-17   Ht: 6'4" Wt: 230 Born: 2/4/1986 Age: 26

Year	Team	Lg	G	GS	CG	GF	IP	BFP	H	R	ER	HR	SH	SF	HB	TBB	IBB	SO	WP	Bk	W	L	Pct	Sh	Sv-Op	Hld	ERC	ERA
2006	Billings	R+	14	14	0	0	68.2	284	58	29	23	3	2	1	6	20	0	49	3	0	6	3	.667	0	0--	-	2.80	3.01
2007	Dayton	A	26	26	0	0	133.2	574	133	74	57	8	1	6	11	40	0	96	8	1	10	8	.556	0	0--	-	3.68	3.84
2008	Srsota	A+	10	10	0	0	67.0	268	61	23	19	2	2	3	7	7	0	44	0	0	7	2	.778	0	0--	-	2.24	2.55
2008	Chatt	AA	11	11	0	0	55.0	255	72	43	33	6	2	4	4	17	1	42	6	1	2	6	.250	0	0--	-	5.78	5.40
2009	Carlina	AA	13	13	0	0	73.1	310	77	37	28	4	5	4	2	21	0	39	1	0	5	3	.625	0	0--	-	3.74	3.44
2010	Carlina	AA	27	0	0	23	28.1	128	38	20	16	3	0	0	1	8	1	14	1	0	1	3	.250	0	9--	-	5.77	5.08
2010	Lsvlle	AAA	3	0	0	1	3.1	16	5	3	3	1	0	0	0	1	0	0	1	0	0	0	-	0	0--	-	8.14	8.10
2011	Lsvlle	AAA	24	0	0	12	26.1	111	25	9	9	2	3	1	1	9	1	13	0	0	0	4	.000	0	7--	-	3.52	3.08
2011	Reds	R	4	3	0	0	6.0	23	6	2	1	1	0	0	0	0	0	2	0	0	0	0	-	0	0--	-	3.02	1.50
2010	Cin	NL	37	0	0	15	42.0	179	45	18	18	7	1	0	2	11	1	26	1	0	3	2	.600	0	1-2	2	4.58	3.86
2011	Cin	NL	17	0	0	1	20.0	94	32	16	16	3	0	3	1	8	1	13	2	1	0	0	-	0	0-1	2	8.77	7.20
	2 ML YEARS		54	0	0	16	62.0	273	77	34	34	10	1	3	3	19	2	39	3	1	3	2	.600	0	1-3	4	5.84	4.94

Seth Smith

Bats: L Throws: L Pos: RF-107; LF-25; PH-25   Ht: 6'3" Wt: 210 Born: 9/30/1982 Age: 29

Year	Team	Lg	G	AB	H	2B	3B	HR	(Hm	Rd)	TB	R	RBI	RC	TBB	IBB	SO	HBP	SH	SF	SB	CS	SB%	GDP	Avg	OBP	Slg
2007	Col	NL	7	8	5	0	1	0	(0	0)	7	4	0	3	0	0	1	0	0	0	0	0	-	0	.625	.625	.875
2008	Col	NL	67	108	28	7	0	4	(2	2)	47	13	15	18	15	0	23	0	0	0	1	0	1.00	0	.259	.350	.435
2009	Col	NL	133	335	98	20	4	15	(8	7)	171	61	55	63	46	3	67	2	1	3	4	1	.80	5	.293	.378	.510
2010	Col	NL	133	358	88	19	5	17	(12	5)	168	55	52	51	35	1	67	2	0	3	2	1	.67	5	.246	.314	.469
2011	Col	NL	147	476	135	32	9	15	(9	6)	230	67	59	73	46	7	93	4	0	7	10	2	.83	9	.284	.347	.483
	Postseason		9	11	4	1	0	0	(0	0)	5	2	2	3	1	1	2	0	0	0	0	0	-	0	.364	.417	.455
	5 ML YEARS		487	1285	354	78	19	51	(31	20)	623	200	181	208	142	11	251	8	1	13	17	4	.81	19	.275	.348	.485

Justin Smoak

Bats: B Throws: L Pos: 1B-108; DH-12; PH-4 SMOKE Ht: 6'4" Wt: 220 Born: 12/5/1986 Age: 25

Year	Team	Lg	G	AB	H	2B	3B	HR	(Hm	Rd)	TB	R	RBI	RC	TBB	IBB	SO	HBP	SH	SF	SB	CS	SB%	GDP	Avg	OBP	Slg
2008	Clinton	A	14	56	17	3	0	3	(-	-)	29	9	6	10	5	0	10	0	0	1	0	0	-	3	.304	.355	.518
2009	Frisco	AA	50	183	60	10	0	6	(-	-)	88	30	29	42	39	2	35	3	0	2	0	0	-	6	.328	.449	.481
2009	Rngrs	R	2	6	4	0	1	2	(-	-)	12	3	5	5	1	0	1	0	0	0	0	0	-	0	.667	.714	2.000
2009	Okla	AAA	54	197	48	11	0	4	(-	-)	71	25	23	29	35	0	45	3	0	2	0	0	-	8	.244	.363	.360
2010	OKCity	AAA	15	50	15	6	0	2	(-	-)	27	10	5	13	16	0	8	0	0	0	0	0	-	0	.300	.470	.540
2010	Tacom	AAA	35	133	36	7	0	7	(-	-)	64	23	25	25	23	0	32	1	0	2	0	0	-	6	.271	.377	.481
2011	Tacom	AAA	4	11	0	0	0	0	(-	-)	0	0	0	0	3	0	1	0	0	0	0	0	-	2	.000	.267	.000
2010	2 Tms	AL	100	348	76	14	0	13	(4	9)	129	40	48	42	46	4	91	0	0	3	1	0	1.00	6	.218	.307	.371
2011	Sea	AL	123	427	100	24	0	15	(10	5)	169	38	55	55	55	4	105	3	0	4	0	0	-	10	.234	.323	.396
10	Tex	AL	70	235	49	10	0	8	(4	4)	83	29	34	30	38	4	57	0	0	2	1	0	1.00	6	.209	.316	.353
10	Sea	AL	30	113	27	4	0	5	(0	5)	46	11	14	12	8	0	34	0	0	1	0	0	-	3	.239	.287	.407
	2 ML YEARS		223	775	176	38	0	28	(14	14)	298	78	103	97	101	8	196	3	0	7	1	0	1.00	19	.227	.316	.385

Travis Snider

Bats: L Throws: L Pos: LF-44; CF-6; RF-3; PH-2; DH-1 Ht: 6'0" Wt: 235 Born: 2/2/1988 Age: 24

Year	Team	Lg	G	AB	H	2B	3B	HR	(Hm	Rd)	TB	R	RBI	RC	TBB	IBB	SO	HBP	SH	SF	SB	CS	SB%	GDP	Avg	OBP	Slg
2011	LsVgs*	AAA	61	248	81	22	2	4	(-	-)	119	47	42	49	25	2	44	3	0	1	12	1	.92	5	.327	.394	.480
2008	Tor	AL	24	73	22	6	0	2	(1	1)	34	9	13	13	5	0	23	0	0	2	0	0	-	0	.301	.338	.466
2009	Tor	AL	77	241	58	14	1	9	(5	4)	101	34	29	30	29	1	78	3	2	1	1	1	.50	5	.241	.328	.419
2010	Tor	AL	82	298	76	20	0	14	(9	5)	138	36	32	40	21	2	79	0	0	0	6	3	.67	3	.255	.304	.463
2011	Tor	AL	49	187	42	14	0	3	(2	1)	65	23	30	21	11	1	56	1	1	2	9	3	.75	5	.225	.269	.348
	4 ML YEARS		232	799	198	54	1	28	(17	11)	338	102	104	104	66	4	236	4	3	5	16	7	.70	13	.248	.307	.423

Brad Snyder

Bats: L Throws: L Pos: PH-6; LF-1; PR-1 Ht: 6'3" Wt: 220 Born: 5/25/1982 Age: 30

Year	Team	Lg	G	AB	H	2B	3B	HR	(Hm	Rd)	TB	R	RBI	RC	TBB	IBB	SO	HBP	SH	SF	SB	CS	SB%	GDP	Avg	OBP	Slg
2003	MhVlly	A-	62	225	64	11	6	6	(-	-)	105	52	31	44	41	1	82	1	1	3	14	5	.74	2	.284	.393	.467
2004	Lk Cty	A	79	304	85	15	5	10	(-	-)	140	52	54	57	48	1	78	5	0	4	11	4	.73	5	.280	.382	.461
2004	Knstn	A+	29	110	39	7	1	6	(-	-)	66	20	21	26	13	1	28	1	0	1	4	2	.67	1	.355	.424	.600
2005	Knstn	A+	58	209	58	10	2	6	(-	-)	90	36	28	36	24	1	64	6	0	2	12	1	.92	2	.278	.365	.431
2005	Akron	AA	75	304	85	21	5	16	(-	-)	164	56	54	56	25	3	94	6	1	1	5	3	.63	3	.280	.345	.539
2006	Akron	AA	135	523	141	28	5	18	(-	-)	233	86	72	88	62	1	158	5	1	3	20	2	.91	12	.270	.351	.446
2007	Buffalo	AAA	86	259	68	12	3	10	(-	-)	116	41	35	45	36	1	91	2	4	2	12	0	1.00	4	.263	.355	.448
2008	Buffalo	AAA	115	411	101	28	5	12	(-	-)	175	52	61	53	27	2	123	4	1	3	7	3	.70	3	.246	.297	.426
2009	Iowa	AAA	69	237	66	16	3	14	(-	-)	130	39	44	44	20	3	68	1	0	2	10	4	.71	5	.278	.335	.549
2009	Cubs	R	5	18	5	1	1	1	(-	-)	11	1	3	3	1	0	7	0	0	0	0	0	-	0	.278	.316	.611
2010	Iowa	AAA	132	477	147	37	6	25	(-	-)	271	97	106	104	56	3	125	4	0	6	19	4	.83	9	.308	.381	.568
2011	Iowa	AAA	102	376	109	27	3	11	(-	-)	175	48	57	60	27	2	109	0	2	2	6	1	.86	2	.290	.336	.465
2010	ChC	NL	12	27	5	1	0	0	(0	0)	6	1	5	2	1	0	12	0	0	0	0	0	-	0	.185	.214	.222
2011	ChC	NL	8	9	1	0	0	0	(0	0)	1	1	0	0	0	0	6	0	0	0	0	0	-	0	.111	.111	.111
	2 ML YEARS		20	36	6	1	0	0	(0	0)	7	2	5	2	1	0	18	0	0	0	0	0	-	0	.167	.189	.194

Brandon Snyder

Bats: R Throws: R Pos: 1B-5; DH-1; PR-1 Ht: 6'2" Wt: 210 Born: 11/23/1986 Age: 25

Year	Team	Lg	G	AB	H	2B	3B	HR	(Hm	Rd)	TB	R	RBI	RC	TBB	IBB	SO	HBP	SH	SF	SB	CS	SB%	GDP	Avg	OBP	Slg
2005	Bluefld	R+	44	144	39	8	0	8	(-	-)	71	26	35	30	28	2	36	1	1	6	7	2	.78	2	.271	.380	.493
2005	Abrdn	A-	8	28	11	2	0	0	(-	-)	13	4	6	5	2	0	7	0	0	1	0	0	-	0	.393	.419	.464
2006	Dlmrva	A	38	144	28	12	0	3	(-	-)	49	12	20	11	9	0	55	0	3	3	0	0	-	3	.194	.237	.340
2006	Abrdn	A-	34	124	29	8	1	1	(-	-)	42	14	11	11	5	0	43	1	0	1	2	1	.67	2	.234	.267	.339
2007	Dlmrva	A	118	448	127	23	3	11	(-	-)	189	63	58	69	44	1	107	6	1	2	0	2	.00	11	.283	.354	.422
2008	Frdrck	A+	116	435	137	33	2	13	(-	-)	213	70	80	77	29	1	83	4	1	7	3	2	.60	14	.315	.358	.490
2009	Bowie	AA	58	201	69	19	1	10	(-	-)	120	24	45	48	27	4	45	2	0	3	0	1	.00	3	.343	.421	.597
2009	Norfolk	AAA	73	262	65	18	2	2	(-	-)	93	36	43	32	24	1	64	5	0	6	3	1	.75	5	.248	.316	.355
2010	Norfolk	AAA	98	339	87	22	1	9	(-	-)	138	36	43	47	28	0	101	7	0	2	4	1	.80	7	.257	.324	.407
2010	Abrdn	A-	3	13	3	1	0	1	(-	-)	7	2	4	1	0	0	2	0	0	0	0	0	-	2	.231	.231	.538
2011	Norfolk	AAA	114	448	117	21	1	14	(-	-)	182	55	71	59	32	0	91	5	0	9	1	2	.33	12	.261	.312	.406
2010	Bal	AL	10	20	6	2	0	0	(0	0)	8	1	3	3	0	0	3	0	0	0	0	1	.00	0	.300	.300	.400
2011	Bal	AL	6	13	3	1	0	0	(0	0)	4	2	1	1	3	0	4	1	0	0	0	0	-	0	.231	.412	.308
	2 ML YEARS		16	33	9	3	0	0	(0	0)	12	3	4	4	3	0	7	1	0	0	0	1	.00	0	.273	.351	.364

Chris Snyder

Bats: R Throws: R Pos: C-33; PH-1 Ht: 6'4" Wt: 245 Born: 2/12/1981 Age: 31

Year	Team	Lg	G	AB	H	2B	3B	HR	(Hm	Rd)	TB	R	RBI	RC	TBB	IBB	SO	HBP	SH	SF	SB	CS	SB%	GDP	Avg	OBP	Slg
2011	Bradtn*	A+	6	20	8	2	0	1	(-	-)	13	6	8	6	6	1	5	0	0	0	0	0	-	1	.400	.538	.650
2004	Ari	NL	29	96	23	6	0	5	(1	4)	44	10	15	11	13	1	25	0	0	1	0	0	-	0	.240	.327	.458
2005	Ari	NL	115	326	66	14	0	6	(2	4)	98	24	28	25	40	5	87	4	3	0	0	1	.00	6	.202	.297	.301
2006	Ari	NL	61	184	51	9	0	6	(2	4)	78	19	32	27	22	4	39	1	1	5	0	0	-	5	.277	.349	.424
2007	Ari	NL	110	326	82	20	0	13	(4	9)	141	37	47	48	40	3	67	7	3	4	0	1	.00	9	.252	.342	.433
2008	Ari	NL	115	334	79	22	1	16	(6	10)	151	47	64	53	56	5	101	4	5	5	0	0	-	7	.237	.348	.452
2009	Ari	NL	61	165	33	7	0	6	(3	3)	58	20	22	17	32	4	47	2	1	2	0	0	-	5	.200	.333	.352

Year	Team	Lg	G	AB	H	2B	3B	HR	(Hm	Rd)	TB	R	RBI	RC	TBB	IBB	SO	HBP	SH	SF	SB	CS	SB%	GDP	Avg	OBP	Slg
2010	2 Tms	NL	105	319	66	9	0	15	(6	9)	120	34	48	38	52	10	94	2	1	2	0	0	-	11	.207	.320	.376
2011	Pit	NL	34	96	26	3	0	3	(0	3)	38	13	17	17	17	0	23	1	2	3	0	1	.00	2	.271	.376	.396
10	Ari	NL	65	195	45	8	0	10	(5	5)	83	22	32	30	36	6	61	1	1	1	0	0	-	5	.231	.352	.426
10	Pit	NL	40	124	21	1	0	5	(1	4)	37	12	16	8	16	4	33	1	0	1	0	0	-	6	.169	.268	.298
	Postseason		6	19	5	2	0	1	(0	1)	10	3	3	2	2	0	6	0	0	0	0	0	-	3	.263	.333	.526
	8 ML YEARS		630	1846	426	90	1	70	(26	44)	728	204	273	236	272	32	483	21	16	22	0	3	.00	45	.231	.333	.394

Eric Sogard

Bats: L Throws: R Pos: SS-14; 3B-10; 2B-3; PH-1; PR-1   SO-guard   **Ht: 5'10" Wt: 180 Born: 5/22/1986 Age: 26**

Year	Team	Lg	G	AB	H	2B	3B	HR	(Hm	Rd)	TB	R	RBI	RC	TBB	IBB	SO	HBP	SH	SF	SB	CS	SB%	GDP	Avg	OBP	Slg
2007	FtWyn	A	22	83	21	2	0	2	(-	-)	29	7	15	9	6	0	13	1	1	1	2	2	.50	5	.253	.308	.349
2007	Eugene	A-	31	125	32	9	0	2	(-	-)	47	20	18	18	19	1	16	0	1	0	4	2	.67	1	.256	.354	.376
2007	Portlnd	AAA	1	3	0	0	0	0	(-	-)	0	0	0	0	0	0	3	1	0	0	0	0	-	0	.000	.250	.000
2008	Lk Els	A+	133	536	165	42	3	10	(-	-)	243	97	87	101	79	3	62	1	0	6	16	7	.70	9	.308	.394	.453
2009	SnAnt	AA	117	458	134	25	3	6	(-	-)	183	79	51	73	58	2	48	2	6	7	10	6	.63	12	.293	.370	.400
2010	Scrmto	AAA	137	514	154	28	6	5	(-	-)	209	82	65	87	75	2	68	4	1	3	14	9	.61	7	.300	.391	.407
2011	Scrmto	AAA	79	315	94	16	2	5	(-	-)	129	55	37	54	40	2	34	4	4	3	13	3	.81	5	.298	.381	.410
2010	Oak	AL	4	7	3	0	0	0	(0	0)	3	0	0	1	2	0	1	0	0	0	0	1	.00	0	.429	.556	.429
2011	Oak	AL	27	70	14	3	0	2	(0	2)	23	7	4	3	4	0	13	0	0	0	0	0	-	2	.200	.243	.329
	2 ML YEARS		31	77	17	3	0	2	(0	2)	26	7	4	4	6	0	14	0	0	0	0	1	.00	2	.221	.277	.338

Andy Sonnanstine

Pitches: R Bats: L Pos: RP-11; SP-4   SAHN-un-styne   **Ht: 6'3" Wt: 190 Born: 3/18/1983 Age: 29**

Year	Team	Lg	G	GS	CG	GF	IP	BFP	H	R	ER	HR	SH	SF	HB	TBB	IBB	SO	WP	Bk	W	L	Pct	Sh	Sv-Op	Hld	ERC	ERA
2011	Drham*	AAA	10	9	0	0	56.0	246	64	37	30	4	1	3	1	15	0	35	0	0	3	6	.333	0	0- -	-	4.16	4.82
2007	TB	AL	22	22	0	0	130.2	554	151	87	85	18	3	5	5	26	2	97	2	0	6	10	.375	1	0-0	0	4.62	5.85
2008	TB	AL	32	32	1	0	193.1	819	212	105	94	21	4	9	5	37	2	124	6	0	13	9	.591	1	0-0	0	3.92	4.38
2009	TB	AL	22	18	0	2	99.2	459	131	85	75	19	0	2	2	34	3	60	3	0	6	9	.400	0	0-0	0	6.38	6.77
2010	TB	AL	41	4	0	23	81.0	355	83	40	40	11	0	1	7	27	3	50	3	0	3	1	.750	0	1-1	0	4.45	4.44
2011	TB	AL	15	4	0	8	35.2	152	40	22	22	10	1	1	1	12	1	12	0	0	0	2	.000	0	0-0	0	6.11	5.55
	Postseason		3	3	0	0	17.0	74	15	11	8	4	0	0	0	5	0	8	0	0	2	1	.667	0	0-0	0	3.64	4.24
	5 ML YEARS		132	80	1	33	540.1	2339	617	339	316	79	8	18	20	136	11	343	14	0	28	31	.475	1	1-1	0	4.74	5.26

Joakim Soria

Pitches: R Bats: R Pos: RP-60   WAH-keem SORE-ee-uh   **Ht: 6'3" Wt: 199 Born: 5/18/1984 Age: 28**

Year	Team	Lg	G	GS	CG	GF	IP	BFP	H	R	ER	HR	SH	SF	HB	TBB	IBB	SO	WP	Bk	W	L	Pct	Sh	Sv-Op	Hld	ERC	ERA
2007	KC	AL	62	0	0	38	69.0	270	46	20	19	3	1	3	1	19	3	75	2	0	2	3	.400	0	17-21	9	1.63	2.48
2008	KC	AL	63	0	0	57	67.1	260	39	13	12	5	2	2	6	19	1	66	1	1	2	3	.400	0	42-45	5	1.72	1.60
2009	KC	AL	47	0	0	41	53.0	222	44	14	13	5	1	2	2	16	1	69	3	0	3	2	.600	0	30-33	0	2.80	2.21
2010	KC	AL	66	0	0	56	65.2	270	53	13	13	4	3	4	2	16	1	71	3	1	1	2	.333	0	43-46	0	2.27	1.78
2011	KC	AL	60	0	0	47	60.1	256	60	29	27	7	3	2	2	17	0	60	1	0	5	5	.500	0	28-35	0	3.80	4.03
	5 ML YEARS		298	0	0	239	315.1	1278	242	89	84	24	10	13	13	87	6	341	10	2	13	15	.464	0	160-180	9	2.35	2.40

Alfonso Soriano

Bats: R Throws: R Pos: LF-128; PH-7; DH-3   **Ht: 6'1" Wt: 195 Born: 1/7/1976 Age: 36**

Year	Team	Lg	G	AB	H	2B	3B	HR	(Hm	Rd)	TB	R	RBI	RC	TBB	IBB	SO	HBP	SH	SF	SB	CS	SB%	GDP	Avg	OBP	Slg
2011	Iowa*	AAA	3	13	1	0	0	0	(-	-)	1	3	0	0	0	0	4	0	0	0	0	0	-	0	.077	.077	.077
1999	NYY	AL	9	8	1	0	0	1	(1	0)	4	2	1	0	0	0	3	0	0	0	0	1	.00	0	.125	.125	.500
2000	NYY	AL	22	50	9	3	0	2	(0	2)	18	5	3	4	1	0	15	0	2	0	2	0	1.00	0	.180	.196	.360
2001	NYY	AL	158	574	154	34	3	18	(8	10)	248	77	73	77	29	0	125	3	3	5	43	14	.75	7	.268	.304	.432
2002	NYY	AL	156	696	209	51	2	39	(17	22)	381	128	102	121	23	1	157	14	1	7	41	13	.76	9	.300	.332	.547
2003	NYY	AL	156	682	198	36	5	38	(15	23)	358	114	91	110	38	7	130	12	0	7	35	8	.81	8	.290	.338	.525
2004	Tex	AL	145	608	170	32	4	28	(12	16)	294	77	91	90	33	4	121	10	0	7	18	5	.78	7	.280	.324	.484
2005	Tex	AL	156	637	171	43	2	36	(25	11)	326	102	104	93	33	3	125	7	0	5	30	2	.94	6	.268	.309	.512
2006	Was	NL	159	647	179	41	2	46	(24	22)	362	119	95	114	67	16	160	9	2	3	41	17	.71	3	.277	.351	.560
2007	ChC	NL	135	579	173	42	5	33	(13	20)	324	97	70	91	31	4	130	4	0	3	19	6	.76	9	.299	.337	.560
2008	ChC	NL	109	453	127	27	0	29	(17	12)	241	76	75	77	43	11	103	3	0	4	19	3	.86	9	.280	.344	.532
2009	ChC	NL	117	477	115	25	1	20	(7	13)	202	64	55	60	40	6	118	3	0	3	9	2	.82	7	.241	.303	.423
2010	ChC	NL	147	496	128	40	3	24	(11	13)	246	67	79	75	45	3	123	3	1	3	5	1	.83	12	.258	.322	.496
2011	ChC	NL	137	475	116	27	1	26	(12	14)	223	50	88	59	27	4	113	4	0	2	2	1	.67	15	.244	.289	.469
	Postseason		44	174	37	3	0	4	(3	1)	52	14	18	14	9	0	53	3	0	0	10	3	.77	3	.213	.263	.299
	13 ML YEARS		1606	6382	1750	401	28	340	(162	178)	3227	978	927	972	410	59	1423	72	9	43	264	73	.78	91	.274	.323	.506

Rafael Soriano

Pitches: R Bats: R Pos: RP-42   **Ht: 6'1" Wt: 220 Born: 12/19/1979 Age: 32**

Year	Team	Lg	G	GS	CG	GF	IP	BFP	H	R	ER	HR	SH	SF	HB	TBB	IBB	SO	WP	Bk	W	L	Pct	Sh	Sv-Op	Hld	ERC	ERA
2011	Tampa*	A+	2	2	0	0	2.1	10	4	3	3	1	1	0	0	1	0	1	0	0	0	1	.000	0	0- -	-	10.10	11.57
2011	S-WB*	AAA	2	0	0	0	2.0	7	1	1	1	0	0	0	0	2	0	2	0	0	1	0	1.000	0	0- -	-	1.73	4.50
2002	Sea	AL	10	8	0	0	47.1	202	45	25	24	8	1	0	0	16	1	32	2	0	0	3	.000	0	1-1	0	3.93	4.56
2003	Sea	AL	40	0	0	12	53.0	201	30	9	9	2	0	1	3	12	1	68	0	0	3	0	1.000	0	1-2	5	1.32	1.53

Year	Team	Lg	G	GS	CG	GF	IP	BFP	H	R	ER	HR	SH	SF	HB	TBB	IBB	SO	WP	Bk	W	L	Pct	Sh	Sv-Op	Hld	ERC	ERA
2004	Sea	AL	6	0	0	0	3.1	23	9	6	5	0	0	0	0	3	0	3	0	0	0	3	.000	0	0-1	0	15.97	13.50
2005	Sea	AL	7	0	0	4	7.1	30	6	2	2	0	0	1	1	1	0	9	0	0	0	0	-	0	0-0	1	2.00	2.45
2006	Sea	AL	53	0	0	14	60.0	241	44	15	15	0	1	1	1	21	0	65	2	0	1	2	.333	0	2-6	18	2.64	2.25
2007	Atl	NL	71	0	0	28	72.0	276	47	26	24	12	0	0	2	15	2	70	0	0	3	3	.500	0	9-12	19	2.05	3.00
2008	Atl	NL	14	0	0	5	14.0	57	7	5	4	1	0	0	1	9	2	16	1	0	0	1	.000	0	3-4	0	2.27	2.57
2009	Atl	NL	77	0	0	52	75.2	307	53	25	25	6	4	2	1	27	4	102	0	0	1	6	.143	0	27-31	6	2.18	2.97
2010	TB	AL	64	0	0	56	62.1	237	36	14	12	4	0	1	1	14	2	57	0	0	3	2	.600	0	**45-48**	0	1.33	1.73
2011	NYY	AL	42	0	0	8	39.1	164	33	18	18	4	1	0	1	18	2	36	0	0	2	3	.400	0	2-5	23	3.51	4.12
Postseason			3	0	0	3	3.0	13	4	3	3	2	0	0	0	0	0	1	0	0	0	0	-	0	1-1	0	8.07	9.00
10 ML YEARS			384	8	0	180	434.1	1738	310	145	138	43	7	6	12	136	14	458	5	0	13	23	.361	0	90-110	72	2.31	2.86

Henry Sosa

Pitches: R Bats: R Pos: SP-10
Ht: 6'2" Wt: 195 Born: 7/28/1985 Age: 26

Year	Team	Lg	G	GS	CG	GF	IP	BFP	H	R	ER	HR	SH	SF	HB	TBB	IBB	SO	WP	Bk	W	L	Pct	Sh	Sv-Op	Hld	ERC	ERA
2006	Giants	R	9	6	0	2	32.1	131	20	15	14	3	1	2	3	12	0	41	1	0	2	1	.667	0	0- -	-	2.27	3.90
2007	Augsta	A	13	10	0	2	62.0	237	30	8	5	2	1	0	3	25	0	61	1	1	6	0	1.000	0	1- -	-	1.44	0.73
2007	SnJos	A+	14	14	0	0	63.2	294	66	36	31	8	1	2	3	36	0	78	3	1	5	5	.500	0	0- -	-	5.25	4.38
2008	SnJos	A+	12	12	0	0	56.1	242	62	28	27	6	2	1	2	18	0	58	2	0	3	4	.429	0	0- -	-	4.59	4.31
2008	Augsta	A	2	0	0	0	1.1	8	1	1	0	0	0	1	1	2	0	0	0	0	0	0	-	0	0- -	-	8.88	0.00
2009	Conn	AA	14	14	0	0	72.1	298	61	22	19	4	3	5	1	25	0	44	2	0	6	0	1.000	0	0- -	-	2.80	2.36
2010	Fresno	AAA	36	14	0	1	115.0	511	113	61	52	20	6	6	2	55	0	83	3	1	7	8	.467	0	0- -	-	4.83	4.07
2011	Fresno	AAA	17	0	0	2	23.1	129	39	30	27	3	1	1	5	17	1	21	0	0	3	1	.750	0	0- -	-	10.87	10.41
2011	Rchmd	AA	8	6	0	1	40.1	167	41	13	12	1	2	1	0	8	1	36	1	1	5	2	.714	0	0- -	-	2.85	2.68
2011	CpChr	AA	3	3	0	0	18.2	76	16	7	6	1	0	0	0	4	0	17	1	0	2	0	1.000	0	0- -	-	2.30	2.89
2011	OKCity	AAA	1	1	0	0	7.0	27	5	0	0	0	0	0	0	3	0	3	0	0	0	0	-	0	0- -	-	2.21	0.00
2011	Hou	NL	10	10	0	0	53.1	231	54	31	31	7	4	2	3	23	1	38	3	1	3	5	.375	0	0-0	-	4.78	5.23

Geovany Soto

Bats: R Throws: R Pos: C-122; PH-5
Ht: 6'1" Wt: 218 Born: 1/20/1983 Age: 29

Year	Team	Lg	G	AB	H	2B	3B	HR	(Hm	Rd)	TB	R	RBI	RC	TBB	IBB	SO	HBP	SH	SF	SB	CS	SB%	GDP	Avg	OBP	Slg
2011	Tenn*	AA	2	7	0	0	0	0	(-	-)	0	0	0	0	0	0	1	0	0	0	0	0	-	0	.000	.000	.000
2005	ChC	NL	1	1	0	0	0	0	(0	0)	0	0	0	0	0	0	0	1	0	0	0	0	-	0	.000	.000	.000
2006	ChC	NL	11	25	5	1	0	0	(0	0)	6	1	2	0	0	0	5	1	0	0	0	0	-	1	.200	.240	.240
2007	ChC	NL	18	54	21	6	0	3	(2	1)	36	12	8	13	5	0	14	0	0	1	0	0	-	1	.389	.433	.667
2008	ChC	NL	141	494	141	35	2	23	(11	12)	249	66	86	81	62	6	121	2	0	5	1	0	1.00	19	.285	.364	.504
2009	ChC	NL	102	331	72	19	1	11	(6	5)	126	27	47	34	50	3	77	3	0	5	1	0	1.00	19	.218	.321	.381
2010	ChC	NL	105	322	90	19	0	17	(12	5)	160	47	53	59	62	4	83	0	0	3	0	0	-	12	.280	.393	.497
2011	ChC	NL	125	421	96	26	0	17	(7	10)	173	46	54	43	45	3	124	6	0	2	0	0	-	12	.228	.310	.411
Postseason			5	17	3	1	0	1	(0	1)	7	1	2	1	3	0	4	0	0	0	0	0	-	0	.176	.300	.412
7 ML YEARS			503	1648	425	106	3	71	(38	33)	750	199	250	230	224	16	424	12	0	16	1	2	.33	48	.258	.348	.455

Denard Span

Bats: L Throws: L Pos: CF-67; PH-2; DH-1
Ht: 6'0" Wt: 205 Born: 2/27/1984 Age: 28

Year	Team	Lg	G	AB	H	2B	3B	HR	(Hm	Rd)	TB	R	RBI	RC	TBB	IBB	SO	HBP	SH	SF	SB	CS	SB%	GDP	Avg	OBP	Slg
2011	Roch*	AAA	10	38	8	1	0	0	(-	-)	9	4	2	2	0	0	5	0	1	0	3	0	1.00	1	.211	.211	.237
2008	Min	AL	93	347	102	16	7	6	(2	4)	150	70	47	68	50	3	60	4	8	2	18	7	.72	3	.294	.387	.432
2009	Min	AL	145	578	180	16	10	8	(5	3)	240	97	68	100	70	3	89	10	12	6	23	10	.70	7	.311	.392	.415
2010	Min	AL	153	629	166	24	10	3	(0	3)	219	85	58	85	60	0	74	4	10	2	26	4	.87	12	.264	.328	.348
2011	Min	AL	70	284	75	11	5	2	(1	1)	102	37	16	32	27	0	36	0	0	0	1	0	1.00	3	.264	.328	.359
Postseason			6	28	10	1	0	0	(0	0)	11	1	1	2	0	0	2	0	0	0	1	0	1.00	1	.357	.357	.393
4 ML YEARS			461	1838	523	67	32	19	(8	11)	711	289	189	285	207	6	259	18	30	10	73	22	.77	25	.285	.361	.387

Nate Spears

Bats: L Throws: R Pos: PH-2; 2B-1; LF-1
Ht: 5'11" Wt: 175 Born: 5/3/1985 Age: 27

Year	Team	Lg	G	AB	H	2B	3B	HR	(Hm	Rd)	TB	R	RBI	RC	TBB	IBB	SO	HBP	SH	SF	SB	CS	SB%	GDP	Avg	OBP	Slg
2003	Orioles	R	56	180	52	7	5	1	(-	-)	72	38	19	37	40	0	32	5	4	2	18	5	.78	2	.289	.427	.400
2004	Orioles	R	97	371	102	12	11	5	(-	-)	151	50	37	57	47	0	63	3	7	3	7	6	.54	3	.275	.358	.407
2005	Frdrck	A+	112	445	131	30	6	6	(-	-)	191	63	41	68	36	1	82	2	14	1	8	4	.67	1	.294	.349	.429
2006	Dytona	A+	97	321	79	15	1	1	(-	-)	99	45	25	35	31	1	53	7	7	3	4	1	.80	2	.246	.323	.308
2007	Dytona	A+	78	249	65	13	3	1	(-	-)	87	36	26	34	28	0	44	6	15	2	2	0	1.00	4	.261	.347	.349
2007	Tenn	AA	38	114	34	2	2	4	(-	-)	52	22	11	21	13	0	19	3	4	1	2	0	1.00	4	.298	.382	.456
2008	Tenn	AA	115	384	115	22	5	7	(-	-)	168	71	51	71	58	3	72	6	19	6	6	5	.55	3	.299	.394	.438
2008	Iowa	AAA	5	18	5	1	0	0	(-	-)	6	1	1	2	3	0	0	0	0	0	1	0	1.00	2	.278	.381	.333
2009	Iowa	AAA	128	368	93	20	4	2	(-	-)	127	48	37	43	35	1	43	2	4	2	6	5	.55	8	.253	.319	.345
2010	Portlnd	AA	136	514	140	30	4	20	(-	-)	238	104	82	99	84	2	93	11	1	10	13	1	.93	3	.272	.380	.463
2011	Pwtckt	AAA	96	315	78	19	2	8	(-	-)	125	49	45	51	49	2	69	6	3	5	13	1	.93	3	.248	.355	.397
2011	Bos	AL	3	4	0	0	0	0	(0	0)	0	0	0	0	0	0	1	0	0	0	0	0	-	0	.000	.000	.000

Josh Spence

Pitches: L Bats: L Pos: RP-40

Ht: 6'1" Wt: 190 Born: 1/22/1988 Age: 24

Year	Team	Lg	G	GS	CG	GF	IP	BFP	H	R	ER	HR	SH	SF	HB	TBB	IBB	SO	WP	Bk	W	L	Pct	Sh	Sv-Op Hld	ERC	ERA
2010	Padres	R	1	0	0	0	1.0	5	1	0	0	0	0	0	0	0	0	3	1	0	0	0		0	0- - -	1.51	0.00
2010	Eugene	A-	2	2	0	0	6.0	21	4	1	1	1	0	0	0	1	0	8	0	0	0	0		0	0- - -	2.11	1.50
2010	FtWyn	A	7	3	0	0	17.0	69	14	7	7	2	0	1	1	6	0	31	1	0	2	2	.500	0	0- - -	3.38	3.71
2011	SnAnt	AA	35	0	0	7	47.1	176	29	9	9	4	3	0	1	11	1	42	0	1	3	1	.750	0	0- - -	1.61	1.71
2011	SD	NL	40	0	0	8	29.2	123	14	9	9	2	1	1	2	19	5	31	0	0	0	2	.000	0	0-2 7	1.99	2.73

Ryan Spilborghs

Bats: R Throws: R Pos: PH-40; LF-29; RF-29; CF-13; PR-1   SPILL-borgs

Ht: 6'1" Wt: 200 Born: 9/5/1979 Age: 32

Year	Team	Lg	G	AB	H	2B	3B	HR	(Hm	Rd)	TB	R	RBI	RC	TBB	IBB	SO	HBP	SH	SF	SB	CS	SB%	GDP	Avg	OBP	Slg
2011	ColSpr*	AAA	10	45	20	3	0	3	(-	-)	32	8	10	12	2	0	6	0	0	0	0	0	-	5	.444	.468	.711
2005	Col	NL	1	4	2	0	0	0	(0	0)	2	0	1	1	0	0	1	0	0	0	0	0	-	0	.500	.500	.500
2006	Col	NL	67	167	48	6	3	4	(3	1)	72	26	21	22	14	0	30	0	2	3	5	2	.71	7	.287	.337	.431
2007	Col	NL	97	264	79	14	1	11	(5	6)	128	40	51	48	28	1	45	2	0	6	4	1	.80	5	.299	.363	.485
2008	Col	NL	89	233	73	14	2	6	(3	3)	109	38	36	42	38	0	41	1	0	3	7	4	.64	8	.313	.407	.468
2009	Col	NL	133	352	85	24	3	8	(4	4)	139	55	48	44	34	0	79	2	3	2	9	5	.64	9	.241	.310	.395
2010	Col	NL	134	341	95	20	2	10	(6	4)	149	41	39	53	39	0	83	5	2	1	4	5	.44	7	.279	.360	.437
2011	Col	NL	98	200	42	8	1	3	(2	1)	61	22	22	15	19	0	49	2	0	2	2	2	.50	10	.210	.283	.305
	Postseason		13	29	5	1	0	0	(0	0)	6	4	0	1	6	1	9	0	0	0	0	0	-	0	.172	.314	.207
7 ML YEARS			619	1561	424	86	12	42	(23	19)	660	222	218	225	172	1	328	12	7	17	31	19	.62	46	.272	.345	.423

Matt Stairs

Bats: L Throws: R Pos: PH-48; DH-5; 1B-4

Ht: 5'9" Wt: 200 Born: 2/27/1968 Age: 44

Year	Team	Lg	G	AB	H	2B	3B	HR	(Hm	Rd)	TB	R	RBI	RC	TBB	IBB	SO	HBP	SH	SF	SB	CS	SB%	GDP	Avg	OBP	Slg
1992	Mon	NL	13	30	5	2	0	0	(0	0)	7	2	5	3	7	0	7	0	0	1	0	0	-	0	.167	.316	.233
1993	Mon	NL	6	8	3	1	0	0	(0	0)	4	1	2	1	0	0	1	0	0	0	0	0	-	0	.375	.375	.500
1995	Bos	AL	39	88	23	7	1	1	(0	1)	35	8	17	9	4	0	14	1	1	1	0	1	.00	4	.261	.298	.398
1996	Oak	AL	61	137	38	5	1	10	(5	5)	75	21	23	27	19	2	23	1	0	1	1	1	.50	2	.277	.367	.547
1997	Oak	AL	133	352	105	19	0	27	(20	7)	205	62	73	77	50	1	60	3	1	4	3	2	.60	6	.298	.386	.582
1998	Oak	AL	149	523	154	33	1	26	(16	10)	267	88	106	96	59	4	93	6	1	4	8	3	.73	13	.294	.370	.511
1999	Oak	AL	146	531	137	26	3	38	(15	23)	283	94	102	101	89	6	124	2	0	1	2	7	.22	8	.258	.366	.533
2000	Oak	AL	143	476	108	26	0	21	(9	12)	197	74	81	69	78	4	122	1	1	6	2	5	.71	7	.227	.358	.414
2001	ChC	NL	128	340	85	21	0	17	(5	12)	157	48	61	57	52	7	76	7	1	3	2	3	.40	7	.250	.358	.462
2002	Mil	NL	107	270	66	15	0	16	(6	10)	129	41	41	38	36	4	50	8	0	1	2	0	1.00	7	.244	.349	.478
2003	Pit	NL	121	305	89	20	1	20	(13	7)	171	49	57	58	45	3	64	5	0	2	1	0	1.00	7	.292	.389	.561
2004	KC	AL	126	439	117	21	3	18	(6	12)	198	48	66	66	49	2	92	5	0	3	1	0	1.00	15	.267	.345	.451
2005	KC	AL	127	396	109	26	1	13	(5	8)	176	55	66	70	60	4	69	5	0	5	0	2	.33	9	.275	.373	.444
2006	3 Tms	AL	117	348	86	21	0	13	(6	7)	146	42	51	51	40	3	86	3	0	2	0	0	-	7	.247	.328	.420
2007	Tor	AL	125	357	103	28	1	21	(7	14)	196	58	64	64	44	5	66	2	0	2	2	1	.67	7	.289	.368	.549
2008	2 Tms	NL	121	337	85	12	1	13	(7	6)	138	46	49	44	42	9	90	5	0	3	1	1	.50	10	.252	.341	.409
2009	Phi	NL	99	103	20	4	0	5	(3	2)	39	15	17	15	23	3	30	3	0	0	1	1	.50	1	.194	.357	.379
2010	SD	NL	78	99	23	6	0	6	(0	6)	47	14	16	16	11	2	32	0	0	0	2	0	1.00	1	.232	.306	.475
2011	Was	NL	56	65	10	1	0	0	(0	0)	11	4	2	1	9	0	23	0	0	0	0	0	-	1	.154	.257	.169
06	KC	AL	77	226	59	14	0	8	(3	5)	97	31	32	35	31	2	52	2	0	2	0	0	-	5	.261	.352	.429
06	Tex	AL	26	81	17	4	0	3	(2	1)	30	6	11	10	6	1	22	1	0	0	0	0	-	1	.210	.273	.370
06	Det	AL	14	41	10	3	0	2	(1	1)	19	5	8	6	3	0	12	0	0	0	0	0	-	1	.244	.295	.463
08	Tor	AL	105	320	80	11	1	11	(6	5)	126	42	44	41	41	9	87	5	0	2	1	1	.50	10	.250	.342	.394
08	Phi	NL	16	17	5	1	0	2	(1	1)	12	4	5	3	1	0	3	0	0	1	0	0	-	0	.294	.316	.706
	Postseason		17	24	3	1	0	1	(0	1)	7	1	3	2	2	0	6	0	0	0	0	0	-	2	.125	.192	.292
19 ML YEARS			1895	5204	1366	294	13	265	(123	142)	2481	770	899	860	717	59	1122	57	5	40	30	24	.56	109	.262	.356	.477

Craig Stammen

Pitches: R Bats: R Pos: RP-7   STAMM-enn

Ht: 6'3" Wt: 200 Born: 3/9/1984 Age: 28

Year	Team	Lg	G	GS	CG	GF	IP	BFP	H	R	ER	HR	SH	SF	HB	TBB	IBB	SO	WP	Bk	W	L	Pct	Sh	Sv-Op Hld	ERC	ERA
2011	Syrcse*	AAA	25	24	1	0	142.0	616	163	80	75	18	5	2	1	40	0	127	6	0	10	7	.588	1	0- - -	4.67	4.75
2009	Was	NL	19	19	1	0	105.2	448	112	67	60	14	4	3	3	24	1	48	7	0	4	7	.364	0	0-0 0	4.03	5.11
2010	Was	NL	35	19	0	3	128.0	562	151	78	73	13	5	6	1	41	4	85	3	0	4	4	.500	0	0-0 0	4.79	5.13
2011	Was	NL	7	0	0	2	10.1	38	3	1	1	0	0	0	0	4	0	12	1	0	1	1	.500	0	0-0 0	0.67	0.87
3 ML YEARS			61	38	1	5	244.0	1048	266	146	134	27	9	9	4	69	5	145	11	0	9	12	.429	0	0-0 2	4.23	4.94

Mike Stanton

Bats: R Throws: R Pos: RF-142; PH-9; CF-1; DH-1

Ht: 6'5" Wt: 233 Born: 11/8/1989 Age: 22

Year	Team	Lg	G	AB	H	2B	3B	HR	(Hm	Rd)	TB	R	RBI	RC	TBB	IBB	SO	HBP	SH	SF	SB	CS	SB%	GDP	Avg	OBP	Slg
2007	Mrlns	R	8	26	7	2	0	0	(-	-)	9	6	1	3	1	0	6	1	0	0	0	0	-	0	.269	.321	.346
2007	Jmstwn	A-	9	30	2	1	0	0	(-	-)	6	2	2	0	3	0	15	0	1	1	0	0	-	0	.067	.147	.200
2008	Grnsbr	A	125	468	137	26	3	39	(-	-)	286	89	97	107	58	7	153	11	0	3	4	2	.67	8	.293	.381	.611
2009	Jupiter	A+	50	180	53	9	3	12	(-	-)	104	27	39	40	28	0	45	1	0	1	2	2	.50	4	.294	.390	.578
2009	Jaxnvl	AA	79	299	69	15	2	16	(-	-)	136	49	53	44	31	1	99	6	0	5	1	1	.50	4	.231	.311	.455

Year Team	Lg	G	AB	H	2B	3B	HR	(Hm Rd)	TB	R	RBI	RC	TBB	IBB	SO	HBP	SH	SF	SB	CS	SB%	GDP	Avg	OBP	Slg
								BATTING								BASERUNNING							AVERAGES		
2010 Jaxnvl	AA	53	192	60	13	2	21	(- -)	140	42	52	59	44	11	53	2	0	2	1	0	1.00	7	.313	.442	.729
2010 Fla	NL	100	359	93	21	1	22	(7 15)	182	45	59	56	34	6	123	2	0	1	5	2	.71	7	.259	.326	.507
2011 Fla	NL	150	516	135	30	5	34	(16 18)	277	79	87	81	70	6	166	9	0	6	5	5	.50	11	.262	.356	.537
2 ML YEARS		250	875	228	51	6	56	(23 33)	459	124	146	137	104	12	289	11	0	7	10	7	.59	18	.261	.344	.525

Tim Stauffer

Pitches: R Bats: R Pos: SP-31   Ht: 6'1" Wt: 223 Born: 6/2/1982 Age: 30

Year Team	Lg	G	GS	CG	GF	IP	BFP	H	R	ER	HR	SH	SF	HB	TBB	IBB	SO	WP	Bk	W	L	Pct	Sh	Sv-Op	Hld	ERC	ERA
				HOW MUCH HE PITCHED							WHAT HE GAVE UP											THE RESULTS					
2005 SD	NL	15	14	0	0	81.0	355	92	50	48	10	2	0	2	29	0	49	0	0	3	6	.333	0	0-0	0	5.00	5.33
2006 SD	NL	1	1	0	0	6.0	21	3	2	1	0	0	0	0	1	0	2	0	0	1	0	1.000	0	0-0	0	0.84	1.50
2007 SD	NL	2	2	0	0	7.2	45	15	18	18	5	0	0	1	6	0	6	0	0	0	1	.000	0	0-0	0	18.32	21.13
2009 SD	NL	14	14	0	0	73.0	316	71	31	29	8	2	1	5	34	1	53	1	0	4	7	.364	0	0-0	0	4.60	3.58
2010 SD	NL	32	7	0	12	82.2	326	65	18	17	3	2	4	5	24	5	61	0	0	6	5	.545	0	0-0	0	2.23	1.85
2011 SD	NL	31	31	0	0	185.2	777	180	81	77	20	14	3	8	53	5	128	4	1	9	12	.429	0	0-0	0	3.67	3.73
6 ML YEARS		95	69	0	12	436.0	1840	426	200	190	46	21	4	18	147	11	299	5	1	23	31	.426	0	0-0	0	3.91	3.92

Mitch Stetter

Pitches: L Bats: L Pos: RP-16   Ht: 6'4" Wt: 212 Born: 1/16/1981 Age: 31

Year Team	Lg	G	GS	CG	GF	IP	BFP	H	R	ER	HR	SH	SF	HB	TBB	IBB	SO	WP	Bk	W	L	Pct	Sh	Sv-Op	Hld	ERC	ERA
				HOW MUCH HE PITCHED							WHAT HE GAVE UP											THE RESULTS					
2011 Brewrs*	R	4	2	0	0	3.2	22	10	6	5	0	0	0	1	1	0	5	0	0	0	0	-	0	0- -		15.89	12.27
2011 Nashv*	AAA	2	0	0	1	1.2	7	2	2	2	1	0	0	0	0	1	1	0	0	0	0	-	0	0- -		6.66	10.80
2007 Mil	NL	6	0	0	2	5.0	20	2	2	2	0	0	1	2	2	0	4	3	0	1	0	1.000	0	0-0	0	1.86	3.60
2008 Mil	NL	30	0	0	7	25.1	109	14	9	9	2	1	0	4	19	1	31	1	0	3	1	.750	0	0-1	4	3.40	3.20
2009 Mil	NL	71	0	0	13	45.0	203	37	19	18	4	0	0	5	27	6	44	2	0	4	1	.800	0	1-2	20	3.90	3.60
2010 Mil	NL	9	0	0	0	3.2	22	7	6	6	1	0	0	1	3	0	3	0	0	0	0	-	0	0-0	3	14.78	14.73
2011 Mil	NL	16	0	0	2	7.0	31	8	4	4	2	1	1	1	1	0	7	1	0	0	0	-	0	0-2	1	5.64	5.14
Postseason		3	0	0	0	1.1	4	0	0	0	0	0	0	0	0	0	2	0	0	0	0	-	0	0-0	1	0.00	0.00
5 ML YEARS		132	0	0	24	86.0	385	68	40	39	9	2	2	13	52	7	89	7	0	8	2	.800	0	1-3	28	4.15	4.08

Jeff Stevens

Pitches: R Bats: R Pos: RP-4   Ht: 6'2" Wt: 205 Born: 9/5/1983 Age: 28

Year Team	Lg	G	GS	CG	GF	IP	BFP	H	R	ER	HR	SH	SF	HB	TBB	IBB	SO	WP	Bk	W	L	Pct	Sh	Sv-Op	Hld	ERC	ERA
				HOW MUCH HE PITCHED							WHAT HE GAVE UP											THE RESULTS					
2011 Iowa*	AAA	17	0	0	6	23.1	121	40	26	26	5	0	2	1	12	1	15	6	0	0	0	-	0	0- -		10.19	10.03
2011 Tenn*	AA	25	0	0	9	41.2	169	34	12	12	1	3	0	1	16	1	52	6	0	3	0	1.000	0	2- -		2.66	2.59
2009 ChC	NL	11	0	0	2	12.2	59	14	10	10	2	1	0	1	8	1	9	0	0	1	0	1.000	0	0-0	0	6.37	7.11
2010 ChC	NL	18	0	0	3	17.2	84	21	15	12	4	0	1	0	10	0	15	3	0	0	0	-	0	0-1	1	6.74	6.11
2011 ChC	NL	4	0	0	1	7.0	31	4	4	4	1	0	2	1	7	0	4	0	0	0	0	-	0	0-0	0	5.11	5.14
3 ML YEARS		33	0	0	6	37.1	174	39	29	26	7	1	3	2	25	1	28	3	0	1	0	1.000	0	0-1	1	6.32	6.27

Chris Stewart

Bats: R Throws: R Pos: C-63; PH-4; 1B-3; PR-1   Ht: 6'4" Wt: 210 Born: 2/19/1982 Age: 30

Year Team	Lg	G	AB	H	2B	3B	HR	(Hm Rd)	TB	R	RBI	RC	TBB	IBB	SO	HBP	SH	SF	SB	CS	SB%	GDP	Avg	OBP	Slg
								BATTING								BASERUNNING							AVERAGES		
2011 Fresno*	AAA	33	95	21	5	0	0	(- -)	26	9	10	9	11	0	16	2	3	1	3	1	.75	2	.221	.312	.274
2006 CWS	AL	6	8	0	0	0	0	(0 0)	0	0	0	0	0	0	2	0	0	0	0	0	-	0	.000	.000	.000
2007 Tex	AL	17	37	9	2	0	0	(0 0)	11	4	3	3	3	0	6	0	3	0	0	0	-	2	.243	.300	.297
2008 NYY	AL	1	3	0	0	0	0	(0 0)	0	0	0	0	0	0	1	0	0	0	0	0	-	0	.000	.000	.000
2010 SD	NL	2	0	0	0	0	0	(0 0)	0	0	0	0	0	0	0	0	0	0	0	0	-	0	-	-	-
2011 SF	NL	67	162	33	8	0	3	(1 2)	50	20	10	10	16	4	18	2	3	0	0	0	-	2	.204	.283	.309
5 ML YEARS		93	210	42	10	0	3	(1 2)	61	24	13	13	19	4	27	2	6	0	0	0	-	4	.200	.273	.290

Ian Stewart

Bats: L Throws: R Pos: 3B-42; PH-10; PR-1   Ht: 6'3" Wt: 215 Born: 4/5/1985 Age: 27

Year Team	Lg	G	AB	H	2B	3B	HR	(Hm Rd)	TB	R	RBI	RC	TBB	IBB	SO	HBP	SH	SF	SB	CS	SB%	GDP	Avg	OBP	Slg
								BATTING								BASERUNNING							AVERAGES		
2011 ColSpr*	AAA	45	171	47	10	1	14	(- -)	101	29	42	36	22	1	51	1	0	1	1	0	1.00	4	.275	.359	.591
2007 Col	NL	35	43	9	4	0	1	(1 0)	16	3	9	5	1	0	17	2	0	0	0	0	-	0	.209	.261	.372
2008 Col	NL	81	266	69	18	2	10	(5 5)	121	33	41	44	30	4	94	7	1	1	1	1	.50	3	.259	.349	.455
2009 Col	NL	147	425	97	19	3	25	(13 12)	197	74	70	59	56	3	138	5	0	5	7	4	.64	7	.228	.322	.464
2010 Col	NL	121	386	99	14	2	18	(6 12)	171	54	61	51	48	8	110	5	0	5	5	2	.71	8	.256	.338	.443
2011 Col	NL	48	122	19	6	1	0	(0 0)	27	14	6	4	14	2	37	0	0	0	3	2	.60	1	.156	.243	.221
Postseason		2	1	0	0	0	0	(0 0)	0	0	0	0	1	0	1	0	0	0	0	0	-	0	.000	.500	.000
5 ML YEARS		432	1242	293	61	8	54	(25 29)	532	178	187	163	146	17	396	19	0	11	16	9	.64	19	.236	.323	.428

Zach Stewart

Pitches: R **Bats:** R **Pos:** SP-11; RP-2   **Ht:** 6'2" **Wt:** 205 **Born:** 9/28/1986 **Age:** 25

			HOW MUCH HE PITCHED						WHAT HE GAVE UP											THE RESULTS							
Year	Team	Lg	G	GS	CG	GF	IP	BFP	H	R	ER	HR	SH	SF	HB	TBB	IBB	SO	WP	Bk	W	L	Pct	Sh	Sv-Op	Hld	ERC	ERA
2008	Dayton	A	11	0	0	10	16.1	61	10	2	1	0	0	0	1	3	0	13	0	0	1	2	.333	0	3--	-	1.27	0.55
2008	Srsota	A+	13	0	0	11	16.2	75	16	5	3	0	1	1	1	11	2	23	0	0	0	2	.000	0	0--	-	4.17	1.62
2009	Srsota	A+	7	7	1	0	42.1	177	47	17	10	1	1	1	1	8	0	32	1	0	1	1	.500	0	0--	-	3.47	2.13
2009	Carlina	AA	7	7	0	0	37.0	145	29	7	6	1	1	0	1	10	0	31	1	0	3	0	1.000	0	0--	-	2.19	1.46
2009	Lsvlle	AAA	9	0	0	4	12.1	55	11	2	1	0	0	0	0	8	0	16	1	0	0	0	-	0	2--	-	3.67	0.73
2009	LsVgs	AAA	11	0	0	3	13.1	62	18	8	5	1	1	0	1	6	0	14	1	0	0	0	-	0	0--	-	6.21	3.38
2010	NHam	AA	26	26	0	0	136.1	575	131	59	55	13	1	2	5	54	0	106	5	2	8	3	.727	0	0--	-	4.05	3.63
2011	NHam	AA	16	16	1	0	94.1	403	106	49	44	6	2	2	1	27	0	75	3	1	5	5	.500	0	0--	-	4.16	4.20
2011	Charltt	AAA	1	1	0	0	6.1	28	10	3	3	0	0	0	0	0	0	5	0	0	1	0	1.000	0	0--	-	5.11	4.26
2011	2 Tms	AL	13	11	1	1	67.1	297	90	44	44	11	2	2	2	18	2	45	2	1	2	6	.250	1	0-0	0	6.25	5.88
11	Tor	AL	3	3	0	0	16.2	75	26	9	9	2	0	1	1	5	1	10	1	1	0	1	.000	0	0-0	0	7.90	4.86
11	CWS	AL	10	8	1	1	50.2	222	64	35	35	9	2	1	1	13	1	35	1	0	2	5	.286	1	0-0	0	5.73	6.22

Josh Stinson

Pitches: R **Bats:** R **Pos:** RP-14   **Ht:** 6'4" **Wt:** 210 **Born:** 3/14/1988 **Age:** 24

			HOW MUCH HE PITCHED						WHAT HE GAVE UP											THE RESULTS							
Year	Team	Lg	G	GS	CG	GF	IP	BFP	H	R	ER	HR	SH	SF	HB	TBB	IBB	SO	WP	Bk	W	L	Pct	Sh	Sv-Op	Hld	ERC	ERA
2006	Mets	R	9	4	0	1	27.0	110	27	10	6	0	3	3	0	5	0	14	1	0	1	2	.333	0	0--	-	2.64	2.00
2006	Hgrstn	A	3	3	0	0	13.1	53	11	2	2	0	1	0	2	4	0	5	0	0	1	0	1.000	0	0--	-	2.83	1.35
2007	Savann	A	26	21	0	2	109.1	491	131	77	59	13	1	4	8	33	0	52	14	0	3	11	.214	0	0--	-	5.24	4.86
2008	Savann	A	21	6	0	10	71.2	319	78	36	28	7	1	2	5	32	0	46	5	0	3	6	.333	0	3--	-	5.10	3.52
2008	StLuci	A+	7	2	0	2	14.2	68	17	12	10	0	1	2	2	5	1	14	3	0	0	2	.000	0	0--	-	4.28	6.14
2009	Savann	A	25	1	0	7	42.1	175	45	17	17	1	3	0	4	10	0	49	3	0	2	2	.500	0	2--	-	3.78	3.61
2009	StLuci	A+	25	0	0	19	36.1	151	22	12	8	0	1	0	0	19	1	35	5	1	3	1	.750	0	6--	-	1.77	1.98
2010	Bnghtn	AA	32	14	0	7	110.1	481	108	57	52	7	5	6	4	50	0	68	10	0	9	3	.750	0	1--	-	4.05	4.24
2010	Buffalo	AAA	4	4	1	0	28.0	112	22	10	8	5	0	0	0	8	0	21	0	0	2	2	.500	0	0--	-	2.99	2.57
2011	Bnghtn	AA	27	2	0	15	47.1	205	46	22	21	1	3	3	4	16	2	39	3	0	4	3	.571	0	6--	-	3.35	3.99
2011	Buffalo	AAA	13	13	0	0	61.2	286	77	54	51	7	4	1	1	33	1	32	4	0	3	7	.300	0	0--	-	6.33	7.44
2011	NYM	NL	14	0	0	3	13.0	57	14	10	10	1	1	0	0	7	0	8	0	0	0	2	.000	0	1-2	4	5.05	6.92

Drew Storen

Pitches: R **Bats:** B **Pos:** RP-73   **Ht:** 6'2" **Wt:** 180 **Born:** 8/11/1987 **Age:** 24

			HOW MUCH HE PITCHED						WHAT HE GAVE UP											THE RESULTS							
Year	Team	Lg	G	GS	CG	GF	IP	BFP	H	R	ER	HR	SH	SF	HB	TBB	IBB	SO	WP	Bk	W	L	Pct	Sh	Sv-Op	Hld	ERC	ERA
2009	Hgrstn	A	11	0	0	4	14.2	59	11	6	6	2	0	0	2	0	0	26	5	0	0	1	.000	0	0--	-	1.91	3.68
2009	Ptomc	A+	7	0	0	7	10.0	37	7	2	2	0	1	0	0	2	0	11	2	0	1	0	1.000	0	2--	-	1.47	1.80
2009	Hrsbrg	AA	10	0	0	10	12.1	45	3	0	0	0	0	0	0	6	0	12	0	0	1	0	1.000	0	9--	-	0.73	0.00
2010	Hrsbrg	AA	7	0	0	6	9.1	32	5	1	1	1	0	0	0	1	0	11	0	0	0	0	-	0	4--	-	1.16	0.96
2010	Syrcse	AAA	6	0	0	1	7.1	29	7	1	1	0	0	0	0	2	0	4	0	0	0	0	-	0	0--	-	2.84	1.23
2010	Was	NL	54	0	0	22	55.1	232	48	24	22	3	6	2	3	22	5	52	3	0	4	4	.500	0	5-7	10	3.19	3.58
2011	Was	NL	73	0	0	52	75.1	303	57	24	23	8	1	1	2	20	4	74	2	0	6	3	.667	0	43-48	3	2.35	2.75
	2 ML YEARS		127	0	0	74	130.2	535	105	48	45	11	7	3	5	42	7	126	5	0	10	7	.588	0	48-55	13	2.70	3.10

Stephen Strasburg

Pitches: R **Bats:** R **Pos:** SP-5   **Ht:** 6'4" **Wt:** 220 **Born:** 7/20/1988 **Age:** 23

			HOW MUCH HE PITCHED						WHAT HE GAVE UP											THE RESULTS							
Year	Team	Lg	G	GS	CG	GF	IP	BFP	H	R	ER	HR	SH	SF	HB	TBB	IBB	SO	WP	Bk	W	L	Pct	Sh	Sv-Op	Hld	ERC	ERA
2010	Hrsbrg	AA	5	5	0	0	22.0	86	13	9	4	0	0	0	1	6	0	27	0	0	3	1	.750	0	0--	-	1.32	1.64
2010	Syrcse	AAA	6	6	0	0	33.1	124	18	5	4	1	0	0	0	7	0	38	1	1	4	1	.800	0	0--	-	1.08	1.08
2011	Hgrstn	A	3	3	0	0	6.1	33	9	8	7	1	0	0	1	3	0	13	1	0	0	1	.000	0	0--	-	7.69	9.95
2011	Ptomc	A+	1	1	0	0	3.0	12	2	0	0	0	0	0	0	0	0	5	0	0	0	0	-	0	0--	-	0.84	0.00
2011	Syrcse	AAA	1	1	0	0	5.0	17	2	1	1	0	0	0	0	0	0	7	0	0	0	0	-	0	0--	-	0.35	1.80
2011	Hrsbrg	AA	1	1	0	0	6.0	19	1	0	0	0	0	0	1	0	0	4	0	0	1	0	1.000	0	0--	-	0.20	0.00
2010	Was	NL	12	12	0	0	68.0	274	56	25	22	5	2	2	0	17	0	92	2	0	5	3	.625	0	0-0	0	2.41	2.91
2011	Was	NL	5	5	0	0	24.0	88	15	5	4	0	1	1	0	2	0	24	0	0	1	1	.500	0	0-0	0	0.97	1.50
	2 ML YEARS		17	17	0	0	92.0	362	71	30	26	5	3	3	0	19	0	116	2	0	6	4	.600	0	0-0	0	1.92	2.54

Huston Street

Pitches: R **Bats:** R **Pos:** RP-62   **Ht:** 6'0" **Wt:** 190 **Born:** 8/2/1983 **Age:** 28

			HOW MUCH HE PITCHED						WHAT HE GAVE UP											THE RESULTS							
Year	Team	Lg	G	GS	CG	GF	IP	BFP	H	R	ER	HR	SH	SF	HB	TBB	IBB	SO	WP	Bk	W	L	Pct	Sh	Sv-Op	Hld	ERC	ERA
2011	ColSpr*	AAA	2	0	0	1	2.0	6	0	0	0	0	0	0	0	0	0	2	0	0	0	0	-	0	0--	-	0.00	0.00
2005	Oak	AL	67	0	0	47	78.1	306	53	17	15	3	3	2	2	26	4	72	1	0	5	1	.833	0	23-27	0	1.87	1.72
2006	Oak	AL	69	0	0	55	70.2	290	64	28	26	4	3	3	2	13	3	67	4	0	4	4	.500	0	37-48	0	2.49	3.31
2007	Oak	AL	48	0	0	35	50.0	199	35	20	16	5	2	1	0	12	3	63	0	0	5	2	.714	0	16-21	5	1.84	2.88
2008	Oak	AL	63	0	0	37	70.0	287	58	29	29	6	3	3	1	27	6	69	2	0	7	5	.583	0	18-25	6	2.98	3.73
2009	Col	NL	64	0	0	52	61.2	240	43	22	21	7	3	2	0	13	4	70	0	0	4	1	.800	0	35-37	2	1.83	3.06
2010	Col	NL	44	0	0	39	47.1	187	39	21	19	5	0	1	2	11	4	45	2	1	4	4	.500	0	20-25	0	2.66	3.61
2011	Col	NL	62	0	0	47	58.1	239	62	28	25	10	3	1	1	9	1	55	0	0	1	4	.200	0	29-33	4	4.03	3.86
	Postseason		8	0	0	7	9.0	43	14	9	9	2	1	1	0	4	0	5	0	0	0	3	.000	0	3-4	0	8.97	9.00
	7 ML YEARS		417	0	0	312	436.1	1748	354	165	151	40	17	13	8	111	25	441	9	1	30	21	.588	0	178-216	18	2.49	3.11

Pedro Strop

Pitches: R Bats: R Pos: RP-23
STROPE
Ht: 6'0" Wt: 175 Born: 6/13/1985 Age: 27

Year Team	Lg	G	GS	CG	GF	IP	BFP	H	R	ER	HR	SH	SF	HB	TBB	IBB	SO	WP	Bk	W	L	Pct	Sh	Sv-Op	Hld	ERC	ERA
2011 RdRck*	AAA	39	0	0	29	47.2	216	53	21	19	2	2	2	1	24	5	55	5	0	4	4	.500	0	11--	-	4.57	3.59
2009 Tex	AL	7	0	0	3	7.0	30	6	6	6	0	0	0	0	4	0	9	0	0	0	0	-	0	0-0	0	3.27	7.71
2010 Tex	AL	15	0	0	5	10.2	60	17	12	12	2	1	0	1	11	0	11	5	1	0	0	-	0	0-0	1	11.92	10.13
2011 2 Tms	AL	23	0	0	6	22.0	90	15	5	5	0	2	1	1	10	0	21	2	2	2	1	.667	0	0-2	4	2.15	2.05
11 Tex	AL	11	0	0	4	9.2	44	7	4	4	0	1	1	1	7	0	9	2	2	0	0	1.000	0	0-1	0	3.34	3.72
11 Bal	AL	12	0	0	2	12.1	46	8	1	1	0	1	0	0	3	0	12	0	0	2	0	1.000	0	0-1	4	1.39	0.73
3 ML YEARS		45	0	0	14	39.2	180	38	23	23	2	3	1	2	25	0	41	7	3	2	1	.667	0	0-2	5	4.56	5.22

Drew Stubbs

Bats: R Throws: R Pos: CF-157; PH-3; PR-1
Ht: 6'4" Wt: 200 Born: 10/4/1984 Age: 27

Year Team	Lg	G	AB	H	2B	3B	HR	(Hm	Rd)	TB	R	RBI	RC	TBB	IBB	SO	HBP	SH	SF	SB	CS	SB%	GDP	Avg	OBP	Slg
2009 Cin	NL	42	180	48	5	1	8	(7	1)	79	27	17	22	15	0	49	0	1	0	10	4	.71	1	.267	.323	.439
2010 Cin	NL	150	514	131	19	6	22	(13	9)	228	91	77	74	55	2	168	5	3	6	30	6	.83	6	.255	.329	.444
2011 Cin	NL	158	604	147	22	3	15	(9	6)	220	92	44	66	63	1	205	7	6	1	40	10	.80	2	.243	.321	.364
Postseason		3	9	1	0	0	0	(0	0)	1	0	0	0	2	0	4	0	0	0	0	0	-	0	.111	.273	.111
3 ML YEARS		350	1298	326	46	10	45	(29	16)	527	210	138	162	133	3	422	12	10	7	80	20	.80	9	.251	.325	.406

Eric Stults

Pitches: L Bats: L Pos: RP-6
Ht: 6'1" Wt: 222 Born: 12/9/1979 Age: 32

Year Team	Lg	G	GS	CG	GF	IP	BFP	H	R	ER	HR	SH	SF	HB	TBB	IBB	SO	WP	Bk	W	L	Pct	Sh	Sv-Op	Hld	ERC	ERA
2011 ColSpr*	AAA	52	0	0	16	68.0	298	76	39	35	11	3	3	0	16	2	69	3	0	4	4	.500	0	1--	-	4.33	4.63
2006 LAD	NL	6	2	0	2	17.2	73	17	12	11	4	2	0	0	7	0	5	0	0	1	0	1.000	0	0-0	-	4.91	5.60
2007 LAD	NL	12	5	0	0	38.2	179	50	26	25	5	1	1	1	17	2	30	2	0	1	4	.200	0	0-0	1	6.25	5.82
2008 LAD	NL	7	7	1	0	38.2	167	38	18	15	6	2	0	1	13	2	30	0	0	2	3	.400	1	0-0	0	4.07	3.49
2009 LAD	NL	10	10	1	0	50.0	223	51	27	27	3	3	0	4	26	2	33	2	0	4	3	.571	1	0-0	0	4.67	4.86
2011 Col	NL	6	0	0	2	12.0	53	11	8	8	4	0	0	1	4	1	7	0	0	0	0	-	0	0-0	0	4.94	6.00
5 ML YEARS		41	24	2	4	157.0	695	167	91	86	22	8	1	7	67	7	105	4	0	8	10	.444	2	0-0	1	4.96	4.93

Michael Stutes

Pitches: R Bats: R Pos: RP-57
STOOTS
Ht: 6'1" Wt: 185 Born: 9/4/1986 Age: 25

Year Team	Lg	G	GS	CG	GF	IP	BFP	H	R	ER	HR	SH	SF	HB	TBB	IBB	SO	WP	Bk	W	L	Pct	Sh	Sv-Op	Hld	ERC	ERA
2008 Wmspt	A-	6	6	0	0	27.0	105	16	5	4	2	0	0	1	11	0	31	1	0	1	1	.667	0	0--	-	2.06	1.33
2008 Lakwd	A	7	7	0	0	42.2	164	20	8	7	1	0	0	1	18	0	53	4	1	5	1	.833	0	0--	-	1.39	1.48
2009 Rdng	AA	27	27	0	0	145.2	632	147	78	69	15	6	5	8	58	0	109	6	1	8	8	.500	0	0--	-	4.39	4.26
2010 Rdng	AA	25	0	0	12	35.2	159	28	15	15	2	1	1	7	21	0	37	2	1	3	0	1.000	0	2--	-	4.05	3.79
2010 LV	AAA	28	0	0	5	40.2	170	29	15	14	5	1	0	1	23	1	42	3	1	4	1	.800	0	1--	-	3.41	3.10
2011 LV	AAA	7	0	0	5	10.0	41	9	3	2	0	0	0	1	4	0	14	1	0	2	1	.667	0	1--	-	2.95	1.80
2011 Phi	NL	57	0	0	11	62.0	259	49	25	25	7	2	2	2	28	2	58	0	0	6	2	.750	0	0-0	13	3.31	3.63

Eric Surkamp

Pitches: L Bats: L Pos: SP-6
Ht: 6'4" Wt: 190 Born: 7/16/1987 Age: 24

Year Team	Lg	G	GS	CG	GF	IP	BFP	H	R	ER	HR	SH	SF	HB	TBB	IBB	SO	WP	Bk	W	L	Pct	Sh	Sv-Op	Hld	ERC	ERA
2008 Giants	R	2	0	0	0	3.1	13	3	1	1	0	0	0	0	0	0	7	0	0	0	0	-	0	0--	-	1.57	2.70
2008 SlmKzr	A-	5	4	0	0	14.0	66	20	10	10	1	3	0	1	5	0	16	0	0	0	2	.000	0	0--	-	6.57	6.43
2009 Augsta	A	23	23	2	0	131.0	551	129	57	48	6	2	4	4	39	0	169	9	0	11	5	.688	0	0--	-	3.36	3.30
2010 SnJos	A+	17	17	1	0	101.1	398	79	39	35	5	4	2	6	22	0	108	5	0	4	2	.667	1	0--	-	2.21	3.11
2011 Rchmd	AA	23	22	1	0	142.1	572	110	37	32	5	6	0	5	44	0	165	5	1	10	4	.714	0	0--	-	2.30	2.02
2011 SnJos	A+	1	1	0	0	6.0	22	4	0	0	0	0	0	0	1	0	5	0	0	1	0	1.000	0	0--	-	1.29	0.00
2011 SF	NL	6	6	0	0	26.2	126	32	18	17	1	2	2	2	17	1	13	0	0	2	2	.500	0	0-0	-	6.03	5.74

Drew Sutton

Bats: B Throws: R Pos: 3B-8; 2B-7; PR-7; PH-6; 1B-5; SS-4; LF-3; DH-1
Ht: 6'3" Wt: 200 Born: 6/30/1983 Age: 29

Year Team	Lg	G	AB	H	2B	3B	HR	(Hm	Rd)	TB	R	RBI	RC	TBB	IBB	SO	HBP	SH	SF	SB	CS	SB%	GDP	Avg	OBP	Slg
2011 Pwtckt*	AAA	45	166	49	13	1	5	(-	-)	79	24	27	30	21	0	38	3	1	1	0	2	.00	4	.295	.382	.476
2009 Cin	NL	42	66	14	4	1	1	(1	0)	23	10	9	12	7	0	20	1	2	0	0	2	.00	1	.212	.297	.348
2010 2 Tms	AL	13	39	10	1	0	2	(1	1)	17	5	8	7	3	0	13	0	0	0	0	0	-	1	.256	.310	.436
2011 Bos	AL	31	54	17	7	0	0	(0	0)	24	11	7	9	3	0	13	1	2	0	0	0	-	0	.315	.362	.444
10 Cin	NL	2	3	2	0	0	1	(1	0)	5	1	4	3	0	0	1	0	0	0	0	0	-	0	.667	.667	1.667
10 Cle	AL	11	36	8	1	0	1	(0	1)	12	4	4	4	3	0	12	0	0	0	0	0	-	1	.222	.282	.333
3 ML YEARS		86	159	41	12	1	3	(2	1)	64	26	24	28	13	0	46	2	4	0	0	2	.00	2	.258	.322	.403

Ichiro Suzuki

Bats: L Throws: R Pos: RF-151; DH-10

Ht: 5'11" Wt: 172 Born: 10/22/1973 Age: 38

Year	Team	Lg	G	AB	H	2B	3B	HR	(Hm	Rd)	TB	R	RBI	RC	TBB	IBB	SO	HBP	SH	SF	SB	CS	SB%	GDP	Avg	OBP	Slg
2001	Sea	AL	157	692	242	34	8	8	(5	3)	316	127	69	124	30	10	53	8	4	4	56	14	.80	3	.350	.381	.457
2002	Sea	AL	157	647	208	27	8	8	(4	4)	275	111	51	110	68	27	62	5	3	5	31	15	.67	8	.321	.388	.425
2003	Sea	AL	159	679	212	29	8	13	(8	5)	296	111	62	107	36	7	69	6	3	1	34	8	.81	3	.312	.352	.436
2004	Sea	AL	161	704	262	24	5	8	(4	4)	320	101	60	125	49	19	63	4	2	3	36	11	.77	6	.372	.414	.455
2005	Sea	AL	162	679	206	21	12	15	(8	7)	296	111	68	109	48	23	66	4	2	6	33	8	.80	5	.303	.350	.436
2006	Sea	AL	161	695	224	20	9	9	(6	3)	289	110	49	107	49	16	71	5	1	2	45	2	.96	2	.322	.370	.416
2007	Sea	AL	161	678	238	22	7	6	(3	3)	292	111	68	128	49	13	77	3	4	2	37	8	.82	7	.351	.396	.431
2008	Sea	AL	162	686	213	20	7	6	(3	3)	265	103	42	100	51	12	65	5	3	4	43	4	.91	8	.310	.361	.386
2009	Sea	AL	146	639	225	31	4	11	(6	5)	297	88	46	111	32	15	71	4	2	1	26	9	.74	1	.352	.386	.465
2010	Sea	AL	162	680	214	30	3	6	(1	5)	268	74	43	96	45	13	86	3	3	1	42	9	.82	3	.315	.359	.394
2011	Sea	AL	161	677	184	22	3	5	(4	1)	227	80	47	80	39	13	69	0	1	4	40	7	.85	11	.272	.310	.335
	Postseason		10	38	16	2	0	0	(0	0)	18	7	3	8	5	2	4	0	0	0	3	2	.60	0	.421	.488	.474
11 ML YEARS			1749	7456	2428	280	74	95	(52	43)	3141	1127	605	1197	496	168	752	47	28	33	423	95	.82	57	.326	.370	.421

Kurt Suzuki

Bats: R Throws: R Pos: C-129; DH-4; PR-3; PH-1

Ht: 5'11" Wt: 196 Born: 10/4/1983 Age: 28

Year	Team	Lg	G	AB	H	2B	3B	HR	(Hm	Rd)	TB	R	RBI	RC	TBB	IBB	SO	HBP	SH	SF	SB	CS	SB%	GDP	Avg	OBP	Slg
2007	Oak	AL	68	213	53	13	0	7	(4	3)	87	27	39	33	24	0	39	3	3	5	0	0	-	4	.249	.327	.408
2008	Oak	AL	148	530	148	25	1	7	(5	2)	196	54	42	66	44	2	69	11	2	1	2	3	.40	20	.279	.346	.370
2009	Oak	AL	147	570	156	37	1	15	(8	7)	240	74	88	77	28	0	59	8	1	7	8	2	.80	14	.274	.313	.421
2010	Oak	AL	131	495	120	18	2	13	(8	5)	181	55	71	54	33	3	49	12	0	4	3	2	.60	22	.242	.303	.366
2011	Oak	AL	134	460	109	26	0	14	(8	6)	177	54	44	42	38	1	64	7	3	7	2	2	.50	14	.237	.301	.385
5 ML YEARS			628	2268	586	119	4	56	(33	23)	881	264	284	272	167	6	280	41	9	24	15	9	.63	74	.258	.318	.388

Anthony Swarzak

Pitches: R Bats: R Pos: RP-16; SP-11

Ht: 6'4" Wt: 208 Born: 9/10/1985 Age: 26

	HOW MUCH HE PITCHED							WHAT HE GAVE UP											THE RESULTS						
Year	Team	Lg	G	GS	CG	GF	IP	BFP	H	R	ER	HR	SH	SF	HB	TBB	IBB	SO	WP	Bk	W	L	Pct	Sh	Sv-Op	Hld	ERC	ERA
2004	Twins	R	11	9	0	2	48.0	193	46	20	14	1	3	0	1	6	0	42	2	1	5	3	.625	0	1- -	-	2.41	2.63
2005	Beloit	A	18	18	0	0	91.1	386	81	48	41	7	4	2	7	32	0	101	3	1	9	5	.643	0	0- -	-	3.40	4.04
2005	FtMyrs	A+	10	10	0	0	59.0	257	72	25	24	3	3	2	1	11	0	55	1	1	3	4	.429	0	0- -	-	4.15	3.66
2006	FtMyrs	A+	27	27	2	0	145.2	613	131	56	53	8	5	5	1	60	0	131	4	3	11	7	.611	1	0- -	-	3.31	3.27
2007	NwBrit	AA	15	14	1	0	86.1	354	78	34	31	6	0	3	5	23	0	76	2	0	5	4	.556	0	0- -	-	3.11	3.23
2007	FtMyrs	A+	3	3	0	0	15.2	66	14	6	4	0	1	1	1	5	0	18	0	0	0	0	-	0	0- -	-	2.75	2.30
2008	NwBrit	AA	20	20	0	0	101.2	462	126	71	64	12	2	6	3	37	0	76	1	0	3	8	.273	0	0- -	-	5.56	5.67
2008	Roch	AAA	7	7	0	0	45.0	189	41	14	9	4	1	1	4	14	0	26	1	0	5	0	1.000	0	0- -	-	3.54	1.80
2009	Roch	AAA	13	13	0	0	79.2	330	79	31	29	4	1	2	3	21	1	45	2	0	4	5	.444	0	0- -	-	3.35	3.28
2010	Roch	AAA	22	22	0	0	111.2	513	143	87	77	14	6	6	5	38	1	69	2	0	5	12	.294	0	0- -	-	5.79	6.21
2011	Roch	AAA	6	6	1	0	32.1	139	35	14	14	3	1	0	0	7	0	25	0	0	2	1	.667	0	0- -	-	3.67	3.90
2009	Min	AL	12	12	0	0	59.0	268	76	43	41	12	1	1	2	20	0	34	0	0	3	7	.300	0	0-0	0	6.50	6.25
2011	Min	AL	27	11	0	2	102.0	441	111	53	49	9	2	3	6	26	1	55	3	1	4	7	.364	0	0-0	0	4.11	4.32
2 ML YEARS			39	23	0	2	161.0	709	187	96	90	21	3	4	8	46	1	89	3	1	7	14	.333	0	0-0	0	4.95	5.03

Ryan Sweeney

Bats: L Throws: L Pos: LF-41; CF-34; RF-23; PH-21; PR-7; DH-2

Ht: 6'4" Wt: 223 Born: 2/20/1985 Age: 27

Year	Team	Lg	G	AB	H	2B	3B	HR	(Hm	Rd)	TB	R	RBI	RC	TBB	IBB	SO	HBP	SH	SF	SB	CS	SB%	GDP	Avg	OBP	Slg
2006	CWS	AL	18	35	8	0	0	0	(0	0)	8	1	5	1	0	0	7	0	0	0	0	0	-	1	.229	.229	.229
2007	CWS	AL	15	45	9	3	0	1	(1	0)	15	5	5	2	4	0	5	0	0	0	0	1	.00	1	.200	.265	.333
2008	Oak	AL	115	384	110	18	2	5	(1	4)	147	53	45	56	38	3	67	3	2	6	9	1	.90	9	.286	.350	.383
2009	Oak	AL	134	484	142	31	3	6	(2	4)	197	68	53	63	40	1	67	3	2	5	6	5	.55	14	.293	.348	.407
2010	Oak	AL	82	303	89	20	2	1	(1	0)	116	41	36	38	24	2	41	0	1	3	1	1	.50	14	.294	.342	.383
2011	Oak	AL	108	264	70	11	3	1	(1	0)	90	34	25	35	33	3	48	0	1	1	1	1	.50	7	.265	.346	.341
6 ML YEARS			472	1515	428	83	10	14	(6	8)	573	202	169	195	139	9	235	6	6	15	17	9	.65	47	.283	.342	.378

Nick Swisher

Bats: B Throws: L Pos: RF-141; 1B-11; DH-5; PH-2

Ht: 5'11" Wt: 210 Born: 11/25/1980 Age: 31

Year	Team	Lg	G	AB	H	2B	3B	HR	(Hm	Rd)	TB	R	RBI	RC	TBB	IBB	SO	HBP	SH	SF	SB	CS	SB%	GDP	Avg	OBP	Slg
2004	Oak	AL	20	60	15	4	0	2	(1	1)	25	11	8	8	8	0	11	2	0	1	0	0	-	2	.250	.352	.417
2005	Oak	AL	131	462	109	32	1	21	(11	10)	206	66	74	62	55	3	110	4	0	1	0	1	.00	9	.236	.322	.446
2006	Oak	AL	157	556	141	24	2	35	(17	18)	274	106	95	95	97	7	152	11	2	6	1	2	.33	13	.254	.372	.493
2007	Oak	AL	150	539	141	36	1	22	(8	14)	245	84	78	89	100	12	131	10	1	9	3	2	.60	13	.262	.381	.455
2008	CWS	AL	153	497	109	21	1	24	(19	5)	204	86	69	69	82	6	135	4	1	4	3	3	.50	14	.219	.332	.410
2009	NYY	AL	150	498	124	35	1	29	(8	21)	248	84	82	84	97	2	126	3	3	6	0	0	-	13	.249	.371	.498
2010	NYY	AL	150	566	163	33	3	29	(15	14)	289	91	89	100	58	0	139	6	3	2	1	2	.33	13	.288	.359	.511
2011	NYY	AL	150	526	137	30	4	23	(11	12)	236	81	85	90	95	6	125	5	1	4	2	2	.50	18	.260	.374	.449
	Postseason		33	105	17	7	0	3	(2	1)	33	15	5	7	20	0	31	1	1	0	0	0	-	2	.162	.302	.314
8 ML YEARS			1061	3704	939	215	9	185	(91	94)	1727	609	580	597	592	36	929	45	11	37	10	12	.45	95	.254	.360	.466

Jose Tabata

Bats: R Throws: R Pos: LF-76; RF-15; CF-2; PH-2   TAH-bah-tah   Ht: 5'11" Wt: 219 Born: 8/12/1988 Age: 23

												BATTING												BASERUNNING				AVERAGES		
Year	Team	Lg	G	AB	H	2B	3B	HR	(Hm	Rd)	TB	R	RBI	RC	TBB	IBB	SO	HBP	SH	SF	SB	CS	SB%	GDP	Avg	OBP	Slg
2005	Yanks	R	44	156	49	5	1	3	(-	-)	65	30	25	27	15	1	14	2	0	0	22	6	.79	3	.314	.382	.417
2006	CtnSC	A	86	319	95	22	1	5	(-	-)	134	50	51	54	30	1	66	12	0	2	15	5	.75	10	.298	.377	.420
2007	Tampa	A+	103	411	126	16	2	5	(-	-)	161	56	54	63	33	4	70	10	1	1	15	7	.68	15	.307	.371	.392
2008	Trntn	AA	78	290	71	9	0	3	(-	-)	89	40	35	32	26	0	48	7	1	4	10	2	.83	15	.245	.318	.307
2008	Pirates	R	4	11	5	1	0	2	(-	-)	12	4	7	5	2	0	0	0	0	0	0	0	-	0	.455	.538	1.091
2008	Altna	AA	22	89	31	6	2	3	(-	-)	50	16	13	20	8	0	18	0	0	0	8	0	1.00	3	.348	.402	.562
2009	Altna	AA	61	228	69	15	1	2	(-	-)	92	31	25	35	20	2	25	5	0	1	7	6	.54	9	.303	.370	.404
2009	Indy	AAA	32	134	37	7	1	3	(-	-)	55	21	10	19	10	1	18	2	1	1	4	2	.67	2	.276	.333	.410
2010	Indy	AAA	53	224	69	13	2	3	(-	-)	95	42	19	39	23	1	35	2	0	3	25	6	.81	5	.308	.373	.424
2011	Bradtn	A+	4	8	1	1	0	0	(-	-)	2	1	1	1	3	0	3	0	0	0	0	0	-	0	.125	.364	.250
2011	Indy	AAA	9	33	11	6	0	0	(-	-)	17	6	2	6	5	0	4	0	0	0	0	2	.00	1	.333	.421	.515
2010	Pit	NL	102	405	121	21	4	4	(3	1)	162	61	35	59	28	0	57	2	5	1	19	7	.73	7	.299	.346	.400
2011	Pit	NL	91	334	89	18	1	4	(3	1)	121	53	21	41	40	1	61	4	1	3	16	7	.70	8	.266	.349	.362
	2 ML YEARS		193	739	210	39	5	8	(6	2)	283	114	56	100	68	1	118	6	6	4	35	14	.71	15	.284	.348	.383

Hisanori Takahashi

Pitches: L Bats: L Pos: RP-61   EES-ah-nore-ee   Ht: 5'10" Wt: 170 Born: 4/2/1975 Age: 37

			HOW MUCH HE PITCHED						WHAT HE GAVE UP										THE RESULTS						
Year	Team	Lg	G	GS	CG	GF	IP	BFP	H	R	ER	HR	SH	SF	HB	TBB	IBB	SO	WP	Bk	W	L	Pct	Sh	Sv-Op	Hld	ERC	ERA
2000	Yomiuri	Jap	24	23	3	0	135.2	563	133	59	48	10	-	-	3	36	-	102	1	0	9	6	.600	2	0- -		3.35	3.18
2001	Yomiuri	Jap	30	23	3	1	134.2	584	126	65	59	20	17	4	3	52	2	99	4	0	9	9	.500	1	0- -		3.98	3.94
2002	Yomiuri	Jap	24	23	2	0	163.1	669	143	58	56	16	-	-	6	39	-	145	4	1	10	4	.714	0	0- -		2.91	3.09
2003	Yomiuri	Jap	13	13	3	0	86.2	364	79	42	37	14	-	-	4	27	1	78	1	1	4	4	.500	0	0- -		3.81	3.84
2004	Yomiuri	Jap	16	16	3	0	91.0	402	107	59	55	18	6	2	3	26	0	61	3	0	5	10	.333	1	0- -		5.45	5.44
2005	Yomiuri	Jap	27	26	4	0	163.0	695	171	88	81	18	14	7	4	48	1	135	1	0	8	12	.400	2	0- -		4.11	4.47
2006	Yomiuri	Jap	35	4	0	0	62.0	266	70	36	34	10	5	0	1	15	2	51	1	0	2	6	.250	0	15- -		4.62	4.94
2007	Yomiuri	Jap	28	27	2	0	186.2	764	168	63	57	21	-	-	2	50	4	141	1	0	14	4	.778	2	0- -		3.13	2.75
2008	Yomiuri	Jap	23	22	0	0	122.0	518	127	63	56	16	7	5	5	30	0	94	2	0	8	5	.615	0	0- -		4.07	4.13
2009	Yomiuri	Jap	25	25	1	0	144.0	610	147	58	47	16	-	-	6	36	1	126	0	2	10	6	.625	0	0- -		3.82	2.94
2010	NYM	NL	53	12	0	21	122.0	516	116	51	49	13	10	3	0	43	7	114	1	1	10	6	.625	0	8-8	3	3.57	3.61
2011	LAA	AL	61	0	0	18	68.0	281	58	30	26	7	3	3	0	25	8	52	1	0	4	3	.571	0	2-5	7	3.01	3.44
	2 ML YEARS		114	12	0	39	190.0	797	174	81	75	20	13	6	0	68	15	166	2	1	14	9	.609	0	10-13	10	3.36	3.55

Mitch Talbot

Pitches: R Bats: R Pos: SP-12   Ht: 6'2" Wt: 200 Born: 10/17/1983 Age: 28

			HOW MUCH HE PITCHED						WHAT HE GAVE UP										THE RESULTS						
Year	Team	Lg	G	GS	CG	GF	IP	BFP	H	R	ER	HR	SH	SF	HB	TBB	IBB	SO	WP	Bk	W	L	Pct	Sh	Sv-Op	Hld	ERC	ERA
2011	Clmbs*	AAA	13	7	0	2	44.1	190	54	24	21	4	0	0	0	10	0	42	4	1	4	2	.667	0	0- -		4.62	4.26
2008	TB	AL	3	1	0	0	9.2	54	16	12	12	3	0	0	1	11	0	5	1	0	0	0	-	0	0-0	0	14.85	11.17
2010	Cle	AL	28	28	1	0	159.1	696	169	88	78	13	2	5	8	69	2	88	3	1	10	13	.435	0	0-0	0	4.68	4.41
2011	Cle	AL	12	12	0	0	63.2	299	90	47	47	10	1	5	3	28	2	36	1	0	2	6	.250	0	0-0	0	7.52	6.64
	3 ML YEARS		43	41	1	0	232.2	1049	275	147	137	26	3	10	12	108	4	129	5	1	12	19	.387	0	0-0	0	5.79	5.30

Brian Tallet

Pitches: L Bats: L Pos: RP-19   TAL-ett   Ht: 6'6" Wt: 220 Born: 9/21/1977 Age: 34

			HOW MUCH HE PITCHED						WHAT HE GAVE UP										THE RESULTS						
Year	Team	Lg	G	GS	CG	GF	IP	BFP	H	R	ER	HR	SH	SF	HB	TBB	IBB	SO	WP	Bk	W	L	Pct	Sh	Sv-Op	Hld	ERC	ERA
2011	QuadC*	A	1	1	0	0	2.0	6	0	0	0	0	0	0	0	0	0	5	0	0	0	0	-	0	0- -	-	0.00	0.00
2011	Dnedin*	A+	4	0	0	0	4.0	16	4	1	1	1	0	0	0	0	0	5	0	0	1	0	1.000	0	0- -	-	3.33	2.25
2002	Cle	AL	2	2	0	0	12.0	47	9	3	2	0	0	0	1	4	0	5	0	0	1	0	1.000	0	0-0	0	2.31	1.50
2003	Cle	AL	5	3	0	1	19.0	87	23	14	10	2	2	0	1	8	0	9	0	0	0	2	.000	0	0-0	0	5.65	4.74
2005	Cle	AL	2	0	0	0	4.2	24	6	4	4	2	0	0	1	3	0	2	0	0	0	0	-	0	0-0	0	10.55	7.71
2006	Tor	AL	44	1	0	8	54.1	229	45	24	23	5	1	5	3	31	4	37	2	1	3	0	1.000	0	0-3	1	3.97	3.81
2007	Tor	AL	48	0	0	11	62.1	267	49	26	24	1	2	3	6	28	7	54	1	0	2	4	.333	0	0-3	1	2.68	3.47
2008	Tor	AL	51	0	0	15	56.1	240	52	19	18	4	1	2	1	22	3	47	0	0	1	2	.333	0	0-0	4	3.39	2.88
2009	Tor	AL	37	25	0	3	160.2	717	169	99	95	20	1	7	6	72	2	120	2	0	7	9	.438	0	0-2	1	4.85	5.32
2010	Tor	AL	34	5	0	5	77.1	356	84	60	55	20	1	6	4	38	3	53	1	0	2	6	.250	0	0-1	1	6.22	6.40
2011	2 Tms		19	0	0	8	13.1	73	22	15	14	4	1	1	2	7	1	10	0	0	0	2	.000	0	0-1	2	10.57	9.45
11	StL	NL	18	0	0	7	13.0	68	20	13	12	4	1	1	2	5	1	9	0	0	0	2	.000	0	0-0	2	9.19	8.31
11	Tor	AL	1	0	0	1	0.1	5	2	2	2	0	0	0	0	2	0	1	0	0	0	0	1.000	0	0-1	0	71.88	54.00
	9 ML YEARS		242	36	0	51	460.0	2040	459	264	245	58	9	23	25	213	20	337	6	1	16	25	.390	0	0-6	13	4.63	4.79

Yoshinori Tateyama

Pitches: R Bats: R Pos: RP-39   YO-shin-nor-ee TAH-tay-yah-mah   Ht: 5'10" Wt: 165 Born: 12/26/1975 Age: 36

			HOW MUCH HE PITCHED						WHAT HE GAVE UP										THE RESULTS						
Year	Team	Lg	G	GS	CG	GF	IP	BFP	H	R	ER	HR	SH	SF	HB	TBB	IBB	SO	WP	Bk	W	L	Pct	Sh	Sv-Op	Hld	ERC	ERA
1999	HNHF	Jap	22	-	1	0	106.0	442	101	43	34	11	-	-	1	29	-	62	0	0	6	5	.545	1	0- -		3.38	2.89
2000	HNHF	Jap	28	-	2	0	89.1	396	106	57	55	15	-	-	2	29	-	55	1	0	6	8	.429	0	0- -		5.45	5.54
2001	HNHF	Jap	10	-	0	0	14.1	72	22	17	17	5	-	-	2	9	-	9	0	0	1	0	1.000	0	0- -		11.80	10.67
2002	HNHF	Jap	45	-	0	0	59.0	231	40	16	16	7	-	-	4	13	-	41	1	0	3	2	.600	0	4- -		2.12	2.29
2003	HNHF	Jap	32	-	0	0	37.1	138	24	9	9	5	-	-	4	5	-	32	0	0	2	1	.667	0	15- -		1.51	2.17
2004	HNHF	Jap	41	-	0	0	46.1	190	39	17	12	4	-	-	2	7	-	39	1	0	1	3	.250	0	0- -		2.30	2.33
2005	HNHF	Jap	45	-	0	0	51.1	211	50	22	21	6	-	-	3	8	-	35	1	0	4	6	.400	0	2- -		3.72	3.68
2006	HNHF	Jap	46	-	0	0	47.0	193	42	18	16	6	-	-	4	11	-	30	1	0	3	3	.500	0	0- -		3.10	3.06

265

Year	Team	Lg	G	GS	CG	GF	IP	BFP	H	R	ER	HR	SH	SF	HB	TBB	IBB	SO	WP	Bk	W	L	Pct	Sh	Sv-Op	Hld	ERC	ERA
2007	HNHF	Jap	7	-	1	-	41.0	167	33	20	19	7	-	-	5	9	-	31	0	0	2	4	.333	0	0- -	-	3.26	4.17
2008	HNHF	Jap	58	-	0	-	67.1	276	61	23	23	3	-	-	4	12	-	53	1	0	1	2	.333	0	2- -	-	2.59	3.07
2009	HNHF	Jap	46	-	0	-	47.2	209	53	24	20	3	-	-	1	15	-	43	1	0	5	7	.417	0	0- -	-	4.15	3.78
2010	HNHF	Jap	58	-	0	-	55.0	218	43	11	11	3	-	-	2	11	-	59	0	0	1	2	.333	0	4- -	-	2.07	1.80
2011	RdRck	AAA	14	0	0	6	21.0	86	17	5	5	1	0	0	3	4	0	26	2	0	1	0	1.000	0	1- -	-	2.47	2.14
2011	Tex	AL	39	0	0	8	44.0	181	37	23	22	8	0	0	2	11	4	43	1	0	2	0	1.000	0	1-1	4	3.16	4.50

Craig Tatum

Bats: R Throws: R Pos: C-30; 1B-1   Ht: 6'1" Wt: 230 Born: 3/18/1983 Age: 29

Year	Team	Lg	G	AB	H	2B	3B	HR	(Hm	Rd)	TB	R	RBI	RC	TBB	IBB	SO	HBP	SH	SF	SB	CS	SB%	GDP	Avg	OBP	Slg
2011	Norfolk*	AAA	21	65	13	3	0	0	(-	-)	16	4	7	5	9	0	13	0	1	2	0	1	.00	1	.200	.289	.246
2009	Cin	NL	26	68	11	1	0	1	(1	0)	15	3	6	4	7	1	10	1	1	0	1	0	-	0	.162	.250	.221
2010	Bal	AL	43	114	32	1	0	0	(0	0)	36	11	9	12	12	0	21	0	0	0	1	0	1.00	5	.281	.349	.316
2011	Bal	AL	31	87	17	3	0	0	(0	0)	20	7	7	3	6	0	21	0	2	1	1	0	1.00	7	.195	.245	.230
	3 ML YEARS		100	269	60	8	0	1	(1	0)	71	21	22	19	25	1	52	1	3	1	2	0	1.00	12	.223	.291	.264

Michael Taylor

Bats: R Throws: R Pos: RF-8; LF-3; PH-1; PR-1   Ht: 6'6" Wt: 250 Born: 12/19/1985 Age: 26

Year	Team	Lg	G	AB	H	2B	3B	HR	(Hm	Rd)	TB	R	RBI	RC	TBB	IBB	SO	HBP	SH	SF	SB	CS	SB%	GDP	Avg	OBP	Slg
2007	Wmspt	A-	66	233	53	14	0	6	(-	-)	85	30	33	27	23	0	53	2	1	2	8	2	.80	10	.227	.300	.365
2008	Lakwd	A	67	249	90	12	3	10	(-	-)	138	40	50	60	31	1	43	6	0	2	10	3	.77	5	.361	.441	.554
2008	Clrwtr	A+	65	243	80	27	1	9	(-	-)	136	36	38	49	19	3	46	2	0	2	5	6	.45	10	.329	.380	.560
2009	Rdng	AA	86	318	106	22	4	15	(-	-)	181	59	65	74	35	7	51	7	0	3	18	4	.82	14	.333	.408	.569
2009	LV	AAA	30	110	31	6	1	5	(-	-)	54	15	19	20	13	0	19	2	0	3	3	1	.75	3	.282	.359	.491
2010	Scrmto	AAA	127	464	126	26	6	6	(-	-)	182	79	78	68	51	1	92	5	0	3	16	5	.76	22	.272	.348	.392
2011	Scrmto	AAA	93	349	95	16	0	16	(-	-)	159	51	64	60	46	1	80	3	0	2	14	5	.74	8	.272	.360	.456
2011	Oak	AL	11	30	6	0	0	1	(1	0)	9	4	1	4	5	0	11	0	0	0	0	0	-	0	.200	.314	.300

Junichi Tazawa

Pitches: R Bats: R Pos: RP-3   joo-NEE-chee tuh-ZAH-wah   Ht: 5'11" Wt: 180 Born: 6/6/1986 Age: 26

Year	Team	Lg	G	GS	CG	GF	IP	BFP	H	R	ER	HR	SH	SF	HB	TBB	IBB	SO	WP	Bk	W	L	Pct	Sh	Sv-Op	Hld	ERC	ERA
2009	Portlnd	AA	18	18	0	0	98.0	394	80	31	28	8	2	3	3	26	0	88	4	2	9	5	.643	0	0- -	-	2.62	2.57
2009	Pwtckt	AAA	2	2	0	0	11.1	41	7	4	3	0	1	0	1	1	0	6	0	0	0	2	.000	0	0- -	-	1.17	2.38
2011	Salem	A+	6	6	0	0	19.1	84	20	13	13	4	3	0	3	6	0	13	0	0	0	1	.000	0	0- -	-	5.41	6.05
2011	Portlnd	AA	8	2	0	2	23.0	99	20	12	12	3	1	1	2	7	0	27	3	0	3	2	.600	0	0- -	-	3.42	4.70
2011	Pwtckt	AAA	8	0	0	1	14.1	58	14	4	4	1	2	0	0	3	0	19	0	0	1	1	.500	0	0- -	-	3.08	2.51
2009	Bos	AL	6	4	0	1	25.1	130	43	23	21	4	0	3	3	9	0	13	0	0	2	3	.400	0	0-0	-	9.14	7.46
2011	Bos	AL	3	0	0	2	3.0	13	3	2	2	1	0	0	0	1	0	4	0	0	0	0	-	0	0-0	1	5.31	6.00
	2 ML YEARS		9	4	0	3	28.1	143	46	25	23	5	0	3	3	10	0	17	0	0	2	3	.400	0	0-0	1	8.73	7.31

Everett Teaford

Pitches: L Bats: L Pos: RP-23; SP-3   Ht: 6'0" Wt: 165 Born: 5/15/1984 Age: 28

Year	Team	Lg	G	GS	CG	GF	IP	BFP	H	R	ER	HR	SH	SF	HB	TBB	IBB	SO	WP	Bk	W	L	Pct	Sh	Sv-Op	Hld	ERC	ERA
2006	Idaho	R+	15	12	0	1	63.0	262	54	29	26	3	1	0	4	20	0	51	5	2	5	1	.833	0	0- -	-	2.89	3.71
2007	Burlgtn	A	27	21	0	1	134.2	578	147	83	70	11	4	10	5	36	0	84	10	2	6	8	.429	0	0- -	-	4.09	4.68
2008	Wilmg	A+	28	23	0	2	144.1	605	135	70	61	15	5	2	3	46	1	116	7	2	8	6	.571	0	1- -	-	3.50	3.80
2009	Wilmg	A+	11	11	0	0	64.0	250	51	19	17	7	2	2	1	12	0	49	2	2	7	1	.875	0	0- -	-	2.37	2.39
2009	NWArk	AA	16	16	1	0	81.0	361	86	53	46	12	3	1	3	34	0	42	2	1	3	7	.300	0	0- -	-	4.97	5.11
2010	NWArk	AA	27	12	0	4	99.0	416	91	39	37	7	3	3	3	32	0	113	4	1	14	3	.824	0	0- -	-	3.25	3.36
2010	Omha	AAA	1	1	0	0	4.2	24	8	7	7	2	0	0	0	1	0	4	0	0	0	1	.000	0	0- -	-	10.29	13.50
2011	Omha	AAA	16	3	0	2	35.0	138	23	14	13	5	0	0	1	11	0	33	1	0	3	2	.600	0	0- -	-	2.35	3.34
2011	KC	AL	26	3	0	7	44.0	175	36	17	16	8	1	3	1	14	0	28	2	0	2	1	.667	0	1-1	1	3.50	3.27

Taylor Teagarden

Bats: R Throws: R Pos: C-14   Ht: 6'1" Wt: 200 Born: 12/21/1983 Age: 28

Year	Team	Lg	G	AB	H	2B	3B	HR	(Hm	Rd)	TB	R	RBI	RC	TBB	IBB	SO	HBP	SH	SF	SB	CS	SB%	GDP	Avg	OBP	Slg
2011	RdRck*	AAA	42	151	43	4	3	12	(-	-)	89	30	22	32	21	0	52	1	0	0	0	0	-	3	.285	.376	.589
2008	Tex	AL	16	47	15	5	0	6	(3	3)	38	10	17	15	5	0	19	1	0	0	0	0	-	0	.319	.396	.809
2009	Tex	AL	60	198	43	13	0	6	(2	4)	74	26	24	16	14	0	76	1	3	2	0	0	-	6	.217	.270	.374
2010	Tex	AL	28	71	11	1	0	4	(1	3)	24	10	6	5	8	0	34	2	4	0	0	0	-	0	.155	.259	.338
2011	Tex	AL	14	34	8	2	0	0	(0	0)	10	3	2	2	2	0	13	0	0	0	0	0	-	0	.235	.278	.294
	4 ML YEARS		118	350	77	21	0	16	(6	10)	146	49	49	38	29	0	142	4	7	2	0	0	-	6	.220	.286	.417

Mark Teahen

Bats: L **Throws:** R **Pos:** 3B-32; PH-27; 1B-18; RF-9; LF-6; DH-6; PR-5   TEE-en   **Ht:** 6'3" **Wt:** 230 **Born:** 9/6/1981 **Age:** 30

								BATTING											BASERUNNING				AVERAGES		
Year	Team	Lg	G	AB	H	2B	3B	HR	(Hm | Rd)	TB	R	RBI	RC	TBB	IBB	SO	HBP	SH	SF	SB	CS	SB%	GDP	Avg	OBP	Slg
2011	Charltt*	AAA	8	31	6	1	0	0	(- | -)	7	1	3	3	7	1	9	0	0	0	0	0	-	1	.194	.342	.226
2005	KC	AL	130	447	110	29	4	7	(3 | 4)	168	60	55	52	40	2	107	1	2	1	7	2	.78	13	.246	.309	.376
2006	KC	AL	109	393	114	21	7	18	(9 | 9)	203	70	69	79	40	2	85	2	2	2	10	0	1.00	5	.290	.357	.517
2007	KC	AL	144	544	155	31	8	7	(6 | 1)	223	78	60	82	55	8	127	3	4	2	13	5	.72	23	.285	.353	.410
2008	KC	AL	149	572	146	31	4	15	(4 | 11)	230	66	59	66	46	4	131	3	0	2	4	3	.57	6	.255	.313	.402
2009	KC	AL	144	524	142	34	1	12	(6 | 6)	214	69	50	60	37	4	123	6	2	2	8	1	.89	12	.271	.325	.408
2010	CWS	AL	77	233	60	13	2	4	(2 | 2)	89	31	25	23	25	0	61	0	2	2	3	5	.38	8	.258	.327	.382
2011	2 Tms	AL	78	160	32	4	0	4	(4 | 0)	48	14	14	11	16	1	45	0	1	0	1	0	1.00	3	.200	.273	.300
11	CWS	AL	51	118	24	3	0	3	(3 | 0)	36	11	11	9	12	1	28	0	0	0	1	0	1.00	3	.203	.277	.305
11	Tor	AL	27	42	8	1	0	1	(1 | 0)	12	3	3	2	4	0	17	0	1	0	0	0	-	0	.190	.261	.286
7 ML YEARS			831	2873	759	163	26	67	(34 | 33)	1175	388	332	373	259	21	679	15	13	11	45	17	.73	70	.264	.327	.409

Julio Teheran

Pitches: R **Bats:** R **Pos:** SP-3; RP-2   tay-RONN   **Ht:** 6'2" **Wt:** 175 **Born:** 1/27/1991 **Age:** 21

			HOW MUCH HE PITCHED					WHAT HE GAVE UP											THE RESULTS						
Year	Team	Lg	G	GS	CG	GF	IP	BFP	H	R	ER	HR	SH	SF	HB	TBB	IBB	SO	WP	Bk	W	L	Pct	Sh	Sv-Op Hld	ERC	ERA
2008	Danvle	R+	6	6	0	0	15.0	66	18	12	11	2	0	1	2	4	0	17	0	0	1	2	.333	0	0- - -	5.63	6.60
2009	Danvle	R+	7	7	0	0	43.2	173	36	17	13	2	2	0	7	7	0	39	1	0	2	1	.667	0	0- - -	2.59	2.68
2009	Rome	A	7	7	0	0	37.2	163	42	20	20	2	0	1	5	11	0	28	4	0	1	3	.250	0	0- - -	4.61	4.83
2010	Rome	A	7	7	0	0	39.1	154	23	8	5	1	1	1	5	10	0	45	1	0	2	2	.500	0	0- - -	1.55	1.14
2010	MrtlBh	A+	10	10	0	0	63.1	260	56	22	21	6	2	0	5	13	1	76	3	1	4	4	.500	0	0- - -	2.95	2.98
2010	Missi	AA	7	7	0	0	40.0	162	29	15	15	2	1	1	1	17	0	38	2	0	3	2	.600	0	0- - -	2.53	3.38
2011	Gwnntt	AAA	25	24	0	0	144.2	590	123	46	41	5	1	6	5	48	2	122	3	1	15	3	.833	0	0- - -	2.75	2.55
2011	Atl	NL	5	3	0	0	19.2	87	21	11	11	4	2	1	0	8	0	10	1	0	1	1	.500	0	0-0 0	5.19	5.03

Mark Teixeira

Bats: B **Throws:** R **Pos:** 1B-147; DH-9; PH-1   tuh-SHARE-uh   **Ht:** 6'3" **Wt:** 220 **Born:** 4/11/1980 **Age:** 32

								BATTING											BASERUNNING				AVERAGES		
Year	Team	Lg	G	AB	H	2B	3B	HR	(Hm	Rd)	TB	R	RBI	RC	TBB	IBB	SO	HBP	SH	SF	SB	CS	SB%	GDP	Avg	OBP	Slg
2003	Tex	AL	146	529	137	29	5	26	(19	7)	254	66	84	78	44	5	120	14	0	2	1	2	.33	14	.259	.331	.480
2004	Tex	AL	145	545	153	34	2	38	(18	20)	305	101	112	120	68	12	117	10	0	2	4	1	.80	6	.281	.370	.560
2005	Tex	AL	162	644	194	41	3	43	(30	13)	370	112	144	148	72	5	124	11	0	3	4	0	1.00	18	.301	.379	.575
2006	Tex	AL	162	628	177	45	1	33	(12	21)	323	99	110	114	89	12	128	4	0	6	2	0	1.00	17	.282	.371	.514
2007	2 Tms	AL	132	494	151	33	2	30	(14	16)	278	86	105	116	72	13	112	7	0	2	0	0	-	7	.306	.400	.563
2008	2 Tms		157	574	177	41	0	33	(19	14)	317	102	121	119	97	13	93	7	0	7	2	0	1.00	17	.308	.410	.552
2009	NYY	AL	156	609	178	43	3	39	(24	15)	344	103	122	112	81	9	114	12	0	5	2	0	1.00	13	.292	.383	.565
2010	NYY	AL	158	601	154	36	0	33	(19	14)	289	113	108	110	93	6	122	13	0	5	0	1	.00	15	.256	.365	.481
2011	NYY	AL	156	589	146	26	1	39	(22	17)	291	90	111	106	76	3	110	11	0	8	4	1	.80	12	.248	.341	.494
07	Tex	AL	78	286	85	24	1	13	(5	8)	150	48	49	58	45	10	66	3	0	1	0	0	-	5	.297	.397	.524
07	Atl	NL	54	208	66	9	1	17	(9	8)	128	38	56	58	27	3	46	4	0	1	0	0	-	2	.317	.404	.615
08	Atl	NL	103	381	108	27	0	20	(11	9)	195	63	78	69	65	9	70	3	0	2	0	0	-	13	.283	.390	.512
08	LAA	AL	54	193	69	14	0	13	(8	5)	122	39	43	50	32	4	23	4	0	5	2	0	1.00	4	.358	.449	.632
Postseason			26	103	22	3	0	3	(2	1)	34	17	12	9	14	1	26	3	0	2	0	0	-	2	.214	.320	.330
9 ML YEARS			1374	5213	1467	328	17	314	(177	137)	2771	872	1017	1023	692	78	1040	89	0	40	19	5	.79	119	.281	.373	.532

Miguel Tejada

Bats: R **Throws:** R **Pos:** 3B-44; SS-42; PH-7; 2B-4   **Ht:** 5'9" **Wt:** 218 **Born:** 5/25/1974 **Age:** 38

								BATTING											BASERUNNING				AVERAGES		
Year	Team	Lg	G	AB	H	2B	3B	HR	(Hm	Rd)	TB	R	RBI	RC	TBB	IBB	SO	HBP	SH	SF	SB	CS	SB%	GDP	Avg	OBP	Slg
1997	Oak	AL	26	99	20	3	2	2	(1	1)	33	10	10	7	2	0	22	3	0	0	2	0	1.00	3	.202	.240	.333
1998	Oak	AL	105	365	85	20	1	11	(5	6)	140	53	45	40	28	0	86	7	4	3	5	6	.45	8	.233	.298	.384
1999	Oak	AL	159	593	149	33	4	21	(12	9)	253	93	84	82	57	3	94	10	9	5	8	7	.53	11	.251	.325	.427
2000	Oak	AL	160	607	167	32	1	30	(16	14)	291	105	115	99	66	6	102	4	2	2	6	0	1.00	15	.275	.349	.479
2001	Oak	AL	162	622	166	31	3	31	(17	14)	296	107	113	94	43	5	89	13	1	4	11	5	.69	14	.267	.326	.476
2002	Oak	AL	162	662	204	30	0	34	(17	17)	336	108	131	123	38	3	84	11	0	4	7	2	.78	21	.308	.354	.508
2003	Oak	AL	162	636	177	42	0	27	(15	12)	300	98	106	103	53	7	65	6	0	8	10	0	1.00	12	.278	.336	.472
2004	Bal	AL	162	653	203	40	2	34	(17	17)	349	107	150	124	48	6	73	10	0	14	4	1	.80	24	.311	.360	.534
2005	Bal	AL	162	654	199	50	5	26	(16	10)	337	89	98	102	40	9	83	7	0	3	5	1	.83	26	.304	.349	.515
2006	Bal	AL	162	648	214	37	0	24	(17	7)	323	99	100	99	46	10	79	9	0	6	6	2	.75	28	.330	.379	.498
2007	Bal	AL	133	514	152	19	1	18	(12	6)	227	72	81	76	41	9	55	10	0	3	2	1	.67	22	.296	.357	.442
2008	Hou	NL	158	632	199	38	3	13	(5	8)	282	92	66	61	24	4	72	6	1	3	7	7	.50	32	.283	.314	.415
2009	Hou	NL	158	635	199	46	1	14	(10	4)	289	83	86	84	19	2	48	11	0	8	5	2	.71	29	.313	.340	.455
2010	2 Tms		156	636	171	26	0	15	(7	8)	242	71	71	73	30	3	67	11	1	3	2	0	1.00	16	.269	.312	.381
2011	SF	NL	91	322	77	16	0	4	(1	3)	105	28	26	24	12	5	35	3	2	4	4	4	.50	10	.239	.270	.326
10	Bal	AL	97	401	108	16	0	7	(5	2)	145	40	39	38	15	3	39	9	0	3	0	0	-	13	.269	.308	.362
10	SD	NL	59	235	63	10	0	8	(2	6)	97	31	32	35	15	0	28	2	1	0	2	0	1.00	3	.268	.317	.413
Postseason			20	85	18	7	0	1	(0	1)	28	9	8	6	3	0	16	1	0	2	1	0	1.00	4	.212	.242	.329
15 ML YEARS			2118	8278	2362	463	23	304	(171	133)	3783	1215	1282	1191	547	72	1054	121	20	70	84	38	.69	271	.285	.336	.457

Ruben Tejada

Bats: R **Throws:** R **Pos:** 2B-55; SS-41; PH-2; PR-1   **Ht:** 5'11" **Wt:** 187 **Born:** 10/27/1989 **Age:** 22

Year	Team	Lg	G	AB	H	2B	3B	HR	(Hm	Rd)	TB	R	RBI	RC	TBB	IBB	SO	HBP	SH	SF	SB	CS	SB%	GDP	Avg	OBP	Slg
2007	Mets	R	35	120	34	4	3	0	(-	-)	44	13	16	17	19	0	16	6	2	2	2	1	.67	4	.283	.401	.367
2008	StLuci	A+	131	497	114	19	4	2	(-	-)	147	55	37	45	41	0	77	5	8	4	8	5	.62	11	.229	.293	.296
2009	Bnghtn	AA	134	488	141	24	3	5	(-	-)	186	59	46	72	37	1	59	11	15	2	19	3	.86	11	.289	.351	.381
2010	Buffalo	AAA	65	218	61	11	0	1	(-	-)	75	25	16	25	14	2	36	3	7	2	1	3	.25	9	.280	.329	.344
2011	Buffalo	AAA	54	207	51	7	3	3	(-	-)	73	26	21	24	19	0	30	2	2	1	4	2	.67	5	.246	.314	.353
2010	NYM	NL	78	216	46	12	0	1	(0	1)	61	28	15	16	22	3	38	8	6	3	2	2	.50	2	.213	.305	.282
2011	NYM	NL	96	328	93	15	1	0	(0	0)	110	31	36	41	35	3	50	6	4	3	5	1	.83	6	.284	.360	.335
	2 ML YEARS		174	544	139	27	1	1	(0	1)	171	59	51	57	57	6	88	14	10	6	7	3	.70	8	.256	.338	.314

Robinson Tejeda

Pitches: R **Bats:** R **Pos:** RP-9   tuh-HAY-duh   **Ht:** 6'2" **Wt:** 243 **Born:** 3/24/1982 **Age:** 30

Year	Team	Lg	G	GS	CG	GF	IP	BFP	H	R	ER	HR	SH	SF	HB	TBB	IBB	SO	WP	Bk	W	L	Pct	Sh	Sv-Op Hld	ERC	ERA
2011	Omha*	AAA	31	0	0	8	45.0	192	40	23	19	8	2	5	4	15	0	43	0	1	0	3	.000	0	1- - -	4.04	3.80
2005	Phi	NL	26	13	0	5	85.2	371	67	36	34	5	3	2	8	51	4	72	3	1	4	3	.571	0	0-0 1	3.64	3.57
2006	Tex	AL	14	14	0	0	73.2	329	83	40	35	10	1	5	3	32	1	40	1	1	5	5	.500	0	0-0 0	5.41	4.28
2007	Tex	AL	19	19	0	0	95.1	454	110	78	70	17	3	6	6	60	2	69	10	0	5	9	.357	0	0-0 0	6.77	6.61
2008	2 Tms	AL	29	1	0	15	45.1	186	27	23	20	4	0	3	1	24	0	45	5	0	2	2	.500	0	0-1 1	2.43	3.97
2009	KC	AL	35	6	0	5	73.2	313	43	30	29	4	2	1	3	50	2	87	6	1	4	2	.667	0	0-0 2	2.68	3.54
2010	KC	AL	54	0	0	12	61.0	258	55	28	24	5	2	3	0	26	1	56	4	1	3	5	.375	0	0-6 12	3.50	3.54
2011	KC	AL	9	0	0	3	7.1	35	12	5	5	2	0	1	0	3	0	2	2	0	0	1	.000	0	0-0 2	9.94	6.14
	08 Tex	AL	4	0	0	1	6.0	29	5	6	6	1	0	1	0	5	0	4	0	0	0	0	-	0	0-1 0	5.04	9.00
	08 KC	AL	25	1	0	14	39.1	157	22	17	14	3	0	2	1	19	0	41	5	0	2	2	.500	0	0-0 1	2.08	3.20
	7 ML YEARS		186	53	0	40	442.0	1946	397	240	217	47	11	21	21	246	10	371	31	4	23	27	.460	0	0-7 18	4.32	4.42

Blake Tekotte

Bats: L **Throws:** R **Pos:** PH-9; CF-7; LF-3; RF-1; PR-1   tee-COAT-ee   **Ht:** 5'11" **Wt:** 175 **Born:** 5/24/1987 **Age:** 25

Year	Team	Lg	G	AB	H	2B	3B	HR	(Hm	Rd)	TB	R	RBI	RC	TBB	IBB	SO	HBP	SH	SF	SB	CS	SB%	GDP	Avg	OBP	Slg
2008	Eugene	A-	47	193	55	15	0	6	(-	-)	88	43	29	35	27	0	45	4	1	3	7	4	.64	0	.285	.379	.456
2009	FtWyn	A	134	530	137	24	5	13	(-	-)	210	83	56	79	68	3	97	4	4	4	30	12	.71	6	.258	.345	.396
2010	Lk Els	A+	59	203	63	17	1	8	(-	-)	106	41	27	46	36	0	46	2	0	0	22	8	.73	2	.310	.419	.522
2010	SnAnt	AA	67	268	67	8	7	10	(-	-)	119	44	37	37	26	2	63	4	2	1	6	9	.40	1	.250	.324	.444
2011	SnAnt	AA	106	414	118	27	2	19	(-	-)	206	77	67	86	67	0	108	8	7	2	36	12	.75	1	.285	.393	.498
2011	SD	NL	19	34	6	1	1	0	(0	0)	9	1	1	1	4	0	21	0	2	0	2	1	.67	0	.176	.263	.265

Kanekoa Texeira

Pitches: R **Bats:** R **Pos:** RP-6   kan-ih-KOE-ah tuh-SHARE-uh   **Ht:** 6'2" **Wt:** 190 **Born:** 2/6/1986 **Age:** 26

Year	Team	Lg	G	GS	CG	GF	IP	BFP	H	R	ER	HR	SH	SF	HB	TBB	IBB	SO	WP	Bk	W	L	Pct	Sh	Sv-Op Hld	ERC	ERA
2006	Bristol	R+	19	0	0	11	23.2	92	15	3	2	0	2	0	1	5	0	29	4	0	1	2	.333	0	3- - -	1.31	0.76
2006	Knapol	A	4	0	0	3	6.0	26	8	3	3	1	0	0	1	1	0	2	0	0	0	0	-	0	0- - -	6.65	4.50
2007	Knapol	A	39	0	0	32	53.2	231	49	24	22	0	1	1	2	22	1	58	4	0	5	2	.714	0	16- - -	3.02	3.69
2008	WinSa	A+	36	0	0	33	38.2	160	28	10	4	0	2	0	0	14	1	36	2	0	3	1	.750	0	20- - -	1.80	0.93
2008	Brham	AA	15	0	0	7	22.1	90	18	5	5	2	1	0	2	7	0	24	2	0	3	2	.600	0	1- - -	3.07	2.01
2009	Trntn	AA	41	6	0	9	101.1	432	90	39	32	7	5	1	2	43	2	88	7	0	9	6	.600	0	2- - -	3.37	2.84
2011	Omha	AAA	8	0	0	6	10.1	49	12	7	6	2	0	0	0	7	0	4	1	0	1	0	1.000	0	1- - -	6.94	5.23
2011	S-WB	AAA	5	0	0	3	4.1	33	16	13	11	1	1	0	0	3	0	4	0	0	0	1	.000	0	0- - -	25.74	22.85
2011	Yanks	R	3	2	0	0	5.0	20	3	2	0	1	0	0	0	1	0	3	0	0	0	0	-	0	0- - -	1.06	0.00
2011	Trntn	AA	11	0	0	5	11.0	60	24	18	13	2	0	3	0	3	0	7	1	0	0	1	.000	0	2- - -	11.73	10.64
2010	2 Tms	AL	43	0	0	10	61.1	277	73	36	33	3	3	6	3	25	1	33	3	1	1	1	.500	0	0-0 2	5.00	4.84
2011	KC	AL	6	0	0	2	6.1	35	13	2	2	0	0	0	0	3	1	0	1	0	0	0	-	0	0-0 1	9.60	2.84
	10 Sea	AL	16	0	0	7	18.2	87	22	12	11	0	0	1	1	10	0	14	2	0	0	1	.000	0	0-0 1	5.06	5.30
	10 KC	AL	27	0	0	3	42.2	190	51	24	22	3	3	5	2	15	1	19	1	1	1	0	1.000	0	0-0 1	4.97	4.64
	2 ML YEARS		49	0	0	12	67.2	312	86	38	35	3	3	7	3	28	2	33	4	1	1	1	.500	0	0-0 3	5.41	4.66

Eric Thames

Bats: L **Throws:** R **Pos:** LF-52; RF-27; DH-13; PH-3   THAIMS   **Ht:** 6'0" **Wt:** 205 **Born:** 11/10/1986 **Age:** 25

Year	Team	Lg	G	AB	H	2B	3B	HR	(Hm	Rd)	TB	R	RBI	RC	TBB	IBB	SO	HBP	SH	SF	SB	CS	SB%	GDP	Avg	OBP	Slg
2009	Dnedin	A+	52	195	61	15	5	3	(-	-)	95	33	38	37	21	1	40	3	0	1	1	1	.50	0	.313	.386	.487
2009	B Jays	R	7	21	6	3	0	0	(-	-)	9	4	1	3	3	0	5	0	0	1	0	0	-	0	.286	.360	.429
2010	NHam	AA	130	496	143	25	6	27	(-	-)	261	95	104	98	50	2	121	18	2	7	9	5	.64	10	.288	.370	.526
2011	LsVgs	AAA	53	210	74	25	4	7	(-	-)	128	38	45	52	23	5	41	5	0	3	5	2	.71	4	.352	.423	.610
2011	Tor	AL	95	362	95	24	5	12	(10	2)	165	58	37	42	23	0	88	5	1	3	2	1	.67	7	.262	.313	.456

Marcus Thames

Bats: R **Throws:** R **Pos:** PH-18; LF-17; DH-2   TIMMS   **Ht:** 6'2" **Wt:** 220 **Born:** 3/6/1977 **Age:** 35

							BATTING																	BASERUNNING				AVERAGES		
Year	Team	Lg	G	AB	H	2B	3B	HR	(Hm	Rd)	TB	R	RBI	RC	TBB	IBB	SO	HBP	SH	SF		SB	CS	SB%	GDP	Avg	OBP	Slg
2011	Albq*	AAA	6	17	3	1	0	2	(-	-)	10	3	4	2	2	0	4	0	0	0		0	0	-	0	.176	.263	.588
2002	NYY	AL	7	13	3	1	0	1	(1	0)	7	2	2	2	0	0	4	0	0	0		0	0	-	0	.231	.231	.538
2003	Tex	AL	30	73	15	2	0	1	(0	1)	20	12	4	5	8	0	18	2	0	1		0	1	.00	2	.205	.298	.274
2004	Det	AL	61	165	42	12	0	10	(5	5)	84	24	33	30	16	0	42	2	0	1		0	1	.00	3	.255	.326	.509
2005	Det	AL	38	107	21	2	0	7	(3	4)	44	11	16	10	9	1	38	1	0	1		0	0	-	1	.196	.263	.411
2006	Det	AL	110	348	89	20	2	26	(11	15)	191	61	60	60	37	0	92	4	0	1		1	1	.50	6	.256	.333	.549
2007	Det	AL	86	269	65	15	0	18	(14	4)	134	37	54	39	13	1	72	1	0	1		2	1	.67	6	.242	.278	.498
2008	Det	AL	103	316	76	12	0	25	(10	15)	163	50	56	44	24	0	95	0	0	2		0	3	.00	6	.241	.292	.516
2009	Det	AL	87	258	65	11	1	13	(6	7)	117	33	36	31	29	2	72	1	0	6		0	2	.00	5	.252	.323	.453
2010	NYY	AL	82	212	61	7	0	12	(4	8)	104	22	33	35	19	0	61	3	0	3		0	0	-	3	.288	.350	.491
2011	LAD	NL	36	66	13	1	1	2	(0	2)	22	4	7	2	4	0	16	0	0	0		0	0	-	4	.197	.243	.333
	Postseason		16	44	9	2	0	1	(1	0)	14	4	4	4	3	1	14	0	0	0		0	0	-	0	.205	.255	.318
	10 ML YEARS		640	1827	450	83	4	115	(54	61)	886	256	301	258	159	4	510	14	0	16		3	9	.25	30	.246	.309	.485

Joe Thatcher

Pitches: L **Bats:** L **Pos:** RP-18   **Ht:** 6'2" **Wt:** 229 **Born:** 10/4/1981 **Age:** 30

				HOW MUCH HE PITCHED						WHAT HE GAVE UP										THE RESULTS						
Year	Team	Lg	G	GS	CG	GF	IP	BFP	H	R	ER	HR	SH	SF	HB	TBB	IBB	SO	WP	Bk	W	L	Pct	Sh	Sv-Op	Hld	ERC	ERA
2011	Lk Els*	A+	1	0	0	0	1.0	3	0	0	0	0	0	0	0	0	0	2	0	0	0	0	-	0	0--	-	0.00	0.00
2011	Tucsn*	AAA	8	0	0	0	7.1	29	3	1	1	0	1	0	1	3	0	10	0	0	0	0	-	0	0--	-	1.24	1.23
2007	SD	NL	22	0	0	5	21.0	85	13	6	3	1	0	0	1	6	2	16	0	0	2	2	.500	0	0-0	2	1.49	1.29
2008	SD	NL	25	0	0	7	25.2	128	42	25	24	4	2	3	0	13	2	17	0	0	0	4	.000	0	0-3	5	8.91	8.42
2009	SD	NL	52	0	0	7	45.0	188	37	14	14	2	1	2	4	18	7	55	2	1	1	0	1.000	0	0-1	9	2.87	2.80
2010	SD	NL	65	0	0	12	35.0	137	23	5	5	1	3	2	1	7	2	45	0	0	1	0	1.000	0	0-0	11	1.37	1.29
2011	SD	NL	18	0	0	5	10.0	44	8	5	5	1	0	0	0	7	1	9	0	0	0	0	-	0	0-0	2	3.96	4.50
	5 ML YEARS		182	0	0	36	136.2	582	123	55	51	9	6	7	6	51	14	142	2	1	4	6	.400	0	0-4	29	3.18	3.36

Dale Thayer

Pitches: R **Bats:** R **Pos:** RP-11   **Ht:** 6'0" **Wt:** 195 **Born:** 12/17/1980 **Age:** 31

				HOW MUCH HE PITCHED						WHAT HE GAVE UP										THE RESULTS						
Year	Team	Lg	G	GS	CG	GF	IP	BFP	H	R	ER	HR	SH	SF	HB	TBB	IBB	SO	WP	Bk	W	L	Pct	Sh	Sv-Op	Hld	ERC	ERA
2011	Buffalo*	AAA	54	0	0	39	71.0	279	54	23	21	8	8	3	1	15	2	66	3	0	4	3	.571	0	21--	-	2.23	2.66
2009	TB	AL	11	0	0	3	13.2	59	18	9	7	3	0	0	0	1	0	8	1	0	0	0	-	0	1-1	0	5.38	4.61
2010	TB	AL	1	0	0	0	2.0	13	7	6	6	1	0	0	0	0	0	2	0	0	0	0	-	0	0-0	0	24.30	27.00
2011	NYM	NL	11	0	0	7	10.1	42	12	4	4	0	1	2	0	0	0	5	0	0	0	3	.000	0	0-0	1	2.78	3.48
	3 ML YEARS		23	0	0	10	26.0	114	37	19	17	4	1	2	0	1	0	15	1	0	0	3	.000	0	1-1	0	5.40	5.88

Ryan Theriot

Bats: R **Throws:** R **Pos:** SS-91; 2B-35; PH-15   TARE-ee-oh   **Ht:** 5'11" **Wt:** 180 **Born:** 12/7/1979 **Age:** 32

							BATTING																	BASERUNNING				AVERAGES		
Year	Team	Lg	G	AB	H	2B	3B	HR	(Hm	Rd)	TB	R	RBI	RC	TBB	IBB	SO	HBP	SH	SF		SB	CS	SB%	GDP	Avg	OBP	Slg
2005	ChC	NL	9	13	2	1	0	0	(0	0)	3	3	0	0	1	0	2	0	0	0		0	0	-	0	.154	.214	.231
2006	ChC	NL	53	134	44	11	3	3	(3	0)	70	34	16	31	17	0	18	2	6	0		13	2	.87	5	.328	.412	.522
2007	ChC	NL	148	537	143	30	2	3	(3	0)	186	80	45	64	49	1	50	0	8	3		28	4	.88	12	.266	.326	.346
2008	ChC	NL	149	580	178	19	4	1	(1	0)	208	85	38	78	73	1	58	3	4	1		22	13	.63	19	.307	.387	.359
2009	ChC	NL	154	602	171	20	5	7	(5	2)	222	81	54	79	51	1	93	6	13	5		21	10	.68	13	.284	.343	.369
2010	2 Tms	NL	150	586	158	15	2	2	(1	1)	183	72	29	58	41	3	74	4	7	2		20	9	.69	13	.270	.321	.312
2011	StL	NL	132	442	120	26	1	1	(0	1)	151	46	47	46	29	0	41	4	6	2		4	6	.40	15	.271	.321	.342
	10 ChC	NL	96	388	110	10	2	1	(0	1)	127	45	21	43	19	3	46	2	2	1		16	6	.73	8	.284	.320	.327
	10 LAD	NL	54	198	48	5	0	1	(1	0)	56	27	8	15	22	0	28	2	5	1		4	3	.57	5	.242	.323	.283
	Postseason		6	23	6	0	0	0	(0	0)	6	0	1	2	2	1	4	0	0	0		1	0	1.00	1	.261	.320	.261
	7 ML YEARS		795	2894	816	122	17	17	(13	4)	1023	401	229	356	261	6	336	19	44	13		108	44	.71	77	.282	.344	.353

Josh Thole

Bats: L **Throws:** R **Pos:** C-102; PH-17   TOE-lee   **Ht:** 6'1" **Wt:** 214 **Born:** 10/28/1986 **Age:** 25

							BATTING																	BASERUNNING				AVERAGES		
Year	Team	Lg	G	AB	H	2B	3B	HR	(Hm	Rd)	TB	R	RBI	RC	TBB	IBB	SO	HBP	SH	SF		SB	CS	SB%	GDP	Avg	OBP	Slg
2009	NYM	NL	17	53	17	2	1	0	(0	0)	21	2	9	9	4	0	5	0	0	2		1	0	1.00	1	.321	.356	.396
2010	NYM	NL	73	202	56	7	1	3	(2	1)	74	17	17	28	24	1	25	1	0	0		1	0	1.00	8	.277	.357	.366
2011	NYM	NL	114	340	91	17	0	3	(1	2)	117	22	40	39	38	6	47	4	1	3		0	2	.00	8	.268	.345	.344
	3 ML YEARS		204	595	164	26	2	6	(3	3)	212	41	66	76	66	7	77	5	1	5		2	2	.50	17	.276	.350	.356

Brad Thomas

Pitches: L **Bats:** L **Pos:** RP-12   **Ht:** 6'4" **Wt:** 234 **Born:** 10/12/1977 **Age:** 34

				HOW MUCH HE PITCHED						WHAT HE GAVE UP										THE RESULTS						
Year	Team	Lg	G	GS	CG	GF	IP	BFP	H	R	ER	HR	SH	SF	HB	TBB	IBB	SO	WP	Bk	W	L	Pct	Sh	Sv-Op	Hld	ERC	ERA
2011	Toledo*	AAA	8	0	0	2	10.1	48	10	4	4	1	1	0	2	6	1	12	1	0	0	1	.000	0	0--	-	5.17	3.48
2001	Min	AL	5	5	0	0	16.1	82	20	17	17	6	1	0	1	14	0	6	2	0	0	2	.000	0	0-0	0	10.12	9.37
2003	Min	AL	3	0	0	1	4.2	22	6	4	4	1	0	0	0	3	1	2	0	0	0	1	.000	0	0-0	0	7.54	7.71

Year	Team	Lg	G	GS	CG	GF	IP	BFP	H	R	ER	HR	SH	SF	HB	TBB	IBB	SO	WP	Bk	W	L	Pct	Sh	Sv-Op	Hld	ERC	ERA
2004	Min	AL	3	0	0	0	2.2	16	7	5	5	1	0	0	0	1	0	0	1	0	0	0	-	0	0-0	0	13.58	16.88
2010	Det	AL	49	2	0	7	69.1	307	77	31	30	4	4	6	4	29	3	30	4	0	6	2	.750	0	0-0	3	4.68	3.89
2011	Det	AL	12	0	0	5	11.0	56	17	12	11	1	0	5	1	6	0	7	0	0	0	1	.000	0	0-0	0	8.33	9.00
5 ML YEARS			72	7	0	13	104.0	483	127	69	67	12	6	11	6	53	4	45	7	0	6	6	.500	0	0-0	3	6.17	5.80

Jim Thome

Bats: L **Throws:** R **Pos:** DH-78; PH-15; 3B-1   TOE-mee   **Ht:** 6'3" **Wt:** 250 **Born:** 8/27/1970 **Age:** 41

							BATTING												BASERUNNING				AVERAGES		
Year	Team	Lg	G	AB	H	2B	3B	HR	(Hm | Rd)	TB	R	RBI	RC	TBB	IBB	SO	HBP	SH	SF	SB	CS	SB%	GDP	Avg	OBP	Slg
1991	Cle	AL	27	98	25	4	2	1	(0 | 1)	36	7	9	9	5	1	16	1	0	0	1	1	.50	4	.255	.298	.367
1992	Cle	AL	40	117	24	3	1	2	(1 | 1)	35	8	12	9	10	2	34	2	0	2	2	0	1.00	3	.205	.275	.299
1993	Cle	AL	47	154	41	11	0	7	(5 | 2)	73	28	22	30	29	1	36	4	0	5	2	1	.67	3	.266	.385	.474
1994	Cle	AL	98	321	86	20	1	20	(10 | 10)	168	58	52	56	46	5	84	0	1	1	3	3	.50	11	.268	.359	.523
1995	Cle	AL	137	452	142	29	3	25	(13 | 12)	252	92	73	109	97	3	113	5	0	3	4	3	.57	8	.314	.438	.558
1996	Cle	AL	151	505	157	28	5	38	(18 | 20)	309	122	116	132	123	8	141	6	0	2	2	2	.50	13	.311	.450	.612
1997	Cle	AL	147	496	142	25	0	40	(17 | 23)	287	104	102	120	120	9	146	3	0	8	1	1	.50	9	.286	.423	.579
1998	Cle	AL	123	440	129	34	2	30	(18 | 12)	257	89	85	104	89	8	141	4	0	4	1	0	1.00	7	.293	.413	.584
1999	Cle	AL	146	494	137	27	2	33	(19 | 14)	267	101	108	116	127	13	171	4	0	4	0	0	-	6	.277	.426	.540
2000	Cle	AL	158	557	150	33	1	37	(21 | 16)	296	106	106	119	118	4	171	4	0	5	1	0	1.00	8	.269	.398	.531
2001	Cle	AL	156	526	153	26	1	49	(30 | 19)	328	101	124	130	111	14	185	4	0	3	0	1	.00	9	.291	.416	.624
2002	Cle	AL	147	480	146	19	2	52	(30 | 22)	325	101	118	139	122	18	139	5	0	6	1	2	.33	5	.304	.445	.677
2003	Phi	NL	159	578	154	30	3	47	(28 | 19)	331	111	131	125	111	11	182	4	0	5	0	3	.00	5	.266	.385	.573
2004	Phi	NL	143	508	139	28	1	42	(19 | 23)	295	97	105	97	104	26	144	2	0	4	0	2	.00	10	.274	.396	.581
2005	Phi	NL	59	193	40	7	0	7	(6 | 1)	68	26	30	25	45	4	59	2	0	2	0	0	-	5	.207	.360	.352
2006	CWS	AL	143	490	141	26	0	42	(25 | 17)	293	108	109	120	107	12	147	6	0	7	0	0	-	4	.288	.416	.598
2007	CWS	AL	130	432	119	19	0	35	(19 | 16)	243	79	96	104	95	11	134	6	0	3	0	1	.00	10	.275	.410	.563
2008	CWS	AL	149	503	123	28	0	34	(19 | 15)	253	93	90	96	91	9	147	4	0	4	1	0	1.00	18	.245	.362	.503
2009	2 Tms		124	362	90	15	0	23	(14 | 9)	174	55	77	65	69	3	123	0	0	3	0	0	-	8	.249	.366	.481
2010	Min	AL	108	276	78	16	2	25	(15 | 10)	173	48	59	61	60	4	82	2	0	2	0	0	-	8	.283	.412	.627
2011	2 Tms		93	277	71	16	0	15	(8 | 7)	132	32	50	54	46	4	92	0	0	1	0	0	-	6	.256	.361	.477
09	CWS	AL	107	345	86	15	0	23	(14 | 9)	170	55	74	65	69	3	116	0	0	3	0	0	-	8	.249	.372	.493
09	LAD	NL	17	17	4	0	0	0	(0 | 0)	4	0	3	0	0	0	7	0	0	0	0	0	-	0	.235	.235	.235
11	Min	AL	71	206	50	12	0	12	(6 | 6)	98	21	40	40	35	3	69	0	0	1	0	0	-	5	.243	.351	.476
11	Cle	AL	22	71	21	4	0	3	(2 | 1)	34	11	10	14	11	1	23	0	0	0	0	0	-	1	.296	.390	.479
Postseason			67	217	47	2	1	17	(13 | 4)	102	35	37	31	29	1	68	4	1	0	0	0	-	3	.217	.320	.470
21 ML YEARS			2485	8259	2287	444	26	604	(337 | 267)	4595	1566	1674	1820	1725	170	2487	68	1	74	19	20	.49	160	.277	.403	.556

Aaron Thompson

Pitches: L **Bats:** L **Pos:** RP-3; SP-1   **Ht:** 6'2" **Wt:** 196 **Born:** 2/28/1987 **Age:** 25

			HOW MUCH HE PITCHED						WHAT HE GAVE UP												THE RESULTS						
Year	Team	Lg	G	GS	CG	GF	IP	BFP	H	R	ER	HR	SH	SF	HB	TBB	IBB	SO	WP	Bk	W	L	Pct	Sh	Sv-Op	Hld	ERC	ERA
2005	Mrlns	R	8	8	0	0	32.0	145	42	20	16	1	1	1	0	10	0	41	4	0	2	4	.333	0	0- -		4.98	4.50
2005	Jmstwn	A-	5	5	0	0	20.1	95	25	13	7	1	1	0	1	10	0	17	0	0	1	2	.333	0	0- -		5.57	3.10
2006	Grnsbr	A	24	24	0	0	134.0	564	139	68	54	12	5	5	5	35	0	114	3	2	8	8	.500	0	0- -		3.85	3.63
2007	Jupiter	A+	20	19	0	0	115.0	502	121	64	43	2	4	4	4	35	1	84	9	0	4	6	.400	0	0- -		3.46	3.37
2008	Carlina	AA	16	16	0	0	81.2	381	111	61	51	9	3	1	2	40	0	53	4	2	2	5	.286	0	0- -		6.94	5.62
2008	Mrlns	R	2	2	0	0	9.0	35	8	2	2	0	0	1	0	1	0	9	0	0	0	0	-	0	0- -		1.88	2.00
2009	Jaxnvl	AA	20	20	0	0	114.0	504	121	63	52	7	4	4	2	43	0	75	5	2	5	9	.357	0	0- -		4.05	4.11
2009	Hrsbrg	AA	6	6	0	0	32.2	138	32	18	12	3	0	1	0	11	0	27	2	0	0	3	.000	0	0- -		3.67	3.31
2010	Hrsbrg	AA	26	26	0	0	136.2	616	164	96	88	16	3	7	5	53	0	95	5	2	4	13	.235	0	0- -		5.49	5.80
2010	Syrcse	AAA	1	1	0	0	5.0	23	5	1	1	0	0	0	0	3	0	4	0	0	1	0	1.000	0	0- -		3.99	1.80
2011	Altna	AA	28	12	0	4	83.2	363	100	55	48	6	10	4	2	20	1	51	9	3	4	7	.364	0	0- -		4.43	5.16
2011	Indy	AAA	5	4	0	0	19.0	88	23	6	6	0	0	1	0	9	0	10	0	0	1	0	1.000	0	0- -		4.73	2.84
2011	Pit	NL	4	1	0	0	7.2	41	13	6	6	2	0	1	0	6	0	1	0	0	0	0	-	0	0-0	0	11.83	7.04

Daryl Thompson

Pitches: R **Bats:** R **Pos:** RP-1   **Ht:** 6'0" **Wt:** 205 **Born:** 11/2/1985 **Age:** 26

			HOW MUCH HE PITCHED						WHAT HE GAVE UP												THE RESULTS						
Year	Team	Lg	G	GS	CG	GF	IP	BFP	H	R	ER	HR	SH	SF	HB	TBB	IBB	SO	WP	Bk	W	L	Pct	Sh	Sv-Op	Hld	ERC	ERA
2003	Expos	R	12	10	0	1	46.0	185	49	16	11	2	2	0	2	11	0	18	2	0	1	2	.333	0	0- -		3.67	2.15
2004	Savann	A	25	21	0	1	102.2	442	117	66	58	13	4	4	9	30	0	79	4	2	4	9	.308	0	0- -		5.14	5.08
2005	Savann	A	11	11	0	0	53.2	225	46	23	20	3	0	2	1	24	0	48	3	1	2	3	.400	0	0- -		3.29	3.35
2006	Vrmnt	A-	4	4	0	0	6.2	31	5	5	5	0	0	0	0	5	0	8	1	0	0	1	.000	0	0- -		3.72	6.75
2006	Reds	R	5	4	0	0	14.0	52	10	4	4	1	0	1	2	4	0	16	0	0	0	0	-	0	0- -		2.80	2.57
2007	Dayton	A	5	5	0	0	28.0	99	16	3	3	1	0	0	0	2	0	24	0	0	5	0	1.000	0	0- -		0.94	0.96
2007	Srsota	A+	22	22	0	0	105.0	446	106	51	44	19	3	2	5	31	0	97	1	3	9	5	.643	0	0- -		4.49	3.77
2008	Chatt	AA	10	10	0	0	61.1	233	43	19	12	2	4	3	0	14	0	56	5	0	3	2	.600	0	0- -		1.64	1.76
2008	Lsvlle	AAA	7	7	0	0	45.2	181	39	15	14	4	2	0	2	9	0	33	1	0	5	0	1.000	0	0- -		2.68	2.76
2008	Reds	R	1	0	0	0	4.0	15	2	1	0	0	0	0	0	3	0	3	0	0	0	0	-	0	0- -		0.00	0.00
2008	Srsota	A+	3	3	0	0	15.2	70	20	12	12	2	3	1	0	7	0	7	0	0	0	2	.000	0	0- -		6.34	6.89
2009	Lsvlle	AAA	8	6	0	0	28.2	129	34	22	21	3	3	1	0	7	1	8	2	0	1	2	.333	0	0- -		4.30	6.59
2009	Reds	R	1	1	0	0	0.2	6	2	3	2	0	0	0	0	2	0	1	1	0	0	0	-	0	0- -		29.63	27.00
2010	Carlina	AA	12	12	0	0	51.0	195	38	25	21	3	0	3	1	11	0	52	2	0	0	5	.000	0	0- -		2.00	3.71
2010	Reds	R	3	3	0	0	11.0	44	10	3	3	1	0	0	0	2	0	17	2	1	1	0	1.000	0	0- -		2.73	2.45
2011	Carlina	AA	9	9	0	0	46.2	200	47	28	23	7	2	2	1	17	0	41	2	0	1	4	.200	0	0- -		4.43	4.44

Year Team	Lg	G	GS	CG	GF	IP	BFP	H	R	ER	HR	SH	SF	HB	TBB	IBB	SO	WP	Bk	W	L	Pct	Sh	Sv-Op	Hld	ERC	ERA
2011 Lsvlle	AAA	17	15	0	1	90.2	392	103	48	42	11	4	3	2	23	0	82	1	1	3	4	.429	0	1--	-	4.49	4.17
2008 Cin	NL	3	3	0	0	14.1	69	20	11	11	3	0	0	1	7	0	6	1	1	0	2	.000	0	0-0	0	8.14	6.91
2011 Cin	NL	1	0	0	0	3.0	20	6	5	5	0	0	1	0	5	0	0	0	0	0	1	.000	0	0-0	0	15.12	15.00
2 ML YEARS		4	3	0	0	17.1	89	26	16	16	3	0	1	1	12	0	6	1	1	0	3	.000	0	0-0	0	9.37	8.31

Rich Thompson

Pitches: R Bats: R Pos: RP-44

Ht: 6'1" Wt: 205 Born: 7/1/1984 Age: 27

Year Team	Lg	G	GS	CG	GF	IP	BFP	H	R	ER	HR	SH	SF	HB	TBB	IBB	SO	WP	Bk	W	L	Pct	Sh	Sv-Op	Hld	ERC	ERA
2007 LAA	AL	7	0	0	2	6.2	32	10	8	8	4	0	0	0	3	0	9	2	0	0	0	-	0	0-0	0	11.85	10.80
2008 LAA	AL	2	0	0	1	2.0	12	4	5	5	0	0	0	0	2	0	1	1	0	0	0	-	0	0-0	0	12.01	22.50
2009 LAA	AL	13	0	0	2	19.1	92	27	11	11	6	1	1	1	7	0	21	5	0	0	0	-	0	0-0	0	8.17	5.12
2010 LAA	AL	13	0	0	7	19.2	75	12	4	3	2	1	0	0	4	0	15	4	0	2	0	1.000	0	0-0	1	1.50	1.37
2011 LAA	AL	44	0	0	16	54.0	228	46	18	18	5	1	2	0	20	0	56	1	1	1	3	.250	0	0-1	3	3.05	3.00
5 ML YEARS		79	0	0	28	101.2	439	99	46	45	17	3	3	1	36	0	102	13	1	3	3	.500	0	0-1	4	4.18	3.98

Matt Thornton

Pitches: L Bats: L Pos: RP-62

Ht: 6'6" Wt: 235 Born: 9/15/1976 Age: 35

Year Team	Lg	G	GS	CG	GF	IP	BFP	H	R	ER	HR	SH	SF	HB	TBB	IBB	SO	WP	Bk	W	L	Pct	Sh	Sv-Op	Hld	ERC	ERA
2004 Sea	AL	19	1	0	8	32.2	148	30	15	15	2	2	1	0	25	1	30	2	0	1	2	.333	0	0-0	0	4.75	4.13
2005 Sea	AL	55	0	0	15	57.0	262	54	33	33	13	1	1	0	42	2	57	7	0	0	4	.000	0	0-1	5	6.06	5.21
2006 CWS	AL	63	0	0	20	54.0	227	46	20	20	5	1	3	1	21	4	49	1	0	5	3	.625	0	2-5	18	3.12	3.33
2007 CWS	AL	68	0	0	13	56.1	249	59	31	30	4	0	2	2	26	6	55	3	0	4	4	.500	0	2-7	17	4.35	4.79
2008 CWS	AL	74	0	0	12	67.1	268	48	20	20	5	1	1	2	19	2	77	3	0	5	3	.625	0	1-6	20	2.07	2.67
2009 CWS	AL	70	0	0	17	72.1	291	58	22	22	5	2	1	1	20	2	87	4	0	6	3	.667	0	4-9	24	2.40	2.74
2010 CWS	AL	61	0	0	13	60.2	239	41	18	18	3	0	2	2	20	5	81	1	0	5	4	.556	0	8-10	21	1.89	2.67
2011 CWS	AL	62	0	0	20	59.2	262	60	34	22	3	3	3	0	21	5	63	2	0	2	5	.286	0	3-7	20	3.32	3.32
Postseason		3	0	0	1	3.1	14	2	0	0	0	0	0	0	2	1	2	0	0	0	0	-	0	0-0	1	1.62	0.00
8 ML YEARS		472	1	0	118	460.0	1946	396	193	180	40	10	14	8	194	27	499	23	0	28	28	.500	0	20-45	125	3.28	3.52

Joe Thurston

Bats: L Throws: R Pos: 2B-1

Ht: 5'11" Wt: 210 Born: 9/29/1979 Age: 32

Year Team	Lg	G	AB	H	2B	3B	HR	(Hm	Rd)	TB	R	RBI	RC	TBB	IBB	SO	HBP	SH	SF	SB	CS	SB%	GDP	Avg	OBP	Slg
2011 NewOr*	AAA	126	453	136	34	3	13	(-	-)	215	68	59	86	48	2	78	17	8	0	12	4	.75	7	.300	.388	.475
2002 LAD	NL	8	13	6	1	0	0	(0	0)	7	1	1	3	0	0	1	0	1	1	0	0	-	0	.462	.429	.538
2003 LAD	NL	12	10	2	0	0	0	(0	0)	2	2	0	0	1	0	1	0	0	0	0	0	-	0	.200	.273	.200
2004 LAD	NL	17	17	3	1	1	0	(0	0)	6	1	1	1	0	0	5	0	0	1	0	0	-	0	.176	.167	.353
2006 Phi	NL	18	18	4	1	0	0	(0	0)	5	3	0	1	1	0	2	1	0	0	0	0	-	0	.222	.300	.278
2008 Bos	AL	4	8	0	0	0	0	(0	0)	0	0	0	0	0	0	1	1	0	0	0	0	-	0	.000	.111	.000
2009 StL	NL	124	267	60	17	4	1	(0	1)	88	27	25	29	33	5	56	3	3	1	4	2	.67	9	.225	.316	.330
2011 Fla	NL	1	4	1	0	0	0	(0	0)	1	0	0	0	0	0	1	0	0	0	1	0	1.00	0	.250	.250	.250
Postseason		1	1	0	0	0	0	(0	0)	0	0	0	0	0	0	1	0	0	0	0	0	-	0	.000	.000	.000
7 ML YEARS		184	337	76	20	5	1	(0	1)	109	34	27	34	35	5	67	5	4	3	5	2	.71	9	.226	.305	.323

Chris Tillman

Pitches: R Bats: R Pos: SP-13

Ht: 6'6" Wt: 210 Born: 4/15/1988 Age: 24

Year Team	Lg	G	GS	CG	GF	IP	BFP	H	R	ER	HR	SH	SF	HB	TBB	IBB	SO	WP	Bk	W	L	Pct	Sh	Sv-Op	Hld	ERC	ERA
2011 Norfolk*	AAA	15	15	0	0	76.1	339	77	50	44	17	1	0	2	38	0	54	4	0	3	6	.333	0	0--	-	5.54	5.19
2009 Bal	AL	12	12	0	0	65.0	285	77	40	39	15	0	0	2	24	1	39	4	0	2	5	.286	0	0-0	0	6.28	5.40
2010 Bal	AL	11	11	0	0	53.2	236	51	37	35	9	1	3	1	31	1	31	2	0	2	5	.286	0	0-0	0	5.12	5.87
2011 Bal	AL	13	13	0	0	62.0	287	77	41	38	5	1	1	4	25	0	46	1	1	3	5	.375	0	0-0	0	5.58	5.52
3 ML YEARS		36	36	0	0	180.2	808	205	118	112	29	2	4	7	80	2	116	7	1	7	15	.318	0	0-0	0	5.69	5.58

Mason Tobin

Pitches: R Bats: R Pos: RP-4

TOE-bin

Ht: 6'3" Wt: 210 Born: 7/8/1987 Age: 24

Year Team	Lg	G	GS	CG	GF	IP	BFP	H	R	ER	HR	SH	SF	HB	TBB	IBB	SO	WP	Bk	W	L	Pct	Sh	Sv-Op	Hld	ERC	ERA
2007 Angels	R	8	7	0	0	28.1	105	17	5	3	1	0	0	0	7	0	32	2	0	2	0	1.000	0	0--	-	1.38	0.95
2007 Orem	R+	6	6	0	0	28.0	112	23	10	10	0	2	0	3	7	0	23	1	0	2	1	.667	0	0--	-	2.40	3.21
2008 CRpds	A	8	8	1	0	37.1	154	29	13	13	2	1	2	4	18	0	18	1	0	2	3	.400	0	0--	-	3.40	3.13
2009 RCuca	A+	3	0	0	0	2.2	14	2	4	0	0	0	0	0	2	0	2	0	0	0	0	-	0	1--	-	2.67	0.00
2011 Tex	AL	4	0	0	1	5.1	24	5	5	4	1	0	0	1	5	0	0	0	0	0	0	-	0	0-0	0	8.25	6.75

Matt Tolbert

Bats: B **Throws:** R **Pos:** 2B-36; SS-31; PH-11; PR-8; 3B-6; DH-3   **Ht:** 6'0" **Wt:** 185 **Born:** 5/4/1982 **Age:** 30

Year	Team	Lg	G	AB	H	2B	3B	HR	(Hm	Rd)	TB	R	RBI	RC	TBB	IBB	SO	HBP	SH	SF	SB	CS	SB%	GDP	Avg	OBP	Slg
2011	Roch*	AAA	17	59	8	1	1	0	(-	-)	11	7	3	2	10	0	11	0	2	2	5	3	.63	2	.136	.254	.186
2008	Min	AL	41	113	32	6	3	0	(0	0)	44	18	6	13	7	0	19	0	2	1	7	1	.88	5	.283	.322	.389
2009	Min	AL	71	198	46	7	1	2	(0	2)	61	28	19	22	21	1	37	0	10	2	6	2	.75	1	.232	.303	.308
2010	Min	AL	48	87	20	4	3	1	(1	0)	33	8	18	12	9	0	18	0	1	3	1	1	.50	2	.230	.293	.379
2011	Min	AL	87	207	41	10	2	0	(0	0)	55	22	11	16	11	0	31	4	4	0	3	2	.60	2	.198	.252	.266
	Postseason		3	5	1	0	0	0	(0	0)	1	0	0	0	0	0	1	1	0	0	0	0	-	0	.200	.333	.200
4 ML YEARS			247	605	139	27	9	3	(1	2)	193	76	54	63	48	1	105	4	17	6	17	6	.74	10	.230	.288	.319

Brett Tomko

Pitches: R **Bats:** R **Pos:** RP-8   **Ht:** 6'4" **Wt:** 220 **Born:** 4/7/1973 **Age:** 39

Year	Team	Lg	G	GS	CG	GF	IP	BFP	H	R	ER	HR	SH	SF	HB	TBB	IBB	SO	WP	Bk	W	L	Pct	Sh	Sv-Op	Hld	ERC	ERA
2011	RdRck*	AAA	21	18	0	0	108.1	505	130	81	74	21	7	3	13	42	0	82	7	0	9	6	.600	0	0- -		6.36	6.15
1997	Cin	NL	22	19	0	1	126.0	519	106	50	48	14	5	9	4	47	4	95	5	0	11	7	.611	0	0-0	0	3.31	3.43
1998	Cin	NL	34	34	1	0	210.2	887	198	111	104	22	12	2	7	64	3	162	9	1	13	12	.520	0	0-0	0	3.50	4.44
1999	Cin	NL	33	26	1	1	172.0	744	175	103	94	31	9	5	4	60	10	132	8	0	5	7	.417	0	0-0	1	4.51	4.92
2000	Sea	AL	32	8	0	10	92.1	401	92	53	48	12	5	5	3	40	4	59	1	1	7	5	.583	0	1-2	3	4.49	4.68
2001	Sea	AL	11	4	0	1	34.2	164	42	24	20	9	1	2	0	15	2	22	1	0	3	1	.750	0	0-1	0	6.31	5.19
2002	SD	NL	32	32	3	0	204.1	871	212	107	102	31	6	8	2	60	9	126	3	0	10	10	.500	0	0-0	0	4.18	4.49
2003	StL	NL	33	32	2	0	202.2	903	252	126	119	35	12	3	5	57	2	114	6	0	13	9	.591	0	0-0	0	5.63	5.28
2004	SF	NL	32	31	2	1	194.0	825	196	98	87	19	7	1	0	64	3	108	10	0	11	7	.611	1	0-0	0	3.82	4.04
2005	SF	NL	33	30	3	1	190.2	823	205	99	95	26	6	5	7	57	11	114	5	0	8	15	.348	0	1-1	1	4.18	4.48
2006	LAD	NL	44	15	0	2	112.1	491	123	67	59	17	7	7	2	29	0	76	3	1	8	7	.533	0	0-3	5	4.37	4.73
2007	2 Tms	NL	40	19	0	9	131.1	588	149	89	81	18	8	6	2	48	1	105	5	0	4	12	.250	0	0-0	0	4.96	5.55
2008	2 Tms		22	10	0	3	70.0	307	83	51	49	11	1	2	0	18	2	49	4	0	2	7	.222	0	0-2	0	4.88	6.30
2009	2 Tms	AL	21	6	1	7	57.1	227	50	24	24	12	1	0	1	13	0	33	2	0	5	3	.625	1	0-0	0	3.56	3.77
2011	Tex	AL	8	0	0	3	17.2	74	15	9	9	4	2	1	0	10	1	14	1	0	0	1	.000	0	0-1	0	4.87	4.58
07	LAD	NL	33	15	0	8	104.0	475	124	75	67	13	5	6	2	42	1	79	3	0	2	11	.154	0	0-0	0	5.39	5.80
07	SD	NL	7	4	0	1	27.1	113	25	14	14	5	3	0	0	6	0	26	2	0	2	1	.667	0	0-0	0	3.37	4.61
08	KC	AL	16	10	0	1	60.2	271	80	49	47	11	1	2	0	13	0	40	4	0	2	7	.222	0	0-2	0	5.73	6.97
08	SD	NL	6	0	0	2	9.1	36	3	2	2	0	0	0	0	5	2	9	0	0	0	0	-	0	0-0	0	0.81	1.93
09	NYY	AL	15	0	0	7	20.2	85	19	12	12	5	1	0	0	7	0	11	1	0	1	2	.333	0	0-0	0	4.42	5.23
09	Oak	AL	6	6	1	0	36.2	142	31	12	12	7	0	0	1	6	0	22	1	0	4	1	.800	1	0-0	0	3.10	2.95
	Postseason		5	0	0	0	8.2	40	8	8	5	0	1	1	0	7	1	4	2	1	0	0	-	0	0-0	0	4.23	5.19
14 ML YEARS			397	266	13	39	1816.0	7824	1898	1011	939	255	82	56	37	582	52	1209	63	3	100	103	.493	2	2-10	10	4.32	4.65

Josh Tomlin

Pitches: R **Bats:** R **Pos:** SP-26   **Ht:** 6'1" **Wt:** 190 **Born:** 10/19/1984 **Age:** 27

Year	Team	Lg	G	GS	CG	GF	IP	BFP	H	R	ER	HR	SH	SF	HB	TBB	IBB	SO	WP	Bk	W	L	Pct	Sh	Sv-Op	Hld	ERC	ERA
2006	MhVlly	A-	15	15	0	0	77.1	307	56	24	18	5	0	3	4	15	0	69	3	0	8	2	.800	0	0- -		1.87	2.09
2007	Lk Cty	A	26	15	0	4	103.2	434	103	44	38	10	2	1	7	19	0	89	5	0	10	3	.769	0	0- -		3.41	3.30
2007	Knstn	A+	6	5	0	0	27.2	119	24	13	11	0	0	3	0	12	0	20	2	0	1	1	.500	0	0- -		2.74	3.58
2008	Knstn	A+	40	9	1	10	102.2	399	82	40	34	10	2	4	7	16	0	109	9	0	9	5	.643	1	3- -		2.41	2.98
2008	Buffalo	AAA	1	1	0	0	7.0	25	6	3	3	2	0	0	0	1	0	3	0	0	1	0	1.000	0	0- -		3.81	3.86
2009	Akron	AA	26	25	0	0	145.0	601	149	81	67	21	4	3	7	27	1	125	3	0	14	9	.609	0	0- -		3.90	4.16
2010	Clmbs	AAA	20	17	1	0	107.1	429	83	34	32	11	1	2	2	33	0	80	4	0	8	4	.667	0	0- -		2.65	2.68
2010	Cle	AL	12	12	1	0	73.0	301	72	38	37	10	3	3	3	19	3	43	1	0	6	4	.600	0	0-0	0	3.89	4.56
2011	Cle	AL	26	26	0	0	165.1	662	157	80	78	24	1	3	3	21	2	89	3	0	12	7	.632	0	0-0	0	3.11	4.25
2 ML YEARS			38	38	1	0	238.1	963	229	118	115	34	4	6	6	40	5	132	4	0	18	11	.621	0	0-0	0	3.34	4.34

Wyatt Toregas

Bats: R **Throws:** R **Pos:** C-2; PH-1   tore-AY-gus   **Ht:** 5'11" **Wt:** 210 **Born:** 12/2/1982 **Age:** 29

Year	Team	Lg	G	AB	H	2B	3B	HR	(Hm	Rd)	TB	R	RBI	RC	TBB	IBB	SO	HBP	SH	SF	SB	CS	SB%	GDP	Avg	OBP	Slg
2004	MhVlly	A-	59	214	63	18	1	7	(-	-)	104	38	48	36	11	1	26	5	1	4	1	0	1.00	4	.294	.338	.486
2005	Lk Cty	A	104	411	95	22	0	5	(-	-)	132	57	42	42	37	1	76	6	2	3	0	1	.00	15	.231	.302	.321
2006	Knstn	A+	44	146	49	14	0	4	(-	-)	75	25	23	31	20	0	28	2	1	2	0	0	-	4	.336	.418	.514
2006	Akron	AA	48	163	42	10	0	4	(-	-)	64	21	29	20	14	0	33	2	2	3	1	3	.25	1	.258	.319	.393
2007	Akron	AA	86	284	71	16	0	6	(-	-)	105	36	39	36	27	1	45	4	2	7	3	1	.75	6	.250	.317	.370
2008	Buffalo	AAA	50	155	34	8	0	2	(-	-)	48	15	25	16	15	0	32	3	5	0	2	0	1.00	1	.219	.301	.310
2008	Akron	AA	47	162	48	9	0	12	(-	-)	93	22	35	34	17	2	20	4	0	3	0	1	.00	2	.296	.371	.574
2009	Clmbs	AAA	60	208	59	10	0	7	(-	-)	90	22	29	31	16	0	43	2	0	3	0	1	.00	7	.284	.336	.433
2010	Akron	AA	17	59	12	3	0	1	(-	-)	18	3	6	5	6	0	8	1	0	2	0	0	-	1	.203	.279	.305
2010	MhVlly	A-	7	19	7	1	0	2	(-	-)	14	9	2	7	8	1	3	0	0	2	0	0	-	2	.368	.556	.737
2010	Clmbs	AAA	15	50	10	1	0	2	(-	-)	17	3	6	3	1	0	9	1	0	1	0	0	-	3	.200	.226	.340
2011	Indy	AAA	22	60	8	3	0	0	(-	-)	11	6	8	1	4	0	15	1	2	0	0	0	-	3	.133	.200	.183
2009	Cle	AL	19	51	9	1	0	0	(0	0)	10	1	6	4	6	0	12	1	0	2	0	0	-	1	.176	.267	.196
2011	Pit	NL	3	4	0	0	0	0	(0	0)	0	0	0	0	0	0	1	0	0	0	0	0	-	0	.000	.000	.000
2 ML YEARS			22	55	9	1	0	0	(0	0)	10	1	6	4	6	0	13	1	0	2	0	0	-	2	.164	.250	.182

Yorvit Torrealba

Bats: R Throws: R Pos: C-98; DH-13; PH-5   yorr-VEET   Ht: 5'11" Wt: 200 Born: 7/19/1978 Age: 33

Year	Team	Lg	G	AB	H	2B	3B	HR	(Hm	Rd)	TB	R	RBI	RC	TBB	IBB	SO	HBP	SH	SF	SB	CS	SB%	GDP	Avg	OBP	Slg
2001	SF	NL	3	4	2	0	1	0	(0	0)	4	0	2	2	0	0	0	0	0	0	0	0	-	0	.500	.500	1.000
2002	SF	NL	53	136	38	10	0	2	(0	2)	54	17	14	16	14	2	20	2	3	0	0	0	-	11	.279	.355	.397
2003	SF	NL	66	200	52	10	2	4	(3	1)	78	22	29	25	14	1	39	2	3	2	1	0	1.00	3	.260	.312	.390
2004	SF	NL	64	172	39	7	3	6	(3	3)	70	19	23	18	17	3	31	2	4	1	2	0	1.00	7	.227	.302	.407
2005	2 Tms		76	201	47	12	0	3	(2	1)	68	32	15	14	16	1	50	2	5	0	1	0	1.00	8	.234	.297	.338
2006	Col	NL	65	223	55	16	3	7	(3	4)	98	23	43	30	11	1	49	4	2	1	4	3	.57	7	.247	.293	.439
2007	Col	NL	113	396	101	22	1	8	(6	2)	149	47	47	34	34	1	73	6	6	1	2	1	.67	19	.255	.323	.376
2008	Col	NL	70	236	58	17	0	6	(5	1)	93	19	31	23	12	0	44	5	5	3	0	4	.00	10	.246	.293	.394
2009	Col	NL	64	213	62	11	1	2	(1	1)	81	27	31	37	21	5	42	1	3	4	1	1	.50	4	.291	.351	.380
2010	SD	NL	95	325	88	14	0	7	(4	3)	123	31	37	41	33	2	67	3	1	1	7	5	.58	12	.271	.343	.378
2011	Tex	AL	113	396	108	27	1	7	(7	0)	158	40	37	41	20	0	65	0	1	2	0	2	.00	11	.273	.306	.399
05	SF	NL	34	93	21	8	0	1	(1	0)	32	18	7	7	9	1	25	1	2	0	1	0	1.00	3	.226	.301	.344
05	Sea		42	108	26	4	0	2	(1	1)	36	14	8	7	7	0	25	1	3	0	0	0	-	5	.241	.293	.333
	Postseason		17	56	15	4	0	2	(1	1)	25	6	13	9	4	1	11	0	3	1	0	0	-	2	.268	.311	.446
	11 ML YEARS		782	2502	650	146	12	52	(34	18)	976	277	309	281	192	16	480	27	33	15	18	16	.53	92	.260	.318	.390

Alex Torres

Pitches: L Bats: L Pos: RP-4   Ht: 5'10" Wt: 175 Born: 12/8/1987 Age: 24

Year	Team	Lg	G	GS	CG	GF	IP	BFP	H	R	ER	HR	SH	SF	HB	TBB	IBB	SO	WP	Bk	W	L	Pct	Sh	Sv-Op Hld	ERC	ERA
2006	Angels	R	14	9	0	1	50.1	219	42	28	24	1	1	1	2	36	0	47	6	0	2	5	.286	0	1- -	4.05	4.29
2007	Angels	R	4	0	0	0	5.2	31	4	6	3	0	1	0	1	8	0	3	7	2	1	0	1.000	0	0- -	5.77	4.76
2008	Angels	R	4	4	0	0	23.1	83	11	4	4	1	0	0	1	10	0	24	2	0	4	0	1.000	0	0- -	1.60	1.54
2008	RCuca	A+	10	10	0	0	53.0	233	52	26	23	1	1	3	3	29	0	62	8	1	3	2	.600	0	0- -	4.24	3.91
2009	RCuca	A+	21	19	0	1	121.1	506	93	43	37	4	6	2	6	63	0	124	9	1	10	3	.769	0	0- -	3.06	2.74
2009	Ark	AA	5	5	0	0	26.0	113	23	10	8	0	0	1	1	17	0	25	1	0	3	1	.750	0	0- -	3.93	2.77
2010	Mont	AA	2	2	0	0	8.2	38	7	6	3	1	1	0	0	5	0	7	1	0	0	2	.000	0	0- -	3.72	3.12
2010	Mont	AA	27	27	0	0	142.2	612	136	63	55	9	5	1	4	70	2	150	12	1	11	6	.647	0	0- -	4.08	3.47
2011	Drham	AAA	27	27	1	0	146.1	636	134	61	50	7	4	5	6	83	0	156	10	3	9	7	.563	0	0- -	4.11	3.08
2011	TB	AL	4	0	0	2	8.0	39	8	4	3	0	0	0	1	7	2	9	0	0	1	1	.500	0	0-0	5.11	3.38

Andres Torres

Bats: B Throws: R Pos: CF-106; PH-9; PR-7; RF-4; LF-1   Ht: 5'9" Wt: 191 Born: 1/26/1978 Age: 34

Year	Team	Lg	G	AB	H	2B	3B	HR	(Hm	Rd)	TB	R	RBI	RC	TBB	IBB	SO	HBP	SH	SF	SB	CS	SB%	GDP	Avg	OBP	Slg
2011	Fresno*	AAA	13	55	15	2	2	4	(-	-)	33	10	11	11	6	0	13	1	0	0	1	0	1.00	1	.273	.355	.600
2002	Det	AL	19	70	14	1	1	0	(0	0)	17	7	3	2	6	0	16	1	0	2	2	2	.50	2	.200	.266	.243
2003	Det	AL	59	168	37	4	3	1	(1	0)	50	23	9	9	10	0	35	0	6	1	5	5	.50	5	.220	.263	.298
2004	Det	AL	3	0	0	0	0	0	(0	0)	0	1	0	0	0	0	0	0	0	0	1	0	1.00	0	-	-	-
2005	Tex	AL	8	19	3	1	0	0	(0	0)	4	2	1	1	1	0	6	0	0	1	1	0	1.00	0	.158	.190	.211
2009	SF	NL	75	152	41	6	8	6	(4	2)	81	30	23	31	16	0	45	1	1	0	6	1	.86	0	.270	.343	.533
2010	SF	NL	139	507	136	43	8	16	(7	9)	243	84	63	87	56	2	128	2	5	0	26	7	.79	10	.268	.343	.479
2011	SF	NL	112	348	77	24	1	4	(1	3)	115	50	19	38	42	0	95	4	4	0	19	6	.76	3	.221	.312	.330
	Postseason		15	58	16	4	0	1	(0	1)	23	6	3	6	3	0	18	1	1	0	2	3	.40	1	.276	.323	.397
	7 ML YEARS		415	1264	308	79	21	27	(13	14)	510	197	118	168	131	2	325	8	16	4	60	21	.74	20	.244	.318	.403

Rene Tosoni

Bats: L Throws: R Pos: LF-38; PH-11; DH-9; RF-4; PR-3   ruh-NAY tuh-SO-nee   Ht: 6'0" Wt: 194 Born: 7/2/1986 Age: 25

Year	Team	Lg	G	AB	H	2B	3B	HR	(Hm	Rd)	TB	R	RBI	RC	TBB	IBB	SO	HBP	SH	SF	SB	CS	SB%	GDP	Avg	OBP	Slg
2007	Elizab	R+	63	236	71	13	4	3	(-	-)	101	58	31	46	32	0	48	13	1	4	13	4	.76	6	.301	.407	.428
2007	Beloit	A	2	11	3	1	0	0	(-	-)	4	1	1	1	0	0	2	0	0	0	0	0	-	0	.273	.273	.364
2008	FtMyrs	A+	42	140	42	7	3	1	(-	-)	58	27	19	24	21	1	30	6	1	2	3	5	.38	3	.300	.408	.414
2008	Twins	R	2	6	4	0	0	1	(-	-)	7	3	3	3	0	0	1	0	0	0	0	0	-	0	.667	.667	1.167
2009	NwBrit	AA	122	425	115	25	4	15	(-	-)	193	64	71	71	45	1	98	16	1	3	8	8	.50	8	.271	.360	.454
2010	NwBrit	AA	52	185	50	8	4	4	(-	-)	78	22	24	31	25	0	52	5	2	2	3	1	.75	1	.270	.369	.422
2011	Roch	AAA	73	275	62	14	0	6	(-	-)	94	30	32	28	20	1	68	2	2	1	4	0	1.00	6	.225	.282	.342
2011	Min	AL	60	172	35	7	1	5	(3	2)	59	20	22	20	14	0	42	3	0	0	0	2	.00	2	.203	.275	.343

J.R. Towles

Bats: R Throws: R Pos: C-51; PH-4; PR-1   TOLLS   Ht: 6'2" Wt: 192 Born: 2/11/1984 Age: 28

Year	Team	Lg	G	AB	H	2B	3B	HR	(Hm	Rd)	TB	R	RBI	RC	TBB	IBB	SO	HBP	SH	SF	SB	CS	SB%	GDP	Avg	OBP	Slg
2011	OKCity*	AAA	35	105	29	4	0	3	(-	-)	42	19	11	21	18	0	11	11	1	1	3	0	1.00	6	.276	.430	.400
2007	Hou	NL	14	40	15	5	0	1	(0	1)	23	9	12	11	3	1	1	1	0	0	0	1	.00	1	.375	.432	.575
2008	Hou	NL	54	146	20	5	0	4	(3	1)	37	10	16	10	16	1	40	6	3	0	0	0	-	3	.137	.250	.253
2009	Hou	NL	16	48	9	2	0	2	(0	2)	17	7	3	7	3	1	16	1	1	0	0	0	-	1	.188	.250	.354
2010	Hou	NL	17	47	9	3	0	1	(0	1)	15	3	8	6	2	0	12	1	0	1	0	0	-	2	.191	.235	.319
2011	Hou	NL	54	147	27	7	0	3	(1	2)	43	11	11	5	13	1	26	2	1	2	0	0	-	3	.184	.256	.293
	5 ML YEARS		155	428	80	22	0	11	(4	7)	135	40	50	34	37	4	95	11	5	3	0	1	.00	10	.187	.267	.315

Matt Treanor

Bats: R **Throws:** R **Pos:** C-72; PH-1 | TRAY-ner | **Ht:** 6'0" **Wt:** 205 **Born:** 3/3/1976 **Age:** 36

								BATTING												BASERUNNING				AVERAGES		
Year	Team	Lg	G	AB	H	2B	3B	HR	(Hm | Rd)	TB	R	RBI	RC	TBB	IBB	SO	HBP	SH	SF	SB	CS	SB%	GDP	Avg	OBP	Slg
2011	NWArk*	AA	7	19	5	1	0	0	(- | -)	6	2	5	3	4	0	2	3	0	0	0	1	.00	2	.263	.462	.316
2004	Fla	NL	29	55	13	2	0	0	(0 | 0)	15	7	1	4	4	0	13	2	0	0	0	0	-	3	.236	.311	.273
2005	Fla	NL	58	134	27	8	0	0	(0 | 0)	35	10	13	13	16	1	28	3	1	0	0	0	-	5	.201	.301	.261
2006	Fla	NL	67	157	36	6	1	2	(0 | 2)	50	12	14	16	19	4	34	5	2	2	0	1	.00	4	.229	.328	.318
2007	Fla	NL	55	171	46	7	1	4	(2 | 2)	67	16	19	26	19	1	29	5	2	1	0	0	-	2	.269	.357	.392
2008	Fla	NL	65	206	49	7	0	2	(1 | 1)	62	18	23	25	18	1	53	3	5	2	1	0	1.00	2	.238	.306	.301
2009	Det	AL	4	13	0	0	0	0	(0 | 0)	0	0	0	0	1	0	4	0	0	0	0	0	-	3	.000	.071	.000
2010	Tex	AL	82	237	50	6	1	5	(4 | 1)	73	22	27	19	22	0	43	5	4	4	1	2	.33	4	.211	.287	.308
2011	2 Tms	AL	72	196	42	6	0	3	(2 | 1)	57	24	22	25	34	0	53	4	5	3	2	2	.50	3	.214	.338	.291
11	KC	AL	65	186	42	6	0	3	(2 | 1)	57	24	21	25	33	0	49	4	5	2	2	2	.50	3	.226	.351	.306
11	Tex	AL	7	10	0	0	0	0	(0 | 0)	0	0	1	0	1	0	4	0	0	1	0	0	-	0	.000	.083	.000
	Postseason		4	10	2	0	0	1	(0 | 1)	5	3	2	2	2	0	2	2	0	0	0	0	-	0	.200	.429	.500
	8 ML YEARS		432	1169	263	42	3	16	(9 | 7)	359	109	119	128	133	7	257	27	19	12	4	5	.44	26	.225	.315	.307

Ramon Troncoso

Pitches: R **Bats:** R **Pos:** RP-18 | tronn-KOE-soe | **Ht:** 6'1" **Wt:** 209 **Born:** 2/16/1983 **Age:** 29

			HOW MUCH HE PITCHED						WHAT HE GAVE UP											THE RESULTS						
Year	Team	Lg	G	GS	CG	GF	IP	BFP	H	R	ER	HR	SH	SF	HB	TBB	IBB	SO	WP	Bk	W	L	Pct	Sh	Sv-Op Hld	ERC	ERA
2011	Albq*	AAA	35	0	0	3	57.0	245	59	36	32	8	5	0	1	26	0	41	2	0	2	4	.333	0	0- --	5.01	5.05
2008	LAD	NL	32	0	0	12	38.0	160	37	19	18	2	4	3	3	12	1	38	2	0	1	1	.500	0	0-0 2	3.60	4.26
2009	LAD	NL	73	0	0	20	82.2	357	83	30	25	3	7	3	3	34	9	55	4	0	5	4	.556	0	6-7 14	3.67	2.72
2010	LAD	NL	52	0	0	13	54.0	234	55	28	26	7	1	2	3	18	5	34	2	0	2	3	.400	0	0-1 8	4.18	4.33
2011	LAD	NL	18	0	0	13	22.2	103	38	18	17	5	1	0	0	4	1	14	2	0	0	0	-	0	0-0 0	8.56	6.75
	Postseason		3	0	0	3	3.0	12	0	0	0	0	1	0	1	3	0	3	0	0	0	0	-	0	0-0 0	1.68	0.00
	4 ML YEARS		175	0	0	58	197.1	854	213	95	86	17	13	8	9	68	16	141	10	0	8	8	.500	0	6-8 24	4.30	3.92

Mike Trout

Bats: R **Throws:** R **Pos:** CF-13; RF-13; LF-10; PH-4; PR-2 | | **Ht:** 6'1" **Wt:** 200 **Born:** 8/7/1991 **Age:** 20

								BATTING												BASERUNNING				AVERAGES		
Year	Team	Lg	G	AB	H	2B	3B	HR	(Hm	Rd)	TB	R	RBI	RC	TBB	IBB	SO	HBP	SH	SF	SB	CS	SB%	GDP	Avg	OBP	Slg
2009	Angels	R	39	164	59	7	7	1	(-	-)	83	29	25	36	18	0	28	0	3	2	13	2	.87	2	.360	.418	.506
2009	CRpds	A	5	15	4	0	0	0	(-	-)	4	1	0	2	4	0	6	0	1	0	0	0	-	0	.267	.421	.267
2010	CRpds	A	81	312	113	19	7	6	(-	-)	164	76	39	79	46	2	52	7	2	1	45	9	.83	1	.362	.454	.526
2010	RCuca	A+	50	196	60	9	2	4	(-	-)	85	30	19	33	27	1	33	1	5	3	11	6	.65	2	.306	.388	.434
2011	Ark	AA	91	353	115	18	13	11	(-	-)	192	82	38	81	45	1	76	9	4	1	33	10	.77	2	.326	.414	.544
2011	LAA	AL	40	123	27	6	0	5	(1	4)	48	20	16	14	9	0	30	2	0	1	4	0	1.00	2	.220	.281	.390

Mark Trumbo

Bats: R **Throws:** R **Pos:** 1B-149; RF-10; PR-2; LF-1; PH-1 | | **Ht:** 6'4" **Wt:** 220 **Born:** 1/16/1986 **Age:** 26

								BATTING												BASERUNNING				AVERAGES		
Year	Team	Lg	G	AB	H	2B	3B	HR	(Hm	Rd)	TB	R	RBI	RC	TBB	IBB	SO	HBP	SH	SF	SB	CS	SB%	GDP	Avg	OBP	Slg
2005	Orem	R+	71	299	82	23	1	10	(-	-)	137	45	45	44	21	4	67	1	0	2	2	2	.50	2	.274	.322	.458
2006	CRpds	A	118	428	94	19	0	13	(-	-)	152	43	59	46	44	1	99	3	0	7	5	5	.50	8	.220	.293	.355
2007	CRpds	A	128	471	128	27	2	14	(-	-)	201	57	76	66	34	1	98	6	0	5	10	8	.56	15	.272	.326	.427
2008	RCuca	A+	103	407	115	28	2	26	(-	-)	225	70	68	74	26	4	67	3	0	2	7	3	.70	12	.283	.329	.553
2008	Ark	AA	32	123	34	7	1	6	(-	-)	61	13	25	18	7	0	29	0	2	2	1	2	.33	5	.276	.311	.496
2009	Ark	AA	137	533	155	35	3	15	(-	-)	241	54	88	82	37	2	100	1	2	8	6	3	.67	22	.291	.333	.452
2010	Salt Lk	AAA	139	532	160	29	5	36	(-	-)	307	103	122	110	58	8	126	1	0	4	3	4	.43	12	.301	.368	.577
2010	LAA	AL	8	15	1	0	0	0	(0	0)	1	2	2	0	1	0	8	0	0	0	0	0	-	0	.067	.125	.067
2011	LAA	AL	149	539	137	31	1	29	(14	15)	257	65	87	69	25	6	120	5	0	4	9	4	.69	17	.254	.291	.477
	2 ML YEARS		157	554	138	31	1	29	(14	15)	258	67	89	69	26	6	128	5	0	4	9	4	.69	17	.249	.287	.466

Ryan Tucker

Pitches: R **Bats:** R **Pos:** RP-5 | | **Ht:** 6'1" **Wt:** 200 **Born:** 12/6/1986 **Age:** 25

			HOW MUCH HE PITCHED						WHAT HE GAVE UP											THE RESULTS						
Year	Team	Lg	G	GS	CG	GF	IP	BFP	H	R	ER	HR	SH	SF	HB	TBB	IBB	SO	WP	Bk	W	L	Pct	Sh	Sv-Op Hld	ERC	ERA
2005	Mrlns	R	8	7	0	0	31.2	137	35	13	13	0	6	2	2	16	0	23	3	0	3	3	.500	0	0- --	4.85	3.69
2005	Jmstwn	A-	4	4	0	0	14.0	76	21	14	13	3	0	1	2	8	0	18	3	0	1	1	.500	0	0- --	8.98	8.36
2006	Grnsbr	A	25	25	2	0	131.1	580	123	86	73	14	4	7	9	67	0	133	11	2	7	13	.350	0	0- --	4.40	5.00
2007	Jupiter	A+	24	24	1	0	138.1	601	142	64	57	6	4	3	11	46	1	104	9	1	5	8	.385	1	0- --	3.85	3.71
2008	Carlina	AA	25	12	0	0	91.0	375	64	17	16	2	2	2	5	37	0	74	6	0	5	3	.625	0	0- --	2.23	1.58
2009	NewOr	AAA	4	4	0	0	15.2	79	18	14	14	1	2	1	1	14	0	7	1	0	1	2	.333	0	0- --	6.87	8.04
2009	Mrlns	R	2	2	0	0	8.0	32	5	2	2	0	0	1	1	2	0	7	0	0	1	0	1.000	0	0- --	1.53	2.25
2010	NewOr	AAA	7	7	0	0	33.2	159	41	26	26	3	2	1	0	17	1	19	2	0	0	5	.000	0	0- --	5.49	6.15
2010	Mrlns	R	2	1	0	0	4.0	16	5	0	0	0	1	0	0	0	0	7	0	0	1	0	1.000	0	0- --	3.37	0.00
2010	Jupiter	A+	23	0	0	13	30.0	143	35	20	20	0	3	3	3	24	3	18	6	0	1	3	.250	0	6- --	6.27	6.00
2011	RdRck	AAA	29	8	0	8	68.1	315	79	45	41	5	5	2	3	31	1	64	7	1	3	5	.375	0	2- --	5.06	5.40
2008	Fla	NL	13	6	0	3	37.0	178	46	34	34	8	1	1	2	23	1	28	1	0	2	3	.400	0	0-1 0	7.63	8.27
2011	Tex	AL	5	0	0	1	5.0	25	6	5	4	1	0	0	0	4	0	4	1	0	0	0	-	0	0-0 0	7.64	7.20
	2 ML YEARS		18	6	0	4	42.0	203	52	39	38	9	1	1	2	27	1	32	2	0	2	3	.400	0	0-1 0	7.63	8.14

Troy Tulowitzki

Bats: R Throws: R Pos: SS-140; PH-3   Ht: 6'3" Wt: 215 Born: 10/10/1984 Age: 27

Year	Team	Lg	G	AB	H	2B	3B	HR	(Hm	Rd)	TB	R	RBI	RC	TBB	IBB	SO	HBP	SH	SF	SB	CS	SB%	GDP	Avg	OBP	Slg
2006	Col	NL	25	96	23	2	0	1	(0	1)	28	15	6	10	10	3	25	1	1	0	3	0	1.00	1	.240	.318	.292
2007	Col	NL	155	609	177	33	5	24	(15	9)	292	104	99	95	57	3	130	9	5	2	7	6	.54	14	.291	.359	.479
2008	Col	NL	101	377	99	24	2	8	(4	4)	151	48	46	42	38	5	56	2	2	2	1	6	.14	16	.263	.332	.401
2009	Col	NL	151	543	161	25	9	32	(17	15)	300	101	92	96	73	4	112	3	0	9	20	11	.65	20	.297	.377	.552
2010	Col	NL	122	470	148	32	3	27	(15	12)	267	89	95	88	48	4	78	5	1	5	11	2	.85	17	.315	.381	.568
2011	Col	NL	143	537	162	36	2	30	(17	13)	292	81	105	101	59	12	79	4	1	5	9	3	.75	16	.302	.372	.544
	Postseason		15	57	12	5	0	1	(0	1)	20	3	6	3	4	0	17	1	0	1	0	1	.00	3	.211	.270	.351
	6 ML YEARS		697	2632	770	152	21	122	(68	54)	1330	438	443	432	285	31	480	24	10	23	51	28	.65	84	.293	.364	.505

Jacob Turner

Pitches: R Bats: R Pos: SP-3   Ht: 6'5" Wt: 210 Born: 5/21/1991 Age: 21

Year	Team	Lg	G	GS	CG	GF	IP	BFP	H	R	ER	HR	SH	SF	HB	TBB	IBB	SO	WP	Bk	W	L	Pct	Sh	Sv-Op	Hld	ERC	ERA
2010	WMich	A	11	10	0	1	54.0	228	53	26	22	4	0	2	1	9	0	51	1	0	2	3	.400	0	0- -	-	2.87	3.67
2010	Lkland	A+	13	13	0	0	61.1	252	53	22	20	3	0	2	7	14	0	51	0	1	4	2	.667	0	0- -	-	2.81	2.93
2011	Erie	AA	17	17	0	0	113.2	473	102	47	44	9	4	4	7	32	1	90	8	0	3	5	.375	0	0- -	-	3.15	3.48
2011	Toledo	AAA	3	3	0	0	17.1	69	15	6	6	1	0	0	0	3	0	20	2	0	1	0	1.000	0	0- -	-	2.27	3.12
2011	Det	AL	3	3	0	0	12.2	60	17	13	12	3	0	1	1	4	0	8	0	0	0	1	.000	0	0-0	0	7.03	8.53

Justin Turner

Bats: R Throws: R Pos: 2B-78; 3B-36; PH-11; SS-1; PR-1   Ht: 6'0" Wt: 210 Born: 11/23/1984 Age: 27

Year	Team	Lg	G	AB	H	2B	3B	HR	(Hm	Rd)	TB	R	RBI	RC	TBB	IBB	SO	HBP	SH	SF	SB	CS	SB%	GDP	Avg	OBP	Slg
2011	Buffalo*	AAA	10	40	12	3	2	0	(-	-)	19	6	2	7	2	0	6	2	0	0	0	0	-	1	.300	.364	.475
2009	2 Tms	AL	12	18	3	0	0	0	(0	0)	3	2	3	1	4	0	3	0	0	0	0	0	-	1	.167	.318	.167
2010	2 Tms		9	17	1	1	0	0	(0	0)	2	1	0	0	1	0	3	0	0	0	0	0	-	0	.059	.111	.118
2011	NYM	NL	117	435	113	30	0	4	(3	1)	155	49	51	59	39	2	59	10	2	1	7	2	.78	9	.260	.334	.356
10	Bal	AL	5	9	0	0	0	0	(0	0)	0	0	0	0	0	0	3	0	0	0	0	0	-	0	.000	.000	.000
10	NYM	NL	4	8	1	1	0	0	(0	0)	2	1	0	0	1	0	0	0	0	0	0	0	-	0	.125	.222	.250
	3 ML YEARS		138	470	117	31	0	4	(3	1)	160	52	54	60	44	2	65	10	2	1	7	2	.78	10	.249	.326	.340

Koji Uehara

Pitches: R Bats: R Pos: RP-65   Ht: 6'1" Wt: 190 Born: 4/3/1975 Age: 37

KOH-jee ooh-ih-HAR-uh

Year	Team	Lg	G	GS	CG	GF	IP	BFP	H	R	ER	HR	SH	SF	HB	TBB	IBB	SO	WP	Bk	W	L	Pct	Sh	Sv-Op	Hld	ERC	ERA
2009	Bal	AL	12	12	0	0	66.2	279	71	33	30	7	1	3	0	12	1	48	0	0	2	4	.333	0	0-0	0	3.56	4.05
2010	Bal	AL	43	0	0	22	44.0	174	37	15	14	5	1	0	0	5	0	55	1	0	1	2	.333	0	13-15	6	2.22	2.86
2011	2 Tms	AL	65	0	0	22	65.0	243	38	17	17	11	1	1	0	9	1	85	0	0	2	3	.400	0	0-1	22	1.48	2.35
11	Bal	AL	43	0	0	19	47.0	174	25	9	9	6	1	1	0	8	1	62	0	0	1	1	.500	0	0-1	13	1.27	1.72
11	Tex	AL	22	0	0	3	18.0	69	13	8	8	5	0	0	0	1	0	23	0	0	1	2	.333	0	0-0	9	2.21	4.00
	3 ML YEARS		120	12	0	44	175.2	696	146	65	61	23	3	4	0	26	2	188	1	0	5	9	.357	0	13-16	28	2.39	3.13

Dan Uggla

Bats: R Throws: R Pos: 2B-159; PH-1; PR-1   Ht: 5'11" Wt: 207 Born: 3/11/1980 Age: 32

Year	Team	Lg	G	AB	H	2B	3B	HR	(Hm	Rd)	TB	R	RBI	RC	TBB	IBB	SO	HBP	SH	SF	SB	CS	SB%	GDP	Avg	OBP	Slg
2006	Fla	NL	154	611	172	26	7	27	(10	17)	293	105	90	97	48	1	123	9	7	8	6	6	.50	5	.282	.339	.480
2007	Fla	NL	159	632	155	49	3	31	(18	13)	303	113	88	81	68	0	167	13	4	11	2	1	.67	14	.245	.326	.479
2008	Fla	NL	146	531	138	37	1	32	(15	17)	273	97	92	93	77	6	171	8	0	3	5	5	.50	10	.260	.360	.514
2009	Fla	NL	158	564	137	27	1	31	(21	10)	259	84	90	81	92	4	150	7	1	4	2	1	.67	10	.243	.354	.459
2010	Fla	NL	159	589	169	31	0	33	(14	19)	299	100	105	101	78	2	149	2	0	5	4	1	.80	10	.287	.369	.508
2011	Atl	NL	161	600	140	22	1	36	(18	18)	272	88	82	78	62	2	156	7	0	3	1	3	.25	9	.233	.311	.453
	6 ML YEARS		937	3527	911	192	13	190	(96	94)	1699	587	547	531	425	15	916	46	12	34	20	17	.54	54	.258	.343	.482

B.J. Upton

Bats: R Throws: R Pos: CF-151; PH-3   Ht: 6'3" Wt: 185 Born: 8/21/1984 Age: 27

Year	Team	Lg	G	AB	H	2B	3B	HR	(Hm	Rd)	TB	R	RBI	RC	TBB	IBB	SO	HBP	SH	SF	SB	CS	SB%	GDP	Avg	OBP	Slg
2004	TB	AL	45	159	41	8	2	4	(2	2)	65	19	12	22	15	0	46	1	1	1	4	1	.80	1	.258	.324	.409
2006	TB	AL	50	175	43	5	0	1	(1	0)	51	20	10	17	13	0	40	1	0	0	11	3	.79	1	.246	.302	.291
2007	TB	AL	129	474	142	25	1	24	(13	11)	241	86	82	93	65	4	154	4	1	4	22	8	.73	14	.300	.386	.508
2008	TB	AL	145	531	145	37	2	9	(4	5)	213	85	67	87	97	4	134	2	3	7	44	16	.73	13	.273	.383	.401
2009	TB	AL	144	560	135	33	4	11	(7	4)	209	79	55	68	57	0	152	3	3	3	42	14	.75	7	.241	.313	.373
2010	TB	AL	154	536	127	38	4	18	(7	11)	227	89	62	74	67	1	164	2	1	4	42	9	.82	13	.237	.322	.424
2011	TB	AL	153	560	136	27	4	23	(9	14)	240	82	81	79	71	4	161	3	4	3	36	12	.75	16	.243	.331	.429
	Postseason		21	87	23	3	1	7	(2	5)	49	16	18	15	5	1	23	0	0	1	8	0	1.00	4	.264	.301	.563
	7 ML YEARS		820	2995	769	173	17	90	(43	47)	1246	460	369	440	385	13	851	17	11	22	201	63	.76	65	.257	.342	.416

Justin Upton

Bats: R **Throws:** R **Pos:** RF-159; PH-2 **Ht:** 6'2" **Wt:** 205 **Born:** 8/25/1987 **Age:** 24

Year Team	Lg	G	AB	H	2B	3B	HR	(Hm Rd)	TB	R	RBI	RC	TBB	IBB	SO	HBP	SH	SF	SB	CS	SB%	GDP	Avg	OBP	Slg
2007 Ari	NL	43	140	31	8	3	2	(2 0)	51	17	11	13	11	4	37	1	0	0	2	0	1.00	3	.221	.283	.364
2008 Ari	NL	108	356	89	19	6	15	(12 3)	165	52	42	47	54	6	121	4	0	3	1	4	.20	3	.250	.353	.463
2009 Ari	NL	138	526	158	30	7	26	(14 12)	280	84	86	94	55	3	137	2	1	4	20	5	.80	10	.300	.366	.532
2010 Ari	NL	133	495	135	27	3	17	(8 9)	219	73	69	73	64	5	152	4	1	7	18	8	.69	20	.273	.356	.442
2011 Ari	NL	159	592	171	39	5	31	(20 11)	313	105	88	103	59	9	126	19	0	4	21	9	.70	8	.289	.369	.529
Postseason		6	14	5	1	1	0	(0 0)	8	2	1	4	3	0	3	2	0	0	1	0	1.00	0	.357	.526	.571
5 ML YEARS		581	2109	584	123	24	91	(56 35)	1028	331	296	330	243	27	573	30	2	18	62	26	.70	44	.277	.357	.487

Juan Uribe

Bats: R **Throws:** R **Pos:** 3B-59; 2B-18; SS-4; PH-4 **Ht:** 5'11" **Wt:** 230 **Born:** 3/22/1979 **Age:** 33

Year Team	Lg	G	AB	H	2B	3B	HR	(Hm Rd)	TB	R	RBI	RC	TBB	IBB	SO	HBP	SH	SF	SB	CS	SB%	GDP	Avg	OBP	Slg
2011 RCuca*	A+	3	8	4	1	0	0	(- -)	5	2	0	2	0	0	2	1	0	0	0	0	-	0	.500	.556	.625
2001 Col	NL	72	273	82	15	11	8	(3 5)	143	32	53	44	8	1	55	2	0	0	3	0	1.00	6	.300	.325	.524
2002 Col	NL	155	566	136	25	7	6	(4 2)	193	69	49	53	34	1	120	5	7	6	9	2	.82	17	.240	.286	.341
2003 Col	NL	87	316	80	19	3	10	(6 4)	135	45	33	45	17	0	60	3	6	1	7	2	.78	3	.253	.297	.427
2004 CWS	AL	134	502	142	31	6	23	(16 7)	254	82	74	81	32	1	96	3	11	5	9	11	.45	10	.283	.327	.506
2005 CWS	AL	146	481	121	23	3	16	(10 6)	198	58	71	59	34	0	77	4	11	10	4	6	.40	7	.252	.301	.412
2006 CWS	AL	132	463	109	28	2	21	(13 8)	204	53	71	52	13	1	82	3	9	7	1	1	.50	10	.235	.257	.441
2007 CWS	AL	150	513	120	18	2	20	(15 5)	202	55	68	52	34	2	112	4	7	5	1	9	.10	6	.234	.284	.394
2008 CWS	AL	110	324	80	22	1	7	(5 2)	125	38	40	43	22	0	64	1	5	1	1	3	.25	5	.247	.296	.386
2009 SF	NL	122	398	115	26	4	16	(9 7)	197	50	55	55	25	2	82	1	3	5	3	1	.75	7	.289	.329	.495
2010 SF	NL	148	521	129	24	2	24	(13 11)	229	64	85	68	45	6	92	4	0	5	1	2	.33	20	.248	.310	.440
2011 LAD	NL	77	270	55	12	0	4	(3 1)	79	21	28	13	17	2	60	6	0	2	2	0	1.00	12	.204	.264	.293
Postseason		30	101	21	5	0	3	(2 1)	35	11	16	11	7	0	27	1	2	1	2	0	1.00	2	.208	.264	.347
11 ML YEARS		1333	4627	1169	243	41	155	(97 58)	1959	567	627	565	281	16	900	36	59	47	41	37	.53	103	.253	.298	.423

Chase Utley

Bats: L **Throws:** R **Pos:** 2B-100; PH-3 UTT-lee **Ht:** 6'1" **Wt:** 200 **Born:** 12/17/1978 **Age:** 33

Year Team	Lg	G	AB	H	2B	3B	HR	(Hm Rd)	TB	R	RBI	RC	TBB	IBB	SO	HBP	SH	SF	SB	CS	SB%	GDP	Avg	OBP	Slg
2011 Clrwtr*	A+	9	32	9	2	0	1	(- -)	14	4	4	5	3	0	6	1	0	0	1	0	1.00	0	.281	.361	.438
2003 Phi	NL	43	134	32	10	1	2	(1 1)	50	13	21	19	11	0	22	6	0	1	2	0	1.00	3	.239	.322	.373
2004 Phi	NL	94	267	71	11	2	13	(8 5)	135	36	57	37	15	1	40	2	1	2	4	1	.80	6	.266	.308	.468
2005 Phi	NL	147	543	158	39	6	28	(12 16)	293	93	105	102	69	5	109	9	0	7	16	3	.84	10	.291	.376	.540
2006 Phi	NL	160	658	203	40	4	32	(16 16)	347	131	102	122	63	1	132	14	0	4	15	4	.79	9	.309	.379	.527
2007 Phi	NL	132	530	176	48	5	22	(14 8)	304	104	103	111	50	1	89	25	1	7	9	1	.90	7	.332	.410	.566
2008 Phi	NL	159	607	177	41	4	33	(20 13)	325	113	104	113	64	14	104	27	1	8	14	2	.88	9	.292	.380	.535
2009 Phi	NL	156	571	161	28	4	31	(16 15)	290	112	93	115	88	3	110	24	0	4	23	0	1.00	5	.282	.397	.508
2010 Phi	NL	115	425	117	20	2	16	(10 6)	189	75	65	83	63	3	63	18	0	5	13	2	.87	4	.275	.387	.445
2011 Phi	NL	103	398	103	21	6	11	(8 3)	169	54	44	57	39	4	47	14	1	2	14	0	1.00	3	.259	.344	.425
Postseason		41	148	36	5	0	10	(5 5)	71	33	24	29	31	3	35	3	0	1	10	1	.91	3	.243	.383	.480
9 ML YEARS		1109	4133	1198	258	34	188	(105 83)	2088	731	694	759	462	32	716	139	4	40	110	13	.89	56	.290	.377	.505

Chris Valaika

Bats: R **Throws:** R **Pos:** PH-5; 3B-4; SS-2; PR-2; 2B-1 vuh-LAKE-uh **Ht:** 6'0" **Wt:** 210 **Born:** 8/14/1985 **Age:** 26

Year Team	Lg	G	AB	H	2B	3B	HR	(Hm Rd)	TB	R	RBI	RC	TBB	IBB	SO	HBP	SH	SF	SB	CS	SB%	GDP	Avg	OBP	Slg
2006 Billings	R+	70	275	89	22	4	8	(- -)	143	58	60	55	24	0	61	8	2	6	2	2	.50	8	.324	.387	.520
2007 Dayton	A	79	300	92	20	3	10	(- -)	148	38	56	51	17	0	72	8	0	6	1	4	.20	9	.307	.353	.493
2007 Srsota	A+	57	217	55	9	1	2	(- -)	72	26	23	22	13	0	42	6	2	3	0	3	.00	7	.253	.310	.332
2008 Srsota	A+	32	135	49	9	0	7	(- -)	79	20	31	30	7	0	28	1	0	2	2	0	1.00	4	.363	.393	.585
2008 Chatt	AA	97	379	114	19	1	11	(- -)	168	58	50	60	28	0	74	3	5	2	7	4	.64	8	.301	.352	.443
2009 Lsvlle	AAA	95	366	86	20	1	6	(- -)	126	32	36	35	16	1	76	4	1	5	1	0	1.00	7	.235	.271	.344
2010 Lsvlle	AAA	118	424	129	28	2	4	(- -)	173	49	53	58	19	0	72	2	4	10	3	3	.50	13	.304	.330	.408
2011 Lsvlle	AAA	109	417	109	18	0	7	(- -)	148	39	37	47	21	1	65	6	3	6	1	0	1.00	10	.261	.302	.355
2010 Cin	NL	19	38	10	1	0	1	(1 0)	14	3	2	2	1	0	9	0	1	0	0	0	-	2	.263	.282	.368
2011 Cin	NL	14	25	7	1	1	0	(0 0)	10	3	0	3	2	0	3	0	0	0	0	0	-	0	.280	.333	.400
2 ML YEARS		33	63	17	2	1	1	(1 0)	24	6	2	5	3	0	12	0	1	0	0	0	-	2	.270	.303	.381

Luis Valbuena

Bats: L **Throws:** R **Pos:** 2B-11; PR-3; LF-2; DH-2; SS-1; PH-1 val-BWAY-nah **Ht:** 5'10" **Wt:** 195 **Born:** 11/30/1985 **Age:** 26

Year Team	Lg	G	AB	H	2B	3B	HR	(Hm Rd)	TB	R	RBI	RC	TBB	IBB	SO	HBP	SH	SF	SB	CS	SB%	GDP	Avg	OBP	Slg
2011 Clmbs*	AAA	113	420	127	22	0	17	(- -)	200	64	75	75	46	1	96	2	1	3	6	3	.67	8	.302	.372	.476
2008 Sea	AL	18	49	12	5	0	0	(0 0)	17	6	1	5	4	0	11	1	0	0	0	0	-	0	.245	.315	.347
2009 Cle	AL	103	368	92	25	3	10	(2 8)	153	52	31	35	26	0	83	0	2	2	2	3	.40	8	.250	.298	.416
2010 Cle	AL	91	275	53	12	0	1	(1 1)	71	22	24	21	28	1	61	3	2	2	1	2	.33	5	.193	.273	.258
2011 Cle	AL	17	43	9	0	0	1	(0 1)	12	4	1	2	1	0	9	0	0	0	1	0	1.00	0	.209	.227	.279
4 ML YEARS		229	735	166	42	3	13	(3 10)	253	84	57	63	59	1	164	4	4	4	4	5	.44	13	.226	.286	.344

Raul Valdes

Pitches: L Bats: L Pos: RP-13   Ht: 5'11" Wt: 190 Born: 11/27/1977 Age: 34

			HOW MUCH HE PITCHED					WHAT HE GAVE UP										THE RESULTS							
Year	Team	Lg	G	GS	CG	GF	IP	BFP	H	R	ER	HR	SH	SF	HB	TBB	IBB	SO	WP	Bk	W	L	Pct	Sh	Sv-Op	Hld	ERC	ERA
2005	WTenn	AA	5	5	0	0	23.0	93	28	13	13	1	1	1	1	3	0	18	2	0	2	0	1.000	0	0--		4.28	5.09
2005	Iowa	AAA	25	17	0	3	98.2	461	135	71	65	7	8	1	4	39	1	73	5	2	6	7	.462	0	0--		6.18	5.93
2006	Iowa	AAA	7	7	0	0	32.0	148	44	27	27	5	4	2	2	11	0	20	1	0	1	3	.250	0	0--		6.88	7.59
2007	StLuci	A+	3	1	0	1	7.1	39	8	5	5	0	1	1	2	6	0	5	0	0	0	1	.000	0	0--		6.19	6.14
2007	Bnghtn	AA	20	0	0	8	29.1	131	35	15	12	3	1	2	2	9	2	27	1	0	0	1	.000	0	1--		4.98	3.68
2010	Buffalo	AAA	9	7	0	1	36.0	148	34	12	12	3	1	1	1	9	0	36	0	0	2	1	.667	0	0--		3.22	3.00
2011	Memp	AAA	27	7	0	3	59.0	248	61	32	31	8	1	0	4	11	0	62	3	0	6	2	.750	0	0--		3.93	4.73
2011	S-WB	AAA	3	0	0	3	3.0	13	5	0	0	0	0	0	0	0	0	2	0	0	1	0	1.000	0	0--		5.88	0.00
2011	Trntn	AA	2	0	0	0	1.2	5	0	0	0	0	0	1	0	0	0	2	0	0	0	0	-	0	0--		0.00	0.00
2010	NYM	NL	38	1	0	8	58.2	262	59	33	32	7	2	2	4	27	1	56	2	0	3	3	.500	0	1-3	1	4.70	4.91
2011	2 Tms	NL	13	0	0	3	12.0	55	14	4	4	1	0	0	1	6	2	15	0	0	0	1	.000	0	0-0		5.42	3.00
11	StL	NL	7	0	0	3	5.1	27	6	2	2	0	0	0	1	4	2	7	0	0	0	1	.000	0	0-0		5.20	3.38
11	NYY	AL	6	0	0	0	6.2	28	8	2	2	1	0	0	0	2	0	8	0	0	0	0	-	0	0-0		5.47	2.70
2 ML YEARS			51	1	0	11	70.2	317	73	37	36	8	2	2	5	33	3	71	2	0	3	4	.429	0	1-3	1	4.82	4.58

Jose Valdez

Pitches: R Bats: R Pos: RP-12   Ht: 6'4" Wt: 200 Born: 1/22/1983 Age: 29

			HOW MUCH HE PITCHED					WHAT HE GAVE UP										THE RESULTS							
Year	Team	Lg	G	GS	CG	GF	IP	BFP	H	R	ER	HR	SH	SF	HB	TBB	IBB	SO	WP	Bk	W	L	Pct	Sh	Sv-Op	Hld	ERC	ERA
2002	StIslnd	A-	4	4	0	0	20.0	88	19	14	12	0	2	0	1	9	0	21	2	0	1	3	.250	0	0--		3.42	5.40
2002	Yanks	R	8	7	0	0	40.1	174	45	19	15	2	1	2	2	10	0	28	1	0	1	4	.200	0	0--		3.96	3.35
2003	Btl Crk	A	22	22	0	0	133.2	568	132	67	54	14	3	5	8	42	1	76	8	4	11	7	.611	0	0--		3.95	3.64
2003	Tampa	A+	3	3	0	0	15.2	61	11	7	7	2	1	1	0	4	0	9	1	1	1	1	.500	0	0--		2.18	4.02
2004	Tampa	A+	23	20	0	1	111.2	482	116	69	53	7	6	4	7	38	1	76	10	2	7	7	.500	0	0--		4.05	4.27
2006	Yanks	R	9	0	0	1	10.1	42	12	7	3	2	0	0	0	1	0	7	0	0	1	1	.500	0	1--		4.52	2.61
2006	CtnSC	A	5	0	0	3	8.1	32	8	1	1	0	0	0	0	2	0	6	0	0	0	0	-	0	2--		2.83	1.08
2007	Tampa	A+	37	0	0	20	59.2	251	54	21	19	4	1	4	0	21	3	60	6	1	3	4	.429	0	3--		3.05	2.87
2008	Tampa	A+	27	0	0	16	36.0	141	30	13	11	4	2	0	0	9	3	32	1	1	6	2	.750	0	3--		2.67	2.75
2008	Trntn	AA	17	0	0	13	24.1	96	17	7	6	4	0	1	1	7	0	23	1	0	1	0	1.000	0	4--		2.64	2.22
2009	Trntn	AA	34	0	0	26	38.1	171	32	17	13	2	5	2	3	23	5	42	14	0	1	1	.500	0	10--		3.61	3.05
2009	S-WB	AAA	9	0	0	3	19.1	86	23	9	9	2	1	0	0	10	1	18	2	0	2	1	.667	0	0--		5.80	4.19
2010	Astros	R	4	0	0	0	4.0	13	2	0	0	0	0	0	0	0	0	4	0	0	0	0	-	0	0--		0.58	0.00
2010	CpChr	AA	9	0	0	6	12.1	48	5	2	2	0	0	0	2	4	0	11	0	0	0	0	-	0	0--		1.12	1.46
2011	OKCity	AAA	20	0	0	13	20.2	99	23	16	13	4	2	1	1	9	3	26	2	0	1	0	1.000	0	9--		5.16	5.66
2011	Astros	R	4	0	0	0	4.0	17	3	3	2	0	0	0	0	1	0	7	1	0	0	1	.000	0	0--		1.55	4.50
2011	Hou	NL	12	0	0	7	14.0	65	17	14	14	2	0	1	1	7	1	15	1	0	0	0	-	0	0-0	1	6.31	9.00

Merkin Valdez

Pitches: R Bats: R Pos: RP-5   Ht: 6'5" Wt: 232 Born: 11/10/1981 Age: 30

			HOW MUCH HE PITCHED					WHAT HE GAVE UP										THE RESULTS							
Year	Team	Lg	G	GS	CG	GF	IP	BFP	H	R	ER	HR	SH	SF	HB	TBB	IBB	SO	WP	Bk	W	L	Pct	Sh	Sv-Op	Hld	ERC	ERA
2011	Albq*	AAA	38	0	0	18	50.1	217	47	23	20	1	2	0	4	24	1	43	2	1	4	2	.667	0	4--		3.77	3.58
2011	RdRck*	AAA	12	0	0	7	15.1	66	14	4	4	1	0	0	0	5	0	14	1	0	1	0	1.000	0	4--		2.97	2.35
2004	SF	NL	2	0	0	0	1.2	12	4	5	5	1	0	0	0	3	0	2	0	0	0	0	-	0	0-0	0	26.50	27.00
2008	SF	NL	17	1	0	3	16.0	69	14	5	3	1	1	0	2	7	2	13	2	1	1	0	1.000	0	0-0	2	3.57	1.69
2009	SF	NL	48	0	0	20	49.1	225	57	33	31	5	1	1	0	28	2	38	5	0	2	1	.667	0	0-3	4	5.67	5.66
2010	Tor	AL	2	0	0	1	1.1	9	2	3	3	0	0	0	0	0	0	0	0	0	0	0	-	0	0-0	0	14.12	20.25
2011	Tex	AL	5	0	0	1	4.1	21	7	3	3	2	0	0	0	1	0	6	0	0	0	0	-	0	0-0	0	9.94	6.23
5 ML YEARS			74	1	0	25	72.2	336	84	49	45	9	2	1	2	42	4	59	7	1	3	1	.750	0	0-3	6	5.96	5.57

Wilson Valdez

Bats: R Throws: R Pos: 2B-45; SS-25; 3B-24; PH-8; PR-5   Ht: 5'11" Wt: 170 Born: 5/20/1978 Age: 34

			BATTING																	BASERUNNING				AVERAGES		
Year	Team	Lg	G	AB	H	2B	3B	HR	(Hm	Rd)	TB	R	RBI	RC	TBB	IBB	SO	HBP	SH	SF	SB	CS	SB%	GDP	Avg	OBP	Slg
2004	CWS	AL	19	43	10	1	0	1	(1	0)	14	8	4	2	2	0	5	0	1	0	1	2	.33	1	.233	.267	.326
2005	2 Tms		51	139	28	7	1	0	(0	0)	37	9	9	8	8	0	26	0	1	0	2	2	.50	2	.201	.245	.266
2007	LAD	NL	41	74	16	2	1	0	(0	0)	20	12	7	7	4	0	12	1	0	1	1	0	1.00	1	.216	.263	.270
2009	NYM	NL	41	86	22	3	2	0	(0	0)	29	11	7	6	8	0	10	1	0	0	0	1	.00	6	.256	.326	.337
2010	Phi	NL	111	333	86	16	3	4	(2	2)	120	37	35	34	21	7	43	2	7	0	7	0	1.00	20	.258	.306	.360
2011	Phi	NL	99	273	68	14	4	1	(1	0)	93	39	30	30	18	3	41	0	7	2	3	3	.50	13	.249	.294	.341
05	Sea	AL	42	126	25	5	1	0	(0	0)	32	9	8	6	6	0	25	0	1	0	2	2	.50	1	.198	.254	.254
05	SD	NL	9	13	3	2	0	0	(0	0)	5	0	1	2	2	0	1	0	0	0	0	0	-	1	.231	.333	.385
Postseason			3	3	1	0	0	0	(0	0)	1	1	0	0	0	0	0	0	0	0	0	0	-	0	.333	.333	.333
6 ML YEARS			362	948	230	43	11	6	(4	2)	313	116	92	87	61	10	137	4	16	3	14	8	.64	42	.243	.290	.330

Danny Valencia

Bats: R Throws: R Pos: 3B-147; DH-4; PH-3   vuh-LENN-see-yah   Ht: 6'2" Wt: 220 Born: 9/19/1984 Age: 27

			BATTING																	BASERUNNING				AVERAGES		
Year	Team	Lg	G	AB	H	2B	3B	HR	(Hm	Rd)	TB	R	RBI	RC	TBB	IBB	SO	HBP	SH	SF	SB	CS	SB%	GDP	Avg	OBP	Slg
2006	Elizab	R+	48	190	59	13	0	8	(-	-)	96	30	29	34	15	2	34	3	0	3	0	2	.00	9	.311	.365	.505
2007	Beloit	A	66	242	73	15	0	11	(-	-)	121	44	35	44	28	0	54	0	1	0	3	3	.50	11	.302	.374	.500
2007	FtMyrs	A+	61	230	67	8	2	6	(-	-)	97	28	31	33	16	0	48	0	0	4	1	0	1.00	10	.291	.332	.422
2008	FtMyrs	A+	60	220	74	19	3	5	(-	-)	114	35	44	45	27	2	43	0	0	4	2	2	.50	6	.336	.402	.518
2008	NwBrit	AA	69	266	77	18	2	10	(-	-)	129	40	32	43	18	1	70	1	0	2	2	1	.67	6	.289	.334	.485

Year	Team	Lg	G	AB	H	2B	3B	HR	(Hm	Rd)	TB	R	RBI	RC	TBB	IBB	SO	HBP	SH	SF	SB	CS	SB%	GDP	Avg	OBP	Slg
2009	NwBrit	AA	57	218	62	14	4	7	(-	-)	105	44	29	40	31	3	40	1	0	2	0	2	.00	8	.284	.373	.482
2009	Roch	AAA	71	269	77	24	4	6	(-	-)	122	35	41	37	8	2	37	1	0	4	0	2	.00	7	.286	.305	.454
2010	Roch	AAA	49	185	54	15	0	0	(-	-)	69	22	24	25	14	0	34	2	0	1	2	0	1.00	6	.292	.347	.373
2010	Min	AL	85	299	93	18	1	7	(4	3)	134	30	40	50	20	0	46	0	0	3	2	0	1.00	11	.311	.351	.448
2011	Min	AL	154	564	139	28	2	15	(9	6)	216	63	72	57	40	2	102	0	0	4	6	2	.25	15	.246	.294	.383
	Postseason		3	9	2	1	0	0	(0	0)	3	1	2	1	1	0	3	0	0	1	0	0	-	0	.222	.273	.333
	2 ML YEARS		239	863	232	46	3	22	(13	9)	350	93	112	107	60	2	148	0	0	7	4	6	.40	26	.269	.314	.406

Jose Valverde

Pitches: R Bats: R Pos: RP-75 val-VARE-day Ht: 6'4" Wt: 254 Born: 3/24/1978 Age: 34

Year	Team	Lg	G	GS	CG	GF	IP	BFP	H	R	ER	HR	SH	SF	HB	TBB	IBB	SO	WP	Bk	W	L	Pct	Sh	Sv-Op	Hld	ERC	ERA
2003	Ari	NL	54	0	0	33	50.1	204	24	16	12	4	0	1	2	26	2	71	2	0	2	1	.667	0	10-11	8	1.77	2.15
2004	Ari	NL	29	0	0	20	29.2	131	23	17	14	7	3	2	1	17	4	38	4	0	1	2	.333	0	8-10	5	4.25	4.24
2005	Ari	NL	61	0	0	34	66.1	268	51	19	18	5	3	1	2	20	1	75	3	0	3	4	.429	0	15-17	7	2.43	2.44
2006	Ari	NL	44	0	0	35	49.1	223	50	32	32	6	1	3	2	22	3	69	2	0	2	3	.400	0	18-22	1	4.42	5.84
2007	Ari	NL	65	0	0	59	64.1	265	46	21	19	7	0	1	3	26	1	78	1	0	1	4	.200	0	47-54	0	2.77	2.66
2008	Hou	NL	74	0	0	71	72.0	303	62	28	27	10	0	2	2	23	6	83	3	2	6	3	.667	0	44-51	0	3.18	3.38
2009	Hou	NL	52	0	0	45	54.0	219	40	15	14	5	1	2	2	21	1	56	1	0	4	2	.667	0	25-29	1	2.76	2.33
2010	Det	AL	60	0	0	55	63.0	259	41	24	21	5	0	1	3	32	1	63	3	0	2	4	.333	0	26-29	0	2.67	3.00
2011	Det	AL	75	0	0	70	72.1	301	52	21	18	5	2	0	3	34	4	69	3	1	2	4	.333	0	49-49	0	2.71	2.24
	Postseason		4	0	0	3	4.2	21	2	1	1	0	0	0	0	4	0	8	0	0	0	1	.000	0	1-1	0	1.91	1.93
	9 ML YEARS		514	0	0	422	521.1	2173	389	193	175	54	10	13	20	221	23	602	22	3	23	27	.460	0	242-272	22	2.89	3.02

Rick VandenHurk

Pitches: R Bats: R Pos: SP-2; RP-2 VANN-denn-herk Ht: 6'5" Wt: 219 Born: 5/22/1985 Age: 27

Year	Team	Lg	G	GS	CG	GF	IP	BFP	H	R	ER	HR	SH	SF	HB	TBB	IBB	SO	WP	Bk	W	L	Pct	Sh	Sv-Op	Hld	ERC	ERA
2011	Norfolk*	AAA	26	26	0	0	154.1	650	141	83	76	23	5	1	13	40	0	108	11	2	9	13	.409	0	0--	-	3.68	4.43
2007	Fla	NL	18	17	0	0	81.2	379	94	63	62	15	5	3	3	48	5	82	4	4	4	6	.400	0	0-0	0	6.50	6.83
2008	Fla	NL	4	4	0	0	14.0	74	20	12	12	1	2	0	1	10	0	20	0	0	1	1	.500	0	0-0	0	8.20	7.71
2009	Fla	NL	11	11	0	0	58.2	256	57	29	28	11	3	2	4	21	3	49	2	0	3	2	.600	0	0-0	0	4.49	4.30
2010	2 Tms		9	1	0	2	17.2	76	16	14	10	2	0	1	2	8	0	18	0	0	1	0	1.000	0	0-0	0	4.38	5.09
2011	Bal	AL	4	2	0	1	9.0	46	12	9	8	4	0	0	1	8	0	7	0	0	0	0	-	0	0-0	0	12.32	8.00
10	Fla	NL	2	0	0	0	1.1	9	3	4	1	0	0	0	0	1	0	1	0	0	0	0	-	0	0-0	0	11.17	6.75
10	Bal	AL	7	1	0	2	16.1	67	13	10	9	2	0	1	2	7	0	17	0	0	0	1	.000	0	0-0	0	3.86	4.96
	5 ML YEARS		46	35	0	3	181.0	831	199	127	120	33	10	6	12	95	8	176	6	4	8	10	.444	0	0-0	0	6.00	5.97

Jason Vargas

Pitches: L Bats: L Pos: SP-32 Ht: 6'0" Wt: 210 Born: 2/2/1983 Age: 29

Year	Team	Lg	G	GS	CG	GF	IP	BFP	H	R	ER	HR	SH	SF	HB	TBB	IBB	SO	WP	Bk	W	L	Pct	Sh	Sv-Op	Hld	ERC	ERA
2005	Fla	NL	17	13	1	0	73.2	325	71	34	33	4	4	1	4	31	4	59	0	0	5	5	.500	0	0-0	0	3.68	4.03
2006	Fla	NL	12	5	0	3	43.0	213	50	39	35	9	4	4	4	30	3	25	2	0	1	2	.333	0	0-0	0	7.30	7.33
2007	NYM	NL	2	2	0	0	10.1	51	17	14	14	4	0	0	0	2	1	4	1	0	0	1	.000	0	0-0	0	8.95	12.19
2009	Sea	AL	23	14	0	4	91.2	385	98	53	50	16	3	6	3	24	1	54	1	0	3	6	.333	0	0-0	0	4.64	4.91
2010	Sea	AL	31	31	0	0	192.2	811	187	86	81	18	4	7	1	54	3	116	1	4	9	12	.429	0	0-0	0	3.37	3.78
2011	Sea	AL	32	32	4	0	201.0	857	205	105	95	22	3	4	4	59	4	131	3	1	10	13	.435	3	0-0	0	3.86	4.25
	6 ML YEARS		117	97	5	7	612.1	2642	628	331	308	73	18	22	16	200	16	389	8	6	28	39	.418	3	0-0	0	4.10	4.53

Jason Varitek

Bats: B Throws: R Pos: C-68 VAIR-uh-teck Ht: 6'2" Wt: 230 Born: 4/11/1972 Age: 40

Year	Team	Lg	G	AB	H	2B	3B	HR	(Hm	Rd)	TB	R	RBI	RC	TBB	IBB	SO	HBP	SH	SF	SB	CS	SB%	GDP	Avg	OBP	Slg
1997	Bos	AL	1	1	1	0	0	0	(0	0)	1	0	0	1	0	0	0	0	0	0	0	0	-	0	1.000	1.000	1.000
1998	Bos	AL	86	221	56	13	0	7	(1	6)	90	31	33	26	17	1	45	2	4	3	2	2	.50	8	.253	.309	.407
1999	Bos	AL	144	483	130	39	2	20	(12	8)	233	70	76	75	46	2	85	2	5	8	1	2	.33	13	.269	.330	.482
2000	Bos	AL	139	448	111	31	1	10	(2	8)	174	55	65	59	60	3	84	6	1	4	1	1	.50	16	.248	.342	.388
2001	Bos	AL	51	174	51	11	1	7	(2	5)	85	19	25	30	21	3	35	1	1	1	0	0	-	6	.293	.371	.489
2002	Bos	AL	132	467	124	27	1	10	(6	4)	183	58	61	52	41	3	95	7	1	3	4	3	.57	13	.266	.332	.392
2003	Bos	AL	142	451	123	31	1	25	(13	12)	231	63	85	79	51	8	106	7	5	7	3	2	.60	10	.273	.351	.512
2004	Bos	AL	137	463	137	30	1	18	(8	10)	223	67	73	79	62	9	126	10	0	1	10	3	.77	11	.296	.390	.482
2005	Bos	AL	133	470	132	30	1	22	(7	15)	230	70	70	78	62	3	117	3	1	3	2	0	1.00	16	.281	.366	.489
2006	Bos	AL	103	365	87	19	2	12	(2	10)	146	46	55	45	46	7	87	2	1	2	1	2	.33	10	.238	.325	.400
2007	Bos	AL	131	435	111	15	3	17	(9	8)	183	57	68	61	71	9	122	8	0	4	1	2	.33	9	.255	.367	.421
2008	Bos	AL	131	423	93	20	0	13	(4	9)	152	37	43	36	52	3	122	6	0	2	0	1	.00	13	.220	.313	.359
2009	Bos	AL	109	364	76	24	0	14	(10	4)	142	41	51	43	54	6	90	3	0	4	0	0	-	6	.209	.313	.390
2010	Bos	AL	39	112	26	6	0	7	(4	3)	53	18	16	11	10	2	35	0	0	1	0	0	-	1	.232	.293	.473
2011	Bos	AL	68	222	49	10	1	11	(5	6)	94	32	36	28	21	0	67	4	3	0	0	0	-	3	.221	.300	.423
	Postseason		63	228	54	12	2	11	(3	8)	103	37	33	27	14	4	56	5	2	3	0	0	-	6	.237	.292	.452
	15 ML YEARS		1546	5099	1307	306	14	193	(85	108)	2220	664	757	703	614	59	1216	61	22	43	25	18	.58	129	.256	.341	.435

Anthony Varvaro

var-VAR-oh

Ht: 6'0" Wt: 195 Born: 10/31/1984 Age: 27

Pitches: R Bats: R Pos: RP-18

			HOW MUCH HE PITCHED					WHAT HE GAVE UP										THE RESULTS						
Year	Team	Lg	G	GS	CG	GF	IP	BFP	H	R	ER	HR	SH	SF	HB	TBB	IBB	SO	WP	Bk	W	L	Pct	Sh	Sv-Op Hld	ERC	ERA
2006	Ms	R	5	3	0	0	11.0	45	7	3	2	0	0	0	2	5	0	15	1	0	0	2	.000	0	0- - -	2.43	1.64
2007	Wisc	A	22	21	0	1	103.2	464	94	67	54	7	0	0	9	51	0	112	16	0	4	11	.267	0	1- - -	3.93	4.69
2008	Hi Dsrt	A+	30	24	0	0	122.2	595	154	105	97	22	5	3	13	82	0	113	10	0	3	9	.250	0	0- - -	8.01	7.12
2009	Hi Dsrt	A+	8	0	0	6	7.2	39	9	6	6	0	0	0	0	6	0	10	1	0	0	0	-	0	4- - -	5.50	7.04
2009	WTenn	AA	36	0	0	20	54.1	240	30	23	17	1	1	4	6	44	5	63	3	1	4	3	.571	0	8- - -	2.82	2.82
2010	WTenn	AA	31	0	0	23	39.1	165	27	15	14	2	2	3	0	21	4	46	2	0	1	3	.250	0	9- - -	2.41	3.20
2010	Tacom	AAA	19	0	0	2	25.2	119	24	17	15	1	0	2	4	14	0	26	3	0	0	0	-	0	0- - -	4.31	5.26
2011	Gwnntt	AAA	38	0	0	14	59.0	245	37	23	19	3	6	2	2	35	4	69	2	0	2	8	.200	0	1- - -	2.53	2.90
2010	Sea	AL	4	0	0	2	4.0	24	6	5	5	2	0	0	0	6	0	1	1	0	0	1	.000	0	0-1 -	16.26	11.25
2011	Atl	NL	18	0	0	9	24.0	96	15	7	7	3	2	1	0	11	4	23	1	0	0	2	.000	0	0-1 -	2.28	2.63
	2 ML YEARS		22	0	0	11	28.0	120	21	12	12	5	2	1	0	17	4	28	2	0	0	3	.000	0	0-1 -	3.81	3.86

Anthony Vasquez

Ht: 6'0" Wt: 175 Born: 9/19/1986 Age: 25

Pitches: L Bats: L Pos: SP-7

			HOW MUCH HE PITCHED					WHAT HE GAVE UP										THE RESULTS						
Year	Team	Lg	G	GS	CG	GF	IP	BFP	H	R	ER	HR	SH	SF	HB	TBB	IBB	SO	WP	Bk	W	L	Pct	Sh	Sv-Op Hld	ERC	ERA
2009	Pulaski	R	8	2	0	4	23.2	101	20	13	10	2	1	2	1	8	0	27	0	0	2	1	.667	0	2- - -	2.96	3.80
2009	Clinton	A	7	7	0	0	35.0	155	47	25	22	4	2	1	2	8	0	24	0	0	3	3	.500	0	0- - -	5.55	5.66
2010	Clinton	A	8	8	1	0	48.2	182	31	11	7	2	0	2	2	7	0	45	0	0	2	2	.500	0	0- - -	1.36	1.29
2010	Hi Dsrt	A+	13	11	2	2	85.0	349	87	38	29	6	3	1	2	12	0	53	1	0	4	6	.636	0	0- - -	3.11	3.07
2010	WTenn	AA	6	6	0	0	38.0	161	44	15	11	2	3	1	4	5	0	27	0	0	2	3	.400	0	0- - -	4.05	2.61
2011	Jacksn	AA	16	16	1	0	100.1	431	125	50	42	6	4	4	8	19	1	59	3	0	5	7	.417	0	0- - -	4.78	3.77
2011	Tacom	AAA	8	8	0	0	53.1	220	51	22	19	6	1	1	0	18	0	32	0	0	4	3	.571	0	0- - -	3.76	3.21
2011	Sea	AL	7	7	0	0	29.1	146	46	35	29	13	1	1	3	10	0	13	0	0	1	6	.143	0	0-0 0	10.65	8.90

Esmerling Vasquez

Ht: 6'1" Wt: 200 Born: 11/7/1983 Age: 28

Pitches: R Bats: R Pos: RP-31

			HOW MUCH HE PITCHED					WHAT HE GAVE UP										THE RESULTS						
Year	Team	Lg	G	GS	CG	GF	IP	BFP	H	R	ER	HR	SH	SF	HB	TBB	IBB	SO	WP	Bk	W	L	Pct	Sh	Sv-Op Hld	ERC	ERA
2011	Reno*	AAA	23	0	0	7	27.2	133	26	19	19	3	0	1	3	21	0	26	6	0	2	2	.500	0	0- - -	5.53	6.18
2009	Ari	NL	53	0	0	10	53.0	238	52	27	26	4	1	3	3	29	2	45	4	0	3	3	.500	0	0-4 4	4.51	4.42
2010	Ari	NL	57	0	0	16	53.2	240	46	32	31	6	0	1	6	38	3	55	3	1	1	6	.143	0	0-2 6	5.04	5.20
2011	Ari	NL	31	0	0	5	30.1	132	27	16	14	2	0	2	4	13	2	20	0	0	1	1	.500	0	0-2 6	3.74	4.15
	3 ML YEARS		141	0	0	31	137.0	610	125	75	71	12	1	4	13	80	7	120	7	1	5	10	.333	0	0-8 16	4.54	4.66

Javier Vazquez

Ht: 6'2" Wt: 210 Born: 7/25/1976 Age: 35

Pitches: R Bats: R Pos: SP-32

			HOW MUCH HE PITCHED					WHAT HE GAVE UP										THE RESULTS						
Year	Team	Lg	G	GS	CG	GF	IP	BFP	H	R	ER	HR	SH	SF	HB	TBB	IBB	SO	WP	Bk	W	L	Pct	Sh	Sv-Op Hld	ERC	ERA
1998	Mon	NL	33	32	0	1	172.1	764	196	121	116	31	9	4	11	68	2	139	2	0	5	15	.250	0	0-0 -	5.79	6.06
1999	Mon	NL	26	26	3	0	154.2	667	154	98	86	20	3	3	4	52	4	113	2	0	9	8	.529	1	0-0 -	4.02	5.00
2000	Mon	NL	33	33	2	0	217.2	945	247	104	98	24	11	3	5	61	10	196	3	0	11	9	.550	1	0-0 -	4.45	4.05
2001	Mon	NL	32	32	5	0	223.2	898	197	92	85	24	9	2	3	44	4	208	3	1	16	11	.593	3	0-0 -	2.75	3.42
2002	Mon	NL	34	34	2	0	230.1	971	243	111	100	28	15	7	4	49	6	179	3	0	10	13	.435	0	0-0 -	3.80	3.91
2003	Mon	NL	34	34	4	0	230.2	938	198	93	83	28	6	6	4	57	5	241	11	1	13	12	.520	1	0-0 -	2.90	3.24
2004	NYY	AL	32	32	0	0	198.0	849	195	114	108	33	4	8	11	60	3	150	12	2	14	10	.583	0	0-0 -	4.00	4.91
2005	Ari	NL	33	33	3	0	215.2	904	223	112	106	35	13	3	5	46	4	192	7	0	11	15	.423	1	0-0 -	4.00	4.42
2006	CWS	AL	33	32	1	0	202.2	872	206	116	109	23	2	4	15	56	2	184	7	0	11	12	.478	1	0-0 -	4.02	4.84
2007	CWS	AL	33	32	2	0	216.2	882	197	95	90	29	5	7	7	50	2	213	5	0	15	8	.652	0	0-0 -	3.29	3.74
2008	CWS	AL	33	33	1	0	208.1	890	214	113	108	25	4	4	6	61	2	200	2	0	12	16	.429	0	0-0 -	4.03	4.67
2009	Atl	NL	32	32	3	0	219.1	890	181	75	70	20	12	2	4	44	4	238	6	0	15	10	.600	0	0-0 -	2.42	2.87
2010	NYY	AL	31	26	0	0	157.1	683	155	96	93	32	2	7	7	65	4	121	8	0	10	10	.500	0	0-0 -	4.94	5.32
2011	Fla	NL	32	32	2	0	192.2	798	178	91	79	21	8	6	2	50	8	162	5	0	13	11	.542	1	0-0 -	3.14	3.69
	Postseason		4	2	0	0	15.2	80	24	18	18	6	0	3	2	10	0	18	0	0	1	1	.500	0	0-0 -	11.90	10.34
	14 ML YEARS		450	443	28	5	2840.0	11935	2784	1431	1331	373	103	66	88	763	58	2536	76	4	165	160	.508	8	0-0 -	3.75	4.22

Gil Velazquez

veh-LAZZ-kezz

Ht: 6'2" Wt: 170 Born: 10/17/1979 Age: 32

Bats: R Throws: R Pos: 2B-2; 3B-2; PH-2

			BATTING																		BASERUNNING				AVERAGES		
Year	Team	Lg	G	AB	H	2B	3B	HR	(Hm	Rd)	TB	R	RBI	RC	TBB	IBB	SO	HBP	SH	SF		SB	CS	SB%	GDP	Avg	OBP	Slg
2011	Salt Lk*	AAA	123	427	140	25	5	8	(-	-)	199	78	58	83	49	2	60	4	10	4		17	6	.74	12	.328	.399	.466
2008	Bos	AL	3	8	1	0	0	0	(0	0)	1	0	1	1	0	0	0	0	0	0		0	0	-	0	.125	.125	.125
2009	Bos	AL	6	2	0	0	0	0	(0	0)	0	0	0	0	0	0	1	0	0	0		0	0	-	0	.000	.333	.000
2011	LAA	AL	4	6	3	0	0	0	(0	0)	3	0	1	1	0	0	0	0	1	1		0	0	-	0	.500	.429	.500
	3 ML YEARS		13	16	4	0	0	0	(0	0)	4	0	2	2	0	0	1	0	1	1		0	0	-	0	.250	.278	.250

Eugenio Velez

Bats: B Throws: R Pos: PH-15; 2B-11; PR-7; LF-4
eh-oo-HEN-ee-oh
Ht: 6'1" Wt: 169 Born: 5/16/1982 Age: 30

Year	Team	Lg	G	AB	H	2B	3B	HR	(Hm	Rd)	TB	R	RBI	RC	TBB	IBB	SO	HBP	SH	SF	SB	CS	SB%	GDP	Avg	OBP	Slg
2011	Albq*	AAA	55	218	74	15	3	2	(-	-)	101	33	31	36	11	0	36	1	3	2	6	6	.50	5	.339	.371	.463
2007	SF	NL	14	11	3	0	2	0	(0	0)	7	5	2	4	2	0	3	0	0	0	4	0	1.00	0	.273	.385	.636
2008	SF	NL	98	275	72	16	7	1	(0	1)	105	32	30	29	14	2	40	1	1	1	15	6	.71	11	.262	.299	.382
2009	SF	NL	84	285	76	13	5	5	(3	2)	114	40	31	33	16	1	55	2	2	2	11	5	.69	6	.267	.308	.400
2010	SF	NL	29	55	9	2	0	2	(1	1)	17	7	8	6	6	0	9	0	5	0	0	0	-	0	.164	.246	.309
2011	LAD	NL	34	37	0	0	0	0	(0	0)	0	5	1	0	2	0	11	1	0	0	1	0	1.00	0	.000	.075	.000
5 ML YEARS			259	663	160	31	14	8	(4	4)	243	89	72	72	40	3	118	4	8	3	31	11	.74	17	.241	.287	.367

Will Venable

Bats: L Throws: L Pos: RF-91; PH-24; CF-14; LF-7; PR-1
Ht: 6'2" Wt: 205 Born: 10/29/1982 Age: 29

Year	Team	Lg	G	AB	H	2B	3B	HR	(Hm	Rd)	TB	R	RBI	RC	TBB	IBB	SO	HBP	SH	SF	SB	CS	SB%	GDP	Avg	OBP	Slg
2011	Tucsn*	AAA	14	58	16	3	2	3	(-	-)	32	14	11	11	5	0	13	0	0	1	3	0	1.00	1	.276	.328	.552
2008	SD	NL	28	110	29	4	2	2	(0	2)	43	16	10	15	13	1	21	0	0	1	1	1	.50	1	.264	.339	.391
2009	SD	NL	95	293	75	14	2	12	(5	7)	129	38	38	34	25	2	89	4	2	0	6	1	.86	6	.256	.323	.440
2010	SD	NL	131	392	96	11	7	13	(6	7)	160	60	51	57	45	8	128	3	0	5	29	7	.81	3	.245	.324	.408
2011	SD	NL	121	370	91	14	7	9	(6	3)	146	49	44	52	31	4	92	5	1	4	26	3	.90	2	.246	.310	.395
4 ML YEARS			375	1165	291	43	18	36	(17	19)	478	163	143	158	114	15	330	12	3	10	62	12	.84	12	.250	.321	.410

Jonny Venters

Pitches: L Bats: L Pos: RP-85
Ht: 6'3" Wt: 195 Born: 3/20/1985 Age: 27

Year	Team	Lg	G	GS	CG	GF	IP	BFP	H	R	ER	HR	SH	SF	HB	TBB	IBB	SO	WP	Bk	W	L	Pct	Sh	Sv-Op	Hld	ERC	ERA
2004	Braves	R	11	8	0	0	42.1	198	53	31	27	3	0	0	7	12	0	54	4	0	1	6	.143	0	0-	-	5.41	5.74
2005	Rome	A	23	12	0	8	103.0	454	100	51	45	4	3	3	8	52	1	66	12	0	8	6	.571	0	3-	-	4.20	3.93
2007	MrtlBh	A+	17	12	0	2	79.2	333	60	39	30	4	3	1	5	38	0	64	10	0	3	3	.500	0	1-	-	2.96	3.39
2008	Braves	R	4	4	0	0	7.2	35	10	6	4	1	0	0	1	2	0	10	0	0	0	0	-	0	0-	-	6.11	4.70
2008	MrtlBh	A+	5	3	0	1	17.2	80	21	12	8	0	0	2	1	7	0	7	2	0	1	2	.333	0	0-	-	4.60	4.08
2008	Missi	AA	3	2	0	1	9.0	42	10	2	1	0	0	0	0	5	0	7	0	0	1	0	1.000	0	1-	-	4.43	1.00
2009	Missi	AA	12	12	1	0	65.1	280	60	24	20	2	2	1	3	35	0	40	3	0	4	4	.500	0	0-	-	3.93	2.76
2009	Gwnntt	AAA	17	17	0	0	91.1	408	103	64	57	7	0	2	3	42	2	58	8	0	4	7	.364	0	0-	-	5.02	5.62
2010	Gwnntt	AAA	2	1	0	0	6.2	25	4	1	1	0	0	0	0	1	0	6	0	0	1	0	1.000	0	0-	-	1.02	1.35
2010	Atl	NL	79	0	0	17	83.0	350	61	30	18	1	2	1	8	39	2	93	4	0	4	4	.500	0	1-5	24	2.64	1.95
2011	Atl	NL	85	0	0	10	88.0	357	53	19	18	2	7	1	5	43	7	96	4	0	6	2	.750	0	5-9	35	1.96	1.84
	Postseason		4	0	0	0	5.1	20	7	0	0	0	0	0	0	0	0	8	0	0	0	0	-	0	0-0	0	4.06	0.00
2 ML YEARS			164	0	0	27	171.0	707	114	49	36	3	9	2	13	82	9	189	8	0	10	6	.625	0	6-14	59	2.28	1.89

Jose Veras

Pitches: R Bats: R Pos: RP-79
Ht: 6'6" Wt: 235 Born: 10/20/1980 Age: 31

Year	Team	Lg	G	GS	CG	GF	IP	BFP	H	R	ER	HR	SH	SF	HB	TBB	IBB	SO	WP	Bk	W	L	Pct	Sh	Sv-Op	Hld	ERC	ERA
2006	NYY	AL	12	0	0	4	11.0	43	8	5	5	2	0	0	0	5	0	6	1	1	0	0	-	0	1-1	1	3.55	4.09
2007	NYY	AL	9	0	0	3	9.1	41	6	6	6	0	0	0	0	7	1	7	1	0	0	0	-	0	2-2	1	2.52	5.79
2008	NYY	AL	60	0	0	15	57.2	252	52	23	23	7	2	1	3	29	6	63	4	0	5	3	.625	0	0-2	10	4.09	3.59
2009	2 Tms		47	0	0	19	50.1	225	42	33	29	8	4	0	6	28	0	40	0	1	4	3	.571	0	0-0	6	4.60	5.19
2010	Fla	NL	48	0	0	11	48.0	201	32	20	20	5	1	0	1	29	0	54	2	0	3	3	.500	0	0-2	19	3.19	3.75
2011	Pit	NL	79	0	0	19	71.0	305	54	32	30	6	2	3	4	34	3	79	5	1	2	4	.333	0	1-8	27	3.06	3.80
09	NYY	AL	25	0	0	10	25.2	118	23	17	17	5	2	0	4	14	0	18	0	0	3	1	.750	0	0-0	3	5.29	5.96
09	Cle	AL	22	0	0	9	24.2	107	19	16	12	3	2	0	2	14	0	22	0	1	1	2	.333	0	0-0	3	3.92	4.38
	Postseason		2	0	0	0	0.2	4	1	0	0	0	0	0	0	1	1	1	0	0	0	0	-	0	0-0	0	6.98	0.00
6 ML YEARS			255	0	0	71	247.1	1068	194	119	113	28	9	4	14	132	10	249	13	3	14	13	.519	0	4-15	64	3.62	4.11

Justin Verlander

Pitches: R Bats: R Pos: SP-34
Ht: 6'5" Wt: 225 Born: 2/20/1983 Age: 29

Year	Team	Lg	G	GS	CG	GF	IP	BFP	H	R	ER	HR	SH	SF	HB	TBB	IBB	SO	WP	Bk	W	L	Pct	Sh	Sv-Op	Hld	ERC	ERA
2005	Det	AL	2	2	0	0	11.1	54	15	9	9	1	0	1	0	5	0	7	1	0	0	2	.000	0	0-0	0	6.41	7.15
2006	Det	AL	30	30	1	0	186.0	776	187	78	75	21	2	4	6	60	1	124	5	1	17	9	.654	1	0-0	0	4.12	3.63
2007	Det	AL	32	32	1	0	201.2	866	181	88	82	20	3	1	19	67	3	183	17	2	18	6	.750	1	0-0	0	3.53	3.66
2008	Det	AL	33	33	1	0	201.0	880	195	119	108	18	4	6	14	87	8	163	6	3	11	17	.393	0	0-0	0	4.17	4.84
2009	Det	AL	35	35	3	0	240.0	982	219	99	92	20	6	4	6	63	5	269	8	4	19	9	.679	1	0-0	0	3.06	3.45
2010	Det	AL	33	33	4	0	224.1	925	190	89	84	14	6	8	6	71	0	219	11	2	18	9	.667	1	0-0	0	2.79	3.37
2011	Det	AL	34	34	4	0	251.0	969	174	73	67	24	2	3	3	57	0	250	7	2	24	5	.828	2	0-0	0	1.92	2.40
	Postseason		4	4	0	0	21.2	100	26	17	14	5	1	0	0	10	0	23	3	1	1	2	.333	0	0-0	0	6.45	5.82
7 ML YEARS			199	199	14	0	1315.1	5452	1161	555	517	118	23	26	55	410	17	1215	55	14	107	57	.652	5	0-0	0	3.19	3.54

Dayan Viciedo

Bats: R Throws: R Pos: RF-21; DH-6; 1B-4; PH-1 DYE-yahn vee-see-AY-doe Ht: 5'11" Wt: 230 Born: 3/10/1989 Age: 23

Year	Team	Lg		G	AB	H	2B	3B	HR	(Hm	Rd)	TB	R	RBI	RC	TBB	IBB	SO	HBP	SH	SF		SB	CS	SB%	GDP		Avg	OBP	Slg
2009	Brham	AA		130	504	141	20	0	12	(-	-)	197	72	78	64	23	4	89	7	0	6		5	2	.71	12		.280	.317	.391
2010	Charltt	AAA		86	343	94	15	0	20	(-	-)	169	42	47	52	11	1	78	6	3	0		1	1	.50	16		.274	.308	.493
2011	Charltt	AAA		119	452	134	28	0	20	(-	-)	222	60	78	82	45	6	83	5	0	3		2	1	.67	10		.296	.364	.491
2010	CWS	AL		38	104	32	7	0	5	(4	1)	54	17	13	15	2	0	25	0	0	0		1	0	1.00	5		.308	.321	.519
2011	CWS	AL		29	102	26	3	0	1	(0	1)	32	11	6	12	9	0	23	2	0	0		1	0	1.00	4		.255	.327	.314
	2 ML YEARS			67	206	58	10	0	6	(4	2)	86	28	19	27	11	0	48	2	0	0		2	0	1.00	9		.282	.324	.417

Shane Victorino

Bats: B Throws: R Pos: CF-130; PH-3 Ht: 5'9" Wt: 190 Born: 11/30/1980 Age: 31

Year	Team	Lg		G	AB	H	2B	3B	HR	(Hm	Rd)	TB	R	RBI	RC	TBB	IBB	SO	HBP	SH	SF		SB	CS	SB%	GDP		Avg	OBP	Slg
2011	Lakwd*	A		2	6	1	0	0	0	(-	-)	1	1	2	0	1	0	2	0	0	0		0	0	-	0		.167	.286	.167
2011	Rdng*	AA		4	15	5	1	0	1	(-	-)	9	2	3	3	1	0	2	1	0	1		1	2	.33	0		.333	.389	.600
2003	SD	NL		36	73	11	2	0	0	(0	0)	13	8	4	1	7	0	17	1	1	1		7	2	.78	5		.151	.232	.178
2005	Phi	NL		21	17	5	0	0	2	(1	1)	11	5	8	4	0	0	3	0	0	2		0	0	-	0		.294	.263	.647
2006	Phi	NL		153	415	119	19	8	6	(3	3)	172	70	46	58	24	0	54	14	8	1		4	3	.57	5		.287	.346	.414
2007	Phi	NL		131	456	128	23	3	12	(6	6)	193	78	46	65	37	1	62	10	5	2		37	4	.90	10		.281	.347	.423
2008	Phi	NL		146	570	167	30	8	14	(6	8)	255	102	58	86	45	2	69	7	5	0		36	11	.77	8		.293	.352	.447
2009	Phi	NL		156	620	181	39	13	10	(4	6)	276	102	62	99	60	1	71	6	4	4		25	8	.76	5		.292	.358	.445
2010	Phi	NL		147	587	152	26	10	18	(13	5)	252	84	69	89	53	5	79	7	0	1		34	6	.85	7		.259	.327	.429
2011	Phi	NL		132	519	145	27	16	17	(6	11)	255	95	61	86	55	1	63	6	6	0		19	3	.86	4		.279	.355	.491
	Postseason			41	156	41	8	2	6	(3	3)	71	23	28	26	15	4	15	4	3	1		8	1	.89	3		.263	.341	.455
	8 ML YEARS			922	3257	908	166	58	79	(39	40)	1427	544	354	488	281	10	418	51	29	11		162	37	.81	44		.279	.344	.438

Carlos Villanueva

Pitches: R Bats: R Pos: RP-20; SP-13 vee-ah-nue-AY-vah Ht: 6'2" Wt: 228 Born: 11/28/1983 Age: 28

	HOW MUCH HE PITCHED						WHAT HE GAVE UP												THE RESULTS						
Year	Team	Lg	G	GS	CG	GF	IP	BFP	H	R	ER	HR	SH	SF	HB	TBB	IBB	SO	WP	Bk	W	L	Pct	Sh	Sv-Op	Hld	ERC	ERA
2011	Dnedin*	A+	1	1	0	0	1.0	5	1	1	0	0	0	0	0	0	0	0	0	0	0	0	-	0	0--	-	1.51	0.00
2006	Mil	NL	10	6	0	2	53.2	215	43	22	22	8	1	0	4	11	1	39	0	0	2	2	.500	0	0-0	0	2.85	3.69
2007	Mil	NL	59	6	0	8	114.1	489	101	52	50	16	4	1	3	53	3	99	3	0	8	5	.615	0	1-3	16	4.03	3.94
2008	Mil	NL	47	9	0	9	108.1	464	112	53	49	18	9	1	3	30	1	93	4	0	4	7	.364	0	1-1	11	4.29	4.07
2009	Mil	NL	64	6	0	23	96.0	422	102	58	57	13	4	0	2	35	8	83	4	0	4	10	.286	0	3-8	9	4.44	5.34
2010	Mil	NL	50	0	0	5	52.2	231	48	27	27	7	0	3	4	22	1	67	5	0	2	0	1.000	0	1-4	14	4.08	4.61
2011	Tor	AL	33	13	0	3	107.0	454	103	49	48	11	1	6	4	32	3	68	4	0	6	4	.600	0	0-0	1	3.57	4.04
	Postseason		2	0	0	0	3.2	11	0	0	0	0	0	0	0	0	0	3	0	0	0	0	-	0	0-0	1	0.00	0.00
	6 ML YEARS		263	40	0	50	532.0	2275	509	261	253	73	19	11	20	183	17	449	20	0	26	28	.481	0	6-17	50	3.95	4.28

Elih Villanueva

Pitches: R Bats: R Pos: SP-1 EE-lye vee-ah-nue-AY-vah Ht: 6'2" Wt: 235 Born: 7/26/1986 Age: 25

	HOW MUCH HE PITCHED						WHAT HE GAVE UP												THE RESULTS						
Year	Team	Lg	G	GS	CG	GF	IP	BFP	H	R	ER	HR	SH	SF	HB	TBB	IBB	SO	WP	Bk	W	L	Pct	Sh	Sv-Op	Hld	ERC	ERA
2008	Mrlns	R	2	1	0	0	6.0	21	4	2	2	0	0	0	1	0	0	9	0	0	0	0	-	0	0--	-	1.35	3.00
2008	Jmstwn	A-	5	1	0	1	19.0	78	15	6	4	2	0	0	0	5	0	20	1	0	2	1	.667	0	0--	-	2.41	1.89
2008	Jupiter	A+	4	2	0	1	11.2	50	7	1	1	0	0	0	4	4	0	12	0	0	1	0	1.000	0	0--	-	2.29	0.77
2009	Jupiter	A+	26	25	2	0	158.0	654	159	68	61	10	4	5	11	18	0	110	5	1	9	12	.429	2	0--	-	3.01	3.47
2009	Jaxnvl	AA	2	2	0	0	10.0	45	12	5	5	0	1	0	0	3	0	5	0	0	1	0	1.000	0	0--	-	3.97	4.50
2010	Jaxnvl	AA	28	28	0	0	179.0	709	137	56	45	15	12	8	8	34	0	115	7	1	14	4	.778	3	0--	-	2.15	2.26
2011	NewOr	AAA	28	28	0	0	165.0	728	199	113	98	24	7	8	2	59	2	105	8	2	7	11	.389	0	0--	-	5.56	5.35
2011	Fla	NL	1	1	0	0	3.0	20	5	8	8	1	0	0	1	5	1	2	0	0	0	1	.000	0	0-0	0	17.31	24.00

Brayan Villarreal

Pitches: R Bats: R Pos: RP-16 BRIAN VEE-yuh-ray-al Ht: 6'0" Wt: 170 Born: 5/10/1987 Age: 25

	HOW MUCH HE PITCHED						WHAT HE GAVE UP												THE RESULTS						
Year	Team	Lg	G	GS	CG	GF	IP	BFP	H	R	ER	HR	SH	SF	HB	TBB	IBB	SO	WP	Bk	W	L	Pct	Sh	Sv-Op	Hld	ERC	ERA
2007	Tigers	R	1	1	0	0	4.1	20	4	4	3	0	0	0	0	3	0	5	0	0	0	0	-	0	0--	-	3.91	6.23
2008	Tigers	R	11	6	1	1	37.0	152	26	19	15	0	2	2	5	11	0	37	2	2	1	5	.167	0	0--	-	1.99	3.65
2008	WMich	A	1	1	0	0	3.1	18	7	7	6	1	0	0	1	1	0	0	0	0	0	1	.000	0	0--	-	14.81	16.20
2009	WMich	A	26	16	0	3	103.1	429	85	40	33	5	7	6	13	34	0	118	6	0	5	5	.500	0	2--	-	3.02	2.87
2010	Lkland	A+	16	16	1	0	85.2	350	73	37	33	8	3	4	6	23	0	90	2	0	7	4	.636	0	0--	-	3.03	3.47
2010	Erie	AA	8	8	0	0	43.2	184	37	21	18	6	2	2	4	16	0	46	4	0	0	4	.000	0	0--	-	3.73	3.71
2011	Toledo	AAA	17	10	0	3	66.0	290	65	40	37	6	0	1	11	29	0	40	6	0	3	5	.375	0	0--	-	4.85	5.05
2011	Det	AL	16	0	0	4	16.0	76	21	12	12	3	1	0	0	10	2	14	1	0	1	1	.500	0	0-0	1	7.53	6.75

Pedro Viola

Pitches: L Bats: R Pos: RP-4 Ht: 6'1" Wt: 185 Born: 6/29/1983 Age: 29

	HOW MUCH HE PITCHED						WHAT HE GAVE UP												THE RESULTS						
Year	Team	Lg	G	GS	CG	GF	IP	BFP	H	R	ER	HR	SH	SF	HB	TBB	IBB	SO	WP	Bk	W	L	Pct	Sh	Sv-Op	Hld	ERC	ERA
2011	Bowie*	AA	40	0	0	14	39.2	153	26	10	9	2	1	3	1	13	1	40	9	0	3	2	.600	0	4--	-	1.88	2.04

			HOW MUCH HE PITCHED			WHAT HE GAVE UP								THE RESULTS						
Year	Team	Lg	G GS CG GF	IP	BFP	H	R	ER	HR SH SF HB	TBB IBB	SO	WP Bk	W	L	Pct	Sh	Sv-Op Hld	ERC	ERA
2009	Cin	NL	9 0 0 1	7.0	30	7	4	4	2 1 0 0	3 0	5	0 0	0	0	-	0	0-0 0	5.60	5.14
2010	Bal	AL	2 0 0 1	1.1	6	1	2	2	1 0 0 0	1 0	3	0 0	0	0	-	0	0-0 0	8.71	13.50
2011	Bal	AL	4 0 0 1	3.2	20	6	4	4	3 0 1 0	2 0	4	0 0	0	0	-	0	0-0 0	14.32	9.82
	3 ML YEARS		15 0 0 3	12.0	56	14	10	10	6 1 1 0	6 0	12	0 0	0	0	-	0	0-0 0	8.45	7.50

Arodys Vizcaino

Pitches: R **Bats:** R **Pos:** RP-17   uh-ROAD-eese   **Ht:** 6'0" **Wt:** 190 **Born:** 11/13/1990 **Age:** 21

			HOW MUCH HE PITCHED			WHAT HE GAVE UP								THE RESULTS						
Year	Team	Lg	G GS CG GF	IP	BFP	H	R	ER	HR SH SF HB	TBB IBB	SO	WP Bk	W	L	Pct	Sh	Sv-Op Hld	ERC	ERA
2008	Yanks	R	12 6 0 2	44.0	186	38	22	18	5 0 1 1	13 0	48	6 1	3	2	.600	0	0- - -	3.01	3.68
2009	StlsInd	A-	10 10 0 0	42.1	179	34	18	10	2 1 1 1	15 0	52	2 2	2	4	.333	0	0- - -	2.52	2.13
2010	Rome	A	14 14 0 0	71.2	292	63	25	19	1 2 3 3	9 0	68	6 2	9	4	.692	0	0- - -	2.01	2.39
2010	MrtlBh	A+	3 3 0 0	13.2	61	16	9	7	1 2 1 1	3 0	11	1 1	0	0	-	0	0- - -	4.31	4.61
2011	Lynbrg	A+	9 9 0 0	40.1	161	31	14	11	3 0 1 0	10 0	37	4 1	2	2	.500	0	0- - -	2.14	2.45
2011	Missi	AA	11 8 0 0	49.2	210	44	21	21	3 1 0 3	18 1	55	4 1	2	3	.400	0	0- - -	3.24	3.81
2011	Gwnntt	AAA	6 0 0 0	7.0	28	7	3	1	1 1 0 0	0 0	8	0 0	1	0	1.000	0	0- - -	2.74	1.29
2011	Atl	NL	17 0 0 2	17.1	77	16	9	9	1 0 0 1	9 1	17	5 0	1	1	.500	0	0-2 5	3.89	4.67

Omar Vizquel

Bats: B **Throws:** R **Pos:** 3B-29; 2B-16; SS-9; PH-7; PR-5; DH-3; 1B-1   vizz-KELL   **Ht:** 5'9" **Wt:** 180 **Born:** 4/24/1967 **Age:** 45

						BATTING														BASERUNNING				AVERAGES		
Year	Team	Lg	G	AB	H	2B	3B	HR	(Hm Rd)	TB	R	RBI	RC	TBB IBB	SO	HBP	SH	SF	SB	CS	SB%	GDP	Avg	OBP	Slg
1989	Sea	AL	143	387	85	7	3	1	(1 0)	101	45	20	25	28 0	40	1	13	2	1	4	.20	6	.220	.273	.261
1990	Sea	AL	81	255	63	3	2	2	(0 2)	76	19	18	22	18 0	22	0	10	2	4	1	.80	7	.247	.295	.298
1991	Sea	AL	142	426	98	16	4	1	(1 0)	125	42	41	39	45 0	37	0	8	3	7	2	.78	8	.230	.302	.293
1992	Sea	AL	136	483	142	20	4	0	(0 0)	170	49	21	54	32 0	38	2	9	1	15	13	.54	14	.294	.340	.352
1993	Sea	AL	158	560	143	14	2	2	(1 1)	167	68	31	53	50 2	71	4	13	3	12	14	.46	7	.255	.319	.298
1994	Cle	AL	69	286	78	10	1	1	(0 1)	93	39	33	32	23 0	23	0	11	2	13	4	.76	4	.273	.325	.325
1995	Cle	AL	136	542	144	28	0	6	(3 3)	190	87	56	70	59 0	59	1	10	10	29	11	.73	4	.266	.333	.351
1996	Cle	AL	151	542	161	36	1	9	(2 7)	226	98	64	87	56 0	42	4	12	9	35	9	.80	10	.297	.362	.417
1997	Cle	AL	153	565	158	23	6	5	(3 2)	208	89	49	75	57 1	58	2	16	2	43	12	.78	16	.280	.347	.368
1998	Cle	AL	151	576	166	30	6	2	(0 2)	214	86	50	82	62 1	64	4	12	6	37	12	.76	10	.288	.358	.372
1999	Cle	AL	144	574	191	36	4	5	(3 2)	250	112	66	106	65 0	50	1	17	7	42	9	.82	8	.333	.397	.436
2000	Cle	AL	156	613	176	27	3	7	(1 6)	230	101	66	92	87 0	72	5	7	5	22	10	.69	13	.287	.377	.375
2001	Cle	AL	155	611	156	26	8	2	(2 0)	204	84	50	66	61 0	72	2	15	4	13	9	.59	14	.255	.323	.334
2002	Cle	AL	151	582	160	31	5	14	(9 5)	243	85	72	91	56 3	64	8	7	10	18	10	.64	7	.275	.341	.418
2003	Cle	AL	64	250	61	13	2	2	(2 0)	84	43	19	25	29 0	20	0	5	1	8	3	.73	11	.244	.321	.336
2004	Cle	AL	148	567	165	28	3	7	(2 5)	220	82	59	86	57 0	62	1	20	6	19	6	.76	12	.291	.353	.388
2005	SF	NL	152	568	154	28	4	3	(0 3)	199	66	45	76	56 0	58	5	20	2	24	10	.71	10	.271	.341	.350
2006	SF	NL	153	579	171	22	10	4	(2 2)	225	88	58	90	56 3	51	6	13	5	24	7	.77	13	.295	.361	.389
2007	SF	NL	145	513	126	18	3	4	(1 3)	162	54	51	53	44 6	48	1	14	3	14	6	.70	14	.246	.305	.316
2008	SF	NL	92	266	59	10	1	0	(0 0)	71	24	23	24	24 9	29	0	7	3	5	4	.56	4	.222	.283	.267
2009	Tex	AL	62	177	47	7	2	1	(0 1)	61	17	14	24	13 0	27	0	5	0	4	0	1.00	6	.266	.316	.345
2010	CWS	AL	108	344	95	11	1	2	(1 1)	114	36	30	41	34 0	45	2	7	4	11	7	.61	8	.276	.341	.331
2011	CWS	AL	58	167	42	7	1	0	(0 0)	51	18	8	11	9 0	18	0	4	2	1	2	.33	2	.251	.287	.305
	Postseason		57	228	57	7	4	0	(0 0)	72	28	20	27	25 0	36	2	7	2	23	3	.88	0	.250	.327	.316
	23 ML YEARS		2908	10433	2841	451	76	80	(35 45)	3684	1432	944	1324	1021 25	1070	49	255	92	401	165	.71	202	.272	.337	.353

Ryan Vogelsong

Pitches: R **Bats:** R **Pos:** SP-28; RP-2   **Ht:** 6'4" **Wt:** 215 **Born:** 7/22/1977 **Age:** 34

			HOW MUCH HE PITCHED			WHAT HE GAVE UP								THE RESULTS						
Year	Team	Lg	G GS CG GF	IP	BFP	H	R	ER	HR SH SF HB	TBB IBB	SO	WP Bk	W	L	Pct	Sh	Sv-Op Hld	ERC	ERA
2011	Fresno*	AAA	2 2 0 0	11.1	47	8	3	2	1 0 1 0	5 0	17	0 0	2	0	1.000	0	0- - -	2.55	1.59
2000	SF	NL	4 0 0 3	6.0	24	4	0	0	0 0 0 0	2 0	6	0 0	0	0	-	0	0-0 1	1.57	0.00
2001	2 Tms	NL	15 2 0 8	34.2	164	39	31	26	6 0 1 2	20 1	24	2 0	0	5	.000	0	0-0 5	6.20	6.75
2003	Pit	NL	6 5 0 0	22.0	108	30	19	16	1 3 1 2	9 3	15	1 0	2	2	.500	0	0-0 5	5.72	6.55
2004	Pit	NL	31 26 0 4	133.0	610	148	97	96	22 8 6 10	67 7	92	3 0	6	13	.316	0	0-0 5	5.89	6.50
2005	Pit	NL	44 0 0 19	81.1	369	82	43	40	5 1 4 8	40 1	52	7 0	2	2	.500	0	0-1 5	4.51	4.43
2006	Pit	NL	20 0 0 7	38.0	178	44	27	27	2 5 4 7	16 2	27	4 1	0	0	-	0	0-0 5	5.31	6.39
2011	SF	NL	30 28 1 1	179.2	752	164	62	54	15 10 3 5	61 6	139	1 1	13	7	.650	1	0-0 5	3.32	2.71
01	SF	NL	13 0 0 8	28.2	130	29	21	18	5 0 1 2	14 0	17	2 0	0	3	.000	0	0-0 5	5.26	5.65
01	Pit	NL	2 2 0 0	6.0	34	10	10	8	1 0 0 0	6 1	7	0 0	0	2	.000	0	0-0 5	11.03	12.00
	7 ML YEARS		150 61 1 42	494.2	2205	511	279	259	51 27 19 34	215 20	355	18 2	23	29	.442	1	0-1 1	4.60	4.71

Edinson Volquez

Pitches: R **Bats:** R **Pos:** SP-20   VOLE-kezz   **Ht:** 6'0" **Wt:** 225 **Born:** 7/3/1983 **Age:** 28

			HOW MUCH HE PITCHED			WHAT HE GAVE UP								THE RESULTS						
Year	Team	Lg	G GS CG GF	IP	BFP	H	R	ER	HR SH SF HB	TBB IBB	SO	WP Bk	W	L	Pct	Sh	Sv-Op Hld	ERC	ERA
2011	Lsville*	AAA	13 13 1 0	87.1	362	72	31	23	5 5 1 4	29 0	83	7 0	4	2	.667	0	0- - -	2.76	2.37
2005	Tex	AL	6 3 0 0	12.2	75	25	22	20	3 0 1 2	10 0	11	0 0	0	4	.000	0	0-0 0	14.15	14.21
2006	Tex	AL	8 8 0 0	33.1	164	52	28	27	7 0 1 1	17 0	15	0 0	1	6	.143	0	0-0 0	9.27	7.29
2007	Tex	AL	6 6 0 0	34.0	149	34	18	17	4 0 2 2	15 0	29	0 0	2	1	.667	0	0-0 0	4.63	4.50
2008	Cin	NL	33 32 0 1	196.0	838	167	82	70	14 6 5 14	93 5	206	10 1	17	6	.739	0	0-0 0	3.61	3.21
2009	Cin	NL	9 9 0 0	49.2	218	34	25	24	6 2 1 5	32 0	47	2 1	4	2	.667	0	0-0 0	3.77	4.35

Year	Team	Lg	G	GS	CG	GF	IP	BFP	H	R	ER	HR	SH	SF	HB	TBB	IBB	SO	WP	Bk	W	L	Pct	Sh	Sv-Op	Hld	ERC	ERA
2010	Cin	NL	12	12	0	0	62.2	275	59	30	30	6	3	1	3	35	0	67	5	0	4	3	.571	0	0-0	0	4.60	4.31
2011	Cin	NL	20	20	0	0	108.2	489	106	72	69	19	5	6	4	65	3	104	5	2	5	7	.417	0	0-0	0	5.42	5.71
Postseason			1	1	0	0	1.2	11	4	4	4	0	0	1	0	2	0	0	0	0	0	1	.000	0	0-0	0	15.90	21.60
7 ML YEARS			94	90	0	1	497.0	2208	477	277	257	59	16	17	31	267	8	479	22	4	33	29	.532	0	0-0	0	4.77	4.65

Chris Volstad

Pitches: R **Bats:** R **Pos:** SP-29 **Ht:** 6'8" **Wt:** 232 **Born:** 9/23/1986 **Age:** 25

Year	Team	Lg	G	GS	CG	GF	IP	BFP	H	R	ER	HR	SH	SF	HB	TBB	IBB	SO	WP	Bk	W	L	Pct	Sh	Sv-Op	Hld	ERC	ERA
2011	NewOr*	AAA	3	3	1	0	18.1	80	20	9	9	1	1	1	0	9	0	14	1	0	1	1	.500	1	0- --		4.75	4.42
2008	Fla	NL	15	14	0	0	84.1	365	76	30	27	3	6	1	5	36	4	52	0	0	6	4	.600	0	0-0	0	3.30	2.88
2009	Fla	NL	29	29	1	0	159.0	682	169	100	92	29	8	3	3	59	3	107	8	0	9	13	.409	1	0-0	0	5.05	5.21
2010	Fla	NL	30	30	2	0	175.0	758	187	94	89	17	8	7	6	60	5	102	8	1	12	9	.571	1	0-0	0	4.38	4.58
2011	Fla	NL	29	29	0	0	165.2	719	187	96	90	23	12	10	1	49	6	117	2	1	5	13	.278	0	0-0	0	4.63	4.89
4 ML YEARS			103	102	3	0	584.0	2524	619	320	298	72	34	21	17	204	18	378	18	2	32	39	.451	2	0-0	0	4.47	4.59

Joey Votto

VAH-toe

Bats: L **Throws:** R **Pos:** 1B-160; PH-2 **Ht:** 6'3" **Wt:** 221 **Born:** 9/10/1983 **Age:** 28

Year	Team	Lg	G	AB	H	2B	3B	HR	Hm	Rd	TB	R	RBI	RC	TBB	IBB	SO	HBP	SH	SF	SB	CS	SB%	GDP	Avg	OBP	Slg
2007	Cin	NL	24	84	27	7	0	4	4	0	46	11	17	17	5	1	15	0	0	0	1	0	1.00	0	.321	.360	.548
2008	Cin	NL	151	526	156	32	3	24	14	10	266	69	84	91	59	9	102	2	0	2	7	5	.58	7	.297	.368	.506
2009	Cin	NL	131	469	151	38	1	25	14	11	266	82	84	99	70	10	106	4	0	1	4	1	.80	8	.322	.414	.567
2010	Cin	NL	150	547	177	36	2	37	18	19	328	106	113	132	91	8	125	7	0	3	16	5	.76	11	.324	**.424**	**.600**
2011	Cin	NL	161	599	185	**40**	3	29	13	16	318	101	103	**131**	110	15	129	4	0	6	8	6	.57	20	.309	.416	.531
Postseason			3	10	1	0	0	0	0	0	1	0	1	0	0	0	2	0	0	1	0	0	-	1	.100	.091	.100
5 ML YEARS			617	2225	696	153	9	119	63	56	1224	369	401	470	335	43	477	17	0	12	36	17	.68	46	.313	.405	.550

Cory Wade

Pitches: R **Bats:** R **Pos:** RP-40 **Ht:** 6'2" **Wt:** 190 **Born:** 5/28/1983 **Age:** 29

Year	Team	Lg	G	GS	CG	GF	IP	BFP	H	R	ER	HR	SH	SF	HB	TBB	IBB	SO	WP	Bk	W	L	Pct	Sh	Sv-Op	Hld	ERC	ERA
2011	Drhm*	AAA	21	0	0	4	36.2	145	34	5	5	4	1	0	1	6	0	34	0	0	2	1	.667	0	0- --		3.03	1.23
2011	S-WB*	AAA	1	0	0	0	1.2	5	2	0	0	0	0	0	0	0	0	1	0	0	1	0	1.000	0	0- --		4.27	0.00
2008	LAD	NL	55	0	0	21	71.1	275	51	22	18	7	2	1	4	15	3	51	2	0	2	1	.667	0	0-1	9	2.11	2.27
2009	LAD	NL	27	0	0	2	27.2	121	28	17	17	3	0	1	1	10	3	18	4	0	2	3	.400	0	0-6	7	3.96	5.53
2011	NYY	AL	40	0	0	8	39.2	157	33	10	9	5	0	0	0	8	0	30	1	0	6	1	.857	0	0-1	8	2.61	2.04
Postseason			7	0	0	1	7.1	28	6	3	3	1	0	0	0	0	0	4	1	0	0	1	.000	0	0-1	2	1.84	3.68
3 ML YEARS			122	0	0	31	138.2	553	112	49	44	15	2	2	5	33	6	99	7	0	10	5	.667	0	0-8	24	2.60	2.86

Neil Wagner

Pitches: R **Bats:** R **Pos:** RP-6 **Ht:** 6'0" **Wt:** 195 **Born:** 1/1/1984 **Age:** 28

Year	Team	Lg	G	GS	CG	GF	IP	BFP	H	R	ER	HR	SH	SF	HB	TBB	IBB	SO	WP	Bk	W	L	Pct	Sh	Sv-Op	Hld	ERC	ERA
2006	MhVlly	A-	26	0	0	24	32.1	122	16	5	5	1	1	0	0	9	0	50	2	0	0	1	.000	0	17- --		1.08	1.39
2007	Lk Cty	A	34	0	0	28	44.0	186	41	21	18	3	1	4	3	11	0	49	1	0	1	4	.200	0	11- --		3.13	3.68
2007	Knstn	A+	16	0	0	9	24.0	92	17	8	8	2	0	0	0	6	0	18	1	0	0	0	-	0	0- --		1.99	3.00
2008	Knstn	A+	41	0	0	17	62.0	274	67	34	31	1	6	2	1	21	0	81	5	1	3	6	.333	0	3- --		3.66	4.50
2008	Akron	AA	7	0	0	1	10.0	44	10	5	4	1	1	0	0	4	0	11	0	0	0	2	.000	0	0- --		3.98	3.60
2009	Akron	AA	46	0	0	24	61.0	262	48	24	20	3	3	2	1	32	2	69	6	0	1	3	.250	0	2- --		3.01	2.95
2010	Akron	AA	13	0	0	9	14.1	70	17	12	10	0	2	0	1	7	0	15	0	0	1	1	.500	0	4- --		4.70	6.28
2010	Mdland	AA	33	0	0	8	48.2	223	55	25	20	1	1	0	0	27	4	45	3	0	6	2	.750	0	1- --		4.66	3.70
2011	Mdland	AA	28	0	0	14	37.1	155	31	18	14	0	3	0	1	13	2	53	2	0	1	3	.250	0	4- --		2.33	3.38
2011	Scrmto	AAA	22	0	0	9	29.0	122	27	10	10	2	0	0	0	10	0	34	0	0	2	1	.667	0	2- --		3.27	3.10
2011	Oak	AL	6	0	0	5	5.0	24	6	7	4	1	0	0	1	3	0	4	0	0	0	0	-	0	0-0	0	7.98	7.20

Adam Wainwright

Pitches: R **Bats:** R **Pos:** P **Ht:** 6'7" **Wt:** 228 **Born:** 8/30/1981 **Age:** 30

Year	Team	Lg	G	GS	CG	GF	IP	BFP	H	R	ER	HR	SH	SF	HB	TBB	IBB	SO	WP	Bk	W	L	Pct	Sh	Sv-Op	Hld	ERC	ERA
2005	StL	NL	2	0	0	1	2.0	9	2	3	3	1	0	0	0	1	0	1	0	0	0	0	-	0	0-0	0	7.30	13.50
2006	StL	NL	61	0	0	10	75.0	309	64	26	26	6	4	1	4	22	2	72	3	0	2	1	.667	0	3-5	17	2.92	3.12
2007	StL	NL	32	32	1	0	202.0	882	212	93	83	13	9	5	9	70	4	136	6	0	14	12	.538	0	0-0	0	4.01	3.70
2008	StL	NL	20	20	1	0	132.0	544	122	51	47	12	6	4	3	34	1	91	3	0	11	3	.786	0	0-0	0	3.14	3.20
2009	StL	NL	34	**34**	1	0	**233.0**	970	216	75	68	17	10	5	3	66	1	212	7	0	19	8	.704	0	0-0	0	3.08	2.63
2010	StL	NL	33	33	5	0	230.1	910	186	68	62	15	13	6	4	56	2	213	2	0	20	11	.645	2	0-0	0	**2.36**	2.42
Postseason			10	1	0	9	17.2	67	10	1	1	1	1	0	0	3	0	22	1	0	0	1	1.000	0	4-5	5	1.27	0.51
6 ML YEARS			182	119	8	11	874.1	3624	802	316	289	64	42	21	23	249	10	724	21	0	66	35	.653	2	3-5	17	3.10	2.97

Tim Wakefield

Pitches: R Bats: R Pos: SP-23; RP-10   Ht: 6'2" Wt: 210 Born: 8/2/1966 Age: 45

Year	Team	Lg	G	GS	CG	GF	IP	BFP	H	R	ER	HR	SH	SF	HB	TBB	IBB	SO	WP	Bk	W	L	Pct	Sh	Sv-Op	Hld	ERC	ERA
1992	Pit	NL	13	13	4	0	92.0	373	76	26	22	3	6	4	1	35	1	51	3	1	8	1	.889	1	0-0	0	2.72	2.15
1993	Pit	NL	24	20	3	1	128.1	595	145	83	80	14	7	5	9	75	2	59	6	0	6	11	.353	2	0-0	0	5.97	5.61
1995	Bos	AL	27	27	6	0	195.1	804	163	76	64	22	3	7	9	68	0	119	11	0	16	8	.667	1	0-0	0	3.28	2.95
1996	Bos	AL	32	32	6	0	211.2	963	238	151	121	38	1	9	12	90	0	140	4	1	14	13	.519	0	0-0	0	5.68	5.14
1997	Bos	AL	35	29	4	2	201.1	866	193	109	95	24	3	7	16	87	5	151	6	0	12	15	.444	2	0-0	1	4.47	4.25
1998	Bos	AL	36	33	2	1	216.0	939	211	123	110	30	1	8	14	79	1	146	6	1	17	8	.680	0	0-0	0	4.30	4.58
1999	Bos	AL	49	17	0	28	140.0	635	146	93	79	19	1	8	5	72	2	104	1	0	6	11	.353	0	15-18	6	5.12	5.08
2000	Bos	AL	51	17	0	13	159.1	706	170	107	97	31	4	8	4	65	3	102	4	0	6	10	.375	0	0-1	3	5.23	5.48
2001	Bos	AL	45	17	0	5	168.2	732	156	84	73	13	3	9	18	73	5	148	5	1	9	12	.429	0	3-5	3	4.02	3.90
2002	Bos	AL	45	15	0	10	163.1	657	121	57	51	15	1	4	9	51	2	134	5	2	11	5	.688	0	3-5	5	2.54	2.81
2003	Bos	AL	35	33	0	0	202.1	872	193	106	92	23	2	4	12	71	0	169	8	0	11	7	.611	0	1-1	0	3.92	4.09
2004	Bos	AL	32	30	0	0	188.1	831	197	121	102	29	2	4	16	63	3	116	9	0	12	10	.545	0	0-0	1	4.73	4.87
2005	Bos	AL	33	33	3	0	225.1	943	210	113	104	35	1	6	11	68	4	151	8	0	16	12	.571	0	0-0	0	3.87	4.15
2006	Bos	AL	23	23	1	0	140.0	610	135	80	72	19	1	3	10	51	0	90	6	0	7	11	.389	0	0-0	0	4.22	4.63
2007	Bos	AL	31	31	0	0	189.0	800	191	104	100	22	2	6	4	64	1	110	10	0	17	12	.586	0	0-0	0	4.14	4.76
2008	Bos	AL	30	30	1	0	181.0	754	154	89	83	25	2	4	13	60	0	117	12	0	10	11	.476	0	0-0	0	3.54	4.13
2009	Bos	AL	21	21	2	0	129.2	572	137	67	66	12	4	1	10	50	0	72	4	0	11	5	.688	0	0-0	0	4.60	4.58
2010	Bos	AL	32	19	0	10	140.0	610	153	92	83	19	3	4	5	36	3	84	11	1	4	10	.286	0	0-0	0	4.32	5.34
2011	Bos	AL	33	23	1	6	154.2	677	163	110	88	25	4	8	8	47	1	93	15	1	7	8	.467	0	0-0	0	4.56	5.12
	Postseason		18	11	2	2	72.0	329	68	56	54	13	1	3	9	38	2	54	1	0	5	7	.417	0	0-0	0	5.25	6.75
	19 ML YEARS		627	463	33	78	3226.1	13939	3152	1791	1582	418	51	109	186	1205	33	2156	134	8	200	180	.526	6	22-30	13	4.26	4.41

Jordan Walden

Pitches: R Bats: R Pos: RP-62   Ht: 6'5" Wt: 235 Born: 11/16/1987 Age: 24

Year	Team	Lg	G	GS	CG	GF	IP	BFP	H	R	ER	HR	SH	SF	HB	TBB	IBB	SO	WP	Bk	W	L	Pct	Sh	Sv-Op	Hld	ERC	ERA
2007	Orem	R+	15	15	0	0	64.1	256	49	27	22	3	1	0	3	17	0	63	3	0	1	1	.500	0	0--	-	2.20	3.08
2008	CRpds	A	18	18	1	0	107.1	426	80	32	26	3	3	1	3	32	0	91	5	1	4	6	.400	0	0--	-	2.07	2.18
2008	RCuca	A+	9	9	0	0	49.0	214	42	30	22	4	1	1	2	24	0	50	3	0	5	2	.714	0	0--	-	3.60	4.04
2009	Ark	AA	13	13	0	0	60.0	274	72	39	35	4	2	1	3	29	1	57	7	1	1	5	.167	0	0--	-	5.56	5.25
2010	Ark	AA	38	0	0	30	43.0	186	44	18	16	2	3	0	0	22	2	38	5	0	1	1	.500	0	8--	-	4.28	3.35
2010	Salt Lk	AAA	6	0	0	2	6.2	29	8	3	3	0	0	0	0	2	0	3	0	0	0	0	--	0	0--	-	4.12	4.05
2010	LAA	AL	16	0	0	5	15.1	65	13	4	4	1	0	0	0	7	0	23	1	1	0	1	.000	0	1-1	6	3.21	2.35
2011	LAA	AL	62	0	0	42	60.1	253	49	22	20	3	4	2	1	26	3	67	6	0	5	5	.500	0	32-42	2	2.82	2.98
	2 ML YEARS		78	0	0	47	75.2	318	62	26	24	4	4	2	1	33	3	90	7	1	5	6	.455	0	33-43	8	2.90	2.85

Kyle Waldrop

Pitches: R Bats: R Pos: RP-7   Ht: 6'5" Wt: 215 Born: 10/27/1985 Age: 26

Year	Team	Lg	G	GS	CG	GF	IP	BFP	H	R	ER	HR	SH	SF	HB	TBB	IBB	SO	WP	Bk	W	L	Pct	Sh	Sv-Op	Hld	ERC	ERA
2004	Twins	R	7	7	0	0	38.0	146	32	9	6	1	1	0	1	4	0	30	1	1	3	2	.600	0	0--	-	1.90	1.42
2004	Elizab	R+	4	4	0	0	25.0	100	21	10	9	1	1	0	1	3	0	25	0	0	2	0	1.000	0	0--	-	1.97	3.24
2005	Beloit	A	27	27	2	0	151.2	667	182	93	84	17	5	5	8	23	1	108	9	0	6	11	.353	1	0--	-	4.40	4.98
2006	Beloit	A	18	18	1	0	110.0	460	110	54	47	8	3	1	14	17	0	62	8	0	6	3	.667	1	0--	-	3.45	3.85
2006	FtMyrs	A+	8	7	1	0	45.1	201	48	27	18	4	2	1	0	17	1	25	2	0	3	2	.600	0	0--	-	4.08	3.57
2007	FtMyrs	A+	16	16	0	0	92.2	383	90	42	35	3	2	2	9	24	0	57	5	1	7	5	.583	0	0--	-	3.38	3.40
2007	NwBrit	AA	11	11	0	0	59.0	274	74	42	35	7	2	1	10	19	1	33	3	0	3	6	.333	0	0--	-	6.06	5.34
2009	FtMyrs	A+	20	0	0	11	35.0	149	43	15	12	0	2	0	2	7	1	20	1	0	3	2	.600	0	0--	-	4.15	3.09
2009	NwBrit	AA	31	0	0	8	55.2	237	51	14	9	2	3	2	7	18	4	30	4	0	2	3	.400	0	3--	-	3.26	1.46
2010	Roch	AAA	59	0	0	20	87.2	369	89	38	25	5	0	2	7	20	4	60	4	1	5	3	.625	0	2--	-	3.46	2.57
2011	Roch	AAA	56	0	0	22	79.0	328	84	39	34	7	1	1	4	18	4	44	4	0	5	5	.500	0	3--	-	3.90	3.87
2011	Min	AL	7	0	0	1	11.0	50	10	7	7	1	1	0	0	6	2	5	1	0	1	0	1.000	0	0-0	0	3.59	5.73

Neil Walker

Bats: B Throws: R Pos: 2B-159; PH-2   Ht: 6'3" Wt: 215 Born: 9/10/1985 Age: 26

Year	Team	Lg	G	AB	H	2B	3B	HR	(Hm	Rd)	TB	R	RBI	RC	TBB	IBB	SO	HBP	SH	SF	SB	CS	SB%	GDP	Avg	OBP	Slg
2009	Pit	NL	17	36	7	1	0	0	(0	0)	8	5	0	2	4	0	11	0	0	0	1	0	1.00	1	.194	.275	.222
2010	Pit	NL	110	426	126	29	3	12	(5	7)	197	57	66	66	34	1	83	3	2	4	2	3	.40	4	.296	.349	.462
2011	Pit	NL	159	596	163	36	4	12	(4	8)	243	76	83	77	54	5	112	4	0	8	9	6	.60	15	.273	.334	.408
	3 ML YEARS		286	1058	296	66	7	24	(9	15)	448	138	149	145	92	6	206	7	2	12	12	9	.57	20	.280	.338	.423

Brett Wallace

Bats: L Throws: R Pos: 1B-96; PH-21   Ht: 6'2" Wt: 250 Born: 8/26/1986 Age: 25

Year	Team	Lg	G	AB	H	2B	3B	HR	(Hm	Rd)	TB	R	RBI	RC	TBB	IBB	SO	HBP	SH	SF	SB	CS	SB%	GDP	Avg	OBP	Slg
2008	QuadC	A	41	153	50	8	1	5	(-	-)	75	28	25	31	17	1	32	7	0	0	0	0	-	2	.327	.418	.490
2008	Sprgfld	AA	13	49	18	5	0	3	(-	-)	32	13	11	13	2	0	7	6	0	0	0	0	-	3	.367	.456	.653
2009	Sprgfld	AA	32	128	36	5	0	5	(-	-)	56	22	16	24	18	2	34	8	0	0	0	0	-	7	.281	.403	.438
2009	Memp	AAA	62	222	65	11	0	6	(-	-)	94	22	19	33	15	1	42	4	0	2	0	1	.00	7	.293	.346	.423
2009	Scrmto	AAA	44	182	55	10	0	9	(-	-)	92	32	28	33	14	4	40	5	0	2	1	1	.50	5	.302	.365	.505
2010	LsVgs	AAA	95	385	116	24	1	18	(-	-)	196	64	61	70	27	1	83	9	0	2	1	1	.50	9	.301	.359	.509

					BATTING																		BASERUNNING				AVERAGES		
Year	Team	Lg	G	AB	H	2B	3B	HR	(Hm	Rd)	TB	R	RBI	RC	TBB	IBB	SO	HBP	SH	SF	SB	CS	SB%	GDP	Avg	OBP	Slg
2011	OKCity	AAA	28	104	37	10	0	1	(-	-)	50	16	24	23	15	0	28	3	0	4	1	0	1.00	2	.356	.437	.481
2010	Hou	NL	51	144	32	6	1	2	(1	1)	46	14	13	10	8	3	50	7	0	0	0	0	-	3	.222	.296	.319
2011	Hou	NL	115	336	87	22	0	5	(2	3)	124	37	29	31	36	4	91	3	1	2	1	1	.50	12	.259	.334	.369
2 ML YEARS			166	480	119	28	1	7	(3	4)	170	51	42	41	44	7	141	10	1	2	1	1	.50	15	.248	.323	.354

P.J. Walters

Pitches: R **Bats:** R **Pos:** RP-5 **Ht:** 6'4" **Wt:** 200 **Born:** 3/12/1985 **Age:** 27

			HOW MUCH HE PITCHED					WHAT HE GAVE UP											THE RESULTS							
Year	Team	Lg	G	GS	CG	GF	IP	BFP	H	R	ER	HR	SH	SF	HB	TBB	IBB	SO	WP	Bk	W	L	Pct	Sh	Sv-Op Hld	ERC	ERA
2011	Memp*	AAA	17	17	1	0	103.1	454	105	51	49	9	2	5	12	42	2	87	0	1	7	4	.636	0	0- -	4.58	4.27
2011	LsVgs*	AAA	7	7	0	0	29.0	147	44	29	27	4	0	2	3	16	0	26	3	1	1	3	.250	0	0- -	8.69	8.38
2009	StL	NL	8	1	0	4	16.0	80	21	19	17	6	1	1	0	9	1	14	0	0	0	0	-	0	0-0 0	8.42	9.56
2010	StL	NL	7	3	0	3	30.0	129	32	20	20	5	1	2	0	10	0	22	0	0	2	0	1.000	0	0-0 0	4.67	6.00
2011	2 Tms		5	0	0	2	5.0	21	3	4	4	1	0	0	0	3	0	4	0	0	0	0	-	0	0-0 0	3.28	7.20
11	StL	NL	4	0	0	2	4.0	18	3	4	4	1	0	0	0	2	0	3	0	0	0	0	-	0	0-0 0	3.76	9.00
11	Tor	AL	1	0	0	0	1.0	3	0	0	0	0	0	0	0	1	0	1	0	0	0	0	-	0	0-0 0	1.26	0.00
3 ML YEARS			20	4	0	9	51.0	230	56	43	41	12	2	3	0	22	1	40	0	0	2	0	1.000	0	0-0 0	5.64	7.24

Chien-Ming Wang

Pitches: R **Bats:** R **Pos:** SP-11
CHENN-MING WONG **Ht:** 6'3" **Wt:** 230 **Born:** 3/31/1980 **Age:** 32

			HOW MUCH HE PITCHED					WHAT HE GAVE UP											THE RESULTS							
Year	Team	Lg	G	GS	CG	GF	IP	BFP	H	R	ER	HR	SH	SF	HB	TBB	IBB	SO	WP	Bk	W	L	Pct	Sh	Sv-Op Hld	ERC	ERA
2011	Hgrstn*	A	1	1	0	0	3.0	15	4	2	2	0	0	0	1	0	0	3	0	0	0	0	-	0	0- -	4.47	6.00
2011	Ptomc*	A+	1	1	0	0	4.0	13	1	0	0	0	0	0	0	2	0	2	1	0	0	0	-	0	0- -	0.87	0.00
2011	Hrsbrg*	A+	2	2	0	0	11.0	39	8	0	0	0	0	0	0	0	0	3	0	0	2	0	1.000	0	0- -	1.12	0.00
2011	Syrcse*	AAA	2	2	0	0	10.2	50	15	8	8	2	2	2	1	2	0	9	1	0	0	1	.000	0	0- -	6.52	6.75
2005	NYY	AL	18	17	0	0	116.1	486	113	58	52	9	3	4	6	32	3	47	3	0	8	5	.615	0	0-0 0	3.47	4.02
2006	NYY	AL	34	33	2	1	218.0	900	233	92	88	12	3	2	2	52	4	76	6	1	19	6	.760	1	1-1 0	3.62	3.63
2007	NYY	AL	30	30	1	0	199.1	823	199	84	82	9	2	3	8	59	1	104	9	1	19	7	.731	0	0-0 0	3.54	3.70
2008	NYY	AL	15	15	1	0	95.0	402	90	44	43	4	0	3	3	35	1	54	0	0	8	2	.800	0	0-0 0	3.39	4.07
2009	NYY	AL	12	9	0	2	42.0	206	66	46	45	7	3	1	2	19	1	29	3	0	1	6	.143	0	0-0 0	8.67	9.64
2011	Was	NL	11	11	0	0	62.1	264	67	35	28	8	2	2	1	13	0	25	2	0	4	3	.571	0	0-0 0	3.97	4.04
Postseason			4	4	0	0	19.0	90	28	19	16	5	2	0	3	5	0	7	0	0	1	3	.250	0	0-0 0	8.53	7.58
6 ML YEARS			120	115	4	3	733.0	3081	768	359	338	49	13	15	22	210	10	335	23	2	59	29	.670	1	1-1 0	3.83	4.15

Tony Watson

Pitches: L **Bats:** L **Pos:** RP-43 **Ht:** 6'4" **Wt:** 223 **Born:** 5/30/1985 **Age:** 27

			HOW MUCH HE PITCHED					WHAT HE GAVE UP											THE RESULTS							
Year	Team	Lg	G	GS	CG	GF	IP	BFP	H	R	ER	HR	SH	SF	HB	TBB	IBB	SO	WP	Bk	W	L	Pct	Sh	Sv-Op Hld	ERC	ERA
2007	StCol	A-	10	10	0	0	53.2	214	47	17	15	4	1	1	1	7	0	40	1	0	6	1	.857	0	0- -	2.32	2.52
2007	Hkry	A	3	3	0	0	14.0	57	14	6	6	2	0	1	2	1	0	18	0	0	1	1	.500	0	0- -	3.70	3.86
2008	Lynbg	A	28	28	0	0	151.2	632	149	70	60	16	8	4	9	36	0	104	1	0	8	12	.400	0	0- -	3.64	3.56
2009	Altna	AA	5	5	0	0	15.1	78	22	18	14	2	1	0	0	11	0	14	0	0	3	0	.000	0	0- -	8.29	8.22
2010	Altna	AA	34	9	0	5	111.1	437	82	33	33	11	3	2	5	24	1	105	2	0	6	4	.600	0	2- -	2.19	2.67
2011	Indy	AAA	26	1	0	6	34.1	140	24	10	9	2	2	1	2	11	2	35	2	0	3	3	.500	0	0- -	2.06	2.36
2011	Pit	NL	43	0	0	6	41.0	174	34	18	18	6	2	1	1	20	4	37	0	0	2	2	.500	0	0-1 10	3.75	3.95

Jered Weaver

Pitches: R **Bats:** R **Pos:** SP-33 **Ht:** 6'7" **Wt:** 215 **Born:** 10/4/1982 **Age:** 29

			HOW MUCH HE PITCHED					WHAT HE GAVE UP											THE RESULTS							
Year	Team	Lg	G	GS	CG	GF	IP	BFP	H	R	ER	HR	SH	SF	HB	TBB	IBB	SO	WP	Bk	W	L	Pct	Sh	Sv-Op Hld	ERC	ERA
2006	LAA	AL	19	19	0	0	123.0	490	94	36	35	15	2	3	3	33	1	105	2	0	11	2	.846	0	0-0 0	2.57	2.56
2007	LAA	AL	28	28	0	0	161.0	695	178	77	70	17	5	5	2	45	3	115	4	0	13	7	.650	0	0-0 0	4.24	3.91
2008	LAA	AL	30	30	0	0	176.2	745	173	88	85	20	1	4	6	54	4	152	3	0	11	10	.524	0	0-0 0	3.80	4.33
2009	LAA	AL	33	33	4	0	211.0	882	196	91	88	26	6	8	4	66	3	174	0	0	16	8	.667	2	0-0 0	3.56	3.75
2010	LAA	AL	34	34	0	0	224.1	905	187	83	75	23	2	5	0	54	0	233	7	1	13	12	.520	0	0-0 0	2.59	3.01
2011	LAA	AL	33	33	4	0	235.2	926	182	65	63	20	5	5	3	56	0	198	8	0	18	8	.692	2	0-0 0	2.27	2.41
Postseason			6	3	0	2	20.2	83	12	6	6	5	0	0	0	10	0	22	0	0	2	1	.667	0	0-0 1	3.04	2.61
6 ML YEARS			177	177	8	0	1131.2	4643	1010	440	416	121	21	29	18	308	11	977	27	1	82	47	.636	4	0-0 0	3.10	3.31

Brandon Webb

Pitches: R **Bats:** R **Pos:** P **Ht:** 6'3" **Wt:** 228 **Born:** 5/9/1979 **Age:** 33

			HOW MUCH HE PITCHED					WHAT HE GAVE UP											THE RESULTS							
Year	Team	Lg	G	GS	CG	GF	IP	BFP	H	R	ER	HR	SH	SF	HB	TBB	IBB	SO	WP	Bk	W	L	Pct	Sh	Sv-Op Hld	ERC	ERA
2011	Frisco*	AA	4	4	0	0	12.0	62	21	13	13	1	0	2	2	6	0	8	1	0	0	2	.000	0	0- -	10.10	9.75
2003	Ari	NL	29	28	1	1	180.2	750	140	65	57	12	9	1	13	68	4	172	9	1	10	9	.526	1	0-0 0	2.80	2.84
2004	Ari	NL	35	35	1	0	208.0	933	194	111	83	17	14	6	11	119	11	164	17	1	7	16	.304	0	0-0 0	4.32	3.59
2005	Ari	NL	33	33	1	0	229.0	943	229	98	90	21	10	7	2	59	4	172	14	1	14	12	.538	0	0-0 0	3.54	3.54
2006	Ari	NL	33	33	5	0	235.0	950	216	91	81	15	10	6	6	50	4	178	5	2	16	8	.667	3	0-0 0	2.81	3.10
2007	Ari	NL	34	34	4	0	236.1	975	209	91	79	12	9	6	5	72	6	194	3	0	18	10	.643	3	0-0 0	2.82	3.01
2008	Ari	NL	34	34	3	0	226.2	944	206	95	83	13	8	9	12	65	5	183	8	1	22	7	.759	0	0-0 0	3.04	3.30
2009	Ari	NL	1	1	0	0	4.0	20	6	6	6	2	0	0	1	2	0	2	0	0	0	0	-	0	0-0 0	12.87	13.50
Postseason			2	2	0	0	13.0	55	11	5	5	0	0	0	1	5	0	13	2	0	1	1	.500	0	0-0 0	2.79	3.46
7 ML YEARS			199	198	15	1	1319.2	5515	1200	557	479	92	60	35	50	435	34	1065	56	6	87	62	.584	8	0-0 0	3.23	3.27

Ryan Webb

Pitches: R Bats: R Pos: RP-53   Ht: 6'6" Wt: 214 Born: 2/5/1986 Age: 26

		HOW MUCH HE PITCHED							WHAT HE GAVE UP											THE RESULTS							
Year	Team	Lg	G	GS	CG	GF	IP	BFP	H	R	ER	HR	SH	SF	HB	TBB	IBB	SO	WP	Bk	W	L	Pct	Sh	Sv-Op	Hld	ERC	ERA
2011	Mrlns*	R	1	1	0	0	2.0	7	2	0	0	0	0	0	0	0	0	2	0	0	0	-	-	0	0--	-	2.31	0.00
2011	Jupiter*	A+	3	1	0	0	3.1	15	4	1	1	0	0	0	0	3	0	3	0	0	1	0	1.000	0	0--	-	7.19	2.70
2009	SD	NL	28	0	0	9	25.2	117	27	14	11	3	2	1	1	11	1	19	4	0	2	1	.667	0	0-0	6	4.54	3.86
2010	SD	NL	54	0	0	15	59.0	253	64	21	19	1	1	1	1	19	5	44	2	1	3	1	.750	0	0-2	9	3.61	2.90
2011	Fla	NL	53	0	0	10	50.2	214	48	20	18	2	3	1	2	20	5	31	1	1	2	4	.333	0	0-4	8	3.39	3.20
	3 ML YEARS		135	0	0	34	135.1	584	139	55	48	6	6	3	4	50	11	94	7	2	7	6	.538	0	0-6	23	3.70	3.19

Jemile Weeks

Bats: B Throws: R Pos: 2B-96; PH-1   jah-MYLE   Ht: 5'9" Wt: 161 Born: 1/26/1987 Age: 25

					BATTING																BASERUNNING				AVERAGES		
Year	Team	Lg	G	AB	H	2B	3B	HR	(Hm	Rd)	TB	R	RBI	RC	TBB	IBB	SO	HBP	SH	SF	SB	CS	SB%	GDP	Avg	OBP	Slg
2008	Kane	A	19	74	22	3	1	1	(-	-)	30	11	8	14	13	0	12	3	0	0	6	2	.75	1	.297	.422	.405
2009	Stcktn	A+	50	201	60	9	2	7	(-	-)	94	29	31	38	26	0	40	3	1	1	5	1	.83	5	.299	.385	.468
2009	Mdland	AA	30	105	25	5	0	2	(-	-)	36	10	13	12	10	0	16	1	4	3	4	0	1.00	0	.238	.303	.343
2010	Mdland	AA	67	273	73	14	7	3	(-	-)	110	43	33	39	28	0	37	3	2	6	11	6	.65	5	.267	.335	.403
2010	As	R	10	36	11	2	1	0	(-	-)	15	9	1	7	7	0	4	1	0	0	5	1	.83	1	.306	.432	.417
2011	Scrmto	AAA	45	184	59	6	4	3	(-	-)	82	30	22	36	29	0	32	2	1	1	10	4	.71	6	.321	.417	.446
2011	Oak	AL	97	406	123	26	8	2	(1	1)	171	50	36	64	21	1	62	4	2	4	22	11	.67	3	.303	.340	.421

Rickie Weeks

Bats: R Throws: R Pos: 2B-115; DH-2; PH-1   Ht: 5'10" Wt: 213 Born: 9/13/1982 Age: 29

					BATTING																BASERUNNING				AVERAGES		
Year	Team	Lg	G	AB	H	2B	3B	HR	(Hm	Rd)	TB	R	RBI	RC	TBB	IBB	SO	HBP	SH	SF	SB	CS	SB%	GDP	Avg	OBP	Slg
2003	Mil	NL	7	12	2	1	0	0	(0	0)	3	1	0	0	1	0	6	1	0	0	0	0	-	0	.167	.286	.250
2005	Mil	NL	96	360	86	13	2	13	(8	5)	142	56	42	49	40	2	96	11	2	1	15	2	.88	11	.239	.333	.394
2006	Mil	NL	95	359	100	15	3	8	(6	2)	145	73	34	53	30	1	92	19	2	3	19	5	.79	6	.279	.363	.404
2007	Mil	NL	118	409	96	21	6	16	(5	11)	177	87	36	65	78	5	116	14	3	2	25	2	.93	3	.235	.374	.433
2008	Mil	NL	129	475	111	22	7	14	(3	11)	189	89	46	67	66	0	115	14	1	4	19	5	.79	5	.234	.342	.398
2009	Mil	NL	37	147	40	5	2	9	(7	2)	76	28	24	27	12	0	39	3	0	0	2	2	.50	1	.272	.340	.517
2010	Mil	NL	160	651	175	32	4	29	(16	13)	302	112	83	110	76	0	184	25	0	2	11	4	.73	5	.269	.366	.464
2011	Mil	NL	118	453	122	26	2	20	(10	10)	212	77	49	68	50	3	107	8	1	3	9	2	.82	6	.269	.350	.468
	Postseason		3	4	0	0	0	0	(0	0)	0	0	0	0	0	0	2	0	0	0	0	0	-	0	.000	.000	.000
	8 ML YEARS		760	2866	732	135	26	109	(55	54)	1246	523	314	439	353	11	755	95	9	15	100	22	.82	37	.255	.354	.435

Kyle Weiland

Pitches: R Bats: L Pos: SP-5; RP-2   WHY-lend   Ht: 6'4" Wt: 195 Born: 9/12/1986 Age: 25

				HOW MUCH HE PITCHED					WHAT HE GAVE UP											THE RESULTS							
Year	Team	Lg	G	GS	CG	GF	IP	BFP	H	R	ER	HR	SH	SF	HB	TBB	IBB	SO	WP	Bk	W	L	Pct	Sh	Sv-Op	Hld	ERC	ERA
2008	Lowell	A-	15	10	0	1	60.0	238	36	17	10	1	2	1	8	10	0	68	1	1	3	3	.500	0	0--	-	1.35	1.50
2009	Salem	A+	26	26	0	0	132.2	575	119	65	51	4	5	2	16	57	0	112	10	3	7	9	.438	0	0--	-	3.60	3.46
2010	Portlnd	AA	25	25	0	0	128.1	543	112	70	63	13	3	1	16	49	0	120	7	2	5	9	.357	0	0--	-	3.86	4.42
2011	Pwtckt	AAA	24	24	0	0	128.1	537	108	54	51	10	7	2	8	55	0	126	9	2	8	10	.444	0	0--	-	3.47	3.58
2011	Bos	AL	7	5	0	2	24.2	118	29	22	21	5	0	1	4	12	0	13	0	0	0	3	.000	0	0-0	0	6.89	7.66

Robbie Weinhardt

Pitches: R Bats: R Pos: RP-2   Ht: 6'2" Wt: 205 Born: 12/8/1985 Age: 26

				HOW MUCH HE PITCHED					WHAT HE GAVE UP											THE RESULTS							
Year	Team	Lg	G	GS	CG	GF	IP	BFP	H	R	ER	HR	SH	SF	HB	TBB	IBB	SO	WP	Bk	W	L	Pct	Sh	Sv-Op	Hld	ERC	ERA
2008	Tigers	R	3	0	0	0	5.2	26	6	3	0	0	0	1	0	2	0	4	0	0	0	0	-	0	0--	-	3.26	0.00
2008	Lkland	A+	21	0	0	10	35.1	139	19	11	8	1	6	3	2	11	2	44	3	0	3	1	.750	0	4--	-	1.31	2.04
2009	Lkland	A+	22	0	0	12	31.2	131	24	5	3	2	0	0	1	10	0	40	2	0	1	1	.500	0	3--	-	2.31	0.85
2009	Erie	AA	20	0	0	9	31.1	141	28	9	8	0	1	0	4	16	1	32	2	0	0	1	.000	0	2--	-	3.54	2.30
2010	Toledo	AAA	24	0	0	12	34.1	131	26	7	6	0	0	0	1	7	0	25	0	0	1	1	.500	0	1--	-	1.72	1.57
2010	Conn	A-	3	0	0	1	4.0	18	2	1	1	0	0	0	1	2	0	5	0	0	1	0	1.000	0	0--	-	1.89	2.25
2011	Toledo	AAA	24	0	0	14	34.2	162	36	31	25	3	0	1	7	14	1	32	3	0	1	4	.200	0	1--	-	4.81	6.49
2011	Erie	AA	16	0	0	8	26.2	113	29	12	12	3	0	1	1	11	0	23	2	0	1	1	.500	0	1--	-	5.13	4.05
2010	Det	AL	28	0	0	4	29.1	135	40	23	20	2	1	1	3	8	2	21	1	0	2	2	.500	0	0-2	5	5.77	6.14
2011	Det	AL	2	0	0	0	1.2	9	4	2	2	0	0	0	0	0	0	1	0	0	0	0	-	0	0-0	0	10.16	10.80
	2 ML YEARS		30	0	0	4	31.0	144	44	25	22	2	1	1	3	8	2	22	1	0	2	2	.500	0	0-2	5	5.99	6.39

Casper Wells

Bats: R Throws: R Pos: RF-58; LF-21; CF-9; DH-8; PH-5; PR-5   Ht: 6'2" Wt: 210 Born: 11/23/1984 Age: 27

					BATTING																BASERUNNING				AVERAGES		
Year	Team	Lg	G	AB	H	2B	3B	HR	(Hm	Rd)	TB	R	RBI	RC	TBB	IBB	SO	HBP	SH	SF	SB	CS	SB%	GDP	Avg	OBP	Slg
2005	Tigers	R	45	141	31	9	5	5	(-	-)	65	25	20	24	18	0	59	8	0	0	6	0	1.00	3	.220	.341	.461
2006	Lkland	A+	11	33	5	1	0	1	(-	-)	9	4	4	3	4	0	9	3	1	0	1	0	1.00	1	.152	.300	.273
2006	Oneont	A-	35	105	24	8	0	1	(-	-)	35	19	14	11	9	0	27	3	1	1	1	1	.50	1	.229	.305	.333
2007	Lkland	A+	2	2	1	1	0	0	(-	-)	2	0	0	0	0	0	1	0	0	0	0	0	-	0	.500	.500	1.000
2007	Oneont	A-	67	260	69	18	11	9	(-	-)	136	46	47	43	18	0	64	6	0	4	8	7	.53	3	.265	.323	.523
2008	WMich	A	50	179	43	7	0	10	(-	-)	80	30	26	31	22	0	39	1	0	1	17	5	.77	2	.240	.351	.447
2008	Erie	AA	75	270	78	18	6	17	(-	-)	159	60	53	59	30	0	66	9	2	2	8	3	.73	5	.289	.376	.589
2009	Erie	AA	86	311	81	18	4	15	(-	-)	152	52	41	56	43	3	103	11	1	1	8	8	.50	5	.260	.369	.489

Year	Team	Lg	G	AB	H	2B	3B	HR	(Hm	Rd)	TB	R	RBI	RC	TBB	IBB	SO	HBP	SH	SF	SB	CS	SB%	GDP	Avg	OBP	Slg
2010	Toledo	AAA	103	387	90	22	6	21	(-	-)	187	56	46	57	34	0	111	9	0	0	7	8	.47	3	.233	.309	.483
2011	Toledo	AAA	7	27	10	2	2	2	(-	-)	22	4	6	8	3	0	8	0	0	0	0	0	-	0	.370	.433	.815
2010	Det	AL	36	93	30	6	1	4	(1	3)	50	14	17	16	6	0	19	0	0	0	0	1	.00	2	.323	.364	.538
2011	2 Tms	AL	95	215	51	11	0	11	(7	4)	95	30	27	30	18	2	71	7	1	0	3	2	.60	3	.237	.317	.442
11	Det	AL	64	113	29	10	0	4	(1	3)	51	16	12	15	9	0	29	2	1	0	1	0	1.00	2	.257	.323	.451
11	Sea	AL	31	102	22	1	0	7	(6	1)	44	14	15	15	9	2	42	5	0	0	2	2	.50	1	.216	.310	.431
2 ML YEARS			131	308	81	17	1	15	(8	7)	145	44	44	46	24	2	90	7	1	0	3	3	.50	5	.263	.330	.471

Randy Wells

Pitches: R Bats: R Pos: SP-23 Ht: 6'5" Wt: 230 Born: 8/28/1982 Age: 29

Year	Team	Lg	G	GS	CG	GF	IP	BFP	H	R	ER	HR	SH	SF	HB	TBB	IBB	SO	WP	Bk	W	L	Pct	Sh	Sv-Op	Hld	ERC	ERA
2011	Peoria*	A	1	1	0	0	3.2	18	6	3	1	0	0	0	0	0	0	1	0	0	0	1	.000	0	0- -	-	4.92	2.45
2011	Iowa*	AAA	1	1	0	0	4.0	21	6	7	6	1	0	0	0	3	0	3	1	0	0	1	.000	0	0- -	-	9.88	13.50
2008	2 Tms		4	0	0	0	5.1	18	0	0	0	0	0	0	0	3	0	1	0	0	0	0	-	0	0-0	0	0.35	0.00
2009	ChC	NL	27	27	0	0	165.1	694	165	67	56	14	7	4	6	46	4	104	3	1	12	10	.545	0	0-0	0	3.62	3.05
2010	ChC	NL	32	32	0	0	194.1	843	209	99	92	19	8	0	6	63	5	144	2	0	8	14	.364	0	0-0	0	4.26	4.26
2011	ChC	NL	23	23	2	0	135.1	583	141	76	75	23	3	6	2	47	4	82	8	0	7	6	.538	1	0-0	0	4.62	4.99
08	Tor	AL	1	0	0	1	1.0	4	0	0	0	0	0	0	0	1	0	0	0	0	0	0	-	0	0-0	0	0.95	0.00
08	ChC	NL	3	0	0	1	4.1	14	0	0	0	0	0	0	0	2	0	1	0	0	0	0	-	0	0-0	0	0.25	0.00
4 ML YEARS			86	82	2	2	500.1	2138	515	240	223	56	18	10	14	159	13	331	13	1	27	30	.474	1	0-0	0	4.08	4.01

Vernon Wells

Bats: R Throws: R Pos: LF-111; CF-12; RF-10; DH-7; PH-1; PR-1 Ht: 6'1" Wt: 230 Born: 12/8/1978 Age: 33

Year	Team	Lg	G	AB	H	2B	3B	HR	(Hm	Rd)	TB	R	RBI	RC	TBB	IBB	SO	HBP	SH	SF	SB	CS	SB%	GDP	Avg	OBP	Slg
2011	InldEm*	A+	2	5	1	1	0	0	(-	-)	2	3	3	1	2	0	1	0	0	0	0	0	-	0	.200	.429	.400
1999	Tor	AL	24	88	23	5	0	1	(1	0)	31	8	8	7	4	0	18	0	0	0	1	1	.50	6	.261	.293	.352
2000	Tor	AL	3	2	0	0	0	0	(0	0)	0	0	0	0	0	0	0	0	0	0	0	0	-	0	.000	.000	.000
2001	Tor	AL	30	96	30	8	0	1	(1	0)	41	14	6	16	5	0	15	1	0	1	5	0	1.00	3	.313	.350	.427
2002	Tor	AL	159	608	167	34	4	23	(10	13)	278	87	100	88	27	0	85	3	2	8	9	4	.69	15	.275	.305	.457
2003	Tor	AL	161	678	215	49	5	33	(13	20)	373	118	117	124	42	2	80	7	0	8	4	1	.80	21	.317	.359	.550
2004	Tor	AL	134	536	146	34	2	23	(14	9)	253	82	67	72	51	2	83	2	0	1	9	2	.82	17	.272	.337	.472
2005	Tor	AL	156	620	167	30	3	28	(14	14)	287	78	97	96	47	3	86	3	0	8	8	3	.73	13	.269	.320	.463
2006	Tor	AL	154	611	185	40	5	32	(24	8)	331	91	106	107	54	0	90	3	0	9	17	4	.81	13	.303	.357	.542
2007	Tor	AL	149	584	143	36	4	16	(8	8)	235	85	80	74	49	4	89	3	0	6	10	4	.71	9	.245	.304	.402
2008	Tor	AL	108	427	128	22	1	20	(11	9)	212	63	78	68	29	5	46	3	0	7	4	2	.67	16	.300	.343	.496
2009	Tor	AL	158	630	164	37	3	15	(8	7)	252	84	66	65	48	2	86	1	0	5	17	4	.81	18	.260	.311	.400
2010	Tor	AL	157	590	161	44	3	31	(20	11)	304	79	88	92	50	5	84	3	0	3	6	4	.60	18	.273	.331	.515
2011	LAA	AL	131	505	110	15	4	25	(8	17)	208	60	66	52	20	0	86	1	0	3	9	4	.69	8	.218	.248	.412
13 ML YEARS			1524	5975	1639	354	34	248	(132	116)	2805	849	879	861	426	23	848	30	2	59	99	33	.75	154	.274	.323	.469

Jayson Werth

Bats: R Throws: R Pos: RF-134; CF-19; PH-2 Ht: 6'5" Wt: 218 Born: 5/20/1979 Age: 33

Year	Team	Lg	G	AB	H	2B	3B	HR	(Hm	Rd)	TB	R	RBI	RC	TBB	IBB	SO	HBP	SH	SF	SB	CS	SB%	GDP	Avg	OBP	Slg
2002	Tor	AL	15	46	12	2	1	0	(0	0)	16	4	6	5	6	0	11	0	0	1	1	0	1.00	4	.261	.340	.348
2003	Tor	AL	26	48	10	4	0	2	(0	2)	20	7	10	6	3	0	22	0	0	0	1	0	1.00	6	.208	.255	.417
2004	LAD	NL	89	290	76	11	3	16	(11	5)	141	56	47	47	30	0	85	4	1	1	4	1	.80	1	.262	.338	.486
2005	LAD	NL	102	337	79	22	2	7	(1	6)	126	46	43	44	48	2	114	6	1	3	11	2	.85	10	.234	.338	.374
2007	Phi	NL	94	255	76	11	3	8	(1	7)	117	43	49	57	44	1	73	2	2	1	7	1	.88	0	.298	.404	.459
2008	Phi	NL	134	418	114	16	3	24	(11	13)	208	73	67	74	57	1	119	4	0	3	20	1	.95	2	.273	.363	.498
2009	Phi	NL	159	571	153	26	1	36	(21	15)	289	98	99	107	91	8	156	8	0	6	20	3	.87	11	.268	.373	.506
2010	Phi	NL	156	554	164	46	2	27	(18	9)	295	106	85	91	82	6	147	7	0	9	13	3	.81	11	.296	.388	.532
2011	Was	NL	150	561	130	26	1	20	(10	10)	218	69	58	74	74	5	160	10	0	4	19	3	.86	10	.232	.330	.389
Postseason			44	153	41	9	2	13	(9	4)	93	30	26	29	27	4	52	1	0	1	5	0	1.00	3	.268	.379	.608
9 ML YEARS			925	3080	814	164	16	140	(73	67)	1430	502	464	505	435	23	887	41	4	28	96	14	.87	49	.264	.360	.464

Jake Westbrook

Pitches: R Bats: R Pos: SP-33 Ht: 6'3" Wt: 215 Born: 9/29/1977 Age: 34

Year	Team	Lg	G	GS	CG	GF	IP	BFP	H	R	ER	HR	SH	SF	HB	TBB	IBB	SO	WP	Bk	W	L	Pct	Sh	Sv-Op	Hld	ERC	ERA
2000	NYY	AL	3	2	0	1	6.2	38	15	10	10	1	0	2	0	4	1	1	0	0	0	2	.000	0	0-0	0	13.53	13.50
2001	Cle	AL	23	6	0	3	64.2	290	79	43	42	6	1	5	4	22	4	48	4	0	4	4	.500	0	0-0	0	5.25	5.85
2002	Cle	AL	11	4	0	1	41.2	185	50	30	27	6	2	1	1	12	1	20	1	0	1	3	.250	0	0-2	1	5.12	5.83
2003	Cle	AL	34	22	1	4	133.0	580	142	70	64	9	4	3	12	56	1	58	3	0	7	10	.412	0	0-0	1	4.78	4.33
2004	Cle	AL	33	30	5	2	215.2	895	208	95	81	19	6	6	5	61	3	116	4	1	14	9	.609	1	0-0	0	3.45	3.38
2005	Cle	AL	34	34	2	0	210.2	895	218	121	105	19	5	4	7	56	3	119	3	0	15	15	.500	0	0-0	0	3.78	4.49
2006	Cle	AL	32	32	3	0	211.1	904	247	106	98	15	5	4	4	55	4	109	5	0	15	10	.600	2	0-0	0	4.39	4.17
2007	Cle	AL	25	25	0	0	152.0	648	159	78	73	13	6	4	6	55	5	93	3	0	6	9	.400	0	0-0	0	4.28	4.32
2008	Cle	AL	5	5	1	0	34.2	139	33	13	12	5	0	2	1	7	0	19	1	0	1	2	.333	0	0-0	0	3.54	3.12
2010	2 Tms		33	33	1	0	202.2	860	203	99	95	16	11	5	2	68	4	128	8	0	10	11	.476	0	0-0	0	3.99	4.22
2011	StL	NL	33	33	0	0	183.1	809	208	103	95	16	11	5	2	73	8	104	3	0	12	9	.571	0	0-0	0	4.75	4.66
10	Cle	AL	21	21	1	0	127.2	543	133	68	66	15	3	3	6	44	4	73	6	0	6	7	.462	0	0-0	0	4.45	4.65
10	StL	NL	12	12	0	0	75.0	317	70	31	29	5	2	2	0	24	0	55	2	0	4	4	.500	0	0-0	0	3.25	3.48
Postseason			3	3	0	0	17.2	74	25	11	11	2	0	1	0	4	1	8	0	0	1	2	.333	0	0-0	0	6.33	5.60
11 ML YEARS			266	226	13	11	1456.1	6243	1562	768	702	129	45	39	50	469	34	815	35	1	85	84	.503	3	0-2	7	4.24	4.34

Dan Wheeler

Pitches: R **Bats:** R **Pos:** RP-47   **Ht:** 6'3" **Wt:** 220 **Born:** 12/10/1977 **Age:** 34

Year	Team	Lg	G	GS	CG	GF	IP	BFP	H	R	ER	HR	SH	SF	HB	TBB	IBB	SO	WP	Bk	W	L	Pct	Sh	Sv-Op	Hld	ERC	ERA
2011	Pwtckt*	AAA	3	0	0	2	4.2	19	3	1	1	1	0	0	0	2	0	7	1	0	0	0	-	0	0--	-	2.95	1.93
1999	TB	AL	6	6	0	0	30.2	136	35	20	20	7	1	0	0	13	1	32	1	0	0	4	.000	0	0-0	0	5.96	5.87
2000	TB	AL	11	2	0	6	23.0	111	29	14	14	2	1	1	2	11	2	17	2	0	1	1	.500	0	0-1	1	5.87	5.48
2001	TB	AL	13	0	0	3	17.2	87	30	17	17	3	0	2	0	5	0	12	1	1	0	1	1.000	0	0-0	0	8.38	8.66
2003	NYM	NL	35	0	0	10	51.0	215	49	23	21	6	0	3	1	17	4	35	1	0	1	3	.250	0	2-3	0	3.69	3.71
2004	2 Tms	NL	46	1	0	11	65.0	287	76	33	31	10	2	1	1	20	2	55	4	1	3	1	.750	0	0-0	5	5.05	4.29
2005	Hou	NL	71	0	0	20	73.1	288	53	18	18	7	5	1	3	19	3	69	0	0	2	3	.400	0	3-5	17	2.22	2.21
2006	Hou	NL	75	0	0	25	71.1	295	58	22	20	5	3	3	2	24	8	68	0	0	3	5	.375	0	9-12	24	2.57	2.52
2007	2 Tms		70	0	0	29	74.2	321	74	48	44	11	3	3	3	23	3	82	2	0	1	9	.100	0	11-18	18	4.04	5.30
2008	TB	AL	70	0	0	26	66.1	264	44	25	23	10	0	2	0	22	4	53	1	0	5	6	.455	0	13-18	26	2.28	3.12
2009	TB	AL	69	0	0	20	57.2	219	41	22	21	11	3	1	0	9	2	45	3	0	4	5	.444	0	2-6	16	2.17	3.28
2010	TB	AL	64	0	0	13	48.1	195	36	20	18	7	1	3	1	16	2	46	3	0	2	4	.333	0	3-6	9	2.77	3.35
2011	Bos	AL	47	0	0	22	49.1	201	47	24	24	7	1	1	0	8	1	39	0	0	2	2	.500	0	0-0	4	3.11	4.38
04	NYM	NL	32	1	0	7	50.2	232	65	29	27	9	2	1	0	17	2	46	4	1	3	1	.750	0	0-0	3	5.91	4.80
04	NYM	NL	14	0	0	4	14.1	55	11	4	4	1	0	0	1	3	0	9	0	0	0	0	-	0	0-0	2	2.35	2.51
07	Hou	NL	45	0	0	25	49.2	205	46	28	28	8	1	1	2	13	1	56	1	0	1	4	.200	0	11-15	6	3.69	4.63
07	TB	AL	25	0	0	4	25.0	116	28	20	16	3	2	2	1	10	2	26	1	0	0	5	.000	0	0-3	12	4.72	5.76
	Postseason		21	0	0	5	26.2	111	21	10	10	3	1	0	3	8	1	28	1	0	1	0	1.000	0	1-3	5	2.98	3.38
12 ML YEARS			577	9	0	185	628.1	2619	572	286	271	86	20	21	13	187	32	553	18	2	25	43	.368	0	43-69	120	3.42	3.88

Kevin Whelan

Pitches: R **Bats:** R **Pos:** RP-2   **Ht:** 6'0" **Wt:** 200 **Born:** 1/8/1984 **Age:** 28

Year	Team	Lg	G	GS	CG	GF	IP	BFP	H	R	ER	HR	SH	SF	HB	TBB	IBB	SO	WP	Bk	W	L	Pct	Sh	Sv-Op	Hld	ERC	ERA
2005	Oneont	A-	11	0	0	11	12.0	46	2	4	3	1	0	0	1	6	0	19	2	1	1	1	.500	0	4--	-	0.95	2.25
2005	WMich	A	14	0	0	14	12.1	43	4	1	1	0	0	0	0	2	0	22	1	0	0	0	-	0	11--	-	0.43	0.73
2006	Lkland	A+	51	0	0	46	54.0	221	33	20	16	1	5	1	1	29	0	69	4	0	4	1	.800	0	27--	-	2.11	2.67
2007	Trntn	AA	31	2	0	11	54.1	236	34	18	18	2	0	3	2	42	4	68	8	1	4	2	.667	0	5--	-	3.01	2.98
2007	Tampa	A+	7	7	0	0	28.0	107	11	6	6	2	0	1	0	12	0	28	2	0	2	0	1.000	0	0--	-	1.24	1.93
2008	Tampa	A+	9	0	0	1	17.1	76	11	9	9	0	1	2	0	14	0	19	2	0	1	0	1.000	0	1--	-	2.88	4.67
2008	Trntn	AA	15	0	0	7	20.2	90	13	10	10	2	0	1	0	15	0	27	7	0	2	0	1.000	0	1--	-	3.21	4.35
2009	Trntn	AA	30	0	0	14	54.2	221	38	17	16	1	0	1	1	28	0	63	5	0	4	0	1.000	0	2--	-	2.49	2.63
2009	S-WB	AAA	14	0	0	6	12.2	58	7	4	4	0	1	0	0	13	1	22	0	0	0	0	-	0	1--	-	3.00	2.84
2010	S-WB	AAA	17	0	0	5	20.0	91	19	15	14	2	1	1	1	10	0	22	3	0	2	1	.667	0	1--	-	4.23	6.30
2010	Trntn	AA	24	0	0	11	29.1	128	20	19	19	1	1	2	1	21	0	40	5	0	3	3	.500	0	3--	-	3.18	5.83
2011	S-WB	AAA	45	0	0	38	52.1	206	38	16	16	5	1	2	1	14	0	54	9	0	2	3	.400	0	23--	-	2.23	2.75
2011	NYY	AL	2	0	0	1	1.2	10	0	1	1	0	0	0	0	5	0	1	0	0	0	0	-	0	0-0	0	7.00	5.40

Alex White

Pitches: R **Bats:** R **Pos:** SP-10   **Ht:** 6'3" **Wt:** 215 **Born:** 8/29/1988 **Age:** 23

Year	Team	Lg	G	GS	CG	GF	IP	BFP	H	R	ER	HR	SH	SF	HB	TBB	IBB	SO	WP	Bk	W	L	Pct	Sh	Sv-Op	Hld	ERC	ERA
2010	Knstn	A+	8	8	0	0	44.0	183	32	18	14	4	5	1	0	19	0	41	1	0	2	3	.400	0	0--	-	2.64	2.86
2010	Akron	AA	18	17	0	0	106.2	439	91	45	27	8	4	4	2	27	0	76	5	0	8	7	.533	0	0--	-	2.61	2.28
2011	Clmbs	AAA	4	4	0	0	23.2	97	19	7	5	1	0	0	2	5	0	28	1	0	1	0	1.000	0	0--	-	2.25	1.90
2011	Tulsa	AA	4	4	0	0	16.1	60	10	3	3	1	0	0	1	1	0	10	0	0	1	1	.500	0	0--	-	1.22	1.65
2011	2 Tms		10	10	0	0	51.1	237	62	42	40	15	2	3	4	25	3	37	5	0	3	4	.429	0	0-0	-	7.55	7.01
11	Cle	AL	3	3	0	0	15.0	66	14	7	6	3	1	1	0	9	2	13	0	0	1	0	1.000	0	0-0	0	5.06	3.60
11	Col	NL	7	7	0	0	36.1	171	48	35	34	12	1	2	4	16	1	24	5	0	2	4	.333	0	0-0	0	8.66	8.42

Eli Whiteside

Bats: R **Throws:** R **Pos:** C-81; PH-2   **Ht:** 6'2" **Wt:** 218 **Born:** 10/22/1979 **Age:** 32

Year	Team	Lg	G	AB	H	2B	3B	HR	(Hm	Rd)	TB	R	RBI	RC	TBB	IBB	SO	HBP	SH	SF	SB	CS	SB%	GDP	Avg	OBP	Slg
2005	Bal	AL	9	12	3	0	0	0	(0	0)	3	1	1	0	0	0	2	0	0	0	0	0	-	1	.250	.250	.250
2009	SF	NL	49	127	29	6	1	2	(1	1)	43	15	13	11	4	1	30	3	0	0	0	0	-	4	.228	.269	.339
2010	SF	NL	56	126	30	6	1	4	(3	1)	50	19	10	9	8	0	35	3	3	0	1	2	.33	4	.238	.299	.397
2011	SF	NL	82	213	42	8	2	4	(3	1)	66	14	17	11	18	3	59	2	1	2	2	1	.67	9	.197	.264	.310
4 ML YEARS			196	478	104	20	4	10	(7	3)	162	49	41	31	30	4	126	8	4	2	3	3	.50	18	.218	.274	.339

Matt Wieters

Bats: B **Throws:** R **Pos:** C-132; PH-5; DH-3; 1B-1   WEE-ters   **Ht:** 6'5" **Wt:** 230 **Born:** 5/21/1986 **Age:** 26

Year	Team	Lg	G	AB	H	2B	3B	HR	(Hm	Rd)	TB	R	RBI	RC	TBB	IBB	SO	HBP	SH	SF	SB	CS	SB%	GDP	Avg	OBP	Slg
2009	Bal	AL	96	354	102	15	0	9	(5	4)	146	35	43	43	28	2	86	1	0	2	0	0	-	11	.288	.340	.412
2010	Bal	AL	130	446	111	22	1	11	(3	8)	168	37	55	47	47	7	94	2	0	7	0	1	.00	13	.249	.319	.377
2011	Bal	AL	139	500	131	28	0	22	(13	9)	225	72	68	76	48	3	84	2	0	1	1	0	1.00	16	.262	.328	.450
3 ML YEARS			365	1300	344	65	2	42	(21	21)	539	144	166	166	123	12	264	5	0	10	1	1	.50	40	.265	.328	.415

Ty Wigginton

Bats: R **Throws:** R **Pos:** 3B-68; 1B-36; LF-21; PH-17; RF-6; PR-1   **Ht:** 6'0" **Wt:** 230 **Born:** 10/11/1977 **Age:** 34

Year	Team	Lg	G	AB	H	2B	3B	HR	(Hm	Rd)	TB	R	RBI	RC	TBB	IBB	SO	HBP	SH	SF	SB	CS	SB%	GDP	Avg	OBP	Slg
2011	ColSpr*	AAA	2	7	2	0	0	0	(-	-)	2	1	1	2	0	1	0	0	0	0	0	0	-	0	.286	.444	.286
2002	NYM	NL	46	116	35	8	0	6	(4	2)	61	18	18	15	8	0	19	2	0	1	2	1	.67	4	.302	.354	.526
2003	NYM	NL	156	573	146	36	6	11	(4	7)	227	73	71	76	46	2	124	9	1	4	12	2	.86	15	.255	.318	.396
2004	2 Tms	NL	144	494	129	30	2	17	(6	11)	214	63	66	59	45	6	82	2	1	3	7	1	.88	15	.261	.324	.433
2005	Pit	NL	57	155	40	9	1	7	(1	6)	72	20	25	22	14	0	30	1	1	0	0	1	.00	3	.258	.324	.465
2006	TB	AL	122	444	122	25	1	24	(18	6)	221	55	79	69	32	3	97	6	1	3	4	3	.57	11	.275	.330	.498
2007	2 Tms	NL	148	547	152	33	0	22	(15	7)	251	71	67	64	41	0	113	8	0	8	3	4	.43	16	.278	.333	.459
2008	Hou	NL	111	386	110	22	1	23	(15	8)	203	50	58	57	32	1	69	8	0	3	4	6	.40	9	.285	.350	.526
2009	Bal	AL	122	410	112	19	0	11	(9	2)	164	44	41	41	23	1	57	2	0	1	1	2	.33	16	.273	.314	.400
2010	Bal	AL	154	581	144	29	1	22	(12	10)	241	63	76	62	50	3	116	8	1	9	0	1	.00	23	.248	.312	.415
2011	Col	NL	130	401	97	21	2	15	(7	8)	167	52	47	38	38	4	84	5	1	1	8	1	.89	10	.242	.315	.416
04	NYM	NL	86	312	89	23	2	12	(5	7)	152	46	42	38	23	4	48	1	1	2	6	1	.86	11	.285	.334	.487
04	Pit	NL	58	182	40	7	0	5	(1	4)	62	17	24	21	22	2	34	1	0	1	1	0	1.00	4	.220	.306	.341
07	TB	AL	98	378	104	21	0	16	(9	7)	173	47	49	42	28	0	73	5	0	6	1	4	.20	8	.275	.329	.458
07	Hou	NL	50	169	48	12	0	6	(6	0)	78	24	18	22	13	0	40	3	0	2	2	0	1.00	8	.284	.342	.462
10 ML YEARS			1190	4107	1087	232	14	158	(91	67)	1821	509	548	503	329	20	791	51	6	33	41	22	.65	122	.265	.325	.443

Tom Wilhelmsen

Pitches: R **Bats:** R **Pos:** RP-25   **Ht:** 6'6" **Wt:** 230 **Born:** 12/16/1983 **Age:** 28

			HOW MUCH HE PITCHED					WHAT HE GAVE UP										THE RESULTS						
Year	Team	Lg	G	GS	CG	GF	IP	BFP	H	R	ER	HR	SH	SF	HB	TBB	IBB	SO	WP	Bk	W	L	Pct	Sh	Sv-Op	Hld	ERC	ERA
2003	Beloit	A	15	15	1	0	88.0	361	78	35	27	6	0	0	4	27	0	63	2	0	5	5	.500	0	0--	-	3.12	2.76
2003	Brewrs	R	2	2	0	0	4.0	22	5	2	2	0	0	0	1	4	0	4	0	0	0	1	.000	0	0--	-	8.02	4.50
2010	Ms	R	5	3	0	0	15.0	54	4	1	1	0	0	0	1	2	0	22	2	0	0	0	-	0	0--	-	0.36	0.60
2010	Everett	A-	3	3	0	0	14.2	59	14	6	6	1	1	0	1	2	0	14	2	0	1	0	1.000	0	0--	-	2.93	3.68
2010	Clinton	A	7	6	1	0	44.1	187	33	16	11	1	1	2	2	15	0	37	4	0	6	1	.857	0	0--	-	2.09	2.23
2011	Jacksn	AA	14	12	0	1	60.2	273	66	45	37	8	2	4	7	26	0	40	6	1	4	5	.444	0	0--	-	5.45	5.49
2011	Sea	AL	25	0	0	10	32.2	136	25	13	12	2	0	2	2	13	0	30	6	1	2	0	1.000	0	0-0	3	2.78	3.31

Adam Wilk

Pitches: L **Bats:** L **Pos:** RP-5   **Ht:** 6'2" **Wt:** 175 **Born:** 12/9/1987 **Age:** 24

			HOW MUCH HE PITCHED					WHAT HE GAVE UP										THE RESULTS						
Year	Team	Lg	G	GS	CG	GF	IP	BFP	H	R	ER	HR	SH	SF	HB	TBB	IBB	SO	WP	Bk	W	L	Pct	Sh	Sv-Op	Hld	ERC	ERA
2009	Oneont	A-	7	7	1	0	37.1	140	23	7	6	0	1	0	1	5	0	34	0	0	2	0	1.000	1	0--	-	1.09	1.45
2009	WMich	A	7	7	0	0	36.1	138	30	7	6	2	0	0	1	2	0	33	1	0	2	1	.667	0	0--	-	1.81	1.49
2010	Lkland	A+	24	24	1	0	143.2	588	139	58	48	8	3	6	4	19	0	100	5	0	9	5	.643	0	0--	-	2.68	3.01
2010	Erie	AA	3	3	0	0	23.2	84	10	3	3	1	0	0	1	5	0	14	0	0	2	0	1.000	0	0--	-	0.92	1.14
2011	Toledo	AAA	18	18	0	0	102.2	422	105	45	37	15	2	2	3	14	0	76	3	0	8	6	.571	0	0--	-	3.58	3.24
2011	Det	AL	5	0	0	1	13.1	57	14	10	8	3	0	0	0	3	0	10	0	0	0	0	-	0	0-0	0	4.40	5.40

Jerome Williams

Pitches: R **Bats:** R **Pos:** SP-6; RP-4   **Ht:** 6'3" **Wt:** 240 **Born:** 12/4/1981 **Age:** 30

			HOW MUCH HE PITCHED					WHAT HE GAVE UP										THE RESULTS						
Year	Team	Lg	G	GS	CG	GF	IP	BFP	H	R	ER	HR	SH	SF	HB	TBB	IBB	SO	WP	Bk	W	L	Pct	Sh	Sv-Op	Hld	ERC	ERA
2011	Salt Lk*	AAA	11	10	1	1	73.2	305	78	36	32	10	1	2	4	15	0	60	2	0	7	2	.778	0	0--	-	4.19	3.91
2003	SF	NL	21	21	2	0	131.0	545	116	54	48	10	6	3	7	49	3	88	2	1	7	5	.583	1	0-0	0	3.42	3.30
2004	SF	NL	22	22	0	0	129.1	559	123	69	61	14	4	9	17	44	1	80	2	1	10	7	.588	0	0-0	0	4.14	4.24
2005	2 Tms	NL	22	20	0	0	122.2	532	119	62	58	14	11	8	10	49	1	70	2	0	6	10	.375	0	0-0	0	4.34	4.26
2006	ChC	NL	5	2	0	1	12.1	61	15	12	10	2	0	3	1	11	1	5	0	0	0	2	.000	0	0-0	0	8.42	7.30
2007	Was	NL	6	6	0	0	30.0	140	34	26	24	6	1	1	0	18	0	15	2	1	0	5	.000	0	0-0	0	6.43	7.20
2011	LAA	AL	10	6	0	1	44.0	184	45	20	18	6	0	1	1	15	0	28	0	0	4	0	1.000	0	0-0	0	4.45	3.68
05	SF	NL	4	3	0	0	16.2	73	21	12	12	2	1	0	1	4	1	11	0	0	0	2	.000	0	0-0	0	5.32	6.48
05	ChC	NL	18	17	0	0	106.0	459	98	50	46	12	10	8	9	45	0	59	2	0	6	8	.429	0	0-0	1	4.19	3.91
Postseason			1	1	0	0	2.0	13	5	3	3	0	1	0	0	1	0	1	0	0	0	0	-	0	0-0	0	12.20	13.50
6 ML YEARS			86	77	2	2	469.1	2021	452	243	219	52	22	25	36	186	6	286	8	3	27	29	.482	1	0-0	1	4.25	4.20

Randy Williams

Pitches: L **Bats:** L **Pos:** RP-7   **Ht:** 6'4" **Wt:** 200 **Born:** 9/18/1975 **Age:** 36

			HOW MUCH HE PITCHED					WHAT HE GAVE UP										THE RESULTS						
Year	Team	Lg	G	GS	CG	GF	IP	BFP	H	R	ER	HR	SH	SF	HB	TBB	IBB	SO	WP	Bk	W	L	Pct	Sh	Sv-Op	Hld	ERC	ERA
2011	Pwtckt*	AAA	27	0	0	17	32.0	133	23	7	5	2	3	0	4	13	0	36	2	0	1	1	.500	0	8--	-	2.83	1.41
2004	Sea	AL	6	0	0	1	4.2	22	3	3	3	0	0	0	0	6	0	4	0	0	0	0	-	0	0-0	1	4.73	5.79
2005	2 Tms	NL	32	0	0	6	26.1	125	33	21	20	5	0	1	1	13	3	21	0	0	3	1	.750	0	0-2	6	6.54	6.84
2009	CWS	AL	25	0	0	6	17.2	80	13	9	9	2	1	1	3	12	4	22	0	0	0	1	.000	0	0-0	3	4.00	4.58
2010	CWS	AL	27	0	0	2	25.0	132	37	17	15	2	0	1	3	21	6	22	0	0	0	1	.000	0	0-1	1	8.81	5.40
2011	Bos	AL	7	0	0	1	8.1	40	10	6	6	0	1	1	0	5	0	6	1	0	0	1	.000	0	0-0	1	5.10	6.48
05	SD	NL	2	0	0	0	4.1	25	7	6	6	1	0	1	1	4	0	2	0	0	1	0	1.000	0	0-0	0	12.46	12.46
05	Col	NL	30	0	0	6	22.0	100	26	15	14	4	0	1	0	9	3	19	0	0	2	1	.667	0	0-2	6	5.48	5.73
5 ML YEARS			97	0	0	16	82.0	399	96	56	53	9	2	4	7	57	13	75	1	0	3	4	.429	0	0-3	10	6.38	5.82

Josh Willingham

Bats: R Throws: R Pos: LF-96; DH-36; PH-6   Ht: 6'2" Wt: 215 Born: 2/17/1979 Age: 33

Year	Team	Lg	G	AB	H	2B	3B	HR	(Hm	Rd)	TB	R	RBI	RC	TBB	IBB	SO	HBP	SH	SF	SB	CS	SB%	GDP	Avg	OBP	Slg
2011	Scrmto*	AAA	2	5	1	0	0	1	(-	-)	4	1	2	1	2	0	2	0	0	0	0	0	-	0	.200	.429	.800
2004	Fla	NL	12	25	5	0	0	1	(0	1)	8	2	1	1	4	0	8	0	0	0	0	0	-	1	.200	.310	.320
2005	Fla	NL	16	23	7	1	0	0	(0	0)	8	3	4	3	2	0	5	2	1	0	0	0	-	1	.304	.407	.348
2006	Fla	NL	142	502	139	28	2	26	(11	15)	249	62	74	74	54	2	109	11	0	6	2	0	1.00	13	.277	.356	.496
2007	Fla	NL	144	521	138	32	4	21	(10	11)	241	75	89	94	66	1	122	16	0	1	8	1	.89	11	.265	.364	.463
2008	Fla	NL	102	351	89	21	5	15	(6	9)	165	54	51	56	48	2	82	14	1	2	3	2	.60	7	.254	.364	.470
2009	Was	NL	133	427	111	29	0	24	(7	17)	212	70	61	61	61	2	104	12	0	2	4	3	.57	11	.260	.367	.496
2010	Was	NL	114	370	99	19	2	16	(11	5)	170	54	56	65	67	3	85	9	0	4	8	0	1.00	8	.268	.389	.459
2011	Oak	AL	136	488	120	26	0	29	(15	14)	233	69	98	86	56	3	150	11	0	8	4	1	.80	6	.246	.332	.477
	8 ML YEARS		799	2707	708	156	13	132	(60	72)	1286	389	434	440	358	13	665	75	2	23	29	7	.81	58	.262	.361	.475

Dontrelle Willis

Pitches: L Bats: L Pos: SP-13   Ht: 6'4" Wt: 225 Born: 1/12/1982 Age: 30

Year	Team	Lg	G	GS	CG	GF	IP	BFP	H	R	ER	HR	SH	SF	HB	TBB	IBB	SO	WP	Bk	W	L	Pct	Sh	Sv-Op Hld	ERC	ERA
2011	Scrmto*	AAA	13	13	0	0	75.1	310	71	29	22	5	3	2	1	20	0	67	5	0	5	2	.714	0	0- -	3.10	2.63
2003	Fla	NL	27	27	2	0	160.2	668	148	61	59	13	3	1	3	58	0	142	7	1	14	6	.700	2	0-0 0	3.49	3.30
2004	Fla	NL	32	32	2	0	197.0	848	210	99	88	20	8	2	8	61	8	139	2	0	10	11	.476	0	0-0 0	4.21	4.02
2005	Fla	NL	34	34	7	0	236.1	960	213	79	69	11	14	5	8	55	3	170	2	1	22	10	.688	5	0-0 0	2.71	2.63
2006	Fla	NL	34	34	4	0	223.1	975	234	106	96	21	11	6	19	83	6	160	6	1	12	12	.500	1	0-0 0	4.53	3.87
2007	Fla	NL	35	35	0	0	205.1	942	241	131	118	29	15	7	14	87	4	146	9	1	10	15	.400	0	0-0 0	5.72	5.17
2008	Det	AL	8	7	0	0	24.0	122	18	25	25	4	0	0	1	35	1	18	5	1	0	2	.000	0	0-0 0	7.65	9.38
2009	Det	AL	7	7	0	0	33.2	160	37	28	28	4	2	3	1	28	0	17	1	0	1	4	.200	0	0-0 0	6.87	7.49
2010	2 Tms		15	13	0	0	65.2	316	72	41	41	6	2	4	5	56	0	47	8	2	2	3	.400	0	0-0 0	6.90	5.62
2011	Cin	NL	13	13	0	0	75.2	334	78	42	42	6	4	3	2	37	2	57	8	0	1	6	.143	0	0-0 0	4.54	5.00
10	Det	AL	9	8	0	0	43.1	202	48	24	24	3	1	0	2	29	0	33	4	0	1	2	.333	0	0-0 0	5.80	4.98
10	Ari	NL	6	5	0	0	22.1	114	24	17	17	3	1	4	3	27	0	14	4	2	1	1	.500	0	0-0 0	9.16	6.85
	Postseason		7	2	0	0	12.2	63	15	12	12	1	1	2	0	10	0	10	1	0	0	1	.000	0	0-0 1	6.43	8.53
	9 ML YEARS		205	202	15	0	1221.2	5325	1251	612	566	114	59	31	61	500	24	896	48	7	72	69	.511	8	0-0 0	4.39	4.17

Reggie Willits

Bats: B Throws: R Pos: LF-19; PH-2; PR-2; RF-1   Ht: 5'11" Wt: 185 Born: 5/30/1981 Age: 31

Year	Team	Lg	G	AB	H	2B	3B	HR	(Hm	Rd)	TB	R	RBI	RC	TBB	IBB	SO	HBP	SH	SF	SB	CS	SB%	GDP	Avg	OBP	Slg
2011	InldEm*	A+	5	20	4	1	0	0	(-	-)	5	1	3	1	3	0	5	0	2	0	0	0	-	0	.200	.304	.250
2011	Salt Lk*	AAA	65	227	59	5	2	0	(-	-)	68	36	15	31	44	0	46	2	7	0	5	4	.56	2	.260	.385	.300
2006	LAA	AL	28	45	12	1	0	0	(0	0)	13	12	2	6	11	0	10	0	2	0	4	3	.57	0	.267	.411	.289
2007	LAA	AL	136	430	126	20	1	0	(0	0)	148	74	34	68	69	2	83	3	11	5	27	8	.77	7	.293	.391	.344
2008	LAA	AL	82	108	21	4	0	0	(0	0)	25	21	7	10	21	0	26	0	5	2	2	1	.67	1	.194	.321	.231
2009	LAA	AL	49	80	17	2	0	0	(0	0)	19	16	6	3	5	0	17	0	6	1	5	1	.83	0	.213	.256	.238
2010	LAA	AL	97	159	41	7	0	0	(0	0)	48	23	8	19	19	0	26	1	3	0	2	4	.33	1	.258	.341	.302
2011	LAA	AL	22	22	1	1	0	0	(0	0)	2	0	1	1	4	0	7	0	2	0	0	0	-	0	.045	.192	.091
	Postseason		10	4	0	0	0	0	(0	0)	0	0	0	0	1	0	2	0	0	0	1	1	.50	0	.000	.200	.000
	6 ML YEARS		414	844	218	35	1	0	(0	0)	255	146	58	107	129	2	169	4	29	8	40	17	.70	9	.258	.356	.302

Bobby Wilson

Bats: R Throws: R Pos: C-47; 1B-6; PH-5; DH-2   Ht: 6'0" Wt: 210 Born: 4/8/1983 Age: 29

Year	Team	Lg	G	AB	H	2B	3B	HR	(Hm	Rd)	TB	R	RBI	RC	TBB	IBB	SO	HBP	SH	SF	SB	CS	SB%	GDP	Avg	OBP	Slg
2008	LAA	AL	7	6	1	0	0	0	(0	0)	1	0	1	0	1	0	3	0	0	0	0	0	-	0	.167	.286	.167
2009	LAA	AL	12	5	1	1	0	0	(0	0)	2	0	0	0	0	0	1	0	1	0	0	0	-	1	.200	.200	.400
2010	LAA	AL	40	96	22	6	0	4	(3	1)	40	12	15	12	8	0	23	0	2	0	0	0	-	3	.229	.288	.417
2011	LAA	AL	57	111	21	8	0	1	(0	1)	32	5	8	7	10	1	16	0	4	2	0	2	.00	2	.189	.252	.288
	4 ML YEARS		116	218	45	15	0	5	(3	2)	75	17	24	19	19	1	43	0	7	2	0	2	.00	6	.206	.268	.344

Brian Wilson

Pitches: R Bats: R Pos: RP-57   Ht: 6'2" Wt: 199 Born: 3/16/1982 Age: 30

Year	Team	Lg	G	GS	CG	GF	IP	BFP	H	R	ER	HR	SH	SF	HB	TBB	IBB	SO	WP	Bk	W	L	Pct	Sh	Sv-Op Hld	ERC	ERA
2006	SF	NL	31	0	0	9	30.0	141	32	19	18	1	1	4	1	21	2	23	0	0	2	3	.400	0	1-2 4	5.11	5.40
2007	SF	NL	24	0	0	9	23.2	93	16	6	6	1	0	0	1	7	0	18	0	0	1	2	.333	0	6-7 9	1.87	2.28
2008	SF	NL	63	0	0	54	62.1	274	62	32	32	7	2	5	3	28	4	67	2	0	3	2	.600	0	41-47 0	4.41	4.62
2009	SF	NL	68	0	0	60	72.1	303	60	27	22	3	4	2	1	27	4	83	4	0	5	6	.455	0	38-45 1	2.61	2.74
2010	SF	NL	70	0	0	59	74.2	311	62	16	15	3	1	0	1	26	5	93	0	0	3	3	.500	0	48-53 0	2.51	1.81
2011	SF	NL	57	0	0	45	55.0	243	50	20	19	2	1	1	2	31	0	54	2	0	6	4	.600	0	36-41 0	3.87	3.11
	Postseason		10	0	0	9	11.2	44	5	1	0	0	1	1	1	4	0	16	0	0	1	0	1.000	0	6-7 0	1.10	0.00
	6 ML YEARS		313	0	0	236	318.0	1365	282	120	112	17	9	12	9	140	15	338	8	0	20	20	.500	0	170-195 14	3.30	3.17

C.J. Wilson

Pitches: L Bats: L Pos: SP-34 Ht: 6'1" Wt: 210 Born: 11/18/1980 Age: 31

Year	Team	Lg	HOW MUCH HE PITCHED						WHAT HE GAVE UP												THE RESULTS							
			G	GS	CG	GF	IP	BFP	H	R	ER	HR	SH	SF	HB	TBB	IBB	SO	WP	Bk	W	L	Pct	Sh	Sv-Op	Hld	ERC	ERA
2005	Tex	AL	24	6	0	5	48.0	220	63	39	37	5	1	2	2	18	1	30	4	1	1	7	.125	0	1-1	4	6.03	6.94
2006	Tex	AL	44	0	0	12	44.1	191	39	23	20	7	1	0	5	18	1	43	0	0	2	4	.333	0	1-2	7	4.25	4.06
2007	Tex	AL	66	0	0	22	68.1	285	50	25	23	4	2	4	6	33	1	63	5	0	2	1	.667	0	12-14	15	3.01	3.03
2008	Tex	AL	50	0	0	41	46.1	214	49	35	31	8	1	1	2	27	2	41	3	0	2	2	.500	0	24-28	1	5.77	6.02
2009	Tex	AL	74	0	0	30	73.2	323	66	29	23	3	3	0	6	32	3	84	3	0	5	6	.455	0	14-18	19	3.40	2.81
2010	Tex	AL	33	33	3	0	204.0	850	161	83	76	10	1	3	10	93	0	170	7	1	15	8	.652	0	0-0	0	3.03	3.35
2011	Tex	AL	34	34	3	0	223.1	915	191	89	73	16	3	5	10	74	0	206	6	0	16	7	.696	1	0-0	0	3.07	2.94
	Postseason		4	4	0	0	24.1	101	17	11	10	4	0	1	1	10	1	17	0	0	1	2	.333	0	0-0	0	2.96	3.70
7 ML YEARS			325	73	6	110	708.0	2998	619	323	283	53	12	15	41	295	8	637	28	2	43	35	.551	1	52-63	46	3.51	3.60

Jack Wilson

Bats: R Throws: R Pos: 2B-45; SS-26; PR-10; 3B-4; PH-4 Ht: 6'0" Wt: 200 Born: 12/29/1977 Age: 34

Year	Team	Lg	BATTING																		BASERUNNING				AVERAGES		
			G	AB	H	2B	3B	HR	(Hm	Rd)	TB	R	RBI	RC	TBB	IBB	SO	HBP	SH	SF	SB	CS	SB%	GDP	Avg	OBP	Slg
2001	Pit	NL	108	390	87	17	1	3	(0	3)	115	44	25	27	16	2	70	1	17	1	1	3	.25	4	.223	.255	.295
2002	Pit	NL	147	527	133	22	4	4	(2	2)	175	77	47	60	37	2	74	4	17	1	5	2	.71	7	.252	.306	.332
2003	Pit	NL	150	558	143	21	3	9	(2	7)	197	58	62	62	36	3	74	4	11	6	5	5	.50	11	.256	.303	.353
2004	Pit	NL	157	652	201	41	12	11	(7	4)	299	82	59	84	26	0	71	3	7	5	8	4	.67	15	.308	.335	.459
2005	Pit	NL	158	587	151	24	7	8	(3	5)	213	60	52	60	31	6	58	6	11	4	7	3	.70	11	.257	.299	.363
2006	Pit	NL	142	543	148	27	1	8	(5	3)	201	70	35	58	33	0	65	4	9	5	4	3	.57	15	.273	.316	.370
2007	Pit	NL	135	477	141	29	2	12	(3	9)	210	67	56	70	38	9	46	6	7	7	2	5	.29	8	.296	.350	.440
2008	Pit	NL	87	305	83	18	1	1	(1	0)	106	24	22	32	13	0	27	5	6	1	2	2	.50	6	.272	.312	.348
2009	2 Tms		106	373	95	23	1	5	(2	3)	135	37	39	40	21	2	48	0	5	3	3	1	.75	6	.255	.292	.362
2010	Sea	AL	61	193	48	11	1	0	(0	0)	61	17	14	16	7	0	35	3	5	3	1	2	.33	2	.249	.282	.316
2011	2 Tms		79	214	52	9	0	0	(0	0)	61	25	11	19	10	0	39	0	6	2	5	2	.71	2	.243	.274	.285
09	Pit	NL	75	266	71	18	1	4	(1	3)	103	26	31	31	15	2	31	0	3	2	2	1	.67	4	.267	.304	.387
09	Sea	AL	31	107	24	5	0	1	(1	0)	32	11	8	9	6	0	17	0	2	1	1	0	1.00	2	.224	.263	.299
11	Sea	AL	62	173	43	8	0	0	(0	0)	51	22	11	18	9	0	27	0	3	2	5	2	.71	2	.249	.283	.295
11	Atl	NL	17	41	9	1	0	0	(0	0)	10	3	0	1	1	0	12	0	3	0	0	0	-	0	.220	.238	.244
11 ML YEARS			1330	4819	1282	242	33	61	(25	36)	1773	561	422	528	268	24	607	36	101	38	43	32	.57	87	.266	.307	.368

Josh Wilson

Bats: R Throws: R Pos: PH-28; 3B-13; SS-11; 2B-10; PR-6; LF-3; 1B-1 Ht: 6'0" Wt: 175 Born: 3/26/1981 Age: 31

Year	Team	Lg	BATTING																		BASERUNNING				AVERAGES		
			G	AB	H	2B	3B	HR	(Hm	Rd)	TB	R	RBI	RC	TBB	IBB	SO	HBP	SH	SF	SB	CS	SB%	GDP	Avg	OBP	Slg
2011	Reno*	AAA	16	57	20	5	2	1	(-	-)	32	11	12	13	4	0	7	2	0	1	2	0	1.00	0	.351	.406	.561
2005	Fla	NL	11	10	1	1	0	0	(0	0)	2	2	0	0	0	0	4	1	0	0	0	0	-	0	.100	.182	.200
2007	2 Tms		105	282	67	15	3	2	(0	2)	94	28	24	24	17	0	57	5	3	3	6	2	.75	5	.238	.290	.333
2009	3 Tms		72	192	42	11	1	3	(1	2)	64	19	13	14	12	1	44	4	3	0	1	2	.33	4	.219	.279	.333
2010	Sea	AL	108	361	82	14	2	2	(1	1)	106	22	25	31	14	0	74	12	0	1	5	0	1.00	6	.227	.278	.294
2011	2 Tms	NL	60	85	19	5	0	2	(0	2)	30	13	5	7	4	0	22	0	3	0	1	0	1.00	0	.224	.258	.353
07	Was	NL	15	19	1	0	0	0	(0	0)	1	3	0	0	5	0	6	1	0	0	0	0	-	0	.053	.280	.053
07	TB	AL	90	263	66	15	3	2	(0	2)	93	25	24	24	12	0	51	4	3	3	6	2	.75	5	.251	.291	.354
09	Ari	NL	11	26	6	1	0	0	(0	0)	7	1	2	4	3	0	3	1	0	0	0	0	-	2	.231	.333	.269
09	SD	NL	16	38	4	2	0	0	(0	0)	6	2	1	1	3	1	9	1	1	0	0	0	-	0	.105	.190	.158
09	Sea	AL	45	128	32	8	1	3	(1	2)	51	16	10	9	6	0	32	2	2	0	1	2	.33	2	.250	.294	.398
11	Ari	NL	6	10	2	1	0	0	(0	0)	3	3	1	1	0	0	1	0	0	0	0	0	-	0	.200	.200	.300
11	Mil	NL	54	75	17	4	0	2	(0	2)	27	10	4	6	4	0	21	0	3	0	1	0	1.00	0	.227	.266	.360
5 ML YEARS			356	930	211	46	6	9	(2	7)	296	84	67	76	47	1	201	22	9	4	13	4	.76	15	.227	.279	.318

Mike Wilson

Bats: R Throws: R Pos: LF-5; RF-2; DH-1; PH-1 Ht: 6'2" Wt: 245 Born: 6/29/1983 Age: 29

Year	Team	Lg	BATTING																		BASERUNNING				AVERAGES		
			G	AB	H	2B	3B	HR	(Hm	Rd)	TB	R	RBI	RC	TBB	IBB	SO	HBP	SH	SF	SB	CS	SB%	GDP	Avg	OBP	Slg
2002	Ms	R	41	143	34	5	0	4	(-	-)	51	28	19	19	18	0	52	9	0	1	4	4	.50	2	.238	.357	.357
2003	Ms	R	48	177	55	9	3	3	(-	-)	79	33	25	31	20	0	46	4	0	1	6	6	.50	1	.311	.391	.446
2004	Everett	A-	66	239	62	15	0	9	(-	-)	104	45	51	39	25	0	61	12	1	1	10	4	.71	4	.259	.357	.435
2005	Wisc	A	127	463	123	29	3	19	(-	-)	215	93	84	83	57	2	107	15	1	6	10	2	.83	6	.266	.360	.464
2006	InldEm	A+	52	200	63	15	3	9	(-	-)	111	38	38	41	22	1	59	3	0	1	4	6	.40	3	.315	.389	.555
2006	SnAnt	AA	67	249	61	12	1	12	(-	-)	111	32	43	38	28	0	85	6	0	0	1	1	.50	7	.245	.336	.446
2007	WTenn	AA	55	208	39	7	2	10	(-	-)	80	30	28	23	17	1	89	8	0	2	3	0	1.00	1	.188	.272	.385
2007	Ms	R	2	10	6	3	0	1	(-	-)	12	4	5	5	2	0	1	0	0	0	1	0	1.00	0	.600	.667	1.200
2008	WTenn	AA	119	407	112	26	2	27	(-	-)	223	76	84	89	61	2	118	14	1	2	9	0	1.00	11	.275	.386	.548
2009	WTenn	AA	26	89	22	7	1	5	(-	-)	41	15	12	17	14	0	31	5	0	0	5	0	1.00	1	.247	.380	.461
2009	Tacom	AAA	40	146	24	4	0	5	(-	-)	43	19	18	12	15	0	50	5	0	3	1	0	1.00	0	.164	.260	.295
2010	WTenn	AA	29	106	30	5	1	8	(-	-)	61	25	22	24	20	0	34	0	0	1	3	1	.75	1	.283	.394	.575
2010	Tacom	AAA	88	286	78	12	1	17	(-	-)	143	52	56	53	38	1	67	3	0	0	10	4	.71	12	.273	.384	.500
2011	Tacom	AAA	87	335	111	27	0	16	(-	-)	186	73	49	76	45	0	86	6	0	2	5	2	.71	6	.331	.418	.555
2011	Sea	AL	8	27	4	1	0	0	(0	0)	5	0	3	1	1	0	7	0	0	0	0	0	-	1	.148	.179	.185

DeWayne Wise

Bats: L **Throws:** L **Pos:** CF-37; PH-20; PR-15; LF-13; RF-2   **Ht:** 5'11" **Wt:** 195 **Born:** 2/24/1978 **Age:** 34

							BATTING													BASERUNNING				AVERAGES		
Year	Team	Lg	G	AB	H	2B	3B	HR	(Hm | Rd)	TB	R	RBI	RC	TBB	IBB	SO	HBP	SH	SF	SB	CS	SB%	GDP	Avg	OBP	Slg
2011	Dnedin*	A+	3	11	3	2	0	1	(- | -)	8	4	2	2	2	0	2	0	0	0	0	0	-	0	.273	.385	.727
2011	LsVgs*	AAA	31	133	45	10	3	4	(- | -)	73	28	19	27	6	1	21	4	0	1	8	3	.73	3	.338	.382	.549
2011	NewOr*	AAA	2	9	3	1	0	0	(- | -)	4	0	0	1	0	0	4	0	0	0	0	0	-	0	.333	.333	.444
2000	Tor	AL	28	22	3	0	0	0	(0 | 0)	3	3	0	0	1	0	5	1	0	0	1	0	1.00	0	.136	.208	.136
2002	Tor	AL	42	112	20	4	1	3	(2 | 1)	35	14	13	8	4	0	15	0	0	0	5	0	1.00	0	.179	.207	.313
2004	Atl	NL	77	162	37	9	4	6	(3 | 3)	72	24	17	20	9	1	28	1	2	1	6	1	.86	1	.228	.272	.444
2006	Cin	NL	31	38	7	2	0	0	(0 | 0)	9	3	1	0	0	0	6	0	2	0	0	0	-	2	.184	.184	.237
2007	Cin	NL	5	5	1	0	1	0	(0 | 0)	3	1	1	1	1	1	1	0	0	0	0	0	-	0	.200	.333	.600
2008	CWS	AL	57	129	32	4	2	6	(2 | 4)	58	20	18	14	8	0	32	1	3	2	9	0	1.00	5	.248	.293	.450
2009	CWS	AL	84	142	32	8	3	2	(2 | 0)	52	17	11	10	3	0	27	4	4	0	4	5	.44	1	.225	.262	.366
2010	Tor	AL	52	112	28	3	2	3	(1 | 2)	44	20	14	17	4	0	29	1	1	0	4	0	1.00	1	.250	.282	.393
2011	2 Tms		69	99	20	2	1	2	(0 | 2)	30	10	7	5	3	0	36	1	0	1	6	2	.75	0	.202	.231	.303
11	Fla	NL	49	67	16	2	0	0	(0 | 0)	18	6	5	5	3	0	21	1	0	1	4	2	.67	0	.239	.278	.269
11	Tor	AL	20	32	4	0	1	2	(0 | 2)	12	4	2	0	0	0	15	0	0	0	2	0	1.00	0	.125	.125	.375
	Postseason		8	12	3	2	0	1	(0 | 1)	8	3	5	3	1	0	4	0	0	0	1	0	1.00	0	.250	.308	.667
	9 ML YEARS		445	821	180	32	14	22	(10 | 12)	306	112	82	75	33	2	179	9	12	4	35	8	.81	10	.219	.256	.373

Randy Wolf

Pitches: L **Bats:** L **Pos:** SP-33   **Ht:** 6'0" **Wt:** 204 **Born:** 8/22/1976 **Age:** 35

			HOW MUCH HE PITCHED						WHAT HE GAVE UP											THE RESULTS						
Year	Team	Lg	G	GS	CG	GF	IP	BFP	H	R	ER	HR	SH	SF	HB	TBB	IBB	SO	WP	Bk	W	L	Pct	Sh	Sv-Op	Hld	ERC	ERA
1999	Phi	NL	22	21	0	0	121.2	552	126	78	75	20	5	1	5	67	0	116	4	0	6	9	.400	0	0-0	0	5.54	5.55
2000	Phi	NL	32	32	1	0	206.1	889	210	107	100	25	10	8	8	83	2	160	1	0	11	9	.550	0	0-0	0	4.54	4.36
2001	Phi	NL	28	25	4	1	163.0	684	150	74	67	15	11	7	10	51	4	152	1	0	10	11	.476	2	0-0	0	3.46	3.70
2002	Phi	NL	31	31	3	0	210.2	855	172	77	75	23	7	6	7	63	5	172	4	0	11	9	.550	2	0-0	0	2.88	3.20
2003	Phi	NL	33	33	2	0	200.0	850	176	101	94	27	8	4	6	78	4	177	6	0	16	10	.615	2	0-0	0	3.67	4.23
2004	Phi	NL	23	23	1	0	136.2	585	145	73	65	20	6	3	5	36	4	89	2	0	5	8	.385	1	0-0	0	4.29	4.28
2005	Phi	NL	13	13	0	0	80.0	346	87	40	39	14	4	1	6	26	2	61	1	0	6	4	.600	0	0-0	0	5.17	4.39
2006	Phi	NL	12	12	0	0	56.2	261	63	37	35	13	2	3	2	33	2	44	2	0	4	0	1.000	0	0-0	0	6.63	5.56
2007	LAD	NL	18	18	0	0	102.2	458	110	55	54	10	5	5	6	39	2	94	4	0	9	6	.600	0	0-0	0	4.52	4.73
2008	2 Tms	NL	33	33	1	0	190.1	823	191	100	91	21	10	4	12	71	4	162	3	0	12	12	.500	1	0-0	0	4.30	4.30
2009	LAD	NL	34	**34**	0	0	214.1	862	178	81	77	24	12	2	6	58	1	160	4	0	11	7	.611	0	0-0	0	2.89	3.23
2010	Mil	NL	34	34	1	0	215.2	936	213	107	100	29	9	6	9	87	6	142	2	0	13	12	.520	1	0-0	0	4.39	4.17
2011	Mil	NL	33	33	0	0	212.1	903	214	95	87	23	13	6	13	66	1	134	4	1	13	10	.565	0	0-0	0	4.10	3.69
08	SD	NL	21	21	0	0	119.2	522	123	69	63	14	6	2	8	47	0	105	2	0	6	10	.375	0	0-0	0	4.63	4.74
08	Hou	NL	12	12	1	0	70.2	301	68	31	28	7	4	2	4	24	4	57	1	0	6	2	.750	1	0-0	0	3.77	3.57
	Postseason		2	2	0	0	9.0	44	10	5	5	1	1	0	1	7	2	4	0	0	0	-	-	0	0-0	0	6.38	5.00
	13 ML YEARS		346	342	13	1	2110.1	9004	2035	1025	959	264	102	56	95	758	37	1663	38	1	127	107	.543	9	0-0	0	4.06	4.09

Blake Wood

Pitches: R **Bats:** R **Pos:** RP-55   **Ht:** 6'5" **Wt:** 230 **Born:** 8/8/1985 **Age:** 26

			HOW MUCH HE PITCHED						WHAT HE GAVE UP											THE RESULTS						
Year	Team	Lg	G	GS	CG	GF	IP	BFP	H	R	ER	HR	SH	SF	HB	TBB	IBB	SO	WP	Bk	W	L	Pct	Sh	Sv-Op	Hld	ERC	ERA
2006	Idaho	R+	12	12	0	0	52.0	224	50	28	26	1	2	3	10	15	0	46	2	0	3	1	.750	0	0- -	-	3.63	4.50
2007	Royals	R	4	4	0	0	9.2	36	9	2	0	0	0	0	0	0	0	15	0	0	0	0	-	0	0- -	-	1.78	0.00
2007	Burlgtn	A	7	7	0	0	35.2	152	32	12	12	3	1	0	3	14	0	26	0	0	2	1	.667	0	0- -	-	3.72	3.03
2007	Wilmg	A+	2	2	0	0	9.2	41	9	5	5	1	0	0	3	3	0	11	0	0	0	1	.000	0	0- -	-	4.84	4.66
2008	Wilmg	A+	10	10	0	0	57.1	212	32	17	17	3	1	3	2	15	0	63	6	0	3	2	.600	0	0- -	-	1.43	2.67
2008	NWArk	AA	18	18	2	0	86.2	383	96	55	51	7	3	2	7	32	0	76	11	0	5	7	.417	2	0- -	-	4.79	5.30
2009	NWArk	AA	17	13	1	3	78.2	338	92	52	51	8	6	1	5	27	1	49	7	0	2	8	.200	0	0- -	-	5.30	5.83
2009	Royals	R	3	2	0	0	4.0	18	4	1	0	0	0	1	0	1	0	4	2	0	0	1	.000	0	0- -	-	2.58	0.00
2010	Omha	AAA	12	0	0	10	16.2	67	12	5	4	0	1	1	0	7	0	12	1	0	2	1	.667	0	5- -	-	2.09	2.16
2011	Omha	AAA	3	0	0	0	5.0	15	2	0	0	0	0	0	0	0	0	6	0	0	0	0	-	0	0- -	-	0.40	0.00
2010	KC	AL	51	0	0	13	49.2	220	54	29	28	6	2	6	1	22	5	31	3	0	1	3	.250	0	0-4	15	4.83	5.07
2011	KC	AL	55	0	0	20	69.2	303	66	30	29	5	5	3	3	32	7	62	2	0	5	3	.625	0	1-3	5	3.82	3.75
	2 ML YEARS		106	0	0	33	119.1	523	120	59	57	11	7	9	4	54	12	93	5	0	6	6	.500	0	1-7	20	4.23	4.30

Brandon Wood

Bats: R **Throws:** R **Pos:** 3B-61; SS-24; PH-16; 1B-10; 2B-3; DH-1   **Ht:** 6'3" **Wt:** 210 **Born:** 3/2/1985 **Age:** 27

							BATTING													BASERUNNING				AVERAGES		
Year	Team	Lg	G	AB	H	2B	3B	HR	(Hm	Rd)	TB	R	RBI	RC	TBB	IBB	SO	HBP	SH	SF	SB	CS	SB%	GDP	Avg	OBP	Slg
2007	LAA	AL	13	33	5	1	0	1	(0	1)	9	2	3	1	0	0	12	0	0	0	0	0	-	0	.152	.152	.273
2008	LAA	AL	55	150	30	4	0	5	(2	3)	49	12	13	7	4	0	43	1	1	1	4	0	1.00	3	.200	.224	.327
2009	LAA	AL	18	41	8	1	0	1	(1	0)	12	5	3	0	3	0	19	1	1	0	0	0	-	3	.195	.267	.293
2010	LAA	AL	81	226	33	2	0	4	(2	2)	47	20	14	4	6	0	71	2	8	1	1	0	1.00	3	.146	.174	.208
2011	2 Tms		105	250	54	10	0	7	(5	2)	85	26	31	22	19	2	73	0	2	1	0	0	-	6	.216	.270	.340
11	LAA	AL	6	14	2	1	0	0	(0	0)	3	1	0	0	0	0	8	0	0	0	0	0	-	1	.143	.143	.214
11	Pit	NL	99	236	52	9	0	7	(5	2)	82	25	31	22	19	2	65	0	2	1	0	0	-	5	.220	.277	.347
	5 ML YEARS		272	700	130	18	0	18	(10	8)	202	65	64	34	32	2	218	4	12	3	5	0	1.00	15	.186	.225	.289

Kerry Wood

Pitches: R **Bats:** R **Pos:** RP-55   **Ht:** 6'5" **Wt:** 211 **Born:** 6/16/1977 **Age:** 35

Year	Team	Lg	G	GS	CG	GF	IP	BFP	H	R	ER	HR	SH	SF	HB	TBB	IBB	SO	WP	Bk	W	L	Pct	Sh	Sv-Op	Hld	ERC	ERA
1998	ChC	NL	26	26	1	0	166.2	699	117	69	63	14	2	4	11	85	1	233	6	3	13	6	.684	1	0-0	0	3.03	3.40
2000	ChC	NL	23	23	1	0	137.0	603	112	77	73	17	7	5	9	87	0	132	5	1	8	7	.533	0	0-0	0	4.43	4.80
2001	ChC	NL	28	28	1	0	174.1	740	127	70	65	16	4	5	10	92	3	217	9	0	12	6	.667	1	0-0	0	3.22	3.36
2002	ChC	NL	33	33	4	0	213.2	895	169	92	87	22	13	5	16	97	5	217	8	1	12	11	.522	1	0-0	0	3.46	3.66
2003	ChC	NL	32	32	4	0	211.0	887	152	77	75	24	11	6	21	100	2	266	10	0	14	11	.560	2	0-0	0	3.31	3.20
2004	ChC	NL	22	22	0	0	140.1	595	127	62	58	16	6	6	11	51	0	144	7	0	8	9	.471	0	0-0	0	3.83	3.72
2005	ChC	NL	21	10	0	4	66.0	273	52	32	31	14	2	1	2	26	0	77	0	0	3	4	.429	0	0-0	4	3.75	4.23
2006	ChC	NL	4	4	0	0	19.2	86	19	13	9	5	0	2	1	8	0	13	1	0	1	2	.333	0	0-0	0	5.17	4.12
2007	ChC	NL	22	0	0	2	24.1	101	18	9	9	0	1	0	0	13	1	24	1	0	1	1	.500	0	0-0	0	2.49	3.33
2008	ChC	NL	65	0	0	56	66.1	276	54	24	24	3	2	2	7	18	4	84	1	0	5	4	.556	0	34-40	0	2.52	3.26
2009	Cle	AL	58	0	0	50	55.0	241	48	26	26	7	1	3	3	28	0	63	5	0	3	3	.500	0	20-26	0	4.16	4.25
2010	2 Tms	AL	47	0	0	19	46.0	201	35	17	16	4	2	0	3	29	4	49	5	1	3	4	.429	0	8-12	11	3.65	3.13
2011	ChC	NL	55	0	0	7	51.0	224	45	23	19	5	3	3	5	21	2	57	5	0	3	5	.375	0	1-7	21	3.69	3.35
10	Cle	AL	23	0	0	18	20.0	93	21	15	14	3	0	0	2	11	2	18	2	1	1	4	.200	0	8-11	1	5.52	6.30
10	NYY	AL	24	0	0	1	26.0	108	14	2	2	1	2	0	1	18	2	31	3	0	2	0	1.000	0	0-1	10	2.36	0.69
	Postseason		15	5	0	2	44.2	190	35	18	17	3	1	1	0	23	3	45	2	0	2	2	.500	0	0-0	3	2.98	3.43
	13 ML YEARS		436	178	11	138	1371.1	5821	1075	591	555	147	54	42	99	655	22	1576	63	6	86	73	.541	5	63-85	36	3.50	3.64

Tim Wood

Pitches: R **Bats:** R **Pos:** RP-13   **Ht:** 6'0" **Wt:** 180 **Born:** 11/16/1982 **Age:** 29

Year	Team	Lg	G	GS	CG	GF	IP	BFP	H	R	ER	HR	SH	SF	HB	TBB	IBB	SO	WP	Bk	W	L	Pct	Sh	Sv-Op	Hld	ERC	ERA
2011	Indy*	AAA	40	0	0	36	44.1	178	32	16	14	1	2	1	0	12	0	32	7	0	2	0	1.000	0	23--	-	1.69	2.84
2011	RdRck*	AAA	4	0	0	2	4.2	23	9	5	5	1	0	0	0	3	0	2	2	0	0	0	-	0	1--	-	13.70	9.64
2009	Fla	NL	18	0	0	8	22.1	97	22	8	7	2	2	3	1	10	1	16	2	0	1	0	1.000	0	0-0	1	4.25	2.82
2010	Fla	NL	26	0	0	8	27.2	129	33	19	17	2	4	2	0	15	1	10	0	0	0	1	.000	0	1-3	3	5.44	5.53
2011	Pit	NL	13	0	0	5	8.0	38	8	5	5	1	0	2	0	8	3	2	1	0	0	3	.000	0	0-0	3	6.16	5.63
	3 ML YEARS		57	0	0	21	58.0	264	63	32	29	5	6	7	1	33	5	28	3	0	1	4	.200	0	1-3	7	5.07	4.50

Travis Wood

Pitches: L **Bats:** R **Pos:** SP-18; RP-4   **Ht:** 5'11" **Wt:** 175 **Born:** 2/6/1987 **Age:** 25

Year	Team	Lg	G	GS	CG	GF	IP	BFP	H	R	ER	HR	SH	SF	HB	TBB	IBB	SO	WP	Bk	W	L	Pct	Sh	Sv-Op	Hld	ERC	ERA
2005	Reds	R	8	7	0	0	24.0	93	13	3	2	0	2	0	1	7	0	45	0	0	0	0	-	0	0--	-	1.21	0.75
2005	Billings	R+	6	4	0	0	24.2	104	15	6	5	0	1	0	4	13	0	22	2	0	2	0	1.000	0	0--	-	2.39	1.82
2006	Dayton	A	27	27	0	0	140.0	582	108	65	57	14	12	2	10	56	2	133	10	0	10	5	.667	0	0--	-	3.10	3.66
2007	Srsota	A+	12	12	0	0	46.1	214	49	33	25	6	1	2	1	27	0	54	0	0	3	2	.600	0	0--	-	5.39	4.86
2008	Srsota	A+	9	9	0	0	46.2	199	39	18	14	2	0	0	2	21	0	41	1	1	3	4	.429	0	0--	-	3.12	2.70
2008	Chatt	AA	17	17	0	0	80.0	380	91	67	63	9	4	2	11	48	3	57	5	1	4	9	.308	0	0--	-	6.32	7.09
2009	Carlina	AA	19	19	1	0	119.0	460	78	23	16	2	3	1	5	37	0	103	0	0	9	3	.750	1	0--	-	1.72	1.21
2009	Lsvlle	AAA	8	8	0	0	48.2	198	43	17	17	4	1	1	1	16	0	32	0	0	4	2	.667	0	0--	-	3.21	3.14
2010	Lsvlle	AAA	16	16	0	0	100.0	404	86	40	34	9	6	1	4	24	0	99	6	0	5	6	.455	0	0--	-	2.84	3.06
2011	Lsvlle	AAA	10	10	0	0	52.1	232	64	33	31	6	1	2	2	17	0	47	2	0	2	3	.400	0	0--	-	5.39	5.33
2010	Cin	NL	17	17	0	0	102.2	419	85	45	40	9	3	3	4	26	1	86	0	1	5	4	.556	0	0-0	0	2.64	3.51
2011	Cin	NL	22	18	0	2	106.0	463	118	57	57	10	9	7	4	40	5	76	2	0	6	6	.500	0	0-0	0	4.73	4.84
	Postseason		1	0	0	0	3.1	12	1	0	0	0	0	0	0	1	1	3	0	0	0	0	-	0	0-0	0	0.38	0.00
	2 ML YEARS		39	35	0	2	208.2	882	203	102	97	19	12	10	8	66	6	162	2	1	11	10	.524	0	0-0	0	3.66	4.18

Chris Woodward

Bats: R **Throws:** R **Pos:** PR-7; 2B-2; 3B-1; SS-1; PH-1   **Ht:** 6'0" **Wt:** 190 **Born:** 6/27/1976 **Age:** 36

Year	Team	Lg	G	AB	H	2B	3B	HR	(Hm	Rd)	TB	R	RBI	RC	TBB	IBB	SO	HBP	SH	SF	SB	CS	SB%	GDP	Avg	OBP	Slg
2011	LsVgs*	AAA	108	422	125	32	2	13	(-	-)	200	67	65	72	39	0	70	1	1	6	4	2	.67	12	.296	.353	.474
1999	Tor	AL	14	26	6	1	0	0	(0	0)	7	1	2	2	2	0	6	0	0	1	0	0	-	1	.231	.276	.269
2000	Tor	AL	37	104	19	7	0	3	(1	2)	35	16	14	9	10	3	28	0	1	0	1	0	1.00	1	.183	.254	.337
2001	Tor	AL	37	63	12	3	2	2	(0	2)	25	9	5	4	1	0	14	0	2	0	0	1	.00	1	.190	.203	.397
2002	Tor	AL	90	312	86	13	4	13	(9	4)	146	48	45	45	26	0	72	3	1	8	3	0	1.00	8	.276	.330	.468
2003	Tor	AL	104	349	91	22	2	7	(4	3)	138	49	45	42	28	0	72	3	0	6	1	2	.33	6	.261	.316	.395
2004	Tor	AL	69	213	50	13	4	1	(0	1)	74	21	24	24	14	0	46	1	2	2	1	2	.33	3	.235	.283	.347
2005	NYM	NL	81	173	49	10	0	3	(2	1)	68	16	18	20	13	0	46	2	2	2	0	0	-	2	.283	.337	.393
2006	NYM	NL	83	222	48	10	1	3	(2	1)	69	25	25	18	23	2	55	1	4	3	1	1	.50	2	.216	.289	.311
2007	Atl	NL	92	136	27	6	1	1	(1	0)	38	16	8	9	10	1	29	0	4	1	1	0	1.00	3	.199	.252	.279
2009	2 Tms	AL	33	79	17	1	0	0	(0	0)	18	7	5	5	7	0	19	2	1	1	1	0	1.00	1	.215	.292	.228
2010	Sea	AL	8	19	3	1	0	0	(0	0)	4	0	0	1	3	0	9	0	0	0	0	0	-	0	.158	.273	.211
2011	Tor	AL	11	10	0	0	0	0	(0	0)	0	3	0	0	0	0	4	0	0	0	0	0	-	0	.000	.000	.000
09	Sea	AL	20	67	16	1	0	0	(0	0)	17	7	5	5	5	0	15	0	1	1	1	0	1.00	1	.239	.288	.254
09	Bos	AL	13	12	1	0	0	0	(0	0)	1	0	0	0	2	0	4	2	0	0	0	0	-	0	.083	.313	.083
	Postseason		1	1	1	1	0	0	(0	0)	2	1	0	1	0	0	0	0	0	0	0	0	-	0	1.000	1.000	2.000
	12 ML YEARS		659	1706	408	87	14	33	(21	12)	622	211	191	179	137	6	400	12	17	24	9	6	.60	28	.239	.296	.365

Vance Worley

Pitches: R Bats: R Pos: SP-21; RP-4
Ht: 6'2" **Wt:** 230 **Born:** 9/25/1987 **Age:** 24

Year	Team	Lg	G	GS	CG	GF	IP	BFP	H	R	ER	HR	SH	SF	HB	TBB	IBB	SO	WP	Bk	W	L	Pct	Sh	Sv-Op	Hld	ERC	ERA
2008	Wmspt	A-	2	2	0	0	8.0	26	3	1	1	0	0	0	0	1	0	8	0	0	0	0	-	0	0- -	-	0.51	1.13
2008	Lakwd	A	11	11	0	0	61.0	249	58	25	18	4	2	2	3	7	0	53	3	0	3	2	.600	0	0- -	-	2.67	2.66
2009	Rdng	AA	27	27	0	0	153.1	660	163	102	91	17	9	4	5	49	0	100	2	1	7	12	.368	0	0- -	-	4.34	5.34
2010	Rdng	AA	19	19	1	0	112.2	478	114	48	40	9	4	3	3	36	0	83	1	0	9	4	.692	1	0- -	-	3.82	3.20
2010	LV	AAA	8	8	0	0	45.1	187	46	19	19	3	1	1	1	10	1	36	1	0	1	3	.250	0	0- -	-	3.33	3.77
2011	LV	AAA	9	9	1	0	50.2	202	41	13	13	5	1	0	2	12	0	50	1	0	5	2	.714	0	0- -	-	2.62	2.31
2010	Phi	NL	5	2	0	2	13.0	51	8	2	2	1	2	0	0	4	0	12	1	0	1	1	.500	0	0-0	0	1.66	1.38
2011	Phi	NL	25	21	1	0	131.2	553	116	47	44	10	9	5	3	46	2	119	2	1	11	3	.786	0	0-0	2	3.12	3.01
	2 ML YEARS		30	23	1	2	144.2	604	124	49	46	11	11	5	3	50	2	131	3	1	12	4	.750	0	0-0	2	2.98	2.86

Mark Worrell

Pitches: R Bats: R Pos: RP-4
Ht: 6'1" **Wt:** 215 **Born:** 3/8/1983 **Age:** 29

Year	Team	Lg	G	GS	CG	GF	IP	BFP	H	R	ER	HR	SH	SF	HB	TBB	IBB	SO	WP	Bk	W	L	Pct	Sh	Sv-Op	Hld	ERC	ERA
2004	JhsCty	R+	17	0	0	17	22.1	86	12	3	3	1	0	0	0	7	0	35	0	0	1	0	1.000	0	7- -	-	1.32	1.21
2004	Peoria	A	12	0	0	11	14.2	60	9	10	7	2	0	0	1	6	0	20	0	0	0	2	.000	0	6- -	-	2.53	4.30
2005	PlmBh	A+	53	0	0	52	56.0	225	38	20	14	6	2	1	4	19	2	53	6	0	2	3	.400	0	35- -	-	2.44	2.25
2006	Sprgfld	AA	57	0	0	51	61.2	257	52	34	31	10	3	3	1	20	2	75	2	0	3	7	.300	0	27- -	-	3.30	4.52
2007	Memp	AAA	49	0	0	17	67.0	289	58	25	23	6	5	6	7	25	5	66	4	0	3	2	.600	0	4- -	-	3.40	3.09
2008	Memp	AAA	53	0	0	18	58.2	249	45	21	14	2	2	1	1	31	2	80	3	0	3	3	.500	0	5- -	-	2.85	2.15
2010	Portlnd	AAA	25	0	0	8	33.0	149	34	28	20	5	1	1	2	11	2	34	2	0	1	4	.200	0	0- -	-	4.29	5.45
2010	Tacom	AAA	4	0	0	0	4.0	21	7	4	4	0	1	1	0	3	0	0	0	0	1	0	1.000	0	0- -	-	9.62	9.00
2011	Norfolk	AAA	52	0	0	41	52.2	224	44	25	20	4	7	2	4	22	1	35	1	0	1	6	.143	0	21- -	-	3.33	3.42
2008	StL	NL	4	0	0	1	5.2	27	8	5	5	1	1	0	0	4	1	4	0	0	0	1	.000	0	0-0	0	8.66	7.94
2011	Bal	AL	4	0	0	0	2.0	14	6	8	8	2	0	0	0	2	1	3	0	0	0	0	-	0	0-0	0	30.68	36.00
	2 ML YEARS		8	0	0	1	7.2	41	14	13	13	3	1	0	0	6	2	7	0	0	0	1	.000	0	0-0	0	13.87	15.26

Danny Worth

Bats: R Throws: R Pos: 2B-15; 3B-13; PR-5; PH-3
Ht: 6'1" **Wt:** 185 **Born:** 9/30/1985 **Age:** 26

Year	Team	Lg	G	AB	H	2B	3B	HR	(Hm	Rd)	TB	R	RBI	RC	TBB	IBB	SO	HBP	SH	SF	SB	CS	SB%	GDP	Avg	OBP	Slg
2007	Lkland	A+	51	171	43	9	2	2	(-	-)	62	22	21	22	18	0	39	1	1	1	6	0	1.00	4	.251	.325	.363
2007	Erie	AA	5	14	6	2	1	0	(-	-)	10	4	4	4	1	0	1	0	0	1	1	0	1.00	0	.429	.438	.714
2008	Erie	AA	79	295	75	18	3	5	(-	-)	114	44	33	42	32	0	59	3	4	2	8	0	1.00	7	.254	.331	.386
2008	Toledo	AAA	1	2	1	0	0	0	(-	-)	1	0	0	0	0	0	0	0	0	0	0	0	-	0	.500	.500	.500
2009	Toledo	AAA	41	151	32	4	1	0	(-	-)	38	9	4	10	11	0	40	0	0	0	3	1	.75	2	.212	.265	.252
2009	Erie	AA	75	285	68	17	3	0	(-	-)	91	33	24	28	26	0	74	3	3	1	4	5	.44	2	.239	.308	.319
2010	Toledo	AAA	45	164	47	5	0	2	(-	-)	58	18	18	21	10	0	29	2	0	1	12	2	.86	1	.287	.333	.354
2011	Toledo	AAA	86	309	79	19	4	8	(-	-)	130	45	37	48	36	0	86	3	8	1	13	2	.87	3	.256	.338	.421
2010	Det	AL	39	106	27	5	0	2	(2	0)	38	10	8	11	6	0	13	0	3	0	1	2	.33	0	.255	.295	.358
2011	Det	AL	30	37	10	2	0	0	(0	0)	12	6	3	3	2	0	9	0	0	0	0	0	-	0	.270	.308	.324
	2 ML YEARS		69	143	37	7	0	2	(2	0)	50	16	11	14	8	0	22	0	3	0	1	2	.33	0	.259	.298	.350

David Wright

Bats: R Throws: R Pos: 3B-101; SS-1; PH-1
Ht: 6'0" **Wt:** 208 **Born:** 12/20/1982 **Age:** 29

Year	Team	Lg	G	AB	H	2B	3B	HR	(Hm	Rd)	TB	R	RBI	RC	TBB	IBB	SO	HBP	SH	SF	SB	CS	SB%	GDP	Avg	OBP	Slg
2011	StLuci*	A+	6	21	10	3	0	0	(-	-)	13	9	2	7	6	0	3	0	0	0	1	0	1.00	0	.476	.593	.619
2004	NYM	NL	69	263	77	17	1	14	(8	6)	138	41	40	42	14	0	40	3	0	3	6	0	1.00	7	.293	.332	.525
2005	NYM	NL	160	575	176	42	1	27	(12	15)	301	99	102	105	72	2	113	7	0	3	17	7	.71	16	.306	.388	.523
2006	NYM	NL	154	582	181	40	5	26	(13	13)	309	96	116	119	66	13	113	5	0	8	20	5	.80	15	.311	.381	.531
2007	NYM	NL	160	604	196	42	1	30	(16	14)	330	113	107	127	94	6	115	6	0	7	34	5	.87	14	.325	.416	.546
2008	NYM	NL	160	626	189	42	2	33	(21	12)	334	115	124	116	94	5	118	4	0	11	15	5	.75	15	.302	.390	.534
2009	NYM	NL	144	535	164	39	3	10	(5	5)	239	88	72	86	74	8	140	3	0	6	27	9	.75	16	.307	.390	.447
2010	NYM	NL	157	587	166	36	3	29	(12	17)	295	87	103	97	69	9	161	2	0	12	19	11	.63	12	.283	.354	.503
2011	NYM	NL	102	389	99	23	1	14	(5	9)	166	60	61	58	52	4	97	3	0	3	13	2	.87	5	.254	.345	.427
	Postseason		10	37	8	3	0	1	(0	1)	14	3	6	5	5	1	8	0	0	0	0	0	-	0	.216	.310	.378
	8 ML YEARS		1106	4161	1248	281	17	183	(92	91)	2112	699	725	750	535	47	897	33	0	53	151	44	.77	100	.300	.380	.508

Jamey Wright

Pitches: R Bats: R Pos: RP-60
Ht: 6'6" **Wt:** 230 **Born:** 12/24/1974 **Age:** 37

Year	Team	Lg	G	GS	CG	GF	IP	BFP	H	R	ER	HR	SH	SF	HB	TBB	IBB	SO	WP	Bk	W	L	Pct	Sh	Sv-Op	Hld	ERC	ERA
1996	Col	NL	16	15	0	0	91.1	406	105	60	50	8	4	2	7	41	1	45	1	2	4	4	.500	0	0-0	1	5.50	4.93
1997	Col	NL	26	26	1	0	149.2	698	198	113	104	19	8	3	11	71	3	59	6	2	8	12	.400	0	0-0	0	6.96	6.25
1998	Col	NL	34	34	1	0	206.1	919	235	143	130	24	8	6	11	95	3	86	6	3	9	14	.391	0	0-0	0	5.57	5.67
1999	Col	NL	16	16	0	0	94.1	423	110	52	51	10	3	4	4	54	3	49	3	0	4	3	.571	0	0-0	0	6.19	4.87
2000	Mil	NL	26	25	0	1	164.2	718	157	81	75	12	4	6	18	88	5	96	9	2	7	9	.438	0	0-0	0	4.67	4.10
2001	Mil	NL	33	33	1	0	194.2	868	201	115	106	26	7	5	20	98	10	129	6	1	11	12	.478	1	0-0	0	5.36	4.90
2002	2 Tms	NL	23	22	1	0	129.1	585	130	80	76	17	9	6	11	75	9	77	9	0	7	13	.350	1	0-0	0	5.35	5.29
2003	KC	AL	4	4	2	0	25.1	106	23	14	12	1	0	1	0	11	0	19	0	0	1	2	.333	1	0-0	0	3.53	4.26
2004	Col	NL	14	14	0	0	78.2	361	82	39	36	8	1	1	6	45	3	41	3	0	2	3	.400	0	0-0	0	5.26	4.12
2005	Col	NL	34	27	0	1	171.1	782	201	119	104	22	4	3	15	81	4	101	2	2	8	16	.333	0	0-1	1	6.02	5.46
2006	SF	NL	34	21	0	0	156.0	676	167	95	90	16	5	4	10	64	4	79	6	0	6	10	.375	0	0-0	0	4.89	5.19

Year	Team	Lg	G	GS	CG	GF	IP	BFP	H	R	ER	HR	SH	SF	HB	TBB	IBB	SO	WP	Bk	W	L	Pct	Sh	Sv-Op	Hld	ERC	ERA
2007	Tex	AL	20	9	0	3	77.0	330	72	35	31	6	3	2	5	41	2	39	4	0	4	5	.444	0	0-0	1	4.44	3.62
2008	Tex	AL	75	0	0	17	84.1	379	93	57	48	5	3	4	8	35	3	60	5	0	8	7	.533	0	0-6	17	4.74	5.12
2009	KC	AL	65	0	0	14	79.0	350	73	51	38	8	4	0	7	44	5	60	7	0	3	5	.375	0	0-3	12	4.56	4.33
2010	2 Tms	AL	46	0	0	17	58.1	249	55	33	27	3	3	3	3	25	1	28	4	1	1	3	.250	0	0-1	9	3.75	4.17
2011	Sea	AL	60	0	0	19	68.1	286	61	26	24	6	2	1	5	30	3	48	4	0	2	3	.400	0	1-5	16	3.89	3.16
02	Mil	NL	19	19	1	0	114.1	515	115	72	68	15	9	6	11	63	8	69	8	0	5	13	.278	1	0-0	0	5.28	5.35
02	StL	NL	4	3	0	0	15.0	70	15	8	8	2	0	0	0	12	1	8	1	0	2	0	1.000	0	0-0	0	5.87	4.80
10	Cle	AL	18	0	0	9	21.1	98	25	18	13	1	1	1	2	9	0	9	1	0	1	2	.333	0	0-0	1	5.10	5.48
10	Sea	AL	28	0	0	8	37.0	151	30	15	14	2	2	2	1	16	1	19	3	1	0	1	.000	0	0-1	8	3.03	3.41
16 ML YEARS			526	246	6	74	1828.2	8136	1963	1113	1002	191	68	50	142	898	59	1016	75	13	85	121	.413	3	1-15	57	5.27	4.93

Wesley Wright

Pitches: L Bats: R Pos: RP-21   **Ht: 5'11" Wt: 175 Born: 1/28/1985 Age: 27**

Year	Team	Lg	G	GS	CG	GF	IP	BFP	H	R	ER	HR	SH	SF	HB	TBB	IBB	SO	WP	Bk	W	L	Pct	Sh	Sv-Op	Hld	ERC	ERA
2011	OKCity*	AAA	39	3	0	6	65.1	265	49	17	15	4	1	1	3	23	2	52	1	0	3	1	.750	0	2- -	-	2.48	2.07
2008	Hou	NL	71	0	0	15	55.2	250	45	34	31	8	1	1	4	34	4	57	2	1	4	3	.571	0	1-1	13	4.21	5.01
2009	Hou	NL	49	0	0	5	44.2	204	53	27	27	9	0	2	0	25	3	47	2	0	3	4	.429	0	0-2	6	6.64	5.44
2010	Hou	NL	14	4	0	3	33.0	148	37	27	21	6	2	1	3	13	0	29	0	0	1	2	.333	0	0-0	0	5.78	5.73
2011	Hou	NL	21	0	0	5	12.0	44	6	2	2	1	0	0	0	5	0	11	1	0	0	0	-	0	0-1	3	1.68	1.50
4 ML YEARS			155	4	0	28	145.1	646	141	90	81	24	3	4	7	77	7	144	5	1	8	9	.471	0	1-4	22	5.03	5.02

Michael Wuertz

Pitches: R Bats: R Pos: RP-39   WURTZ   **Ht: 6'3" Wt: 212 Born: 12/15/1978 Age: 33**

Year	Team	Lg	G	GS	CG	GF	IP	BFP	H	R	ER	HR	SH	SF	HB	TBB	IBB	SO	WP	Bk	W	L	Pct	Sh	Sv-Op	Hld	ERC	ERA
2011	Stcktn*	A+	3	2	0	0	3.0	16	6	4	4	1	0	0	0	1	0	7	1	0	0	0	-	0	0- -	-	12.18	12.00
2011	Scrmto*	AAA	3	1	0	0	3.0	14	3	3	3	0	0	0	0	2	0	5	0	0	0	0	-	0	0- -	-	4.23	9.00
2004	ChC	NL	31	0	0	11	29.0	124	22	14	14	4	4	2	0	17	1	30	2	1	1	0	1.000	0	1-1	5	3.67	4.34
2005	ChC	NL	75	0	0	12	75.2	319	60	36	32	6	3	2	0	40	7	89	7	0	6	2	.750	0	0-3	18	3.17	3.81
2006	ChC	NL	41	0	0	4	40.2	175	35	14	12	5	3	0	1	16	2	42	1	0	3	1	.750	0	0-1	6	3.37	2.66
2007	ChC	NL	73	0	0	19	72.1	312	64	30	28	8	3	1	0	35	6	79	6	0	2	3	.400	0	0-0	8	3.68	3.48
2008	ChC	NL	45	0	0	13	44.2	189	44	23	18	4	1	3	0	20	2	30	2	0	1	1	.500	0	0-3	3	4.15	3.63
2009	Oak	AL	74	0	0	9	78.2	304	52	25	23	6	2	3	0	23	1	102	6	0	6	1	.857	0	4-6	23	1.84	2.63
2010	Oak	AL	48	0	0	14	39.2	171	35	21	19	6	4	0	0	21	5	40	6	0	2	3	.400	0	6-6	11	4.10	4.31
2011	Oak	AL	39	0	0	7	33.2	162	37	25	25	5	3	0	1	26	4	32	0	0	0	0	-	0	0-1	3	6.45	6.68
Postseason			2	0	0	0	1.2	7	0	0	0	0	1	0	0	1	0	2	1	0	0	0	-	0	0-0	0	0.32	0.00
8 ML YEARS			426	0	0	89	414.1	1756	349	188	171	44	23	11	2	198	28	444	30	1	21	11	.656	0	11-21	73	3.47	3.71

Kevin Youkilis

Bats: R Throws: R Pos: 3B-112; 1B-6; DH-4   YOU-kih-liss   **Ht: 6'1" Wt: 220 Born: 3/15/1979 Age: 33**

Year	Team	Lg	G	AB	H	2B	3B	HR	(Hm	Rd)	TB	R	RBI	RC	TBB	IBB	SO	HBP	SH	SF	SB	CS	SB%	GDP	Avg	OBP	Slg
2011	Pwtckt*	AAA	2	8	2	0	0	1	(-	-)	5	2	1	1	1	0	0	0	0	0	0	0	-	0	.250	.333	.625
2004	Bos	AL	72	208	54	11	0	7	(2	5)	86	38	35	36	33	0	45	4	0	3	0	1	.00	1	.260	.367	.413
2005	Bos	AL	44	79	22	7	0	1	(0	1)	32	11	9	13	14	0	19	2	0	0	0	1	.00	0	.278	.400	.405
2006	Bos	AL	147	569	159	42	2	13	(6	7)	244	100	72	104	91	0	120	9	0	11	5	2	.71	12	.279	.381	.429
2007	Bos	AL	145	528	152	35	2	16	(8	8)	239	85	83	101	77	0	105	15	0	5	4	2	.67	9	.288	.390	.453
2008	Bos	AL	145	538	168	43	4	29	(17	12)	306	91	115	120	62	7	108	12	0	9	3	5	.38	11	.312	.390	.569
2009	Bos	AL	136	491	150	36	1	27	(14	13)	269	99	94	114	77	6	125	16	0	4	7	2	.78	9	.305	.413	.548
2010	Bos	AL	102	362	111	26	5	19	(8	11)	204	77	62	77	58	3	67	10	0	5	4	1	.80	4	.307	.411	.564
2011	Bos	AL	120	431	111	32	2	17	(8	9)	198	68	80	81	68	3	100	14	0	4	3	0	1.00	14	.258	.373	.459
Postseason			29	111	34	9	1	6	(2	4)	63	22	17	20	13	0	18	0	0	1	0	0	-	4	.306	.376	.568
8 ML YEARS			911	3206	927	232	16	129	(63	66)	1578	569	550	646	480	19	689	82	0	41	26	14	.65	60	.289	.391	.492

Chris Young

Pitches: R Bats: R Pos: SP-4   **Ht: 6'10" Wt: 262 Born: 5/25/1979 Age: 33**

Year	Team	Lg	G	GS	CG	GF	IP	BFP	H	R	ER	HR	SH	SF	HB	TBB	IBB	SO	WP	Bk	W	L	Pct	Sh	Sv-Op	Hld	ERC	ERA
2004	Tex	AL	7	7	0	0	36.1	158	36	21	19	7	1	0	2	10	0	27	1	0	3	2	.600	0	0-0	0	4.26	4.71
2005	Tex	AL	31	31	0	0	164.2	700	162	84	78	19	2	4	7	45	2	137	3	0	12	7	.632	0	0-0	0	3.71	4.26
2006	SD	NL	31	31	0	0	179.1	735	134	72	69	28	8	3	6	69	4	164	6	1	11	5	.688	0	0-0	0	3.12	3.46
2007	SD	NL	30	30	0	0	173.0	705	118	66	60	10	3	6	7	72	0	167	7	4	9	8	.529	0	0-0	0	2.35	3.12
2008	SD	NL	18	18	1	0	102.1	434	84	46	45	13	4	1	1	48	4	93	3	1	7	6	.538	0	0-0	0	3.50	3.96
2009	SD	NL	14	14	0	0	76.0	336	70	47	44	12	4	5	2	40	3	50	1	0	4	6	.400	0	0-0	0	4.55	5.21
2010	SD	NL	4	4	0	0	20.0	82	10	2	2	1	1	0	1	11	0	15	1	0	2	0	1.000	0	0-0	0	1.72	0.90
2011	NYM	NL	4	4	0	0	24.0	95	12	5	5	3	1	0	1	11	0	22	0	0	1	0	1.000	0	0-0	0	2.04	1.88
Postseason			1	1	0	0	6.2	25	4	0	0	0	0	0	0	2	1	9	0	0	1	0	1.000	0	0-0	0	1.22	0.00
8 ML YEARS			139	139	1	0	775.2	3245	626	343	322	93	24	19	26	306	13	675	22	6	49	34	.590	0	0-0	0	3.23	3.74

Chris Young

Bats: R **Throws:** R **Pos:** CF-155; PH-1 **Ht:** 6'2" **Wt:** 200 **Born:** 9/5/1983 **Age:** 28

Year Team	Lg	G	AB	H	2B	3B	HR	(Hm	Rd)	TB	R	RBI	RC	TBB	IBB	SO	HBP	SH	SF	SB	CS	SB%	GDP	Avg	OBP	Slg
2006 Ari	NL	30	70	17	4	0	2	(1	1)	27	10	10	11	6	0	12	1	0	1	2	1	.67	0	.243	.308	.386
2007 Ari	NL	148	569	135	29	3	32	(14	18)	266	85	68	68	43	1	141	6	1	5	27	6	.82	5	.237	.295	.467
2008 Ari	NL	160	625	155	42	7	22	(9	13)	277	85	85	84	62	2	165	1	6	5	14	5	.74	10	.248	.315	.443
2009 Ari	NL	134	433	92	28	4	15	(7	8)	173	54	42	47	59	2	133	4	3	2	11	4	.73	3	.212	.311	.400
2010 Ari	NL	156	584	150	33	0	27	(20	7)	264	94	91	86	74	0	145	2	1	3	28	7	.80	10	.257	.341	.452
2011 Ari	NL	156	567	134	38	3	20	(14	6)	238	89	71	84	80	4	139	4	1	7	22	9	.71	3	.236	.331	.420
Postseason		7	25	7	1	0	2	(1	1)	14	4	5	7	7	0	13	1	0	0	1	2	.33	0	.280	.455	.560
6 ML YEARS		784	2848	683	174	17	118	(65	53)	1245	417	367	380	324	9	735	18	12	23	104	32	.76	31	.240	.319	.437

Delmon Young

Bats: R **Throws:** R **Pos:** LF-115; DH-7; PH-2; PR-1 **Ht:** 6'3" **Wt:** 240 **Born:** 9/14/1985 **Age:** 26

Year Team	Lg	G	AB	H	2B	3B	HR	(Hm	Rd)	TB	R	RBI	RC	TBB	IBB	SO	HBP	SH	SF	SB	CS	SB%	GDP	Avg	OBP	Slg
2011 Roch*	AAA	9	31	9	3	0	2	(-	-)	18	5	5	5	1	0	5	0	0	0	0	0	-	1	.290	.313	.581
2006 TB	AL	30	126	40	9	1	3	(1	2)	60	16	10	15	1	0	24	3	0	1	2	2	.50	0	.317	.336	.476
2007 TB	AL	**162**	645	186	38	0	13	(9	4)	263	65	93	90	26	2	127	3	0	7	10	3	.77	**23**	.288	.316	.408
2008 Min	AL	152	575	167	28	4	10	(7	3)	233	80	69	74	35	7	105	7	1	5	14	5	.74	19	.290	.336	.405
2009 Min	AL	108	395	112	16	2	12	(7	5)	168	50	60	46	12	1	92	4	0	5	2	5	.29	17	.284	.308	.425
2010 Min	AL	153	570	170	46	1	21	(6	15)	281	77	112	94	28	5	81	6	0	9	5	4	.56	16	.298	.333	.493
2011 2 Tms	AL	124	473	127	21	1	12	(8	4)	186	54	64	57	23	2	85	2	0	5	1	0	1.00	19	.268	.302	.393
11 Min	AL	84	305	81	16	0	4	(1	3)	109	26	32	32	18	2	55	0	0	2	1	0	1.00	12	.266	.305	.357
11 Det	AL	40	168	46	5	1	8	(7	1)	77	28	32	25	5	0	30	2	0	3	0	0	-	7	.274	.298	.458
Postseason		6	24	5	1	1	0	(0	0)	8	2	0	1	2	0	6	1	0	0	1	0	1.00	1	.208	.296	.333
6 ML YEARS		729	2784	802	158	9	71	(38	33)	1191	342	408	376	125	17	514	25	1	32	34	19	.64	94	.288	.321	.428

Eric Young

Bats: B **Throws:** R **Pos:** LF-35; PH-26; 2B-7; PR-6; CF-5; RF-3; DH-1 **Ht:** 5'10" **Wt:** 180 **Born:** 5/25/1985 **Age:** 27

Year Team	Lg	G	AB	H	2B	3B	HR	(Hm	Rd)	TB	R	RBI	RC	TBB	IBB	SO	HBP	SH	SF	SB	CS	SB%	GDP	Avg	OBP	Slg
2011 ColSpr*	AAA	58	223	81	18	9	2	(-	-)	123	61	28	59	39	0	36	2	6	5	17	1	.94	3	.363	.454	.552
2009 Col	NL	30	57	14	1	0	1	(1	0)	18	7	1	2	4	0	12	0	0	0	4	4	.50	1	.246	.295	.316
2010 Col	NL	51	172	42	5	1	0	(0	0)	49	26	8	16	17	0	32	0	0	0	17	6	.74	2	.244	.312	.285
2011 Col	NL	77	198	49	4	3	0	(0	0)	59	34	10	27	26	0	38	3	1	1	27	4	.87	1	.247	.342	.298
Postseason		2	1	0	0	0	0	(0	0)	0	0	0	0	0	0	0	0	0	0	0	0	-	0	.000	.000	.000
3 ML YEARS		158	427	105	10	4	1	(1	0)	126	67	19	45	47	0	82	3	1	1	48	14	.77	4	.246	.324	.295

Matt Young

Bats: L **Throws:** R **Pos:** LF-9; RF-7; PH-7; CF-3; PR-1 **Ht:** 5'8" **Wt:** 175 **Born:** 10/3/1982 **Age:** 29

Year Team	Lg	G	AB	H	2B	3B	HR	(Hm	Rd)	TB	R	RBI	RC	TBB	IBB	SO	HBP	SH	SF	SB	CS	SB%	GDP	Avg	OBP	Slg
2005 Rome	A	114	423	132	15	4	6	(-	-)	173	85	52	75	66	0	65	7	7	2	10	11	.48	3	.312	.412	.409
2006 MrtlBh	A+	118	424	119	30	2	2	(-	-)	159	65	52	71	71	1	55	8	9	6	21	10	.68	11	.281	.389	.375
2006 Missi	AAA	13	50	11	1	0	0	(-	-)	12	3	6	4	7	0	9	0	1	1	1	1	.50	1	.220	.310	.240
2007 MrtlBh	A+	65	243	68	7	3	1	(-	-)	84	29	18	36	37	1	36	4	1	2	14	7	.67	5	.280	.381	.346
2007 Missi	AA	33	95	23	4	1	0	(-	-)	29	6	15	8	10	1	18	0	1	2	0	3	.00	6	.242	.308	.305
2008 Missi	AA	135	491	142	16	11	3	(-	-)	189	74	50	81	68	0	62	9	7	2	30	12	.71	9	.289	.384	.385
2009 Missi	AA	130	460	133	22	10	4	(-	-)	187	81	33	91	94	8	59	12	3	2	42	16	.72	7	.289	.421	.407
2009 Gwnntt	AAA	7	26	5	1	0	1	(-	-)	9	6	3	2	3	0	5	0	0	0	1	1	.50	1	.192	.276	.346
2010 Gwnntt	AAA	134	487	146	33	5	3	(-	-)	198	88	35	85	57	3	53	7	2	2	39	7	.85	13	.300	.380	.407
2011 Gwnntt	AAA	99	366	100	16	4	1	(-	-)	127	64	24	54	57	0	59	2	1	2	17	7	.71	15	.273	.372	.347
2011 Atl	NL	20	48	10	1	0	0	(0	0)	11	4	1	3	4	0	6	0	0	0	0	1	.00	0	.208	.269	.229

Michael Young

Bats: R **Throws:** R **Pos:** DH-69; 3B-40; 1B-36; 2B-14; SS-1 **Ht:** 6'1" **Wt:** 200 **Born:** 10/19/1976 **Age:** 35

Year Team	Lg	G	AB	H	2B	3B	HR	(Hm	Rd)	TB	R	RBI	RC	TBB	IBB	SO	HBP	SH	SF	SB	CS	SB%	GDP	Avg	OBP	Slg
2000 Tex	AL	2	2	0	0	0	0	(0	0)	0	0	0	0	0	0	1	0	0	0	0	0	-	0	.000	.000	.000
2001 Tex	AL	106	386	96	18	4	11	(7	4)	155	57	49	45	26	0	91	3	9	5	3	1	.75	9	.249	.298	.402
2002 Tex	AL	156	573	150	26	8	9	(3	6)	219	77	62	64	41	1	112	0	13	6	6	7	.46	14	.262	.308	.382
2003 Tex	AL	160	666	204	33	9	14	(9	5)	297	106	72	106	36	1	103	1	3	7	13	2	.87	14	.306	.339	.446
2004 Tex	AL	160	690	216	33	9	22	(9	13)	333	114	99	124	44	1	89	1	0	4	12	3	.80	11	.313	.353	.483
2005 Tex	AL	159	668	**221**	40	5	24	(12	12)	343	114	91	131	58	0	91	3	0	3	5	2	.71	20	.331	.385	.513
2006 Tex	AL	**162**	691	217	52	3	14	(8	6)	317	93	103	120	48	0	96	1	0	1	7	3	.70	27	.314	.356	.459
2007 Tex	AL	156	639	201	37	1	9	(8	1)	267	80	94	107	47	5	107	5	0	1	13	3	.81	21	.315	.366	.418
2008 Tex	AL	155	645	183	36	2	12	(8	4)	259	102	82	91	55	0	109	2	0	6	10	0	1.00	19	.284	.339	.402
2009 Tex	AL	135	541	174	36	2	22	(10	12)	280	76	68	87	47	2	90	1	0	4	8	3	.73	16	.322	.374	.518
2010 Tex	AL	157	656	186	36	3	21	(16	5)	299	99	91	85	50	4	115	1	0	11	4	2	.67	21	.284	.330	.444
2011 Tex	AL	159	631	**213**	41	6	11	(10	1)	299	88	106	118	47	7	78	2	0	9	6	2	.75	17	.338	.380	.474
Postseason		16	67	17	3	0	1	(0	1)	23	4	7	5	2	0	15	0	0	0	0	0	-	4	.254	.275	.343
12 ML YEARS		1667	6788	2061	388	52	169	(100	69)	3060	1006	917	1073	499	21	1082	20	25	64	87	28	.76	189	.304	.350	.451

Mike Zagurski

Pitches: L **Bats:** L **Pos:** RP-4 | zah-GURR-skee | **Ht:** 6'0" **Wt:** 221 **Born:** 1/27/1983 **Age:** 29

			HOW MUCH HE PITCHED						WHAT HE GAVE UP										THE RESULTS					
Year	Team	Lg	G	GS	CG	GF	IP	BFP	H	R	ER	HR	SH	SF	HB	TBB	IBB	SO	WP	Bk	W	L	Pct	Sh	Sv-Op	Hld	ERC	ERA
2011	LV*	AAA	46	0	0	20	54.1	224	43	18	16	3	4	0	3	27	1	63	0	1	4	0	1.000	0	11--	-	3.31	2.65
2007	Phi	NL	25	0	0	4	21.1	101	25	14	14	3	1	1	1	11	2	21	2	0	1	0	1.000	0	0-2	5	5.75	5.91
2010	Phi	NL	8	0	0	3	7.0	34	8	8	8	1	1	1	2	5	0	11	1	0	0	0	-	0	0-0	0	8.12	10.29
2011	Phi	NL	4	0	0	1	3.1	17	4	2	2	1	0	0	0	3	0	4	0	0	0	0	-	0	0-0	0	8.99	5.40
	3 ML YEARS		37	0	0	8	31.2	152	37	24	24	5	2	2	3	19	2	36	3	0	1	0	1.000	0	0-2	5	6.58	6.82

Carlos Zambrano

Pitches: R **Bats:** B **Pos:** SP-24 | **Ht:** 6'5" **Wt:** 270 **Born:** 6/1/1981 **Age:** 31

			HOW MUCH HE PITCHED						WHAT HE GAVE UP										THE RESULTS					
Year	Team	Lg	G	GS	CG	GF	IP	BFP	H	R	ER	HR	SH	SF	HB	TBB	IBB	SO	WP	Bk	W	L	Pct	Sh	Sv-Op	Hld	ERC	ERA
2011	Peoria*	A	1	1	0	0	4.0	16	3	1	0	0	1	0	0	3	0	4	0	0	0	0	-	0	0--	-	3.68	0.00
2001	ChC	NL	6	1	0	1	7.2	42	11	13	13	2	1	1	1	8	0	4	1	0	1	2	.333	0	0-1	0	11.86	15.26
2002	ChC	NL	32	16	0	3	108.1	477	94	53	44	9	9	1	4	63	2	93	6	0	4	8	.333	0	0-0	0	4.02	3.66
2003	ChC	NL	32	32	3	0	214.0	907	188	88	74	9	11	6	10	94	12	168	6	1	13	11	.542	1	0-0	0	3.28	3.11
2004	ChC	NL	31	31	1	0	209.2	887	174	73	64	14	10	3	20	81	4	188	6	2	16	8	.667	1	0-0	0	3.20	2.75
2005	ChC	NL	33	33	2	0	223.1	909	170	88	81	21	9	5	8	86	3	202	7	0	14	6	.700	0	0-0	0	2.86	3.26
2006	ChC	NL	33	33	0	0	214.0	917	162	91	81	20	11	4	9	115	4	210	9	1	16	7	.696	0	0-0	0	3.34	3.41
2007	ChC	NL	34	34	1	0	216.1	925	187	100	95	23	6	3	14	101	4	177	3	0	18	13	.581	0	0-0	0	3.88	3.95
2008	ChC	NL	30	30	1	0	188.2	796	172	85	82	18	5	0	6	72	1	130	4	0	14	6	.700	1	0-0	0	3.62	3.91
2009	ChC	NL	28	28	1	0	169.1	733	155	78	71	10	10	5	9	78	6	152	7	0	9	7	.563	1	0-0	0	3.70	3.77
2010	ChC	NL	36	20	0	2	129.2	571	119	55	48	7	9	3	6	69	0	117	7	1	11	6	.647	0	0-0	4	3.97	3.33
2011	ChC	NL	24	24	0	0	145.2	634	154	80	78	19	12	5	5	56	4	101	1	0	9	7	.563	0	0-0	0	4.69	4.82
	Postseason		5	5	0	0	29.0	132	35	19	14	6	1	1	2	8	0	27	1	0	0	2	.000	0	0-0	0	5.72	4.34
	11 ML YEARS		319	282	9	6	1826.2	7798	1586	804	731	152	93	36	92	823	40	1542	57	5	125	81	.607	4	0-1	4	3.60	3.60

Brad Ziegler

Pitches: R **Bats:** R **Pos:** RP-66 | ZIGG-lerr | **Ht:** 6'4" **Wt:** 212 **Born:** 10/10/1979 **Age:** 32

			HOW MUCH HE PITCHED						WHAT HE GAVE UP										THE RESULTS					
Year	Team	Lg	G	GS	CG	GF	IP	BFP	H	R	ER	HR	SH	SF	HB	TBB	IBB	SO	WP	Bk	W	L	Pct	Sh	Sv-Op	Hld	ERC	ERA
2008	Oak	AL	47	0	0	21	59.2	229	47	8	7	2	4	3	1	22	3	30	0	0	3	0	1.000	0	11-13	9	2.60	1.06
2009	Oak	AL	69	0	0	23	73.1	313	82	27	25	2	1	3	1	28	4	54	0	0	2	4	.333	0	7-10	14	4.25	3.07
2010	Oak	AL	64	0	0	12	60.2	257	54	24	22	4	1	1	3	28	9	41	0	1	3	7	.300	0	0-4	18	3.48	3.26
2011	2 Tms		66	0	0	16	58.1	239	53	21	14	0	1	2	1	19	3	44	1	0	3	2	.600	0	1-2	10	2.68	2.16
11	Oak	AL	43	0	0	12	37.2	160	38	14	10	0	1	1	1	13	3	29	1	0	3	2	.600	0	1-2	6	3.21	2.39
11	Ari	NL	23	0	0	4	20.2	79	15	7	4	0	0	1	0	6	0	15	0	0	0	0	-	0	0-0	4	1.77	1.74
	4 ML YEARS		246	0	0	72	252.0	1038	236	80	68	8	7	9	6	97	19	169	1	1	11	13	.458	0	19-29	51	3.29	2.43

Ryan Zimmerman

Bats: R **Throws:** R **Pos:** 3B-97; PH-3; DH-1 | **Ht:** 6'3" **Wt:** 228 **Born:** 9/28/1984 **Age:** 27

			BATTING																		BASERUNNING				AVERAGES		
Year	Team	Lg	G	AB	H	2B	3B	HR	(Hm	Rd)	TB	R	RBI	RC	TBB	IBB	SO	HBP	SH	SF	SB	CS	SB%	GDP	Avg	OBP	Slg
2011	Hgrstn*	A	1	2	2	1	1	0	(-	-)	5	2	1	2	1	0	0	0	0	0	0	0	-	0	1.000	1.000	2.500
2011	Ptomc*	A+	3	10	4	2	0	0	(-	-)	6	0	1	2	1	0	1	0	0	0	0	0	-	0	.400	.455	.600
2011	Syrcse*	AAA	2	9	2	0	0	0	(-	-)	2	1	1	0	0	0	2	0	0	0	0	0	-	0	.222	.222	.222
2005	Was	NL	20	58	23	10	0	0	(0	0)	33	6	6	9	3	0	12	0	0	1	0	0	-	1	.397	.419	.569
2006	Was	NL	157	614	176	47	3	20	(10	10)	289	84	110	101	61	7	120	2	1	4	11	8	.58	15	.287	.351	.471
2007	Was	NL	162	653	174	43	5	24	(11	13)	299	99	91	83	61	3	125	3	0	5	4	1	.80	26	.266	.330	.458
2008	Was	NL	106	428	121	24	1	14	(7	7)	189	51	51	48	31	1	71	3	0	4	1	1	.50	12	.283	.333	.442
2009	Was	NL	157	610	178	37	3	33	(17	16)	320	110	106	96	72	9	119	2	0	9	2	0	1.00	32	.292	.364	.525
2010	Was	NL	142	525	161	32	0	25	(9	16)	268	85	85	97	69	6	98	4	0	5	4	1	.80	16	.307	.388	.510
2011	Was	NL	101	395	114	21	2	12	(7	5)	175	52	49	58	41	4	73	1	0	3	3	1	.75	14	.289	.355	.443
	7 ML YEARS		845	3283	947	214	14	128	(61	67)	1573	487	498	492	338	30	618	15	1	31	25	12	.68	106	.288	.355	.479

Jordan Zimmermann

Pitches: R **Bats:** R **Pos:** SP-26 | **Ht:** 6'2" **Wt:** 218 **Born:** 5/23/1986 **Age:** 26

			HOW MUCH HE PITCHED						WHAT HE GAVE UP										THE RESULTS					
Year	Team	Lg	G	GS	CG	GF	IP	BFP	H	R	ER	HR	SH	SF	HB	TBB	IBB	SO	WP	Bk	W	L	Pct	Sh	Sv-Op	Hld	ERC	ERA
2009	Was	NL	16	16	0	0	91.1	391	95	51	47	10	5	3	4	29	0	92	0	0	3	5	.375	0	0-0	0	4.25	4.63
2010	Was	NL	7	7	0	0	31.0	135	31	20	17	8	1	1	2	10	1	27	0	0	1	2	.333	0	0-0	0	5.02	4.94
2011	Was	NL	26	26	1	0	161.1	662	154	62	57	12	8	2	7	31	2	124	3	1	8	11	.421	0	0-0	0	3.02	3.18
	3 ML YEARS		49	49	1	0	283.2	1188	280	133	121	30	14	6	13	70	3	243	3	1	12	18	.400	0	0-0	0	3.62	3.84

Barry Zito

Pitches: L **Bats:** L **Pos:** SP-9; RP-4 | **Ht:** 6'2" **Wt:** 206 **Born:** 5/13/1978 **Age:** 34

			HOW MUCH HE PITCHED						WHAT HE GAVE UP										THE RESULTS					
Year	Team	Lg	G	GS	CG	GF	IP	BFP	H	R	ER	HR	SH	SF	HB	TBB	IBB	SO	WP	Bk	W	L	Pct	Sh	Sv-Op	Hld	ERC	ERA
2011	SnJos*	A+	3	3	0	0	21.1	82	15	7	6	2	1	0	2	5	0	19	0	0	2	1	.667	0	0--	-	2.33	2.53
2011	Fresno*	AAA	3	3	1	0	17.2	66	10	5	5	1	1	0	0	5	0	17	0	0	2	0	1.000	1	0--	-	1.43	2.55
2000	Oak	AL	14	14	1	0	92.2	376	64	30	28	6	1	0	2	45	2	78	2	0	7	4	.636	1	0-0	0	2.63	2.72
2001	Oak	AL	35	35	3	0	214.1	902	184	92	83	18	5	4	13	80	0	205	6	1	17	8	.680	2	0-0	0	3.33	3.49
2002	Oak	AL	35	35	1	0	229.1	939	182	79	70	24	9	7	9	78	2	182	2	1	23	5	.821	1	0-0	0	2.92	2.75
2003	Oak	AL	35	35	4	0	231.2	957	186	98	85	19	7	4	6	88	3	146	4	0	14	12	.538	1	0-0	0	2.91	3.30

			HOW MUCH HE PITCHED							WHAT HE GAVE UP											THE RESULTS							
Year	Team	Lg	G	GS	CG	GF	IP	BFP	H	R	ER	HR	SH	SF	HB	TBB	IBB	SO	WP	Bk	W	L	Pct	Sh	Sv-Op	Hld	ERC	ERA
2004	Oak	AL	34	34	0	0	213.0	926	216	116	106	28	7	9	9	81	2	163	4	1	11	11	.500	0	0-0	0	4.45	4.48
2005	Oak	AL	35	35	0	0	228.1	953	185	106	98	26	8	7	13	89	0	171	4	0	14	13	.519	0	0-0	0	3.32	3.86
2006	Oak	AL	34	34	0	0	221.0	945	211	99	94	27	7	6	13	99	5	151	4	2	16	10	.615	0	0-0	0	4.47	3.83
2007	SF	NL	34	33	0	0	196.2	850	182	105	99	24	12	4	4	83	4	131	5	0	11	13	.458	0	0-0	0	3.91	4.53
2008	SF	NL	32	32	0	0	180.0	818	186	115	103	16	8	14	4	102	10	120	3	0	10	17	.370	0	0-0	0	4.81	5.15
2009	SF	NL	33	33	1	0	192.0	818	179	89	86	21	11	1	8	81	8	154	2	2	10	13	.435	0	0-0	0	4.00	4.03
2010	SF	NL	34	33	1	1	199.1	848	184	97	92	20	13	7	7	84	7	150	7	0	9	14	.391	0	0-0	0	3.85	4.15
2011	SF	NL	13	9	0	0	53.2	225	51	35	35	10	0	2	0	24	1	32	1	0	3	4	.429	0	0-0	0	4.71	5.87
	Postseason		7	7	0	0	44.1	184	34	16	16	6	1	0	3	17	0	33	1	0	4	3	.571	0	0-0	0	3.24	3.25
	12 ML YEARS		368	362	11	4	2252.0	9557	2010	1061	979	239	88	68	88	934	44	1683	44	7	145	124	.539	4	0-0	0	3.72	3.91

Ben Zobrist

Bats: B **Throws:** R **Pos:** 2B-131; RF-38; DH-3; PH-1; PR-1   ZOH-brist   **Ht:** 6'3" **Wt:** 200 **Born:** 5/26/1981 **Age:** 31

						BATTING															BASERUNNING				AVERAGES		
Year	Team	Lg	G	AB	H	2B	3B	HR	(Hm	Rd)	TB	R	RBI	RC	TBB	IBB	SO	HBP	SH	SF	SB	CS	SB%	GDP	Avg	OBP	Slg
2006	TB	AL	52	183	41	6	2	2	(2	0)	57	10	18	13	10	1	26	0	2	3	2	3	.40	2	.224	.260	.311
2007	TB	AL	31	97	15	2	0	1	(0	1)	20	8	9	0	3	0	21	1	2	2	2	0	1.00	1	.155	.184	.206
2008	TB	AL	62	198	50	10	2	12	(4	8)	100	32	30	31	25	1	37	2	0	2	3	0	1.00	4	.253	.339	.505
2009	TB	AL	152	501	149	28	7	27	(18	9)	272	91	91	109	91	4	104	2	1	4	17	6	.74	7	.297	.405	.543
2010	TB	AL	151	541	129	28	2	10	(3	7)	191	77	75	84	92	1	107	3	7	12	24	3	.89	10	.238	.346	.353
2011	TB	AL	156	588	158	46	6	20	(9	11)	276	99	91	100	77	1	128	2	2	5	19	6	.76	9	.269	.353	.469
	Postseason		12	31	7	2	0	1	(1	0)	12	2	2	2	4	0	6	0	0	0	0	0	-	0	.226	.314	.387
	6 ML YEARS		604	2108	542	120	19	72	(36	36)	916	317	314	337	298	8	423	10	14	28	67	18	.79	33	.257	.348	.435

2011 Fielding Statistics

Last year we did an overhaul of the Fielding Statistics section of the Handbook. We changed the focus of the section from emphasizing range factor and fielding percentage to emphasizing Defensive Runs Saved. In doing so, we believe that we are now highlighting the best defenders in baseball by position by ranking them by Runs Saved.

Some details about this section:

Plus/Minus (PM) and Defensive Runs Saved (Runs Saved for short) numbers are supplied for each player, as well as traditional stats such as putouts, assists, and errors. For lineup regulars we list players by position in order of best-to-worst Runs Saved. The Runs Saved numbers are broken down by component. Eight of the nine positions on the diamond are evaluated on range with Plus/Minus Runs Saved (Runs Saved +/-). Catchers are the exception and they are evaluated on pitcher handling and controlling the running game. Corner infielders are rated on their ability to handle bunts, middle infielders on their double play skills, and outfielders on their throwing arm. A bonus for outfielders is Runs Saved for home run robberies. For a more detailed explanation of Runs Saved, see the glossary.

You can find pitcher fielding data in the "Pitchers Hitting, Fielding, and Holding Runners" section.

First Basemen - Regulars

Player	Tm	G	GS	Inn	PO	A	E	DP	Pct.	PM	Runs Saved Bunts	+/-	Total
Trumbo,Mark	LAA	149	143	1257.1	1281	93	10	117	.993	+11	-1	8	7
Gonzalez,Adrian	Bos	156	155	1352.2	1222	125	4	106	.997	+5	2	4	6
Loney,James	LAD	150	134	1203.2	1129	74	5	90	.996	+7	-1	5	4
Sanchez,Gaby	Fla	153	150	1354.0	1262	101	5	109	.996	+6	0	4	4
Votto,Joey	Cin	160	159	1427.2	1341	173	6	127	.996	+4	1	3	4
Huff,Aubrey	SF	120	119	1032.2	990	72	5	86	.995	+1	3	1	4
Pujols,Albert	StL	146	141	1260.1	1254	165	11	134	.992	+5	-1	4	3
Teixeira,Mark	NYY	147	144	1274.0	1229	73	4	114	.997	+6	-1	4	3
Helton,Todd	Col	119	113	987.2	985	104	3	110	.997	+4	0	3	3
Pena,Carlos	ChC	153	142	1258.1	1116	88	8	104	.993	+3	1	2	3
Lee,Derrek	TOT	113	113	984.0	939	74	8	83	.992	+1	0	1	1
Freeman,Freddie	Atl	156	149	1370.1	1317	92	6	106	.996	0	0	0	0
Kotchman,Casey	TB	146	135	1222.1	1119	80	2	109	.998	+1	-2	1	-1
Fielder,Prince	Mil	159	159	1394.2	1332	84	15	113	.990	-3	1	-2	-1
Smoak,Justin	Sea	108	107	926.2	884	59	7	87	.993	-1	-1	-1	-2
Overbay,Lyle	TOT	109	102	917.0	920	66	8	97	.992	-4	1	-3	-2
Lind,Adam	Tor	109	109	965.1	952	64	4	88	.996	-1	-2	-1	-3
Cabrera,Miguel	Det	152	152	1322.0	1263	103	13	117	.991	-7	-1	-5	-6
Konerko,Paul	CWS	111	110	963.1	975	68	5	89	.995	-5	-3	-4	-7
Howard,Ryan	Phi	149	145	1309.0	1282	70	9	110	.993	-12	0	-9	-9
Hosmer,Eric	KC	127	127	1135.2	1096	78	8	101	.993	-19	-2	-14	-16

Second Basemen - Regulars

Player	Tm	G	GS	Inn	PO	A	E	DP	Pct.	Range	PM	Runs Saved GDP	+/-	Total
Zobrist,Ben	TB	131	118	1058.1	213	316	6	68	.989	4.50	+23	0	17	17
Kinsler,Ian	Tex	144	144	1269.0	268	398	11	103	.984	4.72	+13	6	10	16
Kendrick,Howie	LAA	108	105	937.2	162	317	4	63	.992	4.60	+19	1	14	15
Pedroia,Dustin	Bos	159	158	1392.1	290	425	7	81	.990	4.62	+18	-1	14	13
Ellis,Mark	TOT	123	119	1054.2	250	383	3	92	.995	5.40	+12	1	9	10
Phillips,Brandon	Cin	148	148	1324.0	306	409	6	94	.992	4.86	+13	-3	10	7
Hill,Aaron	TOT	137	133	1198.1	261	367	7	88	.989	4.72	+7	1	6	7
Cano,Robinson	NYY	157	150	1340.0	323	444	10	97	.987	5.15	+7	1	5	6
Utley,Chase	Phi	100	100	887.2	208	275	5	48	.990	4.90	+9	-3	7	4
Beckham,Gordon	CWS	149	147	1307.2	272	443	8	84	.989	4.92	+6	-1	5	4
Espinosa,Danny	Was	158	155	1393.0	305	465	14	101	.982	4.97	+6	-1	5	4
Weeks,Rickie	Mil	115	115	974.0	175	291	15	65	.969	4.31	+2	1	2	3
Getz,Chris	KC	110	97	894.1	189	299	6	69	.988	4.91	+4	-1	3	2
Infante,Omar	Fla	146	145	1283.1	260	466	8	75	.989	5.09	0	-1	0	-1
Johnson,Kelly	TOT	141	138	1224.0	268	349	10	86	.984	4.54	-5	2	-4	-2
Barney,Darwin	ChC	135	124	1110.1	258	349	12	65	.981	4.92	+3	-6	2	-4
Walker,Neil	Pit	159	155	1382.1	333	442	6	108	.992	5.05	-4	-2	-3	-5
Uggla,Dan	Atl	159	157	1431.2	294	440	15	86	.980	4.61	-4	-6	-3	-9
Hudson,Orlando	SD	114	111	959.2	238	308	4	69	.993	5.12	-8	-3	-6	-9

Third Basemen - Regulars

Player	Tm	G	GS	Inn	PO	A	E	DP	Pct.	Range	PM	Runs Saved Bunts	+/-	Total
Sandoval,Pablo	SF	106	101	904.2	71	214	10	16	.966	2.84	+26	2	20	22
Beltre,Adrian	Tex	112	112	980.1	93	208	11	24	.965	2.76	+21	1	16	17
Polanco,Placido	Phi	118	115	1044.2	78	259	8	15	.977	2.90	+20	1	15	16
Longoria,Evan	TB	130	128	1124.2	124	229	14	35	.962	2.82	+12	3	9	12
Callaspo,Alberto	LAA	129	125	1139.1	95	255	15	27	.959	2.76	+7	-1	5	4
Headley,Chase	SD	107	102	895.1	95	166	11	19	.960	2.62	+3	-2	2	0
Zimmerman,Ryan	Was	97	97	866.2	66	200	12	19	.957	2.76	-4	3	-3	0
Morel,Brent	CWS	125	116	1058.0	72	211	14	13	.953	2.41	-1	-1	-1	-2
McGehee,Casey	Mil	147	139	1233.1	72	255	20	17	.942	2.39	-3	0	-2	-2
Roberts,Ryan	Ari	107	102	902.1	74	197	10	15	.964	2.70	-4	-1	-3	-4
Jones,Chipper	Atl	116	111	1006.1	65	177	6	19	.976	2.16	-7	0	-5	-5
Youkilis,Kevin	Bos	112	111	948.2	87	177	9	15	.967	2.50	-8	1	-6	-5
Wright,David	NYM	101	101	893.2	68	180	19	9	.929	2.50	-6	-2	-5	-7
Ramirez,Aramis	ChC	145	143	1241.1	68	216	14	18	.953	2.06	-19	2	-14	-12
Valencia,Danny	Min	147	146	1280.2	73	260	18	20	.949	2.34	-15	-2	-11	-13
Reynolds,Mark	Bal	114	111	984.1	58	169	26	19	.897	2.08	-33	-4	-25	-29

Shortstops - Regulars

Player	Tm	G	GS	Inn	PO	A	E	DP	Pct.	Range	PM	Runs Saved GDP	+/-	Total
Ryan,Brendan	Sea	123	120	1060.2	186	371	15	79	.974	4.73	+22	1	17	18
Gonzalez,Alex	Atl	149	146	1316.0	187	434	12	79	.981	4.25	+22	-2	17	15
Andrus,Elvis	Tex	147	142	1261.1	245	407	25	102	.963	4.65	+14	2	11	13
Barmes,Clint	Hou	122	120	1058.1	171	356	12	69	.978	4.48	+14	1	11	12
Tulowitzki,Troy	Col	140	140	1208.1	261	417	6	98	.991	5.05	+10	3	8	11
Cedeno,Ronny	Pit	125	118	1050.1	191	397	13	72	.978	5.04	+15	-3	11	8
Ramirez,Alexei	CWS	155	154	1382.0	217	457	16	99	.977	4.39	+7	2	5	7
Escobar,Alcides	KC	158	156	1387.1	271	459	15	98	.980	4.74	+12	-4	9	5
Escobar,Yunel	Tor	132	131	1121.0	182	343	14	73	.974	4.21	+8	-1	6	5
Hardy,J.J.	Bal	129	129	1133.0	211	403	6	79	.990	4.88	+7	-2	5	3
Scutaro,Marco	Bos	109	102	928.2	147	269	12	53	.972	4.03	+2	-1	2	1
Aybar,Erick	LAA	142	142	1262.0	239	406	13	102	.980	4.60	-3	2	-2	0
Desmond,Ian	Was	152	146	1317.2	226	437	23	84	.966	4.53	+3	-4	2	-2
Rollins,Jimmy	Phi	138	134	1207.0	181	393	7	79	.988	4.28	-4	1	-3	-2
Peralta,Jhonny	Det	145	140	1245.0	218	383	7	83	.988	4.34	-5	0	-4	-4
Cabrera,Asdrubal	Cle	151	151	1326.2	216	386	15	78	.976	4.08	-5	-1	-4	-5
Betancourt,Yuniesky	Mil	149	146	1278.2	167	418	21	85	.965	4.12	-9	1	-7	-6
Pennington,Cliff	Oak	147	143	1272.1	216	374	22	90	.964	4.17	-10	1	-8	-7
Bartlett,Jason	SD	138	136	1211.0	203	391	18	83	.971	4.41	-10	0	-8	-8
Reyes,Jose	NYM	124	124	1087.0	175	361	18	75	.968	4.44	-13	-1	-10	-11
Castro,Starlin	ChC	158	158	1398.2	267	446	29	82	.961	4.59	-15	-5	-11	-16
Jeter,Derek	NYY	122	121	1047.1	140	280	12	60	.972	3.61	-22	-1	-17	-18

Left Fielders - Regulars

Player	Tm	G	GS	Inn	PO	A	E	DP	Pct.	Range	PM	Runs Saved Throws	HR-Save	+/-	Total
Gardner,Brett	NYY	149	124	1158.2	294	7	4	3	.987	2.34	+31	5		17	22
Parra,Gerardo	Ari	125	117	1018.0	267	12	2	5	.993	2.47	+14	3		8	11
Wells,Vernon	LAA	111	103	930.2	241	4	3	0	.988	2.37	+15	-2		8	6
Gordon,Alex	KC	148	147	1309.0	312	20	3	2	.991	2.28	-14	12		-8	4
Prado,Martin	Atl	100	91	854.0	171	6	3	1	.983	1.87	+2	2		1	3
Holliday,Matt	StL	115	114	990.2	196	4	3	0	.985	1.82	+4	0		2	2
Bay,Jason	NYM	122	121	1053.1	220	4	2	1	.991	1.91	-11	3	2	-6	-1
Morrison,Logan	Fla	119	117	1021.1	207	6	5	0	.977	1.88	-8	2		-4	-2
Braun,Ryan	Mil	147	146	1250.0	259	8	1	2	.996	1.92	+3	-5		2	-3
Pierre,Juan	CWS	155	152	1365.0	278	5	7	1	.976	1.87	-5	-2	2	-3	-3
Young,Delmon	TOT	115	115	994.1	214	7	7	3	.969	2.00	-6	-1		-3	-4
Crawford,Carl	Bos	127	126	1098.1	235	1	3	0	.987	1.93	-8	0		-4	-4
Soriano,Alfonso	ChC	128	126	1007.0	187	8	7	2	.965	1.74	-13	2		-7	-5
Ludwick,Ryan	TOT	117	116	1005.0	190	9	1	3	.995	1.78	-10	-1		-5	-6
Ibanez,Raul	Phi	134	131	1196.2	208	5	1	0	.995	1.60	-29	0		-16	-16

Center Fielders - Regulars

Player	Tm	G	GS	Inn	PO	A	E	DP	Pct.	Range	PM	Runs Saved Throws	HR-Save	+/-	Total
Jackson,Austin	Det	152	142	1264.0	379	8	3	3	.992	2.76	+30	2	3	17	22
Bourjos,Peter	LAA	147	138	1269.1	350	7	4	0	.989	2.53	+24	5	3	13	21
Maybin,Cameron	SD	136	132	1173.0	342	2	5	1	.986	2.64	+19	-1	2	11	12
McCutchen,Andrew	Pit	155	153	1353.2	414	9	7	5	.984	2.81	+11	1		6	7
Ellsbury,Jacoby	Bos	154	152	1358.1	388	6	0	3	1.000	2.61	+14	-2		8	6
Young,Chris	Ari	155	155	1373.1	394	4	3	2	.993	2.61	+13	-3	2	7	6
Rasmus,Colby	TOT	127	122	1092.2	302	4	6	1	.981	2.52	0	-1	2	0	1
Victorino,Shane	Phi	130	128	1150.2	296	0	0	0	1.000	2.32	-1	2		-1	1
Kemp,Matt	LAD	159	158	1380.0	345	11	5	5	.986	2.32	-6	4		-3	1
Crisp,Coco	Oak	133	130	1134.1	321	2	1	1	.997	2.56	+2	-3	2	1	0
Pagan,Angel	NYM	121	119	1045.0	302	5	10	1	.968	2.64	+1	-2		1	-1
Bourn,Michael	TOT	156	154	1359.0	367	6	3	2	.992	2.47	-1	-1		0	-1
Byrd,Marlon	ChC	118	115	998.0	273	8	3	3	.989	2.53	-8	2		-4	-2
Cabrera,Melky	KC	144	143	1265.2	316	13	3	7	.991	2.34	-8	-1	2	-4	-3
Fowler,Dexter	Col	122	119	1072.2	309	6	8	2	.975	2.64	-3	-2		-2	-4
Stubbs,Drew	Cin	157	145	1329.0	366	8	3	2	.992	2.53	-16	5		-9	-4
Upton,B.J.	TB	151	150	1326.1	382	6	3	3	.992	2.63	-10	1		-6	-5
Rios,Alex	CWS	143	136	1230.0	349	5	3	3	.992	2.59	-13	0		-7	-7
Jones,Adam	Bal	148	145	1281.0	379	16	8	5	.980	2.78	-35	9	2	-20	-9
Granderson,Curtis	NYY	155	150	1348.0	354	11	3	1	.992	2.44	-34	4		-19	-15

Right Fielders - Regulars

Player	Tm	G	GS	Inn	PO	A	E	DP	Pct.	Range	PM	Runs Saved Throws	Runs Saved HR-Save	Runs Saved +/-	Total
Heyward,Jason	Atl	122	106	990.1	218	4	6	0	.974	2.02	+30	-2		17	15
Hunter,Torii	LAA	136	133	1179.1	260	15	3	2	.989	2.10	+15	6		9	15
DeJesus,David	Oak	116	114	992.2	231	6	4	1	.983	2.15	+21	1		12	13
Stanton,Mike	Fla	142	140	1219.0	280	10	6	2	.980	2.14	+12	4		7	11
Francoeur,Jeff	KC	153	152	1352.0	327	16	5	4	.986	2.28	-7	8	2	-4	6
Ethier,Andre	LAD	126	124	1091.1	243	8	0	0	1.000	2.07	+8	0		5	5
Joyce,Matt	TB	126	112	1006.1	211	8	3	3	.986	1.96	+2	1	2	1	4
Werth,Jayson	Was	134	131	1172.2	287	10	8	3	.974	2.28	-2	5		-1	4
Quentin,Carlos	CWS	102	100	854.2	177	2	1	0	.994	1.88	+10	-3		6	3
Upton,Justin	Ari	159	156	1366.2	339	5	13	2	.964	2.27	+7	-1		4	3
Beltran,Carlos	TOT	134	134	1153.2	230	10	1	3	.996	1.87	+2	1		1	2
Cruz,Nelson	Tex	109	98	863.2	215	5	5	1	.978	2.29	+2	-1	2	1	2
Suzuki,Ichiro	Sea	151	151	1333.0	263	7	4	5	.985	1.82	+3	-1		2	1
Hart,Corey	Mil	126	123	1087.2	251	3	2	1	.992	2.10	+3	-1		2	1
Swisher,Nick	NYY	141	140	1190.1	273	9	1	1	.996	2.13	-9	5		-5	0
Fukudome,Kosuke	TOT	131	117	1061.0	265	6	3	2	.989	2.30	-10	5		-6	-1
Bautista,Jose	Tor	116	115	1014.0	233	13	6	5	.976	2.18	-13	5	2	-8	-1
Bruce,Jay	Cin	155	151	1371.0	306	10	4	1	.988	2.07	-9	1		-5	-4
Markakis,Nick	Bal	157	157	1389.2	311	14	0	3	1.000	2.10	-18	6		-10	-4
Pence,Hunter	TOT	153	152	1342.2	284	11	6	3	.980	1.98	-19	6		-11	-5
Smith,Seth	Col	107	97	867.1	182	1	5	0	.973	1.90	-2	-6		-1	-7
Berkman,Lance	StL	110	107	865.1	173	3	4	2	.978	1.83	-17	0		-10	-10

Catchers - Regulars

Player	Tm	G	GS	Inn	PO	A	E	DP	PB	Pct.	SBA	CS	PCS	CS%	ER	CERA	Runs Saved SB	Runs Saved Adj-ER	Total
Wieters,Matt	Bal	132	129	1150.0	855	70	5	14	1	.995	92	32	2	.35	583	4.56	5	9	14
Iannetta,Chris	Col	105	105	943.2	733	82	2	7	8	.998	100	26	4	.26	442	4.22	3	4	7
Montero,Miguel	Ari	134	131	1169.1	908	78	11	9	8	.989	80	28	4	.35	468	3.60	3	3	6
Saltalamacchia,J	Bos	101	96	856.0	678	56	6	3	26	.992	120	28	9	.23	439	4.62	4	-2	2
Martin,Russell	NYY	125	118	1044.1	866	96	10	8	4	.990	135	35	5	.26	429	3.70	2	0	2
Avila,Alex	Det	133	130	1157.0	940	73	5	13	7	.995	125	26	14	.21	499	3.88	-2	3	1
Ramos,Wilson	Was	108	106	951.2	684	55	5	7	3	.993	71	19	4	.27	394	3.73	1	-2	-1
Santana,Carlos	Cle	95	88	786.1	580	43	7	4	4	.989	74	15	3	.20	366	4.19	-1	0	-1
Soto,Geovany	ChC	122	119	1041.2	899	82	13	7	5	.987	121	30	6	.25	490	4.31	1	-2	-1
Suzuki,Kurt	Oak	129	127	1132.1	914	55	7	7	5	.993	136	23	15	.17	476	3.78	1	-4	-3
Olivo,Miguel	Sea	127	120	1064.1	835	71	11	7	11	.988	110	25	6	.23	446	3.77	-3	0	-3
Buck,John	Fla	135	129	1144.0	1008	42	5	5	7	.995	100	15	2	.15	496	3.90	-3	0	-3
Arencibia,J.P.	Tor	125	118	1059.2	822	72	6	4	12	.993	115	18	10	.16	507	4.31	-5	1	-4
Lucroy,Jonathan	Mil	132	114	1043.2	976	63	7	6	1	.993	107	21	9	.20	421	3.63	-4	0	-4
Thole,Josh	NYM	102	91	793.1	657	44	2	4	16	.997	82	14	3	.17	373	4.23	-4	-1	-5
McCann,Brian	Atl	126	118	1083.0	978	78	5	14	7	.995	133	22	7	.17	434	3.61	-3	-2	-5
Pierzynski,A.J.	CWS	120	112	1008.0	817	65	4	4	4	.995	118	14	10	.12	453	4.04	-3	-2	-5
Molina,Yadier	StL	138	132	1150.0	857	67	5	5	6	.995	65	15	4	.23	499	3.91	0	-6	-6
Torrealba,Yorvit	Tex	98	95	823.2	685	38	9	4	7	.988	83	21	6	.25	394	4.31	-1	-5	-6
Ruiz,Carlos	Phi	128	113	1051.0	950	68	4	4	8	.996	100	18	5	.18	357	3.06	-2	-4	-6

All Others

Player	Tm	Pos	G	GS	Inn	PO	A	E	DP	Pct.	Rng	+/-	RS
Abreu, B	LAA	LF	18	18	143	20	2	0	0	1.000	1.38	-3	1
	LAA	RF	10	10	81	9	0	1	0	.900	1.00	-5	-3
Ackley, D	Sea	1B	1	0	6	8	0	0	0	1.000	-	0	0
	Sea	2B	86	85	741	144	225	6	49	.984	4.48	+10	10
Adams, R	Bal	2B	26	24	213	47	62	2	16	.982	4.61	-6	-5
Allen, B	TOT	1B	51	49	440	411	24	4	33	.991	-	0	1
Almonte, E	Mil	1B	2	0	2	3	0	0	0	1.000	-	0	0
	Mil	RF	7	6	45	2	0	0	0	1.000	.40	-5	-3
Alonso, Y	Cin	1B	3	1	13	8	3	0	0	1.000	-	0	0
	Cin	3B	1	1	9	0	0	0	0	-	.00	0	0
	Cin	LF	16	14	112	22	1	1	0	.958	1.84	-4	-3
Altuve, J	Hou	2B	57	51	460	80	135	2	25	.991	4.20	-2	-2
Alvarez, P	Pit	3B	66	62	549	55	145	14	15	.935	3.28	-5	-6
Amarista, A	LAA	2B	14	9	93	21	33	2	8	.964	5.19	-3	-2
	LAA	SS	1	0	3	0	0	0	0	-	.00		0
	LAA	LF	8	4	43	9	1	0	0	1.000	2.08	-1	-1
Amezaga, A	TOT	2B	16	14	127	33	40	1	7	.986	5.17	-2	-2
	TOT	3B	2	0	4	0	0	0	0	-	.00	0	0
	TOT	SS	2	1	15	0	6	1	0	.857	3.52	-1	-1
	TOT	LF	4	1	11	1	0	0	0	1.000	.82	0	0
	TOT	RF	2	0	2	0	0	0	0	-	.00	0	0
Anderson, L	Bos	1B	6	0	15	12	3	1	1	.938	-	0	0
Andino, R	Bal	2B	94	81	724	159	239	4	63	.990	4.95	-3	0
	Bal	3B	22	19	172	15	42	1	6	.983	2.98	+1	0
	Bal	SS	30	24	223	31	97	5	17	.962	5.16	-1	0
	Bal	LF	3	2	11	2	0	0	0	1.000	1.64	+1	1
Angle, M	Bal	LF	14	6	65	22	0	2	0	.917	3.05	+3	2
	Bal	CF	16	13	124	37	0	0	0	1.000	2.67	-8	-5
	Bal	RF	2	1	9	3	0	0	0	1.000	3.00	0	0
Ankiel, R	Was	CF	105	84	785	234	8	1	0	.996	2.77	+12	16
	Was	RF	9	6	59	11	1	0	0	1.000	1.81	0	0
Avila, A	Det	3B	1	1	8	0	1	1	0	.500	1.13	0	0
Aviles, M	TOT	2B	27	20	191	50	60	3	17	.973	5.17	0	0
	TOT	3B	46	36	347	20	78	8	4	.925	2.54	-2	-3
	TOT	SS	14	8	91	7	31	1	3	.974	3.76	+1	1
	TOT	LF	1	1	9	4	0	0	0	1.000	4.00	0	0
	TOT	RF	4	1	10	1	0	0	0	1.000	.90	-1	-1
Baker, J	ChC	1B	19	15	126	114	7	0	4	1.000	-	+1	1
	ChC	2B	18	15	119	26	37	1	9	.984	4.74	0	-1
	ChC	3B	11	5	54	4	6	0	0	1.000	1.67	-4	-3
	ChC	LF	1	1	6	2	0	0	0	1.000	3.00	0	0
	ChC	RF	10	6	46	9	0	0	0	1.000	1.76	+2	2
Barney, D	ChC	SS	5	4	35	5	10	0	2	1.000	3.79	+1	1
Barton, D	Oak	1B	65	62	568	596	39	8	72	.988	-	+6	4
Bautista, J	Tor	3B	25	25	205	17	62	2	1	.975	3.47	+9	6
Baxter, M	NYM	LF	3	0	5	2	0	0	0	1.000	3.60	+1	1
	NYM	RF	10	7	68	10	1	0	0	1.000	1.46	0	1
Bell, J	Bal	3B	21	14	134	17	23	3	1	.930	2.69	0	-1
	Bal	LF	1	0	1	0	0	0	0	-	.00	0	0
	Bal	RF	1	0	2	0	0	0	0	-	.00	0	0
Belt, B	SF	1B	31	19	203	201	12	1	8	.995	-	+1	1
	SF	LF	31	30	231	46	1	3	0	.940	1.83	+3	3
	SF	RF	1	1	10	4	1	0	0	1.000	4.22	0	1
Benson, J	Min	LF	11	10	88	19	0	1	0	.950	1.94	-1	-1
	Min	CF	2	2	17	5	0	0	0	1.000	2.65	-2	-1
	Min	RF	7	7	59	20	0	1	0	.952	3.02	0	-1
Berkman, L	StL	1B	21	16	145	154	14	2	18	.988	-	-1	-1
	StL	LF	16	16	131	21	1	0	0	1.000	1.51	+3	2
Bernadina, R	Was	LF	36	15	175	43	2	0	0	1.000	2.31	+7	3
	Was	CF	56	50	420	103	4	0	0	1.000	2.29	-13	-3
	Was	RF	10	6	63	13	0	1	0	.929	1.84	+4	2
Betemit, W	TOT	1B	3	3	27	23	2	0	0	1.000	-	-2	-1
	TOT	2B	1	0	5	2	2	0	1	1.000	7.20	-1	-1
	TOT	3B	87	80	696	49	148	11	12	.947	2.55	-15	-13
Bixler, B	Was	1B	2	0	3	3	0	0	1	1.000	-	0	0
	Was	3B	14	3	48	3	10	1	1	.929	2.42	-1	-1
	Was	SS	2	1	7	1	4	0	0	1.000	6.43	+1	1
	Was	LF	27	6	79	22	0	0	0	1.000	2.50	+5	3
	Was	CF	4	4	31	7	0	0	0	1.000	2.03	-1	0
	Was	RF	6	1	14	2	1	0	0	1.000	1.93	-1	-1
Blackmon, C	Col	LF	25	23	198	39	2	0	0	1.000	1.86	0	0
	Col	CF	2	2	16	4	0	0	0	1.000	2.25	-1	-1

Player	Tm	Pos	G	GS	Inn	PO	A	E	DP	Pct.	Rng	+/-	RS
Blake, C	LAD	1B	8	6	50	45	3	1	2	.980	-	-2	-1
	LAD	3B	45	45	383	37	69	6	6	.946	2.49	+5	3
	LAD	LF	2	0	3	0	0	0	0	-	.00		0
Blanco, A	Tex	2B	5	1	19	6	9	0	1	1.000	7.11	+1	1
	Tex	3B	6	1	18	2	2	1	0	.800	2.00	0	0
	Tex	SS	23	16	147	21	47	3	12	.958	4.16	-1	0
	Tex	RF	1	0	5	0	1	0	0	1.000	1.80	0	1
Blanks, K	SD	1B	13	9	83	67	6	0	6	1.000	-	+1	1
	SD	LF	37	35	300	62	3	1	2	.985	1.95	+4	6
Bloomquist, W	Ari	2B	1	1	8	1	0	0	0	1.000	1.13	-2	-2
	Ari	SS	59	57	501	75	155	5	31	.979	4.13	-2	-3
	Ari	LF	25	22	197	41	0	0	0	1.000	1.87	-7	-5
Blum, G	Ari	3B	14	12	103	5	24	0	3	1.000	2.53	+1	1
Boesch, B	Det	LF	57	54	424	102	4	2	1	.981	2.25	-1	3
	Det	RF	51	45	366	88	3	1	0	.989	2.23	-12	-8
Boggs, B	Mil	LF	2	0	3	0	0	0	0	-	.00	0	0
	Mil	CF	1	1	9	1	0	0	0	1.000	1.00	0	0
	Mil	RF	2	1	10	1	0	0	0	1.000	.90	0	0
Bogusevic, B	Hou	LF	13	4	47	12	0	0	0	1.000	2.30	+1	1
	Hou	RF	40	31	277	68	9	2	4	.975	2.50	+3	7
Bonifacio, E	Fla	2B	5	2	28	5	7	0	1	1.000	3.86	0	0
	Fla	3B	36	30	245	17	47	3	8	.955	2.34	0	1
	Fla	SS	67	61	543	98	154	9	34	.966	4.17	-6	-6
	Fla	LF	32	28	247	54	2	1	0	.982	2.04	+4	4
	Fla	CF	16	9	89	25	0	0	0	1.000	2.53	+1	0
	Fla	RF	15	11	106	26	2	0	0	1.000	2.38	+2	2
Borbon, J	Tex	CF	32	28	243	70	1	1	0	.986	2.63	-6	-1
Bourgeois, J	Hou	2B	2	1	7	1	2	0	1	1.000	3.86	-1	-1
	Hou	LF	34	10	124	28	0	1	0	.966	2.02	-2	0
	Hou	CF	34	27	244	63	0	0	0	1.000	2.32	-4	-3
	Hou	RF	13	11	95	25	1	0	0	1.000	2.45	+1	2
Bowker, J	TOT	1B	2	0	6	4	1	0	0	1.000	-	0	0
	TOT	RF	2	1	8	4	0	0	0	1.000	4.50	+2	1
Bradley, M	Sea	LF	26	26	213	53	0	2	0	.964	2.24	-6	-4
Brantley, M	Cle	LF	66	62	558	118	5	2	2	.984	1.98	+1	5
	Cle	CF	52	46	412	118	0	1	0	.992	2.57	-1	-8
Branyan, R	TOT	1B	25	18	159	150	10	1	17	.994	-	+3	2
	TOT	3B	2	0	3	0	1	0	0	1.000	3.00	0	0
Brignac, R	TB	SS	91	76	680	104	217	7	44	.979	4.24	+11	8
Brown, A	StL	RF	7	5	40	10	0	0	0	1.000	2.25	-2	-1
Brown, D	Phi	RF	52	49	451	78	0	4	0	.951	1.56	-2	-2
Buck, T	Cle	LF	25	22	192	43	0	0	0	1.000	2.02	-1	0
	Cle	CF	1	1	8	5	0	0	0	1.000	5.63	0	0
	Cle	RF	4	4	30	32	0	1	0	.970	2.86	+5	2
Burrell, P	SF	LF	54	50	349	53	2	4	1	.932	1.42	-1	-1
Burriss, M	SF	1B	2	0	8	10	0	0	1	1.000	-	0	0
	SF	2B	39	22	230	62	77	3	24	.979	5.44	+2	3
	SF	3B	2	2	17	3	3	1	0	.857	3.18	-1	-1
	SF	SS	9	4	48	5	12	1	3	.944	3.19	0	0
	SF	LF	2	0	2	2	0	0	0	1.000	9.00	0	0
Burroughs, S	Ari	3B	20	14	132	9	28	1	5	.974	2.52	+2	1
Butler, B	KC	1B	11	11	94	86	8	0	10	1.000	-	-3	-2
Cabrera, E	SD	SS	3	2	17	4	5	0	0	1.000	4.76	-1	-2
Cabrera, M	KC	LF	12	7	63	15	0	0	0	1.000	2.14	+2	2
	KC	RF	2	1	11	0	0	0	0	-	.00	0	0
Cabrera, O	TOT	2B	85	79	709	129	265	6	45	.985	5.00	+3	1
	TOT	3B	5	4	29	2	2	0	0	1.000	1.24	-3	-3
	TOT	SS	39	34	309	55	95	5	19	.968	4.36	+1	0
Cain, L	KC	CF	2	2	17	2	0	0	0	1.000	1.06	-2	-1
	KC	RF	4	4	34	5	0	0	0	1.000	1.30	-1	-1
Cairo, M	Cin	1B	5	0	9	11	0	0	0	1.000	-	0	0
	Cin	2B	13	8	80	10	30	0	6	1.000	4.50	+4	2
	Cin	3B	58	48	432	31	108	4	13	.972	2.89	+3	2
Cameron, M	TOT	LF	4	0	9	2	0	0	0	1.000	2.00	-1	0
	TOT	CF	42	41	350	94	3	0	0	1.000	2.49	+6	2
	TOT	RF	25	23	194	45	0	1	0	.978	2.09	-5	-2
Campana, T	ChC	LF	35	1	68	15	1	1	0	.941	2.10	+3	2
	ChC	CF	29	22	208	54	0	0	0	1.000	2.33	+4	2
	ChC	RF	5	3	26	16	0	0	0	1.000	5.40	+7	4
Cantu, J	SD	1B	26	21	190	198	8	2	10	.990	-	+1	1
	SD	2B	1	0	1	0	0	0	0	-	.00		0
	SD	3B	10	9	84	5	14	1	1	.950	2.04	+1	1
Carp, M	Sea	1B	34	30	263	253	14	2	27	.993	-	-2	-2
	Sea	LF	27	26	216	49	2	4	0	.927	2.12	-4	-2

Player	Tm	Pos	G	GS	Inn	PO	A	E	DP	Pct.	Rng	+/-	RS
	Sea	RF	1	0	3	0	0	0	0	-	.00		0
Carpenter, M	StL	3B	5	4	39	1	12	0	0	1.000	3.00	-1	-1
Carrera, E	Cle	LF	9	6	60	12	0	1	0	.923	1.80	+1	1
	Cle	CF	55	44	426	112	2	3	0	.974	2.41	+8	4
	Cle	RF	6	2	20	4	0	0	0	1.000	1.80	-1	-1
Carroll, B	Mil	CF	1	1	8	3	0	0	0	1.000	3.38	0	0
Carroll, J	LAD	2B	81	57	549	91	160	5	35	.980	4.11	-12	-9
	LAD	SS	66	54	504	78	132	4	27	.981	3.75	-7	-5
Carter, C	Oak	1B	11	9	71	64	4	1	5	.986	-	0	0
Casilla, A	Min	2B	56	53	470	85	174	6	38	.977	4.95	0	1
	Min	SS	36	36	306	56	101	5	23	.969	4.61	-3	-1
Castro, J	LAD	2B	4	2	23	3	11	0	1	1.000	5.48	0	0
	LAD	3B	1	1	7	1	2	0	0	1.000	3.86	0	0
Cedeno, R	Pit	2B	1	1	9	0	3	0	0	1.000	3.00	-1	-1
Cervelli, F	NYY	2B	1	0	2	0	1	0	0	1.000	4.50	0	0
	NYY	3B	2	0	2	0	0	0	0	-	.00		0
Chambers, A	StL	LF	6	0	7	1	0	0	0	1.000	1.29	-1	-1
	StL	CF	5	0	8	5	0	1	0	.833	5.40	-2	-1
	StL	RF	1	0	2	1	0	0	0	1.000	4.50	0	0
Chavez, E	Tex	LF	12	2	32	3	0	0	0	1.000	.84	0	-1
	Tex	CF	66	59	514	126	3	1	0	.992	2.26	+7	4
	Tex	RF	6	5	41	4	0	0	0	1.000	.88	0	0
Chavez, E	NYY	1B	18	12	114	12	1	0	0	1.000	-	0	0
	NYY	3B	42	33	305	26	60	0	9	1.000	2.53	0	1
Chirinos, R	TB	1B	1	0	3	2	1	0	1	1.000	-	0	0
Chisenhall, L	Cle	3B	58	55	461	44	114	10	8	.940	3.08	+1	3
	Cle	LF	1	0	0	0	0	0	0	-	-		0
Choo, S	Cle	RF	85	84	735	172	9	4	2	.978	2.22	-2	2
Christian, J	SF	LF	6	2	29	9	0	0	0	1.000	2.79	+1	1
	SF	CF	10	10	76	17	1	0	0	1.000	2.13	0	0
	SF	RF	3	0	8	1	0	0	0	1.000	1.13	0	0
Ciriaco, P	Pit	3B	2	0	6	1	2	0	1	1.000	4.50	+1	1
	Pit	SS	7	4	34	9	19	1	2	.966	7.34	-1	-1
	Pit	LF	2	0	5	1	0	0	0	1.000	1.69	0	0
Coghlan, C	Fla	CF	65	64	568	157	3	0	1	1.000	2.53	-7	-5
Colvin, T	ChC	1B	4	2	22	21	2	0	1	1.000	-	0	0
	ChC	LF	10	4	43	10	0	0	0	1.000	2.08	+1	0
	ChC	CF	8	8	67	19	0	0	0	1.000	2.55	-1	-1
	ChC	RF	44	35	314	76	2	1	1	.987	2.23	0	3
Conrad, B	Atl	1B	1	0	3	0	0	0	0	1.000	-	0	0
	Atl	2B	10	5	45	8	13	0	4	1.000	4.17	-2	-2
	Atl	3B	8	7	56	6	13	1	0	.950	3.05	+2	2
Constanza, J	Atl	LF	17	13	113	31	0	1	0	.969	2.45	+8	3
	Atl	CF	4	3	28	6	0	0	0	1.000	1.93	-2	-1
	Atl	RF	16	13	114	30	0	0	0	1.000	2.36	+1	0
Cooper, D	Tor	1B	15	11	105	99	7	4	9	.964	-	-1	-1
Cora, A	Was	1B	9	0	16	14	0	2	2	.875	-	-2	-1
	Was	2B	5	3	24	9	0	1	0	.900	3.28	0	-1
	Was	3B	31	18	167	4	41	1	5	.978	2.42	+4	3
	Was	SS	16	13	114	22	47	0	10	1.000	5.42	+2	2
Counsell, C	Mil	2B	25	7	107	18	37	0	9	1.000	4.60	+4	4
	Mil	3B	14	9	86	5	19	1	1	.960	2.51	+3	3
	Mil	SS	23	12	120	19	30	1	6	.980	3.68	+2	2
	Mil	LF	1	0	2	0	0	0	0	-	.00		0
Cousins, S	Fla	LF	4	1	20	2	1	0	1	1.000	1.31	+1	2
	Fla	CF	5	2	25	8	1	0	0	1.000	3.24	0	1
	Fla	RF	12	2	36	10	1	0	0	1.000	2.70	+4	2
Cowgill, C	Ari	LF	18	15	138	43	1	0	0	1.000	2.87	+8	3
	Ari	CF	10	6	60	15	1	0	1	1.000	2.40	+1	2
Cozart, Z	Cin	SS	11	9	77	22	41	0	7	1.000	7.33	+6	5
Craig, A	StL	1B	3	2	6	4	0	0	0	1.000	-	0	0
	StL	2B	8	8	41	7	10	0	1	1.000	3.73	0	0
	StL	3B	2	2	11	0	2	0	0	1.000	1.64	-1	-1
	StL	LF	26	19	190	39	1	0	0	1.000	1.89	+2	1
	StL	CF	5	5	29	9	2	0	0	1.000	3.41	-1	-1
	StL	RF	18	13	106	26	0	0	0	1.000	2.21	+2	1
Crawford, B	SF	SS	65	53	507	74	167	7	29	.972	4.28	+7	6
Crowe, T	Cle	LF	10	4	51	7	0	0	0	1.000	1.24	+1	1
	Cle	CF	7	5	29	9	0	0	0	1.000	2.48	+2	1
Cruz, N	Tex	LF	18	16	135	29	1	1	0	.968	2.00	+2	2
Cruz, T	StL	1B	2	1	10	8	0	0	4	1.000	-	0	0
	StL	2B	1	0	1	0	0	0	0	-	.00		0
	StL	3B	3	1	11	0	2	0	0	1.000	1.64	+1	0
	StL	RF	2	1	6	1	0	0	0	1.000	1.50	0	0
Cuddyer, M	Min	1B	46	41	352	355	23	2	31	.995	-	+1	1
	Min	2B	17	17	140	35	52	1	7	.989	5.59	-2	-3
	Min	RF	77	73	639	142	6	4	1	.974	2.08	-8	-4
Cunningham, A	SD	LF	13	7	61	7	0	0	0	1.000	1.02	+1	0
	SD	RF	18	13	105	28	1	0	0	1.000	2.47	0	0
Damon, J	TB	1B	1	0	1	2	0	0	0	1.000	-		0
	TB	LF	16	11	84	19	0	0	0	1.000	2.04	-3	-2
d'Arnaud, C	Pit	2B	1	0	3	1	1	0	0	1.000	6.00	0	0
	Pit	3B	12	10	95	11	28	3	4	.929	3.69	+3	3
	Pit	SS	29	23	206	27	61	6	14	.936	3.83	-6	-6
Darnell, J	SD	3B	12	10	88	7	13	2	2	.909	2.04	-3	-2
	SD	LF	3	1	15	3	0	0	0	1.000	1.76	0	0
Davis, B	Bal	2B	18	15	140	24	36	2	7	.968	3.86	0	0
	Bal	3B	1	1	8	0	1	2	1	.333	1.13	-4	-3
	Bal	SS	2	0	4	2	2	0	1	1.000	9.00	-1	-1
Davis, C	TOT	1B	31	24	221	231	9	0	25	1.000	-	-5	-4
	TOT	3B	26	25	222	14	35	8	5	.860	1.98	-5	-5
Davis, I	NYM	1B	36	36	317	287	34	1	22	.997	-	+2	2
Davis, R	Tor	LF	4	4	36	5	0	0	0	1.000	1.25	-2	-1
	Tor	CF	79	71	652	174	2	2	0	.989	2.43	-17	-13
	Tor	RF	8	7	62	18	0	0	0	1.000	2.61	+4	2
De Aza, A	CWS	LF	4	2	21	9	0	0	0	1.000	3.86	+1	1
	CWS	CF	19	18	153	49	0	1	0	.980	2.88	+4	1
	CWS	RF	31	21	202	46	2	0	0	1.000	2.14	+4	2
De Jesus, I	LAD	2B	11	7	62	12	21	1	2	.971	4.74	-2	-2
DeJesus, D	Oak	CF	8	6	62	9	0	0	0	1.000	1.29	-6	-3
Denorfia, C	SD	LF	34	11	128	29	0	1	0	.967	2.03	-4	-2
	SD	CF	15	9	86	32	0	0	0	1.000	3.32	-3	0
	SD	RF	62	52	445	101	6	2	2	.982	2.16	-2	0
DeRosa, M	SF	1B	10	3	36	33	3	0	3	1.000	-	0	0
	SF	2B	2	0	2	1	1	0	0	1.000	7.71	+1	1
	SF	3B	16	16	121	10	22	2	2	.941	2.38	-3	-1
Descalso, D	StL	2B	18	9	82	24	34	0	6	1.000	6.31	-1	-1
	StL	3B	117	61	666	51	125	6	18	.967	2.38	-2	-2
	StL	SS	13	11	97	17	35	2	9	.963	4.82	-2	-2
DeWitt, B	ChC	2B	19	15	126	38	40	2	9	.975	5.54	-1	-2
	ChC	3B	14	8	79	6	22	5	3	.848	3.19	-2	-2
	ChC	LF	23	17	155	33	1	0	0	1.000	1.97	-2	1
Diaz, M	TOT	LF	18	11	104	17	0	1	0	.944	1.46	-4	-2
	TOT	RF	54	45	335	61	3	1	0	.985	1.72	-1	2
Dickerson, C	NYY	LF	14	4	43	9	0	0	0	1.000	1.87	0	0
	NYY	RF	42	6	119	25	0	2	0	.926	1.89	+3	2
Dinkelman, B	Min	2B	11	11	89	24	32	0	8	1.000	5.66	-4	-3
	Min	LF	5	5	40	13	0	0	0	1.000	2.88	-1	-2
	Min	RF	5	2	22	7	0	0	0	1.000	2.86	+1	1
Dirks, A	Det	LF	38	25	236	65	1	1	0	.985	2.51	+1	0
	Det	CF	16	14	115	30	1	1	0	.969	2.43	-2	-2
	Det	RF	22	15	140	32	2	0	0	1.000	2.18	+4	3
Dobbs, G	Fla	1B	4	3	28	21	3	0	2	1.000	-	0	0
	Fla	3B	100	84	755	49	132	11	8	.943	2.16	-7	-5
	Fla	LF	3	3	27	9	0	0	0	1.000	3.00	0	0
	Fla	RF	4	3	27	3	0	0	0	1.000	1.00	-2	-1
Dominguez, M	Fla	3B	16	13	122	6	21	2	1	.931	1.99	-5	-4
Donald, J	Cle	2B	19	19	169	35	51	1	10	.989	4.56	-2	-2
	Cle	3B	4	3	30	1	7	0	0	1.000	2.35	+1	1
	Cle	SS	16	10	103	17	30	3	6	.940	4.08	0	1
Downs, M	Hou	1B	13	3	42	37	4	0	1	1.000	-	+2	1
	Hou	2B	27	16	162	37	46	3	9	.965	4.61	-4	-3
	Hou	3B	19	12	126	4	19	2	4	.920	1.64	-3	-3
	Hou	SS	2	1	10	3	1	1	0	.800	3.60	0	0
Drew, J	Bos	RF	76	65	587	146	3	0	0	1.000	2.28	+3	0
Drew, S	Ari	SS	84	83	731	119	219	7	48	.980	4.16	-1	-1
Duda, L	NYM	1B	43	37	323	350	15	2	30	.995	-	-1	-1
	NYM	LF	4	4	29	3	0	0	0	1.000	.93	+1	1
	NYM	RF	42	38	335	72	1	1	0	.986	1.96	-13	-8
Duncan, S	Cle	1B	7	7	52	44	6	1	4	.980	-	+2	1
	Cle	LF	37	34	253	58	2	1	0	.984	2.13	-3	0
	Cle	RF	2	2	16	1	0	0	0	1.000	.56	+1	0
Dunn, A	CWS	1B	35	34	284	259	24	4	21	.986	-	-6	-5
	CWS	RF	2	2	14	1	0	0	0	1.000	.64	-1	-1
Durango, L	Hou	CF	2	2	17	3	0	0	0	1.000	1.59	+1	1
Dyson, J	KC	CF	17	11	98	31	0	0	0	1.000	2.83	+7	4
Ellis, M	TOT	1B	2	2	14	15	3	0	2	1.000	-	+2	2

Player	Tm	Pos	G	GS	Inn	PO	A	E	DP	Pct.	Rng	+/-	RS
Emaus, B	NYM	2B	11	10	83	16	37	0	5	1.000	5.72	0	-1
Encarnacion, E	Tor	1B	25	22	190	192	9	4	16	.980	-	-2	-1
	Tor	3B	36	30	274	23	43	8	2	.892	2.16	-5	-5
Escobar, E	CWS	2B	2	0	3	2	1	0	1	1.000	9.00	0	0
	CWS	SS	3	0	6	0	4	0	0	1.000	6.00	+1	1
Evans, N	NYM	1B	45	38	337	360	35	3	23	.992	-	+7	7
	NYM	3B	2	0	3	0	1	0	0	1.000	3.00	0	0
	NYM	LF	1	0	1	0	0	0	0	-	.00	0	0
	NYM	RF	8	4	45	9	0	0	0	1.000	1.80	-3	-2
Everett, A	Cle	2B	8	5	44	8	17	3	5	.893	5.08	0	0
	Cle	3B	16	12	114	2	28	1	4	.968	2.35	-2	-2
	Cle	SS	4	0	7	4	0	0	0	1.000	5.14	0	0
Field, T	Col	SS	15	12	113	18	47	1	8	.985	5.18	+3	2
	Col	RF	1	0	3	1	0	0	0	1.000	3.00	0	0
Figgins, C	Sea	3B	80	77	679	40	134	11	11	.941	2.30	+1	2
	Sea	LF	2	1	8	2	0	0	0	1.000	2.25	0	0
Florimon, P	Bal	SS	4	2	18	3	6	1	1	.900	4.34	-1	-1
Flowers, T	CWS	1B	3	2	21	17	4	0	2	1.000	-	0	0
Fontenot, M	SF	2B	23	16	155	32	47	3	7	.963	4.57	-2	-3
	SF	3B	8	2	30	1	6	0	0	1.000	1.80	0	0
	SF	SS	37	33	284	38	84	4	18	.968	3.87	+2	3
Ford, D	SF	CF	15	0	43	11	0	0	0	1.000	2.27	+2	1
Forsythe, L	SD	2B	23	15	147	40	40	4	12	.952	4.89	-2	-2
	SD	3B	26	21	184	19	47	1	5	.985	3.23	+8	7
	SD	SS	1	0	2	0	0	0	0	-	.00	0	0
Fox, J	Bal	1B	6	3	34	25	1	0	3	1.000	-	0	0
	Bal	LF	5	4	35	5	0	0	0	1.000	1.29	+1	1
Francisco, B	Phi	LF	14	13	109	17	1	1	0	.947	1.49	-2	0
	Phi	RF	55	49	445	86	3	2	0	.978	1.80	-10	-4
Francisco, J	Cin	3B	24	20	186	14	36	2	1	.962	2.41	+3	2
Frazier, T	Cin	1B	1	1	9	11	0	0	1	1.000	-	-1	-1
	Cin	2B	2	0	8	2	1	0	2	1.000	3.38	0	0
	Cin	3B	27	24	207	19	43	2	1	.969	2.69	0	0
	Cin	SS	2	0	3	2	1	0	0	1.000	9.00	0	0
	Cin	LF	4	2	18	3	1	0	0	1.000	2.00	+2	2
Freese, D	StL	1B	5	1	14	8	0	0	2	1.000	-	-1	-1
	StL	3B	88	87	674	33	159	12	23	.941	2.56	-1	-1
Fukudome, K	TOT	CF	13	12	104	29	1	1	0	.968	2.59	0	2
Fuld, S	TB	LF	75	68	604	162	5	3	0	.982	2.49	+6	9
	TB	CF	7	4	37	14	0	0	0	1.000	3.35	+1	1
	TB	RF	9	4	40	14	0	0	0	1.000	3.15	-1	0
Furcal, R	TOT	SS	85	83	726	130	250	14	54	.964	4.71	-3	-4
Gamel, M	Mil	1B	2	2	15	18	1	0	1	1.000	-	+1	1
	Mil	3B	3	3	19	3	2	1	0	.833	2.37	0	0
	Mil	LF	2	0	3	1	0	0	0	1.000	2.70	0	0
Gardner, B	NYY	CF	18	10	92	28	0	1	0	.966	2.73	0	0
Garner, C	Col	LF	2	1	10	3	0	0	0	1.000	2.70	0	0
	Col	RF	1	1	6	3	0	0	0	1.000	4.26	+1	1
Gathright, J	Bos	LF	4	0	5	2	0	0	0	1.000	3.60	+1	1
Gentry, C	Tex	LF	2	1	9	1	0	0	0	1.000	1.00	0	0
	Tex	CF	55	33	313	103	0	1	0	.990	2.96	+14	7
	Tex	RF	7	4	40	5	0	1	0	.833	1.13	0	0
German, E	Tex	2B	2	1	10	0	3	0	1	1.000	2.70	0	0
	Tex	3B	4	1	13	0	3	0	0	1.000	2.08	-1	-1
Getz, C	KC	SS	4	3	26	6	10	1	2	.941	5.54	+1	1
Giambi, J	Col	1B	23	22	170	203	10	1	13	.995	-	+1	1
Giavotella, J	KC	2B	46	46	385	55	117	5	17	.972	4.02	-4	-3
Gibbons, J	LAD	LF	10	10	71	12	0	0	0	1.000	1.52	-1	0
	LAD	RF	4	4	29	4	1	0	0	1.000	1.55	-3	0
Gillaspie, C	SF	3B	4	2	22	2	1	0	0	1.000	1.23	0	0
Gillespie, C	Ari	LF	2	0	10	3	0	0	0	1.000	2.70	0	0
	Ari	RF	2	0	3	0	0	0	0	-	.00	0	0
Gimenez, C	Sea	1B	2	2	16	15	1	0	5	1.000	-	-1	-1
	Sea	LF	3	1	9	0	0	0	0	-	.00	0	0
Gload, R	Phi	1B	10	7	64	70	3	1	7	.986	-	-2	-1
	Phi	RF	3	3	21	4	0	0	0	1.000	2.14	0	1
Goldschmidt, P	Ari	1B	43	41	368	351	22	0	22	1.000	-	-6	-5
Golson, G	NYY	LF	4	0	8	1	0	0	0	1.000	1.08	0	0
	NYY	CF	3	2	18	5	0	0	0	1.000	2.50	-2	0
	NYY	RF	3	0	8	1	0	0	0	1.000	1.13	0	0
Gomes, J	TOT	LF	73	68	550	114	1	2	0	.983	1.88	0	3
	TOT	RF	11	5	49	13	0	0	0	1.000	2.37	+1	1
Gomez, C	Mil	CF	87	59	569	183	5	0	1	1.000	2.97	+20	16
Gomez, H	Col	SS	2	1	11	1	4	1	0	.833	4.09	-1	-1

Player	Tm	Pos	G	GS	Inn	PO	A	E	DP	Pct.	Rng	+/-	RS
Gonzalez, A	Bos	RF	2	2	13	0	0	0	0	-	.00	0	0
Gonzalez, A	SD	1B	4	1	17	17	1	0	3	1.000	-	0	0
	SD	2B	41	25	243	53	61	2	14	.983	4.22	-1	0
	SD	3B	21	13	129	6	26	1	2	.970	2.23	+3	1
	SD	SS	30	22	199	43	61	1	10	.990	4.70	+4	2
Gonzalez, C	Col	LF	61	60	518	93	5	1	0	.990	1.70	-8	-1
	Col	CF	30	28	248	63	3	0	1	1.000	2.39	+1	3
	Col	RF	34	34	295	63	4	0	1	1.000	2.04	+6	4
Gordon, A	KC	1B	7	2	23	24	3	1	3	.964	-	-2	-1
Gordon, D	LAD	SS	54	51	446	80	128	10	25	.954	4.19	-7	-6
Green, T	Mil	2B	7	3	26	6	9	0	0	1.000	5.19	-1	-1
	Mil	3B	5	4	31	2	7	0	2	1.000	2.61	-1	-1
Greene, T	StL	2B	25	14	136	18	39	3	8	.950	3.76	-5	-4
	StL	SS	20	10	111	13	42	2	7	.965	4.45	0	0
	StL	LF	2	0	3	0	0	0	0	-	.00	0	0
	StL	RF	8	0	14	6	0	0	0	1.000	3.86	+1	1
Guillen, C	Det	1B	1	0	2	2	0	0	0	1.000	-	0	0
	Det	2B	25	25	215	48	69	2	20	.983	4.88	-5	-3
Gutierrez, F	Sea	CF	92	85	763	237	7	0	3	1.000	2.88	+7	8
Guyer, B	TB	LF	3	2	20	7	0	0	0	1.000	3.15	-1	-1
	TB	RF	11	9	74	13	0	0	0	1.000	1.58	+2	1
Guzman, J	SD	1B	53	52	434	380	35	4	28	.990	-	+2	2
	SD	LF	6	6	47	13	0	0	0	1.000	2.49	-1	-1
	SD	RF	1	0	4	0	0	0	0	-	.00	0	0
Gwynn, T	LAD	LF	110	60	624	124	7	1	1	.992	1.89	+4	2
	LAD	CF	12	3	46	16	1	0	1	1.000	3.33	+3	3
	LAD	RF	2	0	6	0	0	0	0	-	.00	-1	-1
Hairston, J	TOT	2B	30	20	199	37	62	3	11	.971	4.46	+1	2
	TOT	3B	49	44	370	31	65	6	4	.941	2.34	-2	-3
	TOT	SS	2	1	9	1	3	0	1	1.000	4.00	+1	1
	TOT	LF	23	13	129	35	0	2	0	.946	2.44	0	0
	TOT	CF	20	14	123	34	2	0	1	1.000	2.63	-9	-2
Hairston, S	NYM	2B	1	0	1	0	0	0	0	-	.00	0	0
	NYM	LF	10	4	48	10	0	1	0	.909	1.86	0	0
	NYM	CF	10	8	59	17	0	0	0	1.000	2.58	-2	-1
	NYM	RF	15	11	85	17	0	1	0	.944	1.79	-2	-2
Hall, B	TOT	2B	51	47	387	114	77	6	23	.970	4.43	-9	-10
	TOT	LF	1	0	4	2	0	0	0	1.000	4.50	+1	1
Halman, G	Sea	LF	29	16	162	39	0	0	0	1.000	2.16	-1	-2
	Sea	CF	8	8	61	20	0	0	0	1.000	2.95	-4	-2
	Sea	RF	2	1	12	0	0	0	0	-	.00	0	0
Hamilton, J	Tex	LF	85	81	709	153	4	4	1	.975	1.99	+4	4
	Tex	CF	35	30	259	71	1	1	0	.986	2.50	-2	-1
Hamilton, M	StL	LF	8	3	25	24	0	1	0	1.000	-	0	0
	StL	LF	2	0	2	0	0	0	0	-	.00	0	0
Hammock, R	Ari	LF	1	0	3	0	0	0	0	-	.00	0	0
Hannahan, J	Cle	1B	8	3	33	30	2	0	1	1.000	-	-1	-1
	Cle	3B	104	88	819	83	208	5	21	.983	3.20	+14	9
Harris, W	NYM	2B	10	7	66	10	22	0	2	1.000	4.34	-1	-2
	NYM	3B	7	5	48	4	11	1	0	.938	2.81	-3	-2
	NYM	LF	33	26	241	48	0	0	0	1.000	1.79	-3	-3
	NYM	CF	7	3	31	9	0	0	0	1.000	2.61	+1	1
	NYM	RF	6	3	22	6	0	0	0	1.000	2.42	-3	-1
Harrison, J	Pit	2B	6	5	41	8	16	2	5	.923	5.27	0	0
	Pit	3B	50	46	363	31	100	6	7	.956	3.24	+7	7
Hawpe, B	SD	1B	44	42	383	368	32	4	46	.990	-	+5	4
	SD	RF	7	7	61	11	0	0	0	1.000	1.62	-1	-1
Hayes, B	Fla	1B	1	0	3	3	0	0	1	1.000	-	0	0
	Fla	LF	1	0	1	0	0	0	0	-	.00	0	0
	Fla	RF	1	0	1	0	0	0	0	-	.00	0	0
Head, J	Cle	LF	9	5	62	15	0	1	0	.938	2.18	+1	1
	Cin	CF	18	15	118	31	0	1	0	.969	2.35	0	1
	Cin	RF	10	8	70	18	1	0	0	1.000	2.43	+6	4
Heisey, C	Cin	LF	88	31	393	85	1	2	0	.977	1.97	+6	2
Helms, W	Fla	1B	5	1	13	7	0	0	0	1.000	-	0	0
	Fla	2B	2	0	7	1	1	0	0	1.000	2.57	-1	-1
	Fla	3B	33	17	179	14	31	3	3	.938	2.26	-5	-3
Hermida, J	TOT	LF	3	3	25	5	0	0	0	1.000	1.80	0	0
	TOT	RF	14	11	104	24	1	0	0	1.000	2.16	+4	3
Hernandez, D	Atl	1B	1	1	7	1	0	0	0	1.000	-	0	0
	Atl	3B	6	4	37	0	5	2	0	.714	1.22	-1	-2
	Atl	SS	3	1	13	1	4	0	1	1.000	3.46	0	0
Hernandez, R	Cin	1B	1	1	9	8	0	0	1	1.000	-	0	0
Herrera, J	Col	2B	62	55	499	94	151	2	30	.992	4.42	0	0

Player	Tm	Pos	G	GS	Inn	PO	A	E	DP	Pct.	Rng	+/-	RS
	Col	3B	9	1	28	1	4	0	0	1.000	1.57	0	0
	Col	SS	21	6	78	11	23	1	5	.971	3.92	+2	2
Hicks, B	Atl	3B	6	1	16	0	2	1	0	.667	1.10	0	0
	Atl	SS	3	3	21	3	7	1	2	.909	4.29	+1	1
Hinske, E	Atl	1B	13	10	83	81	8	0	6	1.000	-	+2	1
	Atl	LF	32	26	211	41	1	0	0	1.000	1.79	+4	5
	Atl	RF	16	13	110	24	1	0	0	1.000	2.05	+2	0
Hoffmann, J	LAD	LF	1	1	8	3	0	0	0	1.000	3.38	-1	-1
Hu, C	NYM	2B	10	2	29	9	7	1	1	.941	4.85	-1	-1
	NYM	SS	1	0	1	1	0	0	0	1.000	9.00		0
Hudson, K	Bal	LF	8	7	60	12	0	1	0	.923	1.78	-1	-1
	Bal	CF	2	1	8	1	0	0	0	1.000	1.13	+1	0
Huff, A	SF	LF	9	2	37	10	0	0	0	1.000	2.39	+2	1
	SF	RF	13	13	86	12	1	0	0	1.000	1.36	-8	-6
Hughes, L	Min	1B	36	30	274	278	13	1	26	.997	-	+2	1
	Min	2B	37	34	301	79	108	2	25	.989	5.59	-1	0
	Min	3B	13	12	104	10	27	2	2	.949	3.20	+2	1
Hunter, C	SD	CF	2	0	3	0	0	0	0	-	.00	0	0
Hunter, T	LAA	CF	1	1	8	4	0	0	0	1.000	4.15	0	0
Iannetta, C	Col	1B	2	0	2	4	0	0	0	1.000	-	0	0
	Col	3B	1	0	1	0	0	0	0	-	.00	0	0
Iglesias, J	Bos	SS	8	1	18	2	3	0	0	1.000	2.41	-1	-1
Inge, B	Det	3B	99	77	730	76	163	9	12	.964	2.94	-1	-2
Inglett, J	Hou	2B	3	2	16	8	7	0	4	1.000	8.44	0	0
	Hou	3B	2	0	4	0	1	0	0	1.000	2.25	-1	-1
Izturis, C	Bal	2B	3	3	22	3	7	1	0	.909	4.03	0	0
	Bal	3B	1	0	1	0	0	0	0	-	.00	0	0
	Bal	SS	12	7	67	17	32	0	11	1.000	6.52	+6	5
Izturis, M	LAA	2B	49	47	422	87	158	4	33	.984	5.22	-10	-6
	LAA	3B	37	35	301	26	55	3	3	.964	2.42	+6	6
	LAA	SS	16	14	132	25	43	1	8	.986	4.64	+1	1
Jackson, C	TOT	1B	53	43	392	354	17	1	27	.997	-	-4	-4
	TOT	3B	7	2	29	4	6	0	0	1.000	3.03	+1	1
	TOT	LF	23	17	162	31	2	0	1	1.000	1.83	+1	0
	TOT	RF	31	26	232	52	2	1	1	.982	2.09	+1	1
Janish, P	Cin	2B	5	5	44	12	9	1	4	.955	4.30	-3	-2
	Cin	3B	8	5	51	1	7	1	0	.889	1.39	-2	-2
	Cin	SS	103	80	743	126	256	10	45	.974	4.63	+14	8
Jay, J	StL	LF	19	12	115	22	0	0	0	1.000	1.72	-4	-3
	StL	CF	75	65	570	167	4	3	3	.983	2.70	+13	8
	StL	RF	56	30	303	84	1	0	1	1.000	2.52	+16	9
Jennings, D	TB	LF	53	53	467	100	3	1	0	.990	1.99	+7	4
	TB	CF	8	7	64	18	0	0	0	1.000	2.53	0	0
	TB	RF	1	0	1	0	0	0	0	-	.00	0	0
Johnson, C	Hou	3B	101	98	841	65	157	15	20	.937	2.37	-23	-16
Johnson, D	TB	1B	21	19	151	151	13	1	10	.994	-	+1	1
	TB	3B	3	0	3	0	2	0	0	1.000	6.00	0	0
Johnson, E	TB	1B	2	0	2	1	0	0	1	1.000	-	0	0
	TB	2B	9	4	38	6	11	1	0	.944	4.03	0	0
	TB	SS	52	37	337	48	100	1	15	.993	3.94	+13	11
	TB	LF	1	0	0	0	0	0	0	-	.00		0
	TB	CF	1	0	1	0	0	0	0	-	.00		0
Johnson, R	ChC	LF	27	5	76	12	0	1	0	.923	1.42	0	-1
	ChC	CF	24	16	153	41	3	1	1	.978	2.58	-8	-4
	ChC	RF	44	28	266	63	2	1	1	.985	2.20	+1	0
Jones, A	NYY	LF	39	34	247	59	0	1	0	.983	2.15	-1	0
	NYY	RF	19	14	123	29	1	0	1	1.000	2.14	-7	-4
Jones, G	Pit	1B	34	29	260	257	17	3	27	.989	-	-1	-2
	Pit	RF	90	78	659	155	2	1	1	.994	2.14	-7	-4
Joyce, M	TB	LF	15	8	86	20	0	0	0	1.000	2.08	+2	0
Ka'aihue, K	KC	1B	19	19	171	181	15	2	14	.990	-	+3	2
Kearns, A	Cle	LF	36	28	264	70	0	0	0	1.000	2.38	+1	2
	Cle	RF	19	16	150	35	1	1	0	.973	2.16	+1	2
Kelly, D	Det	1B	15	4	56	48	7	0	8	1.000	-	+1	1
	Det	3B	45	41	325	30	69	4	7	.961	2.74	+6	5
	Det	LF	17	4	57	16	0	0	0	1.000	2.53	0	0
	Det	CF	4	3	25	9	0	0	0	1.000	3.24	0	0
	Det	RF	39	10	154	34	1	1	0	.972	2.04	+4	3
Kendrick, H	LAA	1B	17	11	113	119	10	1	15	.992	-	+3	2
	LAA	LF	23	20	175	33	1	0	0	1.000	1.75	0	-1
Kennedy, A	Sea	1B	36	23	218	217	24	2	21	.992	-	0	-1
	Sea	2B	34	34	293	47	100	1	20	.993	4.51	-3	0
	Sea	3B	27	24	210	18	37	2	3	.965	2.35	-2	-2
Keppinger, J	TOT	2B	93	92	791	166	219	5	36	.987	4.38	-9	-12
Kipnis, J	Cle	2B	36	34	305	58	100	6	16	.963	4.66	-1	-3
Kotsay, M	Mil	1B	11	1	24	27	1	0	4	1.000	-	+1	1
	Mil	LF	19	13	131	20	2	4	0	.846	1.51	-3	-2
	Mil	CF	10	9	58	11	0	0	0	1.000	1.71	-1	0
	Mil	RF	30	27	223	48	0	1	0	.980	1.93	+4	2
Kouzmanoff, K	TOT	3B	71	66	576	46	122	13	13	.928	2.62	-4	-4
Kozma, P	StL	2B	10	2	28	7	12	0	5	1.000	5.97	0	0
	StL	3B	1	0	1	0	0	0	0	-	.00		0
	StL	SS	3	1	15	2	1	0	0	1.000	1.80	0	0
Kubel, J	Min	LF	9	9	70	15	0	0	0	1.000	1.93	+1	0
	Min	RF	50	48	413	95	9	1	3	.990	2.26	-15	-3
LaHair, B	ChC	1B	4	2	19	15	0	0	3	1.000	-	0	0
	ChC	LF	5	5	41	4	0	0	0	1.000	.88	-1	-1
	ChC	RF	9	9	66	19	0	1	0	.950	2.59	+1	1
Laird, B	NYY	1B	3	2	20	16	5	1	3	.955	-	0	0
	NYY	3B	9	4	40	3	7	0	1	1.000	2.25	+1	1
Laird, G	StL	1B	1	0	1	1	0	0	0	1.000	-		0
Langerhans, R	Sea	LF	5	3	34	8	0	0	0	1.000	2.08	0	0
	Sea	CF	12	11	97	23	0	0	0	1.000	2.13	-9	-6
	Sea	RF	1	1	8	2	0	0	0	1.000	2.25	0	0
LaPorta, M	Cle	1B	97	89	802	807	41	7	69	.992	-	-6	-7
LaRoche, A	Was	1B	43	42	375	380	32	0	34	1.000	-	+6	4
LaRoche, A	Oak	1B	1	1	8	13	2	0	0	1.000	-	0	0
	Oak	2B	8	5	48	7	9	0	2	1.000	3.00	+1	1
	Oak	3B	27	17	159	10	28	4	4	.905	2.15	-5	-4
	Oak	SS	9	5	44	3	25	1	3	.966	5.64	+6	4
Lawrie, B	Tor	3B	43	43	380	38	120	6	10	.963	3.74	+18	14
Lee, C	Hou	1B	79	70	624	578	75	5	59	.992	-	+6	5
	Hou	LF	80	78	645	119	10	2	3	.985	1.80	+3	6
LeMahieu, D	ChC	1B	1	1	8	8	0	0	1	1.000	-	0	0
	ChC	2B	15	8	77	16	22	0	5	1.000	4.40	+1	1
	ChC	3B	11	6	60	6	12	4	5	.818	2.70	0	0
Lewis, F	Cin	LF	45	41	315	76	3	0	1	1.000	2.25	+16	8
	Cin	RF	4	3	21	5	0	1	0	.833	2.11	-1	-1
Liddi, A	Sea	3B	14	13	110	9	25	1	2	.971	2.78	0	0
Lillibridge, B	CWS	1B	22	12	127	114	11	2	9	.984	-	+2	1
	CWS	2B	6	1	19	5	4	0	2	1.000	4.26	-3	-2
	CWS	LF	9	7	60	16	0	0	0	1.000	2.40	+2	1
	CWS	CF	11	8	76	26	0	0	0	1.000	3.05	+2	1
	CWS	RF	43	18	203	45	0	0	0	1.000	2.00	+1	0
Loewen, A	Tor	LF	1	1	7	0	0	1	0	.000	.00	-2	-1
	Tor	CF	3	3	24	7	0	1	0	.875	2.63	-1	-1
	Tor	RF	4	3	28	12	0	1	0	.923	3.86	-1	-1
Lombardozzi, S	Was	2B	3	2	20	6	5	0	0	1.000	4.95	0	0
	Was	3B	3	3	27	2	9	1	0	.917	3.58	+1	1
	Was	SS	1	1	9	1	1	0	0	1.000	2.00	-1	-1
Lopez, F	TOT	1B	6	5	40	39	3	1	2	.977	-	+1	1
	TOT	2B	11	10	82	19	23	1	5	.977	4.61	-1	-1
	TOT	3B	24	19	157	14	27	2	1	.953	2.35	-2	-3
Lopez, J	TOT	1B	8	7	53	40	5	0	2	1.000	-	+1	1
	TOT	2B	20	14	129	26	37	0	10	1.000	4.40	+3	2
	TOT	3B	39	33	288	15	58	5	3	.936	2.28	-1	-1
Lowrie, J	Bos	1B	4	0	12	12	0	0	0	1.000	-	-1	-1
	Bos	2B	1	0	3	0	2	0	0	1.000	6.00	0	0
	Bos	3B	33	29	268	28	64	5	5	.948	3.09	+1	1
	Bos	SS	49	46	398	59	112	10	22	.945	3.87	-8	-7
Ludwick, R	TOT	RF	14	13	106	27	1	1	0	.966	2.38	-3	-3
Lugo, J	Atl	2B	2	0	2	0	0	0	0	-	.00	0	0
	Atl	3B	8	4	53	4	13	0	0	1.000	2.89	+2	2
	Atl	SS	5	4	38	6	6	0	1	1.000	2.82	-3	-2
Maier, M	KC	LF	18	8	79	25	1	0	0	1.000	2.95	+1	2
	KC	CF	9	6	70	24	0	0	0	1.000	3.09	+4	2
	KC	RF	10	5	53	15	1	0	0	1.000	2.68	+6	5
Markakis, N	Bal	1B	3	2	18	15	1	0	2	1.000	-	+1	1
Marrero, C	Was	1B	31	28	264	254	14	2	17	.993	-	-3	-2
Martin, L	Tex	CF	8	1	19	7	0	0	0	1.000	3.32	+1	1
Martin, R	NYY	2B	1	0	2	1	0	0	0	1.000	4.50	0	0
	NYY	3B	3	0	4	0	1	1	0	.500	2.25	0	0
Martinez, F	NYM	LF	1	0	1	0	0	0	0	.000	.00	0	0
	NYM	RF	3	2	17	4	0	0	0	1.000	2.12	-1	-1
Martinez, J	Hou	LF	51	51	436	92	5	1	2	.990	2.00	-4	-1
	Hou	RF	1	1	9	1	0	0	0	1.000	1.00	0	0
Martinez, M	Phi	2B	19	7	83	21	26	1	6	.979	5.10	+5	4
	Phi	3B	26	24	218	20	41	2	2	.968	2.51	-1	-1

Player	Tm	Pos	G	GS	Inn	PO	A	E	DP	Pct.	Rng	+/-	RS
	Phi	SS	13	8	82	15	23	2	5	.950	4.17	+4	3
	Phi	LF	2	1	10	2	1	0	0	1.000	2.70	-2	-1
	Phi	CF	12	8	79	21	0	1	0	.955	2.37	+2	1
Martinez, O	Fla	3B	1	0	1	0	0	0	0	-	.00		0
	Fla	SS	6	1	21	0	3	1	0	.750	1.29	-1	-1
Martinez, V	Det	1B	6	6	52	38	10	0	4	1.000	-	+2	1
Mastroianni, D	Tor	CF	1	1	9	2	0	0	0	1.000	2.00	-1	-1
Mather, J	Atl	1B	1	1	9	11	0	0	2	1.000	-	-1	-1
	Atl	3B	1	0	2	0	1	0	0	1.000	4.50	0	0
	Atl	LF	4	1	12	2	0	0	0	1.000	1.46	0	0
	Atl	CF	3	2	20	11	0	0	0	1.000	4.95	+2	0
	Atl	RF	21	12	122	19	0	1	0	.950	1.40	-4	-1
Matsui, H	Oak	LF	27	27	232	53	3	1	2	.982	2.17	-5	0
Mauer, J	Min	1B	18	16	141	158	11	1	15	.994	-	+4	2
	Min	RF	1	1	9	3	0	0	0	1.000	3.00	0	0
Mayberry, J	Phi	1B	18	10	100	89	6	1	9	.990	-	-1	-1
	Phi	LF	21	17	161	30	1	0	0	1.000	1.73	+3	2
	Phi	CF	32	26	246	62	0	2	0	.969	2.26	+3	2
	Phi	RF	10	7	66	12	1	0	0	1.000	1.76	-1	0
McCoy, M	Tor	2B	10	10	84	16	32	1	4	.980	5.14	+4	3
	Tor	3B	16	5	64	6	10	0	0	1.000	2.23	0	1
	Tor	SS	26	21	211	38	76	4	14	.966	4.86	0	-1
	Tor	CF	16	14	116	36	2	0	0	1.000	2.94	+1	1
	Tor	RF	5	1	15	4	0	0	0	1.000	2.40	0	0
McDonald, D	Bos	LF	23	13	126	28	1	2	0	.935	2.07	0	1
	Bos	CF	13	6	60	23	0	0	0	1.000	3.45	-1	-1
	Bos	RF	37	21	207	39	1	1	0	.976	1.74	+5	1
McDonald, J	TOT	2B	21	16	148	24	57	1	13	.988	4.90	+2	3
	TOT	3B	26	15	162	18	39	1	8	.983	3.16	+1	0
	TOT	SS	38	25	264	49	99	2	22	.987	5.03	+11	9
McGehee, C	Mil	1B	5	0	5	6	0	0	1	1.000	-	0	0
McKenry, M	Pit	3B	1	0	1	0	0	0	0	-	.00		0
McLouth, N	Atl	LF	26	22	202	38	0	0	0	1.000	1.69	+5	2
	Atl	CF	55	55	498	129	0	2	0	.985	2.33	-7	-5
	Atl	RF	3	2	18	2	0	0	0	1.000	1.00	-2	-1
McPherson, D	CWS	1B	6	0	8	7	0	0	0	1.000	-	0	0
	CWS	3B	5	3	28	2	9	0	0	1.000	3.49	0	0
Michaels, J	Hou	LF	26	17	158	36	1	0	0	1.000	2.11	+3	1
	Hou	RF	16	12	95	23	0	0	0	1.000	2.18	+4	2
Miles, A	LAD	2B	72	61	519	119	139	2	28	.992	4.47	-2	-4
	LAD	3B	61	49	459	21	82	8	8	.928	2.02	-5	-4
	LAD	SS	1	0	3	0	0	0	0	-	.00	0	0
Milledge, L	CWS	LF	2	1	11	7	0	0	0	1.000	5.73	-1	-2
Miller, J	Oak	CF	3	0	5	0	0	0	0	-	.00	0	0
	Oak	RF	2	2	17	2	0	0	0	1.000	1.06	0	0
Miranda, J	Ari	1B	46	46	401	367	24	4	36	.990	-	-1	-3
Mitchell, R	LAD	1B	6	5	35	30	1	1	1	.969	-	0	0
	LAD	3B	11	9	82	7	23	0	0	1.000	3.27	+1	2
	LAD	RF	1	0	1	0	0	0	0	-	.00	0	0
Molina, Y	StL	1B	2	0	2	3	0	1	0	.750	-	-1	-1
Montanez, L	ChC	LF	10	2	31	5	0	0	0	1.000	1.44	0	0
	ChC	CF	1	0	0	0	0	0	0	-	.00	0	0
	ChC	RF	14	10	85	20	1	0	0	1.000	2.22	-2	0
Moore, J	LAA	LF	2	1	13	3	1	0	0	1.000	2.77	-1	0
	LAA	RF	3	0	5	1	0	0	0	1.000	1.80	-1	-1
Mora, M	Ari	1B	1	0	1	2	1	0	0	1.000	-	0	0
	Ari	3B	31	30	270	20	63	3	2	.965	2.76	-1	-1
Morales, J	Col	2B	2	0	3	0	2	0	0	1.000	6.00	+1	1
Moreland, M	Tex	1B	99	89	799	731	54	4	88	.995	-	-3	-2
	Tex	RF	34	28	244	55	0	1	0	.982	2.03	-7	-4
Morgan, N	Mil	LF	17	1	35	5	0	0	0	1.000	1.29	-1	-2
	Mil	CF	95	84	724	216	4	2	1	.991	2.73	+15	7
	Mil	RF	20	5	74	23	1	0	0	1.000	2.89	+4	3
Morneau, J	Min	1B	56	55	479	440	44	1	52	.998	-	+1	1
Morrison, L	Fla	1B	1	1	8	6	0	0	0	1.000	-	0	0
Morse, M	Was	1B	85	82	723	732	55	6	63	.992	-	-8	-7
	Was	LF	55	51	421	89	4	1	1	.989	1.99	-1	2
Moss, B	Phi	RF	1	0	4	2	0	0	0	1.000	4.50	0	0
Moustakas, M	KC	3B	89	89	778	60	169	11	14	.954	2.65	+1	0
Murphy, D	NYM	1B	52	46	419	419	36	4	36	.991	-	+6	6
	NYM	2B	24	19	168	36	55	2	5	.978	4.87	0	-2
	NYM	3B	28	25	220	13	43	4	4	.933	2.28	+3	2
	NYM	LF	1	0	2	1	0	0	0	1.000	4.50	-1	0
Murphy, D	Tex	LF	78	62	556	123	2	4	1	.969	2.02	+11	4

Player	Tm	Pos	G	GS	Inn	PO	A	E	DP	Pct.	Rng	+/-	RS
	Tex	CF	13	11	92	21	2	0	1	1.000	2.25	-3	-1
	Tex	RF	32	27	247	47	1	0	0	1.000	1.75	+6	3
Murphy, D	Fla	2B	1	0	1	0	0	0	0	-	.00		0
	Fla	3B	15	8	79	9	17	1	0	.963	2.94	+2	0
	Fla	SS	18	14	140	27	46	1	10	.986	4.68	0	-1
Nady, X	Ari	1B	52	44	391	372	32	3	36	.993	-	+1	1
	Ari	LF	10	5	52	10	1	0	0	1.000	1.90	0	1
Napoli, M	Tex	1B	35	27	246	223	19	1	21	.996	-	-2	-2
Navarro, E	LAA	1B	8	2	29	41	0	0	2	1.000	-	0	0
Navarro, Y	TOT	3B	16	9	100	9	17	2	1	.929	2.34	-3	-3
	TOT	SS	4	3	27	3	3	0	1	1.000	2.00	-1	-1
	TOT	LF	3	3	21	6	0	0	0	1.000	2.57	0	1
Nelson, C	Col	2B	29	23	208	36	58	3	15	.969	4.05	-13	-10
	Col	3B	24	14	130	9	35	4	2	.917	3.03	+1	1
	Col	SS	2	2	22	0	6	1	0	.857	2.45	0	0
Nishioka, T	Min	2B	6	6	49	10	14	2	8	.923	4.35	-2	-1
	Min	SS	60	59	508	96	172	10	34	.964	4.74	-9	-10
Nix, J	Tor	2B	4	2	15	4	6	0	1	1.000	5.87	+1	1
	Tor	3B	41	40	334	32	83	3	8	.975	3.09	+13	10
	Tor	LF	1	0	4	0	0	0	0	-	.00	0	0
Nix, L	Was	1B	9	6	47	44	4	0	5	1.000		0	0
	Was	LF	73	59	504	102	6	2	2	.982	1.93	+3	5
	Was	CF	4	0	8	0	0	0	0	-	.00	-1	-1
	Was	RF	22	12	90	20	1	0	1	1.000	2.10	0	1
Nunez, E	NYY	2B	16	9	82	12	28	0	3	1.000	4.39	+3	2
	NYY	3B	40	33	285	22	46	6	7	.919	2.14	-6	-5
	NYY	SS	50	39	386	46	101	14	17	.913	3.42	-11	-10
	NYY	LF	1	0	1	0	0	0	0	-	.00	0	0
	NYY	RF	3	2	17	4	0	0	0	1.000	2.12	0	0
Oeltjen, T	LAD	LF	13	6	65	15	0	1	0	.938	2.06	0	1
	LAD	CF	1	0	4	1	0	0	0	1.000	2.25	0	0
	LAD	RF	1	1	4	1	0	0	0	1.000	1.64	0	0
Ordonez, M	Det	RF	69	68	471	85	7	0	3	1.000	1.76	-11	-4
Orr, P	Phi	2B	29	22	188	51	61	2	16	.982	5.34	-3	-2
	Phi	3B	3	2	18	2	5	0	0	1.000	3.50	+1	1
Ortiz, D	Bos	1B	2	2	13	18	0	0	4	1.000	-	0	0
Pacheco, J	Col	1B	13	10	97	106	2	1	8	.991	-	-5	-4
	Col	2B	2	2	16	2	2	0	1	1.000	2.25	-2	-2
	Col	3B	7	7	57	6	13	2	0	.905	3.00	0	0
Paredes, J	Hou	3B	46	44	390	31	71	5	6	.953	2.35	-3	-2
Parmelee, C	Min	1B	20	20	173	164	12	2	19	.989	-	+4	2
Parra, G	Ari	CF	2	1	10	2	0	1	0	.667	1.80	-3	-2
	Ari	RF	14	6	73	19	0	0	0	1.000	2.34	+5	3
Parrino, A	SD	2B	3	3	25	6	9	0	2	1.000	5.40	+2	2
	SD	3B	17	7	68	6	16	0	2	1.000	2.90	+6	5
	SD	SS	4	2	20	1	10	0	0	1.000	4.95	+2	2
	SD	LF	1	0	1	0	0	0	0	-	.00	0	0
	SD	RF	4	1	12	5	0	0	0	1.000	3.55	0	0
Pascucci, V	NYM	1B	1	1	7	4	0	1	1	.800	-	-1	-1
Patterson, C	TOT	LF	56	43	396	93	3	0	0	1.000	2.18	-10	-5
	TOT	CF	40	31	287	74	0	0	0	1.000	2.32	-2	-2
	TOT	RF	25	6	82	22	1	1	1	.958	2.50	-1	-1
Patterson, E	SD	2B	10	8	73	20	19	2	8	.951	4.81	0	0
	SD	LF	4	2	18	7	0	0	0	1.000	3.50	+1	1
	SD	CF	7	6	47	12	0	0	0	1.000	2.30	-3	-2
	SD	RF	6	5	45	15	0	0	0	1.000	3.00	+1	1
Paul, X	TOT	LF	27	17	164	31	4	0	0	1.000	1.92	-2	-1
	TOT	CF	9	4	46	11	1	0	0	1.000	2.33	-4	-1
	TOT	RF	72	20	274	60	0	1	0	.984	1.97	-3	0
Pearce, S	Pit	1B	16	9	83	81	9	1	9	.989	-	0	0
	Pit	3B	10	7	57	6	11	2	1	.895	2.67	-1	-1
	Pit		5	2	32	4	0	1	0	.800	1.11	-1	-2
Peguero, C	Sea	LF	40	40	325	79	3	1	2	.988	2.27	-5	-1
	Sea	RF	3	1	11	3	0	0	0	1.000	2.45	0	0
Pena, R	NYY	2B	7	3	31	7	9	0	2	1.000	4.60	-2	-2
	NYY	3B	13	5	59	5	17	3	3	.880	3.34	-3	-1
	NYY	SS	4	2	24	8	5	2	2	.867	4.74	-4	-3
Pena, W	TOT	LF	1	1	8	0	0	0	0	-	.00	-1	-1
Peralta, J	Det	1B	1	0	2	1	0	0	0	1.000	-	0	0
Petersen, B	Fla	LF	22	11	109	19	1	0	0	1.000	1.65	-4	-2
	Fla	CF	42	35	316	71	3	2	2	.974	2.10	+3	4
	Fla	RF	10	5	60	16	1	0	0	1.000	2.55	+2	1
Phelps, C	Cle	2B	20	17	153	28	42	5	10	.933	4.12	-5	-5
Pie, F	Bal	LF	67	31	349	89	1	0	0	1.000	2.32	-16	-11

Player	Tm	Pos	G	GS	Inn	PO	A	E	DP	Pct.	Rng	+/-	RS
	Bal	CF	6	3	33	6	0	0	0	1.000	1.64	0	0
	Bal	RF	3	2	19	5	0	0	0	1.000	2.37	+1	1
Pill, B	SF	1B	14	13	110	105	10	0	5	1.000	-	+3	3
Plouffe, T	Min	1B	1	0	1	0	0	0	0	-	-		0
	Min	2B	17	15	127	32	36	1	10	.986	4.82	-9	-8
	Min	SS	45	45	396	73	111	11	33	.944	4.17	-22	-17
	Min	LF	3	2	19	4	0	0	0	1.000	1.89	-2	-1
	Min	RF	11	9	72	15	1	0	1	1.000	2.00	-4	-1
Polanco, P	Phi	2B	1	0	1	1	0	0	0	1.000	9.00	0	0
Posada, J	NYY	1B	14	11	104	74	6	1	8	.988	-	0	0
	NYY	2B	1	0	1	0	1	0	0	1.000	9.00	0	0
Posey, B	SF	1B	2	2	18	16	2	0	2	1.000	-	+1	1
Powell, L	Oak	1B	1	1	8	8	2	0	1	1.000	-	+1	1
Prado, M	Atl	1B	2	2	13	13	0	0	1	1.000	-	0	0
	Atl	3B	41	34	297	12	84	5	6	.950	2.91	+7	6
Presley, A	Pit	LF	48	47	406	71	2	1	1	.986	1.62	+8	5
	Pit	CF	5	3	32	6	0	0	0	1.000	1.67	-4	-2
Pridie, J	NYM	LF	13	7	67	10	0	0	0	1.000	1.34	-2	-1
	NYM	CF	43	32	312	85	1	2	0	.977	2.48	+4	2
	NYM	RF	21	6	84	25	1	0	0	1.000	2.76	+1	1
Pujols, A	StL	3B	7	4	33	2	12	3	2	.824	3.74	-1	-1
Punto, N	StL	2B	45	23	243	58	91	2	26	.987	5.52	+3	4
	StL	3B	7	3	26	2	10	1	0	.923	4.10	+1	1
	StL	SS	8	6	61	8	15	0	2	1.000	3.38	-2	-2
Quintanilla, O	Tex	2B	5	2	23	5	6	0	2	1.000	4.30	-1	-1
	Tex	3B	3	1	13	1	3	0	0	1.000	2.77	+1	1
	Tex	SS	3	3	25	7	12	0	2	1.000	6.84	+1	1
Raburn, R	Det	1B	2	0	6	6	0	0	2	1.000	-	0	0
	Det	2B	56	55	401	69	122	10	23	.950	4.29	-8	-7
	Det	3B	4	4	30	3	7	1	1	.909	3.00	-3	-2
	Det	LF	52	34	335	89	3	3	1	.968	2.47	+5	6
	Det	CF	2	0	3	2	0	0	0	1.000	6.00	0	0
	Det	RF	20	5	81	15	1	3	1	.842	1.77	-2	-2
Ramirez, H	Fla	SS	86	86	754	127	188	14	38	.957	3.76	-8	-8
Ramirez, W	Atl	LF	5	4	37	4	0	0	0	1.000	.97	-1	-1
	Atl	RF	2	2	17	3	0	1	0	.750	1.59	-1	-1
Ransom, C	Ari	3B	6	4	35	8	11	2	1	.905	4.79	-1	-1
	Ari	SS	8	5	46	4	19	1	2	.958	4.50	0	0
Reddick, J	Bos	LF	21	14	148	36	1	1	0	.974	2.25	+1	2
	Bos	CF	3	2	21	6	0	0	0	1.000	2.57	0	1
	Bos	RF	56	48	432	103	4	4	1	.964	2.23	+9	5
Reimold, N	Bal	LF	73	69	593	147	5	3	0	.981	2.30	-2	2
	Bal	RF	8	2	27	3	0	0	0	1.000	1.00	-1	-1
Renteria, E	Cin	2B	4	0	7	1	5	0	0	1.000	7.71	0	0
	Cin	SS	86	71	628	95	208	13	36	.959	4.34	+1	-1
Repko, J	Min	LF	24	12	128	23	1	0	0	1.000	1.69	-2	0
	Min	CF	5	5	43	11	1	1	0	.923	2.51	-1	0
	Min	RF	27	17	157	44	0	0	0	1.000	2.51	+8	5
Revere, B	Min	LF	13	13	112	33	0	1	0	.971	2.64	+1	0
	Min	CF	89	88	776	243	3	6	0	.976	2.85	+20	8
	Min	RF	5	4	37	9	0	0	0	1.000	2.19	+1	1
Reynolds, M	Bal	1B	44	43	375	370	17	5	45	.987	-	-4	-4
Rhymes, W	Det	2B	24	22	187	31	58	2	12	.978	4.28	-2	-1
Rivera, J	TOT	1B	38	33	303	283	19	3	23	.990	-	0	-1
	TOT	LF	56	54	414	77	3	0	0	1.000	1.74	+1	3
	TOT	RF	17	16	130	30	0	0	0	1.000	2.07	+4	2
Rizzo, A	SD	1B	45	36	341	316	26	2	28	.994	-	+3	3
Roberts, B	Bal	2B	39	39	347	65	123	3	24	.984	4.88	+1	1
Roberts, R	Ari	2B	28	23	212	48	73	4	17	.968	5.12	+4	4
	Ari	SS	1	0	3	0	0	0	0	-	.00	0	0
	Ari	LF	3	2	17	4	0	0	0	1.000	2.12	0	0
Robinson, S	StL	LF	1	0	1	0	0	0	0	-	.00	0	0
	StL	CF	5	1	14	1	0	0	0	1.000	.61	0	0
	StL	RF	3	0	3	1	0	0	0	1.000	3.00	0	0
Robinson, T	Sea	LF	30	25	230	55	2	3	0	.950	2.23	0	2
	Sea	CF	16	13	109	25	1	3	0	.897	2.13	-5	-4
Rodriguez, A	NYY	3B	89	87	762	54	165	6	13	.973	2.59	+12	9
Rodriguez, I	Was	1B	1	0	1	1	0	0	0	1.000	-		0
Rodriguez, J	Pit	2B	1	0	5	1	3	0	0	1.000	7.20	0	0
	Pit	SS	4	3	24	5	6	0	2	1.000	4.13	-1	-1
Rodriguez, L	Sea	1B	1	0	2	3	0	0	0	1.000	-		0
	Sea	2B	7	2	32	11	9	1	3	.952	5.63	-2	-2
	Sea	3B	11	9	88	7	10	0	3	1.000	1.74	-3	-2
	Sea	SS	23	21	185	35	57	3	15	.968	4.46	-4	-2

Player	Tm	Pos	G	GS	Inn	PO	A	E	DP	Pct.	Rng	+/-	RS
Rodriguez, S	TB	1B	5	3	29	24	1	0	1	1.000	-	0	1
	TB	2B	48	40	352	66	112	2	25	.989	4.54	+2	4
	TB	3B	30	16	172	15	45	0	6	1.000	3.13	+2	2
	TB	SS	60	49	430	55	105	9	22	.947	3.34	+2	1
	TB	LF	2	0	3	1	0	0	0	1.000	3.00	0	0
Rolen, S	Cin	3B	63	60	547	38	119	4	11	.975	2.58	+9	7
Romine, A	LAA	3B	3	2	18	1	2	0	1	1.000	1.50	0	0
	LAA	SS	7	2	30	4	15	1	2	.950	5.70	0	0
Rosales, A	Oak	1B	5	4	38	36	2	0	2	1.000	-	-1	-1
	Oak	2B	3	2	19	3	4	0	1	1.000	3.32	0	0
	Oak	3B	6	5	43	4	6	2	1	.833	2.08	-1	-2
	Oak	SS	7	6	51	9	12	2	3	.913	3.66	-1	-1
	Oak	LF	2	1	7	4	0	0	0	1.000	5.14	+1	1
Ross, C	SF	LF	83	56	530	109	4	1	1	.991	1.92	-5	0
	SF	CF	22	19	158	27	2	0	0	1.000	1.64	-4	-2
	SF	RF	35	32	268	47	2	0	0	1.000	1.65	-5	-3
Rottino, V	Fla	LF	1	1	8	0	1	0	0	1.000	1.13	0	0
	Fla	RF	2	1	10	1	0	0	0	1.000	.90	0	0
Rowand, A	SF	LF	46	15	219	32	1	1	0	.971	1.35	0	0
	SF	CF	60	55	413	123	4	0	0	1.000	2.72	-1	-1
	SF	RF	3	3	16	2	0	0	0	1.000	1.08	0	0
Ruggiano, J	TB	LF	27	20	183	49	0	0	0	1.000	2.41	+6	5
	TB	CF	4	1	20	6	1	0	0	1.000	3.15	+1	2
	TB	RF	6	4	38	9	0	0	0	1.000	2.13	0	0
Ruiz, C	Phi	3B	1	0	1	0	0	0	0	-	.00		0
Sanchez, A	Hou	2B	19	14	134	31	48	0	20	1.000	5.29	+5	6
	Hou	3B	10	8	73	4	16	0	2	1.000	2.47	-1	-1
	Hou	SS	46	41	366	58	129	7	22	.964	4.59	-3	-3
Sanchez, F	SF	2B	58	58	514	105	136	3	30	.988	4.22	-5	-5
Sandoval, P	SF	1B	6	6	51	54	6	0	3	1.000	-	+1	1
Sands, J	LAD	1B	6	3	26	28	0	0	3	1.000	-	-1	-1
	LAD	LF	41	34	288	61	4	0	0	1.000	2.03	-6	-2
	LAD	CF	1	0	2	0	0	0	0	-	.00	0	0
	LAD	RF	22	16	153	28	2	0	1	1.000	1.76	+1	3
Santana, C	Cle	1B	66	63	565	622	43	4	43	.994	-	0	0
Santiago, R	Det	2B	75	40	434	93	143	1	27	.996	4.89	+1	0
	Det	3B	5	0	12	0	3	0	0	1.000	2.25	-1	0
	Det	SS	27	22	195	35	80	2	15	.983	5.31	+3	2
Sappelt, D	Cin	LF	31	20	194	44	2	0	1	1.000	2.13	+5	3
	Cin	CF	4	2	20	7	0	0	0	1.000	3.15	0	0
Satin, J	NYM	1B	8	4	44	48	5	0	6	1.000	-	+2	2
	NYM	3B	1	0	5	0	0	0	0	-	.00		0
Saunders, M	Sea	LF	12	5	67	21	0	0	0	1.000	2.82	+1	1
	Sea	CF	46	42	376	118	1	0	0	1.000	2.85	0	0
Schafer, J	TOT	CF	79	72	672	191	1	2	1	.990	2.57	-4	-3
Schafer, L	Mil	CF	1	0	2	0	0	0	0	-	.00	0	0
	Mil	RF	1	0	1	0	0	0	0	-	.00	0	0
Schierholtz, N	SF	LF	8	7	61	15	1	1	1	.941	2.36	0	1
	SF	RF	96	70	703	142	4	2	3	.987	1.92	-9	-5
Schumaker, S	StL	2B	95	89	739	139	251	7	47	.982	4.75	-5	-6
	StL	LF	6	1	16	1	0	0	0	1.000	.56	0	0
	StL	CF	5	1	13	2	0	0	0	1.000	1.38	0	0
	StL	RF	31	3	79	19	1	1	0	.952	2.28	0	2
Scott, L	Bal	1B	12	10	95	84	6	0	8	1.000	-	+1	1
	Bal	LF	45	43	330	82	0	1	0	.988	2.23	-1	-1
Scutaro, M	Bos	2B	2	2	18	3	6	1	1	.900	4.50	-1	1
Seager, K	Sea	2B	3	3	24	2	7	0	0	1.000	3.38	0	0
	Sea	3B	42	38	335	31	85	4	2	.967	3.11	+3	2
	Sea	SS	10	8	74	14	20	2	6	.944	4.14	-3	-1
Sellers, J	LAD	2B	12	11	90	30	19	0	4	1.000	4.86	+2	1
	LAD	3B	5	4	36	4	11	0	0	1.000	3.72	+1	2
	LAD	SS	19	17	151	25	48	1	16	.986	4.33	+4	4
Shuck, J	Hou	LF	6	2	23	4	0	0	0	1.000	1.52	+1	1
	Hou	CF	9	7	58	23	1	1	0	.960	3.68	0	0
	Hou	RF	16	5	73	17	0	0	0	1.000	2.09	+1	0
Sizemore, G	Cle	CF	56	55	479	123	1	2	0	.984	2.33	-7	-3
Sizemore, S	TOT	2B	18	17	151	22	59	3	12	.964	4.82	+2	2
	TOT	3B	91	88	782	54	129	13	10	.934	2.11	-15	-13
Smith, S	Col	1B	25	22	186	34	4	0	0	1.000	1.83	-1	0
Snider, T	Tor	LF	44	39	367	77	3	3	1	.964	1.96	-1	-3
	Tor	CF	6	4	36	11	1	0	0	1.000	3.00	-1	-1
	Tor	RF	3	3	24	3	0	0	0	1.000	1.13	0	0
Snyder, B	ChC	LF	1	1	6	0	0	0	0	-	.00	0	0
Snyder, B	Bal	1B	5	4	40	42	2	1	3	.978	-	-1	-1

Player	Tm	Pos	G	GS	Inn	PO	A	E	DP	Pct.	Rng	+/-	RS
Sogard, E	Oak	2B	3	3	27	5	9	1	2	.933	4.67	0	0
	Oak	3B	10	8	70	5	13	0	0	1.000	2.31	+4	3
	Oak	SS	14	8	79	15	22	1	2	.974	4.22	+2	2
Span, D	Min	CF	67	67	585	206	1	1	0	.995	3.18	+11	4
Spears, N	Bos	2B	1	0	1	0	0	0	0	-	.00		0
	Bos	LF	1	0	5	1	0	0	0	1.000	1.80	+1	1
Spilborghs, R	Col	LF	29	10	126	13	2	0	0	1.000	1.07	+1	1
	Col	CF	13	8	71	30	0	0	0	1.000	3.77	-1	-2
	Col	RF	29	23	209	35	2	0	0	1.000	1.59	-3	-3
Stairs, M	Was	1B	4	3	19	11	1	0	0	1.000	-	0	0
Stanton, M	Fla	CF	1	0	1	2	0	0	0	1.000	18.00	+1	1
Stewart, C	SF	1B	3	0	8	5	0	0	0	1.000	-	0	0
Stewart, I	Col	3B	42	31	284	25	54	6	3	.929	2.50	+2	2
Sutton, D	Bos	1B	5	0	12	13	1	0	0	1.000	-	0	0
	Bos	2B	7	1	18	3	5	1	1	.889	4.00	-3	-2
	Bos	3B	8	4	46	2	13	0	1	1.000	2.93	+4	2
	Bos	SS	4	4	32	6	6	1	2	.923	3.38	-1	-1
	Bos	LF	3	2	16	6	0	1	0	.857	3.38	0	0
Sweeney, R	Oak	LF	41	24	219	41	1	0	0	1.000	1.73	+9	5
	Oak	CF	34	26	245	75	0	0	0	1.000	2.75	-1	-2
	Oak	RF	23	15	153	34	2	0	0	1.000	2.11	-9	-4
Swisher, N	NYY	1B	11	3	44	29	2	0	4	1.000	-	-2	-1
Tabata, J	Pit	LF	76	70	626	140	4	1	2	.993	2.07	+8	2
	Pit	CF	2	2	17	2	0	1	0	.667	1.06	+1	1
	Pit	RF	15	13	106	15	0	0	0	1.000	1.27	-4	-3
Tatum, C	Bal	1B	1	0	2	1	0	0	1	1.000	-	0	0
Taylor, M	Oak	LF	3	2	18	3	0	0	0	1.000	1.50	-1	-2
	Oak	RF	8	7	65	20	0	2	0	.909	2.77	0	0
Teahen, M	TOT	1B	18	2	44	47	2	0	1	1.000	-	-2	-1
	TOT	3B	32	26	219	20	48	0	2	1.000	2.79	+2	2
	TOT	LF	6	1	17	3	0	1	0	.750	1.59	-1	0
	TOT	RF	9	3	38	3	0	0	0	1.000	.71	0	0
Tejada, M	SF	2B	4	4	33	5	13	0	2	1.000	4.91	-1	-1
	SF	3B	44	39	372	29	99	2	12	.985	3.09	+7	7
	SF	SS	42	39	334	44	110	8	12	.951	4.15	-6	-5
Tejada, R	NYM	2B	55	53	457	95	146	4	31	.984	4.74	+2	1
	NYM	SS	41	38	353	53	120	8	18	.956	4.41	+1	-2
Tekotte, B	SD	LF	3	1	11	2	0	0	0	1.000	1.64	0	0
	SD	CF	7	5	46	6	0	0	0	1.000	1.17	-5	-3
	SD	RF	1	1	9	2	0	0	0	1.000	2.00	0	0
Thames, E	Tor	LF	52	51	456	91	1	1	0	.989	1.81	-7	-6
	Tor	RF	27	25	223	55	1	1	1	.982	2.26	-2	0
Thames, M	LAD	LF	17	15	99	26	0	1	0	.963	2.36	-1	-2
Theriot, R	StL	2B	35	17	190	41	71	1	23	.991	5.30	+5	6
	StL	SS	91	87	755	117	254	17	54	.956	4.42	-15	-12
Thome, J	TOT	3B	1	0	0	0	0	0	0	-	-		0
Thurston, J	Fla	2B	1	1	9	3	4	0	1	1.000	7.00	+1	1
Tolbert, M	Min	2B	36	26	244	61	78	3	23	.979	5.13	+1	2
	Min	3B	6	4	37	2	3	0	1	1.000	1.22	-1	-1
	Min	SS	31	22	210	41	66	3	19	.973	4.59	0	1
Torres, A	SF	LF	1	0	4	0	0	0	0	-	.00	0	0
	SF	CF	106	78	776	196	6	3	2	.985	2.34	+8	3
	SF	RF	4	0	11	8	0	0	0	1.000	6.17	+2	1
Tosoni, R	Min	LF	38	36	321	85	4	3	0	.967	2.50	-1	-1
	Min	RF	4	1	11	2	0	0	0	1.000	1.59	0	0
Trout, M	LAA	LF	10	8	75	21	0	0	0	1.000	2.52	+1	1
	LAA	CF	13	12	107	37	0	1	0	.974	3.09	+6	3
	LAA	RF	13	12	109	22	0	1	0	.957	1.82	+3	2
Trumbo, M	LAA	LF	1	0	2	0	0	0	0	-	.00	0	0
	LAA	RF	10	0	21	3	0	0	0	1.000	1.29	0	0
Turner, J	NYM	2B	78	71	642	144	206	8	36	.978	4.90	-8	-11
	NYM	3B	36	31	277	25	50	4	3	.949	2.43	0	0
	NYM	SS	1	0	5	2	1	0	0	.800	7.20	+1	0
Uribe, J	LAD	2B	18	17	137	31	37	0	11	1.000	4.47	0	0
	LAD	3B	59	53	462	37	96	3	3	.978	2.59	+5	5
	LAD	SS	4	3	21	3	5	0	2	1.000	3.32	0	0
Valaika, C	Cin	2B	1	1	4	3	1	0	0	1.000	7.71	-1	-1
	Cin	3B	4	4	33	4	13	0	2	1.000	4.64	+2	2
	Cin	SS	2	2	16	1	2	0	1	1.000	1.69	+1	1
Valbuena, L	Cle	2B	11	9	81	19	24	0	7	1.000	4.78	+1	1
	Cle	SS	1	0	1	0	0	0	0	-	.00	0	0
	Cle	LF	2	1	12	2	0	0	0	1.000	1.46	-1	-1
Valdez, W	Phi	2B	45	33	316	78	95	2	20	.989	4.92	-7	-6
	Phi	3B	24	21	194	13	33	3	4	.939	2.13	-5	-4
	Phi	SS	25	20	188	30	57	4	15	.956	4.16	-3	-1
Velazquez, G	LAA	2B	2	1	11	2	5	0	1	1.000	5.73	+1	1
	LAA	3B	2	0	3	0	2	0	0	1.000	6.00	0	0
Velez, E	LAD	2B	11	6	50	10	13	0	2	1.000	4.11	+1	1
	LAD	LF	4	1	15	4	0	1	0	.800	2.40	+2	1
Venable, W	SD	LF	7	4	38	7	0	0	0	1.000	1.66	-2	-1
	SD	CF	14	10	93	22	1	0	0	1.000	2.23	+2	3
	SD	RF	91	71	662	147	2	2	2	.987	2.02	+15	10
Viciedo, D	CWS	1B	4	2	21	18	1	0	1	1.000	-	0	0
	CWS	RF	21	19	163	26	2	0	1	1.000	1.55	0	2
Vizquel, O	CWS	1B	1	0	3	1	1	0	0	1.000	-	0	0
	CWS	2B	16	14	130	23	37	1	7	.984	4.14	-2	-2
	CWS	3B	29	20	182	13	31	0	2	1.000	2.18	-1	-2
	CWS	SS	9	8	72	8	18	0	3	1.000	3.25	0	0
Wallace, B	Hou	1B	96	89	768	659	77	6	57	.992	-	+1	2
Weeks, J	Oak	2B	96	96	849	148	261	13	49	.969	4.33	-5	-3
Wells, C	TOT	LF	21	20	159	47	3	1	2	.980	2.83	0	2
	TOT	CF	9	6	59	20	2	0	1	1.000	3.36	-1	0
	TOT	RF	58	25	274	61	2	1	1	.984	2.07	0	1
Wells, V	LAA	CF	12	11	79	24	0	0	0	1.000	2.72	-1	-1
	LAA	RF	10	7	66	16	0	0	0	1.000	2.17	-3	-3
Werth, J	Was	CF	19	17	151	55	1	0	0	1.000	3.32	+6	3
Wieters, M	Bal	1B	1	1	8	4	0	0	2	1.000	-	0	0
Wigginton, T	Col	1B	36	17	191	181	12	0	10	1.000	-	-5	-4
	Col	3B	68	62	520	33	96	4	15	.970	2.23	0	-1
	Col	LF	21	16	139	16	0	2	0	.889	1.04	-2	-2
	Col	RF	6	5	46	8	1	0	0	1.000	1.74	+1	2
Willingham, J	Oak	LF	96	94	829	159	3	2	1	.988	1.76	-6	0
Willits, R	LAA	LF	19	8	82	23	0	0	0	1.000	2.50	0	-1
	LAA	RF	1	0	3	0	0	0	0	-	.00	0	0
Wilson, B	LAA	1B	6	0	11	7	0	0	1	1.000	-	0	0
Wilson, J	TOT	2B	45	38	342	79	111	2	28	.990	5.00	+6	6
	TOT	3B	4	2	21	2	5	0	2	1.000	3.00	+1	1
	TOT	SS	26	21	204	42	72	2	14	.983	5.03	+1	-1
Wilson, J	TOT	1B	1	0	1	0	0	0	0	-	-		0
	TOT	2B	10	8	64	12	21	0	4	1.000	4.64	+1	1
	TOT	3B	13	2	33	2	5	1	1	.875	1.89	-2	-2
	TOT	SS	11	5	58	13	19	1	5	.970	4.97	0	0
	TOT	LF	3	2	16	2	0	0	0	1.000	1.13	0	0
Wilson, M	Sea	LF	5	4	42	8	1	0	0	1.000	1.93	-1	0
	Sea	RF	2	2	17	2	0	0	0	1.000	1.06	0	0
Wise, D	TOT	LF	13	1	21	3	0	0	0	1.000	1.29	-2	-1
	TOT	CF	37	19	195	67	1	2	0	.971	3.13	+2	0
	TOT	RF	2	1	8	1	0	0	0	1.000	1.13	0	0
Wood, B	TOT	1B	10	4	41	44	1	0	2	1.000	-	0	0
	TOT	2B	3	1	9	2	1	0	0	1.000	3.00	0	0
	TOT	3B	61	37	377	27	83	3	9	.973	2.62	-2	-3
	TOT	SS	24	18	172	38	50	2	16	.978	4.60	-3	-3
Woodward, C	Tor	2B	2	1	11	0	5	0	1	1.000	4.09	0	0
	Tor	3B	1	1	9	1	1	0	0	1.000	2.00	0	0
	Tor	SS	1	0	1	0	0	0	0	-	.00		0
Worth, D	Det	2B	15	3	53	9	11	0	2	1.000	3.40	+1	1
	Det	3B	13	5	56	5	12	1	3	.944	2.72	-1	-1
Wright, D	NYM	SS	1	0	2	1	0	0	0	1.000	4.50	0	0
Wright, W	Hou	RF	1	0	0	0	0	0	0	-	.00		0
Youkilis, K	Bos	1B	6	5	44	37	5	0	2	1.000	-	+1	1
Young, E	Col	2B	7	5	43	10	11	1	5	.955	4.40	-1	0
	Col	LF	35	30	269	50	0	1	0	.980	1.67	-3	-5
	Col	CF	5	5	39	11	0	1	0	.917	2.54	-5	-3
	Col	RF	3	2	17	4	2	1	0	.857	3.18	-1	0
Young, M	Atl	LF	9	3	35	8	0	0	0	1.000	2.04	0	0
	Atl	CF	3	2	18	3	0	0	0	1.000	1.50	-1	-1
	Atl	RF	7	6	49	7	0	0	0	1.000	1.29	0	0
Young, M	Tex	1B	36	36	302	267	13	3	34	.989	-	-4	-5
	Tex	2B	14	14	120	28	29	0	11	1.000	4.26	-3	-2
	Tex	3B	40	39	342	30	66	5	9	.950	2.53	-6	-6
	Tex	SS	1	1	8	1	2	0	1	1.000	3.38	-1	-1
Zobrist, B	TB	RF	38	33	289	65	1	0	0	1.000	2.05	+8	6

All Other Catchers

Player	Tm	G	GS	Inn	PO	A	E	DP	PB	Pct.	SBA	CS	PCS	CS%	ER	CERA	Runs Saved SB	Adj-ER	Total
Alfonzo,Eliezer	Col	19	18	159.1	128	12	5	2	2	.966	15	5	0	.33	87	4.91	1	0	1
Baker,John	Fla	1	0	3.0	2	0	0	0	0	1.000	0	0	0	-	1	3.00	0	0	0
Barajas,Rod	LAD	88	85	733.1	651	48	2	4	3	.997	80	14	6	.18	291	3.57	-1	-1	-2
Bard,Josh	Sea	25	23	201.0	156	12	2	2	0	.988	24	7	2	.29	88	3.94	0	0	0
Blanco,Henry	Ari	37	31	274.0	178	13	1	0	1	.995	24	8	3	.33	141	4.63	2	-1	1
Boscan,J.C.	Atl	3	2	18.0	18	1	0	0	0	1.000	3	1	0	.33	8	4.00	0	0	0
Brown,Dusty	Pit	10	8	78.0	49	3	0	1	3	1.000	7	1	0	.14	36	4.15	0	0	0
Butera,Drew	Min	93	75	670.2	418	38	5	3	7	.989	70	20	2	.29	369	4.95	3	-6	-3
Cancel,Robinson	Hou	2	2	16.0	14	0	0	0	1	1.000	2	0	0	.00	9	5.06	0	0	0
Castillo,Welington	ChC	4	4	31.2	16	2	2	0	0	.900	3	2	0	.67	21	5.97	0	0	0
Castro,Ramon	CWS	21	20	174.1	117	4	1	0	3	.992	20	2	2	.10	83	4.28	0	0	0
Cervelli,Francisco	NYY	41	35	316.1	278	18	6	1	3	.980	28	4	0	.14	123	3.50	-3	1	-2
Chirinos,Robinson	TB	19	15	132.0	115	8	0	1	0	1.000	23	2	0	.09	65	4.43	-1	0	-1
Clevenger,Steve	ChC	2	1	12.0	13	0	0	0	0	1.000	1	0	0	.00	6	4.50	0	0	0
Conger,Hank	LAA	56	48	450.0	322	27	6	5	1	.983	65	10	2	.15	192	3.84	-3	-1	-4
Corporan,Carlos	Hou	50	46	411.1	371	30	6	5	2	.985	52	9	0	.17	183	4.00	-1	1	0
Cruz,Tony	StL	20	8	99.0	90	6	0	1	1	1.000	4	2	0	.50	33	3.00	0	0	0
Doumit,Ryan	Pit	60	53	461.1	321	26	6	1	4	.983	54	11	2	.20	245	4.78	-1	-3	-4
Ellis,A.J.	LAD	29	25	221.2	167	11	0	2	2	1.000	15	2	2	.13	89	3.61	-1	0	-1
Federowicz,Tim	LAD	7	4	40.0	37	6	1	0	1	.977	5	2	0	.40	14	3.15	1	0	1
Flores,Jesus	Was	22	21	193.0	140	10	1	0	2	.993	20	4	0	.20	72	3.36	0	0	0
Flowers,Tyler	CWS	31	28	256.2	243	15	2	1	3	.992	33	6	2	.18	113	3.96	1	1	2
Fox,Jake	Bal	6	6	57.0	38	1	0	0	2	1.000	5	0	0	.00	49	7.74	-1	0	-1
Fryer,Eric	Pit	8	7	61.2	42	5	1	0	0	.979	10	3	0	.30	21	3.06	2	0	2
Gimenez,Chris	Sea	20	17	152.0	111	9	0	2	0	1.000	20	6	0	.30	83	4.91	1	-1	0
Gimenez,Hector	LAD	1	1	9.0	8	0	0	0	0	1.000	1	0	0	.00	10	10.00	0	0	0
Hanigan,Ryan	Cin	89	73	687.1	541	29	4	6	2	.993	52	13	5	.25	303	3.97	-1	4	3
Hayes,Brett	Fla	50	33	312.2	254	20	0	2	3	1.000	27	5	2	.19	144	4.14	0	0	0
Hernandez,Ramon	Cin	82	76	658.0	507	41	1	6	3	.998	62	18	5	.29	310	4.24	0	-3	-3
Hill,Koyie	ChC	45	38	349.0	319	15	6	5	2	.982	33	7	1	.21	166	4.28	-1	1	0
Holm,Steve	Min	6	5	43.0	33	1	0	1	0	1.000	5	0	0	.00	26	5.44	-1	0	-1
Hundley,Nick	SD	76	73	654.1	501	60	6	8	4	.989	89	24	8	.27	257	3.53	2	-1	1
Jaramillo,Jason	Pit	14	7	73.2	65	2	0	0	0	1.000	6	1	0	.17	31	3.79	0	0	0
Jaso,John	TB	82	67	603.1	479	26	4	4	4	.992	60	8	2	.13	226	3.37	-3	2	-1
Johnson,Rob	SD	63	54	475.0	362	65	2	3	5	.995	64	11	4	.17	173	3.28	-2	1	-1
Kelly,Don	Det	1	1	6.0	3	0	0	0	1	1.000	0	0	0	-	4	6.00	0	0	0
Kottaras,George	Mil	36	31	253.0	171	8	0	0	2	1.000	21	3	0	.14	102	3.63	-2	0	-2
Kratz,Erik	Phi	1	1	10.0	10	0	0	0	1	1.000	1	0	0	.00	4	3.60	0	0	0
Laird,Gerald	StL	31	22	213.0	182	12	3	1	3	.985	20	3	1	.15	83	3.51	-1	0	-1
Lavarnway,Ryan	Bos	8	2	26.2	22	3	0	0	0	1.000	1	1	0	1.00	13	4.39	1	0	1
Lobaton,Jose	TB	14	9	88.0	90	3	1	0	0	.989	10	2	1	.20	24	2.45	0	0	0
Lucy,Donny	CWS	3	2	21.0	23	1	0	1	0	1.000	1	0	1	.00	16	6.86	0	0	0
Maldonado,Martin	Mil	0	0	3.0	4	0	0	0	0	1.000	0	0	0	-	0	0.00	0	0	0
Marson,Lou	Cle	78	74	667.0	476	43	5	6	5	.990	78	24	6	.31	319	4.30	3	0	3
Martinez,Luis	SD	19	16	148.1	122	7	0	0	0	1.000	19	3	2	.16	55	3.34	-2	0	-2
Martinez,Victor	Det	26	26	219.0	141	17	2	3	0	.988	37	7	1	.19	128	5.26	-1	-1	-2
Mathis,Jeff	LAA	91	79	698.0	512	53	3	4	6	.995	66	12	6	.18	252	3.25	1	3	4
Mauer,Joe	Min	52	47	408.2	291	18	4	2	4	.987	40	10	2	.25	201	4.43	0	1	1
McKenry,Michael	Pit	58	54	485.0	359	24	5	2	1	.987	52	10	3	.19	201	3.73	0	0	0
Mesoraco,Devin	Cin	16	13	122.1	103	6	3	1	0	.973	11	2	1	.18	65	4.78	-1	0	-1
Molina,Gustavo	NYY	3	2	19.0	9	1	0	0	0	1.000	2	1	0	.50	5	2.37	0	0	0
Molina,Jose	Tor	48	44	399.0	342	24	1	3	8	.997	36	12	0	.33	194	4.38	1	1	2
Montero,Jesus	NYY	3	3	22.0	12	1	0	0	0	1.000	5	1	0	.20	19	7.77	0	0	0
Moore,Adam	Sea	2	2	15.2	11	1	0	0	0	1.000	2	0	0	.00	6	3.45	0	0	0
Morales,Jose	Col	17	17	151.2	117	8	5	0	3	.962	15	4	2	.27	63	3.74	1	0	1
Napoli,Mike	Tex	61	57	506.1	431	25	2	4	1	.996	33	10	2	.30	178	3.16	1	2	3
Navarro,Dioner	LAD	54	46	428.0	421	27	7	5	2	.985	55	10	4	.18	163	3.43	0	1	1
Nickeas,Mike	NYM	20	15	143.2	118	6	0	0	0	1.000	13	2	2	.15	47	2.94	0	1	1
Nieves,Wil	Mil	17	16	129.0	109	8	1	0	1	.992	10	2	1	.20	55	3.84	0	0	0
Pacheco,Jordan	Col	2	1	10.0	8	1	0	0	0	1.000	2	0	0	.00	5	4.50	0	0	0
Pagnozzi,Matt	TOT	9	9	74.0	44	7	0	0	1	1.000	16	2	3	.13	65	7.91	-1	0	-1
Paulino,Ronny	NYM	68	56	511.0	375	30	7	3	6	.983	59	10	2	.17	254	4.47	-3	-1	-4
Pena,Brayan	KC	69	57	537.0	417	25	2	6	4	.995	75	16	11	.21	268	4.49	2	-1	1
Perez,Salvador	KC	39	39	338.2	290	21	3	2	2	.990	33	5	2	.15	159	4.23	1	-1	0
Phillips,Kyle	SD	24	19	171.2	140	12	3	1	1	.981	29	7	1	.24	67	3.51	0	0	0
Pina,Manny	KC	4	4	36.0	33	1	0	0	0	1.000	2	1	0	.50	11	2.75	1	0	1
Posada,Jorge	NYY	1	0	6.0	7	2	0	0	0	1.000	1	1	0	1.00	5	7.50	1	0	1
Posey,Buster	SF	41	41	361.0	333	24	2	4	3	.994	42	11	4	.26	134	3.34	2	0	2
Powell,Landon	Oak	33	30	273.1	237	15	2	2	1	.992	25	6	3	.24	82	2.70	1	2	3
Quintero,Humberto	Hou	77	73	642.0	541	43	5	9	3	.992	62	11	3	.18	329	4.61	1	1	2
Recker,Anthony	Oak	5	5	42.0	44	1	1	0	0	.978	5	0	0	.00	39	8.36	0	0	0
Rivera,Mike	Mil	1	1	13.0	13	2	0	1	0	1.000	1	1	0	1.00	5	3.46	0	0	0
Rivera,Rene	Min	44	35	299.1	231	16	3	1	1	.988	25	6	4	.24	130	3.91	0	2	2
Rodriguez,Ivan	Was	37	34	304.2	245	18	3	4	3	.989	25	12	1	.48	111	3.28	3	1	4
Romine,Austin	NYY	8	4	50.2	46	3	1	0	0	.980	6	1	1	.17	24	4.26	0	0	0
Rosario,Wilin	Col	14	14	123.0	87	16	1	1	3	.990	8	5	0	.63	66	4.83	1	0	1
Ross,David	Atl	49	42	378.2	337	32	3	2	2	.992	33	10	1	.30	131	3.11	3	1	4
Sanchez,Hector	SF	11	6	63.0	51	3	0	1	2	1.000	14	2	2	.14	37	5.29	-1	0	-1
Santos,Omir	Det	10	6	58.0	48	3	0	0	0	1.000	6	1	0	.17	16	2.48	0	0	0
Sardinha,Dane	Phi	15	12	107.0	86	6	0	3	2	1.000	11	3	0	.27	36	3.03	0	0	0
Schneider,Brian	Phi	40	36	309.0	277	9	1	0	1	.997	23	3	0	.13	99	2.88	-3	1	-2
Shoppach,Kelly	TB	86	71	625.2	485	37	3	7	1	.994	44	15	3	.34	262	3.77	5	-2	3

Player	Tm	G	GS	Inn	PO	A	E	DP	PB	Pct.	SBA	CS	PCS	CS%	ER	CERA	Runs Saved SB	Adj-ER	Total
Snyder,Chris	Pit	33	30	265.2	201	17	0	1	5	1.000	23	5	1	.22	100	3.39	-1	1	0
Stewart,Chris	SF	63	51	460.1	430	48	7	4	2	.986	56	19	3	.34	138	2.70	6	3	9
Tatum,Craig	Bal	30	27	239.2	207	16	3	2	1	.987	28	8	0	.29	159	5.97	1	-1	0
Teagarden,Taylor	Tex	14	8	85.1	63	5	0	0	1	1.000	13	5	2	.38	30	3.16	2	0	2
Toregas,Wyatt	Pit	2	1	10.0	5	1	0	0	0	1.000	3	1	0	.33	4	3.60	0	0	0
Towles,J.R.	Hou	51	41	365.2	284	22	6	3	2	.981	46	6	2	.13	198	4.87	-2	-1	-3
Treanor,Matt	TOT	72	64	565.2	419	24	4	5	2	.991	56	11	3	.20	284	4.52	0	2	2
Varitek,Jason	Bos	68	64	574.2	519	28	4	1	6	.993	85	10	2	.12	228	3.57	-5	2	-3
Whiteside,Eli	SF	81	64	583.2	495	41	5	4	7	.991	71	13	5	.18	214	3.30	-1	-2	-3
Wilson,Bobby	LAA	47	35	317.0	239	26	1	1	0	.996	35	8	2	.23	137	3.89	1	-1	0

The Coyote's After You

Bill James

Victor Martinez in 2011 had 12 home runs and 103 RBI, while Michael Young of Texas had 11 home runs and 106 RBI. It is unusual for a player to have 11 or 12 home runs and 100+ RBI, and there is a related phenomenon that I will tell you about in a moment that is much more unusual than that; in fact, it's borderline unbelievable. But first, who was the last major league player, before Young and Martinez, to have 11 home runs and 100+ RBI?

It was Jeff Cirillo, 11 years ago in 2000. Martinez' and Young's seasons fall into the tradition of a certain type of season, a type of player for whom I have always had a great deal of affection. Other seasons in this class include Edgar Renteria (2003), Cirillo in 2000, Paul Molitor (1996), Keith Hernandez (1979), Wes Parker (1970), Floyd Robinson (1962), George Kell (1950), and Hank Majeski (1948). All of these hitters had 13 or fewer homers, hit .310 or better (usually .330 or better), hit 40+ doubles, and drove in 100 or more runs. All of their seasons look alike; it's what I call a Floyd Robinson season:

Last	YEAR	G	AB	R	H	2B	3B	HR	RBI	BB	SO	Avg
Young	2011	159	631	88	213	41	6	11	106	47	78	.338
Martinez	2011	145	540	76	178	40	0	12	103	46	51	.330
Renteria	2003	157	587	96	194	47	1	13	100	65	54	.330
Cirillo	2000	157	598	111	195	53	2	11	115	67	72	.326
Molitor	1996	161	660	99	225	41	8	9	113	56	72	.341
Hernandez	1979	161	610	116	210	48	11	11	105	80	78	.344
Parker	1970	161	614	84	196	47	4	10	111	79	70	.319
Robinson	1962	156	600	89	187	45	10	11	109	72	47	.312
Kell	1950	157	641	114	218	56	6	8	101	66	18	.340
Majeski	1948	148	590	88	183	41	4	12	120	48	43	.310

You want to know something else about these guys? You don't want to know, but I'm going to tell you anyway.

They all had really disappointing years the next season. Hank Majeski, after driving in 120 runs for the Philadelphia A's in 1948, dropped off to 67 RBI the next season. George Kell, after driving in 101 runs in 1950, dropped off to 59 RBI in 1951. Floyd Robinson, after driving in 109 runs in 1962, fell off to 71 the next season. Wes Parker, after driving in 111 runs in 1970, dropped off to 62 the next season.

Keith Hernandez, co-MVP in 1979 with 105 RBI, came closer to sustaining it than anybody else did; he hit 16 homers and drove in 99 runs in 1980. Paul Molitor, after driving in 113 runs in 1996, dropped off to 89 the next season, although, since he was 40 years old, that really wasn't a bad season, either. Jeff Cirillo, after driving in 115 runs in 2000, fell off to 83 the next year, even though his home runs increased to 17. Edgar Renteria, after driving in 100 runs in 2003, dropped off to 72 the next year.

What these players are doing is essentially unsustainable. Usually, to drive in 100 runs, a player needs to hit 25 or more homers. When a player has a season like this once, your instinct is to think that if he did it once he can do it again. Well. . .maybe. I'm not saying a player absolutely *can't* repeat a season like this. All of these guys were (or are) really good line-drive hitters. If a hitter like that has a season in which he gets to bat a lot of times with runners on base *and* a large number of line drives find the gap when there are runners on base, he can get 100 RBI based on 190 hits, 40 doubles and 10 homers—but it's like a perfect storm, a freakish combination of events. Victor Martinez in 2011 had 270 at bats with the bases empty, and 270 at bats with men on base. With the bases empty he hit .256 with 2 homers. With men on base he hit .404 with 10 homers. Michael Young was .297 (bases empty) and .383 (men on base). Jeff Cirillo hit .281 (bases empty) and .373 (men on base). Floyd Robinson hit .269 (bases empty) and .347 (men on base)—and he hit 8 of his 11 homers with men on base.

These players not only hit really well with men on base, they also had unusual numbers of opportunities with men on base, *and* they had most of their power hits with men on base. Robinson led his league in at bats with runners in scoring position (178). Parker had 182 at bats with runners in scoring position, missed by two of leading his league. It's beautiful when it happens, but it's hard to make it happen year in and year out.

You may be wondering why I am writing about this, in what is supposed to be an article about baserunning. Here's why. Who would you guess led the major leagues in 2011 in the number of times he went first-to-third on a single?

The answer—this is the unbelievable thing I promised you earlier—is Miguel Cabrera. Miguel Cabrera is a wonderful hitter, but. . .fast, he ain't. Usually the major league leader in going first-to-third on a single is somebody like Chone Figgins or Juan Pierre.

Cabrera led the majors in going first-to-third on a single because:

a) he is better at going first-to-third on a single than you would think he is, and

b) he had a huge number of opportunities to do so.

Cabrera was 26-for-69 in first-to-third opportunities. That's a very good percentage, but it's not a Chone Figgins percentage. It's the 69 opportunities that will get you. Figgins had a better percentage (7 for 11), but then, Figgins had only 11 chances. Cabrera had 69. Nobody else in the majors had 50 chances to do that.

Cabrera had a huge number of opportunities, of course, because

a) He led the majors in on base percentage, at .448, and

b) Victor Martinez was batting behind him, and hitting .404 with runners on base.

It's a lethal combination. It's beautiful when it works.

Cabrera went first-to-third, given the chance to do so, almost 40% of the time. That's a very good percentage. It's not a super percentage. The major league norm was 29%. Elvis Andrus led the majors in the number of times going first-to-third on a single in 2010, 20 times. He was 20 for 44. In 2011 he was 25 for 44—but lost his title to Cabrera because Cabrera had 25 additional chances.

The highest percentage going first-to-third on a single (20 or more chances) was 68%, by Brendan Ryan and Chase Utley (they were both 15-for-22). Andrus, however, was still really the best in the majors at doing that, because he was 12 bases better than an average baserunner just in that one category. An average runner would have been 13-for-44; Andrus was 25-for-44. The bottom guy was Billy Butler, who was 1-for-25. That's not a big shock, but here's another surprise in the data. The third-worst in the majors in this category was Michael Bourn; he was 4-for-41. The nine worst in the majors were Billy Butler, Casey McGehee, Ryan Howard, Adam Dunn, Brett Wallace, Raul Ibanez, Jhonny Peralta, Paul Konerko—and Michael Bourn.

Bourn, however, was 25-for-34 at scoring from second base on a single, which is really good. Well. . .it's good. It's not sensational. The norm in that category is 60%. The major league leaders were Ben Revere (15 for 16) and Dexter Fowler (24 for 26). Matt Kemp was 23 for 25, which is impressive for a power hitter. The worst in the majors at that was Billy Butler (5 for 20); Butler, Carlos Lee, Ryan Howard.

OK, our third performance category is "scoring from first on a double"; the norm here is 46%. Butler was the worst in the majors at that, too; he was 2-for-18. With the Red Sox I used to argue against pinch-running for David Ortiz, for two reasons:

1) The gains from using a pinch runner are trivial compared to the loss of his bat, and

2) He's really not a bad baserunner.

David Ortiz last year—and David is getting up in years—but David last year was at 19% going first-to-third on a single, 37% scoring from second on a single, and 20% scoring from first on a double. Butler was at 4%, 25% and 11%. OK, you can pinch run for him.

The next thing we count is "Bases Taken". We credit a runner with taking a base whenever he moves up a base on

a) A Wild Pitch,

b) A Passed Ball,

c) A Balk,

d) A Sacrifice Fly, or

e) Defensive Indifference.

Think about it. These are things that we record as *defensive* events—defensive events only. A pitcher throws a Wild Pitch; we charge it against his record. The batter moves up on the Wild Pitch; we ignore that. "We" don't ignore it; the Official Statistics ignore it.

Almost every event has an offensive and defensive component, and it is unwise to ignore either one. At one time the official records of the game ignored walks by a hitter, treating the walk only as something that was done by the pitcher. Same thing. Into the mid-1970s (with a few exceptions), the Official Statistics ignored Stolen Bases from a defensive standpoint, recording them only as something that was done by the offense.

Ignoring these events (wild pitches, balks, sacrifice flies) . . .ignoring these events, from the standpoint of the offense, tends to cause people to assume that there is no offensive component to them, that one baserunner will take advantage of those opportunities as often as the next. In reality, Bases Taken are more common than Stolen Bases—and the differences between baserunners are huge.

Elvis Andrus led the majors in 2011 in Bases Taken, with 37. Here's another weird stat for you: Billy Butler had more Bases Taken (23) than Jacoby Ellsbury (22). That was just kind of a fluke; in 2009 Butler had only 8 Bases Taken, whereas Ellsbury had 26.

Gerardo Parra was thrown out trying to take an extra base 11 times in 2011, the most of any major league player. Michael Young, who led the majors in hits with 213, was *never* thrown out attempting to advance.

Laynce Nix batted 64 times in double play situations, and grounded into only one double play. Ryan Theriot batted 62 times in double play situations, and grounded into 15 double plays.

Taking into consideration all phases of baserunning including base stealing, the best base runner in the major leagues in 2011 was Elvis Andrus. The top five were Andrus, Ian Kinsler, Michael Bourn, Drew Stubbs and Chase Utley.

The bottom five were Paul Konerko, Jorge Posada, Casey McGehee, Vladimir Guerrero and David Ortiz.   Yeah, I know, but he used to be pretty good; that's all I was trying to tell you.

2011 Baserunning

Player	1st to 3rd Moved	1st to 3rd Chances	2nd to Home Moved	2nd to Home Chances	1st to Home Moved	1st to Home Chances	Bases Taken	Out Adv	Doubled Off	BR Outs	GDP	GDP Opps	BR Gain	SB Gain	Net Gain
Abreu,Bobby	6	32	9	19	3	9	13	4	1	5	8	97	-10	+11	+1
Ackley,Dustin	7	24	6	10	3	6	7	0	1	1	3	70	+7	+6	+13
Allen,Brandon	0	9	5	8	1	1	4	0	0	0	0	24	+4	+3	+7
Altuve,Jose	3	9	8	13	1	6	10	1	0	1	5	48	+5	+1	+6
Alvarez,Pedro	2	13	2	4	0	3	4	2	0	2	11	53	-12	+1	-11
Andino,Robert	11	28	13	21	3	8	18	2	3	5	14	101	0	+7	+7
Andrus,Elvis	25	44	17	25	8	9	37	2	1	3	17	121	+38	+13	+51
Ankiel,Rick	4	14	6	10	1	3	13	1	1	2	7	67	+5	+4	+9
Arencibia,J.P.	4	19	3	9	0	4	6	4	0	4	6	78	-11	-1	-12
Avila,Alex	6	27	8	13	6	10	11	4	4	8	8	112	-12	+1	-11
Aviles,Mike	3	8	4	6	3	4	9	1	3	4	8	54	-5	+6	+1
Aybar,Erick	11	18	10	16	4	7	19	3	4	7	13	99	-1	+18	+17
Baker,Jeff	2	14	5	6	1	3	3	2	0	2	8	39	-9	0	-9
Barajas,Rod	4	8	4	8	2	6	4	3	0	3	5	67	-4	0	-4
Barmes,Clint	5	25	3	10	3	6	12	1	3	4	9	79	-8	+1	-7
Barney,Darwin	14	42	7	14	4	6	19	1	1	2	14	105	+9	+5	+14
Bartlett,Jason	7	36	15	18	6	10	16	4	0	4	13	73	-2	+3	+1
Barton,Daric	3	18	6	11	3	6	7	1	0	1	6	48	-1	0	-1
Bautista,Jose	13	37	9	12	6	7	26	1	3	4	8	136	+23	-1	+22
Bay,Jason	14	39	6	14	2	8	15	1	1	2	8	96	+7	+9	+16
Beckham,Gordon	12	31	6	11	3	8	20	1	3	4	6	95	+11	-1	+10
Belt,Brandon	2	9	3	3	3	4	6	0	1	1	3	37	+5	-1	+4
Beltran,Carlos	10	35	11	21	4	8	18	0	0	1	18	144	+8	0	+8
Beltre,Adrian	10	24	8	15	4	8	14	1	0	1	13	117	+10	-1	+9
Berkman,Lance	9	49	18	26	4	6	15	1	2	3	7	103	+5	-10	-5
Bernadina,Roger	7	20	5	12	2	4	7	1	2	3	7	51	-6	+11	+5
Betancourt,Yuniesky	10	25	7	12	2	3	10	1	2	3	16	109	-3	-4	-7
Betemit,Wilson	2	11	5	13	2	3	8	3	0	3	7	83	-4	+2	-2
Bixler,Brian	0	8	1	2	0	0	5	0	0	0	1	15	+2	-2	0
Blake,Casey	7	24	6	10	1	3	9	1	1	2	9	49	-2	-3	-5
Blanks,Kyle	9	14	3	4	0	3	4	0	0	0	3	32	+8	+2	+10
Bloomquist,Willie	4	12	2	3	7	8	9	2	1	3	3	55	+5	0	+5
Boesch,Brennan	6	27	13	20	3	7	21	2	2	4	7	95	+9	-1	+8
Bogusevic,Brian	1	10	5	8	0	2	5	0	0	0	8	37	-3	0	-3
Bonifacio,Emilio	13	36	10	22	2	4	16	1	2	3	4	83	+8	+18	+26
Bourgeois,Jason	4	13	3	7	1	1	12	1	1	2	5	50	+4	+19	+23
Bourjos,Peter	10	18	11	16	5	6	16	2	1	3	7	82	+14	+4	+18
Bourn,Michael	4	41	25	34	10	12	25	2	1	3	6	79	+16	+33	+49
Brantley,Michael	7	25	10	19	4	6	14	0	0	0	11	74	+8	+3	+11
Braun,Ryan	8	23	13	17	7	11	16	4	3	7	9	132	+2	+21	+23
Brignac,Reid	1	6	5	5	1	4	3	1	1	2	2	45	-1	+1	0
Brown,Domonic	3	10	1	2	5	6	1	2	0	2	2	46	-1	+1	0
Bruce,Jay	8	26	14	18	4	7	12	5	1	6	8	122	0	-6	-6
Buck,John	1	14	8	19	1	2	7	1	0	2	11	91	-9	-2	-11
Buck,Travis	2	6	5	5	2	5	3	2	0	3	3	32	-4	-1	-5
Burrell,Pat	1	6	3	6	0	2	5	1	1	2	2	40	-2	0	-2
Burriss,Manny	7	10	4	8	0	2	8	0	0	0	2	30	+11	+5	+16
Butera,Drew	0	10	3	5	1	4	4	0	0	0	7	53	-2	0	-2
Butler,Billy	1	25	5	20	2	18	23	5	0	5	16	114	-19	0	-19
Byrd,Marlon	8	28	6	8	4	5	15	0	1	1	13	109	+11	-1	+10
Cabrera,Asdrubal	9	27	9	17	6	11	21	4	0	6	10	121	+4	+7	+11
Cabrera,Melky	15	39	17	27	11	16	19	2	2	4	13	135	+13	0	+13
Cabrera,Miguel	26	69	19	31	5	18	24	5	2	7	24	138	-8	0	-8
Cabrera,Orlando	6	23	8	13	1	4	14	2	0	2	12	95	+2	0	+2
Cairo,Miguel	7	19	3	10	4	4	3	0	1	1	3	51	+2	-5	-3
Callaspo,Alberto	12	29	11	13	4	4	9	7	1	8	11	80	-11	+6	-5
Cameron,Mike	3	6	3	7	1	1	7	0	1	2	6	54	0	+1	+1
Campana,Tony	4	8	2	5	1	1	9	1	1	2	1	24	+5	+20	+25
Cano,Robinson	5	21	15	24	5	9	19	2	3	5	18	151	-1	+4	+3
Carp,Mike	5	15	4	9	0	1	4	3	0	3	10	60	-11	-4	-15
Carrera,Ezequiel	4	9	4	6	2	2	9	1	0	1	4	40	+8	0	+8
Carroll,Jamey	10	37	12	19	2	6	9	2	1	3	3	76	+1	+10	+11

2011 Baserunning

Player	1st to 3rd Moved	Chances	2nd to Home Moved	Chances	1st to Home Moved	Chances	Bases Taken	Out Adv	Doubled Off	BR Outs	GDP	GDP Opps	BR Gain	SB Gain	Net Gain
Casilla,Alexi	13	24	12	19	2	4	15	5	2	7	4	74	+3	+7	+10
Castro,Starlin	5	38	13	21	4	9	18	3	3	6	20	124	-17	+4	-13
Cedeno,Ronny	3	12	9	13	3	7	9	0	0	0	11	89	+6	-8	-2
Chavez,Endy	4	15	4	6	3	5	7	1	0	1	7	50	+2	0	+2
Chavez,Eric	3	7	3	5	0	0	4	0	0	0	4	36	+4	0	+4
Chisenhall,Lonnie	3	6	7	11	3	3	5	1	2	3	3	32	-1	+1	0
Choo,Shin-Soo	5	22	6	9	4	5	16	2	1	3	7	68	+6	+2	+8
Coghlan,Chris	4	12	5	10	0	1	9	3	0	3	3	44	-1	-5	-6
Conger,Hank	4	8	0	1	0	0	4	0	0	0	2	30	+5	0	+5
Constanza,Jose	4	6	7	10	0	0	8	1	1	2	1	25	+6	-1	+5
Cora,Alex	0	4	1	2	3	4	5	0	0	0	4	35	+4	+2	+6
Counsell,Craig	4	5	3	5	2	4	8	0	0	0	1	32	+12	0	+12
Craig,Allen	5	13	4	5	1	4	2	0	1	1	7	43	-3	+5	+2
Crawford,Brandon	4	13	1	2	1	1	7	0	0	0	4	42	+7	-5	+2
Crawford,Carl	2	18	10	14	7	11	12	3	1	4	7	107	+2	+6	+8
Crisp,Coco	3	22	16	25	4	9	21	1	0	1	11	101	+12	+31	+43
Cruz,Nelson	2	14	5	14	1	5	14	1	0	1	8	94	+4	-1	+3
Cuddyer,Michael	17	34	10	15	5	8	4	7	0	7	18	119	-16	+9	-7
Cust,Jack	5	17	1	6	0	3	4	0	1	1	3	41	-3	0	-3
Damon,Johnny	9	31	8	12	4	14	18	3	0	3	4	116	+12	+7	+19
Davis,Chris	0	11	6	12	0	1	7	1	0	1	4	42	-1	+1	0
Davis,Ike	0	5	2	4	1	3	5	0	1	1	5	35	-2	0	-2
Davis,Rajai	5	11	5	9	2	2	10	0	0	0	4	49	+12	+12	+24
De Aza,Alejandro	4	11	4	5	0	0	8	2	1	3	2	37	+2	+2	+4
DeJesus,David	14	27	8	12	3	7	15	1	1	2	14	83	+8	-2	+6
Denorfia,Chris	9	21	2	12	1	3	15	2	0	2	10	52	0	-1	-1
Descalso,Daniel	8	16	7	12	1	5	17	2	1	3	3	67	+12	-2	+10
Desmond,Ian	6	20	16	19	4	8	20	3	0	3	9	104	+15	+5	+20
DeWitt,Blake	0	9	5	8	0	0	5	1	0	1	6	50	-2	+1	-1
Diaz,Matt	5	16	5	6	0	1	3	2	2	4	11	53	-14	+1	-13
Dirks,Andy	4	15	5	5	1	2	6	0	0	0	3	61	+10	+1	+11
Dobbs,Greg	4	24	7	12	0	6	12	1	1	2	12	75	-6	0	-6
Donald,Jason	1	8	3	4	1	2	2	0	1	1	2	22	-2	-1	-3
Doumit,Ryan	3	13	0	4	0	2	7	2	0	2	5	44	-5	-2	-7
Downs,Matt	2	9	3	6	2	3	5	4	0	4	3	56	-6	0	-6
Drew,J.D.	4	20	2	6	1	2	3	2	1	3	2	40	-8	-2	-10
Drew,Stephen	5	16	5	9	4	5	16	6	1	7	3	61	-2	-4	-6
Duda,Lucas	4	18	5	8	1	6	6	2	1	4	5	72	-8	+1	-7
Duncan,Shelley	2	15	6	9	0	2	3	0	1	1	7	57	-5	-2	-7
Dunn,Adam	1	29	3	13	0	4	8	1	0	1	10	111	-9	-2	-11
Ellis,Mark	9	21	12	15	3	6	15	1	1	2	8	105	+16	+4	+20
Ellsbury,Jacoby	18	39	24	33	2	6	22	6	1	7	8	112	+11	+9	+20
Encarnacion,Edwin	4	23	7	12	6	14	11	1	0	1	17	107	-4	+4	0
Escobar,Alcides	11	28	11	21	2	4	10	1	1	2	10	126	+6	+8	+14
Escobar,Yunel	13	37	11	14	5	11	16	2	3	5	14	87	-2	-3	-5
Espinosa,Danny	8	37	9	15	1	2	12	2	1	3	6	118	+4	+5	+9
Ethier,Andre	10	49	12	23	4	8	7	3	2	5	8	128	-11	-2	-13
Evans,Nick	1	14	7	8	3	4	4	1	0	1	6	39	-1	-2	-3
Fielder,Prince	8	40	10	24	2	12	15	2	1	3	17	136	-12	-1	-13
Figgins,Chone	7	11	2	8	1	4	10	3	1	4	6	61	-3	-1	-4
Fontenot,Mike	5	12	2	4	2	3	5	0	0	0	3	37	+7	+3	+10
Forsythe,Logan	4	7	1	4	0	0	5	0	0	0	3	29	+5	+1	+6
Fowler,Dexter	20	33	24	26	2	3	19	3	4	8	6	84	+14	-6	+8
Francisco,Ben	3	17	7	10	1	4	2	0	0	0	5	53	-1	-4	-5
Francoeur,Jeff	6	20	10	19	7	11	16	6	2	8	17	143	-12	+2	-10
Freeman,Freddie	4	34	9	18	2	5	9	3	2	5	15	134	-18	-4	-22
Freese,David	7	26	9	13	0	3	4	1	1	2	18	81	-14	+1	-13
Fukudome,Kosuke	5	38	6	19	8	12	14	4	1	5	8	69	-14	-8	-22
Fuld,Sam	2	11	10	12	1	1	10	1	0	1	3	51	+10	+4	+14
Furcal,Rafael	7	18	8	12	0	0	12	1	2	3	3	42	+5	-1	+4
Gardner,Brett	12	34	12	22	5	6	21	0	3	3	5	95	+17	+23	+40
Gentry,Craig	0	10	8	12	0	0	3	0	0	0	2	32	+1	+18	+19
Getz,Chris	7	23	7	13	6	13	11	1	2	3	5	71	+2	+7	+9
Giavotella,Johnny	3	10	2	3	2	5	5	1	1	2	4	31	-3	+1	-2

2011 Baserunning

Player	1st to 3rd Moved	Chances	2nd to Home Moved	Chances	1st to Home Moved	Chances	Bases Taken	Out Adv	Doubled Off	BR Outs	GDP	GDP Opps	BR Gain	SB Gain	Net Gain
Goldschmidt,Paul	1	7	2	7	2	6	7	1	0	1	4	36	-1	+4	+3
Gomes,Jonny	3	13	7	15	3	4	9	1	1	2	2	67	+5	+1	+6
Gomez,Carlos	5	11	8	9	0	0	10	5	2	7	2	50	-5	+12	+7
Gonzalez,Adrian	5	37	11	25	9	23	18	5	0	5	28	157	-24	+1	-23
Gonzalez,Alberto	2	11	9	12	1	1	7	2	1	3	5	41	-3	-3	-6
Gonzalez,Alex	7	20	12	19	1	4	10	4	0	4	19	119	-10	+2	-8
Gonzalez,Carlos	6	22	16	24	6	11	13	1	2	3	11	100	+3	+10	+13
Gordon,Alex	9	44	20	27	2	12	29	1	0	1	9	102	+21	+1	+22
Gordon,Dee	3	14	4	7	2	3	14	1	1	2	1	37	+9	+10	+19
Granderson,Curtis	12	28	14	20	12	17	16	0	2	2	12	142	+20	+5	+25
Greene,Tyler	4	7	3	6	2	3	3	0	0	0	3	20	+3	+11	+14
Guerrero,Vladimir	4	20	7	9	2	7	16	8	1	9	23	106	-27	-2	-29
Gutierrez,Franklin	4	19	7	11	1	4	5	0	0	0	6	56	+1	+9	+10
Guzman,Jesus	4	10	5	8	2	3	7	1	2	3	6	46	-3	+5	+2
Gwynn,Tony	8	19	7	10	1	2	13	2	1	3	2	54	+9	+10	+19
Hafner,Travis	0	17	6	12	3	6	9	2	0	2	7	73	-4	0	-4
Hairston,Jerry	5	16	7	15	2	5	8	4	1	5	7	65	-11	-1	-12
Hall,Bill	1	5	5	6	4	7	2	2	0	2	3	40	-2	-1	-3
Hamilton,Josh	9	30	10	19	6	9	14	2	4	6	8	108	-2	+6	+4
Hanigan,Ryan	2	18	6	7	1	4	7	0	0	0	3	59	+6	0	+6
Hannahan,Jack	6	19	6	15	2	4	7	0	0	0	7	68	+3	0	+3
Hardy,J.J.	8	16	8	15	4	7	17	3	3	6	10	102	+1	0	+1
Harris,Willie	2	18	7	11	1	3	11	0	0	0	6	58	+6	-3	+3
Harrison,Josh	2	6	4	5	2	2	9	1	0	1	6	37	+5	+2	+7
Hart,Corey	8	19	8	16	4	7	15	2	2	4	12	69	-3	-5	-8
Hawpe,Brad	7	18	4	4	1	3	5	1	0	1	7	41	+1	0	+1
Hayes,Brett	1	4	2	5	1	1	4	0	0	0	2	27	+3	0	+3
Headley,Chase	7	31	9	17	3	7	12	3	0	3	6	81	0	+9	+9
Heisey,Chris	1	13	10	13	2	2	7	1	3	4	1	39	-3	+4	+1
Helton,Todd	4	25	10	14	2	7	16	1	1	2	6	82	+7	-2	+5
Hernandez,Ramon	4	27	3	6	0	2	2	2	0	2	11	53	-16	0	-16
Herrera,Jonathan	6	20	5	5	3	7	10	0	0	0	7	59	+10	-4	+6
Heyward,Jason	14	22	7	11	2	4	13	2	0	2	7	85	+15	+5	+20
Hill,Aaron	6	20	12	20	4	7	14	4	0	4	10	101	+1	+7	+8
Hinske,Eric	3	16	4	8	2	2	2	2	1	3	5	51	-9	-2	-11
Holliday,Matt	9	31	14	20	4	4	11	2	3	5	21	106	-12	0	-12
Hosmer,Eric	7	32	16	22	7	11	14	2	2	4	13	115	+1	+1	+2
Howard,Ryan	3	34	7	21	4	13	14	3	1	4	10	116	-13	+1	-12
Hudson,Orlando	4	17	9	14	5	11	5	0	2	2	5	77	0	+13	+13
Huff,Aubrey	3	29	9	16	5	6	8	3	1	4	11	99	-11	-1	-12
Hughes,Luke	5	20	7	8	1	2	5	1	1	2	2	58	+3	-1	+2
Hundley,Nick	3	14	5	7	0	1	10	0	1	1	3	42	+6	-1	+5
Hunter,Torii	12	31	9	17	3	4	21	4	2	6	24	114	-9	-9	-18
Iannetta,Chris	9	20	5	9	2	3	10	0	1	1	10	85	+7	0	+7
Ibanez,Raul	1	30	11	26	6	6	10	2	0	2	13	103	-10	+2	-8
Infante,Omar	7	21	9	16	6	11	14	4	2	6	12	132	-4	0	-4
Inge,Brandon	3	16	1	8	1	1	8	0	1	1	9	71	-3	-1	-4
Izturis,Maicer	5	18	15	20	0	1	6	5	2	7	6	50	-16	-3	-19
Jackson,Austin	4	32	18	27	3	9	22	5	2	7	11	107	-6	+12	+6
Jackson,Conor	5	16	3	10	4	6	8	3	0	3	13	91	-8	+1	-7
Janish,Paul	5	13	6	11	1	3	4	1	0	1	7	86	+2	-1	+1
Jaso,John	5	12	3	4	0	6	3	1	2	3	9	42	-12	-3	-15
Jay,Jon	9	26	13	16	0	1	9	1	0	1	11	90	+6	-8	-2
Jennings,Desmond	2	8	3	4	3	3	13	0	2	2	1	41	+11	+8	+19
Jeter,Derek	4	27	11	15	2	6	22	1	1	3	10	87	+6	+4	+10
Johnson,Chris	2	19	4	9	2	4	9	1	1	2	2	72	+2	-2	0
Johnson,Elliot	1	5	3	8	1	2	3	0	0	0	3	37	+1	-8	-7
Johnson,Kelly	3	23	5	12	4	6	19	4	1	5	3	91	+3	+4	+7
Johnson,Reed	6	14	5	8	2	4	6	3	0	3	4	46	-1	0	-1
Johnson,Rob	0	4	2	4	0	0	1	1	0	1	3	28	-4	+3	-1
Jones,Adam	14	31	10	14	6	7	7	0	0	0	16	126	+11	+4	+15
Jones,Andruw	1	6	4	6	3	8	3	2	1	3	3	55	-5	0	-5
Jones,Chipper	7	29	8	12	2	5	6	2	1	4	10	95	-9	-2	-11
Jones,Garrett	4	21	6	16	1	8	12	4	4	8	7	95	-19	0	-19

2011 Baserunning

Player	1st to 3rd Moved	Chances	2nd to Home Moved	Chances	1st to Home Moved	Chances	Bases Taken	Out Adv	Doubled Off	BR Outs	GDP	GDP Opps	BR Gain	SB Gain	Net Gain
Joyce,Matt	9	20	12	16	6	8	12	1	1	2	7	114	+16	+11	+27
Kearns,Austin	4	12	1	1	1	1	5	0	1	1	2	30	+4	-8	-4
Kelly,Don	3	12	5	9	0	1	9	1	0	1	8	56	+1	0	+1
Kemp,Matt	17	38	23	25	4	8	18	6	3	10	16	157	-1	+18	+17
Kendrick,Howie	13	28	13	16	9	14	8	2	3	5	18	94	-7	+2	-5
Kennedy,Adam	4	14	6	8	1	3	5	1	0	1	3	64	+5	+4	+9
Keppinger,Jeff	5	26	5	10	5	8	12	2	1	3	11	60	-6	-2	-8
Kinsler,Ian	17	30	19	22	5	10	31	1	2	3	17	109	+28	+22	+50
Konerko,Paul	2	39	3	11	0	11	6	5	3	8	14	129	-40	-1	-41
Kotchman,Casey	9	30	8	15	0	4	13	1	1	2	13	87	-3	-2	-5
Kotsay,Mark	2	16	7	9	0	1	7	0	0	0	4	50	+6	+3	+9
Kouzmanoff,Kevin	1	8	6	8	0	4	6	2	1	3	4	44	-5	+2	-3
Kubel,Jason	3	19	6	12	1	3	4	0	2	2	8	71	-8	-1	-9
LaPorta,Matt	6	18	4	13	2	3	5	4	1	5	2	53	-10	+1	-9
LaRoche,Adam	3	8	0	3	0	1	4	0	1	1	2	26	-1	+1	0
Lawrie,Brett	2	6	5	5	1	3	2	0	0	0	0	24	+6	+5	+11
Lee,Carlos	9	28	6	20	2	9	16	8	2	10	9	115	-21	-2	-23
Lee,Derrek	6	24	5	11	2	10	13	2	0	2	14	81	-6	0	-6
Lewis,Fred	4	11	3	4	2	2	7	0	2	2	1	37	+5	-8	-3
Lillibridge,Brent	5	13	5	7	4	4	11	1	3	4	2	37	+4	-2	+2
Lind,Adam	7	25	2	9	0	4	7	1	0	1	12	132	-2	-1	-3
Loney,James	8	21	4	9	4	7	17	1	1	2	8	103	+12	+4	+16
Longoria,Evan	6	29	10	17	2	6	16	0	3	3	11	113	+2	-1	+1
Lopez,Jose	1	4	6	7	1	2	4	1	0	1	6	42	0	+2	+2
Lowrie,Jed	4	18	9	10	3	6	7	1	0	1	6	72	+6	-1	+5
Lucroy,Jonathan	1	12	4	9	2	3	12	4	1	5	7	78	-7	0	-7
Ludwick,Ryan	7	25	6	11	1	6	14	2	2	4	9	119	0	-1	-1
Markakis,Nick	14	41	18	23	5	11	12	5	0	5	16	128	-3	+6	+3
Marson,Lou	5	19	6	11	1	3	8	1	0	1	7	47	0	0	0
Martin,Russell	3	21	8	17	1	2	11	1	0	1	19	98	-8	+4	-4
Martinez,J.D.	2	8	4	8	4	6	2	0	2	2	4	37	-5	-2	-7
Martinez,Michael	3	7	6	7	5	7	3	1	1	2	2	46	+3	+3	+6
Martinez,Victor	8	46	14	29	2	15	19	3	2	5	20	137	-18	+1	-17
Mathis,Jeff	1	6	5	6	1	4	5	2	1	3	3	50	-3	-3	-6
Matsui,Hideki	5	29	10	16	1	7	17	1	0	1	10	108	+7	-1	+6
Mauer,Joe	6	15	8	11	2	5	9	0	1	1	9	56	+4	0	+4
Mayberry,John	3	13	7	11	1	1	6	1	0	1	6	61	+2	+2	+4
Maybin,Cameron	7	18	14	20	7	7	19	4	1	5	6	98	+13	+24	+37
McCann,Brian	1	17	2	7	2	10	2	2	0	2	10	103	-14	-1	-15
McCoy,Mike	8	17	3	4	3	5	10	1	1	2	0	29	+10	+8	+18
McCutchen,Andrew	6	35	16	21	2	8	18	4	1	5	7	89	-1	+3	+2
McDonald,Darnell	4	10	5	5	0	3	9	2	0	2	3	36	+5	-4	+1
McDonald,John	4	8	6	6	2	2	2	2	0	2	1	38	+3	-6	-3
McGehee,Casey	3	32	9	19	1	8	13	6	0	6	19	130	-24	-6	-30
McKenry,Michael	1	7	1	6	1	2	2	1	0	1	3	36	-5	-2	-7
McLouth,Nate	8	14	13	15	3	4	6	0	0	0	4	50	+15	0	+15
Miles,Aaron	11	31	6	6	5	6	12	1	1	2	11	100	+10	-2	+8
Miranda,Juan	5	12	2	5	0	2	2	2	1	3	1	29	-6	-2	-8
Molina,Jose	1	8	0	3	2	2	4	1	0	1	2	23	-2	0	-2
Molina,Yadier	8	25	5	13	2	6	8	2	0	3	21	106	-16	-6	-22
Montero,Miguel	5	26	13	19	3	10	14	5	0	5	14	99	-10	-1	-11
Morel,Brent	4	15	11	19	2	4	12	0	2	2	8	88	+5	-3	+2
Moreland,Mitch	7	27	5	12	4	8	10	0	3	3	9	103	-2	-2	-4
Morgan,Nyjer	10	29	12	18	7	9	21	3	1	4	6	82	+15	+5	+20
Morneau,Justin	2	6	4	8	1	2	8	2	0	2	8	61	-1	0	-1
Morrison,Logan	5	17	4	9	7	10	9	3	0	3	9	109	+1	0	+1
Morse,Michael	6	30	11	17	0	2	10	2	1	3	9	93	-4	-4	-8
Moustakas,Mike	4	19	3	10	0	4	7	4	0	4	5	62	-12	+2	-10
Murphy,Daniel	6	26	7	15	6	6	13	4	0	4	14	81	-7	-5	-12
Murphy,David	3	20	10	18	4	6	12	0	1	1	11	86	+3	-1	+2
Nady,Xavier	1	7	3	6	1	4	7	1	0	1	4	45	+1	+2	+3
Napoli,Mike	5	27	13	20	2	8	7	3	1	4	10	89	-11	0	-11
Navarro,Dioner	1	5	2	5	0	3	4	2	0	2	3	32	-5	0	-5
Nelson,Chris	1	5	3	5	2	2	5	1	1	2	5	37	-2	+1	-1

2011 Baserunning

Player	1st to 3rd		2nd to Home		1st to Home		Bases Taken	Out Adv	Doubled Off	BR Outs	GDP	GDP Opps	BR Gain	SB Gain	Net Gain
	Moved	Chances	Moved	Chances	Moved	Chances									
Nishioka,Tsuyoshi	3	17	6	8	0	1	2	0	0	0	1	40	+3	-6	-3
Nix,Laynce	3	18	6	9	2	3	5	0	0	0	1	64	+8	-2	+6
Nunez,Eduardo	3	16	7	13	0	1	16	5	1	6	6	68	-6	+10	+4
Olivo,Miguel	7	17	9	12	2	3	15	1	2	3	7	104	+13	-4	+9
Ordonez,Magglio	6	27	6	10	0	4	9	0	2	2	10	80	-4	0	-4
Ortiz,David	7	36	7	19	2	10	10	4	0	4	24	134	-26	-1	-27
Overbay,Lyle	3	12	4	8	1	9	8	1	0	1	13	84	-6	0	-6
Pagan,Angel	7	25	12	16	5	11	16	2	0	4	4	93	+9	+18	+27
Paredes,Jimmy	5	12	3	4	1	2	4	1	0	2	3	35	0	-3	-3
Parra,Gerardo	7	18	13	21	3	3	17	11	0	11	8	83	-14	+13	-1
Patterson,Corey	5	15	12	17	3	5	10	3	0	4	8	82	0	-5	-5
Paul,Xavier	3	6	5	9	2	2	7	3	2	5	2	42	-5	+4	-1
Paulino,Ronny	2	11	2	6	0	2	5	0	1	1	9	49	-7	0	-7
Pedroia,Dustin	14	47	10	22	8	20	21	3	2	5	12	135	0	+10	+10
Pena,Brayan	1	12	1	5	1	1	2	1	1	2	6	34	-11	0	-11
Pena,Carlos	14	29	6	11	7	17	17	4	1	5	6	143	+12	-2	+10
Pence,Hunter	11	32	13	15	6	10	19	1	1	2	15	136	+16	+4	+20
Pennington,Cliff	4	27	8	11	2	10	15	2	1	3	5	90	+3	-4	-1
Peralta,Jhonny	3	38	10	17	2	5	8	2	2	4	17	130	-19	-4	-23
Perez,Salvador	1	11	5	10	0	1	6	1	0	1	5	24	-4	0	-4
Petersen,Bryan	1	14	3	7	2	3	6	1	2	3	4	45	-7	+5	-2
Phillips,Brandon	16	35	13	20	5	8	23	6	1	8	15	114	+1	-4	-3
Pie,Felix	4	9	2	5	1	2	5	1	0	1	0	24	+4	-1	+3
Pierre,Juan	16	35	14	17	3	11	34	4	2	6	7	120	+25	-7	+18
Pierzynski,A.J.	5	20	3	12	0	2	11	2	1	3	19	92	-16	0	-16
Plouffe,Trevor	6	14	5	8	3	5	11	1	1	2	6	63	+7	-3	+4
Polanco,Placido	7	24	12	18	2	6	15	3	1	4	15	95	-4	+3	-1
Posada,Jorge	1	18	1	8	1	3	2	4	0	4	17	90	-28	-4	-32
Posey,Buster	3	9	2	2	2	5	3	0	0	0	4	23	+1	+3	+4
Prado,Martin	15	35	14	18	4	10	11	3	2	5	16	88	-6	-12	-18
Presley,Alex	4	6	2	4	1	5	7	2	0	2	1	26	+2	+3	+5
Pridie,Jason	3	9	6	9	1	1	6	0	2	2	2	41	+3	+5	+8
Pujols,Albert	14	42	16	22	0	5	13	6	3	9	29	133	-30	+7	-23
Punto,Nick	3	16	4	5	2	3	6	0	1	1	3	28	+2	-1	+1
Quentin,Carlos	8	25	7	13	0	7	7	2	1	3	7	106	-3	-1	-4
Quintero,Humberto	1	6	3	9	1	2	7	1	0	1	10	61	-4	+1	-3
Raburn,Ryan	6	15	7	12	3	6	11	1	0	1	4	78	+12	-1	+11
Ramirez,Alexei	14	29	12	18	6	11	25	3	3	6	19	137	+7	-3	+4
Ramirez,Aramis	3	21	6	18	6	16	16	5	2	7	12	123	-16	-1	-17
Ramirez,Hanley	6	13	7	11	5	8	14	2	1	3	6	69	+8	0	+8
Ramos,Wilson	13	24	6	14	1	4	6	1	0	1	19	80	-7	-4	-11
Rasmus,Colby	13	35	11	19	3	5	8	3	1	4	10	111	-1	+1	0
Reddick,Josh	8	16	3	7	2	4	8	1	1	2	1	54	+8	-3	+5
Reimold,Nolan	8	20	6	7	1	2	4	0	2	2	4	56	+2	+3	+5
Renteria,Edgar	4	13	6	8	0	5	9	1	0	1	7	68	+4	0	+4
Repko,Jason	2	5	6	8	1	1	4	0	1	1	0	23	+5	+3	+8
Revere,Ben	11	24	15	16	4	7	21	3	1	5	7	66	+14	+16	+30
Reyes,Jose	15	36	19	28	4	7	27	5	2	7	5	70	+13	+25	+38
Reynolds,Mark	6	22	10	19	1	6	18	1	4	5	11	109	-3	-2	-5
Rios,Alex	5	18	10	17	5	8	12	0	0	0	20	111	+2	-1	+1
Rivera,Juan	9	31	7	11	3	7	9	6	3	9	16	99	-26	-1	-27
Roberts,Ryan	18	35	14	17	3	6	17	2	2	4	6	101	+19	0	+19
Rodriguez,Alex	5	20	8	14	4	13	13	2	1	3	13	93	-5	+2	-3
Rodriguez,Sean	9	18	9	12	2	3	13	1	0	1	8	78	+14	-3	+11
Rolen,Scott	0	9	3	7	2	2	7	1	0	2	4	62	0	+1	+1
Rollins,Jimmy	13	33	14	20	3	5	21	4	1	5	9	85	+9	+14	+23
Ross,Cody	5	18	9	14	1	10	14	2	1	3	10	89	-1	+1	0
Ross,David	2	11	2	5	0	1	2	1	0	1	4	32	-5	-2	-7
Rowand,Aaron	10	18	7	12	1	2	17	1	0	1	6	45	+16	-4	+12
Ruiz,Carlos	3	25	15	22	0	4	5	3	2	5	7	84	-15	+1	-14
Ryan,Brendan	15	22	7	8	2	4	16	2	0	2	7	86	+21	+7	+28
Saltalamacchia,J.	4	22	7	12	0	5	11	0	0	0	7	80	+6	+1	+7
Sanchez,Angel	3	22	7	12	2	5	7	0	1	1	3	59	+2	+3	+5
Sanchez,Freddy	1	12	8	9	0	1	9	1	0	1	2	41	+7	-2	+5

2011 Baserunning

Player	1st to 3rd Moved	Chances	2nd to Home Moved	Chances	1st to Home Moved	Chances	Bases Taken	Out Adv	Doubled Off	BR Outs	GDP	GDP Opps	BR Gain	SB Gain	Net Gain
Sanchez,Gaby	14	44	13	19	4	9	16	2	3	5	18	115	-6	+1	-5
Sandoval,Pablo	7	26	7	15	0	4	14	1	2	3	12	81	-5	-6	-11
Sands,Jerry	3	9	2	4	1	1	6	0	1	1	5	39	+2	-3	-1
Santana,Carlos	12	40	10	21	7	12	12	3	2	5	15	140	-7	-1	-8
Santiago,Ramon	5	14	4	7	1	2	9	1	1	2	5	62	+4	0	+4
Schafer,Jordan	6	16	10	15	1	2	15	1	0	1	4	38	+13	+14	+27
Schierholtz,Nate	7	20	5	9	5	6	12	2	0	2	5	72	+10	-1	+9
Schumaker,Skip	11	29	3	10	1	1	21	2	2	4	10	68	+4	-4	0
Scott,Luke	4	10	1	4	1	4	5	1	0	1	2	38	+2	-1	+1
Scutaro,Marco	12	28	11	17	4	11	12	4	1	5	12	88	-5	0	-5
Seager,Kyle	3	6	0	4	2	3	7	0	0	0	4	31	+5	+1	+6
Shoppach,Kelly	0	9	1	3	0	1	1	0	0	0	5	43	-4	0	-4
Sizemore,Grady	2	11	7	11	0	1	12	0	1	1	4	55	+8	-4	+4
Sizemore,Scott	6	22	10	15	5	8	12	1	0	2	8	79	+6	-1	+5
Smith,Seth	6	26	6	11	0	4	16	2	0	2	9	104	+5	+6	+11
Smoak,Justin	5	19	4	7	1	8	7	2	2	4	10	82	-12	0	-12
Snider,Travis	0	5	4	5	3	5	5	0	1	1	5	34	0	+3	+3
Soriano,Alfonso	7	15	0	6	0	5	7	4	2	6	15	117	-19	0	-19
Soto,Geovany	2	11	6	10	3	9	11	4	1	6	12	81	-15	0	-15
Span,Denard	5	15	11	15	1	2	15	1	0	1	3	45	+15	+4	+19
Spilborghs,Ryan	3	7	3	4	2	4	6	2	3	5	10	50	-13	-2	-15
Stanton,Mike	7	25	8	14	2	6	12	2	0	2	11	110	+2	-5	-3
Stewart,Chris	1	7	1	5	3	4	4	0	0	0	2	31	+3	0	+3
Stubbs,Drew	14	25	15	25	7	11	24	1	2	3	2	94	+28	+20	+48
Suzuki,Ichiro	5	36	15	20	7	10	16	2	2	4	11	92	-1	+26	+25
Suzuki,Kurt	7	22	8	17	3	3	11	1	0	1	14	97	+2	-2	0
Sweeney,Ryan	2	13	5	9	1	5	16	3	2	5	7	68	-4	-1	-5
Swisher,Nick	11	40	8	18	5	12	8	4	2	6	18	108	-24	-2	-26
Tabata,Jose	11	26	12	18	2	5	6	1	1	2	8	45	-1	+2	+1
Teahen,Mark	2	9	4	5	0	1	2	0	0	0	3	39	+2	-2	0
Teixeira,Mark	4	30	6	10	2	9	20	0	0	0	12	145	+13	+2	+15
Tejada,Miguel	1	10	4	11	0	4	11	0	0	0	10	72	+1	-4	-3
Tejada,Ruben	6	17	8	14	2	2	9	1	0	1	6	75	+8	+3	+11
Thames,Eric	2	7	13	16	4	6	16	1	0	1	7	89	+18	0	+18
Theriot,Ryan	10	26	11	14	2	6	13	5	1	6	15	62	-12	-8	-20
Thole,Josh	3	20	5	11	2	6	6	4	0	4	8	72	-14	-4	-18
Thome,Jim	2	13	3	7	2	5	3	1	0	1	6	57	-5	0	-5
Tolbert,Matt	6	12	3	7	0	1	4	0	0	0	2	49	+7	-1	+6
Torrealba,Yorvit	2	14	6	17	2	5	6	3	1	4	11	79	-17	-4	-21
Torres,Andres	10	16	7	13	2	3	15	0	1	1	3	41	+17	+7	+24
Tosoni,Rene	1	7	3	8	2	2	2	1	0	1	2	37	-2	-4	-6
Treanor,Matt	4	15	4	6	0	4	2	0	1	1	3	40	-3	-2	-5
Trumbo,Mark	2	9	9	14	0	2	9	2	0	2	17	116	-5	+1	-4
Tulowitzki,Troy	9	34	11	20	3	6	12	5	2	8	16	119	-20	+3	-17
Turner,Justin	9	27	10	19	3	7	9	2	0	3	9	81	-3	+3	0
Uggla,Dan	15	28	13	16	4	5	10	2	2	4	9	124	+11	-5	+6
Upton,B.J.	12	26	9	17	6	11	14	5	2	7	16	130	-8	+12	+4
Upton,Justin	11	30	12	17	9	13	14	0	0	0	8	123	+23	+3	+26
Uribe,Juan	4	8	7	8	1	1	5	1	0	1	12	57	-1	+2	+1
Utley,Chase	15	22	10	11	2	4	15	1	0	1	3	102	+30	+14	+44
Valdez,Wilson	7	19	7	9	2	2	10	1	0	1	13	79	+5	-3	+2
Valencia,Danny	9	36	8	17	6	9	8	4	1	5	15	124	-13	-10	-23
Varitek,Jason	1	14	1	3	2	8	0	3	1	4	3	52	-16	0	-16
Venable,Will	2	11	7	11	2	2	13	0	2	2	2	51	+9	+20	+29
Victorino,Shane	20	39	14	19	2	7	21	1	1	2	4	101	+29	+13	+42
Vizquel,Omar	3	10	4	8	0	3	7	1	2	3	2	39	-3	-3	-6
Votto,Joey	13	46	8	16	2	12	26	5	1	6	20	150	-6	-4	-10
Walker,Neil	12	32	11	15	5	11	17	0	1	1	15	130	+14	-3	+11
Wallace,Brett	1	22	6	14	3	11	8	2	2	4	12	69	-20	-1	-21
Weeks,Jemile	2	19	7	14	4	5	17	5	3	8	3	61	-9	0	-9
Weeks,Rickie	8	26	12	17	1	3	17	6	3	9	6	69	-9	+5	-4
Wells,Casper	1	7	6	7	1	2	4	1	0	1	3	43	+2	-1	+1
Wells,Vernon	7	23	6	13	2	7	12	3	4	7	8	95	-12	+1	-11
Werth,Jayson	15	36	12	16	1	4	17	4	1	5	10	104	+6	+13	+19

2011 Baserunning

Player	1st to 3rd Moved	Chances	2nd to Home Moved	Chances	1st to Home Moved	Chances	Bases Taken	Out Adv	Doubled Off	BR Outs	GDP	GDP Opps	BR Gain	SB Gain	Net Gain
Whiteside,Eli	4	8	2	2	0	0	3	1	0	1	9	49	-2	0	-2
Wieters,Matt	5	28	8	14	2	7	11	1	1	2	16	89	-9	+1	-8
Wigginton,Ty	2	18	5	13	1	2	7	0	1	1	10	83	-5	+6	+1
Willingham,Josh	9	24	7	11	3	9	11	4	3	7	6	116	-5	+2	-3
Wilson,Jack	5	13	6	11	0	1	11	0	2	2	2	46	+7	+1	+8
Wood,Brandon	4	11	4	5	1	2	3	1	1	2	6	62	-2	0	-2
Wright,David	4	25	8	17	9	16	16	4	1	5	5	99	0	+9	+9
Youkilis,Kevin	4	26	8	16	7	8	21	4	2	6	14	123	-3	+3	0
Young,Chris	6	22	16	22	4	7	18	3	1	4	3	114	+15	+4	+19
Young,Delmon	7	30	10	16	7	15	17	4	2	6	19	97	-13	+1	-12
Young,Eric	10	20	6	8	1	3	12	1	0	1	1	25	+14	+19	+33
Young,Michael	9	35	16	25	9	12	12	0	0	0	17	110	+6	+2	+8
Zimmerman,Ryan	11	23	8	14	2	6	8	2	0	2	14	81	-3	+1	-2
Zobrist,Ben	9	33	11	18	10	13	17	1	1	2	9	123	+15	+7	+22

2011 Team Baserunning

Team	1st to 3rd Moved	1st to 3rd Chances	2nd to Home Moved	2nd to Home Chances	1st to Home Moved	1st to Home Chances	Bases Taken	Out Adv	Doubled Off	BR Outs	GDP	GDP Opps	BR Gain	SB Gain	Net Gain
Texas Rangers	96	311	128	217	49	86	179	15	15	30	135	1178	+60	+53	+113
San Diego Padres	83	267	102	165	31	62	145	25	14	39	105	1011	+13	+82	+95
Seattle Mariners	86	267	85	150	25	62	134	19	12	31	82	1039	+42	+45	+87
Tampa Bay Rays	77	253	93	146	38	81	144	16	13	29	101	1112	+54	+31	+85
Toronto Blue Jays	80	261	89	139	44	85	154	24	10	34	108	1141	+50	+27	+77
Philadelphia Phillies	90	324	127	207	37	77	146	25	10	35	108	1166	+26	+48	+74
New York Mets	92	352	118	208	45	91	166	27	10	41	112	1200	+12	+60	+72
Los Angeles Dodgers	108	337	106	167	33	67	148	27	16	44	101	1140	+24	+46	+70
Colorado Rockies	99	313	119	179	30	70	154	23	17	43	112	1147	+21	+34	+55
New York Yankees	71	287	103	182	44	95	166	21	14	36	146	1250	-6	+55	+49
Washington Nationals	91	284	91	157	19	50	128	23	10	33	103	1060	+11	+30	+41
San Francisco Giants	83	265	90	157	30	69	170	16	9	26	118	1036	+55	-17	+38
Oakland Athletics	68	288	103	177	33	80	171	27	12	40	82	1080	-2	+31	+29
Arizona D-Backs	71	254	98	160	46	82	159	45	10	55	82	1080	+5	+23	+28
Florida Marlins	79	265	87	170	35	70	149	21	12	34	111	1119	+14	+13	+27
Kansas City Royals	82	310	111	205	50	112	167	29	13	42	122	1146	-12	+37	+25
Cincinnati Reds	91	301	110	183	36	73	154	27	15	44	97	1157	+23	-3	+20
Cleveland Indians	85	313	112	197	45	80	154	25	10	38	111	1099	+13	+5	+18
Houston Astros	57	294	99	195	40	89	162	28	14	43	111	1103	-38	+52	+14
Milwaukee Brewers	73	272	109	182	34	73	160	35	16	52	114	1102	-29	+32	+3
Minnesota Twins	99	305	118	192	34	71	137	30	15	46	115	1107	-13	+14	+1
Baltimore Orioles	93	289	109	172	31	83	158	29	15	44	154	1111	-32	+31	-1
Boston Red Sox	96	350	120	205	51	122	170	38	12	51	136	1269	-31	+18	-13
Chicago Cubs	76	285	72	148	38	89	149	32	13	46	123	1160	-45	+23	-22
Los Angeles Angels	88	237	101	160	35	67	132	35	20	55	126	993	-54	+31	-23
Detroit Tigers	88	373	128	218	34	92	180	29	19	48	142	1292	-32	+9	-23
Atlanta Braves	95	281	114	175	28	59	105	26	12	39	113	1105	-13	-11	-24
Chicago White Sox	82	294	87	162	28	81	170	24	21	45	125	1199	-16	-25	-41
Pittsburgh Pirates	70	263	95	160	29	85	128	27	16	43	121	1070	-55	+4	-51
St Louis Cardinals	120	374	132	204	27	60	154	27	18	47	169	1156	-45	-21	-66
MLB Totals	2569	8869	3156	5339	1079	2363	4593	795	413	1233	3521	33854			

Relief Pitching

This section documents the bullpen performance of each major league team and every major league reliever. It has been redesigned from last year to make it more readable, but the information remains pretty much the same. We show each relief pitcher's role on his team last year along with his performance in twenty-some bullpen-specific performance categories. A modern bullpen consists of a Closer (CL), a Set Up Man or two set-up men (SU), some left-handers whose job is to get out left-handed hitters (LT), a Long Man (LM), and some auditioning relievers who pitch as they are needed and try to work their way into a better role, categorized as Utilty Relievers. Of course, there's the occasional starting pitcher or position player called to pitch in relief. We call these Emergency Relievers, or ER.

The Relief Pitching chart gets a minor facelift this year. Instead of one continuous table, we've split each team into its own table. Pitchers who appeared in games for more than one team have a role and data unique to that team. That means K-Rod is listed as a closer for the Mets, but a set up-man for the Brewers. The categories haven't changed. As a reminder, they are:

Usage: Games in Relief (Rel G), the number of times the pitcher entered the game before the seventh inning (Early Entry), pitching on consecutive days (Cons Days), long outings (LO), and Leverage Index (Lev Ind). We use the Leverage Index calculated by Tom Tango and published on FanGraphs.com. An average Leverage Index is 1.000. If a pitcher pitches frequently with the game on the line, his Leverage index will be high. If he pitches generally in the 6th inning of 7-2 ballgames, his leverage index will be very low.

Inherited Runners: The total (#), the number that scored (Scrd), and Percentage that scored (Pct).

Saves: A Save is considered "Easy" if the relief pitcher enters the game, pitches one inning or less, and the first batter he faces does not at least represent the tying run. A "Tough" Save is one in which the reliever enters with the tying run on base and a "Regular" Save is a Save Opportunity which is neither easy nor tough.

Relief Results: A Clean Outing (Clean) is any appearance in which a reliever does not allow a run to score and does not allow an inherited run to score. A BS Win is a Blown Save/Win. Sv-Opp is the number of saves and save opportunities. Holds are credited to any pitcher who enters the game with a Save

Opportunity, records at least one out, does not surrender the lead, and passes the ball to another reliever. We also display a pitcher's Save/Hold Percentage, Opponent OPS, and ERA (as a reliever only).

Arizona Diamondbacks

Pitcher	Pos	T	Rel G	Early Entry	Cons Days	Long	Lev Ind	#	Scrd	Pct	Easy	Reg	Tough	Clean	BS Win	Sv-Opp	Holds	Sv/Hld Pct	Opp OPS	Rel ERA
Putz, J.J.	CL	R	60	0	19	2	2.1	10	2	.20	30 - 31	15 - 18	0 - 0	46	1	45 - 49	0	.92	.566	2.17
Hernandez, David	SU	R	74	0	20	5	1.6	13	5	.38	8 - 10	3 - 3	0 - 1	58	0	11 - 14	23	.92	.561	3.38
Paterson, Joe	LT	L	62	7	23	2	1.0	47	11	.23	0 - 0	0 - 0	1 - 1	50	0	1 - 1	10	1.00	.626	2.91
Castillo, Alberto	LT	L	17	1	5	1	0.8	13	3	.23	0 - 0	0 - 0	0 - 0	14	0	0 - 0	3	1.00	.750	2.31
Duke, Zach	LT	L	12	7	0	7	0.3	4	3	.75	0 - 0	0 - 1	0 - 0	5	0	1 - 1	0	1.00	.754	3.86
Kroenke, Zach	LT	L	4	0	0	1	0.1	0	0		0 - 0	0 - 0	0 - 0	2	0	0 - 0	0		.924	9.00
Owings, Micah	LM	R	29	14	6	15	0.8	13	3	.23	0 - 0	0 - 0	0 - 0	18	0	0 - 0	3	1.00	.751	3.59
Demel, Sam	UR	R	34	7	11	2	1.0	27	10	.37	0 - 0	0 - 0	0 - 1	20	0	0 - 1	6	.86	.852	4.21
Shaw, Bryan	UR	R	33	2	7	2	0.8	12	2	.17	0 - 0	0 - 0	0 - 0	25	0	0 - 0	9	1.00	.699	2.54
Heilman, Aaron	UR	R	32	5	4	9	0.7	8	5	.63	0 - 0	0 - 1	0 - 0	17	1	0 - 1	5	.83	.931	6.88
Vasquez, Esmerling	UR	R	31	3	8	4	1.1	14	4	.29	0 - 0	0 - 1	0 - 1	20	0	0 - 2	6	.75	.687	4.15
Ziegler, Brad	UR	R	23	5	6	3	0.7	21	4	.19	0 - 0	0 - 0	0 - 0	18	0	0 - 0	4	1.00	.516	1.74
Gutierrez, Juan	UR	R	20	4	2	5	0.7	6	2	.33	0 - 1	0 - 0	0 - 0	11	0	0 - 1	2	.67	.793	5.40
Cook, Ryan	UR	R	12	1	3	0	0.8	2	1	.50	0 - 0	0 - 0	0 - 0	7	0	0 - 0	1	1.00	.797	7.04
Collmenter, Josh	UR	R	7	3	1	4	0.3	4	0	.00	0 - 0	0 - 0	0 - 0	6	0	0 - 0	0		.438	1.29
Mickolio, Kam	UR	R	6	3	0	1	1.2	3	3	1.00	0 - 0	0 - 0	0 - 0	3	0	0 - 0	1	1.00	.871	6.75
Brazoban, Yhency	UR	R	6	1	1	2	1.2	5	5	1.00	0 - 0	0 - 1	0 - 0	2	0	0 - 1	2	.67	.881	6.00
Miley, Wade	UR	L	1	0	0	0	0.1	0	0		0 - 0	0 - 0	0 - 0	0	0	0 - 0	0		1.667	18.00

Atlanta Braves

Pitcher	Pos	T	Rel G	Early Entry	Cons Days	Long	Lev Ind	#	Scrd	Pct	Easy	Reg	Tough	Clean	BS Win	Sv-Opp	Holds	Sv/Hld Pct	Opp OPS	Rel ERA
Kimbrel, Craig	CL	R	79	0	28	4	1.9	4	0	.00	28 - 31	17 - 22	1 - 1	66	1	46 - 54	0	.85	.499	2.10
Venters, Jonny	SU	L	85	0	33	7	1.8	20	5	.25	3 - 3	2 - 5	0 - 1	69	0	5 - 9	35	.91	.508	1.84
O'Flaherty, Eric	SU	L	78	5	30	4	1.6	31	9	.29	0 - 0	0 - 3	0 - 1	66	0	0 - 4	32	.89	.572	.98
Vizcaino, Arodys	SU	R	17	5	3	4	1.1	11	3	.27	0 - 1	0 - 0	0 - 1	11	0	0 - 2	5	.71	.636	4.67
Sherrill, George	LT	L	51	15	15	3	1.0	37	4	.11	0 - 0	0 - 1	0 - 0	40	0	0 - 1	7	.88	.659	3.00
Martinez, Cristhian	LM	R	46	23	5	17	0.7	27	7	.26	0 - 0	0 - 0	0 - 0	25	0	0 - 0	3	1.00	.586	3.36
Linebrink, Scott	UR	R	64	12	16	6	1.0	33	10	.30	0 - 0	0 - 0	1 - 2	46	0	1 - 2	7	.89	.785	3.64
Proctor, Scott	UR	R	31	4	8	6	1.0	21	7	.33	0 - 0	0 - 2	0 - 0	19	0	0 - 2	4	.67	.888	6.44
Gearrin, Cory	UR	R	18	3	3	4	1.2	8	2	.25	0 - 0	0 - 1	0 - 0	11	0	0 - 1	3	.75	.722	7.85
Varvaro, Anthony	UR	R	18	4	2	5	0.9	9	4	.44	0 - 0	0 - 1	0 - 0	9	0	0 - 1	1	.50	.594	2.63
Moylan, Peter	UR	R	13	4	2	0	1.3	9	0	.00	0 - 0	0 - 0	0 - 0	10	0	0 - 0	2	1.00	.738	3.24
Asencio, Jairo	UR	R	6	1	0	4	0.4	0	0		0 - 1	0 - 0	0 - 0	3	0	0 - 1	0	.00	.914	6.97
Medlen, Kris	UR	R	2	0	0	0	1.8	3	0	.00	0 - 0	0 - 0	0 - 0	2	0	0 - 0	0		.250	.00
Teheran, Julio	UR	R	2	2	0	2	0.2	2	0	.00	0 - 0	0 - 0	0 - 0	0	0	0 - 0	0		.924	7.94

Baltimore Orioles

Pitcher	Pos	T	Rel G	Early Entry	Cons Days	Long	Lev Ind	#	Scrd	Pct	Easy	Reg	Tough	Clean	BS Win	Sv-Opp	Holds	Sv/Hld Pct	Opp OPS	Rel ERA
Gregg, Kevin	CL	R	63	0	8	9	1.8	0	0		11 - 12	11 - 17	0 - 0	44	0	22 - 29	0	.76	.773	4.37
Johnson, Jim	SU	R	69	10	8	12	1.5	22	8	.36	4 - 5	5 - 8	0 - 1	48	1	9 - 14	18	.84	.628	2.67
Uehara, Koji	SU	R	43	0	9	4	1.2	10	4	.40	0 - 0	0 - 1	0 - 0	33	1	0 - 1	13	.93	.477	1.72
Rapada, Clay	LT	L	32	9	8	0	0.8	22	3	.14	0 - 0	0 - 0	0 - 0	22	0	0 - 0	5	1.00	.747	6.06
Phillips, Zach	LT	L	10	5	2	2	0.7	13	1	.08	0 - 0	0 - 0	0 - 0	8	0	0 - 0	0		.597	1.13
Hendrickson, Mark	LT	L	8	4	0	3	0.5	4	2	.50	0 - 0	0 - 0	0 - 0	3	0	0 - 0	0		.955	5.73
Viola, Pedro	LT	L	4	0	0	1	0.1	3	3	1.00	0 - 0	0 - 0	0 - 0	1	0	0 - 0	0		1.341	9.82
Gonzalez, Mike	LM	L	49	7	8	8	0.7	24	6	.25	0 - 0	0 - 1	1 - 1	32	0	1 - 2	6	.88	.766	4.27
Accardo, Jeremy	LM	R	31	12	3	10	1.1	10	3	.30	0 - 0	0 - 1	0 - 0	15	0	0 - 1	2	.67	.848	5.73
Jakubauskas, Chris	LM	R	27	14	2	15	0.3	16	6	.38	0 - 0	0 - 0	0 - 0	14	0	0 - 0	1	1.00	.864	5.00
Bergesen, Brad	LM	R	22	14	1	10	0.2	8	4	.50	0 - 0	0 - 0	0 - 0	12	0	0 - 0	0		.784	5.59

Baltimore Orioles

Pitcher	Pos	T	Usage					Inherited Runners			Saves			Relief Results						
			Rel G	Early Entry	Cons Days	Long	Lev Ind	#	Scrd	Pct	Easy	Reg	Tough	Clean	BS Win	Sv-Opp	Holds	Sv/Hld Pct	Opp OPS	Rel ERA
Patton, Troy	LM	L	20	9	2	8	0.7	14	5	.36	0 - 0	0 - 0	0 - 0	11	0	0 - 0	2	1.00	.567	3.00
Berken, Jason	UR	R	40	12	7	13	0.8	28	15	.54	0 - 0	0 - 1	0 - 2	21	0	0 - 3	4	.57	.943	5.36
Eyre, Willie	UR	R	19	1	3	0	1.0	9	1	.11	0 - 0	0 - 0	0 - 0	13	0	0 - 0	3	1.00	.568	3.44
Strop, Pedro	UR	R	12	0	2	1	1.9	3	0	.00	0 - 0	0 - 0	0 - 1	11	1	0 - 1	4	.80	.483	.73
Rupe, Josh	UR	R	9	3	0	4	0.1	7	5	.71	0 - 0	0 - 0	0 - 0	4	0	0 - 0	0		.933	5.65
Simon, Alfredo	UR	R	7	6	0	6	0.6	9	1	.11	0 - 0	0 - 0	0 - 0	2	0	0 - 0	0		.842	4.64
Reyes, Jo-Jo	UR	L	4	2	0	2	0.7	5	1	.20	0 - 0	0 - 0	0 - 0	2	0	0 - 0	0		.593	3.86
Worrell, Mark	UR	R	4	0	0	0	1.1	7	3	.43	0 - 0	0 - 0	0 - 0	2	0	0 - 0	0		1.655	36.00
VandenHurk, Rick	UR	R	2	1	0	1	0.2	2	0	.00	0 - 0	0 - 0	0 - 0	1	0	0 - 0	0		.774	2.45
Hunter, Tommy	UR	R	1	0	0	0	1.5	0	0		0 - 0	0 - 0	0 - 0	0	0	0 - 0	1	1.00	.900	9.00
Guthrie, Jeremy	ER	R	2	1	0	1	1.1	2	1	.50	0 - 0	0 - 0	0 - 0	0	0	0 - 0	0		.649	2.08

Boston Red Sox

Pitcher	Pos	T	Usage					Inherited Runners			Saves			Relief Results						
			Rel G	Early Entry	Cons Days	Long	Lev Ind	#	Scrd	Pct	Easy	Reg	Tough	Clean	BS Win	Sv-Opp	Holds	Sv/Hld Pct	Opp OPS	Rel ERA
Papelbon, Jonathan	CL	R	63	0	15	7	1.7	10	3	.30	22 - 22	8 - 9	1 - 3	47	0	31 - 34	0	.91	.546	2.94
Bard, Daniel	SU	R	70	1	22	7	1.7	34	5	.15	1 - 3	0 - 1	0 - 2	53	0	1 - 6	34	.88	.546	3.33
Morales, Franklin	LT	L	36	6	9	2	0.9	16	6	.38	0 - 0	0 - 0	0 - 0	26	0	0 - 0	8	1.00	.765	3.62
Doubront, Felix	LT	L	11	4	2	2	0.4	9	3	.33	1 - 1	0 - 0	0 - 0	7	0	1 - 1	0	1.00	.952	6.10
Hill, Rich	LT	L	9	2	1	0	0.9	8	0	.00	0 - 0	0 - 0	0 - 0	9	0	0 - 0	3	1.00	.349	.00
Hottovy, Tommy	LT	L	8	1	2	0	0.5	6	0	.00	0 - 0	0 - 0	0 - 0	6	0	0 - 0	2	1.00	.821	6.75
Okajima, Hideki	LT	L	7	0	1	3	1.6	5	2	.40	0 - 0	0 - 0	0 - 0	4	0	0 - 0	0		.643	4.32
Williams, Randy	LT	L	7	2	0	2	1.1	6	1	.17	0 - 0	0 - 0	0 - 0	3	0	0 - 0	1	1.00	.809	6.48
Reyes, Dennys	LT	L	4	1	2	0	0.5	0	0		0 - 0	0 - 0	0 - 0	3	0	0 - 0	0		.933	16.20
Miller, Trever	LT	L	3	1	0	0	0.6	2	0	.00	0 - 0	0 - 0	0 - 0	3	0	0 - 0	0		.000	.00
Albers, Matt	LM	R	56	19	8	18	0.9	22	10	.45	0 - 1	0 - 1	0 - 1	35	1	0 - 3	10	.77	.733	4.73
Aceves, Alfredo	LM	R	51	20	10	23	1.0	29	11	.38	0 - 0	2 - 3	0 - 2	28	1	2 - 5	11	.81	.596	2.03
Atchison, Scott	LM	R	17	12	4	8	0.3	10	4	.40	0 - 0	1 - 1	0 - 0	10	0	1 - 1	0	1.00	.710	3.26
Wheeler, Dan	UR	R	47	10	8	7	0.4	17	6	.35	0 - 0	0 - 0	0 - 0	31	0	0 - 0	4	1.00	.694	4.38
Jenks, Bobby	UR	R	19	1	3	3	1.5	4	1	.25	0 - 0	0 - 2	0 - 0	13	0	0 - 2	2	.50	.870	6.32
Bowden, Michael	UR	R	14	4	1	8	0.2	6	1	.17	0 - 0	0 - 0	0 - 0	8	0	0 - 0	0		.700	4.05
Wakefield, Tim	UR	R	10	3	1	4	0.1	9	3	.33	0 - 0	0 - 0	0 - 0	4	0	0 - 0	0		.722	3.63
Miller, Andrew	UR	L	5	0	0	3	0.3	3	1	.33	0 - 0	0 - 0	0 - 0	2	0	0 - 0	0		.745	5.40
Tazawa, Junichi	UR	R	3	1	0	1	0.1	2	0	.00	0 - 0	0 - 0	0 - 0	1	0	0 - 0	0		.974	6.00
Weiland, Kyle	UR	R	2	0	0	0	0.0	0	0		0 - 0	0 - 0	0 - 0	2	0	0 - 0	0		.200	.00
Matsuzaka, Daisuke	UR	R	1	0	0	0	3.5	0	0		0 - 0	0 - 0	0 - 0	0	0	0 - 0	0		1.071	18.00
McDonald, Darnell	ER	R	1	0	0	0	0.0	0	0		0 - 0	0 - 0	0 - 0	0	0	0 - 0	0		1.000	18.00

Chicago Cubs

Pitcher	Pos	T	Usage					Inherited Runners			Saves			Relief Results						
			Rel G	Early Entry	Cons Days	Long	Lev Ind	#	Scrd	Pct	Easy	Reg	Tough	Clean	BS Win	Sv-Opp	Holds	Sv/Hld Pct	Opp OPS	Rel ERA
Marmol, Carlos	CL	R	75	0	27	14	2.0	17	5	.29	19 - 23	13 - 17	2 - 4	59	1	34 - 44	2	.78	.643	4.01
Marshall, Sean	SU	L	78	3	23	6	1.6	29	8	.28	3 - 3	1 - 4	1 - 2	61	0	5 - 9	34	.91	.566	2.26
Wood, Kerry	SU	R	55	0	14	6	1.7	21	9	.43	0 - 1	1 - 4	0 - 2	37	1	1 - 7	21	.79	.715	3.35
Russell, James	LT	L	59	14	18	7	0.7	42	11	.26	0 - 0	0 - 0	0 - 2	41	1	0 - 2	6	.75	.666	2.19
Grabow, John	LT	L	58	13	9	8	0.6	17	5	.29	0 - 0	0 - 0	0 - 0	33	0	0 - 0	5	1.00	.811	4.76
Maine, Scott	LT	L	7	3	2	4	0.2	5	1	.20	0 - 0	0 - 0	0 - 0	4	0	0 - 0	1	1.00	1.276	10.29

Chicago Cubs

Pitcher	Pos	T	Usage					Inherited Runners			Saves			Relief Results						
			Rel G	Early Entry	Cons Days	Long	Lev Ind	#	Scrd	Pct	Easy	Reg	Tough	Clean	BS Win	Sv-Opp	Holds	Sv/Hld Pct	Opp OPS	Rel ERA
Gaub, John	LT	L	4	2	1	0	0.4	3	1	.33	0-0	0-0	0-0	2	0	0-0	0		.633	6.75
Ortiz, Ramon	LM	R	20	9	4	4	0.4	5	1	.20	0-0	0-0	0-0	14	0	0-0	1	1.00	.678	3.86
Samardzija, Jeff	UR	R	75	22	19	22	1.0	27	7	.26	0-0	0-1	0-1	54	0	0-2	13	.87	.613	2.97
Mateo, Marcos	UR	R	23	4	7	4	0.7	11	3	.27	0-0	0-0	0-0	17	0	0-0	2	1.00	.741	4.30
Carpenter, Chris	UR	R	10	4	2	2	0.7	11	9	.82	0-0	0-0	0-0	5	0	0-0	0		.878	2.79
Lopez, Rodrigo	UR	R	10	2	1	2	0.4	5	2	.40	0-0	0-0	0-0	5	0	0-0	0		.798	3.72
Berg, Justin	UR	R	8	6	1	2	0.3	8	2	.25	0-0	0-0	0-0	5	0	0-0	0		.797	3.75
Cashner, Andrew	UR	R	6	3	0	0	0.7	1	0	.00	0-0	0-0	0-0	5	0	0-0	1	1.00	.259	1.69
Stevens, Jeff	UR	R	4	3	0	1	0.2	6	0	.00	0-0	0-0	0-0	2	0	0-0	0		.816	5.14
Dolis, Rafael	UR	R	1	1	0	0	0.4	1	0	.00	0-0	0-0	0-0	1	0	0-0	0		.250	.00
Coleman, Casey	ER	R	2	1	0	0	0.2	2	0	.00	0-0	0-0	0-0	1	0	0-0	0		1.500	20.25

Chicago White Sox

Pitcher	Pos	T	Usage					Inherited Runners			Saves			Relief Results						
			Rel G	Early Entry	Cons Days	Long	Lev Ind	#	Scrd	Pct	Easy	Reg	Tough	Clean	BS Win	Sv-Opp	Holds	Sv/Hld Pct	Opp OPS	Rel ERA
Santos, Sergio	CL	R	63	0	10	9	1.8	16	2	.13	16-18	10-14	4-4	49	1	30-36	2	.84	.596	3.55
Crain, Jesse	SU	R	67	1	12	9	1.8	44	14	.32	0-0	0-2	1-5	44	2	1-7	24	.81	.655	2.62
Thornton, Matt	SU	L	62	2	8	12	1.5	36	9	.25	1-2	2-4	0-1	42	0	3-7	20	.85	.649	3.32
Sale, Chris	SU	L	58	4	10	16	1.6	38	7	.18	4-5	1-2	3-3	40	0	8-10	16	.92	.612	2.79
Ohman, Will	LT	L	59	20	12	7	0.6	52	12	.23	0-0	0-0	0-1	37	0	0-1	3	.75	.745	4.22
Santiago, Hector	LT	L	2	1	1	1	0.2	2	0	.00	0-0	0-0	0-0	2	0	0-0	0		.170	.00
Bruney, Brian	UR	R	23	3	5	3	0.5	13	2	.15	0-0	0-0	0-0	17	0	0-0	3	1.00	.981	6.86
Frasor, Jason	UR	R	20	3	3	4	1.0	12	3	.25	0-0	0-0	0-0	11	0	0-0	4	1.00	.871	5.09
Pena, Tony	UR	R	17	6	2	6	0.5	8	2	.25	0-0	0-1	0-0	8	0	0-1	0	.00	.806	6.20
Kinney, Josh	UR	R	13	3	1	5	0.1	8	5	.63	0-0	0-0	0-0	7	0	0-0	0		.881	6.62
Gray, Jeff	UR	R	6	3	0	5	0.2	3	1	.33	0-0	0-0	0-0	4	0	0-0	0		.708	2.70
Reed, Addison	UR	R	6	1	0	2	0.3	3	3	1.00	0-0	0-0	0-0	4	0	0-0	0		.802	3.68
Lindsay, Shane	UR	R	4	1	0	3	0.0	0	0		0-0	0-0	0-0	2	0	0-0	0		1.091	12.00
Harrell, Lucas	UR	R	3	1	0	1	0.1	2	0	.00	0-0	0-0	0-0	2	0	0-0	0		.982	7.20
Stewart, Zach	UR	R	2	1	1	2	0.9	3	0	.00	0-0	0-0	0-0	1	0	0-0	0		.786	4.15
Axelrod, Dylan	UR	R	1	0	0	1	0.6	0	0		0-0	0-0	0-0	1	0	0-0	0		.708	.00
Humber, Philip	ER	R	2	1	0	1	0.2	1	0	.00	0-0	0-0	0-0	1	0	0-0	0		.664	9.00
Floyd, Gavin	ER	R	1	0	0	0	2.4	0	0		0-0	0-0	0-0	0	0	0-0	0		1.400	9.00
Peavy, Jake	ER	R	1	1	0	1	1.3	0	0		0-0	0-0	0-0	1	0	0-0	0		.154	.00

Cincinnati Reds

Pitcher	Pos	T	Usage					Inherited Runners			Saves			Relief Results						
			Rel G	Early Entry	Cons Days	Long	Lev Ind	#	Scrd	Pct	Easy	Reg	Tough	Clean	BS Win	Sv-Opp	Holds	Sv/Hld Pct	Opp OPS	Rel ERA
Cordero, Francisco	CL	R	68	0	21	5	2.1	2	2	1.00	22-24	15-19	0-0	53	0	37-43	0	.86	.591	2.45
Chapman, Aroldis	SU	L	54	3	11	5	1.4	18	3	.17	0-0	1-3	0-0	42	0	1-3	13	.88	.534	3.60
Bray, Bill	LT	L	79	4	28	2	1.3	59	13	.22	0-0	0-0	0-3	61	0	0-3	20	.87	.606	2.98
Horst, Jeremy	LT	L	12	4	1	4	0.3	9	4	.44	0-0	0-0	0-0	5	0	0-0	0		.816	2.93
Maloney, Matt	LT	L	6	4	0	5	0.2	0	0		0-0	0-0	0-0	2	0	0-0	0		.988	6.00
LeCure, Sam	LM	R	39	17	5	14	0.7	28	5	.18	0-0	0-0	0-0	24	0	0-0	5	1.00	.582	3.32
Smith, Jordan	LM	R	17	9	3	3	0.7	11	4	.36	0-1	0-0	0-0	7	0	0-1	2	.67	1.070	7.20
Masset, Nick	UR	R	75	2	18	7	1.3	28	11	.39	1-2	0-3	0-2	51	1	1-7	14	.71	.729	3.71
Ondrusek, Logan	UR	R	66	10	18	6	1.3	35	10	.29	0-1	0-1	0-1	44	0	0-3	14	.82	.676	3.23
Arredondo, Jose	UR	R	53	9	10	9	1.1	13	5	.38	0-0	0-1	0-0	34	1	0-1	4	.80	.720	3.23
Fisher, Carlos	UR	R	17	6	1	5	0.9	3	2	.67	0-0	0-0	0-0	10	0	0-0	0		.732	4.50
Burton, Jared	UR	R	6	3	0	0	0.6	3	2	.67	0-0	0-0	0-0	4	0	0-0	1	1.00	.988	3.86
Thompson, Daryl	UR	R	1	1	0	1	0.7	0	0		0-0	0-0	0-0	0	0	0-0	0		1.050	15.00
Reineke, Chad	UR	R	1	1	0	0	0.5	1	0	.00	0-0	0-0	0-0	1	0	0-0	0		.500	.00
Wood, Travis	ER	L	4	1	0	1	0.8	4	0	.00	0-0	0-0	0-0	4	0	0-0	0		.330	.00
Leake, Mike	ER	R	3	0	0	0	1.1	1	1	1.00	0-0	0-0	0-0	1	0	0-0	0		1.000	4.50

Cleveland Indians

Pitcher	Pos	T	Rel G	Early Entry	Cons Days	Long	Lev Ind	#	Scrd	Pct	Easy	Reg	Tough	Clean	BS Win	Sv-Opp	Holds	Sv/Hld Pct	Opp OPS	Rel ERA
			Usage					**Inherited Runners**			**Saves**			**Relief Results**						
Perez, Chris	CL	R	64	0	16	7	2.2	13	5	.38	17 - 18	18 - 20	1 - 2	44	1	36 - 40	0	.90	.648	3.32
Sipp, Tony	SU	L	69	0	17	4	1.3	36	15	.42	0 - 0	0 - 0	0 - 1	49	0	0 - 1	24	.96	.664	3.03
Pestano, Vinnie	SU	R	68	0	12	5	1.6	23	6	.26	2 - 2	0 - 4	0 - 0	53	0	2 - 6	23	.86	.577	2.32
Perez, Rafael	LT	L	71	13	20	5	1.0	44	7	.16	0 - 0	0 - 1	0 - 1	47	0	0 - 2	12	.86	.650	3.00
Hagadone, Nick	LT	L	9	3	2	4	0.4	8	3	.38	0 - 0	0 - 0	0 - 0	6	0	0 - 0	0		.380	4.09
Durbin, Chad	LM	R	56	23	12	20	0.7	34	10	.29	0 - 0	0 - 0	0 - 1	27	0	0 - 1	3	.75	.872	5.53
Herrmann, Frank	LM	R	40	14	8	16	0.4	16	7	.44	0 - 0	0 - 0	0 - 0	21	0	0 - 0	0		.810	5.11
Smith, Joe	UR	R	71	9	18	4	1.1	37	14	.38	0 - 1	0 - 1	0 - 1	53	0	0 - 3	16	.84	.541	2.01
Judy, Josh	UR	R	12	3	0	4	0.2	7	7	1.00	0 - 0	0 - 0	0 - 0	5	0	0 - 0	0		1.061	7.07
Germano, Justin	UR	R	9	2	1	3	0.3	2	2	1.00	0 - 0	0 - 0	0 - 0	6	0	0 - 0	0		.815	5.68
Putnam, Zach	UR	R	8	1	1	0	0.7	1	0	.00	0 - 0	0 - 1	0 - 0	5	0	0 - 1	0	.00	.915	6.14
Kluber, Corey	UR	R	3	1	0	2	0.0	3	3	1.00	0 - 0	0 - 0	0 - 0	1	0	0 - 0	0		.740	8.31
Gomez, Jeanmar	UR	R	1	1	0	1	1.4	0	0		0 - 0	0 - 0	0 - 0	0	0	0 - 0	0		.641	3.00
Huff, David	UR	L	1	0	0	0	4.8	2	1	.50	0 - 0	0 - 0	0 - 0	0	0	0 - 0	0		2.000	
Masterson, Justin	ER	R	1	0	0	0	0.5	0	0		0 - 0	0 - 0	0 - 0	1	0	0 - 0	0		.250	.00

Colorado Rockies

Pitcher	Pos	T	Rel G	Early Entry	Cons Days	Long	Lev Ind	#	Scrd	Pct	Easy	Reg	Tough	Clean	BS Win	Sv-Opp	Holds	Sv/Hld Pct	Opp OPS	Rel ERA
			Usage					**Inherited Runners**			**Saves**			**Relief Results**						
Street, Huston	CL	R	62	0	17	4	1.8	5	3	.60	19 - 21	10 - 12	0 - 0	43	0	29 - 33	4	.89	.781	3.86
Betancourt, Rafael	SU	R	68	0	20	3	1.2	11	2	.18	5 - 7	3 - 4	0 - 1	51	0	8 - 12	22	.88	.558	2.89
Lindstrom, Matt	SU	R	63	5	14	1	1.4	28	12	.43	1 - 2	0 - 1	1 - 2	43	0	2 - 5	15	.85	.661	3.00
Brothers, Rex	SU	L	48	11	15	3	1.2	18	4	.22	1 - 1	0 - 2	0 - 0	38	0	1 - 3	16	.89	.644	2.88
Reynolds, Matt	LT	L	73	14	21	5	1.0	52	12	.23	0 - 0	0 - 1	0 - 1	53	0	0 - 2	18	.90	.820	4.09
Morales, Franklin	LT	L	14	4	1	2	1.0	5	3	.60	0 - 0	0 - 0	0 - 0	8	0	0 - 0	2	1.00	.739	3.86
Romero, J.C.	LT	L	12	4	2	0	0.5	6	0	.00	0 - 0	0 - 0	0 - 0	8	0	0 - 0	0		.861	4.32
Stults, Eric	LT	L	6	5	0	3	0.2	7	1	.14	0 - 0	0 - 0	0 - 0	1	0	0 - 0	0		.802	6.00
Belisle, Matt	UR	R	74	18	24	13	1.2	44	12	.27	0 - 1	0 - 2	0 - 4	51	3	0 - 7	14	.67	.721	3.25
Roenicke, Josh	UR	R	19	5	5	1	1.1	11	4	.36	0 - 0	0 - 0	0 - 0	15	0	0 - 0	4	1.00	.657	3.78
Paulino, Felipe	UR	R	18	0	4	1	1.1	2	2	1.00	0 - 0	0 - 1	0 - 0	11	0	0 - 1	2	.67	1.041	7.36
Escalona, Edgmer	UR	R	14	6	2	5	0.6	6	0	.00	0 - 0	0 - 0	0 - 0	11	0	0 - 0	0		.586	1.75
Reynolds, Greg	UR	R	10	4	0	4	0.3	4	4	1.00	0 - 0	0 - 0	0 - 0	4	0	0 - 0	0		.911	7.31
Mortensen, Clayton	UR	R	10	4	0	6	0.3	5	1	.20	0 - 0	0 - 0	0 - 0	5	0	0 - 0	0		.781	3.42
Daley, Matt	UR	R	7	1	3	0	0.4	2	0	.00	0 - 0	0 - 0	0 - 0	4	0	0 - 0	0		.954	10.50
Miller, Jim	UR	R	6	2	1	1	0.2	3	1	.33	0 - 0	0 - 0	0 - 0	3	0	0 - 0	0		.546	2.57
Rogers, Esmil	UR	R	5	4	0	5	0.4	0	0		0 - 0	0 - 0	0 - 0	0	0	0 - 0	0		.913	11.91
Hammel, Jason	UR	R	5	2	0	3	1.1	0	0		0 - 0	1 - 1	0 - 0	3	0	1 - 1	0	1.00	.603	1.74
Billings, Bruce	UR	R	1	0	0	1	0.0	0	0		0 - 0	0 - 0	0 - 0	0	0	0 - 0	0		1.222	4.50
Gonzalez, Edgar	UR	R	1	0	0	1	0.3	0	0		0 - 0	0 - 0	0 - 0	0	0	0 - 0	0		1.045	9.00
Cook, Aaron	ER	R	1	0	0	1	0.1	0	0		0 - 0	0 - 0	0 - 0	0	0	0 - 0	0		1.714	27.00

Detroit Tigers

Pitcher	Pos	T	Rel G	Early Entry	Cons Days	Long	Lev Ind	#	Scrd	Pct	Easy	Reg	Tough	Clean	BS Win	Sv-Opp	Holds	Sv/Hld Pct	Opp OPS	Rel ERA
Valverde, Jose	CL	R	75	0	23	5	1.8	6	0	.00	33-33	16-16	0-0	63	0	49-49	0	1.00	.580	2.24
Benoit, Joaquin	SU	R	66	0	15	5	1.5	29	9	.31	0-1	2-5	0-1	53	1	2-7	29	.86	.581	2.95
Schlereth, Daniel	LT	L	49	6	11	9	0.7	29	9	.31	0-0	0-0	0-1	34	0	0-1	7	.88	.699	3.49
Coke, Phil	LT	L	34	3	8	5	1.3	17	7	.41	0-0	1-2	0-0	24	0	1-2	8	.90	.779	3.71
Purcey, David	LT	L	19	2	2	7	0.7	5	4	.80	0-0	0-0	0-0	12	0	0-0	2	1.00	.887	7.23
Below, Duane	LT	L	12	6	1	5	0.8	6	1	.17	0-0	0-0	0-0	6	0	0-0	0		.647	4.19
Thomas, Brad	LT	L	12	3	3	2	0.3	12	10	.83	0-0	0-0	0-0	3	0	0-0	0		.974	9.00
Wilk, Adam	LT	L	5	4	0	4	0.2	1	0	.00	0-0	0-0	0-0	0	0	0-0	0		.780	5.40
Furbush, Charlie	LM	L	15	9	0	7	0.7	12	3	.25	0-0	0-0	0-0	8	0	0-0	1	1.00	.762	2.16
Alburquerque, Al	UR	R	41	8	6	12	1.1	31	3	.10	0-0	0-0	0-0	35	0	0-0	6	1.00	.438	1.87
Perry, Ryan	UR	R	36	8	6	8	0.9	28	8	.29	0-0	0-1	0-0	21	1	0-1	4	.80	.768	5.35
Villarreal, Brayan	UR	R	16	6	4	4	0.8	13	7	.54	0-0	0-0	0-0	7	0	0-0	1	1.00	.921	6.75
Pauley, David	UR	R	14	6	1	6	0.7	7	4	.57	0-0	0-0	0-1	4	0	0-1	1	.50	.900	5.95
Oliveros, Lester	UR	R	9	2	3	0	0.5	4	0	.00	0-0	0-0	0-0	6	0	0-0	1	1.00	.633	5.63
Gonzalez, Enrique	UR	R	8	2	0	4	0.5	5	3	.60	0-0	0-0	0-1	3	0	0-1	0	.00	1.032	10.00
Marte, Luis	UR	R	4	0	1	0	0.5	2	2	1.00	0-0	0-0	0-0	2	0	0-0	0		.849	2.45
Ruffin, Chance	UR	R	2	2	0	1	0.9	3	2	.67	0-0	0-0	0-0	1	0	0-0	0		1.125	4.91
Weinhardt, Robbie	UR	R	2	0	1	0	0.3	1	0	.00	0-0	0-0	0-0	0	0	0-0	0		1.222	10.80
Fister, Doug	UR	R	1	1	0	1	1.1	0	0		0-0	0-0	0-0	0	0	0-0	0		.455	.00
Kelly, Don	ER	R	1	0	0	0	0.0	1	0	.00	0-0	0-0	0-0	1	0	0-0	0		.000	.00

Florida Marlins

Pitcher	Pos	T	Rel G	Early Entry	Cons Days	Long	Lev Ind	#	Scrd	Pct	Easy	Reg	Tough	Clean	BS Win	Sv-Opp	Holds	Sv/Hld Pct	Opp OPS	Rel ERA
Nunez, Leo	CL	R	68	1	23	2	1.9	16	6	.38	24-28	11-12	1-2	49	1	36-42	0	.86	.691	4.06
Mujica, Edward	SU	R	67	9	17	7	1.2	36	9	.25	0-0	0-2	0-1	44	0	0-3	17	.85	.638	2.96
Hensley, Clay	SU	R	28	0	8	1	1.6	2	2	1.00	0-1	0-0	0-1	21	0	0-2	8	.80	.645	3.51
Dunn, Mike	LT	L	72	12	18	13	1.1	46	15	.33	0-0	0-2	0-2	44	0	0-4	15	.79	.723	3.43
Choate, Randy	LT	L	54	3	18	1	1.1	43	6	.14	0-0	0-0	0-0	44	0	0-0	14	1.00	.562	1.82
Sanches, Brian	LM	R	37	22	2	17	0.4	19	0	.00	0-0	0-0	0-0	22	0	0-0	0		.671	3.51
Webb, Ryan	UR	R	53	7	10	7	1.2	30	10	.33	0-0	0-1	0-3	33	0	0-4	8	.67	.693	3.20
Badenhop, Burke	UR	R	50	18	7	13	0.7	30	15	.50	0-0	1-1	0-0	29	0	1-1	5	1.00	.689	4.10
Cishek, Steve	UR	R	45	7	7	12	0.9	16	3	.19	2-2	0-0	1-1	32	0	3-3	2	1.00	.591	2.63
Ceda, Jose	UR	R	17	4	1	6	0.3	4	0	.00	0-0	0-0	0-0	12	0	0-0	0		.608	4.43
Hatcher, Chris	UR	R	11	3	2	2	0.4	10	1	.10	0-0	0-0	0-0	6	0	0-0	0		.960	6.97
Rosario, Sandy	UR	R	4	1	0	0	0.1	2	2	1.00	0-0	0-0	0-0	2	0	0-0	0		.826	2.45
Sanabia, Alex	UR	R	1	0	0	0	0.0	0	0		0-0	0-0	0-0	1	0	0-0	0		1.000	.00
Petersen, Bryan	ER	R	1	0	0	0	0.0	0	0		0-0	0-0	0-0	1	0	0-0	0		.250	.00

Houston Astros

Pitcher	Pos	T	Rel G	Early Entry	Cons Days	Long	Lev Ind	#	Scrd	Pct	Easy	Reg	Tough	Clean	BS Win	Sv- Opp	Holds	Sv/Hld Pct	Opp OPS	Rel ERA
Melancon, Mark	CL	R	71	2	21	8	1.6	17	4	.24	14 - 16	4 - 6	2 - 3	54	1	20 - 25	3	.82	.631	2.78
Abad, Fernando	SU	L	29	7	9	2	1.1	11	5	.45	0 - 1	0 - 0	0 - 1	19	0	0 - 2	7	.78	.946	7.32
Escalona, Sergio	LT	L	49	8	21	1	1.0	35	9	.26	0 - 0	0 - 1	0 - 0	36	0	0 - 1	6	.86	.687	2.93
Wright, Wesley	LT	L	21	2	8	0	1.5	20	4	.20	0 - 0	0 - 0	0 - 0	18	0	0 - 1	3	.75	.583	1.50
Cedeno, Xavier	LT	L	3	1	0	1	0.4	2	0	.00	0 - 0	0 - 0	0 - 0	2	0	0 - 0	0		1.818	27.00
Lopez, Wilton	UR	R	73	14	20	10	1.1	34	16	.47	0 - 0	0 - 4	0 - 2	50	0	0 - 6	14	.70	.686	2.79
Del Rosario, Enerio	UR	R	54	16	9	11	0.6	28	11	.39	0 - 0	0 - 2	0 - 0	33	0	0 - 2	2	.50	.743	4.58
Rodriguez, Fernando	UR	R	47	6	10	14	1.2	21	3	.14	0 - 0	0 - 0	0 - 0	32	0	0 - 0	6	1.00	.781	3.96
Fulchino, Jeff	UR	R	36	3	8	5	0.9	16	7	.44	0 - 0	0 - 1	0 - 2	20	0	0 - 3	4	.57	.804	5.18
Rodriguez, Aneury	UR	R	35	10	6	12	0.3	8	2	.25	0 - 0	0 - 0	0 - 0	17	0	0 - 0	1	1.00	.714	4.80
Carpenter, David	UR	R	34	6	9	1	1.3	19	8	.42	0 - 0	1 - 1	0 - 1	25	0	1 - 2	3	.80	.809	2.93
Lyon, Brandon	UR	R	15	0	2	2	2.4	0	0		1 - 3	3 - 5	0 - 0	7	2	4 - 8	0	.50	1.133	11.48
Valdez, Jose	UR	R	12	1	1	5	0.2	6	2	.33	0 - 0	0 - 0	0 - 0	7	0	0 - 0	1	1.00	.867	9.00
Abreu, Juan	UR	R	7	0	0	0	0.1	0	0		0 - 0	0 - 0	0 - 0	5	0	0 - 0	0		.835	2.70
Lyles, Jordan	UR	R	5	1	1	1	1.0	0	0		0 - 0	0 - 0	0 - 0	2	0	0 - 0	0		.867	12.46
Harrell, Lucas	UR	R	4	1	0	1	1.3	2	0	.00	0 - 0	0 - 0	0 - 0	2	0	0 - 0	0		.425	3.86
Pendleton, Lance	UR	R	4	1	0	1	0.0	0	0		0 - 0	0 - 0	0 - 0	0	0	0 - 0	0		1.525	17.36
Figueroa, Nelson	UR	R	3	1	0	2	0.1	0	0		0 - 0	0 - 0	0 - 0	1	0	0 - 0	0		1.110	11.25
Myers, Brett	ER	R	1	0	0	1	0.0	0	0		0 - 0	0 - 0	0 - 0	0	0	0 - 0	0		.875	4.50

Kansas City Royals

Pitcher	Pos	T	Rel G	Early Entry	Cons Days	Long	Lev Ind	#	Scrd	Pct	Easy	Reg	Tough	Clean	BS Win	Sv- Opp	Holds	Sv/Hld Pct	Opp OPS	Rel ERA
Soria, Joakim	CL	R	60	0	14	7	2.1	10	5	.50	18 - 20	10 - 15	0 - 0	44	1	28 - 35	0	.80	.709	4.03
Holland, Greg	SU	R	46	7	5	14	1.4	33	2	.06	1 - 1	2 - 2	1 - 3	34	0	4 - 6	18	.92	.521	1.80
Collins, Tim	LT	L	68	17	16	14	1.0	42	10	.24	0 - 1	0 - 0	0 - 0	42	0	0 - 1	11	.92	.681	3.63
Teaford, Everett	LT	L	23	4	4	7	0.5	17	5	.29	0 - 1	0 - 0	0 - 0	14	0	1 - 1	1	1.00	.722	3.21
Adcock, Nathan	LM	R	21	14	1	16	0.4	16	3	.19	0 - 0	1 - 2	0 - 0	10	0	1 - 2	0	.50	.730	4.18
Crow, Aaron	UR	R	57	3	3	7	1.7	29	8	.28	0 - 1	0 - 2	0 - 4	40	1	0 - 7	8	.53	.711	2.76
Wood, Blake	UR	R	55	12	5	18	0.9	28	9	.32	0 - 1	1 - 1	0 - 1	31	0	1 - 3	5	.75	.716	3.75
Coleman, Louis	UR	R	48	15	5	13	1.2	39	5	.13	0 - 0	1 - 1	0 - 1	32	0	1 - 2	11	.92	.685	2.87
Jeffress, Jeremy	UR	R	14	2	1	4	1.1	7	5	.71	0 - 0	1 - 2	0 - 0	9	0	1 - 2	0	.50	.706	4.70
Tejeda, Robinson	UR	R	9	0	2	0	1.4	3	0	.00	0 - 0	0 - 0	0 - 0	4	0	0 - 0	2	1.00	1.041	6.14
Texeira, Kanekoa	UR	R	6	2	0	1	0.9	2	1	.50	0 - 0	0 - 0	0 - 0	3	0	0 - 0	1	1.00	.876	2.84
Chavez, Jesse	UR	R	4	1	0	4	0.2	2	2	1.00	0 - 0	0 - 0	0 - 0	1	0	0 - 0	0		1.112	10.57
Mazzaro, Vin	UR	R	3	2	0	2	0.3	4	3	.75	0 - 0	0 - 0	0 - 0	1	0	0 - 0	0		1.145	21.32
Herrera, Kelvin	UR	R	2	0	0	0	1.2	0	0		0 - 0	0 - 0	0 - 0	1	0	0 - 0	1	1.00	1.232	13.50
O'Sullivan, Sean	UR	R	2	1	0	2	1.9	0	0		0 - 0	0 - 1	0 - 0	0	0	0 - 1	0	.00	1.011	11.25
Paulino, Felipe	ER	R	1	1	0	1	0.8	2	0	.00	0 - 0	0 - 0	0 - 0	1	0	0 - 0	0		.143	.00
Maier, Mitch	ER	R	1	0	0	0	0.0	0	0		0 - 0	0 - 0	0 - 0	1	0	0 - 0	0		.750	.00

Los Angeles Angels

Pitcher	Pos	T	Rel G	Early Entry	Cons Days	Long	Lev Ind	#	Scrd	Pct	Easy	Reg	Tough	Clean	BS Win	Sv-Opp	Holds	Sv/Hld Pct	Opp OPS	Rel ERA
Walden, Jordan	CL	R	62	0	10	6	2.5	10	2	.20	18-20	14-19	0-3	47	1	32-42	2	.77	.642	2.98
Downs, Scott	SU	L	60	2	15	1	2.0	36	10	.28	1-1	0-0	0-3	47	0	1-4	26	.90	.539	1.34
Rodney, Fernando	SU	R	39	1	7	3	1.7	12	5	.42	3-4	0-1	0-2	24	1	3-7	10	.76	.672	4.50
Takahashi, Hisanori	LT	L	61	12	13	12	1.0	50	14	.28	0-0	1-2	1-3	36	1	2-5	7	.75	.663	3.44
Ramirez, Horacio	LT	L	12	3	1	1	0.4	6	1	.17	0-0	0-0	0-0	8	0	0-0	0		1.018	6.00
Thompson, Rich	LM	R	44	13	3	17	0.7	25	7	.28	0-0	0-0	0-1	29	0	0-1	3	.75	.637	3.00
Cassevah, Bobby	UR	R	30	7	3	11	0.8	16	4	.25	0-0	0-1	0-0	20	0	0-1	6	.86	.582	2.72
Bell, Trevor	UR	R	19	4	0	9	0.5	7	2	.29	0-0	0-0	0-1	10	0	0-1	0	.00	.760	3.41
Jepsen, Kevin	UR	R	16	1	2	1	1.8	13	1	.08	0-0	0-1	0-0	10	0	0-1	2	.67	.981	7.62
Kohn, Michael	UR	R	14	0	2	2	1.1	5	3	.60	0-0	1-1	0-1	7	0	1-2	1	.67	1.080	7.30
Rodriguez, Francisco	UR	R	10	2	1	5	0.2	5	2	.40	0-0	0-0	0-0	7	0	0-0	1	1.00	.712	4.61
Bulger, Jason	UR	R	5	0	0	3	2.1	3	0	.00	0-0	0-0	0-0	3	0	0-0	0		.736	.96
Williams, Jerome	UR	R	4	3	0	2	0.5	5	2	.40	0-0	0-0	0-0	1	0	0-0	0		1.633	14.40
Richards, Garrett	UR	R	4	0	0	0	0.6	0	0		0-0	0-0	0-0	1	0	0-0	0		1.069	5.40
Pineiro, Joel	ER	R	3	2	0	3	0.1	0	0		0-0	0-0	0-0	1	0	0-0	0		.730	5.63
Chatwood, Tyler	ER	R	2	2	0	2	0.3	4	4	1.00	0-0	0-0	0-0	0	0	0-0	0		.937	3.38
Haren, Dan	ER	R	1	0	0	0	1.7	0	0		0-0	0-0	0-0	1	0	0-0	0		.000	.00

Los Angeles Dodgers

Pitcher	Pos	T	Rel G	Early Entry	Cons Days	Long	Lev Ind	#	Scrd	Pct	Easy	Reg	Tough	Clean	BS Win	Sv-Opp	Holds	Sv/Hld Pct	Opp OPS	Rel ERA
Guerra, Javy	CL	R	47	0	11	7	1.4	8	3	.38	9-10	11-12	1-1	38	0	21-23	0	.91	.608	2.31
Padilla, Vicente	SU	R	9	1	0	1	1.8	0	0		2-2	1-1	0-0	6	0	3-3	5	1.00	.656	4.15
Elbert, Scott	LT	L	47	4	10	1	0.8	33	12	.36	1-1	1-1	0-0	35	0	2-2	7	1.00	.611	2.43
Kuo, Hong-Chih	LT	L	40	8	5	3	0.8	24	4	.17	0-0	0-2	0-0	22	0	0-2	3	.60	.819	9.00
Guerrier, Matt	UR	R	70	7	16	1	1.2	41	19	.46	1-1	0-2	0-1	44	0	1-4	13	.82	.633	4.07
MacDougal, Mike	UR	R	69	11	15	1	1.1	51	17	.33	0-0	1-1	0-0	47	0	1-2	14	.94	.691	2.05
Jansen, Kenley	UR	R	51	12	8	11	1.0	21	1	.05	3-4	1-1	1-1	43	0	5-6	9	.93	.494	2.85
Hawksworth, Blake	UR	R	49	13	8	8	0.9	20	10	.50	0-0	0-1	0-0	27	0	0-1	7	.88	.651	4.08
Lindblom, Josh	UR	R	27	11	5	6	0.8	15	5	.33	0-0	0-1	0-0	18	0	0-1	3	.75	.572	2.73
Troncoso, Ramon	UR	R	18	3	2	7	0.2	10	5	.50	0-0	0-0	0-0	10	0	0-0	0		1.014	6.75
Broxton, Jonathan	UR	R	14	0	5	2	1.7	4	0	.00	6-6	1-2	0-0	7	0	7-8	0	.88	.840	5.68
Cormier, Lance	UR	R	9	0	1	7	0.3	2	0	.00	0-0	0-0	0-0	2	0	0-0	0		1.063	9.88
Eovaldi, Nathan	UR	R	4	0	0	0	0.8	0	0		0-0	0-0	0-0	2	0	0-0	1	1.00	.830	10.13
Ely, John	UR	R	4	1	0	2	0.4	0	0		0-0	0-0	0-0	3	0	0-0	0		.582	2.57
de la Rosa, Rubby	UR	R	3	0	0	2	1.7	0	0		0-0	0-1	0-0	2	1	0-1	1	.50	.458	1.80

Milwaukee Brewers

Pitcher	Pos	T	Rel G	Early Entry	Cons Days	Long	Lev Ind	#	Scrd	Pct	Easy	Reg	Tough	Clean	BS Win	Sv-Opp	Holds	Sv/Hld Pct	Opp OPS	Rel ERA
Axford, John	CL	R	74	0	23	4	1.9	1	0	.00	30-31	16-17	0-0	60	0	46-48	0	.96	.557	1.95
Loe, Kameron	SU	R	72	7	20	4	1.2	34	13	.38	0-0	0-2	1-6	51	0	1-8	16	.71	.638	3.50
Hawkins, LaTroy	SU	R	52	3	8	1	1.0	6	1	.17	0-0	0-0	0-0	41	0	0-0	20	1.00	.624	2.42
Rodriguez, Francisco	SU	R	31	0	12	1	1.8	8	3	.38	0-1	0-2	0-0	25	2	0-3	17	.85	.566	1.86
Saito, Takashi	SU	R	30	3	1	2	1.4	9	3	.33	0-0	0-2	0-0	24	0	0-2	10	.83	.620	2.03
Braddock, Zach	LT	L	25	3	4	2	0.6	6	1	.17	0-0	0-1	0-0	16	0	0-1	3	.75	.757	7.27
Stetter, Mitch	LT	L	16	5	3	0	0.8	12	6	.50	0-0	0-0	0-0	11	0	0-0	1	1.00	.889	5.14

Milwaukee Brewers

Pitcher	Pos	T	Rel G	Early Entry	Cons Days	Long	Lev Ind	#	Scrd	Pct	Easy	Reg	Tough	Clean	BS Win	Sv-Opp	Holds	Sv/Hld Pct	Opp OPS	Rel ERA
Herrera, Daniel	LT	L	2	2	1	1	0.6	2	2	1.00	0 - 0	0 - 0	0 - 0	0	0	0 - 0	0		1.736	21.60
Mitre, Sergio	LM	R	22	9	1	8	0.6	10	2	.20	0 - 0	0 - 0	0 - 1	13	0	0 - 1	1	.50	.683	3.27
Estrada, Marco	UR	R	36	9	5	15	0.8	11	4	.36	0 - 1	0 - 2	0 - 0	21	0	0 - 3	4	.57	.714	4.38
Dillard, Tim	UR	R	24	4	5	3	0.4	11	3	.27	0 - 0	0 - 0	0 - 0	15	0	0 - 0	1	1.00	.658	4.08
Green, Sean	UR	R	14	1	6	2	0.9	5	1	.20	0 - 0	0 - 0	0 - 0	8	0	0 - 0	1	1.00	.737	5.40
de la Cruz, Frankie	UR	R	11	1	2	3	0.2	4	3	.75	0 - 0	0 - 0	0 - 0	8	0	0 - 0	0		.543	2.77
Kintzler, Brandon	UR	R	9	4	1	5	0.5	2	1	.50	0 - 0	0 - 0	0 - 0	3	0	0 - 0	0		.725	3.68
McClendon, Mike	UR	R	9	1	0	5	0.5	1	1	1.00	0 - 0	0 - 0	0 - 0	6	0	0 - 0	0		.686	2.63
DiFelice, Mark	UR	R	3	0	1	0	0.1	0	0		0 - 0	0 - 0	0 - 0	1	0	0 - 0	0		.940	12.00
Fiers, Michael	UR	R	2	0	0	0	0.1	0	0		0 - 0	0 - 0	0 - 0	2	0	0 - 0	0		.786	.00
Narveson, Chris	ER	L	2	1	0	0	0.1	0	0		0 - 0	0 - 0	0 - 0	2	0	0 - 0	0		.100	.00

Minnesota Twins

Pitcher	Pos	T	Rel G	Early Entry	Cons Days	Long	Lev Ind	#	Scrd	Pct	Easy	Reg	Tough	Clean	BS Win	Sv-Opp	Holds	Sv/Hld Pct	Opp OPS	Rel ERA
Capps, Matt	CL	R	69	0	19	3	1.5	34	9	.26	7 - 8	7 - 11	1 - 5	46	2	15 - 24	7	.71	.726	4.25
Nathan, Joe	CL	R	48	1	3	4	1.5	9	4	.44	8 - 9	6 - 7	0 - 1	31	0	14 - 17	8	.88	.705	4.84
Perkins, Glen	SU	L	65	6	15	4	1.4	44	14	.32	0 - 0	0 - 1	2 - 4	42	1	2 - 5	17	.86	.644	2.48
Mijares, Jose	LT	L	58	7	9	10	0.8	43	11	.26	0 - 0	0 - 1	0 - 1	36	0	0 - 2	10	.83	.797	4.59
Dumatrait, Phil	LT	L	45	14	9	10	0.7	37	9	.24	0 - 0	1 - 1	0 - 0	25	0	1 - 1	4	1.00	.822	3.92
Hughes, Dusty	LT	L	15	1	2	4	0.4	10	4	.40	0 - 0	0 - 0	0 - 0	8	0	0 - 0	0		1.125	9.95
James, Chuck	LT	L	8	3	1	6	0.5	8	1	.13	0 - 0	0 - 0	0 - 0	5	0	0 - 0	0		.762	6.10
Swarzak, Anthony	LM	R	16	13	1	11	0.6	14	4	.29	0 - 0	0 - 0	0 - 0	4	0	0 - 0	0		.717	3.99
Burnett, Alex	UR	R	66	14	17	5	0.9	62	10	.16	0 - 0	0 - 0	0 - 2	43	0	0 - 2	10	.83	.749	5.51
Hoey, Jim	UR	R	26	4	4	3	0.7	27	11	.41	0 - 0	0 - 1	0 - 0	12	0	0 - 1	2	.67	.942	5.47
Oliveros, Lester	UR	R	10	3	0	5	0.4	5	2	.40	0 - 0	0 - 0	0 - 0	5	0	0 - 0	0		.698	4.05
Waldrop, Kyle	UR	R	7	5	1	3	0.7	0	0		0 - 0	0 - 0	0 - 0	2	0	0 - 0	0		.652	5.73
Slowey, Kevin	UR	R	6	3	1	2	0.4	2	2	1.00	0 - 0	0 - 0	0 - 0	2	0	0 - 0	0		.811	4.91
Manship, Jeff	UR	R	5	3	0	1	0.3	5	3	.60	0 - 0	0 - 0	0 - 0	2	0	0 - 0	0		1.166	8.10
Hacker, Eric	UR	R	2	2	0	2	0.8	3	3	1.00	0 - 0	0 - 0	0 - 0	1	0	0 - 0	0		.658	.00
Slama, Anthony	UR	R	2	2	0	1	1.4	1	0	.00	0 - 0	0 - 0	0 - 0	2	0	0 - 0	1	1.00	.222	.00
Duensing, Brian	ER	L	4	2	0	1	0.8	0	0		0 - 0	0 - 0	0 - 0	2	0	0 - 0	0		.827	5.06
Baker, Scott	ER	R	2	0	0	1	0.1	0	0		0 - 0	0 - 0	0 - 0	2	0	0 - 0	0		.222	.00
Liriano, Francisco	ER	L	2	2	0	1	0.8	0	0		0 - 0	0 - 0	0 - 0	1	0	0 - 0	0		1.000	19.29
Cuddyer, Michael	ER	R	1	0	0	0	0.0	0	0		0 - 0	0 - 0	0 - 0	1	0	0 - 0	0		1.100	.00

New York Mets

Pitcher	Pos	T	Rel G	Early Entry	Cons Days	Long	Lev Ind	#	Scrd	Pct	Easy	Reg	Tough	Clean	BS Win	Sv-Opp	Holds	Sv/Hld Pct	Opp OPS	Rel ERA
Rodriguez, Francisco	CL	R	42	0	15	6	1.8	13	2	.15	13 - 14	8 - 10	2 - 2	33	1	23 - 26	0	.88	.727	3.16
Parnell, Bobby	SU	R	60	1	16	13	1.4	18	9	.50	5 - 6	1 - 5	0 - 1	36	0	6 - 12	11	.74	.679	3.64
Isringhausen, Jason	SU	R	53	0	13	3	1.9	13	3	.23	4 - 4	3 - 7	0 - 0	36	0	7 - 11	19	.87	.653	4.05
Acosta, Manny	SU	R	44	6	8	7	1.2	17	7	.41	1 - 1	2 - 4	1 - 2	29	1	4 - 7	7	.79	.759	3.45
Byrdak, Tim	LT	L	72	5	26	0	1.1	67	16	.24	0 - 0	0 - 1	0 - 3	49	0	1 - 4	8	.75	.688	3.82
Herrera, Daniel	LT	L	16	4	7	0	1.2	12	3	.25	0 - 0	0 - 0	0 - 0	12	0	0 - 0	1	1.00	.612	1.13
O'Connor, Mike	LT	L	9	2	1	1	0.8	6	5	.83	0 - 0	0 - 0	0 - 1	6	0	0 - 1	2	.67	.550	2.70
Misch, Pat	LT	L	6	3	1	4	0.3	8	4	.50	0 - 0	0 - 0	0 - 0	2	0	0 - 0	0		.995	10.29
Beato, Pedro	UR	R	60	14	11	10	0.9	36	11	.31	0 - 0	0 - 0	0 - 1	36	0	0 - 1	11	.92	.719	4.30
Igarashi, Ryota	UR	R	45	11	13	11	1.0	46	18	.39	0 - 0	0 - 0	0 - 1	26	0	0 - 1	2	.67	.796	4.66

New York Mets

Pitcher	Pos	T	Usage					Inherited Runners			Saves			Relief Results						
			Rel G	Early Entry	Cons Days	Long	Lev Ind	#	Scrd	Pct	Easy	Reg	Tough	Clean	BS Win	Sv-Opp	Holds	Sv/Hld Pct	Opp OPS	Rel ERA
Carrasco, D.J.	UR	R	41	14	7	6	0.5	26	6	.23	0 - 1	0 - 0	0 - 0	23	0	0 - 1	2	.67	.875	5.91
Buchholz, Taylor	UR	R	23	6	4	5	0.9	14	7	.50	0 - 0	0 - 0	0 - 0	13	0	0 - 0	5	1.00	.701	3.12
Stinson, Josh	UR	R	14	1	4	1	1.2	4	2	.50	1 - 1	0 - 0	0 - 1	10	0	1 - 2	4	.83	.824	6.92
Thayer, Dale	UR	R	11	1	3	1	0.7	8	2	.25	0 - 0	0 - 0	0 - 0	5	0	0 - 0	0		.729	3.48
Batista, Miguel	UR	R	5	2	0	0	1.2	2	0	.00	0 - 0	0 - 0	0 - 0	3	0	0 - 0	1	1.00	.646	3.86
Boyer, Blaine	UR	R	5	2	1	2	1.0	2	1	.50	1 - 1	0 - 0	0 - 0	1	0	1 - 1	0	1.00	1.202	10.80
Gee, Dillon	ER	R	3	1	1	2	0.8	2	0	.00	0 - 0	0 - 0	0 - 0	2	0	0 - 0	0		.725	8.31
Capuano, Chris	ER	L	2	1	0	0	0.6	2	0	.00	0 - 0	0 - 0	0 - 0	1	0	0 - 0	1	1.00	1.071	9.00
Pelfrey, Mike	ER	R	1	0	0	0	0.0	0	0		0 - 0	0 - 0	0 - 0	0	0	0 - 0	0		2.000	27.00
Dickey, R.A.	ER	R	1	0	0	0	1.4	0	0		0 - 0	0 - 0	0 - 0	1	0	0 - 0	1	1.00	.500	.00
Niese, Jonathon	ER	L	1	0	0	0	0.4	0	0		0 - 0	0 - 0	0 - 0	0	0	0 - 0	0		1.667	54.00

New York Yankees

Pitcher	Pos	T	Usage					Inherited Runners			Saves			Relief Results						
			Rel G	Early Entry	Cons Days	Long	Lev Ind	#	Scrd	Pct	Easy	Reg	Tough	Clean	BS Win	Sv-Opp	Holds	Sv/Hld Pct	Opp OPS	Rel ERA
Rivera, Mariano	CL	R	64	0	13	4	2.2	17	6	.35	29 - 30	13 - 16	2 - 3	51	0	44 - 49	0	.90	.534	1.91
Robertson, David	SU	R	70	8	14	12	1.7	44	10	.23	0 - 0	1 - 3	0 - 1	57	1	1 - 4	34	.92	.506	1.08
Soriano, Rafael	SU	R	42	0	12	4	1.6	8	2	.25	2 - 2	0 - 3	0 - 0	31	0	2 - 5	23	.89	.645	4.12
Chamberlain, Joba	SU	R	27	1	8	3	1.2	10	2	.20	0 - 0	0 - 1	0 - 0	19	0	0 - 1	12	.92	.628	2.83
Logan, Boone	LT	L	64	18	12	2	1.2	61	13	.21	0 - 0	0 - 0	0 - 2	44	0	0 - 2	10	.83	.746	3.46
Laffey, Aaron	LT	L	11	7	4	2	0.8	5	0	.00	0 - 0	0 - 0	0 - 0	8	0	0 - 0	0		.733	3.38
Valdes, Raul	LT	L	6	3	2	2	0.8	6	1	.17	0 - 0	0 - 0	0 - 0	4	0	0 - 0	0		.819	2.70
Garrison, Steve	LT	L	1	0	0	0	0.0	0	0		0 - 0	0 - 0	0 - 0	1	0	0 - 0	0		.000	.00
Noesi, Hector	LM	R	28	9	1	16	0.8	12	3	.25	0 - 0	0 - 0	0 - 0	15	0	0 - 0	4	1.00	.740	4.01
Ayala, Luis	UR	R	52	13	10	8	0.8	36	12	.33	0 - 0	0 - 0	0 - 1	37	0	0 - 1	4	.80	.708	2.09
Wade, Cory	UR	R	40	15	7	6	0.9	25	5	.20	0 - 0	0 - 1	0 - 0	30	0	0 - 1	8	.89	.624	2.04
Pendleton, Lance	UR	R	11	0	0	5	0.1	3	1	.33	0 - 0	0 - 0	0 - 0	8	0	0 - 0	0		.723	3.21
Proctor, Scott	UR	R	8	3	1	5	1.4	1	0	.00	0 - 0	0 - 0	0 - 0	2	0	0 - 0	0		1.304	9.00
Carlyle, Buddy	UR	R	8	0	2	1	0.8	5	2	.40	0 - 0	0 - 0	0 - 0	5	0	0 - 0	0		.723	4.70
Kontos, George	UR	R	7	3	1	0	0.3	6	0	.00	0 - 0	0 - 0	0 - 0	5	0	0 - 0	0		.625	3.00
Mitre, Sergio	UR	R	4	0	1	2	0.2	1	1	1.00	0 - 0	0 - 0	0 - 0	0	0	0 - 0	0		.967	11.81
Sanit, Amauri	UR	R	4	1	0	2	0.1	4	0	.00	0 - 0	0 - 0	0 - 0	0	0	0 - 0	0		.921	12.86
Brackman, Andrew	UR	R	3	1	0	1	0.0	1	0	.00	0 - 0	0 - 0	0 - 0	3	0	0 - 0	0		.408	.00
Marquez, Jeff	UR	R	3	0	0	1	0.1	0	0		0 - 0	0 - 0	0 - 0	2	0	0 - 0	0		.667	2.25
Hughes, Phil	UR	R	3	2	0	1	1.0	0	0		0 - 0	0 - 0	0 - 0	2	0	0 - 0	0		.854	3.00
Whelan, Kevin	UR	R	2	0	0	1	0.0	0	0		0 - 0	0 - 0	0 - 0	1	0	0 - 0	0		.500	5.40
Betances, Dellin	UR	R	1	0	0	1	0.0	0	0		0 - 0	0 - 0	0 - 0	0	0	0 - 0	0		.714	27.00
Colon, Bartolo	ER	R	3	3	0	3	0.8	1	1	1.00	0 - 0	0 - 0	0 - 0	0	0	0 - 0	0		.641	3.97
Garcia, Freddy	ER	R	1	0	0	0	0.1	0	0		0 - 0	0 - 0	0 - 0	0	0	0 - 0	0		1.167	9.00
Burnett, A.J.	ER	R	1	0	0	0	0.1	0	0		0 - 0	0 - 0	0 - 0	1	0	0 - 0	0		.000	.00
Nova, Ivan	ER	R	1	0	0	0	2.7	0	0		0 - 0	0 - 0	0 - 0	0	0	0 - 0	0		1.250	13.50

Oakland Athletics

Pitcher	Pos	T	Usage					Inherited Runners			Saves			Relief Results						
			Rel G	Early Entry	Cons Days	Long	Lev Ind	#	Scrd	Pct	Easy	Reg	Tough	Clean	BS Win	Sv-Opp	Holds	Sv/Hld Pct	Opp OPS	Rel ERA
Bailey, Andrew	CL	R	42	0	9	4	1.9	3	1	.33	16 - 16	7 - 9	1 - 1	29	0	24 - 26	1	.93	.631	3.24
Fuentes, Brian	SU	L	67	4	19	5	1.5	28	7	.25	6 - 6	4 - 6	2 - 3	47	1	12 - 15	9	.88	.656	3.70
Balfour, Grant	SU	R	62	0	16	7	1.3	15	2	.13	1 - 2	1 - 5	0 - 0	50	0	2 - 7	26	.85	.605	2.47
Devine, Joey	SU	R	26	4	6	0	1.1	10	3	.30	0 - 0	0 - 0	0 - 1	19	1	0 - 1	7	.88	.611	3.52
Breslow, Craig	LT	L	67	14	23	8	0.8	38	8	.21	0 - 0	0 - 1	0 - 2	46	0	0 - 3	8	.73	.773	3.79
Blevins, Jerry	LT	L	26	7	4	6	0.4	14	8	.57	0 - 0	0 - 0	0 - 0	12	0	0 - 0	0		.688	2.86
Purcey, David	LT	L	9	4	1	1	0.4	4	1	.25	0 - 0	0 - 0	0 - 0	6	0	0 - 0	1	1.00	.538	2.13
Norberto, Jordan	LT	L	6	2	0	1	0.1	2	1	.50	0 - 0	0 - 0	0 - 0	2	0	0 - 0	0		.803	8.10
Cramer, Bobby	LT	L	5	1	0	1	0.3	7	0	.00	0 - 0	0 - 0	0 - 0	4	0	0 - 0	0		.526	1.08
Ziegler, Brad	LM	R	43	11	14	4	1.0	38	18	.47	0 - 0	1 - 1	0 - 1	25	0	1 - 2	6	.88	.640	2.39
Wuertz, Michael	UR	R	39	7	8	5	0.9	14	7	.50	0 - 0	0 - 0	0 - 1	25	0	0 - 1	3	.75	.865	6.68
De Los Santos, Fautino	UR	R	34	12	6	7	0.8	21	7	.33	0 - 0	0 - 0	0 - 2	20	0	0 - 2	3	.60	.670	4.32
Magnuson, Trystan	UR	R	9	2	1	3	0.1	4	3	.75	0 - 0	0 - 0	0 - 0	3	0	0 - 0	0		.758	6.14
Carignan, Andrew	UR	R	6	2	0	2	0.2	2	0	.00	0 - 0	0 - 0	0 - 0	4	0	0 - 0	0		.736	4.26
Wagner, Neil	UR	R	6	0	1	1	0.3	3	1	.33	0 - 0	0 - 0	0 - 0	4	0	0 - 0	0		.967	7.20
Outman, Josh	UR	L	4	2	0	2	1.2	0	0		0 - 0	0 - 0	0 - 0	1	0	0 - 0	1	1.00	.842	2.57
Billings, Bruce	UR	R	3	2	0	2	0.1	4	3	.75	0 - 0	0 - 0	0 - 0	1	0	0 - 0	0		1.048	12.60
Ross, Tyson	UR	R	3	0	0	2	1.5	0	0		0 - 0	0 - 0	0 - 0	2	0	0 - 0	0		.641	3.60
Godfrey, Graham	UR	R	1	1	0	1	0.1	0	0		0 - 0	0 - 0	0 - 0	1	0	0 - 0	0		.686	.00
Moscoso, Guillermo	ER	R	2	1	1	1	2.0	1	0	.00	0 - 0	0 - 0	0 - 0	1	0	0 - 0	0		.742	3.00

Philadelphia Phillies

Pitcher	Pos	T	Usage					Inherited Runners			Saves			Relief Results						
			Rel G	Early Entry	Cons Days	Long	Lev Ind	#	Scrd	Pct	Easy	Reg	Tough	Clean	BS Win	Sv-Opp	Holds	Sv/Hld Pct	Opp OPS	Rel ERA
Madson, Ryan	CL	R	62	0	21	2	1.9	8	4	.50	23 - 24	8 - 9	1 - 1	52	0	32 - 34	3	.95	.593	2.37
Bastardo, Antonio	SU	L	64	2	17	4	1.2	32	4	.13	3 - 3	4 - 5	1 - 1	50	0	8 - 9	17	.96	.524	2.64
Lidge, Brad	SU	R	25	1	4	1	1.3	8	1	.13	1 - 1	0 - 0	0 - 0	21	0	1 - 1	8	1.00	.635	1.40
Romero, J.C.	LT	L	24	3	6	1	0.8	7	3	.43	0 - 0	0 - 0	0 - 0	17	0	0 - 0	3	1.00	.736	3.86
Perez, Juan	LT	L	8	1	2	0	1.0	5	1	.20	0 - 0	0 - 0	0 - 0	6	0	0 - 0	1	1.00	.348	3.60
Zagurski, Mike	LT	L	4	2	0	1	0.2	2	2	1.00	0 - 0	0 - 0	0 - 0	1	0	0 - 0	0		.983	5.40
Savery, Joe	LT	L	4	0	1	0	0.8	0	0		0 - 0	0 - 0	0 - 0	4	0	0 - 0	1	1.00	.250	.00
Kendrick, Kyle	LM	R	19	10	0	6	0.9	9	4	.44	0 - 0	0 - 0	0 - 1	9	0	0 - 1	0	.00	.734	3.41
Carpenter, Andrew	LM	R	6	3	0	5	0.8	2	0	.00	0 - 0	0 - 0	0 - 1	2	0	0 - 1	0	.00	1.062	7.71
Stutes, Michael	UR	R	57	7	10	13	1.1	11	0	.00	0 - 0	0 - 0	0 - 0	41	0	0 - 0	13	1.00	.672	3.63
Herndon, David	UR	R	45	10	5	9	1.1	17	8	.47	0 - 0	1 - 1	0 - 1	29	0	1 - 2	4	.83	.774	3.32
Baez, Danys	UR	R	29	2	2	4	0.7	4	1	.25	0 - 0	0 - 0	0 - 0	15	0	0 - 1	0	.00	.811	6.25
Contreras, Jose	UR	R	17	0	3	2	1.3	2	0	.00	3 - 3	2 - 2	0 - 1	14	0	5 - 5	4	1.00	.659	3.86
Schwimer, Michael	UR	R	12	3	2	4	1.3	1	0	.00	0 - 0	0 - 2	0 - 0	7	0	0 - 2	0	.00	.834	5.02
De Fratus, Justin	UR	R	5	0	1	0	1.3	0	0		0 - 0	0 - 0	0 - 0	4	0	0 - 0	0		.396	2.25
Mathieson, Scott	UR	R	4	1	0	2	0.1	1	0	.00	0 - 0	0 - 0	0 - 0	4	0	0 - 0	0		.973	.00
Blanton, Joe	UR	R	3	0	0	0	0.4	0	0		0 - 0	0 - 0	0 - 0	2	0	0 - 0	0		.833	3.00
Worley, Vance	ER	R	4	2	0	2	1.2	2	0	.00	0 - 0	0 - 0	0 - 0	2	0	0 - 0	2	1.00	.796	2.70
Valdez, Wilson	ER	R	1	0	0	0	2.2	0	0		0 - 0	0 - 0	0 - 0	1	0	0 - 0	0		.250	.00
Hamels, Cole	ER	L	1	1	0	1	1.0	0	0		0 - 0	0 - 0	0 - 0	0	0	0 - 0	0		.917	6.00

Pittsburgh Pirates

Pitcher	Pos	T	Usage Rel G	Early Entry	Cons Days	Long	Lev Ind	Inherited Runners #	Scrd	Pct	Saves Easy	Reg	Tough	Clean	BS Win	Sv-Opp	Holds	Sv/Hld Pct	Opp OPS	Rel ERA
Hanrahan, Joel	CL	R	70	0	20	5	1.9	16	2	.13	26 - 26	11 - 13	3 - 5	56	1	40 - 44	0	.91	.543	1.83
Veras, Jose	SU	R	79	2	21	7	1.4	38	9	.24	1 - 1	0 - 5	0 - 2	54	0	1 - 8	27	.80	.636	3.80
Grilli, Jason	SU	R	28	9	6	7	1.6	19	2	.11	0 - 0	1 - 1	0 - 0	21	0	1 - 1	9	1.00	.601	2.48
Watson, Tony	LT	L	43	11	12	5	1.1	27	5	.19	0 - 0	0 - 0	0 - 1	30	0	0 - 1	10	.91	.711	3.95
Beimel, Joe	LT	L	35	2	7	3	0.9	28	10	.36	0 - 0	0 - 0	0 - 2	21	0	0 - 2	7	.78	.936	5.33
Moskos, Daniel	LT	L	31	12	3	3	0.6	19	3	.16	0 - 0	0 - 0	0 - 0	21	0	0 - 0	1	1.00	.723	2.96
Olson, Garrett	LT	L	4	0	1	1	1.8	3	2	.67	0 - 0	0 - 0	0 - 0	1	0	0 - 0	0		.375	2.08
Thompson, Aaron	LT	L	3	3	1	1	0.1	3	3	1.00	0 - 0	0 - 0	0 - 0	1	0	0 - 0	0		1.513	16.20
Burres, Brian	LT	L	3	1	0	2	0.1	0	0		0 - 0	0 - 0	0 - 0	2	0	0 - 0	0		.167	1.80
Leroux, Chris	LM	R	23	13	5	6	1.1	18	6	.33	0 - 0	0 - 0	0 - 1	14	0	0 - 1	2	.67	.599	2.88
Resop, Chris	UR	R	76	16	19	9	1.2	56	18	.32	1 - 2	0 - 2	0 - 2	49	0	1 - 6	15	.76	.756	4.39
McCutchen, Daniel	UR	R	73	22	23	16	0.8	43	8	.19	0 - 0	0 - 0	0 - 0	48	0	0 - 0	10	1.00	.741	3.72
Meek, Evan	UR	R	24	2	3	4	0.8	0	0		0 - 1	0 - 0	0 - 0	18	0	0 - 1	4	.80	.762	3.48
Crotta, Mike	UR	R	15	5	3	1	1.1	12	7	.58	0 - 0	0 - 0	0 - 1	5	0	0 - 1	2	.67	.995	9.28
Wood, Tim	UR	R	13	0	6	0	1.4	5	3	.60	0 - 0	0 - 0	0 - 0	8	0	0 - 0	3	1.00	.814	5.63
Hughes, Jared	UR	R	12	8	3	0	0.6	9	3	.33	0 - 0	0 - 0	0 - 0	9	0	0 - 0	2	1.00	.630	4.09
Ascanio, Jose	UR	R	8	1	1	0	0.3	1	1	1.00	0 - 0	0 - 0	0 - 0	4	0	0 - 0	0		.973	7.11
Lincoln, Brad	UR	R	4	1	0	2	0.4	0	0		0 - 0	0 - 0	0 - 0	1	0	0 - 0	0		.949	7.94
Karstens, Jeff	ER	R	4	2	0	2	1.1	1	0	.00	0 - 0	0 - 0	0 - 0	3	0	0 - 0	0		.608	2.35
Correia, Kevin	ER	R	1	0	0	0	0.2	0	0		0 - 0	0 - 0	0 - 0	1	0	0 - 0	0		.000	.00

San Diego Padres

Pitcher	Pos	T	Usage Rel G	Early Entry	Cons Days	Long	Lev Ind	Inherited Runners #	Scrd	Pct	Saves Easy	Reg	Tough	Clean	BS Win	Sv-Opp	Holds	Sv/Hld Pct	Opp OPS	Rel ERA
Bell, Heath	CL	R	64	0	19	4	2.1	10	1	.10	27 - 29	14 - 16	2 - 3	51	1	43 - 48	0	.90	.588	2.44
Qualls, Chad	SU	R	77	10	19	6	1.4	24	8	.33	0 - 0	0 - 4	0 - 1	58	1	0 - 5	22	.81	.689	3.51
Gregerson, Luke	SU	R	61	5	12	4	1.4	29	7	.24	0 - 1	0 - 0	0 - 2	46	1	0 - 4	16	.80	.681	2.75
Adams, Mike	SU	R	49	0	14	3	1.5	3	3	.60	0 - 0	1 - 2	0 - 1	42	0	1 - 3	23	.92	.453	1.13
Spence, Josh	LT	L	40	5	16	1	1.0	17	2	.12	0 - 0	0 - 1	0 - 1	32	0	0 - 2	7	.78	.507	2.73
Thatcher, Joe	LT	L	18	2	2	1	0.6	16	3	.19	0 - 0	0 - 0	0 - 0	12	0	0 - 0	2	1.00	.665	4.50
Luebke, Cory	LM	L	29	14	5	10	0.8	25	6	.24	0 - 0	0 - 0	0 - 0	22	0	0 - 0	3	1.00	.511	3.23
Bass, Anthony	LM	R	24	8	3	8	0.5	13	5	.38	0 - 0	0 - 0	0 - 0	18	0	0 - 0	4	1.00	.668	1.89
Frieri, Ernesto	UR	R	59	15	9	16	0.7	27	10	.37	0 - 0	0 - 0	0 - 0	43	0	0 - 0	4	1.00	.692	2.71
Neshek, Pat	UR	R	25	5	6	3	0.5	11	3	.27	0 - 0	0 - 0	0 - 0	14	0	0 - 0	0		.742	4.01
Hamren, Erik	UR	R	14	4	3	1	0.5	13	7	.54	0 - 0	0 - 0	0 - 0	6	0	0 - 0	1	1.00	.835	4.38
Scribner, Evan	UR	R	10	3	2	3	0.1	3	3	1.00	0 - 0	0 - 0	0 - 0	6	0	0 - 0	0		.810	7.07
Brach, Brad	UR	R	9	2	0	0	1.4	8	3	.38	0 - 0	0 - 0	0 - 0	3	0	0 - 0	0		.747	5.14
Carpenter, Andrew	UR	R	6	0	0	1	0.3	3	1	.33	0 - 0	0 - 0	0 - 0	4	0	0 - 0	0		.841	8.44
Fulchino, Jeff	UR	R	3	0	0	0	0.2	0	0		0 - 0	0 - 0	0 - 0	2	0	0 - 0	0		1.083	16.20
Deduno, Sam	UR	R	2	0	0	2	0.2	0	0		0 - 0	0 - 0	0 - 0	1	0	0 - 0	0		.899	3.00

San Francisco Giants

Pitcher	Pos	T	Usage					Inherited Runners			Saves			Relief Results						
			Rel G	Early Entry	Cons Days	Long	Lev Ind	#	Scrd	Pct	Easy	Reg	Tough	Clean	BS Win	Sv-Opp	Holds	Sv/Hld Pct	Opp OPS	Rel ERA
Wilson, Brian	CL	R	57	0	19	8	2.2	13	6	.46	20 - 21	16 - 19	0 - 1	43	2	36 - 41	0	.88	.660	3.11
Lopez, Javier	SU	L	70	0	16	5	1.5	43	6	.14	0 - 0	0 - 0	1 - 3	56	0	1 - 3	20	.91	.603	2.72
Romo, Sergio	SU	R	65	0	18	1	1.4	33	6	.18	0 - 0	1 - 2	0 - 0	53	0	1 - 2	23	.96	.458	1.50
Affeldt, Jeremy	LT	L	67	7	16	9	1.1	45	11	.24	0 - 0	2 - 4	1 - 2	46	1	3 - 6	13	.84	.625	2.63
Runzler, Dan	LT	L	30	4	5	5	0.8	14	3	.21	0 - 0	0 - 0	0 - 0	19	0	0 - 0	3	1.00	.698	5.26
Mota, Guillermo	LM	R	52	25	3	21	0.7	39	15	.38	0 - 0	1 - 1	0 - 1	24	0	1 - 2	4	.83	.701	3.81
Ramirez, Ramon	UR	R	66	6	13	11	0.9	39	10	.26	1 - 1	2 - 3	1 - 1	45	0	4 - 5	11	.94	.596	2.62
Casilla, Santiago	UR	R	49	8	15	10	1.0	15	3	.20	4 - 4	2 - 2	0 - 1	39	0	6 - 7	6	.92	.534	1.74
Edlefsen, Steve	UR	R	13	6	2	2	0.4	8	2	.25	0 - 0	0 - 0	0 - 0	7	0	0 - 0	1	1.00	1.038	9.53
Joaquin, Waldis	UR	R	5	2	1	2	0.2	5	4	.80	0 - 0	0 - 0	0 - 0	3	0	0 - 0	0		.725	4.26
Zito, Barry	UR	L	4	1	0	1	0.1	0	0		0 - 0	0 - 0	0 - 0	2	0	0 - 0	0		1.013	9.00
Vogelsong, Ryan	ER	R	2	1	0	1	0.1	4	0	.00	0 - 0	0 - 0	0 - 0	2	0	0 - 0	0		.438	.00

Seattle Mariners

Pitcher	Pos	T	Usage					Inherited Runners			Saves			Relief Results						
			Rel G	Early Entry	Cons Days	Long	Lev Ind	#	Scrd	Pct	Easy	Reg	Tough	Clean	BS Win	Sv-Opp	Holds	Sv/Hld Pct	Opp OPS	Rel ERA
League, Brandon	CL	R	65	0	18	1	1.9	8	4	.50	18 - 19	19 - 23	0 - 0	50	1	37 - 42	0	.88	.601	2.79
Wright, Jamey	SU	R	60	6	7	15	1.1	25	9	.36	1 - 2	0 - 2	0 - 1	40	1	1 - 5	16	.81	.713	3.16
Jimenez, Cesar	LT	L	8	2	1	0	0.6	3	0	.00	0 - 0	0 - 0	0 - 0	6	0	0 - 0			.559	5.40
Pauley, David	LM	R	39	7	5	11	1.1	15	5	.33	0 - 0	0 - 1	0 - 0	28	0	0 - 1	7	.88	.549	2.15
Laffey, Aaron	LM	L	36	9	6	9	0.9	24	11	.46	0 - 0	0 - 0	0 - 1	21	0	0 - 1	5	.83	.856	4.01
Gray, Jeff	LM	R	24	6	2	9	0.8	24	13	.54	0 - 0	1 - 2	0 - 2	10	0	1 - 4	2	.50	.777	4.89
Ray, Chris	UR	R	29	2	3	5	0.8	14	3	.21	0 - 0	0 - 2	0 - 0	17	1	0 - 2	1	.33	.714	4.68
Wilhelmsen, Tom	UR	R	25	6	5	5	0.5	6	5	.83	0 - 0	0 - 0	0 - 0	16	0	0 - 0	3	1.00	.580	3.31
Lueke, Josh	UR	R	25	9	1	8	0.4	7	5	.71	0 - 0	0 - 0	0 - 0	16	0	0 - 0	2	1.00	.717	6.06
Ruffin, Chance	UR	R	13	1	1	7	0.5	1	1	1.00	0 - 0	0 - 0	0 - 0	9	0	0 - 0	1	1.00	.751	3.86
Kelley, Shawn	UR	R	10	3	1	1	0.4	5	1	.20	0 - 0	0 - 0	0 - 0	9	0	0 - 0	1	1.00	.417	.00
Cortes, Dan	UR	R	10	3	0	2	0.8	3	1	.33	0 - 0	0 - 0	0 - 0	5	0	0 - 0	1	1.00	.795	5.91
Delabar, Steve	UR	R	6	1	0	1	1.1	2	0	.00	0 - 0	0 - 0	0 - 0	4	0	0 - 0	0		.792	2.57
Furbush, Charlie	UR	L	1	0	0	0	0.0	0	0		0 - 0	0 - 0	0 - 0	0	0	0 - 0	0		1.400	9.00

St Louis Cardinals

Pitcher	Pos	T	Usage					Inherited Runners			Saves			Relief Results						
			Rel G	Early Entry	Cons Days	Long	Lev Ind	#	Scrd	Pct	Easy	Reg	Tough	Clean	BS Win	Sv-Opp	Holds	Sv/Hld Pct	Opp OPS	Rel ERA
Salas, Fernando	CL	R	68	2	20	8	1.6	30	9	.30	13 - 13	6 - 10	5 - 7	49	1	24 - 30	6	.83	.566	2.28
Motte, Jason	SU	R	78	13	23	8	1.4	56	18	.32	4 - 4	5 - 6	0 - 3	53	0	9 - 13	18	.87	.558	2.25
Rzepczynski, Marc	SU	L	28	4	7	3	1.0	12	4	.33	0 - 0	0 - 0	0 - 1	21	0	0 - 1	8	.89	.692	3.97
Sanchez, Eduardo	SU	R	26	1	3	4	1.5	5	2	.40	4 - 4	1 - 3	0 - 0	20	0	5 - 7	7	.86	.496	1.80
Miller, Trever	LT	L	39	2	8	0	1.2	34	10	.29	0 - 0	1 - 1	0 - 2	26	0	1 - 3	4	.71	.892	4.02
Rhodes, Arthur	LT	L	19	3	4	0	1.4	16	3	.19	0 - 0	0 - 0	0 - 0	13	0	0 - 0	4	1.00	.755	4.15
Tallet, Brian	LT	L	18	3	2	1	0.9	10	2	.20	0 - 0	0 - 0	0 - 0	9	0	0 - 0	2	1.00	1.064	8.31
Valdes, Raul	LT	L	7	2	1	2	1.1	4	2	.50	0 - 0	0 - 0	0 - 0	4	0	0 - 0	0		.771	3.38
Batista, Miguel	LM	R	25	7	1	5	1.3	12	5	.42	0 - 0	0 - 0	0 - 1	15	0	0 - 1	6	.86	.741	4.60

St Louis Cardinals

Pitcher	Pos	T	Usage Rel G	Early Entry	Cons Days	Long	Lev Ind	Inherited Runners #	Scrd	Pct	Saves Easy	Reg	Tough	Clean	BS Win	Sv-Opp	Holds	Sv/Hld Pct	Opp OPS	Rel ERA
Boggs, Mitchell	UR	R	51	11	7	13	0.7	17	3	.18	2-3	1-3	1-2	30	1	4-8	1	.56	.711	3.56
Dotel, Octavio	UR	R	29	2	10	3	1.1	18	3	.17	0-0	0-0	2-2	21	0	2-2	5	1.00	.485	3.28
McClellan, Kyle	UR	R	26	7	4	8	1.1	4	2	.50	0-0	0-0	0-1	14	0	0-1	4	.80	.828	4.14
Franklin, Ryan	UR	R	21	5	2	9	0.9	5	3	.60	0-0	1-4	0-1	5	0	1-5	0	.20	1.103	8.46
Lynn, Lance	UR	R	16	4	2	8	1.6	2	0	.00	0-0	1-2	0-0	12	0	1-2	3	.80	.541	2.22
Augenstein, Bryan	UR	R	5	1	1	2	1.6	0	0		0-0	0-0	0-0	2	0	0-0	0		1.151	9.53
Walters, P.J.	UR	R	4	1	0	2	0.3	2	0	.00	0-0	0-0	0-0	3	0	0-0	0		.653	9.00
Cleto, Maikel	UR	R	3	0	0	2	0.2	2	2	1.00	0-0	0-0	0-0	1	0	0-0	0		1.107	12.46
Dickson, Brandon	UR	R	3	1	0	1	0.2	2	0	.00	0-0	0-0	0-0	3	0	0-0	0		.465	.00
Jackson, Edwin	UR	R	1	0	0	0	0.1	0	0		0-0	0-0	0-0	1	0	0-0	0		.800	.00
Schumaker, Skip	ER	R	1	0	0	0	0.0	0	0		0-0	0-0	0-0	0	0	0-0	0		1.400	18.00

Tampa Bay Rays

Pitcher	Pos	T	Usage Rel G	Early Entry	Cons Days	Long	Lev Ind	Inherited Runners #	Scrd	Pct	Saves Easy	Reg	Tough	Clean	BS Win	Sv-Opp	Holds	Sv/Hld Pct	Opp OPS	Rel ERA
Farnsworth, Kyle	CL	R	63	0	16	1	1.5	25	8	.32	12-13	12-15	1-3	43	1	25-31	0	.81	.608	2.18
Peralta, Joel	SU	R	71	0	22	5	1.3	35	9	.26	2-2	4-5	0-1	47	0	6-8	19	.93	.586	2.93
Ramos, Cesar	LT	L	59	11	18	3	0.6	48	17	.35	0-0	0-0	0-2	37	0	0-2	3	.60	.670	3.92
Howell, J.P.	LT	L	46	6	10	0	1.2	32	8	.25	1-1	0-1	0-0	31	0	1-2	10	.92	.770	6.16
McGee, Jake	LT	L	37	2	11	3	0.7	31	8	.26	0-0	0-0	0-0	21	0	0-0	4	1.00	.801	4.50
Torres, Alex	LT	L	4	1	0	3	1.2	2	2	1.00	0-0	0-0	0-0	1	0	0-0	0		.701	3.38
Moore, Matt	LT	L	2	1	0	2	1.6	1	0	.00	0-0	0-0	0-0	0	0	0-0	1	1.00	.850	6.23
Cruz, Juan	UR	R	56	10	13	7	0.8	30	6	.20	0-0	0-1	0-0	39	0	0-1	6	.86	.671	3.88
Gomes, Brandon	UR	R	40	7	12	4	0.7	25	8	.32	0-0	0-0	0-0	25	0	0-0	5	1.00	.656	2.92
Russell, Adam	UR	R	36	5	9	6	0.5	22	12	.55	0-0	0-0	0-0	21	0	0-0	2	1.00	.741	3.03
Sonnanstine, Andy	UR	R	11	4	0	1	0.3	5	2	.40	0-0	0-0	0-0	6	0	0-0	0		.696	3.12
de la Rosa, Dane	UR	R	7	2	1	2	0.1	5	0	.00	0-0	0-0	0-0	5	0	0-0	0		.834	9.82
Delaney, Rob	UR	R	4	3	0	1	0.3	0	0		0-0	0-0	0-0	2	0	0-0	1	1.00	.793	10.80
Buente, Jay	UR	R	1	0	0	1	0.1	0	0		0-0	0-0	0-0	0	0	0-0	0		.775	9.00
Ekstrom, Mike	UR	R	1	0	0	0	0.0	0	0		0-0	0-0	0-0	1	0	0-0	0		.500	.00

Texas Rangers

Pitcher	Pos	T	Usage Rel G	Early Entry	Cons Days	Long	Lev Ind	Inherited Runners #	Scrd	Pct	Saves Easy	Reg	Tough	Clean	BS Win	Sv-Opp	Holds	Sv/Hld Pct	Opp OPS	Rel ERA
Feliz, Neftali	CL	R	64	0	19	6	1.6	16	5	.31	21-22	11-15	0-1	48	0	32-38	0	.84	.598	2.74
Oliver, Darren	SU	L	61	4	13	5	1.5	33	12	.36	1-1	1-3	0-2	41	1	2-6	16	.82	.591	2.29
Rhodes, Arthur	SU	L	32	2	2	2	1.1	19	3	.16	0-0	1-3	0-0	21	0	1-3	7	.80	.889	4.81
Adams, Mike	SU	R	27	0	9	2	1.0	1	1	1.00	1-1	0-1	0-0	22	0	1-2	9	.91	.574	2.10
Uehara, Koji	SU	R	22	1	4	0	1.1	15	0	.00	0-0	0-0	0-0	15	0	0-0	9	1.00	.673	4.00
Kirkman, Michael	LT	L	15	6	1	8	0.6	8	5	.63	0-0	0-0	0-0	6	0	0-0	1	1.00	.829	6.59
Gonzalez, Mike	LT	L	7	2	0	3	0.7	3	1	.33	0-0	0-0	0-0	3	0	0-0	2	1.00	.536	5.14
Lowe, Mark	UR	R	52	5	11	5	0.9	32	6	.19	1-2	0-0	0-1	37	0	1-3	11	.86	.768	3.80
Tateyama, Yoshinori	UR	R	39	11	10	10	0.6	34	9	.26	0-0	1-1	0-0	24	0	1-1	4	1.00	.681	4.50
ODay, Darren'	UR	R	16	2	1	1	0.6	4	1	.25	0-0	0-0	0-0	10	0	0-0	3	1.00	.929	5.40
Bush, Dave	UR	R	14	5	0	6	0.4	4	0	.00	0-0	0-0	0-0	5	0	0-0	1	1.00	.872	6.49

Texas Rangers

Pitcher	Pos	T	Rel G	Early Entry	Cons Days	Long	Lev Ind	#	Scrd	Pct	Easy	Reg	Tough	Clean	BS Win	Sv-Opp	Holds	Sv/Hld Pct	Opp OPS	Rel ERA
Strop, Pedro	UR	R	11	0	1	2	1.1	6	0	.00	0-0	0-1	0-0	9	0	0-1	0	.00	.555	3.72
Eppley, Cody	UR	R	10	1	2	1	1.6	4	1	.25	0-0	0-0	0-1	6	1	0-1	2	.67	1.016	8.00
Feldman, Scott	UR	R	9	4	0	4	0.3	3	1	.33	0-0	0-0	0-0	5	0	0-0	0		.666	4.29
Hunter, Tommy	UR	R	8	4	1	3	0.9	8	2	.25	0-0	0-1	0-0	4	0	0-1	0	.00	.570	2.93
Tomko, Brett	UR	R	8	4	0	5	0.8	6	3	.50	0-0	0-0	0-1	2	0	0-1	0	.00	.872	4.58
Hamburger, Mark	UR	R	5	4	0	2	0.4	1	0	.00	0-0	0-0	0-0	3	0	0-0	0		.544	4.50
Valdez, Merkin	UR	R	5	1	1	0	0.1	0	0		0-0	0-0	0-0	2	0	0-0	0		1.031	6.23
Tucker, Ryan	UR	R	5	1	1	1	0.7	2	2	1.00	0-0	0-0	0-0	1	0	0-0	0		.924	7.20
Tobin, Mason	UR	R	4	2	0	2	0.5	0	0		0-0	0-0	0-0	2	0	0-0	0		.958	6.75
Ogando, Alexi	ER	R	2	0	0	0	0.0	0	0		0-0	0-0	0-0	2	0	0-0	0		.556	.00
Harrison, Matt	ER	L	1	1	0	1	0.4	0	0		0-0	0-0	0-0	1	0	0-0	0		.000	.00

Toronto Blue Jays

Pitcher	Pos	T	Rel G	Early Entry	Cons Days	Long	Lev Ind	#	Scrd	Pct	Easy	Reg	Tough	Clean	BS Win	Sv-Opp	Holds	Sv/Hld Pct	Opp OPS	Rel ERA
Francisco, Frank	CL	R	54	0	8	5	1.5	11	1	.09	7-7	9-13	1-1	39	0	17-21	2	.83	.721	3.55
Rzepczynski, Marc	SU	L	43	3	5	5	1.3	19	5	.26	0-1	0-0	0-2	31	0	0-3	10	.77	.581	2.97
Perez, Luis	LT	L	33	13	3	12	0.8	29	8	.28	0-0	0-1	0-1	17	0	0-2	4	.67	.775	4.27
Miller, Trever	LT	L	6	0	2	0	0.5	0	0		0-0	0-1	0-0	4	0	0-1	1	.50	1.069	4.91
Lewis, Rommie	LT	L	6	2	0	2	0.1	6	2	.33	0-0	0-0	0-0	1	0	0-0	0		1.220	9.00
Ledezma, Wil	LT	L	5	1	0	3	0.0	1	0	.00	0-0	0-0	0-0	1	0	0-0	0		1.179	15.00
Purcey, David	LT	L	5	0	2	0	0.7	0	0		0-0	0-0	0-0	4	0	0-0	0		.800	11.57
Tallet, Brian	LT	L	1	0	0	0	5.5	0	0		0-0	0-1	0-0	0	0	0-1	0	.00	1.467	54.00
Frasor, Jason	LM	R	44	8	2	6	1.3	27	8	.30	0-0	0-0	0-2	31	0	0-2	10	.83	.723	2.98
Villanueva, Carlos	LM	R	20	10	0	9	0.8	10	4	.40	0-0	0-1	0-0	14	0	0-1	0	.00	.522	1.60
Camp, Shawn	UR	R	67	16	13	9	1.1	37	11	.30	0-0	1-1	0-3	46	1	1-4	5	.67	.821	4.21
Janssen, Casey	UR	R	55	7	6	6	1.0	23	11	.48	1-1	1-2	0-1	42	0	2-4	7	.82	.594	2.26
Rauch, Jon	UR	R	53	0	13	8	1.5	19	3	.16	7-8	3-6	1-2	31	1	11-16	4	.75	.799	4.85
Dotel, Octavio	UR	R	36	4	5	1	0.9	32	5	.16	0-0	1-1	0-0	27	0	1-1	4	1.00	.645	3.68
Litsch, Jesse	UR	R	20	6	2	7	1.0	10	1	.10	0-0	1-2	0-0	10	0	1-2	3	.80	.680	4.08
Carreno, Joel	UR	R	11	2	1	2	0.4	4	0	.00	0-0	0-0	0-0	9	0	0-0	0		.563	1.15
Drabek, Kyle	UR	R	4	1	0	2	0.4	0	0		0-0	0-0	0-0	2	0	0-0	0		1.054	10.50
Farquhar, Danny	UR	R	3	0	0	1	0.0	3	2	.67	0-0	0-0	0-0	2	0	0-0	0		1.170	13.50
Beck, Chad	UR	R	3	0	0	0	0.0	1	0	.00	0-0	0-0	0-0	3	0	0-0	0		.250	.00
Walters, P.J.	UR	R	1	1	0	0	0.7	0	0		0-0	0-0	0-0	1	0	0-0	0		.333	.00
Mills, Brad	UR	L	1	0	0	0	0.0	0	0		0-0	0-0	0-0	0	0	0-0	0		2.500	
McGowan, Dustin	UR	R	1	1	0	1	0.0	0	0		0-0	0-0	0-0	0	0	0-0	0		.988	6.75
Richmond, Scott	UR	R	1	0	0	0	0.4	2	0	.00	0-0	0-0	0-0	1	0	0-0	0		.000	.00
McCoy, Mike	ER	R	1	0	0	0	0.0	0	0		0-0	0-0	0-0	1	0	0-0	0		.000	.00

Washington Nationals

Pitcher	Pos	T	Rel G	Early Entry	Cons Days	Long	Lev Ind	#	Scrd	Pct	Easy	Reg	Tough	Clean	BS Win	Sv-Opp	Holds	Sv/Hld Pct	Opp OPS	Rel ERA
Storen, Drew	CL	R	73	0	24	1	1.8	10	2	.20	23-24	19-22	1-2	57	2	43-48	3	.90	.599	2.75
Clippard, Tyler	SU	R	72	5	15	15	1.5	46	10	.22	0-0	0-3	0-4	54	1	0-7	38	.84	.535	1.83
Burnett, Sean	SU	L	69	6	15	4	1.4	43	19	.44	1-2	2-6	1-3	46	1	4-11	15	.73	.702	3.81
Slaten, Doug	LT	L	31	9	6	1	0.9	32	15	.47	0-0	0-0	0-0	17	0	0-0	3	1.00	1.036	4.41
Severino, Atahualpa	LT	L	6	1	0	0	0.6	4	2	.50	0-0	0-0	0-0	4	0	0-0	1	1.00	.816	3.86
Balester, Collin	LM	R	23	11	4	9	0.7	9	4	.44	0-0	0-1	0-0	9	0	0-1	2	.67	.807	4.54

Washington Nationals

Pitcher	Pos	T	Usage					Inherited Runners			Saves			Relief Results						
			Rel G	Early Entry	Cons Days	Long	Lev Ind	#	Scrd	Pct	Easy	Reg	Tough	Clean	BS Win	Sv-Opp	Holds	Sv/Hld Pct	Opp OPS	Rel ERA
Gorzelanny, Tom	LM	L	15	11	0	6	1.1	9	0	.00	0 - 0	0 - 1	0 - 0	11	0	0 - 1	4	.80	.617	2.42
Coffey, Todd	UR	R	69	16	18	5	0.9	36	7	.19	0 - 0	0 - 1	0 - 1	47	0	0 - 2	10	.83	.656	3.62
Rodriguez, Henry	UR	R	59	9	14	16	1.0	20	7	.35	2 - 2	0 - 1	0 - 2	40	0	2 - 5	10	.80	.596	3.56
Mattheus, Ryan	UR	R	35	6	8	2	0.9	29	8	.28	0 - 0	0 - 0	0 - 0	24	0	0 - 0	8	1.00	.624	2.81
Kimball, Cole	UR	R	12	3	3	3	0.8	5	4	.80	0 - 0	0 - 0	0 - 1	8	1	0 - 1	0	.00	.578	1.93
Broderick, Brian	UR	R	11	4	2	1	0.4	5	5	1.00	0 - 0	0 - 0	0 - 0	4	0	0 - 0	0		.755	6.57
Gaudin, Chad	UR	R	10	4	1	1	0.9	7	1	.14	0 - 0	0 - 0	0 - 0	5	0	0 - 0	2	1.00	.955	6.48
Stammen, Craig	UR	R	7	4	0	1	1.5	9	1	.11	0 - 0	0 - 0	0 - 0	5	0	0 - 0	1	1.00	.272	.87
Maya, Yunesky	UR	R	5	1	0	2	0.3	2	0	.00	0 - 0	0 - 0	0 - 0	3	0	0 - 0	0		.881	4.70
Detwiler, Ross	UR	L	5	4	0	3	0.8	4	1	.25	0 - 0	0 - 0	0 - 0	3	0	0 - 0	1	1.00	.673	1.80
Peacock, Brad	UR	R	1	1	0	1	2.5	2	2	1.00	0 - 0	0 - 1	0 - 0	0	0	0 - 1	0	.00	1.196	6.75

Pitchers Hitting, Fielding & Holding Runners, and Hitters Pitching

Pitchers are notoriously poor hitters and this section displays the carnage. Many pitchers have batting averages well below their weight (and sometimes below their IQ), especially American League pitchers who only get the opportunity to hit through interleague play. 2011 and career hitting statistics for each pitcher are printed in this section.

The best hitting pitcher in 2011 was Carlos Zambrano. The Big Z hit .318 in 44 at-bats with a pair of homers for the Cubs.

This section also includes 2011 fielding statistics for pitchers and data on how well they held runners last season. A pitcher's Runs Saved (RS) is the sum of Plus/Minus Runs Saved to evaluate range and Stolen Base Runs Saved, which measures the ability to control the running game. Mark Buehrle of the White Sox and Jhoulys Chacin of the Rockies led all pitchers with nine Runs Saved.

The final piece of this section is Hitters Pitching. Congratulations to Wilson Valdez of the Phillies for recording the first Win credited to a position player in the history of the *Bill James Handbook*. Career statistics are listed for all active position players who have pitched, as well as any 2011 pitching statistics that they may have accrued.

Pitchers Hitting, Fielding and Holding Runners

Pitcher	T	2011 Hitting Avg	AB	H	HR	RBI	SH	Career Hitting Avg	AB	H	2B	3B	HR	RBI	BB	SO	SH	2011 Fielding and Holding Runners Inn	PO	A	E	DP	Pct	SBA	CS	PCS	PPO	CS%	RS
Abad,Fernando, Hou	L	-	0	0	0	0	0	.000	1	0	0	0	0	0	0	1	0	19.2	1	2	2	0	.600	1	0	0	0	.00	0
Abreu,Juan, Hou	R	-	0	0	0	0	0		0	0	0	0	0	0	0	0	0	6.2	1	0	0	0	1.000	0	0	0	0	-	0
Accardo,Jeremy, Bal	R	-	0	0	0	0	0	.143	7	1	0	0	0	0	0	1	0	37.2	1	5	0	1	1.000	5	0	0	0	.00	-1
Aceves,Alfredo, Bos	R	-	0	0	0	0	0	.000	2	0	0	0	0	0	0	1	0	114.0	6	5	0	1	1.000	9	0	0	0	.00	-1
Acosta,Manny, NYM	R	-	0	0	0	0	0	.000	6	0	0	0	0	0	1	4	0	47.0	3	3	0	1	1.000	8	3	0	0	.38	-3
Adams,Mike, SD-Tex	R	-	0	0	0	0	0	.000	2	0	0	0	0	0	0	0	0	73.2	4	5	0	1	1.000	9	0	0	0	.00	-2
Adcock,Nathan, KC	R	-	0	0	0	0	0		0	0	0	0	0	0	0	0	0	60.1	7	8	0	1	1.000	6	1	0	0	.17	1
Affeldt,Jeremy, SF	L	.000	1	0	0	0	0	.214	14	3	0	0	0	2	2	4	0	61.2	7	11	0	1	1.000	5	1	0	0	.20	1
Albers,Matt, Bos	R	-	0	0	0	0	0	.059	34	2	0	0	0	0	0	21	3	64.2	1	8	1	0	.900	10	4	1	0	.40	0
Alburquerque,Al, Det	R	-	0	0	0	0	0		0	0	0	0	0	0	0	0	0	43.1	3	3	0	1	1.000	6	1	0	0	.17	0
Alvarez,Henderson, Tor	R	-	0	0	0	0	0		0	0	0	0	0	0	0	0	0	63.2	5	13	1	1	.947	3	2	0	0	.67	3
Anderson,Brett, Oak	L	.000	1	0	0	0	0	.000	4	0	0	0	0	0	0	2	0	83.1	0	21	2	1	.913	12	7	5	0	.58	1
Arredondo,Jose, Cin	R	.500	2	1	0	0	0	.500	2	1	0	0	0	0	0	1	0	53.0	10	1	0	0	1.000	6	4	0	0	.67	-1
Arrieta,Jake, Bal	R	.250	4	1	0	1	1	.143	7	1	0	0	0	1	1	2	1	119.1	9	16	3	3	.893	15	4	0	0	.27	1
Arroyo,Bronson, Cin	R	.105	57	6	0	2	8	.128	454	58	15	0	5	26	13	200	56	199.0	22	30	4	2	.929	13	4	0	0	.31	3
Ascanio,Jose, Pit	R	-	0	0	0	0	0	.000	2	0	0	0	0	0	0	1	0	6.1	0	0	0	0	-	0	0	0	0	-	1
Asencio,Jairo, Atl	R	-	0	0	0	0	0		0	0	0	0	0	0	0	0	0	10.1	2	3	0	1	1.000	0	0	0	0	-	1
Atchison,Scott, Bos	R	-	0	0	0	0	0	.000	2	0	0	0	0	0	0	1	0	30.1	2	3	1	0	.833	4	3	0	0	.75	2
Atkins,Mitch, Bal	R	-	0	0	0	0	0	.000	2	0	0	0	0	0	0	1	0	10.2	1	0	0	0	1.000	0	0	0	0	-	0
Augenstein,Bryan, StL	R	1.000	1	1	0	0	0	.250	4	1	0	0	0	0	1	1	0	5.2	0	1	0	0	1.000	1	1	0	0	1.00	0
Axelrod,Dylan, CWS	R	-	0	0	0	0	0		0	0	0	0	0	0	0	0	0	18.2	3	4	0	2	1.000	1	0	0	0	.00	0
Axford,John, Mil	R	-	0	0	0	0	0		0	0	0	0	0	0	0	0	0	73.2	1	7	2	1	.800	8	2	0	0	.25	1
Ayala,Luis, NYY	R	-	0	0	0	0	0	.286	14	4	1	0	0	0	0	3	3	56.0	2	11	0	2	1.000	4	0	0	0	.00	2
Badenhop,Burke, Fla	R	.286	7	2	0	1	0	.100	30	3	1	0	0	2	1	17	5	63.2	4	9	0	1	1.000	3	1	0	1	.33	-1
Baez,Danys, Phi	R	.000	2	0	0	0	0	.167	6	1	0	0	0	0	0	1	0	36.0	3	4	0	1	1.000	7	0	0	0	.00	-1
Bailey,Andrew, Oak	R	-	0	0	0	0	0		0	0	0	0	0	0	0	0	0	41.2	1	4	0	1	1.000	5	0	0	0	.00	-2
Bailey,Homer, Cin	R	.282	39	11	0	2	5	.191	131	25	4	0	0	8	3	53	17	132.0	14	11	1	1	.962	11	2	0	1	.18	0
Baker,Scott, Min	R	.400	5	2	0	0	0	.120	25	3	1	0	0	0	0	9	4	134.2	11	6	0	0	1.000	9	5	0	0	.56	0
Balester,Collin, Was	R	.000	4	0	0	0	1	.148	27	4	0	0	0	1	2	10	11	35.2	0	2	1	0	.667	6	1	0	0	.17	-2
Balfour,Grant, Oak	R	-	0	0	0	0	0	.000	1	0	0	0	0	0	0	1	0	62.0	2	4	0	1	1.000	1	0	0	0	.00	-1
Bard,Daniel, Bos	R	-	0	0	0	0	0		0	0	0	0	0	0	0	0	0	73.0	11	5	1	0	.941	8	1	0	0	.13	-1
Bass,Anthony, SD	R	.000	5	0	0	0	1	.000	5	0	0	0	0	0	0	3	1	48.1	11	7	0	3	1.000	6	1	0	0	.17	2
Bastardo,Antonio, Phi	L	-	0	0	0	0	0	.000	6	0	0	0	0	0	0	3	1	58.0	0	3	1	0	.750	2	0	0	0	.00	1
Batista,Miguel, StL-NYM	R	.000	6	0	0	0	2	.092	305	28	5	0	2	9	11	169	27	60.0	8	4	0	1	1.000	4	0	0	0	.00	1
Beachy,Brandon, Atl	R	.070	43	3	0	1	6	.083	48	4	0	0	0	1	2	26	6	141.2	8	15	0	1	1.000	17	4	1	1	.24	2
Beato,Pedro, NYM	R	-	0	0	0	0	0		0	0	0	0	0	0	0	0	0	67.0	3	14	0	2	1.000	9	3	0	0	.33	2
Beavan,Blake, Sea	R	-	0	0	0	0	0		0	0	0	0	0	0	0	0	0	97.0	5	10	0	0	1.000	9	3	1	0	.33	0
Beck,Chad, Tor	R	-	0	0	0	0	0		0	0	0	0	0	0	0	0	0	2.1	0	0	0	0	-	0	0	0	0	-	0
Beckett,Josh, Bos	R	.000	5	0	0	0	0	.145	221	32	9	0	3	16	10	81	26	193.0	15	18	3	0	.917	35	4	0	0	.11	-4
Bedard,Erik, Sea-Bos	L	.200	5	1	0	0	0	.250	20	5	0	0	1	1	7	7	1	129.1	5	9	1	0	.933	6	3	1	1	.50	2
Beimel,Joe, Pit	L	.000	1	0	0	0	0	.222	45	10	1	0	0	1	2	19	6	25.1	0	1	0	0	1.000	1	0	0	0	.00	0
Belisle,Matt, Col	R	.500	2	1	0	0	1	.088	80	7	3	0	0	3	3	45	18	72.0	2	11	0	0	1.000	4	4	1	0	1.00	3
Bell,Heath, SD	R	-	0	0	0	0	0	.000	6	0	0	0	0	0	0	2	1	62.2	3	5	0	0	1.000	4	0	0	0	.00	-1
Bell,Trevor, LAA	R	-	0	0	0	0	0	.000	1	0	0	0	0	0	0	1	0	34.1	3	2	0	0	1.000	3	3	0	0	1.00	-1
Below,Duane, Det	L	-	0	0	0	0	0		0	0	0	0	0	0	0	0	0	29.0	1	1	0	0	1.000	3	1	1	0	.33	-2
Benoit,Joaquin, Det	R	-	0	0	0	0	0	.000	9	0	0	0	0	0	0	4	0	61.0	1	4	0	1	1.000	5	2	0	0	.40	-1
Berg,Justin, ChC	R	.000	2	0	0	0	0	.000	2	0	0	0	0	0	0	1	0	12.0	0	2	0	0	1.000	1	1	0	0	1.00	0
Bergesen,Brad, Bal	R	-	0	0	0	0	0	.250	8	2	0	0	0	0	0	0	2	101.0	4	12	2	0	.889	8	4	0	0	.50	3
Berken,Jason, Bal	R	-	0	0	0	0	0	.000	1	0	0	0	0	0	0	1	0	47.0	2	6	0	1	1.000	1	0	0	0	.00	-1
Betances,Dellin, NYY	R	-	0	0	0	0	0		0	0	0	0	0	0	0	0	0	2.2	0	0	0	0	-	1	0	0	0	.00	0
Betancourt,Rafael, Col	R	-	0	0	0	0	0	.000	1	0	0	0	0	0	0	1	0	62.1	1	1	0	0	1.000	5	0	0	0	.00	-3
Billings,Bruce, Col-Oak	R	-	0	0	0	0	0		0	0	0	0	0	0	0	0	0	7.0	1	1	0	1	1.000	0	0	0	0	-	0
Billingsley,Chad, LAD	R	.161	56	9	1	4	5	.135	297	40	7	0	2	18	19	144	28	188.0	5	24	2	1	.935	13	4	0	0	.31	1
Blackburn,Nick, Min	R	.000	2	0	0	0	0	.100	10	1	0	0	0	0	0	2	0	148.1	10	30	2	1	.952	20	9	0	3	.45	4
Blanton,Joe, Phi	R	.182	11	2	0	2	1	.119	151	18	0	0	0	5	5	63	24	41.1	1	8	0	2	1.000	4	0	0	0	.00	-1
Blevins,Jerry, Oak	L	-	0	0	0	0	0		0	0	0	0	0	0	0	0	0	28.1	0	3	0	1	1.000	1	0	0	0	.00	1
Boggs,Mitchell, StL	R	.000	2	0	0	0	0	.037	27	1	1	0	0	0	0	14	3	60.2	4	6	1	1	.909	4	2	0	0	.50	-1
Bowden,Michael, Bos	R	-	0	0	0	0	0		0	0	0	0	0	0	0	0	0	20.0	2	1	0	0	1.000	3	1	0	0	.33	-1
Boyer,Blaine, NYM	R	-	0	0	0	0	0	.000	8	0	0	0	0	0	0	6	1	6.2	0	1	0	0	1.000	1	0	0	0	.00	-1
Brach,Brad, SD	R	-	0	0	0	0	0		0	0	0	0	0	0	0	0	0	7.0	0	0	0	0	-	0	0	0	0	-	0
Brackman,Andrew, NYY	R	-	0	0	0	0	0		0	0	0	0	0	0	0	0	0	2.1	0	0	0	0	-	0	0	0	0	-	0
Braddock,Zach, Mil	L	-	0	0	0	0	0		0	0	0	0	0	0	0	0	0	17.1	0	0	0	0	-	2	0	0	0	.00	0
Braden,Dallas, Oak	L	-	0	0	0	0	0	.000	4	0	0	0	0	0	0	2	2	18.0	0	1	0	0	1.000	3	3	0	0	1.00	1
Bray,Bill, Cin	L	-	0	0	0	0	0	.000	1	0	0	0	0	0	0	1	0	48.1	2	2	1	0	.800	6	2	0	0	.33	-1
Brazoban,Yhency, Ari	R	-	0	0	0	0	0	.000	3	0	0	0	0	0	0	1	0	6.0	0	0	0	0	-	0	0	0	0	-	0
Breslow,Craig, Oak	L	-	0	0	0	0	0	.000	1	0	0	0	0	0	0	0	0	59.1	0	9	1	0	.900	10	7	5	0	.70	0
Britton,Zach, Bal	L	.625	8	5	1	2	0	.625	8	5	1	0	1	2	0	1	0	154.1	9	21	2	4	.938	10	3	0	0	.30	-1
Broderick,Brian, Was	R	-	0	0	0	0	0		0	0	0	0	0	0	0	0	0	12.1	2	2	0	1	1.000	2	1	0	0	.50	0

Pitchers Hitting, Fielding and Holding Runners

Pitcher	T	2011 Hitting						Career Hitting										2011 Fielding and Holding Runners											
		Avg	AB	H	HR	RBI	SH	Avg	AB	H	2B	3B	HR	RBI	BB	SO	SH	Inn	PO	A	E	DP	Pct	SBA	CS	PCS	PPO	CS%	RS
Brothers,Rex, Col	L	.000	1	0	0	0	0	.000	1	0	0	0	0	0	0	1	0	40.2	1	0	2	0	.333	7	1	0	0	.14	-1
Broxton,Jonathan, LAD	R	-	0	0	0	0	0	.000	5	0	0	0	0	0	2	2	1	12.2	2	2	0	0	1.000	0	0	0	0	-	1
Bruney,Brian, CWS	R	-	0	0	0	0	0	.000	1	0	0	0	0	0	0	0	0	19.2	1	3	0	0	1.000	5	1	0	0	.20	0
Buchholz,Clay, Bos	R	-	0	0	0	0	0	1.000	1	1	0	0	0	0	0	0	0	82.2	15	14	1	0	.967	9	3	1	0	.33	2
Buchholz,Taylor, NYM	R	.000	2	0	0	0	0	.089	56	5	0	0	0	2	4	22	5	26.0	2	2	0	0	1.000	5	1	0	0	.20	0
Buehrle,Mark, CWS	L	.500	2	1	0	0	0	.106	47	5	1	0	1	2	1	25	8	205.1	15	40	1	4	.982	10	7	4	2	.70	9
Buente,Jay, Fla-TB	R	.000	1	0	0	0	0	.000	1	0	0	0	0	0	0	1	0	5.0	1	2	0	0	1.000	1	1	0	0	1.00	0
Bulger,Jason, LAA	R	-	0	0	0	0	0	-	0	0	0	0	0	0	0	0	0	9.1	2	1	1	0	.750	3	0	1	0	.00	-1
Bumgarner,Madison, SF	L	.119	59	7	0	3	11	.140	100	14	5	0	6	7	30	14	204.2	7	22	3	0	.906	23	11	3	1	.48	0
Burnett,A.J., NYY	R	.000	2	0	0	0	1	.130	269	35	6	3	3	9	12	129	37	190.1	10	23	5	2	.868	31	7	2	3	.23	-3
Burnett,Alex, Min	R	-	0	0	0	0	0	-	0	0	0	0	0	0	0	0	0	50.2	3	6	1	0	.900	8	1	0	0	.13	0
Burnett,Sean, Was	L	1.000	1	1	0	0	0	.069	29	2	1	0	0	0	3	9	2	56.2	7	16	0	1	1.000	2	0	0	0	.00	2
Burres,Brian, Pit	L	.000	3	0	0	0	0	.133	30	4	0	1	0	4	0	16	3	14.0	1	1	0	0	1.000	1	0	0	0	.00	0
Burton,Jared, Cin	R	-	0	0	0	0	0	.000	2	0	0	0	0	0	0	2	0	4.2	0	0	0	0	-	2	0	0	0	.00	0
Bush,Dave, Tex	R	-	0	0	0	0	0	.129	263	34	7	0	0	13	9	96	27	37.1	4	6	0	0	1.000	9	1	0	0	.11	0
Byrdak,Tim, NYM	L	-	0	0	0	0	0	.154	13	2	1	0	0	0	0	4	0	37.2	1	4	0	0	1.000	2	1	1	0	.50	0
Cahill,Trevor, Oak	R	.000	5	0	0	0	0	.100	10	1	0	0	0	0	0	3	2	207.2	12	32	1	1	.978	36	8	1	2	.22	1
Cain,Matt, SF	R	.136	66	9	1	6	8	.117	383	45	8	1	5	18	15	194	49	221.2	14	23	3	0	.925	23	5	0	0	.22	0
Camp,Shawn, Tor	R	-	0	0	0	0	0	1.000	1	1	0	0	0	0	0	0	1	66.1	6	17	1	2	.958	10	2	1	2	.20	0
Capps,Matt, Min	R	-	0	0	0	0	0	.200	5	1	0	0	0	0	1	3	0	65.2	3	12	0	0	1.000	2	0	0	0	.00	2
Capuano,Chris, NYM	L	.071	56	4	0	0	6	.137	292	40	8	0	1	17	7	141	21	186.0	7	28	0	2	1.000	14	5	3	0	.36	2
Carignan,Andrew, Oak	R	-	0	0	0	0	0	-	0	0	0	0	0	0	0	0	0	6.1	0	1	0	0	1.000	1	0	0	0	.00	1
Carlyle,Buddy, NYY	R	-	0	0	0	0	0	.161	56	9	0	0	4	3	17	7	7.2	1	0	0	1.000	1	0	0	0	1.00	0
Carmona,Fausto, Cle	R	.000	3	0	0	0	0	.000	14	0	0	0	0	0	8	2	188.2	9	29	0	2	1.000	21	6	0	0	.29	1
Carpenter,Chris, StL	R	.155	71	11	0	5	9	.118	433	51	8	0	2	21	12	142	47	237.1	28	23	3	3	.944	11	6	0	0	.55	-2
Carpenter,Chris, ChC	R	-	0	0	0	0	0	-	0	0	0	0	0	0	0	0	0	9.2	1	1	1	0	.667	2	1	0	0	.50	0
Carpenter,David, Hou	R	-	0	0	0	0	0	-	0	0	0	0	0	0	0	0	0	27.2	3	5	0	1	1.000	1	0	0	0	.00	0
Carpenter,Drew, Phi-SD	R	-	0	0	0	0	0	.000	4	0	0	0	0	0	0	1	0	14.2	1	0	0	0	1.000	3	1	0	0	.33	-1
Carrasco,Carlos, Cle	R	.000	5	0	0	0	2	.000	5	0	0	0	0	0	0	3	2	124.2	4	15	0	0	1.000	9	3	2	0	.33	3
Carrasco,D.J., NYM	R	-	0	0	0	0	1	.000	15	0	0	0	0	0	0	5	2	49.1	3	5	1	0	.889	8	2	0	0	.25	-1
Carreno,Joel, Tor	R	-	0	0	0	0	0	-	0	0	0	0	0	0	0	0	0	15.2	0	2	0	0	1.000	1	1	0	0	1.00	0
Cashner,Andrew, ChC	R	.000	1	0	0	0	1	.000	3	0	0	0	0	0	0	3	2	10.2	0	1	0	0	-	0	0	0	0	-	0
Casilla,Santiago, SF	R	-	0	0	0	0	0	-	0	0	0	0	0	0	1	0	0	51.2	0	6	0	0	1.000	3	0	0	0	.00	-1
Cassevah,Bobby, LAA	R	-	0	0	0	0	0	-	0	0	0	0	0	0	0	0	0	39.2	3	3	0	1	1.000	6	1	0	0	.17	0
Castillo,Alberto, Ari	L	-	0	0	0	0	0	-	0	0	0	0	0	0	0	0	0	11.2	2	2	0	0	1.000	1	0	0	0	.00	0
Cecil,Brett, Tor	L	-	0	0	0	0	0	.000	4	0	0	0	0	0	0	4	0	123.2	2	11	1	0	.929	6	2	0	0	.33	3
Ceda,Jose, Fla	R	-	0	0	0	0	0	.000	2	0	0	0	0	0	0	2	0	20.1	2	0	0	0	1.000	1	0	0	0	.00	0
Cedeno,Xavier, Hou	L	-	0	0	0	0	0	-	0	0	0	0	0	0	0	0	0	1.2	0	0	0	0	-	0	0	0	0	-	0
Chacin,Jhoulys, Col	R	.164	61	10	0	4	5	.129	101	13	1	0	0	5	2	21	9	194.0	26	39	4	1	.942	11	7	0	1	.64	9
Chamberlain,Joba, NYY	R	-	0	0	0	0	0	.000	5	0	0	0	0	0	1	1	2	28.2	4	3	0	1	1.000	3	1	0	0	.33	-1
Chapman,Aroldis, Cin	L	-	0	0	0	0	0	-	0	0	0	0	0	0	0	0	0	50.0	3	8	4	1	.733	6	4	4	0	.67	0
Chatwood,Tyler, LAA	R	.667	3	2	0	0	2	.667	3	2	0	0	0	0	0	0	2	142.0	11	20	0	2	1.000	19	7	1	1	.37	3
Chavez,Jesse, KC	R	-	0	0	0	0	0	.000	2	0	0	0	0	0	0	2	0	7.2	0	0	0	0	-	1	0	0	0	.00	0
Chen,Bruce, KC	L	.000	1	0	0	0	1	.144	118	17	1	0	0	3	3	54	19	155.0	8	24	0	1	1.000	18	6	4	0	.33	3
Choate,Randy, Fla	L	-	0	0	0	0	0	.000	5	0	0	0	0	0	0	3	0	24.2	5	6	1	1	.917	2	0	0	0	.00	1
Cishek,Steve, Fla	R	-	0	0	0	0	0	-	0	0	0	0	0	0	0	0	0	54.2	4	5	4	0	.692	5	0	0	0	.00	0
Cleto,Maikel, StL	R	.000	1	0	0	0	0	.000	1	0	0	0	0	0	0	1	0	4.1	0	0	0	0	-	0	0	0	0	-	0
Clippard,Tyler, Was	R	.000	2	0	0	0	1	.214	14	3	1	0	0	0	6	3	88.1	0	8	0	1	1.000	8	5	1	0	.63	0
Cobb,Alex, TB	R	-	0	0	0	0	0	-	0	0	0	0	0	0	0	0	0	52.2	5	6	1	0	.917	11	0	0	0	.00	-4
Coffey,Todd, Was	R	-	0	0	0	0	0	.000	7	0	0	0	0	0	0	5	3	59.2	1	6	1	0	.875	3	1	0	0	.33	-2
Coke,Phil, Det	L	.000	2	0	0	0	0	.000	3	0	0	0	0	0	0	3	0	108.2	4	15	2	1	.905	16	6	3	0	.38	-1
Coleman,Casey, ChC	R	.160	25	4	0	0	4	.133	45	6	2	1	0	2	1	17	6	84.1	7	13	0	0	1.000	9	1	0	1	.11	2
Coleman,Louis, KC	R	.000	1	0	0	0	0	.000	1	0	0	0	0	0	0	1	0	59.2	3	3	1	0	.857	6	4	0	0	.67	0
Collins,Tim, KC	L	-	0	0	0	0	0	-	0	0	0	0	0	0	0	0	0	67.0	0	10	0	0	1.000	8	1	0	0	.13	0
Collmenter,Josh, Ari	R	.150	40	6	0	1	4	.150	40	6	0	0	1	2	16	4	154.1	6	18	0	1	1.000	11	7	0	0	.64	1
Colon,Bartolo, NYY	R	.000	1	0	0	0	1	.116	86	10	0	0	0	5	0	50	6	164.1	10	18	1	1	.966	8	3	0	1	.38	2
Contreras,Jose, Phi	R	-	0	0	0	0	0	.000	5	0	0	0	0	0	3	18	1	14.0	0	0	0	0	-	3	1	0	0	.33	0
Cook,Aaron, Col	R	.147	34	5	0	2	1	.152	382	58	7	1	0	19	21	130	67	97.0	14	26	3	4	.930	5	4	0	1	.80	6
Cook,Ryan, Ari	R	-	0	0	0	0	0	-	0	0	0	0	0	0	0	0	0	7.2	1	2	0	0	1.000	3	0	0	1	.00	0
Cordero,Francisco, Cin	R	-	0	0	0	0	0	.000	3	0	0	0	0	0	0	1	0	69.2	8	8	1	2	.941	11	2	0	0	.18	-2
Cormier,Lance, LAD	R	.000	1	0	0	0	0	.106	47	5	1	0	2	2	17	4	13.2	1	5	1	0	.857	0	0	0	0	-	1
Correia,Kevin, Pit	R	.087	46	4	0	3	8	.118	229	27	5	0	0	12	11	95	33	154.0	10	23	0	2	1.000	12	6	1	0	.50	4
Cortes,Dan, Sea	R	-	0	0	0	0	0	-	0	0	0	0	0	0	0	0	0	10.2	2	2	0	0	1.000	3	1	0	0	.33	0
Crain,Jesse, CWS	R	-	0	0	0	0	0	.000	1	0	0	0	0	0	0	1	0	65.1	3	11	1	1	.933	15	2	0	2	.13	-1
Cramer,Bobby, Oak	L	-	0	0	0	0	0	-	0	0	0	0	0	0	0	0	0	8.1	0	0	0	0	-	0	0	0	0	-	0
Crotta,Mike, Pit	R	-	0	0	0	0	0	-	0	0	0	0	0	0	0	0	0	10.2	0	1	0	0	-	4	0	0	0	.33	0
Crow,Aaron, KC	R	-	0	0	0	0	0	-	0	0	0	0	0	0	0	0	0	62.0	5	7	1	1	.923	7	1	0	0	.14	-2
Cruz,Juan, TB	R	-	0	0	0	0	0	.114	70	8	1	1	0	2	4	28	7	48.2	1	6	0	0	1.000	11	3	0	0	.27	-2
Cueto,Johnny, Cin	R	.064	47	3	0	0	7	.089	192	17	0	0	4	8	65	33	156.0	17	24	5	1	.891	5	4	0	2	.80	5
Daley,Matt, Col	R	-	0	0	0	0	0	-	0	0	0	0	0	0	0	0	0	6.0	1	0	0	0	-	0	0	0	0	-	0

Pitchers Hitting, Fielding and Holding Runners

Pitcher	T	2011 Hitting Avg	AB	H	HR	RBI	SH	Career Hitting Avg	AB	H	2B	3B	HR	RBI	BB	SO	SH	2011 Fielding and Holding Runners Inn	PO	A	E	DP	Pct	SBA	CS	PCS	PPO	CS%	RS
Danks,John, CWS	L	.000	3	0	0	0	0	.063	16	1	0	0	0	0	1	6	1	170.1	4	30	0	1	1.000	23	8	6	1	.35	1
Davies,Kyle, KC	R	.000	1	0	0	0	0	.130	69	9	1	0	2	9	4	25	16	61.1	1	9	1	0	.909	10	2	0	0	.20	-1
Davis,Doug, ChC	L	.000	10	0	0	0	3	.083	412	34	4	2	0	13	4	175	48	45.2	2	5	1	0	.875	3	0	0	1	.00	0
Davis,Wade, TB	R	.500	2	1	0	0	2	.333	3	1	0	0	0	0	0	1	2	184.0	11	18	0	4	1.000	6	4	1	1	.67	0
De Fratus,Justin, Phi	R	-	0	0	0	0	0	-	0	0	0	0	0	0	0	0	0	4.0	0	1	0	0	1.000	0	0	0	0	-	0
de la Cruz,Frankie, Mil	R	-	0	0	0	0	0	.000	2	0	0	0	0	0	0	2	0	13.0	0	0	0	0	-	1	0	0	0	.00	0
de la Rosa,Dane, TB	R	-	0	0	0	0	0	-	0	0	0	0	0	0	0	0	0	7.1	0	0	0	0	-	1	1	0	0	1.00	0
de la Rosa,Jorge, Col	L	.238	21	5	0	3	2	.143	175	25	4	0	0	16	1	80	15	59.0	4	8	0	0	1.000	12	2	0	0	.17	0
de la Rosa,Rubby, LAD	R	.214	14	3	0	0	1	.214	14	3	0	0	0	0	1	1	1	60.2	6	10	2	1	.889	13	4	0	0	.31	0
De Los Santos,F., Oak	R	-	0	0	0	0	0	-	0	0	0	0	0	0	0	0	0	33.1	3	2	0	0	1.000	7	1	0	0	.14	-2
Deduno,Sam, SD	R	-	0	0	0	0	0	-	0	0	0	0	0	0	0	0	0	3.0	1	1	0	0	1.000	2	0	0	0	.00	0
Del Rosario,Enerio, Hou	R	-	0	0	0	0	0	-	0	0	0	0	0	0	0	0	0	53.0	7	6	0	0	1.000	11	1	0	0	.09	-3
Delabar,Steve, Sea	R	-	0	0	0	0	0	-	0	0	0	0	0	0	0	0	0	7.0	0	0	0	0	-	2	2	0	0	1.00	0
Delaney,Rob, TB	R	-	0	0	0	0	0	-	0	0	0	0	0	0	0	0	0	5.0	1	0	0	0	1.000	1	0	0	0	.00	0
Delgado,Randall, Atl	R	.000	10	0	0	0	1	.000	10	0	0	0	0	0	0	6	1	35.0	2	8	0	0	1.000	3	1	0	0	.33	-1
Demel,Sam, Ari	R	-	0	0	0	0	0	-	0	0	0	0	0	0	0	0	0	25.2	1	2	0	0	1.000	2	1	0	0	.50	-2
Dempster,Ryan, ChC	R	.086	58	5	0	0	10	.099	556	55	9	1	0	16	13	212	84	202.1	13	36	3	3	.942	27	10	0	0	.37	1
Detwiler,Ross, Was	L	.105	19	2	0	1	3	.067	45	3	0	0	0	2	0	18	3	66.0	3	5	1	0	.889	5	2	0	0	.40	-2
Devine,Joey, Oak	R	-	0	0	0	0	0	.000	1	0	0	0	0	0	0	1	0	23.0	0	0	0	0	-	5	0	0	0	.00	-2
Diamond,Scott, Min	L	-	0	0	0	0	0	-	0	0	0	0	0	0	0	0	0	39.0	1	3	0	0	1.000	2	0	0	0	.00	1
Dickey,R.A., NYM	R	.136	59	8	0	2	9	.200	115	23	2	0	0	7	4	19	16	208.2	7	58	2	5	.970	10	3	1	4	.30	8
Dickson,Brandon, StL	R	.667	3	2	0	0	0	.667	3	2	0	0	0	0	0	1	0	8.1	0	0	0	0	-	0	0	0	0	-	0
DiFelice,Mark, Mil	R	-	0	0	0	0	0	.000	1	0	0	0	0	0	0	1	2	3.0	0	1	0	0	1.000	1	0	0	0	.00	0
Dillard,Tim, Mil	R	-	0	0	0	0	0	.500	2	1	0	0	0	0	0	1	0	28.2	1	9	0	0	1.000	4	2	0	0	.50	2
Dolis,Rafael, ChC	R	-	0	0	0	0	0	-	0	0	0	0	0	0	0	0	0	1.1	0	0	0	0	-	0	0	0	0	-	0
Dotel,Octavio, Tor-StL	R	.000	2	0	0	0	0	.065	77	5	0	0	0	1	5	44	9	54.0	4	1	1	0	.833	2	1	1	0	.50	0
Doubront,Felix, Bos	L	-	0	0	0	0	0	-	0	0	0	0	0	0	0	0	0	10.1	0	2	0	0	1.000	5	3	2	0	.60	1
Downs,Scott, LAA	L	-	0	0	0	0	0	.067	45	3	0	0	0	1	3	17	10	53.2	6	13	0	0	1.000	0	0	0	0	-	1
Drabek,Kyle, Tor	R	-	0	0	0	0	0	-	0	0	0	0	0	0	0	0	0	78.2	6	17	0	1	1.000	11	3	0	4	.27	2
Duensing,Brian, Min	L	.000	4	0	0	0	0	.000	5	0	0	0	0	0	0	3	0	161.2	10	18	4	0	.875	12	6	1	0	.50	-1
Duffy,Danny, KC	L	.000	3	0	0	0	0	.000	3	0	0	0	0	0	0	2	0	105.1	2	15	0	0	1.000	20	9	7	0	.45	1
Duke,Zach, Ari	L	.300	20	6	2	6	2	.176	313	55	7	0	2	23	12	116	42	76.2	6	10	0	0	1.000	4	4	1	0	1.00	0
Dumatrait,Phil, Min	L	-	0	0	0	0	0	.037	27	1	0	0	0	1	0	11	5	41.1	2	7	0	0	1.000	6	1	0	0	.17	0
Dunn,Mike, Fla	L	.000	1	0	0	0	0	.000	1	0	0	0	0	0	0	0	0	63.0	3	7	1	0	.909	2	1	1	0	.50	-1
Durbin,Chad, Cle	R	-	0	0	0	0	0	.083	24	2	0	0	0	1	0	8	1	68.1	3	7	0	0	1.000	9	3	0	0	.33	-2
Edlefsen,Steve, SF	R	.000	1	0	0	0	0	.000	1	0	0	0	0	0	0	1	0	11.1	4	0	0	1	1.000	0	0	0	0	-	0
Ekstrom,Mike, TB	R	-	0	0	0	0	0	.000	2	0	0	0	0	0	0	1	1	1.0	0	0	0	0	-	0	0	0	0	-	0
Elbert,Scott, LAD	L	-	0	0	0	0	0	.167	6	1	1	0	0	1	0	2	0	33.1	1	1	0	0	1.000	2	1	0	0	.50	-2
Ely,John, LAD	R	.000	3	0	0	0	0	.067	30	2	0	0	0	1	2	15	4	12.2	0	1	1	0	.500	3	1	0	0	.33	-1
Enright,Barry, Ari	R	.167	12	2	1	2	1	.222	45	10	1	0	1	8	2	11	4	37.2	1	6	0	0	1.000	1	0	0	0	.00	1
Eovaldi,Nathan, LAD	R	.091	11	1	0	0	0	.091	11	1	0	0	0	0	1	9	0	34.2	1	7	0	0	1.000	3	1	1	1	.33	3
Eppley,Cody, Tex	R	-	0	0	0	0	0	-	0	0	0	0	0	0	0	0	0	9.0	0	5	0	0	1.000	2	1	0	0	.50	1
Escalona,Edgmer, Col	R	.000	3	0	0	0	0	.000	3	0	0	0	0	0	0	3	0	25.2	2	4	0	1	1.000	3	1	0	0	.33	0
Escalona,Sergio, Hou	L	-	0	0	0	0	0	-	0	0	0	0	0	0	0	0	0	27.2	4	4	1	1	.889	6	1	0	0	.17	-1
Estrada,Marco, Mil	R	.250	12	3	0	0	4	.231	13	3	1	0	0	1	5	7	0	92.2	4	12	0	0	1.000	10	2	0	1	.20	0
Eveland,Dana, LAD	L	.000	9	0	0	0	1	.045	22	1	0	0	0	2	13	5	29.2	3	5	0	0	1.000	4	2	1	0	.50	0
Eyre,Willie, Bal	R	-	0	0	0	0	0	.000	1	0	0	0	0	0	0	1	0	18.1	1	3	0	0	1.000	2	1	0	0	.50	0
Farnsworth,Kyle, TB	R	-	0	0	0	0	0	.074	54	4	1	0	0	3	2	18	8	57.2	7	7	1	1	.933	3	1	0	0	.33	0
Farquhar,Danny, Tor	R	-	0	0	0	0	0	-	0	0	0	0	0	0	0	0	0	2.0	0	0	0	0	-	0	0	0	0	-	0
Feldman,Scott, Tex	R	-	0	0	0	0	0	.143	14	2	1	0	0	0	0	5	3	32.0	3	7	0	0	1.000	7	4	0	0	.57	2
Feliz,Neftali, Tex	R	-	0	0	0	0	0	-	0	0	0	0	0	0	0	0	0	62.1	9	4	1	0	.929	4	3	0	2	.75	1
Fiers,Michael, Mil	R	-	0	0	0	0	0	-	0	0	0	0	0	0	0	0	0	2.0	0	2	0	0	1.000	2	1	1	0	.50	0
Figueroa,Nelson, Hou	R	.222	9	2	0	0	1	.172	116	20	2	1	0	8	5	43	15	29.0	2	2	3	0	.571	6	0	0	0	.00	-2
Fisher,Carlos, Cin	R	.000	2	0	0	0	0	.000	7	0	0	0	0	0	0	6	0	24.0	0	5	1	0	.833	3	1	0	0	.33	0
Fister,Doug, Sea-Det	R	.333	6	2	0	1	1	.250	8	2	1	0	0	1	0	3	1	216.1	24	31	3	5	.948	6	2	0	0	.33	5
Floyd,Gavin, CWS	R	.000	3	0	0	0	1	.057	53	3	0	0	0	0	2	29	4	193.2	13	21	1	6	.971	25	2	0	1	.08	0
Francis,Jeff, KC	L	.000	2	0	0	0	0	.125	256	32	6	0	0	15	21	89	45	183.0	4	31	0	3	1.000	23	5	1	0	.22	1
Francisco,Frank, Tor	R	-	0	0	0	0	0	-	0	0	0	0	0	0	0	0	0	50.2	2	2	1	0	.800	14	1	0	0	.07	-3
Franklin,Ryan, StL	R	.000	2	0	0	0	0	.091	22	2	0	0	0	1	2	12	2	27.2	5	6	0	0	1.000	12	2	0	0	.17	0
Frasor,Jason, Tor-CWS	R	-	0	0	0	0	0	-	0	0	0	0	0	0	0	0	0	60.0	1	7	0	0	1.000	12	2	0	0	.17	1
Frieri,Ernesto, SD	R	-	0	0	0	0	0	.000	1	0	0	0	0	0	0	1	0	63.0	2	3	0	1	1.000	12	5	1	0	.42	-1
Fuentes,Brian, Oak	L	-	0	0	0	0	0	.000	1	0	0	0	0	0	0	1	0	58.1	1	9	1	0	.909	7	1	1	0	.14	2
Fulchino,Jeff, Hou-SD	R	-	0	0	0	0	0	.250	4	1	0	0	0	0	1	1	0	34.2	2	4	0	0	1.000	9	0	0	0	.00	0
Furbush,Charlie, Det-Sea	L	-	0	0	0	0	0	-	0	0	0	0	0	0	0	0	0	85.1	3	16	0	1	1.000	17	6	4	0	.35	3
Galarraga,Armando, Ari	R	.000	15	0	0	1	1	.000	23	0	0	0	0	1	3	13	2	42.2	0	7	0	0	1.000	1	0	0	0	.00	1
Gallardo,Yovani, Mil	R	.221	68	15	1	4	7	.218	238	52	14	0	9	28	11	75	15	207.1	12	30	2	3	.955	21	7	1	0	.33	2
Garcia,Freddy, NYY	R	.000	5	0	0	0	3	.176	68	12	2	0	4	2	20	17	146.2	11	19	1	1	.968	29	7	1	0	.24	-3
Garcia,Jaime, StL	L	.097	62	6	1	6	5	.137	117	16	1	0	1	8	5	32	9	194.2	3	22	2	2	.926	18	3	3	0	.17	1
Garland,Jon, LAD	R	.000	11	0	0	0	4	.135	156	21	1	0	1	7	10	60	20	54.0	1	15	0	1	1.000	3	1	0	0	.33	2
Garrison,Steve, NYY	L	-	0	0	0	0	0	-	0	0	0	0	0	0	0	0	0	0.2	0	0	0	0	-	0	0	0	0	-	0

Pitchers Hitting, Fielding and Holding Runners

Pitcher	T	2011 Hitting						Career Hitting										2011 Fielding and Holding Runners											
		Avg	AB	H	HR	RBI	SH	Avg	AB	H	2B	3B	HR	RBI	BB	SO	SH	Inn	PO	A	E	DP	Pct	SBA	CS	PCS	PPO	CS%	RS
Garza,Matt, ChC	R	.094	64	6	0	1	5	.080	75	6	0	0	0	1	2	51	8	198.0	10	15	7	1	.781	15	5	1	0	.33	-1
Gaub,John, ChC	L	-	0	0	0	0	0	-	0	0	0	0	0	0	0	0	0	2.2	1	0	0	0	1.000	0	0	0	0	-	0
Gaudin,Chad, Was	R	-	0	0	0	0	0	.031	32	1	0	0	0	0	2	16	3	8.1	0	0	0	0	-	2	1	0	0	.50	0
Gearrin,Cory, Atl	R	-	0	0	0	0	0	-	0	0	0	0	0	0	0	0	0	18.1	0	1	0	0	1.000	3	0	0	0	.00	0
Gee,Dillon, NYM	R	.109	46	5	0	4	8	.121	58	7	1	0	0	5	2	30	8	160.2	8	21	1	2	.967	15	7	0	0	.47	1
Germano,Justin, Cle	R	-	0	0	0	0	0	.180	50	9	2	0	0	3	3	21	11	12.2	0	5	0	0	1.000	0	0	0	0	-	2
Godfrey,Graham, Oak	R	.000	2	0	0	0	0	.000	2	0	0	0	0	0	0	1	0	25.0	3	4	0	0	1.000	0	0	0	0	-	-1
Gomes,Brandon, TB	R	-	0	0	0	0	0	-	0	0	0	0	0	0	0	0	0	37.0	3	3	0	0	1.000	4	1	0	0	.25	0
Gomez,Jeanmar, Cle	R	-	0	0	0	0	0	-	0	0	0	0	0	0	0	0	0	58.1	4	12	1	1	.941	10	4	1	0	.40	2
Gonzalez,Edgar, Col	R	-	0	0	0	0	0	.175	63	11	1	0	0	2	0	13	7	2.0	0	1	0	0	1.000	0	0	0	0	-	0
Gonzalez,Enrique, Det	R	-	0	0	0	0	0	.281	32	9	1	0	0	3	0	8	3	9.0	2	0	0	0	1.000	1	1	0	0	1.00	-1
Gonzalez,Gio, Oak	L	.000	3	0	0	0	2	.000	7	0	0	0	0	0	0	4	2	202.0	10	23	1	3	.971	23	4	2	0	.17	-1
Gonzalez,Mike, Bal-Tex	L	-	0	0	0	0	0	.333	3	1	1	0	0	2	0	0	0	53.1	0	7	0	1	1.000	4	0	0	0	.00	-1
Gordon,Brian, NYY	R	.000	1	0	0	0	0	.000	1	0	0	0	0	0	1	1	0	10.1	0	1	0	0	1.000	2	2	0	0	1.00	-1
Gorzelanny,Tom, Was	L	.107	28	3	0	1	3	.088	193	17	0	0	0	12	8	91	23	105.0	4	7	2	0	.846	9	1	1	0	.11	-1
Grabow,John, ChC	L	-	0	0	0	0	0	.000	5	0	0	0	0	0	0	1	1	62.1	3	4	1	0	.875	6	3	2	0	.50	-1
Gray,Jeff, CWS-Sea	R	-	0	0	0	0	0	-	0	0	0	0	0	0	0	0	0	48.1	2	9	3	2	.786	6	3	0	0	.50	1
Green,Sean, Mil	R	-	0	0	0	0	0	.000	2	0	0	0	0	0	0	2	0	11.2	0	1	0	0	1.000	3	0	0	0	.00	1
Gregerson,Luke, SD	R	-	0	0	0	0	0	.000	1	0	0	0	0	0	0	0	0	55.2	6	16	2	0	.917	5	0	0	0	.00	1
Gregg,Kevin, Bal	R	-	0	0	0	0	0	.000	6	0	0	0	0	0	0	5	0	59.2	0	11	0	0	1.000	8	2	0	0	.25	0
Greinke,Zack, Mil	R	.143	49	7	1	1	7	.151	73	11	2	0	2	2	3	15	9	171.2	13	22	0	3	1.000	14	6	1	0	.43	2
Grilli,Jason, Pit	R	.000	1	0	0	0	0	.200	15	3	0	0	1	3	0	3	3	32.2	1	9	0	1	1.000	0	0	0	1	-	2
Guerra,Javy, LAD	R	-	0	0	0	0	0	-	0	0	0	0	0	0	1	0	0	46.2	4	7	1	1	.917	1	1	1	0	1.00	-1
Guerrier,Matt, LAD	R	-	0	0	0	1	0	.000	2	0	0	0	0	1	1	1	0	66.1	1	8	0	0	1.000	6	0	0	0	.00	-2
Guthrie,Jeremy, Bal	R	.200	5	1	0	0	0	.091	22	2	2	0	0	0	0	13	0	208.0	11	35	3	5	.939	9	6	1	0	.67	5
Gutierrez,Juan, Ari	R	-	0	0	0	0	0	.000	6	0	0	0	0	0	0	4	1	18.1	1	0	2	0	.333	2	0	0	0	.00	-2
Hacker,Eric, Min	R	-	0	0	0	0	0	-	0	0	0	0	0	0	0	0	0	5.1	0	1	0	0	1.000	0	0	0	0	-	0
Hagadone,Nick, Cle	L	-	0	0	0	0	0	-	0	0	0	0	0	0	0	0	0	11.0	0	1	0	0	1.000	1	1	1	0	1.00	-1
Halladay,Roy, Phi	R	.122	74	9	0	3	16	.123	204	25	2	0	0	9	3	94	21	233.2	12	30	1	0	.977	23	5	1	0	.22	-5
Hamburger,Mark, Tex	R	-	0	0	0	0	0	-	0	0	0	0	0	0	0	0	0	8.0	0	0	0	0	-	1	0	0	0	.00	0
Hamels,Cole, Phi	L	.159	69	11	0	3	3	.160	381	61	9	1	0	18	12	161	30	216.0	11	22	1	4	.971	29	6	1	0	.21	1
Hammel,Jason, Col	R	.152	46	7	1	4	14	.126	159	20	4	0	1	7	4	69	22	170.1	11	27	1	0	.974	22	6	1	1	.27	3
Hamren,Erik, SD	R	-	0	0	0	0	0	-	0	0	0	0	0	0	0	0	0	12.1	1	2	1	0	.750	1	1	0	0	1.00	0
Hand,Brad, Fla	L	.118	17	2	0	1	3	.118	17	2	0	0	0	1	0	7	3	60.0	2	10	1	0	.923	7	4	3	0	.57	3
Hanrahan,Joel, Pit	R	-	0	0	0	0	0	.235	17	4	2	1	0	3	0	5	4	68.2	4	7	2	0	.846	3	0	0	0	.00	-2
Hanson,Tommy, Atl	R	.051	39	2	0	0	6	.072	138	10	0	0	0	5	3	62	22	130.0	2	14	2	0	.889	33	3	1	0	.09	-5
Happ,J.A., Hou	L	.163	43	7	1	4	7	.092	120	11	2	0	1	5	5	46	19	156.1	4	13	0	0	1.000	16	5	3	0	.31	1
Harang,Aaron, SD	R	.089	56	5	0	1	6	.093	494	46	6	0	1	18	3	218	44	170.2	8	17	4	1	.862	34	10	1	1	.29	-1
Harden,Rich, Oak	R	-	0	0	0	0	0	.145	76	11	1	0	0	1	1	31	9	82.2	4	9	2	1	.867	9	5	0	0	.56	-1
Haren,Dan, LAA	R	.333	3	1	0	1	1	.227	260	59	21	0	2	27	8	66	19	238.1	13	35	0	3	1.000	26	5	3	0	.19	1
Harrell,Lucas, CWS-Hou	R	.000	3	0	0	0	0	.000	3	0	0	0	0	0	0	3	0	18.0	2	4	1	0	.857	0	0	0	0	-	1
Harrison,Matt, Tex	L	.000	9	0	0	0	0	.000	11	0	0	0	0	0	1	8	0	185.2	4	32	4	3	.900	6	3	2	0	.50	-1
Hatcher,Chris, Fla	R	-	0	0	0	0	0	.000	6	0	0	0	0	0	2	5	0	10.1	0	0	0	0	-	0	0	0	0	-	-1
Hawkins,LaTroy, Mil	R	-	0	0	0	0	0	.000	6	0	0	0	0	0	0	5	1	48.1	1	10	1	0	.917	3	1	0	0	.33	-1
Hawksworth,Blake, LAD	R	.000	1	0	0	0	0	.000	17	0	0	0	0	0	0	10	2	53.0	1	8	0	1	1.000	6	1	0	0	.17	1
Heilman,Aaron, Ari	R	.000	1	0	0	0	0	.021	47	1	0	0	0	1	2	24	5	35.1	0	7	1	0	.875	1	0	0	0	.00	-1
Hellickson,Jeremy, TB	R	.000	2	0	0	0	0	.000	2	0	0	0	0	0	0	2	0	189.0	15	16	0	0	1.000	11	1	1	2	.09	1
Hendrickson,Mark, Bal	L	-	0	0	0	0	0	.134	97	13	3	1	1	3	6	53	4	11.0	4	2	0	2	1.000	1	0	0	0	.00	-1
Hendriks,Liam, Min	R	-	0	0	0	0	0	-	0	0	0	0	0	0	0	0	0	23.1	0	6	0	0	1.000	0	0	0	0	-	2
Hensley,Clay, Fla	R	.000	14	0	0	0	2	.093	86	8	2	0	0	4	4	46	10	67.2	4	8	0	0	1.000	5	1	0	0	.20	1
Hernandez,David, Ari	R	-	0	0	0	0	0	.000	3	0	0	0	0	0	1	0	0	69.1	3	6	1	0	.900	3	1	0	0	.33	1
Hernandez,Felix, Sea	R	.143	7	1	0	0	0	.125	24	3	0	0	1	5	1	12	4	233.2	27	28	2	4	.965	39	8	0	0	.21	-4
Hernandez,Livan, Was	R	.217	46	10	0	7	15	.222	969	215	38	2	10	85	9	129	123	175.1	11	33	1	7	.978	18	9	1	0	.50	3
Herndon,David, Phi	R	.000	4	0	0	0	0	.000	6	0	0	0	0	0	0	5	0	57.0	4	10	0	1	1.000	5	2	0	0	.40	2
Herrera,Daniel, Mil-NYM	L	-	0	0	0	0	0	.000	3	0	0	0	0	0	1	2	1	9.2	0	2	0	0	1.000	0	0	0	0	-	0
Herrera,Kelvin, KC	R	-	0	0	0	0	0	-	0	0	0	0	0	0	0	0	0	2.0	1	0	0	0	1.000	0	0	0	0	-	0
Herrmann,Frank, Cle	R	.000	1	0	0	0	0	.000	1	0	0	0	0	0	0	0	0	56.1	3	0	3	0	1.000	7	0	0	0	.00	-3
Hill,Rich, Bos	L	-	0	0	0	0	0	.123	114	14	3	0	0	6	2	51	6	8.0	1	0	0	0	1.000	1	0	0	0	.00	0
Hochevar,Luke, KC	R	.000	2	0	0	0	0	.000	11	0	0	0	0	0	0	9	1	198.0	17	22	3	1	.929	23	3	0	0	.13	-3
Hoey,Jim, Min	R	-	0	0	0	0	0	-	0	0	0	0	0	0	0	0	0	24.2	2	2	0	0	1.000	4	1	0	0	.25	-1
Holland,Derek, Tex	L	-	0	0	0	0	0	.000	5	0	0	0	0	0	0	2	0	198.0	7	31	3	2	.927	16	9	5	0	.56	-2
Holland,Greg, KC	R	-	0	0	0	0	0	-	0	0	0	0	0	0	0	0	0	60.0	1	9	0	0	1.000	0	0	0	0	-	1
Horst,Jeremy, Cin	L	1.000	1	1	0	1	0	1.000	1	1	0	0	0	1	0	0	0	15.1	1	1	0	0	1.000	0	0	0	0	-	0
Hottovy,Tommy, Bos	L	-	0	0	0	0	0	-	0	0	0	0	0	0	0	0	0	4.0	0	0	0	0	-	1	0	0	0	.00	0
Howell,J.P., TB	L	-	0	0	0	0	0	.200	10	2	0	0	0	0	2	3	0	30.2	3	0	1	1	1.000	6	1	1	0	.17	1
Hudson,Daniel, Ari	R	.277	65	18	1	14	11	.239	92	22	5	0	1	20	3	28	14	222.0	7	22	2	3	.935	20	10	0	0	.50	-1
Hudson,Tim, Atl	R	.116	69	8	1	4	7	.166	429	71	13	1	2	31	17	127	45	215.0	8	36	2	4	.957	21	5	0	0	.24	1
Huff,David, Cle	L	-	0	0	0	0	0	.000	4	0	0	0	0	0	0	2	2	50.2	0	4	0	0	1.000	4	0	0	0	.00	1
Hughes,Dusty, Min	L	-	0	0	0	0	0	-	0	0	0	0	0	0	0	0	0	12.2	1	1	0	0	1.000	2	2	1	0	1.00	1
Hughes,Jared, Pit	R	-	0	0	0	0	0	-	0	0	0	0	0	0	0	0	0	11.0	0	4	0	0	1.000	2	0	0	0	.00	1

Pitchers Hitting, Fielding and Holding Runners

Pitcher	T	2011 Hitting Avg	AB	H	HR	RBI	SH	Career Avg	AB	H	2B	3B	HR	RBI	BB	SO	SH	Inn	PO	A	E	DP	Pct	SBA	CS	PCS	PPO	CS%	RS
Hughes,Phil, NYY	R	-	0	0	0	0	0	.000	1	0	0	0	0	0	0	0	1	74.2	2	6	0	0	1.000	7	0	0	0	.00	-2
Humber,Philip, CWS	R	.000	5	0	0	0	1	.000	6	0	0	0	0	0	0	2	2	163.0	12	15	1	0	.964	16	3	0	0	.19	-5
Hunter,Tommy, Tex-Bal	R	-	0	0	0	0	0	.000	1	0	0	0	0	0	0	1	0	84.2	7	11	1	2	.947	10	4	1	0	.40	3
Igarashi,Ryota, NYM	R	-	0	0	0	0	0	-	0	0	0	0	0	0	0	0	0	38.2	1	9	0	1	1.000	4	1	0	0	.25	1
Isringhausen,J., NYM	R	-	0	0	0	0	0	.202	104	21	4	1	2	16	5	36	8	46.2	1	6	0	0	1.000	12	2	1	1	.17	-2
Jackson,Edwin, CWS-StL	R	.267	30	8	0	2	2	.184	98	18	0	0	1	7	6	41	8	199.2	12	28	3	2	.930	23	1	0	1	.04	-3
Jakubauskas,Chris, Bal	R	.667	3	2	0	0	0	.400	5	2	0	0	0	0	0	1	0	72.1	2	7	0	1	1.000	4	2	0	0	.50	0
James,Chuck, Min	L	-	0	0	0	0	0	.082	97	8	1	0	0	3	3	34	12	10.1	0	2	0		1.000	0	0	0	0	-	1
Jansen,Kenley, LAD	R	-	0	0	0	0	0	1.000	1	1	0	0	0	0	1	0	0	53.2	2	3	0	1	1.000	7	0	0	0	.00	0
Janssen,Casey, Tor	R	-	0	0	0	0	0	.000	3	0	0	0	0	0	0	2	1	55.2	6	9	2	1	.882	5	3	0	0	.60	1
Jeffress,Jeremy, KC	R	-	0	0	0	0	0	-	0	0	0	0	0	0	0	0	0	15.1	1	3	1	0	.800	2	2	1	0	1.00	1
Jenks,Bobby, Bos	R	-	0	0	0	0	0	-	0	0	0	0	0	0	0	0	0	15.2	1	3	0	1	1.000	2	0	0	0	.00	0
Jepsen,Kevin, LAA	R	-	0	0	0	0	0	-	0	0	0	0	0	0	0	0	0	13.0	1	2	0		1.000	1	0	0	0	.00	-1
Jimenez,Cesar, Sea	L	-	0	0	0	0	0	-	0	0	0	0	0	0	0	0	0	6.2	0	1	0		1.000	0	0	0	0	-	0
Jimenez,Ubaldo, Col-Cle	R	.114	35	4	0	3	5	.117	265	31	0	0	9	16	86	32	188.1	14	28	2	1	.955	30	6	0	2	.20	0
Joaquin,Waldis, SF	R	-	0	0	0	0	0	-	0	0	0	0	0	0	0	0	0	6.1	0	0	0		-	1	1	0	0	1.00	0
Johnson,Alan, Col	R	.000	1	0	0	0	1	.000	1	0	0	0	0	0	0	1	1	4.0	1	1	0		1.000	0	0	0	0	-	0
Johnson,Jim, Bal	R	-	0	0	0	0	0	-	0	0	0	0	0	0	0	0	0	91.0	8	16	1	2	.960	6	2	0	0	.33	-1
Johnson,Josh, Fla	R	.158	19	3	0	4	2	.133	218	29	5	0	3	23	11	111	27	60.1	8	7	0	1	1.000	8	3	0	0	.38	1
Judy,Josh, Cle	R	-	0	0	0	0	0	-	0	0	0	0	0	0	0	0	0	14.0	0	1	0		1.000	2	0	0	0	.00	0
Jurrjens,Jair, Atl	R	.106	47	5	0	1	7	.115	209	24	3	1	0	7	17	69	25	152.0	9	29	0	2	1.000	24	9	1	0	.38	2
Karstens,Jeff, Pit	R	.104	48	5	0	2	7	.085	117	10	1	0	0	2	8	64	14	162.1	15	19	2	2	.944	16	2	0	0	.13	0
Kazmir,Scott, LAA	L	-	0	0	0	0	0	.071	14	1	0	0	0	1	0	6	1	1.2	0	1	0		1.000	2	0	0	0	.00	1
Kelley,Shawn, Sea	R	-	0	0	0	0	0	-	0	0	0	0	0	0	0	0	0	12.2	0	1	0		.000	0	0	0	0	-	-1
Kendrick,Kyle, Phi	R	.208	24	5	0	0	5	.134	172	23	3	0	4	10	71	23	114.2	7	17	1	0	.960	6	3	0	0	.50	2
Kennedy,Ian, Ari	R	.131	61	8	0	4	9	.165	115	19	4	0	0	6	11	48	14	222.0	14	22	0	1	1.000	6	0	0	1	.00	3
Kershaw,Clayton, LAD	L	.225	71	16	0	4	11	.128	203	26	0	0	7	7	59	46	233.1	9	38	0	2	1.000	23	9	7	2	.39	2
Kimball,Cole, Was	R	.000	1	0	0	0	0	.000	1	0	0	0	0	0	1	1	0	14.0	2	0	0		1.000	1	1	0	0	1.00	0
Kimbrel,Craig, Atl	R	-	0	0	0	0	0	-	0	0	0	0	0	0	0	0	0	77.0	4	7	0	0	1.000	4	3	1	0	.75	1
Kinney,Josh, CWS	R	-	0	0	0	0	0	.000	1	0	0	0	0	0	0	1	0	17.2	0	4	0		1.000	0	0	0	0	-	-1
Kintzler,Brandon, Mil	R	.000	1	0	0	0	0	.000	1	0	0	0	0	0	0	1	0	14.2	0	3	0		1.000	0	0	0	0	-	1
Kirkman,Michael, Tex	L	-	0	0	0	0	0	-	0	0	0	0	0	0	0	0	0	27.1	2	4	0		1.000	1	0	0	0	.00	2
Kluber,Corey, Cle	R	-	0	0	0	0	0	-	0	0	0	0	0	0	0	0	0	4.1	0	0	0		-	0	0	0	0	-	0
Kohn,Michael, LAA	R	-	0	0	0	0	0	-	0	0	0	0	0	0	0	0	0	12.1	1	1	1	0	.667	2	0	0	0	.00	-1
Kontos,George, NYY	R	-	0	0	0	0	0	-	0	0	0	0	0	0	0	0	0	6.0	0	0	0		-	2	1	0	0	.50	0
Kroenke,Zach, Ari	L	-	0	0	0	0	0	.000	2	0	0	0	0	0	0	0	0	4.0	0	1	0		1.000	0	0	0	0	-	0
Kuo,Hong-Chih, LAD	L	-	0	0	0	0	0	.185	27	5	2	0	1	1	1	14	8	27.0	1	0	1	0	.500	5	1	0	0	.20	0
Kuroda,Hiroki, LAD	R	.115	61	7	0	1	6	.106	198	21	1	0	0	3	13	68	32	202.0	15	36	0	5	1.000	14	5	1	0	.36	6
Lackey,John, Bos	R	.333	3	1	0	1	0	.105	38	4	2	0	0	2	0	11	2	160.0	19	16	3	4	.921	36	3	0	0	.08	-5
Laffey,Aaron, Sea-NYY	L	-	0	0	0	0	0	.333	3	1	0	0	0	0	0	0	0	53.1	7	11	0	0	1.000	2	0	0	0	.00	1
Lannan,John, Was	L	.088	57	5	1	5	5	.097	217	21	4	0	1	10	13	96	18	184.2	10	31	2	4	.953	10	4	1	0	.40	3
Latos,Mat, SD	R	.071	56	4	1	1	5	.085	129	11	3	0	2	4	1	66	16	194.1	10	28	1	2	.974	33	8	1	0	.24	-1
League,Brandon, Sea	R	-	0	0	0	0	0	-	0	0	0	0	0	0	0	0	0	61.1	1	4	3	0	.625	6	1	0	0	.17	-3
Leake,Mike, Cin	R	.200	55	11	0	2	10	.262	103	27	3	0	0	5	6	38	16	167.2	18	22	0	3	1.000	7	2	0	2	.29	3
LeBlanc,Wade, SD	L	.364	22	8	0	1	3	.287	87	25	0	0	2	3	22	11	79.2	6	13	0	1	1.000	13	6	3	0	.46	2
LeCure,Sam, Cin	R	.111	9	1	0	0	1	.100	20	2	0	0	0	1	7	2	77.2	12	10	0	2	1.000	6	2	1	0	.33	2
Ledezma,Wil, Tor	L	-	0	0	0	0	0	.000	12	0	0	0	0	0	1	6	2	6.0	0	0	0		-	0	0	0	0	-	-1
Lee,Cliff, Phi	L	.200	75	15	2	7	5	.168	143	24	4	0	2	8	2	53	7	232.2	7	26	1	1	.971	15	4	2	0	.27	-1
Leroux,Chris, Pit	R	-	0	0	0	0	0	-	0	0	0	0	0	0	0	0	0	25.0	2	2	0		1.000	3	1	0	0	.33	-1
Lester,Jon, Bos	L	.000	5	0	0	0	0	.000	20	0	0	0	0	1	1	12	0	191.2	9	19	1	2	.966	26	12	4	0	.46	0
Lewis,Colby, Tex	R	.125	8	1	0	0	0	.188	16	3	1	0	2	0	5	1	200.1	3	13	4	1	.800	17	7	0	0	.41	3
Lewis,Rommie, Tor	L	-	0	0	0	0	0	.000	1	0	0	0	0	0	0	1	0	5.0	0	1	0		1.000	0	0	0	0	-	0
Lidge,Brad, Phi	R	-	0	0	0	0	0	.286	7	2	1	0	0	2	0	4	0	19.1	1	2	0		1.000	7	1	0	0	.14	-2
Lilly,Ted, LAD	L	.086	58	5	0	4	5	.104	327	34	6	1	0	17	7	137	33	192.2	7	25	2	0	.941	37	2	1	0	.05	-3
Lincecum,Tim, SF	R	.082	61	5	0	1	8	.121	307	37	3	1	0	14	19	148	46	217.0	12	27	1	0	.975	37	14	2	0	.38	0
Lincoln,Brad, Pit	R	.083	12	1	0	1	1	.259	27	7	1	0	0	4	1	8	4	47.2	9	7	0	1	1.000	6	2	0	0	.33	0
Lindblom,Josh, LAD	R	.000	1	0	0	0	0	.000	1	0	0	0	0	0	0	1	0	29.2	1	4	0		1.000	6	5	0	0	.83	1
Lindsay,Shane, CWS	R	-	0	0	0	0	0	-	0	0	0	0	0	0	0	0	0	6.0	1	1	0		1.000	1	0	0	0	.00	0
Lindstrom,Matt, Col	R	-	0	0	0	0	0	.000	1	0	0	0	0	0	0	1	0	54.0	4	11	1	1	.938	12	2	0	1	.17	-1
Linebrink,Scott, Atl	R	-	0	0	0	0	0	.222	18	4	1	0	0	0	0	10	2	54.1	3	5	2	0	.800	9	3	0	0	.33	-2
Liriano,Francisco, Min	L	.500	2	1	0	1	0	.143	14	2	0	0	0	2	2	7	2	134.1	5	17	0	1	1.000	14	5	3	0	.36	3
Litsch,Jesse, Tor	R	.000	5	0	0	0	0	.000	5	0	0	0	0	0	0	4	0	75.0	11	13	2	2	.885	3	1	0	0	.33	4
Locke,Jeff, Pit	L	.000	5	0	0	0	0	.000	5	0	0	0	0	0	0	0	4	16.2	0	5	0		1.000	4	1	1	0	.25	0
Loe,Kameron, Mil	R	.000	1	0	0	0	0	.200	5	1	0	0	0	0	1	3	0	72.0	3	9	1	0	.923	2	0	0	0	.00	-2
Logan,Boone, NYY	L	-	0	0	0	0	0	-	0	0	0	0	0	0	0	0	0	41.2	2	9	1	0	.917	5	2	2	0	.40	0
Lohse,Kyle, StL	R	.175	63	11	0	3	6	.166	290	48	7	0	0	19	4	82	39	188.1	24	27	0	1	1.000	3	2	0	0	.67	3
Lopez,Javier, SF	L	.000	2	0	0	0	0	.091	11	1	0	0	0	1	0	5	1	53.0	3	17	1	2	.952	5	2	1	0	.40	3
Lopez,Rodrigo, ChC	R	.067	30	2	0	0	2	.062	145	9	0	0	0	1	3	75	9	97.2	7	17	0	2	1.000	13	7	1	1	.54	-1
Lopez,Wilton, Hou	R	-	0	0	0	0	0	.000	5	0	0	0	0	0	0	0	2	71.0	4	16	2	0	.909	3	2	0	0	.67	2
Lowe,Derek, Atl	R	.173	52	9	1	7	9	.146	432	63	13	0	1	25	29	129	67	187.0	12	32	0	1	1.000	30	4	1	0	.13	-2

Pitchers Hitting, Fielding and Holding Runners

Pitcher	T	2011 Hitting						Career Hitting										2011 Fielding and Holding Runners											
		Avg	AB	H	HR	RBI	SH	Avg	AB	H	2B	3B	HR	RBI	BB	SO	SH	Inn	PO	A	E	DP	Pct	SBA	CS	PCS	PPO	CS%	RS
Lowe,Mark, Tex	R	-	0	0	0	0	0	.000	1	0	0	0	0	0	0	1	0	45.0	3	3	0	0	1.000	4	3	0	0	.75	0
Luebke,Cory, SD	L	.212	33	7	0	0	1	.184	38	7	0	0	0	0	2	21	1	139.2	6	26	0	2	1.000	17	6	4	0	.35	2
Lueke,Josh, Sea	R	-	0	0	0	0	0	-	0	0	0	0	0	0	0	0	0	32.2	0	3	0	0	1.000	1	0	0	0	.00	-1
Lyles,Jordan, Hou	R	.120	25	3	0	0	2	.120	25	3	0	0	0	0	2	9	2	94.0	5	18	1	0	.958	4	0	0	1	.00	1
Lynn,Lance, StL	R	.000	4	0	0	0	0	.000	4	0	0	0	0	0	1	1	0	34.2	2	2	0	0	1.000	3	1	0	0	.33	-2
Lyon,Brandon, Hou	R	1.000	1	1	0	1	0	1.000	1	1	1	0	0	1	1	0	0	13.1	4	3	0	1	1.000	2	0	0	0	.00	1
MacDougal,Mike, LAD	R	-	0	0	0	0	0	-	0	0	0	0	0	0	0	0	0	57.0	1	9	3	0	.769	7	2	0	0	.29	-2
Madson,Ryan, Phi	R	-	0	0	0	0	0	.125	48	6	1	0	0	2	2	20	7	60.2	1	5	1	0	.857	5	1	0	0	.20	-1
Magnuson,Trystan, Oak	R	-	0	0	0	0	0	-	0	0	0	0	0	0	0	0	0	14.2	2	3	0	0	1.000	1	0	0	0	.00	1
Maholm,Paul, Pit	L	.109	46	5	0	1	4	.116	354	41	2	0	1	13	19	183	23	162.1	9	28	1	2	.974	10	3	2	1	.30	2
Maine,Scott, ChC	L	-	0	0	0	0	0	-	0	0	0	0	0	0	0	0	0	7.0	0	0	0	0	-	0	0	0	0	-	0
Maloney,Matt, Cin	L	.000	4	0	0	0	0	.211	19	4	0	0	0	0	1	6	4	18.2	1	6	0	1	1.000	0	0	0	0	-	2
Manship,Jeff, Min	R	-	0	0	0	0	0	.000	1	0	0	0	0	0	0	1	0	3.1	1	0	0	0	1.000	1	0	0	0	.00	0
Marcum,Shaun, Mil	R	.153	59	9	1	6	12	.145	69	10	3	0	1	7	6	25	13	200.2	13	26	1	4	.975	14	6	0	1	.43	1
Marmol,Carlos, ChC	R	-	0	0	0	0	0	.200	30	6	1	0	1	1	0	11	3	74.0	6	9	0	1	1.000	13	1	0	0	.08	1
Marquez,Jeff, NYY	R	-	0	0	0	0	0	-	0	0	0	0	0	0	0	0	0	4.0	0	1	0	0	.000	0	0	0	0	-	0
Marquis,Jason, Was-Ari	R	.174	46	8	0	3	3	.197	573	113	30	2	5	53	13	139	37	132.0	11	12	1	2	.958	7	1	0	0	.14	-3
Marshall,Sean, ChC	L	-	0	0	0	0	0	.158	101	16	1	0	1	5	2	48	8	75.2	5	11	1	0	.941	11	2	1	0	.18	-2
Marte,Luis, Det	R	-	0	0	0	0	0	-	0	0	0	0	0	0	0	0	0	3.2	0	0	0	0	-	0	0	0	0	-	0
Martinez,Cristhian, Atl	R	.333	6	2	0	2	2	.167	12	2	1	0	0	2	0	4	2	77.2	9	9	0	1	1.000	0	0	0	0	-	1
Masset,Nick, Cin	R	-	0	0	0	0	0	.000	5	0	0	0	0	0	0	5	1	70.1	7	13	1	0	.952	7	1	0	0	.14	0
Masterson,Justin, Cle	R	.167	6	1	0	0	0	.133	15	2	0	0	0	0	0	7	1	216.0	15	32	2	4	.959	28	14	1	1	.50	0
Mateo,Marcos, ChC	R	.000	1	0	0	0	1	1.000	3	0	0	0	0	0	0	1	1	23.0	0	1	0	0	1.000	4	2	0	0	.50	-1
Mathieson,Scott, Phi	R	-	0	0	0	0	0	.143	7	1	0	0	0	0	0	4	2	5.0	0	1	0	0	1.000	0	0	0	0	-	-1
Matsuzaka,Daisuke, Bos	R	-	0	0	0	0	0	.167	12	2	0	0	0	1	0	4	1	37.1	0	2	0	0	1.000	6	0	0	0	.00	-3
Mattheus,Ryan, Was	R	-	0	0	0	0	0	-	0	0	0	0	0	0	0	0	0	32.0	0	2	0	0	1.000	4	1	0	0	.25	-1
Matusz,Brian, Bal	L	.000	2	0	0	0	0	.000	4	0	0	0	0	0	0	0	0	49.2	1	2	0	1	1.000	10	2	0	0	.20	-2
Maya,Yunesky, Was	R	.000	8	0	0	0	1	.067	15	1	0	0	0	0	0	9	3	32.2	2	5	0	1	1.000	3	2	0	0	.67	-1
Mazzaro,Vin, KC	R	.000	2	0	0	0	0	.000	6	0	0	0	0	0	0	4	4	28.1	1	3	0	0	1.000	5	1	0	1	.20	-2
McAllister,Zach, Cle	R	-	0	0	0	0	0	-	0	0	0	0	0	0	0	0	0	17.2	0	1	1	0	.500	2	1	0	1	.50	-1
McCarthy,Brandon, Oak	R	-	0	0	0	0	0	.000	9	0	0	0	0	0	0	4	1	170.2	12	22	4	1	.895	15	4	1	0	.27	-2
McClellan,Kyle, StL	R	.143	35	5	0	4	5	.133	45	6	1	0	0	4	1	17	6	141.2	14	20	1	3	.971	9	3	0	3	.33	0
McClendon,Mike, Mil	R	-	0	0	0	0	0	.500	2	1	0	0	0	0	0	0	0	13.2	1	3	0	0	1.000	0	0	0	0	-	1
McCutchen,Daniel, Pit	R	.000	5	0	0	0	1	.067	30	2	0	0	0	1	1	8	3	84.2	7	6	2	0	.867	12	3	0	2	.25	0
McDonald,James, Pit	R	.091	55	5	0	3	5	.071	85	6	2	0	0	3	4	47	7	171.0	8	19	1	0	.964	25	8	1	1	.32	-2
McGee,Jake, TB	L	-	0	0	0	0	0	-	0	0	0	0	0	0	0	0	0	28.0	0	3	0	0	1.000	4	0	0	0	.00	-1
McGowan,Dustin, Tor	R	-	0	0	0	0	0	.200	10	2	0	0	0	0	0	4	1	21.0	1	1	0	0	1.000	4	0	0	0	.00	-1
Medlen,Kris, Atl	R	-	0	0	0	0	0	.125	40	5	1	0	0	2	3	21	2	2.1	0	2	0	0	1.000	0	0	0	0	-	1
Meek,Evan, Pit	R	-	0	0	0	0	0	1.000	1	1	0	0	0	0	0	0	1	20.2	2	7	0	0	1.000	0	0	0	0	-	2
Melancon,Mark, Hou	R	-	0	0	0	0	0	-	0	0	0	0	0	0	1	0	0	74.1	12	5	1	0	.944	8	2	0	0	.25	1
Mendoza,Luis, KC	R	-	0	0	0	0	0	.000	1	0	0	0	0	0	0	1	1	14.2	2	3	0	0	1.000	2	2	0	0	1.00	0
Mickolio,Kam, Ari	R	.000	1	0	0	0	0	.000	1	0	0	0	0	0	0	0	0	6.2	0	1	0	0	1.000	1	0	0	0	.00	0
Mijares,Jose, Min	L	-	0	0	0	0	0	-	0	0	0	0	0	0	0	0	0	49.0	2	4	1	0	.857	5	3	2	0	.60	0
Miley,Wade, Ari	L	.077	13	1	0	1	1	.077	13	1	0	0	0	1	2	2	1	40.0	1	4	1	1	.833	5	2	1	0	.40	-1
Miller,Andrew, Bos	L	.000	4	0	0	0	0	.056	72	4	0	0	0	3	0	36	4	65.0	2	9	2	0	.846	9	1	0	0	.11	-2
Miller,Jim, Col	R	-	0	0	0	0	0	-	0	0	0	0	0	0	0	0	0	7.0	0	0	0	0	-	0	0	0	0	-	0
Miller,Trever, StL-Tor-Bos	L	-	0	0	0	0	0	.167	6	1	1	0	0	0	1	1	2	21.1	3	5	0	1	1.000	2	1	0	0	.50	0
Mills,Brad, Tor	L	-	0	0	0	0	0	.000	1	0	0	0	0	0	0	0	0	18.1	1	2	0	0	1.000	0	0	0	0	-	-1
Millwood,Kevin, Col	R	.158	19	3	2	3	3	.122	467	57	15	0	4	27	21	215	55	54.1	7	4	1	0	.917	4	3	0	0	.75	0
Milone,Tom, Was	L	.167	6	1	1	3	4	.167	6	1	0	1	0	3	0	1	4	26.0	1	4	0	1	1.000	2	1	1	0	.50	1
Minor,Mike, Atl	L	.111	27	3	0	0	2	.081	37	3	2	0	0	0	4	22	2	82.2	1	11	0	0	1.000	4	2	0	0	.50	1
Misch,Pat, NYM	L	-	0	0	0	0	0	.077	39	3	0	0	0	1	3	14	8	7.0	3	0	0	0	1.000	0	0	0	0	-	0
Mitre,Sergio, Mil-NYY	R	.000	2	0	0	0	0	.138	80	11	4	0	0	2	3	33	13	38.1	2	7	1	1	.900	9	1	0	0	.11	-2
Moore,Matt, TB	L	-	0	0	0	0	0	-	0	0	0	0	0	0	0	0	0	9.1	1	1	0	0	1.000	0	0	0	0	-	-1
Morales,Fr., Col-Bos	L	-	0	0	0	0	0	.250	28	7	0	0	0	2	1	9	2	46.1	1	8	0	0	1.000	6	0	0	4	.00	0
Morrow,Brandon, Tor	R	.000	6	0	0	0	0	.000	12	0	0	0	0	0	0	4	0	179.1	8	13	3	0	.875	22	5	0	0	.23	-6
Mortensen,Clay, Col	R	.000	13	0	0	1	0	.000	14	0	0	0	0	0	1	9	0	58.1	3	9	1	0	.923	7	3	2	0	.43	1
Morton,Charlie, Pit	R	.080	50	4	0	2	11	.081	124	10	4	0	0	3	1	71	18	171.2	7	31	1	1	.974	22	6	1	1	.27	-2
Moscoso,Guillermo, Oak	R	.000	2	0	0	0	1	.000	2	0	0	0	0	0	0	2	1	128.0	7	6	2	1	.867	7	2	1	0	.29	1
Moseley,Dustin, SD	R	.138	29	4	0	0	6	.138	29	4	0	0	0	0	1	11	6	120.0	8	25	0	1	1.000	22	4	0	1	.18	0
Moskos,Daniel, Pit	L	-	0	0	0	0	0	-	0	0	0	0	0	0	0	0	0	24.1	0	4	2	1	.667	3	0	0	0	.00	0
Mota,Guillermo, SF	R	.100	10	1	0	0	0	.188	48	9	2	0	2	7	0	21	2	80.1	4	10	0	0	1.000	6	2	0	1	.33	1
Motte,Jason, StL	R	.000	1	0	0	0	0	.000	4	0	0	0	0	0	0	4	0	68.0	11	12	0	2	1.000	7	1	0	1	.14	2
Moylan,Peter, Atl	R	-	0	0	0	0	0	.000	7	0	0	0	0	0	1	6	0	8.1	1	1	0	0	1.000	0	0	0	0	-	-1
Mujica,Edward, Fla	R	.000	1	0	0	0	0	.222	9	2	0	0	0	2	2	2	0	76.0	3	17	2	3	.909	8	1	0	2	.13	0
Myers,Brett, Hou	R	.159	63	10	0	4	4	.134	471	63	11	0	12	25	161	60	216.0	33	19	4	2	.929	21	6	0	1	.29	-3
Narveson,Chris, Mil	L	.163	49	8	0	5	7	.234	107	25	3	0	0	12	5	40	15	161.2	7	25	1	0	.970	20	8	6	0	.40	4
Nathan,Joe, Min	R	-	0	0	0	0	0	.159	63	10	3	0	2	4	3	17	10	44.2	5	4	0	0	1.000	8	0	0	0	.00	0
Neshek,Pat, SD	R	-	0	0	0	0	0	-	0	0	0	0	0	0	0	0	0	24.2	0	2	0	0	1.000	3	0	0	0	.00	0
Nicasio,Juan, Col	R	.136	22	3	0	0	1	.136	22	3	2	0	0	0	0	16	1	71.2	5	15	1	1	.952	8	1	1	0	.13	2

Pitchers Hitting, Fielding and Holding Runners

Pitcher	T	2011 Hitting						Career Hitting										2011 Fielding and Holding Runners											
		Avg	AB	H	HR	RBI	SH	Avg	AB	H	2B	3B	HR	RBI	BB	SO	SH	Inn	PO	A	E	DP	Pct	SBA	CS	PCS	PPO	CS%	RS
Niemann,Jeff, TB	R	.333	3	1	0	0	0	.077	13	1	0	0	0	0	0	9	1	135.1	10	21	0	1	1.000	21	5	1	0	.24	0
Niese,Jonathon, NYM	L	.061	49	3	0	0	7	.129	116	15	2	1	0	4	12	67	13	157.1	4	36	0	1	1.000	8	1	0	0	.13	2
Noesi,Hector, NYY	R	-	0	0	0	0	0	-	0	0	0	0	0	0	0	0	0	56.1	1	7	0	1	1.000	9	3	0	0	.33	1
Nolasco,Ricky, Fla	R	.089	56	5	0	1	11	.137	263	36	7	0	1	17	11	120	44	206.0	10	23	1	2	.971	14	2	0	0	.14	-1
Norberto,Jordan, Oak	L	-	0	0	0	0	0	-	0	0	0	0	0	0	0	0	0	6.2	0	0	1	0	.000	0	0	0	0	-	-2
Norris,Bud, Hou	R	.132	53	7	0	5	11	.150	113	17	4	0	0	7	3	42	22	186.0	22	29	3	0	.944	22	6	0	3	.27	1
Nova,Ivan, NYY	R	.000	4	0	0	0	1	.000	4	0	0	0	0	0	0	4	1	165.1	16	21	0	0	1.000	18	8	0	0	.44	3
Nunez,Leo, Fla	R	.000	1	0	0	0	0	.000	1	0	0	0	0	0	0	0	0	64.1	5	6	0	1	1.000	7	1	0	0	.14	1
O'Connor,Mike, NYM	L	-	0	0	0	0	0	.061	33	2	0	0	0	1	1	19	1	6.2	0	0	0	0	-	1	0	0	0	.00	0
O'Day,Darren, Tex	R	-	0	0	0	0	0	-	0	0	0	0	0	0	0	0	0	16.2	2	2	1	0	.800	4	0	0	0	.00	-1
O'Flaherty,Eric, Atl	L	-	0	0	0	0	0	.000	2	0	0	0	0	0	0	2	0	73.2	3	13	0	0	1.000	7	2	1	0	.29	0
Ogando,Alexi, Tex	R	.500	2	1	0	0	0	.667	3	2	0	0	0	0	0	1	0	169.0	8	12	0	1	1.000	5	3	0	0	.60	1
Ohlendorf,Ross, Pit	R	.214	14	3	1	4	1	.085	106	9	0	0	1	4	3	48	7	38.2	1	4	0	0	1.000	9	2	1	0	.22	-2
Ohman,Will, CWS	L	-	0	0	0	0	0	.400	5	2	0	0	0	1	1	2	1	53.1	1	6	0	0	1.000	3	1	1	0	.33	-1
Okajima,Hideki, Bos	L	-	0	0	0	0	0	.000	1	0	0	0	0	0	0	0	0	8.1	2	3	0	0	1.000	2	0	0	0	.00	0
Oliver,Andrew, Det	L	-	0	0	0	0	0	.000	2	0	0	0	0	0	0	1	0	9.2	0	1	0	0	1.000	5	1	0	0	.20	-1
Oliver,Darren, Tex	L	-	0	0	0	0	0	.221	217	48	11	0	1	20	8	74	15	51.0	1	6	2	0	.778	6	2	2	0	.33	-2
Oliveros,Lester, Det-Min	R	-	0	0	0	0	0	-	0	0	0	0	0	0	0	0	0	21.1	0	3	0	1	1.000	0	0	0	0	-	1
Olson,Garrett, Pit	L	-	0	0	0	0	0	.167	6	1	0	0	0	1	0	2	2	4.1	0	0	1	0	.000	0	0	0	0	-	0
Ondrusek,Logan, Cin	R	-	0	0	0	0	0	.000	4	0	0	0	0	0	0	4	0	61.1	4	14	1	2	.947	5	1	0	0	.20	0
Ortiz,Ramon, ChC	R	.000	2	0	0	0	1	.077	143	11	2	0	1	4	5	61	15	33.1	2	6	0	0	1.000	1	0	0	0	.00	1
O'Sullivan,Sean, KC	R	-	0	0	0	0	0	.250	4	1	0	0	0	0	0	1	0	58.1	4	7	1	0	.917	5	4	0	0	.80	2
Oswalt,Roy, Phi	R	.079	38	3	0	2	7	.152	651	99	7	0	1	36	27	179	105	139.0	5	18	1	5	.958	11	0	0	0	.00	-3
Outman,Josh, Oak	L	.000	5	0	0	0	0	.000	7	0	0	0	0	0	0	2	0	58.1	2	11	1	1	.929	5	2	2	0	.40	1
Owings,Micah, Ari	R	.211	19	4	0	1	0	.286	203	58	14	2	9	35	8	70	3	63.0	3	8	1	2	.917	4	2	0	1	.50	2
Padilla,Vicente, LAD	R	-	0	0	0	0	0	.108	250	27	4	1	0	17	16	130	30	8.2	0	1	0	0	1.000	0	0	0	0	-	0
Palmer,Matt, LAA	R	-	0	0	0	0	0	.200	10	2	0	0	0	0	1	5	1	15.2	1	4	0	0	1.000	1	1	0	0	1.00	0
Papelbon,Jonathan, Bos	R	-	0	0	0	0	0	-	0	0	0	0	0	0	0	0	0	64.1	3	2	1	0	.833	6	0	0	0	.00	-2
Parker,Jarrod, Ari	R	.500	2	1	0	0	0	.500	2	1	1	0	0	0	0	1	0	5.2	0	1	0	0	1.000	0	0	0	0	-	0
Parnell,Bobby, NYM	R	-	0	0	0	0	0	.111	9	1	0	0	0	0	0	3	4	59.1	2	10	1	0	.923	9	0	0	0	.00	-3
Paterson,Joe, Ari	L	-	0	0	0	0	0	-	0	0	0	0	0	0	0	0	0	34.0	3	10	1	0	.929	2	0	0	0	.00	2
Patton,Troy, Bal	L	-	0	0	0	0	0	.333	3	1	0	0	0	0	0	1	0	30.0	2	2	0	0	1.000	1	0	0	0	.00	-2
Pauley,David, Sea-Det	R	-	0	0	0	0	0	-	0	0	0	0	0	0	0	0	0	74.0	4	10	0	0	1.000	8	3	0	0	.38	-1
Paulino,Felipe, Col-KC	R	.000	1	0	0	1	3	.143	56	8	1	0	0	1	1	29	9	139.1	8	19	3	3	.900	14	3	1	1	.21	-2
Pavano,Carl, Min	R	.000	6	0	0	0	0	.142	309	44	8	2	2	14	4	122	36	222.0	16	39	2	4	.965	29	5	0	2	.17	1
Peacock,Brad, Was	R	.000	4	0	0	0	0	.000	4	0	0	0	0	0	0	0	0	12.0	1	0	0	0	1.000	1	0	0	0	-	-1
Peavy,Jake, CWS	R	.000	1	0	0	0	0	.179	413	74	14	1	2	26	19	119	45	111.2	9	6	1	0	.938	15	5	0	0	.33	-2
Pelfrey,Mike, NYM	R	.109	55	6	0	4	4	.097	258	25	4	0	0	13	13	70	23	193.2	15	25	1	1	.976	31	2	0	1	.06	-2
Pena,Tony, CWS	R	-	0	0	0	0	0	.143	7	1	0	0	0	1	0	2	0	20.1	0	2	0	0	1.000	2	0	0	0	.00	0
Pendleton,L., NYY-Hou	R	-	0	0	0	0	0	-	0	0	0	0	0	0	0	0	0	18.2	0	1	0	0	1.000	0	0	0	0	-	-1
Penny,Brad, Det	R	.000	4	0	0	0	0	.155	522	81	16	2	3	34	3	170	41	181.2	8	26	1	1	.971	22	6	2	0	.27	-1
Peralta,Joel, TB	R	-	0	0	0	0	0	.250	4	1	1	0	0	2	0	2	0	67.2	7	2	0	1	1.000	7	2	0	1	.29	0
Perez,Chris, Cle	R	-	0	0	0	0	0	.000	1	0	0	0	0	0	0	1	0	59.2	2	11	1	1	.929	8	0	0	0	.00	-2
Perez,Juan, Phi	L	-	0	0	0	0	0	-	0	0	0	0	0	0	0	0	0	5.0	0	0	0	0	-	0	0	0	0	-	0
Perez,Luis, Tor	L	-	0	0	0	0	0	-	0	0	0	0	0	0	0	0	0	65.0	2	6	2	1	.800	5	3	0	0	.60	-1
Perez,Rafael, Cle	L	-	0	0	0	0	0	.000	1	0	0	0	0	0	0	1	0	63.0	6	15	3	0	.875	6	4	0	0	.67	2
Perkins,Glen, Min	L	-	0	0	0	0	0	.000	4	0	0	0	0	0	0	4	3	61.2	3	7	1	0	.909	5	2	1	0	.40	-1
Perry,Ryan, Det	R	-	0	0	0	0	0	-	0	0	0	0	0	0	0	0	0	37.0	3	2	0	1	1.000	3	1	0	0	.33	0
Pestano,Vinnie, Cle	R	-	0	0	0	0	0	-	0	0	0	0	0	0	0	0	0	62.0	2	3	0	0	1.000	1	0	0	0	.00	1
Phillips,Zach, Bal	L	-	0	0	0	0	0	-	0	0	0	0	0	0	0	0	0	8.0	0	1	0	0	1.000	0	0	0	0	-	1
Pineda,Michael, Sea	R	.200	5	1	0	0	0	.200	5	1	0	0	0	0	0	2	0	171.0	8	17	1	1	.962	20	10	0	0	.50	-1
Pineiro,Joel, LAA	R	.000	5	0	0	0	1	.102	167	17	6	0	0	10	11	97	21	145.2	4	17	1	2	.955	8	3	1	0	.38	-1
Pomeranz,Drew, Col	L	.200	5	1	0	0	2	.200	5	1	0	0	0	0	0	3	2	18.1	0	1	0	0	1.000	2	1	0	0	.50	0
Porcello,Rick, Det	R	.167	6	1	0	0	0	.250	12	3	0	0	0	2	0	5	1	182.0	15	21	2	4	.947	20	4	0	0	.20	0
Price,David, TB	L	.000	4	0	0	0	0	.143	14	2	0	0	0	1	7	0	0	224.1	13	23	4	2	.900	25	5	1	0	.20	-4
Proctor,Scott, Atl-NYY	R	.000	2	0	0	1	0	.000	5	0	0	0	0	0	1	0	3	40.1	1	4	0	0	1.000	2	0	0	0	.00	0
Purcey,D., Tor-Oak-Det	L	-	0	0	0	0	0	.000	1	0	0	0	0	0	0	1	0	33.2	1	5	0	0	1.000	4	1	1	0	.25	0
Putnam,Zach, Cle	R	-	0	0	0	0	0	-	0	0	0	0	0	0	0	0	0	7.1	0	0	0	0	-	0	0	0	0	-	0
Putz,J.J., Ari	R	-	0	0	0	0	0	-	0	0	0	0	0	0	0	0	0	58.0	4	9	0	0	1.000	8	1	0	0	.13	-2
Qualls,Chad, SD	R	-	0	0	0	0	0	.000	6	0	0	0	0	0	0	5	0	74.1	4	14	0	1	1.000	14	4	0	1	.29	0
Ramirez,Horacio, LAA	L	-	0	0	0	0	0	.151	179	27	3	1	0	5	2	36	13	9.0	1	4	0	0	1.000	1	0	0	1	.00	1
Ramirez,Ramon, SF	R	.000	1	0	0	0	0	.333	6	2	0	0	0	0	3	1	1	68.2	4	6	2	1	.833	15	2	0	0	.13	-3
Ramos,Cesar, TB	L	-	0	0	0	0	0	.000	4	0	0	0	0	0	0	2	0	43.2	3	9	0	1	1.000	4	0	0	0	.00	2
Rapada,Clay, Bal	L	-	0	0	0	0	0	-	0	0	0	0	0	0	0	0	0	16.1	1	2	0	0	1.000	1	1	1	0	1.00	1
Rauch,Jon, Tor	R	-	0	0	0	0	0	.095	21	2	0	0	1	3	0	15	2	52.0	3	6	0	1	1.000	2	1	0	0	.50	-1
Ray,Chris, Sea	R	-	0	0	0	0	0	-	0	0	0	0	0	0	0	0	0	32.2	2	4	0	1	1.000	7	1	0	0	.14	-1
Reed,Addison, CWS	R	-	0	0	0	0	0	-	0	0	0	0	0	0	0	0	0	7.1	0	0	0	0	-	0	0	0	0	-	-1
Reineke,Chad, Cin	R	.000	2	0	0	0	0	.125	8	1	0	0	0	0	1	5	0	6.2	0	0	0	0	-	2	1	0	0	.50	0
Resop,Chris, Pit	R	-	0	0	0	0	0	.000	1	0	0	0	0	0	0	2	1	69.2	1	4	1	0	.833	12	3	0	0	.25	-3
Reyes,Dennys, Bos	L	-	0	0	0	0	0	.071	56	4	1	0	0	0	2	25	2	1.2	0	1	0	0	1.000	1	1	1	0	1.00	0

Pitchers Hitting, Fielding and Holding Runners

Pitcher	T	2011 Hitting						Career Hitting										2011 Fielding and Holding Runners											
		Avg	AB	H	HR	RBI	SH	Avg	AB	H	2B	3B	HR	RBI	BB	SO	SH	Inn	PO	A	E	DP	Pct	SBA	CS	PCS	PPO	CS%	RS
Reyes,Jo-Jo, Tor-Bal	L	.250	4	1	0	0	0	.143	63	9	2	0	0	2	4	24	7	140.2	4	17	0	1	1.000	16	2	1	0	.13	0
Reynolds,Greg, Col	R	.125	8	1	0	0	4	.174	23	4	2	0	0	1	9	5	5	32.0	3	5	0	0	1.000	1	0	0	0	.00	1
Reynolds,Matt, Col	L	.000	2	0	0	0	0	.000	2	0	0	0	0	0	1	1	0	50.2	0	7	0	0	1.000	8	3	2	0	.38	0
Rhodes,Arthur, Tex-StL	L	.000	1	0	0	0	0	.167	6	1	0	0	0	0	5	0	0	33.0	2	2	0	2	1.000	2	1	0	0	.50	0
Richard,Clayton, SD	L	.107	28	3	0	2	3	.125	112	14	4	0	0	9	2	43	14	99.2	5	21	3	1	.897	10	5	3	2	.50	4
Richards,Garrett, LAA	R	-	0	0	0	0	0	-	0	0	0	0	0	0	0	0	0	14.0	2	3	0	0	1.000	2	1	0	1	.50	1
Richmond,Scott, Tor	R	-	0	0	0	0	0	.000	6	0	0	0	0	0	0	5	0	0.1	0	0	0	0	-	0	0	0	0	-	0
Rivera,Mariano, NYY	R	-	0	0	0	0	0	.000	3	0	0	0	0	1	1	1	0	61.1	1	12	0	1	1.000	6	1	0	0	.17	2
Robertson,David, NYY	R	-	0	0	0	0	0	-	0	0	0	0	0	0	0	0	0	66.2	3	3	1	0	.857	18	2	0	0	.11	-2
Rodney,Fernando, LAA	R	-	0	0	0	0	0	.000	1	0	0	0	0	0	0	0	0	32.0	2	3	1	1	.833	5	0	0	0	.00	-3
Rodriguez,Aneury, Hou	R	.000	9	0	0	0	2	.000	9	0	0	0	0	0	0	5	2	85.1	6	7	2	2	.867	14	1	0	0	.07	-3
Rodriguez,F., Hou	R	.000	1	0	0	0	0	.000	1	0	0	0	0	0	0	1	0	52.1	2	7	0	0	1.000	8	1	1	0	.13	-1
Rodriguez,Fr., NYM-Mil	R	.500	2	1	0	0	0	.500	2	1	0	0	0	0	0	1	0	71.2	8	4	0	0	1.000	12	1	0	0	.08	-3
Rodriguez,Fr., LAA	R	-	0	0	0	0	0	-	0	0	0	0	0	0	0	0	0	13.2	1	1	0	0	1.000	1	0	0	0	.00	0
Rodriguez,Henry, Was	R	.000	2	0	0	0	0	.000	2	0	0	0	0	0	0	2	0	65.2	2	7	0	0	1.000	13	0	0	0	.00	-3
Rodriguez,Wandy, Hou	L	.180	61	11	0	5	6	.144	354	51	10	0	0	18	7	106	43	191.0	15	22	0	3	1.000	23	3	0	0	.13	0
Roenicke,Josh, Col	R	-	0	0	0	0	0	-	0	0	0	0	0	0	0	0	0	16.2	0	1	0	0	1.000	1	0	0	0	.00	0
Rogers,Esmil, Col	R	.259	27	7	0	0	4	.217	46	10	3	0	0	1	0	19	7	83.0	9	12	0	1	1.000	5	3	0	0	.60	1
Romero,J.C., Phi-Col	L	-	0	0	0	0	0	.250	4	1	1	0	0	0	1	0	0	24.2	1	6	0	0	1.000	2	1	1	1	.50	1
Romero,Ricky, Tor	L	.167	6	1	0	2	0	.063	16	1	0	0	0	2	0	9	0	225.0	11	41	1	1	.981	25	7	6	0	.28	3
Romo,Sergio, SF	R	-	0	0	0	0	0	.000	4	0	0	0	0	0	0	3	0	48.0	0	3	0	0	1.000	4	1	0	0	.25	0
Rosario,Sandy, Fla	R	-	0	0	0	0	0	-	0	0	0	0	0	0	0	0	0	3.2	0	1	0	0	-	0	0	0	0	-	0
Ross,Tyson, Oak	R	-	0	0	0	0	0	.000	1	0	0	0	0	0	0	1	0	36.0	2	4	1	0	.857	1	0	0	0	.00	-1
Ruffin,Chance, Det-Sea	R	-	0	0	0	0	0	-	0	0	0	0	0	0	0	0	0	17.2	0	1	0	0	1.000	3	0	0	0	.00	0
Runzler,Dan, SF	L	-	0	0	0	0	0	.000	1	0	0	0	0	0	1	1	0	27.1	0	6	1	0	.857	9	3	2	0	.33	0
Rupe,Josh, Bal	R	-	0	0	0	0	0	-	0	0	0	0	0	0	0	0	0	14.1	1	0	0	0	1.000	0	0	0	0	-	0
Russell,Adam, TB	R	-	0	0	0	0	0	.000	1	0	0	0	0	0	0	0	0	32.2	1	0	0	0	1.000	6	1	0	0	.17	-1
Russell,James, ChC	L	.125	8	1	0	0	0	.083	12	1	0	0	0	0	0	5	0	67.2	3	8	1	1	.917	8	3	2	0	.38	-1
Rzepczynski,M., Tor-StL	L	-	0	0	0	0	0	-	0	0	0	0	0	0	0	0	0	62.0	4	13	2	1	.895	4	2	2	0	.50	4
Sabathia,CC, NYY	L	.000	3	0	0	0	0	.250	100	25	3	0	3	14	1	27	3	237.1	3	21	3	2	.889	17	6	1	0	.35	-5
Saito,Takashi, Mil	R	-	0	0	0	0	0	.000	2	0	0	0	0	0	0	2	0	26.2	0	2	0	0	1.000	1	0	0	0	.00	-1
Salas,Fernando, StL	R	.000	1	0	0	0	0	.000	1	0	0	0	0	0	0	0	0	75.0	5	8	0	1	1.000	2	0	0	0	.00	0
Sale,Chris, CWS	L	-	0	0	0	0	0	-	0	0	0	0	0	0	0	0	0	71.0	5	15	0	0	1.000	7	4	3	0	.57	1
Samardzija,Jeff, ChC	R	.000	4	0	0	0	0	.143	14	2	0	0	1	2	2	7	2	88.0	2	12	1	1	.933	18	2	0	0	.11	-3
Sanabia,Alex, Fla	R	.000	3	0	0	0	1	.040	25	1	0	0	0	0	0	14	4	11.0	0	1	0	0	1.000	1	0	0	0	.00	0
Sanches,Brian, Fla	R	.200	5	1	0	0	0	.100	10	1	0	0	0	1	0	2	1	61.2	3	3	0	0	1.000	14	2	0	0	.14	-1
Sanchez,Anibal, Fla	R	.123	57	7	0	3	9	.089	202	18	0	0	0	6	14	87	25	196.1	18	26	1	1	.978	17	2	0	2	.12	2
Sanchez,Eduardo, StL	R	.000	2	0	0	0	0	.000	2	0	0	0	0	0	0	1	0	30.0	2	1	0	0	1.000	1	0	0	0	.00	0
Sanchez,Jonathan, SF	L	.207	29	6	0	1	1	.121	190	23	6	1	0	9	7	94	22	101.1	5	14	2	1	.905	17	5	3	0	.29	1
Sanit,Amauri, NYY	R	-	0	0	0	0	0	-	0	0	0	0	0	0	0	0	0	7.0	1	1	0	0	1.000	0	0	0	0	-	0
Santana,Ervin, LAA	R	.500	2	1	0	0	0	.176	17	3	1	0	0	2	0	9	0	228.2	11	20	5	3	.861	33	5	0	0	.15	-5
Santiago,Hector, CWS	L	-	0	0	0	0	0	-	0	0	0	0	0	0	0	0	0	5.1	0	1	0	0	1.000	0	0	0	0	-	0
Santos,Sergio, CWS	R	-	0	0	0	0	0	-	0	0	0	0	0	0	0	0	0	63.1	5	4	0	3	1.000	5	0	0	0	.00	0
Saunders,Joe, Ari	L	.197	61	12	0	4	4	.159	88	14	1	0	0	5	3	25	7	212.0	13	36	0	2	1.000	21	12	4	0	.57	5
Savery,Joe, Phi	L	-	0	0	0	0	0	-	0	0	0	0	0	0	0	0	0	2.2	0	0	0	0	-	0	0	0	0	-	0
Scherzer,Max, Det	R	.000	4	0	0	0	0	.167	72	12	2	0	0	3	4	21	6	195.0	11	12	0	2	1.000	21	9	3	0	.43	-3
Schlereth,Daniel, Det	L	-	0	0	0	0	0	-	0	0	0	0	0	0	0	0	0	49.0	3	6	1	0	.900	8	3	1	0	.38	0
Schwimer,Michael, Phi	R	.000	1	0	0	0	0	.000	1	0	0	0	0	0	0	1	0	14.1	0	1	0	0	1.000	1	1	0	0	1.00	0
Schwinden,Chris, NYM	R	.167	6	1	0	0	0	.167	6	1	0	0	0	0	1	2	0	21.0	1	2	1	0	.750	2	0	0	0	.00	0
Scribner,Evan, SD	R	-	0	0	0	0	0	-	0	0	0	0	0	0	0	0	0	14.0	1	2	0	0	1.000	1	0	0	0	.00	0
Severino,Atahualpa, Was	L	-	0	0	0	0	0	-	0	0	0	0	0	0	0	0	0	4.2	0	0	0	0	-	1	0	0	0	.00	0
Shaw,Bryan, Ari	R	-	0	0	0	0	0	-	0	0	0	0	0	0	0	0	0	28.1	5	7	1	0	.923	3	2	1	0	.67	2
Sherrill,George, Atl	L	-	0	0	0	0	0	-	0	0	0	0	0	0	0	1	0	36.0	2	6	0	1	1.000	2	2	1	0	1.00	-1
Shields,James, TB	R	.000	8	0	0	1	0	.188	32	6	0	0	0	2	2	10	1	249.1	19	32	3	2	.944	11	5	1	12	.45	7
Simon,Alfredo, Bal	R	-	0	0	0	0	0	-	0	0	0	0	0	0	0	0	0	115.2	9	14	1	2	.958	18	8	0	0	.44	2
Sipp,Tony, Cle	L	-	0	0	0	0	0	-	0	0	0	0	0	0	0	0	0	62.1	5	9	1	2	.933	15	2	0	0	.13	0
Slama,Anthony, Min	R	-	0	0	0	0	0	-	0	0	0	0	0	0	0	0	0	2.1	0	0	0	0	-	1	0	0	0	.00	0
Slaten,Doug, Was	L	-	0	0	0	0	0	-	0	0	0	0	0	0	0	0	0	16.1	2	3	0	1	1.000	0	0	0	0	-	0
Slowey,Kevin, Min	R	-	0	0	0	0	0	.154	13	2	1	0	0	2	0	3	2	59.1	4	5	0	0	1.000	5	1	0	0	.20	-1
Smith,Joe, Cle	R	-	0	0	0	0	0	.000	2	0	0	0	0	0	0	2	0	67.0	1	24	1	1	.962	7	3	1	2	.43	6
Smith,Jordan, Cin	R	.000	2	0	0	0	0	.000	5	0	0	0	0	0	1	0	0	29.2	0	0	0	0	-	1	1	0	0	1.00	0
Sonnanstine,Andy, TB	R	.000	2	0	0	0	0	.292	24	7	1	0	0	2	3	14	2	35.2	5	4	0	2	1.000	3	2	0	0	.67	0
Soria,Joakim, KC	R	-	0	0	0	0	0	-	0	0	0	0	0	0	0	0	0	60.1	1	11	0	1	1.000	1	1	0	0	1.00	1
Soriano,Rafael, NYY	R	-	0	0	0	0	0	.000	4	0	0	0	0	0	0	1	0	39.1	0	3	0	0	1.000	8	2	0	0	.25	-1
Sosa,Henry, Hou	R	.067	15	1	0	0	1	.067	15	1	1	0	0	2	8	1	53.1	1	12	0	1	1.000	6	3	1	0	.50	0
Spence,Josh, SD	L	-	0	0	0	0	0	-	0	0	0	0	0	0	0	0	0	29.2	2	2	0	0	1.000	2	1	0	0	.50	0
Stammen,Craig, Was	R	.500	2	1	0	0	0	.225	71	16	6	0	0	10	3	25	7	10.1	0	3	0	0	1.000	1	0	0	0	.00	0
Stauffer,Tim, SD	R	.148	54	8	0	6	7	.161	124	20	3	0	0	11	4	57	15	185.2	21	43	1	1	.985	13	8	1	0	.62	4
Stetter,Mitch, Mil	L	-	0	0	0	0	0	.000	1	0	0	0	0	0	0	1	0	7.0	0	0	0	0	-	1	0	0	0	.00	0
Stevens,Jeff, ChC	R	.000	2	0	0	0	0	.000	2	0	0	0	0	0	0	1	0	7.0	2	0	0	0	1.000	2	2	1	0	1.00	0

Pitchers Hitting, Fielding and Holding Runners

Pitcher	T	2011 Hitting						Career Hitting										2011 Fielding and Holding Runners											
		Avg	AB	H	HR	RBI	SH	Avg	AB	H	2B	3B	HR	RBI	BB	SO	SH	Inn	PO	A	E	DP	Pct	SBA	CS	PCS	PPO	CS%	RS
Stewart,Zach, Tor-CWS	R	.000	2	0	0	0	0	.000	2	0	0	0	0	0	0	2	0	67.1	5	9	2	0	.875	8	2	0	0	.25	0
Stinson,Josh, NYM	R	-	0	0	0	0	0	-	0	0	0	0	0	0	1	0	0	13.0	0	0	0	0	-	1	0	0	0	.00	0
Storen,Drew, Was	R	-	0	0	0	0	0	.500	2	1	0	0	0	0	0	1	0	75.1	6	10	0	1	1.000	3	0	0	0	.00	1
Strasburg,Stephen, Was	R	.000	6	0	0	0	2	.038	26	1	0	0	0	1	0	10	4	24.0	0	3	0	0	1.000	1	0	0	0	.00	-1
Street,Huston, Col	R	.000	1	0	0	0	0	.000	2	0	0	0	0	0	0	1	0	58.1	2	13	1	2	.938	3	1	0	0	.33	2
Strop,Pedro, Tex-Bal	R	-	0	0	0	0	0	-	0	0	0	0	0	0	0	0	0	22.0	1	2	0	1	1.000	3	0	0	0	.00	0
Stults,Eric, Col	L	.500	2	1	0	0	0	.224	49	11	3	0	0	4	5	20	3	12.0	1	0	0	0	1.000	0	0	0	0	-	0
Stutes,Michael, Phi	R	-	0	0	0	0	0	-	0	0	0	0	0	0	0	0	0	62.0	3	5	3	0	.727	10	3	0	1	.30	-1
Surkamp,Eric, SF	L	.125	8	1	0	1	0	.125	8	1	0	0	0	1	1	5	0	26.2	1	6	2	0	.778	10	4	1	0	.40	0
Swarzak,Anthony, Min	R	-	0	0	0	0	0	.000	2	0	0	0	0	0	0	2	0	102.0	3	7	0	1	1.000	6	3	0	0	.50	0
Takahashi,Hisanori, LAA	L	-	0	0	0	0	0	.063	16	1	0	0	0	0	0	3	4	68.0	2	12	1	1	.933	9	2	1	0	.22	2
Talbot,Mitch, Cle	R	.000	2	0	0	0	1	.000	7	0	0	0	0	0	0	5	1	63.2	5	7	0	0	1.000	11	4	1	0	.36	-2
Tallet,Brian, StL-Tor	L	-	0	0	0	0	0	.000	5	0	0	0	0	0	0	2	0	13.1	3	3	0	0	1.000	1	0	0	0	.00	1
Tateyama,Yoshinori, Tex	R	-	0	0	0	0	0	-	0	0	0	0	0	0	0	0	0	44.0	3	4	0	0	1.000	5	2	0	0	.40	0
Tazawa,Junichi, Bos	R	-	0	0	0	0	0	-	0	0	0	0	0	0	0	0	0	3.0	0	0	0	0	-	0	0	0	0	-	0
Teaford,Everett, KC	L	-	0	0	0	0	0	-	0	0	0	0	0	0	0	0	0	44.0	1	4	0	0	1.000	4	1	0	0	.25	1
Teheran,Julio, Atl	R	.000	4	0	0	0	1	.000	4	0	0	0	0	0	0	1	1	19.2	4	2	0	1	1.000	3	0	0	0	.00	0
Tejeda,Robinson, KC	R	-	0	0	0	0	0	.080	25	2	0	1	0	0	0	13	7	7.1	0	0	0	0	-	0	0	0	0	-	0
Texeira,Kanekoa, KC	R	-	0	0	0	0	0	.000	1	0	0	0	0	0	0	1	0	6.1	0	1	0	0	1.000	0	0	0	0	-	0
Thatcher,Joe, SD	L	-	0	0	0	0	0	.000	1	0	0	0	0	0	0	0	1	10.0	0	1	0	0	1.000	2	1	1	0	.50	-1
Thayer,Dale, NYM	R	-	0	0	0	0	0	.000	1	0	0	0	0	0	0	0	0	10.1	3	1	0	0	1.000	1	0	0	0	.00	0
Thomas,Brad, Det	R	-	0	0	0	0	0	-	0	0	0	0	0	0	0	0	0	11.0	0	1	0	0	1.000	0	0	0	0	-	-1
Thompson,Aaron, Pit	L	-	0	0	0	0	0	-	0	0	0	0	0	0	1	0	0	7.2	0	2	0	0	1.000	3	0	0	0	.00	0
Thompson,Daryl, Cin	R	.000	1	0	0	0	0	.000	3	0	0	0	0	0	0	1	0	3.0	1	1	0	0	1.000	0	0	0	0	-	0
Thompson,Rich, LAA	R	-	0	0	0	0	0	-	0	0	0	0	0	0	0	0	0	54.0	3	4	0	0	1.000	7	1	1	1	.14	-1
Thornton,Matt, CWS	L	-	0	0	0	0	0	.000	1	0	0	0	0	0	0	1	0	59.2	5	7	0	0	1.000	15	2	1	0	.13	-3
Tillman,Chris, Bal	R	-	0	0	0	0	0	.000	1	0	0	0	0	0	0	1	0	62.0	4	4	0	0	1.000	8	3	0	0	.38	-2
Tobin,Mason, Tex	R	-	0	0	0	0	0	-	0	0	0	0	0	0	0	0	0	5.1	0	0	0	0	-	0	0	0	0	-	0
Tomko,Brett, Tex	R	-	0	0	0	0	0	.156	455	71	9	0	0	29	19	180	71	17.2	0	1	0	0	1.000	1	0	0	0	.00	0
Tomlin,Josh, Cle	R	1.000	2	2	0	1	0	1.000	2	2	0	0	0	1	0	0	0	165.1	16	25	2	1	.953	0	0	0	1	-	4
Torres,Alex, TB	L	-	0	0	0	0	0	-	0	0	0	0	0	0	0	0	0	8.0	0	0	0	0	-	2	1	0	0	.50	0
Troncoso,Ramon, LAD	R	.000	1	0	0	0	0	.000	8	0	0	0	0	1	1	7	1	22.2	1	1	0	1	1.000	2	0	0	0	.00	-1
Tucker,Ryan, Tex	R	-	0	0	0	0	0	.000	7	0	0	0	0	0	0	4	0	5.0	0	0	0	0	-	1	0	0	0	.00	0
Turner,Jacob, Det	R	-	0	0	0	0	0	-	0	0	0	0	0	0	0	0	0	12.2	0	1	0	1	1.000	7	0	0	0	.00	-1
Uehara,Koji, Bal-Tex	R	-	0	0	0	0	0	.000	2	0	0	0	0	0	1	1	0	65.0	2	4	0	0	1.000	0	0	0	1	-	1
Valdes,Raul, StL-NYY	L	-	0	0	0	0	0	.400	10	4	1	0	0	1	0	3	4	12.0	1	2	0	0	1.000	1	1	0	0	1.00	0
Valdez,Jose, Hou	R	-	0	0	0	0	0	-	0	0	0	0	0	0	0	0	0	14.0	2	2	0	2	1.000	1	0	0	0	.00	1
Valdez,Merkin, Tex	R	-	0	0	0	0	0	-	0	0	0	0	0	0	0	0	1	4.1	0	0	0	0	-	1	0	0	0	.00	-1
Valverde,Jose, Det	R	-	0	0	0	0	0	.500	2	1	1	0	0	0	1	0	0	72.1	3	3	1	0	.857	12	3	0	0	.25	-1
VandenHurk,Rick, Bal	R	-	0	0	0	0	0	.021	47	1	0	0	0	0	1	31	6	9.0	0	0	0	0	-	2	1	0	0	.50	0
Vargas,Jason, Sea	L	.000	2	0	0	0	0	.250	56	14	3	0	0	3	2	14	2	201.0	4	24	1	2	.966	23	5	2	0	.22	1
Varvaro,Anthony, Atl	L	-	0	0	0	0	0	-	0	0	0	0	0	0	0	0	0	24.0	2	2	0	0	1.000	3	1	1	0	.33	-1
Vasquez,Anthony, Sea	L	-	0	0	0	0	0	-	0	0	0	0	0	0	0	0	0	29.1	0	3	2	0	.600	2	1	1	0	.50	1
Vasquez,Esmerling, Ari	R	-	0	0	0	0	0	.000	2	0	0	0	0	0	0	1	0	30.1	0	7	1	0	.875	1	0	0	0	.00	2
Vazquez,Javier, Fla	R	.179	56	10	0	2	9	.204	560	114	14	2	1	29	24	95	105	192.2	7	20	1	0	.964	8	0	0	0	.00	0
Venters,Jonny, Atl	L	-	0	0	0	0	0	.000	1	0	0	0	0	0	0	1	0	88.0	6	19	2	1	.926	4	2	0	0	.50	4
Veras,Jose, Pit	R	-	0	0	0	0	0	-	0	0	0	0	0	0	1	0	0	71.0	3	5	0	0	1.000	6	1	0	0	.17	0
Verlander,Justin, Det	R	.000	4	0	0	0	0	.000	20	0	0	0	0	0	0	13	5	251.0	12	33	5	2	.900	15	5	1	1	.33	2
Villanueva,Carlos, Tor	R	.000	4	0	0	0	0	.078	64	5	0	0	0	3	3	31	10	107.0	8	8	1	2	.941	14	1	0	0	.07	0
Villanueva,Elih, Fla	R	.000	1	0	0	0	0	.000	1	0	0	0	0	0	0	1	0	3.0	0	0	0	0	-	0	0	0	0	-	0
Villarreal,Brayan, Det	R	-	0	0	0	0	0	-	0	0	0	0	0	0	0	0	0	16.0	0	6	2	0	.750	4	0	0	2	.00	1
Viola,Pedro, Bal	L	-	0	0	0	0	0	-	0	0	0	0	0	0	0	0	0	3.2	0	0	0	0	-	0	0	0	0	-	0
Vizcaino,Arodys, Atl	R	-	0	0	0	0	0	-	0	0	0	0	0	0	0	0	0	17.1	2	0	0	0	1.000	0	0	0	0	-	0
Vogelsong,Ryan, SF	R	.226	53	12	0	2	5	.205	112	23	5	0	0	5	6	39	17	179.2	9	23	0	4	1.000	15	3	0	1	.20	0
Volquez,Edinson, Cin	R	.115	26	3	0	0	7	.100	120	12	0	0	0	1	2	59	21	108.2	9	5	2	0	.875	20	4	0	0	.20	-3
Volstad,Chris, Fla	R	.196	46	9	0	2	5	.133	173	23	6	0	0	7	2	84	22	165.2	12	22	1	2	.971	14	4	0	1	.29	-1
Wade,Cory, NYY	R	-	0	0	0	0	0	.000	2	0	0	0	0	0	1	1	0	39.2	0	4	0	0	1.000	4	2	0	0	.50	0
Wagner,Neil, Oak	R	-	0	0	0	0	0	-	0	0	0	0	0	0	0	0	0	5.0	0	0	0	0	-	0	0	0	0	-	0
Wakefield,Tim, Bos	R	.000	4	0	0	0	0	.117	111	13	2	0	1	4	3	47	15	154.2	7	19	0	0	1.000	21	9	2	1	.43	3
Walden,Jordan, LAA	R	-	0	0	0	0	0	-	0	0	0	0	0	0	0	0	0	60.1	3	6	1	0	.900	15	2	1	0	.13	-3
Waldrop,Kyle, Min	R	-	0	0	0	0	0	-	0	0	0	0	0	0	0	0	0	11.0	0	2	0	0	1.000	1	0	0	0	.00	0
Walters,P.J., StL-Tor	R	-	0	0	0	0	0	.000	10	0	0	0	0	0	1	6	3	5.0	2	0	0	1	1.000	0	0	0	0	-	0
Wang,Chien-Ming, Was	R	.053	19	1	0	1	0	.030	33	1	0	0	0	1	1	18	1	62.1	3	6	1	0	.900	7	3	0	0	.43	0
Watson,Tony, Pit	L	.000	1	0	0	0	0	.000	1	0	0	0	0	0	0	1	0	41.0	3	8	0	1	1.000	9	1	1	0	.11	0
Weaver,Jered, LAA	R	.000	4	0	0	0	0	.115	26	3	0	0	0	1	1	8	0	235.2	8	24	2	1	.941	17	7	1	5	.41	3
Webb,Ryan, Fla	R	-	0	0	0	0	0	.000	1	0	0	0	0	0	0	1	0	50.2	1	7	1	0	.889	10	1	0	0	.10	0
Weiland,Kyle, Bos	R	-	0	0	0	0	0	-	0	0	0	0	0	0	0	0	0	24.2	1	1	0	0	1.000	1	1	0	0	1.00	-1
Weinhardt,Robbie, Det	R	-	0	0	0	0	0	-	0	0	0	0	0	0	0	0	0	1.2	0	0	0	0	-	0	0	0	0	-	0
Wells,Randy, ChC	R	.140	43	6	0	1	6	.169	142	24	5	0	0	6	5	35	27	135.1	5	12	2	1	.895	17	5	0	0	.29	-2
Westbrook,Jake, StL	R	.106	47	5	1	8	10	.116	86	10	4	0	1	10	5	43	14	183.1	29	43	2	5	.973	17	4	1	3	.24	6

354

Pitchers Hitting, Fielding and Holding Runners

Pitcher	T	2011 Hitting Avg	AB	H	HR	RBI	SH	Career Hitting Avg	AB	H	2B	3B	HR	RBI	BB	SO	SH	2011 Fielding and Holding Runners Inn	PO	A	E	DP	Pct	SBA	CS	PCS	PPO	CS%	RS
Wheeler,Dan, Bos	R	-	0	0	0	0	0	.143	7	1	0	0	0	0	0	1	1	49.1	2	1	0	0	1.000	3	2	0	0	.67	-2
Whelan,Kevin, NYY	R	-	0	0	0	0	0	-	0	0	0	0	0	0	0	0	0	1.2	1	0	0	0	1.000	0	0	0	0	-	0
White,Alex, Cle-Col	R	.077	13	1	0	0	1	.077	13	1	1	0	0	0	0	6	1	51.1	3	2	2	0	.714	7	4	0	0	.57	-3
Wilhelmsen,Tom, Sea	R	-	0	0	0	0	0	-	0	0	0	0	0	0	0	0	0	32.2	1	6	1	1	.875	4	1	1	0	.25	1
Wilk,Adam, Det	L	.000	1	0	0	0	0	.000	1	0	0	0	0	0	0	1	0	13.1	1	0	0	0	1.000	0	0	0	0	-	0
Williams,Jerome, LAA	R	-	0	0	0	0	0	.112	116	13	2	0	0	1	1	54	19	44.0	3	3	2	1	.750	5	2	1	0	.40	-2
Williams,Randy, Bos	L	-	0	0	0	0	0	.000	1	0	0	0	0	0	0	0	0	8.1	0	0	0	0	-	1	0	0	0	.00	0
Willis,Dontrelle, Cin	L	.387	31	12	1	4	3	.244	389	95	13	6	9	39	22	69	33	75.2	3	14	0	1	1.000	4	4	3	0	1.00	3
Wilson,Brian, SF	R	-	0	0	0	0	0	.000	9	0	0	0	0	0	0	2	1	55.0	1	5	0	0	1.000	2	1	0	0	.50	-2
Wilson,C.J., Tex	L	.250	4	1	0	0	1	.125	8	1	0	1	0	0	0	1	2	223.1	6	23	1	0	.967	31	7	0	0	.23	-3
Wolf,Randy, Mil	L	.164	61	10	0	0	4	.187	647	121	33	0	5	54	32	219	74	212.1	8	32	4	3	.909	19	1	1	0	.05	0
Wood,Blake, KC	R	.000	1	0	0	0	0	.000	1	0	0	0	0	0	0	1	0	69.2	4	12	0	1	1.000	9	3	2	0	.33	0
Wood,Kerry, ChC	R	-	0	0	0	0	0	.171	345	59	6	0	7	32	11	113	46	51.0	1	6	1	2	.875	4	1	0	1	.25	0
Wood,Tim, Pit	R	-	0	0	0	0	0	.500	2	1	0	0	0	0	0	0	0	8.0	1	1	0	0	1.000	1	0	0	0	.00	0
Wood,Travis, Cin	L	.067	30	2	0	0	5	.134	67	9	2	1	2	6	0	29	10	106.0	5	14	0	0	1.000	10	5	3	0	.50	2
Worley,Vance, Phi	R	.222	45	10	0	5	2	.208	48	10	1	0	0	5	1	17	2	131.2	8	16	0	2	1.000	2	0	0	0	.00	3
Worrell,Mark, Bal	R	-	0	0	0	0	0	.500	2	1	0	0	1	3	0	0	0	2.0	0	0	0	0	-	1	0	0	0	.00	0
Wright,Jamey, Sea	R	-	0	0	0	0	0	.147	436	64	15	1	1	17	12	175	51	68.1	10	7	1	2	.944	11	3	1	1	.27	-1
Wright,Wesley, Hou	L	.000	1	0	0	0	0	.077	13	1	0	0	0	0	0	5	0	12.0	1	2	0	0	1.000	2	0	0	0	.00	0
Wuertz,Michael, Oak	R	-	0	0	0	0	0	.000	6	0	0	0	0	0	0	5	1	33.2	1	2	0	0	1.000	11	1	0	0	.09	-2
Young,Chris, NYM	R	.333	9	3	0	2	2	.147	170	25	4	1	1	12	9	70	23	24.0	0	2	0	0	1.000	5	1	1	0	.20	0
Zagurski,Mike, Phi	L	-	0	0	0	0	0	-	0	0	0	0	0	0	0	0	0	3.1	0	0	0	0	-	0	0	0	0	-	-1
Zambrano,Carlos, ChC	R	.318	44	14	2	5	2	.241	659	159	26	3	23	69	10	232	35	145.2	8	12	1	5	.952	4	0	0	2	.00	1
Ziegler,Brad, Oak-Ari	R	-	0	0	0	0	0	-	0	0	0	0	0	0	0	0	0	58.1	6	14	3	1	.870	9	3	0	0	.33	2
Zimmermann,J., Was	R	.209	43	9	0	3	11	.188	80	15	1	0	0	5	3	25	17	161.1	18	18	0	1	1.000	9	6	0	3	.67	3
Zito,Barry, SF	L	.000	13	0	0	0	0	.101	257	26	0	0	0	7	12	79	37	53.2	2	9	1	0	.917	8	4	2	0	.50	1

355

Hitters Pitching

Player	2011 Pitching											Career Pitching										
	G	W	L	Sv	IP	H	R	ER	BB	SO	ERA	G	W	L	Sv	IP	H	R	ER	BB	SO	ERA
Ankiel,Rick, Was	0	0	0	0	0.0	0	0	0	0	0	-	51	13	10	1	242.0	198	119	105	130	269	3.90
Brown,Dusty, Pit	0	0	0	0	0.0	0	0	0	0	0	-	1	0	0	0	1.0	2	1	1	0	1	9.00
Burroughs,Sean, Ari	0	0	0	0	0.0	0	0	0	0	0	-	1	0	0	0	1.0	4	3	3	0	0	27.00
Cuddyer,Michael, Min	1	0	0	0	1.0	2	0	0	1	0	0.00	1	0	0	0	1.0	2	0	0	1	0	0.00
Gload,Ross, Phi	0	0	0	0	0.0	0	0	0	0	0	-	1	0	0	0	1.0	0	0	0	2	0	0.00
Hall,Bill, Hou-SF	0	0	0	0	0.0	0	0	0	0	0	-	1	0	0	0	1.0	0	0	0	0	0	0.00
Inglett,Joe, Hou	0	0	0	0	0.0	0	0	0	0	0	-	1	0	0	0	1.0	0	0	0	0	0	0.00
Janish,Paul, Cin	0	0	0	0	0.0	0	0	0	0	0	-	2	0	0	0	2.0	9	11	11	2	3	49.50
Kelly,Don, Det	1	0	0	0	0.1	0	0	0	0	0	0.00	1	0	0	0	0.1	0	0	0	0	0	0.00
Loewen,Adam, Tor	0	0	0	0	0.0	0	0	0	0	0	-	35	8	8	0	164.0	163	105	98	106	134	5.38
Lopez,Felipe, TB-Mil	0	0	0	0	0.0	0	0	0	0	0	-	1	0	0	0	1.0	1	0	0	1	0	0.00
Maier,Mitch, KC	1	0	0	0	1.0	1	0	0	0	0	0.00	1	0	0	0	1.0	1	0	0	0	0	0.00
Mather,Joe, Atl	0	0	0	0	0.0	0	0	0	0	0	-	1	0	1	0	2.0	2	2	2	3	0	9.00
McCoy,Mike, Tor	1	0	0	0	1.0	0	0	0	0	0	0.00	1	0	0	0	1.0	0	0	0	0	0	0.00
McDonald,Darnell, Bos	1	0	0	0	1.0	1	2	2	2	0	18.00	1	0	0	0	1.0	1	2	2	2	0	18.00
Miles,Aaron, LAD	0	0	0	0	0.0	0	0	0	0	0	-	5	0	0	0	5.0	5	2	2	0	0	3.60
Petersen,Bryan, Fla	1	0	0	0	1.0	0	0	0	1	0	0.00	1	0	0	0	1.0	0	0	0	1	0	0.00
Ross,Cody, SF	0	0	0	0	0.0	0	0	0	0	0	-	1	0	0	0	1.0	1	0	0	0	0	0.00
Schumaker,Skip, StL	1	0	0	0	1.0	1	2	2	1	2	18.00	1	0	0	0	1.0	1	2	2	1	2	18.00
Swisher,Nick, NYY	0	0	0	0	0.0	0	0	0	0	0	-	1	0	0	0	1.0	1	0	0	1	1	0.00
Valdez,Wilson, Phi	1	1	0	0	1.0	0	0	0	0	0	0.00	1	1	0	0	1.0	0	0	0	0	0	0.00
Wilson,Josh, Ari-Mil	0	0	0	0	0.0	0	0	0	0	0	-	3	0	1	0	3.0	4	3	3	3	0	9.00

2011 Pitch Repertoire

Bill James

We have a new feature here, a first-time for this book. The pages that follow describe the pitching repertoires of every major league pitcher, answering in particular the questions:

1) How fast is his fastball?
2) How many fastballs does he throw? and
3) What else does he throw?

Bud Norris of the Astros, to pick a pitcher about whom most of us probably don't know a whole lot. . .what does he throw?

He throws 51% fastballs, 36% sliders, 12% change-ups, and 1% curves—a fairly conventional repertoire, similar to that of Edwin Jackson or Manny Acosta. His average fastball was 92.6 miles an hour, which is pretty good. The slider percentage is very high; in fact, now that I look at it, that's the second-highest slider percentage in the majors for a starting pitcher, behind Ervin Santana. Scratch that about conventional; it's too many sliders to be conventional. Brett Anderson of Oakland also had more sliders, but he's usually hurt.

See; we learned something there already. Three minutes ago I didn't know that Ervin Santana throws more sliders than any other major league starting pitcher; now I do.

You may be wondering how we know these things. Baseball Info Solutions, for several years now...I don't know, seven or eight years, maybe more ...has made a practice of electronically recording every major league baseball game, and hiring people to study the video and record things. You can't just hire anybody to do this; you have to hire people who know what they're looking at. We hire people who pitched in college or caught, people who have coaching experience, people who have played minor league ball, people who have been bird-dog scouts for teams. People who know the difference between a slider and a hard curve; people who recognize a cutter when they see one.

This is not as easy as it sounds, even for people who know what they are doing. Sometimes a pitcher will throw a pitch that looks like a slider, but he calls it a cutter, and sometimes he will throw a slider that looks like a curve. It helps to know what the pitcher *calls* his pitches, and we try generally to follow the pitcher's own terminology, but if the pitcher calls his changeup a palm ball, we're still going to call it a change. When Darren Oliver was with the Red Sox, ten years ago, he used to throw a slider, a curve, and a cutter that were indistinguishable from one another. He was at a tough point in his remarkable career; eventually he cleaned that up. Many times a pitcher will throw a slow curve that is used as a change, and the video scout has to decide whether that was a curve or a change.

The terminology is sort of standard, but not really. Twenty years ago some pitchers would throw a slurve, a pitch that was halfway between a slider and a curve. But the terminology changed; the term "slurve" now is just an insult to describe a pitch that isn't exactly fish nor foul, a half-way between pitch. Nobody deliberately throws a slurve anymore.

When I started writing about baseball the dominant change was what was called a straight change. In the 1980s everybody switched from the straight change to the circle change. The circle change dives away from a left-handed hitter (from a right-hander), sort of like a 1970s forkball. The forkball has just about gone away; the forkball was sort of a slow-speed splitter. Nobody much throws it anymore—or if they throw it, they call it a splitter if it comes in over 85 and a change if it doesn't. The last pitcher with a really, really good straight change was Keith Foulke. Greg Maddux would throw three or four different changeups.

I'm rambling, aren't I? Anyway, we at BIS have been tracking this stuff for years, and for years we have included in this book, for example, a list of the pitchers who had the highest average velocity on their fastball, or a list of the pitchers who threw the most curves. This year we decided to add this section, summarizing the repertoires of every pitcher. Let me share with you a few things I have learned from studying this data:

1) Major league pitchers whose average fastball is 94 miles an hour or more average 8.6 strikeouts per nine innings, or anyway did in 2011.

2) Pitchers whose fastball averages 92 to 93.9 miles an hour average 7.5 strikeouts per nine innings.

3) Pitchers whose fastball averages 90 to 91.9 MPH average 7.1 strikeouts per nine innings.

4) Pitchers whose fastball averages 88 to 89.9 MPH average 6.2 strikeouts per nine innings.

5) Pitchers whose fastball averages less than 88 MPH average 6.0 strikeouts per nine innings.

6) Pitchers who throw a lot of splitters do NOT, in fact, throw significantly more Wild Pitches than pitchers who don't throw the splitter. They throw a few more Wild Pitches—15, 20% more—but I would have guessed that they would throw 70 or 80% more. They don't. Pitchers who threw 10% splitters or more in 2011 averaged 9.7 Wild Pitches per 1,000 batters faced; pitchers who threw 5% splitters or less averaged 8.25.

7) Suppose that you sort pitchers into three classes: Those who throw 20% curve balls or more, those who throw 10 to 20% curves, and those who throw less than 10% curve balls.

The "mid-range" group—10 to 20% curves—contains the lion's share of the game's best pitchers. Only about 25% of major league pitchers are in that mid-range group, but that group includes Justin Verlander, Roy Halladay, Ian Kennedy, Jered Weaver, Cliff Lee, C. J. Wilson, Cole Hamels, Josh Beckett, Jon Lester, Felix Hernandez, Zack Greinke, and other stars.

And yet, the pitchers in the mid-range group are significantly *less* effective, on average, than either the pitchers who throw more curve balls or the pitchers who throw less. Pitchers who threw 20% curve balls or more had a 3.88 ERA in 2011, and averaged 7.6 strikeouts per nine innings. Pitchers who threw less than 10% curve balls had a 3.91 ERA and averaged 7.3 strikeouts per nine innings. Pitchers who threw 10 to 20% curves had a 4.01 ERA and averaged 6.7 strikeouts per nine innings.

8) The ten major league pitchers who mix up their pitches the most are 1) Shaun Marcum, 2) Freddy Garcia, 3) Mike Leake, 4) James Shields, 5) D. J. Carrasco, 6) Sean Marshall, 7) Bronson Arroyo, 8) Josh Tomlin, 9) Roy Halladay, and 10) Francisco Cordero.

What does that mean, they "Mix Up" their pitches? It means that they don't have any one or two pitches that they live on. If a pitcher throws 50% fastballs and 50% curves, that would be a pitch mix score of 2.00; if he threw three pitches equally often, that would be a pitch mix score of 3.00. Shaun Marcum threw 34% fastballs, 25% changeups, 16% cutters, 14% curves, and 11% sliders—a pitch mix score of 4.25. I studied this in another forum three or four years ago, and Marcum had the highest score then, too. On the other hand, Zack Britton of the Orioles threw 71% fastballs, 17% changes and 12% sliders—a pitch mix score of 1.83—the lowest of any major league pitcher with a conventional repertoire. Knuckleball pitchers have Pitch Mix scores barely over 1.00, but... they're a different animal.

Player	Fastball Velocity	Pitch Repertoire						
		Fastball	Cutter	Curve	Slider	Change	Splitter	Other
Abad,Fernando	90.2	56%	-	22%	-	21%	-	
Abreu,Juan	95.6	80%	-	16%	-	4%	-	
Accardo,Jeremy	91.8	55%	22%	-	16%	-	7%	
Aceves,Alfredo	92.6	49%	21%	17%	-	13%	-	
Acosta,Manny	94.6	55%	-	-	33%	12%	-	
Adams,Mike	92.7	33%	60%	5%	-	1%	-	
Adcock,Nathan	90.4	61%	-	12%	13%	14%	-	
Affeldt,Jeremy	93.1	63%	-	27%	-	-	10%	
Albers,Matt	93.6	71%	-	2%	27%	-	-	
Alburquerque,Al	95.4	43%	-	-	57%	-	-	
Alvarez,Henderson	93.3	72%	-	-	10%	18%	-	
Anderson,Brett	90.9	47%	-	8%	40%	5%	-	
Arredondo,Jose	91.7	44%	-	-	4%	-	52%	
Arrieta,Jake	92.4	60%	-	15%	17%	7%	-	
Arroyo,Bronson	87.0	46%	8%	13%	16%	18%	-	
Ascanio,Jose	92.5	59%	-	27%	-	14%	-	
Asencio,Jairo	92.5	48%	-	-	19%	33%	-	
Atchison,Scott	90.8	45%	47%	7%	-	-	-	
Atkins,Mitch	90.9	55%	-	15%	25%	5%	-	
Augenstein,Bryan	88.5	53%	-	-	42%	5%	-	
Axelrod,Dylan	89.4	51%	-	4%	41%	4%	-	
Axford,John	95.6	69%	-	22%	9%	-	-	
Ayala,Luis	91.0	63%	17%	-	8%	12%	-	
Badenhop,Burke	89.3	67%	-	-	19%	14%	-	
Baez,Danys	92.4	65%	-	20%	-	-	14%	
Bailey,Andrew	93.4	77%	16%	7%	-	1%	-	
Bailey,Homer	92.2	57%	-	13%	21%	-	9%	
Baker,Scott	91.0	67%	-	15%	14%	5%	-	
Balester,Collin	94.1	69%	-	30%	-	1%	-	
Balfour,Grant	92.8	76%	-	7%	17%	-	-	
Bard,Daniel	97.3	68%	-	-	25%	7%	-	
Bass,Anthony	93.2	57%	-	-	35%	8%	-	
Bastardo,Antonio	92.5	61%	-	-	34%	4%	-	
Batista,Miguel	92.3	71%	26%	-	-	3%	-	
Beachy,Brandon	92.0	61%	-	10%	20%	10%	-	
Beato,Pedro	92.3	62%	12%	21%	-	5%	-	
Beavan,Blake	90.6	66%	-	16%	8%	9%	-	
Beck,Chad	95.1	76%	-	-	16%	-	8%	
Beckett,Josh	93.1	51%	18%	17%	-	14%	-	
Bedard,Erik	90.8	57%	4%	31%	-	8%	-	
Beimel,Joe	86.0	63%	-	23%	-	14%	-	
Belisle,Matt	92.0	68%	-	7%	25%	-	-	
Bell,Heath	94.0	70%	-	29%	-	-	-	
Bell,Trevor	91.1	55%	-	-	28%	16%	-	
Below,Duane	90.4	57%	14%	16%	-	14%	-	
Benoit,Joaquin	93.9	62%	-	-	12%	26%	-	
Berg,Justin	88.5	83%	-	3%	15%	-	-	
Bergesen,Brad	91.0	65%	-	1%	25%	9%	-	
Berken,Jason	92.1	58%	-	-	36%	6%	-	
Betances,Dellin	93.3	70%	-	21%	-	8%	-	
Betancourt,Rafael	92.3	77%	-	-	17%	6%	-	
Billings,Bruce	93.3	73%	-	-	21%	6%	-	
Billingsley,Chad	91.5	55%	22%	16%	-	6%	-	
Blackburn,Nick	89.7	57%	16%	13%	-	14%	-	

Player	Fastball Velocity	Pitch Repertoire						
		Fastball	Cutter	Curve	Slider	Change	Splitter	Other
Blanton,Joe	89.0	47%	11%	10%	16%	16%	-	
Blevins,Jerry	89.0	61%	11%	17%	-	11%	-	
Boggs,Mitchell	95.2	77%	-	-	22%	1%	-	
Bowden,Michael	92.7	69%	5%	-	20%	6%	-	
Boyer,Blaine	93.0	83%	-	1%	8%	8%	-	
Brach,Brad	93.2	65%	-	-	34%	-		1%
Brackman,Andrew	91.6	15%	60%	20%	5%	-	-	
Braddock,Zach	91.5	78%	-	-	21%	1%	-	
Braden,Dallas	87.2	52%	7%	-	8%	33%	-	
Bray,Bill	90.8	51%	-	-	33%	16%	-	
Brazoban,Yhency	92.7	73%	-	-	27%	-	-	
Breslow,Craig	91.1	69%	23%	-	-	8%	-	
Britton,Zach	92.1	71%	-	-	12%	17%	-	
Broderick,Brian	89.5	62%	-	21%	-	17%	-	
Brothers,Rex	95.3	73%	-	-	27%	-	-	
Broxton,Jonathan	94.1	71%	-	-	28%	1%	-	
Bruney,Brian	94.2	68%	-	-	18%	14%	-	
Buchholz,Clay	92.6	50%	20%	13%	-	17%	-	
Buchholz,Taylor	89.4	53%	-	41%	-	7%	-	
Buehrle,Mark	85.6	45%	20%	9%	3%	22%	-	
Buente,Jay	88.6	54%	-	11%	-	-		35%
Bulger,Jason	91.7	28%	-	58%	-	14%	-	
Bumgarner,Madison	91.7	53%	-	11%	32%	4%	-	
Burnett,A.J.	92.7	56%	-	33%	-	11%	-	
Burnett,Alex	92.9	72%	-	6%	21%	1%	-	
Burnett,Sean	91.4	66%	-	-	19%	15%	-	
Burres,Brian	88.6	55%	-	12%	21%	12%	-	
Burton,Jared	90.7	37%	18%	-	17%	28%	-	
Bush,Dave	87.6	47%	14%	24%	12%	3%	-	
Byrdak,Tim	88.8	43%	-	-	50%	7%	-	
Cahill,Trevor	89.1	59%	-	13%	7%	22%	-	
Cain,Matt	91.2	55%	-	13%	16%	17%	-	
Camp,Shawn	87.0	49%	-	-	21%	31%	-	
Capps,Matt	92.9	77%	-	4%	15%	4%	-	
Capuano,Chris	87.9	55%	3%	-	14%	28%	-	
Carignan,Andrew	93.8	83%	-	-	15%	-		2%
Carlyle,Buddy	89.2	64%	33%	-	-	3%	-	
Carmona,Fausto	92.5	68%	-	-	13%	18%	-	
Carpenter,Andrew	90.4	53%	-	-	26%	-		22%
Carpenter,Chris (ChC)	97.1	71%	-	-	29%	-	-	
Carpenter,Chris	92.5	51%	-	20%	26%	2%	-	
Carpenter,David	93.9	79%	-	-	21%	-	-	
Carrasco,Carlos	92.5	58%	-	12%	11%	20%	-	
Carrasco,D.J.	88.1	37%	33%	16%	11%	4%	-	
Carreno,Joel	91.5	42%	-	53%	-	5%	-	
Cashner,Andrew	95.4	71%	-	-	19%	10%	-	
Casilla,Santiago	93.6	68%	-	13%	19%	-	-	
Cassevah,Bobby	92.5	77%	-	-	16%	-		7%
Castillo,Alberto	88.2	49%	-	-	41%	9%	-	
Cecil,Brett	88.5	53%	-	6%	19%	23%	-	
Ceda,Jose	93.4	55%	9%	-	27%	1%		9%
Cedeno,Xavier	88.3	47%	-	42%	-	11%	-	
Chacin,Jhoulys	91.0	60%	-	11%	19%	10%	-	
Chamberlain,Joba	94.3	57%	-	13%	29%	1%	-	
Chapman,Aroldis	97.9	84%	-	-	16%	-	-	
Chatwood,Tyler	93.0	74%	1%	18%	-	7%	-	
Chavez,Jesse	92.5	56%	-	5%	34%	6%	-	

Player	Fastball Velocity	Fastball	Cutter	Curve	Slider	Change	Splitter	Other
Chen,Bruce	85.8	44%	-	11%	29%	16%	-	
Choate,Randy	86.6	62%	-	-	38%	-	-	
Cishek,Steve	92.7	71%	-	-	23%	5%	-	
Cleto,Maikel	98.4	61%	-	9%	18%	12%	-	
Clippard,Tyler	92.7	58%	-	6%	8%	27%	-	
Cobb,Alex	91.3	50%	-	16%	-	34%	-	
Coffey,Todd	93.1	55%	-	-	44%	-	1%	
Coke,Phil	92.0	58%	-	1%	26%	15%	-	
Coleman,Casey	89.6	58%	-	13%	13%	15%	-	
Coleman,Louis	89.6	51%	-	-	46%	3%	-	
Collins,Tim	92.4	62%	-	20%	-	18%	-	
Collmenter,Josh	87.4	68%	-	6%	-	26%	-	
Colon,Bartolo	91.7	83%	1%	-	12%	4%	-	
Contreras,Jose	92.5	58%	-	-	31%	-	11%	
Cook,Aaron	88.2	72%	-	13%	14%	-	-	
Cook,Ryan	94.7	68%	-	-	18%	14%	-	
Cordero,Francisco	93.0	41%	-	10%	30%	19%	-	
Cormier,Lance	88.1	19%	55%	21%	-	4%	-	
Correia,Kevin	90.8	51%	20%	12%	7%	10%	-	
Cortes,Dan	94.7	80%	-	17%	3%	-	-	
Crain,Jesse	94.5	41%	-	2%	48%	8%	-	
Cramer,Bobby	88.7	63%	3%	31%	-	3%	-	
Crotta,Mike	92.7	86%	-	-	14%	-	-	
Crow,Aaron	95.0	59%	-	7%	35%	-	-	
Cruz,Juan	92.8	42%	30%	-	20%	8%	-	
Cuddyer,Michael	86.9	81%	6%	-	6%	6%	-	
Cueto,Johnny	93.4	56%	8%	9%	18%	9%	-	
Daley,Matt	87.9	72%	-	14%	-	15%	-	
Danks,John	91.6	49%	27%	5%	-	19%	-	
Davies,Kyle	92.0	49%	20%	17%	-	14%	-	
Davis,Doug	84.6	32%	40%	16%	-	13%	-	
Davis,Wade	91.4	68%	-	16%	11%	5%	-	
De Fratus,Justin	92.1	62%	-	-	38%	-	-	
de la Cruz,Frankie	91.6	65%	-	7%	-	29%	-	
de la Rosa,Dane	94.0	64%	-	36%	-	-	-	
de la Rosa,Jorge	92.7	47%	-	11%	14%	28%	-	
de la Rosa,Rubby	96.0	71%	-	3%	10%	16%	-	
De Los Santos,Fautino	95.8	66%	-	-	32%	3%	-	
Deduno,Sam	88.9	54%	-	29%	-	17%	-	
Del Rosario,Enerio	89.8	75%	-	-	18%	7%	-	
Delabar,Steve	94.0	77%	-	-	-	-	23%	
Delaney,Rob	89.5	76%	-	-	14%	10%	-	
Delgado,Randall	92.4	66%	-	11%	-	22%	-	
Demel,Sam	91.2	52%	25%	-	22%	1%	-	
Dempster,Ryan	90.3	57%	-	-	31%	-	12%	
Detwiler,Ross	92.2	74%	-	13%	-	14%	-	
Devine,Joey	92.3	75%	-	-	25%	-	-	
Diamond,Scott	88.9	58%	-	28%	-	14%	-	
Dickey,R.A.	84.4	22%	-	-	-	2%	-	Knuckleball 75%
Dickson,Brandon	90.2	58%	-	-	34%	8%	-	
DiFelice,Mark	85.6	17%	77%	6%	-	-	-	
Dillard,Tim	87.3	67%	-	-	31%	1%	-	
Dolis,Rafael	95.4	85%	-	10%	5%	-	-	
Dotel,Octavio	91.5	84%	-	5%	11%	-	-	
Doubront,Felix	93.4	67%	5%	16%	-	11%	-	
Downs,Scott	88.3	79%	-	21%	-	-	-	
Drabek,Kyle	93.5	62%	19%	10%	-	9%	-	

Player	Fastball Velocity	Fastball	Cutter	Curve	Slider	Change	Splitter	Other
Duensing,Brian	91.3	62%	-	9%	15%	14%	-	
Duffy,Danny	93.3	63%	-	20%	2%	14%	-	
Duke,Zach	86.9	60%	-	9%	11%	20%	-	
Dumatrait,Phil	90.9	62%	-	-	32%	6%	-	
Dunn,Mike	93.9	74%	-	-	26%	-	-	
Durbin,Chad	90.0	35%	46%	11%	-	8%	-	
Edlefsen,Steve	90.4	74%	-	-	24%	3%	-	
Ekstrom,Mike	91.1	67%	-	-	33%	-	-	
Elbert,Scott	91.7	58%	-	-	42%	-	-	
Ely,John	87.7	58%	19%	5%	-	19%	-	
Enright,Barry	88.8	65%	-	11%	15%	10%	-	
Eovaldi,Nathan	94.3	69%	-	5%	23%	1%	2%	
Eppley,Cody	87.8	60%	-	-	35%	5%	-	
Escalona,Edgmer	92.5	62%	-	-	32%	7%	-	
Escalona,Sergio	90.1	57%	-	32%	-	11%	-	
Estrada,Marco	91.0	52%	4%	22%	-	22%	-	
Eveland,Dana	87.8	43%	13%	7%	25%	13%	-	
Eyre,Willie	91.4	55%	16%	5%	24%	-	-	
Farnsworth,Kyle	94.7	56%	21%	-	21%	3%	-	
Farquhar,Danny	90.6	70%	-	-	26%	5%	-	
Feldman,Scott	91.9	32%	34%	18%	-	16%	-	
Feliz,Neftali	96.3	80%	-	11%	5%	4%	-	
Fiers,Michael	88.5	67%	5%	7%	-	21%	-	
Figueroa,Nelson	86.9	45%	-	16%	36%	3%	-	
Fisher,Carlos	91.8	50%	28%	-	22%	-	-	
Fister,Doug	90.0	57%	-	15%	17%	11%	-	
Floyd,Gavin	91.2	47%	28%	20%	-	5%	-	
Francis,Jeff	84.7	55%	-	14%	-	31%	-	
Francisco,Frank	94.2	70%	-	10%	-	-	20%	
Franklin,Ryan	91.0	43%	22%	9%	6%	4%	13%	Knuckleball 2%
Frasor,Jason	93.1	71%	-	-	13%	-	16%	
Frieri,Ernesto	92.0	76%	-	21%	2%	1%	-	
Fuentes,Brian	89.3	76%	-	-	6%	18%	-	
Fulchino,Jeff	93.3	64%	-	-	19%	-	17%	
Furbush,Charlie	90.9	55%	14%	20%	-	10%	-	
Galarraga,Armando	90.2	58%	-	-	37%	5%	-	
Gallardo,Yovani	92.7	59%	-	20%	20%	1%	-	
Garcia,Freddy	87.2	36%	-	10%	24%	8%	22%	
Garcia,Jaime	89.8	53%	21%	10%	-	16%	-	
Garland,Jon	88.3	58%	3%	11%	15%	7%	6%	
Garrison,Steve	88.3	44%	-	11%	33%	11%	-	
Garza,Matt	93.7	53%	-	12%	24%	11%	-	
Gaub,John	91.6	43%	-	8%	49%	-	-	
Gaudin,Chad	92.1	66%	-	-	25%	9%	-	
Gearrin,Cory	89.6	67%	-	-	29%	4%	-	
Gee,Dillon	89.8	56%	8%	10%	2%	25%	-	
Germano,Justin	87.7	68%	-	15%	-	17%	-	
Godfrey,Graham	90.9	72%	-	9%	13%	7%	-	
Gomes,Brandon	90.8	60%	-	-	23%	-	17%	
Gomez,Jeanmar	89.8	66%	-	-	20%	14%	-	
Gonzalez,Edgar	91.3	56%	-	3%	12%	29%	-	
Gonzalez,Enrique	92.6	51%	19%	4%	19%	7%	-	
Gonzalez,Gio	92.5	65%	-	28%	-	7%	-	
Gonzalez,Mike	92.6	62%	-	-	34%	4%	-	
Gordon,Brian	88.8	63%	7%	16%	10%	-	5%	
Gorzelanny,Tom	89.6	62%	-	-	18%	19%	-	
Grabow,John	88.0	38%	-	-	32%	31%	-	

Player	Fastball Velocity	Fastball	Cutter	Curve	Slider	Change	Splitter	Other
Gray,Jeff	93.3	68%	-	4%	18%	-	10%	
Green,Sean	84.5	74%	-	26%	-	-	-	
Gregerson,Luke	89.7	38%	-	-	58%	5%	-	
Gregg,Kevin	92.1	45%	25%	-	23%	-	7%	
Greinke,Zack	92.5	56%	-	17%	19%	9%	-	
Grilli,Jason	92.4	61%	-	-	37%	1%	-	
Guerra,Javy	94.0	62%	-	5%	31%	2%	-	
Guerrier,Matt	90.8	47%	-	14%	37%	2%	-	
Guthrie,Jeremy	92.5	63%	-	9%	18%	10%	-	
Gutierrez,Juan	94.0	64%	-	10%	22%	4%	-	
Hacker,Eric	88.5	65%	-	17%	14%	4%	-	
Hagadone,Nick	94.1	82%	-	-	15%	3%	-	
Halladay,Roy	92.0	23%	45%	17%	-	-	16%	
Hamburger,Mark	93.0	62%	-	-	13%	25%	-	
Hamels,Cole	91.7	45%	21%	10%	-	24%	-	
Hammel,Jason	92.9	61%	-	11%	17%	10%	-	
Hamren,Erik	91.6	57%	-	-	37%	-	6%	
Hand,Brad	89.5	64%	-	17%	-	18%	-	
Hanrahan,Joel	97.1	83%	-	-	17%	-	-	
Hanson,Tommy	91.2	54%	-	15%	27%	4%	-	
Happ,J.A.	90.0	67%	-	10%	11%	12%	-	
Harang,Aaron	89.8	59%	-	8%	24%	9%	-	
Harden,Rich	91.7	62%	-	-	2%	37%	-	
Haren,Dan	90.0	34%	48%	5%	-	-	12%	
Harrell,Lucas	92.0	60%	-	5%	25%	10%	-	
Harrison,Matt	92.8	64%	-	13%	9%	14%	-	
Hatcher,Chris	93.6	71%	-	1%	15%	13%	-	
Hawkins,LaTroy	92.6	64%	-	13%	22%	1%	-	
Hawksworth,Blake	95.1	65%	-	16%	-	19%	-	
Heilman,Aaron	90.6	56%	-	-	16%	28%	-	
Hellickson,Jeremy	91.0	56%	1%	11%	-	32%	-	
Hendrickson,Mark	87.5	56%	10%	28%	-	6%	-	
Hendriks,Liam	90.0	62%	-	10%	21%	7%	-	
Hensley,Clay	86.8	59%	-	11%	13%	16%	-	
Hernandez,David	94.6	71%	-	23%	-	6%	-	
Hernandez,Felix	93.3	54%	-	15%	10%	22%	-	
Hernandez,Livan	83.9	48%	-	15%	26%	10%	-	
Herndon,David	91.9	69%	-	-	22%	9%	-	
Herrera,Daniel	82.4	39%	4%	-	25%	32%	-	
Herrera,Kelvin	96.2	72%	-	9%	-	19%	-	
Herrmann,Frank	93.9	78%	-	-	18%	-	5%	
Hill,Rich	90.7	25%	-	75%	-	-	-	
Hochevar,Luke	92.7	54%	16%	12%	11%	7%	-	
Hoey,Jim	95.3	70%	-	-	2%	28%	-	
Holland,Derek	94.2	66%	-	11%	13%	10%	-	
Holland,Greg	94.9	50%	-	6%	39%	-	5%	
Horst,Jeremy	88.7	56%	-	-	24%	20%	-	
Hottovy,Tommy	85.8	53%	-	39%	-	8%	-	
Howell,J.P.	86.5	41%	-	45%	-	14%	-	
Hudson,Daniel	93.2	62%	-	-	16%	22%	-	
Hudson,Tim	90.5	56%	6%	9%	20%	4%	5%	
Huff,David	90.9	68%	5%	9%	4%	15%	-	
Hughes,Dusty	88.9	51%	-	6%	12%	31%	-	
Hughes,Jared	92.9	84%	-	-	15%	1%	-	
Hughes,Phil	91.3	59%	12%	22%	-	7%	-	
Humber,Philip	90.5	46%	-	22%	18%	15%	-	
Hunter,Tommy	92.1	50%	29%	14%	-	6%	-	

Player	Fastball Velocity	Fastball	Cutter	Curve	Slider	Change	Splitter	Other
Igarashi,Ryota	92.3	57%	-	15%	-	-	27%	
Isringhausen,Jason	90.6	46%	31%	23%	-	-	-	
Jackson,Edwin	94.5	55%	-	3%	34%	9%	-	
Jakubauskas,Chris	90.5	66%	-	25%	5%	4%	-	
James,Chuck	88.0	71%	-	-	5%	24%	-	
Jansen,Kenley	93.3	87%	-	1%	12%	1%	-	
Janssen,Casey	92.1	43%	38%	14%	5%	1%	-	
Jeffress,Jeremy	96.8	81%	-	19%	-	-	-	
Jenks,Bobby	94.1	66%	-	5%	20%	9%	-	
Jepsen,Kevin	93.7	71%	15%	14%	-	-	-	
Jimenez,Cesar	90.5	60%	-	1%	14%	25%	-	
Jimenez,Ubaldo	93.5	62%	-	7%	14%	17%	-	
Joaquin,Waldis	94.7	75%	-	-	25%	-	-	
Johnson,Alan	87.6	48%	-	19%	24%	9%	-	
Johnson,Jim	95.1	73%	-	10%	-	17%	-	
Johnson,Josh	93.8	60%	-	8%	25%	7%	-	
Judy,Josh	90.9	61%	-	-	38%	2%	-	
Jurrjens,Jair	89.1	57%	-	-	20%	23%	-	
Karstens,Jeff	88.8	54%	2%	15%	17%	13%	-	
Kazmir,Scott	86.5	68%	-	-	16%	16%	-	
Kelley,Shawn	90.9	60%	-	-	40%	-	-	
Kelly,Don	84.5	80%	-	20%	-	-	-	
Kendrick,Kyle	89.7	53%	29%	3%	-	15%	-	
Kennedy,Ian	90.3	64%	8%	10%	3%	16%	-	
Kershaw,Clayton	93.4	65%	-	5%	26%	4%	-	
Kimball,Cole	93.4	65%	-	29%	-	-	6%	
Kimbrel,Craig	96.2	69%	-	-	31%	-	-	
Kinney,Josh	90.3	46%	-	14%	40%	-	-	
Kintzler,Brandon	93.1	65%	-	-	13%	22%	-	
Kirkman,Michael	93.4	69%	-	-	22%	9%	-	
Kluber,Corey	92.0	44%	-	12%	35%	9%	-	
Kohn,Michael	93.4	68%	-	-	29%	-	3%	
Kontos,George	90.6	61%	-	-	39%	-	-	
Kroenke,Zach	91.2	67%	-	1%	14%	17%	-	
Kuo,Hong-Chih	92.5	73%	-	2%	21%	4%	-	
Kuroda,Hiroki	92.0	61%	-	5%	21%	-	14%	
Lackey,John	91.6	51%	-	18%	24%	7%	-	
Laffey,Aaron	87.5	64%	-	-	23%	13%	-	
Lannan,John	89.8	60%	-	8%	15%	17%	-	
Latos,Mat	92.8	56%	-	13%	24%	7%	-	
League,Brandon	96.5	67%	-	-	5%	-	28%	
Leake,Mike	89.1	35%	32%	7%	15%	11%	-	
LeBlanc,Wade	87.1	45%	27%	7%	-	21%	-	
LeCure,Sam	90.3	63%	-	7%	22%	7%	-	
Ledezma,Wil	93.7	72%	-	-	14%	13%	-	
Lee,Cliff	91.5	54%	23%	11%	-	13%	-	
Leroux,Chris	93.6	64%	-	-	34%	3%	-	
Lester,Jon	92.8	49%	28%	13%	-	9%	-	
Lewis,Colby	89.0	58%	-	8%	27%	7%	-	
Lewis,Rommie	92.2	68%	-	8%	20%	3%	-	
Lidge,Brad	89.0	28%	-	-	72%	-	-	
Lilly,Ted	87.4	54%	-	11%	15%	19%	-	
Lincecum,Tim	92.3	53%	-	7%	16%	24%	-	
Lincoln,Brad	91.8	70%	-	18%	-	12%	-	
Lindblom,Josh	91.7	58%	-	5%	30%	6%	-	
Lindsay,Shane	95.8	71%	13%	8%	-	8%	-	
Lindstrom,Matt	96.0	66%	-	-	31%	-	3%	

Player	Fastball Velocity	Fastball	Cutter	Curve	Slider	Change	Splitter	Other
Linebrink,Scott	93.2	69%	2%	-	5%	7%	17%	
Liriano,Francisco	91.8	52%	-	-	29%	20%	-	
Litsch,Jesse	89.2	51%	13%	5%	19%	12%	-	
Locke,Jeff	89.9	70%	-	14%	-	16%	-	
Loe,Kameron	89.6	80%	-	19%	-	1%	-	
Logan,Boone	92.7	62%	-	-	36%	2%	-	
Lohse,Kyle	89.4	59%	-	6%	16%	19%	-	
Lopez,Javier	87.9	60%	26%	-	9%	5%	-	
Lopez,Rodrigo	88.0	59%	-	1%	25%	15%	-	
Lopez,Wilton	91.7	72%	-	-	8%	21%	-	
Lowe,Derek	88.0	50%	9%	-	25%	16%	-	
Lowe,Mark	96.8	65%	-	-	26%	9%	-	
Luebke,Cory	91.4	67%	-	3%	23%	6%	-	
Lueke,Josh	93.6	62%	-	17%	1%	-	20%	
Lyles,Jordan	89.8	52%	24%	13%	-	12%	-	
Lynn,Lance	93.2	73%	-	22%	2%	3%	-	
Lyon,Brandon	90.1	31%	40%	25%	-	5%	-	
MacDougal,Mike	95.5	71%	-	-	29%	-	-	
Madson,Ryan	94.0	57%	8%	-	-	35%	-	
Magnuson,Trystan	92.9	58%	29%	-	12%	1%	-	
Maholm,Paul	87.4	52%	-	13%	17%	18%	-	
Maier,Mitch	76.8	81%	-	19%	-	-	-	
Maine,Scott	91.2	51%	-	-	18%	31%	-	
Maloney,Matt	87.1	47%	-	10%	11%	32%	-	
Manship,Jeff	90.0	61%	-	20%	8%	11%	-	
Marcum,Shaun	86.9	34%	16%	14%	11%	25%	-	
Marmol,Carlos	91.8	36%	-	-	64%	-	-	
Marquez,Jeff	89.1	52%	-	8%	35%	5%	-	
Marquis,Jason	89.3	52%	11%	-	21%	15%	-	
Marshall,Sean	91.3	25%	19%	40%	15%	-	-	
Marte,Luis	90.3	39%	-	-	43%	18%	-	
Martinez,Cristhian	89.8	44%	-	-	24%	32%	-	
Masset,Nick	94.3	53%	14%	23%	-	-	10%	
Masterson,Justin	92.7	84%	-	-	15%	1%	-	
Mateo,Marcos	93.7	58%	-	-	42%	1%	-	
Mathieson,Scott	93.2	69%	-	8%	12%	2%	9%	
Matsuzaka,Daisuke	90.3	50%	14%	-	24%	7%	5%	
Mattheus,Ryan	93.8	69%	-	-	23%	-	8%	
Matusz,Brian	88.0	63%	-	12%	8%	16%	-	
Maya,Yunesky	89.5	62%	-	10%	18%	7%	3%	
Mazzaro,Vin	91.9	61%	-	8%	25%	7%	-	
McAllister,Zach	91.0	64%	-	7%	22%	7%	-	
McCarthy,Brandon	90.9	42%	36%	17%	2%	2%	-	
McClellan,Kyle	89.1	57%	15%	19%	-	9%	-	
McClendon,Mike	88.2	51%	-	-	41%	9%	-	
McCoy,Mike	76.1	67%	-	33%	-	-	-	
McCutchen,Daniel	91.2	53%	-	2%	25%	-	20%	
McDonald,Darnell	84.8	100%	-	-	-	-	-	
McDonald,James	92.7	69%	-	19%	5%	7%	-	
McGee,Jake	94.8	83%	-	-	14%	4%	-	
McGowan,Dustin	93.0	64%	-	6%	20%	9%	-	
Medlen,Kris	91.1	61%	-	17%	-	22%	-	
Meek,Evan	93.1	43%	34%	10%	14%	-	-	
Melancon,Mark	92.7	52%	17%	28%	-	3%	-	
Mendoza,Luis	90.8	81%	-	11%	-	8%	-	
Mickolio,Kam	91.8	84%	-	-	14%	2%	-	
Mijares,Jose	89.8	65%	-	-	31%	4%	-	

Player	Fastball Velocity	Fastball	Cutter	Curve	Slider	Change	Splitter	Other
Miley,Wade	90.3	67%	-	5%	8%	20%	-	
Miller,Andrew	92.5	61%	-	-	23%	15%	-	
Miller,Jim	92.8	59%	-	17%	23%	-	-	
Miller,Trever	87.0	60%	-	-	32%	9%	-	
Mills,Brad	85.6	63%	9%	10%	-	18%	-	
Millwood,Kevin	89.2	49%	15%	8%	20%	8%	-	
Milone,Tom	87.9	55%	15%	8%	-	22%	-	
Minor,Mike	91.2	59%	-	9%	10%	22%	-	
Misch,Pat	85.6	51%	12%	9%	-	28%	-	
Mitre,Sergio	88.2	70%	-	16%	3%	12%	-	
Moore,Matt	95.7	71%	-	14%	-	14%	-	
Morales,Franklin	94.7	64%	-	19%	5%	11%	-	
Morrow,Brandon	93.9	62%	-	6%	27%	6%	-	
Mortensen,Clayton	86.8	61%	-	-	19%	20%	-	
Morton,Charlie	91.4	70%	6%	17%	1%	6%	-	
Moscoso,Guillermo	90.9	65%	-	18%	5%	13%	-	
Moseley,Dustin	88.9	48%	20%	21%	-	11%	-	
Moskos,Daniel	92.1	62%	-	-	27%	11%	-	
Mota,Guillermo	92.8	58%	-	-	24%	19%	-	
Motte,Jason	96.0	78%	20%	2%	-	1%	-	
Moylan,Peter	90.4	49%	-	-	37%	14%	-	
Mujica,Edward	91.8	55%	-	-	7%	-	38%	
Myers,Brett	88.4	49%	-	23%	19%	9%	-	
Narveson,Chris	87.8	47%	-	13%	6%	35%	-	
Nathan,Joe	92.3	58%	-	20%	22%	-	-	
Neshek,Pat	86.4	45%	-	-	39%	16%	-	
Nicasio,Juan	94.1	74%	-	-	15%	11%	-	
Niemann,Jeff	91.1	61%	-	24%	7%	-	9%	
Niese,Jonathon	90.6	55%	17%	23%	-	5%	-	
Noesi,Hector	93.3	56%	-	14%	21%	9%	-	
Nolasco,Ricky	90.5	52%	-	13%	25%	-	11%	
Norberto,Jordan	92.4	68%	-	1%	23%	9%	-	
Norris,Bud	92.6	51%	-	1%	36%	12%	-	
Nova,Ivan	92.6	61%	-	22%	12%	5%	-	
Nunez,Leo	94.1	63%	-	-	9%	28%	-	
O'Connor,Mike	88.5	72%	-	2%	26%	-	-	
O'Day,Darren	84.2	61%	-	-	39%	-	-	
O'Flaherty,Eric	91.9	69%	-	-	28%	4%	-	
Ogando,Alexi	95.1	67%	-	-	28%	5%	-	
Ohlendorf,Ross	91.2	68%	-	-	24%	8%	-	
Ohman,Will	90.2	59%	-	-	40%	1%	-	
Okajima,Hideki	87.0	50%	-	22%	-	-	28%	
Oliver,Andrew	94.0	60%	-	-	28%	12%	-	
Oliver,Darren	88.6	69%	-	-	30%	-	-	
Oliveros,Lester	93.8	68%	-	-	20%	12%	-	
Olson,Garrett	89.6	69%	-	23%	-	9%	-	
Ondrusek,Logan	92.9	36%	36%	20%	-	-	8%	
Ortiz,Ramon	91.4	34%	-	-	56%	10%	-	
O'Sullivan,Sean	91.5	57%	-	8%	24%	11%	-	
Oswalt,Roy	91.4	61%	-	10%	10%	19%	-	
Outman,Josh	92.0	62%	-	4%	18%	16%	-	
Owings,Micah	87.1	3%	78%	-	13%	6%	-	
Padilla,Vicente	93.0	87%	-	8%	3%	-	2%	
Palmer,Matt	89.8	35%	38%	20%	-	6%	-	
Papelbon,Jonathan	95.0	75%	-	-	10%	-	16%	
Parker,Jarrod	92.7	73%	-	1%	11%	15%	-	
Parnell,Bobby	97.2	73%	-	-	26%	1%	-	

Player	Fastball Velocity	Pitch Repertoire						
		Fastball	Cutter	Curve	Slider	Change	Splitter	Other
Paterson,Joe	85.3	50%	-	-	38%	11%	-	
Patton,Troy	89.1	48%	-	4%	33%	15%	-	
Pauley,David	88.9	54%	-	12%	6%	28%	-	
Paulino,Felipe	95.1	56%	-	6%	28%	10%	-	
Pavano,Carl	89.0	61%	-	-	16%	24%	-	
Peacock,Brad	92.7	65%	-	13%	-	22%	-	
Peavy,Jake	90.7	50%	17%	6%	16%	11%	-	
Pelfrey,Mike	92.2	64%	3%	6%	14%	-	13%	
Pena,Tony	92.7	49%	-	-	34%	17%	-	
Pendleton,Lance	88.8	70%	-	12%	12%	6%	-	
Penny,Brad	92.6	62%	-	13%	3%	9%	14%	
Peralta,Joel	90.6	55%	-	18%	1%	-	25%	
Perez,Chris	93.4	78%	-	-	22%	-	-	
Perez,Juan	94.0	49%	-	-	51%	-		
Perez,Luis	92.6	73%	-	-	19%	9%		
Perez,Rafael	89.3	26%	-	-	61%	14%	-	
Perkins,Glen	94.0	68%	-	-	31%	1%	-	
Perry,Ryan	94.3	63%	-	-	34%	3%		
Pestano,Vinnie	92.7	73%	7%	-	20%	-		
Petersen,Bryan	89.7	83%	6%	-	-	11%		
Phillips,Zach	90.3	58%	-	32%	-	11%		
Pineda,Michael	94.7	62%	-	-	31%	6%	-	
Pineiro,Joel	87.6	63%	-	12%	18%	8%	-	
Pomeranz,Drew	89.6	77%	-	15%	-	8%	-	
Porcello,Rick	90.2	65%	-	3%	19%	12%	-	
Price,David	94.8	70%	-	9%	10%	11%	-	
Proctor,Scott	93.8	67%	-	11%	21%	1%	-	
Purcey,David	92.8	70%	-	-	17%	13%	-	
Putnam,Zach	91.7	53%	-	-	14%	-	33%	
Putz,J.J.	93.0	73%	-	-	7%	-	19%	
Qualls,Chad	92.6	60%	-	-	40%	-	1%	
Ramirez,Horacio	90.7	70%	10%	-	9%	11%	-	
Ramirez,Ramon	92.4	39%	-	-	40%	22%	-	
Ramos,Cesar	92.3	57%	-	16%	8%	19%	-	
Rapada,Clay	85.4	53%	-	-	46%	1%	-	
Rauch,Jon	89.5	58%	-	8%	24%	10%	-	
Ray,Chris	93.7	64%	-	-	27%	-	9%	
Reed,Addison	94.9	70%	-	-	22%	8%	-	
Reineke,Chad	87.0	50%	-	-	44%	6%	-	
Resop,Chris	93.3	77%	-	21%	-	3%	-	
Reyes,Dennys	88.5	69%	-	-	18%	13%	-	
Reyes,Jo-Jo	89.9	72%	-	4%	12%	13%	-	
Reynolds,Greg	88.9	55%	20%	12%	-	13%	-	
Reynolds,Matt	89.4	50%	-	-	31%	5%	14%	
Rhodes,Arthur	89.0	72%	-	-	26%	2%	-	
Richard,Clayton	90.4	60%	21%	3%	4%	12%	-	
Richards,Garrett	94.5	61%	-	-	34%	6%	-	
Richmond,Scott	92.0	50%	-	33%	17%	-	-	
Rivera,Mariano	92.3	13%	87%	-	-	-	-	
Robertson,David	93.1	77%	-	21%	-	2%	-	
Rodney,Fernando	95.5	64%	-	-	10%	26%	-	
Rodriguez,Aneury	91.0	70%	-	2%	23%	4%	-	
Rodriguez,Fernando	92.5	64%	2%	28%	-	7%	-	
Rodriguez,Francisco M.	93.3	63%	35%	3%	-	-	-	
Rodriguez,Francisco	90.3	60%	-	21%	-	19%	-	
Rodriguez,Henry	98.0	69%	-	-	21%	11%	-	
Rodriguez,Wandy	89.1	53%	-	37%	-	10%	-	

Player	Fastball Velocity	Fastball	Cutter	Curve	Slider	Change	Splitter	Other
Roenicke,Josh	93.5	58%	28%	14%	-	-	-	
Rogers,Esmil	94.0	60%	-	14%	17%	9%	-	
Romero,J.C.	89.3	67%	-	-	18%	15%	-	
Romero,Ricky	92.1	61%	9%	9%	1%	20%	-	
Romo,Sergio	89.4	44%	-	-	54%	2%	-	
Rosario,Sandy	95.0	63%	-	-	14%	23%	-	
Ross,Tyson	92.1	67%	-	-	20%	12%	-	
Ruffin,Chance	93.4	63%	-	9%	28%	1%	-	
Runzler,Dan	95.1	75%	-	-	24%	1%	-	
Rupe,Josh	92.0	74%	-	5%	16%	5%	-	
Russell,Adam	94.3	74%	-	2%	21%	3%	-	
Russell,James	88.1	47%	-	5%	37%	11%		
Rzepczynski,Marc	91.3	61%	-	-	29%	10%		
Sabathia,CC	93.8	59%	-	8%	20%	13%		
Saito,Takashi	90.7	59%	-	24%	16%	-	1%	
Salas,Fernando	91.2	60%	-	-	16%	24%	-	
Sale,Chris	95.3	52%	-	-	36%	12%		
Samardzija,Jeff	95.1	59%	7%	-	24%	-	11%	
Sanabia,Alex	89.6	67%	-	-	7%	25%		
Sanches,Brian	87.4	62%	-	1%	14%	-	24%	
Sanchez,Anibal	91.7	54%	-	8%	21%	18%	-	
Sanchez,Eduardo	93.5	67%	-	33%	-	1%	-	
Sanchez,Jonathan	89.9	62%	-	-	18%	20%	-	
Sanit,Amauri	90.6	61%	-	3%	27%	8%	-	
Santana,Ervin	92.8	58%	-	-	38%	3%	-	
Santiago,Hector	93.8	66%	-	-	3%	-	-	Screwball 31%
Santos,Sergio	95.3	59%	-	-	32%	9%	-	
Saunders,Joe	89.6	64%	-	9%	8%	19%	-	
Savery,Joe	90.9	59%	-	-	41%	-	-	
Scherzer,Max	93.1	61%	-	-	18%	20%	-	
Schlereth,Daniel	91.4	53%	-	47%	-	-	-	
Schumaker,Skip	91.0	38%	-	-	-	62%	-	
Schwimer,Michael	91.4	43%	-	-	38%	19%	-	
Schwinden,Chris	89.1	45%	24%	15%	-	16%	-	
Scribner,Evan	89.0	59%	4%	37%	-	-	-	
Severino,Atahualpa	93.6	71%	-	-	28%	1%	-	
Shaw,Bryan	91.3	6%	80%	6%	7%	-	-	
Sherrill,George	87.7	61%	-	-	39%	-	-	
Shields,James	91.0	36%	15%	21%	-	27%	-	
Simon,Alfredo	94.4	52%	-	23%	7%	-	17%	
Sipp,Tony	91.4	67%	-	-	25%	8%	-	
Slama,Anthony	89.8	72%	-	-	28%	-	-	
Slaten,Doug	89.3	59%	-	-	30%	11%	-	
Slowey,Kevin	89.1	65%	-	13%	16%	6%	-	
Smith,Joe	90.2	70%	-	-	30%	-	-	
Smith,Jordan	90.7	52%	-	-	34%	14%	-	
Sonnanstine,Andy	86.3	2%	65%	19%	13%	1%	-	
Soria,Joakim	91.4	75%	-	7%	11%	7%	-	
Soriano,Rafael	92.6	49%	20%	-	31%	-	-	
Sosa,Henry	93.1	62%	-	-	36%	3%	-	
Spence,Josh	83.8	32%	-	-	51%	17%	-	
Stammen,Craig	90.5	62%	-	17%	21%	1%	-	
Stauffer,Tim	90.4	51%	27%	13%	-	9%	-	
Stetter,Mitch	81.6	42%	-	-	58%	-	-	
Stevens,Jeff	89.4	63%	-	15%	22%	-	-	
Stewart,Zach	90.8	64%	-	7%	24%	5%	-	
Stinson,Josh	93.0	64%	-	6%	28%	2%	-	

Player	Fastball Velocity	Pitch Repertoire						
		Fastball	Cutter	Curve	Slider	Change	Splitter	Other
Storen,Drew	95.0	65%	-	-	34%	1%	-	
Strasburg,Stephen	95.8	73%	-	13%	-	13%	-	
Street,Huston	90.1	55%	-	-	28%	17%	-	
Strop,Pedro	94.3	53%	-	-	40%	-	7%	
Stults,Eric	90.6	53%	-	7%	18%	22%	-	
Stutes,Michael	93.1	58%	-	1%	40%	1%	-	
Surkamp,Eric	87.9	51%	10%	25%	-	13%	-	
Swarzak,Anthony	91.3	68%	-	7%	15%	10%	-	
Takahashi,Hisanori	88.9	51%	1%	4%	19%	26%	-	
Talbot,Mitch	89.7	45%	28%	-	13%	14%	-	
Tallet,Brian	88.7	47%	28%	-	13%	12%	-	
Tateyama,Yoshinori	86.9	54%	-	-	32%	14%	-	
Tazawa,Junichi	91.8	59%	-	26%	-	-	15%	
Teaford,Everett	91.7	47%	23%	23%	-	7%	-	
Teheran,Julio	93.0	65%	-	16%	-	19%	-	
Tejeda,Robinson	90.2	62%	-	-	16%	22%	-	
Texeira,Kanekoa	90.1	75%	-	-	12%	12%	-	
Thatcher,Joe	85.4	81%	-	-	19%	-	-	
Thayer,Dale	92.8	77%	-	-	20%	3%	-	
Thomas,Brad	90.0	64%	-	21%	6%	9%	-	
Thompson,Aaron	88.2	58%	-	-	17%	25%	-	
Thompson,Daryl	91.1	56%	-	10%	14%	20%	-	
Thompson,Rich	90.7	33%	45%	20%	-	2%	-	
Thornton,Matt	95.8	86%	7%	-	6%	-	-	
Tillman,Chris	89.5	60%	10%	17%	-	12%	-	
Tobin,Mason	92.6	69%	-	-	10%	21%	-	
Tomko,Brett	90.8	63%	-	12%	21%	4%	-	
Tomlin,Josh	87.9	42%	28%	15%	3%	12%	-	
Torres,Alex	92.2	62%	-	8%	-	30%	-	
Troncoso,Ramon	91.8	70%	-	12%	18%	-	-	
Tucker,Ryan	93.1	73%	-	-	17%	10%	-	
Turner,Jacob	91.7	53%	10%	22%	-	14%	-	
Uehara,Koji	88.8	65%	-	-	-	13%	22%	
Valdes,Raul	87.3	58%	-	-	40%	1%	-	
Valdez,Jose	93.6	60%	-	6%	-	-	34%	
Valdez,Merkin	94.9	66%	-	-	9%	-	25%	
Valdez,Wilson	87.0	90%	-	10%	-	-	-	
Valverde,Jose	93.9	80%	-	-	-	-	20%	
VandenHurk,Rick	93.0	66%	-	9%	17%	9%	-	
Vargas,Jason	87.4	47%	19%	6%	-	28%	-	
Varvaro,Anthony	92.7	69%	-	24%	-	7%	-	
Vasquez,Anthony	85.2	57%	-	11%	-	32%	-	
Vasquez,Esmerling	93.4	72%	-	14%	-	14%	-	
Vazquez,Javier	90.4	60%	-	17%	15%	7%	-	
Venters,Jonny	95.0	80%	-	-	20%	-	-	
Veras,Jose	94.1	49%	-	40%	-	-	11%	
Verlander,Justin	95.0	57%	-	18%	8%	16%	-	
Villanueva,Carlos	89.0	46%	-	13%	19%	21%	-	
Villanueva,Elih	89.1	66%	-	2%	17%	15%	-	
Villarreal,Brayan	94.3	62%	-	-	38%	-	-	
Viola,Pedro	92.7	64%	-	-	35%	1%	-	
Vizcaino,Arodys	95.9	64%	-	33%	-	2%	-	
Vogelsong,Ryan	91.4	56%	15%	20%	-	10%	-	
Volquez,Edinson	93.6	53%	-	21%	-	26%	-	
Volstad,Chris	91.3	59%	-	9%	19%	12%	-	
Wade,Cory	88.8	51%	-	23%	-	26%	-	
Wagner,Neil	95.3	70%	-	-	15%	15%	-	

Player	Fastball Velocity	Fastball	Cutter	Curve	Slider	Change	Splitter	Other
								Pitch Repertoire
Wakefield,Tim	72.9	9%	-	2%	-	-	-	Knuckleball 89%
Walden,Jordan	97.5	81%	-	-	16%	3%	-	
Waldrop,Kyle	88.3	75%	-	19%	-	5%	-	
Walters,P.J.	88.8	52%	6%	2%	21%	19%	-	
Wang,Chien-Ming	90.6	72%	-	7%	14%	7%	-	
Watson,Tony	91.2	77%	-	-	10%	12%	-	
Weaver,Jered	89.1	57%	-	11%	18%	15%	-	
Webb,Ryan	93.8	65%	-	-	23%	11%	-	
Weiland,Kyle	92.5	60%	20%	13%	-	8%	-	
Weinhardt,Robbie	87.5	74%	-	-	26%	-	-	
Wells,Randy	88.1	49%	10%	-	22%	18%	-	
Westbrook,Jake	90.0	64%	16%	-	9%	12%	-	
Wheeler,Dan	89.2	47%	40%	9%	-	3%	-	
Whelan,Kevin	91.1	81%	-	-	2%	-	16%	
White,Alex	92.4	72%	-	-	13%	-	15%	
Wilhelmsen,Tom	95.2	69%	-	25%	6%	-	-	
Wilk,Adam	87.8	53%	21%	5%	-	21%	-	
Williams,Jerome	91.3	44%	34%	5%	-	16%	-	
Williams,Randy	93.0	76%	15%	4%	-	5%	-	
Willis,Dontrelle	87.5	60%	-	14%	19%	8%	-	
Wilson,Brian	94.3	53%	46%	-	1%	-	-	
Wilson,C.J.	91.0	53%	13%	14%	13%	7%	-	
Wolf,Randy	88.4	50%	-	19%	19%	12%	-	
Wood,Blake	95.6	62%	-	-	32%	6%	-	
Wood,Kerry	94.4	50%	38%	12%	-	-	-	
Wood,Tim	94.5	70%	-	-	25%	5%	-	
Wood,Travis	89.9	58%	17%	6%	4%	16%	-	
Worley,Vance	90.2	67%	-	4%	21%	8%	-	
Worrell,Mark	88.5	67%	-	-	33%	-	-	
Wright,Jamey	91.7	47%	25%	25%	3%	-	-	
Wright,Wesley	90.8	75%	-	9%	16%	-	-	
Wuertz,Michael	88.7	37%	-	1%	61%	1%	-	
Young,Chris	84.7	69%	-	2%	18%	12%	-	
Zagurski,Mike	91.8	69%	-	-	31%	-	-	
Zambrano,Carlos	90.2	53%	20%	4%	13%	-	9%	
Ziegler,Brad	85.4	75%	-	-	21%	4%	-	
Zimmermann,Jordan	93.4	61%	-	13%	24%	2%	-	
Zito,Barry	84.1	51%	-	22%	8%	18%	-	

Pinch Hitting

Bill James

1) Russell Branyan now has a career batting average, as a pinch hitter, of .149 (25 for 168). At what point do you say, "You know, maybe we *don't* want you up at the plate right now"?

2) Matt Stairs is one away from having as many career pinch-hit home runs (23) as any other three active players. The next three totals are 9, 8 and 7.

3) Wil Nieves has never had a pinch hit in the majors. He's 0-for-23 as a pinch hitter.

4) Dewayne Wise is 26-for-84 as a pinch hitter (.310).

5) When not pinch hitting, Nieves' batting average is 20 points higher than Wise'. Wise' pinch hitting has increased his career average by 10 points, from .209 to .219; Nieves has lowered his by 7 points, from .228 to .221.

6) The term "pinch" hitter in baseball originally meant a "clutch" hitter; a "pinch" was a tight spot. In 1915, if you said that a player was a good pinch hitter, that meant that he was a good clutch hitter; it didn't necessarily mean that he had ever been used as a substitute batter. Since substitute batters were very often used in "pinch" situations, gradually the term "pinch" hitter came to mean a substitute batter, and the term "clutch" replaced the term "pinch".

7) Wes Helms leads active players with 23 career doubles.

8) There are 43 active players who have 100 or more at bats as a pinch hitter. Nine of those have career pinch hitting averages under .200; four of them are over .300. The four who are over .300 are Jamey Carroll (.350), Seth Smith (.336), Mark Kotsay (.308), and Ryan (Cyborg) Spilborghs (.305).

Pinch Hitting

Batter	B	AB	H	2B	3B	HR	RBI	TBB	IBB	SO	GDP	Avg	OBP	Slg	AB	H	2B	3B	HR	RBI	TBB	IBB	SO	GDP	Avg	OBP	Slg
						2011 Pinch Hitting														**Career Pinch Hitting**								
Bobby Abreu	L	6	0	0	0	0	1	1	0	4	0	.000	.143	.000	52	9	0	1	0	7	11	3	19	0	.173	.317	.212
Dustin Ackley	L	3	1	0	0	0	0	0	0	1	0	.333	.333	.333	3	1	0	0	0	0	0	0	1	0	.333	.333	.333
Ryan Adams	R	2	1	0	0	0	0	0	0	0	0	.500	.500	.500	2	1	0	0	0	0	0	0	0	0	.500	.500	.500
Eliezer Alfonzo	R	6	3	1	0	0	1	0	0	0	0	.500	.500	.667	30	7	2	0	0	5	0	0	12	0	.233	.233	.300
Brandon Allen	L	1	0	0	0	0	0	0	0	1	0	.000	.000	.000	5	1	1	0	0	0	1	0	4	0	.200	.333	.400
Erick Almonte	R	7	0	0	0	0	1	0	0	1	0	.000	.000	.000	7	0	0	0	0	0	0	0	1	0	.000	.000	.000
Yonder Alonso	L	24	6	1	0	1	2	3	0	5	1	.250	.333	.417	40	9	2	0	1	2	3	0	10	1	.225	.279	.350
Jose Altuve	R	2	1	0	0	0	0	0	0	1	0	.500	.500	.500	2	1	0	0	0	0	0	0	1	0	.500	.500	.500
Pedro Alvarez	L	10	2	0	0	0	0	0	0	4	0	.200	.200	.200	10	2	0	0	0	0	1	0	4	0	.200	.273	.200
Alexi Amarista	L	3	0	0	0	0	0	0	0	0	0	.000	.000	.000	3	0	0	0	0	0	0	0	0	0	.000	.000	.000
Alfredo Amezaga	B	13	2	0	0	0	1	0	0	1	0	.154	.154	.154	96	22	3	2	0	3	7	0	21	1	.229	.282	.302
Robert Andino	R	3	2	0	0	0	0	0	0	1	0	.667	.667	.667	34	6	1	0	0	2	3	0	18	0	.176	.243	.206
Elvis Andrus	R	6	2	0	0	0	2	0	0	2	0	.333	.333	.333	9	3	0	0	0	2	1	0	2	0	.333	.400	.333
Matt Angle	L	2	0	0	0	0	0	0	0	1	0	.000	.000	.000	2	0	0	0	0	0	0	0	1	0	.000	.000	.000
Rick Ankiel	L	11	3	0	0	1	2	1	0	2	0	.273	.333	.545	60	14	2	0	4	8	8	1	22	0	.233	.333	.467
J.P. Arencibia	R	3	1	0	0	0	1	0	0	1	0	.333	.333	.333	3	1	0	0	0	1	0	0	1	0	.333	.333	.333
Alex Avila	L	3	1	0	0	1	2	1	0	1	0	.333	.500	1.333	16	4	0	0	1	5	3	0	8	0	.250	.350	.438
Mike Aviles	R	5	1	0	0	0	1	1	0	2	0	.200	.333	.200	9	3	0	0	0	2	2	0	2	0	.333	.455	.333
Jeff Baker	R	30	4	2	0	0	3	0	0	9	3	.133	.133	.200	139	26	5	1	3	12	12	1	52	6	.187	.255	.302
John Baker	L	12	2	0	0	1	2	2	0	3	0	.167	.286	.167	27	4	0	0	1	4	4	0	10	0	.148	.258	.259
Rod Barajas	R	9	1	0	0	0	1	2	0	3	0	.111	.273	.111	35	11	1	0	2	6	5	1	10	0	.314	.390	.514
Clint Barmes	R	1	0	0	0	0	0	0	0	0	0	.000	.000	.000	32	8	2	0	1	6	1	0	6	0	.250	.294	.406
Darwin Barney	R	8	1	0	0	0	0	0	0	2	1	.125	.125	.125	13	2	0	0	0	0	0	0	4	1	.154	.154	.154
Jason Bartlett	R	3	1	0	0	0	0	0	0	0	0	.333	.333	.333	13	3	0	0	1	5	0	0	3	1	.231	.231	.462
Daric Barton	L	2	0	0	0	0	0	1	0	1	0	.000	.333	.000	15	1	0	0	0	2	1	0	9	0	.067	.125	.067
Mike Baxter	L	8	2	2	0	0	1	0	0	1	1	.250	.250	.500	15	2	2	0	0	2	0	0	3	2	.133	.125	.267
Gordon Beckham	R	1	0	0	0	0	0	0	0	0	0	.000	.000	.000	1	0	0	0	0	0	0	0	0	0	.000	.000	.000
Josh Bell	B	2	1	0	0	0	0	0	0	0	0	.500	.500	.500	3	1	0	0	0	0	0	0	1	0	.333	.333	.333
Brandon Belt	L	8	1	0	0	0	0	0	0	4	0	.125	.125	.125	8	1	0	0	0	0	0	0	4	0	.125	.125	.125
Carlos Beltran	B	5	1	0	0	0	0	0	0	0	0	.200	.200	.200	28	5	0	0	1	1	3	1	6	0	.179	.258	.286
Adrian Beltre	R	1	0	0	0	0	0	0	0	0	0	.000	.000	.000	10	3	0	0	2	4	4	0	4	0	.300	.500	.900
Joe Benson	R	1	0	0	0	0	0	0	0	1	0	.000	.000	.000	1	0	0	0	0	0	0	0	1	0	.000	.000	.000
Lance Berkman	B	3	1	0	0	0	1	0	0	1	0	.333	.333	.333	55	8	2	0	1	5	8	2	22	1	.145	.254	.236
Roger Bernadina	L	7	3	0	0	0	0	0	0	1	1	.429	.429	.429	16	6	1	0	0	1	1	0	4	1	.375	.412	.438
Y. Betancourt	R	3	0	0	0	0	1	0	0	0	0	.000	.000	.000	8	1	0	0	0	2	1	0	1	0	.125	.200	.125
Wilson Betemit	B	9	1	0	0	1	4	0	0	6	1	.111	.100	.444	147	36	9	0	5	20	26	0	55	3	.245	.356	.408
Brian Bixler	R	20	4	0	0	0	1	1	0	4	0	.200	.238	.200	26	6	1	0	0	1	2	0	6	0	.231	.286	.269
Charlie Blackmon	L	2	1	0	0	1	1	0	0	0	0	.500	.500	2.000	2	1	0	0	1	1	0	0	0	0	.500	.500	2.000
Casey Blake	R	10	1	1	0	0	3	2	1	4	1	.100	.250	.200	36	6	3	0	0	6	6	1	15	1	.167	.298	.250
Andres Blanco	B	2	0	0	0	0	0	0	0	1	0	.000	.000	.000	12	2	1	0	0	0	0	0	1	0	.167	.167	.250
Henry Blanco	R	1	0	0	0	0	0	0	0	0	0	.000	.000	.000	48	11	1	0	0	6	5	0	13	2	.229	.302	.250
Kyle Blanks	R	7	0	0	0	0	0	2	0	5	0	.000	.222	.000	15	1	1	0	0	0	3	0	8	0	.067	.222	.133
Willie Bloomquist	R	14	1	0	0	0	2	1	1	3	1	.071	.188	.071	72	17	1	0	1	5	5	1	15	2	.236	.282	.292
Geoff Blum	B	7	1	1	0	0	3	3	0	2	0	.143	.455	.286	243	60	12	1	1	35	34	6	49	6	.247	.343	.317
Brennan Boesch	L	5	1	0	0	0	0	1	0	0	0	.200	.333	.200	10	2	0	0	0	0	1	0	0	0	.200	.273	.200
Brandon Boggs	B	11	1	0	0	0	0	1	0	6	0	.091	.167	.091	27	5	1	0	0	2	4	0	14	0	.185	.313	.222
Brian Bogusevic	L	33	10	2	0	1	5	3	0	8	1	.303	.361	.455	42	13	4	0	1	8	4	0	11	1	.310	.370	.476
Emilio Bonifacio	B	8	1	0	0	0	0	2	0	5	0	.125	.300	.125	45	10	2	1	0	2	5	0	16	0	.222	.300	.311
J.C. Boscan	R	1	0	0	0	0	0	0	0	1	0	.000	.000	.000	1	0	0	0	0	0	0	0	1	0	.000	.000	.000
Jason Bourgeois	R	17	5	0	0	0	1	0	0	4	0	.294	.294	.294	52	12	0	0	0	2	5	0	11	1	.231	.298	.231
Peter Bourjos	R	1	0	0	0	0	0	0	0	0	0	.000	.000	.000	1	0	0	0	0	0	0	0	0	0	.000	.000	.000
Michael Bourn	L	2	1	0	0	0	1	0	0	0	0	.500	.500	.500	31	5	1	0	0	1	1	0	8	0	.161	.188	.194
John Bowker	L	26	4	1	0	0	2	2	1	10	0	.154	.214	.192	83	22	4	2	1	12	9	1	25	0	.265	.337	.398
Milton Bradley	B	1	0	0	0	0	0	0	0	1	0	.000	.000	.000	37	6	0	0	1	2	9	1	13	1	.162	.326	.243
Michael Brantley	L	1	0	0	0	0	0	0	0	0	0	.000	.000	.000	4	2	1	0	0	3	1	0	1	0	.500	.600	.750
Russell Branyan	L	28	3	1	0	2	5	5	0	8	0	.107	.242	.357	168	25	5	0	6	19	36	2	80	1	.149	.309	.286
Ryan Braun	R	3	2	1	0	1	3	0	0	0	0	.667	.667	2.000	9	4	3	0	1	5	0	0	2	0	.444	.500	1.111
Andrew Brown	R	5	0	0	0	0	0	0	0	4	0	.000	.000	.000	5	0	0	0	0	0	0	0	4	0	.000	.000	.000
Corey Brown	L	3	0	0	0	0	0	0	0	2	0	.000	.000	.000	3	0	0	0	0	0	0	0	2	0	.000	.000	.000
Domonic Brown	L	5	2	0	0	1	1	0	0	1	0	.400	.400	.400	21	5	1	0	1	3	1	0	10	0	.238	.273	.429
Dusty Brown	R	1	1	0	0	0	0	0	0	0	0	1.000	1.000	1.000	1	1	0	0	0	0	0	0	0	0	1.000	1.000	1.000
Jay Bruce	L	2	1	1	0	0	2	1	1	1	0	.500	.750	1.000	19	8	3	0	0	3	2	1	5	0	.421	.476	.579
John Buck	R	6	2	2	0	0	3	2	0	2	0	.333	.444	.667	25	5	2	0	0	3	4	0	11	2	.200	.300	.280
Travis Buck	L	7	2	2	0	0	0	0	0	1	0	.286	.286	.571	16	3	2	0	0	1	0	0	4	0	.188	.188	.313
M. Bumgarner	R	2	0	0	0	0	0	0	0	0	0	.000	.000	.000	3	0	0	0	0	0	0	0	2	0	.000	.000	.000
Pat Burrell	R	32	6	2	0	0	2	8	0	13	0	.188	.341	.250	83	17	3	0	3	11	21	1	32	1	.205	.358	.349
Manny Burriss	B	8	0	0	0	0	0	0	0	5	0	.000	.000	.000	14	2	0	0	0	0	0	0	6	0	.143	.200	.143
Sean Burroughs	L	56	16	3	0	0	3	2	0	12	4	.286	.310	.339	93	24	4	0	1	8	7	0	20	4	.258	.310	.333

Pinch Hitting

Batter	B	AB	H	2B	3B	HR	RBI	TBB	IBB	SO	GDP	Avg	OBP	Slg	AB	H	2B	3B	HR	RBI	TBB	IBB	SO	GDP	Avg	OBP	Slg
												2011 Pinch Hitting													**Career Pinch Hitting**		
Drew Butera	R	1	0	0	0	0	0	0	0	1	0	.000	.000	.000	3	1	0	0	1	1	0	0	1	0	.333	.333	1.333
Billy Butler	R	6	1	1	0	0	0	0	0	1	0	.167	.167	.333	24	6	2	0	0	0	3	0	5	0	.250	.333	.333
Marlon Byrd	R	1	0	0	0	0	0	0	0	1	0	.000	.000	.000	49	14	6	0	1	5	5	0	12	1	.286	.368	.469
Melky Cabrera	B	1	0	0	0	0	0	0	0	1	0	.000	.000	.000	30	5	0	0	0	1	5	1	9	1	.167	.278	.167
Miguel Cabrera	R	2	1	1	0	0	1	0	0	0	1	.500	.500	1.000	7	3	1	0	0	3	1	0	1	1	.429	.500	.571
Orlando Cabrera	R	4	2	0	0	0	0	0	0	0	0	.500	.500	.500	16	3	0	0	0	3	1	0	2	0	.188	.222	.188
Matt Cain	R	1	0	0	0	0	0	0	0	0	0	.000	.000	.000	2	0	0	0	0	0	0	0	1	0	.000	.000	.000
Miguel Cairo	R	29	11	0	0	1	7	3	0	7	1	.379	.441	.483	252	68	12	2	2	40	21	3	38	5	.270	.327	.357
Alberto Callaspo	B	10	3	0	0	0	0	3	0	3	0	.300	.462	.300	65	13	2	0	0	3	7	0	12	3	.200	.274	.231
Mike Cameron	R	10	1	0	0	0	0	2	0	3	0	.100	.250	.100	30	4	2	0	1	6	6	0	9	0	.133	.297	.300
Tony Campana	L	28	5	0	0	0	0	8	0	8	0	.179	.179	.179	28	5	0	0	0	0	8	0	8	0	.179	.179	.179
Robinson Cano	L	2	0	0	0	0	0	0	0	1	0	.000	.000	.000	15	6	0	0	2	4	0	0	3	0	.400	.400	.800
Jorge Cantu	R	24	6	1	0	0	2	0	0	7	2	.250	.240	.292	57	16	5	0	0	6	3	0	14	2	.281	.323	.368
Russ Canzler	R	2	1	0	0	0	0	1	0	1	0	.500	.667	.500	2	1	0	0	0	0	1	0	1	0	.500	.667	.500
Mike Carp	L	2	0	0	0	0	0	1	0	1	0	.000	.333	.000	8	1	0	0	0	1	3	0	5	0	.125	.333	.125
Matt Carpenter	L	1	0	0	0	0	0	1	0	1	0	.000	.500	.000	1	0	0	0	0	0	1	0	1	0	.000	.500	.000
Ezequiel Carrera	L	4	2	1	0	0	1	1	0	2	0	.500	.600	.750	4	2	1	0	0	1	1	0	2	0	.500	.600	.750
Jamey Carroll	R	11	3	1	0	0	1	0	0	1	0	.273	.273	.364	117	41	4	0	1	14	17	0	23	4	.350	.430	.410
Chris Carter	R	1	0	0	0	0	0	0	0	0	0	.000	.000	.000	2	0	0	0	0	0	0	0	0	0	.000	.000	.000
Alexi Casilla	B	1	0	0	0	0	0	0	0	1	0	.000	.000	.000	110	20	1	1	3	10	6	0	29	2	.182	.224	.291
Juan Castro	R	2	0	0	0	0	0	0	0	1	0	.000	.000	.000	78	20	3	0	3	10	5	0	19	0	.256	.301	.410
Ramon Castro	R	2	1	0	0	0	0	0	0	1	0	.500	.500	.500	59	15	5	0	1	5	6	0	15	0	.254	.343	.390
Ronny Cedeno	R	2	0	0	0	0	0	0	0	2	0	.000	.000	.000	7	1	0	0	0	0	0	0	3	0	.143	.143	.143
Francisco Cervelli	R	2	1	0	0	0	0	0	0	1	0	.500	.500	.500	1	0	0	0	0	0	0	0	0	0	.000	.000	.000
Jhoulys Chacin	R	1	0	0	0	0	0	0	0	0	0	.000	.000	.000	5	2	0	1	0	3	0	0	0	0	.400	.400	.800
Adron Chambers	L	5	2	0	1	0	3	0	0	0	0	.400	.400	.800	112	29	5	3	1	13	7	1	12	3	.259	.303	.384
Endy Chavez	L	11	2	1	0	0	2	0	0	2	0	.182	.182	.273	51	13	4	0	0	9	2	1	12	1	.255	.283	.333
Eric Chavez	L	11	3	0	0	0	2	1	1	3	0	.273	.333	.273	2	1	0	0	0	1	0	0	0	0	.500	.500	.500
Robinson Chirinos	R	2	1	0	0	0	1	0	0	0	0	.500	.500	.500	7	2	0	0	0	0	0	0	2	0	.286	.286	.286
Lonnie Chisenhall	L	7	2	0	0	0	0	0	0	2	0	.286	.286	.286	14	4	1	1	0	1	1	0	3	1	.286	.333	.500
Pedro Ciriaco	R	9	1	0	0	0	0	1	0	1	1	.111	.200	.111	1	1	0	0	0	0	0	0	0	0	1.000	1.000	2.000
Steve Clevenger	L	1	1	1	0	0	0	0	0	0	0	1.000	1.000	2.000	1	0	0	0	0	0	0	0	0	0	.000	.000	.000
Casey Coleman	L	1	0	0	0	0	0	0	0	0	0	.000	.000	.000	40	8	3	0	1	7	3	0	15	0	.200	.250	.350
Tyler Colvin	L	19	3	1	0	0	3	1	0	7	0	.158	.200	.211	9	1	0	0	1	2	0	0	2	0	.111	.273	.111
Hank Conger	B	7	1	0	0	0	0	0	0	1	0	.143	.143	.143	138	27	8	0	7	25	14	1	53	1	.196	.270	.406
Brooks Conrad	B	62	13	4	0	3	10	10	1	29	0	.210	.319	.419	7	1	0	0	0	0	0	0	1	0	.143	.143	.143
Jose Constanza	L	7	1	0	0	0	0	0	0	1	0	.143	.143	.143	7	2	0	0	0	0	0	0	3	0	.286	.286	.286
Aaron Cook	R	1	0	0	0	0	0	0	0	1	0	.000	.000	.000	3	1	1	0	0	2	1	0	0	0	.333	.500	.667
David Cooper	L	3	1	1	0	0	2	1	0	0	0	.333	.500	.667	131	32	4	2	1	12	9	1	19	1	.244	.298	.328
Alex Cora	L	32	6	0	1	0	2	4	0	8	0	.188	.278	.250	4	1	0	0	0	0	0	0	0	0	.250	.250	.250
Carlos Corporan	B	4	1	0	0	0	0	0	0	0	0	.250	.250	.250	263	60	7	1	1	14	46	1	31	4	.228	.351	.274
Craig Counsell	L	40	8	0	0	0	0	9	0	4	0	.200	.353	.200	42	8	2	0	2	2	4	0	16	0	.190	.261	.333
Scott Cousins	L	25	3	0	0	0	0	4	0	9	0	.120	.241	.120	9	1	0	0	0	0	0	0	5	0	.111	.111	.111
Collin Cowgill	R	9	1	0	0	0	0	0	0	5	0	.111	.111	.111	1	0	0	0	0	0	0	0	0	0	.000	.000	.000
Zack Cozart	R	1	0	0	0	0	0	0	0	0	0	.000	.000	.000	29	8	1	0	1	4	2	0	4	2	.276	.323	.414
Allen Craig	R	22	7	1	0	1	4	1	0	1	2	.318	.348	.500	19	2	1	0	0	1	4	1	3	0	.105	.261	.158
Carl Crawford	L	2	1	1	0	0	0	0	0	0	0	.500	.500	1.000	12	3	1	0	0	2	1	0	1	0	.250	.308	.333
Coco Crisp	B	2	1	0	0	0	0	0	0	0	0	.500	.500	.500	8	0	0	0	0	0	2	0	3	0	.000	.200	.000
Trevor Crowe	R	1	0	0	0	0	0	0	0	1	0	.000	.000	.000	18	0	0	0	0	1	1	0	9	0	.000	.053	.000
Nelson Cruz	R	2	0	0	0	0	0	0	0	1	0	.000	.000	.000	15	4	1	0	0	3	2	0	3	0	.267	.333	.333
Tony Cruz	R	15	4	1	0	0	3	2	0	3	0	.267	.353	.333	45	11	4	0	1	3	2	0	9	2	.244	.277	.400
A. Cunningham	R	26	5	1	0	1	0	2	0	5	1	.192	.250	.346	48	9	1	0	0	0	14	0	22	1	.188	.371	.208
Jack Cust	L	4	1	0	0	0	0	0	0	3	0	.250	.250	.250	69	15	3	1	1	8	10	1	18	1	.217	.317	.333
Johnny Damon	L	5	1	0	0	0	2	1	0	1	0	.200	.333	.200	3	1	0	0	0	0	0	0	1	0	.333	.333	.333
Chase d'Arnaud	R	3	1	0	0	0	0	0	0	1	0	.333	.333	.333	3	0	0	0	0	0	0	0	1	0	.000	.000	.000
James Darnell	R	3	0	0	0	0	0	1	0	2	0	.000	.250	.000	3	0	0	0	0	0	1	0	2	0	.000	.250	.000
Blake Davis	L	3	0	0	0	0	0	0	0	1	0	.000	.000	.000	11	4	0	0	1	2	1	0	5	0	.364	.417	.636
Chris Davis	L	3	0	0	0	0	0	2	0	0	0	.000	.000	.000	44	9	2	1	0	2	4	0	12	0	.205	.271	.295
Rajai Davis	R	4	1	0	0	0	0	0	0	1	0	.250	.250	.250	1	1	0	0	0	0	0	0	0	0	1.000	1.000	1.000
Wade Davis	R	1	1	0	0	0	0	0	0	0	0	1.000	1.000	1.000	25	4	1	0	0	2	4	1	5	0	.160	.267	.200
Alejandro De Aza	L	3	1	1	0	0	0	1	1	0	0	.333	.500	.667	7	1	0	0	0	0	0	0	2	0	.143	.143	.143
Ivan De Jesus	R	7	1	0	0	0	0	2	0	4	0	.143	.143	.143	11	2	0	0	0	0	4	0	4	0	.182	.250	.182
David DeJesus	L	5	2	0	0	0	0	2	0	1	0	.400	.400	.400	2	0	0	0	0	0	0	0	1	0	.000	.000	.000
Ryan Dempster	R	1	0	0	0	0	0	0	0	1	0	.000	.000	.000	54	16	3	0	2	9	4	0	11	1	.296	.333	.463
Chris Denorfia	R	22	8	1	0	0	2	4	1	4	0	.364	.400	.409	123	32	4	0	2	19	13	0	22	0	.260	.338	.341
Mark DeRosa	R	19	5	0	0	0	4	3	0	4	0	.263	.364	.263	22	5	2	0	0	2	1	0	5	0	.227	.292	.318
Daniel Descalso	L	21	5	2	0	0	2	1	0	5	0	.238	.304	.333	14	2	1	1	0	3	0	0	4	0	.143	.133	.357
Ian Desmond	R	4	1	0	1	0	0	0	0	1	0	.250	.250	.750	98	23	4	1	3	16	6	0	19	5	.235	.292	.388
Blake DeWitt	L	64	14	2	1	1	10	4	0	12	4	.219	.275	.328	199	52	8	2	1	22	8	0	43	6	.261	.298	.337
Matt Diaz	R	49	12	1	0	0	8	4	0	13	3	.245	.296	.265													

Pinch Hitting

Batter	B	2011 Pinch Hitting													Career Pinch Hitting												
		AB	H	2B	3B	HR	RBI	TBB	IBB	SO	GDP	Avg	OBP	Slg	AB	H	2B	3B	HR	RBI	TBB	IBB	SO	GDP	Avg	OBP	Slg
Chris Dickerson	L	4	1	1	0	0	0	0	0	2	0	.250	.250	.500	40	8	2	1	0	2	10	1	17	1	.200	.360	.300
Brian Dinkelman	L	2	0	0	0	0	0	0	0	2	0	.000	.000	.000	2	0	0	0	0	0	0	0	2	0	.000	.000	.000
Andy Dirks	L	10	3	0	0	1	4	0	0	1	0	.300	.300	.600	10	3	0	0	1	4	0	0	1	0	.300	.300	.600
Greg Dobbs	L	27	10	1	0	1	8	2	0	2	2	.370	.400	.519	286	74	18	2	9	60	25	3	62	6	.259	.316	.430
Matt Dominguez	R	0	0	0	0	0	0	0	0	0	0	-	1.000	-	0	0	0	0	0	0	0	0	0	0	-	1.000	-
Jason Donald	R	3	1	1	0	0	0	0	0	1	0	.333	.333	.667	4	1	1	0	0	0	0	0	0	0	-	1.000	-
Ryan Doumit	B	18	5	0	0	0	0	2	0	8	0	.278	.350	.278	89	25	4	0	3	17	7	1	25	5	.281	.347	.427
Matt Downs	R	43	15	5	0	3	15	7	0	12	0	.349	.462	.674	57	17	5	0	3	17	8	0	16	0	.298	.397	.544
J.D. Drew	L	14	1	0	0	0	0	2	0	2	0	.071	.188	.071	110	25	4	1	4	16	21	3	31	2	.227	.348	.391
Stephen Drew	L	2	2	0	0	0	1	1	0	0	0	1.000	1.000	1.000	21	9	2	0	1	2	4	0	3	0	.429	.520	.667
Lucas Duda	L	17	6	3	0	1	4	2	0	5	0	.353	.421	.706	21	7	4	0	1	7	2	0	5	0	.333	.391	.667
Shelley Duncan	R	8	4	2	0	0	7	2	1	2	1	.500	.600	.750	41	10	2	0	1	12	3	1	10	1	.244	.295	.366
Adam Dunn	L	4	1	0	0	1	2	1	0	2	0	.250	.400	1.000	36	9	1	0	4	12	7	0	14	0	.250	.364	.611
Jarrod Dyson	L	2	0	0	0	0	0	0	0	1	0	.000	.000	.000	2	0	0	0	0	0	0	0	1	0	.000	.333	.000
A.J. Ellis	R	2	1	0	0	0	0	0	0	0	0	.500	.500	.500	4	1	0	0	0	0	0	0	1	0	.250	.250	.250
Mark Ellis	R	7	1	0	0	0	0	0	0	2	0	.143	.143	.143	16	1	0	0	0	1	2	0	5	0	.063	.158	.063
Jacoby Ellsbury	L	3	1	0	0	0	0	0	0	1	0	.333	.333	.333	6	2	0	0	0	0	1	0	2	0	.333	.429	.333
Brad Emaus	R	3	1	0	0	0	0	0	0	2	0	.333	.333	.333	3	1	0	0	0	0	0	0	2	0	.333	.333	.333
E. Encarnacion	R	10	1	0	0	0	1	1	0	3	0	.100	.182	.100	29	7	2	0	1	6	4	0	11	1	.241	.353	.414
Barry Enright	R	1	0	0	0	0	0	0	0	1	0	.000	.000	.000	2	0	0	0	0	0	0	0	2	0	.000	.000	.000
Eduardo Escobar	B	3	0	0	0	0	0	0	0	0	0	.000	.000	.000	3	0	0	0	0	0	0	0	0	0	.000	.000	.000
Yunel Escobar	R	1	1	0	0	0	0	1	0	0	0	1.000	1.000	1.000	15	5	0	0	0	1	7	0	1	0	.333	.545	.333
Danny Espinosa	B	0	0	0	0	0	0	1	0	0	0	-	1.000	-	1	0	0	0	0	0	1	0	0	0	.000	.500	.000
Andre Ethier	L	6	2	0	0	0	2	2	2	2	0	.333	.500	.333	54	15	2	0	2	15	10	2	16	3	.278	.391	.426
Nick Evans	R	8	2	1	0	1	3	5	0	0	0	.250	.500	.750	53	12	4	1	1	7	6	0	20	2	.226	.300	.396
Adam Everett	R	3	0	0	0	0	0	0	0	1	0	.000	.000	.000	16	2	1	0	0	2	2	0	6	0	.125	.300	.188
Eric Farris	R	1	0	0	0	0	0	0	0	0	0	.000	.000	.000	1	0	0	0	0	0	0	0	0	0	.000	.000	.000
Tim Federowicz	R	1	0	0	0	0	0	0	0	0	0	.000	.000	.000	1	0	0	0	0	0	0	0	0	0	.000	.000	.000
Tommy Field	R	1	0	0	0	0	0	0	0	0	0	.000	.000	.000	1	0	0	0	0	0	0	0	0	0	.000	.000	.000
Jesus Flores	R	6	2	0	0	0	0	2	1	3	0	.333	.500	.333	41	10	1	0	1	8	9	1	12	0	.244	.373	.341
Pedro Florimon	B	1	0	0	0	0	0	0	0	1	0	.000	.000	.000	1	0	0	0	0	0	0	0	1	0	.000	.000	.000
Tyler Flowers	R	3	0	0	0	0	0	0	0	1	0	.000	.000	.000	7	0	0	0	0	0	0	0	3	0	.000	.000	.000
Mike Fontenot	L	26	4	2	0	0	2	2	1	5	0	.154	.214	.231	137	30	12	0	2	20	15	1	36	1	.219	.297	.350
Darren Ford	R	2	1	0	0	0	0	0	0	1	0	.500	.500	.500	2	1	0	0	0	0	0	0	1	0	.500	.500	.500
Logan Forsythe	R	16	5	2	0	0	1	2	0	7	0	.313	.400	.438	16	5	2	0	0	1	2	0	7	0	.313	.400	.438
Dexter Fowler	B	4	1	0	0	0	1	0	0	2	0	.250	.250	.250	29	7	2	0	0	2	6	0	8	0	.241	.371	.310
Jake Fox	R	8	3	1	0	0	2	0	0	1	1	.375	.375	.500	50	12	3	0	0	7	4	0	16	3	.240	.322	.300
Ben Francisco	R	26	7	3	0	0	4	5	0	6	1	.269	.375	.385	95	24	9	0	1	16	14	0	24	3	.253	.351	.379
Juan Francisco	L	11	1	0	0	0	0	0	0	4	0	.091	.091	.091	41	10	2	0	2	7	6	0	12	1	.244	.340	.439
Jeff Francoeur	R	0	0	0	0	0	0	1	0	0	0	-	1.000	-	15	2	0	0	0	1	3	0	2	0	.133	.263	.133
Todd Frazier	R	11	2	0	0	1	1	1	0	4	0	.182	.250	.455	11	2	0	0	1	1	1	0	4	0	.182	.250	.455
Freddie Freeman	L	1	0	0	0	0	0	0	0	0	0	.000	.000	.000	12	2	0	0	1	1	0	0	4	0	.167	.167	.417
David Freese	R	9	3	0	0	0	0	0	0	2	0	.333	.333	.333	20	6	1	0	0	1	2	0	4	0	.300	.364	.350
Eric Fryer	R	2	0	0	0	0	0	0	0	2	0	.000	.000	.000	2	0	0	0	0	0	0	0	2	0	.000	.000	.000
K. Fukudome	L	8	1	0	0	0	1	3	0	1	0	.125	.364	.125	50	15	1	0	2	6	8	0	8	0	.300	.397	.440
Sam Fuld	L	15	6	1	0	0	1	6	0	3	0	.400	.571	.467	36	9	1	0	0	1	8	0	6	1	.250	.386	.278
Rafael Furcal	B	2	0	0	0	0	0	0	0	0	0	.000	.000	.000	33	8	0	0	1	2	3	1	6	1	.242	.306	.333
Mat Gamel	L	1	0	0	0	0	0	0	0	0	0	.000	.000	.000	30	5	2	0	0	2	8	1	17	1	.167	.342	.233
Brett Gardner	L	1	0	0	0	0	0	1	0	1	0	.000	.500	.000	11	2	1	0	0	0	1	0	2	0	.182	.250	.273
Cole Garner	R	1	0	0	0	0	0	1	0	0	0	.000	.500	.000	1	0	0	0	0	0	1	0	0	0	.000	.500	.000
Craig Gentry	R	4	2	0	0	0	3	0	0	0	0	.500	.400	.500	7	2	0	0	0	3	0	0	1	0	.286	.250	.286
Esteban German	R	2	1	0	0	1	2	1	0	0	0	.500	.667	2.000	60	13	4	1	1	5	10	0	23	2	.217	.338	.367
Chris Getz	L	2	0	0	0	0	0	0	0	0	0	.000	.000	.000	10	1	0	0	0	1	0	0	0	0	.100	.100	.100
Jason Giambi	L	30	4	0	0	1	5	4	0	17	0	.133	.229	.233	127	31	3	0	7	29	21	4	49	1	.244	.355	.433
Jay Gibbons	L	8	2	0	0	0	0	1	0	2	0	.250	.333	.250	64	10	1	0	1	6	8	0	16	2	.156	.219	.219
Conor Gillaspie	L	10	2	0	0	0	0	2	0	0	0	.200	.333	.200	14	3	0	0	0	0	3	0	0	0	.214	.353	.214
Cole Gillespie	R	1	0	0	0	0	0	0	0	0	0	.000	.000	.000	12	3	2	0	0	0	2	0	2	0	.250	.250	.417
Hector Gimenez	B	3	0	0	0	0	0	0	0	2	0	.000	.000	.000	5	0	0	0	0	0	0	0	3	0	.000	.000	.000
Ross Gload	L	74	18	5	0	0	5	2	0	18	0	.243	.263	.311	300	81	11	1	8	43	20	4	50	4	.270	.317	.393
Paul Goldschmidt	R	6	1	0	0	1	2	0	0	2	2	.167	.167	.667	6	1	0	0	1	2	0	0	2	2	.167	.167	.667
Greg Golson	R	1	0	0	0	0	0	0	0	0	0	.000	.000	.000	2	0	0	0	0	0	0	0	1	0	.000	.000	.000
Jonny Gomes	R	28	0	0	0	0	2	5	0	17	0	.000	.147	.000	101	14	5	0	2	14	11	0	44	1	.139	.241	.248
Carlos Gomez	R	5	2	2	0	0	0	0	0	0	0	.400	.400	.800	28	5	2	0	0	2	2	0	7	0	.179	.233	.250
Hector Gomez	R	1	0	0	0	0	0	0	0	0	0	.000	.000	.000	1	0	0	0	0	0	0	0	0	0	.000	.000	.000
Alberto Gonzalez	R	15	1	1	0	0	1	2	0	3	0	.067	.176	.133	72	15	4	0	0	8	7	0	12	2	.208	.278	.264
Alex Gonzalez	R	2	0	0	0	0	0	0	0	0	0	.000	.000	.000	17	2	0	0	0	1	0	0	9	0	.118	.118	.118
Carlos Gonzalez	L	2	0	0	0	0	0	0	0	0	1	.000	.000	.000	18	2	0	0	0	0	2	0	10	1	.111	.200	.111
Alex Gordon	L	1	0	0	0	0	0	0	0	0	0	.000	.000	.000	5	1	0	0	1	1	2	0	0	0	.200	.429	.800
Dee Gordon	L	2	0	0	0	0	0	0	0	0	0	.000	.000	.000	1	0	0	0	0	0	0	0	0	0	.000	.000	.000
Curtis Granderson	L	4	1	0	0	0	0	0	0	0	0	.250	.250	.250	29	6	0	0	0	1	2	0	12	0	.207	.250	.207

Pinch Hitting

Batter	B	AB	H	2B	3B	HR	RBI	TBB	IBB	SO	GDP	Avg	OBP	Slg	AB	H	2B	3B	HR	RBI	TBB	IBB	SO	GDP	Avg	OBP	Slg
		2011 Pinch Hitting													Career Pinch Hitting												
Taylor Green	L	12	5	1	0	0	0	0	0	3	0	.417	.417	.500	12	5	1	0	0	0	0	0	3	0	.417	.417	.500
Tyler Greene	R	12	2	0	0	0	3	0	0	4	0	.167	.231	.167	22	5	0	0	1	4	3	0	8	0	.227	.393	.364
Zack Greinke	R	0	0	0	0	0	0	0	0	0	0	-	-	-	0	0	0	0	0	0	0	0	0	0	-	-	-
Vladimir Guerrero	R	8	1	0	0	0	1	0	0	1	0	.125	.125	.125	29	8	0	1	0	4	2	2	1	2	.276	.313	.345
Carlos Guillen	B	2	1	0	0	0	0	0	0	1	0	.500	.500	.500	30	7	1	0	0	2	7	1	11	1	.233	.368	.267
Franklin Gutierrez	R	2	0	0	0	0	0	0	0	2	0	.000	.000	.000	34	6	0	0	0	2	2	0	7	2	.176	.222	.176
Brandon Guyer	R	1	0	0	0	0	0	0	0	0	0	.000	.000	.000	1	0	0	0	0	0	0	0	0	0	.000	.000	.000
Jesus Guzman	R	12	4	1	0	1	3	2	0	2	1	.333	.429	.667	21	7	1	0	1	3	2	0	4	3	.333	.391	.524
Tony Gwynn	L	24	8	1	1	0	2	2	1	5	0	.333	.407	.458	111	32	6	2	0	7	13	1	22	2	.288	.368	.378
Travis Hafner	L	7	2	0	0	0	2	2	0	3	0	.286	.500	.286	48	12	2	0	2	13	15	2	11	3	.250	.448	.417
Jerry Hairston	R	11	4	1	0	0	0	1	1	1	0	.364	.417	.455	69	12	3	1	0	2	4	1	12	2	.174	.216	.246
Scott Hairston	R	41	8	1	0	3	6	5	1	17	0	.195	.298	.439	141	25	4	0	6	15	18	1	55	2	.177	.275	.333
Bill Hall	R	8	1	0	0	1	1	0	0	2	0	.125	.125	.500	119	23	5	0	6	19	8	0	46	0	.193	.242	.387
Greg Halman	R	1	0	0	0	0	0	0	0	1	0	.000	.000	.000	1	0	0	0	0	0	0	0	1	0	.000	.000	.000
Cole Hamels	L	1	0	0	0	0	0	0	0	0	0	.000	.000	.000	6	1	0	0	0	0	1	0	1	0	.167	.286	.167
Mark Hamilton	L	28	7	2	0	0	2	1	0	10	0	.250	.276	.321	34	7	2	0	0	2	1	0	12	0	.206	.229	.265
Jason Hammel	R	0	0	0	0	0	0	0	0	0	0	-	-	-	0	0	0	0	0	0	0	0	0	0	-	-	-
Robby Hammock	R	1	0	0	0	0	0	0	0	0	0	.000	.000	.000	26	9	4	0	0	0	0	0	3	1	.346	.370	.500
Ryan Hanigan	R	2	0	0	0	0	0	1	0	0	0	.000	.333	.000	15	5	1	0	1	5	4	0	1	0	.333	.474	.600
Jack Hannahan	L	2	0	0	0	0	0	0	0	1	0	.000	.000	.000	12	2	0	0	0	1	1	0	6	0	.167	.214	.167
J.A. Happ	L	1	0	0	0	0	0	0	0	1	0	.000	.000	.000	1	0	0	0	0	0	0	0	1	0	.000	.000	.000
Willie Harris	L	60	11	2	0	0	5	7	0	15	1	.183	.286	.217	206	44	6	0	4	21	27	0	47	3	.214	.314	.301
Josh Harrison	R	8	0	0	0	0	0	0	0	2	0	.000	.000	.000	8	0	0	0	0	0	0	0	2	0	.000	.000	.000
Corey Hart	R	7	3	2	0	0	2	0	0	2	0	.429	.429	.714	66	23	5	1	3	14	6	1	14	4	.348	.405	.591
Brad Hawpe	L	6	0	0	0	0	0	5	1	4	0	.000	.455	.000	75	15	4	0	3	13	16	1	33	1	.200	.337	.373
Brett Hayes	R	9	1	0	0	0	0	1	0	4	0	.111	.200	.111	19	3	1	0	1	2	1	0	7	1	.158	.238	.368
Jerad Head	R	1	1	0	0	0	0	0	0	0	0	1.000	1.000	1.000	1	1	0	0	0	0	0	0	0	0	1.000	1.000	1.000
Chase Headley	B	7	1	0	0	0	1	0	0	2	0	.143	.143	.143	27	7	1	0	2	3	4	0	10	0	.259	.375	.519
Chris Heisey	R	34	11	1	0	2	11	1	0	11	0	.324	.333	.529	57	19	1	1	6	18	5	0	17	1	.333	.385	.702
Wes Helms	R	33	7	3	0	0	4	5	1	9	1	.212	.316	.303	343	89	23	4	7	56	33	1	102	13	.259	.336	.411
Todd Helton	L	3	0	0	0	0	0	2	0	0	0	.000	.400	.000	47	7	1	0	1	7	8	2	15	1	.149	.273	.234
Jeremy Hermida	L	11	1	0	0	0	1	0	0	6	0	.091	.167	.091	62	14	1	0	2	10	7	0	22	1	.226	.314	.339
Diory Hernandez	R	15	5	1	0	1	4	0	0	3	0	.333	.333	.533	28	6	0	0	2	5	0	0	9	0	.214	.214	.429
Livan Hernandez	R	0	0	0	0	0	0	0	0	0	0	-	-	-	14	1	0	0	0	1	0	0	6	1	.071	.071	.071
R. Hernandez	R	9	4	1	0	0	2	1	0	0	0	.444	.500	.556	68	12	1	0	2	10	4	0	16	3	.176	.222	.279
Jonathan Herrera	R	18	5	1	0	0	0	4	0	2	0	.278	.409	.333	30	6	1	0	0	2	7	0	3	0	.200	.342	.233
Jason Heyward	L	6	0	0	0	0	0	4	1	0	0	.000	.143	.000	9	2	0	0	0	2	1	0	4	1	.222	.364	.222
Brandon Hicks	R	9	1	0	0	0	1	0	0	5	0	.111	.111	.111	13	1	0	0	0	1	1	0	6	0	.077	.143	.077
Aaron Hill	R	1	0	0	0	0	0	1	0	0	0	.000	.500	.000	7	3	1	0	0	1	1	0	0	1	.429	.500	.571
Koyie Hill	B	1	0	0	0	0	0	1	0	0	0	.000	.500	.000	24	4	2	0	0	0	4	1	7	1	.167	.286	.250
Eric Hinske	L	56	9	0	0	2	6	7	0	23	0	.161	.254	.268	205	49	9	1	7	32	31	1	58	3	.239	.344	.395
Jaime Hoffmann	R	1	0	0	0	0	0	0	0	0	0	.000	.000	.000	10	1	0	0	0	0	0	0	0	2	.100	.100	.100
Matt Holliday	R	4	0	0	0	0	0	1	1	2	0	.000	.200	.000	19	4	1	0	0	3	1	0	6	0	.211	.318	.263
Eric Hosmer	L	1	0	0	0	0	0	0	0	0	0	.000	.000	.000	1	0	0	0	0	0	0	0	0	0	.000	.000	.000
Ryan Howard	L	3	2	1	0	1	1	1	0	1	0	.667	.750	2.000	32	14	4	0	6	13	4	0	13	1	.438	.500	1.125
Chin-lung Hu	R	10	0	0	0	0	1	0	0	5	0	.000	.000	.000	14	2	0	0	1	2	0	0	6	0	.143	.133	.357
Orlando Hudson	B	5	0	0	0	0	1	1	0	2	0	.000	.143	.000	29	8	1	0	2	6	5	0	10	1	.276	.371	.517
Aubrey Huff	L	11	2	0	0	0	2	1	0	2	1	.182	.250	.182	52	10	1	1	1	13	5	2	12	1	.192	.271	.308
Luke Hughes	R	9	0	0	0	0	0	1	0	7	0	.000	.100	.000	9	0	0	0	0	0	1	0	7	0	.000	.100	.000
Nick Hundley	R	7	0	0	0	0	1	0	0	3	0	.000	.111	.000	19	4	1	0	1	8	2	0	4	0	.211	.304	.421
Cedric Hunter	L	3	1	0	0	0	0	1	0	0	0	.333	.500	.333	3	1	0	0	0	0	1	0	0	0	.333	.500	.333
Chris Iannetta	R	5	1	1	0	0	0	1	0	0	0	.200	.333	.400	25	8	1	0	2	6	3	0	6	0	.320	.433	.600
Raul Ibanez	L	11	3	1	0	1	3	0	0	5	1	.273	.273	.636	108	17	4	0	2	14	12	1	23	3	.157	.240	.250
Omar Infante	R	2	0	0	0	0	0	0	0	0	0	.000	.000	.000	60	14	2	2	0	12	4	0	17	2	.233	.273	.333
Brandon Inge	R	2	1	1	0	0	1	0	0	0	0	.500	.500	1.000	10	4	3	0	0	2	1	0	1	0	.400	.538	.700
Joe Inglett	L	17	3	0	0	0	1	0	0	4	0	.176	.176	.176	109	28	3	4	1	9	8	0	25	0	.257	.319	.385
Maicer Izturis	B	15	1	0	0	0	2	1	0	3	0	.067	.118	.067	41	8	1	0	0	4	9	2	8	1	.195	.333	.220
Austin Jackson	R	2	1	0	0	0	0	0	0	1	0	.500	.500	.500	6	3	0	0	0	1	1	0	2	0	.500	.625	.500
Conor Jackson	R	16	5	0	0	0	4	1	0	1	1	.313	.368	.313	65	12	0	0	3	16	13	0	7	1	.185	.321	.323
Paul Janish	R	2	0	0	0	0	0	0	0	0	0	.000	.000	.000	12	2	0	0	0	2	0	0	4	0	.167	.333	.167
Jason Jaramillo	B	12	4	2	0	0	2	1	0	3	1	.333	.385	.500	17	4	2	0	0	2	1	0	4	2	.235	.278	.353
John Jaso	L	15	2	0	0	0	0	3	0	3	0	.133	.278	.133	30	3	0	0	0	1	8	0	7	2	.100	.289	.100
Jon Jay	L	23	5	0	0	2	2	4	1	6	0	.217	.379	.478	45	12	1	0	2	5	6	1	12	2	.267	.377	.422
D. Jennings	R	2	1	0	0	0	1	0	0	1	0	.500	.500	.500	3	2	1	0	0	2	1	0	1	0	.667	.750	1.000
Chris Johnson	R	7	3	0	0	1	2	0	0	2	0	.429	.429	.857	16	4	0	0	1	2	0	0	5	0	.250	.250	.438
Dan Johnson	L	7	1	0	0	1	1	0	0	2	1	.143	.143	.571	29	4	0	0	2	5	3	0	7	1	.138	.200	.345
Elliot Johnson	B	13	3	0	0	0	0	2	0	5	0	.231	.333	.231	14	3	0	0	0	0	2	0	5	0	.214	.313	.214
Kelly Johnson	L	7	0	0	0	0	0	1	0	3	0	.000	.125	.000	56	14	2	1	1	8	15	1	13	0	.250	.408	.375
Reed Johnson	R	28	6	1	0	1	3	0	0	10	0	.214	.303	.357	132	32	8	0	3	17	6	1	31	3	.242	.301	.371
Rob Johnson	R	5	1	1	0	0	2	0	0	3	0	.200	.333	.400	5	1	1	0	0	2	0	0	3	0	.200	.333	.400

Pinch Hitting

Batter	B	2011 Pinch Hitting AB	H	2B	3B	HR	RBI	TBB	IBB	SO	GDP	Avg	OBP	Slg	Career Pinch Hitting AB	H	2B	3B	HR	RBI	TBB	IBB	SO	GDP	Avg	OBP	Slg
Andruw Jones	R	10	2	0	0	0	1	1	0	4	0	.200	.273	.200	66	13	3	0	3	14	14	0	20	1	.197	.338	.379
Chipper Jones	B	10	0	0	0	0	0	1	1	1	1	.000	.091	.000	67	15	4	0	2	18	13	5	17	1	.224	.346	.373
Garrett Jones	L	26	7	2	0	0	5	4	0	8	1	.269	.344	.346	35	8	2	0	0	5	4	0	11	2	.229	.293	.286
Matt Joyce	L	14	3	1	0	0	3	2	1	5	0	.214	.313	.286	33	7	2	1	1	11	8	1	11	0	.212	.366	.424
Austin Kearns	R	2	0	0	0	0	0	1	0	1	0	.000	.333	.000	59	14	2	1	2	13	11	0	22	1	.237	.375	.407
Don Kelly	L	9	4	1	0	1	3	0	0	0	0	.444	.444	.889	40	9	1	0	1	3	2	0	7	1	.225	.295	.325
Matt Kemp	R	1	1	0	0	1	1	0	0	0	0	1.000	1.000	4.000	33	7	0	0	2	4	2	0	15	0	.212	.257	.394
Howie Kendrick	R	3	0	0	0	0	0	0	0	1	0	.000	.000	.000	17	4	0	0	0	1	0	0	3	1	.235	.235	.235
Adam Kennedy	L	11	4	1	0	0	2	0	0	3	0	.364	.364	.455	112	25	6	0	1	13	7	1	25	4	.223	.268	.304
Ian Kennedy	R	0	0	0	0	0	0	0	0	0	0	-	-	-	0	0	0	0	0	0	0	0	0	0	-	-	-
Jeff Keppinger	R	7	2	0	0	0	1	0	0	1	0	.286	.286	.286	42	12	1	0	0	4	2	0	4	1	.286	.311	.310
Ian Kinsler	R	1	0	0	0	0	0	0	0	0	0	.000	.000	.000	3	0	0	0	0	0	2	1	1	0	.000	.400	.000
Jason Kipnis	L	1	0	0	0	0	0	0	0	0	0	.000	.000	.000	1	0	0	0	0	0	0	0	0	0	.000	.000	.000
Paul Konerko	R	0	0	0	0	0	0	2	1	0	0	-	1.000	-	53	14	0	0	2	12	9	4	7	2	.264	.365	.377
Casey Kotchman	L	1	0	0	0	0	0	0	0	0	0	.000	.000	.000	48	10	6	0	0	9	12	0	17	2	.208	.367	.333
Mark Kotsay	L	41	12	1	0	0	8	4	0	8	2	.293	.356	.317	133	41	6	0	3	21	10	2	26	3	.308	.357	.421
George Kottaras	L	11	2	0	0	0	2	1	0	1	1	.182	.250	.182	15	2	0	0	0	2	2	0	4	1	.133	.235	.133
Kevin Kouzmanoff	R	4	2	0	0	0	0	0	0	1	0	.500	.500	.500	16	6	1	0	1	7	2	0	3	0	.375	.400	.625
Pete Kozma	R	3	1	1	0	0	1	1	0	0	0	.333	.500	.667	3	1	1	0	0	1	1	0	0	0	.333	.500	.667
Erik Kratz	R	1	1	0	0	0	0	0	0	0	0	1.000	1.000	1.000	1	1	0	0	0	0	0	0	0	0	1.000	1.000	1.000
Jason Kubel	L	5	1	0	0	0	1	0	0	1	0	.200	.200	.200	64	14	3	0	4	9	11	1	21	2	.219	.333	.453
Bryan LaHair	L	3	2	1	0	1	2	0	0	1	0	.667	.667	2.000	7	4	1	0	1	2	0	0	2	1	.571	.571	1.143
Brandon Laird	R	0	0	0	0	0	0	1	0	0	0	-	1.000	-	0	0	0	0	0	0	1	0	0	0	-	1.000	-
Gerald Laird	R	5	1	1	0	0	1	2	0	2	0	.200	.429	.400	20	3	1	0	0	3	6	0	8	0	.150	.346	.200
Ryan Langerhans	L	1	0	0	0	0	0	0	0	1	0	.000	.000	.000	93	22	4	1	4	8	13	0	35	1	.237	.330	.430
Matt LaPorta	R	6	0	0	0	0	0	0	0	3	0	.000	.000	.000	9	1	0	0	0	0	0	0	4	0	.111	.111	.111
Ryan Lavarnway	R	2	0	0	0	0	0	0	0	1	0	.000	.000	.000	2	0	0	0	0	0	0	0	1	0	.000	.000	.000
Mike Leake	R	1	0	0	0	0	0	0	0	1	0	.000	.000	.000	4	0	0	0	0	0	1	0	3	0	.000	.200	.000
Carlos Lee	R	1	0	0	0	0	0	0	0	0	0	.000	.000	.000	19	5	2	0	0	2	1	0	3	1	.263	.300	.368
Cliff Lee	L	2	0	0	0	0	0	0	0	2	0	.000	.000	.000	2	0	0	0	0	0	0	0	2	0	.000	.000	.000
DJ LeMahieu	R	7	1	0	0	0	0	0	0	1	1	.143	.143	.143	7	1	0	0	0	0	0	0	1	1	.143	.143	.143
Fred Lewis	L	30	10	0	0	1	5	2	0	9	0	.333	.394	.433	97	27	7	1	1	16	12	1	34	0	.278	.369	.402
Alex Liddi	R	1	0	0	0	0	0	0	0	1	0	.000	.000	.000	1	0	0	0	0	0	0	0	1	0	.000	.000	.000
Brent Lillibridge	R	7	2	1	0	0	1	1	0	3	0	.286	.444	.429	21	7	4	1	1	7	1	0	6	0	.333	.391	.762
Brad Lincoln	R	1	0	0	0	0	0	0	0	0	0	.000	.000	.000	1	0	0	0	0	0	0	0	0	0	.000	.000	.000
Jose Lobaton	B	2	0	0	0	0	0	1	0	0	0	.000	.333	.000	2	0	0	0	0	0	1	0	0	0	.000	.333	.000
Adam Loewen	L	0	0	0	0	0	0	0	0	0	0	-	1.000	-	0	0	0	0	0	0	0	0	0	0	-	1.000	-
Kyle Lohse	R	2	0	0	0	0	0	0	0	0	0	.000	.000	.000	3	0	0	0	0	0	0	0	0	0	.000	.000	.000
S. Lombardozzi	B	6	1	0	0	0	0	1	0	1	0	.167	.286	.167	6	1	0	0	0	0	1	0	1	0	.167	.286	.167
James Loney	L	12	2	0	0	1	3	1	0	4	0	.167	.231	.417	41	6	1	1	1	6	3	0	9	1	.146	.205	.293
Evan Longoria	R	2	2	0	0	0	1	0	0	0	0	1.000	1.000	1.000	5	3	0	0	0	2	1	1	0	0	.600	.667	.600
Felipe Lopez	B	10	3	1	0	0	0	0	0	3	0	.300	.300	.400	64	12	2	0	0	5	5	1	21	1	.188	.257	.219
Jose Lopez	R	24	3	0	0	0	0	0	0	6	0	.125	.125	.125	31	3	0	0	0	1	0	0	7	0	.097	.097	.097
Jed Lowrie	B	7	1	0	0	0	1	0	0	2	0	.143	.143	.143	17	4	1	0	0	1	2	0	5	0	.235	.316	.294
Jonathan Lucroy	R	13	3	0	0	1	3	0	0	2	0	.231	.231	.462	14	4	0	0	1	3	0	0	2	0	.286	.286	.500
Donny Lucy	R	3	1	0	0	0	0	0	0	1	0	.333	.333	.333	8	3	1	0	0	0	0	0	2	0	.375	.375	.500
Ryan Ludwick	R	4	1	0	0	0	1	1	1	0	0	.250	.400	.250	80	21	5	0	4	12	10	2	20	1	.263	.352	.475
Julio Lugo	R	7	1	0	0	0	1	1	0	2	0	.143	.250	.143	49	10	1	0	0	3	7	0	11	1	.204	.322	.224
Mitch Maier	L	12	3	0	0	0	0	0	0	5	0	.250	.250	.250	22	5	1	0	0	0	1	0	8	0	.227	.261	.273
Martin Maldonado	R	1	0	0	0	0	0	0	0	1	0	.000	.000	.000	1	0	0	0	0	0	0	0	1	0	.000	.000	.000
Jason Marquis	L	2	0	0	0	0	0	0	0	1	0	.000	.000	.000	31	6	1	1	0	0	1	0	9	0	.194	.219	.290
Chris Marrero	R	1	0	0	0	0	0	0	0	1	0	.000	.000	.000	1	0	0	0	0	0	0	0	1	0	.000	.000	.000
Lou Marson	R	1	0	0	0	0	0	0	0	0	0	.000	.000	.000	1	0	0	0	0	0	0	0	0	0	.000	.000	.000
Leonys Martin	L	3	1	0	0	0	0	0	0	1	0	.333	.333	.333	3	1	0	0	0	0	0	0	1	0	.333	.333	.333
Russell Martin	R	3	1	0	0	0	0	0	0	0	0	.333	.333	.333	25	4	0	0	1	2	2	0	2	1	.160	.250	.280
F. Martinez	L	6	1	0	0	1	2	0	0	2	0	.167	.167	.667	11	2	0	0	1	2	0	0	2	0	.182	.182	.455
J.D. Martinez	R	1	1	1	0	0	0	0	0	0	0	1.000	1.000	2.000	1	1	1	0	0	1	0	0	0	0	1.000	1.000	2.000
Luis Martinez	R	4	0	0	0	0	0	0	0	2	0	.000	.000	.000	4	0	0	0	0	0	0	0	2	0	.000	.000	.000
Michael Martinez	B	16	3	0	0	0	2	3	0	3	0	.188	.316	.188	16	3	0	0	0	2	3	0	3	0	.188	.316	.188
Osvaldo Martinez	R	13	2	0	0	0	1	0	0	5	1	.154	.154	.154	16	2	0	0	0	1	1	0	6	1	.125	.176	.125
Victor Martinez	B	1	0	0	0	0	0	0	0	0	0	.000	.000	.000	33	11	2	0	1	9	10	1	1	1	.333	.477	.485
Joe Mather	R	13	2	1	0	0	0	0	0	5	0	.154	.154	.231	45	13	5	0	2	4	1	0	15	0	.289	.304	.533
Jeff Mathis	R	2	0	0	0	0	0	0	0	0	1	.000	.000	.000	13	1	0	0	0	1	0	0	4	1	.077	.077	.077
Hideki Matsui	L	4	0	0	0	0	1	1	0	0	0	.000	.167	.000	40	12	2	0	1	8	8	3	10	2	.300	.400	.425
Joe Mauer	L	4	1	1	0	0	0	0	0	0	0	.250	.250	.500	36	7	1	0	1	7	5	1	8	1	.194	.286	.306
John Mayberry	R	31	7	0	0	1	4	4	1	7	1	.226	.314	.323	47	12	1	0	3	8	6	1	13	2	.255	.340	.468
Cameron Maybin	R	2	0	0	0	0	0	0	0	0	0	.000	.000	.000	14	2	0	0	0	0	0	0	7	0	.143	.200	.143
Brian McCann	L	6	1	0	0	1	1	0	0	3	0	.167	.167	.667	55	14	5	0	2	8	8	4	12	1	.255	.349	.455
Mike McCoy	R	3	0	0	0	0	0	0	0	1	0	.000	.000	.000	11	0	0	0	0	0	0	0	3	0	.000	.000	.000
A. McCutchen	R	1	0	0	0	0	0	1	0	0	0	.000	.500	.000	1	0	0	0	0	0	3	0	0	0	.000	.750	.000

Pinch Hitting

Batter	B	2011 Pinch Hitting AB	H	2B	3B	HR	RBI	TBB	IBB	SO	GDP	Avg	OBP	Slg	Career Pinch Hitting AB	H	2B	3B	HR	RBI	TBB	IBB	SO	GDP	Avg	OBP	Slg
Darnell McDonald	R	6	1	0	0	0	0	2	0	1	0	.167	.444	.167	37	11	2	1	1	5	4	0	9	2	.297	.381	.486
John McDonald	R	3	1	0	0	0	0	0	0	0	0	.333	.333	.333	41	9	0	0	0	2	2	0	8	1	.220	.256	.220
Casey McGehee	R	8	2	0	0	2	5	1	1	3	0	.250	.333	.529	34	8	1	0	3	10	4	2	9	2	.235	.333	.529
Nate McLouth	L	1	0	0	0	0	0	0	0	1	0	.000	.000	.000	97	21	4	1	1	10	5	0	24	0	.216	.267	.309
Dallas McPherson	L	2	1	0	0	0	0	0	0	1	0	.500	.500	.500	18	6	2	0	2	3	1	0	8	0	.333	.368	.778
Devin Mesoraco	R	3	1	1	0	0	0	0	0	1	0	.333	.333	.667	3	1	1	0	0	0	0	0	1	0	.333	.333	.667
Jason Michaels	R	45	8	3	0	0	2	5	1	10	0	.178	.260	.244	372	83	20	2	7	46	49	2	103	4	.223	.315	.344
Aaron Miles	B	16	7	0	0	0	2	0	0	1	0	.438	.444	.438	179	41	5	1	0	15	5	0	23	4	.229	.254	.268
Jai Miller	R	3	2	0	0	0	0	0	0	1	0	.667	.667	.667	5	2	0	0	0	0	0	0	1	0	.400	.400	.400
Juan Miranda	L	16	3	0	1	1	3	2	0	9	0	.188	.316	.500	26	6	0	1	1	5	4	0	13	1	.231	.355	.423
Russ Mitchell	R	7	1	1	0	0	0	1	0	2	0	.143	.250	.286	11	1	1	0	0	0	1	0	4	0	.091	.167	.182
Jose Molina	R	0	0	0	0	0	0	0	0	3	0	.000	.000	.000	17	4	0	0	0	2	0	0	6	0	.235	.235	.235
Yadier Molina	R	2	0	0	0	0	0	0	0	0	0	.000	.000	.000	15	3	0	0	0	1	2	2	1	1	.200	.294	.200
Lou Montanez	R	12	3	1	0	0	3	0	0	4	0	.250	.250	.333	28	4	1	0	0	3	0	0	8	1	.143	.143	.179
Jesus Montero	R	1	0	0	0	0	0	0	0	0	0	.000	.000	.000	1	0	0	0	0	0	0	0	0	0	.000	.000	.000
Miguel Montero	L	7	2	0	0	0	2	2	0	1	0	.286	.444	.286	68	15	2	0	3	14	12	1	20	2	.221	.357	.382
Jeremy Moore	L	1	0	0	0	0	0	0	0	0	0	.000	.000	.000	1	0	0	0	0	0	0	0	0	0	.000	.000	.000
Melvin Mora	R	10	2	0	0	0	2	0	0	2	0	.200	.182	.200	61	11	2	0	2	7	7	1	16	1	.180	.278	.311
Jose Morales	B	3	1	0	0	0	0	1	0	1	0	.333	.500	.333	22	7	1	0	0	4	4	1	6	0	.318	.407	.364
Brent Morel	R	1	0	0	0	0	0	0	0	0	1	.000	.000	.000	3	0	0	0	0	0	0	0	1	1	.000	.000	.000
Mitch Moreland	L	5	0	0	0	0	0	1	0	1	0	.000	.167	.000	8	0	0	0	0	0	2	1	3	1	.000	.200	.000
Nyjer Morgan	L	15	3	0	0	0	1	1	0	4	0	.200	.235	.200	37	9	2	0	0	1	3	0	9	0	.243	.310	.297
Justin Morneau	L	1	0	0	0	0	0	0	0	0	0	.000	.000	.000	22	8	1	0	3	9	4	1	5	2	.364	.462	.818
Logan Morrison	L	2	0	0	0	0	0	1	0	2	0	.000	.333	.000	2	0	0	0	0	0	1	0	2	0	.000	.333	.000
Michael Morse	R	10	1	1	0	0	0	2	0	2	0	.100	.250	.200	55	17	4	1	1	14	5	0	18	1	.309	.361	.473
Brandon Moss	L	4	0	0	0	0	0	0	0	1	1	.000	.000	.000	61	12	3	1	1	7	1	0	21	2	.197	.222	.328
Daniel Murphy	L	19	5	0	0	1	4	0	0	5	1	.263	.263	.421	60	18	1	1	3	16	6	1	12	2	.300	.358	.500
David Murphy	L	9	3	1	0	0	3	1	0	2	0	.333	.400	.444	32	6	1	0	0	4	5	0	7	0	.188	.297	.219
Donnie Murphy	R	7	0	0	0	0	0	0	0	2	0	.000	.000	.000	37	8	4	0	2	9	2	0	17	0	.216	.256	.486
Xavier Nady	R	24	5	1	0	1	5	2	0	7	1	.208	.259	.375	104	24	3	0	4	15	15	0	27	6	.231	.347	.375
Mike Napoli	R	6	1	1	0	0	0	0	0	0	0	.167	.286	.333	29	3	1	0	0	0	7	0	15	1	.103	.297	.138
Dioner Navarro	B	11	1	0	0	0	0	1	0	0	0	.091	.091	.091	36	6	1	0	0	7	1	0	8	2	.167	.211	.194
Efren Navarro	L	2	0	0	0	0	0	0	0	0	0	.000	.000	.000	2	0	0	0	0	0	0	0	0	0	.000	.000	.000
Yamaico Navarro	R	2	1	0	0	1	1	0	0	0	0	.500	.500	2.000	3	2	0	0	1	1	0	0	0	0	.667	.667	1.667
Chris Nelson	R	11	4	1	0	1	4	0	0	1	0	.364	.364	.727	19	8	1	0	1	4	0	0	2	0	.421	.421	.632
Mike Nickeas	R	1	0	0	0	0	0	0	0	1	0	.000	.000	.000	2	0	0	0	0	0	0	0	2	0	.000	.000	.000
Jonathon Niese	L	1	1	0	1	0	0	0	0	0	0	1.000	1.000	3.000	2	1	0	1	0	0	0	0	1	0	.500	.500	1.500
Wil Nieves	R	3	0	0	0	0	0	0	0	1	1	.000	.000	.000	23	0	0	0	0	0	2	0	11	1	.000	.080	.000
Tsuyoshi Nishioka	B	1	0	0	0	0	0	0	0	1	0	.000	.000	.000	1	0	0	0	0	0	0	0	1	0	.000	.000	.000
Laynce Nix	L	29	4	0	0	3	4	1	6	0	0	.138	.235	.138	134	25	5	0	2	11	17	4	40	3	.187	.276	.269
Eduardo Nunez	R	4	0	0	0	0	0	0	0	1	0	.000	.000	.000	4	0	0	0	0	0	0	0	1	0	.000	.000	.000
Trent Oeltjen	L	24	4	1	0	0	1	4	0	7	1	.167	.286	.208	31	5	1	0	0	1	5	0	8	2	.161	.278	.194
Miguel Olivo	R	5	4	0	0	1	2	0	0	0	0	.800	.800	1.400	39	10	1	0	3	9	0	0	10	0	.256	.268	.513
Magglio Ordonez	R	2	0	0	0	0	0	1	0	1	0	.000	.333	.000	28	5	2	0	2	4	6	2	8	1	.179	.306	.464
Pete Orr	L	14	5	1	0	0	2	1	0	2	0	.357	.400	.429	180	48	5	2	1	15	7	0	38	1	.267	.291	.350
David Ortiz	L	7	1	0	0	1	1	1	0	1	1	.143	.250	.571	82	15	3	1	4	17	20	1	21	2	.183	.340	.390
Lyle Overbay	L	12	0	0	0	0	0	2	1	3	0	.000	.143	.000	57	12	4	0	2	14	8	2	18	2	.211	.299	.386
Micah Owings	R	1	0	0	0	0	0	0	0	0	0	.000	.000	.000	45	11	3	0	2	8	3	0	19	1	.244	.292	.444
Jordan Pacheco	R	1	0	0	0	0	0	0	0	0	0	.000	.000	.000	1	0	0	0	0	0	0	0	0	0	.000	.000	.000
Angel Pagan	B	3	1	0	0	0	1	0	0	0	0	.333	.333	.333	61	11	0	1	0	2	1	0	19	1	.180	.194	.213
Matt Pagnozzi	R	3	1	0	0	0	0	0	0	1	0	.333	.333	.333	4	1	0	0	0	0	0	0	1	0	.250	.250	.250
Chris Parmelee	L	1	0	0	0	0	0	0	0	0	0	.000	.000	.000	1	0	0	0	0	0	0	0	1	0	.000	.000	.000
Gerardo Parra	L	9	2	1	0	0	1	0	0	2	0	.222	.222	.333	44	6	1	0	0	2	3	1	12	1	.136	.188	.159
Andy Parrino	B	3	0	0	0	0	0	2	0	0	0	.000	.667	.000	1	0	0	0	0	0	0	0	0	0	.000	.667	.000
Val Pascucci	R	9	3	0	0	1	2	0	0	3	0	.333	.333	.667	19	5	0	0	1	2	3	1	10	1	.263	.364	.421
Corey Patterson	L	22	2	1	0	0	1	1	0	8	1	.091	.130	.136	98	17	5	0	1	6	2	0	36	2	.173	.188	.255
Eric Patterson	L	16	1	0	0	0	2	4	0	8	0	.063	.238	.063	36	3	1	0	1	3	6	0	17	0	.083	.209	.194
Xavier Paul	L	43	4	2	0	0	1	1	0	21	1	.093	.114	.140	59	7	3	0	1	2	1	0	25	2	.119	.133	.220
Ronny Paulino	R	15	1	0	0	0	0	2	0	4	0	.067	.263	.067	52	10	2	0	1	12	6	0	11	2	.192	.276	.288
Steve Pearce	R	23	4	1	0	0	1	2	0	8	1	.174	.240	.217	52	8	4	1	0	2	7	0	18	1	.154	.254	.269
Dustin Pedroia	R	1	0	0	0	0	0	0	0	0	0	.000	.000	.000	8	5	3	0	0	4	0	0	1	0	.625	.625	1.000
Carlos Peguero	L	1	0	0	0	0	0	0	0	0	0	.000	.000	.000	1	0	0	0	0	0	0	0	1	0	.000	.000	.000
Brayan Pena	B	3	0	0	0	0	0	1	0	1	0	.000	.250	.000	70	15	3	0	1	8	7	0	17	2	.214	.282	.300
Carlos Pena	L	4	1	1	0	0	0	2	0	0	0	.250	.500	.500	29	6	3	0	0	3	5	0	17	0	.207	.324	.310
Ramiro Pena	B	1	0	0	0	0	0	0	0	0	0	.000	.000	.000	8	1	0	0	0	1	0	0	2	0	.125	.125	.125
Wily Mo Pena	R	9	3	0	0	2	3	0	0	3	0	.333	.333	1.000	102	21	4	0	5	17	5	0	45	4	.206	.257	.392
Hunter Pence	R	2	0	0	0	0	0	0	0	1	1	.000	.000	.000	6	1	0	0	0	0	1	0	2	1	.167	.286	.167
Jhonny Peralta	R	4	1	0	0	1	2	2	1	1	0	.250	.500	1.000	15	4	0	0	1	4	5	1	4	0	.267	.450	.467
Bryan Petersen	L	15	7	2	0	1	3	1	0	1	1	.467	.500	.800	33	9	2	0	1	5	2	0	6	1	.273	.314	.424
Cord Phelps	B	3	0	0	0	0	0	0	0	1	0	.000	.000	.000	3	0	0	0	0	0	0	0	1	0	.000	.000	.000

379

Pinch Hitting

Batter	B	2011 Pinch Hitting													Career Pinch Hitting												
		AB	H	2B	3B	HR	RBI	TBB	IBB	SO	GDP	Avg	OBP	Slg	AB	H	2B	3B	HR	RBI	TBB	IBB	SO	GDP	Avg	OBP	Slg
Brandon Phillips	R	1	1	0	0	1	1	0	0	0	0	1.000	1.000	4.000	14	5	2	0	2	2	3	1	1	0	.357	.471	.929
Kyle Phillips	L	10	1	0	0	0	2	3	0	4	0	.100	.308	.100	11	2	1	0	0	3	3	0	4	0	.182	.357	.273
Felix Pie	L	11	4	2	0	0	1	0	0	3	0	.364	.364	.545	33	9	3	0	0	2	0	0	15	0	.273	.273	.364
Juan Pierre	L	0	0	0	0	0	0	1	0	0	0	-	1.000	-	90	28	1	2	0	4	10	1	6	0	.311	.386	.367
A.J. Pierzynski	L	7	3	0	0	0	0	1	0	0	1	.429	.500	.429	92	21	4	0	2	15	10	4	14	6	.228	.305	.337
Brett Pill	R	1	0	0	0	0	0	1	0	1	0	.000	.500	.000	1	0	0	0	0	0	1	0	1	0	.000	.500	.000
Trevor Plouffe	R	6	0	0	0	0	0	0	0	3	0	.000	.000	.000	9	0	0	0	0	0	0	0	5	0	.000	.000	.000
Placido Polanco	R	4	1	0	0	0	0	1	0	1	0	.250	.400	.250	79	20	3	0	1	16	6	0	8	2	.253	.302	.329
Jorge Posada	B	13	2	1	0	0	2	5	2	3	2	.154	.389	.231	139	30	4	1	5	28	26	5	47	8	.216	.337	.367
Buster Posey	R	2	0	0	0	0	0	0	0	0	0	.000	.000	.000	6	0	0	0	0	0	0	0	2	0	.000	.000	.000
Landon Powell	B	2	0	0	0	0	0	0	0	1	0	.000	.000	.000	7	0	0	0	0	0	0	0	2	0	.000	.000	.000
Martin Prado	R	1	0	0	0	0	0	0	0	0	0	.000	.000	.000	44	13	5	0	1	12	8	0	7	0	.295	.404	.477
Alex Presley	L	1	1	0	0	0	0	0	0	0	0	1.000	1.000	1.000	7	3	0	0	0	0	0	0	3	0	.429	.429	.429
Jason Pridie	L	24	3	1	0	0	1	5	0	7	0	.125	.276	.167	27	3	1	0	0	1	5	0	8	0	.111	.250	.148
Albert Pujols	R	1	0	0	0	0	0	1	1	0	0	.000	.500	.000	23	8	0	0	2	9	8	3	6	0	.348	.500	.609
Nick Punto	B	10	3	0	0	0	0	3	0	3	0	.300	.462	.300	50	11	1	0	0	0	7	0	14	0	.220	.316	.240
Carlos Quentin	R	4	0	0	0	0	0	0	0	0	0	.000	.000	.000	29	7	4	0	2	10	0	0	6	0	.241	.290	.586
H. Quintero	R	1	0	0	0	0	0	0	0	0	0	.000	.000	.000	20	4	0	0	0	1	0	0	4	3	.200	.200	.200
Ryan Raburn	R	11	2	1	0	1	1	0	0	2	0	.182	.182	.545	62	11	2	0	4	9	7	1	20	1	.177	.278	.403
Alexei Ramirez	R	2	0	0	0	0	0	0	0	0	0	.000	.000	.000	5	1	0	0	0	1	0	0	0	0	.200	.200	.200
Aramis Ramirez	R	2	1	0	0	0	2	0	0	0	0	.500	.333	.500	38	11	1	0	2	16	1	0	8	1	.289	.310	.474
Hanley Ramirez	R	3	1	0	0	0	0	0	0	1	0	.333	.333	.333	14	5	0	0	1	4	2	0	3	0	.357	.438	.571
Manny Ramirez	R	1	0	0	0	0	0	0	0	0	0	.000	.000	.000	43	5	0	0	2	9	9	3	16	0	.116	.278	.256
Wilkin Ramirez	R	10	4	1	0	0	1	0	0	4	0	.400	.400	.500	10	4	1	0	0	1	0	0	4	0	.400	.400	.500
Wilson Ramos	R	4	2	0	0	1	1	0	0	1	1	.500	.500	1.250	4	2	0	0	1	1	0	0	1	1	.500	.500	1.250
Cody Ransom	R	1	0	0	0	0	0	0	0	1	0	.000	.000	.000	29	5	1	0	2	4	5	0	11	1	.172	.294	.414
Colby Rasmus	L	4	0	0	0	0	0	1	0	2	0	.000	.200	.000	36	9	2	0	1	5	5	1	12	1	.250	.341	.389
Josh Reddick	L	11	2	0	0	0	2	0	0	5	0	.182	.182	.182	22	3	0	0	0	2	0	0	9	0	.136	.136	.136
Jeremy Reed	L	7	0	0	0	0	0	0	0	2	0	.000	.000	.000	105	24	4	1	0	9	5	0	28	0	.229	.261	.286
Nolan Reimold	R	5	1	0	0	0	0	0	0	2	0	.200	.333	.200	14	1	0	0	0	0	2	0	8	0	.071	.235	.071
Edgar Renteria	R	13	6	0	0	0	2	2	0	4	0	.462	.533	.462	46	13	1	0	0	8	3	0	17	1	.283	.327	.304
Jason Repko	R	7	1	0	0	0	0	0	0	3	0	.143	.143	.143	38	6	1	0	0	1	3	0	15	0	.158	.214	.184
Ben Revere	L	10	3	0	0	0	0	1	0	1	0	.300	.364	.300	11	3	0	0	0	0	1	0	2	0	.273	.333	.273
Jose Reyes	B	2	1	0	0	0	0	0	0	0	0	.500	.500	.500	9	2	1	0	0	0	2	0	1	0	.222	.417	.333
Mark Reynolds	R	1	0	0	0	0	0	1	0	0	0	.000	.000	.000	16	2	0	0	2	5	2	0	9	2	.125	.211	.500
Will Rhymes	L	4	1	0	0	0	0	0	0	0	0	.250	.250	.250	9	2	1	0	0	2	1	0	2	0	.222	.300	.333
Clayton Richard	L	1	1	0	0	0	0	0	0	0	0	1.000	1.000	1.000	1	1	0	0	0	0	0	0	0	0	1.000	1.000	1.000
A. Richardson	B	4	2	0	0	0	0	0	0	0	0	.500	.500	.500	4	2	0	0	0	0	0	0	0	0	.500	.500	.500
Juan Rivera	R	10	2	0	0	0	1	0	0	2	1	.200	.200	.200	72	15	6	0	1	11	6	2	14	6	.208	.288	.333
Rene Rivera	R	1	0	0	0	0	0	0	0	0	0	.000	.000	.000	5	0	0	0	0	0	0	0	1	0	.000	.000	.000
Anthony Rizzo	L	6	1	1	0	0	1	0	0	2	0	.167	.167	.333	6	1	1	0	0	1	0	0	2	0	.167	.167	.333
Ryan Roberts	R	15	6	0	0	0	1	0	0	6	0	.400	.400	.400	66	17	2	0	0	6	5	0	23	1	.258	.324	.288
Shane Robinson	R	3	0	0	0	0	0	0	0	1	0	.000	.000	.000	8	1	1	0	0	0	0	0	2	0	.125	.125	.250
Trayvon Robinson	B	2	0	0	0	0	0	0	0	2	0	.000	.000	.000	2	0	0	0	0	0	0	0	2	0	.000	.000	.000
Alex Rodriguez	R	0	0	0	0	0	0	1	1	0	0	-	1.000	-	11	0	0	0	0	0	3	1	4	0	.000	.214	.000
Ivan Rodriguez	R	6	1	0	0	0	1	1	1	0	1	.167	.375	.167	85	21	1	0	2	17	7	4	23	5	.247	.313	.329
Josh Rodriguez	R	1	0	0	0	0	0	0	0	1	0	.000	.000	.000	1	0	0	0	0	0	0	0	1	0	.000	.000	.000
Luis Rodriguez	R	3	0	0	0	0	1	1	0	1	0	.000	.200	.000	67	10	0	0	1	8	10	0	6	5	.149	.253	.194
Sean Rodriguez	R	7	0	0	0	0	0	3	0	3	0	.000	.300	.000	24	2	1	0	0	1	3	0	11	0	.083	.185	.125
Ryan Rohlinger	R	1	0	0	0	0	0	0	0	1	0	.000	.000	.000	10	2	0	0	0	2	1	0	3	1	.200	.273	.200
Scott Rolen	R	3	2	1	0	1	2	0	0	0	0	.667	.667	2.000	17	7	1	0	4	7	0	0	4	0	.412	.412	1.176
Jimmy Rollins	B	4	0	0	0	0	0	1	0	1	0	.000	.200	.000	22	2	0	0	1	1	2	0	3	0	.091	.167	.227
Austin Romine	R	1	0	0	0	0	0	0	0	1	0	.000	.000	.000	1	0	0	0	0	0	0	0	1	0	.000	.000	.000
Adam Rosales	R	1	0	0	0	0	0	0	0	1	0	.000	.000	.000	38	7	1	1	2	7	1	0	13	0	.184	.205	.421
Wilin Rosario	R	1	0	0	0	0	1	0	0	1	0	.000	.000	.000	1	0	0	0	0	1	0	0	1	0	.000	.000	.000
Cody Ross	R	6	1	0	0	0	0	2	0	2	0	.167	.375	.167	56	15	4	0	4	10	9	0	18	0	.268	.388	.554
David Ross	R	5	0	0	0	0	0	0	0	2	0	.000	.000	.000	48	9	1	1	3	9	11	0	13	1	.188	.339	.438
Vinny Rottino	R	5	1	0	0	0	0	0	0	1	0	.200	.200	.200	16	2	0	0	0	1	0	0	4	0	.125	.125	.125
Aaron Rowand	R	26	9	2	0	3	4	0	0	7	0	.346	.346	.769	93	23	6	0	5	11	5	0	29	2	.247	.293	.473
Justin Ruggiano	R	10	2	1	0	0	1	2	0	3	0	.200	.333	.300	16	3	1	0	0	3	3	0	5	1	.188	.316	.250
Carlos Ruiz	R	8	3	1	0	1	4	3	0	0	0	.375	.583	.875	34	10	3	0	1	10	5	1	3	1	.294	.400	.471
J. Saltalamacchia	B	2	0	0	0	0	0	0	0	0	0	.000	.000	.000	18	2	0	0	0	1	4	0	9	0	.111	.273	.111
Angel Sanchez	R	32	10	0	0	0	2	4	1	5	0	.313	.389	.313	34	12	0	0	0	2	4	1	5	0	.353	.421	.353
Freddy Sanchez	R	2	0	0	0	0	0	0	0	1	0	.000	.000	.000	58	17	4	2	0	6	9	0	7	1	.293	.388	.431
Gaby Sanchez	R	5	1	0	0	0	0	1	1	1	0	.200	.333	.200	28	6	0	0	2	3	3	1	5	0	.214	.294	.429
Hector Sanchez	B	5	3	0	0	0	1	1	0	1	0	.600	.667	.600	5	3	0	0	0	1	1	0	1	0	.600	.667	.600
Pablo Sandoval	B	7	0	0	0	0	0	0	0	2	0	.000	.000	.000	19	5	2	0	0	7	2	1	3	1	.263	.318	.368
Jerry Sands	R	4	0	0	0	0	0	1	0	2	0	.000	.200	.000	4	0	0	0	0	0	1	0	2	0	.000	.200	.000
Carlos Santana	B	3	1	0	0	1	1	0	0	0	0	.333	.333	1.333	3	1	0	0	1	1	0	0	0	0	.333	.500	1.333
Ramon Santiago	B	6	1	0	0	0	0	0	0	1	0	.167	.167	.167	43	12	1	0	0	0	3	0	10	0	.279	.380	.302

Pinch Hitting

Batter	B	AB	H	2B	3B	HR	RBI	TBB	IBB	SO	GDP	Avg	OBP	Slg	AB	H	2B	3B	HR	RBI	TBB	IBB	SO	GDP	Avg	OBP	Slg
						2011 Pinch Hitting														Career Pinch Hitting								
Omir Santos	R	2	1	0	0	0	0	0	0	1	0	.500	.500	.500	13	4	0	0	1	2	0	0	2	0	.308	.308	.538
Dave Sappelt	R	5	1	0	0	0	0	3	0	0	0	.200	.500	.200	5	1	0	0	0	0	3	0	0	0	.200	.500	.200
Dane Sardinha	R	1	0	0	0	0	0	0	0	1	0	.000	.000	.000	6	0	0	0	0	0	0	0	4	0	.000	.000	.000
Josh Satin	R	9	2	1	0	0	2	0	0	2	1	.222	.222	.333	9	2	1	0	0	2	0	0	2	1	.222	.222	.333
Jordan Schafer	L	3	0	0	0	0	0	0	0	2	0	.000	.000	.000	3	0	0	0	0	0	0	0	2	0	.000	.000	.000
Logan Schafer	L	3	1	0	0	0	0	0	0	1	0	.333	.333	.333	3	1	0	0	0	0	0	0	1	0	.333	.333	.333
Nate Schierholtz	L	22	6	1	0	1	6	0	0	4	0	.273	.273	.455	97	31	7	0	2	15	7	0	21	1	.320	.358	.454
Brian Schneider	L	3	0	0	0	0	0	0	0	1	0	.000	.000	.000	57	12	2	0	1	10	7	2	10	4	.211	.308	.298
Skip Schumaker	L	14	6	1	0	0	2	1	0	1	0	.429	.467	.500	110	29	5	0	1	10	3	0	18	2	.264	.293	.336
Luke Scott	L	7	3	0	0	1	2	0	0	0	1	.429	.429	.857	80	19	8	0	2	10	8	1	23	1	.238	.307	.413
Marco Scutaro	R	2	0	0	0	0	0	0	0	0	0	.000	.000	.000	47	7	0	1	0	4	3	0	10	2	.149	.200	.191
Kyle Seager	L	3	0	0	0	0	0	0	0	2	0	.000	.000	.000	3	0	0	0	0	0	0	0	2	0	.000	.000	.000
Justin Sellers	R	2	0	0	0	0	0	1	0	1	0	.000	.333	.000	2	0	0	0	0	0	1	0	1	0	.000	.333	.000
Kelly Shoppach	R	4	2	0	0	0	2	1	0	1	0	.500	.600	.500	25	8	1	0	1	7	7	0	9	0	.320	.455	.480
J.B. Shuck	L	11	4	0	0	0	1	3	0	2	1	.364	.500	.364	11	4	0	0	0	1	3	0	2	1	.364	.500	.364
Grady Sizemore	L	4	0	0	0	0	0	0	0	1	0	.000	.000	.000	15	4	0	0	0	0	0	0	3	0	.267	.267	.267
Scott Sizemore	R	4	3	1	0	1	7	0	0	0	0	.750	.750	1.750	8	4	1	0	2	10	0	0	0	0	.500	.500	1.375
Seth Smith	L	22	8	1	0	0	2	2	0	7	1	.364	.400	.409	137	46	11	5	5	34	25	2	34	2	.336	.430	.599
Justin Smoak	B	1	0	0	0	0	1	2	0	1	0	.000	.750	.000	4	1	0	0	0	3	2	0	1	1	.250	.571	.250
Travis Snider	L	2	1	1	0	0	2	0	0	0	0	.500	.500	1.000	10	2	2	0	0	2	0	0	5	0	.200	.200	.400
Brad Snyder	L	5	1	0	0	0	0	0	0	3	0	.200	.200	.200	11	3	1	0	0	2	0	0	6	0	.273	.273	.364
Chris Snyder	R	0	0	0	0	0	0	0	0	0	0	-	-	-	18	2	0	0	1	4	2	1	3	0	.111	.190	.278
Eric Sogard	L	1	1	0	0	0	0	0	0	0	0	1.000	1.000	1.000	2	1	0	0	0	0	1	0	1	0	.500	.667	.500
Alfonso Soriano	R	7	2	2	0	0	3	0	0	2	0	.286	.286	.571	24	5	3	0	1	6	4	1	6	0	.208	.321	.458
Geovany Soto	R	4	1	0	0	1	3	1	0	0	0	.250	.400	1.000	22	6	1	0	1	5	5	2	6	0	.273	.407	.455
Denard Span	L	2	1	1	0	0	0	0	0	0	0	.500	.500	1.000	4	2	1	0	0	2	0	0	1	0	.500	.500	.750
Nate Spears	L	2	0	0	0	0	0	0	0	0	0	.000	.000	.000	2	0	0	0	0	0	0	0	0	0	.000	.000	.000
Ryan Spilborghs	R	33	7	0	0	1	6	7	0	11	2	.212	.350	.303	174	53	13	1	2	39	32	0	44	8	.305	.411	.425
Matt Stairs	L	39	6	0	0	0	1	7	0	10	0	.154	.283	.154	416	105	20	2	23	87	64	10	109	5	.252	.357	.476
Mike Stanton	R	5	1	0	0	0	1	3	0	3	1	.200	.556	.200	7	1	0	0	0	1	3	0	4	1	.143	.455	.143
Tim Stauffer	R	1	0	0	0	0	0	0	0	1	0	.000	.000	.000	1	0	0	0	0	0	0	0	1	0	.000	.000	.000
Chris Stewart	R	2	0	0	0	0	0	0	0	0	0	.000	.000	.000	5	0	0	0	0	0	0	0	0	0	.000	.000	.000
Ian Stewart	L	10	1	0	0	0	0	0	0	4	0	.100	.100	.100	70	16	7	0	2	10	5	0	28	1	.229	.299	.414
Drew Stubbs	R	2	1	1	0	0	1	1	0	0	0	.500	.667	1.000	6	3	2	0	0	1	3	0	1	0	.500	.667	.833
Drew Sutton	B	4	1	0	0	0	0	1	0	2	0	.250	.400	.250	27	6	1	0	1	7	2	0	10	0	.222	.300	.370
Kurt Suzuki	R	0	0	0	0	0	0	1	0	0	0	-	1.000	-	15	7	1	0	2	6	3	0	0	0	.467	.579	.933
Ryan Sweeney	L	18	4	0	1	0	2	3	0	4	1	.222	.333	.333	34	6	0	1	0	2	6	1	11	2	.176	.300	.235
Nick Swisher	B	1	1	1	0	0	0	1	0	0	0	1.000	1.000	2.000	22	3	3	0	0	3	3	0	5	2	.136	.240	.273
Jose Tabata	R	2	0	0	0	0	0	0	0	1	0	.000	.000	.000	3	0	0	0	0	0	0	0	1	0	.000	.000	.000
Michael Taylor	R	1	0	0	0	0	0	0	0	1	0	.000	.000	.000	1	0	0	0	0	0	0	0	1	0	.000	.000	.000
Mark Teahen	L	26	4	0	0	1	4	1	0	11	0	.154	.185	.269	42	8	1	0	1	6	4	0	15	0	.190	.261	.286
Mark Teixeira	B	0	0	0	0	0	0	1	1	0	0	-	1.000	-	4	0	0	0	0	0	3	2	0	0	.000	.429	.000
Miguel Tejada	R	6	3	0	0	0	0	0	0	1	0	.500	.500	.500	12	5	0	0	0	1	0	0	2	0	.417	.417	.417
Ruben Tejada	R	2	0	0	0	0	0	1	0	0	0	.000	.000	.000	3	0	0	0	0	0	1	0	0	0	.000	.000	.000
Blake Tekotte	L	9	0	0	0	0	0	0	0	7	0	.000	.000	.000	9	0	0	0	0	0	0	0	7	0	.000	.000	.000
Eric Thames	L	3	0	0	0	0	0	0	0	2	0	.000	.000	.000	3	0	0	0	0	0	0	0	2	0	.000	.000	.000
Marcus Thames	R	18	4	0	0	2	4	0	0	5	0	.222	.222	.556	92	26	2	0	7	19	13	2	31	1	.283	.371	.533
Ryan Theriot	R	12	3	2	1	0	7	2	0	1	1	.250	.357	.583	49	10	4	1	1	13	7	0	10	1	.204	.316	.388
Josh Thole	L	14	1	1	0	0	1	3	1	6	0	.071	.235	.143	29	6	1	0	0	4	5	1	8	0	.207	.324	.241
Jim Thome	L	13	3	1	0	0	1	2	0	9	0	.231	.333	.308	120	28	9	0	4	14	21	1	52	2	.233	.354	.408
Matt Tolbert	B	7	1	1	0	0	0	4	0	1	0	.143	.455	.286	16	3	1	0	0	0	6	0	4	0	.188	.409	.250
Wyatt Toregas	R	1	0	0	0	0	0	0	0	0	1	.000	.000	.000	1	0	0	0	0	0	0	0	0	1	.000	.000	.000
Yorvit Torrealba	R	5	0	0	0	0	0	0	0	2	0	.000	.000	.000	27	1	0	0	0	1	2	0	14	0	.037	.133	.037
Andres Torres	R	6	1	0	0	0	1	3	0	2	0	.167	.444	.167	32	9	0	0	1	9	5	0	12	0	.281	.378	.375
Rene Tosoni	L	9	2	1	0	0	1	0	0	2	0	.222	.222	.333	9	2	1	0	0	1	0	0	2	0	.222	.222	.333
J.R. Towles	R	4	0	0	0	0	0	0	0	2	0	.000	.000	.000	9	0	0	0	0	0	0	0	3	0	.000	.000	.000
Matt Treanor	R	1	0	0	0	0	0	0	0	0	0	.000	.000	.000	20	4	0	1	0	3	0	0	4	0	.200	.200	.300
Mike Trout	R	3	1	0	0	0	0	1	0	2	0	.333	.500	.333	3	1	0	0	0	0	1	0	2	0	.333	.500	.333
Mark Trumbo	R	1	1	1	0	0	0	0	0	0	0	1.000	1.000	2.000	2	1	1	0	0	0	0	0	1	0	.500	.500	1.000
Troy Tulowitzki	R	3	0	0	0	0	0	0	0	2	0	.000	.000	.000	5	0	0	0	0	0	0	0	3	0	.000	.000	.000
Justin Turner	R	10	4	2	0	0	3	1	0	1	0	.400	.455	.600	16	5	2	0	0	3	1	0	2	0	.313	.389	.438
Dan Uggla	R	1	1	0	0	1	2	0	0	0	0	1.000	1.000	4.000	5	1	0	0	1	2	2	0	0	0	.200	.429	.800
B.J. Upton	R	2	0	0	0	0	0	1	0	2	0	.000	.333	.000	12	5	0	1	1	2	1	0	4	1	.417	.462	.833
Justin Upton	R	2	0	0	0	0	1	0	0	0	0	.000	.000	.000	14	4	2	0	0	1	0	0	6	1	.286	.286	.429
Juan Uribe	R	3	1	1	0	0	1	1	0	0	0	.333	.500	.667	38	13	5	0	1	9	3	0	9	1	.342	.390	.553
Chase Utley	L	1	1	0	0	0	0	2	2	0	0	1.000	1.000	1.000	45	14	1	0	4	15	7	3	16	0	.311	.407	.622
Chris Valaika	R	5	2	0	0	0	0	0	0	1	0	.400	.400	.400	10	3	0	0	0	0	1	0	2	0	.300	.364	.300
Luis Valbuena	L	1	0	0	0	0	0	0	0	0	0	.000	.000	.000	7	2	0	1	0	0	0	0	0	0	.286	.286	.571
Wilson Valdez	R	7	0	0	0	0	0	0	0	3	0	.000	.000	.000	29	3	1	0	0	2	0	0	6	0	.103	.188	.138
Danny Valencia	R	2	0	0	0	0	1	1	0	1	0	.000	.333	.000	5	1	0	0	0	1	1	0	1	0	.200	.333	.200

Pinch Hitting

Batter	B	2011 Pinch Hitting													Career Pinch Hitting												
		AB	H	2B	3B	HR	RBI	TBB	IBB	SO	GDP	Avg	OBP	Slg	AB	H	2B	3B	HR	RBI	TBB	IBB	SO	GDP	Avg	OBP	Slg
Javier Vazquez	R	2	1	0	0	0	0	0	0	1	0	.500	.500	.500	4	1	0	0	0	0	1	0	2	0	.250	.400	.250
Gil Velazquez	R	2	1	0	0	0	0	0	0	0	0	.500	.500	.500	2	1	0	0	0	0	0	0	0	0	.500	.500	.500
Eugenio Velez	B	13	0	0	0	0	1	1	0	3	0	.000	.133	.000	67	13	2	2	0	7	3	0	15	2	.194	.239	.284
Will Venable	L	19	1	0	0	0	0	4	1	4	0	.053	.217	.053	55	9	2	1	0	5	6	1	19	0	.164	.242	.236
Dayan Viciedo	R	0	0	0	0	0	0	1	0	0	0	-	1.000	-	7	2	0	0	0	1	2	0	3	0	.286	.444	.286
Shane Victorino	B	2	1	0	0	0	1	0	0	0	1	.500	.500	.500	85	23	1	1	3	23	7	0	16	2	.271	.326	.412
Omar Vizquel	B	5	1	0	0	0	0	2	0	2	0	.200	.429	.200	60	7	3	0	0	3	6	0	13	1	.117	.197	.167
Joey Votto	L	1	0	0	0	0	0	1	0	0	0	.000	.500	.000	14	3	0	0	1	4	5	2	5	0	.214	.421	.429
Neil Walker	B	1	0	0	0	0	0	1	0	0	0	.000	.500	.000	10	2	1	0	0	0	1	0	0	1	.200	.273	.300
Brett Wallace	L	17	1	0	0	0	2	2	0	4	1	.059	.158	.059	20	2	0	0	0	3	2	0	4	1	.100	.182	.100
Jemile Weeks	B	1	0	0	0	0	0	0	0	1	0	.000	.000	.000	1	0	0	0	0	0	0	0	1	0	.000	.000	.000
Rickie Weeks	R	0	0	0	0	0	0	1	0	0	0	-	1.000	-	15	4	0	1	1	1	5	0	6	1	.267	.450	.600
Casper Wells	R	3	1	0	0	0	0	0	0	2	0	.333	.600	.333	10	3	0	0	0	0	0	0	5	0	.300	.417	.300
Vernon Wells	R	1	0	0	0	0	0	0	0	1	0	.000	.000	.000	11	2	0	0	0	4	0	0	2	0	.182	.182	.182
Jayson Werth	R	2	0	0	0	0	0	0	0	1	0	.000	.000	.000	55	12	1	0	3	11	8	0	22	0	.218	.317	.400
Jake Westbrook	R	1	0	0	0	0	0	0	0	1	0	.000	.000	.000	1	0	0	0	0	0	0	0	1	0	.000	.000	.000
Eli Whiteside	R	2	0	0	0	0	0	0	0	1	0	.000	.000	.000	3	0	0	0	0	0	0	0	2	0	.000	.000	.000
Matt Wieters	B	4	1	0	0	0	0	1	0	1	1	.250	.400	.250	11	3	1	0	0	1	2	0	4	2	.273	.385	.364
Ty Wigginton	R	13	2	0	0	0	0	3	1	7	0	.154	.313	.154	70	19	2	0	3	21	10	2	16	2	.271	.373	.429
Josh Willingham	R	6	1	0	0	1	2	0	0	1	0	.167	.167	.667	52	12	2	0	3	12	5	0	16	0	.231	.310	.442
Dontrelle Willis	L	3	0	0	0	0	0	0	0	2	0	.000	.000	.000	21	6	1	1	0	0	1	0	6	1	.286	.318	.429
Reggie Willits	B	2	0	0	0	0	0	0	0	1	0	.000	.000	.000	40	7	0	0	0	0	5	0	12	0	.175	.267	.175
Bobby Wilson	R	4	0	0	0	0	1	0	0	1	0	.000	.000	.000	5	1	0	0	0	1	0	0	1	0	.200	.167	.200
Jack Wilson	R	4	0	0	0	0	0	0	0	1	0	.000	.000	.000	35	14	2	0	1	2	1	0	8	0	.400	.417	.543
Josh Wilson	R	22	3	1	0	1	2	3	0	8	0	.136	.240	.318	41	8	2	0	1	5	4	0	14	1	.195	.267	.317
Mike Wilson	R	1	0	0	0	0	0	0	0	0	0	.000	.000	.000	1	0	0	0	0	0	0	0	0	0	.000	.000	.000
DeWayne Wise	L	19	6	1	0	0	2	1	0	3	0	.316	.350	.368	84	26	3	1	3	14	1	0	18	1	.310	.314	.476
Brandon Wood	R	15	3	0	0	1	2	1	0	5	1	.200	.250	.400	22	5	1	0	2	5	1	0	5	1	.227	.292	.545
Chris Woodward	R	1	0	0	0	0	0	0	0	0	0	.000	.000	.000	72	16	2	0	2	11	8	0	18	0	.222	.305	.333
Danny Worth	R	3	2	0	0	0	1	0	0	0	0	.667	.667	.667	5	2	0	0	0	1	1	0	0	0	.400	.500	.400
David Wright	R	1	0	0	0	0	0	0	0	0	0	.000	.000	.000	5	1	0	0	0	0	1	0	1	0	.200	.200	.200
Chris Young	R	1	1	0	0	0	0	0	0	0	0	1.000	1.000	1.000	16	5	3	0	0	6	4	1	4	0	.313	.450	.500
Delmon Young	R	2	1	0	0	0	0	0	0	0	0	.500	.500	.500	8	4	1	0	0	1	0	0	0	0	.500	.500	.625
Eric Young	B	20	4	0	0	0	0	6	0	1	1	.200	.385	.200	40	10	1	1	0	0	10	0	4	2	.250	.400	.325
Matt Young	L	7	0	0	0	0	0	0	0	0	0	.000	.000	.000	7	0	0	0	0	0	0	0	0	0	.000	.000	.000
Carlos Zambrano	B	1	1	0	0	0	2	0	0	0	0	1.000	1.000	1.000	29	3	0	0	0	2	0	0	14	1	.103	.103	.103
Ryan Zimmerman	R	2	2	0	0	0	2	1	0	0	0	1.000	1.000	1.000	15	6	2	0	1	7	1	0	1	1	.400	.412	.733
J. Zimmermann	R	1	0	0	0	0	0	0	0	1	0	.000	.000	.000	1	0	0	0	0	0	0	0	1	0	.000	.000	.000
Ben Zobrist	B	1	0	0	0	0	0	0	0	1	0	.000	.000	.000	31	5	0	0	3	9	3	1	9	0	.161	.235	.452

Manufactured Run Contributions

Bill James

Be honest now: If you met Daniel Descalso on the street, would you know it?

Daniel Descalso is a rather unusual player. In 2011—a rookie—he played in 148 games for the St. Louis Cardinals, but had only 326 at bats. The only other player in major league history to play in that many games with that few at bats was Michael Tucker in 2000.

Of course, this did not happen because Descalso is an unusual player as much as it happened because Tony LaRussa is an unusual manager. LaRussa chose to get Descalso into almost every game, but very often in a limited role. He started 81 games; he came into 67 others as a defensive replacement, pinch hitter, or pinch runner. He didn't do a lot of pinch running; he's not fast. Even when he started the game, very often he wouldn't finish it. Sometimes somebody else would pinch hit for him.

Very often he bunts. Sometimes he is used as a pinch bunter. Because of this, and some other things, Descalso contributed to 18 Manufactured Runs—the most of any major league third baseman.

The best team in baseball at Manufacturing a Run is the Texas Rangers, and the two players who are key to that are Ian Kinsler and Elvis Andrus. The Rangers in 2011 (regular season) manufactured 203 runs. This

a) was easily the most in the majors, and

b) was still way down from their number in 2010, when they led the majors with 230.

Kinsler and Andrus were 1-2 in the majors in the number of manufactured runs that they contributed to; probably a few of these were the same runs, although most of them quite certainly were not. The Rangers Manufactured Run total was way down because nobody on the 2011 Rangers was actually very good at manufacturing a run, other than Kinsler and Andrus, who are great at it, and Julio Borbon, who didn't play much.

Usually I spend some space here defining a Manufactured Run, but I've decided this year to skip that; if you want to know how we define a Manufactured Run, you can look it up in the glossary or on the internet. The internet is a series of tubes; it's not a dump truck. If you need a dump truck, you can rent that from Hertz Equipment Rentals; you will need a Class B Commercial Driver's License. In order to get a Class B CDL, you will need to know how to maintain air brakes.

No, we define a Manufactured Run, or try to, exactly the same way any announcer would use the term; the only difference is that to count them we have to think through the definition to its logical conclusion.

There were 4,678 Manufactured Runs in the major leagues in 2011, which is about one per team per game. The critical element to manufacturing runs is speed—also bunting and bat control, but mostly speed—and so the players who are best at that are almost all outfielders and middle infielders. Here is an All-Star team of guys who are good at manufacturing runs: Catcher, Miguel Olivo (contributed to 14 Manufactured Runs), First Base, Miguel Cabrera or Albert Pujols (19 each), Second Base, Kinsler (45), Third Base, Descalso (18), Shortstop, Andrus (43), Left Field, Juan Pierre (39), Center Field, Michael Bourn to Run (36), Right Field, Ichiro Suzuki (33). Honorable mention, Brett Gardner (36). Four of these players were also on this team in 2010: Andrus, Pierre, Bourn and Suzuki.

What may be more critical to the success of a team than the ability to Manufacture a run is the ability to stop the opposition from doing the same. The team that is really, really good at that is the Tampa Bay Rays. The Rays allowed their opponents to manufacture only 118 runs in 2011—ten fewer than any other major league team. The Rays also led the American League in this category in 2010.

2011 Manufactured Runs

American League

Team	MR
Texas Rangers	203
Kansas City Royals	186
Los Angeles Angels	170
Detroit Tigers	158
Seattle Mariners	157
Minnesota Twins	157
New York Yankees	156
Chicago White Sox	156
Toronto Blue Jays	154
Tampa Bay Rays	154
Boston Red Sox	150
Baltimore Orioles	148
Oakland Athletics	146
Cleveland Indians	138

American League Opponents

Team	MR
Minnesota Twins	207
Oakland Athletics	197
Cleveland Indians	179
Boston Red Sox	166
Kansas City Royals	161
Detroit Tigers	160
Chicago White Sox	159
Los Angeles Angels	159
Toronto Blue Jays	146
New York Yankees	146
Seattle Mariners	145
Baltimore Orioles	145
Texas Rangers	128
Tampa Bay Rays	118

National League

Team	MR
Los Angeles Dodgers	170
New York Mets	169
Milwaukee Brewers	168
Cincinnati Reds	167
St Louis Cardinals	166
San Diego Padres	165
Colorado Rockies	162
Washington Nationals	159
Atlanta Braves	158
San Francisco Giants	149
Houston Astros	148
Pittsburgh Pirates	145
Arizona Diamondbacks	145
Philadelphia Phillies	140
Chicago Cubs	118
Florida Marlins	116

National League Opponents

Team	MR
Pittsburgh Pirates	187
New York Mets	182
Colorado Rockies	170
Chicago Cubs	169
Washington Nationals	158
Houston Astros	157
San Diego Padres	155
Florida Marlins	152
San Francisco Giants	151
St Louis Cardinals	149
Atlanta Braves	146
Arizona Diamondbacks	143
Los Angeles Dodgers	142
Milwaukee Brewers	138
Philadelphia Phillies	135
Cincinnati Reds	128

2011 Manufactured Runs

Top Three From Each Team

American League Leaders

Player	Tm	MRC
Kinsler, Ian	Tex	45
Andrus, Elvis	Tex	43
Pierre, Juan	CWS	39
Gardner, Brett	NYY	36
Suzuki, Ichiro	Sea	33
Jackson, Austin	Det	32
Ellsbury, Jacoby	Bos	31
Revere, Ben	Min	30
Bourjos, Peter	LAA	28
Crisp, Coco	Oak	27
Gordon, Alex	KC	25

National League Leaders

Player	Tm	MRC
Bourn, Michael	2 Tms	36
Reyes, Jose	NYM	35
Bonifacio, Emilio	Fla	32
Maybin, Cameron	SD	32
Fowler, Dexter	Col	31
Kemp, Matt	LAD	30
Phillips, Brandon	Cin	29
Braun, Ryan	Mil	27
Young, Chris	Ari	24
Desmond, Ian	Was	24
Stubbs, Drew	Cin	24

MRC = Manufactured Runs Contribution

Arizona Diamondbacks

Player	MRC
Young, Chris	24
Upton, Justin	19
Roberts, Ryan	19

Atlanta Braves

Player	MRC
Uggla, Dan	21
Prado, Martin	17
Heyward, Jason	14
Constanza, Jose	14
Gonzalez, Alex	14

Baltimore Orioles

Player	MRC
Andino, Robert	23
Hardy, J.J.	19
Markakis, Nick	13
Jones, Adam	13

Boston Red Sox

Player	MRC
Ellsbury, Jacoby	31
Pedroia, Dustin	15
Youkilis, Kevin	14

Chicago Cubs

Player	MRC
Castro, Starlin	17
Barney, Darwin	17
Campana, Tony	13

Chicago White Sox

Player	MRC
Pierre, Juan	39
Beckham, Gordon	20
Ramirez, Alexei	19

Cincinnati Reds

Player	MRC
Phillips, Brandon	29
Stubbs, Drew	24
Bruce, Jay	16

Cleveland Indians

Player	MRC
Cabrera, Asdrubal	20
Santana, Carlos	13
Brantley, Michael	12

Colorado Rockies

Player	MRC
Fowler, Dexter	31
Young, Eric	19
Gonzalez, Carlos	17

Detroit Tigers

Player	MRC
Jackson, Austin	32
Cabrera, Miguel	19
Martinez, Victor	12
Peralta, Jhonny	12

Florida Marlins

Player	MRC
Bonifacio, Emilio	32
Buck, John	11
Ramirez, Hanley	11

Houston Astros

Player	MRC
Bourn, Michael	24
Lee, Carlos	12
Sanchez, Angel	12

Kansas City Royals

Player	MRC
Gordon, Alex	25
Getz, Chris	23
Escobar, Alcides	19
Cabrera, Melky	19

Los Angeles Angels

Player	MRC
Bourjos, Peter	28
Aybar, Erick	24
Kendrick, Howie	21

Los Angeles Dodgers

Player	MRC
Kemp, Matt	30
Carroll, Jamey	21
Gwynn, Tony	15

Milwaukee Brewers

Player	MRC
Braun, Ryan	27
Weeks, Rickie	23
Morgan, Nyjer	22

Minnesota Twins

Player	MRC
Revere, Ben	30
Casilla, Alexi	19
Span, Denard	12

New York Mets

Player	MRC
Reyes, Jose	35
Pagan, Angel	23
Wright, David	15

New York Yankees

Player	MRC
Gardner, Brett	36
Granderson, Curtis	24
Cano, Robinson	13
Jeter, Derek	13

Oakland Athletics

Player	MRC
Crisp, Coco	27
DeJesus, David	14
Weeks, Jemile	12
Willingham, Josh	12
Pennington, Cliff	12

Philadelphia Phillies

Player	MRC
Rollins, Jimmy	22
Victorino, Shane	19
Valdez, Wilson	14
Utley, Chase	14

Pittsburgh Pirates

Player	MRC
McCutchen, Andrew	20
Walker, Neil	19
Tabata, Jose	15

San Diego Padres

Player	MRC
Maybin, Cameron	32
Bartlett, Jason	18
Venable, Will	15
Hudson, Orlando	15

San Francisco Giants

Player	MRC
Torres, Andres	22
Rowand, Aaron	15
Schierholtz, Nate	15

Seattle Mariners

Player	MRC
Suzuki, Ichiro	33
Ryan, Brendan	15
Olivo, Miguel	14

St Louis Cardinals

Player	MRC
Pujols, Albert	19
Descalso, Daniel	18
Holliday, Matt	16

Tampa Bay Rays

Player	MRC
Upton, B.J.	19
Zobrist, Ben	19
Rodriguez, Sean	18

Texas Rangers

Player	MRC
Kinsler, Ian	45
Andrus, Elvis	43
Chavez, Endy	14

Toronto Blue Jays

Player	MRC
Escobar, Yunel	21
Davis, Rajai	19
Bautista, Jose	18

Washington Nationals

Player	MRC
Desmond, Ian	24
Werth, Jayson	23
Espinosa, Danny	17

The Manager's Record

The purpose of this section is to document and quantify, as much as we can, the objective differences between managers. Is a manager quick to go to his bullpen, or slow? Is he willing to bring back a reliever he used yesterday, or not so much? Does he like to have runners in motion, or not?

The tools we have to evaluate managers are divided into several categories:

Lineups: Number of Different Lineups Used (LUp), the percentage of players who had the platoon advantage at the start of the game (PL%).

Substitution: Pinch Hitters Used (PH), Pinch Runners Used (PR), Defensive Substitutes Used (DS).

Pitchers Usage: Quick Hooks (Quick), Slow Hooks (Slow), Long Outings by Starting Pitchers (LO), Relievers Used on Consecutive Days (RCD), Long Saves (LS), Relievers Used (Rel).

For Quick Hooks, we calculate a "Damage Score" for each pitcher and each game, which is his pitches thrown, plus 10 times his runs allowed. The bottom 25% of the games in each league are Quick Hooks. If the manager takes his pitcher out after 92 pitches and 1 run allowed (102), that will be a quick hook. The top 25% are Slow Hooks. If a pitcher throws 114 pitches and gives up 4 runs (154), that will be a Slow Hook. If a pitcher throws more than 110 pitches in a start, that's a Long Outing. Yes, this *is* redundant of Slow Hooks; thanks for noticing.

Tactics: Stolen Base Attempts (SBA), Sacrifice Bunts Attempts (SacA), Runners Moving with the Pitch (RM), Pitchouts ordered (PO).

Intentional Walks: Intentional Walks issued (#), Intentional Walks resulting in a Good Outcome (Good), Intentional Walks resulting Not in a Good Outcome (NG), Intentional Walks Blowing up on the Manager (Bomb).

A good result is 1) The next hitter grounds into a double play, or 2) The team in the field gets out of the inning without additional runs scoring. A "Bomb" means that *Multiple* runs score in the inning after the intentional walk. If the hitter after the IBB grounds into a double play, then we count that intentional walk as a success, even if multiple runs score after the IBB.

Results: Wins (W), Losses (L) and Winning Percentage (Pct.).

Manny Acta

Year	Team	Lg	G	LINEUPS		SUBSTITUTION			PITCHER USAGE						TACTICS				INTENTIONAL BB				RESULTS		
				LUp	PL%	PH	PR	DS	Quick	Slow	LO	RCD	LS	Rel	SBA	SacA	RM	PO	#	Good	NG	Bomb	W	L	Pct
2007	Nationals	NL	162	101	.65	295	32	78	53	28	5	183	1	588	92	86	70	28	44	28	16	8	73	89	.451
2008	Nationals	NL	161	133	.62	293	31	39	38	46	6	119	4	517	124	95	63	24	44	27	17	8	59	102	.366
2009	Nationals	NL	87	66	.62	145	11	20	14	25	1	91	1	282	54	43	62	5	26	13	13	6	26	61	.299
2010	Indians	AL	162	142	.63	79	20	39	44	49	18	81	6	470	124	41	142	20	36	17	19	10	69	93	.426
2011	Indians	AL	162	134	.71	76	44	43	47	49	20	107	0	483	131	40	144	29	34	20	14	10	80	82	.494
162-Game Average				127	.65	196	30	48	43	43	11	128	3	516	116	67	106	23	41	23	17	9	68	94	.420

Dusty Baker

Year	Team	Lg	G	LINEUPS		SUBSTITUTION			PITCHER USAGE						TACTICS				INTENTIONAL BB				RESULTS		
				LUp	PL%	PH	PR	DS	Quick	Slow	LO	RCD	LS	Rel	SBA	SacA	RM	PO	#	Good	NG	Bomb	W	L	Pct
1994	Giants	NL	115	76	.53	177	16	9	29	25	2	86	12	288	154	88		78	40	24	16	8	55	60	.478
1995	Giants	NL	144	96	.41	230	36	13	32	50	8	90	8	381	184	101		77	51	32	19	14	67	77	.465
1996	Giants	NL	162	129	.51	250	17	15	24	58	15	94	8	425	166	103		96	60	37	23	15	68	94	.420
1997	Giants	NL	162	114	.71	212	17	22	46	25	17	132	4	481	170	85		93	57	36	21	12	90	72	.556
1998	Giants	NL	163	130	.62	224	20	12	43	38	8	113	5	433	153	111		41	68	42	26	9	89	74	.546
1999	Giants	NL	162	120	.62	233	16	16	30	51	27	111		450	165	113		40	41	25	16	10	86	76	.531
2000	Giants	NL	162	82	.56	233	26	22	38	50	25	91	3	384	118	86		37	26	17	9	2	97	65	.599
2001	Giants	NL	162	122	.48	261	22	19	40	48	10	114	4	439	99	95		45	49	33	16	6	90	72	.556
2002	Giants	NL	162	118	.43	223	32	38	29	56	53	106	8	417	95	89	42	41	44	28	16	10	95	66	.590
2003	Cubs	NL	162	114	.49	272	25	43	24	58	65	111	3	420	104	93	31	24	36	23	13	4	88	74	.543
2004	Cubs	NL	162	113	.44	254	16	19	37	41	42	129	8	460	94	108	71	62	33	22	11	7	89	73	.549
2005	Cubs	NL	162	121	.59	240	21	29	40	46	36	103	2	457	104	88	107	70	48	27	21	7	79	83	.488
2006	Cubs	NL	162	133	.56	271	9	26	45	39	22	165	2	542	170	108	139	46	44	28	16	11	66	96	.407
2008	Reds	NL	162	119	.58	285	28	27	26	63	39	124	2	507	132	100	101	37	40	28	12	4	74	88	.457
2009	Reds	NL	162	130	.45	252	15	35	30	62	35	115	1	478	136	120	118	23	36	29	7	4	78	84	.481
2010	Reds	NL	162	120	.46	258	19	49	36	41	22	140	0	502	136	91	157	13	32	22	10	9	91	71	.562
2011	Reds	NL	162	142	.42	240	29	42	34	51	20	115	0	502	147	102	226	33	47	26	21	5	79	83	.488
162-Game Average				119	.52	248	22	26	35	48	27	117	4	456	140	101	110	52	45	29	16	8	83	79	.512

Bud Black

Year	Team	Lg	G	LINEUPS		SUBSTITUTION			PITCHER USAGE						TACTICS				INTENTIONAL BB				RESULTS		
				LUp	PL%	PH	PR	DS	Quick	Slow	LO	RCD	LS	Rel	SBA	SacA	RM	PO	#	Good	NG	Bomb	W	L	Pct
2007	Padres	NL	163	115	.62	279	18	13	63	28	13	122	0	485	79	85	73	56	48	28	20	11	89	74	.546
2008	Padres	NL	162	113	.63	286	25	20	55	36	17	109	0	491	53	75	78	31	61	30	31	17	63	99	.389
2009	Padres	NL	162	137	.64	264	8	34	50	37	8	118	5	527	111	99	84	55	58	42	16	6	75	87	.463
2010	Padres	NL	162	135	.61	285	16	45	55	33	10	132	7	499	174	99	135	31	51	35	16	8	90	72	.556
2011	Padres	NL	162	140	.58	288	20	43	40	36	10	110	2	490	214	69	184	41	56	31	25	13	71	91	.438
162-Game Average				128	.62	280	17	31	53	34	12	118	3	498	126	85	111	43	55	33	22	11	78	84	.481

Bruce Bochy

Year	Team	Lg	G	LINEUPS		SUBSTITUTION			PITCHER USAGE						TACTICS				INTENTIONAL BB				RESULTS		
				LUp	PL%	PH	PR	DS	Quick	Slow	LO	RCD	LS	Rel	SBA	SacA	RM	PO	#	Good	NG	Bomb	W	L	Pct
1995	Padres	NL	144	96	.59	262	30	23	44	41	17	38	3	337	170	68		38	37	19	18	11	70	74	.486
1996	Padres	NL	162	114	.52	289	29	15	51	33	10	67	12	411	164	73		65	47	29	18	12	91	71	.562
1997	Padres	NL	162	111	.60	291	26	9	45	45	3	81	11	426	200	84		58	37	20	17	11	76	86	.469
1998	Padres	NL	162	110	.65	280	62	44	44	45	9	81	12	369	116	84		27	45	31	14	10	98	64	.605
1999	Padres	NL	162	137	.60	298	51	21	44	36	4	68	5	403	241	60		29	48	29	19	13	74	88	.457
2000	Padres	NL	162	134	.52	285	44	14	41	47	14	105	5	443	184	52		27	50	21	29	11	76	86	.469
2001	Padres	NL	162	116	.60	255	54	27	32	47	6	85	10	422	173	43		23	54	31	23	13	79	83	.488
2002	Padres	NL	162	123	.66	259	44	56	39	43	17	106	4	459	115	63	74	14	61	38	23	14	66	96	.407
2003	Padres	NL	162	134	.58	339	20	29	34	43	16	100	3	473	115	63	41	6	52	33	19	12	64	98	.395
2004	Padres	NL	162	96	.54	261	28	47	47	32	15	76	3	437	77	75	96	14	39	24	15	10	87	75	.537
2005	Padres	NL	162	128	.58	285	31	49	46	36	23	87	1	456	143	89	111	16	45	33	12	8	82	80	.506
2006	Padres	NL	162	111	.60	264	64	48	43	42	24	111	2	475	154	77	110	21	63	43	20	10	88	74	.543
2007	Giants	NL	162	128	.72	264	50	45	26	50	36	132	2	496	152	86	119	10	41	29	12	3	71	91	.438
2008	Giants	NL	162	134	.68	276	32	39	24	59	42	97	6	478	154	77	155	5	59	40	19	8	72	90	.444
2009	Giants	NL	162	134	.65	231	21	52	42	40	32	84	8	457	106	93	118	5	49	32	17	4	88	74	.543
2010	Giants	NL	162	126	.55	224	45	70	29	37	40	118	12	477	87	102	144	12	58	41	17	8	92	70	.568
2011	Giants	NL	162	138	.62	245	49	42	38	38	44	108	3	480	136	79	175	11	46	36	10	6	86	76	.531
162-Game Average				123	.60	273	40	37	40	42	21	91	6	444	147	75	114	23	49	31	18	10	81	81	.500

Daren Brown

Year	Team	Lg	G	LINEUPS		SUBSTITUTION			PITCHER USAGE						TACTICS				INTENTIONAL BB				RESULTS		
				LUp	PL%	PH	PR	DS	Quick	Slow	LO	RCD	LS	Rel	SBA	SacA	RM	PO	#	Good	NG	Bomb	W	L	Pct
2010	Mariners	AL	50	39	.60	9	12	2	15	8	6	14	2	104	52	19	71	9	8	5	3	2	19	31	.380
162-Game Average				126	.60	29	39	6	49	26	19	45	6	337	168	62	230	29	26	16	10	6	62	100	.383

Dave Clark

Year	Team	Lg	G	LUp	PL%	PH	PR	DS	Quick	Slow	LO	RCD	LS	Rel	SBA	SacA	RM	PO	#	Good	NG	Bomb	W	L	Pct
2009	Astros	NL	13	9	.63	28	1	4	3	5	0	15	0	48	7	5	8	0	3	1	2	1	4	9	.308
162-Game Average				112	.63	349	12	50	37	62	0	187	0	598	87	62	100	0	37	12	25	12	50	112	.309

Terry Collins

Year	Team	Lg	G	LUp	PL%	PH	PR	DS	Quick	Slow	LO	RCD	LS	Rel	SBA	SacA	RM	PO	#	Good	NG	Bomb	W	L	Pct
1994	Astros	NL	115	74	.54	185	20	13	6	6	0	37	4	268	168	90		37	28	17	11	5	66	49	.574
1995	Astros	NL	144	106	.49	302	38	11	15	7	8	100	8	394	236	97		44	39	27	12	8	76	68	.528
1996	Astros	NL	162	111	.41	257	30	38	13	12	9	70	10	371	243	94		35	42	30	12	6	82	80	.506
1997	Angels	AL	162	117	.70	86	34	22	10	16	15	67	8	400	198	55		60	25	13	12	4	84	78	.519
1998	Angels	AL	162	119	.57	100	64	33	15	11	28	86	11	415	138	69		38	16	6	10	4	85	77	.525
1999	Angels	AL	133	113	.56	93	26	16	10	16	10	68	2	315	93	39		7	10	1	9	3	51	82	.383
2011	Mets	NL	162	121	.68	312	18	28	32	44	23	126	5	514	165	88	151	9	48	35	13	9	77	85	.475
162-Game Average				119	.57	208	36	25	16	17	14	86	7	417	193	83	151	36	32	20	12	6	81	81	.500

Cecil Cooper

Year	Team	Lg	G	LUp	PL%	PH	PR	DS	Quick	Slow	LO	RCD	LS	Rel	SBA	SacA	RM	PO	#	Good	NG	Bomb	W	L	Pct
2007	Astros	NL	31	26	.42	63	8	23	10	5	2	11	0	88	19	16	20	4	14	8	6	4	15	16	.484
2008	Astros	NL	161	115	.58	252	16	47	60	35	14	108	2	488	166	81	112	5	53	35	18	11	86	75	.534
2009	Astros	NL	149	94	.54	238	26	36	48	34	14	116	6	449	150	86	77	8	53	30	23	12	70	79	.470
162-Game Average				112	.55	263	24	50	56	35	14	112	4	487	159	87	99	8	57	35	22	13	81	81	.500

Don Cooper

Year	Team	Lg	G	LUp	PL%	PH	PR	DS	Quick	Slow	LO	RCD	LS	Rel	SBA	SacA	RM	PO	#	Good	NG	Bomb	W	L	Pct
2011	White Sox	AL	2	2	.39	0	1	0	1	0	0	2	1	6	1	1	1	0	1	0	1	1	1	1	.500
162-Game Average				162	.39	0	81	0	81	0	0	162	81	486	81	81	81	0	81	0	81	81	81	81	.500

Bobby Cox

Year	Team	Lg	G	LUp	PL%	PH	PR	DS	Quick	Slow	LO	RCD	LS	Rel	SBA	SacA	RM	PO	#	Good	NG	Bomb	W	L	Pct
1994	Braves	NL	114	64	.60	163	30	25	22	31	5	60	5	244	79	83		44	52	33	19	9	68	46	.596
1995	Braves	NL	144	59	.56	224	48	40	41	34	13	60	6	339	116	77		41	46	31	15	4	90	54	.625
1996	Braves	NL	162	89	.62	254	32	27	48	43	19	110	9	408	126	90		34	64	38	26	14	96	66	.593
1997	Braves	NL	162	87	.64	276	58	29	40	37	23	90	4	374	166	112		13	56	42	14	10	101	61	.623
1998	Braves	NL	162	80	.64	245	28	25	44	33	14	70	1	354	141	97		40	37	22	15	8	106	56	.654
1999	Braves	NL	162	76	.58	272	51	34	44	39	13	99	6	394	214	89		54	55	35	20	11	103	59	.636
2000	Braves	NL	162	103	.59	252	72	11	52	41	6	81	13	376	204	109		59	52	35	17	5	95	67	.586
2001	Braves	NL	162	113	.57	278	50	23	49	40	4	93	8	412	131	84		90	77	49	28	13	88	74	.543
2002	Braves	NL	161	105	.48	282	33	44	46	30	20	113	9	469	115	89	47	51	63	41	22	12	101	59	.631
2003	Braves	NL	162	69	.52	262	49	45	40	45	23	113	10	489	90	85	23	49	69	51	18	11	101	61	.623
2004	Braves	NL	162	105	.70	243	57	28	50	34	25	128	16	483	118	105	87	25	50	30	20	14	96	66	.593
2005	Braves	NL	162	110	.69	247	54	35	46	27	20	125	7	484	124	104	93	11	52	34	18	11	90	72	.556
2006	Braves	NL	162	85	.58	299	24	35	44	38	24	144	3	522	87	99	58	24	69	48	21	12	79	83	.488
2007	Braves	NL	162	86	.68	290	33	21	60	24	10	143	1	528	94	77	68	28	89	58	31	16	84	78	.519
2008	Braves	NL	162	117	.67	294	31	17	59	34	6	134	6	545	85	90	77	23	80	45	35	20	72	90	.444
2009	Braves	NL	162	112	.62	252	37	32	48	34	19	142	1	488	84	125	47	21	59	35	24	14	86	76	.531
2010	Braves	NL	162	109	.65	263	51	50	49	31	9	140	1	490	92	89	121	48	64	36	28	14	91	71	.562
162-Game Average				95	.61	265	45	31	48	36	15	112	6	446	125	97	69	40	62	40	22	12	93	69	.574

John Farrell

Year	Team	Lg	G	LUp	PL%	PH	PR	DS	Quick	Slow	LO	RCD	LS	Rel	SBA	SacA	RM	PO	#	Good	NG	Bomb	W	L	Pct
2011	Blue Jays	AL	162	131	.43	64	48	22	40	41	26	62	3	474	183	40	181	22	28	17	11	5	81	81	.500
162-Game Average				131	.43	64	48	22	40	41	26	62	3	474	183	40	181	22	28	17	11	5	81	81	.500

Terry Francona

Year	Team	Lg	G	LUp	PL%	PH	PR	DS	Quick	Slow	LO	RCD	LS	Rel	SBA	SacA	RM	PO	#	Good	NG	Bomb	W	L	Pct
1997	Phillies	NL	162	98	.66	288	19	28	28	54	22	102	9	409	148	91		30	42	23	19	9	68	94	.420
1998	Phillies	NL	162	84	.53	256	20	19	34	57	20	88	7	385	142	85		16	27	10	17	8	75	87	.463
1999	Phillies	NL	162	85	.51	239	13	31	29	41	16	111	7	441	160	81		27	24	14	10	6	77	85	.475

Year	Team	Lg	G	LINEUPS LUp	PL%	SUBSTITUTION PH	PR	DS	PITCHER USAGE Quick	Slow	LO	RCD	LS	Rel	TACTICS SBA	SacA	RM	PO	INTENTIONAL BB #	Good	NG	Bomb	RESULTS W	L	Pct
2000	Phillies	NL	162	108	.53	278	17	14	38	43	25	102	5	414	132	89		16	32	22	10	7	65	97	.401
2004	Red Sox	AL	162	141	.65	116	65	58	41	48	32	105	8	437	98	18	91	28	28	22	6	4	98	64	.605
2005	Red Sox	AL	162	104	.67	110	46	37	25	55	30	99	3	442	57	21	79	11	28	18	10	5	95	67	.586
2006	Red Sox	AL	162	116	.59	93	54	49	36	44	13	94	9	454	74	33	98	16	25	11	14	7	86	76	.531
2007	Red Sox	AL	162	109	.60	84	34	23	41	35	32	89	4	451	120	45	90	14	20	14	6	4	96	66	.593
2008	Red Sox	AL	162	131	.59	62	40	40	50	30	20	90	11	466	155	40	87	8	17	10	7	4	95	67	.586
2009	Red Sox	AL	162	113	.58	85	47	28	36	50	30	68	6	463	165	29	68	9	24	15	9	6	95	67	.586
2010	Red Sox	AL	162	143	.62	125	48	34	32	63	49	84	3	443	85	36	125	26	30	17	13	4	89	73	.549
2011	Red Sox	AL	162	123	.67	89	44	11	52	46	27	89	4	444	144	29	163	34	11	6	5	2	90	72	.556
	162-Game Average			113	.60	152	37	31	37	47	26	93	6	437	123	50	100	20	26	15	11	6	86	76	.531

Ron Gardenhire

Year	Team	Lg	G	LINEUPS LUp	PL%	SUBSTITUTION PH	PR	DS	PITCHER USAGE Quick	Slow	LO	RCD	LS	Rel	TACTICS SBA	SacA	RM	PO	INTENTIONAL BB #	Good	NG	Bomb	RESULTS W	L	Pct
2002	Twins	AL	161	111	.69	141	36	42	54	25	10	84	1	435	141	48	44	11	24	16	8	4	94	67	.584
2003	Twins	AL	162	126	.63	144	50	26	49	33	13	85	2	399	138	59	37	14	35	16	19	6	90	72	.556
2004	Twins	AL	162	131	.59	129	45	29	56	21	20	106	4	435	162	66	121	18	27	15	12	7	92	70	.568
2005	Twins	AL	162	135	.58	104	45	26	50	21	5	87	1	396	146	59	138	16	38	28	10	3	83	79	.512
2006	Twins	AL	162	97	.62	93	36	21	60	31	3	82	5	421	143	48	130	11	25	14	11	4	96	66	.593
2007	Twins	AL	162	139	.63	104	42	25	45	30	8	99	4	438	142	45	148	11	33	14	19	9	79	83	.488
2008	Twins	AL	163	103	.64	109	26	12	47	29	5	115	3	485	144	73	143	17	38	25	13	8	88	75	.540
2009	Twins	AL	163	129	.63	83	54	34	43	25	12	115	3	480	117	62	100	21	20	9	11	6	87	76	.534
2010	Twins	AL	162	112	.62	86	55	30	57	28	5	106	1	465	96	47	140	14	19	12	7	4	94	68	.580
2011	Twins	AL	162	150	.58	93	48	21	34	44	17	82	1	457	131	44	170	5	37	21	16	9	63	99	.389
	162-Game Average			123	.62	109	44	27	49	29	10	96	2	441	136	55	117	14	30	17	13	6	87	75	.537

Cito Gaston

Year	Team	Lg	G	LINEUPS LUp	PL%	SUBSTITUTION PH	PR	DS	PITCHER USAGE Quick	Slow	LO	RCD	LS	Rel	TACTICS SBA	SacA	RM	PO	INTENTIONAL BB #	Good	NG	Bomb	RESULTS W	L	Pct
1994	Blue Jays	AL	115	59	.55	41	16	21	7	14	2	23	5	221	105	44		48	23	15	8	6	55	60	.478
1995	Blue Jays	AL	144	82	.65	85	24	7	15	27	40	29	10	265	91	47		57	42	24	18	10	56	88	.389
1996	Blue Jays	AL	162	87	.70	126	23	11	12	27	23	41	4	303	154	63		34	37	23	14	9	74	88	.457
1997	Blue Jays	AL	157	90	.59	71	19	6	13	22	36	74	6	322	177	50		30	29	20	9	2	72	85	.459
2008	Blue Jays	AL	88	65	.59	36	18	30	18	19	25	40	0	216	37	41	37	11	16	8	8	6	51	37	.580
2009	Blue Jays	AL	162	105	.49	48	36	18	36	47	25	83	3	445	96	32	64	25	26	15	11	6	75	87	.463
2010	Blue Jays	AL	162	103	.45	40	40	13	51	33	12	77	4	455	78	22	88	23	35	19	16	6	85	77	.525
	162-Game Average			97	.57	73	29	17	25	31	27	60	5	364	121	49	74	37	34	20	14	7	77	85	.475

Bob Geren

Year	Team	Lg	G	LINEUPS LUp	PL%	SUBSTITUTION PH	PR	DS	PITCHER USAGE Quick	Slow	LO	RCD	LS	Rel	TACTICS SBA	SacA	RM	PO	INTENTIONAL BB #	Good	NG	Bomb	RESULTS W	L	Pct
2007	Athletics	AL	162	140	.57	64	31	24	39	43	14	112	9	446	72	31	91	22	60	38	22	10	76	86	.469
2008	Athletics	AL	161	133	.59	91	57	37	49	32	5	87	8	441	109	44	62	18	45	25	20	10	75	86	.466
2009	Athletics	AL	162	129	.59	77	27	40	54	40	5	108	11	488	181	37	71	5	30	15	15	7	75	87	.463
2010	Athletics	AL	162	126	.63	108	28	26	57	30	19	81	8	423	194	58	138	11	29	16	13	3	81	81	.500
2011	Athletics	AL	63	47	.62	42	9	3	25	11	7	50	2	177	57	18	54	9	15	7	8	4	27	36	.429
	162-Game Average			131	.60	87	35	30	51	36	11	100	9	451	140	43	95	15	41	23	18	8	76	86	.469

John Gibbons

Year	Team	Lg	G	LINEUPS LUp	PL%	SUBSTITUTION PH	PR	DS	PITCHER USAGE Quick	Slow	LO	RCD	LS	Rel	TACTICS SBA	SacA	RM	PO	INTENTIONAL BB #	Good	NG	Bomb	RESULTS W	L	Pct
2004	Blue Jays	AL	50	36	.68	42	3	2	16	8	7	22	1	130	34	2	47	21	11	5	6	3	20	30	.400
2005	Blue Jays	AL	162	124	.66	148	11	37	55	18	9	77	12	432	107	28	128	45	29	13	16	9	80	82	.494
2006	Blue Jays	AL	162	120	.53	112	32	40	59	33	17	94	16	482	98	20	127	40	56	32	24	12	87	75	.537
2007	Blue Jays	AL	162	131	.46	139	48	33	45	37	31	75	9	420	79	35	99	37	34	17	17	6	83	79	.512
2008	Blue Jays	AL	74	60	.48	53	15	18	12	20	12	43	0	205	70	23	39	10	26	16	10	6	35	39	.473
	162-Game Average			125	.56	131	29	35	50	31	20	83	10	443	103	29	117	41	41	22	19	10	81	81	.500

Kirk Gibson

Year	Team	Lg	G	LINEUPS LUp	PL%	SUBSTITUTION PH	PR	DS	PITCHER USAGE Quick	Slow	LO	RCD	LS	Rel	TACTICS SBA	SacA	RM	PO	INTENTIONAL BB #	Good	NG	Bomb	RESULTS W	L	Pct
2010	Diamondbacks	NL	83	57	.64	154	7	11	25	21	8	43	1	247	69	28	62	19	19	13	6	2	34	49	.410
2011	Diamondbacks	NL	162	118	.57	253	9	13	33	51	15	116	2	463	188	74	143	12	16	10	6	3	94	68	.580
	162-Game Average			116	.59	269	11	16	38	48	15	105	2	469	170	67	136	20	23	15	8	3	85	77	.525

Joe Girardi

Year	Team	Lg	G	LINEUPS		SUBSTITUTION			PITCHER USAGE						TACTICS				INTENTIONAL BB				RESULTS		
				LUp	PL%	PH	PR	DS	Quick	Slow	LO	RCD	LS	Rel	SBA	SacA	RM	PO	#	Good	NG	Bomb	W	L	Pct
2006	Marlins	NL	162	117	.50	250	44	**66**	46	40	28	76	3	438	168	97	108	42	58	37	21	7	78	84	.481
2008	Yankees	AL	162	114	.63	97	37	42	**60**	37	12	88	10	475	157	38	**173**	**36**	37	22	15	8	89	73	.549
2009	Yankees	AL	162	106	**.73**	97	61	42	36	45	27	88	**13**	461	139	44	83	33	28	14	14	9	**103**	59	.636
2010	Yankees	AL	162	114	**.72**	117	44	31	43	39	33	76	3	430	133	47	152	20	37	26	11	6	95	67	.586
2011	Yankees	AL	162	94	.69	72	41	53	51	36	21	88	2	465	193	50	151	26	43	30	13	4	**97**	65	.599
	162-Game Average			109	.65	127	45	47	47	39	24	83	6	454	158	55	133	31	41	26	15	7	92	70	.568

Fredi Gonzalez

Year	Team	Lg	G	LINEUPS		SUBSTITUTION			PITCHER USAGE						TACTICS				INTENTIONAL BB				RESULTS		
				LUp	PL%	PH	PR	DS	Quick	Slow	LO	RCD	LS	Rel	SBA	SacA	RM	PO	#	Good	NG	Bomb	W	L	Pct
2007	Marlins	NL	162	96	.50	284	29	34	33	**56**	20	138	5	560	139	91	79	22	60	36	24	**16**	71	91	.438
2008	Marlins	NL	161	106	.51	255	38	49	38	39	8	120	3	511	104	61	75	17	66	42	24	14	84	77	.522
2009	Marlins	NL	162	97	.58	281	28	49	48	26	12	116	0	**530**	110	86	88	20	60	38	22	15	87	75	.537
2010	Marlins	NL	70	31	.41	104	12	16	14	13	11	35	1	193	56	33	64	10	18	11	7	5	34	36	.486
2011	Braves	NL	162	120	.60	260	27	29	53	36	21	**144**	0	510	121	95	139	19	**73**	**49**	24	13	89	73	.549
	162-Game Average			102	.54	268	30	40	42	38	16	125	2	521	120	83	101	20	63	40	23	14	82	80	.506

Ozzie Guillen

Year	Team	Lg	G	LINEUPS		SUBSTITUTION			PITCHER USAGE						TACTICS				INTENTIONAL BB				RESULTS		
				LUp	PL%	PH	PR	DS	Quick	Slow	LO	RCD	LS	Rel	SBA	SacA	RM	PO	#	Good	NG	Bomb	W	L	Pct
2004	White Sox	AL	162	134	.58	**132**	35	15	28	**65**	48	86	8	399	129	**84**	97	17	36	15	**21**	6	83	79	.512
2005	White Sox	AL	162	112	.51	100	32	21	31	56	35	114	5	412	204	68	148	15	**42**	27	15	6	**99**	63	.611
2006	White Sox	AL	162	87	.60	**135**	42	38	28	68	35	83	7	398	141	61	85	27	**59**	**39**	20	9	90	72	.556
2007	White Sox	AL	162	124	.56	100	26	23	26	53	33	131	2	463	123	54	92	13	50	24	**26**	**15**	72	90	.444
2008	White Sox	AL	163	100	.52	75	49	37	42	48	14	100	3	463	101	44	98	8	42	29	13	6	89	74	.546
2009	White Sox	AL	162	124	.52	105	48	19	50	37	16	70	4	415	162	45	114	15	41	23	**18**	**10**	79	83	.488
2010	White Sox	AL	162	115	.51	85	46	36	41	51	24	61	**8**	407	**234**	60	220	25	41	26	15	**10**	88	74	.543
2011	White Sox	AL	160	111	.52	73	47	28	34	45	28	63	**8**	404	133	65	172	40	**49**	**35**	14	7	78	82	.488
	162-Game Average			113	.54	101	41	27	35	53	29	89	6	420	153	60	128	20	45	27	18	9	85	77	.525

Trey Hillman

Year	Team	Lg	G	LINEUPS		SUBSTITUTION			PITCHER USAGE						TACTICS				INTENTIONAL BB				RESULTS		
				LUp	PL%	PH	PR	DS	Quick	Slow	LO	RCD	LS	Rel	SBA	SacA	RM	PO	#	Good	NG	Bomb	W	L	Pct
2008	Royals	AL	162	134	.55	71	44	34	35	48	19	78	2	439	117	50	96	15	15	9	6	3	75	87	.463
2009	Royals	AL	162	141	.63	90	34	38	41	**54**	34	72	7	426	117	51	110	27	28	13	15	**10**	65	97	.401
2010	Royals	AL	35	24	.57	12	12	1	9	13	4	21	2	109	38	25	41	8	3	2	1	1	12	23	.343
	162-Game Average			135	.59	78	41	33	38	52	26	77	5	440	123	57	111	23	21	11	10	6	69	93	.426

A.J. Hinch

Year	Team	Lg	G	LINEUPS		SUBSTITUTION			PITCHER USAGE						TACTICS				INTENTIONAL BB				RESULTS		
				LUp	PL%	PH	PR	DS	Quick	Slow	LO	RCD	LS	Rel	SBA	SacA	RM	PO	#	Good	NG	Bomb	W	L	Pct
2009	Diamondbacks	NL	133	115	.63	222	10	13	24	50	24	61	5	392	113	64	41	5	24	12	12	6	58	75	.436
2010	Diamondbacks	NL	79	56	.53	120	7	4	12	40	21	39	1	207	58	19	51	7	19	9	10	9	31	48	.392
	162-Game Average			131	.59	261	13	13	28	69	34	76	5	458	131	63	70	9	33	16	17	11	68	94	.420

Clint Hurdle

Year	Team	Lg	G	LINEUPS		SUBSTITUTION			PITCHER USAGE						TACTICS				INTENTIONAL BB				RESULTS		
				LUp	PL%	PH	PR	DS	Quick	Slow	LO	RCD	LS	Rel	SBA	SacA	RM	PO	#	Good	NG	Bomb	W	L	Pct
2002	Rockies	NL	140	100	.52	274	28	41	33	45	17	104	3	437	139	46	50	13	38	22	16	11	67	73	.479
2003	Rockies	NL	162	108	.47	317	17	32	35	40	5	87	4	500	100	82	26	16	51	31	20	13	74	88	.457
2004	Rockies	NL	162	131	.57	289	18	35	36	**63**	20	74	1	473	77	**128**	67	12	**84**	**54**	**30**	12	68	94	.420
2005	Rockies	NL	162	135	.60	273	21	40	42	**60**	17	89	2	459	97	114	119	22	54	28	26	**15**	67	**95**	.414
2006	Rockies	NL	162	111	.49	259	17	22	34	**52**	17	107	2	499	135	**156**	114	28	81	45	**36**	**23**	76	86	.469
2007	Rockies	NL	163	96	.51	283	32	29	45	37	13	112	1	529	131	112	109	26	61	30	**31**	14	**90**	73	.552
2008	Rockies	NL	162	131	.49	253	20	31	40	43	16	85	2	485	**178**	111	116	**43**	49	31	18	6	74	88	.457
2009	Rockies	NL	46	42	.60	73	8	10	11	14	3	31	0	135	45	26	34	3	11	8	3	1	18	28	.391
2011	Pirates	NL	162	134	.60	278	26	63	**58**	27	1	134	3	**549**	160	101	173	20	65	39	**26**	13	72	90	.444
	162-Game Average			121	.53	282	23	37	41	47	13	101	2	499	130	107	99	22	61	35	25	13	74	88	.457

Brandon Hyde

Year	Team	Lg	G	LUp	PL%	PH	PR	DS	Quick	Slow	LO	RCD	LS	Rel	SBA	SacA	RM	PO	#	Good	NG	Bomb	W	L	Pct
2011	Marlins	NL	1	1	.44	0	0	0	0	0	1	1	0	3	0	0	1	0	1	1	0	0	0	1	.000
	162-Game Average			162	.44	0	0	0	0	0	162	162	0	486	0	0	162	0	162	162	0	0	0	162	.000

Davey Johnson

Year	Team	Lg	G	LUp	PL%	PH	PR	DS	Quick	Slow	LO	RCD	LS	Rel	SBA	SacA	RM	PO	#	Good	NG	Bomb	W	L	Pct
1994	Reds	NL	115	79	.54	195	22	12	13	5	2	56	12	261	170	74		47	22	14	8	1	66	48	.579
1995	Reds	NL	144	106	.55	258	18	31	21	7	1	60	16	330	258	87		8	25	9	16	10	85	59	.590
1996	Orioles	AL	163	100	.69	85	33	38	15	28	13	67	9	378	116	46		13	27	5	22	11	88	74	.543
1997	Orioles	AL	162	109	.57	104	36	43	21	12	5	84	11	400	89	59		31	24	9	15	9	98	64	.605
1999	Dodgers	NL	162	108	.54	236	22	9	16	16	8	67	4	399	235	89		28	18	9	9	7	77	85	.475
2000	Dodgers	NL	162	89	.59	252	26	11	20	15	10	96	1	371	137	80	51	11	14	8	6	2	86	76	.531
2011	Nationals	NL	83	59	.45	143	20	23	40	13	1	51	1	271	58	51	85	6	19	10	9	6	40	43	.482
	162-Game Average			106	.57	209	29	27	24	16	7	63	10	395	174	80	265	24	24	10	14	8	88	74	.543

Tony LaRussa

Year	Team	Lg	G	LUp	PL%	PH	PR	DS	Quick	Slow	LO	RCD	LS	Rel	SBA	SacA	RM	PO	#	Good	NG	Bomb	W	L	Pct
1994	Athletics	AL	114	97	.62	89	28	14	43	21	5	60	4	308	130	31		32	30	20	10	4	51	63	.447
1995	Athletics	AL	144	120	.54	113	38	24	33	38	19	46	7	358	158	42		42	26	18	8	4	67	77	.465
1996	Cardinals	NL	162	120	.52	246	25	13	32	48	24	90	8	413	207	117		41	43	28	15	7	88	74	.543
1997	Cardinals	NL	162	146	.54	307	17	18	34	42	16	81	2	399	224	77		79	34	26	8	2	73	89	.451
1998	Cardinals	NL	162	146	.52	259	7	18	62	31	13	82	14	429	174	85		34	38	25	13	8	83	79	.512
1999	Cardinals	NL	161	138	.47	264	32	28	50	41	13	96	14	454	182	103		30	38	20	18	11	75	86	.466
2000	Cardinals	NL	162	137	.53	240	35	25	40	31	11	63	18	386	138	107		34	28	21	7	6	95	67	.586
2001	Cardinals	NL	162	117	.47	256	26	13	46	36	7	140	7	485	126	102		25	36	21	15	4	93	69	.574
2002	Cardinals	NL	162	117	.52	340	27	41	58	33	23	110	6	472	128	106	75	13	39	25	14	8	97	65	.599
2003	Cardinals	NL	162	126	.50	352	28	51	38	49	36	113	9	460	114	108	56	9	36	28	8	2	85	77	.525
2004	Cardinals	NL	162	119	.53	275	25	69	30	48	31	120	16	469	158	88	158	9	24	17	7	4	105	57	.648
2005	Cardinals	NL	162	138	.55	270	25	48	40	38	22	88	4	436	119	92	153	9	27	16	11	7	100	62	.617
2006	Cardinals	NL	161	131	.56	272	11	53	50	34	21	95	6	469	91	86	123	13	35	21	14	3	83	78	.516
2007	Cardinals	NL	162	150	.60	317	19	37	46	44	8	102	5	516	89	85	120	23	25	10	15	11	78	84	.481
2008	Cardinals	NL	162	153	.64	275	26	57	52	40	16	101	11	506	105	87	114	18	21	13	8	1	86	76	.531
2009	Cardinals	NL	162	131	.52	289	12	51	55	38	17	92	8	481	106	93	91	17	23	15	8	1	91	71	.562
2010	Cardinals	NL	162	147	.55	292	16	28	52	40	16	80	5	455	120	87	151	22	32	17	15	8	86	76	.531
2011	Cardinals	NL	162	127	.57	262	36	86	47	44	20	94	8	468	96	101	179	17	44	23	21	14	90	72	.556
	162-Game Average			134	.54	268	25	38	46	40	18	95	9	453	140	91	122	27	33	21	12	6	87	75	.537

Jim Leyland

Year	Team	Lg	G	LUp	PL%	PH	PR	DS	Quick	Slow	LO	RCD	LS	Rel	SBA	SacA	RM	PO	#	Good	NG	Bomb	W	L	Pct
1994	Pirates	NL	114	94	.56	170	16	13	12	9	1	48	4	285	78	48		38	52	29	23	15	53	61	.465
1995	Pirates	NL	144	124	.56	282	8	4	13	12	11	71	4	391	139	69		51	50	30	20	10	58	86	.403
1996	Pirates	NL	162	117	.53	299	18	14	27	8	11	60	11	422	175	101		46	50	23	27	13	73	89	.451
1997	Marlins	NL	162	105	.59	258	36	31	21	12	18	65	2	404	173	91		38	41	25	16	9	92	70	.568
1998	Marlins	NL	162	96	.59	277	13	15	18	24	31	73	8	420	172	91		31	61	36	25	11	54	108	.333
1999	Rockies	NL	162	124	.56	294	11	12	11	29	21	72	5	421	113	88		11	46	24	22	14	72	90	.444
2006	Tigers	AL	162	120	.53	81	34	38	52	32	16	52	3	390	100	57	128	9	35	23	12	9	95	67	.586
2007	Tigers	AL	162	108	.53	77	31	49	46	43	14	70	5	443	133	35	123	20	41	24	17	13	88	74	.543
2008	Tigers	AL	162	131	.51	66	25	50	29	47	20	72	7	440	94	40	114	10	63	37	26	13	74	88	.457
2009	Tigers	AL	163	126	.55	125	52	50	47	47	38	86	3	439	105	60	132	19	42	26	16	6	86	77	.528
2010	Tigers	AL	162	129	.58	130	11	47	36	54	45	70	6	416	99	54	174	31	29	14	15	9	81	81	.500
2011	Tigers	AL	162	127	.63	86	42	87	43	39	39	84	1	421	69	62	172	7	34	17	17	10	95	67	.586
	162-Game Average			121	.56	185	26	35	31	31	23	71	5	422	125	69	140	27	47	27	20	11	79	83	.488

Ken Macha

Year	Team	Lg	G	LUp	PL%	PH	PR	DS	Quick	Slow	LO	RCD	LS	Rel	SBA	SacA	RM	PO	#	Good	NG	Bomb	W	L	Pct
2003	Athletics	AL	162	111	.57	140	29	23	44	38	30	72	12	364	62	31	28	9	42	25	17	10	96	66	.593
2004	Athletics	AL	162	119	.60	123	13	14	37	47	39	94	5	414	69	30	63	2	49	31	18	9	91	71	.562
2005	Athletics	AL	162	127	.62	83	17	11	43	36	30	79	13	410	53	29	53	13	42	27	15	6	88	74	.543
2006	Athletics	AL	162	121	.58	62	33	23	39	47	28	104	8	444	81	29	70	22	47	26	11	11	93	69	.574
2009	Brewers	NL	162	111	.48	267	7	32	35	51	19	120	1	512	105	70	90	12	60	35	25	17	80	82	.494
2010	Brewers	NL	162	95	.47	226	14	22	42	55	27	102	9	495	107	52	138	5	42	27	15	11	77	85	.475
	162-Game Average			114	.55	150	19	21	40	46	29	95	8	440	80	40	74	11	47	29	19	11	88	74	.543

Joe Maddon

Year	Team	Lg	G	LINEUPS		SUBSTITUTION			PITCHER USAGE						TACTICS				INTENTIONAL BB				RESULTS		
				LUp	PL%	PH	PR	DS	Quick	Slow	LO	RCD	LS	Rel	SBA	SacA	RM	PO	#	Good	NG	Bomb	W	L	Pct
1996	Angels	AL	22	19	.64	21	5	0	7	6	6	10	3	48	11	20		6	4	3	1	1	8	14	.364
1998	Angels	AL	8	4	.57	2	4	0	1	5	3	5	3	12	2	7		0	1	0	1	0	6	2	.750
1999	Angels	AL	29	19	.58	29	4	1	6	0	4	20	0	85	23	12		7	3	1	2	1	19	10	.655
2006	Devil Rays	AL	162	145	.54	81	26	51	41	39	16	79	10	444	186	51	132	48	39	19	20	13	61	101	.377
2007	Devil Rays	AL	162	122	.53	80	19	16	31	56	19	113	1	483	179	40	118	50	31	18	13	4	66	96	.407
2008	Rays	AL	162	115	.69	133	16	39	48	37	14	112	7	448	192	31	113	26	29	15	14	8	97	65	.599
2009	Rays	AL	162	123	.66	140	21	18	28	51	23	139	3	510	255	29	99	15	22	10	12	7	84	78	.519
2010	Rays	AL	162	129	.67	174	31	18	41	34	26	135	2	491	219	45	166	12	34	28	6	3	96	66	.593
2011	Rays	AL	162	130	.67	137	16	31	34	36	47	112	6	438	217	42	187	4	38	23	15	6	91	71	.562
	162-Game Average			127	.63	125	22	27	37	41	25	114	5	465	202	44	136	26	32	18	13	7	83	79	.512

Charlie Manuel

Year	Team	Lg	G	LINEUPS		SUBSTITUTION			PITCHER USAGE						TACTICS				INTENTIONAL BB				RESULTS		
				LUp	PL%	PH	PR	DS	Quick	Slow	LO	RCD	LS	Rel	SBA	SacA	RM	PO	#	Good	NG	Bomb	W	L	Pct
2000	Indians	AL	162	102	.64	73	40	26	21	12	20	104	7	462	147	59		30	45	28	17	9	90	72	.556
2001	Indians	AL	162	114	.61	105	30	49	28	17	10	120	3	484	120	67		43	44	30	14	11	91	71	.562
2002	Indians	AL	86	67	.61	57	10	19	14	17	25	47	0	222	57	21	34	3	21	12	9	4	39	47	.453
2005	Phillies	NL	162	80	.64	265	36	19	42	28	13	119	6	442	143	86	76	11	51	35	16	9	88	74	.543
2006	Phillies	NL	162	81	.65	301	42	49	28	43	22	126	2	500	117	79	74	16	63	35	28	12	85	77	.525
2007	Phillies	NL	162	87	.64	264	56	75	40	40	19	128	6	498	157	84	90	30	62	41	21	16	89	73	.549
2008	Phillies	NL	162	77	.65	291	62	60	33	42	24	124	1	468	161	88	92	34	64	46	18	11	92	70	.568
2009	Phillies	NL	162	68	.67	283	20	16	32	55	32	107	3	459	147	74	65	3	31	19	12	3	93	69	.574
2010	Phillies	NL	162	94	.64	276	17	19	37	50	39	114	1	451	129	64	120	3	42	27	15	6	97	65	.599
2011	Phillies	NL	162	105	.69	264	26	22	49	39	48	74	1	395	120	80	141	5	41	31	10	5	102	60	.630
	162-Game Average			92	.65	229	36	37	34	36	26	112	3	460	136	74	92	19	49	32	17	9	91	71	.562

Jerry Manuel

Year	Team	Lg	G	LINEUPS		SUBSTITUTION			PITCHER USAGE						TACTICS				INTENTIONAL BB				RESULTS		
				LUp	PL%	PH	PR	DS	Quick	Slow	LO	RCD	LS	Rel	SBA	SacA	RM	PO	#	Good	NG	Bomb	W	L	Pct
1998	White Sox	AL	162	110	.56	65	19	31	43	35	6	72	14	405	173	54		26	20	14	6	4	80	82	.494
1999	White Sox	AL	161	109	.58	79	35	39	35	42	9	78	8	409	160	69		22	31	20	11	7	75	86	.466
2000	White Sox	AL	162	84	.53	84	35	20	41	31	8	91	18	466	161	75		32	27	16	11	10	95	67	.586
2001	White Sox	AL	162	115	.53	104	34	50	45	39	5	93	16	406	182	95		41	38	24	14	9	83	79	.512
2002	White Sox	AL	162	104	.55	86	10	39	50	44	17	86	10	423	106	73	38	18	31	17	14	11	81	81	.500
2003	White Sox	AL	162	105	.55	146	40	71	39	36	27	74	10	361	106	66	39	20	30	18	12	7	86	76	.531
2008	Mets	NL	93	58	.76	167	7	31	12	30	23	95	2	324	89	54	81	6	37	18	19	6	55	38	.591
2009	Mets	NL	162	117	.72	289	11	37	34	51	22	137	2	511	166	112	104	3	60	38	22	14	70	92	.432
2010	Mets	NL	162	124	.67	290	19	25	39	47	32	145	6	491	174	100	169	9	55	42	13	6	79	83	.488
	162-Game Average			108	.60	153	25	40	39	41	17	102	10	443	154	81	94	21	38	24	14	9	82	80	.506

Don Mattingly

Year	Team	Lg	G	LINEUPS		SUBSTITUTION			PITCHER USAGE						TACTICS				INTENTIONAL BB				RESULTS		
				LUp	PL%	PH	PR	DS	Quick	Slow	LO	RCD	LS	Rel	SBA	SacA	RM	PO	#	Good	NG	Bomb	W	L	Pct
2011	Dodgers	NL	161	140	.57	233	29	44	45	40	30	86	1	461	166	93	181	13	48	27	21	12	82	79	.509
	162-Game Average			141	.57	234	29	44	45	40	30	87	1	464	167	94	182	13	48	27	21	12	83	79	.512

Jack McKeon

Year	Team	Lg	G	LINEUPS		SUBSTITUTION			PITCHER USAGE						TACTICS				INTENTIONAL BB				RESULTS		
				LUp	PL%	PH	PR	DS	Quick	Slow	LO	RCD	LS	Rel	SBA	SacA	RM	PO	#	Good	NG	Bomb	W	L	Pct
1997	Reds	NL	63	50	.46	102	18	7	23	11	5	44	3	154	79	42		18	16	6	10	7	33	30	.524
1998	Reds	NL	162	132	.55	288	30	25	49	25	10	107	20	366	137	98		7	42	29	13	8	77	85	.475
1999	Reds	NL	163	95	.50	251	30	38	58	23	9	93	28	381	218	88		14	46	30	16	5	96	67	.589
2000	Reds	NL	163	117	.51	270	31	41	52	27	10	96	24	387	137	82		24	53	36	17	10	85	77	.525
2003	Marlins	NL	124	57	.43	171	26	21	32	35	33	63	6	280	150	92	41	17	28	16	12	10	75	49	.605
2004	Marlins	NL	162	90	.48	224	27	34	42	37	20	95	12	404	139	104	96	19	61	40	21	13	83	79	.512
2005	Marlins	NL	162	82	.43	246	24	36	44	35	36	103	7	449	134	106	106	16	57	37	20	10	83	79	.512
2011	Marlins	NL	90	65	.53	146	22	16	29	15	13	63	0	278	87	74	67	10	43	25	18	10	40	50	.444
	162-Game Average			102	.49	253	31	32	49	31	20	99	15	402	161	102	93	19	52	33	19	11	85	77	.525

John McLaren

Year	Team	Lg	G	LINEUPS		SUBSTITUTION			PITCHER USAGE						TACTICS				INTENTIONAL BB				RESULTS		
				LUp	PL%	PH	PR	DS	Quick	Slow	LO	RCD	LS	Rel	SBA	SacA	RM	PO	#	Good	NG	Bomb	W	L	Pct
2007	Mariners	AL	84	52	.48	55	40	18	17	23	19	49	6	247	56	20	76	18	19	10	9	5	43	41	.512

Year	Team	Lg	G	LUp	PL%	PH	PR	DS	Quick	Slow	LO	RCD	LS	Rel	SBA	SacA	RM	PO	#	Good	NG	Bomb	W	L	Pct
2008	Mariners	AL	72	48	.50	31	16	4	17	24	9	45	1	197	65	17	63	11	12	6	6	5	25	47	.347
2011	Nationals	NL	3	3	.56	2	0	1	1	0	2	3	0	12	6	2	8	1	2	1	1	0	2	1	.667
	162-Game Average			105	.49	90	57	23	36	48	31	99	7	465	129	40	150	31	34	17	16	10	71	91	.438

Bob Melvin

Year	Team	Lg	G	LUp	PL%	PH	PR	DS	Quick	Slow	LO	RCD	LS	Rel	SBA	SacA	RM	PO	#	Good	NG	Bomb	W	L	Pct
2003	Mariners	AL	162	111	.62	81	62	33	27	46	43	56	6	366	145	44	37	5	24	14	10	4	93	69	.574
2004	Mariners	AL	162	151	.59	109	66	26	26	63	43	82	5	414	152	56	123	24	32	18	14	8	63	99	.389
2005	Diamondbacks	NL	162	120	.68	310	26	38	26	56	36	123	11	458	93	93	101	30	43	27	16	9	77	85	.475
2006	Diamondbacks	NL	162	114	.72	278	11	35	37	42	15	86	0	461	106	83	61	30	44	28	16	8	76	86	.469
2007	Diamondbacks	NL	162	146	.57	243	11	61	35	42	31	96	2	469	133	74	70	25	38	30	8	4	90	72	.556
2008	Diamondbacks	NL	162	134	.57	263	27	30	41	39	16	102	0	444	81	87	79	28	41	27	14	9	82	80	.506
2009	Diamondbacks	NL	29	29	.62	47	6	8	7	4	3	17	0	91	29	17	13	3	3	1	2	2	12	17	.414
2011	Athletics	AL	99	87	.71	33	13	17	24	23	18	59	2	283	103	34	87	23	9	5	4	3	47	52	.475
	162-Game Average			131	.63	201	33	37	33	46	30	91	4	440	124	72	84	25	34	22	12	7	80	82	.494

Brad Mills

Year	Team	Lg	G	LUp	PL%	PH	PR	DS	Quick	Slow	LO	RCD	LS	Rel	SBA	SacA	RM	PO	#	Good	NG	Bomb	W	L	Pct
2010	Astros	NL	162	128	.50	280	17	51	29	52	41	121	1	507	136	90	122	8	39	30	9	5	76	86	.469
2011	Astros	NL	162	121	.49	284	31	31	25	65	38	125	2	503	151	95	135	11	59	38	21	9	56	106	.346
	162-Game Average			125	.50	282	24	41	27	59	40	123	2	505	144	93	129	10	49	34	15	7	66	96	.407

Lou Piniella

Year	Team	Lg	G	LUp	PL%	PH	PR	DS	Quick	Slow	LO	RCD	LS	Rel	SBA	SacA	RM	PO	#	Good	NG	Bomb	W	L	Pct
1994	Mariners	AL	112	98	.49	113	24	6	30	35	4	54	9	252	69	54		37	39	21	18	9	49	63	.438
1995	Mariners	AL	145	98	.56	137	41	22	37	39	30	58	20	324	151	66		40	37	18	19	12	79	66	.545
1996	Mariners	AL	161	99	.55	190	28	14	56	21	15	91	14	403	129	65		40	52	31	21	13	85	76	.528
1997	Mariners	AL	162	84	.57	147	35	27	38	47	25	79	11	392	129	61		32	36	18	18	10	90	72	.556
1998	Mariners	AL	161	111	.53	99	38	43	38	54	32	81	4	368	154	58		20	23	8	15	7	76	85	.472
1999	Mariners	AL	162	130	.46	122	38	30	31	40	21	51	10	346	175	49		31	39	15	24	8	79	83	.488
2000	Mariners	AL	162	130	.50	109	43	52	51	37	1	64	11	383	178	73		22	37	20	17	8	91	71	.562
2001	Mariners	AL	162	115	.64	121	44	64	55	33	5	62	9	392	216	62		35	28	19	9	3	116	46	.716
2002	Mariners	AL	162	129	.64	95	129	50	49	39	34	52	7	343	195	61	43	26	34	15	19	11	93	69	.574
2003	Devil Rays	AL	162	124	.60	188	43	26	38	41	29	59	5	372	184	53	52	23	37	21	16	10	63	99	.389
2004	Devil Rays	AL	161	137	.63	97	25	36	51	34	23	57	15	401	174	45	104	16	35	16	19	9	70	91	.435
2005	Devil Rays	AL	162	135	.64	127	18	52	38	54	32	67	10	401	200	53	128	16	41	19	22	13	67	95	.414
2007	Cubs	NL	162	125	.51	263	52	51	35	38	33	98	3	478	119	60	89	17	46	28	18	4	85	77	.525
2008	Cubs	NL	161	112	.47	286	22	31	42	37	27	111	3	478	121	93	98	15	45	28	17	9	97	64	.602
2009	Cubs	NL	161	131	.57	277	14	55	47	40	20	127	3	480	90	81	92	23	46	21	25	13	83	78	.516
2010	Cubs	NL	125	101	.53	192	10	37	31	41	32	93	6	371	68	65	103	16	33	17	16	9	51	74	.408
	162-Game Average			121	.55	167	39	39	44	41	24	79	8	403	153	65	91	26	40	21	19	10	83	79	.512

Mike Quade

Year	Team	Lg	G	LUp	PL%	PH	PR	DS	Quick	Slow	LO	RCD	LS	Rel	SBA	SacA	RM	PO	#	Good	NG	Bomb	W	L	Pct
2010	Cubs	NL	37	32	.52	44	1	15	10	11	6	20	3	111	18	14	16	4	9	8	1	0	24	13	.649
2011	Cubs	NL	162	125	.50	259	30	66	30	56	35	125	4	495	92	78	113	23	45	32	13	9	71	91	.438
	162-Game Average			128	.50	247	25	66	33	55	33	118	6	493	90	75	105	22	44	33	11	7	77	85	.475

Willie Randolph

Year	Team	Lg	G	LUp	PL%	PH	PR	DS	Quick	Slow	LO	RCD	LS	Rel	SBA	SacA	RM	PO	#	Good	NG	Bomb	W	L	Pct
2005	Mets	NL	162	105	.64	222	10	51	47	34	20	74	5	392	193	89	118	18	43	28	15	9	83	79	.512
2006	Mets	NL	162	101	.68	247	9	24	40	40	15	119	4	474	181	102	106	16	39	25	14	9	97	65	.599
2007	Mets	NL	162	102	.68	269	21	28	26	44	27	122	3	499	246	97	100	10	40	26	14	7	88	74	.543
2008	Mets	NL	69	46	.77	104	3	11	12	20	11	73	1	233	85	44	48	4	16	10	6	2	34	35	.493
	162-Game Average			103	.68	246	13	33	36	40	21	113	4	466	206	97	109	14	40	26	14	8	88	74	.543

Jim Riggleman

Year	Team	Lg	G	LUp	PL%	PH	PR	DS	Quick	Slow	LO	RCD	LS	Rel	SBA	SacA	RM	PO	#	Good	NG	Bomb	W	L	Pct
1994	Padres	NL	117	93	.63	184	28	19	11	5	3	53	10	273	116	80		52	62	34	28	11	47	70	.402
1995	Cubs	NL	144	92	.56	196	9	30	15	8	13	119	12	414	142	90		53	68	45	23	12	73	71	.507
1996	Cubs	NL	162	87	.54	326	34	21	17	11	7	114	11	439	158	79		65	55	33	22	10	76	86	.469
1997	Cubs	NL	162	127	.50	280	40	44	13	5	2	113	9	441	176	103		74	51	38	13	6	68	94	.420
1998	Cubs	NL	163	104	.60	273	26	35	16	14	20	133	6	449	109	89		26	48	22	26	15	90	73	.552
1999	Cubs	NL	162	122	.61	312	25	30	16	19	8	105	4	441	104	94		20	48	21	27	15	67	95	.414
2008	Mariners	AL	90	70	.60	75	30	22	21	25	19	50	4	272	57	27	88	10	25	17	8	3	36	54	.400
2009	Nationals	NL	75	60	.51	115	15	33	24	16	4	63	6	250	59	44	36	8	33	17	16	8	33	42	.440
2010	Nationals	NL	162	131	.58	271	33	67	50	32	9	101	5	494	151	101	158	13	57	37	20	10	69	93	.426
2011	Nationals	NL	75	61	.58	105	22	23	24	15	2	54	5	220	80	47	89	3	22	16	6	3	38	37	.507
	162-Game Average			117	.57	264	32	40	26	19	11	112	9	456	142	93	150	40	58	35	23	11	74	88	.457

Edwin Rodriguez

Year	Team	Lg	G	LUp	PL%	PH	PR	DS	Quick	Slow	LO	RCD	LS	Rel	SBA	SacA	RM	PO	#	Good	NG	Bomb	W	L	Pct
2010	Marlins	NL	92	60	.42	152	12	20	22	23	13	72	1	288	62	37	69	9	24	17	7	3	46	46	.500
2011	Marlins	NL	71	50	.51	114	10	10	14	17	14	49	0	227	49	47	62	5	28	19	9	4	32	39	.451
	162-Game Average			109	.46	264	22	30	36	40	27	120	1	512	110	83	130	14	52	36	16	7	78	84	.481

Ron Roenicke

Year	Team	Lg	G	LUp	PL%	PH	PR	DS	Quick	Slow	LO	RCD	LS	Rel	SBA	SacA	RM	PO	#	Good	NG	Bomb	W	L	Pct
2011	Brewers	NL	162	105	.45	260	31	36	36	43	31	92	1	434	125	104	141	14	16	9	7	4	96	66	.593
	162-Game Average			105	.45	260	31	36	36	43	31	92	1	434	125	104	141	14	16	9	7	4	96	66	.593

John Russell

Year	Team	Lg	G	LUp	PL%	PH	PR	DS	Quick	Slow	LO	RCD	LS	Rel	SBA	SacA	RM	PO	#	Good	NG	Bomb	W	L	Pct
2008	Pirates	NL	162	128	.51	290	17	13	29	47	15	111	0	497	76	92	54	19	31	21	10	4	67	95	.414
2009	Pirates	NL	161	121	.60	251	3	5	44	45	12	89	0	456	122	78	97	15	37	20	17	10	62	99	.385
2010	Pirates	NL	162	119	.60	275	13	10	48	44	8	122	0	517	123	81	124	32	40	26	14	4	57	105	.352
	162-Game Average			123	.57	273	11	9	40	45	12	108	0	491	107	84	92	22	36	22	14	6	62	100	.383

Juan Samuel

Year	Team	Lg	G	LUp	PL%	PH	PR	DS	Quick	Slow	LO	RCD	LS	Rel	SBA	SacA	RM	PO	#	Good	NG	Bomb	W	L	Pct
2010	Orioles	AL	51	39	.63	27	14	3	11	17	6	33	0	157	40	18	39	2	18	12	6	5	17	34	.333
	162-Game Average			124	.63	86	44	10	35	54	19	105	0	499	127	57	124	6	57	38	19	16	54	108	.333

Mike Scioscia

Year	Team	Lg	G	LUp	PL%	PH	PR	DS	Quick	Slow	LO	RCD	LS	Rel	SBA	SacA	RM	PO	#	Good	NG	Bomb	W	L	Pct
2000	Angels	AL	162	75	.62	110	41	4	56	42	6	95	9	441	145	63		40	44	28	16	7	82	80	.506
2001	Angels	AL	162	130	.62	118	30	8	29	41	5	81	9	384	168	66		50	47	22	25	12	75	87	.463
2002	Angels	AL	162	102	.64	162	57	26	36	33	34	88	8	400	168	62	52	30	24	15	9	5	99	63	.611
2003	Angels	AL	162	130	.64	134	54	40	50	48	11	60	4	375	190	64	79	25	38	26	12	3	77	85	.475
2004	Angels	AL	162	126	.57	94	32	44	37	40	22	61	11	343	189	70	229	33	27	18	9	3	92	70	.568
2005	Padres	AL	162	124	.65	92	37	37	47	37	24	88	9	379	218	58	160	43	24	15	9	4	95	67	.586
2006	Angels	AL	162	114	.63	103	45	38	38	49	21	99	9	380	205	37	166	22	27	18	9	6	89	73	.549
2007	Angels	AL	162	127	.66	103	26	19	39	40	14	94	4	396	194	41	166	44	22	12	10	5	94	68	.580
2008	Angels	AL	162	125	.63	74	30	36	37	48	21	87	1	383	177	39	151	31	32	22	10	6	100	62	.617
2009	Angels	AL	162	123	.69	80	26	37	47	47	33	91	1	434	211	55	137	40	35	22	13	6	97	65	.599
2010	Angels	AL	162	133	.59	96	31	23	41	52	48	76	0	410	156	58	223	28	33	17	16	8	80	82	.494
2011	Angels	AL	162	129	.64	88	14	24	31	37	55	57	1	386	187	69	212	46	34	25	9	5	86	76	.531
	162-Game Average			120	.63	105	35	28	41	43	25	81	6	393	184	57	158	36	32	20	12	6	89	73	.549

Buck Showalter

Year	Team	Lg	G	LUp	PL%	PH	PR	DS	Quick	Slow	LO	RCD	LS	Rel	SBA	SacA	RM	PO	#	Good	NG	Bomb	W	L	Pct
1994	Yankees	AL	113	79	.59	95	31	3	24	30	0	38	7	241	95	34		22	24	13	11	4	70	43	.619
1995	Yankees	AL	145	107	.68	124	30	20	29	42	37	57	6	302	80	27		29	21	14	7	1	79	65	.549
1998	Diamondbacks	NL	162	124	.62	252	17	15	34	40	7	43	6	368	111	68		13	32	16	16	9	65	97	.401
1999	Diamondbacks	NL	162	97	.63	220	20	17	37	48	25	74	3	382	176	75		15	48	29	19	8	100	62	.617

Year	Team	Lg	G	LUp	PL%	PH	PR	DS	Quick	Slow	LO	RCD	LS	Rel	SBA	SacA	RM	PO	#	Good	NG	Bomb	W	L	Pct
				LINEUPS		SUBSTITUTION			PITCHER USAGE						TACTICS				INTENTIONAL BB				RESULTS		
2000	Diamondbacks	NL	162	99	.60	250	32	11	46	26	18	74	12	390	141	89		10	53	28	25	16	85	77	.525
2003	Rangers	AL	162	133	.61	88	51	41	35	33	12	93	7	494	90	35	80	12	45	24	21	14	71	91	.438
2004	Rangers	AL	162	120	.64	86	15	24	53	30	12	82	10	468	105	30	88	5	29	19	10	3	89	73	.549
2005	Rangers	AL	162	98	.59	57	22	11	42	39	17	79	8	454	82	11	103	5	31	10	21	16	79	83	.488
2006	Rangers	AL	162	95	.57	39	34	22	41	27	10	85	4	489	77	30	72	8	18	11	7	5	80	82	.494
2010	Orioles	AL	57	42	.74	20	11	13	23	9	10	24	1	144	38	13	31	1	10	9	1	1	34	23	.596
2011	Orioles	AL	162	117	.53	60	39	27	43	40	14	61	2	478	106	32	133	6	42	31	11	5	69	93	.426
162-Game Average				112	.61	130	30	21	41	37	16	71	7	424	111	45	95	13	36	21	15	8	83	79	.512

Dale Sveum

Year	Team	Lg	G	LUp	PL%	PH	PR	DS	Quick	Slow	LO	RCD	LS	Rel	SBA	SacA	RM	PO	#	Good	NG	Bomb	W	L	Pct
				LINEUPS		SUBSTITUTION			PITCHER USAGE						TACTICS				INTENTIONAL BB				RESULTS		
2008	Brewers	NL	12	3	.48	32	2	1	7	2	1	12	0	46	5	13	6	1	2	1	1	0	7	5	.583
162-Game Average				41	.48	432	27	14	95	27	14	162	0	621	68	176	81	14	27	14	14	0	94	68	.580

Joe Torre

Year	Team	Lg	G	LUp	PL%	PH	PR	DS	Quick	Slow	LO	RCD	LS	Rel	SBA	SacA	RM	PO	#	Good	NG	Bomb	W	L	Pct
				LINEUPS		SUBSTITUTION			PITCHER USAGE						TACTICS				INTENTIONAL BB				RESULTS		
1994	Cardinals	NL	115	79	.68	192	9	0	36	29	6	106	4	330	122	57		33	28	18	10	6	53	61	.465
1995	Cardinals	NL	47	36	.51	99	6	4	17	11	1	41	2	146	42	26		14	16	10	6	2	20	27	.426
1996	Yankees	AL	162	131	.57	92	62	55	59	23	22	97	10	411	142	53		19	35	17	18	14	92	70	.568
1997	Yankees	AL	162	118	.61	75	70	23	35	41	19	84	14	368	157	54		14	41	23	18	10	96	66	.593
1998	Yankees	AL	162	96	.62	94	36	28	43	38	27	71	17	334	216	44		9	25	17	8	4	114	48	.704
1999	Yankees	AL	162	95	.63	114	63	10	29	51	26	80	12	359	161	31		12	27	17	10	8	98	64	.605
2000	Yankees	AL	161	112	.63	86	49	27	43	53	27	92	16	382	147	22		8	23	9	14	7	87	74	.540
2001	Yankees	AL	161	94	.56	76	33	14	37	45	10	77	17	362	214	41		21	29	20	9	6	95	65	.594
2002	Yankees	AL	161	108	.58	89	53	31	39	49	44	86	13	334	138	35	46	18	44	33	11	4	103	58	.640
2003	Yankees	AL	162	104	.65	118	48	18	26	51	52	75	10	367	131	39	69	33	36	21	15	8	101	61	.623
2004	Yankees	AL	162	116	.65	86	35	46	48	35	29	129	10	436	117	50	126	36	32	16	16	9	101	61	.623
2005	Yankees	AL	162	117	.64	94	65	47	44	45	28	92	7	418	111	40	123	50	25	11	14	9	95	67	.586
2006	Yankees	AL	162	120	.66	108	50	59	50	30	9	109	7	489	174	48	118	50	41	22	19	4	97	65	.599
2007	Yankees	AL	162	102	.68	99	34	22	51	29	10	113	13	522	163	51	152	41	33	17	16	7	94	68	.580
2008	Dodgers	NL	162	124	.53	277	43	66	61	30	17	94	8	461	169	75	133	38	58	46	12	5	84	78	.519
2009	Dodgers	NL	162	113	.59	263	22	22	62	23	18	125	8	526	164	107	163	17	68	45	23	12	95	67	.586
2010	Dodgers	NL	162	127	.55	255	18	47	42	37	30	92	5	475	142	108	192	8	75	53	22	11	80	82	.494
162-Game Average				112	.61	139	44	33	45	39	23	98	11	421	157	55	125	26	40	25	15	8	94	68	.580

Jim Tracy

Year	Team	Lg	G	LUp	PL%	PH	PR	DS	Quick	Slow	LO	RCD	LS	Rel	SBA	SacA	RM	PO	#	Good	NG	Bomb	W	L	Pct
				LINEUPS		SUBSTITUTION			PITCHER USAGE						TACTICS				INTENTIONAL BB				RESULTS		
2001	Dodgers	NL	162	111	.50	264	34	20	46	42	8	84	4	409	131	81		10	37	19	18	9	86	76	.531
2002	Dodgers	NL	162	102	.52	317	39	37	49	36	21	118	9	423	133	81	46	18	45	31	14	5	92	70	.568
2003	Dodgers	NL	162	103	.64	269	22	64	52	29	22	148	11	438	116	97	32	10	35	23	12	8	85	77	.525
2004	Dodgers	NL	162	94	.70	295	25	19	49	34	16	128	16	459	143	81	93	7	47	32	15	8	93	69	.574
2005	Dodgers	NL	162	129	.64	303	31	37	44	40	20	126	2	459	93	76	97	17	34	21	13	6	71	91	.438
2006	Pirates	NL	162	121	.43	264	22	22	37	43	12	156	3	505	91	80	75	12	62	39	23	15	67	95	.414
2007	Pirates	NL	162	124	.49	240	12	26	33	40	13	113	0	495	98	80	90	12	55	30	25	11	68	94	.420
2009	Rockies	NL	116	87	.63	186	25	28	28	27	27	83	3	349	116	73	82	9	40	28	12	7	74	42	.638
2010	Rockies	NL	162	135	.65	257	30	41	38	40	34	128	0	513	141	64	135	11	54	34	20	10	83	79	.512
2011	Rockies	NL	162	134	.62	252	21	30	35	47	21	129	1	517	160	94	231	18	47	27	20	11	73	89	.451
162-Game Average				117	.58	272	27	33	42	39	20	125	5	470	126	83	101	13	47	29	18	9	82	80	.506

Dave Trembley

Year	Team	Lg	G	LUp	PL%	PH	PR	DS	Quick	Slow	LO	RCD	LS	Rel	SBA	SacA	RM	PO	#	Good	NG	Bomb	W	L	Pct
				LINEUPS		SUBSTITUTION			PITCHER USAGE						TACTICS				INTENTIONAL BB				RESULTS		
2007	Orioles	AL	93	71	.60	63	29	16	21	25	16	47	3	279	124	32	83	32	29	15	14	8	40	53	.430
2008	Orioles	AL	161	119	.58	117	36	25	41	44	11	87	4	492	118	38	143	11	44	18	26	12	68	93	.422
2009	Orioles	AL	162	132	.68	99	26	21	43	39	11	66	4	484	113	20	86	6	45	28	17	9	64	98	.395
2010	Orioles	AL	54	50	.62	24	14	7	6	16	10	33	1	153	32	10	24	2	17	7	10	5	15	39	.278
162-Game Average				128	.62	104	36	24	38	43	17	80	4	485	133	34	116	18	47	23	23	12	64	98	.395

Don Wakamatsu

Year	Team	Lg	G	LUp	PL%	PH	PR	DS	Quick	Slow	LO	RCD	LS	Rel	SBA	SacA	RM	PO	#	Good	NG	Bomb	W	L	Pct
2009	Mariners	AL	162	138	.51	58	31	19	50	27	18	76	1	410	122	61	91	4	13	3	10	6	85	77	.525
2010	Mariners	AL	112	93	.61	49	21	12	37	21	20	39	2	254	129	40	124	17	25	11	14	7	42	70	.375
162-Game Average				137	.55	63	31	18	51	28	22	68	2	393	148	60	127	12	22	8	14	8	75	87	.463

Ron Washington

Year	Team	Lg	G	LUp	PL%	PH	PR	DS	Quick	Slow	LO	RCD	LS	Rel	SBA	SacA	RM	PO	#	Good	NG	Bomb	W	L	Pct
2007	Rangers	AL	162	139	.60	89	30	53	47	46	4	78	9	467	113	76	67	13	38	19	19	11	75	87	.463
2008	Rangers	AL	162	129	.64	118	16	14	31	53	11	85	3	458	106	53	74	20	44	19	25	20	79	83	.488
2009	Rangers	AL	162	123	.55	48	11	11	39	47	28	80	9	436	185	44	80	5	14	9	5	3	87	75	.537
2010	Rangers	AL	162	112	.52	86	39	31	46	42	35	110	4	481	188	68	132	9	24	15	9	0	90	72	.556
2011	Rangers	AL	162	106	.48	66	18	23	43	39	40	76	2	417	188	52	182	3	21	12	9	6	96	66	.593
162-Game Average				122	.56	81	23	26	41	45	24	86	5	452	153	59	113	10	28	15	13	8	85	77	.525

Eric Wedge

Year	Team	Lg	G	LUp	PL%	PH	PR	DS	Quick	Slow	LO	RCD	LS	Rel	SBA	SacA	RM	PO	#	Good	NG	Bomb	W	L	Pct
2003	Indians	AL	162	145	.67	117	43	27	47	34	18	89	5	428	147	67	54	12	37	22	15	8	68	94	.420
2004	Indians	AL	162	114	.72	91	34	20	44	38	22	121	0	479	149	57	129	28	47	26	21	18	80	82	.494
2005	Indians	AL	162	111	.66	88	18	16	45	45	15	90	3	409	98	53	79	9	20	11	9	7	93	69	.574
2006	Indians	AL	162	111	.59	98	13	13	31	52	27	48	1	377	78	40	83	15	35	21	14	11	78	84	.481
2007	Indians	AL	162	117	.60	116	41	25	34	38	20	79	2	395	113	40	108	16	42	24	18	9	96	66	.593
2008	Indians	AL	162	136	.54	112	31	18	40	35	17	78	4	399	106	56	98	5	28	6	22	11	81	81	.500
2009	Indians	AL	162	148	.59	63	28	11	32	41	21	67	3	445	115	52	74	8	31	14	17	9	65	97	.401
2011	Mariners	AL	162	152	.68	52	30	22	39	45	30	50	1	351	165	43	161	7	27	20	7	6	67	95	.414
162-Game Average				129	.63	92	30	19	39	41	21	78	2	410	121	51	98	13	33	18	15	10	78	84	.481

Ned Yost

Year	Team	Lg	G	LUp	PL%	PH	PR	DS	Quick	Slow	LO	RCD	LS	Rel	SBA	SacA	RM	PO	#	Good	NG	Bomb	W	L	Pct
2003	Brewers	NL	162	97	.44	304	22	39	23	59	18	90	6	460	138	85	40	23	43	28	15	9	68	94	.420
2004	Brewers	NL	161	131	.60	283	25	20	39	41	27	63	2	423	178	79	108	8	27	16	11	8	67	94	.416
2005	Brewers	NL	162	99	.46	259	18	35	26	41	42	71	2	395	113	89	97	50	52	23	29	10	81	81	.500
2006	Brewers	NL	162	106	.48	238	12	14	33	44	18	77	4	427	108	80	82	16	34	14	20	12	75	87	.463
2007	Brewers	NL	162	109	.60	259	11	41	37	42	18	117	7	492	128	74	94	19	37	28	9	9	83	79	.512
2008	Brewers	NL	150	93	.48	217	5	16	37	39	23	69	5	399	141	61	105	31	30	17	13	7	83	67	.553
2010	Royals	AL	127	80	.57	56	25	6	22	39	20	65	0	332	127	40	128	18	25	16	9	5	55	72	.433
2011	Royals	AL	162	87	.58	36	28	16	42	42	21	56	7	420	211	65	203	19	42	27	15	5	71	91	.438
162-Game Average				104	.53	214	19	24	34	45	24	79	4	435	149	74	111	24	38	22	16	8	76	86	.469

Categories of this record are Games Managed (G), Number of Different Lineups Used (LUp), the percentage of players who had the platoon advantage at the start of the game (PL%), Pinch Hitters Used (PH), Pinch Runners Used (PR), Defensive Substitutes Used (DS), Quick Hooks (Quick), Slow Hooks (Slow), Long Outings by Starting Pitchers (LO), Relievers Used on Consecutive Days (RCD), Long Saves (LS), Relievers Used (Rel), Stolen Base Attempts (SBA), Sacrifice Bunts Attempts (SacA), Runners Moving with the Pitch (RM), Pitchouts ordered (PO), Intentional Walks issued (#), Intentional Walks resulting in a Good Outcome (Good), Intentional Walks resulting Not in a Good Outcome (NG), Intentional Walks Blowing up on the Manager (Bomb), Wins (W), Losses (L) and Winning Percentage (Pct.).

2011 American League Managers

Manager	G	LUp	PL%	PH	PR	DS	Quick	Slow	LO	RCD	LS	Rel	SBA	SacA	RM	PO	#	Good	NG	Bomb	W	L	Pct
Mike Scioscia, LAA	162	129	.64	88	14	24	31	37	**55**	57	1	386	187	**69**	**212**	46	34	25	9	5	86	76	.531
Buck Showalter, Bal	162	117	.53	60	39	27	43	40	14	61	2	478	106	32	133	6	42	31	11	5	69	93	.426
Terry Francona, Bos	162	123	.67	89	44	11	**52**	46	27	89	4	444	144	29	163	34	11	6	5	2	90	72	.556
Ozzie Guillen, CWS	160	111	.52	73	47	28	34	45	28	63	8	404	133	65	172	40	49	**35**	14	7	78	82	.488
Manny Acta, Cle	162	134	**.71**	76	44	43	47	**49**	20	107	0	**483**	131	40	144	29	34	20	14	**10**	80	82	.494
Jim Leyland, Det	162	127	.63	86	42	**87**	43	39	39	84	1	421	69	62	172	7	34	17	**17**	**10**	95	67	.586
Ned Yost, KC	162	87	.58	36	28	16	42	42	21	56	7	420	211	65	203	19	42	27	15	5	71	91	.438
Ron Gardenhire, Min	162	150	.58	93	**48**	21	34	44	17	82	1	457	131	44	170	5	37	21	16	9	63	**99**	.389
Joe Girardi, NYY	162	94	.69	72	41	53	51	36	21	88	2	465	193	50	151	26	43	30	13	4	**97**	65	.599
Eric Wedge, Sea	162	**152**	.68	52	30	22	39	45	30	50	1	351	165	43	161	7	27	20	7	6	67	95	.414
Joe Maddon, TB	162	130	.67	**137**	16	31	34	36	47	**112**	6	438	**217**	42	187	4	38	23	15	6	91	71	.562
Ron Washington, Tex	162	106	.48	66	18	23	43	39	40	76	2	417	188	52	182	3	21	12	9	6	96	66	.593
John Farrell, Tor	162	131	.43	64	**48**	22	40	41	26	62	3	474	183	40	181	22	28	17	11	5	81	81	.500
162-Game Average		126	.60	72	37	28	45	38	27	86	8	440	153	51	162	19	36	19	17	11	81	81	.500

Manager	G	LUp	PL%	PH	PR	DS	Quick	Slow	LO	RCD	LS	Rel	SBA	SacA	RM	PO	#	Good	NG	Bomb	W	L	Pct
Don Cooper, CWS	2	2	.39	0	1	0	1	0	0	2	1	6	1	1	1	0	1	0	1	1	1	1	.500
Bob Geren, Oak	63	47	.62	42	9	3	25	11	7	50	2	177	57	18	54	9	15	7	8	4	27	36	.429
Bob Melvin, Oak	99	87	.71	33	13	17	24	23	18	59	2	283	103	34	87	23	9	5	4	3	47	52	.475

2011 National League Managers

Manager	G	LUp	PL%	PH	PR	DS	Quick	Slow	LO	RCD	LS	Rel	SBA	SacA	RM	PO	#	Good	NG	Bomb	W	L	Pct
Kirk Gibson, Ari	162	118	.57	253	9	13	33	51	15	116	2	463	188	74	143	12	16	10	6	3	94	68	.580
Fredi Gonzalez, Atl	162	120	.60	260	27	29	53	36	21	**144**	0	510	121	95	139	19	**73**	**49**	24	13	89	73	.549
Mike Quade, ChC	162	125	.50	259	30	66	30	56	35	125	4	495	92	78	113	23	45	32	13	9	71	91	.438
Dusty Baker, Cin	162	**142**	.42	240	29	42	34	51	20	115	0	502	147	102	226	33	47	26	21	5	79	83	.488
Jim Tracy, Col	162	134	.62	252	21	30	35	47	21	129	1	517	160	94	**231**	18	47	27	20	11	73	89	.451
Brad Mills, Hou	162	121	.49	284	31	31	25	**65**	38	125	2	503	151	95	135	11	59	38	21	9	56	**106**	.346
Don Mattingly, LAD	161	140	.57	233	29	44	45	40	30	86	1	461	166	93	181	13	48	27	21	12	82	79	.509
Ron Roenicke, Mil	162	105	.45	260	31	36	36	43	31	92	1	434	125	**104**	141	14	16	9	7	4	96	66	.593
Terry Collins, NYM	162	121	.68	**312**	18	28	32	44	23	126	5	514	165	88	151	9	48	35	13	9	77	85	.475
Charlie Manuel, Phi	162	105	**.69**	264	26	22	49	39	**48**	74	1	395	120	80	141	5	41	31	10	5	**102**	60	.630
Clint Hurdle, Pit	162	134	.60	278	26	63	**58**	27	1	134	3	**549**	160	101	173	20	65	39	**26**	13	72	90	.444
Tony LaRussa, StL	162	127	.57	262	36	**86**	47	44	20	94	**8**	468	96	101	179	17	44	23	21	**14**	90	72	.556
Bud Black, SD	162	140	.58	288	20	43	40	36	10	110	2	490	**214**	69	184	**41**	56	31	25	13	71	91	.438
Bruce Bochy, SF	162	138	.62	245	**49**	42	38	38	44	108	3	480	136	79	175	11	46	36	10	6	86	76	.531
162-Game Average		129	.55	241	27	39	41	37	34	117	2	497	146	90	176	17	57	39	19	9	78	84	.481

Manager	G	LUp	PL%	PH	PR	DS	Quick	Slow	LO	RCD	LS	Rel	SBA	SacA	RM	PO	#	Good	NG	Bomb	W	L	Pct
Brandon Hyde, Fla	1	1	.44	0	0	0	0	0	1	1	0	3	0	0	1	0	1	1	0	0	0	1	.000
Edwin Rodriguez, Fla	71	50	.51	114	10	10	14	17	14	49	0	227	49	47	62	5	28	19	9	4	32	39	.451
Jack McKeon, Fla	90	65	.53	146	22	16	29	15	13	63	0	278	87	74	67	10	43	25	18	10	40	50	.444
Davey Johnson, Was	83	59	.45	143	20	23	40	13	1	51	1	271	58	51	85	6	19	10	9	6	40	43	.482
Jim Riggleman, Was	75	61	.58	105	22	23	24	15	2	54	5	220	80	47	89	3	22	16	6	3	38	37	.507
John McLaren, Was	3	3	.56	2	0	1	1	0	2	3	0	12	6	2	8	1	2	1	1	0	2	1	.667

2011 Park Indices

A Park Index tells you whether a given park is favorable to hitters or pitchers compared to other MLB parks. For example, Coors Field in Colorado has a park index for scoring runs of 132 over the last three years, meaning 32% more runs are scored there than other parks. U.S. Cellular Field in Chicago has a home run park index of 132 (just coincidentally the same index) making it the easiest home run park in baseball.

Park indices are calculated in a way that neutralizes the effect of a team's makeup and isolates the effects of the park. The isolation is figured by comparing what both the team and its opponents accomplished at home, and comparing that to what the same team and its opponents accomplished on the road.

To calculate the park index for home runs in a given ballpark, we take the total home runs of both the home team and its opponents at the ballpark and compare it to the total home runs of the home team and its opponents in other games. We then divide each of those totals by the at-bats in the equivalent situations, so that if there are more at-bats in either situation the index is not skewed. The result is then multiplied by 100 to yield the familiar form.

The park indices for doubles, triples, walks, strikeouts and home runs by lefties and righties are determined like home runs above—relative to at-bats. Indices of at-bats, runs, hits, errors and infield fielding errors (E-Infield) are calculated relative to games. The three batting average indices are calculated as is, since these are already relative to at-bats.

A park with an index of exactly 100 is neutral and can be said to have had no effect on that particular stat. An index above 100 means the ballpark favors that statistic. For example, if a park has a home run index of 120, it was 20% easier to hit home runs in that park then the rest of the parks in that team's league.

There were no new stadiums this year, but there was one oddity. Due to a scheduling conflict with a U2 concert, the Marlins played home games in Safeco Field in Seattle against the Mariners. As far as the park indices are concerned, those were home games for the Mariners.

Arizona Diamondbacks - Chase Field

	2011 Season							2009-2011						
	Home Games			Away Games				Home Games			Away Games			
	D'Backs	Opp	Total	D'Backs	Opp	Total	Index	D'Backs	Opp	Total	D'Backs	Opp	Total	Index
G	81	81	162	81	81	162		243	243	486	243	243	486	
Avg	.262	.257	.259	.239	.257	.248	105	.264	.263	.264	.238	.264	.251	105
AB	2672	2826	5498	2749	2672	5421	101	8102	8560	16662	8357	8070	16427	101
R	400	344	744	331	318	649	115	1170	1184	2354	994	1096	2090	113
H	699	727	1426	658	687	1345	106	2142	2255	4397	1989	2132	4121	107
2B	162	151	313	131	141	272	113	493	455	948	408	406	814	115
3B	23	17	40	14	15	29	136	77	62	139	39	44	83	165
HR	93	80	173	79	79	158	108	278	270	548	247	267	514	105
BB	269	199	468	262	243	505	91	876	691	1567	815	824	1639	94
SO	595	544	1139	654	514	1168	96	1936	1713	3649	2140	1573	3713	97
E	41	35	76	49	43	92	83	155	115	270	161	137	298	91
E-Infield	15	11	26	16	19	35	74	66	41	107	55	57	112	96
LHB-Avg	.248	.242	.245	.257	.260	.258	95	.273	.262	.267	.251	.261	.255	105
LHB-HR	32	29	61	34	28	62	98	99	118	217	107	105	212	104
RHB-Avg	.271	.268	.269	.226	.255	.241	112	.258	.264	.261	.227	.267	.247	106
RHB-HR	61	51	112	45	51	96	115	179	152	331	140	162	302	106

Atlanta Braves - Turner Field

	2011 Season							2009-2011						
	Home Games			Away Games				Home Games			Away Games			
	Braves	Opp	Total	Braves	Opp	Total	Index	Braves	Opp	Total	Braves	Opp	Total	Index
G	81	81	162	81	81	162		243	243	486	243	243	486	
Avg	.256	.230	.243	.231	.252	.241	101	.261	.237	.249	.249	.257	.253	98
AB	2724	2819	5543	2804	2722	5526	100	8088	8369	16457	8442	8075	16517	100
R	325	283	608	316	322	638	95	1048	896	1944	1066	979	2045	95
H	698	647	1345	647	685	1332	101	2112	1983	4095	2103	2074	4177	98
2B	127	107	234	117	121	238	98	412	372	784	444	413	857	92
3B	6	13	19	10	20	30	63	35	47	82	26	67	93	88
HR	90	55	145	83	70	153	94	233	170	403	228	200	428	95
BB	272	256	528	232	265	497	106	877	780	1657	863	776	1639	101
SO	623	732	1355	637	600	1237	109	1686	2055	3741	1778	1750	3528	106
E	48	56	104	35	43	78	133	162	154	316	143	140	283	112
E-Infield	19	29	48	19	25	44	109	82	77	159	59	67	126	126
LHB-Avg	.267	.244	.257	.248	.254	.251	102	.257	.246	.252	.257	.264	.260	97
LHB-HR	49	27	76	45	26	71	111	132	76	208	122	87	209	102
RHB-Avg	.244	.220	.230	.210	.250	.232	99	.265	.230	.246	.242	.251	.246	100
RHB-HR	41	28	69	38	44	82	81	101	94	195	106	113	219	88

Baltimore Orioles - Oriole Park at Camden Yards

	2011 Season							2009-2011						
	Home Games			Away Games				Home Games			Away Games			
	Orioles	Opp	Total	Orioles	Opp	Total	Index	Orioles	Opp	Total	Orioles	Opp	Total	Index
G	81	81	162	81	81	162		243	243	486	243	243	486	
Avg	.255	.272	.264	.259	.282	.270	98	.271	.277	.274	.253	.279	.266	103
AB	2746	2928	5674	2839	2736	5575	102	8282	8789	17071	8475	8143	16618	103
R	360	422	782	348	438	786	99	1093	1248	2341	969	1273	2242	104
H	699	797	1496	735	771	1506	99	2241	2437	4678	2141	2272	4413	106
2B	147	180	327	126	174	300	107	439	498	937	405	510	915	100
3B	6	11	17	7	16	23	73	25	38	63	28	49	77	80
HR	106	108	214	85	102	187	112	274	323	597	210	291	501	116
BB	228	276	504	224	259	483	103	701	788	1489	692	813	1505	96
SO	546	523	1069	574	521	1095	96	1519	1548	3067	1670	1436	3106	96
E	43	39	82	67	50	117	70	140	113	253	165	159	324	78
E-Infield	23	16	39	36	18	54	72	73	47	120	75	62	137	88
LHB-Avg	.249	.278	.267	.245	.258	.252	106	.277	.282	.279	.253	.277	.264	106
LHB-HR	23	53	76	19	42	61	123	116	155	271	86	125	211	122
RHB-Avg	.257	.267	.262	.266	.304	.283	93	.265	.273	.270	.253	.281	.267	101
RHB-HR	83	55	138	66	60	126	107	158	168	326	124	166	290	111

Boston Red Sox - Fenway Park

| | 2011 Season | | | | | | | 2009-2011 | | | | | | |
| | Home Games | | | Away Games | | | | Home Games | | | Away Games | | | |
	Red Sox	Opp	Total	Red Sox	Opp	Total	Index	Red Sox	Opp	Total	Red Sox	Opp	Total	Index
G	81	81	162	81	81	162		243	243	486	243	243	486	
Avg	.296	.262	.279	.265	.231	.248	112	.285	.260	.272	.261	.252	.256	106
AB	2837	2870	5707	2873	2659	5532	103	8249	8511	16760	8650	8159	16809	100
R	460	410	870	415	327	742	117	1360	1154	2514	1205	1063	2268	111
H	840	752	1592	760	614	1374	116	2351	2210	4561	2255	2052	4307	106
2B	199	163	362	153	123	276	127	586	516	1102	459	390	849	130
3B	22	9	31	13	14	27	111	43	32	75	39	43	82	92
HR	91	77	168	112	79	191	85	303	220	523	323	255	578	91
BB	276	276	552	302	264	566	95	894	805	1699	930	845	1775	96
SO	540	619	1159	568	594	1162	97	1637	1820	3457	1731	1830	3561	97
E	60	54	114	32	47	79	144	163	156	319	122	139	261	122
E-Infield	28	25	53	14	25	39	136	65	67	132	50	70	120	110
LHB-Avg	.296	.252	.277	.273	.228	.255	109	.277	.259	.268	.257	.260	.258	104
LHB-HR	53	25	78	79	31	110	68	137	83	220	160	115	275	81
RHB-Avg	.296	.270	.281	.252	.233	.241	117	.292	.261	.276	.264	.244	.254	109
RHB-HR	38	52	90	33	48	81	110	166	137	303	163	140	303	100

Chicago Cubs - Wrigley Field

| | 2011 Season | | | | | | | 2009-2011 | | | | | | |
| | Home Games | | | Away Games | | | | Home Games | | | Away Games | | | |
	Cubs	Opp	Total	Cubs	Opp	Total	Index	Cubs	Opp	Total	Cubs	Opp	Total	Index
G	81	81	162	81	81	162		242	242	484	243	243	486	
Avg	.257	.255	.256	.256	.269	.262	98	.262	.256	.259	.250	.253	.251	103
AB	2710	2813	5523	2839	2689	5528	100	8086	8421	16507	8461	8005	16466	101
R	324	357	681	330	399	729	93	1064	1132	2196	982	1063	2045	108
H	697	717	1414	726	722	1448	98	2121	2152	4273	2114	2025	4139	104
2B	132	133	265	153	156	309	86	438	386	824	438	399	837	98
3B	22	15	37	14	14	28	132	50	50	100	42	45	87	115
HR	73	81	154	75	81	156	99	229	246	475	229	230	459	103
BB	224	290	514	201	290	491	105	762	896	1658	734	875	1609	103
SO	590	668	1258	612	556	1168	108	1700	1978	3678	1923	1786	3709	99
E	68	60	128	66	48	114	112	191	161	352	174	146	320	110
E-Infield	25	33	58	25	23	48	121	81	78	159	68	62	130	123
LHB-Avg	.234	.261	.250	.232	.268	.253	99	.241	.260	.252	.229	.256	.243	103
LHB-HR	24	25	49	24	28	52	101	66	87	153	70	78	148	111
RHB-Avg	.266	.251	.259	.265	.269	.267	97	.272	.253	.263	.261	.251	.256	103
RHB-HR	49	56	105	51	53	104	97	163	159	322	159	152	311	99

Chicago White Sox - U.S. Cellular Field

| | 2011 Season | | | | | | | 2009-2011 | | | | | | |
| | Home Games | | | Away Games | | | | Home Games | | | Away Games | | | |
	White Sox	Opp	Total	White Sox	Opp	Total	Index	White Sox	Opp	Total	White Sox	Opp	Total	Index
G	81	81	162	81	81	162		243	243	486	243	243	486	
Avg	.252	.254	.253	.252	.268	.260	97	.259	.258	.258	.260	.265	.262	98
AB	2681	2839	5520	2821	2774	5595	99	7997	8485	16482	8452	8222	16674	99
R	314	363	677	340	343	683	99	1084	1117	2201	1046	1025	2071	106
H	675	720	1395	712	743	1455	96	2068	2192	4260	2196	2180	4376	97
2B	116	126	242	136	139	275	89	354	435	789	407	406	813	98
3B	9	10	19	7	21	28	69	27	29	56	30	45	75	76
HR	86	80	166	68	67	135	125	300	248	548	215	204	419	132
BB	258	247	505	217	192	409	125	791	783	1574	685	653	1338	119
SO	496	670	1166	493	550	1043	113	1430	1888	3318	1503	1600	3103	108
E	43	36	79	36	50	86	92	152	133	285	143	144	287	99
E-Infield	17	15	32	14	22	36	89	60	54	114	61	57	118	97
LHB-Avg	.257	.255	.256	.247	.274	.262	98	.265	.260	.262	.266	.265	.266	99
LHB-HR	20	35	55	8	32	40	135	65	99	164	38	96	134	122
RHB-Avg	.249	.252	.251	.255	.263	.259	97	.255	.257	.256	.256	.265	.260	98
RHB-HR	66	45	111	60	35	95	121	235	149	384	177	108	285	138

Cincinnati Reds - Great American Ballpark

| | 2011 Season | | | | | | | 2009-2011 | | | | | | |
| | Home Games | | | Away Games | | | | Home Games | | | Away Games | | | |
	Reds	Opp	Total	Reds	Opp	Total	Index	Reds	Opp	Total	Reds	Opp	Total	Index
G	81	81	162	81	81	162		243	243	486	243	243	486	
Avg	.261	.252	.256	.252	.258	.255	101	.263	.254	.258	.253	.258	.256	101
AB	2710	2827	5537	2902	2719	5621	99	8100	8445	16545	8553	8134	16687	99
R	388	368	756	347	352	699	108	1116	1069	2185	1082	1059	2141	102
H	706	713	1419	732	701	1433	99	2134	2142	4276	2168	2096	4264	100
2B	116	134	250	148	145	293	87	393	411	804	444	417	861	94
3B	11	8	19	8	19	27	71	40	28	68	34	40	74	93
HR	105	104	209	78	81	159	133	301	279	580	228	252	480	122
BB	255	258	513	280	281	561	93	788	816	1604	800	824	1624	100
SO	601	580	1181	649	532	1181	102	1744	1762	3506	1853	1549	3402	104
E	46	56	102	45	56	101	101	111	153	264	141	162	303	87
E-Infield	29	25	54	14	25	39	138	59	62	121	52	65	117	103
LHB-Avg	.270	.258	.263	.285	.260	.270	97	.269	.260	.264	.290	.253	.268	98
LHB-HR	35	44	79	39	39	78	105	108	124	232	102	108	210	109
RHB-Avg	.257	.248	.253	.239	.256	.247	102	.261	.249	.256	.240	.261	.249	103
RHB-HR	70	60	130	39	42	81	161	193	155	348	126	144	270	132

Cleveland Indians - Progressive Field

| | 2011 Season | | | | | | | 2009-2011 | | | | | | |
| | Home Games | | | Away Games | | | | Home Games | | | Away Games | | | |
	Indians	Opp	Total	Indians	Opp	Total	Index	Indians	Opp	Total	Indians	Opp	Total	Index
G	81	81	162	81	81	162		243	243	486	243	243	486	
Avg	.252	.259	.256	.249	.268	.258	99	.252	.265	.259	.256	.277	.266	97
AB	2668	2888	5556	2841	2740	5581	100	8067	8578	16645	8497	8156	16653	100
R	348	369	717	356	391	747	96	1032	1112	2144	1091	1265	2356	91
H	673	748	1421	707	734	1441	99	2033	2271	4304	2177	2258	4435	97
2B	132	172	304	158	151	309	99	426	503	929	468	438	906	103
3B	13	9	22	13	22	35	63	33	34	67	41	53	94	71
HR	89	69	158	65	84	149	107	219	211	430	224	272	496	87
BB	252	219	471	242	244	486	97	821	778	1599	800	855	1655	97
SO	616	532	1148	653	492	1145	101	1785	1540	3325	1879	1437	3316	100
E	52	34	86	58	35	93	92	152	147	299	165	119	284	105
E-Infield	22	11	33	27	11	38	87	72	62	134	78	42	120	112
LHB-Avg	.258	.275	.266	.241	.298	.264	101	.263	.269	.266	.261	.294	.275	97
LHB-HR	71	40	111	42	34	76	146	134	115	249	121	107	228	107
RHB-Avg	.243	.242	.242	.265	.241	.250	97	.239	.261	.251	.251	.263	.257	98
RHB-HR	18	29	47	23	50	73	65	85	96	181	103	165	268	69

Colorado Rockies - Coors Field

| | 2011 Season | | | | | | | 2009-2011 | | | | | | |
| | Home Games | | | Away Games | | | | Home Games | | | Away Games | | | |
	Rockies	Opp	Total	Rockies	Opp	Total	Index	Rockies	Opp	Total	Rockies	Opp	Total	Index
G	81	81	162	81	81	162		243	243	486	243	243	486	
Avg	.274	.281	.278	.242	.247	.245	113	.286	.270	.278	.235	.251	.243	114
AB	2756	2905	5661	2788	2646	5434	104	8206	8567	16773	8266	7910	16176	104
R	439	427	866	296	347	643	135	1382	1185	2567	927	1021	1948	132
H	754	817	1571	675	654	1329	118	2349	2314	4663	1940	1989	3929	119
2B	147	166	313	127	126	253	119	466	480	946	378	372	750	122
3B	24	25	49	16	27	43	109	94	69	163	50	59	109	144
HR	94	101	195	69	75	144	130	300	254	554	226	202	428	125
BB	304	241	545	251	281	532	98	941	749	1690	859	826	1685	97
SO	552	544	1096	649	574	1223	86	1681	1770	3451	2071	1736	3807	87
E	56	55	111	42	47	89	125	143	165	308	143	134	277	111
E-Infield	23	22	45	18	25	43	105	62	60	122	55	65	120	102
LHB-Avg	.287	.290	.289	.258	.246	.252	114	.294	.279	.287	.248	.252	.250	115
LHB-HR	43	50	93	32	38	70	128	154	104	258	113	86	199	129
RHB-Avg	.262	.274	.268	.229	.248	.238	113	.279	.264	.271	.222	.251	.237	114
RHB-HR	51	51	102	37	37	74	132	146	150	296	113	116	229	121

Detroit Tigers - Comerica Park

| | 2011 Season | | | | | | | 2009-2011 | | | | | | |
| | Home Games | | | Away Games | | | | Home Games | | | Away Games | | | |
	Tigers	Opp	Total	Tigers	Opp	Total	Index	Tigers	Opp	Total	Tigers	Opp	Total	Index
G	81	81	162	81	81	162		243	243	486	244	244	488	102
Avg	.288	.261	.274	.267	.252	.259	106	.280	.254	.267	.258	.268	.263	102
AB	2690	2805	5495	2873	2673	5546	99	8155	8397	16552	8591	8100	16691	100
R	413	358	771	374	353	727	106	1225	1035	2260	1056	1164	2220	102
H	774	733	1507	766	673	1439	105	2283	2133	4416	2215	2167	4382	101
2B	143	137	280	154	122	276	102	422	379	801	428	394	822	98
3B	23	21	44	11	8	19	234	59	57	116	42	46	88	133
HR	94	64	158	75	85	160	100	256	222	478	248	251	499	97
BB	245	225	470	276	267	543	87	802	760	1562	805	863	1668	94
SO	511	525	1036	632	590	1222	86	1540	1628	3168	1864	1645	3509	91
E	61	45	106	42	48	90	118	162	167	329	138	133	271	122
E-Infield	29	14	43	15	21	36	119	60	67	127	52	59	111	115
LHB-Avg	.291	.263	.275	.272	.241	.255	108	.272	.252	.260	.254	.265	.260	100
LHB-HR	34	32	66	32	41	73	90	91	100	191	85	128	213	89
RHB-Avg	.285	.260	.273	.263	.263	.263	104	.285	.256	.272	.260	.270	.264	103
RHB-HR	60	32	92	43	44	87	108	165	122	287	163	123	286	102

Florida Marlins - Sun Life Stadium

| | 2011 Season | | | | | | | 2009-2011 | | | | | | |
| | Home Games | | | Away Games | | | | Home Games | | | Away Games | | | |
	Marlins	Opp	Total	Marlins	Opp	Total	Index	Marlins	Opp	Total	Marlins	Opp	Total	Index
G	78	78	156	84	84	168		237	237	474	249	249	498	99
Avg	.247	.249	.248	.246	.257	.251	99	.256	.255	.256	.256	.259	.257	99
AB	2603	2724	5327	2905	2830	5735	100	7967	8347	16314	8644	8241	16885	102
R	299	337	636	326	365	691	99	1035	1115	2150	1081	1070	2151	105
H	644	677	1321	714	726	1440	99	2043	2130	4173	2211	2131	4342	101
2B	126	145	271	148	151	299	98	406	443	849	458	396	854	103
3B	18	20	38	12	21	33	124	50	50	100	42	73	115	90
HR	72	67	139	77	82	159	94	222	208	430	238	235	473	94
BB	283	254	537	259	246	505	114	859	868	1727	765	782	1547	116
SO	610	666	1276	634	552	1186	116	1929	1984	3913	1916	1650	3566	114
E	46	50	96	47	57	104	99	175	148	323	147	169	316	107
E-Infield	21	17	38	18	16	34	120	63	53	116	58	64	122	100
LHB-Avg	.242	.256	.250	.264	.252	.257	97	.251	.258	.255	.261	.253	.256	100
LHB-HR	22	32	54	21	45	66	81	45	99	144	49	103	152	92
RHB-Avg	.251	.242	.247	.236	.260	.247	100	.259	.253	.256	.254	.263	.258	99
RHB-HR	50	35	85	56	37	93	104	177	109	286	189	132	321	96

Houston Astros - Minute Maid Park

| | 2011 Season | | | | | | | 2009-2011 | | | | | | |
| | Home Games | | | Away Games | | | | Home Games | | | Away Games | | | |
	Astros	Opp	Total	Astros	Opp	Total	Index	Astros	Opp	Total	Astros	Opp	Total	Index
G	81	81	162	81	81	162		243	243	486	243	243	486	99
Avg	.263	.264	.263	.252	.269	.261	101	.260	.260	.260	.250	.275	.263	99
AB	2765	2870	5635	2833	2673	5506	102	8104	8506	16610	8382	8099	16481	101
R	325	414	739	290	382	672	110	956	1085	2041	913	1210	2123	96
H	727	757	1484	715	720	1435	103	2106	2213	4319	2099	2231	4330	100
2B	165	162	327	144	132	276	116	411	447	858	420	441	861	99
3B	16	13	29	12	18	30	94	51	48	99	34	58	92	107
HR	46	106	152	49	82	131	113	187	258	445	158	246	404	109
BB	216	279	495	185	281	466	104	656	808	1464	608	846	1454	100
SO	569	634	1203	595	557	1152	102	1549	1900	3449	1630	1645	3275	104
E	56	49	105	60	50	110	95	141	152	293	156	132	288	102
E-Infield	25	21	46	25	19	44	105	61	70	131	74	57	131	100
LHB-Avg	.280	.276	.277	.250	.265	.258	107	.262	.270	.266	.243	.264	.254	105
LHB-HR	6	41	47	8	25	33	133	39	102	141	35	84	119	113
RHB-Avg	.257	.256	.257	.253	.272	.262	98	.259	.254	.257	.254	.282	.267	96
RHB-HR	40	65	105	41	57	98	107	148	156	304	123	162	285	108

Kansas City Royals - Kauffman Stadium

| | 2011 Season | | | | | | | 2009-2011 | | | | | | |
| | Home Games | | | Away Games | | | | Home Games | | | Away Games | | | |
	Royals	Opp	Total	Royals	Opp	Total	Index	Royals	Opp	Total	Royals	Opp	Total	Index
G	81	81	162	81	81	162		243	243	486	243	243	486	
Avg	.278	.264	.271	.273	.271	.272	100	.278	.273	.276	.261	.268	.264	104
AB	2778	2863	5641	2894	2700	5594	101	8273	8667	16940	8535	8062	16597	102
R	371	372	743	359	390	749	99	1098	1213	2311	994	1236	2230	104
H	771	756	1527	789	731	1520	100	2300	2367	4667	2226	2159	4385	106
2B	150	164	314	175	137	312	100	431	486	917	449	409	858	105
3B	27	22	49	14	21	35	139	82	59	141	41	45	86	161
HR	53	68	121	76	95	171	70	178	219	397	216	286	502	77
BB	235	289	524	207	268	475	109	722	831	1553	648	877	1525	100
SO	463	531	994	543	549	1092	90	1380	1655	3035	1622	1613	3235	92
E	53	61	114	42	61	103	111	172	149	321	160	146	306	105
E-Infield	16	24	40	13	19	32	125	76	67	143	57	58	115	124
LHB-Avg	.282	.264	.274	.277	.272	.275	100	.280	.275	.278	.259	.265	.261	106
LHB-HR	23	23	46	42	37	79	57	75	77	152	113	121	234	64
RHB-Avg	.273	.264	.268	.268	.270	.269	100	.276	.272	.274	.263	.270	.267	103
RHB-HR	30	45	75	34	58	92	82	103	142	245	103	165	268	89

Los Angeles Angels - Angel Stadium of Anaheim

| | 2011 Season | | | | | | | 2009-2011 | | | | | | |
| | Home Games | | | Away Games | | | | Home Games | | | Away Games | | | |
	Angels	Opp	Total	Angels	Opp	Total	Index	Angels	Opp	Total	Angels	Opp	Total	Index
G	81	81	162	81	81	162		243	243	486	243	243	486	
Avg	.248	.244	.246	.257	.259	.258	95	.261	.253	.257	.263	.267	.265	97
AB	2676	2812	5488	2837	2713	5550	99	8072	8508	16580	8551	8135	16686	99
R	305	287	592	362	346	708	84	1068	995	2063	1163	1101	2264	91
H	664	685	1349	730	703	1433	94	2109	2154	4263	2252	2169	4421	96
2B	130	136	266	159	151	310	87	402	414	816	456	484	940	87
3B	14	7	21	20	13	33	64	34	25	59	52	51	103	58
HR	62	69	131	93	73	166	80	221	241	462	262	229	491	95
BB	219	231	450	223	245	468	97	722	764	1486	733	800	1533	98
SO	511	570	1081	575	488	1063	103	1509	1718	3227	1701	1532	3233	100
E	44	57	101	49	62	111	91	148	168	316	143	176	319	99
E-Infield	19	15	34	24	26	50	68	59	55	114	63	74	137	83
LHB-Avg	.242	.248	.246	.277	.262	.268	92	.275	.254	.263	.271	.279	.275	95
LHB-HR	10	31	41	23	31	54	76	74	99	173	79	110	189	93
RHB-Avg	.251	.238	.246	.248	.256	.251	98	.253	.253	.253	.259	.255	.257	98
RHB-HR	52	38	90	70	42	112	82	147	142	289	183	119	302	96

Los Angeles Dodgers - Dodger Stadium

| | 2011 Season | | | | | | | 2009-2011 | | | | | | |
| | Home Games | | | Away Games | | | | Home Games | | | Away Games | | | |
	Dodgers	Opp	Total	Dodgers	Opp	Total	Index	Dodgers	Opp	Total	Dodgers	Opp	Total	Index
G	81	81	162	80	80	160		243	243	486	242	242	484	
Avg	.251	.238	.244	.262	.243	.253	97	.258	.234	.246	.261	.245	.253	97
AB	2653	2720	5373	2783	2625	5408	98	8015	8283	16298	8439	7912	16351	99
R	300	311	611	344	301	645	94	987	924	1911	1104	991	2095	91
H	665	648	1313	730	639	1369	95	2069	1938	4007	2205	1937	4142	96
2B	114	132	246	123	131	254	97	383	378	761	402	382	784	97
3B	15	3	18	13	16	29	62	43	18	61	53	71	124	49
HR	53	67	120	64	65	129	94	184	191	375	198	202	400	94
BB	254	260	514	244	247	491	105	786	791	1577	852	839	1691	94
SO	510	652	1162	577	613	1190	98	1575	1977	3552	1764	1834	3598	99
E	44	47	91	41	53	94	96	124	154	278	142	173	315	88
E-Infield	17	15	32	18	21	39	81	42	57	99	65	72	137	72
LHB-Avg	.260	.236	.249	.261	.257	.259	96	.266	.232	.250	.262	.246	.255	98
LHB-HR	18	26	44	16	23	39	114	74	73	147	65	74	139	104
RHB-Avg	.243	.240	.241	.264	.235	.249	97	.252	.235	.243	.261	.244	.252	96
RHB-HR	35	41	76	48	42	90	85	110	118	228	133	128	261	89

Milwaukee Brewers - Miller Park

	2011 Season							2009-2011						
	Home Games			Away Games			Index	Home Games			Away Games			Index
	Brewers	Opp	Total	Brewers	Opp	Total		Brewers	Opp	Total	Brewers	Opp	Total	
G	81	81	162	81	81	162		243	243	486	243	243	486	
Avg	.277	.244	.260	.246	.248	.247	105	.264	.256	.260	.260	.265	.262	99
AB	2661	2821	5482	2786	2660	5446	101	8062	8542	16604	8501	8097	16598	100
R	389	304	693	332	334	666	104	1120	1105	2225	1136	1155	2291	97
H	737	687	1424	685	661	1346	106	2131	2188	4319	2209	2145	4354	99
2B	145	136	281	131	127	258	108	424	484	908	426	440	866	105
3B	19	14	33	12	14	26	126	54	36	90	47	47	94	96
HR	102	69	171	83	78	161	106	302	266	568	247	261	508	112
BB	260	219	479	221	221	442	108	850	809	1659	787	820	1607	103
SO	527	671	1198	556	586	1142	104	1718	1962	3680	1812	1657	3469	106
E	55	51	106	56	53	109	97	152	138	290	158	149	307	94
E-Infield	26	21	47	29	21	50	94	72	51	123	69	70	139	88
LHB-Avg	.264	.241	.251	.267	.245	.255	98	.257	.258	.257	.266	.265	.266	97
LHB-HR	27	26	53	25	30	55	95	90	119	209	80	94	174	116
RHB-Avg	.283	.245	.265	.236	.251	.243	109	.268	.255	.262	.257	.265	.261	100
RHB-HR	75	43	118	58	48	106	111	212	147	359	167	167	334	109

Minnesota Twins - Target Field

	2011 Season							2010-2011						
	Home Games			Away Games			Index	Home Games			Away Games			Index
	Twins	Opp	Total	Twins	Opp	Total		Twins	Opp	Total	Twins	Opp	Total	
G	81	81	162	81	81	162		162	162	324	162	162	324	
Avg	.252	.275	.264	.243	.287	.264	100	.267	.269	.268	.254	.278	.266	101
AB	2683	2874	5557	2804	2697	5501	101	5366	5716	11082	5689	5458	11147	99
R	290	401	691	329	403	732	94	689	714	1403	711	761	1472	95
H	677	791	1468	680	773	1453	101	1433	1539	2972	1445	1518	2963	100
2B	129	136	265	130	155	285	92	295	297	592	282	301	583	102
3B	10	23	33	15	20	35	93	37	37	74	29	41	70	106
HR	46	80	126	57	81	138	90	98	144	242	147	172	319	76
BB	215	235	450	225	245	470	95	511	424	935	488	439	927	101
SO	514	499	1013	534	441	975	103	939	1029	1968	1076	959	2035	97
E	63	56	119	56	59	115	103	104	100	204	93	112	205	100
E-Infield	23	25	48	16	25	41	117	39	43	82	24	48	72	114
LHB-Avg	.261	.250	.256	.255	.290	.271	94	.275	.259	.268	.262	.275	.268	100
LHB-HR	17	26	43	27	33	60	72	47	49	96	77	66	143	68
RHB-Avg	.244	.296	.272	.230	.284	.258	105	.258	.277	.269	.245	.281	.264	102
RHB-HR	29	54	83	30	48	78	104	51	95	146	70	106	176	83

New York Mets - Citi Field

	2011 Season							2009-2011						
	Home Games			Away Games			Index	Home Games			Away Games			Index
	Mets	Opp	Total	Mets	Opp	Total		Mets	Opp	Total	Mets	Opp	Total	
G	81	81	162	81	81	162		243	243	486	243	243	486	
Avg	.262	.256	.259	.265	.275	.270	96	.264	.249	.256	.258	.277	.268	96
AB	2754	2853	5607	2846	2742	5588	100	8066	8438	16504	8452	8185	16637	99
R	328	367	695	390	375	765	91	1005	999	2004	1040	1152	2192	91
H	722	729	1451	755	753	1508	96	2129	2102	4231	2181	2270	4451	95
2B	160	140	300	149	162	311	96	429	422	851	441	473	914	94
3B	22	19	41	17	17	34	120	79	42	121	49	49	98	124
HR	50	58	108	58	89	147	73	162	186	348	169	254	423	83
BB	286	267	553	285	247	532	104	809	846	1655	790	829	1619	103
SO	551	581	1132	534	545	1079	105	1507	1713	3220	1601	1550	3151	103
E	66	47	113	50	58	108	105	155	147	302	145	170	315	96
E-Infield	30	20	50	19	24	43	116	69	60	129	61	74	135	96
LHB-Avg	.283	.266	.275	.278	.249	.266	104	.271	.247	.260	.266	.266	.266	98
LHB-HR	25	25	50	29	35	64	80	71	81	152	71	104	175	90
RHB-Avg	.242	.249	.246	.252	.291	.273	90	.257	.251	.253	.249	.285	.269	94
RHB-HR	25	33	58	29	54	83	68	91	105	196	98	150	248	78

New York Yankees - Yankee Stadium

| | 2011 Season | | | | | | | 2009-2011 | | | | | | |
| | Home Games | | | Away Games | | | | Home Games | | | Away Games | | | |
	Yankees	Opp	Total	Yankees	Opp	Total	Index	Yankees	Opp	Total	Yankees	Opp	Total	Index
G	81	81	162	81	81	162		243	243	486	243	243	486	
Avg	.274	.253	.263	.252	.259	.256	103	.279	.250	.264	.264	.254	.259	102
AB	2713	2841	5554	2805	2720	5525	101	8187	8440	16627	8558	8055	16613	100
R	471	338	809	396	319	715	113	1404	1063	2467	1237	1040	2277	108
H	744	719	1463	708	704	1412	104	2284	2113	4397	2257	2045	4302	102
2B	132	146	278	135	146	281	98	428	386	814	439	426	865	94
3B	12	14	26	21	10	31	83	33	27	60	53	35	88	68
HR	122	87	209	100	65	165	126	373	296	669	294	216	510	131
BB	332	242	574	295	265	560	102	998	812	1810	954	809	1763	103
SO	550	626	1176	588	596	1184	99	1577	1856	3433	1711	1780	3491	98
E	49	55	104	53	35	88	118	119	157	276	138	126	264	105
E-Infield	19	23	42	26	15	41	102	44	66	110	56	55	111	99
LHB-Avg	.268	.256	.262	.253	.263	.258	102	.280	.250	.266	.263	.257	.260	102
LHB-HR	77	47	124	58	27	85	147	245	145	390	178	92	270	143
RHB-Avg	.282	.251	.265	.251	.255	.253	105	.278	.250	.262	.265	.251	.258	102
RHB-HR	45	40	85	42	38	80	104	128	151	279	116	124	240	117

Oakland Athletics - O.co Coliseum

| | 2011 Season | | | | | | | 2009-2011 | | | | | | |
| | Home Games | | | Away Games | | | | Home Games | | | Away Games | | | |
	Athletics	Opp	Total	Athletics	Opp	Total	Index	Athletics	Opp	Total	Athletics	Opp	Total	Index
G	81	81	162	81	81	162		243	243	486	243	243	486	
Avg	.249	.235	.242	.239	.265	.252	96	.256	.240	.248	.252	.267	.259	96
AB	2630	2758	5388	2822	2755	5577	97	7970	8297	16267	8514	8198	16712	97
R	335	309	644	310	370	680	95	1091	933	2024	976	1133	2109	96
H	655	649	1304	675	731	1406	93	2044	1995	4039	2146	2186	4332	93
2B	145	113	258	135	132	267	100	431	358	789	432	424	856	95
3B	17	9	26	12	17	29	93	49	31	80	31	40	71	116
HR	50	60	110	64	76	140	81	167	191	358	191	254	445	83
BB	272	258	530	237	261	498	110	822	741	1563	741	813	1554	103
SO	497	610	1107	597	550	1147	100	1520	1754	3274	1681	1600	3281	103
E	69	50	119	55	45	100	119	169	166	335	159	155	314	107
E-Infield	25	20	45	21	22	43	105	63	56	119	60	68	128	93
LHB-Avg	.253	.247	.250	.253	.260	.256	98	.256	.248	.252	.255	.277	.265	95
LHB-HR	15	21	36	27	38	65	59	70	76	146	86	121	207	73
RHB-Avg	.245	.228	.235	.225	.270	.248	95	.257	.235	.245	.249	.259	.255	96
RHB-HR	35	39	74	37	38	75	99	97	115	212	105	133	238	91

Philadelphia Phillies - Citizens Bank Park

| | 2011 Season | | | | | | | 2009-2011 | | | | | | |
| | Home Games | | | Away Games | | | | Home Games | | | Away Games | | | |
	Phillies	Opp	Total	Phillies	Opp	Total	Index	Phillies	Opp	Total	Phillies	Opp	Total	Index
G	81	81	162	81	81	162		246	246	492	240	240	480	
Avg	.256	.228	.242	.249	.252	.250	97	.261	.247	.254	.253	.259	.256	99
AB	2743	2812	5555	2836	2690	5526	101	8287	8579	16866	8451	8039	16490	100
R	367	253	620	346	276	622	100	1185	939	2124	1120	939	2059	101
H	703	642	1345	706	678	1384	97	2163	2119	4282	2136	2082	4218	99
2B	134	124	258	124	128	252	102	441	423	864	419	408	827	102
3B	21	8	29	17	19	36	80	59	26	85	48	49	97	86
HR	77	56	133	76	64	140	95	279	244	523	264	233	497	103
BB	284	191	475	255	213	468	101	864	648	1512	824	661	1485	100
SO	518	679	1197	506	620	1126	106	1576	1932	3508	1667	1703	3370	102
E	41	50	91	33	51	84	108	117	147	264	116	148	264	98
E-Infield	18	21	39	12	33	45	87	57	57	114	53	72	125	89
LHB-Avg	.252	.239	.247	.241	.248	.244	101	.258	.248	.254	.249	.258	.253	100
LHB-HR	56	26	82	42	19	61	130	179	93	272	160	84	244	109
RHB-Avg	.262	.222	.238	.259	.254	.257	93	.265	.247	.254	.258	.259	.259	98
RHB-HR	21	30	51	34	45	79	66	100	151	251	104	149	253	97

Pittsburgh Pirates - PNC Park

| | 2011 Season | | | | | | | 2009-2011 | | | | | | |
| | Home Games | | | Away Games | | | | Home Games | | | Away Games | | | |
	Pirates	Opp	Total	Pirates	Opp	Total	Index	Pirates	Opp	Total	Pirates	Opp	Total	Index
G	81	81	162	81	81	162		243	243	486	242	242	484	
Avg	.247	.269	.258	.242	.272	.257	100	.257	.267	.262	.236	.285	.260	101
AB	2627	2855	5482	2794	2741	5535	99	7969	8481	16450	8255	8083	16338	100
R	287	360	647	323	352	675	96	980	1117	2097	853	1229	2082	100
H	648	767	1415	677	746	1423	99	2047	2266	4313	1945	2305	4250	101
2B	136	141	277	141	134	275	102	425	499	924	417	485	902	102
3B	15	9	24	20	13	33	73	50	43	93	46	61	107	86
HR	49	66	115	58	86	144	81	188	200	388	170	271	441	87
BB	219	261	480	270	274	544	89	700	803	1503	751	833	1584	94
SO	558	514	1072	750	517	1267	85	1601	1501	3102	2056	1475	3531	87
E	62	47	109	50	54	104	105	167	139	306	145	134	279	109
E-Infield	24	27	51	22	22	44	116	72	75	147	62	62	124	118
LHB-Avg	.247	.283	.265	.243	.307	.273	97	.255	.275	.264	.231	.296	.260	102
LHB-HR	21	23	44	30	36	66	71	101	78	179	95	106	201	92
RHB-Avg	.247	.260	.254	.242	.251	.247	103	.259	.263	.261	.240	.279	.260	100
RHB-HR	28	43	71	28	50	78	89	87	122	209	75	165	240	84

San Diego Padres - PETCO Park

| | 2011 Season | | | | | | | 2009-2011 | | | | | | |
| | Home Games | | | Away Games | | | | Home Games | | | Away Games | | | |
	Padres	Opp	Total	Padres	Opp	Total	Index	Padres	Opp	Total	Padres	Opp	Total	Index
G	81	81	162	81	81	162		243	243	486	243	243	486	
Avg	.221	.234	.228	.252	.257	.254	90	.227	.230	.229	.256	.265	.260	88
AB	2613	2761	5374	2804	2647	5451	99	7840	8310	16150	8436	8064	16500	98
R	255	287	542	338	324	662	82	855	870	1725	1041	1091	2132	81
H	578	645	1223	706	679	1385	88	1781	1912	3693	2156	2139	4295	86
2B	111	133	244	136	134	270	92	318	353	671	430	404	834	82
3B	23	20	43	19	12	31	141	53	44	97	44	43	87	114
HR	46	54	100	45	71	116	87	166	188	354	198	243	441	82
BB	261	253	514	240	268	508	103	885	822	1707	740	819	1559	112
SO	669	591	1260	651	548	1199	107	1858	1933	3791	1827	1688	3515	110
E	43	52	95	51	59	110	86	126	137	263	134	158	292	90
E-Infield	19	21	40	23	25	48	83	50	52	102	54	69	123	83
LHB-Avg	.220	.251	.239	.236	.276	.260	92	.225	.241	.234	.263	.271	.267	88
LHB-HR	16	14	30	11	31	42	67	62	64	126	100	100	200	63
RHB-Avg	.222	.220	.221	.258	.242	.251	88	.228	.221	.225	.251	.261	.256	88
RHB-HR	30	40	70	34	40	74	100	104	124	228	98	143	241	98

San Francisco Giants - AT&T Park

| | 2011 Season | | | | | | | 2009-2011 | | | | | | |
| | Home Games | | | Away Games | | | | Home Games | | | Away Games | | | |
	Giants	Opp	Total	Giants	Opp	Total	Index	Giants	Opp	Total	Giants	Opp	Total	Index
G	81	81	162	81	81	162		243	243	486	243	243	486	
Avg	.240	.225	.232	.244	.240	.242	96	.257	.228	.242	.247	.242	.244	99
AB	2663	2748	5411	2823	2672	5495	98	7960	8236	16196	8507	7976	16483	98
R	236	251	487	334	327	661	74	941	817	1758	983	955	1938	91
H	638	618	1256	689	642	1331	94	2049	1878	3927	2100	1929	4029	97
2B	141	136	277	141	136	277	102	416	384	800	425	377	802	102
3B	13	14	27	11	15	26	105	58	41	99	39	61	100	101
HR	42	39	81	79	57	136	60	182	167	349	223	203	426	83
BB	215	263	478	233	296	529	92	661	799	1460	666	922	1588	94
SO	549	702	1251	573	614	1187	107	1600	2054	3654	1779	1895	3674	101
E	45	51	96	59	58	117	82	140	145	285	125	153	278	103
E-Infield	23	18	41	28	19	47	87	64	47	111	55	57	112	99
LHB-Avg	.243	.208	.227	.252	.230	.242	94	.259	.221	.241	.254	.237	.246	98
LHB-HR	21	9	30	47	20	67	47	76	48	124	103	83	186	68
RHB-Avg	.237	.234	.235	.237	.247	.242	97	.256	.232	.243	.242	.245	.243	100
RHB-HR	21	30	51	32	37	69	74	106	119	225	120	120	240	96

Seattle Mariners - Safeco Field

| | 2011 Season | | | | | | | 2009-2011 | | | | | | |
| | Home Games | | | Away Games | | | | Home Games | | | Away Games | | | |
	Mariners	Opp	Total	Mariners	Opp	Total	Index	Mariners	Opp	Total	Mariners	Opp	Total	Index
G	84	84	168	78	78	156		246	246	492	240	240	480	
Avg	.222	.240	.231	.244	.263	.253	91	.238	.240	.239	.247	.262	.254	94
AB	2703	2865	5568	2718	2590	5308	97	8073	8496	16569	8300	7961	16261	99
R	265	325	590	291	350	641	85	817	964	1781	892	1101	1993	87
H	599	689	1288	664	680	1344	89	1918	2043	3961	2049	2087	4136	93
2B	111	118	229	142	135	277	79	350	385	735	410	420	830	87
3B	10	9	19	12	15	27	67	29	21	50	28	41	69	71
HR	57	77	134	52	68	120	106	168	226	394	202	248	450	86
BB	245	217	462	190	219	409	108	712	708	1420	603	714	1317	106
SO	706	589	1295	574	499	1073	115	1859	1650	3509	1698	1454	3152	109
E	41	40	81	67	54	121	62	135	137	272	188	144	332	80
E-Infield	19	18	37	25	25	50	69	67	54	121	89	67	156	76
LHB-Avg	.225	.250	.236	.252	.262	.256	92	.244	.246	.245	.251	.261	.255	96
LHB-HR	38	29	67	28	24	52	127	98	93	191	92	96	188	101
RHB-Avg	.216	.234	.227	.233	.263	.250	91	.232	.237	.234	.243	.263	.253	92
RHB-HR	19	48	67	24	44	68	91	70	133	203	110	152	262	75

St Louis Cardinals - Busch Stadium

| | 2011 Season | | | | | | | 2009-2011 | | | | | | |
| | Home Games | | | Away Games | | | | Home Games | | | Away Games | | | |
	Cardinals	Opp	Total	Cardinals	Opp	Total	Index	Cardinals	Opp	Total	Cardinals	Opp	Total	Index
G	81	81	162	81	81	162		243	243	486	243	243	486	
Avg	.270	.242	.256	.277	.279	.278	92	.268	.247	.257	.265	.270	.267	96
AB	2646	2801	5447	2886	2807	5693	96	7986	8371	16357	8553	8203	16756	98
R	350	337	687	412	355	767	90	1077	932	2009	1151	1041	2192	92
H	715	679	1394	798	782	1580	88	2139	2064	4203	2266	2216	4482	94
2B	140	130	270	168	165	333	85	427	386	813	460	449	909	92
3B	9	13	22	13	22	35	66	36	33	69	33	60	93	76
HR	67	63	130	95	73	168	81	200	172	372	272	220	492	77
BB	267	231	498	275	217	492	106	845	683	1528	766	702	1468	107
SO	437	562	999	541	536	1077	97	1403	1676	3079	1643	1565	3208	98
E	59	38	97	57	52	109	89	161	148	309	150	147	297	104
E-Infield	27	16	43	32	20	52	83	77	63	140	74	62	136	103
LHB-Avg	.263	.245	.254	.274	.268	.271	94	.260	.257	.258	.265	.266	.265	97
LHB-HR	23	28	51	35	25	60	93	56	80	136	77	89	166	86
RHB-Avg	.275	.241	.257	.278	.286	.282	91	.272	.239	.256	.265	.274	.269	95
RHB-HR	44	35	79	60	48	108	74	144	92	236	195	131	326	73

Tampa Bay Rays - Tropicana Field Surface: FieldTurf

| | 2011 Season | | | | | | | 2009-2011 | | | | | | |
| | Home Games | | | Away Games | | | | Home Games | | | Away Games | | | |
	Rays	Opp	Total	Rays	Opp	Total	Index	Rays	Opp	Total	Rays	Opp	Total	Index
G	81	81	162	81	81	162		243	243	486	243	243	486	
Avg	.236	.225	.230	.251	.244	.247	93	.251	.235	.243	.251	.256	.254	96
AB	2632	2760	5392	2804	2635	5439	99	7925	8353	16278	8412	8081	16493	99
R	310	284	594	397	330	727	82	1094	922	2016	1218	1095	2313	87
H	621	620	1241	703	643	1346	92	1988	1962	3950	2113	2069	4182	94
2B	127	118	245	146	142	288	86	406	398	804	459	435	894	91
3B	16	12	28	21	18	39	72	56	49	105	54	39	93	114
HR	81	77	158	91	84	175	91	262	243	505	269	276	545	94
BB	286	241	527	285	263	548	97	929	727	1656	956	770	1726	97
SO	559	606	1165	634	537	1171	100	1784	1832	3616	1930	1625	3555	103
E	41	41	82	32	66	98	84	119	129	248	137	186	323	77
E-Infield	13	19	32	12	27	39	82	46	48	94	51	78	129	73
LHB-Avg	.253	.218	.237	.248	.241	.245	97	.252	.232	.242	.251	.255	.253	96
LHB-HR	37	37	74	35	33	68	107	135	103	238	122	125	247	98
RHB-Avg	.214	.230	.223	.254	.247	.250	89	.250	.237	.243	.251	.257	.254	96
RHB-HR	44	40	84	56	51	107	82	127	140	267	147	151	298	91

Texas Rangers - Rangers Ballpark in Arlington

| | 2011 Season | | | | | | | 2009-2011 | | | | | | |
| | Home Games | | | Away Games | | | | Home Games | | | Away Games | | | |
	Rangers	Opp	Total	Rangers	Opp	Total	Index	Rangers	Opp	Total	Rangers	Opp	Total	Index
G	81	81	162	81	81	162		243	243	486	243	243	486	
Avg	.296	.256	.276	.269	.230	.251	110	.286	.255	.270	.261	.244	.253	107
AB	2800	2834	5634	2859	2610	5469	103	8264	8509	16773	8556	7960	16516	102
R	498	398	896	357	279	636	141	1354	1104	2458	1072	1000	2072	119
H	829	726	1555	770	601	1371	113	2362	2172	4534	2229	1942	4171	109
2B	168	141	309	142	118	260	115	457	434	891	417	387	804	109
3B	23	12	35	9	6	15	226	54	33	87	30	33	63	136
HR	126	102	228	84	68	152	146	341	276	617	255	227	482	126
BB	242	233	475	233	228	461	100	761	761	1522	697	782	1479	101
SO	434	572	1006	496	607	1103	89	1477	1682	3159	1692	1694	3386	92
E	65	71	136	49	58	107	127	177	194	371	148	163	311	119
E-Infield	33	36	69	20	26	46	150	86	97	183	52	66	118	155
LHB-Avg	.276	.268	.271	.273	.234	.253	107	.274	.258	.265	.268	.245	.256	104
LHB-HR	34	51	85	27	28	55	143	116	126	242	91	90	181	131
RHB-Avg	.306	.248	.279	.268	.228	.250	112	.293	.253	.274	.257	.244	.251	109
RHB-HR	92	51	143	57	40	97	147	225	150	375	164	137	301	123

Toronto Blue Jays - Rogers Centre Surface: FieldTurf

| | 2011 Season | | | | | | | 2009-2011 | | | | | | |
| | Home Games | | | Away Games | | | | Home Games | | | Away Games | | | |
	Blue Jays	Opp	Total	Blue Jays	Opp	Total	Index	Blue Jays	Opp	Total	Blue Jays	Opp	Total	Index
G	81	81	162	81	81	162		240	240	480	246	246	492	
Avg	.254	.269	.262	.244	.242	.243	108	.256	.260	.258	.253	.261	.257	100
AB	2757	2929	5686	2802	2662	5464	104	8094	8480	16574	8656	8217	16873	101
R	387	418	805	356	343	699	115	1163	1136	2299	1133	1124	2257	104
H	701	788	1489	683	645	1328	112	2072	2201	4273	2192	2148	4340	101
2B	152	186	338	133	121	254	128	468	491	959	475	449	924	106
3B	20	22	42	14	11	25	161	36	52	88	32	38	70	128
HR	103	95	198	83	84	167	114	353	266	619	299	244	543	116
BB	267	264	531	258	276	534	96	771	779	1550	773	851	1624	97
SO	579	616	1195	605	553	1158	99	1630	1839	3469	1746	1695	3441	103
E	52	62	114	58	52	110	104	133	151	284	145	137	282	103
E-Infield	22	29	51	20	27	47	109	44	66	110	47	62	109	103
LHB-Avg	.238	.279	.262	.242	.255	.249	105	.253	.253	.253	.249	.266	.259	98
LHB-HR	31	37	68	28	27	55	114	98	103	201	90	98	188	107
RHB-Avg	.262	.261	.262	.245	.232	.239	109	.257	.264	.261	.255	.258	.256	102
RHB-HR	72	58	130	55	57	112	114	255	163	418	209	146	355	121

Washington Nationals - Nationals Park

| | 2011 Season | | | | | | | 2009-2011 | | | | | | |
| | Home Games | | | Away Games | | | | Home Games | | | Away Games | | | |
	Nationals	Opp	Total	Nationals	Opp	Total	Index	Nationals	Opp	Total	Nationals	Opp	Total	Index
G	80	80	160	81	81	162		242	242	484	243	243	486	
Avg	.252	.257	.254	.234	.255	.244	104	.256	.260	.258	.244	.272	.258	100
AB	2619	2771	5390	2822	2714	5536	99	7998	8469	16467	8354	8094	16448	101
R	311	304	615	313	339	652	96	1007	1089	2096	982	1170	2152	98
H	659	712	1371	660	691	1351	103	2050	2204	4254	2040	2201	4241	101
2B	130	126	256	127	132	259	102	392	451	843	386	443	829	102
3B	9	9	18	13	14	27	68	51	38	89	40	61	101	88
HR	83	65	148	71	64	135	113	233	227	460	226	226	452	102
BB	228	174	402	242	303	545	76	794	716	1510	796	902	1698	89
SO	607	492	1099	716	557	1273	89	1748	1538	3286	2003	1490	3493	94
E	47	49	96	57	55	112	87	185	142	327	189	138	327	100
E-Infield	22	19	41	25	25	50	83	73	56	129	83	61	144	90
LHB-Avg	.228	.252	.241	.214	.242	.228	106	.250	.267	.258	.236	.272	.254	102
LHB-HR	32	21	53	20	27	47	119	99	87	186	82	98	180	104
RHB-Avg	.265	.260	.262	.246	.263	.254	103	.261	.256	.258	.250	.272	.261	99
RHB-HR	51	44	95	51	37	88	109	134	140	274	144	128	272	100

2011 American League Ballpark Index Rankings - Runs

Home Park	TOTALS											LHB		RHB	
	Avg	AB	R	H	2B	3B	HR	BB	SO	E	E-Inf	Avg	HR	Avg	HR
Rangers (Rangers Ballpark in Arlington)	110	103	141	113	115	226	146	100	89	127	150	107	143	112	147
Red Sox (Fenway Park)	112	103	117	116	127	111	85	95	97	144	136	109	68	117	110
Blue Jays (Rogers Centre)	108	104	115	112	128	161	114	96	99	104	109	105	114	109	114
Yankees (Yankee Stadium)	103	101	113	104	98	83	126	102	99	118	102	102	147	105	104
Tigers (Comerica Park)	106	99	106	105	102	234	100	87	86	118	119	108	90	104	108
Orioles (Oriole Park at Camden Yards)	98	102	99	99	107	73	112	103	96	70	72	106	123	93	107
Royals (Kauffman Stadium)	100	101	99	100	100	139	70	109	90	111	125	100	57	100	82
White Sox (U.S. Cellular Field)	97	99	99	96	89	69	125	125	113	92	89	98	135	97	121
Indians (Progressive Field)	99	100	96	99	99	63	107	97	101	92	87	101	146	97	65
Athletics (O.co Coliseum)	96	97	95	93	100	93	81	110	100	119	105	98	59	95	99
Twins (Target Field)	100	101	94	101	92	93	90	95	103	103	117	94	72	105	104
Mariners (Safeco Field)	91	97	85	89	79	67	106	108	115	62	69	92	127	91	91
Angels (Angel Stadium of Anaheim)	95	99	84	94	87	64	80	97	103	91	68	92	76	98	82
Rays (Tropicana Field)	93	99	82	92	86	72	91	97	100	84	82	97	107	89	82

2011 National League Ballpark Index Rankings - Runs

Home Park	TOTALS											LHB		RHB	
	Avg	AB	R	H	2B	3B	HR	BB	SO	E	E-Inf	Avg	HR	Avg	HR
Rockies (Coors Field)	113	104	135	118	119	109	130	98	86	125	105	114	128	113	132
Diamondbacks (Chase Field)	105	101	115	106	113	136	108	91	96	83	74	95	98	112	115
Astros (Minute Maid Park)	101	102	110	103	116	94	113	104	102	95	105	107	133	98	107
Reds (Great American Ballpark)	101	99	108	99	87	71	133	93	102	101	138	97	105	102	161
Brewers (Miller Park)	105	101	104	106	108	126	106	108	104	97	94	98	95	109	111
Phillies (Citizens Bank Park)	97	101	100	97	102	80	95	101	106	108	87	101	130	93	66
Marlins (Sun Life Stadium)	99	100	99	99	98	124	94	114	116	99	120	97	81	100	104
Pirates (PNC Park)	100	99	96	99	102	73	81	89	85	105	116	97	71	103	89
Nationals (Nationals Park)	104	99	96	103	102	68	113	76	89	87	83	106	119	103	109
Braves (Turner Field)	101	100	95	101	98	63	94	106	109	133	109	102	111	99	81
Dodgers (Dodger Stadium)	97	98	94	95	97	62	94	105	98	96	81	96	114	97	85
Cubs (Wrigley Field)	98	100	93	98	86	132	99	105	108	112	121	99	101	97	97
Mets (Citi Field)	96	100	91	96	96	120	73	104	105	105	116	104	80	90	68
Cardinals (Busch Stadium)	92	96	90	88	85	66	81	106	97	89	83	94	93	91	74
Padres (PETCO Park)	90	99	82	88	92	141	87	103	107	86	83	92	67	88	100
Giants (AT&T Park)	96	98	74	94	102	105	60	92	107	82	87	94	47	97	74

2011 AL Home Runs

Home Park	Index
Rangers	146
Yankees	126
White Sox	125
Blue Jays	114
Orioles	112
Indians	107
Mariners	106
Tigers	100
Rays	91
Twins	90
Red Sox	85
Athletics	81
Angels	80
Royals	70

2011 AL LHB Home Runs

Home Park	Index
Yankees	147
Indians	146
Rangers	143
White Sox	135
Mariners	127
Orioles	123
Blue Jays	114
Rays	107
Tigers	90
Angels	76
Twins	72
Red Sox	68
Athletics	59
Royals	57

2011 AL RHB Home Runs

Home Park	Index
Rangers	147
White Sox	121
Blue Jays	114
Red Sox	110
Tigers	108
Orioles	107
Yankees	104
Twins	104
Athletics	99
Mariners	91
Royals	82
Rays	82
Angels	82
Indians	65

2011 NL Home Runs

Home Park	Index
Reds	133
Rockies	130
Astros	113
Nationals	113
Diamondbacks	108
Brewers	106
Cubs	99
Phillies	95
Braves	94
Marlins	94
Dodgers	94
Padres	87
Cardinals	81
Pirates	81
Mets	73
Giants	60

2011 NL LHB Home Runs

Home Park	Index
Astros	133
Phillies	130
Rockies	128
Nationals	119
Dodgers	114
Braves	111
Reds	105
Cubs	101
Diamondbacks	98
Brewers	95
Cardinals	93
Marlins	81
Mets	80
Pirates	71
Padres	67
Giants	47

2011 NL RHB Home Runs

Home Park	Index
Reds	161
Rockies	132
Diamondbacks	115
Brewers	111
Nationals	109
Astros	107
Marlins	104
Padres	100
Cubs	97
Pirates	89
Dodgers	85
Braves	81
Cardinals	74
Giants	74
Mets	68
Phillies	66

2011 AL Avg	
Home Park	Index
Red Sox	112
Rangers	110
Blue Jays	108
Tigers	106
Yankees	103
Twins	100
Royals	100
Indians	99
Orioles	98
White Sox	97
Athletics	96
Angels	95
Rays	93
Mariners	91

2011 AL LHB Avg	
Home Park	Index
Red Sox	109
Tigers	108
Rangers	107
Orioles	106
Blue Jays	105
Yankees	102
Indians	101
Royals	100
Athletics	98
White Sox	98
Rays	97
Twins	94
Mariners	92
Angels	92

2011 AL RHB Avg	
Home Park	Index
Red Sox	117
Rangers	112
Blue Jays	109
Twins	105
Yankees	105
Tigers	104
Royals	100
Angels	98
White Sox	97
Indians	97
Athletics	95
Orioles	93
Mariners	91
Rays	89

2011 NL Avg	
Home Park	Index
Rockies	113
Brewers	105
Diamondbacks	105
Nationals	104
Astros	101
Braves	101
Reds	101
Pirates	100
Marlins	99
Cubs	98
Phillies	97
Dodgers	97
Mets	96
Giants	96
Cardinals	92
Padres	90

2011 NL LHB Avg	
Home Park	Index
Rockies	114
Astros	107
Nationals	106
Mets	104
Braves	102
Phillies	101
Cubs	99
Brewers	98
Reds	97
Pirates	97
Marlins	97
Dodgers	96
Diamondbacks	95
Giants	94
Cardinals	94
Padres	92

2011 NL RHB Avg	
Home Park	Index
Rockies	113
Diamondbacks	112
Brewers	109
Nationals	103
Pirates	103
Reds	102
Marlins	100
Braves	99
Astros	98
Giants	97
Cubs	97
Dodgers	97
Phillies	93
Cardinals	91
Mets	90
Padres	88

2011 AL Doubles	
Home Park	Index
Blue Jays	128
Red Sox	127
Rangers	115
Orioles	107
Tigers	102
Athletics	100
Royals	100
Indians	99
Yankees	98
Twins	92
White Sox	89
Angels	87
Rays	86
Mariners	79

2011 AL Triples	
Home Park	Index
Tigers	234
Rangers	226
Blue Jays	161
Royals	139
Red Sox	111
Twins	93
Athletics	93
Yankees	83
Orioles	73
Rays	72
White Sox	69
Mariners	67
Angels	64
Indians	63

2011 AL Errors	
Home Park	Index
Red Sox	144
Rangers	127
Athletics	119
Yankees	118
Tigers	118
Royals	111
Blue Jays	104
Twins	103
Indians	92
White Sox	92
Angels	91
Rays	84
Orioles	70
Mariners	62

2011 NL Doubles	
Home Park	Index
Rockies	119
Astros	116
Diamondbacks	113
Brewers	108
Phillies	102
Pirates	102
Giants	102
Nationals	102
Braves	98
Marlins	98
Dodgers	97
Mets	96
Padres	92
Reds	87
Cubs	86
Cardinals	85

2011 NL Triples	
Home Park	Index
Padres	141
Diamondbacks	136
Cubs	132
Brewers	126
Marlins	124
Mets	120
Rockies	109
Giants	105
Astros	94
Phillies	80
Pirates	73
Reds	71
Nationals	68
Cardinals	66
Braves	63
Dodgers	62

2011 NL Errors	
Home Park	Index
Braves	133
Rockies	125
Cubs	112
Phillies	108
Pirates	105
Mets	105
Reds	101
Marlins	99
Brewers	97
Dodgers	96
Astros	95
Cardinals	89
Nationals	87
Padres	86
Diamondbacks	83
Giants	82

2009-2011 American League Ballpark Index Rankings - Runs

Home Park	TOTALS											LHB		RHB	
	Avg	AB	R	H	2B	3B	HR	BB	SO	E	E-Inf	Avg	HR	Avg	HR
Rangers (Rangers Ballpark in Arlington)	107	102	119	109	109	136	126	101	92	119	155	104	131	109	123
Red Sox (Fenway Park)	106	100	111	106	130	92	91	96	97	122	110	104	81	109	100
Yankees (Yankee Stadium)	102	100	108	102	94	68	131	103	98	105	99	102	143	102	117
White Sox (U.S. Cellular Field)	98	99	106	97	98	76	132	119	108	99	97	99	122	98	138
Orioles (Oriole Park at Camden Yards)	103	103	104	106	100	80	116	96	96	78	88	106	122	101	111
Blue Jays (Rogers Centre)	100	101	104	101	106	128	116	97	103	103	103	98	107	102	121
Royals (Kauffman Stadium)	104	102	104	106	105	161	77	100	92	105	124	106	64	103	89
Tigers (Comerica Park)	102	100	102	101	98	133	97	94	91	122	115	100	89	103	102
Athletics (O.co Coliseum)	96	97	96	93	95	116	83	103	103	107	93	95	73	96	91
Twins (Target Field) *	101	99	95	100	102	106	76	101	97	100	114	100	68	102	83
Angels (Angel Stadium of Anaheim)	97	99	91	96	87	58	95	98	100	99	83	95	93	98	96
Indians (Progressive Field)	97	100	91	97	103	71	87	97	100	105	112	97	107	98	69
Mariners (Safeco Field)	94	99	87	93	87	71	86	106	109	80	76	96	101	92	75
Rays (Tropicana Field)	96	99	87	94	91	114	94	97	103	77	73	96	98	96	91

2009-2011 National League Ballpark Index Rankings - Runs

Home Park	TOTALS											LHB		RHB	
	Avg	AB	R	H	2B	3B	HR	BB	SO	E	E-Inf	Avg	HR	Avg	HR
Rockies (Coors Field)	114	104	132	119	122	144	125	97	87	111	102	115	129	114	121
Diamondbacks (Chase Field)	105	101	113	107	115	165	105	94	97	91	96	105	104	106	106
Cubs (Wrigley Field)	103	101	108	104	98	115	103	103	99	110	123	103	111	103	99
Marlins (Sun Life Stadium)	99	102	105	101	103	90	94	116	114	107	100	100	92	99	96
Reds (Great American Ballpark)	101	99	102	100	94	93	122	100	104	87	103	98	109	103	132
Phillies (Citizens Bank Park)	99	100	101	99	102	86	103	100	102	98	89	100	109	98	97
Pirates (PNC Park)	101	100	101	101	102	86	87	94	87	109	118	102	92	100	84
Nationals (Nationals Park)	100	101	98	101	102	88	102	89	94	100	90	102	104	99	100
Brewers (Miller Park)	99	100	97	99	105	96	112	103	106	94	88	97	116	100	109
Astros (Minute Maid Park)	99	101	96	100	99	107	109	100	104	102	100	105	113	96	108
Braves (Turner Field)	98	100	95	98	92	88	95	101	106	112	126	97	102	100	88
Cardinals (Busch Stadium)	96	98	92	94	92	76	77	107	98	104	103	97	86	95	73
Mets (Citi Field)	96	99	91	95	94	124	83	103	103	96	96	98	90	94	78
Dodgers (Dodger Stadium)	97	99	91	96	97	49	94	94	99	88	72	98	104	96	89
Giants (AT&T Park)	99	98	91	97	102	101	83	94	101	103	99	98	68	100	96
Padres (PETCO Park)	88	98	81	86	82	114	82	112	110	90	83	88	63	88	98

2009-2011 AL Home Runs	
Home Park	Index
White Sox	132
Yankees	131
Rangers	126
Blue Jays	116
Orioles	116
Tigers	97
Angels	95
Rays	94
Red Sox	91
Indians	87
Mariners	86
Athletics	83
Royals	77
Twins *	76

2009-2011 AL LHB Home Runs	
Home Park	Index
Yankees	143
Rangers	131
Orioles	122
White Sox	122
Indians	107
Blue Jays	107
Mariners	101
Rays	98
Angels	93
Tigers	89
Red Sox	81
Athletics	73
Twins *	68
Royals	64

2009-2011 AL RHB Home Runs	
Home Park	Index
White Sox	138
Rangers	123
Blue Jays	121
Yankees	117
Orioles	111
Tigers	102
Red Sox	100
Angels	96
Athletics	91
Rays	91
Royals	89
Twins *	83
Mariners	75
Indians	69

2009-2011 NL Home Runs	
Home Park	Index
Rockies	125
Reds	122
Brewers	112
Astros	109
Diamondbacks	105
Cubs	103
Phillies	103
Nationals	102
Braves	95
Marlins	94
Dodgers	94
Pirates	87
Giants	83
Mets	83
Padres	82
Cardinals	77

2009-2011 NL LHB Home Runs	
Home Park	Index
Rockies	129
Brewers	116
Astros	113
Cubs	111
Reds	109
Phillies	109
Dodgers	104
Diamondbacks	104
Nationals	104
Braves	102
Marlins	92
Pirates	92
Mets	90
Cardinals	86
Giants	68
Padres	63

2009-2011 NL RHB Home Runs	
Home Park	Index
Reds	132
Rockies	121
Brewers	109
Astros	108
Diamondbacks	106
Nationals	100
Cubs	99
Padres	98
Phillies	97
Marlins	96
Giants	96
Dodgers	89
Braves	88
Pirates	84
Mets	78
Cardinals	73

* Data since 2010

414

2009-2011 AL Avg	
Home Park	Index
Rangers	107
Red Sox	106
Royals	104
Orioles	103
Yankees	102
Tigers	102
Twins *	101
Blue Jays	100
White Sox	98
Indians	97
Angels	97
Athletics	96
Rays	96
Mariners	94

2009-2011 AL LHB Avg	
Home Park	Index
Royals	106
Orioles	106
Rangers	104
Red Sox	104
Yankees	102
Tigers	100
Twins *	100
White Sox	99
Blue Jays	98
Indians	97
Mariners	96
Rays	96
Angels	95
Athletics	95

2009-2011 AL RHB Avg	
Home Park	Index
Rangers	109
Red Sox	109
Tigers	103
Royals	103
Twins *	102
Yankees	102
Blue Jays	102
Orioles	101
Angels	98
White Sox	98
Indians	98
Athletics	96
Rays	96
Mariners	92

2009-2011 NL Avg	
Home Park	Index
Rockies	114
Diamondbacks	105
Cubs	103
Reds	101
Pirates	101
Nationals	100
Marlins	99
Phillies	99
Giants	99
Brewers	99
Astros	99
Braves	98
Dodgers	97
Cardinals	96
Mets	96
Padres	88

2009-2011 NL LHB Avg	
Home Park	Index
Rockies	115
Diamondbacks	105
Astros	105
Cubs	103
Nationals	102
Pirates	102
Phillies	100
Marlins	100
Reds	98
Giants	98
Dodgers	98
Mets	98
Cardinals	97
Braves	97
Brewers	97
Padres	88

2009-2011 NL RHB Avg	
Home Park	Index
Rockies	114
Diamondbacks	106
Reds	103
Cubs	103
Brewers	100
Pirates	100
Giants	100
Braves	100
Marlins	99
Nationals	99
Phillies	98
Dodgers	96
Astros	96
Cardinals	95
Mets	94
Padres	88

2009-2011 AL Doubles	
Home Park	Index
Red Sox	130
Rangers	109
Blue Jays	106
Royals	105
Indians	103
Twins *	102
Orioles	100
Tigers	98
White Sox	98
Athletics	95
Yankees	94
Rays	91
Angels	87
Mariners	87

2009-2011 AL Triples	
Home Park	Index
Royals	161
Rangers	136
Tigers	133
Blue Jays	128
Athletics	116
Rays	114
Twins *	106
Red Sox	92
Orioles	80
White Sox	76
Indians	71
Mariners	71
Yankees	68
Angels	58

2009-2011 AL Errors	
Home Park	Index
Red Sox	122
Tigers	122
Rangers	119
Athletics	107
Indians	105
Royals	105
Yankees	105
Blue Jays	103
Twins *	100
White Sox	99
Angels	99
Mariners	80
Orioles	78
Rays	77

2009-2011 NL Doubles	
Home Park	Index
Rockies	122
Diamondbacks	115
Brewers	105
Marlins	103
Phillies	102
Pirates	102
Nationals	102
Giants	102
Astros	99
Cubs	98
Dodgers	97
Reds	94
Mets	94
Braves	92
Cardinals	92
Padres	82

2009-2011 NL Triples	
Home Park	Index
Diamondbacks	165
Rockies	144
Mets	124
Cubs	115
Padres	114
Astros	107
Giants	101
Brewers	96
Reds	93
Marlins	90
Braves	88
Nationals	88
Pirates	86
Phillies	86
Cardinals	76
Dodgers	49

2009-2011 NL Errors	
Home Park	Index
Braves	112
Rockies	111
Cubs	110
Pirates	109
Marlins	107
Cardinals	104
Giants	103
Astros	102
Nationals	100
Phillies	98
Mets	96
Brewers	94
Diamondbacks	91
Padres	90
Dodgers	88
Reds	87

* Data since 2010

2011 Lefty/Righty Statistics

The following section contains lefty/righty splits for each batter and pitcher who appeared during the 2011 season. The batting side of each hitter is shown below his name; for pitchers, the hand that he throws with is indicated.

For each batter, we show his batting average, on-base percentage, and slugging percentage along with a count of his at-bats, hits, doubles, triples, home runs, RBI, walks, and strikeouts. The results of opposing batters, broken out into the same categories, are displayed for pitchers.

Batters vs. Left-Handed and Right-Handed Pitchers

Batter	vs	Avg	AB	H	2B	3B	HR	RBI	BB	SO	OBP	Slg
Abreu,Bobby	L	.238	147	35	6	0	0	15	18	43	.319	.279
Bats Left	R	.259	355	92	24	1	8	45	60	70	.366	.400
Ackley,Dustin	L	.224	85	19	4	1	2	8	8	27	.287	.365
Bats Left	R	.290	248	72	12	6	4	28	32	52	.369	.435
Adams,Ryan	L	.370	27	10	1	0	0	2	0	6	.370	.407
Bats Right	R	.242	62	15	3	0	0	5	6	19	.319	.290
Alfonzo,Eliezer	L	.300	20	6	0	0	0	0	1	2	.333	.300
Bats Right	R	.255	55	14	1	0	1	9	2	11	.293	.327
Allen,Brandon	L	.151	53	8	1	0	1	4	3	19	.196	.226
Bats Left	R	.221	122	27	8	2	5	14	15	49	.309	.443
Almonte,Erick	L	.158	19	3	0	0	1	3	0	1	.158	.316
Bats Right	R	.000	10	0	0	0	0	0	0	3	.000	.000
Alonso,Yonder	L	.154	13	2	0	0	1	3	2	3	.267	.385
Bats Left	R	.360	75	27	4	0	4	12	8	18	.422	.573
Altuve,Jose	L	.321	53	17	2	0	1	5	3	7	.351	.415
Bats Right	R	.262	168	44	8	1	1	7	2	22	.279	.339
Alvarez,Pedro	L	.158	38	6	2	0	1	3	3	20	.256	.289
Bats Left	R	.198	197	39	7	1	3	16	21	60	.275	.289
Amarista,Alexi	L	.000	6	0	0	0	0	1	0	1	.000	.000
Bats Left	R	.174	46	8	3	1	0	4	2	7	.208	.283
Amezaga,Alfredo	L	.143	28	4	0	0	0	4	3	6	.219	.143
Bats Both	R	.204	49	10	1	0	0	0	4	8	.264	.224
Anderson,Lars	L	.000	3	0	0	0	0	0	2	0	.000	.000
Bats Left	R	.000	2	0	0	0	0	0	0	1	.000	.000
Andino,Robert	L	.306	144	44	7	0	0	3	14	25	.367	.354
Bats Right	R	.243	313	76	15	0	5	33	27	58	.308	.339
Andrus,Elvis	L	.282	142	40	5	0	2	15	15	16	.354	.359
Bats Right	R	.279	445	124	22	3	3	45	41	58	.344	.362
Angle,Matt	L	.167	6	1	1	0	0	1	0	3	.167	.333
Bats Left	R	.178	73	13	3	0	1	6	12	10	.302	.260
Ankiel,Rick	L	.228	79	18	3	0	1	9	6	21	.282	.304
Bats Left	R	.243	301	73	17	0	8	28	23	75	.300	.379
Arencibia,J.P.	L	.259	108	28	2	0	9	23	8	31	.310	.528
Bats Right	R	.206	335	69	18	4	14	55	28	102	.273	.409
Avila,Alex	L	.273	128	35	9	1	3	17	14	37	.349	.430
Bats Left	R	.304	336	102	24	3	16	65	59	94	.403	.536
Aviles,Mike	L	.318	85	27	11	1	3	18	4	11	.348	.576
Bats Right	R	.229	201	46	6	2	4	21	9	33	.263	.338
Aybar,Erick	L	.216	176	38	8	1	3	17	13	20	.284	.324
Bats Both	R	.308	380	117	25	7	7	42	18	48	.341	.466
Baker,Jeff	L	.314	121	38	7	1	3	17	7	16	.349	.463
Bats Right	R	.200	80	16	5	0	0	6	3	30	.229	.263
Baker,John	L	-	0	0	0	0	0	0	0	0	-	-
Bats Left	R	.154	13	2	0	0	0	1	2	3	.267	.154
Barajas,Rod	L	.267	90	24	4	0	5	13	9	23	.340	.478
Bats Right	R	.214	215	46	9	0	11	34	13	48	.265	.409
Bard,Josh	L	.125	16	2	1	0	0	2	1	5	.176	.188
Bats Both	R	.231	65	15	3	0	2	9	4	15	.275	.369
Barmes,Clint	L	.226	115	26	6	0	2	9	15	19	.318	.330
Bats Right	R	.251	331	83	21	0	10	30	23	69	.310	.405
Barney,Darwin	L	.290	100	29	5	2	1	8	4	15	.324	.410
Bats Right	R	.273	429	117	18	4	1	35	18	52	.310	.340
Bartlett,Jason	L	.279	140	39	5	0	1	8	15	31	.348	.336
Bats Right	R	.234	414	97	17	3	1	32	33	67	.295	.297
Barton,Daric	L	.253	75	19	8	0	0	8	13	15	.360	.360
Bats Left	R	.193	161	31	5	0	0	13	26	32	.309	.224
Bautista,Jose	L	.336	119	40	7	0	11	21	33	24	.484	.672
Bats Right	R	.292	394	115	17	2	32	82	99	87	.436	.589
Baxter,Mike	L	.000	2	0	0	0	0	0	1	2	.333	.000
Bats Left	R	.250	32	8	2	1	1	4	4	7	.351	.469
Bay,Jason	L	.300	110	33	5	1	5	17	22	32	.418	.500
Bats Right	R	.228	334	76	14	0	7	40	34	77	.297	.332
Beckham,Gordon	L	.195	123	24	4	0	2	8	9	25	.265	.276
Bats Right	R	.242	376	91	19	0	8	36	26	86	.307	.356
Bell,Josh	L	.188	16	3	0	0	1	2	7	7	.278	.188
Bats Both	R	.156	45	7	0	0	0	5	2	18	.191	.156
Belt,Brandon	L	.348	46	16	2	0	2	4	4	15	.412	.522
Bats Left	R	.184	141	26	4	2	7	14	12	42	.272	.376
Beltran,Carlos	L	.286	147	42	11	3	9	28	11	28	.338	.585
Bats Both	R	.306	373	114	28	3	13	56	60	60	.402	.501
Beltre,Adrian	L	.315	111	35	11	0	10	28	12	10	.391	.685
Bats Right	R	.290	376	109	22	0	22	77	13	43	.312	.524
Benson,Joe	L	.118	17	2	0	0	0	1	1	8	.167	.118
Bats Right	R	.278	54	15	6	1	0	2	2	13	.304	.426
Berkman,Lance	L	.277	101	28	6	0	4	14	9	21	.348	.455
Bats Both	R	.307	387	119	17	2	27	80	83	72	.427	.571

Batter	vs	Avg	AB	H	2B	3B	HR	RBI	BB	SO	OBP	Slg
Bernadina,Roger	L	.191	68	13	0	0	1	4	1	15	.225	.235
Bats Left	R	.257	241	62	12	2	6	23	21	48	.322	.398
Betancourt,Yuniesky	L	.229	118	27	3	0	3	14	2	14	.246	.331
Bats Right	R	.258	438	113	24	3	10	54	14	49	.277	.395
Betemit,Wilson	L	.236	89	21	2	0	2	8	6	36	.281	.326
Bats Both	R	.303	234	71	20	4	6	38	25	69	.365	.500
Bixler,Brian	L	.212	52	11	0	0	0	1	3	11	.255	.212
Bats Right	R	.194	31	6	1	2	0	1	4	8	.286	.355
Blackmon,Charlie	L	.400	20	8	1	0	0	3	2	0	.455	.450
Bats Left	R	.218	78	17	0	0	1	5	1	8	.228	.256
Blake,Casey	L	.283	53	15	4	0	1	8	8	12	.365	.415
Bats Right	R	.242	149	36	6	1	3	18	18	38	.333	.356
Blanco,Andres	L	.190	21	4	0	0	1	1	1	3	.227	.333
Bats Both	R	.236	55	13	3	0	1	2	3	11	.276	.345
Blanco,Henry	L	.266	64	17	3	0	6	8	6	10	.329	.594
Bats Right	R	.222	36	8	0	1	2	4	6	11	.333	.444
Blanks,Kyle	L	.185	54	10	0	1	1	4	5	11	.250	.278
Bats Right	R	.250	116	29	7	0	6	22	11	40	.323	.466
Bloomquist,Willie	L	.303	109	33	2	2	7	9	13	16	.361	.376
Bats Both	R	.249	241	60	8	2	2	19	14	38	.296	.324
Blum,Geoff	L	.000	9	0	0	0	0	0	1	3	.100	.000
Bats Both	R	.275	40	11	3	0	2	10	4	6	.356	.500
Boesch,Brennan	L	.302	106	32	7	0	1	14	9	22	.356	.396
Bats Left	R	.276	322	89	18	1	15	40	26	61	.336	.478
Boggs,Brandon	L	.167	6	1	0	0	1	1	0	4	.167	.667
Bats Both	R	.154	13	2	0	0	1	1	3	4	.313	.385
Bogusevic,Brian	L	.154	13	2	0	0	0	0	1	3	.267	.154
Bats Left	R	.298	151	45	14	1	4	15	14	37	.355	.483
Bonifacio,Emilio	L	.333	147	49	11	2	1	9	19	29	.407	.456
Bats Both	R	.282	418	118	15	5	4	27	40	100	.343	.371
Borbon,Julio	L	.300	30	9	1	1	0	5	1	4	.333	.400
Bats Left	R	.254	59	15	0	2	0	6	2	5	.290	.322
Boscan,J.C.	L	-	0	0	0	0	0	0	0	0	-	-
Bats Right	R	.333	9	3	0	0	0	0	0	5	.333	.333
Bourgeois,Jason	L	.396	101	40	5	1	1	10	6	7	.430	.495
Bats Right	R	.219	137	30	3	1	0	6	4	17	.241	.255
Bourjos,Peter	L	.289	173	50	10	6	5	19	10	45	.337	.503
Bats Right	R	.261	329	86	16	5	7	24	22	79	.321	.404
Bourn,Michael	L	.254	197	50	6	5	1	14	10	55	.295	.350
Bats Left	R	.312	459	143	28	5	1	36	43	85	.371	.401
Bowker,John	L	-	0	0	0	0	0	0	0	0	-	-
Bats Left	R	.133	30	4	1	0	0	2	2	11	.188	.167
Bradley,Milton	L	.255	51	13	3	1	0	5	2	9	.296	.353
Bats Both	R	.180	50	9	3	0	2	8	11	22	.328	.360
Brantley,Michael	L	.214	140	30	4	0	0	11	12	33	.282	.243
Bats Left	R	.289	311	90	20	4	7	35	22	43	.335	.447
Branyan,Russell	L	.182	11	2	0	0	0	2	5	3	.308	.182
Bats Left	R	.198	116	23	7	0	5	14	16	36	.293	.388
Braun,Ryan	L	.350	120	42	8	0	8	22	19	21	.433	.617
Bats Right	R	.327	443	145	30	6	25	89	39	72	.387	.591
Brignac,Reid	L	.150	40	6	0	0	0	0	2	12	.190	.150
Bats Left	R	.201	209	42	4	0	1	15	8	51	.234	.234
Brown,Andrew	L	.167	12	2	1	0	0	2	0	6	.167	.250
Bats Right	R	.200	10	2	0	0	0	1	0	2	.200	.200
Brown,Corey	L	-	0	0	0	0	0	0	0	0	-	-
Bats Left	R	.000	3	0	0	0	0	0	0	2	.000	.000
Brown,Domonic	L	.281	32	9	2	0	0	0	4	7	.361	.344
Bats Left	R	.237	152	36	8	1	5	19	21	28	.328	.401
Brown,Dusty	L	.000	5	0	0	0	0	0	0	0	.000	.000
Bats Right	R	.130	23	3	0	0	0	0	1	8	.167	.130
Bruce,Jay	L	.240	175	42	9	1	11	35	17	59	.313	.491
Bats Left	R	.263	410	108	18	1	21	62	54	99	.353	.466
Buck,John	L	.189	122	23	3	0	5	16	10	35	.250	.336
Bats Right	R	.241	344	83	12	1	11	41	44	80	.338	.378
Buck,Travis	L	.067	15	1	1	0	0	1	0	5	.167	.133
Bats Left	R	.246	134	33	10	0	2	17	8	25	.289	.366
Burrell,Pat	L	.219	64	14	3	1	1	6	11	26	.342	.344
Bats Right	R	.235	119	28	6	0	6	15	22	41	.357	.437
Burriss,Manny	L	.143	28	4	0	0	0	1	1	1	.200	.143
Bats Both	R	.220	109	24	1	0	0	3	5	16	.267	.229
Burroughs,Sean	L	.286	14	4	1	0	0	0	0	2	.286	.357
Bats Left	R	.271	96	26	3	0	1	8	3	13	.290	.333
Butera,Drew	L	.215	65	14	3	0	1	7	4	11	.261	.308
Bats Right	R	.148	169	25	6	1	1	16	7	31	.190	.213
Butler,Billy	L	.306	147	45	12	0	6	27	24	26	.407	.510
Bats Right	R	.287	450	129	32	0	13	68	42	69	.345	.444

418

Batters vs. Left-Handed and Right-Handed Pitchers

Batter	vs	Avg	AB	H	2B	3B	HR	RBI	BB	SO	OBP	Slg
Byrd,Marlon	L	.219	105	23	5	0	4	10	5	20	.268	.381
Bats Right	R	.293	341	100	17	2	5	25	20	58	.341	.399
Cabrera,Asdrubal	L	.291	196	57	12	0	6	27	14	28	.333	.444
Bats Both	R	.265	408	108	20	3	19	65	30	91	.331	.468
Cabrera,Everth	L	.500	2	1	0	0	0	0	0	0	.500	.500
Bats Both	R	.000	6	0	0	0	0	0	1	3	.143	.000
Cabrera,Melky	L	.304	207	63	11	0	7	29	9	30	.329	.459
Bats Both	R	.306	451	138	33	5	11	58	26	64	.344	.475
Cabrera,Miguel	L	.319	141	45	12	0	6	23	38	23	.459	.532
Bats Right	R	.353	431	152	36	0	24	82	70	66	.444	.603
Cabrera,Orlando	L	.248	137	34	6	0	4	15	8	15	.290	.380
Bats Right	R	.233	313	73	10	0	1	36	9	42	.257	.275
Cain,Lorenzo	L	.000	5	0	0	0	0	0	1	1	.167	.000
Bats Right	R	.353	17	6	1	0	0	1	0	3	.353	.412
Cairo,Miguel	L	.319	47	15	3	1	2	9	2	5	.365	.553
Bats Both	R	.253	198	50	5	1	6	24	16	31	.321	.379
Callaspo,Alberto	L	.306	147	45	7	0	1	12	12	18	.356	.374
Bats Both	R	.280	328	92	16	0	5	34	46	30	.370	.375
Cameron,Mike	L	.165	91	15	2	0	5	13	13	23	.267	.352
Bats Right	R	.226	146	33	8	0	4	14	15	36	.296	.363
Campana,Tony	L	.231	26	6	0	0	0	1	1	5	.259	.231
Bats Left	R	.265	117	31	3	0	1	5	7	25	.312	.316
Cancel,Robinson	L	.000	1	0	0	0	0	0	0	1	.000	.000
Bats Right	R	.000	5	0	0	0	0	0	1	3	.167	.000
Cano,Robinson	L	.314	204	64	13	3	8	45	11	31	.354	.525
Bats Left	R	.296	419	124	33	4	20	73	27	65	.347	.537
Cantu,Jorge	L	.204	54	11	1	0	1	7	3	6	.237	.278
Bats Right	R	.189	90	17	3	0	2	9	4	22	.229	.289
Canzler,Russ	L	.500	2	1	0	0	0	0	0	1	.500	.500
Bats Right	R	.000	1	0	0	0	0	0	0	0	.333	.000
Carp,Mike	L	.306	72	22	3	1	4	17	4	17	.342	.542
Bats Left	R	.266	218	58	14	0	8	29	15	64	.321	.440
Carpenter,Matt	L	.000	1	0	0	0	0	0	1	0	.500	.000
Bats Left	R	.071	14	1	1	0	0	0	3	4	.235	.143
Carrera,Ezequiel	L	.191	68	13	1	0	0	3	7	14	.276	.206
Bats Left	R	.269	134	36	7	3	0	11	9	21	.315	.366
Carroll,Brett	L	.000	3	0	0	0	0	0	0	1	.000	.000
Bats Right	R	-	0	0	0	0	0	0	0	0	-	
Carroll,Jamey	L	.304	125	38	4	3	0	3	13	11	.367	.384
Bats Right	R	.284	327	93	10	3	0	14	34	47	.355	.333
Carter,Chris	L	.050	20	1	0	0	0	0	1	9	.095	.050
Bats Right	R	.208	24	5	0	0	0	1	1	11	.240	.208
Casilla,Alexi	L	.236	106	25	8	0	0	7	5	10	.268	.311
Bats Both	R	.272	217	59	13	4	2	14	23	35	.347	.396
Castillo,Welington	L	.000	3	0	0	0	0	0	0	2	.000	.000
Bats Right	R	.200	10	2	0	0	0	0	0	2	.200	.200
Castro,Juan	L	.286	7	2	0	0	0	0	1	1	.375	.286
Bats Right	R	.286	7	2	0	0	0	1	0	3	.286	.286
Castro,Ramon	L	.289	45	13	3	0	3	6	6	16	.373	.556
Bats Right	R	.130	23	3	0	0	1	4	1	7	.167	.261
Castro,Starlin	L	.342	155	53	10	2	3	19	9	21	.376	.471
Bats Right	R	.297	519	154	26	7	8	53	26	75	.331	.420
Cedeno,Ronny	L	.220	91	20	6	0	0	5	10	23	.291	.286
Bats Right	R	.258	322	83	19	3	2	27	20	70	.299	.354
Cervelli,Francisco	L	.276	29	8	0	0	1	4	4	5	.364	.379
Bats Right	R	.263	95	25	4	0	3	18	5	24	.311	.400
Chambers,Adron	L	-	0	0	0	0	0	0	0	0	-	
Bats Left	R	.375	8	3	0	1	0	4	0	1	.375	.625
Chavez,Endy	L	.357	42	15	2	0	0	4	4	5	.413	.405
Bats Left	R	.290	214	62	9	3	5	23	6	25	.305	.430
Chavez,Eric	L	.304	23	7	0	0	0	5	0	9	.304	.304
Bats Left	R	.255	137	35	7	1	2	21	14	25	.322	.365
Chirinos,Robinson	L	.333	3	1	0	0	0	0	1	1	.500	.333
Bats Right	R	.212	52	11	2	0	1	7	4	12	.268	.308
Chisenhall,Lonnie	L	.260	50	13	2	0	5	11	2	14	.288	.600
Bats Left	R	.253	162	41	11	0	2	11	6	35	.282	.358
Choo,Shin-Soo	L	.269	108	29	2	2	1	7	6	30	.336	.352
Bats Left	R	.254	205	52	9	1	7	29	30	48	.347	.410
Christian,Justin	L	.370	27	10	4	0	0	3	0	3	.370	.519
Bats Right	R	.100	20	2	1	0	0	1	2	5	.182	.150
Ciriaco,Pedro	L	.222	9	2	0	0	0	0	0	3	.222	.222
Bats Right	R	.333	24	8	2	1	0	6	1	3	.360	.500
Clevenger,Steve	L	1.000	1	1	1	0	0	0	0	0	1.000	2.000
Bats Left	R	.000	3	0	0	0	0	0	0	0	.000	.000
Coghlan,Chris	L	.107	75	8	3	0	0	3	3	16	.160	.147
Bats Left	R	.278	194	54	17	1	5	19	19	33	.347	.454

Batter	vs	Avg	AB	H	2B	3B	HR	RBI	BB	SO	OBP	Slg
Colvin,Tyler	L	.057	35	2	1	0	0	1	1	12	.083	.086
Bats Left	R	.170	171	29	7	3	6	19	13	46	.227	.351
Conger,Hank	L	.182	11	2	0	0	0	2	3	3	.357	.182
Bats Both	R	.211	166	35	8	0	6	17	14	34	.276	.367
Conrad,Brooks	L	.292	24	7	2	0	1	4	4	11	.393	.500
Bats Both	R	.203	79	16	3	0	3	9	11	30	.304	.354
Constanza,Jose	L	.385	39	15	0	0	0	6	2	5	.415	.385
Bats Left	R	.257	70	18	1	1	2	4	4	9	.297	.386
Cooper,David	L	.286	14	4	2	0	0	2	0	2	.286	.429
Bats Left	R	.193	57	11	5	0	2	10	7	12	.284	.386
Cora,Alex	L	.300	10	3	1	0	0	0	1	4	.364	.400
Bats Left	R	.219	146	32	5	1	0	6	11	19	.281	.267
Corporan,Carlos	L	.243	37	9	3	0	0	1	5	14	.349	.324
Bats Both	R	.171	117	20	5	1	0	10	5	35	.220	.231
Counsell,Craig	L	.333	6	2	1	0	0	2	0	1	.333	.500
Bats Left	R	.172	151	26	1	1	1	7	20	20	.278	.212
Cousins,Scott	L	.000	8	0	0	0	0	0	1	6	.111	.000
Bats Left	R	.159	44	7	1	0	1	4	5	15	.245	.250
Cowgill,Collin	L	.275	40	11	1	0	1	2	4	12	.341	.375
Bats Right	R	.212	52	11	2	0	0	7	4	16	.268	.250
Cozart,Zack	L	.333	12	4	0	0	0	0	0	1	.333	.333
Bats Right	R	.320	25	8	0	0	2	3	0	5	.320	.560
Craig,Allen	L	.313	67	21	8	0	5	16	3	12	.343	.657
Bats Right	R	.316	133	42	7	0	6	24	12	28	.372	.504
Crawford,Brandon	L	.133	30	4	1	1	0	3	3	12	.212	.233
Bats Left	R	.217	166	36	4	1	3	18	20	19	.301	.307
Crawford,Carl	L	.195	164	32	9	1	3	22	10	41	.249	.317
Bats Left	R	.284	342	97	20	6	8	34	13	63	.309	.447
Crisp,Coco	L	.211	171	36	9	0	3	18	16	24	.277	.316
Bats Both	R	.289	360	104	18	5	5	36	25	41	.332	.408
Crowe,Trevor	L	.200	15	3	1	0	0	0	1	5	.250	.267
Bats Both	R	.231	13	3	0	0	0	2	3	4	.375	.231
Cruz,Nelson	L	.340	100	34	6	0	10	22	10	27	.396	.700
Bats Right	R	.243	375	91	22	1	19	65	23	89	.289	.459
Cruz,Tony	L	.269	26	7	2	0	0	2	2	1	.321	.346
Bats Right	R	.256	39	10	3	0	0	4	4	12	.341	.333
Cuddyer,Michael	L	.311	151	47	12	0	10	22	24	28	.403	.589
Bats Right	R	.272	378	103	17	2	10	48	24	67	.321	.407
Cunningham,Aaron	L	.205	44	9	5	0	1	4	4	5	.265	.386
Bats Right	R	.152	46	7	1	1	2	5	5	12	.250	.348
Cust,Jack	L	.246	65	16	3	0	0	7	9	22	.338	.292
Bats Left	R	.200	160	32	12	1	3	16	35	65	.347	.344
Damon,Johnny	L	.277	166	46	6	3	6	28	16	23	.354	.458
Bats Left	R	.255	416	106	23	4	10	45	35	69	.314	.401
d'Arnaud,Chase	L	.255	47	12	2	2	0	3	1	14	.286	.383
Bats Right	R	.198	96	19	4	0	0	3	3	22	.220	.240
Darnell,James	L	.143	21	3	0	0	1	4	1	2	.182	.286
Bats Right	R	.292	24	7	2	0	0	3	4	5	.379	.375
Davis,Blake	L	.222	9	2	1	0	0	0	0	2	.222	.333
Bats Left	R	.260	50	13	2	1	1	6	6	11	.339	.400
Davis,Chris	L	.350	40	14	4	0	1	5	2	10	.381	.525
Bats Left	R	.245	159	39	8	0	4	14	9	53	.286	.371
Davis,Ike	L	.163	43	7	1	1	0	4	5	18	.260	.233
Bats Left	R	.372	86	32	7	0	7	21	12	13	.444	.698
Davis,Rajai	L	.288	80	23	8	3	0	5	9	17	.367	.463
Bats Right	R	.221	240	53	13	3	1	24	6	46	.239	.313
De Aza,Alejandro	L	.263	19	5	2	0	0	4	2	4	.333	.368
Bats Left	R	.338	133	45	9	3	4	19	15	30	.409	.541
De Jesus,Ivan	L	.286	7	2	0	0	0	1	2	2	.444	.286
Bats Right	R	.160	25	4	0	0	0	0	0	9	.160	.160
DeJesus,David	L	.174	121	21	4	0	1	8	7	31	.227	.231
Bats Left	R	.265	321	85	16	5	9	38	38	55	.357	.430
Denorfia,Chris	L	.328	119	39	8	0	4	9	13	16	.391	.496
Bats Right	R	.245	188	46	5	2	1	10	15	33	.302	.309
DeRosa,Mark	L	.263	38	10	1	0	0	3	6	8	.378	.289
Bats Right	R	.292	48	14	1	0	0	9	2	10	.327	.313
Descalso,Daniel	L	.190	58	11	3	0	0	3	6	11	.277	.241
Bats Left	R	.280	268	75	17	3	1	25	27	54	.347	.377
Desmond,Ian	L	.216	125	27	6	1	3	7	12	28	.290	.352
Bats Right	R	.264	459	121	21	4	5	42	23	111	.300	.359
DeWitt,Blake	L	.406	32	13	3	2	0	1	3	5	.472	.625
Bats Left	R	.242	198	48	8	2	5	25	9	26	.275	.379
Diaz,Matt	L	.295	132	39	6	1	0	9	8	22	.336	.356
Bats Right	R	.227	119	27	7	0	0	11	4	30	.264	.286
Dickerson,Chris	L	.333	12	4	0	0	0	3	0	4	.385	.333
Bats Left	R	.237	38	9	2	0	1	4	2	13	.268	.368

Batters vs. Left-Handed and Right-Handed Pitchers

Batter	vs	Avg	AB	H	2B	3B	HR	RBI	BB	SO	OBP	Slg
Dinkelman,Brian	L	.273	11	3	0	0	0	0	0	1	.273	.273
Bats Left	R	.306	62	19	1	0	0	4	4	13	.358	.323
Dirks,Andy	L	.323	31	10	1	0	2	9	0	2	.323	.548
Bats Left	R	.239	188	45	12	0	5	19	11	34	.292	.383
Dobbs,Greg	L	.216	37	8	1	0	0	5	3	12	.275	.243
Bats Left	R	.281	374	105	22	0	8	44	19	71	.315	.404
Dominguez,Matt	L	.389	18	7	3	0	0	0	0	3	.389	.556
Bats Right	R	.148	27	4	1	0	0	2	2	5	.233	.185
Donald,Jason	L	.377	61	23	4	1	1	5	5	12	.424	.525
Bats Right	R	.268	71	19	2	0	0	3	2	23	.312	.296
Doumit,Ryan	L	.315	54	17	5	0	2	10	6	6	.393	.519
Bats Both	R	.299	164	49	7	1	6	20	10	29	.339	.463
Downs,Matt	L	.340	47	16	4	0	3	11	3	11	.415	.617
Bats Right	R	.257	152	39	14	0	7	30	14	36	.325	.487
Drew,J.D.	L	.167	48	8	1	1	1	3	6	16	.259	.292
Bats Left	R	.235	200	47	5	0	3	19	27	42	.328	.305
Drew,Stephen	L	.224	85	19	6	2	1	17	9	29	.295	.376
Bats Left	R	.263	236	62	15	3	4	28	21	45	.326	.403
Duda,Lucas	L	.274	62	17	5	1	0	11	3	14	.328	.387
Bats Left	R	.297	239	71	16	2	10	39	30	43	.380	.506
Duncan,Shelley	L	.245	102	25	9	0	1	18	11	23	.316	.363
Bats Right	R	.273	121	33	8	0	10	29	8	33	.331	.587
Dunn,Adam	L	.064	94	6	1	0	0	3	20	39	.235	.074
Bats Left	R	.187	321	60	15	0	11	39	55	138	.310	.336
Durango,Luis	L	-	0	0	0	0	0	0	0	0	-	-
Bats Both	R	.167	6	1	0	0	0	1	1	1	.286	.167
Dyson,Jarrod	L	.000	2	0	0	0	0	0	1	1	.333	.000
Bats Left	R	.214	42	9	1	0	0	3	6	13	.306	.238
Ellis,A.J.	L	.360	25	9	1	0	2	3	3	4	.429	.640
Bats Right	R	.233	60	14	0	1	0	8	11	12	.378	.267
Ellis,Mark	L	.268	123	33	6	0	3	6	5	12	.302	.390
Bats Right	R	.241	357	86	18	1	4	35	17	63	.283	.331
Ellsbury,Jacoby	L	.284	197	56	17	3	6	22	15	25	.348	.492
Bats Left	R	.337	463	156	29	2	26	83	37	73	.388	.577
Emaus,Brad	L	.250	8	2	0	0	0	1	0	2	.250	.250
Bats Right	R	.138	29	4	0	0	0	0	4	7	.265	.138
Encarnacion,Edwin	L	.276	123	34	10	0	6	14	12	24	.341	.504
Bats Right	R	.271	358	97	26	0	11	41	31	53	.332	.436
Escobar,Alcides	L	.244	135	33	5	0	0	8	10	17	.295	.281
Bats Right	R	.257	413	106	16	8	4	38	15	56	.288	.363
Escobar,Eduardo	L	.333	3	1	0	0	0	0	0	0	.333	.333
Bats Both	R	.250	4	1	0	0	0	0	0	1	.250	.250
Escobar,Yunel	L	.330	115	38	9	2	3	13	13	17	.408	.522
Bats Right	R	.279	398	111	15	1	8	35	48	53	.358	.382
Espinosa,Danny	L	.283	127	36	9	0	6	16	13	33	.361	.496
Bats Both	R	.222	446	99	20	5	15	50	44	133	.312	.390
Ethier,Andre	L	.220	141	31	9	0	1	13	7	41	.258	.305
Bats Left	R	.321	346	111	21	0	10	49	51	62	.410	.468
Evans,Nick	L	.236	55	13	0	1	3	7	7	15	.323	.436
Bats Right	R	.264	121	32	10	1	1	18	8	33	.310	.388
Everett,Adam	L	.143	21	3	0	0	0	3	5	5	.250	.143
Bats Right	R	.256	39	10	1	0	0	1	2	9	.293	.282
Farris,Eric	L	-	0	0	0	0	0	0	0	0	-	-
Bats Right	R	.000	1	0	0	0	0	0	0	0	.000	.000
Federowicz,Tim	L	.200	5	1	0	0	0	1	0	0	.200	.200
Bats Right	R	.125	8	1	0	0	0	0	2	4	.364	.125
Field,Tommy	L	.364	11	4	0	0	0	0	0	2	.364	.364
Bats Right	R	.243	37	9	0	0	0	3	3	12	.300	.243
Fielder,Prince	L	.282	170	48	7	1	7	31	22	40	.363	.459
Bats Left	R	.306	399	122	29	0	31	89	85	66	.435	.612
Figgins,Chone	L	.152	92	14	5	1	1	9	4	17	.186	.261
Bats Both	R	.204	196	40	6	0	0	6	17	25	.266	.235
Flores,Jesus	L	.200	20	4	2	0	0	0	1	9	.238	.300
Bats Right	R	.212	66	14	4	0	1	2	4	18	.257	.318
Florimon,Pedro	L	-	0	0	0	0	0	0	1	0	1.000	-
Bats Both	R	.125	8	1	1	0	0	2	0	6	.125	.250
Flowers,Tyler	L	.135	37	5	0	0	1	5	3	14	.214	.216
Bats Right	R	.247	73	18	5	1	4	11	11	24	.356	.507
Fontenot,Mike	L	.255	47	12	3	1	1	7	8	13	.357	.426
Bats Left	R	.220	173	38	12	2	3	14	17	35	.289	.364
Ford,Darren	L	1.000	2	2	0	0	0	0	1	0	1.000	1.000
Bats Right	R	.167	12	2	0	0	0	0	0	5	.231	.167
Forsythe,Logan	L	.217	46	10	3	0	0	1	3	11	.265	.283
Bats Right	R	.212	104	22	6	1	0	11	9	22	.288	.288
Fowler,Dexter	L	.254	126	32	8	3	1	10	23	21	.373	.389
Bats Both	R	.270	355	96	27	12	4	35	45	109	.360	.448
Fox,Jake	L	.156	32	5	2	0	0	2	2	3	.206	.219
Bats Right	R	.345	29	10	2	1	2	4	2	5	.424	.690
Francisco,Ben	L	.245	110	27	3	0	2	17	14	16	.333	.327
Bats Right	R	.243	140	34	7	1	4	17	19	26	.345	.393
Francisco,Juan	L	.143	14	2	0	0	0	1	0	5	.143	.143
Bats Left	R	.278	79	22	7	1	3	14	4	19	.313	.506
Francoeur,Jeff	L	.302	149	45	11	1	9	30	12	27	.363	.570
Bats Right	R	.279	452	126	36	3	11	57	25	96	.318	.445
Frazier,Todd	L	.360	25	9	3	0	1	4	1	4	.385	.600
Bats Right	R	.195	87	17	2	0	5	11	6	23	.263	.391
Freeman,Freddie	L	.247	186	46	8	0	7	22	13	55	.304	.403
Bats Left	R	.299	385	115	24	0	14	54	40	87	.367	.400
Freese,David	L	.347	75	26	3	0	3	14	6	14	.393	.507
Bats Right	R	.283	258	73	13	1	7	41	18	61	.337	.422
Fryer,Eric	L	.250	8	2	0	0	0	0	2	2	.400	.250
Bats Right	R	.278	18	5	0	0	0	0	1	5	.316	.278
Fukudome,Kosuke	L	.262	130	34	4	2	2	11	7	31	.304	.369
Bats Left	R	.263	400	105	23	1	6	24	54	79	.353	.370
Fuld,Sam	L	.192	73	14	2	2	0	9	5	13	.280	.274
Bats Left	R	.255	235	60	16	3	3	23	23	36	.323	.387
Furcal,Rafael	L	.235	81	19	4	0	2	10	4	12	.276	.358
Bats Both	R	.230	252	58	11	0	6	18	24	27	.305	.345
Gamel,Mat	L	.000	6	0	0	0	0	0	0	3	.000	.000
Bats Left	R	.150	20	3	1	0	0	2	1	1	.190	.200
Gardner,Brett	L	.233	103	24	4	0	0	6	16	15	.344	.272
Bats Left	R	.265	407	108	15	8	7	30	44	78	.345	.393
Garner,Cole	L	.000	3	0	0	0	0	1	1	2	.250	.000
Bats Right	R	.333	6	2	0	0	0	2	0	4	.333	.333
Gathright,Joey	L	-	0	0	0	0	0	0	1	0	1.000	-
Bats Left	R	-	0	0	0	0	0	0	0	0	-	-
Gentry,Craig	L	.265	68	18	4	1	1	10	6	13	.338	.397
Bats Right	R	.277	65	18	1	0	0	3	4	14	.356	.292
German,Esteban	L	.500	4	2	0	0	1	3	1	1	.500	.500
Bats Right	R	.429	7	3	1	0	0	1	0	0	.429	.571
Getz,Chris	L	.286	98	28	0	1	0	7	6	14	.330	.306
Bats Left	R	.245	282	69	6	2	0	19	24	31	.307	.280
Giambi,Jason	L	.219	32	7	0	0	3	6	5	13	.359	.500
Bats Left	R	.273	99	27	6	0	10	26	12	32	.354	.636
Giavotella,Johnny	L	.262	42	11	0	2	1	5	3	6	.311	.429
Bats Right	R	.243	136	33	9	2	1	16	3	26	.261	.360
Gibbons,Jay	L	.444	9	4	1	0	1	2	0	2	.444	.889
Bats Left	R	.217	46	10	1	0	0	3	5	12	.302	.239
Gillaspie,Conor	L	.333	3	1	0	0	0	0	0	1	.333	.333
Bats Left	R	.250	16	4	0	0	1	2	2	0	.333	.438
Gillespie,Cole	L	.000	2	0	0	0	0	0	0	1	.000	.000
Bats Right	R	.500	4	2	0	0	1	4	1	0	.600	1.250
Gimenez,Chris	L	.313	16	5	0	0	1	3	3	2	.421	.500
Bats Right	R	.163	43	7	1	0	0	3	7	11	.275	.186
Gimenez,Hector	L	.333	3	1	0	0	0	0	0	1	.333	.333
Bats Both	R	.000	4	0	0	0	0	0	0	2	.000	.000
Gload,Ross	L	.000	4	0	0	0	0	0	0	0	.000	.000
Bats Left	R	.266	109	29	8	0	0	8	3	21	.286	.339
Goldschmidt,Paul	L	.162	37	6	2	0	2	4	6	13	.279	.378
Bats Right	R	.277	119	33	7	1	6	22	14	40	.351	.504
Golson,Greg	L	.167	6	1	0	0	0	0	1	1	.286	.167
Bats Right	R	.200	5	1	0	0	0	0	0	1	.200	.200
Gomes,Jonny	L	.311	90	28	4	0	3	13	15	26	.407	.456
Bats Right	R	.167	221	37	8	1	11	30	33	79	.292	.362
Gomez,Carlos	L	.278	90	25	5	1	6	12	3	25	.301	.556
Bats Right	R	.191	141	27	6	2	2	12	12	39	.261	.305
Gomez,Hector	L	.000	3	0	0	0	0	0	1	1	.250	.000
Bats Right	R	.667	3	2	0	0	0	0	0	1	.667	.667
Gonzalez,Adrian	L	.321	215	69	8	0	3	31	21	47	.387	.400
Bats Left	R	.347	415	144	37	3	24	86	53	72	.422	.624
Gonzalez,Alberto	L	.257	70	18	4	1	0	6	6	10	.312	.343
Bats Right	R	.198	177	35	6	1	1	26	7	27	.233	.260
Gonzalez,Alex	L	.267	146	39	10	0	5	13	4	34	.287	.438
Bats Right	R	.232	418	97	17	1	10	43	18	92	.264	.349
Gonzalez,Carlos	L	.272	158	43	5	1	7	26	13	39	.329	.449
Bats Left	R	.307	323	99	22	2	19	66	35	66	.379	.563
Gordon,Alex	L	.278	187	52	10	1	8	28	21	47	.358	.471
Bats Left	R	.314	424	133	35	3	15	59	46	92	.384	.517
Gordon,Dee	L	.275	69	19	1	0	0	5	3	13	.306	.290
Bats Left	R	.316	155	49	8	2	0	6	4	14	.333	.394
Granderson,Curtis	L	.272	191	52	6	4	16	44	15	59	.347	.597
Bats Left	R	.258	392	101	26	6	25	75	70	110	.372	.531

Batters vs. Left-Handed and Right-Handed Pitchers

Batter	vs	Avg	AB	H	2B	3B	HR	RBI	BB	SO	OBP	Slg
Green,Taylor	L	-	0	0	0	0	0	0	0	0	-	-
Bats Left	R	.270	37	10	3	0	0	1	0	6	.270	.351
Greene,Tyler	L	.209	43	9	2	0	1	3	4	11	.306	.326
Bats Right	R	.213	61	13	3	0	0	8	9	20	.333	.262
Guerrero,Vladimir	L	.288	153	44	9	0	2	13	7	20	.323	.386
Bats Right	R	.291	409	119	21	1	11	50	10	36	.315	.428
Guillen,Carlos	L	.185	27	5	0	0	0	2	0	7	.179	.185
Bats Both	R	.250	68	17	2	1	3	11	5	9	.297	.441
Gutierrez,Franklin	L	.224	67	15	1	0	1	1	5	13	.278	.284
Bats Right	R	.224	255	57	12	0	0	18	11	43	.257	.271
Guyer,Brandon	L	.207	29	6	1	0	2	3	0	6	.207	.448
Bats Right	R	.167	12	2	0	0	0	0	1	3	.231	.167
Guzman,Jesus	L	.333	93	31	8	1	2	13	8	16	.386	.505
Bats Right	R	.299	154	46	14	1	3	31	14	27	.359	.461
Gwynn,Tony	L	.200	70	14	4	1	0	5	4	22	.250	.286
Bats Left	R	.273	242	66	8	5	2	17	19	39	.324	.372
Hafner,Travis	L	.233	103	24	3	0	4	19	2	24	.259	.379
Bats Left	R	.302	222	67	13	0	9	38	34	54	.404	.482
Hairston,Jerry	L	.228	101	23	7	0	2	9	19	8	.350	.356
Bats Right	R	.288	236	68	14	1	3	22	14	38	.341	.394
Hairston,Scott	L	.247	81	20	7	1	1	9	7	21	.307	.395
Bats Right	R	.216	51	11	1	0	6	15	4	13	.298	.588
Hall,Bill	L	.245	53	13	5	0	0	5	4	23	.298	.340
Bats Right	R	.197	132	26	4	2	2	9	7	40	.246	.303
Halman,Greg	L	.258	31	8	1	0	1	3	0	13	.281	.387
Bats Right	R	.214	56	12	1	1	1	3	2	19	.241	.321
Hamilton,Josh	L	.260	146	38	5	3	10	31	6	34	.284	.541
Bats Left	R	.314	341	107	26	2	15	63	33	59	.371	.534
Hamilton,Mark	L	.182	11	2	0	0	0	2	0	3	.182	.182
Bats Left	R	.222	36	8	3	0	0	2	4	13	.300	.306
Hammock,Robby	L	-	0	0	0	0	0	0	0	0	-	-
Bats Right	R	.000	2	0	0	0	0	0	0	0	.000	.000
Hanigan,Ryan	L	.275	40	11	2	0	2	10	8	4	.396	.475
Bats Right	R	.265	226	60	4	0	4	21	27	28	.349	.336
Hannahan,Jack	L	.296	108	32	8	1	2	19	11	29	.367	.444
Bats Left	R	.226	212	48	8	1	6	21	27	51	.314	.358
Hardy,J.J.	L	.268	123	33	9	0	5	17	12	26	.331	.463
Bats Right	R	.270	404	109	18	0	25	63	19	66	.303	.500
Harris,Willie	L	.355	31	11	1	0	0	5	6	10	.500	.387
Bats Left	R	.230	209	48	10	0	2	18	30	52	.325	.306
Harrison,Josh	L	.226	62	14	4	2	0	3	1	7	.238	.355
Bats Right	R	.293	133	39	9	0	1	13	2	17	.301	.383
Hart,Corey	L	.333	102	34	3	0	9	20	16	19	.430	.627
Bats Right	R	.272	390	106	22	4	17	43	35	95	.335	.479
Hawpe,Brad	L	.190	21	4	0	0	0	0	4	8	.320	.190
Bats Left	R	.236	174	41	10	0	4	19	15	60	.298	.362
Hayes,Brett	L	.207	29	6	3	0	1	1	3	12	.281	.414
Bats Right	R	.238	101	24	6	0	4	15	8	27	.294	.416
Head,Jerad	L	.250	12	3	1	0	0	1	0	2	.308	.333
Bats Right	R	.000	12	0	0	0	0	0	0	3	.000	.000
Headley,Chase	L	.352	105	37	11	1	0	14	12	19	.415	.476
Bats Both	R	.264	276	73	17	0	4	30	40	73	.359	.370
Heisey,Chris	L	.197	61	12	3	0	1	9	4	24	.258	.295
Bats Right	R	.271	218	59	6	1	17	41	15	54	.324	.541
Helms,Wes	L	.212	66	14	4	0	0	4	5	17	.268	.273
Bats Right	R	.159	44	7	1	0	0	2	6	18	.288	.182
Helton,Todd	L	.292	144	42	6	0	5	19	15	32	.356	.438
Bats Left	R	.307	277	85	21	0	9	50	44	39	.399	.480
Hermida,Jeremy	L	.400	5	2	0	0	0	0	1	1	.500	.400
Bats Left	R	.170	53	9	2	1	2	9	6	25	.267	.358
Hernandez,Diory	L	.091	11	1	0	0	0	0	0	2	.091	.091
Bats Right	R	.273	22	6	1	0	1	4	0	3	.273	.455
Hernandez,Ramon	L	.323	62	20	4	0	0	6	9	5	.403	.387
Bats Right	R	.271	236	64	9	0	12	30	14	36	.324	.462
Herrera,Jonathan	L	.250	68	17	0	1	1	2	4	12	.292	.324
Bats Both	R	.239	213	51	5	0	2	12	24	28	.319	.291
Heyward,Jason	L	.192	104	20	4	1	2	7	10	23	.270	.308
Bats Left	R	.240	292	70	14	1	12	35	41	70	.336	.418
Hicks,Brandon	L	.111	9	1	0	0	0	1	1	4	.200	.111
Bats Right	R	.000	12	0	0	0	0	0	0	5	.000	.000
Hill,Aaron	L	.241	116	28	5	0	4	19	8	14	.290	.388
Bats Right	R	.248	404	100	22	3	4	42	27	58	.301	.347
Hill,Koyie	L	.091	22	2	0	0	0	3	2	5	.167	.091
Bats Both	R	.214	112	24	3	1	2	6	12	35	.288	.313
Hinske,Eric	L	.118	34	4	0	0	2	4	1	8	.167	.294
Bats Left	R	.252	202	51	10	0	8	24	25	63	.333	.421

Batter	vs	Avg	AB	H	2B	3B	HR	RBI	BB	SO	OBP	Slg
Hoffmann,Jamie	L	.000	4	0	0	0	0	0	0	1	.000	.000
Bats Right	R	-	0	0	0	0	0	0	0	0	-	-
Holliday,Matt	L	.256	86	22	6	0	4	10	22	20	.418	.465
Bats Right	R	.306	360	110	30	0	18	65	38	73	.379	.539
Holm,Steve	L	.000	2	0	0	0	0	0	0	0	.000	.000
Bats Right	R	.133	15	2	1	0	0	0	1	4	.188	.200
Hosmer,Eric	L	.237	152	36	5	1	1	13	10	27	.282	.303
Bats Left	R	.315	371	117	22	2	18	65	24	55	.355	.531
Howard,Ryan	L	.224	170	38	10	1	3	28	12	55	.286	.347
Bats Left	R	.266	387	103	20	0	30	88	63	117	.370	.550
Hu,Chin-lung	L	.067	15	1	0	0	0	1	1	10	.118	.067
Bats Right	R	.000	5	0	0	0	0	0	0	1	.000	.000
Hudson,Kyle	L	.000	4	0	0	0	0	0	0	0	.000	.000
Bats Left	R	.167	24	4	0	0	0	2	0	6	.167	.167
Hudson,Orlando	L	.224	125	28	4	0	3	14	7	25	.263	.328
Bats Both	R	.256	273	70	11	3	4	29	42	59	.356	.363
Huff,Aubrey	L	.270	137	37	5	0	3	21	10	23	.318	.372
Bats Left	R	.237	384	91	22	1	9	38	37	67	.301	.370
Hughes,Luke	L	.196	92	18	3	0	3	14	10	25	.282	.326
Bats Right	R	.236	195	46	9	0	4	16	14	54	.292	.344
Hundley,Nick	L	.286	63	18	4	1	2	6	1	21	.292	.476
Bats Right	R	.289	218	63	12	4	7	23	21	53	.362	.477
Hunter,Cedric	L	-	0	0	0	0	0	0	0	0	-	-
Bats Left	R	.250	4	1	0	0	0	0	1	0	.400	.250
Hunter,Torii	L	.287	167	48	6	1	9	27	29	33	.389	.497
Bats Right	R	.252	413	104	18	1	14	55	33	92	.313	.402
Iannetta,Chris	L	.241	83	20	6	0	7	18	26	20	.423	.566
Bats Right	R	.237	262	62	11	1	7	37	44	69	.351	.366
Ibanez,Raul	L	.211	133	28	5	1	4	24	3	38	.232	.353
Bats Left	R	.256	402	103	26	0	16	60	30	68	.307	.440
Iglesias,Jose	L	1.000	1	1	0	0	0	0	0	0	1.000	1.000
Bats Right	R	.200	5	1	0	0	0	0	0	2	.200	.200
Infante,Omar	L	.273	150	41	10	2	3	10	7	16	.302	.427
Bats Right	R	.277	429	119	14	6	4	39	27	51	.319	.366
Inge,Brandon	L	.245	98	24	4	0	3	6	14	18	.339	.378
Bats Right	R	.170	171	29	6	2	0	17	10	56	.220	.228
Inglett,Joe	L	1.000	1	1	0	0	0	0	0	0	1.000	1.000
Bats Left	R	.192	26	5	1	0	0	1	0	7	.192	.231
Izturis,Cesar	L	.333	9	3	0	0	0	1	0	1	.333	.333
Bats Both	R	.143	21	3	0	0	0	0	2	9	.217	.143
Izturis,Maicer	L	.295	166	49	17	0	2	14	9	22	.346	.434
Bats Both	R	.265	283	75	18	0	3	24	24	43	.327	.360
Jackson,Austin	L	.257	179	46	10	3	3	12	21	57	.335	.397
Bats Right	R	.245	412	101	12	8	7	33	35	124	.308	.364
Jackson,Conor	L	.244	131	32	10	1	0	10	15	18	.324	.336
Bats Right	R	.244	221	54	7	0	5	33	17	35	.302	.344
Janish,Paul	L	.210	62	13	2	0	0	4	2	10	.234	.242
Bats Right	R	.215	274	59	12	1	0	19	16	36	.264	.266
Jaramillo,Jason	L	.364	11	4	2	0	0	2	1	1	.417	.545
Bats Both	R	.313	32	10	1	0	0	4	1	11	.333	.344
Jaso,John	L	.161	31	5	1	1	0	2	7	8	.316	.258
Bats Left	R	.233	215	50	14	0	5	25	18	28	.295	.367
Jay,Jon	L	.287	94	27	5	1	1	8	6	16	.333	.394
Bats Left	R	.299	361	108	19	1	9	29	22	65	.347	.432
Jennings,Desmond	L	.256	78	20	4	2	2	5	9	21	.356	.436
Bats Right	R	.260	169	44	5	2	8	20	22	38	.356	.456
Jeter,Derek	L	.349	149	52	11	0	5	19	17	15	.423	.523
Bats Right	R	.277	397	110	13	4	1	42	29	66	.329	.338
Johnson,Chris	L	.260	96	25	10	0	1	12	3	17	.291	.344
Bats Right	R	.248	282	70	16	3	6	30	13	80	.291	.390
Johnson,Dan	L	.200	30	6	0	0	1	3	1	8	.226	.300
Bats Left	R	.074	54	4	1	0	1	1	5	10	.167	.148
Johnson,Elliot	L	.213	75	16	4	1	1	4	11	29	.314	.333
Bats Both	R	.176	85	15	3	1	3	13	3	24	.202	.341
Johnson,Kelly	L	.224	152	34	5	1	5	17	6	40	.258	.368
Bats Left	R	.221	393	87	22	6	16	41	54	123	.320	.430
Johnson,Reed	L	.305	105	32	11	0	2	12	1	23	.330	.467
Bats Right	R	.312	141	44	11	1	3	16	4	40	.361	.468
Johnson,Rob	L	.229	70	16	4	1	2	9	8	15	.313	.400
Bats Right	R	.165	109	18	2	0	1	7	6	43	.222	.211
Jones,Adam	L	.242	153	37	8	0	4	14	10	31	.293	.373
Bats Right	R	.295	414	122	18	2	21	69	19	82	.329	.500
Jones,Andruw	L	.286	126	36	8	0	8	25	18	39	.384	.540
Bats Right	R	.172	64	11	0	0	5	8	11	23	.303	.406
Jones,Chipper	L	.268	142	38	8	0	4	22	17	23	.342	.408
Bats Both	R	.278	313	87	25	1	14	48	34	57	.345	.498

Batters vs. Left-Handed and Right-Handed Pitchers

Batter	vs	Avg	AB	H	2B	3B	HR	RBI	BB	SO	OBP	Slg
Jones,Garrett	L	.147	68	10	3	0	2	8	2	20	.181	.279
Bats Left	R	.262	355	93	27	1	14	50	46	84	.346	.462
Joyce,Matt	L	.217	92	20	5	0	3	15	8	31	.287	.370
Bats Left	R	.292	370	108	27	2	16	60	41	75	.361	.505
Ka'aihue,Kila	L	.130	23	3	3	0	0	4	2	8	.192	.261
Bats Left	R	.220	59	13	1	0	2	2	10	18	.333	.339
Kearns,Austin	L	.235	68	16	1	0	0	2	7	19	.316	.250
Bats Right	R	.171	82	14	4	1	2	5	11	29	.292	.317
Kelly,Don	L	.190	21	4	0	0	0	1	0	6	.190	.190
Bats Left	R	.250	236	59	8	3	7	27	14	26	.299	.398
Kemp,Matt	L	.341	132	45	12	0	11	32	30	29	.461	.682
Bats Right	R	.319	470	150	21	4	28	94	44	130	.380	.560
Kendrick,Howie	L	.295	183	54	13	1	7	24	11	38	.348	.492
Bats Right	R	.280	354	99	17	5	11	39	22	81	.332	.449
Kennedy,Adam	L	.191	68	13	2	0	0	8	5	19	.243	.221
Bats Left	R	.244	312	76	21	1	7	30	17	48	.284	.385
Keppinger,Jeff	L	.290	93	27	9	0	3	14	0	4	.292	.484
Bats Right	R	.273	286	78	11	0	3	21	12	20	.302	.343
Kinsler,Ian	L	.263	160	42	7	0	11	24	27	18	.367	.513
Bats Right	R	.344	460	116	27	4	21	53	62	53	.350	.465
Kipnis,Jason	L	.263	38	10	2	0	1	5	5	10	.349	.395
Bats Left	R	.276	98	27	7	1	6	14	6	24	.327	.551
Konerko,Paul	L	.292	130	38	4	0	6	15	20	18	.386	.462
Bats Right	R	.303	413	125	21	0	25	90	57	71	.389	.535
Kotchman,Casey	L	.289	149	43	6	0	2	13	5	23	.340	.369
Bats Left	R	.313	351	110	18	2	8	35	43	43	.394	.444
Kotsay,Mark	L	.462	13	6	0	0	0	1	2	1	.500	.462
Bats Left	R	.259	220	57	13	1	3	30	19	26	.318	.368
Kottaras,George	L	.174	23	4	0	0	1	1	1	7	.208	.304
Bats Left	R	.273	88	24	6	1	4	16	9	19	.337	.500
Kouzmanoff,Kevin	L	.259	58	15	3	0	2	6	2	9	.295	.414
Bats Right	R	.227	176	40	8	0	5	27	10	37	.281	.358
Kozma,Pete	L	.250	8	2	0	0	0	0	1	1	.333	.250
Bats Right	R	.111	9	1	1	0	0	1	3	3	.333	.222
Kratz,Erik	L	.000	4	0	0	0	0	0	0	1	.000	.000
Bats Right	R	1.000	2	2	1	0	0	0	0	0	1.000	1.500
Kubel,Jason	L	.254	122	31	8	0	4	17	10	32	.313	.418
Bats Left	R	.283	244	69	13	1	8	41	22	54	.341	.443
LaHair,Bryan	L	.250	12	3	2	0	0	1	2	4	.357	.417
Bats Left	R	.298	47	14	3	1	2	5	7	14	.382	.532
Laird,Brandon	L	.273	11	3	0	0	0	1	0	2	.273	.273
Bats Right	R	.100	10	1	0	0	0	0	3	2	.308	.100
Laird,Gerald	L	.286	14	4	2	0	0	2	5	2	.474	.429
Bats Right	R	.222	81	18	5	1	1	10	4	17	.264	.346
Langerhans,Ryan	L	.286	21	6	0	0	2	4	1	6	.318	.571
Bats Left	R	.097	31	3	0	0	1	2	10	16	.317	.194
LaPorta,Matt	L	.207	87	18	6	1	1	9	5	19	.263	.333
Bats Right	R	.260	265	69	17	0	10	44	18	68	.310	.438
LaRoche,Adam	L	.098	41	4	0	0	1	5	7	14	.224	.171
Bats Left	R	.200	110	22	4	0	2	10	18	23	.313	.291
LaRoche,Andy	L	.286	28	8	4	0	0	1	5	3	.412	.429
Bats Right	R	.231	65	15	2	1	0	4	3	16	.275	.292
Lavarnway,Ryan	L	.294	17	5	0	0	2	5	1	2	.333	.647
Bats Right	R	.182	22	4	2	0	0	3	3	8	.280	.273
Lawrie,Brett	L	.295	44	13	3	0	1	6	4	10	.354	.432
Bats Right	R	.292	106	31	5	4	8	19	12	21	.380	.642
Lee,Carlos	L	.348	135	47	13	1	7	32	16	14	.413	.615
Bats Right	R	.253	450	114	25	3	11	62	43	46	.319	.396
Lee,Derrek	L	.287	101	29	2	0	2	9	11	21	.363	.366
Bats Right	R	.260	334	87	15	2	17	50	22	89	.313	.470
LeMahieu,DJ	L	.292	24	7	2	0	0	2	0	4	.292	.375
Bats Right	R	.222	36	8	0	0	0	2	1	8	.243	.222
Lewis,Fred	L	.000	13	0	0	0	0	0	0	6	.000	.000
Bats Left	R	.247	170	42	7	0	3	19	22	32	.342	.341
Liddi,Alex	L	.429	14	6	2	0	2	4	3	4	.529	1.000
Bats Right	R	.115	26	3	1	0	1	2	0	13	.148	.269
Lillibridge,Brent	L	.287	94	27	1	0	9	18	7	29	.346	.585
Bats Right	R	.228	92	21	4	1	4	11	10	33	.333	.424
Lind,Adam	L	.243	140	34	8	0	3	20	5	36	.275	.364
Bats Left	R	.253	359	91	8	0	23	67	27	71	.303	.468
Lobaton,Jose	L	.150	20	3	1	0	0	0	1	2	.190	.200
Bats Both	R	.071	14	1	0	0	0	0	1	2	.278	.071
Loewen,Adam	L	.000	5	0	0	0	0	1	1	2	.286	.000
Bats Left	R	.222	27	6	1	0	1	3	2	11	.300	.370
Lombardozzi,Steve	L	.000	1	0	0	0	0	0	0	0	.000	.000
Bats Both	R	.200	30	6	1	0	0	1	1	4	.226	.233

Batter	vs	Avg	AB	H	2B	3B	HR	RBI	BB	SO	OBP	Slg
Loney,James	L	.213	127	27	6	0	2	14	8	21	.254	.307
Bats Left	R	.312	404	126	24	1	10	51	34	46	.365	.450
Longoria,Evan	L	.258	120	31	5	1	10	33	24	25	.376	.567
Bats Right	R	.240	363	87	21	0	21	66	56	68	.348	.471
Lopez,Felipe	L	.208	48	10	1	0	2	5	1	16	.220	.354
Bats Both	R	.204	93	19	3	0	0	6	7	19	.260	.237
Lopez,Jose	L	.203	74	15	5	0	2	7	3	5	.231	.351
Bats Right	R	.223	157	35	7	0	6	14	4	23	.252	.382
Lowrie,Jed	L	.330	109	36	7	1	4	22	5	12	.353	.523
Bats Both	R	.210	200	42	7	3	2	14	18	48	.277	.305
Lucroy,Jonathan	L	.291	86	25	0	0	6	18	4	16	.322	.547
Bats Right	R	.259	344	89	12	1	6	41	25	83	.310	.352
Lucy,Donny	L	1.000	1	1	1	0	0	1	0	0	1.000	2.000
Bats Right	R	.111	9	1	0	0	0	0	1	5	.200	.111
Ludwick,Ryan	L	.264	121	32	6	0	4	20	17	21	.350	.413
Bats Right	R	.228	369	84	17	0	9	55	34	103	.297	.347
Lugo,Julio	L	.115	26	3	0	0	0	2	3	7	.207	.115
Bats Right	R	.167	18	3	0	0	0	1	1	4	.211	.167
Maier,Mitch	L	.229	35	8	2	0	0	2	6	12	.341	.286
Bats Left	R	.233	60	14	2	3	0	5	10	20	.347	.367
Maldonado,Martin	L	.000	1	0	0	0	0	0	0	1	.000	.000
Bats Right	R	.000	0	0	0	0	0	0	0	0	-	-
Markakis,Nick	L	.261	188	49	4	0	1	14	17	24	.330	.298
Bats Left	R	.294	453	133	27	1	14	59	45	51	.359	.450
Marrero,Chris	L	.313	16	5	2	0	0	4	0	4	.294	.438
Bats Right	R	.237	93	22	3	0	0	6	4	23	.270	.269
Marson,Lou	L	.297	91	27	5	1	1	9	14	24	.387	.407
Bats Right	R	.191	152	29	4	1	0	10	10	44	.244	.230
Martin,Leonys	L	.000	0	0	0	0	0	0	0	0	-	-
Bats Left	R	.375	8	3	1	0	0	0	0	1	.375	.500
Martin,Russell	L	.211	114	24	3	0	5	23	16	29	.316	.368
Bats Right	R	.248	303	75	14	0	13	42	34	52	.327	.422
Martinez,Fernando	L	.250	4	1	1	0	0	0	0	1	.250	.500
Bats Left	R	.222	18	4	1	0	1	2	1	6	.263	.444
Martinez,J.D.	L	.360	50	18	7	0	3	14	6	11	.439	.680
Bats Right	R	.247	158	39	6	0	3	21	7	37	.278	.342
Martinez,Luis	L	.214	14	3	1	1	0	1	1	5	.313	.429
Bats Right	R	.200	45	9	0	0	1	9	7	9	.308	.267
Martinez,Michael	L	.176	51	9	1	0	0	4	1	9	.189	.196
Bats Both	R	.203	158	32	4	2	3	20	17	26	.278	.310
Martinez,Osvaldo	L	.200	10	2	0	0	0	1	0	2	.200	.200
Bats Right	R	.077	13	1	0	0	0	0	0	7	.077	.077
Martinez,Victor	L	.311	148	46	10	0	4	34	15	15	.363	.459
Bats Both	R	.337	392	132	30	0	8	69	31	36	.386	.474
Mastroianni,Darin	L	-	0	0	0	0	0	0	0	0	-	-
Bats Right	R	.000	2	0	0	0	0	0	0	1	.000	.000
Mather,Joe	L	.250	24	6	3	0	0	2	3	7	.333	.375
Bats Right	R	.196	51	10	1	0	1	7	3	16	.241	.275
Mathis,Jeff	L	.180	100	18	6	0	0	6	6	29	.229	.240
Bats Right	R	.170	147	25	6	0	3	16	9	46	.222	.272
Matsui,Hideki	L	.273	154	42	6	0	8	29	14	22	.327	.468
Bats Left	R	.242	363	88	22	0	4	43	42	62	.318	.336
Mauer,Joe	L	.234	111	26	2	0	0	13	11	19	.310	.252
Bats Left	R	.319	185	59	13	0	3	17	21	19	.391	.438
Mayberry,John	L	.306	111	34	8	0	8	21	8	18	.358	.595
Bats Right	R	.250	156	39	9	1	7	28	18	37	.330	.455
Maybin,Cameron	L	.296	142	42	3	2	3	6	10	32	.342	.408
Bats Right	R	.251	374	94	21	6	6	34	34	93	.316	.388
McCann,Brian	L	.265	151	40	6	0	9	32	10	30	.311	.483
Bats Left	R	.273	315	86	13	0	15	39	47	59	.369	.457
McCoy,Mike	L	.190	63	12	0	0	0	1	9	18	.292	.190
Bats Right	R	.201	134	27	8	0	2	9	16	23	.291	.306
McCutchen,Andrew	L	.277	141	39	9	1	10	27	23	28	.377	.567
Bats Right	R	.253	431	109	24	4	13	62	66	98	.360	.420
McDonald,Darnell	L	.260	104	27	5	1	5	18	10	20	.333	.471
Bats Right	R	.189	53	10	1	0	1	6	4	13	.241	.264
McDonald,John	L	.241	58	14	2	0	0	8	2	7	.262	.276
Bats Right	R	.225	169	38	6	1	2	14	10	20	.271	.320
McGehee,Casey	L	.169	124	21	0	1	0	12	10	22	.228	.185
Bats Right	R	.239	422	101	24	1	13	55	35	82	.295	.393
McKenry,Michael	L	.167	42	7	3	0	0	2	6	15	.260	.238
Bats Right	R	.239	138	33	9	0	2	9	8	34	.281	.348
McLouth,Nate	L	.179	84	15	4	1	0	2	11	20	.281	.250
Bats Left	R	.251	183	46	8	1	4	14	33	32	.372	.372
McPherson,Dallas	L	-	0	0	0	0	0	0	0	0	-	-
Bats Left	R	.133	15	2	0	0	0	0	0	7	.133	.133

Batters vs. Left-Handed and Right-Handed Pitchers

Batter	vs	Avg	AB	H	2B	3B	HR	RBI	BB	SO	OBP	Slg
Mesoraco,Devin	L	.250	8	2	1	0	0	0	0	1	.250	.375
Bats Right	R	.167	42	7	2	0	2	6	3	9	.222	.357
Michaels,Jason	L	.221	86	19	6	0	1	6	6	15	.280	.326
Bats Right	R	.171	70	12	3	0	1	4	5	16	.227	.257
Miles,Aaron	L	.293	99	29	4	0	2	8	5	16	.327	.394
Bats Both	R	.270	355	96	13	3	1	37	20	33	.311	.332
Milledge,Lastings	L	.000	3	0	0	0	0	0	0	1	.000	.000
Bats Right	R	1.000	1	1	1	0	0	0	0	0	1.000	2.000
Miller,Jai	L	.500	6	3	0	0	1	2	0	1	.500	1.000
Bats Right	R	.000	6	0	0	0	0	0	0	4	.000	.000
Miranda,Juan	L	.242	33	8	1	1	2	3	4	11	.359	.515
Bats Left	R	.206	141	29	7	1	5	20	19	37	.304	.376
Mitchell,Russ	L	.115	26	3	0	0	0	1	4	5	.233	.115
Bats Right	R	.200	25	5	1	0	2	2	3	5	.286	.480
Molina,Gustavo	L	.000	3	0	0	0	0	0	0	0	.000	.000
Bats Right	R	.333	3	1	1	0	0	0	0	0	.333	.667
Molina,Jose	L	.276	58	16	3	0	2	4	4	16	.323	.431
Bats Right	R	.283	113	32	9	1	1	11	11	28	.352	.407
Molina,Yadier	L	.284	102	29	6	0	4	8	16	12	.381	.461
Bats Right	R	.311	373	116	26	1	10	57	17	32	.339	.466
Montanez,Lou	L	.250	40	10	3	0	1	9	2	5	.302	.400
Bats Right	R	.143	14	2	1	0	0	0	0	4	.143	.214
Montero,Jesus	L	.500	24	12	3	0	0	7	3	6	.556	.625
Bats Right	R	.216	37	8	1	0	4	5	4	11	.310	.568
Montero,Miguel	L	.195	113	22	6	0	1	9	6	31	.260	.274
Bats Left	R	.308	380	117	30	1	17	77	41	66	.378	.526
Moore,Adam	L	.200	5	1	1	0	0	0	0	2	.200	.400
Bats Right	R	.000	1	0	0	0	0	0	0	0	.000	.000
Moore,Jeremy	L	.250	4	1	0	0	0	0	0	2	.250	.250
Bats Left	R	.000	4	0	0	0	0	0	0	0	.000	.000
Mora,Melvin	L	.263	38	10	4	0	0	4	1	8	.293	.368
Bats Right	R	.213	89	19	2	0	0	12	1	16	.223	.236
Morales,Jose	L	.250	16	4	0	0	0	0	2	2	.333	.250
Bats Both	R	.273	44	12	3	0	0	7	7	10	.358	.341
Morel,Brent	L	.240	129	31	4	1	5	14	5	17	.279	.403
Bats Right	R	.246	284	70	14	0	5	27	17	40	.290	.349
Moreland,Mitch	L	.234	111	26	2	0	1	9	7	25	.298	.279
Bats Left	R	.266	353	94	20	1	15	42	32	67	.326	.456
Morgan,Nyjer	L	.209	43	9	1	1	0	3	2	13	.261	.279
Bats Left	R	.316	335	106	19	5	4	34	17	57	.370	.439
Morneau,Justin	L	.144	90	13	3	0	1	5	3	15	.189	.211
Bats Left	R	.270	174	47	13	0	3	25	16	29	.332	.397
Morrison,Logan	L	.241	133	32	6	0	5	26	13	36	.325	.398
Bats Left	R	.249	329	82	19	4	18	46	41	63	.332	.495
Morse,Michael	L	.297	118	35	9	0	6	21	12	32	.366	.525
Bats Right	R	.304	404	123	27	0	25	74	24	94	.358	.557
Moss,Brandon	L	.000	1	0	0	0	0	0	0	0	.000	.000
Bats Left	R	.000	5	0	0	0	0	0	0	2	.000	.000
Moustakas,Mike	L	.191	89	17	4	0	0	6	7	15	.258	.236
Bats Left	R	.289	249	72	14	1	5	24	15	36	.327	.414
Murphy,Daniel	L	.299	87	26	6	0	2	16	2	13	.319	.437
Bats Left	R	.326	304	99	22	2	4	33	22	29	.374	.451
Murphy,David	L	.215	107	23	2	0	0	5	9	18	.274	.234
Bats Left	R	.296	297	88	12	2	11	41	24	43	.348	.461
Murphy,Donnie	L	.160	25	4	0	1	1	3	2	7	.267	.360
Bats Right	R	.194	67	13	4	0	1	6	2	19	.229	.299
Nady,Xavier	L	.248	105	26	5	0	4	24	7	23	.292	.410
Bats Right	R	.248	101	25	6	0	0	11	3	23	.282	.307
Napoli,Mike	L	.319	113	36	7	0	9	28	22	30	.430	.619
Bats Right	R	.320	256	82	18	0	21	47	36	55	.407	.637
Navarro,Dioner	L	.179	28	5	1	0	1	3	5	5	.294	.321
Bats Both	R	.196	148	29	5	1	4	14	15	30	.273	.324
Navarro,Efren	L	.333	3	1	0	0	0	0	0	0	.333	.333
Bats Left	R	.143	7	1	1	0	0	0	1	1	.250	.286
Navarro,Yamaico	L	.276	29	8	1	0	1	7	1	5	.290	.414
Bats Right	R	.226	31	7	2	0	0	2	4	9	.314	.290
Nelson,Chris	L	.245	53	13	3	1	1	2	1	12	.259	.396
Bats Right	R	.252	127	32	7	0	3	14	6	23	.289	.378
Nickeas,Mike	L	.115	26	3	1	0	1	3	3	3	.207	.269
Bats Right	R	.259	27	7	0	0	0	3	1	8	.286	.259
Nieves,Wil	L	.118	17	2	1	0	0	0	1	4	.167	.176
Bats Right	R	.152	33	5	1	0	0	0	2	8	.200	.182
Nishioka,Tsuyoshi	L	.203	79	16	3	0	0	5	2	15	.222	.241
Bats Both	R	.239	142	34	2	0	0	14	13	28	.308	.254
Nix,Jayson	L	.273	22	6	1	0	2	4	5	5	.407	.591
Bats Right	R	.149	114	17	4	1	2	12	7	37	.210	.254

Batter	vs	Avg	AB	H	2B	3B	HR	RBI	BB	SO	OBP	Slg
Nix,Laynce	L	.111	27	3	2	0	0	1	4	11	.226	.185
Bats Left	R	.263	297	78	11	1	16	43	19	71	.306	.475
Nunez,Eduardo	L	.277	112	31	6	1	3	16	6	11	.314	.429
Bats Right	R	.259	197	51	12	1	2	14	16	26	.313	.360
Oeltjen,Trent	L	.250	12	3	0	1	1	1	1	5	.308	.667
Bats Left	R	.186	59	11	1	0	1	5	12	25	.324	.254
Olivo,Miguel	L	.236	123	29	5	0	4	13	7	35	.269	.374
Bats Right	R	.220	354	78	14	1	15	49	13	105	.247	.393
Ordonez,Magglio	L	.292	130	38	6	0	2	11	8	13	.331	.385
Bats Right	R	.231	199	46	4	0	3	21	15	28	.284	.296
Orr,Pete	L	.167	6	1	0	0	0	0	0	3	.286	.167
Bats Left	R	.222	90	20	3	0	0	4	6	16	.278	.256
Ortiz,David	L	.329	173	57	17	0	8	33	27	33	.423	.566
Bats Left	R	.298	352	105	23	1	21	63	51	50	.386	.548
Overbay,Lyle	L	.241	108	26	6	0	2	7	8	31	.299	.352
Bats Left	R	.231	286	66	15	1	7	40	34	57	.314	.364
Pacheco,Jordan	L	.385	26	10	1	0	1	8	1	3	.407	.538
Bats Right	R	.241	58	14	0	0	1	6	2	6	.279	.293
Pagan,Angel	L	.262	122	32	9	0	0	13	13	19	.336	.336
Bats Both	R	.261	356	93	15	4	7	43	31	43	.317	.385
Pagnozzi,Matt	L	.375	8	3	0	0	0	1	0	1	.375	.375
Bats Right	R	.238	21	5	0	0	0	2	1	9	.304	.238
Paredes,Jimmy	L	.216	37	8	1	0	0	3	2	9	.256	.243
Bats Both	R	.305	131	40	7	2	2	15	7	38	.338	.435
Parmelee,Chris	L	.316	19	6	4	0	0	4	3	4	.409	.526
Bats Left	R	.368	57	21	7	0	4	10	9	9	.455	.614
Parra,Gerardo	L	.277	94	26	2	0	4	15	10	18	.364	.426
Bats Left	R	.296	351	104	18	8	4	31	33	64	.355	.427
Parrino,Andy	L	.143	7	1	0	0	1	1	1	3	.300	.143
Bats Both	R	.189	37	7	1	0	0	3	8	14	.333	.216
Pascucci,Val	L	.333	9	3	0	0	1	2	0	2	.333	.667
Bats Right	R	.000	2	0	0	0	0	0	0	1	.000	.000
Patterson,Corey	L	.298	84	25	6	0	2	9	4	20	.330	.440
Bats Left	R	.222	284	63	14	3	4	27	13	57	.257	.335
Patterson,Eric	L	.250	4	1	0	0	0	1	3	2	.500	.250
Bats Left	R	.176	85	15	2	1	2	7	9	20	.253	.294
Paul,Xavier	L	.071	28	2	0	0	0	1	1	12	.103	.071
Bats Left	R	.279	215	60	6	5	2	19	12	50	.316	.381
Paulino,Ronny	L	.289	90	26	6	0	1	8	10	14	.363	.389
Bats Right	R	.254	138	35	7	0	1	11	5	24	.276	.326
Pearce,Steve	L	.213	47	10	1	0	1	6	5	9	.291	.298
Bats Right	R	.191	47	9	1	0	0	4	2	12	.224	.213
Pedroia,Dustin	L	.358	179	64	11	1	7	19	36	25	.463	.547
Bats Right	R	.287	456	131	26	2	14	72	50	60	.355	.445
Peguero,Carlos	L	.286	7	2	0	0	0	1	1	3	.375	.286
Bats Left	R	.191	136	26	3	2	6	18	7	51	.245	.375
Pena,Brayan	L	.250	68	17	1	0	1	5	4	4	.292	.309
Bats Both	R	.247	154	38	10	0	2	19	8	20	.286	.351
Pena,Carlos	L	.133	120	16	3	0	7	19	22	46	.260	.333
Bats Left	R	.255	373	95	24	3	21	61	79	115	.388	.504
Pena,Ramiro	L	.071	14	1	0	0	0	1	1	3	.133	.071
Bats Both	R	.115	26	3	0	0	1	3	1	8	.172	.231
Pena,Wily Mo	L	.242	33	8	0	0	2	4	2	11	.306	.424
Bats Right	R	.188	80	15	3	0	5	11	3	28	.226	.413
Pence,Hunter	L	.317	139	44	8	3	8	24	19	18	.400	.590
Bats Right	R	.313	467	146	30	2	14	73	37	106	.360	.475
Pennington,Cliff	L	.270	148	40	8	0	1	13	13	23	.325	.345
Bats Both	R	.262	367	96	18	2	7	45	29	81	.316	.379
Peralta,Jhonny	L	.240	150	36	8	1	7	26	18	35	.318	.447
Bats Right	R	.323	375	121	17	2	14	60	22	60	.357	.491
Perez,Salvador	L	.484	31	15	3	1	1	6	4	1	.543	.742
Bats Right	R	.291	117	34	5	1	2	15	3	19	.309	.402
Petersen,Bryan	L	.294	51	15	4	0	1	2	6	9	.379	.431
Bats Left	R	.255	153	39	9	3	1	8	20	40	.350	.373
Pettit,Chris	L	-	0	0	0	0	0	0	0	0	-	-
Bats Right	R	-	0	0	0	0	0	0	0	0	-	-
Phelps,Cord	L	.100	10	1	0	0	0	0	2	4	.250	.100
Bats Both	R	.164	61	10	2	1	1	6	8	13	.239	.279
Phillips,Brandon	L	.316	136	43	10	1	3	14	16	21	.381	.471
Bats Right	R	.295	474	140	28	1	15	68	28	64	.344	.454
Phillips,Kyle	L	.200	5	1	0	0	1	1	1	2	.333	.800
Bats Left	R	.169	71	12	3	0	1	9	7	17	.253	.254
Pie,Felix	L	.063	16	1	1	0	0	0	1	3	.118	.125
Bats Left	R	.236	148	35	7	1	0	7	9	29	.280	.297
Pierre,Juan	L	.329	146	48	1	0	0	10	21	9	.430	.336
Bats Left	R	.264	493	130	16	4	2	40	22	32	.296	.325

Batters vs. Left-Handed and Right-Handed Pitchers

Batter	vs	Avg	AB	H	2B	3B	HR	RBI	BB	SO	OBP	Slg
Pierzynski,A.J.	L	.305	82	25	11	1	0	12	4	7	.345	.463
Bats Left	R	.283	382	108	18	0	8	36	19	26	.319	.393
Pill,Brett	L	.250	28	7	3	0	1	4	1	7	.276	.464
Bats Right	R	.364	22	8	0	2	1	5	1	1	.375	.682
Pina,Manny	L	.333	3	1	1	0	0	0	0	1	.333	.667
Bats Right	R	.182	11	2	1	0	0	0	1	1	.250	.273
Plouffe,Trevor	L	.308	78	24	8	0	1	8	3	18	.333	.449
Bats Right	R	.212	208	44	10	1	7	23	22	53	.295	.370
Polanco,Placido	L	.336	119	40	6	0	2	17	12	8	.391	.437
Bats Right	R	.257	350	90	8	0	3	33	30	36	.316	.306
Posada,Jorge	L	.092	65	6	1	0	0	3	6	24	.169	.108
Bats Both	R	.269	279	75	13	0	14	41	33	52	.348	.466
Posey,Buster	L	.205	44	9	3	0	1	6	7	8	.340	.341
Bats Right	R	.314	118	37	2	0	3	15	11	22	.379	.407
Powell,Landon	L	.185	27	5	0	0	1	1	2	7	.241	.296
Bats Both	R	.167	84	14	3	0	0	3	9	25	.247	.202
Prado,Martin	L	.245	143	35	8	1	2	13	15	21	.316	.357
Bats Right	R	.265	408	108	18	1	11	44	19	31	.297	.395
Presley,Alex	L	.231	65	15	2	1	1	8	3	18	.261	.338
Bats Left	R	.327	150	49	10	5	3	12	10	22	.373	.520
Pridie,Jason	L	.194	31	6	1	1	1	2	2	9	.242	.387
Bats Left	R	.237	177	42	10	2	3	18	22	55	.320	.367
Pujols,Albert	L	.295	112	33	8	0	9	23	9	12	.339	.607
Bats Right	R	.300	467	140	21	0	28	76	52	46	.372	.525
Punto,Nick	L	.273	44	12	2	2	0	6	9	5	.389	.409
Bats Both	R	.281	89	25	6	2	1	14	16	16	.387	.427
Quentin,Carlos	L	.297	101	30	5	0	7	18	11	18	.388	.554
Bats Right	R	.241	320	77	26	0	17	59	23	66	.323	.481
Quintanilla,Omar	L	.000	11	0	0	0	0	0	0	3	.000	.000
Bats Left	R	.091	11	1	0	1	0	2	0	6	.091	.273
Quintero,Humberto	L	.268	56	15	3	1	0	1	2	14	.293	.357
Bats Right	R	.233	206	48	9	0	2	24	4	39	.249	.306
Raburn,Ryan	L	.274	146	40	10	0	7	13	10	39	.321	.486
Bats Right	R	.245	241	59	12	2	7	36	11	75	.283	.398
Ramirez,Alexei	L	.268	142	38	6	0	3	14	15	20	.342	.373
Bats Right	R	.269	472	127	25	2	12	56	36	64	.324	.407
Ramirez,Aramis	L	.305	128	39	8	1	4	16	9	15	.348	.477
Bats Right	R	.307	437	134	27	0	22	77	34	54	.365	.519
Ramirez,Hanley	L	.315	73	23	10	0	3	12	12	12	.419	.575
Bats Right	R	.223	265	59	6	0	7	33	32	54	.309	.325
Ramirez,Manny	L	.000	3	0	0	0	0	0	0	0	.000	.000
Bats Right	R	.071	14	1	0	0	0	1	0	4	.071	.071
Ramirez,Wilkin	L	.222	18	4	1	0	0	1	4	7	.364	.278
Bats Right	R	.250	8	2	1	0	0	1	0	4	.250	.375
Ramos,Wilson	L	.276	87	24	4	0	3	13	12	18	.364	.425
Bats Right	R	.265	302	80	18	1	12	39	26	58	.325	.450
Ransom,Cody	L	.125	16	2	0	0	1	2	2	5	.222	.313
Bats Right	R	.176	17	3	2	0	0	2	1	4	.263	.294
Rasmus,Colby	L	.215	130	28	6	2	3	21	18	29	.309	.362
Bats Left	R	.229	341	78	18	4	11	32	32	87	.293	.402
Recker,Anthony	L	.286	7	2	0	0	0	0	2	3	.444	.286
Bats Right	R	.100	10	1	1	0	0	0	2	5	.250	.200
Reddick,Josh	L	.275	40	11	3	0	1	3	3	11	.341	.425
Bats Left	R	.280	214	60	15	3	6	25	16	39	.325	.463
Reed,Jeremy	L	.000	1	0	0	0	0	0	0	0	.000	.000
Bats Left	R	.000	6	0	0	0	0	0	0	2	.000	.000
Reimold,Nolan	L	.225	89	20	1	0	5	14	7	24	.276	.404
Bats Right	R	.258	178	46	9	3	8	31	21	33	.353	.478
Renteria,Edgar	L	.304	56	17	4	0	1	13	6	9	.354	.429
Bats Right	R	.239	243	58	10	0	4	23	18	56	.294	.329
Repko,Jason	L	.292	48	14	1	0	0	5	1	9	.320	.313
Bats Right	R	.188	85	16	1	0	2	6	5	29	.242	.271
Revere,Ben	L	.265	151	40	5	0	0	11	8	15	.311	.298
Bats Left	R	.268	299	80	4	5	0	19	18	26	.309	.314
Reyes,Jose	L	.325	126	41	8	2	1	9	12	8	.397	.444
Bats Both	R	.341	411	140	23	14	6	31	28	29	.379	.509
Reynolds,Mark	L	.208	130	27	6	1	8	25	22	47	.327	.454
Bats Right	R	.225	404	91	21	0	29	61	53	149	.321	.493
Rhymes,Will	L	.143	7	1	0	0	0	0	2	1	.333	.143
Bats Left	R	.244	78	19	3	0	0	2	9	11	.322	.282
Richardson,Antoan	L	.500	4	2	0	0	0	0	0	0	.500	.500
Bats Both	R	-	0	0	0	0	0	0	0	0	-	-
Rios,Alex	L	.287	150	43	8	0	3	18	5	15	.304	.400
Bats Right	R	.204	387	79	14	2	10	26	22	53	.250	.328
Rivera,Juan	L	.289	114	33	7	0	4	21	12	17	.349	.456
Bats Right	R	.247	352	87	16	1	7	53	31	59	.309	.358
Rivera,Mike	L	-	0	0	0	0	0	0	0	0	-	-
Bats Right	R	.333	6	2	0	0	0	0	0	1	.333	.333
Rivera,Rene	L	.179	28	5	1	0	1	2	2	5	.233	.321
Bats Right	R	.132	76	10	2	0	0	3	6	27	.202	.158
Rizzo,Anthony	L	.172	29	5	2	0	1	3	3	9	.273	.345
Bats Left	R	.131	99	13	6	1	0	6	18	37	.283	.212
Roberts,Brian	L	.188	48	9	2	1	1	8	4	7	.250	.333
Bats Both	R	.235	115	27	5	0	2	11	8	14	.282	.330
Roberts,Ryan	L	.278	133	37	7	0	7	18	25	21	.392	.489
Bats Right	R	.238	349	83	18	2	12	47	41	77	.320	.404
Robinson,Shane	L	.000	4	0	0	0	0	0	1	1	.200	.000
Bats Right	R	.000	3	0	0	0	0	0	0	1	.000	.000
Robinson,Trayvon	L	.158	38	6	3	0	0	4	2	13	.200	.237
Bats Both	R	.229	105	24	9	0	2	10	6	48	.268	.371
Rodriguez,Alex	L	.277	94	26	4	0	2	10	14	17	.367	.383
Bats Right	R	.276	279	77	10	0	14	52	33	63	.361	.481
Rodriguez,Ivan	L	.238	21	5	2	0	0	4	2	6	.304	.333
Bats Right	R	.214	103	22	5	0	2	15	8	22	.277	.320
Rodriguez,Josh	L	-	0	0	0	0	0	0	1	0	1.000	-
Bats Right	R	.083	12	1	0	0	0	1	0	8	.154	.083
Rodriguez,Luis	L	.172	29	5	3	0	0	1	3	4	.242	.276
Bats Both	R	.205	88	18	7	0	2	13	13	17	.317	.352
Rodriguez,Sean	L	.273	139	38	10	3	4	20	20	27	.389	.475
Bats Right	R	.192	234	45	10	0	4	16	18	60	.280	.286
Rohlinger,Ryan	L	-	0	0	0	0	0	0	0	0	-	-
Bats Right	R	.000	1	0	0	0	0	0	0	1	.000	.000
Rolen,Scott	L	.246	57	14	7	0	2	9	2	5	.295	.474
Bats Right	R	.241	195	47	13	2	3	27	8	31	.274	.374
Rollins,Jimmy	L	.240	146	35	4	0	3	13	9	13	.280	.329
Bats Both	R	.278	421	117	18	2	13	50	49	46	.357	.423
Romine,Andrew	L	.000	5	0	0	0	0	0	0	0	.000	.000
Bats Both	R	.182	11	2	0	0	0	0	1	5	.250	.182
Romine,Austin	L	.000	3	0	0	0	0	0	1	1	.250	.000
Bats Right	R	.188	16	3	0	0	0	0	1	4	.188	.188
Rosales,Adam	L	.114	35	4	0	0	2	5	3	5	.200	.286
Bats Right	R	.077	26	2	0	0	0	3	1	8	.107	.077
Rosario,Wilin	L	.286	14	4	1		1	1	2	4	.375	.714
Bats Right	R	.175	40	7	2	0	2	7	0	16	.171	.375
Ross,Cody	L	.234	94	22	6	0	2	10	14	23	.336	.362
Bats Right	R	.241	311	75	19	0	12	42	35	73	.322	.418
Ross,David	L	.240	50	12	2	0		6	7	18	.333	.280
Bats Right	R	.275	102	28	5	0	6	17	9	33	.333	.500
Rottino,Vinny	L	.400	5	2	0	0	0	0	2	0	.571	.400
Bats Right	R	.000	7	0	0	0	0	0	0	4	.000	.000
Rowand,Aaron	L	.286	105	30	8	1	1	4	4	26	.309	.410
Bats Right	R	.208	226	47	14	1	3	17	6	58	.257	.319
Ruggiano,Justin	L	.217	46	10	2	0	1	5	2	12	.250	.326
Bats Right	R	.271	59	16	2	0	3	8	2	14	.290	.458
Ruiz,Carlos	L	.265	98	26	7	0	0	6	14	12	.379	.337
Bats Right	R	.288	312	90	16	0	6	34	34	36	.368	.397
Ryan,Brendan	L	.255	106	27	4	2	1	9	10	24	.350	.358
Bats Right	R	.245	330	81	15	1	2	30	21	63	.301	.315
Saltalamacchia,J.	L	.209	115	24	5	0	5	17	7	32	.252	.383
Bats Both	R	.247	243	60	18	3	11	39	17	87	.304	.481
Sanchez,Angel	L	.270	63	17	2	0	0	4	12	8	.387	.302
Bats Right	R	.231	225	52	8	0	1	24	15	36	.280	.280
Sanchez,Freddy	L	.222	54	12	6	0	0	4	7	10	.323	.333
Bats Right	R	.308	185	57	9	1	3	20	6	25	.335	.416
Sanchez,Gaby	L	.295	129	38	9	0	5	19	26	19	.420	.481
Bats Right	R	.257	443	114	26	0	14	59	48	78	.331	.411
Sanchez,Hector	L	.091	11	1	1	0	0	0	1	3	.167	.182
Bats Both	R	.350	20	7	1	0	0	1	2	3	.409	.400
Sandoval,Pablo	L	.281	96	27	3	1	3	6	2	19	.296	.427
Bats Both	R	.324	330	107	23	2	20	64	30	44	.373	.588
Sands,Jerry	L	.367	60	22	7	0	3	14	7	8	.433	.633
Bats Right	R	.203	138	28	8	0	1	12	18	43	.297	.283
Santana,Carlos	L	.318	179	57	20	2	5	25	34	25	.428	.536
Bats Both	R	.201	373	75	15	0	22	54	63	108	.314	.418
Santiago,Ramon	L	.320	50	16	2	0	2	7	2	9	.352	.480
Bats Both	R	.245	208	51	9	3	3	23	15	29	.301	.361
Santos,Omir	L	.364	11	4	0	0	0	0	0	1	.364	.364
Bats Right	R	.091	11	1	0	0	0	0	0	3	.091	.091
Sappelt,Dave	L	.267	30	8	4	0	0	0	2	7	.313	.400
Bats Right	R	.234	77	18	4	0	0	5	5	10	.280	.286
Sardinha,Dane	L	.333	9	3	0	0	0	0	5	2	.571	.333
Bats Right	R	.174	23	4	0	0	1	5	1	11	.345	.217

Batters vs. Left-Handed and Right-Handed Pitchers

Batter	vs	Avg	AB	H	2B	3B	HR	RBI	BB	SO	OBP	Slg
Satin,Josh	L	.300	10	3	1	0	0	2	0	2	.300	.400
Bats Right	R	.133	15	2	0	0	0	0	1	9	.235	.133
Saunders,Michael	L	.143	56	8	1	0	0	4	2	21	.169	.161
Bats Left	R	.152	105	16	4	0	2	4	10	35	.226	.248
Schafer,Jordan	L	.213	75	16	5	0	0	2	7	21	.280	.280
Bats Left	R	.251	227	57	5	3	2	11	21	49	.319	.326
Schafer,Logan	L	-	0	0	0	0	0	0	0	0	-	-
Bats Left	R	.333	3	1	0	0	0	0	1	1	.500	.333
Schierholtz,Nate	L	.234	64	15	4	0	0	7	3	13	.265	.297
Bats Left	R	.288	271	78	18	1	9	34	18	48	.340	.461
Schneider,Brian	L	.125	24	3	0	0	0	1	2	9	.222	.125
Bats Left	R	.188	101	19	4	0	2	8	9	26	.252	.287
Schumaker,Skip	L	.250	36	9	2	0	1	6	5	6	.326	.389
Bats Left	R	.287	331	95	17	0	1	32	22	44	.334	.347
Scott,Luke	L	.167	36	6	2	0	4	7	3	12	.225	.556
Bats Left	R	.231	173	40	9	0	5	15	21	42	.316	.370
Scutaro,Marco	L	.303	109	33	10	0	1	13	9	10	.353	.422
Bats Right	R	.297	286	85	16	1	6	41	29	26	.361	.423
Seager,Kyle	L	.229	35	8	0	0	0	3	5	7	.341	.229
Bats Left	R	.265	147	39	13	0	3	10	8	29	.304	.415
Sellers,Justin	L	.300	30	9	3	0	0	2	4	2	.382	.400
Bats Right	R	.172	93	16	6	0	1	11	8	19	.250	.269
Shoppach,Kelly	L	.241	108	26	1	0	7	15	13	32	.344	.444
Bats Right	R	.115	113	13	2	0	4	7	6	47	.192	.239
Shuck,J.B.	L	.455	11	5	0	0	0	0	0	1	.455	.455
Bats Left	R	.243	70	17	2	1	0	3	11	6	.346	.300
Sizemore,Grady	L	.183	71	13	3	1	2	7	3	24	.244	.338
Bats Left	R	.239	197	47	18	0	8	25	15	61	.300	.452
Sizemore,Scott	L	.294	119	35	11	0	2	16	19	29	.391	.437
Bats Right	R	.221	249	55	11	1	9	40	34	83	.318	.382
Smith,Seth	L	.217	92	20	3	1	1	12	7	19	.272	.304
Bats Left	R	.299	384	115	29	8	14	47	39	74	.365	.526
Smoak,Justin	L	.252	127	32	6	0	4	13	21	26	.326	.394
Bats Both	R	.227	300	68	18	0	11	42	42	84	.322	.397
Snider,Travis	L	.116	43	5	0	0	1	6	0	16	.114	.186
Bats Left	R	.257	144	37	14	0	2	24	11	40	.312	.396
Snyder,Brad	L	-	0	0	0	0	0	0	0	0	-	-
Bats Left	R	.111	9	1	0	0	0	0	0	6	.111	.111
Snyder,Brandon	L	.300	10	3	1	0	0	0	1	3	.364	.400
Bats Right	R	.000	3	0	0	0	0	0	1	2	.500	.000
Snyder,Chris	L	.310	29	9	0	0	1	5	5	8	.412	.414
Bats Right	R	.254	67	17	3	0	2	12	12	15	.361	.388
Sogard,Eric	L	.000	11	0	0	0	0	1	2	3	.154	.000
Bats Left	R	.237	59	14	3	0	2	3	2	10	.262	.390
Soriano,Alfonso	L	.271	118	32	6	0	7	21	7	27	.312	.500
Bats Right	R	.235	357	84	21	1	19	67	20	86	.282	.459
Soto,Geovany	L	.296	98	29	5	0	7	16	16	22	.410	.561
Bats Right	R	.207	323	67	21	0	10	39	29	102	.277	.365
Span,Denard	L	.240	75	18	1	1	1	6	11	11	.337	.320
Bats Left	R	.273	209	57	10	4	1	10	16	25	.324	.373
Spears,Nate	L	-	0	0	0	0	0	0	0	0	-	-
Bats Left	R	.000	4	0	0	0	0	0	0	1	.000	.000
Spilborghs,Ryan	L	.207	82	17	6	1	1	8	7	17	.264	.341
Bats Right	R	.212	118	25	2	0	2	14	12	32	.295	.280
Stairs,Matt	L	.333	3	1	0	0	0	1	0	2	.333	.333
Bats Left	R	.145	62	9	1	0	0	1	9	21	.254	.161
Stanton,Mike	L	.293	116	34	9	2	9	27	19	29	.404	.638
Bats Right	R	.253	400	101	21	3	25	60	51	137	.341	.508
Stewart,Chris	L	.295	44	13	2	0	1	2	7	3	.392	.409
Bats Right	R	.169	118	20	6	0	2	8	9	15	.240	.271
Stewart,Ian	L	.091	22	2	1	0	0	1	3	10	.200	.136
Bats Left	R	.170	100	17	5	1	0	5	11	27	.252	.240
Stubbs,Drew	L	.319	113	36	7	1	3	12	20	36	.418	.478
Bats Right	R	.226	491	111	15	2	12	32	43	169	.298	.338
Sutton,Drew	L	.214	14	3	1	0	0	1	1	4	.267	.286
Bats Both	R	.350	40	14	6	0	0	6	2	9	.395	.500
Suzuki,Ichiro	L	.281	192	54	5	0	1	16	13	19	.325	.323
Bats Left	R	.268	485	130	17	3	4	31	26	50	.304	.340
Suzuki,Kurt	L	.233	133	31	4	0	2	6	14	19	.309	.308
Bats Right	R	.239	327	78	22	0	12	38	24	45	.298	.416
Sweeney,Ryan	L	.159	44	7	0	0	0	2	5	11	.245	.159
Bats Left	R	.286	220	63	11	3	1	23	28	37	.365	.377
Swisher,Nick	L	.327	159	52	12	0	6	21	34	33	.442	.516
Bats Both	R	.232	367	85	18	0	17	64	61	92	.343	.420
Tabata,Jose	L	.297	74	22	6	0	1	5	13	12	.400	.419
Bats Right	R	.258	260	67	12	1	3	16	27	49	.333	.346

Batter	vs	Avg	AB	H	2B	3B	HR	RBI	BB	SO	OBP	Slg
Tatum,Craig	L	.278	18	5	1	0	0	2	4	4	.409	.333
Bats Right	R	.174	69	12	2	0	0	5	2	17	.194	.203
Taylor,Michael	L	.211	19	4	0	0	1	1	3	7	.318	.368
Bats Right	R	.182	11	2	0	0	0	0	2	4	.308	.182
Teagarden,Taylor	L	.000	6	0	0	0	0	0	0	5	.000	.000
Bats Right	R	.286	28	8	2	0	0	2	2	8	.333	.357
Teahen,Mark	L	.143	28	4	1	0	0	5	3	8	.226	.179
Bats Left	R	.212	132	28	3	0	4	9	13	37	.283	.326
Teixeira,Mark	L	.302	189	57	7	1	15	41	22	25	.380	.587
Bats Both	R	.223	400	89	19	0	24	70	54	85	.323	.450
Tejada,Miguel	L	.247	89	22	4	0	2	8	5	11	.284	.360
Bats Right	R	.236	233	55	12	0	2	18	7	24	.264	.313
Tejada,Ruben	L	.266	79	21	5	0	0	11	15	13	.375	.329
Bats Right	R	.289	249	72	10	1	0	25	20	37	.355	.337
Tekotte,Blake	L	.000	4	0	0	0	0	0	1	4	.200	.000
Bats Left	R	.200	30	6	1	1	0	1	3	17	.273	.300
Thames,Eric	L	.209	86	18	3	2	3	9	4	20	.242	.395
Bats Left	R	.279	276	77	21	3	9	28	19	68	.334	.475
Thames,Marcus	L	.167	36	6	0	1	1	3	3	10	.231	.306
Bats Both	R	.233	30	7	1	0	1	4	1	6	.258	.367
Theriot,Ryan	L	.310	126	39	11	1	0	12	8	8	.356	.413
Bats Right	R	.256	316	81	15	0	1	35	21	33	.307	.313
Thole,Josh	L	.167	36	6	2	0	0	4	6	7	.302	.222
Bats Left	R	.280	304	85	15	0	3	36	32	40	.351	.359
Thome,Jim	L	.253	75	19	3	0	5	18	16	30	.385	.493
Bats Left	R	.257	202	52	13	0	10	32	30	62	.352	.470
Thurston,Joe	L	-	0	0	0	0	0	0	0	0	-	-
Bats Left	R	.250	4	1	0	0	0	0	0	1	.250	.250
Tolbert,Matt	L	.200	50	10	1	0	0	2	4	7	.273	.220
Bats Both	R	.197	157	31	9	2	0	9	7	24	.246	.280
Toregas,Wyatt	L	.000	1	0	0	0	0	0	0	0	.000	.000
Bats Right	R	.000	3	0	0	0	0	0	0	1	.000	.000
Torrealba,Yorvit	L	.256	117	30	7	0	0	8	7	16	.296	.316
Bats Right	R	.280	279	78	20	1	7	29	13	49	.311	.434
Torres,Andres	L	.170	47	8	3	0	0	1	9	12	.316	.234
Bats Both	R	.229	301	69	21	1	4	18	33	83	.312	.346
Tosoni,Rene	L	.286	28	8	2	0	1	3	1	8	.333	.464
Bats Left	R	.188	144	27	5	1	4	19	13	34	.264	.319
Towles,J.R.	L	.149	47	7	4	0	1	3	5	5	.226	.298
Bats Right	R	.200	100	20	3	0	2	8	8	21	.270	.290
Treanor,Matt	L	.186	43	8	0	0	1	4	10	10	.345	.256
Bats Right	R	.222	153	34	6	0	2	18	24	43	.335	.301
Trout,Mike	L	.245	49	12	3	0	3	9	3	12	.283	.490
Bats Right	R	.203	74	15	3	0	2	7	6	18	.280	.324
Trumbo,Mark	L	.264	178	47	10	0	8	31	8	46	.293	.455
Bats Right	R	.249	361	90	21	1	21	56	17	74	.291	.488
Tulowitzki,Troy	L	.349	149	52	15	0	9	30	18	20	.418	.631
Bats Right	R	.284	388	110	21	2	21	75	41	59	.354	.510
Turner,Justin	L	.234	124	29	8	0	0	9	15	18	.331	.298
Bats Right	R	.270	311	84	22	0	4	42	24	41	.335	.379
Uggla,Dan	L	.201	164	33	8	0	6	13	20	49	.288	.360
Bats Right	R	.245	436	107	14	1	30	69	42	107	.320	.489
Upton,B.J.	L	.238	147	35	7	0	5	16	28	37	.358	.388
Bats Right	R	.245	431	101	20	4	18	65	43	124	.320	.443
Upton,Justin	L	.268	138	37	7	1	10	20	24	24	.378	.551
Bats Right	R	.295	454	134	32	4	21	68	35	102	.367	.522
Uribe,Juan	L	.159	69	11	2	0	1	7	8	15	.253	.232
Bats Right	R	.219	201	44	10	0	3	21	9	45	.269	.313
Utley,Chase	L	.187	107	20	5	1	2	9	9	22	.298	.308
Bats Left	R	.285	291	83	16	5	9	35	30	25	.362	.467
Valaika,Chris	L	.800	5	4	0	0	0	0	0	0	.800	.800
Bats Right	R	.150	20	3	1	1	0	0	2	3	.227	.300
Valbuena,Luis	L	.250	12	3	0	0	1	1	0	2	.250	.500
Bats Left	R	.194	31	6	0	0	0	0	1	7	.219	.194
Valdez,Wilson	L	.250	92	23	7	1	0	7	9	15	.317	.348
Bats Right	R	.249	181	45	7	3	1	23	9	26	.281	.337
Valencia,Danny	L	.309	149	46	10	1	4	22	10	21	.352	.470
Bats Right	R	.224	415	93	18	1	11	50	30	81	.274	.352
Varitek,Jason	L	.264	72	19	2	1	2	11	8	17	.346	.403
Bats Both	R	.200	150	30	8	0	9	25	13	50	.277	.433
Velazquez,Gil	L	.500	2	1	0	0	0	1	0	0	.333	.500
Bats Right	R	.500	4	2	0	0	0	0	0	0	.500	.500
Velez,Eugenio	L	.000	15	0	0	0	0	1	1	5	.063	.000
Bats Both	R	.000	22	0	0	0	0	0	1	6	.083	.000
Venable,Will	L	.174	46	8	1	0	0	4	2	11	.240	.196
Bats Left	R	.256	324	83	13	7	9	40	29	81	.319	.423

Batters vs. Left-Handed and Right-Handed Pitchers

Batter	vs	Avg	AB	H	2B	3B	HR	RBI	BB	SO	OBP	Slg
Viciedo,Dayan	L	.406	32	13	2	0	1	3	3	5	.457	.563
Bats Right	R	.186	70	13	1	0	0	3	6	18	.269	.200
Victorino,Shane	L	.308	120	37	8	2	8	17	20	11	.424	.608
Bats Both	R	.271	399	108	19	14	9	44	35	52	.333	.456
Vizquel,Omar	L	.200	20	4	0	0	0	0	0	6	.200	.200
Bats Both	R	.259	147	38	7	1	0	8	9	12	.297	.320
Votto,Joey	L	.333	174	58	16	2	7	32	24	40	.418	.569
Bats Left	R	.299	425	127	24	1	22	71	86	89	.415	.515
Walker,Neil	L	.269	160	43	8	1	1	15	11	23	.322	.350
Bats Both	R	.275	436	120	28	3	11	68	43	89	.338	.429
Wallace,Brett	L	.211	57	12	3	0	0	2	5	15	.286	.263
Bats Left	R	.269	279	75	19	0	5	27	31	76	.344	.391
Weeks,Jemile	L	.287	129	37	9	2	0	11	6	17	.316	.388
Bats Both	R	.310	277	86	17	6	2	25	15	45	.351	.437
Weeks,Rickie	L	.261	92	24	6	0	4	10	16	24	.375	.457
Bats Right	R	.271	361	98	20	2	16	39	34	83	.343	.471
Wells,Casper	L	.260	96	25	7	0	5	13	10	32	.349	.490
Bats Right	R	.218	119	26	4	0	6	14	8	39	.290	.403
Wells,Vernon	L	.284	162	46	6	2	10	22	9	25	.320	.531
Bats Right	R	.187	343	64	9	2	15	44	11	61	.213	.356
Werth,Jayson	L	.184	114	21	9	0	4	16	20	36	.307	.368
Bats Right	R	.244	447	109	17	1	16	42	54	124	.336	.394
Whiteside,Eli	L	.250	36	9	3	0	2	7	6	9	.342	.500
Bats Right	R	.186	177	33	5	2	2	10	12	50	.240	.271
Wieters,Matt	L	.339	121	41	10	0	11	26	20	32	.430	.694
Bats Both	R	.237	379	90	18	0	11	42	28	52	.293	.372
Wigginton,Ty	L	.259	108	28	3	0	5	12	17	25	.370	.426
Bats Right	R	.235	293	69	18	2	10	35	21	59	.292	.413
Willingham,Josh	L	.208	159	33	5	0	12	31	23	51	.317	.465
Bats Right	R	.264	329	87	21	0	17	67	33	99	.340	.483
Willits,Reggie	L	.000	10	0	0	0	0	0	2	3	.167	.000
Bats Both	R	.083	12	1	1	0	0	1	2	4	.214	.167
Wilson,Bobby	L	.250	56	14	7	0	1	7	5	3	.302	.429
Bats Right	R	.127	55	7	1	0	0	1	5	13	.200	.145
Wilson,Jack	L	.242	91	22	4	0	0	5	4	13	.271	.286
Bats Right	R	.244	123	30	5	0	0	6	6	26	.277	.285
Wilson,Josh	L	.208	48	10	1	0	2	4	4	17	.269	.354
Bats Right	R	.243	37	9	4	0	0	1	0	5	.243	.351
Wilson,Mike	L	.105	19	2	1	0	0	2	1	5	.150	.158
Bats Right	R	.250	8	2	0	0	0	1	0	2	.250	.250
Wise,DeWayne	L	.150	20	3	0	0	0	1	0	9	.150	.150
Bats Left	R	.215	79	17	2	1	2	6	3	27	.250	.342
Wood,Brandon	L	.241	87	21	6	0	2	14	7	29	.298	.379
Bats Right	R	.202	163	33	4	0	5	17	12	44	.256	.319
Woodward,Chris	L	.000	2	0	0	0	0	0	0	1	.000	.000
Bats Right	R	.000	8	0	0	0	0	0	0	3	.000	.000
Worth,Danny	L	.333	21	7	2	0	0	2	1	4	.364	.429
Bats Right	R	.188	16	3	0	0	0	1	1	5	.235	.188
Wright,David	L	.256	78	20	6	0	2	11	17	21	.396	.410
Bats Right	R	.254	311	79	17	1	12	50	35	76	.330	.431
Youkilis,Kevin	L	.311	132	41	15	0	6	20	25	37	.426	.561
Bats Right	R	.234	299	70	17	2	11	60	43	63	.349	.415
Young,Chris	L	.285	130	37	7	0	9	23	25	31	.392	.546
Bats Right	R	.222	437	97	31	3	11	48	55	108	.312	.382
Young,Delmon	L	.301	133	40	5	1	3	20	8	18	.338	.421
Bats Right	R	.256	340	87	16	0	9	44	15	67	.288	.382
Young,Eric	L	.234	77	18	2	2	0	3	8	12	.306	.312
Bats Both	R	.256	121	31	2	1	0	7	18	26	.364	.289
Young,Matt	L	.125	8	1	0	0	0	0	1	1	.222	.125
Bats Left	R	.225	40	9	1	0	0	1	3	5	.279	.250
Young,Michael	L	.361	158	57	10	3	2	27	11	20	.402	.500
Bats Right	R	.330	473	156	31	3	9	79	36	58	.373	.465
Zimmerman,Ryan	L	.338	65	22	7	0	1	6	10	11	.427	.492
Bats Right	R	.279	330	92	14	2	11	43	31	62	.340	.433
Zobrist,Ben	L	.303	185	56	16	3	7	38	21	48	.372	.535
Bats Both	R	.253	403	102	30	3	13	53	56	80	.344	.439
AL	L	.262	-	-	-	-	-	-	-	-	.329	.408
	R	.256	-	-	-	-	-	-	-	-	.320	.408
NL	L	.251	-	-	-	-	-	-	-	-	.320	.391
	R	.253	-	-	-	-	-	-	-	-	.318	.391
MLB	L	.256	-	-	-	-	-	-	-	-	.325	.399
	R	.255	-	-	-	-	-	-	-	-	.319	.399

Pitchers vs. Left-Handed and Right-Handed Batters

Pitcher	vs	Avg	AB	H	2B	3B	HR	RBI	BB	SO	OBP	Slg
Abad,Fernando	L	.273	44	12	3	0	0	3	1	9	.289	.341
Throws Left	R	.381	42	16	2	0	5	18	8	6	.472	.786
Abreu,Juan	L	.125	8	1	0	0	1	1	2	4	.462	.500
Throws Right	R	.278	18	5	0	1	0	1	1	8	.381	.389
Accardo,Jeremy	L	.257	70	18	4	0	2	7	11	10	.366	.400
Throws Right	R	.329	76	25	7	0	3	12	7	13	.386	.539
Aceves,Alfredo	L	.190	184	35	11	0	3	15	16	41	.278	.299
Throws Right	R	.216	227	49	13	0	5	22	26	39	.317	.339
Acosta,Manny	L	.247	81	20	6	1	1	6	5	21	.291	.383
Throws Right	R	.286	105	30	4	0	5	16	10	25	.356	.467
Adams,Mike	L	.189	148	28	8	1	2	10	10	42	.241	.297
Throws Right	R	.143	112	16	5	0	3	6	4	32	.171	.268
Adcock,Nathan	L	.260	104	27	7	0	3	19	8	10	.319	.413
Throws Right	R	.281	128	36	9	1	2	10	18	26	.376	.414
Affeldt,Jeremy	L	.144	90	13	2	0	1	7	5	24	.206	.200
Throws Left	R	.248	137	34	9	1	4	16	19	30	.348	.416
Albers,Matt	L	.263	99	26	8	0	4	17	15	27	.364	.465
Throws Right	R	.243	148	36	5	0	3	19	16	41	.329	.338
Alburquerque,Al	L	.176	68	12	0	0	0	3	9	32	.291	.176
Throws Right	R	.113	80	9	1	0	0	3	20	35	.287	.125
Alvarez,Henderson	L	.252	131	33	8	1	3	12	7	22	.301	.397
Throws Right	R	.274	113	31	3	1	5	12	1	18	.287	.451
Anderson,Brett	L	.303	109	33	1	0	4	15	3	17	.339	.422
Throws Left	R	.252	210	53	10	1	4	21	22	44	.333	.367
Arredondo,Jose	L	.238	80	19	4	2	1	4	11	21	.330	.375
Throws Right	R	.218	110	24	4	1	4	14	20	27	.348	.382
Arrieta,Jake	L	.253	241	61	12	3	13	40	42	54	.366	.490
Throws Right	R	.252	214	54	8	0	8	27	17	39	.314	.402
Arroyo,Bronson	L	.317	375	119	23	3	27	64	26	44	.365	.611
Throws Right	R	.258	418	108	24	0	19	47	19	64	.293	.452
Ascanio,Jose	L	.294	17	5	0	0	1	4	0	2	.294	.471
Throws Right	R	.417	12	5	1	0	1	2	2	3	.500	.750
Asencio,Jairo	L	.250	16	4	0	0	0	2	2	1	.333	.250
Throws Right	R	.387	31	12	3	1	1	8	3	7	.441	.645
Atchison,Scott	L	.289	45	13	6	0	0	8	4	5	.347	.422
Throws Right	R	.273	66	18	6	0	0	7	2	12	.306	.364
Atkins,Mitch	L	.440	25	11	3	0	2	5	3	4	.483	.800
Throws Right	R	.385	26	10	0	0	3	5	0	3	.407	.731
Augenstein,Bryan	L	.600	10	6	2	0	1	3	2	2	.692	1.100
Throws Right	R	.294	17	5	2	0	0	2	1	4	.333	.412
Axelrod,Dylan	L	.256	43	11	1	0	1	4	6	10	.333	.349
Throws Right	R	.259	27	7	3	0	0	1	3	9	.355	.370
Axford,John	L	.188	128	24	1	1	1	8	10	45	.246	.234
Throws Right	R	.233	150	35	2	1	3	10	15	41	.301	.320
Ayala,Luis	L	.250	104	26	4	0	3	16	11	30	.319	.375
Throws Right	R	.263	95	25	4	0	2	10	9	9	.355	.368
Badenhop,Burke	L	.264	91	24	4	1	0	12	16	17	.376	.330
Throws Right	R	.266	154	41	8	2	1	25	8	34	.313	.364
Baez,Danys	L	.327	55	18	4	0	3	12	7	8	.413	.564
Throws Right	R	.272	92	25	4	0	2	15	6	10	.330	.380
Bailey,Andrew	L	.227	88	20	8	0	3	15	8	22	.289	.420
Throws Right	R	.206	68	14	3	1	0	2	4	19	.250	.279
Bailey,Homer	L	.274	234	64	9	2	10	34	15	52	.320	.457
Throws Right	R	.256	281	72	11	0	8	32	14	54	.306	.381
Baker,Scott	L	.267	318	85	14	2	11	27	21	79	.315	.428
Throws Right	R	.215	191	41	8	1	4	16	11	44	.265	.330
Balester,Collin	L	.235	51	12	1	0	2	7	9	12	.361	.373
Throws Right	R	.286	91	26	7	0	5	14	5	22	.320	.527
Balfour,Grant	L	.191	110	21	6	0	3	6	9	27	.252	.327
Throws Right	R	.207	111	23	1	0	5	10	11	32	.279	.351
Bard,Daniel	L	.211	147	31	5	1	4	17	11	29	.270	.340
Throws Right	R	.136	110	15	3	2	1	10	13	45	.234	.227
Bass,Anthony	L	.243	74	18	4	0	1	9	6	10	.309	.338
Throws Right	R	.230	100	23	2	1	2	3	15	14	.330	.330
Bastardo,Antonio	L	.145	69	10	1	2	2	4	10	31	.253	.304
Throws Left	R	.143	126	18	4	0	4	10	16	39	.236	.270
Batista,Miguel	L	.277	83	23	7	3	2	13	16	8	.400	.506
Throws Right	R	.193	135	26	6	0	0	10	21	23	.304	.237
Beachy,Brandon	L	.236	212	50	13	2	6	19	20	70	.306	.401
Throws Right	R	.237	317	75	8	1	10	35	26	99	.297	.363
Beato,Pedro	L	.261	88	23	5	2	1	14	18	9	.389	.398
Throws Right	R	.228	158	36	13	1	4	25	9	30	.277	.399
Beavan,Blake	L	.314	207	65	19	1	8	25	6	22	.330	.531
Throws Right	R	.236	174	41	7	1	5	18	9	20	.280	.374
Beck,Chad	L	.500	2	1	0	0	0	0	0	0	.500	.500
Throws Right	R	.000	6	0	0	0	0	0	0	3	.000	.000
Beckett,Josh	L	.186	403	75	17	0	10	31	37	102	.260	.303
Throws Right	R	.245	290	71	6	0	11	30	15	73	.292	.379
Bedard,Erik	L	.245	139	34	4	1	3	14	14	35	.318	.353
Throws Left	R	.239	351	84	16	0	11	42	34	90	.306	.379
Beimel,Joe	L	.302	43	13	2	1	1	7	2	8	.333	.465
Throws Left	R	.333	63	21	3	0	5	15	7	9	.408	.619
Belisle,Matt	L	.250	104	26	5	1	1	12	8	21	.310	.346
Throws Right	R	.291	175	51	11	1	4	30	6	37	.326	.434
Bell,Heath	L	.283	113	32	4	0	2	11	13	28	.354	.372
Throws Right	R	.164	116	19	2	0	2	7	8	23	.218	.233
Bell,Trevor	L	.281	64	18	5	0	0	4	8	10	.370	.359
Throws Right	R	.300	70	21	6	0	2	12	2	7	.315	.471
Below,Duane	L	.255	47	12	1	0	1	5	4	9	.321	.340
Throws Left	R	.250	64	16	3	0	1	8	7	5	.315	.344
Benoit,Joaquin	L	.248	113	28	2	0	2	15	12	38	.320	.319
Throws Right	R	.184	103	19	2	0	3	14	5	25	.226	.291
Berg,Justin	L	.294	17	5	2	0	1	4	3	2	.400	.588
Throws Right	R	.222	27	6	3	0	0	2	3	4	.344	.333
Bergesen,Brad	L	.310	216	67	23	2	7	34	16	32	.359	.532
Throws Right	R	.264	197	52	12	1	9	41	16	29	.322	.472
Berken,Jason	L	.391	87	34	6	1	5	24	12	21	.465	.655
Throws Right	R	.261	111	29	6	2	5	19	9	20	.317	.486
Betances,Dellin	L	.167	6	1	0	0	0	1	2	2	.444	.167
Throws Right	R	.000	2	0	0	0	0	1	4	0	.571	.000
Betancourt,Rafael	L	.220	100	22	4	0	2	11	7	26	.269	.320
Throws Right	R	.189	127	24	2	1	5	11	1	47	.194	.339
Billings,Bruce	L	.462	13	6	0	0	1	7	3	2	.563	.692
Throws Right	R	.368	19	7	3	0	0	4	3	5	.455	.526
Billingsley,Chad	L	.282	330	93	20	0	8	45	51	80	.382	.415
Throws Right	R	.248	387	96	22	2	6	43	33	72	.309	.362
Blackburn,Nick	L	.295	312	92	13	4	7	31	35	37	.365	.429
Throws Right	R	.316	288	91	15	2	12	50	19	39	.362	.507
Blanton,Joe	L	.299	67	20	5	0	2	9	3	18	.329	.463
Throws Right	R	.333	96	32	5	1	3	13	6	17	.373	.500
Blevins,Jerry	L	.256	43	11	1	0	2	11	6	15	.340	.419
Throws Left	R	.220	59	13	2	2	0	8	8	11	.314	.322
Boggs,Mitchell	L	.247	81	20	5	1	2	9	8	13	.308	.407
Throws Right	R	.276	152	42	6	1	2	14	13	35	.341	.368
Bowden,Michael	L	.258	31	8	0	0	1	2	3	5	.324	.355
Throws Right	R	.229	48	11	1	0	2	5	8	12	.339	.375
Boyer,Blaine	L	.286	14	4	1	0	1	4	1	0	.375	.571
Throws Right	R	.563	16	9	2	0	1	5	0	1	.563	.875
Brach,Brad	L	.333	3	1	0	0	0	0	0	3	.500	.333
Throws Right	R	.286	21	6	0	0	0	5	4	9	.423	.286
Brackman,Andrew	L	.000	3	0	0	0	0	0	1	0	.250	.000
Throws Right	R	.143	7	1	0	0	0	0	2	0	.333	.143
Braddock,Zach	L	.250	28	7	2	0	2	4	5	6	.389	.536
Throws Left	R	.231	39	9	3	0	0	5	6	12	.326	.308
Braden,Dallas	L	.333	12	4	2	0	1	4	0	2	.333	.750
Throws Left	R	.250	56	14	3	1	1	5	3	13	.311	.393
Bray,Bill	L	.180	89	16	2	1	2	13	10	29	.265	.292
Throws Left	R	.226	84	19	9	0	1	5	7	15	.290	.369
Brazoban,Yhency	L	.444	9	4	0	0	0	3	2	3	.583	.444
Throws Right	R	.235	17	4	1	0	1	5	2	5	.316	.471
Breslow,Craig	L	.352	91	32	6	1	1	11	6	13	.394	.473
Throws Left	R	.261	142	37	8	0	3	21	15	31	.333	.380
Britton,Zach	L	.260	154	40	2	0	5	17	17	34	.328	.370
Throws Left	R	.281	434	122	29	1	7	62	45	63	.347	.401
Broderick,Brian	L	.400	25	10	3	0	0	5	3	2	.464	.520
Throws Right	R	.240	25	6	0	0	0	3	0	2	.286	.240
Brothers,Rex	L	.193	57	11	2	0	1	5	10	28	.313	.281
Throws Left	R	.232	95	22	2	1	3	4	10	31	.305	.368
Broxton,Jonathan	L	.238	21	5	1	0	0	3	5	5	.385	.286
Throws Right	R	.313	32	10	0	0	2	4	4	5	.389	.563
Bruney,Brian	L	.389	36	14	3	0	1	5	3	5	.425	.556
Throws Right	R	.293	41	12	2	0	3	10	9	11	.420	.561
Buchholz,Clay	L	.241	162	39	9	1	5	17	15	32	.305	.401
Throws Right	R	.242	153	37	8	0	5	16	16	28	.314	.392
Buchholz,Taylor	L	.324	37	12	1	0	4	8	6	7	.409	.676
Throws Right	R	.175	57	10	1	0	1	7	1	19	.197	.246
Buehrle,Mark	L	.251	235	59	5	1	9	30	5	34	.270	.413
Throws Left	R	.288	563	162	25	5	12	54	40	75	.332	.414
Buente,Jay	L	.167	12	2	1	1	0	3	2	0	.286	.417
Throws Right	R	.500	10	5	2	0	0	3	3	2	.643	.700
Bulger,Jason	L	.250	16	4	0	0	1	1	4	4	.400	.438
Throws Right	R	.118	17	2	0	0	0	1	3	5	.348	.294

Pitchers vs. Left-Handed and Right-Handed Batters

Pitcher	vs	Avg	AB	H	2B	3B	HR	RBI	BB	SO	OBP	Slg
Bumgarner,Madison	L	.243	148	36	7	1	1	18	6	39	.277	.324
Throws Left	R	.264	629	166	33	2	11	59	40	152	.310	.375
Burnett,A.J.	L	.256	383	98	27	2	13	47	45	96	.338	.439
Throws Right	R	.264	348	92	21	2	18	57	38	77	.339	.491
Burnett,Alex	L	.263	80	21	6	1	0	16	9	13	.330	.363
Throws Right	R	.264	110	29	3	1	4	19	12	20	.371	.418
Burnett,Sean	L	.200	95	19	1	1	3	17	7	16	.267	.326
Throws Left	R	.297	118	35	5	0	3	21	14	17	.373	.415
Burres,Brian	L	.167	6	1	0	0	1	1	2	1	.375	.667
Throws Left	R	.234	47	11	0	0	3	5	2	9	.260	.426
Burton,Jared	L	.500	6	3	0	0	1	2	2	0	.625	1.000
Throws Right	R	.231	13	3	2	0	0	2	1	3	.286	.385
Bush,Dave	L	.293	82	24	2	0	3	13	5	13	.341	.427
Throws Right	R	.329	70	23	2	0	3	8	4	10	.382	.486
Byrdak,Tim	L	.222	99	22	5	0	2	15	6	36	.271	.333
Throws Left	R	.279	43	12	3	0	1	5	13	11	.439	.419
Cahill,Trevor	L	.264	421	111	18	3	13	45	48	76	.341	.413
Throws Right	R	.274	376	103	22	0	6	49	34	71	.340	.380
Cain,Matt	L	.185	416	77	19	2	4	29	35	90	.254	.269
Throws Right	R	.250	400	100	27	3	5	41	28	89	.304	.370
Camp,Shawn	L	.347	124	43	14	1	1	15	13	10	.413	.500
Throws Right	R	.263	137	36	10	2	2	27	9	22	.329	.409
Capps,Matt	L	.264	121	32	6	0	6	22	6	14	.302	.463
Throws Right	R	.260	131	34	2	1	4	16	7	20	.308	.382
Capuano,Chris	L	.224	165	37	5	1	6	21	10	34	.277	.376
Throws Left	R	.283	569	161	46	2	21	67	43	134	.336	.482
Carignan,Andrew	L	.143	7	1	0	0	0	0	2	1	.333	.143
Throws Right	R	.318	22	7	1	0	1	3	0	4	.318	.500
Carlyle,Buddy	L	.000	8	0	0	0	0	0	4	4	.333	.000
Throws Right	R	.263	19	5	2	0	1	5	3	5	.364	.526
Carmona,Fausto	L	.296	398	118	30	1	10	61	29	51	.349	.452
Throws Right	R	.252	345	87	22	0	12	50	31	58	.327	.420
Carpenter,Drew	L	.296	27	8	2	0	2	8	4	9	.387	.593
Throws Right	R	.344	32	11	3	1	1	6	3	7	.400	.594
Carpenter,Chris	L	.259	432	112	19	2	7	36	27	78	.304	.361
Throws Right	R	.268	489	131	14	2	9	52	28	113	.313	.360
Carpenter,Chris (ChC)	L	.143	14	2	0	0	1	5	3	5	.278	.357
Throws Right	R	.417	24	10	3	0	0	7	4	3	.483	.542
Carpenter,David	L	.190	42	8	4	0	1	3	8	11	.340	.357
Throws Right	R	.328	61	20	2	1	2	11	5	18	.397	.492
Carrasco,Carlos	L	.318	255	81	14	2	10	37	29	36	.382	.506
Throws Right	R	.216	227	49	13	0	5	26	11	49	.261	.339
Carrasco,D.J.	L	.354	82	29	3	1	1	11	11	11	.459	.451
Throws Right	R	.325	117	38	8	0	6	23	5	16	.358	.547
Carreno,Joel	L	.250	24	6	0	0	1	1	2	7	.308	.375
Throws Right	R	.161	31	5	3	0	0	1	2	7	.212	.258
Cashner,Andrew	L	.083	12	1	0	0	0	0	2	3	.083	.083
Throws Right	R	.087	23	2	0	0	1	1	4	6	.222	.217
Casilla,Santiago	L	.234	64	15	5	0	0	3	8	13	.319	.313
Throws Right	R	.155	116	18	1	1	1	9	17	32	.274	.207
Cassevah,Bobby	L	.222	54	12	2	0	1	7	13	7	.368	.315
Throws Right	R	.198	81	16	2	1	0	5	6	17	.261	.247
Castillo,Alberto	L	.300	20	6	3	0	0	4	3	4	.417	.450
Throws Left	R	.190	21	4	3	0	0	2	4	2	.308	.333
Cecil,Brett	L	.186	129	24	3	2	0	9	16	22	.282	.240
Throws Left	R	.282	347	98	21	1	22	55	26	65	.337	.539
Ceda,Jose	L	.185	27	5	1	0	1	3	6	6	.333	.333
Throws Right	R	.224	49	11	2	0	0	3	6	15	.309	.265
Cedeno,Xavier	L	.500	4	2	0	0	0	0	0	0	.500	.500
Throws Left	R	.714	7	5	0	0	2	5	0	0	.714	1.571
Chacin,Jhoulys	L	.232	370	86	21	6	13	39	53	73	.332	.427
Throws Right	R	.230	357	82	18	3	7	30	34	77	.298	.356
Chamberlain,Joba	L	.250	48	12	0	0	1	3	4	14	.315	.313
Throws Right	R	.208	53	11	3	0	2	9	3	10	.250	.377
Chapman,Aroldis	L	.077	52	4	1	0	1	1	11	27	.238	.154
Throws Left	R	.180	111	20	3	0	1	14	30	44	.364	.234
Chatwood,Tyler	L	.321	312	100	19	2	6	42	44	44	.410	.452
Throws Right	R	.281	235	66	11	0	8	36	27	30	.356	.430
Chavez,Jesse	L	.214	14	3	0	1	1	5	3	3	.353	.571
Throws Right	R	.450	20	9	0	0	2	6	2	5	.500	.750
Chen,Bruce	L	.259	174	45	6	0	3	17	19	31	.333	.345
Throws Left	R	.258	415	107	25	1	15	48	31	66	.316	.431
Choate,Randy	L	.145	69	10	2	0	2	7	3	28	.192	.261
Throws Left	R	.167	18	3	1	0	1	4	10	3	.483	.389
Cishek,Steve	L	.225	80	18	7	0	1	6	10	22	.311	.350
Throws Right	R	.218	124	27	3	1	0	8	9	33	.287	.258

Pitcher	vs	Avg	AB	H	2B	3B	HR	RBI	BB	SO	OBP	Slg
Cleto,Maikel	L	.364	11	4	1	0	1	5	2	3	.462	.727
Throws Right	R	.300	10	3	0	0	0	1	3	2	.417	.600
Clippard,Tyler	L	.169	142	24	4	1	6	14	8	53	.211	.338
Throws Right	R	.156	154	24	4	0	5	12	18	51	.243	.279
Cobb,Alex	L	.259	116	30	4	0	3	11	9	18	.312	.371
Throws Right	R	.224	85	19	6	0	0	5	12	19	.323	.294
Coffey,Todd	L	.338	80	27	7	0	1	9	9	11	.404	.463
Throws Right	R	.193	145	28	5	0	3	13	11	35	.250	.290
Coke,Phil	L	.215	149	32	6	2	2	15	15	36	.289	.295
Throws Left	R	.314	274	86	19	2	3	45	25	33	.375	.431
Coleman,Casey	L	.336	143	48	16	1	4	25	19	24	.418	.545
Throws Right	R	.274	197	54	10	1	6	30	27	51	.366	.426
Coleman,Louis	L	.257	74	19	4	0	3	10	14	16	.371	.432
Throws Right	R	.180	139	25	7	0	6	12	12	48	.260	.360
Collins,Tim	L	.210	105	22	4	0	2	15	29	27	.378	.305
Throws Left	R	.221	136	30	9	0	3	12	35	53	.325	.353
Collmenter,Josh	L	.250	292	73	13	1	10	25	18	40	.304	.404
Throws Right	R	.225	285	64	13	0	7	27	10	60	.250	.344
Colon,Bartolo	L	.297	323	96	25	5	15	42	20	66	.335	.545
Throws Right	R	.238	320	76	11	1	6	35	20	69	.286	.334
Contreras,Jose	L	.056	18	1	1	0	0	1	7	8	.320	.111
Throws Right	R	.313	32	10	4	0	3	1	5	.353	.438
Cook,Aaron	L	.349	192	67	12	5	4	33	19	23	.404	.526
Throws Right	R	.303	198	60	13	1	5	29	18	25	.365	.455
Cook,Ryan	L	.313	16	5	0	0	0	2	3	3	.421	.313
Throws Right	R	.353	17	6	0	0	0	3	5	4	.500	.353
Cordero,Francisco	L	.243	115	28	5	1	5	16	10	23	.302	.435
Throws Right	R	.159	132	21	5	0	1	6	12	19	.245	.220
Cormier,Lance	L	.179	28	5	3	0	0	1	2	2	.233	.286
Throws Right	R	.459	37	17	5	1	4	16	1	5	.500	.973
Correia,Kevin	L	.277	260	72	9	2	8	23	19	37	.326	.419
Throws Right	R	.294	350	103	19	1	16	55	20	40	.334	.491
Cortes,Dan	L	.200	20	4	1	0	1	6	3	2	.304	.400
Throws Right	R	.391	23	9	0	0	1	3	1	.481	.391
Crain,Jesse	L	.184	87	16	1	0	0	6	16	29	.311	.195
Throws Right	R	.233	146	34	8	1	7	23	15	41	.299	.445
Cramer,Bobby	L	.000	8	0	0	0	0	0	1	1	.111	.000
Throws Left	R	.273	22	6	0	0	1	1	0	5	.273	.409
Crotta,Mike	L	.353	17	6	2	0	0	5	4	2	.476	.471
Throws Right	R	.412	34	14	0	0	2	8	1	5	.429	.588
Crow,Aaron	L	.311	106	33	7	1	5	13	12	24	.381	.538
Throws Right	R	.175	126	22	1	0	3	10	19	41	.283	.254
Cruz,Juan	L	.171	70	12	2	0	1	6	11	23	.284	.243
Throws Right	R	.238	101	24	3	2	4	13	17	23	.345	.426
Cueto,Johnny	L	.209	254	53	8	0	5	25	24	45	.289	.299
Throws Right	R	.229	306	70	15	0	3	22	23	59	.290	.307
Daley,Matt	L	.375	8	3	0	1	0	2	2	2	.500	.625
Throws Right	R	.313	16	5	1	0	1	5	0	5	.294	.563
Danks,John	L	.270	189	51	8	0	5	20	12	27	.312	.392
Throws Left	R	.275	476	131	25	6	14	57	34	108	.329	.441
Davies,Kyle	L	.338	139	47	15	2	4	23	16	28	.400	.561
Throws Right	R	.325	114	37	7	0	3	23	10	22	.382	.465
Davis,Doug	L	.326	46	15	2	1	0	9	6	9	.404	.413
Throws Right	R	.310	142	44	7	0	2	16	20	21	.395	.401
Davis,Wade	L	.289	350	101	21	4	8	39	26	55	.339	.440
Throws Right	R	.246	362	89	22	2	15	46	37	50	.323	.442
De Fratus,Justin	L	.200	5	1	0	0	0	0	2	1	.500	.200
Throws Right	R	.000	7	0	0	0	0	0	1	2	.125	.000
de la Cruz,Frankie	L	.185	27	5	0	0	0	4	2	8	.281	.185
Throws Right	R	.250	20	5	1	0	0	1	3	1	.348	.300
de la Rosa,Dane	L	.385	13	5	1	0	0	1	1	3	.429	.462
Throws Right	R	.278	18	5	0	0	1	3	2	5	.350	.444
de la Rosa,Jorge	L	.111	36	4	0	0	0	0	6	13	.238	.111
Throws Left	R	.244	180	44	11	0	4	22	16	39	.312	.372
de la Rosa,Rubby	L	.235	119	28	9	1	4	16	17	35	.345	.429
Throws Right	R	.255	102	26	2	0	2	9	14	25	.345	.333
De Los Santos,F.	L	.173	52	9	0	0	2	10	5	24	.241	.288
Throws Right	R	.254	71	18	3	1	2	14	12	19	.361	.408
Deduno,Sam	L	.333	6	2	1	0	0	0	1	2	.429	.500
Throws Right	R	.375	8	3	0	0	0	1	2	2	.500	.375
Del Rosario,Enerio	L	.311	74	23	4	0	1	10	15	6	.422	.405
Throws Right	R	.263	137	36	5	0	2	24	16	25	.353	.343
Delabar,Steve	L	.125	8	1	1	0	0	1	2	4	.364	.250
Throws Right	R	.267	15	4	1	0	1	2	2	3	.353	.533
Delaney,Rob	L	.400	10	4	0	1	0	3	4	1	.533	.600
Throws Right	R	.000	7	0	0	0	0	0	3	2	.300	.000

Pitchers vs. Left-Handed and Right-Handed Batters

Pitcher	vs	Avg	AB	H	2B	3B	HR	RBI	BB	SO	OBP	Slg
Delgado,Randall	L	.196	56	11	1	0	3	4	9	10	.308	.375
Throws Right	R	.237	76	18	2	0	2	7	5	8	.293	.342
Demel,Sam	L	.379	29	11	0	1	1	6	6	2	.500	.552
Throws Right	R	.278	72	20	1	0	3	14	7	13	.350	.417
Dempster,Ryan	L	.303	346	105	27	5	8	49	45	92	.382	.480
Throws Right	R	.245	433	106	24	3	15	52	37	99	.311	.418
Detwiler,Ross	L	.167	48	8	1	0	1	2	7	10	.298	.250
Throws Left	R	.281	196	55	9	0	6	22	13	31	.324	.418
Devine,Joey	L	.268	41	11	5	1	0	5	7	8	.380	.439
Throws Right	R	.163	43	7	0	0	0	3	4	12	.245	.163
Diamond,Scott	L	.323	31	10	2	1	1	6	7	4	.447	.548
Throws Left	R	.315	130	41	7	0	2	12	10	15	.362	.415
Dickey,R.A.	L	.263	316	83	20	3	11	43	26	59	.325	.449
Throws Right	R	.251	474	119	18	1	7	39	28	75	.297	.338
Dickson,Brandon	L	.182	11	2	0	0	0	0	1	4	.250	.182
Throws Right	R	.350	20	7	1	0	2	3	2	3	.409	.700
DiFelice,Mark	L	.167	6	1	0	0	0	1	2	1	.375	.167
Throws Right	R	.333	6	2	1	0	1	3	0	2	.333	1.000
Dillard,Tim	L	.300	40	12	3	0	2	9	2	10	.349	.525
Throws Right	R	.206	68	14	1	1	1	7	2	17	.236	.294
Dolis,Rafael	L	.000	2	0	0	0	0	0	1	1	.333	.000
Throws Right	R	.000	1	0	0	0	0	0	0	0	.000	.000
Dotel,Octavio	L	.236	72	17	4	0	5	14	10	17	.345	.500
Throws Right	R	.154	123	19	2	1	1	10	7	45	.198	.211
Doubront,Felix	L	.412	17	7	2	1	1	7	4	2	.524	.824
Throws Left	R	.238	21	5	1	0	0	2	4	4	.346	.286
Downs,Scott	L	.179	84	15	3	0	1	10	6	22	.233	.250
Throws Left	R	.214	112	24	3	1	2	8	9	13	.268	.313
Drabek,Kyle	L	.304	171	52	13	1	6	28	37	33	.427	.497
Throws Right	R	.269	130	35	7	0	4	22	18	18	.351	.415
Duensing,Brian	L	.217	175	38	4	2	1	12	6	38	.242	.280
Throws Left	R	.330	470	155	40	4	20	81	46	77	.387	.560
Duffy,Danny	L	.266	109	29	5	2	4	16	13	30	.352	.459
Throws Left	R	.295	305	90	19	6	11	46	38	57	.378	.505
Duke,Zach	L	.225	71	16	1	0	2	7	1	12	.247	.324
Throws Left	R	.353	241	85	19	2	4	35	18	20	.393	.498
Dumatrait,Phil	L	.237	76	18	2	1	1	11	7	14	.298	.329
Throws Left	R	.310	87	27	4	0	6	15	18	15	.422	.563
Dunn,Mike	L	.198	101	20	3	1	2	17	15	32	.308	.307
Throws Left	R	.244	127	31	9	0	7	19	16	36	.329	.480
Durbin,Chad	L	.289	121	35	8	1	4	22	16	23	.364	.471
Throws Right	R	.319	160	51	11	0	8	26	10	36	.362	.538
Edlefsen,Steve	L	.533	15	8	3	0	1	5	5	1	.650	.933
Throws Right	R	.265	34	9	2	0	1	6	5	5	.375	.412
Ekstrom,Mike	L	.000	2	0	0	0	0	0	0	0	.000	.000
Throws Right	R	.500	2	1	0	0	0	0	0	1	.500	.500
Elbert,Scott	L	.191	68	13	2	1	0	9	7	18	.267	.250
Throws Left	R	.255	55	14	4	0	1	4	7	16	.344	.382
Ely,John	L	.217	23	5	3	0	0	1	3	6	.308	.348
Throws Right	R	.269	26	7	1	0	2	4	4	7	.367	.538
Enright,Barry	L	.309	68	21	5	0	4	12	13	11	.415	.559
Throws Right	R	.337	86	29	4	0	7	18	2	10	.356	.628
Eovaldi,Nathan	L	.275	51	14	2	0	1	4	6	10	.362	.373
Throws Right	R	.197	71	14	3	0	1	8	14	13	.337	.282
Eppley,Cody	L	.385	13	5	0	0	1	2	3	2	.500	.615
Throws Right	R	.261	23	6	2	0	2	6	2	4	.346	.609
Escalona,Edgmer	L	.135	37	5	1	0	1	2	6	6	.256	.243
Throws Right	R	.222	54	12	4	0	2	3	1	8	.236	.407
Escalona,Sergio	L	.188	64	12	0	1	2	5	8	16	.278	.313
Throws Left	R	.333	36	12	1	0	1	7	3	9	.415	.444
Estrada,Marco	L	.204	157	32	8	2	4	17	22	42	.304	.357
Throws Right	R	.276	185	51	7	0	7	27	7	46	.306	.427
Eveland,Dana	L	.278	18	5	0	0	0	2	1	2	.316	.278
Throws Left	R	.253	91	23	6	0	1	7	5	14	.306	.352
Eyre,Willie	L	.120	25	3	0	1	0	1	2	3	.179	.200
Throws Right	R	.231	39	9	1	0	2	5	3	7	.279	.410
Farnsworth,Kyle	L	.194	93	18	5	1	4	12	10	30	.280	.398
Throws Right	R	.225	120	27	7	0	1	11	2	21	.244	.308
Farquhar,Danny	L	.667	3	2	1	0	0	4	1	0	.750	1.000
Throws Right	R	.400	5	2	0	0	0	2	1	1	.429	.400
Feldman,Scott	L	.155	58	9	1	0	0	8	5	11	.219	.172
Throws Right	R	.276	58	16	3	0	3	5	5	11	.354	.483
Feliz,Neftali	L	.189	127	24	6	0	3	12	11	36	.254	.307
Throws Right	R	.200	90	18	7	0	1	11	19	18	.333	.311
Fiers,Michael	L	.500	2	1	0	0	0	0	2	1	.750	.500
Throws Right	R	.200	5	1	0	0	0	0	1	1	.333	.200

Pitcher	vs	Avg	AB	H	2B	3B	HR	RBI	BB	SO	OBP	Slg
Figueroa,Nelson	L	.278	36	10	3	0	1	4	7	7	.395	.444
Throws Right	R	.380	92	35	4	1	2	23	9	10	.431	.511
Fisher,Carlos	L	.294	34	10	1	0	0	8	5	4	.375	.324
Throws Right	R	.246	61	15	2	0	3	9	6	13	.324	.426
Fister,Doug	L	.239	456	109	22	5	8	40	25	89	.280	.362
Throws Right	R	.235	357	84	18	0	3	29	12	57	.275	.311
Floyd,Gavin	L	.272	427	116	18	3	16	62	27	86	.324	.440
Throws Right	R	.211	303	64	9	2	6	28	18	65	.258	.314
Francis,Jeff	L	.277	177	49	12	1	3	17	2	28	.286	.407
Throws Left	R	.309	567	175	35	5	16	78	37	63	.352	.473
Francisco,Frank	L	.292	120	35	5	0	5	12	13	29	.361	.458
Throws Right	R	.177	79	14	7	0	2	5	5	24	.226	.342
Franklin,Ryan	L	.326	46	15	2	1	2	8	3	8	.367	.543
Throws Right	R	.392	74	29	7	1	7	19	4	9	.425	.797
Frasor,Jason	L	.279	104	29	6	2	3	16	17	26	.379	.462
Throws Right	R	.238	122	29	9	0	4	15	9	31	.296	.410
Frieri,Ernesto	L	.258	93	24	6	2	1	10	23	29	.425	.398
Throws Right	R	.196	138	27	9	2	12	11	47		.277	.319
Fuentes,Brian	L	.265	83	22	3	0	2	13	4	17	.315	.373
Throws Left	R	.221	136	30	1	1	4	16	16	25	.306	.331
Fulchino,Jeff	L	.207	58	12	3	0	3	8	14	16	.356	.414
Throws Right	R	.321	78	25	7	0	2	14	8	17	.379	.487
Furbush,Charlie	L	.293	92	27	2	1	2	15	8	25	.356	.402
Throws Left	R	.294	238	70	13	0	14	40	22	42	.361	.525
Galarraga,Armando	L	.279	61	17	5	0	4	11	14	12	.410	.557
Throws Right	R	.283	106	30	6	0	9	22	8	16	.325	.594
Gallardo,Yovani	L	.257	366	94	10	2	12	35	34	101	.317	.393
Throws Right	R	.235	422	99	17	1	15	50	25	106	.277	.386
Garcia,Freddy	L	.284	261	74	18	2	8	23	27	36	.347	.460
Throws Right	R	.255	306	78	17	2	8	36	18	60	.299	.402
Garcia,Jaime	L	.308	146	45	8	1	2	19	10	29	.352	.418
Throws Left	R	.264	613	162	29	4	13	70	40	127	.309	.388
Garland,Jon	L	.351	97	34	7	0	5	13	7	17	.383	.577
Throws Right	R	.206	102	21	3	1	1	9	13	11	.305	.284
Garrison,Steve	L	-	0	0	0	0	0	0	0	0	-	-
Throws Left	R	.000	2	0	0	0	0	0	0	0	.000	.000
Garza,Matt	L	.247	361	89	14	2	5	35	24	102	.296	.338
Throws Right	R	.243	399	97	18	1	9	42	39	95	.311	.361
Gaub,John	L	.000	6	0	0	0	0	0	1	2	.250	.000
Throws Left	R	.500	4	2	1	0	0	0	0	1	.500	.750
Gaudin,Chad	L	.429	14	6	2	0	0	3	4	3	.556	.571
Throws Right	R	.273	22	6	1	0	1	3	4	7	.385	.455
Gearrin,Cory	L	.393	28	11	1	3	0	10	6	7	.514	.643
Throws Right	R	.143	42	6	1	0	0	5	6	18	.260	.167
Gee,Dillon	L	.224	263	59	10	3	10	38	43	45	.344	.399
Throws Right	R	.265	343	91	21	1	8	40	28	69	.332	.402
Germano,Justin	L	.273	33	9	0	0	1	2	4	3	.351	.364
Throws Right	R	.316	19	6	5	0	0	8	1	2	.409	.579
Godfrey,Graham	L	.267	60	16	2	0	1	5	3	8	.302	.350
Throws Right	R	.356	45	16	5	0	2	3	2	5	.396	.600
Gomes,Brandon	L	.291	55	16	1	0	2	12	7	12	.359	.418
Throws Right	R	.217	83	18	2	0	1	6	9	20	.298	.277
Gomez,Jeanmar	L	.319	113	36	9	1	2	12	12	11	.386	.469
Throws Right	R	.289	128	37	9	0	4	17	3	20	.303	.453
Gonzalez,Edgar	L	.500	4	2	0	0	0	1	0	0	.500	.500
Throws Right	R	.500	6	3	0	0	0	1	1	1	.571	.500
Gonzalez,Enrique	L	.381	21	8	3	1	1	6	2	2	.435	.762
Throws Right	R	.286	14	4	1	0	0	6	5	1	.429	.357
Gonzalez,Gio	L	.253	174	44	5	1	5	18	19	52	.333	.379
Throws Left	R	.224	586	131	18	2	12	46	72	145	.314	.323
Gonzalez,Mike	L	.214	103	22	4	0	2	6	6	27	.264	.311
Throws Left	R	.287	101	29	9	0	5	17	15	24	.375	.525
Gordon,Brian	L	.231	13	3	0	0	0	0	2	1	.333	.231
Throws Right	R	.333	27	9	1	0	3	6	1	3	.400	.704
Gorzelanny,Tom	L	.157	89	14	3	1	2	10	5	29	.216	.281
Throws Left	R	.287	307	88	19	0	13	37	28	66	.351	.476
Grabow,John	L	.244	90	22	7	0	3	15	7	14	.293	.422
Throws Left	R	.287	157	45	12	1	6	24	21	24	.374	.490
Gray,Jeff	L	.270	89	24	5	0	2	19	5	8	.302	.393
Throws Right	R	.280	100	28	7	1	2	14	16	15	.381	.430
Green,Sean	L	.353	17	6	1	0	0	1	2	2	.421	.412
Throws Right	R	.242	33	8	4	0	0	6	4	5	.324	.364
Gregerson,Luke	L	.329	85	28	4	0	0	10	8	15	.394	.376
Throws Right	R	.225	129	29	6	1	2	17	11	19	.289	.333
Gregg,Kevin	L	.259	116	30	7	2	4	16	26	29	.399	.457
Throws Right	R	.250	112	28	3	0	3	14	14	24	.336	.348

Pitchers vs. Left-Handed and Right-Handed Batters

Pitcher	vs	Avg	AB	H	2B	3B	HR	RBI	BB	SO	OBP	Slg
Greinke,Zack	L	.245	327	80	15	5	14	37	18	91	.288	.450
Throws Right	R	.245	331	81	26	1	5	31	27	110	.305	.375
Grilli,Jason	L	.238	42	10	1	1	1	3	8	13	.385	.381
Throws Right	R	.179	78	14	2	0	1	4	7	24	.264	.244
Guerra,Javy	L	.164	73	12	4	0	0	3	10	18	.271	.219
Throws Right	R	.258	97	25	3	1	2	11	8	20	.327	.371
Guerrier,Matt	L	.204	103	21	4	1	2	10	16	30	.311	.320
Throws Right	R	.253	150	38	5	1	2	29	9	20	.294	.340
Guthrie,Jeremy	L	.270	429	116	33	1	12	50	38	79	.331	.436
Throws Right	R	.263	369	97	22	3	14	55	28	51	.320	.453
Gutierrez,Juan	L	.351	37	13	3	0	2	7	4	8	.415	.595
Throws Right	R	.209	43	9	1	0	1	5	5	15	.306	.302
Hacker,Eric	L	.125	8	1	0	0	0	2	3	0	.333	.125
Throws Right	R	.333	9	3	1	0	0	1	1	2	.400	.444
Hagadone,Nick	L	.071	14	1	0	0	0	1	2	3	.176	.071
Throws Left	R	.150	20	3	0	0	0	2	4	8	.320	.150
Halladay,Roy	L	.273	421	115	14	4	4	34	17	76	.305	.354
Throws Right	R	.206	451	93	13	0	6	26	18	144	.236	.275
Hamburger,Mark	L	.167	12	2	1	0	0	0	3	3	.333	.250
Throws Right	R	.188	16	3	2	0	0	3	0	3	.188	.313
Hamels,Cole	L	.249	181	45	7	2	4	15	10	43	.286	.376
Throws Right	R	.204	608	124	21	4	15	50	34	151	.251	.326
Hammel,Jason	L	.268	287	77	11	2	11	48	46	42	.372	.436
Throws Right	R	.271	361	98	21	4	10	40	22	52	.316	.435
Hamren,Erik	L	.077	13	1	0	0	1	4	4	4	.294	.308
Throws Right	R	.321	28	9	2	0	1	10	5	6	.444	.500
Hand,Brad	L	.300	50	15	2	0	2	10	3	4	.352	.460
Throws Left	R	.224	170	38	11	1	8	20	32	34	.341	.441
Hanrahan,Joel	L	.195	113	22	6	0	1	3	9	32	.254	.274
Throws Right	R	.241	141	34	5	0	0	14	7	29	.278	.277
Hanson,Tommy	L	.244	221	54	13	3	10	31	22	66	.317	.466
Throws Right	R	.198	263	52	13	0	7	22	24	76	.266	.327
Happ,J.A.	L	.270	115	31	9	1	2	15	12	29	.333	.417
Throws Left	R	.264	477	126	31	3	19	78	71	105	.358	.461
Harang,Aaron	L	.277	303	84	17	2	9	30	33	63	.351	.436
Throws Right	R	.261	348	91	20	1	11	37	25	61	.312	.420
Harden,Rich	L	.232	151	35	9	2	5	20	12	42	.283	.417
Throws Right	R	.297	175	52	4	2	12	26	19	49	.372	.549
Haren,Dan	L	.226	523	118	32	1	11	40	23	125	.263	.354
Throws Right	R	.248	375	93	19	2	9	38	10	67	.267	.381
Harrell,Lucas	L	.421	19	8	0	0	0	3	1	5	.476	.421
Throws Right	R	.268	56	15	2	0	0	7	7	10	.344	.304
Harrison,Matt	L	.275	207	57	11	1	5	22	13	44	.318	.411
Throws Left	R	.249	494	123	26	2	8	47	44	82	.309	.358
Hatcher,Chris	L	.263	19	5	0	1	0	3	0	3	.250	.368
Throws Right	R	.409	22	9	2	0	2	6	4	5	.464	.773
Hawkins,LaTroy	L	.207	82	17	4	1	1	7	7	14	.267	.317
Throws Right	R	.300	110	33	4	0	0	6	3	14	.319	.336
Hawksworth,Blake	L	.193	88	17	3	0	3	11	7	21	.253	.330
Throws Right	R	.250	112	28	5	1	3	19	10	22	.311	.393
Heilman,Aaron	L	.328	64	21	5	3	3	13	4	15	.368	.641
Throws Right	R	.310	87	27	2	0	5	16	7	18	.368	.506
Hellickson,Jeremy	L	.230	365	84	22	4	11	34	47	39	.323	.403
Throws Right	R	.188	330	62	16	2	10	22	25	78	.246	.339
Hendrickson,Mark	L	.240	25	6	1	0	1	4	3	5	.310	.400
Throws Left	R	.500	18	9	4	0	0	2	3	0	.571	.722
Hendriks,Liam	L	.333	54	18	3	2	0	7	4	9	.379	.463
Throws Right	R	.282	39	11	3	0	3	9	2	7	.310	.590
Hensley,Clay	L	.171	129	22	2	1	2	13	17	26	.265	.248
Throws Right	R	.305	131	40	11	0	7	21	13	20	.385	.550
Hernandez,David	L	.171	117	20	5	0	1	9	7	29	.222	.239
Throws Right	R	.212	137	29	5	0	3	19	23	48	.327	.314
Hernandez,Felix	L	.252	476	120	19	3	7	47	42	103	.314	.349
Throws Right	R	.243	404	98	9	2	12	44	25	119	.292	.364
Hernandez,Livan	L	.297	317	94	14	5	7	42	26	44	.352	.438
Throws Right	R	.286	367	105	20	3	9	43	20	55	.324	.431
Herndon,David	L	.354	79	28	4	2	6	13	16	12	.463	.684
Throws Right	R	.200	130	26	2	0	3	13	8	27	.255	.285
Herrera,Daniel	L	.294	17	5	1	0	1	3	2	3	.368	.529
Throws Left	R	.381	21	8	3	0	0	4	1	2	.391	.524
Herrera,Kelvin	L	.500	2	1	0	0	1	2	0	0	.500	2.000
Throws Right	R	.200	5	1	1	0	0	1	0	0	.333	.400
Herrmann,Frank	L	.386	114	44	8	1	5	24	9	11	.431	.605
Throws Right	R	.223	121	27	7	0	2	9	7	23	.266	.331
Hill,Rich	L	.071	14	1	0	0	0	0	2	7	.188	.071
Throws Left	R	.167	12	2	0	0	0	0	1	5	.286	.167
Hochevar,Luke	L	.269	412	111	28	7	8	46	37	65	.336	.430
Throws Right	R	.231	350	81	16	4	15	47	25	63	.286	.429
Hoey,Jim	L	.326	46	15	2	0	2	15	3	5	.360	.500
Throws Right	R	.333	57	19	6	1	2	10	10	9	.426	.579
Holland,Derek	L	.235	196	46	5	1	3	16	11	31	.284	.316
Throws Left	R	.272	570	155	31	0	19	72	56	131	.339	.426
Holland,Greg	L	.181	94	17	5	1	0	4	11	38	.267	.255
Throws Right	R	.171	117	20	3	1	3	10	8	36	.228	.291
Horst,Jeremy	L	.316	19	6	2	0	1	2	3	3	.409	.579
Throws Left	R	.279	43	12	3	0	1	8	3	6	.319	.419
Hottovy,Tommy	L	.286	7	2	1	0	0	1	1	0	.375	.429
Throws Right	R	.250	8	2	1	0	0	1	2	2	.455	.375
Howell,J.P.	L	.222	63	14	2	0	1	9	4	16	.279	.302
Throws Left	R	.302	53	16	0	0	4	13	14	10	.449	.528
Hudson,Daniel	L	.251	375	94	23	5	7	33	27	76	.303	.395
Throws Right	R	.258	476	123	30	2	10	54	23	93	.299	.393
Hudson,Tim	L	.249	370	92	15	2	8	35	33	74	.327	.365
Throws Right	R	.226	430	97	15	0	6	43	23	84	.268	.302
Huff,David	L	.268	56	15	6	0	1	9	7	9	.349	.429
Throws Left	R	.265	151	40	10	1	5	19	10	27	.305	.444
Hughes,Dusty	L	.360	25	9	3	0	1	5	3	5	.448	.600
Throws Left	R	.370	27	10	1	0	3	10	5	6	.455	.741
Hughes,Jared	L	.214	14	3	0	0	1	2	3	1	.353	.429
Throws Right	R	.222	27	6	2	0	0	4	1	9	.250	.296
Hughes,Phil	L	.312	186	58	12	3	4	26	15	24	.368	.473
Throws Right	R	.234	111	26	5	0	5	15	12	23	.315	.414
Humber,Philip	L	.268	381	102	19	1	8	37	22	76	.315	.386
Throws Right	R	.203	241	49	8	0	6	22	19	40	.261	.311
Hunter,Tommy	L	.316	187	59	8	1	9	25	8	21	.350	.513
Throws Right	R	.261	157	41	11	0	3	20	7	24	.298	.389
Igarashi,Ryota	L	.208	48	10	1	0	0	5	16	22	.415	.229
Throws Right	R	.306	108	33	10	1	2	29	12	20	.390	.472
Isringhausen,Jason	L	.257	70	18	2	1	4	9	15	16	.384	.486
Throws Right	R	.178	101	18	1	0	2	9	9	28	.250	.248
Jackson,Edwin	L	.304	385	117	22	5	6	38	39	70	.366	.434
Throws Right	R	.276	391	108	20	6	10	48	23	78	.317	.419
Jakubauskas,Chris	L	.348	132	46	9	1	6	24	15	21	.412	.568
Throws Right	R	.290	162	47	12	0	5	24	14	31	.352	.457
James,Chuck	L	.357	14	5	0	0	0	4	0	2	.333	.357
Throws Left	R	.259	27	7	0	1	1	2	4	6	.355	.444
Jansen,Kenley	L	.163	80	13	2	0	1	10	12	35	.269	.225
Throws Right	R	.156	109	17	2	0	2	6	14	61	.264	.229
Janssen,Casey	L	.216	111	24	6	0	0	10	7	23	.269	.270
Throws Right	R	.242	95	23	5	0	2	14	7	30	.301	.358
Jeffress,Jeremy	L	.222	27	6	2	0	1	5	7	6	.382	.407
Throws Right	R	.222	27	6	0	0	0	8	4	7	.323	.296
Jenks,Bobby	L	.278	36	10	2	0	1	8	11	10	.447	.417
Throws Right	R	.387	31	12	2	0	0	3	2	7	.424	.452
Jepsen,Kevin	L	.333	30	10	2	0	1	3	3	5	.394	.500
Throws Right	R	.423	26	11	0	0	1	5	6	1	.529	.538
Jimenez,Cesar	L	.214	14	3	1	0	0	0	0	6	.214	.286
Throws Left	R	.231	13	3	0	0	0	0	3	3	.375	.231
Jimenez,Ubaldo	L	.239	356	85	23	4	9	44	32	102	.308	.402
Throws Right	R	.269	375	101	22	8	8	57	46	78	.356	.435
Joaquin,Waldis	L	.250	4	1	0	0	0	2	1	0	.333	.250
Throws Right	R	.263	19	5	1	1	0	5	2	3	.333	.421
Johnson,Alan	L	.000	3	0	0	0	0	0	0	0	.250	.000
Throws Right	R	.462	13	6	1	0	0	3	2	3	.533	.538
Johnson,Jim	L	.220	173	38	8	2	2	15	5	35	.243	.324
Throws Right	R	.258	163	42	6	1	3	20	16	23	.328	.362
Johnson,Josh	L	.209	115	24	6	0	1	6	14	26	.292	.287
Throws Right	R	.156	96	15	2	0	1	5	6	30	.214	.208
Judy,Josh	L	.318	22	7	4	0	1	5	2	4	.375	.636
Throws Right	R	.324	34	11	3	0	3	12	2	6	.415	.676
Jurrjens,Jair	L	.270	252	68	12	4	6	21	26	32	.339	.421
Throws Right	R	.233	318	74	13	1	8	25	18	58	.279	.355
Karstens,Jeff	L	.288	281	81	15	0	12	32	23	38	.346	.470
Throws Right	R	.242	339	82	16	0	10	34	10	58	.263	.378
Kazmir,Scott	L	1.000	3	3	2	0	0	3	1	0	1.000	1.667
Throws Left	R	.286	7	2	0	0	1	2	1	0	.500	.714
Kelley,Shawn	L	.278	18	5	1	0	0	1	2	2	.350	.333
Throws Right	R	.077	26	2	1	0	0	0	1	8	.111	.115
Kendrick,Kyle	L	.234	188	44	13	2	7	19	24	28	.327	.436
Throws Right	R	.270	244	66	13	0	7	32	6	31	.298	.410
Kennedy,Ian	L	.237	414	98	23	4	8	40	28	111	.287	.370
Throws Right	R	.218	404	88	21	0	11	28	27	87	.274	.351

Pitchers vs. Left-Handed and Right-Handed Batters

Pitcher	vs	Avg	AB	H	2B	3B	HR	RBI	BB	SO	OBP	Slg
Kershaw,Clayton	L	.178	146	26	4	0	3	13	12	53	.245	.267
Throws Left	R	.213	696	148	26	1	12	46	42	195	.259	.305
Kimball,Cole	L	.211	19	4	1	0	0	3	6	5	.400	.263
Throws Right	R	.148	27	4	0	1	0	3	5	6	.294	.222
Kimbrel,Craig	L	.157	127	20	1	0	1	7	16	60	.253	.189
Throws Right	R	.196	143	28	3	1	2	12	16	67	.277	.273
Kinney,Josh	L	.353	34	12	4	1	0	10	4	7	.436	.529
Throws Right	R	.289	38	11	3	0	1	8	3	13	.357	.447
Kintzler,Brandon	L	.200	15	3	0	0	1	2	2	6	.278	.400
Throws Right	R	.268	41	11	2	0	2	6	1	9	.279	.463
Kirkman,Michael	L	.214	42	9	4	0	0	6	4	9	.313	.310
Throws Left	R	.274	62	17	6	0	5	15	8	12	.356	.613
Kluber,Corey	L	.400	15	6	0	0	0	5	2	3	.500	.400
Throws Right	R	.000	5	0	0	0	0	0	1	2	.286	.000
Kohn,Michael	L	.286	21	6	0	0	3	5	2	2	.375	.714
Throws Right	R	.276	29	8	2	0	3	6	7	7	.417	.655
Kontos,George	L	.200	5	1	0	0	0	0	0	2	.200	.200
Throws Right	R	.188	16	3	0	0	1	1	3	4	.316	.375
Kroenke,Zach	L	.000	4	0	0	0	0	1	0	2	.000	.000
Throws Left	R	.429	14	6	1	0	1	3	1	1	.467	.714
Kuo,Hong-Chih	L	.289	45	13	3	0	2	9	7	17	.396	.489
Throws Left	R	.204	54	11	3	0	2	8	16	19	.394	.370
Kuroda,Hiroki	L	.264	375	99	24	5	12	32	27	67	.316	.451
Throws Right	R	.244	398	97	19	0	12	38	22	94	.285	.382
Lackey,John	L	.343	362	124	28	5	8	59	28	52	.401	.514
Throws Right	R	.265	298	79	10	2	12	47	28	56	.345	.433
Laffey,Aaron	L	.242	99	24	5	0	3	14	9	14	.321	.384
Throws Left	R	.358	120	43	8	0	4	18	12	16	.414	.525
Lannan,John	L	.211	185	39	9	0	3	17	16	55	.281	.308
Throws Left	R	.293	529	155	26	2	12	54	60	100	.305	.392
Latos,Mat	L	.258	388	100	17	7	7	39	28	100	.305	.392
Throws Right	R	.204	333	68	11	2	9	30	34	85	.277	.330
League,Brandon	L	.254	118	30	6	0	2	11	8	21	.302	.356
Throws Right	R	.224	116	26	5	0	1	3	2	24	.250	.293
Leake,Mike	L	.262	302	79	15	1	11	31	21	61	.316	.427
Throws Right	R	.240	333	80	15	2	12	37	17	57	.282	.405
LeBlanc,Wade	L	.408	71	29	7	0	1	9	4	10	.447	.549
Throws Left	R	.236	233	55	16	0	6	25	24	41	.304	.382
LeCure,Sam	L	.186	102	19	5	0	5	13	13	31	.278	.382
Throws Right	R	.216	176	38	6	3	5	21	8	42	.266	.369
Ledezma,Wil	L	.500	14	7	3	1	0	4	1	0	.533	.857
Throws Left	R	.286	14	4	0	0	1	5	6	6	.476	.500
Lee,Cliff	L	.196	204	40	7	1	4	11	4	49	.219	.299
Throws Left	R	.239	658	157	28	2	14	53	38	189	.283	.351
Leroux,Chris	L	.368	38	14	1	0	0	1	1	7	.400	.395
Throws Right	R	.190	63	12	2	0	0	12	6	17	.261	.222
Lester,Jon	L	.207	184	38	6	1	3	18	18	52	.281	.299
Throws Left	R	.244	525	128	25	3	17	51	37	130	.328	.400
Lewis,Colby	L	.274	434	119	23	3	21	58	44	86	.343	.486
Throws Right	R	.204	333	68	12	2	14	37	12	83	.237	.378
Lewis,Rommie	L	.500	10	5	3	0	0	2	1	3	.583	.800
Throws Left	R	.412	17	7	1	0	1	6	1	2	.474	.647
Lidge,Brad	L	.097	31	3	1	0	0	1	6	10	.243	.129
Throws Right	R	.325	40	13	3	0	0	3	7	13	.438	.400
Lilly,Ted	L	.210	157	33	5	0	7	16	6	26	.256	.357
Throws Left	R	.246	566	139	34	2	22	62	45	132	.305	.429
Lincecum,Tim	L	.217	396	86	21	2	6	31	49	103	.303	.326
Throws Right	R	.226	398	90	27	0	9	35	37	117	.302	.362
Lincoln,Brad	L	.349	83	29	8	1	0	10	9	12	.409	.470
Throws Right	R	.236	106	25	5	0	4	14	7	17	.293	.396
Lindblom,Josh	L	.370	27	10	4	0	0	2	6	3	.500	.519
Throws Right	R	.153	72	11	3	0	0	7	4	25	.200	.194
Lindsay,Shane	L	.385	13	5	3	0	0	3	5	1	.556	.615
Throws Right	R	.375	16	6	1	0	1	5	0	5	.375	.625
Lindstrom,Matt	L	.253	83	21	2	2	2	14	5	9	.300	.398
Throws Right	R	.258	120	31	5	0	1	17	9	27	.311	.325
Linebrink,Scott	L	.304	79	24	3	0	2	11	9	18	.363	.418
Throws Right	R	.268	127	34	6	2	4	19	12	24	.347	.441
Liriano,Francisco	L	.235	119	28	5	1	1	7	17	30	.350	.319
Throws Left	R	.253	384	97	11	2	13	60	58	82	.350	.393
Litsch,Jesse	L	.279	154	43	10	2	6	26	20	29	.358	.487
Throws Right	R	.203	128	26	7	0	4	13	8	37	.266	.352
Locke,Jeff	L	.300	10	3	2	0	0	1	2	0	.417	.500
Throws Left	R	.327	55	18	3	0	3	11	8	5	.415	.545
Loe,Kameron	L	.250	112	28	7	1	2	14	9	20	.306	.384
Throws Right	R	.233	159	37	9	0	2	23	7	41	.274	.327

Pitcher	vs	Avg	AB	H	2B	3B	HR	RBI	BB	SO	OBP	Slg
Logan,Boone	L	.260	104	27	7	1	4	18	7	34	.328	.462
Throws Left	R	.262	61	16	5	0	0	4	6	12	.328	.344
Lohse,Kyle	L	.249	325	81	25	1	7	31	21	54	.299	.397
Throws Right	R	.248	391	97	24	1	9	43	21	57	.284	.384
Lopez,Javier	L	.163	92	15	0	1	0	8	9	25	.245	.185
Throws Left	R	.276	98	27	9	0	0	10	17	15	.393	.367
Lopez,Rodrigo	L	.295	173	51	10	1	5	15	11	26	.341	.451
Throws Right	R	.302	215	65	17	0	13	30	18	28	.364	.563
Lopez,Wilton	L	.330	100	33	7	0	1	12	7	13	.374	.430
Throws Right	R	.225	173	39	4	0	5	23	11	43	.283	.335
Lowe,Derek	L	.285	358	102	17	4	5	41	33	53	.348	.397
Throws Right	R	.286	385	110	21	1	9	59	37	84	.347	.416
Lowe,Mark	L	.256	78	20	5	1	3	10	10	23	.341	.462
Throws Right	R	.268	97	26	5	0	3	17	9	19	.327	.412
Luebke,Cory	L	.157	140	22	6	0	0	13	11	46	.222	.200
Throws Left	R	.229	362	83	19	1	12	36	33	108	.293	.387
Lueke,Josh	L	.220	59	13	4	1	0	6	9	16	.324	.322
Throws Right	R	.313	67	21	2	0	2	14	4	13	.347	.433
Lyles,Jordan	L	.271	166	45	10	2	6	20	13	32	.331	.464
Throws Right	R	.295	210	62	11	3	8	31	13	35	.344	.490
Lynn,Lance	L	.229	48	11	2	0	2	6	7	17	.327	.396
Throws Right	R	.187	75	14	3	0	1	3	4	23	.238	.267
Lyon,Brandon	L	.652	23	15	5	0	4	12	2	1	.680	1.391
Throws Right	R	.279	43	12	1	0	0	4	3	5	.326	.302
MacDougal,Mike	L	.278	79	22	4	0	1	13	12	13	.376	.367
Throws Right	R	.244	131	32	4	0	2	15	17	28	.338	.321
Madson,Ryan	L	.198	96	19	4	0	0	5	9	28	.267	.240
Throws Right	R	.278	126	35	2	0	2	13	7	34	.319	.341
Magnuson,Trystan	L	.091	22	2	1	0	0	1	3	3	.200	.136
Throws Right	R	.342	38	13	2	0	3	12	2	8	.375	.632
Maholm,Paul	L	.265	113	30	5	2	1	12	9	26	.325	.372
Throws Left	R	.261	498	130	32	2	10	51	41	71	.320	.394
Maine,Scott	L	.125	8	1	1	0	0	0	1	2	.222	.250
Throws Left	R	.417	24	10	1	1	4	8	4	3	.500	1.042
Maloney,Matt	L	.346	26	9	2	0	3	7	2	3	.393	.769
Throws Left	R	.435	62	27	7	0	4	12	2	10	.448	.742
Manship,Jeff	L	.500	6	3	2	0	0	1	1	0	.571	.833
Throws Right	R	.286	7	2	0	1	0	4	3	2	.417	.571
Marcum,Shaun	L	.271	369	100	19	2	11	45	32	66	.327	.423
Throws Right	R	.195	384	75	14	1	11	34	25	92	.243	.323
Marmol,Carlos	L	.192	120	23	3	0	1	12	21	46	.319	.242
Throws Right	R	.215	144	31	7	0	4	20	27	53	.363	.347
Marquez,Jeff	L	.125	8	1	1	0	0	1	0	0	.125	.250
Throws Right	R	.400	10	4	1	0	0	0	0	2	.400	.500
Marquis,Jason	L	.306	235	72	16	0	7	36	25	27	.376	.464
Throws Right	R	.284	289	82	21	0	4	27	18	49	.328	.328
Marshall,Sean	L	.206	97	20	5	0	0	10	5	31	.245	.258
Throws Left	R	.249	185	46	6	0	1	13	12	48	.302	.297
Marte,Luis	L	.375	8	3	1	0	0	0	1	1	.444	.500
Throws Right	R	.375	8	3	0	0	0	3	0	2	.375	.375
Martinez,Cristhian	L	.222	126	28	5	1	3	13	8	19	.269	.349
Throws Right	R	.177	158	28	7	0	5	21	11	39	.244	.316
Masset,Nick	L	.284	102	29	6	0	1	13	14	24	.368	.373
Throws Right	R	.267	176	47	9	0	4	24	17	38	.335	.386
Masterson,Justin	L	.291	475	138	28	2	9	50	27	68	.331	.415
Throws Right	R	.210	347	73	11	0	2	18	38	90	.300	.259
Mateo,Marcos	L	.353	34	12	2	0	0	7	0	6	.353	.412
Throws Right	R	.226	53	12	2	0	2	4	10	19	.349	.377
Mathieson,Scott	L	.615	13	8	1	0	0	0	3	3	.688	.692
Throws Right	R	.111	9	1	0	0	0	0	0	2	.273	.111
Matsuzaka,Daisuke	L	.259	85	22	2	0	3	16	18	18	.388	.388
Throws Right	R	.172	58	10	1	0	1	5	5	8	.250	.241
Mattheus,Ryan	L	.170	53	9	2	0	1	6	7	8	.262	.264
Throws Right	R	.279	61	17	3	0	0	10	8	4	.380	.328
Matusz,Brian	L	.327	55	18	2	0	6	17	4	15	.367	.691
Throws Left	R	.387	163	63	14	0	12	36	20	23	.451	.693
Maya,Yunesky	L	.283	60	17	5	0	1	8	4	8	.333	.417
Throws Right	R	.359	64	23	4	0	2	7	6	7	.423	.516
Mazzaro,Vin	L	.388	49	19	3	0	4	19	11	3	.484	.694
Throws Right	R	.333	60	20	7	0	0	6	4	7	.375	.450
McAllister,Zach	L	.421	19	8	4	0	1	7	3	5	.463	.605
Throws Right	R	.256	39	10	3	0	0	5	4	7	.326	.333
McCarthy,Brandon	L	.256	348	89	20	2	8	33	13	65	.281	.394
Throws Right	R	.260	304	79	17	2	3	30	12	58	.282	.359
McClellan,Kyle	L	.206	223	46	12	0	8	29	19	32	.270	.368
Throws Right	R	.297	327	97	17	1	13	39	24	44	.353	.474

431

Pitchers vs. Left-Handed and Right-Handed Batters

Pitcher	vs	Avg	AB	H	2B	3B	HR	RBI	BB	SO	OBP	Slg
McClendon,Mike	L	.208	24	5	1	0	0	2	3	4	.296	.250
Throws Right	R	.323	31	10	1	0	1	4	0	6	.344	.452
McCutchen,Daniel	L	.308	120	37	7	1	3	17	15	18	.381	.458
Throws Right	R	.250	200	50	10	0	4	15	18	29	.321	.360
McDonald,James	L	.302	262	79	15	0	11	35	38	48	.390	.485
Throws Right	R	.246	395	97	18	1	13	44	40	94	.321	.395
McGee,Jake	L	.164	61	10	2	0	2	7	4	18	.215	.295
Throws Left	R	.400	50	20	4	0	3	11	8	9	.483	.660
McGowan,Dustin	L	.326	43	14	3	0	2	6	8	8	.442	.535
Throws Right	R	.158	38	6	1	1	2	7	5	12	.250	.395
Medlen,Kris	L	.000	4	0	0	0	0	0	0	1	.000	.000
Throws Right	R	.250	4	1	0	0	0	0	0	1	.250	.250
Meek,Evan	L	.324	37	12	0	0	0	1	3	3	.375	.324
Throws Right	R	.300	50	15	2	0	1	5	9	14	.407	.400
Melancon,Mark	L	.243	111	27	4	0	3	18	17	28	.344	.360
Throws Right	R	.228	167	38	7	0	2	10	9	38	.275	.305
Mendoza,Luis	L	.200	25	5	1	0	0	0	3	4	.310	.240
Throws Right	R	.222	27	6	1	0	0	2	2	3	.290	.259
Mickolio,Kam	L	.500	8	4	1	0	0	4	1	2	.500	.625
Throws Right	R	.300	20	6	0	0	3	2	5	5	.364	.400
Mijares,Jose	L	.253	87	22	5	1	1	14	8	19	.330	.368
Throws Left	R	.292	106	31	9	0	3	17	22	11	.412	.462
Miley,Wade	L	.391	23	9	0	0	0	1	5	1	.417	.391
Throws Left	R	.289	135	39	13	0	6	16	17	20	.366	.519
Miller,Andrew	L	.312	77	24	6	1	1	11	6	25	.357	.455
Throws Left	R	.298	178	53	6	1	7	30	35	25	.414	.461
Miller,Jim	L	.167	6	1	0	1	0	1	0	1	.143	.500
Throws Right	R	.118	17	2	0	1	0	2	4	4	.273	.235
Miller,Trever	L	.276	58	16	5	0	1	7	8	9	.382	.414
Throws Left	R	.346	26	9	2	1	1	5	4	3	.406	.615
Mills,Brad	L	.345	29	10	2	0	1	5	5	6	.457	.517
Throws Left	R	.271	48	13	3	1	3	12	7	12	.375	.563
Millwood,Kevin	L	.296	81	24	2	1	4	9	4	15	.329	.494
Throws Right	R	.260	131	34	4	1	5	13	4	21	.281	.420
Milone,Tom	L	.300	10	3	2	0	1	1	0	3	.364	.800
Throws Left	R	.281	89	25	4	1	1	8	4	12	.313	.382
Minor,Mike	L	.316	57	18	5	1	1	8	3	16	.344	.491
Throws Left	R	.279	269	75	20	1	6	23	27	61	.347	.428
Misch,Pat	L	.357	14	5	1	0	1	5	1	1	.438	.643
Throws Left	R	.333	18	6	3	0	0	6	3	4	.429	.500
Mitre,Sergio	L	.283	60	17	6	1	0	10	11	4	.389	.417
Throws Right	R	.247	89	22	4	0	3	13	3	12	.284	.393
Moore,Matt	L	.222	9	2	1	0	0	1	2	3	.364	.333
Throws Left	R	.250	28	7	0	0	1	2	1	12	.276	.357
Morales,Franklin	L	.238	84	20	5	2	3	14	11	24	.337	.452
Throws Left	R	.235	85	20	7	0	3	12	8	18	.301	.424
Morrow,Brandon	L	.220	391	86	20	2	9	43	38	127	.291	.350
Throws Right	R	.260	292	76	14	2	12	49	31	76	.345	.445
Mortensen,Clayton	L	.281	89	25	5	0	5	17	12	14	.373	.506
Throws Right	R	.240	125	30	9	0	4	12	12	16	.312	.408
Morton,Charlie	L	.364	280	102	15	4	5	34	49	44	.460	.500
Throws Right	R	.220	381	84	17	1	1	35	28	66	.289	.278
Moscoso,Guillermo	L	.225	249	56	13	0	6	23	20	36	.283	.349
Throws Right	R	.197	233	46	8	1	8	29	18	38	.257	.343
Moseley,Dustin	L	.262	221	58	15	2	5	29	20	34	.324	.416
Throws Right	R	.249	237	59	10	3	5	20	16	30	.298	.380
Moskos,Daniel	L	.364	44	16	5	0	0	5	2	6	.391	.477
Throws Left	R	.250	52	13	1	0	0	4	7	5	.333	.269
Mota,Guillermo	L	.234	94	22	2	0	6	17	13	24	.324	.447
Throws Right	R	.243	202	49	8	2	4	26	17	53	.306	.361
Motte,Jason	L	.270	89	24	7	1	1	13	8	18	.333	.404
Throws Right	R	.162	154	25	6	1	1	18	8	45	.220	.234
Moylan,Peter	L	.571	7	4	0	0	0	1	1	2	.625	.571
Throws Right	R	.286	28	8	0	0	0	1	2	8	.333	.286
Mujica,Edward	L	.220	132	29	3	0	3	10	7	30	.259	.311
Throws Right	R	.245	143	35	8	2	4	16	7	33	.288	.413
Myers,Brett	L	.278	371	103	20	2	14	51	29	68	.330	.456
Throws Right	R	.259	474	123	22	2	17	63	28	92	.303	.422
Narveson,Chris	L	.212	99	21	4	1	2	10	20	20	.345	.333
Throws Left	R	.265	524	139	30	4	15	64	45	106	.322	.424
Nathan,Joe	L	.198	86	17	4	0	3	9	8	22	.271	.349
Throws Right	R	.247	85	21	6	1	4	14	6	21	.309	.482
Neshek,Pat	L	.209	43	9	0	0	1	5	12	11	.382	.279
Throws Right	R	.222	45	10	1	0	3	6	10	9	.375	.444
Nicasio,Juan	L	.313	147	46	8	0	6	17	13	28	.369	.490
Throws Right	R	.205	132	27	10	2	2	15	5	30	.239	.356

Pitcher	vs	Avg	AB	H	2B	3B	HR	RBI	BB	SO	OBP	Slg
Niemann,Jeff	L	.253	289	73	10	3	12	37	18	62	.294	.433
Throws Right	R	.247	235	58	16	3	6	22	19	43	.315	.417
Niese,Jonathon	L	.259	143	37	8	0	2	13	8	39	.307	.357
Throws Left	R	.291	484	141	27	4	12	62	36	99	.343	.438
Noesi,Hector	L	.302	106	32	7	0	3	12	8	15	.353	.453
Throws Right	R	.272	114	31	7	0	3	16	14	30	.354	.412
Nolasco,Ricky	L	.305	400	122	27	3	12	51	33	64	.358	.478
Throws Right	R	.285	428	122	23	2	8	52	11	84	.304	.404
Norberto,Jordan	L	.333	9	3	0	0	0	2	3	2	.462	.333
Throws Left	R	.294	17	5	1	0	0	2	1	4	.455	.353
Norris,Bud	L	.280	361	101	23	2	13	46	38	81	.348	.463
Throws Right	R	.220	346	76	15	0	11	37	32	95	.292	.358
Nova,Ivan	L	.240	313	75	19	1	6	26	33	48	.317	.364
Throws Right	R	.275	320	88	18	1	7	40	24	50	.327	.403
Nunez,Leo	L	.270	115	31	5	2	6	19	14	25	.349	.504
Throws Right	R	.203	128	26	6	0	2	13	7	30	.246	.297
O'Connor,Mike	L	.308	13	4	1	0	0	5	2	4	.400	.385
Throws Left	R	.083	12	1	0	0	0	0	1	4	.214	.083
O'Day,Darren	L	.233	30	7	1	0	4	6	0	8	.233	.667
Throws Right	R	.286	35	10	0	0	3	5	5	10	.395	.543
O'Flaherty,Eric	L	.195	87	17	2	1	1	8	2	25	.237	.276
Throws Left	R	.233	180	42	8	0	1	8	19	42	.305	.294
Ogando,Alexi	L	.255	384	98	17	3	12	49	22	61	.300	.409
Throws Right	R	.202	253	51	10	0	4	19	21	65	.271	.289
Ohlendorf,Ross	L	.352	54	19	4	0	4	13	10	15	.462	.648
Throws Right	R	.369	111	41	7	2	5	17	5	12	.411	.604
Ohman,Will	L	.234	107	25	1	1	4	13	8	34	.299	.374
Throws Left	R	.277	101	28	6	1	4	19	9	20	.345	.475
Okajima,Hideki	L	.364	11	4	1	0	0	3	2	2	.462	.455
Throws Left	R	.158	19	3	1	0	0	1	3	4	.273	.211
Oliver,Andrew	L	.250	12	3	3	0	0	1	3	2	.412	.500
Throws Left	R	.308	26	8	1	0	3	6	5	3	.438	.692
Oliver,Darren	L	.227	88	20	2	0	2	11	4	23	.269	.318
Throws Left	R	.243	111	27	4	0	1	7	7	21	.288	.306
Oliveros,Lester	L	.233	30	7	1	0	0	4	6	4	.351	.267
Throws Right	R	.292	48	14	3	0	0	6	5	9	.352	.354
Olson,Garrett	L	.286	7	2	0	0	0	2	1	3	.333	.286
Throws Left	R	.000	9	0	0	0	0	2	1	1	.182	.000
Ondrusek,Logan	L	.232	82	19	3	0	1	7	12	22	.330	.305
Throws Right	R	.242	149	36	4	1	5	19	16	19	.316	.383
Ortiz,Ramon	L	.296	54	16	4	1	3	8	7	7	.377	.574
Throws Right	R	.205	73	15	1	0	3	9	4	18	.241	.342
O'Sullivan,Sean	L	.321	131	42	7	2	6	22	18	12	.405	.542
Throws Right	R	.336	107	36	7	1	4	23	8	7	.376	.533
Oswalt,Roy	L	.276	257	71	14	1	3	20	17	50	.327	.374
Throws Right	R	.284	289	82	23	1	7	36	14	43	.324	.443
Outman,Josh	L	.217	60	13	2	0	0	7	4	14	.258	.250
Throws Left	R	.299	164	49	11	1	4	19	19	21	.370	.451
Owings,Micah	L	.291	86	25	8	2	3	6	11	14	.378	.535
Throws Right	R	.211	147	31	7	1	5	22	12	30	.273	.374
Padilla,Vicente	L	.462	13	6	1	1	0	3	1	4	.500	.692
Throws Right	R	.056	18	1	0	0	0	1	4	5	.227	.056
Palmer,Matt	L	.286	21	6	3	0	0	4	1	2	.304	.429
Throws Right	R	.317	41	13	1	0	0	6	3	5	.370	.415
Papelbon,Jonathan	L	.156	122	19	6	1	1	8	4	42	.183	.246
Throws Right	R	.261	119	31	5	0	2	16	6	45	.310	.353
Parker,Jarrod	L	.143	7	1	0	0	0	0	0	0	.143	.143
Throws Right	R	.250	12	3	1	0	0	0	1	1	.308	.333
Parnell,Bobby	L	.239	92	22	4	0	1	6	17	35	.369	.315
Throws Right	R	.270	141	38	3	0	3	29	10	29	.318	.355
Paterson,Joe	L	.205	78	16	4	1	0	9	8	20	.292	.282
Throws Left	R	.255	47	12	1	0	1	8	7	8	.368	.340
Patton,Troy	L	.264	53	14	0	0	0	6	2	7	.286	.264
Throws Left	R	.186	59	11	4	0	2	7	3	15	.226	.356
Pauley,David	L	.194	129	25	4	0	1	11	6	20	.235	.248
Throws Right	R	.277	141	39	6	1	5	24	16	24	.342	.440
Paulino,Felipe	L	.270	282	76	14	2	8	34	34	73	.345	.418
Throws Right	R	.289	242	70	7	2	5	34	21	60	.360	.397
Pavano,Carl	L	.289	485	140	22	7	12	61	14	61	.316	.433
Throws Right	R	.300	406	122	27	2	11	49	26	41	.339	.458
Peacock,Brad	L	.148	27	4	0	0	0	2	2	2	.207	.148
Throws Right	R	.200	15	3	0	0	0	1	4	2	.368	.200
Peavy,Jake	L	.259	243	63	10	0	6	22	11	46	.295	.374
Throws Right	R	.278	194	54	9	3	4	37	13	49	.322	.418
Pelfrey,Mike	L	.277	368	102	17	4	12	51	31	51	.333	.443
Throws Right	R	.294	402	118	20	3	9	45	34	54	.353	.425

432

Pitchers vs. Left-Handed and Right-Handed Batters

Pitcher	vs	Avg	AB	H	2B	3B	HR	RBI	BB	SO	OBP	Slg
Pena,Tony	L	.200	30	6	1	0	0	2	7	6	.351	.233
Throws Right	R	.358	53	19	4	0	2	12	3	11	.386	.547
Pendleton,Lance	L	.345	29	10	2	0	2	6	3	5	.394	.621
Throws Right	R	.227	44	10	2	1	4	8	8	8	.357	.591
Penny,Brad	L	.264	349	92	20	3	10	41	40	39	.337	.424
Throws Right	R	.345	377	130	25	3	14	65	22	35	.385	.538
Peralta,Joel	L	.155	110	17	4	1	1	3	6	34	.198	.236
Throws Right	R	.218	124	27	9	0	6	23	12	27	.283	.435
Perez,Chris	L	.198	111	22	7	0	1	12	17	27	.310	.288
Throws Right	R	.233	103	24	3	1	4	16	9	12	.304	.398
Perez,Juan	L	.000	9	0	0	0	0	0	3	6	.250	.000
Throws Left	R	.143	7	1	0	0	0	0	2	2	.333	.143
Perez,Luis	L	.260	104	27	6	0	2	18	5	29	.322	.375
Throws Left	R	.305	154	47	10	1	7	27	22	25	.388	.519
Perez,Rafael	L	.237	118	28	5	0	1	14	9	16	.289	.305
Throws Left	R	.270	115	31	8	1	1	10	10	17	.325	.383
Perkins,Glen	L	.222	90	20	3	0	1	5	9	20	.300	.289
Throws Left	R	.259	135	35	11	0	1	17	12	45	.318	.363
Perry,Ryan	L	.292	65	19	6	1	1	13	9	9	.373	.462
Throws Right	R	.263	76	20	4	1	0	10	12	15	.370	.342
Pestano,Vinnie	L	.280	93	26	4	2	3	15	8	14	.350	.462
Throws Right	R	.115	130	15	0	2	2	5	16	70	.218	.192
Phillips,Zach	L	.100	20	2	1	0	0	0	0	8	.100	.150
Throws Left	R	.364	11	4	1	0	1	2	2	0	.462	.727
Pineda,Michael	L	.237	325	77	13	1	8	35	25	74	.296	.357
Throws Right	R	.184	304	56	11	1	10	29	30	99	.261	.326
Pineiro,Joel	L	.322	304	98	21	2	7	36	25	28	.372	.474
Throws Right	R	.299	281	84	15	0	9	38	13	34	.330	.448
Pomeranz,Drew	L	.222	9	2	0	0	0	1	0	1	.300	.222
Throws Left	R	.279	61	17	7	0	0	3	7	12	.333	.393
Porcello,Rick	L	.321	430	138	20	5	14	57	29	65	.368	.488
Throws Right	R	.248	290	72	15	2	4	32	17	39	.295	.355
Price,David	L	.171	210	36	6	1	5	28	13	48	.227	.281
Throws Left	R	.250	625	156	37	3	17	58	50	170	.309	.400
Proctor,Scott	L	.281	64	18	1	1	4	14	13	12	.405	.516
Throws Right	R	.333	96	32	7	1	7	23	18	17	.435	.646
Purcey,David	L	.327	49	16	0	0	0	3	7	12	.411	.327
Throws Left	R	.215	79	17	9	0	2	14	20	10	.374	.405
Putnam,Zach	L	.231	13	3	1	1	0	1	0	4	.231	.462
Throws Right	R	.368	19	7	2	0	1	3	0	5	.429	.632
Putz,J.J.	L	.179	112	20	6	1	2	6	4	35	.205	.304
Throws Right	R	.214	98	21	5	1	2	9	8	26	.282	.347
Qualls,Chad	L	.320	122	39	8	1	4	13	12	15	.381	.500
Throws Right	R	.218	156	34	1	0	3	21	8	28	.255	.282
Ramirez,Horacio	L	.318	22	7	1	0	0	3	1	4	.348	.364
Throws Left	R	.600	15	9	1	0	1	5	1	0	.588	.867
Ramirez,Ramon	L	.250	68	17	1	0	0	7	9	14	.346	.265
Throws Right	R	.203	182	37	9	1	3	22	17	52	.277	.313
Ramos,Cesar	L	.221	86	19	3	0	2	16	9	20	.313	.326
Throws Left	R	.227	75	17	3	0	2	12	16	11	.359	.347
Rapada,Clay	L	.104	48	5	0	0	1	4	4	18	.170	.167
Throws Left	R	.692	13	9	2	1	2	4	3	0	.750	1.462
Rauch,Jon	L	.267	105	28	6	0	3	10	12	19	.347	.410
Throws Right	R	.272	103	28	5	0	8	17	2	17	.286	.553
Ray,Chris	L	.308	52	16	3	0	0	3	5	7	.356	.365
Throws Right	R	.243	70	17	3	1	2	13	7	15	.308	.400
Reed,Addison	L	.313	16	5	1	0	1	5	0	5	.313	.563
Throws Right	R	.313	16	5	1	0	0	1	1	7	.353	.375
Reineke,Chad	L	.250	4	1	0	0	0	1	3	1	.625	.250
Throws Right	R	.211	19	4	0	0	2	4	3	2	.318	.526
Resop,Chris	L	.255	94	24	5	0	1	16	8	31	.376	.340
Throws Right	R	.277	177	49	10	0	7	29	10	48	.323	.452
Reyes,Dennys	L	.333	3	1	0	0	0	0	2	1	.667	.333
Throws Left	R	.333	3	1	0	0	0	0	0	0	.500	.333
Reyes,Jo-Jo	L	.294	163	48	9	3	3	24	13	27	.356	.442
Throws Left	R	.307	417	128	26	2	18	68	35	60	.365	.508
Reynolds,Greg	L	.328	67	22	5	0	6	15	4	6	.361	.672
Throws Right	R	.277	65	18	4	1	0	11	6	12	.347	.369
Reynolds,Matt	L	.292	96	28	5	1	6	14	6	30	.324	.552
Throws Left	R	.217	92	20	8	1	4	14	12	20	.305	.457
Rhodes,Arthur	L	.245	53	13	1	1	4	9	8	10	.344	.528
Throws Left	R	.288	73	21	6	0	4	12	3	11	.312	.534
Richard,Clayton	L	.261	92	24	4	1	0	9	6	12	.313	.326
Throws Left	R	.276	290	80	17	1	8	42	32	41	.349	.424
Richards,Garrett	L	.367	30	11	3	1	2	6	2	4	.406	.733
Throws Right	R	.200	25	5	1	0	2	3	5	5	.333	.480

Pitcher	vs	Avg	AB	H	2B	3B	HR	RBI	BB	SO	OBP	Slg
Richmond,Scott	L	-	0	0	0	0	0	0	0	0	-	-
Throws Right	R	.000	1	0	0	0	0	0	0	0	.000	.000
Rivera,Mariano	L	.240	104	25	3	0	2	7	3	24	.269	.327
Throws Right	R	.191	115	22	4	0	1	11	5	36	.228	.252
Robertson,David	L	.156	122	19	3	1	0	7	19	58	.270	.197
Throws Right	R	.186	113	21	5	0	1	9	16	42	.292	.257
Rodney,Fernando	L	.273	55	15	4	0	0	7	13	16	.420	.345
Throws Right	R	.180	61	11	0	0	1	8	15	10	.359	.230
Rodriguez,Aneury	L	.269	119	32	7	2	6	17	22	23	.383	.513
Throws Right	R	.243	210	51	12	2	7	25	10	41	.280	.419
Rodriguez,Fernando	L	.225	71	16	2	0	3	8	17	22	.375	.380
Throws Right	R	.287	122	35	6	1	3	14	13	35	.370	.426
Rodriguez,Francisco	L	.282	156	44	10	2	3	15	16	44	.347	.429
Throws Right	R	.192	120	23	4	0	1	10	10	35	.265	.250
Rodriguez,Fr. M.	L	.212	33	7	1	0	1	6	1	4	.235	.333
Throws Right	R	.286	21	6	2	0	1	3	4	3	.400	.524
Rodriguez,Henry	L	.238	105	25	0	0	0	9	20	19	.370	.238
Throws Right	R	.206	141	29	5	1	1	18	25	51	.323	.262
Rodriguez,Wandy	L	.233	150	35	8	3	1	12	8	41	.281	.347
Throws Left	R	.256	574	147	29	2	24	65	61	126	.329	.439
Roenicke,Josh	L	.158	19	3	2	0	0	0	2	5	.238	.263
Throws Right	R	.268	41	11	1	0	1	8	5	7	.362	.366
Rogers,Esmil	L	.318	154	49	7	4	8	27	26	33	.420	.571
Throws Right	R	.321	190	61	9	0	6	28	21	30	.397	.463
Romero,J.C.	L	.237	38	9	0	0	0	0	5	14	.326	.237
Throws Left	R	.317	60	19	8	0	1	9	5	16	.423	.500
Romero,Ricky	L	.269	238	64	15	2	9	21	31	45	.372	.462
Throws Left	R	.194	578	112	23	1	17	50	49	133	.263	.325
Romo,Sergio	L	.229	48	11	3	0	1	2	1	9	.245	.354
Throws Right	R	.150	120	18	4	1	1	9	4	61	.177	.225
Rosario,Sandy	L	.273	11	3	0	0	0	1	1	1	.333	.273
Throws Right	R	.400	5	2	0	0	0	2	1	1	.500	.800
Ross,Tyson	L	.250	68	17	2	0	2	9	9	9	.338	.279
Throws Right	R	.254	63	16	1	0	1	5	4	15	.299	.317
Ruffin,Chance	L	.333	27	9	2	0	2	4	4	6	.419	.630
Throws Right	R	.214	42	9	2	0	2	7	5	12	.298	.405
Runzler,Dan	L	.244	45	11	1	0	0	4	1	11	.255	.267
Throws Left	R	.310	58	18	5	1	0	11	15	14	.452	.431
Rupe,Josh	L	.259	27	7	1	0	2	6	3	5	.333	.519
Throws Right	R	.290	31	9	1	0	3	8	3	2	.389	.613
Russell,Adam	L	.135	37	5	1	0	0	4	9	6	.304	.162
Throws Right	R	.306	85	26	7	0	2	14	11	7	.404	.459
Russell,James	L	.250	112	28	6	1	4	15	2	24	.256	.429
Throws Left	R	.312	154	48	11	0	8	26	12	19	.363	.539
Rzepczynski,Marc	L	.163	104	17	3	0	1	7	10	37	.256	.221
Throws Left	R	.275	120	33	7	2	11	16	24	31	.365	.383
Sabathia,CC	L	.207	246	51	6	1	5	33	25	63	.253	.301
Throws Left	R	.273	656	179	33	2	12	56	50	142	.324	.384
Saito,Takashi	L	.279	43	12	3	0	0	4	4	9	.340	.349
Throws Right	R	.167	54	9	2	0	2	4	5	14	.250	.315
Salas,Fernando	L	.214	117	25	2	2	4	14	11	31	.281	.368
Throws Right	R	.164	152	25	8	0	3	13	10	44	.226	.276
Sale,Chris	L	.208	120	25	6	0	1	7	10	39	.275	.283
Throws Left	R	.199	136	27	8	0	5	15	17	40	.292	.368
Samardzija,Jeff	L	.208	120	25	6	1	1	14	27	33	.360	.300
Throws Right	R	.195	200	39	8	0	4	20	23	54	.286	.295
Sanabia,Alex	L	.200	25	5	2	0	0	1	1	7	.231	.280
Throws Right	R	.400	20	8	3	1	2	3	2	1	.455	.950
Sanches,Brian	L	.257	113	29	7	2	5	15	25	19	.393	.487
Throws Right	R	.198	116	23	7	1	2	12	11	34	.271	.328
Sanchez,Anibal	L	.243	374	91	19	5	6	30	28	95	.302	.369
Throws Right	R	.257	374	96	18	2	14	50	36	107	.324	.428
Sanchez,Eduardo	L	.158	38	6	0	0	0	3	5	11	.283	.158
Throws Right	R	.136	59	8	2	1	1	5	11	24	.278	.254
Sanchez,Jonathan	L	.188	96	18	5	1	0	12	8	23	.266	.260
Throws Left	R	.231	268	62	14	1	9	33	58	79	.372	.392
Sanit,Amauri	L	.500	18	9	0	0	3	1	1	1	.526	.667
Throws Right	R	.188	16	3	1	0	0	1	3	2	.381	.250
Santana,Ervin	L	.245	465	114	26	2	13	51	44	93	.310	.394
Throws Right	R	.237	393	93	17	1	13	39	28	85	.296	.384
Santiago,Hector	L	.000	8	0	0	0	0	0	0	1	.000	.000
Throws Left	R	.111	9	1	0	0	0	0	1	1	.200	.111
Santos,Sergio	L	.234	111	26	6	1	3	11	17	35	.336	.387
Throws Right	R	.130	115	15	3	1	3	12	12	57	.229	.243
Saunders,Joe	L	.212	170	36	2	1	6	16	6	40	.240	.341
Throws Left	R	.281	620	174	33	6	23	67	61	68	.345	.465

433

Pitchers vs. Left-Handed and Right-Handed Batters

Pitcher	vs	Avg	AB	H	2B	3B	HR	RBI	BB	SO	OBP	Slg
Savery,Joe	L	.000	4	0	0	0	0	0	0	1	.000	.000
Throws Left	R	.250	4	1	0	0	0	0	0	1	.250	.250
Scherzer,Max	L	.281	417	117	21	6	19	54	41	84	.345	.496
Throws Right	R	.262	343	90	17	1	10	40	15	90	.301	.405
Schlereth,Daniel	L	.174	86	15	1	0	2	9	8	27	.273	.256
Throws Left	R	.244	86	21	6	0	4	15	23	17	.409	.453
Schwimer,Michael	L	.400	25	10	2	0	2	5	1	6	.423	.720
Throws Right	R	.172	29	5	2	0	0	3	6	10	.333	.241
Schwinden,Chris	L	.216	37	8	3	0	1	6	4	7	.302	.378
Throws Right	R	.319	47	15	4	1	0	7	2	10	.340	.447
Scribner,Evan	L	.379	29	11	2	1	0	8	2	4	.419	.517
Throws Right	R	.226	31	7	3	0	1	6	2	6	.273	.419
Severino,Atahualpa	L	.222	9	2	1	0	0	2	1	3	.300	.333
Throws Left	R	.333	9	3	0	0	1	2	0	4	.333	.667
Shaw,Bryan	L	.244	45	11	1	0	0	3	5	8	.320	.267
Throws Right	R	.292	65	19	2	0	2	6	5	16	.361	.415
Sherrill,George	L	.256	78	20	3	0	1	5	1	32	.275	.333
Throws Left	R	.236	55	13	1	0	2	9	11	6	.358	.364
Shields,James	L	.219	484	106	17	1	12	38	33	127	.270	.333
Throws Right	R	.215	413	89	18	2	14	34	32	98	.277	.370
Simon,Alfredo	L	.282	234	66	17	3	6	29	25	44	.351	.457
Throws Right	R	.287	216	62	22	1	9	35	15	39	.339	.523
Sipp,Tony	L	.229	96	22	3	0	4	12	7	25	.279	.385
Throws Left	R	.180	128	23	9	0	6	19	17	32	.274	.391
Slama,Anthony	L	.000	1	0	0	0	0	0	0	0	.000	.000
Throws Right	R	.000	6	0	0	0	0	0	0	2	.250	.000
Slaten,Doug	L	.333	36	12	3	1	2	13	1	9	.368	.639
Throws Left	R	.378	37	14	4	0	1	6	8	4	.489	.568
Slowey,Kevin	L	.345	113	39	12	1	5	25	3	16	.361	.602
Throws Right	R	.300	130	39	5	1	5	18	2	18	.316	.469
Smith,Joe	L	.152	79	12	2	0	1	6	9	19	.244	.215
Throws Right	R	.248	161	40	5	0	0	19	12	26	.303	.280
Smith,Jordan	L	.538	26	14	5	0	2	10	2	3	.552	.962
Throws Right	R	.321	56	18	4	1	1	10	6	10	.385	.482
Sonnanstine,Andy	L	.299	67	20	3	0	6	14	9	6	.390	.612
Throws Right	R	.286	70	20	3	0	4	9	3	6	.311	.500
Soria,Joakim	L	.242	120	29	5	1	1	14	10	33	.306	.325
Throws Right	R	.277	112	31	4	0	6	19	7	27	.319	.473
Soriano,Rafael	L	.302	63	19	2	0	2	9	13	15	.421	.429
Throws Right	R	.173	81	14	0	0	2	7	5	21	.230	.247
Sosa,Henry	L	.297	74	22	9	0	3	13	12	10	.404	.541
Throws Right	R	.256	125	32	9	0	4	15	11	28	.319	.424
Spence,Josh	L	.158	57	9	0	0	2	4	7	18	.262	.263
Throws Left	R	.116	43	5	2	0	0	2	12	13	.316	.163
Stammen,Craig	L	.067	15	1	0	0	0	0	1	5	.125	.067
Throws Right	R	.105	19	2	0	0	0	1	3	7	.227	.105
Stauffer,Tim	L	.276	351	97	24	2	10	33	27	60	.332	.442
Throws Right	R	.239	347	83	16	2	10	37	26	68	.300	.383
Stetter,Mitch	L	.211	19	4	1	0	1	3	1	6	.273	.421
Throws Left	R	.500	8	4	0	0	1	5	0	1	.500	.875
Stevens,Jeff	L	.000	4	0	0	0	0	0	2	2	.429	.000
Throws Right	R	.235	17	4	2	0	1	4	5	2	.375	.529
Stewart,Zach	L	.341	135	46	10	0	4	20	13	21	.396	.504
Throws Right	R	.321	137	44	10	1	7	23	5	24	.352	.562
Stinson,Josh	L	.333	15	5	0	0	0	1	2	2	.412	.333
Throws Right	R	.265	34	9	3	1	1	4	5	6	.359	.500
Storen,Drew	L	.198	121	24	4	0	2	10	9	33	.260	.281
Throws Right	R	.209	158	33	7	1	6	11	11	41	.263	.380
Strasburg,Stephen	L	.125	40	5	1	0	0	1	1	16	.146	.150
Throws Right	R	.227	44	10	1	0	0	3	1	8	.239	.250
Street,Huston	L	.284	88	25	4	2	3	10	6	23	.333	.477
Throws Right	R	.270	137	37	5	1	7	19	3	32	.286	.474
Strop,Pedro	L	.176	34	6	1	0	0	2	7	8	.310	.206
Throws Right	R	.214	42	9	1	0	0	1	3	13	.283	.238
Stults,Eric	L	.158	19	3	0	0	1	3	2	4	.273	.316
Throws Left	R	.276	29	8	1	0	3	6	2	3	.323	.621
Stutes,Michael	L	.212	24	5	0	0	4	12	17	21	.322	.384
Throws Right	R	.222	126	28	3	2	3	12	11	37	.295	.349
Surkamp,Eric	L	.429	7	3	0	0	0	3	1	1	.500	.429
Throws Left	R	.302	96	29	9	1	1	11	16	12	.405	.448
Swarzak,Anthony	L	.253	221	56	7	2	6	29	17	29	.306	.385
Throws Right	R	.301	183	55	12	0	3	21	9	26	.350	.415
Takahashi,Hisanori	L	.261	119	31	8	0	4	15	8	23	.305	.429
Throws Left	R	.206	131	27	4	0	3	16	17	29	.293	.305
Talbot,Mitch	L	.388	129	50	10	1	4	20	17	15	.456	.574
Throws Right	R	.301	133	40	4	1	6	22	11	21	.356	.481

Pitcher	vs	Avg	AB	H	2B	3B	HR	RBI	BB	SO	OBP	Slg
Tallet,Brian	L	.261	23	6	2	1	2	7	2	4	.370	.696
Throws Left	R	.410	39	16	3	0	2	9	5	6	.467	.641
Tateyama,Yoshinori	L	.260	73	19	2	0	7	20	7	16	.333	.575
Throws Right	R	.189	95	18	5	0	1	11	4	27	.230	.274
Tazawa,Junichi	L	.500	4	2	2	0	1	0	0	0	.500	1.000
Throws Right	R	.125	8	1	0	0	1	1	1	4	.222	.500
Teaford,Everett	L	.197	61	12	2	0	1	8	8	9	.292	.279
Throws Left	R	.253	95	24	3	0	7	13	6	19	.294	.505
Teheran,Julio	L	.340	47	16	2	1	2	4	6	5	.415	.553
Throws Right	R	.172	29	5	0	0	2	7	2	5	.219	.379
Tejeda,Robinson	L	.222	9	2	1	0	0	1	1	0	.300	.333
Throws Right	R	.455	22	10	0	0	2	4	2	2	.480	.727
Texeira,Kanekoa	L	.438	16	7	0	0	0	2	2	0	.500	.438
Throws Right	R	.400	15	6	0	0	0	1	1	0	.412	.400
Thatcher,Joe	L	.158	19	3	0	0	0	2	3	7	.273	.158
Throws Left	R	.278	18	5	1	0	1	3	4	2	.409	.500
Thayer,Dale	L	.500	12	6	2	1	0	2	0	0	.462	.833
Throws Right	R	.222	27	6	1	0	0	3	0	5	.214	.259
Thomas,Brad	L	.400	20	8	3	0	0	7	3	4	.480	.550
Throws Left	R	.375	24	9	1	0	1	13	3	3	.387	.542
Thompson,Aaron	L	.500	10	5	1	0	1	5	0	1	.500	.900
Throws Left	R	.333	24	8	0	1	1	4	6	0	.467	.542
Thompson,Daryl	L	.364	11	4	1	0	0	5	2	0	.429	.455
Throws Right	R	.667	3	2	0	0	0	0	3	0	.833	.667
Thompson,Rich	L	.237	97	23	5	1	0	11	11	29	.312	.309
Throws Right	R	.213	108	23	3	0	5	13	9	27	.271	.380
Thornton,Matt	L	.260	104	27	4	0	1	16	6	34	.292	.327
Throws Left	R	.252	131	33	6	0	2	19	15	29	.329	.344
Tillman,Chris	L	.300	150	45	11	0	3	23	14	30	.364	.433
Throws Right	R	.302	106	32	10	0	2	15	11	16	.380	.453
Tobin,Mason	L	.429	7	3	0	0	1	2	5	0	.692	.857
Throws Right	R	.182	11	2	1	0	0	1	0	0	.182	.273
Tomko,Brett	L	.333	27	9	1	1	3	7	8	6	.486	.778
Throws Right	R	.176	34	6	2	0	1	5	2	8	.216	.324
Tomlin,Josh	L	.267	337	90	20	4	12	33	13	46	.296	.457
Throws Right	R	.226	297	67	15	3	12	38	8	43	.248	.418
Torres,Alex	L	.200	15	3	0	0	0	0	1	5	.250	.200
Throws Left	R	.313	16	5	1	0	0	5	6	4	.522	.375
Troncoso,Ramon	L	.350	40	14	4	0	1	4	1	9	.366	.525
Throws Right	R	.414	58	24	2	0	4	19	3	5	.443	.655
Tucker,Ryan	L	.300	10	3	1	0	1	1	2	2	.417	.700
Throws Right	R	.273	11	3	1	0	0	5	2	2	.385	.364
Turner,Jacob	L	.400	25	10	0	1	0	1	1	2	.423	.480
Throws Right	R	.241	29	7	1	0	3	8	3	6	.324	.586
Uehara,Koji	L	.130	115	15	2	0	5	6	9	43	.194	.278
Throws Right	R	.197	117	23	4	1	6	15	0	42	.195	.402
Valdes,Raul	L	.296	27	8	2	0	0	4	3	10	.387	.370
Throws Left	R	.286	21	6	1	0	1	2	3	5	.375	.476
Valdez,Jose	L	.318	22	7	1	0	1	7	2	6	.375	.500
Throws Right	R	.294	34	10	3	0	1	6	5	9	.390	.471
Valdez,Merkin	L	.462	13	6	0	0	1	2	0	3	.462	.692
Throws Right	R	.143	7	1	0	0	0	1	1	3	.250	.571
Valverde,Jose	L	.230	148	34	6	0	3	15	29	39	.356	.331
Throws Right	R	.158	114	18	1	0	2	4	5	30	.213	.219
VandenHurk,Rick	L	.286	21	6	2	0	2	4	5	5	.423	.667
Throws Right	R	.375	16	6	2	0	2	4	3	2	.500	.875
Vargas,Jason	L	.278	198	55	11	0	4	31	14	28	.326	.394
Throws Left	R	.255	589	150	27	2	18	63	45	103	.310	.399
Varvaro,Anthony	L	.189	37	7	2	0	1	2	6	6	.302	.324
Throws Right	R	.178	45	8	0	0	2	7	5	17	.255	.311
Vasquez,Anthony	L	.480	25	12	2	1	4	6	2	4	.536	1.120
Throws Right	R	.321	106	34	7	0	9	22	8	9	.376	.642
Vasquez,Esmerling	L	.217	46	10	3	0	2	6	6	11	.315	.413
Throws Right	R	.254	67	17	2	1	0	9	7	9	.346	.313
Vazquez,Javier	L	.245	351	86	20	2	12	40	34	77	.314	.416
Throws Right	R	.241	381	92	18	4	9	42	16	85	.269	.381
Venters,Jonny	L	.127	79	10	1	0	1	7	7	38	.225	.177
Throws Left	R	.194	222	43	4	1	1	15	36	58	.310	.234
Veras,Jose	L	.184	103	19	3	1	5	10	19	30	.311	.379
Throws Right	R	.220	159	35	8	1	1	26	15	49	.298	.302
Verlander,Justin	L	.174	495	86	14	2	10	35	38	145	.233	.271
Throws Right	R	.215	409	88	17	1	14	33	19	105	.253	.364
Villanueva,Carlos	L	.259	216	56	7	2	6	28	20	44	.320	.394
Throws Right	R	.241	195	47	11	1	5	21	12	24	.292	.385
Villanueva,Elih	L	.400	10	4	2	0	1	5	1	1	.500	.900
Throws Right	R	.250	4	1	0	0	0	3	4	1	.625	.750

Pitchers vs. Left-Handed and Right-Handed Batters

Pitcher	vs	Avg	AB	H	2B	3B	HR	RBI	BB	SO	OBP	Slg
Villarreal,Brayan	L	.375	32	12	3	0	1	6	6	7	.474	.563
Throws Right	R	.273	33	9	0	0	2	7	4	7	.351	.455
Viola,Pedro	L	.222	9	2	0	0	2	2	1	0	.300	.889
Throws Left	R	.500	8	4	1	0	1	4	1	4	.500	1.000
Vizcaino,Arodys	L	.286	28	8	1	0	0	3	4	6	.375	.321
Throws Right	R	.205	39	8	0	0	1	3	5	11	.311	.282
Vogelsong,Ryan	L	.258	299	77	17	1	7	30	34	57	.335	.391
Throws Right	R	.233	374	87	7	4	8	27	27	82	.289	.337
Volquez,Edinson	L	.274	168	46	11	1	6	23	37	38	.404	.458
Throws Right	R	.249	241	60	13	2	13	38	28	66	.330	.481
Volstad,Chris	L	.305	321	98	17	1	19	52	34	58	.367	.542
Throws Right	R	.273	326	89	23	1	4	36	15	59	.303	.387
Wade,Cory	L	.246	65	16	2	0	4	8	2	11	.269	.462
Throws Right	R	.202	84	17	4	0	1	3	6	19	.256	.286
Wagner,Neil	L	.429	7	3	1	0	0	3	1	2	.500	.571
Throws Right	R	.231	13	3	1	0	1	5	2	2	.375	.538
Wakefield,Tim	L	.246	256	63	21	1	7	31	19	38	.306	.418
Throws Right	R	.282	354	100	24	1	18	67	28	55	.337	.508
Walden,Jordan	L	.227	119	27	8	1	1	14	15	44	.314	.336
Throws Right	R	.218	101	22	6	0	2	6	11	23	.295	.337
Waldrop,Kyle	L	.056	18	1	1	0	0	0	3	1	.190	.111
Throws Right	R	.360	25	9	0	0	1	5	3	4	.429	.480
Walters,P.J.	L	.143	7	1	0	0	0	0	0	1	.143	.143
Throws Right	R	.182	11	2	0	0	1	4	3	3	.357	.455
Wang,Chien-Ming	L	.368	117	43	4	0	4	14	9	10	.406	.504
Throws Right	R	.186	129	24	4	0	4	20	4	15	.216	.310
Watson,Tony	L	.279	61	17	2	0	1	7	6	19	.348	.361
Throws Left	R	.193	88	17	4	0	5	14	14	18	.304	.409
Weaver,Jered	L	.216	468	101	20	2	8	27	28	108	.260	.318
Throws Right	R	.208	389	81	18	2	12	35	28	90	.264	.357
Webb,Ryan	L	.276	87	24	4	1	2	9	10	15	.357	.414
Throws Right	R	.238	101	24	6	1	0	12	10	16	.310	.317
Weiland,Kyle	L	.178	45	8	2	0	0	6	5	7	.283	.222
Throws Right	R	.375	56	21	3	1	5	16	7	6	.462	.732
Weinhardt,Robbie	L	.400	5	2	1	0	0	0	0	1	.400	.600
Throws Right	R	.500	4	2	2	0	0	0	0	0	.500	1.000
Wells,Randy	L	.263	228	60	8	1	7	24	24	41	.332	.399
Throws Right	R	.273	297	81	10	0	16	48	23	41	.324	.468
Westbrook,Jake	L	.260	335	87	19	2	7	37	42	53	.343	.391
Throws Right	R	.316	383	121	21	6	9	57	31	51	.365	.473
Wheeler,Dan	L	.278	72	20	5	0	2	12	6	12	.333	.431
Throws Right	R	.227	119	27	7	0	5	15	2	27	.238	.412
Whelan,Kevin	L	.000	5	0	0	0	0	1	4	1	.444	.000
Throws Right	R	-	0	0	0	0	0	0	1	0	1.000	-
White,Alex	L	.325	83	27	5	1	7	15	7	9	.374	.663
Throws Right	R	.292	120	35	8	0	8	26	18	28	.396	.558
Wilhelmsen,Tom	L	.200	60	12	0	0	1	9	5	14	.258	.250
Throws Right	R	.220	59	13	3	0	1	7	8	16	.329	.322
Wilk,Adam	L	.286	21	6	0	0	1	3	2	4	.348	.429
Throws Left	R	.242	33	8	3	0	2	5	1	6	.265	.515
Williams,Jerome	L	.235	85	20	4	0	2	9	5	15	.275	.353
Throws Right	R	.305	82	25	6	0	4	13	10	13	.387	.524
Williams,Randy	L	.250	16	4	2	0	0	2	3	2	.368	.375
Throws Left	R	.353	17	6	2	0	0	2	2	4	.400	.471
Willis,Dontrelle	L	.127	55	7	1	0	1	4	2	20	.169	.200
Throws Left	R	.305	233	71	11	2	5	34	35	37	.395	.433
Wilson,Brian	L	.223	103	23	3	0	0	7	19	29	.347	.252
Throws Right	R	.257	105	27	7	0	2	13	12	25	.339	.381
Wilson,C.J.	L	.251	179	45	7	1	2	17	17	51	.323	.335
Throws Left	R	.227	644	146	36	2	14	57	57	155	.296	.354
Wolf,Randy	L	.246	134	33	10	1	1	17	13	31	.333	.358
Throws Left	R	.270	671	181	35	2	22	68	53	103	.328	.426
Wood,Blake	L	.252	123	31	8	0	3	23	16	27	.347	.390
Throws Right	R	.255	137	35	5	2	2	11	16	35	.331	.365
Wood,Kerry	L	.227	66	15	5	1	0	9	7	24	.316	.333
Throws Right	R	.240	125	30	2	3	5	19	14	33	.326	.424
Wood,Tim	L	.286	14	4	0	0	1	6	4	0	.421	.500
Throws Right	R	.286	14	4	0	0	0	1	4	2	.421	.286
Wood,Travis	L	.316	76	24	6	1	0	6	7	14	.386	.421
Throws Left	R	.287	327	94	22	3	10	44	33	62	.350	.465
Worley,Vance	L	.201	244	49	13	1	3	20	24	66	.271	.299
Throws Right	R	.272	246	67	18	1	7	25	22	53	.336	.439
Worrell,Mark	L	.500	2	1	0	0	0	0	2	1	.750	.500
Throws Right	R	.500	10	5	1	0	2	9	0	2	.500	1.200
Wright,Jamey	L	.226	124	28	7	1	4	16	13	26	.304	.395
Throws Right	R	.266	124	33	5	0	2	12	17	22	.370	.355

Pitcher	vs	Avg	AB	H	2B	3B	HR	RBI	BB	SO	OBP	Slg
Wright,Wesley	L	.038	26	1	0	0	0	0	4	11	.167	.038
Throws Left	R	.385	13	5	2	1	1	6	1	0	.429	.923
Wuertz,Michael	L	.241	58	14	4	0	2	10	13	14	.380	.414
Throws Right	R	.311	74	23	5	0	3	17	13	18	.420	.500
Young,Chris	L	.104	48	5	2	0	0	8	16	.232	.146
Throws Right	R	.206	34	7	1	0	3	5	3	6	.289	.500
Zagurski,Mike	L	.167	6	1	0	0	0	1	2	.286	.167
Throws Left	R	.375	8	3	1	0	1	4	2	2	.500	.875
Zambrano,Carlos	L	.289	249	72	8	3	10	33	36	41	.376	.466
Throws Right	R	.268	306	82	18	1	9	43	20	60	.320	.422
Ziegler,Brad	L	.373	67	25	3	1	0	7	9	8	.442	.448
Throws Right	R	.188	149	28	5	0	0	22	10	36	.242	.221
Zimmermann,Jordan	L	.252	286	72	19	3	7	29	16	58	.290	.413
Throws Right	R	.251	327	82	10	3	5	20	15	66	.297	.346
Zito,Barry	L	.294	34	10	4	0	2	12	6	4	.390	.588
Throws Left	R	.248	165	41	7	2	8	21	18	28	.321	.461
AL	L	.259	-	-	-	-	-	-	-	-	.324	.403
	R	.255	-	-	-	-	-	-	-	-	.320	.406
NL	L	.256	-	-	-	-	-	-	-	-	.328	.399
	R	.252	-	-	-	-	-	-	-	-	.314	.390
MLB	L	.257	-	-	-	-	-	-	-	-	.326	.401
	R	.253	-	-	-	-	-	-	-	-	.316	.397

2011 Leader Boards

This section contains all the leader boards you traditionally see, but way more of those that you never see. For example, the three longest home runs in baseball were hit by two relative newcomers: Mitch Moreland of Texas and Mark Trumbo both hit 472-foot bombs, and Trumbo threw in another of 471 feet for good measure.

Some of the leader boards derive from the complex pitch data collected by Baseball Info Solutions. For example, the two best curveball hitters in baseball in 2011 were two right-handed hitters from the same team: Chris Young and Justin Upton from the Arizona Diamondbacks.

Bill James provides his own leader boards including Runs Created, Tough Losses and Power/Speed Numbers. The pitcher with the most Tough Losses in 2011 was Hiroki Kuroda of the Dodgers. Half of his 16 losses were in games in which he pitched very well and didn't deserve the loss. If the Dodgers could have scored a few more runs in just four of those games, Kuroda's record would have been 17-12 instead of 13-16.

In short, if there's any kind of leader board that we thought would be interesting, we put it here.

Some details:

Our home run distance leader boards are fueled by Hit Tracker data. Please check out www.hittrackeronline.com and thank you ESPN Stats & Information Group.

In the past we measured hitter performance against various pitch types by result only. The problem with that approach was that if a hitter regularly looked silly on non-result-pitch curveballs, but mashed just a few along the way, he could look like a great curveball hitter, even though nothing was further from the truth. Bill James designed a formula to rate hitters not only on the result pitches, but on every pitch the batter faced. The hitters you'll now see in these leader boards are a much better representation of the guys who mastered each pitch type this past year.

Here are some definitions to help clarify parts of the leader boards that may not be familiar to all readers:

BPS stands for "Batting Average plus Slugging Percentage." We feel that BPS makes more sense than OPS for some leader boards that involve pitches.

OutZ is "Pitches Outside the Strike Zone."

Holds Adjusted Save Percentage is calculated by dividing holds plus saves by holds plus save opportunities.

2011 American League Batting Leaders

Batting Average
(minimum 502 PA)

Cabrera,Miguel, Det	.344
Gonzalez,Adrian, Bos	.338
Young,Michael, Tex	.338
Martinez,Victor, Det	.330
Ellsbury,Jacoby, Bos	.321
Ortiz,David, Bos	.309
Pedroia,Dustin, Bos	.307
Kotchman,Casey, TB	.306
Cabrera,Melky, KC	.305
Gordon,Alex, KC	.303

On Base Percentage
(minimum 502 PA)

Cabrera,Miguel, Det	.448
Bautista,Jose, Tor	.447
Gonzalez,Adrian, Bos	.410
Ortiz,David, Bos	.398
Avila,Alex, Det	.389
Konerko,Paul, CWS	.388
Pedroia,Dustin, Bos	.387
Young,Michael, Tex	.380
Martinez,Victor, Det	.380
Kotchman,Casey, TB	.378

Slugging Average
(minimum 502 PA)

Bautista,Jose, Tor	.608
Cabrera,Miguel, Det	.586
Beltre,Adrian, Tex	.561
Ortiz,David, Bos	.554
Granderson,Curtis, NYY	.552
Ellsbury,Jacoby, Bos	.552
Gonzalez,Adrian, Bos	.548
Hamilton,Josh, Tex	.536
Cano,Robinson, NYY	.533
Konerko,Paul, CWS	.517

Home Runs

Bautista,Jose, Tor	43
Granderson,Curtis, NYY	41
Teixeira,Mark, NYY	39
Reynolds,Mark, Bal	37
Beltre,Adrian, Tex	32
Ellsbury,Jacoby, Bos	32
Kinsler,Ian, Tex	32
Konerko,Paul, CWS	31
Longoria,Evan, TB	31
3 tied with	30

Games

Cabrera,Miguel, Det	161
Suzuki,Ichiro, Sea	161
Markakis,Nick, Bal	160
Butler,Billy, KC	159
Cano,Robinson, NYY	159
Gardner,Brett, NYY	159
Gonzalez,Adrian, Bos	159
Pedroia,Dustin, Bos	159
Young,Michael, Tex	159
4 tied with	158

Plate Appearances

Ellsbury,Jacoby, Bos	732
Pedroia,Dustin, Bos	731
Kinsler,Ian, Tex	723
Suzuki,Ichiro, Sea	721
Markakis,Nick, Bal	716
Gonzalez,Adrian, Bos	715
Pierre,Juan, CWS	711
Cabrera,Melky, KC	706
Granderson,Curtis, NYY	691
Gordon,Alex, KC	690

At Bats

Suzuki,Ichiro, Sea	677
Ellsbury,Jacoby, Bos	660
Cabrera,Melky, KC	658
Markakis,Nick, Bal	641
Pierre,Juan, CWS	639
Pedroia,Dustin, Bos	635
Young,Michael, Tex	631
Gonzalez,Adrian, Bos	630
Cano,Robinson, NYY	623
Kinsler,Ian, Tex	620

Hits

Gonzalez,Adrian, Bos	213
Young,Michael, Tex	213
Ellsbury,Jacoby, Bos	212
Cabrera,Melky, KC	201
Cabrera,Miguel, Det	197
Pedroia,Dustin, Bos	195
Cano,Robinson, NYY	188
Gordon,Alex, KC	185
Suzuki,Ichiro, Sea	184
Markakis,Nick, Bal	182

Singles

Pierre,Juan, CWS	155
Young,Michael, Tex	155
Suzuki,Ichiro, Sea	154
Gonzalez,Adrian, Bos	138
Markakis,Nick, Bal	135
Cabrera,Melky, KC	134
Pedroia,Dustin, Bos	134
Andrus,Elvis, Tex	129
Ellsbury,Jacoby, Bos	129
Jeter,Derek, NYY	128

Doubles

Cabrera,Miguel, Det	48
Francoeur,Jeff, KC	47
Cano,Robinson, NYY	46
Ellsbury,Jacoby, Bos	46
Zobrist,Ben, TB	46
Gonzalez,Adrian, Bos	45
Gordon,Alex, KC	45
Butler,Billy, KC	44
Cabrera,Melky, KC	44
Young,Michael, Tex	41

Triples

Bourjos,Peter, LAA	11
Jackson,Austin, Det	11
Granderson,Curtis, NYY	10
Aybar,Erick, LAA	8
Escobar,Alcides, KC	8
Gardner,Brett, NYY	8
Weeks,Jemile, Oak	8
4 tied with	7

Total Bases

Ellsbury,Jacoby, Bos	364
Gonzalez,Adrian, Bos	345
Cabrera,Miguel, Det	335
Cano,Robinson, NYY	332
Granderson,Curtis, NYY	322
Bautista,Jose, Tor	312
Cabrera,Melky, KC	309
Gordon,Alex, KC	307
Pedroia,Dustin, Bos	301
Young,Michael, Tex	299

Runs Scored

Granderson,Curtis, NYY	136
Kinsler,Ian, Tex	121
Ellsbury,Jacoby, Bos	119
Cabrera,Miguel, Det	111
Gonzalez,Adrian, Bos	108
Bautista,Jose, Tor	105
Cano,Robinson, NYY	104
Cabrera,Melky, KC	102
Pedroia,Dustin, Bos	102
Gordon,Alex, KC	101

RBI

Granderson,Curtis, NYY	119
Cano,Robinson, NYY	118
Gonzalez,Adrian, Bos	117
Teixeira,Mark, NYY	111
Young,Michael, Tex	106
Beltre,Adrian, Tex	105
Cabrera,Miguel, Det	105
Ellsbury,Jacoby, Bos	105
Konerko,Paul, CWS	105
2 tied with	103

Walks

Bautista,Jose, Tor	132
Cabrera,Miguel, Det	108
Santana,Carlos, Cle	97
Swisher,Nick, NYY	95
Kinsler,Ian, Tex	89
Pedroia,Dustin, Bos	86
Granderson,Curtis, NYY	85
Longoria,Evan, TB	80
Abreu,Bobby, LAA	78
Ortiz,David, Bos	78

Strikeouts

Reynolds,Mark, Bal	196
Jackson,Austin, Det	181
Dunn,Adam, CWS	177
Granderson,Curtis, NYY	169
Upton,B.J., TB	161
Willingham,Josh, Oak	150
Olivo,Miguel, Sea	140
Gordon,Alex, KC	139
Arencibia,J.P., Tor	133
Santana,Carlos, Cle	133

2011 American League Batting Leaders

Intentional Walks

Bautista,Jose, Tor	24
Cabrera,Miguel, Det	22
Gonzalez,Adrian, Bos	20
Konerko,Paul, CWS	17
Butler,Billy, KC	15
Hamilton,Josh, Tex	13
Suzuki,Ichiro, Sea	13
Ortiz,David, Bos	12
Cano,Robinson, NYY	11
2 tied with	9

BA Bases Loaded
(minimum 10 PA)

Cabrera,Asdrubal, Cle	.636
Peralta,Jhonny, Det	.563
Hafner,Travis, Cle	.500
Martinez,Victor, Det	.500
Zobrist,Ben, TB	.500
Valencia,Danny, Min	.471
Santana,Carlos, Cle	.462
Cano,Robinson, NYY	.444
Damon,Johnny, TB	.429
Ramirez,Alexei, CWS	.429

Sacrifice Hits

Pierre,Juan, CWS	19
Escobar,Alcides, KC	18
Andrus,Elvis, Tex	16
Getz,Chris, KC	14
Jackson,Austin, Det	14
Mathis,Jeff, LAA	14
Santiago,Ramon, Det	11
Andino,Robert, Bal	9
Aybar,Erick, LAA	9
Ryan,Brendan, Sea	9

Sacrifice Flies

Jones,Adam, Bal	12
Konerko,Paul, CWS	11
Francoeur,Jeff, KC	10
Hamilton,Josh, Tex	10
Matsui,Hideki, Oak	9
Peralta,Jhonny, Det	9
Young,Michael, Tex	9
8 tied with	8

BA Close & Late
(minimum 50 PA)

Young,Michael, Tex	.406
Napoli,Mike, Tex	.358
Konerko,Paul, CWS	.345
Cabrera,Miguel, Det	.341
Crisp,Coco, Oak	.338
Getz,Chris, KC	.333
Smoak,Justin, Sea	.324
Markakis,Nick, Bal	.323
Hafner,Travis, Cle	.322
Hamilton,Josh, Tex	.322

Batting Average w/ RISP
(minimum 100 PA)

Martinez,Victor, Det	.394
Cabrera,Miguel, Det	.388
Young,Michael, Tex	.377
Napoli,Mike, Tex	.372
Ellsbury,Jacoby, Bos	.366
Sizemore,Scott, Det-Oak	.360
Pennington,Cliff, Oak	.348
Gonzalez,Adrian, Bos	.337
Pierre,Juan, CWS	.331
Betemit,Wilson, KC-Det	.329

SLG vs. LHP
(minimum 125 PA)

Wieters,Matt, Bal	.694
Beltre,Adrian, Tex	.685
Bautista,Jose, Tor	.672
Napoli,Mike, Tex	.619
Granderson,Curtis, NYY	.597
Cuddyer,Michael, Min	.589
Teixeira,Mark, NYY	.587
Francoeur,Jeff, KC	.570
Longoria,Evan, TB	.567
Ortiz,David, Bos	.566

SLG vs. RHP
(minimum 377 PA)

Gonzalez,Adrian, Bos	.624
Cabrera,Miguel, Det	.603
Bautista,Jose, Tor	.589
Ellsbury,Jacoby, Bos	.577
Ortiz,David, Bos	.548
Cano,Robinson, NYY	.537
Avila,Alex, Det	.536
Konerko,Paul, CWS	.535
Hamilton,Josh, Tex	.534
Hosmer,Eric, KC	.531

Leadoff Hitters OBP
(minimum 150 PA)

Gordon,Alex, KC	.383
Ellsbury,Jacoby, Bos	.381
Escobar,Yunel, Tor	.366
Kinsler,Ian, Tex	.356
Jennings,Desmond, TB	.355
Damon,Johnny, TB	.343
Izturis,Maicer, LAA	.340
Weeks,Jemile, Oak	.338
Jeter,Derek, NYY	.337
Span,Denard, Min	.331

Cleanup Hitters SLG
(minimum 150 PA)

Cabrera,Miguel, Det	.582
Konerko,Paul, CWS	.574
Beltre,Adrian, Tex	.529
Cano,Robinson, NYY	.521
Cuddyer,Michael, Min	.500
Carp,Mike, Sea	.482
Willingham,Josh, Oak	.477
Wells,Vernon, LAA	.477
Youkilis,Kevin, Bos	.477
Hosmer,Eric, KC	.476

BA vs. LHP
(minimum 125 PA)

Young,Michael, Tex	.361
Pedroia,Dustin, Bos	.358
Jeter,Derek, NYY	.349
Wieters,Matt, Bal	.339
Bautista,Jose, Tor	.336
Escobar,Yunel, Tor	.330
Ortiz,David, Bos	.329
Pierre,Juan, CWS	.329
Swisher,Nick, NYY	.327
Gonzalez,Adrian, Bos	.321

BA vs. RHP
(minimum 377 PA)

Cabrera,Miguel, Det	.353
Gonzalez,Adrian, Bos	.347
Ellsbury,Jacoby, Bos	.337
Martinez,Victor, Det	.337
Young,Michael, Tex	.330
Peralta,Jhonny, Det	.323
Hosmer,Eric, KC	.315
Hamilton,Josh, Tex	.314
Gordon,Alex, KC	.314
Kotchman,Casey, TB	.313

Home BA
(minimum 251 PA)

Young,Michael, Tex	.353
Cabrera,Miguel, Det	.349
Gonzalez,Adrian, Bos	.347
Ortiz,David, Bos	.342
Gordon,Alex, KC	.329
Ellsbury,Jacoby, Bos	.326
Martinez,Victor, Det	.326
Escobar,Yunel, Tor	.321
Pedroia,Dustin, Bos	.321
Youkilis,Kevin, Bos	.320

Away BA
(minimum 251 PA)

Cabrera,Miguel, Det	.339
Martinez,Victor, Det	.333
Gonzalez,Adrian, Bos	.329
Young,Michael, Tex	.322
Cabrera,Melky, KC	.321
Izturis,Maicer, LAA	.319
Ellsbury,Jacoby, Bos	.316
Zobrist,Ben, TB	.311
Cano,Robinson, NYY	.310
Callaspo,Alberto, LAA	.309

OBP vs. LHP
(minimum 125 PA)

Bautista,Jose, Tor	.484
Pedroia,Dustin, Bos	.463
Cabrera,Miguel, Det	.459
Swisher,Nick, NYY	.442
Pierre,Juan, CWS	.430
Napoli,Mike, Tex	.430
Wieters,Matt, Bal	.430
Santana,Carlos, Cle	.428
Youkilis,Kevin, Bos	.426
Ortiz,David, Bos	.423

OBP vs. RHP
(minimum 377 PA)

Cabrera,Miguel, Det	.444
Bautista,Jose, Tor	.436
Gonzalez,Adrian, Bos	.422
Avila,Alex, Det	.403
Kotchman,Casey, TB	.394
Konerko,Paul, CWS	.389
Ellsbury,Jacoby, Bos	.388
Martinez,Victor, Det	.386
Ortiz,David, Bos	.386
Gordon,Alex, KC	.384

2011 American League Batting Leaders

Stolen Bases

Crisp,Coco, Oak	49
Gardner,Brett, NYY	49
Suzuki,Ichiro, Sea	40
Ellsbury,Jacoby, Bos	39
Andrus,Elvis, Tex	37
Upton,B.J., TB	36
Davis,Rajai, Tor	34
Revere,Ben, Min	34
Aybar,Erick, LAA	30
Kinsler,Ian, Tex	30

Caught Stealing

Pierre,Juan, CWS	17
Ellsbury,Jacoby, Bos	15
Gardner,Brett, NYY	13
Andrus,Elvis, Tex	12
Upton,B.J., TB	12
Davis,Rajai, Tor	11
Weeks,Jemile, Oak	11
Cabrera,Melky, KC	10
Francoeur,Jeff, KC	10
Granderson,Curtis, NYY	10

Highest SB Success Pct
(minimum 20 SBA)

Kinsler,Ian, Tex	88.2
Suzuki,Ichiro, Sea	85.1
Crisp,Coco, Oak	84.5
Aybar,Erick, LAA	83.3
Jackson,Austin, Det	81.5
Abreu,Bobby, LAA	80.8
Revere,Ben, Min	79.1
Gardner,Brett, NYY	79.0
Nunez,Eduardo, NYY	78.6
Cabrera,Asdrubal, Cle	77.3

Lowest SB Success Pct
(minimum 20 SBA)

Pennington,Cliff, Oak	60.9
Pierre,Juan, CWS	61.4
Patterson,Corey, Tor	61.9
Cabrera,Melky, KC	66.7
Weeks,Jemile, Oak	66.7
Gordon,Alex, KC	68.0
Francoeur,Jeff, KC	68.8
Kendrick,Howie, LAA	70.0
Bourjos,Peter, LAA	71.0
2 tied with	71.4

Steals of Third

Davis,Rajai, Tor	17
Crisp,Coco, Oak	11
Pierre,Juan, CWS	10
Gardner,Brett, NYY	9
Suzuki,Ichiro, Sea	9
Escobar,Alcides, KC	7
Andrus,Elvis, Tex	6
Ellsbury,Jacoby, Bos	5
Getz,Chris, KC	5
Upton,B.J., TB	5

Grounded Into DP

Gonzalez,Adrian, Bos	28
Cabrera,Miguel, Det	24
Hunter,Torii, LAA	24
Ortiz,David, Bos	24
Guerrero,Vladimir, Bal	23
Martinez,Victor, Det	20
Rios,Alex, CWS	20
4 tied with	19

Grounded Into DP Pct
(minimum 50 GIDP Ops)

Reddick,Josh, Bos	1.85
Damon,Johnny, TB	3.45
Hughes,Luke, Min	3.45
LaPorta,Matt, Cle	3.77
Ackley,Dustin, Sea	4.29
Kennedy,Adam, Sea	4.69
Dirks,Andy, Det	4.92
Weeks,Jemile, Oak	4.92
Raburn,Ryan, Det	5.13
Willingham,Josh, Oak	5.17

Hit By Pitch

Quentin,Carlos, CWS	23
Rodriguez,Sean, TB	18
Youkilis,Kevin, Bos	14
Beckham,Gordon, CWS	13
Cano,Robinson, NYY	12
Granderson,Curtis, NYY	12
Kotchman,Casey, TB	12
4 tied with	11

Pitches Seen

Pedroia,Dustin, Bos	3077
Granderson,Curtis, NYY	3069
Kinsler,Ian, Tex	2852
Santana,Carlos, Cle	2839
Ellsbury,Jacoby, Bos	2818
Teixeira,Mark, NYY	2818
Bautista,Jose, Tor	2805
Markakis,Nick, Bal	2784
Gordon,Alex, KC	2765
Gonzalez,Adrian, Bos	2735

At Bats Per Home Run
(minimum 502 PA)

Bautista,Jose, Tor	11.9
Granderson,Curtis, NYY	14.2
Reynolds,Mark, Bal	14.4
Teixeira,Mark, NYY	15.1
Beltre,Adrian, Tex	15.2
Longoria,Evan, TB	15.6
Cruz,Nelson, Tex	16.4
Willingham,Josh, Oak	16.8
Konerko,Paul, CWS	17.5
Hardy,J.J., Bal	17.6

Highest GB/FB Ratio
(minimum 502 PA)

Jeter,Derek, NYY	3.36
Suzuki,Ichiro, Sea	2.84
Andrus,Elvis, Tex	2.65
Escobar,Yunel, Tor	2.32
Kotchman,Casey, TB	2.16
Pierre,Juan, CWS	2.06
Kendrick,Howie, LAA	1.94
Escobar,Alcides, KC	1.86
Gardner,Brett, NYY	1.85
Young,Michael, Tex	1.79

Lowest GB/FB Ratio
(minimum 502 PA)

Granderson,Curtis, NYY	0.71
Willingham,Josh, Oak	0.72
Teixeira,Mark, NYY	0.75
Kinsler,Ian, Tex	0.75
Bautista,Jose, Tor	0.79
Peralta,Jhonny, Det	0.81
Suzuki,Kurt, Oak	0.81
Reynolds,Mark, Bal	0.82
Encarnacion,Edwin, Tor	0.82
Wells,Vernon, LAA	0.82

Pitches Per Plate App
(minimum 502 PA)

Granderson,Curtis, NYY	4.44
Abreu,Bobby, LAA	4.36
Santana,Carlos, Cle	4.31
Bautista,Jose, Tor	4.28
Reynolds,Mark, Bal	4.22
Pedroia,Dustin, Bos	4.21
Gardner,Brett, NYY	4.19
Youkilis,Kevin, Bos	4.18
Teixeira,Mark, NYY	4.12
Willingham,Josh, Oak	4.10

Pct Pitches Taken
(minimum 1500 Pitches)

Abreu,Bobby, LAA	65.9
Gardner,Brett, NYY	63.9
Scutaro,Marco, Bos	62.9
Santana,Carlos, Cle	62.8
Youkilis,Kevin, Bos	62.7
Bautista,Jose, Tor	62.5
Kinsler,Ian, Tex	62.3
Brantley,Michael, Cle	61.9
Ackley,Dustin, Sea	61.3
DeJesus,David, Oak	60.9

Best BPS on OutZ
(minimum 502 PA)

Martinez,Victor, Det	.793
Young,Michael, Tex	.782
Francoeur,Jeff, KC	.680
Cabrera,Miguel, Det	.671
Bautista,Jose, Tor	.651
Guerrero,Vladimir, Bal	.649
Hosmer,Eric, KC	.644
Gordon,Alex, KC	.625
DeJesus,David, Oak	.615
Cabrera,Melky, KC	.606

Worst BPS on OutZ
(minimum 502 PA)

Reynolds,Mark, Bal	.284
Abreu,Bobby, LAA	.288
Olivo,Miguel, Sea	.348
Upton,B.J., TB	.360
Crisp,Coco, Oak	.364
Pennington,Cliff, Oak	.368
Bourjos,Peter, LAA	.370
Rios,Alex, CWS	.377
Swisher,Nick, NYY	.387
Wieters,Matt, Bal	.397

2011 American League Batting Leaders

Best OPS vs Fastballs
(minimum 251 PA)

Gonzalez,Adrian, Bos	1.036
Ortiz,David, Bos	1.022
Napoli,Mike, Tex	1.017
Granderson,Curtis, NYY	1.004
Bautista,Jose, Tor	1.002
Cabrera,Miguel, Det	.995
Konerko,Paul, CWS	.964
Beltre,Adrian, Tex	.962
Gordon,Alex, KC	.958
Young,Michael, Tex	.953

Best OPS vs Curveballs
(minimum 50 PA)

Markakis,Nick, Bal	1.088
Cabrera,Miguel, Det	1.012
Arencibia,J.P., Tor	.992
Kotchman,Casey, TB	.967
Francoeur,Jeff, KC	.951
Cabrera,Melky, KC	.947
Cabrera,Asdrubal, Cle	.907
Jones,Adam, Bal	.887
Cano,Robinson, NYY	.845
Hamilton,Josh, Tex	.830

Best OPS vs Changeups
(minimum 50 PA)

Cuddyer,Michael, Min	1.339
Ellsbury,Jacoby, Bos	1.171
Avila,Alex, Det	1.166
Cabrera,Miguel, Det	1.127
Gonzalez,Adrian, Bos	1.053
Bautista,Jose, Tor	1.052
Raburn,Ryan, Det	1.026
Boesch,Brennan, Det	1.002
Thames,Eric, Tor	.995
Kinsler,Ian, Tex	.955

Best OPS vs Sliders
(minimum 32 PA)

Izturis,Maicer, LAA	1.345
Carp,Mike, Sea	1.172
Bautista,Jose, Tor	1.069
Weeks,Jemile, Oak	1.061
Wieters,Matt, Bal	1.026
Lind,Adam, Tor	1.021
Ellsbury,Jacoby, Bos	1.007
Teixeira,Mark, NYY	.997
Cano,Robinson, NYY	.988
Cabrera,Miguel, Det	.984

OPS
(minimum 502 PA)

Bautista,Jose, Tor	1.056
Cabrera,Miguel, Det	1.033
Gonzalez,Adrian, Bos	.957
Ortiz,David, Bos	.953
Ellsbury,Jacoby, Bos	.928
Granderson,Curtis, NYY	.916
Konerko,Paul, CWS	.906
Avila,Alex, Det	.895
Beltre,Adrian, Tex	.892
2 tied with	.882

OPS First Half
(minimum 260 PA)

Bautista,Jose, Tor	1.170
Gonzalez,Adrian, Bos	1.006
Cabrera,Miguel, Det	.980
Ortiz,David, Bos	.965
Konerko,Paul, CWS	.954
Granderson,Curtis, NYY	.935
Youkilis,Kevin, Bos	.911
Peralta,Jhonny, Det	.891
Avila,Alex, Det	.876
Teixeira,Mark, NYY	.871

OPS Second Half
(minimum 201 PA)

Napoli,Mike, Tex	1.171
Cabrera,Miguel, Det	1.100
Ellsbury,Jacoby, Bos	1.000
Ortiz,David, Bos	.936
Gordon,Alex, KC	.918
Avila,Alex, Det	.916
Longoria,Evan, TB	.907
Cano,Robinson, NYY	.905
Bautista,Jose, Tor	.896
Gonzalez,Adrian, Bos	.893

OPS by Catchers
(minimum 251 PA)

Avila,Alex, Det	.887
Santana,Carlos, Cle	.822
Wieters,Matt, Bal	.774
Saltalamacchia,J, Bos	.741
Martin,Russell, NYY	.736
Pierzynski,A.J., CWS	.728
Arencibia,J.P., Tor	.727
Torrealba,Yorvit, Tex	.721
Suzuki,Kurt, Oak	.684
Jaso,John, TB	.667

OPS by First Basemen
(minimum 251 PA)

Cabrera,Miguel, Det	1.060
Gonzalez,Adrian, Bos	.960
Konerko,Paul, CWS	.873
Teixeira,Mark, NYY	.836
Kotchman,Casey, TB	.802
Hosmer,Eric, KC	.800
Santana,Carlos, Cle	.789
Trumbo,Mark, LAA	.759
Smoak,Justin, Sea	.748
LaPorta,Matt, Cle	.743

OPS by Second Basemen
(minimum 251 PA)

Cano,Robinson, NYY	.886
Pedroia,Dustin, Bos	.862
Kinsler,Ian, Tex	.818
Zobrist,Ben, TB	.816
Kendrick,Howie, LAA	.806
Weeks,Jemile, Oak	.763
Ackley,Dustin, Sea	.755
Andino,Robert, Bal	.639
Beckham,Gordon, CWS	.634
Cabrera,Orlando, Cle	.617

OPS by Third Basemen
(minimum 251 PA)

Beltre,Adrian, Tex	.870
Longoria,Evan, TB	.852
Rodriguez,Alex, NYY	.840
Youkilis,Kevin, Bos	.826
Betemit,Wilson, KC-Det	.792
Reynolds,Mark, Bal	.766
Sizemore,Scott, Det-Oak	.758
Hannahan,Jack, Cle	.741
Callaspo,Alberto, LAA	.740
Moustakas,Mike, KC	.675

OPS by Shortstops
(minimum 251 PA)

Peralta,Jhonny, Det	.818
Hardy,J.J., Bal	.801
Cabrera,Asdrubal, Cle	.792
Scutaro,Marco, Bos	.785
Escobar,Yunel, Tor	.779
Jeter,Derek, NYY	.745
Aybar,Erick, LAA	.743
Ramirez,Alexei, CWS	.731
Andrus,Elvis, Tex	.710
Pennington,Cliff, Oak	.687

OPS by Left Fielders
(minimum 251 PA)

Hamilton,Josh, Tex	.916
Gordon,Alex, KC	.892
Willingham,Josh, Oak	.821
Reimold,Nolan, Bal	.734
Gardner,Brett, NYY	.715
Crawford,Carl, Bos	.701
Young,Delmon, Min-Det	.694
Wells,Vernon, LAA	.683
Fuld,Sam, TB	.675
Brantley,Michael, Cle	.668

OPS by Center Fielders
(minimum 251 PA)

Ellsbury,Jacoby, Bos	.928
Granderson,Curtis, NYY	.921
Cabrera,Melky, KC	.823
Jones,Adam, Bal	.785
Bourjos,Peter, LAA	.766
Upton,B.J., TB	.761
Span,Denard, Min	.693
Crisp,Coco, Oak	.692
Jackson,Austin, Det	.689
Davis,Rajai, Tor	.651

OPS by Right Fielders
(minimum 251 PA)

Bautista,Jose, Tor	1.033
Cruz,Nelson, Tex	.883
Quentin,Carlos, CWS	.838
Swisher,Nick, NYY	.823
Joyce,Matt, TB	.813
Francoeur,Jeff, KC	.804
Cuddyer,Michael, Min	.803
Markakis,Nick, Bal	.769
Hunter,Torii, LAA	.747
Choo,Shin-Soo, Cle	.733

OPS by Designated Hitters
(minimum 125 PA)

Konerko,Paul, CWS	.995
Ortiz,David, Bos	.964
Martinez,Victor, Det	.903
Encarnacion,Edwin, Tor	.855
Thome,Jim, Min-Cle	.847
Butler,Billy, KC	.833
Young,Michael, Tex	.821
Hafner,Travis, Cle	.810
Willingham,Josh, Oak	.775
Kubel,Jason, Min	.768

2011 American League Batting Leaders

OPS Batting Left vs. LHP
(minimum 125 PA)

Ortiz,David, Bos	.989
Granderson,Curtis, NYY	.944
Cano,Robinson, NYY	.879
Ellsbury,Jacoby, Bos	.841
Gordon,Alex, KC	.829
Hamilton,Josh, Tex	.825
Damon,Johnny, TB	.812
Matsui,Hideki, Oak	.795
Gonzalez,Adrian, Bos	.787
Avila,Alex, Det	.779

OPS Batting Left vs. RHP
(minimum 377 PA)

Gonzalez,Adrian, Bos	1.046
Ellsbury,Jacoby, Bos	.965
Avila,Alex, Det	.939
Ortiz,David, Bos	.934
Hamilton,Josh, Tex	.904
Granderson,Curtis, NYY	.902
Gordon,Alex, KC	.901
Hosmer,Eric, KC	.886
Cano,Robinson, NYY	.884
Joyce,Matt, TB	.866

OPS Batting Right vs. LHP
(minimum 125 PA)

Bautista,Jose, Tor	1.156
Wieters,Matt, Bal	1.124
Beltre,Adrian, Tex	1.075
Napoli,Mike, Tex	1.049
Pedroia,Dustin, Bos	1.010
Cuddyer,Michael, Min	.993
Cabrera,Miguel, Det	.990
Youkilis,Kevin, Bos	.987
Teixeira,Mark, NYY	.967
Santana,Carlos, Cle	.964

OPS Batting Right vs. RHP
(minimum 377 PA)

Cabrera,Miguel, Det	1.047
Bautista,Jose, Tor	1.025
Konerko,Paul, CWS	.924
Peralta,Jhonny, Det	.848
Young,Michael, Tex	.838
Beltre,Adrian, Tex	.836
Jones,Adam, Bal	.829
Willingham,Josh, Oak	.823
Longoria,Evan, TB	.819
Kinsler,Ian, Tex	.815

OPS vs. LHP
(minimum 125 PA)

Bautista,Jose, Tor	1.156
Wieters,Matt, Bal	1.124
Beltre,Adrian, Tex	1.075
Napoli,Mike, Tex	1.049
Pedroia,Dustin, Bos	1.010
Cuddyer,Michael, Min	.993
Cabrera,Miguel, Det	.990
Ortiz,David, Bos	.989
Youkilis,Kevin, Bos	.987
Teixeira,Mark, NYY	.967

OPS vs. RHP
(minimum 377 PA)

Cabrera,Miguel, Det	1.047
Gonzalez,Adrian, Bos	1.046
Bautista,Jose, Tor	1.025
Ellsbury,Jacoby, Bos	.965
Avila,Alex, Det	.939
Ortiz,David, Bos	.934
Konerko,Paul, CWS	.924
Hamilton,Josh, Tex	.904
Granderson,Curtis, NYY	.902
Gordon,Alex, KC	.901

RC Per 27 Outs vs. LHP
(minimum 125 PA)

Napoli,Mike, Tex	10.6
Bautista,Jose, Tor	10.3
Wieters,Matt, Bal	10.2
Young,Michael, Tex	10.0
Cabrera,Miguel, Det	9.1
Butler,Billy, KC	8.6
Pedroia,Dustin, Bos	8.6
Zobrist,Ben, TB	8.2
Teixeira,Mark, NYY	8.1
Beltre,Adrian, Tex	7.9

RC Per 27 Outs vs. RHP
(minimum 377 PA)

Cabrera,Miguel, Det	9.3
Bautista,Jose, Tor	9.2
Gonzalez,Adrian, Bos	8.8
Ellsbury,Jacoby, Bos	8.4
Martinez,Victor, Det	7.7
Avila,Alex, Det	7.5
Konerko,Paul, CWS	7.0
Gordon,Alex, KC	6.7
Hamilton,Josh, Tex	6.5
Joyce,Matt, TB	6.5

Highest RBI %
(minimum 502 PA)

Beltre,Adrian, Tex	12.20
Granderson,Curtis, NYY	11.57
Hamilton,Josh, Tex	11.27
Longoria,Evan, TB	11.25
Bautista,Jose, Tor	11.23
Cano,Robinson, NYY	10.99
Teixeira,Mark, NYY	10.89
Cruz,Nelson, Tex	10.89
Willingham,Josh, Oak	10.79
Konerko,Paul, CWS	10.46

Lowest RBI %
(minimum 502 PA)

Gardner,Brett, NYY	4.28
Suzuki,Ichiro, Sea	4.58
Andino,Robert, Bal	4.62
Escobar,Alcides, KC	4.77
Jackson,Austin, Det	4.77
Pierre,Juan, CWS	4.85
Rios,Alex, CWS	5.03
Beckham,Gordon, CWS	5.18
Bourjos,Peter, LAA	5.33
Suzuki,Kurt, Oak	5.67

Highest Strikeout per PA
(minimum 502 PA)

Reynolds,Mark, Bal	.316
Olivo,Miguel, Sea	.276
Jackson,Austin, Det	.271
Willingham,Josh, Oak	.266
Upton,B.J., TB	.252
Granderson,Curtis, NYY	.245
Avila,Alex, Det	.238
Cruz,Nelson, Tex	.226
Bourjos,Peter, LAA	.225
Trumbo,Mark, LAA	.209

Lowest Strikeout per PA
(minimum 502 PA)

Pierre,Juan, CWS	.058
Martinez,Victor, Det	.086
Callaspo,Alberto, LAA	.090
Guerrero,Vladimir, Bal	.095
Suzuki,Ichiro, Sea	.096
Kinsler,Ian, Tex	.098
Beltre,Adrian, Tex	.101
Markakis,Nick, Bal	.105
Andrus,Elvis, Tex	.111
Crisp,Coco, Oak	.111

Home Runs At Home

Beltre,Adrian, Tex	23
Teixeira,Mark, NYY	22
Granderson,Curtis, NYY	21
Bautista,Jose, Tor	20
Cruz,Nelson, Tex	19
Jones,Adam, Bal	19
Konerko,Paul, CWS	19
Reynolds,Mark, Bal	17
Cano,Robinson, NYY	16
Kinsler,Ian, Tex	16

Home Runs Away

Bautista,Jose, Tor	23
Granderson,Curtis, NYY	20
Reynolds,Mark, Bal	20
Ellsbury,Jacoby, Bos	17
Gonzalez,Adrian, Bos	17
Longoria,Evan, TB	17
Napoli,Mike, Tex	17
Quentin,Carlos, CWS	17
Teixeira,Mark, NYY	17
Wells,Vernon, LAA	17

Longest Avg Home Run
(min 10 over the wall)

Moreland,Mitch, Tex	422
Gordon,Alex, KC	415
Butler,Billy, KC	414
Carp,Mike, Sea	413
Hunter,Torii, LAA	412
Cruz,Nelson, Tex	412
Hamilton,Josh, Tex	411
Jones,Andruw, NYY	409
Thames,Eric, Tor	409
Trumbo,Mark, LAA	409

Shortest Avg Home Run
(min 10 over the wall)

Kotchman,Casey, TB	376
Suzuki,Kurt, Oak	377
Damon,Johnny, TB	378
Aybar,Erick, LAA	379
Zobrist,Ben, TB	380
Rios,Alex, CWS	381
Beckham,Gordon, CWS	382
Pedroia,Dustin, Bos	382
LaPorta,Matt, Cle	384
3 tied with	385

2011 American League Batting Leaders

Under Age 26: AB Per HR
(minimum 502 PA)

Longoria,Evan, TB	15.6
Trumbo,Mark, LAA	18.6
Santana,Carlos, Cle	20.4
Wieters,Matt, Bal	22.7
Cabrera,Asdrubal, Cle	24.2
Avila,Alex, Det	24.4
Hosmer,Eric, KC	27.5
Butler,Billy, KC	31.4
Bourjos,Peter, LAA	41.8
Beckham,Gordon, CWS	49.9

Under Age 26: OPS
(minimum 502 PA)

Avila,Alex, Det	.895
Longoria,Evan, TB	.850
Butler,Billy, KC	.822
Santana,Carlos, Cle	.808
Hosmer,Eric, KC	.799
Cabrera,Asdrubal, Cle	.792
Wieters,Matt, Bal	.778
Trumbo,Mark, LAA	.768
Bourjos,Peter, LAA	.765
Andrus,Elvis, Tex	.708

Under Age 26: RC/27 Outs
(minimum 502 PA)

Avila,Alex, Det	6.7
Longoria,Evan, TB	6.4
Cabrera,Asdrubal, Cle	5.8
Butler,Billy, KC	5.6
Wieters,Matt, Bal	5.3
Santana,Carlos, Cle	4.9
Hosmer,Eric, KC	4.9
Bourjos,Peter, LAA	4.5
Andrus,Elvis, Tex	4.4
Trumbo,Mark, LAA	4.3

Longest Home Run

Moreland,Mitch, Tex, 6/20	472
Trumbo,Mark, LAA, 5/30	472
Trumbo,Mark, LAA, 8/7	471
Pena,Wily Mo, Sea, 8/21	468
Thome,Jim, Min, 7/17	464
Reynolds,Mark, Bal, 8/7	463
Konerko,Paul, CWS, 4/5	462
Cruz,Nelson, Tex, 8/26	461
Hunter,Torii, LAA, 3/31	461
Rodriguez,Alex, NYY, 6/10	460

Swing and Miss %
(minimum 1500 Pitches Seen)

Reynolds,Mark, Bal	36.2
Olivo,Miguel, Sea	35.0
Dunn,Adam, CWS	31.3
Saltalamacchia,J, Bos	30.2
Cruz,Nelson, Tex	27.9
Arencibia,J.P., Tor	26.8
Raburn,Ryan, Det	26.5
Rodriguez,Sean, TB	26.4
Napoli,Mike, Tex	26.3
Hamilton,Josh, Tex	26.1

Highest First Swing %
(minimum 502 PA)

Hamilton,Josh, Tex	45.6
Olivo,Miguel, Sea	42.3
Guerrero,Vladimir, Bal	41.2
Cabrera,Miguel, Det	39.5
Francoeur,Jeff, KC	39.5
Upton,B.J., TB	38.7
Cano,Robinson, NYY	35.9
Young,Delmon, Min-Det	35.7
Joyce,Matt, TB	32.8
2 tied with	32.6

Lowest First Swing %
(minimum 502 PA)

Hardy,J.J., Bal	7.9
Abreu,Bobby, LAA	8.3
Gardner,Brett, NYY	10.3
Youkilis,Kevin, Bos	10.4
Pedroia,Dustin, Bos	10.6
Granderson,Curtis, NYY	10.7
Suzuki,Kurt, Oak	13.2
Callaspo,Alberto, LAA	13.5
Pierre,Juan, CWS	14.2
DeJesus,David, Oak	15.7

Home RC Per 27 Outs
(minimum 251 PA)

Cabrera,Miguel, Det	9.3
Bautista,Jose, Tor	9.1
Ortiz,David, Bos	8.5
Escobar,Yunel, Tor	8.3
Young,Michael, Tex	8.3
Youkilis,Kevin, Bos	8.2
Avila,Alex, Det	8.0
Ellsbury,Jacoby, Bos	7.8
Cruz,Nelson, Tex	7.6
Gordon,Alex, KC	7.4

Road RC Per 27 Outs
(minimum 251 PA)

Bautista,Jose, Tor	9.7
Cabrera,Miguel, Det	9.4
Zobrist,Ben, TB	8.0
Martinez,Victor, Det	7.5
Longoria,Evan, TB	7.4
Ellsbury,Jacoby, Bos	7.2
Gonzalez,Adrian, Bos	7.2
Granderson,Curtis, NYY	6.7
Pennington,Cliff, Oak	6.5
Markakis,Nick, Bal	6.2

2011 National League Batting Leaders

Batting Average
(minimum 502 PA)

Reyes,Jose, NYM	.337
Braun,Ryan, Mil	.332
Kemp,Matt, LAD	.324
Pence,Hunter, Hou-Phi	.314
Votto,Joey, Cin	.309
Castro,Starlin, ChC	.307
Ramirez,Aramis, ChC	.306
Molina,Yadier, StL	.305
Morse,Michael, Was	.303
Tulowitzki,Troy, Col	.302

On Base Percentage
(minimum 502 PA)

Votto,Joey, Cin	.416
Fielder,Prince, Mil	.415
Berkman,Lance, StL	.412
Kemp,Matt, LAD	.399
Braun,Ryan, Mil	.397
Holliday,Matt, StL	.388
Beltran,Carlos, NYM-SF	.385
Reyes,Jose, NYM	.384
Tulowitzki,Troy, Col	.372
Pence,Hunter, Hou-Phi	.370

Slugging Average
(minimum 502 PA)

Braun,Ryan, Mil	.597
Kemp,Matt, LAD	.586
Fielder,Prince, Mil	.566
Morse,Michael, Was	.550
Berkman,Lance, StL	.547
Tulowitzki,Troy, Col	.544
Pujols,Albert, StL	.541
Stanton,Mike, Fla	.537
Votto,Joey, Cin	.531
Upton,Justin, Ari	.529

Home Runs

Kemp,Matt, LAD	39
Fielder,Prince, Mil	38
Pujols,Albert, StL	37
Uggla,Dan, Atl	36
Stanton,Mike, Fla	34
Braun,Ryan, Mil	33
Howard,Ryan, Phi	33
Bruce,Jay, Cin	32
3 tied with	31

Games

Fielder,Prince, Mil	162
Kemp,Matt, LAD	161
Uggla,Dan, Atl	161
Votto,Joey, Cin	161
Jay,Jon, StL	159
Sanchez,Gaby, Fla	159
Upton,Justin, Ari	159
Walker,Neil, Pit	159
6 tied with	158

Plate Appearances

Bourn,Michael, Hou-Atl	722
Votto,Joey, Cin	719
Castro,Starlin, ChC	715
Fielder,Prince, Mil	692
Kemp,Matt, LAD	689
Stubbs,Drew, Cin	681
McCutchen,Andrew, Pit	678
Phillips,Brandon, Cin	675
Upton,Justin, Ari	674
Uggla,Dan, Atl	672

At Bats

Castro,Starlin, ChC	674
Bourn,Michael, Hou-Atl	656
Phillips,Brandon, Cin	610
Pence,Hunter, Hou-Phi	606
Stubbs,Drew, Cin	604
Kemp,Matt, LAD	602
Uggla,Dan, Atl	600
Votto,Joey, Cin	599
Walker,Neil, Pit	596
Upton,Justin, Ari	592

Hits

Castro,Starlin, ChC	207
Kemp,Matt, LAD	195
Bourn,Michael, Hou-Atl	193
Pence,Hunter, Hou-Phi	190
Braun,Ryan, Mil	187
Votto,Joey, Cin	185
Phillips,Brandon, Cin	183
Reyes,Jose, NYM	181
Pujols,Albert, StL	173
Ramirez,Aramis, ChC	173

Singles

Castro,Starlin, ChC	152
Bourn,Michael, Hou-Atl	147
Bonifacio,Emilio, Fla	129
Reyes,Jose, NYM	127
Pence,Hunter, Hou-Phi	125
Phillips,Brandon, Cin	125
Infante,Omar, Fla	121
Kemp,Matt, LAD	119
Barney,Darwin, ChC	115
Votto,Joey, Cin	113

Doubles

Votto,Joey, Cin	40
Beltran,Carlos, NYM-SF	39
Upton,Justin, Ari	39
Braun,Ryan, Mil	38
Lee,Carlos, Hou	38
Pence,Hunter, Hou-Phi	38
Phillips,Brandon, Cin	38
Young,Chris, Ari	38
7 tied with	36

Triples

Reyes,Jose, NYM	16
Victorino,Shane, Phi	16
Fowler,Dexter, Col	15
Bourn,Michael, Hou-Atl	10
Castro,Starlin, ChC	9
Smith,Seth, Col	9
Infante,Omar, Fla	8
Maybin,Cameron, SD	8
Parra,Gerardo, Ari	8
2 tied with	7

Total Bases

Kemp,Matt, LAD	353
Braun,Ryan, Mil	336
Fielder,Prince, Mil	322
Votto,Joey, Cin	318
Pujols,Albert, StL	313
Upton,Justin, Ari	313
Pence,Hunter, Hou-Phi	304
Tulowitzki,Troy, Col	292
Castro,Starlin, ChC	291
Ramirez,Aramis, ChC	288

Runs Scored

Kemp,Matt, LAD	115
Braun,Ryan, Mil	109
Pujols,Albert, StL	105
Upton,Justin, Ari	105
Reyes,Jose, NYM	101
Votto,Joey, Cin	101
Fielder,Prince, Mil	95
Victorino,Shane, Phi	95
Bourn,Michael, Hou-Atl	94
Phillips,Brandon, Cin	94

RBI

Kemp,Matt, LAD	126
Fielder,Prince, Mil	120
Howard,Ryan, Phi	116
Braun,Ryan, Mil	111
Tulowitzki,Troy, Col	105
Votto,Joey, Cin	103
Pujols,Albert, StL	99
Bruce,Jay, Cin	97
Pence,Hunter, Hou-Phi	97
Morse,Michael, Was	95

Walks

Votto,Joey, Cin	110
Fielder,Prince, Mil	107
Pena,Carlos, ChC	101
Berkman,Lance, StL	92
McCutchen,Andrew, Pit	89
Young,Chris, Ari	80
Howard,Ryan, Phi	75
Kemp,Matt, LAD	74
Sanchez,Gaby, Fla	74
Werth,Jayson, Was	74

Strikeouts

Stubbs,Drew, Cin	205
Howard,Ryan, Phi	172
Espinosa,Danny, Was	166
Stanton,Mike, Fla	166
Pena,Carlos, ChC	161
Werth,Jayson, Was	160
Kemp,Matt, LAD	159
Bruce,Jay, Cin	158
Uggla,Dan, Atl	156
Freeman,Freddie, Atl	142

2011 National League Batting Leaders

Intentional Walks

Fielder,Prince, Mil	32
Kemp,Matt, LAD	24
Berkman,Lance, StL	17
Howard,Ryan, Phi	16
Parra,Gerardo, Ari	16
Pujols,Albert, StL	15
Votto,Joey, Cin	15
Bruce,Jay, Cin	14
McCann,Brian, Atl	14
Tulowitzki,Troy, Col	12

BA Bases Loaded
(minimum 10 PA)

Fowler,Dexter, Col	.600
Pagan,Angel, NYM	.571
Tejada,Ruben, NYM	.545
Reyes,Jose, NYM	.500
Rollins,Jimmy, Phi	.500
Roberts,Ryan, Ari	.462
Soto,Geovany, ChC	.417
Theriot,Ryan, StL	.412
Morrison,Logan, Fla	.400
Ruiz,Carlos, Phi	.385

Sacrifice Hits

Infante,Omar, Fla	17
Halladay,Roy, Phi	16
Hernandez,Livan, Was	15
Morgan,Nyjer, Mil	15
Hammel,Jason, Col	14
Marcum,Shaun, Mil	12
9 tied with	11

Sacrifice Flies

Betancourt,Yuniesky, Mil	10
Huff,Aubrey, SF	9
Helton,Todd, Col	8
Infante,Omar, Fla	8
McGehee,Casey, Mil	8
Polanco,Placido, Phi	8
Ramirez,Aramis, ChC	8
Walker,Neil, Pit	8
7 tied with	7

BA Close & Late
(minimum 50 PA)

Reyes,Jose, NYM	.407
Descalso,Daniel, StL	.356
Parra,Gerardo, Ari	.347
Roberts,Ryan, Ari	.347
Victorino,Shane, Phi	.347
Braun,Ryan, Mil	.342
Denorfia,Chris, SD	.338
Montero,Miguel, Ari	.329
McGehee,Casey, Mil	.329
Wallace,Brett, Hou	.322

Batting Average w/ RISP
(minimum 100 PA)

Votto,Joey, Cin	.383
Murphy,Daniel, NYM	.364
Berkman,Lance, StL	.360
Freese,David, StL	.354
Braun,Ryan, Mil	.351
Turner,Justin, NYM	.350
Pence,Hunter, Hou-Phi	.339
Gonzalez,Carlos, Col	.339
Jones,Chipper, Atl	.337
Kemp,Matt, LAD	.335

SLG vs. LHP
(minimum 125 PA)

Kemp,Matt, LAD	.682
Stanton,Mike, Fla	.638
Tulowitzki,Troy, Col	.631
Braun,Ryan, Mil	.617
Lee,Carlos, Hou	.615
Victorino,Shane, Phi	.608
Pence,Hunter, Hou-Phi	.590
Beltran,Carlos, NYM-SF	.585
Votto,Joey, Cin	.569
McCutchen,Andrew, Pit	.567

SLG vs. RHP
(minimum 377 PA)

Fielder,Prince, Mil	.612
Braun,Ryan, Mil	.591
Berkman,Lance, StL	.571
Kemp,Matt, LAD	.560
Morse,Michael, Was	.557
Howard,Ryan, Phi	.550
Holliday,Matt, StL	.539
Montero,Miguel, Ari	.526
Smith,Seth, Col	.526
Pujols,Albert, StL	.525

Leadoff Hitters OBP
(minimum 150 PA)

Phillips,Brandon, Cin	.417
Reyes,Jose, NYM	.383
Bonifacio,Emilio, Fla	.376
Tabata,Jose, Pit	.373
Castro,Starlin, ChC	.370
Fukudome,Kosuke, ChC	.370
Hart,Corey, Mil	.366
Fowler,Dexter, Col	.363
McCutchen,Andrew, Pit	.352
Presley,Alex, Pit	.347

Cleanup Hitters SLG
(minimum 150 PA)

Uggla,Dan, Atl	.586
Kemp,Matt, LAD	.569
Fielder,Prince, Mil	.566
Tulowitzki,Troy, Col	.547
Berkman,Lance, StL	.545
Morse,Michael, Was	.532
Holliday,Matt, StL	.524
Beltran,Carlos, NYM-SF	.511
McCann,Brian, Atl	.510
Ramirez,Hanley, Fla	.500

BA vs. LHP
(minimum 125 PA)

Braun,Ryan, Mil	.350
Tulowitzki,Troy, Col	.349
Lee,Carlos, Hou	.348
Castro,Starlin, ChC	.342
Kemp,Matt, LAD	.341
Polanco,Placido, Phi	.336
Bonifacio,Emilio, Fla	.333
Votto,Joey, Cin	.333
Denorfia,Chris, SD	.328
Reyes,Jose, NYM	.325

BA vs. RHP
(minimum 377 PA)

Reyes,Jose, NYM	.341
Braun,Ryan, Mil	.327
Ethier,Andre, LAD	.321
Kemp,Matt, LAD	.319
Morgan,Nyjer, Mil	.316
Pence,Hunter, Hou-Phi	.313
Loney,James, LAD	.312
Bourn,Michael, Hou-Atl	.312
Molina,Yadier, StL	.311
Montero,Miguel, Ari	.308

Home BA
(minimum 251 PA)

Braun,Ryan, Mil	.351
Reyes,Jose, NYM	.348
Upton,Justin, Ari	.333
Ramirez,Aramis, ChC	.332
Gonzalez,Carlos, Col	.331
Pence,Hunter, Hou-Phi	.330
Kemp,Matt, LAD	.329
Fielder,Prince, Mil	.326
Molina,Yadier, StL	.325
Pujols,Albert, StL	.321

Away BA
(minimum 251 PA)

Votto,Joey, Cin	.334
Carroll,Jamey, LAD	.329
Reyes,Jose, NYM	.327
Kemp,Matt, LAD	.319
Braun,Ryan, Mil	.315
Castro,Starlin, ChC	.309
Ruiz,Carlos, Phi	.308
Berkman,Lance, StL	.307
Jay,Jon, StL	.305
Morse,Michael, Was	.303

OBP vs. LHP
(minimum 125 PA)

Kemp,Matt, LAD	.461
Braun,Ryan, Mil	.433
Victorino,Shane, Phi	.424
Sanchez,Gaby, Fla	.420
Bay,Jason, NYM	.418
Stubbs,Drew, Cin	.418
Votto,Joey, Cin	.418
Tulowitzki,Troy, Col	.418
Lee,Carlos, Hou	.413
Bonifacio,Emilio, Fla	.407

OBP vs. RHP
(minimum 377 PA)

Fielder,Prince, Mil	.435
Berkman,Lance, StL	.427
Votto,Joey, Cin	.415
Ethier,Andre, LAD	.410
Beltran,Carlos, NYM-SF	.402
Pena,Carlos, ChC	.388
Braun,Ryan, Mil	.387
Kemp,Matt, LAD	.380
Holliday,Matt, StL	.379
Reyes,Jose, NYM	.379

2011 National League Batting Leaders

Stolen Bases		Caught Stealing		Highest SB Success Pct (minimum 20 SBA)		Lowest SB Success Pct (minimum 20 SBA)	
Bourn,Michael, Hou-Atl	61	Bourn,Michael, Hou-Atl	14	Campana,Tony, ChC	92.3	Fowler,Dexter, Col	57.1
Bonifacio,Emilio, Fla	40	Bonifacio,Emilio, Fla	11	Venable,Will, SD	89.7	Phillips,Brandon, Cin	60.9
Kemp,Matt, LAD	40	Kemp,Matt, LAD	11	Young,Eric, Col	87.1	Bloomquist,Willie, Ari	66.7
Maybin,Cameron, SD	40	Bartlett,Jason, SD	10	Hudson,Orlando, SD	86.4	Ramirez,Hanley, Fla	66.7
Stubbs,Drew, Cin	40	Bloomquist,Willie, Ari	10	Victorino,Shane, Phi	86.4	Roberts,Ryan, Ari	66.7
Reyes,Jose, NYM	39	Desmond,Ian, Was	10	Werth,Jayson, Was	86.4	Tabata,Jose, Pit	69.6
Braun,Ryan, Mil	33	McCutchen,Andrew, Pit	10	Bernadina,Roger, Was	85.0	Bartlett,Jason, SD	69.7
Pagan,Angel, NYM	32	Ramirez,Hanley, Fla	10	Reyes,Jose, NYM	84.8	McCutchen,Andrew, Pit	69.7
Bourgeois,Jason, Hou	31	Stubbs,Drew, Cin	10	Braun,Ryan, Mil	84.6	Upton,Justin, Ari	70.0
Rollins,Jimmy, Phi	30	6 tied with	9	Schafer,Jordan, Atl-Hou	84.6	2 tied with	71.0

Steals of Third		Grounded Into DP		Grounded Into DP Pct (minimum 50 GIDP Ops)		Hit By Pitch	
Bourn,Michael, Hou-Atl	14	Pujols,Albert, StL	29	Nix,Laynce, Was	1.56	Espinosa,Danny, Was	19
Reyes,Jose, NYM	8	Holliday,Matt, StL	21	Stubbs,Drew, Cin	2.13	Upton,Justin, Ari	19
Rollins,Jimmy, Phi	8	Molina,Yadier, StL	21	Young,Chris, Ari	2.63	Morgan,Nyjer, Mil	14
Werth,Jayson, Was	7	Castro,Starlin, ChC	20	Johnson,Chris, Hou	2.78	Utley,Chase, Phi	14
Braun,Ryan, Mil	6	Votto,Joey, Cin	20	Utley,Chase, Phi	2.94	Morse,Michael, Was	13
6 tied with	5	Gonzalez,Alex, Atl	19	Gomes,Jonny, Cin-Was	2.99	Johnson,Reed, ChC	11
		McGehee,Casey, Mil	19	Gwynn,Tony, LAD	3.70	5 tied with	10
		Ramos,Wilson, Was	19	Venable,Will, SD	3.92		
		3 tied with	18	Carroll,Jamey, LAD	3.95		
				Victorino,Shane, Phi	3.96		

Pitches Seen		At Bats Per Home Run (minimum 502 PA)		Highest GB/FB Ratio (minimum 502 PA)		Lowest GB/FB Ratio (minimum 502 PA)	
Votto,Joey, Cin	2888	Fielder,Prince, Mil	15.0	Jay,Jon, StL	2.32	Soriano,Alfonso, ChC	0.57
Werth,Jayson, Was	2833	Stanton,Mike, Fla	15.2	Bonifacio,Emilio, Fla	2.31	Young,Chris, Ari	0.65
McCutchen,Andrew, Pit	2832	Kemp,Matt, LAD	15.4	Bourn,Michael, Hou-Atl	2.22	Ludwick,Ryan, SD-Pit	0.72
Bourn,Michael, Hou-Atl	2820	Pujols,Albert, StL	15.6	Bartlett,Jason, SD	2.03	Bruce,Jay, Cin	0.78
Kemp,Matt, LAD	2704	Berkman,Lance, StL	15.7	Maybin,Cameron, SD	1.93	Pena,Carlos, ChC	0.79
Stubbs,Drew, Cin	2697	Uggla,Dan, Atl	16.7	Carroll,Jamey, LAD	1.88	Lee,Carlos, Hou	0.79
Howard,Ryan, Phi	2666	Morse,Michael, Was	16.8	Barney,Darwin, ChC	1.73	Ramirez,Aramis, ChC	0.79
Walker,Neil, Pit	2638	Howard,Ryan, Phi	16.9	Desmond,Ian, Was	1.70	Sanchez,Gaby, Fla	0.80
Fielder,Prince, Mil	2629	Braun,Ryan, Mil	17.1	Pence,Hunter, Hou-Phi	1.67	McCann,Brian, Atl	0.81
2 tied with	2627	Pena,Carlos, ChC	17.6	Castro,Starlin, ChC	1.55	Upton,Justin, Ari	0.82

Pitches Per Plate App (minimum 502 PA)		Pct Pitches Taken (minimum 1500 Pitches)		Best BPS on OutZ (minimum 502 PA)		Worst BPS on OutZ (minimum 502 PA)	
Werth,Jayson, Was	4.37	Carroll,Jamey, LAD	63.5	Prado,Martin, Atl	.676	Stubbs,Drew, Cin	.251
Carroll,Jamey, LAD	4.28	Zimmerman,Ryan, Was	61.5	Reyes,Jose, NYM	.664	McCutchen,Andrew, Pit	.263
McCutchen,Andrew, Pit	4.18	Soto,Geovany, ChC	61.4	Kemp,Matt, LAD	.662	Buck,John, Fla	.291
Howard,Ryan, Phi	4.14	Werth,Jayson, Was	61.1	Smith,Seth, Col	.630	Roberts,Ryan, Ari	.297
Pena,Carlos, ChC	4.13	Morrison,Logan, Fla	60.8	Fielder,Prince, Mil	.625	Gonzalez,Alex, Atl	.304
Bonifacio,Emilio, Fla	4.03	Utley,Chase, Phi	59.8	Berkman,Lance, StL	.624	Bruce,Jay, Cin	.312
Votto,Joey, Cin	4.02	Tulowitzki,Troy, Col	59.7	Pujols,Albert, StL	.610	Weeks,Rickie, Mil	.338
Morrison,Logan, Fla	3.99	Victorino,Shane, Phi	59.3	Braun,Ryan, Mil	.608	Werth,Jayson, Was	.356
Young,Chris, Ari	3.99	Rollins,Jimmy, Phi	59.1	Polanco,Placido, Phi	.600	Hart,Corey, Mil	.371
Walker,Neil, Pit	3.98	Helton,Todd, Col	59.1	Victorino,Shane, Phi	.595	Bartlett,Jason, SD	.371

2011 National League Batting Leaders

Best OPS vs Fastballs
(minimum 251 PA)

Braun,Ryan, Mil	1.091
Kemp,Matt, LAD	1.070
Votto,Joey, Cin	1.039
Fielder,Prince, Mil	1.021
Beltran,Carlos, NYM-SF	1.005
Upton,Justin, Ari	.994
Berkman,Lance, StL	.986
Howard,Ryan, Phi	.945
Tulowitzki,Troy, Col	.932
Montero,Miguel, Ari	.931

Best OPS vs Curveballs
(minimum 50 PA)

Young,Chris, Ari	1.149
Upton,Justin, Ari	1.148
Gonzalez,Carlos, Col	1.090
Ramirez,Aramis, ChC	1.071
Uggla,Dan, Atl	1.011
Freeman,Freddie, Atl	.934
Victorino,Shane, Phi	.934
Fielder,Prince, Mil	.925
Sandoval,Pablo, SF	.906
Castro,Starlin, ChC	.890

Best OPS vs Changeups
(minimum 50 PA)

Stanton,Mike, Fla	1.291
Schierholtz,Nate, SF	1.172
Gonzalez,Carlos, Col	1.024
Tulowitzki,Troy, Col	1.024
Sandoval,Pablo, SF	.989
Ramirez,Aramis, ChC	.954
Pence,Hunter, Hou-Phi	.952
Weeks,Rickie, Mil	.942
Duda,Lucas, NYM	.936
Reyes,Jose, NYM	.932

Best OPS vs Sliders
(minimum 32 PA)

Berkman,Lance, StL	1.210
Victorino,Shane, Phi	1.111
Holliday,Matt, StL	1.104
Mayberry,John, Phi	1.060
Rollins,Jimmy, Phi	1.060
Craig,Allen, StL	1.049
Hanigan,Ryan, Cin	1.036
Bruce,Jay, Cin	1.025
Heisey,Chris, Cin	1.014
McKenry,Michael, Pit	.982

OPS
(minimum 502 PA)

Braun,Ryan, Mil	.994
Kemp,Matt, LAD	.986
Fielder,Prince, Mil	.981
Berkman,Lance, StL	.959
Votto,Joey, Cin	.947
Tulowitzki,Troy, Col	.916
Holliday,Matt, StL	.912
Morse,Michael, Was	.910
Beltran,Carlos, NYM-SF	.910
Pujols,Albert, StL	.906

OPS First Half
(minimum 260 PA)

Berkman,Lance, StL	1.006
Holliday,Matt, StL	.995
Fielder,Prince, Mil	.990
Kemp,Matt, LAD	.982
Braun,Ryan, Mil	.961
Votto,Joey, Cin	.945
Reyes,Jose, NYM	.927
Victorino,Shane, Phi	.900
3 tied with	.894

OPS Second Half
(minimum 201 PA)

Tulowitzki,Troy, Col	1.060
Braun,Ryan, Mil	1.034
Kemp,Matt, LAD	.990
Fielder,Prince, Mil	.968
Sandoval,Pablo, SF	.963
Stanton,Mike, Fla	.962
Beltran,Carlos, NYM-SF	.960
Pujols,Albert, StL	.960
Duda,Lucas, NYM	.957
2 tied with	.948

OPS by Catchers
(minimum 251 PA)

Hundley,Nick, SD	.844
McCann,Brian, Atl	.827
Montero,Miguel, Ari	.821
Molina,Yadier, StL	.819
Iannetta,Chris, Col	.788
Hernandez,Ramon, Cin	.775
Ramos,Wilson, Was	.773
Ruiz,Carlos, Phi	.739
Barajas,Rod, LAD	.727
Hanigan,Ryan, Cin	.717

OPS by First Basemen
(minimum 251 PA)

Morse,Michael, Was	1.002
Fielder,Prince, Mil	.985
Votto,Joey, Cin	.947
Pujols,Albert, StL	.911
Helton,Todd, Col	.854
Lee,Carlos, Hou	.828
Howard,Ryan, Phi	.825
Pena,Carlos, ChC	.818
Freeman,Freddie, Atl	.796
Sanchez,Gaby, Fla	.774

OPS by Second Basemen
(minimum 251 PA)

Phillips,Brandon, Cin	.803
Weeks,Rickie, Mil	.800
Utley,Chase, Phi	.763
Uggla,Dan, Atl	.757
Walker,Neil, Pit	.742
Espinosa,Danny, Was	.736
Sanchez,Freddy, SF	.735
Ellis,Mark, Col	.717
Johnson,Kelly, Ari	.708
Infante,Omar, Fla	.699

OPS by Third Basemen
(minimum 251 PA)

Sandoval,Pablo, SF	.933
Ramirez,Aramis, ChC	.876
Jones,Chipper, Atl	.847
Roberts,Ryan, Ari	.821
Zimmerman,Ryan, Was	.798
Freese,David, StL	.786
Headley,Chase, SD	.782
Wright,David, NYM	.772
Wigginton,Ty, Col	.771
Polanco,Placido, Phi	.680

OPS by Shortstops
(minimum 251 PA)

Tulowitzki,Troy, Col	.921
Reyes,Jose, NYM	.877
Castro,Starlin, ChC	.773
Bonifacio,Emilio, Fla	.759
Rollins,Jimmy, Phi	.744
Ramirez,Hanley, Fla	.711
Drew,Stephen, Ari	.703
Barmes,Clint, Hou	.700
Bloomquist,Willie, Ari	.675
Betancourt,Yuniesky, Mil	.656

OPS by Left Fielders
(minimum 251 PA)

Braun,Ryan, Mil	.989
Holliday,Matt, StL	.926
Morrison,Logan, Fla	.808
Parra,Gerardo, Ari	.785
Lee,Carlos, Hou	.780
Gomes,Jonny, Cin-Was	.774
Soriano,Alfonso, ChC	.764
Gonzalez,Carlos, Col	.757
Prado,Martin, Atl	.719
Ibanez,Raul, Phi	.707

OPS by Center Fielders
(minimum 251 PA)

Kemp,Matt, LAD	.980
Victorino,Shane, Phi	.846
McCutchen,Andrew, Pit	.826
Fowler,Dexter, Col	.798
Morgan,Nyjer, Mil	.767
Rasmus,Colby, StL	.759
Young,Chris, Ari	.749
Bourn,Michael, Hou-Atl	.734
Jay,Jon, StL	.733
Byrd,Marlon, ChC	.721

OPS by Right Fielders
(minimum 251 PA)

Berkman,Lance, StL	.932
Beltran,Carlos, NYM-SF	.915
Upton,Justin, Ari	.901
Stanton,Mike, Fla	.893
Pence,Hunter, Hou-Phi	.874
Hart,Corey, Mil	.864
Bruce,Jay, Cin	.810
Ethier,Andre, LAD	.790
Smith,Seth, Col	.789
Schierholtz,Nate, SF	.784

OPS by Pitchers
(minimum 50 PA)

Hudson,Daniel, Ari	.678
Gallardo,Yovani, Mil	.577
Lowe,Derek, Atl	.540
Lee,Cliff, Phi	.528
Vogelsong,Ryan, SF	.513
Kershaw,Clayton, LAD	.492
Zimmermann,Jordan, Was	.488
Billingsley,Chad, LAD	.485
Happ,J.A., Hou	.484
Leake,Mike, Cin	.459

2011 National League Batting Leaders

OPS Batting Left vs. LHP
(minimum 125 PA)

Votto,Joey, Cin	.987
Fielder,Prince, Mil	.822
Bruce,Jay, Cin	.804
McCann,Brian, Atl	.794
Helton,Todd, Col	.794
Gonzalez,Carlos, Col	.779
Morrison,Logan, Fla	.723
Freeman,Freddie, Atl	.707
Huff,Aubrey, SF	.690
Bourn,Michael, Hou-Atl	.645

OPS Batting Left vs. RHP
(minimum 377 PA)

Fielder,Prince, Mil	1.046
Berkman,Lance, StL	.998
Votto,Joey, Cin	.930
Howard,Ryan, Phi	.921
Beltran,Carlos, NYM-SF	.908
Montero,Miguel, Ari	.904
Pena,Carlos, ChC	.892
Smith,Seth, Col	.891
Reyes,Jose, NYM	.890
Ethier,Andre, LAD	.878

OPS Batting Right vs. LHP
(minimum 125 PA)

Kemp,Matt, LAD	1.142
Braun,Ryan, Mil	1.049
Tulowitzki,Troy, Col	1.049
Stanton,Mike, Fla	1.042
Victorino,Shane, Phi	1.032
Lee,Carlos, Hou	1.028
Pence,Hunter, Hou-Phi	.990
McCutchen,Andrew, Pit	.945
Young,Chris, Ari	.939
Upton,Justin, Ari	.929

OPS Batting Right vs. RHP
(minimum 377 PA)

Braun,Ryan, Mil	.979
Kemp,Matt, LAD	.940
Holliday,Matt, StL	.918
Morse,Michael, Was	.915
Pujols,Albert, StL	.897
Upton,Justin, Ari	.889
Ramirez,Aramis, ChC	.884
Tulowitzki,Troy, Col	.864
Stanton,Mike, Fla	.849
Pence,Hunter, Hou-Phi	.836

OPS vs. LHP
(minimum 125 PA)

Kemp,Matt, LAD	1.142
Braun,Ryan, Mil	1.049
Tulowitzki,Troy, Col	1.049
Stanton,Mike, Fla	1.042
Victorino,Shane, Phi	1.032
Lee,Carlos, Hou	1.028
Pence,Hunter, Hou-Phi	.990
Votto,Joey, Cin	.987
McCutchen,Andrew, Pit	.945
Young,Chris, Ari	.939

OPS vs. RHP
(minimum 377 PA)

Fielder,Prince, Mil	1.046
Berkman,Lance, StL	.998
Braun,Ryan, Mil	.979
Kemp,Matt, LAD	.940
Votto,Joey, Cin	.930
Howard,Ryan, Phi	.921
Holliday,Matt, StL	.918
Morse,Michael, Was	.915
Montero,Miguel, Ari	.904
Beltran,Carlos, NYM-SF	.903

RC Per 27 Outs vs. LHP
(minimum 125 PA)

Kemp,Matt, LAD	11.9
Braun,Ryan, Mil	9.1
Tulowitzki,Troy, Col	8.8
Young,Chris, Ari	8.4
Lee,Carlos, Hou	8.0
Roberts,Ryan, Ari	7.9
Victorino,Shane, Phi	7.7
Pence,Hunter, Hou-Phi	7.7
Polanco,Placido, Phi	7.6
Votto,Joey, Cin	7.6

RC Per 27 Outs vs. RHP
(minimum 377 PA)

Berkman,Lance, StL	8.9
Fielder,Prince, Mil	8.7
Braun,Ryan, Mil	8.3
Votto,Joey, Cin	7.8
Montero,Miguel, Ari	7.5
Ethier,Andre, LAD	7.2
Kemp,Matt, LAD	6.8
Beltran,Carlos, NYM-SF	6.7
Pena,Carlos, ChC	6.6
Morse,Michael, Was	6.6

Highest RBI %
(minimum 502 PA)

Braun,Ryan, Mil	11.75
Kemp,Matt, LAD	11.66
Fielder,Prince, Mil	11.45
Howard,Ryan, Phi	11.32
Gonzalez,Carlos, Col	11.28
Berkman,Lance, StL	10.89
Tulowitzki,Troy, Col	10.86
Morse,Michael, Was	10.72
Soriano,Alfonso, ChC	10.40
Pujols,Albert, StL	10.20

Lowest RBI %
(minimum 502 PA)

Carroll,Jamey, LAD	2.35
Bonifacio,Emilio, Fla	4.07
Stubbs,Drew, Cin	4.61
Bartlett,Jason, SD	4.66
Infante,Omar, Fla	4.90
Maybin,Cameron, SD	4.90
Barney,Darwin, ChC	4.97
Bourn,Michael, Hou-Atl	5.00
Jay,Jon, StL	5.15
Desmond,Ian, Was	5.36

Highest Strikeout per PA
(minimum 502 PA)

Stubbs,Drew, Cin	.301
Stanton,Mike, Fla	.276
Howard,Ryan, Phi	.267
Pena,Carlos, ChC	.266
Espinosa,Danny, Was	.252
Werth,Jayson, Was	.247
Bruce,Jay, Cin	.238
Uggla,Dan, Atl	.232
Fowler,Dexter, Col	.231
Kemp,Matt, LAD	.231

Lowest Strikeout per PA
(minimum 502 PA)

Reyes,Jose, NYM	.070
Polanco,Placido, Phi	.084
Molina,Yadier, StL	.085
Prado,Martin, Atl	.088
Pujols,Albert, StL	.089
Lee,Carlos, Hou	.092
Rollins,Jimmy, Phi	.094
Infante,Omar, Fla	.105
Betancourt,Yuniesky, Mil	.108
Victorino,Shane, Phi	.108

Home Runs At Home

Fielder,Prince, Mil	24
Upton,Justin, Ari	20
Kemp,Matt, LAD	19
Uggla,Dan, Atl	18
Hart,Corey, Mil	17
Howard,Ryan, Phi	17
Tulowitzki,Troy, Col	17
5 tied with	16

Home Runs Away

Berkman,Lance, StL	22
Pujols,Albert, StL	21
Kemp,Matt, LAD	20
Morse,Michael, Was	20
Stanton,Mike, Fla	18
Uggla,Dan, Atl	18
Braun,Ryan, Mil	17
Pence,Hunter, Hou-Phi	17
5 tied with	16

Longest Avg Home Run
(min 10 over the wall)

Upton,Justin, Ari	424
Stanton,Mike, Fla	417
Gonzalez,Carlos, Col	414
Duda,Lucas, NYM	413
Freeman,Freddie, Atl	413
Morse,Michael, Was	413
Rasmus,Colby, StL	412
Kemp,Matt, LAD	412
Uggla,Dan, Atl	411
Smith,Seth, Col	411

Shortest Avg Home Run
(min 10 over the wall)

Downs,Matt, Hou	371
Lee,Carlos, Hou	376
Barmes,Clint, Hou	377
Rollins,Jimmy, Phi	382
Utley,Chase, Phi	382
Hinske,Eric, Atl	384
Roberts,Ryan, Ari	384
Barajas,Rod, LAD	385
Freese,David, StL	386
2 tied with	387

2011 National League Batting Leaders

Under Age 26: AB Per HR

(minimum 502 PA)

Stanton,Mike, Fla	15.2
Bruce,Jay, Cin	18.3
Gonzalez,Carlos, Col	18.5
Upton,Justin, Ari	19.1
Morrison,Logan, Fla	20.1
McCutchen,Andrew, Pit	24.9
Freeman,Freddie, Atl	27.2
Espinosa,Danny, Was	27.3
Maybin,Cameron, SD	57.3
Castro,Starlin, ChC	67.4

Under Age 26: OPS

(minimum 502 PA)

Upton,Justin, Ari	.898
Stanton,Mike, Fla	.893
Gonzalez,Carlos, Col	.889
McCutchen,Andrew, Pit	.820
Bruce,Jay, Cin	.814
Morrison,Logan, Fla	.797
Fowler,Dexter, Col	.796
Freeman,Freddie, Atl	.795
Castro,Starlin, ChC	.773
Espinosa,Danny, Was	.737

Under Age 26: RC/27 Outs

(minimum 502 PA)

Gonzalez,Carlos, Col	7.1
Upton,Justin, Ari	6.3
McCutchen,Andrew, Pit	6.1
Bruce,Jay, Cin	5.7
Fowler,Dexter, Col	5.7
Stanton,Mike, Fla	5.4
Castro,Starlin, ChC	5.0
Freeman,Freddie, Atl	4.9
Espinosa,Danny, Was	4.9
Maybin,Cameron, SD	4.7

Longest Home Run

Fielder,Prince, Mil, 4/29	486
Francisco,Juan, Cin, 9/12	482
Upton,Justin, Ari, 4/12	478
Stanton,Mike, Fla, 8/15	474
Smith,Seth, Col, 8/23	472
Fielder,Prince, Mil, 7/30	471
Howard,Ryan, Phi, 5/13	470
Johnson,Kelly, Ari, 5/24	466
Morse,Michael, Was, 8/9	466
Stanton,Mike, Fla, 8/17	466

Swing and Miss %

(minimum 1500 Pitches Seen)

Stanton,Mike, Fla	34.5
Howard,Ryan, Phi	33.4
Pena,Carlos, ChC	31.4
Johnson,Kelly, Ari	29.6
Soto,Geovany, ChC	29.6
Hart,Corey, Mil	28.9
Stubbs,Drew, Cin	28.6
Maybin,Cameron, SD	28.0
Ankiel,Rick, Was	27.8
Kemp,Matt, LAD	27.7

Highest First Swing %

(minimum 502 PA)

Molina,Yadier, StL	40.7
Ramirez,Aramis, ChC	40.6
Freeman,Freddie, Atl	40.1
Buck,John, Fla	38.6
Montero,Miguel, Ari	38.1
Ludwick,Ryan, SD-Pit	36.8
Berkman,Lance, StL	36.1
Betancourt,Yuniesky, Mil	36.0
Morse,Michael, Was	35.4
Pena,Carlos, ChC	34.7

Lowest First Swing %

(minimum 502 PA)

Carroll,Jamey, LAD	6.9
Prado,Martin, Atl	9.8
Barney,Darwin, ChC	12.9
Victorino,Shane, Phi	13.9
Werth,Jayson, Was	13.9
Polanco,Placido, Phi	15.1
Bonifacio,Emilio, Fla	15.4
Morrison,Logan, Fla	15.9
Ibanez,Raul, Phi	16.0
Pujols,Albert, StL	17.1

Home RC Per 27 Outs

(minimum 251 PA)

Braun,Ryan, Mil	10.5
Gonzalez,Carlos, Col	9.9
Upton,Justin, Ari	8.7
Fielder,Prince, Mil	8.6
Kemp,Matt, LAD	8.4
Ramirez,Aramis, ChC	8.1
Hart,Corey, Mil	7.9
Pence,Hunter, Hou-Phi	7.7
Reyes,Jose, NYM	7.6
Tulowitzki,Troy, Col	7.6

Road RC Per 27 Outs

(minimum 251 PA)

Votto,Joey, Cin	9.2
Berkman,Lance, StL	8.6
Morse,Michael, Was	7.9
Kemp,Matt, LAD	7.3
Holliday,Matt, StL	7.0
McCutchen,Andrew, Pit	6.9
Braun,Ryan, Mil	6.8
Fielder,Prince, Mil	6.7
Beltran,Carlos, NYM-SF	6.5
Carroll,Jamey, LAD	6.4

2011 American League Pitching Leaders

Earned Run Average
(minimum 162 IP)

Verlander,Justin, Det	2.40
Weaver,Jered, LAA	2.41
Shields,James, TB	2.82
Fister,Doug, Sea-Det	2.83
Beckett,Josh, Bos	2.89
Romero,Ricky, Tor	2.92
Wilson,C.J., Tex	2.94
Hellickson,Jeremy, TB	2.95
Sabathia,CC, NYY	3.00
Gonzalez,Gio, Oak	3.12

Winning Percentage
(minimum 15 Decisions)

Verlander,Justin, Det	.828
Nova,Ivan, NYY	.800
Holland,Derek, Tex	.762
Sabathia,CC, NYY	.704
Wilson,C.J., Tex	.696
Weaver,Jered, LAA	.692
Beckett,Josh, Bos	.650
Tomlin,Josh, Cle	.632
Lester,Jon, Bos	.625
Scherzer,Max, Det	.625

Opponent Batting Average
(minimum 162 IP)

Verlander,Justin, Det	.192
Hellickson,Jeremy, TB	.210
Beckett,Josh, Bos	.211
Pineda,Michael, Sea	.211
Weaver,Jered, LAA	.212
Romero,Ricky, Tor	.216
Shields,James, TB	.217
Price,David, TB	.230
Gonzalez,Gio, Oak	.230
Wilson,C.J., Tex	.232

Baserunners Per 9 IP
(minimum 162 IP)

Verlander,Justin, Det	8.39
Weaver,Jered, LAA	9.20
Haren,Dan, LAA	9.40
Shields,James, TB	9.57
Beckett,Josh, Bos	9.65
Tomlin,Josh, Cle	9.85
Fister,Doug, Sea-Det	10.07
Pineda,Michael, Sea	10.16
McCarthy,Brandon, Oak	10.18
Hellickson,Jeremy, TB	10.57

Games

Valverde,Jose, Det	75
Peralta,Joel, TB	71
Perez,Rafael, Cle	71
Smith,Joe, Cle	71
Bard,Daniel, Bos	70
Robertson,David, NYY	70
Capps,Matt, Min	69
Johnson,Jim, Bal	69
Sipp,Tony, Cle	69
2 tied with	68

Games Started

Cahill,Trevor, Oak	34
Haren,Dan, LAA	34
Price,David, TB	34
Verlander,Justin, Det	34
Wilson,C.J., Tex	34
8 tied with	33

Complete Games

Shields,James, TB	11
Hernandez,Felix, Sea	5
McCarthy,Brandon, Oak	5
Haren,Dan, LAA	4
Holland,Derek, Tex	4
Romero,Ricky, Tor	4
Santana,Ervin, LAA	4
Vargas,Jason, Sea	4
Verlander,Justin, Det	4
Weaver,Jered, LAA	4

Shutouts

Holland,Derek, Tex	4
Shields,James, TB	4
Haren,Dan, LAA	3
Vargas,Jason, Sea	3
Romero,Ricky, Tor	2
Verlander,Justin, Det	2
Weaver,Jered, LAA	2
19 tied with	1

Wins

Verlander,Justin, Det	24
Sabathia,CC, NYY	19
Weaver,Jered, LAA	18
Gonzalez,Gio, Oak	16
Haren,Dan, LAA	16
Holland,Derek, Tex	16
Nova,Ivan, NYY	16
Shields,James, TB	16
Wilson,C.J., Tex	16
3 tied with	15

Losses

Guthrie,Jeremy, Bal	17
Francis,Jeff, KC	16
Carmona,Fausto, Cle	15
Cahill,Trevor, Oak	14
Duensing,Brian, Min	14
Hernandez,Felix, Sea	14
5 tied with	13

No Decisions

Holland,Derek, Tex	11
Masterson,Justin, Cle	11
Pavano,Carl, Min	11
Wilson,C.J., Tex	11
7 tied with	10

Wild Pitches

Burnett,A.J., NYY	25
Cahill,Trevor, Oak	15
Wakefield,Tim, Bos	15
Floyd,Gavin, CWS	12
Hernandez,Felix, Sea	12
Morrow,Brandon, Tor	12
Porcello,Rick, Det	12
Scherzer,Max, Det	12
3 tied with	11

Strikeouts

Verlander,Justin, Det	250
Sabathia,CC, NYY	230
Shields,James, TB	225
Hernandez,Felix, Sea	222
Price,David, TB	218
Wilson,C.J., Tex	206
Morrow,Brandon, Tor	203
Weaver,Jered, LAA	198
Gonzalez,Gio, Oak	197
Haren,Dan, LAA	192

Walks Allowed

Gonzalez,Gio, Oak	91
Burnett,A.J., NYY	83
Cahill,Trevor, Oak	82
Romero,Ricky, Tor	80
Lester,Jon, Bos	75
Liriano,Francisco, Min	75
Wilson,C.J., Tex	74
Hellickson,Jeremy, TB	72
Santana,Ervin, LAA	72
Chatwood,Tyler, LAA	71

Intentional Walks Allowed

Camp,Shawn, Tor	9
Hellickson,Jeremy, TB	8
Ramos,Cesar, TB	8
Takahashi,Hisanori, LAA	8
Wood,Blake, KC	7
Coleman,Louis, KC	6
Robertson,David, NYY	6
Simon,Alfredo, Bal	6
15 tied with	5

Hit Batters

Lackey,John, Bos	19
Aceves,Alfredo, Bos	15
Carmona,Fausto, Cle	14
Romero,Ricky, Tor	14
Fister,Doug, Sea-Det	12
Morrow,Brandon, Tor	12
Floyd,Gavin, CWS	11
Lester,Jon, Bos	11
Masterson,Justin, Cle	11
Wilson,C.J., Tex	10

2011 American League Pitching Leaders

Runs Allowed		Hits Allowed		Doubles Allowed		Home Runs Allowed	
Carmona,Fausto, Cle	125	Pavano,Carl, Min	262	Guthrie,Jeremy, Bal	55	Lewis,Colby, Tex	35
Pavano,Carl, Min	123	Sabathia,CC, NYY	230	Carmona,Fausto, Cle	52	Burnett,A.J., NYY	31
Lackey,John, Bos	119	Francis,Jeff, KC	224	Haren,Dan, LAA	51	Scherzer,Max, Det	29
Penny,Brad, Det	117	Penny,Brad, Det	222	Pavano,Carl, Min	49	Guthrie,Jeremy, Bal	26
Burnett,A.J., NYY	115	Buehrle,Mark, CWS	221	Burnett,A.J., NYY	48	Romero,Ricky, Tor	26
Guthrie,Jeremy, Bal	113	Hernandez,Felix, Sea	218	Francis,Jeff, KC	47	Santana,Ervin, LAA	26
Hochevar,Luke, KC	110	Cahill,Trevor, Oak	214	Penny,Brad, Det	45	Shields,James, TB	26
Wakefield,Tim, Bos	110	Guthrie,Jeremy, Bal	213	Wakefield,Tim, Bos	45	Wakefield,Tim, Bos	25
Vargas,Jason, Sea	105	Haren,Dan, LAA	211	Duensing,Brian, Min	44	3 tied with	24
3 tied with	103	Masterson,Justin, Cle	211	Hochevar,Luke, KC	44		

Run Support Per Nine IP		% Pitches In Strike Zone		Pitches Per Start		Pitches Per Batter	
(minimum 162 IP)		(minimum 162 IP)		(minimum 30 GS)		(minimum 162 IP)	
Holland,Derek, Tex	7.64	McCarthy,Brandon, Oak	49.9	Verlander,Justin, Det	115.9	Pavano,Carl, Min	3.54
Lester,Jon, Bos	6.86	Tomlin,Josh, Cle	47.9	Weaver,Jered, LAA	113.5	Tomlin,Josh, Cle	3.58
Nova,Ivan, NYY	6.70	Masterson,Justin, Cle	47.3	Haren,Dan, LAA	110.6	McCarthy,Brandon, Oak	3.62
Scherzer,Max, Det	6.42	Danks,John, CWS	47.0	Hernandez,Felix, Sea	109.4	Carmona,Fausto, Cle	3.63
Porcello,Rick, Det	6.38	Vargas,Jason, Sea	46.6	Sabathia,CC, NYY	109.2	Santana,Ervin, LAA	3.64
Lewis,Colby, Tex	6.15	Pineda,Michael, Sea	46.1	Price,David, TB	108.7	Nova,Ivan, NYY	3.64
Sabathia,CC, NYY	5.95	Holland,Derek, Tex	45.9	Shields,James, TB	108.4	Porcello,Rick, Det	3.65
Tomlin,Josh, Cle	5.77	Shields,James, TB	45.8	Gonzalez,Gio, Oak	106.5	Fister,Doug, Sea-Det	3.65
Ogando,Alexi, Tex	5.70	Humber,Philip, CWS	45.1	Wilson,C.J., Tex	105.6	Sabathia,CC, NYY	3.66
Burnett,A.J., NYY	5.44	Hochevar,Luke, KC	45.0	Romero,Ricky, Tor	105.4	Colon,Bartolo, NYY	3.66

Quality Starts		Batters Faced		Innings Pitched		Most Pitches in a Game	
Verlander,Justin, Det	28	Sabathia,CC, NYY	985	Verlander,Justin, Det	251.0	Verlander,Justin, Det	132
Weaver,Jered, LAA	28	Shields,James, TB	975	Shields,James, TB	249.1	Moscoso,Guillermo, Oak	129
Haren,Dan, LAA	26	Verlander,Justin, Det	969	Haren,Dan, LAA	238.1	Santana,Ervin, LAA	129
Romero,Ricky, Tor	25	Hernandez,Felix, Sea	964	Sabathia,CC, NYY	237.1	Verlander,Justin, Det	129
Shields,James, TB	25	Pavano,Carl, Min	955	Weaver,Jered, LAA	235.2	Wilson,C.J., Tex	129
Wilson,C.J., Tex	23	Haren,Dan, LAA	953	Hernandez,Felix, Sea	233.2	Hernandez,Felix, Sea	128
Buehrle,Mark, CWS	22	Santana,Ervin, LAA	949	Santana,Ervin, LAA	228.2	Sabathia,CC, NYY	128
Hernandez,Felix, Sea	22	Weaver,Jered, LAA	926	Romero,Ricky, Tor	225.0	Weaver,Jered, LAA	128
Masterson,Justin, Cle	22	Price,David, TB	918	Price,David, TB	224.1	Weaver,Jered, LAA	128
Sabathia,CC, NYY	22	Romero,Ricky, Tor	917	Wilson,C.J., Tex	223.1	8 tied with	127

Stolen Bases Allowed		Caught Stealing Off		Stolen Base Pct Allowed		Pickoffs	
				(minimum 162 IP)			
Lackey,John, Bos	33	Masterson,Justin, Cle	14	Buehrle,Mark, CWS	30.0	Shields,James, TB	13
Beckett,Josh, Bos	31	Lester,Jon, Bos	12	Davis,Wade, TB	33.3	Danks,John, CWS	7
Hernandez,Felix, Sea	31	Pineda,Michael, Sea	10	Guthrie,Jeremy, Bal	33.3	Duffy,Danny, KC	7
Cahill,Trevor, Oak	28	Blackburn,Nick, Min	9	Ogando,Alexi, Tex	40.0	Buehrle,Mark, CWS	6
Santana,Ervin, LAA	28	Duffy,Danny, KC	9	Holland,Derek, Tex	43.8	Romero,Ricky, Tor	6
Burnett,A.J., NYY	24	Holland,Derek, Tex	9	Harrison,Matt, Tex	50.0	Weaver,Jered, LAA	6
Pavano,Carl, Min	24	Scherzer,Max, Det	9	Masterson,Justin, Cle	50.0	Anderson,Brett, Oak	5
Wilson,C.J., Tex	24	Wakefield,Tim, Bos	9	Pineda,Michael, Sea	50.0	Breslow,Craig, Oak	5
Floyd,Gavin, CWS	23	5 tied with	8	Lester,Jon, Bos	53.8	Burnett,A.J., NYY	5
Garcia,Freddy, NYY	22			Shields,James, TB	54.5	Holland,Derek, Tex	5

2011 American League Pitching Leaders

Strikeouts Per 9 IP	
(minimum 162 IP)	
Morrow,Brandon, Tor	10.19
Pineda,Michael, Sea	9.11
Verlander,Justin, Det	8.96
Gonzalez,Gio, Oak	8.78
Price,David, TB	8.75
Sabathia,CC, NYY	8.72
Hernandez,Felix, Sea	8.55
Lester,Jon, Bos	8.55
Wilson,C.J., Tex	8.30
Burnett,A.J., NYY	8.18

Opp On-Base Percentage	
(minimum 162 IP)	
Verlander,Justin, Det	.242
Weaver,Jered, LAA	.262
Haren,Dan, LAA	.265
Beckett,Josh, Bos	.273
Shields,James, TB	.273
Tomlin,Josh, Cle	.274
Fister,Doug, Sea-Det	.278
Pineda,Michael, Sea	.279
McCarthy,Brandon, Oak	.281
Hellickson,Jeremy, TB	.287

Opp Slugging Average	
(minimum 162 IP)	
Verlander,Justin, Det	.313
Beckett,Josh, Bos	.335
Gonzalez,Gio, Oak	.336
Weaver,Jered, LAA	.336
Fister,Doug, Sea-Det	.339
Pineda,Michael, Sea	.342
Masterson,Justin, Cle	.349
Wilson,C.J., Tex	.350
Shields,James, TB	.350
Hernandez,Felix, Sea	.356

Opponent OPS	
(minimum 162 IP)	
Verlander,Justin, Det	.555
Weaver,Jered, LAA	.598
Beckett,Josh, Bos	.608
Fister,Doug, Sea-Det	.617
Pineda,Michael, Sea	.621
Shields,James, TB	.623
Haren,Dan, LAA	.630
Ogando,Alexi, Tex	.649
Humber,Philip, CWS	.651
Wilson,C.J., Tex	.651

Home Runs Per Nine IP	
(minimum 162 IP)	
Fister,Doug, Sea-Det	0.46
Masterson,Justin, Cle	0.46
McCarthy,Brandon, Oak	0.58
Harrison,Matt, Tex	0.63
Sabathia,CC, NYY	0.64
Wilson,C.J., Tex	0.64
Nova,Ivan, NYY	0.71
Hernandez,Felix, Sea	0.73
Haren,Dan, LAA	0.76
Gonzalez,Gio, Oak	0.76

Batting Average vs. LHB	
(minimum 125 BF)	
Papelbon,Jonathan, Bos	.156
Robertson,David, NYY	.156
Price,David, TB	.171
Verlander,Justin, Det	.174
Cecil,Brett, Tor	.186
Beckett,Josh, Bos	.186
Feliz,Neftali, Tex	.189
Aceves,Alfredo, Bos	.190
Pauley,David, Sea-Det	.194
Perez,Chris, Cle	.198

Batting Average vs. RHB	
(minimum 225 BF)	
Pineda,Michael, Sea	.184
Hellickson,Jeremy, TB	.188
Romero,Ricky, Tor	.194
Moscoso,Guillermo, Oak	.197
Ogando,Alexi, Tex	.202
Humber,Philip, CWS	.203
Lewis,Colby, Tex	.204
Weaver,Jered, LAA	.208
Masterson,Justin, Cle	.210
Floyd,Gavin, CWS	.211

Opp BA w/ RISP	
(minimum 125 BF)	
Aceves,Alfredo, Bos	.165
Hellickson,Jeremy, TB	.167
Romero,Ricky, Tor	.171
Gonzalez,Gio, Oak	.182
Scherzer,Max, Det	.188
Garcia,Freddy, NYY	.193
Beckett,Josh, Bos	.193
Jackson,Edwin, CWS	.203
Verlander,Justin, Det	.211
Arrieta,Jake, Bal	.214

OBP vs. Leadoff Hitter	
(minimum 150 BF)	
Verlander,Justin, Det	.228
Vargas,Jason, Sea	.251
Pineda,Michael, Sea	.251
Weaver,Jered, LAA	.253
Tomlin,Josh, Cle	.257
Shields,James, TB	.260
Santana,Ervin, LAA	.266
Haren,Dan, LAA	.270
Wilson,C.J., Tex	.276
Colon,Bartolo, NYY	.279

Strikeouts / Walks Ratio	
(minimum 162 IP)	
Haren,Dan, LAA	5.82
McCarthy,Brandon, Oak	4.92
Verlander,Justin, Det	4.39
Tomlin,Josh, Cle	4.24
Fister,Doug, Sea-Det	3.95
Sabathia,CC, NYY	3.77
Weaver,Jered, LAA	3.54
Shields,James, TB	3.46
Price,David, TB	3.46
Colon,Bartolo, NYY	3.38

Highest GB/FB Ratio	
(minimum 162 IP)	
Cahill,Trevor, Oak	2.21
Masterson,Justin, Cle	2.06
Carmona,Fausto, Cle	2.06
Nova,Ivan, NYY	1.83
Romero,Ricky, Tor	1.76
Porcello,Rick, Det	1.73
Hernandez,Felix, Sea	1.64
Pavano,Carl, Min	1.63
Hochevar,Luke, KC	1.55
Wilson,C.J., Tex	1.55

Lowest GB/FB Ratio	
(minimum 162 IP)	
Weaver,Jered, LAA	0.67
Lewis,Colby, Tex	0.70
Hellickson,Jeremy, TB	0.78
Pineda,Michael, Sea	0.81
Vargas,Jason, Sea	0.83
Davis,Wade, TB	0.85
Morrow,Brandon, Tor	0.87
Ogando,Alexi, Tex	0.91
Beckett,Josh, Bos	0.95
Tomlin,Josh, Cle	0.95

Sacrifice Flies Allowed	
Burnett,A.J., NYY	10
Guthrie,Jeremy, Bal	10
Fister,Doug, Sea-Det	9
McCarthy,Brandon, Oak	9
Morrow,Brandon, Tor	9
Pavano,Carl, Min	9
Floyd,Gavin, CWS	8
Francis,Jeff, KC	8
Wakefield,Tim, Bos	8
12 tied with	7

Sacrifice Hits Allowed	
Haren,Dan, LAA	12
Carmona,Fausto, Cle	9
Beckett,Josh, Bos	8
Britton,Zach, Bal	8
Cahill,Trevor, Oak	8
Harrison,Matt, Tex	8
Sabathia,CC, NYY	8
4 tied with	7

GIDP Induced	
Wilson,C.J., Tex	31
Harrison,Matt, Tex	30
Romero,Ricky, Tor	28
Chatwood,Tyler, LAA	26
Britton,Zach, Bal	25
Hernandez,Felix, Sea	25
Penny,Brad, Det	25
Sabathia,CC, NYY	24
Pineiro,Joel, LAA	23
Porcello,Rick, Det	23

GIDP Per Nine IP	
(minimum 162 IP)	
Harrison,Matt, Tex	1.45
Wilson,C.J., Tex	1.25
Penny,Brad, Det	1.24
Porcello,Rick, Det	1.14
Romero,Ricky, Tor	1.12
Hernandez,Felix, Sea	0.96
Holland,Derek, Tex	0.95
Sabathia,CC, NYY	0.91
Guthrie,Jeremy, Bal	0.91
Nova,Ivan, NYY	0.87

2011 American League Pitching Leaders

Saves

Valverde,Jose, Det	49
Rivera,Mariano, NYY	44
League,Brandon, Sea	37
Perez,Chris, Cle	36
Feliz,Neftali, Tex	32
Walden,Jordan, LAA	32
Papelbon,Jonathan, Bos	31
Santos,Sergio, CWS	30
Soria,Joakim, KC	28
Farnsworth,Kyle, TB	25

Blown Saves

Walden,Jordan, LAA	10
Capps,Matt, Min	9
Crow,Aaron, KC	7
Gregg,Kevin, Bal	7
Soria,Joakim, KC	7
Crain,Jesse, CWS	6
Farnsworth,Kyle, TB	6
Feliz,Neftali, Tex	6
Santos,Sergio, CWS	6
7 tied with	5

Save Pct
(minimum 20 Save Ops)

Valverde,Jose, Det	100.0
Bailey,Andrew, Oak	92.3
Papelbon,Jonathan, Bos	91.2
Perez,Chris, Cle	90.0
Rivera,Mariano, NYY	89.8
League,Brandon, Sea	88.1
Feliz,Neftali, Tex	84.2
Santos,Sergio, CWS	83.3
Francisco,Frank, Tor	81.0
Farnsworth,Kyle, TB	80.6

Save Opportunities

Rivera,Mariano, NYY	49
Valverde,Jose, Det	49
League,Brandon, Sea	42
Walden,Jordan, LAA	42
Perez,Chris, Cle	40
Feliz,Neftali, Tex	38
Santos,Sergio, CWS	36
Soria,Joakim, KC	35
Papelbon,Jonathan, Bos	34
Farnsworth,Kyle, TB	31

Easy Saves

Valverde,Jose, Det	33
Rivera,Mariano, NYY	29
Papelbon,Jonathan, Bos	22
Feliz,Neftali, Tex	21
League,Brandon, Sea	18
Soria,Joakim, KC	18
Walden,Jordan, LAA	18
Perez,Chris, Cle	17
Bailey,Andrew, Oak	16
Santos,Sergio, CWS	16

Regular Saves

League,Brandon, Sea	19
Perez,Chris, Cle	18
Valverde,Jose, Det	16
Walden,Jordan, LAA	14
Rivera,Mariano, NYY	13
Farnsworth,Kyle, TB	12
Feliz,Neftali, Tex	11
Gregg,Kevin, Bal	11
Santos,Sergio, CWS	10
Soria,Joakim, KC	10

Tough Saves

Santos,Sergio, CWS	4
Sale,Chris, CWS	3
Fuentes,Brian, Oak	2
Perkins,Glen, Min	2
Rivera,Mariano, NYY	2
11 tied with	1

Holds Adjusted Save %
(minimum 20 Save Ops)

Valverde,Jose, Det	100.0
Bailey,Andrew, Oak	92.6
Papelbon,Jonathan, Bos	91.2
Perez,Chris, Cle	90.0
Rivera,Mariano, NYY	89.8
League,Brandon, Sea	88.1
Feliz,Neftali, Tex	84.2
Santos,Sergio, CWS	84.2
Francisco,Frank, Tor	82.6
Farnsworth,Kyle, TB	80.6

Relief Wins

Aceves,Alfredo, Bos	9
Crain,Jesse, CWS	8
Alburquerque,Al, Det	6
Camp,Shawn, Tor	6
Downs,Scott, LAA	6
Janssen,Casey, Tor	6
Johnson,Jim, Bal	6
Sipp,Tony, Cle	6
Wade,Cory, NYY	6
13 tied with	5

Relief Losses

Bard,Daniel, Bos	9
Fuentes,Brian, Oak	8
Capps,Matt, Min	7
Perez,Chris, Cle	7
Pauley,David, Sea-Det	6
9 tied with	5

Relief Games

Valverde,Jose, Det	75
Peralta,Joel, TB	71
Perez,Rafael, Cle	71
Smith,Joe, Cle	71
Bard,Daniel, Bos	70
Robertson,David, NYY	70
Capps,Matt, Min	69
Johnson,Jim, Bal	69
Sipp,Tony, Cle	69
2 tied with	68

Holds

Bard,Daniel, Bos	34
Robertson,David, NYY	34
Benoit,Joaquin, Det	29
Balfour,Grant, Oak	26
Downs,Scott, LAA	26
Crain,Jesse, CWS	24
Sipp,Tony, Cle	24
Pestano,Vinnie, Cle	23
Soriano,Rafael, NYY	23
Uehara,Koji, Bal-Tex	22

Relief Innings

Aceves,Alfredo, Bos	93.0
Johnson,Jim, Bal	91.0
Pauley,David, Sea-Det	74.0
Bard,Daniel, Bos	73.0
Valverde,Jose, Det	72.1
Sale,Chris, CWS	71.0
Wood,Blake, KC	69.2
Durbin,Chad, Cle	68.1
Wright,Jamey, Sea	68.1
Takahashi,Hisanori, LAA	68.0

Inherited Runners Scrd %
(minimum 30 IR)

Holland,Greg, KC	6.1
Alburquerque,Al, Det	9.7
Coleman,Louis, KC	12.8
Bard,Daniel, Bos	14.7
Dotel,Octavio, Tor	15.6
Perez,Rafael, Cle	15.9
Burnett,Alex, Min	16.1
Sale,Chris, CWS	18.4
Lowe,Mark, Tex	18.8
Cruz,Juan, TB	20.0

Relief Opp On Base Pct
(minimum 50 IP)

Uehara,Koji, Bal-Tex	.194
Peralta,Joel, TB	.244
Holland,Greg, KC	.246
Rivera,Mariano, NYY	.247
Papelbon,Jonathan, Bos	.247
Downs,Scott, LAA	.254
Bard,Daniel, Bos	.254
Farnsworth,Kyle, TB	.261
Balfour,Grant, Oak	.266
Pestano,Vinnie, Cle	.272

Relief Opp Slugging Avg
(minimum 50 IP)

Robertson,David, NYY	.226
Smith,Joe, Cle	.258
Holland,Greg, KC	.275
Valverde,Jose, Det	.282
Downs,Scott, LAA	.286
Rivera,Mariano, NYY	.288
Bard,Daniel, Bos	.292
Papelbon,Jonathan, Bos	.299
Pestano,Vinnie, Cle	.305
Benoit,Joaquin, Det	.306

2011 American League Pitching Leaders

Relief Opp BA Vs LHB (minimum 50 AB)	
Uehara,Koji, Bal-Tex	.130
Smith,Joe, Cle	.152
Swarzak,Anthony, Min	.154
Peralta,Joel, TB	.155
Papelbon,Jonathan, Bos	.156
Robertson,David, NYY	.156
Rzepczynski,Marc, Tor	.159
McGee,Jake, TB	.164
Cruz,Juan, TB	.171
De Los Santos,F., Oak	.173

Relief Opp BA Vs RHB (minimum 50 AB)	
Alburquerque,Al, Det	.113
Pestano,Vinnie, Cle	.115
Villanueva,Carlos, Tor	.123
Santos,Sergio, CWS	.130
Bard,Daniel, Bos	.136
Valverde,Jose, Det	.158
Dotel,Octavio, Tor	.159
Holland,Greg, KC	.171
Soriano,Rafael, NYY	.173
Crow,Aaron, KC	.175

Relief Opp Batting Average (minimum 50 IP)	
Uehara,Koji, Bal-Tex	.164
Robertson,David, NYY	.170
Holland,Greg, KC	.175
Bard,Daniel, Bos	.179
Santos,Sergio, CWS	.181
Pestano,Vinnie, Cle	.184
Peralta,Joel, TB	.188
Aceves,Alfredo, Bos	.193
Feliz,Neftali, Tex	.194
Valverde,Jose, Det	.198

Relief Earned Run Average (minimum 50 IP)	
Robertson,David, NYY	1.08
Downs,Scott, LAA	1.34
Holland,Greg, KC	1.80
Rivera,Mariano, NYY	1.91
Smith,Joe, Cle	2.01
Aceves,Alfredo, Bos	2.03
Ayala,Luis, NYY	2.09
Farnsworth,Kyle, TB	2.18
Valverde,Jose, Det	2.24
Janssen,Casey, Tor	2.26

Rel OBP 1st Batter Faced (minimum 40 BF)	
Peralta,Joel, TB	.099
Wheeler,Dan, Bos	.149
Benoit,Joaquin, Det	.152
Bailey,Andrew, Oak	.167
Farnsworth,Kyle, TB	.175
Downs,Scott, LAA	.200
Wade,Cory, NYY	.200
Santos,Sergio, CWS	.210
Rauch,Jon, Tor	.212
Uehara,Koji, Bal-Tex	.215

Rel Opp BA w/ Runners On (minimum 50 IP)	
Uehara,Koji, Bal-Tex	.128
Holland,Greg, KC	.144
Balfour,Grant, Oak	.151
Robertson,David, NYY	.153
Bard,Daniel, Bos	.157
Coleman,Louis, KC	.158
Crain,Jesse, CWS	.165
Valverde,Jose, Det	.172
Aceves,Alfredo, Bos	.172
Sale,Chris, CWS	.179

Relief Opp BA w/ RISP (minimum 50 IP)	
Balfour,Grant, Oak	.125
Holland,Greg, KC	.125
Downs,Scott, LAA	.127
Aceves,Alfredo, Bos	.130
Uehara,Koji, Bal-Tex	.140
Robertson,David, NYY	.141
Coleman,Louis, KC	.152
Collins,Tim, KC	.164
Bard,Daniel, Bos	.169
Farnsworth,Kyle, TB	.172

Fastest Avg Fastball-Relief (minimum 50 IP)	
Walden,Jordan, LAA	97.5
Bard,Daniel, Bos	97.3
League,Brandon, Sea	96.5
Feliz,Neftali, Tex	96.3
Thornton,Matt, CWS	95.8
Wood,Blake, KC	95.6
Santos,Sergio, CWS	95.3
Sale,Chris, CWS	95.3
Johnson,Jim, Bal	95.1
Papelbon,Jonathan, Bos	95.0

Fastest Average Fastball (minimum 162 IP)	
Ogando,Alexi, Tex	95.1
Verlander,Justin, Det	95.0
Price,David, TB	94.8
Pineda,Michael, Sea	94.7
Holland,Derek, Tex	94.2
Morrow,Brandon, Tor	93.9
Sabathia,CC, NYY	93.8
Hernandez,Felix, Sea	93.3
Scherzer,Max, Det	93.1
Beckett,Josh, Bos	93.1

Slowest Average Fastball (minimum 162 IP)	
Francis,Jeff, KC	84.7
Buehrle,Mark, CWS	85.6
Vargas,Jason, Sea	87.4
Tomlin,Josh, Cle	87.9
Lewis,Colby, Tex	89.0
Pavano,Carl, Min	89.0
Cahill,Trevor, Oak	89.1
Weaver,Jered, LAA	89.1
Haren,Dan, LAA	90.0
Fister,Doug, Sea-Det	90.0

Pitches 100+ Velocity	
Walden,Jordan, LAA	49
Verlander,Justin, Det	39
Feliz,Neftali, Tex	21
Bard,Daniel, Bos	12
Jeffress,Jeremy, KC	4
League,Brandon, Sea	4
Lowe,Mark, Tex	2
Pineda,Michael, Sea	2
Farnsworth,Kyle, TB	1
Rodney,Fernando, LAA	1

Pitches 95+ Velocity	
Price,David, TB	1647
Verlander,Justin, Det	1264
Ogando,Alexi, Tex	1188
Paulino,Felipe, KC	928
Pineda,Michael, Sea	911
Jackson,Edwin, CWS	880
Holland,Derek, Tex	867
Walden,Jordan, LAA	856
Thornton,Matt, CWS	811
Bard,Daniel, Bos	725

Pitches Less Than 80 MPH	
Wakefield,Tim, Bos	2379
Bedard,Erik, Sea-Bos	1588
Francis,Jeff, KC	1288
Weaver,Jered, LAA	1018
Fister,Doug, Sea-Det	958
Buehrle,Mark, CWS	807
Garcia,Freddy, NYY	739
Shields,James, TB	697
Chen,Bruce, KC	676
Furbush,Charlie, Det-Sea	656

Lowest % Fastballs (minimum 162 IP)	
Haren,Dan, LAA	34.5
Shields,James, TB	36.4
McCarthy,Brandon, Oak	42.0
Tomlin,Josh, Cle	42.3
Buehrle,Mark, CWS	45.3
Humber,Philip, CWS	45.8
Floyd,Gavin, CWS	47.2
Vargas,Jason, Sea	47.4
Danks,John, CWS	48.9
Lester,Jon, Bos	49.5

Highest % Fastballs (minimum 162 IP)	
Masterson,Justin, Cle	84.4
Colon,Bartolo, NYY	82.9
Price,David, TB	70.5
Carmona,Fausto, Cle	68.4
Davis,Wade, TB	68.3
Ogando,Alexi, Tex	67.4
Holland,Derek, Tex	66.1
Porcello,Rick, Det	65.4
Gonzalez,Gio, Oak	64.7
Harrison,Matt, Tex	64.3

Highest % Curveballs (minimum 162 IP)	
Burnett,A.J., NYY	33.2
Gonzalez,Gio, Oak	27.8
Nova,Ivan, NYY	22.4
Humber,Philip, CWS	21.6
Shields,James, TB	21.0
Floyd,Gavin, CWS	19.9
Verlander,Justin, Det	18.3
McCarthy,Brandon, Oak	17.1
Beckett,Josh, Bos	16.9
Davis,Wade, TB	16.3

2011 American League Pitching Leaders

Highest % Changeups
(minimum 162 IP)

Hellickson,Jeremy, TB	31.7
Francis,Jeff, KC	30.8
Vargas,Jason, Sea	28.0
Shields,James, TB	27.2
Pavano,Carl, Min	23.6
Buehrle,Mark, CWS	22.3
Cahill,Trevor, Oak	22.0
Hernandez,Felix, Sea	21.5
Scherzer,Max, Det	20.3
Romero,Ricky, Tor	19.8

Highest % Sliders
(minimum 162 IP)

Santana,Ervin, LAA	38.3
Pineda,Michael, Sea	31.5
Ogando,Alexi, Tex	27.7
Lewis,Colby, Tex	26.8
Morrow,Brandon, Tor	26.6
Sabathia,CC, NYY	19.7
Porcello,Rick, Det	19.5
Scherzer,Max, Det	18.3
Humber,Philip, CWS	18.0
Weaver,Jered, LAA	17.7

Balks

Aceves,Alfredo, Bos	2
Hochevar,Luke, KC	2
Howell,J.P., TB	2
James,Chuck, Min	2
Pavano,Carl, Min	2
Simon,Alfredo, Bal	2
Strop,Pedro, Tex-Bal	2
Verlander,Justin, Det	2
47 tied with	1

Strikeout/Hit Ratio
(minimum 50 IP)

Robertson,David, NYY	2.50
Santos,Sergio, CWS	2.24
Uehara,Koji, Bal-Tex	2.24
Pestano,Vinnie, Cle	2.05
Holland,Greg, KC	2.00
Papelbon,Jonathan, Bos	1.74
Bard,Daniel, Bos	1.61
Sale,Chris, CWS	1.52
Coleman,Louis, KC	1.45
Verlander,Justin, Det	1.44

Opp OPS vs Fastballs
(minimum 251 BF)

Moscoso,Guillermo, Oak	.534
Verlander,Justin, Det	.555
Beckett,Josh, Bos	.594
Weaver,Jered, LAA	.604
Wilson,C.J., Tex	.615
Fister,Doug, Sea-Det	.620
Swarzak,Anthony, Min	.621
Baker,Scott, Min	.630
Pineda,Michael, Sea	.636
Price,David, TB	.636

Opp OPS vs Curveballs
(minimum 100 BF)

Tomlin,Josh, Cle	.418
Shields,James, TB	.482
Verlander,Justin, Det	.496
Hernandez,Felix, Sea	.545
Humber,Philip, CWS	.569
McCarthy,Brandon, Oak	.617
Burnett,A.J., NYY	.629
Bedard,Erik, Sea-Bos	.656
Niemann,Jeff, TB	.675
Gonzalez,Gio, Oak	.696

Opp OPS vs Changeups
(minimum 100 BF)

Hernandez,Felix, Sea	.474
Price,David, TB	.503
Weaver,Jered, LAA	.505
Romero,Ricky, Tor	.532
Verlander,Justin, Det	.587
Hellickson,Jeremy, TB	.598
Shields,James, TB	.628
Fister,Doug, Sea-Det	.629
Pavano,Carl, Min	.635
Buehrle,Mark, CWS	.637

Opp OPS vs Sliders
(minimum 64 BF)

Alburquerque,Al, Det	.354
Holland,Greg, KC	.355
Sale,Chris, CWS	.373
Perkins,Glen, Min	.403
Crow,Aaron, KC	.477
Hochevar,Luke, KC	.480
Coleman,Louis, KC	.512
Santos,Sergio, CWS	.524
O'Sullivan,Sean, KC	.531
Coke,Phil, Det	.539

Earned Runs

Lackey,John, Bos	114
Carmona,Fausto, Cle	110
Burnett,A.J., NYY	109
Penny,Brad, Det	107
Pavano,Carl, Min	106
Hochevar,Luke, KC	103
Guthrie,Jeremy, Bal	100
Francis,Jeff, KC	98
Lewis,Colby, Tex	98
3 tied with	96

Hits Per Nine Innings
(minimum 162 IP)

Verlander,Justin, Det	6.24
Beckett,Josh, Bos	6.81
Hellickson,Jeremy, TB	6.95
Weaver,Jered, LAA	6.95
Pineda,Michael, Sea	7.00
Romero,Ricky, Tor	7.04
Shields,James, TB	7.04
Price,David, TB	7.70
Wilson,C.J., Tex	7.70
Lester,Jon, Bos	7.79

2011 National League Pitching Leaders

Earned Run Average
(minimum 162 IP)

Kershaw,Clayton, LAD	2.28
Halladay,Roy, Phi	2.35
Lee,Cliff, Phi	2.40
Vogelsong,Ryan, SF	2.71
Lincecum,Tim, SF	2.74
Hamels,Cole, Phi	2.79
Kennedy,Ian, Ari	2.88
Cain,Matt, SF	2.88
Kuroda,Hiroki, LAD	3.07
Bumgarner,Madison, SF	3.21

Winning Percentage
(minimum 15 Decisions)

Kennedy,Ian, Ari	.840
Kershaw,Clayton, LAD	.808
Halladay,Roy, Phi	.760
Greinke,Zack, Mil	.727
Gee,Dillon, NYM	.684
Jurrjens,Jair, Atl	.684
Lee,Cliff, Phi	.680
Harang,Aaron, SD	.667
3 tied with	.650

Opponent Batting Average
(minimum 162 IP)

Kershaw,Clayton, LAD	.207
Hamels,Cole, Phi	.214
Cain,Matt, SF	.217
Lincecum,Tim, SF	.222
Kennedy,Ian, Ari	.227
Lee,Cliff, Phi	.229
Chacin,Jhoulys, Col	.231
Marcum,Shaun, Mil	.232
Latos,Mat, SD	.233
Hudson,Tim, Atl	.236

Baserunners Per 9 IP
(minimum 162 IP)

Kershaw,Clayton, LAD	8.91
Hamels,Cole, Phi	9.08
Lee,Cliff, Phi	9.48
Halladay,Roy, Phi	9.51
Cain,Matt, SF	10.11
Kennedy,Ian, Ari	10.14
Marcum,Shaun, Mil	10.41
Lohse,Kyle, StL	10.66
Latos,Mat, SD	10.70
Vazquez,Javier, Fla	10.74

Games

Venters,Jonny, Atl	85
Bray,Bill, Cin	79
Kimbrel,Craig, Atl	79
Veras,Jose, Pit	79
Marshall,Sean, ChC	78
Motte,Jason, StL	78
O'Flaherty,Eric, Atl	78
Qualls,Chad, SD	77
Resop,Chris, Pit	76
3 tied with	75

Games Started

Carpenter,Chris, StL	34
Dempster,Ryan, ChC	34
Lowe,Derek, Atl	34
17 tied with	33

Complete Games

Halladay,Roy, Phi	8
Lee,Cliff, Phi	6
Kershaw,Clayton, LAD	5
Carpenter,Chris, StL	4
Cueto,Johnny, Cin	3
Hamels,Cole, Phi	3
Hudson,Daniel, Ari	3
Sanchez,Anibal, Fla	3
11 tied with	2

Shutouts

Lee,Cliff, Phi	6
Carpenter,Chris, StL	2
Garcia,Jaime, StL	2
Kershaw,Clayton, LAD	2
Sanchez,Anibal, Fla	2
22 tied with	1

Wins

Kennedy,Ian, Ari	21
Kershaw,Clayton, LAD	21
Halladay,Roy, Phi	19
Gallardo,Yovani, Mil	17
Lee,Cliff, Phi	17
Greinke,Zack, Mil	16
Hudson,Daniel, Ari	16
Hudson,Tim, Atl	16
3 tied with	14

Losses

Lowe,Derek, Atl	17
Kuroda,Hiroki, LAD	16
Happ,J.A., Hou	15
Chacin,Jhoulys, Col	14
Dempster,Ryan, ChC	14
Latos,Mat, SD	14
Lilly,Ted, LAD	14
Lincecum,Tim, SF	14
Maholm,Paul, Pit	14
Myers,Brett, Hou	14

No Decisions

Beachy,Brandon, Atl	15
Sanchez,Anibal, Fla	15
Carpenter,Chris, StL	14
Norris,Bud, Hou	14
Marcum,Shaun, Mil	13
McDonald,James, Pit	13
Pelfrey,Mike, NYM	13
Garcia,Jaime, StL	12
Myers,Brett, Hou	12
Westbrook,Jake, StL	12

Wild Pitches

Rodriguez,Henry, Was	14
Gallardo,Yovani, Mil	12
Garcia,Jaime, StL	12
Kuroda,Hiroki, LAD	12
Beachy,Brandon, Atl	11
Kennedy,Ian, Ari	11
Greinke,Zack, Mil	10
Hudson,Tim, Atl	10
3 tied with	9

Strikeouts

Kershaw,Clayton, LAD	248
Lee,Cliff, Phi	238
Halladay,Roy, Phi	220
Lincecum,Tim, SF	220
Gallardo,Yovani, Mil	207
Sanchez,Anibal, Fla	202
Greinke,Zack, Mil	201
Kennedy,Ian, Ari	198
Garza,Matt, ChC	197
Hamels,Cole, Phi	194

Walks Allowed

Chacin,Jhoulys, Col	87
Lincecum,Tim, SF	86
Billingsley,Chad, LAD	84
Happ,J.A., Hou	83
Dempster,Ryan, ChC	82
McDonald,James, Pit	78
Morton,Charlie, Pit	77
Lannan,John, Was	76
Westbrook,Jake, StL	73
Gee,Dillon, NYM	71

Intentional Walks Allowed

Beachy,Brandon, Atl	9
Resop,Chris, Pit	9
Lilly,Ted, LAD	8
Madson,Ryan, Phi	8
Nolasco,Ricky, Fla	8
O'Flaherty,Eric, Atl	8
Sanchez,Anibal, Fla	8
Vazquez,Javier, Fla	8
Westbrook,Jake, StL	8
8 tied with	7

Hit Batters

Hudson,Tim, Atl	15
Gee,Dillon, NYM	14
Morton,Charlie, Pit	13
Wolf,Randy, Mil	13
Cueto,Johnny, Cin	10
6 tied with	9

2011 National League Pitching Leaders

Runs Allowed		Hits Allowed		Doubles Allowed		Home Runs Allowed	
Arroyo,Bronson, Cin	119	Nolasco,Ricky, Fla	244	Hudson,Daniel, Ari	53	Arroyo,Bronson, Cin	46
Nolasco,Ricky, Fla	117	Carpenter,Chris, StL	243	Capuano,Chris, NYM	51	Myers,Brett, Hou	31
Myers,Brett, Hou	116	Arroyo,Bronson, Cin	227	Dempster,Ryan, ChC	51	Saunders,Joe, Ari	29
Dempster,Ryan, ChC	111	Myers,Brett, Hou	226	Nolasco,Ricky, Fla	50	Lilly,Ted, LAD	28
Pelfrey,Mike, NYM	111	Pelfrey,Mike, NYM	220	Lohse,Kyle, StL	49	Capuano,Chris, NYM	27
Lowe,Derek, Atl	110	Hudson,Daniel, Ari	217	Lincecum,Tim, SF	48	Gallardo,Yovani, Mil	27
Happ,J.A., Hou	103	Wolf,Randy, Mil	214	Arroyo,Bronson, Cin	47	Rodriguez,Wandy, Hou	25
Westbrook,Jake, StL	103	Lowe,Derek, Atl	212	Cain,Matt, SF	46	4 tied with	24
Garcia,Jaime, StL	100	Dempster,Ryan, ChC	211	Wolf,Randy, Mil	45		
Hammel,Jason, Col	100	Saunders,Joe, Ari	210	Kennedy,Ian, Ari	44		

Run Support Per Nine IP (minimum 162 IP)		% Pitches In Strike Zone (minimum 162 IP)		Pitches Per Start (minimum 30 GS)		Pitches Per Batter (minimum 162 IP)	
Garcia,Jaime, StL	5.92	Lee,Cliff, Phi	53.1	Lincecum,Tim, SF	109.3	Karstens,Jeff, Pit	3.53
Greinke,Zack, Mil	5.87	Dickey,R.A., NYM	51.0	Halladay,Roy, Phi	108.4	Morton,Charlie, Pit	3.56
Leake,Mike, Cin	5.80	Lilly,Ted, LAD	49.8	Lee,Cliff, Phi	106.3	Maholm,Paul, Pit	3.57
Gallardo,Yovani, Mil	5.77	Karstens,Jeff, Pit	48.7	Carpenter,Chris, StL	106.3	Dickey,R.A., NYM	3.58
Billingsley,Chad, LAD	5.55	Kennedy,Ian, Ari	47.4	Cain,Matt, SF	105.7	Hernandez,Livan, Was	3.58
Lohse,Kyle, StL	5.30	Vazquez,Javier, Fla	46.7	Kershaw,Clayton, LAD	105.1	Nolasco,Ricky, Fla	3.59
Harang,Aaron, SD	5.17	Bumgarner,Madison, SF	46.5	Gallardo,Yovani, Mil	104.9	Volstad,Chris, Fla	3.61
Westbrook,Jake, StL	5.11	Billingsley,Chad, LAD	46.3	Rodriguez,Wandy, Hou	104.8	Garcia,Jaime, StL	3.62
Capuano,Chris, NYM	5.03	Sanchez,Anibal, Fla	46.2	Hudson,Daniel, Ari	104.1	Lohse,Kyle, StL	3.62
Vazquez,Javier, Fla	4.86	Hamels,Cole, Phi	46.0	Kennedy,Ian, Ari	103.8	Hudson,Tim, Atl	3.62

Quality Starts		Batters Faced		Innings Pitched		Most Pitches in a Game	
Cain,Matt, SF	26	Carpenter,Chris, StL	996	Carpenter,Chris, StL	237.1	Lincecum,Tim, SF	133
Halladay,Roy, Phi	25	Halladay,Roy, Phi	933	Halladay,Roy, Phi	233.2	Carpenter,Chris, StL	132
Kershaw,Clayton, LAD	25	Hudson,Daniel, Ari	921	Kershaw,Clayton, LAD	233.1	Halladay,Roy, Phi	130
Lee,Cliff, Phi	25	Lee,Cliff, Phi	920	Lee,Cliff, Phi	232.2	Dempster,Ryan, ChC	128
Hamels,Cole, Phi	24	Myers,Brett, Hou	917	Hudson,Daniel, Ari	222.0	Zambrano,Carlos, ChC	128
Kennedy,Ian, Ari	24	Kershaw,Clayton, LAD	912	Kennedy,Ian, Ari	222.0	Lincecum,Tim, SF	127
Bumgarner,Madison, SF	23	Cain,Matt, SF	907	Cain,Matt, SF	221.2	Lincecum,Tim, SF	127
Gallardo,Yovani, Mil	23	Wolf,Randy, Mil	903	Lincecum,Tim, SF	217.0	4 tied with	126
Hudson,Tim, Atl	23	Kennedy,Ian, Ari	900	Hamels,Cole, Phi	216.0		
Lincecum,Tim, SF	23	Lincecum,Tim, SF	900	Myers,Brett, Hou	216.0		

Stolen Bases Allowed		Caught Stealing Off		Stolen Base Pct Allowed (minimum 162 IP)		Pickoffs	
Lilly,Ted, LAD	35	Lincecum,Tim, SF	14	Lohse,Kyle, StL	33.3	Kershaw,Clayton, LAD	9
Hanson,Tommy, Atl	30	Saunders,Joe, Ari	12	Chacin,Jhoulys, Col	36.4	Narveson,Chris, Mil	6
Pelfrey,Mike, NYM	29	Bumgarner,Madison, SF	11	Stauffer,Tim, SD	38.5	Dickey,R.A., NYM	5
Lowe,Derek, Atl	26	Dempster,Ryan, ChC	10	Saunders,Joe, Ari	42.9	Richard,Clayton, SD	5
Latos,Mat, SD	25	Harang,Aaron, SD	10	Carpenter,Chris, StL	45.5	Bumgarner,Madison, SF	4
Harang,Aaron, SD	24	Hudson,Daniel, Ari	10	Hernandez,Livan, Was	50.0	Chapman,Aroldis, Cin	4
Hamels,Cole, Phi	23	Hernandez,Livan, Was	9	Hudson,Daniel, Ari	50.0	Luebke,Cory, SD	4
Lincecum,Tim, SF	23	Jurrjens,Jair, Atl	9	Bumgarner,Madison, SF	52.2	Saunders,Joe, Ari	4
Rodriguez,Wandy, Hou	20	Kershaw,Clayton, LAD	9	Greinke,Zack, Mil	57.1	Westbrook,Jake, StL	4
4 tied with	18	4 tied with	8	Marcum,Shaun, Mil	57.1	12 tied with	3

2011 National League Pitching Leaders

Strikeouts Per 9 IP (minimum 162 IP)		Opp On-Base Percentage (minimum 162 IP)		Opp Slugging Average (minimum 162 IP)		Opponent OPS (minimum 162 IP)	
Greinke,Zack, Mil	10.54	Kershaw,Clayton, LAD	.256	Kershaw,Clayton, LAD	.298	Kershaw,Clayton, LAD	.554
Kershaw,Clayton, LAD	9.57	Hamels,Cole, Phi	.259	Halladay,Roy, Phi	.313	Halladay,Roy, Phi	.582
Sanchez,Anibal, Fla	9.26	Lee,Cliff, Phi	.268	Cain,Matt, SF	.319	Hamels,Cole, Phi	.596
Lee,Cliff, Phi	9.21	Halladay,Roy, Phi	.269	Hudson,Tim, Atl	.331	Cain,Matt, SF	.597
Lincecum,Tim, SF	9.12	Cain,Matt, SF	.279	Hamels,Cole, Phi	.337	Lee,Cliff, Phi	.607
Gallardo,Yovani, Mil	8.99	Kennedy,Ian, Ari	.281	Lee,Cliff, Phi	.339	Hudson,Tim, Atl	.627
Garza,Matt, ChC	8.95	Marcum,Shaun, Mil	.284	Lincecum,Tim, SF	.344	Kennedy,Ian, Ari	.641
Latos,Mat, SD	8.57	Lohse,Kyle, StL	.291	Garza,Matt, ChC	.350	Lincecum,Tim, SF	.646
Norris,Bud, Hou	8.52	Vazquez,Javier, Fla	.291	Carpenter,Chris, StL	.360	Garza,Matt, ChC	.654
Dempster,Ryan, ChC	8.50	Latos,Mat, SD	.292	Kennedy,Ian, Ari	.361	Latos,Mat, SD	.655

Home Runs Per Nine IP (minimum 162 IP)		Batting Average vs. LHB (minimum 125 BF)		Batting Average vs. RHB (minimum 225 BF)		Opp BA w/ RISP (minimum 125 BF)	
Morton,Charlie, Pit	0.31	Luebke,Cory, SD	.157	Venters,Jonny, Atl	.194	Kennedy,Ian, Ari	.141
Cain,Matt, SF	0.37	Kimbrel,Craig, Atl	.157	Samardzija,Jeff, ChC	.195	Hanson,Tommy, Atl	.164
Halladay,Roy, Phi	0.39	Clippard,Tyler, Was	.169	Marcum,Shaun, Mil	.195	Chacin,Jhoulys, Col	.173
Bumgarner,Madison, SF	0.53	Hensley,Clay, Fla	.171	Hanson,Tommy, Atl	.198	Worley,Vance, Phi	.175
Kershaw,Clayton, LAD	0.58	Hernandez,David, Ari	.171	Hamels,Cole, Phi	.204	Cain,Matt, SF	.190
Hudson,Tim, Atl	0.59	Kershaw,Clayton, LAD	.178	Latos,Mat, SD	.204	Kershaw,Clayton, LAD	.193
Carpenter,Chris, StL	0.61	Cain,Matt, SF	.185	Halladay,Roy, Phi	.206	Kuroda,Hiroki, LAD	.194
Maholm,Paul, Pit	0.61	Axford,John, Mil	.189	Kershaw,Clayton, LAD	.213	Cueto,Johnny, Cin	.198
Lincecum,Tim, SF	0.62	Marmol,Carlos, ChC	.192	Kennedy,Ian, Ari	.218	Stauffer,Tim, SD	.199
Garza,Matt, ChC	0.64	Lee,Cliff, Phi	.196	Norris,Bud, Hou	.220	2 tied with	.200

OBP vs. Leadoff Hitter (minimum 150 BF)		Strikeouts / Walks Ratio (minimum 162 IP)		Highest GB/FB Ratio (minimum 162 IP)		Lowest GB/FB Ratio (minimum 162 IP)	
Hamels,Cole, Phi	.247	Halladay,Roy, Phi	6.29	Morton,Charlie, Pit	3.10	Lilly,Ted, LAD	0.72
Zimmermann,Jordan, Was	.249	Lee,Cliff, Phi	5.67	Lowe,Derek, Atl	2.62	Vazquez,Javier, Fla	0.74
Carpenter,Chris, StL	.250	Kershaw,Clayton, LAD	4.59	Westbrook,Jake, StL	2.61	Marcum,Shaun, Mil	0.87
Chacin,Jhoulys, Col	.256	Greinke,Zack, Mil	4.47	Hudson,Tim, Atl	2.29	Arroyo,Bronson, Cin	0.91
Cain,Matt, SF	.260	Hamels,Cole, Phi	4.41	Lannan,John, Was	2.15	McDonald,James, Pit	0.92
Narveson,Chris, Mil	.265	Bumgarner,Madison, SF	4.15	Chacin,Jhoulys, Col	1.99	Wolf,Randy, Mil	0.94
Vazquez,Javier, Fla	.268	Kennedy,Ian, Ari	3.60	Garcia,Jaime, StL	1.92	Kennedy,Ian, Ari	0.98
Kershaw,Clayton, LAD	.271	Gallardo,Yovani, Mil	3.51	Volstad,Chris, Fla	1.89	Harang,Aaron, SD	0.99
Hudson,Tim, Atl	.277	Carpenter,Chris, StL	3.47	Stauffer,Tim, SD	1.82	Norris,Bud, Hou	1.01
Kuroda,Hiroki, LAD	.278	Hudson,Daniel, Ari	3.38	Maholm,Paul, Pit	1.77	Latos,Mat, SD	1.04

Sacrifice Flies Allowed		Sacrifice Hits Allowed		GIDP Induced		GIDP Per Nine IP (minimum 162 IP)	
Maholm,Paul, Pit	10	Dickey,R.A., NYM	16	Saunders,Joe, Ari	29	Morton,Charlie, Pit	1.31
Volstad,Chris, Fla	10	Niese,Jonathon, NYM	16	Lannan,John, Was	26	Lannan,John, Was	1.27
Kennedy,Ian, Ari	9	Halladay,Roy, Phi	15	Garcia,Jaime, StL	25	Saunders,Joe, Ari	1.23
Billingsley,Chad, LAD	8	Stauffer,Tim, SD	14	Morton,Charlie, Pit	25	Garcia,Jaime, StL	1.16
Cook,Aaron, Col	8	Billingsley,Chad, LAD	13	Hudson,Tim, Atl	24	Westbrook,Jake, StL	1.08
Happ,J.A., Hou	8	Lincecum,Tim, SF	13	Wolf,Randy, Mil	23	Hudson,Tim, Atl	1.00
Pelfrey,Mike, NYM	8	Wolf,Randy, Mil	13	Dickey,R.A., NYM	22	Rodriguez,Wandy, Hou	0.99
6 tied with	7	8 tied with	12	Westbrook,Jake, StL	22	Wolf,Randy, Mil	0.97
				Rodriguez,Wandy, Hou	21	Dickey,R.A., NYM	0.95
				3 tied with	20	Maholm,Paul, Pit	0.94

2011 National League Pitching Leaders

Saves		Blown Saves		Save Pct (minimum 20 Save Ops)		Save Opportunities	
Axford,John, Mil	46	Marmol,Carlos, ChC	10	Axford,John, Mil	95.8	Kimbrel,Craig, Atl	54
Kimbrel,Craig, Atl	46	Kimbrel,Craig, Atl	8	Madson,Ryan, Phi	94.1	Putz,J.J., Ari	49
Putz,J.J., Ari	45	Belisle,Matt, Col	7	Putz,J.J., Ari	91.8	Axford,John, Mil	48
Bell,Heath, SD	43	Clippard,Tyler, Was	7	Guerra,Javy, LAD	91.3	Bell,Heath, SD	48
Storen,Drew, Was	43	Loe,Kameron, Mil	7	Hanrahan,Joel, Pit	90.9	Storen,Drew, Was	48
Hanrahan,Joel, Pit	40	Veras,Jose, Pit	7	Bell,Heath, SD	89.6	Hanrahan,Joel, Pit	44
Cordero,Francisco, Cin	37	9 tied with	6	Storen,Drew, Was	89.6	Marmol,Carlos, ChC	44
Nunez,Leo, Fla	36			Street,Huston, Col	87.9	Cordero,Francisco, Cin	43
Wilson,Brian, SF	36			Wilson,Brian, SF	87.8	Nunez,Leo, Fla	42
Marmol,Carlos, ChC	34			Cordero,Francisco, Cin	86.0	Wilson,Brian, SF	41

Easy Saves		Regular Saves		Tough Saves		Holds Adjusted Save % (minimum 20 Save Ops)	
Axford,John, Mil	30	Storen,Drew, Was	19	Salas,Fernando, StL	5	Axford,John, Mil	95.8
Putz,J.J., Ari	30	Kimbrel,Craig, Atl	17	Hanrahan,Joel, Pit	3	Madson,Ryan, Phi	94.6
Kimbrel,Craig, Atl	28	Axford,John, Mil	16	Bell,Heath, SD	2	Putz,J.J., Ari	91.8
Bell,Heath, SD	27	Wilson,Brian, SF	16	Dotel,Octavio, StL	2	Guerra,Javy, LAD	91.3
Hanrahan,Joel, Pit	26	Cordero,Francisco, Cin	15	Marmol,Carlos, ChC	2	Hanrahan,Joel, Pit	90.9
Nunez,Leo, Fla	24	Putz,J.J., Ari	15	Melancon,Mark, Hou	2	Storen,Drew, Was	90.2
Madson,Ryan, Phi	23	Bell,Heath, SD	14	Rodriguez,Fr., NYM-Mil	2	Bell,Heath, SD	89.6
Storen,Drew, Was	23	Marmol,Carlos, ChC	13	19 tied with	1	Street,Huston, Col	89.2
Cordero,Francisco, Cin	22	3 tied with	11			Wilson,Brian, SF	87.8
Wilson,Brian, SF	20					Rodriguez,Fr., NYM-Mil	87.0

Relief Wins		Relief Losses		Relief Games		Holds	
Belisle,Matt, Col	10	Qualls,Chad, SD	8	Venters,Jonny, Atl	85	Clippard,Tyler, Was	38
Mujica,Edward, Fla	9	Loe,Kameron, Mil	7	Bray,Bill, Cin	79	Venters,Jonny, Atl	35
Melancon,Mark, Hou	8	9 tied with	6	Kimbrel,Craig, Atl	79	Marshall,Sean, ChC	34
Samardzija,Jeff, ChC	8			Veras,Jose, Pit	79	O'Flaherty,Eric, Atl	32
9 tied with	6			Marshall,Sean, ChC	78	Veras,Jose, Pit	27
				Motte,Jason, StL	78	Adams,Mike, SD	23
				O'Flaherty,Eric, Atl	78	Hernandez,David, Ari	23
				Qualls,Chad, SD	77	Romo,Sergio, SF	23
				Resop,Chris, Pit	76	Betancourt,Rafael, Col	22
				3 tied with	75	Qualls,Chad, SD	22

Relief Innings		Inherited Runners Scrd % (minimum 30 IR)		Relief Opp On Base Pct (minimum 50 IP)		Relief Opp Slugging Avg (minimum 50 IP)	
Clippard,Tyler, Was	88.1	Sherrill,George, Atl	10.8	Clippard,Tyler, Was	.228	Chapman,Aroldis, Cin	.209
Samardzija,Jeff, ChC	88.0	Bastardo,Antonio, Phi	12.5	Betancourt,Rafael, Col	.228	Venters,Jonny, Atl	.219
Venters,Jonny, Atl	88.0	Choate,Randy, Fla	14.0	Bastardo,Antonio, Phi	.242	Jansen,Kenley, LAD	.228
McCutchen,Daniel, Pit	84.2	Lopez,Javier, SF	14.0	Putz,J.J., Ari	.242	Kimbrel,Craig, Atl	.233
Mota,Guillermo, SF	80.1	Romo,Sergio, SF	18.2	Salas,Fernando, StL	.250	Casilla,Santiago, SF	.244
Martinez,Cristhian, Atl	77.2	McCutchen,Daniel, Pit	18.6	Martinez,Cristhian, Atl	.255	Rodriguez,Henry, Was	.252
Kimbrel,Craig, Atl	77.0	Coffey,Todd, Was	19.4	LeCure,Sam, Cin	.259	Hanrahan,Joel, Pit	.276
Mujica,Edward, Fla	76.0	Clippard,Tyler, Was	21.7	Storen,Drew, Was	.262	Lopez,Javier, SF	.279
Marshall,Sean, ChC	75.2	Bray,Bill, Cin	22.0	Motte,Jason, StL	.262	Hernandez,David, Ari	.280
Storen,Drew, Was	75.1	Reynolds,Matt, Col	23.1	Kimbrel,Craig, Atl	.266	Axford,John, Mil	.281

2011 National League Pitching Leaders

Relief Opp BA Vs LHB
(minimum 50 AB)

Chapman,Aroldis, Cin	.077
Venters,Jonny, Atl	.127
Affeldt,Jeremy, SF	.144
Bastardo,Antonio, Phi	.145
Choate,Randy, Fla	.145
Kimbrel,Craig, Atl	.157
Spence,Josh, SD	.158
Jansen,Kenley, LAD	.163
Lopez,Javier, SF	.163
Guerra,Javy, LAD	.164

Relief Opp BA Vs RHB
(minimum 50 AB)

Adams,Mike, SD	.107
Sanchez,Eduardo, StL	.136
Bastardo,Antonio, Phi	.143
Dotel,Octavio, StL	.148
Romo,Sergio, SF	.150
Lindblom,Josh, LAD	.153
Casilla,Santiago, SF	.155
Clippard,Tyler, Was	.156
Jansen,Kenley, LAD	.156
Cordero,Francisco, Cin	.159

Relief Opp Batting Average
(minimum 50 IP)

Bastardo,Antonio, Phi	.144
Chapman,Aroldis, Cin	.147
Jansen,Kenley, LAD	.159
Clippard,Tyler, Was	.162
Venters,Jonny, Atl	.176
Kimbrel,Craig, Atl	.178
Casilla,Santiago, SF	.183
Salas,Fernando, StL	.186
LeCure,Sam, Cin	.189
Hernandez,David, Ari	.193

Relief Earned Run Average
(minimum 50 IP)

O'Flaherty,Eric, Atl	0.98
Casilla,Santiago, SF	1.74
Clippard,Tyler, Was	1.83
Hanrahan,Joel, Pit	1.83
Venters,Jonny, Atl	1.84
Axford,John, Mil	1.95
MacDougal,Mike, LAD	2.05
Kimbrel,Craig, Atl	2.10
Putz,J.J., Ari	2.17
Motte,Jason, StL	2.25

Rel OBP 1st Batter Faced
(minimum 40 BF)

Clippard,Tyler, Was	.155
Adams,Mike, SD	.167
Salas,Fernando, StL	.179
Stutes,Michael, Phi	.193
Axford,John, Mil	.203
Bastardo,Antonio, Phi	.203
Storen,Drew, Was	.205
Betancourt,Rafael, Col	.206
Bray,Bill, Cin	.215
Jansen,Kenley, LAD	.216

Rel Opp BA w/ Runners On
(minimum 50 IP)

Clippard,Tyler, Was	.101
Bastardo,Antonio, Phi	.143
Casilla,Santiago, SF	.164
Salas,Fernando, StL	.165
Kimbrel,Craig, Atl	.168
Putz,J.J., Ari	.171
Venters,Jonny, Atl	.173
Cordero,Francisco, Cin	.179
Ondrusek,Logan, Cin	.181
Chapman,Aroldis, Cin	.186

Relief Opp BA w/ RISP
(minimum 50 IP)

Clippard,Tyler, Was	.086
Bastardo,Antonio, Phi	.132
Arredondo,Jose, Cin	.136
Putz,J.J., Ari	.137
Venters,Jonny, Atl	.141
Axford,John, Mil	.153
MacDougal,Mike, LAD	.157
Frieri,Ernesto, SD	.158
Storen,Drew, Was	.158
Ondrusek,Logan, Cin	.159

Fastest Avg Fastball-Relief
(minimum 50 IP)

Rodriguez,Henry, Was	98.0
Chapman,Aroldis, Cin	97.9
Parnell,Bobby, NYM	97.2
Hanrahan,Joel, Pit	97.1
Kimbrel,Craig, Atl	96.2
Motte,Jason, StL	96.0
Lindstrom,Matt, Col	96.0
Axford,John, Mil	95.6
MacDougal,Mike, LAD	95.5
Boggs,Mitchell, StL	95.2

Fastest Average Fastball
(minimum 162 IP)

Garza,Matt, ChC	93.7
Kershaw,Clayton, LAD	93.4
Hudson,Daniel, Ari	93.2
Hammel,Jason, Col	92.9
Latos,Mat, SD	92.8
McDonald,James, Pit	92.7
Gallardo,Yovani, Mil	92.7
Norris,Bud, Hou	92.6
Greinke,Zack, Mil	92.5
Carpenter,Chris, StL	92.5

Slowest Average Fastball
(minimum 162 IP)

Hernandez,Livan, Was	83.9
Dickey,R.A., NYM	84.4
Marcum,Shaun, Mil	86.9
Arroyo,Bronson, Cin	87.0
Maholm,Paul, Pit	87.4
Lilly,Ted, LAD	87.4
Capuano,Chris, NYM	87.9
Lowe,Derek, Atl	88.0
Wolf,Randy, Mil	88.4
Myers,Brett, Hou	88.4

Pitches 100+ Velocity

Chapman,Aroldis, Cin	158
Rodriguez,Henry, Was	127
Parnell,Bobby, NYM	84
Carpenter,Chris, ChC	13
de la Rosa,Rubby, LAD	9
Cleto,Maikel, StL	8
Kimbrel,Craig, Atl	5
Cashner,Andrew, ChC	1
Eovaldi,Nathan, LAD	1
Hanrahan,Joel, Pit	1

Pitches 95+ Velocity

Paulino,Felipe, Col	928
Jackson,Edwin, StL	880
Hanrahan,Joel, Pit	829
Rodriguez,Henry, Was	818
Kimbrel,Craig, Atl	779
Motte,Jason, StL	734
Parnell,Bobby, NYM	718
Axford,John, Mil	697
Chapman,Aroldis, Cin	689
Venters,Jonny, Atl	657

Pitches Less Than 80 MPH

Dickey,R.A., NYM	2063
Rodriguez,Wandy, Hou	1154
Arroyo,Bronson, Cin	1150
Hernandez,Livan, Was	1029
Wolf,Randy, Mil	959
Marcum,Shaun, Mil	901
Capuano,Chris, NYM	805
Myers,Brett, Hou	753
Collmenter,Josh, Ari	752
Carpenter,Chris, StL	726

Lowest % Fastballs
(minimum 162 IP)

Dickey,R.A., NYM	22.4
Halladay,Roy, Phi	22.6
Marcum,Shaun, Mil	34.3
Leake,Mike, Cin	35.4
Hamels,Cole, Phi	45.2
Arroyo,Bronson, Cin	46.2
Hernandez,Livan, Was	48.2
Myers,Brett, Hou	49.1
Wolf,Randy, Mil	49.7
Lowe,Derek, Atl	50.0

Highest % Fastballs
(minimum 162 IP)

Morton,Charlie, Pit	69.7
McDonald,James, Pit	69.2
Kershaw,Clayton, LAD	65.3
Pelfrey,Mike, NYM	64.4
Saunders,Joe, Ari	64.0
Westbrook,Jake, StL	63.6
Kennedy,Ian, Ari	63.5
Hudson,Daniel, Ari	61.6
Hammel,Jason, Col	60.9
Kuroda,Hiroki, LAD	60.8

Highest % Curveballs
(minimum 162 IP)

Rodriguez,Wandy, Hou	37.2
Myers,Brett, Hou	22.9
Carpenter,Chris, StL	20.4
Gallardo,Yovani, Mil	19.8
Vogelsong,Ryan, SF	19.7
McDonald,James, Pit	19.2
Wolf,Randy, Mil	19.1
Halladay,Roy, Phi	17.1
Vazquez,Javier, Fla	17.0
Greinke,Zack, Mil	16.7

2011 National League Pitching Leaders

Highest % Changeups
(minimum 162 IP)

Capuano,Chris, NYM	27.7
Marcum,Shaun, Mil	24.8
Hamels,Cole, Phi	24.1
Lincecum,Tim, SF	24.1
Hudson,Daniel, Ari	22.1
Lohse,Kyle, StL	19.2
Lilly,Ted, LAD	19.0
Saunders,Joe, Ari	18.9
Maholm,Paul, Pit	17.7
Sanchez,Anibal, Fla	17.7

Highest % Sliders
(minimum 162 IP)

Norris,Bud, Hou	36.2
Bumgarner,Madison, SF	32.4
Dempster,Ryan, ChC	31.1
Hernandez,Livan, Was	26.4
Carpenter,Chris, StL	26.0
Kershaw,Clayton, LAD	25.5
Lowe,Derek, Atl	25.3
Nolasco,Ricky, Fla	25.1
Latos,Mat, SD	24.4
Harang,Aaron, SD	23.8

Balks

Sanchez,Anibal, Fla	5
Masset,Nick, Cin	4
Grabow,John, ChC	3
Hamels,Cole, Phi	3
13 tied with	2

Strikeout/Hit Ratio
(minimum 50 IP)

Jansen,Kenley, LAD	3.20
Chapman,Aroldis, Cin	2.96
Kimbrel,Craig, Atl	2.65
Bastardo,Antonio, Phi	2.50
Clippard,Tyler, Was	2.17
Marmol,Carlos, ChC	1.83
Venters,Jonny, Atl	1.81
Betancourt,Rafael, Col	1.59
Hernandez,David, Ari	1.57
Salas,Fernando, StL	1.50

Opp OPS vs Fastballs
(minimum 251 BF)

Venters,Jonny, Atl	.483
Lee,Cliff, Phi	.541
Stauffer,Tim, SD	.588
Kershaw,Clayton, LAD	.589
Luebke,Cory, SD	.591
Kennedy,Ian, Ari	.598
Cueto,Johnny, Cin	.604
Hudson,Tim, Atl	.623
Worley,Vance, Phi	.625
Hamels,Cole, Phi	.629

Opp OPS vs Curveballs
(minimum 100 BF)

Halladay,Roy, Phi	.394
Veras,Jose, Pit	.427
Vazquez,Javier, Fla	.484
Myers,Brett, Hou	.572
Rodriguez,Wandy, Hou	.572
Vogelsong,Ryan, SF	.580
Marshall,Sean, ChC	.590
Hernandez,Livan, Was	.594
Wolf,Randy, Mil	.615
McDonald,James, Pit	.616

Opp OPS vs Changeups
(minimum 100 BF)

Cain,Matt, SF	.442
Hamels,Cole, Phi	.445
Garcia,Jaime, StL	.509
Lohse,Kyle, StL	.540
Lincecum,Tim, SF	.586
Lilly,Ted, LAD	.595
Collmenter,Josh, Ari	.596
Jimenez,Ubaldo, Col	.597
Saunders,Joe, Ari	.605
Maholm,Paul, Pit	.611

Opp OPS vs Sliders
(minimum 64 BF)

Cordero,Francisco, Cin	.331
Kimbrel,Craig, Atl	.394
Romo,Sergio, SF	.394
Cueto,Johnny, Cin	.453
Bailey,Homer, Cin	.478
Kershaw,Clayton, LAD	.482
Coffey,Todd, Was	.483
LeCure,Sam, Cin	.488
Zambrano,Carlos, ChC	.498
Ortiz,Ramon, ChC	.516

Earned Runs

Arroyo,Bronson, Cin	112
Dempster,Ryan, ChC	108
Myers,Brett, Hou	107
Nolasco,Ricky, Fla	107
Lowe,Derek, Atl	105
Pelfrey,Mike, NYM	102
Westbrook,Jake, StL	95
Capuano,Chris, NYM	94
Happ,J.A., Hou	93
Carpenter,Chris, StL	91

Hits Per Nine Innings
(minimum 162 IP)

Kershaw,Clayton, LAD	6.71
Hamels,Cole, Phi	7.04
Cain,Matt, SF	7.19
Lincecum,Tim, SF	7.30
Kennedy,Ian, Ari	7.54
Lee,Cliff, Phi	7.62
Latos,Mat, SD	7.78
Chacin,Jhoulys, Col	7.79
Marcum,Shaun, Mil	7.85
Hudson,Tim, Atl	7.91

2011 American League Fielding Leaders

2B Pivot %
(minimum 98 G)

Kendrick,Howie, LAA	0.722
Zobrist,Ben, TB	0.708
Kinsler,Ian, Tex	0.688
Cano,Robinson, NYY	0.635
Hill,Aaron, Tor	0.606
Getz,Chris, KC	0.593
Pedroia,Dustin, Bos	0.590
Beckham,Gordon, CWS	0.580

SS Pivot %
(minimum 98 G)

Ramirez,Alexei, CWS	0.689
Pennington,Cliff, Oak	0.679
Andrus,Elvis, Tex	0.677
Aybar,Erick, LAA	0.656
Ryan,Brendan, Sea	0.610
Jeter,Derek, NYY	0.610
Scutaro,Marco, Bos	0.604
Cabrera,Asdrubal, Cle	0.583
Peralta,Jhonny, Det	0.581
Escobar,Yunel, Tor	0.577

Highest Pct CS by Catchers
(minimum 600 INN or 50 SBA)

Shoppach,Kelly, TB	36.6
Wieters,Matt, Bal	35.6
Marson,Lou, Cle	33.3
Butera,Drew, Min	29.4
Torrealba,Yorvit, Tex	27.3
Martin,Russell, NYY	26.9
Saltalamacchia,J, Bos	25.2
Pena,Brayan, KC	25.0
Olivo,Miguel, Sea	24.0
Avila,Alex, Det	23.4

Lowest Pct CS by Catchers
(minimum 600 INN or 50 SBA)

Varitek,Jason, Bos	12.0
Pierzynski,A.J., CWS	13.0
Jaso,John, TB	13.8
Conger,Hank, LAA	15.9
Arencibia,J.P., Tor	17.1
Suzuki,Kurt, Oak	19.0
Mathis,Jeff, LAA	20.0
Treanor,Matt, KC-Tex	20.8
Santana,Carlos, Cle	21.1
Avila,Alex, Det	23.4

2B Double Play %
(minimum 98 G)

Kinsler,Ian, Tex	0.632
Hill,Aaron, Tor	0.556
Kendrick,Howie, LAA	0.536
Cano,Robinson, NYY	0.524
Zobrist,Ben, TB	0.504
Beckham,Gordon, CWS	0.485
Pedroia,Dustin, Bos	0.478
Getz,Chris, KC	0.473

3B Double Play %
(minimum 98 G)

Longoria,Evan, TB	0.484
Beltre,Adrian, Tex	0.451
Callaspo,Alberto, LAA	0.417
Inge,Brandon, Det	0.393
Reynolds,Mark, Bal	0.340
Valencia,Danny, Min	0.328
Hannahan,Jack, Cle	0.291
Youkilis,Kevin, Bos	0.289
Morel,Brent, CWS	0.257

SS Double Play %
(minimum 98 G)

Ramirez,Alexei, CWS	0.644
Aybar,Erick, LAA	0.630
Andrus,Elvis, Tex	0.624
Pennington,Cliff, Oak	0.616
Ryan,Brendan, Sea	0.602
Peralta,Jhonny, Det	0.598
Scutaro,Marco, Bos	0.563
Cabrera,Asdrubal, Cle	0.560
Escobar,Yunel, Tor	0.557
Jeter,Derek, NYY	0.549

Errors

Reynolds,Mark, Bal	31
Andrus,Elvis, Tex	25
Pennington,Cliff, Oak	22
Nunez,Eduardo, NYY	20
Valencia,Danny, Min	18
Raburn,Ryan, Det	17
Ramirez,Alexei, CWS	16
Sizemore,Scott, Det-Oak	16
5 tied with	15

Fielding Errors

Reynolds,Mark, Bal	20
Andrus,Elvis, Tex	19
Lowrie,Jed, Bos	13
Nunez,Eduardo, NYY	12
Raburn,Ryan, Det	12
Cabrera,Miguel, Det	11
Pennington,Cliff, Oak	11
Callaspo,Alberto, LAA	10
3 tied with	9

Throwing Errors

Escobar,Alcides, KC	13
Pennington,Cliff, Oak	11
Reynolds,Mark, Bal	11
Martin,Russell, NYY	10
Sizemore,Scott, Det-Oak	10
Valencia,Danny, Min	10
Longoria,Evan, TB	9
4 tied with	8

Range Factor for 2B
(minimum 98 games)

Cano,Robinson, NYY	5.15
Beckham,Gordon, CWS	4.92
Getz,Chris, KC	4.91
Kinsler,Ian, Tex	4.72
Hill,Aaron, Tor	4.65
Pedroia,Dustin, Bos	4.62
Kendrick,Howie, LAA	4.60
Zobrist,Ben, TB	4.50

Range Factor for 3B
(minimum 98 games)

Hannahan,Jack, Cle	3.20
Inge,Brandon, Det	2.94
Longoria,Evan, TB	2.82
Beltre,Adrian, Tex	2.76
Callaspo,Alberto, LAA	2.76
Youkilis,Kevin, Bos	2.50
Morel,Brent, CWS	2.41
Valencia,Danny, Min	2.34
Reynolds,Mark, Bal	2.08

Range Factor for SS
(minimum 98 games)

Hardy,J.J., Bal	4.88
Escobar,Alcides, KC	4.74
Ryan,Brendan, Sea	4.73
Andrus,Elvis, Tex	4.65
Aybar,Erick, LAA	4.60
Ramirez,Alexei, CWS	4.39
Peralta,Jhonny, Det	4.34
Escobar,Yunel, Tor	4.21
Pennington,Cliff, Oak	4.17
Cabrera,Asdrubal, Cle	4.08

2011 National League Fielding Leaders

2B Pivot %
(minimum 98 G)

Infante,Omar, Fla	0.695
Johnson,Kelly, Ari	0.694
Weeks,Rickie, Mil	0.672
Espinosa,Danny, Was	0.671
Uggla,Dan, Atl	0.621
Hudson,Orlando, SD	0.615
Walker,Neil, Pit	0.613
Phillips,Brandon, Cin	0.589
Barney,Darwin, ChC	0.569
Utley,Chase, Phi	0.500

SS Pivot %
(minimum 98 G)

Rollins,Jimmy, Phi	0.716
Tulowitzki,Troy, Col	0.678
Betancourt,Yuniesky, Mil	0.625
Barmes,Clint, Hou	0.623
Reyes,Jose, NYM	0.614
Cedeno,Ronny, Pit	0.563
Bartlett,Jason, SD	0.556
Gonzalez,Alex, Atl	0.552
Castro,Starlin, ChC	0.525
Desmond,Ian, Was	0.522

Highest Pct CS by Catchers
(minimum 600 INN or 50 SBA)

Montero,Miguel, Ari	36.8
Stewart,Chris, SF	35.8
Hernandez,Ramon, Cin	31.6
Hundley,Nick, SD	29.6
Ramos,Wilson, Was	28.4
Hanigan,Ryan, Cin	27.7
Iannetta,Chris, Col	27.1
Soto,Geovany, ChC	26.1
Molina,Yadier, StL	24.6
Lucroy,Jonathan, Mil	21.4

Lowest Pct CS by Catchers
(minimum 600 INN or 50 SBA)

Buck,John, Fla	15.3
Corporan,Carlos, Hou	17.3
McCann,Brian, Atl	17.5
Paulino,Ronny, NYM	17.5
Thole,Josh, NYM	17.7
Johnson,Rob, SD	18.3
Quintero,Humberto, Hou	18.6
Barajas,Rod, LAD	18.9
Ruiz,Carlos, Phi	18.9
Navarro,Dioner, LAD	19.6

2B Double Play %
(minimum 98 G)

Johnson,Kelly, Ari	0.526
Weeks,Rickie, Mil	0.526
Espinosa,Danny, Was	0.476
Walker,Neil, Pit	0.471
Infante,Omar, Fla	0.469
Phillips,Brandon, Cin	0.448
Hudson,Orlando, SD	0.432
Utley,Chase, Phi	0.407
Uggla,Dan, Atl	0.402
Barney,Darwin, ChC	0.363

3B Double Play %
(minimum 98 G)

Descalso,Daniel, StL	0.483
Headley,Chase, SD	0.400
Johnson,Chris, Hou	0.400
Roberts,Ryan, Ari	0.400
McGehee,Casey, Mil	0.340
Jones,Chipper, Atl	0.326
Ramirez,Aramis, ChC	0.314
Sandoval,Pablo, SF	0.279
Dobbs,Greg, Fla	0.242
Polanco,Placido, Phi	0.234

SS Double Play %
(minimum 98 G)

Tulowitzki,Troy, Col	0.653
Rollins,Jimmy, Phi	0.628
Barmes,Clint, Hou	0.610
Betancourt,Yuniesky, Mil	0.603
Bartlett,Jason, SD	0.586
Reyes,Jose, NYM	0.555
Gonzalez,Alex, Atl	0.535
Cedeno,Ronny, Pit	0.504
Desmond,Ian, Was	0.500
Janish,Paul, Cin	0.482

Errors

Castro,Starlin, ChC	29
Desmond,Ian, Was	23
Betancourt,Yuniesky, Mil	21
McGehee,Casey, Mil	20
Wright,David, NYM	19
Bartlett,Jason, SD	18
Reyes,Jose, NYM	18
Theriot,Ryan, StL	18
4 tied with	15

Fielding Errors

Desmond,Ian, Was	19
Bartlett,Jason, SD	13
Castro,Starlin, ChC	13
Fielder,Prince, Mil	13
Theriot,Ryan, StL	12
Wright,David, NYM	12
Janish,Paul, Cin	11
McGehee,Casey, Mil	11
Pujols,Albert, StL	11
Upton,Justin, Ari	11

Throwing Errors

Castro,Starlin, ChC	16
Betancourt,Yuniesky, Mil	11
Soto,Geovany, ChC	11
Montero,Miguel, Ari	10
McGehee,Casey, Mil	9
Ramirez,Aramis, ChC	9
Ramirez,Hanley, Fla	9
5 tied with	8

Range Factor for 2B
(minimum 98 games)

Hudson,Orlando, SD	5.12
Infante,Omar, Fla	5.09
Walker,Neil, Pit	5.05
Espinosa,Danny, Was	4.97
Barney,Darwin, ChC	4.92
Utley,Chase, Phi	4.90
Phillips,Brandon, Cin	4.86
Uggla,Dan, Atl	4.61
Johnson,Kelly, Ari	4.58
Weeks,Rickie, Mil	4.31

Range Factor for 3B
(minimum 98 games)

Polanco,Placido, Phi	2.90
Sandoval,Pablo, SF	2.84
Roberts,Ryan, Ari	2.70
Headley,Chase, SD	2.62
Wright,David, NYM	2.50
McGehee,Casey, Mil	2.39
Descalso,Daniel, StL	2.38
Johnson,Chris, Hou	2.37
Dobbs,Greg, Fla	2.16
Jones,Chipper, Atl	2.16

Range Factor for SS
(minimum 98 games)

Tulowitzki,Troy, Col	5.05
Cedeno,Ronny, Pit	5.04
Janish,Paul, Cin	4.63
Castro,Starlin, ChC	4.59
Desmond,Ian, Was	4.53
Barmes,Clint, Hou	4.48
Reyes,Jose, NYM	4.44
Bartlett,Jason, SD	4.41
Rollins,Jimmy, Phi	4.28
Gonzalez,Alex, Atl	4.25

2011 Active Career Batting Leaders

Batting Average (minimum 1000 PA)		On Base Percentage (minimum 1000 PA)		Slugging Average (minimum 1000 PA)		Home Runs	
Pujols,Albert	.328	Helton,Todd	.421	Pujols,Albert	.617	Rodriguez,Alex	629
Suzuki,Ichiro	.326	Pujols,Albert	.420	Ramirez,Manny	.585	Thome,Jim	604
Mauer,Joe	.323	Ramirez,Manny	.411	Rodriguez,Alex	.567	Ramirez,Manny	555
Helton,Todd	.323	Berkman,Lance	.409	Braun,Ryan	.563	Jones,Chipper	454
Guerrero,Vladimir	.318	Votto,Joey	.405	Howard,Ryan	.560	Guerrero,Vladimir	449
Cabrera,Miguel	.317	Giambi,Jason	.404	Thome,Jim	.556	Pujols,Albert	445
Holliday,Matt	.315	Mauer,Joe	.403	Cabrera,Miguel	.555	Giambi,Jason	428
Jeter,Derek	.313	Thome,Jim	.403	Guerrero,Vladimir	.553	Jones,Andruw	420
Votto,Joey	.313	Jones,Chipper	.402	Votto,Joey	.550	Konerko,Paul	396
Ramirez,Manny	.312	Abreu,Bobby	.397	Helton,Todd	.550	Ortiz,David	378

Games		At Bats		Hits		Total Bases	
Vizquel,Omar	2908	Vizquel,Omar	10433	Jeter,Derek	3088	Rodriguez,Alex	5215
Rodriguez,Ivan	2543	Jeter,Derek	9868	Rodriguez,Ivan	2844	Ramirez,Manny	4826
Thome,Jim	2485	Rodriguez,Ivan	9592	Vizquel,Omar	2841	Thome,Jim	4595
Damon,Johnny	2426	Damon,Johnny	9529	Rodriguez,Alex	2775	Jones,Chipper	4579
Jeter,Derek	2426	Rodriguez,Alex	9199	Damon,Johnny	2723	Guerrero,Vladimir	4506
Rodriguez,Alex	2402	Jones,Chipper	8597	Jones,Chipper	2615	Rodriguez,Ivan	4451
Jones,Chipper	2387	Tejada,Miguel	8278	Guerrero,Vladimir	2590	Jeter,Derek	4430
Ramirez,Manny	2302	Thome,Jim	8259	Ramirez,Manny	2574	Damon,Johnny	4146
Abreu,Bobby	2247	Ramirez,Manny	8244	Suzuki,Ichiro	2428	Helton,Todd	4028
Renteria,Edgar	2152	Guerrero,Vladimir	8155	Abreu,Bobby	2384	Abreu,Bobby	3906

Doubles		Triples		Runs Scored		RBI	
Rodriguez,Ivan	572	Crawford,Carl	112	Rodriguez,Alex	1824	Rodriguez,Alex	1893
Abreu,Bobby	554	Damon,Johnny	107	Jeter,Derek	1769	Ramirez,Manny	1831
Helton,Todd	554	Rollins,Jimmy	100	Damon,Johnny	1643	Thome,Jim	1674
Ramirez,Manny	547	Reyes,Jose	99	Thome,Jim	1566	Jones,Chipper	1561
Jones,Chipper	526	Pierre,Juan	86	Jones,Chipper	1561	Guerrero,Vladimir	1496
Damon,Johnny	516	Vizquel,Omar	76	Ramirez,Manny	1544	Giambi,Jason	1397
Rolen,Scott	500	Granderson,Curtis	74	Vizquel,Omar	1432	Rodriguez,Ivan	1332
Rodriguez,Alex	495	Suzuki,Ichiro	74	Abreu,Bobby	1412	Pujols,Albert	1329
Jeter,Derek	492	Beltran,Carlos	73	Rodriguez,Ivan	1354	Abreu,Bobby	1325
Guerrero,Vladimir	477	2 tied with	65	Helton,Todd	1329	Helton,Todd	1308

Walks		Intentional Walks		Hit By Pitch		Strikeouts	
Thome,Jim	1725	Pujols,Albert	251	Giambi,Jason	173	Thome,Jim	2487
Jones,Chipper	1455	Guerrero,Vladimir	250	Jeter,Derek	158	Rodriguez,Alex	1916
Abreu,Bobby	1419	Ramirez,Manny	216	Rodriguez,Alex	157	Cameron,Mike	1901
Ramirez,Manny	1329	Helton,Todd	183	Utley,Chase	139	Ramirez,Manny	1813
Giambi,Jason	1314	Jones,Chipper	171	Rowand,Aaron	126	Dunn,Adam	1809
Helton,Todd	1256	Thome,Jim	170	Rolen,Scott	124	Abreu,Bobby	1763
Rodriguez,Alex	1166	Suzuki,Ichiro	168	Tejada,Miguel	121	Jones,Andruw	1677
Berkman,Lance	1149	Berkman,Lance	154	Mora,Melvin	117	Jeter,Derek	1653
Dunn,Adam	1065	Cabrera,Miguel	144	Johnson,Reed	113	Lee,Derrek	1622
Vizquel,Omar	1021	Howard,Ryan	132	Ramirez,Manny	109	Burrell,Pat	1564

2011 Active Career Batting Leaders

Sacrifice Hits

Vizquel,Omar	255
Pierre,Juan	144
Hernandez,Livan	123
Oswalt,Roy	105
Vazquez,Javier	105
Wilson,Jack	101
Renteria,Edgar	99
Cairo,Miguel	86
Dempster,Ryan	84
Hairston,Jerry	84

Sacrifice Flies

Rodriguez,Alex	96
Jones,Chipper	94
Lee,Carlos	92
Vizquel,Omar	92
Cabrera,Orlando	90
Ramirez,Manny	90
Rolen,Scott	90
Giambi,Jason	88
Helton,Todd	85
Abreu,Bobby	82

Stolen Bases

Pierre,Juan	554
Crawford,Carl	427
Suzuki,Ichiro	423
Damon,Johnny	404
Vizquel,Omar	401
Abreu,Bobby	393
Rollins,Jimmy	373
Reyes,Jose	370
Jeter,Derek	339
Figgins,Chone	333

Seasons Played

Vizquel,Omar	23
Rodriguez,Ivan	21
Thome,Jim	21
Rhodes,Arthur	20
Ramirez,Manny	19
Stairs,Matt	19
Wakefield,Tim	19
Jones,Chipper	18
Oliver,Darren	18
Rodriguez,Alex	18

At Bats Per Home Run
(minimum 1000 AB)

Howard,Ryan	13.3
Thome,Jim	13.7
Pujols,Albert	14.2
Rodriguez,Alex	14.6
Dunn,Adam	14.8
Ramirez,Manny	14.9
Branyan,Russell	15.1
Fielder,Prince	15.3
Napoli,Mike	15.7
Thames,Marcus	15.9

Grounded Into DP

Rodriguez,Ivan	337
Guerrero,Vladimir	277
Tejada,Miguel	271
Konerko,Paul	247
Jeter,Derek	245
Ramirez,Manny	243
Ordonez,Magglio	242
Renteria,Edgar	241
Jones,Chipper	238
Pujols,Albert	232

Highest SB Success Pct
(minimum 100 SBA)

Utley,Chase	89.4
Beltran,Carlos	87.7
Werth,Jayson	87.3
Kinsler,Ian	86.1
Bay,Jason	85.3
McLouth,Nate	85.3
Gardner,Brett	82.8
Rollins,Jimmy	82.7
Bourn,Michael	82.1
Weeks,Rickie	82.0

Lowest SB Success Pct
(minimum 100 SBA)

Hall,Bill	60.8
Guillen,Carlos	61.2
Kotsay,Mark	62.0
Mora,Melvin	62.8
Berkman,Lance	63.6
Ordonez,Magglio	65.3
Guerrero,Vladimir	65.8
Hart,Corey	66.1
Rodriguez,Ivan	66.5
Hunter,Torii	66.8

Strikeouts / Walks Ratio
(minimum 1000 AB)

Pujols,Albert	.722
Helton,Todd	.831
Mauer,Joe	.832
Pedroia,Dustin	.894
Keppinger,Jeff	.916
Jones,Chipper	.933
Ruiz,Carlos	.979
Pierre,Juan	.993
Callaspo,Alberto	1.012
Vizquel,Omar	1.048

At Bats Per GIDP
(minimum 1000 AB)

Stubbs,Drew	144.2
Bourn,Michael	140.6
Suzuki,Ichiro	130.8
Coghlan,Chris	125.7
Gwynn,Tony	123.6
Bonifacio,Emilio	116.5
Granderson,Curtis	109.9
Drew,Stephen	107.0
Damon,Johnny	101.4
Mathis,Jeff	100.1

OPS
(minimum 1000 PA)

Pujols,Albert	1.037
Ramirez,Manny	.996
Helton,Todd	.971
Thome,Jim	.959
Votto,Joey	.955
Berkman,Lance	.954
Rodriguez,Alex	.953
Cabrera,Miguel	.950
Jones,Chipper	.935
Braun,Ryan	.933

Secondary Average
(minimum 1000 PA)

Thome,Jim	.491
Dunn,Adam	.468
Pujols,Albert	.456
Berkman,Lance	.450
Ramirez,Manny	.439
Giambi,Jason	.437
Howard,Ryan	.430
Rodriguez,Alex	.425
Fielder,Prince	.422
Pena,Carlos	.420

Highest Strikeout per PA
(minimum 1000 PA)

Reynolds,Mark	.331
Shoppach,Kelly	.330
Branyan,Russell	.329
Cust,Jack	.317
Davis,Chris	.315
Pena,Wily Mo	.303
Stubbs,Drew	.289
Saltalamacchia,J	.288
Stewart,Ian	.279
Dunn,Adam	.276

Lowest Strikeout per PA
(minimum 1000 PA)

Pierre,Juan	.057
Keppinger,Jeff	.062
Polanco,Placido	.067
Callaspo,Alberto	.079
Pedroia,Dustin	.084
Molina,Yadier	.085
Cabrera,Orlando	.090
Vizquel,Omar	.090
3 tied with	.093

Plate Appearances

Vizquel,Omar	11850
Jeter,Derek	11155
Damon,Johnny	10693
Rodriguez,Alex	10634
Rodriguez,Ivan	10270
Jones,Chipper	10166
Thome,Jim	10127
Ramirez,Manny	9774
Abreu,Bobby	9669
Renteria,Edgar	9066

At Bats Per RBI
(minimum 1000 AB)

Howard,Ryan	4.4
Ramirez,Manny	4.5
Pujols,Albert	4.7
Rodriguez,Alex	4.9
Ortiz,David	4.9
Thome,Jim	4.9
Giambi,Jason	5.0
Cabrera,Miguel	5.1
Teixeira,Mark	5.1
Berkman,Lance	5.2

2011 Active Career Pitching Leaders

Earned Run Average (minimum 750 IP)	
Rivera,Mariano	2.21
Wainwright,Adam	2.97
Lincecum,Tim	2.98
Santana,Johan	3.10
Cordero,Francisco	3.17
Oswalt,Roy	3.21
Halladay,Roy	3.23
Hernandez,Felix	3.24
Webb,Brandon	3.27
Weaver,Jered	3.31

Winning Percentage (minimum 100 Decisions)	
Lester,Jon	.691
Halladay,Roy	.671
Santana,Johan	.658
Wainwright,Adam	.653
Verlander,Justin	.652
Hudson,Tim	.651
Sabathia,CC	.647
Weaver,Jered	.636
Lee,Cliff	.633
Oswalt,Roy	.631

Opponent Batting Average (minimum 750 IP)	
Rivera,Mariano	.210
Wood,Kerry	.216
Dotel,Octavio	.216
Young,Chris	.218
Lincecum,Tim	.223
Santana,Johan	.226
Cain,Matt	.227
Harden,Rich	.228
Jimenez,Ubaldo	.233
Peavy,Jake	.234

Baserunners Per 9 IP (minimum 750 IP)	
Rivera,Mariano	9.32
Santana,Johan	10.25
Hamels,Cole	10.46
Weaver,Jered	10.63
Halladay,Roy	10.75
Haren,Dan	10.77
Lincecum,Tim	10.91
Cain,Matt	10.99
Peavy,Jake	11.02
Wainwright,Adam	11.06

Games	
Rivera,Mariano	1042
Rhodes,Arthur	901
Hawkins,LaTroy	823
Farnsworth,Kyle	776
Cordero,Francisco	753
Mota,Guillermo	717
Dotel,Octavio	695
Miller,Trever	694
Isringhausen,Jason	674
Reyes,Dennys	673

Games Started	
Hernandez,Livan	474
Wakefield,Tim	463
Vazquez,Javier	443
Millwood,Kevin	415
Hudson,Tim	377
Buehrle,Mark	365
Zito,Barry	362
Lowe,Derek	356
Sabathia,CC	355
Halladay,Roy	352

Complete Games	
Halladay,Roy	66
Hernandez,Livan	50
Carpenter,Chris	33
Sabathia,CC	33
Wakefield,Tim	33
Colon,Bartolo	32
Vazquez,Javier	28
Buehrle,Mark	27
Lee,Cliff	26
Hudson,Tim	24

Shutouts	
Halladay,Roy	20
Carpenter,Chris	15
Hudson,Tim	12
Sabathia,CC	12
Lee,Cliff	11
Burnett,A.J.	9
Colon,Bartolo	9
Hernandez,Livan	9
Wolf,Randy	9
8 tied with	8

Wins	
Wakefield,Tim	200
Halladay,Roy	188
Hudson,Tim	181
Sabathia,CC	176
Hernandez,Livan	174
Lowe,Derek	166
Vazquez,Javier	165
Millwood,Kevin	163
Buehrle,Mark	161
Colon,Bartolo	161

Losses	
Wakefield,Tim	180
Hernandez,Livan	176
Vazquez,Javier	160
Lowe,Derek	146
Millwood,Kevin	140
Zito,Barry	124
Wright,Jamey	121
Buehrle,Mark	119
Garland,Jon	119
Dempster,Ryan	116

Innings Pitched	
Wakefield,Tim	3226.1
Hernandez,Livan	3121.2
Vazquez,Javier	2840.0
Millwood,Kevin	2559.1
Halladay,Roy	2531.0
Lowe,Derek	2515.2
Hudson,Tim	2503.1
Buehrle,Mark	2476.2
Sabathia,CC	2364.1
Zito,Barry	2252.0

Batters Faced	
Wakefield,Tim	13939
Hernandez,Livan	13524
Vazquez,Javier	11935
Millwood,Kevin	10927
Lowe,Derek	10661
Hudson,Tim	10408
Halladay,Roy	10359
Buehrle,Mark	10317
Sabathia,CC	9789
Zito,Barry	9557

Strikeouts	
Vazquez,Javier	2536
Wakefield,Tim	2156
Sabathia,CC	2017
Millwood,Kevin	1976
Halladay,Roy	1934
Hernandez,Livan	1928
Santana,Johan	1877
Burnett,A.J.	1791
Dempster,Ryan	1765
Oswalt,Roy	1759

Walks Allowed	
Wakefield,Tim	1205
Hernandez,Livan	1050
Dempster,Ryan	940
Zito,Barry	934
Wright,Jamey	898
Batista,Miguel	866
Burnett,A.J.	826
Zambrano,Carlos	823
Millwood,Kevin	787
Davis,Doug	783

Hit Batters	
Wakefield,Tim	186
Wright,Jamey	142
Padilla,Vicente	106
Lackey,John	101
Hudson,Tim	99
Wood,Kerry	99
Burnett,A.J.	98
Wolf,Randy	95
Zambrano,Carlos	92
Oliver,Darren	90

Wild Pitches	
Wakefield,Tim	134
Burnett,A.J.	124
Batista,Miguel	101
Lackey,John	97
Garcia,Freddy	84
Vazquez,Javier	76
Wright,Jamey	75
Hudson,Tim	73
3 tied with	72

2011 Active Career Pitching Leaders

Saves	
Rivera,Mariano	603
Cordero,Francisco	327
Isringhausen,Jason	300
Rodriguez,Francisco	291
Nathan,Joe	261
Valverde,Jose	242
Lidge,Brad	223
Papelbon,Jonathan	219
Fuentes,Brian	199
Street,Huston	178

Save Pct	
(minimum 50 Save Ops)	
Axford,John	93.4
Rivera,Mariano	89.3
Bailey,Andrew	89.3
Nathan,Joe	89.1
Valverde,Jose	89.0
Soria,Joakim	88.9
Papelbon,Jonathan	88.3
Feliz,Neftali	88.1
Storen,Drew	87.3
Wilson,Brian	87.2

Home Runs Allowed	
Wakefield,Tim	418
Vazquez,Javier	373
Hernandez,Livan	347
Lilly,Ted	286
Millwood,Kevin	283
Colon,Bartolo	277
Buehrle,Mark	274
Wolf,Randy	264
Arroyo,Bronson	256
Tomko,Brett	255

Strikeouts Per 9 IP	
(minimum 750 IP)	
Dotel,Octavio	10.91
Wood,Kerry	10.34
Lincecum,Tim	9.87
Harden,Rich	9.20
Farnsworth,Kyle	8.97
Santana,Johan	8.85
Peavy,Jake	8.84
Cordero,Francisco	8.77
Bedard,Erik	8.76
Kazmir,Scott	8.74

Opp On-Base Percentage	
(minimum 750 IP)	
Rivera,Mariano	.262
Santana,Johan	.282
Hamels,Cole	.288
Weaver,Jered	.289
Haren,Dan	.292
Halladay,Roy	.293
Lincecum,Tim	.297
Young,Chris	.298
Peavy,Jake	.298
Cain,Matt	.298

Opp Slugging Average	
(minimum 750 IP)	
Rivera,Mariano	.290
Lincecum,Tim	.333
Cordero,Francisco	.344
Isringhausen,Jason	.348
Webb,Brandon	.352
Jimenez,Ubaldo	.354
Zambrano,Carlos	.358
Hernandez,Felix	.359
Wood,Kerry	.360
Wainwright,Adam	.361

Hits Per Nine Innings	
(minimum 750 IP)	
Rivera,Mariano	6.94
Wood,Kerry	7.06
Dotel,Octavio	7.14
Young,Chris	7.26
Lincecum,Tim	7.37
Cain,Matt	7.53
Harden,Rich	7.57
Santana,Johan	7.59
Jimenez,Ubaldo	7.76
Zambrano,Carlos	7.81

Home Runs Per Nine IP	
(minimum 750 IP)	
Rivera,Mariano	0.48
Lincecum,Tim	0.58
Jimenez,Ubaldo	0.61
Webb,Brandon	0.63
Cordero,Francisco	0.63
Wainwright,Adam	0.66
Billingsley,Chad	0.67
Hudson,Tim	0.71
Pelfrey,Mike	0.72
Isringhausen,Jason	0.73

Strikeouts / Walks Ratio	
(minimum 750 IP)	
Haren,Dan	4.04
Rivera,Mariano	4.04
Hamels,Cole	3.74
Halladay,Roy	3.72
Nolasco,Ricky	3.69
Shields,James	3.64
Santana,Johan	3.55
Oswalt,Roy	3.52
Greinke,Zack	3.48
Baker,Scott	3.44

Stolen Base Pct Allowed	
(minimum 750 IP)	
Carpenter,Chris	37.4
Buehrle,Mark	41.9
Duke,Zach	50.6
Zambrano,Carlos	52.0
Colon,Bartolo	52.4
Garland,Jon	52.5
Santana,Johan	52.6
Greinke,Zack	53.0
Franklin,Ryan	54.5
Capuano,Chris	56.1

GIDP Induced	
Hernandez,Livan	291
Lowe,Derek	288
Buehrle,Mark	278
Hudson,Tim	273
Wright,Jamey	255
Garland,Jon	245
Halladay,Roy	238
Wakefield,Tim	229
Carpenter,Chris	220
Sabathia,CC	216

GIDP Per Nine IP	
(minimum 750 IP)	
Cook,Aaron	1.28
Wright,Jamey	1.26
Westbrook,Jake	1.21
Maholm,Paul	1.20
Lannan,John	1.19
Saunders,Joe	1.17
Carmona,Fausto	1.15
Garland,Jon	1.06
Duke,Zach	1.05
Lowe,Derek	1.03

Complete Game %	
(minimum 100 GS)	
Halladay,Roy	0.19
Hernandez,Livan	0.11
Lee,Cliff	0.10
Carpenter,Chris	0.10
Sabathia,CC	0.09
Colon,Bartolo	0.09
Hernandez,Felix	0.09
Shields,James	0.09
Webb,Brandon	0.08
Willis,Dontrelle	0.07

Quality Start Pct	
(minimum 100 GS)	
Lincecum,Tim	72.9
Wainwright,Adam	69.7
Oswalt,Roy	68.4
Johnson,Josh	68.1
Weaver,Jered	67.2
Halladay,Roy	67.0
Hernandez,Felix	66.8
Webb,Brandon	66.7
Haren,Dan	66.4
Santana,Johan	66.2

Walks Per 9 IP	
(minimum 750 IP)	
Halladay,Roy	1.85
Haren,Dan	1.89
Rivera,Mariano	2.04
Buehrle,Mark	2.05
Shields,James	2.07
Nolasco,Ricky	2.08
Oswalt,Roy	2.09
Baker,Scott	2.10
Lee,Cliff	2.15
Pavano,Carl	2.17

Games Finished	
Rivera,Mariano	883
Cordero,Francisco	557
Isringhausen,Jason	482
Rodriguez,Francisco	445
Valverde,Jose	422
Nathan,Joe	408
Fuentes,Brian	367
Lidge,Brad	364
Papelbon,Jonathan	334
Gregg,Kevin	313

2011 American League Bill James Leaders

Top Game Scores

Pitcher	Date	Opp	IP	H	R	ER	BB	SO	GS
Santana,Ervin, LAA	7/27	Cle	9.0	0	1	0	1	10	94
Stewart,Zach, CWS	9/5	Min	9.0	1	0	0	0	9	94
Verlander,Justin, Det	6/14	Cle	9.0	2	0	0	1	12	94
Shields,James, TB	5/22	Fla	9.0	3	0	0	1	13	93
Haren,Dan, LAA	7/5	Det	9.0	2	0	0	0	9	92
Beckett,Josh, Bos	6/15	TB	9.0	1	0	0	0	6	91
Haren,Dan, LAA	4/12	Cle	9.0	1	0	0	2	8	91
McCarthy,Brandon, Oak	9/3	Sea	9.0	3	0	0	0	10	91
Danks,John, CWS	8/27	Sea	9.0	3	0	0	1	10	90
Verlander,Justin, Det	5/7	Tor	9.0	0	0	0	1	4	90

Worst Game Scores

Pitcher	Date	Opp	IP	H	R	ER	BB	SO	GS
Cahill,Trevor, Oak	7/22	NYY	2.0	9	10	10	2	2	-2
O'Sullivan,Sean, KC	5/28	Tex	5.2	15	10	10	2	1	-2
Shields,James, TB	7/27	Oak	4.0	12	10	10	2	2	-2
Floyd,Gavin, CWS	8/3	NYY	2.1	9	10	10	1	2	0
Carmona,Fausto, Cle	4/1	CWS	3.0	11	10	10	1	5	1
Chen,Bruce, KC	7/27	Bos	4.0	10	10	10	3	3	2
Talbot,Mitch, Cle	5/25	Bos	3.0	12	8	8	2	1	2
Stewart,Zach, CWS	9/23	KC	4.0	12	9	9	0	1	3
Perez,Luis, Tor	9/6	Bos	2.2	10	8	8	2	1	5
5 tied with									6

Runs Created

Cabrera,Miguel, Det	141
Ellsbury,Jacoby, Bos	134
Bautista,Jose, Tor	133
Gonzalez,Adrian, Bos	121
Young,Michael, Tex	118
Pedroia,Dustin, Bos	114
Granderson,Curtis, NYY	113
Cano,Robinson, NYY	111
Teixeira,Mark, NYY	106
2 tied with	103

Runs Created Per 27 Outs

Bautista,Jose, Tor	9.5
Cabrera,Miguel, Det	9.3
Ellsbury,Jacoby, Bos	7.5
Gonzalez,Adrian, Bos	7.2
Martinez,Victor, Det	7.1
Young,Michael, Tex	7.1
Ortiz,David, Bos	6.7
Avila,Alex, Det	6.7
Konerko,Paul, CWS	6.6
Granderson,Curtis, NYY	6.6

Offensive Winning %

Bautista,Jose, Tor	.808
Cabrera,Miguel, Det	.807
Ellsbury,Jacoby, Bos	.720
Martinez,Victor, Det	.708
Longoria,Evan, TB	.704
Gonzalez,Adrian, Bos	.704
Konerko,Paul, CWS	.687
Avila,Alex, Det	.680
Zobrist,Ben, TB	.673
Joyce,Matt, TB	.672

Secondary Average
(minimum 502 PA)

Bautista,Jose, Tor	.581
Granderson,Curtis, NYY	.479
Cabrera,Miguel, Det	.434
Longoria,Evan, TB	.422
Kinsler,Ian, Tex	.415
Reynolds,Mark, Bal	.414
Santana,Carlos, Cle	.402
Ortiz,David, Bos	.396
Teixeira,Mark, NYY	.382
Upton,B.J., TB	.377

Isolated Power
(minimum 502 PA)

Bautista,Jose, Tor	.306
Granderson,Curtis, NYY	.290
Beltre,Adrian, Tex	.265
Reynolds,Mark, Bal	.262
Longoria,Evan, TB	.251
Cruz,Nelson, Tex	.246
Teixeira,Mark, NYY	.246
Ortiz,David, Bos	.246
Cabrera,Miguel, Det	.241
Hamilton,Josh, Tex	.238

Power / Speed Number
(minimum 502 PA)

Ellsbury,Jacoby, Bos	35.2
Granderson,Curtis, NYY	31.1
Kinsler,Ian, Tex	31.0
Upton,B.J., TB	28.1
Pedroia,Dustin, Bos	23.2
Francoeur,Jeff, KC	21.0
Cabrera,Asdrubal, Cle	20.2
Gordon,Alex, KC	19.6
Zobrist,Ben, TB	19.5
Cabrera,Melky, KC	18.9

Speed Scores (2010-2011)

Crawford,Carl, Bos	8.34
Gardner,Brett, NYY	8.29
Jackson,Austin, Det	8.22
Crisp,Coco, Oak	7.92
Davis,Rajai, Tor	7.73
Granderson,Curtis, NYY	7.67
Span,Denard, Min	7.65
Upton,B.J., TB	7.21
Pierre,Juan, CWS	7.07
Suzuki,Ichiro, Sea	7.00

Cheap Wins

Penny,Brad, Det	6
Lackey,John, Bos	5
Arrieta,Jake, Bal	4
Hochevar,Luke, KC	4
9 tied with	3

Tough Losses

Price,David, TB	8
Shields,James, TB	8
Fister,Doug, Sea-Det	6
Guthrie,Jeremy, Bal	6
Hellickson,Jeremy, TB	6
Hernandez,Felix, Sea	6
McCarthy,Brandon, Oak	6
Pineda,Michael, Sea	6
4 tied with	5

2011 National League Bill James Leaders

Top Game Scores

Pitcher	Date	Opp	IP	H	R	ER	BB	SO	GS
Capuano,Chris, NYM	8/26	Atl	9.0	2	0	0	0	13	96
Carpenter,Chris, StL	9/28	Hou	9.0	2	0	0	1	11	93
Kershaw,Clayton, LAD	6/20	Det	9.0	2	0	0	1	11	93
Sanchez,Anibal, Fla	9/10	Pit	9.0	1	0	0	3	11	93
Jurrjens,Jair, Atl	7/1	Bal	9.0	1	0	0	1	8	92
Kershaw,Clayton, LAD	5/29	Fla	9.0	2	0	0	1	10	92
Lee,Cliff, Phi	4/14	Was	9.0	3	0	0	1	12	92
Kennedy,Ian, Ari	9/19	Pit	8.0	1	0	0	1	12	91
Kennedy,Ian, Ari	4/25	Phi	9.0	3	0	0	0	10	91
Garcia,Jaime, StL	5/6	Mil	9.0	2	0	0	1	8	90
Hudson,Tim, Atl	5/4	Mil	9.0	1	0	0	1	6	90

Worst Game Scores

Pitcher	Date	Opp	IP	H	R	ER	BB	SO	GS
Garcia,Jaime, StL	5/28	Col	3.1	11	12	11	4	6	-6
Nolasco,Ricky, Fla	8/17	Col	3.0	11	11	11	1	2	-6
Davis,Doug, ChC	6/28	SF	4.1	12	10	10	3	3	-1
Nolasco,Ricky, Fla	7/20	SD	1.1	9	9	9	2	3	1
Bailey,Homer, Cin	7/28	NYM	4.0	12	9	9	2	2	2
Bumgarner,Madison, SF	6/21	Min	0.1	9	8	8	0	1	2
Arroyo,Bronson, Cin	5/23	Phi	2.2	10	9	9	1	2	3
Correia,Kevin, Pit	8/2	ChC	2.0	10	8	8	0	2	6
Karstens,Jeff, Pit	8/5	SD	3.1	9	9	9	1	2	7
Narveson,Chris, Mil	7/2	Min	4.2	14	7	7	2	1	7
Willis,Dontrelle, Cin	9/12	ChC	3.1	9	8	8	3	0	7

Runs Created

Votto,Joey, Cin	131
Kemp,Matt, LAD	129
Braun,Ryan, Mil	124
Fielder,Prince, Mil	120
Berkman,Lance, StL	107
Upton,Justin, Ari	103
McCutchen,Andrew, Pit	102
Pence,Hunter, Hou-Phi	102
Tulowitzki,Troy, Col	101
Pujols,Albert, StL	100

Runs Created Per 27 Outs

Braun,Ryan, Mil	8.5
Berkman,Lance, StL	8.1
Votto,Joey, Cin	7.9
Kemp,Matt, LAD	7.9
Fielder,Prince, Mil	7.6
Gonzalez,Carlos, Col	7.1
Morse,Michael, Was	6.8
Tulowitzki,Troy, Col	6.8
Beltran,Carlos, NYM-SF	6.7
Reyes,Jose, NYM	6.5

Offensive Winning %

Berkman,Lance, StL	.802
Braun,Ryan, Mil	.797
Kemp,Matt, LAD	.791
Votto,Joey, Cin	.763
Fielder,Prince, Mil	.761
Beltran,Carlos, NYM-SF	.740
Morse,Michael, Was	.734
Holliday,Matt, StL	.722
Reyes,Jose, NYM	.717
Ramirez,Aramis, ChC	.706

Secondary Average
(minimum 502 PA)

Fielder,Prince, Mil	.457
Kemp,Matt, LAD	.452
Pena,Carlos, ChC	.446
Berkman,Lance, StL	.439
Braun,Ryan, Mil	.426
Stanton,Mike, Fla	.421
Votto,Joey, Cin	.419
McCutchen,Andrew, Pit	.393
Upton,Justin, Ari	.375
Gonzalez,Carlos, Col	.372

Isolated Power
(minimum 502 PA)

Stanton,Mike, Fla	.275
Fielder,Prince, Mil	.267
Braun,Ryan, Mil	.265
Kemp,Matt, LAD	.262
Morse,Michael, Was	.247
Berkman,Lance, StL	.246
Tulowitzki,Troy, Col	.242
Pujols,Albert, StL	.242
Upton,Justin, Ari	.240
Pena,Carlos, ChC	.237

Power / Speed Number
(minimum 502 PA)

Kemp,Matt, LAD	39.5
Braun,Ryan, Mil	33.0
Upton,Justin, Ari	25.0
McCutchen,Andrew, Pit	23.0
Gonzalez,Carlos, Col	22.6
Stubbs,Drew, Cin	21.8
Young,Chris, Ari	21.0
Rollins,Jimmy, Phi	20.9
Werth,Jayson, Was	19.5
Espinosa,Danny, Was	18.8

Speed Scores (2010-2011)

Reyes,Jose, NYM	8.25
Victorino,Shane, Phi	8.24
Bourn,Michael, Hou-Atl	8.17
Maybin,Cameron, SD	8.15
Stubbs,Drew, Cin	7.84
Morgan,Nyjer, Mil	7.72
Fowler,Dexter, Col	7.65
Pagan,Angel, NYM	7.55
Torres,Andres, SF	7.14
Utley,Chase, Phi	7.04

Cheap Wins

Harang,Aaron, SD	4
Narveson,Chris, Mil	4
Westbrook,Jake, StL	4
Capuano,Chris, NYM	3
Chacin,Jhoulys, Col	3
Garcia,Jaime, StL	3
Minor,Mike, Atl	3
Niese,Jonathon, NYM	3
Vogelsong,Ryan, SF	3
Zambrano,Carlos, ChC	3

Tough Losses

Kuroda,Hiroki, LAD	8
Dickey,R.A., NYM	7
Latos,Mat, SD	7
Lincecum,Tim, SF	7
Bumgarner,Madison, SF	6
Chacin,Jhoulys, Col	6
Dempster,Ryan, ChC	6
Lilly,Ted, LAD	6
Volstad,Chris, Fla	6
Zimmermann,Jordan, Was	6

Additional Bill James Leaders

AL Batters Win Shares
(2011)

Cabrera,Miguel, Det	38
Bautista,Jose, Tor	36
Ellsbury,Jacoby, Bos	34
Cano,Robinson, NYY	30
Zobrist,Ben, TB	28
Avila,Alex, Det	27
Gonzalez,Adrian, Bos	27
Pedroia,Dustin, Bos	27
Granderson,Curtis, NYY	26
2 tied with	25

NL Batters Win Shares
(2011)

Braun,Ryan, Mil	37
Kemp,Matt, LAD	37
Fielder,Prince, Mil	33
Votto,Joey, Cin	33
Berkman,Lance, StL	30
Montero,Miguel, Ari	29
McCutchen,Andrew, Pit	28
4 tied with	26

AL Pitchers Win Shares
(2011)

Verlander,Justin, Det	27
Weaver,Jered, LAA	24
Romero,Ricky, Tor	20
Shields,James, TB	20
Wilson,C.J., Tex	20
Sabathia,CC, NYY	19
Fister,Doug, Sea-Det	18
Haren,Dan, LAA	18
Beckett,Josh, Bos	16
Hernandez,Felix, Sea	16

NL Pitchers Win Shares
(2011)

Kershaw,Clayton, LAD	23
Halladay,Roy, Phi	22
Lee,Cliff, Phi	22
Kennedy,Ian, Ari	20
Hamels,Cole, Phi	17
Kimbrel,Craig, Atl	17
Hudson,Daniel, Ari	16
Lincecum,Tim, SF	16
5 tied with	15

Batters Win Shares
(Career)

Rodriguez,Alex	457
Ramirez,Manny	408
Jones,Chipper	401
Jeter,Derek	380
Thome,Jim	379
Pujols,Albert	373
Abreu,Bobby	347
Rodriguez,Ivan	338
Guerrero,Vladimir	324
Giambi,Jason	320

Pitchers Win Shares
(Career)

Rivera,Mariano	255
Halladay,Roy	216
Hudson,Tim	192
Sabathia,CC	180
Buehrle,Mark	176
Wakefield,Tim	176
Oswalt,Roy	171
Lowe,Derek	170
Vazquez,Javier	170
Santana,Johan	169

AL Component ERA
(minimum 162 IP)

Verlander,Justin, Det	1.92
Weaver,Jered, LAA	2.27
Haren,Dan, LAA	2.45
Fister,Doug, Sea-Det	2.53
Beckett,Josh, Bos	2.56
Shields,James, TB	2.58
Pineda,Michael, Sea	2.73
McCarthy,Brandon, Oak	2.80
Hellickson,Jeremy, TB	2.89
Price,David, TB	2.97

NL Component ERA
(minimum 162 IP)

Kershaw,Clayton, LAD	2.00
Hamels,Cole, Phi	2.23
Halladay,Roy, Phi	2.26
Cain,Matt, SF	2.31
Lee,Cliff, Phi	2.44
Kennedy,Ian, Ari	2.71
Hudson,Tim, Atl	2.91
Lincecum,Tim, SF	2.92
Latos,Mat, SD	2.93
Marcum,Shaun, Mil	2.97

ALHighest Avg Game Score
(minimum 30 GS)

Verlander,Justin, Det	65.94
Weaver,Jered, LAA	62.94
Shields,James, TB	62.85
Beckett,Josh, Bos	60.00
Romero,Ricky, Tor	59.03
Sabathia,CC, NYY	58.76
Haren,Dan, LAA	58.47
Fister,Doug, Sea-Det	58.10
Wilson,C.J., Tex	57.76
Price,David, TB	57.35

AL Lowest Avg Game Score
(minimum 30 GS)

Penny,Brad, Det	42.61
Carmona,Fausto, Cle	45.59
Francis,Jeff, KC	45.77
Porcello,Rick, Det	46.77
Pavano,Carl, Min	47.45
Burnett,A.J., NYY	48.31
Guthrie,Jeremy, Bal	49.34
Hochevar,Luke, KC	49.68
Cahill,Trevor, Oak	50.00
Vargas,Jason, Sea	50.22

AL Lowest Offensive Win %

Rios,Alex, CWS	.183
Escobar,Alcides, KC	.271
Suzuki,Kurt, Oak	.316
Olivo,Miguel, Sea	.335
Beckham,Gordon, CWS	.339
Crawford,Carl, Bos	.379
Guerrero,Vladimir, Bal	.381
Valencia,Danny, Min	.383
Moreland,Mitch, Tex	.397
Wells,Vernon, LAA	.403

NL Highest Avg Game Score
(minimum 30 GS)

Kershaw,Clayton, LAD	64.79
Lee,Cliff, Phi	64.06
Halladay,Roy, Phi	63.31
Hamels,Cole, Phi	62.06
Kennedy,Ian, Ari	59.91
Lincecum,Tim, SF	59.61
Cain,Matt, SF	58.88
Hudson,Tim, Atl	56.15
Latos,Mat, SD	56.06
Bumgarner,Madison, SF	55.91

NL Lowest Avg Game Score
(minimum 30 GS)

Westbrook,Jake, StL	46.15
Lowe,Derek, Atl	46.35
Pelfrey,Mike, NYM	46.36
Arroyo,Bronson, Cin	46.44
Nolasco,Ricky, Fla	48.12
Lannan,John, Was	48.97
McDonald,James, Pit	49.26
Dempster,Ryan, ChC	49.76
Billingsley,Chad, LAD	50.00
Myers,Brett, Hou	50.18

NL Lowest Offensive Win %

Betancourt,Yuniesky, Mil	.305
McGehee,Casey, Mil	.324
Gonzalez,Alex, Atl	.349
Bartlett,Jason, SD	.378
Stubbs,Drew, Cin	.418
Prado,Martin, Atl	.430
Desmond,Ian, Was	.452
Infante,Omar, Fla	.468
Bay,Jason, NYM	.470
Huff,Aubrey, SF	.474

Win Shares

Bill James devised Win Shares as a way to relate a player's individual statistics to the number of wins he contributed to his team. As a single number, Win Shares allows us to easily compare the accomplishments of each player to other players and to compare players across positions.

We credit a team with three Win Shares for each win. If a team wins 100 games, the players on the team will be credited with 300 Win Shares—or 300 thirds-of-a-win. If a team wins 70 games, the players on the team will be credited with 210 Win Shares, and so on.

The following pages contain the sum of a player's Win Shares prior to 2002, followed by his individual season totals from 2002 through 2011. Career totals are also included for each player.

The quality of the team does not affect an individual player's Win Shares. A great player on a bad team will rate just as well as a great player on a good team.

Win Shares are also a great tool for evaluating award voting and Hall of Fame credentials. Generally, 30 Win Shares indicates an MVP-caliber season; 20 Win Shares indicates a season worthy of the Cy Young Award.

Win Shares also adjusts for offensive environment, so it is a great tool to use for looking at the greatest individual seasons in baseball history, as well as the greatest players of all time.

Player	<02	02	03	04	05	06	07	08	09	10	11	Career
Aardsma,David				0		4	1	1	16	8		30
Abad,Fernando										2	0	2
Abreu,Bobby	107	29	28	33	25	27	18	22	23	20	15	347
Abreu,Juan											1	1
Accardo,Jeremy				2	4	14	0	2	0	1		23
Aceves,Alfredo								3	7	2	12	24
Ackley,Dustin											14	14
Acosta,Manny							2	4	1	4	3	14
Adams,Mike				5	1	0		6	5	10	12	39
Adams,Ryan											2	2
Adcock,Nathan											2	2
Affeldt,Jeremy		5	12	4	1	3	5	6	10	3	6	55
Albers,Matt						0	0	4	2	5	3	14
Alburquerque,Al											6	6
Alfonzo,Eliezer						9	1	0	1	0	1	12
Allen,Brandon									1	1	3	5
Almonte,Erick	1		2									3
Alonso,Yonder										0	4	4
Altuve,Jose											2	2
Alvarez,Henderson											4	4
Alvarez,Pedro										14	3	17
Amarista,Alexi											1	1
Amezaga,Alfredo		2	1	1	0	5	5	9	1		1	25
Anderson,Brett									8	9	4	21
Anderson,Lars										1	0	1
Andino,Robert					0	0	0	1	3	0	11	15
Andrus,Elvis									17	20	18	55
Angle,Matt											1	1
Ankiel,Rick	17			0				8	13	5	4	7 → 54
Arencibia,J.P.										1	14	15
Arredondo,Jose								11	1		4	16
Arrieta,Jake										5	5	10
Arroyo,Bronson	3	2	2	11	11	20	11	10	13	14	3	100
Ascanio,Jose								0	1	0	0	0
Asencio,Jairo									0	0	0	0
Atchison,Scott			2	0			2			2	2	8
Atkins,Mitch									0	0	0	0
Augenstein,Bryan									0	0	0	0
Avila,Alex									3	7	27	37
Aviles,Mike								17	2	10	5	34
Axelrod,Dylan											2	2
Axford,John									1	11	15	27
Ayala,Luis		11	10	8		4	2	2			5	42
Aybar,Erick					1		2	15	20	9	20	67
Badenhop,Burke								0	5	4	4	13
Baez,Danys	6	11	9	10	10	6	1		5	0	0	58
Bailey,Andrew									17	11	6	34
Bailey,Homer							2	0	5	5	5	17
Baker,Jeff					1	3	1	7	7	4	3	26
Baker,John								9	13	1	0	23
Baker,Scott					4	0	8	13	12	8	11	56
Balester,Collin								1	0	2	0	3
Balfour,Grant	0		2	3			0	11	5	6	8	35
Barajas,Rod	2	3	5	9	11	7	3	10	12	13	8	83
Bard,Daniel									4	11	7	22
Bard,Josh		1	7	2	2	10	16	2	4	2	2	48
Barmes,Clint			1	3	9	6	0	12	13	10	11	65
Barney,Darwin										1	14	15
Bartlett,Jason				0	6	13	16	14	23	16	11	99
Barton,Daric							3	9	6	21	4	43
Bass,Anthony											5	5
Bastardo,Antonio									0	1	10	11
Batista,Miguel	23	9	14	11	8	10	12	0	5	5	4	101
Bautista,Jose				0	0	9	12	8	6	34	36	105
Baxter,Mike										0	1	1
Bay,Jason			5	15	30	21	12	24	29	11	10	157
Beachy,Brandon										0	7	7
Beato,Pedro											2	2
Beavan,Blake											5	5
Beck,Chad											0	0
Beckett,Josh	3	5	11	9	12	11	18	11	16	2	16	114
Beckham,Gordon									12	11	14	37
Bedard,Erik		0		6	8	13	17	6	8		6	64

Player	<02	02	03	04	05	06	07	08	09	10	11	Career
Beimel,Joe	4	3	2	0	1	7	6	7	4	4	0	38
Belisle,Matt			0		4	3	5	0	1	11	7	31
Bell,Heath			2	0	1	13	6	12	15	11		60
Bell,Josh										1	0	1
Bell,Trevor									0	2	2	4
Below,Duane											1	1
Belt,Brandon											5	5
Beltran,Carlos	52	20	28	29	21	34	25	29	14	8	26	286
Beltre,Adrian	53	16	13	33	13	17	16	13	10	26	16	226
Beltre,Omar										0		0
Benoit,Joaquin	0	3	5	4	6	4	10	2		9	8	51
Benson,Joe										0		0
Berg,Justin									2	1	1	4
Bergesen,Brad									9	6	0	15
Berken,Jason									1	6	1	8
Berkman,Lance	43	29	25	30	20	31	24	36	22	14	30	304
Bernadina,Roger								1	0	10	7	18
Betances,Dellin										0		0
Betancourt,Rafael			4	5	7	5	16	3	8	8	10	66
Betancourt,Yuniesky					3	13	19	8	8	12	11	74
Betemit,Wilson	0		1	7	9	8	2	0		12	11	50
Billings,Bruce										0		0
Billingsley,Chad						6	12	16	9	11	6	60
Bixler,Brian								1	0	0	0	1
Blackburn,Nick							0	10	12	3	5	30
Blackmon,Charlie											1	1
Blake,Casey	2	0	11	17	9	11	11	18	19	13	5	116
Blanco,Andres			3	1	2				2	4	1	13
Blanco,Henry	21	4	2	5	5	6	0	3	6	3	4	59
Blanks,Kyle									5	2	3	10
Blanton,Joe				0	13	10	13	7	11	4	1	59
Blevins,Jerry							0	3	1	3	2	9
Bloomquist,Willie		3	3	2	4	5	2	5	7	3	8	42
Blum,Geoff	21	15	5	3	7	6	9	9	6	7	0	88
Boesch,Brennan										11	12	23
Boggs,Brandon								5	0	0	0	5
Boggs,Mitchell								0	2	4	3	9
Bogusevic,Brian										0	4	4
Bonifacio,Emilio							1	2	7	5	20	35
Borbon,Julio									5	11	3	19
Boscan,J.C.									0	0	0	0
Bourgeois,Jason								0	0	0	6	6
Bourjos,Peter										3	16	19
Bourn,Michael						0	4	7	23	18	21	73
Bowden,Michael								1	0	0	1	2
Bowker,John								7	1	2	0	10
Boyer,Blaine					4	0	0	1	3	3	0	11
Brach,Brad											0	0
Brackman,Andrew											0	0
Braddock,Zach										3	0	3
Braden,Dallas							0	4	8	12	1	25
Bradley,Milton	6	6	18	16	10	13	11	19	11	3	2	115
Brantley,Michael									3	5	11	19
Branyan,Russell	16	8	5	5	9	6	5	5	14	8	2	83
Braun,Ryan							22	23	36	25	37	143
Bray,Bill						3	1	4		1	6	15
Brazoban,Yhency			4	4	0	0	0				0	8
Breslow,Craig					1	1		6	6	8	3	25
Brignac,Reid								0	2	10	4	16
Britton,Zach											6	6
Broderick,Brian											0	0
Brothers,Rex											4	4
Brown,Andrew										0		0
Brown,Corey										0		0
Brown,Domonic										0	4	4
Brown,Dusty									0	0	0	0
Broxton,Jonathan					0	9	10	10	16	6	0	51
Bruce,Jay								7	9	16	22	54
Bruney,Brian		2	0	3		2	6	3	0	0		16
Buchholz,Clay							3	0	6	18	6	33
Buchholz,Taylor					1	5	9			1	2	18
Buck,John				4	10	8	7	8	6	17	14	74
Buck,Travis							10	5	1	0	3	19

Player	<02	02	03	04	05	06	07	08	09	10	11	Career
Buehrle,Mark	22	17	13	17	22	9	17	16	16	12	15	176
Buente,Jay										0	0	0
Bulger,Jason				1	0	1	0	7	0	1		10
Bumgarner,Madison									1	8	12	21
Burnett,A.J.	17	14	0	7	11	9	11	14	12	4	5	104
Burnett,Alex										1	1	2
Burnett,Sean			2					2	5	7	5	21
Burrell,Pat	29	25	8	14	24	15	20	20	6	14	6	181
Burres,Brian						1	3	2	0	2	1	9
Burriss,Manny								4	2	0	2	8
Burroughs,Sean			3	16	16	6	1				1	43
Burton,Jared							5	6	3	1	0	15
Bush,Dave				7	6	12	6	8	0	4	0	43
Butera,Drew										3	3	6
Butler,Billy							7	8	18	20	17	70
Byrd,Marlon		0	16	5	6	2	13	12	20	19	8	101
Byrdak,Tim	0				1	0	4	4	5	3	2	19
Cabrera,Asdrubal							7	12	18	9	25	71
Cabrera,Everth									14	3	0	17
Cabrera,Melky					0	13	12	5	14	8	19	71
Cabrera,Miguel		12	19	27	33	29	20	25	30	38		233
Cabrera,Orlando	49	14	19	11	15	18	25	19	14	9	4	197
Cahill,Trevor									7	16	9	32
Cain,Lorenzo										6	0	6
Cain,Matt					5	11	12	14	20	15	15	92
Cairo,Miguel	34	3	3	14	5	5	4	4	0	5	8	85
Callaspo,Alberto						1	1	6	17	11	17	53
Cameron,Mike	90	18	21	15	11	25	20	17	17	4	5	243
Camp,Shawn				4	0	5	0	3	5	7	4	28
Campana,Tony											3	3
Cancel,Robinson	0							0	0	0	0	0
Cano,Robinson					12	17	21	12	18	34	30	144
Cantu,Jorge				4	18	5	1	19	17	9	0	73
Canzler,Russ											0	0
Capps,Matt					0	7	14	7	2	13	7	50
Capuano,Chris			2	4	13	14	5			3	5	46
Carignan,Andrew											0	0
Carlyle,Buddy	0			0			3	4	0		0	7
Carmona,Fausto						1	22	3	0	12	2	40
Carp,Mike									2	0	7	9
Carpenter,Andrew								0	0	0	0	0
Carpenter,Chris	40	3		12	20	19	0	1	21	14	11	141
Carpenter,Chris (ChC)											1	1
Carpenter,David											2	2
Carpenter,Matt											0	0
Carrasco,Carlos									0	3	5	8
Carrasco,D.J.			6	1	4			3	7	4	0	25
Carreno,Joel											2	2
Carrera,Ezequiel											5	5
Carroll,Brett							0	0	5	0	0	5
Carroll,Jamey		3	3	6	9	13	5	10	8	14	14	85
Carter,Chris									0	0	0	0
Cashner,Andrew										2	1	3
Casilla,Alexi						0	1	9	4	6	7	27
Casilla,Santiago				0	0	0	4	3	0	8	8	23
Cassevah,Bobby										1	4	5
Castillo,Alberto								2	1	0	1	4
Castillo,Welington										1	0	1
Castro,Juan	10	2	7	5	7	6	1	2	2	2	0	44
Castro,Ramon	4	4	2	1	7	2	6	6	4	5	2	43
Castro,Starlin										12	25	37
Cecil,Brett									3	10	4	17
Ceda,Jose										0	0	0
Cedeno,Ronny					2	5	1	5	7	9	10	39
Cedeno,Xavier											0	0
Cervelli,Francisco								0	3	7	4	14
Chacin,Jhoulys									0	10	12	22
Chamberlain,Joba							5	11	6	5	3	30
Chambers,Adron											1	1
Chapman,Aroldis										2	4	6
Chatwood,Tyler											3	3
Chavez,Endy	0	3	9	10	1	13	4	3	3		6	52
Chavez,Eric	53	24	23	18	20	16	6	3	0	0	6	169

Player	<02	02	03	04	05	06	07	08	09	10	11	Career
Chavez,Jesse								0	4	0	0	4
Chen,Bruce	17	1	0	4	13	0	0		1	9	9	54
Chirinos,Robinson										1	1	1
Chisenhall,Lonnie											6	6
Choate,Randy	5	0	0	3	0	1	0		5	2	4	20
Choo,Shin-Soo					0	4	1	16	23	27	8	79
Christian,Justin								1			1	2
Ciriaco,Pedro										1	2	3
Cishek,Steve										1	6	7
Cleto,Maikel										0	0	0
Clevenger,Steven											0	0
Clippard,Tyler							1	1	5	9	13	29
Cobb,Alex											3	3
Coffey,Todd					3	9	1	7	1		5	27
Coghlan,Chris									21	8	4	33
Coke,Phil								3	5	6	4	18
Coleman,Casey										3	0	3
Coleman,Louis											5	5
Collins,Tim											4	4
Collmenter,Josh											10	10
Colon,Bartolo	63	22	17	10	18	1	1	2	3		8	145
Colvin,Tyler									0	9	1	10
Conger,Hank										1	4	5
Conrad,Brooks							0	1	8	2		11
Constanza,Jose										3		3
Contreras,Jose			7	6	17	13	5	7	4	6	2	67
Cook,Aaron		2	3	6	6	12	9	15	11	4	0	68
Cook,Ryan										0	0	0
Cooper,David											2	2
Cora,Alex	13	13	12	17	5	6	4	5	5	3	2	85
Cordero,Francisco	5	8	12	17	11	12	12	11	13	10	13	124
Cormier,Lance				0	4	2	0	4	6	3	0	19
Corporan,Carlos										0	1	1
Correia,Kevin			3	0	2	6	8	0	8	1	4	32
Cortes,Dan										0	0	0
Counsell,Craig	42	15	5	10	22	9	6	6	15	6	2	138
Cousins,Scott										1	0	1
Cowgill,Collin											2	2
Cozart,Zack											1	1
Craig,Allen										2	10	12
Crain,Jesse				4	10	7	0	5	4	6	10	46
Cramer,Bobby										2	1	3
Crawford,Brandon											5	5
Crawford,Carl		6	13	20	22	21	20	11	19	32	8	172
Crisp,Coco		3	8	14	20	9	16	11	4	14	15	114
Crotta,Mike											0	0
Crow,Aaron											5	5
Crowe,Trevor									2	7	1	10
Cruz,Juan	4	3	0	7	0	6	6	6	2	0	3	37
Cruz,Nelson					0	3	4	7	16	19	16	65
Cruz,Tony											2	2
Cuddyer,Michael	0	3	1	10	7	22	16	7	17	15	17	115
Cueto,Johnny								6	7	12	12	37
Cunningham,Aaron								3	0	3	1	7
Cust,Jack	0	0	4	0		0	19	17	14	12	4	70
Daley,Matt									4	1	0	5
Damon,Johnny	104	22	19	26	25	21	15	23	21	13	15	304
Danks,John							4	17	16	16	8	61
D'Arnaud,Chase											1	1
Darnell,James											0	0
Davies,Kyle					4	0	1	7	5	4	0	21
Davis,Blake											1	1
Davis,Chris								8	7	1	4	20
Davis,Doug	13	3	7	16	12	8	11	7	10	0	0	87
Davis,Ike										16	6	22
Davis,Rajai						0	5	5	13	14	6	43
Davis,Wade									2	8	6	16
De Aza,Alejandro							1		1	1	9	12
De Fratus,Justin											0	0
De Jesus,Ivan											0	0
de la Cruz,Frankie								0	0	0	1	1
de la Rosa,Dane											0	0
de la Rosa,Jorge			0	2	2	3	5	12	8	4		36

Player	<02	02	03	04	05	06	07	08	09	10	11	Career
de la Rosa,Rubby											3	3
De Los Santos,F.											2	2
Deduno,Sam										0	0	0
DeJesus,David			0	9	16	14	15	22	16	11	8	111
Del Rosario,Enerio										1	1	2
Delabar,Steve											1	1
Delaney,Rob										0	0	0
Delgado,Randall											2	2
Demel,Sam										1	1	2
Dempster,Ryan	30	4	0	2	14	6	8	18	12	12	5	111
Denorfia,Chris					0	2		2	0	10	7	21
DeRosa,Mark	7	7	5	2	4	14	16	23	13	1	3	95
Descalso,Daniel										1	10	11
Desmond,Ian								2	11	16		29
Detwiler,Ross							0		2	0	4	6
Devine,Joey				0	0	1	9				2	12
DeWitt,Blake								12	0	15	5	32
Diamond,Scott											1	1
Diaz,Matt			0	0	2	7	11	1	15	6	2	44
Dickerson,Chris								5	7	0	1	13
Dickey,R.A.	0		7	4	0	0		3	3	15	11	43
Dickson,Brandon											0	0
DiFelice,Mark								2	3		0	5
Dillard,Tim								0	0		1	1
Dinkelman,Brian											2	2
Dirks,Andy											6	6
Dobbs,Greg				1	2	1	7	8	2	1	7	29
Dolis,Rafael											0	0
Dominguez,Matt											0	0
Donald,Jason										6	4	10
Dotel,Octavio	22	17	12	14	2	0	3	6	6	6	5	93
Doubront,Felix										1	0	1
Doumit,Ryan					6	2	6	20	4	9	9	56
Downs,Matt									1	2	9	12
Downs,Scott	3		0	0	5	6	8	11	6	8	10	57
Drabek,Kyle										0	1	1
Drew,J.D.	53	15	13	31	12	19	12	16	18	13	4	206
Drew,Stephen						6	16	21	16	20	10	89
Duda,Lucas										0	11	11
Duensing,Brian									6	13	4	23
Duffy,Danny											1	1
Duke,Zach					10	10	2	3	12	1	4	42
Dumatrait,Phil							0	1	0		2	3
Duncan,Shelley							3	0	0	6	9	18
Dunn,Adam	10	20	13	29	25	18	18	21	24	18	1	197
Dunn,Mike									0	2	5	7
Durango,Luis									1	0	0	1
Durbin,Chad	8	0	0	1		1	6	8	3	5	1	33
Dyson,Jarrod										2	2	4
Edlefsen,Steve											0	0
Ekstrom,Mike								0	0	1	0	1
Elbert,Scott								0	1	0	4	5
Ellis,A.J.								0	0	4	3	7
Ellis,Mark		14	18		21	14	20	13	11	19	9	139
Ellsbury,Jacoby						6	16	21	1	34		78
Ely,John										0	0	0
Emaus,Brad											0	0
Encarnacion,Edwin					4	14	16	14	6	8	11	73
Enright,Barry										6	0	6
Eovaldi,Nathan											2	2
Eppley,Cody											0	0
Escalona,Edgmer										1	3	4
Escalona,Sergio									1		2	3
Escobar,Alcides								0	4	12	8	24
Escobar,Eduardo											0	0
Escobar,Yunel							12	13	24	14	20	83
Espinosa,Danny										4	22	26
Estrada,Marco								0	0	0	4	4
Ethier,Andre						11	13	23	21	22	18	108
Evans,Nick								1	1		5	8
Eveland,Dana				0	0	0	8	0	0		2	10
Everett,Adam	0	1	11	12	14	13	4	4	6	1	1	67
Eyre,Willie					2	2		1			2	7

Player	<02	02	03	04	05	06	07	08	09	10	11	Career
Farnsworth,Kyle	14	0	7	3	14	5	3	3	2	5	12	68
Farquhar,Danny											0	0
Farris,Eric											0	0
Federowicz,Tim											0	0
Feldman,Scott					1	3	1	4	14	2	2	27
Feliz,Neftali								6	15	12		33
Field,Tommy											1	1
Fielder,Prince					2	16	27	23	36	23	33	160
Fiers,Michael										0		0
Figgins,Chone		0	9	20	22	17	21	12	26	11	1	139
Figueroa,Nelson	6	1	3	0				2	4	8	0	24
Fisher,Carlos									2	0		2
Fister,Doug									4	7	18	29
Flores,Jesus							6	9	3		1	19
Florimon,Pedro										0		0
Flowers,Tyler									0	0	3	3
Floyd,Gavin				2	0	0	2	15	13	12	11	55
Fontenot,Mike					0		5	12	7	7	5	36
Ford,Darren										0	1	1
Forsythe,Logan											3	3
Fowler,Dexter								0	15	13	16	44
Fox,Jake								0	6	1	1	8
Francis,Jeff				2	6	13	14	5		4	5	49
Francisco,Ben							1	9	10	5	6	31
Francisco,Frank				6		0	3	6	9	5	7	36
Francisco,Juan									2	0	2	4
Francoeur,Jeff					12	15	20	5	9	8	17	86
Franklin,Ryan	6	6	13	6	6	4	8	8	14	10	0	81
Frasor,Jason				9	6	4	3	2	10	5	5	44
Frazier,Todd											3	3
Freeman,Freddie										0	19	19
Freese,David									1	8	13	22
Frieri,Ernesto									0	4	4	8
Fryer,Eric											0	0
Fuentes,Brian	1	2	10	2	14	12	10	12	9	9	5	86
Fukudome,Kosuke								15	17	13	13	58
Fulchino,Jeff						0		0	7	1	1	9
Fuld,Sam							0		4	1	9	14
Furbush,Charlie											1	1
Furcal,Rafael	26	20	26	20	26	27	15	8	17	19	7	211
Galarraga,Armando							0	13	3	5	0	21
Gallardo,Yovani							9	2	10	11	13	45
Gamel,Mat								0	5	0	0	5
Garcia,Freddy	42	11	8	15	17	14	1	1	4	9	10	132
Garcia,Jaime								1		12	7	20
Gardner,Brett								3	9	17	16	45
Garland,Jon	9	8	10	11	20	15	13	9	10	12	1	118
Garner,Cole											0	0
Garrison,Steve											0	0
Garza,Matt						1	4	12	12	10	10	49
Gathright,Joey				0	4	7	6	6	0		0	23
Gaub,John											0	0
Gaudin,Chad			3	1	0	7	9	5	3	2	0	30
Gearrin,Cory											0	0
Gee,Dillon										3	5	8
Gentry,Craig									0	0	5	5
German,Esteban		0	0	2	1	11	8	5	1	1	1	30
Germano,Justin				0		0	4	0		0	2	6
Getz,Chris								0	10	4	8	22
Giambi,Jason	167	34	27	8	24	22	6	14	7	6	5	320
Giavotella,Johnny											2	2
Gibbons,Jay	4	12	18	4	15	9	1			3	1	67
Gillaspie,Conor								0		1	1	1
Gillespie,Cole										1	1	2
Gimenez,Chris									1	1	1	3
Gimenez,Hector							0			0	0	0
Gload,Ross	0	0		7	0	4	7	5	4	5	0	32
Godfrey,Graham											1	1
Goldschmidt,Paul											6	6
Golson,Greg								0	0	1	0	1
Gomes,Brandon											3	3
Gomes,Jonny			0	0	14	6	8	2	10	18	6	64
Gomez,Carlos							2	13	6	4	7	32

WIN SHARES BY YEAR

Player	<02	02	03	04	05	06	07	08	09	10	11	Career
Gomez,Hector											0	0
Gomez,Jeanmar										2	3	5
Gonzalez,Adrian				1	1	16	25	24	34	35	27	163
Gonzalez,Alberto							0	3	5	2	4	14
Gonzalez,Alex	25	3	20	15	14	10	10		8	19	13	137
Gonzalez,Carlos								6	9	25	20	60
Gonzalez,Edgar		1	0	0	3	5	0	1		0		10
Gonzalez,Enrique						3	0	0	0	1	0	4
Gonzalez,Gio								0	2	15	15	32
Gonzalez,Mike			0	8	6	11	3	3	9	3	2	45
Gordon,Alex							12	15	2	3	24	56
Gordon,Brian											0	0
Gordon,Dee											6	6
Gorzelanny,Tom					0	3	11	0	2	7	4	27
Grabow,John			0	1	2	5	3	6	7	0	2	26
Granderson,Curtis				0	6	20	25	20	20	16	26	133
Gray,Jeff								0	1	0	2	3
Green,Sean						2	5	4	3	0	0	14
Green,Taylor											1	1
Greene,Tyler									1	2	3	6
Gregerson,Luke									5	9	4	18
Gregg,Kevin			2	6	2	4	10	11	7	9	4	55
Greinke,Zack				9	3	1	9	15	26	11	10	84
Grilli,Jason	1		0	1	4	4	7	2				23
Guerra,Javy											8	8
Guerrero,Vladimir	119	28	18	27	27	24	29	22	7	17	6	324
Guerrier,Matt				0	5	5	9	2	11	7	4	43
Guillen,Carlos	24	12	12	22	8	25	19	13	6	5	1	147
Guthrie,Jeremy				1	0	0	12	13	7	15	8	56
Gutierrez,Franklin					0	1	6	5	21	14	4	51
Gutierrez,Juan							0		7	3	0	10
Guyer,Brandon											0	0
Guzman,Jesus										0	13	13
Gwynn,Tony						1	3	0	13	6	7	30
Hacker,Eric										0	1	1
Hafner,Travis		1	7	21	26	24	16	2	8	11	15	131
Hagadone,Nick											1	1
Hairston,Jerry	19	12	7	8	9	1	2	12	8	13	10	101
Hairston,Scott				3	0	0	7	9	14	5	3	41
Hall,Bill		1	3	7	17	20	10	8	4	11	1	82
Halladay,Roy	21	21	23	9	15	20	16	23	21	25	22	216
Halman,Greg										0	1	1
Hamburger,Mark											1	1
Hamels,Cole						8	15	18	10	16	17	84
Hamilton,Josh							11	26	11	30	15	93
Hamilton,Mark										0	1	1
Hammel,Jason						0	2	3	10	8	5	28
Hammock,Robby			7	3		0	1	1			0	12
Hamren,Erik											0	0
Hand,Brad											1	1
Hanigan,Ryan							1	4	8	13	11	37
Hannahan,Jack						0	5	5	4		14	28
Hanrahan,Joel							2	7	3	7	15	34
Hanson,Tommy									10	12	8	30
Happ,J.A.							0	2	15	6	1	24
Harang,Aaron		4	3	5	11	18	17	6	7	1	8	80
Harden,Rich			4	14	12	4	2	16	7	2	2	63
Hardy,J.J.					11	3	19	20	6	10	22	91
Haren,Dan			1	2	13	14	17	19	20	14	18	118
Harrell,Lucas										1	0	1
Harris,Willie	0	2	2	10	4	1	9	10	9	4	5	56
Harrison,Josh											5	5
Harrison,Matt								3	1	3	15	22
Hart,Corey				0	0	5	21	16	9	18	21	90
Hatcher,Chris										0	0	0
Hawkins,LaTroy	26	11	13	16	5	4	5	6	10	0	6	102
Hawksworth,Blake									5	1	2	8
Hawpe,Brad				1	8	15	20	16	19	5	2	86
Hayes,Brett									0	2	3	5
Head,Jerad											0	0
Headley,Chase							0	8	16	15	16	55
Heilman,Aaron			0	0	10	8	8	2	5	4	0	37
Heisey,Chris										4	8	12

WIN SHARES BY YEAR

Player	<02	02	03	04	05	06	07	08	09	10	11	Career
Hellickson,Jeremy										3	15	18
Helms,Wes	6	1	14	4	5	10	2	5	5	7	0	59
Helton,Todd	93	27	35	30	25	21	22	8	23	7	13	304
Hendrickson,Mark		4	5	7	4	8	3	3	6	2	0	42
Hendriks,Liam											0	0
Hensley,Clay					5	11	0	0		11	1	28
Hermida,Jeremy					3	6	13	13	11	4	2	52
Hernandez,David									3	6	10	19
Hernandez,Diory									1	0	0	1
Hernandez,Felix					8	8	14	13	26	23	16	108
Hernandez,Livan	43	7	22	19	13	10	10	3	3	11	5	146
Hernandez,Ramon	29	12	18	13	10	21	11	11	11	13	10	159
Herndon,David										2	3	5
Herrera,Daniel								0	5	1	1	7
Herrera,Jonathan									1	6	3	10
Herrera,Kelvin											0	0
Herrmann,Frank										2	2	4
Heyward,Jason										23	11	34
Hicks,Brandon										0	0	0
Hill,Aaron					9	14	20	5	25	12	12	97
Hill,Koyie			0	1	1		1	0	7	3	1	14
Hill,Rich					0	5	13	1	0	1	1	21
Hinske,Eric		22	12	6	11	7	3	10	5	8	5	89
Hochevar,Luke							1	3	1	4	7	16
Hoey,Jim							0	0		0	0	0
Hoffmann,Jamie									0		0	0
Holland,Derek									2	3	14	19
Holland,Greg										0	9	9
Holliday,Matt				9	17	19	27	21	25	25	21	164
Holm,Steve								2	1		0	3
Horst,Jeremy											1	1
Hosmer,Eric											13	13
Hottovy,Tommy											0	0
Howard,Ryan				1	10	29	26	24	26	20	21	157
Howell,J.P.						1	2	0	11	11	0	25
Hu,Chin-lung							1	1	0	0	0	2
Hudson,Daniel									1	9	16	26
Hudson,Kyle											0	0
Hudson,Orlando		7	17	16	15	20	21	17	20	14	14	161
Hudson,Tim	44	23	23	16	14	7	17	10	4	20	14	192
Huff,Aubrey	8	12	21	20	14	9	12	21	8	28	12	165
Huff,David									3	0	1	4
Hughes,Dusty									0	3	0	3
Hughes,Jared											1	1
Hughes,Luke										0	6	6
Hughes,Phil						4	0	10	11	1		26
Humber,Philip						0	0	0	0	2	11	13
Hundley,Nick								3	10	10	12	35
Hunter,Cedric											0	0
Hunter,Tommy								0	8	10	3	21
Hunter,Torii	32	20	16	13	11	17	22	21	20	23	17	212
Iannetta,Chris						1	5	17	10	3	16	52
Ibanez,Raul	15	12	15	12	17	25	23	21	17	19	12	188
Igarashi,Ryota										0	2	2
Iglesias,Jose											0	0
Infante,Omar		3	3	12	7	5	4	9	7	19	18	87
Inge,Brandon	3	4	4	13	17	17	12	10	13	13	3	109
Inglett,Joe						6	1	12	2	4	0	25
Isringhausen,Jason	42	13	7	15	12	8	12	1	1		4	115
Izturis,Cesar	4	4	10	25	6	3	5	9	8	6	1	81
Izturis,Maicer				1	6	13	16	11	17	7	13	84
Jackson,Austin										18	14	32
Jackson,Conor					0	12	13	17	1	4	5	52
Jackson,Edwin			2	0	0	1	2	10	17	9	12	53
Jakubauskas,Chris									3	0	2	5
James,Chuck						1	8	8	0		0	17
Janish,Paul								1	4	8	3	16
Jansen,Kenley										6	6	12
Janssen,Casey						4	10		0	5	8	27
Jaramillo,Jason									2	0	2	4
Jaso,John									0	16	5	21
Jay,Jon										8	13	21
Jeffress,Jeremy										1	1	2

Player	<02	02	03	04	05	06	07	08	09	10	11	Career
Jenks,Bobby					6	12	16	13	8	7	0	62
Jennings,Desmond										0	11	11
Jepsen,Kevin								0	4	5	0	9
Jeter,Derek	151	24	19	26	26	32	24	18	28	19	13	380
Jimenez,Cesar						0		2			0	2
Jimenez,Ubaldo						0	4	11	19	22	6	62
Joaquin,Waldis									1	0	1	2
Johnson,Alan											0	0
Johnson,Chris									0	15	8	23
Johnson,Dan				9	5	10	1			4	0	29
Johnson,Elliot							0			2		2
Johnson,Jim				0	0	8	7	3			11	29
Johnson,Josh					1	12	0	6	19	16	7	61
Johnson,Kelly					9		19	19	6	21	16	90
Johnson,Reed			11	9	10	16	3	13	3	3	8	76
Johnson,Rob							0	0	9	3	3	15
Jones,Adam						1	0	9	13	15	16	54
Jones,Andruw	122	27	23	17	21	22	15	2	6	9	8	272
Jones,Chipper	186	31	26	18	18	22	25	23	20	13	19	401
Jones,Garrett								0	10	13	12	35
Joyce,Matt								6	1	10	19	36
Judy,Josh											0	0
Jurrjens,Jair							2	11	17	4	12	46
Ka'aihue,Kila									1	1	0	2
Karstens,Jeff						3	0	1	2	3	9	18
Kazmir,Scott				1	10	13	13	12	6	0	0	55
Kearns,Austin	16	12	5	10	17	20	3	2	10	1		96
Kelley,Shawn									3	2	2	7
Kelly,Don							0		1	5	5	11
Kemp,Matt						3	10	19	26	15	37	110
Kendrick,Howie						6	9	15	15	19	18	82
Kendrick,Kyle							9	3	2	5	7	26
Kennedy,Adam	21	17	13	13	17	15	2	8	18	7	6	137
Kennedy,Ian							2	0	0	11	20	33
Keppinger,Jeff			2		1	9	10	5	21	8		56
Kershaw,Clayton								5	12	15	23	55
Kimball,Cole											2	2
Kimbrel,Craig										4	17	21
Kinney,Josh						2		1	0		0	3
Kinsler,Ian						12	17	24	24	13	22	112
Kintzler,Brandon										0	1	1
Kipnis,Jason											6	6
Kirkman,Michael										2	0	2
Kluber,Corey											0	0
Kohn,Michael										3	0	3
Konerko,Paul	48	17	4	20	24	21	16	10	18	29	24	231
Kontos,George											0	0
Kotchman,Casey				2	4	0	15	14	10	6	17	68
Kotsay,Mark	48	22	13	21	19	11	3	9	4	4	7	161
Kottaras,George								0	1	4	4	9
Kouzmanoff,Kevin						1	15	14	16	7	4	57
Kozma,Pete											1	1
Kratz,Erik										0	0	0
Kroenke,Zach										0	0	0
Kubel,Jason				3		1	12	12	19	12	13	72
Kuo,Hong-Chih					0	3	0	10	3	15	0	31
Kuroda,Hiroki								10	5	11	12	38
Lackey,John		7	7	10	16	16	21	13	12	11	1	114
Laffey,Aaron							3	4	5	2	3	17
LaHair,Bryan								2			2	4
Laird,Brandon											0	0
Laird,Gerald			1	3	1	5	10	9	14	6	3	52
Langerhans,Ryan		0	0	12	8	5	4	2	2	1		34
Lannan,John							2	9	9	4	8	32
LaPorta,Matt									3	6	10	19
LaRoche,Adam				7	11	16	16	16	17	16	1	100
LaRoche,Andy							2	2	12	2	1	19
Latos,Mat									1	13	8	22
Lavarnway,Ryan											0	0
Lawrie,Brett											10	10
League,Brandon				1	0	5	0	4	3	8	11	32
Leake,Mike										7	9	16
LeBlanc,Wade								0	2	6	2	10

WIN SHARES BY YEAR

Player	<02	02	03	04	05	06	07	08	09	10	11	Career
LeCure,Sam										2	4	6
Ledezma,Wil			2	3	0	4	2	2	0	0		13
Lee,Carlos	39	17	20	22	21	22	21	22	18	15	17	234
Lee,Cliff		1	3	6	13	10	1	24	17	16	22	113
Lee,Derrek	45	22	25	19	34	4	21	17	24	13	9	233
LeMahieu,DJ											0	0
Leroux,Chris										0	2	2
Lester,Jon						5	4	18	17	17	14	75
Lewis,Colby	0		1	1			0	0		13	11	26
Lewis,Fred						1	5	13	7	10	2	38
Lewis,Rommie									0	0		0
Liddi,Alex										2		2
Lidge,Brad		1	8	22	15	7	10	15	0	8	3	89
Lillibridge,Brent								1	1	2	7	11
Lilly,Ted	3	6	10	15	4	11	15	12	14	11	8	109
Lincecum,Tim							8	25	22	14	16	85
Lincoln,Brad										1	1	2
Lind,Adam						3	7	7	21	9	11	58
Lindblom,Josh											3	3
Lindsay,Shane											0	0
Lindstrom,Matt							5	6	2	4	5	22
Linebrink,Scott	2	0	6	10	11	8	5	5	3	3	4	57
Liriano,Francisco						0	16	4	2	14	4	40
Litsch,Jesse							7	12	0	0	4	23
Lobaton,Jose									0		1	1
Locke,Jeff											0	0
Loe,Kameron					0	8	2	3	2	5	5	25
Loewen,Adam						4	2	0				6
Logan,Boone						0	3	1	0	4	3	11
Lohse,Kyle	3	11	11	6	10	4	9	12	3	0	9	78
Lombardozzi,Steve											0	0
Loney,James						3	16	14	18	18	16	85
Longoria,Evan								19	24	28	25	96
Lopez,Felipe	5	6	3	9	21	16	11	10	23	9	1	114
Lopez,Javier			6	0	0	2	4	6	0	6	6	30
Lopez,Jose				3	5	16	10	18	12	7	2	73
Lopez,Rodrigo	0	15	2	14	8	4	4		0	3	3	53
Lopez,Wilton									0	8	5	13
Lowe,Derek	57	22	12	6	11	15	11	16	7	11	2	170
Lowe,Mark						3	0	1	8	1	3	16
Lowrie,Jed								7	1	8	5	21
Lucroy,Jonathan										4	15	19
Lucy,Donny							0			1	0	1
Ludwick,Ryan		0	6	0	0		10	24	19	17	12	88
Luebke,Cory										1	7	8
Lueke,Josh											0	0
Lugo,Julio	18	9	15	20	24	13	11	2	9	3	0	124
Lyles,Jordan											0	0
Lynn,Lance											2	2
Lyon,Brandon	4	0	5		0	6	11	6	11	14	0	57
MacDougal,Mike	1	0	9	0	8	5	0	2	5	0	6	36
Madson,Ryan			0	9	6	4	5	8	10	8	12	62
Magnuson,Trystan											0	0
Maholm,Paul					4	7	5	9	8	4	7	44
Maier,Mitch							0	1	9	11	3	24
Maine,Scott										1	0	1
Maldonado,Martin											0	0
Maloney,Matt									1	2	0	3
Manship,Jeff									1	1	0	2
Marcum,Shaun					1	3	10	12		14	13	53
Markakis,Nick						12	20	23	16	22	19	112
Marmol,Carlos						1	11	12	10	16	8	58
Marquez,Jeff										0	0	0
Marquis,Jason	9	3	1	14	12	2	8	8	15	0	6	78
Marrero,Chris											0	0
Marshall,Sean						2	6	4	5	10	11	38
Marson,Lou								1	1	5	5	12
Marte,Luis											1	1
Martin,Leonys											0	0
Martin,Russell						14	22	20	16	9	14	95
Martinez,Cristhian									1	1	5	7
Martinez,Fernando									0	0	0	0
Martinez,J.D.											6	6

Player	<02	02	03	04	05	06	07	08	09	10	11	Career
Martinez,Luis											3	3
Martinez,Michael											4	4
Martinez,Osvaldo										2	0	2
Martinez,Victor		1	3	20	22	18	29	7	21	17	24	162
Masset,Nick						1	0	4	10	7	4	26
Masterson,Justin								7	5	5	15	32
Mastroianni,Darin											0	0
Mateo,Marcos										0	1	1
Mather,Joe								4		0	2	6
Mathieson,Scott					0					0	1	1
Mathis,Jeff					0	0	2	7	4	3	4	20
Matsui,Hideki			19	28	23	6	16	10	18	20	10	150
Matsuzaka,Daisuke							12	16	2	7	1	38
Mattheus,Ryan											3	3
Matusz,Brian									3	10	0	13
Mauer,Joe				6	22	30	21	30	32	27	10	178
Maya,Yunesky										0	0	0
Mayberry,John									1	1	11	13
Maybin,Cameron							0	3	2	8	17	30
Mazzaro,Vin									2	4	0	6
McAllister,Zach											0	0
McCann,Brian					6	22	15	18	20	19	23	123
McCarthy,Brandon					5	5	3	1	5		11	30
McClellan,Kyle								4	6	8	5	23
McClendon,Mike										2	2	4
McCoy,Mike									0	1	3	4
McCutchen,Andrew									18	22	28	68
McCutchen,Daniel									2	0	5	7
McDonald,Darnell				0				0	1	10	3	14
McDonald,James								1	3	4	6	14
McDonald,John	0	5	3	1	4	3	8	1	3	5	6	39
McGee,Jake										0	2	2
McGehee,Casey								0	17	23	10	50
McGowan,Dustin					0	0	11	5			0	16
McKenry,Michael										0	2	2
McLouth,Nate					1	2	10	24	19	4	9	69
McPherson,Dallas				1	6	3	0					10
Medlen,Kris									3	7	0	10
Meek,Evan								0	4	9	1	14
Melancon,Mark									1	2	10	13
Mendoza,Luis							2	0	0	0	2	4
Mesoraco,Devin											1	1
Michaels,Jason	0	3	4	10	12	9	7	7	3	6	1	62
Mickolio,Kam									0	1	0	1
Mijares,Jose								1	8	2	1	12
Miles,Aaron			1	12	8	10	10	9	2	3	12	67
Miley,Wade											2	2
Milledge,Lastings						4	6	11	4	10	0	35
Miller,Andrew						0	2	0	2	0	2	6
Miller,Jai									0	0	0	0
Miller,Jim							1				1	2
Miller,Trever	6		4	4	2	6	2	3	6	2	0	35
Mills,Brad									0	1	0	1
Millwood,Kevin	50	19	12	5	14	13	5	6	15	5	3	147
Milone,Tom											2	2
Minor,Mike										0	3	3
Miranda,Juan								1	0	1	3	5
Misch,Pat						0	2	1	3	1	0	7
Mitchell,Russ										0	1	1
Mitre,Sergio			0	0	2	0	4		0	3	2	11
Molina,Gustavo							0	0		0	0	0
Molina,Jose	1	2	2	6	7	5	4	9	4	4	7	51
Molina,Yadier				5	14	9	12	15	20	17	18	110
Montanez,Lou								3	1	0	2	6
Montero,Jesus											2	2
Montero,Miguel						0	3	4	13	9	29	58
Moore,Adam									1	3	0	4
Moore,Jeremy											0	0
Moore,Matt											1	1
Mora,Melvin	23	16	15	24	20	18	10	17	7	9	1	160
Morales,Franklin							4	0	4	0	3	11
Morales,Jose								1	4	1	1	7
Morales,Kendrys						2	2	0	23	8		35

Player	<02	02	03	04	05	06	07	08	09	10	11	Career
Morel,Brent										0	4	4
Moreland,Mitch										6	8	14
Morgan,Nyjer							4	3	15	9	17	48
Morneau,Justin			1	9	7	26	18	28	18	17	4	128
Morrison,Logan										9	11	20
Morrow,Brandon							5	7	4	7	7	30
Morse,Michael					5	2	2	0	2	9	25	45
Mortensen,Clay									0	0	3	3
Morton,Charlie								0	4	0	8	12
Moscoso,Guillermo									1	0	8	9
Moseley,Dustin						0	6	0	1	2	4	13
Moskos,Daniel											2	2
Moss,Brandon							1	5	5	0		11
Mota,Guillermo	8	2	14	12	3	3	1	4	4	2	4	57
Motte,Jason								2	2	6	9	19
Moustakas,Mike											4	4
Moylan,Peter						1	9	1	7	6	1	25
Mujica,Edward						1	0	0	4	4	8	17
Murphy,Daniel								6	10		14	30
Murphy,David						0	5	11	11	15	9	51
Murphy,Donnie				0	0	3	1			3	1	8
Myers,Brett		3	9	4	14	12	9	7	3	17	6	84
Nady,Xavier	0		7	1	8	12	10	20	0	5	4	67
Napoli,Mike						10	8	12	10	12	23	75
Narveson,Chris						0			2	7	6	15
Nathan,Joe	7	1	11	19	17	20	16	16	16		5	128
Navarro,Dioner				0	4	5	6	17	5	2	3	42
Navarro,Efren											0	0
Navarro,Yamaico										0	2	2
Nelson,Chris										0	2	2
Neshek,Pat						6	8	1		0	1	16
Nicasio,Juan											4	4
Nickeas,Mike										0	1	1
Niemann,Jeff								0	12	7	7	26
Niese,Jonathon								0	1	6	4	11
Nieves,Wil	1				0	0	1	4	4	2	1	13
Nishioka,Tsuyoshi											3	3
Nix,Jayson								1	6	6	2	15
Nix,Laynce			4	7	4	0	0	0	6	4	7	32
Noesi,Hector											2	2
Nolasco,Ricky						5	0	14	6	7	5	37
Norberto,Jordan										0	0	0
Norris,Bud									3	3	7	13
Nova,Ivan										2	11	13
Nunez,Eduardo										2	8	10
Nunez,Leo					0	1	3	5	9	10	8	36
O'Connor,Mike						3	0				1	4
O'Day,Darren								2	9	9	0	20
Oeltjen,Trent									0	0	1	1
O'Flaherty,Eric						0	4	0	4	5	12	25
Ogando,Alexi										6	13	19
Ohlendorf,Ross							1	0	11	4	0	16
Ohman,Will	0			4	5	2	5	0	4		3	23
Okajima,Hideki							11	8	7	2	1	29
Oliver,Andrew										0	0	0
Oliver,Darren	53	3	10	1		6	5	9	9	6	7	109
Oliveros,Lester											1	1
Olivo,Miguel		1	8	7	7	13	7	7	9	11	10	80
Olson,Garrett							0	1	1	1	1	4
Ondrusek,Logan										5	5	10
Ordonez,Magglio	83	25	23	8	10	19	34	16	13	11	3	245
Orr,Pete					3	2	0	1	1		2	9
Ortiz,David	26	11	14	24	30	27	27	15	11	18	18	221
Ortiz,Ramon	19	14	5	7	3	3	3			0	1	55
O'Sullivan,Sean									2	2	0	4
Oswalt,Roy	15	20	10	18	21	20	17	16	9	18	7	171
Outman,Josh									1	4	3	8
Overbay,Lyle	0	0	6	17	17	17	6	14	12	15	6	110
Owings,Micah							13	2	4	1	5	25
Pacheco,Jordan											2	2
Padilla,Vicente	9	14	13	5	6	12	2	8	5	5	1	83
Pagan,Angel						3	5	3	12	23	15	61
Pagnozzi,Matt									0	2	0	2

Player	<02	02	03	04	05	06	07	08	09	10	11	Career
Palmer,Matt								0	10	1	0	11
Papelbon,Jonathan				4	19	15	15	15	10	12		90
Paredes,Jimmy											5	5
Parker,Jarrod											1	1
Parmelee,Chris											6	6
Parnell,Bobby								0	2	2	4	8
Parra,Gerardo									9	6	19	34
Parrino,Andy											1	1
Pascucci,Val			0								0	0
Paterson,Joe											3	3
Patterson,Corey	3	8	13	17	4	13	8	2	0	7	5	80
Patterson,Eric							0	2	3	4	1	10
Patton,Troy				1						0	3	4
Paul,Xavier									0	0	4	4
Pauley,David				0		0				4	7	11
Paulino,Felipe						0			0	1	5	6
Paulino,Ronny				0	14	10	3	8	8	3		46
Pavano,Carl	17	3	9	19	3		1	1	7	15	9	84
Peacock,Brad											2	2
Pearce,Steve							2	2	2	1	0	7
Peavy,Jake		3	7	15	16	12	21	13	6	6	5	104
Pedroia,Dustin						2	18	26	24	12	27	109
Peguero,Carlos											2	2
Pelfrey,Mike						0	1	12	4	12	3	32
Pena,Brayan				0	1	0	0		2	4	5	12
Pena,Carlos	3	11	9	11	7	0	28	22	17	16	18	142
Pena,Ramiro									4	3	1	8
Pena,Tony						1	11	6	6	4	0	28
Pena,Wily Mo		0	1	14	6	8	5	1			1	36
Pence,Hunter							18	19	17	21	24	99
Pendleton,Lance											1	1
Pennington,Cliff								3	7	19	18	47
Penny,Brad	17	4	10	10	9	11	20	0	7	3	4	95
Peralta,Jhonny			5	0	25	15	21	19	10	16	22	133
Peralta,Joel				2	5	6	0	0		5	8	26
Perez,Chris								4	3	13	10	30
Perez,Juan				0	0						1	1
Perez,Luis											2	2
Perez,Rafael					1	9	8	0	6	6		30
Perez,Salvador											7	7
Perkins,Glen						1	2	7	2	0	8	20
Perry,Ryan									4	5	1	10
Pestano,Vinnie										0	8	8
Petersen,Bryan										0	6	6
Pettit,Chris								0	0			0
Phelps,Cord											0	0
Phillips,Brandon		1	4	0	0	14	17	19	19	18	22	114
Phillips,Kyle									0		1	1
Phillips,Zach											1	1
Pie,Felix						5	2	5	6	1		19
Pierre,Juan	20	15	20	22	14	15	12	9	12	14	14	167
Pierzynski,A.J.	19	18	22	12	11	14	8	8	10	12	11	145
Pill,Brett											2	2
Pina,Manny											0	0
Pineda,Michael											10	10
Pineiro,Joel	7	14	13	5	3	0	5	3	13	10	2	75
Plouffe,Trevor										0	6	6
Polanco,Placido	30	16	18	17	22	14	24	15	21	16	14	207
Pomeranz,Drew											1	1
Porcello,Rick									13	5	8	26
Posada,Jorge	83	22	28	21	19	24	24	5	19	10	3	258
Posey,Buster									0	20	9	29
Powell,Landon									5	2	2	9
Prado,Martin						2	1	9	12	22	12	58
Presley,Alex										0	8	8
Price,David								1	6	17	13	37
Pridie,Jason									0	0	4	4
Proctor,Scott				1	0	9	6	0		0	0	16
Pujols,Albert	29	32	41	37	34	37	32	34	39	32	26	373
Punto,Nick	0	0	1	4	6	12	5	10	11	5	8	62
Purcey,David								1	0	2	1	4
Putnam,Zach											0	0
Putz,J.J.			0	3	5	17	20	5	1	8	13	72

Player	<02	02	03	04	05	06	07	08	09	10	11	Career
Qualls,Chad				4	7	9	9	11	8	0	5	53
Quentin,Carlos					5	5	23	8	15	16		72
Quintanilla,Omar						1	0	1	3	1	1	7
Quintero,Humberto		0	1	1	0	1	3	4	6	1		17
Raburn,Ryan				0			4	3	9	11	10	37
Ramirez,Alexei								18	15	20	20	73
Ramirez,Aramis	32	6	20	19	18	21	21	25	15	13	25	215
Ramirez,Hanley					0	25	27	32	34	22	10	150
Ramirez,Horacio		9	5	8	3	0	2	0			0	27
Ramirez,Manny	192	29	28	25	33	27	14	31	18	11	0	408
Ramirez,Ramon						7	0	9	8	7	7	38
Ramirez,Wilkin									1		0	1
Ramos,Cesar									1	0	1	2
Ramos,Wilson										3	13	16
Ransom,Cody	0	0	0	2			2	3	1	1	1	10
Rapada,Clay							0	2	0	1	1	4
Rasmus,Colby									13	17	11	41
Rauch,Jon		0		4	2	8	10	9	7	9	4	53
Ray,Chris				4	12	6			0	5	1	28
Recker,Anthony											0	0
Reddick,Josh									0	1	7	8
Reed,Addison											0	0
Reed,Jeremy			3	9	1	0	4	1	0	0		18
Reimold,Nolan									10	0	11	21
Reineke,Chad								1	0		0	1
Renteria,Edgar	82	26	25	16	15	19	19	11	10	6	7	236
Repko,Jason					5	4		0	0	2	2	13
Resop,Chris					0	1	0	0		2	4	7
Revere,Ben										0	9	9
Reyes,Dennys	12	4	0	4	1	9	2	6	3	3	0	44
Reyes,Jo-Jo							0	0	0	0	2	2
Reyes,Jose			12	4	16	28	24	28	5	19	26	162
Reynolds,Greg								0			1	1
Reynolds,Mark							14	17	20	16	16	83
Reynolds,Matt										2	3	5
Rhodes,Arthur	53	11	4	2	6	3		6	7	8	2	102
Rhymes,Will										6	1	7
Richard,Clayton								0	8	10	2	20
Richards,Garrett											0	0
Richardson,Antoan											0	0
Richmond,Scott								1	3		0	4
Rios,Alex				7	9	18	22	20	11	18	4	109
Rivera,Juan	0	1	4	12	9	18	1	4	16	10	10	85
Rivera,Mariano	101	9	17	18	19	16	12	20	15	14	14	255
Rivera,Mike	0	1	0			4	0	4	4	0	0	13
Rivera,Rene						0	2	2			2	6
Rizzo,Anthony											0	0
Roberts,Brian	3	2	14	16	28	13	22	20	20	7	3	148
Roberts,Ryan						0	0	0	8	1	19	28
Robertson,David								2	3	4	11	20
Robinson,Shane									0	0	0	0
Robinson,Trayvon											1	1
Rodney,Fernando		0	1			6	8	3	4	10	6	39
Rodriguez,Alex	185	35	31	29	34	25	37	23	23	21	14	457
Rodriguez,Aneury											0	0
Rodriguez,Fernando										0	2	2
Rodriguez,Francisco		1	9	17	14	17	15	16	10	11	10	120
Rodriguez,Fr. M.										2	0	2
Rodriguez,Henry									0	1	4	5
Rodriguez,Ivan	206	11	25	22	10	24	12	11	5	8	4	338
Rodriguez,Josh											0	0
Rodriguez,Luis					6	1	1	4	4		3	19
Rodriguez,Sean								3	0	9	10	22
Rodriguez,Wandy				2	2	7	9	16	11	10		57
Roenicke,Josh								0	1	0	1	2
Rogers,Esmil									0	0	0	0
Rohlinger,Ryan								0	0	0	0	0
Rolen,Scott	123	26	24	35	5	21	11	11	17	18	5	296
Rollins,Jimmy	21	17	18	24	21	25	28	24	19	14	25	236
Romero,J.C.	2	14	3	8	5	0	8	7	1	3	1	52
Romero,Ricky									10	14	20	44
Romine,Andrew										0	0	0
Romine,Austin											0	0

Player	<02	02	03	04	05	06	07	08	09	10	11	Career
Romo,Sergio								4	4	8	9	25
Rosales,Adam								0	3	8	0	11
Rosario,Sandy										0	0	0
Rosario,Wilin											1	1
Ross,Cody			1		0	6	10	16	16	14	14	77
Ross,David	1	4	2	3	13	7	5	6	6	7		54
Ross,Tyson										0	3	3
Rottino,Vinny									0	0	0	0
Rowand,Aaron	5	7	6	20	18	7	21	14	15	7	4	124
Ruffin,Chance											1	1
Ruggiano,Justin						0	1				4	5
Ruiz,Carlos						2	13	6	13	19	18	71
Runzler,Dan									1	3	0	4
Rupe,Josh			1	2		3	0	0	0			6
Russell,Adam						2	1	0	2			5
Russell,James										1	2	3
Ryan,Brendan							5	2	14	8	13	42
Rzepczynski,Marc									4	2	5	11
Sabathia,CC	12	13	13	11	12	15	24	23	18	20	19	180
Saito,Takashi						18	17	9	6	5	4	59
Salas,Fernando										1	12	13
Sale,Chris										5	11	16
Saltalamacchia,J							5	6	6	0	7	24
Samardzija,Jeff								3	0	0	7	10
Sanabia,Alex										4	1	5
Sanches,Brian					0	0	0		6	6	3	15
Sanchez,Angel						0				7	5	12
Sanchez,Anibal						10	1	0	5	11	10	37
Sanchez,Eduardo											5	5
Sanchez,Freddy	0	1	0	12	23	21	11	13	14	9		104
Sanchez,Gaby								1	1	17	16	35
Sanchez,Hector											0	0
Sanchez,Jonathan						2	0	6	7	14	2	31
Sandoval,Pablo								6	27	9	23	65
Sands,Jerry											6	6
Sanit,Amauri											0	0
Santana,Carlos										7	22	29
Santana,Ervin					6	12	3	19	6	14	14	74
Santana,Johan	4	10	16	26	23	24	17	21	14	14		169
Santiago,Hector											1	1
Santiago,Ramon	4	5	0	0	1	2	6	7	9	5		39
Santos,Omir									0	7	0	7
Santos,Sergio										5	12	17
Sappelt,Dave											1	1
Sardinha,Dane			0		0			1	1	1	1	4
Satin,Josh											0	0
Saunders,Joe					0	4	7	18	11	6	12	58
Saunders,Michael									1	6	2	9
Savery,Joe											1	1
Schafer,Jordan										2	8	10
Schafer,Logan											0	0
Scherzer,Max								4	9	13	10	36
Schierholtz,Nate							2	3	8	5	13	31
Schlereth,Daniel									0	2	4	6
Schneider,Brian	3	7	13	17	16	9	11	10	4	4	2	96
Schumaker,Skip					0	0	7	16	18	14	11	66
Schwimer,Michael											0	0
Schwinden,Chris											0	0
Scott,Luke					0	11	11	11	11	14	4	62
Scribner,Evan											0	0
Scutaro,Marco	0	2	11	11	11	8	15	21	15	11		105
Seager,Kyle											3	3
Sellers,Justin											4	4
Severino,Atahualpa											0	0
Shaw,Bryan											3	3
Sherrill,George			1	2	3	8	7	13	0	3		37
Shields,James						6	12	15	11	3	20	67
Shoppach,Kelly					0	3	7	14	7	4	4	39
Shuck,J.B.											2	2
Simon,Alfredo								0	0	4	3	7
Sipp,Tony									3	4	7	14
Sizemore,Grady				5	24	24	29	26	13	1	5	127
Sizemore,Scott										2	14	16

Player	<02	02	03	04	05	06	07	08	09	10	11	Career
Slama,Anthony										0	0	0
Slaten,Doug						1	4	1	0	3	0	9
Slowey,Kevin							3	10	5	8	0	26
Smith,Joe							3	6	2	3	8	22
Smith,Jordan										3	0	3
Smith,Seth							1	3	14	9	13	40
Smoak,Justin										7	10	17
Snider,Travis								3	4	8	3	18
Snyder,Brad										0	0	0
Snyder,Brandon										1	0	1
Snyder,Chris				2	4	7	16	15	3	8	5	60
Sogard,Eric										0	1	1
Sonnanstine,Andy							3	10	0	3	0	16
Soria,Joakim							13	17	12	15	7	64
Soriano,Alfonso	16	28	27	16	16	26	20	16	10	15	11	201
Soriano,Rafael	1	7	0	1	7	9	2	12	14	4		57
Sosa,Henry											1	1
Soto,Geovany					0	0	3	21	8	15	10	57
Span,Denard								16	21	20	6	63
Spears,Nate											0	0
Spence,Josh											2	2
Spilborghs,Ryan					0	3	9	8	7	9	1	37
Stairs,Matt	82	7	12	11	14	7	13	6	3	3	0	158
Stammen,Craig									3	3	2	8
Stanton,Mike										13	19	32
Stauffer,Tim					0	1	0		3	9	7	20
Stetter,Mitch							1	3	4	0	0	8
Stevens,Jeff									0	0	0	0
Stewart,Chris					0	1	0			0	3	4
Stewart,Ian							1	9	11	8	1	30
Stewart,Zach											1	1
Stinson,Josh											0	0
Storen,Drew										5	15	20
Strasburg,Stephen										5	2	7
Street,Huston					16	14	10	10	15	9	7	81
Strop,Pedro									0	0	3	3
Stubbs,Drew									5	18	13	36
Stults,Eric						1	1	2	2		0	6
Stutes,Michael											5	5
Surkamp,Eric											0	0
Sutton,Drew									3	2	2	7
Suzuki,Ichiro	36	26	23	27	22	24	33	19	28	23	15	276
Suzuki,Kurt							7	17	17	10	8	59
Swarzak,Anthony									0	4	0	4
Sweeney,Ryan						0	0	12	12	8	7	39
Swisher,Nick				1	12	20	18	12	18	22	19	122
Tabata,Jose										14	8	22
Takahashi,Hisanori										9	5	14
Talbot,Mitch									0	6	0	6
Tallet,Brian	2	0		0	4	4	5	4	0	0		19
Tateyama,Yoshinori											3	3
Tatum,Craig									1	3	1	5
Taylor,Michael										1	1	1
Tazawa,Junichi									0	0	0	0
Teaford,Everett											3	3
Teagarden,Taylor								4	3	1	1	9
Teahen,Mark					9	18	15	11	9	3	1	66
Teheran,Julio										0	0	0
Teixeira,Mark			12	24	33	21	25	28	26	24	22	215
Tejada,Miguel	76	32	26	28	26	23	14	14	22	18	5	284
Tejada,Ruben										3	10	13
Tejeda,Robinson					5	4	0	3	6	4	0	22
Tekotte,Blake											0	0
Texeira,Kanekoa										2	0	2
Thames,Eric											7	7
Thames,Marcus		0	0	6	1	11	6	7	4	7	0	42
Thatcher,Joe							2	0	3	5	0	10
Thayer,Dale									0	0	0	0
Theriot,Ryan					0	6	11	16	17	11	10	71
Thole,Josh									2	8	9	19
Thomas,Brad	0	0	0							5	0	5
Thome,Jim	192	33	29	20	4	25	21	17	11	14	13	379
Thompson,Aaron											0	0

Player	<02	02	03	04	05	06	07	08	09	10	11	Career
Thompson,Daryl									0		0	0
Thompson,Rich							0	0	1	3	4	8
Thornton,Matt			2	1	7	4	10	12	12	5		53
Thurston,Joe		1	0	0		0		0	5			6
Tillman,Chris									2	1	1	4
Tobin,Mason											0	0
Tolbert,Matt								3	5	3	2	13
Tomko,Brett	31	6	6	10	8	5	1	1	4		1	73
Tomlin,Josh										4	9	13
Toregas,Wyatt									1	0		1
Torrealba,Yorvit	1	4	7	4	4	6	6	4	9	12	7	64
Torres,Alex											1	1
Torres,Andres		0	0	0	0			8	23	10		41
Tosoni,Rene											3	3
Towles,J.R.						3	2	0	2	1		8
Treanor,Matt			1	2	5	6	5	0	3	6		28
Troncoso,Ramon								2	8	2	0	12
Trout,Mike											3	3
Trumbo,Mark										0	14	14
Tucker,Ryan									0			0
Tulowitzki,Troy						1	24	9	24	25	25	108
Turner,Jacob											0	0
Turner,Justin									0	0	15	15
Uehara,Koji									4	9	8	21
Uggla,Dan						23	16	24	18	24	21	126
Upton,B.J.				4		2	22	23	13	18	20	102
Upton,Justin							1	8	19	14	26	68
Uribe,Juan	7	10	9	18	17	11	13	11	13	16	2	127
Utley,Chase			5	8	25	27	28	30	32	25	18	198
Valaika,Chris										0	1	1
Valbuena,Luis							1	6	4	0		11
Valdes,Raul										2	1	3
Valdez,Jose										0		0
Valdez,Merkin			0				2	1	0	0		3
Valdez,Wilson				1	2		2		1	9	9	24
Valencia,Danny										12	10	22
Valverde,Jose			11	3	13	4	14	14	11	10	15	95
VandenHurk,Rick							0	0	3	0	0	3
Vargas,Jason				4	1	0			3	10	8	26
Varitek,Jason	32	12	16	18	18	7	14	8	7	3	6	141
Varvaro,Anthony										0	2	2
Vasquez,Anthony											0	0
Vasquez,Esmerling									3	1	1	5
Vazquez,Javier	43	13	21	9	12	11	18	11	16	5	11	170
Velazquez,Gil								0	0	0		0
Velez,Eugenio							1	4	6	1	0	12
Venable,Will								3	8	15	12	38
Venters,Jonny										9	15	24
Veras,Jose						1	1	5	2	4	5	18
Verlander,Justin					0	15	16	8	21	17	27	104
Viciedo,Dayan										3	2	5
Victorino,Shane			0		1	11	11	20	22	23	23	111
Villanueva,Carlos						4	8	6	2	2	7	29
Villanueva,Elih											0	0
Villarreal,Brayan											0	0
Viola,Pedro									0	0	0	0
Vizcaino,Arodys											1	1
Vizquel,Omar	166	21	5	18	20	20	12	5	6	7	1	281
Vogelsong,Ryan	1		0	0	3	0					14	18
Volquez,Edinson					0	0	2	16	2	3	0	23
Volstad,Chris								7	4	6	2	19
Votto,Joey							3	19	24	33	33	112
Wade,Cory								7	1		5	13
Wagner,Neil										0		0
Wainwright,Adam					0	9	13	11	21	20		74
Wakefield,Tim	86	15	12	8	15	7	10	10	8	2	3	176
Walden,Jordan										2	11	13
Waldrop,Kyle											0	0
Walker,Neil									0	16	20	36
Wallace,Brett										1	4	5
Walters,P.J.									0	0	0	0
Wang,Chien-Ming					7	16	15	7	0		2	47
Watson,Tony											2	2

Player	<02	02	03	04	05	06	07	08	09	10	11	Career
Weaver,Jered						14	12	11	17	19	24	97
Webb,Brandon			17	11	17	20	22	21	0			108
Webb,Ryan									1	4	4	9
Weeks,Jemile											15	15
Weeks,Rickie			0		9	10	14	16	7	29	18	103
Weiland,Kyle											0	0
Weinhardt,Robbie										0	0	0
Wells,Casper										4	6	10
Wells,Randy							1	13	9	3		26
Wells,Vernon	4	18	26	13	20	24	15	15	8	21	10	174
Werth,Jayson		1	1	11	9		13	17	26	22	17	117
Westbrook,Jake	2	1	6	15	8	13	9	3		9	4	70
Wheeler,Dan	2		3	3	10	12	4	12	6	4	3	59
Whelan,Kevin										0		0
White,Alex											1	1
Whiteside,Eli			0						3	2	3	8
Wieters,Matt									9	12	23	44
Wigginton,Ty		3	14	10	4	13	11	14	4	8	4	85
Wilhelmsen,Tom											3	3
Wilk,Adam										0		0
Williams,Jerome		9	7	6	0	0					3	25
Williams,Randy			0	1				1	0	0		2
Willingham,Josh				0	0	14	19	13	11	14	18	89
Willis,Dontrelle		14	9	22	13	7	0	0	1	2		68
Willits,Reggie						1	14	1	0	4	0	20
Wilson,Bobby								0	0	3	2	5
Wilson,Brian						1	5	9	15	17	9	56
Wilson,C.J.					0	3	9	2	11	15	20	60
Wilson,Jack	5	12	12	22	14	12	19	7	9	4	6	122
Wilson,Josh				0		3		3	7	1		14
Wilson,Mike										0		0
Wise,DeWayne	0	1		3		0	0	2	2	4	1	13
Wolf,Randy	28	15	12	6	4	2	5	7	14	9	12	114
Wood,Blake										2	4	6
Wood,Brandon						0	2	0	2	5		9
Wood,Kerry	34	12	18	9	4	2	2	12	6	4	4	107
Wood,Tim									2	0	0	2
Wood,Travis										6	3	9
Woodward,Chris	3	10	9	4	4	3	1		1	0	0	35
Worley,Vance										2	11	13
Worrell,Mark								0				0
Worth,Danny										3	0	3
Wright,David			9	26	30	34	27	20	25	14		185
Wright,Jamey	39	2	2	5	4	4	5	3	4	3	6	77
Wright,Wesley								3	1	0	1	5
Wuertz,Michael			2	6	4	6	3	10	3	0		34
Youkilis,Kevin				8	3	22	20	27	28	19	18	145
Young,Chris			2	10	12	12	5	1	3	3		48
Young,Chris				2	14	17	8	19	21			81
Young,Delmon					2	17	13	7	22	10		71
Young,Eric									0	2	4	6
Young,Matt										0		0
Young,Michael	7	11	22	25	29	26	23	20	17	16	23	219
Zagurski,Mike							1			0	0	1
Zambrano,Carlos	0	5	18	20	18	17	16	16	10	11	6	137
Ziegler,Brad								12	7	5	6	30
Zimmerman,Ryan					2	24	20	9	21	23	15	114
Zimmermann,Jordan									3	1	11	15
Zito,Barry	24	25	18	12	13	17	8	5	10	7	0	139
Zobrist,Ben						2	1	8	27	21	28	87

Instant Replay

Established just before the end of the season in 2008, instant replay has become a big part of baseball. Umpires review disputable home run calls to determine whether the ball left the playing field, was fair or foul, or was interfered with by a fan. Since replay's inception, 32% of the 201 reviewed calls have been overturned.

The chart below summarizes the results. The next few pages provide the details of every instant replay review since 2008.

Instant Replay Summary

Season	Instant Replays	Calls Overturned	Percentage
2008	7	2	29%
2009	59	22	37%
2010	69	24	34%
2011	66	17	26%
Totals	201	65	32%

Date	Matchup	Pitcher	Hitter	Inning	Outs	Men On	Score	Initial Ruling	Video Ruling
9/3/2008	NYA@TB	Troy Percival	Alex Rodriguez	9	2	_2_	6-3	HR	HR
9/9/2008	PIT@HOU	Jesse Chavez	Hunter Pence	6	2	12_	8-2	2B	2B
9/19/2008	MIN@TB	Boof Bonser	Carlos Pena	4	2	12_	6-0	2B	2B
9/23/2008	CIN@HOU	Chris Sampson	Joey Votto	7	2	1__	2-1	1B	1B
9/24/2008	LAA@SEA	Felix Hernandez	Vladimir Guerrero	5	1	___	2-2	Foul	Foul
9/26/2008	LAN@SF	Scott Proctor	Bengie Molina	6	1	1__	0-2	1B	HR
9/26/2008	WAS@PHI	Joe Blanton	Kory Casto	6	2	___	3-7	HR	HR
4/19/2009	CLE@NYA	Jensen Lewis	Jorge Posada	7	1	1__	2-3	HR	HR
4/22/2009	OAK@NYA	CC Sabathia	Kurt Suzuki	2	0	12_	0-0	HR	HR
4/24/2009	SF@ARI	Tim Lincecum	Eric Byrnes	3	2	___	0-1	2B	2B
4/25/2009	SEA@LAA	Carlos Silva	Gary Matthews Jr.	3	0	___	0-3	2B	2B
4/29/2009	FLA@NYN	Josh Johnson	Fernando Tatis	6	0	___	2-2	HR	HR
5/13/2009	FLA@MIL	Braden Looper	Ross Gload	6	2	_2_	5-8	HR	Foul
5/13/2009	STL@PIT	Joel Pineiro	Adam LaRoche	1	2	__3	0-0	HR	2B
5/23/2009	NYN@BOS	Jonathan Papelbon	Omir Santos	9	2	1__	1-2	2B	HR
5/23/2009	TEX@HOU	Scott Feldman	Miguel Tejada	1	1	___	0-0	HR	HR
5/24/2009	NYN@BOS	Tim Redding	Kevin Youkilis	5	0	___	3-5	Foul	Foul
5/25/2009	WAS@NYN	John Lannan	Gary Sheffield	6	0	12_	1-1	HR	HR
5/27/2009	WAS@NYN	Jordan Zimmermann	Daniel Murphy	6	0	1__	3-3	2B	HR
5/28/2009	TB@CLE	Jensen Lewis	Willy Aybar	6	1	___	0-2	HR	HR
6/3/2009	BAL@SEA	Jason Vargas	Aubrey Huff	1	2	1__	0-0	HR	Foul
6/4/2009	BOS@DET	Tim Wakefield	Jeff Larish	6	1	1__	3-6	Foul	Foul
6/6/2009	TEX@BOS	Derek Holland	Mike Lowell	2	1	___	0-0	2B	HR
6/9/2009	SEA@BAL	Jason Vargas	Melvin Mora	1	2	1__	1-0	HR	FO
6/9/2009	LAA@TB	James Shields	Howie Kendrick	5	0	___	2-0	3B	3B
6/10/2009	PIT@ATL	Jeff Karstens	Brian McCann	6	2	_2_	0-2	2B	2B
6/13/2009	CIN@KC	Bronson Arroyo	Billy Butler	4	0	___	5-3	Foul	Foul
6/19/2009	MIL@DET	Braden Looper	Dusty Ryan	4	2	1__	3-4	HR	2B
6/19/2009	MIL@DET	Braden Looper	Miguel Cabrera	3	2	___	2-3	1B	HR
6/21/2009	LAN@LAA	John Lackey	James Loney	8	2	__3	2-0	HR	HR
6/25/2009	PHI@TB	Jack Taschner	Pat Burrell	7	2	1__	10-4	GR 2B	GR 2B
7/1/2009	SEA@NYA	Jarrod Washburn	Melky Cabrera	5	1	___	1-1	HR	HR
7/3/2009	HOU@SF	Felipe Paulino	Travis Ishikawa	2	2	1_3	6-0	2B	HR
7/6/2009	PIT@HOU	Virgil Vasquez	Geoff Blum	1	2	12_	0-0	3B	3B
7/12/2009	WAS@HOU	Jordan Zimmermann	Carlos Lee	4	0	1__	1-0	2B	2B
7/17/2009	LAA@OAK	Trevor Cahill	Kendry Morales	2	1	___	0-0	HR	HR
7/19/2009	MIN@TEX	Francisco Liriano	Andruw Jones	4	1	___	1-3	HR	Foul
7/20/2009	CIN@LAN	Jason Schmidt	Willy Taveras	1	0	___	0-0	3B	3B
7/22/2009	MIL@PIT	Jeff Suppan	Ryan Doumit	3	1	___	4-2	2B	HR
7/29/2009	WAS@MIL	Garrett Mock	Ryan Braun	3	1	1__	0-4	HR	3B
7/29/2009	PHI@ARI	Tyler Walker	Gerardo Parra	8	0	___	3-0	2B	2B
7/31/2009	BOS@BAL	John Smoltz	Nolan Reimold	3	1	_2_	1-3	HR	HR
8/2/2009	LAA@MIN	Shane Loux	Joe Mauer	8	2	___	4-13	2B	2B
8/10/2009	CHN@COL	Esmailin Caridad	Troy Tulowitzki	2	2	123	4-0	Foul	Foul
8/11/2009	PHI@CHN	Angel Guzman	Carlos Ruiz	9	2	___	3-2	HR	Foul
8/11/2009	TOR@NYA	Jesse Carlson	Jorge Posada	8	0	___	4-4	HR	HR
8/14/2009	NYA@SEA	R. Rowland-Smith	Jorge Posada	2	0	___	0-2	2B	2B
8/16/2009	HOU@MIL	Braden Looper	Hunter Pence	6	1	___	4-2	HR	Foul
8/20/2009	MIN@TEX	Bobby Keppel	Michael Young	6	1	_2_	7-1	2B	2B
8/25/2009	DET@LAA	John Lackey	Curtis Granderson	7	0	___	3-3	3B	3B
8/25/2009	TEX@NYA	Kevin Millwood	Robinson Cano	4	0	___	4-7	HR	HR
8/26/2009	OAK@SEA	Luke French	Jack Cust	6	1	___	3-4	Foul	Foul
8/28/2009	NYN@CHN	Pat Misch	Aramis Ramirez	6	0	___	1-1	Foul	Foul
8/28/2009	OAK@LAA	Craig Breslow	Kendry Morales	6	2	1__	1-6	Foul	Foul
8/31/2009	PIT@CIN	Paul Maholm	Brandon Phillips	5	0	___	4-0	HR	Foul
9/5/2009	NYA@TOR	Andy Pettitte	Randy Ruiz	2	0	___	0-1	HR	Foul
9/10/2009	ATL@HOU	Derek Lowe	Lance Berkman	3	1	12_	1-6	HR	HR
9/10/2009	DET@KC	Eddie Bonine	Alberto Callaspo	8	1	___	6-4	HR	HR
9/12/2009	SEA@TEX	Brandon Morrow	Chris Davis	5	0	___	2-5	HR	2B
9/22/2009	SF@ARI	Matt Cain	Gerardo Parra	3	1	1__	5-4	HR	2B
9/23/2009	SF@ARI	Jonathan Sanchez	Rusty Ryal	6	1	1__	0-3	3B	3B
9/27/2009	SD@ARI	Edward Mujica	Chad Tracy	6	1	___	2-3	HR	HR
9/29/2009	ARI@SF	Jonathan Sanchez	Ryan Roberts	4	2	___	1-2	HR	2B
9/30/2009	HOU@PHI	Pedro Martinez	J.R. Towels	2	0	___	1-1	2B	HR
9/30/2009	NYN@WAS	John Lannan	Jeff Francoeur	2	0	1__	0-0	2B	2B
10/31/2009	NYA@PHI	Cole Hames	Alex Rodriguez	4	1	1__	0-3	2B	HR
4/06/2010	SF@HOU	Barry Zito	Jeff Keppinger	6	1	___	0-3	2B	2B
4/11/2010	WAS@NYN	Johan Santana	Josh Willingham	1	1	123	0-0	3B	HR
4/12/2010	BOS@MIN	Carl Pavano	Mike Cameron	5	0	___	1-4	Foul	Foul
4/13/2010	CIN@FLA	Nate Robertson	Jay Bruce	2	0	___	3-0	HR	1B

482

Date	Matchup	Pitcher	Hitter	Inning	Outs	Men On	Score	Initial Ruling	Video Ruling
4/20/2010	CLE@MIN	Kevin Slowey	Austin Kearns	5	1	___	1-5	2B	2B
4/23/2010	CHN@MIL	Ryan Dempster	Prince Fielder	1	2	1__	0-2	2B	2B
4/28/2010	CLE@LAA	Ervin Santana	Lou Marson	6	0	___	1-0	2B	2B
5/03/2010	STL@PHI	Jaime Garcia	Chase Utley	1	2	___	0-0	Foul	Foul
5/04/2010	NYN@CIN	Fernando Nieve	Scott Rolen	8	2	___	3-4	HR	HR
5/07/2010	CHN@CIN	Carlos Fisher	Marlon Byrd	8	1	1__	10-4	2B	2B
5/10/2010	TOR@BOS	John Lackey	Alex Gonzalez	2	0	1__	0-2	2B	2B
5/11/2010	WAS@NYN	Miguel Batista	Ike Davis	8	2	123	8-6	Foul	Foul
5/16/2010	TEX@TOR	Colby Lewis	John Buck	4	2	123	1-1	2B	2B
5/18/2010	CHA@DET	Freddy Garcia	Brandon Inge	6	1	___	2-4	HR	Foul
5/19/2010	MIN@BOS	Scott Baker	David Ortiz	4	1	_2_	0-1	3B	HR
5/21/2010	LAA@STL	Joel Pineiro	Felipe Lopez	3	2	___	8-4	HR	HR
5/23/2010	NYA@NYN	Johan Santana	Francisco Cervelli	7	2	1__	0-6	1B	1B
5/27/2010	WAS@SF	Barry Zito	Adam Dunn	7	1	1__	3-2	2B	2B
5/28/2010	LAN@COL	Carlos Monasterios	Clint Barmes	4	1	___	3-0	HR	HR
5/28/2010	TEX@MIN	Kevin Slowey	Ian Kinsler	4	1	___	0-1	HR	Foul
5/29/2010	TEX@MIN	C.J. Wilson	Delmon Young	3	0	___	0-1	Foul	Foul
6/01/2010	LAA@KC	Brian Bannister	Hideki Matsui	6	1	1__	3-5	2B	2B
6/03/2010	OAK@BOS	Jerry Blevins	Marco Scutaro	8	0	___	6-9	HR	HR
6/05/2010	BOS@BAL	Jeremy Guthrie	Marco Scutaro	6	1	___	0-0	Foul	Foul
6/08/2010	BOS@CLE	David Huff	Kevin Youkilis	4	2	_2_	0-1	2B	2B
6/08/2010	SD@NYN	Clayton Richard	Jose Reyes	7	2	___	0-1	2B	HR
6/16/2010	SEA@STL	Jason Vargas	Albert Pujols	4	1	___	0-1	2B	2B
6/18/2010	LAN@BOS	Carlos Monasterios	J.D. Drew	1	2	___	2-0	2B	HR
7/01/2010	NYN@WAS	Johan Santana	Ian Desmond	5	0	___	0-1	2B	2B
7/03/2010	BAL@BOS	Robert Manuel	Jake Fox	9	2	1__	1-9	2B	HR
7/03/2010	NYN@WAS	Francisco Rodriguez	Adam Dunn	9	1	123	3-5	2B	2B
7/03/2010	PHI@PIT	Paul Maholm	Jayson Werth	4	0	1__	7-1	2B	2B
7/05/2010	CLE@TEX	Joe Smith	Nelson Cruz	7	1	1_3	3-9	HR	Foul
7/07/2010	KC@SEA	Chad Cordero	Billy Butler	9	2	___	6-3	2B	HR
7/10/2010	SF@WAS	Miguel Batista	Buster Posey	9	0	1__	8-5	HR	HR
7/11/2010	CIN@PHI	Matt Maloney	Jayson Werth	4	0	___	1-0	2B	2B
7/11/2010	CIN@PHI	Matt Maloney	Carlos Ruiz	3	0	___	0-0	2B	2B
7/16/2010	COL@CIN	Bronson Arroyo	Miguel Olivo	8	0	___	1-3	HR	HR
7/19/2010	CLE@MIN	Aaron Laffey	Delmon Young	4	0	_2_	0-2	1B	1B
7/22/2010	WAS@CIN	Edinson Volquez	Willie Harris	3	1	___	5-0	3B	3B
7/24/2010	TB@CLE	Mitch Talbot	Ben Zobrist	5	2	12_	0-3	3B	HR
7/26/2010	BOS@LAA	Scott Atchison	Hideki Matsui	8	2	1__	1-4	HR	HR
7/26/2010	FLA@SF	Taylor Tankersley	Aaron Rowand	7	1	1__	0-3	HR	HR
7/30/2010	SEA@MIN	Doug Fister	Alexi Casilla	5	2	__3	3-0	3B	HR
8/01/2010	SEA@MIN	Francisco Liriano	Josh Wilson	2	2	___	0-0	Foul	Foul
8/05/2010	PHI@FLA	Will Ohman	Ben Francisco	10	1	___	5-4	Foul	Foul
8/06/2010	MIN@CLE	Chris Perez	Jim Thome	9	0	1__	4-6	2B	2B
8/06/2010	COL@PIT	Joel Hanrahan	Dexter Fowler	9	0	___	4-3	HR	3B
8/07/2010	COL@PIT	Huston Street	Andrew McCutchen	10	0	___	5-7	HR	2B
8/12/2010	FLA@WAS	Livan Hernandez	Mike Stanton	2	1	1__	0-0	3B	HR
8/13/2010	PHI@NYN	Cole Hamels	Mike Hessman	5	0	___	0-0	HR	3B
8/16/2010	TEX@TB	David Price	Bengie Molina	7	0	___	0-2	2B	2B
8/23/2010	MIN@TEX	Nick Blackburn	David Murphy	1	2	12_	0-0	3B	3B
8/25/2010	ARI@SD	Wade LeBlanc	Stephen Drew	1	0	___	0-0	2B	HR
8/29/2010	FLA@ATL	Leo Nunez	Brian McCann	9	2	___	6-6	2B	HR
9/02/2010	DET@MIN	Scott Baker	Austin Jackson	2	2	___	2-0	3B	3B
9/04/2010	COL@SD	Jason Hammel	Adrian Gonzalez	1	2	1__	0-0	2B	2B
9/04/2010	TB@BAL	James Shields	Luke Scott	5	1	___	5-2	2B	2B
9/06/2010	CHA@DET	Chris Sale	Brandon Inge	8	2	1__	4-4	HR	Foul
9/07/2010	TEX@TOR	Scott Feldman	John Buck	2	2	___	0-0	2B	HR
9/07/2010	CLE@LAA	Trevor Bell	Travis Hafner	6	0	___	1-1	HR	HR
9/14/2010	DET@TEX	Jeremy Bonderman	David Murphy	4	0	___	1-4	HR	HR
9/15/2010	DET@TEX	Colby Lewis	Ryan Raburn	1	2	1__	1-0	2B	2B
9/20/2010	KC@DET	Zack Greinke	Will Rhymes	6	2	1__	4-5	3B	HR
9/28/2010	OAK@LAA	Dallas Braden	Peter Bourjos	7	0	_23	3-2	HR	Foul
10/02/2010	MIL@CIN	Brandon Kintzler	Jay Bruce	5	0	___	3-1	HR	HR
10/03/2010	PIT@FLA	Brian Burres	Wes Helms	6	2	12_	2-2	HR	2B
10/10/2010	PHI@CIN	Johnny Cueto	Chase Utley	5	2	___	1-0	HR	HR
10/19/2010	TEX@NYA	Tommy Hunter	Lance Berkman	2	2	___	1-0	HR	Foul
4/01/2011	CHA@CLE	Fausto Carmona	Carlos Quentin	3	1	1__	4-0	HR	HR
4/01/2011	CHA@CLE	Will Ohman	Carlos Santana	7	2	_2_	5-14	HR	HR
4/02/2011	DET@NYA	Brad Penny	Robinson Cano	5	0	___	6-3	2B	2B
4/06/2011	WAS@FLA	Livan Hernandez	John Buck	5	2	123	1-4	3B	3B
4/07/2011	WAS@FLA	Josh Johnson	Jayson Werth	4	1	___	0-2	HR	HR
4/10/2011	KC@DET	Luke Hochevar	Alex Avila	6	0	___	1-5	HR	HR
4/11/2011	CHN@HOU	Ryan Dempster	Michael Bourn	7	1	___	2-5	2B	2B
4/14/2011	COL@NYN (2)	Jorge de la Rosa	Scott Hairston	2	0	1__	0-0	2B	2B

483

Date	Matchup	Pitcher	Hitter	Inning	Outs	Men On	Score	Initial Ruling	Video Ruling
4/15/2011	TOR@BOS	Clay Buchholz	Adam Lind	1	1	12_	0-0	HR	Foul
4/17/2011	LAA@CHA	Mark Buehrle	Vernon Wells	6	1	___	3-0	3B	3B
4/19/2011	ARI@CIN	Sam LeCure	Justin Upton	5	2	___	4-3	3B	3B
4/22/2011	ARI@NYN	Esmerling Vasquez	Ike Davis	7	2	_2_	0-1	2B	HR
4/24/2011	CLE@MIN	Carl Pavano	Michael Brantley	4	1	_23	1-2	HR	2B
5/01/2011	STL@ATL	Jaime Garcia	Dan Uggla	7	0	___	3-4	2B	2B
5/03/2011	LAA@BOS	Hisanori Takahashi	Marco Scutaro	8	1	1__	5-1	HR	HR
5/08/2011	MIN@BOS	Daisuke Matsuzaka	Danny Valencia	4	0	___	3-5	HR	HR
5/09/2011	LAN@PIT	Chad Billingsley	Garrett Jones	1	2	___	0-1	2B	2B
5/12/2011	TB@CLE	Joel Peralta	Asdrubal Cabrera	8	1	___	2-5	3B	3B
5/17/2011	NYA@TB	Amauri Sanit	Kelly Shoppach	9	1	___	1-6	FO	FO
5/19/2011	ATL@ARI	Jair Jurrjens	Juan Miranda	6	2	1__	1-0	3B	3B
5/20/2011	MIN@ARI	Aaron Heilman	Jason Kubel	8	2	12_	2-6	3B	3B
5/24/2011	ATL@PIT	Charlie Morton	Chipper Jones	5	2	1__	2-0	2B	2B
5/25/2011	CIN@PHI	Antonio Bastardo	Jay Bruce	10	0	___	3-3	HR	HR
6/01/2011	LAA@KC	Scott Downs	Billy Butler	9	1	1__	0-0	2B	HR
6/03/2011	MIN@KC	Carl Pavano	Eric Hosmer	3	2	1__	0-3	2B	2B
6/05/2011	PHI@PIT	Daniel Moskos	Domonic Brown	7	2	___	4-2	2B	2B
6/09/2011	CHN@PHI	Ryan Madson	Tyler Colvin	9	1	___	3-3	HR	GR2B
6/11/2011	WAS@SD	John Lannan	Ryan Ludwick	4	0	___	1-2	HR	Foul
6/17/2011	PIT@CLE	Daniel Moskos	Travis Hafner	8	0	12_	2-1	2B	2B
6/21/2011	OAK@NYN	Brian Fuentes	Jason Bay	8	2	1__	2-7	3B	3B
6/22/2011	TOR@ATL	Jon Rauch	Brooks Conrad	7	1	___	4-1	2B	HR
6/24/2011	TB@HOU	Wandy Rodriguez	B.J. Upton	3	2	___	3-0	HR	HR
6/26/2011	TB@HOU	Wilton Lopez	Evan Longoria	6	1	_3	5-7	1B	HR
6/29/2011	MIL@NYA	Tim Dillard	Jorge Posada	6	1	___	4-2	1B	HR
7/04/2011	KC@CHA	Sergio Santos	Eric Hosmer	9	0	___	3-4	3B	HR
7/10/2011	CIN@MIL	Dontrelle Willis	Randy Wolf	2	1	___	1-2	Foul	Foul
7/16/2011	LAA@OAK (1)	Scott Downs	Hideki Matsui	8	1	___	2-3	2B	2B
7/17/2011	CLE@BAL	Mitch Atkins	Carlos Santana	1	2	___	1-0	HR	HR
7/19/2011	OAK@DET	Guillermo Moscoso	Carlos Guillen	5	2	1__	5-3	HR	HR
7/20/2011	MIL@ARI	Bryan Shaw	Ryan Braun	8	2	___	2-0	HR	Foul
7/26/2011	HOU@STL	Brett Myers	Albert Pujols	1	1	1__	0-0	HR	HR
7/28/2011	LAA@DET	Brad Penny	Mark Trumbo	2	2	1__	0-0	3B	HR
7/31/2011	CHN@STL	Ryan Dempster	David Freese	5	1	___	0-0	2B	2B
8/01/2011	CLE@BOS	Daniel Bard	Asdrubal Cabrera	8	0	1__	5-5	1B	HR
8/03/2011	BAL@KC	Luke Hochevar	Felix Pie	8	1	1__	2-6	2B	2B
8/03/2011	OAK@SEA	Charlie Furbush	Conor Jackson	5	1	___	0-2	2B	2B
8/13/2011	DET@BAL	Max Scherzer	Blake Davis	2	1	12_	2-0	HR	HR
8/17/2011	TEX@LAA	C.J. Wilson	Mark Trumbo	1	2	1__	1-0	2B	2B
8/17/2011	NYA@KC	Bartolo Colon	Billy Butler	3	1	___	3-2	HR	HR
8/18/2011	NYA@MIN	CC Sabathia	Justin Morneau	1	2	1__	0-0	HR	Foul
8/21/2011	SEA@TB	Jeff Gray	Johnny Damon	7	1	123	4-5	HR	2B
8/23/2011	BOS@TEX	Mark Lowe	Marco Scutaro	8	2	_23	7-4	2B	2B
8/27/2011	TB@TOR	Shawn Camp	B.J. Upton	6	0	___	2-2	Foul	Foul
8/31/2011	TOR@BAL	Zach Phillips	Edwin Encarnacion	8	1	1__	13-0	2B	2B
9/03/2011	CHA@DET	Gavin Floyd	Miguel Cabrera	1	2	1__	0-1	2B	2B
9/04/2011	PHI@FLA	Anibal Sanchez	Hunter Pence	6	0	1__	2-2	2B	FO
9/06/2011	BAL@NYA	Tommy Hunter	Francisco Cervelli	7	2	___	3-3	HR	HR
9/08/2011	PHI@MIL	Chris Narveson	Shane Victorino	6	2	___	0-1	2B	2B
9/11/2011	LAN@SF	Hiroki Kuroda	Aubrey Huff	2	0	___	0-1	2B	2B
9/13/2011	TOR@BOS	Tim Wakefield	J.P. Arencibia	2	0	12_	0-2	HR	HR
9/16/2011	TB@BOS	Josh Beckett	Evan Longoria	1	1	_2_	0-0	HR	HR
9/17/2011	CHA@KC	Zach Stewart	Mike Moustakas	5	2	_2_	3-1	HR	HR
9/18/2011	TEX@SEA	Felix Hernandez	Ian Kinsler	3	1	1__	0-0	HR	Foul
9/18/2011	HOU@CHN	Brett Myers	Carlos Pena	8	2	1__	2-3	HR	2B
9/19/2011	PIT@ARI	Jeff Karstens	Justin Upton	6	0	___	0-0	HR	HR
9/22/2011	NYN@STL	Jake Westbrook	Willie Harris	4	2	_2_	0-2	Foul	Foul

The Hall of Fame Monitor

Bill James

There are certain things that ballplayers do that tend to identify them as future Hall of Famers. Hall of Fame players hit .300, they hit between 30 home runs and 40, they drive in 100 runs and score 100, they win Gold Gloves, they win MVP Awards. They win 20 games, if they are pitchers, and strike out 200 batters, and save 40 games, and they play in the World Series, and they steal 50 bases and win batting titles. If you do *enough* of those kind of things, you become a Hall of Famer.

This is not an "opinion" book; this is a book of facts. However, the fact that it is a book of facts does not mean that we cannot wrestle a little bit with interesting questions, even if we may not be able to reduce every little wrinkle in them to a flat fact. We all know that Albert Pujols and Lance Berkman have done in their careers a great many things that would be characteristic of Hall of Famers. We summarize those things in our count as Pujols 152, Berkman 71. You can make up a different system if you want to; you can make up a better system if you can figure out how. That's our best effort to reduce that particular complex problem to a simple count.

What does Pujols 152, Berkman 71 mean? It means that Albert Pujols, based on what he has already done and without any projection of what he is likely to do in the future, is a fully qualified Hall of Fame player, whereas Lance Berkman is at this point, in the words of the old hymn, standin' in the need of prayer. 100 points is the standard of a fully qualified, few-questions-asked, might-have-to-wait-through-a-few-elections Hall of Famer. We're not saying that Lance *can't* make the Hall of Fame or that he won't; we're saying that he is, at this point, not obviously or overwhelmingly qualified. Many players have been elected who were not obviously or overwhelmingly qualified; maybe he'll make that list. At this point it's a live question.

As best we are able to determine this, there are eight active players who are fully qualified Hall of Famers: Pujols, A-Rod, Vladimir, Jeter, Ichiro, Chipper, Pudge and the Sand Man. You can almost make an All-Star team out of them; A-Rod has to play second and we need a third outfielder. We'll get Ken Griffey or Manny as the third outfielder. Jim Thome is very close to being an obviously qualified Hall of Famer; Todd Helton is very close to that standard. Everybody else needs to keep working on it.

I believe that the player who made the *most* strides toward being a Hall of Famer in 2011 was Miguel Cabrera. We had Miggy pegged a year ago at 55 points—half-qualified for the Hall of Fame. Now we have him at 72. That's assuming—because I am writing this on October 12—that the Tigers don't win the World Series and that Cabrera doesn't win the MVP Award. If the Tigers do win the World Series and/or Cabrera does win the MVP Award, then that gives him another point or two.

There are lots of other players who are doing well. . .Teixeira, Verlander, Sabathia, Lincecum, Longoria, King Felix. They're all making steady strides toward the Hall of Fame, although none of them needs to start working on his acceptance speech just yet. I need to explain one other thing. Hitters' careers are, compared to pitchers', relatively predictable. If you take the best 25-year-old hitters in baseball today and look in on them in ten years, you will find that they're now the best 35-year-old hitters in baseball. The same is not true of pitchers. Byung-Hyun Kim is only 32 years old now; ten years ago everybody was very excited about him. Roy Halladay is the same age as Kerry Wood. Ten years ago, nobody in the world would have traded Kerry Wood for Roy Halladay; the whole idea would have been considered crazy. Pitchers go up and down.

Because pitchers go up and down, our system to evaluate pitchers' careers has to be back-loaded onto career accomplishments (200 careers wins, 250 wins, etc.) to a greater extent than for hitters. We kind of have to hold our breath to see whether a pitcher is going to make it past the standards. For that reason, the numbers for outstanding pitchers (Halladay, Sabathia, Verlander, Tim Hudson) may seem to be lower than the numbers for position players of the same age and the same stature. It's just the nature of the problem. If Tim Hudson can get past 200 career wins, his numbers will start to race forward.

We all like to think about who in the game is making progress on a Hall of Fame career. This is not an argument about who *should* be in the Hall of Fame; it is merely an attempt to mark off the floor and measure the progress.

The following is a summary of the leading Hall of Fame candidates by year of birth.

Leading Hall of Fame Candidates Born in
1990

Player	Points
Starlin Castro	11

Leading Hall of Fame Candidates Born in
1989

Player	Points
Mike Stanton	3
Jason Heyward	3
Freddie Freeman	2

Leading Hall of Fame Candidates Born in
1988

Player	Points
Clayton Kershaw	12
Neftali Feliz	12
Craig Kimbrel	9
Elvis Andrus	7
Trevor Cahill	4

Leading Hall of Fame Candidates Born in
1987

Player	Points
Justin Upton	9
Alex Avila	6
Drew Storen	6
Jay Bruce	4
Buster Posey	4
Jordan Walden	4
Austin Jackson	4
Ivan Nova	1
Pedro Alvarez	1

Leading Hall of Fame Candidates Born in
1986

Player	Points
Felix Hernandez	20
Pablo Sandoval	10

Leading Hall of Fame Candidates Born in
1986

Player	Points
Billy Butler	9
Andrew McCutchen	9
Matt Wieters	6
Yovani Gallardo	5
Jair Jurrjens	5

Leading Hall of Fame Candidates Born in
1985

Player	Points
Evan Longoria	20
Carlos Gonzalez	12
Asdrubal Cabrera	9
David Price	8
Chris Perez	7
Delmon Young	7
Jon Jay	1
Carlos Gomez	1
Daniel Bard	1

Leading Hall of Fame Candidates Born in
1984

Player	Points
Prince Fielder	37
Brian McCann	29
Tim Lincecum	26
Troy Tulowitzki	25
Joakim Soria	25
Matt Kemp	23
Ryan Zimmerman	18
Jon Lester	14
B.J. Upton	13
Andrew Bailey	12
Melky Cabrera	11
Ubaldo Jimenez	10
Jonathan Broxton	10
Matt Cain	10
Jeff Francoeur	9
Scott Kazmir	8
Josh Johnson	8
Alex Gordon	8
James Loney	8
Ian Kennedy	7
Denard Span	7

Leading Hall of Fame Candidates Born in
1983

Player	Points
Miguel Cabrera	72
Joe Mauer	59
Hanley Ramirez	44
Jose Reyes	39
Dustin Pedroia	38
Ryan Braun	38
Justin Verlander	32
Joey Votto	29
Jacoby Ellsbury	19
Nick Markakis	19
Huston Street	17
Russell Martin	15
Cole Hamels	15
Hunter Pence	13
Zack Greinke	13
John Axford	11
Matt Capps	11
Mark Reynolds	11
Martin Prado	10
Howie Kendrick	9
Stephen Drew	8
Leo Nunez	8
Chris Young	8
Miguel Montero	8
Geovany Soto	8

Leading Hall of Fame Candidates Born in
1982

Player	Points
Francisco Rodriguez	49
Robinson Cano	43
David Wright	42
Adrian Gonzalez	40
Brian Wilson	26
Yadier Molina	25
Grady Sizemore	23
Ian Kinsler	20
Jhonny Peralta	17
Andre Ethier	14
Aaron Hill	13
Dontrelle Willis	12
Rickie Weeks	12
Jered Weaver	12
Carlos Marmol	12
Shin-Soo Choo	11

Leading Hall of Fame Candidates Born in 1982

Player	Points
Corey Hart	10
J.J. Hardy	9
Michael Bourn	9
Ervin Santana	9
Jorge Cantu	9

Leading Hall of Fame Candidates Born in 1981

Player	Points
Carl Crawford	29
Curtis Granderson	26
Josh Hamilton	26
Justin Morneau	26
Bobby Jenks	24
Carlos Zambrano	22
Jake Peavy	19
Brandon Phillips	18
Adam Wainwright	16
Ben Zobrist	16
Alex Rios	12
James Shields	10

Leading Hall of Fame Candidates Born in 1980

Player	Points
Albert Pujols	152
Mark Teixeira	61
CC Sabathia	44
Matt Holliday	43
Jonathan Papelbon	41
Dan Uggla	25
Jose Bautista	24
Josh Beckett	22
Dan Haren	18
Shane Victorino	18
Nick Swisher	15
Felipe Lopez	10

Leading Hall of Fame Candidates Born in 1979

Player	Points
Ryan Howard	51
Johan Santana	45
Adrian Beltre	42
Adam Dunn	42
Mark Buehrle	28
Kevin Youkilis	23
Brandon Webb	22
Jayson Werth	14
Jason Bartlett	13
Jon Garland	12
Michael Cuddyer	12
Carlos Ruiz	12
Rafael Soriano	12
Coco Crisp	11
Juan Uribe	11
Adam LaRoche	10
David DeJesus	10

Leading Hall of Fame Candidates Born in 1978

Player	Points
Chase Utley	55
Jimmy Rollins	54
Victor Martinez	42
Aramis Ramirez	41
Vernon Wells	33
Jason Bay	31
Jose Valverde	31
Cliff Lee	27
Barry Zito	23
Carlos Pena	20
Chone Figgins	19
John Lackey	17
Brad Penny	13
Ryan Ludwick	11
Kevin Gregg	11

Leading Hall of Fame Candidates Born in 1977

Player	Points
Carlos Beltran	63
Andruw Jones	63

Leading Hall of Fame Candidates Born in 1977

Player	Points
Roy Halladay	61
Juan Pierre	35
Roy Oswalt	33
Rafael Furcal	29
Brian Roberts	26
Eric Chavez	26
Heath Bell	24
Travis Hafner	24
J.J. Putz	23
Orlando Hudson	21
Freddy Sanchez	20
Ryan Dempster	18
Kerry Wood	15
Aaron Rowand	15
Jack Wilson	13
Mark Ellis	13
Lyle Overbay	12
Danys Baez	12
Bronson Arroyo	11
Marlon Byrd	10
A.J. Burnett	10

Leading Hall of Fame Candidates Born in 1976

Player	Points
Lance Berkman	71
Michael Young	70
Alfonso Soriano	50
Carlos Lee	48
Paul Konerko	45
Brad Lidge	29
Aubrey Huff	25
A.J. Pierzynski	22
Pat Burrell	21
Javier Vazquez	18
Freddy Garcia	17
Ramon Hernandez	16
Adam Kennedy	13
Kyle Farnsworth	10
Ted Lilly	10

Leading Hall of Fame Candidates Born in 1975

Player	Points
Alex Rodriguez	189
Vladimir Guerrero	108
Scott Rolen	60
David Ortiz	53
Edgar Renteria	51
Francisco Cordero	47
Derrek Lee	43
Placido Polanco	34
Tim Hudson	33
Chris Carpenter	28
Brian Fuentes	27
Torii Hunter	27
J.D. Drew	25
Carlos Guillen	22
Livan Hernandez	19
Mark Kotsay	13
Julio Lugo	10

Leading Hall of Fame Candidates Born in 1974

Player	Points
Derek Jeter	151
Miguel Tejada	83
Bobby Abreu	79
Magglio Ordonez	62
Jason Kendall	55
Joe Nathan	51
Jose Vidro	33
Jermaine Dye	32
Orlando Cabrera	29
Mike Lowell	27
Hideki Matsui	25
Darin Erstad	25
Kevin Millwood	18

Leading Hall of Fame Candidates Born in 1973

Player	Points
Ichiro Suzuki	110
Todd Helton	95
Nomar Garciaparra	70
Johnny Damon	56

Leading Hall of Fame Candidates Born in 1973

Player	Points
Edgardo Alfonzo	37
Mike Cameron	28
Bartolo Colon	27
Mike Sweeney	26
Derek Lowe	26
Jason Schmidt	21
Ryan Franklin	11
Octavio Dotel	10

Leading Hall of Fame Candidates Born in 1972

Player	Points
Manny Ramirez	125
Chipper Jones	107
Carlos Delgado	76
Andy Pettitte	53
Shawn Green	46
Armando Benitez	45
Garret Anderson	43
Jason Isringhausen	41
Keith Foulke	34
Raul Ibanez	26
Jason Varitek	21
Melvin Mora	18
LaTroy Hawkins	15

Leading Hall of Fame Candidates Born in 1971

Player	Points
Ivan Rodriguez	111
Billy Wagner	92
Pedro Martinez	87
Jason Giambi	75
Jorge Posada	64
Brian Giles	52
Ryan Klesko	30

Leading Hall of Fame Candidates Born in 1970

Player	Points
Jim Thome	95

Leading Hall of Fame Candidates Born in 1970

Player	Points
Jim Edmonds	64
Javier Lopez	41
Takashi Saito	13
Craig Counsell	12

Leading Hall of Fame Candidates Born in 1969

Player	Points
Mariano Rivera	154
Ken Griffey Jr.	114
Robb Nen	58
Troy Percival	57
Arthur Rhodes	13

Leading Hall of Fame Candidates Born in 1968

Player	Points
Frank Thomas	121
Mike Piazza	120
Gary Sheffield	101
Sammy Sosa	100
Bernie Williams	83
Jeff Kent	77
Mike Mussina	60
John Olerud	59
Matt Stairs	12

Leading Hall of Fame Candidates Born in 1967

Player	Points
Trevor Hoffman	112
Omar Vizquel	48

Leading Hall of Fame Candidates Born in 1966

Player	Points
Tim Wakefield	16

Nostradamus with Numbers

Bill James

In these pages last year, when we projected the 2011 performance of every major league hitter, we had 73 projections for hitters that, in retrospect, I would grade at an "F". Two of these were projections for young left-handed center fielders who simply hit a great deal better than we had anticipated that they would hit:

Jacoby Ellsbury

	G	AB	R	H	D	T	HR	RBI	BB	SO	SB	Avg	Slg
Actual	158	660	119	212	46	5	32	105	52	98	39	.321	.552
Projected	157	624	102	187	32	6	8	58	50	69	59	.300	.409

Melky Cabrera

	G	AB	R	H	D	T	HR	RBI	BB	SO	SB	Avg	Slg
Actual	155	658	102	201	44	5	18	87	35	94	20	.305	.470
Projected	136	329	41	88	17	2	6	39	30	44	6	.267	.386

That happens a couple of times every year—last year it was Jose Bautista and Carlos Gonzalez—and there was a third one that we could sort of put into that class, which was Michael Morse:

Mike Morse, of Course

	G	AB	R	H	D	T	HR	RBI	BB	SO	SB	Avg	Slg
Actual	146	522	73	158	36	0	31	95	36	126	2	.303	.550
Projected	96	284	36	79	17	1	11	44	23	58	1	.278	.461

In our defense we weren't *totally* blindsided by how good a hitter Inspector Morse turned out to be, but. . .it's an "F" projection.

Those, however, were the only cases in the majors in which we had very bad projections because players simply had much better seasons than we had expected them to have. Of our 73 "F" projections, four were for players who had better years than we had projected for them (those three, and Emilio Bonifacio), and the other 69 were for players who had much worse seasons than we had projected for them. These could be sorted into five classes:

1) Ruinous injury seasons,

2) Older players whose ability suddenly left them,

3) Players who just had awful years,

4) Players who did not get anything like the playing time we had projected for them, and

5) "Half and half" players—players who did not get anything like the playing time we had projected for them because they just didn't play as well as we thought they would play.

The "ruinous injury" category includes Buster Posey, Grady Sizemore, Hanley Ramirez, Joe Mauer, David Wright and Justin Morneau, and possibly some other guys who had very bad seasons to which injuries certainly contributed (ie, Daric Barton). I will skip the stat layouts on these players because you probably already know what kind of players these men usually are and what kind of seasons they had, and, if you are a fair-minded and reasonable person, you probably don't hold it against us too much that we failed to anticipate these injuries.

That leaves about 60 "F" projections for which you may still ridicule us. In the category of "older players whose ability suddenly skedaddled" we have Melvin Mora, Miguel Tejada, Russell Branyan, Magglio Ordonez, Juan Uribe, Felipe Lopez, J.D. Drew, Julio Lugo, Adam Dunn (I suppose), Adam LaRoche, and Manny Ramirez:

Melvin Mora

	G	AB	R	H	D	T	HR	RBI	BB	SO	SB	Avg	Slg
Actual	42	127	5	29	6	0	0	16	2	24	0	.228	.276
Projected	104	298	38	81	14	1	8	40	27	49	2	.272	.406

Magglio

	G	AB	R	H	D	T	HR	RBI	BB	SO	SB	Avg	Slg
Actual	92	329	33	84	10	0	5	32	23	41	2	.255	.331
Projected	131	497	70	152	30	1	17	82	53	67	2	.306	.473

J.D. Drew

	G	AB	R	H	D	T	HR	RBI	BB	SO	SB	Avg	Slg
Actual	81	248	23	55	6	1	4	22	33	58	0	.222	.302
Projected	145	513	86	135	29	3	22	77	84	120	3	.263	.460

Manny Ramirez

	G	AB	R	H	D	T	HR	RBI	BB	SO	SB	Avg	Slg
Actual	5	17	0	1	0	0	0	1	0	4	0	.059	.059
Projected	128	455	74	132	28	0	23	84	77	106	1	.290	.503

Adam Dunn, of course, had the captain of all I-don't-think-he-is-old-enough-to-explain-this type seasons, but he was by no means the only sailor on that ship:

Adam Dunn

	G	AB	R	H	D	T	HR	RBI	BB	SO	SB	Avg	Slg
Actual	122	415	36	66	16	0	11	42	75	177	0	.159	.277
Projected	160	567	90	140	31	1	39	102	107	197	2	.247	.511

Chone Figgins

	G	AB	R	H	D	T	HR	RBI	BB	SO	SB	Avg	Slg
Actual	81	288	24	54	11	1	1	15	21	42	11	.188	.243
Projected	146	528	77	146	21	4	3	42	67	99	32	.277	.348

Jack Cust

	G	AB	R	H	D	T	HR	RBI	BB	SO	SB	Avg	Slg
Actual	67	225	19	48	15	1	3	23	44	87	0	.213	.329
Projected	134	430	66	104	20	0	20	64	91	160	1	.242	.428

Andres Torres

	G	AB	R	H	D	T	HR	RBI	BB	SO	SB	Avg	Slg
Actual	112	348	50	77	24	1	4	19	42	95	19	.221	.330
Projected	152	521	84	141	30	8	14	53	54	125	25	.271	.440

There are players who just have inexplicably awful years, like Jason Heyward, Franklin Gutierrez and Travis Snider:

Jason Heyward

	G	AB	R	H	D	T	HR	RBI	BB	SO	SB	Avg	Slg
Actual	128	396	50	90	18	2	14	42	51	93	9	.227	.389
Projected	156	572	101	169	35	6	22	88	105	121	13	.295	.493

Franklin Gutierrez

	G	AB	R	H	D	T	HR	RBI	BB	SO	SB	Avg	Slg
Actual	92	322	26	72	13	0	1	19	16	56	13	.224	.273
Projected	151	559	77	146	32	2	14	63	49	131	20	.261	.401

Travis Snider

	G	AB	R	H	D	T	HR	RBI	BB	SO	SB	Avg	Slg
Actual	49	187	23	42	14	0	3	30	11	56	9	.225	.348
Projected	97	311	46	85	21	0	16	48	29	84	6	.273	.495

There are many more players who just have inexplicably awful years than there are players who fool us by displaying ability we never suspected that they had.

This leaves two categories of "F" projections from last season:

a) Players who did not get anything like the playing time we had projected for them, and

b) "Half and half" players—players who did not get anything like the playing time we had projected for them because they just didn't play as well as we thought they would play.

It is our philosophy, if such may be called philosophy. . .it is our practice, when we cannot know whether a player will or will not get playing time next season, to project that he will.   Very often there is a situation in which, looking ahead to next season, the regular at a position may be Player X, Y or Z, and there is no way in the world that anyone can say which player will win the job.   The manager doesn't know; the general manager doesn't know, no one knows.

In that situation, our position is that rather than making a guess as to who will win the job, we project both players (or all three players) as if they will play. Our job, as we see it, is to tell you what kind of a hitter the player should be *if* he gets a chance to play.   Sometimes this leads us to project playing time for young players that does not materialize.   Like Lorenzo Cain, Luis Durango, Adam Moore and Cole Gillespie:

Lorenzo Cain

	G	AB	R	H	D	T	HR	RBI	BB	SO	SB	Avg	Slg
Actual	6	22	4	6	1	0	0	1	1	4	0	.273	.318
Projected	135	512	75	143	24	6	5	46	50	109	33	.279	.379

Luis Durango

	G	AB	R	H	D	T	HR	RBI	BB	SO	SB	Avg	Slg
Actual	2	6	0	1	0	0	0	1	1	1	0	.167	.167
Projected	129	371	46	97	5	1	0	20	46	62	39	.261	.280

Adam Moore

	G	AB	R	H	D	T	HR	RBI	BB	SO	SB	Avg	Slg
Actual	2	6	0	1	1	0	0	0	0	2	0	.167	.333
Projected	118	409	40	104	23	1	10	44	26	88	1	.254	.389

Cole Gillespie

	G	AB	R	H	D	T	HR	RBI	BB	SO	SB	Avg	Slg
Actual	5	6	2	2	0	0	1	4	1	1	0	.333	.833
Projected	84	199	26	50	13	2	5	26	23	42	6	.251	.412

These are all "F" projections. You may agree with this practice; you may criticize it. That's the way we do it.

There are, finally, the players who do not get the playing time that we project for them because frankly, they suck. Some of these guys, I'm sure, were injured and will bounce back strong in 2012. Others of them just suck, and will continue to suck in 2012. We probably don't know which is which in all cases, but this group from 2011 includes Ian Stewart, Pedro Alvarez, Tyler Colvin and Luke Scott:

Ian Stewart

	G	AB	R	H	D	T	HR	RBI	BB	SO	SB	Avg	Slg
Actual	48	122	14	19	6	1	0	6	14	37	3	.156	.221
Projected	142	534	84	139	30	4	26	86	61	142	7	.260	.478

Pedro Alvarez

	G	AB	R	H	D	T	HR	RBI	BB	SO	SB	Avg	Slg
Actual	74	235	18	45	9	1	4	19	24	80	1	.191	.289
Projected	149	537	78	149	35	2	27	103	62	154	4	.277	.501

Tyler Colvin

	G	AB	R	H	D	T	HR	RBI	BB	SO	SB	Avg	Slg
Actual	80	206	17	31	8	3	6	20	14	58	0	.150	.306
Projected	149	514	76	133	25	6	24	75	35	116	9	.259	.471

Luke Scott

	G	AB	R	H	D	T	HR	RBI	BB	SO	SB	Avg	Slg
Actual	64	209	24	46	11	0	9	22	24	54	1	.220	.402
Projected	142	493	70	131	31	2	27	80	62	114	2	.266	.501

To this point in our review, you might have concluded that all of our projections from last year were pretty terrible. Actually, many of them were pretty good. We had more than 400 projections from last seasons; 73 of them were "F"s and none of them deserves an "A+", but I credit us with 23 "A"s, 36 "A-"s, and 51 grades of "B+". We had projected that Gerardo Parra would play in 141 games, and he did:

Gerardo Parra

	G	AB	R	H	D	T	HR	RBI	BB	SO	SB	Avg	Slg
Actual	141	445	55	130	20	8	8	46	43	82	15	.292	.427
Projected	141	405	49	117	22	7	5	45	30	70	8	.289	.415

We had projected that Troy of the Witskis would have 537 at bats, and he did:

Troy Tulowitzki

	G	AB	R	H	D	T	HR	RBI	BB	SO	SB	Avg	Slg
Actual	143	537	81	162	36	2	30	105	59	79	9	.302	.544
Projected	142	537	96	159	34	4	27	93	60	95	11	.296	.525

We had projected that Jimmy Rollins would score 87 runs and would have 59 strikeouts, and he did:

Jimmy Rollins

	G	AB	R	H	D	T	HR	RBI	BB	SO	SB	Avg	Slg
Actual	142	567	87	152	22	2	16	63	58	59	30	.268	.399
Projected	136	556	87	148	33	5	15	61	49	59	25	.266	.424

We had projected that Nick Swisher would get 137 hits, and he did:

Nick Swisher

	G	AB	R	H	D	T	HR	RBI	BB	SO	SB	Avg	Slg
Actual	150	526	81	137	30	0	23	85	95	125	2	.260	.449
Projected	153	534	87	137	32	1	27	83	80	136	1	.257	.472

We had projected that Mark Reynolds should hit 27 doubles, and he did:

Mark Reynolds

	G	AB	R	H	D	T	HR	RBI	BB	SO	SB	Avg	Slg
Actual	155	534	84	118	27	1	37	86	75	196	6	.221	.483
Projected	150	529	89	123	27	2	35	94	77	212	9	.233	.490

We had projected that John McDonald would have 10 doubles, 1 triple and 22 RBI, and he did:

John McDonald

	G	AB	R	H	D	T	HR	RBI	BB	SO	SB	Avg	Slg
Actual	84	227	21	52	10	1	2	22	12	27	2	.229	.308
Projected	91	220	27	51	10	1	4	22	9	35	3	.232	.341

Actually we had projected the right triples total for more than a hundred major league hitters. It's not that hard; most players hit zero to five triples in a year, so you have a good chance to pick the right number at random. We had projected that Freddie Freeman, a rookie, would hit .282, and he did:

Freddie Freeman

	G	AB	R	H	D	T	HR	RBI	BB	SO	SB	Avg	Slg
Actual	157	571	67	161	32	0	21	76	53	142	4	.282	.448
Projected	148	511	68	144	34	1	16	83	41	93	6	.282	.446

We had projected that Billy Butler would hit 44 doubles, one triple and 18 homers; actually it was 44-0-19:

Billy Butler

	G	AB	R	H	D	T	HR	RBI	BB	SO	SB	Avg	Slg
Actual	159	597	74	174	44	0	19	95	66	95	2	.291	.461
Projected	156	590	78	181	44	1	18	89	63	80	0	.307	.476

It was the home run that he hit off of Wade Davis on July 22 that got us; we had expected that one to be a triple. So far I have shown you 22 bad projections and 8 good ones, which is not the actual ratio, but let me show you some in the middle. Let's see. . .we had 405 projections last year for players who actually played, so the middle would be the 202nd, 203rd and 204th most accurate projections. That would be Adam Lind, David Ortiz and Danny Valencia:

Adam Lind

	G	AB	R	H	D	T	HR	RBI	BB	SO	SB	Avg	Slg
Actual	125	499	56	125	16	0	26	87	32	107	1	.251	.439
Projected	149	551	72	155	37	2	26	92	44	115	1	.281	.497

David Ortiz

	G	AB	R	H	D	T	HR	RBI	BB	SO	SB	Avg	Slg
Actual	146	525	84	162	40	1	29	96	78	83	1	.309	.554
Projected	151	564	91	147	39	1	33	112	91	146	0	.261	.509

Danny Valencia

	G	AB	R	H	D	T	HR	RBI	BB	SO	SB	Avg	Slg
Actual	154	564	63	139	28	2	15	72	40	102	2	.246	.383
Projected	137	479	61	139	35	2	10	62	34	78	3	.290	.434

Those are "C+" projections; we got some things right, we got some things wrong. A player's in-play batting average is pretty unpredictable; it's random, whether he hits the ball at fielders or away from them. We had projected Valencia's in-play batting average at .330; it was actually .277—and yet we were not entirely wrong about him. We were half right for all of these guys, which is the normal fare. Our most accurate projection, as we score these things, was actually for Shelley Duncan:

Shelley Duncan

	G	AB	R	H	D	T	HR	RBI	BB	SO	SB	Avg	Slg
Actual	76	223	29	58	17	0	11	47	19	56	0	.260	.484
Projected	81	217	32	55	12	0	12	40	26	53	1	.253	.475

Although why that one scores as more accurate than the projection for Brendan Ryan or Will Venable, I couldn't tell you:

Brendan Ryan

	G	AB	R	H	D	T	HR	RBI	BB	SO	SB	Avg	Slg
Actual	123	436	51	108	19	3	3	39	34	87	13	.248	.326
Projected	133	398	53	101	18	3	3	31	29	52	11	.254	.337

Will Venable

	G	AB	R	H	D	T	HR	RBI	BB	SO	SB	Avg	Slg
Actual	121	370	49	91	14	7	9	44	31	92	26	.246	.395
Projected	109	321	45	80	12	3	10	40	32	86	16	.249	.399

Carlos Pena bounces between MVP-candidate seasons and hitting .196. When a player bounces up and down we project that he will land in the middle. Surprisingly often this turns out to be almost exactly right:

Carlos Pena

	G	AB	R	H	D	T	HR	RBI	BB	SO	SB	Avg	Slg
Actual	153	493	72	111	27	3	28	80	101	161	2	.225	.462
Projected	138	469	73	107	23	1	30	86	84	156	3	.228	.473

Jacoby Ellsbury last year was projected to hit 8 home runs but actually hit 32, so next year we project that he will hit 19. That's how we do this. We do take pride in our ability to occasionally produce very accurate projections for young players, like Freddie Freeman. Mike Stanton last year was a first-year regular, but we projected him pretty good:

Mike Stanton

	G	AB	R	H	D	T	HR	RBI	BB	SO	SB	Avg	Slg
Actual	150	516	79	135	30	5	34	87	70	166	5	.262	.537
Projected	152	522	85	140	32	2	38	104	69	162	5	.268	.556

Ben Revere had only 28 at bats before last season, hitting .179, but we had a pretty accurate projection for him:

Ben Revere

	G	AB	R	H	D	T	HR	RBI	BB	SO	SB	Avg	Slg
Actual	117	450	56	120	9	5	0	30	26	41	34	.267	.309
Projected	92	341	33	96	9	3	1	18	26	39	34	.282	.334

We do the best we can, and we try not to claim to do more than we can do. I hope you'll take it for whatever it's worth.

2012 Hitter Projections

Hitter	Team	Age	G	AB	H	2B	3B	HR	R	RBI	RC	RC27	BB	SO	SB	CS	SB%	Avg	OBP	Slg	OPS
Abreu,Bobby	LAA	38	129	423	110	26	1	11	61	61	63	5.13	67	97	15	6	.71	.260	.364	.404	.768
Ackley,Dustin	Sea	24	158	616	157	33	8	11	82	60	82	4.59	81	112	14	5	.74	.255	.341	.388	.729
Adams,Ryan	Bal	25	59	186	50	13	0	5	22	18	25	4.74	13	47	2	1	.67	.269	.320	.419	.739
Allen,Brandon	Oak	26	137	486	118	26	4	22	71	70	71	4.95	61	142	11	5	.69	.243	.327	.449	.776
Alonso,Yonder	Cin	25	107	336	93	22	1	11	37	44	51	5.39	35	61	5	3	.62	.277	.345	.446	.791
Altuve,Jose	Hou	22	144	538	160	27	5	10	64	46	71	4.75	16	61	19	11	.63	.297	.320	.422	.742
Alvarez,Pedro	Pit	25	131	496	125	27	2	19	61	76	70	4.89	58	148	2	1	.67	.252	.332	.429	.761
Anderson,Lars	Bos	24	46	113	29	9	0	3	14	15	16	4.95	15	28	1	0	1.00	.257	.344	.416	.760
Andino,Robert	Bal	28	98	277	70	13	1	4	34	24	29	3.59	19	52	7	3	.70	.253	.303	.350	.653
Andrus,Elvis	Tex	23	153	572	161	23	4	4	93	54	73	4.48	56	75	39	13	.75	.281	.351	.357	.707
Ankiel,Rick	Was	32	106	298	70	15	1	10	38	38	34	3.83	24	82	5	3	.62	.235	.296	.393	.689
Arencibia,J.P.	Tor	26	129	455	105	27	2	24	54	73	58	4.31	30	117	1	0	1.00	.231	.281	.457	.738
Avila,Alex	Det	25	141	459	127	31	2	19	62	76	82	6.38	71	113	3	2	.60	.277	.376	.477	.853
Aviles,Mike	Bos	31	101	319	89	18	2	8	41	37	41	4.52	14	40	11	6	.65	.279	.311	.423	.735
Aybar,Erick	LAA	28	146	551	151	28	6	8	74	53	68	4.31	32	71	26	10	.72	.274	.320	.390	.710
Baker,Jeff	ChC	31	76	164	46	11	1	4	21	22	24	5.29	12	35	1	0	1.00	.280	.333	.433	.766
Barajas,Rod	LAD	36	117	397	89	20	0	17	43	55	43	3.63	23	83	0	0	.00	.224	.274	.403	.677
Barmes,Clint	Hou	33	142	496	123	29	2	13	58	52	57	3.94	33	94	4	3	.57	.248	.303	.393	.696
Barney,Darwin	ChC	26	98	306	84	15	2	2	36	25	34	3.95	15	36	6	2	.75	.275	.317	.356	.673
Bartlett,Jason	SD	32	140	496	132	25	3	4	66	44	57	3.98	44	88	17	8	.68	.266	.333	.353	.686
Barton,Daric	Oak	26	86	233	58	14	1	4	33	26	31	4.58	40	41	2	1	.67	.249	.364	.369	.733
Bautista,Jose	Tor	31	157	568	149	31	2	38	103	108	113	6.95	107	127	7	4	.64	.262	.385	.525	.909
Bay,Jason	NYM	33	143	486	125	26	2	19	73	77	75	5.36	69	131	10	3	.77	.257	.355	.436	.792
Beckham,Gordon	CWS	25	152	507	130	33	1	13	70	61	63	4.30	42	97	6	4	.60	.256	.326	.402	.728
Belt,Brandon	SF	24	151	527	140	29	5	25	73	79	90	5.94	75	142	11	7	.61	.266	.358	.482	.840
Beltran,Carlos	SF	35	128	481	134	31	3	20	75	79	85	6.31	67	86	8	3	.73	.279	.369	.480	.849
Beltre,Adrian	Tex	33	140	534	154	35	1	26	77	90	89	6.06	34	76	4	2	.67	.288	.337	.504	.841
Berkman,Lance	StL	36	146	516	144	30	1	27	82	92	101	7.00	97	108	4	3	.57	.279	.396	.498	.894
Bernadina,Roger	Was	28	96	268	70	12	2	7	36	25	35	4.46	24	56	18	6	.75	.261	.327	.399	.726
Betancourt,Yuniesky	Mil	30	149	528	137	29	3	11	54	60	58	3.83	18	57	4	3	.57	.259	.285	.388	.673
Betemit,Wilson	Det	30	108	359	95	24	1	12	43	52	52	5.08	37	108	3	2	.60	.265	.333	.437	.771
Blackmon,Charlie	Col	25	40	119	33	7	1	3	14	14	16	4.67	6	14	7	3	.70	.277	.312	.429	.741
Blake,Casey	LAD	38	48	171	42	9	0	5	22	22	21	4.20	18	45	1	1	.50	.246	.338	.386	.724
Blanco,Henry	Ari	40	75	212	47	9	0	7	19	21	22	3.47	19	46	0	0	.00	.222	.286	.363	.649
Blanks,Kyle	SD	25	100	302	78	17	2	12	45	50	44	5.06	32	85	3	2	.60	.258	.335	.447	.782
Bloomquist,Willie	Ari	34	75	184	48	5	1	2	24	13	19	3.53	12	30	9	4	.69	.261	.313	.332	.645
Boesch,Brennan	Det	27	119	409	114	23	2	17	61	62	64	5.60	32	79	5	2	.71	.279	.337	.469	.807
Bogusevic,Brian	Hou	28	64	150	39	9	1	3	19	15	20	4.60	15	34	9	2	.82	.260	.327	.393	.721
Bonifacio,Emilio	Fla	27	132	446	123	19	5	2	64	29	55	4.29	41	91	27	10	.73	.276	.338	.354	.692
Borbon,Julio	Tex	26	77	233	67	8	3	2	34	22	29	4.36	14	29	19	7	.73	.288	.333	.373	.707
Bourgeois,Jason	Hou	30	79	162	45	7	1	2	21	13	20	4.26	10	18	14	5	.74	.278	.320	.370	.690
Bourjos,Peter	LAA	25	147	514	137	22	9	13	77	49	68	4.57	33	108	27	10	.73	.267	.317	.420	.737
Bourn,Michael	Atl	29	152	583	160	25	6	3	87	40	73	4.33	55	127	50	15	.77	.274	.339	.353	.692
Brantley,Michael	Cle	25	131	523	140	23	3	6	76	47	63	4.19	49	69	23	8	.74	.268	.332	.358	.689
Branyan,Russell	LAA	36	80	206	47	11	0	12	25	30	30	4.88	28	75	2	1	.67	.228	.326	.456	.783
Braun,Ryan	Mil	28	157	615	195	43	4	35	111	115	134	8.16	59	108	25	7	.78	.317	.382	.571	.953
Brignac,Reid	TB	26	91	225	55	12	1	5	27	25	24	3.63	15	48	3	2	.60	.244	.295	.373	.668
Brown,Domonic	Phi	24	141	510	140	29	3	19	79	71	83	5.68	64	110	24	10	.71	.275	.355	.455	.810
Bruce,Jay	Cin	25	150	537	145	27	3	32	85	88	94	6.16	62	137	7	5	.58	.270	.349	.510	.859
Buck,John	Fla	31	128	443	106	22	1	17	47	61	54	4.17	39	115	0	0	.00	.239	.309	.409	.718
Burrell,Pat	SF	35	110	305	70	15	0	14	37	49	44	4.87	54	97	0	0	.00	.230	.349	.416	.765
Butler,Billy	KC	26	160	612	184	46	1	20	81	96	108	6.55	67	91	1	1	.50	.301	.372	.477	.850
Byrd,Marlon	ChC	34	146	556	153	33	2	13	70	66	73	4.67	36	103	5	3	.62	.275	.329	.412	.741
Cabrera,Asdrubal	Cle	26	143	566	158	35	3	16	86	75	83	5.21	48	105	15	6	.71	.279	.342	.436	.778
Cabrera,Melky	KC	27	150	516	144	30	3	11	69	64	70	4.81	39	72	13	6	.68	.279	.332	.413	.745
Cabrera,Miguel	Det	29	159	596	196	44	1	35	108	120	145	9.40	92	103	2	1	.67	.329	.422	.582	1.004
Cabrera,Orlando	SF	37	130	465	120	24	0	5	55	47	47	3.50	27	55	8	4	.67	.258	.302	.342	.644
Cain,Lorenzo	KC	26	146	531	151	28	6	10	73	58	75	5.03	42	110	22	8	.73	.284	.337	.416	.753
Cairo,Miguel	Cin	38	52	154	39	7	1	3	20	16	17	3.81	10	23	2	1	.67	.253	.315	.370	.686
Callaspo,Alberto	LAA	29	144	505	141	27	3	7	61	51	66	4.68	47	44	6	3	.67	.279	.342	.386	.728
Campana,Tony	ChC	26	85	135	39	5	1	0	19	8	16	4.16	8	24	16	4	.80	.289	.333	.341	.674
Cano,Robinson	NYY	29	161	632	191	45	4	25	96	101	108	6.31	39	86	5	4	.56	.302	.350	.505	.854
Cantu,Jorge	SD	30	76	211	55	14	0	6	23	31	26	4.33	13	38	0	0	.00	.261	.316	.412	.728
Carp,Mike	Sea	26	79	267	69	14	1	11	34	40	38	4.94	25	62	2	2	.50	.258	.327	.442	.768
Carrera,Ezequiel	Cle	25	53	112	30	4	1	0	16	9	13	3.98	11	19	10	3	.77	.268	.339	.321	.660
Carroll,Jamey	LAD	38	94	325	89	12	2	1	45	21	38	4.13	37	51	6	3	.67	.274	.353	.332	.686
Casilla,Alexi	Min	27	109	329	87	15	3	2	48	28	38	3.98	31	42	15	6	.71	.264	.331	.347	.678
Castro,Jason	Hou	25	129	452	107	18	1	6	59	37	45	3.38	50	77	2	1	.67	.237	.313	.321	.634
Castro,Starlin	ChC	22	158	631	197	39	9	8	84	66	97	5.68	38	82	21	10	.68	.312	.354	.441	.795
Cedeno,Ronny	Pit	29	133	429	107	22	3	6	44	39	45	3.60	28	96	5	3	.62	.249	.297	.357	.654
Cervelli,Francisco	NYY	26	92	294	79	12	1	5	37	43	36	4.29	28	54	5	3	.62	.269	.336	.367	.704
Chavez,Endy	Tex	34	85	254	70	11	2	3	31	22	30	4.15	15	27	9	4	.69	.276	.316	.370	.686
Chavez,Eric	NYY	34	52	107	26	6	0	3	12	14	13	4.17	12	25	0	0	.00	.243	.319	.383	.703
Chisenhall,Lonnie	Cle	23	126	452	112	26	2	13	66	64	54	4.12	34	85	2	1	.67	.248	.302	.400	.702
Choo,Shin-Soo	Cle	29	149	568	160	32	3	18	82	80	92	5.74	74	138	19	9	.68	.282	.371	.444	.815
Coghlan,Chris	Fla	27	101	355	98	24	3	6	56	37	50	4.94	37	57	12	6	.67	.276	.351	.411	.762
Colvin,Tyler	ChC	26	84	189	44	9	2	7	24	24	21	3.74	11	46	2	1	.67	.233	.279	.413	.691
Conger,Hank	LAA	24	72	222	57	11	1	6	24	29	29	4.57	23	38	0	0	.00	.257	.329	.396	.726
Conrad,Brooks	Atl	32	81	122	28	7	1	5	18	17	16	4.38	13	34	1	0	1.00	.230	.309	.426	.735
Cowgill,Collin	Ari	26	99	205	58	12	2	5	31	26	31	5.34	18	35	14	4	.78	.283	.341	.434	.775

2012 Hitter Projections

Hitter	Team	Age	G	AB	H	2B	3B	HR	R	RBI	RC	RC27	BB	SO	SB	CS	SB%	Avg	OBP	Slg	OPS
Cozart,Zack	Cin	26	131	503	129	31	2	13	71	50	63	4.33	36	88	16	4	.80	.256	.306	.404	.710
Craig,Allen	StL	27	93	295	85	19	1	13	43	50	49	6.04	23	54	3	1	.75	.288	.340	.492	.831
Crawford,Brandon	SF	25	83	259	60	12	2	4	30	22	26	3.33	24	51	6	4	.60	.232	.297	.340	.637
Crawford,Carl	Bos	30	155	608	174	30	8	15	93	73	88	5.14	38	112	34	11	.76	.286	.332	.436	.768
Crisp,Coco	Oak	32	119	428	116	23	3	8	62	46	58	4.70	39	60	32	9	.78	.271	.333	.395	.728
Cruz,Nelson	Tex	31	136	516	143	29	1	31	76	92	90	6.17	47	126	14	6	.70	.277	.339	.517	.856
Cuddyer,Michael	Min	33	152	586	161	34	3	21	86	85	91	5.53	60	108	8	3	.73	.275	.347	.451	.798
Cust,Jack	Sea	33	60	152	36	7	0	6	21	21	23	5.16	32	58	0	0	.00	.237	.376	.401	.778
Damon,Johnny	TB	38	131	445	119	23	2	12	69	52	62	4.88	48	74	12	4	.75	.267	.343	.409	.752
d'Arnaud,Chase	Pit	25	51	113	26	6	1	1	15	9	11	3.21	8	21	8	2	.80	.230	.287	.327	.614
Darnell,James	SD	25	39	125	31	7	0	4	16	18	17	4.70	16	24	1	0	1.00	.248	.333	.400	.733
Davis,Chris	Bal	26	103	366	97	24	1	20	54	63	58	5.59	27	106	2	1	.67	.265	.316	.500	.816
Davis,Ike	NYM	25	141	520	150	35	1	25	80	87	98	6.87	73	124	1	1	.50	.288	.377	.504	.881
Davis,Rajai	Tor	31	115	361	96	20	3	3	49	31	41	3.82	22	64	37	14	.73	.266	.313	.363	.676
De Aza,Alejandro	CWS	28	79	220	64	16	2	5	35	23	34	5.46	20	43	13	6	.68	.291	.353	.450	.803
DeJesus,David	Oak	32	124	424	115	22	4	8	58	46	57	4.75	42	73	4	3	.57	.271	.349	.399	.748
Denorfia,Chris	SD	31	97	253	68	13	1	5	33	25	32	4.40	22	38	8	4	.67	.269	.330	.387	.717
Descalso,Daniel	StL	25	90	208	55	13	1	2	27	23	25	4.22	19	31	2	1	.67	.264	.332	.365	.697
Desmond,Ian	Was	26	143	526	141	28	4	10	62	54	65	4.29	35	109	21	9	.70	.268	.317	.394	.711
DeWitt,Blake	ChC	26	87	175	45	9	2	4	20	21	22	4.37	16	26	1	1	.50	.257	.326	.400	.726
Diaz,Matt	Atl	34	100	241	67	13	1	5	26	28	30	4.43	13	52	4	2	.67	.278	.328	.402	.731
Dirks,Andy	Det	26	104	351	95	19	1	11	52	44	48	4.78	24	54	16	5	.76	.271	.321	.425	.745
Dobbs,Greg	Fla	33	103	223	56	12	1	5	22	28	25	3.89	14	47	1	0	1.00	.251	.298	.381	.679
Dominguez,Matt	Fla	22	106	341	79	21	1	8	35	43	37	3.67	28	61	0	0	.00	.232	.292	.370	.661
Donald,Jason	Cle	27	86	276	75	17	1	4	37	23	35	4.46	23	61	9	3	.75	.272	.332	.384	.716
Doumit,Ryan	Pit	31	113	397	109	26	1	13	46	55	58	5.22	32	74	1	1	.50	.275	.335	.443	.778
Downs,Matt	Hou	28	76	152	37	11	0	5	19	21	19	4.26	12	28	1	1	.50	.243	.311	.414	.726
Drew,J.D.	Bos	36	107	318	80	17	1	11	48	43	47	5.11	51	75	1	1	.50	.252	.360	.415	.775
Drew,Stephen	Ari	29	134	518	137	32	7	13	70	61	73	4.94	51	104	6	3	.67	.264	.332	.429	.760
Duda,Lucas	NYM	26	100	330	92	25	1	14	44	53	58	6.34	40	65	1	0	1.00	.279	.364	.488	.852
Duncan,Shelley	Cle	32	89	241	60	13	0	13	35	45	37	5.29	29	56	1	1	.50	.249	.335	.465	.799
Dunn,Adam	CWS	32	116	350	77	18	0	20	48	55	54	5.14	67	135	1	0	1.00	.220	.355	.443	.797
Ellis,Mark	Col	35	126	420	107	22	1	8	49	45	47	3.85	30	65	9	4	.69	.255	.314	.369	.683
Ellsbury,Jacoby	Bos	28	158	586	178	34	5	19	102	72	102	6.33	48	82	38	11	.78	.304	.362	.476	.838
Encarnacion,Edwin	Tor	29	115	368	98	24	0	16	52	53	57	5.45	37	65	4	2	.67	.266	.341	.462	.803
Escobar,Alcides	KC	25	155	536	143	21	7	5	72	49	60	3.87	30	69	27	10	.73	.267	.309	.360	.669
Escobar,Yunel	Tor	29	146	556	158	28	2	10	80	58	78	5.06	64	74	4	3	.57	.284	.364	.396	.760
Espinosa,Danny	Was	25	158	568	141	27	5	25	83	74	79	4.71	55	145	19	9	.68	.248	.329	.445	.774
Ethier,Andre	LAD	30	149	560	161	38	2	19	79	82	94	6.11	64	113	2	1	.67	.288	.366	.464	.830
Evans,Nick	NYM	26	61	135	36	9	1	4	18	17	19	4.99	12	29	1	0	1.00	.267	.331	.437	.768
Fielder,Prince	Mil	28	153	562	160	34	1	38	93	109	122	7.87	101	118	1	1	.50	.285	.404	.552	.956
Figgins,Chone	Sea	34	94	283	74	11	2	2	38	22	33	3.97	33	50	16	7	.70	.261	.341	.336	.676
Flowers,Tyler	CWS	26	80	266	64	15	1	15	39	38	44	5.64	43	94	2	1	.67	.241	.350	.474	.824
Fontenot,Mike	SF	32	81	207	53	13	1	4	25	21	26	4.33	21	43	3	2	.60	.256	.330	.386	.717
Fowler,Dexter	Col	26	142	512	140	35	12	7	88	47	79	5.39	70	121	16	9	.64	.273	.364	.430	.794
Francisco,Ben	Phi	30	113	311	83	20	1	9	41	40	44	4.93	31	53	7	4	.64	.267	.341	.424	.765
Francisco,Juan	Cin	25	64	178	51	12	1	9	23	28	29	5.94	7	42	1	0	1.00	.287	.314	.517	.830
Francoeur,Jeff	KC	28	152	592	159	37	3	18	73	87	78	4.60	35	115	14	8	.64	.269	.317	.432	.749
Frazier,Todd	Cin	26	59	153	38	10	1	6	20	20	21	4.67	13	36	6	2	.75	.248	.311	.444	.756
Freeman,Freddie	Atl	22	157	542	155	34	0	20	70	82	86	5.73	50	115	4	3	.57	.286	.350	.459	.809
Freese,David	StL	29	110	394	118	22	1	12	52	66	63	5.91	32	84	2	1	.67	.299	.357	.452	.808
Fukudome,Kosuke	Cle	35	140	453	116	28	2	10	57	46	62	4.73	64	100	5	4	.56	.256	.352	.393	.745
Fuld,Sam	TB	30	65	117	29	6	1	1	16	9	13	3.71	14	14	6	3	.67	.248	.333	.342	.675
Furcal,Rafael	StL	34	124	485	131	24	3	10	74	44	64	4.61	48	67	15	7	.68	.270	.338	.394	.732
Gamel,Mat	Mil	26	118	443	125	27	1	19	63	72	72	5.87	40	94	3	1	.75	.282	.342	.476	.818
Gardner,Brett	NYY	28	156	516	141	19	7	6	99	43	75	5.03	73	90	50	13	.79	.273	.369	.372	.741
Gentry,Craig	Tex	28	68	150	40	6	1	2	22	13	18	4.14	12	25	12	3	.80	.267	.333	.360	.693
Getz,Chris	KC	28	94	263	69	9	1	1	34	22	26	3.68	24	29	13	4	.76	.262	.329	.316	.644
Giambi,Jason	Col	41	79	186	41	7	0	10	23	33	27	4.84	34	55	0	0	.00	.220	.364	.419	.783
Giavotella,Johnny	KC	24	147	515	152	35	4	7	65	60	73	5.13	36	68	12	7	.63	.295	.342	.419	.762
Gload,Ross	Phi	36	85	125	33	7	0	2	13	15	14	3.96	7	20	0	0	.00	.264	.308	.368	.676
Goldschmidt,Paul	Ari	24	148	545	145	32	4	32	93	99	103	6.61	87	162	9	5	.64	.266	.367	.516	.883
Gomes,Jonny	Was	31	120	342	82	18	1	16	48	53	48	4.75	40	107	6	3	.67	.240	.333	.439	.772
Gomez,Carlos	Mil	26	100	240	58	11	3	5	36	24	27	3.75	16	61	16	5	.76	.242	.297	.375	.672
Gonzalez,Adrian	Bos	30	160	604	182	38	1	30	93	105	120	7.39	80	118	1	0	1.00	.301	.387	.517	.903
Gonzalez,Alberto	SD	29	86	164	41	8	1	1	17	17	16	3.35	10	20	1	1	.50	.250	.301	.329	.630
Gonzalez,Alex	Atl	35	145	514	122	30	1	14	55	60	53	3.51	25	112	1	1	.50	.237	.278	.381	.659
Gonzalez,Carlos	Col	26	141	535	163	34	6	28	97	97	106	7.27	46	108	19	7	.73	.305	.364	.548	.912
Gordon,Alex	KC	28	156	602	166	43	3	22	96	81	100	5.87	75	145	14	7	.67	.276	.361	.467	.827
Gordon,Dee	LAD	24	146	556	150	18	5	0	72	30	56	3.48	25	78	42	12	.78	.270	.301	.320	.621
Granderson,Curtis	NYY	31	155	585	152	28	8	31	107	84	99	5.84	73	156	19	8	.70	.260	.348	.494	.842
Greene,Tyler	StL	28	90	248	62	12	1	7	39	25	32	4.40	23	67	16	3	.84	.250	.321	.391	.712
Guerrero,Vladimir	Bal	37	133	470	139	25	1	17	62	73	73	5.70	30	53	3	2	.60	.296	.347	.462	.809
Gutierrez,Franklin	Sea	29	150	560	143	30	2	11	70	57	66	4.06	44	119	18	6	.75	.255	.312	.375	.687
Guyer,Brandon	TB	26	67	199	55	15	2	6	32	25	30	5.31	13	37	9	3	.75	.276	.321	.462	.783
Guzman,Jesus	SD	28	122	420	120	27	2	10	51	61	61	5.20	35	72	9	5	.64	.286	.341	.431	.772
Gwynn,Tony	LAD	29	93	199	49	7	2	1	25	13	20	3.38	20	37	11	4	.73	.246	.318	.317	.635
Hafner,Travis	Cle	35	106	377	101	23	0	15	51	63	61	5.75	53	92	0	0	.00	.268	.368	.448	.817
Hairston,Jerry	Mil	36	87	287	73	16	1	5	38	28	33	3.97	24	40	4	2	.67	.254	.323	.369	.692
Hairston,Scott	NYM	32	81	188	46	10	1	8	24	25	24	4.55	14	44	2	1	.67	.245	.314	.436	.750
Hall,Bill	SF	32	94	254	58	16	1	8	30	30	28	3.68	21	84	3	2	.60	.228	.292	.394	.686

2012 Hitter Projections

Hitter	Team	Age	G	AB	H	2B	3B	HR	R	RBI	RC	RC27	BB	SO	SB	CS	SB%	Avg	OBP	Slg	OPS
Hamilton,Josh	Tex	31	133	503	156	33	3	27	83	95	101	7.50	44	100	8	3	.73	.310	.369	.549	.918
Hanigan,Ryan	Cin	31	108	357	98	15	0	6	40	39	47	4.72	47	40	0	0	.00	.275	.362	.367	.729
Hannahan,Jack	Cle	32	81	197	48	11	0	4	23	24	23	3.99	26	47	1	1	.50	.244	.335	.360	.695
Hardy,J.J.	Bal	29	134	503	132	26	1	21	69	68	70	4.91	39	86	0	0	.00	.262	.317	.443	.760
Harris,Willie	NYM	34	88	137	31	6	1	3	20	12	15	3.61	20	34	3	2	.60	.226	.342	.350	.692
Harrison,Josh	Pit	24	57	133	37	9	1	1	16	14	16	4.24	6	14	5	2	.71	.278	.309	.383	.693
Hart,Corey	Mil	30	144	551	151	35	4	25	85	80	89	5.71	48	128	10	5	.67	.274	.338	.488	.826
Hawpe,Brad	SD	33	82	216	56	13	1	8	27	34	33	5.36	30	67	0	0	.00	.259	.355	.440	.795
Hayes,Brett	Fla	28	67	158	35	9	0	4	16	16	15	3.17	10	39	0	0	.00	.222	.268	.354	.622
Headley,Chase	SD	28	141	496	137	33	2	10	62	58	73	5.23	60	122	12	4	.75	.276	.358	.411	.769
Heisey,Chris	Cin	27	107	266	71	14	1	14	41	40	41	5.41	20	62	6	2	.75	.267	.328	.485	.813
Helton,Todd	Col	38	132	441	126	28	1	12	61	60	75	6.19	75	78	0	0	.00	.286	.393	.435	.828
Hernandez,Ramon	Cin	36	81	273	73	13	0	8	26	39	36	4.68	23	40	0	0	.00	.267	.336	.403	.738
Herrera,Jonathan	Col	27	81	193	48	6	1	1	22	13	18	3.18	17	25	4	2	.67	.249	.310	.306	.615
Heyward,Jason	Atl	22	149	540	145	31	4	21	86	74	92	5.98	86	114	14	5	.74	.269	.374	.457	.831
Hill,Aaron	Ari	30	133	481	123	28	1	14	62	61	59	4.21	35	70	11	6	.65	.256	.314	.405	.720
Hill,Koyie	ChC	33	60	133	30	7	0	2	13	13	12	3.03	11	34	1	0	1.00	.226	.285	.323	.608
Hinske,Eric	Atl	34	105	211	49	12	1	8	27	28	27	4.31	24	61	1	1	.50	.232	.319	.412	.732
Holliday,Matt	StL	32	149	563	173	42	2	27	98	100	114	7.54	67	108	7	3	.70	.307	.390	.533	.923
Hosmer,Eric	KC	22	153	605	188	34	4	23	86	92	108	6.65	48	87	14	5	.74	.311	.362	.494	.857
Howard,Ryan	Phi	32	155	594	158	30	2	40	92	128	110	6.54	81	189	1	1	.50	.266	.360	.525	.885
Hudson,Orlando	SD	34	138	505	133	27	4	8	68	51	65	4.48	56	99	13	5	.72	.263	.340	.380	.721
Huff,Aubrey	SF	35	125	391	102	22	1	13	47	55	54	4.82	39	67	3	2	.60	.261	.334	.422	.756
Hughes,Luke	Min	27	74	196	49	11	1	6	26	25	25	4.39	17	44	2	1	.67	.250	.313	.408	.721
Hundley,Nick	SD	28	107	383	96	21	3	13	44	52	51	4.60	36	93	1	1	.50	.251	.318	.423	.741
Hunter,Torii	LAA	36	154	584	154	32	1	23	80	88	84	5.02	56	124	8	5	.62	.264	.333	.440	.773
Iannetta,Chris	Col	29	113	386	96	22	2	18	56	64	64	5.70	69	89	4	2	.67	.249	.371	.456	.827
Ibanez,Raul	Phi	40	136	462	120	26	1	17	61	71	64	4.85	43	95	2	1	.67	.260	.325	.431	.756
Iglesias,Jose	Bos	22	50	141	34	5	0	0	14	10	11	2.62	7	24	5	2	.71	.241	.277	.277	.554
Infante,Omar	Fla	30	143	526	153	26	4	8	62	54	70	4.84	34	68	4	3	.57	.291	.335	.401	.736
Inge,Brandon	Det	35	112	327	74	14	2	10	36	41	36	3.69	32	94	2	1	.67	.226	.307	.373	.680
Izturis,Maicer	LAA	31	122	434	118	27	1	5	59	48	54	4.37	39	58	10	5	.67	.272	.338	.373	.711
Jackson,Austin	Det	25	154	607	164	30	8	9	98	58	81	4.68	57	179	25	7	.78	.270	.335	.390	.725
Jackson,Brett	ChC	23	77	251	63	13	3	9	39	26	37	4.98	31	78	15	5	.75	.251	.333	.434	.768
Janish,Paul	Cin	29	101	261	60	14	0	2	28	21	23	2.96	22	35	3	1	.75	.230	.297	.307	.604
Jaso,John	TB	28	100	303	77	17	1	6	41	38	39	4.47	42	39	2	1	.67	.254	.347	.376	.723
Jay,Jon	StL	27	129	394	113	22	2	8	53	39	54	4.91	29	60	8	5	.62	.287	.340	.414	.754
Jennings,Desmond	TB	25	157	634	169	33	8	17	116	65	97	5.31	75	127	47	10	.82	.267	.347	.424	.771
Jeter,Derek	NYY	38	151	621	181	29	2	10	95	65	87	5.07	58	99	15	6	.71	.291	.360	.393	.752
Johnson,Chris	Hou	27	101	315	86	19	2	9	34	41	42	4.75	16	75	2	1	.67	.273	.316	.432	.748
Johnson,Elliot	TB	28	71	186	47	9	2	5	24	20	23	4.18	15	48	9	4	.69	.253	.308	.403	.712
Johnson,Kelly	Tor	30	148	526	132	32	5	19	78	62	76	4.93	63	141	13	7	.65	.251	.334	.439	.774
Johnson,Reed	ChC	35	111	269	72	17	1	4	34	28	30	3.92	12	65	2	2	.50	.268	.323	.383	.706
Johnson,Rob	SD	29	66	155	34	9	0	2	14	14	14	2.98	13	37	2	1	.67	.219	.288	.316	.604
Jones,Adam	Bal	26	152	591	166	29	4	24	85	84	87	5.25	34	122	11	6	.65	.281	.329	.465	.794
Jones,Andruw	NYY	35	63	175	39	8	0	10	24	29	24	4.55	24	51	1	1	.50	.223	.330	.440	.770
Jones,Chipper	Atl	40	110	356	99	21	1	14	53	56	62	6.25	57	63	2	1	.67	.278	.378	.461	.838
Jones,Garrett	Pit	31	138	452	118	30	1	18	57	69	66	5.09	42	94	7	3	.70	.261	.325	.451	.777
Joyce,Matt	TB	27	124	427	115	31	2	19	65	69	73	5.99	56	95	10	5	.67	.269	.357	.485	.841
Kearns,Austin	Cle	32	68	144	34	8	0	4	19	17	17	3.98	19	41	1	1	.50	.236	.353	.375	.728
Kelly,Don	Det	32	99	208	54	9	1	4	26	21	24	4.00	15	26	4	2	.67	.260	.316	.370	.686
Kemp,Matt	LAD	27	161	616	180	34	5	31	103	104	114	6.66	62	159	32	11	.74	.293	.362	.516	.878
Kendrick,Howie	LAA	29	149	571	164	38	4	14	80	74	81	5.10	30	111	13	6	.68	.287	.329	.441	.771
Kennedy,Adam	Sea	36	88	223	56	11	1	3	24	22	24	3.69	17	38	5	2	.71	.251	.313	.350	.663
Keppinger,Jeff	SF	32	105	342	97	19	1	5	39	33	44	4.65	24	23	1	1	.50	.284	.334	.389	.723
Kinsler,Ian	Tex	30	146	575	156	34	2	25	108	78	97	5.92	72	75	25	7	.78	.271	.358	.468	.826
Kipnis,Jason	Cle	25	133	508	138	28	6	18	89	69	79	5.49	49	107	18	4	.82	.272	.337	.457	.794
Konerko,Paul	CWS	36	154	575	162	28	0	32	79	102	105	6.61	76	106	1	0	1.00	.282	.372	.497	.870
Kotchman,Casey	TB	29	120	351	94	21	1	8	36	43	47	4.74	34	44	1	1	.50	.268	.344	.402	.746
Kotsay,Mark	Mil	36	79	166	43	9	0	3	16	18	19	3.98	14	19	1	1	.50	.259	.317	.367	.684
Kottaras,George	Mil	29	90	288	71	20	1	10	38	39	41	4.91	38	69	0	0	.00	.247	.334	.427	.761
Kouzmanoff,Kevin	Col	30	106	342	88	21	1	12	38	52	43	4.38	17	63	1	1	.50	.257	.308	.430	.738
Kubel,Jason	Min	30	135	485	133	29	2	20	64	84	77	5.67	50	107	1	1	.50	.274	.343	.466	.809
LaHair,Bryan	ChC	29	104	289	79	19	0	13	37	43	46	5.67	27	72	1	1	.50	.273	.335	.474	.809
LaPorta,Matt	Cle	27	92	256	65	16	1	10	32	37	36	4.90	25	52	1	0	1.00	.254	.327	.441	.769
LaRoche,Adam	Was	32	87	263	67	17	0	11	34	41	39	5.17	30	72	1	0	1.00	.255	.333	.445	.778
Lavarnway,Ryan	Bos	24	77	207	57	13	0	13	31	41	38	6.59	24	50	0	0	.00	.275	.351	.527	.877
Lawrie,Brett	Tor	22	153	584	166	37	10	13	92	75	97	5.89	44	118	30	10	.75	.284	.337	.495	.831
Lee,Carlos	Hou	36	148	532	146	31	1	21	63	87	80	5.36	44	57	4	2	.67	.274	.333	.455	.788
Lee,Derrek	Pit	36	133	475	128	28	1	20	66	68	75	5.59	54	116	3	2	.60	.269	.349	.459	.808
Lewis,Fred	Cin	31	98	257	67	15	2	5	40	24	34	4.56	30	62	7	4	.64	.261	.347	.393	.740
Lillibridge,Brent	CWS	28	85	166	40	7	1	5	25	19	19	3.80	14	45	10	4	.71	.241	.311	.386	.697
Lind,Adam	Tor	28	144	557	149	32	1	27	69	94	84	5.34	42	123	1	1	.50	.268	.322	.474	.796
Loney,James	LAD	28	153	540	153	33	2	12	62	76	77	5.13	49	75	5	3	.62	.283	.345	.419	.764
Longoria,Evan	TB	26	151	570	157	39	2	35	101	116	111	6.94	81	119	6	3	.67	.275	.370	.535	.906
Lopez,Felipe	Mil	32	53	132	44	9	1	3	22	17	21	4.23	17	37	2	1	.67	.256	.326	.372	.698
Lopez,Jose	Fla	28	89	261	69	16	0	8	29	34	32	4.31	10	30	2	1	.67	.264	.299	.418	.717
Lowrie,Jed	Bos	28	101	332	90	27	2	8	47	47	50	5.35	38	58	1	1	.50	.271	.348	.437	.784
Lucroy,Jonathan	Mil	26	136	478	126	24	1	12	53	64	61	4.48	45	88	3	2	.60	.264	.328	.393	.722
Ludwick,Ryan	Pit	33	122	385	96	21	1	15	50	62	52	4.66	38	101	1	1	.50	.249	.325	.426	.751
Markakis,Nick	Bal	28	161	639	190	43	2	17	88	87	107	6.14	72	87	10	4	.71	.297	.372	.451	.823

2012 Hitter Projections

Hitter	Team	Age	G	AB	H	2B	3B	HR	R	RBI	RC	RC27	BB	SO	SB	CS	SB%	Avg	OBP	Slg	OPS
Marrero,Chris	Was	23	45	100	28	6	0	2	11	13	13	4.69	8	19	0	0	.00	.280	.339	.400	.739
Marson,Lou	Cle	26	76	195	46	10	1	2	24	18	21	3.62	24	44	4	2	.67	.236	.323	.328	.651
Martin,Leonys	Tex	24	115	396	107	22	3	5	56	43	47	4.03	28	44	28	14	.67	.270	.318	.379	.697
Martin,Russell	NYY	29	128	457	117	22	1	14	67	61	64	4.84	64	82	10	4	.71	.256	.355	.400	.755
Martinez,J.D.	Hou	24	146	526	156	35	1	16	69	90	85	5.96	45	104	1	1	.50	.297	.353	.458	.811
Martinez,Victor	Det	33	149	573	174	38	0	17	76	100	97	6.32	58	65	1	0	1.00	.304	.371	.459	.830
Mathis,Jeff	LAA	29	59	114	23	5	0	2	12	12	9	2.57	8	30	1	0	1.00	.202	.266	.298	.564
Matsui,Hideki	Oak	38	127	392	103	20	0	13	49	61	56	5.04	48	69	1	0	1.00	.263	.346	.413	.759
Mauer,Joe	Min	29	124	470	153	31	1	11	77	71	90	7.36	67	55	2	1	.67	.326	.412	.466	.878
Mayberry,John	Phi	28	72	148	38	9	0	6	20	21	20	4.68	11	32	4	1	.80	.257	.313	.439	.752
Maybin,Cameron	SD	25	137	480	133	23	6	11	79	50	71	5.19	48	113	32	9	.78	.277	.345	.419	.764
McCann,Brian	Atl	28	139	504	139	33	0	24	62	88	86	6.09	62	91	3	2	.60	.276	.360	.484	.844
McCoy,Mike	Tor	31	85	205	50	9	1	2	28	16	23	3.74	25	36	14	5	.74	.244	.326	.327	.653
McCutchen,Andrew	Pit	25	154	585	162	35	6	19	97	74	97	5.81	79	104	27	11	.71	.277	.368	.455	.822
McDonald,Darnell	Bos	33	113	321	86	19	2	9	43	40	44	4.79	26	68	8	4	.67	.268	.325	.424	.748
McDonald,John	Ari	37	95	244	56	11	1	3	27	23	20	2.74	11	34	2	2	.50	.230	.266	.320	.585
McGehee,Casey	Mil	29	132	424	112	24	1	12	47	63	56	4.67	35	71	0	0	.00	.264	.322	.410	.732
McKenry,Michael	Pit	27	61	165	40	11	0	4	16	16	20	4.16	16	37	1	0	1.00	.242	.309	.382	.691
McLouth,Nate	Atl	30	99	305	74	18	1	9	47	33	40	4.44	39	60	7	3	.70	.243	.340	.397	.737
Mesoraco,Devin	Cin	24	91	302	79	21	1	12	39	43	45	5.25	28	59	1	0	1.00	.262	.324	.457	.781
Michaels,Jason	Hou	36	78	110	26	6	0	3	13	13	12	3.71	10	23	1	0	1.00	.236	.311	.373	.684
Miles,Aaron	LAD	35	104	254	68	10	1	1	28	21	25	3.48	14	29	2	1	.67	.268	.311	.327	.638
Miranda,Juan	Ari	29	61	123	31	7	1	5	17	20	19	5.37	16	31	0	0	.00	.252	.343	.447	.790
Molina,Jose	Tor	37	84	252	58	13	0	4	23	21	23	3.07	17	62	2	1	.67	.230	.284	.329	.613
Molina,Yadier	StL	29	140	497	140	26	0	10	46	64	66	4.77	41	48	4	3	.57	.282	.340	.394	.734
Montero,Jesus	NYY	22	144	505	146	29	1	26	65	83	89	6.45	47	109	0	0	.00	.289	.351	.505	.856
Montero,Miguel	Ari	28	130	468	128	32	1	17	60	73	72	5.49	47	93	1	1	.50	.274	.345	.455	.800
Mora,Melvin	Ari	40	76	199	52	9	0	5	23	26	24	4.22	16	34	1	1	.50	.261	.335	.382	.717
Morales,Kendrys	LAA	29	141	506	150	31	1	24	69	86	86	6.26	33	81	1	1	.50	.296	.341	.504	.845
Morel,Brent	CWS	25	136	447	122	25	2	12	53	50	58	4.58	25	66	6	4	.60	.273	.314	.418	.733
Moreland,Mitch	Tex	26	98	296	80	17	1	11	40	42	44	5.27	29	53	2	1	.67	.270	.339	.446	.785
Morgan,Nyjer	Mil	31	130	445	128	19	4	2	65	32	54	4.28	30	71	25	11	.69	.288	.345	.362	.707
Morneau,Justin	Min	31	87	271	78	18	1	12	39	51	49	6.60	32	46	0	0	.00	.288	.369	.494	.864
Morrison,Logan	Fla	24	123	442	117	29	5	18	64	67	75	5.96	64	82	3	2	.60	.265	.363	.475	.838
Morse,Michael	Was	30	140	515	150	33	1	25	68	87	88	6.25	38	109	2	1	.67	.291	.347	.505	.852
Moustakas,Mike	KC	23	149	557	155	38	1	18	68	84	80	5.16	36	84	3	1	.75	.278	.323	.447	.770
Murphy,Daniel	NYM	27	122	461	139	35	3	10	60	64	73	5.82	36	49	6	4	.60	.302	.355	.456	.810
Murphy,David	Tex	30	132	423	118	25	2	12	54	58	62	5.20	40	74	10	5	.67	.279	.341	.433	.774
Nady,Xavier	Ari	33	65	120	31	7	0	4	14	17	15	4.38	7	28	1	0	1.00	.258	.326	.417	.742
Napoli,Mike	Tex	30	131	458	124	27	1	31	77	83	88	6.79	62	123	5	3	.62	.271	.364	.537	.901
Navarro,Dioner	LAD	28	69	172	40	8	0	3	17	17	17	3.32	17	29	1	1	.50	.233	.309	.331	.640
Nelson,Chris	Col	26	83	263	69	15	2	6	32	31	32	4.24	14	44	4	2	.67	.262	.300	.403	.703
Nishioka,Tsuyoshi	Min	27	120	469	113	13	0	0	30	43	37	2.67	37	81	4	4	.50	.241	.298	.269	.566
Nix,Jayson	Tor	29	70	167	38	9	0	6	20	18	18	3.57	12	39	4	2	.67	.228	.291	.389	.680
Nix,Laynce	Was	31	121	306	76	17	1	14	39	44	41	4.61	23	81	2	1	.67	.248	.303	.448	.751
Nunez,Eduardo	NYY	24	112	368	106	20	1	6	49	40	49	4.72	24	42	23	8	.74	.288	.332	.397	.728
Olivo,Miguel	Sea	33	121	408	95	18	2	16	47	55	43	3.54	18	124	5	3	.62	.233	.269	.404	.673
Ordonez,Magglio	Det	38	70	220	64	11	0	6	28	33	33	5.46	21	31	1	1	.50	.291	.355	.423	.778
Ortiz,David	Bos	36	150	538	149	37	1	30	86	104	104	6.93	85	114	1	1	.50	.277	.378	.517	.894
Overbay,Lyle	Ari	35	113	327	81	22	1	9	40	41	44	4.63	41	76	1	1	.50	.248	.335	.404	.739
Pacheco,Jordan	Col	26	104	271	67	12	1	3	24	30	25	3.17	13	32	1	1	.50	.247	.284	.332	.616
Pagan,Angel	NYM	30	136	504	140	27	5	8	71	55	68	4.73	42	78	28	10	.74	.278	.335	.399	.733
Paredes,Jimmy	Hou	23	126	391	101	20	3	7	50	36	42	3.62	15	91	26	12	.68	.258	.286	.379	.664
Parra,Gerardo	Ari	25	151	518	152	26	8	9	65	58	78	5.45	45	88	15	6	.71	.293	.352	.427	.779
Patterson,Corey	StL	32	74	153	38	8	1	3	19	15	16	3.53	8	34	6	3	.67	.248	.294	.373	.667
Paul,Xavier	Pit	27	79	149	40	8	1	2	19	15	17	3.91	10	33	8	4	.67	.268	.314	.376	.690
Paulino,Ronny	NYM	31	100	312	83	18	0	5	30	35	37	4.20	24	55	1	0	1.00	.266	.320	.372	.692
Pedroia,Dustin	Bos	28	143	572	171	42	2	17	95	73	102	6.52	70	65	17	6	.74	.299	.378	.469	.847
Pena,Brayan	KC	30	65	178	49	11	0	3	17	20	22	4.40	11	19	1	1	.50	.275	.321	.388	.709
Pena,Carlos	ChC	34	140	448	100	22	1	27	68	79	71	5.29	86	151	2	1	.67	.223	.356	.458	.813
Pena,Wily Mo	Sea	30	57	147	38	7	0	7	19	23	20	4.73	10	44	1	1	.50	.259	.314	.449	.763
Pence,Hunter	Phi	29	158	613	179	36	4	25	86	91	103	6.10	53	120	10	5	.67	.292	.349	.486	.835
Pennington,Cliff	Oak	28	146	521	133	26	3	6	65	50	61	4.02	55	91	20	7	.74	.255	.328	.351	.679
Peralta,Jhonny	Det	30	153	580	159	34	2	19	76	86	85	5.25	52	117	1	0	1.00	.274	.336	.438	.774
Perez,Salvador	KC	22	119	380	109	22	1	8	42	51	50	4.80	16	42	0	0	.00	.287	.317	.413	.731
Petersen,Bryan	Fla	26	74	230	63	13	2	4	28	18	32	4.87	26	45	6	4	.60	.274	.353	.400	.753
Phillips,Brandon	Cin	31	156	619	173	33	3	19	91	79	87	4.98	44	89	15	8	.65	.279	.334	.435	.769
Pie,Felix	Bal	27	77	165	44	9	2	3	22	17	20	4.19	11	31	5	3	.62	.267	.313	.400	.713
Pierre,Juan	CWS	34	147	562	157	18	4	1	74	38	61	3.79	36	39	30	13	.70	.279	.333	.331	.664
Pierzynski,A.J.	CWS	35	116	429	119	23	0	9	42	48	52	4.36	19	41	1	0	1.00	.277	.317	.394	.711
Plouffe,Trevor	Min	26	81	276	68	17	2	9	39	34	34	4.21	21	57	3	2	.60	.246	.304	.420	.725
Polanco,Placido	Phi	36	131	486	138	22	1	6	61	49	59	4.38	33	42	3	2	.60	.284	.337	.370	.708
Posada,Jorge	NYY	40	110	317	78	18	0	12	36	47	45	4.90	43	77	1	0	1.00	.246	.343	.416	.760
Posey,Buster	SF	25	138	523	159	28	2	19	71	80	91	6.45	52	80	5	3	.62	.304	.370	.474	.844
Powell,Landon	Oak	30	47	100	22	3	0	3	12	11	11	3.67	13	24	0	0	.00	.220	.310	.340	.650
Prado,Martin	Atl	28	144	515	149	32	2	11	72	56	73	5.14	38	61	4	3	.57	.289	.339	.423	.763
Presley,Alex	Pit	26	125	452	136	24	7	9	62	51	69	5.50	30	69	22	10	.69	.301	.346	.445	.790
Pridie,Jason	NYM	28	58	101	25	4	1	2	13	10	11	3.71	7	23	4	1	.80	.248	.296	.366	.663
Pujols,Albert	StL	32	157	592	187	40	0	41	115	120	144	9.15	94	65	10	4	.71	.316	.414	.591	1.005
Punto,Nick	StL	34	99	267	65	12	2	1	34	23	28	3.55	34	49	6	3	.67	.243	.329	.315	.644
Quentin,Carlos	CWS	29	136	498	127	33	1	27	75	88	78	5.45	50	93	2	1	.67	.255	.343	.488	.831

2012 Hitter Projections

Hitter	Team	Age	G	AB	H	2B	3B	HR	R	RBI	RC	RC27	BB	SO	SB	CS	SB%	Avg	OBP	Slg	OPS
Quintero,Humberto	Hou	32	76	192	47	9	0	3	15	18	17	3.05	6	36	0	0	.00	.245	.275	.339	.614
Raburn,Ryan	Det	31	135	440	116	27	2	18	64	66	64	5.10	36	120	4	2	.67	.264	.324	.457	.780
Ramirez,Alexei	CWS	30	158	604	167	28	2	17	82	77	81	4.75	44	82	9	6	.60	.276	.329	.414	.743
Ramirez,Aramis	ChC	34	140	520	148	32	1	26	74	94	89	6.20	45	75	1	1	.50	.285	.350	.500	.850
Ramirez,Hanley	Fla	28	136	521	155	33	2	21	94	69	96	6.62	63	95	28	11	.72	.298	.379	.489	.868
Ramos,Wilson	Was	24	113	397	106	24	1	13	48	49	54	4.82	28	66	0	0	.00	.267	.317	.431	.748
Rasmus,Colby	Tor	25	137	444	113	25	3	18	77	56	66	5.14	52	103	8	3	.73	.255	.334	.446	.780
Reddick,Josh	Bos	25	121	453	113	29	4	19	66	59	63	4.76	40	84	5	4	.56	.249	.312	.457	.769
Reimold,Nolan	Bal	28	119	388	100	19	1	17	52	55	58	5.18	46	81	8	3	.73	.258	.341	.443	.784
Renteria,Edgar	Cin	36	118	411	106	20	1	6	51	43	46	3.88	34	77	5	3	.62	.258	.316	.355	.671
Revere,Ben	Min	24	152	567	159	13	5	1	66	37	63	3.88	36	50	45	14	.76	.280	.325	.326	.651
Reyes,Jose	NYM	29	133	548	166	29	10	10	92	51	90	5.97	46	52	36	10	.78	.303	.358	.447	.805
Reynolds,Mark	Bal	28	153	542	126	28	2	37	90	94	88	5.45	78	206	8	4	.67	.232	.335	.496	.832
Rios,Alex	CWS	31	140	513	138	30	3	15	70	63	68	4.63	33	79	16	7	.70	.269	.318	.427	.745
Rivera,Juan	LAD	33	119	381	99	19	0	13	43	58	49	4.49	31	57	2	2	.50	.260	.319	.412	.731
Rivera,Rene	Min	28	51	118	27	7	0	3	10	13	12	3.43	7	27	0	0	.00	.229	.272	.364	.636
Rizzo,Anthony	SD	22	109	398	94	31	1	14	46	62	51	4.29	41	110	8	5	.62	.236	.312	.425	.737
Roberts,Brian	Bal	34	86	296	81	21	1	5	44	29	42	4.99	34	48	13	4	.76	.274	.350	.402	.752
Roberts,Ryan	Ari	31	133	419	107	24	2	14	61	51	60	4.89	53	81	14	7	.67	.255	.340	.422	.763
Rodriguez,Alex	NYY	36	134	509	141	25	0	29	86	100	92	6.45	70	113	8	3	.73	.277	.373	.497	.870
Rodriguez,Luis	Sea	32	75	199	48	10	0	4	21	20	22	3.76	22	23	1	1	.50	.241	.320	.352	.672
Rodriguez,Sean	TB	27	129	421	106	24	3	15	66	57	57	4.62	41	101	12	6	.67	.252	.331	.430	.761
Rolen,Scott	Cin	37	109	369	99	26	1	11	51	56	52	4.99	33	59	2	1	.67	.268	.338	.434	.772
Rollins,Jimmy	Phi	33	140	573	150	31	5	16	89	62	79	4.78	53	62	25	7	.78	.262	.328	.417	.745
Rosario,Wilin	Col	23	76	240	59	11	0	13	27	29	31	4.45	10	52	1	0	1.00	.246	.276	.458	.734
Ross,Cody	SF	31	130	425	108	26	1	16	57	60	58	4.73	39	102	5	2	.71	.254	.324	.433	.757
Ross,David	Atl	35	91	289	67	15	1	11	30	40	37	4.33	37	93	0	0	.00	.232	.321	.405	.726
Rowand,Aaron	SF	34	105	300	75	18	1	7	36	32	33	3.78	16	74	3	2	.60	.250	.314	.387	.701
Ruggiano,Justin	TB	30	53	116	32	7	0	4	17	18	17	5.14	10	32	6	2	.75	.276	.333	.440	.773
Ruiz,Carlos	Phi	33	132	442	120	28	1	9	50	54	62	4.99	55	58	1	1	.50	.271	.360	.400	.760
Ryan,Brendan	Sea	30	129	401	98	18	2	3	50	31	39	3.29	30	70	11	5	.69	.244	.305	.322	.627
Saltalamacchia,Jarrod	Bos	27	95	319	78	20	1	13	44	45	43	4.62	30	91	1	1	.50	.245	.311	.436	.747
Sanchez,Angel	Hou	28	98	293	75	13	1	1	35	27	29	3.43	24	42	3	2	.60	.256	.314	.317	.632
Sanchez,Freddy	SF	34	116	462	131	28	1	6	53	47	57	4.46	25	69	1	1	.50	.284	.326	.387	.713
Sanchez,Gaby	Fla	28	153	555	153	36	1	20	72	83	89	5.73	69	86	5	2	.71	.276	.360	.452	.812
Sandoval,Pablo	SF	25	144	537	167	37	3	24	74	86	102	7.13	43	69	3	2	.60	.311	.363	.525	.888
Santana,Carlos	Cle	26	155	513	150	33	2	25	101	103	94	5.74	87	121	6	3	.67	.262	.360	.457	.817
Santiago,Ramon	Det	32	121	353	88	14	2	6	42	35	38	3.71	27	60	2	1	.67	.249	.310	.351	.661
Sappelt,Dave	Cin	25	52	120	36	7	1	2	15	12	18	5.44	9	16	3	2	.60	.300	.349	.425	.774
Saunders,Michael	Sea	25	62	127	28	5	1	3	17	12	13	3.35	14	37	5	2	.71	.220	.298	.346	.644
Schafer,Jordan	Hou	25	118	380	91	16	2	4	49	30	39	3.40	38	83	22	9	.71	.239	.310	.324	.634
Schierholtz,Nate	SF	28	122	294	82	20	3	7	38	35	41	4.96	18	47	6	3	.67	.279	.327	.439	.766
Schneider,Brian	Phi	35	57	132	29	6	0	2	11	14	12	3.03	14	27	0	0	.00	.220	.299	.311	.610
Schumaker,Skip	StL	32	138	468	132	24	1	4	60	38	57	4.38	39	64	2	2	.50	.282	.340	.363	.703
Scott,Luke	Bal	34	135	458	116	28	2	25	63	71	75	5.69	58	113	2	1	.67	.253	.340	.487	.827
Scutaro,Marco	Bos	36	143	564	153	31	1	9	80	59	72	4.52	58	65	5	3	.62	.271	.341	.378	.719
Seager,Kyle	Sea	24	93	342	98	27	1	6	43	36	49	5.12	28	53	9	5	.64	.287	.344	.424	.768
Sellers,Justin	LAD	26	36	119	28	6	0	3	15	12	13	3.67	11	22	2	1	.67	.235	.305	.361	.667
Shoppach,Kelly	TB	32	85	216	49	11	0	11	28	31	27	4.20	21	73	0	0	.00	.227	.318	.431	.749
Shuck,J.B.	Hou	25	78	165	45	5	1	0	20	10	18	3.74	20	17	8	5	.62	.273	.351	.315	.667
Sizemore,Grady	Cle	29	82	268	67	17	2	10	42	33	39	4.97	31	70	6	3	.67	.250	.343	.440	.783
Sizemore,Scott	Oak	27	128	404	110	28	2	12	62	54	64	5.58	54	100	8	4	.67	.272	.359	.441	.800
Smith,Seth	Col	29	149	467	131	31	4	17	68	63	77	5.91	47	81	8	3	.73	.281	.349	.473	.822
Smoak,Justin	Sea	25	150	537	131	29	0	20	63	74	75	4.80	79	119	0	0	.00	.244	.343	.410	.753
Snider,Travis	Tor	24	77	221	60	10	0	8	30	33	33	5.23	18	54	9	3	.75	.271	.329	.452	.782
Soriano,Alfonso	ChC	36	130	433	109	26	1	22	57	63	61	4.87	31	109	6	2	.75	.252	.308	.469	.777
Soto,Geovany	ChC	29	127	440	111	28	1	19	52	67	69	5.29	59	120	0	0	.00	.252	.345	.450	.795
Span,Denard	Min	28	115	417	120	16	5	4	64	41	57	4.88	45	53	16	7	.70	.288	.361	.379	.740
Spilborghs,Ryan	Col	32	93	194	52	11	1	5	26	24	27	4.88	20	44	3	2	.60	.268	.343	.412	.755
Stanton,Mike	Fla	22	150	532	145	32	4	39	88	103	108	7.20	73	160	5	3	.62	.273	.366	.568	.933
Stewart,Ian	Col	27	90	239	59	13	2	10	34	35	34	4.86	26	65	4	2	.67	.247	.328	.444	.772
Stubbs,Drew	Cin	27	136	476	123	21	3	14	75	48	66	4.74	52	141	31	9	.77	.258	.336	.403	.740
Suzuki,Ichiro	Sea	38	162	679	206	23	3	7	85	47	91	4.91	43	77	32	9	.78	.303	.347	.377	.724
Suzuki,Kurt	Oak	28	137	502	127	28	1	14	61	63	61	4.21	41	64	3	2	.60	.253	.319	.396	.716
Sweeney,Ryan	Oak	27	105	309	88	17	2	4	42	36	42	4.90	31	46	2	2	.50	.285	.352	.392	.743
Swisher,Nick	NYY	31	155	564	144	33	1	27	91	88	94	5.81	93	141	2	1	.67	.255	.366	.461	.827
Tabata,Jose	Pit	23	153	568	161	32	3	7	88	48	77	4.78	55	83	29	12	.71	.283	.349	.387	.736
Taylor,Michael	Oak	26	108	362	89	18	1	11	47	51	45	4.21	35	79	14	5	.74	.246	.312	.392	.705
Teahen,Mark	Tor	30	69	159	41	9	1	3	20	18	20	4.37	16	41	1	1	.50	.258	.333	.384	.717
Teixeira,Mark	NYY	32	159	613	166	38	1	38	103	120	116	6.73	87	120	3	1	.75	.271	.370	.522	.892
Tejada,Miguel	SF	38	108	361	99	19	0	8	42	44	43	4.23	17	39	3	2	.60	.274	.319	.393	.713
Tejada,Ruben	NYM	22	84	223	57	10	1	1	24	20	22	3.56	20	32	4	2	.67	.256	.333	.323	.656
Thames,Eric	Tor	25	111	366	102	27	4	14	58	52	58	5.65	27	83	5	3	.62	.279	.333	.489	.822
Theriot,Ryan	StL	32	121	421	117	18	2	2	52	34	48	4.04	35	49	9	5	.64	.278	.338	.344	.682
Thole,Josh	NYM	25	114	385	107	24	1	3	33	42	40	4.66	43	46	1	1	.50	.278	.353	.369	.722
Thome,Jim	Cle	41	87	265	63	13	0	15	37	46	44	5.66	51	88	0	0	.00	.238	.365	.457	.821
Tolbert,Matt	Min	30	67	128	31	6	1	1	15	11	12	3.15	10	19	4	2	.67	.242	.302	.328	.630
Torrealba,Yorvit	Tex	33	117	425	110	25	1	8	43	48	50	4.11	31	80	2	1	.67	.259	.312	.379	.691
Torres,Andres	SF	34	119	353	90	21	4	8	54	32	48	4.64	39	86	16	6	.73	.255	.332	.405	.738
Towles,J.R.	Hou	28	51	111	26	6	0	3	14	14	13	3.93	12	18	2	1	.67	.234	.320	.369	.689
Treanor,Matt	Tex	36	66	150	33	5	0	2	15	16	13	2.86	19	32	1	1	.50	.220	.320	.293	.613

2012 Hitter Projections

PLAYER			BATTING												BASERUNNING			AVERAGES			
Hitter	Team	Age	G	AB	H	2B	3B	HR	R	RBI	RC	RC27	BB	SO	SB	CS	SB%	Avg	OBP	Slg	OPS
Trout,Mike	LAA	20	71	272	79	14	5	9	56	30	48	6.27	29	59	23	6	.79	.290	.363	.478	.841
Trumbo,Mark	LAA	26	138	535	144	32	2	28	69	94	81	5.32	32	112	8	5	.62	.269	.313	.493	.806
Tulowitzki,Troy	Col	27	147	558	167	36	3	29	94	99	109	7.16	63	92	10	5	.67	.299	.374	.530	.905
Turner,Justin	NYM	27	101	362	98	25	1	5	45	39	46	4.48	31	45	6	3	.67	.271	.335	.387	.722
Uggla,Dan	Atl	32	161	601	151	32	1	33	95	92	94	5.41	72	158	2	2	.50	.251	.337	.473	.810
Upton,B.J.	TB	27	153	561	141	34	3	19	89	70	83	4.98	76	161	37	13	.74	.251	.344	.424	.768
Upton,Justin	Ari	24	153	582	171	37	6	30	101	92	113	6.98	68	137	20	10	.67	.294	.377	.533	.910
Uribe,Juan	LAD	33	96	279	67	14	1	9	30	37	32	3.91	19	57	1	1	.50	.240	.298	.394	.692
Utley,Chase	Phi	33	134	510	143	30	3	21	85	79	87	6.10	60	80	14	4	.78	.280	.375	.475	.849
Valdez,Wilson	Phi	34	99	259	66	10	1	2	31	21	25	3.32	18	33	4	3	.57	.255	.306	.324	.630
Valencia,Danny	Min	27	114	374	104	24	1	9	46	50	52	4.99	28	61	2	1	.67	.278	.328	.420	.748
Varitek,Jason	Bos	40	59	192	43	9	0	8	23	26	24	4.19	24	57	0	0	.00	.224	.323	.396	.719
Venable,Will	SD	29	116	330	84	13	3	10	45	41	43	4.45	30	81	18	5	.78	.255	.322	.403	.725
Viciedo,Dayan	CWS	23	132	484	133	24	0	21	61	67	71	5.24	34	96	3	1	.75	.275	.324	.455	.778
Victorino,Shane	Phi	31	149	592	164	30	8	17	97	64	89	5.31	54	77	24	8	.75	.277	.344	.441	.784
Vizquel,Omar	CWS	45	73	177	44	6	1	1	18	14	17	3.27	15	21	3	2	.60	.249	.311	.311	.622
Votto,Joey	Cin	28	156	583	181	41	2	31	98	105	130	8.30	97	128	9	5	.64	.310	.412	.547	.959
Walker,Neil	Pit	26	159	598	163	41	3	15	77	88	84	4.96	51	103	9	5	.64	.273	.332	.426	.758
Wallace,Brett	Hou	25	117	437	117	26	1	10	52	48	57	4.62	38	108	2	1	.67	.268	.331	.400	.731
Weeks,Jemile	Oak	25	153	542	151	29	9	4	68	51	69	4.43	41	81	28	14	.67	.279	.332	.387	.719
Weeks,Rickie	Mil	29	136	539	141	29	4	22	95	62	84	5.43	66	139	12	4	.75	.262	.355	.453	.808
Wells,Casper	Sea	27	87	229	57	13	2	12	33	30	33	4.90	20	65	4	3	.57	.249	.317	.480	.798
Wells,Vernon	LAA	33	140	507	132	27	2	22	65	70	70	4.80	35	91	8	4	.67	.260	.311	.452	.762
Werth,Jayson	Was	33	146	506	131	26	1	23	78	72	82	5.63	73	146	15	4	.79	.259	.360	.451	.811
Whiteside,Eli	SF	32	77	183	40	8	1	4	17	20	16	2.89	11	45	1	1	.50	.219	.270	.339	.609
Wieters,Matt	Bal	26	135	498	140	28	1	21	66	76	82	5.96	53	85	1	0	1.00	.281	.353	.468	.820
Wigginton,Ty	Col	34	136	450	112	24	1	17	51	56	58	4.42	38	93	5	3	.62	.249	.314	.420	.734
Willingham,Josh	Oak	33	142	500	124	29	1	25	71	82	78	5.37	70	142	4	2	.67	.248	.352	.460	.812
Wilson,Bobby	LAA	29	60	120	30	8	0	2	11	15	14	4.04	10	18	0	0	.00	.250	.308	.367	.674
Wilson,Jack	Atl	34	91	262	67	14	1	2	26	20	26	3.43	14	40	3	2	.60	.256	.299	.340	.638
Wood,Brandon	Pit	27	68	126	29	6	0	5	15	16	14	3.75	9	34	1	0	1.00	.230	.287	.397	.684
Wright,David	NYM	29	141	538	154	38	2	22	86	90	97	6.45	72	132	17	7	.71	.286	.375	.487	.862
Youkilis,Kevin	Bos	33	135	499	140	37	2	21	87	86	92	6.63	77	113	3	2	.60	.281	.389	.489	.878
Young,Chris	Ari	28	156	568	139	38	3	24	87	75	85	5.06	73	144	20	8	.71	.245	.334	.449	.783
Young,Delmon	Det	26	125	425	122	25	2	13	55	66	60	5.11	20	75	4	2	.67	.287	.325	.447	.772
Young,Eric	Col	27	78	158	42	7	2	1	25	9	20	4.33	17	27	16	4	.80	.266	.341	.354	.695
Young,Michael	Tex	35	152	588	180	35	2	13	81	82	92	5.83	45	90	5	2	.71	.306	.357	.439	.796
Zimmerman,Ryan	Was	27	139	537	156	35	2	22	81	81	94	6.38	59	101	3	2	.60	.291	.363	.486	.849
Zobrist,Ben	TB	31	156	562	147	36	4	18	88	80	88	5.42	84	118	18	7	.72	.262	.360	.436	.796

Pitcher Projections

Bill James

Did you expect Justin Verlander to go 24-5 in 2011? If you did, you're a better man than I am, Gunga Din. We had him projected to go 15-10:

Verlander

	G	GS	IP	H	HR	BB	SO	W	L	Pct	Sv	ERA
Actual	34	34	251	174	24	57	250	24	5	.828	0	2.40
Projected	33	33	226	207	19	74	209	15	10	.600	0	3.46

Which, come to think of it, I don't know why we had him at 15-10; he had gone 19-9 and 18-9 the previous two seasons and had won 17 to 19 games four times in five years; I don't know why we didn't think he would do that again. Anyway, my point was that we're not in the business of predicting the unusual. Predicting the unusual is the province of mystics and savants who foresee miracles, natural disasters, no-hitters and what Manny Ramirez is up to; we just look for predictable patterns.

We didn't predict that any pitcher would win 20 games in 2011, not because we didn't expect anybody to win 20 but because we didn't know who it would be. We predicted that Man Mountain Sabathia would win 18:

Sabathia

	G	GS	IP	H	HR	BB	SO	W	L	Pct	Sv	ERA
Actual	33	33	237	230	17	61	230	19	8	.704	0	3.00
Projected	34	34	236	215	19	65	202	18	8	.692	0	3.32

And we projected that Roy Halladay would win 18:

Roy Halladay

	G	GS	IP	H	HR	BB	SO	W	L	Pct	Sv	ERA
Actual	32	32	234	208	10	35	220	19	6	.760	0	2.35
Projected	32	32	245	234	21	38	190	18	9	.667	0	3.16

We were one game away from getting Sabathia's won-lost record exactly right, which happens a lot. It's annoying. We had Jon Lester at 14-9; he went 15-9. We had Wandy Rodriguez at 12-11; he went 11-11. We had Tim Hudson at 15-10; he went 16-10. We had Joe Saunders at 11-13; he went 12-13. We went Jonathon Niese at 10-11; he went 11-11. We had Cole Hamels at 15-9; he went 14-9. We had Ervin Santana at 11-13; he went 11-12.

We get lots of won-lost records exactly right for relievers, because relievers very often go 2-3 and 4-4, and sometimes you'll be exactly right by dumb luck. The only starter whose won-lost record we nailed was Chad (Willingly) Billingsley, and that actually wasn't a very good projection; we just happened to get the won-lost right:

Billingsley

	G	GS	IP	H	HR	BB	SO	W	L	Pct	Sv	ERA
Actual	32	32	188	189	14	84	152	11	11	.500	0	4.21
Projected	31	31	201	182	15	84	189	11	11	.500	0	3.63

Javier Vazquez was a good projection for us:

Vazquez

	G	GS	IP	H	HR	BB	SO	W	L	Pct	Sv	ERA
Actual	32	32	193	178	21	50	162	13	11	.542	0	3.69
Projected	30	30	198	188	27	55	183	13	9	.591	0	3.73

And Jason Vargas was good:

Vargas

	G	GS	IP	H	HR	BB	SO	W	L	Pct	Sv	ERA
Actual	32	32	201	205	22	59	131	10	13	.435	0	4.25
Projected	31	31	195	205	24	67	135	8	14	.364	0	4.29

We're sorry there were no pitchers named Jamie Vatgas or Jackie Valquez; we're sure we would have nailed those, too. Our best projection was for Joaquin Benoit:

Benoit

	G	GS	IP	H	HR	BB	SO	W	L	Pct	Sv	ERA
Actual	66	0	61	47	5	17	63	4	3	.571	2	2.95
Projected	65	0	65	50	7	24	67	4	3	.571	0	2.91

While our worst was for Scott Kazmir.

Scott Kazmir

	G	GS	IP	H	HR	BB	SO	W	L	Pct	Sv	ERA
Actual	1	1	2	5	1	2	0	0	0	.000	0	27.00
Projected	29	29	162	153	20	75	151	8	10	.444	0	4.22

I think Kazmir's Lebanese.   You can't predict the Lebanese.

Pitchers in general are more predictable than I thought they were before we started running these predictions.   Here's a list of the pitchers that we predicted to have 200 strikeouts in 2011:

> Gallardo, Yovani
> Gonzalez, Gio
> Hamels, Cole
> Hanson, Tommy
> Haren, Dan
> Hernandez, Felix
> Kershaw, Clayton
> Lincecum, Tim
> Sabathia, CC
> Sanchez, Jonathan
> Scherzer, Max
> Verlander, Justin

And here's a list of those who actually did:

> Gallardo, Yovani
> Greinke, Zack
> Halladay, Roy
> Hernandez, Felix
> Kershaw, Clayton
> Lee, Cliff
> Lincecum, Tim
> Morrow, Brandon
> Price, David
> Sabathia, CC
> Sanchez, Anibal
> Shields, James
> Verlander, Justin
> Wilson, C.J.

We got about half of them right, and the others are almost all borderline calls. We projected Gio Gonzalez with 212 strikeouts; he actually struck out 197:

Gonzalez

	G	GS	IP	H	HR	BB	SO	W	L	Pct	Sv	ERA
Actual	32	32	202	175	17	91	197	16	12	.571	0	3.12
Projected	33	33	212	192	21	97	212	13	10	.565	0	3.99

We projected Cole Hamels for 209; he had 194. We projected Greinke for 193; he had 201. We projected David Price for 191; he had 218.

Well, here are our projections for 2012. We predict that in 2012 there will be a half-dozen starting pitchers whose won-lost records we have predicted almost exactly correctly, and one who, by dumb luck, we will get exactly right. We predict that three pitchers will pitch dramatically better than we have projected for them, and 25 will pitch much worse and be released in May. We predict that somebody will win 22 games, but we don't know who it will be; maybe Felix Hernandez. We predict that Manny will do something extremely eccentric, but we don't know what it will be. We predict that Mariano Rivera will be really good. Here was our projection for him last year:

Mariano Rivera

	G	GS	IP	H	HR	BB	SO	W	L	Pct	Sv	ERA
Actual	64	0	61	47	3	8	60	1	2	.333	44	1.91
Projected	61	0	62	47	3	11	58	5	2	.714	33	1.89

Thanks for reading, and may the best man win your Fantasy League. Rather than the un-employed plumber who usually wins it.

2012 Pitcher Projections

Pitcher	Team	Age	G	GS	IP	H	HR	BB	SO	HB	W	L	Pct	Sv	BR/9	ERA
Aardsma,David	Sea	30	31	0	32	28	3	18	32	1	1	2	.333	0	13.2	3.94
Aceves,Alfredo	Bos	30	61	2	118	103	12	43	85	10	8	5	.615	0	11.9	3.43
Acosta,Manny	NYM	31	59	0	66	61	7	32	62	2	4	4	.500	2	13.0	3.95
Adams,Mike	Tex	33	76	0	75	56	5	18	77	0	7	2	.778	0	8.9	1.92
Affeldt,Jeremy	SF	33	54	0	53	48	4	22	43	3	3	3	.500	0	12.4	3.57
Albers,Matt	Bos	29	57	0	65	68	6	30	49	3	3	4	.429	0	14.0	4.57
Alburquerque,Al	Det	26	34	0	37	29	0	23	48	2	3	2	.600	0	13.1	3.16
Anderson,Brett	Oak	24	6	6	42	42	4	11	34	2	2	2	.500	0	11.8	3.64
Arredondo,Jose	Cin	28	60	0	63	55	5	34	59	2	4	3	.571	0	13.0	3.71
Arrieta,Jake	Bal	26	20	20	119	121	15	58	92	6	5	8	.385	0	14.0	4.76
Arroyo,Bronson	Cin	35	31	31	207	209	32	51	131	8	11	12	.478	0	11.7	4.00
Atchison,Scott	Bos	36	20	0	38	36	3	8	33	1	3	2	.600	0	10.7	3.08
Axford,John	Mil	29	69	0	72	57	3	28	87	1	5	3	.625	45	10.8	2.63
Ayala,Luis	NYY	34	56	0	63	68	6	21	43	5	3	4	.429	0	13.4	4.43
Badenhop,Burke	Fla	29	49	0	71	72	4	27	51	4	4	4	.500	0	13.1	3.93
Bailey,Andrew	Oak	28	49	0	50	39	4	14	48	1	4	2	.667	26	9.7	2.34
Bailey,Homer	Cin	26	27	27	166	172	19	48	137	5	9	10	.474	0	12.2	3.96
Baker,Scott	Min	30	24	22	140	145	19	35	114	4	7	8	.467	0	11.8	3.99
Balester,Collin	Was	26	33	0	51	58	7	23	40	3	2	4	.333	0	14.8	5.47
Balfour,Grant	Oak	34	57	0	60	45	5	21	68	1	4	2	.667	0	10.0	2.40
Bard,Daniel	Bos	27	64	0	70	49	6	25	79	3	6	2	.750	2	9.9	2.31
Bastardo,Antonio	Phi	26	60	0	56	43	6	24	62	2	4	2	.667	0	11.1	3.05
Batista,Miguel	NYM	41	30	8	76	79	8	41	47	4	3	5	.375	0	14.7	4.86
Beachy,Brandon	Atl	25	27	27	155	130	13	48	183	5	11	6	.647	0	10.6	3.14
Beato,Pedro	NYM	25	59	0	66	67	8	25	43	3	3	4	.429	0	13.0	4.36
Beavan,Blake	Sea	23	23	23	154	177	15	26	83	4	7	10	.412	0	12.1	3.97
Beckett,Josh	Bos	32	29	29	186	173	22	53	169	8	12	9	.571	0	11.3	3.63
Bedard,Erik	Bos	33	23	23	122	109	12	46	119	3	8	5	.615	0	11.7	3.54
Belisle,Matt	Col	32	72	0	74	81	7	14	56	3	4	4	.500	0	11.9	3.77
Bell,Heath	SD	34	60	0	60	49	3	21	62	1	4	2	.667	42	10.5	2.55
Bell,Trevor	LAA	25	20	10	64	70	5	18	43	2	3	4	.429	0	12.7	4.08
Below,Duane	Det	26	24	1	44	45	6	16	31	1	2	3	.400	0	12.7	4.30
Benoit,Joaquin	Det	34	65	0	65	51	6	16	68	2	5	2	.714	0	9.6	2.49
Bergesen,Brad	Bal	26	37	6	83	91	10	26	44	3	4	5	.444	0	13.0	4.55
Berken,Jason	Bal	28	32	0	38	44	5	15	27	1	2	3	.400	0	14.2	5.21
Betancourt,Rafael	Col	37	63	0	62	51	7	9	68	0	4	3	.571	32	8.7	2.32
Billingsley,Chad	LAD	27	30	30	174	161	13	73	158	7	9	10	.474	0	12.5	3.67
Blackburn,Nick	Min	30	28	28	162	193	21	52	80	4	6	12	.333	0	13.8	5.00
Blanton,Joe	Phi	31	26	26	161	177	20	40	109	4	8	10	.444	0	12.4	4.25
Blevins,Jerry	Oak	28	27	0	32	30	3	11	32	1	2	2	.500	0	11.8	3.66
Boggs,Mitchell	StL	28	48	0	60	65	5	23	42	3	3	4	.429	0	13.6	4.50
Bowden,Michael	Bos	25	18	0	30	30	4	12	24	0	2	2	.500	0	12.6	4.20
Braden,Dallas	Oak	28	26	26	149	149	13	36	101	3	8	8	.500	0	11.4	3.56
Bray,Bill	Cin	29	71	0	44	37	4	15	46	1	3	2	.600	0	10.8	3.07
Breslow,Craig	Oak	31	63	0	62	55	5	23	54	2	4	3	.571	0	11.6	3.34
Britton,Zach	Bal	24	27	27	152	158	12	56	109	3	8	9	.471	0	12.8	4.03
Brothers,Rex	Col	24	57	0	50	38	4	27	70	1	3	2	.600	0	11.9	3.06
Broxton,Jonathan	LAD	28	47	0	45	37	3	22	56	1	3	2	.600	0	12.0	3.20
Buchholz,Clay	Bos	27	30	30	191	170	18	73	162	5	13	8	.619	0	11.7	3.53
Buehrle,Mark	CWS	33	31	31	208	227	22	46	112	3	12	11	.522	0	11.9	3.98
Bumgarner,Madison	SF	22	32	32	214	208	15	51	176	6	14	10	.583	0	11.1	3.36
Burnett,A.J.	NYY	35	32	30	173	167	22	75	160	10	9	10	.474	0	13.1	4.32
Burnett,Alex	Min	24	65	0	50	52	4	23	40	4	2	3	.400	0	14.2	4.50
Burnett,Sean	Was	29	60	0	55	55	5	20	35	2	3	3	.500	0	12.6	3.93
Byrdak,Tim	NYM	38	71	0	36	31	4	19	35	1	2	2	.500	0	12.8	4.00
Cahill,Trevor	Oak	24	32	32	200	190	21	75	128	7	10	12	.455	0	12.2	3.83
Cain,Matt	SF	27	32	32	225	188	18	64	188	6	16	9	.640	0	10.3	3.04
Camp,Shawn	Tor	36	64	0	65	70	6	20	44	4	3	4	.429	0	13.0	4.29
Capps,Matt	Min	28	68	0	63	66	8	15	46	2	3	4	.429	3	11.9	3.86
Capuano,Chris	NYM	33	32	31	190	197	25	54	159	7	10	11	.476	0	12.2	4.12
Carmona,Fausto	Cle	28	31	31	192	202	19	65	116	12	9	12	.429	0	13.1	4.27
Carpenter,Chris	StL	37	31	31	216	200	15	52	169	8	16	8	.667	0	10.8	3.25
Carrasco,D.J.	NYM	35	43	0	51	57	5	19	35	3	2	3	.400	0	13.9	4.76
Cashner,Andrew	ChC	25	26	20	137	120	8	54	121	5	9	6	.600	0	11.8	3.35
Casilla,Santiago	SF	31	58	0	63	54	4	30	60	3	4	3	.571	4	12.4	3.43
Cassevah,Bobby	LAA	26	43	0	56	56	3	26	32	3	3	3	.500	0	13.7	4.18
Cecil,Brett	Tor	25	30	30	191	197	25	61	146	6	9	12	.429	0	12.4	4.19
Ceda,Jose	Fla	25	27	0	33	25	2	17	42	2	2	1	.667	0	12.0	3.00
Chacin,Jhoulys	Col	24	29	29	188	166	18	85	161	8	11	10	.524	0	12.4	3.73
Chamberlain,Joba	NYY	26	32	0	33	31	3	11	35	2	2	2	.500	0	12.0	3.55
Chapman,Aroldis	Cin	24	58	0	54	39	4	37	73	2	3	3	.500	0	13.0	3.33
Chatwood,Tyler	LAA	23	19	19	109	123	10	54	59	5	4	8	.333	0	15.0	5.12
Chavez,Jesse	KC	28	40	0	40	44	6	13	33	0	2	3	.400	0	12.8	4.73
Chen,Bruce	KC	35	29	29	194	195	27	65	133	7	10	12	.455	0	12.4	4.22
Cishek,Steve	Fla	26	52	0	67	58	1	26	66	6	5	3	.625	0	12.1	2.96
Clippard,Tyler	Was	27	70	0	86	69	11	31	88	2	6	4	.600	0	10.7	3.03
Cobb,Alex	TB	24	13	13	70	68	5	23	68	4	4	4	.500	0	12.0	3.60
Coffey,Todd	Was	31	70	0	57	59	6	19	45	2	3	3	.500	0	12.6	4.11
Coke,Phil	Det	29	57	7	84	84	6	31	67	2	5	4	.556	0	12.5	3.75
Coleman,Casey	ChC	24	21	20	105	110	10	43	66	3	5	7	.417	0	13.4	4.29

2012 Pitcher Projections

Pitcher	Team	Age	G	GS	IP	H	HR	BB	SO	HB	W	L	Pct	Sv	BR/9	ERA
Coleman,Louis	KC	26	45	0	61	47	6	23	68	4	4	3	.571	0	10.9	2.95
Collins,Tim	KC	22	62	0	58	44	4	35	68	1	4	3	.571	0	12.4	3.26
Collmenter,Josh	Ari	26	29	26	165	153	16	39	118	4	11	7	.611	0	10.7	3.33
Colon,Bartolo	NYY	39	29	27	165	177	24	41	118	4	9	9	.500	0	12.1	4.25
Contreras,Jose	Phi	40	34	0	33	34	3	13	24	2	2	2	.500	2	13.4	4.36
Cook,Aaron	Col	33	22	20	116	134	10	41	53	3	5	8	.385	0	13.8	4.73
Cordero,Francisco	Cin	37	68	0	71	60	5	27	66	2	4	4	.500	39	11.3	3.04
Correia,Kevin	Pit	31	26	24	149	158	18	47	101	4	7	10	.412	0	12.6	4.29
Crain,Jesse	CWS	30	61	0	61	55	5	28	51	4	3	3	.500	0	12.5	3.54
Cruz,Juan	TB	33	53	0	46	37	4	27	49	2	3	2	.600	0	12.9	3.72
Cueto,Johnny	Cin	26	30	30	198	187	21	62	156	13	11	11	.500	0	11.9	3.77
Danks,John	CWS	27	28	28	180	178	22	54	143	5	9	11	.450	0	11.8	3.85
Davies,Kyle	KC	28	6	6	31	34	3	12	22	1	1	2	.333	0	13.6	4.65
Davis,Wade	TB	26	29	29	196	192	23	70	144	6	10	11	.476	0	12.4	3.99
de la Rosa,Jorge	Col	31	12	12	70	68	8	29	63	3	4	4	.500	0	12.9	4.11
De Los Santos,Fautino	Oak	26	50	0	46	37	3	25	61	1	3	2	.600	0	12.3	3.33
Del Rosario,Enerio	Hou	26	43	0	40	45	3	18	23	2	1	3	.250	0	14.6	4.95
Delgado,Randall	Atl	22	20	20	114	107	13	50	100	4	6	7	.462	0	12.7	4.03
Dempster,Ryan	ChC	35	32	32	203	195	21	80	185	7	11	12	.478	0	12.5	3.95
Detwiler,Ross	Was	26	20	18	109	122	8	41	75	3	5	7	.417	0	13.7	4.46
Devine,Joey	Oak	28	34	0	33	24	1	14	40	3	2	1	.667	0	11.2	2.73
Diamond,Scott	Min	25	12	12	68	86	5	27	50	1	2	5	.286	0	15.1	5.29
Dickey,R.A.	NYM	37	30	30	206	217	21	52	123	8	12	11	.522	0	12.1	3.89
Dotel,Octavio	StL	38	69	0	60	48	8	24	73	4	3	3	.571	0	11.2	3.30
Downs,Scott	LAA	36	58	0	53	46	4	14	42	2	4	2	.667	5	10.5	2.72
Drabek,Kyle	Tor	24	24	20	128	132	15	69	94	2	5	9	.357	0	14.3	4.85
Duensing,Brian	Min	29	31	25	143	162	16	46	92	3	6	10	.375	0	13.3	4.53
Duke,Zach	Ari	29	23	4	66	80	7	18	33	2	3	5	.375	0	13.6	4.91
Dumatrait,Phil	Min	30	48	0	43	48	5	26	27	2	1	3	.250	0	15.9	5.65
Dunn,Mike	Fla	27	70	0	50	40	4	29	62	2	3	3	.500	0	12.8	3.60
Durbin,Chad	Cle	34	53	0	75	76	10	31	58	5	3	5	.375	0	13.4	4.56
Elbert,Scott	LAD	26	55	0	40	34	4	21	46	2	2	2	.500	0	12.8	3.83
Escalona,Edgmer	Col	25	24	0	49	44	8	16	41	3	3	3	.500	0	11.6	3.86
Estrada,Marco	Mil	28	40	8	91	91	9	29	74	2	5	5	.500	0	12.1	3.76
Eveland,Dana	LAD	28	10	10	59	63	4	22	42	3	3	4	.429	0	13.4	4.27
Eyre,Willie	Bal	33	37	0	37	38	2	15	25	1	2	2	.500	0	13.1	4.14
Farnsworth,Kyle	TB	36	57	0	53	47	6	13	52	2	4	2	.667	23	10.5	3.06
Feldman,Scott	Tex	29	17	4	60	63	7	18	34	3	3	3	.500	0	12.6	4.05
Feliz,Neftali	Tex	24	66	0	67	52	4	27	68	3	4	3	.571	37	11.0	2.69
Fister,Doug	Det	28	30	30	214	228	18	37	141	10	13	10	.565	0	11.6	3.70
Floyd,Gavin	CWS	29	29	29	186	189	22	49	142	9	10	11	.476	0	12.0	3.92
Francis,Jeff	KC	31	28	28	162	183	18	35	101	5	8	10	.444	0	12.4	4.22
Francisco,Frank	Tor	32	51	0	52	45	5	18	58	1	3	2	.600	21	11.1	3.12
Frasor,Jason	CWS	34	57	0	54	49	5	22	52	2	3	3	.500	0	12.2	3.67
Frieri,Ernesto	SD	26	50	0	54	41	4	29	58	3	3	3	.500	0	12.2	3.17
Fuentes,Brian	Oak	36	60	0	53	43	5	20	52	4	3	3	.500	13	11.4	3.23
Fulchino,Jeff	SD	32	37	0	37	39	4	17	30	2	1	3	.250	0	14.1	4.62
Furbush,Charlie	Sea	26	28	20	121	121	23	41	107	5	5	9	.357	0	12.4	4.54
Gallardo,Yovani	Mil	26	30	30	203	182	20	69	215	3	14	9	.609	0	11.3	3.46
Garcia,Freddy	NYY	35	25	25	144	153	19	43	95	3	8	8	.500	0	12.4	4.25
Garcia,Jaime	StL	25	30	30	183	181	15	55	150	4	12	9	.571	0	11.8	3.64
Garland,Jon	LAD	32	10	10	63	66	7	25	34	2	3	4	.429	0	13.3	4.43
Garza,Matt	ChC	28	31	31	214	204	22	69	185	8	12	12	.500	0	11.8	3.70
Gee,Dillon	NYM	26	29	28	160	158	19	62	130	13	8	10	.444	0	13.1	4.33
Gomes,Brandon	TB	27	50	0	44	33	2	17	56	1	3	1	.750	0	10.4	2.45
Gomez,Jeanmar	Cle	24	14	14	81	89	9	30	58	2	4	5	.444	0	13.4	4.56
Gonzalez,Gio	Oak	26	31	31	209	187	22	97	208	6	11	13	.458	0	12.5	3.83
Gonzalez,Mike	Tex	34	52	0	53	44	5	23	60	2	4	2	.667	0	11.7	3.23
Gorzelanny,Tom	Was	29	35	7	83	82	8	32	68	3	4	5	.444	0	12.7	4.01
Grabow,John	ChC	33	47	0	58	58	7	27	45	2	3	4	.429	0	13.5	4.50
Gray,Jeff	Sea	30	35	0	52	57	4	21	33	3	2	4	.333	0	14.0	4.67
Gregerson,Luke	SD	28	58	0	55	46	4	18	55	2	4	2	.667	0	10.8	2.62
Gregg,Kevin	Bal	34	61	0	58	53	6	35	54	2	3	4	.429	5	14.0	4.34
Greinke,Zack	Mil	28	31	31	202	197	18	51	187	6	13	9	.591	0	11.3	3.52
Grilli,Jason	Pit	35	48	0	54	53	4	24	46	3	3	3	.500	0	13.3	4.17
Guerra,Javy	LAD	26	55	0	57	50	3	26	51	2	3	3	.500	29	12.3	3.32
Guerrier,Matt	LAD	33	64	0	62	56	7	21	42	2	4	3	.571	0	11.5	3.34
Guthrie,Jeremy	Bal	33	30	30	200	203	26	58	123	10	11	11	.500	0	12.2	4.05
Halladay,Roy	Phi	35	32	32	232	219	18	32	188	6	17	8	.680	0	10.0	3.03
Hamels,Cole	Phi	28	31	31	215	190	25	50	200	5	14	10	.583	0	10.3	3.22
Hammel,Jason	Col	29	31	22	149	163	16	51	108	6	7	10	.412	9	13.3	4.53
Hanrahan,Joel	Pit	30	69	0	67	62	6	23	67	2	4	3	.571	37	11.7	3.36
Hanson,Tommy	Atl	25	25	25	153	126	14	49	153	8	10	7	.588	0	10.8	3.18
Happ,J.A.	Hou	29	24	24	140	136	18	72	121	2	5	10	.333	0	13.5	4.50
Harang,Aaron	SD	34	28	28	176	189	24	58	144	5	7	12	.368	0	12.9	4.50
Harden,Rich	Oak	30	22	22	121	105	18	56	130	5	6	8	.429	0	12.3	4.02
Haren,Dan	LAA	31	33	32	234	221	26	39	202	5	16	10	.615	0	10.2	3.27
Harrison,Matt	Tex	26	31	29	183	198	17	62	117	2	10	11	.476	0	12.9	4.23
Hawkins,LaTroy	Mil	39	51	0	50	50	4	12	33	1	3	2	.600	0	11.3	3.42
Hawksworth,Blake	LAD	29	45	0	51	54	6	18	36	2	2	4	.333	0	13.1	4.41
Hellickson,Jeremy	TB	25	29	29	194	164	21	69	168	8	13	9	.591	0	11.2	3.39

2012 Pitcher Projections

Pitcher	Team	Age	G	GS	IP	H	HR	BB	SO	HB	W	L	Pct	Sv	BR/9	ERA
Hensley,Clay	Fla	32	38	13	87	84	8	36	64	3	5	5	.500	0	12.7	3.93
Hernandez,David	Ari	27	69	0	67	60	9	30	67	2	4	4	.500	0	12.4	4.03
Hernandez,Felix	Sea	26	33	33	234	209	18	67	216	7	14	12	.538	0	10.9	3.23
Hernandez,Livan	Was	37	24	24	148	169	16	42	79	3	7	10	.412	0	13.0	4.50
Herndon,David	Phi	26	45	0	62	68	8	21	39	2	3	4	.429	0	13.2	4.65
Herrmann,Frank	Cle	28	44	0	61	68	6	17	39	1	3	4	.429	0	12.7	4.13
Hochevar,Luke	KC	28	28	28	189	201	22	61	129	8	9	12	.429	0	12.9	4.33
Holland,Derek	Tex	25	30	30	188	187	24	65	156	6	10	11	.476	0	12.4	4.07
Holland,Greg	KC	26	54	0	68	58	5	29	74	1	5	3	.625	0	11.6	3.04
Howell,J.P.	TB	29	51	0	33	31	4	18	32	2	2	2	.500	0	13.9	4.36
Hudson,Daniel	Ari	25	32	32	224	201	21	58	199	10	15	10	.600	0	10.8	3.29
Hudson,Tim	Atl	36	32	32	218	205	17	61	138	10	14	11	.560	0	11.4	3.43
Huff,David	Cle	27	18	16	82	91	10	28	54	2	4	6	.400	0	13.3	4.61
Hughes,Phil	NYY	26	23	17	102	95	11	35	91	3	6	5	.545	0	11.7	3.71
Humber,Philip	CWS	29	25	24	150	161	20	38	108	7	7	10	.412	0	12.4	4.26
Hunter,Tommy	Bal	25	27	21	146	164	20	33	83	4	7	9	.438	0	12.4	4.38
Igarashi,Ryota	NYM	33	55	0	52	48	4	28	51	2	3	3	.500	0	13.5	3.98
Isringhausen,Jason	NYM	39	42	0	38	32	4	22	32	2	2	2	.500	0	13.3	4.03
Jackson,Edwin	StL	28	33	31	206	219	22	68	153	4	11	12	.478	0	12.7	4.24
Jakubauskas,Chris	Bal	33	38	3	69	77	9	26	47	2	3	5	.375	0	13.7	4.83
Jansen,Kenley	LAD	24	49	0	52	27	2	27	90	1	5	1	.833	11	9.5	1.73
Janssen,Casey	Tor	30	58	0	64	67	5	17	49	3	4	4	.500	0	12.2	3.80
Jimenez,Ubaldo	Cle	28	31	31	192	172	14	79	173	9	11	10	.524	0	12.2	3.56
Johnson,Jim	Bal	29	67	0	89	95	8	20	60	4	5	5	.500	23	12.0	3.84
Johnson,Josh	Fla	28	25	25	160	143	9	46	146	4	12	6	.667	0	10.9	3.09
Jurrjens,Jair	Atl	26	29	29	181	176	16	58	125	4	10	10	.500	0	11.8	3.68
Karstens,Jeff	Pit	29	25	23	135	147	19	30	84	2	7	8	.467	0	11.9	4.13
Kelley,Shawn	Sea	28	40	0	40	34	5	14	38	2	2	2	.500	0	11.2	3.38
Kendrick,Kyle	Phi	27	29	14	110	118	13	29	52	5	6	7	.462	0	12.4	4.25
Kennedy,Ian	Ari	27	32	32	222	190	22	63	200	10	15	9	.625	0	10.7	3.24
Kershaw,Clayton	LAD	24	32	32	218	167	13	66	229	4	17	8	.680	0	9.8	2.72
Kimbrel,Craig	Atl	24	74	0	74	41	3	39	121	3	6	3	.667	44	10.1	1.95
Kinney,Josh	CWS	33	25	0	35	32	3	12	34	3	2	2	.500	0	12.1	3.60
Kuo,Hong-Chih	LAD	30	45	0	34	26	2	19	41	1	2	2	.500	0	13.3	3.18
Kuroda,Hiroki	LAD	37	31	31	204	199	23	49	145	3	11	11	.500	0	11.1	3.57
Lackey,John	Bos	33	29	29	174	183	17	57	134	11	9	10	.474	0	13.0	4.24
Laffey,Aaron	NYY	27	43	0	46	54	3	22	26	2	2	3	.400	0	15.3	5.28
Lannan,John	Was	27	32	32	180	192	17	68	96	7	8	12	.400	0	13.4	4.40
Latos,Mat	SD	24	31	31	211	174	17	64	206	2	15	9	.625	0	10.2	2.99
League,Brandon	Sea	29	63	0	62	60	5	15	47	4	3	4	.429	41	11.5	3.34
Leake,Mike	Cin	24	29	29	178	183	26	46	123	6	9	10	.474	0	11.9	4.04
LeBlanc,Wade	SD	27	21	21	127	123	16	39	103	3	6	8	.429	0	11.7	3.83
LeCure,Sam	Cin	28	48	2	80	81	11	25	69	5	4	5	.444	0	12.5	4.28
Lee,Cliff	Phi	33	32	32	232	223	19	35	194	5	17	9	.654	0	10.2	3.18
Leroux,Chris	Pit	28	36	0	41	42	1	14	37	2	2	2	.500	0	12.7	3.73
Lester,Jon	Bos	28	31	31	192	174	17	74	180	8	15	9	.625	0	12.0	3.61
Lewis,Colby	Tex	32	31	31	198	185	27	58	170	6	12	10	.545	0	11.3	3.73
Lidge,Brad	Phi	35	43	0	35	29	4	20	45	2	2	2	.500	2	13.1	3.86
Lilly,Ted	LAD	36	32	32	200	178	30	50	168	6	12	11	.522	0	10.5	3.47
Lincecum,Tim	SF	28	32	32	220	180	14	83	239	6	15	9	.625	0	11.0	3.11
Lincoln,Brad	Pit	27	22	14	86	93	8	22	63	5	4	5	.444	0	12.6	4.08
Lindblom,Josh	LAD	25	38	0	40	39	3	13	37	3	2	2	.500	0	12.4	3.83
Lindstrom,Matt	Col	32	54	0	47	51	4	14	39	2	2	3	.400	0	12.8	4.02
Linebrink,Scott	Atl	35	51	0	45	45	7	16	39	2	2	3	.400	0	12.6	4.40
Liriano,Francisco	Min	28	29	29	180	173	17	85	175	7	9	11	.450	0	13.2	4.05
Litsch,Jesse	Tor	27	41	4	79	85	10	25	52	5	4	5	.444	0	13.1	4.56
Locke,Jeff	Pit	24	8	8	33	34	3	13	28	2	2	2	.500	0	13.4	4.36
Loe,Kameron	Mil	30	62	0	69	74	7	18	44	2	4	4	.500	0	12.3	3.91
Logan,Boone	NYY	27	64	0	41	41	4	15	40	4	2	2	.500	0	13.2	4.17
Lohse,Kyle	StL	33	28	28	170	184	18	43	103	5	10	9	.526	0	12.3	4.02
Lopez,Javier	SF	34	60	0	44	43	2	20	29	2	2	3	.400	0	13.3	3.68
Lopez,Rodrigo	ChC	36	20	15	94	111	14	26	58	2	4	7	.364	0	13.3	4.98
Lopez,Wilton	Hou	28	73	0	68	77	6	13	46	1	3	5	.375	0	12.0	3.97
Lowe,Derek	Atl	39	32	32	180	193	16	63	119	3	9	11	.450	0	13.0	4.15
Lowe,Mark	Tex	29	50	0	44	43	4	18	40	1	2	2	.500	0	12.7	4.09
Luebke,Cory	SD	27	30	30	178	140	15	56	168	4	13	7	.650	0	10.1	2.88
Lueke,Josh	Sea	27	31	0	50	43	2	15	50	2	3	2	.600	0	10.8	2.70
Lyles,Jordan	Hou	21	23	13	87	100	10	26	70	5	3	7	.300	0	13.6	4.76
Lynn,Lance	StL	25	12	12	79	78	6	29	67	3	5	4	.556	0	12.5	3.76
Lyon,Brandon	Hou	32	39	0	41	41	3	16	27	1	2	3	.400	0	12.7	3.95
MacDougal,Mike	LAD	35	65	0	57	56	4	31	46	3	2	4	.333	0	14.2	4.26
Madson,Ryan	Phi	31	65	0	65	62	5	17	59	3	4	3	.571	36	11.4	3.32
Maholm,Paul	Pit	30	24	24	147	161	12	47	90	6	7	9	.438	0	13.1	4.22
Marcum,Shaun	Mil	30	32	32	207	192	27	54	168	5	13	10	.565	0	10.9	3.52
Marmol,Carlos	ChC	29	74	0	76	52	5	52	97	8	5	4	.556	36	13.3	3.43
Marquis,Jason	Ari	33	21	21	118	127	12	41	65	6	6	8	.429	0	13.3	4.42
Marshall,Sean	ChC	29	78	0	75	71	6	21	65	2	5	4	.556	2	11.3	3.24
Martinez,Cristhian	Atl	30	57	0	86	83	8	18	63	2	6	4	.600	0	10.8	3.14
Masset,Nick	Cin	30	60	0	62	64	6	26	52	1	3	4	.429	0	13.2	4.35
Masterson,Justin	Cle	27	32	32	205	204	14	70	164	12	11	12	.478	0	12.6	3.82
Matsuzaka,Daisuke	Bos	31	12	12	74	68	8	37	66	3	4	4	.500	0	13.1	4.14

513

2012 Pitcher Projections

PLAYER			HOW MUCH			WHAT HE WILL GIVE UP					THE RESULTS					
Pitcher	Team	Age	G	GS	IP	H	HR	BB	SO	HB	W	L	Pct	Sv	BR/9	ERA
Mattheus,Ryan	Was	28	37	0	30	31	3	13	21	2	1	2	.333	0	13.8	4.20
Matusz,Brian	Bal	25	25	25	148	159	21	57	119	4	7	10	.412	0	13.4	4.74
McCarthy,Brandon	Oak	28	27	27	190	185	21	34	139	4	11	10	.524	0	10.6	3.41
McClellan,Kyle	StL	28	54	8	114	108	13	36	77	4	7	6	.538	0	11.7	3.71
McCutchen,Daniel	Pit	29	73	0	82	88	11	28	52	3	4	6	.400	0	13.1	4.50
McDonald,James	Pit	27	29	29	170	160	18	75	157	8	9	10	.474	0	12.9	4.02
McGee,Jake	TB	25	44	0	36	32	3	13	38	0	2	2	.500	6	11.2	3.25
McGowan,Dustin	Tor	30	20	20	112	110	12	59	97	4	5	7	.417	0	13.9	4.50
Medlen,Kris	Atl	26	20	20	118	112	10	28	111	3	8	5	.615	0	10.9	3.36
Melancon,Mark	Hou	27	66	0	75	70	6	31	71	5	3	5	.375	13	12.7	3.84
Mijares,Jose	Min	27	57	0	56	54	6	29	48	2	3	4	.429	0	13.7	4.34
Miley,Wade	Ari	25	15	14	80	79	8	30	61	1	4	5	.444	0	12.4	3.94
Miller,Andrew	Bos	27	21	12	70	75	6	47	58	4	3	5	.375	0	16.2	5.40
Millwood,Kevin	Col	37	17	17	109	122	14	36	78	4	5	7	.417	0	13.4	4.71
Milone,Tom	Was	25	10	10	52	53	4	7	48	1	3	2	.600	0	10.6	3.29
Minor,Mike	Atl	24	20	20	115	112	13	40	120	2	6	7	.462	0	12.1	3.83
Morales,Franklin	Bos	26	56	0	51	48	6	26	42	3	3	3	.500	0	13.6	4.41
Morrow,Brandon	Tor	27	30	30	191	169	19	79	209	8	11	10	.524	0	12.1	3.68
Morton,Charlie	Pit	28	29	29	176	190	12	73	122	11	8	12	.400	0	14.0	4.50
Moscoso,Guillermo	Oak	28	26	25	157	151	16	53	124	4	8	9	.471	0	11.9	3.78
Moseley,Dustin	SD	30	10	10	60	68	8	19	36	2	2	4	.333	0	13.4	4.80
Moskos,Daniel	Pit	26	61	0	59	65	4	25	37	2	3	4	.429	0	14.0	4.58
Mota,Guillermo	SF	38	50	0	65	59	7	25	53	2	4	4	.500	0	11.9	3.60
Motte,Jason	StL	30	80	0	74	62	6	21	81	3	5	3	.625	29	10.5	2.80
Mujica,Edward	Fla	28	61	0	74	73	10	12	65	1	5	4	.556	0	10.5	3.28
Myers,Brett	Hou	31	32	30	212	211	29	59	176	5	10	14	.417	0	11.7	3.91
Narveson,Chris	Mil	30	26	22	133	132	16	51	108	3	7	8	.467	0	12.6	4.13
Nathan,Joe	Min	37	48	0	46	34	4	16	54	1	4	2	.667	33	10.0	2.35
Neshek,Pat	SD	31	35	0	35	30	5	20	34	1	2	2	.500	0	13.1	4.11
Niemann,Jeff	TB	29	26	26	159	153	20	49	127	7	9	9	.500	0	11.8	3.85
Niese,Jonathon	NYM	25	29	29	166	182	16	51	142	6	9	10	.474	0	13.0	4.28
Nolasco,Ricky	Fla	29	30	30	192	205	24	41	165	4	10	11	.476	0	11.7	3.94
Norris,Bud	Hou	27	29	29	177	175	20	74	173	7	7	13	.350	0	13.0	4.22
Nova,Ivan	NYY	25	28	28	183	195	17	67	124	5	10	10	.500	0	13.1	4.28
Nunez,Leo	Fla	28	56	0	56	53	7	19	47	2	3	3	.500	35	11.9	3.70
O'Flaherty,Eric	Atl	27	72	0	73	67	3	23	61	5	5	3	.625	0	11.7	3.08
Ogando,Alexi	Tex	28	31	27	150	127	12	42	124	5	11	5	.688	0	10.4	3.06
Ohlendorf,Ross	Pit	29	14	14	64	71	9	24	44	3	2	5	.286	0	13.8	4.92
Ohman,Will	CWS	34	62	0	56	52	7	22	55	2	3	3	.500	0	12.2	3.86
Oliver,Darren	Tex	41	60	0	48	45	4	11	39	2	3	2	.600	0	10.9	3.00
Ondrusek,Logan	Cin	27	51	0	47	43	4	18	32	1	3	2	.600	0	11.9	3.45
Ortiz,Ramon	ChC	39	35	1	44	48	5	11	29	1	2	3	.400	0	12.3	4.30
O'Sullivan,Sean	KC	24	7	6	37	42	5	12	22	1	2	3	.400	0	13.4	4.86
Oswalt,Roy	Phi	34	28	26	171	165	15	43	133	6	11	8	.579	0	11.3	3.47
Outman,Josh	Oak	27	14	6	47	45	4	24	36	1	2	3	.400	0	13.4	4.21
Owings,Micah	Ari	29	38	2	67	66	8	27	48	6	3	4	.429	0	13.3	4.43
Papelbon,Jonathan	Bos	31	58	0	63	50	5	16	73	3	4	3	.571	31	9.9	2.43
Parnell,Bobby	NYM	27	70	0	70	74	6	29	62	2	3	4	.429	29	13.5	4.37
Paterson,Joe	Ari	26	55	0	32	29	1	14	28	2	2	2	.500	0	12.7	3.38
Patton,Troy	Bal	26	30	0	47	53	6	14	30	3	2	3	.400	0	13.4	4.79
Pauley,David	Det	29	46	0	66	75	8	21	42	4	3	4	.429	0	13.6	4.91
Paulino,Felipe	KC	28	33	24	157	167	16	67	143	7	7	10	.412	0	13.8	4.59
Pavano,Carl	Min	36	32	32	226	234	27	42	125	8	11	14	.440	0	11.3	4.22
Peavy,Jake	CWS	31	19	19	123	117	12	29	121	4	8	5	.615	0	11.0	3.51
Pelfrey,Mike	NYM	28	34	32	188	207	16	63	110	9	9	11	.450	0	13.4	4.36
Penny,Brad	Det	34	29	29	173	192	19	54	103	5	9	10	.474	0	13.1	4.42
Peralta,Joel	TB	36	62	0	63	53	7	16	54	2	5	2	.714	1	10.1	2.86
Perez,Chris	Cle	26	66	0	64	47	6	28	64	5	4	3	.571	37	11.2	2.95
Perez,Luis	Tor	27	37	8	77	79	7	38	58	7	3	5	.375	0	14.5	4.79
Perez,Rafael	Cle	30	71	0	62	63	4	22	48	1	3	3	.500	0	12.5	3.77
Perkins,Glen	Min	29	63	0	62	73	7	20	45	2	2	4	.333	0	13.8	4.94
Perry,Ryan	Det	25	41	0	40	37	3	18	32	2	2	2	.500	0	12.8	3.83
Pestano,Vinnie	Cle	27	68	0	66	51	4	25	82	2	5	2	.714	0	10.6	2.59
Pineda,Michael	Sea	23	29	29	176	144	16	53	184	7	11	8	.579	0	10.4	3.07
Pineiro,Joel	LAA	33	28	22	143	159	15	33	76	3	7	9	.438	0	12.3	4.09
Porcello,Rick	Det	23	31	31	190	210	20	49	105	7	10	11	.476	0	12.6	4.22
Price,David	TB	26	34	34	226	193	23	73	207	8	15	10	.600	0	10.9	3.31
Proctor,Scott	NYY	35	36	0	43	45	7	25	39	1	2	3	.400	0	14.9	5.65
Putz,J.J.	Ari	35	62	0	60	48	4	15	64	2	4	3	.571	44	9.8	2.40
Qualls,Chad	SD	33	72	0	70	72	7	20	54	2	3	4	.429	0	12.1	3.86
Ramirez,Ramon	SF	30	65	0	71	60	6	28	60	2	5	3	.625	0	11.4	3.17
Ramos,Cesar	TB	28	47	0	39	41	4	20	25	1	2	3	.400	0	14.3	4.85
Rauch,Jon	Tor	33	37	0	38	37	4	10	30	1	2	2	.500	1	11.4	3.55
Resop,Chris	Pit	29	70	0	66	61	5	30	67	2	4	4	.500	0	12.7	3.68
Reyes,Jo-Jo	Bal	27	27	19	116	132	16	41	84	4	5	8	.385	0	13.7	5.04
Reynolds,Greg	Col	26	16	1	30	37	3	7	16	1	1	2	.333	0	13.5	5.10
Reynolds,Matt	Col	27	69	0	47	42	6	15	48	1	3	2	.600	0	11.1	3.45
Rhodes,Arthur	StL	42	52	0	30	25	3	10	27	0	2	1	.667	0	10.5	3.00
Richard,Clayton	SD	28	9	9	50	51	4	20	34	1	2	3	.400	0	13.0	3.96
Rivera,Mariano	NYY	42	63	0	62	47	3	9	58	3	5	2	.714	35	8.6	1.89
Robertson,David	NYY	27	70	0	70	53	4	37	96	2	5	3	.625	1	11.8	2.83

2012 Pitcher Projections

Pitcher	Team	Age	G	GS	IP	H	HR	BB	SO	HB	W	L	Pct	Sv	BR/9	ERA
Rodriguez,Aneury	Hou	24	43	4	72	71	9	30	55	3	3	5	.375	0	13.0	4.38
Rodriguez,Fernando	Hou	28	56	0	65	74	7	33	52	4	2	5	.286	0	15.4	5.40
Rodriguez,Francisco	Mil	30	69	0	67	53	4	26	80	2	4	3	.571	34	10.9	2.69
Rodriguez,Henry	Was	25	68	0	74	61	3	46	88	2	4	4	.500	1	13.3	3.41
Rodriguez,Wandy	Hou	33	30	30	199	196	22	70	171	7	9	13	.409	0	12.3	3.93
Roenicke,Josh	Col	29	37	0	33	31	2	14	31	2	2	2	.500	0	12.8	3.82
Rogers,Esmil	Col	26	25	19	124	146	13	51	97	8	5	9	.357	0	14.9	5.37
Romero,Ricky	Tor	27	31	31	221	213	22	83	175	11	12	13	.480	0	12.5	3.91
Romo,Sergio	SF	29	55	0	43	31	3	7	51	2	4	1	.800	0	8.4	1.67
Russell,James	ChC	26	60	2	54	63	11	13	39	2	2	4	.333	0	13.0	5.17
Rzepczynski,Marc	StL	26	73	0	62	61	5	27	62	3	4	3	.571	0	13.2	4.06
Sabathia,CC	NYY	31	33	33	235	217	19	65	207	8	17	9	.654	0	11.1	3.33
Saito,Takashi	Mil	42	41	0	37	30	3	12	41	2	3	1	.750	0	10.7	2.68
Salas,Fernando	StL	27	68	0	75	61	8	23	79	2	6	3	.667	5	10.3	2.88
Sale,Chris	CWS	23	54	0	70	53	8	28	87	1	5	3	.625	2	10.5	2.83
Samardzija,Jeff	ChC	27	75	0	87	83	10	51	71	3	4	6	.400	0	14.2	4.66
Sanches,Brian	Fla	33	29	1	43	38	5	22	40	2	2	3	.400	0	13.0	3.98
Sanchez,Anibal	Fla	28	30	30	187	182	16	65	165	6	11	10	.524	0	12.2	3.75
Sanchez,Jonathan	SF	29	30	29	159	130	16	90	166	8	9	9	.500	0	12.9	3.79
Santana,Ervin	LAA	29	32	32	221	217	28	71	175	11	11	13	.458	0	12.2	3.95
Santana,Johan	NYM	33	28	28	189	163	20	52	174	3	14	7	.667	0	10.4	3.19
Santos,Sergio	CWS	28	59	0	59	50	4	29	74	4	3	3	.500	37	12.7	3.51
Saunders,Joe	Ari	31	32	32	212	222	27	67	123	5	10	13	.435	0	12.5	4.20
Scherzer,Max	Det	27	32	32	192	179	22	60	188	8	12	9	.571	0	11.6	3.66
Schlereth,Daniel	Det	26	50	0	56	45	3	36	62	4	3	3	.500	0	13.7	3.70
Schwinden,Chris	NYM	25	8	8	42	44	4	14	37	3	2	3	.400	0	13.1	4.29
Shaw,Bryan	Ari	24	49	0	43	43	3	16	32	4	2	3	.400	0	13.2	3.98
Shields,James	TB	30	32	32	228	226	29	58	193	6	13	12	.520	0	11.4	3.79
Simon,Alfredo	Bal	31	29	25	164	192	26	59	115	8	6	12	.333	0	14.2	5.43
Sipp,Tony	Cle	28	64	0	60	47	9	28	65	1	4	3	.571	0	11.4	3.45
Slowey,Kevin	Min	28	18	15	97	111	14	15	73	4	5	6	.455	0	12.1	4.27
Smith,Joe	Cle	28	73	0	72	61	4	28	58	3	5	3	.625	0	11.5	3.00
Soria,Joakim	KC	28	51	0	52	43	4	14	56	2	4	2	.667	37	10.2	2.77
Soriano,Rafael	NYY	32	57	0	55	40	5	19	58	1	5	2	.714	1	9.8	2.45
Sosa,Henry	Hou	26	19	19	107	112	12	44	76	4	4	8	.333	0	13.5	4.54
Stauffer,Tim	SD	30	28	28	166	165	16	49	113	7	9	10	.474	0	12.0	3.80
Stewart,Zach	CWS	25	21	17	110	124	11	37	88	3	5	8	.385	0	13.4	4.58
Storen,Drew	Was	24	69	0	72	58	6	21	69	2	5	3	.625	40	10.1	2.63
Street,Huston	Col	28	49	0	46	40	5	8	46	1	3	2	.600	30	9.6	2.74
Strop,Pedro	Bal	27	29	0	30	29	1	15	32	1	2	2	.500	0	13.5	3.90
Stutes,Michael	Phi	25	57	0	68	63	8	34	60	4	3	4	.429	0	13.4	4.24
Swarzak,Anthony	Min	26	29	14	123	147	15	37	77	6	5	9	.357	0	13.9	4.98
Takahashi,Hisanori	LAA	37	57	0	68	62	7	25	58	0	4	3	.571	0	11.5	3.44
Talbot,Mitch	Cle	28	7	7	40	47	4	16	29	2	2	3	.400	0	14.6	5.18
Teaford,Everett	KC	28	26	6	64	62	8	21	50	2	3	4	.429	0	12.0	3.94
Thatcher,Joe	SD	30	50	0	35	30	2	14	39	2	2	2	.500	0	11.8	3.09
Thompson,Rich	LAA	27	39	0	48	41	6	16	48	2	3	2	.600	0	11.1	3.38
Thornton,Matt	CWS	35	62	0	65	56	5	22	72	1	4	3	.571	1	10.9	2.91
Tillman,Chris	Bal	24	9	9	46	49	7	20	37	1	2	3	.400	0	13.7	4.89
Tomlin,Josh	Cle	27	27	27	176	175	26	34	117	5	10	10	.500	0	10.9	3.73
Uehara,Koji	Tex	37	62	0	58	50	7	8	55	0	5	2	.714	0	9.0	2.64
Valverde,Jose	Det	34	75	0	77	58	7	37	83	3	5	3	.625	42	11.5	3.04
Vargas,Jason	Sea	29	30	30	192	199	23	55	130	4	8	13	.381	0	12.1	3.98
Varvaro,Anthony	Atl	27	33	0	45	33	3	29	50	2	3	2	.600	0	12.8	3.40
Vasquez,Anthony	Sea	25	14	14	59	71	8	15	35	4	2	5	.286	0	13.7	5.03
Vazquez,Javier	Fla	35	31	31	213	201	28	62	192	6	13	11	.542	0	11.4	3.72
Venters,Jonny	Atl	27	79	0	81	71	3	40	73	5	5	4	.556	3	12.9	3.44
Veras,Jose	Pit	31	74	0	69	58	7	36	74	4	4	4	.500	0	12.8	3.78
Verlander,Justin	Det	29	33	33	240	206	21	61	226	8	18	8	.692	0	10.3	3.08
Villanueva,Carlos	Tor	28	28	8	72	69	9	24	61	3	4	4	.500	0	12.0	3.88
Vogelsong,Ryan	SF	34	30	29	196	194	18	81	161	9	10	12	.455	0	13.0	4.09
Volquez,Edinson	Cin	28	25	25	155	137	17	77	150	8	8	9	.471	0	12.9	3.95
Volstad,Chris	Fla	25	27	27	164	174	19	55	108	4	8	10	.444	0	12.8	4.34
Wade,Cory	NYY	29	56	0	53	49	7	10	41	2	4	2	.667	0	10.4	3.23
Wainwright,Adam	StL	30	30	30	209	195	16	53	174	5	15	8	.652	0	10.9	3.27
Wakefield,Tim	Bos	45	15	12	80	81	11	24	48	4	4	4	.500	0	12.3	4.16
Walden,Jordan	LAA	24	55	0	56	55	3	26	58	1	3	3	.500	31	13.2	3.86
Wang,Chien-Ming	Was	32	20	20	119	128	9	24	56	3	7	6	.538	0	11.7	3.78
Watson,Tony	Pit	27	50	0	48	42	5	17	43	2	3	2	.600	0	11.4	3.38
Weaver,Jered	LAA	29	32	32	224	196	23	55	197	3	15	10	.600	0	10.2	3.17
Webb,Ryan	Fla	26	52	0	50	54	4	18	37	1	3	3	.500	0	13.1	4.14
Weiland,Kyle	Bos	25	11	7	34	32	4	16	30	3	2	2	.500	0	13.5	4.50
Wells,Randy	ChC	29	27	27	174	183	20	59	126	5	8	11	.421	0	12.8	4.24
Westbrook,Jake	StL	34	32	32	183	197	17	69	105	5	10	11	.476	0	13.3	4.33
Wheeler,Dan	Bos	34	43	0	45	37	7	10	40	1	3	2	.600	0	9.6	2.80
Williams,Jerome	LAA	30	19	12	88	102	13	25	54	6	3	6	.333	0	13.6	5.11
Willis,Dontrelle	Cin	30	19	19	117	122	11	58	85	6	5	8	.385	0	14.3	4.69
Wilson,Brian	SF	30	60	0	61	52	3	28	65	2	4	3	.571	41	12.1	3.10
Wilson,C.J.	Tex	31	32	32	215	184	14	80	194	12	15	9	.625	0	11.6	3.31
Wolf,Randy	Mil	35	32	32	217	212	26	73	155	10	12	12	.500	0	12.2	3.94
Wood,Blake	KC	26	56	0	73	79	6	31	55	4	3	5	.375	0	14.1	4.68

2012 Pitcher Projections

PLAYER			HOW MUCH			WHAT HE WILL GIVE UP					THE RESULTS					
Pitcher	Team	Age	G	GS	IP	H	HR	BB	SO	HB	W	L	Pct	Sv	BR/9	ERA
Wood,Kerry	ChC	35	56	0	52	45	5	26	57	4	3	3	.500	0	13.0	3.81
Wood,Travis	Cin	25	19	12	72	70	7	24	59	3	4	4	.500	0	12.1	3.75
Worley,Vance	Phi	24	28	23	147	147	15	48	118	4	8	8	.500	0	12.2	3.86
Wright,Jamey	Sea	37	55	0	69	71	6	32	43	5	3	5	.375	0	14.1	4.57
Wright,Wesley	Hou	27	42	0	39	37	5	17	35	2	2	3	.400	0	12.9	4.15
Zambrano,Carlos	ChC	31	30	30	181	167	16	78	149	8	10	10	.500	0	12.6	3.83
Ziegler,Brad	Ari	32	65	0	60	59	3	22	40	2	4	3	.571	0	12.4	3.60
Zimmermann,Jordan	Was	26	28	28	175	164	18	38	147	7	11	8	.579	0	10.7	3.39
Zito,Barry	SF	34	12	4	33	31	4	14	24	1	2	2	.500	0	12.5	3.82

Career Targets

This section is designed to give probabilities on players achieving important career milestones. The method (formerly under the name of "The Favorite Toy") was developed by Bill James and takes into account a player's age and performance level in predicting the probability that he will accumulate certain career stats. A detailed explanation of how the system works can be found in the glossary.

Congratulations to Derek Jeter who earned his 3,000th career hit on a home run on July 9th. Jim Thome also entered the record books as the eighth member of the 600 home run club.

Looking forward:

- A healthy and productive 2012 season would make Alex Rodriguez just the fourth player in baseball history to record 2,000 RBI. A-Rod is 107 RBI away from the mark. If he makes it, he would join Hank Aaron, Babe Ruth, and Cap Anson as the only players in history with 2,000 RBI.

- A-Rod is also 225 hits away from 3,000 but he's only had three 200 hit seasons in his career, so 3,000 probably won't come until 2013.

- Albert Pujols finished the 2011 regular season with 445 career home runs, making him 55 shy of 500. He'll need a monster season in 2012 to get there.

- There are some new names on the "Most Likely No-Hitter" board. Welcome 2011 rookies Brandon Beachy and Michael Pineda. After recording his second career no-hitter in 2011, Justin Verlander enters the list with a 15% chance for a third.

3,000 Hits	
% chance to reach milestone	
Jeter,Derek	done
Rodriguez,Alex	94%
Damon,Johnny	86%
Guerrero,Vladimir	67%
Pujols,Albert	56%
Cabrera,Miguel	46%
Suzuki,Ichiro	38%
Young,Michael	34%
Beltre,Adrian	30%
Cano,Robinson	28%
Pierre,Juan	27%
Crawford,Carl	23%
Markakis,Nick	22%
Butler,Billy	19%
Braun,Ryan	18%
Kemp,Matt	16%
Gonzalez,Adrian	16%
Lee,Carlos	14%
Rodriguez,Ivan	14%
Reyes,Jose	12%
Fielder,Prince	12%
Upton,Justin	12%
Castro,Starlin	11%
Andrus,Elvis	11%
Cabrera,Melky	10%
Konerko,Paul	9%
Rollins,Jimmy	8%
Pence,Hunter	8%
Votto,Joey	8%
Francoeur,Jeff	7%
Vizquel,Omar	7%
Abreu,Bobby	7%
Tulowitzki,Troy	6%
Jones,Adam	6%
Teixeira,Mark	5%
Pedroia,Dustin	5%
Phillips,Brandon	5%
Zimmerman,Ryan	5%
Sandoval,Pablo	4%
Young,Delmon	4%
Loney,James	3%
Wright,David	3%
Holliday,Matt	3%
McCutchen,Andrew	2%
Ramirez,Aramis	2%
Bourn,Michael	1%
Peralta,Jhonny	1%
Gonzalez,Carlos	< 1%
Polanco,Placido	< 1%
Cabrera,Asdrubal	< 1%
Moyer, Steve	< 1%

Career Targets

762 Home Runs
% chance to break record

Pujols,Albert	20%
Rodriguez,Alex	11%
Fielder,Prince	3%

2,298 RBI
% chance to break record

Rodriguez,Alex	27%
Pujols,Albert	13%
Cabrera,Miguel	9%
Fielder,Prince	< 1%

2,296 Runs Scored
% chance to break record

Pujols,Albert	11%
Rodriguez,Alex	3%
Cabrera,Miguel	3%

4,257 Hits
% chance to break record

Cabrera,Miguel	< 1%

900 Home Runs
% chance to reach milestone

2,000 RBI
% chance to reach milestone

Rodriguez,Alex	96%
Pujols,Albert	41%
Cabrera,Miguel	27%
Teixeira,Mark	13%
Fielder,Prince	12%
Howard,Ryan	7%
Kemp,Matt	7%
Cano,Robinson	6%
Braun,Ryan	6%
Longoria,Evan	5%

6,857 Total Bases
% chance to break record

Pujols,Albert	12%
Cabrera,Miguel	8%

4,000 Hits
% chance to reach milestone

Cabrera,Miguel	6%
Pujols,Albert	< 1%

800 Home Runs
% chance to reach milestone

Pujols,Albert	12%

600 Home Runs
% chance to reach milestone

Rodriguez,Alex	done
Thome,Jim	done
Pujols,Albert	89%
Fielder,Prince	26%
Cabrera,Miguel	22%
Teixeira,Mark	21%
Reynolds,Mark	12%
Howard,Ryan	10%
Dunn,Adam	7%
Konerko,Paul	7%

793 Doubles
% chance to break record

Cabrera,Miguel	20%
Butler,Billy	14%
Cano,Robinson	12%
Pujols,Albert	7%
Beltre,Adrian	1%
Markakis,Nick	1%
Braun,Ryan	< 1%

Most Likely No-Hitter
% chance to reach milestone

Kershaw,Clayton	20%
Beachy,Brandon	19%
Greinke,Zack	18%
Morrow,Brandon	16%
Lincecum,Tim	15%
Verlander,Justin	15%
Sanchez,Anibal	14%
Price,David	14%
Pineda,Michael	13%
Gallardo,Yovani	13%

700 Home Runs
% chance to reach milestone

Rodriguez,Alex	63%
Pujols,Albert	37%
Fielder,Prince	10%
Cabrera,Miguel	5%
Teixeira,Mark	3%
Reynolds,Mark	< 1%

500 Home Runs
% chance to reach milestone

Rodriguez,Alex	done
Thome,Jim	done
Ramirez,Manny	done
Pujols,Albert	96%
Konerko,Paul	62%
Guerrero,Vladimir	60%
Teixeira,Mark	59%
Cabrera,Miguel	55%
Fielder,Prince	54%
Dunn,Adam	50%

1,000 Stolen Bases
% chance to reach milestone

Bourn,Michael	3%

Pitchers on Course
For 300 Wins

Bill James

Name	2011 Age	R/L	W	L	EWL	Momentum	Chance
Halladay, Roy	34	R	188	92	17.5	.894	.49
Sabathia, CC	30	L	176	96	17.7	.901	.48
Verlander, Justin	28	R	107	57	19.6	.887	.31
Lee, Cliff	32	L	119	69	15.7	.883	.24
Haren, Dan	30	R	107	84	14.1	.885	.19
Hernandez, Felix	25	R	85	67	13.8	.870	.11
Shields, James	29	R	72	63	14.6	.840	.07
Hudson, Tim	35	R	181	97	13.3	.717	.05
Weaver, Jered	28	R	82	47	15.1	.811	.05
Vazquez, Javier	34	R	165	160	11.7	.751	.04
Carpenter, Chris	36	R	144	92	11.7	.780	.04
Santana, Ervin	28	R	87	67	11.9	.821	.03
Buehrle, Mark	32	L	161	119	11.1	.759	.03
Burnett, A.J.	34	R	121	111	11.2	.770	.02
Lowe, Derek	38	R	166	146	10.3	.715	.01
Wolf, Randy	34	L	127	107	11.4	.731	.01
Dempster, Ryan	34	R	112	116	11.7	.744	.01
Beckett, Josh	31	R	125	81	11.5	.716	.01
Lilly, Ted	35	L	125	110	11.3	.714	.01
Penny, Brad	33	R	119	99	7.6	.569	< .01
Arroyo, Bronson	34	R	112	105	9.9	.731	< .01
Myers, Brett	30	R	94	85	8.9	.764	< .01
Pavano, Carl	35	R	106	102	9.2	.738	< .01
Hernandez, Livan	36	R	174	176	7.9	.619	< .01
Wakefield, Tim	44	R	200	180	6.5	.578	< .01
Colon, Bartolo	38	R	161	113	6.6	.623	< .01

Note: EWL = Established Win Level

It is likely that two pitchers now active will eventually win 300 games. It is likely that one of those two will be either Roy Halladay or CC Sabathia, and the other one will be somebody else.

We estimate the chance that a pitcher will win 300 games by asking three questions:

1) How many more wins does he need?
2) How old is he?
3) How fast is he moving?

In the chart below the heading "EWL" stands for "Established Win Level". How many games per-season is the pitcher winning? If the pitcher has been winning 15 to 20 games per season, that gives him an established Win Level between 15 and 20.

We combine the answers to these three questions with some other data into a "momentum" number. The momentum number will be higher for a strikeout pitcher than for a finesse-type pitcher, since strikeout pitchers last longer than finesse pitchers, and it will be much higher for a pitcher with a record of being consistently healthy than for a pitcher who has spent time on the disabled list. It will be higher for a younger pitcher than an older, if the rest of the data is the same.

You may ask "Why is Zack Greinke not here?", or "Why is David Price not here?", or "Why is Jordan Lyles not here?" The answer is that we do not consider any pitcher to be *established* as a 300-win candidate unless the sum of his career wins and his (2011) innings pitched is at least 300. Zack Greinke has 76 career wins; he pitched 172 innings in 2011. That's 248. Basically, he's too far away from 300 wins for us to start worrying about him yet. If he wins 18 games and pitches 206 innings in 2012, then we'll add him to the list.

Through 2008 (thus, in the 2009 Handbook) the leading 300-win candidates were Randy Johnson, Mike Mussina, Jamie Moyer, Johan Santana and Brandon Webb. Johnson—then at 295 wins—did go on to get 300. Mussina and Moyer retired without reaching the goal, and Santana and Webb had injuries that wiped them out of the competition. Thus, by one year later (2009, 2010 Handbook), Roy Halladay and CC Sabathia had emerged as the leading 300-win candidates in baseball.

All that has really happened since then is that Halladay and Sabathia have stepped further forward from the group. At that time (2009) Halladay was at 33% and Sabathia was at 23%--the highest percentages in baseball. Now they're at 49% and 48% (and Justin Verlander, who at that time was at 7%, is now at 31%). This is the typical pattern: A pitcher walks forward a few inches at a time, going from 6% to 10%, from 10% to 13, from 13 to 16, from 16 to 25, from 25 to 28, from 28 to 34, etc., and then something happens, he has an injury, and he goes from 34 to zero in a year or two. That's the normal pattern.

But a few pitchers are exceptions to the normal patterns, and it is those exceptions who get to 300 wins. Sabathia and Halladay have now come so far that they're basically 50/50 candidates. Everybody else is a long shot.

Baseball Glossary

% Inherited Scored

The percentage of inherited baserunners a relief pitcher allows to score.

% Pitches Taken

The percentage of pitches that a batter does not swing at out of the total number of pitches thrown to him.

1st Batter Average

The Batting Average that a relief pitcher allows to the first batter he faces when he enters a game.

1st Batter OBP

The On-Base Percentage that a relief pitcher allows to the first batter he faces when he enters a game.

1st to 3rd (Baserunning)

"Moved" is the number of times a runner goes from 1st base to 3rd base on a SINGLE. "Chances" are the number of times a runner is on 1st base and a batter is credited with a SINGLE.

1st to Home (Baserunning)

"Moved" is the number of times a runner goes from 1st base to home on a DOUBLE. "Chances" are the number of times a runner is on 1st base and a batter is credited with a DOUBLE.

2nd to Home (Baserunning)

"Moved" is the number of times a runner goes from 2nd base to home on a SINGLE. "Chances" are the number of times a runner is on 2nd base and a batter is credited with a SINGLE.

Active Career Batting Leaders

A list of batting leaders among active (appearing in the most recent season) players. An active player is eligible when he meets the minimum requirements for the following categories:

> 1,000 At Bats—Batting Average, On-Base Percentage, Slugging Average, At Bats Per HR, At Bats Per GDP, At Bats Per RBI, Strikeout to Walk Ratio
> 100 Stolen Base Attempts—Stolen Base Success Percentage

Active Career Pitching Leaders

A list of pitching leaders among active (appearing in the most recent season) players. An active player is eligible when he meets the minimum requirements for the following categories:

750 Innings Pitched—Earned Run Average, Opponent Batting Average, all "Per 9 Innings" categories, Strikeout to Walk Ratio
250 Games Started—Complete Game Frequency
100 Decisions—Win-Loss Percentage

AVG Allowed ScPos
The Batting Average allowed by a pitcher while pitching with runners in scoring position.

AVG Bases Loaded
The Batting Average of a hitter while batting with the bases loaded.

Base Taken
A player is credited with a Base Taken whenever he moves up a base on a Wild Pitch, Passed Ball, Balk, Sacrifice Fly, or Defensive Indifference.

Batting Average
Hits divided by at bats.

Blown Save
When a relief pitcher enters a game in a Save Situation (see definition for Save Situation) and allows the other team to score the tying or go-ahead run.

Bomb (Intentional Walk)
An Intentional Walk is counted as a "Bomb" if
1) The next batter, after the IBB, does not ground into a double play, and
2) Multiple runs are scored in the inning, after the intentional walk.

BR Gain (Baserunning)
BR Gain (or Loss if a negative number) is the total of all the types of extra baserunning advances minus the (triple) penalty for all the BR Outs compared with what would be expected based on the MLB averages.

BR Outs (Baserunning)
BR Outs include the sum of Outs Advancing, Doubled Offs, and when a runner is tagged out on the bases when another runner moves up on a Wild Pitch, Passed Ball, or scores on a Sacrifice Fly.

BS Win
A Blown Save Win is a "win" credited to a reliever who has blown a save opportunity.

Career Targets
This method, once called the Favorite Toy, is a way to estimate the probability that a player will achieve a specific career goal. In this example, 3,000 hits will be used. The four components of the formula are Needed Hits, Years Remaining, Established Hit Level and Projected Remaining Hits.

Needed Hits. This is the number of Hits (or any statistic) that a player needs to reach a desired goal.

Years Remaining. This is the estimated number of years remaining in the player's career. It is determined using the player's age (on June 30th of the previous year; use 2011 when making the calculation after the 2011 season is complete). The formula is (42 - age) divided by two. This means a player who is 20 years old will have 11 remaining seasons, a player who is 25 years old will have 8.5 remaining seasons and a player who is 35 years old will have 3.5 remaining seasons. If the player is a catcher, then multiply his remaining seasons by .7. The only stipulation is that years remaining must always be greater than or equal to 1.5.

Established Hit Level. The Established Hit Level is a weighted average of the player's hits over the past three seasons. To calculate the Established Hit Level after the 2011 season is complete, add 2009 Hits, (2010 Hits multiplied by two) and (2011 Hits multiplied by three), then divide by six. If the Established Hit Level is less than 75% of the most recent performance (2011 Hits in this case), then the Established Hit Level is equal to .75 times the most recent performance.

Projected Remaining Hits. This is calculated by multiplying Years Remaining by the Established Hit Level.

The probability of achieving the specified goal is found by dividing Projected Remaining Hits by Needed Hits, then subtracting .5. The maximum that any player has of achieving a goal is .97 raised to the power of (Need Hits / Established Hit Level). This prevents the possibility of a player reaching a goal from being higher than 100 percent, which is impossible.

Catcher's ERA
The ERA for a catcher is equal to the ERA of pitchers pitching while the catcher is playing behind the plate. It is calculated exactly like ERA for pitchers. Take the number of earned runs allowed while the catcher is playing, multiply it by 9 and then divide it by the total number of defensive innings that the catcher was behind the plate.

Cheap Win
A starting pitcher who wins the game with a game score under 50 gets credit for a cheap win. See Game Score.

Clean Outing
A Clean Outing is a game in which the reliever is not charged with a run (earned or otherwise) AND does not allow an inherited runner to score.

Cleanup Slugging Average
The Slugging Average of a batter when he bats in the cleanup spot, or fourth, in the batting order.

Close and Late
A situation in a game that is very similar to a Save Situation. The following requirements are necessary for a Close and Late game:
1. The game is in the seventh inning or later AND

2.The batting team is either leading by one run or tied OR

3.The tying run is on base, at bat, or on deck.

Component ERA (ERC)

A statistic that estimates what a pitcher's ERA should have been, based on his pitching performance. The ERC formula is calculated as follows:

1.Subtract the pitcher's Home Runs Allowed from his Hits Allowed.

2.Multiply Step 1 by 1.255.

3.Multiply his Home Runs Allowed by four.

4.Add Steps 2 and 3 together.

5.Multiply Step 4 by .89.

6.Add his Walks and Hit Batsmen.

7.Multiply Step 6 by .475.

8.Add Steps 5 and 7 together.

This yields the pitcher's total base estimate (PTB), which is:

$$PTB = 0.89 \times (1.255 \times (H - HR) + 4 \times HR) + 0.475 \times (BB + HB)$$

For those pitchers for whom there is intentional walk data, use this formula instead:

$$PTB = 0.89 \times (1.255 \times (H - HR) + 4 \times HR) + 0.56 \times (BB + HB - IBB)$$

9.Add Hits and Walks and Hit Batsmen.

10.Multiply Step 9 by PTB.

11.Divide Step 10 by Batters Facing Pitcher. If BFP data is unavailable, approximate it by multiplying Innings Pitched by 2.9, then adding Step 9.

12.Multiply Step 11 by 9.

13.Divide Step 12 by Innings Pitched.

14.Subtract .56 from Step 13.

This is the pitcher's ERC, which is:

$$\frac{(H + BB + HB) \times PTB}{BFP \times IP} \times 9 - 0.56$$

If the result after Step 13 is less than 2.24, adjust the formula as follows:

$$\frac{(H + BB + HB) \times PTB}{BFP \times IP} \times 9 \times 0.75$$

Consecutive Days

A count of how many times the pitcher was used after having pitched on the previous day or (in a few cases) in an earlier game on the same day.

Defensive Runs Saved (Runs Saved, for short) is the innovative metric introduced by John Dewan in *The Fielding Bible—Volume II*. The Runs Saved value indicates how many runs a player saved or hurt his team in the field compared to the average player at his position. A player near zero Runs Saved is about average; a positive number of runs saved indicates above-average defense, below-average fielders post negative Runs Saved totals. There are eight components of Runs Saved:

Plus Minus Runs Saved (all positions except Catcher)
Earned Runs Saved (Catchers)
Stolen Base Runs Saved (Catchers)
Stolen Base Runs Saved (Pitchers)
Bunt Runs Saved (Corner Infielders)
Double Play Runs Saved (Middle Infielders)
Outfield Arm Runs Saved (Outfielders)
Home Run Saving Catch Runs Saved (Outfielders)

Double Play %
Successful Double Plays divided by the number of Double Play opportunities. This statistic includes both the fielder who started the play and the pivot man.

Double Play Opportunity
A fielder is considered to have a double play opportunity when a ground ball is hit with a runner on first base and less than 2 outs and that fielder is involved in the play. This is used to calculate Double Play % and Pivot %.

Doubled Off
A runner is Doubled Off when he is out for failing to get back to his base before he, or the base, is tagged after a ball hit in the air is caught.

Early Entry
A count of the number of times the reliever entered the game in the sixth inning or earlier.

Earned Run Average
The number of earned runs that a pitcher surrenders per nine innings that he pitches. It is calculated by multiplying the total earned runs allowed by nine and dividing by the total number of innings pitched.

Easy Save
This label is used to separate Saves by difficulty level (Easy or Tough). A Save is considered Easy if the relief pitcher enters the game, pitches one inning or less, and the first batter he faces does not at least represent the tying run.

Fielding Percentage
The percentage of plays a player makes in the field without making an error out of the total number of opportunities. It is calculated by adding (Putouts plus Assists) and dividing by (Putouts plus Assists plus Errors).

Games Finished

The relief pitcher who is in the game for each team when the game ends is credited with a Game Finished.

Game Score

To determine the starting pitcher's Game Score:
Start with 50.
Add 1 point for each out recorded by the starting pitcher.
Add 2 points for each inning the pitcher completes after the fourth inning.
Add 1 point for each strikeout.
Subtract 2 points for each hit allowed.
Subtract 4 points for each earned run allowed.
Subtract 2 points for an unearned run.
Subtract 1 point for each walk.

GDP

Grounded into Double Play

GDP Opportunity

This is a situation where the batter has a chance to ground into a double play. It occurs with at least a runner on first base and less than two outs.

Ground / Fly Ratio (Grd/Fly, GB/FB)

Calculated for both batters and pitchers. For batters, it is the number of groundballs hit divided by the number of flyballs hit. For pitchers, it is exactly the same but uses the number of groundballs and flyballs allowed. Every fair batted ball is included except for bunts and line drives.

Hold

A relief pitcher is given a Hold anytime he enters the game in a Save Situation (see definition for Save Situation), records one out or more, and exits the game without giving up the lead. If the pitcher finishes the game, then he will only earn credit for a Save. He cannot receive credit for both a Hold and a Save.

Holds Adjusted Save Percentage (same as Save/Hold Percentage)

Holds plus Saves divided by Holds plus Saves Opportunities.

Inherited Runner

When a relief pitcher enters the game, any runner who was on base at the time is considered an Inherited Runner.

Isolated Power

Slugging Average minus Batting Average.

K/BB Ratio

Strikeouts divided by Walks.

Leadoff On-Base Percentage

The On-Base Percentage of a batter when he bats leadoff, or first, in the batting order.

Leverage Index

Leverage is the amount of swing in the possible change in win probability, compared to the average swing in all situations. The average swing value, by definition, is indexed to 1.00.

If the score of the game is 12-0 or 14-1 the possible changes in win probability will be very close to negligible. Whether the pitcher gives up a home run or gets a double play ball doesn't really change the outcome of the game. There won't be much swing in either direction for the probability of the win. But in the late innings of a close game, the change in win probability among the various events will have rather wild swings. With a runner on first, two outs, down by one, and in the bottom of the ninth, the game can hinge on one swing of that bat. A home run and an out will both end the game, but with different outcomes for the teams involved. The Leverage Index we use (LI) was developed at the website Tangotiger.net, and compiled at the website Fangraphs.com.

Long Outing

A Long Outing is one in which the starting pitcher throws more than 110 pitches. Prior to 2002, we used 120 pitches as the cutoff in the Manager's Record section.

Long Save

A Long Save is when the pitcher credited with a save pitches more than one inning.

Manufactured Runs

1) A run that scores without a hit, or a run on which the only hit(s) is/are infield hits, is always scored as a Manufactured Run.

2) A run which is driven in by a home run is never scored a Manufactured Run, under any circumstance.

3) A run which is driven in by a double or a triple is scored as a Manufactured Run only if *two* of the four bases result from advancing on one of these four acts: a sacrifice bunt, a stolen base, a hit and run, or a bunt single.

4) Otherwise, a run is considered to be a Manufactured Run if two of the four bases do not result from the runner being forced along by a walk, a hit batsman, or a safe hit reaching the outfield.

5) A forceout or fielder's choice which does not improve the position of the base runners should not be counted as contributing toward a Manufactured Run. Advancing on a forceout or a fielder's choice DOES count toward a manufactured run, if the play is one which improves the position of the baserunners.

6) A base "gained" on a double play does not count as a contribution to a Manufactured Run. A run scored on a double play is a Manufactured Run only if two of the OTHER bases are not attributable to forced advancement.

Not Good Outcome (Intentional Walk)

A Not Good Outcome (NG) for an Intentional Walk occurs when one run scored in the inning after the intentional walk (and the next batter after the intentional walk did not ground into a double play).

Offensive Winning Percentage (OWP)

A player's Offensive Winning Percentage is the winning percentage of a hypothetical team which has an offense consisting of nine of that player, and pitching and defense which is average for the player's league. It is calculated by taking the square of RC/27 (see the definition for Runs Created per 27 Outs), dividing it by the sum of the square of RC/27 and the square of the average runs scored per game in the league.

On-Base Percentage

(Hits plus Walks plus Hit by Pitcher) divided by (At Bats plus Walks plus Hit by Pitcher plus Sacrifice Flies).

$$\frac{H + BB + HBP}{AB + BB + HBP + SF}$$

Opponent Batting Average

Hits Allowed divided by (Batters Faced minus Walks minus Hit Batsmen minus Sacrifice Hits minus Sacrifice Flies minus Catcher's Interference).

$$\frac{H}{BFP - BB - HBP - SH - SF - CI}$$

Opposition OPS

The OPS of the hitters facing the pitcher.

Out Advancing

A runner is out advancing when he is tagged out attempting to score from 2nd base on a single or from 1st base on a double, or attempting to go from 1st base to 3rd base on a single.

PA*

Used in the denominator for the calculation of On-Base Percentage. It is calculated by subtracting (Sacrifice Hits plus Times Reached Base on Defensive Interference) from Plate Appearances (see definition for Plate Appearances).

Park Index

To calculate the park index for home runs in a given ballpark, we take the total home runs of both the home team and its opponents at the ballpark and compare it to the total home runs of the home team and its opponents in other games. We then divide each of those totals by the at-bats in the equivalent situations, so that if there are more at-bats in either situation the index is not skewed. The result is then multiplied by 100 to yield the familiar form.

The park indices for doubles, triples, walks, strikeouts and home runs by lefties and righties are determined like home runs above—relative to at-bats. Indices of at-bats, runs, hits, errors and infield fielding errors (E-Infield) are calculated relative to games. The three batting average indices are calculated as is, since these are already relative to at-bats.

PCS (Pitchers' Caught Stealing)

The number of runners officially scored as Caught Stealing where the pitcher initiated the play. The normal Caught Stealing is when a runner is out attempting to steal a base but the play was initiated by the catcher. PCS plays are often referred to as pickoffs, but differ when the runner breaks towards the next base as opposed to returning to the base he was currently on. Pickoffs occur when the pitcher throws to a base that a runner is leading from, and the runner is out attempting to return to that base. Pickoffs are not an official statistic.

Pitches per PA

The total number of pitches a hitter sees divided by his total Plate Appearances.

Pivot %

Successful Double Plays turned by pivot man divided by the number of Double Play opportunities with that pivot man involved.

Plate Appearances

At Bats plus Total Walks plus Hit By Pitcher plus Sacrifice Hits plus Sacrifice Flies plus Times Reached on Defensive Interference.

Platoon Advantage %

Platoon Advantage % is the percentage of players in the starting lineup who have the platoon advantage (i.e. bats right against a left-handed pitcher or bats left against a right-hander) against the starting pitcher; e.g. if the opposing starting pitcher is right handed and the batting team has six left-handed batters in its lineup, the platoon advantage for that game would be 67%.

Plus/Minus System

The Plus/Minus System is a method for evaluating defensive play on batted balls. It is made possible by a game scoring system in which each batted ball is rated for type (line drive, grounder, etc.), velocity within its type (hard, medium or soft), and location on the field. A player gets credit (a "plus" number) if he makes a play that at least one other player at his position missed during the season and he loses credit (a "minus" number") if he misses a play that at least one player made. The size of the credits are proportional to the percentage of times all players make the play. All plays for each player at his position are summed to get his total plus/minus for the season. A total of zero would be average and any other number would approximate how many plays more or less the player made than the average player at the position for the number of chances the player had to field batted balls.

Power/Speed Number

A single number that reflects a combination of power and speed. To achieve a high Power/Speed Number, a player must score high in both power and speed. To calculate the Power/Speed Number, multiply Home Runs by Stolen Bases by two, and divide by the sum of Home Runs and Stolen Bases.

$$\frac{2 \times HR \times SB}{HR + SB}$$

PPO (Pitcher Pickoff)

The number of baserunners thrown out when a pitcher throws to a base with a leading baserunner, and the runner is tagged out attempting to return to the base. PPO is not an official statistic and does not count toward Caught Stealing totals.

Quality Start

A game where the starting pitcher pitches for at least six innings and allows no more than three earned runs.

Quality Start Percentage

Quality Starts divided by Games Started (see the definition for Quality Start).

Quick Hooks

Used in the Manager's Record. For Quick Hooks and Slow Hooks a score is calculated for each game that is the sum of the number of Pitches plus 10 times the number of Runs Allowed. The bottom 25% of scores in the league are considered to be Quick Hooks.

Range Factor

The number of Successful Chances (Putouts plus Assists) times nine divided by the number of Defensive Innings Played. The average for a player at each position in 2011:

      Second Base: 4.76
      Third Base: 2.57
      Shortstop: 4.39
      Left Field: 1.99
      Center Field: 2.58
      Right Field: 2.07

RBI %

The percentage of all potential runs driven in by a certain hitter. Simply put, it's RBIs divided by RBI Opportunities. An RBI Opportunity is any runner on base when the hitter steps up to the plate. We also count the hitter himself, as he can drive in a runner with no one on base via the solo home run. Here's the full formula:

A = Runs Batted In
B = Men On Base + Plate Appearances – Walks – Hit By Pitch – Reaches on Catcher's Interference + C
C = Walks, Hit By Pitch, or Reaches on Catcher's Interference with the bases loaded (resulting in a Run Batted In)

Regular Saves

Any save which does not meet the definition either of an Easy Save or a Tough Save is a "Regular" Save.

Run Support Per 9 IP

The total number of runs scored by a pitcher's team while he is in the game multiplied by nine and divided by total Innings Pitched.

Runs Created

"Runs Created" is an estimate of the number of a team's runs which are created by each individual hitter. The Cincinnati Reds scored 820 runs last year, let us say. How many of those were created by Joey Votto? How many by Brandon Phillips? How many by Jay Bruce?

There are many different formulas for estimating runs created. . .did you want the one that involves swinging a dead cat in the cemetery under a full moon? Yeah, I don't blame you. . .worm-eaten persimmons are so hard to find in the modern world.

This is the one we use now; it is complicated enough. First, there is an "A" Factor in the formula, a "B" Factor, and a "C" factor. The "A" Factor, which represents the number of times the hitter is on base, is Hits, Plus Walks, Plus Hit Batsmen, Minus Caught Stealing, Minus Grounded Into Double Play. The "B" Factor, which represents the hitter's ability to advance other runners, is 1.125 times the player's Singles, plus 1.69 times his Doubles, plus 3.02 times his Triples, plus 3.73 times his Home Runs, plus .29 times his Walks and Hit Batsmen, not counting intentional walks, plus .492 times Sacrifice Hits, Sacrifice Flies and Stolen Bases, minus .04 times Strikeouts. The "C" Factor, which represents opportunities, is At Bats, Plus Walks, Plus Hit By Pitch, Plus Sacrifice Hits, Plus Sacrifice Flies.

Having made these initial calculations of the A, B and C factors, we then change the "A" factor to "A plus 2.4 times C".

We change the "B" factor to "B plus 3 times C".

We change the "C" factor to "9 times C".

Multiply A times B, divide by then new C ("9 times C"), and subtract .90 times by the original C.

This is our first, temporary estimate of the player's runs created. We what we have done here is to ask these questions:
> 1. How many runs would a team probably score that consisted of eight "ordinary" type of hitters, plus this particular hitter?
> 2. How many of those runs would be created by the eight ordinary type of hitters?
> 3. What is the difference-and thus, how many runs did our player create?

To estimate this, we have placed our player in the context of eight hitters with a .300 on base percentage (2.4 divided by 8) and a .375 advancement percentage (3 divided by 8). For each trip through the batting order, the eight ordinary-type hitters would produce 9/10 of a run (2.4 times 3, divided by 8). The "9" in the denominator is eight ordinary hitters plus our man. The "-.9" being subtracted at the end is the runs created by the "ordinary" hitters. In essence, we have placed the hitter in a neutral solution, measured the neutral solution without our hitter, measured it with our hitter, and then estimated the contribution of this hitter as being the difference between the two.

We're not quite done. After that, we adjust the player's runs created estimate for his performance in two "run-sensitive" situations. Suppose that a player whose overall batting average is .250 has batted 100 times with runners in scoring position, and has gone 30-for-100. That's five hits better than expected, 30 hits where we would have expected 25. His team will score an extra five runs because he has done that, and so we increase the player's runs created estimate by five runs. If the player has hit poorly with runners in scoring position, we decrease it by the shortfall in the same way.

Suppose that a player has batted 250 times with runners on base, 250 times with the bases empty, and that he has hit 20 home runs overall. We would expect him to have hit 10 with men on base, 10 with the bases empty, right?

Suppose that he didn't. Suppose that he hit 12 with the bases empty, 8 with men on base. His team would score two runs less than expected because he did this, and we would thus penalize him two runs for the shortfall.

This is our second runs created estimate-the player's runs created, adjusted for his batting performance in run-sensitive situations.

Suppose, however, that we figure the runs created for all of the individuals on a team, and we add them up, and it doesn't match the runs actually scored by the team? What if the formulas say that the team should have scored 800 runs, but they actually scored 820?

Then obviously, the formulas missed. We're trying to measure the runs ACTUALLY created by each hitter as best we can, in the real world, not the theoretical impact of some combination of singles, doubles, triples and walks. If the actual number is different than the estimates, we have to adjust the estimates to fit the facts. In this case-820 runs scored with only 800 runs created-we would multiply each runs created estimate by 820/800, or 1.025. Then we round it off to an integer, and that's the player's estimated runs created.

Let go of that cat, Arthur. Heck, the moon isn't full for three weeks, anyway.

Runs Created per 27 Outs (RC/27)
This statistic estimates the number of runs per game that a team made up of nine of the same player would score. To calculate RC/27, multiply Runs Created by league outs per team game, divide the result by outs made by the player (the sum of at bats plus sacrifice hits plus sacrifice flies plus caught stealing plus grounded into double plays, minus hits). The formula written out is:

$$\frac{\frac{RC \times 3 \times LgIP}{2 \times LgG}}{AB - H + SH + SF + CS + GDP}$$

Runs Saved
See Defensive Runs Saved.

Save Opportunities

The sum of Saves and Blown Saves (see Save Situation).

Save/Hold Percentage (same as Holds Adjusted Saves Percentage)

The sum of Saves and Holds, divided by the sum of Saves, Holds, and Blown Saves.

For several years we figured "Save Percentage", which is simply Saves divided by Save Opportunities, and this stat has some currency in the game. But the Save Percentage severely discriminates against middle relievers, who have no real chance to be credited with the Save, since they will be taken out of the game and replaced by the Closer even if they throw 110 miles an hour and strike out everybody they see. Middle relievers typically have Save Percentages of zero, even if they pitch well. The Save/Hold Percentage is a much more realistic evaluation of a pitcher's success in Save situations.

Save Percentage

A pitcher's Saves divided by the total number of Save Situations he faces (see definition for Save Situation).

Save Situation

A relief pitcher is in a Save Situation when he enters the game with his team in the lead, has the opportunity to finish the game, is not the winning pitcher of record at the time, and meets any one of the three following conditions:

> 1.The pitcher's team is leading by no more than three runs and the pitcher has the chance to pitch for at least one inning,
>
> OR
>
> 2.The pitcher enters the game with the potential tying run on base, at bat, or on deck,
>
> OR
>
> 3.The pitcher pitches three or more effective innings regardless of the lead. The determination of a save in this situation is made by the official scorer.
>
> It is not possible to have more than one save credited to a single team in a game.

SB Gain (Baserunning)

Stolen Base attempts must be successful greater than about two thirds of the time to have a positive result on the number of runs scored. SB gain is therefore the number of bases stolen minus two times the number of caught stealing (SB Gain = SB - 2CS). For example, a runner steals 30 bases and is caught stealing 7 times. His SB Gain would be 30 - 2*7 = +16. Another runner steals 10 bases and is caught stealing 6 times. His SB Gain (actually a loss) would be 10 - 2*6 = -2.

SB Success Percentage

Stolen Bases divided by the number of Stolen Base attempts (Stolen Bases plus Caught Stealing).

$$\frac{SB}{SB + CS}$$

Secondary Average

A number meant to reflect everything else except for batting average. A player will have a high Secondary Average if he hits for power, takes walks and steals bases. It is calculated with the following formula:

$$\frac{TB - H + BB + SB}{AB}$$

Similarity Score

A number which reflects the similarity between two different statistical lines, either for a player or for a team. A score of 1,000 means that the statistical lines are identical.

Slow Hooks

Used in the Manager's Record. For Quick Hooks and Slow Hooks a score is calculated for each game that is the sum of the number of Pitches plus 10 times the number of Runs Allowed. The top 25% of scores in the league are considered to be Slow Hooks.

Slugging Average

Total Bases divided by At Bats.

$$\frac{TB}{AB}$$

Speed Score

Speed Score is a number which evaluates how fast a player is. To calculate the Speed Score, start with the player's statistics over the last two seasons combined. A value will be found for each of the following six categories and will be combined for a final score at the end:

1. Stolen Base Percentage. The value of this category is:

$$\left(\frac{SB + 3}{SB + CS + 7} - 0.4 \right) \times 20$$

2. Frequency of Stolen Base Attempts. The value of this category is:

$$\frac{\sqrt{\dfrac{SB + CS}{Singles + BB + HBP}}}{0.07}$$

3. Percentage of Triples. This is calculated by taking the percentage of triples out of the number of balls put in play. To get the percentage, use this formula:

$$\frac{3B}{AB - HR - SO}$$

From this assign an integer from 0 to 10, based on the following chart:

Less than .001   0
.001   - .0023   1
.0023 - .0039   2
.0039 - .0058   3
.0058 - .0080   4
.0080 - .0105   5
.0105 - .013   6
.013   - .0158   7
.0158 - .0189   8
.0189 - .0223   9
.0223 or more   10

4. Runs Scored Percentage. This is calculated by taking the percentage of times the player scores a run out of the number of times the player is on base. To get the percentage, use this formula:

$$\frac{\left(\dfrac{R-HR}{H+HBP+BB-HR}-0.1\right)}{0.04}$$

5. Grounded Into Double Play Frequency. To get the frequency, use this formula:

$$\frac{0.055-\left(\dfrac{GIDP}{AB-HR-SO}\right)}{0.005}$$

6. Range Factor. The value of this category depends on the players position:

Catcher—1
First Baseman—2
Designated Hitter—1.5
Second Baseman—1.25 x Range Factor
Third Baseman—1.51 x Range Factor
Shortstop—1.52 x Range Factor
Outfield—3 x Range Factor

For an explanation on Range Factor, consult the definition in this glossary. Remember to figure range factors over a two-year period.

If any category value is greater than 10, then reduce it to 10. If any value is less than zero, then increase the value to zero. All category values must fall within the zero to 10 range. The Speed Score is then calculated by discarding the lowest of the six values, and taking the average of the remaining five.

Total Bases

Hits plus Doubles plus (2 times Triples) plus (3 times Home Runs).

$$H + 2B + (2 \times 3B) + (3 \times HR)$$

Tough Loss

A starting pitcher who loses the game with a game score over 50 gets credit for a tough loss. See Game Score.

Tough Save

This label is used to separate Saves by difficulty level (Easy or Tough). A Save is considered Tough if the relief pitcher enters the game with the tying run on base.

Win Probability

The probability of a team winning the game determined at any time during the game based on the score, inning, outs and base situation.

Winning Percentage

Wins divided by (Wins plus Losses).

Minor League Abbreviation Key

Abbreviation	Team	Level	League	MLB Affiliate	First Year	Last Year
Abrdn	Aberdeen IronBirds	A-	New York-Penn League	Baltimore Orioles	2002	2011
Akron	Akron Aeros	AA	Eastern League	Cleveland Indians	1997	2011
Albq	Albuquerque Isotopes	AAA	Pacific Coast League	Florida Marlins	2003	2008
Albq	Albuquerque Isotopes	AAA	Pacific Coast League	Los Angeles Dodgers	2009	2011
Altna	Altoona Curve	AA	Eastern League	Pittsburgh Pirates	1999	2011
Angels	AZL Angels	R	Arizona League	Los Angeles Angels	2001	2011
Ark	Arkansas Travelers	AA	Texas League	Los Angeles Angels	2001	2011
As	AZL Athletics	R	Arizona League	Oakland Athletics	1988	2011
Ashvll	Asheville Tourists	A	South Atlantic League	Colorado Rockies	1994	2011
Astros	GCL Astros	R	Gulf Coast League	Houston Astros	2009	2011
Auburn	Auburn Doubledays	A-	New York-Penn League	Toronto Blue Jays	2001	2010
Augsta	Augusta GreenJackets	A	South Atlantic League	San Francisco Giants	2005	2011
Augsta	Augusta Greenjackets	A	South Atlantic League	Boston Red Sox	1999	2004
B Jays	GCL Blue Jays	R	Gulf Coast League	Toronto Blue Jays	2007	2011
Batvia	Batavia Muckdogs	A-	New York-Penn League	St Louis Cardinals	2007	2011
Batvia	Batavia Muckdogs	A-	New York-Penn League	Philadelphia Phillies	1998	2006
Beloit	Beloit Snappers	A	Midwest League	Minnesota Twins	2005	2011
Beloit	Beloit Snappers	A	Midwest League	Milwaukee Brewers	1995	2004
BG	Bowling Green Hot Rods	A	Midwest League	Tampa Bay Rays	2010	2011
BG	Bowling Green Hot Rods	A	South Atlantic League	Tampa Bay Rays	2009	2009
Billings	Billings Mustangs	R+	Pioneer League	Cincinnati Reds	1974	2011
Bklyn	Brooklyn Cyclones	A-	New York-Penn League	New York Mets	2001	2011
Bkrsfld	Bakersfield Blaze	A+	California League	Texas Rangers	2005	2010
Bkrsfld	Bakersfield Blaze	A+	California League	Tampa Bay Rays	2001	2004
Bluefld	Bluefield Orioles	R+	Appalachian League	Baltimore Orioles	1963	2010
Bnghtn	Binghamton Mets	AA	Eastern League	New York Mets	1992	2011
Boise	Boise Hawks	A-	Northwest League	Chicago Cubs	2001	2011
Bowie	Bowie Baysox	AA	Eastern League	Baltimore Orioles	1993	2011
Bradtn	Bradenton Marauders	A+	Florida State League	Pittsburgh Pirates	2010	2011
Braves	GCL Braves	R	Gulf Coast League	Atlanta Braves	1976	2011
Brewrs	AZL Brewers	R	Arizona League	Milwaukee Brewers	2001	2011
Brham	Birmingham Barons	AA	Southern League	Chicago White Sox	1986	2011
Bristol	Bristol White Sox	R+	Appalachian League	Chicago White Sox	1995	2011
BrvdCt	Brevard County Manatees	A+	Florida State League	Washington Nationals	2002	2004
BrvdCt	Brevard County Manatees	A+	Florida State League	Milwaukee Brewers	2005	2011
Btl Crk	Battle Creek Yankees	A	Midwest League	New York Yankees	2003	2004
Buffalo	Buffalo Bisons	AAA	International League	Cleveland Indians	1995	2008
Buffalo	Buffalo Bisons	AAA	International League	New York Mets	2009	2011
Burlgtn	Burlington Royals	R+	Appalachian League	Kansas City Royals	2007	2011
Burlgtn	Burlington Bees	A	Midwest League	Kansas City Royals	2001	2010
CapeF	Cape Fear Crocs	A	South Atlantic League	Washington Nationals	1997	2000
Cards	GCL Cardinals	R	Gulf Coast League	St Louis Cardinals	2007	2011
Carlina	Carolina Mudcats	AA	Southern League	Florida Marlins	2003	2008
Carlina	Carolina Mudcats	AA	Southern League	Cincinnati Reds	2009	2011
Carlina	Carolina Mudcats	AA	Southern League	Colorado Rockies	1999	2002
Casper	Casper Ghosts	R+	Pioneer League	Colorado Rockies	2008	2011
Casper	Casper Rockies	R+	Pioneer League	Colorado Rockies	2001	2007
Charltt	Charlotte Knights	AAA	International League	Chicago White Sox	1999	2011
Charltt	Charlotte Stone Crabs	A+	Florida State League	Tampa Bay Rays	2009	2011
Chatt	Chattanooga Lookouts	AA	Southern League	Cincinnati Reds	1988	2008
Chatt	Chattanooga Lookouts	AA	Southern League	Los Angeles Dodgers	2009	2011
Clinton	Clinton LumberKings	A	Midwest League	Seattle Mariners	2009	2011
Clinton	Clinton LumberKings	A	Midwest League	Texas Rangers	2003	2008
Clmbs	Columbus Catfish	A	South Atlantic League	Los Angeles Dodgers	2004	2006
Clmbs	Columbus Clippers	AAA	International League	Cleveland Indians	2009	2011
Clmbs	Columbus Catfish	A	South Atlantic League	Tampa Bay Rays	2007	2008
Clmbs	Columbus Clippers	AAA	International League	New York Yankees	1979	2006
Clrwtr	Clearwater Threshers	A+	Florida State League	Philadelphia Phillies	2004	2011
ColSpr	Colorado Springs Sky Sox	AAA	Pacific Coast League	Colorado Rockies	1993	2011
Conn	Connecticut Defenders	AA	Eastern League	San Francisco Giants	2006	2009
Conn	Connecticut Tigers	A-	New York-Penn League	Detroit Tigers	2010	2011

Minor League Abbreviation Key

Abbreviation	Team	Level	League	MLB Affiliate	First Year	Last Year
CpChr	Corpus Christi Hooks	AA	Texas League	Houston Astros	2005	2011
CRpds	Cedar Rapids Kernels	A	Midwest League	Los Angeles Angels	1993	2011
CtnSC	Charleston RiverDogs	A	South Atlantic League	New York Yankees	2005	2011
CtnSC	Charleston - SC RiverDogs	A	South Atlantic League	Tampa Bay Rays	1997	2004
CtnWV	Charleston - WV Alley Cats	A	South Atlantic League	Toronto Blue Jays	2001	2004
Cubs	AZL Cubs	R	Arizona League	Chicago Cubs	1993	2011
Danvle	Danville Braves	R+	Appalachian League	Atlanta Braves	1993	2011
Dayton	Dayton Dragons	A	Midwest League	Cincinnati Reds	2000	2011
DBcks	AZL Diamondbacks	R	Arizona League	Arizona Diamondbacks	2011	2011
Ddgrs	GCL Dodgers	R	Gulf Coast League	Los Angeles Dodgers	2001	2008
Ddgrs	AZL Dodgers	R	Arizona League	Los Angeles Dodgers	2009	2011
Dlmrva	Delmarva Shorebirds	A	South Atlantic League	Baltimore Orioles	1997	2011
Dnedin	Dunedin Blue Jays	A+	Florida State League	Toronto Blue Jays	1990	2011
Drham	Durham Bulls	AAA	International League	Tampa Bay Rays	1998	2011
Dytona	Daytona Cubs	A+	Florida State League	Chicago Cubs	1993	2011
Edmtn	Edmonton Trappers	AAA	Pacific Coast League	Washington Nationals	2003	2004
Edmtn	Edmonton Trappers	AAA	Pacific Coast League	Minnesota Twins	2001	2002
Elizab	Elizabethton Twins	R+	Appalachian League	Minnesota Twins	1974	2011
ElPaso	El Paso Diablos	AA	Texas League	Arizona Diamondbacks	1999	2004
Erie	Erie SeaWolves	AA	Eastern League	Detroit Tigers	2001	2011
Eugene	Eugene Emeralds	A-	Northwest League	San Diego Padres	2001	2011
Everett	Everett AquaSox	A-	Northwest League	Seattle Mariners	1995	2011
Expos	GCL Expos	R	Gulf Coast League	Washington Nationals	1986	2004
Frdrck	Frederick Keys	A+	Carolina League	Baltimore Orioles	1990	2011
Fresno	Fresno Grizzlies	AAA	Pacific Coast League	San Francisco Giants	1998	2011
Frisco	Frisco RoughRiders	AA	Texas League	Texas Rangers	2003	2011
FtMyrs	Fort Myers Miracle	A+	Florida State League	Minnesota Twins	1993	2011
FtWyn	Fort Wayne Wizards	A	Midwest League	San Diego Padres	1999	2008
FtWyn	Fort Wayne TinCaps	A	Midwest League	San Diego Padres	2009	2011
Giants	AZL Giants	R	Arizona League	San Francisco Giants	2000	2011
Gr Falls	Great Falls Voyagers	R+	Pioneer League	Chicago White Sox	2008	2011
Gr Falls	Great Falls White Sox	R+	Pioneer League	Chicago White Sox	2003	2007
Grnsbr	Greensboro Grasshoppers	A	South Atlantic League	Florida Marlins	2005	2011
Grnville	Greenville Braves	AA	Southern League	Atlanta Braves	1984	2004
Grnville	Greenville Drive	A	South Atlantic League	Boston Red Sox	2006	2011
Grnville	Greenville Bombers	A	South Atlantic League	Boston Red Sox	2005	2005
Grnville	Greeneville Astros	R+	Appalachian League	Houston Astros	2004	2011
Gt Lks	Great Lakes Loons	A	Midwest League	Los Angeles Dodgers	2007	2011
Gwnntt	Gwinnett Braves	AAA	International League	Atlanta Braves	2009	2011
Helena	Helena Brewers	R+	Pioneer League	Milwaukee Brewers	2003	2011
Hgrstn	Hagerstown Suns	A	South Atlantic League	Washington Nationals	2007	2011
Hgrstn	Hagerstown Suns	A	South Atlantic League	San Francisco Giants	2001	2004
Hi Dsrt	High Desert Mavericks	A+	California League	Seattle Mariners	2007	2011
Hi Dsrt	High Desert Mavericks	A+	California League	Milwaukee Brewers	2001	2004
Hkry	Hickory Crawdads	A	South Atlantic League	Texas Rangers	2009	2011
Hkry	Hickory Crawdads	A	South Atlantic League	Pittsburgh Pirates	1999	2008
Hntsvl	Huntsville Stars	AA	Southern League	Milwaukee Brewers	1999	2011
Hrsbrg	Harrisburg Senators	AA	Eastern League	Washington Nationals	1991	2011
HudVal	Hudson Valley Renegades	A-	New York-Penn League	Tampa Bay Rays	1997	2011
Idaho	Idaho Falls Padres	R+	Pioneer League	San Diego Padres	1995	2003
Idaho	Idaho Falls Chukars	R+	Pioneer League	Kansas City Royals	2004	2011
Indns	GCL Indians	R	Gulf Coast League	Cleveland Indians	2006	2008
Indns	AZL Indians	R	Arizona League	Cleveland Indians	2009	2011
Indy	Indianapolis Indians	AAA	International League	Pittsburgh Pirates	2005	2011
InldEm	Inland Empire 66ers	A+	California League	Los Angeles Dodgers	2007	2010
InldEm	Inland Empire 66ers	A+	California League	Seattle Mariners	2003	2006
Iowa	Iowa Cubs	AAA	Pacific Coast League	Chicago Cubs	1982	2011
Jacksn	Jackson Generals	AA	Southern League	Seattle Mariners	2011	2011
Jaxnvl	Jacksonville Suns	AA	Southern League	Los Angeles Dodgers	2001	2008
Jaxnvl	Jacksonville Suns	AA	Southern League	Florida Marlins	2009	2011
JhsCty	Johnson City Cardinals	R+	Appalachian League	St Louis Cardinals	1975	2011
Jmstwn	Jamestown Jammers	A-	New York-Penn League	Florida Marlins	2002	2011
Jupiter	Jupiter Hammerheads	A+	Florida State League	Florida Marlins	2002	2011
Kane	Kane County Cougars	A	Midwest League	Oakland Athletics	2003	2010

Minor League Abbreviation Key

Abbreviation	Team	Level	League	MLB Affiliate	First Year	Last Year
Knapol	Kannapolis Intimidators	A	South Atlantic League	Chicago White Sox	2001	2011
Kngspt	Kingsport Mets	R+	Appalachian League	New York Mets	1984	2011
Knstn	Kinston Indians	A+	Carolina League	Cleveland Indians	1990	2011
Lakwd	Lakewood BlueClaws	A	South Atlantic League	Philadelphia Phillies	2001	2011
Lancst	Lancaster JetHawks	A+	California League	Houston Astros	2009	2011
Lancst	Lancaster Jethawks	A+	California League	Arizona Diamondbacks	2001	2006
Lansng	Lansing Lugnuts	A	Midwest League	Chicago Cubs	1999	2004
Lk Cty	Lake County Captains	A	South Atlantic League	Cleveland Indians	2003	2009
Lk Cty	Lake County Captains	A	Midwest League	Cleveland Indians	2010	2011
Lk Els	Lake Elsinore Storm	A+	California League	San Diego Padres	2001	2011
Lkland	Lakeland Flying Tigers	A+	Florida State League	Detroit Tigers	1990	2006
Lkland	Lakeland Tigers	A+	Florida State League	Detroit Tigers	2007	2011
Lnsng	Lansing Lugnuts	A	Midwest League	Toronto Blue Jays	2005	2011
Lowell	Lowell Spinners	A-	New York-Penn League	Boston Red Sox	1996	2011
LsVgs	Las Vegas 51s	AAA	Pacific Coast League	Los Angeles Dodgers	2001	2008
LsVgs	Las Vegas 51s	AAA	Pacific Coast League	Toronto Blue Jays	2009	2011
Lsvlle	Louisville Bats	AAA	International League	Cincinnati Reds	2000	2011
LV	Lehigh Valley IronPigs	AAA	International League	Philadelphia Phillies	2008	2011
Lxngtn	Lexington Legends	A	South Atlantic League	Houston Astros	2001	2011
Lynbrg	Lynchburg Hillcats	A+	Carolina League	Cincinnati Reds	2010	2010
Lynbrg	Lynchburg Hillcats	A+	Carolina League	Pittsburgh Pirates	1995	2009
Macon	Macon Braves	A	South Atlantic League	Atlanta Braves	1991	2002
Mdest	Modesto A's	A+	California League	Oakland Athletics	1990	2004
Mdest	Modesto Nuts	A+	California League	Colorado Rockies	2005	2011
MdHat	Medicine Hat Blue Jays	R+	Pioneer League	Toronto Blue Jays	1978	2002
Mdland	Midland RockHounds	AA	Texas League	Oakland Athletics	1999	2011
Memp	Memphis Redbirds	AAA	Pacific Coast League	St Louis Cardinals	1998	2011
Mets	GCL Mets	R	Gulf Coast League	New York Mets	2004	2011
MhVlly	Mahoning Valley Scrappers	A-	New York-Penn League	Cleveland Indians	1999	2011
Mich	Michigan Battle Cats	A	Midwest League	Houston Astros	1999	2002
Missi	Mississippi Braves	AA	Southern League	Atlanta Braves	2005	2011
Mobile	Mobile BayBears	AA	Southern League	Arizona Diamondbacks	2007	2011
Mont	Montgomery Biscuits	AA	Southern League	Tampa Bay Rays	2004	2011
Mrlns	GCL Marlins	R	Gulf Coast League	Florida Marlins	1992	2011
MrtlBh	Myrtle Beach Pelicans	A+	Carolina League	Atlanta Braves	1999	2010
Ms	AZL Mariners	R	Arizona League	Seattle Mariners	1989	2011
Msoula	Missoula Osprey	R+	Pioneer League	Arizona Diamondbacks	1999	2011
Nashv	Nashville Sounds	AAA	Pacific Coast League	Milwaukee Brewers	2005	2011
Nats	GCL Nationals	R	Gulf Coast League	Washington Nationals	2005	2011
NewOr	New Orleans Zephyrs	AAA	Pacific Coast League	Houston Astros	1997	2004
NewOr	New Orleans Zephyrs	AAA	Pacific Coast League	Florida Marlins	2009	2011
NewOr	New Orleans Zephyrs	AAA	Pacific Coast League	New York Mets	2007	2008
NHam	New Hampshire Fisher Cats	AA	Eastern League	Toronto Blue Jays	2004	2011
Norfolk	Norfolk Tides	AAA	International League	New York Mets	1993	2006
Norfolk	Norfolk Tides	AAA	International League	Baltimore Orioles	2007	2011
Nrwich	Norwich Navigators	AA	Eastern League	San Francisco Giants	2003	2005
NWArk	Northwest Arkansas Naturals	AA	Texas League	Kansas City Royals	2008	2011
NwBrit	New Britain Rock Cats	AA	Eastern League	Minnesota Twins	1997	2011
NwHav	New Haven Ravens	AA	Eastern League	Toronto Blue Jays	2003	2003
Ogden	Ogden Raptors	R+	Pioneer League	Los Angeles Dodgers	2003	2011
OKCity	Oklahoma City RedHawks	AAA	Pacific Coast League	Texas Rangers	2009	2010
Okla	Oklahoma RedHawks	AAA	Pacific Coast League	Texas Rangers	1998	2008
Omha	Omaha Royals	AAA	Pacific Coast League	Kansas City Royals	1969	2010
Omha	Omaha Storm Chasers	AAA	Pacific Coast League	Kansas City Royals	2011	2011
Oneont	Oneonta Tigers	A-	New York-Penn League	Detroit Tigers	1999	2009
Orem	Orem Owlz	R+	Pioneer League	Los Angeles Angels	2005	2011
Orioles	GCL Orioles	R	Gulf Coast League	Baltimore Orioles	2007	2011
Padres	AZL Padres	R	Arizona League	San Diego Padres	2004	2011
Peoria	Peoria Chiefs	A	Midwest League	St Louis Cardinals	1995	2004
Peoria	Peoria Chiefs	A	Midwest League	Chicago Cubs	2005	2011
Phillies	GCL Phillies	R	Gulf Coast League	Philadelphia Phillies	1999	2011
Pirates	GCL Pirates	R	Gulf Coast League	Pittsburgh Pirates	1968	2011
PlmBh	Palm Beach Cardinals	A+	Florida State League	St Louis Cardinals	2003	2011
Portlnd	Portland Beavers	AAA	Pacific Coast League	San Diego Padres	2001	2010

Minor League Abbreviation Key

Abbreviation	Team	Level	League	MLB Affiliate	First Year	Last Year
Portlnd	Portland Sea Dogs	AA	Eastern League	Boston Red Sox	2003	2011
Princtn	Princeton Rays	R+	Appalachian League	Tampa Bay Rays	2008	2011
Princtn	Princeton Devil Rays	R+	Appalachian League	Tampa Bay Rays	1997	2007
Provo	Provo Angels	R+	Pioneer League	Los Angeles Angels	2001	2004
Ptomc	Potomac Nationals	A+	Carolina League	Washington Nationals	2005	2011
Ptomc	Potomac Cannons	A+	Carolina League	Cincinnati Reds	2003	2004
Pulaski	Pulaski Mariners	R+	Appalachian League	Seattle Mariners	2008	2011
Pulaski	Pulaski Blue Jays	R+	Appalachian League	Toronto Blue Jays	2003	2006
Pwtckt	Pawtucket Red Sox	AAA	International League	Boston Red Sox	1977	2011
QuadC	Quad Cities River Bandits	A	Midwest League	St Louis Cardinals	2008	2011
QuadC	Quad City Swing	A	Midwest League	St Louis Cardinals	2005	2007
QuadC	Quad City Swing	A	Midwest League	Minnesota Twins	2004	2004
Rays	GCL Rays	R	Gulf Coast League	Tampa Bay Rays	2009	2011
Rchmd	Richmond Flying Squirrels	AA	Eastern League	San Francisco Giants	2010	2011
Rchmd	Richmond Braves	AAA	International League	Atlanta Braves	1966	2008
RCuca	Rancho Cucamonga Quakes	A+	California League	Los Angeles Angels	2001	2010
Rdng	Reading Phillies	AA	Eastern League	Philadelphia Phillies	1967	2011
RdRck	Round Rock Express	AA	Texas League	Houston Astros	2000	2004
RdRck	Round Rock Express	AAA	Pacific Coast League	Houston Astros	2005	2010
Reds	GCL Reds	R	Gulf Coast League	Cincinnati Reds	1999	2009
Reds	AZL Reds	R	Arizona League	Cincinnati Reds	2010	2011
RedSx	GCL Red Sox	R	Gulf Coast League	Boston Red Sox	1989	2011
Reno	Reno Aces	AAA	Pacific Coast League	Arizona Diamondbacks	2009	2011
Rngrs	AZL Rangers	R	Arizona League	Texas Rangers	2003	2011
Roch	Rochester Red Wings	AAA	International League	Minnesota Twins	2003	2011
Rome	Rome Braves	A	South Atlantic League	Atlanta Braves	2003	2011
Royals	AZL Royals	R	Arizona League	Kansas City Royals	2004	2011
Salem	Salem Red Sox	A+	Carolina League	Boston Red Sox	2009	2011
Salem	Salem Avalanche	A+	Carolina League	Houston Astros	2003	2008
Salt Lk	Salt Lake Bees	AAA	Pacific Coast League	Los Angeles Angels	2006	2011
Salt Lk	Salt Lake Stingers	AAA	Pacific Coast League	Los Angeles Angels	2001	2005
Savann	Savannah Sand Gnats	A	South Atlantic League	Washington Nationals	2003	2006
Savann	Savannah Sand Gnats	A	South Atlantic League	New York Mets	2007	2011
Sbend	South Bend Silver Hawks	A	Midwest League	Arizona Diamondbacks	1997	2011
Scrmto	Sacramento River Cats	AAA	Pacific Coast League	Oakland Athletics	2000	2011
SlmKzr	Salem-Keizer Volcanoes	A-	Northwest League	San Francisco Giants	1997	2011
SnAnt	San Antonio Missions	AA	Texas League	Seattle Mariners	2006	2006
SnAnt	San Antonio Missions	AA	Texas League	San Diego Padres	2007	2011
SnJos	San Jose Giants	A+	California League	San Francisco Giants	1990	2011
Spkane	Spokane Indians	A-	Northwest League	Texas Rangers	2003	2011
Sprgfld	Springfield Cardinals	AA	Texas League	St Louis Cardinals	2005	2011
Srsota	Sarasota Reds	A+	Florida State League	Cincinnati Reds	2005	2009
Srsota	Sarasota Red Sox	A+	Florida State League	Boston Red Sox	1995	2004
Stcktn	Stockton Ports	A+	California League	Oakland Athletics	2005	2011
Stcktn	Stockton Ports	A+	California League	Texas Rangers	2003	2004
StCol	State College Spikes	A-	New York-Penn League	Pittsburgh Pirates	2007	2011
StIslnd	Staten Island Yankees	A-	New York-Penn League	New York Yankees	1999	2011
StLuci	St. Lucie Mets	A+	Florida State League	New York Mets	1990	2011
S-WB	Scranton/Wikes-Barre Red Barons	AAA	International League	Philadelphia Phillies	1989	2006
S-WB	Scranton/Wikes-Barre Yankees	AAA	International League	New York Yankees	2007	2011
SWMch	Southwest Michigan Devil Rays	A	Midwest League	Tampa Bay Rays	2005	2006
Syrcse	Syracuse Chiefs	AAA	International League	Washington Nationals	2009	2011
Syrcse	Syracuse SkyChiefs	AAA	International League	Toronto Blue Jays	1978	2006
Syrcse	Syracuse Chiefs	AAA	International League	Toronto Blue Jays	2007	2008
Tacom	Tacoma Rainiers	AAA	Pacific Coast League	Seattle Mariners	1995	2011
Tampa	Tampa Yankees	A+	Florida State League	New York Yankees	1994	2011
Tenn	Tennessee Smokies	AA	Southern League	Chicago Cubs	2007	2011
Tigers	GCL Tigers	R	Gulf Coast League	Detroit Tigers	1995	2011
Toledo	Toledo Mud Hens	AAA	International League	Detroit Tigers	1987	2011
TriCity	Tri-City ValleyCats	A-	New York-Penn League	Houston Astros	2002	2011
TriCity	Tri-City Dust Devils	A-	Northwest League	Colorado Rockies	2001	2011
Trntn	Trenton Thunder	AA	Eastern League	New York Yankees	2003	2011
Trntn	Trenton Thunder	AA	Eastern League	Boston Red Sox	1995	2002
Tucsn	Tucson Sidewinders	AAA	Pacific Coast League	Arizona Diamondbacks	1998	2008

Minor League Abbreviation Key

Abbreviation	Team	Level	League	MLB Affiliate	First Year	Last Year
Tucsn	Tucson Padres	AAA	Pacific Coast League	San Diego Padres	2011	2011
Tulsa	Tulsa Drillers	AA	Texas League	Colorado Rockies	2003	2011
Twins	GCL Twins	R	Gulf Coast League	Minnesota Twins	1989	2011
Vancvr	Vancouver Canadians	A-	Northwest League	Oakland Athletics	1999	1999
VeroB	Vero Beach Devil Rays	A+	Florida State League	Tampa Bay Rays	2007	2008
VeroB	Vero Beach Dodgers	A+	Florida State League	Los Angeles Dodgers	1990	2006
Visalia	Visalia Oaks	A+	California League	Colorado Rockies	2003	2004
Visalia	Visalia Rawhide	A+	California League	Arizona Diamondbacks	2007	2011
Vrmnt	Vermont Expos	A-	New York-Penn League	Washington Nationals	1994	2005
Vrmnt	Vermont Lake Monsters	A-	New York-Penn League	Washington Nationals	2006	2010
Wilmg	Wilmington Blue Rocks	A+	Carolina League	Kansas City Royals	2007	2011
WinSa	Winston-Salem Warthogs	A+	Carolina League	Chicago White Sox	1997	2008
WinSa	Winston-Salem Dash	A+	Carolina League	Chicago White Sox	2009	2011
Wisc	Wisconsin Timber Rattlers	A	Midwest League	Milwaukee Brewers	2009	2011
Wisc	Wisconsin Timber Rattlers	A	Midwest League	Seattle Mariners	1995	2008
WMich	West Michigan Whitecaps	A	Midwest League	Detroit Tigers	1997	2011
Wmspt	Williamsport Crosscutters	A-	New York-Penn League	Philadelphia Phillies	2007	2011
Wmspt	Williamsport Crosscutters	A-	New York-Penn League	Pittsburgh Pirates	1999	2006
WTenn	West Tenn Diamond Jaxx	AA	Southern League	Chicago Cubs	1998	2006
WTenn	West Tenn Diamond Jaxx	AA	Southern League	Seattle Mariners	2007	2010
WV	West Virginia Power	A	South Atlantic League	Pittsburgh Pirates	2009	2011
WV	West Virginia Power	A	South Atlantic League	Milwaukee Brewers	2005	2008
Yakima	Yakima Bears	A-	Northwest League	Arizona Diamondbacks	2001	2011
Yanks	GCL Yankees	R	Gulf Coast League	New York Yankees	1984	2011

Baseball Info Solutions

Baseball Info Solutions has been supplying top notch, timely, and in-depth baseball data and analytics to its customers for the last ten years. BIS collects a statistical snapshot of every important moment of every Major League Baseball game with the most advanced technology, resulting in a database that includes traditional data, pitch-by-pitch data, and defensive positioning data. The company also has the highest quality pitch charting data available anywhere, including pitch type, location, and velocity.

BIS provides comprehensive services to about half of the 30 Major League Baseball teams, as well as many sports agents, media, fantasy services, game companies and private individuals.

John Dewan, the principal owner of BIS, has been on the cutting edge of baseball analysis for over 25 years. His experience goes all the way back to his days as Executive Director of Project Scoresheet, the Bill James-led effort that pioneered the new wave of baseball statistics that are now common terminology.

President Steve Moyer brings 20 years of baseball industry experience to BIS. His hands-on, can-do business demeanor helps set BIS apart from its competition.

The rest of the BIS team includes former professional and collegiate baseball players as well as research, programming and database management experts. Over the last five seasons, BIS has more than tripled its full-time staff.

BIS continues to grow within the industry while emphasizing personal attention to its customers. This focus on personal attention is evidenced by the fact that if you contact the office with an inquiry you may very well find yourself speaking directly to the company president.

To contact BIS:

Baseball Info Solutions
41 S. 2nd Street
Coplay, PA 18037
610-261-2370
www.baseballinfosolutions.com

Acknowledgements

Bill James is the brains behind the majority of what you see in this book, thus the title.

John Dewan is a primary owner of Baseball Info Solutions and is also a pioneer in the analysis of baseball data. John's specialty is defensive data. Sue Dewan is another primary owner of Baseball Info Solutions and is lending her talents to the BIS team more than ever before.

For the first time we are naming Rob Burckhard the Production Manager of the Handbook. His hard work and organizational skills have (hopefully) put the days of Handbook sleepovers in the rear view mirror. Rob's main job is in the R&D department. Ben Jedlovec is the other half of R&D. I like to call them the BIS "baseball scientists." Joe Rosales and Michael Schatz interned for them in 2011.

The leaders of the Operations department at Baseball Info Solutions are Dan Casey, Mike Piekarski and Todd Radcliffe. The volume and accuracy of our data can be attributed in great part to these three.

The leader of the IT department is Jeff Spoljaric. Along with Patrick Coyle and Andrew Gibson, they keep the BIS databases in good hands.

Jim Swavely and Jon Vrecsics are the primary caretakers of our invaluable Minor League operation.

Mark Alken, Tani Cohen, Will Cohen, Maxwell Cook, Dennen Cuthbertson, Kyle Donnelly, Jason Eisele, Mike Fecteau, Justin Goot, Adam Hayes, Andy Johnson, Brady Johnston, Christian Karayannides, Ian Kenyon, Alex Lewin, Matt Sinise, Andy Tworischuk, Craig Vanderkam, Mark Wierichs, and Jack Yerxa were the 2011 Video Scout crew. I doubt anyone watches more major league baseball over the course of a season than these guys.

Jim Capuano is the head of Business Development.

The ACTA Publications crew is headed by Greg Pierce, along with Donna Ryding, Mary Eggert, Richard Struben, Brendan Gaughan, and Amanda Modelski.

Our friends in the baseball industry include: Greg Ambrosius, Andy Andres, David Appelman, Matthew Berry, Jim Callis, Doug Dennis, Jeff Erickson, Peter Gammons, Steve Gardner, Jason Grey, Durward Hamil, Eric Karabell, Peter Kreutzer, Michael Lehrer, Chris Liss, Gene McCaffrey, Deric McKamey, Sig Mejdal, John Menna, Bob Meyerhoff, Lawr Michaels, Mike Murphy, Patrick Newman, Rob Neyer, Alex Patton, Scott Pianowski, Mike Phillips, David Pinto, Joe Posnanski, Nate Ravitz, Hal Richman, Steve Ruskowski, Mike Salfino, Peter Schoenke, Ron Shandler, Joe Sheehan, John Sickels, Dave Studenmund, Tom Tango, Mark Watson, Rick Wilton, Trace Wood, Don Zminda, and Todd Zola.

Thank you for the things you have done to make our book the industry standard.

Sincerely,
Steve Moyer
President
Baseball Info Solutions

NOTES

NOTES

Free Bill James Daily Match-Ups
E-mailed to You
Every Day of the Season

ACTA Sports is offering our customers a free subscription to *The Bill James Daily Match-Ups*. Each day you'll receive a PDF file in your e-mail inbox showing lifetime batter vs. pitcher statistics for your favorite team against your team's next opponent. These match-ups are updated daily throughout the season.

If you would like to receive a free subscription to *The Bill James Daily Match-Ups* for the 2012 season, please send an email to **matchups@actasports.com** with your name and favorite team and where you usually buy your sports books. Limit one team per customer.

Oh, and you might ask: is there an app for that? Yes, there is! Look for *Bill James Daily Match-Ups* on your iPhone or iPad. Only $1.99 for the whole 2012 season. An even more powerful app for iPhone/iPad is *Bill James Baseball IQ* at only $14.95 a year. Check them both out.

Thanks for your patronage.

Play ball!

Greg Pierce
Co-Publisher